Eighth Edition

AF773706

Business Law and the Regulation of Business

Richard A. Mann
Professor of Business Law
The University of North Carolina at Chapel Hill
Member of the North Carolina Bar

Barry S. Roberts
Professor of Business Law
The University of North Carolina at Chapel Hill
Member of the North Carolina and Pennsylvania Bar

THOMSON
SOUTH-WESTERN
WEST

Australia · Canada · Mexico · Singapore · Spain · United Kingdom · United States

THOMSON
SOUTH-WESTERN
WEST

Business Law and the Regulation of Business, **8e**
Richard A. Mann and Barry S. Roberts

VP/Editorial Director:
Jack W. Calhoun

VP/Editor-in-Chief:
George Werthman

Publisher:
Rob Dewey

Developmental Editor:
Bob Sandman

Marketing Manager:
Steven Silverstein, Esq.

Production Editor:
Chris Hudson

Technology Project Editor:
Christine Wittmer

Media Editor:
Amy Wilson

Manufacturing Coordinator:
Rhonda Utley

Production House/Compositor:
DPS Associates, Inc.

Printer:
QuebecorWorld
Taunton, Massachusetts

Cover and Internal Designer:
Anne Marie Rekow

COPYRIGHT © 2005
by West Legal Studies in Business, part of the Thomson Corporation. West Legal Studies in Business, Thomson, and the Thomson logo are trademarks used herein under license.

Printed in the United States of America
1 2 3 4 5 07 06 05 04

ISBN: 0-324-27074-7

International Student Edition:
0-324-22545-8

Library of Congress Control Number:
2003112843

ALL RIGHTS RESERVED.
No part of this work covered by the copyright hereon may be reproduced or used in any form or by any means–graphic, electronic, or mechanical, including photocopying, recording, taping, Web distribution or information storage and retrieval systems–without the written permission of the publisher.

For permission to use material from this text or product, submit a request online at *http://www.thomsonrights.com.*
For more information contact
West Legal Studies in Business,
5191 Natorp Boulevard,
Mason, Ohio 45040.
Or you can visit our Internet site at
http://www.westbuslaw.com

About the Authors

Richard A. Mann received a B.S. in Mathematics from the University of North Carolina at Chapel Hill and a J.D. from Yale Law School. He is currently professor of Business Law at the Kenan-Flagler School of Business, University of North Carolina at Chapel Hill. Richard Mann is past president of the Southeastern Regional Business Law Association. He is a member of Who's Who in America, Who's Who in American Law, Outstanding Young Men of America, and the North Carolina Bar.

Professor Mann has written extensively on a number of legal topics including bankruptcy, sales, secured transactions, real property, insurance law, and business associations. He has received the *American Business Law Journal's* award both for best article and best comment and has, in addition, served as a reviewer and staff editor for the publication. He teaches in several executive education programs and is a founder, managing director, and instructor in the Carolina CPA Review. He is a co-author of *Smith and Roberson's Business Law* (Twelfth Edition), as well as *Essentials of Business Law and the Legal Environment* (Eighth Edition) and *Contemporary Business Law*.

Barry S. Roberts received a B.S. in Business Administration from Pennsylvania State University, a J.D. from the University of Pennsylvania, and an LL.M. from Harvard Law School. He served as a judicial clerk for the Pennsylvania Supreme Court prior to practicing law in Pittsburgh. Barry Roberts is currently professor of Business Law at the Kenan-Flagler School of Business, University of North Carolina at Chapel Hill. He is a member of Who's Who in American Law, Outstanding Young Men in America, and the North Carolina and Pennsylvania Bars.

Professor Roberts has written numerous articles on such topics as antitrust, products liability, constitutional law, banking law, employment law, and business associations. He has been a reviewer and staff editor for the *American Business Law Journal*. Professor Roberts is a founder, managing director, and instructor in the Carolina CPA Review. He is a co-author of *Smith and Roberson's Business Law* (Twelfth Edition), as well as *Essentials of Business Law and the Legal Environment* (Eighth Edition) and *Contemporary Business Law*.

Brief Contents

Table of Contents

PART IV

Sales 345

PART V

Negotiable Instruments 453

PART VIII

Debtor and Creditor Relations 771

PART IX

Regulation of Business 831

PART X

Property 1039

Table of Cases

G

H

I

J

K

L

M

N

O

P

Table of Figures

Preface

The Tradition Continues

The eighth edition of *Business Law and the Regulation of Business* continues the tradition of accuracy, comprehensiveness, and authoritativeness associated with its earlier editions. This text covers its subject material in a nontechnical but authoritative manner. It covers the material succinctly yet provides depth sufficient to ensure easy comprehension by today's students.

CPA Preparation

This text is designed for use in business law and legal environment courses generally offered in universities, colleges, and schools of business and management. By reason of the broad coverage and variety of the material, instructors may readily adapt this volume to specially designed courses in business law by assigning and emphasizing different combinations of the subject matter. All topics included in the business law section of the CPA exam are covered by the text. Portions of the text covering commonly tested areas on the CPA exam are marked to aid students in exam preparation.

Uniform CPA Examination Content Specifications

(Effective Upon the Launch of the Computer-Based Uniform CPA Examination)

The AICPA Board of Examiners has approved and adopted content specification outlines (CSOs) for the four sections of the new computer-based Uniform CPA Examination: Auditing & Attestation, Financial Accounting & Reporting, Regulation, and Business Environment & Concepts. These revised CSOs become effective upon the launch of the computer-based Uniform CPA Examination (targeted for early 2004). The CSOs include the following topics covered in this textbook:

Regulation Section

I. Ethics and professional and legal responsibilities
   A. Legal responsibilities and liabilities [of accountants]
      1. Common law liability to clients and third parties
      2. Federal statutory liability
   B. Privileged communications and confidentiality [of accountants]

II. Business Law
   A. Agency
      1. Formation and termination
      2. Duties and authority of agents and principals
      3. Liabilities and authority of agents and principals
   B. Contracts
      1. Formation
      2. Performance
      3. Third-party assignments
      4. Discharge, breach, and remedies
   C. Debtor-creditor relationships
      1. Rights, duties, and liabilities of debtors, creditors, and guarantors
      2. Bankruptcy
   D. Government regulation of business
      1. Federal securities acts
      2. Other government regulation (antitrust, pension and retirement plans, union and employee relations, and legal liability for payroll and social security taxes)
   E. Uniform Commercial Code
      1. Negotiable instruments and letters of credit
      2. Sales
      3. Secured transactions
      4. Documents of title and title transfer
   F. Real property, including insurance

Business Environment & Concepts Section

I. Business Structure
   A. Advantages, implications, and constraints of legal structures for business
      1. Sole proprietorships and general and limited partnerships
      2. Limited liability companies (LLC), limited liability partnerships (LLP), and joint ventures
      3. Subchapter C and subchapter S corporations
   B. Formation, operation, and termination of businesses
   C. Financial structure, capitalization, profit and loss allocation, and distributions
   D. Rights, duties, legal obligations, and authority of owners and management (directors, officers, stockholders, partners, and other owners)

For more information, visit http://www.cpa-exam.org/.

Business Ethics Emphasis

To supplement the chapter on business ethics, we have included five managerial case studies in business ethics. These case studies require the student to make the value trade-offs that confront business people in their professional lives. (We gratefully acknowledge the assistance of James Leis in writing the Mykon's Dilemma case.) More than half of the chapters also contain an "Ethical Dilemma," which presents a managerial situation involving ethical issues. A series of questions leads the student to explore the ethical dimensions of each situation. We wish to acknowledge and thank the following professors for their contribution in preparing the Ethical Dilemmas: Sandra K. Miller, Associate Professor of Accounting and Taxation, Widener University and Gregory P. Cermignano, Associate Professor of Accounting, Widener University. In addition, to provide further application of ethics in different business contexts, an ethics question follows many cases. These questions encourage students to consider the ethical dimensions of the facts in the case or of the legal issue invoked by the facts.

Up-to-Date Statutes

In the partnership chapters, discussion is based on the Revised Uniform Partnership Act. In the secured transactions chapter, coverage is based on the Revised Article 9 of the UCC.

FEATURES RETAINED

Excerpted Cases

From long classroom experience we are of the opinion that fundamental legal principles can be learned more effectively from text and case materials having at least a degree of human interest. Accordingly, we have included a large number of recent cases. Landmark cases, on the other hand, have not been neglected. All of the cases have the facts and decisions summarized for clarity and the opinions edited to preserve the language of the court. Each case is followed by an interpretation, which explains the significance of the case and how it relates to the textual material.

Case Critical Thinking Questions

Each case is followed by a critical thinking question to encourage students to examine the legal policy or reasoning behind the legal principle of the case or to apply it in a real world context.

Insights

As in the previous edition, we have included Managerial and Consumer Insights. Managerial Insights provide both future and current managers legal information relevant to their decision making. Consumer Insights complement the Managerial Insights by exploring business regulations from a consumer's perspective. We wish to thank Linda Haac, Ginger Travis and Beth Woods for their contribution to the managerial and consumer insights.

Internet Research Questions

These end-of-chapter questions lead students to the rich resources of the World Wide Web to obtain additional knowledge about the law. One caveat for students is that they should examine the reliability and currency of the information found; not all of it is current or accurate.

Practical Advice

Each chapter contains a number of statements that illustrate how legal concepts can be applied to common business situations.

Chapter Objectives

Each chapter begins with a list of learning objectives for the student.

Law and You

In a number of chapters we have provided a listing of consumer-oriented brochures available on the World Wide Web. These brochures, which have been prepared by state bar associations, state attorney generals, and/or federal governmental agencies, provide students with practical information about how the law affects them in their professional and personal lives. Topics include buying a car, tenants' and landlords' rights, applying for credit, what to do if involved in an automobile accident, what to do if arrested, and buying a home.

Law on the Internet

Throughout the text we provide references to Web sites containing primary legal materials, such as statutes, cases, and administrative regulations as well as Web sites that are directly relevant to the material in the text, cases, and problems.

ENHANCED READABILITY

To improve readability throughout the text, all unnecessary "legalese" has been eliminated while necessary legal terms have been printed in boldface and clearly defined, explained, and illustrated. The text is enriched by numerous illustrative hypothetical and case examples that help students relate material to real-life experiences.

CLASSROOM-TESTED END-OF-CHAPTER MATERIALS

Classroom-tested problems appear at the end of the chapters to test the students' understanding of major concepts. We have used the problems and consider them excellent stimulants to classroom discussion. Students, in turn, have found the problems—many of which are taken from reported court decisions—helpful in enabling them to apply the basic rules of law to factual situations. Besides serving as a springboard for discussion, the problems readily suggest other and related problems to the inquiring, analytical mind.

AMPLE ILLUSTRATIONS

We have incorporated approximately 160 classroom-tested figures, charts, and diagrams. The diagrams help the students conceptualize the many abstract concepts in the law; the charts not only summarize prior discussions but also indicate relationships between different legal rules. In addition, each chapter ends with a summary in the form of an annotated outline of the entire chapter, including key terms.

CYBERLAW CHAPTER

In this chapter we identify the legal and regulatory issues that have arisen or are likely to arise from the widespread usage of the Internet for business transactions. We also describe the extent to which the law has responded or is in the process of responding. This chapter covers the following areas of the law that have been most significantly affected by e-commerce and the evolution of the Internet: defamation, intellectual property, contract and sales law, privacy, securities regulation, and cybercrime.

PEDAGOGICAL BENEFITS

Classroom use and study of this book should provide the following benefits and skills for the student:

1. Perception and appreciation of the scope, extent, and importance of the law.
2. Basic knowledge of the fundamental concepts, principles, and rules of law that apply to business transactions.
3. Knowledge of the function and operation of courts and governmental administrative agencies.
4. Ability to recognize the potential legal problems that may arise in a doubtful or complicated situation, and the necessity of consulting a lawyer and obtaining competent professional legal advice.
5. Development of analytical skills and reasoning power.

We express our gratitude to the following professors for their helpful comments:

J. Lenora Bresler
University of South Florida

Kurt E. Erickson
Southwestern Michigan College

Susan Glatthorn Johnson
University of South Florida

Ruth B. Kraft
Audrey Cohen College

Brad McDonald
Northern Illinois University

Russell A. Meade
Virginia Tidewater Community College

Radlyn Mendoza
Old Dominion University

We also are grateful to those who provided us with comments regarding earlier editions of the book:

William Dennis Ames
Indiana University—Purdue

Denise Bartles
Missouri Western State College

Joseph Boucher
University of Wisconsin—Madison

Susan Cabral
Salisbury State University

Elizabeth A. Cameron
Alma College

Ronald R. Caplette
Western Piedmont Community College

Theresa Clark
Methodist College

David Cooper
Fullerton College

Patricia DeFrain
Glendale College

Bruce Farrel Dorn
Oakton Community College

Kurt E. Erickson
Southwestern Michigan College

Vincent A. Errante
University of North Dakota

Robert A. Fidrych
University of Wisconsin—Platteville

Steven J. Green
University of California-Berkeley

Gary A. Hanson
Pepperdine University

Bruce L. Harms
University of Wisconsin—Madison

Charles Hartmann
Wright State University

Gregory T. Hinton
Fairmont State College

Clay Hipp
New Mexico State University

Georgia L. Holmes
Mankato State University

Robert J. Hotopp
Indiana University—Southeast

Neely S. Inlow
Lynchburg College

Uldis E. Inveiss
Carroll College

Susan S. Jarvis
Pan American University

John R. Jozwiak
Loyola University of Chicago

Jack E. Karns
East Carolina University

Robert H. Kieserman
Philadelphia College of Textiles and Science

Karl H. Kline
Lafayette College

Richard G. Kunkel
University of St. Thomas

Logan Langwith
College of St. Thomas

Anne Lawton
Miami University

Stephen M. Maple
University of Indianapolis

Keith A. Maxwell
University of Puget Sound

Douglas E. McClelland
Montana State University

Brad McDonald
Northern Illinois University

Sharlene McEvoy
Fairfield University

Debbie L. Mescon
Salisbury State University

D. Lynn Morison
Michigan State University

Gregory C. Mosier
Oklahoma State University

Darwin H. Mueller
Tacoma Community College

Lee J. Ness
University of North Dakota

Robert L. Peace
North Carolina State University

James L. Porter
University of New Mexico

Daniel L. Reynolds
Middle Tennessee State University

Ellen Blumberg Rubert
College of Lake County

Linda B. Samuels
George Mason University

Pamella A. Seay
Edison Community College

Harold Silverman
Bridgewater State College

Beverly Stanis
Oakton Community College

Dorothy L. Steele
Montclair State College

Stanley E. Stettz
Lafayette College

Rene Thomas
Holyoke Community College

John T. Wendt
University of St. Thomas

Keith E. Werner
Wesleyan College

Scott White
University of Wisconsin—Platteville

John G. Williams
Northwestern State University

Raymond Wyrsch
Catholic University

Joseph Zavaglia, Jr.
Brookdale Community College

Raymond C. Zumoff
Camden County College

We express our thanks and appreciation to Peggy Pickard for administrative assistance. For their support we extend our thanks to Karlene Fogelin Knebel and Joanne Erwick Roberts. And we are grateful to Crystal Bullen of DPS, and Rob Dewey, Bob Sandman, and Chris Hudson of West Legal Studies in Business for their invaluable assistance and cooperation in connection with the preparation of this text.

This text is dedicated also to our children Lilli-Marie Knebel Mann, Justin Erwick Roberts, and Matthew Charles Roberts.

Richard A. Mann

Barry S. Roberts

Total Learning Solutions

For more information about any of the ancillaries listed below, contact your local Thomson Learning/West Legal Studies in Business sales representative or visit the Mann and Roberts *Business Law and the Regulation of Business* Web site at http://mann.westbuslaw.com.

The Student Study Guide (ISBN: 0-324-27075-5), prepared by Ronald L. Taylor of Metropolitan State College of Denver, provides a brief statement of purpose, chapter checkpoints, chapter outlines, key terms lists, and true/false, multiple choice, and short essay questions for each chapter. Each part has a sample test bank of 20 cumulative test questions. The Study Guide also includes a CPA exam business law review.

The Instructor's Manual (ISBN: 0-324-27076-3), prepared by Richard A. Mann, Barry S. Roberts, and Beth D. Woods, contains chapter outlines, teaching notes, answers to problems, key terms, recommendations for transparency masters and acetates, and part openers, which provide suggested research and outside activities for students.

The Test Bank (ISBN: 0-324-27077-1), prepared by Carol Cromer, is bound in a separate volume and includes true/false, multiple choice, short essay, and challenge test questions.

ExamView Testing Software—Computerized Testing Software (ISBN: 0-324-27079-8) contains all of the questions in the printed test bank. This program is an easy-to-use test-creation software compatible with Microsoft Windows. Instructors can add or edit questions, instructions, and answers, and select questions by previewing them on the screen, selecting them randomly, or selecting them by number. Instructors can also create and administer quizzes online, whether over the Internet, a local area network (LAN), or a wide area network (WAN).

Microsoft PowerPoint Lecture Review Slides are available for use by students as an aid to note-taking and by instructors for enhancing their lectures. Download these slides at http://mann.westbuslaw.com/.

Transparency Masters and Acetates (ISBN: 0-324-15857-2) highlight text illustrations. Recommendations for using these items appear in the Instructor's Manual.

InfoTrac College Edition is an online library that contains hundreds of scholarly and popular periodicals, including *American Business Law Journal, Journal of International Business Studies, Environmental Law,* and *Ethics.* Students can be provided free access to InfoTrac College Edition when they purchase this textbook. Contact your local Thomson Learning/West Legal Studies in Business sales representative to set up a package for your course.

Videos are available to qualified adopters using this text. You may access the entire library of West videos, a vast selection covering most business law issues. There are some restrictions and, if you have questions, please contact your local Thomson Learning/West Legal studies sales representative or visit http://www.westbuslaw.com/video_library.html.

eCoursepacks provide a tailor-made, easy to use, online companion for your course. eCoursepacks give educators access to content from thousands of current popular, professional, and academic periodicals; business and industry information from Gale; and the ability to easily add your own material. Permissions for all eCoursepack content are already secured, saving you the time and worry of securing rights.

eCoursepacks online publishing tools also save you time, allowing you to quickly search the databases and make selections, organize all your content, and publish the final online product in a clean, uniform, and full color format. eCoursepacks are the best way to provide your audience with current information easily, quickly, and inexpensively. To learn more visit http://ecoursepacks.swlearning.com.

Enron Web Project. West Legal Studies in Business and South-Western have created a special Web project entitled "Inside Look," focusing on Enron. You will find in-depth articles and expert analysis concerning the events leading to Enron's collapse and the continuing investigation of that company. Inside Look provides analysis from all angles by using an interdisciplinary approach emphasizing accounting, business law, and management. For more information, visit http://insidelook.westbuslaw.com.

PART I

INTRODUCTION TO LAW AND ETHICS

U.S. Constitution
http://www.law.cornell.edu/constitution/constitution.table.html

State Constitutions
http://www.law.cornell.edu/states/listing.html

Supreme Court Decisions
http://supct.law.cornell.edu/supct

Federal Case Law
http://www.ll.georgetown.edu/federal/judicial/index.cfm

State Case Law
http//www.law.cornell.edu/opinions.html#state

The American Law Institute
http://www.ali.org

U.S. Code
http://www4.law.cornell.edu/uscode/

State Statutes
http://www.law.cornell.edu/states/listing.html

The National Conference of Commissioners on Uniform State Laws
http://www.nccusl.org/

Uniform Laws
http://www.law.upenn.edu/bll/ulc/ulc_frame.htm

Online Treaties
http://www.asil.org/resource/treaty1.htm#sect21

Executive Orders
http://www.archives.gov/federal_register/executive_orders/disposition_tables.html

Council for Ethics in Economics
http://www.businessethics.org/

Business for Social Responsibility
http://www.bsr.org/

International Business Ethics Institute
http://www.business-ethics.org/

Centre for Applied Ethics
http://www.ethics.ubc.ca/resources/business/

CHAPTER I

Introduction to Law

The life of law has not been logic; it has been experience.

OLIVER WENDELL HOLMES (1881)

Learning Objectives

After reading this chapter you should be able to:

1. Identify and describe the basic functions of law.
2. Distinguish between (a) law and justice and (b) law and morals.
3. Distinguish between (a) substantive and procedural law, (b) public and private law, and (c) criminal law.
4. Identify and describe the sources of law.
5. Explain the principle of *stare decisis*.

Law concerns the relations between individuals as such relations affect the social and economic order. It is both the product of civilization and the means by which civilization is maintained. As such, law reflects the social, economic, political, religious, and moral philosophy of society.

Law is an instrument of social control. Its function is to regulate, within certain limitations, human conduct and human relations. Accordingly, the laws of the United States affect the life of every U.S. citizen. At the same time, the laws of each state influence the life of each of its citizens and the lives of many noncitizens as well. The rights and duties of all individuals, as well as the safety and security of all people and their property, depend on the law.

The law is pervasive. It permits, forbids, and/or regulates practically every known human activity and affects all persons either directly or indirectly. Law is, in part, prohibitory: certain acts must not be committed. For example, one must not steal; one must not murder. Law is also partly mandatory: certain acts must be done or be done in a prescribed way. Thus, taxes must be paid; corporations must make and file certain reports with state authorities; traffic must keep to the right. Finally, law is permissive: certain acts may be done. For instance, one may or may not enter into a contract; one may or may not dispose of one's estate by will.

Because the areas of law are so highly interrelated, you will find it helpful to begin the study of the different areas of business law by first considering the nature, classification, and sources of law. This will enable you not only to understand better each specific area of law but also to understand its relationship to other areas of law.

NATURE OF LAW

The law has evolved slowly, and it will continue to change. It is not a pure science based on unchanging and universal truths. Rather, it results from a continuous striving to develop a workable set of rules that balance the individual and group rights of a society.

DEFINITION OF LAW

Scholars and citizens in general often ask a fundamental but difficult question regarding law: What is it? Numerous philosophers and jurists (legal scholars) have attempted to define it. American jurists and Supreme

Court Justices Oliver Wendell Holmes and Benjamin Cardozo defined law as predictions of the way in which a court will decide specific legal questions. The English jurist Blackstone, on the other hand, defined law as "a rule of civil conduct prescribed by the supreme power in a state, commanding what is right, and prohibiting what is wrong."

Because of its great complexity, many legal scholars have attempted to explain the law by outlining its essential characteristics. Roscoe Pound, a distinguished American jurist and former dean of the Harvard Law School, described law as having multiple meanings:

> First we may mean the legal order, that is, the régime of ordering human activities and relations through systematic application of the force of politically organized society, or through social pressure in such a society backed by such force. We use the term "law" in this sense when we speak of "respect for law" or for the "end of law."
>
> Second we may mean the aggregate of laws or legal precepts; the body of authoritative grounds of judicial and administrative action established in such a society. We may mean the body of received and established materials on which judicial and administrative determinations proceed. We use the term in this sense when we speak of "systems of law" or of "justice according to law."
>
> Third we may mean what Justice Cardozo has happily styled "the judicial process." We may mean the process of determining controversies, whether as it actually takes place, or as the public, the jurists, and the practitioners in the courts hold it ought to take place.

FUNCTIONS OF LAW

At a general level the primary function of law is to maintain stability in the social, political, and economic system while simultaneously permitting change. The law accomplishes this basic function by performing a number of specific functions, among them dispute resolution, protection of property, and preservation of the state.

Disputes, which arise inevitably in any modern society, may involve criminal matters, such as theft, or noncriminal matters, such as an automobile accident. Because disputes threaten social stability, the law has established an elaborate and evolving set of rules to resolve them. In addition, the legal system has instituted societal remedies, usually administered by the courts, in place of private remedies such as revenge.

A second crucial function of law is to protect the private ownership of property and to assist in the making of voluntary agreements (called contracts) regarding exchanges of property and services. Accordingly, a significant portion of law, as well as this text, involves property and its disposition, including the law of property, contracts, sales, commercial paper, and business associations.

A third essential function of the law is preservation of the state. In our system, law ensures that changes in political structure and leadership are brought about by political action, such as elections, legislation, and referenda, rather than by revolution, sedition, and rebellion.

LAW AND MORALS

Although moral concepts greatly influence the law, morals and law are not the same. You might think of them as two intersecting circles (see Figure 1-1). The more darkly shaded area common to both circles includes the vast body of ideas that are both moral and legal. For instance, "Thou shall not kill" and "Thou shall not steal" are both moral precepts and legal constraints.

On the other hand, that part of the legal circle that does not intersect the morality circle (the lightly shaded portion) includes many rules of law that are completely unrelated to morals, such as the rules stating that you must drive on the right side of the road and that you must register before you can vote. Likewise, the part of the morality circle that does not intersect the legal circle includes moral precepts not enforced by legal sanctions, such as the idea that you should not silently stand by and watch a blind man walk off a cliff or that you should not foreclose a poor widow's mortgage.

LAW AND JUSTICE

Law and justice represent separate and distinct concepts. Without law, however, there can be no justice. Although defining justice is at least as difficult as defining law, justice generally may be defined as the fair, equitable, and impartial treatment of the competing interests and desires of individuals and groups with due regard for the common good.

On the other hand, law is no guarantee of justice. Some of history's most monstrous acts have been committed pursuant to "law." For example, recall the actions of Nazi Germany during the 1930s and 1940s. Totalitarian societies often have shaped formal legal systems around the atrocities they have sanctioned.

CLASSIFICATION OF LAW

Because the subject is vast, classifying the law into categories is helpful. Though a number of categories is possible, the most useful ones are (1) substantive and procedural,

Figure 1-1
Law and Morals

(2) public and private, and (3) civil and criminal. See Figure 1-2, which illustrates a classification of law.

Basic to understanding these classifications are the terms *right* and *duty*. A **right** is the capacity of a person, with the aid of the law, to require another person or persons to perform, or to refrain from performing, a certain act. Thus, if Alice sells and delivers goods to Bob for the agreed price of $500 payable at a certain date, Alice is capable, with the aid of the courts, of enforcing the payment by Bob of the $500. A **duty** is the obligation the law imposes upon a person to perform, or to refrain from performing, a certain act. Duty and right are correlatives: no right can rest upon one person without a corresponding duty resting upon some other person, or in some cases upon all other persons.

SUBSTANTIVE AND PROCEDURAL LAW

Substantive law creates, defines, and regulates legal rights and duties. Thus, the rules of contract law that determine a binding contract are rules of substantive law. On the other hand, **procedural law** sets forth the rules for enforcing those rights that exist by reason of the substantive law. Thus, procedural law defines the method by which to obtain a remedy in court.

PUBLIC AND PRIVATE LAW

Public law is the branch of substantive law that deals with the government's rights and powers and its relationship to individuals or groups. Public law consists of constitutional, administrative, and criminal law. **Private law** is that part of substantive law governing individuals and legal entities (such as corporations) in their relationships with one another. Business law is primarily private law.

CIVIL AND CRIMINAL LAW

The **civil law** defines duties the violation of which constitutes a wrong against the party injured by the violation. In contrast, the **criminal law** establishes duties the violation of which is a wrong against the whole community. Civil law is a part of private law, whereas criminal law is a part of public law. (The term *civil law* should be distinguished from the concept of a civil law *system*, which is discussed later in this chapter.) In a civil action the injured party **sues** to recover *compensation* for the damage and injury sustained as a result of the **defendant's** wrongful conduct. The party bringing a civil action (the **plaintiff**) has the burden of proof, which the plaintiff must sustain by a *preponderance* (greater weight) *of the evidence*. The purpose of the civil law is to compensate the injured party, not, as in the case of criminal law, to punish the wrongdoer. The principal forms of relief the civil law affords are a judgment for money damages and a decree ordering the defendant to perform a specified act or to desist from specified conduct.

A crime is any act prohibited or omission required by public law in the interest of protecting the public and made punishable by the government in a judicial proceeding brought (**prosecuted**) by it. The government must prove criminal guilt *beyond a reasonable* doubt, which is a significantly higher burden of proof than that required in a civil action. Crimes are prohibited and punished on the grounds of public policy, which may include the safeguarding of government, human life, or private property.

Figure 1-2 *Classification of Law*

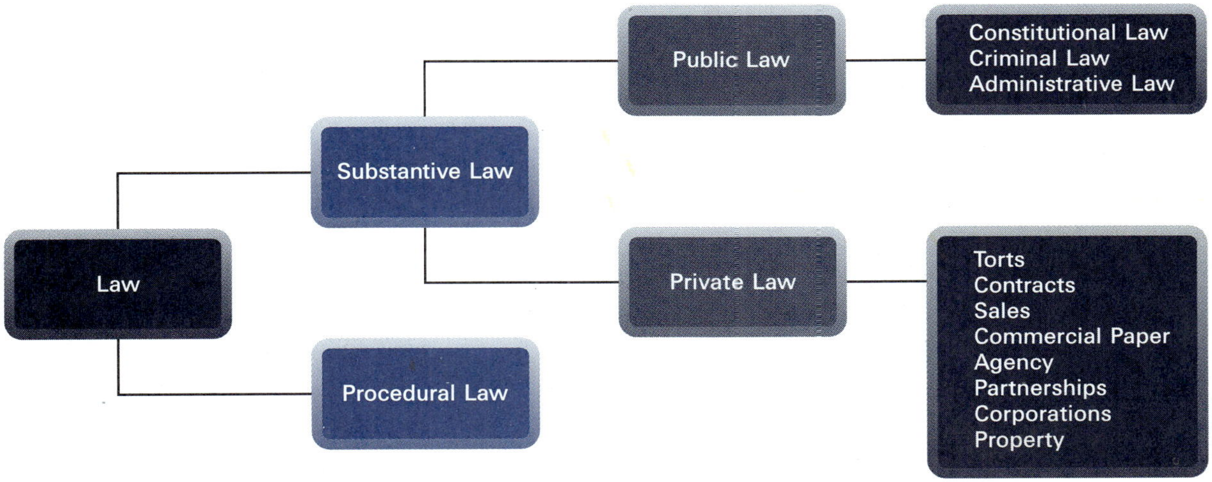

Additional purposes of the criminal law include deterrence and rehabilitation. See Concept Review: Comparison of Civil and Criminal Law.

SOURCES OF LAW

The sources of law in the U.S. legal system are the federal and state constitutions, federal treaties, interstate compacts, federal and state statutes and executive orders, the ordinances of countless local municipal governments, the rules and regulations of federal and state administrative agencies, and an ever-increasing volume of reported federal and state court decisions.

The ***supreme law*** of the land is the U.S. Constitution, which provides in turn that federal statutes and treaties shall be paramount to state constitutions and statutes. Federal legislation is of great significance as a source of law. Other federal actions having the force of law are executive orders by the President and rules and regulations set by federal administrative officials, agencies, and commissions. The federal courts also contribute considerably to the body of law in the United States.

The same pattern exists in every state. The paramount law of each state is contained in its written constitution. (Although a state constitution cannot deprive citizens of federal constitutional rights, it can guarantee rights beyond those provided in the U.S. Constitution.) Subordinate to the state constitution are the statutes enacted by the state's legislature and the case law developed by its judiciary. Likewise, rules and regulations of state administrative agencies have the force of law, as do executive orders issued by the governor. In addition, cities, towns, and villages have

CONCEPT REVIEW

Comparison of Civil and Criminal Law

	Civil Law	Criminal Law
Commencement of action	Aggrieved individual (plaintiff) sues	State or federal government prosecutes
Purpose	Compensation Deterrence	Punishment Deterrence Rehabilitation Preservation of peace
Burden of proof	Preponderance of the evidence	Beyond a reasonable doubt
Principal sanctions	Monetary damages Equitable remedies	Capital punishment Imprisonment Fines

limited legislative powers to pass ordinances and resolutions within their respective municipal areas. See Figure 1-3, which illustrates this hierarchy.

CONSTITUTIONAL LAW

A **constitution**—the fundamental law of a particular level of government—establishes the governmental structure and allocates power among governmental levels, thereby defining political relationships. One of the fundamental principles on which our government is founded is that of separation of powers. As incorporated into our Constitution, this means that government consists of three distinct and independent branches—the federal judiciary, the Congress, and the executive branch.

A constitution also restricts the powers of government and specifies the rights and liberties of the people. For example, the Constitution of the United States not only specifically states what rights and authority are vested in the national government but also specifically enumerates certain rights and liberties of the people. Moreover, the Ninth Amendment to the U.S. Constitution makes it clear that this enumeration of rights does not in any way deny or limit other rights that the people retain.

All other law in the United States is subordinate to the federal Constitution. No law, federal or state, is valid if it violates the federal Constitution. Under the principle of **judicial review**, the Supreme Court of the United States determines the constitutionality of *all* laws.

Figure 1-3
Hierarchy of Law

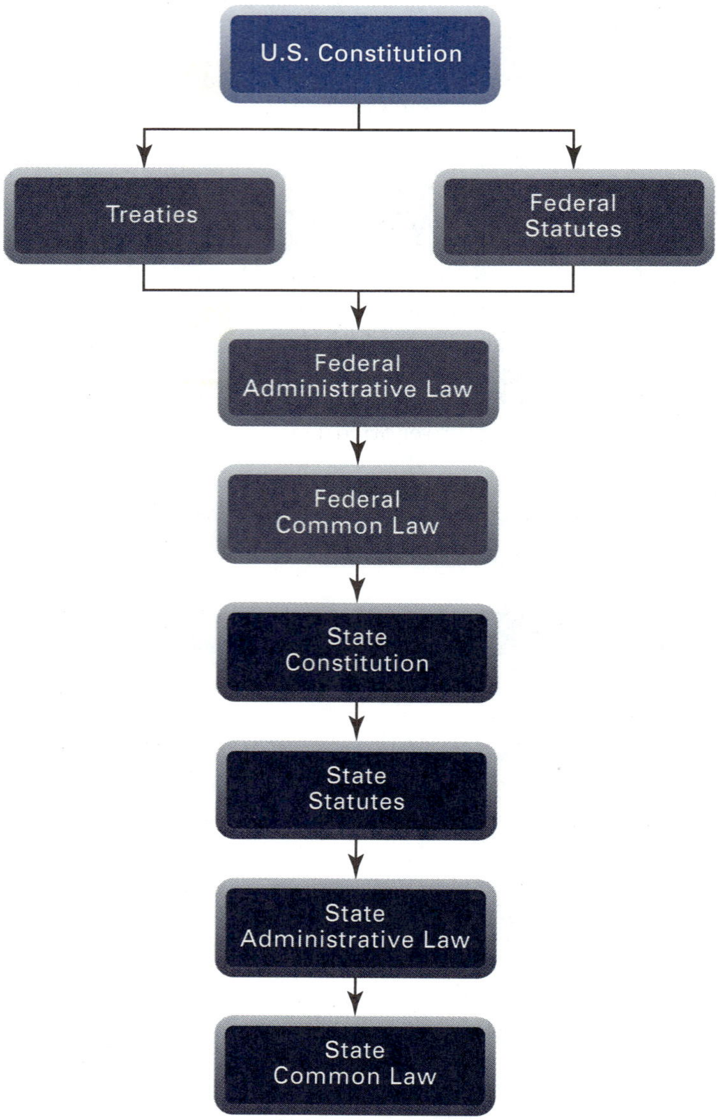

http:// U.S. Constitution: http://www.law.cornell.edu/constitution/constitution.table.html
State constitutions: http://www.law.cornell.edu/states.listing.html
Supreme Court decisions: http://supct.law.cornell.edu/supct/

JUDICIAL LAW

The U.S. legal system, a **common law system** like the system first developed in England, relies heavily on the judiciary as a source of law and on the adversary system for settling disputes. In an **adversary system** the parties, not the court, must initiate and conduct litigation. This approach is based on the belief that the truth is more likely to emerge from the investigation and presentation of evidence by two opposing parties, both motivated by self-interest, than from judicial investigation motivated only by official duty. In addition to the United States and England, the common law system is used in other English-speaking countries, including Canada and Australia.

In distinct contrast to the common law system are civil law systems, which are based on Roman law. **Civil law systems** depend on comprehensive legislative enactments (called codes) and an **inquisitorial system** of determining disputes. In the inquisitorial system, the judiciary initiates litigation, investigates pertinent facts, and conducts the presentation of evidence. The civil law system prevails in most of Europe, Scotland, the state of Louisiana, the province of Quebec, Latin America, and parts of Africa and Asia.

Common Law The courts in common law systems have developed a body of law that serves as precedent for determining later controversies. In this sense, common law, also called case law or judge-made law, is distinguished from other sources of law, such as legislation and administrative rulings.

To evolve in a stable and predictable manner, the common law has developed by application of *stare decisis*. Under the principle of ***stare decisis*** ("to stand by the decisions"), courts adhere to and rely on rules of law that they or superior courts relied on and applied in prior similar decisions. Judicial decisions thus have two uses: to determine with finality the case currently being decided and to indicate how the court will decide similar cases in the future. *Stare decisis* does not, however, preclude courts from correcting erroneous decisions or from choosing among conflicting precedents. Thus, the doctrine allows sufficient flexibility for the common law to change. The strength of the common law is its ability to adapt to change without losing its sense of direction.

http:// Federal case law: http://www.ll.georgetown.edu/federal/judicial/index.cfm
State case law: http://www.law.cornell.edu/opinions.html#state

Equity As the common law developed in England, it became overly rigid and beset with technicalities. As a consequence, in many cases no remedies were provided because the judges insisted that a claim must fall within one of the recognized forms of action. Moreover, courts of common law could provide only limited remedies; the principal type of relief obtainable was a money judgment. Consequently, individuals who could not obtain adequate relief from monetary awards began to petition the king directly for justice. He, in turn, came to delegate these petitions to his chancellor.

Gradually, there evolved what was in effect a new and supplementary system of needed judicial relief for those who could not receive adequate remedies through the common law. This new system, called **equity**, was administered by a court of chancery presided over by the chancellor. The chancellor, deciding cases on "equity and good conscience," regularly provided relief where common law judges had refused to act or where the remedy at law was inadequate. Thus, there grew up, side by side, two systems of law administered by different tribunals, the common law courts and courts of equity.

An important difference between common law and equity is that the chancellor could issue a **decree**, or order, compelling a defendant to do, or refrain from doing, a specified act. A defendant who did not comply with this order could be held in contempt of court and punished by fine or imprisonment. This power of compulsion available in a court of equity opened the door to many needed remedies not available in a court of common law.

Courts of equity in some cases recognized rights that were enforceable at common law, but they provided more effective remedies. For example, in a court of equity, for breach of a land contract the buyer could obtain a decree of **specific performance** commanding the defendant seller to perform his part of the contract by transferring title to the land. Another powerful and effective remedy available only in the courts of equity was the **injunction**, a court order requiring a party to do or refrain from doing a specified act. Another remedy not available elsewhere was **reformation**, where, upon the ground of mutual mistake, an action could be brought to reform or change the language of a written agreement to conform to the actual intention of the contracting parties. An action for **rescission** of a contract, which allowed a party to invalidate a contract under certain circumstances, was another remedy.

Although courts of equity provided remedies not available in courts of law, they granted such remedies only at their discretion, not as a matter of right. This discretion was exercised according to the general legal principles, or **maxims**, formulated by equity courts over the years.

In nearly every jurisdiction in the United States, courts of common law and equity have merged into a single court

CONCEPT REVIEW

Comparison of Law and Equity

	Law	Equity
Availability	Generally	Discretionary: if remedy at law is inadequate
Precedents	*Stare decisis*	Equitable maxims
Jury	If either party demands	None in federal and almost all states
Remedies	Judgment for monetary damages	Decree of specific performance, injunction, reformation, rescission

that administers both systems of law. Vestiges of the old division remain, however. For example, the right to a trial by jury applies only to actions at law, but not under federal law and in almost every state to suits filed in equity.

Restatements of Law The common law of the United States results from the independent decisions of the state and federal courts. The rapid increase in the number of decisions by these courts led to the establishment of the American Law Institute (ALI) in 1923. The ALI is composed of a distinguished group of lawyers, judges, and law teachers who set out to prepare "an orderly restatement of the general common law of the United States, including in that term not only the law developed solely by judicial decision, but also the law that has grown from the application by the courts of statutes that were generally enacted and were in force for many years."

Regarded as the authoritative statement of the common law of the United States, the Restatements cover many important areas of the common law, including torts, contracts, agency, property, and trusts. Although not law in themselves, they are highly persuasive, and courts frequently have used them to support their opinions. Because they provide a concise and clear statement of much of the common law, relevant portions of the Restatements are relied on frequently in this book.

http:// The American Law Institute: http://www.ali.org

LEGISLATIVE LAW

Since the end of the nineteenth century, legislation has become the primary source of new law and ordered social change in the United States. The annual volume of legislative law is enormous. Justice Felix Frankfurter's remarks to the New York City Bar in 1947 are even more appropriate today:

> Inevitably the work of the Supreme Court reflects the great shift in the center of gravity of law-making. Broadly speaking, the number of cases disposed of by opinions has not changed from term to term. But even as late as 1875 more than 40 percent of the controversies before the Court were common-law litigation, fifty years later only 5 percent, while today cases not resting on statutes are reduced almost to zero. It is therefore accurate to say that courts have ceased to be the primary makers of law in the sense in which they "legislated" the common law. It is certainly true of the Supreme Court that almost every case has a statute at its heart or close to it.

This emphasis on legislative or statutory law has occurred because common law, which develops evolutionarily and haphazardly, is not well suited for making drastic or comprehensive changes. Moreover, while courts tend to be hesitant about overruling prior decisions, legislatures commonly repeal prior enactments. In addition, legislatures may choose the issues they wish to address, whereas courts may deal only with those issues presented by actual cases. As a result, legislatures are better equipped to make the dramatic, sweeping, and relatively rapid changes in the law that technological, social, and economic innovations compel.

While some business law topics, such as contracts, agency, property, and trusts, still are governed principally by the common law, most areas of commercial law, including partnerships, corporations, sales, commercial paper, secured transactions, insurance, securities regulation, antitrust, and bankruptcy have become largely statutory. Because most states enacted their own statutes dealing with these branches of commercial law, a great diversity developed among the states and hampered the conduct of commerce on a national scale. The increased need for greater uniformity brought about the formation of the National Conference of Commissioners on Uniform State Laws to prepare legislation that would reduce the conflicts among state laws.

The most successful example is the ***Uniform Commercial Code*** (UCC), which was prepared under the joint sponsorship and direction of the National Conference of Commissioners on Uniform State Laws and the American Law Institute. All fifty states (although Louisiana has adopted only Articles 1, 3, 4, 5, 7, and 8), the District of Columbia, and the Virgin Islands have adopted the Uniform Commercial Code.

Other uniform laws include the Uniform Partnership Act, the Uniform Limited Partnership Act, the Model Business Corporation Act, and the Uniform Probate Code.

http:// U.S. Code: http://www4.law.cornell.edu/uscode/
State statutes: http://www.law.cornell.edu/states/listing.html
The National Conference of Commissioners on Uniform State Laws: http://www.nccusl.org/
Uniform Commercial Code: http://www.law.cornell.edu/uniform/ucc.html
Other Uniform Laws: http://www.law.upenn.edu/bll/ulc/ulc_frame.htm

Treaties A **treaty** is an agreement between or among independent nations. The United States Constitution authorizes the President to enter into treaties with the advice and consent of the Senate, "providing two thirds of the Senators present concur."

Treaties may be entered into only by the federal government, not by the states. A treaty signed by the President and approved by the Senate has the legal force of a federal statute. Accordingly, a federal treaty may supersede a prior federal statute, while a federal statute may supersede a prior treaty. Like statutes, treaties are subordinate to the federal Constitution and subject to judicial review.

http:// Online treaties: http:// www.asil.org/resource/treaty1.htm#sect21

Executive Orders In addition to the executive functions, the President of the United States also has authority to issue laws, which are called **executive orders.** This authority typically derives from specific delegation by federal legislation. An executive order may amend, revoke, or supersede a prior executive order. An example of an executive order is the one issued by President Johnson in 1965 prohibiting discrimination by federal contractors on the basis of race, color, sex, religion, or national origin in employment on any work the contractor performed during the period of the federal contract.

The governors of the states enjoy comparable authority to issue executive orders.

http:// Executive orders: http://www.archives.gov/federal_register/executive_orders/disposition_tables.html

ADMINISTRATIVE LAW

Administrative law is the branch of public law that is created by administrative agencies in the form of rules, regulations, orders, and decisions to carry out the regulatory powers and duties of those agencies. It also deals with controversies arising among individuals and these public officials and agencies. Administrative functions and activities concern general matters of public health, safety, and welfare, including the establishment and maintenance of military forces, police, citizenship and naturalization, taxation, environmental protection, the regulation of transportation, interstate highways, waterways, television, radio, and trade and commerce.

Because of the increasing complexity of the nation's social, economic, and industrial life, the scope of administrative law has expanded enormously. In 1952 Justice Jackson stated that "the rise of administrative bodies has been the most significant legal trend of the last century, and perhaps more values today are affected by their decisions than by those of all the courts, review of administrative decisions apart." This is evidenced by the great increase in the number and activities of federal government boards, commissions, and other agencies. Certainly, agencies create more legal rules and decide more controversies than all the legislatures and courts combined.

http:// Code of Federal Regulations: http://www4.law.cornell.edu/cfr/

LEGAL ANALYSIS

Decisions in state trial courts generally are not reported or published. The precedent a trial court sets is not sufficiently weighty to warrant permanent reporting. Except in New York and a few other states where selected opinions of trial courts are published, decisions in trial courts are simply filed in the office of the clerk of the court, where they are available for public inspection. Decisions of state courts of appeals are published in consecutively numbered volumes called "reports." In most states, court decisions are found in the official state reports of that state. In addition, state reports are published by West Publishing Company in a regional reporter called the National Reporter System, composed of the following: Atlantic (A. or A.2d); South Eastern (S.E. or S.E.2d); South Western (S.W. or S.W.2d); New York Supplement (N.Y.S. or N.Y.S.2d); North Western (N.W. or N.W.2d); North Eastern (N.E. or N.E.2d); Southern (So. or So.2d); and Pacific (P. or P.2d). A number of states no longer publish official reports and have designated a commercial reporter as the authoritative source of state case law. After they are published, these opinions, or "cases," are referred to ("cited") by giving the name of the case; the volume, name, and page of the official state report, if any, in which it is published; the volume, name, and page of the particular set and series of the National Reporter System; and the volume, name, and page of any other selected case series. For instance, *Lefkowitz v. Great*

Across the Globe: Four Major Legal Systems

Today, in an ever closer international world, nations and businesses find themselves dealing more and more with legal systems other than their own. As a result, they no longer can afford to ignore different types of legal reasoning.

Whereas national legal systems often differ in their particulars, they tend to fall into one of four major legal traditions, each of which represents a different approach to keeping the peace, maintaining stability, providing justice, and interpreting social reality. The four systems are

1. civil law,
2. common law,
3. socialist law, and
4. religious/customary law.

According to today's comparative legal scholars, civil law remains the oldest and most influential legal system operating in the modern Western world. The system derives from the Roman-Germanic tradition, which had its origins in the ancient Roman Empire. Sometime around 450 B.C., the Romans produced their first written legal code, known as the Twelve Tables of Rome. Later, as the Roman Empire spread from Greece to Gaul, the Romans carried with them their legal system, defined by administrative order, attention to detail, and official edict.

Once Rome crumpled under the invasion of Germanic tribes, however, this system of law might have been lost forever if the Byzantine Emperor Justinian I had not ordered the making of a written compilation in the sixth century. The Corpus Juris Civilis, or the Body of Civil Law, was completed around 534 A.D.

During the Renaissance, European scholars, such as those at the University of Bologna in Italy, eventually rediscovered the Justinian compilation when they turned to classical antiquity for intellectual models. So impressed were they with the Corpus Juris Civilis that they lauded it as "written reason."

Hundreds of years later, when Europe began to produce stronger, more centralized governments, Roman law served as the foundation for national codes of law. In the seventeenth century, the Scandinavian countries developed the first such codes. Then, in 1804, under Napoleon Bonaparte, France enacted its Code Napoleon, which embodied the principles of the French Revolution and which came to represent the first modern civil law code. In 1896, Germany also enacted a civil code.

England, on the other hand, followed a course completely different from that of continental Europe. Even as part of the Roman Empire, England had managed to retain its local customs, which did not provide for a national, unified body of law. Not until William of Normandy invaded the island country in 1066 did Britain begin to develop a centralized legal system. That system would become known as the common law.

During the rule of William the Conqueror, English law grew out of the royal courts, where royal judges decided specific disputes of interest to the crown. Often, these disputes involved arguments over taxes, since William I was the first ruler of his time to impose a national tax on landed property. In fact, the Court of Exchequer, the first common law court, mainly decided tax disputes.

Unlike Europe's civil law, then, which developed as a law of principle and a systematic codification of justice, England's common law evolved as a law of procedure and precedent, used to solve practical problems. Judges, rather than university scholars, created and furthered the system. Because of the nature of their courtrooms, they relied heavily on trial procedure, evidence, and case law, rather than code.

Today, England, Canada, Australia, New Zealand, and the United States all use a form of common law. Continental Europe, Latin America, Japan, South Korea, and large areas of Africa employ a system of civil law.

In the twentieth century, still another legal system, socialism, played an important role in such places as the former Soviet Union, the countries of Eastern Europe, the People's Republic of China, North Korea, and Cuba.

Socialism, largely the product of German and Russian thought of the late nineteenth and early twentieth centuries, is the youngest of the four major legal systems. Until 1917, Russia relied on a form of civil law; then, with the Bolshevik revolution, the country embraced a legal concept unlike anything the industrial world had seen before. Based on the philosophy of Karl Marx and Frederich Engels, socialism centered on a revolutionary idea: the turning of society's economic base away from capitalism would lead to a new social order, marked by collective ownership of the means of production and a proletarian equality. Law, then, could serve a revolutionary purpose, in that the state could use it not only to settle disputes or provide justice, but also to transform society.

Finally, religious law continues to be an important legal force in the world today, especially in Muslim countries. The Islamic religion, which calls on its believers to follow strict rules of conduct, is the national law in such places as Iran and Saudi Arabia. The law of Islam is known as Shari'a, which in Arabic translates as "jurisprudence." It is based primarily on the Koran, on sayings of the Prophet Muhammad, and on the writings of Islamic scholars.

THE LAW AND YOU

State Bar Asssociations

Alabama: http://www.alabar.org/brochures/fees.cfm ("Lawyers and Legal Fees")

Arizona: http://www.azbar.org/PublicResources/pubinfo.asp ("Tips for Hiring and Working with a Lawyer")

California: http://www.calbar.ca.gov/state/calbar/calbar_home.jsp ("How Can I Find and Hire the Right Lawyer?")

Colorado: http://www.cobar.org/group/display.cfm?GenID=417 ("How to Choose and Use a Lawyer")

Florida: http://www.flabar.org/ ("Attorney-Client")

Georgia: http://www.gabar.org/ ("Lawyers and Legal Fees")

Illinois: http://www.illinoislawyerfinder/home.html ("Know Your Illinois Lawyer")

Iowa: http://www.iowabar.org/pamphlet.nsf/$about!OpenAbout ("The Legal Profession")

Louisiana: http://www.lsba.org/Public_Resources/consumer_brochures.html ("Answers to Commonly Asked Questions About Lawyers")

Maine: http://www.mainebar.org/ (legal information pamphlets) ("What Should I Know About Lawyers and Their Fees?")

Maryland: http://www.msba.org/public/ brochure.htm ("When You Need a Lawyer"; "Lawyers and Legal Fees")

Minnesota: http://www.mnbar.org/consumer.htm ("Selecting a Lawyer"; "Helping Your Lawyer Help You")

Mississippi: http://www.msbar.org/ ("How to Choose a Lawyer")

Missouri: http://www.mobar.org/ (brochures on legal topics) ("The Client Resource Guide")

Montana: http://www.montanabar.org/ ("When You Need a Lawyer")

Nevada: http://www.nvbar.org/ (public services) ("Lawyer Referral and Information Service")

New Hampshire: http://www.nhbar.org/?area/15.html ("What to Expect from Your Lawyer")

New Jersey: http://www.ng.org/cgi-bin/redir.cgi?url=http://www.nisba.com ("Finding a Lawyer")

New York: http://www.nysba.org/ ("You and Your Lawyer")

Ohio: http://www.ohiobar.org/conres/pamphlets/ ("Attorneys")

Oklahoma: http://www.okbar.org/publicinfo/brochures/ ("Lawyers and Legal Fees")

Oregon: http://www.osbar.org/1legallinks/Public/legalinfo/specinfo.html ("Lawyers")

Rhode Island: http://www.ribar.com/public/default.asp/ ("How to Choose and Use a Lawyer")

South Carolina: http://www.scbar.org/Free_Publications/free_publications.htm ("Working with Your Lawyer")

South Dakota: http://www.sdbar.org/public/default.htm ("Selecting a Lawyer")

Tennessee: http://www.tba.org/LawBytes/LawBytes.html ("Attorneys/Legal Services")

Washington: http://www.wsba.org/public/consumer/default.html ("Legal Fees")

Wisconsin: http://www.legalexplorer.com/legal/legalQA.asp?PositionPoint=5&Sid=5&Qid=1#quest ("Answering Your Questions About Hiring & Working with a Lawyer")

Minneapolis Surplus Store, Inc., 251 Minn. 188, 86 N.W.2d 689 (1957), indicates that the opinion in this case may be found in Volume 251 of the official Minnesota Reports at page 188 and in Volume 86 of the North Western Reporter, Second Series, at page 689, and that the opinion was delivered in 1957.

The decisions of courts in the federal system are found in a number of reports. Federal District Court opinions appear in the Federal Supplement (F.Supp.). Decisions of the U.S. Court of Appeals are found in the Federal Reporter (Fed., F.2d, or F.3d), while the U.S. Supreme Court's opinions are published in the United States Supreme Court Reports (U.S.), Supreme Court Reporter (S.Ct.), and Lawyers Edition (L.Ed.).

In reading the title of a case, such as *"Jones v. Brown,"* the *"v."* or *"vs."* means versus or against. In the trial court, Jones is the **plaintiff**, the person who filed the suit, and Brown is the **defendant**, the person against whom the suit was brought. When the case is appealed, some, but not all, courts of appeals or appellate courts place the name of the party who appeals, or the **appellant**, first, so that *"Jones v. Brown"* in the trial court becomes, if Brown loses and hence becomes the appellant, *"Brown v. Jones"* in the appellate court. Therefore, it is not always possible to determine from the title itself who was the plaintiff and who was the defendant. You must carefully read the facts of each case and clearly identify each party in your mind to understand the discussion by the appellate court. In a criminal case the caption in the trial court will first designate the prosecuting governmental unit and then will indicate the defendant, as in *"State v. Jones"* or *"Commonwealth v. Brown."*

The study of reported cases requires an understanding and application of legal analysis. Normally, the reported opinion in a case sets forth (a) the essential facts, the nature of the action, the parties, what happened to bring about the controversy, what happened in the lower court, and what pleadings are material to the issues; (b) the issues of law or fact; (c) the legal principles involved; (d) the application of these principles; and (e) the decision.

A serviceable method of analyzing and briefing cases after a careful reading and comprehension of the opinion is for students to write in their own language a brief containing the following:

1. the facts of the case
2. the issue or question involved
3. the decision of the court
4. the reasons for the decision

The following excerpt from Professor Karl Llewellyn's *The Bramble Bush* contains a number of useful suggestions for reading cases.

> The first thing to do with an opinion, then, is read it. The next thing is to get clear the actual decision, the judgment rendered. Who won, the plaintiff or defendant? And watch your step here. You are after in first instance the plaintiff and defendant *below*, in the trial court. In order to follow through what happened you must therefore first know the outcome *below*; else you do not see what was appealed from, nor by whom. You now follow through in order to see exactly what *further* judgment has been rendered on appeal. The stage is then clear of form—although of course you do not yet know all that these forms mean, that they imply. You can turn now to what you want peculiarly to know. Given the actual judgments below and above as your indispensable framework—what has the case decided, and what can you derive from it as to what will be decided later?
>
> You will be looking, in the opinion, or in the preliminary matter plus the opinion, for the following: a statement of the facts the court assumes; a statement of the precise way the question has come before the court—which includes what the plaintiff wanted below, and what the defendant did about it, the judgement below, and what the trial court did that is complained of; then the outcome on appeal, the judgment; and, finally the reasons this court gives for doing what it did. This does not look so bad. But it is much worse than it looks.
>
> For all our cases are decided, all our opinions are written, all our predictions, all our arguments are made, on certain four assumptions. They are the first presuppositions of our study. They must be rutted into you till you can juggle with them standing on your head and in your sleep.
>
> 1. *The court must decide the dispute that is before it.* It cannot refuse because the job is hard, or dubious, or dangerous.
> 2. *The court can decide only the particular dispute which is before it.* When it speaks to that question it speaks *ex cathedra*, with authority, with finality, with an almost magic power. When it speaks to the question before it, it announces *law*, and if what it announces is new, it legislates, it *makes* the law. But when it speaks to any other question at all, it says mere words, which no man needs to follow. Are such words worthless? They are not. We know them as judicial *dicta*; when they are wholly off the point at issue we call them *obiter dicta*—words dropped along the road, wayside remarks. Yet even wayside remarks shed light on the remarker. They may be very useful in the future to him, or to us. But he will not feel bound to them, as to his *ex cathedra* utterance. They came not hallowed by a Delphic frenzy. He may be slow to change them; but not so slow as in the other case.
> 3. *The court can decide the particular dispute only according to a* general *rule which covers a whole class of like disputes.* Our legal theory does not admit of single decisions standing on their own. If judges are free, are indeed forced, to decide new cases for which there is no rule, they must at least make a new rule as they decide. So far, good. But how wide, or how narrow, is the general rule in this particular case? That is a troublesome matter. The practice of our case-law, however, is I think fairly stated thus: it pays to be suspicious of general rules which look too wide; it pays to go slow in feeling *certain* that a wide rule has been laid down at all, or that, if seemingly laid down, it will be followed. For there is a fourth accepted canon:
> 4. *Everything, everything, everything, big or small, a judge may say in an opinion, is to be read with primary reference to the particular dispute, the particular question before him.* You are not to think that the words mean what they might if they stood alone. You are to have your eye on the case in hand, and to learn how to interpret all that has been said merely as a reason for deciding *that* case *that* way.

By way of example, the following edited case of *Caldwell v. Bechtel, Inc.* is presented and then briefed using the suggested format. (Note: The cases in the rest of this text have their facts and decision summarized for the reader's convenience. The edited portion of the case begins with the judge's name.)

Caldwell v. Bechtel, Inc.

United States Court of Appeals, District of Columbia Circuit, 1980
631 F.2d 989

OPINION MacKinnon, J. We are here concerned with a claim for damages by a worker who allegedly contracted silicosis while he was mucking in a tunnel under construction as part of the metropolitan subway system [Washington Metropolitan Area Transit Authority (WMATA) **(http://www.wmata.com)**]. The basic issue is whether a consultant engineering firm owed the worker a duty to protect him against unreasonable risk of harm.

* * *

In attempting to convince the court that it owes no duty of reasonable care to protect appellant's safety, Bechtel **(http://www.bechtel.com)** argues that by its contract with WMATA it assumed duties only to WMATA. Appellant has not brought action, however, for breach of contract but rather seeks damages for an asserted breach of the duty of reasonable care. Unlike contractual duties, which are imposed by agreement of the parties to a contract, a duty of due care under tort law is based primarily upon social policy. The law imposes upon individuals certain expectations of conduct, such as the expectancy that their actions will not cause foreseeable injury to another. These societal expectations, as formed through the common law, comprise the concept of duty.

Society's expectations, and the concomitant duties imposed, vary in response to the activity engaged in by the defendant. If defendant is driving a car, he will be held to exercise the degree of care normally exercised by a reasonable person in like circumstances. Or if defendant is engaged in the practice of his profession, he will be held to exercise a degree of care consistent with his superior knowledge and skill. Hence, when defendant Bechtel engaged in consulting engineering services, the company was required to observe a standard of care ordinarily adhered to by one providing such services, possessing such skill and expertise.

A secondary but equally important principle involved in a determination of duty is to whom the duty is owed. The answer to this question is usually framed in terms of the foreseeable plaintiff, in other words, one who might foreseeably be injured by defendant's conduct. This secondary principle also serves to distinguish tort law from contract law. While in contract law, only one to whom the contract specifies that a duty be rendered will have a cause of action for its breach, in tort law, society, not the contract, specifies to whom the duty is owed, and this has traditionally been the foreseeable plaintiff.

It is important to keep these differences between contract and tort duties in mind when examining whether Bechtel's undertaking of contractual duties to WMATA created a duty of reasonable care toward Caldwell. Dean Prosser expressed the relationship in this terse fashion.

> [B]y entering into a contract with A, the defendant may place himself in such a relation toward B that the law will impose upon him an obligation, sounding in tort and not in contract, to act in such a way that B will not be injured. The incidental fact of the existence of the contract with A does not negative the responsibility of the actor when he enters upon a course of affirmative conduct which may be expected to affect the interests of another person.

* * *

Analyzing the common law, Prosser noted that courts have found a duty to act for the protection of another when certain relationships exist, such as carrier-passenger, innkeeper-guest, shipper-seaman, employer-employee, shopkeeper-visitor, host-social guest, jailer-prisoner, and school-pupil. These holdings suggest that courts have been eroding the general rule that there is no duty to act to help another in distress, by creating exceptions based upon a relationship between the actors.

* * *

We find that case law provides many such analogous situations from which the principles deserving of application to this case may be culled. The foregoing concepts of duty converge in this case, as the facts include both the WMATA-Bechtel contractual relationship from which it was foreseeable that a negligent undertaking by Bechtel might injure the appellant, and a special relationship established between Bechtel and the appellant because of Bechtel's superior skills, knowledge of the dangerous condition, and ability to protect appellant.

We reverse the summary judgment of the district court, and hold that as a matter of law, on the record as we are required to view it at this time, Bechtel owed Caldwell a duty of due care to take reasonable steps to protect him from the foreseeable risk of harm to his health posed by the excessive concentration of silica dust in the Metro tunnels. We remand so that Caldwell will have an opportunity to prove, if he can, the other elements of his negligence action.

Brief of Caldwell v. Bechtel, Inc.

FACTS Caldwell was a laborer who now suffers from silicosis. He claims that he contracted the disease while working in a tunnel under construction as part of the Washington Metropolitan Area Transportation Authority (WMATA). He brought his action for damages against Bechtel, Inc., a consultant engineering firm under contract with WMATA for the project.

ISSUE Did Bechtel breach a duty of due care owed to Caldwell to take reasonable steps to protect him from the foreseeable risk of harm to his health posed by the excessive concentration of silica dust in the subway tunnels?

DECISION In favor of Caldwell. Summary judgment reversed and case remanded to the district court.

REASONS Caldwell has not brought an action for breach of contract as Bechtel seems to believe. Rather, he seeks damages for an alleged breach of the duty of reasonable care. Unlike contractual duties, which are imposed by agreement of the parties to a contract, a duty of due care under tort law is based primarily on social policy. That is, the law imposes upon individuals the expectation that their actions will not cause foreseeable injury to another. These societal expectations comprise the concept of duty—a concept that varies in response to the activity engaged in by the individual. Moreover, the duty is owed to anyone who might foreseeably be injured by the conduct of the actor in question. In contrast, under contract law, a duty is owed only to those parties specified in the contract. Here, by entering into a contract with WMATA, Bechtel placed itself in such a relation toward Caldwell that the law will impose upon it an obligation in tort, and not in contract, to act in such a way that Caldwell would not be injured.

Chapter Summary

Nature of Law

Definition of Law "a rule of civil conduct prescribed by the supreme power in a state, commanding what is right, and prohibiting what is wrong" (Blackstone)

Functions of Law to maintain stability in the social, political, and economic system through dispute resolution, protection of property, and the preservation of the state, while simultaneously permitting ordered change

Laws and Morals are different but overlapping: law provides sanctions while morals do not

Law and Justice are separate and distinct concepts; justice is the fair, equitable, and impartial treatment of competing interests with due regard for the common good

Classification of Law

Substantive and Procedural
- *Substantive Law* law creating rights and duties
- *Procedural Law* rules for enforcing substantive law

Public and Private
- *Public Law* law dealing with the relationship between government and individuals
- *Private Law* law governing the relationships among individuals and legal entities

Civil and Criminal

- *Civil Law* law dealing with rights and duties the violation of which constitutes a wrong against an individual or other legal entity
- *Criminal Law* law establishing duties that, if violated, constitute a wrong against the entire community

Sources of Law

Constitutional Law fundamental law of a government establishing its powers and limitations

Judicial Law

- *Common Law* body of law developed by the courts that serves as precedent for determination of later controversies
- *Equity* body of law based upon principles distinct from common law and providing remedies not available at law

Legislative Law statutes adopted by legislative bodies

- *Treaties* agreements between or among independent nations
- *Executive Orders* laws issued by the President or by the governor of a state

Administrative Law is created by administrative agencies in the form of rules, regulations, orders, and decisions to carry out the regulatory powers and duties of those agencies

http://

Internet Exercise For the federal government and for your state, find examples of the following sources of law: (a) constitutional law, (b) judicial law, (c) legislative law, and (d) administrative law. (If such information on your state is not available, choose another state.)

CHAPTER 2

Business Ethics

Our characters are the result of our conduct.

ARISTOTLE, IN *NICOMACHEAN ETHICS* (C. 335 B.C.)

Learning Objectives

After reading this chapter you should be able to:

1. Describe the difference between law and ethics.
2. Compare the various ethical theories.
3. Describe cost-benefit analysis and explain when it should be used and when it should be avoided.
4. Explain Kohlberg's stages of moral development.
5. Explain the ethical responsibilities of business.

Business ethics is a subset of ethics: no special set of ethical principles applies only to the world of business. Immoral acts are immoral, whether or not a businessperson has committed them. In the last few years, countless business wrongs, such as insider trading, the Beech-Nut adulterated apple juice scandal, the Bhopal disaster, the Dalkon Shield tragedy, and the savings and loan industry collapse have been reported almost daily.

Ethics can be defined broadly as the study of what is right or good for human beings. It attempts to determine what people ought to do, or what goals they should pursue. **Business ethics**, as a branch of applied ethics, is the study and determination of what is right and good in business settings. Business ethics seeks to understand the moral issues that arise from business practices, institutions, and decision making and their relationship to generalized human values. Unlike legal analyses, analyses of ethics have no central authority, such as courts or legislatures, upon which to rely; nor do they follow clear-cut, universal standards. Nonetheless, despite these inherent limitations, it still may be possible to make meaningful ethical judgments. To improve ethical decision making, it is important to understand how others have approached the task.

Some examples of the many business ethics questions may help to clarify the definition of business ethics. In the employment relationship, countless ethical issues arise regarding the safety and compensation of workers, their civil rights (such as equal treatment, privacy, and freedom from sexual harassment), and the legitimacy of whistleblowing. In the relationship between business and its customers, ethical issues permeate marketing techniques, product safety, and consumer protection. The relationship between business and its owners bristles with ethical questions involving corporate governance, shareholder voting, and management's duties to the shareholders. The relationship among competing businesses involves numerous ethical matters, including fair competition and the effects of collusion. The interaction between business and society at large presents additional ethical dimensions: pollution of the physical environment, commitment to the community's economic and social infrastructure, and depletion of natural resources. Not only do all of these issues recur at the international level, but additional ones present themselves, such as bribery of foreign officials, exploitation of less-developed countries, and conflicts among differing cultures and value systems. (See "The Aftermath of Bhopal.")

In resolving the ethical issues raised by business conduct, it is helpful to use a seeing-knowing-doing model. First, the decision maker should ***see*** (identify) the ethical issues involved in the proposed conduct, including the ethical implications of the various available options. Second, the decision maker should ***know*** (resolve) what to do by choosing the best option. Finally, the decision maker should *do* (implement) the chosen option by developing implementing strategies.

This chapter first surveys the most prominent ethical theories (the knowing part of the decision, on which the great majority of philosophers and ethicists have focused). The chapter then examines ethical standards in business and the ethical responsibilities of business. It concludes with five ethical business cases, which give the student the opportunity to apply the seeing-knowing-doing model. The student (1) identifies the ethical issues presented in these cases; (2) resolves these issues by using one of the ethical theories described in the chapter, some other ethical theory, or a combination of the theories; and (3) develops strategies for implementing the ethical resolution.

http://

Ethics Resource Center: http://www.ethics.org/
DePaul University Institute for Business and Professional Ethics: http://commerce.depaul.edu/ethics/
Council for Ethics in Economics: http://www.businessethics.org/
Business for Social Responsibility: http://www.bsr.org/
International Business Ethics Institute: http://www.business-ethics.org/
EthicsWeb.ca: http://www.ethicsweb.ca
Business Enterprise Trust: http://www.banyansociety.org/commmoral/busethres/busethlinks/guidetobusinessethicssites. htm.

LAW VERSUS ETHICS

As discussed in Chapter 1, moral concepts strongly affect the law, but law and morality are not the same. Although it is tempting to say that "if it's legal, it's moral," such a proposition is generally too simplistic. For example, it would seem gravely immoral to stand by silently while a blind man walks off a cliff if one could prevent the fall by shouting a warning, even though one would not be legally obligated to do so. Similarly, moral questions arise concerning "legal" business practices, such as failing to fulfill a promise that is not legally binding; exporting products banned in the United States to third world countries where they are not prohibited; or slaughtering baby seals for fur coats. The mere fact that these practices are legal does not prevent them from being challenged on moral grounds.

Just as it is possible for legal acts to be immoral, it is equally possible for illegal acts to seem morally preferable to following the law. For example, it is the moral conviction of the great majority of people that those who sheltered Jews in violation of Nazi edicts during World War II and those who committed acts of civil disobedience in the 1950s and 1960s to challenge segregation laws in the United States were acting properly and that the laws themselves were immoral.

ETHICAL THEORIES

Philosophers have sought for centuries to develop dependable and universal methods for making ethical judgments. In earlier times, some thinkers analogized the discovery of ethical principles with the derivation of mathematical proofs. They asserted that people could discover fundamental ethical rules by applying careful reasoning *a priori*. (*A priori* reasoning is based on theory rather than experimentation and deductively draws conclusions from cause to effect and from generalizations to particular instances.) In more recent times, many philosophers have concluded that although careful reasoning and deep thought assist substantially in moral reasoning, experience reveals that the complexities of the world defeat most attempts to fashion precise, *a priori* guidelines. Nevertheless, a review of the most significant ethical theories is useful in the analysis of issues of business ethics.

ETHICAL FUNDAMENTALISM

Under **ethical fundamentalism,** or absolutism, individuals look to a central authority or set of rules to guide them in ethical decision making. Some look to the Bible; others look to the Koran or the writings of Karl Marx or to any number of living or deceased prophets. The essential characteristic of this approach is a reliance upon a central repository of wisdom. In some cases, such reliance is total. In others, followers of a religion or a spiritual leader may believe that all members of the group are obligated to assess moral dilemmas independently, according to each person's understanding of the dictates of the fundamental principles.

ETHICAL RELATIVISM

Ethical relativism is a doctrine asserting that actions must be judged by what individuals feel is right or wrong for themselves. It holds that when any two individuals or cultures differ regarding the morality of a particular issue or action, they are both correct because morality is relative. However, though ethical relativism promotes openmindedness and tolerance, it has limitations. If each person's actions are always correct for that person, then his behavior is, by definition, moral and, therefore, exempt from criticism. Once a person concludes that criticizing or punishing behavior in some cases is appropriate, he abandons ethical relativism and faces the task of developing a broader ethical methodology.

Although bearing a surface resemblance to ethical relativism, situational ethics actually differs substantially. **Situational ethics** holds that developing precise guidelines for effectively navigating ethical dilemmas is difficult because real-life decision making is so complex. To judge the morality of someone's behavior, the person judging must actually put herself in the other person's shoes to understand what motivated the other to choose a particular course of action. Situational ethics, however, does not cede the ultimate judgment of the propriety of an action to the actor; rather, it insists that, prior to evaluation, a person's decision or act be viewed from the actor's perspective.

UTILITARIANISM

Utilitarianism is a doctrine that assesses good and evil in terms of the consequences of actions. Those actions that produce the greatest net pleasure compared with net pain are better in a moral sense than those that produce less net pleasure. As Jeremy Bentham (http://www.utm.edu/research/iep/b/bentham.htm), one of the most influential proponents of utilitarianism, proclaimed, a good or moral act is one that results in "the greatest happiness for the greatest number."

The two major forms of utilitarianism are act utilitarianism and rule utalitarianism. **Act utalitarianism** asseses each separate act according to whether it maximizes pleasure over pain. For example, if telling a lie in a particular situation produces more overall pleasure than pain, then an act utilitarian would support lying as the moral thing to do. **Rule utilitarians**, disturbed by the unpredictability of act utilitarianism and its potential for abuse, follow a different approach. Rule utilitarianism holds that general rules must be established and followed even though, in some instances, following rules may produce less overall pleasure than not following them. It applies utilitarian principles in developing rules; thus, it supports rules that on balance produce the greatest satisfaction. Determining whether telling a lie in a given instance would produce greater pleasure than telling the truth is less important to the rule utilitarian than deciding whether a general practice of lying would maximize society's pleasure. If lying would not maximize pleasure generally, then one should follow a rule of not lying even though on occasion telling a lie would produce greater pleasure than would telling the truth.

Utilitarian notions underlie cost-benefit analysis, an analytical tool used by many business and government managers today. **Cost-benefit analysis** first quantifies in monetary terms and then compares the direct and indirect costs and benefits of program alternatives for meeting a specified objective. Cost-benefit analysis seeks the greatest economic efficiency, according to the underlying notion that, given two potential acts, the act achieving the greatest output at the least cost promotes the greatest marginal happiness over the less-efficient act, other things being equal.

The chief criticism of utilitarianism is that in some important instances it ignores justice. A number of situations would maximize the pleasure of the majority at great social cost to a minority. Another major criticism of utilitarianism is that measuring pleasure and pain in the fashion its supporters advocate is extremely difficult, if not impossible.

DEONTOLOGY

Deontological theories (from the Greek word *deon*, meaning duty or obligation) address the practical problems of utilitarianism by holding that certain underlying principles are right or wrong regardless of any pleasure or pain calculations. Believing that actions cannot be measured simply by their results but must be judged by means and motives as well, deontologists judge the morality of acts not so much by their consequences but by the motives that lead to them. A person not only must achieve just results but also must employ the proper means.

The best known deontological theory was proffered by the eighteenth-century philosopher Immanuel Kant (http://www.utm.edu/research/iep/k/kantmeta/htm). Under Kant's ***categorical imperative***, for an action to be moral, it (1) must potentially be a universal law that could be applied consistently and (2) must respect the autonomy and rationality of all human beings and not treat them as an expedient. That is, one should not do anything that he or she would not have everyone do in a similar situation. For example, you should not lie to colleagues unless you support the right of all colleagues to lie to one another. Similarly, you should not cheat others unless you advocate everyone's right to cheat. We apply Kantian reasoning when we challenge someone's behavior by asking: What if everybody acted that way?

Under Kant's approach, it would be improper to assert a principle to which one claimed personal exception, such as insisting that it was acceptable for you to cheat but not for anyone else to do so. This principle could not be universalized because everyone would then insist on similar rules from which only they were exempt.

Kant's philosophy also rejects notions of the end justifying the means. To Kant, every person is an end in himself or herself. Each person deserves respect simply because of his or her humanity. Thus, any sacrifice of a person for the greater good of society would be unacceptable to Kant.

In many respects, Kant's categorical imperative is a variation of the Golden Rule; and, like the Golden Rule, the categorical imperative appeals to the individual's self-centeredness.

MANAGERIAL insight

The Aftermath of Bhopal

When corporations operate internationally, they confront ethical issues related to political, social, and cultural differences among countries. Take, for example, the case of Union Carbide.

In 1984, the multinational chemical company had interests in thirty-five countries and, at least in the United States, boasted one of the best safety records among major manufacturers of chemical products. That was before the tragedy at Bhopal, India.

Union Carbide owned nearly 51 percent of Union Carbide India Limited (UCIL), a publicly traded corporation in India that ranked at the time as the country's twenty-first largest company. At the urging of the Indian government, UCIL went into the pesticide business in the 1960s, a time when India was attempting to modernize its agricultural base and produce more food. Also, at the government's urging, UCIL located in India's Bhopal region, a densely populated but extremely impoverished area. In addition, the subsidiary installed a manually operated safety system at the Bhopal plant, rather than an automatic one. (The manual system provided more jobs, a goal of the Indian government.) By the early 1980s, the UCIL plant was losing money. Squeezed by a drop in the demand for pesticides, the plant was operating at only 40 percent of its capacity. It also had taken steps to cut costs. One was to manufacture the commonly used pesticide, Sevin, in bulk quantities, from start to finish, at the plant. This required UCIL not only to make large quantities of methyl isocyanate (MIC) but also to store the highly dangerous, extremely volatile chemical on-site. The company also cut its workforce, which impaired plant maintenance.

Not long before midnight on Sunday, December 2, 1984, a Bhopal plant engineer, Suman Dey, noticed that the pressure and temperature gauges on tank E610, which held some forty-five tons of MIC, had climbed to the boiling point. The normally refrigerated tank held the chemical, deadly in its gaseous state, in a cool, liquid form. But now the tank had lost its refrigeration. Employees had reason to believe that the gauges did not work properly, yet they searched for a leak anyway. Then, shortly after midnight, Dey heard what sounded like an explosion in the tank. Within seconds, a toxic cloud of MIC escaped. The silent, deadly fog enveloped the area close to the plant and then rolled down toward Bhopal's railroad station and its main city.

The UCIL plant had been built in what was, at the time, an open area, but by the time of the accident, a large, densely populated shantytown had grown up around it. Squatters had moved in as close as the plant's gate. In the early morning hours of December 3, many of these squatters died where they fell, their lungs seared by MIC. Others were killed in the stampede to escape the deadly gas. As the cloud drifted over Bhopal, more victims fell in its wake. Of those who survived, many were permanently blinded or otherwise disabled. In all, approximately 200,000 people were injured. Today, estimates of the death toll range from more than 2,000 victims to as many as 30,000 victims.

When Union Carbide's chairperson, Warren M. Anderson, arrived in Bhopal shortly after the disaster, he was arrested and charged with homicide. In the United States, the company faced a takeover bid from GAF Corporation, which it avoided only by selling off its consumer products division, maker of Prestone antifreeze, Eveready batteries, and Glad Bags.

In 1989, the Indian Supreme Court ordered Union Carbide, now only a shadow of its former self, to pay $470 million to compensate Bhopal victims. Criminal charges against the company and its officials, though, were dropped.

For a multinational corporation like Union Carbide, the lesson of Bhopal is simple: Be careful. Yet how careful should a company be? Should multinational corporations maintain in their overseas plants safety standards the same as those they maintain in their U.S. operations? Or should the governments of host countries determine required safety standards?

Whatever the answers, any corporation doing business in another country should consider the following: To operate successfully in a foreign land requires a deep understanding of the political, social, and cultural differences among countries. Often, such an enterprise also demands a keen sense of advanced technology's impact on underdeveloped nations.

As does every theory, Kantian ethics has its critics. Just as deontologists criticize utilitarians for excessive pragmatism and flexible moral guidelines, utilitarians and others criticize deontologists for rigidity and excessive formalism. For example, if one inflexibly adopts as a rule to tell the truth, one ignores situations in which lying might well be justified. A person hiding a terrified wife from her angry, abusive husband would seem to be acting morally by falsely denying that the wife is at the person's house. Yet a deontologist, feeling bound to tell the truth, might ignore the consequences of truthfulness, tell the husband where his wife is, and create the possibility of a terrible tragedy. Another criticism of deontological theories is that the proper course may be difficult to determine when values or assumptions conflict.

SOCIAL ETHICS THEORIES

Social ethics theories assert that special obligations arise from the social nature of human beings. Such theories focus not only on each person's obligations to other members of society but also on the individual's rights and obligations within the society. For example, **social egalitarians** believe that society should provide each person with equal amounts of goods and services regardless of the contribution each makes to increase society's wealth.

Two other ethics theories have received widespread attention in recent years. One is the theory of **distributive justice** proposed by Harvard philosopher John Rawls (http://www.geocities.com/Athens/Parthenon/1643/rawls.html), which seeks to analyze the type of society that people in a "natural state" would establish if they could not determine in advance whether they would be talented, rich, healthy, or ambitious, relative to other members of society. According to distributive justice, the society contemplated through this "veil of ignorance" is the one that should be developed because it considers the needs and rights of all its members. Rawls did not argue that such a society would be strictly egalitarian, or that it would unfairly penalize those who turned out to be the most talented and ambitious. Instead, Rawls suggested that such a society would stress equality of opportunity, not of results. On the other hand, Rawls stressed that society would pay heed to the least advantaged to ensure that they did not suffer unduly and that they enjoyed society's benefits. To Rawls, society must be premised on justice. Everyone is entitled to his or her fair share in society, a fairness all must work to guarantee.

In contrast to Rawls, another Harvard philosopher, Robert Nozick (http://www.fasharvard.edu/~phildept/html/faculty_pages_7.html), stressed liberty, not justice, as the most important obligation that society owes its members. **Libertarians** stress market outcomes as the basis for distributing society's rewards. Only to the extent that one meets market demands does one deserve society's benefits. Libertarians oppose social interference in the lives of those who do not violate the rules of the marketplace, that is, in the lives of those who do not cheat others and who disclose honestly the nature of their transactions with others. The fact that some end up with fortunes while others accumulate little simply proves that some can play in the market effectively while others cannot. To libertarians, this is not unjust. What is unjust to them is any attempt by society to take wealth earned by citizens and distribute it to those who did not earn it.

These theories and others (e.g., Marxism) judge society in moral terms by its organization and by the way in which it distributes goods and services. They demonstrate the difficulty of ethical decision making in the context of a social organization: behavior that is consistently ethical from individual to individual may not necessarily produce a just society.

OTHER THEORIES

The preceding theories do not exhaust the possible approaches to evaluating ethical behavior; several other theories also deserve mention. **Intuitionism** holds that a rational person possesses inherent powers to assess the correctness of actions. Though an individual may refine and strengthen these powers, they are just as basic to humanity as our instincts for survival and self-defense. Just as some people are better artists or musicians, some people have more insight into ethical behavior than others. Consistent with intuitionism is the **good person philosophy**, which declares that if individuals wish to act morally, they should seek out and emulate those who always seem to know the right choice in any given situation and who always seem to do the right thing. One variation of these ethical approaches is the **"Television Test,"** which directs us to imagine that every ethical decision we make is being broadcast on nationwide television. An appropriate decision is one we would be comfortable broadcasting on national television for all to witness.

ETHICAL STANDARDS IN BUSINESS

In this section we will explore the application of the theories of ethical behavior to the world of business.

CHOOSING AN ETHICAL SYSTEM

In their efforts to resolve the moral dilemmas facing humankind, philosophers and other thinkers have struggled for years to refine the various systems previously discussed. All of the systems are limited, however, in terms of applicability and tend to produce unacceptable prescriptions for action in some circumstances. But to say that each system has limits is not to say it is useless. On the contrary, a number of these systems provide insight into ethical decision making and help us formulate issues and resolve moral dilemmas. Furthermore, concluding that moral standards are difficult to articulate and that moral boundaries are imprecise is not the same as concluding that moral standards are unnecessary or nonexistent.

Research by the noted psychologist Lawrence Kohlberg provides some insight into ethical decision making and lends credibility to the notion that moral growth, like physical growth, is part of the human condition. **Kohlberg** observed that people progress through sequential **stages of moral development** according to two major variables: age and reasoning. During the first level—the ***preconventional level***—a child's conduct is a reaction to the fear of punishment and, later, to the pleasure of reward. Although people who operate at this level may behave in a moral manner, they do so without understanding why their behavior is moral. The rules are imposed upon them. During adolescence—Kohlberg's ***conventional level***—people conform their behavior to meet the expectations of groups, such as family, peers, and eventually society. The motivation for conformity is loyalty, affection, and trust.

Figure 2-1
Kohlberg's Stages of Moral Development

Levels	Perspective	Justification
Preconventional (Childhood)	Self	Punishment/Reward
Conventional (Adolescent)	Group	Group Norms
Postconventional (Adult)	Universal	Moral Principles

Most adults operate at this level. According to Kohlberg, some reach the third level—the ***postconventional level***—where they accept and conform to moral principles because they understand *why* the principles are right and binding. At this level, moral principles are voluntarily internalized, not externally imposed. Moreover, individuals at this stage develop their own universal ethical principles and may even question the laws and values that society and others have adopted (see Figure 2-1 for Kohlberg's stages of moral development).

Kohlberg believed that not all people reach the third, or even the second, stage. He therefore argued that essential to the study of ethics was the exploration of ways to help people achieve the advanced stage of postconventional thought. Other psychologists assert that individuals do not pass sequentially from stage to stage but rather function in all three stages simultaneously.

Whatever the source of our ethical approach, we cannot avoid facing moral dilemmas that challenge us to recognize and to do the right thing. Moreover, for those who plan business careers, such dilemmas necessarily will have implications for many others—employees, shareholders, suppliers, customers, and society at large.

CORPORATIONS AS MORAL AGENTS

Because corporations are not persons but artificial entities created by the state, whether they can or should be held morally accountable is difficult to determine. Though, clearly, individuals within corporations can be held morally responsible, the corporate entity presents unique problems.

Commentators are divided on the issue. Some insist that only people can engage in behavior that can be judged in moral terms. Opponents of this view concede that corporations are not persons in any literal sense but insist that the attributes of responsibility inherent in corporations are sufficient to justify judging corporate behavior from a moral perspective.

ETHICAL RESPONSIBILITIES OF BUSINESS

Many people assert that the only responsibility of business is to maximize profit and that this obligation overrides any ethical or social responsibility. Although our economic system of modified capitalism is based on the pursuit of self-interest, it also contains components to check this motivation of greed. Our system has always recognized the need for some form of regulation, whether it be by the "invisible hand" of competition, the self-regulation of business, or government regulation.

REGULATION OF BUSINESS

As explained and justified by Adam Smith in *The Wealth of Nations* (1776) (http://www.socsci.mcmaster.ca/~econ/ugcm/3ll3/smith/), the capitalistic system is composed of six "institutions": economic motivation, private productive property, free enterprise, free markets, competition, and limited government. As long as all these constituent institutions continue to exist and operate in balance, the factors of production—land, capital, and labor—combine to produce an efficient allocation of resources for individual consumers and for the economy as a whole. To achieve this outcome, however, Smith's model requires that a number of conditions be satisfied: "standardized products, numerous firms in markets, each firm with a small share and unable by its actions alone to exert significant influence over price, no barriers to entry, and output carried to the point where each seller's marginal cost equals the going market price." E. Singer, *Antitrust Economics and Legal Analysis*.

History has demonstrated that the actual operation of the economy has satisfied almost none of these assumptions. More specifically, the actual competitive process falls considerably short of the assumptions of the classic economic model of perfect competition:

> Competitive industries are never perfectly competitive in this sense. Many of the resources they employ cannot be shifted to other employments without substantial cost and delay. The allocation of those resources, as between industries or as to relative proportions within a single industry, is unlikely to have been made in a way that affords the best possible expenditure of economic effort. Information is incomplete, motivation confused, and decision therefore ill informed and often unwise. Variations in efficiency are not directly reflected in variations of profit. Success is derived in large part from competitive selling efforts, which in the aggregate may be wasteful, and from differentiation of products, which may be undertaken partly by methods designed to impair the opportunity of the buyer to compare quality and price.
>
> C. Edwards, *Maintaining Competition*

In addition to capitalism's failure to allocate resources efficiently, it cannot be relied on to achieve all of the social and public policy objectives a pluralistic democracy requires. For example, the free enterprise model simply does not address equitable distribution of wealth, national defense, conservation of natural resources, full employment, stability in economic cycles, protection against economic dislocations, health and safety, social security, and other important social and economic goals. Increased **regulation of business** has occurred not only to preserve the competitive process in our economic system but also to achieve social goals extrinsic to the efficient allocation of resources, the "invisible hand" and self-regulation by business having failed to bring about these desired results. Such intervention attempts (1) to regulate both "legal" monopolies, such as those conferred by law through copyrights, patents, and trade symbols, and "natural" monopolies, such as utilities, transportation, and communications; (2) to preserve competition by correcting imperfections in the market system; (3) to protect specific groups, especially labor and agriculture, from marketplace failures; and (4) to promote other social goals. Successful government regulation involves a delicate balance between regulations that attempt to preserve competition and those that attempt to advance other social objectives. The latter should not undermine the basic competitive processes that provide an efficient allocation of economic resources.

CORPORATE GOVERNANCE

In addition to the broad demands of maintaining a competitive and fair marketplace, another factor demanding the ethical and social responsibility of business is the sheer size and power of individual corporations. The five thousand largest U.S. firms currently produce more than half of the nation's gross national product.

In a classic study published in 1932, Adolf Berle and Gardner Means concluded that great amounts of economic power had been concentrated in a relatively few large corporations, that the ownership of these corporations had become widely dispersed, and that the shareholders had become far removed from active participation in management. Since their original study, these trends have continued steadily. Thus, vast amounts of wealth and power are controlled by a small number of corporations, which are in turn controlled by a small group of corporate officers.

These developments raise a large number of social, policy, and ethical issues about the governance of large, publicly owned corporations. Many observers insist that companies playing such an important economic role should have a responsibility to undertake projects that benefit society in ways that go beyond mere financial efficiency in producing goods and services. In some instances, the idea of corporate obligations comes from industrialists themselves.

http:// Corporate Governance OECD: http://www.oecd.org/department/0,2688,en_2649_34795_1_1_1_1_1,00.html
Corporate Governance Network: http://www.corpgov.net/
The Business Roundtable: http://www.brtable.org/issue.cfm/2

ARGUMENTS AGAINST SOCIAL RESPONSIBILITY

A number of arguments oppose business involvement in socially responsible activities: profitability, unfairness, accountability, and expertise.

Profitability As Milton Friedman (http://www-hoover.stanford.edu/BIOS/friedman.html) and others have argued, businesses are artificial entities established to permit people to engage in profit-making, not social, activities. Without profits, they assert, there is little reason for a corporation to exist and no real way to measure the effectiveness of corporate activities. Businesses are not organized to engage in social activities; they are structured to produce goods and services for which they receive money. Their social obligation is to return as much of this money as possible to their direct stakeholders. In a free market with significant competition, the selfish pursuits of corporations will lead to maximizing output, minimizing costs, and establishing fair prices. All other concerns distract companies and interfere with achieving these goals.

Unfairness Whenever companies stray from their designated role of profit-maker, they take unfair advantage of company employees and shareholders. For example, a company may support the arts or education or spend excess funds on health and safety; however, these funds rightfully belong to the shareholders or employees. The company's decision to disburse these funds to others who may well be less deserving than the shareholders and employees is unfair. Furthermore, consumers can express their desires through the marketplace, and shareholders and employees can decide privately if they wish to make charitable contributions. In most cases, senior management consults the board of directors about supporting social concerns but does not seek the approval of the company's major stakeholders, thereby effectively disenfranchising these shareholders from actions that reduce their benefits from the corporation.

Accountability Corporations, as previously noted, are private institutions that are subject to a lower standard of accountability than are public bodies. Accordingly, a company may decide to support a wide range of social causes and yet submit to little public scrutiny. But a substantial potential for abuse exists in such cases. For one thing, a company could provide funding for a variety of causes its employees or shareholders did not support. It also could provide money "with strings attached," thereby controlling the recipients' agendas for less than socially beneficial purposes. For example, a drug company that contributes to a consumer group might implicitly or explicitly condition its assistance on the group's agreement never to criticize the company or the drug industry.

This lack of accountability warrants particular concern because of the enormous power corporations wield in modern society. Many large companies, like General Motors or Exxon, generate and spend more money in a year than all but a handful of the world's countries. If these companies suddenly began to vigorously pursue their own social agendas, their influence might well rival, and perhaps undermine, that of their national government. In a country like the United States, founded on the principles of limited government and the balance of powers, too much corporate involvement in social affairs might well present substantial problems. Without clear guidelines and accountability, companies pursuing their private visions of socially responsible behavior might well distort the entire process of governance.

There is a clear alternative to corporations engaging in socially responsible action. If society wishes to increase the resources devoted to needy causes, it has the power to do so. Let the corporations seek profits without the burden of a social agenda, let the consumers vote in the marketplace for the products and services they desire, and let the government tax a portion of corporate profits for socially beneficial causes.

Expertise Even though a corporation has an expertise in producing and selling its product, it may not possess a talent for recognizing or managing socially useful activities. Corporations become successful in the market because they can identify and meet the needs of their customers. Nothing suggests that this talent spills over into nonbusiness arenas. In fact, critics of corporate participation in social activities worry that corporations will prove unable to distinguish the true needs of society from their own narrow self-interests.

ARGUMENTS IN FAVOR OF SOCIAL RESPONSIBILITY

First, it should be recognized that even the critics of business acknowledge that the prime responsibility of business is to make a reasonable return on its investment by producing a quality product at a reasonable price. They do not suggest that business entities be charitable institutions. They do assert, however, that business has certain obligations beyond making a profit or not harming society. Such critics contend that business must help to resolve societal problems, and they offer a number of arguments in support of their position.

http:// Institute of Business Ethics, Codes of Conduct: http://www.ibe.org.uk/codesofconduct.html

The Social Contract Society creates corporations and gives them a special social status, including the granting of limited liability, which insulates owners from liability for debts their organizations incur. Supporters of social roles for corporations assert that limited liability and other rights granted to companies carry a responsibility: corporations, just like other members of society, must contribute to its betterment. Therefore, companies owe a moral debt to society to contribute to its overall well-being. Society needs a host of improvements, such as pollution control, safe products, a free marketplace, quality education, cures for illness, and freedom from crime. Corporations can help in each of these areas. Granted, deciding which social needs deserve corporate attention is difficult; however, this challenge does not lessen a company's obligation to choose a cause. Corporate America cannot ignore the multitude of pressing needs that remain, despite the efforts of government and private charities.

A derivative of the social contract theory is the **stakeholder model** for the societal role of the business corporation. Under the stakeholder model a corporation has fiduciary responsibilities—duty of utmost loyalty and good faith—to all of its stakeholders, not just its stockholders. Historically, the stockholder model for the role of business has been the norm. Under this theory, a corporation is viewed as private property owned by and for the benefit of its owners—the stockholders of the corporation. (For a full discussion of this legal model, see Chapter 36.) The stakeholder model, on the other hand, holds that corporations are responsible to society at large and more directly to all those constituencies on which they depend for their survival. Thus, it is argued that a corporation should be managed for the benefit of all of its stakeholders—stockholders, employees, customers, suppliers, and managers, as well as the local communities in which it operates. (See Figure 2-2 for the stakeholder model of corporate responsibility; compare it with Figure 36-1.)

Less Government Regulation According to another argument in favor of corporate social responsibility, the more responsibly companies act, the less the government

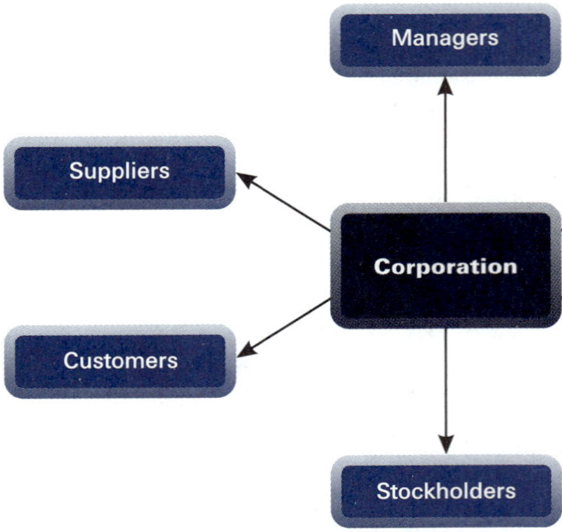

Figure 2-2
The Stakeholder Model

must regulate them. This idea, if accurate, would likely appeal to those corporations that typically view regulation with distaste, perceiving it as a crude and expensive way of achieving social goals. To them, regulation often imposes inappropriate, overly broad rules that hamper productivity and require extensive recordkeeping procedures to document compliance. If companies can use more flexible, voluntary methods of meeting a social norm such as pollution control, then government will be less tempted to legislate norms.

The argument can be taken further. Not only does anticipatory corporate action lessen the likelihood of government regulation, but also social involvement by companies creates a climate of trust and respect that reduces the overall inclination of government to interfere in company business. For example, a government agency is much more likely to show some leniency toward a socially responsible company than toward one that ignores social plights.

Long-Run Profits Perhaps the most persuasive argument in favor of corporate involvement in social causes is that such involvement actually makes good business sense. Consumers often support good corporate images and avoid bad ones. For example, consumers generally prefer to patronize stores with "easy return" policies. Even though such policies are not required by law, companies institute them because they create goodwill—an intangible though indispensable asset for ensuring repeat customers. In the long run, enhanced goodwill often rebounds to stronger profits. Moreover, corporate actions to improve the well-being of their communities make these communities more attractive to citizens and more profitable for business.

CHAPTER SUMMARY

Definitions

Ethics study of what is right or good for human beings

Business Ethics study of what is right and good in a business setting

Ethical Theories

Ethical Fundamentalism individuals look to a central authority or set of rules to guide them in ethical decision making

Ethical Relativism asserts that actions must be judged by what individuals subjectively feel is right or wrong for themselves

Situational Ethics one must judge a person's actions by first putting oneself in the actor's situation

Utilitarianism moral actions are those that produce the greatest net pleasure compared with net pain

- ***Act Utilitarianism*** assesses each separate act according to whether it maximizes pleasure over pain
- ***Rule Utilitarianism*** supports rules that on balance produce the greatest pleasure for society
- ***Cost-Benefit Analysis*** quantifies the benefits and costs of alternatives

Deontology holds that actions must be judged by their motives and means as well as their results

Social Ethics Theories focus on a person's obligations to other members in society and on the individual's rights and obligations within society

- ***Social Egalitarians*** believe that society should provide all its members with equal amounts of goods and services regardless of their relative contributions
- ***Distributive Justice*** stresses equality of opportunity rather than results
- ***Libertarians*** stress market outcomes as the basis for distributing society's rewards

Other Theories

- ***Intuitionism*** a rational person possesses inherent power to assess the correctness of actions
- ***Good Person*** individuals should seek out and emulate good role models

Ethical Standards in Business

Choosing an Ethical System Kohlberg's stages of moral development is a widely accepted model (See Figure 2-1.)

Corporations as Moral Agents because a corporation is a statutorily created entity, it is not clear whether it should be held morally responsible

Ethical Responsibilities of Business

Regulation of Business governmental regulation has been necessary because all the conditions for perfect competition have not been satisfied and free competition cannot by itself achieve other societal objectives

Corporate Governance vast amounts of wealth and power have become concentrated in a small number of corporations, which are in turn controlled by a small group of corporate officers

Arguments Against Social Responsibility

- ***Profitability*** because corporations are artificial entities established for profit-making activities, their only social obligation should be to return as much money as possible to shareholders
- ***Unfairness*** whenever corporations engage in social activities, such as supporting the arts or education, they divert funds rightfully belonging to shareholders and/or employees to unrelated third parties
- ***Accountability*** a corporation is subject to less public accountability than public bodies are
- ***Expertise*** although a corporation may have a high level of expertise in selling its goods and services, there is absolutely no guarantee that any promotion of social activities will be carried on with the same degree of competence

Arguments in Favor of Social Responsibility
- *The Social Contract* because society allows for the creation of corporations and gives them special rights, including a grant of limited liability, corporations owe a responsibility to society
- ***Less Government Regulation*** by taking a more proactive role in addressing society's problems, corporations create a climate of trust and respect that has the effect of reducing government regulation
- ***Long-Run Profits*** corporate involvement in social causes creates goodwill, which simply makes good business sense

QUESTIONS

1. You have an employee who has a chemical imbalance in the brain that causes him to be severely unstable. The medication that is available to deal with this schizophrenic condition is extremely powerful and decreases the taker's life span by one to two years for every year that the user takes it. You know that his doctors and family believe that it is in his best interest to take the medication. What course of action should you follow?

2. You have an employee from another country who is very shy. After a period of time, you notice that the quality of her performance is deteriorating rapidly. You find an appropriate time to speak with her and determine that she is extremely distraught. She informs you that her family has arranged a marriage for her and that she refuses to obey their contract. She further informs you that she is contemplating suicide. Two weeks later, after her poor performance continues, you determine that she is on the verge of a nervous breakdown; and once again she informs you that she is going to commit suicide. What should you do? Consider further that you can petition a court to have her involuntarily committed to a mental hospital. You know, however, that such a commitment would be considered an extreme insult by her family and that they might seek retribution. Does this alter your decision?

3. You receive a telephone call from a company you never do business with requesting a reference on one of your employees, Mary Sunshine. You believe Mary performs in a generally incompetent manner and would be delighted to see her take another job. You give her a glowing reference. Is this right? Explain.

4. You have just received a report suggesting that a chemical your company uses in its manufacturing process is very dangerous. You have not read the report, but you are generally aware of its contents. You believe that the chemical can be replaced fairly easily, but that if word gets out, panic may set in among employees and community members. A reporter asks if you have seen the report, and you say no. Is your behavior right or wrong? Explain.

5. Joe Jones, your neighbor and friend, and you bought lottery tickets at the corner drugstore. While watching the lottery drawing on TV with you that night, Joe leaped from the couch, waved his lottery ticket, and shouted, "I've got the winning number!" Suddenly, he clutched his chest, keeled over, and died on the spot. You are the only living person who knows that Joe, not you, bought the winning ticket. If you substitute his ticket for yours, no one will know of the switch and you will be $10 million richer. Joe's only living relative is a rich aunt whom he despised. Will you switch his ticket for yours? Explain.

6. Omega, Inc., a publicly held corporation, has assets of $100 million and annual earnings in the range of $13 to $15 million. Omega owns three aluminum plants, which are profitable, and one plastics plant, which is losing $4 million a year. Because of its very high operating costs, the plastics plant shows no sign of ever becoming profitable, and there is no evidence that the plant and the underlying real estate will increase in value. Omega decides to sell the plastics plant. The only bidder for the plant is Gold, who intends to use the plant for a new purpose, to introduce automation, and to replace all existing employees. Would it be ethical for Omega to turn down Gold's bid and keep the plastics plant operating indefinitely, for the purpose of preserving the employees' jobs? Explain.

7. You are the sales manager of a two-year-old electronics firm. At times, the firm has seemed on the brink of failure, but recently it has begun to be profitable. In large part, the profitability is due to the aggressive and talented sales force you have recruited. Two months ago, you hired Alice North, an honors graduate from the State University, who decided that she was tired of the Research Department and wanted to try sales.

   Almost immediately after you sent Alice out for training with Brad West, your best salesperson, he began reporting to you an unexpected turn of events. According to Brad, "Alice is terrific: she's confident, smooth, and persistent. Unfortunately, a lot of our buyers are good old boys who just aren't comfortable around young, bright women. Just last week, Hiram Jones, one of our biggest customers, told me that he simply won't continue to do business with 'young chicks' who think they invented the world. It's not that Alice is a know-it-all. She's not. It's just that these guys like to booze it up a bit, tell some off-color jokes, and then get down to business. Alice doesn't drink, and, although she never objects to the jokes, it's clear she thinks they're offensive." Brad felt that several potential deals had fallen through "because the mood just wasn't right with Alice there." Brad added, "I don't like a lot of these guys' styles myself, but I go along to make the sales. I just don't think Alice is going to make it."

When you call Alice in to discuss the situation, she concedes the accuracy of Brad's report but indicates that she's not to blame and insists that she be kept on the job. You feel committed to equal opportunity but don't want to jeopardize your company's ability to survive. What should you do?

8. Major Company subcontracted the development of part of a large technology system to Start-up Company, a small corporation specializing in custom computer systems. The contract, which was a major breakthrough for Start-up Company and crucial to its future, provided for an initial development fee and subsequent progress payments, as well as a final date for completion.

   Start-up Company provided Major Company with periodic reports indicating that everything was on schedule. After several months, however, the status reports stopped coming, and the company missed delivery of the schematics, the second major milestone. As an in-house technical consultant for Major Company, you visited Start-up Company and found not only that it was far behind schedule but that it had lied about its previous progress. Moreover, you determined that this slippage put the schedule for the entire project in severe jeopardy. The cause of Start-up's slippage was the removal of personnel from your project to work on short-term contracts to obtain money to meet the weekly payroll.

   Your company decided that you should stay at Start-up Company to monitor its work and to assist in the design of the project. After six weeks and some progress, Start-up is still way behind its delivery dates. Nonetheless, you are now familiar enough with the project to complete it in-house with Major's personnel.

   Start-up is still experiencing severe cash flow problems and repeatedly requests payment from Major. But your CEO, furious with Start-up's lies and deceptions, wishes to "bury" Start-up and finish the project using Major Company's internal resources. She knows that withholding payment to Start-up will put it out of business. What do you do? Explain.

9. A customer requested certain sophisticated tests on equipment he purchased from your factory. Such tests are very expensive and must be performed by a third party. The equipment met all of the industry standards but showed anomalies, which could not be explained.

   Though the problem appeared to be very minor, you decided to inspect the unit to try to understand the test data—a very expensive and time-consuming process. You informed the customer of this decision. A problem was found, but it was minor and was highly unlikely ever to cause the unit to fail. Rebuilding the equipment would be very expensive and time consuming; moreover, notifying the customer that you were planning to rebuild the unit would also put your overall manufacturing procedures in question. What should you do—fix it, ship it, inform the customer?

10. a. You are a project manager for a company making a major proposal to a Middle Eastern country. Your major competition is from Japan. Your local agent, who is closely tied to a very influential sheik, would receive a 5 percent commission if the proposal were accepted. Near the date for the decision, the agent asks you for $150,000 to grease the skids so that your proposal is accepted. What do you do?

    b. What if, after you say no, the agent goes to your vice president, who provides the money? What do you do?

    c. Your overseas operation learns that most other foreign companies in this Middle Eastern location bolster their business by exchanging currency on the gray market. You discover that your division is twice as profitable as budgeted due to the amount of domestic currency you have received on the gray market. What do you do?

http:// **Internet Exercise** Find and identify some Websites pertaining to business ethics that contain (a) political, social, or economic bias, (b) codes of conduct for companies, associations, or users, and (c) other significant material.

Business Ethics Cases

The business ethics cases that follow are based on the kinds of situations that companies regularly face in conducting business. You should first read each case carefully and in its entirety before attempting to analyze it. Second, you should identify the most important ethical issues arising from the situation. Often it is helpful to prioritize these issues. Third, you should identify the viable options for addressing these issues and the ethical implications of the identified options. This might include examining the options from the perspectives of the various ethical theories as well as the affected stakeholders. Fourth, you should reach a definite resolution of the ethical issues by choosing what you think is the best option. You should have a well-articulated rationale for your resolution. Finally, develop a strategy for implementing your resolution.

PHARMAKON DRUG COMPANY

Background

William Wilson, senior vice president of research, development, and medical (R, D & M) at Pharmakon Drug Company, received both his Ph.D. in biochemistry and his M.D. from the University of Oklahoma. Upon completion of his residency, Dr. Wilson joined the faculty at Harvard Medical School. He left Harvard after five years to join the research group at Merck & Co. Three years later, he went to Burroughs-Wellcome as director of R, D & M, and, after eight years, Dr. Wilson joined Pharmakon in his current position.

William Wilson has always been highly respected as a scientist, a manager, and an individual. He has also been an outstanding leader in the scientific community, particularly in the effort to attract more minorities into the field.

Pharmakon concentrates its research efforts in the areas of antivirals (with a focus on HIV), cardiovascular, respiratory, muscle relaxants, gastrointestinal, the central nervous system, and consumer health care (that is, nonprescription or over-the-counter medicines). Dr. Wilson is on the board of directors of Pharmakon and the company's executive committee. He reports directly to the chairman of the board and CEO, Mr. Jarred Swenstrum.

Declining Growth

During the previous eight years, Pharmakon experienced tremendous growth: 253 percent overall with yearly growth ranging from 12 percent to 25 percent. During this period, Pharmakon's R, D & M budget grew from $79 million to $403 million, and the number of employees rose from 1,192 to 3,273 (see Figure 2-3). During the previous two years, however, growth in revenue and earnings had slowed considerably. Moreover, in the current year, Pharmakon's revenues of $3.55 billion and earnings before taxes of $1.12 billion were up only 2 percent from the previous year. Furthermore, both revenues and earnings are projected to be flat or declining for the next five years.

The cessation of this period's tremendous growth and the likelihood of future decline have been brought about principally by two causes. First, a number of Pharmakon's most important patents have expired, and competition from generics has begun and could continue to erode its products' market shares. Second, as new types of health-care delivery organizations evolve, pharmaceutical companies' revenues and earnings will in all likelihood be adversely affected.

Figure 2-3 *Pharmakon Employment*

ATTRIBUTE/YEARS AGO	1	2	3	4	5	6	7	8
Total Employment	3,273	3,079	2,765	2,372	1,927	1,619	1,306	1,192
Minority Employment	272 (8.35%)	238 (7.7%)	196 (7.15%)	143 (6.0%)	109 (5.7%)	75 (4.6%)	53 (4.1%)	32 (2.7%)
Revenue ($ million)	3,481	3,087	2,702	2,184	1,750	1,479	1,214	986
Profit ($ million)	1,106	1,021	996	869	724	634	520	340
R, D & M Budget ($ million)	403	381	357	274	195	126	96	79

Problem and Proposed Solutions

In response, the board of directors has decided that the company must emphasize two conflicting goals: increase the number of new drugs brought to market and cut back on the workforce in anticipation of rising labor and marketing costs and declining revenues. Accordingly, Dr. Wilson has been instructed to cut costs significantly and to reduce his workforce by 15 percent over the next six months.

Dr. Wilson called a meeting with his management team to discuss the workforce reduction. One of his managers, Leashia Harmon, argued that the layoffs should be made "so that recent gains in minority hiring are not wiped out." The percentage of minority employees had increased from 2.7 percent eight years ago to 8.3 percent in the previous year (see Figure 2-3). The minority population in communities in which Pharmakon has major facilities has remained over the years at approximately 23 percent. About 20 percent of the R, D & M workforce have a Ph.D. in a physical science or in pharmacology, and another 3 percent have an M.D.

Dr. Harmon, a Ph.D. in pharmacology and head of clinical studies, is the only minority on Dr. Wilson's seven-member management team. Dr. Harmon argued that R, D & M has worked long and hard to increase minority employment and has been a leader in promoting Pharmakon's affirmative action plan (see Figure 2-4). Therefore, she asserted, all layoffs should reflect this commitment, even if it meant disproportionate layoffs of nonminorities.

Dr. Anson Peake, another member of Dr. Wilson's management team and director of new products, argued that Pharmakon's R, D & M division has never discharged a worker except for cause and should adhere as closely as possible to that policy by terminating individuals solely based on merit. Dr. Rachel Waugh, director of product development, pointed out that the enormous growth in employment over the last eight years—almost a trebling of the workforce—had made the company's employee performance evaluation system less than reliable. Consequently, she contended that because laying off 15 percent of her group would be extremely difficult and subjective, she preferred to follow a system of seniority.

Dr. Wilson immediately recognized that any system of reducing the workforce would be difficult to implement. Moreover, he was concerned about fairness to employees and maintaining the best qualified group to carry out the area's mission. He was very troubled by a merit or seniority system if it could not maintain the minority gains. In fact, he had even thought about the possibility of using this difficult situation to increase the percentage of minorities to bring it more in line with the minority percentage of the communities in which Pharmakon had major facilities.

Figure 2-4
Pharmakon Affirmative Action Program

Pharmakon Drug Company
Equal Employment Opportunity

POLICY

It is the policy of Pharmakon Drug Co. to provide equal employment opportunities without regard to race, color, religion, sex, national origin, sexual preference, disability and veteran status. The Company will also take affirmative action to employ and advance individual applicants from all segments of our society. This policy relates to all phases of employment, including, but not limited to, recruiting, hiring, placement, promotion, demotion, layoff, recall, termination, compensation, and training. In communities where Pharmakon has facilities, it is our policy to be a leader in providing equal employment for all of its citizens.

RESPONSIBILITY FOR IMPLEMENTATION

The head of each division is ultimately responsible for initiating, administering, and controlling activities within all areas of responsibility necessary to ensure full implementation of this policy.

The managers of each location or area are responsible for the implementation of this policy.

All other members of management are responsible for conducting day-to-day activities in a manner to ensure compliance with this policy.

MYKON'S DILEMMA

Jack Spratt, the newly appointed CEO of Mykon Pharmaceuticals, Inc., sat at his desk and scratched his head for the thousandth time that night. His friends never tired of telling him that unless he stopped this habit he would remove what little hair he had left. Nevertheless, he had good reason to be perplexed—the decisions he made would determine the future of the company and, literally, the life or death of thousands of people.

As a young, ambitious scientist, Spratt had gained international fame and considerable fortune while rising quickly through the ranks of the scientists at Mykon. After receiving a degree from the Executive MBA program at the Kenan-Flagler Business School, University of North Carolina at Chapel Hill, he assumed, in rapid succession, a number of administrative positions at the company, culminating in his appointment as CEO. But no one had told him that finding cures for previously incurable diseases would be fraught with moral dilemmas. Although it was 3:00 in the morning, Spratt remained at his desk, unable to stop thinking about his difficult choices. His preoccupation was made worse by the knowledge that pressure from governments and consumers would only increase each day he failed to reach a decision. This pressure had mounted relentlessly since the fateful day he had announced that Mykon had discovered the cure for AIDS. But the cure brought with it a curse: there was not enough to go around.

Company Background

Mykon, a major international research-based pharmaceutical group, engages in the research, development, manufacture, and marketing of human health-care products for sale in both the prescription and over-the-counter (OTC) markets. The company's principal prescription medicines include a range of products in the following areas: antiviral, neuromuscular blocking, cardiovascular, anti-inflammatory, immunosuppressive, systemic antibacterial, and central nervous system. Mykon also manufactures other products such as muscle relaxants, antidepressants, anticonvulsants, and respiratory stimulants. In addition, the company markets drugs for the treatment of congestive heart failure and the prevention of organ rejection following transplant.

Mykon's OTC business primarily consists of cough and cold preparations and several topical antibiotics. The company seeks to expand its OTC business in various ways, including the reclassification of some of its prescription drugs to OTC status. Mykon's OTC sales represented 14 percent of the company's sales during last year.

Mykon has a long tradition of excellence in research and development (R&D). The company's expenditures on R&D for the last three financial years constituted 15 percent of its sales.

Mykon focuses its R&D on the following selected therapeutic areas, listed in descending order of expenditure amount: antivirals and other antibiotics, cardiovascular, central nervous system, anti-cancer, anti-inflammatory, respiratory, and neuromuscular.

Mykon sells its products internationally in more than 120 countries and has a significant presence in two of the largest pharmaceutical markets—the United States and Europe—and a growing presence in Japan. It generated approximately 43 percent and 35 percent of the company's sales from the previous year in the United States and Europe, respectively. The company sells essentially the same range of products throughout the world.

Production

Mykon carries out most of its production in Rotterdam in the Netherlands and in Research Triangle Park, North Carolina, in the United States. The latter is the company's world headquarters. The company's manufacturing processes typically consist of three stages: the manufacture of active chemicals, the incorporation of these chemicals into products designed for use by the consumer, and packaging. The firm has an ongoing program of capital expenditure to provide up-to-date production facilities and relies on advanced technology, automation, and computerization of its manufacturing capability to help maintain its competitive position.

Production facilities are also located in ten other countries to meet the needs of local markets and to overcome legal restrictions on the importation of finished products. These facilities principally engage in product formulation and packaging, although plants in certain countries manufacture active chemicals. Last year, Mykon had more than 17,000 employees, 27 percent of whom were in the United States. Approximately 21 percent of Mykon's employees were engaged in R&D, largely in the Netherlands and the United States. Although unions represent a number of the firm's employees, the firm has not experienced any significant labor disputes in recent years, and it considers its employee relations to be good.

Research and Development

In the pharmaceutical industry, R&D is both expensive and prolonged, entailing considerable uncertainty. The process of producing a commercial drug typically takes between eight and twelve years as it proceeds from discovery through development to regulatory approval and finally to the product launch. No assurance exists that new compounds will survive the development process or obtain the requisite regulatory approvals. In addition, research conducted by other pharmaceutical companies may lead at any time to the introduction of competing or improved treatments.

Last year Mykon incurred approximately 95 percent of its R&D expenditures in the Netherlands and the United States. Figure 2-5 sets out the firm's annual expenditure on R&D in dollars and as a percentage of sales for each of the last three financial years.

Jack Spratt

> Every society, every institution, every company, and most important, every individual should follow those precepts that society holds most dear. The pursuit of profits must be consistent with and subordinate to these ideals, the most important of which is the Golden Rule. To work for the betterment of humanity is the reason I became a scientist in the first place. As a child, Banting and Best were my heroes. I could think of no vocation that held greater promise to help mankind. Now that I am CEO I intend to have these beliefs included in our company's mission statement.

These sentiments, expressed by Jack Spratt in a newsmagazine interview, capture the intensity and drive that animate the man. None who knew him was surprised when he set out years ago—fueled by his prodigious energy, guided by his brilliant mind, and financed by Mykon—for the inner reaches of the Amazon Basin to find naturally occurring medicines. Spratt considered it to be his manifest destiny to discover the cure for some dread disease.

His search was not totally blind. Some years earlier, Frans Berger, a well-known but eccentric scientist, had written extensively about the variety of plant life and fungi that flourished in the jungles of the Bobonaza River region deep in the Amazon watershed. Although he spent twenty years there and discovered nothing of medical significance, the vast number and intriguing uniqueness of his specimens convinced Spratt that it was just a matter of time before a major breakthrough would occur.

Spratt also had some scientific evidence. While working in Mykon's laboratory to finance his graduate education in biology and genetics, Spratt and his supervisors had noticed that several fungi could not only restore damaged skin but, when combined with synthetic polymers, had significant effects on internal cells. Several more years of scientific expeditions and investigations proved promising enough for Mykon to send Spratt and a twenty-person exploration team to the Amazon Basin for two years. Two years became five, and the enormous quantity of specimens sent back eventually took over an entire wing of the company's sizable laboratories in Research Triangle Park, North Carolina.

Upon Spratt's return, he headed up a group of Mykon scientists who examined the Amazonian fungi for pharmacological activity. After several years of promising beginnings and disappointing endings, they discovered that one fungus destroyed the recently identified virus HIV. Years later, the company managed to produce enough of the drug (code named Sprattalin) derived from the fungus to inform the Food and Drug Administration (FDA) that it was testing what appeared to be a cure for HIV. It was the happiest moment of Jack Spratt's life. The years of determined effort, not to mention the $800 million Mykon had invested, would now be more than fully rewarded.

Spratt's joy was short lived, though. Public awareness of the drug quickly spread, and groups pressured the FDA to shorten or eliminate its normal approval process, which ordinarily

Figure 2-5
Mykon R & D Expenditures

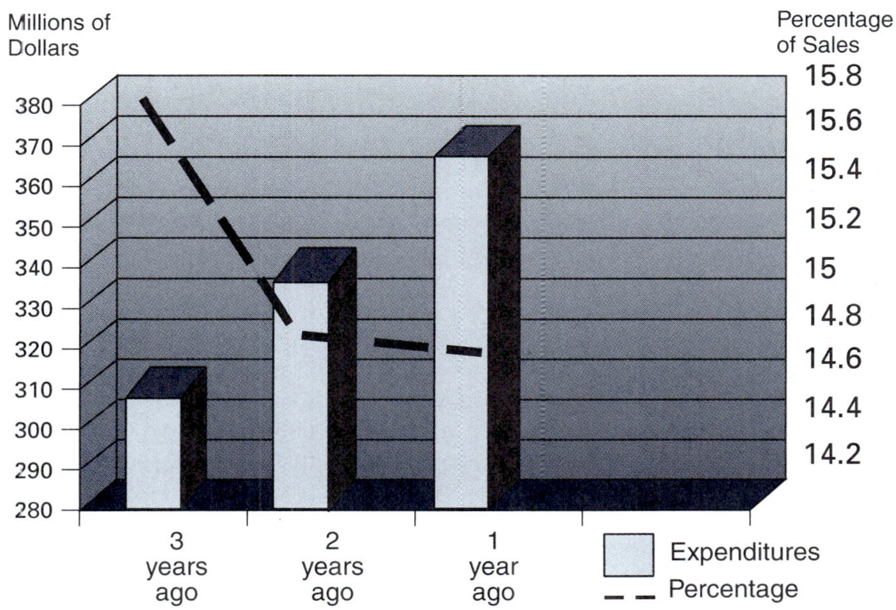

takes more than seven years. People dying from the virus's effects demanded immediate access to the drug.

The Drug

Mirroring the insidiousness of HIV itself, the structure of Sprattalin is extraordinarily complex. Consequently, it takes four to seven months to produce a small quantity, only 25 percent of which is usable. It is expensive; each unit of Sprattalin costs Mykon $20,000 to produce. The projected dosage ranges from ten units for asymptomatic HIV-positive patients who have normal white blood cell counts to fifty units for patients with low white blood cell counts and full-blown AIDS. The drug appears to eliminate the virus from all patients regardless of their stage of the disease. However, it does not have any restorative effect on patients' compromised immune systems. Accordingly, it is expected that asymptomatic HIV-positive patients will revert to their normal life expectancies. It is not clear what the life expectancy will be of patients with full-blown AIDS, although it is almost certain that their life expectancy would be curtailed.

Supply of Sprattalin The company has estimated that the first two years of production would yield enough Sprattalin to cure 6 percent of all asymptomatic HIV-positive patients. Alternatively, the supply would be sufficient to treat 4 percent of all patients with full-blown AIDS. Children constitute 3 percent of all people living with HIV/AIDS.

Interested parties have argued that the solution to production problems is clear: build larger facilities. However, even with production levels as low as they are, the bottleneck in supply occurs elsewhere. The fungus on which the whole process depends is incredibly rare, growing only in two small regions near Jatun Molino, Ecuador, along the Bobonaza River. At current harvesting rates, scientists predict that all known deposits will be depleted in three years, and many of them insist that production should be scaled back to allow the fungus to regenerate itself.

Presently there are no known methods of cultivating the fungus in the laboratory. Apparently, the delicate ecology that allows it to exist in only one region of the earth is somehow distressed enough by either transport or lab conditions to render it unable to grow and produce the drug's precursor. Scientists are feverishly trying to discover those factors that will support successful culture. However, with limited quantities of the starting material and most of that pressured into production, the company has enjoyed no success in this endeavor. Because of Sprattalin's complexity, attempts to synthesize the drug have failed completely, mainly because, like aspirin, it is not known how the drug works; thus, Sprattalin's effectiveness remains shrouded in mystery.

Allocation of Sprattalin In response to the insufficient supply, a number of powerful consumer groups have made public their suggestions regarding the allocation of Sprattalin. One proposition advanced would use medical records to establish a waiting list of possible recipients based on the length of time they have been in treatment for the virus. The argument is that those people who have waited the longest and are most in danger of dying should be the first to find relief.

Other groups propose an opposite approach, arguing that because supply is so drastically short, Mykon should make Sprattalin available only to asymptomatic HIV patients. They require the least concentrations of the drug to become well, thus extending the drug's supply. They also have the greatest likelihood of returning to full life expectancies. Under this proposal, people who have full-blown AIDS would be ineligible for treatment. Such patients have previously come to terms with their impending mortality, have fewer psychological adjustments to make, and represent, on a dosage basis, two to five healthier patients. In meting the drug out in this manner, proponents argue, the drug can more readily meet the highest public health objectives to eradicate the virus and prevent further transmission.

Others propose that only patients who contracted the virus through no fault of their own should have priority. This approach would first make Sprattalin available to children who were born with the virus, hemophiliacs and others who got the virus from blood transfusions, rape victims, and health-care workers.

One member of Sprattalin's executive committee has suggested a free market approach: the drug should go to the highest bidder.

Pricing of Sprattalin In addition to supply problems, Mykon has also come under considerable criticism for its proposed pricing structure. Because of extraordinarily high development and production costs, the company has tentatively priced the drug at levels unattainable for most people afflicted with HIV. Perhaps never before in the history of medicine has the ability to pay been so starkly presented as those who can pay, live, while those who cannot, die.

Even at these prices, though, demand far exceeds supply. Jack Spratt and the rest of the Mykon executives predict that the company could easily sell available supplies at twice the proposed price.

A growing number of Mykon executives disagree with the passive stance the company has taken in pricing the product. In their view, a 20 percent markup represents a meager return for the prolonged risk and high levels of spending that the company incurred to develop the drug. Moreover, it leaves little surplus for future investment. Furthermore, eight years is too long to amortize the R&D expenses because Sprattalin, though the first, is unlikely to be the last anti-HIV drug, now that Mykon has blazed a path. Other, more heavily capitalized companies are racing to reverse engineer the drug, and the availability of competing drugs remains only a matter of time. Accordingly, the company cannot realistically count on an eight-year window of opportunity.

Foreign markets further exacerbate the pricing perplexity. Other countries, with less privatized health care, have already promised their citizens access to Sprattalin at any price. Some first world countries, for instance, are willing to pay up to $2 million per patient. They do not, however, wish to subsidize the drug for the United States. At the same time, some voices in the United States insist that supplies should go first to U.S. citizens.

On the other hand, countries with the most severe concentration of the HIV infection cannot afford to pay even Mykon's actual costs. Some regions in Africa and Asia have experienced rapid growth of the disease, reporting 50 percent to 80 percent of their population at some stage in the HIV cycle. Jack Spratt feels a very real moral obligation to help at least some of these people, whether they can pay or not.

Making the Decision

In the last few months, Jack Spratt had seen many aspects of the most important project in his life become not only public knowledge but also public domain. Because of the enormous social and political consequences of the discovery, it is unlikely that the government will allow Mykon to control the destiny of either Sprattalin or ultimately the company.

Addressing the public's concern over access to the drug while ensuring future prosperity of his company had become like walking a tightrope with strangers holding each end of the rope. He knew of no way to satisfy everyone. As Jack Spratt sat at his desk, sleep remained an eon away.

OLIVER WINERY, INC.

Background

Paul Oliver, Sr., immigrated to the United States in 1930 from Greece. After working for several wineries, he started Oliver Winery, Inc., which eventually found a market niche in nonvarietal jug wines. Through mass-marketing techniques, the company established a substantial presence in this segment of the market. Ten years ago, Paul, Jr., joined the firm after receiving a degree in enology (the study of wine making). He convinced his father of the desirability of entering a different segment of the wine market: premium varietals. To do this, the company needed a large infusion of capital to purchase appropriate vineyards. Reluctantly, Paul, Sr., agreed to take the company public. The initial public offering succeeded and 40 percent of the company's stock went into outsiders' hands. Also, for the first time, outsiders served on the board of directors. Although Paul, Jr., wanted to use a new name for the premium varietal to appeal to a more upscale market, his father insisted on using the name Oliver.

Board Meeting

The board of directors met, along with Janet Stabler, the director of marketing of Oliver Winery, Inc. In attendance were:

Paul Oliver, Sr.,
Chairman of the board and founder of the company
Paul Oliver, Jr., CEO,
has an advanced degree in enology
Cyrus Abbott, CFO,
has an MBA
Arlene Dale, comptroller
has a CPA with a master's degree in accounting
Raj Ray, COO,
has a master's degree in industrial engineering
LaTasha Lane, VP Legal,
has a J.D. degree
Elisabeth Constable,
union representative to the board, has a GED degree
Rev. John W. Calvin,
outside director, has a Doctor of Divinity degree
Carlos Menendez, outside director,
has an MFA degree

Oliver, Sr.: The next item on the agenda is a proposal to develop a new line of wines. Janet Stabler will briefly present the proposal.

Stabler: Thank you. The proposal is to enter the fortified wine market. It's the only type of wine in which unit sales are increasing. We'll make the wines cheaply and package them in pint bottles with screw-on caps. Our chief competitors are Canandaigua with Richard's Wild Irish Rose, Gallo with Thunderbird and Night Train Express, and Mogen David with MD 20/20. We'll market the wine with little or no media advertising by strategically sampling the product to targeted consumers. That's it in a nutshell.

Oliver, Sr.: Any questions before we vote?

Menendez: Who'll buy this wine?

Calvin: From what I know about the consumers of your competitors, it appears to me that it's bought by homeless winos.

Stabler: Not entirely. For example, pensioners on a fixed income would find the price of the wine appealing. Thunderbird has been recently introduced into England and has become very popular with the yuppie crowd.

Calvin: Then why put it in pint bottles?

Stabler: For the convenience of consumers.

Menendez: Why would pensioners want a small bottle?

Calvin: Homeless people want it in pints so they can fit it in their hip pockets. They obviously don't have a wine cellar to lay away their favorite bottles of Mad Dog.

Stabler: The pint size also keeps the price as low as possible.

Calvin: Translation: The homeless don't have to panhandle as long before they can make a purchase. Also, why would you increase the alcoholic content to 18 percent and make it so sweet if it weren't for the wino market?

Stabler: Many people like sweet dessert wines and 18 percent is not that much more than other types of wines that have 12 percent alcohol.

Menendez: Is it legal?

Lane: Sure. We sell to the retailers. It may be against the law to sell to intoxicated persons, but that's the retailers' business. We cannot control what they do.

Calvin: Isn't this product intended for a perpetually intoxicated audience that many people consider to be ill? Wouldn't we be taking advantage of their illness by selling highly sugared alcohol that suppresses their appetite? I've spoken to drinkers who claim to live on a gallon of this type of product a day.

Oliver, Jr.: What will this do to our image? We're still trying to get our premium wines accepted.

Stabler: Of course we won't use the Oliver name on these wines. We will use another name.

Menendez: Is it OK to do that?

Stabler: Why not? Canandaigua, Gallo, and Mogen David all do the same thing. None of them put their corporate name on this low-end product.

Abbott: We're getting away from the crux of the matter. Profit margins would be at least 10 percent higher on this line than our others. Moreover, unit sales might increase over time. Our other lines are stagnant or decreasing. The public shareholders are grousing.

Dale: Not to mention that our stock options have become almost worthless. I'm only a few years from retirement. We need to increase the profitability of the company.

Ray: Operationally, this proposal is a great fit. We can use the grapes we reject from the premium line. It will also insulate us from bad grape years because any grape will do for this wine. We can fill a lot of our unused capacity.

Constable: And hire back some of the workers who were laid off!

Stabler: It's a marketing dream. Just give out some samples to "bell cows."

Menendez: What are bell cows?

Stabler: Opinion leaders who will induce other consumers to switch to our brand.

Calvin: You mean wino gurus?

Oliver, Sr.: Look, if we don't do it, others will. In fact, they already have.

Abbott: And they'll get richer and we'll get poorer.

Lane: Gallo pulled out of several of these skid row markets as did Canandaigua. Little good it did. The alcoholics just switched to malt liquor, vodka, or anything they could get their hands on.

Dale: I think our concern is misplaced. These people are the dregs of society. They contribute nothing.

Calvin: They're human beings who need help. We're profiting off their misfortune and misery.

Oliver, Sr.: We can take that up when we decide on what charities to support. Anyone opposed to the proposal?

Calvin: Is this a done deal? I believe we should contribute half of our profits from this product to support homeless shelters and other programs that benefit indigent and homeless people. If not, I must resign from this board.

Sources

Carrie Dolan, "Gallo Conducts Test to Placate Critics of Its Cheap Wine," *The Wall Street Journal,* June 16, 1989, p. B3.

Alix M. Freedman, "Winos and Thunderbird Are a Subject Gallo Doesn't Like to Discuss," *The Wall Street Journal,* February 25, 1988, p. 1.

Frank J. Prial, "Experiment by a Wine Maker Fails to Thwart Street Drunks," *The New York Times,* February 11, 1990, p. A29.

JLM INC.

Background

Sitting in her office, Ellen Fulbright, director of human resources for JLM, Inc., thought over the decisions confronting her. To help her decide, she mentally reviewed how they had arisen.

After receiving her MBA and J.D. degrees from a highly regarded university, she joined a prestigious New York law firm where she specialized in employment law. After seven years at the law firm, she was hired by one of the firm's clients as general counsel. When that company was acquired by JLM, she joined its legal staff and within a few years had been promoted to her current position.

Fulbright's rapid advancement resulted from her having made a positive impression on Rasheed Raven, JLM's CEO. Raven is a hard-driving, bottom-line-oriented pragmatist in his early forties. Raven, a graduate of Howard University, had begun his business career on Wall Street, which he astounded by his aggressive but successful takeover strategies. After acquiring fifteen unrelated manufacturing companies, he decided to try his hand at the turnaround business. He organized JLM as an umbrella for his acquired companies. Soon he earned the reputation as the best in the business by transforming JLM into the leader in the industry.

JLM is a highly successful turnaround company. Typically, JLM purchases companies that are in serious financial trouble and manages them until they become successful companies. At that time, JLM either retains them in its own portfolio of companies or sells them off to other enterprises.

Reference Letter Policy

About a year after Fulbright had become director of human resources (HR), Raven called her into his office and showed her a newspaper article. It reported, in somewhat sensational fashion, that several defamation suits had resulted in multimillion dollar judgments against companies that had written negative letters of references about former employees. Raven told her that he was concerned about this and that he wanted her to develop an HR policy covering letters of reference.

In researching the issue, she discovered several articles in which the authors decried the recent spate of companies that had decided to stop writing letters of reference. According to their data, they believed that these companies had overreacted to the actual risk posed by defamation suits. Based on these articles and her own inclination toward full disclosure, she proposed that the company continue to permit letters of reference but that all letters with negative comments must be reviewed by her.

Raven did not receive her proposal favorably and sought a second opinion from her old law firm. His analysis of the firm's advice was: "We get nothing but brownie points for writing reference letters, but we face the possibility of incurring the cost of a legal defense or, worse yet, a court judgment. This is a 'no-brainer.' We have no upside and all downside." Raven ordered that, henceforth, company employees would no longer write letters of reference but would simply verify dates of employment.

Although Fulbright was personally and professionally miffed by his decision, she drew up the policy statement as directed. Fulbright believed that because JLM frequently took over companies that needed immediate downsizing, this policy would be unfair and extremely detrimental to longtime employees of newly purchased companies.

Takeover of Diversified Manufacturing, Inc.

After a number of years of steady growth, Diversified Manufacturing began experiencing huge financial losses and its immediate survival was in serious doubt. After careful consideration, Raven decided that Diversified was an ideal takeover target in that its core businesses were extremely strong and presented great long-term economic viability.

Upon acquiring Diversified, JLM quickly decided that it had to rid Diversified of some of its poorly performing companies and that it had to reduce the size of Diversified's home office staff by 25 percent. Raven relentlessly orchestrated the reduction in force, but at Fulbright's urging he provided the discharged executives with above average severance packages, including excellent outplacement services.

The Problem

The reduction in force was disruptive and demoralizing in all the usual ways. But for Fulbright there was a further complication: the no reference letter policy. She was extremely troubled by its application to three discharged Diversified employees and to one discharged JLM employee.

The Salacious Sales Manager Soon after taking over Diversified, Fulbright became all too aware of the story of Ken Byrd, Diversified's then national sales manager. Ken is an affable man of fifty who had been an unusually effective sales manager. Throughout his career, his sales figures had always doubled those of his peers. He achieved rapid advancement despite a fatal flaw: he is an inveterate and indiscreet womanizer. He could not control his hands, which slapped backs so well, nor his tongue, which persuaded so eloquently. He had two approaches to women. With a woman of equal or superior rank in the company, he would politely, but inexorably, attempt to sweep her off her feet. With these women, he would be extremely charming and attentive, taking great care to avoid being offensive or harassing. In contrast, with a woman of subordinate rank, he would physically harass her. Less openly, but much too often, he would come up behind a woman, reach around her, and grab her. He invariably found this amusing—his victims, however, did not.

Fulbright could not believe that such a manager had stayed employed at Diversified so long, let alone been continually promoted to positions of greater responsibility and power. As Fulbright investigated the situation, she discovered that numerous sexual harassment complaints had been filed with Diversified concerning Byrd's behavior. To protect Byrd, Diversified dealt with these complaints by providing money and undeserved promotions to the complainants to smooth over their anger. Thus, Diversified successfully kept the complaints in-house and away from the courts and the Equal Employment Opportunity Commission.

After JLM's takeover of Diversified, Fulbright quickly discharged Byrd. Her satisfaction in getting rid of him was short lived, however. His golden tongue and stellar sales record had landed him several job offers. Her dilemma was that she was uncomfortable about loosing this deviant on an unsuspecting new employer. But JLM's policy forbade her from writing any letters or answering questions from prospective employers.

The Fruitless Juice Melissa Cuthbertson had been a vice president in procurement for Diversified's Birch-Wood division with direct responsibility over the ordering of supplies and raw materials. Birch-Wood manufactured a full line of baby food products, including fruit juices that were labeled "100% fruit juice." To cut costs, Stanley Aker, the division's president, had arranged for an unscrupulous supplier to provide high-fructose corn syrup labeled as juice concentrate. Because standard testing in the industry was unable to detect the substitution, the company did not get caught. Emboldened, Aker gradually increased the proportion of corn syrup until there were only trace amounts of fruit juice left in the "juice." A company employee discovered the practice and after the takeover brought the matter to Fulbright's attention through JLM's internal whistle-blowing channel, which Fulbright had established. She referred the matter to Raven, who called Aker and Cuthbertson in and confronted them with the accusation. They admitted it all, explaining that nutritionally the corn syrup was equivalent to the fruit juice. But at 60 percent of the cost of fruit juice, the corn syrup made a big difference to the bottom line. Raven told them that such conduct was not permitted and that they must properly dispose of the adulterated juice.

That night Aker and Cuthbertson had the juice moved from Birch-Wood's New York warehouse and shipped to its Puerto Rico warehouse. Over the course of the next few days, the "juice" was sold in Latin America as "apple juice." Aker reported to Raven that the juice had been properly disposed of and that Birch-Wood had sustained only a small loss during that quarter. When Raven discovered the truth, he immediately discharged Aker and Cuthbertson, telling them "that if he had anything to do with it, neither of them would ever work again." Fulbright was to meet soon with Raven to discuss what should be done about Aker and Cuthbertson.

The Compassionate CFO Jackson Cobb, JLM's former chief financial officer, is a brilliant analyst. Through hard work he had earned an excellent education that honed his innate mathematical gifts. His natural curiosity led him to read widely, and this enabled him to bring disparate facts and concepts to bear on his often novel analyses of financial matters. But he had no interest in implementing his insights, for his only enjoyment was the process of discovering connections. Fortune—or fate—had brought him together with Raven, who is twenty years younger than Cobb. Theirs was definitely a case of opposites attracting. Raven cared little about ideas; he cared primarily about money. Cobb cared little about money; he cared primarily about ideas. Raven took Cobb's insights and translated them into action with spectacular success. Their relationship brought new meaning to the concept of synergy. When Raven formed JLM, he brought Cobb on as chief financial officer and installed him in an adjoining office.

Their relationship continued to flourish, as did JLM's bottom line, until Cobb's wife became terminally ill. During the eighteen months she languished, Cobb spent as much time as he could taking care of her. After forty years of marriage, he was unwilling to leave her welfare to the "kindness of strangers." At his own expense, he installed a state-of-the-art communication center in his home. By virtue of computers, modems, video cameras, faxes, copiers, mobile telephones, and the like, he had available to him the same data and information as he had at his office. He could be reached by telephone at all times. But he was not in the office next to Raven; he was not present at Raven's daily breakfast meetings; he was not on the corporate jet en route to business meetings. After their many years of working together, Raven was enraged at the loss of immediate access to Cobb. He felt that Cobb had betrayed him and demanded that Cobb resume his old working hours. Cobb refused, and Raven fired him. Because of his age, Cobb was experiencing difficulty in finding new employment, and Fulbright wanted to write a letter on his behalf.

SWORD TECHNOLOGY, INC.

Background

Sitting in his office, Stephen Hag, CEO of Sword Technology, Inc., contemplated the problems that had been perplexing him for some time now. They had begun when he took his company international, and they kept coming. But today he was no more successful in devising a solution than he had been previously. Slowly, his thoughts drifted to those early days years ago when he and his sister Marian started the company.

The company's first product was an investment newsletter stressing technical analysis in securities investing. A few years later, he developed what became a "killer app": a computer program that defines an entirely new market and through customer loyalty substantially dominates that market. His software program enabled investors to track their investments in stocks, bonds, and futures. By combining powerful analytical tools with an accessible graphical interface, it appealed to both professional and amateur investors. Moreover, it required users to download information from the company's database. With one of the most extensive databases and the cheapest downloading rates in the industry, the company soon controlled the U.S. market. Sword then went public through a highly successful IPO (an initial public offering of the company's common stock), and its stock is traded on the over-the-counter market. The company is required to file periodic reports with the Securities and Exchange Commission.

The company used cash from sales of software, online charges, and the IPO to try to enter the hardware side of the computer industry. It began manufacturing modems and other computer peripherals. A nagging problem, however, plagued the company's manufacturing efforts. Although Sword's modem could convert data more quickly and efficiently than most of its competitors, because of high labor costs it was unable to market its modem successfully. To reduce manufacturing costs, especially labor costs, the company decided to move its manufacturing facilities overseas. And that's when the trouble began.

Stephen's thoughts returned to the present. He reopened the folder labeled "Confidential: International Issues" and began perusing its contents.

Transfer Pricing

The first item he saw was an opinion letter from the company's tax attorney. It dealt with Excalibur Technology, the first overseas company Sword established. Excalibur, a wholly owned subsidiary of Sword, is incorporated in Tolemac, an emerging country with a rapidly growing economy. To encourage foreign investment, Tolemac taxes corporate profits at a significantly lower rate than the United States and other industrialized nations. Excalibur manufactures modems for Sword pursuant to a licensing agreement under which Excalibur pays Sword a royalty equal to a specified percentage of the modems' gross sales. Excalibur sells all of its output at a fair market price to Sword, which then markets the modems in the United States. Stephen had been closely involved in structuring this arrangement and had insisted on keeping the royalty rate low to minimize taxable income for Sword. Stephen reread the opinion letter:

> Section 482 of the Internal Revenue Code authorizes the Internal Revenue Service to allocate gross income, deductions, credits, and other common allowances among two or more organizations, trades, or businesses under common ownership or control whenever it determines that this action is necessary "in order to prevent evasion of taxes or clearly to reflect the income of any such organizations, trades, or businesses." IRS Regulation 1.482–2(e) governing the sale or trade of intangibles between related persons mandates an appropriate allocation to reflect the price that an unrelated party under the same circumstances would have paid, which normally includes profit to the seller. The Regulations provide four methods for determining an arm's length price. In our opinion, under the only method applicable to the circumstances of Sword Technology, Inc., and Excalibur Technology, the royalty rate should be at least three times the current one. If the IRS were to reach the same conclusion, then the company would be liable for the taxes it underpaid because of the understatement of income. Moreover, the company would be liable for a penalty of either 20 percent or 40 percent of the tax deficiency, unless the company can show that it had reasonable cause and acted in good faith.

Stephen had spoken to the tax attorney at length and learned that the probability of an audit was about 10 percent and that many multinational companies play similar "games" with their transfer pricing. The attorney also told him that he believed that if the company were audited, there was at least a 90 percent probability that the IRS would agree with his conclusion and at least a 70 percent probability that it would impose a penalty. Because the dollar amount of the contingent tax liability was not an insignificant amount, Stephen had been concerned about it for the six weeks since he had received the letter.

Customs and Customs

Soon after Excalibur had manufactured the first shipment of modems, a new problem arose: getting them out of Tolemac. It took far too long to clear customs, thus undermining their carefully planned just-in-time manufacturing schedules. Stephen hired a local export broker, who distributed cash gifts to customs officials. Miraculously, the clearance time shortened and manufacturing schedules were maintained. The export broker billed the company for his services and the amount of the cash gifts. Although the broker assured Stephen that such gifts were entirely customary, Stephen was not entirely comfortable with the practice.

The Thorn in His Side

Tolemac was not Stephen's only problem. Six months after commencing operations in Tolemac, Sword began serious negotiations to enter the Liarg market. Liarg is an undeveloped country with a large population and a larger national debt. Previously, Sword had encountered great difficulties in exporting products to Liarg. Stephen's sister, Marian, COO of Sword, took on the challenge of establishing a Liarg presence.

They decided that setting up a manufacturing facility in Liarg would achieve two objectives: greater access to the Liarg marketplace and lower-cost modems. At first, the Liarg government insisted that Sword enter into a joint venture, with the government having a 51 percent interest. Sword was unwilling to invest in such an arrangement, countering with a proposal for a wholly owned subsidiary. Marian conducted extensive negotiations with the government, assisted by a Liarg consulting firm that specialized in lobbying governmental officials. As part of these negotiations, Sword made contributions to the reelection campaigns of key Liarg legislators who were opposed to wholly owned subsidiaries of foreign corporations. After the legislators' reelection, the negotiations quickly reached a successful conclusion. On closing the contract, Sword flew several Liarg officials and their wives to Lake Tahoe for a lavish, three-day celebration. All of these expenses were reported in the company's financial statements as payments for legal and consulting fees.

Marian then hired an international engineering firm to help design the manufacturing plant. Two weeks later, they submitted plans for the plant and its operations that fully complied with Liarg regulations regarding worker health and safety as well as environmental protection. But, as Marian had explained to Stephen, the plant's design fell far short of complying with U.S. requirements. Marian noted that, under the proposed design, the workers would face exposure to moderately high levels of toxic chemicals and hazardous materials. The design also would degrade the water supply of nearby towns. However, the design would generate very significant savings in capital and operational costs as compared with the design used in their U.S. facility. Marian assured Stephen that all quality control systems were in place so the modems produced in this plant would be indistinguishable from their U.S. counterparts. Stephen and Marian have had long discussions about what to do about the plant.

Stephen then took from the folder an article that had appeared in a number of U.S. newspapers.

Children and Chips

A twelve-year-old Liarg child recently spoke at an international conference in New York denouncing the exploitation of children in the Liarg computer chip industry. The child informed the outraged audience that he had worked in such a plant from age four to age ten. He asserted that he was just one of many children who were so employed. He described the deplorable working conditions: poor ventilation, long hours, inadequate food, and substandard housing. The pay was low. But, because their families could not afford to keep them at home, the children were hired out to the factory owners, who especially wanted young children because their small fingers made them adept at many assembly processes.

Stephen had read the article countless times, thinking about his own children. He knew that if they set up a plant in Liarg, they would have to buy chip components from Liarg suppliers. He also knew that there would be no way for Sword to ensure that the chips had not been made with child labor.

He was also troubled by another labor issue. Marian told him that she had met considerable resistance from the Liarg executives they had hired when she suggested that women should be hired at the supervisory level. They maintained that it was not done and would make it impossible to hire and control a satisfactory workforce at the plant. Moreover, they insisted on hiring their relatives as supervisors. When Marian protested this nepotism, they assured her that it was customary and asserted that they could not trust anyone not related to them.

On top of all these concerns had come a letter from the company's outside legal counsel regarding payments made to foreign officials.

Memorandum of Law

The Foreign Corrupt Practices Act makes it unlawful for any domestic company or any of its officers, directors, employees, or agents or its stockholders acting on its behalf to offer or give anything of value directly or indirectly to any foreign official, political party, or political official for the purpose of

1. influencing any act or decision of that person or party in his or its official capacity,
2. inducing an act or omission in violation of his or its lawful duty, or
3. inducing such person or party to use its influence to affect a decision of a foreign government in order to assist the domestic concern in obtaining or retaining business.

An offer or promise to make a prohibited payment is a violation even if the offer is not accepted or the promise is not performed. The 1988 amendments explicitly excluded facilitating or expediting payments made to expedite or secure the performance of routine governmental actions by a foreign official, political party, or party official. Routine governmental action does not include any decision by a foreign official regarding the award of new business or the continuation of old business. The amendments also added an affirmative defense for payments that are lawful under the written laws or regulations of the foreign official's country. Violations are punishable by fines of up to $2 million for companies; individuals may be fined a maximum of $100,000 or imprisoned up to five years, or both. Fines imposed upon individuals may not be paid directly or indirectly by the domestic company on whose behalf they acted. In addition, the courts may impose civil penalties of up to $10,000.

The statute also imposes internal control requirements on all reporting companies. Such companies must

1. make and keep books, records, and accounts, that in reasonable detail, accurately and fairly reflect the transactions and dispositions of the assets of the company; and
2. devise and maintain a system of internal controls that ensure that transactions are executed as authorized and recorded in conformity with generally accepted accounting principles, thereby establishing accountability with regard to assets and ensuring that access to those assets is permitted only with management's authorization.

Any person who knowingly circumvents or knowingly fails to implement a system of internal accounting controls or knowingly falsifies any book, record, or account is subject to criminal liability.

PART II

THE LEGAL ENVIRONMENT OF BUSINESS

Information About Federal Courts
http://www.uscourts.gov/about.html

Information About and Cases Decided by the U.S. District Courts
http://www.law.cornell.edu/federal/districts.html#circuit

Cases Decided by the U.S. Court of Appeals
http://www.law.emory.edu/FEDCTS/

Information About the U.S. Supreme Court
http://supct.law.cornell.edu/supct/

Cases Decided by the U.S. Court of Federal Claims
http://www.uscfc.uscourts.gov/opinions.htm

Information About and Cases Decided by the U.S. Bankruptcy Courts
http://www.law.cornell.edu/federal/districts.html#circuit

Cases Decided by the U.S. Court of Appeals for the Federal Circuit
http://www.law.emory.edu/fedcircuit/

Information About and Cases Decided by State Courts
http://ncsconline.org/D_KIS/info_court_web_sites.html

State Court Decisions
http://www.law.cornell.edu/opinions.html#state

State Civil Procedure Laws
http://www.law.cornell.edu/topics/state_statutes.html#civil_procedure

Information About Alternate Dispute Resolution
http://www.abanet.org/dispute/ and http://www.adr.org/

Federal Agencies
http://www.findlaw.com/10fedgov/agencies/index.htm

Federal Register
http://www.archives.gov/federal_register

Code of Federal Regulations
http://www.access.gpo.gov/nara/cfr/cfr-table-search.html

U.S. Department of Justice
http://www.ojp.usdoj.gov

FBI, Uniform Crime Reports
http://www.fbi.gov/ucr/ucr.htm?topic_id=0&sect_id=1&indv_proj_id=&CFID=56680&CFTOKEN=61273708

CHAPTER 3

Civil Dispute Resolution

Laws are a dead letter without courts to expound and define their true meaning and operation.

ALEXANDER HAMILTON, IN *THE FEDERALIST* (1788)

Learning Objectives

After reading this chapter you should be able to:

1. List and describe the courts in the federal court system and in a typical state court system.
2. Distinguish among exclusive federal jurisdiction, concurrent federal jurisdiction, and exclusive state jurisdiction.
3. Distinguish between (a) subject matter jurisdiction and jurisdiction over the parties and (b) the three types of jurisdiction over the parties.
4. List and explain the various stages of a civil proceeding.
5. Compare and contrast litigation, arbitration, conciliation, and mediation.

As we discussed in Chapter 1, substantive law sets forth the rights and duties of individuals and other legal entities, whereas procedural law determines how these rights are asserted. Procedural law attempts to accomplish two competing objectives: (1) to be fair and impartial and (2) to operate efficiently. The judicial process in the United States represents a balance between these two objectives as well as a commitment to the adversary system.

In the first part of this chapter, we will describe the structure and function of the federal and state court systems. The second part deals with jurisdiction; the third part discusses civil dispute resolution, including the procedure in civil lawsuits.

THE COURT SYSTEM

Courts are impartial tribunals (seats of judgment) established by governmental bodies to settle disputes. A court may render a binding decision only when it has jurisdiction over the dispute and the parties to that dispute; that is, when it has a right to hear and make a judgment in a case. The United States has a dual court system: the federal government has its own independent system, as does each of the fifty states and the District of Columbia.

THE FEDERAL COURTS

Article III of the U.S. Constitution states that the judicial power of the United States shall be vested in one Supreme Court and such lower courts as Congress may establish. Congress has established a lower federal court system consisting of a number of special courts, district courts, and courts of appeals. Judges in the federal court system are appointed for life by the President, subject to confirmation by the Senate. The structure of the federal court system is illustrated in Figure 3-1.

http:// Information about federal courts: http://www.uscourts.gov/about.html

Figure 3-1 *Federal Judicial System*

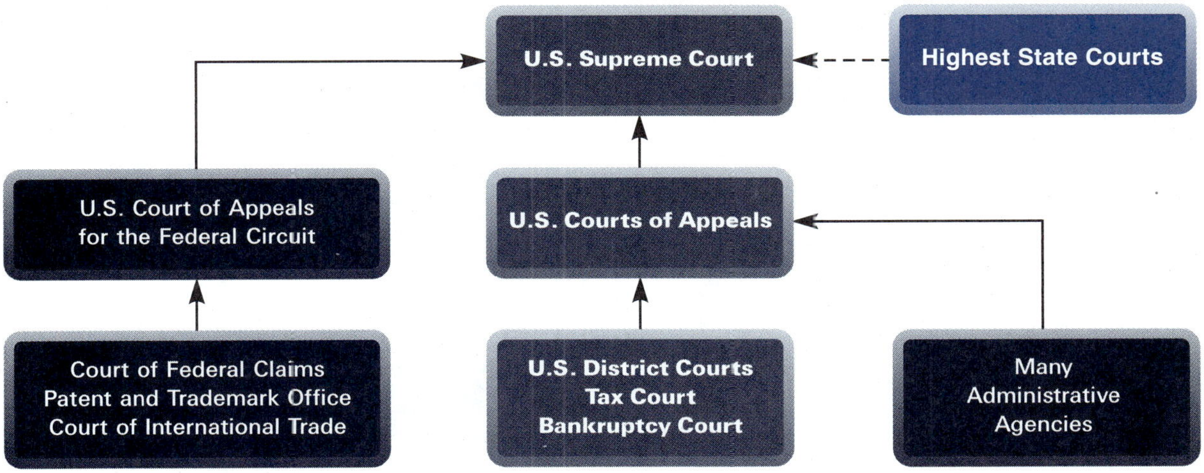

DISTRICT COURTS

The **district courts** are general trial courts in the federal system. Most federal cases begin in the district court, and it is here that issues of fact are decided. The district court is generally presided over by *one* judge, although in certain cases three judges preside. In a few cases, an appeal from a judgment or decree of a district court is taken directly to the Supreme Court. In most cases, however, appeals go to the Circuit Court of Appeals of the appropriate circuit, the decision of which is final in most cases.

Congress has established judicial districts, each of which is located entirely in a particular state. All states have at least one district, while certain states contain more than one district. For instance, New York has four districts, Illinois has three, and Wisconsin has two, while a number of less populated states each make up a single district.

http:// Information about and cases decided by the U.S. district courts: http://www.law.cornell.edu/federal/districts.html#circuit

COURTS OF APPEALS

Congress has established twelve judicial circuits (eleven numbered circuits plus the D.C. circuit), each having a court known as the Court of Appeals, which primarily hears appeals from the district courts located within its circuit (see Figure 3-2). In addition, these courts review decisions of many administrative agencies, the Tax Court, and the Bankruptcy Courts. Congress has also established the U.S. Court of Appeals for the Federal Circuit, which is discussed later in the section on "Special Courts." The U.S. Courts of Appeals generally hear cases in panels of three judges, although in some instances all judges of the circuit will sit *en banc* to decide a case.

The function of appellate courts is to examine the record of a case on appeal and to determine whether the trial court committed prejudicial error (error substantially affecting the appellant's rights and duties). If so, the appellate court will **reverse** or **modify** the judgment of the lower court and, if necessary, **remand** or send it back to the lower court for further proceeding. If there is no prejudicial error, the appellate court will **affirm** the decision of the lower court.

http:// Cases decided by the U.S Court of Appeals: http://www.law.emory.edu/FEDCTS/

THE SUPREME COURT

The nation's highest tribunal is the U.S. Supreme Court, which consists of nine justices (a Chief Justice and eight Associate Justices) who sit as a group in Washington, D.C. A quorum consists of any six justices. In certain types of cases, the U.S. Supreme Court has original jurisdiction (the right to hear a case first). The Court's principal function, nonetheless, is to review decisions of the Federal Courts of Appeals and, in some instances, those of the highest state courts or other tribunals. Cases reach the Supreme Court under its appellate jurisdiction by one of two routes. Very few come by way of **appeal by right.** The Court must hear these cases if one of the parties requests the review. In 1988 Congress enacted legislation that almost completely eliminated the right to appeal to the U.S. Supreme Court.

The second way in which the Supreme Court may review a decision of a lower court is by the discretionary **writ of *certiorari***, which requires a lower court to produce the records of a case it has tried. Now almost all cases reaching the Supreme Court come to it by means of writs of *certiorari*. If four Justices vote to hear the case, the Court grants writs when there is a federal question of substantial importance or a conflict in the decisions of the U.S. Circuit Courts of Appeals. Only a small percentage of the petitions to the Supreme Court for review by *certiorari* are granted,

Figure 3-2 *Circuit Courts of the United States*

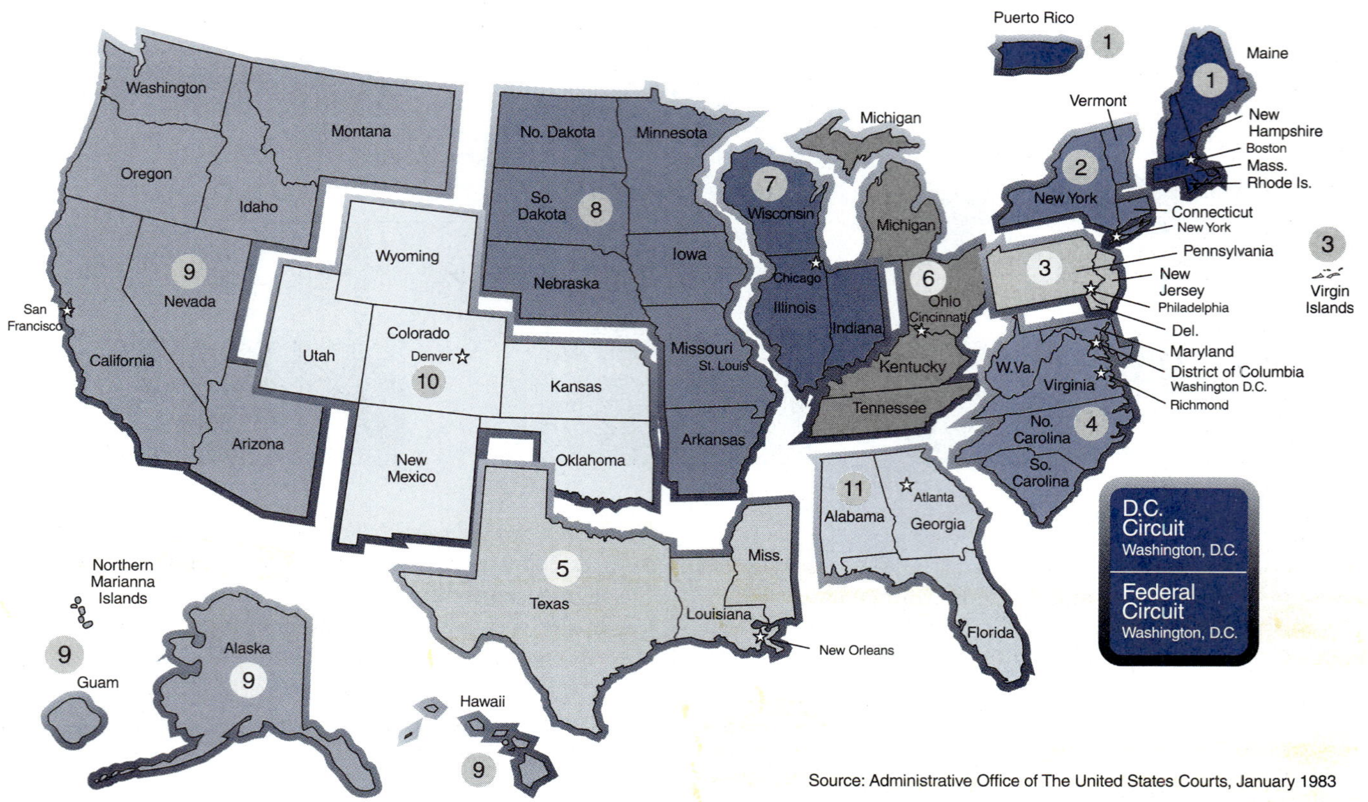

however, because the Court uses the writ as a device to choose which cases it wishes to hear.

http:// Information about the U.S. Supreme Court: http://supct.law.cornell.edu/supct/index.html

SPECIAL COURTS

The **special courts** in the federal judicial system include the U.S. Court of Federal Claims, the U.S. Bankruptcy Courts, the U.S. Tax Court, and the U.S. Court of Appeals for the Federal Circuit. These courts have jurisdiction over particular areas. The U.S. Court of Federal Claims hears claims against the United States. The U.S. Bankruptcy Courts hear and decide certain matters under the Federal Bankruptcy Code, subject to review by the U.S. District Court. The U.S. Tax Court has jurisdiction over certain cases involving federal taxes. The U.S. Court of Appeals for the Federal Circuit reviews decisions of the Court of Federal Claims, the Patent and Trademark Office, patent cases decided by U.S. District Courts, the United States Court of International Trade, the Merit Systems Protection Board, and the U.S. Court of Veterans Appeals.

http:// Cases decided by the U.S. Court of Federal Claims: http://www.uscfc.uscourts.gov/opinions.htm
Information about and cases decided by the U.S. Bankruptcy Courts: http://www.law.cornell.edu/federal/districts.html#circuit
Cases decided by the U.S. Court of Appeals for the Federal Circuit: http://www. law.emory.edu/fedcircuit/

STATE COURTS

Each of the fifty states and the District of Columbia has its own independent court system. In most states, the voters elect judges for a stated term. The structure of state court systems varies from state to state. Figure 3-3 shows a typical system.

INFERIOR TRIAL COURTS

At the bottom of the state court system are the **inferior trial courts**, which decide the least serious criminal and civil matters. Usually, inferior trial courts do not keep a complete written record of trial proceedings. Minor criminal cases such as traffic offenses are heard in inferior trial courts, which are referred to as municipal courts, justice of the

Figure 3-3
State Court System

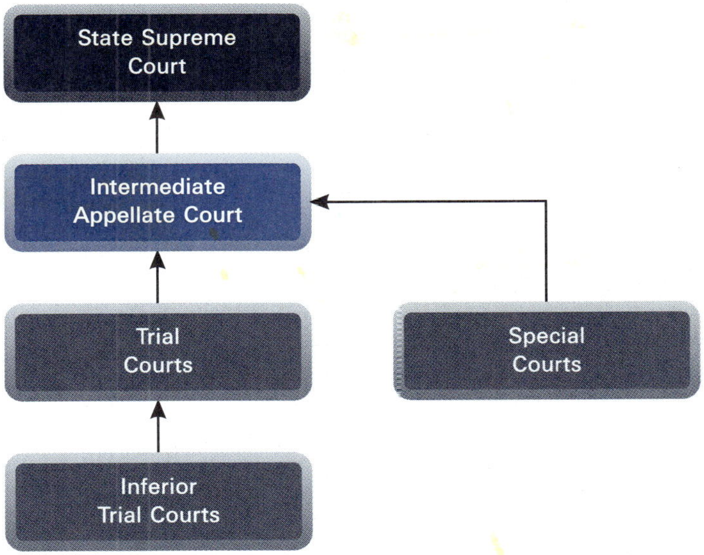

peace courts, or traffic courts. These courts also conduct preliminary hearings in more serious criminal cases.

Small claims courts are inferior trial courts that hear civil cases involving a limited amount of money. Usually there is no jury, the procedure is informal, and neither side employs an attorney. An appeal from a small claims court is taken to the trial court of general jurisdiction, where a new trial (called a trial *de novo*), in which the small claims court's decision is given no weight, is begun.

Trial Courts

Each state has **trial courts** of general jurisdiction, which may be called county, district, superior, circuit, or common pleas courts. (In New York the trial court is called the Supreme Court.) These courts do not have a dollar limitation on their jurisdiction in civil cases and hear all criminal cases other than minor offenses. Unlike the inferior trial courts, these trial courts of general jurisdiction maintain formal records of their proceedings as procedural safeguards.

Many states have **special trial courts** that have jurisdiction over particular areas. For example, many states have probate courts with jurisdiction over the administration of wills and estates and family courts with jurisdiction over divorce and child custody cases.

Appellate Courts

At the summit of the state court system is the state's court of last resort, a reviewing court generally called the supreme court of the state. Except for those cases in which review by the U.S. Supreme Court is available, the decision of the highest state tribunal is final. In addition, most states also have created intermediate **appellate courts** to handle the large volume of cases in which review is sought. Review by such a court is usually by right. Further review is in most cases at the highest court's discretion.

http:// Information about and cases decided by state courts: http://ncsconline.org/D_KIS/info_court_web_sites.html
State court decisions: http://www.law.cornell.edu/opinions.html#state

JURISDICTION

Jurisdiction means the power or authority of a court to hear and decide a given case. To resolve a lawsuit, a court must have two kinds of jurisdiction. The first is jurisdiction over the subject matter of the lawsuit. Where a court lacks jurisdiction over the subject matter of a case, no action it takes in the case will have legal effect.

The second kind of jurisdiction is over the parties to a lawsuit. This jurisdiction is required for the court to render an enforceable judgment that affects the parties' rights and duties. A court usually may obtain jurisdiction over the defendant in a lawsuit if the defendant lives and is present in the court's territory or the transaction giving rise to the case has a substantial connection to the court's territory. The court obtains jurisdiction over the plaintiff when the plaintiff voluntarily submits to the court's power by filing a complaint with the court.

Subject Matter Jurisdiction

Subject matter jurisdiction refers to the authority of a particular court to judge a controversy of a particular kind.

Federal courts have *limited* subject matter jurisdiction. State courts have jurisdiction over *all* matters that the Constitution or Congress neither denies them nor gives exclusively to the federal courts.

FEDERAL JURISDICTION

The federal courts have, to the exclusion of the state courts, subject matter jurisdiction over some areas. Such jurisdiction is called **exclusive federal jurisdiction.** Federal jurisdiction is exclusive only if Congress so provides, either explicitly or implicitly. If Congress does not so provide and the area is one over which federal courts have subject matter jurisdiction, they share this jurisdiction with the state courts. Such jurisdiction is known as **concurrent federal jurisdiction.**

Exclusive Federal Jurisdiction The federal courts have exclusive jurisdiction over federal criminal prosecutions; admiralty, bankruptcy, antitrust, patent, trademark, and copyright cases; suits against the United States; and cases arising under certain federal statutes that expressly provide for exclusive federal jurisdiction.

Concurrent Federal Jurisdiction There are two types of concurrent federal jurisdiction: federal question jurisdiction and diversity jurisdiction. The first arises whenever there is a federal question over which the federal courts do not have exclusive jurisdiction. A **federal question** is any case arising under the Constitution, statutes, or treaties of the United States. There is no minimum dollar requirement in federal question cases.

The second type of concurrent federal jurisdiction occurs in a civil suit where there is diversity of citizenship and the amount in controversy exceeds $75,000. As the following case explains, the jurisdictional requirement is satisfied if the claim for the amount is made in good faith, unless it is clear to a legal certainty that the claim does not meet or exceed the required amount. *Diversity of citizenship* exists (1) when the plaintiffs are citizens of a state or states different from the state or states of which the defendants are citizens; (2) when a foreign country brings an action against citizens of the United States; or (3) when the controversy is between citizens of the United States and citizens of a foreign country. The citizenship of an individual litigant (party in a lawsuit) is the state in which the individual resides or is domiciled, whereas that of a corporate litigant is both the state of incorporation and the state in which its principal place of business is located. For example, if the amount in controversy exceeds $75,000, then diversity of citizenship jurisdiction would be satisfied if Ada, a citizen of California, sues Bob, a citizen of Idaho. If, however, Carol, a citizen of Virginia, and Dianne, a citizen of North Carolina, sue Evan, a citizen of Georgia, and Farley, a citizen of North Carolina, there is *not* diversity of citizenship, because both Dianne, a plaintiff, and Farley, a defendant, are citizens of North Carolina.

When a federal district court hears a case solely under diversity of citizenship jurisdiction, no federal question is involved; and, accordingly, the federal courts must apply substantive state law. The conflict of law rules of the state in which the district court is located determine which state's substantive law is to be used in the case. (Conflict of laws is discussed later.) Federal courts apply federal procedural rules in diversity cases.

In any case involving concurrent jurisdiction, the plaintiff has the choice of bringing the action in either an appropriate federal court or state court. If the plaintiff brings the case in a state court, however, the defendant usually may have it removed (shifted) to a federal court for the district in which the state court is located.

Practical Advice

If you have the option, consider whether you want to bring your lawsuit in a federal or state court.

Ram Products Co. v. Chauncey

United States District Court, N.D. Indiana, South Bend Division, 1997
967 F.Supp. 1071

FACTS Defendant, Warren C. Chauncey (Chauncey), is an Indiana resident, who briefly held the position of Vice President of Sales and Marketing while employed at RAM Products. He is fifty-nine years old and has been in the plastics industry for twenty-five years. Defendant, Replex Plastics (Replex), is an Ohio Corporation now employing Chauncey in a management position. Plaintiff, RAM Products (RAM), a Michigan corporation, and Replex (**http://www.replex.com**) are both in the plastics industry. The employment contract in controversy was entered into between Chauncey and RAM in St. Joseph County, Michigan, on November 18, 1991, and contained a clause prohibiting former employees from competing against RAM for a period of one year after termination of employment with RAM. On December 3, 1996, Chauncey was released from his employment at RAM and soon after began employment with Replex.

The plaintiff contends that this was a breach of its former employment contract's covenant not to compete, that Chauncey has converted and continues to convert RAM's property and trade secrets, and that he has made derogatory remarks regarding RAM to its customers and the general public. The plaintiff argues that Chauncey's breach of contract causes irreparable harm to it through the disclosure of confidential information, the loss of client confidence, loss of goodwill, and loss of business reputation. The plaintiff seeks a preliminary injunction requiring Chauncey to cease his employment with Replex until the one-year time period required by the contract has expired, an injunction restraining Chauncey from working for any other competitor during the one-year period, and damages originally in the amount of $50,000, the jurisdictional amount when the plaintiff filed this suit. The defendant Chauncey asserts that he is not violating his former employment contract, that the contract is void due to RAM's failure to perform certain provisions of the contract, that the noncompetition clause is overly broad and unenforceable, and that he has not disclosed any trade secrets or confidential information.

DECISION Federal diversity jurisdiction satisfied.

OPINION Sharp, C. J. The court heard oral argument regarding the issues on February 5, 1997, at which time the court directed the parties to brief the issues. Subsequently, the parties entered into settlement negotiations with the Magistrate and requested several extensions for the filing of their briefs. The settlement conferences were ultimately unsuccessful. On March 18, 1997 the court received the parties' briefs addressing the preliminary injunction. At that time, the court expressed serious reservations regarding jurisdictional issues and requested the parties to supplement the record by briefing those issues. [Court's footnote: Specifically, the court questioned the amount in controversy. Plaintiff's complaint alleged an amount of $50,000. At the time plaintiff filed, the increased jurisdictional amount of $75,000 was required, as the amendment to 28 U.S.C. 1332 [the diversity jurisdiction statute] became effective on January 16, 1997. Additionally, the complaint contained only unsupported allegations of potential lost profits and sales. Plaintiff has since filed an amended complaint and a brief on the jurisdictional issue.]

This court has subject matter jurisdiction over this case pursuant to 28 U.S.C. § 1332, as amended October 19, 1996, because the matter in controversy exceeds the sum or value of $75,000 and is between citizens of different states. [Court's footnote: While this court still has concerns regarding the amount of actual damages attributable to defendant, the court finds that plaintiff has alleged sufficient facts to proceed with the case. However, close attention should be given to 18 U.S.C. § 1332(G), which authorizes cost to be assessed against the plaintiff where the recovery is less than the jurisdictional amount. It has been this court's practice to do such.] * * * If the right of recovery is uncertain, the doubt should be resolved, for jurisdictional purposes, in favor of the subjective good faith of the plaintiff. [Citation.] Moreover, even where those allegations leave "grave doubt about the likelihood of a recovery of the requisite amount, dismissal is not warranted." [Citation.] Applying this rationale, this court resolves the jurisdictional conflict in favor of Plaintiff. [Only] if it appears to a legal certainty that the plaintiff cannot recover the jurisdictional amount will the case be dismissed for want of jurisdiction. [Citation.]

This action is based on an employment contract with no express choice of law provision. * * * Therefore, prior to determining the merits of plaintiff's request for an injunction, this court must determine which state's law applies to the substantive contract issues.

As a rule, a court in a diversity case must apply the substantive law of the forum in which it sits, [*Erie v. Tomkins*, citation], including that pertaining to choice of law. [Citation.] Therefore, if the laws of more than one jurisdiction arguably are in issue, *Erie* requires the federal court to apply the choice of law rules of the state in which it sits. [Citation.] Accordingly, this court will apply Indiana's choice of law rules in making its determination of which state's law governs the substantive issues.

The characterization of the nature of an action bears upon the choice-of-law question. The present action arises from a breach of contract claim. Formerly, in contract cases, Indiana courts applied the law of the state in which the alleged contract was made or was to be performed. [Citation.] The focus upon performance, in most instances, resulted in application of the law where the breach took place. That rule was modified, however, to allow application of the law of the state with the most significant contacts to the subject matter of the litigation be applied, regardless of the place of the breach. [Citation.] The test requires that a court analyze "all acts of the parties touching the transaction in relation to the several states involved" and apply "the law of the state with which the facts are in most intimate contact." [Citation.] * * * Applying the above principles this court now considers the relevant factors to determine whether Michigan or Indiana substantive law applies to the claims at issue.

Indiana maintains at least some interest in the present action. Defendant Chauncey is an Indiana resident. Indiana has an interest in protecting its citizens' rights to earn a livelihood. [Citation.] Furthermore, Indiana's public policy disfavors noncompetition clauses. [Citation.] In addition, both the plaintiff, RAM, and one of the defendants, Replex, transact business in Indiana. Indiana has an economic interest in the ability of companies to conduct business there. Certainly, the final resolution of the case may have some economic impact on Indiana.

In determining the state where the facts are in "most intimate contact" the court notes that defendant RAM is a Michigan corporation. Additionally, both RAM and Replex transact business in Michigan. Similar to Indiana, Michigan has an interest in protecting its corporations and in protecting the ability of companies to conduct business in the state. As a result, Michigan also has an economic interest in this case. Furthermore, while there is no indication of where the negotiations for this contract occurred, the "home office" for which Chauncey worked was located in Michigan. In addition, the employment agreement in question was formed in Michigan. Moreover, Michigan public policy and statutes favor noncompetition covenants as long as they are reasonable. [Citation.]

Based on the above facts, this court finds that the balance of factors tips slightly in favor of Michigan's interests, therefore, this court will apply Michigan law to resolve the substantive contract issues.

INTERPRETATION If it is not clear to a legal certainty that the damages claimed would not satisfy the jurisdictional amount requirement, the plaintiff is entitled to have its claim heard in a federal court.

ETHICAL QUESTION Is it ethical for a plaintiff to inflate the amount of damages requested in order to obtain federal diversity jurisdiction? Explain.

CRITICAL THINKING QUESTION Why has Congress imposed a jurisdictional minimum for diversity of citizenship cases?

EXCLUSIVE STATE JURISDICTION

The state courts have exclusive jurisdiction over all other matters. All matters not granted to the federal courts in the Constitution or by Congress are solely within the jurisdiction of the states. Accordingly, exclusive state jurisdiction would include cases involving diversity of citizenship where the amount in controversy is $75,000 or less. In addition, the state courts have exclusive jurisdiction over all cases to which the federal judicial power does not reach, including, but by no means limited to, property, torts, contract, agency, commercial transactions, and most crimes.

A court in one state may be a proper forum for a case even though some or all of the relevant events occurred in another state. For example, a California plaintiff may sue a Washington defendant in Washington over a car accident that occurred in Oregon. Because of Oregon's connections to the accident, Washington may choose, under its ***conflict of laws*** rules, to apply the substantive law of Oregon. Conflict of laws rules vary from state to state. See *RAM Products Co. v. Chauncey* above.

The jurisdiction of the federal and state courts is illustrated in Figure 3-4. Also, see the following Concept Review.

Practical Advice

Consider including in your contracts a choice-of-law provision specifying which jurisdiction's law will apply.

STARE DECISIS IN THE DUAL COURT SYSTEM

The doctrine of *stare decisis* presents certain problems when there are two parallel court systems. As a consequence, in the United States, *stare decisis* works approximately as follows (also illustrated in Figure 3-5):

Figure 3-4
Federal and State Jurisdiction

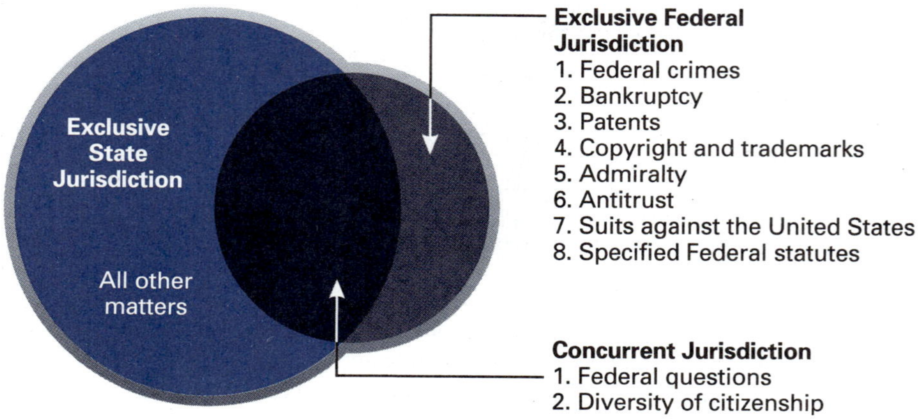

CONCEPT REVIEW

Subject Matter Jurisdiction

Type of Jurisdiction	Court	Law Applied
Exclusive federal	Federal	Federal
Concurrent: federal question	Federal or state	Federal
Concurrent: diversity	Federal or state	State
Exclusive state	State	State

1. The U.S. Supreme Court has never held itself to be bound rigidly by its own decisions, and lower federal courts and state courts have followed that course with respect to their own decisions.
2. A decision of the U.S. Supreme Court on a federal question is binding on all other courts, federal or state.
3. On a federal question, although a decision of a federal court other than the Supreme Court may be persuasive in a state court, it is not binding.
4. A decision of a state court may be persuasive in the federal courts, but it is not binding except where federal jurisdiction is based on diversity of citizenship. In such a case, the federal courts must apply state law as determined by the highest state tribunal.
5. Decisions of the federal courts (other than the U.S. Supreme Court) are not binding on other federal courts of equal or inferior rank unless the latter owe obedience to the deciding court. For example, a decision of the Fifth Circuit Court of Appeals binds district courts in the fifth circuit but binds no other federal court.
6. A decision of a state court is binding on all courts inferior to it in its jurisdiction. Thus, the decision of the supreme court in a state binds all other courts in that state.
7. A decision of a state court is not binding on courts in another state except where the latter courts are required, under their conflict of laws rules, to apply the law of the first state as determined by the highest court in that state. For example, if a North Carolina court is required to apply Virginia law, it must follow decisions of the Virginia Supreme Court.

JURISDICTION OVER THE PARTIES

The second essential type of jurisdiction a court must have is the power to bind the parties involved in the dispute. This type of jurisdiction is called **jurisdiction over the parties**, and its requirements may be met in any of three ways: (1) *in personam* jurisdiction, (2) *in rem* jurisdiction, or (3) attachment jurisdiction. In addition, the exercise of jurisdiction must satisfy the constitutionally imposed requirements of reasonable notification and a reasonable opportunity to be heard. Moreover, the court's exercise of jurisdiction is valid under the due process clause of the U.S. Constitution only if the defendant has minimum contacts with the state sufficient to prevent the

Figure 3-5
Stare Decisis *in the Dual Court System*

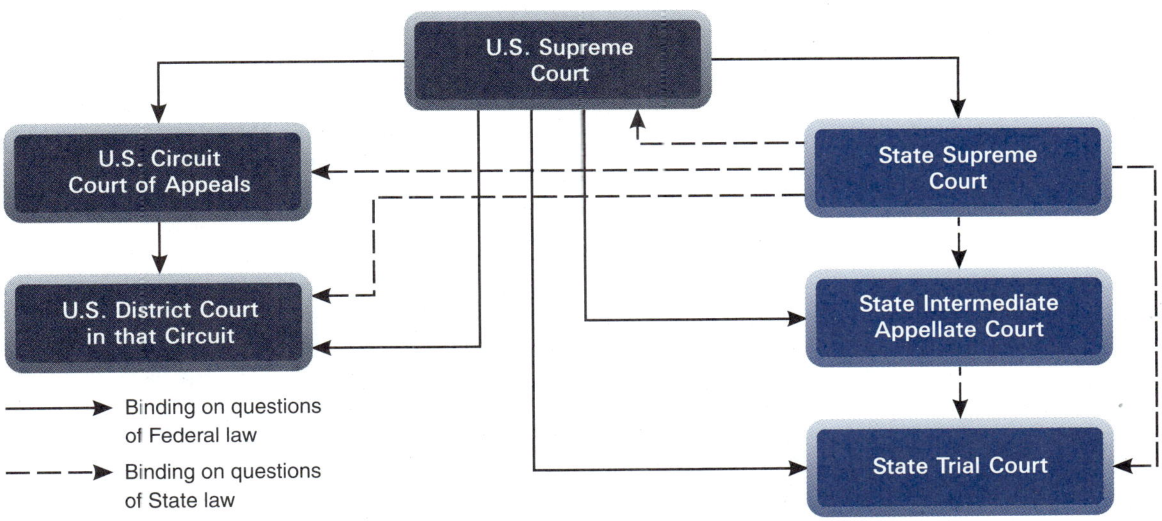

court's assertion of jurisdiction from offending "traditional notions of fair play and substantial justice." For a court constitutionally to assert jurisdiction over a defendant, the defendant must have engaged in either purposeful acts in the state or acts outside the state that are of such a nature that the defendant could reasonably foresee being sued in that state, as discussed in the next case.

World-Wide Volkswagen Corp. v. Woodson

Supreme Court of the United States, 1980
44 U.S. 286, 100 S.Ct. 559, 62 L.Ed.2d 490
http://laws.findlaw.com/us/444/286.html

FACTS Harry and Kay Robinson purchased a new Audi automobile from Seaway Volkswagen, Inc. (Seaway) in Massena, New York. The Robinsons, who had resided in New York for years, left for a new home in Arizona. As they drove through Oklahoma, another car struck their Audi from behind, causing a fire that severely burned Kay and her two children.

The Robinsons brought a products-liability suit in the District Court in Oklahoma, claiming their injuries resulted from defective design of the Audi gas tank and fuel system. They joined as defendants the manufacturer (Audi) **(http://www.audiusa.com/index)**, the regional distributor (World-Wide Volkswagen Corp.) **(http://www.vw.com)**, and the retail distributor (Seaway).

World-Wide and Seaway entered special appearances, asserting that Oklahoma's exercise of jurisdiction over them offended limitations on state jurisdiction imposed by the due process clause of the Fourteenth Amendment. The Oklahoma Supreme Court upheld the assertion of state jurisdiction, and World-Wide and Seaway appealed.

DECISION Judgment of Oklahoma Supreme Court reversed.

OPINION White, J. The Due Process Clause of the Fourteenth Amendment limits the power of a state court to render a valid personal judgment against a nonresident defendant. [Citation.] A judgment rendered in violation of due process is void in the rendering State and is not entitled to full faith and credit elsewhere. [Citation.] Due process requires that the defendant be given adequate notice of the suit, [citation], and be subject to the personal jurisdiction of the court, [citation]. In the present case, it is not contended that notice was inadequate; the only question is whether these particular petitioners were subject to the jurisdiction of the Oklahoma courts.

As has long been settled, and as we reaffirm today, a state court may exercise personal jurisdiction over a nonresident defendant only so long as there exist "minimum contacts" between the defendant and the forum State. [Citation.] The concept of minimum contacts, in turn, can be seen to perform two related, but distinguishable, functions. It protects the defendant against the burdens of litigating in a distant or inconvenient forum. And it acts to ensure that the States, through their courts, do not reach out beyond the limits imposed on them by their status as coequal sovereigns in a federal system.

The protection against inconvenient litigation is typically described in terms of "reasonableness" or "fairness." We have said that the defendant's contacts with the forum State must be such that maintenance of the suit "does not offend 'traditional notions of fair play and substantial justice.'" [Citation.] The relationship between the defendant and the forum must be such that it is "reasonable * * * to require the corporation to defend the particular suit which is brought there." [Citation.] Implicit in this emphasis on reasonableness is the understanding that the burden on the defendant, while always a primary concern, will in an appropriate case be considered in light of other relevant factors, including the forum State's interest in adjudicating the dispute, [citation]; the plaintiff's interest in obtaining convenient and effective relief, [citation], at least when that interest is not adequately protected by the plaintiff's power to choose the forum, [citation]; the interstate judicial system's interest in obtaining the most efficient resolution of controversies; and the shared interest of the several States in furthering fundamental substantive social policies, [citation].

* * *

Applying these principles to the case at hand, we find in the record before us a total absence of those affiliating circumstances that are a necessary predicate to any exercise of state-court jurisdiction. Petitioners carry on no activity whatsoever in Oklahoma. They close no sales and perform no services there. They avail themselves of none of the privileges and benefits of Oklahoma law. They solicit no business there either through salespersons or through advertising reasonably calculated to reach the State. Nor does the record show that they regularly sell cars at wholesale or retail to Oklahoma customers or residents or that they indirectly, through others, serve or seek to serve the Oklahoma market. In short, respondents seek to base jurisdiction on one, isolated occurrence and whatever inferences can be drawn therefrom: the fortuitous circumstance that a single Audi automobile, sold in New York to New York residents, happened to suffer an accident while passing through Oklahoma.

INTERPRETATION Sufficient minimal contacts between the defendant and the state must exist for a state to exercise jurisdiction.

CRITICAL THINKING QUESTION Explain the public policy reasons for subjecting nonresidents doing business in a state to the *in personam* jurisdiction of the courts within that state.

IN PERSONAM JURISDICTION

***In personam* jurisdiction**, or personal jurisdiction, is the jurisdiction of a court over the parties to a lawsuit, in contrast to its jurisdiction over their property. A court obtains *in personam* jurisdiction over a person either (1) by serving process on the party within the state in which the court is located or (2) by reasonable notification to a party outside the state in those instances where a "long-arm statute" applies. To *serve process* means to deliver a summons, which is an order to respond to a complaint lodged against a party. (The terms *summons* and *complaint* are explained more fully later in this chapter.)

Personal jurisdiction may be obtained by personally serving process upon a person within a state if that person is domiciled in that state. The U.S. Supreme Court has held that a state may exercise personal jurisdiction over a nonresident defendant who is temporarily present if the defendant is personally served in that state. Personal jurisdiction may also arise from a party's consent. For example, parties to a contract may agree that any dispute concerning that contract will be subject to the jurisdiction of a specific court.

Most states have adopted ***long-arm statutes*** to expand their jurisdictional reach beyond those persons who may be personally served within the state. These statutes allow courts to obtain jurisdiction over nonresident defendants under the following conditions, as long as the exercise of jurisdiction does not offend traditional notions of fair play and substantial justice: if the defendant (1) has committed a tort (civil wrong) within the state, (2) owns property within the state and if that property is the subject matter of the lawsuit, (3) has entered into a contract within the state, or (4) has transacted business within the state and if that business is the subject matter of the lawsuit.

Practical Advice

Consider including in your contracts a choice-of-forum provision specifying what court will have jurisdiction over any litigation arising from the contract.

IN REM JURISDICTION

Courts in a state have the jurisdiction to adjudicate claims to property situated within the state if the plaintiff gives those persons who have an interest in the property reasonable notice and an opportunity to be heard. Such jurisdiction over property is called ***in rem* jurisdiction.** For example, if Carpenter and Miller are involved in a lawsuit over property located in Kansas, then an appropriate court in Kansas would have *in rem* jurisdiction to adjudicate claims over this property as long as both parties are given notice of the lawsuit and a reasonable opportunity to contest the claim.

ATTACHMENT JURISDICTION

Attachment jurisdiction, or ***quasi in rem* jurisdiction**, like *in rem* jurisdiction, is jurisdiction over property rather than over a person. But attachment jurisdiction is invoked by seizing the defendant's property located within the state to obtain payment of a claim against the defendant that is *unrelated* to the property seized. For example, Allen, a resident of Ohio, has obtained a valid judgment in the amount of $20,000 against Bradley, a citizen of Kentucky. Allen can attach Bradley's automobile, which is located in Ohio, to satisfy his court judgment against Bradley.

See Figure 3-6, which outlines the concepts of subject matter and party jurisdiction.

VENUE

Venue, which often is confused with jurisdiction, concerns the geographical area in which a lawsuit should be brought. The purpose of venue is to regulate the distribution of cases within a specific court system and to identify a convenient forum. In the federal court system, venue determines the district or districts in a given state in which suit may be brought. State rules of venue typically require that a suit be initiated in a county where one of the defendants lives. In matters involving real estate, most venue rules require that a suit be initiated in the county where the property is situated.

CIVIL DISPUTE RESOLUTION

As mentioned in Chapter 1, one of the primary functions of law is to provide for the peaceful resolution of disputes. Accordingly, our legal system has established an elaborate set of governmental mechanisms to settle disputes. The

Figure 3-6 *Jurisdiction*

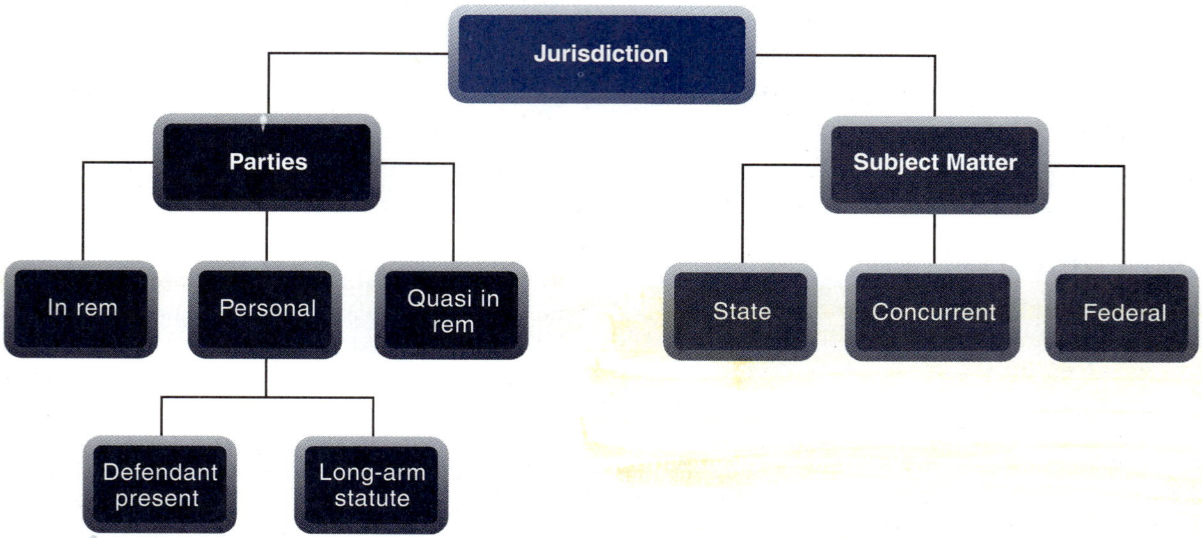

most prominent of these is judicial dispute resolution, called *litigation*. Judicial resolution of civil disputes is governed by the rules of civil procedure, which we will discuss in the first part of this section. Judicial resolution of criminal cases is governed by the rules of criminal procedure, which are covered in Chapter 6. Dispute resolution by administrative agencies, which is also very common, is discussed in Chapter 5.

As an alternative to governmental dispute resolution, several nongovernmental methods of dispute resolution, such as arbitration, have developed. We will discuss these in the second part of this section.

> **Practical Advice**
>
> If you become involved in litigation, make full disclosure to your attorney and do not discuss the lawsuit without consulting your attorney.

CIVIL PROCEDURE

A civil dispute that enters the judicial system must follow the rules of civil procedure. These rules are designed to resolve the dispute justly, promptly, and inexpensively.

To acquaint you with civil procedure, we will carry a hypothetical action through the trial court to the highest court of review in the state. Although there are technical differences in trial and appellate procedure among the states and the federal courts, the following illustration will give you a general understanding of the trial and appeal of cases. Assume that Pam Pederson, a pedestrian, is struck while crossing a street in Chicago by an automobile driven by David Dryden. Pederson suffers serious personal injuries, incurs heavy medical and hospital expenses, and is unable to work for several months. She desires that Dryden pay her for the loss and damages she sustained. After attempts at settlement fail, Pederson brings an action at law against Dryden. Thus, Pederson is the plaintiff and Dryden the defendant. Each is represented by a lawyer. Let us follow the progress of the case.

http:// State civil procedure laws: http://www.law.cornell.edu/topics/statestatutes.html#civil_procedure

THE PLEADINGS

The **pleadings** are a series of responsive, formal, written statements in which each side to a lawsuit states its claims and defenses. The purpose of pleadings is to give notice and to establish the issues of fact and law the parties dispute. An "issue of fact" is a dispute between the parties regarding the events that gave rise to the lawsuit. In contrast, an "issue of law" is a dispute between the parties as to what legal rules apply to these facts. Issues of fact are decided by the jury, or by the judge when there is no jury, whereas issues of law are decided by the judge.

Complaint and Summons A lawsuit begins when Pederson, the plaintiff, files with the clerk of the trial court a **complaint** against Dryden that contains (1) a statement of the claim and supporting facts showing that she is entitled to relief and (2) a demand for that relief. Pederson's complaint alleges that while exercising due and reasonable care for her own safety, she was struck by Dryden's automobile, which was being driven negligently by Dryden, causing her personal injuries and damages of $50,000, for which Pederson requests judgment.

Once the plaintiff has filed a complaint, the clerk issues a **summons** to be served upon the defendant to notify him that a suit has been brought against him. If the defendant has contacts with the state sufficient to show that the state's assertion of jurisdiction over the defendant is constitutional, proper service of the summons establishes the court's jurisdiction over the person of the defendant. The county sheriff or a deputy sheriff serves a summons and a copy of the complaint on Dryden, the defendant, commanding him to file his appearance and answer with the clerk of the court within a specific time, usually thirty days from the date the summons was served.

Responses to Complaint At this point, Dryden has several options. If he fails to respond at all, a **default judgment** will be entered against him. He may make ***pretrial motions*** contesting the court's jurisdiction over him or asserting that the action is barred by the statute of limitations, which requires suits to be brought within a specified time. Dryden also may move, or request, that the complaint be made more definite and certain, or he may instead move that the complaint be dismissed for failure to state a claim on which relief may be granted. Such a motion is sometimes called a **demurrer**; it essentially asserts that even if all of Pederson's allegations were true, she still would not be entitled to the relief she seeks and that therefore there is no need for a trial of the facts. The court rules on this motion as a matter of law. If it rules in favor of the defendant, the plaintiff may appeal the ruling.

If he does not make any pretrial motions, or if they are denied, Dryden will respond to the complaint by filing an **answer**, which may contain denials, admissions, affirmative defenses, and counterclaims. Dryden might answer the complaint by denying its allegations of negligence and stating that he was driving his car at a low speed and with reasonable care (a ***denial***) when his car struck Pederson (an ***admission***), who had dashed across the street in front of his car without looking in any direction to see whether cars or other vehicles were approaching; that, accordingly, Pederson's injuries were caused by her own negligence (an ***affirmative defense***); and that, therefore, she should not be permitted to recover any damages. Dryden might further state that Pederson caused damage to his car and request a judgment for $2,000 (a ***counterclaim***). These pleadings create an issue of fact regarding whether Dryden or Pederson, or both, failed to exercise due and reasonable care under the circumstances and were thus negligent and liable for their carelessness.

If the defendant counterclaims, the plaintiff must respond through a **reply**, which also may contain admissions, denials, or affirmative defenses.

PRETRIAL PROCEDURE

Judgment on the Pleadings After the pleadings, either party may move for **judgment on the pleadings**, which requests the judge to rule as a matter of law whether the facts as alleged in the pleadings of the nonmoving party are sufficient to warrant granting the requested relief.

Discovery In preparation for trial and even before completion of the pleadings stage, each party has the right to obtain relevant evidence, or information that may lead to evidence, from the other party. This procedure, known as **discovery**, includes (1) pretrial *depositions* consisting of sworn testimony, taken out of court, of the opposing party or other witnesses; (2) sworn answers by the opposing party to *written interrogatories*, or questions; (3) *production* of documents and physical objects in the possession of the opposing party; (4) *court-ordered examination* by a physician of the opposing party, as needed; and (5) admissions of facts set forth in a *request for admissions* submitted to the opposing party. By using discovery properly, each party may become fully informed of relevant evidence and avoid surprise at trial. Another purpose of this procedure is to facilitate settlements by giving both parties as much relevant information as possible.

Pretrial Conference Also furthering these objectives is the pretrial conference between the judge and the attorneys representing the parties. The basic purposes of the **pretrial conference** are (1) to simplify the issues in dispute by amending the pleadings, admitting or stipulating facts, and limiting the number of expert witnesses; and (2) to encourage settlement of the dispute without trial. (More than 90 percent of all cases are settled before going to trial.) If no settlement occurs, the judge will enter a pretrial order containing all of the amendments, stipulations, admissions, and other matters agreed to during the pretrial conference. The order supersedes the pleadings and controls the remainder of the trial.

Summary Judgment The evidence disclosed by discovery may be so clear that a trial to determine the facts becomes unnecessary. If this is so, either party may move for a summary judgment, which requests the judge to rule that, because there are no issues of fact to be determined by trial, the party thus moving should prevail as a matter of law. A **summary judgment** is a final binding determination on the merits made by the judge before a trial. The following case involving actress Shirley MacLaine explains the rules courts use to determine whether to grant summary judgment.

Parker v. Twentieth Century-Fox Film Corp.

Supreme Court of California, 1970
3 Cal.3d 176, 89 Cal.Rptr. 737, 474 P.2d 689

FACTS Shirley MacLaine Parker, a well-known actress, contracted with Twentieth Century-Fox Film Corporation **(http://www.newscorp.com/)** in August 1965 to play the female lead in Fox's upcoming production of *Bloomer Girl*, a motion picture musical that was to be filmed in California. Fox agreed to pay Parker $750,000 for fourteen weeks of her services. Fox decided to cancel its plans for *Bloomer Girl* before production had begun and, instead, offered Parker the female lead in another film, *Big Country, Big Man*, a dramatic western to be filmed in Australia. The compensation offered was identical, but Parker's right to approve the director and screenplay would have been eliminated or altered by the *Big Country* proposal. She refused to accept and brought suit to recover the $750,000 for Fox's breach of the *Bloomer Girl* contract. Fox's sole defense in its answer was that it owed no money to Parker because she had deliberately failed to mitigate or reduce her damages by unreasonably refusing to accept the *Big Country* lead. Parker filed a motion for summary judgment. Fox, in opposition to the motion, claimed, in effect, only that the *Big Country* offer was not employment different from or inferior to that under the *Bloomer Girl* contract. The trial court granted Parker a summary judgment and Fox appealed.

DECISION Summary judgment affirmed.

OPINION Burke, J. The familiar rules are that the matter to be determined by the trial court on a motion for summary judgment is whether facts have been presented which give rise to a triable factual issue. The court may not pass upon the issue itself. Summary judgment is proper only if the affidavits or declarations in support of the moving party would be sufficient to sustain a judgment in his favor and his opponent does not by affidavit show facts sufficient to present a triable issue of fact. The affidavits of the moving party are strictly construed, and doubts as to the propriety of summary judgment should be resolved against granting the motion. Such summary procedure is drastic and should be used with caution so that it does not become a substitute for the open trial method of determining facts. The moving party cannot depend upon allegations in his own pleadings to cure deficient affidavits, nor can his adversary rely upon his own pleadings in lieu or in support of affidavits in opposition to a motion; however, a party can rely on his adversary's pleadings to establish facts not contained in his own affidavits. [Citations.] Also, the court may consider facts stipulated to by the parties and facts which are properly the subject of judicial notice. [Citations.]

* * *

Applying the foregoing rules to the record in the present case, with all intendments in favor of the party opposing the summary judgment motion—here, defendant—it is clear that the trial court correctly ruled that plaintiff's failure to accept defendant's tendered substitute employment could not be applied in mitigation of damages because the offer of the *Big Country* lead was of employment both different and inferior, and that no factual dispute was presented on that issue. The mere circumstance that *Bloomer Girl* was to be a musical review calling upon plaintiff's talents as a dancer as well as an actress, and was to be produced in the City of Los Angeles, whereas, *Big Country* was a straight dramatic role in a "Western Type" story taking place in an opal mine in Australia, demonstrates the difference in kind between the two employments; the female lead as a dramatic actress in a western style motion picture can by no stretch of imagination be considered the equivalent of or substantially similar to the lead in a song-and-dance production.

Additionally, the substitute *Big Country* offer proposed to eliminate or impair the director and screenplay approvals accorded to plaintiff under the original *Bloomer Girl* contract * * * and thus constituted an offer of inferior employment. No expertise or judicial notice is required in order to hold that the deprivation or infringement of an employee's rights held under an original employment contract converts the available "other employment" relied upon by the employer to mitigate damages, into inferior employment which the employee need not seek or accept. [Citation.]

INTERPRETATION A court will grant summary judgment when there are no issues of fact to be determined by trial.

CRITICAL THINKING QUESTION When should a court grant summary judgment? Explain.

TRIAL

In all federal civil cases at common law involving more than $20, the U.S. Constitution guarantees the right to a jury trial. In addition, nearly every state constitution provides a similar right. Under federal law and in almost all states, jury trials are *not* available in equity cases. Even in cases where a jury trial is available, the parties may waive (choose not to have) a trial by jury. When a trial is conducted without a jury, the judge serves as the fact finder and will make separate findings of fact and conclusions of law. When a trial is conducted *with* a jury, the judge determines issues of law and the jury determines questions of fact.

Jury Selection Assuming a timely demand for a jury has been made, the trial begins with the selection of a jury. The jury selection process involves a ***voir dire***, an examination by the parties' attorneys (or in some courts by the judge) of the potential jurors. Each party has an unlimited number of ***challenges for cause***, which allow the party to prevent a prospective juror from serving if the juror is biased or cannot be fair and impartial. In addition, each party has a limited number of ***peremptory challenges*** for which no cause is required to disqualify a prospective juror. The Supreme Court has held that the U.S. Constitution prohibits discrimination in jury selection on the basis of race or gender.

Edmonson v. Leesville Concrete Company, Inc.

Supreme Court of the United States, 1991
500 U.S. 614, 111 S.Ct. 2077, 114 L.Ed.2d 660
http://laws.findlaw.com/us/500/614.html

FACTS Thaddeus Donald Edmonson, a construction worker, was injured in a job-site accident at Fort Polk, Louisiana. Edmonson sued Leesville Concrete Company for negligence in the U.S. District Court for the Western District of Louisiana, claiming that a Leesville employee permitted one of the company's trucks to roll backward and pin him against some construction equipment. Edmonson invoked his Seventh Amendment right to a trial by jury. During *voir dire*, Leesville used two of its three peremptory challenges authorized by statute to remove black persons from the prospective jury. When Edmonson, who is himself black, requested that the District Court require Leesville to articulate a race-neutral explanation for striking the two jurors, the District Court ruled that the precedent on which Edmonson's request relied applied only to criminal cases and allowed the strikes to stand. A jury of eleven whites and one black brought in a verdict for Edmonson, assessing total damages at $90,000. It also attributed 80 percent of the fault to Edmonson's contributory negligence and awarded him only $18,000. On appeal, a divided *en banc* panel affirmed the judgment of the District Court, concluding that the use of peremptory challenges by private litigants did not constitute state action and, as a result, did not violate constitutional guarantees against racial discrimination. The U.S. Supreme Court granted *certiorari*.

DECISION Judgment for Edmonson.

OPINION Kennedy, J. We must decide in the case before us whether a private litigant in a civil case may use peremptory challenges to exclude jurors on account of their race. * * *

* * *

* * * Although the conduct of private parties lies beyond the Constitution's scope in most instances, governmental authority may dominate an activity to such an extent that its participants must be deemed to act with the authority of the government and, as a result, be subject to constitutional constraints. * * *

* * * Our precedents establish that, in determining whether a particular action or course or conduct is governmental in character, it is relevant to examine the following: the extent to which the actor relies on governmental assistance and benefits, [citations]; whether the actor is performing a traditional governmental function, [citations]; and whether the injury caused is aggravated in a unique way by the incidents of governmental authority, [citation]. Based on our application of these three principles to the circumstances here, we hold that the exercise of peremptory challenges by the defendant in the District Court was pursuant to a course of state action.

* * * It cannot be disputed that, without the overt, significant participation of the government, the peremptory challenge system, as well as the jury trial system of which it is a part, simply could not exist. As discussed above, peremptory challenges have no utility outside the jury system, a system which the government alone administers. In the federal system, Congress has established the qualifications for the jury service, [citation], and has outlined the procedures by which jurors are selected. * * *

* * *

The trial judge exercises substantial control over *voir dire* in the federal system. [Citation.] * * * Without the direct and indispensable participation of the judge, who beyond all question is a state actor, the peremptory challenge system would serve no purpose. By enforcing a discriminatory peremptory challenge, the court "has not only made itself a party to the [biased act], but has elected to place its power, property and prestige behind the [alleged] discrimination." [Citation.] * * *

* * * The peremptory challenge is used in selecting an entity that is a quintessential governmental body, having no attributes of a private actor. The jury exercises the power of the court and of the government that confers the court's jurisdiction. * * * In the federal system, the Constitution itself commits the trial of facts in a civil cause to the jury. Should either party to a cause invoke its Seventh Amendment right, the jury becomes the principal factfinder, charged with weighing the evidence, judging the credibility of witnesses, and reaching a verdict. The jury's factual determinations as a general rule are final. [Citation.] In some civil cases, as we noted earlier this Term, the jury can weigh the gravity of a wrong and determine the degree of the government's interest in punishing and deterring willful misconduct. * * * And in all jurisdictions a true verdict will be incorporated in a judgment enforceable by the court. These are traditional functions of government, not of a select, private group beyond the reach of the Constitution.

* * *

Finally, we note that the injury caused by the discrimination is made more severe because the government permits it to occur within the courthouse itself. Few places are a more real expression of the constitutional authority of the government than a courtroom, where the law itself unfolds. * * * To permit racial exclusion in this official forum compounds the racial insult inherent in judging a citizen by the color of his or her skin.

INTERPRETATION The U.S. Constitution imposes restrictions against racial discrimination in the jury selection process.

ETHICAL QUESTION What are ethical grounds for an attorney to exercise a peremptory challenge? Explain.

CRITICAL THINKING QUESTION What grounds should be disallowed in the exercise of peremptory challenges? Explain.

Conduct of Trial After the jury has been selected, both attorneys make an ***opening statement*** about the facts that they expect to prove in the trial. The plaintiff and plaintiff's witnesses then testify on ***direct examination*** by the plaintiff's attorney. Each is subject to ***cross-examination*** by the defendant's attorney. Pederson and her witnesses testify that the traffic light at the street intersection where she was struck was green for traffic in the direction in which she was crossing but changed to yellow when she was about one-third of the way across the street.

During the trial, the judge rules on the admission and exclusion of evidence. If the judge does not allow certain evidence to be introduced or certain testimony to be given, the attorney must make an ***offer of proof*** to preserve for review on appeal the question of its admissibility. The offer of proof is not regarded as evidence, and the offer, which consists of oral statements of counsel or witnesses showing for the record the evidence that the judge has ruled inadmissible, is not heard by the jury.

After cross-examination, followed by redirect examination of each of her witnesses, Pederson rests her case. At this time, Dryden may move for a directed verdict in his favor. A **directed verdict** is a final binding determination on the merits made by the judge after a trial has begun but before the jury renders a verdict. If the judge concludes that the evidence introduced by Pederson, which is assumed for the purposes of the motion to be true, would not be sufficient for the jury to find in favor of the plaintiff, then the judge will grant the directed verdict in favor of the defendant. In some states, the judge will deny the motion for a directed verdict if there is *any* evidence on which the jury might possibly render a verdict for the plaintiff.

If the judge denies the motion for a directed verdict, however, the defendant then has the opportunity to present evidence. Dryden and his witnesses testify that he was driving his car at a low speed when it struck Pederson and that Dryden at the time had the green light at the intersection. After the defendant has presented his evidence and both parties have rested (concluded), then either party may move for a directed verdict. By this motion the party contends that the evidence is so clear that reasonable persons could not differ about the outcome of the case. If the judge grants the motion for a directed verdict, he takes the case away from the jury and enters a judgment for the party making the motion.

If these motions are denied, then Pederson's attorney makes a ***closing argument*** to the jury, reviewing the evidence and urging a verdict in favor of Pederson. Then Dryden's attorney makes a closing argument, summarizing the evidence and urging a verdict in favor of Dryden. Pederson's attorney is permitted to make a short argument in rebuttal.

THE LAW AND YOU

State Bar Associations

Alabama: http://www.alabar.org/ ("Mediation")

Arizona: http://www.azbar.org/PublicResources/pubinfo.asp ("Alternatives to Trial")

Arkansas: http://www.arkbar.com/publications/publication_public.html ("Small Claims Court")

California: http://www.calbar.ca.gov/state/calbar/calbar_home.jsp ("How Do I Use the Small Claims Court?")

Colorado: http://www.cobar.org/group/index.cfm?category=55&EntityID=dpwfp ("What in the World Is ADR?")

Florida: http://www.flabar.org/tfbtemplates.nsf/newwebsite?openframeset&frame=content&src=/tfb/flabarwe.nsf ("Guide to Florida's Court System"; "Handbook for Jurors"; "So You're Going to Be a Witness")

Georgia: http://www.gabar.org/cps.asp?Header=CPS ("How to Be a Good Witness"; "Juror's Manual")

Iowa: http://www.iowabar.org/pamphlet.nsf/$about!OpenAbout ("Iowa's New Court System")

Louisiana: http://www.lsba.org/Public_Resources/consumer_brochures.html ("The Judicial System"; "Preparing to Be a Witness")

Maine: http://www.mainebar.org/ (legal information pamphlets) ("How to Be a Good Witness"; "Mediation and Other Settlement Procedures")

Maryland: http://www.msba.org/public/brochure.htm/ ("Being a Witness")

Minnesota: http://www.mnbar.org/consumer.htm ("So You're Going to Be a Witness")

Mississippi: http://www.msbar.org/ aw_you_can_use.htm ("A Citizen's Role in the Courts") http://www.msbar.org/jurors_guide.htm ("Juror's Guide")

Missouri: http://www.mobar.org/ (brochures on legal topics) ("Small Claims Court"; "Dispute Resolution Alternatives: What You Need to Know")

Montana: http://www.montanabar.org/ ("Dispute Resolution"; "Small Claims Court")

New Hampshire: http://www.nhbar.org/?area/15.html ("Alternative Dispute Resolution")

New Jersey: http://njsbf.org/njsbf/programs/courts.cfm ("Small Claims Court")

North Carolina: http://www.ncbar.org/legal_prof/divisions/yld/publications/Consumer_pub.asp ("Serving on a North Carolina Jury")

Ohio: http://www.ohiobar.org/conres/pamphlets ("Being a Witness"; "Resolving Disputes Without a Trial")

Oklahoma: http://www.okbar.org/publicinfo/brochures/ ("Information for Trial Jurors"; "Methods for Resolving Conflicts and Dispute"; "Should You Go to Small Claims Court?")

Oregon: http://www.osbar.org/1legallinks/Public/legalinfo/specinfo.html ("Resolving Disputes: Arbitration and Mediation"; "Courts")

Rhode Island: http://www.ribar.com/resources/default.asp ("Serving on a Rhode Island Jury")

South Carolina: http://www.scbar.org/Free_Publications/free_publications.htm ("Alternative Ways to Resolve Disputes")

South Dakota: http://www.sdbar.org/public/Default.htm ("Law and the Courts"; "So You're Going to Be a Witness")

Tennessee: http://www.tba.org/LawBytes/LawBytes.html ("General Procedures")

Texas: http://www.texasbar.com/public/consumerinfo/helpfulinfo/pamphlets.asp ("How to Sue in Small Claims Court")

Washington: http://www.wsba.org/public/consumer/default.html ("Alternatives to Court")

Wisconsin: http://www.legalexplorer.com/legal/legal-QA.asp ("Small Claims Court"; "Alternative Dispute Resolution")

State Attorney Generals

Colorado: http://www.ago.state.co.us/CONSPROT.stm ("Small Claims Court")

Florida: http://doacs.state.fl.us/consumer/ ("Court Is Your Last Resort")

Kansas: http://www.accesskansas.org/ksag/contents/consumer/main.htm ("Filing a Lawsuit in Small Claims Court")

Maine: http://www.maine.gov/portal/living/consumerprotection.html#resources ("A Consumer's Guide to Small Claims Court")

New Hampshire: http://www.state.nh.us/nhdoj/Consumer/cpb.html ("Effective Negotiation"; "Small Claims Court")

New Jersey: http://www.state.nj.us/lps/ca/home.htm ("Alternative Dispute Resolution")

North Carolina: http://www.jus.state.nc.us/cpframe.htm ("Small Claims Court")

South Dakota: http://www.state.sd.us/attorney/office/divisions/consumer/complaints/court.asp ("Small Claims Court")

Jury Instructions The attorneys have previously given written ***jury instructions*** on the applicable law to the trial judge, who gives to the jury those instructions that he approves and denies those that he considers incorrect. The judge also may give the jury instructions of his own. These instructions (called "charges" in some states) advise the jury of the particular rules of law that apply to the facts the jury determines from the evidence.

Verdict The jury then retires to the jury room to deliberate and to reach its **verdict** in favor of one party or the other. If the jury finds the issues in favor of Dryden, its verdict is that he is not liable. If, however, it finds the issues for Pederson and against Dryden, its verdict will be that the defendant is liable and will specify the amount of the plaintiff's damages. In this case, the jury found that Pederson's damages were $35,000. On returning to the jury box, the foreperson either announces the verdict or hands it in written form to the clerk to give to the judge, who reads the verdict in open court. In some jurisdictions, a ***special verdict***, by which the jury makes specific written findings on each factual issue, is used. The judge then applies the law to these findings and renders a judgment.

Motions Challenging Verdict The unsuccessful party may then file a written motion for a new trial or for judgment notwithstanding the verdict. A ***motion for a new trial*** may be granted if (1) the judge committed prejudicial error during the trial, (2) the verdict is against the weight of the evidence, (3) the damages are excessive, or (4) the trial was not fair. The judge has the discretion to grant a motion for a new trial (on grounds 1, 3, or 4 above) even if the verdict is supported by substantial evidence. On the other hand, the motion for judgment notwithstanding the verdict (also called a judgment n.o.v.) must be denied if there is any substantial evidence supporting the verdict. This motion is similar to a motion for a directed verdict, only it is made after the jury's verdict. To grant the motion for **judgment notwithstanding the verdict**, the judge must decide that the evidence is so clear that reasonable people could not differ as to the outcome of the case. If the judge denies the motions for a new trial or for a judgment notwithstanding the verdict, he enters ***judgment on the verdict*** for $35,000 in favor of the plaintiff.

APPEAL

The purpose of an appeal is to determine whether the trial court committed prejudicial error. As a general rule, only errors of law are reviewed by an appellate court. Errors of law include the judge's decisions to admit or exclude evidence; the judge's instructions to the jury; and the judge's actions in denying or granting a motion for a demurrer, a summary judgment, a directed verdict, or a judgment notwithstanding the verdict. Appellate courts review errors of law *de novo*. Errors of fact will be reversed only if they are so clearly erroneous that they are considered to be an error of law.

Let us assume that Dryden directs his attorney to appeal. The attorney files a notice of appeal with the clerk of the trial court within the prescribed time. Later, Dryden, as appellant, files in the reviewing court the record on appeal, which contains the pleadings, a transcript of the testimony, rulings by the judge on motions made by the parties, arguments of counsel, jury instructions, the verdict, posttrial motions, and the judgment from which the appeal is taken. In states having an intermediate court of appeals, such court will usually be the reviewing court. In states having no intermediate court of appeal, a party may appeal directly from the trial court to the state supreme court.

Dryden, as appellant, is required to prepare a condensation of the record, known as an abstract, or pertinent excerpts from the record, which he files with the reviewing court together with a brief and argument. His ***brief*** contains a statement of the facts, the issues, the rulings by the trial court that Dryden contends are erroneous and prejudicial, grounds for reversal of the judgment, a statement of the applicable law, and arguments on his behalf. Pederson, the appellee, files an answering brief and argument. Dryden may, but is not required to, file a reply brief. The case is now ready to be considered by the reviewing court.

The appellate court does not hear any evidence; rather, it decides the case on the record, abstracts, and briefs. After ***oral argument*** by the attorneys, if the court elects to hear one, the court takes the case under advisement, or begins deliberations. Then, having made a decision based on majority rule, the appellate court prepares a written opinion containing the reasons for its decision, the rules of law that apply, and its judgment. The judgment may affirm the judgment of the trial court, or, if the appellate court finds that reversible error was committed, the judgment may be reversed or modified or returned to the lower court (remanded) for a new trial. In some instances the appellate court will affirm the lower court's decision in part and will reverse it in part. The losing party may file a petition for rehearing, which is usually denied.

If the reviewing court is an intermediate appellate court, the party losing in that court may decide to seek a reversal of its judgment by filing within a prescribed time a notice of appeal, if the appeal is by right, or a petition for leave to appeal to the state supreme court, if the appeal is by discretion. This petition corresponds to a petition for a writ of *certiorari* in the U.S. Supreme Court. The party winning in the appellate court may file an answer to the petition for leave to appeal. If the petition is granted, or if the appeal is by right, the record is certified to the Supreme Court, where each party files a new brief and argument. The Supreme Court may hear oral argument or simply review the record; it then takes the case under advisement. If the Supreme Court concludes that the judgment of the appellate court is correct, it affirms. If it decides otherwise, it reverses the judgment of the appellate court and enters a reversal or an order of remand. The unsuccessful party may again file a petition for a rehearing, which is likely to be denied. Barring the remote possibility of an application for still further review by the United States Supreme Court, the case either has reached its termination or, on remand, is about to start its second journey through the courts, beginning, as it did originally, in the trial court.

ENFORCEMENT

If Dryden does not appeal, or if the reviewing court affirms the judgment if he does appeal, and Dryden does not pay the judgment, the task of enforcement will remain. Pederson must request the clerk to issue a ***writ of execution*** demanding payment of the judgment, which is served by the sheriff on the defendant. If the writ is returned "unsatisfied," that is, if Dryden still does not pay, Pederson may post bond or other security and order a levy on and sale of specific nonexempt property belonging to the defendant, which is then seized by the sheriff, advertised for sale, and sold at a public sale under the writ of execution. If the sale does not produce enough money to pay the judgment, Pederson's attorney may begin another proceeding in an attempt to locate money or other property belonging to Dryden. In an attempt to collect the judgment, Pederson's attorney may also proceed by ***garnishment*** against Dryden's employer to collect from his wages or against a bank in which he has an account.

If Pederson cannot satisfy the judgment with Dryden's property located within Illinois (the state where the judgment was obtained), Pederson will have to bring an action on the original judgment in other states where Dryden owns property. Because the U.S. Constitution requires each state to accord judgments of other states ***full faith and credit***, Pederson will be able to obtain a local judgment that may be enforced by the methods described above.

The various stages in civil procedure are illustrated in Figure 3-7.

ALTERNATIVE DISPUTE RESOLUTION

Litigation is complex, time consuming, and expensive. Furthermore, court adjudications involve long delays, lack special expertise in substantive areas, and provide only a limited range of remedies. Additionally, litigation is

Figure 3-7
Stages in Civil Procedure

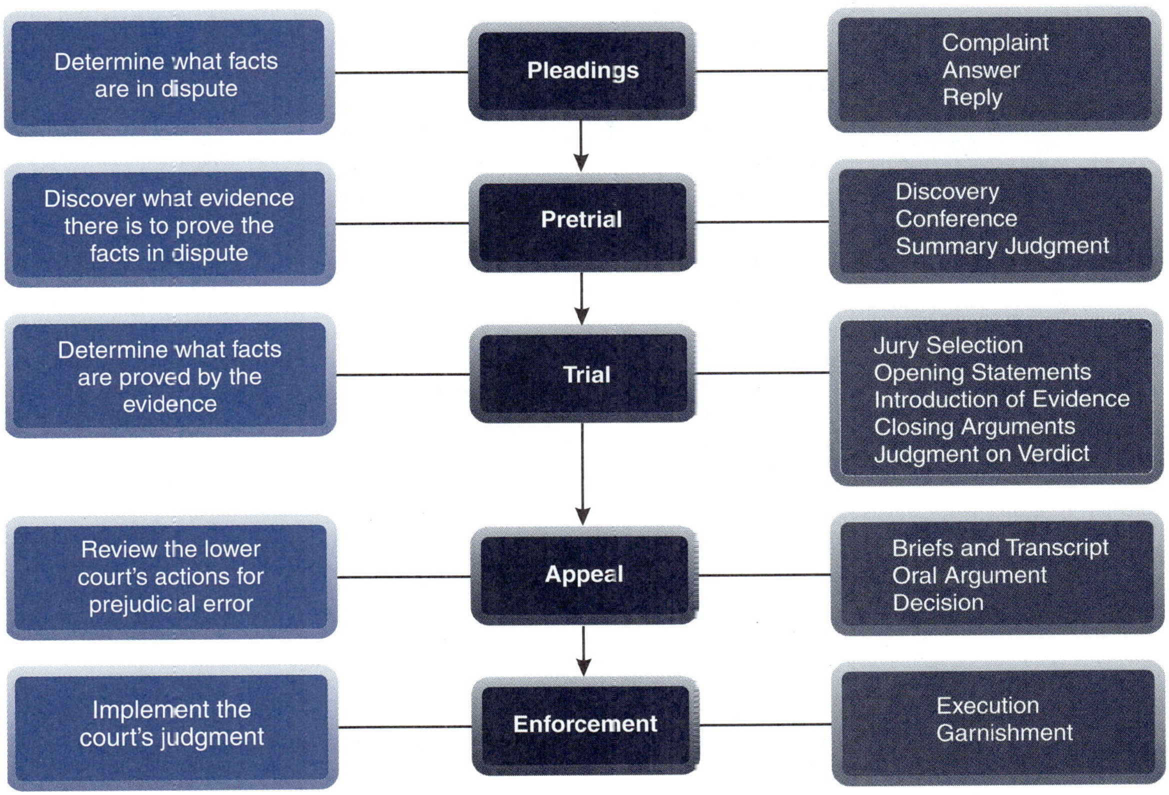

structured so that one party takes all with little opportunity for compromise and often causes animosity between the disputants. Consequently, in an attempt to overcome some of the disadvantages of litigation, several nonjudicial methods of dealing with disputes have developed. The most important of these alternatives to litigation is arbitration. Others include conciliation, mediation, and "mini-trials."

The various techniques differ in a number of ways, including (1) whether the process is voluntary, (2) whether the process is binding, (3) whether the disputants represent themselves or are represented by attorneys, (4) whether the decision is made by the disputants or by a third party, (5) whether the procedure used is formal or informal, and (6) whether the basis for the decision is law or some other criterion.

Which method of civil dispute resolution—litigation or one of the nongovernmental methods—is better for a particular dispute depends on several factors, including the financial circumstances of the disputants, the nature of the relationship (commercial or personal, ongoing or limited) between them, and the urgency of a quick resolution. Alternative dispute resolution methods are especially suitable when privacy, speed, preservation of continuing relations, and control over the process—including the flexibility to compromise—are important to the parties. Nevertheless, the disadvantages of using alternative dispute mechanisms may make court adjudication more appropriate. For example, with the exception of arbitration, only courts can compel participation and provide a binding resolution. In addition, only courts can establish precedents and create public duties. Furthermore, the courts provide greater due process protections and uniformity of outcome. Finally, the courts are independent of the parties and are publicly funded.

See the following Concept Review for a comparison of adjudication, arbitration, and mediation/conciliation.

http:// Information about alternate dispute resolution: http://www.abanet.org/dispute/ and http://www.adr.org/

Practical Advice

Consider including in your contracts a provision specifying what means of dispute resolution will apply to the contract.

ARBITRATION

In **arbitration**, the parties select a *neutral* third person or persons—the arbitrator(s)—who render(s) a binding decision after hearing arguments and reviewing evidence. Because the presentation of the case is less formal and the rules of evidence are more relaxed, arbitration usually takes less time and costs less than litigation. Moreover, in many arbitration cases the parties are able to select an arbitrator with special expertise concerning the subject of the dispute. Thus, the quality of the arbitrator's decision may be higher than that available through the court system. In addition, arbitration normally is conducted in private, thus avoiding unwanted publicity. Arbitration is commonly used in commercial and labor management disputes.

CONCEPT REVIEW

Comparison of Adjudication, Arbitration, and Mediation/Conciliation

	Court Adjudication	Arbitration	Mediation/Conciliation
Advantages	Binding Public norms Precedents Uniformity Publicly funded Compels participation	Binding Parties control process Privacy Special expertise Speedy resolution	Preserves relations Parties control process Privacy Flexible
Disadvantages	Expensive Time-consuming Long delays Limited remedies Lacks special expertise No compromise Disrupts relationships Publicity	No public norms No precedent No uniformity	Not binding Lacks finality No compelled participation No precedent No uniformity

Source: Adapted from Table 4 of *Report of the Ad Hoc Panel on Dispute Resolution and Public Policy,* prepared by the National Institute for Dispute Resolution.

Types of Arbitration There are two basic types of arbitration—consensual, which is by far the most common, and compulsory. **Consensual arbitration** occurs whenever the parties to a dispute agree to submit the controversy to arbitration. They may do this in advance by agreeing in their contract that disputes arising out of their contract will be resolved by arbitration. Or they may do so after a dispute arises by then agreeing to submit the dispute to arbitration. In either instance, such agreements are enforceable under the Federal Arbitration Act (FAA) and statutes in more than forty states. The great majority of these states have adopted the Uniform Arbitration Act (UAA); the others have adopted substantially similar legislation. (In 2000, the National Conference of Commissioners on Uniform State Laws promulgated the Revised Uniform Arbitration Act to provide state legislatures with a more up-to-date statute to resolve disputes through arbitration. To date, only a few states have adopted the Revised UAA.) In **compulsory arbitration**, which is relatively infrequent, a federal or state statute requires arbitration for specific types of disputes, such as those involving public employees including police officers, teachers, and firefighters.

http:// Federal Arbitration Act: http://caselaw.lp.findlaw.com/casecode/uscodes/9/toc.html
Uniform Arbitration Act: http://www.law.upenn.edu/bll/ulc/ulc_frame.htm
Revised Uniform Arbitration Act: http://www.law.upenn.edu/bll/ulc/ulc_frame.htm

Procedure Usually the parties' agreement to arbitrate specifies how the arbitrator or arbitrators will be chosen. If it does not, the Federal Arbitration Act and state statutes provide methods for selecting arbitrators. Although the requirements for arbitration hearings vary from state to state, they generally consist of opening statements, case presentation, and closing statements. Case presentations may include witnesses, documentation, and site inspections. The parties may cross-examine witnesses and may be represented by attorneys.

The decision of the arbitrator, called an **award**, is binding on the parties. Nevertheless, it is subject to *very* limited judicial review. Under the Federal Arbitration Act and the Revised UAA these include (1) the award was procured by corruption, fraud, or other undue means; (2) the arbitrators were partial or corrupt; (3) the arbitrators were guilty of misconduct prejudicing the rights of a party to the arbitration proceeding; and (4) the arbitrators exceeded their powers. Historically, the courts were unfriendly to arbitration; however, they have dramatically changed their attitude and now favor arbitration.

International Arbitration Arbitration is a commonly used means for resolving international disputes. The United Nations Committee on International Trade Law (UNCITRAL) and the International Chamber of Commerce have promulgated arbitration rules, which have won broad international adherence. The Federal Arbitration Act has provisions implementing the United Nations Convention on the Recognition and Enforcement of Foreign Arbitral Awards. A number of states have enacted laws specifically governing international arbitration; some of the statutes have been based on the Model Law on International Arbitration drafted by UNCITRAL.

Court-Annexed Arbitration A growing number of federal and state courts have adopted "court-annexed arbitration" in civil cases where the parties seek limited amounts of damages. The arbitrators are usually attorneys. Appeal from this type of *nonbinding* arbitration is by trial *de novo*. Many states have enacted statutes requiring the arbitration of medical malpractice disputes.

Circuit City Stores, Inc. v. Saint Clair Adams

Supreme Court of the United States, 2001
532 U.S. 105, 121 S.Ct. 1302, 149 L.Ed.2d 234
http://laws.findlaw.com/us/000/99-1379.html

FACTS In October 1995, Saint Clair Adams applied for a job at Circuit City Stores **(http://www.circuitcity.com/init.jsp)**, Inc. Adams [Respondant] signed an employment application, which included the following provision:

> I agree that I will settle any and all previously unasserted claims, disputes or controversies arising out of or relating to my application or candidacy for employment, employment and/or cessation of employment with Circuit City, *exclusively* by final and binding *arbitration* before a neutral Arbitrator. By way of example only, such claims include claims under federal, state, and local statutory or common law, such as the Age Discrimination in Employment Act, Title VII of the Civil Rights Act of 1964, as amended, including the

amendments of the Civil Rights Act of 1991, the Americans with Disabilities Act, the law of contract and the law of tort.

Adams was hired as a sales counselor in Circuit City's store in Santa Rosa, California. Two years later, Adams filed an employment discrimination lawsuit against Circuit City in state court, asserting claims under California's Fair Employment and Housing Act, and other claims based on general tort theories under California law. Circuit City filed suit in the United States District Court, seeking to enjoin the state-court action and to compel arbitration of Adams's claims pursuant to the Federal Arbitration Act (FAA). The District Court entered the requested order, concluding that Adams was obligated by the arbitration agreement to submit his claims against Circuit City to binding arbitration. Adams appealed.

While the appeal was pending in the Court of Appeals for the Ninth Circuit, that court ruled on the key issue in an unrelated case, holding that the FAA does not apply to contracts of employment and so was not subject to the FAA. Circuit City petitioned the United States Supreme Court, noting that the Ninth Circuit's conclusion that all employment contracts are excluded from the FAA conflicts with every other Court of Appeals to have addressed the question. The United States Supreme Court granted *certiorari* to resolve the issue.

DECISION The judgment of the Court of Appeals for the Ninth Circuit is reversed, and the case is remanded for further proceedings consistent with this opinion.

OPINION Kennedy, J. Congress enacted the FAA in 1925. * * * the FAA was a response to hostility of American courts to the enforcement of arbitration agreements, a judicial disposition inherited from then-longstanding English practice. See, e.g., *Allied-Bruce Terminix Cos. v. Dobson,* [citation]; [citation]. To give effect to this purpose, the FAA compels judicial enforcement of a wide range of written arbitration agreements. The FAA's coverage provision, § 2, provides that

> "[a] written provision in any maritime transaction or a contract evidencing a transaction involving commerce to settle by arbitration a controversy thereafter arising out of such contract or transaction, or the refusal to perform the whole or any part thereof, or an agreement in writing to submit to arbitration an existing controversy arising out of such a contract, transaction, or refusal, shall be valid, irrevocable, and enforceable, save upon such grounds as exist at law or in equity for the revocation of any contract." [Citation.]

* * *

The instant case * * * involves not the basic coverage authorization under § 2 of the Act, but the exemption from coverage under § 1. The exemption clause provides the Act shall not apply "to contracts of employment of seamen, railroad employees, or any other class of workers engaged in foreign or interstate commerce." [Citation.] Most Courts of Appeals conclude the exclusion provision is limited to transportation workers, defined, for instance, as those workers "actually engaged in the movement of goods in interstate commerce." [Citation.] * * * the Court of Appeals for the Ninth Circuit takes a different view and interprets the § 1 exception to exclude all contracts of employment from the reach of the FAA. * * *

* * *

Respondent, endorsing the reasoning of the Court of Appeals for the Ninth Circuit that the provision excludes all employment contracts, relies on the asserted breadth of the words "contracts of employment of * * * any other class of workers engaged in * * * commerce." Referring to our construction of § 2's coverage provision in *Allied-Bruce*—concluding that the words "involving commerce" evidence the congressional intent to regulate to the full extent of its commerce power—respondent contends § 1's interpretation should have a like reach, thus exempting all employment contracts. * * *

This reading of § 1, however, runs into an immediate and, in our view, insurmountable textual obstacle. Unlike the "involving commerce" language in § 2, the words "any other class of workers engaged in * * * commerce" constitute a residual phrase, following, in the same sentence, explicit reference to "seamen" and "railroad employees." Construing the residual phrase to exclude all employment contracts fails to give independent effect to the statute's enumeration of the specific categories of workers which precedes it; there would be no need for Congress to use the phrases "seamen" and "railroad employees" if those same classes of workers were subsumed within the meaning of the "engaged in * * * commerce" residual clause. The wording of § 1 calls for * * * the statutory canon that "where general words follow specific words in a statutory enumeration, the general words are construed to embrace only objects similar in nature to those objects enumerated by the preceding specific words." [Citations.] Under this rule of construction the residual clause should be read to give effect to the terms "seamen" and "railroad employees," and should itself be controlled and defined by reference to the enumerated categories of workers which are recited just before it; the interpretation of the clause pressed by respondent fails to produce these results.

* * *

In sum, the text of the FAA forecloses the construction of § 1 followed by the Court of Appeals in the case under review, a construction which would exclude all employment contracts from the FAA. * * * the text of § 1 precludes interpreting the exclusion provision to defeat the language of

§ 2 as to all employment contracts. Section 1 exempts from the FAA only contracts of employment of transportation workers.

* * *

Furthermore, for parties to employment contracts not involving the specific exempted categories set forth in § 1, it is true here, just as it was for the parties to the contract at issue in *Allied-Bruce*, that there are real benefits to the enforcement of arbitration provisions. We have been clear in rejecting the supposition that the advantages of the arbitration process somehow disappear when transferred to the employment context. [Citation.] Arbitration agreements allow parties to avoid the costs of litigation, a benefit that may be of particular importance in employment litigation, which often involves smaller sums of money than disputes concerning commercial contracts. These litigation costs to parties (and the accompanying burden to the Courts) would be compounded by the difficult choice-of-law questions that are often presented in disputes arising from the employment relationship, [citation], and the necessity of bifurcation of proceedings in those cases where state law precludes arbitration of certain types of employment claims but not others. The considerable complexity and uncertainty that the construction of § 1 urged by respondent would introduce into the enforceability of arbitration agreements in employment contracts would call into doubt the efficacy of alternative dispute resolution procedures adopted by many of the Nation's employers, in the process undermining the FAA's proarbitration purposes and "breeding litigation from a statute that seeks to avoid it." * * *

INTERPRETATION Arbitration agreements in employment contracts are binding except for contracts of employment of transportation workers engaged in interstate commerce.

CRITICAL THINKING QUESTION What policy reasons support using arbitration over litigation as a means of dispute resolution?

Conciliation

Conciliation is a nonbinding, informal process in which a third party (the conciliator) selected by the disputing parties attempts to help them reach a mutually acceptable agreement. The duties of the conciliator include improving communications, explaining issues, scheduling meetings, discussing differences of opinion, and serving as an intermediary between the parties when they are unwilling to meet.

Mediation

Mediation is a process in which a third party (the mediator) selected by the disputants helps them to resolve their disagreement. In addition to employing conciliation techniques to improve communications, the mediator, unlike the conciliator, proposes possible solutions for the parties to consider. Like the conciliator, the mediator does not have the power to render a binding decision. Mediation has become commonly used by the judicial system in such tribunals as small claims courts, housing courts, family courts, and neighborhood justice centers. In 2001 the National Conference of Commissioners on Uniform State Laws promulgated the Uniform Mediation Act, which establishes a privilege of confidentiality for mediators and participants. To date no states have adopted it.

Sometimes the techniques of arbitration and mediation are combined in a procedure called "med-arb." In **med-arb**, the neutral third party serves first as a mediator and, if all issues are not resolved through such mediation, then serves as an arbitrator authorized to render a binding decision on the remaining issues.

http:// Uniform Mediation Act: http://www.nccusl.org/nccusl/Annual_Meeting_2001/MED01AM.pdf

Mini-Trial

A mini-trial is a structured settlement process that combines elements of negotiation, mediation, and trials. Mini-trials are most commonly used when both disputants are corporations. In a **mini-trial**, attorneys for the two corporations conduct limited discovery and then present evidence to a panel consisting of managers from each company, as well as to a neutral third party, who may be a retired judge or other attorney. After the lawyers complete their presentations, the managers try to negotiate a settlement without the attorneys. The managers may consult the third party on how a court might resolve the issues in dispute.

Summary Jury Trial

A **summary jury trial** is a mock trial in which the parties present their case to a jury. Though not binding, the jury's verdict does influence the negotiations in which the parties must participate following the mock trial. If the parties do not reach a settlement, they may have a full trial *de novo*.

Negotiation

Negotiation is a consensual bargaining process in which the parties attempt to reach an agreement resolving their dispute. Negotiation differs from other methods of alternate dispute resolution in that there are no third parties.

CHAPTER SUMMARY

The Court System

Federal Courts

District Courts trial courts of general jurisdiction that can hear and decide most legal controversies in the federal system

Courts of Appeals hear appeals from the district courts and review orders of certain administrative agencies

The Supreme Court nation's highest court whose principal function is to review decisions of the Federal Courts of Appeals and the highest state courts

Special Courts have jurisdiction over cases in a particular area of federal law and include the U.S. Court of Federal Claims, the Tax Court, the U.S. Bankruptcy Courts, and the U.S. Court of Appeals for the Federal Circuit

State Courts

Inferior Trial Courts hear minor criminal cases such as traffic offenses and civil cases involving small amounts of money and conduct preliminary hearings in more serious criminal cases

Trial Courts have general jurisdiction over civil and criminal cases

Special Courts trial courts, such as probate courts and family courts, have jurisdiction over a particular area of state law

Appellate Courts include one or two levels; the highest court's decisions are final except in those cases reviewed by the U.S. Supreme Court

Jurisdiction

Subject Matter Jurisdiction

Definition authority of a court to decide a particular kind of case

Federal Jurisdiction
- ***Exclusive Federal Jurisdiction*** federal courts have sole jurisdiction over federal crimes, bankruptcy, antitrust, patent, trademark, copyright, and other special cases
- ***Concurrent Federal Jurisdiction*** authority of more than one court to hear the same case; state and federal courts have concurrent jurisdiction over (1) federal question cases (cases arising under the Constitution, statutes, or treaties of the United States) which do not involve exclusive federal jurisdiction and (2) diversity of citizenship cases involving more than $75,000

State Jurisdiction state courts have exclusive jurisdiction over all matters to which the federal judicial power does not reach

Jurisdiction over the Parties

Definition the power of a court to bind the parties to a suit

***In Personam* Jurisdiction** jurisdiction based upon claims against a person in contrast to jurisdiction over his property

***In Rem* Jurisdiction** jurisdiction based on claims against property

Attachment Jurisdiction jurisdiction over a defendant's property to obtain payment of a claim not related to the property

Venue geographical area in which a lawsuit should be brought

Civil Dispute Resolution

Civil Procedure

The Pleadings series of statements that give notice and establish the issues of fact and law presented and disputed

- ***Complaint*** initial pleading by the plaintiff stating his case
- ***Summons*** notice given to inform a person of a lawsuit against her
- ***Answer*** defendant's pleading in response to the plaintiff's complaint
- ***Reply*** plaintiff's pleading in response to the defendant's answer

Pretrial Procedure process requiring the parties to disclose what evidence is available to prove the disputed facts; designed to encourage settlement of cases or to make the trial more efficient

- ***Judgment on Pleadings*** a final ruling in favor of one party by the judge based on the pleadings
- ***Discovery*** right of each party to obtain evidence from the other party
- ***Pretrial Conference*** a conference between the judge and the attorneys to simplify the issues in dispute and to attempt to settle the dispute without trial
- ***Summary Judgment*** final ruling by the judge in favor of one party based on the evidence disclosed by discovery

Trial determines the facts and the outcome of the case

- ***Jury Selection*** each party has an unlimited number of challenges for cause and a limited number of peremptory challenges
- ***Conduct of Trial*** consists of opening statements by attorneys, direct and cross-examination of witnesses, and closing arguments
- ***Jury Instructions*** judge gives the jury the particular rules of law that apply to the case
- ***Verdict*** the jury's decision based on those facts the jury determines the evidence proves
- ***Motions Challenging Verdict*** include motions for a new trial and a motion for judgment notwithstanding the verdict

Appeal determines whether the trial court committed prejudicial error

Enforcement plaintiff with an unpaid judgment may resort to a writ of execution to have the sheriff seize property of the defendants and to garnishment to collect money owed to the defendant by a third party

Alternative Dispute Resolution

Arbitration nonjudicial proceeding in which a neutral third party selected by the disputants renders a binding decision (award)

Conciliation nonbinding process in which a third party acts as an intermediary between the disputing parties

Mediation nonbinding process in which a third party acts as an intermediary between the disputing parties and proposes solutions for them to consider

Mini-Trial nonbinding process in which attorneys for the disputing parties (typically corporations) present evidence to managers of the disputing parties and a neutral third party, after which the managers attempt to negotiate a settlement in consultation with the third party

Summary Jury Trial mock trial followed by negotiations

Negotiation consensual bargaining process in which the parties attempt to reach an agreement resolving their dispute without the involvement of third parties.

QUESTIONS

1. On June 15 a newspaper columnist predicted that the coast of State X would be flooded on the following September 1. Relying on this pronouncement, Gullible quit his job and sold his property at a loss so as not to be financially ruined. When the flooding did not occur, Gullible sued the columnist in a State X court for damages. The court dismissed the case for failure to state a cause of action under applicable state law. On appeal, the State X Supreme Court upheld the lower court. Three months after this ruling, the State Y Supreme Court heard an appeal in which a lower court had ruled that a reader could sue a columnist for falsely predicting flooding.
   a. Must the State Y Supreme Court follow the ruling of the State X Supreme Court as a matter of *stare decisis*?
   b. Should the State Y lower court have followed the ruling of the State X Supreme Court until the State Y Supreme Court issued a ruling on the issue?
   c. Once the State X Supreme Court issued its ruling, could the U.S. Supreme Court overrule the State X Supreme Court?
   d. If the State Y Supreme Court and the State X Supreme Court rule in exactly opposite ways, must the U.S. Supreme Court resolve the conflict between the two courts?

2. State Senator Bowdler convinced the legislature of State Z to pass a law requiring all professors to submit their class notes and transparencies to a board of censors to be sure that no "lewd" materials were presented to students at state universities. Professor Rabelais would like to challenge this law as being violative of his First Amendment rights under the U.S. Constitution.
   a. May Professor Rabelais challenge this law in State Z courts?
   b. May Professor Rabelais challenge this law in a federal district court?

3. While driving his car in Virginia, Carpe Diem, a resident of North Carolina, struck Butt, a resident of Alaska. As a result of the accident, Butt suffered more than $80,000 in medical expenses. Butt would like to know if he personally serves the proper papers to Diem whether he can obtain jurisdiction against Diem for damages in the following courts:
   a. Alaska state trial court
   b. Federal Circuit Court of Appeals for the Ninth Circuit (includes Alaska)
   c. Virginia state trial court
   d. Virginia federal district court
   e. Federal Circuit Court of Appeals for the Fourth Circuit (includes Virginia and North Carolina)
   f. Virginia equity court
   g. North Carolina state trial court

4. Sam Simpleton, a resident of Kansas, and Nellie Naive, a resident of Missouri, each bought $85,000 in stock at local offices in their home states from Evil Stockbrokers, Inc. (Evil), a business incorporated in Delaware with its principal place of business in Kansas. Both Simpleton and Naive believe that they were cheated by Evil and would like to sue it for fraud. Assuming that no federal question is at issue, assess the accuracy of the following statements:
   a. Simpleton can sue Evil in a Kansas state trial court.
   b. Simpleton can sue Evil in a federal district court in Kansas.
   c. Naive can sue Evil in a Missouri state trial court.
   d. Naive can sue Evil in a federal district court in Missouri.

5. The Supreme Court of State A ruled that, under the law of State A, pit bull owners must either keep their dogs fenced or pay damages to anyone bitten by the dogs. Assess the accuracy of the following statements:
   a. It is likely that the U.S. Supreme Court would issue a writ of *certiorari* in the "pit bull" case.
   b. If a case similar to the "pit bull" case were to come before the Supreme Court of State B in the future, the doctrine of *stare decisis* would leave the court no choice but to rule the same way as the "pit bull" case.

6. The Supreme Court of State G decided that the U.S. Constitution requires professors to warn students of their right to remain silent before questioning the students about cheating. This ruling directly conflicts with a decision of the Federal Court of Appeals for the circuit that includes State G.
   a. Must the Federal Circuit Court of Appeals withdraw its ruling?
   b. Must the Supreme Court of State G withdraw its ruling?

CASE PROBLEMS

7. Thomas Clements brought an action to recover damages for breach of warranty against defendant, Signa Corporation. (A warranty is an obligation that the seller of goods assumes with respect to the quality of the goods sold.) Clements had purchased a motorboat from Barney's Sporting Goods, an Illinois corporation. The boat was manufactured by Signa Corporation, an Indiana corporation with its principal place of business in Decatur, Indiana. Signa has no office in Illinois and no agent authorized to do business on its behalf within Illinois. Clements saw Signa's boats on display at the Chicago Boat Show. In addition, literature on Signa's boats was distributed at the Chicago Boat Show. Several boating magazines, delivered to Clements in Illinois, contained advertisements for Signa's boats. Clements had also seen Signa's boats on display at Barney's Sporting Goods Store in Palatine, Illinois, where he eventually purchased the boat. A written warranty issued by Signa was delivered to Clements in Illinois. Although Signa was served with a summons, it failed to enter an appearance in this case. A default order was entered against Signa and subsequently a judgment of $6,220 was entered against Signa. Signa appealed. Decision?

8. Vette sued Aetna (http://www.aetna.com/index1.htm) under a fire insurance policy. Aetna moved for summary judgment on the basis that the pleadings and discovered evidence showed a lack of an insurable interest in Vette. An "insurable interest" exists when the insured derives a monetary benefit or advantage from the preservation or continued existence of the property or would sustain an economic loss from its destruction. Aetna provided ample evidence to infer that Vette had no insurable interest in the contents of the burned building. Vette also provided sufficient evidence to put in dispute this factual issue. The trial court granted the motion for summary judgment. Vette appealed. Decision?

9. Mark Womer and Brian Perry were members of the U.S. Navy (http://www.navy.mil/) and were stationed in Newport, Rhode Island. On April 10, Womer allowed Perry to borrow his automobile so that Perry could visit his family in New Hampshire. Later that day, while operating Womer's vehicle, Perry was involved in an accident in Manchester, New Hampshire. As a result of the accident, Tzannetos Tavoularis was injured. Tavoularis brought this action against Womer in a New Hampshire superior court, contending that Womer was negligent in lending the automobile to Perry when he knew or should have known that Perry did not have a valid driver's license. Womer sought to dismiss the action on the ground that the New Hampshire courts lacked jurisdiction over him, citing the following facts: (1) he lived and worked in Georgia; (2) he had no relatives in New Hampshire; (3) he neither owned property nor possessed investments in New Hampshire; and (4) he had never conducted business in New Hampshire. Decision?

10. Mariana Deutsch worked as a knitwear mender and attended a school for beauticians. The sink in her apartment collapsed on her foot, fracturing her big toe and making it painful for her to stand. She claims that as a consequence of the injury she was compelled to abandon her plans to become a beautician because that job requires long periods of standing. She also asserts that she was unable to work at her current job for a month. She filed a tort claim against Hewes Street Realty for negligence in failing properly to maintain the sink. She brought the suit in federal district court, claiming damages of $85,000. Her medical expenses and actual loss of salary were less than $7,500; the rest of her alleged damages were for loss of future earnings as a beautician. Hewes Street moved to dismiss the suit on the basis that Deutsch's claim fell short of the jurisdictional requirement and therefore the federal court lacked subject matter jurisdiction over her claim. The district court dismissed the suit, and Deutsch appealed. Did the New Hampshire courts have jurisdiction?

11. Kenneth Thomas brought suit against his former employer, Kidder, Peabody & Company, and two of its employees, Barclay Perry and James Johnston, in a dispute over commissions on sales of securities. When he applied to work at Kidder, Peabody, Thomas had filled out a form, which contained an arbitration agreement clause. Thomas had also registered with the New York Stock Exchange (NYSE) (http://www.nyse.com/). Rule 347 of the NYSE provides that any controversy between a registered representative and a member company shall be settled by arbitration. Kidder, Peabody is a member of the NYSE. Thomas refused to arbitrate, relying on Section 229 of the California Labor Code, which provides that actions for the collection of wages may be maintained "without regard to the existence of any private agreement to arbitrate." Perry and Johnston filed a petition in a California state court to compel arbitration under Section 2 of the Federal Arbitration Act. Should the petition of Perry and Johnson be granted?

12. Steven Gwin bought a lifetime Termite Protection Plan for his home from the local office of Allied-Bruce, a franchise of Terminix International Company (http://www.terminix.com/). The plan provided that Allied-Bruce would "protect" Gwin's house against termite infestation, reinspect periodically, provide additional treatment if necessary, and repair damage caused by new termite infestations. Terminix International guaranteed the fulfillment of these contractual provisions. The plan also provided that all disputes arising out of the contract would be settled exclusively by arbitration. Four years later, Gwin had Allied-Bruce reinspect the house in anticipation of selling it. Allied-Bruce gave the house a "clean bill of health." Gwin then sold the house and transferred the Termite Protection Plan to Dobson. Shortly thereafter, Dobson found the house to be infested with termites. Allied-Bruce attempted to treat and repair the house, using materials from out of state, but these efforts failed to satisfy Dobson. Dobson then sued Gwin, Allied-Bruce, and Terminix International in an Alabama state court. Allied-Bruce and Terminix International asked for a stay of these proceedings until arbitration could be carried out as stipulated in the contract. The trial court refused to grant the stay. The Alabama Supreme Court upheld that ruling, citing a state statute that makes predispute arbitration agreements unenforceable. The court found that the Federal Arbitration Act, which preempts conflicting state law, did not apply to this contract because its connection to interstate commerce was too slight. Was the Alabama Supreme Court correct? Explain.

http:// **Internet Exercise** Find information about the structure and operations of (1) the federal court system and (2) your own state's court system. (If such information on your state is not available, choose another state.)

CHAPTER 4

Constitutional Law

I have always regarded [the American] Constitution as the most remarkable work known to me in modern times to have been produced by the human intellect, at a single stroke (so to speak), in its application to political affairs.

WILLIAM GLADSTONE (BRITISH PRIME MINISTER)

Learning Objectives

After reading this chapter you should be able to:

1. Explain the basic principles of constitutional law.
2. Describe the sources and extent of the power of the federal and state governments to regulate business and commerce.
3. Distinguish the three levels of scrutiny used by the courts to determine the constitutionality of governmental action.
4. Explain the effect of the First Amendment on (a) corporate political speech, (b) commercial speech, and (c) defamation.
5. Explain the difference between substantive and procedural due process.

You will recall from Chapter 1 that a constitution is the fundamental law of a particular level of government. It establishes the structure of government and defines the political relationships within it. It also places restrictions on the powers of government and guarantees the rights and liberties of the people.

The Constitution of the United States was adopted on September 17, 1787, by representatives of the thirteen newly created states. Its purpose is stated in the preamble:

> We the People of the United States, in Order to form a more perfect Union, establish Justice, insure domestic Tranquility, provide for the common defense, promote the general Welfare, and secure the Blessings of Liberty to ourselves and our Posterity, do ordain and establish this Constitution for the United States of America.

Although the framers of the U.S. Constitution stated precisely what rights and authority were vested in the new national government, they considered it unnecessary to list those liberties the people were to keep for themselves. Nonetheless, during the state conventions ratifying the document, people expressed fear that the federal government might abuse its powers. To calm these concerns, the first Congress approved ten amendments to the U.S. Constitution, now known as the Bill of Rights, which were adopted on December 15, 1791.

The Bill of Rights restricts the powers and authority of the federal government and establishes many of the civil and political rights enjoyed in the United States, including the right to due process of law and freedoms of speech, press, religion, assembly, and petition. Though the Bill of Rights does not apply directly to the states, the Supreme Court has held that the Fourteenth Amendment incorporates most of the principal guarantees of the Bill of Rights, thus making them applicable to the states.

This chapter concerns constitutional law as it applies to business and commerce. We will begin by surveying some of the basic principles of constitutional law, and will then examine the allocation of power between the federal and state governments with respect to the regulation of business. Finally, we will discuss the constitutional restrictions on the power of government to regulate business.

http:// The U.S. Constitution: http://www.house.gov/Constitution/Constitution.html

Basic Principles

Constitutional law in the United States involves several basic concepts. These fundamental principles, which apply both to the powers of and to the limitations on government, are (1) federalism, (2) federal supremacy and preemption, (3) judicial review, (4) separation of powers, and (5) state action.

Federalism

Federalism is the division of governing power between the federal government and the states. The U.S. Constitution enumerates the powers of the federal government and specifically reserves to the states or the people the powers not expressly delegated to the federal government. Accordingly, the federal government is a government of enumerated, or limited, powers; and a specified power must authorize each of its acts. The doctrine of enumerated powers is not, however, a significant limitation on the federal government because a number of these enumerated powers, in particular the power to regulate interstate and foreign commerce, have been broadly interpreted.

Furthermore, the Constitution grants Congress not only specified powers but also the power "[t]o make all Laws which shall be necessary and proper for carrying into Execution the foregoing Powers, and all other Powers vested by this Constitution in the Government of the United States, or in any Department or Officer thereof." U.S. Const. art. I, § 8, cl. 18. In the Supreme Court's view, the "necessary and proper" clause enables Congress to legislate in areas not mentioned in the list of enumerated powers as long as such legislation reasonably relates to some enumerated power.

Federal Supremacy and Preemption

Although under our federalist system the states retain significant powers, the **supremacy clause** of the U.S. Constitution provides that within its own sphere, federal law is supreme and that state law must, in case of conflict, yield. Accordingly, any state constitutional provision or law that conflicts with the U.S. Constitution or valid federal laws or treaties is unconstitutional and may not be given effect.

Under the supremacy clause, whenever Congress enacts legislation within its constitutional powers, the federal action **preempts** (overrides) any conflicting state legislation. Even if a state regulation is not in conflict, it must still give way if Congress clearly has intended its action to preempt state legislation. This intent may be specifically stated in the legislation or inferred from the scope of the legislation, the need for uniformity, or the danger of conflict between coexisting federal and state regulation.

When Congress has *not* intended to displace all state legislation, then nonconflicting state legislation is permitted. The case of *Silkwood v. Kerr-McGee Corporation* illustrates this point. When Congress has not acted, the fact that it has the power to act does not prevent the states from acting. Until Congress exercises its power to preempt, state regulation is permitted.

Silkwood v. Kerr-Mcgee Corporation

Supreme Court of the United States, 1984
464 U.S. 238, 104 S.Ct. 615, 78 L.Ed.2d 443
http://laws.findlaw.com/us/464/238.html

FACTS Karen Silkwood was a laboratory analyst for Kerr-McGee Corporation **(http://www.kerr-mcgee.com/)** at its Cimarron plant in Oklahoma. The plant made plutonium fuel pins for use as reactor fuel in nuclear power plants. Accordingly, the plant was subject to licensing and extensive federal regulation by the Nuclear Regulatory Commission (NRC), pursuant to the Atomic Energy Act, which preempts Oklahoma's regulation of the safety aspects of nuclear energy. During a three-day work period in 1974, Silkwood was contaminated by plutonium at the plant. After high levels of contamination were detected on her when she arrived at work on the third day, Kerr-McGee ordered a decontamination squad to Silkwood's apartment, resulting in the unavoidable destruction of many of her personal belongings. Silkwood was sent to the Los Alamos Scientific Laboratory to determine the extent of the contamination in her body's vital organs. A week later she returned to work but died that night in an unrelated automobile accident. Her father, as administrator of her estate, filed a claim against Kerr-McGee under Oklahoma tort law for Karen's personal injuries and property damage resulting from her contamination. On the basis of the jury's verdict, the trial court awarded Silkwood $505,000 ($500,000 for personal injuries and $5,000 for property damage) plus punitive damages of $10,000,000. The appellate court held that because federal statutes regulate nuclear energy, punitive damages could not be awarded. Silkwood appealed.

DECISION Judgement of appellate court reversed.

OPINION White, J. As we recently observed in *Pacific Gas & Electric Co. v. State Energy, Resources Conservation & Development Comm'n,* [citation], state law can be preempted in either of two general ways. If Congress evidences an intent to occupy a given field, any state law falling within that field is preempted. [Citations.] If Congress has not entirely displaced state regulation over the matter in question, state law is still preempted to the extent it actually conflicts with federal law, that is, when it is impossible to comply with both state and federal law, [citation], or where the state law stands as an obstacle to the accomplishment of the full purposes and objectives of Congress, [citation]. Kerr-McGee contends that the award in this case is invalid under either analysis. We consider each of these contentions in turn.

In *Pacific Gas & Electric*, an examination of the statutory scheme and legislative history of the Atomic Energy Act convinced us that "Congress * * * intended that the federal government regulate the radiological safety aspects involved * * * in the construction and operation of a nuclear plant." [Citation.] Thus, we concluded that "the federal government has occupied the entire field of nuclear safety concerns, except the limited powers expressly ceded to the states." [Citation.]

* * *

Congress' decision to prohibit the states from regulating the safety aspects of nuclear development was premised on its belief that the Commission was more qualified to determine what type of safety standards should be enacted in this complex area. As Congress was informed by the AEC, the 1959 legislation provided for continued federal control over the more hazardous materials because "the technical safety considerations are of such complexity that it is not likely that any State would be prepared to deal with them during the foreseeable future." [Citation.] If there were nothing more, this concern over the states' inability to formulate effective standards and the foreclosure of the states from conditioning the operation of nuclear plants on compliance with state-imposed safety standards arguably would disallow resort to state-law remedies by those suffering injuries from radiation in a nuclear plant. There is, however, ample evidence that Congress had no intention of forbidding the states from providing such remedies.

Indeed, there is no indication that Congress even seriously considered precluding the use of such remedies either when it enacted the Atomic Energy Act in 1954 and/or when it amended it in 1959. This silence takes on added significance in light of Congress' failure to provide any federal remedy for persons injured by such conduct. It is difficult to believe that Congress would, without comment, remove all means of judicial recourse for those injured by illegal conduct. [Citation.] More importantly, the only congressional discussion concerning the relationship between the Atomic Energy Act and state tort remedies indicates that Congress assumed that such remedies would be available. After the 1954 law was enacted, private companies contemplating entry into the nuclear industry expressed concern over potentially bankrupting state-law suits arising out of a nuclear incident. As a result, in 1957 Congress passed the Price-Anderson Act, an amendment to the Atomic Energy Act. [Citation.] That Act established an indemnification scheme under which operators of licensed nuclear facilities could be required to obtain up to $60 million in private financial protection against such suits. The government would then provide indemnification for the next $500 million of liability, and the resulting $560 million would be the limit of liability for any one nuclear incident.

In sum, it is clear that in enacting and amending the Price-Anderson Act, Congress assumed that state-law remedies, in whatever form they might take, were available to those injured by nuclear incidents. * * *

We do not suggest that there could never be an instance in which the federal law would preempt the recovery of damages based on state law. But insofar as damages for radiation injuries are concerned, preemption should not be judged on the basis that the federal government has so completely occupied the field of safety that state remedies are foreclosed but on whether there is an irreconcilable conflict between the federal and state standards or whether the imposition of a state standard in a damages action would frustrate the objectives of the federal law. We perceive no such conflict or frustration in the circumstances of this case.

* * *

We conclude that the award of punitive damages in this case is not preempted by federal law.

INTERPRETATION When Congress has not intended to displace all state legislation, then nonconflicting state legislation is permitted.

CRITICAL THINKING QUESTION What policy reasons support the federal government's power to preempt state law?

JUDICIAL REVIEW

Judicial review describes the process by which the courts examine governmental actions to determine whether they conform to the U.S. Constitution. If governmental action violates the U.S. Constitution, under judicial review the courts will invalidate that action. Judicial review extends to legislation, acts of the executive branch, and the decisions of inferior courts; such review scrutinizes actions of both the federal and state governments and applies to both the same standards of constitutionality. The U.S. Supreme Court is the final authority as to the constitutionality of any federal and state law.

SEPARATION OF POWERS

Another basic principle on which our government is founded is that of **separation of powers**. Our Constitution vests power in three distinct and independent branches of government—the executive, legislative, and judicial branches. The purpose of the doctrine of separation of powers is to prevent any branch of government from gaining too much power. The doctrine also permits each branch to function without interference from any other branch. Basically, the legislative branch is granted the power to make the law, the executive branch to enforce the law, and the judicial branch to interpret the law. This separation of powers is not complete, however. For example, the executive branch has veto power over legislation enacted by Congress; the legislative branch must approve a great number of executive appointments; and the judicial branch may declare both legislation and executive actions unconstitutional. Nevertheless, our government generally operates under a three-branch scheme that provides for separation of powers and places checks and balances on the power of each branch, as illustrated by Figure 4-1.

STATE ACTION

Most of the protections provided by the U.S. Constitution and its amendments apply only to governmental, or state, action. **State action** includes any actions of the federal and state governments and their subdivisions, such as city or county governments and agencies. Only the Thirteenth Amendment, which abolishes slavery or involuntary servitude, applies to the actions of private individuals. The protections that guard against state action may, however, be extended by statute to apply to private activity.

Additionally, action taken by private citizens may constitute state action if the state exercises coercive power over the challenged private action or has encouraged the action significantly. For example, the Supreme Court found state action when the Supreme Court of Missouri ordered a lower court to enforce an agreement among white property owners that prohibited the transfer of their property to nonwhites. Moreover, if "private" individuals or entities engage in public functions, their actions may be considered state action subject to constitutional limitations. For example, the U.S. Supreme Court held that a company town was subject to the First Amendment because the state had allowed the company to exercise all of the public functions and activities usually conducted by a town government. Since that case, the Supreme Court has been less willing to find state action based upon the performance of public functions by private entities; the Court now limits such a finding to those functions "traditionally exclusively reserved to the state."

Figure 4-1
Separation of Powers: Checks and Balances

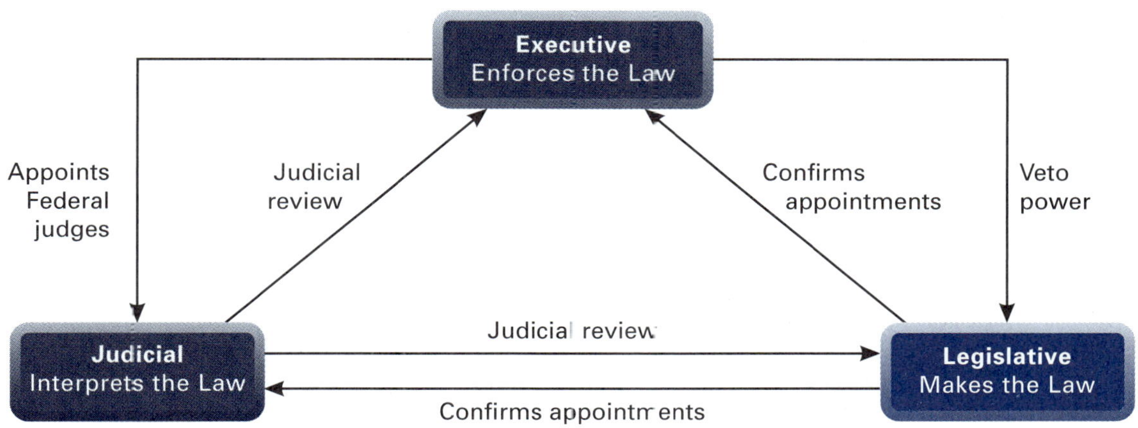

Brentwood Academy v. Tennessee Secondary School Athletic Association

Supreme Court of the United States, 2001
531 U.S. 288, 121 S.Ct. 924, 148 L.Ed.2d 807
http://laws.findlaw.com/us/000/99-901.html

FACTS The Tennessee Secondary School Athletic Association (Association) **(http://www.tssaa.org/)** is a not-for-profit membership corporation organized to regulate interscholastic sport among the public and private high schools in Tennessee. No school is forced to join, but since there is no other authority regulating interscholastic athletics, it enjoys the memberships of almost all the state's public high schools (some 290 of them or 84 percent of the Association's voting membership), far outnumbering the 55 private schools that belong.

The Association's rulemaking arm is its legislative council, while its board of control tends to administration. The voting membership of each of these nine-person committees is limited under the Association's bylaws to high school principals, assistant principals, and superintendents elected by the member schools, and the public school administrators who so serve typically attend meetings during regular school hours. Although the Association's staff members are not paid by the state, they are eligible to join the state's public retirement system for its employees. Member schools pay dues to the Association, though the bulk of its revenue is gate receipts at member teams' football and basketball tournaments. The constitution, bylaws, and rules of the Association set standards of school membership and the eligibility of students to play in interscholastic games. In 1997, a regulatory enforcement proceeding was brought against Brentwood Academy, a private parochial high school member of the Association. The Association's board of control found that Brentwood violated a rule prohibiting "undue influence" in recruiting athletes, when it wrote to incoming students and their parents about spring football practice. The Association placed Brentwood's athletic program on probation for four years, declared its football and boys' basketball teams ineligible to compete in playoffs for two years, and imposed a $3,000 fine.

Brentwood sued the Association and its executive director claiming that enforcement of the Rule was state action and a violation of the First and Fourteenth Amendments. The District Court entered summary judgment for Brentwood and enjoined the Association from enforcing the Rule. The United States Court of Appeals for the Sixth Circuit reversed, saying that the District Court was mistaken in seeing a symbiotic relationship between the state and the Association. It emphasized that the Association was neither engaging in a traditional and exclusive public function nor responding to state compulsion. The United States Supreme Court granted *certiorari* to resolve the conflict.

DECISION The judgment of the Court of Appeals for the Sixth Circuit is reversed, and the case is remanded for further proceedings consistent with this opinion.

OPINION Souter, J. Thus, we say that state action may be found if, though only if, there is such a "close nexus between the State and the challenged action" that seemingly private behavior "may be fairly treated as that of the State itself." [Citation.]

* * *

Our cases have identified a host of facts that can bear on the fairness of such an attribution. We have, for example, held that a challenged activity may be state action when it results from the State's exercise of "coercive power," [citation], when the State provides "significant encouragement, either overt or covert," [citation], or when a private actor operates as a "willful participant in joint activity with the State or its agents," [citation]. We have treated a nominally private entity as a state actor when it is controlled by an "agency of the State," [citation], when it has been delegated a public function by the State, [citations], when it is "entwined with governmental policies" or when government is "entwined in [its] management or control," [citation].

* * *

* * * [T]he "necessarily fact-bound inquiry," [citation], leads to the conclusion of state action here. The nominally private character of the Association is overborne by the pervasive entwinement of public institutions and public officials in its composition and workings, and there is no substantial reason to claim unfairness in applying constitutional standards to it.

The Association is not an organization of natural persons acting on their own, but of schools, and of public schools to the extent of 84% of the total. Under the Association's bylaws, each member school is represented by its principal or a faculty member, who has a vote in selecting members of the governing legislative council and board of control from eligible principals, assistant principals and superintendents.

Although the findings and prior opinions in this case include no express conclusion of law that public school officials act within the scope of their duties when they represent their institutions, no other view would be rational, the official nature of their involvement being shown in any number of ways. Interscholastic athletics obviously play an integral part in the public education of Tennessee, where nearly every public high school spends money on competitions among schools. Since a pickup system of interscholastic games would not do, these public teams need some mechanism to produce rules and regulate competition. The mechanism is an organization overwhelmingly composed of public school officials who select representatives (all of them public officials at the time in question here), who in turn adopt and enforce the rules that make the system work. Thus, by giving these jobs to the Association, the 290 public schools of Tennessee belonging to it can sensibly be seen as exercising their own authority to meet their own responsibilities. Unsurprisingly, then, the record indicates that half the council or board meetings documented here were held during official school hours, and that public schools have largely provided for the Association's financial support. A small portion of the Association's revenue comes from membership dues paid by the schools, and the principal part from gate receipts at tournaments among the member schools. Unlike mere public buyers of contract services, whose payments for services rendered do not convert the service providers into public actors, [citation], the schools here obtain membership in the service organization and give up sources of their own income to their collective association. The Association thus exercises the authority of the predominantly public schools to charge for admission to their games; the Association does not receive this money from the schools, but enjoys the schools' moneymaking capacity as its own.

In sum, to the extent of 84% of its membership, the Association is an organization of public schools represented by their officials acting in their official capacity to provide an integral element of secondary public schooling. There would be no recognizable Association, legal or tangible, without the public school officials, who do not merely control but overwhelmingly perform all but the purely ministerial acts by which the Association exists and functions in practical terms. Only the 16% minority of private school memberships prevents this entwinement of the Association and the public school system from being total and their identities totally indistinguishable.

To complement the entwinement of public school officials with the Association from the bottom up, the State of Tennessee has provided for entwinement from top down. State Board members are assigned ex officio to serve as members of the board of control and legislative council, and the Association's ministerial employees are treated as state employees to the extent of being eligible for membership in the state retirement system.

* * *

INTERPRETATION If an association involves the pervasive entwinement of state school officials in its structure, the association's regulatory activity will be treated as state action.

CRITICAL THINKING QUESTION Should the actions of private parties be immune from federal constitutional limitations? Explain.

POWERS OF GOVERNMENT

The U.S. Constitution created a federal government of enumerated powers. Moreover, as the Tenth Amendment declares, "[t]he powers not delegated to the United States by the Constitution, nor prohibited by it to the States, are reserved to the States respectively, or to the people." Consequently, the legislation Congress enacts must be based on a specific power the Constitution grants to the federal government or be reasonably necessary for carrying out an enumerated power.

Some governmental powers may be exercised only by the federal government. These exclusive federal powers include the power to establish laws regarding bankruptcy, to establish post offices, to grant patents and copyrights, to coin currency, to wage war, and to enter into treaties. Conversely, both the federal government and the states may exercise concurrent governmental powers, which include taxation, spending, and police power (regulation of public health, safety, and welfare).

In this part of the chapter, we will examine the sources and extent of the powers of the federal government—as well as the power of the states—to regulate business and commerce.

FEDERAL COMMERCE POWER

The U.S. Constitution provides that Congress has the power to regulate commerce with other nations and among the states. This commerce clause has two important effects: (1) it provides a broad source of **commerce power** for the federal government to regulate the economy and (2) it restricts state regulations that obstruct or unduly burden interstate commerce.

The U.S. Supreme Court interprets the commerce clause as granting virtually complete power to Congress to regulate the economy and business. A court may invalidate legislation enacted under the commerce clause only if it is clear (1) that the activity the legislation regulates does not affect interstate commerce or (2) that there is no reasonable connection between the selected regulatory means and the stated ends. For example, activities conducted solely within one state, such as the practice of law or real estate brokerage agreements, are subject to federal antitrust laws under the power granted by the commerce clause if those activities (1) substantially affect interstate commerce or (2) are in the flow of commerce.

Because of the broad and permissive interpretation of the commerce power, Congress currently regulates a vast range of activities. Many of the activities discussed in this text are regulated by the federal government through its exercise of the commerce power; such activities include federal crimes, consumer warranties and credit transactions, electronic funds transfers, trademarks, unfair trade practices, other consumer transactions, residential real estate transactions, consumer and employee safety, labor relations, civil rights in employment, transactions in securities, and environmental protection.

STATE REGULATION OF COMMERCE

The commerce clause, as we have previously discussed, specifically grants to Congress the power to regulate commerce among the states. In addition to acting as a broad source of federal power, the clause also implicitly restricts the states' power to regulate activities if the result obstructs or unduly burdens interstate commerce.

Regulations The Supreme Court ultimately decides the extent to which state regulation may affect interstate commerce. In doing so, the Court weighs and balances several factors: (1) the necessity and importance of the state regulation, (2) the burden it imposes on interstate commerce, and (3) the extent to which it discriminates against interstate commerce in favor of local concerns. The application of these factors involves case-by-case analysis. In general, where a state statute regulates evenhandedly to accomplish a legitimate state interest and its effects on interstate commerce are only incidental, the Court will uphold the statute unless the burden imposed on interstate commerce is excessive compared to the local benefits. The Court will uphold a discriminatory regulation only if no other reasonable method of achieving a legitimate local interest exists. *Chemical Waste Management, Inc. v. Hunt* illustrates the application of this test.

Chemical Waste Management, Inc. v. Hunt

Supreme Court of the United States, 1992
504 U.S. 334, 112 S.Ct. 2009, 119 L.Ed. 2d 121
http://laws.findlaw.com/US/504/334.html

FACTS Alabama law imposes a fee of $97.60 per ton for hazardous wastes generated outside the state and disposed of at a commercial facility in Alabama. The fee for hazardous wastes generated within Alabama is $25.60 per ton. Chemical Waste Management, Inc., which operates a commercial hazardous waste land disposal facility in Emelle, Alabama, filed suit requesting a declaratory judgment that the Alabama law violated the commerce clause of the U.S. Constitution. Alabama argued that the additional fee of $72.00 served a legitimate local purpose related to its citizens' health and safety, given recent large increases in the hazardous waste received into the state and the possible adverse effects of such waste. The trial court found the additional fee to be in violation of the U.S. Constitution, but the Alabama Supreme Court reversed that decision.

DECISION Decision of the Alabama Supreme Court reversed.

OPINION White, J. No state may attempt to isolate itself from a problem common to the several States by raising barriers to the free flow of interstate trade. * * *

* * *

The Act's additional fee facially discriminates against hazardous waste generated in States other than Alabama, and the Act overall has plainly discouraged the full operation of petitioner's Emelle facility. Such burdensome taxes imposed on interstate commerce alone are generally forbidden: "[A] State may not tax a transaction or incident more heavily when it crosses state lines than when it occurs entirely within the State." [Citations.] Once a state tax is found to discriminate against out-of-state commerce, it is typically struck down without further inquiry. [Citations.]

The State, however, argues that the additional fee imposed on out-of-state hazardous waste serves legitimate local purposes related to its citizens' health and safety. Because the additional fee discriminates both on its face and in practical effect, the burden falls on the State "to justify it both in terms of the local benefits flowing from the statute and the unavailability of nondiscriminatory alternatives adequate to preserve the local interests at stake." [Citations.] "At a minimum such facial discrimination invokes the strictest scrutiny of any purported legitimate local purpose and of the absence of nondiscriminatory alternatives." [Citation.]

* * *

Ultimately, the State's concern focuses on the volume of the waste entering the Emelle facility. Less discriminatory alternatives, however, are available to alleviate this concern, not the least of which are a generally applicable per-ton additional fee on all hazardous waste disposed of within Alabama, [citation], or a per-mile tax on all vehicles transporting hazardous waste across Alabama roads, [citation], or an evenhanded cap on the total tonnage landfilled at Emelle, [citation], which would curtail volume from all sources. To the extent Alabama's concern touches environmental conservation and the health and safety of its citizens, such concern does not vary with the point of origin of the waste, and it remains within the State's power to monitor and regulate more closely the transportation and disposal of all hazardous waste within its borders. Even with the possible future financial and environmental risks to be borne by Alabama, such risks likewise do not vary with the waste's State of origin in a way allowing foreign, but not local, waste to be burdened. In sum, we find the additional fee to be "an obvious effort to saddle those outside the State" with most of the burden of slowing the flow of waste into the Emelle facility. [Citation.] "That legislative effort is clearly impermissible under the Commerce Clause of the Constitution." [Citation.]

INTERPRETATION The U.S. Constitution permits states to discriminate against interstate commerce only if there is no other reasonable method of achieving a legitimate local interest.

ETHICAL QUESTION Did the state of Alabama act fairly? Explain.

CRITICAL THINKING QUESTION What is your assessment of the Court's less discriminatory alternatives? Can you suggest any others? Explain.

Taxation The commerce clause, in conjunction with the import-export clause, also limits the power of the state to tax. The import-export clause provides: "No State shall, without the Consent of the Congress, lay any Imposts or Duties on Imports or Exports." U.S. Const. art. I, § 10, cl. 2. Together, the commerce clause and the import-export clause exempt from state taxation goods that have entered the stream of commerce, whether they are interstate or foreign and whether they are imports or exports. The purpose of this immunity is to protect goods in commerce from both discriminatory and cumulative state taxes. Once the goods enter the stream of interstate or foreign commerce, the power of the state to tax ceases and does not resume until the goods are delivered to the purchaser or the owner terminates the movement of the goods through commerce.

The due process clause of the Fourteenth Amendment also restricts the power of states to tax. Under the due process clause, for a state tax to be constitutional, a sufficient nexus must exist between the state and the person, thing, or activity to be taxed.

FEDERAL FISCAL POWERS

The federal government exerts a dominating influence over the national economy through its control of financial matters. Much of this impact results from the exercise of its regulatory powers under the commerce clause, as previously discussed. In addition, the government derives a substantial portion of its influence from powers that are independent of the commerce clause. These include (1) the power to tax, (2) the power to spend, (3) the power to borrow and coin money, and (4) the power of eminent domain.

Taxation The federal government's power to tax, although extremely broad, has three major limitations: (1) direct taxes must be apportioned among the states, (2) all custom duties and excise taxes must be uniform throughout the United States, and (3) no duties may be levied on exports from any state.

Besides raising revenues, taxes also have regulatory and socioeconomic effects. For example, import taxes and custom duties can protect domestic industry from foreign competition. Graduated or progressive tax rates and exemptions may further social policies seeking the redistribution of wealth. Tax credits encourage investment in favored enterprises to the disadvantage of unfavored businesses. A tax that does more than just raise revenue will be upheld "so long as the motive of Congress and the effect of its legislative action are to secure revenue for the benefit of the general government. . . ."

Spending Power The Constitution authorizes the federal government to pay debts and to spend for the common defense and general welfare of the United States. Like the power to tax, the spending power of Congress is extremely broad; this power will be upheld so long as it does not violate a specific constitutional limitation on federal power.

Furthermore, through its spending power, Congress may accomplish indirectly what it may not do directly. For example, the Supreme Court has held that Congress may condition a state's receipt of federal highway funds on that state's mandating twenty-one as the minimum drinking age, even though the Twenty-first Amendment grants the states significant powers with respect to consumption within their respective borders. As the Court noted, "Constitutional limitations on Congress when exercising its spending power are less exacting than those on its authority to regulate directly." Whether directly or indirectly, the power of the federal government to spend money represents an important regulatory force in the economy and significantly affects the general welfare of the United States.

Borrowing and Coining Money The U.S. Constitution also grants Congress the power to borrow money on the credit of the United States and to coin money. These two powers have enabled the federal government to establish a national banking system, the Federal Reserve System, and specialized federal lending programs such as the Federal Land Bank. Through these and other institutions and agencies, the federal government wields extensive control over national fiscal and monetary policies and exerts considerable influence over interest rates, the money supply, and foreign exchange rates.

Eminent Domain The government's power to take private property for public use, known as the power of **eminent domain**, is recognized, in the federal Constitution and in the constitutions of the states, as one of the inherent powers of government. At the same time, however, the power is carefully limited. The Fifth Amendment to the federal Constitution contains a "takings clause" that provides that private property shall not be taken for public use without just compensation. Although this amendment applies only to the federal government, the Supreme Court has held that the takings clause is incorporated through the Fourteenth Amendment and is therefore applicable to the states. Moreover, similar or identical provisions are found in the constitutions of the states.

As the language of the takings clause indicates, the taking must be for a public use. Public use has been held to be synonymous with public purpose. Thus, private entities, such as railroads and housing authorities, may use the government's power of eminent domain so long as the entity's use of the property benefits the public. When the government or a private entity properly takes property under the power of eminent domain, the owners of the property must receive just compensation, which has been interpreted as the fair market value of the property. Eminent domain is discussed further in Chapter 51.

Figure 4-2 summarizes the powers granted to the federal government, the states, and the people.

LIMITATIONS ON GOVERNMENT

As we have discussed, the U.S. Constitution grants certain specified powers to the federal government, while reserving other, unspecified powers to the states. The Constitution and its amendments, however, impose limits on the powers of both the federal government and the states. In this part of the chapter, we will discuss those limitations most applicable to business: (1) the contract clause, (2) the First Amendment, (3) due process, and (4) equal protection. The

Figure 4-2
Powers of Government

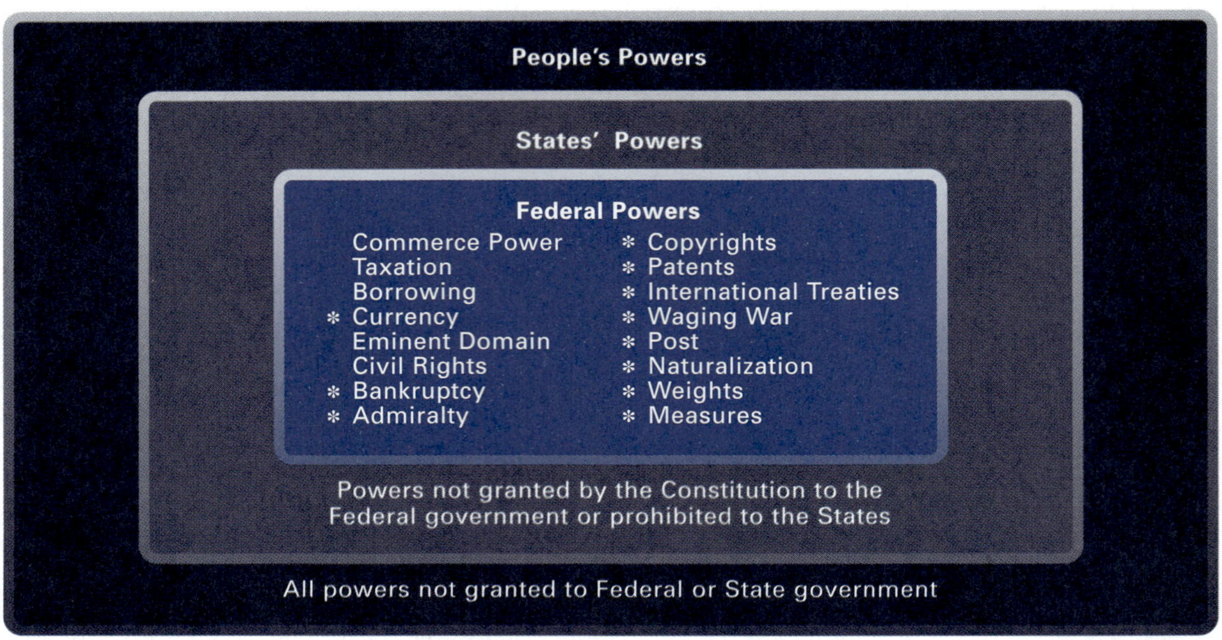

*Exclusive power

first of these—the contract clause—applies only to the actions of state governments, whereas the other three apply to both the federal government and the states.

None of these restrictions operates as an absolute limitation but instead triggers review or scrutiny by the courts to determine whether the governmental power exercised encroaches impermissibly upon the interest the Constitution protects. The U.S. Supreme Court has used different levels of scrutiny, depending on the interest affected and the nature of the governmental action. Although this differentiation among levels of scrutiny is most fully developed in the area of equal protection, it also occurs in other areas, including substantive due process and protection of free speech.

The least rigorous level of scrutiny is the **rational relationship test**, which requires that the regulation conceivably bear some rational relationship to a legitimate governmental interest that the regulation will attempt to further. The most exacting level of scrutiny is the **strict scrutiny test**, which requires that the regulation be necessary to promote a compelling governmental interest. Finally, under the **intermediate test**, the regulation must have a substantial relationship to an important governmental objective. These standards will be more fully explained below. See the Concept Review illustrating these limitations on government.

CONTRACT CLAUSE

Article I, Section 10, of the Constitution provides: "No State shall . . . pass any . . . Law impairing the Obligation of Contracts, . . . " The Supreme Court has used the contract clause to restrict states from retroactively modifying public charters and private contracts. However, the Court, holding that the contract clause does *not* preclude the states from exercising eminent domain or their police powers, has ruled: "No legislature can bargain away the public health or the public morals." Although the contract clause does not apply to the federal government, due process limits the federal government's power to impair contracts.

Practical Advice

The Federal Constitution protects you from a state law that impairs a preexisting contract.

FIRST AMENDMENT

The First Amendment states:

> Congress shall make no law respecting an establishment of religion, or prohibiting the free exercise thereof; or abridging the freedom of speech, or of the press; or the right of the people peaceably to assemble, and to petition the Government for a redress of grievances.

The First Amendment's protection of **free speech** is not absolute. Some forms of speech, such as obscenity, receive no protection. Most forms of speech, however, are protected by the strict or exacting scrutiny standard, which requires the existence of a compelling and legitimate state interest to justify a restriction of speech. If such an interest exists, the legislature must use means that least restrict free speech. We will examine the application of the First Amendment's guarantee of free speech to (1) corporate political speech, (2) commercial speech, and (3) defamation.

Corporate Political Speech Freedom of speech is indispensable to the discovery and spread of political truth; indeed, "the best test of truth is the power of the thought to get itself accepted in the competition of the market." To promote this competition of ideas, the First Amendment's guarantee of free speech applies not only to individuals but also to corporations. Accordingly, corporations may not be prohibited from speaking out on political issues. For example, the Supreme Court has held unconstitutional a Massachusetts criminal statute that prohibited banks and business corporations from making contributions and expenditures with regard to most referenda issues. The Court held that if speech is otherwise protected, the fact that the speaker is a corporation does not alter the speech's protected status.

CONCEPT REVIEW

Limitations on Government

Test/Interest	Equal Protection	Substantive Due Process	Free Speech
Strict Scrutiny	Fundamental Rights Suspect Classifications	Fundamental Rights	Protected Noncommercial Speech
Intermediate	Gender Legitimacy		Commercial Speech
Rational Relationship	Economic Regulation	Economic Regulation	Nonprotected Speech

The Supreme Court retreated somewhat from this holding when it upheld a state statute prohibiting corporations, except media corporations, from using general treasury funds to make independent expenditures in elections for public office but permitting such expenditures from segregated funds used solely for political purposes. The Court held that the statute did not violate the First Amendment because the burden on corporations' exercise of political expression was justified by a compelling state interest in preventing corruption in the political arena: "the corrosive and distorting effects of immense aggregations of wealth that are accumulated with the help of the corporate form and that have little or no correlation to the public's support for the corporation's political ideas." The Court held that the statute was sufficiently narrowly tailored because it "is precisely targeted to eliminate the distortion caused by corporate spending while also allowing corporations to express their political views" by making expenditures through segregated funds.

Commercial Speech Commercial speech is expression related to the economic interests of the speaker and his audience, such as advertisements for a product or service. Since the mid-1970s, U.S. Supreme Court decisions have eliminated the doctrine that commercial speech is wholly outside the protection of the First Amendment. Rather, the Court has established the principle that speech proposing a commercial transaction is entitled to protection, which, although less than that accorded political speech, is still extensive. Protection is accorded commercial speech because of the interest such communication holds for the advertiser, consumer, and general public. Advertising and other similar messages convey important information for the proper and efficient distribution of resources in our free market system. At the same time, however, commercial speech is less valuable and less vulnerable than other varieties of speech and therefore does not merit complete First Amendment protection.

In cases determining the protection to be afforded commercial speech, a four-part analysis has developed. First, the court must determine whether the expression is protected by the First Amendment. For commercial speech to come within that provision, such speech, at the least, must concern lawful activity and not be misleading. Second, the court must determine whether the asserted governmental interest is substantial. If both inquiries yield positive answers, then, third, the court must determine whether the regulation directly advances the governmental interest asserted and, fourth, whether the regulation is not more extensive than is necessary to serve that interest. The Supreme Court recently held that governmental restrictions of commercial speech need not be absolutely

Ethical Dilemma

Who Is Responsible for Commercial Speech?

FACTS Jane Stewart is an assistant manager of advertising for *Dazzling Magazine*, a fashion magazine aimed primarily at women between the ages of twenty-five and thirty-five. Offering regular columns on health, beauty, fashion, and current events, the magazine has a small circulation and handles its advertising internally.

Having experienced declining sales in recent years, the magazine has downsized its operations by eliminating jobs and implementing cost-cutting measures. To prevent further declines in revenue, *Dazzling's* marketing and editorial staffs are attempting to expand the magazine's appeal to include younger audiences between the ages of sixteen and twenty-four. Jane is in charge of making recommendations to the advertising manager with regard to new advertisements. The advertising manager, in turn, makes the final recommendation to the head of the advertising department. Because of the magazine's overall decline in sales, the advertising unit has come under increased pressure to generate revenue from advertisements. Compensation of advertising unit employees is based in part on the earning of "bonus points" related to first-year revenues from new clients.

Jane has received advertisement offers from two cigarette companies and from one swimsuit manufacturer. Although the cigarette advertisements would generate twice as much revenue as the swimsuit advertisement, Jane is concerned that the cigarette advertisements would lure young women to smoke. She has recommended to her supervisor, Agnes Scott, that the cigarette advertisements be rejected. Scott adamantly disagrees. She strongly recommends to the head of the advertising department that the cigarette advertisements be accepted.

SOCIAL, POLICY, AND ETHICAL CONSIDERATIONS

1. What should Jane do? What is best for (a) her company and (b) society? Should Jane raise her concerns to the department head?
2. Identify the competing social values at stake with regard to cigarette advertising. What role should the government play in regulating speech that promotes products such as tobacco and alcohol?
3. Should the age of *Dazzling*'s prospective audience influence the choice of advertisements? Explain.

the least severe so long as they are "narrowly tailored" to achieve the governmental objective.

Because the constitutional protection extended to commercial speech is based on the informational function of advertising, governments may regulate or suppress commercial messages that do not accurately inform the public about lawful activity. "The government may ban forms of communication more likely to deceive the public than to inform it, or commercial speech related to illegal activity." Therefore, governmental regulation of false and misleading advertising is permissible under the First Amendment.

Thompson v. Western States Medical Center

Supreme Court of the United States, 2002
535 U.S. 357, 122 S.Ct. 1497, 152 L.Ed.2d 563
http://laws.findlaw.com/us/000/01-344.html

FACTS Drug compounding is a process by which a pharmacist or doctor combines, mixes, or alters ingredients to create a medication tailored to the needs of an individual patient. Compounding is typically used to prepare medications that are not commercially available, such as medication for a patient who is allergic to an ingredient in a mass-produced product.

The Federal Food, Drug, and Cosmetic Act of 1938 (FDCA) regulates drug manufacturing, marketing, and distribution, providing that no person may sell any new drug unless approved by the Food and Drug Administration (FDA). The Food and Drug Administration Modernization Act of 1997 (FDAMA), which amends the FDCA, exempts compounded drugs from the FDCA's requirements provided the drugs satisfy a number of restrictions, including that the prescription must be "unsolicited," and the provider compounding the drug may "not advertise or promote the compounding of any particular drug, class of drug, or type of drug." The provider may, however, "advertise and promote the compounding service."

The plaintiffs are a group of licensed pharmacies that specialize in drug compounding. They filed a complaint in the United States District Court for the District of Nevada, arguing that the Act's requirement that they refrain from advertising and promoting their products if they wish to continue compounding violates the Free Speech Clause of the First Amendment. The District Court agreed with the plaintiffs and granted their motion for summary judgment, holding that the provisions do not meet the test for acceptable government regulation of commercial speech set forth in *Central Hudson Gas & Elec. Corp. v. Public Serv. Comm'n of N. Y.* The Court of Appeals for the Ninth Circuit affirmed in relevant part agreeing that the provisions regarding advertisement and promotion are unconstitutional.

DECISION Judgment affirmed.

OPINION O'Connor, J. The parties agree that the advertising and soliciting prohibited by the FDAMA constitute commercial speech. In *Virginia Bd. of Pharmacy v. Virginia Citizens Consumer Council, Inc.*, [citation], the first case in which we explicitly held that commercial speech receives First Amendment protection, we explained the reasons for this protection: "It is a matter of public interest that [economic] decisions, in the aggregate, be intelligent and well-informed. To this end, the free flow of commercial information is indispensable." [Citation.]

* * *

Although commercial speech is protected by the First Amendment, not all regulation of such speech is unconstitutional. [Citation]. In *Central Hudson*, [citation], we articulated a test for determining whether a particular commercial speech regulation is constitutionally permissible. Under that test we ask as a threshold matter whether the commercial speech concerns unlawful activity or is misleading. If so, then the speech is not protected by the First Amendment. If the speech concerns lawful activity and is not misleading, however, we next ask "whether the asserted governmental interest is substantial." [Citation.] If it is, then we "determine whether the regulation directly advances the governmental interest asserted," and, finally, "whether it is not more extensive than is necessary to serve that interest." [Citation.] Each of these latter three inquiries must be answered in the affirmative for the regulation to be found constitutional.

* * *

The Government asserts that three substantial interests underlie the FDAMA. The first is an interest in "preserving the effectiveness and integrity of the FDCA's new drug approval process and the protection of the public health that it provides." [Citation.] The second is an interest in "preserving the availability of compounded drugs for those individual patients who, for particularized medical reasons, cannot use commercially available products that have been approved by the FDA." [Citation.] Finally, the Government argues that "achieving the proper balance between those two independently compelling but competing interests is itself a substantial governmental interest." [Citation.]

* * *

Preserving the effectiveness and integrity of the FDCA's new drug approval process is clearly an important governmental interest, and the Government has every reason to want as many drugs as possible to be subject to that approval process. The Government also has an important interest, however, in permitting the continuation of the practice of compounding so that patients with particular needs may obtain medications suited to those needs. And it would not make sense to require compounded drugs created to meet the unique needs of individual patients to undergo the testing required for the new drug approval process. Pharmacists do not make enough money from small-scale compounding to make safety and efficacy testing of their compounded drugs economically feasible, so requiring such testing would force pharmacists to stop providing compounded drugs. Given this, the Government needs to be able to draw a line between small-scale compounding and large-scale drug manufacturing. That line must distinguish compounded drugs produced on such a small scale that they could not undergo safety and efficacy testing from drugs produced and sold on a large enough scale that they could undergo such testing and therefore must do so.

The Government argues that the FDAMA's speech-related provisions provide just such a line, i.e., that, in the terms of *Central Hudson*, they "directly advance the governmental interests asserted." [Citation.] Those provisions use advertising as the trigger for requiring FDA approval—essentially, as long as pharmacists do not advertise particular compounded drugs, they may sell compounded drugs without first undergoing safety and efficacy testing and obtaining FDA approval. If they advertise their compounded drugs, however, FDA approval is required. * * *

* * * Assuming it is true that drugs cannot be marketed on a large scale without advertising, the FDAMA's prohibition on advertising compounded drugs might indeed "directly advance" the Government's interests. *Central Hudson,* [citation]. Even assuming that it does, however, the Government has failed to demonstrate that the speech restrictions are "not more extensive than is necessary to serve [those] interests." [Citation.] In previous cases addressing this final prong of the *Central Hudson* test, we have made clear that if the Government could achieve its interests in a manner that does not restrict speech, or that restricts less speech, the Government must do so.

Several non-speech-related means of drawing a line between compounding and large-scale manufacturing might be possible here. First, it seems that the Government could use the very factors the FDA relied on to distinguish compounding from manufacturing in its 1992 Compliance Policy Guide. For example, the Government could ban the use of "commercial scale manufacturing or testing equipment for compounding drug products." [Citation.] It could prohibit pharmacists from compounding more drugs in anticipation of receiving prescriptions than in response to prescriptions already received. [Citation.] It could prohibit pharmacists from "offering compounded drugs at wholesale to other state licensed persons or commercial entities for resale." [Citation.] Alternately, it could limit the amount of compounded drugs, either by volume or by numbers of prescriptions, that a given pharmacist or pharmacy sells out of state. * * *

* * *

Even if the Government had argued that the FDAMA's speech-related restrictions were motivated by a fear that advertising compounded drugs would put people who do not need such drugs at risk by causing them to convince their doctors to prescribe the drugs anyway, that fear would fail to justify the restrictions. Aside from the fact that this concern rests on the questionable assumption that doctors would prescribe unnecessary medications * * * this concern amounts to a fear that people would make bad decisions if given truthful information about compounded drugs * * * We have previously rejected the notion that the Government has an interest in preventing the dissemination of truthful commercial information in order to prevent members of the public from making bad decisions with the information. In *Virginia Bd. of Pharmacy*, the State feared that if people received price advertising from pharmacists,they would "choose the low-cost, low-quality service and drive the 'professional' pharmacist out of business" and would destroy the pharmacist-customer relationship" by going from one pharmacist to another. We found these fears insufficient to justify a ban on such advertising. [Citation.] We explained:

> "There is, of course, an alternative to this highly paternalistic approach. That alternative is to assume that this information is not in itself harmful, that people will perceive their own best interests if only they are well enough informed, and that the best means to that end is to open the channels of communication rather than to close them * * *[Citation.]

* * *

If the Government's failure to justify its decision to regulate speech were not enough to convince us that the FDAMA's advertising provisions were unconstitutional, the amount of beneficial speech prohibited by the FDAMA would be. Forbidding the advertisement of compounded drugs would affect pharmacists other than those interested in producing drugs on a large scale. It would prevent pharmacists with no interest in mass-producing medications, but who serve clienteles with special medical needs, from telling the doctors treating those clients about the alternative drugs available through compounding.* * *

INTERPRETATION A governmental restriction on nonmisleading commercial speech concerning lawful activity is invalid under the First Amendment if the regulation is more extensive than necessary to directly advance a substantial governmental interest.

CRITICAL THINKING QUESTION Do you agree that the Court's suggested non-speech-related means of drawing a line between compounding and large-scale manufacturing would be effective? Explain.

Defamation Defamation is a civil wrong or tort that consists of disgracing or diminishing a person's reputation through the communication of a false statement. An example would be the publication of a statement that a person had committed a crime or had a loathsome disease. (Defamation is also discussed in Chapter 7.)

Because defamation involves a communication, it receives the protection extended to speech by the First Amendment. Moreover, the Supreme Court has ruled that a public official who is defamed in regard to his conduct, fitness, or role as public official may not recover in a defamation action unless the statement was made with *actual malice*, which requires clear and convincing proof that the defendant had knowledge of the falsity of the communication or acted in reckless disregard of its truth or falsity. This restriction on the right to recover for defamation is based on "a profound national commitment to the principle that debate on public issues should be uninhibited, robust and wide-open, and that it may well include vehement, caustic, and sometimes unpleasantly sharp attacks on government and public officials." The communication may deal with the official's qualifications for and performance in office, which would likely include most aspects of character and public conduct. In addition, the Supreme Court has extended the same rule to public figures and candidates for public office. (The Court, however, has not precisely defined the term *public figure*.)

In a defamation suit brought by a private person (one who is neither a public official nor a public figure) against a member of the news media, the plaintiff must prove that the defendant published the defamatory and false comment with malice or negligence. In contrast, when a private person brings suit against a defendant who is not a member of the news media, it is currently unresolved whether the plaintiff must prove anything beyond the fact that a defamatory and false statement has been made.

DUE PROCESS

The Fifth and Fourteenth Amendments prohibit the federal and state governments, respectively, from depriving any person of life, liberty, or property without **due process** of law. Due process has two different aspects: substantive and procedural. As we discussed in Chapter 1, substantive law creates, defines, or regulates legal rights, whereas procedural law establishes the rules for enforcing those rights. Accordingly, substantive due process concerns the compatibility of a law or governmental action with fundamental constitutional rights such as free speech. In contrast, procedural due process involves the review of the decision-making process that enforces substantive laws and results in depriving a person of life, liberty, or property.

Substantive Due Process Substantive due process, which involves a court's determination of whether a particular governmental action is compatible with individual liberties, addresses the constitutionality of a legal rule, not the fairness of the process by which the rule is applied. Legislation affecting economic and social interests satisfies substantive due process so long as the legislation is rationally related to legitimate governmental objectives. Where a rule affects individuals' fundamental rights under the Constitution, however, the Court will carefully scrutinize the legislation to determine if it is necessary to promote a compelling or overriding state interest.

Procedural Due Process Procedural due process pertains to the governmental decision-making process that results in depriving a person of life, liberty, or property. As the Supreme Court has interpreted procedural due process, the government is required to provide an individual with a fair procedure if, but only if, the person faces deprivation of life, liberty, or property. When governmental action adversely affects an individual but does not deny life, liberty, or property, the government is not required to give the person any hearing at all.

For the purposes of procedural due process, **liberty** generally includes the ability of individuals to engage in freedom of action and choice regarding their personal lives. **Property** includes not only all forms of real and personal property but also certain benefits (entitlements) conferred by the government, such as social security payments and food stamps.

When applicable, procedural due process requires that a court use a fair and impartial procedure in resolving the factual and legal basis for a governmental action that results in a deprivation of life, liberty, or property.

EQUAL PROTECTION

The Fourteenth Amendment provides that "nor shall any State . . . deny to any person within its jurisdiction the equal protection of the laws." Although this amendment applies only to the actions of state governments, the Supreme Court has interpreted the due process clause of the Fifth Amendment to subject federal actions to the same standards of review. The most important constitutional concept protecting individual rights, the guarantee of **equal protection** basically requires that similarly situated persons be treated similarly by governmental actions.

When governmental action involves classification of people, the equal protection guarantee comes into play. In determining whether governmental action satisfies the equal protection guarantee, the Supreme Court uses one of three standards of review, depending on the nature of the right involved. The three standards are (1) the rational relationship test, (2) the strict scrutiny test, and (3) the intermediate test.

Rational Relationship Test The rational relationship test, which applies to economic regulation, simply requires that the classification *conceivably* bear some rational relationship to a legitimate governmental interest the classification seeks to further. Under this standard of review, the governmental action is permitted to attack part of the evil to which the action is addressed. Moreover, there is a strong presumption that the action is constitutional. Therefore, the courts will overturn the governmental action *only* if clear and convincing evidence shows that there is *no* reasonable basis justifying the action.

Strict Scrutiny Test The strict scrutiny test is far more exacting than the rational relationship test. Under this test, the courts do not defer to the government; rather, they independently determine whether a classification of persons is constitutionally permissible. This determination requires that the classification be necessary to promote a compelling or overriding governmental interest.

The strict scrutiny test is applied when governmental action affects fundamental rights or involves suspect classifications. Fundamental rights include most of the provisions of the Bill of Rights and certain other rights, such as interstate travel, voting, and access to criminal justice. Suspect classifications include those made on the basis of race or national origin. A classic and important example of strict scrutiny applied to classifications based upon race is found in the 1954 school desegregation case of *Brown v. Board of Education of Topeka*, in which the Supreme Court ruled that segregated public school systems violated the equal protection guarantee. Subsequently, the Court has invalidated segregation in public beaches, municipal golf courses, buses, parks, public golf courses, and courtroom seating.

http:// Brown v. Board of Education National Historic Site: http://www.nps.gov/brvb/home.htm

Brown v. Board of Education of Topeka

Supreme Court of the United States, 1954
347 U.S. 483, 74 S.Ct. 686, 98 L.Ed. 873
http://laws.findlaw.com/US/347/483.html

FACTS These were consolidated cases from Kansas, South Carolina, Virginia, and Delaware, each with a different set of facts and local conditions but also presenting a common legal question. Black minors, through their legal representatives, sought court orders to obtain admission to the public schools in their community on a nonsegregated basis. They had been denied admission to schools attended by white children under laws requiring or permitting segregation according to race. The Supreme Court had previously upheld such laws under the "separate but equal" doctrine, which provided that there was equality of treatment of the races through substantially equal, though separate, facilities; and the lower courts had found that the white schools and the black schools involved had been or were being equalized with respect to buildings, curricula, qualifications and salaries of teachers, and other "tangible" factors. The black minors contended, however, that segregated public schools were not and could not be made "equal," and that hence they had been deprived of the equal protection of the laws guaranteed by the Fourteenth Amendment.

DECISION Judgment for plaintiffs.

OPINION Warren, C. J. Today, education is perhaps the most important function of state and local governments. Compulsory school attendance laws and the great expenditures for education both demonstrate our recognition of the importance of education to our democratic society. It is required in the performance of our most basic public responsibilities, even service in the armed forces. It is the very foundation of good citizenship. Today it is a principal instrument in awakening the child to cultural values, in preparing him for later professional training, and in helping him to adjust normally to his environment. In these days, it is doubtful that any child may reasonably be expected to succeed in life if he is denied the opportunity of an education. Such an opportunity, where the state has undertaken to provide it, is a right which must be made available to all on equal terms.

We come then to the question presented: Does segregation of children in public schools solely on the basis of race, even though the physical facilities and other "tangible" factors may be equal, deprive the children of the minority group of equal educational opportunities? We believe that it does.

In *Sweatt v. Painter*, [citation], in finding that a segregated law school for Negroes could not provide them equal educational opportunities, this Court relied in large part on "those qualities which are incapable of objective measurement but which make for greatness in a law school." In *McLaurin v. Oklahoma State Regents*, [citation], the Court in requiring that a Negro admitted to a white graduate school be treated like all other students, again resorted to intangible considerations: "* * * his ability to study, to engage in discussions and exchange views with other students, and, in general, to learn his profession." Such considerations apply with added force to children in grade and high schools. To separate them from others of similar age and qualifications solely because of their race generates a feeling of inferiority as to their status in the community that may affect their hearts and minds in a way unlikely ever to be undone. The effect of this separation on their educational opportunities was well stated by a finding in the Kansas case by a court which nevertheless felt compelled to rule against the Negro plaintiffs:

"Segregation of white and colored children in public schools has a detrimental effect upon the colored children. The impact is greater when it has the sanction of the law, for the policy of separating the races is usually interpreted as denoting the inferiority of the Negro group. A sense of inferiority affects the motivation of a child to learn. Segregation with the sanction of law, therefore, has a tendency to (retard) the educational and mental development of Negro children and to deprive them of some of the benefits they would receive in a racial(ly) integrated school system."

* * *

We conclude that in the field of public education the doctrine of "separate but equal" has no place. Separate educational facilities are inherently unequal. Therefore, we hold that the plaintiffs and others similarly situated for whom the actions have been brought are, by reason of the segregation complained of, deprived of the equal protection of the laws guaranteed by the Fourteenth Amendment. This disposition makes unnecessary any discussion whether such segregation also violates the Due Process Clause of the Fourteenth Amendment.

INTERPRETATION When a governmentally imposed classification involves fundamental rights or suspect classifications, equal protection requires the classification to be necessary to promote a compelling or overriding governmental interest.

CRITICAL THINKING QUESTION Is the equal protection clause of the U.S. Constitution violated when different public school districts spend significantly different amounts of money per student? Explain.

Intermediate Test An intermediate test has been applied to governmental action based on gender and legitimacy. Under this test, the classification must have a substantial relationship to an important governmental objective. The intermediate standard eliminates the strong presumption of constitutionality to which the rational relationship test adheres. For example, the Court invalidated an Alabama law that allowed courts to grant alimony awards only from husbands to wives and not from wives to husbands. Similarly, where an Idaho statute gave preference to males over females in qualifying for selection as administrators of estates, the Court invalidated the statute because the preference did not bear a fair and substantial relationship to any legitimate legislative objective. More recently, the Court invalidated a state university's (Virginia Military Institute) admission policy excluding women. *U.S. v. Virginia*, 518 U.S. 515, (1996). On the other hand, not all legislation based on gender is invalid. For example, the Court has upheld a California statutory rape law that imposed penalties only on males, as well as the federal military selective service act, that exempted women from registering for the draft.

CHAPTER SUMMARY

Basic Principles

Federalism the division of governing power between the federal government and the states

Federal Supremacy federal law takes precedence over conflicting state law

Federal Preemption right of federal government to regulate matters within its power to the exclusion of regulation by the states

Judicial Review examination of governmental actions to determine whether they conform to the U.S. Constitution

Separation of Powers allocation of powers among executive, legislative, and judicial branches of government

State Action actions of governments to which constitutional provisions apply

Powers of Government

Federal Commerce Power exclusive power of federal government to regulate commerce with other nations and among the states

State Regulation of Commerce the commerce clause of the Constitution restricts the states' power to regulate activities if the result obstructs interstate commerce

Federal Fiscal Powers
- ***Taxation and Spending*** the Constitution grants Congress broad powers to tax and spend; such powers are important to federal government regulation of the economy
- ***Borrowing and Coining Money*** enables the federal government to establish a national banking system and to control national fiscal and monetary policy
- ***Eminent Domain*** the government's power to take private property for public use with the payment of just compensation

Limitations on Government

Contract Clause restricts states from retroactively modifying contracts

Freedom of Speech First Amendment protects most speech by using a strict scrutiny standard
- ***Corporate Political Speech*** First Amendment protects a corporation's right to speak out on political issues
- ***Commercial Speech*** expression related to the economic interests of the speaker and its audience; such expression receives a lesser degree of protection
- ***Defamation*** a tort consisting of a false communication that injures a person's reputation; such a communication receives limited constitutional protection

Due Process Fifth and Fourteenth Amendments prohibit the federal and state governments from depriving any person of life, liberty, or property without due process of law
- ***Substantive Due Process*** determination of whether a particular governmental action is compatible with individual liberties
- ***Procedural Due Process*** requires the governmental decision-making process to be fair and impartial if it deprives a person of life, liberty, or property

Equal Protection requires that similarly situated persons be treated similarly by governmental actions
- ***Rational Relationship Test*** standard of review used to determine whether economic regulation satisfies the equal protection guarantee
- ***Strict Scrutiny Test*** exacting standard of review applicable to regulation affecting a fundamental right or involving a suspect classification
- ***Intermediate Test*** standard of review applicable to regulation based on gender and legitimacy

QUESTIONS

1. In May, Patricia Allen left her automobile on the shoulder of a road in the city of Erewhon after the car stopped running. A member of the Erewhon city police department found the car later that day and placed on it a sticker stating that unless the car were moved, it would be towed. When after a week the car had not been removed, the police department authorized Baldwin Auto Wrecking Co. to tow it away and to store it on its property. Allen was told by a friend that her car was at Baldwin's. Allen asked Baldwin to allow her to take possession of her car, but Baldwin refused to relinquish the car until the $70 towing fee was paid. Allen could not afford to pay the fee, and the car remained at Baldwin's for six weeks. At that time, Baldwin requested the police department for a permit to dispose of the automobile. After the police department tried unsuccessfully to telephone Allen, the department issued the permit. In late July, Baldwin destroyed the automobile. Allen brings an action against the city and Baldwin for damages for loss of the vehicle, arguing that she was denied due process. Decision?

CASE PROBLEMS

2. In 1967, large oil reserves were discovered in the Prudhoe Bay area of Alaska. As a result, state revenues increased from $124 million in 1969 to $3.7 billion in 1981. In 1980, the state legislature enacted a dividend program (http://www.pfd.state.ak.us) that would distribute annually a portion of these earnings to the state's adult residents. Under the plan, each citizen eighteen years of age or older receives one unit for each year of residency subsequent to 1959, the year Alaska became a state. The state advanced three purposes justifying the distinctions made by the dividend program: (a) creation of a financial incentive for individuals to establish and maintain residence in Alaska; (b) encouragement of prudent management of the earnings; and (c) apportionment of benefits in recognition of undefined "contributions of various kinds, both tangible and intangible, which residents have made during their years of residency." Crawford, a resident since 1978, brings suit challenging the dividend distribution plan as violative of the equal protection guarantee. Did the dividend program violate equal protection? Explain.

3. Maryland enacted a statute prohibiting any producer or refiner of petroleum products from operating retail service stations within the state. The statute also required that any producer or refiner discontinue operating its company-owned retail service stations. Approximately 3,800 retail service stations in Maryland sell more than twenty different brands of gasoline. No petroleum products are produced or refined in Maryland, however, and only 5 percent of the total number of retailers are operated by a producer or refiner. Maryland enacted the statute because a survey conducted by the state comptroller indicated that gasoline stations operated by producers or refiners had received preferential treatment during periods of gasoline shortage. Seven major producers and refiners brought an action challenging the statute on the ground that it discriminated against interstate commerce in violation of the commerce clause of the U.S. Constitution. Are they correct? Explain.

4. The Federal Aviation Act provides that "The United States of America is declared to possess and exercise complete and exclusive national sovereignty in the airspace of the United States" The city of Orion adopted an ordinance that makes it unlawful for jet aircraft to take off from its airport between 11 P.M. of one day and 7 A.M. of the next day. Jordan Airlines, Inc., is adversely affected by this ordinance and brings suit challenging it under the supremacy clause of the U.S. Constitution as conflicting with the Federal Aviation Act or preempted by it. Is the ordinance valid? Explain.

5. The Public Service Commission of State X issued a regulation completely banning all advertising that "promotes the use of electricity" by any electric utility company in State X. The commission issued the regulation in order to conserve energy. Central Electric Corporation of State X challenges the order in the state courts, arguing that the commission had restrained commercial speech in violation of the First Amendment. Was their freedom of speech unconstitutionally infringed? Explain.

6. E-Z-Rest Motel is a motel with 216 rooms located in the center of a large city in State Y. It is readily accessible from two interstate highways and three major state highways. The motel solicits patronage from outside State Y through various national advertising media, including magazines of national circulation. It accepts convention trade from outside State Y, and approximately 75 percent of its registered guests are from out of State Y. An action under the Federal Civil Rights Act of 1964 has been brought against E-Z-Rest Motel alleging that the motel discriminates on the basis of race and color. The motel contends that the statute cannot be applied to it because it is not engaged in interstate commerce. Can the federal government regulate this activity under the interstate commerce clause? Why?

7. State Z enacted a Private Pension Benefits Protection Act requiring private employers with 100 or more employees to pay a pension funding charge for terminating a pension plan or closing an office in State Z. Acme Steel Company closed its offices in State Z, whereupon the state assessed the company $185,000 under the vesting provisions of the act. Acme challenged the constitutionality of the act under the contract clause (Article I, Section 10) of the U.S. Constitution. Was the act constitutional? Explain.

8. A state statute empowered public school principals to suspend students for up to ten days without any notice or hearing. A student who was suspended for ten days challenges the constitutionality of his suspension on the ground that he was denied due process. Was due process denied? Explain.

9. Iowa enacted a statute prohibiting the use of sixty-five-foot double trailer truck combinations. All of the other midwestern and western states permit such trucks to be used on their roads. Consolidated Freightways is adversely affected by this statute and brings suit against Iowa, alleging that the statute violates the commerce clause. Decision?

10. Metropolitan Edison Company (http://www.firstenergcorp.com) is a privately owned and operated Pennsylvania corporation subject to extensive regulation by the Pennsylvania Public Utility Commission (http://puc.paonline.com/). Under a provision of its general tariff filed with the commission, Edison had the right to discontinue electric service to any customer on reasonable notice of nonpayment of bills. Catherine Jackson had been receiving electricity from Metropolitan Edison when her account was terminated in 1970 because of her delinquency in payments. Edison later opened a new account for her residence in the name of James Dodson, another occupant of Jackson's residence. In August 1971, Dodson moved away and no further payments were made to the account. Finally, in October 1971, Edison disconnected Jackson's service without any prior notice. Jackson brought suit claiming that her electric service could not be terminated without notice and a hearing. She further argued that such action, allowed by a provision of Edison's tariff filed with the commission, constituted "state action" depriving her of property in violation of the Fourteenth Amendment's guarantee of due process of law. Should Edison's actions be considered state action? Explain.

11. The McClungs own Ollie's Barbecue, a restaurant located a few blocks from the interstate highway in Birmingham, Alabama, with dining accommodations for whites only and a take-out service for blacks. In the year preceding the passage of the Civil Rights Act of 1964, the restaurant had purchased a substantial portion of the food it served from outside the state. The restaurant has refused to serve blacks since its original opening in 1927 and asserts that if it were required to serve blacks it would lose much of its business. The McClungs sought a declaratory judgment to render unconstitutional the application of the Civil Rights Act to their restaurant because their admitted racial discrimination did not restrict or significantly impede interstate commerce. Decision?

12. Miss Horowitz was admitted as an advanced medical student at the University of Missouri-Kansas City (http://www.umkc.edu). During the spring of her first year, several faculty members expressed dissatisfaction with Miss Horowitz's clinical performance, noting that it was below that of her peers, that she was erratic in attendance at her clinical sessions, and that she lacked a critical concern for personal hygiene. Upon the recommendation of the school's Council on Evaluation, she was advanced to her second and final year on a probationary basis. After subsequent unfavorable reviews during her second year and a negative evaluation of her performance by seven practicing physicians, the council recommended that Miss Horowitz be dismissed from the school for her failure to meet academic standards. The decision was approved by the dean and later affirmed by the provost after an appeal by Miss Horowitz. She brought suit against the school's Board of Curators, claiming that her dismissal violated her right to procedural due process under the Fourteenth Amendment and deprived her of "liberty" by substantially impairing her opportunities to continue her medical education or return to employment in a medically related field. Is her claim correct? Explain.

13. CompuServe Incorporated ("CompuServe") (http://www.compuserve.com/corporate/cs_overview.html) is one of the major national commercial online services. It operates a computer communication service through a proprietary nationwide computer network. In addition to allowing access to the content available on its own network, CompuServe also provides its subscribers with a link to the much larger resources of the Internet. This allows its subscribers to send and receive electronic messages, known as "e-mail," by the Internet. Cyber Promotions, Inc. is in the business of sending unsolicited e-mail advertisements on behalf of itself and its clients to hundreds of thousands of Internet users, many of whom are CompuServe subscribers. CompuServe has notified Cyber Promotions that it is prohibited from using CompuServe's computer equipment to process and store the unsolicited e-mail and has requested that Cyber Promotions terminate the practice. Instead, Cyber Promotions has sent an increasing volume of e-mail solicitations to CompuServe subscribers. CompuServe has attempted to employ technological means to block the flow of Cyber Promotions e-mail transmissions but to no avail. CompuServe seeks an injunction preventing Cyber Promotions from sending unsolicited advertisements to CompuServe subscribers. In response, Cyber Promotions argues that it has the right to continue to send unsolicited commercial e-mail to CompuServe's computer systems under the First Amendment to the United States Constitution. Decision?

http:// **Internet Exercise** Find your state's constitution and compare its protection of individual rights with that of the U.S. Constitution. (If such information on your state is not available, choose another state.)

CHAPTER 5

Administrative Law

In all tyrannical governments,. . . the right both of making and enforcing the law is vested in . . . one and the same body of men; and wherever these two powers are united together, there can be no public liberty.

WILLIAM BLACKSTONE (BRITISH JURIST, 1775)

Learning Objectives

After reading this chapter you should be able to:

1. Explain the three basic functions of administrative law.
2. Distinguish among the three types of rules promulgated by administrative agencies.
3. Explain the difference between formal and informal methods of adjudication
4. Identify (a) the questions of law determined by a court in conducting a review of a rule or order of an administrative agency and (b) the three standards of judicial review of factual determinations made by administrative agencies.
5. Describe the limitations imposed on administrative agencies by the legislative branch, the executive branch, and the legally required disclosure of information.

Administrative law is the branch of public law that is created by administrative agencies in the form of rules, regulations, orders, and decisions, to carry out the regulatory powers and duties of those agencies. **Administrative agencies** are governmental entities—other than courts and legislatures—having authority to affect the rights of private parties through their operations. Administrative agencies, referred to by names such as commission, board, department, agency, administration, government corporation, bureau, or office, regulate a vast array of important matters involving national safety, welfare, and convenience. For instance, federal administrative agencies are charged with responsibility for national security, citizenship and naturalization, law enforcement, taxation, currency, elections, environmental protection, consumer protection, regulation of transportation, telecommunications, labor relations, trade, commerce, and securities markets, as well as providing health and social services.

Because of the increasing complexity of the social, economic, and industrial life of the nation, the scope of administrative law has expanded enormously. In 1952, Justice Jackson observed that "the rise of administrative bodies has been the most significant legal trend of the last century, and perhaps more values today are affected by their decisions than by those of all the courts, review of administrative decisions apart." This observation is even more true today, as evidenced by the great increase in the number and activities of federal government boards, commissions, and other agencies. Certainly, agencies create more legal rules and adjudicate more controversies than all the nation's legislatures and courts combined.

State agencies also play a significant role in the functioning of our society. Among the more important state boards and commissions are those that supervise and regulate banking, insurance, communications, transportation, public utilities, pollution control, and workers' compensation.

Much of the federal, state, and local law in this country is established by countless administrative agencies. These agencies, which many label the "fourth branch of government," possess tremendous power and have long been criticized as being "in reality miniature independent governments . . . which are a haphazard deposit of irresponsible agencies. . . ." 1937 Presidential Task Force Report.

Despite such criticism, these administrative entities clearly play a significant and necessary role in our society. Administrative agencies relieve legislatures from the impossible burden of fashioning legislation that deals with every detail of a specific problem. As a result, Congress can enact legislation, such as the Federal Trade Commission Act, which prohibits unfair and deceptive trade practices, without having to define such a phrase specifically or to anticipate all the particular problems that may arise. Instead, Congress may pass an enabling statute that creates an agency—in this example, the Federal Trade Commission—to which it can delegate the power to issue rules, regulations, and guidelines to carry out the statutory mandate. In addition, the establishment of separate, specialized bodies enables administrative agencies to be staffed by individuals with expertise in the field being regulated. Administrative agencies can thus develop the knowledge and devote the time necessary to provide continuous and flexible solutions to evolving regulatory problems.

In this chapter, we will discuss federal administrative agencies. Such agencies can be classified as either independent or executive. Executive agencies are those housed within the executive branch of government, while independent agencies are not. Many federal agencies are discussed in other parts of the text. More specifically, the Federal Trade Commission (FTC) and Department of Justice are discussed in Chapter 43; the FTC and the Consumer Product Safety Commission in Chapter 45; the Department of Labor, National Labor Relations Board (NLRB), and Equal Employment Opportunity Commission (EEOC) in Chapter 42; the Securities and Exchange Commission (SEC) in Chapters 40 and 44; and the Environmental Protection Agency (EPA) in Chapter 46.

http:// American Bar Association's Administrative Law Section: http://abanet.org/adminlaw/home.html
Federal Agencies: http://www.fedworld.gov

OPERATION OF ADMINISTRATIVE AGENCIES

Most administrative agencies perform three basic functions: (1) rulemaking, (2) enforcement, and (3) adjudication of controversies. The term **administrative process** refers to the entire set of activities in which administrative agencies engage while carrying out these functions. Administrative agencies exercise powers that have been allocated by the Constitution to the three separate branches of government. More specifically, an agency exercises legislative power when it makes rules, executive power when it enforces its enabling statute and its rules, and judicial power when it adjudicates disputes. This concentration of power has raised questions regarding the propriety of having the same bodies that establish the rules also act as prosecutors and judges in determining whether those rules have been violated. To address this issue and to bring about certain additional procedural reforms, the Administrative Procedure Act (APA) was enacted in 1946.

http:// Administrative Procedure Act: http://www.archives.gov/federal_register/publiclaws/acts.html#apa

RULEMAKING

Rulemaking is the process by which an administrative agency enacts or promulgates rules of law. Under the APA, a **rule** is "the whole or a part of an agency statement of general or particular applicability and future effect designed to implement, interpret, or process law or policy." Once promulgated, rules are applicable to all parties. Moreover, the process of rulemaking notifies all parties that the impending rule is being considered and provides concerned individuals with an opportunity to be heard. Administrative agencies promulgate three types of rules: legislative rules, interpretative rules, and procedural rules.

Legislative Rules Legislative rules, often called regulations, are in effect "administrative statutes." **Legislative rules** are those issued by an agency having the ability, under a legislative delegation of power, to make rules having the force and effect of law. For example, the FTC has rulemaking power with which to elaborate upon its enabling statute's prohibition of unfair or deceptive acts or practices.

Legislative rules have the force of law if they are constitutional, within the power granted to the agency by the legislature, and issued according to proper procedure. To be constitutional, regulations must not violate any provisions of the U.S. Constitution, such as due process or equal protection. In addition, they may not involve an unconstitutional delegation of legislative power from the legislature to the agency. To be constitutionally permissible, the enabling statute granting power to an agency must establish reasonable standards to guide the agency in implementing the statute. This requirement has been met by statutory language such as "to prohibit unfair methods of competition," "fair and equitable," "public interest, convenience, and necessity," and other equally broad expressions. In any event, agencies may not exceed the actual authority granted by the enabling statute.

Diersen v. Chicago Car Exchange

United States Court of Appeals, Seventh Circuit, 1997
110 F.3d 481, *cert. denied*, 522 U.S. 868, 118 S.Ct. 178, 139 L.Ed.2d 119 (1997)
http://laws.findlaw.com/7th/961588.html

FACTS David Diersen filed a complaint against the Chicago Car Exchange ("CCE"), an automobile dealership, alleging that the CCE fraudulently furnished him an inaccurate odometer reading when it sold him a 1968 Dodge Charger, in violation of the Vehicle Information and Cost Savings Act ("the Odometer Act" or "the Act"). The Odometer Act requires all persons transferring a motor vehicle to give an accurate, written odometer reading to the purchaser or recipient of the transferred vehicle. Under the Act, those who disclose an inaccurate odometer reading with the intent to defraud are subject to a private cause of action by the purchaser and may be held liable for treble damages or $1,500, whichever is greater. The CCE had purchased the vehicle from Joseph Slaski, who certified to the CCE that the mileage was approximately 22,600. The CCE did not suspect that the odometer reading was inaccurate. After purchasing the vehicle, Diersen conducted an extensive investigation and discovered that the vehicle's title documents previously listed its mileage as 75,000. Before Diersen filed this lawsuit, the CCE offered to have Diersen return the car for a complete refund. Diersen refused this offer and decided instead to sue the CCE under the Act. The district court granted the defendant's motion for summary judgment, relying upon a regulation promulgated by the National Highway Traffic Safety Administration ("NHTSA") **(http://www.nhtsa.dot.gov)**, which purports to exempt vehicles that are at least ten years old (such as the one Diersen purchased from the CCE) from the Act's odometer disclosure requirements. Diersen then filed a motion for reconsideration of the court's summary judgment order, arguing that the older-car exemption created by the NHTSA lacked any basis in the Act and was therefore invalid. The court denied Diersen's motion to reconsider and Diersen appealed.

DECISION That portion of the district court opinion which relied upon the NHTSA regulation as a ground for ruling in favor of the CCE is reversed, but the grant of summary judgment is affirmed on other grounds.

OPINION Coffey, C. J. The CCE argues that in considering the validity of the NHTSA regulation, we must defer to the NHTSA's interpretation of the Act, because the NHTSA is the agency charged with administering the Act and thus has familiarity and expertise that we do not possess. We do defer to an administrative agency's reasonable construction of a statute if (as is not the case here) the statute is silent or ambiguous. On the other hand, "[i]f the intent of Congress is clear, that is the end of the matter; for the court, as well as the agency must give effect to the unambiguously expressed intent of Congress." *Chevron, U.S.A., Inc. v. Natural Resources Defense Council, Inc.*, [citation]. Because the text of the Odometer Act does not even suggest—much less explicitly state—a legislative intent to exempt entire classes of vehicles from the disclosure requirements of the Act, we hold that the regulation is invalid and that the district court erred in relying upon this exemption when it granted summary judgment to the CCE.

Our holding is in accord with a number of decisions by other courts on a closely analogous issue: whether the NHTSA exceeded its statutory authority in promulgating an exemption to the odometer disclosure requirements of the Odometer Act for so-called "heavy trucks" (i.e., trucks with a gross weight in excess of 16,000 pounds). [Citation.] A number of courts, including the Court of Appeals for the Ninth Circuit, have held that the NHTSA's "heavy truck" exemption, like the older-car exemption, has no basis in the text of the Odometer Act and represents an invalid exercise of regulatory authority. [Citations.] The principle behind these cases also applies to the exemption for older cars. That principle is that "legislative power rests in Congress and * * * the will of Congress as unambiguously expressed in a properly enacted statute cannot be amended or altered by regulation. * * * [A] regulation to the extent it is in direct variance with an unambiguous statutory provision is void." [Citation.]

Our holding that the older-car exemption is invalid also comports with the broad purposes of the Act, which are "to prohibit tampering with motor vehicle odometers; and to provide safeguards to protect purchasers in the sale of motor vehicles with altered or reset odometers." [Citation.] There is nothing in this statement of purpose to suggest that the purchasers of older vehicles are less deserving of protection than consumers who buy newer vehicles. The statutory statement of purpose, read concomitantly with the language of the Act (which, to reiterate, does not specify any exemptions) establishes that Congress intended to protect all purchasers of motor vehicles from odometer tampering.

Finally, we observe that the Act provides for the levying of civil and criminal fines against violators at the discretion of the NHTSA. [Citation.] In the exercise of prosecutorial discretion, the NHTSA may opt to conserve its resources by declining to prosecute certain classes of vehicles (e.g., those cases involving older vehicles). However, the NHTSA does not, without statutory authority, have jurisdiction to tell victims of odometer fraud that they are without a remedy if the car they purchased was ten or more years old. This effectively removes a cause of action that Congress has unambiguously provided to all victims of odometer fraud, regardless of the age of the vehicle being purchased. As one member of this panel observed at oral argument, the regulation issued by the NHTSA, in effect, repeals a portion of the statute. There may be good policy reasons for exempting older vehicles from the requirements of the Act, but that determination is legislative in nature and is properly made by Congress, and not by regulatory fiat. [Citation] ("[R]ationality is not enough. The Secretary need[s] Authority.").

To summarize, we hold that the NHTSA regulation is invalid. This means that the odometer disclosure requirements of the Act apply regardless of the age of the vehicle, and thus the defendant may be held liable under the Act if, when it sold the 1968 Charger to Diersen, it provided an inaccurate odometer disclosure statement with the intent to defraud Diersen.

Although we agree with Diersen that the NHTSA regulation is invalid, this does not end our inquiry, for the CCE argues that it is entitled to summary judgment even if the odometer disclosure requirements of the Act do apply to the sale of the 1968 Dodge Charger. In order to succeed on his claim of odometer fraud, Diersen must demonstrate two essential elements: (1) a violation of the Act's odometer disclosure requirements (i.e., the providing of an inaccurate odometer reading), and (2) an intent to defraud. [Citation.] Our review of the summary judgment record persuades us that a rational trier of fact could not find in Diersen's favor as to the second element (intent to defraud); therefore, we affirm the entry of summary judgment in the defendant's favor.

INTERPRETATION To be valid, legislative rules must not exceed the actual authority granted to the agency by the enabling statute.

ETHICAL QUESTION Did Diersen act fairly in refusing the CCE's offer of a full refund? Explain.

CRITICAL THINKING QUESTION Do you agree with the court's distinction between the agency's power to exercise prosecutorial discretion and its lack of power to deprive purchasers of a statutory remedy? Explain.

Legislative rules must be promulgated in accordance with the procedural requirements of the APA, although the enabling statute may impose more stringent requirements. Most legislative rules are issued in accordance with the ***informal rulemaking*** procedures of the APA, which require that the agency provide the following:

1. prior notice of a proposed rule, usually by publication in the Federal Register
2. an opportunity for interested parties to participate in the rulemaking
3. publication of a final draft containing a concise general statement of the rule's basis and purpose at least thirty days before its effective date

http:// Federal Register: http://www.gpoaccess.gov/fr/index/.html
Code of Federal Regulations: http://www.access.gpo.gov/nara/cfr/cfr-table-search.html

Practical Advice

Keep informed of the regulations issued by administrative agencies that affect your business.

In some instances the enabling statute requires that certain rules be made only after the opportunity for an agency hearing. This formal rulemaking procedure is far more complex than the informal procedures and is governed by the same APA provisions that govern an adjudication, discussed later in this chapter. In ***formal rulemaking***, the agency must consider the record of the trial-like agency hearing and include a statement of "findings and conclusions, and the reasons or basis therefore, on all the material issues of fact, law, or discretion presented on the record" when making rules.

Some enabling statutes direct that the agency, in making rules, use certain procedures more formal than those in informal rulemaking but do not compel the full hearing that formal rulemaking requires. This intermediate procedure, known as ***hybrid rulemaking***, results from combining the informal procedures of the APA with the additional procedures specified by the enabling statute. For example, an agency may be required to conduct a legislative-type hearing (formal) that permits no cross-examination (informal).

In 1990, Congress enacted the Negotiated Rulemaking Act to encourage the involvement of affected parties in the initial stages of the policy-making process prior to the publication of notice of a proposed rule. The Act authorizes agencies to use negotiated rulemaking but does not require it. If an agency decides to use negotiated rulemaking, the affected parties and the agency develop an agreement and offer it to the agency. If accepted, the agreement becomes a basis for the proposed regulation, which is then published for comment.

Interpretative Rules

Interpretative rules are agency-issued statements that explain how the agency construes its governing statute. For instance, the Securities and Exchange Commission "renders administrative interpretations of the law and regulations thereunder to members of the public, prospective registrants and others, to help them decide legal questions about the application of the law and the regulations to particular situations and to aid them in complying with the law." *The Work of the SEC* (1980).

These interpretative rules, however, which are exempt from the APA's procedural requirements of notice and comment, are *not* automatically binding on the private parties the agency regulates or on the courts, although they are given substantial weight. As the Supreme Court has stated, "The weight of such [an interpretative rule] in a particular case will depend upon the thoroughness evident in its consideration, the validity of its reasoning, its consistency with earlier and later pronouncements, and all those factors which give it power to persuade. . . . "

> **Practical Advice**
>
> Participate as early as possible in the rulemaking process of administrative agencies that affect your business.

Procedural Rules **Procedural rules** are also exempt from the notice and comment requirements of the APA and are not law. These rules establish rules of conduct for practice before the agency, identify an agency's organization, and describe its method of operation. For example, the Securities and Exchange Commission's Rules of Practice deal with matters such as who may appear before the commission; business hours and notice of proceedings and hearings; settlements, agreements, and conferences; presentation of evidence and the taking of depositions and interrogatories; and review of hearings.

ENFORCEMENT

Agencies also investigate conduct to determine whether the enabling statute or the agency's legislative rules have been violated. In carrying out this executive function, the agencies traditionally have been accorded great discretion, subject to constitutional limitations, to compel the disclosure of information. These limitations require that (1) the investigation is authorized by law and undertaken for a legitimate purpose, (2) the information sought is relevant, (3) the demand for information is sufficiently specific and not unreasonably burdensome, and (4) the information sought is not privileged.

For example, the following explains some of the investigative and enforcement functions of the Securities and Exchange Commission:

> Most of the Commission's investigations are conducted privately. Facts are developed to the fullest extent possible through informal inquiry, interviewing witnesses, examining brokerage records and other documents, reviewing and trading data, and similar means. The Commission is empowered to issue subpoenas requiring sworn testimony and the production of books, records, and other documents pertinent to the subject matter under investigation. In the event of refusal to respond to a subpoena, the Commission may apply to a Federal court for an order compelling obedience. *The Work of the SEC* (1986).

ADJUDICATION

After concluding an investigation, the agency may use informal or formal methods to resolve the matter. Because the caseload of administrative agencies is vast, far greater than that of the judicial system, most matters are informally adjudicated. Informal procedures include advising, negotiating, and settling. In 1990, Congress enacted the Administrative Dispute Resolution Act to authorize and encourage federal agencies to use mediation, conciliation, arbitration, and other techniques for the prompt and informal resolution of disputes. The Act does not, however, require agencies to use alternative dispute resolution and the affected parties must consent to its use.

> **Practical Advice**
>
> When available, consider using alternative methods of dispute resolution with administrative agencies.

The formal procedure by which an agency resolves a matter (called **adjudication**) involves finding facts, applying legal rules to the facts, and formulating orders. An **order** "means the whole or a part of a final disposition, whether

CONCEPT REVIEW

Administrative Rulemaking

Rule	Procedure	Effect
Legislative	Subject to APA	Binding
Interpretative	Exempt from APA	Persuasive
Procedural	Exempt from APA	Persuasive

affirmative, negative, injunctive or declaratory in form, of an agency." In essence an administrative trial, adjudication is used when the enabling statute so requires.

The procedures employed by the various administrative agencies to adjudicate cases are nearly as varied as the agencies themselves. Nevertheless, the APA does establish certain mandatory standards for those federal agencies the act covers. For example, an agency must give notice of a hearing. The APA also requires that the agency give all interested parties the opportunity to submit and consider "facts, arguments, offers of settlement, or proposals of adjustment." In many cases this involves testimony and cross-examination of witnesses. If no settlement is reached, then a hearing must be held.

The hearing is presided over by an administrative law judge (ALJ) and is prosecuted by the agency. ALJs are appointed by the agency through a professional merit selection system and may be removed only for good cause. There are more than twice as many administrative law judges as there are federal judges. Juries are never used. Thus, the agency serves as both the prosecutor and decision maker. To reduce the potential for a conflict of interest, the APA provides for a separation of functions between those agency members engaged in investigation and prosecution and those involved in decision making.

Oral and documentary evidence may be introduced by either party, and all sanctions, rules, and orders must be based upon "consideration of the whole record or those parts cited by a party and supported by and in accordance with the reliable, probative, and substantial evidence." All decisions must include a statement of findings of fact and conclusions of law and the reasons or basis for them, as well as a statement of the appropriate rule, order, sanction, or relief.

If such are authorized by law and within its delegated jurisdiction, an agency may impose in its orders sanctions such as penalties; fines; the seizing of property; the assessment of damages, restitution, compensation, or fees; and the act of requiring, revoking, or suspending a license. In most instances, orders are final unless appealed; and failure to comply with an order subjects the party to a statutory penalty. If the order is appealed, the governing body of the agency may decide the case de novo. Thus, the agency may hear additional evidence and arguments in deciding whether to revise the findings and conclusions it made in the initial decision.

Although administrative adjudications mirror to a large extent the procedures of judicial trials, there are many differences between the two.

> Agency hearings, especially those dealing with rulemaking, often tend to produce evidence of general conditions as distinguished from facts relating solely to the respondent. Administrative agencies in rulemaking and occasionally in formal adversarial adjudications more consciously formulate policy than do courts. Consequently, administrative adjudications may require that the administrative law judge consider more consciously the impact of his decision upon the public interest as well as upon the particular respondent. . . . An administrative hearing is tried to an ***administrative law judge***, never to a jury. Since many of the rules governing the admission of proof in judicial trials are designed to protect the jury from unreliable and possibly confusing evidence, it has long been asserted that such rules need not be applied at all or with the same vigor in proceedings solely before an administrative law judge. . . . Consequently, the technical common law rules governing the admissibility of evidence have generally been abandoned by administrative agencies. *McCormick on Evidence*, 4th ed., Section 350, p. 605.

American Airlines, Incorporated v. Department of Transportation

United States Court of Appeals, Fifth Circuit, 2000

202 F.3d 788, *cert. denied*, 530 U.S. 1284, 120 S.Ct. 2762, 147 L.Ed.2d 1022 (2000)

http://laws.findlaw.com/5th/9960008cv0v3.html

FACTS Prior to 1968, Dallas and Fort Worth operated independent and competing airports, one of which was Dallas's Love Field. The Department of Transportation's (DOT's) **(http://www.dot.gov)** predecessor agency, the Civil Aeronautics Board ("CAB"), found that the competition between Dallas's and Fort Worth's airports was harmful and in 1964 ordered the cities to build a jointly operated airport that would serve as the region's primary airport. The cities responded by creating the DFW Board and by jointly adopting the 1968 Regional Airport Concurrent Bond Ordinance (the "Ordinance"). The Ordinance authorized the issuance of bonds to finance the Dallas–Fort Worth Airport ("DFW") and contained the cities' agreement to phase-out operations at the old airports and to transfer these activities to the DFW Regional Airport **(http://www.dfwairport.com)**. The eight CAB-certified air carriers who were using the Dallas and Fort Worth airports first signed "letter agreements" and then later signed "use agreements" with the DFW Board, agreeing to move their air services to DFW as specified in the Ordinance. Southwest Airlines

(http://www.southwest.com), which was solely running intrastate flights from Love Field and thus was exempt from CAB certification and pressure, refused to move to DFW and did not sign a use agreement. Litigation ensued over efforts to force Southwest from Love Field, terminating with a decision by the Fifth Circuit Court of Appeals that Southwest Airlines Co. has a federally declared right to the continued use of and access to Love Field, so long as Love Field remains open.

Shortly after Congress deregulated the airline industry in 1978 Southwest applied for permission to provide interstate service between Love Field and New Orleans. The CAB granted the application, concluding that it lacked power to deny it. Congress responded by enacting the Wright Amendment, which generally bans interstate service from Love Field. However, it and the 1997 Shelby Amendments provide certain exemptions from this ban, including: (1) the commuter airline exemption which allows interstate "air transportation provided by commuter airlines operating aircraft with a passenger capacity of 56 passengers or less" and (2) the contiguous state exemption which allows flights to and from Louisiana, Arkansas, Oklahoma, New Mexico, Kansas, Alabama, and Mississippi if the flights do not "provide any through service or ticketing with another air carrier" and do not "offer for sale transportation to or from.* * * any point which is outside any such State."

The airlines began offering additional flights from and to Love Field. Lawsuits to block the proposed additional service from Love Field were brought in state and federal court. At the urging of several of the parties, and while both the federal and state actions were pending, DOT initiated an interpretative proceeding and ultimately issued a "Declaratory Order" ruling that included the following provisions: (1) services at Love Field authorized by federal law may not be restricted by the cities of Dallas and Fort Worth; (2) the Wright and Shelby Amendments preempt the ability of the City of Dallas to limit the type of airline service operated at Love Field; (3) the commuter airline exemption overrides any agreement between the Cities of Dallas and Fort Worth; and (4) the Dallas–Fort Worth International Airport Board may not enforce any contract provision that allegedly bars an airline from operating interstate airline service at another airport in the Dallas–Fort Worth metropolitan area. In an accompanying "Procedural Order," DOT rejected various procedural objections raised by the parties. DOT subsequently reaffirmed its rulings on reconsideration. Several of the parties appealed challenging DOT's declaratory order on procedural grounds that DOT violated the Administrative Procedure Act ("APA").

DECISION DOT's orders affirmed.

OPINION Garza, J. DOT issued its declaratory order after conducting an informal adjudication, pursuant to its authority under § 554(e) to "issue a declaratory ruling to terminate a controversy or remove uncertainty." [Citations.] Several parties object to DOT's failure to adhere to the APA's notice requirements for formal adjudications. However, in the absence of a statute requiring an agency to conduct its adjudication "on the record after opportunity for agency hearing," [citation], an agency can define its own procedures for conducting an informal adjudication. [Citation.]

While the APA does not expressly require notice in informal adjudications, courts have inferred a requirement that there be "some sort of procedures for notice [and] comment * * * as a necessary means of carrying out our responsibility for a thorough and searching review [of agency action]." [Citation.] Here, DOT issued an order in which it specified the legal issues on which it would rule, allowed the parties to submit comments on these issues, and extended the comment period at the request of several parties. It then ruled on precisely the issues that it identified. We find that DOT's actions satisfied the minimum procedural notice requirements. [Citation.]

Fort Worth contends that DOT failed to comply with § 554(b) by neglecting to notify parties that DOT would also be considering a factual issue: the effect of increased service at Love Field on DFW Airport. This argument fails for two reasons. First, as noted, the formal notice requirement of § 554(b) does not apply to an informal adjudication. Second, the parties were effectively on notice of this issue since it was one that they could reasonably expect to arise given the issues of which DOT gave notice. [Citation.] The fact that Dallas, Continental Express, and Legend all submitted factual evidence to DOT should also have put Fort Worth on notice that it could submit its own factual evidence.

We also note the absence of anything in the record to indicate that Fort Worth possesses any information bearing on the impact of increased service at Love Field. Fort Worth has had three opportunities to present or identify such evidence—during the comment period, in its motion for reconsideration, and in its brief on appeal—but has not demonstrated that it possesses relevant factual information not considered by DOT. This continued failure to identify the evidence it would have submitted indicates that Fort Worth was not prejudiced by any inadequacy in DOT's notice. [Citations.]

We also reject the DFW Board's argument that DOT's order amounts to a substantive rule subject to the notice and comment provision of § 553. Agencies have discretion to choose between adjudication and rulemaking as a means of setting policy. [Citation.] In determining whether an agency action constituted adjudication or rulemaking, we look to the product of the agency action. We also accord significant deference to an agency's characterization of its own action. [Citation.] Since the APA defines "adjudication" as the "agency process for formulating an order," 5 U.S.C. § 551(7), and DOT classifies its ruling as a declaratory order, we find that the agency engaged in adjudication rather than rulemaking. Furthermore, because DOT's order interpreted the rights of a small number of parties properly before it, DOT did not abuse its discretion by acting through an adjudicatory proceeding. [Citation.]

INTERPRETATION While the APA does not expressly require notice in informal adjudications, courts have inferred there must be some procedures for notice and comment.

CRITICAL THINKING QUESTION Why is it so important that administrative agencies provide prior notice of proposed rules and adjudications?

LIMITS ON ADMINISTRATIVE AGENCIES

An important and fundamental part of administrative law is the limits imposed by judicial review upon the activities of administrative agencies. On matters of policy, however, courts are not supposed to substitute their judgment for the agency's. Additional limitations arise from the legislature and the executive branch, which, unlike the judiciary, may address the wisdom and correctness of an agency's decision or action. See Figure 5-1, which illustrates the limits on administrative agencies. Moreover, legally required disclosure of agency actions provides further protection for the public.

JUDICIAL REVIEW

As discussed in Chapter 4, judicial review describes the process by which the courts examine governmental action. Judicial review, which is available unless a statute precludes such review or the agency action is committed to agency discretion by law, acts as a control or check on a particular rule or order of an administrative agency.

General Requirements Parties seeking to challenge agency action must have standing and must have exhausted their administrative remedies. Standing requires that the agency action injure the party in fact and that the party assert an interest that is in the "zone of interests to be protected or regulated by the statute in question." Judicial review is ordinarily available only for *final* agency action. Accordingly, if a party seeks review while an agency proceeding is in progress, a court will usually dismiss the action because the party has failed to exhaust his administrative remedies.

Practical Advice

Be sure to exhaust all of your administrative remedies before seeking judicial review of actions taken by an administrative agent.

Figure 5-1
Limits on Administrative Agencies

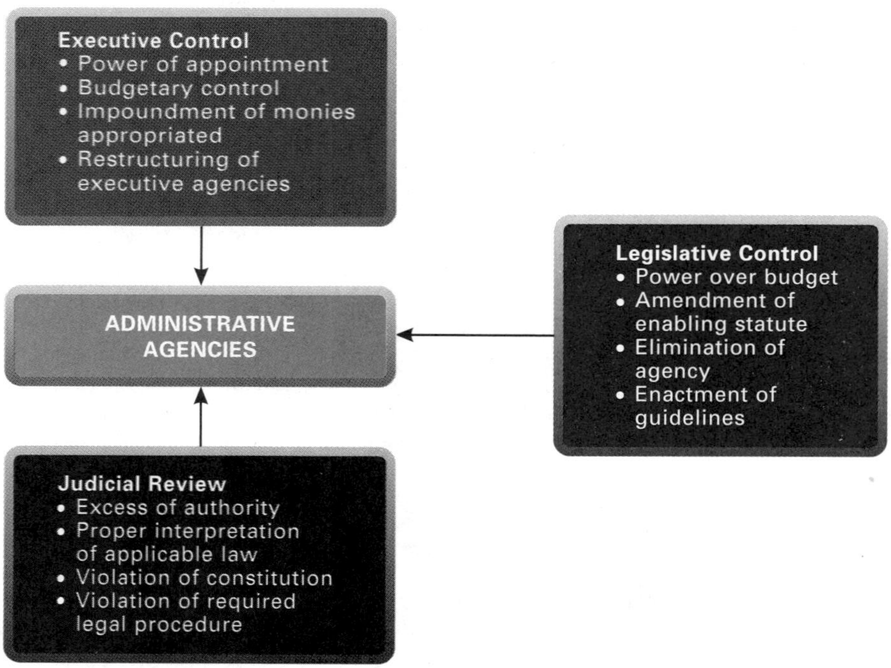

Lujan v. Defenders of Wildlife

Supreme Court of the United States, 1992
504 U.S. 555, 112 S.Ct. 2130, 119 L.Ed.2d 351
http://laws.findlaw.com/US/504/555.html

FACTS This case involves a challenge to a rule promulgated by the Secretary of the Interior interpreting Section 7 of the Endangered Species Act of 1973 (ESA) **(http://www4.law.cornell.edu/uscode/16/1531.html)**. Section 7(a)(2) of the Act provides (in relevant part) that "[e]ach Federal agency shall, in consultation with and with the assistance of the Secretary (of the Interior), insure that any action authorized, funded, or carried out by such agency * * * is not likely to jeopardize the continued existence of any endangered species or threatened species or result in the destruction or adverse modification of habitat of such species which is determined by the Secretary, after consultation as appropriate with affected States, to be critical." In 1978, the Fish and Wildlife Service **(http://www.fws.gov)** and the National Marine Fisheries Service **(http://www.nmfs.noaa.gov)**, on behalf of the Secretary of the Interior **(http://www.doi.gov/secretary)** and the Secretary of Commerce **(http://www.doc.gov)** respectively, promulgated a joint regulation stating that the obligations imposed by Section 7(a)(2) extend to actions taken in foreign nations. In 1983, the Interior Department proposed a revised joint regulation that would require consultation only for actions taken in the United States or on the high seas. Shortly thereafter, Defenders of Wildlife (Defenders) **(http://www.defenders.org)** and other organizations filed this action against the Secretary of the Interior, seeking a declaratory judgment that the new regulation is in error as to the geographic scope of Section 7(a)(2) and an injunction requiring the Secretary to promulgate a new regulation restoring the initial interpretation. The District Court granted the Secretary's motion to dismiss for lack of standing. The Court of Appeals for the Eighth Circuit reversed and remanded for judicial review of the regulation. On remand, the district court denied summary judgment on the standing issue based on the Eighth Circuit's earlier ruling and ordered the Secretary to publish a revised regulation.

DECISION Judgment reversed.

OPINION Scalia, J. Over the years, our cases have established that the irreducible constitutional minimum of standing contains three elements: First, the plaintiff must have suffered an "injury in fact"—an invasion of a legally-protected interest which is (a) concrete and particularized, [citations] and (b) "actual or imminent, not 'conjectural' or 'hypothetical,'" [citations]. Second, there must be a causal connection between the injury and the conduct complained of—the injury has to be "fairly * * * trace[able] to the challenged action of the defendant, and not * * * th[e] result [of] the independent action of some third party not before the court." [Citation.] Third, it must be "likely," as opposed to merely "speculative," that the injury will be "redressed by a favorable decision." [Citation.]

The party invoking federal jurisdiction bears the burden of establishing these elements. * * *

When the suit is one challenging the legality of government action or inaction, the nature and extent of facts that must be averred (at the summary judgment stage) or proved (at the trial stage) in order to establish standing depends considerably upon whether the plaintiff is himself an object of the action (or forgone action) at issue. If he is, there is ordinarily little question that the action or inaction has caused him injury, and that a judgment preventing or requiring the action will redress it. When, however, as in this case, a plaintiff's asserted injury arises from the government's allegedly unlawful regulation (or lack of regulation) of someone else, much more is needed. In that circumstance, causation and redressability ordinarily hinge on the response of the regulated (or regulable) third party to the government action or inaction—and perhaps on the response of others as well. The existence of one or more of the essential elements of standing "depends on the unfettered choices made by independent actors not before the courts and whose exercise of broad and legitimate discretion the courts cannot presume either to control or to predict," [citation] and it becomes the burden of the plaintiff to adduce facts showing that those choices have been or will be made in such manner as to produce causation and permit redressability of injury. [Citation.] Thus, when the plaintiff is not himself the object of the government action or inaction he challenges, standing is not precluded, but it is ordinarily "substantially more difficult" to establish. [Citation.]

* * *

Respondents' claim to injury is that the lack of consultation with respect to certain funded activities abroad "increas[es] the rate of extinction of endangered and threatened species." [Citation.] Of course, the desire to use or observe an animal species, even for purely aesthetic purposes, is undeniably a cognizable interest for purpose of standing. [Citation.] "But the 'injury in fact' test requires more than an injury to a cognizable interest. It requires that the party seeking review be himself among the injured." To survive the Secretary's summary judgment motion, respondents had to submit affidavits or other evidence showing, through specific facts, not only that listed species were in fact being threatened by funded activities abroad, but also that one or more of respondents' members would thereby be "directly" affected apart from their "'special interest' in th[e] subject." [Citations.]

With respect to this aspect of the case, the Court of Appeals focused on the affidavits of two Defenders' members—Joyce Kelly and Amy Skilbred. * * *

We shall assume for the sake of argument that these affidavits contain facts showing that certain agency-funded projects threaten listed species—though that is questionable. They plainly contain no facts, however, showing how damage to the species will produce "imminent" injury to Mss. Kelly and Skilbred. That the women "had visited" the areas of the projects before the projects commenced proves nothing. As we have said in a related context, "'[p]ast exposure to illegal conduct does not in itself show a present case or controversy regarding injunctive relief * * * if unaccompanied by any continuing, present adverse effects.'" [Citation.] And the affiants' profession of an "inten[t]" to return to the places they had visited before—where they will presumably, this time, be deprived of the opportunity to observe animals of the endangered species—is simply not enough. Such "some day" intentions—without any description of concrete plans, or indeed even any specification of when the some day will be—do not support a finding of the "actual or imminent" injury that our cases require. [Citation.]

Besides relying upon the Kelly and Skilbred affidavits, respondents propose a series of novel standing theories. The first, inelegantly styled "ecosystem nexus," proposes that any person who uses any part of a "contiguous ecosystem" adversely affected by a funded activity has standing even if the activity is located a great distance away. This approach, as the Court of Appeals correctly observed, is inconsistent with our opinion in National Wildlife Federation, which held that a plaintiff claiming injury from environmental damage must use the area affected by the challenged activity and not an area roughly "in the vicinity" of it. [Citation.] It makes no difference that the general-purpose section of the ESA states that the Act was intended in part "to provide a means whereby the ecosystems upon which endangered species and threatened species depend may be conserved," [citation]. To say that the Act protects ecosystems is not to say that the Act creates (if it were possible) rights of action in persons who have not been injured in fact, that is, persons who use portions of an ecosystem not perceptibly affected by the unlawful action in question.

Respondents' other theories are called, alas, the "animal nexus" approach, whereby anyone who has an interest in studying or seeing the endangered animals anywhere on the globe has standing; and the "vocational nexus" approach, under which anyone with a professional interest in such animals can sue. Under these theories, anyone who goes to see Asian elephants in the Bronx Zoo, and anyone who is a keeper of Asian elephants in the Bronx Zoo, has standing to sue because the Director of AID did not consult with the Secretary regarding the AID-funded project in Sri Lanka. This is beyond all reason. Standing is not "an ingenious academic exercise in the conceivable," [citation], but as we have said requires, at the summary judgment stage, a factual showing of perceptible harm. It is clear that the person who observes or works with a particular animal threatened by a federal decision is facing perceptible harm, since the very subject of his interest will no longer exist. It is even plausible—though it goes to the outermost limit of plausibility—to think that a person who observes or works with animals of a particular species in the very area of the world where that species is threatened by a federal decision is facing such harm, since some animals that might have been the subject of his interest will no longer exist, [citation]. It goes beyond the limit, however, and into pure speculation and fantasy, to say that anyone who observes or works with an endangered species, anywhere in the world, is appreciably harmed by a single project affecting some portion of that species with which he has no more specific connection.

INTERPRETATION Parties seeking to challenge agency action must have standing, which requires that the agency action injure the party in fact and that the party assert an interest that is in the zone of interests to be protected or regulated by the statute in question.

CRITICAL THINKING QUESTION What policy reasons support and which oppose the standing requirement?

In exercising judicial review, the court may decide either to compel agency action unlawfully withheld or to set aside impermissible agency action. In making its determination, the court must review the whole record and may set aside agency action only if the error is prejudicial.

Questions of Law When conducting a review, a court decides all relevant questions of law, interprets constitutional and statutory provisions, and determines the meaning or applicability of the terms of an agency action. This review of questions of law includes determining whether the agency has (1) exceeded its authority, (2) properly interpreted the applicable law, (3) violated any constitutional provision, or (4) acted contrary to the procedural requirements of the law.

Questions of Fact When reviewing factual determinations, the courts use one of three different standards.

Ethical Dilemma

Should the Terminally Ill Be Asked to Await FDA Approval of Last-Chance Treatments?

FACTS Mrs. Barnett is a 63-year-old widow who has just been diagnosed with ovarian cancer. Because of the lack of adequate screening procedures for this type of cancer, Mrs. Barnett's cancer has long gone undetected and has progressed considerably.

Dr. Jason, Mrs. Barnett's doctor, will perform immediate surgery, but the surgery will not effectively cure the cancer. He has recommended that she undergo rigorous chemotherapy on a monthly basis for eighteen months following surgery. Thereafter, an exploratory operation can be conducted to assess the success of the treatment. The proposed chemotherapy, which involves the use of platinum, will cause severe side effects, including nausea, oral lesions, and complete hair loss.

Dr. Jason has informed Mrs. Barnett and her two daughters, June and Sarina, that although chemotherapy will defer their mother's immediate death, her chances of a recovery are slim. Dr. Jason stated that while, on average, one in three patients undergoing such treatment could expect to recover, he believed Mrs. Barnett's recovery was highly unlikely. A second opinion from a reputable cancer treatment center confirmed Dr. Jason's diagnosis and recommendations for treatment.

Sarina has heard of an experimental cancer drug being tested in Europe and Scandinavia. Thus far the results seem promising. Though the drug may be obtained in Norway, it is not yet legal in the United States. The Food and Drug Administration has just begun to review the drug, but it will be years before the drug could receive FDA approval.

Sarina is strongly opposed to the painful regimen of chemotherapy that has been proposed, particularly because the treatment seems futile. She wants to fly to Norway, obtain the experimental drug, and return with it to the United States. Mrs. Barnett is much too ill to travel. June, on the other hand, is opposed to any course of treatment that does not have the approval of the FDA. Mrs. Barnett, who is weak and confused, is looking to her daughters for guidance.

Social, Policy, and Ethical Considerations

1. If Mrs. Barnett were your mother, what recommendation would you make? Under the circumstances, is it unethical to use a drug that has not been approved by the Food and Drug Administration?
2. As a policy matter, how should the FDA handle drugs for life-threatening diseases?
3. Should individuals be allowed absolute freedom to take risks with drug therapy?
4. Should the FDA apply different drug approval standards with regard to children who suffer from life-threatening diseases?
5. As a policy matter, how should the government and nonprofit organizations allocate resources among research groups competing for funding? How should the government, through its administrative agencies, establish priorities for funding research on various illnesses?

Where informal rulemaking or informal adjudication has occurred, the standard generally is the **arbitrary and capricious** test, which requires only that the agency had a rational basis for reaching its decision. Where there has been a formal hearing, the **substantial evidence** test usually applies. It also applies to informal or hybrid rulemaking if the enabling statute so requires. The substantial evidence test requires the conclusions reached to be supported by "such relevant evidence as a reasonable mind might accept as adequate to support a conclusion." Finally, in rare instances the reviewing court may apply the **unwarranted by the facts** standard, which permits the court to try the facts *de novo*. This strict review is available only when the enabling statute so provides, when the agency has conducted an adjudication with inadequate fact-finding procedures, or when issues that were not before the agency are raised in a proceeding to enforce nonadjudicative agency action.

http:// Recent administrative law decisions: http://www4.law.cornell.edu/cgi-bin/empower?DB=SupctSyllabi&TOPDOC=0&Query00=administrative and http://www4.law.cornell.edu/cgi-bin/fx?DB=Circuits&P=administrative

Legislative Control

The legislature may exercise control over administrative agencies in various ways. Through its budgetary power, it may greatly restrict or expand an agency's operations. Congress may amend an enabling statute to increase, modify, or decrease an agency's authority. Even more drastically, it may completely eliminate an agency. Or, Congress may establish general guidelines to govern agency action, as it did by enacting the Administrative Procedure Act. Moreover, it may reverse or change an agency rule or decision by specific legislation. In addition, each house of Congress has oversight committees that review the operations of administrative agencies. Finally, the Senate has the power of confirmation over some high-level appointments to administrative agencies.

In 1996 Congress enacted the Congressional Review Act, which subjects most rules to a new, extensive form of legislative control. With limited exceptions, the Act requires agencies to submit newly adopted rules to each house of Congress before they can take effect. If the rule is a major rule, it does not become final until Congress has had an opportunity to disapprove it. A ***major rule*** is any rule that the Office of Management and Budget (OMB) finds has resulted in or is likely to result in (1) an annual effect on the economy of at least $100 million, (2) a major increase in costs or prices, or (3) a significant adverse effect on competition, employment, investment, productivity, innovation, or international competitiveness of U.S. enterprises. If the rule is not a major rule, it takes effect as it otherwise would have after its submission to Congress; it is subject to possible disapproval by Congress. All rules covered by the Act shall not take effect if Congress adopts a joint resolution of disapproval. The President may veto the joint resolution, but Congress may then vote to override the veto. A rule that has been disapproved is treated as though it had never taken effect.

CONTROL BY EXECUTIVE BRANCH

By virtue of his power to appoint and remove their chief administrators, the President has significant control over the administrative agencies housed within the executive branch. With respect to independent agencies, however, the President has less control because commissioners serve for a fixed term that is staggered with the President's term of office. Nevertheless, his power to appoint agency chairs and to fill vacancies confers considerable control, as does his power to remove commissioners for statutorily defined cause. The President's central role in the budgeting process of agencies also enables him to exert great control over agency policy and operations. Even more extreme is the President's power to impound monies appropriated to an agency by Congress. In addition, the President may radically alter, combine, or even abolish agencies of the executive branch unless either house of Congress disapproves such an act within a prescribed time.

DISCLOSURE OF INFORMATION

Requiring administrative agencies to disclose information about their actions makes them more accountable to the public. Accordingly, Congress has enacted disclosure statutes to enhance public and political oversight of agency activities. These statutes include the Freedom of Information Act and the Government in the Sunshine Act.

Freedom of Information Act First enacted in 1966, the Freedom of Information Act (FOIA) gives the public access to most records in the files of federal administrative agencies. Once a person has requested files, an agency must indicate within ten working days whether it intends to comply with the request and must within a reasonable time respond to the request. The agency may charge a fee for providing the records.

The FOIA permits agencies to deny access to nine categories of records: (1) records specifically authorized in the interest of national defense or foreign policy to be kept secret; (2) records that relate solely to the internal personnel rules and practices of an agency; (3) records specifically exempted by statute from disclosure; (4) trade secrets and commercial or financial information that is privileged or confidential; (5) inter- or intraagency memorandums; (6) personnel and medical files, the disclosure of which would constitute a clearly unwarranted invasion of personal privacy; (7) investigatory records compiled for law enforcement purposes; (8) records that relate to the regulation or supervision of financial institutions; and (9) certain geological and geophysical information and data.

The Electronic Freedom of Information Act Amendments require agencies to provide public access to information in an electronic format. Agencies must, within one year after their creation, make records available by computer telecommunications or other electronic means.

http:// Freedom of Information Act: http://www.usdoj/04foia/foiastat.htm
Electronic Freedom of Information Act Amendments: http://www.usdoj.gov/oip/foia_updates/Vol_XVII_4/page2.htm

Practical Advice

Be aware that the Freedom of Information Act may give the public access to information you provide to administrative agencies.

Government in the Sunshine Act The Government in the Sunshine Act requires meetings of many federal agencies to be open to the public. This act applies to multimember bodies whose members the President appoints with the advice and consent of the Senate, such as the Securities and Exchange Commission, the Federal Trade Commission, the Federal Communications Commission, the Consumer Product Safety Commission, and the Commodity Futures Trading Commission. The act does not cover executive agencies such as the Environmental Protection Agency, the Food and Drug Administration, and the National Highway Safety Administration.

Agencies generally may close meetings on the same grounds upon which they may refuse disclosure of records under the Freedom of Information Act. In addition, agencies such as the SEC and the Federal Reserve Board may close meetings to protect information the disclosure of which would lead to financial speculation or endanger the stability of financial institutions. The Sunshine Act also permits agencies to close meetings that concern agency participation in pending or anticipated litigation.

CHAPTER SUMMARY

Operation of Administrative Agencies

Rulemaking process by which an administrative agency promulgates rules of law

- ***Legislative Rules*** substantive rules issued by an administrative agency under the authority delegated to it by the legislature
- ***Interpretative Rules*** statements issued by an administrative agency indicating how it construes its governing statute
- ***Procedural Rules*** rules issued by an administrative agency establishing its organization, method of operation, and rules of conduct for practice before it

Enforcement process by which agencies determine whether their rules have been violated

Adjudication formal methods by which an agency resolves disputes

Limits on Administrative Agencies

Judicial Review acts as a control or check by a court on a particular rule or order of an administrative agency

Legislative Control includes control over the agency's budget and enabling statute

Control by Executive Branch includes the President's power to appoint members of the agency

Disclosure of Information congressionally required public disclosure enhances oversight of agency activities

CASE PROBLEMS

1. Congress passed the Emergency Price Control Act in the interest of national defense and security. The stated purpose of the act was "to stabilize prices and to prevent speculative, unwarranted and abnormal increases in prices and rents. . . ." The act established the Office of Price Administration, which was authorized to establish maximum prices and rents that were to be "generally fair and equitable and [were to] effectuate the purposes of this Act." Stark was convicted for selling beef at prices in excess of those set by the agency. Stark appeals on the ground that the act unconstitutionally delegated to the agency the legislative power of Congress to control prices. Is Stark correct in this contention?

2. The Secretary of Commerce (Secretary) (http://www.commerce.gov) published notice in the *Federal Register* inviting comments regarding flammability standards for mattresses. Statistical data were compiled, consultant studies were conducted, and seventy-five groups submitted comments. The Secretary then determined that all mattresses, including crib mattresses, must pass a cigarette test, consisting of bringing a mattress in contact with a burning cigarette. Bunny Bear, Inc. now challenges the cigarette flammability test, asserting that the standard was not shown to be applicable to crib mattresses, as "infants and young children obviously do not smoke." Bunny Bear argues that the Secretary has not satisfied the burden of proof justifying the inclusion of crib mattresses within this general safety standard. Is Bunny Bear correct? Explain.

3. National Airport (http://www.metwashairports.com/National/index.html) in Washington, D.C., is one of the busiest and

most crowded airports in the nation. Accordingly, the Federal Aviation Administration (FAA) (http://www.faa.gov) has restricted the number of commercial landing and takeoff slots at National to 40 per hour. Allocation of the slots among the air carriers serving National had been by voluntary agreement through an airline scheduling committee (ASC). When a new carrier requested twenty slots during peak hours, National's ASC was unable to agree on a slot allocation schedule. The FAA invited public comment as a means to solve the slot allocation dilemma. The FAA then issued Special Federal Aviation Regulation 43 (SFAR 43) based on public comments and a proposal made at the last National ASC meeting, thereby decreasing the number of slots held by current carriers and shifting some slots to less desirable times. SFAR 43 also granted eighteen slots to New York Air. Northwest Airlines (http://www.nwa.com) seeks judicial review of SFAR 43, claiming that it is arbitrary, capricious, and not a product of reasoned decision making, and that it capriciously favors the Washington–New York market as well as the new carrier. Will Northwest prevail? Explain.

4. Bachowski was defeated in a United Steelworkers of America (http://www.uswa.org) union election. After exhausting his union remedies, Bachowski filed a complaint with Secretary of Labor (http://www.dol.gov) Dunlop. Bachowski invoked the Labor-Management Reporting and Disclosure Act, which required Dunlop to investigate the complaint and determine whether to bring a court action to set aside the election. Dunlop decided such action was unwarranted. Bachowski then filed an action in a federal district court to have Dunlop's decision declared arbitrary and capricious and to order Dunlop to file suit to set aside the election. Should Dunlop prevail? Explain.

5. The Federal Crop Insurance Corporation (FCIC) (http://www.act.fcic.usda.gov/aboutrma/fcic/) was created as a wholly government-owned corporation to insure wheat producers against unavoidable crop failure. As required by law, the FCIC published in the *Federal Register* conditions for crop insurance. Specifically, the FCIC published that spring wheat reseeded on winter wheat acreage was ineligible for coverage. When farmer Merrill applied for insurance on his wheat crop, he informed the local FCIC agent that 400 of his 460 acres of spring wheat were reseeded on the winter acreage. The agent advised Merrill that his entire crop was insurable. When drought destroyed Merrill's wheat, Merrill tried to collect the insurance, but the FCIC refused to pay, asserting that Merrill is bound by the notice provided by publication of the regulation in the *Federal Register*. Is the FCIC correct? Explain.

6. David Fenster, president and part owner of Utica Packing Company, was convicted of bribing a meat inspector. After an administrative hearing filed by the U.S. Department of Agriculture (USDA) (http://www.usda.gov), the administrative law judge ordered withdrawal of inspection services from Utica. Upon judicial review of this decision, the court ordered Davis, the judicial officer for the USDA, to consider several mitigating circumstances. For example, there had been improper conduct by the inspectors, virulent anti-Semitic remarks by an inspector (Fenster is a Jewish survivor of the Holocaust), Fenster's serious health problems, and the fact that, despite the bribe, the Utica plant was clean. Davis ruled to reinstate inspection services to Utica. The USDA moved for reconsideration and replaced judicial officer Davis with Franke, who, unlike Davis, had no judicial background, could be fired at will, and who was assigned a legal adviser who worked with the prosecutors in the case. Fenster claims this violates his Fifth Amendment due process rights. The USDA responds that separation of investigative, prosecutorial, and adjudicative functions is relaxed in an administrative setting. Decision?

7. The Department of Energy (DOE) (http://www.doe.gov) issued a subpoena requesting information regarding purchases, sales, exchanges, and other transactions in crude oil from Phoenix Petroleum Company (Phoenix). The aim of the DOE audit was to uncover violations of the Emergency Petroleum Allocation Act of 1973 (EPAA). The EPAA contained provisions for summary, or expedited, enforcement of DOE decisions. However, after the subpoena was issued but before Phoenix had responded, the EPAA expired. Furthermore, during this time, the President of the United States had ordered deregulation of DOE price and allocation controls. Using the summary enforcement provisions of the now-defunct EPAA, the DOE sues to enforce the subpoena. Phoenix argues that because the EPAA has expired, the DOE lacks the authority either to issue the subpoena or to use the summary enforcement provisions. Is Phoenix correct? Why?

8. In May 1976, the Federal Communications Commission (http://www.fcc.gov) issued rules requiring cable television systems of a designated size (1) to develop a minimum ten-channel capacity by 1986, (2) to make available on a first-come, nondiscriminatory basis certain channels for access by third parties, and (3) to furnish equipment and facilities for such access. The purpose of these rules was to ensure public access to the cable systems. Midwest Video Corporation claimed that the access rules exceeded the Commission's jurisdiction granted it by the Communications Act of 1934, because the rules infringe upon the cable systems' journalistic freedom by in effect treating the cable operators as "common carriers." A common carrier is one that "makes a public offering to provide [communication facilities] whereby all members of the public who choose to employ such facilities may communicate or transmit. . . ." The Commission contended that its expansive mandate under the Communications Act to supervise and regulate broadcasting encompassed the access rules because they were intended to promote these broad objectives. Decision?

9. Congress enacted the National Traffic and Motor Vehicle Safety Act of 1966 (the Act) for the purpose of reducing the number of traffic accidents that result in death or personal injury. The Act directs the Secretary of Transportation to issue motor vehicle safety standards in order to improve the design and safety features of cars. The Secretary has

delegated authority to promulgate safety standards to the National Highway Traffic Safety Administration (NHTSA) (http://www.nhtsa.dot.gov/). The Act also authorizes judicial review under the provisions of the Administrative Procedure Act (APA) of all orders establishing, amending, or revoking a federal motor vehicle safety standard issued by the NHTSA.

Pursuant to the Act, the NHTSA issued Motor Vehicle Safety Standard 208, which required all cars made after September 1982 to be equipped with passive restraints (either automatic seatbelts or airbags). The cost of implementing the standard was estimated to be around $1 billion. However, early in 1981, due to changes in economic circumstances and particularly due to complaints from the automotive industry, the NHTSA rescinded Standard 208. The NHTSA had originally assumed that car manufacturers would install airbags in 60 percent of new cars and passive seatbelts in 40 percent. However, by 1981 it appeared that manufacturers were planning to install seatbelts in 99 percent of all new cars.

Moreover, the majority of passive seatbelts could be easily and permanently detached by consumers. Therefore, the NHTSA felt that Standard 208 would not result in any significant safety benefits. State Farm Mutual Automobile Insurance Company (State Farm) (http://www.statefarm.com/) and the National Association of Independent Insurers (NAII) filed petitions in Federal court for review of the NHTSA's rescission of Standard 208 arguing that it was arbitrary and capricious. Decision?

http:// **Internet Exercise** Find and explore several federal administrative agencies to learn about their (a) organization, (b) purpose, and (c) operations.

CHAPTER 6

Criminal Law

These guys commit their crimes with a pencil instead of a gun.

BRONX DISTRICT ATTORNEY, SPEAKING ABOUT CORPORATE CRIME TO *THE NEW YORK TIMES*

Learning Objectives

After reading this chapter you should be able to:

1. Describe criminal intent and the various degrees of mental fault.
2. Identify the significant features of white-collar crimes, corporate crimes, and RICO.
3. List and define the crimes against business.
4. Describe the defenses of person or property, duress, mistake of fact, and entrapment.
5. List and explain the constitutional amendments affecting criminal procedure.

As we discussed in Chapter 1, the civil law defines duties the violation of which constitutes a wrong against the injured party. The criminal law, on the other hand, establishes duties the violation of which is a societal wrong against the whole community. Civil law is a part of private law, whereas criminal law is a part of public law. In a civil action, the injured party sues to recover compensation for the damage and injury that he has sustained as a result of the defendant's wrongful conduct. The party bringing a civil action (the plaintiff) has the burden of proof, which he must sustain by a preponderance (greater weight) of the evidence. The purpose of the civil law is to compensate the aggrieved party.

Criminal law is designed to prevent harm to society by defining criminal conduct and establishing punishment for such conduct. In a criminal case, the defendant is prosecuted by the government, which must prove the defendant's guilt beyond a reasonable doubt, a significantly higher burden of proof than that required in a civil action. Moreover, under our legal system, guilt is never presumed. Indeed, the law presumes the innocence of the accused, and this presumption is unaffected by the defendant's failure to testify in her own defense. The government still has the burden of affirmatively proving the guilt of the accused beyond a reasonable doubt.

Of course, the same conduct may, and often does, constitute both a crime and a tort, which is a civil wrong. (We will discuss torts in Chapters 7 and 8.) But an act may be criminal without being tortious; by the same token, an act may be a tort but not a crime.

Because of the increasing use of criminal sanctions to enforce governmental regulation of business, criminal law is an essential part of business law. Moreover, businesses sustain considerable loss as victims of criminal actions. Accordingly, this chapter covers the general principles of criminal law and criminal procedure as well as specific crimes and defenses relevant to business.

http://

U.S. Department of Justice, Bureau of Justice Statistics: http://www.ojp.usdoj.gov/bjs/welcome.html
U.S. Department of Justice, Bureau of Justice Statistics Crime and Justice Electronic Data Abstracts: http://www.ojp.usdoj.gov/bjs/dtdata.htm
FBI, Uniform Crime Reports: http://www.fbi.gov/ucr/ucr.htm

NATURE OF CRIMES

A **crime** is any act or omission forbidden by public law in the interest of protecting society and made punishable by the government in a judicial proceeding brought by it. Punishment for criminal conduct includes fines, imprisonment, probation, and death. In addition, some states and the federal government have enacted victim indemnification statutes, which establish funds, financed by criminal fines, to provide indemnification in limited amounts to victims of criminal activity. Crimes are prohibited and punished on grounds of public policy, which may include the protection and safeguarding of government (as in treason), human life (as in murder), or private property (as in larceny). Additional purposes for criminal law include deterrence, rehabilitation, and retribution.

Historically, criminal law was primarily common law. Today, however, criminal law is almost exclusively statutory. All states have enacted comprehensive criminal law statutes (or codes) covering most, if not all, of the common law crimes. Moreover, these statutes have made the number of crimes defined in criminal law far greater than the number of crimes defined under common law. Some codes expressly limit crimes to those the code includes, thus abolishing common law crimes. Nonetheless, some states do not define all crimes statutorily; therefore, the courts must rely on common law definitions. Because there are no federal common law crimes, all federal crimes are statutory.

Within recent times the scope of the criminal law has increased greatly. The scope of traditional criminal behavior has been expanded by numerous regulations and laws, pertaining to nearly every phase of modern living, that contain criminal penalties. Typical examples in the field of business law are those laws concerning the licensing and conduct of a business, antitrust laws, and the laws governing the sales of securities.

ESSENTIAL ELEMENTS

In general, a crime consists of two elements: (1) the wrongful or overt act (**actus reus**) and (2) the criminal or mental intent (**mens rea**). For example, to support a larceny conviction it is not enough to show that the defendant stole another's goods; it must also be established that he intended to steal the goods. Conversely, criminal intent without an overt act is not a crime. For instance, Ann decides to rob the neighborhood grocery store and then really "live it up." Without more than the thought, Ann has committed no crime.

Actus reus refers to all the nonmental elements of a crime, including the physical act that must be performed, the circumstances under which it must be performed, and the consequences of that act. The *actus reus* required for specific crimes will be discussed later in this chapter.

Mens rea, or mental fault, refers to the mental element of a crime. Most common law and some statutory crimes require subjective fault, whereas other crimes require objective fault; some statutory crimes require no fault at all. The American Law Institute's proposed Model Penal Code and most modern criminal statutes recognize three possible types of **subjective fault**: purposeful, knowing, and reckless. A person acts *purposely* or *intentionally* if his conscious object is to engage in the prohibited conduct or to cause the prohibited result. Thus, if Arthur, with the desire to kill Donna, shoots his rifle at Donna, who is seemingly out of gunshot range, and in fact does kill her, Arthur had the purpose or intent to kill Donna. If Benjamin, desiring to poison Paula, places a toxic chemical in the water cooler in Paula's office and unwittingly poisons Gail and Ram, Benjamin will be found to have purposefully killed Gail and Ram because Benjamin's intent to kill Paula is transferred to Gail and Ram, regardless of Benjamin's feelings toward Gail and Ram.

A person acts *knowingly* if he is aware that his conduct is of a prohibited type or is practically certain to cause a prohibited result. A person acts *recklessly* if he consciously disregards a substantial and unjustifiable risk that his conduct is prohibited or that it will cause a prohibited result.

Johnson v. Florida
Supreme Court of Florida, 1992
597 So.2d 798

FACTS Raymond Johnson snatched a purse that had been left in an unattended car at a gas station. The purse contained both money and a firearm. Johnson was convicted for the crimes of grand theft of property (cash and payroll check) and grand theft of a firearm. Johnson appealed, arguing that this conviction is a double jeopardy violation in that it constitutes multiple convictions for a single act.

DECISION Case remanded. Johnson cannot be separately convicted for grand theft of property and grand theft of a firearm.

OPINION Per Curiam. We * * * phrase the question as follows:

May a defendant be separately convicted and sentenced for grand theft of cash and grand theft of a firearm accomplished by means of snatching a purse that contained both cash and a firearm when the defendant did not know the nature of the purse's contents?

* * * We answer the * * * question in the negative and remand for further proceedings.

Raymond Johnson was convicted and sentenced for the crimes of burglary of a conveyance, grand theft of property (i.e., cash and payroll checks), and grand theft of a firearm. All of these crimes allegedly were committed when Johnson snatched a purse left in an unattended car at a gas station. That purse contained both money and a firearm, among other items. A filling station attendant identified Johnson as the man he had seen near the victim's car immediately before and after the snatching. An eyewitness saw Johnson fleeing the scene.

The theft occurred when Johnson wrongfully took the property of another. He did this in one swift motion. The degree of the crime of theft depends on what was taken. Because of the value of the property, his crime was a third-degree felony. Because part of the goods he took was a firearm, his crime additionally is defined as a third-degree felony. [Citation.] We conclude that the value of the goods or the taking of a firearm merely defines the degree of the felony and does not constitute separate crimes. A separate crime occurs only when there are separate distinct acts of seizing the property of another.

We recognize that our views herein appear to be contrary to *State v. Getz*, [citation], wherein we upheld a third-degree felony conviction for the taking of a gun and a petit theft conviction for the taking of a calculator when both takings occurred during a household burglary. In *Getz*, however, there was a separate intent and act to take each item. In this case there was one intent and one act of taking the handbag. Had the gun been picked up separately from the taking of the handbag, *Getz* would allow separate convictions. However, * * * *Getz* * * * should [not] apply where an enclosed bag and its contents are the subject of the theft in one swift action. Accordingly, there could be only one theft conviction in this case.

INTERPRETATION An essential element of a crime is the mental intent (mens rea) to commit the crime.

ETHICAL QUESTION Is it appropriate to hold the defendant guilty of both crimes? Explain.

CRITICAL THINKING QUESTION When should crimes be considered as separate offenses? Explain.

Objective fault involves a gross deviation from the standard of care that a reasonable person would observe under given circumstances. Criminal statutes refer to objective fault by terms such as carelessness or negligence. Such conduct occurs when a person *should* be aware of a substantial and unjustifiable risk that his conduct is prohibited or will cause a prohibited result. Examples of crimes requiring objective fault are involuntary manslaughter (negligently causing the death of another), carelessly driving an automobile, and, in some states, issuing a bad check.

Many regulatory statutes have totally dispensed with the mental element of a crime by imposing criminal **liability without fault.** Without regard to the care that a person exercises, criminal liability without fault makes it a crime for that person to do a specified act or to bring about a certain result. Statutory crimes imposing liability without fault include the sale of adulterated food, the sale of narcotics without a prescription, and the sale of alcoholic beverages to a minor. Most of these crimes involve regulatory statutes dealing with health and safety and impose only fines for violations.

See Concept Review for an overview of degree of mental fault.

CLASSIFICATION

Historically, crimes have been classified ***mala in se*** (wrongs in themselves or morally wrong, such as murder) or ***mala prohibita*** (not morally wrong but declared wrongful by law, such as the failure to drive on the right side of the road). From the standpoint of the seriousness of the offense, crimes are also classified as a **felony**, or serious crime (any crime punishable by death or imprisonment in the penitentiary), or as a **misdemeanor**, a less serious crime (any crime punishable by a fine or imprisonment in a local jail).

VICARIOUS LIABILITY

Vicarious liability is liability imposed upon one person for the acts of another. Employers are vicariously liable for the authorized criminal acts of their employees if the employer directed, participated in, or approved of the act. For example, if an employer directs its vice president of marketing to fix prices with its company's competitors, and the employee does so, both the employer and employee have criminally violated the Sherman Antitrust Act. On the other hand, employers ordinarily are not liable for the unauthorized criminal acts of their employees. As

CONCEPT REVIEW

Degrees of Mental Fault

Type	Fault Required	Examples
Subjective Fault	Purposeful Knowing Reckless	Larceny Embezzlement
Objective Fault	Negligent Careless	Careless driving Issuing bad checks (some states)
Liability without Fault	None	Sale of alcohol to a minor Sale of adulterated food

previously discussed, most crimes require mental fault; this element is not present, so far as criminal responsibility of the employer is concerned, where the employee's criminal act was not authorized.

Employers may, however, be subject to a criminal penalty for the unauthorized act of an adviser or manager acting in the scope of employment. Moreover, an employer may be criminally liable under a liability without fault statute for certain unauthorized acts of an employee, whether the employee is managerial or not. For example, many states have statutes that punish "every person who by himself or his employee or agent sells anything at short weight," or "whoever sells liquor to a minor and any sale by an employee shall be deemed the act of the employer as well."

Practical Advice

Because employees may be criminally liable for the acts of their employees, you should exercise due diligence in adequately checking the backgrounds of prospective employees.

LIABILITY OF A CORPORATION

Historically, corporations were not held criminally liable because, under the traditional view, a corporation could not possess the requisite criminal intent and, therefore, was incapable of committing a crime. The dramatic growth in size and importance of corporations changed this view. Under the modern approach, a corporation may be liable for violation of statutes imposing liability without fault. In addition, a corporation may be liable when the offense is perpetrated by a high corporate officer or the board of directors. The American Law Institute's Model Penal Code provides that a corporation may be convicted of a criminal offense for the conduct of its employees if

1. the legislative purpose of the statute defining the offense is to impose liability on corporations and the conduct is within the scope of the agent's office or employment;
2. the offense consists of an omission to discharge a specific, affirmative duty imposed upon corporations by law; or
3. the offense was authorized, requested, commanded, performed, or recklessly tolerated by the board of directors or by a high managerial agent of the corporation.

By necessity, punishment of a corporation for crimes is by fine rather than imprisonment. Nonetheless, those individuals bearing responsibility for the criminal act face either fines or imprisonment, or both. The Model Penal Code provides that the corporate agent having primary responsibility for the discharge of a duty imposed by law on the corporation is as accountable for the corporation's reckless omission to perform the required act as if the duty were imposed by law directly upon him.

On November 1, 1991, the Federal Organizational Corporate Sentencing Guidelines took effect. The overall purpose of the guidelines is to impose sanctions that will provide just punishment and adequate deterrence. To that end, the guidelines require corporations to formulate and implement compliance programs reasonably designed to prevent potential legal violations by the corporation and its employees.

The guidelines provide for a base corporate fine for each criminal offense, calculated by one of the following: (a) the amount listed in the guidelines' offense-level fine table (fines range from $5,000 to $72.5 million), (b) the pecuniary gain to the organization, or (c) the pecuniary loss as a result of the offense, to the extent that the loss was intentionally, knowingly, or recklessly caused. In addition, restitution is available to victims whenever possible. In the most extreme case, a corporation's charter can be revoked. For a corporation that has implemented an adequate compliance program, the fine can be reduced to as little as 5 percent of the scheduled amount. On the other hand, if a company does not have a proper program in place, the fine can be multiplied by up to four times.

An adequate compliance program should include the following:

1. a written code of conduct,
2. assignment of a senior corporate official to be responsible for the overall compliance program,
3. effective communication of the program to all employees and agents,
4. ongoing monitoring of the program,
5. proper delegation of program-related authority within the organization,
6. disciplinary measures appropriate to enforce the program, and
7. periodic reviews of the program.

http:// United States Sentencing Commission: http://www.ussc.gov/

Practical Advice

Companies should ensure that they have a satisfactory corporate compliance program.

WHITE-COLLAR CRIME

White-collar crime has been defined in various ways. The Justice Department defines it as nonviolent crime involving deceit, corruption, or breach of trust. It includes crimes committed by individuals—such as embezzlement and forgery—as well as crimes committed on behalf of a corporation—such as commercial bribery, product safety and health crimes, false advertising, and antitrust violations. Regardless of the definition, white-collar crime clearly costs society billions of dollars (estimates range from $40 billion to more than $200 billion per year). Historically, prosecution of white-collar crime was de-emphasized because such crime was not considered violent. Now, however, many contend that white-collar crime often inflicts violence but does so impersonally. For example, unsafe products cause injury and death to consumers, while unsafe working conditions cause injury and death to employees. Indeed, many contend that white-collar criminals should receive stiff prison sentences due to the magnitude of their crimes.

In response to the business scandals involving companies such as Enron, WorldCom, Global Crossing, and Arthur Andersen, in 2002 Congress passed the Sarbanes-Oxley Act, which is more fully discussed in Chapter 40—Securities Regulation. The Act, according to President George W. Bush, constitutes "the most far-reaching reforms of American business practices since the time of Franklin Delano Roosevelt [President from 1932 until 1945]." The legislation seeks to prevent these types of scandals by increasing corporate responsibility; adding new financial disclosure requirements; creating new criminal offenses and increasing the penalties of existing federal crimes; and creating a powerful new five-person Accounting Oversight Board with authority to review and discipline auditors.

The Act establishes new criminal penalties including: (1) making it a crime to defraud any person or to obtain any money or property fraudulently in connection with any security of a public company with penalties of a fine and/or up to twenty-five years imprisonment, and (2) imposing fines and/or imprisonment of up to twenty years for knowingly altering, destroying, mutilating, or falsifying any document with the intent of impeding a federal investigation. In addition, the Act substantially increases the penalties for existing crimes including: (1) mail and wire fraud (five-year maximum increased to twenty-five year maximum) and (2) violation of the Securities and Exchange Act (ten-year maximum increased to twenty-year maximum).

http:// Department of Justice: http://www.usdoj.gov/
National White Collar Crime Center: http://www.nw3c.org

People v. Farell

Supreme Court of California, 2002
28 Cal.4th 381, 121 Cal.Rptr.2d 603

FACTS On April 18, 1997 the defendant, Farell, was charged with the theft of a trade secret, in violation of Section 499c. It was further alleged as a sentence enhancement that the loss exceeded $2.5 million and, as a restriction on the granting of probation, that the theft was of an amount exceeding $100,000 within the meaning of Sections 1203.044 and 1203.045. Defendant pleaded no contest to the theft charge, a charge based upon evidence that he had printed out confidential design specifications for certain computer chips on the last day of his employment as an electrical engineer at Digital Equipment Corporation and also had done so on the following day. Defendant waived preliminary hearing and jury trial on the enhancement allegation. He objected, however, to the potential application of Section 1203.044 to his sentence. The trial court, in sentencing the defendant, placed him on probation conditioned on the service of a term in county jail under section 1203.044, which requires a 90-day county jail sentence as condition of probation for theft of an amount exceeding $ 50,000.

A hearing was held in the superior court on the limited question of whether the amount of the theft applies to the theft of property other than money, including trade secrets. The court concluded that the provision applies to the theft of all property of a certain value, including trade secrets. The court suspended imposition of sentence and placed defendant on probation for a period of three years on condition that he serve three months in county jail, with credit for time served of seven days. The court granted a stay of the jail term pending appeal.

The Court of Appeal reversed, held the statute applies only to the theft of what it termed "monetary property." The California Supreme Court granted the government's petition for review.

DECISION The judgment of the Court of Appeals is reversed.

OPINION George, C. J. Defendant stands convicted of theft, specifically a violation of [California statute] which provides: "(b) Every person is guilty of theft who, with intent to deprive or withhold the control of a trade secret from its owner, or with an intent to appropriate a trade secret to his or her own use or to the use of another, does any of the following: (1) Steals, takes, carries away, or uses without authorization, a trade secret." The statute defines the term "trade secret" as follows: "information, including a formula, pattern, compilation, program, device, method, technique, or process, that: (A) Derives independent economic value, actual or potential, from not being generally known to the public or to other persons who can obtain economic value from its disclosure or use; and (B) Is the subject of efforts that are reasonable under the circumstances to maintain its secrecy." [Citation.]

The trial court determined that Section 1203.044 applies to such a theft. This statute, entitled The Economic Crime Law of 1992, requires that a defendant who is convicted of certain theft offenses and is granted probation shall be sentenced to at least 90 days in the county jail as a condition of probation. * * * As relevant to the present case, the statute provides:

> This section shall apply only to a defendant convicted of a felony for theft of an amount exceeding fifty thousand dollars ($50,000) in a single transaction or occurrence. This section shall not apply unless the fact that the crime involved the theft of an amount exceeding fifty thousand dollars ($50,000) in a single transaction or occurrence is charged in the accusatory pleading and either admitted by the defendant in open court or found to be true by the trier of fact. * * *

The Court of Appeal determined that Section 1203.044 may not be applied to persons convicted of the theft of trade secrets. It examined the words of the statute and the legislative history of the enactment and, concluding that the statute is at best ambiguous, applied the so-called rule of lenity to give defendant the benefit of the doubt. Our task is one of statutory interpretation and, "as with any statute, [it] is to ascertain and effectuate legislative intent." [Citations.] We turn first to the words of the statute themselves, recognizing that 'they generally provide the most reliable indicator of legislative intent.' [Citation.] We examine the meaning of the phrase "convicted of a felony for theft of an amount exceeding fifty thousand dollars," keeping in mind that the words must be interpreted in context. [Citation.] In outlining the circumstances under which a person given a probationary term for a theft offense must be sentenced to a minimum period in custody * * * does not specify that the theft must involve cash—or that it must involve what is referred to by the Court of Appeal as "monetary property" and by defendant as a "cash equivalent."

The crime of theft, of course, is not limited to an unlawful taking of money. * * * The crime of theft may involve the theft of trade secrets; indeed, * * * the Legislature specified that the theft of trade secrets is akin to the theft of any other property. * * * In the absence of evidence to the contrary, we may infer that when the Legislature referred in Section 1203.044 to persons "convicted of a felony for theft," it had in mind the general definition of theft, including the broad categories of property that may be the subject of theft * * * .

* * *

To interpret Section 1203.044 as limited to the theft of cash or cash equivalents also would be inconsistent with express legislative intent. The Legislature addressed problems of certain white collar crimes, specifically theft, in enacting Section 1203.044. As the Legislature's own statement of intent discloses, that body intended to remedy the perceived relative unfairness arising from the light probationary sentences meted out to white collar criminals, as well as to provide reliable tools to ensure that victims of white collar criminals receive restitution, and to provide financial support for investigation and prosecution of white collar crime.

The Legislature declared in enacting Section 1203.044: "[M]ajor economic or 'white collar' crime is an increasing threat to California's economy and the well-being of its citizens. The Legislature intends to deter that crime by ensuring that every offender, without exception, serves at least some time in jail and by requiring the offenders to divert a portion of their future resources to the payment of restitution to their victims. White collar criminals granted probation too often complete their probation without having compensated their victims or society. Probation accompanied by a restitution order is often ineffective because county financial officers are often unaware of the income and assets enjoyed by white collar offenders. * * * Thus, it is the Legislature's intent that the financial reporting requirements of this act be utilized to achieve satisfactory disclosure to permit an appropriate restitution order. White collar criminal investigations and prosecutions are unusually expensive. These high costs sometimes discourage vigorous enforcement of white collar crime laws by local agencies. Thus, it is necessary to require white collar offenders to assist in funding this enforcement activity.

* * *

We observe that the term "white collar crime" is a relatively broad one and is not limited to losses involving cash or cash equivalents. It generally is defined as "[a] nonviolent crime usu[ally] involving cheating or dishonesty in commercial matters. Examples include fraud, embezzlement, bribery, and insider trading." [Citation.] The Legislature has applied the term "white collar crime" to fraud and embezzlement * * * , a statute that provides for enhanced prison terms for recidivists committing these offenses when the offense involves a pattern of "taking of more than one hundred thousand dollars." Like the crime of theft, fraud and embezzlement are not limited to the unlawful acquisition of cash or cash equivalents. [Citations.] Indeed, frequently fraud and embezzlement simply are methods by which a charged theft is accomplished. [Citations.] Because the crime of theft includes a wide range of property and the term "white collar crime" has a broad meaning, we find it improbable that the Legislature intended to address only the theft of cash or cash equivalents * * * . It is far more reasonable to conclude that the Legislature intended the provision to apply to all thefts of property of a particular value. Any other interpretation would permit many white collar thieves to continue to receive light probationary sentences and to evade strict restitution requirements. From the usual meaning of the terms used in Section 1202.044, the purpose of the enactment, and the Legislature's parallel use of the same terms in other statutes, one must conclude that Section 1203.044 is not limited to thefts of cash or cash equivalents.

INTERPRETATION The requirement imposing a minimum term in county jail applies to the theft of property other than money, including trade secrets.

CRITICAL THINKING QUESTION Should the penalty for a crime vary depending on (1) the dollar value of the crime or (2) whether the crime is of money or its equivalent? Explain.

COMPUTER CRIME

One special type of white-collar crime is computer crime. **Computer crime** involves the use of a computer to steal money or services, to remove personal or business information, and to tamper with information. Computer crimes fall into five general categories: (1) theft of computer hardware, software, or secrets; (2) unauthorized use of computer services; (3) theft of money by computer; (4) vandalism of computer hardware or software; and (5) theft of computer data. For a more complete discussion of computer crime, see Chapter 48, CyberLaw.

Detection of crimes involving computers is extremely difficult. In addition, computer crimes often are not reported because businesses do not want to give the impression that their security is lax. Nonetheless, losses due to computer crimes are estimated to be in the tens of billions of dollars. Moreover, given society's ever-increasing dependence upon computers, this type of crime will in all likelihood continue to increase.

Already, computer crimes have become commonplace. Examples abound: software piracy (the unauthorized copying of copyrighted software) is now so widespread that two out of every three copies of software are estimated to be illegally obtained. A computer consultant hired by Security Pacific Bank wrongfully transferred $10 million from the bank to his own Swiss bank account. Six employees stole TRW's credit-rating data and offered to "repair" poor credit ratings for a fee. Disgruntled or discharged employees have used computer programs to destroy software.

As a consequence, enterprises are spending large sums of money to increase computer security. In addition, nearly all of the states have enacted computer crime laws. And though, despite numerous attempts, the federal government has not passed comprehensive legislation prohibiting computer crime, in 1984 Congress enacted specific legislation (the Counterfeit Access Device and Computer Fraud and Abuse Act) making unauthorized access to a computer a federal crime.

http://
Department of Justice Computer Crime: http://www.usdoj.gov/criminal/cybercrime/
National Security Institute: http://www.nsi.org/ (federal legislation); http://nsi.org/Library/Compsec/computerlaw/statelaws.html (state legislation)
High Tech Crime Investigation Association: http://htcia.org/
Counterfeit Access Device and Computer Fraud and Abuse Act: http://www4.law.cornell.edu/uscode/18/1001.html

Practical Advice

Adequately protect the safety and security of all company data and records.

RACKETEER INFLUENCED AND CORRUPT ORGANIZATIONS ACT (RICO)

The **Racketeer Influenced and Corrupt Organizations Act (RICO)** was enacted in 1970 with the stated purpose of terminating the infiltration by organized crime into legitimate business. The act subjects to severe civil and criminal penalties enterprises that engage in a pattern of racketeering, defined as the commission of two or more predicate acts within a period of ten years. A "predicate act" is any of several criminal offenses listed in RICO. Included are nine major categories of state crimes and more than thirty federal crimes, such as murder, kidnapping, arson, extortion, drug dealing, mail fraud, and bribery. The most controversial issue concerning RICO is its application to businesses that are not engaged in organized crime but that do meet the "pattern of racketeering" test under the act. Criminal conviction under the law may result in a prison term of up to twenty years plus a fine of up to $25,000 per violation. In addition, businesses forfeit any property obtained due to a RICO violation, and individuals harmed by RICO violations may invoke the statute's civil remedies, which include treble damage and attorneys' fees.

Other areas of federal law that impose both civil and criminal penalties include bankruptcy (Chapter 39), antitrust (Chapter 43), securities regulation (Chapter 44), and environmental regulation (Chapter 46).

http:// RICO: http://www4.law.cornell.edu/uscode/18/1961.html

CRIMES AGAINST BUSINESS

Criminal offenses against property greatly affect businesses, amounting to losses worth hundreds of billions of dollars each year. In this section we will discuss the following crimes against property: (1) larceny, (2) embezzlement, (3) false pretenses, (4) robbery, (5) burglary, (6) extortion and bribery, (7) forgery, and (8) bad checks.

LARCENY

The crime of **larceny** is the (1) trespassory (2) taking and (3) carrying away of (or exercising dominion or control over) (4) personal property (5) of another (6) with the intent to deprive the victim permanently of the goods. All six elements must be present for the crime to exist. Thus, if Carol takes Dan's 1968 automobile without Dan's permission, intending to use it for a joyride and to then return it to Dan, Carol has not committed larceny because she did not intend to deprive Dan permanently of the automobile. (Carol nevertheless has committed the offense of unauthorized use of an automobile, which is a crime in most states.) On the other hand, if Carol left Dan's 1968 car in a junkyard after the joyride, Carol most likely would be held to have committed a larceny because of the high risk that Dan would be permanently deprived of the car.

EMBEZZLEMENT

Embezzlement is the fraudulent conversion of another's property by one who was in lawful possession of it. A conversion is any act that seriously interferes with the owner's rights in the property; such acts may include exhausting the resources of the property, selling it, giving it away, or refusing to return it to its rightful owner. The key distinction between larceny and embezzlement, therefore, is whether the thief is in lawful possession of the property. Although both situations concern misuse of the property of another, in embezzlement, the thief lawfully possesses the property; in larceny, she does not.

FALSE PRETENSES

False pretenses is the crime of obtaining title to property of another by making materially false representations of an existing fact with knowledge of their falsity and with the intent to defraud. Larceny does not cover this situation because here the victim voluntarily transfers the property to the thief. For example, a con artist who goes door to door and collects money by saying he is selling stereo equipment, when he is not, is committing the crime of false pretenses.

Other specialized crimes that are similar to false pretenses include mail, wire, and bank fraud as well as securities fraud. ***Mail fraud***, unlike the crime of false pretenses, does not require the victim to be actually defrauded; it simply requires the defendant to use the mails (or private carrier) to carry out a scheme that attempts to defraud others. Due to its breadth and ease of use, mail fraud has been employed extensively by federal prosecutors. The ***wire fraud*** statute prohibits the transmittal by wire, radio, or television in interstate or foreign commerce of any information with the intent to defraud. The federal statute prohibiting ***bank fraud*** makes it a crime knowingly to execute or attempt to execute a scheme to defraud a financial institution or to obtain by false pretenses funds under the control or custody of a financial institution. ***Securities fraud*** is discussed in Chapter 40.

ROBBERY

Robbery is a larceny with these additional elements: (1) the property is taken directly from the victim or in the immediate presence of the victim and (2) the act is accomplished through either force or the threat of force. The defendant's force or threat of force need not be against the person from whom the property is taken. For example, a robber threatens Sam that unless Sam opens up his employer's safe, the robber will shoot Maria.

Many statutes distinguish between simple robbery and aggravated robbery. Robbery can be aggravated by any of several factors, including (1) robbery with a deadly weapon, (2) robbery where the robber has the intent to kill or would kill if faced with resistance, (3) robbery that involves serious bodily injury, or (4) robbery by two or more persons.

BURGLARY

At common law, **burglary** was defined as breaking and entering the dwelling of another at night with the intent to commit a felony. Modern statutes differ from the common law definition. Many of them simply require that there be (1) an entry (2) into a building (3) with the intent to commit a felony in the building. Nevertheless, the modern statutes vary so greatly it is nearly impossible to generalize.

EXTORTION AND BRIBERY

Although extortion and bribery are frequently confused, they are two distinct crimes. **Extortion**, or blackmail as it is sometimes called, is generally held to be the making of threats for the purpose of obtaining money or property. For example, Lindsey tells Jason that unless Jason pays her $10,000, she will tell Jason's customers that Jason was once arrested for disturbing the peace. Lindsey has committed the crime of extortion. In a few jurisdictions, however, the crime of extortion occurs only if the defendant actually causes the victim to relinquish money or property.

Bribery, on the other hand, is the offer of money or property to a public official to influence the official's decision. The crime of bribery is committed when the illegal offer is made, whether accepted or not. Thus, if Andrea offered Edward, the mayor of Allentown, a 20 percent interest in Andrea's planned real estate development if Edward would use his influence to have the development proposal approved, Andrea would be guilty of criminal bribery. In contrast, if Edward had threatened Andrea that unless he received a 20 percent interest in Andrea's development, he would use his influence to prevent the approval of the development, Edward would be guilty of criminal extortion. Bribery of foreign officials is covered by the Foreign Corrupt Practices Act, discussed in Chapter 40.

Some jurisdictions have gone beyond the traditional bribery law to adopt statutes that make ***commercial bribery*** illegal. Commercial bribery is the use of bribery to acquire new business, obtain secret information or processes, or obtain kickbacks.

FORGERY

Forgery is the intentional falsification or false making of a document with the intent to defraud. Accordingly, if William prepares a false certificate of title to a stolen automobile, he is guilty of forgery. Likewise, if an individual alters some receipts in order to increase her income tax deductions, she has committed the crime of forgery. The most common type of forgery is the signing of another's name to a financial document.

BAD CHECKS

All jurisdictions have enacted laws making it a crime to issue **bad checks**; that is, writing a check when there is not enough money in the account to cover the check. Most jurisdictions simply require that the check be issued; they do not require that the issuer receive anything in return for the check. Also, though most jurisdictions require that defendants issue a check with knowledge that they do not have enough money to cover the check, a few jurisdictions require only that there be insufficient funds.

State v. Kelm

Superior Court of New Jersey, 1996

289 N.J.Super. 55, 672 A.2d 1261, cert. denied 146 N.J. 68, 679 A.2d 655 (1996)

http://lawlibrary.rutgers.edu/decisions/appellate/a1118-94.opn.html

FACTS On February 10, 1991, defendant Kelm secured a loan for $6,000 from Ms. Joan Williams. Kelm told Williams that the loan was to finance a real estate transaction. Five days later, Ms. Williams received a check drawn by Kelm in the amount of $6,000 from Kelm's attorney. Although the check was dated February 15, 1991, Kelm claims that she delivered the check to her attorney on February 10, 1991. The following week, Ms. Williams learned the check was uncollectible. Subsequently, Williams received assurances from Kelm but was unsuccessful in her efforts to obtain money from the drawee's bank. When Williams deposited the check, it was returned with a notation that it should not be presented again and that no account was on file. Bank records show that the account was closed on March 8, 1991, and that it had negative balances since February 10, 1991. Following a jury trial, Kelm was found guilty of issuing a bad check. Kelm appeals, asserting that an intent to defraud is an element of the statutory offense of issuing a bad check and that the statutory provision exempts postdated checks.

DECISION The jury verdict is affirmed.

OPINION Bilder, J. The principal issue on appeal is whether an intent to defraud the victim is an element of N.J.S.A. 2C:21-5 [issuing a bad check]. Defendant contends that the issuance of a post-dated check cannot be found to be a violation of the criminal statute and that proof of an intent to defraud is required for a conviction.In support of that defendant relies heavily on a predecessor bad check statute, N.J.S.A. 2A: 111-15, and case law interpreting that former law.

N.J.S.A. 2C:21-5, in pertinent part, reads as follows:

> A person who issues or passes a check or similar sight order for the payment of money, knowing that it will not be honored by the drawee, commits an offense * * * For the purposes of this section as well as in any prosecution for theft committed by means of a bad check, an issuer is presumed to know that the check or money order (other than a post-dated check or order) would not be paid, if:
>
> * * *
>
> (b) Payment was refused by the drawee for lack of funds, upon presentation within 30 days after issue, and the issuer failed to make good within 10 days after receiving notice of that refusal or after notice has been sent to the issuer's last known address. Notice of refusal may be given to the issuer orally or in writing in any reasonable manner by that person.

Defendant's reliance on N.J.S.A. 2A:111-15 [the old bad check statute] is misplaced. The need to show that the check was drawn "with intent to defraud" was specifically set forth in the statute. N.J.S.A. 2C:21-5 does not contain any such requirement, merely knowledge at the time the check is issued or passed that it will not be honored by the drawee. Cases involving the requirement of an intent to defraud under the old statute are irrelevant.

Defendant's contention that the statute's reference to a post-dated check exempts such checks from its operation is similarly without merit. This provision merely excludes post-dated checks from the statutory presumption of knowledge that the check will not be paid. When the instrument is post-dated the presumption is inapplicable; the State must show that the drawer knew at the time the post-dated check was drawn that it would not be honored on the later date when presented.

In his charge the trial judge instructed the jury:

> The State must prove the following elements beyond a reasonable doubt in order to convict the defendant under this [bad check] count. The State must prove that the defendant knowingly issued or passed the check for the payment of money and, two, that the defendant knew at the time that she issued or passed the check that it would not be honored by the drawee. Two things must occur at the same time: the defendant knowingly passed the check for the payment of the money and knew at the time she gave the check over to Mrs. Williams that it would not be honored by the bank.
>
> * * *
>
> There is some argument that has been made that the testimony allows you and compels you to infer that there was a post-dated check situation. It is for you to determine when this particular check was issued; was it issued on the 15th, the date it was dated, or was it issued on the 10th? You should examine the evidence carefully to determine whether or not you can make such an inference. If you do come to the conclusion that the check was issued on the 10th, that is that it is a post-dated check, then the element that the defendant knew that it would not be honored by the bank requires proof again beyond a reasonable doubt, that the defendant knew at the time the check was issued that it would not be honored in the future on the 15th. * * * Now, the State is not required to prove under the statute that there was any intent to defraud; the State need only prove that the defendant knew that the check would not be honored in the future.

INTERPRETATION The New Jersey statute requires mere knowledge at the time the check is issued or passed that the check will not be honored by the drawee for the offense of issuing a bad check to exist.

CRITICAL THINKING QUESTION What elements do you believe are essential to a bad check law? Explain

DEFENSES TO CRIMES

Even though a defendant is found to have committed a criminal act, he will not be convicted if he has a valid defense. The defenses most relevant to white-collar crimes and crimes against business include defense of property, duress, mistake of fact, and entrapment. In some instances, a defense proves the absence of a required element of the crime; other defenses provide a justification or excuse that bars criminal liability.

DEFENSE OF PERSON OR PROPERTY

Individuals may use reasonable force to protect themselves, other individuals, and their property. This defense enables a person to commit, without any criminal liability, what would otherwise be considered the crime of assault, battery, manslaughter, or murder. Under the majority rule, deadly force is never reasonable to protect property because life is deemed more important than the protection of property. For this reason, individuals cannot use a deadly mechanical device, such as a spring gun, to protect their property. If, however, the defender's use of reasonable force in protecting his property is met with an attack upon his person, he then may use deadly force if the attack threatens him with death or serious bodily harm.

DURESS

A person who is threatened with immediate, serious bodily harm to himself or another unless he engages in criminal activity has the valid defense of **duress** (sometimes referred to as compulsion or coercion) to criminal conduct other than murder. For example, Ann threatens to kill Ben if Ben does not assist her in committing larceny. Ben complies. Because of duress, he would not be guilty of the larceny.

MISTAKE OF FACT

If a person reasonably believes the facts surrounding an act to be such that his conduct would not constitute a crime, then the law will treat the facts as he reasonably believes them to be. Accordingly, an honest and reasonable **mistake of fact** will justify the defendant's conduct. For example, if Ann gets into a car that she reasonably believes to be hers—the car is the same color, model, and year as hers, is parked in the same parking lot, and is started by her key—she will be relieved of criminal responsibility for taking Ben's automobile.

ENTRAPMENT

The defense of **entrapment** arises when a law enforcement official induces a person to commit a crime when that person would not have done so without the persuasion of the police official. The rationale behind the rule, which applies only to government officials and agents, not to private individuals, is to prevent law enforcement officials from provoking crime and from engaging in improper conduct.

CRIMINAL PROCEDURE

Each of the states and the federal government have procedures for initiating and coordinating criminal prosecutions. In addition, the first ten amendments to the U.S. Constitution (called the Bill of Rights) guarantee many defenses and rights of an accused. The Fourth Amendment prohibits unreasonable searches and seizures to obtain incriminating evidence. The Fifth Amendment requires indictment by a grand jury for capital crimes, prevents double jeopardy, protects against self-incrimination, and prohibits deprivation of life or liberty without due process of law. The Sixth Amendment requires that an accused receive a speedy and public trial by an impartial jury and that he be informed of the nature of the accusation, be confronted with the witnesses who testify against him, be given the power to obtain witnesses in his favor, and have the right to competent counsel for his defense. The Eighth Amendment prohibits excessive bail, excessive fines, and cruel or unusual punishment.

Most state constitutions have similar provisions to protect the rights of accused persons. In addition, the Fourteenth Amendment prohibits state governments from depriving any person of life, liberty, or property without due process of law. Moreover, the U.S. Supreme Court has held that most of the constitutional protections just discussed apply to the states through the operation of the Fourteenth Amendment.

Although various jurisdictions may differ in actual operational details, their criminal processes have a number of common objectives. The primary purpose of the process in any jurisdiction is the effective enforcement of the criminal law, but this purpose must be accomplished within the limitations imposed by other goals. These goals include advancing an adversary system of adjudication, requiring the government to bear the burden of proof, minimizing both erroneous convictions and the burdens of defense, respecting individual dignity, maintaining the appearance of fairness, and achieving equality in the administration of the process.

We will first discuss the steps in a criminal prosecution; we will then focus on the major constitutional protections for the accused in our system of criminal justice.

STEPS IN CRIMINAL PROSECUTION

Although the particulars of criminal procedure vary from state to state, the following provides a basic overview. After arrest, the accused is booked and appears before the magistrate, commissioner, or justice of the peace, where he is given formal notice of the charges and is advised of his rights and where bail is set. Next, a **preliminary hearing** is held to determine whether there is probable cause to believe the defendant is the one who committed the crime. The defendant is usually entitled to be represented by counsel.

If the magistrate concludes that there is probable cause, she will bind the case over to the next stage, which is either an indictment or information, depending upon the jurisdiction. The federal system and about one-third of the states require indictments for all felony prosecutions (unless waived by the defendant), while the other states permit, but do not mandate, indictments. A grand jury issues an **indictment** or true bill if it finds sufficient evidence to justify a trial on the charge brought. The grand jury, which traditionally consists of no fewer than sixteen and not more than twenty-three people, is not bound by the magistrate's decision at the preliminary hearing. Unlike the preliminary hearing, the grand jury does not hear evidence from the defendant, nor does the defendant appear before the grand jury. In contrast, an **information** is a formal accusation of a crime brought by a prosecuting officer, not a grand jury. Such a procedure is used in misdemeanor cases and in some felony cases in those states that do not require indictments. The indictment or information at times precedes the actual arrest.

At the **arraignment**, the defendant is brought before the trial court, where he is informed of the charge against him and where he enters his plea. The arraignment must be held promptly after the indictment or information has been filed. If his plea is "not guilty," the defendant must stand trial. He is entitled to a jury trial for all felonies and for misdemeanors punishable by more than six months' imprisonment. Most states also permit a defendant to request a jury trial for lesser misdemeanors. If the defendant chooses, however, he may have his guilt or innocence determined by the court sitting without a jury, which is called a "bench trial."

A criminal trial is similar to a civil trial, but there are some significant differences: (1) the defendant is presumed innocent, (2) the burden of proof on the prosecution is to prove criminal guilt **beyond a reasonable doubt** (proof that is entirely convincing, satisfied to a moral certainty), and (3) the defendant is not required to testify. The trial begins with the selection of the jury and the opening statements by the prosecutor and the attorney for the defense. The prosecution presents evidence first; then the defendant presents his. At the conclusion of the testimony, closing statements are made and the jury is instructed as to the applicable law and retires to arrive at a verdict. If the verdict is "not guilty," the matter ends there. The state has no right to appeal from an acquittal; and the accused, having been placed in "jeopardy," cannot be tried a second time for the same offense. If the verdict is "guilty," the judge will enter a judgment of conviction and set the case for sentencing. The defendant may make a motion for a new trial, asserting that prejudicial error occurred at his original trial, thus requiring a retrial of the case. He may appeal to a reviewing court, alleging error by the trial court and asking for either his discharge or a remandment of the case for a new trial.

FOURTH AMENDMENT

The **Fourth Amendment**, which protects all individuals against unreasonable searches and seizures, is designed to guard the privacy and security of individuals against arbitrary invasions by government officials. Although the Fourth Amendment by its terms applies only to acts of the federal government, the Fourteenth Amendment makes it applicable to state government actions as well.

When a violation of the Fourth Amendment has occurred, the general rule prohibits the introduction of the illegally seized evidence at trial. The purpose of this **exclusionary rule** is to discourage illegal police conduct and to protect individual liberty, not to hinder the search for the truth. Nonetheless, in recent years the Supreme Court has limited the exclusionary rule.

To obtain a warrant to search a particular person, place, or thing, a law enforcement official must demonstrate to a magistrate that he has probable cause to believe that the search will reveal evidence of criminal activity. **Probable cause** means "[t]he task of the issuing magistrate is simply to make a practical, common-sense decision whether, given all the circumstances set forth . . . before him, . . . there is a fair probability that contraband or evidence of a crime will be found in a particular place." *Illinois v. Gates*, 462 U.S. 213 (1983).

Even though the Fourth Amendment requires that a search and seizure generally be made after a valid search warrant has been obtained, in some instances a search warrant is not necessary. For example, it has been held that a warrant is not necessary where (1) there is hot pursuit of a fugitive, (2) the subject of the search voluntarily consents, (3) an emergency requires such action, (4) there has been a lawful arrest, (5) evidence of a crime is in plain view of the law enforcement officer, or (6) delay would present a significant obstacle to the investigation.

http:// U.S. Constitution: http://www.law.cornell.edu/constitution/constitution.table.html

THE LAW AND YOU

State Bar Associations

Florida: http://www.flabar.org/newflabar/consumerservices/General/Consumer.Pam/ ("If You Are Arrested in Florida"; "Juvenile Arrest")

Illinois: http://www.illinoislawyerfinder.com/publicinfo/home.html ("If You're Arrested")

Maine: http://www.mainebar.org/ (legal information pamphlets) ("Domestic Abuse")

Maryland: http://www.msba.org/public/brochure.htm ("Domestic Violence: You Can Live Without It"; "Juvenile Court"; "Your Legal Rights If Arrested"; "So, You've Received a Traffic Ticket")

Minnesota: http://www.mnbar.org/consumer.htm ("Child Abuse and Neglect")

Missouri: http://www.mobar.org/ (brochures on legal topics) ("Your Rights If Arrested"; "Your Rights in Traffic Court"; "Domestic Violence and the Law"; "You Can Stop Child Abuse")

Nevada: http://www.nvbar.org/pamphlets.htm (public services) ("DUI")

New Hampshire: http://www.nhbar.org/?area/15.html ("The Rights of Juveniles")

New Mexico: http://www.nmbar.org/ ("Rights and Obligations of Parents in Juvenile Court")

New York: http://www.nysba.org/templatecfm?Section=Public_Resources ("Your Rights If Arrested"; "Your Rights as a Crime Victim")

North Carolina: http://www.ncbar.org/legal_prof/divisions/yld/publications/consumer_pub.asp ("Family Violence")

Ohio: http://www.ohiobar.org/public/conres/pamphlets.html ("Your Rights If Questioned, Stopped, or Arrested by Police")

Oregon: http://www.osbar.org/public/legallinks.html ("Restraining Orders and Domestic Violence"; "Your Rights If You Are Arrested"; "Your Right to a Free Attorney If Charged with a Crime"; "Help for Crime Victims"; "Clearing Your Record"; "Are You a Victim of Mail Order Fraud?"; "Must I Take a Chemical Breath Test?"; "Should I Fight My Traffic Ticket?"; "DUI"; "Driving with a Suspended License")

Rhode Island: http://www.ribar.com/public/default.asp ("What If You Are Arrested"; "What If Drunk Drivers Get Caught?")

South Dakota: http://www.sdbar.org/public/Default.htm ("Protection Orders")

Tennessee: http://www.tba.org/LawBytes/LawBytes.html ("Criminal Law")

Texas: http://www.texasbar.com/public/consumerinfo/helpfulinfo/pamphlets. asp ("The Texas Criminal Justice Process: A Citizen's Guide")

Washington: http://www.wsba.org/public/consumer/default.htm ("Criminal Law")

Wisconsin: http://www.wisbar.org/asp/titles.asp ("Arrest")

State Attorney Generals

Illinois: http://www.ag.state.il.us/publications/pubs.htm ("Financial Aid for Crime Victims")

Maine: http://www.maine.gov/ag/?r=protection ("The Maine Attorney General's Consumer Law Guide")

Maryland: http://www.oag.state.md.us/ ("Victim Assistance")

Nevada: http://ag.state.nv.us/dv/dom_vio.htm ("Domestic Violence")

Texas: http://www.texasag.org/alerts_view.asp?type=1/ ("Crime Victim Services"; "Criminal Justice")

Wisconsin: http://www.doj.state.wi.us/CVS/ ("Crime Victim Services")

FIFTH AMENDMENT

The **Fifth Amendment** protects persons against self-incrimination, double jeopardy, and being charged with a capital or infamous crime except by grand jury indictment. The prohibitions against self-incrimination and double jeopardy also apply to the states through the due process clause of the Fourteenth Amendment; however, the grand jury clause does not.

The privilege against self-incrimination extends only to testimonial evidence, not to physical evidence. The Fifth Amendment privilege "protects an accused only from being compelled to testify against himself, or otherwise provide the state with evidence of a testimonial or communicative nature." Therefore, a person can be forced to stand in an identification lineup, provide a handwriting sample, or take a blood test. Significantly, the Fifth Amendment does not protect the records of a business entity, such as a corporation or partnership; it applies only to papers of individuals. Moreover, the Fifth Amendment does not prohibit examination of an individual's business records as long as the individual is not compelled to testify against himself.

SIXTH AMENDMENT

The **Sixth Amendment** provides that the federal government shall provide the accused with a speedy and public

CONCEPT REVIEW

Constitutional Protection for the Criminal Defendant

Amendment	Protection Conferred
Fourth	Freedom from unreasonable search and seizure
Fifth	Right to due process Right to indictment by grand jury for capital crimes* Freedom from double jeopardy Freedom from self-incrimination
Sixth	Right to a speedy, public trial by jury Right to present witnesses Right to competent counsel
Eighth	Freedom from excessive bail Freedom from cruel and unusual punishment

*This right has *not* been applied to the states through the Fourteenth Amendment

trial by an impartial jury, inform him of the nature and cause of the accusation, confront him with the witnesses against him, have compulsory process for obtaining witnesses in his favor, and allow him to obtain the assistance of counsel for his defense. The Fourteenth Amendment extends these guarantees to the states.

See Concept Review for a presentation of the constitutional protections provided the defendant in a criminal action.

Practical Advice

A defendant has the right not to testify against himself and a jury cannot consider this against him.

CHAPTER SUMMARY

Nature of Crimes

Definition any act or omission forbidden by public law

Essential Elements
- *Actus reus* wrongful or overt act
- *Mens rea* criminal intent or mental fault

Classification
- *Felony* a serious crime
- *Misdemeanor* a less serious crime

Vicarious Liability liability imposed for acts of his or her employees if the employer directed, participated in, or approved of the acts

Liability of a Corporation under certain circumstances a corporation may be convicted of crimes and punished by fines

White-Collar Crime

Definition nonviolent crime involving deceit, corruption, or breach of trust

Computer Crime use of a computer to commit a crime

RICO federal law intended to stop organized crime from infiltrating legitimate businesses

Crimes Against Business

Larceny trespassory taking, and carrying away of personal property of another with the intent to deprive the victim permanently of the property

Embezzlement taking of another's property by a person who was in lawful possession of the property

False Pretenses obtaining title to property of another by means of representations one knows to be materially false, made with intent to defraud

Robbery committing larceny with the use or threat of force

Burglary under most modern statutes, an entry into a building with the intent to commit a felony

Extortion the making of threats to obtain money or property

Bribery offering money or property to a public official to influence the official's decision

Forgery intentional falsification of a document in order to defraud

Bad Checks knowingly issuing a check without funds sufficient to cover the check

Defenses to Crime

Defense of Person or Property individuals may use reasonable force to protect themselves, other individuals, and their property

Duress coercion by threat of serious bodily harm is a defense to criminal conduct other than murder

Mistake of Fact honest and reasonable belief that conduct is not criminal is a defense

Entrapment inducement by a law enforcement official to commit a crime is a defense

Criminal Procedure

Steps in Criminal Prosecution generally include arrest, booking, formal notice of charges, preliminary hearing to determine probable cause, indictment or information, arraignment, and trial

Fourth Amendment protects individuals against unreasonable searches and seizures

Fifth Amendment protects persons against self-incrimination, double jeopardy, and being charged with a capital crime except by grand jury indictment

Sixth Amendment provides the accused with the right to a speedy and public trial, the opportunity to confront witnesses, process for obtaining witnesses, and the right to counsel

QUESTIONS

1. Sam said to Carol, "Kim is going to sell me a good used car next Monday and then I'll deliver it to you in exchange for your microcomputer, but I'd like to have the computer now." Relying on this statement, Carol delivered the computer to Sam. Sam knew Kim had no car and would have none in the future, and he had no such arrangement with her. The appointed time of exchange passed, and Sam failed to deliver the car to Carol. Has a crime been committed? Discuss.
2. Sara, a lawyer, drew a deed for Robert by which Robert was to convey land to Rick. The deed was correct in every detail. Robert examined and verbally approved it but did not sign it. Sara erased Rick's name and substituted her own. Robert signed the deed with all required legal formalities without noticing the change. Was Sara guilty of forgery? Discuss.
3. Ann took Bonnie's watch before Bonnie was aware of the theft. Bonnie discovered her loss immediately and pursued Ann. Ann pointed a loaded pistol at Bonnie, who, in fear of being shot, allowed Ann to escape. Was Ann guilty of robbery? Of any other crime?

4. Jones and Wilson were on trial, separately, for larceny of a $1,000 bearer bond (payable to the holder of the bond, not a named individual) issued by Brown, Inc. The commonwealth's evidence showed that the owner of the bond put it in an envelope bearing his name and address and dropped it accidentally in the street; that Jones found the envelope with the bond in it; that Jones could neither read nor write; that Jones presented the envelope and bond to Wilson, an educated man, and asked Wilson what he should do with it; that Wilson told Jones that the finder of lost property becomes the owner of it; that Wilson told Jones that the bond was worth $100 but that the money could be collected only at the issuer's home office; that Jones then handed the bond to Wilson, who redeemed it at the corporation's home office and received $1,000; that Wilson gave Jones $100 of the proceeds. What rulings?

5. Truck drivers for a hauling company, while loading a desk, found a $100 bill that had fallen out of the desk. They agreed to get it exchanged for small bills and divide the proceeds. En route to the bank, one of them changed his mind and refused to proceed with the scheme, whereupon the other pulled a knife and demanded the bill. A police officer intervened. It turned out that the bill was counterfeit money. What crimes have been committed?

6. Peter, an undercover police agent, was trying to locate a laboratory where it was believed that methamphetamine, or "speed"—a controlled substance—was being manufactured illegally. Peter went to Mary's home and said that he represented a large organization that was interested in obtaining methamphetamine. Peter offered to supply a necessary ingredient for the manufacture of the drug, which was very difficult to obtain, in return for one-half of the drug produced. Mary agreed and processed the chemical given to her by Peter in Peter's presence. Later Peter returned with a search warrant and arrested Mary. Mary was charged with various narcotics law violations. Mary asserted the defense of entrapment. Should Mary prevail? Why?

7. The police obtained a search warrant based on an affidavit that contained the following allegations: (a) Donald was seen crossing a state line on four occasions during a five-day period and going to a particular apartment; (b) telephone records disclosed that the apartment had two telephones; (c) Donald had a reputation as a bookmaker and as an associate of gamblers; and (d) the FBI was informed by a "confidential reliable informant" that Donald was conducting gambling operations. When a search was made based on the warrant, evidence was obtained that resulted in Donald's conviction of violating certain gambling laws. Donald challenged the constitutionality of the search warrant. Were Donald's constitutional rights violated? Explain your answer.

8. A national bank was robbed by a man with a small strip of tape on each side of his face. An indictment was returned against David. David was then arrested, and counsel was appointed to represent him. Two weeks later, without notice to David's lawyer, an FBI agent arranged to have the two bank employees observe a lineup, including David and five or six other prisoners. Each person in the lineup wore strips of tape, as had the robber, and each was directed to repeat the words "Put the money in the bag," as had the robber. Both of the bank employees identified David as the robber. At David's trial he was again identified by the two, in the courtroom, and the prior lineup identification was elicited on cross-examination by David's counsel. David's counsel moved the court either to grant a judgment of acquittal or alternatively to strike the courtroom identifications on the ground that the lineup had violated David's Fifth Amendment privilege against self-incrimination and his Sixth Amendment right to counsel. Decision?

CASE PROBLEMS

9. Waronek owned and operated a trucking rig, transporting goods for L.T.L. Perishables, Inc., of St. Paul, Minnesota. He accepted an offer to haul a trailer load of beef from Illini Beef Packers, Inc., in Joslin, Illinois, to Midtown Packing Company in New York City. After his truck was loaded with ninety-five forequarters and ninety-five hindquarters of beef in Joslin, Waronek drove north to his home in Watertown, Wisconsin, rather than east to New York. While in Watertown, he asked employees of the Royal Meat Company to butcher and prepare four hindquarters of beef—two for himself and two for his friends. He also offered to sell ten hindquarters to one employee of the company at an alarmingly reduced rate. The suspicious employee contacted the authorities, who told him to proceed with the deal. When Waronek arrived in New York with his load short nineteen hindquarters, Waronek telephoned L.T.L. Perishables in St. Paul. He notified them "that he was short nineteen hindquarters, that he knew where the beef went, and that he would make good on it out of future settlements." L.T.L. told him to contact the New York police but he failed to do so. Shortly thereafter, he was arrested by the Federal Bureau of Investigation and indicted for the embezzlement of goods moving in interstate commerce. Explain whether Waronek was guilty of the crime of embezzlement.

10. Four separate cases involving similar fact situations were consolidated because they presented the same constitutional question. In each case, police officers, detectives, or prosecuting attorneys took a defendant into custody and interrogated him in a police station to obtain a confession. In none

of these cases did the officials fully and effectively advise the defendant of his rights at the outset of the interrogation. The interrogations produced oral admissions of guilt from each defendant, as well as signed statements from three of them, which were used to convict them at their trials. The defendants appealed, arguing that the officials should have warned them of their constitutional rights and the consequences of waiving them before the questioning began. It was contended that to permit any statements obtained without such a warning violated their Fifth Amendment privilege against self-incrimination. Were the defendants' constitutional rights violated? Discuss.

11. The Racketeer Influenced and Corrupt Organization Act (RICO) is directed at "racketeering activity"—defined to encompass acts indictable under specific federal criminal provisions, including mail and wire fraud. Petitioner corporation, Sedima, which had entered into a joint business venture with respondent company, Imrex, and which believed that it was being cheated by alleged overbilling, filed suit in district court, asserting RICO claims against respondent company and two of its officers (also respondents) based on predicate acts of mail and wire fraud. The court dismissed the RICO counts for failure to state a claim. The Court of Appeals affirmed, holding that under RICO, a plaintiff must allege a "racketeering injury"—an injury "caused by an activity which RICO was designed to deter," not just an injury occurring as a result of the predicate acts themselves. Sedima appealed. Discuss who will prevail and why.

12. Officer Cyril Rombach of the Burbank Police Department, an experienced and well-trained narcotics officer, applied for a warrant to search several residences and automobiles for cocaine, methaqualone, and other narcotics. Rombach supported his application with information given to another police officer by a confidential informant of unproven reliability. He also based the warrant application on his own observations made during an extensive investigation: known drug offenders visiting the residences and leaving with small packages as well as a suspicious trip to Miami by two of the suspects. A state superior court judge issued a search warrant to Rombach based on this information. Rombach's searches netted large quantities of drugs and other evidence, which produced indictments of several suspects on charges of conspiracy to possess and distribute cocaine. The defendants moved to suppress the evidence on the grounds that the search warrant was defective in that Rombach had failed to establish the informant's credibility and that the information provided by the informant about the suspect's criminal activity was fatally stale. The district court declared that the search lacked probable cause, that the warrant was invalid, and that the obtained evidence must be excluded from the prosecution's case under the Fourth Amendment's exclusionary rule. The Court of Appeals for the Ninth Circuit affirmed. Should the evidence be excluded? Why?

13. Olivo was in the hardware area of a department store. A security guard saw him look around, take a set of wrenches, and conceal it in his clothing. Olivo looked around once more and proceeded toward an exit, passing several cash registers. The guard stopped him short of the exit. Olivo testified at trial that he was waiting in line at a cashier with the tools under his arm when he was seized by the guard. A jury found him guilty of larceny. Olivo then brought this appeal, maintaining that larceny is not legally established unless the defendant leaves a place of business without paying for merchandise in his possession. Decision?

http:// **Internet Exercise** Find and review (a) the Bureau of Justice's data for the burglary, theft, and motor vehicle theft rates for the last five years and (b) information on computer crime and its trend.

Chapter 7

Intentional Torts

Torts are infinitely various, not limited or confined, for there is nothing in nature but may be an instrument for mischief.

CHARLES PRATT, QUOTED IN *THE GUIDE TO AMERICAN LAW*, VOL. 10

Learning Objectives

After reading this chapter you should be able to:

1. Identify and describe the torts that protect against intentional harm to personal rights.
2. Explain the application of the various privileges to defamation suits and how they are affected by whether the plaintiff is (a) a public figure, (b) a public official, or (c) a private person.
3. Describe and distinguish the four torts comprising invasion of privacy.
4. Identify and describe the torts that protect against harm to property.
5. Distinguish among interference with contractual relations, disparagement, and fraudulent misrepresentation.

All forms of civil liability are either (1) voluntarily assumed, as by contract, or (2) involuntarily assumed, as imposed by law. **Tort** liability is of the second type. Tort law gives persons relief from civil wrongs or injuries to their persons, property, and economic interests. This law has three principal objectives: (1) to compensate persons who sustain harm or loss resulting from another's conduct, (2) to place the cost of that compensation only on those parties who should bear it, and (3) to prevent future harms and losses. Thus, the law of torts reallocates losses caused by human misconduct. In general, a tort is committed when (1) a duty owed by one person to another (2) is breached, (3) proximately causing (4) injury or damage to the owner of a legally protected interest.

Each person is legally responsible for the damages proximately caused by his tortious conduct. Moreover, as we will discuss in Chapter 30, businesses that conduct their business activities through employees are also liable for the torts their employees commit in the course of employment. The tort liability of employers makes the study of tort law essential to business managers.

Injuries may be inflicted intentionally, negligently, or without fault (strict liability). We will discuss intentional torts in this chapter and cover negligence and strict liability in Chapter 8.

The same conduct may, and often does, constitute both a crime and a tort. For example, let us assume that Johnson has committed an assault and battery against West. For the commission of this crime, the state may take appropriate action against Johnson. In addition, Johnson has violated West's right to be secure in his person, and so has committed a tort against West. Regardless of the criminal action brought by the state against Johnson, West may bring a civil tort action against Johnson for damages. But an act may be criminal without being tortious; by the same token, an act may be a tort but not a crime.

In a tort action, the injured party sues to recover compensation for the injury sustained as a result of the defendant's wrongful conduct. The purpose of tort law, unlike criminal law, is to compensate the injured party, not to punish the wrongdoer. In certain cases, however, courts may award exemplary or **punitive damages**, which are damages over and above the amount necessary to compensate the plaintiff. Where the defendant's tortious conduct has been intentional and outrageous, showing malice or a fraudulent or evil motive, most courts permit a jury to award punitive damages. The allowance of punitive damages is designed to punish and make an example of the defendant and thus deter others from similar conduct.

State Farm Mutual Automobile Insurance v. Campbell

Supreme Court of the United States, 2003
__ U.S. __, 123 S.Ct. 1513, 155 L.Ed.2d 585

FACTS In 1981, Curtis Campbell was driving with his wife, Inez Preece Campbell, in Cache County, Utah. He decided to pass six vans traveling ahead of them on a two-lane highway. Todd Ospital was driving a small car approaching from the opposite direction. To avoid a head-on collision with Campbell, who by then was driving on the wrong side of the highway and toward oncoming traffic, Ospital swerved onto the shoulder, lost control of his automobile, and collided with a vehicle driven by Robert G. Slusher. Ospital was killed, and Slusher was rendered permanently disabled. The Campbells escaped uninjured.

In the wrongful death and tort action brought by Ospital's estate and Slusher, Campbell denied fault. The investigators and witnesses all concluded that Mr. Campbell's unsafe pass had caused the crash. Campbell's insurance company, petitioner State Farm Mutual Automobile Insurance Company (State Farm), nevertheless, decided to contest liability and refused offers by Slusher and Ospital's estate to settle the claims for the policy limit of $50,000 ($25,000 per claimant). State Farm also ignored the advice of one of its own investigators and took the case to trial, assuring the Campbells that "their assets were safe, that they had no liability for the accident, that [State Farm] would represent their interests, and that they did not need to procure separate counsel." A jury determined that Campbell was 100 percent at fault, and a judgment was returned for $185,849.

At first State Farm refused to cover the $135,849 in excess liability. Its counsel made this clear to the Campbells: "You may want to put for sale signs on your property to get things moving." State Farm also refused to post a bond to allow Campbell to appeal the judgment against him. Campbell obtained his own counsel to appeal the verdict. In 1989, the Utah Supreme Court denied Campbell's appeal in the wrongful death and tort actions. State Farm then paid the entire judgment, including the amounts in excess of the policy limits.

The Campbells filed a complaint against State Farm alleging bad faith, fraud, and intentional infliction of emotional distress. The trial court initially granted State Farm's motion for summary judgment because State Farm had paid the excess verdict, but that ruling was reversed on appeal. On remand the trial court denied State Farm's motion to exclude evidence of alleged conduct that occurred in unrelated cases outside of Utah. The jury determined that State Farm's decision not to settle was unreasonable because there was a substantial likelihood of an excess verdict. The jury awarded the Campbells $2.6 million in compensatory damages and $145 million in punitive damages, which the trial court reduced to $1 million and $25 million respectively. The Utah Supreme Court reinstated the $145 million punitive damages award. The U.S. Supreme Court granted certiorari.

DECISION The judgment of the Utah Supreme Court is reversed, and the case is remanded.

OPINION Kennedy, J. We recognized in [citation], that in our judicial system compensatory and punitive damages, although usually awarded at the same time by the same decisionmaker, serve different purposes. [Citation.] Compensatory damages "are intended to redress the concrete loss that the plaintiff has suffered by reason of the defendant's wrongful conduct." [Citation.] By contrast, punitive damages serve a broader function; they are aimed at deterrence and retribution. [Citations.]

* * * The Due Process Clause of the Fourteenth Amendment prohibits the imposition of grossly excessive or arbitrary punishments on a tortfeasor. [Citations.] The reason is that "elementary notions of fairness enshrined in our constitutional jurisprudence dictate that a person receive fair notice not only of the conduct that will subject him to punishment, but also of the severity of the penalty that a State may impose." [Citations.] To the extent an award is grossly excessive, it furthers no legitimate purpose and constitutes an arbitrary deprivation of property. [Citation.]

Although these awards serve the same purposes as criminal penalties, defendants subjected to punitive damages in civil cases have not been accorded the protections applicable in a criminal proceeding. This increases our concerns over the imprecise manner in which punitive damages systems are administered. We have admonished that "punitive damages pose an acute danger of arbitrary deprivation of property. Jury instructions typically leave the jury with wide discretion in choosing amounts, and the presentation of evidence of a defendant's net worth creates the potential that juries will use their verdicts to express biases against big businesses, particularly those without strong local presences." * * * Our concerns are heightened when the decisionmaker is presented, as we shall discuss, with evidence that has little bearing as to the amount of punitive damages that should be awarded. Vague instructions, or those that merely inform the jury to avoid "passion or prejudice," [citation], do little to aid the decisionmaker in its task of assigning appropriate weight to evidence that is relevant and evidence that is tangential or only inflammatory.

In light of these concerns, in *Gore*, [citation], we instructed courts reviewing punitive damages to consider three guideposts: (1) the degree of reprehensibility of the defendant's misconduct; (2) the disparity between the actual or potential harm suffered by the plaintiff and the punitive damages award; and (3) the difference between the punitive damages awarded by the jury and the civil penalties authorized or imposed in comparable cases. [Citation.] We reiterated the importance of these three guideposts in [citation] and mandated appellate courts to conduct *de novo* [a new] review of a trial court's application of them to the jury's award. [Citation.] Exacting appellate review ensures that an award of punitive damages is based upon an "'application of law, rather than a decisionmaker's caprice.'" [Citation.]

Under the principles outlined in *BMW of North America, Inc. v. Gore*, this case is neither close nor difficult. It was error to reinstate the jury's $145 million punitive damages award. We address each guidepost of *Gore* in some detail.

"The most important indicium of the reasonableness of a punitive damages award is the degree of reprehensibility of the defendant's conduct." [Citation.] We have instructed courts to determine the reprehensibility of a defendant by considering whether: the harm caused was physical as opposed to economic; the tortious conduct evinced an indifference to or a reckless disregard of the health or safety of others; the target of the conduct had financial vulnerability; the conduct involved repeated actions or was an isolated incident; and the harm was the result of intentional malice, trickery, or deceit, or mere accident. [Citation.] The existence of any one of these factors weighing in favor of a plaintiff may not be sufficient to sustain a punitive damages award; and the absence of all of them renders any award suspect. It should be presumed a plaintiff has been made whole for his injuries by compensatory damages, so punitive damages should only be awarded if the defendant's culpability, after having paid compensatory damages, is so reprehensible as to warrant the imposition of further sanctions to achieve punishment or deterrence. [Citation.]

Applying these factors in the instant case, we must acknowledge that State Farm's handling of the claims against the Campbells merits no praise. The trial court found that State Farm's employees altered the company's records to make Campbell appear less culpable. State Farm disregarded the overwhelming likelihood of liability and the near-certain probability that, by taking the case to trial, a judgment in excess of the policy limits would be awarded. State Farm amplified the harm by at first assuring the Campbells their assets would be safe from any verdict and by later telling them, postjudgment, to put a for-sale sign on their house. While we do not suggest there was error in awarding punitive damages based upon State Farm's conduct toward the Campbells, a more modest punishment for this reprehensible conduct could have satisfied the State's legitimate objectives, and the Utah courts should have gone no further.

This case, instead, was used as a platform to expose, and punish, the perceived deficiencies of State Farm's operations throughout the country. The Utah Supreme Court's opinion makes explicit that State Farm was being condemned for its nationwide policies rather than for the conduct direct toward the Campbells. * * *

* * *

A State cannot punish a defendant for conduct that may have been lawful where it occurred. [Citations.] * * * Nor, as a general rule, does a State have a legitimate concern in imposing punitive damages to punish a defendant for unlawful acts committed outside of the State's jurisdiction. * * *

For a more fundamental reason, however, the Utah courts erred in relying upon this and other evidence: The courts awarded punitive damages to punish and deter conduct that bore no relation to the Campbells' harm. A defendant's dissimilar acts, independent from the acts upon which liability was premised, may not serve as the basis for punitive damages. A defendant should be punished for the conduct that harmed the plaintiff, not for being an unsavory individual or business. * * *

* * *

Turning to the second *Gore* guidepost, we have been reluctant to identify concrete constitutional limits on the ratio between harm, or potential harm, to the plaintiff and the punitive damages award. [Citation.] We decline again to impose a bright-line ratio which a punitive damages award cannot exceed. Our jurisprudence and the principles it has now established demonstrate, however, that, in practice, few awards exceeding a single-digit ratio between punitive and compensatory damages, to a significant degree, will satisfy due process. In [citation], in upholding a punitive damages award, we concluded that an award of more than four times the amount of compensatory damages might be close to the line of constitutional impropriety. [Citation.] We cited that 4-to-1 ratio again in *Gore*. [Citation.] The Court further referenced a long legislative history, dating back over 700 years and going forward to today, providing for sanctions of double, treble, or quadruple damages to deter and punish. [Citation.] While these ratios are not binding, they are instructive. They demonstrate what should be obvious: Single-digit multipliers are more likely to comport with due process, while still achieving the State's goals of deterrence and retribution, than awards with ratios in range of 500 to 1, [citation], or, in this case, of 145 to 1.

Nonetheless, because there are no rigid benchmarks that a punitive damages award may not surpass, ratios greater than those we have previously upheld may comport with due process where "a particularly egregious act has resulted in only a small amount of economic damages." [Citation.] The converse is also true, however. When compensatory damages are substantial, then a lesser ratio, perhaps only equal to compensatory damages, can reach the outermost limit of the due process guarantee. The precise award in any case, of course, must be based upon the facts and circumstances of the defendant's conduct and the harm to the plaintiff.

In sum, courts must ensure that the measure of punishment is both reasonable and proportionate to the amount of harm to the plaintiff and to the general damages recovered. In the context of this case, we have no doubt that there is a presumption against an award that has a 145-to-1 ratio. The compensatory award in this case was substantial; the Campbells were awarded $1 million for a year and a half of emotional distress. This was complete compensation. The harm arose from a transaction in the economic realm, not from some physical assault or trauma; there were no physical injuries; and State Farm paid the excess verdict before the complaint was filed, so the Campbells suffered only minor economic injuries for the 18-month period in which State Farm refused to resolve the claim against them. The compensatory damages for the injury suffered here, moreover, likely were based on a component which was duplicated in the punitive award. Much of the distress was caused by the outrage and humiliation the Campbells suffered at the actions of their insurer; and it is a major role of punitive damages to condemn such conduct. Compensatory damages, however, already contain this punitive element. [Citation.]

* * *

The third guidepost in *Gore* is the disparity between the punitive damages award and the "civil penalties authorized or imposed in comparable cases." * * * Punitive damages are not a substitute for the criminal process, and the remote possibility of a criminal sanction does not automatically sustain a punitive damages award.

* * * The most relevant civil sanction under Utah state law for the wrong done to the Campbells appears to be a $10,000 fine for an act of fraud, [citation], an amount dwarfed by the $145 million punitive damages award. The Supreme Court of Utah speculated about the loss of State Farm's business license, the disgorgement of profits, and possible imprisonment, but here again its references were to the broad fraudulent scheme drawn from evidence of out-of-state and dissimilar conduct. This analysis was insufficient to justify the award.

* * * The punitive award of $145 million * * * was neither reasonable nor proportionate to the wrong committed, and it was an irrational and arbitrary deprivation of the property of the defendant. The proper calculation of punitive damages under the principles we have discussed should be resolved, in the first instance, by the Utah courts.

INTERPRETATION In most states a jury may award punitive damages if a defendant's tortious conduct is intentional and outrageous, but the amount of damages must not be grossly excessive.

ETHICAL QUESTION Did State Farm act ethically in this case? Explain.

CRITICAL THINKING QUESTION What would have been an appropriate amount of punitive damages? Explain.

Practical Advice

When bringing a lawsuit for an intentional tort, consider whether it is appropriate to ask for punitive damages.

Tort law is primarily common law, and, as we mentioned in Chapter 1, the Restatements, prepared by the American Law Institute, present many important areas of the common law, including torts. You will recall that although they are not law in themselves, the Restatements are highly persuasive in the courts.

Intent, as used in tort law, does not require a hostile or evil motive. Rather, it means that the actor desires to cause the consequences of his act or that he believes the consequences are substantially (almost) certain to result from it. (See Figure 7-1, which illustrates intent.) The following examples illustrate the definition of intent: (1) If Mark fires a gun in the middle of the Mojave Desert, he intends to fire the gun; but when the bullet hits Steven, who is in the desert without Mark's knowledge, Mark does not intend that result. (2) Mark throws a bomb into Steven's office in order to kill Steven. Mark knows that Carol is in Steven's office and that the bomb is substantially certain to injure Carol, although Mark has no desire to harm her. Mark is, nonetheless, liable to Carol for any injury caused Carol. Mark's intent to injure Steven is *transferred* to Carol.

Infants (persons who have not reached the age of majority) are held liable for their intentional torts. The infant's age and knowledge, however, are critical in determining whether the infant had sufficient intelligence to form the required intent. Incompetents, like infants, are generally not held liable for their intentional torts.

Even though the defendant has intentionally invaded the interests of the plaintiff, the defendant will not be liable if such conduct was privileged. A defendant's conduct is ***privileged*** if it furthers an interest of such social importance that the law grants immunity from tort liability for damage

Figure 7-1
Intent

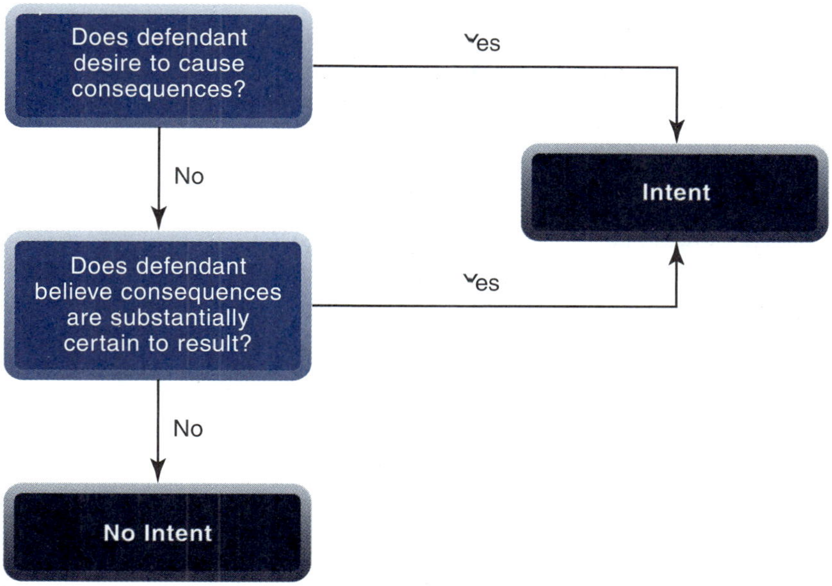

to others. Examples of privilege include self-defense, defense of property, and defense of others. In addition, the plaintiff's consent to the defendant's conduct is a defense to intentional torts.

HARM TO THE PERSON

The law provides protection against harm to the person. Generally, intentional torts to the person entitle the injured party to recover damages for bodily harm, emotional distress, loss or impairment of earning capacity, reasonable medical expenses, and harm the tortious conduct caused to property or business.

BATTERY

Battery is an intentional infliction of harmful or offensive bodily contact. It may consist of contact causing serious injury, such as a gunshot wound or a blow on the head with a club. Or it may involve contact causing little or no physical injury, such as knocking a hat off of a person's head or flicking a glove in another's face. Bodily contact is offensive if it would offend a reasonable person's sense of dignity. Such contact may be accomplished through the use of objects, such as Gustav's throwing a rock at Hester with the intention of hitting her. If the rock hits Hester or any other person, Gustav has committed a battery.

ASSAULT

Assault is intentional conduct by one person directed at another that places the other in apprehension of immediate bodily harm or offensive contact. It is usually committed immediately before a battery, but if the intended battery fails, the assault remains. Assault is essentially a mental rather than a physical intrusion. Accordingly, damages for it may include compensation for fright and humiliation. The person in danger of immediate bodily harm must have *knowledge* of the danger and be apprehensive of its imminent threat to his safety.

FALSE IMPRISONMENT

The tort of **false imprisonment** or **false arrest** is the act of intentionally confining a person against her will within fixed boundaries if the person is conscious of the confinement or harmed by it. Such restraint may be brought about by physical force, the threat of physical force, or by force directed against a person's property. Damages for false imprisonment may include compensation for loss of time, physical discomfort, inconvenience, physical illness, and mental suffering. Merely obstructing a person's freedom of movement is not false imprisonment so long as a reasonable alternative exit is available.

Merchants occasionally encounter potential liability for false imprisonment when they seek to question a suspected shoplifter. A merchant who detains an innocent person may face a lawsuit for false imprisonment. However, most states have statutes protecting the merchant, provided she detains the suspect with probable cause, in a reasonable manner, and for not more than a reasonable time.

> **Practical Advice**
>
> When detaining a suspected shoplifter, be careful to conform with the limitations of your state's statutory privilege.

Vaughn v. Wal-Mart Stores, Inc.

Court of Appeal of Louisiana, Fifth Circuit, 1999
734 So.2d 156

FACTS On July 31, 1994, Amanda Vaughn and Jason Vaughn accompanied their mother, Emma Simpson Vaughn, to a Wal-Mart store **(http://www.walmartstores.com)** located in Jefferson Parish. Amanda's friend, Kimberly Dickerson, was also with them. Once they entered the store, Mrs. Vaughn and Jason went into separate areas of the store. The two girls remained together in the front of the store and selected a stamp album to purchase. Kimberly took the album to the check-out register, and while she was at the register, she also selected a pack of gum. Once Kimberly paid for her two items, they were placed in a bag and she was given her change. Kimberly testified that she did not immediately put the change in her wallet while she was at the register. Instead, Kimberly walked back into the merchandise area where Amanda had remained. Kimberly was in the merchandise area, away from the registers, when she placed her change in her purse. Kimberly proceeded to place her hand in the Wal-Mart bag to retrieve the gum she had just purchased.

At this time, Ms. Clara Lynn Neal, a customer service manager, observed Kimberly's hand coming out of her Wal-Mart bag. According to Ms. Neal, because the two girls were in a somewhat secluded area of the store, Ms. Neal walked past the two girls twice to observe them before she walked over to them.

Ms. Neal testified that she asked Kimberly if she could see her bag and her receipt and that Kimberly voluntarily gave her the bag. Plaintiffs alleged that Ms. Neal "detained the girls, snatched Kimberly's bag from her, searched the bag, discovered a receipt, tied the bag, and then personally escorted the girls to an area near the front door away from the registers. * * *" However, Kimberly's testimony stated that "[Ms. Neal] said she was going to have to check my bag because she doesn't know if I'm stealing something. So I didn't say anything. I didn't really give it to her because I was shocked. So she took it, and she was like searching through it."

Once Ms. Neal checked the purchases with the receipt, the girls were told to go to the front of the store and wait for their party. The girls were never told that they could not leave the store and the girls were not detained by anyone else. According to all parties, from the time Ms. Neal walked up to the girls, verified the purchases, and returned the bag to Kimberly, the entire incident only lasted about one minute.

While the girls were waiting at the front of the store, Jason was asked by his mother to inform the girls that she was ready to go. Jason approached the girls, and they responded that they could not leave. When Jason reported to his mother that the girls stated they could not leave the area, Mrs. Vaughn then went to the front of the store to investigate.

Before Mrs. Vaughn took the children home, she explained to a store manager what had occurred. Mrs. Vaughn returned to the store with Sandra Dickerson, Kimberly's mother, to make further inquiries. Mrs. Vaughn, Mrs. Dickerson, Ms. Neal and the manager then went into an office to discuss the incident. Mrs. Vaughn testified that, at this meeting, Ms. Neal informed her she searched Kimberly because Kimberly had her hand in her bag and looked suspicious. Although Mrs. Vaughn also claims that Ms. Neal stated that she thought Jason was a "look out" person, this claim was refuted later by Ms. Neal.

Plaintiffs, Woodrow Wilson, on behalf of his minor children, Amanda Vaughn and Jason Vaughn, and Whitney Dickerson, on behalf of his minor daughter, Kimberly Dickerson, filed suit against the defendant, Wal-Mart, to recover damages for wrongful detention. The trial court awarded the amount of $500.00 in damages to each child, plus court costs. The defendant appealed this judgment.

DECISION The trial court's judgment is reversed.

OPINION Grisbaum, J. Under normal circumstances, private citizens have no authority to detain individuals for petty theft. * * * However, [Louisiana law] gives quasi-police powers to merchants and their agents to protect against shoplifting and gives them immunity from liability for malicious prosecution when the detainer has reasonable cause to believe that a theft of goods has occurred on their premises. [Citation.]

Therefore, the test for false imprisonment claims is a plaintiff must prove either (1) unreasonable force was used, or (2) no reasonable cause existed for the belief that the suspect had committed a theft of goods, or (3) the detention lasted more than 60 minutes, unless it was reasonable under the circumstances that the suspect be detained longer. [Citation.]

First, we determine that Jason Vaughn's claim is without merit. The element of detention is an essential component of the tort of false imprisonment. [Citation.] Here, Jason was not even present at the time of the alleged incident. Jason subsequently was not stopped nor spoken to by Ms. Neal nor any other personnel. There is no evidence to support his claim that he was ever detained. * * *

Next, we also find Amanda Vaughn's claim is without merit. Although Amanda was with Kimberly when they were both approached by Ms. Neal, there is no evidence

Ms. Neal even spoke with Amanda individually, except to tell her and Kimberly to "go to the front of the store and stay there." Ms. Neal stated that the girls were given the option to go to the front of the store and wait for their party or to check their bag at the service desk. Importantly, Amanda testified that, at no time, did Ms. Neal ever ask her any questions. Consequently, we find that appellee, Amanda Vaughn, has also failed to demonstrate she was detained by appellant's employee. Ergo, we conclude Amanda has also failed to show a right to relief.

Finally, we address Kimberly Dickerson's claim that she was wrongfully detained by Ms. Neal. It is undisputed that no unreasonable force was used or that the detention lasted more than 60 minutes. Rather, the evidence establishes Kimberly was only stopped by Ms. Neal and handed her bag to Ms. Neal. Once Ms. Neal verified the purchases with the receipt, the two girls were told to go to the front of the store and to wait for their party.

The test of liability is not based upon the store patron's actual guilt or innocence, but rather on the reasonableness of the store employee's action under all the circumstances. [Citation.] Therefore, we must determine whether, under all of the circumstances, Ms. Neal acted reasonably in detaining Kimberly.

The trial court must decide whether reasonable cause existed to believe that the suspect committed a theft of goods. [Citation.] Reasonable cause is defined as something less than probable cause and requires that the detaining officer have articulable knowledge of particular facts sufficiently reasonable to suspect the detained person of criminal activity. [Citation.]

However, the inquiry does not end with that finding. Our jurisprudence recognizes that

> "[t]he purpose of [Louisiana law] is to provide merchants with authority to detain and question persons suspected of shoplifting without subjecting them to suits by those detained persons on the basis of false imprisonment when the merchant has reasonable cause to believe a theft of goods has occurred."

[Citation.] Furthermore, the statute provides immunity only to those merchants who have conducted a reasonable post detention inquiry of a person. [Citation.]

At this time, it is appropriate to review the factual scenario regarding the action of the merchant in question. The record shows Ms. Neal testified that she saw the two girls standing near a closed register, in a secluded part of the store, where merchandise was held for sale, and saw Kimberly reaching into a bag. This was supported by the testimony of Amanda, who confirmed that Kimberly had her hand in a bag getting out gum when Ms. Neal stopped and approached her.

According to Ms. Neal, this is not an area where Kimberly should be standing. Furthermore, Ms. Neal testified that it is against Wal-Mart policy to allow customers to walk around the store with bags. The policy is to have customers either check the bag at the service desk or exit the store with the bag.

Consequently, Ms. Neal approached the girls and asked Kimberly to see her bag and receipt. Once the purchases were verified, the girls were not accused of stealing. Rather, they were told to "step to the front of the store and wait for your party or go check your bag at the service desk."

* * *

* * * [W]e are compelled here to find the trial court was manifestly erroneous in failing to find that appellant had reasonable cause to detain Kimberly for questioning * * *. However, different from [citation], once Ms. Neal confirmed that a theft had not taken place, the girls had the option of going to the front of the store and waiting for their party or checking the bag at the customer service desk. At no time was Kimberly told that she could not leave the store. Again, we note the detention did not involve unreasonable force given that none of the girls was touched or threatened in anyway. Furthermore, according to all parties, the detention lasted approximately one minute, well below the proscribed period of time. Considering the facts and circumstances presented, we find the actions of appellant's employee were reasonable.

Because we find the actions of appellant's employee were reasonable and, thus, meet the requirements of an authorized detention * * *, appellant is immune from civil liability.

INTERPRETATION Under statutes in many states, a merchant is not liable for false imprisonment for detaining a shoplifting suspect if the merchant has probable or reasonable cause and the detention is conducted in a reasonable manner and for a reasonable length of time.

CRITICAL THINKING QUESTION What public policy supports granting merchants immunity from false imprisonment for detaining innocent persons?

INFLICTION OF EMOTIONAL DISTRESS

Infliction of emotional distress occurs when a person by extreme and outrageous conduct intentionally or recklessly causes severe emotional distress to another, thereby imposing liability upon himself for such emotional distress as well as for any resulting bodily harm. **Recklessness** is conduct that evidences a conscious disregard of or an indifference to the consequences of the act committed. Damages may be recovered for severe emotional distress even in the absence of any physical injury.

This cause of action does not protect a person from abusive language or rudeness but rather from atrocious, intolerable conduct beyond all bounds of decency. Examples of this tort include sexual harassment on the job and outrageous and prolonged bullying tactics employed by creditors or collection agencies attempting to collect a debt, or by insurance adjusters trying to force a settlement of an insurance claim.

HARM TO THE RIGHT OF DIGNITY

The law also protects a person against intentional interference with, or harm to, his right of dignity. This protection covers a person's reputation, privacy, and right to freedom from unjustifiable litigation.

DEFAMATION

As we discussed in Chapter 4, the tort of **defamation** is a false communication that injures a person's reputation by disgracing him and diminishing the respect in which he is held. An example would be the publication of a false statement that a person had committed a crime or had a loathsome disease.

Elements of Defamation The elements of a defamation action are (1) a false and defamatory statement concerning another, (2) an unprivileged publication (communication) to a third party, (3) in some cases, depending on the status of the defendant, some degree of fault on her part in knowing or failing to ascertain the falsity of the statement, and (4) in some cases, proof of special harm caused by the publication. The burden of proof is on the plaintiff to prove the falsity of the defamatory statement.

If the defamatory communication is handwritten, typewritten, printed, pictorial, or in any other medium with similar communicative power, such as a television or radio broadcast, it is designated as **libel**. If it is spoken or oral, it is designated as **slander**. In either case, it must be communicated to a person or persons other than the one who is defamed, a process referred to as its ***publication***. Thus, if Maurice writes a defamatory letter about Pierre's character that he hands or mails to Pierre, this is not a publication because it is intended only for Pierre.

A significant trend affecting business has been the bringing of defamation suits against former employers by discharged employees. It has been reported that such suits comprise approximately one third of all defamation lawsuits. The following case demonstrates the consequences of failing to be careful in discharging an employee.

Practical Advice

Consider whether you should provide employment references for current employees, and if you decide to do so, take care in what you say. See the "Managerial Insight" feature in this chapter.

Frank B. Hall & Co., Inc. v. Buck

Court of Appeals of Texas, Fourteenth District, 1984

678 S.W.2d 612, *cert. denied*, 472 U.S. 1009, 105 S.Ct. 2704, 86 L.Ed.2d 720 (1985)

FACTS On June 1, 1976, Larry W. Buck, an established salesman in the insurance business, began working for Frank B. Hall & Co. In the course of the ensuing months, Buck brought several major accounts to Hall and produced substantial commission income for the firm. In October 1976, Mendel Kaliff, then president of Frank B. Hall & Co. of Texas, informed Buck that his salary and benefits were being reduced because of his failure to generate sufficient income for the firm. On March 31, 1977, Kaliff and Lester Eckert, Hall's office manager, fired Buck. Buck was unable to procure subsequent employment with another insurance firm. He hired an investigator, Lloyd Barber, to discover the true reasons for his dismissal and for his inability to find other employment.

Barber contacted Kaliff, Eckert, and Virginia Hilley, a Hall employee, and told them he was an investigator and was seeking information about Buck's employment with the firm. Barber conducted tape-recorded interviews with the three in September and October of 1977. Kaliff accused Buck of being disruptive, untrustworthy, paranoid, hostile, untruthful, and of padding his expense account. Eckert referred to Buck as "a zero" and a "classical sociopath" who was ruthless, irrational, and disliked by other employees. Hilley stated that Buck could have been charged with theft for certain materials he brought with him from his former employer to Hall. Buck sued Hall for damages for defamation and was awarded over $1.9 million by a jury—$605,000 for actual damages and $1,300,000 for punitive damages. Hall then brought this appeal.

DECISION Judgment for Buck affirmed.

OPINION Junell, J. Any act wherein the defamatory matter is intentionally or negligently communicated to a third person is a publication. In the case of slander, the act is usually the speaking of the words. Restatement (Second) Torts § 577 comment a (1977). There is ample support in the record to show that these individuals intentionally communicated disparaging remarks to a third person. The jury was instructed that "Publication means to communicate defamatory words to some third person in such a way that he understands the words to be defamatory. A statement is not published if it was unauthorized, invited or procured by Buck and if Buck knew in advance the contents of the invited communication." In response to special issues, the jury found that the slanderous statements were made and published to Barber.

* * *

A defamer cannot escape liability by showing that, although he desired to defame the plaintiff, he did not desire to defame him to the person to whom he in fact intentionally published the defamatory communication. The publication is complete although the publisher is mistaken as to the identity of the person to whom the publication is made. Restatement (Second) of Torts § 577 comment l (1977). Likewise, communication to an agent of the person defamed is a publication, unless the communication is invited by the person defamed or his agent. Restatement § 577 comment e (1977). We have already determined that the evidence is sufficient to show that Buck did not know what Kaliff, Eckert or Hilley would say and that he did not procure the defamatory statements to create a lawsuit. Thus, the fact that Barber may have been acting at Buck's request is not fatal to Buck's cause of action. There is absolutely no proof that Barber induced Kaliff, Eckert or Hilley to make any of the defamatory comments.

* * *

When an ambiguity exists, a fact issue is presented. The court, by submission of proper fact issues, should let the jury render its verdict on whether the statements were fairly susceptible to the construction placed thereon by the plaintiff. [Citation.] Here, the jury found (1) Eckert made a statement calculated to convey that Buck had been terminated because of serious misconduct; (2) the statement was slanderous or libelous; (3) the statement was made with malice; (4) the statement was published; and (5) damage directly resulted from the statement. The jury also found the statements were not substantially true. The jury thus determined that these statements, which were capable of a defamatory meaning, were understood as such by Barber.

* * *

We hold that the evidence supports the award of actual damages and the amount awarded is not manifestly unjust. Furthermore, in responding to the issue on exemplary damages, the jury was instructed that exemplary damages must be based on a finding that Hall "acted with ill will, bad intent, malice or gross disregard to the rights of Buck." Although there is no fixed ratio between exemplary and actual damages, exemplary damages must be reasonably apportioned to the actual damages sustained. [Citation.] Because of the actual damages [$605,000] and the abundant evidence of malice, we hold that the award of punitive damages [$1,300,000] was not unreasonable. * * *

INTERPRETATION The key elements of defamation are that the statements made are false, injure the plaintiff's reputation, and are published.

ETHICAL QUESTION Did Hall's employees act ethically? Did Buck act ethically in hiring an investigator to obtain the information? Explain.

CRITICAL THINKING QUESTION How should a company respond to inquiries for information about former or current employees? Explain.

Defenses to Defamation Privilege is an immunity from tort liability granted when the defendant's conduct furthers a societal interest of greater importance than the injury inflicted upon the plaintiff. Three kinds of privileges apply to defamation: absolute, conditional, and constitutional.

Absolute privilege, which protects the defendant regardless of his motive or intent, has been confined to those few situations where public policy clearly favors complete freedom of speech. Such privilege includes (1) statements made by participants in a judicial proceeding regarding that proceeding; (2) statements made by members of Congress on the floor of Congress; (3) statements made by certain executive branch officers while performing their governmental duties; and (4) statements regarding a third party made between spouses when they are alone.

Qualified or ***conditional privilege*** depends on proper use of the privilege. A person has a conditional privilege to publish defamatory matter to protect her own legitimate interests or, in some cases, the interests of another. Conditional privilege also extends to many communications in which the publisher and the recipient have a common interest, such as letters of reference. Conditional privilege, however, is forfeited by a publisher who acts in an excessive manner, without probable cause, or for an improper purpose.

The First Amendment to the U.S. Constitution guarantees freedom of speech and freedom of the press. The U.S. Supreme Court has applied these rights to the law of defamation by extending a form of ***constitutional privilege*** to defamatory and false statements about public officials or public figures so long as it is done without malice. For these purposes, *malice* is not ill will but clear and convincing proof of the publisher's knowledge of falsity or reckless disregard of the truth. Thus, under constitutional privilege, the public official or public figure must prove that the defendant published the defamatory and false

MANAGERIAL insight

Employee References and Liability for Defamation

If you own or manage a business, you can expect employees to leave for a variety of reasons. When your present or former employees apply for work elsewhere, their potential new employers may well call you to verify their employment history and ask your opinion of them as employees. Should you give that information?

In the 1980s, many employers stopped giving meaningful references for former employees. Some employers would verify only employment dates and job titles of former employees. Others would give no information at all. The reason? Fear of liability for defamation and of incurring large legal expenses to defend a lawsuit.

Are those fears justified? Does the benefit of minimizing risk outweigh the cost of shutting down a legitimate and valuable information system?

Two researchers surveyed all published employee defamation cases in state and federal trial and appeals courts for 1965–69 and 1985–89, taking special note of cases involving employment references. They concluded that employers faced less risk in the 1980s. Although the number of lawsuits went up, plaintiffs won less often in the 1980s than in the 1960s, and damage awards decreased slightly. The researchers suggest that employers who stopped giving references may have overreacted to sensational newspaper accounts of large damage awards.

Points to Consider

- At least half of the states have enacted statutes that provide varying degrees of protection against liability for defamation to companies that give job references for current or former employees.
- The law actually offers employers more protection since a key Supreme Court decision in 1974. Before that decision, an employer who published an employee-related statement that turned out to be untrue was strictly liable. Now the employer is liable for a false statement only if she was negligent in attempting to establish its truth.
- Employment references enjoy qualified privilege, unless the employer communicates the statements to people with no need to know their contents or publishes them out of spite.
- Employment references are valuable. Employers who expect to get useful information about job applicants should also be willing to give it.

You can reduce the risk of liability when giving employment references if you. . . .

- Endeavor to ensure that all statements you publish about an employee are true. Your effort can be used as a defense against negligence.
- Make sure you publish statements only to people with a legitimate need to know (i.e., potential employers).
- Regulate the giving of references in your company. Make sure people who work for you understand who may give references and who may not. And make sure they know that no one is ever to publish statements maliciously.
- Ask your existing employees to give you written consent to provide references for them.

Source: Ramona L. Paetzold and Steven L. Wilborn, "Employer (Ir)rationality and the Demise of Employment References," *American Business Law Journal*, May 1992, 123–42.

comment with knowledge or in reckless disregard of the comment's falsity and its defamatory character.

In a defamation suit brought by a private person (one who is neither a public official nor a public figure) against a member of the news media, the plaintiff must prove that the defendant published the defamatory and false comment with malice *or* negligence. By comparison, in a suit brought by a private person against a defendant who is *not* a member of the news media, the question whether the plaintiff must prove anything beyond the fact that a defamatory statement has been made is currently unresolved.

Congress enacted legislation granting immunity to Internet service providers (ISPs) from liability for defamation when publishing information originating from a third party. See Chapter 48.

INVASION OF PRIVACY

The invasion of a person's right to privacy actually consists of four distinct torts: (1) appropriation of a person's name or likeness; (2) unreasonable intrusion on the seclusion of another; (3) unreasonable public disclosure of private facts; or (4) unreasonable publicity that places another in a false light in the public eye. See Chapter 48 for a discussion of the impact of the Internet on these torts.

It is entirely possible and not uncommon for a person's right of privacy to be invaded in a manner entailing two or more of these related torts. For example, Bart forces his way into Cindy's hospital room, takes a photograph of Cindy, and publishes it to promote his cure for Cindy's illness along with false statements about Cindy that would be highly objectionable to a reasonable person. Cindy would be entitled to recover on any or all of the four torts comprising invasion of privacy.

Appropriation **Appropriation** is the unauthorized use of another person's name or likeness for one's own benefit, as, for example, in promoting or advertising a product or service. The tort of appropriation, which seeks to protect the individual's right to the exclusive use of his identity, is also known as the "right of publicity." In the example above, Bart's use of Cindy's photograph to promote Bart's business constitutes the tort of appropriation. The following case involving Vanna White is also an example of appropriation.

White v. Samsung Electronics

United States Court of Appeals, Ninth Circuit, 1992

971 F.2d 1395, *cert. denied*, 508 U.S. 951, 113 S.Ct. 2443, 124 L.Ed.2d 660 (1993)

FACTS Plaintiff, Vanna White, is the hostess of *Wheel of Fortune* **(http://www.spe.sony.com/tv/shows/wheel)**, one of the most popular game shows in television history. Samsung Electronics **(http://samsungelectronics.com)** and David Deutsch Associates ran an advertisement for videocassette recorders that depicted a robot dressed in a wig, gown, and jewelry chosen to resemble White's hair and dress. The robot was posed in a stance, for which White is famous, next to a game board, which is instantly recognizable as the *Wheel of Fortune* game show set. The caption of the ad read: "Longest-running game show. 2012 a.d." Defendants referred to the ad as the "Vanna White" ad. White neither consented to the ads, nor was she paid for them. White sued Samsung and Deutsch under the California common law right of publicity. The district court granted summary judgment against White on this claim.

DECISION Judgment reversed.

OPINION Goodwin, J. White argues that the district court erred in granting summary judgment to defendants on White's common law right of publicity claim. In *Eastwood v. Superior Court*, [citation], the California court of appeal stated that the common law right of publicity cause of action "may be pleaded by alleging (1) the defendant's use of the plaintiff's identity; (2) the appropriation of plaintiff's name or likeness to defendant's advantage, commercially or otherwise; (3) lack of consent, and (4) resulting injury." [Citation.] The district court dismissed White's claim for failure to satisfy *Eastwood's* second prong, reasoning that defendants had not appropriated White's "name or likeness" with their robot ad. We agree that the robot ad did not make use of White's name or likeness. However, the common law right of publicity is not so confined.

The *Eastwood* court did not hold that the right of publicity cause of action could be pleaded only by alleging an appropriation of name or likeness. *Eastwood* involved an unauthorized use of photographs of Clint Eastwood and of his name. Accordingly, the *Eastwood* court had no occasion to consider the extent beyond the use of name or likeness to which the right of publicity reaches. That court held only that the right of publicity cause of action "may be" pleaded by alleging, *inter alia*, appropriation of name or likeness, not that the action may be pleaded only in those terms.

The "name or likeness" formulation referred to in *Eastwood* originated not as an element of the right of publicity cause of action, but as a description of the types of cases in which the cause of action had been recognized. The source of this formulation is Prosser, *Privacy*, 48 Cal.L.Rev. 383, 401–07 (1960), one of the earliest and most enduring articulations of the common law right of publicity cause of action. In looking at the case law to that point, Prosser recognized that right of publicity cases involved one of two basic factual scenarios: name appropriation, and picture or other likeness appropriation. [Citation.]

Even though Prosser focused on appropriations of name or likeness in discussing the right of publicity, he noted that "[i]t is not impossible that there might be appropriation of the plaintiff's identity, as by impersonation, without use of either his name of his likeness, and that this would be an invasion of his right of privacy." [Citation.] At the time Prosser wrote, he noted however, that "[n]o such case appears to have arisen." [Citation.]

Since Prosser's early formulation, the case law has borne out his insight that the right of publicity is not limited to the appropriation of name or likeness. In *Motschenbacher v. R.J. Reynolds Tobacco Co.*, [citation], the defendant had used a photograph of the plaintiff's race car in a television commercial. Although the plaintiff appeared driving the car in the photograph, his features were not visible. Even though the defendant had not appropriated the plaintiff's name or likeness, this court held that plaintiff's California right of publicity claim should reach the jury.

In *Midler*, this court held that, even though the defendants had not used Midler's name or likeness, Midler had stated a claim for violation of her California common law right of publicity because "the defendants * * * for their own profit in selling their product did appropriate part of her identity" by using a Midler sound-alike. [Citation.]

In *Carson v. Here's Johnny Portable Toilets, Inc.*, [citation], the defendant had marketed portable toilets under the brand name "Here's Johnny"—Johnny Carson's signature "Tonight Show" introduction—without Carson's permission. The district court had dismissed Carson's Michigan common law right of publicity claim because the defendants had not used Carson's "name or likeness."

[Citation.] In reversing the district court, the sixth circuit found "the district court's conception of the right of publicity * * * too narrow" and held that the right was implicated because the defendant had appropriated Carson's identity by using, *inter alia*, the phrase "Here's Johnny." [Citation.]

These cases teach not only that the common law right of publicity reaches means of appropriation other than name or likeness, but that the specific means of appropriation are relevant only for determining whether the defendant has in fact appropriated the plaintiff's identity. The right of publicity does not require that appropriations of identity be accomplished through particular means to be actionable. It is noteworthy that the Midler and Carson defendants not only avoided using the plaintiff's name or likeness, but they also avoided appropriating the celebrity's voice, signature, and photograph. The photograph in Motschenbacher did include the plaintiff, but because the plaintiff was not visible the driver could have been an actor or dummy and the analysis in the case would have been the same.

Although the defendants in these cases avoided the most obvious means of appropriating the plaintiffs' identities, each of their actions directly implicated the commercial interests which the right of publicity is designed to protect. As the Carson court explained:

> [t]he right of publicity has developed to protect the commercial interest of celebrities in their identities. The theory of the right is that a celebrity's identity can be valuable in the promotion of products, and the celebrity has an interest that may be protected from the unauthorized commercial exploitation of that identity. * * * If the celebrity's identity is commercially exploited, there has been an invasion of his right whether or not his "name or likeness" is used.

[Citation.] It is not important how the defendant has appropriated the plaintiff's identity, but whether the defendant has done so. *Motschenbacher*, *Midler*, and *Carson* teach the impossibility of treating the right of publicity as guarding only against a laundry list of specific means of appropriating identity. A rule which says that the right of publicity can be infringed only through the use of nine different methods of appropriating identity merely challenges the clever advertising strategist to come up with the tenth.

Indeed, if we treated the means of appropriation as dispositive in our analysis of the right of publicity, we would not only weaken the right but effectively eviscerate it. The right would fail to protect those plaintiffs most in need of its protection. Advertisers use celebrities to promote their products. The more popular the celebrity, the greater the number of people who recognize her, and the greater the visibility for the product. The identities of the most popular celebrities are not only the most attractive for advertisers, but also the easiest to evoke without resorting to obvious means such as name, likeness, or voice.

Consider a hypothetical advertisement which depicts a mechanical robot with male features, an African-American complexion, and a bald head. The robot is wearing black hightop Air Jordan basketball sneakers, and a red basketball uniform with black trim, baggy shorts, and the number 23 (though not revealing "Bulls" or "Jordan" lettering). The ad depicts the robot dunking a basketball one-handed, stiff-armed, legs extended like open scissors, and tongue hanging out. Now envision that this ad is run on television during professional basketball games. Considered individually, the robot's physical attributes, its dress, and its stance tells us little. Taken together, they lead to the only conclusion that any sports viewer who has registered a discernible pulse in the past five years would reach: the ad is about Michael Jordan.

Viewed separately, the individual aspects of the advertisement in the present case say little. Viewed together, they leave little doubt about the celebrity the ad is meant to depict. The female shaped robot is wearing a long gown, blond wig, and large jewelry. Vanna White dresses exactly like this at times, but so do many other women. The robot is in the process of turning a block letter on a game-board. Vanna White dresses like this while turning letters on a game-board but perhaps similarly attired Scrabble-playing women do this as well. The robot is standing on what looks to be the *Wheel of Fortune* game show set. Vanna White dresses like this, turns letters, and does this on the *Wheel of Fortune* game show. She is the only one. Indeed, defendants themselves referred to their ad as the "Vanna White" ad. We are not surprised.

Television and other media create marketable celebrity identity value. Considerable energy and ingenuity are expended by those who have achieved celebrity value to exploit it for profit. The law protects the celebrity's sole right to exploit this value whether the celebrity has achieved her fame out of rare ability, dumb luck, or a combination thereof. We decline Samsung and Deutsch's invitation to permit the evisceration of the common law right of publicity through means as facile as those in this case. Because White has alleged facts showing that Samsung and Deutsch had appropriated her identity, the district court erred by rejecting, on summary judgment, White's common law right of publicity claim.

INTERPRETATION The tort of appropriation protects a person's exclusive right to exploit the value of her identity.

CRITICAL THINKING QUESTION What are the interests protected by this tort?

Practical Advice

When using another person's identity for your own, be sure to obtain that person's written consent.

Intrusion **Intrusion** is the unreasonable and highly offensive interference with the solitude or seclusion of another. Such unreasonable interference includes improper entry into another's dwelling, unauthorized eavesdropping on another's private conversations, and unauthorized examination of another's private papers and records. The intrusion must be offensive or objectionable to a reasonable person and must involve private matters. Thus, there is no liability if the defendant examines public records or observes the plaintiff in a public place. This form of invasion of privacy is committed once the intrusion occurs—publicity is not required.

Public Disclosure of Private Facts Under the tort of **public disclosure of private facts**, liability is imposed for publicity given to private information about another, if the matter made public would be highly offensive and objectionable to a reasonable person. Like intrusion, this tort applies only to private, not public, information about an individual; unlike intrusion, it requires publicity. Under the Restatement, the publicity required differs in degree from "publication" as used in the law of defamation. This tort requires that private facts be communicated to the public at large or that they become public knowledge, whereas publication of a defamatory statement need be made only to a single third party. Thus Kathy, a creditor of Gary, will not invade Gary's privacy by writing a letter to Gary's employer informing the employer of Gary's failure to pay the debt, but Kathy would be liable if she posted in the window of her store a statement that Gary will not pay a debt owed to her. Some courts, however, have allowed recovery where the disclosure was made to only one person. Also, unlike defamation, this tort applies to truthful private information if the matter published would be offensive and objectionable to a reasonable person of ordinary sensibilities.

False Light The tort of **false light** imposes liability for highly offensive publicity placing another in a false light if the defendant knew that the matter publicized was false or acted in reckless disregard of the truth. For example, Edgar includes Jason's name and photograph in a public "rogues' gallery" of convicted criminals. Because Jason has never been convicted of any crime, Edgar is liable to Jason for placing him in a false light.

As with defamation, the matter must be untrue; unlike defamation, it must be "publicized," not merely "published." Although the matter must be objectionable to a reasonable person, it need not be defamatory. In many instances, the same facts will give rise to actions both for defamation and for false light.

Defenses The defenses of absolute, conditional, and constitutional privilege apply to publication of any matter that is an invasion of privacy to the same extent that such defenses apply to defamation.

MISUSE OF LEGAL PROCEDURE

Three torts comprise the **misuse of legal procedure**: malicious prosecution, wrongful civil proceedings, and abuse of process. Each protects an individual from being subjected to unjustifiable litigation. ***Malicious prosecution*** and ***wrongful civil proceedings*** impose liability for damages caused by improperly brought proceedings, including harm to reputation, credit, or standing; emotional distress; and the expenses incurred in defending against the wrongfully brought lawsuit. ***Abuse of process*** consists of using a legal proceeding (criminal or civil) to accomplish a purpose for which the proceeding is not designed. This misuse of procedure applies even when there is probable cause or when the plaintiff or prosecution succeeds in the litigation.

HARM TO PROPERTY

The law also provides protection against invasions of a person's interests in property. Intentional harm to property includes the torts of (1) trespass to real property, (2) nuisance, (3) trespass to personal property, and (4) conversion.

CONCEPT REVIEW

Privacy

	Appropriation	Intrusion	Public Disclosure	False Light
Publicity	Yes	No	Yes	Yes
Private Facts	No	Yes	Yes	No
Offensiveness	No	Yes	Yes	Yes
Falsity	No	No	No	Yes

REAL PROPERTY

Real property is land and anything attached to it, such as buildings, trees, and minerals. The law protects the possessor's rights to the exclusive use and quiet enjoyment of the land. Accordingly, damages for harm to land include compensation for the resulting diminution in the value of the land, the loss of use of the land, and the discomfort caused to the possessor of the land.

Trespass A person is liable for **trespass to real property** if he intentionally (1) enters or remains on land in the possession of another, (2) causes a thing or a third person to so enter or remain, or (3) fails to remove from the land a thing that he is under a duty to remove. Liability exists even though no actual damage is done to the land.

It is no defense that the intruder acted under the mistaken belief of law or fact that he was not trespassing. If the intruder intended to be on the particular property, his reasonable belief that he owned the land or had permission to enter on it is irrelevant. However, an intruder is not liable if his presence on the land of another is not caused by his own actions. For example, if Shirley is thrown onto Roy's land by Jimmy, Shirley is not liable to Roy for trespass, although Jimmy is.

A trespass may be committed on, beneath, or above the surface of the land, although the law regards the upper air, above a prescribed minimum altitude for flight, as a public highway. No aerial trespass occurs unless the aircraft enters into the lower reaches of the airspace and substantially interferes with the landowner's use and enjoyment.

Nuisance A **nuisance** is a nontrespassory invasion of another's interest in the private use and enjoyment of land. In contrast to trespass, nuisance does not require interference with another's right to exclusive possession of land but imposes liability for significant and unreasonable harm to another's use or enjoyment of land. Examples of nuisances include the emission of unpleasant odors, smoke, dust, or gas, as well as the pollution of a stream, pond, or underground water supply.

> **Practical Advice**
>
> In using, manufacturing, and disposing of dangerous, noxious, or toxic materials, take care not to create a nuisance.

PERSONAL PROPERTY

Personal property is any type of property other than an interest in land. The law protects a number of interests in the possession of personal property, including an interest in the property's physical condition and usability, an interest in the retention of possession, and an interest in the property's availability for future use.

Trespass **Trespass to personal property** consists of the intentional dispossession or unauthorized use of the personal property of another. Although the interference with the right to exclusive use and possession may be direct or indirect, liability is limited to instances in which the trespasser (1) dispossesses the other of the property; (2) substantially impairs the condition, quality, or value of the property; or (3) deprives the possessor of use of the property for a substantial time. For example, Albert parks his car in front of his house. Later, Ronald pushes Albert's car around the corner. Albert subsequently looks for his car but cannot find it for several hours. Ronald is liable to Albert for trespass.

Conversion **Conversion** is an intentional exercise of dominion or control over another's personal property that so seriously interferes with the other's right of control as justly to require the payment of full value for the property. Thus, all conversions are trespasses, but not all trespasses are conversions. Conversion may consist of the intentional destruction of the personal property or the use of the property in an unauthorized manner. For example, Barbara entrusts an automobile to Ken, a dealer, for sale. After he drives the car 8,000 miles on his own business, Ken is liable to Barbara for conversion. On the other hand, in the example in which Ronald pushed Albert's car around the corner, Ronald would not be liable to Albert for conversion.

HARM TO ECONOMIC INTERESTS

Economic interests comprise a fourth set of interests the law protects against intentional interference. Economic or pecuniary interests include a person's existing and prospective contractual relations, a person's business reputation, a person's name and likeness (previously discussed under appropriation), and a person's freedom from deception. In this section, we will discuss business torts—those torts that protect a person's economic interests.

INTERFERENCE WITH CONTRACTUAL RELATIONS

Interference with contractual relations involves interfering intentionally and improperly with the performance of a contract by inducing one of the parties not to perform it. (Contracts are discussed extensively in Part Three of this text.) The injured party may recover the economic loss resulting from the breach of the contract. The law imposes similar liability for intentional and improper interference with another's prospective contractual relation, such as a lease renewal or financing for construction.

In either case, the rule requires that a person act with the purpose or motive of interfering with another's contract or with the knowledge that such interference is substantially certain to occur as a natural consequence of her actions. The interference may be by prevention through the use of physical force or by threats. Frequently, the interference is accomplished by inducement, such as the offer of a better contract. For instance, Calvin may offer Becky, an employee of Fran under a contract that has two years left, a yearly salary of $5,000 per year more than the contractual arrangement between Becky and Fran. If Calvin is aware of the contract between Becky and Fran and of the fact that his offer to Becky will interfere with that contract, then Calvin is liable to Fran for intentional interference with contractual relations.

Practical Advice

Recognize that inducing another person's employees to breach a valid agreement not to compete or not to disclose confidential information may be improper interference with contractual relations.

Texaco, Inc. v. Pennzoil, Co.

Court of Appeals of Texas, First District, 1987
729 S.W.2s 768, *cert denied,* 485 U.S. 994, 108 S.Ct. 1305,99 L.Ed.2d 686 (1988)

FACTS Pennzoil **(http://www.pennzoil.com)** negotiated with Gordon Getty and the J. Paul Getty Museum **(http://www.getty.edu/museum)** over the purchase by Pennzoil of all the Getty Oil stock held by each. Gordon Getty, who was also a director of Getty Oil, held about 40.2 percent of the outstanding shares of Getty Oil. The Museum held 11.8 percent. On January 2, a Memorandum of Agreement was drafted, setting forth the terms reached by Pennzoil, Gordon Getty, and the Museum. After increasing the offering price to $110 per share plus a $5 "stub" or bonus, the board of directors of Getty Oil voted on January 3 to accept the Pennzoil deal. Accordingly, on January 4 both Getty Oil and Pennzoil issued press releases, announcing an agreement in principle on the terms of the Memorandum of Agreement but at the higher price.

Having learned of the impending sale of Getty Oil stock to Pennzoil, Texaco **(http://www.texaco.com)** hurriedly called several in-house meetings, and hired an investment banker as well, to determine a feasible price range for acquiring Getty Oil. On January 5, Texaco decided on $125 per share and authorized its officers to take any steps necessary to conclude a deal. Texaco met first with a lawyer for the Museum, then with Gordon Getty. Texaco stressed to Getty that if he hesitated in selling his shares, he might be "locked out" in a minority position. On January 6, the Getty Oil board of directors voted to withdraw from the Pennzoil deal and unanimously voted to accept the $125-per-share Texaco offer. Pennzoil sued and won an award of $7.53 billion in compensatory damages and $3 billion in punitive damages based on tortious interference with a contract. Texaco appealed.

DECISION Judgment of trial court affirmed.

OPINION Warren, J. New York law requires knowledge by a defendant of the existence of contractual rights as an element of the tort of inducing a breach of that contract. [Citation.] However, the defendant need not have full knowledge of all the detailed terms of the contract. [Citations.]

* * *

The element of knowledge by the defendant is a question of fact, and proof may be predicated on circumstantial evidence. [Citation.] Since there was no direct evidence of Texaco's knowledge of a contract in this case, the question is whether there was legally and factually sufficient circumstantial evidence from which the trier of fact reasonably could have inferred knowledge.

* * *

We find that an inference could arise that Texaco had some knowledge of Pennzoil's agreement with the Getty entities, given the evidence of Texaco's detailed studies of the Pennzoil plan, its knowledge that some members of the Getty board were not happy with Pennzoil's price, and its subsequent formulation of strategy to "stop the [Pennzoil] train" * * *.

* * *

A necessary element of the plaintiff's cause of action is a showing that the defendant took an active part in persuading a party to a contract to breach it. [Citation.] Merely entering into a contract with a party with the knowledge of that party's contractual obligations to someone else is not the same as inducing a breach. [Citation.] It is necessary that there be some act of interference or of persuading a party to breach, for example by offering better terms or other incentives, for tort liability to arise. [Citations.] The issue of whether a defendant affirmatively took steps to induce the breach of an existing contract is a question of fact for the jury. [Citation.]

* * *

The evidence discussed above on Texaco's calculated formulation and implementation of its ideal strategy to acquire Getty is also inconsistent with its contention that it was merely the passive target of Getty's aggressive solicitation campaign and did nothing more than to accept terms that Getty Oil and the Museum had proposed. The evidence showed that Texaco knew it had to act quickly, and that it had "24 hours" to "stop the train." Texaco's strategy was to approach the Museum first, through its "key person" Lipton, to obtain the Museum's shares, and then to "talk to Gordon." It knew that the Trust instrument permitted Gordon Getty to sell the Trust shares only to avoid a loss, and it knew of the trustee's fear of being left in a powerless minority ownership position at Getty Oil. Texaco notes indicated a deliberate strategy to "create concern that he will take a loss;" "if there's a tender offer and Gordon doesn't tender, then he could wind up with paper"; and "pressure." This evidence contradicts the contention that Texaco passively accepted a deal proposed by the other parties.

INTERPRETATION The tort of interference with contractual relations protects a party to a contract from a third party who intentionally and improperly induces the other contracting party not to perform the contract.

ETHICAL QUESTION Did Getty or Texaco act unethically? Explain.

CRITICAL THINKING QUESTION Does the protection afforded by this tort conflict with society's interest in free competition? Explain.

Ethical Dilemma

What May One Do to Attract Clients from a Previous Employer?

FACTS Carl Adle and Louise Bart formed a law firm as partners, and Anne Lily, Marvin Thomas, and Tim Jones joined the newly formed firm of Adle & Bart as associates (nonpartner employees). After about five years, Lily, Thomas, and Jones became disenchanted with the law firm and decided to form their own, to be called Lily, Thomas & Jones.

Lily and Thomas suggested to Jones that they contact approximately five hundred of Adle & Bart's current clients. Lily and Thomas had prepared a model letter to inform clients about the new law firm (Lily, Thomas & Jones) and to encourage them to leave Adle & Bart and to become clients of the new firm. The letter also indicated that Lily, Thomas & Jones would offer legal services far better than those of Adle & Bart: billing rates would be more reasonable, service more prompt, and legal representation more effective and successful. The reference to success was aimed, in part, at three large clients who recently lost lawsuits under Adle & Bart representation. Although the losses had not resulted from malpractice or mishandling by Adle & Bart, Lily and Thomas knew that significant amounts of money had been at issue and that the clients were sensitive about the results of the lengthy litigation.

The letter included two postage-paid form letters for the prospective client to sign and mail. One form letter was addressed to Adle & Bart, informing them of the client's desire to discontinue the client-attorney relationship and requesting the firm to forward all files to Lily, Thomas & Jones. The other form letter, addressed to Lily, Thomas & Jones, requested representation.

Jones is reluctant about the proposed mailing. Lily and Thomas, in turn, argue that their new firm is not doing as well as they expected. They essentially give Jones an ultimatum: join in the letter or leave the firm. Jones, who has thoroughly alienated Adle & Bart, does not believe he has any immediate alternative job opportunities.

SOCIAL, POLICY, AND ETHICAL CONSIDERATIONS

1. Should Jones agree to the proposed mailing? Is it ethical for those forming the new firm to use a client list of their former employer when seeking clients?
2. What practical steps could Jones take to assist him in his decision?
3. What are the competing social interests at stake in this controversy?
4. How would your answers differ, if at all, if the firms were accounting firms rather than law firms?
5. In what manner, if at all, should the law protect existing businesses from competition? Under what circumstances might competition become unfair, and how should laws be tailored to deter unfair practices?
6. Should Jones be concerned about the comparisons the letter makes between the new firm and Adle & Bart?

CONCEPT REVIEW

Intentional Torts

Interest Protected	Tort
Person	
Freedom from contact	Battery
Freedom from apprehension	Assault
Freedom of movement	False imprisonment
Freedom from distress	Infliction of emotional distress
Dignity	
Reputation	Defamation
Privacy	Appropriation
	Intrusion
	Public disclosure of private facts
	False light
Freedom from wrongful legal actions	Misuse of legal procedure
Property	
Real	Trespass
	Nuisance
Personal	Trespass
	Conversion
Economic	
Contracts	Interference with contractual rights
Goodwill	Disparagement
Freedom from deception	Fraudulent misrepresentation

DISPARAGEMENT

The tort of **disparagement** or injurious falsehood imposes liability upon one who publishes a false statement that results in harm to another's monetary interests if the publisher knows that the statement is false or acts in reckless disregard of its truth or falsity. This tort most commonly involves intentionally false statements that cast doubt on another's right of ownership in or on the quality of another's property or products. Thus Simon, while contemplating the purchase of a stock of merchandise that belongs to Marie, reads an advertisement in a newspaper in which Ernst falsely asserts he owns the merchandise. Ernst has disparaged Marie's property in the goods.

Absolute, conditional, and constitutional privileges apply to the same extent to the tort of disparagement as they do to defamation. In addition, a competitor has conditional privilege to compare her products favorably with those of a rival, even though she does not believe that her products are superior. No privilege applies, however, if the comparison contains false assertions of specific unfavorable facts about the competitor's property.

> **Practical Advice**
>
> When commenting on the products or services offered by a competitor, take care not to make any false statements.

The pecuniary loss an injured person may recover is that which directly and immediately results from impairment of the marketability of the property disparaged. Damages may also be recovered for expenses necessary to counteract the false publication, including litigation expenses, the cost of notifying customers, and the cost of publishing denials.

FRAUDULENT MISREPRESENTATION

Fraudulent misrepresentation imposes liability for the monetary loss caused by a justifiable reliance on a misrepresentation of fact intentionally made for the purpose of inducing the relying party to act. For example, Smith misrepresents to Jones that a tract of land in Texas is located in an area where oil drilling has recently commenced. Smith makes this statement knowing it is not true. In reliance upon the statement, Jones purchases the land from Smith. Smith is liable to Jones for intentional or fraudulent misrepresentation. Although fraudulent misrepresentation is a tort action, it is closely connected with contractual negotiations; we will discuss its relationship to contracts in Chapter 11.

> **Practical Advice**
>
> When describing your products or services, take care not to make any false statements.

CHAPTER SUMMARY

Harm to the Person

Battery intentional infliction of harmful or offensive bodily contact

Assault intentional infliction of apprehension of immediate bodily harm or offensive contact

False Imprisonment intentional confining of a person against her will

Infliction of Emotional Distress extreme and outrageous conduct intentionally or recklessly causing severe emotional distress

Harm to the Right of Dignity

Defamation false communication that injures a person's reputation
- *Libel* written or electronically transmitted defamation
- *Slander* spoken defamation

Invasion of Privacy
- *Appropriation* unauthorized use of a person's identity
- *Intrusion* unreasonable and offensive interference with the seclusion of another
- *Public Disclosure of Private Facts* offensive publicity of private information
- *False Light* offensive and false publicity about another

Misuse of Legal Procedure torts of malicious prosecution, wrongful civil proceeding, and abuse of process that protect an individual from unjustifiable litigation

Harm to Property

Real Property land and anything attached to it
- *Trespass* wrongfully entering on land of another
- *Nuisance* a nontrespassory interference with another's use and enjoyment of land

Personal Property any property other than land
- *Trespass* an intentional taking or use of another's personal property
- *Conversion* intentional exercise of control over another's personal property

Harm to Economic Interests

Interference with Contractual Relations intentionally causing one of the parties to a contract not to perform

Disparagement publication of false statements about another's property or products

Fraudulent Misrepresentation a false statement, made with knowledge of its falsity, intended to induce another to act

QUESTIONS

1. The Penguin intentionally hits Batman with his umbrella. Batman, stunned by the blow, falls backward, knocking Robin down. Robin's leg is broken in the fall, and he cries out, "Holy broken bat bones! My leg is broken." Who, if anyone, has liability to Robin? Why?

2. CEO was convinced by his employee, M. Ploy, that a co-worker, A. Cused, had been stealing money from the company. At lunch that day in the company cafeteria, CEO discharged Cused from her employment, accused her of stealing from the company, searched through her purse over her objections, and finally forcibly escorted her to his office to await the arrival of the police, whom he had his secretary summon. Cused is indicted for embezzlement but subsequently is acquitted upon establishing her innocence. What rights, if any, does Cused have against CEO?

3. Ralph kisses Edith while she is asleep but does not waken or harm her. Edith sues Ralph for battery. Has a battery been committed?

4. Claude, a creditor seeking to collect a debt, calls on Dianne and demands payment in a rude and insolent manner. When Dianne says that she cannot pay, Claude calls Dianne a deadbeat and says that he will never trust Dianne again. Is Claude liable to Dianne? If so, for what tort?

5. Lana, a ten-year-old child, is run over by a car negligently driven by Mitchell. Lana, at the time of the accident, was acting reasonably and without negligence. Clark, a newspaper reporter, photographs Lana while she is lying in the street in great pain. Two years later, Perry, the publisher of a newspaper, prints Clark's picture of Lana in his newspaper as a lead to an article concerning the negligence of children. The caption under the picture reads: "They ask to be killed." Lana, who has recovered from the accident, brings suit against Clark and Perry. What is the result?

6. The *Saturday Evening Post* (http://www.satevepost.org) featured an article entitled "The Story of a College Football Fix," characterized in the subtitle as "A Shocking Report of How Wally Butts and Bear Bryant Rigged a Game Last Fall." Butts was athletic director of the University of Georgia (http://www.uga.edu), and Bryant was head coach of the University of Alabama (http://www.ua.edu). The article was based on a claim by one George Burnett that he had accidentally overheard a long-distance telephone conversation between Butts and Bryant in the course of which Butts divulged information on plays Georgia would use in the upcoming game against Alabama. The writer assigned to the story by the *Post* was not a football expert, did not interview either Butts or Bryant, and did not personally see the notes Burnett had made of the telephone conversation. Butts admitted that he had a long-distance telephone conversation with Bryant but denied that any advance information on prospective football plays was given. Has Butts been defamed by the *Post*?

7. A patient confined in a hospital, Joan, has a rare disease that is of great interest to the public. Carol, a television reporter, requests Joan to consent to an interview. Joan refuses, but Carol, nonetheless, enters Joan's room over her objection and photographs her. Joan brings a suit against Carol. Is Carol liable? If so, for what tort?

8. Owner has a place on his land where he piles trash. The pile has been there for three months. John, a neighbor of Owner, without Owner's consent or knowledge, throws trash onto the trashpile. Owner learns that John has done this and sues him. What tort, if any, has John committed?

9. Chris leaves her car parked in front of a store. There are no signs that say Chris cannot park there. The store owner, however, needs the car moved to enable a delivery truck to unload. He releases the brake and pushes Chris's car three or four feet, doing no harm to the car. Chris returns and sees that her car has been moved and is very angry. She threatens to sue the store owner for trespass to her personal property. Can she recover?

10. Carr borrowed John's brand-new Ford for the purpose of going to the store. He told John he would be right back. Carr then decided, however, to go to the beach while he had the car. Can John recover from Carr the value of the automobile? If so, for what tort?

CASE PROBLEMS

11. Marcia Samms, a respectable married woman, claimed that David Eccles had repeatedly and persistently called her at various hours, including late at night, from May to December, soliciting her to have illicit sexual relations with him. She also claimed that on one occasion Eccles came over to her residence to again solicit sex and indecently exposed himself to her. Mrs. Samms had never encouraged Eccles but had continuously repulsed his "insulting, indecent, and obscene" proposals. She brought suit against Eccles, claiming she suffered great anxiety and fear for her personal safety and severe emotional distress, demanding actual and punitive damages. Can she recover? If so, for what tort?

12. National Bond and Investment Company sent two of its employees to repossess Whithorn's car after he failed to complete the payments. The two repossessors located Whithorn while he was driving his car. They followed him and hailed him down in order to make the repossession. Whithorn refused to abandon his car and demanded evidence of their authority. The two repossessors became impatient and called a wrecker. They ordered the driver of the wrecker to hook Whithorn's car and move it down the street while Whithorn was still inside the vehicle. Whithorn started the car and tried to escape, but the wrecker lifted the car off the road and progressed seventy-five to one hundred feet until Whithorn managed to stall the wrecker. Has National Bond committed the tort of false imprisonment?

13. William Proxmire, a United States senator from Wisconsin, initiated the "Golden Fleece of the Month Award" (http://www.taxpayer.net/TCS/proxmire.html) to publicize what he believed to be wasteful government spending. The second of these awards was given to the federal agencies that had for seven years funded Dr. Hutchinson's research on stress levels in animals. The award was made in a speech Proxmire gave in the Senate (http://www.senate.gov); the text was also incorporated into an advance press release that was sent to 275 members of the national news media. Proxmire also referred to the research again in two subsequent newsletters sent to 100,000 constituents and during a television interview. Hutchinson then brought this action alleging defamation resulting in personal and economic injury. Assuming that Hutchinson proved that the statements were false and defamatory, would he prevail?

14. Capune was attempting a trip from New York to Florida on an eighteen-foot-long paddleboard. The trip was being covered by various media to gain publicity for Capune and certain products he endorsed. Capune approached a pier by water. The pier was owned by Robbins, who had posted signs prohibiting surfing and swimming around the pier. Capune was unaware of these notices and attempted to continue his journey by passing under the pier. Robbins ran up yelling and threw two bottles at Capune. Capune was frightened and tried to maneuver his paddleboard to go around the pier. Robbins then threw a third bottle that hit Capune on the head. Capune had to be helped out of the water and taken to the hospital. He suffered a physical wound that required twenty-four sutures and, as a result, had to discontinue his trip. Capune brought suit in tort against Robbins. Is Robbins liable? If so, for which tort or torts?

15. Ralph Nader (http://www.pbs.org/newshour/bb/politics/jan-june00/nader_bio.html), who has been a critic of General Motors (http://www.gm.com/flash_homepage/) for many years, claims that when General Motors learned that Nader was about to publish a book entitled *Unsafe at Any Speed*, criticizing one of its automobiles, the company decided to conduct a campaign of intimidation against him. Specifically, Nader claims that GMC (1) conducted a series of interviews with Nader's acquaintances, questioning them about his political, social, racial, and religious views; (2) kept him under surveillance in public places for an unreasonable length of time; (3) caused him to be accosted by women for the purpose of entrapping him into illicit relationships; (4) made threatening, harassing, and obnoxious telephone calls to him; (5) tapped his telephone and eavesdropped by means of mechanical and electronic equipment on his private conversations with others; and (6) conducted a "continuing" and harassing investigation of him. Nader brought suit against GMC for invasion of privacy. Which, if any, of the alleged actions would constitute invasion of privacy?

16. Bill Kinsey was charged with murdering his wife while working for the Peace Corps (http://www.peacecorps.gov/home.html) in Tanzania. After waiting six months in jail, he was acquitted at a trial that attracted wide publicity. Five years later, while a graduate student at Stanford University, Kinsey had a brief affair with Mary Macur. He abruptly ended the affair by telling Macur he would no longer be seeing her because another woman, Sally Allen, was coming from England to live with him. A few months later, Kinsey and Allen moved to Africa and were subsequently married. Soon after Bill ended their affair, Macur began a letter-writing campaign designed to expose Bill and his mistreatment of her. Macur sent several letters to both Bill and Sally Kinsey, their former spouses, their parents, their neighbors, their parents' neighbors, members of Bill's dissertation committee, other faculty, and the president of Stanford University. The letters contained statements accusing Bill of murdering his first wife, spending six months in jail for the crime, being a rapist, and other questionable behavior. The Kinseys brought an action for invasion of privacy, seeking damages and a permanent injunction. Will the Kinseys prevail? If so, for what tort?

17. Plaintiff, John W. Carson, was the host and star of *The Tonight Show* (http://www.timvp.com/carson.html), a well-known television program broadcast by the National Broadcasting Company (http://www.nbc.com). Carson also

appears as an entertainer in nightclubs and theaters around the country. From the time he began hosting *The Tonight Show*, he had been introduced on the show each night with the phrase "Here's Johnny." The phrase "Here's Johnny" is still generally associated with Carson by a substantial segment of the television viewing public. To earn additional income, Carson began authorizing use of this phrase by outside business ventures.

Defendant, Here's Johnny Portable Toilets, Inc., is a Michigan corporation engaged in the business of renting and selling "Here's Johnny" portable toilets. Defendant's founder was aware at the time he formed the corporation that "Here's Johnny" was the introductory slogan for Carson on *The Tonight Show*. He indicated that he coupled the phrase with a second one, "The World's Foremost Commodian," to make "a good play on a phrase." Carson brought suit for invasion of privacy. Should Carson recover? If so, for which tort?

18. Lemmie L. Ruffin, Jr., was an Alabama licensed agent for Pacific Mutual Life Insurance and for Union Fidelity Life Insurance Company. Union wrote group health insurance policies for municipalities, while Pacific did not. Plaintiffs Cleopatra Haslip, Cynthia Craig, Alma M. Calhoun, and Eddie Hargrove were employees of Roosevelt City, Alabama. Ruffin gave the city a single proposal for health and life insurance for its employees, which the city approved. Both companies provided the coverage, however, Union provided the health insurance and Pacific the life insurance. This packaging of coverage by two different and unrelated insurers was not unusual. Union would send its billings for health premiums to Ruffin at Pacific Mutual's office. The city clerk each month issued a check for those premiums and sent it to Ruffin. Ruffin, however, did not remit to Union the premium payments he received from the city; instead, he misappropriated most of them. When Union did not receive payment from the city, it sent notices of lapsed health coverage to the plaintiffs, who did not know that their health policies had been canceled.

    Plaintiff Haslip was subsequently hospitalized and because the hospital could not confirm her health coverage, it required her to make a partial payment on her bill. Her physician, when he was not paid, placed her account with a collection agency, which obtained against Haslip a judgment that damaged her credit. Plaintiffs sued Pacific Mutual and Ruffin for fraud. The case was submitted to a jury, which was instructed that if it found liability for fraud, it could award punitive damages. The jury returned verdicts for the plaintiffs and awarded Haslip $1,040,000, of which at least $840,000 was punitive damages. The Supreme Court of Alabama affirmed the trial court's judgment. Pacific Mutual appealed. Decision?

19. Susan Jungclaus Peterson was a twenty-one-year-old student at Moorhead State University (http://www.mnstate.edu) who had lived most of her life on her family farm in Minnesota. Though Susan was a dean's list student her first year, her academic performance declined after she became deeply involved in an international religious cult organization known locally as The Way of Minnesota, Inc. The cult demanded an enormous psychological and monetary commitment from Susan. Near the end of her junior year, her parents became alarmed by the changes in Susan's physical and mental well-being and concluded that she had been "reduced to a condition of psychological bondage by The Way." They sought help from Kathy Mills, a self-styled "deprogrammer" of minds brainwashed by cults.

    On May 24, Norman Jungclaus, Susan's father, picked up Susan at Moorhead State. Instead of returning home, they went to the residence of Veronica Morgel, where Kathy Mills attempted to deprogram Susan. For the first few days of her stay, Susan was unwilling to discuss her involvement. She lay curled in a fetal position in her bedroom, plugging her ears and hysterically screaming and crying while her father pleaded with her to listen. By the third day, however, Susan's demeanor changed completely. She became friendly and vivacious and communicated with her father. Susan also went roller skating and played softball at a nearby park over the following weekend. She spent the next week in Columbus, Ohio, with a former cult member who had shared her experiences of the previous week. While in Columbus, she spoke daily by telephone with her fiancé, a member of The Way, who begged her to return to the cult. Susan expressed the desire to get her fiancé out of the organization, but a meeting between them could not be arranged outside the presence of other members of The Way. Her parents attempted to persuade Susan to sign an agreement releasing them from liability for their actions, but Susan refused. After nearly sixteen days of "deprogramming" Susan left the Morgel residence and returned to her fiancé and The Way. Upon the direction of The Way ministry, she brought this action against her parents for false imprisonment. Will Susan prevail? Explain.

20. Debra Agis was a waitress in a restaurant owned by the Howard Johnson Company (http://www.hojo.com/ctg/cgi-bin/HowardJohnson). On May 23, 1975, Roger Dionne, manager of the restaurant, called a meeting of all waitresses at which he informed them "there was some stealing going on." Dionne also stated that the identity of the party or parties responsible was not known and that he would begin firing all waitresses in alphabetical order until the guilty party or parties were detected. He then fired Debra Agis, who allegedly "became greatly upset, began to cry, sustained emotional distress, mental anguish, and loss of wages and earnings." Mrs. Agis brought this complaint against the Howard Johnson Company and Roger Dionne, alleging that the defendants acted recklessly and outrageously, intending to cause emotional distress and anguish. The defendants argued that damages for emotional distress are not recoverable unless physical injury occurs as a result of the distress. Will Agis be successful on her complaint?

21. The plaintiff, Edith Mitchell, was forcibly stopped as she exited a Wal-Mart (http://www.walmartstores.com) (defendant) store. The plaintiff, accompanied by her 13-year-old daughter, went through the checkout and purchased several items at the defendant's store. As she exited, the plaintiff

passed through an electronic antitheft device, which sounded an alarm. Robert Canady, employed by the defendant as a "people greeter" and security guard, forcibly stopped the plaintiff at the exit, grabbed the plaintiff's bag, and told her to step back inside, but never touched the plaintiff or her daughter and never threatened to touch either of them. Nevertheless, the plaintiff described the security guard's actions in her affidavit as "gruff, loud, rude behavior." This security guard removed every item the plaintiff had just purchased and ran it through the security gate. One of the items still had a security code unit on it, which an employee admitted could have been the one that the employee had forgotten to pull off at the cash register. When the security guard finished examining the contents of the plaintiffs' bag, he put it on the checkout counter. This examination of her bag took ten or fifteen minutes. Once her bag had been checked, no employee of defendant ever told plaintiff she could not leave. The plaintiff was never threatened with arrest. The plaintiff brought a tort action against the Wal-Mart alleging false imprisonment, assault, battery, and intentional infliction of emotional distress. Is the defendant liable for any of these torts? Explain.

http:// **Internet Exercise** Find information about punitive damages and review the proposed Model Punitive Damages Act.

CHAPTER 8

Negligence and Strict Liability

Nothing is so easy as to be wise after the event.

B. BRANWELL (1859)

Learning Objectives

After reading this chapter you should be able to:

1. List and describe the three required elements of an action for negligence.
2. Explain the duty of care that is imposed on (a) adults, (b) children, (c) persons with a physical disability, (d) persons with a mental deficiency, (e) persons with superior knowledge, and (f) persons acting in an emergency.
3. Differentiate among the duties that possessors of land owe to trespassers, licensees, and invitees.
4. Identify the defenses that are available to a tort action in negligence and those that are available to a tort action is strict liability.
5. Identify and describe those activities giving rise to a tort action in strict liability.

Whereas intentional torts deal with conduct that has a substantial certainty of causing harm, negligence involves conduct that creates an unreasonable risk of harm. The basis of liability for negligence is the failure to exercise reasonable care under the circumstances for the safety of another person or his property, which failure proximately causes injury to such person or damage to his property, or both. Thus, if the driver of an automobile intentionally runs down a person, she has committed the intentional tort of battery. If, on the other hand, the driver hits and injures a person while driving with no reasonable regard for the safety of others, she is negligent.

Strict liability is not based on the negligence or intent of the defendant but rather on the nature of the activity in which he is engaging. Under this doctrine, defendants who engage in certain activities, such as keeping animals or maintaining abnormally dangerous conditions, are held liable for injuries they cause, even if they have exercised the utmost care. The law imposes this liability in order to bring about a just reallocation of loss, given that the defendant engaged in the activity for his own benefit and probably is better prepared than the plaintiff is to manage the risk inherent in the activity through insurance or otherwise.

NEGLIGENCE

The Restatement defines **negligence** as "conduct that falls below the standard established by law for the protection of others against unreasonable risk of harm." The standard established by law is the conduct of a reasonable person acting prudently and with due care under the circumstances. The general rule is that a person is under a duty to all others at all times to exercise reasonable care for the safety of other persons and their property. This rule is subject to certain exceptions, however, which we will discuss below.

Except when strict liability applies, a person is not liable for injury caused to another by an unavoidable accident—an occurrence the person had not intended and could not have prevented by the exercise of reasonable care. Thus, no liability results from the loss of control of an automobile because the driver suddenly and unforeseeably suffers a heart attack, stroke, or fainting spell. If, however, the driver had warning of the imminent heart attack or other infirmity, it would be negligent for him to drive at all.

An action for negligence consists of three elements, each of which the plaintiff must prove:

1. Breach of duty of care: that a legal duty required the defendant to conform to the standard of conduct established for the protection of others *and* that the defendant failed to conform to that standard
2. Proximate cause: that the defendant's failure to conform to the required standard of conduct proximately caused the injury and harm the plaintiff sustained
3. Injury: that the injury and harm is of a type protected against the defendant's negligent conduct

BREACH OF DUTY OF CARE

Negligence consists of conduct that creates an unreasonable risk of harm. In determining whether a given risk of harm was unreasonable, the following factors are considered: (1) the probability that the harm would occur, (2) the gravity or seriousness of the resulting harm, (3) the social utility of the conduct creating the risk, and (4) the cost of taking precautions that would have reduced the risk. Thus, the standard of conduct, which is the basis for the law of negligence, is usually determined by a cost-benefit analysis.

REASONABLE PERSON STANDARD

The duty of care imposed by law is measured by the degree of carefulness that a reasonable person would exercise in a given situation. The **reasonable person** is a fictitious individual who is always careful and prudent and never negligent. What the judge or jury determines a reasonable person would have done in light of the facts revealed by the evidence in a particular case sets the standard of conduct for that case. The reasonable person standard is thus *external* and *objective*.

Children The standard of conduct to which a child must conform to avoid being negligent is that of a reasonable person of like age, intelligence, and experience under like circumstances. The law applies a test that acknowledges these three factors, because children do not have the judgment, intelligence, knowledge, and experience of adults. Moreover, children as a general rule do not engage in activities entailing high risk to others, and their conduct normally does not involve a potential for harm as great as that of adult conduct. A child who engages in an adult activity, however, such as flying an airplane or driving a boat or car, is held in about half the states to the standard of care applicable to adults.

Physical Disability If a person is ill or otherwise physically disabled, the standard of conduct to which he or she must conform to avoid being negligent is that of a reasonable person having a like disability. Thus, a blind person must act as a reasonable person who is blind.

Mental Deficiency The law does not allow for the insanity, voluntary intoxication, or other mental deficiency (in terms, for example, of intelligence, judgment, memory, or emotional stability) of the defendant in a negligence case; rather, the defendant is held to the standard of conduct of a reasonable person who is *not* insane, intoxicated, or mentally deficient, even though the defendant is, in fact, incapable of conforming to the standard.

Superior Skill or Knowledge Persons who are qualified and who practice a profession or trade that requires special skill and expertise are required to use the same care and skill that members of their profession or trade normally possess. This standard applies to such professionals as physicians, dentists, attorneys, pharmacists, architects, accountants, and engineers and to those who perform a skilled trade such as an airline pilot, electrician, carpenter, and plumber. If a member of a profession or skilled trade possesses greater skill than that common to the profession or trade, she is required to exercise that greater degree of skill.

Emergencies An **emergency** is a sudden and unexpected event that calls for immediate action and permits no time for deliberation. In determining whether a defendant's conduct was reasonable, the fact that he was at the time confronted with an emergency is taken into consideration. The standard is still that of a reasonable person under the circumstances—the emergency is simply part of the circumstances. If, however, the defendant's own negligent or tortious conduct created the emergency, he is liable for the consequences of this conduct even if he acted reasonably in the resulting emergency situation.

Violation of Statute The reasonable person standard of conduct may be established by legislation. Some statutes do so by expressly imposing civil liability on violators. Where a statute does not expressly provide for civil liability, courts may adopt the requirements of the statute as the standard of conduct if the statute is intended to protect a class of persons that includes the plaintiff against the particular hazard and kind of harm that resulted.

If the statute is found to apply, the great majority of the courts hold that an unexcused violation is **negligence *per se***; that is, the violation conclusively shows negligent conduct (breach of duty of care). In a minority of states, the violation is considered merely to be evidence of negligence. In either event, the plaintiff must also prove legal causation and injury.

For example, a statute enacted to protect employees from injuries requires that all factory elevators be equipped with specified safety devices. Arthur, an employee in Leonard's factory, and Marian, a business visitor to the factory, are injured when the elevator falls because the safety devices have not been installed. The court may adopt the statute as a standard of conduct as to Arthur, and hold Leonard negligent *per se* as to Arthur, but not as to Marian, because Arthur, not Marian, is within the class of persons the statute is intended to protect. Marian would have to establish that a reasonable person in the position of Leonard under the circumstances would have installed the safety device. (See Figure 8-1 illustrating negligence and negligence *per se*.)

On the other hand, compliance with a legislative enactment or administrative regulation does not prevent a finding of negligence if a reasonable person would have taken additional precautions. For instance, driving at the speed limit may not constitute due care when traffic or road conditions require a lower speed. Legislative or administrative rules normally establish *minimum* standards.

> **Practical Advice**
>
> Assess the potential liability for negligence arising from your activities and obtain adequate liability insurance to cover your exposure.

Figure 8-1
Negligence and Negligence per se

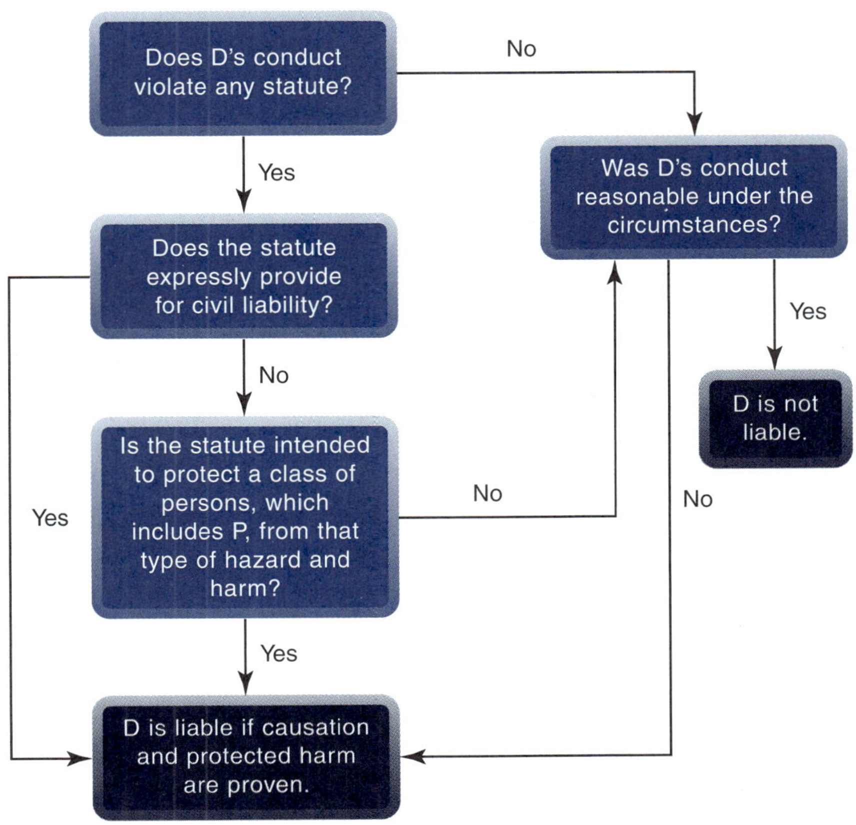

Ryan v. Friesenhahn

Court of Appeals of Texas, 1995
911 S.W.2d 113, *aff'd*, 41 Tex.Sup.J. 261, 960 S.W.2d 656 (1998)

FACTS Todd Friesenhahn, son of Nancy and Frederick Friesenhahn, held an "open invitation" party at his parents' home that encouraged guests to "bring your own bottle." Sabrina Ryan attended the party, became intoxicated, and was involved in a fatal accident after she left the party. Sandra and Stephen Ryan, Sabrina's parents, sued the Friesenhahns for negligence, alleging that the Friesenhahns were aware of the underage drinking at the party and of Sabrina's condition when she left the party. The trial court granted summary judgment for the Friesenhahns.

DECISION Judgment reversed.

OPINION Rickhoff, J. ***Negligence Per Se*** Accepting the petition's allegations as true, the Friesenhahns were aware that minors possessed and consumed alcohol on their property and specifically allowed Sabrina to become intoxicated. The Texas Alcoholic Beverage Code provides that one commits an offense if, with criminal negligence, he "makes available an alcoholic beverage to a minor." [Citation.] The exception for serving alcohol to a minor applies only to the minor's adult parent. [Citation.]

An unexcused violation of a statute constitutes negligence *per se* if the injured party is a member of the class protected by the statute. [Citation.] The Alcoholic Beverage Code was designed to protect the general public and minors in particular and must be liberally construed. [Citation.] We conclude that Sabrina is a member of the class protected by the Code.

In viewing the Ryans' allegations in the light most favorable to them, we find that they stated a cause of action against the Friesenhahns for the violation of the Alcoholic Beverage Code.

Common Law Negligence The elements of negligence include (1) a legal duty owed by one person to another; (2) breach of that duty; and (3) damages proximately caused by the breach. [Citation.] To determine whether a common law duty exists, we must consider several factors, including risk, foreseeability, and likelihood of injury weighed against the social utility of the defendant's conduct, the magnitude of the burden of guarding against the injury and consequences of placing that burden on the defendant. [Citation.] We may also consider whether one party has superior knowledge of the risk, and whether one party has the right to control the actor whose conduct precipitated the harm. [Citation.]

As the Supreme Court in [citation] explained, there are two practical reasons for not imposing a third-party duty on social hosts who provide alcohol to adult guests: first, the host cannot reasonably know the extent of his guests' alcohol consumption level; second, the host cannot reasonably be expected to control his guests' conduct. [Citation.] The Tyler court in [citation] relied on these principles in holding that a minor "had no common law duty to avoid making alcohol available to an intoxicated guest [another minor] who he knew would be driving." [Citation.]

We disagree with the Tyler court because the rationale expressed [by the Supreme Court] in [citation] does not apply to the relationship between minors, or adults and minors. The adult social host need not estimate the extent of a minor's alcohol consumption because serving minors any amount of alcohol is a criminal offense. [Citation.] Furthermore, the social host may control the minor, with whom there is a special relationship, analogous to that of parent-child. [Citation.]

For similar reasons, we distinguish [citation], which held that a social host has no duty to an intoxicated adult guest who injures himself. The Amarillo court discussed the social host's inability to monitor adults and also noted that statutes do not regulate the adults' relationship. [Citation.]

As this case demonstrates, serving minors alcohol creates a risk of injury or death. Under the pled facts, a jury could find that the Friesenhahns, as the adult social hosts, allowed open invitations to a beer bust at their house and they could foresee, or reasonably should have foreseen, that the only means of arriving at their property would be by privately operated vehicles; once there, the most likely means of departure would be by the same means. That adults have superior knowledge of the risk of drinking should be apparent from the legislature's decision to allow persons to become adults on their eighteenth birthday for all purposes but the consumption of alcohol. [Citations.]

While one adult has no general duty to control the behavior of another adult, one would hope that adults would exercise special diligence in supervising minors—even during a simple swimming pool party involving potentially dangerous but legal activities. We may have no special duty to watch one adult to be sure he can swim, but it would be ill-advised to turn loose young children without insuring they can swim. When the "party" is for the purpose of engaging in dangerous and illicit activity, the consumption of alcohol by minors, adults certainly have a greater duty of care. [Citation.]

We are aware that three of our former colleagues in [citation], deferred to the legislature or the Supreme Court to determine social policy regarding adult social hosts serving adult guests. In view of the legislature's determination that minors are not competent to understand the effects of alcohol, we find sufficient legislative intent to support our holding that, taken from the pleadings before us, a duty exists between the adult social host and the minor guest. Accordingly, we find that the Ryans' petition stated a common-law cause of action.

INTERPRETATION A violation of a statute constitutes negligence *per se* if the injured party is a member of the class protected by the statute.

ETHICAL QUESTION When should a parent be held liable for her child's negligence? Explain.

CRITICAL THINKING QUESTION Should a court extend social host liability for providing alcohol to an adult guest? Explain.

DUTY TO ACT

Except in special circumstances, no one is required to aid another in peril. For example, Adolf, an adult standing at the edge of a steep cliff, observes a baby carriage with a crying infant in it slowly heading toward the edge and certain doom. Adolf could easily prevent the baby's fall at no risk to his own safety. Nonetheless, Adolf does nothing, and the baby falls to its death. Adolf is under no legal duty to act and therefore incurs no liability for failing to do so. However, special relations that impose a duty on the defendant to aid or protect the other may exist between the parties. Thus, if Adolf were the baby's parent or babysitter, Adolf would be under a duty to act and would therefore be liable for not taking action. The special relations giving rise to the duty to aid or protect another include common carrier–passenger, innkeeper–guest, employer–employee, store–customer, and parent–child.

A duty to act is also imposed on those whose conduct, whether tortious or innocent, has injured another and left him helpless and in danger of further harm. For example, Alice drives her car into Frank, rendering him unconscious. Alice leaves Frank lying in the middle of the road, where he is run over by a second car driven by Rebecca. Alice is liable to Frank for the additional injuries inflicted by Rebecca. Moreover, a person voluntarily coming to the assistance of another in need of aid incurs a duty to exercise care. In other words, the actor

Ethical Dilemma

What Are the Obligations of a Bartender to His Patrons?

FACTS John Campbell, age 22, was recently hired as a management trainee for the Stanton Hotel. The Stanton features a health club, swimming pool, ski slopes, and boating facilities. The management trainee program is an eighteen-month program during which the trainees rotate jobs to gain exposure to all phases of hotel operations. There is no formal orientation, and each trainee is randomly assigned to jobs.

John's first assignment was at the restaurant/bar working with Mr. Arnold, a bartender who was 50 years old and quite experienced. Mr. Arnold commented to John that John was lucky to be working the bar during the skiing season. Mr. Arnold explained that skiers frequently come in from the slopes to warm up. He told John that all tips are shared equally and that the more it snows and the colder it gets, the better the bar business.

One day, John observed that Mr. Arnold was serving drinks to two young men who appeared to be about 22 or 23. John overheard the men planning to ski an hour or so more and then drive over to meet friends at a neighboring hotel. One of the men appeared self-contained and unaffected by the drinks. His friend, however, was gradually getting louder, although he was not making a disturbance.

John noticed that Mr. Arnold had already served three rounds of bourbon to the men. When Mr. Arnold was preparing the fourth round, John said to him, "Don't you think they've had enough? They're going back on the slopes." Mr. Arnold replied, "Kid, you've got a lot to learn."

SOCIAL, POLICY, AND ETHICAL CONSIDERATIONS

1. What action, if any, should John take?
2. What are the potential risks to the two men who are drinking? Are public safety issues involved?
3. What management policies should the hotel institute with regard to its liquor policies and athletic operations?
4. Do the drinking companions bear an ethical responsibility for each other's drinking?
5. How should society balance the interests of freedom of business and individual conduct (i.e., drinking) with the competing interests of protecting public safety?

is liable if his failure to exercise reasonable care increases the risk of harm, causes harm, or leaves the other in a worse position. For example, Ann finds Ben drunk and stumbling along a dark sidewalk. Ann leads Ben halfway up a steep and unguarded stairway, where she then abandons him. Ben attempts to climb the stairs but trips and falls, suffering serious injury. Ann is liable to Ben for having left him in a worse position.

Soldano v. O'Daniels

California Court of Appeals, Fifth District, 1983
141 Cal.App.3d.443, 190 Cal.Rptr. 310

FACTS On August 9, the plaintiff's father, Darrell Soldano, was shot and killed at the Happy Jack Saloon. The defendant owns and operates the Circle Inn, an eating establishment across the street from the Happy Jack Saloon. On the night of the shooting, a patron of the Happy Jack Saloon came into the Circle Inn and informed the Circle Inn bartender that a man had been threatened at Happy Jack's. The patron requested that the Circle Inn bartender either call the police or allow the patron to use the Circle Inn phone to call the police. The bartender refused either to make the call or to allow the Happy Jack patron to use the phone. The plaintiff alleges that the actions of the Circle Inn employee were a breach of the legal duty that the Circle Inn owed to the decedent. The defendant maintains that there was no legal obligation to take any action, and therefore there was no duty owed to the decedent. The trial court dismissed the case on the defendant's motion for summary judgment.

DECISION The appellate court reversed and remanded the case for trial.

OPINION Andreen, J. There is a distinction, well rooted in the common law, between action and nonaction. [Citation.] It has found its way into the prestigious Restatement Second of Torts (hereafter cited as "Restatement"), which provides in section 314:

> The fact that the actor realizes or should realize that action on his part is necessary for another's aid or protection does nor of itself impose upon him a duty to take such action.

* * *

As noted in [citation], the courts have increased the instances in which affirmative duties are imposed not by direct rejection of the common law rule, but by expanding the list of special relationships which will justify departure from that rule.

* * *

Section 314A of the Restatement lists other special relationships which create a duty to render aid, such as that of a common carrier to its passengers, an innkeeper to his guest, possessors of land who hold it open to the public, or one who has a custodial relationship to another. A duty may be created by an undertaking to give assistance. [Citation.]

Here there was no special relationship between the defendant and the deceased. It would be stretching the concept beyond recognition to assert there was a relationship between the defendant and the patron from Happy Jack's Saloon who wished to summon aid. But this does not end the matter.

It is time to re-examine the common law rule of nonliability for nonfeasance in the special circumstances of the instant case.

* * *

We turn now to the concept of duty in a tort case. The [California] Supreme Court has identified certain factors to be considered in determining whether a duty is owed to third persons. These factors include:

> the foreseeability of harm to the plaintiff, the degree of certainty that the plaintiff suffered injury, the closeness of the connection between the defendant's conduct and the injury suffered, the moral blame attached to the defendant's conduct, the policy of preventing future harm, the extent of the burden to the defendant and consequences to the community of imposing a duty to exercise care with resulting liability for breach, and the availability, cost, and prevalence of insurance for the risk involved. [Citation.]

We examine those factors in reference to this case. (1) The harm to the decedent was abundantly foreseeable; it was imminent. The employee was expressly told that a man had been threatened. The employee was a bartender. As such he knew it is foreseeable that some people who drink alcohol in the milieu of a bar setting are prone to violence. (2) The certainty of decedent's injury is undisputed. (3) There is arguably a close connection between the employee's conduct and the injury: the patron wanted to use the phone to summon the police to intervene. The employee's refusal to allow the use of the phone prevented this anticipated intervention. If permitted to go to trial, the plaintiff may be able to show that the probable response time of the police would have been shorter than the time between the prohibited telephone call and the fatal shot. (4) The employee's conduct displayed a disregard for human life that can be characterized as morally wrong: he was callously indifferent to the possibility that Darrell

Soldano would die as the result of his refusal to allow a person to use the telephone. Under the circumstances before us the bartender's burden was minimal and exposed him to no risk: all he had to do was allow the use of the telephone. It would have cost him or his employer nothing. It could have saved a life. (5) Finding a duty in these circumstances would promote a policy of preventing future harm. A citizen would not be required to summon the police but would be required, in circumstances such as those before us, not to impede another who has chosen to summon aid. (6) We have no information on the question of the availability, cost, and prevalence of insurance for the risk, but note that the liability which is sought to be imposed here is that of employee negligence, which is covered by many insurance policies. (7) The extent of the burden on the defendant was minimal, as noted.

* * *

We acknowledge that defendant contracted for the use of his telephone, and its use is a species of property. But if it exists in a public place as defined above, there is no privacy or ownership interest in it such that the owner should be permitted to interfere with a good faith attempt to use it by a third person to come to the aid of another.

* * *

We conclude that the bartender owed a duty to the plaintiff's decedent to permit the patron from Happy Jack's to place a call to the police or to place the call himself. It bears emphasizing that the duty in this case does not require that one must go to the aid of another. That is not the issue here. The employee was not the good samaritan intent on aiding another. The patron was.

INTERPRETATION Although a person may not have a duty to help another, in a case such as this, a person has a duty not to hinder others who are trying to help.

CRITICAL THINKING QUESTION Should the courts go beyond the rule of this case and impose an affirmative duty to go to the aid of another person who is in peril if it can be done without endangerment? Explain.

DUTIES OF POSSESSORS OF LAND

The right of possessors of land to use that land for their own benefit and enjoyment is limited by their duty to do so in a reasonable manner. By the use of their land, possessors of land cannot cause unreasonable risks of harm to others. Liability for breach of this obligation may arise from conduct in any of the three areas of torts discussed in this and the preceding chapter: intentional harm, negligence, or strict liability. Most of these cases fall within the classification of negligence.

In conducting activities on her land, the possessor of land is required to exercise reasonable care to protect others who are not on her property. For example, a property owner who constructs a factory on her premises must take reasonable care that it is not unreasonably dangerous to people off the site.

The duty of a possessor of land to persons who come on the land usually depends on whether those persons are trespassers, licensees, or invitees. A few states have abandoned these distinctions, however, and simply apply ordinary negligence principles of foreseeable risk and reasonable care.

Duty to Trespassers

A **trespasser** is a person who enters or remains on the land of another without permission or privilege to do so. The lawful possessor of the land is not liable to adult trespassers for his failure to maintain the land in a reasonably safe condition. Nonetheless, the lawful possessor is not free to inflict intentional injury on a trespasser. Moreover, most courts hold that upon discovery of the presence of trespassers on the land, the lawful possessor is required to exercise reasonable care for their safety in carrying on her activities and to warn the trespassers of potentially dangerous conditions that the trespassers are not likely to discover.

Duty to Licensees

A **licensee** is a person who is privileged to enter or remain on land only by virtue of the lawful possessor's consent. Licensees include members of the possessor's household, social guests, and salespersons calling at private homes. A licensee will become a trespasser, however, if he enters a portion of the land to which he is not invited or remains on the land after his invitation has expired.

The possessor owes a higher duty of care to licensees than to trespassers. The possessor must warn the licensee of dangerous activities and conditions of which the possessor has knowledge and the licensee does not and is not likely to discover. If he is not warned, the licensee may recover if the activity or dangerous condition resulted from the possessor's failure to exercise reasonable care to protect him from the danger. To illustrate: Henry invites a friend, Anne, to his place in the country at 8 P.M. on a winter evening. Henry knows that a bridge in his driveway is in a dangerous condition that is not noticeable in the dark. Henry does not inform Anne of this fact. The bridge gives way under Anne's car, causing serious harm to Anne. Henry is liable to Anne.

Some states have extended to licensees the same protection traditionally accorded invitees. A number of states have included social guests in the invitee category.

Figure 8-2
Duties of Possessors of Land

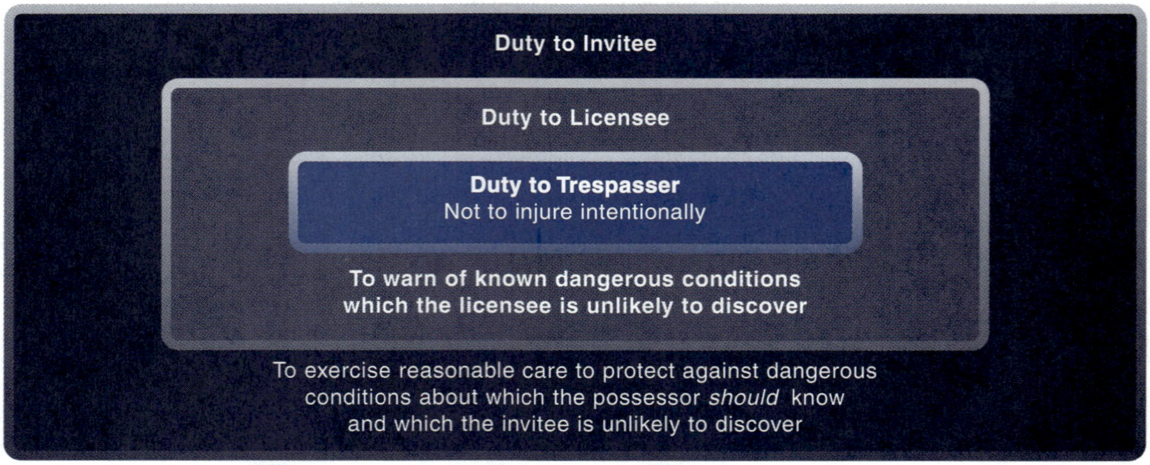

Duty to Invitees An **invitee** is a person invited upon land as a member of the public or for a business purpose. A ***public invitee*** is a person who is invited to enter or remain on land as a member of the public for a purpose for which the land is held open to the public. Such invitees include those who use public parks, beaches, or swimming pools, as well as those who use governmental facilities, such as a post office or an office of the recorder of deeds, where business with the public is transacted openly. A ***business visitor*** is a person invited to enter or remain on premises for a purpose directly or indirectly concerning business dealings with the possessor of the land, such as one who enters a store or a worker who enters a residence to make repairs.

With respect to the condition of the premises, the possessor of land is under a duty to exercise reasonable care to protect invitees against dangerous conditions they are unlikely to discover. This liability extends not only to those conditions of which the possessor actually knows but also to those of which he *should* reasonably know. For example, David's store has a large glass front door that is well lighted and plainly visible. Maxine, a customer, mistakes the glass for an open doorway and walks into the glass, injuring herself. David is not liable to Maxine. If, on the other hand, the glass was difficult to see and a person foreseeably might have mistaken the glass for an open doorway, then David would be liable to Maxine if Maxine crashed into the glass while exercising reasonable care.

These three kinds of duties are illustrated in Figure 8-2.

Practical Advice

Take care of your premises regularly to detect any dangerous conditions and either remedy the danger or post prominent warnings of any dangerous conditions you discover.

Love v. Hardee's Food Systems, Inc.

Court of Appeals of Missouri, Eastern District, Division Two, 2000
16 S.W.3d 739
http://caselaw.lp.findlaw.com/scripts/getcase.pl?court=mo&vol=/appeals/052000/&invol=5050200_2000

FACTS At about 3:15 P.M. on November 15, 1995, plaintiff, Jason Love, and his mother, Billye Ann Love, went to the Hardee's Restaurant in Arnold, Missouri, owned by defendant, Hardee's Food Systems, Inc. **(http://www.hardeesrestaurants.com/)**. There were no other customers in the restaurant between 3:00 P.M. and 4:00 P.M., but two or three workmen were in the back doing construction. The workmen reported that they did not use the restroom and did not see anyone use the restroom. When Jason went to use the restroom, he slipped on water on the restroom floor. He fell backwards, hit his head, and felt a shooting pain down his right leg. He found himself lying in an area of dirty water, which soaked his clothes. There were no barricades, warning cones, or anything else that would either restrict access to the bathroom or warn of the danger.

Jason stated after the fall that his back and leg were "hurting pretty bad." His mother reported the fall. The supervisor filled out an accident report form, which reported that the accident occurred at 3:50 P.M. The supervisor testified that the water appeared to have come from someone shaking his hands after washing them. The supervisor could not recall the last time the restroom had been checked. Love was taken to a hospital emergency room. As a result of his injuries, he underwent two back surgeries, missed substantial time from work, and suffered from continuing pain and limitations on his physical activities.

Hardee's had a policy requiring that the restroom be checked and cleaned every hour by a maintenance person, who was scheduled to work until 3:00 P.M., but normally left at 1:00 P.M. The supervisor could not recall whether the maintenance person left at 1:00 P.M. or 3:00 P.M. on November 15, and the defendant was unable to produce the time clock report for that day.

It was also a store policy that whenever employees cleaned the tables, they would check the restroom. If an employee had to use the restroom, then that employee was also supposed to check the restroom. The restaurant supervisor did not ask if any employees had been in the restroom, or if they had checked it in the hour prior to the accident, and did not know if the restroom was actually inspected or cleaned at 3:00 P.M. The restaurant had shift inspection checklists on which the manager would report on the cleanliness of the restrooms and whether the floors were clean and dry. However, the checklists for November 15 were thrown away.

Jason Love filed a lawsuit against Hardee's Food Systems, Inc. to recover damages for negligence. The jury returned a verdict in the plaintiff's favor in the amount of $125,000.

DECISION The judgment of the trial court is affirmed.

OPINION Crane, J. In order to have made a submissible case, plaintiff had to show that defendant knew or, by using ordinary care, could have known of the dangerous condition and failed to use ordinary care to remove it, barricade it, or warn of it, and plaintiff sustained damage as a direct result of such failure. [Citation.]

"In order to establish constructive notice, the condition must have existed for a sufficient length of time or the facts must be such that the defendant should have reasonably known of its presence." [Citation.] [Prior] cases * * * placed great emphasis on the length of time the dangerous condition had been present and held that times of 20 or 30 minutes, absent proof of other circumstances, were insufficient to establish constructive notice as a matter of law. [Citations.]

* * *

Defendant's liability is predicated on the foreseeability of the risk and the reasonableness of the care taken, which is a question of fact to be determined by the totality of the circumstances, including the nature of the restaurant's business and the method of its operation. [Citations.]

In this case the accident took place in the restaurant's restroom which is provided for the use of employees and customers. The cause of the accident was water, which is provided in the restroom. The restaurant owner could reasonably foresee that anyone using the restroom, customers or employees, would use the tap water provided in the restroom and could spill, drop, or splash water on the floor. Accordingly, the restaurant owner was under a duty to use due care to guard against danger from water on the floor.

There was substantial evidence to support submissibility. First, there was evidence from which the jury could infer that the water came from the use of the restroom. It was on the floor of the restroom and the supervisor testified it appeared that someone had shaken water from his hands on the floor.

Next, there was evidence from which the jury could infer that, if the water was caused by a non-employee, the water was on the floor for at least 50 minutes, or longer, because there was evidence that no other customers were in the store to use the restroom after 3:00 P.M. and the workmen on the site advised that they had not used the restroom.

In addition, plaintiff adduced evidence from which the jury could have found that defendants' employees had the opportunity to observe the hazard. The restroom was to be used by the employees and was supposed to be checked by them when they used it; employees cleaning tables were supposed to check the restroom when they cleaned the tables; and a maintenance man was supposed to check and clean the restroom every hour.

There was evidence from which the jury could have inferred that the maintenance man charged with cleaning the restroom every hour did not clean the restroom at 3:00 P.M. as scheduled on the day of the accident. There was testimony that the maintenance man usually left at 1:00 P.M. The supervisor could not recall what time the maintenance man left that day and defendant was unable to produce the time clock reports for that day which would have shown when the maintenance man clocked out. This could have created a span of 2 hours and 50 minutes during which there was no employee working at the restaurant whose primary responsibility was to clean the restroom. [Citation.]

There was also evidence from which the jury could have inferred that the restroom was not inspected by any employee who had the responsibility to inspect it during that same time period. The supervisor testified that he could not recall the last time the restroom had been checked and did not ask any employees if they had been in the restroom or had checked it in the hour before the accident. * * *

INTERPRETATION The owner or possessor of property is liable to an invitee if the owner knew or, by using ordinary care, could have known of the dangerous condition and failed to use ordinary care to remove it, barricade it, or warn of it, and the invitee sustained damage as a direct result of such failure.

CRITICAL THINKING QUESTION Should customers be required to look for dangers?

RES IPSA LOQUITUR

A rule has developed that permits the jury to infer both negligent conduct and causation from the mere occurrence of certain types of events. This rule, called ***res ipsa loquitur***, meaning "the thing speaks for itself," applies when the event is of a kind that ordinarily would not occur in the absence of negligence and other possible causes are sufficiently eliminated by the evidence. For example, Camille rents a room in Leo's motel. During the night, a large piece of plaster falls from the ceiling and injures Camille. In the absence of other evidence, the jury may infer that the harm resulted from Leo's negligence in permitting the plaster to become defective. Leo is permitted, however, to introduce evidence to contradict the inference of negligence.

PROXIMATE CAUSE

Liability for the negligent conduct of a defendant requires not only that the conduct in fact caused injury to the plaintiff but also that it was the proximate cause of the injury. Most simply expressed, proximate cause consists of the judicially imposed limitations on a person's liability for the consequences of his negligence. As a matter of social policy, the courts have not permitted legal responsibility to follow all the consequences of a negligent act. Rather, they have limited responsibility—to a greater extent than with intentional torts—to those persons and results that are closely connected with the negligent conduct. Moreover, in strict liability cases the courts impose a narrower rule of proximate cause than they do in negligence cases.

CAUSATION IN FACT

To support a finding that the defendant's negligence was the proximate cause of the plaintiff's injury, it is first necessary to show that the defendant's conduct was the cause in fact (that is, the actual cause) of the injury. A widely applied test for causation in fact is the **but for rule**: A person's conduct is a cause of an event if the event would not have occurred but for the person's negligent conduct. Under this test, an act or omission to act is not a cause of an event if that event would have occurred regardless of the act or omission. For instance, Arnold fails to erect a barrier around an excavation. Doyle is driving a truck when its accelerator becomes stuck. Arnold's negligence is not a cause in fact of Doyle's death if the runaway truck would have crashed through the barrier even if it had been erected. Similarly, failure to install a proper fire escape to a hotel is not the cause in fact of the death of a person who is suffocated by the smoke while sleeping in bed.

The "but for" test, however, is not useful when two or more forces, each of which is sufficient to bring about the harm in question, are actively operating. For example, Wilson and Hart negligently set fires that combine to destroy Kennedy's property. Either fire would have destroyed the property. Under the "but for" test, either Wilson or Hart, or both, could argue that the fire caused by the other would have destroyed the property and that he, therefore, is not liable. The ***substantial factor*** test addresses this problem by stating that negligent conduct is a legal cause of harm to another if the conduct is a substantial factor in bringing about the harm. Under this test the conduct of both Wilson and Hart would be found to be a cause in fact of the destruction of Kennedy's property.

LIMITATIONS ON CAUSATION IN FACT

As a matter of policy, the law imposes limitations on the causal connection between the defendant's negligence and the plaintiff's injury. Two of the principal factors that the courts consider in determining such limitations are (a) unforeseeable consequences and (b) superseding causes.

Unforeseeable Consequences Determining the liability of a negligent defendant for unforeseeable consequences has proved to be troublesome and controversial. The Restatement and a majority of the courts have adopted the following position: even if the defendant's negligent conduct is a cause in fact of harm to the plaintiff, the conduct is not a proximate cause unless the defendant could reasonably have anticipated injuring the plaintiff or a class of persons of which the plaintiff is a member. Proximate cause involves recognizing the risk of harm to the plaintiff individually or to a class of persons of which the plaintiff is a member.

For example, Steven, while negligently driving an automobile, collides with a car carrying dynamite. Steven is unaware of the contents of the other car and has no reason to know about them. The collision causes the dynamite to explode, shattering glass in a building a block away. The shattered glass injures Doria, who is inside the building. The explosion also injures Walter, who is walking on the sidewalk near the collision. Steven would be liable to Walter because Steven should have realized that his negligent driving might result in a collision that would endanger pedestrians nearby; and the fact that the actual harm resulted in an unforeseeable manner does not affect his liability. Doria, however, was beyond the zone of danger created by Steven's negligence, and Steven is therefore not liable to Doria. Steven's negligent driving is not deemed to be the "proximate cause" of Doria's injury because, looking back from the harm to Steven's negligence, it appears highly extraordinary that Steven's conduct should have brought about the harm to Doria. See Figure 8-3 summarizing proximate cause.

Figure 8-3
Proximate Cause

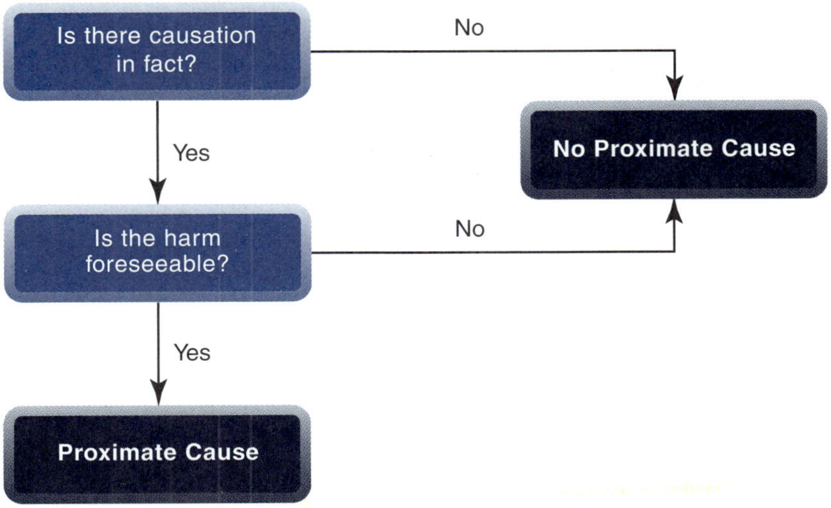

Palsgraf v. Long Island Railroad Co.

Court of Appeals of New York, 1928
248 N.Y. 339, 162 N.E.99

FACTS Palsgraf was on the railroad station platform buying a ticket when a train stopped at the station. As it began to depart, two men ran to catch it. After the first was safely aboard, the second jumped onto the moving car. When he started to fall, a guard on the train reached to grab him and another guard on the platform pushed the man from behind. They helped the man to regain his balance, but in the process they knocked a small package out of his arm. The package, which contained fireworks, fell onto the rails and exploded. The shock from the explosion knocked over a scale resting on the other end of the platform, and it landed on Mrs. Palsgraf. She then brought an action against the Long Island Railroad Company **(http://www.mta.nyc.ny.us/lirr)** to recover for the injuries she sustained. The railroad appealed from the trial and appellate courts' decisions in favor of Palsgraf.

DECISION Judgment for Palsgraf reversed.

OPINION Cardozo, C. J. The conduct of the defendant's guard, if a wrong in its relation to the holder of the package, was not a wrong in its relation to the plaintiff, standing far away. Relatively to her it was not negligence at all. Nothing in the situation gave notice that the falling package had in it the potency of peril to persons thus removed. Negligence is not actionable unless it involves the invasion of a legally protected interest, the violation of a right. "Proof of negligence in the air, so to speak, will not do." [Citations.] "Negligence is the absence of care, according to the circumstances." [Citations.]

* * *

If no hazard was apparent to the eye of ordinary vigilance, an act innocent and harmless, at least to outward seeming, with reference to her, did not take to itself the quality of a tort because it happened to be wrong, though apparently not one involving the risk of bodily insecurity, with reference to some one else. "In every instance, before negligence can be predicated of a given act, back of the act must be sought and found a duty to the individual complaining, the observance of which would have averted or avoided the injury." [Citations.]

* * *

A different conclusion will involve us, and swiftly too, in a maze of contradictions. A guard stumbles over a package which has been left upon a platform. It seems to be a bundle of newspapers. It turns out to be a can of dynamite. To the eye of ordinary vigilance, the bundle is abandoned waste, which may be kicked or trod on with impunity. Is a passenger at the other end of the platform protected by the law against the unsuspected hazard concealed beneath the waste? If not, is the result to be any different, so far as the distant passenger is concerned, when the guard stumbles over a valise which a truckman or a porter has left upon the walk? The passenger far away, if the victim of a wrong at all, has a cause of action, not derivative, but original and primary. His claim to be protected against invasion of his bodily security is neither greater nor less because the act resulting in the invasion is a wrong to another far removed. In this case, the rights that are said to have been violated, the interests said to have been invaded, are not even of the same order. The man was not injured in his person nor even put in danger. The purpose of the act, as well as its effect, was to make his person safe. If there was wrong to him at all, which may very well be doubted, it was wrong to a property interest only, the safety of his package. Out of this wrong to property, which threatened injury to nothing else, there has passed, we are told, to the plaintiff by derivation or succession a right of action for the invasion of an interest of another order, the right to bodily security. The diversity of interests emphasizes the futility of the effort to build the plaintiff's right upon the basis of a wrong to some one else. * * * One who jostles one's neighbor in a crowd does not invade the rights of others standing at the outer fringe when the unintended contact casts a bomb upon the ground. The wrongdoer as to them is the man who carries the bomb, not the one who explodes it without suspicion of the danger.

INTERPRETATION Even if the defendant's negligent conduct in fact caused harm to the plaintiff, the defendant is not liable if the defendant could not have foreseen injuring the plaintiff or a class of persons to which the plaintiff belonged.

CRITICAL THINKING QUESTION Should a person be held liable for all injuries that her negligence in fact causes? Explain.

Superseding Cause An intervening cause is an event or act that occurs after the defendant's negligent conduct and with that negligence causes the plaintiff's harm. If the intervening cause is deemed a **superseding cause**, it relieves the defendant of liability for that harm.

For example, Adams negligently leaves in a public sidewalk an excavation without a fence or warning lights, into which Bogues falls at night. Darkness is an intervening, but not a superseding, cause of harm to Bogues because it is a normal consequence of the situation caused by Adams's negligence. Therefore, Adams is liable to Bogues. In contrast, if Adams negligently leaves an excavation in a public sidewalk into which Carson intentionally hurls Bogues, Adams is not liable to Bogues because Carson's conduct is a superseding cause that relieves Adams of liability.

Petition of Kinsman Transit Co.

United States Court of Appeals, Second Circuit, 1964
338 F.2d 708

FACTS The *MacGilvray Shiras* was a ship owned by the Kinsman Transit Company. During the winter months when Lake Erie was frozen, the ship and others moored at docks on the Buffalo River. As oftentimes happened, one night an ice jam disintegrated upstream, sending large chunks of ice downstream. Chunks of ice began to pile up against the *Shiras*, which at that time was without power and manned only by a shipman. The ship broke loose when a negligently constructed "deadman" to which one mooring cable was attached pulled out of the ground. The "deadman" was operated by Continental Grain Company. The ship began moving down the S-shaped river stern first and struck another ship, the *Tewksbury*. The *Tewksbury* also broke loose from its mooring, and the two ships floated down the river together. Although the crew manning the Michigan Avenue Bridge downstream had been notified of the runaway ships, they failed to raise the bridge in time to avoid a collision because of a mixup in the shift changeover. As a result, both ships crashed into the bridge and were wedged against the bank of the river. The two vessels substantially dammed the flow of the river, causing ice and water to back up and flood installations as far as three miles upstream. The injured parties brought this action for damages against Kinsman, Continental, and the city of Buffalo. The trial court found the three defendants liable, and they appealed from that decree.

DECISION Decree of trial court affirmed as to liability.

OPINION Friendly, J. The very statement of the case suggests the need for considering *Palsgraf v. Long Island RR*, [citation], and the closely related problem of liability for unforeseeable consequences.

* * *

We see little similarity between the *Palsgraf* case and the situation before us. The point of *Palsgraf* was that the appearance of the newspaper-wrapped package gave no notice that its dislodgement could do any harm save to itself and those nearby, and this impact, perhaps with consequent breakage, and not by explosion. In contrast, a ship insecurely moored in a fast flowing river is a known danger not only to herself but to the owners of all other ships and structures down river, and to persons upon them. No one would dream of saying that a shipowner who "knowingly and wilfully" failed to secure his ship at a pier on such a river "would not have threatened" persons and owners of property downstream in some manner. The shipowner and the wharfinger in this case having thus owed a duty of care to all within the reach of the ship's known destructive power, the impossibility of advance identification of the particular person who would be hurt is without legal consequence. [Citations.] Similarly the foreseeable consequences of the City's failure to raise the bridge were not limited to the *Shiras* and the *Tewksbury*. Collision plainly created a danger that the bridge towers might fall onto adjoining property, and the crash of two uncontrolled lake vessels, one 425 feet and the other 525 feet long, into a bridge over a swift ice-ridden stream, with a channel only 177 feet wide, could well result in a partial damming that would flood property upstream.

* * *

All the claimants here met the *Palsgraf* requirement of being persons to whom the actors owed a "duty of care," * * * . But this does not dispose of the alternative argument that the manner in which several of the claimants were harmed, particularly by flood damage, was unforeseeable and that recovery for this may not be had—whether the argument is put in the forthright form that unforeseeable damages are not recoverable or is concealed under a formula of lack of "proximate cause."

* * *

Foreseeability of danger is necessary to render conduct negligent; where as here the damage was caused by just those forces whose existence required the exercise of greater care than what was taken—the current, the ice, and the physical mass of the *Shiras*, the incurring of consequences other and greater than foreseen does not make the conduct less culpable or provide a reasoned basis for insulation. [Citation.] The oft encountered argument that failure to limit liability to foreseeable consequences may subject the defendant to a loss wholly out of proportion to his fault seems scarcely consistent with the universally accepted rule that the defendant takes the plaintiff as he finds him and will be responsible for the full extent of the injury even though a latent susceptibility of the plaintiff renders this far more serious than could reasonably have been anticipated. [Citation.]

The weight of authority in this country rejects the limitation of damages to consequences foreseeable at the time of the negligent conduct when the consequences are "direct," and the damage, although other and greater than expectable, is of the same general sort that was risked.

INTERPRETATION The unforeseeability of the exact manner and extent of a loss will not limit liability where the persons injured and the general nature of the damage were foreseeable.

CRITICAL THINKING QUESTION Compare this decision with that in the *Palsgraf* case and attempt to reconcile the two decisions.

INJURY

The plaintiff must prove that the defendant's negligent conduct proximately caused **harm to a legally protected interest.** Certain interests receive little or no protection against such conduct, while others receive full protection. The courts determine the extent of protection for a particular interest as a matter of law on the basis of social policy and expediency. For example, negligent conduct that is the proximate cause of harmful contact with the person of another is actionable. Thus, if Bob negligently runs into Julie, a pedestrian, who is carefully crossing the street, Bob is liable for physical injuries Julie sustains as a result of the collision. On the other hand, if Bob's careless conduct causes only offensive contact with Julie's person, Bob is not liable because Julie did not sustain harm to a legally protected interest.

The courts traditionally have been reluctant to allow recovery for negligently inflicted emotional distress. This view has gradually changed, and the majority of courts now hold a person liable for negligently causing emotional distress if bodily harm—such as a heart attack—results from the distress. And though, in the great majority of states, a defendant is not liable for conduct resulting solely in emotional disturbance, a few courts have recently allowed recovery of damages for negligently inflicted emotional distress even in the absence of resultant physical harm.

DEFENSES TO NEGLIGENCE

Although a plaintiff has established by a preponderance of the evidence all the required elements of a negligence action, he may nevertheless fail to recover damages if the defendant proves a valid defense. As a general rule, any defense to an intentional tort is also available in an action in negligence. In addition, certain defenses are available in negligence cases that are not defenses to intentional torts. These are contributory negligence, comparative negligence, and assumption of risk. (See Figure 8-4 illustrating the defenses to a negligence action.)

CONTRIBUTORY NEGLIGENCE

Contributory negligence is defined as conduct on the part of the plaintiff that falls below the standard to which he should conform for his own protection and that is a legal cause of the plaintiff's harm. If negligence of the plaintiff together with negligence of the defendant proximately

Figure 8-4
Defenses to a Negligence Action

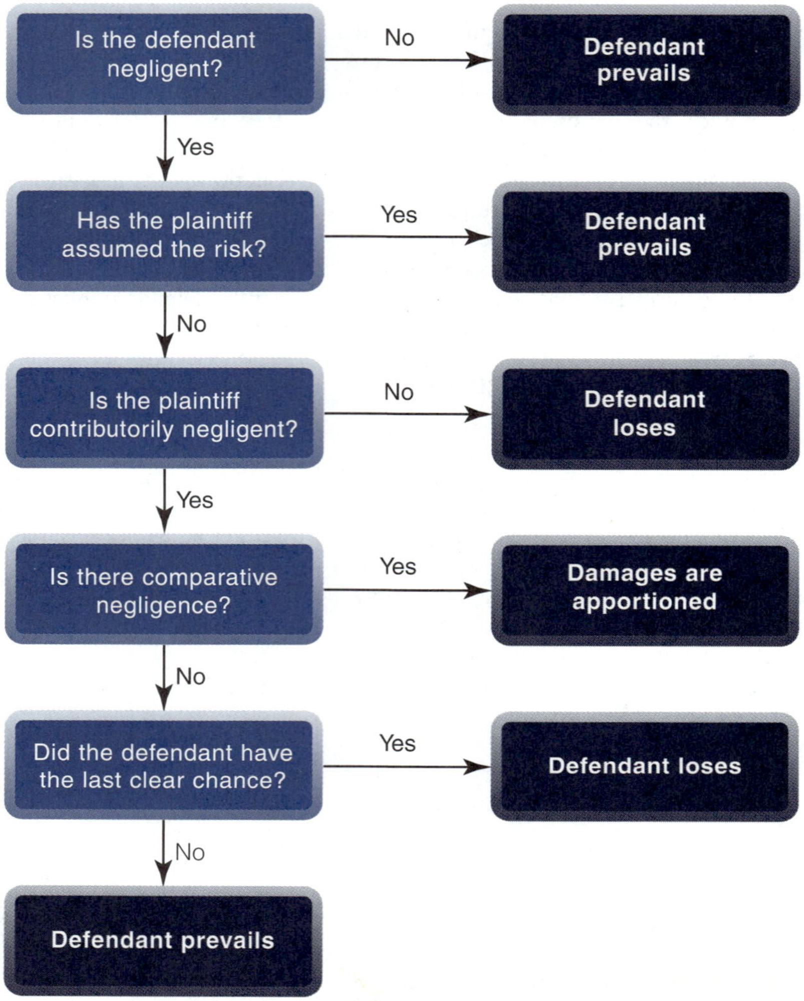

caused the injury and damage the plaintiff sustained, he cannot recover any damages from the defendant in those few states where contributory negligence is still recognized, no matter how slight the plaintiff's contributory negligence was.

Notwithstanding the contributory negligence of the plaintiff, if the defendant had a **last clear chance** to avoid injury to the plaintiff but did not avail himself of such a chance, the contributory negligence of the plaintiff does not bar his recovery of damages.

COMPARATIVE NEGLIGENCE

The harshness of the contributory negligence doctrine has caused all but a few states to reject its all-or-nothing rule and to substitute the doctrine of comparative negligence, which is also called comparative fault or comparative responsibility. (In states adopting **comparative negligence**, the doctrine of last clear chance has been abandoned.)

Approximately a dozen states have judicially or legislatively adopted "pure" comparative negligence systems. Under ***pure comparative negligence*** damages are divided between the parties in proportion to the degree of fault or negligence found against them. For instance, Matthew negligently drives his automobile into Nancy, who is crossing against the light. Nancy sustains damages in the amount of $10,000 and sues Matthew. If the trier of fact (the jury or judge, depending on the case) determines that Matthew's negligence contributed 70 percent to Nancy's injury and that Nancy's contributory negligence contributed 30 percent to her injury, then Nancy would recover $7,000.

Most states have adopted the doctrine of "modified" comparative negligence. Under ***modified comparative negligence*** the plaintiff recovers as in pure comparative negligence unless her contributory negligence was equal to or greater than that of the defendant, in which case the plaintiff recovers nothing. Thus, in the example above, if the trier of fact determined that Matthew's negligence and

Nancy's contributory negligence contributed 40 percent and 60 percent, respectively, to her injury, then Nancy would not recover anything from Matthew.

ASSUMPTION OF RISK

A plaintiff who has voluntarily and knowingly assumed the risk of harm arising from the negligent or reckless conduct of the defendant cannot recover for such harm. In **express assumption of the risk**, the plaintiff expressly agrees to assume the risk of harm from the defendant's conduct. Usually, but not always, such an agreement is by contract. Courts usually construe these exculpatory contracts strictly and will hold that the plaintiff has assumed the risk only if the terms of the agreement are clear and unequivocal. Moreover, some contracts for assumption of risk are considered unenforceable as a matter of public policy. See Chapter 13.

In **implied assumption of the risk** the plaintiff voluntarily proceeds to encounter a known danger. Thus, a spectator entering a baseball park may be regarded as consenting that the players may proceed with the game without taking precautions to protect him from being hit by the ball. The next case involves both contributory negligence and implied assumption of risk. Most states have abolished or modified the defense of implied assumption of risk. Some have abandoned it entirely while others have merged implied assumption of risk into their comparative negligence systems.

The American Law Institute recently adopted The Third Restatement of Torts: Apportionment Liability. Reflecting this general trend, the new Restatement has abandoned the doctrine of implied voluntary assumption of risk: it is no longer a defense that the plaintiff was aware of a risk and voluntarily confronted it. But if a plaintiff's conduct in the face of a known risk is unreasonable it might constitute contributory negligence, thereby reducing the plaintiff's recovery under comparative negligence. The new Restatement limits the defense of assumption of risk to express assumption of risk, which consists of a contract between the plaintiff and another person to absolve the other person from liability for future harm. Contractual assumption of risk may occur by written agreement, express oral agreement, or conduct that creates an implied-in-fact contract, as determined by the applicable rules of contract law. Some contractual assumptions of risk, however, are not enforceable under other areas of substantive law or as against public policy.

Practical Advice

Consider having customers and clients sign waivers of liability and assumption of risk forms, but realize that many courts limit their effectiveness

Dukat v. Leiserv, Inc.

Court of Appeals of Nebraska, 1998
6 Neb.App. 905, 578 N.W.2d 486, *aff'd*, 255 Neb. 750, 587 N.W.2d 96 (1998)

FACTS Rebecca S. Dukat arrived at Mockingbird Lanes, a bowling alley in Omaha, Nebraska, at approximately 6 P.M. on February 2, 1994, to bowl in her league game. The bowling alley's parking lot and adjacent sidewalk were snow and ice covered. Dukat proceeded to walk into the bowling alley on the only sidewalk provided in and out of the building. She testified that she noticed the sidewalk was icy. After bowling three games and drinking three beers, Dukat left the bowling alley at approximately 9 P.M. She retraced her steps on the same sidewalk, which was still ice covered and in a condition that, according to Frank Jameson, general manager of Mockingbird Lanes, was "unacceptable" if the bowling alley were open to customers. As Dukat proceeded along the sidewalk to her car, she slipped, attempted to catch herself by reaching toward a car, and fell. She suffered a fracture of both bones in her left ankle as well as a ruptured ligament.

Dukat sued Leiserv, Inc., doing business as Mockingbird Lanes, alleging that Leiserv was negligent in failing to keep the sidewalk in a reasonably safe condition, in failing to warn her of a dangerous condition, and in failing to take adequate and reasonable measures to protect her. Leiserv alleged two affirmative defenses: (1) Dukat was contributorily negligent and (2) Dukat had assumed the risk of injury. The jury returned a verdict for Leiserv and the judge entered judgment for Leiserv.

DECISION Judgment for Leiserv reversed and case remanded for a new trial.

OPINION Sievers, J. Assumption of Risk.
Before the defense of assumption of risk may be submitted to a jury, the defendant has the burden to establish the elements of assumption of risk, which are that the plaintiff

knew of the danger, understood the danger, and voluntarily exposed himself or herself to the danger which proximately caused the plaintiff's injury. [Citation.] Dukat argues that Leiserv failed to meet its burden of establishing the elements of assumption of risk. Specifically, she argues that Leiserv failed to prove that she knew, understood, and voluntarily exposed herself to the danger of walking unassisted on an icy sidewalk. Dukat's argument focuses primarily on the "voluntary" element of assumption of risk. She maintains that because the sidewalk was the only route into and out of the bowling alley, she did not "voluntarily" expose herself to the danger, rather, according to Nebraska case law, she merely "encountered" it.

Leiserv maintains that Dukat "knew full well that the sidewalk and parking lot were icy," because on her way into the bowling alley she had noticed the sidewalk was slippery. Leiserv contends that Dukat voluntarily exposed herself to the danger when she failed to (1) ask someone to assist her to her car or (2) tell a Mockingbird Lanes employee about the icy conditions and that the sidewalk needed sand or "ice melt."

The standard to be applied in determining whether a plaintiff has assumed the risk of injury is a subjective one based upon the particular facts and circumstances of the event. [Citation.] The subjective standard involves what "the particular plaintiff in fact sees, knows, understands and appreciates. In this it differs from the objective standard which is applied to contributory negligence." [Citation.] If one who knows and comprehends the danger chooses to expose himself or herself thereto, even though the choice is not negligent, he or she will be deemed to have assumed the risk of injury and be precluded from recovery. [Citations.] Thus, it was Leiserv's burden to show that Dukat knowingly and voluntarily exposed herself to the risk of walking on the sidewalk, but a subjective standard is employed.

* * *

In [citation], * * * [the plaintiff] argued that the court should have given the following instruction: "A plaintiff does not assume a risk of harm unless he or she voluntarily accepts the risk. A plaintiff's acceptance of a risk is not voluntary if the defendant's conduct has left plaintiff no reasonable alternative course of conduct in order to avert harm to plaintiff." [Citation.] The court, finding that [the plaintiff's] proposed instruction should have been given, stated:

> "(1) A plaintiff does not assume a risk of harm unless he voluntarily accepts the risk. (2) The plaintiff's acceptance of a risk is not voluntary if the defendant's tortious conduct has left him no reasonable alternative course of conduct in order to (a) avert harm to himself or another, or (b) exercise or protect a right or privilege of which the defendant has no right to deprive him." [Citation], quoting the Restatement [(Second) of Torts] § 496E [(1965)].

* * *

The doctrine of a safer choice as used in [citation] and as illustrated by § 496E suggests something other than retreat from where a person needs to be or wants to be. * * * To further amplify our point, we quote two illustrations from the Restatement, supra, comment d. at 579:

> 8. A illegally carries on blasting operations next to the public highway. B, approaching in a car, ignores a conspicuous warning sign and a flagman who tries to stop him and informs him that there will be a delay of five minutes. B insists upon proceeding along the highway, and is injured by the blasting. B assumes the risk.
> 9. The A City clears the snow and ice from the sidewalk on one side of the street, leaving the sidewalk on the other side covered with ice, slippery, and visibly dangerous. B, having a free choice of either side, and fully understanding the risk, elects to walk on the icy sidewalk, slips, and is injured. B assumes the risk.

In each illustration, there is a reasonable safe choice readily available, and one which allows the "traveler" to reach his or her destination. When the "traveler" rejects the safe and reasonable choice, then there is assumption of risk. * * *

* * *

Contributory Negligence.

* * *

A plaintiff is contributorily negligent if (1) the plaintiff fails to protect himself or herself from injury; (2) the plaintiff's conduct concurs and cooperates with the defendant's actionable negligence; and (3) the plaintiff's conduct contributes to the plaintiff's injuries as a proximate cause. [Citation.] Contributory negligence is an affirmative defense which must be proved by the party asserting such defense. [Citation.] The distinction between assumption of risk and contributory negligence presents a difference which prevents interchangeable use of those defenses in a negligence action. [Citation.]

The Supreme Court of Nebraska has frequently held: "Where different minds may reasonably draw different conclusions or inferences from the evidence adduced concerning the issues of negligence or contributory negligence and the degree thereof when one is compared with the other, such issues must be submitted to the jury." [Citations.]

Minds could reasonably differ on the evidence introduced with respect to Dukat's contributory negligence. It is a permissible inference from the record that the ice alone would not have caused the accident. It is clear from Dukat's testimony that she knew of the icy condition of the sidewalk as she entered the bowling alley and despite this knowledge may have done things a reasonably careful person might not have done. For example, the evidence shows that Dukat drank three beers while she was at the bowling alley and that she did not recall eating dinner that night. Dukat also decided to navigate the same icy path she had come in on without asking the assistance of one of her friends who remained inside the bowling alley. A reasonable person might also have asked management to spread an ice melting substance on the sidewalk and delayed their departure.

* * *

In view of our determination that the district court committed reversible error by submitting the defense of assumption of risk, the judgment of the district court is reversed, and the cause is remanded to the district court for a new trial.

INTERPRETATION A plaintiff who has proven all of the elements of a negligence action nevertheless will be denied a full recovery if the plaintiff voluntarily and knowingly assumed the risk or negligently contributed to her injuries.

CRITICAL THINKING QUESTION What policy reasons support denying a plaintiff recovery where she has been contributorily negligent or has assumed the risk of harm?

STRICT LIABILITY

In some instances a person may be held liable for injuries he has caused even though he has not acted intentionally or negligently. Such liability is called **strict liability**, absolute liability, or liability without fault. The courts have determined that certain types of otherwise socially desirable activities pose sufficiently high risks of harm regardless of how carefully they are conducted, and that therefore those who carry on these activities should bear the cost of any harm that such activities cause. The doctrine of strict liability is not based on any particular fault of the defendant but on the nature of the activity in which he is engaging.

ACTIVITIES GIVING RISE TO STRICT LIABILITY

We will discuss in this section the following activities that give rise to strict liability: (1) performing abnormally dangerous activities, (2) keeping animals, and (3) selling defective, unreasonably dangerous products.

ABNORMALLY DANGEROUS ACTIVITIES

The courts impose strict liability for harm resulting from extraordinary, unusual, abnormal, or exceptional activities, as determined in light of the place, time, and manner in which the activity was conducted. An **abnormally dangerous activity** is one that (1) necessarily involves a high degree of risk of serious harm to the persons and/or chattels of others, which risk cannot be eliminated by the exercise of reasonable care, *and* (2) is not a matter of common usage. Activities to which the rule has been applied include storing explosives or flammable liquids in large quantities; blasting or pile driving; crop dusting; drilling for or refining oil in populated areas; and emitting noxious gases or fumes into a settled community. On the other hand, courts have refused to apply the rule where the activity is a "natural" use of the land, such as drilling for oil in the oil fields of Texas or transmitting gas through a gas pipe or electricity through electric wiring.

Practical Advice

Determine if any of your activities involve abnormally dangerous activities for which strict liability is imposed and be sure to obtain adequate insurance.

Klein v. Pyrodyne Corporation

Supreme Court of Washington, 1991

117 Wash.2d 1, 810 P.2d 917

FACTS Pyrodyne Corporation contracted to display the fireworks at the Western Washington State Fairgrounds **(http://www.thefair.com)** in Puyallup, Washington, on July 4, 1987. During the fireworks display, one of the five-inch mortars was knocked into a horizontal position. A shell inside ignited and discharged, flying five hundred feet parallel to the earth and exploding near the crowd of onlookers. Danny and Marion Klein were injured by the explosion. Mr. Klein suffered facial burns and serious injuries to his eyes. The parties provided conflicting explanations for the improper discharge, and because all the evidence had exploded, there was no means of proving the cause of the misfire. The Kleins brought suit against Pyrodyne under the theory of strict liability for participating in an abnormally dangerous activity.

DECISION Judgment for the Kleins.

OPINION Guy, J. The modern doctrine of strict liability for abnormally dangerous activities derives from *Fletcher v. Rylands*, [citation], in which the defendant's reservoir flooded mine shafts on the plaintiff's adjoining land. *Rylands v. Fletcher* has come to stand for the rule that "the defendant will be liable when he damages another by a thing or activity unduly dangerous and inappropriate to the place where it is maintained, in the light of the character of that place and its surroundings." [Citation.]

The basic principle of *Rylands v. Fletcher* has been accepted by the Restatement (Second) of Torts (1977). [Citation.] Section 519 of the Restatement provides that any party carrying on an "abnormally dangerous activity" is strictly liable for ensuing damages. The test for what constitutes such an activity is stated in section 520 of the Restatement. Both Restatement sections have been adopted by this court, and determination of whether an activity is an "abnormally dangerous activity" is a question of law. [Citations.]

Section 520 of the Restatement lists six factors that are to be considered in determining whether an activity is "abnormally dangerous." The factors are as follows: (a) existence of a high degree of risk of some harm to the person, land or chattels of others; (b) likelihood that the harm that results from it will be great; (c) inability to eliminate the risk by the exercise of reasonable care; (d) extent to which the activity is not a matter of common usage; (e) inappropriateness of the activity to the place where it is carried on; and (f) extent to which its value to the community is outweighed by its dangerous attributes. Restatement (Second) of Torts § 520 (1977). As we previously recognized in [citation], the comments to section 520 explain how these factors should be evaluated: Any one of them is not necessarily sufficient of itself in a particular case, and ordinarily several of them will be required for strict liability. On the other hand, it is not necessary that each of them be present, especially if others weigh heavily. Because of the interplay of these various factors, it is not possible to reduce abnormally dangerous activities to any definition. The essential question is whether the risk created is so unusual, either because of its magnitude or because of the circumstances surrounding it, as to justify the imposition of strict liability for the harm that results from it, even though it is carried on with all reasonable care. Restatement (Second) of Torts § 520, comment f (1977). Examination of these factors persuades us that fireworks displays are abnormally dangerous activities justifying the imposition of strict liability.

We find that the factors stated in clauses (a), (b), and (c) are all present in the case of fireworks displays. Any time a person ignites aerial shells or rockets with the intention of sending them aloft to explode in the presence of large crowds of people, a high risk of serious personal injury or property damage is created. That risk arises because of the possibility that a shell or rocket will malfunction or be misdirected. Furthermore, no matter how much care pyrotechnicians exercise, they cannot entirely eliminate the high risk inherent in setting off powerful explosives such as fireworks near crowds.

* * *

The factor expressed in clause (d) concerns the extent to which the activity is not a matter "of common usage." The Restatement explains that "[a]n activity is a matter of common usage if it is customarily carried on by the great mass of mankind or by many people in the community." Restatement (Second) of Torts § 520, comment i (1977). As examples of activities that are not matters of common usage, the Restatement comments offer driving a tank, blasting, the manufacture, storage, transportation, and use of high explosives, and drilling for oil. The deciding characteristic is that few persons engage in these activities. Likewise, relatively few persons conduct public fireworks displays. Therefore, presenting public fireworks displays is not a matter of common usage.

* * *

The factor stated in clause (e) requires analysis of the appropriateness of the activity to the place where it was carried on. In this case, the fireworks display was conducted at the Puyallup Fairgrounds. Although some locations—such as over water—may be safer, the Puyallup Fairgrounds is an appropriate place for a fireworks show because the audience can be seated at a reasonable distance from the display. Therefore, the clause (e) factor is not present in this case.

The factor stated in clause (f) requires analysis of the extent to which the value of fireworks to the community outweighs its dangerous attributes. We do not find that this factor is present here. This country has a long-standing tradition of fireworks on the 4th of July. That tradition suggests that we as a society have decided that the value of fireworks on the day celebrating our national independence and unity outweighs the risks of injuries and damage.

In sum, we find that setting off public fireworks displays satisfies four of the six conditions under the Restatement test; that is, it is an activity that is not "of common usage" and that presents an ineliminably high risk of serious bodily injury or property damage. We therefore hold that conducting public fireworks displays is an abnormally dangerous activity justifying the imposition of strict liability.

INTERPRETATION The courts impose strict liability for harm resulting from an abnormally dangerous activity, as determined in light of the place, time, and manner in which the activity was conducted.

CRITICAL THINKING QUESTION If an activity is abnormally dangerous, should the law abolish it? Explain.

KEEPING OF ANIMALS

Strict liability for harm caused by animals existed at common law and continues today with some modification. As a general rule, those who possess animals for their own purposes do so at their peril and must protect against harm those animals may cause to people and property.

Trespassing Animals Keepers of animals are generally held strictly liable for any damage their animals cause by trespassing on the property of another. There are three exceptions to this rule: (1) keepers of cats and dogs are liable only for negligence, except where a statute or ordinance has imposed strict liability; (2) keepers of animals are not strictly liable for animals straying from a highway on which they are being lawfully driven, although the owner may be liable for negligence if he fails to control them properly; and (3) in some western states, keepers of farm animals, typically cattle, are not strictly liable for harm caused by their trespassing animals that are allowed to graze freely.

Nontrespassing Animals Keepers of wild animals are strictly liable for harm caused by such animals, whether or not they are trespassing. ***Wild animals*** are defined as those that, in the particular region in which they are kept, are known to be likely to inflict serious damage and that cannot be considered safe, no matter how domesticated they are. Animals included in this category are bears, lions, elephants, monkeys, tigers, deer, and raccoons.

Domestic animals are those animals that are traditionally devoted to the service of humankind and that as a class are considered safe. Examples of domestic animals are dogs, cats, horses, cattle, and sheep. Keepers of domestic animals are liable if they knew, or should have known, of an animal's dangerous propensity. The animal's dangerous propensity must be the cause of the harm. For example, a keeper is not liable for a dog that bites a human merely because he knows that the dog has a propensity to fight with other dogs. On the other hand, a person whose 150-pound Old English sheepdog has a propensity to jump enthusiastically on visitors would be liable for any damage caused by the dog's playfulness.

PRODUCTS LIABILITY

A recent and important trend in the law is the imposition of a limited form of strict liability on manufacturers and merchants who sell goods in a defective condition unreasonably dangerous to the user or consumer. Such liability, imposed regardless of the seller's due care, applies to all merchant sellers. Nearly all states have adopted some version of strict products liability, a topic we will cover in Chapter 22.

DEFENSES TO STRICT LIABILITY

Because the strict liability of one who carries on an abnormally dangerous activity, keeps animals, or sells products is *not* based on his negligence, the ordinary **contributory negligence** of the plaintiff is not a defense to such liability. The law in imposing strict liability places the full responsibility for preventing harm on the defendant. Nevertheless, some states apply the doctrine of **comparative negligence** to some types of strict liability. Moreover, most states apply comparative negligence to strict products liability cases.

Voluntary **assumption of risk** is a defense to an action based on strict liability. If the owner of an automobile knowingly and voluntarily parks the vehicle in a blasting zone, he may not recover for harm to his automobile. The assumption of risk, however, must be voluntary. Where blasting operations are established, for example, the possessor of nearby land is not required to move away and may recover for harm suffered.

THE LAW AND YOU

State Bar Associations

California: http://www.calbar.ca.gov/tate/calbar/calbar_home.jsp ("What Should I Do If I Have an Auto Accident?")

Florida: http://www.flabar.org/ ("What to Do in Case of an Automobile Accident")

Georgia: http://www.gabar.org/cps.htm ("Auto Accidents")

Illinois: http://www.illinoislawyerfinder.com/publicinfo/home.html ("Auto Accidents")

Iowa: http://www.iowabar.org/pamphlet.nsf/$about!OpenAbout ("Auto Accidents")

Maine: http://www.mainebar.org/lawyer_pamphlets.asp (legal information pamphlets) ("If You Are in a Vehicle Collision")

Maryland: http://www.msba.org/public/brochure.htm ("What to Do in Case of an Auto Accident")

Missouri: http://www.mobar.org/pamphlet/ broindex.htm (brochures on legal topics) ("What to Do in Case of an Auto Accident")

Montana: http://www.montanabar.org/forthepublic/index.html ("What to Do in an Auto Accident")

New Mexico: http://www.nmbar.org/public/publicresources/publiceducation.htm ("What to Do in Case of an Auto Accident")

New York: http://www.nysba.org/Template.cfm?Section=Public_Resources ("If You Have an Auto Accident")

North Carolina: http://www.barlinc.org/public/pamphlets/accident.pdf ("What to Do in Case of an Auto Accident")

Ohio: http://www.ohiobar.org/conres/pamphlets ("Auto Accidents")

Oregon: http://www.osbar.org/public/legalinfo/traffic.html ("Auto Accidents")

Rhode Island: http://www.ribar.com/public/accident.asp ("An Accident! What Do I Do Now?")

South Carolina: http://www.scbar.org/Free_publications/free_publications.htm ("Auto Accidents and the Law")

Wisconsin: http://www.legalexplorer.com/legal/legal-QA.asp ("Traffic Accidents")

CHAPTER SUMMARY

Negligence

Breach of Duty of Care

Definition of Negligence conduct that falls below the standard established by law for the protection of others against unreasonable risk of harm

Reasonable Person standard degree of care that a reasonable person would exercise in a given situation
- *Children* must conform to conduct of a reasonable person of like age, intelligence, and experience
- *Physical Disability* a disabled person's conduct must conform to that of a reasonable person under like disability
- *Mental Deficiency* a mentally deficient person is held to the reasonable person standard of a reasonable person who is not mentally deficient
- *Superior Skill or Knowledge* professionals must exercise the same care and skill normally possessed by members of their profession
- *Emergencies* the reasonable person standard applies, but the emergency is considered part of the circumstances
- *Violation of Statute* if the statute applies, the violation is negligence *per se*

Duty to Act except in special circumstances, no one is required to aid another in peril

Duties of Possessors of Land
- *Duty to Trespassers* not to injure intentionally
- *Duty to Licensees* to warn of known dangerous conditions licensees are unlikely to discover for themselves

- *Duty to Invitees* to exercise reasonable care to protect invitees against dangerous conditions possessor should know of but invitees are unlikely to discover

Res Ipsa Loquitur permits the jury to infer both negligent conduct and causation

Proximate Cause

Causation in Fact the defendant's conduct was the actual cause of, or a substantial factor in causing, the injury

Limitations on Causation in Fact
- *Unforeseeable Consequences* no liability if defendant could not reasonably have anticipated injuring the plaintiff or a class of persons to which the plaintiff belongs
- *Superseding Cause* an intervening act that relieves the defendant of liability

Injury

Burden of Proof plaintiff must prove that defendant's negligent conduct caused harm to a legally protected interest

Harm to Legally Protected Interest courts determine which interests are protected from negligent interference

Defenses to Negligence

Contributory Negligence failure of a plaintiff to exercise reasonable care for his own protection, which in a few states prevents the plaintiff from recovering anything

Comparative Negligence damages are divided between the parties in proportion to their degree of negligence; applies in almost all states

Assumption of Risk plaintiff's express consent to encounter a known danger; some states still apply implied assumption of the risk

Strict Liability

Activities Giving Rise to Strict Liability

Definition of Strict Liability liability for nonintentional and nonnegligent conduct

Abnormally Dangerous Activities involve a high degree of risk of serious harm and are not matters of common usage

Keeping of Animals strict liability is imposed for wild animals and usually for trespassing domestic animals

Products Liability imposed upon manufacturers and merchants who sell goods in a defective condition unreasonably dangerous to the user or consumer

Defenses to Strict Liability

Contributory Negligence is not a defense to strict liability

Comparative Negligence most states apply this doctrine to products liability cases

Assumption of Risk is a defense to an action based upon strict liability

QUESTIONS

1. A statute that requires railroads to fence their tracks is construed as intended solely to prevent injuries to animals straying onto the right-of-way. B & A Railroad Company fails to fence its tracks. Two of Calvin's cows wander onto the track. Nellie is hit by a train. Elsie is poisoned by weeds growing beside the track. For which cows, if any, is B & A Railroad Company liable to Calvin? Why?

2. Martha invites John to come to lunch. Martha knows that her private road is dangerous to travel, having been guttered by recent rains. She doesn't warn John of the condition,

reasonably believing that he will notice the gutters and exercise sufficient care. John's attention, while driving over, is diverted from the road by the screaming of his child, who has been stung by a bee. He fails to notice the condition of the road, hits a gutter, and skids into a tree. If John is not contributorily negligent, is Martha liable to John?

3. Nathan is run over by a car and left lying in the street. Sam, seeing Nathan's helpless state, places him in his car for the purpose of taking him to the hospital. Sam drives negligently into a ditch, causing additional injury to Nathan. Is Sam liable to Nathan?

4. Vance was served liquor while he was an intoxicated patron of the Clear Air Force Station Noncommissioned Officers' Club. He later injured himself as a result of his intoxication. An Alaska state statute makes it a crime to give or to sell liquor to intoxicated persons. Vance has brought an action seeking damages for the injuries he suffered. Could Vance successfully argue that the United States was negligent per se by its employee's violation of the statute?

5. A statute requires all vessels traveling on the Great Lakes to provide lifeboats. One of Winston Steamship Company's boats is sent out of port without a lifeboat. Perry, a sailor, falls overboard in a storm so heavy that had there been a lifeboat it could not have been launched. Perry drowns. Is Winston liable to Perry's estate?

6. Lionel is negligently driving an automobile at excessive speed. Reginald's negligently driven car crosses the center line of the highway and scrapes the side of Lionel's car, damaging its fenders. As a result, Lionel loses control of his car, which goes into the ditch, wrecking the car and causing personal injuries to Lionel. What can Lionel recover?

7. a. Ellen, the owner of a baseball park, is under a duty to the entering public to provide a reasonably sufficient number of screened seats to protect those who desire such protection against the risk of being hit by batted balls. Ellen fails to do so. Frank, a customer entering the park, is unable to find a screened seat and, although fully aware of the risk, sits in an unscreened seat. Frank is struck and injured by a batted ball. Is Ellen liable?

   b. Gretchen, Frank's wife, has just arrived from Germany and is viewing baseball for the first time. Without asking any questions, she follows Frank to a seat. After the batted ball hits Frank, it caroms into Gretchen, injuring her. Is Ellen liable to Gretchen?

8. CC Railroad is negligent in failing to give warning of the approach of its train to a crossing and thereby endangers Larry, a blind man who is about to cross. Mildred, a bystander, in a reasonable effort to save Larry, rushes onto the track to push Larry out of danger. Although Mildred acts as carefully as possible, she is struck and injured by the train.
   a. Can Mildred recover from Larry?
   b. Can Mildred recover from CC Railroad?

9. Two thugs in an alley in Manhattan held up an unidentified man. When the thieves departed with his possessions, the man quickly gave chase. He had almost caught one when the thief managed to force his way into an empty taxicab stopped at a traffic light. The Peerless Transport Company owned the cab. The thief pointed his gun at the driver's head and ordered him to drive on. The driver started to follow the directions while closely pursued by a posse of good citizens, but then suddenly jammed on the brakes and jumped out of the car to safety. The thief also jumped out, but the car traveled on, injuring Mrs. Cordas and her two children. The Cordases then brought an action for damages, claiming that the cab driver was negligent in jumping to safety and leaving the moving vehicle uncontrolled. Was the cab driver negligent? Explain.

10. Timothy keeps a pet chimpanzee that is thoroughly tamed and accustomed to playing with its owner's children. The chimpanzee escapes, despite every precaution to keep it on the owner's premises. It approaches a group of children. Wanda, the mother of one of the children, erroneously thinking the chimpanzee is about to attack the children, rushes to her child's assistance. In her hurry and excitement, she stumbles and falls, breaking her leg. Can Wanda recover from Timothy for her personal injuries?

CASE PROBLEMS

11. Hawkins slipped and fell on a puddle of water just inside the automatic door to the H. E. Butt Grocery Company's store (http://www.hebgrocery.com/). The water had been tracked into the store by customers and blown through the door by a strong wind. The store manager was aware of the puddle and had mopped it up several times earlier in the day. Still, no signs had been placed to warn store patrons of the danger. Hawkins brought an action to recover damages for injuries sustained in the fall. Was the store negligent in its conduct?

12. Escola, a waitress, was injured when a bottle of Coca-Cola (http://www.coke.com/flashIndex1.html) exploded in her hand while she was putting it into the restaurant's cooler. The bottle came from a shipment that had remained under the counter for thirty-six hours after being delivered by the bottling company. The bottler had subjected the bottle to the method of testing for defects commonly used in the industry, and there is no evidence that Escola or anyone else did anything to damage the bottle between its delivery and the explosion. Escola brought an action against the bottler for

damages. Because she is unable to show any specific acts of negligence on its part, she seeks to rely on the doctrine of *res ipsa loquitur*. Should she be able to recover on this theory? Explain.

13. Hunn injured herself when she slipped and fell on a loose plank while walking down some steps that the hotel had repaired the day before. The night before, while entering the hotel, she had noticed that the steps were dangerous, and although she knew from her earlier stays at the hotel that another exit was available, she chose that morning to leave via the dangerous steps. The hotel was aware of the hazard, as one of three other guests who had fallen that night had reported his accident to the desk clerk then on duty. Still, there were no cautionary signs on the steps to warn of the danger, and they were not roped off or otherwise excluded from use. Hunn brought an action against the hotel for injuries she sustained as a result of her fall. Should she recover? Explain.

14. Fredericks, a hotel owner, had a dog named Sport that he had trained as a watchdog. When Vincent Zarek, a guest at the hotel, leaned over to pet the dog, it bit him. Although Sport had never bitten anyone before, Fredericks was aware of the dog's violent tendencies and, therefore, did not allow it to roam around the hotel alone. Vincent brought an action for injuries sustained when the dog bit him. Is Fredericks liable for the actions of his dog? Explain.

15. Led Foot drives his car carelessly into another car. The second car contains dynamite, a fact which Led had no way of knowing. The collision causes an explosion that shatters a window of a building half a block away on another street. The flying glass inflicts serious cuts on Sally, who is working at a desk near the window. The explosion also harms Vic, who is walking on the sidewalk near the point of the collision. Toward whom is Led Foot negligent?

16. A foul ball struck Marie Uzdavines on the head while she was watching the Metropolitan Baseball Club (The Mets) (http://www.nymets.com) play the Philadelphia Phillies (http://www.phillies.com) at the Mets' home stadium in New York. The ball came through a hole in a screen designed to protect spectators sitting behind home plate. The screen contained several holes that had been repaired with baling wire, a lighter weight wire than that used in the original screen. Although the manager of the stadium makes no formal inspections of the screen, his employees do try to repair the holes as they find them. Weather conditions, rust deterioration, and baseballs hitting the screen are the chief causes of these holes. The owner of the stadium, the city of New York, leases the stadium to the Mets and replaces the entire screen every two years. Uzdavines sued the Mets for negligence under the doctrine of *res ipsa loquitur*. Is this an appropriate case for *res ipsa loquitur*? Explain.

17. Two-year-old David Allen was bitten by Joseph Whitehead's dog while he was playing on the porch at the Allen residence. Allen suffered facial cuts, a severed muscle in his left eye, a hole in his left ear, and scarring over his forehead. Through his father, David sued Whitehead, claiming that, as owner, Whitehead is responsible for his dog's actions. Whitehead admitted that (1) the dog was large, mean-looking, and frequently barked at neighbors; (2) the dog was allowed to roam wild; and (3) the dog frequently chased and barked at cars. He stated, however, that (1) the dog was friendly and often played with his and neighbors' children; (2) he had not received previous complaints about the dog; (3) the dog was neither aggressive nor threatening; and (4) the dog had never bitten anyone before this incident. Is Whitehead liable?

18. Larry VanEgdom, in an intoxicated state, bought alcoholic beverages from the Hudson Municipal Liquor Store in Hudson, South Dakota. Immediately following the purchase, VanEgdom, while driving a car, struck and killed Guy William Ludwig, who was stopped on his motorcycle at a stop sign. Lela Walz, as special administrator of Ludwig's estate, brought an action against the city of Judson, which operated the liquor store, for the wrongful death of Ludwig. Walz alleged that the store employee was negligent in selling intoxicating beverages to VanEgdom when he knew or could have observed that VanEgdom was drunk. Decision?

19. Carolyn Falgout accompanied William Wardlaw as a social guest to Wardlaw's brother's camp. After both parties had consumed intoxicating beverages, Falgout walked onto a pier that was then only partially completed. Wardlaw had requested that she not go on the pier. Falgout said, "Don't tell me what to do," and proceeded to walk on the pier. Wardlaw then asked her not to walk past the completed portion of the pier. She ignored his warnings and walked to the pier's end. When returning to the shore, Falgout got her shoe caught between the boards. She fell, hanging by her foot, with her head and arms in the water. Wardlaw rescued Falgout, who had seriously injured her knee and leg. She sued Wardlaw for negligence. Decision?

20. Joseph Yania and Boyd Ross visited a coal strip-mining operation owned by John Bigan to discuss a business matter with Bigan. On Bigan's property there were several cuts and trenches he had dug to remove the coal underneath. While there, Bigan asked the two men to help him pump water from one of these cuts in the earth. This particular cut contained water eight to ten feet in depth with sidewalls or embankments sixteen to eighteen feet in height. The two men agreed, and the process began with Ross and Bigan entering the cut and standing at the point where the pump was located. Yania stood at the top of one of the cut's sidewalls. Apparently, Bigan taunted Yania into jumping into the water from the top of the sidewall—a height of sixteen to eighteen feet. As a result, Yania drowned. His widow brought a negligence action against Bigan. She claims that Bigan was negligent "(1) by urging, enticing, taunting and inveigling Yania to jump into the water; (2) by failing to warn Yania of a dangerous condition on the land; and (3) by failing to go to Yania's rescue after he jumped into the water." Was Bigan negligent?

http:// Internet Exercise Find and review information about tort reform.

PART III

CONTRACTS

American Law Institute
http://www.ali.org/

Uniform Commercial Code
http://www.law.cornell.edu/uniform/ucc.html

U.S. Treasury Auctions
http://www.treas.gov/auctions/

National Fraud Information Center
http://www.fraud.org/welcome.htm

Gamblers Anonymous
http://www.gamblersanonymous.org/

National Gambling Impact Study Commission
http://govinfo.library.unt.edu/ngisc/index.html

Economic Statistics
http://www.whitehouse.gov/fsbr/money.html

Federal Reserve System
http://www.federalreserve.gov

CHAPTER 9

Introduction to Contracts

A promise is a debt, and I certainly wish to keep all my promises to the letter; I can give no better advice.
THE MAN OF LAW IN THE *CANTERBURY TALES* BY GEOFFREY CHAUCER (14TH CENTURY)

Learning Objectives

After reading this chapter you should be able to:

1. Distinguish between contracts that are covered by the Uniform Commercial Code and those covered by the common law.
2. List the essential elements of a contract.
3. Distinguish among (a) express and implied contracts; (b) unilateral and bilateral contracts; (c) valid, void, voidable, and unenforceable agreements; and (d) executed and executory contracts.
4. Explain the doctrine of promissory estoppel.
5. Identify the three elements of enforceable quasi contract and explain how it differs from a contract.

Every business enterprise, whether large or small, must enter into contracts with its employees, its suppliers of goods and services, and its customers in order to conduct its business operations. Thus, contract law is an important subject for the business manager. Contract law is also basic to fields of law treated in other parts of this book, such as agency, partnerships, corporations, sales of personal property, commercial paper, and secured transactions.

Even the most common transaction may involve many contracts. For example, in a typical contract for the sale of land, the seller promises to transfer title, or right of ownership, to the land; and the buyer promises to pay an agreed-upon purchase price. In addition, the seller may promise to pay certain taxes, and the buyer may promise to assume a mortgage on the property or to pay the purchase price to a creditor of the seller. If the parties have lawyers, they very likely have contracts with these lawyers. If the seller deposits the proceeds of the sale in a bank, he enters into a contract with the bank. If the buyer rents the property, he enters into a contract with the tenant. When one of the parties leaves his car in a parking lot to attend to any of these matters, he assumes a contractual relationship with the owner of the lot. In short, nearly every business transaction is based on contract and the expectations the agreed-upon promises create. It is, therefore, essential that you know the legal requirements for making binding contracts.

CPA DEVELOPMENT OF THE LAW OF CONTRACTS

Contract law, like the law as a whole, is not static. It has undergone—and is still undergoing—enormous changes. In the nineteenth century, almost total freedom in forming contracts was the rule. However, contract formation also involved many technicalities, and the courts imposed contract liability only when the parties complied strictly with the required formalities.

During the twentieth century, many of the formalities of contract formation were relaxed. Today, contractual obligations are usually recognized whenever the parties clearly intend to be bound. In addition, an increasing number of promises are now enforced in certain circumstances, even though such promises do not comply strictly with the basic requirements of a contract. In brief, the twentieth century has left its mark on contract law by limiting the absolute freedom of contract and, at the same time, by relaxing the requirements of contract formation. Accordingly, we can say that it is considerably easier now both to get into a contract and to get out of one.

COMMON LAW

Contracts are primarily governed by state common law. An orderly presentation of this law is found in the Restatements of the Law of Contracts, a valuable authoritative reference work extensively relied on and quoted in reported judicial opinions.

THE UNIFORM COMMERCIAL CODE

The sale of personal property is a large part of commercial activity. Article 2 of the **Uniform Commercial Code** (the Code, or UCC) governs such sales in all states except Louisiana. A **sale** consists in the passing of title to goods from seller to buyer for a price. A contract for sale includes both a present sale of goods and a contract to sell goods at a future time. The Code essentially defines **goods** as tangible personal property. **Personal property** is any property other than an interest in real property (land). For example, the purchase of a television set, an automobile, or a textbook is a sale of goods. All such transactions are governed by Article 2 of the Code, but where the Code has not specifically modified general contract law, the common law of contracts continues to apply. In other words, the law of sales is a specialized part of the general law of contracts, and the law of contracts governs unless specifically displaced by the Code. See *Pittsley v. Houser* in Chapter 19.

http:// Uniform Commercial Code: http://www.law.cornell.edu.uniform/ucc.html

TYPES OF CONTRACTS OUTSIDE THE CODE

General contract law (**common law**) governs all contracts outside the scope of the Code. Such contracts play a significant role in commercial activities. For example, the Code does *not* apply to employment contracts, service contracts, insurance contracts, contracts involving **real property** (land and anything attached to it, including buildings), and contracts for the sale of intangibles such as patents and copyrights. These transactions continue to be governed by general contract law. Figure 9-1 summarizes the types of law governing contracts.

See *Fox v. Mountain West Electric, Inc.* later in this chapter.

CPA DEFINITION OF CONTRACT

Put simply, a **contract** is a binding agreement that the courts will enforce. The Restatement, Second, of Contracts more precisely defines a contract as "a promise or a set of promises for the breach of which the law gives a remedy, or

Figure 9-1
Law Governing Contracts

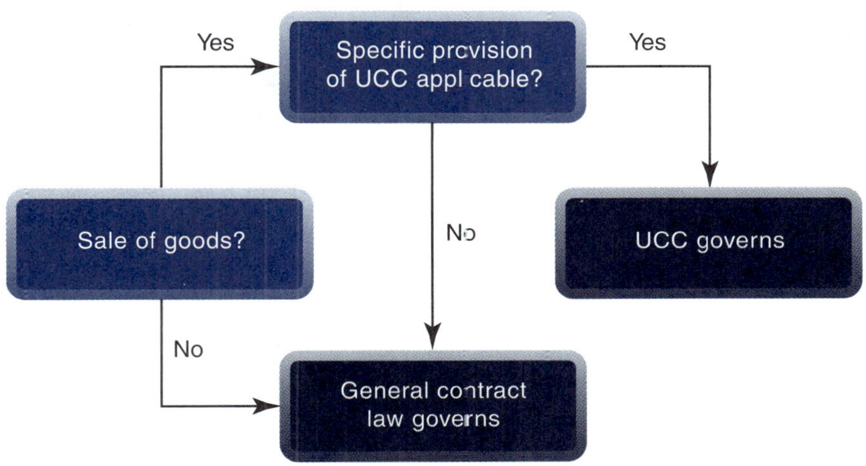

the performance of which the law in some way recognizes a duty." A ***promise*** manifests or demonstrates the intention to act or to refrain from acting in a specified manner.

Those promises that meet *all* of the essential requirements of a binding contract are contractual and will be enforced. All other promises are *not* contractual, and usually no legal remedy is available for a **breach** of, or a failure to properly perform, these promises. (The remedies provided for breach of contract, which include compensatory damages, equitable remedies, reliance damages, and restitution, are discussed in Chapter 18.) Thus, a promise may be contractual (and therefore binding) or noncontractual. In other words, all contracts are promises, but not all promises are contracts as illustrated by Figure 9-2.

CPA REQUIREMENTS OF A CONTRACT

The four basic requirements of a contract are as follows:

1. **Mutual assent.** The parties to a contract must manifest by words or conduct that they have agreed to enter into a contract. The usual method of showing mutual assent is by offer and acceptance.
2. **Consideration.** Each party to a contract must intentionally exchange a legal benefit or incur a legal detriment as an inducement to the other party to make a return exchange.
3. **Legality of object.** The purpose of a contract must not be criminal, tortious, or otherwise against public policy.
4. **Capacity.** The parties to a contract must have contractual capacity. Certain persons, such as adjudicated incompetents, have no legal capacity to contract, while others, such as minors, incompetent persons, and intoxicated persons, have limited capacity to contract. All others have full contractual capacity.

In addition, though in a limited number of instances a contract must be evidenced by a writing to be enforceable, in most cases an oral contract is binding and enforceable. Moreover, there must be an *absence* of invalidating conduct, such as duress, undue influence, misrepresentation, or mistake. (See Figure 9-3.) As the following case shows, a promise meeting all of these requirements is contractual and legally binding. However, if any requirement is unmet, the promise is noncontractual. We will consider these requirements separately in succeeding chapters.

Figure 9-2
Contractual and Noncontractual Promises

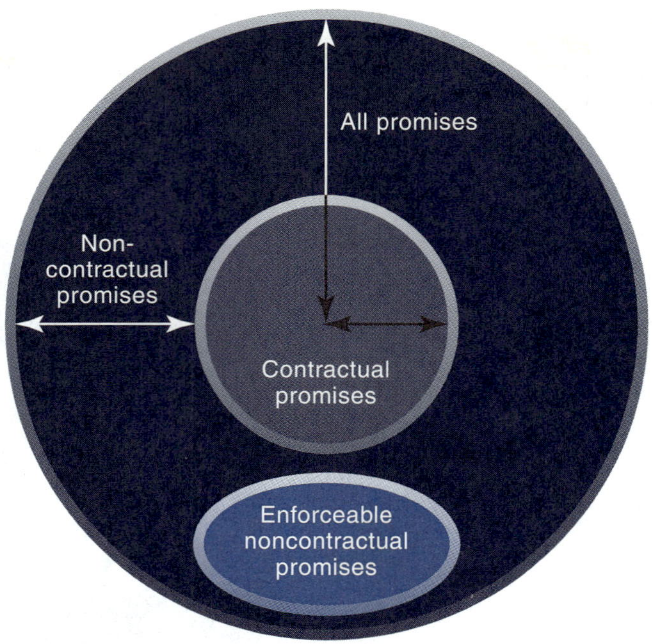

Figure 9-3
Validity of Agreements

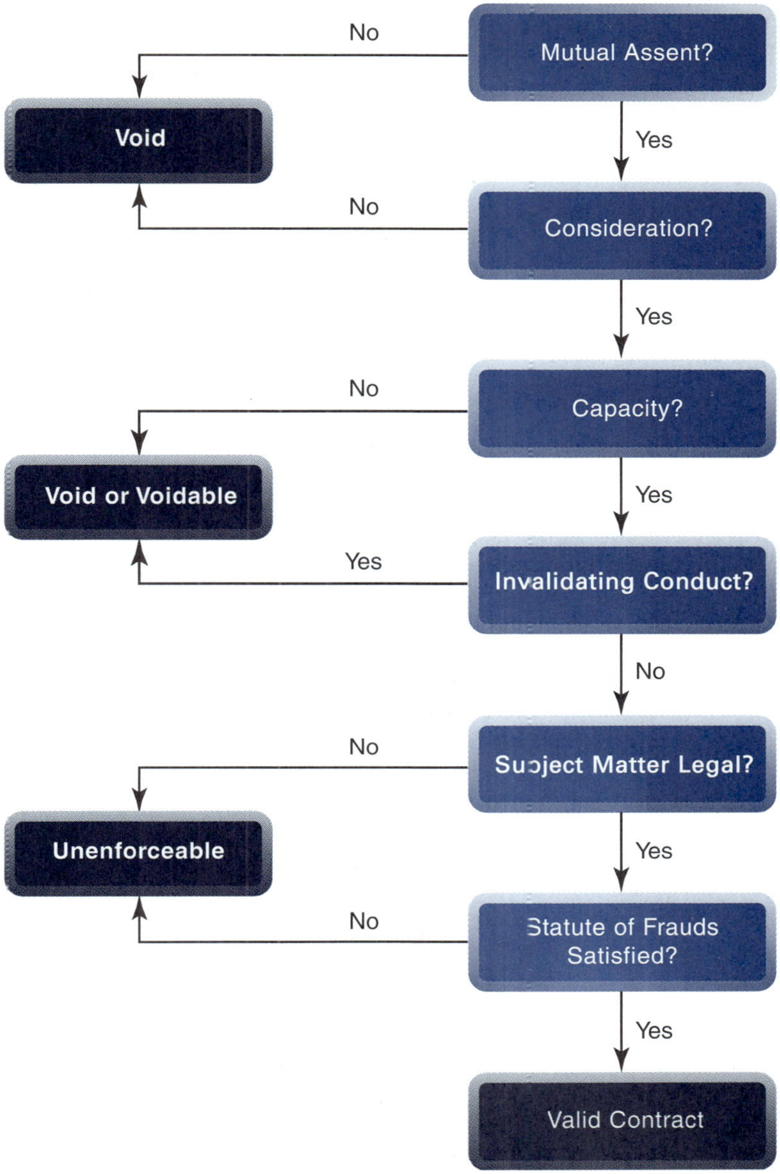

Steinberg v. Chicago Medical School

Illinois Court of Appeals, 1976
41 Ill.App.3d 804, 354 N.E.2d 586

FACTS Robert Steinberg applied for admission to the Chicago Medical School (**http://www.finchcms.edu/**) as a first-year student and paid an application fee of $15. The school, a private educational institution, rejected his application. Steinberg brought an action against the school, claiming that it did not evaluate his and other applications according to the academic entrance criteria printed in the school's bulletin. Instead, he argues, the school based its decisions primarily on nonacademic considerations, such as family connections between the applicant and the school's faculty and members of its board of trustees and the ability of the applicant or his family to donate large sums of money to the school. Steinberg asserts that by evaluating his application according to these unpublished criteria, the school breached the contract it had created when it accepted his application fee. The trial court granted the defendant's motion to dismiss, and Steinberg appealed.

DECISION Trial court's dismissal reversed and case remanded.

OPINION Dempsey, J. A contract is an agreement between competent parties, based upon a consideration sufficient in law, to do or not do a particular thing. It is a promise or a set of promises for the breach of which the law gives a remedy, or the performance of which the law in some way recognizes as a duty. [Citation.] A contract's essential requirements are: competent parties, valid subject matter, legal consideration, mutuality of obligation and mutuality of agreement. Generally, parties may contract in any situation where there is no legal prohibition, since the law acts by restraint and not by conferring rights. [Citation.] However, it is basic contract law that in order for a contract to be binding the terms of the contract must be reasonably certain and definite. [Citation.]

A contract, in order to be legally binding, must be based on consideration. [Citation.] Consideration has been defined to consist of some right, interest, profit or benefit accruing to one party or some forbearance, disadvantage, detriment, loss or responsibility given, suffered, or undertaken by the other [Citation.] Money is a valuable consideration and its transfer or payment or promises to pay it or the benefit from the right to its use, will support a contract.

In forming a contract, it is required that both parties assent to the same thing in the same sense [citation] and that their minds meet on the essential terms and conditions. [Citation.] Furthermore, the mutual consent essential to the formation of a contract must be gathered from the language employed by the parties or manifested by their words or acts. The intention of the parties gives character to the transaction, and if either party contracts in good faith he is entitled to the benefit of his contract no matter what may have been the secret purpose or intention of the other party. [Citation.]

Steinberg contends that the Chicago Medical School's informational brochure constituted an invitation to make an offer; that his subsequent application and the submission of his $15 fee to the school amounted to an offer; that the school's voluntary reception of his fee constituted an acceptance and because of these events a contract was created between the school and himself. He contends that the school was duty bound under the terms of the contract to evaluate his application according to its stated standards and that the deviation from these standards not only breached the contract, but amounted to an arbitrary selection which constituted a violation of due process and equal protection. He concludes that such a breach did in fact take place each and every time during the past ten years that the school evaluated applicants according to their relationship to the school's faculty members or members of its board of trustees, or in accordance with their ability to make or pledge large sums of money to the school. Finally, he asserts that he is a member and a proper representative of the class that has been damaged by the school's practice.

The school counters that no contract came into being because informational brochures, such as its bulletin, do not constitute offers, but are construed by the courts to be general proposals to consider, examine and negotiate. The school points out that this doctrine has been specifically applied in Illinois to university informational publications.

* * *

We agree with Steinberg's position. We believe that he and the school entered into an enforceable contract; that the school's obligation under the contract was stated in the school's bulletin in a definitive manner and that by accepting his application fee—a valuable consideration—the school bound itself to fulfill its promises. Steinberg accepted the school's promises in good faith and he was entitled to have his application judged according to the school's stated criteria.

INTERPRETATION An agreement meeting all of the requirements of a contract is binding and legally enforceable.

ETHICAL QUESTION Is it ethical for a school to consider any factors other than an applicant's merit? Explain.

CRITICAL THINKING QUESTION Should the courts resolve this type of dispute on the basis of contract law? Explain.

CPA CLASSIFICATION OF CONTRACTS

Contracts can be classified according to various characteristics, such as method of formation, content, and legal effect. The standard classifications are (1) express or implied contracts; (2) bilateral or unilateral contracts; (3) valid, void, voidable, or unenforceable contracts; and (4) executed or executory contracts. These classifications are not mutually exclusive. For example, a contract may be express, bilateral, valid, executory, and informal.

EXPRESS AND IMPLIED CONTRACTS

Parties to a contract may indicate their assent either in words or by conduct implying such willingness. For instance, a regular customer known to have an account at a drugstore might pick up an item at the drugstore, show it to the clerk, and walk out. This is a perfectly valid contract. The clerk knows from the customer's conduct that she is buying the item at the specified price and wants it charged to her account. Her actions speak as effectively as words. Such a contract, formed by conduct, is an implied or, more precisely, an **implied in fact contract**; in contrast, a contract in which the parties manifest assent in words is an **express contract**. Both are contracts, equally enforceable. The difference between them is merely the manner in which the parties manifest their assent.

Practical Advice

Whenever possible, try to use written express contracts that specify all of the important terms rather than using implied in fact contracts.

Fox v. Mountain West Electric, Inc.

Supreme Court of Idaho, 2002
137 Idaho 703, 52 P.3d 848 2002; rehearing denied, 2002

FACTS Lockheed Martin Idaho Technical Company ("LMITCO") (**http://www.lockheedmartin.com/**) requested bids for a comprehensive fire alarm system in its twelve buildings located in Idaho Falls. Mountain West Electric, Inc. (MWE) and Fox met and discussed working together on the project. MWE was in the business of installing electrical wiring, conduit and related hookups and attachments. Fox provided services in designing, drafting, testing, and assisting in the installation of fire alarm systems, and in ordering specialty equipment necessary for such projects. The parties decided that it would be better for them to work together on the project than for each of them to bid separately for the entire job. They further agreed that Fox would work under MWE. The parties prepared a document defining each of their roles entitled "Scope and Responsibilities."

Fox prepared a bid for the materials and services that he would provide, which was incorporated into MWE's bid to LMITCO. MWE was the successful bidder and was awarded the LMITCO fixed price contract. In May 1996, Fox began performing various services at the direction of MWE's manager. During the course of the project, many changes and modifications to the LMITCO contract were made.

MWE presented a written contract to Fox on August 7, 1996. MWE and Fox subsequently disagreed on the procedure for the compensation of the change orders. MWE proposed a flow-down procedure, whereby Fox would receive whatever compensation LMITCO decided to pay MWE. Fox found this unacceptable and suggested a bidding procedure to which MWE objected. On December 5, 1996, Fox met with MWE to discuss the contract but the parties agreed upon no compensation arrangement with respect to change orders. Fox left the project on December 9, 1996, after delivering the remaining equipment and materials to MWE. MWE contracted with Life Safety Systems to complete the LMITCO project.

Fox filed a complaint in July 1998 seeking monetary damages representing money due and owing for materials and services provided by Fox to MWE. MWE answered and counterclaimed seeking monetary damages resulting from the alleged breach of the parties' agreement by Fox. Following a court trial, the district court found that an implied-in-fact contract existed between the parties based on the industry standard's flow-down method of compensation. The court found in favor of MWE. Fox appealed.

DECISION The decision of the district court is affirmed.

OPINION Walters, J.

IMPLIED-IN-FACT CONTRACT

This Court has recognized three types of contractual relationships:

> First is the express contract wherein the parties expressly agree regarding a transaction. Secondly, there is the implied in fact contract wherein there is no express agreement, but the conduct of the parties implies an agreement from which an obligation in contract exists. The third category is called an implied in law contract, or quasi contract. However, a contract implied in law is not a contract at all, but an obligation imposed by law for the purpose of bringing about justice and equity without reference to the intent or the agreement of the parties and, in some cases, in spite of an agreement between the parties. It is a non-contractual obligation that is to be treated procedurally as if it were a contract, and is often refered (sic) to as quasi contract, unjust enrichment, implied in law contract or restitution.

[Citation.]

"An implied in fact contract is defined as one where the terms and existence of the contract are manifested by the conduct of the parties with the request of one party and the performance by the other often being inferred from the circumstances attending the performance." [Citation.] The implied-in-fact contract is grounded in the parties' agreement and tacit understanding. [Citation.] "The general rule is that where the conduct of the parties allows the dual inferences that one performed at the other's request and that the requesting party promised payment, then the court may find a contract implied in fact." [Citations.]

[UCC §] 1–205(1) defines "course of dealing" as "a sequence of previous conduct between the parties to a particular transaction which is fairly to be regarded as establishing a common basis of understanding for interpreting their expressions and other conduct."

* * *

Although the procedure was the same for each change order, in that MWE would request a pricing from Fox for the work, which was then presented to LMITCO, each party treated the pricings submitted by Fox for the change orders in a different manner. This treatment is not sufficient to establish a meeting of the minds or to establish a course of dealing when there was no "common basis of understanding for interpreting [the parties'] expressions" under [UCC §] 1–205(1).

* * * After a review of the record, it appears that the district court's findings are supported by substantial and competent, albeit conflicting, evidence. This Court will not substitute its view of the facts for the view of the district court.

Using the district court's finding that pricings submitted by Fox were used by MWE as estimates for the change orders, the conclusion made by the district court that an implied-in-fact contract allowed for the reasonable compensation of Fox logically follows and is grounded in the law in Idaho. [Citation.]

This Court holds that the district court did not err in finding that there was an implied-in-fact contract using the industry standard's flow-down method of compensation for the change orders rather than a series of fixed price contracts between MWE and Fox.

UNIFORM COMMERCIAL CODE

Fox contends that the district court erred by failing to consider previous drafts of the proposed contract between the parties to determine the terms of the parties' agreement. Fox argues the predominant factor of this transaction was the fire alarm system, not the methodology of how the system was installed, which would focus on the sale of goods and, therefore, the Uniform Commercial Code ("UCC") should govern. Fox argues that in using the UCC various terms were agreed upon by the parties in the prior agreement drafts, including terms for the timing of payments, payments to Fox's suppliers and prerequisites to termination.

MWE contends that the UCC should not be used, despite the fact that goods comprised one-half of the contract price, because the predominant factor at issue is services and not the sale of goods. MWE points out that the primary issue is the value of Fox's services under the change orders and the cost of obtaining replacement services after Fox left the job. MWE further argues that the disagreement between the parties over material terms should prevent the court from using UCC gap fillers. Rather, MWE contends the intent and relationship of the parties should be used to resolve the conflict.

This Court in [citation], pointed out "in determining whether the UCC applies in such cases, a majority of courts look at the entire transaction to determine which aspect, the sale of goods or the sale of services, predominates." [Citation.] It is clear that if the underlying transaction to the contract involved the sale of goods, the UCC would apply. [Citation.] However, if the contract only involved services, the UCC would not apply. [Citation.] This Court has not directly articulated the standard to be used in mixed sales of goods and services, otherwise known as hybrid transactions.

The Court of Appeals in *Pittsley v. Houser,* [citation], focused on the applicability of the UCC to hybrid transactions. The court held that the trial court must look at the predominant factor of the transaction to determine if the UCC applies. [Citation.]

The test for inclusion or exclusion is not whether they are mixed, but, granting that they are mixed, whether their predominant factor, their thrust, their purpose, reasonably stated, is the rendition of service, with goods incidentally involved (e.g., contract with artist for painting) or is a transaction of sale, with labor incidentally involved (e.g., installation of a water heater in a bathroom). This test essentially involves consideration of the contract in its entirety, applying the UCC to the entire contract or not at all.

[Citation.] This Court agrees with the Court of Appeals' analysis and holds that the predominant factor test should be used to determine whether the UCC applies to transactions involving the sale of both goods and services.

One aspect that the Court of Appeals noted in its opinion in *Pittsley*, in its determination that the predominant factor in that case was the sale of goods, was that the purchaser was more concerned with the goods and less concerned with the installation, either who would provide it or the nature of the work. MWE and Fox decided to work on this project together because of their differing expertise. MWE was in the business of installing electrical wiring, while Fox designed, tested and assisted in the installation of fire alarm systems, in addition to ordering specialty equipment for fire alarm projects.

The district court found that the contract at issue in this case contained both goods and services; however, the predominant factor was Fox's services. The district court found that the goods provided by Fox were merely incidental to the services he provided, and the UCC would provide no assistance in interpreting the parties' agreement.

This Court holds that the district court did not err in finding that the predominant factor of the underlying transaction was services and that the UCC did not apply.

INTERPRETATION An implied in fact contract is formed by the conduct of the parties; where a contract provides for both goods and services, the common law applies if the predominate factor of the contract is the provision of services.

CRITICAL THINKING QUESTION Why should the legal rights of contracting parties depend on whether a contract is or is not for the sale of goods?

BILATERAL AND UNILATERAL CONTRACTS

In the typical contractual transaction, each party makes at least one promise. For example, if Adelle says to Byron, "If you promise to mow my lawn, I will pay you $10," and Byron agrees to mow Adelle's lawn, Adelle and Byron have made mutual promises, each agreeing to do something in exchange for the promise of the other. When a contract is formed by the exchange of promises, each party is under a duty to the other. This kind of contract is called a **bilateral contract**, because each party is both a **promisor** (a person making a promise) and a **promisee** (the person to whom a promise is made).

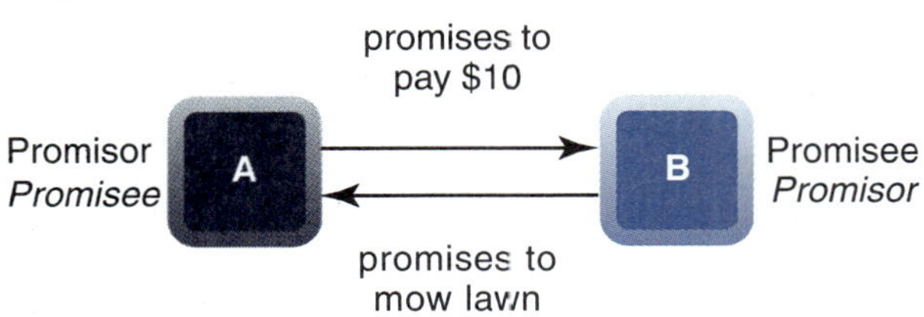

But suppose that only one of the parties makes a promise. Adelle says to Byron, "If you will mow my lawn, I will pay you $10." A contract will be formed when Byron has finished mowing the lawn and not before. At that time, Adelle becomes contractually obligated to pay $10 to Byron. Adelle's offer was in exchange for Byron's act of mowing the lawn, not for his promise to mow it. Because Byron never made a promise to mow the lawn, he was under no duty to mow it. This is a **unilateral contract** because only one of the parties has made a promise.

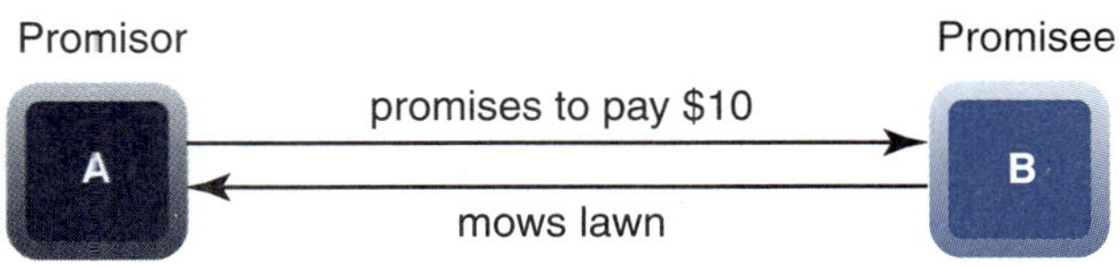

Thus, whereas a bilateral contract results from the exchange of a promise for a return promise, a unilateral contract results from the exchange of a promise either for performing an act or for refraining from doing an act. Where it is not clear whether a unilateral or bilateral contract has been formed, the courts presume that the parties intended a bilateral contract. Thus, if Adelle says to Byron, "If you will mow my lawn, I will pay you $10," and Byron replies, "OK, I will mow your lawn," a bilateral contract is formed.

Practical Advice

Because it is uncertain whether the offeree in a unilateral contract will choose to perform, use bilateral contracts wherever possible.

MANAGERIAL insight

Can You Contract by Fax?

Roberta Maxwell is trying to buy a new home. She and her husband have made an offer on a two-story contemporary house in Chapel Hill, North Carolina. In fact, this dream home is the one for which Roberta and her husband have been searching for more than two years.

Now, after a few days of negotiation, the owner agrees to Roberta's price. There's only one glitch. The owner's wife, whose name is on the deed, has already moved to Ohio, and she will not be returning. The owner suggests that he fax the contract to his wife, who will sign it and zap it back. But will the contract be legal?

The answer is probably yes. Still, Roberta and her husband will need to be careful.

As fax machines proliferate, more and more business transactions, including contract negotiations, are being conducted long-distance. For the first time in history, parties can exchange written agreements within minutes, even if they are separated by an ocean or two, or one or more continents. With the invention of the fax, however, came a number of vexing legal questions, and so far, the courts have yet to address fully the issues raised. To protect yourself, consider the following when attempting to contract by fax:

- *Is the faxed document a copy of the original contract or the original contract itself?* To ensure that the fax serves as an original contract, have it signed. You may want to protect yourself even further by having any signature on the document notarized before the fax is sent. You also should state in the contract that both the faxed contract and the faxed signature are intended to serve as originals.
- *Is the fax a written contract or an oral contract?* Again, make certain that the fax document is signed if you want it to serve as a written contract. You should also include language in your faxed document that defines the document as a written contract. This is important because the statute of frauds requires certain contracts to be in writing and to be signed.
- *Will the printing on the faxed contract deteriorate over time?* If so, follow the fax up with an original hard copy sent by mail. To avoid any questions about the original nature of the faxed contract, add language to the contract that defines the hard copy as an original counterpart of the faxed contract.
- *Is the faxed contract a final agreement?* Because of the ease of transmission, faxed documents tend to fly back and forth between parties. To ensure that your faxed contract serves as the final agreement, state in the contract that it is the final and complete agreement of the parties. Also, be certain to date the faxed contract and to keep on file all faxed documents related to the negotiation.
- *Will the faxed contract stand up in court?* Most likely, if you have followed the steps outlined above. Section 2-206 of the Uniform Commercial Code allows for the acceptance of contracts by any reasonable manner and method under the circumstances. This part of the Code is meant to offer flexibility to contracting parties and to allow them to use new technologies. The Restatement of Contracts, Section 65, takes a similar approach.
- *Are there circumstances under which faxed contracts won't work?* Yes, there are times when you cannot contract by fax. For example, some states require that any land transfer be accompanied by a signed and sealed deed, which eliminates the use of a fax. In addition, a corporate seal is usually invalid if faxed. In the United States, different states have enacted different laws related to contracts, as have different countries. Therefore, always check appropriate legal requirements before you attempt to contract by fax.

Valid, Void, Voidable, and Unenforceable Contracts

By definition a **valid contract** is one that meets all of the requirements of a binding contract. It is an enforceable promise or agreement.

A **void contract** is an agreement that does not meet all of the requirements of a binding contract. Thus, it is no contract at all; it is merely a promise or agreement that has no legal effect. An example of a void agreement is an agreement entered into by a person whom the courts have declared incompetent.

A **voidable contract**, on the other hand, though defective, is not wholly lacking in legal effect. A voidable contract is a contract; however, because of the manner in which the contract was formed or a lack of capacity of a party to it, the law permits one or more of the parties to avoid the legal duties the contract creates. If the contract is voided, both of the parties are relieved of their legal duties under the agreement. For instance, through intentional misrepresentation of a material fact (fraud), Thomas induces Regina to enter into a contract. Regina may, upon discovery of the fraud, notify Thomas that by reason of the misrepresentation, she will not perform her promise, and the law will support Regina. Although the contract induced by fraud is not void, it is voidable at the election of Regina, the defrauded party. Thomas, the fraudulent party, may make no such election. If Regina elects to avoid the contract, Thomas will be released from his promise under the agreement, although he may be liable for damages under tort law for fraud.

A contract that is neither void nor voidable may nonetheless be unenforceable. An **unenforceable contract** is one for the breach of which the law provides no remedy. For example, a contract may be unenforceable because of a failure to satisfy the requirements of the statute of frauds, which requires certain kinds of contracts to be evidenced by a writing to be enforceable. Also, the statute of limitations imposes restrictions on the time during which a party has the right to bring a lawsuit for breach of contract. After the statutory time period has passed, a contract is referred to as unenforceable, rather than void or voidable. Figure 9-3 lists the requirements of a binding contract and the consequences of failing to satisfy each requirement.

Practical Advice

Be careful to avoid entering into void, voidable, and unenforceable contracts.

EXECUTED AND EXECUTORY CONTRACTS

A contract that has been fully carried out by all of the parties to it is an **executed contract**. Strictly speaking, an executed contract is no longer a contract, because all of the duties under it have been performed; but having a term for such a completed contract is useful. By comparison, the term **executory contract** applies to contracts that are still partially or entirely unperformed by one or more of the parties.

CPA PROMISSORY ESTOPPEL

As a general rule, promises are not enforceable if they do not meet all the requirements of a contract. Nevertheless, in certain circumstances, the courts enforce noncontractual promises under the doctrine of **promissory estoppel** in order to avoid injustice. A noncontractual promise is enforceable when it is made under circumstances that should lead the promisor reasonably to expect that the promisee, in reliance on the promise, would be induced by it to take definite and substantial action or to forbear, and the promisee does take such action or does forbear. (See Figure 9-2). For example, Gordon promises Constance not to foreclose for a period of six months on a mortgage Gordon owns on Constance's land. Constance then expends $100,000 to construct a building on the land. His promise not to foreclose is binding on Gordon under the doctrine of promissory estoppel.

Practical Advice

Take care not to make promises on which others may detrimentally rely.

Gorham v. Benson Optical

Court of Appeals of Minnesota, 1995
539 N.W.2d 798

FACTS In early September 1993, Carl Gorham received a phone call from Ed Iwinski about a job opportunity with Benson Optical. At that time, Gorham earned $38,000 annually as a store manager for LensCrafters, but indicated he was interested in employment with Benson Optical. Iwinski, who had been offered the job of chief operating officer (COO) for Benson Optical but was not yet part of the decision-making process on hiring, told Gorham that he would forward Gorham's name to Benson Optical. The next day, Benson Optical's eastern regional manager, Sue Opahle, called Gorham to schedule an interview for an area manager position.

On September 15, 1993, Opahle interviewed Gorham in Chicago. During this interview, Gorham came to believe that Iwinski was Opahle's boss and the COO at Benson Optical. On September 18, Opahle telephoned Gorham and offered him the job of area manager for half of North Carolina and some stores in Florida and Kentucky at a $50,000 annual salary and discussed relocation. After describing the terms of employment Opahle promised to send a confirming letter and employee packet in two days. Gorham told Opahle that he accepted the position provisionally, and unless he notified her otherwise within two days, he would give LensCrafters his notice of termination.

When Gorham did not receive the packet on September 20, he called Benson Optical where someone informed him that the packet was in the mail and reassured him that the deal was finalized so he could give LensCrafters notice. On September 21, Gorham gave LensCrafters his two-week notice of resignation. LensCrafters attempted to keep Gorham in its employment with an offer of a raise, but Gorham declined. When Gorham received the packet a few days later, it contained two shortcomings, which he called to Benson's attention. Gorham received a corrected letter, which asked that he sign and return it as acceptance of the terms of employment. Gorham signed this letter, but never returned it because he had started having reservations about his employment with Benson Optical.

On about September 30, Iwinski informed Benson Optical's vice president of human resources, Fran Scibora, that he was declining the COO position. Scibora, Opahle, and Benson Optical's chief financial officer, Dominic Sblendorio, immediately contacted Gorham and three other new employees who had been recommended by Iwinski, asking for their reactions to the fact that Iwinski would not be working for Benson Optical. Gorham responded that Iwinski's absence did not change his decision to accept the job. When Gorham asked if Iwinski's departure affected Gorham's job, Scibora assured him that it would not.

Gorham's last day of work for LensCrafters was October 1. On October 3, he flew to Minneapolis for Benson Optical's national sales meeting. The meeting then turned into another interview in which they reviewed Gorham's skills and aptitudes. Scibora finally told Gorham that he did not possess the skills necessary for the area manager position. Gorham had the clear impression that he had been or would be terminated. This group also met with and terminated three other employees whom Opahle had hired at Iwinski's suggestion. In a letter to Gorham dated October 15, Benson Optical explained that it had terminated his position because Iwinski had declined the job as COO, because of a "change [in] the requirements of the Area Manager's position," and because Gorham's "skills and abilities did not satisfy the requirements for the new direction in which the company is going." Gorham brought suit claiming breach of contract and promissory estoppel. The district court granted Benson Optical's motion for summary judgment on all claims, and Gorham appealed.

DECISION The district court's summary judgment on Gorham's promissory estoppel claim reversed and remanded.

OPINION Davies, J. A party may manifest acceptance of an agreement by written or spoken words, or by conduct and actions. [Citation.] The record establishes that a contract existed here before October 4 because, even though Gorham did not return the acceptance letter to Benson Optical, he demonstrated his acceptance by verbally agreeing to take the job, resigning his former employment, flying to Chicago at his own expense, and reporting for the sales meeting on October 3. He also admitted that, at that time, he considered himself hired.

The hiring letter, however, fell short as a matter of law of guaranteeing Gorham employment for 90 days as he claims. The relevant statement merely informed Gorham that he needed to produce in 90 days or face termination. Because the contract was at-will and there are no issues of fact as to its terms, the district court properly granted summary judgment on Gorham's breach of contract claim.

Gorham alternatively contends that the district court erred in granting summary judgment for Benson Optical on the promissory estoppel claim. We agree.

The elements of promissory estoppel are: A promise which the promisor should reasonably expect to induce action or forbearance * * * on the part of the promisee and which does induce such action or forbearance is binding if injustice can be avoided only by enforcement of the promise. Restatement of Contracts § 90 [citation], quoted in *Grouse v. Group Health Plan*.

Respondents argue that promissory estoppel is not available when a contract exists. This is true (but with one exception). [Citation.]

In *Grouse*, however, the supreme court in effect found an exception to this rule. The exception applies when the contract is of a type that provides no basis for a contract recovery, i.e., an at-will employment contract. Then there is no bar to a promissory estoppel claim.

In *Grouse*, the supreme court applied the doctrine of promissory estoppel to facts very similar to the present case and allowed the plaintiff to recover reliance damages. There, a pharmacy offered a pharmacist a job and, after the pharmacist accepted, resigned his current position, and declined another job offer, the pharmacy hired someone else. * * *

Significant to this case, the Grouse court stated, in dictum: "[U]nder appropriate circumstances we believe section 90 [of the Restatement] would apply even after employment has begun." [Citation.] Gorham presents the specific hypothetical situation the Grouse court's dictum addressed—a short time actually on the job. And, independent of the hypothetical and like Grouse himself, Gorham relied on the promise of a new job when he quit his job with LensCrafters and declined any renegotiations with them. Gorham came to Minneapolis to begin work on October 4, believing that he had been hired. Within a day, Benson Optical terminated him. These facts show Gorham's reasonable reliance on Benson Optical's promise of employment, his declining any other job in deference to his new job with Benson Optical, and the injustice to him when, on his first day of "employment," he went through a hostile reinterview process that led to his immediate termination.

We see no relevant difference between Gorham, who reported to the national sales meeting on his first day of employment, and Grouse, who was denied even one day on the job. Both men relied to their detriment on the promise of a new job, only to discover that the opportunity had disintegrated before they ever actually started working. Neither man had a "good faith opportunity to perform his duties." [Citation.] Given these facts, Gorham's claim fits squarely within the spirit of Grouse and is entitled to the benefit of promissory estoppel leading to reliance damages.

* * *

The district court erred when it granted summary judgment against Gorham's promissory estoppel claim.

* * *

* * * The doctrine of promissory estoppel allows Gorham to recover good faith reliance damages when Benson Optical terminated him on his first day of employment, after Gorham had detrimentally and reasonably relied on the promise of new employment. Summary judgment on the promissory estoppel claim is reversed and remanded for further proceedings.

INTERPRETATION The courts will enforce a promise that the promisor should reasonably expect to induce detrimental reliance by the promisee if the promisee takes such action and justice requires enforcement.

ETHICAL QUESTION Did Benson Optical act ethically in terminating Gorham and the three other employees hired at Iwinski's suggestion? Explain.

CRITICAL THINKING QUESTION What could Gorham have done to better protect his interests? Explain.

CPA QUASI CONTRACTS

In addition to express and implied in fact contracts, there are implied in law or quasi contracts, which were not included in the previous classification of contracts for the reason that a quasi (meaning "as if") contract is not a contract at all. The term *quasi contract* is used because the remedy granted for quasi contract is similar to one of the remedies available for breach of contract.

A quasi contract is not a contract because it is based neither on an express nor on an implied promise. Rather, a **contract implied in law** or **quasi contract** is an obligation imposed by law to avoid injustice. For example, Willard by mistake delivers to Roy a plain, unaddressed envelope containing $100 intended for Lucia. Roy is under no contractual obligation to return it, but Willard is permitted to recover the $100 from Roy. The law imposes a quasi-contractual obligation on Roy in order to prevent his unjust enrichment at the expense of Willard. Such a recovery requires three essential elements: (1) a benefit conferred upon the defendant (Roy) by the plaintiff (Willard); (2) the defendant's (Roy's) appreciation or knowledge of the benefit; and (3) acceptance or retention of the benefit by the defendant (Roy) under circumstances making it inequitable for him to retain the benefit without compensating the plaintiff for its value.

Not infrequently, quasi contracts are used to provide a remedy when the parties enter into a void contract, an unenforceable contract, or a voidable contract that is avoided. In such a case, the law of quasi contracts will determine what recovery is permitted for any performance rendered by the parties under the invalid, unenforceable, or invalidated agreement.

Weichert Co. Realtors v. Ryan

Supreme Court of New Jersey, 1992

128 N.J. 427, 608 A.2d 280

FACTS In March 1987, William Tackaberry, a real estate agent for Weichert Co. Realtors, informed Thomas Ryan, a local developer, that he knew of property Ryan might be interested in purchasing. Ryan indicated he was interested in knowing more about the property. Tackaberry disclosed the property's identity and the seller's proposed price. Tackaberry also stated that the purchaser would have to pay Weichert a 10 percent commission. Tackaberry met with the property owner and gathered information concerning the property's current leases, income, expenses, and development plans. Tackaberry also collected tax and zoning documents relevant to the property. In a face-to-face meeting on April 4, Tackaberry gave Ryan the data he had gathered and presented Ryan with a letter calling for a 10 percent finder's fee to be paid to Weichert by Ryan upon "successfully completing and closing of title." Tackaberry arranged a meeting, held three days later, where Ryan contracted with the owner to buy the land. Ryan refused, however, to pay the 10 percent finder's fee to Weichert. The trial and appellate courts found that Ryan and Weichert had entered into a binding contract. Ryan appealed.

DECISION Judgment for Weichert modified and remanded to the trial court to determine the amount of plaintiff's recovery.

OPINION Stein, J. We consider two issues: whether Ryan and Tackaberry entered into an enforceable agreement and, if not, whether Weichert is entitled to recover the reasonable value of Tackaberry's services on a theory of quantum meruit. A contract arises from offer and acceptance, and must be sufficiently definite "that the performance to be rendered by each party can be ascertained with reasonable certainty." [Citations.] Thus, if parties agree on essential terms and manifest an intention to be bound by those terms, they have created an enforceable contract. [Citations.] Where the parties do not agree to one or more essential terms, however, courts generally hold that the agreement is unenforceable. [Citations.]

* * *

In some circumstances, however, courts will allow recovery even though the parties' words and actions are insufficient to manifest an intention to agree to the proffered terms. Recovery based on quasi-contract, sometimes referred to as a contract implied-in-law, "is wholly unlike an express or implied-in-fact contract in that it is 'imposed by the law for the purpose of bringing about justice without reference to the intention of the parties.' " [Citations.] ("In the case of actual contracts, the agreement defines the duty, while in the case of quasi-contracts the duty defines the contract.") Courts generally allow recovery in quasi-contract when one party has conferred a benefit on another, and the circumstances are such that to deny recovery would be unjust. See, e.g., [citation]; Restatement of Restitution § 53 (1937). Quasi-contractual liability "rests on the equitable principle that a person shall not be allowed to enrich himself unjustly at the expense of another." [Citation.]

Applying that principle, courts have allowed quasi-contractual recovery for services rendered when a party confers a benefit with a reasonable expectation of payment. [Citations.] That type of quasi-contractual recovery is known as quantum meruit ("as much as he deserves"), and entitles the performing party to recoup the reasonable value of services rendered. [Citations.]

Accordingly, a broker seeking recovery on a theory of quantum meruit must establish that the services were performed with an expectation that the beneficiary would pay for them, and under circumstances that should have put the beneficiary on notice that the plaintiff expected to be paid. [Citation.] Courts have allowed brokers to recover in quantum meruit when a principal accepts a broker's services but the contract proves unenforceable for lack of agreement on essential terms—for instance, the amount of the broker's commission. [Citations.] Thus, a broker who makes a sufficient showing can recover fees for services rendered even absent express or implied agreement concerning the amount of the fee.

Application of the foregoing principles to the transaction between Weichert and Ryan demonstrates that the record is insufficient to support a finding that Tackaberry and Ryan mutually manifested assent to the essential terms of the contract. First, Ryan never expressly assented to the terms of Tackaberry's offer. Although Ryan expressed interest in learning more about the Pitt property during the initial March phone call, neither his expression of interest nor his agreement to meet with Tackaberry to learn more about the transaction was sufficient to establish the "unqualified acceptance" necessary to manifest express assent. [Citation.] Moreover, Ryan refused to agree to the ten-percent figure during the April 4th meeting, and thereafter consistently rejected that term. Thus, the parties never formed an express contract.

* * *

The record clearly establishes, however, that Tackaberry is entitled to recover in quantum meruit for the reasonable value of his services. The trial court's factual finding that Tackaberry was the procuring cause of the sale is supported by substantial evidence. Further, the proofs adduced at trial firmly establish that Tackaberry furnished Ryan with information about the Pitt property with an expectation that Ryan would pay a brokerage fee, and Ryan himself admitted throughout the trial that he had always intended to compensate Tackaberry for his services. Given those circumstances, to deny Tackaberry compensation for services rendered would unjustly enrich Ryan * * *. [Citation.]

INTERPRETATION The courts impose a quasi-contractual obligation to pay the reasonable value of a benefit conferred in order to avoid unjust enrichment.

CRITICAL THINKING QUESTION Why does the law allow a recovery in quasi contract?

CONCEPT REVIEW

Contracts, Promissory Estoppel, and Quasi Contracts

	Contract	Promissory Estoppel	Quasi Contract
Type of Promise	Contractual	Noncontractual	None Void Unenforceable Invalidated
Requirements	All of the essential elements of a contract	Detrimental and justifiable reliance	Benefit conferred and knowingly accepted
Remedies	Equitable Compensatory Reliance Restitution	Promise enforced to the extent necessary to avoid injustice	Reasonable value of benefit conferred

CHAPTER SUMMARY

Law of Contracts

Definition of Contract a binding agreement that the courts will enforce

Common Law most contracts are primarily governed by state common law, including contracts involving employment, services, insurance, real property (land and anything attached to it), patents, and copyrights

The Uniform Commercial Code Article 2 of the UCC governs the sales of goods

- *Sale* the transfer of title from seller to buyer
- *Goods* tangible personal property (personal property is all property other than an interest in land)

Requirements of a Contract

Mutual Assent the parties to a contract must manifest by words or conduct that they have agreed to enter into a contract

Consideration each party to a contract must intentionally exchange a legal benefit or incur a legal detriment as an inducement to the other party to make a return exchange

Legality of Object the purpose of a contract must not be criminal, tortious, or otherwise against public policy

Capacity the parties to a contract must have contractual capacity

Classification of Contracts

Express and Implied Contracts

- *Implied in Fact Contract* contract where the agreement of the parties is inferred from their conduct
- *Express Contract* an agreement that is stated in words either orally or in writing

Bilateral and Unilateral Contracts

- *Bilateral Contract* contract in which both parties exchange promises
- *Unilateral Contract* contract in which only one party makes a promise

Valid, Void, Voidable, and Unenforceable Contracts
- *Valid Contract* one that meets all of the requirements of a binding contract
- *Void Contract* no contract at all; without legal effect
- *Voidable Contract* contract capable of being made void
- *Unenforceable Contract* contract for the breach of which the law provides no remedy

Executed and Executory Contracts
- *Executed Contract* contract that has been fully performed by all of the parties
- *Executory Contract* contract that has yet to be fully performed

Promissory Estoppel doctrine enforcing noncontractual promises where there has been justifiable reliance on the promise and justice requires the enforcement of the promise

Quasi Contract an obligation not based upon contract that is imposed by law to avoid injustice; also called an implied in law contract

QUESTIONS

1. Owen telephones an order to Hillary's store for certain goods which Hillary delivers to Owen. Nothing is said by either party about price or payment terms. What are the legal obligations of Owen and Hillary?
2. Minth is the owner of the Hiawatha Supper Club, which he leased during 1972 and 1973 to Piekarski. During the period of the lease, Piekarski contracted with Puttkammer for the resurfacing of the access and service areas of the supper club. The work, including labor and materials, had a reasonable value of $2,540, but Puttkammer was never paid because Piekarski went bankrupt. Puttkammer brought an action against Minth to recover the amount owed to him by Piekarski. Will Puttkammer prevail? Explain.
3. Jonathan writes to Willa, stating, "I'll pay you $150 if you reseed my lawn." Willa reseeds Jonathan's lawn as requested. Has a contract been formed? If so, what kind?
4. Calvin uses fraud to induce Maria to promise to pay money in return for goods he has delivered to her. Has a contract been formed? If so, what kind? What are the rights of Calvin and Maria?
5. Anna is about to buy a house on a hill. Prior to the purchase, she obtains a promise from Betty, the owner of the adjacent property, that Betty will not build any structure that would block Anna's view. In reliance on this promise, Anna buys the house. Is Betty's promise binding? Why or why not?

CASE PROBLEMS

6. Mary Dobos was admitted to Boca Raton Community Hospital (http://www.brch.com) in serious condition with an abdominal aneurysm. The hospital called upon Nursing Care Services, Inc., to provide around-the-clock nursing services for Mrs. Dobos. She received two weeks of in-hospital care, forty-eight hours of postrelease care, and two weeks of at-home care. The total bill was $3,723.90. Mrs. Dobos refused to pay, and Nursing Care Services, Inc., brought an action to recover. Mrs. Dobos maintained that she was not obligated to render payment in that she never signed a written contract, nor did she orally agree to be liable for the services. The necessity for the services, reasonableness of the fee, and competency of the nurses were undisputed. After Mrs. Dobos admitted that she or her daughter authorized the forty-eight hours of postrelease care, the trial court ordered compensation of $248 for that period. It did not allow payment of the balance, and Nursing Care Services, Inc., appealed. Decision?
7. St. Charles Drilling Co. contracted with Osterholt to install a well and water system that would produce a specified quantity of water. The water system failed to meet its warranted capacity, and Osterholt sued for breach of contract. Does the UCC apply to this contract?
8. On March 4, 1970, Helvey brought suit against the Wabash County REMC (REMC) (http://www.wvpa.com/Distribution Co-ops/wabashco/wabash.html) for breach of implied and express warranties. He alleged that REMC furnished electricity in excess of 135 volts to Helvey's home, damaging his 110-volt household appliances. This incident occurred on January 10, 1966. In defense, REMC pleads that the Uniform Commercial Code's Article 2 statute of limitations of four

years has passed, thereby barring Helvey's suit. Helvey argues that providing electrical energy is not a transaction in goods under the UCC but rather a furnishing of services that would make applicable the general contract six-year statute of limitations. Is the contract governed by the UCC? Why?

9. In April, Jack Duran, president of Colorado Carpet Installation, Inc., began negotiations with Fred and Zuma Palermo for the sale and installation of carpeting, carpet padding, tile, and vinyl floor covering in their home. Duran drew up a written proposal that referred to Colorado Carpet as "the seller" and to the Palermos as the "customer." The proposal listed the quantity, unit cost, and total price of each item to be installed. The total price of the job was $4,777.75. Although labor was expressly included in this figure, Duran estimated the total labor cost at $926. Mrs. Palermo orally accepted Duran's written proposal soon after he submitted it to her. After Colorado Carpet delivered the tile to the Palermo home, however, Mrs. Palermo had a disagreement with Colorado Carpet's tile man and arranged for another contractor to perform the job. Colorado Carpet brought an action against the Palermos for breach of contract. Does the UCC apply to this contract?

10. On November 1, the Kansas City Post Office Employees Credit Union merged into the Kansas City Telephone Credit Union to form the Communications Credit Union (Credit Union) (http://www.cccreditu.org). Systems Design and Management Information (SDMI) develops computer software programs for credit unions, using Burroughs (now Unisys) (http://www.unisys.com) hardware. SDMI and Burroughs together offered to sell to Credit Union both a software package, called the Generic System, and Burroughs hardware. Later in November, a demonstration of the software was held at SDMI's offices, and the Credit Union agreed to purchase the Generic System software. This agreement was oral. After Credit Union was converted to the SDMI Generic System, major problems with the system immediately became apparent. SDMI filed suit against Credit Union to recover the outstanding contract price for the software. Credit Union counterclaimed for damages based upon breach of contract and negligent and fraudulent misrepresentation. Does the UCC apply to this contract?

11. Insul-Mark is the marketing arm of Kor-It Sales, Inc. (http://www.korit.com). Kor-It manufactures roofing fasteners and Insul-Mark distributes them nationwide. In late 1985, Kor-It contracted with Modern Materials, Inc. (http://www.plantfloor.com/in/modernmaterialsinc.htm) to have large volumes of screws coated with a rust-proofing agent. The contract specified that the coated screws must pass a standard industry test and that Kor-It would pay according to the pound and length of the screws coated. Kor-It had received numerous complaints from customers that the coated screws were rusting, but Modern Materials unsuccessfully attempted to remedy the problem. Kor-It terminated its relationship with Modern Materials and brought suit for the deficient coating. Modern Materials counterclaimed for the labor and materials it had furnished to Kor-It. The trial court held that the contract (1) was for performance of a service, (2) not governed by the UCC, (3) governed by the common law of contracts, and (4) therefore, barred by a two-year statute of limitations. Insul-Mark appealed. Decision?

12. Max E. Pass, Jr. and his wife, Martha N. Pass, departed in an aircraft owned and operated by Mr. Pass from Plant City, Florida, bound for Clarksville, Tennessee. Somewhere over Alabama the couple encountered turbulence, and Mr. Pass lost control of the aircraft. The plane crashed killing both Mr. and Mrs. Pass. Approximately four and a half months prior to the flight in which he was killed, Mr. Pass had taken his airplane to Shelby Aviation, an aircraft service company, for inspection and service. In servicing the aircraft, Shelby Aviation replaced both rear wing attach point brackets on the plane. Three and one half years after the crash, Max E. Pass, Sr., father of Mr. Pass and administrator of his estate, and Shirley Williams, mother of Mrs. Pass and administratrix of her estate, filed suit against Shelby Aviation. The lawsuit alleged that the rear wing attach point brackets sold and installed by Shelby Aviation were defective because they lacked the bolts necessary to secure them properly to the airplane. The plaintiffs asserted claims against the defendant for breach of express and implied warranties under Article 2 of the Uniform Commercial Code ("UCC"), which governs the sale of goods. Shelby Aviation contended that the transaction with Mr. Pass had been primarily for the sale of services, rather than of goods, and that consequently Article 2 of the UCC did not cover the transaction. Does the UCC apply to this transaction? Explain.

13. Richardson hired J. C. Flood Company, a plumbing contractor, to correct a stoppage in the sewer line of her house. The plumbing company's "snake" device, used to clear the line leading to the main sewer, became caught in the underground line. To release it, the company excavated a portion of the sewer line in Richardson's backyard. In the process, the company discovered numerous leaks in a rusty, defective water pipe that ran parallel with the sewer line. To meet public regulations, the water pipe, of a type no longer approved for such service, had to be replaced either then or later, when the yard would have to be excavated again. The plumbing company proceeded to repair the water pipe. Though Richardson inspected the company's work daily and did not express any objection to the extra work involved in replacing the water pipe, she refused to pay any part of the total bill after the company completed the entire operation. J. C. Flood Company then sued Richardson for the costs of labor and material it had furnished. Richardson argued that she requested correction only of a sewer obstruction and had never agreed to the replacement of the water pipe. For what, if anything, is Richardson liable? Explain.

http:// **Internet Exercises** Find several samples of contracts.

Chapter 10

Mutual Assent

It is elementary that for a contract to exist there must be an offer and acceptance.
Zeller v. First National Bank and Trust, 79 Ill.App.3d 170, 34 Ill.Dec. 473, 398 N.E.2d 148

Learning Objectives

After reading this chapter you should be able to:

1. Identify the three essentials of an offer and explain briefly the requirements associated with each.
2. State the seven ways by which an offer may be terminated other than by acceptance.
3. Compare the traditional and modern theories of definiteness of acceptance of an offer, as shown by the common law "mirror image" rule and by the rule of the Uniform Commercial Code.
4. Describe the five situations limiting an offeror's right to revoke her offer.
5. Explain the various rules that determine when an acceptance takes effect.

Though each of the requirements for forming a contract is essential to its existence, mutual assent is so basic that frequently a contract is referred to as an agreement between the parties. Enforcing the contract means enforcing the agreement; indeed, the agreement between the parties is the very core of the contract. As we discussed in Chapter 9, a contractual agreement always involves either a promise exchanged for a promise (*bilateral contract*) or a promise exchanged for a completed act or forbearance to act (*unilateral contract*).

The way in which parties usually show mutual assent is by offer and acceptance. One party makes a proposal (offer) by words or conduct to the other party, who agrees by words or conduct to the proposal (acceptance).

A contract may be formed by conduct. Thus, though there may be no definite offer and acceptance, or definite acceptance of an offer, a contract exists if both parties' actions manifest (indicate) a recognition by each of them of the existence of a contract. To form a contract, the agreement must be objectively manifested. The important thing is what the parties indicate to one another by spoken or written words or by conduct. The law, therefore, applies an ***objective*** standard and is concerned only with the assent, agreement, or intention of a party as it reasonably appears from his words or actions. The law of contracts is not concerned with what a party may have actually thought or the meaning that he intended to convey even if his subjective understanding or intention differed from the meaning he objectively indicated by word or conduct. For example, if Joanne seemingly offers to sell to Bruce her Chevrolet automobile but intended to offer and believes that she is offering her Ford automobile, and Bruce accepts the offer, reasonably believing it was for the Chevrolet, a contract has been formed for the sale of the Chevrolet. Subjectively, Joanne and Bruce are not in agreement as to the subject matter. Objectively, however, there is agreement; and the objective manifestation is binding.

The Code's treatment of mutual assent is covered in greater detail in Chapter 19.

OFFER

An **offer** is a definite undertaking or proposal made by one person to another indicating a willingness to enter into a contract. The person making the proposal is the **offeror**. The person to whom it is made is the **offeree**. When it is received, the offer confers on the offeree the power to create a contract by acceptance, which is an expression of the offeree's willingness to comply with the terms of the offer. Until the offeree exercises this power, the outstanding offer creates neither rights nor liabilities.

CPA ESSENTIALS OF AN OFFER

An offer need not take any particular form to have legal effect. To be effective, however, it must (1) be communicated to the offeree; (2) manifest an intent to enter into a contract; and (3) be sufficiently definite and certain. If these essentials are present and the offer has not terminated, the offer gives the offeree the power to form a contract by accepting the offer.

COMMUNICATION

To provide his part of the mutual assent required to form a contract, the offeree must know about the offer; he cannot agree to something about which he has no knowledge. Accordingly, the offeror must communicate the offer in an intended manner. For example, Oscar signs a letter containing an offer to Ellen and leaves it on top of the desk in his office. Later that day, Ellen, without prearrangement, goes to Oscar's office, discovers that he is away, notices the letter on his desk, reads it, and then writes on it an acceptance that she dates and signs. No contract is formed because the offer never became effective: Ellen became aware of the offer by chance, not by Oscar's intentional communication of it.

Not only must the offer be communicated to the offeree, but the communication must also be made or authorized by the offeror. If Jones tells Black that she plans to offer White $600 for a piano, and Black promptly informs White of Jones's intention, no offer has been made. There was no authorized communication of any offer by Jones to White. By the same token, if David should offer to sell to Lou his diamond ring, an acceptance of this offer by Tia would not be effective, as David made no offer to Tia.

An offer need not be stated or communicated by words. Conduct from which a reasonable person may infer a proposal in return for either an act or a promise amounts to an offer.

An offer may be made to the general public. No person can accept such an offer, however, until and unless he knows that the offer exists. For example, if a person, without knowing of an advertised reward for information leading to the return of a lost watch, gives information leading to the return of the watch, he is not entitled to the reward. His act was not an acceptance of the offer because he could not accept something of which he had no knowledge.

INTENT

To have legal effect, an offer must manifest an intent to enter into a contract. The intent of an offer is determined objectively from the words or conduct of the parties. The meaning of either party's manifestation is based on what a reasonable person in the other party's position would have believed.

Occasionally, a person exercises her sense of humor by speaking or writing words that—taken literally and without regard to context or surrounding circumstances—could be construed as an offer. The promise is intended as a joke, however, and the promisee as a reasonable person should understand it to be such. Therefore, it is not an offer. Because the person to whom it is made realizes or should realize that it is not made in earnest, it should not create a reasonable expectation in his mind. No contractual intent exists on the part of the promisor, and the promisee is or reasonably ought to be aware of that fact. If, however, the intended joke is so real that the promisee as a reasonable person under all the circumstances believes that the joke is in fact an offer, and so believing accepts, the objective standard applies and the parties have entered into a contract.

> **Practical Advice**
>
> Make sure that you indicate by words or conduct what agreement you wish to enter.

A promise made under obvious excitement or emotional strain is likewise not an offer. For example, Charlotte, after having her month-old Cadillac break down for the third time in two days, screams in disgust, "I will sell this car to anyone for $10!" Lisa hears Charlotte and hands her a $10 bill. Under the circumstances, Charlotte's statement was not an offer if a reasonable person in Lisa's position would have recognized it merely as an excited, nonbinding utterance.

It is important to distinguish language that constitutes an offer from that which merely solicits or invites offers. Such proposals, although made in earnest, lack the intent to enter into a contract and are therefore not deemed offers. As a result, a purported acceptance does not bring about a contract but operates only as an offer. Proposals that invite offers include preliminary negotiations, advertisements, and auctions.

City of Everett v. Estate of Sumstad

Supreme Court of Washington, 1981
95 Wash.2d 853, 631 P.2d 366

FACTS On August 12, 1978, Mr. and Mrs. Mitchell, the owners of a small secondhand store, attended Alexander's Auction, where they bought a used safe for $50. The safe, part of the Sumstad estate, contained a locked inside compartment. Both the auctioneer and the Mitchells knew this fact. Soon after the auction, the Mitchells had the compartment opened by a locksmith, who discovered $32,207 inside. The Everett Police Department impounded the money. The City of Everett (**http://www.ci.everett.wa.us/**) brought an action against the Sumstad estate and the Mitchells to determine the owner of the money. Both parties moved for summary judgment. The trial court entered summary judgment for the estate, and the court of appeals affirmed. The Mitchells appealed.

DECISION Case remanded to trial court for entry of summary judgment in favor of the Mitchells.

OPINION Dolliver, J. A sale is a consensual transaction. The subject matter which passes is to be determined by the intent of the parties as revealed by the terms of their agreement in light of the surrounding circumstances. [Citation.] The objective manifestation theory of contracts, which is followed in this state [citation] lays stress on the outward manifestation of assent made by each party to the other. The subjective intention of the parties is irrelevant.

> A contract has, strictly speaking, nothing to do with the personal, or individual, intent of the parties. A contract is an obligation attached by the mere force of law to certain acts of the parties, usually words, which ordinarily accompany and represent a known intent. If, however, it were proved by twenty bishops that either party, when he used the words, intended something else than the usual meaning which the law imposes upon them, he would still be held, unless there were some mutual mistake, or something else of the sort. [Citation.]

* * *

The inquiry, then, is into the outward manifestations of intent by a party to enter into a contract. We impute an intention corresponding to the reasonable meaning of a person's words and acts. [Citation.] If the offeror, judged by a reasonable standard manifests an intention to agree in regard to the matter in question, that agreement is established. [Citation.]

* * *

In the case before us, * * * the Mitchells were aware of the rule of the auction that all sales were final. Furthermore, the auctioneer made no statement reserving rights to any contents of the safe to the estate. Under these circumstances, we hold reasonable persons would conclude that the auctioneer manifested an objective intent to sell the safe and its contents and that the parties mutually assented to enter into that sale of the safe and the contents of the locked compartment.

INTERPRETATION The intent of an offer is determined by an objective standard of what a reasonable offeree would have believed.

ETHICAL QUESTION Who should have received the money? Explain.

CRITICAL THINKING QUESTION Does the decision rendered by the court establish a policy that is best for society? Explain.

Preliminary Negotiations If a communication creates in the mind of a reasonable person in the position of the offeree an expectation that his acceptance will conclude a contract, then the communication is an offer. If it does not, then the communication is a preliminary negotiation. Initial communications between potential parties to a contract often take the form of preliminary negotiations, through which the parties either request or supply the terms of an offer that may or may not be made. A statement that may indicate a willingness to make an offer is not in itself an offer. For instance, if Brown writes to Young, "Will you buy my automobile for $3,000?" and Young replies, "Yes," there is no contract. Brown has not made an offer to sell her automobile to Young for $3,000. The offeror must demonstrate an intent to enter into a contract, not merely a willingness to enter into a negotiation.

Advertisements Merchants desire to sell their merchandise and thus are interested in informing potential customers about the goods, the terms of sale, and price. But if they make widespread promises to sell to each person on their mailing list, the number of acceptances and resulting contracts might conceivably exceed their ability to perform. Consequently, a merchant might refrain from making offers by merely announcing that he has goods for sale, describing the goods, and quoting prices. He is simply inviting his customers and, in the case of published advertisements, the public, to make offers to him to buy his goods. His advertisements, circulars, quotation sheets, and displays of merchandise are *not* offers because (1) they do not contain a promise and (2) they leave unexpressed many terms that would be necessary to the making of a contract. Accordingly, his customers' responses are not acceptances because no offer to sell has been made.

Nonetheless, a seller is not free to advertise goods at one price and then raise the price once demand has been stimulated. Although as far as contract law is concerned, the seller has made no offer, such conduct is prohibited by the Federal Trade Commission as well as by legislation in most states. Moreover, in some circumstances a public announcement or advertisement may constitute an offer if the advertisement or announcement contains a definite promise of something in exchange for something else and confers a power of acceptance on a specified person or class of persons. The typical offer of a reward is an example of a definite offer, as is the situation presented in the landmark *Lefkowitz* case, which follows.

Lefkowitz v. Great Minneapolis Surplus Store, Inc.

Supreme Court of Minnesota, 1957
251 Minn. 188, 86 N.W.2d 689

FACTS On April 6, 1956, Great Minneapolis Surplus Store published an advertisement in a Minneapolis newspaper reporting that "Saturday, 9:00 A.M. sharp; 3 brand new fur coats worth up to $100; first come, first served, $1 each." Lefkowitz was the first to arrive at the store, but the store refused to sell him the fur coats because the "house rule" was that the offers were intended for women only and sales would not be made to men. The following week, Great Minneapolis published a similar advertisement for the sale of two mink scarves and a black lapin stole. Again Lefkowitz was the first to arrive at the store on Saturday morning, and once again the store refused to sell to him, this time because Lefkowitz knew of the house rule. This appeal was from a judgment awarding the plaintiff the sum of $138.50 as damages for breach of contract.

DECISION Judgment for Lefkowitz affirmed.

OPINION Murphy, J. The defendant * * * relies upon authorities which hold that, where an advertiser publishes in a newspaper that he has a certain quantity or quality of goods which he wants to dispose of at certain prices and on certain terms, such advertisements are not offers which become contracts as soon as any person to whose notice they may come signifies his acceptance by notifying the other that he will take a certain quantity of them. Such advertisements have been construed as an invitation for an offer of sale on the terms stated which offer, when received, may be accepted or rejected and which, therefore does not become a contract of sale until accepted by the seller; and until a contract has been so made, the seller may modify or revoke such prices or terms. [Citations.] * * *

On the facts before us we are concerned with whether the advertisement constituted an offer.

* * *

The test of whether a binding obligation may originate in advertisements addressed to the general public is "whether the facts show that some performance was promised in positive terms in return for something requested."

* * *

Whether in any individual instance a newspaper advertisement is an offer rather than an invitation to make an offer depends on the legal intention of the parties and the surrounding circumstances. [Citations.] We are of the view on the facts before us that the offer by the defendant of the sale * * * was clear, definite, and explicit, and left nothing open for negotiation. The plaintiff having successfully managed to be the first one to appear at the seller's place of business to be served, as requested by the advertisement, and having offered the stated purchase price of the article, he was entitled to performance on the part of the defendant. We think the trial court was correct in holding that there was in the conduct of the parties a sufficient mutuality of obligation to constitute a contract of sale.

INTERPRETATION Although advertisements generally do not constitute offers, under some circumstances they do.

ETHICAL QUESTION Should Lefkowitz be entitled to damages? Why?

CRITICAL THINKING QUESTION Should an advertisement generally be construed as not constituting an offer? Explain.

Auction Sales The auctioneer at an auction sale does not make offers to sell the property being auctioned but invites offers to buy. The classic statement by the auctioneer is, "How much am I offered?" The persons attending the auction may make progressively higher bids for the property, and each bid or statement of a price or a figure is an offer to buy at that figure. If the bid is accepted, customarily indicated by the fall of the hammer in the auctioneer's hand, a contract results. A bidder is free to withdraw his bid at any time prior to its acceptance. The auctioneer is likewise free to withdraw the goods from sale *unless* the sale is advertised or announced to be without reserve.

If the auction sale is advertised or announced in explicit terms to be **without reserve**, the auctioneer may not withdraw an article or lot put up for sale unless no bid is made within a reasonable time. Unless so advertised or announced, the sale is with reserve. A bidder at either type of sale may retract his bid at any time prior to its acceptance by the auctioneer; such retraction, however, does not revive any previous bid.

http:// U.S. Treasury Auctions: http://www.treas.gov/auctions/

DEFINITENESS

The terms of a contract, all of which are usually contained in the offer, must be clear enough to provide a court with a reasonable basis for determining the existence of a breach and for giving an appropriate remedy. It is a fundamental policy that contracts should be made by the parties, not by the courts; accordingly, remedies for a breach must in turn have their basis in the parties' contract.

Where the parties have intended to form a contract, the courts will attempt to find a basis for granting a remedy. Missing terms may be supplied by course of dealing, usage of trade, or inference. Thus, uncertainty as to incidental matters seldom will be fatal so long as the parties intended to form a contract. Nevertheless, the more terms the parties leave open, the less likely it is that they have intended to form a contract. Moreover, given the great variety of contracts, stating the terms that are essential to all contracts is impossible. In most cases, however, material terms would include the subject matter, price, quantity, quality, terms of payment, and duration.

Open Terms With respect to agreements for the sale of goods, the Uniform Commercial Code provides standards by which the courts may determine omitted terms, provided the parties intended to enter into a binding contract. The Code provides missing terms in a number of instances, where, for example, the contract fails to specify the price, the time or place of delivery, or payment terms. The Restatement has adopted an approach similar to the Code's in supplying terms omitted from the parties' contract.

Practical Advice

To make an offer that will result in an enforceable contract, make sure you include all the necessary terms.

Under the Code, an offer for the purchase or sale of goods may leave open particulars of performance to be specified by one of the parties. Any such specification must be made in good faith and within limits set by commercial reasonableness. **Good faith** is defined as honesty in fact in the conduct or transaction concerned. **Commercial reasonableness** is a standard determined in terms of the business judgment of reasonable persons familiar with the practices customary in the type of transaction involved and in terms of the facts and circumstances of the case.

Output and Requirements Contracts An **output contract** is an agreement of a buyer to purchase a seller's entire output for a stated period. In comparison, a **requirements contract** is an agreement of a seller to supply a buyer with all his requirements for certain goods. Even though the exact quantity of goods is not specified and the seller may have some degree of control over his output and the buyer over his requirements, under the Code and the Restatement, such agreements are enforceable by the application of an objective standard based on the good faith of both parties. Thus, a seller who operated a factory only eight hours a day before the agreement was made cannot operate the factory twenty-four hours a day and insist that the buyer take all of the output. Nor can the buyer expand his business abnormally and insist that the seller still supply all of his requirements.

CPA DURATION OF OFFERS

An offer confers upon the offeree a power of acceptance, which continues until the offer terminates. The ways in which an offer may be terminated, other than by acceptance, are through (1) lapse of time; (2) revocation; (3) rejection; (4) counteroffer; (5) death or incompetency of the offeror or offeree; (6) destruction of the subject matter to which the offer relates; and (7) subsequent illegality of the type of contract the offer proposes.

LAPSE OF TIME

The offeror may specify the time within which the offer is to be accepted, just as he may specify any other term or condition in the offer. Unless otherwise terminated, the offer remains open for the *specified* time. Upon the expiration of that time, as demonstrated by *Newman v. Schiff*, the offer no longer exists and cannot be accepted. Any purported acceptance of an expired offer will serve only as a new offer.

If the offer does not state the time within which the offeree may accept, the offer will terminate after a *reasonable* time. Determining a "reasonable" time is a question of fact, depending on the nature of the contract proposed, the usages of business, and other circumstances of the case (including whether the offer was communicated by electronic means). For instance, an offer to sell a perishable good would be open for a far shorter period of time than an offer to sell undeveloped real estate.

Practical Advice

Because of the uncertainty as to what is a "reasonable time," it is advisable to specify clearly the duration of offers you make.

Newman v. Schiff

United States Court of Appeals, Eighth Circuit, 1985
778 F.2d 460

FACTS Irwin Schiff is a self-styled "tax rebel" who has made a career, and substantial profit, out of his tax protest activities. On February 7, 1983, Schiff appeared live on CBS News (**http://cbsnews.cbs.com**) *Nightwatch*, a late-night program with a viewer participation format. During the broadcast Schiff repeated his assertion that nothing in the Internal Revenue Code stated that an individual was legally required to pay federal income tax. Schiff then challenged "if anybody calls this show—I have the Code—and cites any section of this Code that says an individual is required to file a tax return, I will pay them $100,000." Call-in telephone numbers were periodically flashed on the screen. John Newman, an attorney, did not see Schiff's live appearance on *Nightwatch*. Newman did, however, see a two-minute videotaped segment, including Schiff's challenge, that was rebroadcast several hours later on the *CBS Morning News*. Newman researched the matter that same day, and on the following day, February 9, 1983, placed a call using directory assistance to *CBS Morning News* stating that the call was performance of the consideration requested by Mr. Schiff in exchange for his promise to pay $100,000. When Schiff refused to pay, Newman sued.

DECISION Judgment for Schiff.

OPINION Bright, J.

A. THE REQUIREMENT OF MUTUAL ASSENT

* * * It is a basic legal principle that mutual assent is necessary for the formation of a contract. A significant doctrinal struggle in the development of contract law revolved around whether it was a party's actual or apparent assent that was necessary. This was a struggle between subjective and objective theorists. The subjectivists looked to actual assent. Both parties had to actually assent to an agreement for there to be a contract. External acts were merely necessary evidence to prove or disprove the requisite state of mind. The familiar cliché was that a contract required a "meeting of the minds" of the parties. [Citation.] The objectivists, on the other hand, looked to apparent assent. The expression of mutual assent, and not the assent itself, was the essential element in the formation of a contract. * * *

By the end of the nineteenth century the objective approach to the mutual assent requirement had become predominant, and courts continue to use it today. [Citation.]

* * *

B. THE MECHANICS OF MUTUAL ASSENT: OFFER AND ACCEPTANCE

Courts determine whether the parties expressed their assent to a contract by analyzing their agreement process in terms of offer and acceptance. An offer is the "manifestation of willingness to enter into a bargain, so made as to justify another person in understanding that his assent to that bargain is invited and will conclude it." [Citations.]

The present case concerns a special type of offer: an offer for a reward. * * *

* * *

1. The *Nightwatch* Offer
In the present case, Schiff's statement on *Nightwatch* that he would pay $100,000 to anyone who called the show and cited any section of the Internal Revenue Code "that says an individual is required to file a tax return" constituted a valid offer for a reward. In our view, if anyone had called the show and cited the code sections that Newman produced, a contract would have been formed and Schiff would have been obligated to pay the $100,000 reward, for his bluff would have been properly called.

2. The *CBS Morning News* Rebroadcast
Newman, however, never saw the live CBS *Nightwatch* program upon which Schiff appeared and this lawsuit is not predicated on Schiff's *Nightwatch* offer. Newman saw the *CBS Morning News* rebroadcast of Schiff's *Nightwatch* appearance. This rebroadcast served not to renew or extend Schiff's offer, but rather only to inform viewers that Schiff had made an offer on *Nightwatch*. * * * An offeror is the master of his offer and it is clear that Schiff by his words, "If anybody calls this show * * * ," limited his offer in time to remain open only until the conclusion of the live Nightwatch broadcast. A reasonable person listening to the news rebroadcast could not conclude that the above language—"calls this show"—constituted a new offer; rather than what it actually was, a news report of the offer previously made, which had already expired.

* * *

INTERPRETATION An offeror may limit the duration of an offer, either directly or by implied language.

ETHICAL QUESTION Was Schiff morally obligated to pay Newman? Explain.

CRITICAL THINKING QUESTION Should the courts consider the social and public policy in a case such as this? Explain.

REVOCATION

The offeror generally may cancel or ***revoke*** an offer (**revocation**) at any time *prior* to its acceptance. If the offeror originally promises that the offer will be open for thirty days but wishes to terminate it after five days, he may do so merely by giving the offeree notice that he is withdrawing the offer. This notice may be given by any means of communication and effectively terminates the offer when ***received*** by the offeree. A very few states, however, have adopted a rule that treats revocations the same as acceptances, thus making them effective upon dispatch. An offer made to the general public is revoked only by giving to the revocation publicity equivalent to that given the offer.

Notice of revocation may be communicated indirectly to the offeree through reliable information from a third person that the offeror has disposed of the property he has offered for sale or has otherwise placed himself in a position indicating an unwillingness or inability to perform the promise contained in the offer. For example, Aaron offers to sell his portable television set to Ted and tells Ted that he has ten days in which to accept. One week later, Ted observes the television set in Celia's house and is informed that Celia purchased it from Aaron. The next day, Ted sends to Aaron an acceptance of the offer. There is no contract because Aaron's offer was effectively revoked when Ted learned of Aaron's inability to sell the television set to Ted because he had sold it to Celia.

Certain limitations, however, restrict the offeror's power to revoke the offer at any time prior to its acceptance. These limitations apply to the following five situations.

Option Contracts An **option** is a contract by which the offeror is bound to hold open an offer for a specified period of time. It must comply with all of the requirements of a contract, including the offeree's giving of consideration to the offeror. (**Consideration**, or the inducement to enter into a contract consisting of an act or promise that has legal value, is discussed in Chapter 12.) For example, if Ellen, in return for the payment of $500 to her by Barry, grants Barry an option, exercisable at any time within thirty days, to buy Blackacre at a price of $80,000, Ellen's offer is irrevocable. Ellen is legally bound to keep the offer open for thirty days, and any communication by Ellen to Barry giving notice of withdrawal of the offer is ineffective. Though Barry is not bound to accept the offer, the option contract entitles him to thirty days in which to accept.

Firm Offers under the Code The Code provides that a ***merchant*** is bound to keep an offer to buy or sell ***goods*** open for a stated period (or, if no time is stated, for a reasonable time) not exceeding three months if the merchant gives assurance in a ***signed writing*** that the offer will be held open. The Code, therefore, makes a merchant's **firm offer** (written promise not to revoke an offer for a stated period of time) enforceable even though no consideration is given the offeror for that promise (i.e., an option contract does not exist). A ***merchant*** is defined as a person (1) who is a dealer in a given type of goods, or (2) who by his occupation holds himself out as having knowledge or skill peculiar to the goods or practices involved, or (3) who employs an agent or broker whom he holds out as having such knowledge or skill.

Statutory Irrevocability Certain offers, such as bids made to the state, municipality, or other governmental body for the construction of a building or some public work, are made irrevocable by statute. Another example is preincorporation stock subscription agreements, which are irrevocable for a period of six months under many state corporation statutes.

Irrevocable Offers of Unilateral Contracts Where the offer contemplates a *unilateral* contract—that is, a promise for an act—injustice to the offeree may result if revocation is permitted after the offeree has started to perform the act requested in the offer and has substantially but not completely accomplished it. Such an offer is not accepted and no contract is formed until the offeree has completed the requested act. By simply starting performance, the offeree does not bind himself to complete performance; historically, he did not bind the offeror to keep the offer open, either. Thus, the offeror could revoke the offer at any time before the offeree's completion of performance. For example, Jordan offers Karlene $300 if Karlene will climb to the top of the flagpole in the center of campus. Karlene starts to climb, but when she is five feet from the top, Jordan yells to her, "I revoke."

The Restatement deals with this problem by providing that where the performance of the requested act necessarily requires the offeree to expend time and effort, the offeror is obligated not to revoke the offer for a reasonable time. This obligation arises when the offeree begins performance. If, however, the offeror does not know of the offeree's performance and has no adequate means of learning of it within a reasonable time, the offeree must exercise reasonable diligence to notify the offeror of the performance.

> **Practical Advice**
>
> When making an offer, be careful to make it irrevocable only if you so desire.

Promissory Estoppel As discussed in the previous chapter, a noncontractual promise may be enforced when it is made under circumstances that should lead the promisor reasonably to expect that the promise will induce the promisee to take action in reliance on it. This doctrine has been used in some cases to prevent an offeror from revoking an offer prior to its acceptance.

Thus, Ramanan Plumbing Co. submits a written offer for plumbing work to be used by Resolute Building Co. as part of Resolute's bid as a general contractor. Ramanan knows that Resolute is relying on Ramanan's bid, and in fact Resolute submits Ramanan's name as the plumbing subcontractor in the bid. Ramanan's offer is irrevocable until Resolute has a reasonable opportunity to notify Ramanan that Resolute's bid has been accepted.

REJECTION

An offeree is at liberty to accept or reject the offer as he sees fit. If he decides not to accept it, he is not required to reject it formally but may simply wait until the offer terminates by lapse of time. A **rejection** of an offer is a manifestation by the offeree of his unwillingness to accept. A communicated rejection terminates the power of acceptance. From the effective moment of rejection, which is the receipt of the rejection by the offeror, the offeree may no longer accept the offer. Rejection by the offeree may consist of express language or may be implied from language or conduct.

COUNTEROFFER

A **counteroffer** is a counterproposal from the offeree to the offeror that indicates a willingness to contract but on terms or conditions different from those contained in the original offer. It is not an unequivocal acceptance of the original offer, and by indicating an unwillingness to agree to the terms of the offer, it generally operates as a rejection. It also operates as a new offer. To illustrate further, assume that Worthy writes Joanne a letter stating that he will sell to Joanne a secondhand color television set for $300. Joanne replies that she will pay Worthy $250 for the set. This is a counteroffer that, on *receipt* by Worthy, terminates the original offer. Worthy may, if he wishes, accept the counteroffer and thereby create a contract for $250. If, on the other hand, Joanne in her reply states that she wishes to consider the $300 offer but is willing to pay $250 at once for the set, she is making a counteroffer that does not terminate Worthy's original offer. In the first instance, after making the $250 counteroffer, Joanne may not accept the $300 offer. In the second instance, she may do so, because the counteroffer was stated in such a manner as not to indicate an unwillingness to accept the original offer; Joanne therefore did not terminate it. In addition, a mere inquiry about the possibility of obtaining different or new terms is not a counteroffer and does not terminate the original offer.

Another common type of counteroffer is the **conditional acceptance**, which claims to accept the offer but expressly makes the acceptance contingent on the offeror's assent to additional or different terms. Nonetheless, it is a counteroffer and generally terminates the original offer. The Code's treatment of acceptances containing terms that vary from the offer is discussed later in this chapter.

Practical Advice

Consider whether you want to make a counterproposal that terminates the original offer or whether you merely wish to discuss alternative possibilities.

Giannetti v. Cornillie

Court of Appeals of Michigan, 1994
204 Mich. App. 234, 514 N.W.2d 221

FACTS Defendants listed with a real estate agent a home for sale. Plaintiffs, Patrick and Anne Giannetti, offered $155,000 for the home and submitted a deposit in the amount of $2,500. The defendants countered the offer with an offer to sell the house for $160,000. The plaintiffs then inquired whether certain equipment and items of furniture could be included with the sale of the house. The defendants refused to include the questioned items in the sale. The plaintiffs then accepted the $160,000 offer, but changed the mortgage amount from $124,000 to $128,000. The agent failed to show this change to the defendants but instead told the defendants that the plaintiffs had accepted their counteroffer. Defendants then signed all papers, but before the closing sought to invalidate the agreement. The plaintiffs brought this action for specific performance to enforce the sale. The trial court granted plaintiffs' motion and the defendants appealed.

DECISION Judgment for the defendants.

OPINION Hood, J. Defendants' main argument is that the trial court clearly erred in finding that there was a contract where defendants never agreed to plaintiffs' change in the mortgage amount. We reluctantly agree.

As argued by defendants, "[a]n offer is a unilateral declaration of intention, and is not a contract. A contract is made when both parties have executed or accepted it, and not before. A counterproposition is not an acceptance." [Citations.] An acceptance must be "unambiguous and in strict conformance with an offer." [Citation.]

"'[A] proposal to accept, or an acceptance, upon terms varying from those offered, is a rejection of the offer, and puts an end to the negotiation, unless the party who made the original offer renews it, or assents to the modification suggested.'" [Citation.] Thus, "'a]ny material departure from the terms of an offer invalidates the offer as made and results in a counter proposition, which, unless accepted, cannot be enforced.'" [Citation.]

Plaintiffs argue that the modification of the mortgage amount did not vitiate their purported acceptance because the mortgage amount, unlike the purchase price, was not a material term of the contract. We disagree.

* * *

In other words, before the change, plaintiffs were obligated to buy the property if they obtained a mortgage for $124,000; after the change, no obligation to buy arose unless they obtained a $128,000 mortgage. Thus, the modification and the legal effect of widening the door through which plaintiffs could escape the contract and it was therefore material. [Citation.]

INTERPRETATION A counteroffer generally operates as a rejection and thus terminates the power of acceptance.

ETHICAL QUESTION Was the defendant morally obligated to sell the property? Explain.

CRITICAL THINKING QUESTION What could the plaintiffs have done to protect themselves while at the same time seeking different terms?

DEATH OR INCOMPETENCY

The death or incompetency of either the offeror or the offeree ordinarily terminates an offer. On his death or incompetency, the offeror no longer has the legal capacity to enter into a contract; thus, all outstanding offers are terminated. Death or incompetency of the offeree also terminates the offer, because an ordinary offer is not assignable (transferable) and may be accepted only by the person to whom it was made. When the offeree dies or ceases to have legal capability to enter into a contract, no one else has the power to accept the offer. Therefore, the offer necessarily terminates.

The death or incompetency of the offeror or offeree, however, does *not* terminate an offer contained in an option.

DESTRUCTION OF SUBJECT MATTER

Destruction of the specific subject matter of an offer terminates the offer. Suppose that Sarah, owning a Buick, offers to sell the car to Barbara and allows Barbara five days in which to accept. Three days later the car is destroyed by fire. On the following day, Barbara, without knowledge of the destruction of the car, notifies Sarah that she accepts Sarah's offer. There is no contract. The destruction of the car terminated Sarah's offer.

SUBSEQUENT ILLEGALITY

One of the essential requirements of a contract, as we previously mentioned, is legality of purpose or subject matter. If performance of a valid contract is subsequently made illegal, the obligations of both parties under the contract are discharged. Illegality taking effect after the making of an offer but prior to acceptance has the same effect: the offer is legally terminated.

For an illustration of the duration of revocable offers, see Figure 10-1.

ACCEPTANCE OF OFFER

The acceptance of an offer is essential to the formation of a contract. Once an effective acceptance has been given, the contract is formed. **Acceptance** of an offer for a bilateral contract is some overt act by the offeree that manifests his assent to the terms of the offer, such as speaking or sending a letter, a telegram, or other explicit or implicit communication to the offeror. If the offer is for a unilateral contract, acceptance is the performance of the requested act with the intention of accepting. For example, if Joy publishes an offer of a reward to anyone who returns the diamond ring that she has lost (an offer to enter into a unilateral contract) and Bob, with knowledge of the offer, finds and returns the ring to Joy, Bob has accepted the offer.

CPA COMMUNICATION OF ACCEPTANCE

GENERAL RULE

Because acceptance is the manifestation of the offeree's assent to the offer, it must necessarily be communicated to the offeror. This is the rule as to all offers to enter into bilateral contracts. In the case of unilateral offers, however, notice of acceptance to the offeror usually is not required. If, however, the offeree in a unilateral contract has reason to know that the offeror has no adequate

Figure 10-1
Duration of Revocable Offers

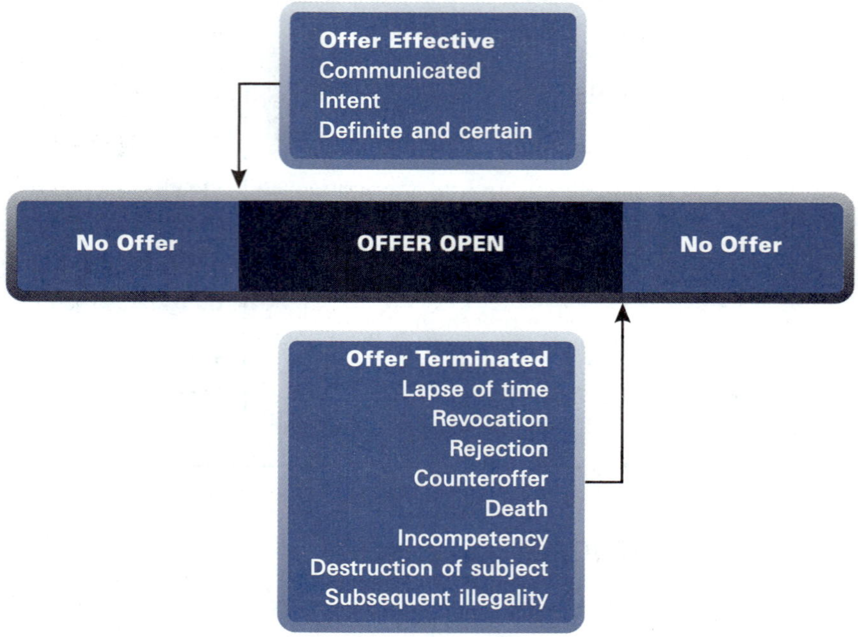

means of learning of the offeree's performance with reasonable promptness and certainty, then the offeree must make reasonable efforts to notify the offeror of acceptance or lose the right to enforce the contract.

SILENCE AS ACCEPTANCE

An offeree is generally under no legal duty to reply to an offer. Silence or inaction therefore does *not* indicate acceptance of the offer. By custom, usage, or course of dealing, however, the offeree's silence or inaction may operate as an acceptance. Thus, the silence or inaction of an offeree who fails to reply to an offer operates as an acceptance and causes a contract to be formed where by previous dealings the offeree has given the offeror reason to understand that the offeree will accept all offers unless the offeree sends notice to the contrary. Another example of silence operating as an acceptance occurs when the prospective member of a mail-order club agrees that his failure to return a notification card rejecting offered goods will constitute his acceptance of the club's offer to sell the goods.

Furthermore, if an offeror sends unordered or unsolicited merchandise to a person, stating that the goods may be purchased at a specified price and that the offer will be deemed to have been accepted unless the goods are returned within a stated period of time, the offer is one for an inverted unilateral contract (i.e., an act for a promise). This practice has led to abuse, however, prompting the federal government as well as most states to enact statutes that provide that in such cases the offeree-recipient of the goods may keep them as a gift and is under no obligation either to return them or to pay for them.

EFFECTIVE MOMENT

As we discussed previously, an offer, a revocation, a rejection, and a counteroffer are effective when they are *received*. An acceptance is generally effective upon *dispatch*. This is true unless the offer specifically provides otherwise, the offeree uses an unauthorized means of communication, or the acceptance follows a prior rejection.

Stipulated Provisions in the Offer If the offer specifically stipulates the means of communication to be used by the offeree, the acceptance must conform to that specification. Thus, if an offer states that acceptance must be made by registered mail, any purported acceptance not made by registered mail would be ineffective. Moreover, the rule that an acceptance is effective when dispatched or sent does not apply where the offer provides that the acceptance must be received by the offeror. If the offeror states that a reply must be received by a certain date or that he must hear from the offeree or uses other language indicating that the acceptance must be received by him, the effective moment of the acceptance is when the offeror receives it, not when the offeree sends or dispatches it.

Practical Advice

Consider whether you should specify in your offers that acceptances are valid only upon receipt.

Authorized Means Historically, an authorized means of communication was either the means the offeror expressly authorized in the offer or, if none was authorized, the means the offeror used in presenting the offer. If in reply to an offer by mail, the offeree places in the mail a letter of acceptance properly stamped and addressed to the offeror, a contract is formed at the time and place that the offeree mails the letter. This assumes, of course, that the offer was open at that time and had not been terminated by any of the methods previously discussed. The reason for this rule is that the offeror, by using the mail, impliedly authorized the offeree to use the same means of communication. It is immaterial if the letter of acceptance goes astray in the mails and is never received.

The Restatement and the Code both now provide that where the language in the offer or the circumstances do not otherwise indicate, an offer to make a contract shall be construed as authorizing acceptance in any reasonable manner. Thus, an **authorized means** is usually any ***reasonable*** means of communication. These provisions are intended to allow flexibility of response and the ability to keep pace with new modes of communication.

See Figure 10-2 for an overview of offer and acceptance.

Figure 10-2
Mutual Assent

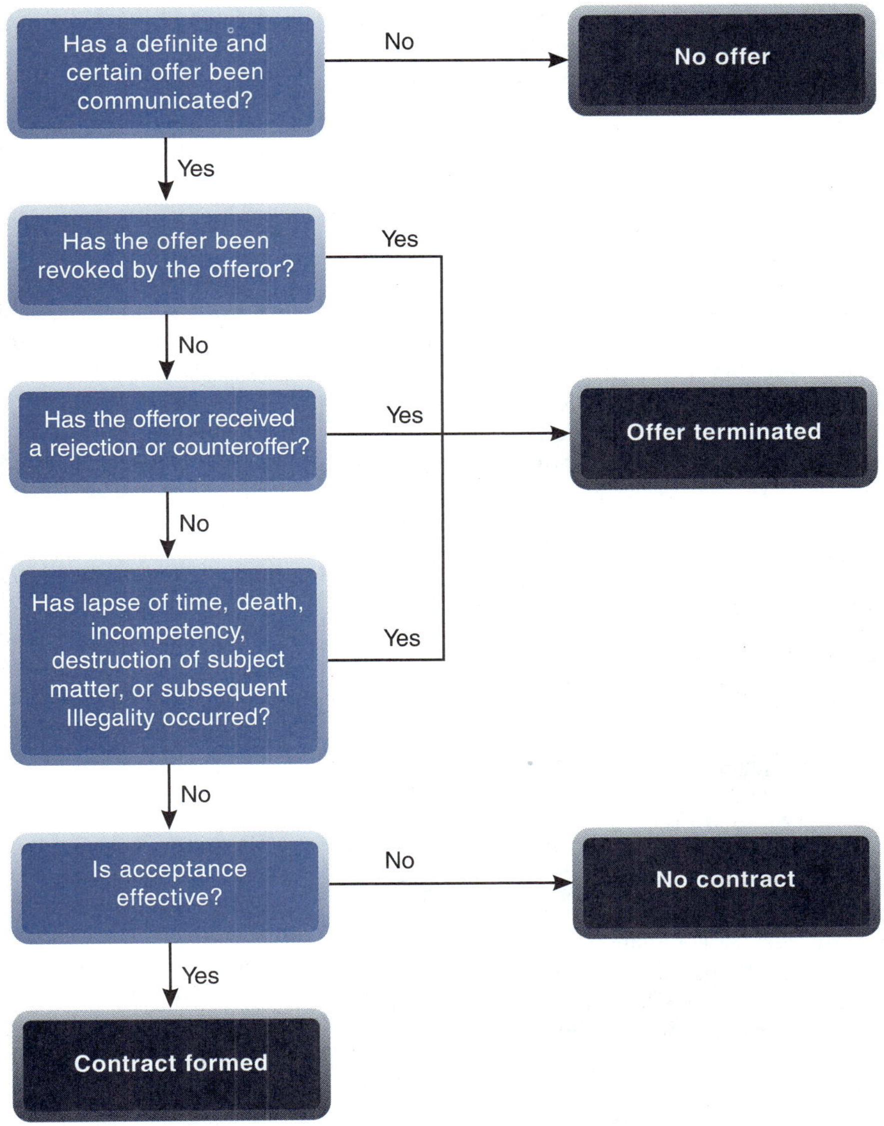

Osprey L.L.C. v. Kelly-Moore Paint Co., Inc.

Supreme Court of Oklahoma 1999

1999 OK 50, 984 P.2d 194

http://caselaw.findlaw.com/scripts/getcase.pl?court=OK&vol=/supreme/1999/&invol=1999OK50

FACTS In 1977, the defendant, Kelly-Moore Paint Company **(http://www.kellymoore.com)**, entered into a 15 year commercial lease with the plaintiff, Osprey, for a property in Edmond, Oklahoma. The lease contained two five-year renewal options. The lease required that the lessee give notice of its intent to renew at least six months prior to its expiration. It also provided that the renewal "may be delivered either personally or by depositing the same in United States mail, first class postage prepaid, registered or certified mail, return receipt requested." Upon expiration of the original fifteen-year lease, Kelly-Moore timely informed the lessor by certified letter of its intent to extend the lease an additional five years. The first five-year extension was due to expire on August 31, 1997. On the last day of the six-month notification deadline, Kelly-Moore faxed a letter of renewal notice to Osprey's office at 5:28 P.M. In addition, Kelly-Moore sent a copy of the faxed renewal notice letter by Federal Express that same day. Osprey denies ever receiving the fax, but it admits receiving the Federal Express copy of the notice on the following business day. Osprey rejected the notice, asserting that it was late, and it filed an action to remove the defendant from the premises. After a trial on the merits, the trial court granted judgment in favor of Kelly-Moore, finding that the faxed notice was effective. Osprey appealed. The Court of Civil Appeals reversed, determining that the plain language of the lease required that it be renewed by delivering notice either personally or by mail, and that Kelly-Moore had done neither. Kelly-Moore appealed.

DECISION The decision of the Court of Appeals is vacated and the decision of the trial court is affirmed.

OPINION Kauger, J. Under the facts presented, the faxed delivery of the written notice of renewal timely exercised the renewal option of the lease.

The precise issue of whether a faxed or facsimile delivery of a written notice to renew a commercial lease is sufficient to exercise timely the renewal option of the lease is one of first impression in Oklahoma. Neither party has cited to a case from another jurisdiction which has decided this question, or to any case which has specifically defined "personal delivery" as including facsimile delivery.

* * *

Osprey argues that: 1) the lease specifically prescribed limited means of acceptance of the option, and it required that the notice of renewal be delivered either personally or sent by United States mail, registered or certified; 2) Kelly-Moore failed to follow the contractual requirements of the lease when it delivered its notice by fax; and 3) because the terms for extending the lease specified in the contract were not met, the notice was invalid and the lease expired on August 31, 1997. Kelly-Moore counters that: 1) the lease by the use of the word "shall" mandates that the notice be written, but the use of the word "may" is permissive; and 2) although the notice provision of the lease permits delivery personally or by United States mail, it does not exclude other modes of delivery or transmission which would include delivery by facsimile. * * *

A lease is a contract and in construing a lease, the usual rules for the interpretation of contractual writings apply. * * *

Language in a contract is given its plain and ordinary meaning, unless some technical term is used in a manner meant to convey a specific technical concept. A contract term is ambiguous only if it can be interpreted as having two different meanings. * * * The lease does not appear to be ambiguous.

"Shall" is ordinarily construed as mandatory and "may" is ordinarily construed as permissive. The contract clearly requires that notice "shall" be in writing. The provision for delivery, either personally or by certified or registered mail, uses the permissive "may" and it does not bar other modes of transmission which are just as effective.

The purpose of providing notice by personal delivery or registered mail is to insure the delivery of the notice, and to settle any dispute which might arise between the parties concerning whether the notice was received. A substituted method of notice which performs the same function and serves the same purpose as an authorized method of notice is not defective.

Here, the contract provided that time was of the essence. Although Osprey denies that it ever received the fax, the fax activity report and telephone company records confirm that the fax was transmitted successfully, and that it was sent to Osprey's correct facsimile number on the last day of the deadline to extend the lease. The fax provided immediate written communication similar to personal delivery and, like a telegram, would be timely if it were properly transmitted before the expiration of the deadline to renew. Kelly-Moore's use of the fax served the same function and the same purpose as the two methods suggested by the lease and it was transmitted before the expiration of the deadline to renew. Under these facts, we hold that the faxed or facsimile delivery of the written notice to renew the commercial lease was sufficient to exercise timely the renewal option of the lease.

* * *

INTERPRETATION Where the language in the offer or the circumstances does not otherwise indicate, an offer to make a contract shall be construed as authorizing acceptance in any reasonable manner.

CRITICAL THINKING QUESTION Are there instances when an offeror should require a certain mode for acceptance? When?

Unauthorized Means When the method of communication used by the offeree is unauthorized, the traditional rule is that acceptance is effective when and if received by the offeror, provided that it is received within the time during which the authorized means would have arrived. The Restatement goes further by providing that if these conditions are met, then the effective time for the acceptance is the moment of dispatch.

Acceptance Following a Prior Rejection An acceptance sent after a prior rejection is not effective when sent by the offeree, but only when and if ***received*** by the offeror before he receives the rejection. Thus, when an acceptance follows a prior rejection, the *first communication* the offeror receives is the effective one. For example, Carlos in New York sends by airmail to Paula in San Francisco an offer that is expressly stated to be open for one week. On the fourth day, Paula sends to Carlos by airmail a letter of rejection, which is delivered on the morning of the sixth day. At noon on the fifth day, Paula dispatches a telegram of acceptance that Carlos receives before the close of business on that day. A contract was formed when Carlos received Paula's telegram of acceptance—it was the first communication he received.

DEFECTIVE ACCEPTANCES

A late or defective acceptance does not create a contract. After the offer has expired, it cannot be accepted. However, a late or defective acceptance does manifest a willingness on the part of the offeree to enter into a contract and therefore constitutes a new offer. In order to create a contract based on this offer, the original offeror must accept the new offer by manifesting his assent to it.

CPA VARIANT ACCEPTANCES

A variant acceptance—one that contains terms different from or additional to those in the offer—receives distinctly different treatment under the common law and under the Code.

COMMON LAW

An acceptance must be *positive* and *unequivocal*. It may not change, add to, subtract from, or qualify in any way the provisions of the offer. In other words, it must be the **mirror image** of the offer. Any communication by the offeree that attempts to modify the offer is not an acceptance but a counteroffer, which does not create a contract.

CODE

The common law mirror image rule, by which the acceptance cannot vary or deviate from the terms of the offer, is modified by the Code. This modification is necessitated by the realities of modern business practices. A vast number of business transactions use standardized business forms. For example, a merchant buyer sends to a merchant seller on the buyer's order form a purchase order for one thousand dozen cotton shirts at $60 per dozen with delivery by October 1 at the buyer's place of business. On the reverse side of this standard form are twenty-five numbered paragraphs containing provisions generally favorable to the buyer. When the seller receives the buyer's order, he agrees to the buyer's quantity, price, and delivery terms and sends to the buyer on his acceptance form an unequivocal acceptance of the offer. However, on the back of his acceptance form, the seller has thirty-two numbered paragraphs generally favorable to himself and in significant conflict with the provisions on the buyer's form. Under the common law's *mirror image* rule, no contract would exist; for the seller has not accepted unequivocally all of the material terms of the buyer's offer.

The Code attempts to alleviate this ***battle of the forms*** by focusing on the intent of the parties. If the offeree does not expressly make her acceptance conditional upon the offeror's assent to the additional or different terms, a contract is formed. The issue then becomes whether the

THE LAW AND YOU

State Bar Associations

Florida: http://www.flabar.org/newflabar/consumerservices/General/Consumer.Pam/ ("Marriage")

Illinois: http://www.illinoislawyerfinder.com/publicinfo/home.html ("Newlyweds")

Minnesota: http://www.mnbar.org/consumer.htm ("Getting Married")

Missouri: http://www.mobar.org/ (public information brochures) ("Marriage")

North Carolina: http://www.ncbar.org/legal_prof/divisions/yld/publications/consumer_pub.asp ("Marriage in North Carolina")

Ohio: http://www.ohiobar.org/conres/pamphlets/ ("Ohio's Marriage Laws")

Oregon: http://www.osbar.org/public/legallinks.html ("Marriage in Oregon")

South Dakota: http://www.sdbar.org/public/pamphlets/pamphlets.htm ("Marriage")

Washington: http://www.wsba.org/public/ default.htm ("Marriage")

State Attorney Generals

Alabama: http://www.ago.state.al.us/consumer_info.cfm ("Unordered Merchandise")

California: http://www.dca.ca.gov/r_r/conspub1.htm ("Contracts")

Maine: http://www.state.me.us/ag/?=protection ("The Maine Attorney General's Consumer Law Guide")

New Hampshire: http://www.state.nh.us/nhdoj/Consumer/brochures.html ("Unordered Merchandise")

North Dakota: http://www.ag.state.nd.us/cpat/pdf files/unordered.pdf ("Unordered Merchandise Is a Free Gift")

South Dakota: http://www.state.sd.us/attorney/office/divisions/consumer/links.asp ("Contracts Chapter in Consumer Handbook")

Tennessee: http://www.state.tn.us/consumer/brochure.html

Texas: http://www.oag.state.tx.us/

Utah: http://www.dfi.state.ut.us/ConsTips.htm

Vermont: http://www.state.vt.us/atg/consumer.htm

Virginia: http://www.oag.state.va.us/Protecting/Consumer Fraud/consumer_assistance.htm

Washington: http://www.wa.gov/ago/consumer/ http://www.wa.gov/ago/consumer/cp_publications.html

West Virginia: http://www.state.wv.us/wvag/

Wisconsin: http://www.doj.state.wi.us/

U.S. Government

U.S. Consumer Information Center
http://www.pueblo.gsa.gov/smbuss.htm

offeree's different or additional terms become part of the contract. If both offeror and offeree are merchants, such *additional* terms may become part of the contract provided that they do not materially alter the agreement and are not objected to either in the offer itself or within a reasonable period of time. If either of the parties is not a merchant or if the additional terms materially alter the offer, then the additional terms are merely construed as proposals to the contract. *Different* terms proposed by the offeree will not become part of the contract unless accepted by the offeror. The courts are divided over what terms to include when the terms differ or conflict. Most courts hold that the offeror's terms govern; other courts hold that the terms cancel each other out and look to the Code to provide the missing terms. Some states follow a third alternative and apply the additional terms test to different terms. (See Figure 19-1 in Chapter 19.)

Let us apply the Code to the previous example involving the seller and the buyer: because both parties are merchants and the seller's acceptance was not conditional upon assent to the seller's additional or different terms, then either (1) the contract will be formed without the seller's different terms unless the buyer specifically accepts them; (2) the contract will be formed without the seller's additional terms (unless they are specifically accepted by the buyer) because the additional terms materially alter the offer; or (3) depending upon the jurisdiction, either (a) the buyer's conflicting terms will be included in the contract, (b) the Code will provide the missing terms, because the conflicting terms cancel each other out, or (c) the additional terms test is applied.

See the following Concept Review explicating the effective time and effect of communications involved in offer and acceptances.

Concept Review

Offer and Acceptance

	Time Effective	Effect
Communication by Offeror		
• Offer	Received by offeror	Creates power to form a contact
• Revocation	Received by offeree	Terminates power
Communication by Offeree		
• Rejection	Received by offeror	Terminates offer
• Counteroffer	Received by offeror	Terminates offer
• Acceptance	Sent by offeree	Forms a contract
• Acceptance after prior rejection	Received by offeror	If received before rejection forms a contract

Chapter Summary

Offer

Essentials of an Offer

Definition indication of willingness to enter into a contract

Communication offeree must have knowledge of the offer and the offer must be made by the offeror or her authorized agent to the offeree

Intent determined by an objective standard of what a reasonable offeree would have believed

Definiteness offer's terms must be clear enough to provide a court with a basis for giving an appropriate remedy

Duration of Offers

Lapse of Time offer remains open for the time period specified or, if no time is stated, for a reasonable period of time

Revocation generally, an offer may be terminated at any time before it is accepted, subject to the following exceptions

- *Option Contracts* contract that binds offeror to keep an offer open for a specified time
- *Firm Offer* a merchant's irrevocable offer to sell or buy goods in a signed writing that ensures that the offer will not be terminated for up to three months
- *Statutory Irrevocability* offer made irrevocable by statute
- *Irrevocable Offer of Unilateral Contracts* a unilateral offer may not be revoked for a reasonable time after performance is begun
- *Promissory Estoppel* noncontractual promise that binds the promisor because she should reasonably expect that the promise will induce the promisee (offeree) to take action in reliance on it

Rejection refusal to accept an offer terminates the power of acceptance

Counteroffer counterproposal to an offer that generally terminates the original offer

Death or Incompetency of either the offeror or the offeree terminates the offer

Destruction of Subject Matter of an offer terminates the offer

Subsequent Illegality of the purpose or subject matter of the offer terminates the offer

Acceptance of Offer

Requirements

Definition positive and unequivocal expression of a willingness to enter into a contract on the terms of the offer

Mirror Image Rule except as modified by the Code, an acceptance cannot deviate from the terms of the offer

Communication of Acceptance

General Rule acceptance effective upon dispatch unless the offer specifically provides otherwise or the offeree uses an unauthorized means of communication

Silence as Acceptance generally does not indicate acceptance of the offer

Effective Moment generally upon dispatch
- ***Stipulated Provisions in the Offer*** the communication of acceptance must conform to the specifications in the offer
- ***Authorized Means*** Restatement and the Code provide that, unless the offer provides otherwise, acceptance is authorized to be in any reasonable manner
- ***Unauthorized Means*** acceptance effective when received, provided that it is received within the time within which the authorized means would have arrived
- ***Acceptance Following a Prior Rejection*** first communication received by the offeror is effective

Defective Acceptance does not create a contract but serves as a new offer

QUESTIONS

1. Ames, seeking business for his lawn maintenance firm, posted the following notice in the meeting room of the Antlers, a local lodge: "To the members of the Antlers—Special this month. I will resod your lawn for $4.00 per square foot using Fairway brand sod. This offer expires July 15."

   The notice also included Ames's name, address, and signature and specified that the acceptance was to be in writing.

   Bates, a member of the Antlers, and Cramer, the janitor, read the notice and were interested. Bates wrote a letter to Ames saying he would accept the offer if Ames would use Putting Green brand sod. Ames received this letter July 14 and wrote to Bates saying he would not use Putting Green sod. Bates received Ames's letter on July 16 and promptly wrote Ames that he would accept Fairway sod. Cramer wrote to Ames on July 10 saying he accepted Ames's offer.

   By July 15, Ames had found more profitable ventures and refused to resod either lawn at the specified price. Bates and Cramer brought an appropriate action against Ames for breach of contract. Decisions as to the respective claims of Bates and Cramer?

2. Justin owned four speedboats named *Porpoise*, *Priscilla*, *Providence*, and *Prudence*. On April 2, Justin made written offers to sell the four boats in the order named for $4,200 each to Charles, Diane, Edward, and Fran, respectively, allowing ten days for acceptance. In which, if any, of the following four situations was a contract formed?

   a. Five days later, Charles received notice from Justin that he had contracted to sell *Porpoise* to Mark. The next day, April 8, Charles notified Justin that he accepted Justin's offer.

   b. On the third day, April 5, Diane mailed a rejection to Justin that reached Justin on the morning of the fifth day. At 10 A.M. on the fourth day, Diane sent an acceptance by telegram to Justin, who received it at noon the same day.

   c. Edward, on April 3, replied that he was interested in buying *Providence* but declared the price appeared slightly excessive and wondered if, perhaps, Justin would be willing to sell the boat for $3,900. Five days later, having received no reply from Justin, Edward accepted Justin's offer by letter, and enclosed a certified check for $4,200.

   d. Fran was accidentally killed in an automobile accident on April 9. The following day, the executor of her estate mailed an acceptance of Justin's offer to Justin.

3. Alpha Rolling Mill Corporation (Alpha Corporation), by letter dated June 8, offered to sell Brooklyn Railroad

Company (Brooklyn Company) 2,000 to 5,000 tons of fifty-pound iron rails on certain specified terms and added that, if the offer was accepted, Alpha Corporation would expect to be notified prior to June 20. Brooklyn Company, on June 16, by telegram, referring to Alpha Corporation's offer of June 8, directed Alpha Corporation to enter an order for 1,200 tons of fifty-pound iron rails on the terms specified. The same day, June 16, Brooklyn Company, by letter to Alpha Corporation, confirmed the telegram. On June 18, Alpha Corporation, by telegram, declined to fulfill the order. Brooklyn Company, on June 19, telegraphed Alpha Corporation: "Please enter an order for 2,000 tons of rails as per your letter of the eighth. Please forward written contract. Reply." In reply to Brooklyn Company's repeated inquiries concerning whether the order for 2,000 tons of rails had been entered, Alpha denied the existence of any contract between Brooklyn Company and itself. Thereafter, Brooklyn Company sued Alpha Corporation for breach of contract. Decision?

4. On April 8, Crystal received a telephone call from Akers, a truck dealer, who told Crystal that a new model truck in which Crystal was interested would arrive in one week. Although Akers initially wanted $10,500, the conversation ended after Akers agreed to sell and Crystal agreed to purchase the truck for $10,000, with a $1,000 down payment and the balance on delivery. The next day, Crystal sent Akers a check for $1,000, which Akers promptly cashed.

   One week later, when Crystal called Akers and inquired about the truck, Akers informed Crystal he had several prospects looking at the truck and would not sell for less than $10,500. The following day Akers sent Crystal a properly executed check for $1,000 with the following notation thereon: "Return of down payment on sale of truck."

   After notifying Akers that she will not cash the check, Crystal sues Akers for damages. Should Crystal prevail? Explain.

5. On November 15, Gloria, Inc., a manufacturer of crystalware, mailed to Benny Buyer a letter stating that Gloria would sell to Buyer one hundred crystal "A" goblets at $100 per goblet and that "the offer would remain open for fifteen (15) days." On November 18, Gloria, noticing the sudden rise in the price of crystal "A" goblets, decided to withdraw its offer to Buyer and so notified Buyer. Buyer chose to ignore Gloria's letter of revocation and gleefully watched as the price of crystal "A" goblets continued to skyrocket. On November 30, Buyer mailed to Gloria a letter accepting Gloria's offer to sell the goblets. The letter was received by Gloria on December 4. Buyer demands delivery of the goblets. What is the result?

6. On May 1, Melforth Realty Company offered to sell Greenacre to Dallas, Inc., for $1,000,000. The offer was made by telegraph and stated that the offer would expire on May 15. Dallas decided to purchase the property and sent a registered letter to Melforth on May 10 accepting the offer. As a result of unexplained delays in the postal service, the letter was not received by Melforth until May 22. Melforth wishes to sell Greenacre to another buyer who is offering $1,200,000 for the tract of land. Has a contract resulted between Melforth and Dallas?

7. Rowe advertised in newspapers of wide circulation and otherwise made known that she would pay $5,000 for a complete set, consisting of ten volumes, of certain rare books. Ford, not knowing of the offer, gave Rowe all but one of the set of rare books as a Christmas present. Ford later learned of the offer, obtained the one remaining book, tendered it to Rowe, and demanded the $5,000. Rowe refused to pay. Is Ford entitled to the $5,000?

8. Scott, manufacturer of a carbonated beverage, entered into a contract with Otis, owner of a baseball park, whereby Otis rented to Scott a large signboard on top of the center field wall. The contract provided that Otis should letter the sign as Scott desired and would change the lettering from time to time within forty-eight hours after receipt of written request from Scott. As directed by Scott, the signboard originally stated in large letters that Scott would pay $100 to any ballplayer hitting a home run over the sign.

   In the first game of the season, Hume, the best hitter in the league, hit one home run over the sign. Scott immediately served written notice on Otis instructing Otis to replace the offer on the signboard with an offer to pay $50 to every pitcher who pitched a no-hit game in the park. A week after receipt of Scott's letter, Otis had not changed the wording on the sign; and on that day, Perry, a pitcher for a scheduled game, pitched a no-hit game and Todd, one of his teammates, hit a home run over Scott's sign.

   Scott refuses to pay any of the three players. What are the rights of Scott, Hume, Perry, and Todd?

9. Barney accepted Clark's offer to sell to him a portion of Clark's coin collection. Clark forgot at the time of the offer and acceptance that her prized $20 gold piece was included in the portion that she offered to sell to Barney. Clark did not intend to include the gold piece in the sale. Barney, at the time of inspecting the offered portion of the collection, and prior to accepting the offer, saw the gold piece. Is Barney entitled to the $20 gold piece?

10. Small, admiring Jasper's watch, asked Jasper where and at what price he had purchased it. Jasper replied, "I bought it at West Watch Shop about two years ago for around $85, but I am not certain as to that." Small then said, "Those fellows at West are good people and always sell good watches. I'll buy that watch from you." Jasper replied, "It's a deal." The next morning, Small telephoned Jasper and said he had changed his mind and did not wish to buy the watch.

    Jasper sued Small for breach of contract. In defense, Small has pleaded that he made no enforceable contract with Jasper because (a) the parties did not agree on the price to be paid for the watch and (b) the parties did not agree on the place and time of delivery of the watch to Small. Are either, or both, of these defenses good?

11. Jeff says to Brenda, "I offer to sell you my IBM PC for $900." Brenda replies, "If you do not hear otherwise from

me by Thursday, I have accepted your offer." Jeff agrees and does not hear from Brenda by Thursday. Does a contract exist between Jeff and Brenda? Explain.

12. On November 19, Hoover Motor Express Company sent to Clements Paper Company a written offer to purchase certain real estate. Sometime in December, Clements authorized Williams to accept. Williams, however, attempted to bargain with Hoover to obtain a better deal, specifically that Clements would retain easements on the property. In a telephone conversation on January 13 of the following year, Williams first told Hoover of his plan to obtain the easements. Hoover replied, "Well, I don't know if we are ready. We have not decided, we might not want to go through with it." On January 20, Clements sent a written acceptance of Hoover's offer. Hoover refused to buy, claiming it had revoked its offer through the January 13 phone conversation. Clements then brought suit to compel the sale or obtain damages. Did Hoover successfully revoke its offer?

13. Walker leased a small lot to Keith for ten years at $100 a month, with a right for Keith to extend the lease for another ten-year term under the same terms except as to rent. The renewal option provided:

> Rental will be fixed in such amount as shall actually be agreed upon by the lessors and the lessee with the monthly rental fixed on the comparative basis of rental values as of the date of the renewal with rental values at this time reflected by the comparative business conditions of the two periods.

Keith sought to exercise the renewal right and, when the parties were unable to agree on the rent, brought suit against Walker. Who prevails? Why?

CASE PROBLEMS

14. The Brewers contracted to purchase Dower House from McAfee. Then, several weeks before the May 7 settlement date for the purchase of the house, the two parties began to negotiate for the sale of certain items of furniture in the house. On April 30, McAfee sent the Brewers a letter containing a list of the furnishings to be purchased at specific prices; a payment schedule including a $3,000 payment due on acceptance; and a clause reading: "If the above is satisfactory, please sign and return one copy with the first payment."

    On June 3, the Brewers sent a letter to McAfee stating that enclosed was a $3,000 check; that the original contract had been misplaced and could another be furnished; that they planned to move into Dower House on June 12; and that they wished that the red desk be included in the contract. McAfee then sent a letter dated June 8 to the Brewers listing the items of furniture they had purchased.

    The Brewers moved into Dower House in the middle of June. Soon after they moved in, they tried to contact McAfee at his office to tell him that there had been a misunderstanding relating to their purchase of the listed items. They then refused to pay him any more money, and he brought this action to recover the outstanding balance. Will McAfee be able to collect the additional money from the Brewers?

15. The Thoelkes were owners of real property located in Orange County, which the Morrisons agreed to purchase. The Morrisons signed a contract for the sale of that property and mailed it to the Thoelkes in Texas on November 26. The next day, the Thoelkes executed the contract and placed it in the mail addressed to the Morrisons' attorney in Florida. After the executed contract was mailed but before it was received in Florida, the Thoelkes called the Morrisons' attorney in Florida and attempted to repudiate the contract. Does a contract exist between the Thoelkes and the Morrisons? Discuss.

16. On December 20, Lucy and Zehmer met while having drinks in a restaurant. During the course of their conversation, Lucy apparently offered to buy Zehmer's 471.6-acre farm for $50,000 cash. Although Zehmer claims that he thought the offer was made in jest, he wrote the following on the back of a pad: "We hereby agree to sell to W. O. Lucy the Ferguson Farm complete for $50,000, title satisfactory to buyer." Zehmer then signed the writing and induced his wife Ida to do the same. She claims, however, that she signed only after Zehmer assured her that it was only a joke. Finally, Zehmer claims that he was "high as a Georgia pine" at the time but admits that he was not too drunk to make a valid contract. Explain whether the contract is enforceable.

17. On July 31, Lee Calan Imports advertised a used Volvo station wagon for sale in the *Chicago Sun-Times*. As part of the information for the advertisement, Lee Calan Imports instructed the newspaper to print the price of the car as $1,795. However, due to a mistake made by the newspaper, without any fault on the part of Lee Calan Imports, the printed ad listed the price of the car as $1,095. After reading the ad and then examining the car, O'Brien told a Lee Calan Imports salesman that he wanted to purchase the car for the advertised price of $1,095. Calan Imports refuses to sell the car to O'Brien for $1,095. Is there a contract? If so, for what price?

18. On May 20, cattle rancher Oliver visited his neighbor Southworth, telling him, "I know you're interested in buying the land I'm selling." Southworth replied, "Yes, I do

want to buy that land, especially because it adjoins my property." Although the two men did not discuss the price, Oliver told Southworth he would determine the value of the property and send that information to Southworth so that he would have "notice" of what Oliver "wanted for the land." On June 13, Southworth called Oliver to ask if he still planned to sell the land. Oliver answered, "Yes, and I should have the value of the land determined soon." On June 17, Oliver sent a letter to Southworth listing a price quotation of $324,000. Southworth then responded to Oliver by letter on June 21, stating that he accepted Oliver's offer. However, on June 24 Oliver wrote back to Southworth saying, "There has never been a firm offer to sell, and there is no enforceable contract between us." Oliver maintains that a price quotation alone is not an offer. Southworth claims a valid contract has been made. Who wins? Discuss.

19. Cushing filed an application with the office of the Adjutant General of the State of New Hampshire (http://www.nharmyguard.com/chain/tag.htm) for the use of the Portsmouth Armory to hold a dance on the evening of April 29. The application, made on behalf of the Portsmouth Area Clamshell Alliance, was received by the Adjutant General's office on or about March 30. On March 31 the Adjutant General mailed a signed contract after agreeing to rent the armory for the evening requested. The agreement required acceptance by the renter affixing his signature to the agreement and then returning the copy to the Adjutant General within five days after receipt. Cushing received the contract offer, signed it on behalf of the alliance, and mailed it on April 3. At 6:30 on the evening of April 4, Cushing received a telephone call from the Adjutant General revoking the rental offer. Cushing stated during the conversation that he had already signed and mailed the contract. The Adjutant General sent a written confirmation of the withdrawal on April 5. On April 6 the Adjutant General's office received by mail the signed contract dated April 3 and postmarked April 5. Does a binding contract exist? Explain.

http:// **Internet Exercise** Go to several retail Websites and auction sites and determine: (1) who is the offeror and the offeree, (2) what are the terms of the offer, and (3) when can the offer be revoked.

CHAPTER 11

Conduct Invalidating Assent

Fraud—A generic term embracing all multifarious means which human ingenuity can devise, and which are resorted to by one individual to get advantage over another by false suggestion or by suppression of the truth.

JOHNSON V. MCDONALD, 170 OKL. 117, 39 P.2D 150

Learning Objectives

After reading this chapter you should be able to:

1. Identify the types of duress and describe the legal effect of each.
2. Define undue influence and identify some of the situations giving rise to a confidential relationship.
3. Identify the types of fraud and the elements that must be shown to establish the existence of each.
4. Define the two types of nonfraudulent misrepresentation.
5. Identify and explain the situations involving voidable mistakes.

In addition to requiring offer and acceptance, the law requires that the agreement be voluntary and knowing. If these requirements are not met, then the agreement is either voidable or void. This chapter deals with situations in which the consent manifested by one of the parties to the contract is not effective because it was not knowingly and voluntarily given. We consider five such situations in this chapter: duress, undue influence, fraud, nonfraudulent misrepresentation, and mistake.

CPA DURESS

A person should not be held to an agreement he has not entered voluntarily. Accordingly, the law will not enforce any contract induced by **duress**, which in general is any wrongful or unlawful act or threat that overcomes the free will of a party.

PHYSICAL COMPULSION

Duress is of two basic types. The first type, **physical duress**, occurs when one party compels another to manifest assent to a contract through actual physical force, such as pointing a gun at a person or taking a person's hand and compelling him to sign a written contract. This type of duress, while extremely rare, renders the agreement ***void***.

IMPROPER THREATS

The second and more common type of duress involves the use of **improper threats** or acts, including economic and social coercion, to compel a person to enter into a contract. Though the threat may be explicit or may be inferred from words or conduct, in either case it must leave the victim with no reasonable alternative. This type of duress makes the contract ***voidable*** at the option of the coerced party. For example, if Ellen, a landlord, induces Vijay, an infirm, bedridden tenant, to enter into a new lease on the same apartment at a greatly increased rent by wrongfully threatening to terminate Vijay's lease and evict him, Vijay can escape or *avoid* the new lease by reason of the duress exerted on him.

The fact that the act or threat would not affect a person of average strength and intelligence is not important if it places fear in the person actually affected and induces her to act against her will. The test is ***subjective***, and the question is this: Did the threat actually induce assent on the part of the person claiming to be the victim of duress?

Ordinarily, the acts or threats constituting duress are themselves crimes or torts. But this is not true in all cases. The acts need not be criminal or tortious in order to be *wrongful*; they merely need to be contrary to public policy or morally reprehensible. For example, if the threat involves a breach of a contractual duty of good faith and fair dealing, it is improper.

Moreover, it generally has been held that contracts induced by threats of criminal prosecution are voidable, regardless of whether the coerced party had committed an unlawful act. Similarly, threatening the criminal prosecution of a close relative is also duress. To be distinguished from such threats of prosecution are threats that resort to ordinary civil remedies to recover a debt due from another. It is not wrongful to threaten a civil suit against an individual to recover a debt. What is prohibited is threatening to bring a civil suit when bringing such a suit would be abuse of process.

Practical Advice

If you entered into a contract due to improper threats, consider whether you wish to void the contract. If you decide to do so, act promptly.

Berardi v. Meadowbrook Mall Company

Supreme Court of Appeals of West Virginia, 2002

212 W.Va.377; 572 S.E.2d 900

FACTS Between 1985 and 1987, Jerry A. Berardi , Betty J. Berardi, and Bentley Corporation, plaintiffs/appellants (collectively referred to as "the Berardis") leased space for three restaurants from Meadowbrook Mall Company (Meadowbrook). In 1990, the Berardis were delinquent in their rent. Meadowbrook informed him that a lawsuit would be filed in Ohio requesting judgment for the total amount of the arrearages. Mr. Berardi thereafter entered into a consent judgment with Meadowbrook granting judgment for the full amount of arrearages. Meadowbrook in return promised that no steps to enforce the judgment would be undertaken providing the Berardis continued to operate their three restaurants.

In April 1996, Meadowbrook filed in the Circuit Court of Harrison County, West Virginia, the judgment of the Ohio lawsuits and obtained a lien on a building that was owned by the Berardis, the Goff Building. By so doing, Meadowbrook impeded the then pending refinancing of the building by the Berardis.

In June 1997, the Berardis and Meadowbrook signed a "Settlement Agreement and Release" settling the 1990 Ohio judgments. In this document, the Berardis acknowledged the validity of the 1990 Ohio judgments and that the aggregate due under them was $814,375.97. The Berardis agreed to pay Meadowbrook $150,000 on the date the Goff Building refinancing occurred, and also to pay Meadowbrook $100,000 plus 8.5% interest per year on the third anniversary of the initial $150,000 payment. These payments would discharge the Berardis from all other amounts due and owing. The payment of the initial $150,000 would also result in Meadowbrook releasing the lien against the Goff Building.

The agreement additionally recited:

> "Berardis hereby release and forever discharge Meadowbrook, its employees, agents, successors, and assigns from any and all claims, demands, damages, actions, and causes of action of any kind or nature that have arisen or may arise as a result of the leases, * * *."

Nevertheless, on October 2, 2000, the Berardis filed a complaint against Meadowbrook alleging that Meadowbrook breached the October 1990 agreement by attempting to enforce the 1990 Ohio judgments and that Meadowbrook extorted by duress and coercion the 1997 agreement. Meadowbrook filed a motion to dismiss under the 1997 settlement. Meadowbrook sought summary judgment, which the circuit court granted. From this summary judgment, Berardi now appeals.

DECISION Summary judgment affirmed.

OPINION The Berardis contend that because the 1997 agreement was coerced by economic duress, the circuit erred in finding it was enforceable. * * *

Meadowbrook retorts that the 1997 settlement agreement is valid and was not the result of economic duress in a legal sense. It contends the release was an arms-length transaction between sophisticated business people represented by counsel which is indisputably valid.

* * *

"We begin our discussion of this issue by reiterating, at the outset, that settlements are highly regarded and scrupulously enforced, so long as they are legally sound." [Citation.] "The law favors and encourages the resolution of controversies by contracts of compromise and settlement rather than by litigation; and it is the policy of the law to uphold and enforce such contracts if they are fairly made and are not in contravention of some law or public policy." [Citations.] Those who seek to avoid a settlement "face a heavy burden" [citation] and "since * * * settlement agreements, when properly executed, are legal and binding, this Court will not set aside such agreements on allegations of duress * * * absent clear and convincing proof of such claims." [Citation.]

The Berardis contend the 1997 settlement is invalid as it was procured by "economic duress:"

The concept of "economic or business duress" may be generally stated as follows: Where the plaintiff is forced into a transaction as a result of unlawful threats or wrongful, oppressive, or unconscionable conduct on the part of the defendant which leaves the plaintiff no reasonable alternative but to acquiesce, the plaintiff may void the transaction and recover any economic loss.

[Citation.] In [citation], we emphasized that there appears to be general acknowledgment that duress is not shown because one party to the contract has driven a hard bargain or that market or other conditions now make the contract more difficult to perform by one of the parties or that financial circumstances may have caused one party to make concessions.

"Duress is not readily accepted as an excuse" to avoid a contract. [Citation.] Thus, to establish economic duress, "in addition to their own * * * statements, the plaintiffs must produce objective evidence of their duress. The defense of economic duress does not turn only upon the subjective state of mind of the plaintiffs, but it must be reasonable in light of the objective facts presented." [Citation.]

Mr. Berardi is a sophisticated businessman who has operated a number of commercial enterprises. As of 1997, the Berardis had substantial assets and a considerable net worth. While economic duress may reach large business entities as well as the "proverbial little old lady in tennis shoes," [citation], when the parties are sophisticated business entities, releases should be voided only in "extreme and extraordinary cases." [Citation.] Indeed, "where an experienced businessman takes sufficient time, seeks the advice of counsel and understands the content of what he is signing he cannot claim the execution of the release was a product of duress." [Citation.] While the presence of counsel will not *per se* defeat a claim of economic duress, "a court must determine if the attorneys had an opportunity for meaningful input under the circumstances." [Citation.]

Here, the Berardis were represented by Attorneys John Farmer and Louis E. Enderle, Jr. in negotiations leading up to the June 1997 agreement. These negotiations apparently commenced at least as of April 22 and culminated in the June 1997 agreement. It also appears Mr. Berardi communicated with Attorney Enderle during negotiations. * * * Mr. Enderle stated in his deposition that he was unaware of any reason why the 1997 settlement agreement was unenforceable. The Berardis testified in their depositions they understood they would be bound by the terms of the agreement. * * *

Further, Mr. Berardi testified at his deposition that he never became aware of any new facts relative to the 1997 agreement that prompted him to sue Meadowbrook. The Berardis stated in their answers to Meadowbrook's requests for admission that there were no new facts which came to light after the 1997 agreement.

"No case can be found, we apprehend, where a party who, without force or intimidation and with full knowledge of all the facts of the case, accepts on account of an unlitigated and controverted demand a sum less than what he claims and believes to be due him, and agrees to accept that sum in full satisfaction, has been permitted to avoid his act on the ground that this is duress." [Citations.]

Moreover, the Berardis did not file their complaint until October 2, 2000. A party seeking to repudiate a release must act promptly in disavowing it once the putative duress ends or else the party will be deemed to have ratified the agreement. [Citations.] * * *

Finally, we do not believe that any relative economic inequality between the Berardis and Meadowbrook sufficiently factor into the summary judgment calculation. We have recognized that, "in most commercial transactions it may be assumed that there is some inequality of bargaining power. * * * " [Citation.] Indeed, even when one sophisticated business entity enjoys "a decided economic advantage" over another such entity, economic duress is extremely circumscribed:

> "Because an element of economic duress is * * * present when many contracts are formed or releases given, the ability of a party to disown his obligations under a

contract or release on that basis is reserved for extreme and extraordinary cases. Otherwise, the stronger party to a contract or release would routinely be at risk of having its rights under the contract or release challenged long after the instrument became effective." [Citation.]

Given the facts, the law's disfavor of economic duress, its approbation of settlements, the sophisticated nature of the parties, and the extremely high evidentiary burden the Berardis must overcome, we harbor no substantial doubt nor do we believe the circuit court abused its discretion.

* * *

INTERPRETATION An act that is not wrongful or unfair does not constitute duress.

ETHICAL QUESTION Did Meadowbrook act in a proper manner? Explain.

CRITICAL THINKING QUESTION Did Berardi really have a reasonable alternative to signing the release? Explain.

CPA UNDUE INFLUENCE

Undue influence is the unfair persuasion of a person by a party in a dominant position based on a *confidential relationship*. The law very carefully scrutinizes contracts between those in a relationship of trust and confidence that is likely to permit one party to take unfair advantage of the other. Examples are the relationships of guardian–ward, trustee–beneficiary, agent–principal, spouses, parent–child, attorney–client, physician–patient, and clergy–parishioner.

A transaction induced by undue influence on the part of the dominant party is ***voidable.*** The ultimate question in undue influence cases is whether the transaction was induced by dominating either or both the mind or emotions of a submissive party. The weakness or dependence of the person persuaded is a strong indicator of whether the persuasion may have been unfair. For example, Abigail, a person without business experience, has for years relied on Boris, who is experienced in business, for advice on business matters. Boris, without making any false representations of fact, induces Abigail to enter into a contract with Boris's confederate, Cassius, that is disadvantageous to Abigail, as both Boris and Cassius know. The transaction is voidable on the grounds of undue influence.

Practical Advice

If you are in a confidential relationship with another person, when you enter into a contract with that person, make sure that (1) you fully disclose all relevant information about that transaction, (2) the contract is fair, and (3) the other party obtains independent advice about the transaction.

Rea v. Paulson

Court of Appeals of Oregon, 1994
131 Or.App. 743, 887 P.2d 355

FACTS Plaintiff (Ken Rea), as personal representative of his mother's estate, brought this action to set aside a deed from his mother to defendant Larry Paulson, a son of decedent by a second marriage. Decedent died on January 31, 1988, leaving four children: Ken, Donald, Barbara, and Larry. She had purchased a home in Rainier, the property that is the subject of this lawsuit, in 1983, for $21,300. At that time, she had a will that she had executed in 1967, leaving all of her property to her four children in equal shares. That will was never changed. After she moved into the house in Rainier, Ken and his wife, and Barbara and Don, helped decedent, who suffered from arthritis in both hands, renal failure, congestive heart failure, and diabetes, as a result of which she had trouble getting around and, during the last part of her life, used an electric cart. She was taking several medications, including Prozac, Prednisone, Zantac, and Procardia, and was receiving insulin daily and dialysis an average of three times a week. Although there is no evidence that she was mentally incompetent, the medications and treatments made her drowsy, tired, and depressed, and caused mood swings. It is undisputed that she was dependent on the help of others in her daily living.

Larry was not in the Rainier area when his mother moved there and did not visit her. The other children and her neighbor helped her. The other children reroofed the house for her, picked fruit and stored it, and mowed the lawn; her daughter helped her with her finances and had a joint account with her, which the daughter never used. All of those children visited her frequently, and at least one of them saw her every day. Decedent expressed concern about losing the house because of her medical bills and suggested that she put the house in Ken's name; he and Barbara looked into the situation and concluded that it was not necessary, and so advised their mother. At some point—it is not clear when—Larry was told by state welfare authorities, as Ken and Barbara had learned, that so long as his mother maintained her house as her primary residence and was not receiving Medicaid, she was not in danger of losing her house to the state.

Some time in early 1987, Larry and his then girlfriend (later his wife) moved in with decedent and took over her care. Larry expressed his concern to his mother that the state might take her house. Not long thereafter, Larry rented a house in Longview in his name and persuaded his mother to move in with him, his girlfriend, and her child. After decedent moved to Longview, she rented her house in Rainier; the rent was used to maintain the house in Longview. At that time decedent had a savings account with approximately $2,000 in it; Larry held his mother's power of attorney. At the time of her death in January 1988, that account was exhausted, although her medical expenses were being paid by Medicare. Larry admitted that he used some of that money to buy a bicycle and a guitar. He had also used her credit card, on which there was a substantial balance after her death, which he did not pay. He said that that debt "died with his mother." On numerous occasions, Larry expressed to his mother his concern that the state would take her house if she kept it in her name. She was fearful of that, in spite of what she had been told by Ken and Barbara. Larry told her that they were wrong, and frequently urged her to make up her mind "about the deed."

Decedent was hospitalized three times during 1987. Finally, on September 30, 1987, Larry suggested to his mother that they go to a title company in Rainier to get a deed. Decedent signed the deed and gave up all of her rights in the property. Larry then had it recorded. He did not mention it to any of his half-brothers or -sister until two months later when he boasted of it to his half-sister.

The trial court, sitting in equity, found in favor of plaintiff on his complaint.

DECISION Judgment affirmed in favor of plaintiff.

OPINION Buttler, J. Clearly, decedent had trust and confidence in Larry and was completely dependent on him in her daily life. He helped her with her finances and held her power of attorney. She was unable to write checks; Larry wrote them for her, and "she signed them as best she could." She was unable to come and go, as she wished; after she moved in with Larry, she depended on him to take her places. Because Larry made it clear to decedent's other children that they were not welcome in his home, he succeeded in driving a wedge between them and their mother, with whom they had had a very close relationship until he appeared on the scene and took control of her life. He did not advise them of her death. We conclude that there was a confidential relationship between decedent and Larry and that, under the circumstances, he held a position of dominance over her; he was, literally, in the driver's seat. [Citation.]

Although one who claims that another has asserted undue influence has the burden to prove it, an inference of undue influence arises when, in addition to a confidential relationship, there are suspicious circumstances. [Citation.] That inference, if unexplained, may be sufficient, although the burden of proof remains with the one asserting undue influence. [Citation.] Circumstances that give rise to suspicions of undue influence are set out in [citation], and several are present here. Larry * * * not only procured the deed, he also participated in its preparation. Although he contends that it was his mother's idea, if it was, it was the result of his having persuaded her that she would lose the house if she did not deed the property to him, and of his repeatedly telling her to make up her mind "about the deed." At that time, Larry knew that the state would not take her home away from her as long as it was her primary residence, * * *. Therefore, his persistence in raising the question was false, and he knew it was false.

He did not argue that, because the Rainier house was no longer her primary residence, there was a risk that the state would take it. That argument would have been disingenuous, given that it was he who had suggested that she rent her house and move in with him.

Another important factor is the absence of independent advice. Although Ken and Barbara had advised decedent long before the deed was executed that she would not lose her house to the state if she maintained it in her name instead of deeding it to Ken, as she was contemplating at the time, Larry had persuaded her that Ken was wrong and that she should deed it to him. Under the circumstances, independent advice was essential, and Larry breached his fiduciary duty to her by not seeing to it that she get independent advice.

We also consider the change in attitude of decedent toward her other children after Larry took charge of his mother. Larry conceded that he had little good to say to his mother about his half-brothers and -sister. More than that, the record shows that he told them that they were not welcome at his home, and that when Barbara tried to call her mother on the telephone, he would get on another line to interfere with the call. As a result, the relations between decedent and her other children deteriorated after Larry took over the care of their mother.

We have no reason to doubt that decedent was grateful to Larry for his having helped her during her final days, or that she loved him. However, the circumstances leading up to the conveyance, and the preparation and signing of the deed, lead us to conclude that it was the product of undue influence exerted by Larry on his mother.

INTERPRETATION Undue influence is the unfair persuasion of a person by a party in a dominant position based upon a confidential relationship.

ETHICAL QUESTION Did the court correctly decide this case? Explain.

CRITICAL THINKING QUESTION Should the courts get involved in this type of controversy? Explain.

CPA FRAUD

Another factor affecting the validity of consent given by a contracting party is fraud, which prevents assent from being knowingly given. There are two distinct types of fraud: fraud in the execution and fraud in the inducement.

FRAUD IN THE EXECUTION

Fraud in the execution, which is extremely rare, consists of a misrepresentation that deceives the defrauded person as to the very nature of the contract. Such fraud occurs when a person does not know, or does not have reasonable opportunity to know, the character or essence of a proposed contract because the other party misrepresents its character or essential terms. Fraud in the execution renders the transaction *void*.

For example, Melody delivers a package to Ray, requests that Ray sign a receipt for it, holds out a simple printed form headed "Receipt," and indicates the line on which Ray is to sign. This line, which appears to Ray to be the bottom line of the receipt, is actually the signature line of a promissory note cleverly concealed underneath the receipt. Ray signs where directed without knowing that he is signing a note. This is fraud in the execution. The note is void and of no legal effect, for, although the signature is genuine and appears to manifest Ray's assent to the terms of the note, there is no actual assent. The nature of Melody's fraud precluded consent to the signing of the note because it prevented Ray from reasonably knowing what he was signing.

FRAUD IN THE INDUCEMENT

Fraud in the inducement, generally referred to as fraud or deceit, is an intentional misrepresentation of material fact by one party to the other, who consents to enter into a contract in justifiable reliance on the misrepresentation. Fraud in the inducement renders the contract *voidable* by the defrauded party. For example, Alice, in offering to sell her dog to Bob, tells Bob that the dog won first prize in its class in the recent national dog show. In truth, the dog had not even been entered in the show. However, Alice's statement induces Bob to accept the offer and pay a high price for the dog. There is a contract, but it is voidable by Bob because Alice's fraud induced his assent.

The requisites for fraud in the inducement are

1. a false representation
2. of a fact
3. that is material and
4. made with knowledge of its falsity and the intention to deceive (scienter) and
5. which representation is justifiably relied on.

http:// Federal Trade Commission: http://www.ftc.gov/ftc/consumer.htm
Federal Consumer Focus: http://www.pueblo.gsa.gov
National Fraud Information Center: http://www.fraud.org/welcome.htm

False Representation A basic element of fraud is a false representation or a **misrepresentation** (i.e., misleading conduct or an assertion not in accord with the facts, made through a positive statement). In contrast, **concealment** is an action intended or known to be likely to keep another from learning a fact he otherwise would have learned. Active concealment can form the basis for fraud, as, for example, when a seller puts heavy oil or grease in a car engine to conceal a knock. Truth may be suppressed by concealment as much as by misrepresentation. Expressly denying knowledge of a fact that a party knows to exist is a misrepresentation if it leads the other party to believe that the fact does not exist or cannot be discovered. Moreover, a statement of misleading half-truth is considered the equivalent of a false representation.

Generally, *silence* or nondisclosure alone does not amount to fraud when the parties deal at arm's length. An ***arm's-length transaction*** is one in which the parties owe each other no special duties and each is acting in his or her self-interest. In most business or market transactions, the parties deal at arm's length and generally have no obligation to tell the other party everything they know about the subject of the contract. Thus, it is not fraud when a buyer possesses advantageous information about the seller's property, information of which he knows the seller to be ignorant, and does not disclose such information to the seller. A buyer is under no duty to inform the seller of the greater value or other advantages of the property for sale. Assume, for example, that Sid owns a farm that, as a farm, is worth $10,000. Brenda, who knows that there is oil under Sid's farm, also knows that Sid is ignorant of this fact. Without disclosing this information to Sid, Brenda makes an offer to Sid to buy the farm for $10,000. Sid accepts the offer and a contract is duly made. Sid, on later learning the facts, can do nothing about the matter, either at law or in equity. As one case puts it, "a purchaser is not bound by our laws to make the man he buys from as wise as himself."

Although nondisclosure usually does not constitute a misrepresentation, in certain situations it does. One such situation arises when (1) a person fails to disclose a fact known to him; (2) he knows that the disclosure of that fact would correct a mistake of the other party as to a basic assumption on which that party is making the contract; and (3) nondisclosure of the fact amounts to a failure to act in good faith and in accordance with reasonable standards of fair dealing. Accordingly, if the property at issue in the contract contains a substantial latent (hidden) defect, one that would not be discovered through an ordinary examination, the seller may be obliged to reveal it. Suppose, for example, that Judith owns a valuable horse, which she knows is suffering from a disease discoverable only by a competent veterinary surgeon. Judith offers to sell this horse to Curt but does not inform him about the condition of her horse. Curt makes a reasonable examination of the horse and, finding it in apparently normal condition, purchases it from Judith. Curt, on later discovering the disease in question, can have the sale set aside. Judith's silence, under the circumstances, was a misrepresentation.

> **Practical Advice**
>
> Consider bargaining with the other party to promise to give you full disclosure.

There are other situations in which the law imposes a duty of disclosure. For example, one may have a duty of disclosure because of prior representations innocently made before entering into the contract, which are later discovered to be untrue. Another instance in which silence may constitute fraud is a transaction involving a fiduciary. A **fiduciary** is a person in a confidential relationship who owes a duty of trust, loyalty, and confidence to another. For example, an agent owes a fiduciary duty to his principal, as does a trustee to the beneficiary of the trust and a partner to her copartners. A fiduciary may not deal at *arm's length*, as a party in most everyday business or market transactions may, but owes a duty to disclose fully all relevant facts when entering into a transaction with the other party to the relationship.

> **Practical Advice**
>
> When entering into contract negotiations, first determine what duty of disclosure you owe to the other party.

Fact The basic element of fraud is the misrepresentation of a material fact. A **fact** is an event that actually took place or a thing that actually exists. Suppose that Dale induces Mike to purchase shares in a company unknown to Mike at a price of $100 per share by representing that she had paid $150 per share for them during the preceding year, when in fact she had paid only $50. This representation of a past event is a misrepresentation of fact.

Actionable fraud rarely can be based upon what is merely a statement of **opinion**. A representation is one of opinion if it expresses only the uncertain belief of the representer as to the existence of a fact or his judgment as to quality, value, authenticity, or other matters of judgment.

The line between fact and opinion is not an easy one to draw and in close cases presents an issue for the jury. The solution often will turn upon the superior knowledge of the person making the statement and the information available to the other party. Thus, if Dale said to Mike that the shares were "a good investment," she was merely stating her opinion; and normally Mike ought to regard it as no more than that. Other common examples of opinion are statements of value, such as "This is the best car for the money in town" or "This deluxe model will give you twice the wear of a cheaper model." Such exaggerations and commendations of articles offered for sale are to be expected from dealers, who are merely **puffing** their wares with "sales talk." If the representer is a professional advising a client, the courts are more likely to regard an untrue statement of opinion as actionable. Such a statement expresses the opinion of one holding himself out as having expert knowledge, and the tendency is to grant relief to those who have sustained loss by reasonable reliance on expert evaluation, as the next case shows.

Also to be distinguished from a representation of fact is a *prediction*. Predictions are similar to opinions, as no one can know with certainty what will happen in the future, and normally they are not regarded as factual statements. Likewise, promissory statements ordinarily do not constitute a basis of fraud, because a breach of promise does not necessarily indicate that the promise was fraudulently made. However, a promise that the promisor, at the time of making, had no intention of keeping is a misrepresentation of fact.

Historically, courts held that representations of *law* were not statements of fact but of opinion. The present trend is to recognize that a statement of law may have the effect of either a statement of fact or a statement of opinion. For example, a statement asserting that a particular statute has been enacted or repealed has the effect of a statement of fact. On the other hand, a statement as to the legal consequences of a particular set of facts is a statement of opinion.

Vokes v. Arthur Murray, Inc.

Court of Appeal of Florida, 1968
212 So.2d 906

FACTS Mrs. Audrey E. Vokes, a widow of fifty-one years and without family, purchased fourteen separate dance courses from J. P. Davenport's Arthur Murray, Inc., School of Dance **(http://www.arthurmurray.com/)**. The fourteen courses totaled in the aggregate 2,302 hours of dancing lessons at a cost to Mrs. Vokes of $31,090.45. Mrs. Vokes was induced continually to reapply for new courses by representations made by Mr. Davenport that her dancing ability was improving, that she was responding to instruction, that she had excellent potential, and that they were developing her into an accomplished dancer. In fact, she had no dancing ability or aptitude and had trouble "hearing the musical beat." Mrs. Vokes brought action to have the contracts set aside. The plaintiff's complaint was dismissed for failure to state a cause of action, and she appealed.

DECISION Judgment reversed.

OPINION Pierce, J. It is true that "generally a misrepresentation, to be actionable, must be one of fact rather than of opinion." [Citation.] But this rule has significant qualifications, applicable here. * * *

"A statement of a party having * * * superior knowledge may be regarded as a statement of fact although it would be considered as opinion if the parties were dealing on equal terms."

It could be reasonably supposed here that defendants had "superior knowledge" as to whether plaintiff had "dance potential" and as to whether she was noticeably improving in the art of terpsichore. And it would be a reasonable inference from the undenied averments of the complaint that the flowery elogiums heaped upon her by defendants as a prelude to her contracting for 1,944 additional hours of instruction in order to attain the rank of the Bronze Standard, thence to the bracket of the Silver Standard, thence to the class of the Gold Bar Standard, and finally to the crowning plateau of a Life Member of the Studio, proceeded as much or more from the urge to "ring the cash register" as from any honest or realistic appraisal of her dancing prowess or a factual representation of her progress.

Even in contractual situations where a party to a transaction owes no duty to disclose facts within his knowledge or to answer inquiries respecting such facts, the law is if he undertakes to do so he must disclose the whole truth. [Citations.] From the face of the complaint, it should have been reasonably apparent to defendants that her vast outlay of cash for the many hundreds of additional hours of instruction was not justified by her slow and awkward progress, which she would have been made well aware of if they had spoken the "whole truth."

INTERPRETATION Because of his superior knowledge, Davenport's statements regarding Mrs. Vokes' dancing ability and potential may be taken as statements of fact.

ETHICAL QUESTION Did Arthur Murray, Inc., act in an unethical manner by attempting to retain business by this conduct, or were its employees trying to make Mrs. Vokes feel better about herself? Explain.

CRITICAL THINKING QUESTION Is this the type of dispute that courts should decide? Explain.

Materiality In addition to the requirement that a misrepresentation be one of fact, it must also be material. A misrepresentation is **material** if (1) it would be likely to induce a reasonable person to manifest assent or (2) the maker knows that it would be likely to induce the recipient to do so. Thus, in the sale of a racehorse, it may not be material whether the horse was ridden in its most recent race by a certain jockey, but its running time for the race probably would be. The Restatement of Contracts provides that a contract justifiably induced by a misrepresentation is voidable if the misrepresentation is *either* fraudulent *or* material. Therefore, a fraudulent misrepresentation does not have to be material to obtain rescission, but it must be material to recover damages.

The following case presents an unusual factual situation involving the duty to disclose a "material" fact.

Reed v. King

California Court of Appeals, 1983
145 Cal.App.3d 261, 193 Cal.Rptr. 130

FACTS Dorris Reed bought a house from Robert King for $76,000. King and his real estate agent knew that a woman and her four children had been murdered in the house ten years earlier and allegedly knew that the event had materially affected the market value of the house. They said nothing about the murders to Reed, and King asked a neighbor not to inform her of them. After the sale, neighbors told Reed about the murders and informed her that the house was consequently worth only $65,000. Reed brought an action against King and the real estate agent, alleging fraud and seeking rescission and damages. The complaint was dismissed, and Reed appealed.

DECISION Judgment reversed.

OPINION Blease, J. Does Reed's pleading state a cause of action? Concealed within this question is the nettlesome problem of the duty of disclosure of blemishes on real property which are not physical defects or legal impairments to use.

Reed seeks to state a cause of action sounding in contract, i.e., rescission, or in tort, i.e., deceit. In either event her allegations must reveal a fraud. [Citation.] * * *

The trial court perceived the defect in Reed's complaint to be a failure to allege concealment of a material fact. * * *

Concealment is a term of art which includes mere nondisclosure when a party has a duty to disclose. [Citation.] Rest.2d Contracts, § 161; Rest.2d Torts, § 551; Reed's complaint reveals only nondisclosure despite the allegation King asked a neighbor to hold his peace. There is no allegation the attempt at suppression was a cause in fact of Reed's ignorance. (See Rest.2d Contracts, §§ 160, 162–164; Rest.2d Torts, § 550; Rest. Restitution, § 9.) Accordingly, the critical question is: does the seller have a duty to disclose here? Resolution of this question depends on the materiality of the fact of the murders.

In general, a seller of real property has a duty to disclose: "where the seller knows of facts *materially* affecting the value or desirability of the property which are known or accessible only to him and also knows that such facts are not known to, or within the reach of the diligent attention and observation of the buyer, the seller is under a duty to disclose them to the buyer." [Citation.] This broad statement of duty has led one commentator to conclude: "The ancient maxim *caveat emptor* ('let the buyer beware.') has little or no application to California real estate transactions." [Citation.]

Whether information "is of sufficient materiality to affect the value or desirability of the property * * * depends on the facts of the particular case." [Citation.] Materiality "is a question of law, and is part of the concept of right to rely or justifiable reliance." [Citation.] * * * Three considerations bear on this legal conclusion: the gravity of the harm inflicted by nondisclosure; the fairness of imposing a duty of discovery on the buyer as an alternative to compelling disclosure, and the impact on the stability of contracts if rescission is permitted.

Numerous cases have found nondisclosure of physical defects and legal impediments to use of real property are material. [Citation.] However, to our knowledge, no prior real estate sale case has faced an issue of nondisclosure of the kind presented here.

* * *

The murder of innocents is highly unusual in its potential for so disturbing buyers they may be unable to reside in a home where it has occurred. This fact may foreseeably deprive a buyer of the intended use of the purchase. Murder is not such a common occurrence that *buyers* should be charged with anticipating and discovering this disquieting possibility. Accordingly, the fact is not one for which a duty of inquiry and discovery can sensibly be imposed upon the buyer.

Reed alleges the fact of the murders has a quantifiable effect on the market value of the premises. We cannot say this allegation is inherently wrong and, in the pleading posture of the case, we assume it to be true.

* * *

Whether Reed will be able to prove her allegation that the decade-old multiple murder has a significant effect on market value we cannot determine. If she is able to do so by competent evidence, she is entitled to a favorable ruling on the issues of materiality and duty to disclose.

INTERPRETATION A representation is material if it is likely to influence or affect a reasonable person.

ETHICAL QUESTION Should King have revealed the information to Reed? Explain.

CRITICAL THINKING QUESTION What is material information, and how should it be determined?

Knowledge of Falsity and Intention to Deceive To establish fraud, the misrepresentation must have been known by the one making it to be false and must be made with an intent to deceive. This element of fraud is known as ***scienter.*** Knowledge of falsity can consist of (a) actual knowledge, (b) lack of belief in the statement's truthfulness, or (c) reckless indifference as to its truthfulness.

Justifiable Reliance A person is not entitled to relief unless she has **justifiably relied** on the misrepresentation. If the complaining party's decision was in no way influenced by the misrepresentation, she must abide by the terms of the contract. She is not deceived if she does not rely on the misrepresentation. Justifiable reliance requires that the misrepresentation contribute substantially to the misled party's decision to enter into the contract. If the complaining party knew or it was obvious that the representation of the defendant was untrue, but she still entered into the contract, she has not justifiably relied on that representation. Moreover, where the misrepresentation is fraudulent, the party who relies on it is entitled to relief even though she does not investigate the statement or is contributorily negligent in relying on it. Not knowing or discovering the facts before making a contract does not make a person's reliance unjustified unless her reliance amounts to a failure to act in good faith and in accordance with reasonable standards of fair dealing. Thus, most courts will not allow a person who concocts a deliberate and elaborate scheme to defraud—one that the defrauded party should readily detect—to argue that the defrauded party did not justifiably rely upon the misrepresentation.

CPA NONFRAUDULENT MISREPRESENTATION

Nonfraudulent misrepresentation is a material, false statement that induces another to rely justifiably but is made *without* scienter. Such representation may occur in one of two ways. **Negligent misrepresentation** is a false representation that is made without due care in ascertaining its truthfulness; such representation renders an agreement voidable. **Innocent misrepresentation**, which also renders a contract voidable, is a false representation made without knowledge of its falsity but with due care. To obtain relief for nonfraudulent misrepresentation, all of the other elements of fraud must be present *and* the misrepresentation must be material. The remedies that may be available for nonfraudulent misrepresentation are rescission and damages (see Chapter 18).

CPA MISTAKE

A **mistake** is a belief that is not in accord with the facts. Where the mistaken facts relate to the basis of the parties' agreement, the law permits the adversely affected party to avoid or reform the contract under certain circumstances. But because permitting avoidance for mistake undermines the objective approach to mutual assent, the law has experienced considerable difficulty in specifying those circumstances that justify permitting the subjective matter of mistake to invalidate an otherwise objectively satisfactory agreement. As a result, establishing clear rules to govern the effect of mistake has proven elusive.

The Restatement and modern cases treat mistakes of law in existence at the time of making the contract no

CONCEPT REVIEW

Misrepresentation

	Fraudulent	Negligent	Innocent
False Statement of Fact	Yes	Yes	Yes
Materiality	Yes for damages No for rescission	Yes	Yes
Fault	Scienter (knowledge and intent)	Without due care	Without knowledge and due care
Reliance	Yes	Yes	Yes
Injury	Yes for damages No for rescission	Yes for damages No for rescission	Yes for damages No for rescission
Remedies	Damages Rescission	Damages Rescission	Damages Rescission

differently than mistakes of fact. For example, Susan contracts to sell a parcel of land to James with the mutual understanding that James will build an apartment house on the land. Both Susan and James believe that such a building is lawful. Unknown to them, however, three days before they entered into their contract, the town in which the land was located had enacted an ordinance precluding such use of the land. In states that regard mistakes of law and fact in the same light, this mistake of law would be treated as a mistake of fact that would lead to the consequences discussed below.

MUTUAL MISTAKE

Mutual mistake occurs when *both* parties are mistaken as to the same set of facts. If the mistake relates to a basic assumption on which the contract is made and has a material effect on the agreed exchange, then it is *voidable* by the adversely affected party unless he bears the risk of the mistake.

Usually, market conditions and the financial situation of the parties are not considered basic assumptions. Thus, if Gail contracts to purchase Pete's automobile under the belief that she can sell it at a profit to Jesse, she is not excused from liability if she is mistaken in this belief. Nor can she rescind the agreement simply because she was mistaken as to her estimate of what the automobile was worth. These are the ordinary risks of business, and courts do not undertake to relieve against them. But suppose that the parties contract upon the assumption that the automobile is a 1992 Cadillac with fifteen thousand miles of use, when in fact the engine is that of a cheaper model and has been run in excess of fifty thousand miles. Here, a court likely would allow a rescission because of mutual mistake of a material fact. In a New Zealand case, the plaintiff purchased a "stud bull" at an auction. There were no express warranties as to "sex, condition, or otherwise." Actually, the bull was sterile. Rescission was allowed, the court observing that it was a "bull in name only."

Lesher v. Strid

Court of Appeals of Oregon, 2000
165 Or.App. 34, 996 P.2d 988
http://caselaw.findlaw.com/scripts/getcase.pl?court=OR&vol=A99602&invol=1

FACTS In May 1995, the plaintiffs, Vernon and Janene Lesher, agreed to purchase an eighteen-acre parcel of real property from defendant with the intention of using it to raise horses. In purchasing the property, the plaintiffs relied on their impression that at least four acres of the subject property had a right to irrigation from Slate Creek. The earnest money agreement to the contract provided:

"* * * **D. Water Rights** are being conveyed to Buyer at the close of escrow. * * * Seller will provide Buyer with a written explanation of the operation of the irrigation system, water right certificates, and inventory of irrigation equipment included in sale."

The earnest money agreement also provided:

"**THE SUBJECT PROPERTY IS BEING SOLD 'AS IS'** subject to the Buyer's approval of the tests and conditions as stated herein. Buyer declares that Buyer is not depending on any other statement of the Seller or licensees that is not incorporated by reference in this earnest money contract" [Bold in original].

Before signing the earnest money agreement, the defendants presented to the plaintiffs a 1977 Water Resources Department water rights certificate and a map purporting to show an area of the subject property to be irrigated ("area to be irrigated" map), which indicated that the property carried a four-acre water right. Both parties believed that the property carried the irrigation rights and that the plaintiffs needed such rights for their horse farm. The plaintiffs did not obtain the services of an attorney or a water rights examiner before purchasing the property.

After purchasing the property and before establishing a pasture, the plaintiffs learned that the property did not carry a four-acre water right. The plaintiffs sought rescission of the contract for sale, alleging mutual mistake of fact or innocent misrepresentation regarding existence of water rights. The trial court ruled in favor of the plaintiffs and the defendant appeals.

DECISION Judgment of the trial court affirmed.

OPINION Wollheim, J. Grounds for rescission on the basis of a mutual mistake of fact or innocent misrepresentation must be proved by clear and convincing evidence. [Citations.] An innocent misrepresentation of fact renders a contract voidable by a party if the party's "manifestation of assent is induced by * * * a material misrepresentation by the other party upon which the recipient is justified in relying[.]" [Citations.] A mutual mistake of fact renders a contract voidable by the adversely affected party, "where the parties are mistaken as to the facts existing at the time of the contract, if the mistake is so fundamental that it frustrates the purpose of the contract," [citation], and where the adversely affected party does not bear the risk of the mistake, [citation]. A mistake "is a state of mind which is not in accord with the facts." [Citation].

Even though it appears that the trial court did not apply the clear and convincing standard, * * * , we find that plaintiffs' evidence meets that standard. Both defendant and plaintiffs testified that they believed that the four acres of water rights were appurtenant to the subject property. Defendant does not dispute that the 1977 water rights certificate and the "area to be irrigated" map are her representation about the water right.

* * *

Plaintiffs also established by clear and convincing evidence that the existence of the four-acre water right was material and essential to the contract. Vernon testified that the motivation for the purchase was to expand his ability to raise horses from property they already owned where they had a two-acre irrigation right and that the subject property's water right was essential to the contract. Certainly, a smaller water right would limit, not expand, plaintiffs' ability to raise horses. The mistake, therefore, goes to the very essence of the contract.

We next consider defendant's arguments that plaintiffs bore the risk of that mistake. The Restatement (Second) of Contracts § 154 explains that a party bears the risk of a mistake, in part, if the risk is allocated to the party by agreement of the parties, or if the risk is allocated to the party "by the court on the ground that it is reasonable in the circumstances to do so." We find nothing in the contract that would allocate to plaintiffs the risk of a mistake as to the existence of a four-acre water right.

Defendant argues in the alternative that plaintiffs' mistake of fact is the result of defendant's misrepresentation, on which plaintiffs could not reasonably rely. An "innocent misrepresentation may support a claim for rescission of a real estate agreement if the party who relied on the misrepresentations of another establishes a right to have done so." [Citations.]

Defendant argues that her representations about the four-acre water right were extrinsic to the contract and that the contract's "as is" clause expressly excluded reliance on such extrinsic representations. * * * The "as is" clause specifically contemplated reliance on any statements by the seller that were "incorporated by reference" in the earnest money agreement. The earnest money agreement specifically referred to the conveyance of water rights.

* * *

INTERPRETATION If both parties to a contract have a common but erroneous belief as to a basic assumption on which the contract is made, the contract is voidable.

CRITICAL THINKING QUESTION Should all contracts provide for this type of situation and, if so, how? Explain.

CONCEPT REVIEW

Conduct Invalidating Assent

Conduct	Effect
Duress by physical force	Void
Duress by improper threat	Voidable
Undue influence	Voidable
Fraud in the execution	Void
Fraud in the inducement	Voidable

UNILATERAL MISTAKE

Unilateral mistake occurs when only one of the parties is mistaken. Courts have been hesitant to grant relief for unilateral mistake, even though it relates to a basic assumption on which a party entered into the contract and has a material effect on the agreed exchange. Nevertheless, relief will be granted where the nonmistaken party knows, or reasonably should know, that such a mistake has been made (palpable unilateral mistake) or where the mistake was caused by the fault of the nonmistaken party. For example, suppose a building contractor makes a serious error in his computations and consequently submits a job bid that is one-half the amount it should be. If the other party knows that the contractor made such an error, or reasonably should have known it, she cannot, as a general rule, take advantage of the other's mistake by accepting the offer. In addition, many courts and the Restatement allow rescission where the effect of unilateral mistake makes enforcement of the contract unconscionable.

ASSUMPTION OF RISK OF MISTAKE

A party who has undertaken to bear the risk of a mistake will not be able to avoid the contract, even though the mistake (which may be either mutual or unilateral) would have otherwise permitted the party to do so. This allocation of risk may occur by agreement of the parties. For instance, a ship at sea may be sold "lost or not lost." In such case the buyer is liable whether the ship was lost or not lost at the time the contract was made. There is no mistake; instead, there is a conscious allocation of risk.

The risk of mistake also may be allocated by conscious ignorance when the parties recognize that they have limited knowledge of the facts. For example, the Supreme Court of Wisconsin refused to set aside the sale of a stone for which the purchaser paid one dollar but that was subsequently discovered to be an uncut diamond valued at $700. The parties did not know at the time of sale what the stone was and knew they did not know. Each consciously assumed the risk that the value might be more or less than the selling price.

Practical Advice

If you are unsure about the nature of a contract, consider allocating the risk of the uncertainties in your contract.

EFFECT OF FAULT UPON MISTAKE

The Restatement provides that a mistaken party's fault in not knowing or discovering a fact before making a contract does not prevent him from avoiding the contract "unless his fault amounts to a failure to act in good faith and in accordance with reasonable standards of fair dealing." This rule does not, however, apply to a failure to read a contract. As a general proposition, a party is held to what she signs. Her signature authenticates the writing, and she cannot repudiate that which she has voluntarily approved. Generally, one who assents to a writing is presumed to know its contents and cannot escape being bound by its terms merely by contending that she did not read them; her assent is deemed to cover unknown as well as known terms.

MISTAKE IN MEANING OF TERMS

Somewhat related to mistakes of fact is the situation in which the parties misunderstand their manifestations of mutual assent. A famous case involving this problem is *Raffles v. Wichelhaus*, 2 Hurlstone & Coltman 906 (1864),

THE LAW AND YOU

State Bar Associations

Montana: http://www.montanabar.org/ ("Living Trust Scams")

Oregon: http://www.osbar.org/public/legalinfo/consumer.html ("Are You a Victim of Mail Order Fraud?")

State Attorney Generals

Alabama: http://www.ago.state.al.us/consumer_info.cfm ("Consumer Laws and Information")

Arizona: http://www.attorney_general.state.az.us/consumer/help.html ("Telemarketing Scams"; "Three Day Right of Cancellation"; "Credit Reporting"; "Living Trust Scam"; "Home Improvement Schemes"; "Pyramid Schemes"; "Top 10 Consumer Myths")

Arkansas: http://www.ag.state.ar.us/ ("Credit Repair Scams")

California: http://www.dca.ca.gov/legal ("Contracts"; "Prizes, Promotions, Giveaways, and Lotteries")

Colorado: http://www.state.co.us/consprot.stm ("Ripped Off? Dealing with Consumer Fraud")

Connecticut: http://www.cslib.org/attygenl/mainlinks/tabindex7.htm ("Telemarketing"; "Telephone Scams"; "Consumer Credit"; "Product Recalls"; "Travel Scams")

Delaware: http://www.state.de.us/attgen/fraud/consumerprotection/tips.htm ("Tips to Protect Yourself from Becoming a Victim of Consumer Fraud")

Florida: http://doacs.state.fl.us./consumer/ ("Multi-Level Marketing vs. Illegal Pyramid Schemes"; "Recognize & Avoid Telemarketing Fraud")

Idaho: http://www2.state.id.us/ag/consumer/tipsandinfo.htm ("Telephone Solicitations"; "Consumer Protection Manual")

Illinois: http://www.ag.state.il.us/consumer/consume.htm (consumer protection information) ("Magazine Sales")

Iowa: http://www.state.ia.us/government/ag/consumer/consumer_tips.html ("Nigerian Letter Scam"; "Multilevel Marketing")

Kansas: http://www.accesskansas.org/ksag/contents/consumer/main.htm ("How to Remove Your Name from Mail and Telephone Lists"; "Pyramid Schemes")

Kentucky: http://www.law.state.ky.us/cp/resource.htm ("Home Solicitation Sales"; "Telemarketers, Telephone Solicitations")

Louisiana: http://www.ag.state.la.us/consumereducation.shtml ("Charity Fraud"; "Credit Card Fraud"; "Credit Repair Scams"; "Elderly Fraud"; "Telemarketing Fraud"; "Sweepstakes Fraud"; "Pyramid Schemes")

Maine: http://www.maine.gov/portal/living/consumer_protection.html ("The Maine Attorney Generals Consumer Law Guide")

Maryland: http://www.oag.state.md.us/ ("Consumer Protection")

Massachusetts: http://www.magnet.state.ma.us/cns.htm ("Scams!!!")

Michigan: http://www.michigan.gov/ag ("Consumer Alerts"; "Telemarketing"; "Home Services")

Minnesota: http://www.ag.state.mn.us ("Fraud"; "Personal Finance"; "Senior Center")

Mississippi: http://www.ago.state.ms.us/divisions/consumer/consumer-protection.html ("Recognizing Disaster Fraud")

Nebraska: http://www.nol.org/home/ago/brochures.htm ("Don't Be a Victim"; "Sweepstakes Fraud"; "Charity Fraud")

Nevada: http://www.state.nv.us/pubs/C1.htm ("Telephone Scams and Older Consumers"; "Stay Alert to Sweepstakes Fraud")

New Hampshire: http://www.state.nh.us/nhdoj/Consumer/cpb.html ("Cyber Scams"; "Schemes, Swindles & Other Scams"; "Mail & Telephone Order Scams")

New Jersey: http //www.state.nj.us/lps/ca/dcapub.htm ("Don't Be Taken for a Ride Guide to Auto Repair"; "The Consumer Fraud Act")

New York: http://www.consumer.state.ny.publications ("Home Improvement Factsheet"; "Senior Citizens")

North Carolina: http://www.jus.state.nc.us/cpframe.htm ("Know Your Rights"; "Tips for Consumers"; "Consumer Alerts")

North Dakota: http://www.ag.state.nd.us ("Your Rights"; "Computer/Internet"; "Telemarketing"; "Marketplace"; "Cars"; "Telephone Scams"; "Business"; "Privacy/Identity Theft"; "Home Solicitation"; "Students"; "Home Improvement"; "Common Scams")

Ohio: http://www2.ag.state.oh.us/sections/consumer/ccapsplus/store.asp ("Ohio Auto Repairs and Services Law"; "Ohio Home Improvement Law")

Oklahoma: http://www.oag.state.ok.us/ ("Disaster Scam Prevention"; "Home Repair Fraud Prevention Tips")

Oregon: http://www.doj.state.or.us/FinFraud/Info2.htm ("Sweepstakes and Other Prize Promotions")

Pennsylvania: http://www.attorneygeneral.gov/pei/bei.cfm ("Pyramid Schemes"; "Telemarketing Fraud—How to Spot It—How to Avoid It")

Rhode Island: http://www.riag.state.ri.us/consumer/default.htm ("Know Your Consumer Rights"; "Mail Call"; "Telemarketing")

South Carolina: http://www.state.sc.us/consumer/ ("Information about Fraud"; "Automobiles")

South Dakota: http://www.state.sd.us/attorney/office/divisions/consumer/ (consumer protection publications)

Tennessee: http://www.state.tn.us/consumer/brochure.html ("Scams"; "Shopping"; "Sweepstakes and Contests"; "Telemarketing/Telecommunications")

Texas: http://www.oag.state.tx.us/ ("Telephone Fraud")

Utah: http://attorneygeneral.utah.gov/brochures.html ("Medicaid Fraud")

THE LAW AND YOU

Vermont: http://www.state.vt.us/atg/consumer.htm ("Scam Alert")

Virginia: http://www.oag.state.va.us/Protecting/Consumer Fraud/default.htm ("Preventing Consumer Fraud"; "New Telemarketing Rules"; "Credit Reports and Practices"; "Gold and Platinum Card Scams"; "Checking Account Scams")

Washington: http://www.wa.gov/ago/consumer/ ("Telemarketing Fraud"; "Direct Mail Advertising")

http://www.wa.gov/ago/consumer/cp_publications.html ("Senior Scams"; "Telemarketing Fraud"; "Pyramid Schemes")

West Virginia: http://www.wvs.state.wv.us/wvag/ ("Home Improvement"; "Telemarketing Scams"; "Online/Internet")

U.S. Government

At-Home Shopping Rights: http://www.pueblo.gsa.gov/specpubs.htm#NM

Getting What You Pay For: Weights & Measures Tips for Consumers: http://www.pueblo.gsa.gov/specpubs.htm#NM

Choosing & Using Credit Cards: http://www.pueblo.gsa.gov/cic_text/money/credit_card.htm

Consumer Handbook to Credit Protection Laws: http://www.pueblo.gsa.gov/money.htm

Credit and Divorce: http://www.pueblo.gsa.gov/specpubs.htm#NM

Fair Credit Reporting: http://www.pueblo.gsa.gov/money.htm

Fair Debt Collection: http://www.pueblo.gsa.gov/money.htm

Shop...The Card You Pick Can Save You Money: http://www.pueblo.gsa.gov/specpubs.htm#NM

What Savvy Consumers Need to Know About Debit Cards: http://www. pueblo.gsa.gov/specpubs.htm#NM

Can Your Kitchen Pass the Food Safety Test?: http://www.pueblo.gsa.gov/food.htm

Consumer's Guide to Fats: http://www.pueblo.gsa.gov/specpubs.htm#FO

Keep Your Food Safe: http://www.pueblo.gsa.gov/specpubs.htm#FO

Making Healthy Food Choices: http://www.pueblo.gsa.gov/food.htm

2004 Consumer Action Handbook: http://www.pueblo.gsa.gov/misc.htm

Funerals: A Consumer Guide: http://www.pueblo.gsa.gov/misc.htm

Swindlers Are Calling: http://www.pueblo.gsa.gov/specpubs.htm#XX

Federal Trade Commission: http://www.ftc.gov/bcp/menu-tmark.htm ("Advance-Fee Loan Scams Campaign"; "Are You a Target of . . . Telephone Scams?"; "Automatic Debit Scam"; "Border-Line Scams Are the Real Thing Alert"; "Catch the Bandit in Your Mailbox"; "Easy Credit, Not So Fast. The Truth About Advance Fee Loan Scams"; "FTC Names Its Dirty Dozen: 12 Scams Most Likely to Arrive via Bulk Email Alert"; "International Lottery Scams"; "Magazine Subscription Scams"; "Reloading Scams: Double Trouble for Consumers"; "Telemarketing Recovery Scams"; "Telemarketing Travel Fraud")

popularly known as the "*Peerless*" case. A contract of purchase was made for 125 bales of cotton to arrive on the *Peerless* from Bombay. It happened, however, that there were two ships by the name of *Peerless* each sailing from Bombay, one in October and the other in December. The buyer had in mind the ship that sailed in October, while the seller reasonably believed the agreement referred to the *Peerless* sailing in December. Neither party was at fault, but both believed in good faith that a different ship was intended. The English court held that no contract existed.

The Restatement is in accord: There is no manifestation of mutual assent where the parties attach materially different meanings to their manifestations and neither party knows or has reason to know the meaning attached by the other. If blame can be ascribed to either party, however, that party will be held responsible. Thus, if the seller knew of the sailing from Bombay of two ships by the name of *Peerless*, then he would be at fault, and the contract would be for the ship sailing in October as the buyer expected. If neither party is to blame or both are to blame, there is no contract at all; that is, the agreement is void.

CHAPTER SUMMARY

Duress

Definition wrongful act or threat that overcomes the free will of a party

Physical Compulsion coercion involving physical force renders the agreement void

Improper Threats improper threats or acts, including economic and social coercion, render the contract voidable

Undue Influence

Definition taking unfair advantage of a person by reason of a dominant position based on a confidential relationship

Effect renders contract voidable

Fraud

Fraud in the Execution a misrepresentation that deceives the other party as to the nature of a document evidencing the contract; renders agreement void

Fraud in the Inducement renders the agreement voidable if the following elements are present:
- *False Representation* positive statement or conduct that misleads
- *Fact* an event that occurred or thing that exists
- *Materiality* of substantial importance
- *Knowledge of Falsity and Intention to Deceive* (called *scienter*) and includes (a) actual knowledge, (b) lack of belief in statement's truthfulness, or (c) reckless indifference to its truthfulness
- *Justifiable Reliance* a defrauded party is reasonably influenced by the misrepresentation

Nonfraudulent Misrepresentation

Negligent Misrepresentation misrepresentation made without due care in ascertaining its truthfulness; renders agreement voidable

Innocent Misrepresentation misrepresentation made without knowledge of its falsity but with due care; renders contract voidable

Mistake

Definition an understanding that is not in accord with existing fact

Mutual Mistake both parties have a common but erroneous belief forming the basis of the contract; renders the contract voidable by either party

Unilateral Mistake courts are unlikely to grant relief unless the error is known or should be known by the nonmistaken party

Assumption of Risk of Mistake a party may assume the risk of a mistake

Effect of Fault upon Mistake not a bar to avoidance unless the fault amounts to a failure to act in good faith

QUESTIONS

1. Anita and Barry were negotiating, and Anita's attorney prepared a long and carefully drawn contract that was given to Barry for examination. Five days later and prior to its execution, Barry's eyes became so infected that it was impossible for him to read. Ten days thereafter and during the continuance of the illness, Anita called Barry and urged him to sign the contract, telling him that time was running out. Barry signed the contract despite the fact he was unable to read it. In a subsequent action by Anita, Barry claimed that the contract was not binding on him because it was impossible for him to read and he did not know what it contained prior to his signing it. Should Barry be held to the contract?

2. a. William tells Carol that he paid $150,000 for his farm in 2000 and that he believes it is now worth twice that. Relying on these statements, Carol buys the farm from William for $225,000. William did pay $150,000 for the farm in 2000, but its value has increased only slightly, and it is presently not worth $300,000. On discovering this, Carol offers to reconvey the farm to William and sues for the return of her $225,000. Result?
   b. Modify the facts in (a) by assuming that William had paid $100,000 for the property in 2000. What is the result?

3. On September 1, Adams in Portland, Oregon, wrote a letter to Brown in New York City offering to sell to Brown 1,000 tons of chromite at $48 per ton, to be shipped by *S.S. Malabar* sailing from Portland, Oregon, to New York City via the Panama Canal. Upon receiving the letter on September 5, Brown immediately mailed to Adams a letter stating that she accepted the offer. There were two ships by the name of *S.S. Malabar* sailing from Portland to New York City via the Panama Canal, one sailing in October and the other sailing in December. At the time of mailing her letter of acceptance, Brown knew of both sailings and further knew that Adams knew only of the December sailing. Is there a contract? If so, to which *S.S. Malabar* does it relate?

4. Adler owes Perreault, a police captain, $500. Adler threatens Perreault that unless Perreault gives him a discharge from the debt, Adler will disclose the fact that Perreault has on several occasions become highly intoxicated and has been seen in the company of certain disreputable persons. Perreault, induced by fear that such a disclosure would cost him his position or in any event lead to social disgrace, gives Adler a release but subsequently sues to set it aside and recover on his claim. Will Adler be able to enforce the release?

5. Harris owned a farm that was worth about $600 an acre. By false representations of fact, Harris induced Pringle to buy the farm at $1,500 an acre. Shortly after taking possession of the farm, Pringle discovered oil under the land. Harris, on learning this, sues to have the sale set aside on the ground that it was voidable because of fraud. Result?

6. On February 2, Phillips induced Mallor to purchase from her fifty shares of stock in the XYZ Corporation for $10,000, representing that the actual book value of each share was $200. A certificate for fifty shares was delivered to Mallor. On February 16, Mallor discovered that the February 2 book value was only $50 per share. Thereafter, Mallor sues Phillips. Will Mallor be successful in a lawsuit against Phillips? Why?

7. Dorothy mistakenly accused Fred's son, Steven, of negligently burning down Dorothy's barn. Fred believed that his son was guilty of the wrong and that he, Fred, was personally liable for the damage, because Steven was only fifteen years old. Upon demand made by Dorothy, Fred paid Dorothy $2,500 for the damage to Dorothy's barn. After making this payment, Fred learned that his son had not caused the burning of Dorothy's barn and was in no way responsible for its burning. Fred then sued Dorothy to recover the $2,500 that he had paid her. Will he be successful?

8. Jones, a farmer, found an odd-looking stone in his fields. He went to Smith, the town jeweler, and asked him what he thought it was. Smith said he did not know but thought it might be a ruby. Jones asked Smith what he would pay for it, and Smith said $200, whereupon Jones sold it to Smith for $200. The stone turned out to be an uncut diamond worth $3,000. Jones brought an action against Smith to recover the stone. On trial, it was proved that Smith actually did not know the stone was a diamond when he bought it, but he thought it might be a ruby. Can Jones void the sale? Explain.

9. Decedent, Joan Jones, a bedridden, lonely woman, eighty-six years old, owned outright Greenacre, her ancestral estate. Biggers, her physician and friend, visited her weekly and was held in the highest regard by Joan. Joan was extremely fearful of pain and suffering and depended on Biggers to ease her anxiety and pain. Several months before her death, Joan deeded Greenacre to Biggers for $5,000. The fair market value of Greenacre at this time was $125,000. Joan was survived by two children and six grandchildren. Joan's children challenged the validity of the deed. Should the deed be declared invalid due to Biggers' undue influence? Explain.

CASE PROBLEMS

10. In February, Gardner, a schoolteacher with no experience in running a tavern, entered into a contract to purchase for $40,000 the Punjab Tavern from Meiling. The contract was contingent upon Gardner's obtaining a five-year lease for the tavern's premises and a liquor license from the state. Prior to the formation of the contract, Meiling had made no representations to Gardner concerning the gross income of the tavern. Approximately three months after the contract was signed, Gardner and Meiling met with an inspector from the Oregon Liquor Control Commission (OLCC) (http://www.olcc.state.or.us/) to discuss transfer of the liquor license. Meiling reported to the agent, in Gardner's presence, that the tavern's gross income figures for February, March, and April were $5,710, $4,918, and $5,009 respectively. The OLCC granted the required license, the transaction was closed, and Gardner took possession on June 10. After discovering that the tavern's income was very low and that the tavern had very few female patrons, Gardner contacted Meiling's bookkeeping service and learned that the actual gross income for those three months had been approximately $1,400 to $2,000. Will a court grant Gardner rescission of the contract? Explain.

11. Dorothy and John Huffschneider listed their house and lot for sale with C. B. Property. The asking price was $165,000, and the owners told C. B. that the property contained 6.8 acres. Dean Olson, a salesman for C. B., advertised the property in local newspapers as consisting of six acres. James and Jean Holcomb signed a contract to purchase the property through Olson after first inspecting the property with Olson and being assured by Olson that the property was at least 6.6 acres. The Holcombs never asked for nor received a copy of the survey. In actuality, the lot was only 4.6 acres. Can the Holcombs rescind the contract? Explain.

12. Christine Boyd was designated as the beneficiary of a life insurance policy issued by Aetna Life Insurance Company (http://www.aetna.com/index1.htm) on the life of Christine's husband, Jimmie Boyd. The policy insured against Jimmie's permanent total disability and provided for a death benefit to be paid on Jimmie's death. Several years after the policy was issued, Jimmie and Christine separated. Jimmie began to travel extensively, and, therefore, Christine was unable to keep track of his whereabouts or his state of health. Jimmie, nevertheless continued to pay the premiums on the policy until Christine tried to cash in the policy to alleviate her financial distress. A loan had previously been made on the policy, however, leaving its cash surrender value, and thus the amount Christine received, at only $4.19. Shortly thereafter, Christine learned that Jimmie had been permanently and totally disabled before the surrender of the policy. Aetna also was unaware of Jimmie's condition, and Christine requested the surrendered policy be reinstated and that the disability payments be made. Jimmie died soon thereafter, and Christine then requested that Aetna pay the death benefit. Decision?

13. Beginning in 1971, Treasure Salvors and the state of Florida entered into a series of four annual contracts governing the salvage of the *Nuestra Senora de Atocha*. The *Atocha* is a Spanish galleon that sank in 1622, carrying a treasure now worth well over $250 million. Both parties had contracted under the impression that the seabed on which the *Atocha* lay was land owned by Florida. Treasure Salvors agreed to relinquish 25 percent of the items recovered in return for the right to salvage on state lands. In accordance with these contracts, Treasure Salvors delivered to Florida its share of the salvaged artifacts. In 1975 the United States Supreme Court held that the part of the continental shelf on which the *Atocha* was resting had *never* been owned by Florida. Treasure Salvors then brought suit to rescind the contracts and to recover the artifacts it had delivered to the state of Florida. Should Treasure Salvors prevail?

14. Jane Francois married Victor H. Francois. At the time of the marriage, Victor was a fifty-year-old bachelor living with his elderly mother, and Jane was a thirty-year-old, twice-divorced mother of two. Victor had a relatively secure financial portfolio; Jane, on the other hand, brought no money or property to the marriage.

The marriage deteriorated quickly over the next couple of years, with disputes centered on financial matters. During this period, Jane systematically gained a joint interest and took control of most of Victor's assets. Three years after they married, Jane contracted Harold Monoson, an attorney, to draw up divorce papers. Victor was unaware of Jane's decision until he was taken to Monoson's office, where Monoson presented for Victor's signature a "Property Settlement and Separation Agreement." Monoson told Victor that he would need an attorney, but Jane vetoed Victor's choice. Monoson then asked another lawyer, Gregory Ball, to come into the office. Ball read the agreement and strenuously advised Victor not to sign it because it would commit him to financial suicide. The agreement transferred most of Victor's remaining assets to Jane. Victor, however, signed it because Jane and Monoson persuaded him that it was the only way that his marriage could be saved. In October of the following year, Jane informed Victor that she had sold most of his former property and that she was leaving him permanently. Can Victor have the agreement set aside as a result of undue influence?

15. Iverson owned Iverson Motor Company, an enterprise engaged in the repair and sale of Oldsmobile, Rambler, and International Harvester Scout automobiles. Forty percent of the business's sales volume and net earnings came from the Oldsmobile franchise. Whipp contracted to buy Iverson Motors, which Iverson said included the Oldsmobile franchise. After the sale, however, General Motors refused to transfer the franchise to Whipp. Whipp then returned the

property to Iverson and brought this action seeking rescission of the contract. Should the contract be rescinded? Explain.

16. On February 10, Mrs. Sunderhaus purchased a diamond ring from Perel & Lowenstein for $6,990. She was told by the company's salesman that the ring was worth its purchase price, and she also received at that time a written guarantee from the company attesting to the diamond's value, style, and trade-in value. When Mrs. Sunderhaus went to trade the ring for another, however, she was told by two jewelers that the ring was valued at $3,000 and $3,500, respectively. Mrs. Sunderhaus knew little about the value of diamonds and claims to have relied on the oral representation of the Perel & Lowenstein's salesman and the written representation as to the ring's value. Mrs. Sunderhaus seeks rescission of the contract or damages in the amount of the sales price over the ring's value. Will she prevail? Explain.

17. Division West Chinchilla Ranch advertised on television that a five-figure income could be earned by raising chinchillas with an investment of only $3.75 per animal per year and only thirty minutes of maintenance per day. The minimum investment was $2,150 for one male and six female chinchillas. Division West represented to the plaintiffs that chinchilla ranching would be easy and that no experience was required to make ranching profitable. The plaintiffs, who had no experience raising chinchillas, each invested $2,150 or more to purchase Division's chinchillas and supplies. After three years without earning a profit, the plaintiffs sued Division West for fraud. Do these facts sustain an action for fraud in the inducement?

18. William Schmalz entered into an employment contract with Hardy Salt Company. The contract granted Schmalz six months' severance pay for involuntary termination but none for voluntary separation or termination for cause. Schmalz was asked to resign from his employment. He was informed that if he did not resign he would be fired for alleged misconduct. When Schmalz turned in his letter of resignation, he signed a release prohibiting him from suing his former employer as a consequence of his employment. Schmalz consulted an attorney before signing the release and, upon signing it, received $4,583.00 (one month's salary) in consideration. Schmalz now sues his former employer for the severance pay, claiming that he signed the release under duress. Is Schmalz correct in his assertion?

19. Glen Haumont, who owned an equipment retail business in Broken Bow, Nebraska, owed the Security State Bank more than $628,000 due to improper selling practices as well as business and inventory loans. Several times Glen tried to persuade his parents, Lee and Letha Haumont, to financially back his business debts, but each time they refused. Glen then told his parents that, according to his attorney and the bank, Glen could be prosecuted and sent to jail. Soon afterward, David Schweitz, the president of the bank, drove out to the elder Haumonts' farm to convince them to sign as guarantors of Glen's debt. Both Schweitz and Glen stressed to the Haumonts that unless they agreed to guarantee his debt, Glen would go to jail. Letha asked that her attorney be allowed to read over the guaranty agreement, but Schweitz told her that he did not have time to wait and that she must decide right then whether Glen was to go to jail. As a result, the Haumonts signed the agreement, encumbering their previously debt-free family farm for more than $628,000. Should the guarantee agreement be set aside due to duress?

20. Conrad Schaneman was a Russian immigrant who could neither read nor write the English language. In 1975, Conrad deeded (conveyed) a farm he owned to his eldest son, Laurence, for $23,500, which was the original purchase price of the property in 1945. The value of the farm in 1975 was between $145,000 and $160,000. At the time he executed the deed, Conrad was an eighty-two-year-old invalid, severely ill, and completely dependent on others for his personal needs. He weighed between 325 and 350 pounds, had difficulty breathing, could not walk more than fifteen feet, and needed a special jackhoist to get in and out of the bathtub. Conrad enjoyed a long-standing, confidential relationship with Laurence, who was his principal adviser and handled Conrad's business affairs. Laurence also obtained a power of attorney from Conrad and made himself a joint owner of Conrad's bank account and $20,000 certificate of deposit. Conrad brought this suit to cancel the deed, claiming it was the result of Laurence's undue influence. Explain whether the deed was executed as a result of undue influence.

21. At the time of her death in August 1984, Olga Mestrovic was the owner of a large number of works of art created by her late husband, Ivan Mestrovic, an internationally known sculptor and artist whose works were displayed throughout Europe and the United States. By the terms of Olga's will, all the works of art created by her husband were to be sold and the proceeds distributed to members of the Mestrovic family. Also included in the estate of Olga Mestrovic was certain real property which 1st Source Bank (the Bank), as personal representative of the estate of Olga Mestrovic, agreed to sell to Terrence and Antoinette Wilkin. The agreement of purchase and sale made no mention of any works of art, although it did provide for the sale of such personal property as a dishwasher, drapes, and French doors stored in the attic. Immediately after closing on the real estate, the Wilkins complained to the Bank of the clutter left on the premises; the Bank gave the Wilkins an option of cleaning the house themselves and keeping any personal property they desired, to which the Wilkins agreed. At the time these arrangements were made, neither the Bank nor the Wilkins suspected that any works of art remained on the premises. During cleanup, however, the Wilkins found eight drawings and a sculpture created by Ivan Mestrovic to which the Wilkins claimed ownership based upon their agreement with the Bank that, if they cleaned the real property, they could keep such personal property as they desired. Who is entitled to ownership of the works of art?

22. Frank Berryessa stole funds from his employer, the Eccles Hotel Company. His father, W. S. Berryessa, learned of his son's trouble and, thinking the amount involved was about $2,000, gave the hotel a promissory note for $2,186 to cover the shortage. In return, the hotel agreed not to publicize the incident or notify the bonding company. (A bonding company is an insurer that is paid a premium for agreeing to reimburse an employer for thefts by an employee.) Before this note became due, however, the hotel discovered that Frank had actually misappropriated $6,865. The hotel then notified its bonding company, Great American Indemnity Company, to collect the entire loss. W. S. Berryessa claims that the agent for Great American told him that unless he paid them $2,000 in cash and signed a note for the remaining $4,865, Frank would be prosecuted. Berryessa agreed, signed the note, and gave the agent a cashier's check for $1,500 and a personal check for $500. He requested that the agent not cash the personal check for about a month. Subsequently, Great American sued Berryessa on the note. He defends against the note on the grounds of duress and counterclaims for the return of the $1,500 and the cancellation of the uncashed $500 check. Who should prevail? Explain.

http:// **Internet Exercise** Find information on how businesses and consumers can avoid and detect fraud and scams (including online, credit card, and telemarketing misuse).

CHAPTER 12

Consideration

Nuda pactio obligationem non parit. *(A naked agreement, that is, one without consideration, does not beget an obligation.)*

LEGAL MAXIM

Learning Objectives

After reading this chapter you should be able to:

1. Define *consideration* and explain what is meant by legal sufficiency.
2. Describe illusory promises, output contracts, requirements contracts, exclusive dealing contracts, and conditional contracts.
3. Explain whether preexisting public and contractual obligations satisfy the legal requirement of consideration.
4. Explain the concept of bargained-for exchange and whether this element is present with past consideration and third-party beneficiaries.
5. Identify and discuss those contracts that are enforceable even though they are not supported by consideration.

Consideration is the primary—but not the only—basis for the enforcement of promises in our legal system. **Consideration** is the inducement to make a promise enforceable. The doctrine of consideration ensures that promises are enforced only where the parties have exchanged something of value in the eye of the law. **Gratuitous** (gift) **promises**—those made without consideration—are not legally enforceable, except under certain circumstances, which are discussed later in the chapter.

Consideration, or that which is exchanged for a promise, is present only when the parties intend an exchange. The consideration exchanged for the promise may be an act, a forbearance to act, or a promise to do either of these. Thus, there are two basic elements to consideration: (1) legal sufficiency (something of value in the eye of the law) and (2) bargained-for exchange. Both must be present to satisfy the requirement of consideration.

CPA LEGAL SUFFICIENCY

To be **legally sufficient**, the consideration for the promise must be either a legal detriment to the promisee or a legal benefit to the promisor. In other words, the promisee must give up something of legal value, or the promisor must receive something of legal value in return for the promise.

Legal detriment means (1) the doing of (or the undertaking to do) that which the promisee was under no prior legal obligation to do or (2) the refraining from the doing of (or the undertaking to refrain from doing) that which he was previously under no legal obligation to refrain from doing. On the other hand, legal benefit means the obtaining by the promisor of that which he had no prior legal right to obtain. In most, if not all, cases where there is legal detriment to the promisee, there is also a **legal benefit** to the promisor. However, the presence of either is sufficient.

Pearsall v. Alexander

District of Columbia Court of Appeals, 1990
572 A.2d 113

FACTS Harold Pearsall and Joe Alexander were friends for over twenty-five years. About twice a week they would get together after work and proceed to a liquor store, where they would purchase what the two liked to refer to as a "package"—a half-pint of vodka, orange juice, two cups, and two lottery tickets. Occasionally these lottery tickets would yield modest rewards of two or three dollars, which the pair would then "plow back" into the purchase of additional tickets. On December 16, 1982, Pearsall and Alexander visited the liquor store twice, buying their normal "package" on both occasions. For the first package, Pearsall went into the store alone, and when he returned to the car, he said to Alexander, in reference to the tickets, "Are you in on it?" Alexander said, "Yes." When Pearsall asked him for his half of the purchase price, though, Alexander replied that he had no money. When they went to Alexander's home, Alexander snatched the tickets from Pearsall's hand and "scratched" them, only to find that they were both worthless. Later that same evening Alexander returned to the liquor store and bought a second "package." This time, Pearsall snatched the tickets from Alexander and said that he would "scratch" them. Instead, he gave one to Alexander, and each man scratched one of the tickets. Alexander's was a $20,000 winner. Alexander cashed the ticket and refused to give Pearsall anything. Pearsall brought suit against Alexander, claiming breach of an agreement to share the proceeds. The trial court dismissed Pearsall's complaint, and Pearsall appealed.

DECISION Judgment reversed and remanded with instructions to enter judgment in favor of Pearsall.

OPINION Newman, J. It is also clear to us that, by exchanging mutual promises to share in the proceeds of winning tickets, adequate consideration was given by both parties. An exchange of promises is consideration, so long as it is bargained-for. [Citation.] Moreover, consideration may consist of detriment to the promisee. [Citation.] The giving of one-half of the proceeds of a winning ticket would be detriment to either man. Therefore, Pearsall's promise to share, as expressed in his question to Alexander, "Are you in on it?" induced a detriment in Alexander. Likewise, Alexander's promise to share, as contained in his assent, induced a detriment in Pearsall.

The record supports the trial court's finding that an agreement existed between Pearsall and Alexander to share equally in the proceeds of the winning ticket at issue.

The conduct of the two men on the evening of December 16, 1982, when the ticket was purchased, clearly demonstrates a meeting of the minds. After purchasing the first pair of tickets, Pearsall asked Alexander if he was "in on it." Not only did Alexander give his verbal assent, but later, when the two reached Alexander's home, Alexander, who had contributed nothing to the purchase price of the tickets, snatched *both* tickets from Pearsall and anxiously "scratched" them. It is evident from this that Alexander considered himself "in on" an agreement to share in the fortunes of the tickets purchased by his friend. It is equally clear that in giving over tickets he had purchased, Pearsall gave his assent to the agreement he had proposed earlier in the car. Moreover, this conduct took place within the context of a long-standing pattern of similar conduct, analogous to a "course of conduct" as described in the Uniform Commercial Code, which included their practice of "plowing back" small returns from winning tickets into the purchase of additional tickets.

In conclusion we find that there was a valid, enforceable agreement between Pearsall and Alexander to share in the proceeds of the $20,000 ticket purchased by Alexander on the evening of December 16, 1982.

INTERPRETATION Consideration can either be a legal benefit to the promisor or a legal detriment to the promisee.

CRITICAL THINKING QUESTION Would it have been preferable to have this continuing agreement put in writing? Explain.

ADEQUACY

Legal sufficiency has nothing to do with **adequacy of consideration**. The items or actions that the parties agree to exchange do not need to have the same value. Rather, the law will regard the consideration as adequate if the parties have freely agreed to the exchange. The requirement of legally sufficient consideration is, therefore, *not* at all concerned with whether the bargain was good or bad or whether one party received disproportionately more or less than what he gave or promised in exchange. (Such facts, however, may be relevant to the availability of certain defenses—such as fraud, duress, or undue influence—or certain remedies—such as specific performance.) The requirement of legally sufficient consideration is simply (1) that the parties have agreed to an exchange and (2) that, with respect to each party, the subject matter exchanged, or promised in exchange, either imposed a legal detriment on the promisee or conferred a legal benefit on the promisor. If the purported consideration is clearly without value, however, such that the transaction is a sham, many courts would hold that consideration is lacking.

> **Practical Advice**
>
> Be sure you are satisfied with your agreed-upon exchange because courts will not invalidate a contract for absence of adequate consideration.

UNILATERAL CONTRACTS

In a unilateral contract, a promise is exchanged for a completed act or a forbearance to act. Because only one promise exists, only one party, the ***offeror***, makes a promise, and is therefore the **promisor** while the other party, the **offeree**, is the person receiving the promise and, thus, is the **promisee**. For example, A promises to pay B $2,000 if B paints A's house. B paints A's house.

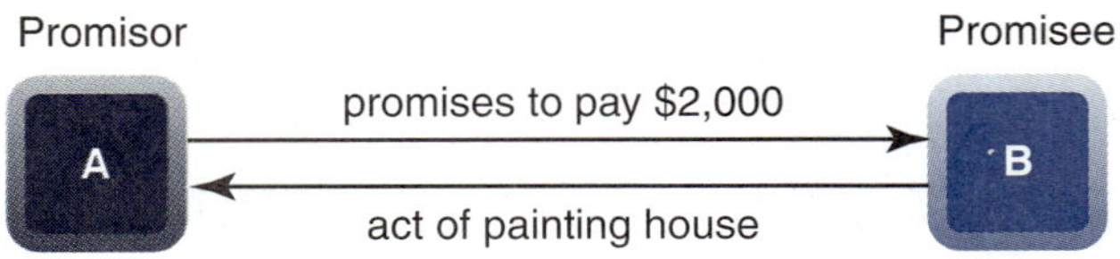

A's promise is binding only if it is supported by consideration consisting of either a legal detriment to B, the promisee (offeree), or a legal benefit to A, the promisor (offeror). B's painting the house is a legal detriment to B, the promisee, because she was under no prior legal duty to paint A's house. Also, B's painting of A's house is a legal benefit to A, the promisor, because A had no prior legal right to have his house painted by B.

A unilateral contract may also consist of a promise exchanged for a forbearance. To illustrate, A negligently injures B, for which B may recover damages in a tort action. A promises B $5,000 if B forbears from bringing suit. B accepts by not suing.

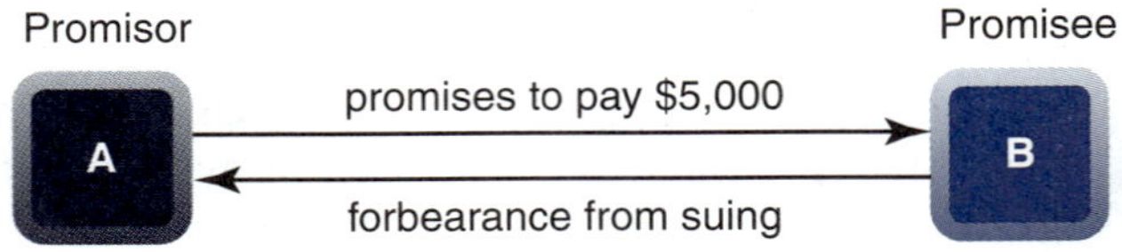

A's promise to pay B $5,000 is binding because it is supported by consideration; B, the promisee (offeree), has incurred a legal detriment by refraining from bringing suit, which he was under no prior legal obligation to refrain from doing. A, the promisor (offeror), has received a legal benefit because she had no prior legal right to B's forbearance from bringing suit.

BILATERAL CONTRACTS

In a bilateral contract there is an exchange of promises. Thus, each party is *both* a promisor and a promisee. For example, if A (the offeror) promises (offers) to purchase an automobile from B for $20,000 and B (the offeree) promises to sell the automobile to A for $20,000 (accepts the offer), the following relationship exists:

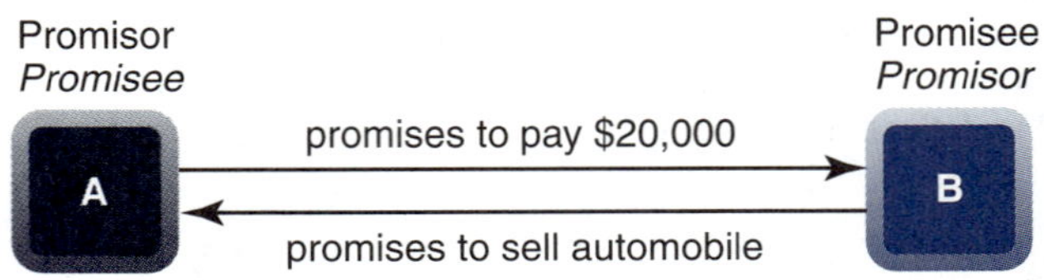

A (offeror) as promisor: A's promise (the offer) to pay B $20,000 is binding if that promise is supported by legal consideration from B (offeror), which may consist of either a legal detriment to B, the *promisee,* or a legal benefit to A, the *promisor*. B's promise to sell A the automobile is a legal detriment to B because he was under no prior legal duty to sell the automobile to A. Moreover, B's promise is also a legal benefit to A because A had no prior legal right to that automobile. Consequently, A's promise to pay $20,000 to B is supported by consideration and is enforceable.

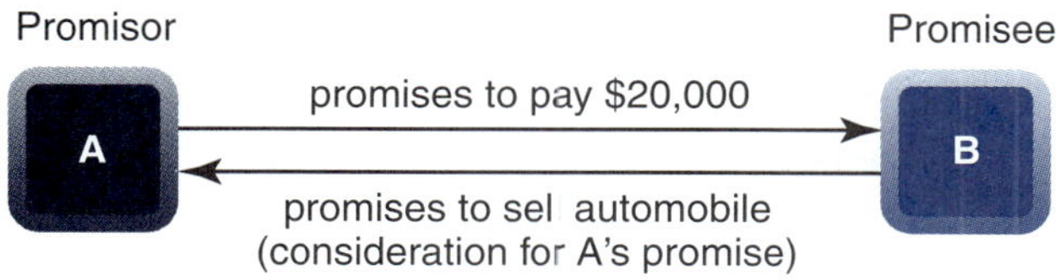

B* (offeree) *as promisor: For *B's promise (the acceptance)* to sell the automobile to A to be binding, it likewise must be supported by consideration from A (offeror), which may be either a legal detriment to A, the *promisee*, or a legal benefit to B, the *promisor*. A's promise to pay B $20,000 is a legal detriment to A because he was under no prior legal duty to pay $20,000 to B. At the same time, A's promise is also a legal benefit to B because B had no prior legal right to the $20,000. Thus, B's promise to sell the automobile is supported by consideration and is enforceable.

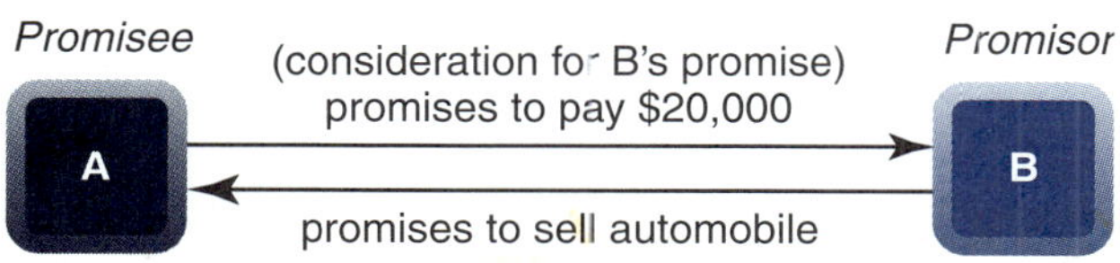

To summarize, for A's *promise* to B to be binding, it must be supported by legally sufficient consideration, which requires that the promise A receives from B in exchange either provides a legal benefit to A or constitutes a legal detriment to B. B's return promise to A must also be supported by consideration. Thus, in a bilateral contract, each promise is the consideration for the other, a relationship that has been referred to as ***mutuality of obligation***. A general consequence of mutuality of obligation is that each promisor in a bilateral contract must be bound or neither is bound. See Concept Review for an overview of consideration in both unilateral and bilateral contracts. Also see the Ethical Dilemma for a situation dealing with the disputed enforceability of a promise.

ILLUSORY PROMISES

Words of promise that make the performance of the purported promisor entirely optional do not constitute a promise at all. Consequently, they cannot serve as consideration. In this section, we will distinguish such illusory promises from promises that do impose obligations of performance upon the promisor and thus can be legally sufficient consideration.

An **illusory promise** is a statement that is in the form of a promise but imposes no obligation upon the maker of the statement. An illusory promise is not consideration for a return promise. Thus, a statement committing the promisor to purchase such quantity of goods as he may "desire" or "want" or "wish to buy" is an illusory promise because its performance is entirely optional. For example, if Exxon offers to sell to Gasco as many barrels of oil as Gasco shall choose at $40 per barrel, there is no contract for lack of consideration. An offer containing such a promise, although accepted by the offeree, does not create a contract because the promise is illusory—Gasco's performance is entirely optional and no constraint is placed on its freedom. It is not bound to do anything, nor can Exxon reasonably expect it to do anything. Thus, Gasco, by its promise, suffers no legal detriment and confers no legal benefit.

> **Practical Advice**
>
> Because an agreement under which one party may perform at his discretion is not a binding contract, be sure that you make a promise and receive a promise that is not optional.

Output and Requirements Contracts The agreement of a seller to sell her entire production to a particular purchaser is called an **output contract**. It gives the seller an ensured market for her product. Conversely, a purchaser's agreement to purchase from a particular seller all the

CONCEPT REVIEW

Consideration in Unilateral and Bilateral Contracts

Type of Contract	Offer	Acceptance	Consideration
Unilateral	Promise by A	Performance of requested act or forbearance by B	*Promise* by A *Performance* of requested act or forbearance by B
Bilateral	Promise by A	Return promise by B to perform requested act or forbearance	*Promise* by A *Return promise* by B to perform requested act or forbearance

Ethical Dilemma

Should a Spouse's Promise Be Legally Binding?

FACTS Joan Kantor is a social worker for the employees of Surf & Co., a towel manufacturer. Stan Koronetsky, a Surf employee, has confided the following problems to Kantor.

Koronetsky and his wife, Paula, have been married for ten years. Koronetsky states that three years ago his wife was unfaithful and Koronetsky began a divorce proceeding. When Paula Koronetsky promised to refrain from further infidelity and to attend marital counseling sessions, Koronetsky agreed to stop the divorce proceeding. However, although Stan dropped the divorce proceeding, his wife never attended counseling.

Koronetsky is also upset because he and his wife had agreed that she would attend medical school while he worked to support her. In exchange for his promise to put her through medical school, Paula promised that she would support him while he obtained his M.B.A. degree. But after Paula became a doctor, she refused to support him; consequently, Stan never got his master's degree.

Social, Policy, and Ethical Considerations

1. What should Joan Kantor do in this situation? What is the scope of her counseling responsibilities?
2. Should agreements between married parties be enforced in a court of law? If so, what types of agreements should be enforceable?
3. What are the individual interests at stake in this situation? Is it reasonable to assume that spouses make many private agreements, and that generally these agreements are made without the intention of their being legally binding?

materials of a particular kind that the purchaser needs is called a **requirements contract.** It ensures the buyer of a ready source of inventory or supplies. These contracts are *not* illusory. The buyer under a requirements contract does not promise to buy as much as she desires to buy, but to buy as much as she *needs*. Similarly, under an output contract, the seller promises to sell to the buyer the seller's entire production, not merely as much as the seller desires.

Furthermore, the Code imposes a good faith limitation upon the quantity to be sold or purchased under an output or requirements contract. Thus, this type of contract involves such actual output or requirements as may occur in good faith, except that no quantity unreasonably disproportionate to any stated estimate or, in the absence of a stated estimate, to any normal prior output or requirements may be tendered or demanded. Therefore, after contracting to sell to Adler, Inc., its entire output, Benevito Company cannot increase its production from one eight-hour shift per day to three eight-hour shifts per day.

> **Practical Advice**
>
> If you use an output or requirements contract, be sure to act in good faith and do not take unfair advantage of the situation.

Exclusive Dealing Contracts An **exclusive dealing** agreement is a contract in which a manufacturer of goods grants to a distributor an exclusive right to sell its products in a designated market. Unless otherwise agreed, an implied obligation is imposed on the manufacturer to use its best efforts to supply the goods and on the distributor to use her best efforts to promote their sale. These implied obligations are sufficient consideration to bind both parties to the exclusive dealing contract.

Conditional Promises A **conditional promise** is a promise the performance of which depends upon the happening or nonhappening of an event not certain to occur (the condition). A conditional promise is sufficient consideration *unless* the promisor knows at the time of making the promise that the condition cannot occur.

Thus, if Joanne offers to pay Barry $8,000 for Barry's automobile, provided that Joanne receives such amount as an inheritance from the estate of her deceased uncle, and Barry accepts the offer, the duty of Joanne to pay $8,000 to Barry is *conditioned* on her receiving $8,000 from her deceased uncle's estate. The consideration moving from Barry to Joanne is the transfer of title to the automobile. The consideration moving from Joanne to Barry is the promise of $8,000 subject to the condition.

Preexisting Obligations

The law does not regard the performance of, or the promise to perform, a preexisting legal duty, public or private, as either a legal detriment or a legal benefit. A public duty does not arise out of a contract; rather, it is imposed on members of society by force of the common law or by statute. Illustrations, as found in the law of torts, include the duty not to commit assault, battery, false imprisonment, or defamation. The criminal law also imposes many public duties. Thus, if Norton promises to pay Holmes, the village ruffian, $100 not to injure him, Norton's promise is unenforceable because both tort and criminal law impose a preexisting public obligation on Holmes to refrain from such abuse.

Public officials, such as the mayor of a city, members of a city council, police, and firefighters, are under a preexisting obligation to perform their duties by virtue of their public office. See *Denney v. Reppert* below.

The performance of, or the promise to perform, a **preexisting contractual duty**, a duty the terms of which are neither doubtful nor the subject of honest dispute, is also legally insufficient consideration because the doing of what one is legally bound to do is neither a detriment to a promisee nor a benefit to the promisor. For example, if Anita employs Ben for one year at a salary of $1,000 per month, and at the end of six months promises Ben that in addition to the salary she will pay Ben $3,000 if Ben remains on the job for the remainder of the period originally agreed on, Anita's promise is not binding for lack of legally sufficient consideration. However, if Ben's duties were by agreement changed in nature or amount, Anita's promise would be binding because Ben's new duties are a legal detriment to Ben and a legal benefit to Anita.

The following case deals with both preexisting public and contractual obligations.

Denney v. Reppert

Court of Appeals of Kentucky, 1968
432 S.W.2d 647

FACTS In June, three armed men entered and robbed the First State Bank of Eubank, Kentucky, of $30,000. Acting on information supplied by four employees of the bank, Denney, Buis, McCollum, and Snyder, three law enforcement officials apprehended the robbers. Two of the arresting officers, Godby and Simms, were state policemen, and the third, Reppert, was a deputy sheriff in a neighboring county. All seven claimed the reward for the apprehension and conviction of the bank robbers. The trial court held that only Reppert was entitled to the reward, and Denney appealed.

DECISION Judgment affirmed.

OPINION Myre, J. The first question for determination is whether the employees of the robbed bank are eligible to receive or share in the reward. The great weight of authority answers in the negative. * * *

"To the general rule that, when a reward is offered to the general public for the performance of some specified act, such reward may be claimed by any person who performs such act, is the exception of agents, employees and public officials who are acting within the scope of their employment or official duties. * * *"

* * *

At the time of the robbery the claimants Murrell Denney, Joyce Buis, Rebecca McCollum, and Jewell Snyder were employees of the First State Bank of Eubank. They were under duty to protect and conserve the resources and moneys of the bank, and safeguard every interest of the institution furnishing them employment. Each of these employees exhibited great courage, and cool bravery, in a time of stress and danger. The community and the county have recompensed them in commendation, admiration and high praise, and the world looks on them as heroes. But in making known the robbery and assisting in acquainting the public and the officers with details of the crime and with identification of the robbers, they performed a duty to the bank and the public, for which they cannot claim a reward.

State Policemen Garret Godby, Johnny Simms, and [deputy sheriff] Tilford Reppert made the arrest of the bank robbers and captured the stolen money. All participated in the prosecution. At the time of the arrest, it was the duty of the state policemen to apprehend the criminals. Under the law they cannot claim or share in the reward and they are interposing no claim to it.

This leaves * * * Tilford Reppert the sole eligible claimant. The record shows that at the time of the arrest he was a deputy sheriff in Rockcastle County, but the arrest and recovery of the stolen money took place in Pulaski County. He was out of his jurisdiction, and was thus under no legal duty to make the arrest, and is thus eligible to claim and receive the award.

* * *

It is manifest from the record that Tilford Reppert is the only claimant qualified and eligible to receive the reward. Therefore, it is the judgment of the circuit court that he is entitled to receive payment of the $1,500.00 reward now deposited with the Clerk of this Court.

INTERPRETATION The law does not regard the performance of a preexisting duty as either a legal detriment or a legal benefit.

ETHICAL QUESTION Did the court treat all the parties fairly? Explain.

CRITICAL THINKING QUESTION Do you agree with the preexisting duty rule? Explain.

Modification of a Preexisting Contract A modification of a contract occurs when the parties to the contract mutually agree to change one or more of its terms. Under the common law, as shown in the following case, a modification of an existing contract must be supported by mutual consideration to be enforceable. In other words, the modification must be supported by some new consideration beyond that which is already owed under the original contract. Thus, there must be a separate and distinct modification contract. For example, Diane and Fred agree that Diane shall put in a gravel driveway for Fred at a cost of $2,000. Subsequently, Fred agrees to pay an additional $3,000 if Diane will blacktop the driveway. Because Diane was not bound by the original contract to provide blacktop, she would incur a legal detriment in doing so and is therefore entitled to the additional $3,000. Similarly, consideration may consist of the promisee's refraining from exercising a legal right.

The Code has modified the common law rule for contract modification by providing that the parties can effectively modify a contract for the sale of goods without new consideration, provided they both intend to modify the contract and act in good faith. Moreover, the Restatement has moved toward this position by providing that a modification of an executory contract is binding if it is fair and equitable in the light of surrounding facts that the parties had not anticipated when the contract was made. Figure 12-1 demonstrates when consideration is required to modify an existing contract.

Practical Advice

If you modify a contract governed by the common law, be sure to provide additional consideration to make the other party's new promise enforceable.

Figure 12-1 *Modification of a Preexisting Contract*

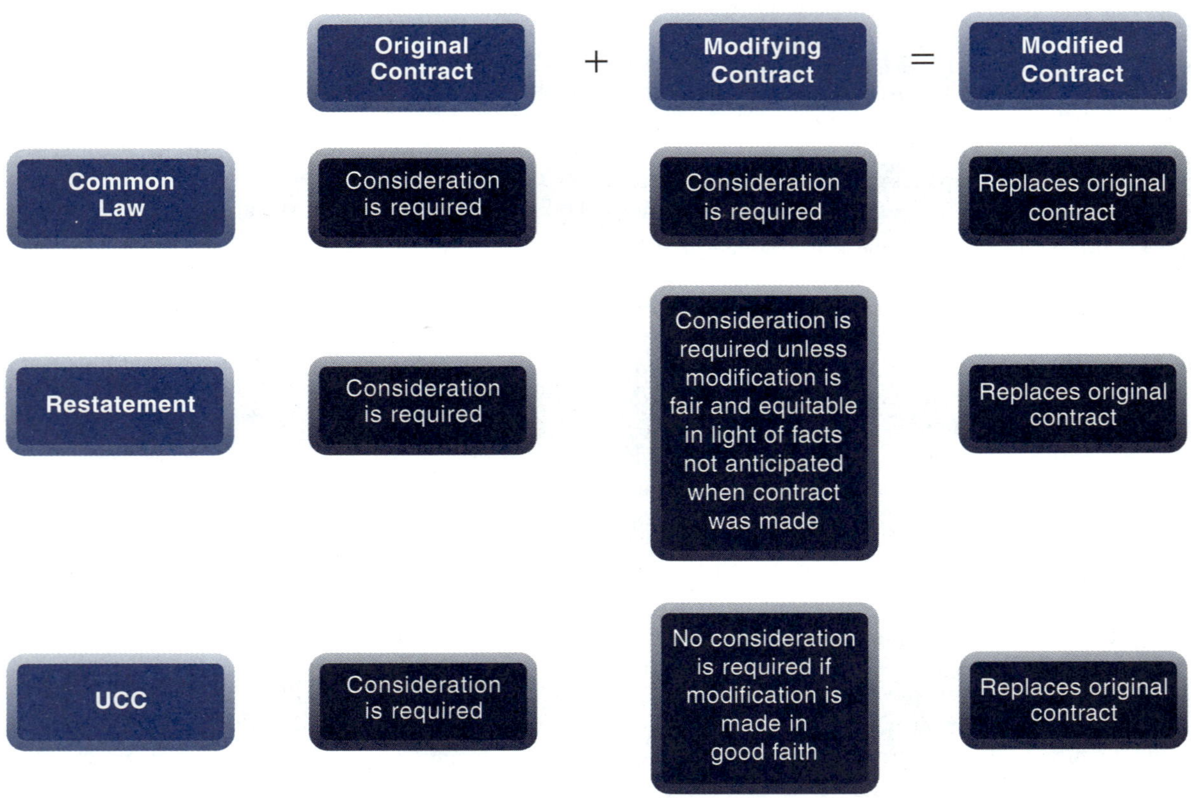

New England Rock Services, Inc. v Empire Paving, Inc.

Appellate Court of Connecticut, 1999
53 Conn.App. 771, 731 A.2d 784, *cert. denied*, 250 Conn. 921, 738 A.2d 658

FACTS On October 26, 1995, the defendant, Empire Paving, Inc., entered into a contract with Rock Services under which Rock Services would provide drilling and blasting services as a subcontractor on the Niles Hill Road sewer project on which Empire was the general contractor and the city of New London was the owner. Rock Services was to be paid an agreed upon price of $29 per cubic yard with an estimated amount of 5,000 cubic yards, or on a time and materials basis, whichever was less. From the outset, Rock Services experienced problems on the job, the primary problem being the presence of a heavy concentration of water on the site. The water problem hindered Rock Services' ability to complete its work as anticipated. It is the responsibility of the general contractor to control the water on the work site and, on this particular job, Empire failed to control the water on the site properly. Rock Services attempted alternative methods of dealing with the problem, but was prevented from using them by the city. Thereafter, in order to complete its work, Rock Services was compelled to use a more costly and time-consuming method.

In late November, 1995, Rock Services advised Empire that it would be unable to complete the work as anticipated because of the conditions at the site and requested that Empire agree to amend the contract to allow Rock Services to complete the project on a time and materials basis. On December 8, Empire signed a purchase order that so modified the original agreement. Upon completion of the work, Empire refused to pay Rock Services for the remaining balance due on the time and materials agreement in the amount of $58,686.63, and Rock Services instituted this action. The trial court concluded that the modified agreement was valid and ruled in favor of Rock Services. Empire brings this appeal.

DECISION Judgment in favor of Rock Services affirmed.

OPINION Schaller, J. In concluding that the modification was valid and enforceable, the trial court determined that the later agreement was supported by sufficient consideration. * * *

"The doctrine of consideration is fundamental in the law of contracts, the general rule being that in the absence of consideration an executory promise is unenforceable." [Citation.] While mutual promises may be sufficient consideration to bind parties to a modification [citations]; a promise to do that which one is already bound by his contract to do is not sufficient consideration to support an additional promise by the other party to the contract. [Citations.]

"A modification of an agreement must be supported by valid consideration and requires a party to do, or promise to do, something further than, or different from, that which he is already bound to do. [Citations.] It is an accepted principle of law in this state that when a party agrees to perform an obligation for another to whom that obligation is already owed, although for lesser remuneration, the second agreement does not constitute a valid, binding contract. [Citations.] The basis of the rule is generally made to rest upon the proposition that in such a situation he who promises the additional [work] receives nothing more than that to which he is already entitled and he to whom the promise is made gives nothing that he was not already under legal obligation to give. [Citations.]

Our Supreme Court in [citation], however, articulated an exception to the preexisting duty rule: "[W]here a contract must be performed under burdensome conditions not anticipated, and not within the contemplation of the parties at the time when the contract was made, and the promisee measures up to the right standard of honesty and fair dealing, and agrees, in view of the changed conditions, to pay what is then reasonable, just, and fair, such new contract is not without consideration within the meaning of that term, either in law or in equity." * * * "What unforeseen difficulties and burdens will make a party's refusal to go forward with his contract equitable, so as to take the case out of the general rule and bring it within the exception, must depend upon the facts of each particular case. They must be substantial, unforeseen, and not within the contemplation of the parties when the contract was made. They need not be such as would legally justify the party in his refusal to perform his contract, unless promised extra pay, or to justify a court of equity in relieving him from the contract; for they are sufficient if they are of such a character as to render the party's demand for extra pay manifestly fair, so as to rebut all inference that he is seeking to be relieved from an unsatisfactory contract, or to take advantage of the necessities of the opposite party to coerce from him a promise for further compensation. Inadequacy of the contract price which is the result of an error of judgment, and not of some excusable mistake of fact, is not sufficient." [Citation.] * * *

Empire argues strenuously that the water conditions on the site cannot qualify as a new circumstance that was not anticipated at the time the original contract was signed. * * *

Empire's argument, however, is misplaced. Rock Services does not argue that it was unaware of the water conditions on the site but, rather, that Empire's failure to control or remove the water on the site constituted the new or changed circumstance. Rock Services argues that Empire's duty to control or remove the water on the job site arose in accordance with the custom and practice in the industry and, therefore, Empire's failure to control or remove the water on the site constituted a new circumstance that Rock Services did not anticipate at the time the original contract was signed.

* * *

INTERPRETATION The Restatement provides that a modification of an executory contract is binding if it is fair and equitable in the light of surrounding facts that the parties had not anticipated when the contract was made.

CRITICAL THINKING QUESTION Which rule for contract modification do you believe is the best: the common law, the Restatement's, or the Code's ? Why?

Substituted Contracts A **substituted contract** results when the parties to a contract mutually agree to rescind their original contract and enter into a new one. This situation actually involves three separate contracts: the original contract, the contract of rescission, and the substitute contract. Substituted contracts are perfectly valid, allowing the parties to effectively discharge the original contract and to impose obligations under the new one. The rescission is binding in that, as long as each party still had rights under the original contract, each has, by giving up those rights, provided consideration to the other.

Settlement of an Undisputed Debt An **undisputed debt** is an obligation that is not contested as to its existence or its amount. Under the common law, the payment of a lesser sum of money than is owed in consideration of a promise to discharge a fully matured, undisputed debt is legally insufficient to support the promise of discharge. To illustrate, assume that Barbara owes Arnold $100, and in consideration of Barbara's paying him $50, Arnold agrees to discharge the debt. In a subsequent suit by Arnold against Barbara to recover the remaining $50, at common law Arnold is entitled to a judgment for $50 on the ground that Arnold's promise of discharge is not binding because Barbara's payment of $50 was no legal detriment to the promisee, Barbara, because she was under a ***preexisting legal obligation*** to pay that much and more. Consequently, the consideration for Arnold's promise of discharge was legally insufficient, and Arnold is not bound by his promise. If, however, Arnold had accepted from Barbara any new or different consideration, such as the sum of $40 and a fountain pen worth $10 or less, or even the fountain pen with no payment of money, in full satisfaction of the $100 debt, the consideration moving from Barbara would be legally sufficient because Barbara was under no legal obligation to give a fountain pen to Arnold. In this example, consideration would also exist if Arnold had agreed to accept $50 *before* the debt became due, in full satisfaction of the debt. Barbara was under no legal obligation to pay any of the debt before its due date. Consequently, Barbara's early payment would constitute a legal detriment to Barbara as well as a legal benefit to Arnold. The common law is not concerned with the amount of the discount, because that is simply a question of adequacy. Likewise, Barbara's payment of a lesser amount on the due date at an agreed-upon different place of payment would be legally sufficient consideration. The Restatement, however, requires that the new consideration "differ[s] from what was required by the duty in a way which reflects more than a pretense of bargain."

Settlement of a Disputed Debt A **disputed debt** is an obligation whose existence or amount is contested. A promise to settle a validly disputed claim in exchange for an agreed payment or other performance is supported by consideration. Where the dispute is based on contentions without merit or not made in good faith, the debtor's surrender of such contentions is not a legal detriment to the claimant. The Restatement adopts a different position by providing that the settlement of a claim that proves invalid is consideration if at the time of the settlement (1) the claimant honestly believed that the claim was valid *or* (2) the claim was in fact doubtful because of uncertainty as to the facts or the law.

For example, where a person has requested professional services from an accountant or a lawyer and no agreement has been made about the amount of the fee to be charged, the client has a legal obligation to pay the reasonable value of the services performed. Because no definite amount was agreed on, the client's obligation is uncertain. When the accountant or lawyer sends the client a bill for services rendered, even though the amount stated in the bill is an estimate of the reasonable value of the services, the debt does not become undisputed until and unless the client agrees to pay the amount of the bill. If the client honestly disputes the amount that is owing and offers in full settlement an amount less than the bill, acceptance of the lesser amount by the accountant or lawyer discharges the debt. Thus, if Andy sends to Bess, an accountant, a check for $120 in full payment of his debt to Bess for services rendered, which services Andy considered worthless but for which Bess billed Andy $600, Bess's acceptance (cashing) of the check releases Andy from any further liability. Andy has given up his right to dispute the billing further, and Bess has forfeited her right to further collection. Thus, there is mutuality of consideration.

Practical Advice

If your contract is validly disputed, carefully consider whether to accept any payment marked "payment in full."

Mathis v. St. Alexis Hospital

Court of Appeals of Ohio, 1994
99 Ohio App.3d 159, 650 N.E.2d 141

FACTS Rodney and Donna Mathis (Mathis) filed a wrongful death action against St. Alexis Hospital and several physicians, arising out of the death of their mother, Mary Mathis. Several weeks before trial, an expert consulted by Mathis notified the trial court and Mathis's counsel that, in his opinion, Mary Mathis's death was not proximately caused by the negligence of the physicians. Shortly thereafter, Mathis voluntarily dismissed the wrongful death action. Mathis and St. Alexis entered into a covenant-not-to-sue in which Mathis agreed not to pursue any claims against St. Alexis or its employees in terms of the medical care of Mary Mathis. St. Alexis, in return, agreed not to seek sanctions, including attorney fees and costs incurred in defense of the previously dismissed wrongful death action. Subsequently, Mathis filed a second wrongful death action against St. Alexis Hospital, among others. Mathis asked the court to rescind the covenant-not-to-sue, arguing that because St. Alexis was not entitled to sanctions in connection with the first wrongful death action, there was no consideration for the covenant-not-to-sue. The trial court granted summary judgment for St. Alexis. Mathis appeals.

DECISION Judgment affirmed.

OPINION Nahra, J. Mathis argued that the covenant not to sue was unsupported by sufficient consideration and was consequently non-binding. However, St. Alexis argued that the consideration for the covenant not to sue was St. Alexis' agreement not to file a motion for attorney fees incurred in the defense of Mathis' previously dismissed action.

A covenant not to sue is governed by the same principles as a contract and must meet all requirements for a valid contract, including consideration. [Citation.] A promise not to prosecute a valid claim may be valuable consideration, where the promisor has the right to sue on the claim and the claim is valid. [Citation.]

Mathis argued that St. Alexis did not have a valid claim for sanctions against the plaintiffs. Mathis argued that any sanctions award should have been against Mathis' attorney. Mathis argued that since St. Alexis had no claim against Mathis, St. Alexis' promise to forbear prosecution of its claim was not sufficient consideration for Mathis' promise not to sue St. Alexis for medical negligence.

St. Alexis' proposed claim for sanctions was under * * * R.C.2323.51.

* * *

R.C. 2323.51 provides:

> "(B) (1) * * * [A]t any time prior to the commencement of the trial in a civil action or within twenty-one days after the entry of judgment in a civil action, the court may award reasonable attorney's fees to any party to that action adversely affected by frivolous conduct."

According[ly] * * *, sanctions could have been awarded against Mathis. Mathis argued that St. Alexis has not shown that Mathis engaged in any frivolous conduct. However, we must note that the standard for evaluating the validity of the forborne claim is a subjective one. [Citation.] A promise to forbear pursuit of a legal claim can be sufficient consideration to support a contract when the promisor has a good faith belief in the validity of the claim. [Citation.]

> The modern trend of authority is to move still further away from an objective view of the actual validity of the surrendered claim and to focus primarily on whether the claimant's subjective belief in its legitimacy is honest and sincere; the only remnants of an objective standard are that the asserted claim must not be "frivolous, vexatious, or unlawful" and that asserted good faith belief "would affront the intelligence of ordinary and reasonable layman." Compared to the first cases on the subject, the most recent ones clearly require a minimal

degree of objective certainty in the existent validity of the surrendered claim. [Citation.]

We find that St. Alexis sufficiently asserted a good faith belief in the validity of its sanctions claim. In its motion for summary judgment and brief in opposition to Mathis' motion for summary judgment, St. Alexis asserted that its belief in the validity of its sanctions claim was based on Mathis' complete failure to produce any expert testimony on the issue of proximate cause. The only expert testimony presented on the issue indicated that St. Alexis' actions did not proximately cause Mary Mathis' death. St. Alexis' belief in the validity of its sanctions claim was reasonable.

INTERPRETATION A promise to settle a validly disputed claim in exchange for an agreed payment or other performance is supported by consideration.

ETHICAL QUESTION Did the parties act ethically? Explain.

CRITICAL THINKING QUESTION When should a claim be considered to be frivolous and therefore not consideration for a promise? Explain.

CPA BARGAINED-FOR EXCHANGE

The central idea behind consideration is that the parties have intentionally entered into a **bargained-for exchange** with each other and have each given to the other something in a mutually agreed-upon exchange for his promise or performance. Thus, a promise to give someone a birthday present is without consideration, because the promisor received nothing in exchange for her promise of a present.

Practical Advice

Because a promise to make a gift is generally not legally enforceable, obtain delivery of something that shows your control or ownership of the item to make it an executed gift.

PAST CONSIDERATION

Consideration, as previously defined, is the inducement for a promise or performance. The element of exchange is absent where a promise is given for an act already done. Therefore, unbargained-for past events are not consideration, despite their designation as **past consideration**. A promise made on account of something that the promisee has already done is not enforceable. For example, Diana installs Tom's complex new car stereo and speakers. Tom subsequently promises to reimburse Diana for her expenses, but his promise is not binding because there is no bargained-for exchange.

THIRD PARTIES

Consideration to support a promise may be given to a person other than the promisor if the promisor bargains for that exchange. For example, A promises to pay B $15 if B delivers a specified book to C.

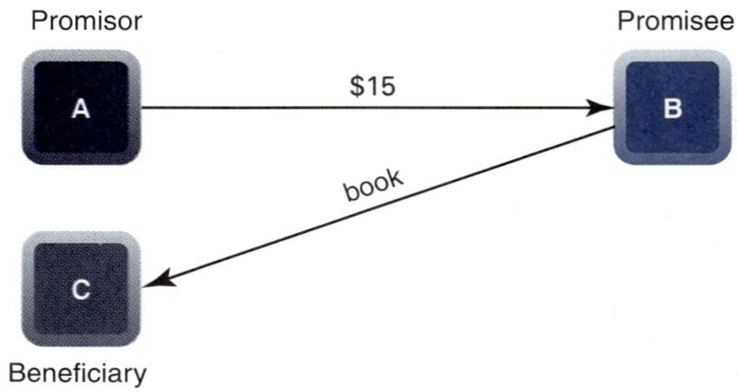

A's promise is binding because B incurred a legal detriment by delivering the book to C, because B was under no prior legal obligation to do so, and A had no prior legal right to have the book given to C. A and B have bargained for A to pay B $15 in return for B's delivering to C the book. A's promise to pay $15 is also consideration for B's promise to give C the book.

Conversely, consideration may be given by some person other than the promisee. For example, A promises to pay B $25 in return for D's promise to give A a radio. A's promise to pay $25 to B is consideration for D's promise to give A a radio and *vice versa*.

CPA CONTRACTS WITHOUT CONSIDERATION

Certain transactions are enforceable even though they are not supported by consideration.

PROMISES TO PERFORM PRIOR UNENFORCEABLE OBLIGATIONS

In certain circumstances the courts will enforce new promises to perform an obligation that originally was not enforceable or that has become unenforceable by operation of law. These situations include promises to pay debts barred by the statute of limitations, debts discharged in bankruptcy, and voidable obligations. In addition, some courts will enforce promises to pay moral obligations.

Promise to Pay Debt Barred by the Statute of Limitations Every state has a **statute of limitations** stating that legal actions to enforce a debt must be brought within a prescribed period of time after the rights to bring the action arose. Actions not begun within the specified period—such periods vary among the states and also with the nature of the legal action—will be dismissed.

An exception to the past consideration rule extends to promises to pay all or part of a contractual or quasi-contractual debt barred by the statute of limitations. The new promise is binding according to its terms, without consideration, for a second statutory period. Any recovery under the new promise is limited to the terms contained in the new promise. Most states require that new promises falling under this rule, except those partially paid, must be in writing to be enforceable.

Promise to Pay Debt Discharged in Bankruptcy A promise to pay a debt that has been discharged in bankruptcy is also enforceable without consideration. The Bankruptcy Code, however, imposes a number of requirements that must be met before such a promise may be enforced. These requirements are discussed in Chapter 39.

Voidable Promises Another promise that is enforceable without new consideration is a new promise to perform a voidable obligation that has not previously been avoided. The power of avoidance may be based on lack of capacity, fraud, misrepresentation, duress, undue influence, or mistake. For instance, a promise to perform an antecedent obligation made by a minor upon reaching the age of majority is enforceable without new consideration. To be enforceable, the promise itself must not be voidable. For example, if the new promise is made without knowledge of the original fraud or by a minor before reaching the age of majority, then the new promise is not enforceable.

Moral Obligation Under the common law and in most states, a promise made in order to satisfy a preexisting moral obligation is made for past consideration and therefore is unenforceable for lack of consideration. Instances involving such moral obligations include promises to pay another for board and lodging the other previously furnished to one's needy relative and promises to pay debts owed by a relative.

The Restatement and a minority of states recognize moral obligations as consideration. The Restatement provides that a promise made for "a benefit previously received by the promisor from the promisee is binding to the extent necessary to prevent injustice." For instance, under the Restatement, Tim's subsequent promise to Donna to reimburse her for expenses she incurred in rendering emergency services to Tim's son is binding even though it is not supported by new consideration.

PROMISSORY ESTOPPEL

As discussed in Chapter 10, in certain circumstances where there has been detrimental reliance, the courts enforce noncontractual promises under the doctrine of promissory estoppel. When applicable, the doctrine makes gratuitous promises enforceable to the extent necessary to avoid injustice. The doctrine applies when a promise that the promisor should reasonably expect to induce detrimental reliance does induce such action or forbearance.

Promissory estoppel does not mean that a promise given without consideration is binding simply because it is followed by a change of position on the part of the promisee. Such a change of position in justifiable reliance on the promise creates liability if injustice can be avoided only by the enforcement of the promise. For example, Ann promises Larry not to foreclose for a period of six months on a mortgage Ann owns on Larry's land. Larry then changes his position by spending $100,000 to construct a building on the land. Ann's promise not to foreclose is binding on her under the doctrine of promissory estoppel.

The most common application of the doctrine of promissory estoppel is to charitable subscriptions. Numerous churches, memorials, college buildings, stadiums, hospitals, and other structures used for religious, educational, or charitable purposes have been built with the assistance of contributions made through fulfillment of pledges or promises to contribute to particular worthwhile causes. Although the pledgor regards herself as making a gift for a charitable purpose and gift promises tend not to be enforceable, the courts have generally enforced charitable subscription promises. Although various reasons and theories have been advanced in support of liability, the one most commonly accepted is that the subscription has induced a change of position by the promisee (the church, school, or charitable organization) in reliance on the promise. The Restatement, moreover, has relaxed the reliance requirement for charitable subscriptions so that actual reliance need not be shown; the probability of reliance is sufficient.

Feinberg v. Pfeiffer Co.

St. Louis Court of Appeals, Missouri, 1959
322 S.W.2d 163

FACTS Anna Feinberg began working for the Pfeiffer Company in 1910 at age seventeen. By 1947, she had attained the position of bookkeeper, office manager, and assistant treasurer. In appreciation for her skill, dedication, and long years of service, the Pfeiffer board of directors resolved to increase Feinberg's monthly salary to $400 and to create for her a retirement plan. The plan allowed that Feinberg would be given the privilege of retiring from active duty at any time she chose and that she would receive retirement pay of $200 per month, although the Board expressed the hope that Feinberg would continue to serve the company for many years. Feinberg, however, chose to retire two years later, in 1949. The Pfeiffer Company paid Feinberg her retirement pay until 1956. The company thereafter discontinued payments, alleging that no contract had been made by the board of directors, because Feinberg had paid no consideration, and that the resolution was merely a promise to make a gift. Feinberg sued.

DECISION Judgment for Feinberg.

OPINION Doerner, C. J. Appellant's * * * complaint is that there was insufficient evidence to support the court's findings that plaintiff would not have quit defendant's employ had she not known and relied upon the promise of defendant to pay her $200 a month for life, and the finding that, from her voluntary retirement until April 1, 1956, plaintiff relied upon the continued receipt of the pension installments. The trial court so found, and, in our opinion, justifiably so.

* * *

It is defendant's contention, in essence, that the resolution adopted by its Board of Directors was a mere promise to make a gift, and that no contract resulted either thereby, or when plaintiff retired, because there was no consideration given or paid by the plaintiff. It urges that a promise to make a gift is not binding unless supported by a legal consideration; that the only apparent consideration for the adoption of the foregoing resolution was the "many years of long and faithful service" expressed therein; and that past services are not a valid consideration for a promise. Defendant argues further that there is nothing in the resolution which made its effectiveness conditional upon plaintiff's continued employment, that she was not under contract to work for any length of time but was free to quit whenever she wished, and that she had no contractual right to her position and could have been discharged at any time.

Plaintiff concedes that a promise based upon past services would be without consideration, but contends that there were two other elements which supplied the required element: First, the continuation by plaintiff in the employ of the defendant for the period from December 27, 1947, the date when the resolution was adopted, until the date of her retirement on June 30, 1949. And, second, her change of position, i.e., her retirement, and the abandonment by her of her opportunity to continue in gainful employment, made in reliance on defendant's promise to pay her $200 per month for life.

We must agree with the defendant that the evidence does not support the first of these contentions. There is no language in the resolution predicating plaintiff's right to a pension upon her continued employment. * * *

But as to the second of these contentions we must agree with plaintiff.

* * *

Section 90 of the Restatement of the Law of Contracts states that: "A promise which the promisor should reasonably expect to induce action or forbearance of a definite and substantial character on the part of the promisee and which does induce such action or forbearance is binding if injustice can be avoided only by enforcement of the promise." This doctrine has been described as that of "promissory estoppel." * * *

* * *

Was there such an act on the part of plaintiff, in reliance upon the promise contained in the resolution, as will estop the defendant, and therefore create an enforceable contract under the doctrine of promissory estoppel? We think there was. * * * At the time she retired plaintiff was 57 years of age. At the time the payments were discontinued she was over 63 years of age. It is a matter of common knowledge that it is virtually impossible for a woman of that age to find satisfactory employment, much less a position comparable to that which plaintiff enjoyed at the time of her retirement.

INTERPRETATION A court may enforce noncontractual promises under the doctrine of promissory estoppel when failure to do so will result in injustice.

ETHICAL QUESTION Did Pfeiffer Co. act in an ethical manner? Explain.

CRITICAL THINKING QUESTION Under what circumstances should the doctrine of promissory estoppel be employed? Explain.

CONTRACTS UNDER SEAL

Under the common law, when a person desired to bind himself by bond, deed, or solemn promise, he executed his promise under seal. He did not have to sign the document; rather, his delivery of a document to which he had affixed his seal was sufficient. No consideration for his promise was necessary. In some states a promise under seal is still binding without consideration.

Nevertheless, most states have abolished by statute the distinction between contracts under seal and written unsealed contracts. In these states, the seal is no longer recognized as a substitute for consideration. The Code also has adopted this position, specifically eliminating the use of seals in contracts for the sale of goods.

PROMISES MADE ENFORCEABLE BY STATUTE

Some gratuitous promises that would otherwise be unenforceable have been made binding by statute. Most significant among these are (1) contract modifications, (2) renunciations, and (3) irrevocable offers.

Contract Modifications As mentioned previously, the Uniform Commercial Code has abandoned the common law rule requiring that a modification of an existing contract be supported by consideration to be valid. Instead, the Code provides that a contract for the sale of goods can be effectively modified without new consideration, provided the modification is made in good faith.

Renunciations Under the Code, any claim or right arising out of an alleged breach of contract can be discharged in whole or in part without consideration by a written waiver or renunciation signed and delivered by the aggrieved party.

Firm Offers Under the Code, a firm offer, a written offer signed by a merchant offeror to buy or sell goods, is not revocable for lack of consideration during the time within which it is stated to be open, not to exceed three months, or, if no time is stated, for a reasonable time. For a summary of consideration, see Figure 12-2.

CHAPTER SUMMARY

Consideration

Definition the inducement to enter into a contract

Elements legal sufficiency and bargained-for exchange

Legal Sufficiency of Consideration

Definition consists of either a benefit to the promisor or a detriment to the promisee
- ***Legal Benefit*** obtaining something to which one had no prior legal right
- ***Legal Detriment*** doing an act one is not legally obligated to do or not doing an act that one has a legal right to do

Adequacy of Consideration not required where the parties have freely agreed to the exchange

Illusory Promise promise that imposes no obligation on the promisor; the following promises are not illusory
- ***Output Contract*** agreement to sell all of one's production to a single buyer
- ***Requirements Contract*** agreement to buy all of one's needs from a single producer
- ***Exclusive Dealing Contract*** grant to a franchisee or licensee by a manufacturer of the sole right to sell goods in a defined market
- ***Conditional Contract*** one where the obligations are contingent upon the occurrence of a stated event

Preexisting Public Obligations public duties such as those imposed by tort or criminal law are neither a legal detriment nor a legal benefit

Figure 12-2 *Consideration*

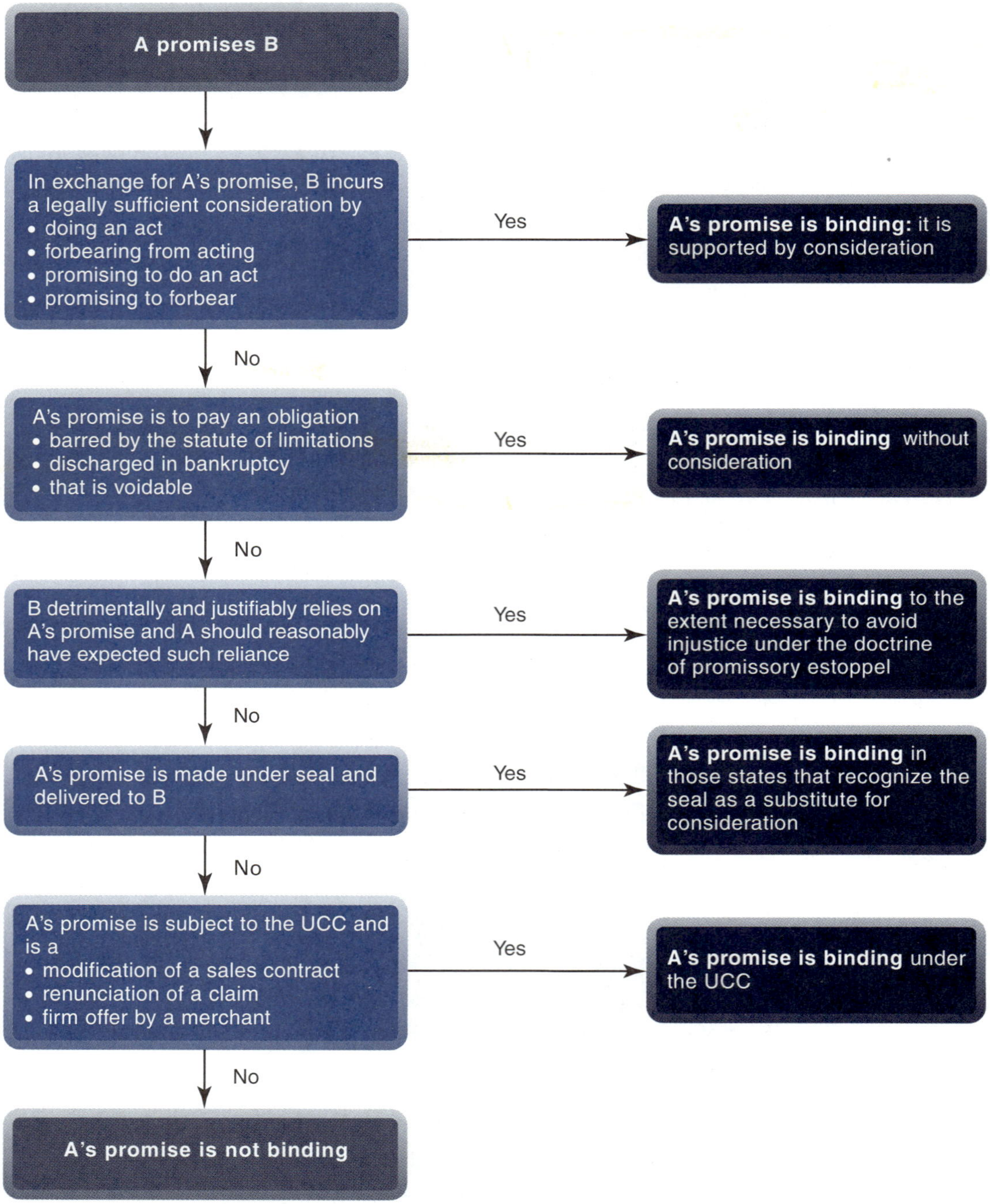

Preexisting Contractual Obligation performance of a preexisting contractual duty is not consideration
- *Modification of a Preexisting Contract* under the common law a modification of a preexisting contract must be supported by mutual consideration; under the Code a contract can be modified without new consideration
- *Substituted Contracts* the parties agree to rescind their original contract and to enter into a new one; rescission and new contract are supported by consideration
- *Settlement of an Undisputed Debt* payment of a lesser sum of money to discharge an undisputed debt (one whose existence and amount are not contested) does not constitute legally sufficient consideration
- *Settlement of a Disputed Debt* payment of a lesser sum of money to discharge a disputed debt (one whose existence or amount is contested) is legally sufficient consideration

Bargained-For Exchange

Definition a mutually agreed-upon exchange

Past Consideration an act done before the contract is made is not consideration

Contracts Without Consideration

Promises to Perform Prior Unenforceable Obligations
- *Promise to Pay Debt Barred by the Statute of Limitations* a new promise by the debtor to pay the debt renews the running of the statute of limitations for a second statutory period
- *Promise to Pay Debt Discharged in Bankruptcy* may be enforceable without consideration
- *Voidable Promises* a new promise to perform a voidable obligation that has not been previously avoided is enforceable
- *Moral Obligation* a promise made to satisfy a preexisting moral obligation is generally unenforceable for lack of consideration

Promissory Estoppel doctrine that prohibits a party from denying his promise when the promisee takes action or forbearance to his detriment reasonably based upon the promise

Contracts under Seal where still recognized, the seal acts as a substitute for consideration

Promises Made Enforceable by Statute some gratuitous promises have been made enforceable by statute; the Code makes enforceable (1) contract modifications, (2) renunciations, and (3) firm offers

QUESTIONS

1. In consideration of $800 paid to him by Joyce, Hill gave Joyce a written option to purchase his house for $80,000 on or before April 1. Prior to April 1, Hill verbally agreed to extend the option until July 1. On May 18, Hill sold the house to Gray, who was ignorant of the unrecorded option. On May 20 Joyce sent an acceptance to Hill who received it on May 25. Is there a contract between Joyce and Hill? Explain.

2. a. Ann owed $500 to Barry for services Barry rendered to Ann. The debt was due June 30, 2003. In March 2004, the debt was still unpaid. Barry was in urgent need of ready cash and told Ann that if she would pay $150 on the debt at once, Barry would release her from the balance. Ann paid $150 and stated to Barry that all claims had been paid in full. In August 2004, Barry demanded the unpaid balance and subsequently sued Ann for $350. Result?

   b. Modify the facts in (a) by assuming that Barry gave Ann a written receipt stating that all claims had been paid in full. Result?

   c. Modify the facts in (a) by assuming that Ann owed Barry the $500 on Ann's purchase of a motorcycle from Barry. Result?

3. a. Judy orally promises her daughter, Liza, that she will give her a tract of land for her home. Liza, as intended by Judy, gives up her homestead and takes possession of the

land. Liza lives there for six months and starts construction of a home. Is Judy bound to convey the real estate?

b. Ralph, knowing that his son, Ed, desires to purchase a tract of land, promises to give him the $25,000 he needs for the purchase. Ed, relying on this promise, buys an option on the tract of land. Can Ralph rescind his promise?

4. George owed Keith $800 on a personal loan. Neither the amount of the debt nor George's liability to pay the $800 was disputed. Keith had also rendered services as a carpenter to George without any agreement as to the price to be paid. When the work was completed, an honest and reasonable difference of opinion developed between George and Keith with respect to the value of Keith's services. Upon receiving Keith's bill for the carpentry services for $600, George mailed in a properly stamped and addressed envelope his check for $800 to Keith. In an accompanying letter, George stated that the enclosed check was in full settlement of both claims. Keith endorsed and cashed the check. Thereafter, Keith unsuccessfully sought to collect from George an alleged unpaid balance of $600. May Keith recover the $600 from George?

5. The Snyder Mfg. Co., being a large user of coal, entered into separate contracts with several coal companies. In each contract, it was agreed that the coal company would supply coal during the year in such amounts as the manufacturing company might desire to order, at a price of $49 per ton. In February of that year, the Snyder Company ordered 1,000 tons of coal from Union Coal Company, one of the contracting parties. Union Coal Company delivered 500 tons of the order and then notified Snyder Company that no more deliveries would be made and that it denied any obligation under the contract. In an action by Union Coal to collect $49 per ton for the 500 tons of coal delivered, Snyder files a counterclaim, claiming damages of $1,500 for failure to deliver the additional 500 tons of the order and damages of $4,000 for breach of agreement to deliver coal during the balance of the year. What contract, if any, exists between Snyder and Union?

6. On February 5, Devon entered into a written agreement with Gordon whereby Gordon agreed to drill a well on Devon's property for the sum of $5,000 and to complete the well on or before April 15. Before entering into the contract, Gordon had made test borings and had satisfied himself as to the character of the subsurface. After two days of drilling, Gordon struck hard rock. On February 17, Gordon removed his equipment and advised Devon that the project had proved unprofitable and that he would not continue. On March 17, Devon went to Gordon and told Gordon that he would assume the risk of the enterprise and would pay Gordon $100 for each day required to drill the well, as compensation for labor, the use of Gordon's equipment, and Gordon's services in supervising the work, provided Gordon would furnish certain special equipment designed to cut through hard rock. Gordon said that the proposal was satisfactory. The work was continued by Gordon and completed in an additional fifty-eight days. Upon completion of the work, Devon failed to pay, and Gordon brought an action to recover $5,800. Devon answered that he had never become obligated to pay $100 a day and filed a counterclaim for damages in the amount of $500 for the month's delay based on an alleged breach of contract by Gordon. Explain who will prevail and why.

7. Discuss and explain whether there is valid consideration for each of the following promises:
   a. A and B entered into a contract for the purchase and sale of goods. A subsequently promised to pay a higher price for the goods when B refused to deliver at the contract price.
   b. A promised in writing to pay a debt, which was due from B to C, on C's agreement to extend the time of payment for one year.
   c. A orally promised to pay $150 to her son, B, solely in consideration of past services rendered to A by B, for which there had been no agreement or request to pay.

8. Alan purchased shoes from Barbara on open account. Barbara sent Alan a bill for $10,000. Alan wrote back that 200 pairs of the shoes were defective and offered to pay $6,000 and give Barbara his promissory note for $1,000. Barbara accepted the offer, and Alan sent his check for $6,000 and his note in accordance with the agreement. Barbara cashed the check, collected on the note, and one month later sued Alan for $3,000. Is Barbara bound by her acceptance of the offer?

9. Nancy owed Sharon $1,500, but Sharon did not initiate a lawsuit to collect the debt within the time period prescribed by the statute of limitations. Nevertheless, Nancy promises Sharon that she will pay the barred debt. Thereafter, Nancy refuses to pay. Sharon brings suit to collect on this new promise. Is Nancy's new promise binding? Explain.

10. Anthony lends money to Frank, who dies without having repaid the loan. Frank's widow, Carol, promises Anthony to repay the loan. Upon Carol's refusal to pay the loan, Anthony brings suit against Carol for payment. Is Carol bound by her promise to pay the loan?

11. The parties entered into an oral contract in June under which the plaintiff agreed to construct a building for the defendant on a time and materials basis, at a maximum cost of $56,146, plus sales tax and extras ordered by the defendant. When the building was 90 percent completed, the defendant told the plaintiff he was unhappy with the whole job as "the thing just wasn't being run right." The parties then, on October 17, signed a written agreement lowering the maximum cost to $52,000 plus sales tax. The plaintiff thereafter completed the building at a cost of $64,155. The maximum under the June oral agreement, plus extras and sales tax, totaled $61,040. Explain whether the defendant is obligated to pay only the lower maximum fixed by the October 17 agreement.

CASE PROBLEMS

12. Taylor assaulted his wife, who then took refuge in Ms. Harrington's house. The next day, Mr. Taylor entered the house and began another assault on his wife. Taylor's wife knocked him down and, while he was lying on the floor, attempted to cut his head open or decapitate him with an axe. Harrington intervened to stop the bloodshed and was hit by the axe as it was descending. The axe fell upon her hand, mutilating it badly, but sparing Taylor his life. Afterwards, Taylor orally promised to compensate Harrington for her injury. Is Taylor's promise enforceable? Explain.

13. Jonnel Enterprises, Inc. contracted to construct a student dormitory at Clarion State College. On May 6, Jonnel entered into a written agreement with Graham and Long as electrical contractors to perform the electrical work and to supply materials for the dormitory. The contract price was $70,544.66. Graham and Long claim that they believed the May 6 agreement obligated them to perform the electrical work on only one wing of the building, but that three or four days after work was started, a second wing of the building was found to be in need of wiring. At that time, Graham and Long informed Jonnel that they would not wire both wings of the building under the present contract, so the parties orally agreed upon a new contract. Under the new contract, Graham and Long were obligated to wire both wings and were to be paid only $65,000, but they were relieved of the obligations to supply entrances and a heating system. Graham and Long resumed their work, and Jonnel made seven of the eight progress payments called for. When Jonnel did not pay the final payment, Graham and Long brought this action. Jonnel claims that the May 6 contract is controlling. Is Jonnel correct in its assertion? Why?

14. Baker entered into an oral agreement with Healey, the state distributor of Ballantine & Sons's liquor products, that Ballantine would supply Baker with its products on demand and that Baker would have the exclusive agency for Ballantine within a certain area of Connecticut. Shortly thereafter, the agreement was modified to give Baker the right to terminate at will. Eight months later, Ballantine & Sons revoked its agency. May Baker enforce the oral agreement? Explain.

15. PLM, Inc. entered into an oral agreement with Quaintance Associates, an executive "headhunter" service, for the recruitment of qualified candidates to be employed by PLM. As agreed, PLM's obligation to pay Quaintance did not depend on PLM actually hiring a qualified candidate presented by Quaintance. After several months Quaintance sent a letter to PLM, admitting that it had so far failed to produce a suitable candidate, but included a bill for $9,806.61, covering fees and expenses. PLM responded that Quaintance's services were only worth $6,060.48, and that payment of the lesser amount was the only fair way to handle the dispute. Accordingly, PLM enclosed a check for $6,060.48, writing on the back of the check "IN FULL PAYMENT OF ANY CLAIMS QUAINTANCE HAS AGAINST PLM, INC." Quaintance cashed the check and then sued PLM for the remaining $3,746.13. Decision?

16. Red Owl Stores told the Hoffman family that upon the payment of approximately $18,000 a grocery store franchise would be built for them in a new location. On the advice of Red Owl, the Hoffmans bought a small grocery store in their hometown in order to get management experience. After the Hoffmans operated at a profit for three months, Red Owl advised them to sell the small grocery, assuring them that Red Owl would find them a larger store elsewhere. Although selling at that point would cost them much profit, the Hoffmans followed Red Owl's directions. Additionally, to raise the required money for the deal, the Hoffmans sold their bakery business in their hometown. The Hoffmans also sold their house and moved to a new home in the city where their new store was to be located. Red Owl then informed the Hoffmans that it would take $24,100, not $18,000, to complete the deal. The family scrambled to find the additional funds. However, when told by Red Owl that it would now cost them $34,000 to get their new franchise, the Hoffmans decided to sue instead. Should Red Owl be held to its promises? Explain.

17. The plaintiff, Brenner, entered into a contract with the defendant, Little Red School House, Ltd., which stated that in return for a nonrefundable tuition of $1,080, Brenner's son could attend the defendant's school for a year. When Brenner's ex-wife refused to enroll their son, the plaintiff sought and received a verbal promise of a refund. The defendant now refuses to refund the plaintiff's money for lack of consideration. Did mutual consideration exist between the parties? Explain.

18. Tender Loving Care, Inc. (TLC), a corporation owned and operated by Virginia Bryant, eventually went out of business. The Secretary of State canceled its corporate charter, and a check drawn on TLC's account made out to the Department of Human Resources (DHR) to pay state unemployment taxes was returned for insufficient funds. Subsequently, Bryant filed individually for bankruptcy, listing the DHR as a creditor. This claim was not allowed, because Bryant was held not to be personally liable on the debts of TLC to the DHR. The DHR later called Bryant to its offices, where she was told that she needed to pay the debt owed to the DHR by TLC. Unable to contact her lawyer, Bryant eventually was persuaded to sign a personal guarantee to cover the debt. Later, when Bryant refused to pay, the DHR filed suit. Decision?

19. Ben Collins was a full professor with tenure at Wisconsin State University in 1996. In March 1996 Parsons College, in an attempt to lure Dr. Collins from Wisconsin State,

offered him a written contract promising him the rank of full professor with tenure and a salary of $55,000 for the 1996–97 academic year. The contract further provided that the College would increase his salary by $2,000 each year for the next five years. In return, Collins was to teach two trimesters of the academic year beginning in October 1996. In addition, the contract stipulated, by reference to the College's faculty bylaws, that tenured professors could be dismissed only for just cause and after written charges were filed with the Professional Problems Committee. The two parties signed the contract, and Collins resigned his position at Wisconsin State.

In February 1998, the College tendered a different contract to Collins to cover the following year. This contract reduced his salary to $45,000 with no provision for annual increments, but left his rank of full professor intact. It also required that Collins waive any and all rights or claims existing under any previous employment contracts with the College. Collins refused to sign this new contract and Parsons College soon notified him that he would not be employed the following year. The College did not give any grounds for his dismissal; nor did it file charges with the Professional Problems Committee. As a result, Collins was forced to take a teaching position at the University of North Dakota at a substantially reduced salary. He sued to recover the difference between the salary Parsons College promised him until 2001 and the amount he earned. Will he prevail? Explain.

http:// **Internet Exercise** Find several sample contracts and determine what consideration is given by the parties.

Chapter 13

Illegal Bargains

Pactis privatorum juri publico non derogatur. *(Private contracts do not derogate from public law.)*

Legal Maxim

Learning Objectives

After reading this chapter you should be able to:

1. Identify and explain the types of contracts that may violate a statute and distinguish between the two types of licensing statutes.
2. Describe when a covenant not to compete will be enforced and identify the two situations in which these types of covenants most frequently arise.
3. Explain when exculpatory agreements, agreements involving the commitment of a tort, and agreements involving public officials will be held to be illegal.
4. Distinguish between procedural and substantive unconscionability.
5. Explain the usual effects of illegality and the major exceptions to this rule.

A legal objective is essential for a promise or agreement to be binding. When the formation or performance of an agreement is criminal, tortious, or otherwise contrary to public policy, the agreement is illegal and ***unenforceable*** (as opposed to being void). The law does *not* provide a remedy for the breach of an unenforceable agreement and thus "leaves the parties where it finds them." (It is preferable to use the term *illegal bargain* or *illegal agreement* rather than *illegal contract*, because the word *contract*, by definition, denotes a legal and enforceable agreement.) The illegal bargain is made unenforceable (1) to discourage such undesirable conduct in the future and (2) to avoid the inappropriate use of the judicial process in carrying out the socially undesirable bargain.

In this chapter, we will discuss (a) agreements in violation of a statute, (b) agreements contrary to public policy, and (c) the effect of illegality on agreements.

CPA Violations of Statutes

The courts will not enforce an agreement declared illegal by statute. For example, "wagering or gambling contracts" are specifically declared unenforceable in most states. Likewise, an agreement induced by criminal conduct will not be enforced. For example, if Alice enters into an agreement with Brent Co. through the bribing of Brent Co.'s purchasing agent, the agreement would be unenforceable.

Licensing Statutes

Every jurisdiction has laws requiring a **license** for those who engage in certain trades, professions, or businesses. Common examples are licensing statutes that apply to lawyers, doctors, dentists, accountants, brokers, plumbers, and contractors. Some licensing statutes mandate schooling and/or examination, while others require only financial responsibility and/or good moral character. Whether a person who has failed to comply with a licensing requirement may recover for services rendered depends on the terms or type of licensing statute.

The statute itself may expressly provide that an unlicensed person engaged in a business or profession for which a license is required shall not recover for services rendered. Where there is no express statutory provision, the courts commonly distinguish between regulatory statutes and those enacted merely to raise revenue through the issuance of licenses. If the statute is regulatory, a person cannot recover for professional services unless he has the required license as long as the public policy behind the regulatory purpose clearly outweighs the person's interest in being paid for his services. Some courts balance the penalty suffered by the unlicensed party against the benefit received by the other party. In contrast, if the law is for revenue purposes only, agreements for unlicensed services are enforceable.

A **regulatory license** is a measure designed to protect the public from unqualified practitioners. Examples are licenses issued under statutes prescribing standards for those who seek to practice law or medicine or, as demonstrated by the case below, to engage in the construction business. A **revenue license**, on the other hand, does not seek to protect against incompetent or unqualified practitioners but serves simply to raise money. An example is a statute requiring a license of plumbers but not establishing standards of competence for those who practice the trade. The courts regard this as a taxing measure lacking any expression of legislative intent to prevent unlicensed plumbers from enforcing their business contracts.

Practical Advice

Obtain all necessary licenses before beginning to operate your business.

Pacific Custom Pools, Inc. v. Turner Construction Company

Court of Appeal, Second District, Division 4, California, 2000
79 Cal.App.4th 1254, 94 Cal.Rptr.2d 756
http://www.courtinfo.ca.gov/opinions/archive/B122853.DOC

FACTS Universal City Studios, Inc. ("Universal") entered into a general contract with Turner Construction Company ("Turner") for the construction of the Jurassic Park ride. Turner entered into a subcontract with Pacific Custom Pools, Inc. ("PCP"), for PCP to furnish and install all water treatment work for the project for the contract price of $959,131. PCP performed work on the project from April 1995 until June 1996 for which it was paid $897,719. PCP's contractor's license, however, was under suspension from October 12, 1995 to March 14, 1996. In addition, PCP's license had expired as of January 31, 1996, and it was not renewed until May 5, 1996. PCP brought suit against Universal and Turner, the defendants, for the remainder of the contract price. The trial court granted the defendants' motion for summary judgment on the basis that PCP had not been licensed in California and thus could not bring suit. PCP appealed.

DECISION Summary judgment in favor of defendants affirmed.

OPINION Berle, J. Section 7031, subdivision (a) provides that a contractor may not maintain an action for the recovery of compensation for the performance of work requiring a license unless it was "a duly licensed contractor at all times during the performance of that" work. In [citation], the [California] Supreme Court set forth the social policy underpinning section 7031:

> "The purpose of the licensing law is to protect the public from incompetence and dishonesty in those who provide building and construction services. [Citation.] The licensing requirements provide minimal assurance that all persons offering such services in California have the requisite skill and character, understand applicable local laws and codes, and know the rudiments of administering a contracting business. [Citation.]
>
> "Section 7031 advances this purpose by withholding judicial aid from those who seek compensation for unlicensed contract work. The obvious statutory intent is to discourage persons who have failed to comply with the

licensing law from offering or providing their unlicensed services for pay.

"Because of the strength and clarity of this policy, it is well settled that section 7031 applies despite injustice to the unlicensed contractor. 'Section 7031 represents a legislative determination that the importance of deterring unlicensed persons from engaging in the contracting business outweighs any harshness between the parties, and that such deterrence can best be realized by denying violators the right to maintain any action for compensation in the courts of this state. [Citation.] * * *'"

Through a series of cases beginning in 1966, the courts attempted to alleviate the severity of the application of section 7031 by allowing recovery to a contractor who has substantially complied with the licensing statutory scheme. [Citations.]

In reaction to this development in the law, the Legislature amended section 7031 in 1989 to add a subsection (d) which provided that the substantial compliance doctrine shall not apply to that statute. [Citations.] In 1991, the Legislature further amended section 7031 to provide an exception to the prohibition of the substantial compliance doctrine where noncompliance with licensure requirements was the result of inadvertent clerical error or other error or delay not caused by the negligence of the licensee. [Citation.]

* * *

An unlicensed contractor may thus avoid the consequences of the prohibition against the substantial compliance doctrine under section 7031, subd. (d) if the contractor proves that it had been licensed before performing work, acted reasonably in trying to maintain a license and did not know or reasonably should not have known that it was not licensed. The parties concur that PCP was licensed before commencing work on the project. However, the parties dispute whether PCP acted reasonably and in good faith to maintain its license, and whether PCP knew or should have reasonably known that it was not licensed.

* * *

In * * * the case at bar: (a) PCP was aware in November 1995 that its license was suspended for failure to file a judgment bond and that the deadline date for license renewal was January 31, 1996; (b) PCP knew shortly after February 23, 1996 that a renewal application sent in February 1996 was untimely; and (c) that PCP was advised on April 22, 1996 that its license had not been renewed because PCP's filing fee check had been dishonored. These facts do not suggest that PCP acted reasonably or in good faith to maintain licensure or that PCP did not know or reasonably should not have known that it was not duly licensed, to support a claim of substantial compliance within the meaning of section 7031.

* * *

INTERPRETATION A regulatory license is a measure to protect the public from unqualified practitioners; the failure to comply with such a regulation prevents the noncomplying party from recovering for services rendered.

CRITICAL THINKING QUESTION When should the failure to obtain a license to operate a business prevent the owner or operator from receiving compensation for services?

GAMBLING STATUTES

In a **wager**, the parties stipulate that one shall win and the other lose depending on the outcome of an event in which their only "interest" is the possibility of such gain or loss. All states have legislation on gambling or wagering, and U.S. courts generally refuse to recognize the enforceability of a gambling agreement. Thus, if Smith makes a bet with Brown on the outcome of a ball game, the agreement is unenforceable by either party. Some states, however, now permit certain kinds of regulated gambling. Wagering conducted by governmental agencies, principally state-operated lotteries, has come to constitute an increasingly important source of public revenues.

http:// Gamblers Anonymous: http://www.gamblersanonymous.org/
National Gambling Impact Study Commission: http://standup.quiknet.com/ngisc.html

Practical Advice

Make sure that your promotions that offer prizes do not fall under state gambling statutes.

USURY STATUTES

A **usury statute** is a law establishing a maximum rate of permissible interest for which a lender and borrower of money may contract. Although, historically every state had a usury statute, the recent trend is to limit or relax such statutes. Maximum permitted rates vary greatly from state to state and among types of transactions. These statutes typically are general in their application, and certain types of transactions are exempted altogether. For example, many states impose no limit on the rate of interest that may be charged on loans to corporations. Furthermore, some states permit the parties to contract for any rate of interest on loans made to individual proprietorships or partnerships for the purpose of carrying on a business.

In addition to the exceptions affecting certain designated types of borrowers, a number of states have exempted specific lenders. For example, the majority of states have enacted installment loan laws, which permit eligible lenders a higher return on installment loans than would otherwise be permitted under the applicable general interest statute. These specific lender usury statutes, which have all but eliminated general usury statutes, vary greatly but generally encompass small consumer loans, retail installment sales acts, corporate loans, loans by small lenders, real estate mortgages, and numerous other transactions.

For a transaction to be usurious, courts usually require evidence of the following factors: (a) a loan (b) of money (c) that is repayable absolutely and in all events (d) for which an interest charge is exacted in excess of the interest rate allowed by law. Nevertheless, the law does permit certain expenses or charges in addition to the maximum legal interest, such as payments made by a borrower to the lender for expenses incurred or for services rendered in good faith in making a loan or in obtaining security for its repayment. Permissible expenses commonly incurred by a lender include the costs of examining title, investigating the borrower's credit rating, drawing necessary documents, and inspecting the property. If not excessive, such expenses are not considered in determining the rate of interest under the usury statutes. As shown in the following case, however, payments made to the lender from which he derives an advantage are considered if they exceed the reasonable value of services he actually rendered.

http:// Economic Statistics: http://www.whitehouse.gov/news/fsbr.html
Federal Reserve System: http://www.federalreserve.gov

Dunnam v. Burns

Court of Appeals of Texas, El Paso, 1995
901 S.W.2d 628

FACTS Defendant (Louis Dunnam) and Steve Oualline jointly borrowed $35,000 from plaintiff (Ken Burns) and agreed to repay the principal plus $5,000 six months later. After defendant defaulted on the loan, plaintiff sued to recover. Dunnam defended by claiming the loan was usurious. The trial court ruled in favor of the plaintiff, and defendant appealed.

DECISION Judgment for defendant.

OPINION Barajas, J. Appellant [Dunnam] attacks the judgment of the trial court in two points of error, claiming that the trial court erred by refusing to submit his usury defense to the jury and by holding that he was personally obligated on the note which he signed.

* * *

In his first point of error, Appellant claims the trial court erred by refusing to submit his usury defense to the jury. Usury is interest in excess of the amount permitted by law. [Citation.] Interest is compensation for the use or forbearance of money. [Citation.] For most transactions between private persons, the maximum allowable rate of interest is 18 percent if the parties agree on a rate of interest [citation], and 6 percent if they do not, [citation]. Usurious contracts are against public policy, [citation] and persons who contract for or collect usurious interest are subject to penalties that may exceed the total value of the contract, [citation].

We must initially determine whether the $5,000 additional sum contained in the promissory note constitutes interest. Interest need not be denominated interest. [Citation.] When money is advanced in exchange for an obligation to repay the advance plus an additional amount, the added amount is interest that may not exceed the statutory maximum. [Citations.] The foregoing principles instruct that Appellant's absolute obligation to pay $5,000 in addition to the principal renders the additional amount interest.

Appellee [Burns] does not contest that the $5,000 is interest. Neither does he claim that the amount of interest was not usurious, although we note that the promissory note effectively charges a 28.57 percent interest rate, which exceeds even the highest rate permitted by statute [citation] (permitting 28 percent interest on certain transactions). He argues, rather, that he did not "charge" such interest because the instrument was drafted by Appellant and because Appellee was actually interested in collecting only the principal amount. In so arguing, Appellee misapprehends the significance of his intent and of the identity of the drafter of the promissory note.

A document that contains an absolute obligation to repay a loan together with interest in excess of the amount permitted by statute is usurious on its face. [Citations.] "It is not the lender's subjective intent to charge usury that makes a loan usurious, but rather his intent to make the bargain that was made." [Citations.] The specific intent of the lender is immaterial because it is presumed to be reflected in the document he signs. [Citations.] Further, "once the agreed terms have been reduced to writing in the form of a compulsory contract, the test of alleged usury is not concerned with which party might have originated the alleged[ly] usurious provisions." [Citations.]

The foregoing principles foreclose Appellee's arguments. The drafter of the usurious promissory note is simply irrelevant. * * * The instrument embodies a usurious transaction, and Appellee, as the lender, contracted for usurious interest. Appellant's first point of error is sustained.

INTERPRETATION Usury statutes establish a maximum rate of interest for which a lender may charge a borrower.

CRITICAL THINKING QUESTION Should the law establish maximum rates of interest? If so, in what situations?

The legal effect of a usurious loan varies from state to state. In a few states, the lender forfeits both principal and interest. In some jurisdictions, the lender can recover the principal but forfeits all interest. In other states, only that portion of interest exceeding the permitted maximum is forfeited, whereas in still other states, the amount forfeited is a multiple (double or treble) of the interest charged. How the states deal with usurious interest already paid also varies. Some states do not allow the borrower to recover any of the usurious interest she has paid; others allow recovery of such interest or a multiple of it.

Practical Advice

When calculating interest, consider all charges, including service fees, that exceed the actual reasonable expense of making the loan.

SUNDAY STATUTES

In the absence of a statutory prohibition, the common law does not prohibit entering into contracts on Sunday. Some states, however, have legislation, referred to as **blue laws**, modifying this common law rule and prohibiting certain types of commercial activity on Sunday. Even in a state that prohibits contracts on Sunday, a court nonetheless will enforce a subsequent weekday ratification of a loan made on Sunday or a promise to pay for goods sold and delivered on Sunday. In addition, blue laws usually do not apply to activities of "necessity" and "charity."

CPA VIOLATIONS OF PUBLIC POLICY

The reach of a statute may extend beyond its language. Sometimes the courts, by analogy, use a statute and the policy it embodies as a guide in determining a person's rights under a private contract. Conversely, the courts frequently must express the "public policy" of the state without significant help from statutory sources. This judicially declared public policy is very broad in scope, it often being said that agreements having "a tendency to be injurious to the public or the public good" are contrary to public policy. Contracts raising questions of public policy include agreements that (1) restrain trade, (2) excuse or exculpate a party from liability for his own negligence, (3) are unconscionable, (4) involve tortious conduct, (5) tend to corrupt public officials or impair the legislative process, (6) tend to obstruct the administration of justice, or (7) impair family relationships. This section will focus on the first five of these types of agreements.

COMMON LAW RESTRAINT OF TRADE

A **restraint of trade** is any contract or agreement that eliminates or tends to eliminate competition or otherwise obstructs trade or commerce. One type of restraint of trade is a **covenant not to compete**, which is an agreement to refrain from entering into a competing trade, profession, or business.

Today, an agreement to refrain from a particular trade, profession, or business is enforceable if (1) the purpose of the restraint is to protect a property interest of the promisee and (2) the restraint is no more extensive than is reasonably necessary to protect that interest. Restraints typically arise in two situations: (a) the sale of a business and (b) employment contracts.

Sale of a Business As part of an agreement to sell a business, the seller frequently promises not to compete in that particular type of business in a defined area for a stated period of time in order to protect the business's goodwill (an asset that the buyer has purchased). The courts will enforce such a covenant (promise) if the restraint is within reasonable limitations. The reasonableness of the restraint depends on the geographic area the restraint covers, the period for which it is to be effective, and the hardship it imposes on the promisor and the public.

For example, the promise of a person selling a service station business in Detroit not to enter the service station business in Michigan for the next twenty-five years is unreasonable as to both area and time. The business interest would not include the entire state, so the protection of the purchaser does not require that the seller be prevented from engaging in the service station business in all of Michigan or perhaps, for that matter, in the entire city of Detroit. Limiting the area to the neighborhood in which the station is located or to a radius of a few miles would probably be adequate protection. However, in the case of a citywide business, such as a laundry or cleaning establishment with neighborhood outlets, a covenant restraining competition anywhere in the city might well be reasonable.

The same type of inquiry must be made about time limitations. In the sale of a service station, a twenty-five-year ban on competition from the seller would be unreasonable, but a one-year ban probably would not. The courts consider each case on its own facts to determine what is reasonable under the particular circumstances.

Employment Contracts Salespeople, management personnel, and other employees are frequently required to sign employment contracts prohibiting them from competing with their employers during their employment and for some additional stated period after their termination. The same is also frequently true among corporations or partnerships involving professionals such as accountants, lawyers, investment brokers, stockbrokers, or doctors. Though the courts readily enforce a covenant not to compete during the period of employment, they subject the promise not to compete after termination of employment to a test of reasonableness stricter even than that applied to noncompetition promises included in a contract for the sale of a business.

A court order enjoining (prohibiting) a former employee from competing in a described territory for a stated period of time is the usual way in which an employer seeks to enforce an employee's promise not to compete. However, before the courts will grant such injunctions, the employer must demonstrate that the restriction is necessary to protect his legitimate interests, such as trade secrets or customer lists. Because the injunction may have the practical effect of placing the employee out of work, the courts must carefully balance the public policy favoring the employer's right to protect his business interests against the public policy favoring full opportunity for individuals to gain employment. Some courts, rather than refusing to enforce an unreasonable restraint, will modify the restrictive covenant to make it reasonable under the circumstances.

Thus, one court has held unreasonable a contract covenant requiring a travel agency employee after termination of her employment to not engage in a like business in any capacity in either of two named towns or within a sixty-mile radius of those towns for two years. There was no indication that the employee had enough influence over customers to cause them to move their business to her new agency, nor was it shown that any trade secrets were involved.

Non-compete agreements drafted for employees of Internet companies have been held to be subject to shorter periods of reasonable duration. Since it is generally agreed that "Internet time" is much faster than calendar time, some courts consider a noncompete clause of one year to be unreasonable. (For additional discussion on this issue, see Chapter 48.)

Practical Advice

If you include a covenant not to compete to protect your property interests, be careful to select a reasonable duration and geographic scope.

EarthWeb, Inc. v. Schlack

United States District Court for the Southern District of New York, 1999
71 F.Supp.2d 299, *aff'd*, 2000 WL 1093320, 2000 U.S. App. LEXIS 11446
http://www.nysd.uscourts.gov/courtweb/pdf/D02NYSC/99-06890.PDF

FACTS EarthWeb provides online products and services to business professionals in the information technology ("IT") industry. EarthWeb operates through a family of websites offering information, products, and services for IT professionals to use for facilitating tasks and solving technology problems in a business setting. EarthWeb obtains this content primarily through licensing agreements with third parties.

Schlack began his employment with EarthWeb in its New York City office on October 19, 1998. His title at

EarthWeb was Vice President, Worldwide Content, and as the name suggests, Schlack was responsible for the content of all of EarthWeb's websites.

Although Schlack's employment contract stated that he was an employee at will, it also included a section titled "Limited Agreement Not To Compete." That section provides:

> (c) For a period of twelve (12) months after the termination of Schlack's employment with EarthWeb, Schlack shall not, directly or indirectly:
>
> (1) work as an employee, employer, consultant, agent, principal, partner, manager, officer, director, or in any other individual or representative capacity for any person or entity that directly competes with EarthWeb. For the purpose of this section, the term "directly competing" is defined as a person or entity or division of an entity that is
>
> > (i) an online service for Information Professionals whose primary business is to provide Information Technology Professionals with a directory of third party technology, software, and/or developer resources; and/or an online reference library, and or
> >
> > (ii) an online store, the primary purpose of which is to sell or distribute third party software or products used for Internet site or software development.

On September 22, 1999, Schlack tendered his letter of resignation to EarthWeb senior vice president William F. Gollan. Upon inquiry by Gollan, Schlack revealed that he had accepted a position with ITworld.com, a subsidiary of IDG. EarthWeb brought this action to enforce the noncompete agreement in Schlack's employment agreement. EarthWeb brought this action claiming breach of contract and misappropriation of trade secrets. EarthWeb moved for preliminary injunctive relief enjoining defendant Schlack from: (1) commencing employment with IDG, and (2) disclosing or revealing EarthWeb's trade secrets to IDG or any third parties.

DECISION Plaintiff's motion for a preliminary injunction is denied.

OPINION Pauley III, J. EarthWeb describes Schlack as one of its most important officers, while Schlack claims that EarthWeb has inflated the nature of his duties and responsibilities. Schlack also argues that the position waiting for him at IDG is so different that he would have no occasion to divulge any trade secrets belonging to EarthWeb. * * *

EarthWeb claims that Schlack's primary job responsibilities involved making all significant strategic decisions relating to content. The company also asserts that Schlack either authored or supervised the creation of the content plans for a number of EarthWeb websites within the last year. Thus, Schlack was involved in deciding what content EarthWeb licensed and how that content would be structured on its websites in order to reach specific types of IT professionals. Schlack was also involved in determining whether the users of a particular EarthWeb website should pay for access to the site, and if so, what the appropriate price should be. As a result, Schlack knows the specific target audience for each website, how EarthWeb aggregated content on those websites to reach the targeted audience, and how EarthWeb may intend to improve the content and delivery of particular websites.

Schlack * * * contends that whatever he knows about EarthWeb's strategic planning is likely to become obsolete rather quickly because the company's websites are constantly changing.

During his employment, Schlack was involved in negotiating at least two licensing agreements with third parties, and he was generally aware of the terms and conditions of other such agreements. Schlack also knows of companies whose content EarthWeb is interested in licensing. As vice president for content, Schlack often played a key role in determining whether particular content should be licensed, and if so, what the terms of the deal would be. With respect to acquisitions, Schlack analyzed and evaluated websites and companies that EarthWeb later acquired. Schlack also knows of at least four companies that EarthWeb continues to view as desirable acquisitions.

Schlack contends, and EarthWeb does not dispute, that the terms of EarthWeb's licensing agreements are frequently revealed by licensors as they continue to search for better deals. * * *

It should be noted that EarthWeb does not allege that Schlack has retained copies of any licensing agreements or other sensitive documents concerning licensors. * * *

Schlack was also involved, albeit less directly, with EarthWeb's marketing and sales efforts. Schlack describes his role as "explaining EarthWeb's editorial focus and how [it] might relate to the advertiser's customer." * * *

Schlack's job responsibilities required him to be familiar with the software and hardware infrastructure that supports EarthWeb's websites. Thus, Schlack has general knowledge of how EarthWeb customized and deployed the products of outside vendors and consultants in order to fit EarthWeb's programming needs. Schlack also gained an understanding of the technical problems that EarthWeb successfully tackled in order to make its websites operate efficiently.

However, Schlack had no access to EarthWeb's source codes or configuration files, so his knowledge of

EarthWeb's proprietary software and infrastructure is necessarily limited. In addition, EarthWeb plans to revamp its software infrastructure in the near future, so any knowledge Schlack has may soon become obsolete. * * *

At the moment, ITworld.com does not exist; the website is scheduled to be launched in January 2000. According to its president and CEO, William Reinstein, ITworld.com will consolidate four online publications of IDG—Computerworld, Network World, InfoWorld and CIO—and three additional wholly-owned websites. When operational, ITworld.com will be a single website for IT professionals that contains news, product information and editorial opinions written primarily by an internal staff of more than 275 journalists.

Thus, in contrast to EarthWeb's emphasis on obtaining the products and services of third parties through acquisitions and licensing agreements and then making those materials readily accessible on its websites, ITworld.com will rely on original content for over 70% of its website's material. Content such as product reviews and technical research will be created in-house by ITworld.com's staff.

Schlack contends that ITworld.com will also be distinguishable from EarthWeb in the type of audience it targets. While both EarthWeb and ITworld.com are intended to appeal to IT professionals, Schlack argues that the products and services offered by EarthWeb are aimed at programmers and technicians, while ITworld.com will focus on upper level executives, such as technology managers and chief information officers. EarthWeb disputes this assertion, and claims that it offers "a wide range of technology-related content" tailored to, * * * , IT managers and chief information officers. * * *

Given the dynamics of the Internet, such comparisons may be ephemeral. This underscores the difficulty in assessing the characteristics of ITworld.com, an embryonic business entity that will compete in a nascent industry which is evolving and re-inventing itself with breathtaking speed. * * *

* * *

Even if the terms of EarthWeb's restrictive covenant reached Schlack's prospective employment at ITworld.com, EarthWeb would still have to establish that the restraint is reasonable and necessary to protect its legitimate interests. In New York, non-compete covenants will be enforced only if reasonably limited in scope and duration, and only "to the extent necessary (1) to prevent an employee's solicitation or disclosure of trade secrets, (2) to prevent an employee's release of confidential information regarding the employer's customers, or (3) in those cases where the employee's services to the employer are deemed special or unique." [Citations.]

The policy underlying this strict approach rests on notions of employee mobility and free enterprise. "Once the term of an employment agreement has expired, the general public policy favoring robust and uninhibited competition should not give way merely because a particular employer wishes to insulate himself from competition." [Citation.] "Important, too, are the 'powerful considerations of public policy which militate against sanctioning the loss of a man's livelihood.'" [Citation.] On the other hand, "the employer is entitled to protection from unfair or illegal conduct that causes economic injury." [Citations.]

Applying these principles here, EarthWeb's restrictive covenant would fail to pass muster even if Schlack's position at ITworld.com fell within the provision's relatively narrow parameters.

As a threshold matter, this Court finds that the one-year duration of EarthWeb's restrictive covenant is too long given the dynamic nature of this industry, its lack of geographical borders, and Schlack's former cutting-edge position with EarthWeb where his success depended on keeping abreast of daily changes in content on the Internet. By comparison, the court in DoubleClick enjoined the defendants for only a six-month period. The DoubleClick court observed that "given the speed with which the Internet advertising industry apparently changes, defendants' knowledge of DoubleClick's operation will likely lose value to such a degree that the purpose of a preliminary injunction will have evaporated before the year is up." [Citation.] Similar considerations predominate here, making a one-year restrictive covenant unreasonably long. While courts may "blue pencil" such provisions to make them shorter and hence enforceable, [citation], this Court would decline to exercise its discretion to do so in this case because, as discussed above, the employment agreement as a whole overreaches. [Citation.]

Contrary to EarthWeb's contention, Schlack's services are not "unique and extraordinary." Such characteristics have traditionally been associated with "various categories of employment where the services are dependent on an employee's special talents; such categories include musicians, professional athletes, actors and the like." [Citations.] However, in order to justify a enforcement of a restrictive covenant,

> more must * * * be shown to establish such a quality than that the employee excels at his work or that his performance is of high value to his employer. It must also appear that his services are of such character as to make his replacement impossible or that the loss of such services would cause the employer irreparable injury.

[Citations.] EarthWeb has not shown that the nature of Schlack's services are unique or that he cultivated the type of special client relationships that the Second Circuit found worthy of protection in [citation].

INTERPRETATION An employment contract prohibiting an employee from competing with his employer for a reasonable period following termination is enforceable provided the restriction is reasonable and necessary to protect legitimate interests of the employer.

ETHICAL QUESTION Is it unethical for Schlack to use what he has learned at EarthWeb to benefit his new employer? Explain.

CRITICAL THINKING QUESTION How should courts balance the protection of employers with the freedom of employees to change jobs? Explain.

EXCULPATORY CLAUSES

Some contracts contain an **exculpatory clause** that excuses one party from liability for her own tortious conduct. Although there is general agreement that exculpatory clauses relieving a person from tort liability for harm caused intentionally or recklessly are unenforceable as violating public policy, exculpatory clauses that excuse a party from liability for harm caused by negligent conduct undergo careful scrutiny by the courts, which often require that the clause be conspicuously placed in the contract and clearly written. Accordingly, an exculpatory clause on the reverse side of a parking lot claim check, which attempts to relieve the parking lot operator of liability for negligently damaging the customer's automobile, will generally be held unenforceable as against public policy.

Where one party's superior bargaining position has enabled him to impose an exculpatory clause upon the other party, the courts are inclined to nullify the provision. Such a situation, as shown in the case that follows, may arise in residential leases exempting a landlord from liability for his negligence. Moreover, an exculpatory clause may be unenforceable for unconscionability.

Practical Advice

Because many courts do not favor exculpatory clauses, carefully limit its applicability, make sure that it is clear and understandable, put it in writing, and have it signed.

Henrioulle v. Marin Ventures, Inc.

Supreme Court of California, 1978
20 Cal.3d 512, 573 P.2d 465, 143 Cal.Rptr. 247

FACTS Henrioulle, an unemployed widower with two children, received public assistance in the form of a rent subsidy. He entered into an apartment lease agreement with Marin Ventures that provided "INDEMNIFICATION: Owner shall not be liable for any damage or injury to the tenant, or any other person, or to any property, occurring on the premises, or any part thereof, and Tenant agrees to hold Owner harmless for any claims for damages no matter how caused." Henrioulle fractured his wrist when he tripped over a rock on a common stairway in the apartment building. At the time of the accident, the landlord had been having difficulty keeping the common areas of the apartment building clean. Henrioulle appealed from the trial court's orders granting Marin Ventures a judgment notwithstanding the jury's verdict and a new trial.

DECISION Orders of the trial court reversed and case remanded with directions to enter a judgment for Henrioulle on the verdict.

OPINION Bird, C. J. In *Tunkl v. Regents of the University of California* [citation], this court held invalid a clause in a hospital admission form which released the hospital from liability for future negligence. This court noted that although courts have made "diverse" interpretations of [California] Civil Code section 1668, which invalidates contracts which exempt one from responsibility for certain willful or negligent acts, all the decisions were in accord that exculpatory clauses affecting the public interest are invalid. [Citation.]

In *Tunkl*, six criteria are used to identify the kind of agreement in which an exculpatory clause is invalid as contrary to public policy: "[1] It concerns a business of a type generally thought suitable for public regulation. [2] The party seeking exculpation is engaged in performing a service of great importance to the public, which is often a matter of practical necessity for some members of the public. [3] The party holds himself out as willing to perform this service for any member of the public who seeks it, or at least any member coming within certain established standards. [4] As a result of the essential nature of the service, in the economic setting of the transaction, the party invoking exculpation possesses a decisive advantage of bargaining strength against any member of the public who seeks his services. [5] In exercising a superior bargaining power the party confronts the public with a standardized adhesion contract of exculpation, and makes no provision whereby a purchaser may pay additional fees and obtain protection against negligence. [6] Finally, as a result of the transaction, the person or property of the purchaser is placed under the control of the seller, subject to the risk of carelessness by the seller or his agents." [Citation.]

The transaction before this court, a residential rental agreement, meets the *Tunkl* criteria.

* * *

In holding that exculpatory clauses in residential leases violate public policy, this court joins an increasing number of jurisdictions. [Citations.]

INTERPRETATION An exculpatory clause is valid only if it is not contrary to public policy.

ETHICAL QUESTION Did Marin Ventures, Inc. act unethically? Explain.

CRITICAL THINKING QUESTION When should an exculpatory clause be held invalid? Explain.

UNCONSCIONABLE CONTRACTS

The Uniform Commercial Code provides that a court may scrutinize every contract for the sale of goods to determine whether in its commercial setting, purpose, and effect the contract is unconscionable, or unfair. The court may refuse to enforce an **unconscionable** contract or any part of the contract it finds to be unconscionable. The Restatement has a similar provision.

Though neither the Code nor the Restatement defines the word *unconscionable*, the term is defined in the *New Webster's Dictionary* (Deluxe Encyclopedic Edition) as "contrary to the dictates of conscience; unscrupulous or unprincipled; exceeding that which is reasonable or customary; inordinate, unjustifiable."

The doctrine of unconscionability has been justified on the basis that it permits the courts to resolve issues of unfairness explicitly in terms of that unfairness without recourse to formalistic rules or legal fictions. In policing contracts for fairness, the courts have again demonstrated their willingness to limit freedom of contract to protect the less advantaged from overreaching by dominant contracting parties. The doctrine of unconscionability has evolved through its application by the courts to include both procedural and substantive unconscionability. **Procedural unconscionability** involves scrutiny for the presence of "bargaining naughtiness." In other words, was the negotiation process fair? Or were there procedural irregularities, such as burying important terms of the agreement in fine print or obscuring the true meaning of the contract with impenetrable legal jargon?

By comparison, in searching for **substantive unconscionability**, the courts examine the actual terms of a contract for oppressive or grossly unfair provisions such as exorbitant prices or unfair exclusions or limitations of contractual remedies. An all-too-common example of such a provision involves a buyer in pressing need who is in an unequal bargaining position with a seller who consequently obtains an exorbitant price for his product or service. In one case, a price of $749 ($920 if the purchaser wished to pay on credit over time) for a vacuum cleaner that cost the seller $140 was held unconscionable. In another case, the buyers, welfare recipients, purchased by a time payment contract a home freezer unit for $900 that, when time credit charges, credit life insurance, credit property insurance, and sales tax were added, cost $1,235. The purchase resulted from a visit to the buyers' home by a salesperson representing Your Shop At Home Service, Inc.; the maximum retail value of the freezer unit at the time of purchase was $300. The court held the contract unconscionable and reformed it by reducing the price to the total payment ($620) the buyers had managed to make. Another landmark case follows.

Closely akin to the concept of unconscionability is the doctrine of contracts of adhesion. An *adhesion contract*, a standard-form contract prepared by one party, generally involves the preparer offering the other party the contract on a "take-it-or-leave-it" basis. Such contracts are not automatically unenforceable but are subject to greater scrutiny for procedural or substantive unconscionability. See the Ethical Dilemma later in this chapter.

Practical Advice

When negotiating a contract, keep in mind that if your bargaining techniques or the contract terms are oppressive, a court may refuse to enforce the contract in part or in full.

Williams v. Walker-Thomas Furniture Co.

United States Court of Appeals, District of Columbia Circuit, 1965
350 F.2d 445

FACTS Between 1957 and 1962, Williams purchased a number of household items on credit from Walker-Thomas Furniture Co., a retail furniture store. Walker-Thomas retained the right in its contracts to repossess an item if Williams defaulted on an installment payment. Each contract also provided that each installment payment by Williams would be credited *pro rata* to all outstanding accounts or bills owed to Walker-Thomas. As a result of this provision, an unpaid balance would remain on every item purchased until the entire balance due on all items, whenever purchased, was paid in full. Williams defaulted on a monthly installment payment in 1962, and Walker-Thomas sought to repossess all the items that Williams had purchased since 1957. Williams claimed that the contracts were unconscionable and therefore unenforceable. The trial court granted judgment for Walker-Thomas, and the District of Columbia Court of Appeals affirmed.

DECISION Judgment reversed and remanded to determine the possible unconscionability of the contracts.

OPINION Wright, C. J. Unconscionability has generally been recognized to include an absence of meaningful choice on the part of one of the parties together with contract terms which are unreasonably favorable to the other party. Whether a meaningful choice is present in a particular case can only be determined by consideration of all the circumstances surrounding the transaction. In many cases the meaningfulness of the choice is negated by a gross inequality of bargaining power. The manner in which the contract was entered is also relevant to this consideration. Did each party to the contract, considering his obvious education or lack of it, have a reasonable opportunity to understand the terms of the contract, or were the important terms hidden in a maze of fine print and minimized by deceptive sales practices? Ordinarily, one who signs an agreement without full knowledge of its terms might be held to assume the risk that he has entered a one-sided bargain. But when a party of little bargaining power, and hence little real choice, signs a commercially unreasonable contract with little or no knowledge of its terms, it is hardly likely that his consent, or even an objective manifestation of his consent, was ever given to all the terms. In such a case the usual rule that the terms of the agreement are not to be questioned should be abandoned and the court should consider whether the terms of the contract are so unfair that enforcement should be withheld.

In determining reasonableness or fairness, the primary concern must be with the terms of the contract considered in light of the circumstances existing when the contract was made. The test is not simple, nor can it be mechanically applied. The terms are to be considered "in the light of the general commercial background and the commercial needs of the particular trade or case." Corbin suggests the test as being whether the terms are "so extreme as to appear unconscionable according to the mores and business practices of the time and place." [Citation.] We think this formulation correctly states the test to be applied to those cases where no meaningful choice was exercised upon entering the contract.

Because the trial court and the appellate court did not feel that enforcement could be refused, no findings were made on the possible unconscionability of the contracts in these cases. Since the record is not sufficient for our deciding the issue as a matter of law, the cases must be remanded to the trial court for further proceedings.

INTERPRETATION The doctrine of unconscionability includes both procedural and substantive unconscionability.

ETHICAL QUESTION Did Walker-Thomas Furniture Co. act unethically? Explain.

CRITICAL THINKING QUESTION What is the appropriate penalty to apply in this type of situation? Explain.

TORTIOUS CONDUCT

An agreement that requires a person to commit a tort is an illegal agreement and thus is unenforceable. The courts will not permit contract law to violate the law of torts. Any agreement attempting to do so is considered contrary to public policy. For example, Ada and Bernard enter into an agreement under which Ada promises Bernard that in return for $5,000, she will disparage the product of Bernard's competitor, Cone, in order to provide Bernard with a competitive advantage. Ada's promise is to commit the tort of disparagement and is unenforceable as contrary to public policy.

Ethical Dilemma

Is It Fair to Reserve the Right to Withhold Test Scores?

FACTS Professor Cramer teaches business law at State University. She also serves as a prelaw adviser. Ed Brinter, a 21-year-old college senior, is one of her advisees. Last semester, Ed applied to five law schools. Because he was uncertain whether he wanted to attend law school or to pursue an M.B.A., Professor Cramer suggested that he also apply to three graduate business schools.

As required for admission, Ed took the GMAT and the LSAT, both administered by the Educational Testing Service (ETS). He obtained a good, but not outstanding, score on the GMAT and an excellent score on his LSAT. ETS, however, has refused to send either set of test scores to any of the schools to which Ed applied. According to an ETS testing specialist, Ed's correct and incorrect answers so closely correlated to those of another student that ETS is requiring both students to retake the LSAT before any test scores will be forwarded. ETS also refuses to forward Ed's GMAT scores.

The ETS maintains that Ed entered into a contract when he registered for the exams. The application form included a clause that states that ETS reserves the right to cancel any test score if there is adequate reason to question its validity.

Ed has come to Professor Cramer for advice. Professor Cramer has known Ed for two years and has never seen him do anything dishonest. Yet she has lingering doubts. She knows how desperately Ed wants to attend graduate school and is aware of the significant pressure he has been under from his family.

Social, Policy, and Ethical Considerations

1. Should Professor Cramer attempt to intervene on Ed's behalf? What actions should she take?
2. Is it fair for the Educational Testing Service to take the position that all applicants agree to specific terms and conditions by virtue of the application process?
3. What policy interests does ETS serve through such procedures? What competing issues do such procedures present?
4. What justification, if any, is there for withholding the second set of Ed's test scores?

Corrupting Public Officials

Agreements that may adversely affect the public interest through the corruption of public officials or the impairment of the legislative process are unenforceable. Examples include using improper means to influence legislation, to secure some official action, or to procure a government contract. Contracts to pay lobbyists for services to obtain or defeat official action by means of persuasive argument are to be distinguished from illegal influence-peddling agreements.

For example, a bargain by a candidate for public office to make a certain appointment following his election is illegal. In addition, an agreement to pay a public officer something extra for performing his official duty, such as promising a bonus to a police officer for strictly enforcing the traffic laws on her beat, is illegal. The same is true of an agreement in which a citizen promises to perform, or to refrain from performing, duties imposed on her by citizenship. Thus, a promise by Carl to pay $50 to Rachel if she will register and vote is opposed to public policy and illegal.

CPA Effect of Illegality

With few exceptions, illegal contracts are ***unenforceable.*** In most cases, neither party to an illegal agreement can sue the other for breach or recover for any performance rendered. It is often said that where parties are *in pari delicto* (in pa'·re de·lik'tow)—in equal fault—a court will leave them where it finds them. The law will provide neither with any remedy. This strict rule of unenforceability is subject to certain exceptions, however, which are discussed as follows.

Party Withdrawing Before Performance

A party to an illegal agreement may, before performance, withdraw from the transaction and recover whatever she has contributed, if the party has not engaged in serious misconduct. A common example is recovery of money left with a stakeholder for a wager before it is paid over to the winner.

THE LAW AND YOU

State Bar Associations

Alabama: http://www.ago.state.al.us/ ("Fraudulent Telemarketing Tips")

Kansas: http://www.accesskansas.org/ksag/contents/consumer/ ("Internet Gambling Warning!")

Massachusetts: http://www.state.ma.us/consumerindex.htm ("Licensing")

PARTY PROTECTED BY STATUTE

Sometimes an agreement is illegal because it violates a statute designed to protect persons from the effects of the prohibited agreement. For example, state and federal statutes prohibiting the sale of unregistered securities are designed primarily to protect investors. In such case, even though there is an unlawful agreement, the statutes usually expressly give the purchaser a right to withdraw from the sale and recover the money paid.

PARTY NOT EQUALLY AT FAULT

Where one of the parties is less at fault than the other, he may be allowed to recover payments made or property transferred. For example, this exception would apply where one party induces the other to enter into an illegal bargain through the exercise of fraud, duress, or undue influence.

EXCUSABLE IGNORANCE

An agreement that appears to be entirely permissible on its face may, nevertheless, be illegal by reason of facts and circumstances of which one of the parties is completely unaware. For example, a man and woman make mutual promises to marry, but unknown to the woman, the man is already married. This is an agreement to commit the crime of bigamy, and the marriage, if entered into, is void. In such case, the courts permit the party who is ignorant of the illegality to maintain a lawsuit against the other party for damages.

A party may also be excused for ignorance of legislation of a minor character. For instance, Jones and Old South Building Co. enter into a contract to build a factory that contains specifications in violation of the town's building ordinance. Jones did not know of the violation and had no reason to know. Old South's promise to build would not be rendered unenforceable on grounds of public policy, and Jones consequently would have a claim against Old South for damages for breach of contract.

PARTIAL ILLEGALITY

A contract may be partly unlawful and partly lawful. The courts view such a contract in one of two ways. First, the partial illegality may be held to taint the entire contract with illegality, so that it is wholly unenforceable. Second, the court may determine it possible to separate the illegal from the legal part, in which case the illegal part only will be held unenforceable, while the legal part will be enforced. For example, if a contract contains an illegal covenant not to compete, the covenant will not be enforced, though the rest of the contract may be.

CHAPTER SUMMARY

Violations of Statutes

General Rule the courts will not enforce agreements declared illegal by statute

Licensing Statutes require formal authorization to engage in certain trades, professions, or businesses
- *Regulatory License* licensing statute that is intended to protect the public against unqualified persons; an unlicensed person may not recover for services he has performed
- *Revenue License* licensing statute that seeks to raise money; an unlicensed person may recover for services he has performed

Gambling Statutes prohibit wagers, which are agreements that one party will win and the other lose depending on the outcome of an event in which their only interest is the gain or loss

Usury Statutes establish a maximum rate of interest

Sunday Statutes prohibition of certain types of commercial activity on Sunday (also called blue laws)

Violations of Public Policy

Common Law Restraint of Trade unreasonable restraints of trade are not enforceable
- *Sale of a Business* the promise by the seller of a business not to compete in that particular business in a reasonable geographic area for a reasonable period of time is enforceable
- *Employment Contracts* an employment contract prohibiting an employee from competing with his employer for a reasonable period following termination is enforceable provided the restriction is necessary to protect legitimate interests of the employer

Exculpatory Clauses the courts generally disapprove of contractual provisions excusing a party from liability for his own tortious conduct

Unconscionable Contracts unfair or unduly harsh agreements are not enforceable
- *Procedural Unconscionability* unfair or irregular bargaining
- *Substantive Unconscionability* oppressive or grossly unfair contractual terms

Tortious Conduct an agreement that requires a person to commit a tort is unenforceable

Corrupting Public Officials agreements that corrupt public officials are not enforceable

Effect of Illegality

Unenforceability neither party may recover (unenforceable) under an illegal agreement where both parties are *in pari delicto* (in equal fault)

Exceptions permit one party to recover payments
- *Party Withdrawing Before Performance*
- *Party Protected by Statute*
- *Party Not Equally at Fault*
- *Excusable Ignorance*
- *Partial Illegality*

Questions

1. Johnson and Wilson were the principal shareholders in XYZ Corporation, located in the city of Jonesville, Wisconsin. This corporation was engaged in the business of manufacturing paper novelties, which were sold over a wide area in the Midwest. The corporation was also in the business of binding books. Johnson purchased Wilson's shares in XYZ Corporation and, in consideration thereof, Wilson agreed that for a period of two years he would not (a) manufacture or sell in Wisconsin any paper novelties of any kind that would compete with those sold by XYZ Corporation or (b) engage in the bookbinding business in the city of Jonesville. Discuss the validity and effect, if any, of this agreement.

2. Wilkins, a Texas resident licensed by that state as a certified public accountant, rendered service in his professional capacity in Louisiana to Coverton Cosmetics Company. He was not registered as a certified public accountant in Louisiana. His service under his contract with the cosmetics company was not the only occasion on which he had practiced his profession in that state. The company denied liability and refused to pay him, relying on a Louisiana statute declaring it unlawful for any person to perform or offer to perform services as a CPA for compensation until he has been registered by the designated agency of the state and holds an unrevoked registration card. The statute provides that a CPA certificate may be issued without examination to any applicant who holds a valid unrevoked certificate as a CPA under the laws of any other state. The statute provides further that rendering services of the kind performed by Wilkins, without registration, is a misdemeanor punishable by a fine or imprisonment in the county jail or by both fine and imprisonment. Discuss whether Wilkins would be successful in an action against Coverton seeking to recover a fee in the amount of $1,500 as the reasonable value of his services.

3. Michael is interested in promoting the passage of a bill in the state legislature. He agrees with Christy, an attorney, to pay Christy for her services in writing the required bill, obtaining its introduction in the legislature, and making an argument for its passage before the legislative committee to which it will be referred. Christy renders these services. Subsequently, on Michael's refusal to pay Christy, Christy sues Michael for damages for breach of contract. Will Christy prevail? Explain.

4. Anthony promises to pay McCarthy $10,000 if McCarthy reveals to the public that Washington is a communist. Washington is not a communist and never has been. McCarthy successfully persuades the media to report that Washington is a communist and now seeks to recover the $10,000 from Anthony, who refuses to pay. McCarthy initiates a lawsuit against Anthony. What will be the result?

5. The Dear Corporation was engaged in the business of making and selling harvesting machines. It sold everything pertaining to its business to the HI Company, agreeing "not again to go into the manufacture of harvesting machines anywhere in the United States." The Dear Corporation, which had a national and international goodwill in its business, now begins the manufacture of such machines contrary to its agreement. Should the court stop it from doing so? Explain.

6. Charles Leigh, engaged in the industrial laundry business in Central City, employed Tim Close, previously employed in the home laundry business, as a route salesperson. Leigh rents linens and industrial uniforms to commercial customers; the soiled linens and uniforms are picked up at regular intervals by the route drivers and replaced with clean ones. Every employee is assigned a list of customers whom she services. The contract of employment stated that in consideration of being employed, on termination of his employment, Close would not "directly or indirectly engage in the linen supply business or any competitive business within Central City, Illinois, for a period of one year from the date when his employment under this contract ceases." On May 10 of the following year, Close's employment was terminated by Leigh for valid reasons. Close then accepted employment with Ajax Linen Service, a direct competitor of Leigh in Central City. He began soliciting former customers he had called on for Leigh and obtained some of them as customers for Ajax. Will Leigh be able to enforce the provisions of the contract?

7. On July 5, 1988, Barbara and Kitty entered into a bet on the outcome of the 1988 presidential election. On January 28, 1989, Barbara, who bet on the winner, approached Kitty, seeking to collect the $3,000 Kitty had wagered. Kitty paid Barbara the wager but now seeks to recover the funds from Barbara. Result?

8. Carl, a salesperson for Smith, comes to Benson's home and sells him a complete set of "gourmet cooking utensils" that are worth approximately $300. Benson, an eighty-year-old man who lives alone in a one-room efficiency apartment, signs a contract to buy the utensils for $1,450 plus a credit charge of $145 and to make payments in ten equal monthly installments. Three weeks after Carl leaves with the signed contract, Benson decides he cannot afford the cooking utensils and has no use for them. What can Benson do? Explain.

9. Consider the facts in problem 8 but assume that the price was $350. Assume further that Benson wishes to avoid the contract based on the allegation that Carl befriended and tricked him into the purchase. Discuss.

10. Adrian rents a bicycle from Barbara. The bicycle rental contract Adrian signed provides that Barbara is not liable for any injury to the renter caused by any defect in the bicycle or the negligence of Barbara. Adrian is injured when she is involved in an accident due to Barbara's improper maintenance of the bicycle. Adrian sues Barbara for damages. Will Barbara be protected from liability by the provision in their contract?

CASE PROBLEMS

11. Merrill Lynch (http://www.ml.com/) employed Post and Maney as account executives beginning on April 20, 1959, and May 15, 1961, respectively. Both men elected to be paid a salary and to participate in the firm's pension and profit-sharing plans rather than take a straight commission. Merrill Lynch terminated the employment of both Post and Maney on August 30, 1974. On September 4, 1974, both began working for Bache & Company, a competitor of Merrill Lynch. Merrill Lynch then informed them that all of their rights in the company-funded pension plan had been forfeited pursuant to a provision of the plan that permitted forfeiture in the event an employee directly or indirectly competed with the firm. Is Merrill Lynch correct in its assertion?

12. Tovar applied for the position of resident physician in Paxton Community Memorial Hospital. The hospital examined his background and licensing and assured him that he was qualified for the position. Relying upon the hospital's promise of permanent employment, Tovar resigned from his job and began work at the hospital. He was discharged two weeks later, however, because he did not hold a license to practice medicine in Illinois as required by state law. He had taken the examination but had never passed it. Tovar claims that the hospital promised him a position of permanent employment and that by discharging him, it breached their employment contract. Who is correct? Discuss.

13. Carolyn Murphy, a welfare recipient with four minor children, responded to an advertisement that offered the opportunity to purchase televisions without a deposit or credit history. She entered into a rent-to-own contract for a twenty-five-inch console color television set that required seventy-eight weekly payments of $16 (a total of $1,248, which was two and one-half times the retail value of the set). Under the contract, the renter could terminate the agreement by returning the television and forfeiting any payments already made. After Murphy had paid $436 on the television, she read a newspaper article criticizing the lease plan. She stopped payment and sued the television company. In response, the television company has attempted to take possession of the set. What will be the outcome?

14. Albert Bennett, an amateur cyclist, participated in a bicycle race conducted by the United States Cycling Federation. During the race, Bennett was hit by an automobile. He claims that employees of the Federation improperly allowed the car onto the course. The Federation claims that it cannot be held liable to Bennett because Bennett signed a release exculpating the Federation from responsibility for any personal injury resulting from his participation in the race. Is the exculpatory clause effective?

15. In February 1980, Brady, a general contractor, signed a written contract with the Fulghums to build for them a house in North Carolina. The contract price of the house was $106,850, and construction was to begin in March of 1980. Neither during the contract negotiations nor during the commencement of construction was Brady licensed as a general contractor as required by North Carolina law. In fact, Brady did not obtain his license until late October 1980, at which time he had completed more than two-thirds of the construction on the Fulghums' house. The Fulghums submitted to Brady total payments of $104,000 on the house. Brady sues for $2,850 on the original contract and $29,000 for additions and changes requested by the Fulghums during construction. Is Fulghum liable to Brady? Explain.

16. Robert McCart owned and operated an H&R Block tax preparation franchise. When Robert became a district manager for H&R Block (http://www.hrblock.com/), in accordance with company policy, he signed over his franchise to his wife June. June signed the new franchise agreement, which included a covenant not to compete for a two-year period within a 50-mile radius of the franchise territory should the H&R Block franchise be terminated, transferred, or otherwise disposed of. At all times Robert was aware of the terms of this agreement. Shortly after terminating her franchise agreement, June sent out letters to H&R Block customers, criticizing H&R Block's fees and informing them that she and Robert would establish their own tax preparation services at the same address as the former franchise location. Each letter included a separate letter from Robert detailing the tax services to be offered by the McCarts' new business. Should H&R Block be able to obtain an injunction against Robert?

17. Abramowitz obtained a one-year mortgage loan from Barnett Bank for $400,000 at 9 percent interest with a 1 percent "point" or service fee. The maximum lawful rate of interest on such a loan is 10 percent. The bank deducted the $4,000 service fee from the loan proceeds, actually disbursing only $396,000 to Abramowitz. During the one-year term of his loan, Abramowitz was charged and he paid $36,347.78 in interest. He claims the loan was usurious because the $4,000 "service fee" plus the $36,347.78 interest charge exceeded the 10 percent limit on total interest. Abramowitz appealed from a judgment denying him any relief. Is the loan usurious? Explain.

18. In 1964 Michelle Marvin and actor Lee Marvin began living together, holding themselves out to the general public as man and wife without actually being married. The two orally agreed that while they lived together, they would share equally any and all property and earnings accumulated as a result of their individual and combined efforts. In addition, Michelle promised to render her services as "companion, homemaker, housekeeper, and cook" to Lee. Shortly thereafter, she gave up her lucrative career as an entertainer in order to devote her full time to being Lee's companion, homemaker, housekeeper, and cook. In return

he agreed to provide for all of her financial support and needs for the rest of her life. In 1970, Lee compelled Michelle to leave his household but continued to provide for her support. In late 1971, however, he refused to provide further support. Michelle sued to recover support payments and half of their accumulated property. Lee contends that their agreement is so closely related to the supposed "immoral" character of their relationship that its enforcement would violate public policy. Explain who is correct in this situation.

19. Richard Brobston was hired by Insulation Corporation of America (ICA) (http://www.insulcorp.com/) in 1982. Initially, he was hired as a territory sales manager but was promoted to national account manager in 1986 and to general manager in 1990. In 1992, ICA was planning to acquire computer-assisted design (CAD) technology to upgrade its product line. Prior to acquiring this technology, ICA required that Brobston and certain other employees sign employment contracts that contained restrictive covenants or be terminated. These restrictive covenants provided that in the event of Brobston's termination for any reason, Brobston would not reveal any of ICA's trade secrets or sales information and would not enter into direct competition with ICA within three hundred miles of Allentown, Pennsylvania, for a period of two years from the date of termination. The purported consideration for Brobston's agreement was a $2,000 increase in his base salary and proprietary information concerning the CAD system, customers, and pricing. Brobston signed the proffered employment contract. In October 1992, Brobston became vice president of special products, which included responsibility for sales of the CAD system products as well as other products. Over the course of the next year, Brobston failed in several respects to properly perform his employment duties and on August 13, 1993, ICA terminated Brobston's employment. In December 1993, Brobston was hired by a competitor of ICA who was aware of ICA's restrictive covenants. Can ICA enforce the employment agreement by enjoining Brobston from disclosing proprietary information about ICA and by restraining him from competing with ICA? If so, for what duration and over what geographic area?

http:// **Internet Exercise** Find and review information on lotteries, including which states have them and how the proceeds are used.

Chapter 14

Contractual Capacity

Youth is a blunder, manhood a struggle, old age a regret.
BENJAMIN DISRAELI (1805–1881), *CONINGSBY*, BOOK III, CH.I

Learning Objectives

After reading this chapter you should be able to:

1. Explain how and when a minor may ratify a contract.
2. Describe the liability of a minor who (a) disaffirms a contract or (b) misrepresents his age.
3. Define a necessary and explain how it affects the contracts of a minor.
4. Distinguish between the legal capacity of a person under guardianship and a mentally incompetent person who is not under guardianship.
5. Explain the rule governing an intoxicated person's capacity to enter into a contract and contrast this rule with the law governing minors and incompetent persons.

A binding promise or agreement requires that the parties to the agreement have contractual capacity. Everyone is regarded as having such capacity unless the law, for public policy reasons, holds that the individual lacks such capacity. We will consider this essential ingredient of a contract by discussing those classes and conditions of persons who are legally limited in their capacity to contract: minors, incompetent persons, and intoxicated persons.

CPA MINORS

A **minor**, also called an infant, is a person who has not attained the age of legal majority. At common law, a minor was an individual who had not reached the age of twenty-one years. Today the age of majority has been changed by statute in nearly all jurisdictions, usually to age eighteen. Almost without exception a minor's contract, whether executory or executed, is ***voidable*** at his guardian's option. Thus, the minor is in a favored position by having the option to disaffirm the contract or to enforce it. Even an "emancipated" minor, one who, because of marriage or other reasons, is no longer subject to strict parental control, may nevertheless avoid contractual liability in most jurisdictions. Consequently, businesspeople deal at their peril with minors and in situations of consequence generally require an adult to co-sign or guarantee the performance of the contract. Nevertheless, most states recognize special categories of contracts that cannot be avoided (such as student loans or contracts for medical care) or that have a lower age for capacity (such as bank accounts, marriage, and insurance contracts).

LIABILITY ON CONTRACTS

A minor's contract is not entirely void and of no legal effect; rather, as we have said, it is voidable at the minor's option. The exercise of this power of avoidance, called a **disaffirmance**, releases the minor from any liability on the contract. On the other hand, after the minor comes of age, he may choose to adopt or ratify the contract, in which case he surrenders his power of avoidance and becomes bound by his **ratification.**

Disaffirmance As we stated earlier, a minor has the power to avoid liability. The minor or, in some jurisdictions, her guardian, may exercise the power to disaffirm a contract through words or conduct showing an intention not to abide by it.

A minor may disaffirm a contract at any time before reaching the age of majority. Moreover, a minor generally may disaffirm a contract within a reasonable time after coming of age as long as she has not already ratified the contract. A notable exception is that a minor cannot disaffirm a sale of land until after reaching her majority.

In most states, determining a reasonable time depends on circumstances such as the nature of the transaction, whether either party has caused the delay, and the extent to which either party has been injured by the delay. Some states, however, statutorily prescribe a time period, generally one year, in which the minor may disaffirm the contract.

Disaffirmance may be either *express* or *implied*. No particular form of language is essential, so long as it shows an intention not to be bound. This intention also may be manifested by acts or by conduct. For example, a minor agrees to sell property to Andy and then sells the property to Betty. The sale to Betty constitutes a disaffirmance of the contract with Andy.

A troublesome yet important problem in this area pertains to the minor's duty upon disaffirmance. The courts do not agree on this question. The majority hold that the minor must return any property received from the other party to the contract, provided she is in possession of it at the time of disaffirmance. Nothing more is required. If the minor disaffirms the purchase of an automobile and the vehicle has been wrecked, she need only return the wrecked vehicle. Other states require at least the payment of a reasonable amount for the use of the property or of the amount by which the property depreciated while in the hands of the minor. (See *Dodson v. Shrader* below.) A few states, however, either by statute or court ruling, recognize a duty on the part of the minor to make *restitution*; that is, to return an equivalent of what has been received so that the seller will be in approximately the same position he would have occupied had the sale not occurred.

Dodson v. Shrader

Supreme Court of Tennessee, 1992
824 S.W.2d 545

FACTS Joseph Eugene Dodson, age sixteen, purchased a used pickup truck from Burns and Mary Shrader. The Shraders owned and operated Shrader's Auto Sales in Columbia, Tennessee. Dodson paid $4,900 in cash for the truck. At the time of sale, the Shraders did not question Mr. Dodson's age, but thought he was eighteen or nineteen. Dodson made no misrepresentation concerning his age. Nine months after the date of purchase, the truck began to develop mechanical problems. A mechanic diagnosed the problem as a burnt valve but could not be certain. Dodson, who could not afford the repairs, continued to drive the truck until one month later, when the engine "blew up." Dodson parked the vehicle in the front yard of his parents' home and contacted the Shraders to rescind the purchase of the truck and to request a full refund. The Shraders refused. Dodson filed an action, seeking to rescind the contract and to obtain a full refund of the money he had paid. Before the case was heard, a hit-and-run driver hit the truck. The trial judge granted the rescission and ordered the Shraders to reimburse the $4,900. The Court of Appeals affirmed.

DECISION Case remanded to determine the proper amount to be refunded.

OPINION O'Brien, J. The law on the subject of the protection of infant's rights has been slow to evolve. However, in *Human v. Hartsell*, [citation] (1940) the Court of Appeals noted:

> * * * the modern rule that contracts of infants are not void but only voidable and subject to be disaffirmed by the minor either before or after attaining majority appears to have been favored. * * *

As noted by the Court of Appeals, the rule in Tennessee * * * is in accord with the majority rule on the issue among our sister states. This rule is based upon the underlying purpose of the "infancy doctrine" which is to protect minors from their lack of judgment and "from squandering their wealth through improvident contracts with crafty adults who would take advantage of them in the marketplace." [Citation.]

There is, however, a modern trend among the states, either by judicial action or by statute, in the approach to the problem of balancing the rights of minors against those of innocent merchants. As a result, two (2) minority rules have developed which allow the other party to a contract with a minor to refund less than the full consideration paid in the event of rescission.

The first of these minority rules is called the "Benefit Rule." [Citations.] The rule holds that, upon rescission, recovery of the full purchase price is subject to a deduction for the minor's use of the merchandise. * * * to the extent of the benefit actually derived by [the minor]. * * *

The other minority rule holds that the minor's recovery of the full purchase price is subject to a deduction for the minor's "use" of the consideration he or she received under the contract, or for the "depreciation" or "deterioration" of the consideration in his or her possession. [Citations.]

* * * At a time when we see young persons between 18 and 21 years of age demanding and assuming more responsibilities in their daily lives; when we see such persons emancipated, married, and raising families; when we see such persons charged with the responsibility for committing crimes; when we see such persons being sued in tort claims for acts of negligence; when we see such persons subject to military service; when we see such persons engaged in business and acting in almost all other respects as an adult, it seems timely to re-examine the case law pertaining to contractual rights and responsibilities of infants to see if the law as pronounced and applied by the courts should be redefined.

* * *

We state the rule to be followed hereafter, in reference to a contract of a minor, to be where the minor has not been overreached in any way, and there has been no undue influence, and the contract is a fair and reasonable one, and the minor has actually paid money on the purchase price, and taken and used the article purchased, that he ought not to be permitted to recover the amount actually paid, without allowing the vendor of the goods reasonable compensation for the use of, depreciation, and willful or negligent damage to the article purchased, while in his hands. If there has been any fraud or imposition on the part of the seller or if the contract is unfair, or any unfair advantage has been taken of the minor inducing him to make the purchase, then the rule does not apply. Whether there has been such an overreaching on the part of the seller, and the fair market value of the property returned, would always, in any case, be a question for the trier of fact. This rule will fully and fairly protect the minor against injustice or imposition, and at the same time it will be fair to a business person who has dealt with such minor in good faith.

* * *

We note that in this case, some nine (9) months after the date of purchase, the truck purchased by the plaintiff began to develop mechanical problems. Plaintiff was informed of the probable nature of the difficulty which apparently involved internal problems in the engine. He continued to drive the vehicle until the engine "blew up" and the truck became inoperable. Whether or not this involved gross negligence or intentional conduct on his part is a matter for determination at the trial level. * * * After the first tender of the vehicle was made by plaintiff, and refused by the defendant, the truck was damaged by a hit-and-run driver while parked on plaintiff's property. The amount of that damage and the liability for that amount between the purchaser and the vendor, as well as the fair market value of the vehicle at the time of tender, is also an issue for the trier of fact.

INTERPRETATION Under the majority rule, a minor may disaffirm her contracts during minority and for a reasonable time thereafter; this case also presents two minority views.

ETHICAL QUESTION Should Dodson have received all of his money back? Explain.

CRITICAL THINKING QUESTION Under what circumstances should minors be able to disaffirm their contracts and receive their full consideration? Explain.

Finally, can a minor disaffirm and recover property that he has sold to a buyer who in turn has sold it to a good-faith purchaser for value? Traditionally, the minor could avoid the contract and recover the property, even though the third person gave value for it and had no notice of the minority. Thus, in the case of the sale of real estate, a minor could take back a deed of conveyance even against a third-party good-faith purchaser of the land who did not know of the minority. The Uniform Commercial Code, however, has changed this principle in connection with sales of goods by providing that a person with voidable title (e.g., the person buying goods from a minor) has power to transfer valid title to a good-faith purchaser for value. For example, a minor sells his car to an individual who resells it to a used-car dealer, a good-faith purchaser for value. The used-car dealer would acquire legal title even though he bought the car from a seller who had only voidable title.

Practical Advice

In all significant contracts entered into with a minor, have an adult cosign or guarantee the written agreement.

Ratification A minor has the option of ratifying a contract after reaching the age of majority. Ratification makes the contract binding *ab initio* (from the beginning). That is, the result is the same as if the contract had been valid and binding from its inception. Ratification, once effected, is final and cannot be withdrawn; furthermore, it must be in total, validating the entire contract. The minor can ratify the contract only as a whole, both as to burdens and benefits. He cannot, for example, ratify so as to retain the consideration received and escape payment or other performance on his part; nor can the minor retain part of the contract and disaffirm another part.

Note that a minor has *no* power to ratify a contract while still a minor. A ratification based on words or conduct occurring while the minor is still underage is no more effective than his original contractual promise. The ratification must take place after the individual has acquired contractual capacity by attaining his majority.

Ratification can occur in three ways: (1) through express language, (2) as implied from conduct, and (3) through failure to make a timely disaffirmance. Suppose that a minor makes a contract to buy property from an adult. The contract is voidable by the minor, and she can escape liability. But suppose that after reaching her majority she promises to go through with the purchase. The minor has *expressly* ratified the contract she entered when she was a minor. Her promise is binding, and the adult can recover for breach if the minor fails to carry out the terms of the contract.

Ratification also may be *implied* from a person's conduct. Suppose that the minor, after attaining majority, uses the property involved in the contract, undertakes to sell it to someone else, or performs some other act showing an intention to affirm the contract. She may not thereafter disaffirm the contract but is bound by it. Perhaps the most common form of implied ratification occurs when a minor, after attaining majority, continues to use the property purchased as a minor. This use is obviously inconsistent with the nonexistence of a contract. Whether the contract is performed or still partly executory, the continued use of the property amounts to a ratification and prevents a disaffirmance by the minor. Simply keeping the goods for an unreasonable time after attaining majority has also been construed as a ratification.

In re The Score Board, Inc.

United States District Court, District of New Jersey, 1999

238 B.R. 585

http://lawlibrary.rutgers.edu/fed/html/ca99-259-1.html

FACTS During the Spring of 1996, Kobe Bryant ("Bryant") **(http://www.nba.com/playerfile/kobe_bryant/?nav=page)**, then a seventeen-year old star high school basketball player, declared his intention to forgo college and enter the 1996 National Basketball Association lottery draft. The Score Board Inc., a company in the business of licensing, manufacturing, and distributing sports and entertainment-related memorabilia, entered into negotiations with Bryant's agent, Arn Tellem ("Agent") and Bryant's father, former NBA star Joe "Jelly Bean" Bryant, to sign Bryant to a contract. In early July 1996, Score Board sent Bryant a signed written licensing agreement ("agreement"). The agreement granted Score Board the right to produce licensed products, such as trading cards, with Bryant's image. Bryant was obligated to make two personal appearances on behalf of Score Board and provide between a minimum of 15,000 and a maximum of 32,500 autographs. Bryant was to receive a $2.00 stipend for each autograph, after the first 7,500. Under the agreement, Bryant could receive a maximum of $75,000 for the autographs. In addition to being compensated for the autographs, Bryant was entitled to receive a base compensation of $10,000.

Bryant rejected this proposed agreement, and on July 11, 1996, while still a minor, made a counter-offer ("counter-offer"), signed it, and returned it to Score Board. The counter-offer made several changes to Score Board's agreement, including the number of autographs. Score Board claimed that they signed the counter-offer and placed it into its files. The copy signed by Score Board was subsequently misplaced and has never been produced by Score Board during these proceedings. Rather, Score Board has produced a copy signed only by Bryant.

On August 23, 1996, Bryant turned eighteen. Three days later, Bryant deposited the check for $10,000 into his account. Bryant subsequently performed his contractual duties for about a year and a half. By late 1997, Bryant grew reluctant to sign any more autographs under the agreement and his Agent came to the conclusion that a fully executed contract did not exist. By this time, Agent became concerned with Score Board's financial condition because it failed to make certain payments to several other players. Score Board claims that the true motivation for Bryant's reluctance stems from his perception that he was becoming a "star" player, and that his autograph was "worth" more than $2.00.

On March 17, 1998, Score Board mistakenly sent Bryant a check for $1,130 as compensation for unpaid autographs. Bryant was actually entitled to $10,130 and the check for $1,130 was based on a miscalculation.

On March 18, 1998, Score Board filed a voluntary Chapter 11 bankruptcy petition. On March 23, 1998, Agent returned the $1,130 check. Included with the check was a letter that directed Score Board to "immediately cease and desist from any use of" Kobe Bryant's name, likeness or other publicity rights. Subsequently, Score Board began to sell its assets, including numerous executory contracts with major athletes, including Bryant. Bryant argued that Score Board could not do this, because he believed that a contract never existed. In the alternative, if a contract had been created, Bryant contended that it was voidable because it had been entered into while he was a minor. The Bankruptcy Court ruled in favor of Score Board. Bryant appealed.

DECISION Judgment affirmed.

OPINION Irenas, J. Bryant challenges the Bankruptcy Court's finding that he ratified the agreement upon attaining majority. Contracts made during minority are voidable at the minor's election within a reasonable time after the minor attains the age of majority. [Citations]

The right to disaffirm a contract is subject to the infant's conduct which, upon reaching the age of majority, may amount to ratification. [Citation.] "Any conduct on the part of the former infant which evidences his decision that the transaction shall not be impeached is sufficient for this purpose." [Citation.]

On August 23, 1996, Bryant reached the age of majority, approximately six weeks after the execution of the agreement. On August 26, 1996, Bryant deposited the $10,000 check sent to him from Debtor [Score Board]. Bryant also performed his contractual duties by signing autographs.

The Bankruptcy Court did not presume ratification from inaction as Bryant asserts. It is clear that Bryant ratified the contract from the facts, because Bryant consciously performed his contractual duties.

Bryant asserts that he acted at the insistence of his Agent, who believed that he was obligated to perform by contract. Yet, neither Bryant nor his Agent disputed the existence of a contract until the March 23, 1998, letter by Tellem [Agent]. That Bryant may have relied on his Agent is irrelevant to this Court's inquiry and is proper evidence only in a suit against the Agent. To the contrary, by admitting that he acted because he was under the belief that a contract existed, Bryant confirms the existence of the contract. Moreover, it was Bryant who deposited the check, signed the autographs, and made personal appearances.

* * *

INTERPRETATION Ratification of a contract may be implied from a person's conduct after the person attains his majority.

CRITICAL THINKING QUESTION What criteria should a court employ in determining what is a reasonable period of time for disaffirmance by a person who has attained majority?

LIABILITY FOR NECESSARIES

Contractual incapacity does not excuse a minor from an obligation to pay for **necessaries**, those things, such as food, shelter, medicine, and clothing, that suitably and reasonably supply his personal needs. Even here, however, the minor is not contractually liable for the agreed price but for the *reasonable* value of the items furnished. Recovery is based on quasi-contract. Thus, if a clothier sells a minor a suit that the minor needs, the clothier can successfully sue the minor. The clothier's recovery, however, is limited to the reasonable value of the suit only, even if this amount is much less than the agreed-upon selling price. In addition, a minor is not liable for anything on the ground that the item is a necessary unless it has been actually furnished to him and used or consumed by him. In other words, a minor may disaffirm his executory contracts for necessaries and refuse to accept such clothing, lodging, or other items.

Defining "necessaries" is a difficult task. In general, the states regard as necessary those things that the minor needs to maintain himself in his particular station in life. Items necessary for subsistence and health, such as food, lodging, clothing, medicine, and medical services, are included. But other less essential items, such as textbooks, school instruction, and legal advice, may be included as well. Further, some states enlarge the concept of necessaries to include articles of property and services that a minor needs to earn the money required to provide the necessities of life for himself and his dependents. Nevertheless, many states limit necessaries to items that are not provided to the minor. Thus, if a minor's guardian provides her with an adequate wardrobe, a blouse the minor purchased would not be considered a necessary.

The following is the leading case on the rights and obligations of minors for the purchase of "necessaries."

Zelnick v. Adams

Supreme Court of Virginia, 2002
263 Va. 601, 561 S.E.2d 711
http://caselaw.lp.findlaw.com/scripts/getcase.pl?court=va&vol=1011390&invol=1

FACTS Jonathan Ray Adams ("Jonathan") was born on April 5, 1980, the son of Mildred A. Adams ("Adams" or "mother") and Cecil D. Hylton, Jr. ("Hylton" or "father"). Jonathan's parents were never married. Nevertheless, the Florida courts did determine Hylton's paternity of Jonathan. Jonathan's grandfather, Cecil D. Hylton, Sr. ("Hylton Sr."), died in 1989 and established certain trusts under his will, which provided that the trustees had sole discretion to determine who qualified as "issue" under the will.

In 1996, Adams met with an attorney, Robert J. Zelnick ("Zelnick"), about protecting Jonathan's interest as a beneficiary of the trusts after she had unsuccessfully attempted to get Jonathon recognized as an heir. Adams explained that she could not afford to pay Zelnick's hourly fee and requested legal services on her son's behalf on a contingency fee basis. Zelnick subsequently informed Adams that he had examined a copy of the will and that he was willing to accept the case. Adams went to Zelnick's office the next day, where Zelnick explained that the gross amount of the estate was very large. Nevertheless, Adams signed a retainer agreement ("the contract") for Zelnick's firm to represent Jonathan on a one-third contingency fee.

In May 1997, Zelnick initiated a legal action on Jonathan's behalf to have Jonathan recognized as the grandchild and "issue" of Hylton Sr. for the purposes of the will and trusts. A consent decree was entered on January 23, 1998, which ordered that Jonathan was "declared to be the grandchild and issue of Cecil D. Hylton" and was "entitled to all bequests, devises, distributions and benefits under the Last Will and Testament of Cecil D. Hylton and the trusts created."

In March 1998, Jonathan's father brought suit against Adams and Zelnick, on Jonathan's behalf, to have the contract with Zelnick declared void. Upon reaching the age of majority, Jonathan filed a petition to intervene, in which he disaffirmed the contract. On April 6, 2000, Jonathan filed a motion for summary judgment. He asserted that the contract was "void as a matter of law" because it was not a contract for necessaries. Jonathan argued that the 1997 suit was unnecessary due to the Florida paternity decree which conclusively established Hylton's paternity.

The trial court granted Jonathan's motion for summary judgment and ruled that the contingency fee agreement was void. The trial court held that the contract was not binding on Jonathan because he was "in his minority" when the contract was executed. Furthermore, according to the trial court, the doctrine of necessaries did not apply to the contract "because the matter could have been adjudicated after the majority of [Jonathan], who was within a few years of his majority at the time that all of this came out."

DECISION Judgment reversed and remanded.

OPINION Lemons, J. In this appeal, we consider whether a contract for legal services entered into on behalf of a minor is voidable upon a plea of infancy or subject to enforcement as an implied contract for necessaries and, if enforceable, the basis for determining value of services rendered.

Under well and long-established Virginia law, a contract with an infant is not void, only voidable by the infant upon attaining the age of majority. [Citation.] This oft-cited rule is subject to the relief provided by the doctrine of necessaries which received thorough analysis in the case of *Bear's Adm'x v. Bear*, [citation].

In *Bear*, we explained that when a court is faced with a defense of infancy, the court has the initial duty to determine, as a matter of law, whether the "things supplied" to the infant under a contract may fall within the general class of necessaries. [Citation.] The court must further decide whether there is sufficient evidence to allow the finder of fact to determine whether the "things supplied" were in fact necessary in the instant case. If either of these preliminary inquiries is answered in the negative, the party who provided the goods or services to the infant under the disaffirmed contract cannot recover. If the preliminary inquiries are answered in the affirmative, then the finder of fact must decide, under all the circumstances, whether the "things supplied" were actually necessary to the "position and condition of the infant." If so, the party who provided the goods or services to the infant is entitled to the "reasonable value" of the things furnished. In contracts for necessaries, an infant is not bound on the express contract, but rather is bound under an implied contract to pay what the goods or services furnished were reasonably worth. [Citation.]

"Things supplied," which fall into the class of necessaries, include "board, clothing and education." [Citation.] Things that are "necessary to [an infant's] subsistence and comfort, and to enable [an infant] to live according to his real position in society" are also considered part of the class of necessaries. [Citation.] * * *

Certainly, the provision of legal services may fall within the class of necessaries for which a contract by or on behalf of an infant may not be avoided or disaffirmed on the grounds of infancy. Generally, contracts for legal services related to prosecuting personal injury actions, and protecting an infant's personal liberty, security, or reputation are considered contracts for necessaries. [Citation.] "Whether attorney's services are to be considered necessaries or not depends on whether or not there is a necessity therefor. If such necessity exists, the infant may be bound. * * * If there is no necessity for services, there can be no recovery" for the services. [Citation.]

The Supreme Court of Appeals of West Virginia recently addressed this issue in a paternity action against the estate of an infant's father, brought by the infant's mother on the infant's behalf. [Citation.] The court held that contracts for legal services by infants should be regarded as contracts for necessaries in some instances because "if minors are not required to pay for legal representation, they will not be able to protect their various interests." [Citation.]

Other states have also broadened the definition of "necessaries" to include contracts for legal services for the protection of an infant's property rights. * * *

In determining whether the doctrine of necessaries may be applied to defeat an attempt to avoid or disaffirm a contract on the grounds of infancy, the trial court must first determine as a matter of law if the class of "things supplied" falls within the "general classes of necessaries." We hold that a contract for legal services falls within this class. However, the inquiry does not end with this determination. The ultimate determination is an issue of fact. The trier of fact must conclude that "under all the circumstances, the things furnished were actually necessary to the position and condition of the infant * * * and whether the infant was already sufficiently supplied." [Citation.] If the contract does not fall within the "general classes of necessaries," the trial court must, as a matter of law, sustain the plea of infancy and permit the avoidance of the contract. Similarly, if the contract does fall within the "general classes of necessaries," but upon consideration of all of the circumstances, the trier of fact determines that the provision of the particular services or things was not actually necessary, the plea of infancy must be sustained. Where there is a successful avoidance of the contract, the trial court may not circumvent the successful plea of infancy by affording a recovery to the claimant on the theory of *quantum meruit*. However, if the plea of infancy is not sustained, the claimant is not entitled to enforcement of the express contract. Rather, as we have previously held, "even in contracts for necessaries, the infant is not bound on the express contract but on the implied contract to pay what they are reasonably worth." [Citation.]

* * *

Upon review of the record, we hold that the * * * reason stated by the trial court for holding that the necessaries doctrine did not apply, namely that the contract "was conducted while he was in his minority and he's not bound by that," is an error of law. We hold that a contract for legal services is within the "general classes of necessaries" that may defeat a plea of infancy. * * *

* * *

The trial court's determination that the necessaries doctrine did not apply was made upon motion for summary judgment filed by Jonathan. Nowhere in Jonathan's motion for summary judgment is the issue raised that the services were unnecessary at the time rendered * * *. Although Jonathan argues that the services were not necessary at all because he alleges that the Florida litigation resolved the question of his inclusion as a beneficiary under the will of Hylton Sr., the timing of the services was not even mentioned as an issue, much less as a reason for granting summary judgment. * * *

Because the trial court erred in its determination, on this record, on summary judgment, that the doctrine of necessaries did not apply, we will reverse the judgment of the trial court and remand for further proceedings, including the taking of evidence on the issue of the factual determination of necessity "under all of the circumstances." Consistent with this opinion, should the trial court upon remand hold that the doctrine of necessaries does not apply because the evidence adduced does not support the claim, the contract is avoided and no award shall be made.

Should the trial court upon remand hold that the evidence is sufficient to defeat Jonathan's plea of infancy, the trial court shall receive evidence of the reasonable value of the services rendered. * * *

INTERPRETATION Contractual incapacity does not excuse a minor from an obligation to pay a reasonable value for a necessary.

CRITICAL THINKING QUESTION What factors should a court use in determining whether goods or services are necessary? Explain.

Ordinarily, luxury items, such as cameras, tape recorders, stereo equipment, television sets, and motorboats, do not qualify as necessaries. The question concerning whether automobiles and trucks are necessaries has caused considerable controversy, but some courts have recognized that under certain circumstances, an automobile may be a necessary where it is used by the minor for his business activities.

LIABILITY FOR MISREPRESENTATION OF AGE

The states do not agree whether a minor who fraudulently misrepresents her age when entering into a contract has the power to disaffirm. Suppose a contracting minor says that she is eighteen years of age (or twenty-one, if that is the year of attaining majority) and actually looks that old or even older. By the prevailing view in this country, despite her misrepresentation, the minor may nevertheless disaffirm the contract. Some states, however, prohibit disaffirmance if a minor misrepresented her age to an adult who, in good faith, reasonably relied on the misrepresentation. As shown in the following case, other states not following the majority rule either (a) require the minor to restore the other party to the position he occupied before making the contract or (b) allow the defrauded party to recover damages against the minor in tort.

Keser v. Chagnon

Supreme Court of Colorado, 1966

159 Colo. 209, 410 P.2d 637

FACTS On June 11, 1964, Chagnon bought a 1959 Edsel **(http://www.edsel.com)** from Keser for $995. Chagnon, who was then a twenty-year-old minor, obtained the contract by falsely advising Keser that he was over twenty-one years old, the age of majority. On September 25, 1964, two months and four days after his twenty-first birthday, Chagnon disaffirmed the contract and, ten days later, returned the Edsel to Keser. He then brought suit to recover the money he had paid for the automobile. Keser counterclaimed that he suffered damages as the direct result of Chagnon's false representation of his age. A trial was had to the court, sitting without a jury, all of which culminated in a judgment in favor of Chagnon against Keser in the sum of $655.78. This particular sum was arrived at by the trial court in the following manner: the trial court found that Chagnon initially purchased the Edsel for the sum of $995 and that he was entitled to the return of his $995; and then, by way of setoff, the trial court subtracted from the $995 the sum of $339.22, apparently representing the difference between the purchase price paid for the vehicle and the reasonable value of the Edsel on October 5, 1964, the date when the Edsel was returned to Keser.

DECISION Judgment affirmed except as to the calculation of damages for misrepresentation.

OPINION McWilliams, J. Before considering each of these several matters, it is deemed helpful to allude briefly to some of the general principles pertaining to the long-standing policy of the law to protect a minor from at least some of his childish foibles by affording him the right, under certain circumstances, to avoid his contract, not only during his minority but also within a reasonable time after reaching his majority. In [citation] we held that when a minor elects to disaffirm and avoid his contract, the "contract" becomes invalid ab initio and that the parties thereto then revert to the same position as if the contract had never been made. In that case we went on to declare that when a minor thus sought to avoid his contract and had in his possession the specific property received by him in the transaction, he was in such circumstance required to return the same as a prerequisite to any avoidance.

In [citation] it is said that a minor failing to disaffirm within a "reasonable time" after reaching his majority loses the right to do so and that just what constitutes a "reasonable time" is ordinarily a question of fact. As regards the necessity for restoration of consideration, in [citation] it is stated that the minor after disaffirming is "usually required * * * to return the consideration, if he can, or the part remaining in his possession or control."

* * *

Keser's * * * contention that Chagnon upon attaining his majority ratified the contract by his failure to disaffirm within a reasonable time after becoming twenty-one and by his retention and use of the Edsel prior to its return to the seller is equally untenable. In this connection it is pointed out that Chagnon did not notify Keser of his desire to disaffirm until 66 days after he became twenty-one and that he did not return the Edsel until 10 days after his notice to disaffirm, during all of which time Chagnon had the possession and use of the vehicle in question. As already noted, when an infant attains his majority he has a reasonable time within which he may thereafter disaffirm a contract entered into during his minority. And this rule is not as strict where, as here, we are dealing with an executed contract. There is no hard and fast rule as to just what constitutes a "reasonable" time within which the infant may disaffirm. * * * Suffice it to say, that under the circumstances disclosed by the record we are not prepared to hold that as a matter of law Chagnon ratified the contract either by his actions or by his alleged failure to disaffirm within a reasonable time after reaching his majority. * * *

Finally, error is predicated upon the trial court's finding in connection with Keser's setoff for the damage occasioned him by Chagnon's admitted false representation of his age. In this regard the trial court apparently found that the reasonable value of the Edsel when it was returned to Keser by Chagnon was $655.78, and accordingly went on to allow Keser a setoff in the amount of $339.22, this latter sum representing the difference between the purchase price, $995, and the value of the vehicle on the date it was returned. Finding, then, that Chagnon was entitled to the return of the $995 which he had theretofore paid Keser for the Edsel, the trial court then subtracted therefrom Keser's setoff in the amount of $339.22, and accordingly entered judgment for Chagnon against Keser in the sum of $655.78. Whether it was by accident or design we know not, but $655.78 is apparently the exact amount which Chagnon "owed" the Public Finance Corporation on his note with that company.

INTERPRETATION States vary on the rights of a minor and a defrauded party when a minor fraudulently misrepresents her age when entering into a contract.

ETHICAL QUESTION If a minor misrepresents his age, should he forfeit the right to avoid the contract? Explain.

CRITICAL THINKING QUESTION What rule would you apply in this case? Explain.

Practical Advice

In all significant contracts, if you have doubts about the age of your customers, have them prove that they are of legal age.

LIABILITY FOR TORT CONNECTED WITH CONTRACT

It is well settled that minors are generally liable for their torts. There is, however, a legal doctrine that if a tort and a contract are so "interwoven" that the court must enforce the contract to enforce the tort action, the minor is not liable in tort. Thus, a minor who rents an automobile from an adult enters into a contractual relationship obliging him to exercise reasonable care to protect the property from injury. By negligently damaging the automobile, he breaches that contractual undertaking. But his contractual immunity protects him from an action by the adult based on the contract. By the majority view, the adult cannot successfully sue the minor for damages on a tort theory. For, it is reasoned, a tort recovery would, in effect, be an enforcement of the contract and would defeat the protection that contract law gives the minor. Should the minor depart, however, from the terms of the agreement (by using a rental automobile for an unauthorized purpose, for example) and in so doing negligently cause damage to the automobile, most courts would hold that the tort is independent and that the adult can collect from the minor.

CPA INCOMPETENT PERSONS

In this section, we will discuss the contract status of incompetent persons who are under court-appointed guardianship and those who are not adjudicated incompetents.

PERSON UNDER GUARDIANSHIP

If a person is under **guardianship** by ***court order***, her contracts are ***void*** and of no legal effect. A court appoints a *guardian*, generally under the terms of a statute, to control and preserve the property of a person (the *ward* or ***adjudicated incompetent***) whose impaired capacity prevents her from managing her own property. Nonetheless, a party dealing with an individual under guardianship may be able to recover the fair value of any necessaries provided to the incompetent. Moreover, the contracts of the ward may be ratified by her guardian during the period of guardianship or by the ward on termination of the guardianship.

Ethical Dilemma

Should a Merchant Sell to One Who Lacks Capacity?

FACTS Alice Richards is a salesclerk for an exclusive department store in Connecticut. She was working in the children's clothing department when an elderly woman, Carrie Johnson, entered the area and began to browse. Because part of her compensation is based on commissions and it had been a slow season, Richards was eager to help her. However, when Richards asked Johnson if she needed any help, Johnson replied, "No, I'm just looking for a new pocketbook." When Richards attempted to direct Johnson to the pocketbooks, Johnson did not appear to respond. Puzzled, Richards began to wonder whether the woman was mentally alert.

Johnson picked out infants clothing and accessories worth approximately $250. At the cashier's counter she exclaimed how lovely everything was and explained that the jumpers and bath toys would go well with the other new clothes she had purchased for her son, who would soon be back from a cruise in the Bahamas.

Worried that the woman did not know what she was purchasing, Richards asked her manager for assistance. The manager said that the sale should be completed, as long as the store's credit policies were satisfied.

Social, Policy, and Ethical Considerations

1. What would you do?
2. What responsibility does a retail store have in stopping a sale where a reasonable person would assume that the customer lacks capacity? What business policies are appropriate?
3. What are the dangers in assuming a protective position? How can a retailer avoid discrimination and extend appropriate protection?
4. What alternatives does a family have when an elderly member begins to lose capacity?

Mental Illness or Defect

Because a contract is a consensual transaction, the parties to a valid contract must have a certain level of mental capacity. If a person lacks such capacity, or is **mentally incompetent**, the agreement is ***voidable***.

Under the traditional cognitive ability test, a person is mentally incompetent if he is unable to comprehend the subject of the contract, its nature, and its probable consequences. Though he need not be proved permanently incompetent to avoid the contract, his mental defect must be something more than a weakness of intellect or a lack of average intelligence. In short, a person is competent unless he is unable to understand the nature and effect of his actions, in which case he may disaffirm the contract even if the other party did not know or had no reason to know of the incompetent's mental condition.

A second type of mental incompetence recognized by the Restatement and some states is a mental condition that impairs a person's ability to act in a reasonable manner. In other words, the person understands what he is doing but cannot control his behavior in order to act in a reasonable and rational way. If the contract he enters is entirely executory or grossly unfair, it is voidable. If, however, the contract is executed and fair and the competent party had no reason to suspect the incompetency of the other, the incompetent must restore the competent party to the *status quo* by returning the consideration he has received or its equivalent in money. If restoration to the *status quo* is impossible, avoidance will depend upon the equities of the situation.

Like minors and persons under guardianship, an incompetent person is liable on the principle of quasi-contract for *necessaries* furnished him, the amount of recovery being the reasonable value of the goods or services. Moreover, an incompetent person may *ratify* or *disaffirm* voidable contracts during a lucid period or when he becomes competent.

CPA Intoxicated Persons

A person may *avoid* any contract that he enters into if the other party has reason to know that the person, because of his intoxication, is unable to understand the nature and consequences of his actions or unable to act in a reasonable manner. Such contracts, as in the case that follows, are ***voidable***, although they may be ratified when the intoxicated person regains his capacity. Slight intoxication will not destroy one's contractual capacity; on the other hand, to make a contract voidable, a person need not be so drunk that he is totally without reason or understanding.

The effect that the courts allow intoxication to have on contractual capacity is similar to the effect they allow contracts that are voidable because of incompetency, although the courts are even more strict with intoxication due to its voluntary nature. Most courts, therefore, require that, to avoid a contract, the intoxicated person on regaining his capacity must act promptly to disaffirm and generally must offer to restore the consideration he has received. Individuals who are taking prescribed medication or who are involuntarily intoxicated are treated the same as those who are incompetent under the cognitive ability test. As with incompetent persons, intoxicated persons are liable in quasi-contract for necessaries furnished during their incapacity.

First State Bank of Sinai v. Hyland

Supreme Court of South Dakota, 1987
399 N.W.2d 894

FACTS Randy Hyland, unable to pay two promissory notes due September 19, 1981, negotiated with The First State Bank of Sinai (Bank) **(http://www.siteit.com/sinaibank/)** for an extension. The Bank agreed on the condition that Randy's father, Mervin, act as cosigner. Mervin, a good customer of the Bank, had executed and paid on time over sixty promissory notes within a seven-year period. Accordingly, the Bank drafted a new promissory note with an April 20, 1982, due date, which Randy took home for Mervin to sign. On April 20, 1982, the new note was unpaid. Randy, on May 5, 1982, brought the Bank a check signed by Mervin to cover the interest owed on the unpaid note and asked for another extension. The Bank agreed to a second extension, again on the condition that Mervin act as cosigner. Mervin, however, refused to sign the last note; and Randy subsequently declared bankruptcy. The Bank sued Mervin on December 19, 1982. Mervin responded that he was not liable since he had been incapacitated by liquor at the time he signed the note. He had been drinking heavily throughout this period, and in fact had been involuntarily committed to an alcoholism treatment hospital twice during the time of these events. In between commitments, however, Mervin had executed and paid his own promissory note with the Bank and had transacted business in connection with his farm. The trial court held that Mervin's contract as cosigner was void due to alcohol-related incapacity, and the Bank appealed.

DECISION Judgment for the Bank.

OPINION Henderson, J. Historically, the void contract concept has been applied to nullify agreements made by mental incompetents who have contracted * * * after a judicial determination of incapacity had been entered. [Citations.] * * *

Mervin had numerous and prolonged problems stemming from his inability to handle alcohol. However, he was not judicially declared incompetent during the note's signing.

* * *

Contractual obligations incurred by intoxicated persons may be voidable. [Citation.] Voidable contracts (contracts other than those entered into following a judicial determination of incapacity) * * * may be rescinded by the previously disabled party. [Citation.] However, disaffirmance must be prompt, upon the recovery of the intoxicated party's mental abilities, and upon his notice of the agreement, if he had forgotten it. [Citation.] * * *

A voidable contract may also be ratified by the party who had contracted while disabled. Upon ratification, the contract becomes a fully valid legal obligation. [Citation.] Ratification can either be express or implied by conduct. [Citations.] In addition, failure of a party to disaffirm a contract over a period of time may, by itself, ripen into a ratification, especially if rescission will result in prejudice to the other party. [Citations.]

Mervin received both verbal notice from Randy and written notice from Bank on or about April 27, 1982, that the note was overdue. On May 5, 1982, Mervin paid the interest owing with a check which Randy delivered to Bank. This by itself could amount to ratification through conduct. If Mervin wished to avoid the contract, he should have then exercised his right of rescission. We find it impossible to believe that Mervin paid almost $900 in interest without, in his own mind, accepting responsibility for the note. His assertion that paying interest on the note relieved his obligation is equally untenable in light of his numerous past experiences with promissory notes.

* * *

We conclude that Mervin's obligation to Bank was not void. * * * Mervin's obligation on the note was voidable and his subsequent failure to disaffirm (lack of rescission) and his payment of interest (ratification) then transformed the voidable contract into one that is fully binding upon him.

Figure 14-1
Incapacity: Minors, Nonadjudicated Incompetents, and Intoxicated Persons

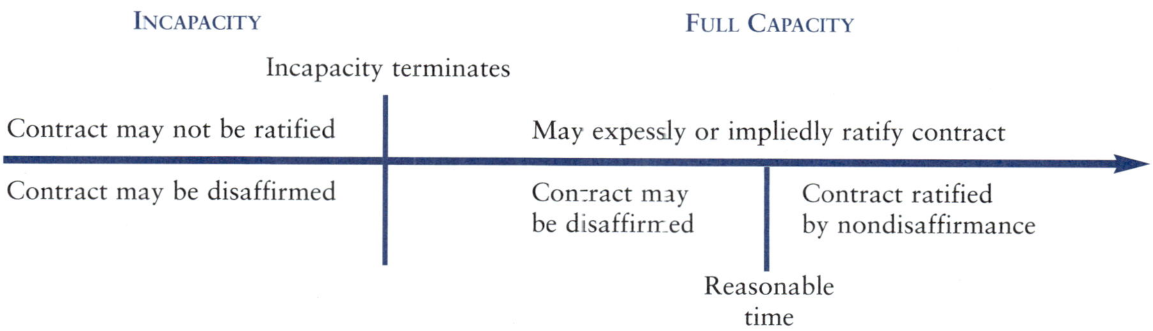

INTERPRETATION An intoxicated party ratifies a contract by not disaffirming it when she is not intoxicated and learns of its existence and by making interest payments on it when she is not intoxicated.

CRITICAL THINKING QUESTION When should a person be allowed to invalidate an agreement because of intoxication? Explain.

Practical Advice

If you have doubts about the capacity of the other party to a contract, have an individual with full legal capacity cosign the contract.

Figure 14-1 summarizes the voidability of contracts made by persons with contractual incapacity.

THE LAW AND YOU

State Bar Associations

Arizona: http://www.azbar.org/PublicResources/pubinfo.asp ("A Guide to Guardianships and Conservatorships")

Colorado: http://www.cobar.org/ ("So Now You Are a Guardian"; "So Now You Are a Conservator")

Florida: http://www.flabar.org/newflabar/consumerservices/General/Consumer.Pam/ ("What Is Guardianship?"; "Legal Guide for New Adults")

Iowa: http://www.iowabar.org/pamphlet.nsf/$about!OpenAbout ("So Now You Are a Conservator, a Guardian"; "The Rights of Young People")

Maryland: http://www.msba.org/public/brochure.htm ("Appointing a Guardian")

Minnesota: http://www.mnbar.org/consumer.htm ("Coming of Age")

Missouri: http://www.mobar.org/pamphlet/broindex.htm (brochures on legal topics) ("Juveniles and the Law")

Ohio: http://www.ohiobar.org/conres/pamphlets ("Guardianships")

South Dakota: http://www.sdbar.org/public/Default.htm ("As You Turn 18")

Texas: http://www.texasbar.com/public/consumerinfo/helpfulinfo/elder/aging/guardianship.asp ("Guardianship")

CHAPTER SUMMARY

Minors

Definition person who is under the age of majority (usually 18 years)

Liability on Contracts minor's contracts are voidable at the minor's option
- *Disaffirmance* avoidance of the contract; may be done during minority and for a reasonable time after reaching majority
- *Ratification* affirmation of the entire contract; may be done upon reaching majority

Liability for Necessaries a minor is liable for the reasonable value of necessary items (those that reasonably supply a person's needs)

Liability for Misrepresentation of Age prevailing view is that a minor may disaffirm the contract

Liability for Tort Connected with Contract if a tort and a contract are so intertwined that to enforce the tort the court must enforce the contract, the minor is not liable in tort

Incompetent and Intoxicated Persons

Person Under Guardianship contracts made by a person placed under guardianship by court order are void

Mental Illness or Defect a contract entered into by a mentally incompetent person (one who is unable to understand the nature and consequences of his acts) is voidable

Intoxicated Persons a contract entered into by an intoxicated person (one who cannot understand the nature and consequence of her actions) is voidable

QUESTIONS

1. Mark, a minor, operates a one-man automobile repair shop. Rose, having heard of Mark's good work on other cars, takes her car to Mark's shop for a thorough engine overhaul. Mark, while overhauling Rose's engine, carelessly fits an unsuitable piston ring on one of the pistons, with the result that Rose's engine is seriously damaged. Mark offers to return the sum that Rose paid him for his work, but refuses to make good on the damage. Rose sues Mark in tort for the damage to her engine. Can Rose recover from Mark in tort for the damage to her engine? Why?

2. a. On March 20, Andy Small became seventeen years old, but he appeared to be at least eighteen (the age of majority). On April 1, he moved into a rooming house in Chicago and orally agreed to pay the landlady $300 a month for room and board, payable at the end of each month.

   b. On April 4, he went to Honest Hal's Carfeteria and signed a contract to buy a used car on credit with a small down payment. He made no representation as to his age, but Honest Hal represented the car to be in top condition, which it subsequently turned out not to be.

   c. On April 7, Andy sold and conveyed to Adam Smith a parcel of real estate that he owned. On April 30, Andy refused to pay his landlady for his room and board for the month of April; he returned the car to Honest Hal and demanded a refund of his down payment; and he demanded that Adam Smith reconvey the land, although the purchase price, which Andy received in cash, had been spent in riotous living. Decisions as to each claim?

3. Jones, a minor, owned a 2000 automobile. She traded it to Stone for a 2001 car. Jones went on a three-week trip and found that the 2001 car was not as good as the 2000 car. She asked Stone to return the 2000 car but was told that it had been sold to Tate, who did not know that the car had been obtained by Stone from a minor. Jones thereupon sued Tate for the return of the 2000 car. Is Jones entitled to regain ownership of the 2000 car? Explain.

4. On May 7, Roy, a minor, a resident of Smithton, purchased an automobile from Royal Motors, Inc., for $7,750 in cash. On the same day, he bought a motor scooter from Marks, also a minor, for $750 and paid him in full. On June 5, two days before attaining his majority, Roy disaffirmed the contracts and offered to return the car and the motor scooter to the respective sellers. Royal Motors and Marks each refused the offers. On June 16, Roy brought separate appropriate actions against Royal Motors and Marks to recover the purchase price of the car and the

motor scooter. By agreement on July 30, Royal Motors accepted the automobile. Royal then filed a counterclaim against Roy for the reasonable rental value of the car between June 5 and July 30. The car was not damaged during this period. Royal knew that Roy lived twenty-five miles from his place of employment in Smithton and that he would probably use the car, as he did, for transportation. What is the decision as to (a) Roy's action against Royal Motors, Inc. and its counterclaim against Roy; (b) Roy's action against Marks?

5. On October 1, George Jones, who was then a minor, entered into a contract with Johnson Motor Company, a dealer in automobiles, to buy a car for $7,600. He paid $1,100 down and agreed to make monthly payments thereafter of $325 each. Although he made the first payment on November 1, he failed to make any more payments. Though Jones was seventeen years old at the time he made the contract, he represented to the company that he was twenty-one years old because he was afraid the company would not sell the car to him if it knew his real age. His appearance was that of a man of twenty-one years of age. On December 15, the company repossessed the car under the terms provided in the contract. At that time, the car had been damaged and was in need of repairs. On December 20, George Jones became of age and at once disaffirmed the contract and demanded the return of the $1,425 paid on the contract. When the company refused to do so, Jones brought an action to recover the $1,425; and the company set up a counterclaim of $1,500 for expenses it incurred in repairing the car. Who will prevail? Why?

6. Rebecca entered into a written contract to sell certain real estate to Mary, a minor, for $80,000, payable $4,000 on the execution of the contract and $800 on the first day of each month thereafter until paid. Mary paid the $4,000 down payment and eight monthly installments before attaining her majority. Thereafter, Mary made two additional monthly payments and caused the contract to be recorded in the county where the real estate was located. Mary was then advised by her lawyer that the contract was voidable. After being so advised, Mary immediately tendered the contract to Rebecca, together with a deed reconveying all of Mary's interest in the property to Rebecca. Also, Mary demanded that Rebecca return the money paid under the contract. Rebecca refused the tender and declined to repay any portion of the money paid to her by Mary. Can Mary cancel the contract and recover the amount paid to Rebecca? Explain.

7. Anita sold and delivered an automobile to Marvin, a minor. Marvin, during his minority, returned the automobile to Anita, saying that he disaffirmed the sale. Anita accepted the automobile and said she would return the purchase price to Marvin the next day. Later in the day, Marvin changed his mind, took the automobile without Anita's knowledge, and sold it to Chris. Anita had not returned the purchase price when Marvin took the car. On what theory, if any, can Anita recover from Marvin? Explain.

8. Ira, who in 2000 had been found not guilty of a criminal offense because of insanity, was released from a hospital for the criminally insane during the summer of 2001 and since that time has been a reputable and well-respected citizen and businessperson. On February 1, 2002, Ira and Shirley entered into a contract in which Ira would sell his farm to Shirley for $100,000. Ira now seeks to void the contract. Shirley insists that Ira is fully competent and has no right to avoid the contract. Who will prevail? Why?

9. Daniel, while under the influence of alcohol to the extent that he did not know the nature and consequences of his acts, agreed to sell his 1995 automobile to Belinda for $8,000. The next morning when Belinda went to Daniel's house with the $8,000 in cash, Daniel stated that he did not remember the transaction but that "a deal is a deal." One week after completing the sale, Daniel decides that he wishes to avoid the contract. What is the result?

CASE PROBLEMS

10. Langstraat, age seventeen, owned a motorcycle that he insured against liability with Midwest Mutual Insurance Company. He signed a notice of rejection attached to the policy indicating that he did not desire to purchase uninsured motorists' coverage from the insurance company. Later he was involved in an accident with another motorcycle owned and operated by a party who was uninsured. Langstraat now seeks to recover from the insurance company, asserting that his rejection was not valid because he is a minor. Can Langstraat recover from Midwest? Explain.

11. G.A.S. married his wife, S.I.S., on January 19, 1957. He began to have mental health problems in 1970; that year, he was hospitalized at the Delaware State Hospital for eight weeks. Similar illnesses occurred in 1972 and in the early part of 1974, with G.A.S. suffering from symptoms such as paranoia and loss of a sense of reality. In early 1975, G.A.S. was still committed to the Delaware State Hospital, attending a regular job during the day and returning to the hospital at night. During this time, he entered into a separation agreement prepared by his wife's attorney. G.A.S., however, never spoke with the attorney about the contents of the agreement; nor did he read it prior to signing. Moreover, G.A.S. was not independently represented by counsel when he executed this agreement. Can G.A.S. disaffirm the separation agreement? Explain.

12. L. D. Robertson bought a pickup truck from King and Julian, who did business as the Julian Pontiac Company. At the time of purchase, Robertson was seventeen years old, living at home with his parents, and driving his father's truck around the county to different construction jobs.

According to the sales contract, he traded in a passenger car for the truck and was given $723 credit toward the truck's $1,743 purchase price, agreeing to pay the remainder in monthly installments. After he paid the first month's installment, the truck caught fire and was rendered useless. The insurance agent, upon finding that Robertson was a minor, refused to deal with him. Consequently, Robertson sued to exercise his right as a minor to rescind the contract and to recover the purchase price he had already paid ($723 credit for the car traded in plus the one month's installment). The defendants argue that Robertson, even as a minor, cannot rescind the contract because it was for a necessary item. Are they correct?

13. A fifteen-year-old minor was employed by Midway Toyota, Inc., of Great Falls, Montana. On August 18, 1975, the minor, while engaged in lifting heavy objects, injured his lower back. In October 1975 he underwent surgery to remove a herniated disk. Midway Toyota paid him the appropriate amount of temporary total disability payments ($53.36 per week) from August 18, 1975, through November 15, 1976. In February 1977 a final settlement was reached for 150 weeks of permanent partial disability benefits totaling $6,136.40. Tom Mazurek represented Midway Toyota in the negotiations leading up to the agreement and negotiated directly with the minor and his mother, Hermoine Parrent. The final settlement agreement was signed by the minor only. Mrs. Parrent was present at the time and did not object to the signing, but neither she nor anyone else of "legal guardian status" co-signed the agreement. The minor later sought to disaffirm the agreement and reopen his workers' compensation case. The workers' compensation court denied his petition, holding that Mrs. Parrent "participated fully in consideration of the offered final settlement and . . . ratified and approved it on behalf of her ward . . . to the same legal effect as if she had actually signed [it]. . . ." The minor appealed. Decision?

14. Rose, a minor, bought a new Buick Riviera from Sheehan Buick. Seven months later, while still a minor, he attempted to disaffirm the purchase. Sheehan Buick refused to accept the return of the car or to refund the purchase price. Rose, at the time of the purchase, gave all the appearance of being of legal age. The car had been used by him to carry on his school, business, and social activities. Can Rose successfully disaffirm the contract?

15. Haydocy Pontiac sold Jennifer Lee an automobile for $1,552, of which $1,402 was financed with a note and security agreement. At the time of the sale, Lee, age twenty, represented to Haydocy that she was twenty-one years old, the age of majority, and capable of contracting. After receiving the car, Lee allowed John Roberts to take possession of it. Roberts took the car and has not returned. Lee has failed to make any further payments on the car. Haydocy has sued to recover on the note, but Lee disaffirms the contract, claiming that she was too young to enter into a valid contract. Can Haydocy recover the money from Lee? Explain.

16. Carol White ordered a $225 pair of contact lenses through an optometrist. White, an emancipated minor, paid $100 by check and agreed to pay the remaining $125 at a later time. The doctor ordered the lenses, incurring a debt of $110. After the lenses were ordered, White called to cancel her order and stopped payment on the $100 check. The lenses could be used by no one but White. The doctor sued White for the value of the lenses. Will the doctor be able to recover the money from White? Explain.

17. Williamson, her mortgage in default, was threatened with foreclosure on her home. She decided to sell the house. The Matthewses learned of this and contacted her about the matter. Williamson claims that she offered to sell her equity for $17,000 and that the Matthewses agreed to pay off the mortgage. The Matthewses contend that the asking price was $1,700. On September 27, 1978, the parties signed a contract of sale, which stated the purchase price to be $1,800 ($100 increase to account for furniture in the house) plus the unpaid balance of the mortgage. The parties met again on October 10 to sign the deed. Later that day, Williamson, concerned that she had not received her full $17,000 consideration, contacted an attorney. Can Williamson set aside the sale based upon inadequate consideration and mental weakness due to intoxication?

18. Halbman, a minor, purchased a 1968 Oldsmobile from Lemke for $1,250. Under the terms of the contract, Halbman would pay $1,000 down and the balance in $25 weekly installments. Upon making the down payment, Halbman received possession of the car, but Lemke retained the title until the balance was paid. After Halbman had made his first four payments, a connecting rod in the car's engine broke. Lemke denied responsibility but offered to help Halbman repair the engine if Halbman would provide the parts. Halbman, however, placed the car in a garage where the repairs cost $637.40. Halbman never paid the repair bill.

Hoping to avoid any liability for the vehicle, Lemke transferred title to Halbman even though Halbman never paid the balance owed. Halbman returned the title with a letter disaffirming the contract and demanded return of the money paid. Lemke refused. As the repair bill remained unpaid, the garage removed the car's engine and transmission and towed the body to Halbman's father's house. Vandalism during the period of storage rendered the car unsalvageable. Several times Halbman requested Lemke to remove the car. Lemke refused. Halbman sued Lemke for the return of his consideration, and Lemke countersued for the amount still owed on the contract. Decision?

19. On April 29, 1991, Kirsten Fletcher and John E. Marshall III jointly signed a lease to rent an apartment for the term beginning on July 1, 1991, and ending on June 30, 1992, for a monthly rent of $525. At the time the lease was signed, Marshall was not yet eighteen years of age. Marshall turned eighteen on May 30, 1991. Two weeks later, the couple moved into the apartment. About two months later, Marshall moved out to attend college, but Fletcher

remained. She paid the rent herself for the remaining ten months of the lease and then sought contribution for Marshall's share of the rent plus court costs in the amount of $2,500. Can Fletcher collect from Marshall?

20. Rogers was a nineteen-year-old (the age of majority then being twenty-one) high school graduate pursuing a civil engineering degree when he learned that his wife was expecting a child. As a result, he quit school and sought assistance from Gastonia Personnel Corporation in finding a job. Rogers signed a contract with the employment agency providing that he would pay the agency a service charge if it obtained suitable employment for him. The employment agency found him such a job, but Rogers refused to pay the service charge, asserting that he was a minor when he signed the contract. Gastonia sued to recover the agreed-upon service charge from Rogers. Should Rogers be liable under his contract? If so, for how much?

http:// **Internet Exercise** Find and review information on (a) laws governing the employment of minors, (b) gifts to minors, and (c) Uniform Guardianship and Protective Proceedings Act.

Chapter 15

Contracts in Writing

To break an oral agreement which is not legally binding is morally wrong.

TALMUD

Learning Objectives

After reading this chapter you should be able to:

1. Identify and explain the five types of contracts covered by the general contract statute of frauds and the contracts covered by the Uniform Commercial Code (UCC) statute of frauds provision.
2. Describe the writings that are required to satisfy the general contract and the UCC statute of frauds provisions.
3. Identify and describe the other methods of complying with the general contract and the UCC statute of frauds provisions.
4. Explain the parol evidence rule and identify the situations to which the rule does not apply.
5. Discuss the rules that aid in the interpretation of a contract.

An *oral* contract, that is, one not in writing, is in every way as enforceable as a written contract *unless* otherwise provided by statute. Although most contracts do not need to be in writing to be enforceable, it is highly desirable that significant contracts be written. Written contracts avoid many problems that proving the terms of oral contracts inevitably involve. The process of setting down the contractual terms in a written document also tends to clarify the terms and bring to light problems the parties might not otherwise foresee. Moreover, the terms of a written contract do not change over time, whereas the parties' recollections of the terms might.

When the parties do reduce their agreement to a complete and final written expression, the law (under the parol evidence rule) honors this document by not allowing the parties to introduce any evidence in a lawsuit that would alter, modify, or vary the terms of the written contract. Nevertheless, the parties may differ as to the proper or intended meaning of language contained in the written agreement where such language is ambiguous or susceptible to different interpretations. To determine the proper meaning requires an interpretation, or construction, of the contract. The rules of construction permit the parties to introduce evidence to resolve ambiguity and to show the meaning of the language employed and the sense in which both parties used it.

In this chapter, we will examine (1) the types of contracts that must be in writing to be enforceable, (2) the parol evidence rule, and (3) the rules of contractual interpretation.

STATUTE OF FRAUDS

The **statute of frauds** requires that certain designated types of contracts be evidenced by a writing to be enforceable. Many more types of contracts are *not* subject to the statute of frauds than are subject to it. Most oral contracts, as previously indicated, are as enforceable and valid as written contracts. If, however, a given contract subject to the statute of frauds is said to be *within* the statute, to be enforceable it must comply with the requirements of the statute. All other types of contracts are said to be "not within" or "outside" the statute and need not comply with its requirements to be enforceable.

The statute of frauds has no relation whatever to any kind of fraud practiced in the making of contracts. The rules relating to such fraud are rules of common law and are discussed in Chapter 11. The purpose of the statute is to prevent fraud in the proof of certain oral contracts by perjured testimony in court. This purpose is accomplished by requiring certain contracts to be proved by a signed writing. On the other hand, the statute does not prevent the performance of oral contracts if the parties are willing to perform. In brief, the statute relates only to the proof or evidence of a contract. It has nothing to do with the circumstances surrounding the making of a contract or with the validity of a contract.

Practical Advice

Significant contracts should be memorialized in a writing signed by both parties.

CPA Contracts Within the Statute of Frauds

The following five kinds of contracts are within the statute of frauds as most states have adopted it. Compliance requires a writing signed by the party to be charged (the party against whom the contract is to be enforced).

1. Promises to answer for the duty of another
2. Promises of an executor or administrator to answer personally for a duty of the decedent whose funds he is administering
3. Agreements upon consideration of marriage
4. Agreements for the transfer of an interest in land
5. Agreements not to be performed within one year

A sixth type of contract within the original English statute of frauds applied to contracts for the sale of goods. The Uniform Commercial Code now governs the enforceability of contracts of this kind.

The various provisions of the statute of frauds apply independently. Accordingly, a contract for the sale of an interest in land may also be a contract in consideration of marriage, a contract not to be performed in one year, *and* a contract for the sale of goods.

In addition to those contracts specified in the original statute, most states require that other contracts be evidenced by a writing as well—for example, a contract to make a will, to authorize an agent to sell real estate, or to pay a commission to a real estate broker. Moreover, the UCC requires that contracts for the sale of securities, contracts creating certain types of security interests, and contracts for the sale of all other personal property for more than $5,000 be in writing.

Suretyship Provision

The **suretyship** provision applies to a contractual promise by a **surety** (*promisor*) to a **creditor** (*promisee*) to perform the duties or obligations of a third person (**principal debtor**) if the principal debtor does not perform. Thus, if a mother tells a merchant to extend $1,000 worth of credit to her son and says, "If he doesn't pay, I will," the promise is a suretyship and must be evidenced by a writing to be enforceable. The factual situation can be reduced to the simple idea that "If X doesn't pay, I will." The promise is said to be a **collateral promise**, in that the promisor is not primarily liable. The mother does not promise to pay in any event; her promise is to pay only if the one primarily obligated, the son, defaults.

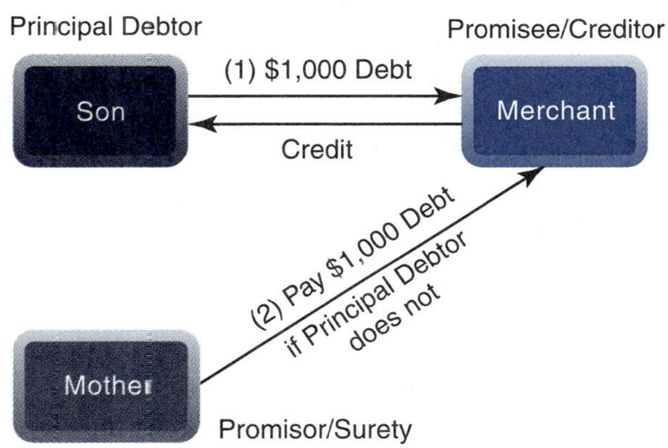

Thus, a suretyship involves three parties and two contracts. The primary contract, between the principal debtor and the creditor, creates the indebtedness. The collateral contract is made by the third person (surety) directly with the creditor, whereby the surety promises to pay the debt to the creditor in case the principal debtor fails to do so. For a complete discussion of suretyship, see Chapter 38.

Original Promise If the promisor makes an **original promise** by undertaking to become primarily liable, then the statute of frauds does not apply. For example, a father tells a merchant to deliver certain items to his daughter and says, "I will pay $400 for them." The father is not promising to answer for the debt of another; rather, he is making the debt his own. It is to the father, and to the father alone, that the merchant extends credit; to the father alone the creditor may look for payment. The statute of frauds does not apply, and the promise may be oral.

The following case further illustrates the distinction between suretyship and original promise.

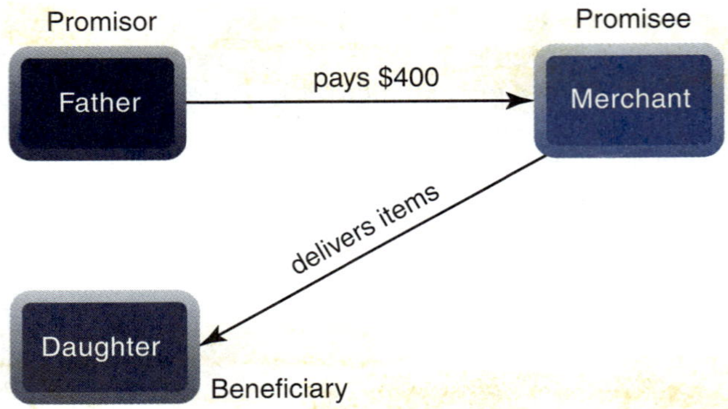

Carter v. Allstate Insurance Company

Court of Appeals of Texas, Houston (1st. Dist.), 1998
962 S.W.2d 268

FACTS Plaintiffs/appellants, Jesse Carter and Jesse Thomas, had an auto accident with Allstate's insured. Plaintiffs hired attorney Joseph Onwuteaka to represent them. On April 11, 1994, Mr. Onwuteaka sent a demand letter for settlement of plaintiffs' claims to Allstate's adjustor, Ms. Gracie Weatherly. Mr. Onwuteaka claims Ms. Weatherly made, and he orally accepted, settlement terms on behalf of the plaintiffs. When Allstate **(http://www.allstate.com/Home/Home.asp)** did not honor the agreements, plaintiffs filed this suit for breach of contract.

Allstate filed for summary judgment based on the statute of frauds. The trial court granted defendant's request for summary judgment without stating a particular basis. The plaintiffs/appellants appeal this judgment.

DECISION Judgment reversed and remanded.

OPINION Taft, J. [T]he appellants contend the alleged oral agreement is not governed by the Statute of Frauds. Allstate claims the Statute of Frauds is applicable to the alleged agreement as "a promise by another person to answer for the debt, default, or miscarriage of another person." [Citation.] This provision of the Statute of Frauds is commonly referred to as the "suretyship provision." [Citation.]

One test for determining whether a promise to pay the debt of another is within or without the Statute of Frauds is whether the promisor is a surety, only secondarily liable, or has accepted primary responsibility for the debt. [Citations.] If the party is primarily liable, its promise to pay a debt is not required to be in writing by the Statute of Frauds [Citation.] However, if the party is a surety, the promise to pay the debt of a third party is required to be in writing. [Citation.]

If Allstate were merely a surety, its obligation would have been to pay its insured's debt upon default by its insured. However, as an insurer, Allstate contracted with its insured to assume responsibility for the liability of its insured, at least to the limits of the insurance policy. By Allstate's oral promise to settle, it was settling not only its insured's potential liability but its own possible obligation to pay and its own duty to defend its insured. The oral promise to settle was an original undertaking, not a promise to answer for the debt of the insured. Therefore, the suretyship provision of the Statute of Frauds does not apply to Allstate's promise to settle. [Citation.]

INTERPRETATION If the promisor makes an original promise to become primarily liable, then the statute of frauds does not apply.

CRITICAL THINKING QUESTION Should the contracts of a surety have to be in writing? Explain

Main Purpose Doctrine The courts have developed an exception to the suretyship provision called the "main purpose doctrine" or "leading object rule." Where the **main purpose** of the promisor is to obtain an economic benefit for herself that she did not previously have, then the promise comes within the exception and is *outside* the statute. The expected benefit to the surety "must be such as to justify the conclusion that his main purpose in making the promise is to advance his own interest." The fact that the surety received consideration for his promise or that he might receive a slight and indirect advantage is insufficient to bring the promise within the main purpose doctrine.

> **Practical Advice**
>
> When entering into a contract with two parties promising you that they will perform, make them both original promisors and avoid having a surety. In any event, if the contract is for a significant amount of money, have both parties sign a written agreement.

Suppose that a supply company has refused to furnish materials on the credit of a building contractor. Faced with a possible slowdown in the construction of his building, the owner of the land promises the supplier that if the supplier will extend credit to the contractor, the owner will pay if the contractor does not. Here, the purpose of the promisor was to serve an economic interest of his own, even though the performance of the promise would discharge the duty of another. The intent to benefit the contractor was at most incidental, and courts will enforce oral promises of this type.

Promise Made to Debtor The suretyship provision has been interpreted *not* to include promises made to a *debtor*. For example, D owes a debt to C. S promises D to pay D's debt. Because the promise of S was made to the debtor (D), not the creditor, the promise is enforceable even if it is oral.

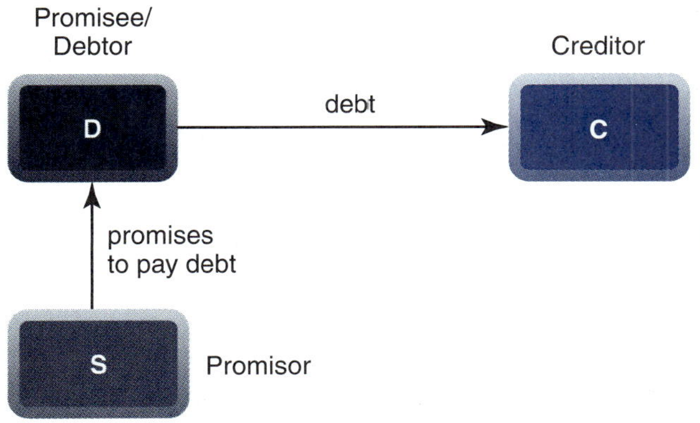

EXECUTOR-ADMINISTRATOR PROVISION

The executor-administrator provision applies to the promises of an executor of a decedent's will, or to those of the administrator of the estate if there is no will, to answer personally for a duty of the decedent. An **executor** or **administrator** is a person appointed by a court to carry out, subject to order of court, the administration of the estate of a deceased person. If the will of a decedent nominates a certain person as executor, the court usually appoints that person. (For a more detailed discussion of executors, administrators, and the differences between the two, see Chapter 52.) If an executor or administrator promises to answer personally for a duty of the decedent, the promise is unenforceable unless it is in writing. For example, Edgar, who is Donna's son and executor of Donna's will, recognizes that Donna's estate will not have enough funds to pay all of the decedent's debts. He orally promises Clark, one of Donna's creditors, that he will personally pay all of his mother's debts in full. Edgar's oral promise is not enforceable. This provision does not apply, however, to promises to pay debts of the deceased out of assets of the estate.

The executor-administrator provision is thus a specific application of the suretyship provision. Accordingly, the exceptions to the suretyship provision also apply to this provision.

MARRIAGE PROVISION

The notable feature of the marriage provision is that it does not apply to mutual promises to marry. Rather, the provision applies only if a promise to marry is made in consideration for some promise other than a mutual promise to marry. Therefore, this provision covers Adams's promise to convey title to a certain farm to Barnes if Barnes accepts Adams's proposal of marriage.

LAND CONTRACT PROVISION

The land contract provision covers promises to transfer any **interest in land**, which includes any right, privilege, power, or immunity in real property. Thus, all promises to transfer, buy, or pay for an interest in land, including ownership interests, leases, mortgages, options, and easements, are within the provision.

The land contract provision does not include contracts to transfer an interest in personal property. It also does not cover short-term leases, which by statute in most states are those for one year or less; contracts to build a building on a piece of land; contracts to do work on the land; or contracts to insure a building.

An oral contract for the transfer of an interest in land may be enforced if the party seeking enforcement has so changed his position in reasonable reliance on the contract that a court can prevent injustice only by enforcing the contract. In applying this ***part performance*** exception, many states require the transferee to have paid a portion or all of the purchase price *and* either to have taken possession of the real estate or to have started to make valuable improvements on the land. Payment of part or all of the price is not sufficient in itself to make the contract enforceable under this exception. For example, Jane orally agrees to sell land to Jack for $30,000. With Jane's consent, Jack takes possession of the land, pays Jane $10,000, builds a house on the land, and occupies it. Several years later, Jane repudiates the contract. The courts will enforce the contract against Jane.

An oral promise by a purchaser is also enforceable if the seller fully performs by conveying the property to the purchaser.

ONE-YEAR PROVISION

The statute of frauds requires that all contracts that ***cannot*** be fully performed within one year of the making of the contract be in writing.

The Possibility Test To determine whether a contract falls within the one-year provision, the courts ask whether it is *possible* for the performance of the contract to be completed within a year. Under the majority rule, the **possibility test** does not ask whether the agreement is likely to be performed within one year from the date it was formed; nor does it ask whether the parties think that performance will occur within the year. The enforceability of the contract depends *not* on probabilities or on actual subsequent events but on whether the terms of the contract make it possible for performance to occur within one year. For example, an oral contract between Alice and Bill for Alice to build a bridge, which should reasonably take three years, is generally enforceable if it is possible, although extremely unlikely and difficult, for Alice to perform the contract in one year. Similarly, if Alice agrees to employ Bill for life, this contract is also not within the statute of frauds. It is possible that Bill may die within the year, in which case the contract would be completely performed. The contract is therefore one that is *fully performable* within a year. Contracts of indefinite duration are likewise excluded from the provision. On the other hand, an oral contract to employ another person for thirteen months could not possibly be performed within a year and is therefore unenforceable.

Iacono v. Lyons
Court of Appeals of Texas, 2000
16 S.W.3d 92

FACTS The plaintiff, Mary Iacono, and the defendant, Carolyn Lyons, had been friends for almost 35 years. In late 1996, the defendant invited the plaintiff to join her on a trip to Las Vegas, Nevada, for which the defendant paid. The plaintiff contended she was invited to Las Vegas by the defendant because the defendant thought the plaintiff was lucky. Sometime before the trip, the plaintiff had a dream about winning on a Las Vegas slot machine. The plaintiff's dream convinced her to go to Las Vegas, and she accepted the defendant's offer to split "50–50" any gambling winnings. The defendant provided the plaintiff with money for the gambling.

The plaintiff and defendant started to gamble but after losing $47, the defendant wanted to leave to see a show. The plaintiff begged the defendant to stay, and the defendant agreed on the condition that the defendant put the coins into the machines because doing so took the plaintiff, who suffers from advanced rheumatoid arthritis and was in a wheelchair, too long. The plaintiff agreed and took the defendant to a dollar slot machine that looked like the machine in her dream. The machine did not pay on the first try. The plaintiff then said, "Just one more time," and the defendant looked at the plaintiff and said, "This one's for you, Puddin." They hit the jackpot, and the slot machine paid $1,908,064. The defendant refused to share the winnings with the plaintiff and denied they had an agreement to split any winnings. The defendant told Caesar's Palace that she was the sole winner and to pay her all the winnings.

The plaintiff sued the defendant for breach of contract. The defendant moved for summary judgment on the grounds that any oral agreement was unenforceable under the statute of frauds. The trial court entered summary judgment in favor of the defendant. The plaintiff appeals.

DECISION Summary judgment reversed and remanded.

OPINION O'Connor, J. The defendant asserted the agreement, if any, was unenforceable under the statute of frauds because it could not be performed within one year. There is no dispute that the winnings were to be paid over a period of 20 years.

* * *

[The one year provision of the statute of frauds] does not apply if the contract, from its terms, could possibly be performed within a year—however improbable performance within one year may be. [Citations.]

To determine the applicability of the statute of frauds with indefinite contracts, this Court may use any reasonably clear method of ascertaining the intended length of performance. [Citation.] The method is used to determine the parties' intentions at the time of contracting. [Citation.] The fact that the entire performance within one year is not required, or expected, will not bring an agreement within the statute. [Citations.]

Assuming without deciding that the parties agreed to share their gambling winnings, such an agreement possibly could have been performed within one year. For example, if the plaintiff and defendant had won $200, they probably would have received all the money in one pay-out and could have split the winnings immediately.* * *

Therefore, the defendant was not entitled to summary judgment based on her affirmative defense of the statute of frauds.

INTERPRETATION If a contract is possible to perform fully within one year, it does not fall within the statute of frauds.

ETHICAL QUESTION Is this result fair? Explain.

CRITICAL THINKING QUESTION Do you agree with the one-year provision? Explain.

Computation of Time The year runs from the time the *agreement is made*, not from the time when the performance is to begin. For example, on January 1, 2003, A hires B to work for eleven months starting on May 1, 2003, under the terms of an oral contract. That contract will be fully performed on March 31, 2004, which is more than one year after January 1, 2003, the date the contract was made. Consequently, the contract is *within* the statute of frauds and unenforceable because it is oral.

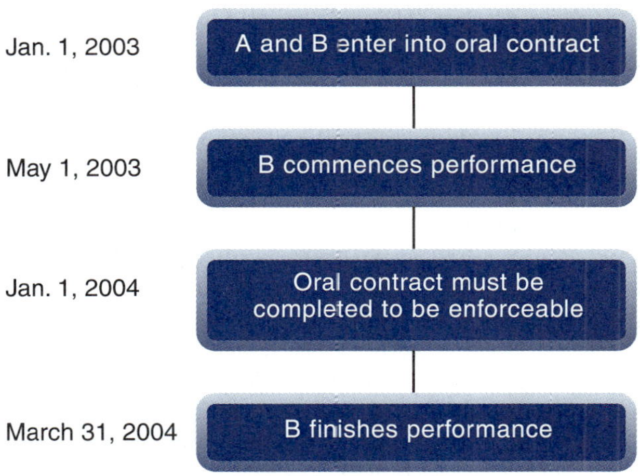

Similarly, a contract for a year's performance that is to begin three days after the date of the making of the contract is within the statute and, if oral, is unenforceable. If, however, the performance is to begin the day following the making or, under the terms of the agreement, *could* have begun the following day, it is not within the statute and need not be in writing.

Full Performance by One Party Where a contract has been fully performed by one party, most courts hold that the promise of the other party is enforceable even though by its terms its performance was not possible within one year. For example, Jane borrows $4,800 from Tom. Jane orally promises to pay Tom $4,800 in three annual installments of $1,600. Jane's promise is enforceable, despite the one-year provision, because Tom has fully performed by making the loan.

SALES OF GOODS

The English statute of frauds, which applied to contracts for the sale of goods, has been used as a prototype for the UCC, Article 2, statute of frauds provision. The UCC provides that a contract for the sale of goods for the price of ***$500 or more*** is not enforceable unless there is some writing sufficient to indicate that a contract for sale has been made between the parties. The Code defines *goods* as movable personal property.

Admission The Code permits an oral contract for the sale of goods to be enforced against a party who, in his pleading, testimony, or otherwise, admits in court that a contract was made; but the Code limits enforcement to the quantity of goods he admits. Moreover, some courts hold that, by performing over a period of time, for example, a party may implicitly admit the existence of a contract. Some courts now apply this exception to other statute of frauds provisions.

Specially Manufactured Goods The Code permits enforcement of an oral contract for goods specially manufactured for a buyer, but only if evidence indicates that the goods were made for the buyer and the seller can show that he has made a *substantial beginning* of their manufacture before receiving any notice of repudiation. If the goods, although manufactured on special order, may be readily resold in the ordinary course of the seller's business, this exception does not apply.

Kalas v. Cook

Appellate Court of Connecticut, 2002
70 Conn.App. 477, 800 A.2d 553, 47 U.C.C. Rep.Serv.2d 1307

FACTS The plaintiff, Barbara H. Kalas, doing business as Clinton Press of Tolland, operated a printing press and, for several decades, provided written materials, including books and pamphlets, for Adelma G. Simmons. Simmons ordered these materials for use and sale at her farm, known as Caprilands Herb Farm (Caprilands). The defendant has not suggested that these materials could have been sold on the open market. Due to limited space at Caprilands, the plaintiff and Simmons agreed that the written materials would remain stored at the plaintiff's print shop until Simmons decided that delivery was necessary. The materials were delivered either routinely or upon request by Simmons and were paid for according to the invoice from Kalas.

In early 1997, the plaintiff decided to close her business. The plaintiff and Simmons agreed that the materials printed for Caprilands and stored at the plaintiff's print shop would be delivered and paid for upon delivery. On December 3, 1997, Simmons died. The plaintiff submitted a claim against the estate for $24,599.38 for unpaid deliveries to Caprilands. (The defendant, Edward W. Cook, is the executor of the estate of Simmons). The defendant denied these allegations and interposed a defense under the statute of frauds.

The trial court held that the transaction between the plaintiff and the deceased was a sale of goods as that term is defined in § 2–105. Furthermore, the trial ruled that as a contract for the sale of goods, its enforcement was not precluded by the UCC statute of frauds provision. Accordingly, the court rendered a judgment in favor of the plaintiff in the amount of $24,599.38. The defendant appealed.

DECISION Judgment affirmed.

OPINION Peters, J. On appeal, the defendant argues that the oral contract was invalid * * * because a writing was required by § 2–201. This argument is unpersuasive * * *.

* * *

* * * Contracts for the sale of goods * * * are governed by § 2–201. [Citations.]

Under § 2–201, oral agreements for the sale of goods at a price of $500 or more are presumptively unenforceable. [Citations.] The applicable provisions in this case, however, are other subsections of § 2–201.

Under § 2–201(3)(a), an oral contract for the sale of goods is enforceable if the goods in question are "specially manufactured." In determining whether the specially manufactured goods exception applies, courts generally apply a four part standard:

> "(1) the goods must be specially made for the buyer; (2) the goods must be unsuitable for sale to others in the ordinary course of the seller's business; (3) the seller must have substantially begun to have manufactured the goods or to have a commitment for their procurement; and (4) the manufacture or commitment must have been commenced under circumstances reasonably indicating that the goods are for the buyer and prior to the seller's receipt of notification of contractual repudiation." [Citation.]

In applying this standard, "courts have traditionally looked to the goods themselves. The term 'specially manufactured,' therefore, refers to the nature of the particular goods in question and not to whether the goods were made in an unusual, as opposed to the regular, business operation or manufacturing process of the seller." [Citations.]

Printed material, particularly that, as in this case, names the buyer, has been deemed by both state and federal courts to fall within the exception set out for specially manufactured goods. [Citations.]

It is inherent in the court's findings that the printed materials in the present case were specially manufactured goods. The materials were printed specifically for Caprilands. The materials included brochures and labels with the Caprilands name, as well as books that were written and designed by Simmons. The plaintiff testified that the books were printed, as Simmons had requested, in a rustic style with typed inserts and hand-drawn pictures. Therefore, none of these materials was suitable for sale to others. It is undisputed that, at the time of breach of the alleged contract, goods printed for Simmons already had been produced.

We conclude that, in light of the nature of the goods at issue * * * this case falls within the exception for specially manufactured goods. To be enforceable, the agreement for their production was, therefore, not required to be in writing under § 2–201(3)(a).

INTERPRETATION An oral contract for the sale of goods is enforceable if the goods in question are specially manufactured.

CRITICAL THINKING QUESTION Do you agree with the court's decision? Explain

Delivery or Payment and Acceptance Under the Code, delivery and acceptance of part of the goods, or payment and acceptance of part of the price, validates the contract but only for the goods that have been accepted or for which payment has been accepted. To illustrate, Liz orally agrees to buy 1,000 watches from David for $15,000. David delivers 300 watches to Liz, who receives and accepts the watches. The oral contract is enforceable to the extent of 300 watches ($4,500)—those received and accepted—but is unenforceable to the extent of 700 watches ($10,500).

A summary of the contracts within, and the exceptions to, the statute of frauds is provided in the Concept Review.

MODIFICATION OR RESCISSION OF CONTRACTS WITHIN THE STATUTE OF FRAUDS

Oral contracts modifying previously existing contracts are unenforceable if the resulting contract is within the statute of frauds. The reverse is also true: an oral modification of a prior contract is enforceable if the new contract is not within the statute of frauds.

Thus, examples of unenforceable oral contracts include an oral promise to guarantee the additional duties of another, an oral agreement to substitute different land for that described in the original contract, and an oral agreement to extend an employee's contract for six months to a total of two years. On the other hand, an oral agreement to modify an employee's contract from two years to six months at a higher salary is not within the statute of frauds and is enforceable.

Under the UCC, the decisive point is the contract price *after* modification. If the parties enter into an oral contract to sell for $450 a motorcycle to be delivered to the buyer and later, prior to delivery, orally agree that the seller shall paint the motorcycle and install new tires and that the buyer shall pay a price of $550, the modified contract is unenforceable. Conversely, if the parties have a written contract for the sale of 200 bushels of wheat at a price of $4 per bushel and later orally agree to decrease the quantity to 100 bushels at the same price per bushel, the agreement as modified is for a total price of $400 and thus is enforceable.

An oral rescission is effective and discharges all unperformed duties under the original contract. For example, Jones and Brown enter into a written contract

CONCEPT REVIEW

The Statute of Frauds

Contracts Within the Statue of Frauds	Exceptions
Suretyship—a promise to answer for the duty of another	• Main purpose rule • Original promise • Promise made to debtor
Executor–Administrator—a promise to answer personally for debt of decedent	• Main purpose rule • Original promise • Promise made to debtor
Agreements made upon consideration of marriage	• Mutual promises to marry
Agreements for the transfer of an interest in land	• Part performance plus detrimental reliance • Seller conveys property
Agreements not to be performed within one year	• Full performance by one party • Possibility of performance within one year
Sale of goods for $500 or more	• Admission • Specially manufactured goods • Delivery or payment and acceptance

of employment for a two-year term. Later they orally agree to rescind the contract. The oral agreement is effective, and the written contract is rescinded. Where land has been transferred, however, an agreement to rescind the transaction is a contract to retransfer the land and is within the statute of frauds.

> **Practical Advice**
>
> When significantly modifying an existing common law contract, make sure that consideration is given and that the modification is in writing and signed by both parties.

CPA

COMPLIANCE WITH THE STATUTE OF FRAUDS

Even a contract within the statute of frauds will be enforced if it is contained in a *writing* or *memorandum* sufficient to satisfy the statute's requirements. As long as the writing meets those requirements, it need not be in any specific form, nor be an attempt by the parties to enter into a binding contract, nor represent their entire agreement.

GENERAL CONTRACT PROVISIONS

The English statute of frauds and most modern statutes of frauds require that the agreement be evidenced by a writing to be enforceable. The statute's purpose in requiring a writing is to ensure that the parties have actually entered into a contract. It is, therefore, not necessary that the writing be in existence when the parties initiate litigation; it is sufficient to show that the memorandum existed at one time. The note or memorandum, which may be formal or informal, must:

1. specify the parties to the contract;
2. specify with reasonable certainty the subject matter and the essential terms of the unperformed promises; and
3. be signed by the party to be charged or by her agent.

The memorandum may be such that the parties themselves view it as having no legal significance whatever. For example, a personal letter between the parties, an interdepartmental communication, an advertisement, or the record books of a business may serve as a memorandum. The writing need not have been delivered to the party who seeks to take advantage of it, and it may even contain a repudiation of the oral agreement. For example, Sid and Gail enter into an oral agreement that Sid will sell Blackacre to Gail for $5,000. Sid subsequently receives a better offer and sends Gail a signed letter, which begins by reciting all the material terms of the oral agreement. The letter concludes: "Because my agreement to sell Blackacre to you for $5,000 was oral, I am not bound by my promise. I have since received a better offer and will accept that one." Sid's letter constitutes a sufficient memorandum for Gail to enforce Sid's promise to sell Blackacre. Because Gail did not sign the memorandum, however, the writing does not bind her. Thus, a contract may be enforceable against only one of the parties.

The "signature" may be initials or may even be typewritten or printed, as long as the party intended it to authenticate the writing. Furthermore, the signature need not be at the bottom of the page or at the customary place for a signature. In 2000, Congress passed the Electronic Signatures in Global and National Commerce Act, which took effect on October 1, 2000. The Act provides that all electronic transactions and signatures will be valid and enforceable and, furthermore, are not unenforceable because of the statute of frauds. (For more information on this statute, see Chapter 47).

The memorandum may consist of several papers or documents, none of which would be sufficient by itself. The several memoranda, however, must together satisfy all of the requirements of a writing to comply with the statute of frauds and must clearly indicate that they relate to the same transaction. The latter requirement can be satisfied if (a) the writings are physically connected, (b) the writings refer to each other, or (c) an examination of the writings shows them to be in reference to each other.

> **Practical Advice**
>
> To avoid becoming solely liable by signing a contract before the other party signs, include a provision to the effect that no party is bound to the contract until all parties sign the contract.

http:// Washington: ("Signing Documents")
http://www.wsba.org/public/default.htm

Estate of Jackson v. Devenyns

Supreme Court of Wyoming, 1995
892 P.2d.786

FACTS On February 9, 1993, George Jackson and his neighbors, Karen and Steve Devenyn, drafted and signed a document that purports to convey a seventy-nine-acre parcel of land owned by Jackson. By the terms of the agreement, Jackson wished to reserve a 1.3 acre portion of the parcel. Although the agreement contained a drawing and dimensions of the conveyance, it did not contain a specific description of the parcel. Jackson died on May 8, 1993, and his estate refused to honor the agreement. The Devenyns then filed a petition with the probate court to order a conveyance. Based on the parol evidence rule, the estate of Jackson objected to the admission of the witnesses' testimony that they could point out the specific area based on conversations with Jackson. However, the probate court heard the testimony and determined that, with the witnesses' testimony, a sufficient description of the parcel could be determined. Accordingly, it granted the petition. The estate appeals.

DECISION Judgment reversed.

OPINION Golden, J. A written memorandum purporting to convey real estate must sufficiently describe the property so as to comply with the requirements of the statute of frauds and permit specific performance. [Citation.] Wyoming [statute of frauds] states:

> (a) In the following cases every agreement shall be void [unenforceable in most states] unless such agreement, or some note or memorandum thereof be in writing, and subscribed by the party to be charged therewith:
>
> * * *
>
> (v) Every agreement or contract for the sale of real estate, or the lease thereof, for more than one (1) year[.]

The question of what constitutes a memorandum sufficient to satisfy the statute of frauds is set forth in Restatement (Second) of Contracts, § 131 (1979) as follows:

> § 131. General Requisites of a Memorandum
>
> Unless additional requirements are prescribed by the particular statute, a contract within the Statute of Frauds is enforceable if it is evidenced by any writing, signed by or on behalf of the party to be charged, which
>
> (a) reasonably identifies the subject matter of the contract,
>
> (b) is sufficient to indicate that a contract with respect thereto has been made between the parties or offered by the signer to the other party, and
>
> (c) states with reasonable certainty the essential terms of the unperformed promises in the contract.

* * * This Court's decision in *Noland* [citation] concluded that a valid contract to convey land must expressly contain a description of the land, certain in itself or capable of being rendered certain by reference to an extrinsic source which the writing itself designates. [Citation.] *Noland* expressly prohibited supplying the writing's essential provisions by inferences or presumptions deduced from oral testimony. [Citation.]

* * *

The parties both recognize that the central issue is the adequacy of the property description supplied in the agreement to satisfy the statute of frauds. The estate contends the probate court improperly relied upon parol evidence in deciding the document had sufficiently described Jackson's property in satisfaction of the statute of frauds. The general rule for Wyoming is that parol evidence is admissible to identify described property, but parol evidence may not supply a portion of the description. [Citation.]

This writing insufficiently describes the property it purports to convey, to reserve, and for which it grants an option to purchase. All three of these transactions fall under the statute of frauds and each must be sufficiently definite in description to satisfy the statute of frauds or, as a matter of law, the contract is void because an essential term has been omitted. [Citation.] We also note that if the description of the property reserved out of the tract to be conveyed is indefinite and uncertain, then the general description of the land to be conveyed is indefinite and the entire conveyance must fail. [Citation.]

* * *

Nevertheless, the Devenyns urge the writing's of words such as "remain," "retain," and "keep" was correctly found by the probate court to indicate that Jackson was selling property he owned at that time and that these words are a "key" or "index finger" which, under *Noland*, permits parol evidence that Jackson only owned this property in all of the world and, therefore, the location of conveyed property is described. However, *Noland* determined that Wyoming required greater certainty in the description provided by the writing extrinsic evidence is permitted to supplement. [Citation.] * * *

When a writing only states the total acreage without any description of the location of the land involved, the statute of frauds' requirement that the subject matter be reasonably certain is not satisfied and the contract is void. [Citation.] Without the prohibited supplied inference of ownership, the present description only provides the total acreage, does not provide any certainty that this particular tract was intended to be conveyed and, consequently, is too uncertain to be enforced. [Citations.]

The descriptions for the property reserved and for the option also fail to satisfy the statute of frauds. The reserved property boundaries can only be ascertained by witnesses actually directing a surveyor on-site according to the witnesses' memory of Jackson's boundary description. Parol evidence cannot supply a portion of the description. [Citation.] The option granted in the document does not provide any description at all, leaving unclear for what property an option was granted.

INTERPRETATION A writing to comply with the general contract statute of frauds must (1) specify the parties to the contract, (2) specify with reasonable certainty the subject matter and the essential terms of the promises, and (3) be signed by the party to be charged or by her agent.

CRITICAL THINKING QUESTION Should the statute of frauds provision mandate that the writing contain a reasonably certain description of the land? Explain.

SALE OF GOODS

The statute of frauds provision under Article 2 (Sales) of the UCC is more liberal. For a sale of goods, the Code requires merely a writing (a) sufficient to indicate that a contract has been made between the parties; (b) signed by the party against whom enforcement is sought or by her authorized agent or broker; and (c) specifying the ***quantity*** of goods or securities to be sold. The writing is sufficient even if it omits or incorrectly states an agreed-upon term; however, if the quantity term is misstated, the contract can be enforced only to the extent of the quantity stated in the writing.

As with general contracts, several related documents may satisfy the writing requirement. Moreover, the "signature" may be by initials or even typewritten or printed, so long as the party intended to authenticate the writing.

In addition, between merchants, if one party, within a reasonable time after entering into the oral contract, sends a written confirmation of the contract for a sale of goods to the other party and the written confirmation is sufficient against the sender, it is also sufficient against the recipient of the confirmation unless the recipient gives written notice of his objection within ten days after receiving the confirmation.

For example, Brown Co. and ANM Industries enter into an oral contract that provides that ANM will deliver 12,000 shirts to Brown at $6 per shirt. Brown sends a letter to ANM acknowledging the agreement. The letter is signed by Brown's president, contains the quantity term but not the price, and is mailed to ANM's vice president for sales. Brown is bound by the contract once its authorized agent signs the letter, while ANM cannot raise the defense of the statute of frauds ten days after receiving the letter if it does not object within that time.

Practical Advice

Merchants should examine written confirmations carefully and promptly to make certain that they are accurate.

CPA EFFECT OF NONCOMPLIANCE

Under both the statute of frauds and the Code, the basic legal effect is the same: a contracting party has a defense to an action by the other party for enforcement of an ***unenforceable*** oral contract—that is, an oral contract that falls within the statute and does not comply with its requirements. For example, if Kirkland, a painter, and Riggsbee, a homeowner, make an oral contract under which Riggsbee is to give Kirkland a certain tract of land in return for the painting of Riggsbee's house, the contract is unenforceable under the statute of frauds. It is a contract for the sale of an interest in land. Either party can repudiate and has a defense to an action by the other to enforce the contract.

FULL PERFORMANCE

After *all* the promises of an oral contract have been *performed* by all the parties, the statute of frauds no longer applies. Accordingly, neither party may ask the court to rescind the executed oral contract on the basis that it did not meet the statute's requirements. Thus, the statute applies to executory contracts only.

RESTITUTION

A party to a contract that is unenforceable because of the statute of frauds may have, nonetheless, acted in reliance upon the contract. In such a case, the party may recover in restitution the benefits he conferred upon the other in relying upon the unenforceable contract. Thus, if Wilton makes an oral contract to furnish services to Rochelle that are not to be performed within a year and Rochelle discharges Wilton after three months, Wilton may recover as restitution the value of the services he rendered during the three months. Most courts require, however, that the party seeking restitution not be in default.

PROMISSORY ESTOPPEL

A growing number of courts have used the doctrine of promissory estoppel to displace the requirement of a writing by enforcing oral contracts within the statute of frauds where the party seeking enforcement has reasonably and foreseeably relied upon a promise in such a way that the court can avoid injustice only by enforcing the promise. The remedy granted is limited, as justice requires, and depends on such factors as the availability of other remedies; the foreseeability, reasonableness, and substantiality of the reliance; and the extent to which reliance corroborates evidence of the promise. The use of promissory estoppel, however, to avoid the writing requirement of the statute of frauds has gained little acceptance in cases involving the sale of goods.

PAROL EVIDENCE RULE

A contract reduced to writing and signed by the parties is frequently the result of many conversations, conferences, proposals, counterproposals, letters, and memoranda; and sometimes it is also the product of negotiations conducted, or partly conducted, by agents of the parties. At some stage in the negotiations, the parties or their agents may have reached tentative agreements that were superseded (or regarded as such by one of the parties) by subsequent negotiations. Offers may have been made and withdrawn, either expressly or by implication, or forgotten in the give-and-take of negotiations. Ultimately, though, the parties prepare and sign a final draft of the written contract, which may or may not include all of the points that they discussed and agreed on in the course of the negotiations. By signing the agreement, despite its potential omissions, the parties have declared it to be their contract; and the terms as contained in it represent the contract they have made. As a rule of substantive law, neither party is later permitted to show that the contract they made is different from the terms and provisions that appear in the written agreement. This rule, which also applies to wills and deeds, is called the "parol evidence" rule.

CPA THE RULE

When the parties express their contract in a writing that is intended to be the complete and final expression of their rights and duties, the **parol evidence rule** excludes ***prior*** oral or written negotiations or agreements of the parties or their ***contemporaneous*** oral agreements that ***vary*** or ***change*** an integrated written contract. The word *parol* literally means "speech" or "words." The term *parol evidence* refers to any evidence, whether oral or in writing, that is outside the written contract and not incorporated into it either directly or by reference.

The parol evidence rule applies only to an **integrated contract**, that is, one contained in a certain writing or writings to which the parties have assented as being the statement of the complete and exclusive agreement or contract between them. When there is such an integration of a contract, the courts will not permit parol evidence of any prior or contemporaneous agreement to vary, change, alter, or modify any of the terms or provisions of the written contract.

The reason for the rule is that the parties, by reducing their entire agreement to writing, are regarded as having intended the writing that they signed to include the whole of their agreement. The terms and provisions contained in the writing are there because the parties intended them to be in their contract. Conversely, the courts regard the parties as having omitted intentionally any provision not in the writing. The rule, by excluding evidence that would tend to change, alter, vary, or modify the terms of the written agreement, safeguards the contract as made by the parties. The rule, which applies to all integrated written contracts, deals with what terms are part of the contract. The rule differs from the statute of frauds, which governs what contracts must be evidenced by a writing to be enforceable. Does the parol evidence rule or the statute of frauds apply to the situation presented in the Ethical Dilemma later in this chapter?

Leitz v. Thorson

Court of Appeals of Oregon, 1992

113 Or.App. 557, 833 P.2d 343

FACTS Plaintiffs leased commercial space from the defendant to open a florist shop. After the lease was executed, the plaintiffs learned that they could not place a freestanding sign along the highway to advertise their business because the Deschutes County Code allowed only one freestanding sign on the property, and the defendant already had one in place. The plaintiffs filed this action, alleging that defendant had breached the lease by failing to provide them with space in which they could erect a freestanding sign. Paragraph 16 of the lease provides as follows: "Tenant shall not erect or install any signs * * * visible from outside the leased premises with out [sic] the previous written consent of the Landlord." The trial court allowed the plaintiffs to introduce evidence that, before the lease was executed, the defendant told them that they could have a freestanding sign. The defendant objected to the testimony on the basis of the parol evidence rule and brought this appeal.

DECISION Affirmed; the evidence was properly admitted.

OPINION Edmonds, J. Our review is to determine whether the trial court's conclusion that the lease is not a fully integrated agreement is supported by the evidence. [Citation.] We start with a presumption that the writing is intended to be a complete integration. [Citation.] The integration clause in this lease is an indication that the lease was intended to be a complete integration, but it is not conclusive. [Citation.] Oral admissions of a party may be probative of whether the agreement is integrated. [Citation.]

Defendant testified that the written form that he had used for the lease was not drafted to be used specifically for this property. Although the lease required attachment of exhibits, he admitted that no exhibits were attached to the lease. He conceded that he told plaintiffs that they could have a sign and that he did not require his written consent, despite the words in paragraph 16 of the lease. He admitted that, during the lease negotiations, the parties had discussed plaintiffs' renovations. He said that he did not require those plans to be in writing, even though the lease required his written consent before alterations, additions or installations on the premises. Defendant also testified: "Usually our detail comes later, after they've, you know, gotten their lease signed, and they're—they get it figured out, and they measure and come up with information on saying: well, this is what we're going to do."

There was evidence to support the trial court's conclusion that the parties did not intend the written lease to reflect their entire agreement, thereby overcoming the presumption of integration.

The next question is whether a separate oral agreement to allow a freestanding sign was inconsistent with the written lease. Although defendant admitted that he told plaintiffs they could have a sign, he disputes whether he told them that the sign could be "freestanding." No provision of the lease prohibits a freestanding sign. The disputed parol evidence was not inconsistent with the written agreement.

* * *

There is evidence to support the trial court's finding that the parties did not intend the written lease to be their complete agreement, that the oral agreement is not inconsistent with the written agreement and that the oral agreement would have been made naturally as a separate agreement.

INTERPRETATION The parol evidence rule applies only to an integrated contract (i.e., one where the parties intend the writing to represent their complete agreement).

CRITICAL THINKING QUESTION Do you agree with the parol evidence rule? Explain.

Practical Advice

If your contract is intended to be the complete and final agreement, make sure that all terms are included and state your intention that the writing is complete and final. If you do not intend the writing to be complete or final, make sure that you so indicate in the writing itself.

CPA SITUATIONS TO WHICH THE RULE DOES NOT APPLY

The parol evidence rule, in spite of its name, is not an exclusionary rule of evidence; nor is it a rule of construction or interpretation. Rather, it is a rule of substantive law that defines the limits of a contract. Bearing this in mind, as well as the reason underlying the rule, you will readily understand that the rule does ***not*** apply to any of the following situations (see Figure 15-1 for an overview of the parol evidence rule):

1. a contract that is *partly written* and partly oral; that is, a contract in which the parties do not intend the writing to be their entire agreement. See *Leitz v. Thorson*, above.
2. a clerical or *typographical error* that obviously does not represent the agreement of the parties. Where, for example, a written contract for the services of a skilled mining engineer provides that his rate of compensation

Figure 15-1 *Parol Evidence Rule*

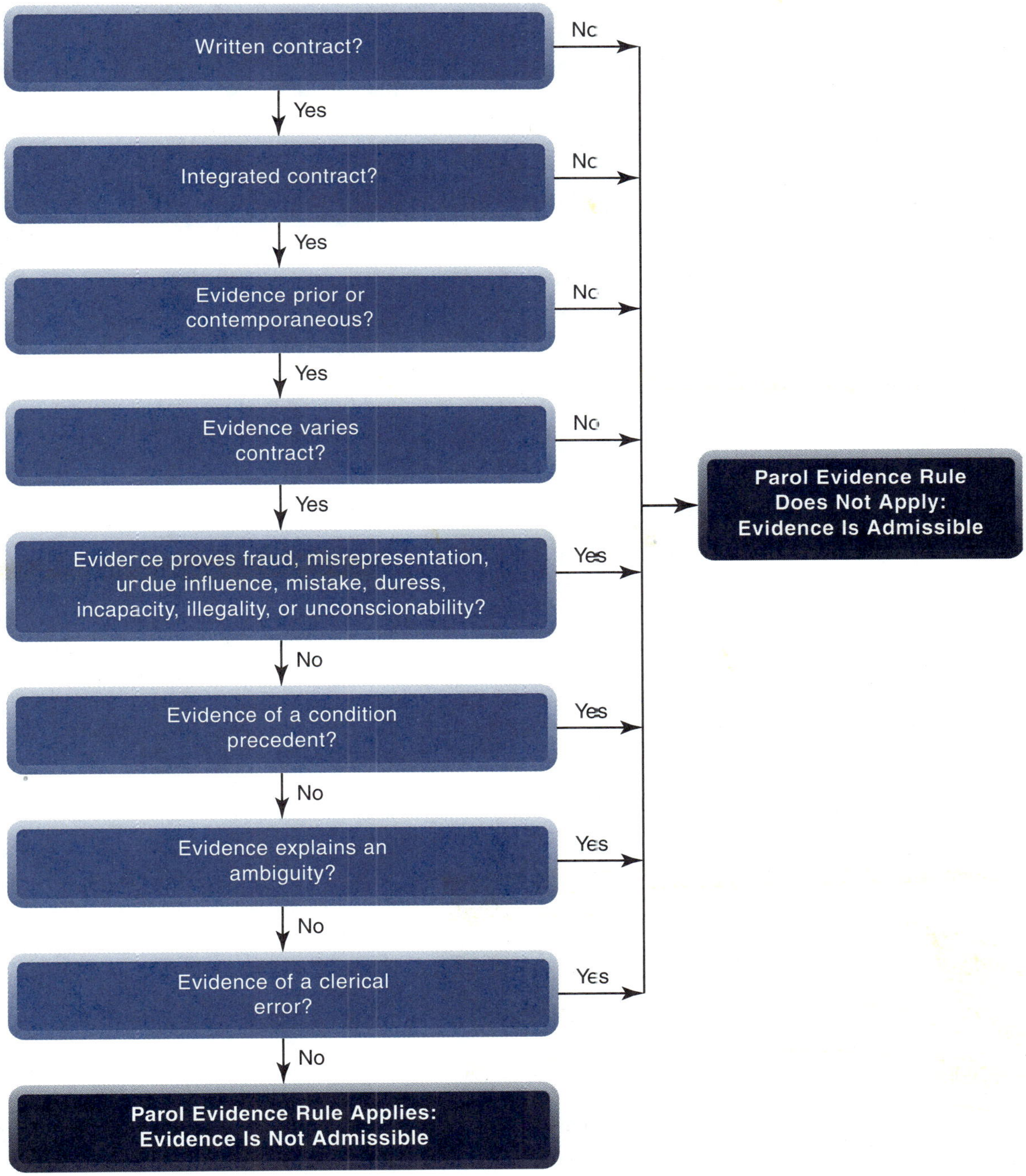

is to be $2 per day, a court of equity would permit reformation (correction) of the contract to correct the mistake if both parties intended the rate to be $200 per day.

3. the lack of *contractual capacity* of one of the parties through, for instance, minority, intoxication, or mental incompetency. Such evidence would not tend to vary, change, or alter any of the terms of the written agreement but rather would show that the written agreement was voidable or void.
4. a *defense* of fraud, misrepresentation, duress, undue influence, mistake, illegality, lack of consideration, or other invalidating cause. Evidence establishing any of these defenses would not purport to vary, change, or alter any of the terms of the written agreement but rather would show such agreement to be voidable, void, or unenforceable.
5. a *condition precedent* to which the parties agreed orally at the time of the execution of the written agreement and to which the entire agreement was made subject. Such evidence does not tend to vary, alter, or change any of the terms of the agreement; rather, it shows whether the entire unchanged written agreement ever became effective.
6. a *subsequent mutual rescission* or *modification* of the written contract. Parol evidence of a later agreement does not tend to show that the integrated writing did not represent the contract between the parties at the time the writing was made.
7. *parol evidence* is admissible to explain *ambiguous* terms in the contract. To enforce a contract, it is necessary to understand its intended meaning. Nevertheless, such interpretation is not to alter, change, or vary the terms of the contract.
8. a *separate contract*; the rule does not prevent a party from proving the existence of a separate, distinct contract between the same parties.

CPA SUPPLEMENTAL EVIDENCE

Although a written agreement cannot be contradicted by evidence of a prior agreement or of a contemporaneous agreement, under the Restatement and the Code, a written contract may be explained or supplemented by (1) course of dealing between the parties; (2) usage of trade; (3) course of performance; or (4) evidence of consistent additional terms, unless the writing was intended by the parties to be a complete and exclusive statement of their agreement.

A **course of dealing** is a sequence of previous conduct between the parties that a court may fairly regard as having established a common basis of understanding for interpreting their expressions and other conduct.

A **usage of trade** is a practice or method of dealing regularly observed and followed in a place, vocation, or trade.

Course of performance refers to the manner in which and the extent to which the respective parties to a contract have accepted without objection successive tenders of performance by the other party.

The Restatement and the Code permit *supplemental consistent evidence* to be introduced into a court proceeding. Such evidence, however, is admissible only if it does not contradict a term or terms of the original agreement and would probably not have been included in the original contract.

INTERPRETATION OF CONTRACTS

Although parol evidence may not change the written words or language in which the parties embodied their agreement or contract, the ascertainment (determination) of the meaning to be given to the written language is outside the scope of the parol evidence rule. Though the written words embody the terms of the contract, these words are but symbols; and, if their meaning is ambiguous, the courts may clarify this meaning by applying rules of interpretation or construction and by using extrinsic (external) evidence where necessary.

The Restatement defines **interpretation** as the ascertainment of the meaning of a promise or agreement or of a term of the promise or agreement. Where the language in a contract is unambiguous, a court will not accept extrinsic evidence tending to show a meaning different from that which the words clearly convey. To perform its function of interpreting and construing written contracts and documents, the court adopts rules of interpretation to apply a legal standard to the words contained in the agreement. These are among the rules that aid interpretation:

1. words and other conduct are interpreted in the light of all the circumstances, and if the principal purpose of the parties is ascertainable, it is given great weight.
2. a writing is interpreted as a whole, and all writings that are part of the same transaction are interpreted together.
3. unless the parties manifest a different intention, language that has a commonly accepted meaning is interpreted in accordance with that meaning.
4. unless a different intention is manifested, technical terms and words of art are given their technical meanings.

Ethical Dilemma

What's (Wrong) in a Contract?

FACTS Rick Davidson was an All-American point guard on Donaldson University's varsity basketball team. He was a four-year starter and, through the cooperation of several accommodating professors, was able to graduate on time-with one small catch: he really couldn't read or write. But his classroom experiences helped convince him that he could handle any situation, and when he was drafted in the first round by an NBA team, he decided to act as his own agent.

During the negotiations, John Stock, general manager for the team, made Rick an offer of $2,400,000 to play for the team for three years. After seeing that other first-round draft choices were receiving closer to $3,000,000 for the same three years, Rick made it known to Stock that the team's offer was unacceptable. Stock told Rick that because of the salary cap (each NBA team has a limit on the total amount of salaries it can pay its players), he would be willing to raise the offer to $2,800,000 but that the extra $400,000 could not be written into the contract. This would be an oral agreement that would avoid disclosing the salary cap violation to the league. After considering the offer, Rick signed the contract for $2,400,000 for three years' service, and he and Stock shook hands on the deal for the additional $400,000 for the same three years. The contract stated that it was the complete and final agreement between the parties.

After Rick's first year, it was obvious to the team that Rick was not worth the money, and Stock decided not to pay him the first year's portion of the extra $400,000. Stock claimed that because this agreement was not in writing, it was not enforceable.

Social, Policy, and Ethical Considerations

1. What would you do?
2. Is the team legally obligated to pay the additional $400,000? Is it ethically obligated to do so?
3. What policy interests are served by the team's decision not to pay Rick the extra money? Would the fact that NBA policy makes it impossible for a player to leave a team and play for another NBA team change your answer?
4. What responsibility does the university bear in this situation?
5. What is the nature of Rick's responsibility with respect to the above facts? What should he do?

5. wherever reasonable, the parties' manifestations of intention regarding a promise or agreement are interpreted as consistent with each other and with any relevant course of performance, course of dealing, or usage of trade.
6. an interpretation that gives a reasonable, lawful, and effective meaning to all the terms is preferred over an interpretation that leaves a part unreasonable, unlawful, or of no effect.
7. specific and exact terms are given greater weight than general language.
8. separately negotiated or added terms are given greater weight than standardized terms or other terms not separately negotiated.
9. express terms, course of performance, course of dealing, and usage of trade are weighted in that order.
10. where a term or promise has several possible meanings, it will be interpreted against the party who supplied the contract or the term.
11. where written provisions are inconsistent with typed or printed provisions, the written provision is given preference. Likewise, typed provisions are given preference to printed provisions.
12. if the amount payable is set forth in both figures and words and the amounts differ, the words control the figures.

We may observe that, through the application of the parol evidence rule (where properly applicable) and the above rules of interpretation and construction, the law not only enforces a contract but also, in so doing, exercises great care both that the contract being enforced is the one the parties made and that the sense and meaning of the parties' intentions are carefully ascertained and given effect.

Practical Advice

Take care to ensure that your contracts are complete and understandable, especially if you drafted the contract.

CHAPTER SUMMARY

Statute of Frauds

Contracts Within the Statute of Frauds

Rule contracts within the statute of frauds must be evidenced by a writing to be enforceable

Suretyship Provision applies to promises to pay the debt of another
- ***Promise Must Be Collateral*** promisor must be secondarily, not primarily, liable
- ***Main Purpose Doctrine*** if primary object is to provide an economic benefit to the surety, then the promise is not within the statute

Executor-Administrator Provision applies to promises to answer personally for a duty of the decedent

Marriage Provision applies to promises in consideration of marriage but not to mutual promises to marry

Land Contract Provision applies to promises to transfer any right, privilege, power, or immunity in real property

One-Year Provision applies to contracts that cannot be performed within one year
- ***The Possibility Test*** the criterion is whether it is possible, not likely, for the agreement to be performed within one year
- ***Computation of Time*** the year runs from the time the agreement is made
- ***Full Performance by One Party*** makes the promise of the other party enforceable under majority view

Sale of Goods a contract for the sale of goods for the price of $500 or more must be evidenced by a writing to be enforceable
- ***Admission*** an admission in pleadings, testimony, or otherwise in court makes the contract enforceable for the quantity of goods admitted
- ***Specially Manufactured Goods*** an oral contract for specially manufactured goods is enforceable
- ***Delivery or Payment and Acceptance*** validates the contract only for the goods that have been accepted or for which payment has been accepted

Modification or Rescission of Contracts within the Statute of Frauds oral contracts modifying existing contracts are unenforceable if the resulting contract is within the statute of frauds

Methods of Compliance

General Contract Law the writing or writings must:
- specify the parties to the contract
- specify the subject matter and essential terms
- be signed by the party to be charged or by her agent

Sale of Goods provides a general method of compliance for all parties and an additional one for merchants
- ***Writing or Writings Must:*** (1) be sufficient to indicate that a contract has been made between the parties, (2) be signed by the party against whom enforcement is sought or by her authorized agent, and (3) specify the quantity of goods to be sold
- ***Written Confirmation*** between merchants, a written confirmation that is sufficient against the sender is also sufficient against the recipient unless the recipient gives written notice of his objection within ten days

Effect of Noncompliance

Oral Contract Within Statute of Frauds is unenforceable

Full Performance statute does not apply to executed contracts

Restitution is available in quasi-contract for benefits conferred in reliance on the oral contract

Promissory Estoppel oral contracts will be enforced where the party seeking enforcement has reasonably and justifiably relied on the promise and the court can avoid injustice only by enforcement

Parol Evidence Rule and Interpretation of Contracts

Parol Evidence

Statement of Rule when parties express a contract in a writing that they intend to be the final expression of their rights and duties, evidence of their prior oral or written negotiations or agreements of their contemporaneous oral agreements that vary or change the written contract are not admissible

Situations to Which the Rule Does Not Apply
- a contract that is not an integrated document
- correction of a typographical error
- showing that a contract was void or voidable
- showing whether a condition has in fact occurred
- showing a subsequent mutual rescission or modification of the contract

Supplemental Evidence may be admitted
- *Course of Dealing* previous conduct between the parties
- *Usage of Trade* practice engaged in by the trade or industry
- *Course of Performance* conduct between the parties concerning performance of the particular contract
- *Supplemental Consistent Evidence*

Interpretation of Contracts

Definition the ascertainment of the meaning of a promise or agreement or a term of the promise or agreement

Rules of Interpretation
- all the circumstances are considered and the principal purpose of the parties is given great weight
- a writing is interpreted as a whole
- commonly accepted meanings are used unless the parties manifest a different intention
- wherever possible, the intentions of the parties are interpreted as consistent with each other and with course of performance, course of dealing, or usage of trade
- technical terms are given their technical meaning
- specific terms are given greater weight than general language
- separately negotiated terms are given greater weight than standardized terms or those not separately negotiated
- the order for interpretation is express terms, course of performance, course of dealing, and usage of trade
- where a term has several possible meanings, the term will be interpreted against the party who supplied the contract or term
- written provisions are given preference over typed or printed provisions and typed provisions are given preference over printed provisions
- if an amount is set forth in both words and figures and they differ, words control the figures

QUESTIONS

1. Rafferty was the principal shareholder in Continental Corporation, and, as a result, he received the lion's share of Continental Corporation's dividends. Continental Corporation was anxious to close an important deal for iron ore products to use in its business. A written contract was on the desk of Stage Corporation for the sale of the iron ore to Continental Corporation. Stage Corporation, however, was cautious about signing the contract; and it did not sign until Rafferty called Stage Corporation on the telephone and stated that if Continental Corporation did not pay for the ore, he would pay. Business reversals struck Continental Corporation, and it failed. Stage Corporation sued Rafferty. What defense, if any, has Rafferty?

2. Green was the owner of a large department store. On Wednesday, January 26, he talked to Smith and said, "I will hire you to act as sales manager in my store for one year at a salary of $38,000. You are to begin work next Monday." Smith accepted and started work on Monday, January 31. At the end of three months, Green discharged Smith. On May 15, Smith brought an action against Green to recover the unpaid portion of the $38,000 salary. Is Smith's employment contract enforceable?

3. Rowe was admitted to the hospital suffering from a critical illness. He was given emergency treatment and later underwent surgery. On at least four occasions, Rowe's two sons discussed with the hospital the payment for services to be rendered by the hospital. The first of these four conversations took place the day after Rowe was admitted. The sons informed the treating physician that their father had no financial means but that they themselves would pay for such services. During the other conversations, the sons authorized whatever treatment their father needed, assuring the hospital that they would pay for the services. After Rowe's discharge, the hospital brought this action against the sons to recover the unpaid bill for the services rendered to their father. Are the sons' promises to the hospital enforceable? Explain.

4. Ames, Bell, Cain, and Dole each orally ordered color television sets from Marvel Electronics Company, which accepted the orders. Ames's set was to be specially designed and encased in an ebony cabinet. Bell, Cain, and Dole ordered standard sets described as "Alpha Omega Theatre." The price of Ames's set was $1,800, and the sets ordered by Bell, Cain, and Dole were $700 each. Bell paid the company $75 to apply on his purchase; Ames, Cain, and Dole paid nothing. The next day, Marvel sent Ames, Bell, Cain, and Dole written confirmations captioned "Purchase Memorandum," numbered 12345, 12346, 12347, and 12348 respectively, containing the essential terms of the oral agreements. Each memorandum was sent in duplicate with the request that one copy be signed and returned to the company. None of the four purchasers returned a signed copy. Ames promptly sent the company a repudiation of the oral contract, which it received before beginning manufacture of the set for Ames or making commitments to carry out the contract. Cain sent the company a letter reading in part, "Referring to your Contract No. 12347, please be advised I have canceled this contract. Yours truly, (Signed) Cain." The four television sets were duly tendered by Marvel to Ames, Bell, Cain, and Dole, all of whom refused to accept delivery. Marvel brings four separate actions against Ames, Bell, Cain, and Dole for breach of contract. Decide each claim.

5. Moriarity and Holmes enter into an oral contract by which Moriarity promises to sell and Holmes promises to buy Blackacre for $10,000. Moriarity repudiates the contract by writing a letter to Holmes in which she states accurately the terms of the bargain, but adds "our agreement was oral. It, therefore, is not binding upon me, and I shall not carry it out." Thereafter, Holmes sues Moriarity for specific performance of the contract. Moriarity interposes the defense of the statute of frauds, arguing that the contract is within the statute and hence unenforceable. What will be the result? Discuss.

6. On March 1, Lucas called Craig on the telephone and offered to pay him $90,000 for a house and lot that Craig owned. Craig accepted the offer immediately on the telephone. Later in the same day, Lucas told Annabelle that if she would marry him, he would convey to her the property then owned by Craig that was the subject of the earlier agreement. On March 2 Lucas called Penelope and offered her $16,000 if she would work for him for the year commencing March 15, and she agreed. Lucas and Annabelle were married on June 25. By this time, Craig had refused to convey the house to Lucas. Thereafter, Lucas renounced his promise to convey the property to Annabelle. Penelope, who had been working for Lucas, was discharged without cause on July 5; Annabelle left Lucas and instituted divorce proceedings in July.

   What rights, if any, have (a) Lucas against Craig for his failure to convey the property; (b) Annabelle against Lucas for failure to convey the house to her; (c) Penelope against Lucas for discharging her before the end of the agreed term of employment?

7. Blair orally promises Clay to sell him five crops of potatoes to be grown on Blackacre, a farm in Idaho; and Clay promises to pay a stated price for them on delivery. Is the contract enforceable?

8. Rachel leased an apartment to Bertha for a one-year term beginning May 1, at $800 a month, "payable in advance on the first day of each and every month of said term." At the time the lease was signed, Bertha told Rachel that she received her salary on the tenth of the month, and that she would be unable to pay the rent before that date each month. Rachel replied that would be satisfactory. On June 2, Bertha not having paid the June rent, Rachel sued Bertha for the rent. At the trial, Bertha offered to prove the oral agreement as to the date of payment each month. Is the oral evidence admissible?

9. Ann bought a car from the Used Car Agency (Used) under a written contract. She purchased the car in reliance on Used's agent's oral representations that it had never been in a wreck and could be driven at least 2,000 miles without adding oil. Thereafter, Ann discovered that the car had, in fact, been previously wrecked and rebuilt, that it used excessive quantities of oil, and that Used's agent was aware of these facts when the car was sold. Ann brought an action to rescind the contract and recover the purchase price. Used objected to the introduction of oral testimony concerning representations of its agent, contending that the written contract alone governed the rights of the parties. Should Ann succeed?

10. In a contract drawn up by Goldberg Company, it agreed to sell and Edwards Contracting Company agreed to buy wood shingles at $650. After the shingles were delivered and used, Goldberg Company billed Edwards Company at $650 per bunch of 900 shingles. Edwards Company refused to pay because it thought the contract meant $650 per thousand shingles. Goldberg Company brought action to recover on the basis of $650 per bunch. The evidence showed that there was no applicable custom or usage in the trade and that each party held its belief in good faith. Decision?

11. Amos orally agrees to hire Elizabeth for an eight-month trial period. Elizabeth performs the job magnificently, and after several weeks Amos orally offers Elizabeth a six-month extension at a salary increase of 20 percent. Elizabeth accepts the offer. At the end of the eight-month trial period, Amos discharges Elizabeth, who brings suit against Amos for breach of contract. Is Amos liable? Why?

CASE PROBLEMS

12. Halsey, a widower, was living without family or housekeeper in his house in Howell, New York. Burns and his wife claim that Halsey invited them to give up their house and business in Andover, New York, to live in his house and care for him. In return, they allege, he promised them the house and its furniture upon his death. Acting upon this proposal, the Burnses left Andover, moved into Halsey's house, and cared for him until he died five months later. No deed, will, or memorandum exists to authenticate Halsey's promise. McCormick, the administrator of the estate, claims the oral promise is unenforceable under the statute of frauds. Explain whether McCormick is correct.

13. Ethel Greenberg acquired the ownership of the Carlyle Hotel on Miami Beach but had little experience in the hotel business. She asked Miller to participate in and counsel her operation of the hotel, which he did. He claims that, because his efforts produced a substantial profit, Ethel made an oral agreement for the continuation of his services. Miller alleges that in return for his services, Ethel promised to marry him and to share the net income resulting from the operation of the hotel. Miller maintains that he rendered his services to Ethel in reliance upon her promises and that the couple planned to wed in the fall of 1955. Ethel, due to physical illness, decided not to marry. Miller sued for damages for Ethel's breach of agreement. Is the oral contract enforceable? Discuss.

14. Dean was hired on February 12, 1962, as a sales manager of the Co-op Dairy for a minimum period of one year with the dairy agreeing to pay his moving expenses. By February 26, 1962, Dean had signed a lease, moved his family from Oklahoma to Arizona, and reported for work. After he worked for a few days, he was fired. Dean then brought this action against the dairy for his salary for the year, less what he was paid. The dairy argues that the statute of frauds bars enforcement of the oral contract because the contract was not to be performed within one year. Is the dairy correct in its assertion?

15. Yokel, a grower of soybeans, had sold soybeans to Campbell Grain and Seed Company and other grain companies in the past. Campbell entered into an oral contract with Yokel to purchase soybeans from him. Promptly after entering into the oral contract, Campbell signed and mailed to Yokel a written confirmation of the oral agreement. Yokel received the written confirmation but did not sign it or object to its content. Campbell now brings this action against Yokel for breach of contract upon Yokel's failure to deliver the soybeans. Is the agreement binding?

16. Presti claims that he reached an oral agreement with Wilson by telephone in October 1970 to buy a horse for $60,000. Presti asserts that he sent Wilson a bill of sale and a postdated check, which Wilson retained. Presti also claims that Wilson told him that he wished not to consummate the transaction until January 1, 1971, for tax reasons. The check was neither deposited nor negotiated. Wilson denies that he ever agreed to sell the horse or that he received the check and bill of sale from Presti. Presti's claim is supported by a copy of his check stub and by the affidavit of his executive assistant, who says that he monitored the telephone call and prepared and mailed both the bill of sale and the check. Wilson argues that the statute of frauds governs this transaction and that because there was no writing, the contract claim is barred. Is Wilson correct? Explain.

17. Louie E. Brown worked for the Phelps Dodge Corporation (http://www.phelpsdodge.com) under an oral contract for approximately twenty-three years. In 1967, he was suspended from work for unauthorized possession of company property. In 1968, Phelps Dodge fired Brown after discovering that he was using company property without permission and building a trailer on company time. Brown sued Phelps Dodge for benefits under an unemployment benefit plan. According to the plan, "in order to be eligible for unemployment benefits, a laid-off employee must: (1) Have completed 2 or more years of continuous service

with the company, and (2) Have been laid off from work because the company had determined that work was not available for him." The trial court held that the wording of the second condition was ambiguous and should be construed against Phelps Dodge, the party who chose the wording. A reading of the entire contract, however, indicates that the plan was not intended to apply to someone who was fired for cause. What is the correct interpretation of this contract?

18. Katz offered to purchase land from Joiner, and, after negotiating the terms, Joiner accepted. On October 13, over the telephone, both parties agreed to extend the time period for completing and mailing the written contract until October 20. Although the original paperwork deadline in the offer was October 14, Katz stated he had inserted that provision "for my purpose only." All other provisions of the contract remained unchanged. Accordingly, Joiner completed the contract and mailed it on October 20. Immediately after, however, Joiner sent Katz a telegram stating that "I have signed and returned contract, but have changed my mind. Do not wish to sell property." Joiner now claims an oral modification of a contract within the statute of frauds is unenforceable. Katz counters that the modification is not material, and therefore does not affect the underlying contract. Explain who is correct.

19. When Mr. McClam died, he left the family farm, heavily mortgaged, to his wife and children. In order to save the farm from foreclosure, Mrs. McClam planned to use insurance proceeds and her savings to pay off the debts. She was unwilling to do so, however, unless she had full ownership of the property. Mrs. McClam wrote her daughter, stating that the daughter should deed over her interest in the family farm to her mother. Mrs. McClam promised that upon her death all the children would inherit the farm from their mother equally. The letter further explained that if foreclosure occurred, each child would receive very little, but if they complied with their mother's plan, each would eventually receive a valuable property interest upon her death. Finally, the letter stated that all the other children had agreed to this plan. The daughter also agreed. Years later, Mrs. McClam tried to convey the farm to her son Donald. The daughter challenged, arguing that the mother was contractually bound to convey the land equally to all children. Donald says this was an oral agreement to sell land, and is unenforceable. The daughter says the letter satisfies the statute of frauds, making the contract enforceable. Who gets the farm? Explain.

20. Butler Brothers Building Company sublet all of the work in a highway construction contract to Ganley Brothers, Inc. Soon thereafter, Ganley brought this action against Butler for fraud in the inducement of the contract. The contract, however, provided: "The contractor [Ganley] has examined the said contracts . . . , knows all the requirements, and is not relying upon any statement made by the company in respect thereto." Can Ganley introduce into evidence the oral representations made by Butler?

21. Alice solicited an offer from Robett Manufacturing Company to manufacture certain clothing that Alice intended to supply to the government. Alice contends that in a telephone conversation Robett made an oral offer that she immediately accepted. She then received the following letter from Robett, which, she claims, confirmed their agreement:

> Confirming our telephone conversation, we are pleased to offer the 3,500 shirts at $4.00 each and the trousers at $3.80 each with delivery approximately ninety days after receipt of order. We will try to cut this to sixty days if at all possible.
>
> This, of course, is quoted f.o.b. Atlanta and the order will not be subject to cancellation, domestic pack only.
>
> Thanking you for the opportunity to offer these garments, we are
>
> Very truly yours,
> ROBETT MANUFACTURING CO., INC.

Is the agreement enforceable?

22. Enrique Gittes was a financial consultant for NCC, an English holding company that invested capital in other businesses in return for a stake in those businesses. One of NCC's investments was a substantial holding in Simplicity Pattern Company. Gittes's consulting contract was subsequently transferred to Simplicity, and Gittes was elected to the Simplicity board of directors.

When NCC fell into serious financial straits, it became imperative that it sell its interest in Simplicity. Accordingly, a buyer was found. The buyer insisted that before closing the deal all current Simplicity directors, including Gittes, must resign. Gittes, however, refused to resign. Edward Cook, the largest shareholder of NCC and the one with the most to lose if the Simplicity sale was not completed, orally offered Gittes a five-year, $50,000-per-year consulting contract with Cook International if Gittes would resign from the Simplicity board.

Gittes and Cook never executed a formal contract. However, Cook International did issue two writings, a prospectus and a memo, that mentioned the employment of Gittes for five years at $50,000 per year. Neither writing described the nature of Gittes's job or any of his duties. In fact, Gittes was given no responsibilities, and was never paid. Gittes sued to enforce the employment contract. Cook International contended that the statute of frauds made the oral contract unenforceable. Decision?

23. The defendant, Shane Quadri, contacted Don Hoffman, an employee of defendant Al J. Hoffman & Co., to procure car insurance. Later, Quadri's car was stolen on October 25 or 26, 1977. Quadri contacted Hoffman, who arranged with Budget Rent-a-Car, a plaintiff in this case, for a rental car for Quadri until his car was recovered. Hoffman authorized Budget Rent-a-Car (http://www.budget.com/) to bill the Hoffman Agency. Later, when the stolen car was recovered, Hoffman telephoned the plaintiff, Goodyear (http://www.goodyear.com/), and arranged to have four new tires put on

Quadri's car to replace those damaged during the theft. The plaintiffs (Budget and Goodyear) sued the defendants (Quadri and Hoffman) for payment of the car rental and tires. Is Hoffman liable on his oral promise to pay for the four new tires?

24. Stuart Studio, an art studio, prepared a new catalog for the National School of Heavy Equipment, a school run by Gilbert and Donald Shaw. When the artwork was virtually finished, Gilbert Shaw requested Stuart Studio to purchase and supervise the printing of 25,000 catalogs. Shaw told the art studio that payment of the printing costs would be made within ten days after billing and that if the "National School would not pay the full total that he would stand good for the entire bill." Shaw was chairman of the board of directors of the school, and he owned 100 percent of its voting stock and 49 percent of its nonvoting stock. The school became bankrupt, and Stuart Studio was unable to recover the sum from the school. Stuart Studio then brought this action against Shaw on the basis of his promise to pay the bill. Is Shaw obligated to pay the debt in question? Explain.

25. On July 5, 1970, Richard Price signed a written employment contract as a new salesman with the Mercury Supply Company. The contract was of indefinite duration and could be terminated by either party for any reason upon fifteen days' notice. Between 1970 and 1978, Price was promoted several times. In 1975, Price was made vice president of sales. In September of 1978, however, Price was told that his performance was not satisfactory and that if he did not improve he would be fired. In February of 1981, Price received notice of termination. Price claims that in 1975 he entered into a valid oral employment contract with Mercury Supply Company in which he was made vice president of sales for life or until he should retire. Is the alleged oral contract barred by the one-year provision of the statute of frauds?

http:// **Internet Exercise** Search the Internet for information on why it is advantageous to have a written contract.

CHAPTER 16

Third Parties to Contracts

The establishment of [the third-party beneficiary] doctrine . . .
is a victory of practical utility over theory, of equity over technical subtlety.

BRANTLY ON CONTRACTS, 2D EDITION

Learning Objectives

After reading this chapter you should be able to:

1. Distinguish between an assignment of rights and a delegation of duties.
2. Identify (a) the requirements of an assignment of contract rights and (b) those rights that are not assignable.
3. Identify those situations in which a delegation of duties is not permitted.
4. Distinguish between an intended beneficiary and an incidental beneficiary.
5. Explain when the rights of an intended beneficiary vest.

In prior chapters, we considered situations that essentially involved only two parties. In this chapter, we deal with the rights and duties of third parties, namely, persons who are not parties to the contract but who have a right to or an obligation for its performance. These rights and duties arise either by (1) an assignment of the rights of a party to the contract, (2) a delegation of the duties of a party to the contract, or (3) the express terms of a contract entered into for the benefit of a third person. In an assignment or delegation, the third party's rights or duties arise after the original contract is made, whereas in the third situation the third-party beneficiary's rights arise at the time the contract is formed. We will consider these three situations in that order.

CPA ASSIGNMENT OF RIGHTS

Every contract creates both rights and duties. A person who owes a duty under a contract is an **obligor**, while a person to whom a contractual duty is owed is an **obligee**. For instance, Ann promises to sell to Bart an automobile for which Bart promises to pay $10,000 by monthly installments over the next three years. Ann's right under the contract is to receive payment from Bart, whereas Ann's duty is to deliver the automobile. Bart's right is to receive the automobile; his duty is to pay for it.

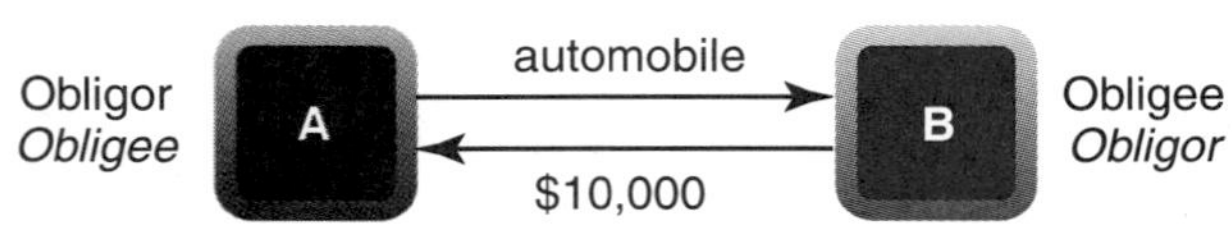

An **assignment of rights** is the voluntary transfer to a third party of the rights arising from the contract. In the above example, if Ann were to transfer her right under the contract (the installment payments due from Bart) to Clark for $8,500 in cash, this would constitute a valid assignment of rights. In this case, Ann would be the **assignor**, Clark would be the **assignee**, and Bart would be the ***obligor***.

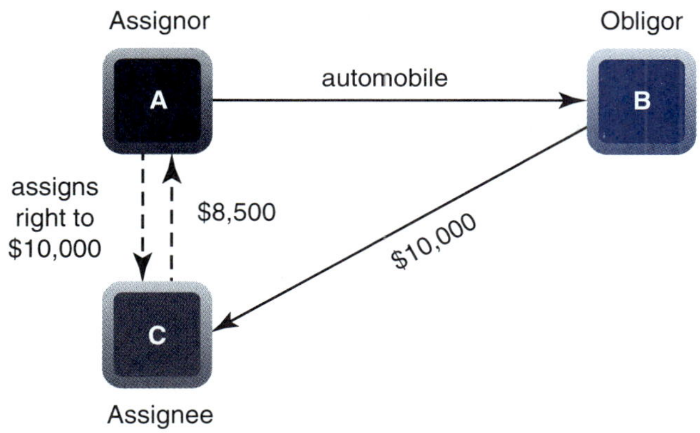

An effective assignment terminates the assignor's right to receive performance by the obligor. After an assignment, only the assignee has a right to the obligor's performance.

On the other hand, if Ann and Doris agree that Doris should deliver the automobile to Bart, this would constitute a delegation, not an assignment, of duties between Ann and Doris. A **delegation of duties** is a transfer to a third party of a contractual obligation. In this instance, Ann would be the **delegator**, Doris would be the **delegatee**, and Bart would be the ***obligee***.

REQUIREMENTS OF AN ASSIGNMENT

The Restatement defines an assignment of a right as a manifestation of the assignor's intention to transfer the right so that the assignor's right to the performance of the obligor is extinguished either in whole or in part and the assignee acquires a right to such performance. No special form or particular words are necessary to create an assignment. Any words that fairly indicate an intention to make the assignee the owner of the right are sufficient.

Unless otherwise provided by statute, an assignment may be oral. The UCC imposes a writing requirement on all assignments beyond $5,000. In addition, Article 9 requires certain assignments to be in writing.

Consideration is not required for an effective assignment. Consequently, gratuitous assignments are valid and enforceable. By giving value, or consideration, for the assignment, the assignee indicates his assent to the assignment as part of the bargained-for exchange. On the other hand, when the assignment is gratuitous, the assignee's assent is not always required. Any assignee who has not assented to an assignment may, however, disclaim the assignment within a reasonable time after learning of its existence and terms.

Revocability of Assignments When the assignee gives consideration in exchange for an assignment, a contract exists between the assignor and the assignee. Consequently, the assignor may not revoke the assignment without the assignee's assent. In contrast, a gratuitous assignment is revocable by the assignor and is terminated by the assignor's death, incapacity, or subsequent assignment of the right, unless the assignor has made an effective delivery of the assignment to the assignee, as in the case of *Speelman v. Pascal*. Such delivery can be accomplished by transferring a deed or other document evidencing the right, such as a stock certificate or savings passbook. Delivery may also consist of physically delivering a signed, written assignment of the contract right. A gratuitous assignment is also made irrevocable if, before the attempted revocation, the donee-assignee receives payment of the claim from the obligor, obtains a judgment against the obligor, or obtains a new contract with the obligor.

Practical Advice

Be sure to make irrevocable assignments of only those rights you wish to transfer.

Speelman v. Pascal

Court of Appeals of New York, 1961
10 N.Y.2d 313, 222 N.Y.S.2d 324, 178 N.E.2d 723

FACTS In 1952, the estate of George Bernard Shaw granted to Gabriel Pascal Enterprises, Limited, the exclusive rights to produce a musical play and a motion picture based on Shaw's play *Pygmalion*. The agreement contained a provision terminating the license if Gabriel Pascal Enterprises did not arrange for well-known composers, such as Lerner and Loewe, to write the musical and produce it within a specified period of time. George Pascal, owner of 98 percent of Gabriel Pascal Enterprises' stock, attempted to meet these requirements but died in July 1954 before negotiations had been completed. In February 1954, however, while the license had two years yet to run, Pascal had sent a letter to Kingman, his executive secretary, granting to her certain percentages of his share of the profits from the expected stage and screen productions of *Pygmalion*. Subsequently, Pascal's estate arranged for the writing and production of the highly successful *My Fair Lady*, based on Shaw's *Pygmalion*. Kingman then sued to enforce Pascal's gift assignment of the future royalties. The trial court entered judgment for Kingman.

DECISION Judgment for Kingman affirmed.

OPINION Desmond, C. J. The only real question is as to whether the 1954 letter * * * operated to transfer to plaintiff an enforceable right to the described percentages of the royalties to accrue to Pascal on the production of a stage or film version of a musical play based on *Pygmalion*. We see no reason why this letter does not have that effect. It is true that at the time of the delivery of the letter there was no musical stage or film play in existence but Pascal, who owned and was conducting negotiations to realize on the stage and film rights, could grant to another a share of the moneys to accrue from the use of those rights by others. There are many instances of courts enforcing assignments of rights to sums which were expected thereafter to become due to the assignor. * * * In every such case the question must be as to whether there was a completed delivery of a kind appropriate to the subject property. * * * In our present case there was nothing left for Pascal to do in order to make an irrevocable transfer to plaintiff of part of Pascal's right to receive royalties from the productions.

INTERPRETATION A gratuitous assignment becomes irrevocable upon the assignor's making an effective delivery of the assignment to the assignee.

CRITICAL THINKING QUESTION Should the law enforce assignments of contractual rights not in existence at the time of the assignment? Explain.

Partial Assignments A **partial assignment** is a transfer of a portion of the contractual rights to one or more assignees, as in the case above. The obligor, however, may require all the parties entitled to the promised performance to litigate the matter in one action, thus ensuring that all parties are present and avoiding the undue hardship of multiple lawsuits. For example, Jack owes Richard $2,500. Richard assigns $1,000 to Mildred. Neither Richard nor Mildred can maintain an action against Jack if Jack objects, unless the other is joined in the proceeding against Jack.

RIGHTS THAT ARE ASSIGNABLE

As a general rule, most contract rights, including rights under an option contract, are assignable. The most common contractual right that may be assigned is the right to the payment of money. A contract right to other property, such as land or goods, is likewise assignable.

RIGHTS THAT ARE NOT ASSIGNABLE

To protect the obligor or the public interest, some contract rights are not assignable. These nonassignable contract rights include those that (1) materially increase the duty, risk, or burden upon the obligor; (2) transfer highly personal contract rights; (3) are expressly prohibited by the contract; or (4) are prohibited by law.

Assignments That Materially Increase the Duty, Risk, or Burden An assignment is ineffective if performance by the obligor to the assignee would differ materially from the obligor's performance to the assignor, that is, if the assignment would significantly change the nature or extent of the obligor's duty. Thus, an automobile liability insurance policy issued to Alex is not assignable by Alex to Betty. The risk assumed by the insurance company was liability for Alex's negligent operation of the automobile. Liability for Betty's operation of the same automobile would be a risk entirely different from the one the insurance company had assumed. Similarly, Candice would not be allowed to assign to Eunice, the owner of a twenty-five room mansion, Candice's contractual right to have David paint her small, two-bedroom house. Clearly, such an assignment would materially increase David's duty of performance. By comparison, the right to receive monthly payments under a contract may be assigned; for mailing the check to the assignee costs no more than mailing it to the assignor. Moreover, if a contract explicitly provides that it may be assigned, then rights under it are assignable even if the assignment would change the duty, risk, or burden of performance on the obligor.

Reiser v. Dayton Country Club Company

United States Court of Appeals, 1992
972 F.2d 689

FACTS The Dayton Country Club Company (the Club) **(http://cincinnati.teemaster.com/course_detail.asp?RegionShortName=&c=33410)** offers many social activities to its members. However, the privilege to play golf at the Club is reserved to a special membership category for which additional fees are charged. The Club chooses golfing memberships from a waiting list of members according to detailed rules, regulations, and procedures. Magness and Redman were golfing members of the Club. Upon their filing for bankruptcy, their trustee sought to assign by sale their rights under these memberships to (1) other members on the waiting list, (2) other members not on the waiting list, or (3) the general public, provided the purchaser first acquired membership in the Club. The bankruptcy court found that the Club's rules governing golf membership were essentially anti-assignment provisions and therefore the estate could not assign rights contained in the membership agreement. On appeal to the district court, the bankruptcy court's ruling was affirmed. The district court added that this case was not a lease but rather a "non-commercial dispute over the possession of a valuable membership in a recreational and social club."

DECISION Judgment affirmed.

OPINION Joiner, J. * * * [T]he contracts involve complex issues and multiple parties: the members of the club, in having an orderly procedure for the selection of full golfing members; the club itself, in demonstrating to all who would become members that there is a predictable and orderly method of filling vacancies in the golfing roster; and more particularly, persons on the waiting list who have deposited substantial sums of money based on an expectation and a developed procedure that in due course they, in turn, would become full golfing members.

If the trustee is permitted to assume and assign the full golf membership, the club would be required to breach its agreement with the persons on the waiting list, each of whom has contractual rights with the club. It would require the club to accept performance from and render performance to a person other than the debtor. * * *

* * *

The contracts creating the complex relationships among the parties and others are not in any way commercial. They create personal relationships among individuals who play golf, who are waiting to play golf, who eat together, swim and play together. They are personal contracts and Ohio law does not permit the assignment of personal contracts. [Citation.]

So-called personal contracts, or contracts in which the personality of one of the parties is material, are not assignable. Whether the personality of one or both parties is material depends on the intention of the parties, as shown by the language which they have used, and upon the nature of the contract.

The claim that the assignment will be made only to those who are already members of the club is not relevant. "Nor would the fact that a particular person it attempted to designate [assign] was personally unexceptionable affect the nature of the contract." [Citation.]

Therefore, we believe that the trustee's motion to assign the full golf membership should be denied. We reach this conclusion because the arrangements for filling vacancies proscribe assignment, the club did not consent to the assignment and sale, and applicable law excuses the club from accepting performance from or rendering performance to a person other than the debtor.

INTERPRETATION When rights under a contract are personal, they may not be assigned.

ETHICAL QUESTION Is the court's decision fair to the creditors of Magness and Redman? Explain.

CRITICAL THINKING QUESTION Which type of contracts should not be assignable because of their personal nature? Explain.

Assignments of Personal Rights When the rights under a contract are highly personal, in that they are limited to the person of the obligee, such rights are not assignable. An extreme example of such a contract is an agreement of two persons to marry one another. The prospective groom obviously may not transfer the prospective bride's promise to marry to some third party. A more typical example of contract involving personal rights would be a contract between a teacher and a school. The teacher could not assign her right to a faculty position to another teacher.

Similarly, a student who is awarded a scholarship cannot assign his right to some other person.

Express Prohibition Against Assignment Though contract terms prohibiting assignment of rights under the contract are strictly construed, most courts interpret a general prohibition against assignments as a mere promise not to assign. As a consequence, the general prohibition, if violated, gives the obligor a right to damages for breach of the terms forbidding assignment but does not render the assignment ineffective.

The Restatement provides that, unless circumstances indicate the contrary, a contract term prohibiting assignment of the *contract* bars only the delegation to the assignee (delegatee) of the assignor's (delegator's) duty of performance, not the assignment of *rights*. Thus, Norman and Lucy contract for the sale of land by Lucy to Norman for $30,000 and provide in their contract that Norman may not assign the contract. Norman pays Lucy $30,000, thereby fulfilling his duty of performance under the contract. Norman then assigns his rights to George, who consequently is entitled to receive the land from Lucy (the obligor) despite the contractual prohibition of assignment.

Article 2 of the Code provides that a right to damages for breach of the whole contract or a right arising out of the assignor's due performance of his entire obligation can be assigned despite a contractual provision to the contrary. Article 2 also provides that, unless circumstances indicate the contrary, a contract term prohibiting assignment of the *contract* bars only the delegation to the assignee (delegatee) of the assignor's (delegator's) *duty* of performance, not the assignment of *rights*. Article 9 of the Code makes ineffective any term in a contract prohibiting the assignment of any right to payment for goods sold or leased or for services rendered.

Practical Advice

Consider including in your contract a provision prohibiting the assignment of any contractual rights without your written consent and making ineffective any such assignment.

Aldana v. Colonial Palms Plaza, Inc.

District Court of Appeal of Florida, Third District, 1991

591 So.2d 953

FACTS Colonial Palms Plaza, Inc. (Landlord) entered into a lease agreement with Abby's Cakes On Dixie, Inc. (Tenant). The lease included a provision in which Landlord agreed to pay Tenant a construction allowance of up to $11,250 after Tenant completed certain improvements. Prior to completion of the improvements, Tenant assigned its right to receive the first $8,000 of the construction allowance to Robert Aldana in return for a loan of $8,000 to finance the construction. Aldana sent notice of the assignment to Landlord. When Tenant completed the improvements, Landlord ignored the assignment and paid Tenant the construction allowance. Aldana sued Landlord for the money due pursuant to the assignment. Landlord relied on an anti-assignment clause in the lease to argue that the assignment was void. That clause states in part: "TENANT agrees not to assign, mortgage, pledge, or encumber this Lease, in whole or in part, to sublet in whole or any part of the DEMISED PREMISES * * * without first obtaining the prior, specific written consent of the LANDLORD at LANDLORD'S sole discretion. * * * Any such assignment * * * without such consent shall be void." The trial court granted Landlord summary judgment.

DECISION Summary judgment reversed and case remanded.

OPINION Per Curiam. Assignee argues * * * that under ordinary contract principles, the lease provision at issue here does not prevent the assignment of the right to receive contractual payments. We agree.

So far as pertinent here, the lease provides that "TENANT agrees not to assign * * * this Lease, in whole or in part. * * *" Tenant did not assign the lease, but instead assigned a right to receive the construction allowance.

The law in this area is summarized in Restatement (Second) of Contracts, § 322(1), as follows:

> (1) Unless the circumstances indicate the contrary, a contract term prohibiting assignment of "the contract" bars only the delegation to an assignee of the performance by the assignor of a duty or condition.

As a rule of construction, in other words, a prohibition against assignment of the contract (or in this case, the lease) will prevent assignment of contractual duties, but does not prevent assignment of the right to receive payments due—unless the circumstances indicate the contrary. [Citations.]

Landlord was given notice of the assignment. Delivery of the notice of the assignment to the debtor fixes accountability of the debtor to the assignee. [Citation.] Therefore, Landlord was bound by the assignment. [Citation.] The trial court improperly granted final summary judgment in favor of Landlord and the judgment must be reversed.

INTERPRETATION Unless circumstances indicate the contrary, a contract term prohibiting assignment of the contract bars only delegation of the assignor's contractual duties.

ETHICAL QUESTION If the landlord had inadvertently ignored the notice of assignment, would the outcome of the case have been fair? Explain.

CRITICAL THINKING QUESTION Should the courts honor contractual prohibitions of assignments by rendering such assignments ineffective? Explain.

Assignments Prohibited by Law Various federal and state statutes, as well as public policy, prohibit or regulate the assignment of certain types of contract rights. For instance, assignments of future wages are subject to such statutes, some of which prohibit these assignments altogether, whereas others require the assignments to be in writing and subject them to certain restrictions. Moreover, an assignment that violates public policy will be unenforceable even in the absence of a prohibiting statute.

RIGHTS OF THE ASSIGNEE

Obtains Rights of Assignor The general rule is that an assignee ***stands in the shoes*** of the assignor. She acquires the rights of the assignor but no new or additional rights, and she takes with the assigned rights all of the defenses, defects, and infirmities to which they would be subject in an action against the obligor by the assignor. Thus, in an action brought by the assignee against the obligor, the obligor may plead fraud, duress, undue influence, failure of consideration, breach of contract, or any other defense arising out of the original contract against the assignor. The obligor may also assert rights of **setoff** or counterclaim arising out of entirely separate matters that he may have against the assignor, as long as they arose before he had notice of the assignment.

The Code permits the buyer under a contract of sale to agree as part of the contract that he will not assert against an assignee any claim or defense that the buyer may have against the seller if the assignee takes the assignment for value and in good faith. Such a provision in an agreement renders the seller's rights more marketable. The Federal Trade Commission, however, has invalidated such waiver of defense provisions in consumer credit transactions. This rule is discussed more fully in Chapter 26. Most states also have statutes protecting buyers in consumer transactions by prohibiting waiver of defenses.

Notice The obligor need not receive notice for an assignment to be valid. Giving notice of assignment is advisable, however, because an assignee will lose his rights against the obligor if the obligor, without notice of the assignment, pays the assignor. Compelling an obligor to pay a claim a second time, when she was unaware that a new party was entitled to payment, would be unfair. For example, Donald owes Gary $1,000 due on September 1. Gary assigns the debt to Paula on August 1, but neither Gary nor Paula informs Donald. On September 1, Donald pays Gary. Donald is fully discharged from his obligation, whereas Gary is liable for $1,000 to Paula. On the other hand, if Paula had given notice of the assignment to Donald before September 1 and Donald had paid Gary nevertheless, Paula would then have the right to recover the $1,000 from either Donald or Gary. Furthermore, notice cuts off any defenses based on subsequent agreements between the obligor and assignor and, as already indicated, subsequent setoffs and counterclaims of the obligor that may arise out of entirely separate matters.

Practical Advice

Upon receiving an assignment of a contractual right, promptly notify the obligor of the assignment.

IMPLIED WARRANTIES OF ASSIGNOR

An **implied warranty** is an obligation imposed by law upon the transferor of property or contract rights. In the absence of an express intention to the contrary, an assignor who receives value makes the following implied warranties to the assignee with respect to the assigned right:

1. that he will do nothing to defeat or impair the assignment;

2. that the assigned right actually exists and is subject to no limitations or defenses other than those stated or apparent at the time of the assignment;
3. that any writing that evidences the right and that is delivered to the assignee or exhibited to him as an inducement to accept the assignment is genuine and what it purports to be; and
4. that the assignor has no knowledge of any fact that would impair the value of the assignment.

Thus, Eric has a right against Julia and assigns it for value to Gwen. Later, Eric gives Julia a release. Gwen may recover damages from Eric for breach of the first implied warranty.

EXPRESS WARRANTIES OF ASSIGNOR

An **express warranty** is an explicitly made contractual promise regarding the property or contract rights transferred. The assignor is further bound by any specific express warranties he makes to the assignee about the right assigned. Unless he explicitly states as much, however, the assignor does not guarantee that the obligor will pay the assigned debt or otherwise perform.

Practical Advice

Consider obtaining from the assignor an express warranty that the contractual right is assignable and guaranteeing that the obligor will perform the assigned obligation.

SUCCESSIVE ASSIGNMENTS OF THE SAME RIGHT

The owner of a right could conceivably make successive assignments of the same claim to different persons. Although this action is morally and legally inappropriate, it raises the question of what rights successive assignees have. Assume, for example, that B owes A $1,000. On June 1, A for value assigns the debt to C. Thereafter, on June 15, A assigns it to D, who in good faith gives value and has no knowledge of the prior assignment by A to C. If the assignment is subject to Article 9, then the article's priority rules will control, as discussed in Chapter 38. Otherwise, the priority is determined by the common law. The majority rule in the United States is that the first assignee in point of time (C) prevails over later assignees. By way of contrast, in England and in a minority of the states, the first assignee to notify the obligor prevails.

The Restatement adopts a third view: A prior assignee is entitled to the assigned right and its proceeds to the exclusion of a subsequent assignee, *except* where the prior assignment is revocable or voidable by the assignor or the subsequent assignee in good faith and without knowledge of the prior assignment gives value and obtains one of the following: (1) payment or satisfaction of the obligor's duty, (2) a judgment against the obligor, (3) a new contract with the obligor, or (4) possession of a writing of a type customarily accepted as a symbol or evidence of the right assigned.

CPA DELEGATION OF DUTIES

As we indicated earlier, contractual ***duties*** are not assignable, but their performance generally may be delegated to a third person. A delegation of duties is a transfer of a contractual obligation to a third party. For example, A promises to sell B a new automobile, for which B promises to pay $10,000 by monthly installments over the next three years. If A and D agree that D should deliver the automobile to B, this would not constitute an assignment but would be a delegation of duties between A and D. In this instance, A would be the ***delegator***, D would be the ***delegatee***, and B would be the ***obligee***. A delegation of duty does not extinguish the delegator's obligation to perform because A remains liable to B. When the delegatee accepts, or **assumes**, the delegated duty, *both* the delegator and delegatee are liable for performance of the contractual duty to the obligee.

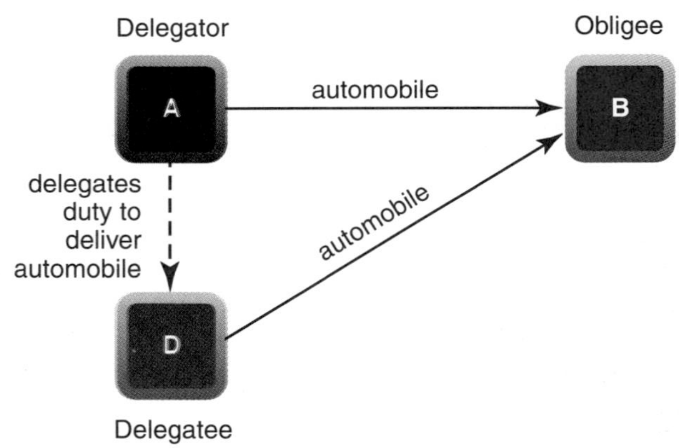

DELEGABLE DUTIES

Though contractual duties generally are delegable, a delegation will not be permitted if

1. the nature of the duties are personal in that the obligee has a substantial interest in having the delegator perform the contract;
2. the performance is expressly made nondelegable; or
3. the delegation is prohibited by statute or public policy.

The courts will examine a delegation more closely than an assignment because a delegation compels the nondelegating party to the contract (the obligee) to receive performance from a party with whom she has not dealt.

For example, a schoolteacher may not delegate her performance to another teacher, even if the substitute is equally competent, for this contract is personal in nature. On the other hand, under a contract in which performance by a party involves no special skill and in which no personal trust or confidence is involved, the party may delegate performance of his duty. For example, the duty to pay money, to deliver fungible goods such as corn, or to mow a lawn is usually delegable. The next case deals with this type of delegation.

Practical Advice

When it is important that the other party to a contract personally perform his contractual obligations, consider including a term in the contract prohibiting any delegation of duties without written consent.

Macke Company v. Pizza of Gaithersburg, Inc.

Court of Appeals of Maryland, 1970
259 Md. 479, 270 A.2d 645

FACTS In 1966, Pizza of Gaithersburg and The Pizza Shops contracted with Virginia Coffee Service to have vending machines installed in each of their pizza establishments. One year later, the Macke Company purchased Virginia's assets, and the vending machine contracts were assigned to Macke. When The Pizza Shops attempted to terminate their contracts for vending services, Macke brought suit for damages for breach of contract. The Pizza Shops argued that they had dealt with Macke before but had chosen Virginia because they preferred the way it conducted its business. They contended that because there was a material difference between the performance of Virginia and that of Macke, they were justified in refusing to recognize Virginia's delegation of its duties to Macke. Macke appealed from a judgment for the defendants.

DECISION Judgment reversed.

OPINION Singley, J. In the absence of a contrary provision—and there was none here—rights and duties under an executory bilateral contract may be assigned and delegated, subject to the exception that duties under a contract to provide personal services may never be delegated, nor rights be assigned under a contract where *delectus personae* [choice of person] was an ingredient of the bargain. [Citations.] *Crane Ice Cream Co. v. Terminal Freezing & Heating Co.*, [citation] held that the right of an individual to purchase ice under a contract which by its terms reflected a knowledge of the individual's needs and reliance on his credit and responsibility could not be assigned to the corporation which purchased his business. In [citation], our predecessors held that an advertising agency could not delegate its duties under a contract which had been entered into by an advertiser who had relied on the agency's skill, judgment and taste.

* * *

We cannot regard the agreements as contracts for personal services. They were either a license or concession granted Virginia by the appellees, or a lease of a portion of the appellees' premises, with Virginia agreeing to pay a percentage of gross sales as a license or concession fee or as rent, [citations], and were assignable by Virginia unless they imposed on Virginia duties of a personal or unique character which could not be delegated, [citation].

The appellees earnestly argue that they had dealt with Macke before and had chosen Virginia because they preferred the way it conducted its business. Specifically, they say that service was more personalized, since the president of Virginia kept the machines in working order, that commissions were paid in cash, and that Virginia permitted them to keep keys to the machines so that minor adjustments could be made when needed. Even if we assume all this to be true, the agreements with Virginia were silent as to the details of the working arrangements and contained only a provision requiring Virginia to "install * * * the above listed equipment and * * * maintain the equipment in good operating order and stocked with merchandise." We think the Supreme Court of California put the problem of personal service in proper focus a century ago when it upheld the assignment of a contract to grade a San Francisco street:

All painters do not paint portraits like Sir Joshua Reynolds, nor landscapes like Claude Lorraine, nor do all writers write dramas like Shakespeare or fiction like Dickens. Rare genius and extraordinary skill are not transferable, and contracts for their employment are therefore personal, and cannot be assigned. But rare genius and extraordinary skill are not indispensable to the workmanlike digging down of a sand hill or the filling up of a depression to a given level, or the construction of brick sewers with manholes and covers, and contracts for such work are not personal, and may be assigned. [Citation.]

* * * Moreover, the difference between the service The Pizza Shops happened to be getting from Virginia and what they expected to get from Macke did not mount up to such a material change in the performance of obligations under the agreements as would justify the appellees' refusal to recognize the assignment, [citation].

* * *

As we see it, the delegation of duty by Virginia to Macke was entirely permissible under the terms of the agreements.

INTERPRETATION Contractual duties, unless otherwise stated, are delegable if the quality of performance remains materially the same.

ETHICAL QUESTION Should the court have given more weight to the fact that the defendant had previously been dissatisfied with Macke's performance and had chosen not to deal with Macke? Explain.

CRITICAL THINKING QUESTION In determining whether the quality of performance will remain the same despite a delegation of duties, should the court use an objective standard or a subjective standard? Explain.

DUTIES OF THE PARTIES

Even when permitted, a **delegation** of a duty to a third person leaves the delegator bound to perform. If the delegator desires to be discharged of the duty, she may enter into an agreement by which she obtains the consent of the obligee to substitute a third person (the delegatee) in her place. This is a **novation**, whereby the delegator is discharged and the third party becomes directly bound on his promise to the obligee.

Though a delegation authorizes a third party to perform a duty for the delegator, the delegatee becomes liable for performance only if he assents to perform the delegated duties. Thus, if Frank owes a duty to Grace, and Frank delegates that duty to Henry, Henry is not obligated to either Frank or Grace to perform the duty unless Henry agrees to do so. If, however, Henry promises either Frank (the delegator) or Grace (the obligee) that he will perform Frank's duty, Henry is said to have **assumed the delegated duty** and becomes liable for nonperformance to both Frank and Grace. Accordingly, when there is both a delegation of duties *and* an assumption of the delegated duties, *both* the delegator and the delegatee are liable to the obligee for proper performance of the original contractual duty. The delegatee's promise to perform creates contract rights in the obligee, who may bring an action against the delegatee as a third-party beneficiary of the contract between the delegator and the delegatee. (Third-party contracts are discussed later in this chapter.)

The question of whether a party has assumed contractual duties frequently arises in the following ambiguous situation: Marty and Carol agree to an assignment of Marty's contract with Bob. The Restatement and the Code clearly resolve this ambiguity by providing that unless the language or circumstances indicate the contrary, an assignment of "the contract" or of "all my rights under the contract" or an assignment in similar general terms is an assignment of rights *and* a delegation of performance of the duties of the assignor, and its acceptance by the assignee constitutes a promise to perform those duties. For example, Cooper Oil Company has a contract to deliver oil to Halsey. Cooper makes a written assignment to Lowell Oil Company "of all Cooper's rights under the contract." Lowell is under a duty to Halsey to deliver the oil called for by the contract, and Cooper is liable to Halsey if Lowell does not perform. You should also recall that the Restatement and the Code provide that a clause prohibiting an assignment of "the contract" is to be construed as barring only the delegation to the assignee (delegatee) of the assignor's (delegator's) performance, unless the circumstances indicate the contrary.

THIRD-PARTY BENEFICIARY CONTRACTS

CPA

A contract in which a party (the ***promisor***) promises to render a certain performance not to the other party (the promisee) but to a third person (the beneficiary) is called a **third-party beneficiary contract**. The third person is merely a beneficiary of the contract, not a party to it. The law divides such contracts into two types: (1) intended beneficiary contracts and (2) incidental beneficiary contracts. An **intended beneficiary** is intended by the two parties to the contract (the promisor and promisee) to receive a benefit from the performance of their agreement. Accordingly, the courts generally permit intended beneficiaries to enforce third-party contracts. For example, Abbot promises Baldwin to deliver an automobile to Carson if Baldwin promises to pay $10,000. Carson is the intended beneficiary.

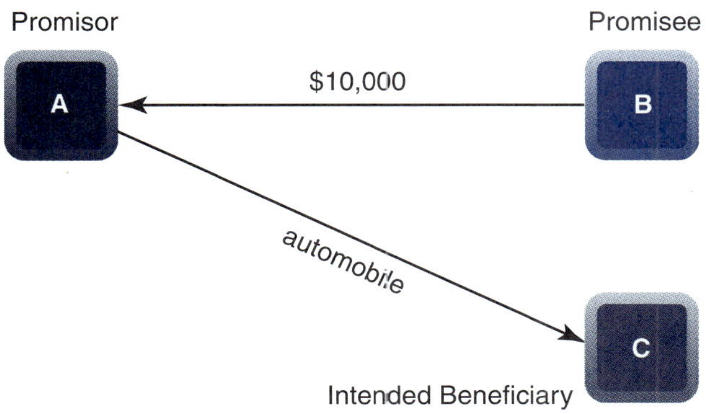

In an **incidental beneficiary** contract the third party is not intended to receive a benefit under the contract. Accordingly, courts do not enforce the third party's right to the benefits of the contract. For example, Abbot promises to purchase and deliver to Baldwin an automobile for $10,000. In all probability Abbot would acquire the automobile from Davis. Davis would be an incidental beneficiary and would have no enforceable rights against either Abbot or Baldwin.

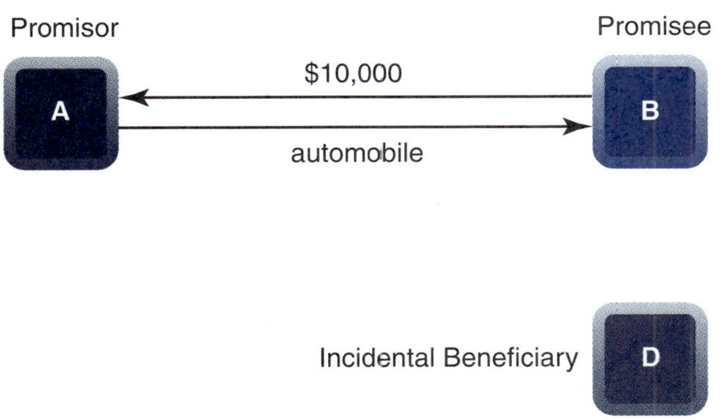

INTENDED BENEFICIARY

Unless otherwise agreed between the promisor and promisee, a beneficiary of a promise is an intended beneficiary if the parties intended this to be the result of their agreement. Thus, there are two types of intended beneficiaries: (1) donee beneficiaries and (2) creditor beneficiaries.

Donee Beneficiary A third party is an intended donee beneficiary if the promisee's purpose in bargaining for and obtaining the contract with the promisor was to make a gift of the promised performance to the beneficiary. The ordinary life insurance policy illustrates this type of intended beneficiary third-party contract. The insured (the promisee) makes a contract with an insurance company (the promisor), which promises, in consideration of premiums paid to it by the insured, to pay upon the death of the insured a stated sum of money to the named beneficiary (generally a relative or close friend), who is an intended donee beneficiary.

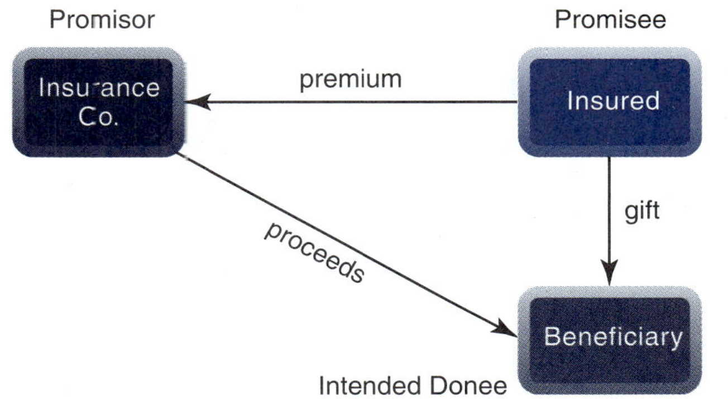

Creditor Beneficiary A third person is an intended creditor beneficiary if the promisee intends the performance of the promise to satisfy a legal duty owed to the beneficiary, who is a creditor of the promisee. The contract involves consideration moving from the promisee to the promisor in exchange for the promisor's engaging to pay a debt or to discharge an obligation the promisee owes to the third person.

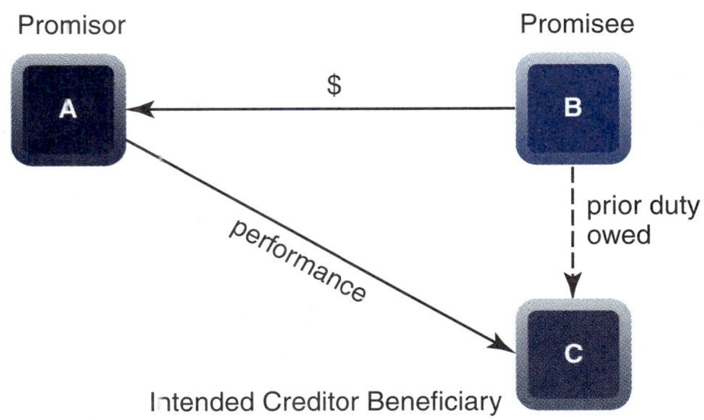

To illustrate: in the contract for the sale by Wesley of his business to Susan, she promises Wesley that she will pay all of his outstanding business debts, as listed in the contract. Wesley's creditors are intended creditor beneficiaries.

Stine v. Stewart

Supreme Court of Texas, 2002
80 S.W.3d 586
http://caselaw.lp.findlaw.com/scripts/getcase.pl?court=tx&vol=/sc/010896&invol=1

FACTS On April 26, 1984, Mary Stine (Stine) loaned her daughter (Mary Ellen) and son-in-law William Stewart $100,000 to purchase a home. In return, the Stewarts jointly executed a promissory note for $100,000, payable on demand to Stine. The note required interest payments at a floating rate adjusted every six months to one percent below the prime rate. The Stewarts did not give a security interest or mortgage to secure the note. The Stewarts eventually paid $50,000 on the note, leaving $50,000, plus unpaid accrued interest, due.

The Stewarts divorced on October 2, 1992. The couple executed an Agreement Incident to Divorce, which disposed of marital property, including the home (the agreement identifies the home as the Lago Vista property). The agreement provides that if Stewart sold the home, he agreed that "any monies owing to [Stine] are to be paid in the current principal sum of $50,000.00." The agreement further states:

> The parties agree that with regard to the note to Mary Nelle Stine, after application of the proceeds of the [Lago Vista property], if there are any amounts owing to [Stine] the remaining balance owing to her will be appropriated 50% to NANCY KAREN STEWART and 50% to WILLIAM DEAN STEWART, JR. and said 50% from each party will be due and payable upon the determination that the proceeds from the sale of said residence are not sufficient to repay said $50,000.00 in full.

Stine did not sign the agreement.

On November 17, 1995, Stewart sold the Lago Vista property for $125,000, leaving $6,820.21 in net proceeds. Stewart did not pay these proceeds to Stine and did not make any further payments on the $50,000 principal. Consequently, on July 27, 1998, Stine sued Stewart for breaching the agreement.

The trial court concluded that Stine was an intended third-party beneficiary of the agreement and that Stewart breached the agreement when he refused to pay Stine. The trial court awarded Stine $28,410 in damages from Stewart. The court of appeals reversed the judgment, concluding that Stine was neither an intended third-party donee beneficiary of the agreement nor an intended third-party creditor beneficiary of the agreement.

DECISION The court of appeals' judgment is reversed and case remanded.

OPINION Per Curiam. A third party may recover on a contract made between other parties only if the parties intended to secure a benefit to that third party, and only if the contracting parties entered into the contract directly for the third party's benefit. [Citation.] A third party does not have a right to enforce the contract if she received only an incidental benefit. [Citation.] "A court will not create a third-party beneficiary contract by implication." [Citation.] Rather, an agreement must clearly and fully express an intent to confer a direct benefit to the third party. [Citation.] To determine the parties' intent, courts must examine the entire agreement when interpreting a contract and give effect to all the contract's provisions so that none are rendered meaningless. [Citation.]

To qualify as an intended third-party beneficiary, a party must show that she is either a "donee" or "creditor" beneficiary of the contract. [Citation.] An agreement benefits a "donee" beneficiary if, under the contract, "the performance promised will, when rendered, come to him as a pure donation." [Citations.] In contrast, an agreement benefits a "creditor" beneficiary if, under the agreement, "that performance will come to him in satisfaction of a legal duty owed to him by the promisee." [Citations.] This duty may be an indebtedness, contractual obligation or other legally enforceable commitment owed to the third party. [Citation.]

Stine contends that she has standing to sue for breach of the agreement as a third-party beneficiary, because the Stewarts intended to secure a benefit to her—that is, the payment of the remaining balance under the note. Stine also argues that whether or not limitations expired on enforcing the note, she was still a third-party creditor beneficiary because the debt remained an existing, legal obligation. Moreover, Stine contends, the agreement "acknowledges" the $50,000 debt owed to her because it recognizes that the note exists and requires the Stewarts to pay any amounts due under the note when Stewart sells the Lago Vista property. * * *

Stewart responds that Stine does not have standing to sue under the agreement, because she is only an incidental beneficiary. Stewart argues that the agreement was not entered into directly and primarily for Stine's benefit, and the agreement does not fully and clearly express the intent to confer a benefit to Stine. * * * Moreover, Stewart contends that the agreement does not acknowledge the original note, because it does not contain unequivocal language that revives the expired debt. * * *

We agree with the court of appeals' determination that Stine was not an intended third-party donee beneficiary of the agreement. [Citation.] But, we conclude that Stine is a third-party creditor beneficiary. The agreement expressly provides that the Stewarts intended to satisfy an obligation to repay Stine the $50,000 that the Stewarts owed her. Specifically, the agreement refers to the monies owed to Stine as "the current principal sum of $50,000." Then, the agreement states that Stewart agreed to pay the property sale net proceeds "with regard to the note" to Stine. The agreement further provides that, if the property sale net proceeds did not cover the amount owed to Stine, the remainder would be immediately due and payable from the Stewarts, with each owing one half. Thus, the agreement expressly requires the Stewarts to satisfy their existing obligation to pay Stine. [Citation.]

* * *

Furthermore, contrary to Stewart's argument, a third-party beneficiary does not have to show that the signatories executed the contract *solely* to benefit her as a non-contracting party. Rather, the focus is on whether the contracting parties intended, at least in part, to discharge an obligation owed to the third party. [Citation.] Here, the entire agreement is obviously not for Stine's sole benefit. However, certain provisions in the agreement expressly state the Stewarts' intent to pay Stine the money due to her.

* * *

The agreement's language clearly shows that Stewart intended to secure a benefit to Stine as a third-party creditor beneficiary. The agreement also acknowledges the existence of a legal obligation owed to Stine and thus revives it as an enforceable obligation. Consequently, Stewart breached the agreement when he refused to pay Stine the money owed to her as the agreement requires.

INTERPRETATION An intended third-party beneficiary of a contract may enforce that contract.

CRITICAL THINKING QUESTION Why did the court conclude that Stine was not an intended third-party donee beneficiary?

Rights of Intended Beneficiary Though an intended creditor beneficiary may sue either or both parties, an intended donee beneficiary may enforce the contract against the promisor only. He cannot maintain an action against the promisee, as the promisee was under no legal obligation to him.

Vesting of Rights A contract for the benefit of an intended beneficiary confers upon that beneficiary rights that the beneficiary may enforce. Until these rights vest (take effect), however, the promisor and promisee may, by later agreement, vary or completely discharge them. There is considerable variation among the states as to when vesting occurs. Some states hold that vesting takes place immediately upon the making of the contract. In other states, vesting occurs when the third party learns of the contract and assents to it. In another group of states, vesting requires the third party to change his position in reliance upon the promise made for his benefit. The Restatement has adopted the following position: If the contract between the promisor and promisee provides that its terms may not be varied without the consent of the beneficiary, such a provision will be upheld. If there is no such provision, the parties to the contract may rescind or vary the contract unless the intended beneficiary (1) has brought an action on the promise, (2) has changed her position in reliance on it, or (3) has assented to the promise at the request of the promisor or promisee.

On the other hand, the promisor and promisee may provide that the benefits will never vest. For example, Mildred purchases an insurance policy on her own life, naming her husband as beneficiary. The policy, as such policies commonly do, reserves to Mildred the right to change her beneficiary or even to cancel the policy entirely.

Defenses Against Beneficiary In an action by the intended beneficiary to enforce the promise, the promisor may assert any defense that would be available to her if the action had been brought by the promisee. The rights of the third party are based upon the promisor's contract with the promisee. Thus, the promisor may assert the absence of mutual assent or consideration, lack of capacity, fraud, mistake, and the like against the intended beneficiary. Once an intended beneficiary's rights have vested, however, the promisor may not assert the defense of contractual modification or rescission entered into with the promisee.

INCIDENTAL BENEFICIARY

An incidental third-party beneficiary is a person to whom the parties to a contract did not intend a benefit but who nevertheless would derive some benefit by its performance. For instance, a contract to raze an old, unsightly building and to replace it with a costly modern house would benefit the owner of the adjoining property by increasing his property's value. He would have no rights under the contract, however, as the benefit to him would be unintended and incidental.

A third person who may benefit incidentally by the performance of a contract to which he is not a party has no rights under the contract, as neither the promisee nor the promisor intended that the third person benefit. Assume that for a stated consideration Charles promises Madeline that he will purchase and deliver to Madeline a new Sony television of the latest model. Madeline performs. Charles does not. Reiner, the local exclusive Sony dealer, has no rights under the contract, although performance by Charles would produce a sale from which Reiner would derive a benefit, for Reiner is only an incidental beneficiary.

Practical Advice

To avoid uncertainty, consider specifying in the contract whether there are any third-party beneficiaries and, if so, who they are, what their rights are, and when their rights vest.

CHAPTER SUMMARY

Assignment of Rights

Definition of Assignment voluntary transfer to a third party of the rights arising from a contract so that the assignor's right to performance is extinguished
- *Assignor* party making an assignment
- *Assignee* party to whom contract rights are assigned
- *Obligor* party owing a duty to the assignor under the original contract
- *Obligee* party to whom a duty of performance is owed under a contract

Requirements of an Assignment include intent but not consideration
- *Revocability of Assignment* when the assignee gives consideration, the assignor may not revoke the assignment without the assignee's consent
- *Partial Assignment* transfer of a portion of contractual rights to one or more assignees

Assignability most contract rights are assignable *except*:
- Assignments that materially increase the duty, risk, or burden upon the obligor
- Assignments of personal rights
- Assignments expressly forbidden by the contract
- Assignments prohibited by law

Rights of Assignee the assignee stands in the shoes of the assignor
- *Defenses of obligor* may be asserted against the assignee
- *Notice* is not required but is advisable

Implied Warranties obligation imposed by law upon the assignor of a contract right

Express Warranty explicitly made contractual promise regarding contract rights transferred

Successive Assignments the majority rule is that the first assignee in point of time prevails over later assignees; minority rule is that the first assignee to notify the obligor prevails

Delegation of Duties

Definition of Delegation transfer to a third party of a contractual obligation
- *Delegator* party delegating his duty to a third party
- *Delegatee* third party to whom the delegator's duty is delegated
- *Obligee* party to whom a duty of performance is owed by the delegator and delegatee

Delegability most contract duties may be delegated except:
- Duties that are personal
- Duties that are expressly nondelegable
- Duties whose delegation is prohibited by statute or public policy

Duties of Parties
- ***Delegation*** delegator is still bound to perform original obligation
- ***Novation*** contract, to which the obligee is a party, substituting a new promisor for an existing promisor, who is consequently no longer liable on the original contract and is not liable as a delegator

Third-Party Beneficiary Contracts

Definition a third-party beneficiary contract is one in which one party promises to render a performance to a third person (the beneficiary)

Intended Beneficiaries third parties intended by the two contracting parties to receive a benefit from their contract
- ***Donee Beneficiary*** a third party intended to receive a benefit from the contract as a gift
- ***Creditor Beneficiary*** a third person intended to receive a benefit from the contract to satisfy a legal duty owed to him
- ***Rights of Intended Beneficiaries*** an intended donee beneficiary may enforce the contract against the promisor; an intended creditor beneficiary may enforce the contract against either or both the promisor and the promisee
- ***Vesting of Rights*** if the beneficiary's rights vest, the promisor and promisee may not thereafter vary or discharge these vested rights

Defenses Against Beneficiary in an action by the intended beneficiary to enforce the promise, the promisor may assert any defense that would be available to her if the action had been brought by the promisee

Incidental Beneficiary third party whom the two parties to the contract have no intention of benefitting by their contract and who acquires no rights under the contract

QUESTIONS

1. On December 1, Euphonia, a famous singer, contracted with Boito to sing at Boito's theater on December 31 for a fee of $25,000 to be paid immediately after the performance.
   a. Euphonia, for value received, assigns this fee to Carter.
   b. Euphonia, for value received, assigns this contract to sing to Dumont, an equally famous singer.
   c. Boito sells his theater to Edmund and assigns his contract with Euphonia to Edmund.

   State the effect of each of these assignments.

2. The Smooth Paving Company entered into a paving contract with the city of Chicago. The contract contained the clause "contractor shall be liable for all damages to buildings resulting from the work performed." In the process of construction, one of the bulldozers of the Smooth Paving Company struck and broke a gas main, causing an explosion and a fire that destroyed the house of John Puff. Puff brought an action for breach of the paving contract against the Smooth Paving Company to recover damages for the loss of his house. Can Puff recover under this contract? Explain.

3. Anne, who was unemployed, registered with the Speedy Employment Agency. A contract was then made under which Anne, in consideration of such position as the agency would obtain for her, agreed to pay the agency one half of her first month's salary. The contract also contained an assignment by Anne to the agency of one half of her first month's salary. Two weeks later, the agency obtained a permanent position for Anne with the Bostwick Co. at a monthly salary of $900. The agency also notified Bostwick Co. of the assignment by Anne. At the end of the first month, Bostwick Co. paid Anne her salary in full. Anne then quit and disappeared. The agency now sues Bostwick Co. for $450 under the assignment. Who will prevail? Explain.

4. Georgia purchased an option on Blackacre from Pamela for $1,000. The option contract contained a provision by which Georgia promised not to assign the option contract without Pamela's permission. Georgia, without Pamela's permission, assigned the contract to Michael. Michael now seeks to exercise the option, and Pamela refuses to sell Blackacre to him. Must Pamela sell the land to Michael?

5. Julia contracts to sell to Hayden, an ice cream manufacturer, the amount of ice Hayden may need in his business for the ensuing three years to the extent of not more than 250 tons a week at a stated price per ton. Hayden makes a corresponding promise to Julia to buy such an amount of ice. Hayden sells his ice cream plant to Reed and assigns to Reed all Hayden's rights under the contract with Julia. On learning of the sale, Julia refuses to furnish ice to Reed. Can Reed successfully collect damages from Julia? Explain.

6. Brown enters into a written contract with Ideal Insurance Company under which, in consideration of Brown's payment of her premiums, the insurance company promises to pay XYZ College the face amount of the policy, $100,000, on Brown's death. Brown pays the premiums until her death. Thereafter, XYZ College makes demand for the $100,000, which the insurance company refuses to pay on the ground that XYZ College was not a party to the contract. Can XYZ successfully enforce the contract?

7. Grant and Debbie enter into a contract binding Grant personally to do some delicate cabinetwork. Grant assigns his rights and delegates performance of his duties to Clarence.
   a. On being informed of this, Debbie agrees with Clarence, in consideration of Clarence's promise to do the work, that Debbie will accept Clarence's work, if properly done, instead of the performance promised by Grant. Later, without cause, Debbie refuses to allow Clarence to proceed with the work, though Clarence is ready to do so, and makes demand on Grant that Grant perform. Grant refuses. Can Clarence recover damages from Debbie? Can Debbie recover from Grant?
   b. Debbie refuses to permit Clarence to do the work, employs another carpenter, and brings an action against Grant, claiming as damages the difference between the contract price and the cost to employ the other carpenter. Explain whether Debbie will prevail.

8. Rebecca owes Lewis $2,500 due on November 1. On August 15, Lewis assigns this right for value received to Julia, who gives notice on September 10 of the assignment to Rebecca. On August 25, Lewis assigns the same right to Wayne, who in good faith gives value and has no prior knowledge of the assignment by Lewis to Julia. Wayne gives Rebecca notice of the assignment on August 30. What are the rights and obligations of Rebecca, Lewis, Julia, and Wayne?

9. Lisa hired Jay in the spring, as she had for many years, to set out in beds the flowers Lisa had grown in her greenhouses during the winter. The work was to be done in Lisa's absence for $300. Jay became ill the day after Lisa departed and requested his friend, Curtis, to set out the flowers, promising to pay Curtis $250 when Jay received his payment. Curtis agreed. On completion of the planting, an agent of Lisa's, who had authority to dispense the money, paid Jay, and Jay paid Curtis. Within two days, it became obvious that the planting was a disaster. Because he did not operate Lisa's automatic watering system properly, everything set out by Curtis had died of water rot.

   May Lisa recover damages from Curtis? May Lisa recover damages from Jay, and, if so, does Jay have an action against Curtis?

10. Caleb, operator of a window-washing business, dictated a letter to his secretary addressed to Apartments, Inc., stating, "I will wash the windows of your apartment buildings at $4.10 per window to be paid on completion of the work." The secretary typed the letter, signed Caleb's name, and mailed it to Apartments, Inc. Apartments, Inc., replied, "Accept your offer."

    Caleb wrote back, "I will wash them during the week starting July 10 and direct you to pay the money you will owe me to my son, Bernie. I am giving it to him as a wedding present." Caleb sent a signed copy of the letter to Bernie.

    Caleb washed the windows during the time stated and demanded payment to him of $8,200 (2,000 windows at $4.10 each), informing Apartments, Inc., that he had changed his mind about having the money paid to Bernie.

    What are the rights of the parties?

CASE PROBLEMS

11. On April 1, members of Local 100, Transport Workers Union of America (TWU) (http://www.twu.org), began an eleven-day mass transit strike that paralyzed the life and commerce of the city of New York (http://www.ci.nyc.ny.us). Jackson, Lewis, Schnitzler & Krupman (http://www.jacksonlewis.com), a Manhattan law firm, brought a class action suit against the TWU for the direct and foreseeable damages it suffered as a result of the union's illegal strike. The law firm sought to recover as a third-party beneficiary of the collective bargaining agreement between the union and New York City. The agreement contains a no-strike clause and states that the TWU agreed to cooperate with the city to provide a safe, efficient, and dependable mass transit system. The law firm argues that its members are a part of the general public that depends on the mass transit system to go to and from work. Therefore, they are in the class of persons for whose benefit the union has promised to provide dependable transportation service. Are the members of the class action suit entitled to recover? Explain.

12. Northwest Airlines (http://www.nwa.com) leased space in the terminal building at the Portland Airport (http://www.portlandairportpdx.com/web_pop/PDXHOme.htm) from the Port of Portland. Crosetti entered into a contract

with the Port to furnish janitorial services for the building, which required Crosetti to keep the floor clean, to indemnify the Port against loss due to claims or lawsuits based upon Crosetti's failure to perform, and to provide public liability insurance for the Port and Crosetti. A patron of the building who was injured by a fall caused by a foreign substance on the floor at Northwest's ticket counter brought suit for damages against Northwest, the Port, and Crosetti. Upon settlement of this suit, Northwest sued Crosetti to recover the amount of its contribution to the settlement and other expenses on the grounds that Northwest was a third-party beneficiary of Crosetti's contract with the Port to keep the floors clean and, therefore, within the protection of Crosetti's indemnification agreement. Will Northwest prevail? Why?

13. Tompkins-Beckwith, as the contractor on a construction project, entered into a subcontract with a division of Air Metal Industries. Air Metal procured American Fire and Casualty Company to be surety on certain bonds in connection with contracts it was performing for Tompkins-Beckwith and others. As security for these bonds, on January 3, 1962, Air Metal executed an assignment to American Fire of all accounts receivable under the Tompkins-Beckwith subcontract. On November 26, 1962, Boulevard National Bank lent money to Air Metal. To secure the loans, Air Metal purported to assign to the bank certain accounts receivable it had under its subcontract with Tompkins-Beckwith.

    In June 1963, Air Metal defaulted on various contracts bonded by American Fire. On July 1, 1963, American Fire served formal notice on Tompkins-Beckwith of Air Metal's assignment. Tompkins-Beckwith acknowledged the assignment and agreed to pay. In August 1963, Boulevard National Bank notified Tompkins-Beckwith of its assignment. Tompkins-Beckwith refused to recognize the bank's claim and, instead, paid all remaining funds that had accrued to Air Metal to American Fire. The bank then sued to enforce its claim under Air Metal's assignment. Is the assignment effective? Why?

14. The International Association of Machinists (the union) (http://www.iamaw.org) was the bargaining agent for the employees of Powder Power Tool Corporation. On August 24, the union and the corporation executed a collective bargaining agreement providing for retroactively increased wage rates for the corporation's employees effective as of the previous April 1. Three employees who were working for Powder before and for several months after April 1, but who were not employed by the corporation when the agreement was executed on August 24, were paid to the time their employment terminated at the old wage scale. The three employees assigned their claims to Springer, who brought this action against the corporation for the extra wages. Decision?

15. In March 1998, Adrian Saylor sold government bonds owned exclusively by him and with $6,450 of the proceeds opened a savings account in a bank in the name of "Mr. or Mrs. Adrian M. Saylor." In June 1999 Saylor deposited the additional sum of $2,132 of his own money in the account. There were no other deposits and no withdrawals prior to the death of Saylor in May 2000. Is the balance of the account on Saylor's death payable wholly to Adrian Saylor's estate, wholly to his widow, or half to each?

16. Linda King was found liable to Charlotte Clement as the result of an automobile accident. King, who was insolvent at the time, declared bankruptcy and directed her attorney, Prestwich, to list Clement as an unsecured creditor. The attorney failed to carry out this duty, and consequently King sued him for legal malpractice. When Clement pursued her judgment against King, she received a written assignment of King's legal malpractice claim against Prestwich. Clement has attempted to bring the claim, but Prestwich alleges that a claim for legal malpractice is not assignable. Decision?

17. Rensselaer Water Company contracted with the city of Rensselaer to provide water to the city for use in homes, public buildings, industry, and fire hydrants. During the term of the contract a building caught fire. The fire spread to a nearby warehouse and destroyed it and its contents. The water company knew of the fire but failed to supply adequate water pressure at the fire hydrant to extinguish the fire. The warehouse owner sued the water company for failure to fulfill its contract with the city. Can the owner of the warehouse enforce the contract? Explain.

18. McDonald's (http://www.mcdonalds.com) granted to Copeland a franchise in Omaha, Nebraska. In a separate letter, it also granted him a right of first refusal for future franchises to be developed in the Omaha-Council Bluffs area. Copeland then sold all rights in his six McDonald's franchises to Schupack. When McDonald's offered a new franchise in the Omaha area to someone other than Schupack, he attempted to exercise the right of first refusal. McDonald's would not recognize the right in Schupack, claiming that it was personal to Copeland and, therefore, nonassignable without its consent. Schupack brought an action for specific performance, requiring McDonald's to accord him the right of first refusal. Is Schupack correct in its contention?

19. While under contract to play professional basketball for the Philadelphia 76ers (http://www.nba.com/sixers), Billy Cunningham negotiated a three-year contract with the Carolina Cougars, another professional basketball team. The contract with the Cougars was to begin at the expiration of the contract with the 76ers. In addition to a signing bonus of $125,000, Cunningham was to receive under the new contract a salary of $100,000 for the first year, $110,000 for the second, and $120,000 for the third. The contract also stated that Cunningham "had special, exceptional and unique knowledge, skill and ability as a basketball player" and that Cunningham therefore agreed the Cougars could enjoin him from playing basketball for any other team for the term of the contract. In addition, the contract contained a clause prohibiting its assignment to

another club without Cunningham's consent. In 1971, the ownership of the Cougars changed, and Cunningham's contract was assigned to Munchak Corporation, the new owners, without his consent. When Cunningham refused to play for the Cougars, Munchak Corporation sought to enjoin his playing for any other team. Cunningham asserts that his contract was not assignable. Was the contract assignable? Explain.

20. Pauline Brown was shot and seriously injured by an unknown assailant in the parking lot of National Supermarkets. Pauline and George Brown brought a negligence action against National, Sentry Security Agency, and T. G. Watkins, a security guard and Sentry employee. The Browns maintained that the defendants have a legal duty to protect National's customers, both in the store and in the parking lot, and that this duty was breached. The defendants denied this allegation. Decision?

http:// **Internet Exercise** Find a sample of one of the following: (a) an assignment of a contract, (b) a delegation of a contractual duty, or (c) a third-party beneficiary contract.

Chapter 17

Performance, Breach, and Discharge

Because contracting parties ordinarily expect that they will perform their obligations, they are usually more explicit in defining those obligations than in stating the consequences of their nonperformance.

RESTATEMENT OF CONTRACTS, INTRODUCTORY NOTE

Learning Objectives

After reading this chapter you should be able to:

1. Identify and distinguish among the various types of conditions.
2. Distinguish between full performance and tender of performance.
3. Explain the difference between material breach and substantial performance.
4. Distinguish among a mutual rescission, substituted contract, accord and satisfaction, and novation.
5. Identify and explain the ways discharge may be brought about by operation of law.

The subject of discharge of contracts concerns the termination of contractual duties. In earlier chapters we saw how parties may become contractually bound by their promises. It is also important to know how a person may become unbound from a contract. Although contractual promises are made for a purpose and the parties reasonably expect this purpose to be fulfilled by performance, performance of a contractual duty is only one method of discharge.

Whatever causes a binding promise to cease to be binding is a discharge of the contract. In general, there are four kinds of discharge: (1) performance by the parties, (2) material breach by one or both of the parties, (3) agreement of the parties, and (4) operation of law. Moreover, many contractual promises are not absolute promises to perform but are conditional—that is, they depend on the happening or nonhappening of a specific event. After we discuss the subject of conditions, we will cover the four kinds of discharge.

CPA CONDITIONS

A **condition** is an event whose happening or nonhappening affects a duty of performance under a contract. Some conditions must be satisfied before any duty to perform arises; others terminate the duty to perform; still others either limit or modify the duty to perform. A condition is inserted in a contract to protect and benefit the promisor. The more conditions to which a promise is subject, the less content the promise has. For example, a promise to pay $8,000 provided that such sum is realized from the sale of an automobile, provided the automobile is sold within sixty days, and provided that the automobile, which has been stolen, can be found, is clearly different from, and worth considerably less than, an unconditional promise by the same promisor to pay $8,000.

A fundamental difference exists between the breach or nonperformance of a contractual promise and the failure or nonhappening of a condition. A breach of contract subjects the promisor to liability. It may or may not, depending on its materiality, excuse the nonbreaching party's nonperformance of his duty under the contract. The happening or nonhappening of a condition, on the other hand, either prevents a party from acquiring a right or deprives him of a right but subjects neither party to any liability.

Conditions may be classified by *how* they are imposed: express conditions, implied-in-fact conditions, or implied-in-law conditions (also called constructive conditions). They also may be classified by *when* they affect a duty of performance: conditions concurrent, conditions precedent, or conditions subsequent. These two ways of classifying conditions are not mutually exclusive; for example, a condition may be constructive and concurrent or express and precedent.

Practical Advice

Consider using conditions to place the risk of the nonoccurrence of critical, uncertain events on the other party to the contract.

EXPRESS CONDITIONS

An **express condition** is explicitly set forth in language. No particular form of words is necessary to create an express condition, as long as the event to which the performance of the promise is made subject is clearly expressed. An express condition is usually preceded by words such as "provided that," "on condition that," "if," "while," "after," "upon," or "as soon as."

The basic rule applied to express conditions is that they must be fully and literally performed before the conditional duty to perform arises. However, when application of the full and literal performance test would result in a forfeiture, the courts usually apply to the completed portion of the condition a *substantial satisfaction* test, as discussed in this chapter under "Substantial Performance."

Satisfaction of a Contracting Party The parties to a contract may agree that performance by one of them shall be to the **satisfaction** of the other, who will not be obligated to perform unless he is satisfied. This is an express condition to the duty to perform. Assume that tailor Ken contracts to make a suit of clothes to Dick's satisfaction, and that Dick promises to pay Ken $350 for the suit if he is satisfied with it when completed. Ken completes the suit using materials ordered by Dick. The suit fits Dick beautifully, but Dick tells Ken that he is not satisfied with it and refuses to accept or pay for it. Ken is not entitled to recover $350 or any amount from Dick because the express condition did not happen. This is so if Dick's dissatisfaction is honest and in good faith, even if it is unreasonable. Where satisfaction relates to a matter of personal taste, opinion, or judgment, the law applies the **subjective satisfaction** standard; and the condition has not occurred if the promisor is in good faith dissatisfied.

If the contract does not clearly indicate that satisfaction is subjective, or if the performance contracted for relates to mechanical fitness or utility, the law assumes an **objective satisfaction** standard. For example, the objective standard of satisfaction would apply to the sale of a building or standard goods. In such cases, the question would not be whether the promisor was actually satisfied with the performance by the other party but whether, as a reasonable person, he ought to be satisfied.

Practical Advice

In your contracts based on satisfaction, specify which standard—the subjective satisfaction or objective satisfaction—should apply to each contractual duty of performance.

Kohler v. Leslie Hindman, Inc.

United States Court of Appeals, Seventh Circuit, 1996
80 F.3d 1181
http://laws.findlaw.com/7th/951752.html

FACTS An artist once produced a painting now called *The Plains of Meudon* (**http://www.maineantiquedigest.com/articles/hindman.htm**). For a while, the parties in this case thought that the artist was Theodore Rousseau, a prominent member of the Barbizon school, and that the painting was quite valuable. With this idea in mind, the Kohlers consigned the painting to Leslie Hindman, Inc., an auction house (**http://www.lesliehindman.com**). Among other things, the consignment agreement between the Kohlers and Hindman, Inc. defined the scope of Hindman, Inc.'s authority as agent. First, Hindman, Inc. was obliged to sell the painting according to the conditions of sale spelled out in the auction catalog. Those conditions provided that neither the consignors nor Hindman, Inc. made any warranties of authenticity. Second, Paragraph 14 of the consignment agreement gave Hindman, Inc. extensive and exclusive discretionary authority to rescind sales if in its "sole discretion" it determined that the sale subjected the company or the Kohlers to any liability under a warranty of authenticity.

Despite having some doubts about its authenticity, Thune was still interested in the painting but wanted to have it authenticated before committing to its purchase. Unable to obtain an authoritative opinion about its authenticity before the auction, Leslie Hindman and Thune made a verbal agreement that Thune could return the painting within approximately thirty days of the auction if he was the successful bidder and if an expert then determined that Rousseau had not painted it. Neither Leslie Hindman nor anyone else at Hindman, Inc. told the Kohlers about the questions concerning the painting or about the side agreement between Thune and Hindman, Inc. At the auction on October 13, 1991, Thune prevailed in the bidding with a high bid of $90,000, and he took possession of the painting without paying. He then sent it to an expert in Paris who decided that it was not a Rousseau. Thune returned the painting to Hindman, Inc. in March 1992.

The Kohlers sued both Hindman, Inc. and Thune. They claimed that Hindman, Inc. had breached the consignment agreement with them. They also claimed that they had an implied contract with Thune himself for the painting, and that Thune had breached that contract by failing to pay the $90,000. The district court ruled that Hindman, Inc. and Thune were entitled to judgment on all of the Kohlers' claims against them. The Kohlers contend that the district court erred in its interpretation of the contracts, and they appeal.

DECISION Judgment of the district court affirmed.

OPINION Cudahy, J. Indeed, all of the Kohlers' claims depend upon how the consignment agreement defined the scope of Hindman, Inc.'s authority as the Kohlers' agent. If Hindman, Inc. acted at all times within its authority, the Kohlers cannot prevail on any of their claims. Defining the scope of that authority requires an interpretation of the consignment agreement.

* * *

* * * The district court concluded that this grant of discretion allowed Hindman, Inc. to rescind a sale whenever it perceived the threat of such liability, notwithstanding the auction catalog's emphatic disclaimers. In the district court's reading of the consignment agreement, once the questions about the authenticity of the painting arose, Hindman, Inc. had open-ended authority to avoid a lawsuit arising from a claim under a warranty of authenticity. Hindman, Inc. had the power to rescind or to make a conditional promise to rescind in side agreements with prospective buyers. * * *

* * *

Interpretation would be easier if we could find a customary meaning for "sole discretion" as used in auctioneers' consignment agreements. * * * [Other courts have] found that such a contract provision is highly analogous to a satisfaction clause (typically conditioning one party's performance on that party's satisfaction with the other party's performance). [Citation.] Through a satisfaction clause, a party's exercise of judgment or discretion is a condition for its duty to perform. [Citations.] Because satisfaction clauses involve the same principles of contract law as apply here, we will treat Paragraph 14 as a satisfaction clause.

* * * [S]atisfaction clauses * * * come in two categories: those that make the exercise of discretion purely subjective and those that require the exercise of discretion according to objective factors. [Citations.] The first category includes satisfaction clauses invoking the feelings, taste or judgment of the party exercising discretion. [Citations.] When a satisfaction clause conveys this sort of subjective discretion, it does not, however, remove all limitations on the exercise of discretion. The party that has the right to act according to its personal judgment or within its sole discretion must still act in good faith. [Citation.]

On the other hand, a satisfaction clause may fall into the second category when it involves matters susceptible to objective evaluation; mechanical utility is a stereotype of such matters. [Citations.] When objective considerations control the exercise of discretion, the party to be satisfied must exercise its authority in a just and reasonable way. [Citation.]

These rules do not apply easily to Paragraph 14. By giving Hindman, Inc. "sole discretion," this provision suggests that the consignment agreement had defined Hindman, Inc.'s authority subjectively. The consignment agreement did not define any objective criteria that would control Hindman, Inc.'s exercise of judgment. Nevertheless, the object of Hindman, Inc.'s discretion was not a purely subjective phenomenon like taste or feeling. Rather, Hindman, Inc. had to evaluate risk, and demanding such an evaluation impliedly invoked rational analysis. The Kohlers were not giving Hindman, Inc. a contract right to emulate Chicken Little. Viewing all of these conditions together, the grant of "sole discretion" to assess risk is somewhat ambiguous as between objective and subjective satisfaction.

Ultimately, for lack of objective criteria, we must conclude that Hindman, Inc.'s exercise of its authority is bounded only by its satisfaction as limited, of course, by good faith. The principal factor leading us to this conclusion is the agreement's use of the phrase "sole discretion." This phrase denotes subjectivity. Moreover, this conclusion corresponds with the theoretical understanding of contract bargaining. The consignment agreement made the interests of the Kohlers and Hindman, Inc. largely coincident. The Kohlers and Hindman, Inc. would each profit most from the same set of circumstances, namely the sale of the painting for the highest possible price. Given this identity of interests, the Kohlers could trust Hindman, Inc.'s subjective decision making. For the purposes of analyzing the risk of liability, Hindman, Inc. and the Kohlers had the same perspective. Therefore, the Kohlers did not have to hold Hindman, Inc. to some external standard as a means of making the auctioneer's interests coincide with its own. At least in theory, it would be rational for the Kohlers to accept Hindman, Inc.'s good faith subjective judgments as part of a bargain. Because the language of the contract clearly implies that the Kohlers did trust Hindman, Inc.'s subjective judgment, we conclude the consignment agreement held the auctioneer to a subjective standard.

Hindman, Inc.'s actions towards Thune, before and after the auction, meet the standard of good faith. * * *

INTERPRETATION Under the subjective satisfaction standard, the party has the right to act according to her personal judgment or sole discretion, but she must act in good faith.

CRITICAL THINKING QUESTION If the painting had been authentic but Thune learned after the sale that it was not worth what he had paid, could Thune have rescinded the sale? Explain.

Satisfaction of a Third Party A contract may condition the performance of a party on the approval of a third party. For example, building contracts commonly provide that before the owner is required to pay, the builder shall furnish the architect's certificate stating that the building has been constructed according to the plans and specifications on which the builder and the owner agreed. For even though the price is being paid for the building, not for the certificate, the owner must have both the building and the certificate before she will be obliged to pay. The duty of payment was made expressly conditional on the presentation of the certificate.

IMPLIED-IN-FACT CONDITIONS

Implied-in-fact conditions are similar to express conditions in that they must fully and literally occur and in that they are understood by the parties to be part of the agreement. They differ in that they are not stated in express language; rather, they are necessarily inferred from the terms of the contract, the nature of the transaction, or the conduct of the parties. Thus, if Edna, for $750, contracts to paint Sy's house any color Sy desires, it is necessarily implied in fact that Sy will inform Edna of the desired color before Edna begins to paint. The notification of choice of color is an implied-in-fact condition, an operative event that must occur before Edna is subject to the duty of painting the house.

IMPLIED-IN-LAW CONDITIONS

An **implied-in-law condition**, or a constructive condition, is imposed by law to accomplish a just and fair result. It differs from an express condition and an implied-in-fact condition in two ways: (1) it is not contained in the language of the contract or necessarily inferred from the contract and (2) it need only be substantially performed. For example, Fernando contracts to sell a certain tract of land to Marie for $18,000, but the contract is silent as to the time of delivery of the deed and payment of the price. According to the law, the contract implies that payment and delivery of the deed are not independent of each other. The courts will treat the promises as mutually dependent and will therefore hold that a delivery or tender of the deed by Fernando to Marie is a condition to the duty of Marie to pay the price. Conversely, payment or tender of $18,000 by Marie to Fernando is a condition to the duty of Fernando to deliver the deed to Marie.

CONCURRENT CONDITIONS

Concurrent conditions occur when the mutual duties of performance are to take place simultaneously. As we indicated in the section above, in the absence of agreement to the contrary, the law assumes that the respective performances under a contract are concurrent conditions.

CONDITION PRECEDENT

A **condition precedent** is an event that must occur before performance is due under a contract. In other words, the immediate duty of one party to perform is subject to the condition that some event must first occur. For instance, Steve is to deliver shoes to Nancy on June 1, and Nancy is to pay for the shoes on July 15. Steve's delivery of the shoes is a condition precedent to Nancy's performance. Similarly, if Rachel promises to buy Justin's land for $50,000, provided Rachel can obtain financing in the amount of $40,000 at 10 percent or less for thirty years within sixty days of signing the contract, Rachel's obtaining the specified financing is a condition precedent to her duty. If the condition is satisfied, Rachel is bound to perform; if it is not met, she is not bound to perform. Rachel, however, is under an implied-in-law duty to use her best efforts to obtain financing under these terms.

CONDITION SUBSEQUENT

A **condition subsequent** is an event that terminates an existing duty. For example, when goods are sold under terms of "sale or return," the buyer has the right to return the goods to the seller within a stated period but is under an immediate duty to pay the price unless the parties have agreed on credit. The duty to pay the price is terminated by a return of the goods, which operates as a condition subsequent. Conditions subsequent occur very infrequently in contract law; conditions precedent are quite common.

CPA DISCHARGE BY PERFORMANCE

Discharge is the termination of a contractual duty. **Performance** is the fulfillment of a contractual obligation. Discharge by performance is undoubtedly the most frequent method of discharging a contractual duty. If a promisor exactly performs his duty under the contract, the promisor is no longer subject to that duty.

Every contract imposes upon each party a duty of good faith and fair dealing in its performance and its enforcement. As discussed in Chapter 19, the UCC imposes a comparable duty.

Tender is an offer by one party—who is ready, willing, and able to perform—to the other party to perform his obligation according to the terms of the contract. Under a bilateral contract, the refusal or rejection of a tender, or offer of performance, by one party may be treated as a repudiation, excusing or discharging the tendering party from further duty of performance under the contract.

CPA DISCHARGE BY BREACH

A **breach** of a contract is a wrongful failure to perform its terms. Breach of contract always gives rise to a cause of action for damages by the aggrieved (injured) party. It may, however, have a more important effect: an uncured (uncorrected) *material* breach by one party operates as an excuse for nonperformance by the other party and discharges the aggrieved party from any further duty under the contract. If, on the other hand, the breach is not material, the aggrieved party is not discharged from the contract, although she may recover money damages. Under the Code's perfect tender rule, which applies only to sales transactions, *any* deviation discharges the aggrieved party.

MATERIAL BREACH

An unjustified failure to perform *substantially* the obligations promised in a contract is a **material breach**. The key is whether the aggrieved party obtained substantially what he had bargained for, despite the breach, or whether the breach significantly impaired his rights under the contract. A material breach discharges the aggrieved party from his duty of performance. For instance, Joe orders a custom-made, tailored suit from Peggy to be made of wool; but Peggy makes the suit of cotton instead. Assuming that the labor component of this contract predominates and thus the contract is not considered a sale of goods, Peggy has materially breached the contract. Consequently, Joe is discharged from his duty to pay for the suit; and he may also recover money damages from Peggy for her breach.

Although there are no clear-cut rules as to what constitutes a material breach, several basic principles apply. First, partial performance is a material breach of a contract if it omits some essential part of the contract. Second, the courts will consider a breach material if it is quantitatively or qualitatively serious. Third, an intentional breach of contract is generally held to be material. Fourth, a failure to perform a promise promptly is a material breach if time is of the essence; that is, if the parties have clearly indicated that a failure to perform by a stated time is material; otherwise, the aggrieved party may recover damages only for loss caused by the delay. Fifth, the parties to a contract may, within limits, specify what breaches are to be considered material.

> **Practical Advice**
>
> If the timely performance of a contractual duty is important, use a "time-is-of-the-essence" clause to make failure to perform promptly a material breach.

Prevention of Performance One party's substantial interference with, or prevention of, performance by the other generally constitutes a material breach that discharges the other party to the contract. For instance, Dale prevents an architect from giving Lucy a certificate that is a condition to Dale's liability to pay Lucy a certain sum of money. Dale may not then use Lucy's failure to produce a certificate as an excuse for nonpayment. Likewise, if

Maude has contracted to grow a certain crop for Harold and Harold plows the field and destroys the seedlings Maude has planted, his interference with Maude's performance discharges Maude from her duty under the contract. It does not, however, discharge Harold from his duty under the contract.

Perfect Tender Rule The Code greatly alters the common law doctrine of material breach by adopting what is known as the **perfect tender rule.** The perfect tender rule, which we will discuss more fully in Chapter 20, essentially provides that *any* deviation from the promised performance in a sales contract under the Code constitutes a material breach of the contract and discharges the aggrieved party from his duty of performance.

SUBSTANTIAL PERFORMANCE

Substantial performance is performance that, though incomplete, does not defeat the purpose of the contract. If a party substantially, but not completely, performs her obligations under a contract, the common law generally will allow her to obtain the other party's performance, less any damages the partial performance caused. If no harm has been caused, the breaching party will obtain the other party's full contractual performance. Thus, in the specially ordered suit illustration, if Peggy, the tailor, used the correct fabric but improperly used black buttons instead of blue, she would be permitted to collect from Joe the contract price of the suit less the damage, if any, caused to Joe by the substitution of the wrongly colored buttons. The doctrine of substantial performance assumes particular importance in the construction industry in cases in which a structure is built on the aggrieved party's land. Consider the following: Adam builds a $300,000 house for Betty but deviates from the specifications, causing Betty $10,000 in damages. If the courts considered this a material breach, Betty would not have to pay for the house that is now on her land, a result that would clearly constitute an unjust forfeiture on Adam's part. Therefore, because Adam's performance has been substantial, the courts would probably not deem the breach material, and he would be able to collect $290,000 from Betty.

See *Associated Builders, Inc. v. William M. Coggins* later in this chapter.

ANTICIPATORY REPUDIATION

A breach of contract, as previously discussed, is a failure to perform the terms of a contract. Although it is logically and physically impossible to fail to perform a duty before the date on which that performance is due, a party may announce before the due date that she will not perform, or she may commit an act that makes her unable to perform. Either act is a repudiation of the contract, which notifies the other party that a breach is imminent. Such repudiation before the date fixed by the contract for performance is called an **anticipatory repudiation.** The courts, as shown in the leading case that follows, view it as a breach that discharges the nonrepudiating party's duty to perform and permits her to bring suit immediately. Nonetheless, the nonbreaching party may wait until the time the performance is due, to see if the repudiator will retract his repudiation and perform his contractual duties. If the repudiator does perform, then there is a discharge by performance; if the repudiator does not perform, there is a material breach.

Practical Advice

If the other party to a contract commits an anticipatory breach, carefully consider whether it is better to sue immediately or to wait until the time performance is due.

Hochster v. De La Tour

Queen's Bench of England, 1853
2 Ellis and Blackburn Reports 678

FACTS On April 12, 1852, Hochster contracted with De La Tour to serve as a guide for De La Tour on his three-month trip to Europe, beginning on June 1 at an agreed-upon salary. On May 11, De La Tour notified Hochster that he would not need Hochster's services. He also refused to pay Hochster any compensation. Hochster brought this action to recover damages for breach of contract.

DECISION Judgment for Hochster.

OPINION Lord Campbell, C. J. On this motion * * * the question arises, Whether, if there be an agreement between A. and B., whereby B. engages to employ A. on and from a future day for a given period of time, to travel with him into a foreign country as a [guide], and to start with him in that capacity on that day, A. being to receive a monthly salary during the continuance of such service, B. may, before the day, refuse to perform the agreement and break and renounce it, so as to entitle A. before the day to commence an action against B. to recover damages for breach of the agreement; A. having been ready and willing to perform it, till it was broken and renounced by B.

* * *

If the plaintiff has no remedy for breach of the contract unless he treats the contract as in force, and acts upon it down to the 1st June, 1852, it follows that, till then, he must enter into no employment which will interfere with his promise "to start with the defendant on such travels on the day and year," and that he must then be properly equipped in all respects as a [guide] for a three months' tour on the continent of Europe. But it is surely much more rational, and more for the benefit of both parties, that, after the renunciation of the agreement by the defendant, the plaintiff should be at liberty to consider himself absolved from any future performance of it, retaining his right to sue for any damage he has suffered from the breach of it. Thus, instead of remaining idle and laying out money in preparations which must be useless, he is at liberty to seek service under another employer, which would go in mitigation of the damages to which he would otherwise be entitled for a breach of the contract. It seems strange that the defendant, after renouncing the contract, and absolutely declaring that he will never act under it, should be permitted to object that faith is given to his assertion, and that an opportunity is not left to him of changing his mind.

* * *

The man who wrongfully renounces a contract into which he has deliberately entered cannot justly complain if he is immediately sued for a compensation in damage by the man whom he has injured: and it seems reasonable to allow an option to the injured party, either to sue immediately, or to wait till the time when the act was to be done, still holding it as prospectively binding for the exercise of the option, which may be advantageous to the innocent party, and cannot be prejudicial to the wrongdoer.

INTERPRETATION An anticipatory breach discharges the injured party and entitles her to bring suit immediately.

CRITICAL THINKING QUESTION What policy reasons support an injured party's right to bring suit immediately upon an anticipatory repudiation? Explain.

MATERIAL ALTERATION OF WRITTEN CONTRACT

An unauthorized alteration or change of any of the material terms or provisions of a written contract or document is a discharge of the entire contract. An alteration is material if it would vary any party's legal relations with the maker of the alteration or would adversely affect that party's legal relations with a third person. To constitute a discharge, the alteration must be material and fraudulent and must be the act of either a party to the contract or someone acting on his behalf. An unauthorized change in the terms of a written contract by a person who is not a party to the contract does not discharge the contract.

CPA DISCHARGE BY AGREEMENT OF THE PARTIES

By agreement, the parties to a contract may discharge each other from performance under the contract. They may do this by rescission, substituted contract, accord and satisfaction, or novation.

MUTUAL RESCISSION

A **mutual rescission** is an agreement between the parties to terminate their respective duties under the contract. It is, literally, a contract to end a contract; and it must contain all of the essentials of a contract. In rescinding an executory, bilateral contract, each party furnishes consideration in giving up his rights under the contract in exchange for the other party's doing the same. If one party has already fully performed, however, a mutual rescission is not binding at common law because of lack of consideration.

SUBSTITUTED CONTRACTS

A **substituted contract** is a new contract accepted by both parties in satisfaction of the parties' duties under the original contract. A substituted contract immediately discharges the original contract and imposes new obligations under its own terms.

ACCORD AND SATISFACTION

An **accord** is a contract by which an obligee promises to accept a stated performance in satisfaction of the obligor's existing contractual duty. The performance of the accord, called a **satisfaction**, discharges the original duty. Thus, if Dan owes Sara $500, and the parties agree that Dan will paint Sara's house in satisfaction of the debt, the agreement is an executory accord. When Dan performs the accord by painting Sara's house, he will by satisfaction discharge the $500 debt.

Associated Builders, Inc. v. William M. Coggins et al.

Supreme Judicial Court of Maine, 1999
1999 ME 12; 722 A.2d 1278
http://caselaw.lp.findlaw.com/scripts/getcase.pl?court=me&vol=99me12as&invol=1

FACTS Associated Builders, Inc. provided labor and materials to the defendants William M. Coggins and Benjamin W. Coggins, d/b/a Ben & Bill's Chocolate Emporium, to complete a structure on Main Street in Bar Harbor, Maine. After a dispute arose regarding compensation, Associated and the Cogginses executed an agreement stating that there existed an outstanding balance of $70,005.54 and setting forth the following terms of repayment:

> It is agreed that, two payments will be made by [the Cogginses] to [Associated] as follows: Twenty Five Thousand Dollars ($25,000.00) on or before June 1, 1996 and Twenty Five Thousand Dollars ($25,000.00) on or before June 1, 1997. No interest will be charged or paid providing payments are made as agreed. If the payments are not made as agreed then interest shall accrue at 10% per annum figured from the date of default. * * * It is further agreed that Associated Builders will forfeit the balance of Twenty Thousand and Five Dollars and Fifty Four Cents ($20,005.54) providing the above payments are made as agreed.

The Cogginses made their first payment in accordance with the agreement. The second payment, however, was delivered three days late on June 4, 1997. Claiming a breach of the contract, Associated filed a complaint demanding the balance on the original contract of $20,005.54, plus interest and cost. The Cogginses answered the complaint raising the affirmative defense of an accord and satisfaction and waiver. Both parties moved for a summary judgment. The court granted the Cogginses' motion and Associated appealed.

DECISION Judgment for the Cogginses affirmed.

OPINION Dana, J. "An accord 'is a contract under which an obligee promises to accept a substituted performance in future satisfaction of the obligor's duty.'" [Citation.] Settlement of a disputed claim is sufficient consideration for an accord and satisfaction. [Citation.] Here, the court correctly found the June 15, 1995 agreement to be an accord.

Satisfaction is the execution or performance of the accord. [Citation.] If the obligor breaches the accord, the obligee may enforce either the original duty or any duty pursuant to the accord. [Citations.] The obligor's breach of the accord, however, must be material. [Citations.] The question before the court, therefore, was whether the Cogginses' late payment constituted a material breach of the accord. The court found that it was not.

We apply traditional contract principles to determine if a party has committed a material breach. [Citation.] A material breach "is a nonperformance of a duty that is so material and important as to justify the injured party in regarding the whole transaction as at an end." [Citation]; see RESTATEMENT (SECOND) OF CONTRACTS § 241 (1981). [Court's footnote: The Restatement lists five factors as significant in determining if a failure to render performance is material: (a) the extent to which the injured party will be deprived of the benefit which he reasonably expected; (b) the extent to which the injured party can be adequately compensated for the part of the benefit of which he will be deprived; (c) the extent to which the party failing to perform * * * will suffer forfeiture; (d) the likelihood that the party failing to perform * * * will cure his failure * * *; (e) the extent to which the behavior of the party failing to perform or to offer to perform comports with standards of good faith and fair dealing.]

"Time of performance" is merely one element in determining whether a defective or incomplete or belated performance is "substantial [performance]." [Citation.] Applying these principles, courts have found that a slight delay of payment that causes no detriment or prejudice to the obligee is not a material breach. [Citations.]

We discern no error in the Superior Court's finding that the Cogginses' payment to Associated after a three-day delay was not a material breach and, therefore, satisfied the June 15, 1995 accord. [Citation.] By receiving the second and final payment of $25,000, Associated was not deprived of the benefit that it reasonably expected.

[Citation.] Moreover, Associated has not alleged any prejudice from this three-day delay. [Citations.] Further, the Cogginses' late payment was not made in bad faith. [Citations.] Finally, neither the purpose of the June 15, 1995 accord nor the language of the accord suggests that time was of the essence. [Citation.] Because the late payment was not a material breach of the June 15, 1995 accord, the Cogginses have complied with the June 15, 1995 agreement relieving them of further liability to Associated.

INTERPRETATION Satisfaction is the performance of an accord; but if the obligor materially breaches the accord, the obligee may enforce either the original duty or any duty under the accord.

CRITICAL THINKING QUESTION Should courts hold contracting parties strictly to the letter of a contract? Why or why not?

NOVATION

A **novation** is a substituted contract that involves an agreement among *three* parties to substitute a new promisee for the existing promisee or to replace the existing promisor with a new one. A novation discharges the old obligation by creating a new contract in which there is either a new promisee or a new promisor. Thus, if B owes A $500, and A, B, and C agree that C will pay the debt and B will be discharged, the novation is the substitution of the new promisor C for B. Alternatively, if the three parties agree that B will pay $500 to C instead of to A, the novation is the substitution of a new promisee (C for A). In each instance, the debt B owes A is discharged.

DISCHARGE BY OPERATION OF LAW

CPA

In this chapter, we have considered various ways by which contractual duties may be discharged. In all of these cases, the discharge resulted from the action of one or both of the parties to the contract. In this section, we will examine discharge brought about by the operation of law.

IMPOSSIBILITY

If a particular contracting party is unable to perform because of financial inability or lack of competence, for instance, this **subjective impossibility** does not excuse the promisor from liability for breach of contract, as the next case shows. Historically, the common law excused a party from contractual duties only for **objective impossibility**; that is, for situations where no one could render performance. Thus, the death or illness of a person who has contracted to render personal services is a discharge of his contractual duty. Furthermore, the contract is discharged if, for example, a jockey contracts to ride a certain horse in the Kentucky Derby and the horse dies prior to the derby, for it is objectively impossible for this or any other jockey to perform the contract. Also, if Ken contracts to lease to Karlene a certain ballroom for a party on a scheduled future date, destruction of the ballroom by fire without Ken's fault before the scheduled event discharges the contract. Destruction of the subject matter or of the agreed-upon means of performance of a contract, without the fault of the promisor, is excusable impossibility.

Practical Advice

Use a clause in your contract specifying which events will excuse the nonperformance of the contract.

Christy v. Pilkinton

Supreme Court of Arkansas, 1954
224 Ark. 407, 273 S.W.2d 533

FACTS The Christys entered into a written contract to purchase an apartment house from Pilkinton for $30,000. Pilkinton tendered a deed to the property and demanded payment of the unpaid balance of $29,000 due on the purchase price. As a result of a decline in the Christy's used car business, the Christys did not possess and could not borrow the unpaid balance and, thus, asserted that it was impossible for them to perform their contract. This suit was brought by Pilkinton to enforce the sale of the apartment house.

DECISION Judgment for Pilkinton.

OPINION Smith, J. Proof of this kind [an inability to pay the purchase price] does not establish the type of impossibility that constitutes a defense. There is a familiar distinction between objective impossibility, which amounts to saying, "The thing cannot be done," and subjective impossibility—"I cannot do it." [Citations.] The latter, which is well illustrated by a promisor's financial inability to pay, does not discharge the contractual duty and is therefore not a bar to a [judgment in favor of the plaintiff.]

INTERPRETATION Subjective impossibility (the promisor, but not all promisors, cannot perform) does not discharge the promisor's contractual duty.

ETHICAL QUESTION Is it fair to make contracting parties strictly liable for breach of contract? Explain.

CRITICAL THINKING QUESTION What type of fact situation would have excused the Christys' duty to perform? Explain.

Subsequent Illegality If the performance of a contract that was legal when formed becomes illegal or impractical because of a subsequently enacted law, the duty of performance is discharged. For example, Linda contracts to sell and deliver to Carlos ten cases of a certain whiskey each month for one year. A subsequent prohibition law makes the manufacture, transportation, or sale of intoxicating liquor unlawful. The contractual duties that Linda has yet to perform are discharged.

Frustration of Purpose Where, after a contract is made, a party's principal purpose is substantially frustrated without his fault by the occurrence of an event whose nonoccurrence was a basic assumption on which the contract was made, his remaining duties to render performance are discharged, unless the party has assumed the risk. This rule developed from the so-called "coronation cases." When, on the death of his mother, Queen Victoria, Edward VII became King of England, impressive coronation ceremonies were planned, including a procession along a designated route through London. Owners and lessees of buildings along the route made contracts to permit the use of rooms on the day scheduled for the procession. The king became ill, however, and the procession did not take place. Consequently, the rooms were not used. Numerous suits were filed, some by landowners seeking to hold the would-be viewers liable on their promises, and some by the would-be viewers seeking to recover money they had paid in advance for the rooms. Though the principle involved was novel, from these cases evolved the **frustration of purpose** doctrine, under which a contract is discharged if supervening circumstances make impossible the fulfillment of the purpose that both parties had in mind, unless one of the parties has contractually assumed that risk.

Commercial Impracticability The Restatement and Code have relaxed the traditional test of objective impossibility by providing that performance need not be actually or literally impossible; rather, **commercial impracticability**, or unforeseen and unjust hardship, will excuse nonperformance. This does not mean mere hardship or an unexpectedly increased cost of performance. A party will be discharged from performing her duty only when her performance is made impracticable by a supervening event not caused by her own fault. Moreover, the nonoccurrence of the subsequent event must have been a "basic assumption" made by both parties when entering into the contract, neither party having assumed the risk that the event would occur.

Practical Advice

Clearly state the basic assumptions of your contract and which risks are assumed by each of the parties.

Northern Corporation v. Chugach Electrical Association

Supreme Court of Alaska, 1974

518 P.2d 76

FACTS Northern Corporation (Northern) entered into a contract with Chugach Electrical Association (Chugach) **(http://www.chugachelectric.com)** in August 1966 to repair and upgrade the upstream face of Cooper Lake Dam in

Alaska. The contract required Northern to obtain rock from a quarry site at the opposite end of the lake and to transport the rock to the dam during the winter across the ice on the lake. In December 1966, Northern cleared a road on the ice to permit deeper freezing, but thereafter water overflowed on the ice, preventing use of the road. Northern complained of the unsafe conditions of the lake ice, but Chugach insisted on performance. In March 1967, one of Northern's loaded trucks broke through the ice and sank. Northern continued to encounter difficulties and ceased operations with the approval of Chugach. However, on January 8, 1968, Chugach notified Northern that it would be in default unless all rock was hauled by April 1. After two more trucks broke through the ice, causing the deaths of the drivers, Northern ceased operations and notified Chugach that it would make no more attempts to haul across the lake. Northern advised Chugach that it considered the contract terminated for impossibility of performance and commenced suit to recover the cost incurred in attempting to complete the contract. The trial court found for Northern.

DECISION Judgment for Northern affirmed.

OPINION Boochever, J. The focal question is whether the * * * contract was impossible of performance. The September 27, 1966 directive specified that the rock was to be transported "across Cooper Lake to the dam site when such lake is frozen to a sufficient depth to permit heavy vehicle traffic thereon," and * * * specified that the hauling to the dam site would be done during the winter of 1966–67. It is therefore clear that the parties contemplated that the rock would be transported across the frozen lake by truck. Northern's repeated efforts to perform the contract by this method during the winter of 1966–67 and subsequently in February 1968, culminating in the tragic loss of life, abundantly support the trial court's finding that the contract was impossible of performance by this method.

Chugach contends, however, that Northern was nevertheless bound to perform, and that it could have used means other than hauling by truck across the ice to transport the rock. The answer to Chugach's contention is that * * * the parties contemplated that the rock would be hauled by truck once the ice froze to a sufficient depth to support the weight of the vehicles. The specification of this particular method of performance presupposed the existence of ice frozen to the requisite depth. Since this expectation of the parties was never fulfilled, and since the provisions relating to the means of performance were clearly material, Northern's duty to perform was discharged by reason of impossibility.

There is an additional reason for our holding that Northern's duty to perform was discharged because of impossibility. It is true that in order for a defendant to prevail under the original common law doctrine of impossibility he had to show that no one else could have performed the contract. However, this harsh rule has gradually been eroded, and the Restatement of Contracts has departed from the early common law rule by recognizing the principle of "commercial impracticability." Under this doctrine, a party is discharged from his contract obligations, even if it is technically possible to perform them, if the costs of performance would be so disproportionate to that reasonably contemplated by the parties as to make the contract totally impractical in a commercial sense. * * * Removed from the strictures of the common law, "impossibility" in its modern context has become a coat of many colors, including among its hues the point argued here—namely, impossibility predicated upon "commercial impracticability." This concept—which finds expression both in case law * * * and in other authorities * * * is grounded upon the assumption that in legal contemplation something is impracticable when it can only be done at an excessive and unreasonable cost.

* * * The doctrine ultimately represents the ever-shifting line, drawn by courts hopefully responsive to commercial practices and mores, at which the community's interest in having contracts enforced according to their terms is outweighed by the commercial senselessness of requiring performance. * * *

In the case before us the detailed opinion of the trial court clearly indicates that the appropriate standard was followed. There is ample evidence to support its findings that "[t]he ice haul method of transporting riprap ultimately selected was within the contemplation of the parties and was part of the basis of the agreement which ultimately resulted in amendment No. 1 in October 1966," and that that method was not commercially feasible within the financial parameters of the contract. We affirm the court's conclusion that the contract was impossible of performance.

INTERPRETATION Commercial impracticability (unforeseen and unjust hardship) will excuse performance.

ETHICAL QUESTION Did Chugach act ethically in insisting on performance by Northern in face of dangerous conditions? Explain.

CRITICAL THINKING QUESTION Do you think that the court used the proper standard in this case? Explain.

Figure 17-1
Discharge of Contracts

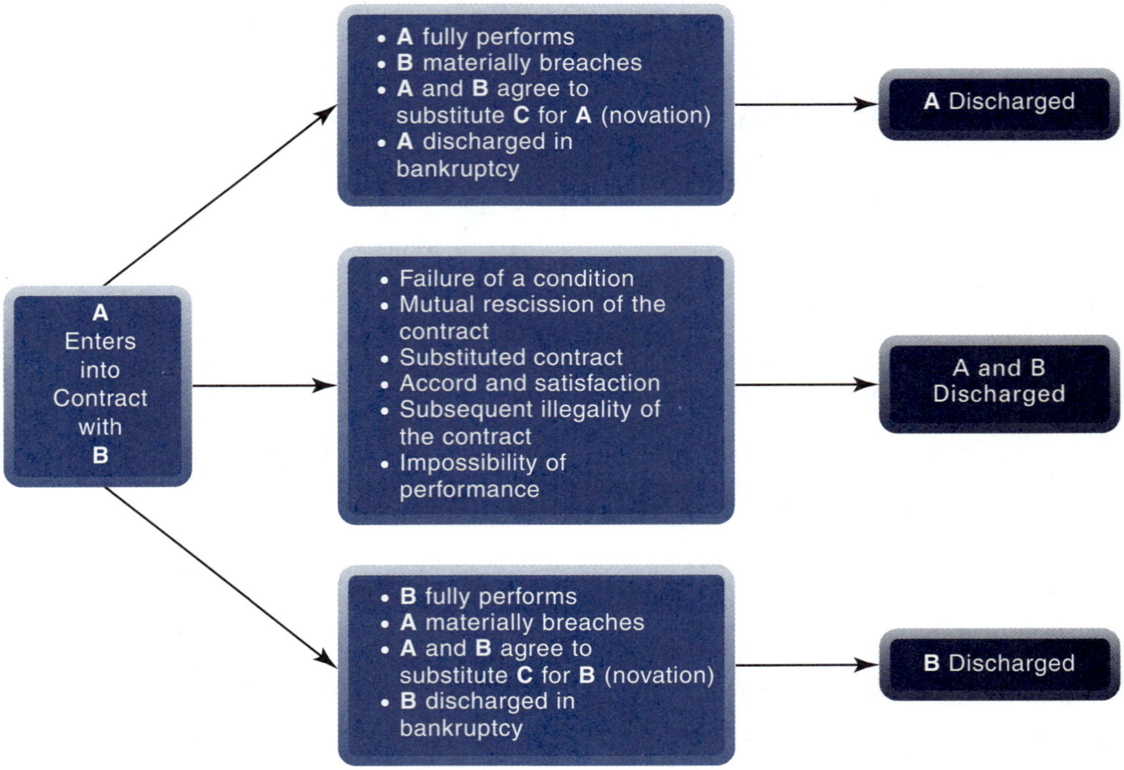

BANKRUPTCY

Bankruptcy is a discharge of a contractual duty by operation of law available to a debtor who, by compliance with the requirements of the Bankruptcy Code, obtains an order of discharge by the bankruptcy court. It applies only to obligations that the Bankruptcy Code provides are dischargeable in bankruptcy. (We will treat the subject of bankruptcy in Chapter 39.)

STATUTE OF LIMITATIONS

At common law a plaintiff was not subject to any time limitation within which to bring an action. Now, however, all states have statutes providing such a limitation. The majority of courts hold that the running of the period of the statute of limitations does not operate to discharge the obligation but only to bar the creditor's right to bring an action.

For a summary of discharge of contracts, see Figure 17-1.

CHAPTER SUMMARY

Conditions

Definition of a Condition an event whose happening or nonhappening affects a duty of performance

Express Condition contingency explicitly set forth in language
- *Satisfaction* express condition making performance contingent on one party's approval of the other's performance
- *Subjective Satisfaction* approval based on a party's honestly held opinion
- *Objective Satisfaction* approval based on whether a reasonable person would be satisfied

Implied-in-Fact Condition contingency understood by the parties to be part of the agreement, though not expressed

Implied-in-Law Condition contingency not contained in the language of the contract but imposed by law; also called a constructive condition

Concurrent Conditions conditions that are to take place at the same time

Condition Precedent an event that must or must not occur before performance is due

Condition Subsequent an event that terminates a duty of performance

Discharge by Performance

Discharge termination of a contractual duty

Performance fulfillment of a contractual obligation resulting in a discharge

Discharge by Breach

Definition of Breach a wrongful failure to perform the terms of a contract that gives rise to a right to damages by the injured party

Material Breach nonperformance that significantly impairs the injured party's rights under the contract and discharges the injured party from any further duty under the contract

- *Prevention of Performance* one party's substantial interference with or prevention of performance by the other constitutes a material breach and discharges the other party to the contract
- *Perfect Tender Rule* standard under the UCC that a seller's performance under a sales contract must strictly comply with contractual duties and that any deviation discharges the injured party

Substantial Performance performance that is incomplete but that does not defeat the purpose of the contract; does not discharge the injured party but entitles him to damages

Anticipatory Repudiation an inability or refusal to perform, before performance is due, that is treated as a breach, allowing the nonrepudiating party to bring suit immediately

Material Alteration a material and fraudulent alteration of a written contract by a party to the contract discharges the entire contract

Discharge by Agreement of the Parties

Mutual Rescission an agreement between the parties to terminate their respective duties under the contract

Substituted Contract a new contract accepted by both parties in satisfaction of the parties' duties under the original contract

Accord and Satisfaction substituted duty under a contract (accord) and the discharge of the prior contractual obligation by performance of the new duty (satisfaction)

Novation a substituted contract involving a new third-party promisor or promisee

Discharge by Operation of Law

Impossibility performance of contract cannot be done

- *Subjective Impossibility* the promisor—but not all promisors—cannot perform; does not discharge the promisor
- *Objective Impossibility* no promisor is able to perform; generally discharges the promisor
- *Subsequent Illegality* if performance becomes illegal or impractical as a result of a change in the law, the duty of performance is discharged

- *Frustration of Purpose* principal purpose of a contract cannot be fulfilled because of a subsequent event
- *Commercial Impracticability* where performance can be accomplished only under unforeseen and unjust hardship, the contract is discharged under the Code and the Restatement

Bankruptcy discharge available to a debtor who obtains an order of discharge by the bankruptcy court

Statute of Limitations after the statute of limitations has run, the debt is not discharged, but the creditor cannot maintain an action against the debtor

QUESTIONS

1. A-1 Roofing Co. entered into a written contract with Jaffe to put a new roof on the latter's residence for $1,800, using a specified type of roofing, and to complete the job without unreasonable delay. A-1 undertook the work within a week thereafter, and when all the roofing material was at the site and the labor 50 percent completed, the premises were totally destroyed by fire caused by lightning. A-1 submitted a bill to Jaffe for $1,200 for materials furnished and labor performed up to the time of the destruction of the premises. Jaffe refused to pay the bill, and A-1 now seeks payment from Jaffe. Should A-1 prevail? Explain.

2. By contract dated January 5, Rebecca agreed to sell to Nancy, and Nancy agreed to buy from Rebecca, a certain parcel of land then zoned commercial. The specific intent of Nancy, which was known to Rebecca, was to erect a storage plant on the land; and the contract stated that the agreement was conditioned on Nancy's ability to construct such a plant on the land. The closing date for the transaction was set for April 1. On February 15, the city council rezoned the land from commercial to residential, which precluded the erection of the storage plant. As the closing date drew near, Nancy made it known to Rebecca that she did not intend to go through with the purchase because the land could no longer be used as intended. On April 1, Rebecca tendered the deed to Nancy, who refused to pay Rebecca the agreed purchase price. Rebecca brought an action against Nancy for breach of contract. Can Rebecca enforce the contract?

3. The Perfection Produce Company entered into a written contract with Hiram Hodges for the purchase of 200 tons of potatoes to be grown on Hodges's farm in Maine at a stipulated price per ton. Though the land would ordinarily produce 1,000 tons and although the planting and cultivation were properly done, Hodges was able to deliver only 100 tons because an unprecedented drought caused a partial crop failure. Hodges sued the produce company to recover an unpaid balance of the agreed price for 100 tons of potatoes. The produce company counterclaimed against Hodges for his failure to deliver the additional 100 tons. Who will prevail? Why?

4. On November 23, Sally agreed to sell to Bart her Pontiac automobile for $7,000, delivery and payment to be made on December 1. On November 26, Bart informed Sally that he wished to rescind the contract and would pay Sally $350 if Sally agreed. Sally agreed and took the $350 in cash. On December 1, Bart tendered to Sally $6,650 and demanded that Sally deliver the automobile. Sally refused, and Bart initiated a lawsuit. May Bart enforce the original contract?

5. Webster, Inc., dealt in automobile accessories at wholesale. Although it manufactured a few items in its own factory, among them windshield wipers, Webster purchased most of its inventory from a large number of other manufacturers. In January, Webster entered into a written contract to sell Hunter 2,000 windshield wipers for $1,900, delivery to be made June 1. In April, Webster's factory burned to the ground and Webster failed to make delivery on June 1. Hunter, forced to buy windshield wipers elsewhere at a higher price, is now trying to recover damages from Webster. Will Hunter be successful in its claim?

6. Erwick Construction Company contracted to build a house for Charles. The specifications called for the use of Karlene Pipe for all plumbing. Erwick, nevertheless, got a better price on Boynton Pipe and substituted the equally good Boynton Pipe for Karlene Pipe. Charles's inspection revealed the change, and Charles now refuses to make the final payment. The contract price was for $200,000, and the final payment is $20,000. Erwick now brings suit seeking the $20,000. Will Erwick succeed in its claim?

7. Green owed White $3,500, which was due and payable on June 1. White owed Brown $3,500, which was due and payable on August 1. On May 25, White received a letter signed by Green stating, "If you will cancel my debt to you, in the amount of $3,500, I will pay, on the due date, the debt you owe Brown, in the amount of $3,500." On May 28, Green received a letter signed by White stating, "I received your letter and agree to the proposals recited therein. You may consider your debt to me canceled as of the date of this letter." On June 1, White, needing money to pay his income taxes, made a demand upon Green to pay him the $3,500 due on that date. Is Green obligated to pay the money demanded by White?

8. By written contract, Ames agreed to build a house on Bowen's lot for $45,000, commencing within ninety days of the date of the contract. Prior to the date for beginning construction, Ames informed Bowen that he was repudiating the contract and would not perform. Bowen refused to accept

the repudiation and demanded fulfillment of the contract. Eighty days after the date of the contract, Bowen entered into a new contract with Curd for $42,000. The next day, without knowledge or notice of Bowen's contract with Curd, Ames began construction. Bowen ordered Ames from the premises and refused to allow him to continue. Will Ames be able to collect damages from Bowen? Explain.

9. Judy agreed in writing to work for Northern Enterprises, Inc., for three years as superintendent of Northern's manufacturing establishment and to devote herself entirely to the business, giving it her full time, attention, and skill, for which she was to receive $24,000 per annum in monthly installments of $2,000. Judy worked and was paid for the first twelve months, when, through no fault of her own or Northern's, she was arrested and imprisoned for one month. It became imperative for Northern to employ another, and it treated the contract with Judy as breached and abandoned, refusing to permit Judy to resume work on her release from jail. What rights, if any, does Judy have under the contract?

10. The Park Plaza Hotel awarded its valet and laundry concession to Larson for a three-year term. The contract contained the following provision: "It is distinctly understood and agreed that the services to be rendered by Larson shall meet with the approval of the Park Plaza Hotel, which shall be the sole judge of the sufficiency and propriety of the services." After seven months, the hotel gave a month's notice to discontinue services based on the failure of the services to meet its approval. Larson brought an action against the hotel, alleging that its dissatisfaction was unreasonable. The hotel defended on the ground that subjective or personal satisfaction may be the sole justification for termination of the contract. Who is correct? Explain.

11. Schlosser entered into an agreement to purchase a cooperative apartment from Flynn Company. The written agreement contained the following provision: "This entire agreement is conditioned on Purchaser's being approved for occupancy by the board of directors of the Cooperative. In the event approval of the Purchaser shall be denied, this agreement shall thereafter be of no further force or effect." When Schlosser unilaterally revoked her "offer," Flynn sued for breach of contract. Schlosser claims the approval provision was a condition precedent to the existence of a binding contract and, thus, she was free to revoke. Decision?

12. Jacobs, owner of a farm, entered into a contract with Earl Walker in which Walker agreed to paint the buildings on the farm. Walker purchased the paint from Jones. Before the work was completed, however, Jacobs without good cause ordered Walker to stop. Walker made offers to complete the job, but Jacobs declined to permit Walker to fulfill his contract. Explain whether Walker would be successful in an action against Jacobs for breach of contract.

13. Barta entered into a written contract to buy the K&K Pharmacy, located in a local shopping center. Included in the contract was a provision stating that "this Agreement shall be contingent upon Buyer's ability to obtain a new lease from Landlord for the premises presently occupied by Seller. In the event Buyer is unable to obtain a lease satisfactory to Buyer, this Agree-ment shall be null and void." Barta planned to sell "high-traffic" grocery items, such as bread, milk, and coffee, in order to attract customers to his drugstore. A grocery store in the shopping center, however, already held the exclusive right to sell grocery items. Barta, therefore, could not obtain a leasing agreement meeting his approval. Barta refused to close the sale. In a suit by K&K Pharmacy against Barta for breach of contract, who will prevail? Explain.

14. Victor Packing Co. (Victor) contracted to supply Sun Maid Raisin Growers (http://www.sun-maid.com) 1,800 tons of raisins from the current year's crop. After delivering 1,190 tons of raisins by August, Victor refused to supply any more. Although Victor had until the end of the crop season to ship the remaining 610 tons of raisins, Sun Maid treated Victor's repeated refusals to ship any more raisins as a repudiation of the contract. In order to prevent breaching its own contracts, Sun Maid went into the marketplace to "cover" and bought the raisins needed. Unfortunately, between the time Victor refused delivery and Sun Maid entered the market, disastrous rains had caused the price of raisins to skyrocket. May Sun Maid recover from Victor the difference between the contract price and the market price before the end of the current crop year?

CASE PROBLEMS

15. On August 20, Hildebrand entered into a written contract with the city of Douglasville (http://www.ci.douglasville.ga.us) whereby he was to serve as community development project engineer for three years at a monthly fee of $1,583.33. This salary figure could be changed without affecting the other terms of the contract. One of the provisions for termination of the contract was written notice by either party to the other at any time at least ninety days prior to the intended date of termination. The contract listed a number of services and duties Hildebrand was to perform for the city, among which were (1) keeping the community development director (Hildebrand's supervisor) informed at all times of his whereabouts and how he could be contacted and (2) attending meetings at which his presence was requested. Two years later, by which time Hildebrand's fee had risen to $1,915.83 per month, the city fired Hildebrand effective immediately, citing "certain material breaches . . . of the . . . agreement." The city specifically charged that he did not attend the necessary meetings although requested to do so and seldom if ever kept his supervisor informed of his whereabouts and how he could be contacted. Will Hildebrand prevail in a suit against the mayor and city for the amount of $5,747.49 for breach of his employment contract because

of the city's failure to give him ninety days' notice prior to termination?

16. Walker & Co. contracted to provide a sign for Harrison to place above his dry cleaning business. According to the contract, Harrison would lease the sign from Walker, making monthly payments for thirty-six months. In return, Walker agreed to maintain and service the sign at its own expense. Walker installed the sign in July 1953, and Harrison made the first rental payment. Shortly thereafter, someone hit the sign with a tomato. Harrison also claims he discovered rust on its chrome and little spiderwebs in its corners. Harrison repeatedly called Walker for the maintenance work promised under the contract, but Walker did not respond. Harrison then telegraphed Walker that, due to Walker's failure to perform the maintenance services, he held Walker in material breach of the contract. A week later, Walker sent out a crew, which did all of the requested maintenance services. Harrison sued Walker for breach of contract. Explain whether Harrison will prevail.

17. In May, Watts was awarded a construction contract, based on its low bid, by the Cullman County Commission (http://www.co.cullman.al.us). The contract provided that it would not become effective until approved by the state director of the Farmers Home Administration, now part of the USDA Rural Development Office—(http://www.rurdev.usda.gov/). In September, construction still had not been authorized and Watts wrote to the County Commission requesting a 5 percent price increase to reflect seasonal and inflationary price increases. The County Commission countered with an offer of 3.5 percent. Watts then wrote the commission, insisting on a 5 percent increase and stating that if this was not agreeable, it was withdrawing its original bid. The commission obtained another company to perform the project, and on October 14, informed Watts that it had accepted the withdrawal of the bid. Watts sued for breach of contract. Explain whether Watts will prevail and why or why not.

18. K & G Construction Co. was the owner of and the general contractor for a housing subdivision project. Harris contracted with the company to do excavating and earth-moving work on the project. Certain provisions of the contract stated that (1) K & G was to make monthly progress payments to Harris; (2) no such payments were to be made until Harris obtained liability insurance; and (3) all of Harris's work on the project must be performed in a workmanlike manner. On August 9, a bulldozer operator, working for Harris, drove too close to one of K & G's houses, causing the collapse of a wall and other damage. When Harris and his insurance carrier denied liability and refused to pay for the damage, K & G refused to make the August monthly progress payment. Harris, nonetheless, continued to work on the project until mid-September, when the excavator ceased its operations due to K & G's refusal to make the progress payment. K & G had another excavator finish the job at an added cost of $450. It then sued Harris for the bulldozer damage, alleging negligence, and for the $450 damages for breach of contract. Harris claims that K & G defaulted first, having no legal right to refuse the August progress payment. Did K&G default first? Explain.

19. Mountain Restaurant Corporation (Mountain) leased commercial space in the ParkCenter Mall to operate a restaurant called Zac's Grill. The lease specified that the shopping center should always have as a part of it, or upon premises immediately next to it, a minimum of 500 parking spaces at all times. While developing the mall, ParkCenter entered into two agreements that restricted the amount of parking at their mall to fewer than 500 spaces. Neither agreement was shown to Mountain before it signed the lease.

Zac's Grill was to be a fast-food restaurant where tables were anticipated to "turn over" twice during lunch. Zac's operated successfully until parking close to the restaurant became restricted. Two other restaurants opened and began competing for parking spaces, and the parking lot would become full between 12:00 and 12:30 P.M. Parking, however, was always available at other areas of the mall. Business declined for Zac's, which fell behind on the rent due to ParkCenter until finally the restaurant closed. Mountain claims that it was discharged from its obligations under the lease because of material breach. Is Mountain correct? Explain.

20. In late 1989 or early 1990, the plaintiff, Lan England, agreed to sell 258,363 shares of stock to the defendant, Eugene Horbach, for $2.75 per share, resulting in a total price of $710,498.25. Although the purchase money was to be paid in the first quarter of 1990, the defendant made periodic payments on the stock at least through September 1990. The parties met in May of 1991 to finalize the transaction. At this time, the plaintiff believed that the defendant owed at least $25,000 of the original purchase price. The defendant did not dispute that amount. The parties then reached a second agreement whereby the defendant agreed to pay to the plaintiff an additional $25,000 and to hold in trust 2 percent of the stock for the plaintiff. In return, the plaintiff agreed to transfer the stock and to forgo his right to sue the defendant for breach of the original agreement.

In December 1992, the plaintiff made a demand for the 2 percent stock, but the defendant refused, contending that the 2 percent agreement was meant only to secure his payment of the additional $25,000. The plaintiff sued for breach of the 2 percent agreement. Prior to trial, the defendant discovered additional business records documenting that he had, before entering into the second agreement, actually overpaid the plaintiff for the purchase of the stock. The defendant asserts the plaintiff could not enforce the second agreement as an accord and satisfaction because (1) it was not supported by consideration and (2) it was based upon a mutual mistake that the defendant owed additional money on the original agreement. Is the defendant correct in his assertions? Explain.

http:// **Internet Exercise** Compare the provisions governing performance and breach of contract contained in the Principles of European Contract Law with the provisions of the U.S. common law.

Chapter 18

Contract Remedies

The traditional goal of the law of contract remedies has not been the compulsion of the promisor to perform his promise but compensation of the promisee for the loss resulting from breach.

Restatement of Contracts

Learning Objectives

After reading this chapter you should be able to:

1. Explain how compensatory damages and reliance damages are computed.
2. Define (a) nominal damages, (b) incidental damages, (c) consequential damages, (d) foreseeability of damages, (e) punitive damages, (f) liquidated damages, and (g) mitigation of damages.
3. Define the various types of equitable relief and explain when the courts will grant such relief.
4. Explain how restitutionary damages are computed and identify the situations in which restitution is available as a contractual remedy.
5. Identify and explain the limitations on contractual remedies.

When one party to a contract breaches the contract by failing to perform his contractual duties, the law provides a remedy for the injured party. Although the primary objective of contract remedies is to compensate the injured party for the loss resulting from the breach, it is impossible for any remedy to equal the promised performance. The relief a court can give an injured party is what it regards as an *equivalent* of the promised performance.

Practical Advice

Consider including in your contracts a provision for the recovery of attorneys' fees in the event of breach of contract.

In this chapter, we will examine the most common remedies available for breach of contract: (1) monetary damages, (2) the equitable remedies of specific performance and injunction, and (3) restitution. Article 2 of the Uniform Commercial Code, which provides specialized remedies that we will discuss in Chapter 23, governs sales of goods. Contract remedies are available to protect one or more of the following interests of the injured parties:

1. their ***expectation interest***, which is their interest in having the benefit of their bargain by being put in a position as good as the one they would have been in had the contract been performed;
2. their ***reliance interest***, which is their interest in being reimbursed for loss caused by reliance on the contract by being put in a position as good as the one they would have been in had the contract not been made; or
3. their ***restitution interest***, which is their interest in having restored to them any benefit that they had conferred on the other party.

The contract remedies of compensatory damages, specific performance, and injunction protect the expectation interest. The contractual remedy of reliance damages protects the reliance interest, while the contractual remedy of restitution protects the restitution interest.

> **Practical Advice**
>
> Consider including in your contracts a provision for the arbitration of contract disputes.

CPA MONETARY DAMAGES

A judgment awarding monetary damages is the most frequently granted judicial remedy for breach of contract. Monetary damages, however, will be awarded only for losses that are foreseeable, established with reasonable certainty, and not avoidable. The equitable remedies discussed in this chapter are discretionary and are available only if monetary damages are inadequate.

COMPENSATORY DAMAGES

The right to recover compensatory damages for breach of contract is always available to the injured party. The purpose in allowing **compensatory damages** is to place the injured party in a position as good as the one he would have been in had the other party performed under the contract. This involves compensating the injured party for the dollar value of the benefits he would have received had the contract been performed less any savings he experienced by not having to perform his own obligations under the contract. These damages are intended to protect the injured party's ***expectation interest***, which is the value he expected to derive from the contract. Thus, the amount of compensatory damages is the loss of value to the injured party caused by the other party's failure to perform or by the other's deficient performance *minus* the loss or cost avoided by the injured party *plus* incidental damages *plus* consequential damages.

Loss of Value In general, **loss of value** is the *difference between the value of the promised performance* of the breaching party *and the value of the actual performance* rendered by the breaching party. If no performance is rendered at all, the loss of value is the value of the promised performance. If defective or partial performance is rendered, the loss of value is the difference between the value that the full performance would have had and the value of the performance actually rendered. Thus, when there has been a breach of warranty, the injured party may recover the difference between the value the goods would have had, had they been as warranted, and the value of the goods in the condition in which the buyer actually received them. To illustrate, Jacob sells an automobile to Juliet, expressly warranting that it will get 45 miles per gallon; but the automobile gets only 20 miles per gallon. The automobile would have been worth $8,000 if as warranted, but it is worth only $6,000 as delivered. Juliet would recover $2,000 in damages for loss of value.

Cost Avoided The recovery by the injured party is reduced, however, by any cost or loss she has avoided by not having to perform. For example, Clinton agrees to build a hotel for Debra for $1,250,000 by September 1. Clinton breaches by not completing construction until October 1. As a consequence, Debra loses revenues for one month in the amount of $10,000 but saves operating expenses of $6,000. Therefore, she may recover damages for $4,000. Similarly, in a contract in which the injured party has not fully performed, the injured party's recovery is reduced by the value to the injured party of the performance the injured party promised but did not render. For example, Victor agrees to convey land to Joan in return for Joan's promise to work for Victor for two years. Joan repudiates the contract before Victor has conveyed the land to Joan. Victor's recovery for loss from Joan is reduced by the value to Victor of the land.

Incidental Damages **Incidental damages** are damages that arise directly out of the breach, such as costs incurred to acquire the nondelivered performance from some other source. For example, Agnes employs Benton for nine months for $20,000 to supervise construction of a factory. She then fires Benton without cause after three weeks. Benton, who spends $350 in reasonable fees attempting to find comparable employment, may recover $350 in incidental damages in addition to any other actual loss he has suffered.

Consequential Damages **Consequential damages** are damages not arising directly out of a breach but arising as a foreseeable result of the breach. Consequential damages include lost profits and injury to person or property. Thus, if Tracy leases to Sean a defective machine that causes $4,000 in property damage and $12,000 in personal injuries, Sean may recover, in addition to damages for loss of value and incidental damages, $16,000 as consequential damages.

> **Practical Advice**
>
> If you are the provider of goods or services, consider including a contractual provision for the limitation or exclusion of consequential damages. If you are the purchaser of goods or services, avoid such limitations.

RELIANCE DAMAGES

Instead of seeking compensatory damages, the injured party may seek reimbursement for foreseeable loss caused by her reliance on the contract. The purpose of **reliance damages** is to place the injured party in a position as good as the one she would have been in had the contract *not been made*. Reliance damages include expenses incurred in preparing to perform, in actually performing, or in forgoing opportunities to enter into other contracts. An injured party may prefer damages for reliance to compensatory damages when she is unable to establish her lost profits with reasonable certainty. For example, Donald agrees to sell his retail store to Gary, who spends $50,000 in acquiring inventory and fixtures. Donald then repudiates the contract, and Gary sells the inventory and fixtures for $35,000. Because neither party can establish with reasonable certainty what profit Gary would have made, Gary may recover from Donald as damages the loss of $15,000 he sustained on the sale of the inventory and fixtures plus any other costs he incurred in entering into the contract. An injured party may choose reliance damages instead of compensatory damages when the agreed upon contract would be unprofitable. In such a case, however, if the breaching party can prove with reasonable certainty the amount of the loss, it will be subtracted from the injured party's reliance damages.

NOMINAL DAMAGES

An action to recover damages for breach of contract may be maintained even though the plaintiff has not sustained or cannot prove any injury or loss resulting from the breach. In such case he will be permitted to recover **nominal damages**—a small sum fixed without regard to the amount of loss. Such a judgment may also include an award of court costs.

DAMAGES FOR MISREPRESENTATION

The basic remedy for misrepresentation is rescission (avoidance) of the contract. When appropriate, restitution will also be required. At common law, an alternative remedy to rescission is a suit for damages. The Code liberalizes the common law by not restricting a defrauded party to an election of remedies. That is, the injured party may both rescind the contract by restoring the other party to the status quo and recover damages or obtain any other remedy available under the Code. In most states, the measure of damages for misrepresentation depends on whether the misrepresentation was fraudulent or nonfraudulent.

Fraud A party who has been induced by fraud to enter into a contract may recover general damages in a tort action. A minority of states allow the injured party to recover, under the **"out-of-pocket"** rule, general damages equal to the difference between the value of what she has received and the value of what she has given for it. The great majority of states, however, permit the intentionally defrauded party to recover, under the **"benefit-of-the-bargain"** rule, general damages that are equal to the difference between the value of what she has received and the value of the fraudulent party's performance as represented. The Restatement of Torts provides the fraudulently injured party with the option of either out-of-pocket or benefit-of-the-bargain damages. To illustrate, Emily intentionally misrepresents the capabilities of a printing press and thereby induces Melissa to purchase the machine for $20,000. Though the value of the press as delivered is $14,000, the machine would be worth $24,000 if it performed as represented. Under the out-of-pocket rule, Melissa would recover $6,000, whereas under the benefit-of-the-bargain rule, she would recover $10,000. In addition to a recovery of general damages under one of the measures just discussed, consequential damages may be recovered to the extent they are proved with reasonable certainty and to the extent they do not duplicate general damages. Moreover, where the fraud is gross, oppressive, or aggravated, punitive damages are permitted. See *Merritt v. Craig* later in this chapter.

Nonfraudulent Misrepresentation When the misrepresentation is negligent, the deceived party may recover general damages (under the out-of-pocket measure) and consequential damages. Furthermore, some states permit the recovery of general damages under the benefit-of-the-bargain measure. When the misrepresentation is neither fraudulent nor negligent, however, the Restatement of Torts limits damages to the out-of-pocket measure.

PUNITIVE DAMAGES

Punitive damages are monetary damages in addition to compensatory damages awarded to a plaintiff in certain situations involving willful, wanton, or malicious conduct. Their purpose is to punish the defendant and thus discourage him, and others, from similar wrongful conduct. The purpose of allowing contract damages, on the other hand, is to compensate the plaintiff for the loss sustained because of the defendant's breach of contract. Accordingly, the Restatement provides that punitive damages are not recoverable for a breach of contract unless the conduct constituting the breach is also a tort for which the plaintiff may recover punitive damages. See *Merritt v. Craig* later in this chapter.

LIQUIDATED DAMAGES

A contract may contain a **liquidated damages** provision by which the parties agree in advance to the damages to be paid in event of a breach. Such a provision will be enforced if it amounts to a reasonable forecast of the loss that may or does result from the breach. If, however, the sum agreed on as liquidated damages bears no reasonable relationship to the amount of probable loss, it is unenforceable as a penalty. (A penalty is a contractual provision designed to deter a party from breaching her contract and to punish her for doing so.) Such equivalence is required because the objective of contract remedies is compensatory, not punitive. By examining the substance of the provision, the nature of the contract, and the extent of probable harm that a breach may reasonably be expected to cause the promisee, the courts will determine whether the agreed amount is proper as liquidated damages or unenforceable as a penalty. If a liquidated damages provision is not enforceable, the injured party nevertheless is entitled to the ordinary remedies for breach of contract.

Practical Advice

Consider including a contractual provision for reasonable liquidated damages, especially where damages will be difficult to prove.

Westhaven Associates, Ltd. v. C.C. of Madison, Inc.

Court of Appeals of Wisconsin, District Four, 2002
257 Wis.2d 789, 652 N.W.2d 819
http://www.courts.state.wi.us/html/ca/01/01-1953.htm

FACTS Westhaven Associates, Ltd. (Westhaven) owns the Westhaven Village Shopping Center (Shopping Center). On July 28, 1997, C.C. of Madison, Inc. (Cost Cutters) entered into a ten-year lease with Westhaven. Cost Cutters leased about 17% of the available rentable space in the Shopping Center. On October 9, 1999, Cost Cutters closed its store without Westhaven's approval. At this time, the lease rate was $49.58 per day. Before the parties entered into the lease on July 28, 1997, the Shopping Center's occupancy rate was 71%. The Shopping Center's occupancy rate fluctuated after the parties signed the lease, dropping to 53% in October 1999 prior to Cost Cutters' departure. By March 2000, the occupancy rate increased to 72%. In accordance with the lease, Westhaven attempted to find a new tenant for the Cost Cutters space. The space remained vacant until it was leased to a third party beginning December 1, 2000.

Westhaven then sued Cost Cutters. Westhaven sought relief under paragraph 14.00 of the lease entitled "Default by Tenant." Westhaven exercised the second option under that paragraph, entitling it to the lease rate of $49.58 for each day between October 9, 1999, when Cost Cutters vacated, and December 1, 2000, when the space was sublet. In addition, Westhaven's exercise of the second option under paragraph 14.00 permitted Westhaven to seek stipulated damages under the "failure to do business" provisions contained in paragraphs 3.02 and 8.00(n) of the lease. Paragraph 3.02 requires Cost Cutters to pay Westhaven $20 per day if Cost Cutters fails to keep its premises open for business during "normal business hours." Westhaven claimed that it was entitled to $20 per day for each violation of paragraph 3.02 from October 14, 1999, to November 30, 2000. Paragraph 8.00(n) of the lease requires Cost Cutters to pay a sum equal to Cost Cutters' normal daily rent for each day Cost Cutters fails to keep its premises open for business during specified "minimum hours." Westhaven claimed that it was entitled to an amount equal to the daily rent for each violation of paragraph 8.00(n) from October 14, 1999, to November 30, 2000.

The trial court ruled that paragraphs 3.02 and 8.00(n) were unreasonable and, therefore, unenforceable. Westhaven appealed.

DECISION Judgment reversed and case remanded with directions.

OPINION Lundsten, J. The parties dispute whether stipulated damages provisions in the lease are reasonable, and thus enforceable liquidated damages provisions, or unreasonable, and thus unenforceable penalty provisions. Following the terminology used in the seminal case on this topic, [citation], we use the term "stipulated damages" to mean the damages specified in the lease and "liquidated damages" to mean reasonable and enforceable stipulated damages.

* * *

A stipulated damages provision will be enforced if it is reasonable under the totality of the circumstances. [Citation.] The court looks at several factors to determine reasonableness: "(1) Did the parties intend to provide for damages or for a penalty? (2) Is the injury caused by the breach one that is difficult or incapable of accurate estimation at the time of contract? and (3) Are the stipulated damages a reasonable forecast of the harm caused by the breach?" [Citation.] Essentially, we must look at both the "harm anticipated at the time of contract formation and the actual harm at the time of breach." [Citation.] The factors are not meant to be mechanically applied, and courts may give some factors greater weight than others. [Citation.]

* * *

The first factor we examine when determining the reasonableness of a stipulated damages provision is whether the parties intended the provision to provide liquidated damages or to provide a penalty. As explained in [citation], this factor is "rarely helpful" because the parties' intent has "little relevance to what is reasonable in law." * * *

* * *

The second factor used to determine the reasonableness of a stipulated damages provision examines whether the damages can be estimated *at the time of contracting*. The third factor examines whether the stipulated damages provisions are a reasonable forecast of the *harm caused by the breach*. * * *

Although the second and third factors both use a prospective-retrospective approach, the fact remains that they require two distinct inquiries: the reasonableness of the stipulated damages provision at the time of contracting and the reasonableness of the provision when compared with actual damages after a breach. [Citations.] We first address whether the "failure to do business" provisions were reasonable at the time of contracting.

* * *

As tenants vacate, a shopping center receives less customer traffic, potentially causing other tenants to vacate or go out of business [as well as decreasing the value of the landlord's property]. These consequential damages are often difficult to prove, but that does not prevent sophisticated parties from including consequential damages when estimating the damages at the time of contracting. [Citation.]

* * *

Cost Cutters has failed to persuade us that the "failure to do business" fees were an unreasonable estimation of Westhaven's damages. Cost Cutters did not, for example, present expert testimony that the stipulated damages provisions were unusually harsh as compared with stipulated damages provisions found in other multi-tenant retail commercial leases. To the contrary, in this case Cost Cutters' president, in his deposition testimony, admitted that similar "failure to do business" provisions are common in leases with other shopping malls.

Next, we turn to the question whether the stipulated damages are reasonable in light of the actual damages caused by the breach. [Citation.] As stated above, it is incumbent on Cost Cutters to persuade us that the damages it must pay under the contract do not reasonably relate to the actual harm suffered by Westhaven. Cost Cutters fails to meet this burden.

* * *

Cost Cutters * * * argues that because the occupancy rate at the Shopping Center was low before Cost Cutters departed and actually rose after Cost Cutters left, it is obvious that Westhaven suffered no harm as a result of Cost Cutters' departure. The occupancy rate just prior to Cost Cutters' departure was 53%. About five months later, occupancy had risen to 72%. However, we are not persuaded by the occupancy rate information. Simply because the occupancy rate rose after Cost Cutters' breach does not mean that the breach caused Westhaven no harm. Based on the record before us, the most reasonable inference is that occupancy would have been even higher had Cost Cutters remained in the Shopping Center. When a mall has a low occupancy rate, it does not follow that the mall suffers no harm when a significant tenant vacates. * * *

* * *

We conclude that Cost Cutters has failed to meet its burden of persuasion. Cost Cutters has not shown that the stipulated damages provisions in the lease were unreasonable under the totality of the circumstances.

INTERPRETATION A liquidated damages provision is enforceable if it is a reasonable forecast of the harm caused by the breach.

CRITICAL THINKING QUESTION What limitations, if any, should the law impose upon liquidated damages? Explain.

LIMITATIONS ON DAMAGES

To accomplish the basic purposes of contract remedies, the limitations of foreseeability, certainty, and mitigation have been imposed upon monetary damages. These limitations are intended to ensure that damages can be taken into account at the time of contracting, that they are compensatory and not speculative, and that they do not include loss that could have been avoided by reasonable efforts.

Foreseeability of Damages Contracting parties are generally expected to consider foreseeable risks at the time they enter into the contract. Therefore, compensatory or reliance damages are recoverable only for loss that the party in breach had reason to foresee as a *probable* result of a breach when the contract was made. The breaching party is not liable for loss that was not foreseeable at the time of entering into the contract. The test of **foreseeable damages** is *objective*, based on what the breaching party had reason to foresee. Loss may be deemed foreseeable as a probable result of a breach because it followed from the breach (a) in the ordinary course of events or (b) as a result of special circumstances, beyond the ordinary course of events, about which the party in breach had reason to know.

The leading case on the subject of foreseeability of damages is *Hadley v. Baxendale*, decided in England in 1854. In this case, the plaintiffs operated a flour mill at Gloucester. Their mill was compelled to cease operating because of a broken crankshaft attached to the steam engine that furnished power to the mill. It was necessary to send the broken shaft to a foundry located at Greenwich so that a new shaft could be made. The plaintiffs delivered the broken shaft to the defendants, who were common carriers, for immediate transportation from Gloucester to Greenwich, but did not inform the defendants that operation of the mill had ceased because of the nonfunctioning crankshaft. The defendants received the shaft, collected the freight charges in advance, and promised to deliver the shaft for repairs the following day. The defendants, however, did not make delivery as promised; as a result, the mill did not resume operations for several days, causing the plaintiffs to lose profitable sales. The defendants contended that the loss of profits was too remote, and therefore unforeseeable, to be recoverable. Nonetheless, the jury, in awarding damages to the plaintiffs, was permitted to take into consideration the loss of these profits. The appellate court reversed the decision and ordered a new trial on the ground that the plaintiffs had never communicated to the defendants the special circumstances that caused the loss of profits, namely, the continued stoppage of the mill while awaiting the return of the repaired crankshaft. A common carrier, the court reasoned, would not reasonably have foreseen that the plaintiffs' mill would be shut down as a result of delay in transporting the broken crankshaft. On the other hand, if the defendants had been informed that the shaft was necessary for the operation of the mill, or otherwise had reason to know this fact, they would be liable for the plaintiffs' loss of profit during that period of the shutdown caused by their delay. Under these circumstances, the loss would be the "foreseeable" and "natural" result of the breach.

Should a plaintiff's expected profit be extraordinarily large, the general rule is that the breaching party will be liable for such special loss only if he had reason to know of it. In any event, the plaintiff may recover for any ordinary loss resulting from the breach. Thus, if Madeline breaches a contract with Jane, causing Jane, due to special circumstances, $10,000 in damages when ordinarily such a breach would result in only $6,000 in damages, Madeline would be liable to Jane for $6,000, not $10,000, provided that Madeline was unaware of the special circumstances causing Jane the unusually large loss.

Practical Advice

Be sure to inform the other party to the contract of any "special circumstances" beyond the ordinary course of events that could result from a breach of contract.

Certainty of Damages Damages are not recoverable for loss beyond an amount that the injured party can establish with reasonable certainty. If the injured party cannot prove a particular element of her loss with reasonable certainty, she nevertheless will be entitled to recover the portion of her loss that she can prove with reasonable certainty. The certainty requirement creates the greatest challenge for plaintiffs seeking the recovery of consequential damages for lost profits on related transactions. Similar difficulty arises in proving lost profits caused by breach of a contract to produce a sporting event or to publish a new book, for example.

Mitigation of Damages Under the doctrine of **mitigation of damages**, the injured party may not recover damages for loss that he could have avoided with reasonable effort and without undue risk, burden, or humiliation. Thus, if Earl is under a contract to manufacture goods for Karl and Karl repudiates the contract after Earl has begun performance, Earl will not be allowed to recover for losses he sustains by continuing to manufacture the goods, if to do so would increase the amount of damages. The amount of loss that could reasonably have been avoided is deducted from the amount that would otherwise be recoverable as damages. On the other hand, if the goods were almost completed when Karl repudiated the contract, completing the goods might reduce the damages, because the finished goods may be resalable whereas the unfinished goods may not.

Similarly, if Harvey contracts to work for Olivia for one year for a weekly salary and after two months is wrongfully discharged by Olivia, Harvey must use reasonable efforts to mitigate his damages by seeking other employment. If, after such effort, he cannot obtain other employment of the same general character, he is entitled to recover full pay for the contract period during which he is unemployed. He is not obliged to accept a radically different type of employment or to accept work at a distant place. For example, a person employed as a schoolteacher or accountant who is wrongfully discharged is not obliged to accept employment as a chauffeur or truck driver. The next case involving Shirley MacLaine turns on whether acting in a western is employment equivalent to singing and dancing in a musical.

Practical Advice

If the other party to the contract breaches, be sure to make reasonable efforts to avoid or mitigate damages.

Parker v. Twentieth Century-Fox Film Corp.

Supreme Court of California, 1970
3 Ca.3d 176, 89 Cal.Rptr. 737, 474 P.2d 689

FACTS Shirley MacLaine Parker, a well-known actress, contracted with Twentieth Century-Fox Film Corporation (Fox) in August 1965 to play the female lead in Fox's upcoming production of *Bloomer Girl*, a motion picture musical that was to be filmed in California. The contract provided that Fox would pay Parker a minimum "guaranteed compensation" of $750,000 for fourteen weeks of Parker's services, beginning May 23, 1966. By letter dated April 4, 1966, Fox notified Parker of its intention not to produce the film and, instead, offered to employ Parker in the female lead of another film entitled *Big Country, Big Man*, a dramatic western to be filmed in Australia. The compensation offered and most of the other provisions in the substitute contract were identical to the *Bloomer Girl* provisions, except that Parker's right to approve the director and screenplay would have been eliminated or reduced under the *Big Country* contract. Parker refused to accept and brought suit against Fox to recover $750,000 for breach of the *Bloomer Girl* contract. Fox contended that it owed no money to Parker because she had deliberately failed to mitigate or reduce her damages by unreasonably refusing to accept the *Big Country* lead. The trial court granted Parker a summary judgment. [The court's opinion with respect to the rules for determining whether to grant summary judgment appears in Chapter 3.]

DECISION Judgment for Parker affirmed.

OPINION Burke, J. The general rule is that the measure of recovery by a wrongfully discharged employee is the amount of salary agreed upon for the period of service, less the amount which the employer affirmatively proves the employee has earned or with reasonable effort might have earned from other employment. [Citations.] However, before projected earnings from other employment opportunities not sought or accepted by the discharged employee can be applied in mitigation, the employer must show that the other employment was comparable, or substantially similar, to that of which the employee has been deprived; the employee's rejection of or failure to seek other available employment of a different or inferior kind may not be resorted to in order to mitigate damages. [Citations.]

* * *

Applying the foregoing rules to the record in the present case, with all intendments in favor of the party opposing the summary judgment motion—here, defendant—it is clear that the trial court correctly ruled that plaintiff's failure to accept defendant's tendered substitute employment could not be applied in mitigation of damages because the offer of the *Big Country* lead was of employment both different and inferior, and that no factual dispute was presented on that issue. The mere circumstance that *Bloomer Girl* was to be a musical review calling upon plaintiff's talents as a dancer as well as an actress, and was to be produced in the City of Los Angeles, whereas *Big Country* was a straight dramatic role in a "Western Type" story taking place in an opal mine in Australia, demonstrates the difference in kind between the two employments; the female lead as a dramatic actress in a western style motion picture can by no stretch of the imagination be considered the equivalent of or substantially similar to the lead in a song-and-dance production.

Additionally, the substitute *Big Country* offer proposed to eliminate or impair the director and screenplay approvals accorded to plaintiff under the original *Bloomer Girl* contract * * * and thus constituted an offer of inferior employment. No expertise or judicial notice is required in order to hold that the deprivation or infringement of an employee's rights held under an original employment contract converts the available "other employment" relied upon by the employer to mitigate damages, into inferior employment which the employee need not seek or accept. [Citation.]

INTERPRETATION An injured party's damages may not be reduced by mitigation for her failure to accept or seek other employment of a different or inferior kind.

ETHICAL QUESTION Was it fair for Twentieth Century-Fox Film Corporation to expect Parker to act in the substitute film? Explain.

CRITICAL THINKING QUESTION Why should an injured party be required to mitigate damages? Explain.

CPA REMEDIES IN EQUITY

At times, damages will not adequately compensate an injured party. In these cases, equitable relief in the form of specific performance or an injunction may be available to protect the injured party's interest. Such remedies are not a matter of right but rest in the discretion of the court. Consequently, they will not be granted when there is an adequate remedy at law; when it is impossible to enforce them, as when the seller has already transferred the subject matter of the contract to an innocent third person; when the terms of the contract are unfair; when the consideration is grossly inadequate; when the contract is tainted with fraud, duress, undue influence, mistake, or unfair practices; or when the relief would cause the defendant unreasonable hardship. See *Tamarind Lithography Workshop v. Sanders* later in this chapter.

On the other hand, a court may grant specific performance or an injunction despite a provision for liquidated damages. Moreover, a court will grant specific performance or an injunction even though a term of the contract prohibits equitable relief, if denying such relief would cause the injured party unreasonable hardship.

Another equitable remedy is **reformation**, a process whereby the court "rewrites" or "corrects" a written contract to make it conform to the true agreement of the parties. The purpose of reformation is not to make a new contract for the parties but to express adequately the contract they have made for themselves. The remedy of reformation is granted when the parties agree on a contract but write it in a way that inaccurately reflects their actual agreement. For example, Acme Insurance Co. and Bell agree that for good consideration, Acme will issue an annuity paying $500 per month. Because of a clerical error, the annuity policy is issued for $50 per month. A court of equity, upon satisfactory proof of the mistake, will reform the policy to provide for the correct amount—$500 per month. In addition, as discussed in Chapter 13, when a covenant not to compete is unreasonable, some courts will reform the agreement to make it reasonable and enforceable.

SPECIFIC PERFORMANCE

Specific performance is the equitable remedy that compels the defaulting party to perform her contractual obligations. As with all equitable remedies, it is available only when there is no adequate remedy at law. Ordinarily, for instance, in a case in which a seller breaches a contract for the sale of personal property, the buyer has a sufficient remedy at law. When, however, the personal property contracted for is rare or unique, this remedy is inadequate. Examples of such property would include a famous painting or statue, an original manuscript or a rare edition of a book, a patent, a copyright, shares of stock in a closely held corporation, or an heirloom. Articles of this kind cannot be purchased elsewhere. Accordingly, on breach by the seller of the contract for the sale of any such article, money damages will not adequately compensate the buyer. Consequently, the buyer may avail herself of the equitable remedy of specific performance.

Although courts of equity will grant specific performance in connection with contracts for the sale of personal property only in exceptional circumstances, they will always grant it in case of breach of contract for the sale of real property. The reason for this is that every parcel of land is regarded as unique. Consequently, if the seller refuses to convey title to the real estate contracted for, the buyer may seek the aid of a court of equity to compel the seller to convey the title. Most courts of equity will likewise compel the buyer in a real estate contract to perform at the suit of the seller.

Courts of equity will not grant specific performance of contracts for personal services. In the first place, there is the practical difficulty, if not impossibility, of enforcing such a decree. In the second place, it is against the policy of the courts to force one person to work for or to serve another against his will, even though the person has contracted to do so. Such enforcement would closely resemble involuntary servitude. For example, if Carmen, an accomplished concert pianist, agrees to appear at a certain time and place to play a specified program for Rudolf, a court would not issue a decree of specific performance upon her refusal to appear.

Tamarind Lithography Workshop, Inc. v. Sanders

Court of Appeal of California, Second District, 1983
143 Cal.App.3d 571, 193 Cal.Rptr. 409

FACTS In 1969, Sanders agreed in writing to write, direct, and produce a motion picture on the subject of lithography for the Tamarind Lithography Workshop. After the completion of this film, *Four Stones for Kanemitsu*, litigation arose concerning the parties' rights and obligations under their 1969 agreement. Tamarind and Sanders resolved this dispute by a written settlement agreement, whereby Tamarind promised to provide Sanders a screen credit stating: "A Film by Terry Sanders." Tamarind did not comply with this agreement and failed to include a screen credit for Sanders in the prints it subsequently distributed. In the ensuing litigation, Sanders sought damages for Tamarind's breach of the settlement agreement and specific performance to compel Tamarind's compliance with its obligation to provide a screen credit. The trial court denied Sanders's request for specific performance, and he brought his case to the Court of Appeal.

DECISION Decision for Sanders granting specific performance.

OPINION Stephens, J. The availability of the remedy of specific performance is premised upon well established requisites. These requisites include: A showing by plaintiff of (1) the inadequacy of his legal remedy; (2) an underlying contract that is both reasonable and supported by adequate consideration; (3) the existence of a mutuality of remedies; (4) contractual terms which are sufficiently definite to enable the court to know what it is to enforce; and (5) a substantial similarity of the requested performance to that promised in the contract. [Citation.]

It is manifest that the legal remedies available to Sanders for harm resulting from the future exhibition of the film are inadequate as a matter of law. The primary reasons are two-fold: (1) that an accurate assessment of damages would be far too difficult and require much speculation, and (2) that any future exhibitions might be deemed to be a continuous breach of contract and thereby create the danger of an untold number of lawsuits.

There is no doubt that the exhibition of a film, which is favorably received by its critics and the public at large, can result in valuable advertising or publicity for the artists responsible for that film's making. Likewise, it is unquestionable that the nonappearance of an artist's name or likeness in the form of screen credit on a successful film can result in a loss of that valuable publicity. However, whether that loss of publicity is measurable dollar wise is quite another matter.

By its very nature, public acclaim is unique and very difficult, if not sometimes impossible, to quantify in monetary terms. * * *

* * *

We return to the remaining requisites for Sanders' entitlement to specific performance. The need for our finding the contract to be reasonable and supported by adequate consideration is obviated by the jury's determination of respondent's [Tamarind's] breach of that contract. The requisite of mutuality of remedy has been satisfied in that Sanders had fully performed his obligations pursuant to the agreement (i.e., release of all claims of copyright to the film and dismissal of his then pending action against respondents). [Citation.] Similarly, we find the terms of the agreement sufficiently definite to permit enforcement of the respondent's performance as promised.

INTERPRETATION Specific performance is an appropriate remedy when there is no adequate remedy at law.

CRITICAL THINKING QUESTION Should specific performance be available for all breaches of contract? Explain.

INJUNCTIONS

The **injunction**, as used as a contract remedy, is a formal court order enjoining (commanding) a person to refrain from doing a specific act or to cease engaging in specific conduct. A court of equity, at its discretion, may grant an injunction against breach of a contractual duty when damages for a breach would be inadequate. For example, Clint enters into a written contract to give Janice the right of first refusal on a tract of land owned by Clint. Clint, however, subsequently offers the land to Blake without first offering it to Janice. A court of equity may properly enjoin Clint from selling the land to Blake. Similarly, valid covenants not to compete may be enforced by an injunction.

An employee's promise of exclusive personal services may be enforced by an injunction against serving another employer as long as the probable result will not deprive the employee of other reasonable means of making a living. Suppose, for example, that Allan makes a contract with Marlene, a famous singer, under which Marlene agrees to sing at Allan's theater on certain dates for an agreed-upon fee. Before the date of the first performance, Marlene makes a contract with Craig to sing for Craig at his theater on the same dates. Although, as we have already discussed, Allan cannot obtain specific performance of his contract by Marlene, a court of equity will, on suit by Allan against Marlene, issue an injunction against her ordering her not to sing for Craig. This is the situation in the case of *Madison Square Garden Corp., Ill. v. Carnera*.

When the services contracted for are *not* unusual or extraordinary in character, the injured party cannot obtain injunctive relief. His only remedy is an action at law for damages.

Madison Square Garden Corp., Ill. v. Carnera

Circuit Court of Appeals, Second Circuit, 1931
52 F.2d 47

FACTS Carnera (defendant) agreed with Madison Square Garden (plaintiff) to render services as a boxer in his next contest with the winner of the Schmeling-Stribling contest for the heavyweight championship title. The contract also provided that prior to the match Carnera would not engage in any major boxing contest without the permission of Madison Square Garden. Without obtaining such permission, Carnera contracted to engage in a major boxing contest with Sharkey. Madison Square Garden brought suit requesting an injunction against Carnera's performing his contract to box Sharkey. The trial court granted a preliminary injunction.

DECISION Order for Madison Square Garden affirmed.

OPINION Chase, J. The District Court has found on affidavits which adequately show it that the defendant's services are unique and extraordinary. A negative covenant in a contract for such personal services is enforceable by injunction where the damages for a breach are incapable of ascertainment. [Citations.]

The defendant points to what is claimed to be lack of consideration for his negative promise, in that the contract is inequitable and contains no agreement to employ him. It is true that there is no promise in so many words to employ the defendant to box in a contest with Stribling or Schmeling, but the agreement read as a whole binds the plaintiff to do just that, providing either Stribling or Schmeling becomes the contestant as the result of the match between them and can be induced to box the defendant. The defendant has agreed to "render services as a boxer" for the plaintiff exclusively, and the plaintiff has agreed to pay him a definite percentage of the gate receipts as his compensation for so doing. The promise to employ the defendant to enable him to earn the compensation agreed upon is implied to the same force and effect as though expressly stated. * * * [Citations.]

As we have seen, the contract is valid and enforceable. It contains a restrictive covenant which may be given effect. Whether a preliminary injunction shall be issued under such circumstances rests in the sound discretion of the court. [Citations.] The District Court, in its discretion, did issue the preliminary injunction and required the plaintiff as a condition upon its issuance to secure its own performance of the contract in suit with a bond for $25,000 and to give a bond in the sum of $35,000 to pay the defendant such damages as he may sustain by reason of the injunction. Such an order is clearly not an abuse of discretion.

INTERPRETATION When damages are not adequate, an injunction may be used to enforce an agreement to perform exclusive services that are unusual and extraordinary.

CRITICAL THINKING QUESTION Should money damages have been an adequate remedy in this case? Explain.

CPA RESTITUTION

One of the remedies that may be available to a party to a contract is restitution. **Restitution** is the act of returning to the aggrieved party the consideration, or its value, that he gave to the other party. The purpose of restitution is to restore the injured party to the position he was in before the contract was made. Therefore, the party seeking restitution must return what has been received from the other party.

Restitution is available in several contractual situations: (1) for a party injured by breach, as an alternative remedy; (2) for a party in default; (3) for a party who may not enforce a contract because of the statute of frauds; and (4) for a party wishing to rescind (avoid) a voidable contract.

Party Injured by Breach

A party is entitled to restitution if the other party totally breaches the contract by nonperformance or repudiation. For example, Benedict agrees to sell land to Beatrice for $60,000. After Beatrice makes a partial payment of $15,000, Benedict wrongfully refuses to transfer title. As an alternative to damages or specific performance, Beatrice may recover the $15,000 in restitution.

Party in Default

Where a party, after having partly performed, commits a breach by nonperformance or repudiation that discharges the other party's duty to perform, the party in default is entitled to restitution for any benefit she has conferred in excess of the loss she has caused by the breach. For example, Nathan agrees to sell land to Milly for $60,000, and Milly makes a partial payment of $15,000. Milly then repudiates the contract. Nathan sells the land to Murray in good faith for $55,000. Milly may recover from Nathan in restitution the part payment of the $15,000 less the $5,000 damages Nathan sustained because of Milly's breach, which equals $10,000.

Statute of Frauds

A party to a contract that is unenforceable because of the statute of frauds may, nonetheless, have acted in reliance on the contract. In such a case, that party may recover in restitution the benefits he conferred on the other in relying on the unenforceable contract. In most states the party seeking restitution must not be in default. Thus, if Wilton makes an oral contract to furnish services to Rochelle that are not to be performed within a year, and Rochelle discharges Wilton after three months, Wilton may recover as restitution the value of the services rendered during the three months.

Voidable Contracts

A party who has rescinded or avoided a contract for lack of capacity, duress, undue influence, fraud in the inducement, nonfraudulent misrepresentation, or mistake is entitled to restitution for any benefit he has conferred on the other. For example, Samuel fraudulently induces Edith to sell land for $60,000. Samuel pays the purchase price, and Edith conveys the land. She then discovers the fraud. Edith may disaffirm the contract and recover the land as restitution. Generally, the party seeking restitution must return any benefit that he has received under the agreement; however, as we found in our discussion of contractual capacity (Chapter 14), this is not always the case.

Figure 18-1 summarizes the remedies for breach of contract.

CPA Limitations on Remedies

Election of Remedies

If a party injured by a breach of contract has more than one remedy available, her manifestation of a choice of one remedy, such as bringing suit, does not prevent seeking another unless the remedies are inconsistent and the other party materially changes his position in reliance on the manifestation. For example, a party who seeks specific performance, an injunction, or restitution may be entitled to incidental damages, such as those brought about by delay in performance. Damages for total breach, however, are inconsistent with the remedies of specific performance, injunction, and restitution. Likewise, the remedy of specific performance or an injunction is inconsistent with that of restitution.

With respect to contracts for the sale of goods, the Code rejects any doctrine of election of remedies. Thus, the remedies it provides, which are essentially cumulative, include all of the remedies available for breach. Under the Code, whether one remedy prevents the use of another depends on the facts of the individual case.

Loss of Power of Avoidance

A party with a power of avoidance for lack of capacity, duress, undue influence, fraud, misrepresentation, or mistake may lose that power if (1) she affirms the contract, (2) she delays unreasonably in exercising the power of disaffirmance, or (3) the rights of third parties intervene.

Affirmance A party who has the power to avoid a contract for lack of capacity, duress, undue influence, fraud in the inducement, nonfraudulent misrepresentation, or mistake will lose that power by affirming the contract.

Figure 18-1
Contract Remedies

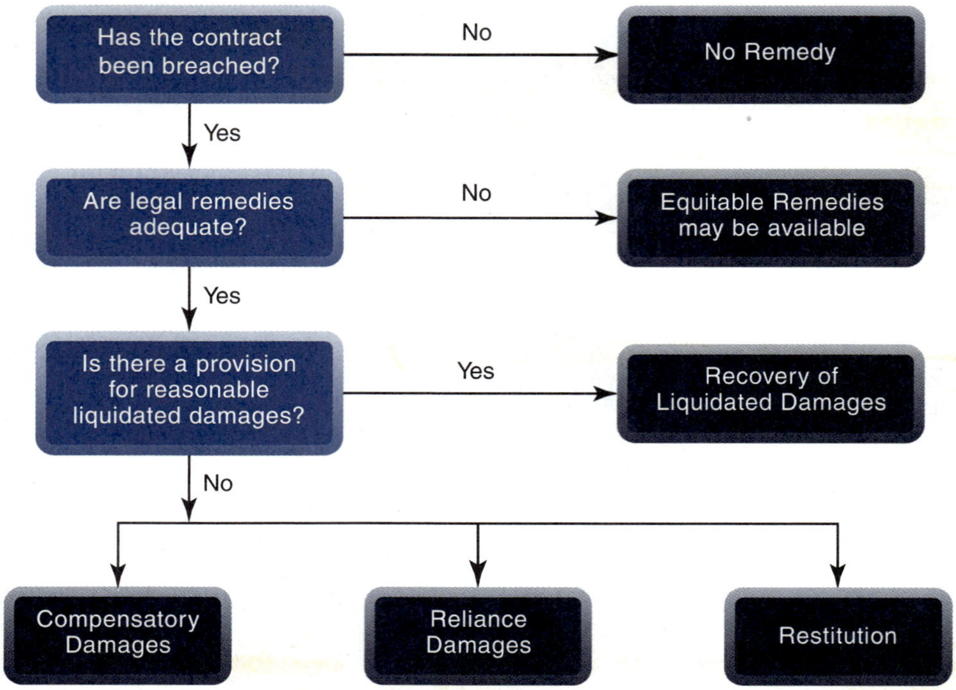

Affirmance occurs where the party, with full knowledge of the facts, either declares the intention to proceed with the contract or takes some other action from which such intention may reasonably be inferred. Thus, suppose that Pam was induced to purchase a ring from Sally through Sally's fraudulent misrepresentation. If, after learning the truth, Pam undertakes to sell the ring to Janet or does something else that is consistent only with her ownership of the ring, she may no longer rescind the transaction with Sally. In the case of incapacity, duress, or undue influence, affirmance is effective only after the circumstances that made the contract voidable cease to exist. When there has been fraudulent misrepresentation, the defrauded party may affirm only after he knows of the misrepresentation; if the misrepresentation is nonfraudulent or a mistake is involved, affirmance may occur only after the defrauded party knows or should know of the misrepresentation or mistake.

Practical Advice

If you have the power to avoid a contract, do not affirm the contract unless you are sure you wish to relinquish your right to rescind the contract.

Merritt v. Craig

Court of Special Appeals of Maryland, 2000

130 Md.App. 350, 746 A.2d 923, *cert. denied*, 359 Md. 29, 753 A.2d 2 (2000)

http://www.courts.state.md.us/opinions.html

FACTS In the fall of 1995, during their search for a new residence, the plaintiffs, Benjamin K. and Julie S. Merritt, advised the defendant, Virginia Craig, that they were interested in purchasing Craig's property contingent upon a satisfactory home inspection. On November 5, 1995, the plaintiffs, their inspector, and the defendant's husband Mark Craig conducted an inspection of the cistern and water supply pipes in the basement. The examination revealed that the cistern had been used to store a water supply reserve, but was not currently utilized. There were also two water lines that entered into the basement. One of the lines came from an 800-foot well that was located on the property, and the other line came from a well located on the adjacent property. The well located on the adjacent property supplied water to both the residence for sale and a guesthouse owned by Craig. The existence of the adjacent well was not disclosed to the plaintiffs.

On December 2, 1995, plaintiffs and Craig executed a contract of sale for the property, along with a "Disclosure Statement" signed by Craig and acknowledged by the plaintiffs affirming that there were no problems with the water supply to the house. Between November 5, 1995, and June 1996, Craig caused the water line from the guesthouse to the house purchased by the plaintiffs to be cut, and the cistern reactivated to store water from the existing well. On May 18, 1996, Craig's husband advised Dennis Hannibal, one of the real estate agents involved in the deal, that he had spent $4,196.79 to upgrade the water system on the property. On June 14, 1996, the plaintiffs and Craig closed the sale of the property. Later that afternoon, Craig's husband, without the plaintiffs' knowledge, excavated the inside wall of the house and installed a cap to stop a leaking condition on the water line that he had previously cut.

Upon taking possession of the house the plaintiffs noticed that the water supply in their well had depleted. The plaintiffs met with Craig to discuss a solution to the water failure problem, agreeing with Craig to conduct a flow test to the existing well and to contribute money for the construction of a new well. On October 29, 1996, the well was drilled and produced only one-half gallon of water per minute. Subsequently plaintiffs paid for the drilling of a second well on their property, but it failed to produce water. In January 1997, appellants contacted a plumber, who confirmed that the line from the guesthouse well had been cut flush with the inside surface of the basement wall and cemented closed. Plaintiffs continued to do further work on the house in an effort to cure the water problem. The plaintiffs brought suit against Craig, seeking rescission of the deed to the property and contract of sale, along with compensatory and punitive damages. The trial judge dismissed plaintiffs' claim for rescission on the ground that they had effectively waived their right to rescission. The jury returned a verdict in favor of the plaintiffs, awarding compensatory damages in the amount of $42,264.76 and punitive damages in the amount of $150,000. The plaintiffs appealed the trial court's judgment denying their right to rescind the contract. The defendant cross-appealed on the award of punitive damages.

DECISION Judgment of the trial court reversed, and the case is remanded.

OPINION Davis, J. Under Maryland law, when a party to a contract discovers that he or she has been defrauded, the party defrauded has either "a right to retain the contract and collect damages for its breach, or a right to rescind the contract and recover his or her own expenditures," not both. [Citations.] "These rights [are] inconsistent and mutually exclusive, and the discovery put[s] the purchaser to a prompt election." [Citation.] "A plaintiff seeking rescission must demonstrate that he [or she] acted promptly after discovery of the ground for rescission," otherwise the right to rescind is waived. [Citations.] * * *

In [this] case * * *, appellants [plaintiffs] claim that they were entitled to a rescission of the subject contract of sale and deed and incidental damages. Appellants also claim that they were entitled to compensatory and punitive damages arising from Craig's actions. Appellants, however, may not successfully rescind the contract while simultaneously recovering compensatory and punitive damages. Restitution is "a party's unilateral unmaking of a contract for a legally sufficient reason, such as the other party's material breach" and it in effect "restores the parties to their pre-contractual position." [Citation.] The restoration of the parties to their original position is incompatible with the circumstance when the complaining party is, at once, relieved of all obligations under the contract while simultaneously securing the windfall of compensatory and punitive damages beyond incidental expenses.

* * *

In sum, although whether appellants promptly repudiated the contract was not squarely before the court, we are not persuaded by appellees' assertion that appellants did not seek rescission in a timely fashion. We hold that, under the facts of this case, appellants must elect the form of relief, i.e., damages or rescission * * *

Although we remand for the trial court to permit appellants to elect which remedy they wish to pursue, for the guidance of the court, we shall address the question presented by Craig in her cross appeal, i.e., whether the trial court erred by allowing the jury verdict awarding appellants punitive damages in the amount of $150,000 to stand. * * *

We hold that * * * the appellants are entitled to be awarded punitive damages resulting from Craig's actions. A "[p]laintiff seeking to recover punitive damages must allege in detail in the complaint the facts that indicate the entertainment by defendant of evil motive or intent." [Citation.] The Court of Appeals has held that "punitive damages may only be awarded in such cases where 'the plaintiff has established that the defendant's conduct was characterized by evil motive, intent to injure, ill will or fraud * * * '". [Citation.] In cases of fraud that arise out of a contractual relationship, the plaintiff would have to establish actual malice to recover punitive damages. [Citation.] Finally, we have stated that "actual or express malice requires an intentional or willful act (or omission) * * * and 'has been characterized as the performance of an act without legal justification or excuse, but with an evil or rancorous motive influenced by hate, the purpose being to deliberately and willfully injure the plaintiff.' " [Citation.]

In the instant case, the jury found that appellants had been induced by fraud to enter into a contract for the sale of Craig's property. * * *

The jury believed that the representations made by Craig were undertaken with actual knowledge that the representations were false and with the intention to deceive appellants. The Court of Appeals, in [citation], held that a person's actual knowledge that the statement is false, coupled with his or her intent to deceive the plaintiffs by means of that statement, constitutes the actual malice required to support an award for punitive damages. [Citation.] Moreover, the record reflects that the jury could reasonably infer Craig's intention to defraud appellants by her representation in the Disclosure Statement that there were no problems with the water supply, and by subsequently making substantial changes in the water system by cutting off a water line which supplied water to appellants' residence immediately after appellants' inspector examined the system. Therefore, we hold that the circuit court was not in error in finding facts from the record sufficient to support an award of punitive damages.

Craig also challenges the punitive damages award on the basis that the amount of the award was excessive. * * *

In the case at hand, the trial judge undertook the appropriate review of the jury's award. It is clear from the court's comments at the hearing that the court's decision not to disturb the jury's verdict was based on the evidence presented at trial and was not excessive under the criteria set forth in [citation]. Craig's conduct toward appellants was reprehensible and fully warranted punitive damages. Her conduct in willfully misrepresenting the condition of the water system in the Disclosure Statement, coupled with her actions and those of her husband in interfering and diverting the water flow subsequent to the inspection and sale of the property, constitute egregious conduct. As a result of Craig's conduct, appellants were forced to employ extreme water conservation practices due to an insufficient water supply and they attempted to ameliorate the problem by having two new wells drilled on the property which proved to be unproductive. Moreover, the lack of water supply to appellants' property clearly reduced its market value. * * *

INTERPRETATION A defrauded party may rescind a contract induced by fraud but may lose that power if he affirms the contract or delays unreasonably in exercising the power of rescission.

CRITICAL THINKING QUESTION What is the policy reason for requiring a defrauded party to elect between rescission and damages? Explain

Delay The power of avoidance may be lost if the party who has the power to do so does not rescind within a reasonable time after the circumstances that made the contract voidable have ceased to exist. Determining a reasonable time depends on all the circumstances, including the extent to which the delay enables the party with the power of avoidance to speculate at the other party's risk. To illustrate, a defrauded purchaser of stock cannot wait unduly to see if the market price or value of the stock appreciates sufficiently to justify retaining the stock.

Practical Advice

If you have the power to avoid a contract, be sure to rescind within a reasonable time or you will forfeit your right to do so.

Rights of Third Parties The intervening rights of third parties further limit the power of avoidance and the accompanying right to restitution. If A transfers property to B in a transaction that is voidable by A, and B sells the property to C (a good faith purchaser for value) before A exercises the power of avoidance, A will lose the right to recover the property.

Thus, if a third party (C), who is a good faith purchaser for value, acquires an interest in the subject matter of the contract before A has elected to rescind, no rescission is permitted. Because the transaction is voidable, B acquires a voidable title to the property. Upon a sale of the property by B to C, who is a purchaser in good faith and for value, C obtains good title and is allowed to retain the property. Because both A and C are innocent, the law will not disturb the title held by C, the good faith purchaser. In this case, as in all cases where rescission is not available, A's only recourse is against B.

The one notable exception to this rule is the situation involving a sale, *other than a sale of goods*, by a minor who subsequently wishes to avoid the transaction, in which the property has been retransferred to a good faith purchaser. Under this special rule, a good faith purchaser is deprived of the protection generally provided such third parties. Therefore, the third party in a transaction not involving goods, real property being the primary example, is no more protected from the minor's disaffirmance than is the person dealing directly with the minor.

CHAPTER SUMMARY

Monetary Damages

Compensatory Damages contract damages placing the injured party in a position as good as the one he would have held had the other party performed; equals loss of value minus loss avoided by injured party plus incidental damages plus consequential damages
- *Loss of Value* value of promised performance minus value of actual performance
- *Cost Avoided* loss or costs the injured party avoids by not having to perform
- *Incidental Damages* damages arising directly out of a breach of contract
- *Consequential Damages* damages not arising directly out of a breach but arising as a foreseeable result of the breach

Reliance Damages contract damages placing the injured party in as good a position as she would have been in had the contract not been made

Nominal Damages a small sum awarded where a contract has been breached but the loss is negligible or unproved

Damages for Misrepresentation
- *Benefit-of-the-Bargain Damages* difference between the value of the fraudulent party's performance as represented and the value the defrauded party received
- *Out-of-Pocket Damages* difference between the value given and the value received

Punitive Damages are generally not recoverable for breach of contract

Liquidated Damages reasonable damages agreed to in advance by the parties to a contract

Limitations on Damages
- *Foreseeability of Damages* potential loss that the party now in default had reason to know of when the contract was made
- *Certainty of Damages* damages are not recoverable beyond an amount that can be established with reasonable certainty
- *Mitigation of Damages* injured party may not recover damages for loss he could have avoided by reasonable effort

Remedies in Equity

Availability only where there is no adequate remedy at law

Types
- *Specific Performance* court decree ordering breaching party to render promised performance
- *Injunction* court order prohibiting a party from doing a specific act
- *Reformation* court order correcting a written contract to conform with the intent of the contracting parties

Restitution

Definition of Restitution restoration of the injured party to the position she was in before the contract was made

Availability
- *Party Injured by Breach* if the other party totally breaches the contract by nonperformance or repudiation
- *Party in Default* for any benefit conferred in excess of the loss caused by the breach

- *Statute of Frauds* where a contract is unenforceable because of the statute of frauds, a party may recover the benefits conferred on the other party in reliance on the contract
- *Voidable Contracts* a party who has avoided a contract is entitled to restitution for any benefit conferred on the other party

Limitations on Remedies

Election of Remedies if remedies are not inconsistent, a party injured by a breach of contract may seek more than one remedy

Loss of Power of Avoidance a party with the power to avoid a contract may lose that power by
- Affirming the contract
- Delaying unreasonably in exercising the power of avoidance
- Being subordinated to the intervening rights of third parties

QUESTIONS

1. Edward contracted to buy 1,000 barrels of sugar from Marcia. Marcia failed to deliver, and because Edward could not buy any sugar in the market, he was forced to shut down his candy factory. (a) What damages is Edward entitled to recover? (b) Would it make any difference if Marcia had been told by Edward that he wanted the sugar to make candies for the Christmas trade and that he had accepted contracts for delivery by certain dates?

2. Daniel agreed to erect an apartment building for Steven for $750,000, and that Daniel would suffer a deduction of $1,000 per day for every day of delay. Daniel was twenty days late in finishing the job, losing ten days because of a strike and ten days because the material suppliers were late in furnishing him with materials. Daniel claims that he is entitled to payment in full (a) because the agreement as to $1,000 a day is a penalty and (b) because Steven has not shown that he has sustained any damage. Discuss each contention and decide.

3. Sharon contracted with Jane, a shirtmaker, for 1,000 shirts for men. Jane manufactured and delivered 500 shirts, for which Sharon paid. At the same time, Sharon notified Jane that she could not use or dispose of the other 500 shirts and directed Jane not to manufacture any more under the contract. Nevertheless, Jane made up the other 500 shirts and tendered them to Sharon. Sharon refused to accept the shirts. Jane then sued for the purchase price. Is she entitled to the purchase price? If not, is she entitled to any damages? Explain.

4. Stuart contracts to act in a comedy for Charlotte and to comply with all theater regulations for four seasons. Charlotte promises to pay Stuart $800 for each performance and to allow Stuart one benefit performance each season. It is expressly agreed "Stuart shall not be employed in any other production for the period of the contract." Stuart and Charlotte, during the first year of the contract, have a terrible quarrel. Thereafter, Stuart signs a contract to perform in Elaine's production and ceases performing for Charlotte. Charlotte seeks (a) to prevent Stuart from performing for Elaine and (b) to require Stuart to perform his contract with Charlotte. Will she succeed?

5. Louis leased a building to Pam for five years at a rental of $1,000 per month. Pam was to deposit $10,000 as security for performance of all her promises in the lease, which was to be retained by Louis in case of any breach on Pam's part. Pam defaulted in the payment of rent for the last two months of the lease. Louis refused to return any of the deposit, claiming it as liquidated damages. Pam sued Louis to recover $8,000 (the $10,000 deposit less the amount of rent due Louis for the last two months). What amount of damages should Pam be allowed to collect from Louis? Explain.

6. In which of the following situations is specific performance available as a remedy?
   a. Mary and Anne enter into a written agreement under which Mary agrees to sell and Anne agrees to buy for $10 per share 100 shares of the 300 shares outstanding of the capital stock of the Infinitesimal Steel Corporation, whose shares are not listed on any exchange and are closely held. Mary refuses to deliver when tendered the $1,000.
   b. Modifying (a) above, assume that the subject matter of the agreement is stock of the United States Steel Corporation, which is traded on the New York Stock Exchange.
   c. Modifying (a) above, assume that the subject matter of the agreement is undeveloped farmland of little commercial value.

7. On March 1, Joseph sold to Sandra fifty acres of land in Oregon that Joseph at the time represented to be fine black loam, high, dry, and free of stumps. Sandra paid Joseph the agreed price of $40,000 and took from Joseph a deed to the

land. Sandra subsequently discovered that the land was low, swampy, and not entirely free of stumps. Sandra, nevertheless, undertook to convert the greater part of the land into cranberry bogs. After one year of cranberry culture, Sandra became entirely dissatisfied, tendered the land back to Joseph, and demanded from Joseph the return of the $40,000. On Joseph's refusal to repay the money, Sandra brought an action at law against him to recover the $40,000. What judgment?

8. James contracts to make repairs to Betty's building in return for Betty's promise to pay $12,000 on completion of the repairs. After partially completing the repairs, James is unable to continue. Betty hires another builder, who completes the repairs for $5,000. The building's value to Betty has increased by $10,000 as a result of the repairs by James, but Betty has lost $500 in rents because of the delay caused by James's breach. James sues Betty. How much, if any, may James recover in restitution from Betty?

9. Linda induced Sally to enter into a purchase of a stereo amplifier by intentionally misrepresenting the power output to be sixty watts at rated distortion, when in fact it delivered only twenty watts. Sally paid $450 for the amplifier. Amplifiers producing twenty watts generally sell for $200, whereas amplifiers producing sixty watts generally sell for $550. Sally decides to keep the amp and sue for damages. How much may Sally recover in damages from Linda?

10. Virginia induced Charles to sell Charles's boat to Virginia by misrepresentation of material fact on which Charles reasonably relied. Virginia promptly sold the boat to Donald, who paid fair value for it and knew nothing concerning the transaction between Virginia and Charles. Upon discovering the misrepresentation, Charles seeks to recover the boat. What are Charles's rights against Virginia and Donald?

CASE PROBLEMS

11. Felch was employed as a member of the faculty of Findlay College on a continuing basis. He was dismissed by action of the president and board of trustees, who did not comply with a contractual provision for dismissal that requires a hearing. Felch requested the court to enjoin Findlay College to continue Felch as a member of the faculty and to pay him the salary agreed upon. Should Felch be entitled to injunctive relief? Explain.

12. Copenhaver, the owner of a laundry business, contracted with Berryman, the owner of a large apartment complex, to allow Copenhaver to own and operate the laundry facilities within the apartment complex. Berryman terminated the five-year contract with Copenhaver with forty-seven months remaining. Within six months, Copenhaver placed the equipment into use in other locations. He then filed suit, claiming that he was entitled to conduct the laundry operations for an additional forty-seven months and that, through such operations, he would have earned a profit of $13,886.58, after deducting Berryman's share of the gross receipts and other operating expenses. Decision?

13. Billy Williams Builders and Developers (Williams) entered into a contract with Hillerich under which Williams agreed to sell to Hillerich a certain lot and to construct on it a house according to submitted plans and specifications. The house built by Williams was defectively constructed. Hillerich brought suit for specific performance of the contract and for damages resulting from the defective construction and delay in performance. Williams argued that Hillerich was not entitled to have both specific performance and damages for breach of the contract because the remedies were inconsistent and Hillerich had to elect one or the other. Explain whether Williams is correct in this assertion.

14. Developers under a plan approved by the city of Rye had constructed six luxury cooperative apartment buildings and were to construct six more. In order to obtain certificates of occupancy for the six completed buildings, the developers were required to post a bond with the city to insure completion of the remaining buildings. The developers posted a $100,000 bond upon which the defendant, Public Service Mutual Insurance Company (http://www.psmins.com/overview.htm), as guarantor or surety, agreed to pay $200 for each day after April 1, that the remaining buildings were not completed. After the April deadline, more than 500 days passed without completion of the buildings. Should the city prevail in its suit against the developers and the insurance company to recover $100,000 on the bond? Explain.

15. Kerr Steamship Company sent a telegram to the Philippines through the Radio Corporation of America (http://www.rca.com). The telegram, which contained instructions for loading cargo on one of Kerr's ships, was mislaid and never delivered. Consequently, the ship was improperly loaded and the cargo was lost. Kerr sued the Radio Corporation for the $6,675.29 in profits the company lost on the cargo because of the Radio Corporation's failure to deliver the telegram. Should Kerr be allowed to recover damages from Radio? Explain.

16. El Dorado Tire Company fired Bill Ballard, a sales executive. Ballard had a five-year contract with El Dorado but was fired after only two years of employment. Ballard sued El Dorado for breach of contract. El Dorado claims that any damages due to breach of the contract should be mitigated because of Ballard's failure to seek other employment after he was fired. Explain whether El Dorado is correct in its contention.

17. California and Hawaiian Sugar Company (C and H) is an agricultural cooperative in the business of growing sugarcane in Hawaii and transporting the raw sugar to its refinery in California for processing. Because of the seasonal nature of the sugarcane crop, availability of ships to transport the raw sugar immediately after harvest is imperative. In 1999, C and H lost the services of the shipping company it previously used. To fill the void, C and H decided to build its own ship, a Macababoo, which had two components, a tug and a barge. C and H contracted with Halter Marine to build the tug and with Sun Ship to build the barge. In finalizing the contract for construction of the barge, both C and H and Sun Ship were represented by senior management and by legal counsel. The resulting contract called for a liquidated damages payment of $17,000 per day that delivery of the completed barge was delayed. Delivery of both the barge and the tug was significantly delayed. Sun Ship paid the $17,000 per day liquidated damages amount and then sued to recover it, claiming that without the liquidated damages provision, C and H's legal remedy for money damages would have been significantly less than that paid by Sun Ship pursuant to the liquidated damages provision. Decision?

18. Bettye Gregg offered to purchase a house from Head & Seeman, Inc. (seller). Though she represented in writing that she had between $15,000 and $20,000 in equity in another home that she would pay to the seller after she sold the other home, she knew that she did not have such equity. In reliance upon these intentionally fraudulent representations, the seller accepted Gregg's offer and the parties entered into a land contract. After taking occupancy, Gregg failed to make any of the contract payments. The seller's investigations then revealed the fraud. Head & Seeman then brought suit seeking rescission of the contract, return of the real estate, and restitution. Restitution was sought for the rental value for the five months of lost use of the property and the seller's out-of-pocket expenses made in reliance upon the bargain. Gregg contends that under the election of remedies doctrine, the seller cannot both rescind the contract and recover damages for its breach. Is Gregg correct? Explain.

19. Watson agreed to buy Ingram's house for $355,000. The contract provided that Watson deposit $15,000 as earnest money and that "in the event of default by the Buyer, earnest money shall be forfeited to Seller as liquidated damages, unless Seller elects to seek actual damages or specific performance." The contract also stipulated that the "Buyer represents that Buyer has sufficient funds available to close this sale in accordance with this agreement, and is not relying on any contingent source of funds unless otherwise set forth in this agreement." In fact, Watson did not have sufficient funds available but planned to assume Ingram's mortgage on the house. When this arrangement did not materialize, Watson sought to modify the terms of sale to defer payment in exchange for giving Ingram a lien on certain real estate owned by Watson. Ingram rejected this modification and stated that he intended to strictly enforce the original terms. Watson secured other, contingent financing, but Ingram refused to grant Watson an extension, and the sale to Watson was not completed. Finally, nine months after the Watson sale was to occur, Ingram sold the house to a third party for $355,000. Is Ingram entitled to Watson's $15,000 earnest money as liquidated damages?

http:// **Internet Exercise** Find information about or examples of liquidated damages provisions.

PART IV

SALES

Uniform Commercial Code, Article 2
http://www.law.cornell.edu/ucc/2/overview.html

Uniform Commercial Code, Article 2A
http://www.law.cornell.edu/ucc/2A/overview.html

Uniform Law Commissioners
http://www.law.upenn.edu/bll/ulc/ulc_frame.htm

United Nations Commission on International Trade Law
http://www.uncitral.org/en-index.htm

Consumer Product Safety Commission
http://www.cpsc.gov/

Consumers Union
http://www.consumersunion.org/

Magnuson-Moss Federal Warranty Act
http://home.cinci.rr.com/asktherep/MagMoss-UniformCode.pdf

Federal Trade Commission
http://www.ftc.gov/

American Law Institute
http://www.ali.org/

CHAPTER 19

Introduction to Sales and Leases

The propensity to truck, barter, and exchange one thing for another . . .
is common to all men, and to be found in no other race of animals.

ADAM SMITH (1723–1790) IN *THE WEALTH OF NATIONS*, 1776

Learning Objectives

After reading this chapter you should be able to:

1. Distinguish a sale from a lease and describe the governing law for both.
2. Identify and explain the fundamental principles of Article 2 and Article 2A of the Uniform Commercial Code (UCC).
3. Compare and contrast the manifestation of mutual assent under both the common law and under Article 2.
4. Determine how Article 2 deals with (a) the necessity of consideration to modify a contract and (b) irrevocable offers.
5. Describe the UCC's approach to requiring that certain contracts be in writing and identify the alternative methods of compliance under the Code.

Sales are the most common and important of all commercial transactions. In an exchange economy such as ours, sales are the essential means by which the various units of production exchange their outputs, thereby providing the opportunity for specialization and enhanced productivity. An advanced, complex, industrialized economy with highly coordinated manufacturing and distribution systems requires a reliable mechanism for ensuring that *future* exchanges can be entered into today and fulfilled later. Because practically everyone in our economy is a purchaser of both durable and consumable goods, the manufacture and distribution of goods involve numerous sales transactions. The critical role of the law of sales is to establish a framework in which these present and future exchanges may take place in a predictable, certain, and orderly fashion with a minimum of transaction costs.

Leases of personal property, also of great economic significance, exceed $100 billion annually. Leases range from a consumer's renting an automobile or a lawn mower to a Fortune 500 corporation's leasing heavy industrial machinery. Despite the frequent and widespread use of personal property leases, the law governing these transactions had been patched together from the common law of personal property, real estate leasing law, and the Uniform Commercial Code (Articles 2 and 9). Except for several provisions, the UCC did not directly apply to leases. Although some courts have held, nevertheless, that the UCC is applicable to leases of goods because a lease is a transaction in goods, other courts have refused to apply the Code to leases because actual title to the goods never passed. Still other courts have applied the Code to lease by analogy. Even in states in which Article 2 was extended to leases, which provisions were to be applied remained unclear. In any event, no unified or uniform statutory law governed leases of personal property for most of the twentieth century.

To fill this void, the drafters of the Code approved Article 2A—Leases in 1987 and subsequently amended the Article in 1990. An analogue of Article 2, the new article adopts many of the same rules. Article 2A is an attempt to codify in one statute all the rules governing the leasing of personal property. One state has enacted the 1987 version of Article 2A while more than forty-five other states and the District of Columbia have adopted the 1990 version.

This part of the book covers both the sale of goods and the lease of goods. All chapters in this part will cover Article 2A in addition to Article 2 by stating "Article 2A" wherever Article 2A's provision is either identical or essentially the same as the Article 2 provision. When Article 2A significantly deviates from Article 2, both rules will be discussed. In this chapter we will discuss the nature and formation of sales and lease contracts and the fundamental principles of sales and leases of goods.

http:// Uniform Commercial Code, Article 2: http://www.law.cornell.edu/ucc/2/overview.html
Uniform Commercial Code, Article 2A: http://www.law.cornell.edu/ucc/ 2A/overview.html
Uniform Law Commissioners: http://www.law.upenn.edu/bll/ulc/ ulc_frame.htm
United Nations Commission on International Trade Law: http://www. uncitral.org/en-index.htm

NATURE OF SALES AND LEASES

The law of sales, which governs contracts involving the sale of goods, is a specialized branch of both the law of contracts (discussed in Chapters 9–18) and the law of personal property (discussed in Chapter 49). This section will cover the definition of sales and leases and the fundamental principles of Article 2 and Article 2A of the UCC.

CPA DEFINITIONS

GOODS

Goods are essentially defined as movable, tangible, personal property. For example, the sale of a bicycle, stereo set, or this textbook is considered a sale of goods. Goods also include the unborn young of animals, growing crops, and, if removed by the seller, timber, minerals, or a building attached to real property. Under Article 2A, minerals cannot be leased prior to their extraction.

SALE

The Code defines a **sale** as the transfer of title to goods from seller to buyer for a price. The price can be money, other goods, real estate, or services.

LEASE

Article 2A defines a **lease** of goods as a "transfer of the right to possession and use of goods for a term in return for consideration, but . . . retention or creation of a security interest is not a lease." A transaction within this definition of a lease is governed by Article 2A, but if the transaction is a security interest disguised as a lease, it is governed by Article 9. Categorizing a transaction as a lease has significant implications not only for the parties to the lease but for third parties as well. If the transaction is deemed to be a lease, the residual interest in the goods belongs to the lessor, who need not file publicly to protect this interest. On the other hand, if the transaction is a security interest, then the provisions of Article 9 regarding enforceability, perfection, priority, and remedies apply.

Consumer Leases Article 2A affords special treatment for consumer leases. The definition of a **consumer lease** requires that (1) the transaction meet the definition of a lease under Article 2A; (2) the lessor be regularly engaged in the business of leasing *or* selling goods; (3) the lessee be an individual, not an organization; (4) the lessee take the lease interest primarily for a personal, family, or household purpose; and (5) the total payments under the lease do not exceed $25,000. Although consumer protection for lease transactions is primarily left to other state and federal law, Article 2A does contain a number of provisions that apply to consumer leases and that may *not* be varied by agreement of the parties.

Finance Leases A **finance lease** is a special type of lease transaction generally involving three parties instead of two. Whereas in the typical lease situation the lessor also supplies the goods, in a finance lease arrangement, the lessor and the supplier are separate parties. The lessor's primary function in a finance lease is to provide financing to the lessee for a lease of goods provided by the supplier. For example, under a finance lease arrangement, a manufacturer supplies goods pursuant to the lessee's instructions or specifications. The party functioning as the lessor will then either purchase those goods from the supplier or act as the prime lessee in leasing them from the supplier. In turn, the lessor will lease or sublease the goods to the lessee. Because the finance lessor functions merely as a source of credit, she typically will have no special expertise as to the goods. Due to the limited role the finance lessor usually plays, Article 2A treats finance leases differently from ordinary leases.

Carter v. Tokai Financial Services, Inc.

Court of Appeals of Georgia, 1998
231 Ga.App. 755, 500 S.E.2d 638

FACTS On January 3, 1996, Tokai's (now part of De Lage Landen Leasing and Trade Finance) **(http://www.delagelandenus.com/)** predecessor in interest, Mitel Financial, entered into a "Master Equipment Lease Agreement" (Agreement) with Applied Radiological Control, Inc. (ARC) for the lease of certain telephone equipment valued at $42,000. Randy P. Carter of ARC personally guaranteed ARC's obligations under the Agreement. ARC made four rental payments and then defaulted on its obligations. Thereafter, Tokai repossessed the telephone equipment and sold it for $5,900. Tokai then brought this suit against Carter, and the trial court awarded Tokai $56,765.74. Carter appeals.

DECISION Judgment reversed.

OPINION Blackburn, J. As an initial matter, we note that Paragraph 13 of the Agreement states that each lease contemplated therein is a finance lease as defined by Article 2A of the UCC. "A 'finance lease' involves three parties—the lessee/business, the finance lessor, and the equipment supplier. The lessee/business selects the equipment and negotiates particularized modifications with the equipment supplier. Instead of purchasing the equipment from the supplier, the lessee/business has a finance lessor purchase the selected equipment, and then leases the equipment from the finance lessor." [Citation.]

Carter contends, nonetheless, that the true intent of the parties was to enter into a security agreement. "Whether a transaction creates a lease or security interest is determined by the facts of each case; however, a transaction creates a security interest if the consideration the lessee is to pay the lessor for the right to possession and use of the goods is an obligation for the term of the lease not subject to termination by the lessee, and (a) [t]he original term of the lease is equal to or greater than the remaining economic life of the goods, (b) [t]he lessee is bound to renew the lease for the remaining economic life of the goods or is bound to become the owner of the goods, (c) [t]he lessee has an option to renew the lease for the remaining economic life of the goods for no additional consideration or nominal additional consideration upon compliance with the lease agreement, or (d) [t]he lessee has an option to become the owner of the goods for no additional consideration or nominal additional consideration upon compliance with the lease agreement." [UCC §] 1–201(37).

Here, the Agreement's initial term was for five years, ARC was not required to renew the lease or purchase the telephone equipment at the end of the term, and ARC did not have the option to renew the lease or purchase the property at the end of the term for nominal consideration. Therefore, the Agreement does not fit within the definition of a secured transaction provided by [UCC §] 1–201(37).

Furthermore, "it is commonly held that the 'best test' for determining the intent of an agreement which provides for an option to buy is a comparison of the option price with the market value of the equipment at the time the option is to be exercised. * * * If, upon compliance with the terms of the 'lease,' the lessee has an option to become the owner of the property for no additional or for a nominal consideration, the lease is deemed to be intended for security." [Citations.] ARC was given the option to purchase the telephone equipment in this case at the end of the lease term for its fair market value. "Additional consideration is not nominal if * * * when the option to become the owner of the goods is granted to the lessee the price is stated to be the fair market value of the goods determined at the time the option is to be performed." [UCC Section 1–201(37)(x).] Accordingly, the agreement in this case must be considered a true lease, not a secured transaction. As a result, the procedural safeguards of Article 9 of the UCC are inapplicable to the matter at hand, and Carter's claims under this enumeration must fail. [Citations.]

* * *

"In Georgia, all lease contracts for 'goods,' including finance leases, first made or first effective on or after July 1, 1993, are governed by Article 2A of the Uniform Commercial Code. [Citations.] The Agreement was entered into by the parties on January 3, 1996; therefore, it is subject to Article 2A of the UCC."

INTERPRETATION A lease will be governed by Article 2A unless in compliance with the terms of the "lease" the lessee has the option to become the owner of the property for no additional or for a nominal consideration, in which case, the lease is deemed to be intended for security and governed by Article 9.

CRITICAL THINKING QUESTION Why might the parties attempt to disguise a security agreement as a lease?

GOVERNING LAW

Although sales transactions are governed by Article 2 of the Code, general contract law continues to apply where the Code has not specifically modified such law. In other words, the law of sales is a specialized part of the general law of contracts, and the law of contracts continues to govern unless specifically displaced by the Code.

General contract law also continues to govern all contracts outside the scope of the Code. Transactions not within the scope of Article 2 include employment contracts, service contracts, insurance contracts, contracts involving real property, and contracts for the sale of intangibles such as stocks, bonds, patents, and copyrights. For an illustration of the law governing contracts, see Figure 9-1. In determining whether a contract containing both a sale of goods and a service is a UCC contract or general contract, the majority of states follow the predominant purpose test. This test, as in *Pittsley v. Houser*, which follows, and in *Pass v. Shelby Aviation, Inc.* in Chapter 9 holds that if the predominant purpose of the whole transaction is a sale of goods, Article 2 applies to the entire transaction. If, on the other hand, the predominant purpose is the nongood or service portion, Article 2 does not apply. A few states apply Article 2 only to the goods part of a transaction and general contract law to the nongoods or service part of the transaction.

CISG

The United Nations Convention on Contracts for the International Sales of Goods (CISG), which has been ratified by the United States and more than forty other countries, governs all contracts for the international sales of goods between parties located in different nations that have ratified the CISG. Because treaties are federal law, the CISG supersedes the Uniform Commercial Code in any situation to which either could apply. The CISG includes provisions dealing with interpretation, trade usage, contract formation, obligations and remedies of sellers and buyers, and risk of loss. Parties to an international sales contract may, however, expressly exclude CISG governance from their contract. The CISG specifically excludes sales of (1) goods bought for personal, family, or household use; (2) ships or aircraft; and (3) electricity. In addition, it does not apply to contracts in which the primary obligation of the party furnishing the goods consists of supplying labor or services.

Pittsley v. Houser

Idaho Court of Appeals, 1994
875 P.2d 232

FACTS Jane Pittsley contracted with Donald Houser, who was doing business as Hilton Contract Co. (Hilton), to install carpet in her home. The total contract price was $4,402. From this sum, Hilton paid the installers $700 to put the carpet in Pittsley's home. Following installation, Pittsley complained to Hilton that the installation was defective in several respects. Hilton attempted to fix the installation but was unable to satisfy Pittsley. Eventually, Pittsley refused any further efforts to fix the carpet. She sued for rescission of the contract and return of the $3,500 she had previously paid on the contract plus incidental damages. Hilton counterclaimed for the balance due on the contract. The magistrate determined that the breach was not so material as to justify rescission of the contract and awarded Pittsley $250 in repair costs plus $150 in expenses. The magistrate also awarded Hilton the balance of $902 remaining on the contract. Pittsley appealed to the district court, which reversed and remanded the case to the magistrate for additional findings of fact and to apply the UCC to the transaction. Hilton appeals this ruling, asserting that application of the UCC is inappropriate because the only defects alleged were in the installation of the carpet, not in the carpet itself.

DECISION The judgment of the magistrate is vacated and the case remanded.

OPINION Swanstrom, J. The single question upon which this appeal depends is whether the UCC is applicable to the subject transaction. If the underlying transaction involved the sale of "goods," then the UCC would apply. If the transaction did not involve goods, but rather was for services, then application of the UCC would be erroneous.

Idaho Code § 2–105(l) defines "goods" as "all things (including specially manufactured goods) which are movable at the time of identification to the contract for sale. * * *" Although there is little dispute that carpets are "goods," the transaction in this case also involved installation, a service. Such hybrid transactions, involving both goods and services, raise difficult questions about the applicability of the UCC. Two lines of authority have emerged to deal with such situations.

The first line of authority, and the majority position, utilizes the "predominant factor" test. The Ninth Circuit, applying the Idaho Uniform Commercial Code to the subject transaction, restated the predominant factor test as:

> The test for inclusion or exclusion is not whether they are mixed, but, granting that they are mixed, whether their predominant factor, their thrust, their purpose, reasonably stated, is the rendition of service, with goods incidentally involved (e.g., contract with artist for painting) or is a transaction of sale, with labor incidentally involved (e.g., installation of a water heater in a bathroom).

[Citations.] This test essentially involves consideration of the contract in its entirety, applying the UCC to the entire contract or not at all.

The second line of authority, which Hilton urges us to adopt, allows the contract to be severed into different parts, applying the UCC to the goods involved in the contract, but not to the nongoods involved, including services as well as other nongoods assets and property. Thus, an action focusing on defects or problems with the goods themselves would be covered by the UCC, while a suit based on the service provided or some other nongoods aspect would not be covered by the UCC. * * *

We believe the predominant factor test is the more prudent rule. Severing contracts into various parts, attempting to label each as goods or nongoods and applying different law to each separate part clearly contravenes the UCC's declared purpose "to simplify, clarify and modernize the law governing commercial transactions." § 1–102(2)(a). As the Supreme Court of Tennessee suggested in [citation], such a rule would, in many contexts, present "difficult and in some instances insurmountable problems of proof in segregating assets and determining their respective values at the time of the original contract and at the time of resale, in order to apply two different measures of damages."

Applying the predominant factor test to the case before us, we conclude that the UCC was applicable to the subject transaction. The record indicates that the contract between the parties called for "165 yds Masterpiece No. 2122—Installed" for a price of $4319.50. There was an additional charge for removing the existing carpet. The record indicates that Hilton paid the installers $700 for the work done in laying Pittsley's carpet. It appears that Pittsley entered into this contract for the purpose of obtaining carpet of a certain quality and color. It does not appear that the installation, either who would provide it or the nature of the work, was a factor in inducing Pittsley to choose Hilton as the carpet supplier. On these facts, we conclude that the sale of the carpet was the predominant factor in the contract, with the installation being merely incidental to the purchase. Therefore, in failing to consider the UCC, the magistrate did not apply the correct legal principles to the facts as found.

INTERPRETATION If the predominant purpose of the whole transaction is a sale of goods, then Article 2 applies to the whole transaction; if the predominant purpose is the nongood or service component, then Article 2 does not apply.

CRITICAL THINKING QUESTION Which test do you prefer? Explain.

Although Article 2 governs sales, the drafters of the article have invited the courts to extend Code principles to nonsale transactions in goods. To date, a number of courts have accepted this invitation and have applied Code provisions by analogy to other transactions in goods not expressly included within the Act, most frequently to leases and bailments. The Code has also greatly influenced the revision of the Restatement, Second, Contracts, which, as previously discussed, has great effect upon all contracts.

Although lease transactions are governed by Article 2A of the Code, general contract law continues to apply where the Code has not specifically modified such law. In other words, the law of leases is a specialized part of the general law of contracts, and the law of contracts continues to govern unless specifically displaced by the Code.

Practical Advice

Because it is unclear which law will govern certain contracts, be careful to specify the particulars of your agreement in your written contract.

FUNDAMENTAL PRINCIPLES OF ARTICLE 2 AND ARTICLE 2A

CPA

The purpose of Article 2 is to modernize, clarify, simplify, and make uniform the law of sales. Furthermore, the article is to be interpreted according to these principles and not according to some abstraction such as the passage of title. The Code "is drawn to provide flexibility so that, since it is intended to be a semi-permanent piece of legislation, it will provide its own machinery for expansion of commercial practices. It is intended to make it possible for the law embodied in this Act to be developed by the courts in the light of unforeseen and new circumstances and practices. However, the proper construction of the Act requires that its interpretation and application be limited to its reason." (*General Provisions* in Comment to Section 1–102). This open-ended drafting includes the following fundamental concepts.

> **CISG**
>
> The CISG governs only the formation of the contract of sales and the rights and obligations of the seller and buyer arising from such contract. It does not cover the validity of the contract or any of its provisions. In addition, one of the purposes of the CISG is to promote uniformity of the law of sales.

GOOD FAITH

All parties who enter into a contract or duty within the scope of the Code must perform their obligations in good faith. The Code defines **good faith** as "honesty in fact in the conduct or transaction concerned." For a merchant, good faith also requires the observance of reasonable commercial standards of fair dealing in the trade. For instance, if the parties agree that the seller is to set the price term, the seller must establish the price in good faith.

> **CISG**
>
> The CISG is also designed to promote the observation of good faith in international trade.

UNCONSCIONABILITY

The courts may scrutinize every contract of sale to determine whether in its commercial setting, purpose, and effect it is unconscionable. The reviewing court may refuse to enforce a contract (or any part of it) found to be unconscionable or may limit its application to prevent an unconscionable result. The Code does not define ***unconscionable***; however, the term is defined in the *New Webster's Dictionary* (Deluxe Encyclopedic Edition) as "contrary to the dictates of conscience; unscrupulous or unprincipled; exceeding that which is reasonable or customary; inordinate, unjustifiable."

The Code denies or limits enforcement of an unconscionable contract for the sale of goods to promote fairness and decency and to correct harshness or oppression in contracts resulting from the unequal bargaining positions of the parties.

The doctrine of unconscionability permits the courts to resolve issues of unfairness explicitly on that basis without recourse to formalistic rules or legal fictions. In policing contracts for fairness, the courts have demonstrated their willingness to limit freedom of contract to protect the less advantaged from the overreaching of dominant contracting parties.

The doctrine of unconscionability has evolved through its application by the courts to include both procedural and substantive unconscionability. **Procedural unconscionability** involves scrutiny for the presence of "bargaining naughtiness." In other words, was the negotiation process fair? Or were there procedural irregularities such as burying important terms of the agreement in fine print or obscuring the true meaning of the contract with impenetrable legal jargon?

In the search for **substantive unconscionability**, the court examines the actual terms of the contract, seeking oppressive or grossly unfair provisions such as an exorbitant price or an unfair exclusion or limitation of contractual remedies. An all-too-common example involves a necessitous buyer in an unequal bargaining position with a seller who consequently has obtained an exorbitant price for his product or service.

> **Practical Advice**
>
> Refrain from entering into contracts with provisions that are oppressively harsh or that were negotiated under unfair circumstances.

As to *all* leases, Article 2A provides that a court faced with an unconscionable contract or clause may refuse to enforce either the entire contract or just the unconscionable clause or may limit the application of the unconscionable clause to avoid an unconscionable result. This is similar to Article 2's treatment of unconscionable clauses in sales contracts. A lessee under a consumer lease, however, is provided with additional protection against unconscionability. In the case of a consumer lease, if a court as a matter of law finds that any part of the lease contract has been induced by unconscionable conduct, the court is expressly empowered to grant appropriate relief. The same is true when unconscionable conduct occurs in the collection of a claim arising from a consumer lease contract. The *explicit* availability of relief for consumers subjected to unconscionable conduct (procedural unconscionability)—in addition to a provision regarding unconscionable contracts (substantive unconscionability)—represents a departure from Article 2. An additional remedy that Article 2A provides for consumers is the award of attorney's fees. If the court finds unconscionability with respect to a consumer lease, it shall award reasonable attorney's fees to the lessee.

The following case illustrates the application of the doctrine of unconscionability, as does *Williams v. Walker-Thomas Furniture Co.* in Chapter 13.

Construction Associates, Inc. v. Fargo Water Equipment Co.

North Dakota Supreme Court, 1989
446 N.W.2d 237

FACTS Construction Associates (CA) was the successful bidder to construct a water supply line for the city of Breckenridge, Minnesota. CA purchased a large amount of polyvinyl chloride pipe manufactured by the Johns-Manville Sales Corporation (J-M) in order to construct the pipeline. CA, however, did not have any direct contact with J-M; instead, it purchased the pipe through a supply company (Fargo Water Equipment). J-M shipped the pipe directly to the work site, and included with each shipment an installation guide written for those who actually directed the installation of the pipe. On page three of the installation guide, J-M expressly warranted the pipe to be free from defects in workmanship and materials. In addition, J-M set forth a limitation of liability clause, which stated there would be no liability except for breach of the express warranty, and that J-M would be responsible only for resupplying a like quantity of nondefective pipe. J-M stated that it would not be liable for any incidental, consequential, or other damages.

Eventually the Breckenridge pipeline developed more than seventy leaks. The only way these leaks could be repaired was to remove the defective joints and replace them with stainless steel sleeves. After incurring more than $140,000 in repairs to the pipeline, CA sued J-M and Fargo. CA won a jury award of more than $140,000 in damages from J-M. J-M appealed, claiming that the limitation of liability clause should be enforced.

DECISION Judgment for CA affirmed.

OPINION Ericksted, J. [UCC § 2–719] specifically allows the parties to an agreement to limit the remedies available upon breach and to exclude consequential damages:

* * *

By its terms § 2–302 [unconscionable contract or clause] applies to any clause of the contract. Courts thus have construed §§ 2–302 and 2–719 together in holding that a general limitation of remedies clause, including those limiting liability to repair or replacement, may be subject to unconscionability analysis under the Code. [Citations.]

The determination whether a particular contractual provision is unconscionable is a question of law for the court. [Citations.] The court is to look at the contract from the perspective of the time it was entered into, without the benefit of hindsight.* * *

Courts and commentators have generally viewed the Code's unconscionability provisions within a two-pronged framework: procedural unconscionability, which encompasses factors relating to unfair surprise, oppression, and inequality of bargaining power, and substantive unconscionability, which focuses upon the harshness or one-sidedness of the contractual provision in question. [Citations.]

Procedural Unconscionability We initially note that this case presents a commercial, rather than a consumer, transaction. Although courts have generally been more reluctant to find unconscionability in purely commercial settings, [citation], under appropriate circumstances a contractual provision may be found unconscionable even in a commercial setting. [Citations.]

* * *

The circumstances presented in this case demonstrate a substantial inequality in bargaining power between J-M and Construction Associates. Construction Associates is a relatively small local construction firm, while J-M is part of an enormous, highly diversified, international conglomerate. The limitation of remedies and exclusion of damages were part of a pre-printed installation guide included with all shipments of J-M Pipe. J-M has continually stressed on appeal that those limitations and exclusions are included in all of its brochures and guides. It is obvious that there is no room for bargaining or negotiation as to the warranty provisions.

We also note that the facts in this case demonstrate an actual lack of negotiation coupled with elements of unfair surprise. * * *

The limitations and exclusions clause in this case can hardly be described as "bargained for." The clauses were included on page three of a pre-printed installation guide expressly directed to the worker in the field, rather than to officers of Construction Associates. Construction Associates was not apprised at the time of contracting that their remedies under the Code were being limited or excluded. It would be within J-M's control to do so by, for example, requiring its dealers to accept orders for pipe only upon a J-M form which included the limitations and exclusions and which required the purchaser's signature. Clearly an element of procedural unconscionability is present where through a pre-printed guide which was not provided to Construction Associates (and then only to field workers) until long after the sales contract had been finalized.

Substantive Unconscionability Substantive unconscionability focuses upon the harshness of the particular contractual terms:

* * *

The clause at issue here would limit Construction Associates' remedy for J-M's breach to a like quantity of replacement pipe, with no recovery of consequential damages. Construction Associates argues, with support in the evidence, that replacement pipe is not used when making repairs to leaking joints on a completed underground water pipeline. Because the accepted method of repair is to cut out the leaking joint and repair it with a stainless steel sleeve, Construction Associates argues, the replacement pipe would be useless in effecting repairs upon the line. The trial court determined that J-M's limited remedy "amount[ed] to nothing whatsoever." * * *

Numerous courts, in a variety of commercial and consumer contexts, have held limitations and exclusions unconscionable when they leave the non-breaching party with no effective remedy. [Citations.] This is particularly true where the defect in the product is latent, so that the buyer is unable to discover the defect until additional damages are incurred. [Citations.]. In this case, Construction Associates did not discover the defects until the pipe was assembled and placed underground.

INTERPRETATION A court can override a term of a contract if it finds that term to be unconscionable or the result of an unconscionable negotiation process.

ETHICAL QUESTION Is unconscionable conduct always unethical? Explain.

CRITICAL THINKING QUESTION How active should courts be in finding contracts or clauses to be unconscionable? Explain.

EXPANSION OF COMMERCIAL PRACTICES

An underlying policy of the Code is "to permit the continued expansion of commercial practices through custom, usage and agreement of the parties." In particular, the Code emphasizes the course of dealing and the usage of trade in interpreting agreements.

A **course of dealing** is a sequence of previous conduct between the parties that may fairly be regarded as establishing a common basis of understanding for interpreting their expressions and agreement.

A **usage of trade** is a practice or method of dealing regularly observed and followed in a place, vocation, or trade. To illustrate: Connie contracts to sell Ward 1,000 feet of San Domingo mahogany. By usage of dealers in mahogany, known to Connie and Ward, good figured mahogany of a certain density is known as San Domingo mahogany, though it does not come from San Domingo. Unless otherwise agreed, the usage is part of the contract.

CISG

The parties are bound by any usage or practices that they have agreed to or established between themselves. In addition, the parties are considered, unless otherwise agreed, to be bound by any usage of international trade that is widely known and regularly observed in the particular trade.

SALES BY AND BETWEEN MERCHANTS

The Code establishes some separate rules that apply to transactions between merchants or to transactions involving a merchant as a party. A **merchant** is defined as a person (1) who is a dealer in a particular type of goods, (2) who by his occupation holds himself out as having knowledge or skill peculiar to certain goods or practices, or (3) who employs an agent or broker whom he holds out as having such knowledge or skill. (Article 2A.) These rules exact higher standards of conduct from merchants because of their knowledge of trade and commerce and because merchants as a class generally set these standards for themselves. The more significant of these merchant provisions are good faith, confirmation of oral contracts, firm offers, "battle of the forms," warranty of title, warranty of merchantability, sales on approval, retention of possession of goods by seller, entrusting of goods, risk of loss, and duties after rightful rejection.

LIBERAL ADMINISTRATION OF REMEDIES

The Code provides that its remedies shall be liberally administered in order to place the aggrieved party in a position as good as the one she would have held, had the defaulting party fully performed. The Code does make it clear, however, that remedies are limited to compensation and may not include consequential or punitive damages, unless specifically provided by the Code. According to its provisions, for cases in which the Code itself does not expressly provide a remedy for a right or obligation, the courts should provide an appropriate remedy. Remedies are discussed in Chapter 23.

FREEDOM OF CONTRACT

Most of the Code's provisions are not mandatory but permit the parties by agreement to vary or displace them altogether. However, the obligations of good faith, diligence, reasonableness, and care may not be disclaimed by agreement, although the parties may by agreement determine the standards by which to measure the performance of these obligations, as long as the standards are not obviously unreasonable.

VALIDATION AND PRESERVATION OF SALES CONTRACTS

One of the requirements of commercial law is the establishment of rules that determine when an agreement is valid. The Code approaches this requirement by reducing formal requisites to the bare minimum and by attempting to preserve agreements whenever the parties manifest an intent to enter into a contract.

FORMATION OF SALES AND LEASE CONTRACTS

As we have stated previously, the Code's basic approach to validation is to recognize contracts whenever the parties manifest such an intent. This is so whether or not the parties can identify the precise moment at which they formed the contract. (Article 2A.)

CPA MANIFESTATION OF MUTUAL ASSENT

In order for a contract to exist, there must be an objective manifestation of mutual assent: an offer and an acceptance. In this section, we will examine the UCC rules that affect offers and acceptances.

DEFINITENESS OF AN OFFER

At common law, the terms of a contract were required to be definite and complete. The Code has rejected the strict approach of the common law by recognizing an agreement as valid, despite missing terms, if there is any reasonably certain basis for granting a remedy. Accordingly, the Code provides that even though a contract may omit one or more terms, the contract need not fail for indefiniteness. (Article 2A.) The Code provides standards by which the courts may ascertain and supply omitted essential terms, provided the parties intended to enter into a binding agreement. Nevertheless, the more terms the parties leave open, the less likely their intent to enter into a binding contract. Article 2A generally does not provide the same gap-filling provisions.

> **CISG**
> An offer to contract is sufficiently definite if it indicates the goods and fixes or makes provision, expressly or implicitly, for determining price and quality.

Open Price The parties may enter into a contract for the sale of goods even though they have reached no agreement on the price. In such a case, the price is reasonable at the time for delivery. A contract has an open price term if the agreement (1) says nothing as to price; (2) provides that the parties shall agree later as to the price and they fail to so agree; or (3) fixes the price in terms of some agreed market or other standard, as set by a third person or agency, and the price is not so set. An agreement that the price is to be fixed by the seller or buyer means that it must be fixed in good faith.

Open Quantity: Output and Requirements Contracts As we discussed in Chapters 10 and 12, an output contract is the agreement of a buyer to purchase the entire output of a seller for a stated period, whereas a requirements contract is an agreement of a seller to supply a buyer with all her requirements for certain goods. Even though the exact quantity of goods is not specified and even though the seller may have some control over his

Ethical Dilemma

What Constitutes Unconscionability in a Business?

FACTS Frank's Maintenance and Repair, Inc. orally placed with C. A. Roberts Co. an order for steel tubing to use in manufacturing front fork tubes for motorcycles. Front fork tubes bear the bulk of a motorcycle's weight, so Frank's had to use high-quality steel.

Soon, Frank's received from Roberts Co. an acknowledgment of the order. This acknowledgment included the conditions of sale, which limited consequential damages, as well as a description of restricted remedies that were available upon the contract's breach. The sale conditions required that the buyer make any claim for defective equipment promptly upon receipt of the goods. These conditions were printed on the back of the acknowledgment. On the front, a legend that read "conditions of sale on reverse side" had been stamped over in such a way that the words at first appeared to read "No conditions of sale on reverse side."

Roberts delivered the steel to Frank's in December 1975. The steel had no visible defects. When Frank's began using the material in its manufacturing process in the summer of 1976, however, the company discovered that the steel was hopelessly pitted and cracked. Frank's Maintenance and Repair informed Roberts Co. of the defects, revoked its acceptance of the steel, and sued for breach of the warranty of merchantability.

Social, Policy, and Ethical Considerations

1. Did Frank's Maintenance and Repair have a reasonable opportunity to understand the terms of its contract with C. A. Roberts Co.? Given the contract that Frank's received, was the company able to make a meaningful choice with regard to the terms of the agreement? Why or why not?
2. Who bears the responsibility in a situation such as this when both parties are businesspersons and thus should know enough to read all contracts carefully and thoroughly?
3. With or without the stamp, did Roberts act unconscionably in drawing up its contract? Moreover, should Roberts have the right to restrict a buyer's remedies if its steel may have a latent defect?

output and the buyer over her requirements, such agreements are enforceable through the application of an objective standard based on the good faith of both parties. Moreover, the parties may not produce or request quantities disproportionate to any stated estimate of need or production or to prior output or requirements.

Irrevocable Offer

An offeror generally may withdraw an offer at any time prior to its acceptance. To be effective, the notice revoking the offer must reach the offeree before he has accepted.

An **option** is a contract by which the offeror is bound to hold open an offer for a specified time. It must comply with all of the requirements of a contract, including consideration. Option contracts apply to all types of contracts, including sales of goods.

The Code has made certain offers—called **firm offers**—irrevocable without the offeree giving any consideration for the promise to keep the offer open. The Code provides that a merchant is bound to keep an offer open for a maximum of three months if the merchant gives assurance in a signed writing that it will be held open. (Article 2A.) The Code, therefore, makes a merchant's written promise not to revoke an offer for a stated period of time enforceable even though no consideration is given the merchant-offeror for that promise.

CISG

An offer may not be revoked if it indicates that it is irrevocable; it need not be in writing.

Variant Acceptances

The common law ***mirror image*** rule, by which the acceptance cannot vary or deviate from the terms of the offer, has been modified by the Code. This modification has been necessitated by the realities of modern business practices, notably by the fact that a vast number of businesses use standardized business forms. For example, a buyer sends to the seller on the buyer's order form a purchase order for 1,000 dozen cotton shirts at $60 per dozen with delivery by October 1 at the buyer's place of business. On the reverse side of this standard form are twenty-five numbered paragraphs containing provisions generally favorable to the buyer. When the seller receives the buyer's order and agrees to the buyer's quantity, price, and delivery terms, he sends to the buyer an unequivocal acceptance of the offer on his acceptance form. On the back of his acceptance form, however, the seller has thirty-two numbered paragraphs generally favorable to himself and in significant conflict with the provisions in the buyer's form. Under the common law's "mirror image" rule, no contract would exist, for the seller has not accepted unequivocally all of the material terms of the buyer's offer.

The Code attempts to reconcile this ***"battle of the forms"*** by focusing on the intent of the parties. If the offeree expressly makes his acceptance conditional upon assent to the additional or different terms, no contract is formed. If, however, the offeree does not expressly require such a condition, a contract is formed. The issue then becomes whether the offeree's different or ***additional*** terms become part of the contract. If both offeror and offeree are merchants, additional terms (terms the offeree proposed for the contract for the first time) will become part of the contract if they do not materially alter the agreement and are not objected to either in the offer itself or within a reasonable time. If either of the parties is not a merchant, or if the terms materially alter the offer, the additional terms are merely construed as proposals for addition to the contract. ***Different*** terms (terms that contradict or conflict with terms of the offer) proposed by the offeree also will generally not become part of the contract unless specifically accepted by the offeror.

The courts are divided over what terms are included when the terms conflict. The majority of courts hold that the terms cancel each other out and look to the Code to provide the missing terms; other courts hold that the offeror's terms govern. Some states follow a third alternative and apply the additional terms test to different terms. See Figure 19-1 on page 359 for a summary of the battle of the forms.

Applying Section 2–207 to the previous example: because both parties are merchants and the seller did not condition acceptance upon the buyer's assent to the additional or different terms, (1) the contract will be formed without the *seller's different terms* unless the buyer specifically accepts them; (2) the contract will be formed without the *seller's additional terms* unless (a) the buyer specifically accepts or (b) the additional terms do not materially alter the offer and the buyer does not object to them; and (3) depending on the jurisdiction, (a) the conflicting terms cancel each other out and the Code provides the missing terms, (b) the *buyer's conflicting terms* are included in the contract, or (c) the additional terms test is applied.

CISG

A reply to an offer that contains additions, limitations, or other modifications is a counteroffer that rejects the original offer. Nevertheless, a purported acceptance that contains additional or different terms acts as an acceptance if the terms do not materially alter the contract unless the offeror objects to the change. Changes in price, payment, quality, quantity, place and time of delivery, terms of delivery, liability of the parties, and settlement of a dispute are always considered to be material alterations.

Finally, subsection 3 of 2–207 deals with those situations in which the writings do not form a contract but the conduct of the parties recognizes the existence of one. For instance, Ernest makes an offer to Gwen, who replies with a conditional acceptance. Although no contract has been formed, Gwen ships the ordered goods and Ernest accepts the goods. Subsection 3 provides that in this instance the contract consists of the written terms to which both parties agreed together with supplementary provisions of the Code.

Practical Advice

In negotiating a contract, try to be the offeror and consider providing in your offer that your terms control and that any new or different terms will be made part of the contract only if you specifically agree to them in a signed writing.

McJunkin Corporation v. Mechanicals, Inc.

United States Court of Appeals, Sixth Circuit, 1989
888 F.2d 481

FACTS Emery Industries (Emery) contracted with Mechanicals, Inc. (Mechanicals) to install a pipe system to carry chemicals and fatty acids under high pressure and temperature. The system required stainless steel "stub ends" (used to connect pipe segments), which Mechanicals ordered from McJunkin Corporation (McJunkin). McJunkin in turn ordered the stub ends from the Alaskan Copper Companies, Inc. (Alaskan). McJunkin's purchase order required the seller to certify the goods and to relieve the buyer of liabilities that might arise from defective goods. After shipment of the goods to McJunkin, Alaskan sent written acknowledgment of the order, containing terms and conditions of sale different from those in McJunkin's purchase order. The acknowledgment provided a disclaimer of warranty and a requirement for inspection of the goods within ten days of receipt. The acknowledgment also contained a requirement that the buyer accept all of the seller's terms.

The stub ends were delivered to Mechanicals in several shipments over a five-month period. Each shipment included a document reciting terms the same as those on Alaskan's initial acknowledgment. Apparently, McJunkin never objected to any of the terms contained in any of Alaskan's documents.

After the stub ends were installed, they were found to be defective. Mechanicals had to remove and replace them, causing Emery to close its plant for several days. McJunkin filed a complaint alleging that Mechanicals had failed to pay $26,141.88 owed on account for the stub ends McJunkin supplied. Mechanicals filed an answer and counterclaim against McJunkin, alleging $93,586.13 in damages resulting from the replacement and repair of the defective stub ends. McJunkin filed a third-party complaint against Alaskan, alleging that Alaskan was liable for any damages Mechanicals incurred as a result of the defective stub ends. The district court entered a $68,000 judgment for Mechanicals against McJunkin ($87,000 in damages minus $19,000 owed McJunkin on its account). The court granted Alaskan a judgment against McJunkin based on Alaskan's liability limitation provision. McJunkin appealed the judgment in favor of Alaskan.

DECISION Judgment for Alaskan vacated and remanded.

OPINION Engel, J. To determine the contractual obligations of McJunkin and Alaskan, we consider both the parties' actions and the forms exchanged, viewing the totality of circumstances surrounding the transaction. [Citation.] We must determine: (1) whether McJunkin and Alaskan assumed any contractual obligations; (2) how such obligations arose; and (3) the nature of those obligations.

There are several possible interpretations of Alaskan's and McJunkin's contractual relationship. First, by shipping the stub ends, Alaskan accepted McJunkin's offer (made in McJunkin's purchase order) and therefore was bound by the terms of McJunkin's offer, with any remedy limitation contained in Alaskan's acknowledgment being excluded from the contract. Second, McJunkin's acquiescence to the shipments and failure to object to the terms in the acknowledgment constituted an acceptance of Alaskan's terms contained in the acknowledgment, thereby giving effect to Alaskan's remedy limitation under Ohio Rev.Code § [2–207(2)(C)]. Third, Alaskan's acknowledgment was a seasonable, yet conditional, response to McJunkin's purchase order, thereby vitiating formation of a contract based upon the forms alone, although the conduct of the parties may have established a contract under Ohio Rev.Code § 2–207(3). We now address these contentions.

* * *

First, Alaskan's shipment of stub ends prior to acknowledgment might be considered an acceptance upon McJunkin's terms alone. * * * Nevertheless, although Alaskan's acknowledgment was sent five days after the initial shipment, we hold that the more reasonable interpretation of the parties' actions is that Alaskan, through its shipment and transmission of an acknowledgment within a few short days, did not intend to bind itself to McJunkin's terms, but instead sought to incorporate its own terms into a contract with McJunkin. * * *

[Secondly,] [i]t is urged that McJunkin's failure to object to the remedy limitation [in Alaskan's acknowledgment forms] indicates that McJunkin accepted that limitation. § [2–207(2)(C)] (additional or different terms become part of contract between merchants unless objection made within reasonable time). Although Alaskan's contract terms might indicate that McJunkin's failure to object within a reasonable time constituted McJunkin's acceptance of Alaskan's terms, we find that McJunkin did not accept Alaskan's terms. McJunkin never explicitly accepted the terms of Alaskan's acknowledgment. Given McJunkin's silence in the face of Alaskan's acknowledgment, McJunkin was not bound by those terms. [Citations.]

Instead, under Ohio Rev.Code § 2–207(1), a seasonable expression of acceptance, such as that made by Alaskan, does not create a contract based upon the terms contained in the forms if "acceptance is expressly made conditional on assent to the additional or different terms." It is clear that Alaskan's acknowledgment expressly conditioned Alaskan's acceptance upon McJunkin's assent to Alaskan's terms of sale: * * *

However, although we find that no contract was created by virtue of the exchanged document, "A contract for sale of goods may be made in any manner sufficient to show agreement, *including conduct* by both parties which recognizes the existence of such contract." Ohio Rev.Code § [2–207(1)]. Moreover, under Ohio Rev.Code § 2–207(3), "Conduct by both parties which recognizes the existence of a contract is sufficient to establish a contract for sale although the writings of the parties do not otherwise establish a contract. In such case the terms of the particular contract consist of those terms on which the writings of the parties agree, together with any supplementary terms incorporated under any other provisions of [Article 2]."

Abundantly clear from McJunkin's and Alaskan's actions is that they had entered a contract within the meaning of Ohio Rev.Code §§ [2–207(1) & 2–207(3)]. Alaskan sent numerous shipments of stub ends, and McJunkin paid for them before they were shipped directly to Mechanicals. Indeed, both Alaskan and McJunkin do not dispute that they had contracted; instead, they disagree about who should be obligated to bear the loss for the defective stub ends. We can thus say with confidence that McJunkin's and Alaskan's course of conduct established a contract enforceable under Ohio law.

Under Ohio Rev.Code § [2–207(3)], the terms of McJunkin's and Alaskan's contract "consist of those terms on which the writings of the parties agree, together with any supplementary terms incorporated under any other provisions of [Article2]." Because the remedy limitation was contained only in Alaskan's form and not agreed upon by both parties' documents, Alaskan's remedy limitation did not bind McJunkin, and, contrary to the district court judgment, Alaskan could not take advantage of this provision.

[We conclude] that the remedy limitation was unenforceable.

INTERPRETATION Subsection 3 of Section 2–207 deals with those situations in which the writings do not form a contract but the conduct of the parties recognizes the existence of one: the contract consists of the written terms to which both parties agreed, together with supplementary provisions of the UCC.

CRITICAL THINKING QUESTION Do you agree with the Code's approach to dealing with the battle of the forms? Explain.

MANNER OF ACCEPTANCE

As is true of contracts under common law, the offeror may specify the manner in which the offer must be accepted. If the offeror does not so specify and the circumstances do not otherwise clearly indicate, an offer to make a sales contract invites acceptance, effective upon dispatch, in any manner and in any medium reasonable in the circumstances. (Article 2A.) The Code therefore allows flexibility of response and the ability to keep pace with new modes of communication.

An offer to buy goods for prompt or current shipment may be accepted either by a prompt promise to ship or by prompt shipment. Acceptance by performance requires notice within a reasonable time, or the offer may be treated as lapsed. (Article 2A.)

AUCTIONS

The Code provides that if an auction sale is advertised or announced in explicit terms to be ***without reserve***, the auctioneer may not withdraw the article put up for sale unless no bid is made within a reasonable time. Unless the sale is advertised as being without reserve, the sale is ***with reserve***, and the auctioneer may withdraw the goods at any time until he announces completion of the sale. Whether with or without reserve, a bidder may retract his bid at any time prior to acceptance by the auctioneer. Such retraction, however, does not revive any previous bid.

If the auctioneer knowingly receives a bid by or on behalf of the seller, and notice has not been given that the seller reserves the right to bid at the auction sale, the bidder to whom the goods are sold can either avoid the sale or take the goods at the price of the last good faith bid.

CISG
The CISG does not apply to sales by auctions.

CPA CONSIDERATION

In several respects, the Code has relaxed the common law requirements regarding consideration. For example, the Code provides that a contract for the sale of goods can be modified without new consideration, provided the modification is made in good faith. (Article 2A.) In addition, any claim of right arising out of an alleged breach of contract can be discharged in whole or in part without consideration by a written waiver or renunciation signed and delivered by the aggrieved party. As previously noted, a firm offer is not revocable for lack of consideration.

CISG
Consideration is not needed to modify a contract.

CPA FORM OF THE CONTRACT

STATUTE OF FRAUDS

The original statute of frauds, which applied to contracts for the sale of goods, has been used as a prototype for the Article 2 statute of frauds provision. The Code provides that a contract for the sale of goods costing ***$500 or more*** is not enforceable unless there is some writing sufficient to evidence the existence of a contract between the parties ($1,000 or more for leases—Article 2A).

Figure 19-1
Battle of the Forms

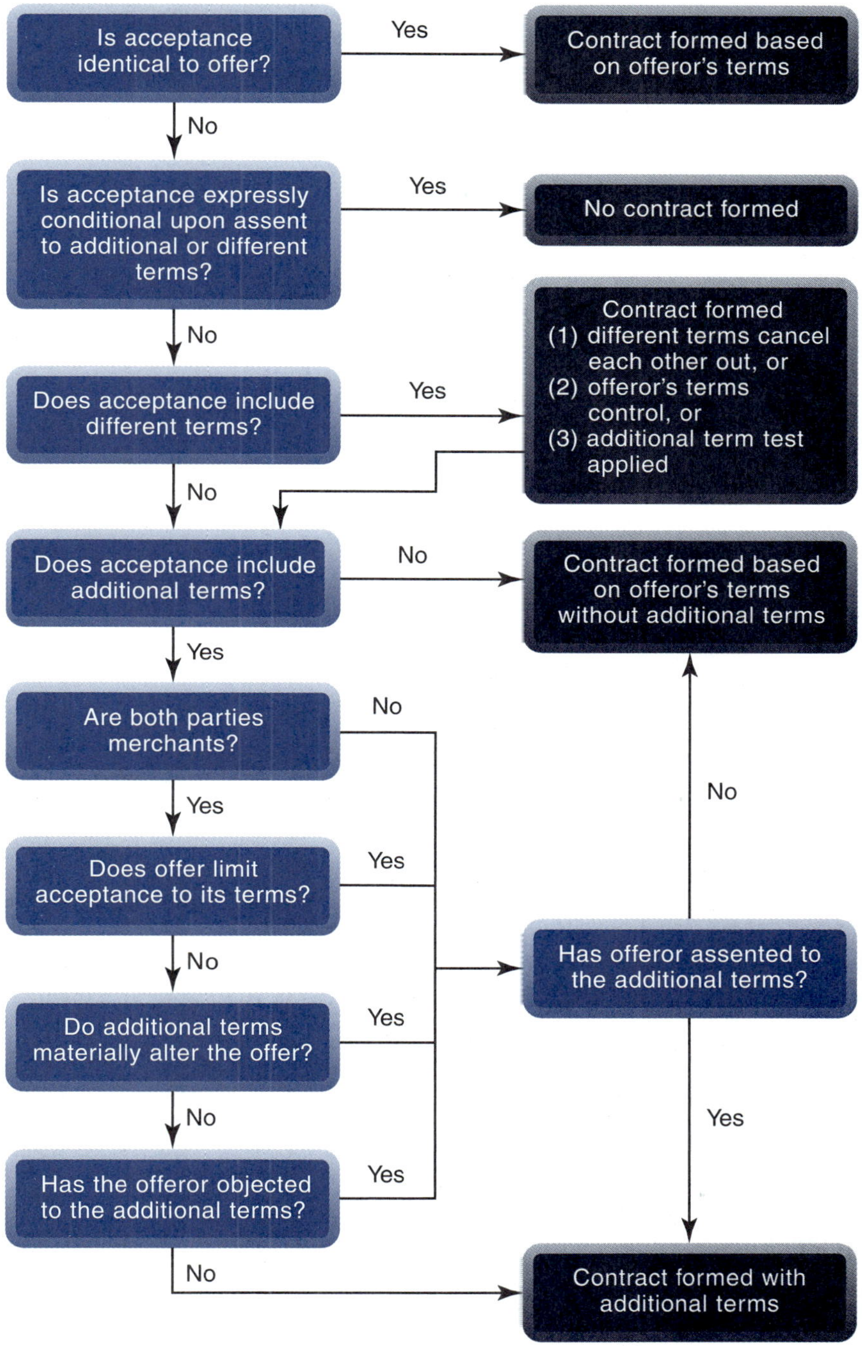

> **CISG**
> A contract must be evidenced by a writing, unless one of the parties has its place of business in a country that provides otherwise.

Modification of Contracts An agreement modifying a contract must be in writing if the resulting contract is within the statute of frauds (Article 2A omits this provision). Conversely, if a contract that was previously within the statute of frauds is modified so as to no longer fall within it, the modification is enforceable even if it is oral. Thus, if the parties enter into an oral contract to sell for

CONCEPT REVIEW

Contract Law Compared with Law of Sales

Section of UCC	Contract Law	Law of Sales
Definiteness	Contract must include all material terms.	Open terms permitted if parties intend to make a contract. (Article 2, 2A)
Counteroffers	Acceptance must be a mirror image of offer. Counteroffer and conditional acceptance are rejections.	Battle of the Forms. See Figure 19-1. (Article 2)
Modification of Contract	Consideration is required.	Consideration is not required. (Article 2, 2A)
Irrevocable Offers	Options.	Options. Firm offers up to three months' binding without consideration. (Article 2, 2A)
Statute of Frauds	Writing must include all material terms.	Writing must include quantity term. Specially manufactured goods. Confirmation by merchants. Delivery or payment and acceptance. Admissions. (Article 2, Article 2A *except* merchant confirmation.)

$450 a dining room table, to be delivered to the buyer, and later, prior to delivery, *orally* agree that the seller shall stain the table and that the buyer shall pay a price of $550, the modified contract is unenforceable. In contrast, if the parties have a written contract for the sale of 150 bushels of wheat at a price of $4.50 per bushel and, later, orally agree to decrease the quantity to 100 bushels at the same price per bushel, the agreement, as modified, is enforceable.

A signed agreement that requires modifications or rescissions of it to be in a signed writing cannot be otherwise modified or rescinded. (Article 2A.) If this requirement is on a form provided by a merchant, the other party must separately sign it unless the other party is a merchant.

Written Compliance The statute of frauds compliance provisions under the Code are more liberal than the rules under general contract law. The Code requires merely some writing (1) sufficient to indicate that a contract has been made between the parties, (2) signed by the party against whom enforcement is sought or by her authorized agent or broker, and (3) including a term specifying the quantity of goods to be exchanged. Whereas general contract law requires that the writing include all essential terms, under the Code a writing may be sufficient even if it omits or incorrectly states an agreed-upon term. This is consistent with other provisions of the Code that permit contracts to be enforced even though material terms are omitted. Nevertheless, the contract is enforceable only to the extent of the quantity of goods stated. Given proof that a contract was intended and that a signed writing describes the goods, the quantity of goods, and the names of the parties, the court, under the Code, can supply omitted terms such as price and particulars of performance. Moreover, several related documents together may satisfy the writing requirement.

Between merchants, a written confirmation, if sufficient against the sender, is also sufficient against the recipient unless the recipient gives written notice of her objection within ten days after receiving the confirmation. (Article 2A does not have a comparable rule.)

> **Practical Advice**
>
> Be aware that if you receive a signed written confirmation of a contract, you have ten business days to object if the confirmation is inaccurate.

Exceptions A contract that does not satisfy the writing requirement but is otherwise valid is enforceable in the following instances:

The Code permits an oral contract for the sale of goods to be enforced against a party who in his pleading, testimony, or otherwise in court ***admits*** that a contract was made; but the Code limits enforcement to the quantity of

THE LAW AND YOU

State Bar Associations

Alabama: http://www.alabar.org/ ("Consumer Finance or Buying on Time")

Illinois: http://www.illinoislawyerfinder.com/publicinfo/home.html ("Buying a Car")

Louisiana: http://www.lsba.org/Public_Resources/consumer_brochures.html ("Is Your Car a Lemon?")

New Hampshire: http://www.nhbar.org/?area/15.html

North Carolina: http://www.ncbar.org/legal_prof/divisions/yld/publications/consumer_pub.asp ("Buying on Time")

State Attorney Generals

Alabama: http://www.ago.state.al.us/ (consumer affairs and other information)

Arizona: http://www.attorney_general.state.az.us/consumer/help.html ("New Car Buying Tips"; "Used Car Buying Tips")

Arkansas: http://www.ag.state.ar.us/ ("Home Solicitation Sales Tip Sheet")

California: http://www.dca.ca.gov/r_r/conspub1.htm ("Sales")

Colorado: http://www.ago.state.co.us/consprot.stm ("Automobile Information")

Connecticut: http://www.cslib.org/attygenl/mainlinks/tabindex7.htm ("Auto Issues")

Florida: http://doacs.state.fl.us./consumer/ ("How to Buy a New Car"; "How to Buy a Used Car")

Idaho: http://www2.state.id.us/ag/consumer/tipsandinfo.htm ("Automobiles")

Illinois: http://www.ag.state.il.us/consumer/consumer.htm ("Auto Buying and Repair")

Iowa: http://www.state.ia.us/government/ag/consumer.html ("Car Buying Made Easier")

Kansas: http://www.ksag.org/contents/consumer/main.htm ("Planning Your Next Used Vehicle Purchase")

Kentucky: http://www.law.state.ky.us/cp/resource.htm ("Mobile Home Buying Tips")

Louisiana: http://www.ag.state.la.us/consumereducation.shtml (consumer protection brochures)

Michigan: http://www.ag.state.mi.us/ ("Rental Purchase Agreement Act"; "Automobiles"; "Truth in Renting"; "Keys to Vehicle Leasing")

Minnesota: http://www.ag.state.mn.us/ ("Car Shop")

New Hampshire: http://www.state.nh.us/nhdoj/Consumer/brochures.html (consumer protection brochures)

New York: http://www.consumer.state.ny.us/publications.htm ("Rent Smarts"; "A Guide to New York State's Lemon Law")

North Dakota: http://www.ag.state.nd.us ("Computer/Internet"; "Marketplace"; "Cars")

Ohio: http://www.ag.state.oh.us/online%5Fpublications/consumer%5Fprotection/index.htm ("Ohio Auto Repairs and Services Law")

Oregon: http://www.doj.state.or.us/FinFraud/welcome3htm ("Used Car Sales"; "New Car Sales")

Rhode Island: http://www.riag.ri.gov/consumer/protect%20yourself.php ("Cars")

South Carolina: http://www.state.sc.us/consumer/ ("Automobiles")

South Dakota: http://www.state.sd.us/attorney/office/divisions/consumer ("Consumer Handbook")

Tennessee: http://www.state.tn.us/consumer/consinfo.html ("Automobile Repair Tips"; "Shopping Safe Online"; "Mail Order Rule")

Texas: http://www.oag.state.tx.us/ ("Buying a Used Car")

Washington: http://www.wa.gov/ago/consumer/ ("Auto Repair") http:// www.wa.gov/ago/consumer/cp_publications.html ("Buying Cars"; "Auto Repair"; "Buying, Leasing Cars")

U.S. Government

http://www.pueblo.gsa.gov/cars.htm ("Buying a New Car")

http://www.pueblo.gsa.gov/cars.htm ("Buying a Used Car")

http://www.pueblo.gsa.gov/specpubs.htm#CA ("Keys to Vehicle Leasing")

http://www.pueblo.gsa.gov/specpubs.htm ("Cybershopping")

http://www.pueblo.gsa.gov/cic_text/money/athome/rights.htm ("At Home Shopping Rights")

http://www.pueblo.gsa.gov/cic_text/misc/buy-computer/buycomp.htm ("Buying a Computer")

goods he admits. (Article 2A.) This provision recognizes that the policy behind the statute of frauds does not apply when the party seeking to avoid the oral contract admits under oath the existence of the contract.

The Code also permits enforcement of an oral contract for goods ***specially manufactured*** for the buyer. (Article 2A.) Nevertheless, if the goods are readily marketable in the ordinary course of the seller's business, even though they were manufactured on special order, the contract is not enforceable unless it is in writing.

Under the Code, delivery and acceptance of part of the goods or payment and acceptance of part of the price validates the contract, but only for the goods that have been ***delivered and accepted*** or for which ***payment*** has been ***accepted***. (Article 2A.) To illustrate, Debra orally agrees to buy 1,000 watches from Brian for $15,000. Brian delivers 300 watches to Debra, who receives and accepts them. The oral contract is enforceable to the extent of 300 watches ($4,500)—those received and accepted—but is unenforceable to the extent of 700 watches ($10,500).

PAROL EVIDENCE

Contractual terms that are set forth in a writing intended by the parties as a final expression of their agreement may not be contradicted by evidence of any prior agreement or of a contemporaneous oral agreement, but, under the Code, the terms may be explained or supplemented by (a) course of dealing, usage of trade, or course of performance and (b) evidence of consistent additional terms, unless the writing was intended as the complete and exclusive statement of the terms of the agreement. (Article 2A.)

CISG

The CISG permits a court to consider all relevant circumstances of the agreement, including the negotiations, any course of performance between the parties, and trade usage, and any subsequent conduct.

CHAPTER SUMMARY

Nature of Sales and Leases

Definitions

Goods movable personal property

Sale transfer of title to goods from seller to buyer for a price

Lease a transfer of right to possession and use of goods in return for consideration
- *Consumer Leases* leases by a merchant to an individual who leases for personal, family, or household purposes for no more than $25,000
- *Finance Leases* special type of lease transaction generally involving three parties: the lessor, the supplier, and the lessee

Governing Law
- *Sales Transactions* governed by Article 2 of the Code, except where general contract law has not been specifically modified by the Code, general contract law continues to apply
- *Lease Transactions* governed by Article 2A of the Code, but where general contract law has not been specifically modified by the Code, general contract law continues to apply
- *Transactions Outside the Code* include employment contracts, service contracts, insurance contracts, contracts involving real property, and contracts for the sale of tangibles

Fundamental Principles of Article 2 and Article 2A

Purpose to modernize, clarify, simplify, and make uniform the law of sales and leases

Good Faith the Code requires all sales and lease contracts to be performed in good faith, which means honesty in fact in the conduct or transaction concerned; in the case of a merchant, it also includes the observance of reasonable commercial standards

Unconscionability a court may refuse to enforce an unconscionable contract or any part of a contract found to be unconscionable
- *Procedural Unconscionability* unfairness of the bargaining process
- *Substantive Unconscionability* oppressive or grossly unfair contractual provisions

Expansion of Commercial Practices
- *Course of Dealing* a sequence of previous conduct between the parties establishing a common basis for interpreting their agreement
- *Usage of Trade* a practice or method of dealing regularly observed and followed in a place, vocation, or trade

Sales by and Between Merchants the Code establishes separate rules that apply to transactions between merchants or involving a merchant (a dealer in goods or a person who by his occupation holds himself out as having knowledge or skill peculiar to the goods or practices involved, or who employs an agent or broker whom he holds out as having such knowledge or skill)

Liberal Administration of Remedies
- *Freedom of Contract* most provisions of the Code may be varied by agreement
- *Validation and Preservation of Sales Contracts* the Code reduces formal requisites to the bare minimum and attempts to preserve agreements whenever the parties manifest an intention to enter into a contract

Formation of Sales and Lease Contracts

Manifestation of Mutual Assent

Definiteness of an Offer the Code provides that a contract does not fail for indefiniteness even though one or more terms may have been omitted; the Code provides standards by which missing essential terms may be supplied

Irrevocable Offers
- *Option* a contract to hold open an offer
- *Firm Offer* a signed writing by a merchant to hold open an offer for the purchase or sale of goods (or lease of goods) for a maximum of three months

Variant Acceptances the inclusion of different or additional terms in an acceptance is addressed by focusing on the intent of the parties

Manner of Acceptance an acceptance can be made in any reasonable manner and is effective upon dispatch

Auction auction sales are generally with reserve, permitting the auctioneer to withdraw the goods at any time prior to sale.

Consideration

Contractual Modifications the Code provides that a contract for the sale or lease of goods may be modified without new consideration if the modification is made in good faith

Firm Offers are not revocable for lack of consideration

Form of the Contract

Statute of Frauds sale of goods costing $500 or more (or lease of goods for $1,000 or more) must be evidenced by a signed writing to be enforceable
- *Written Compliance* the Code requires some writing or writings sufficient to indicate that a contract has been made between the parties, signed by the party against whom enforcement is sought or by her authorized agent or broker, and including a term specifying the quantity of goods
- *Alternative Methods of Compliance* written confirmation between merchants, admission, specially manufactured goods, and delivery or payment and acceptance

Parol Evidence contractual terms that are set forth in a writing intended by the parties as a final expression of their agreement may not be contradicted by evidence of any prior agreement or of a contemporaneous oral agreement, but such terms may be explained or supplemented by course of dealing, usage of trade, course of performance, or consistent additional evidence

QUESTIONS

1. Dickison orders 1,000 widgets at $5 per widget from International Widget to be delivered within sixty days. After the contract is consummated and signed, Dickison orally requests that International deliver the widgets within thirty days rather than sixty days. International agrees. Is the contractual modification binding?

2. In Question 1, what effect, if any, would the following telegram have?

   International Widget:

   In accordance with our agreement of this date you will deliver the 1,000 previously ordered widgets within thirty days. Thank you for your cooperation in this matter.

   (signed) Dickison

3. Hicks, a San Francisco company, orders from U.S. Electronics, a New York company, 10,000 electronic units. Hicks's order form provides that any dispute would be resolved by an arbitration panel located in San Francisco. U.S. Electronics executes and delivers to Hicks its acknowledgment form accepting the order and containing the following provision: "All disputes will be resolved by the state courts of New York." A dispute arises concerning the workmanship of the parts, and Hicks wishes the case to be arbitrated in San Francisco. What would be the result?

4. Explain how the result in Question 3 might change if the U.S. Electronics form contained the following provisions:
   a. "The seller's acceptance of the purchase order to which this acknowledgment responds is expressly made conditional on the buyer's assent to any or different terms contained in this acknowledgment."
   b. "The seller's acceptance of the purchase order is subject to the terms and conditions on the face and reverse side hereof, which the buyer accepts by accepting the goods described herein."
   c. "The seller's terms govern this agreement—this acknowledgment merely constitutes a counteroffer."

5. Reinfort executed a written contract with Bylinski to purchase an assorted collection of shoes for $3,000. A week before the agreed shipment date, Bylinski called Reinfort and said, "We cannot deliver at $3,000; unless you agree to pay $4,000, we will cancel the order." After considerable discussion, Reinfort agreed to pay $4,000 if Bylinski would ship as agreed in the contract. After the shoes had been delivered and accepted by Reinfort, Reinfort refused to pay $4,000 and insisted on paying only $3,000. Is the contractual modification binding? Explain.

6. On November 23, Blackburn, a dress manufacturer, mailed to Conroy a written and signed offer to sell 1,000 sundresses at $50 per dress. The offer stated that it would "remain open for ten days" and that it could "not be withdrawn prior to that date."

   Two days later, Blackburn, noting a sudden increase in the price of sundresses, changed his mind. Blackburn therefore sent Conroy a letter revoking the offer. The letter was sent on November 25 and received by Conroy on November 28.

   Conroy chose to disregard the letter of November 25; instead, she happily continued to watch the price of sundresses rise. On December 1, Conroy sent a letter accepting the original offer. The letter, however, was not received by Blackburn until December 9, due to a delay in the mails.

   Conroy has demanded delivery of the goods according to the terms of the offer of November 23, but Blackburn has refused. Does a contract exist between Conroy and Blackburn? Explain.

7. Henry and Wilma, an elderly immigrant couple, agreed to purchase from Harris a refrigerator with a fair market value of $450 for twenty-five monthly installments of $60 per month. Henry and Wilma now wish to void the contract, asserting that they did not realize the exorbitant price they were paying. Result?

8. Courts Distributors needed 200 compact refrigerators on a rush basis. It contacted Eastinghouse Corporation, a manufacturer of refrigerators. Eastinghouse said it would take some time to quote a price on an order of that size. Courts replied, "Send the refrigerators immediately and bill us later." The refrigerators were delivered three days later, and the invoice arrived ten days after that. The invoice price was $140,000. Courts believes that the wholesale market price of the refrigerators is only $120,000. Do the parties have a contract? If so, what is the price? Explain.

CASE PROBLEMS

9. While adjusting a television antenna beside his mobile home and underneath a high-voltage electric transmission wire, Prince received an electric shock resulting in personal injury. He claims the high-voltage electric current jumped from the transmission wire to the antenna. The wire, which carried some 7,200 volts of electricity, did not serve his mobile home but ran directly above it. Prince sued the Navarro County Electric Co-Op, the owner and operator of the wire, for breach of implied warranty of merchantability under the Uniform Commercial Code. He contends that the Code's implied warranty of merchantability extends to the container of a product—in this instance, the wiring—and that the escape of the current shows that the wiring was unfit for its purpose of transporting electricity. The electric company argues that the electricity passing through the transmission wire was not being sold to Prince and that, therefore, there was no sale of goods to Prince. Is the contract covered by the UCC?

10. HMT, already in the business of marketing agricultural products, decided to try its hand at marketing potatoes for processing. Nine months before the potato harvest, HMT contracted to supply Bell Brand with 100,000 sacks of potatoes. At harvest time, Bell Brand would accept only 60,000 sacks. HMT sues for breach of contract. Bell Brand argues that custom and usage in marketing processing potatoes allows buyers to give estimates in contracts, not fixed quantities, as the contracts are established so far in advance. HMT responds that the quantity term in the contract was definite and unambiguous. Can custom and trade usage be used to interpret an unambiguous contract? Discuss.

11. Schreiner, a cotton farmer, agreed over the telephone to sell 150 bales of cotton to Loeb & Co. Schreiner had sold cotton to Loeb & Co. for the past five years. Written confirmation of the date, parties, price, and conditions was mailed to Schreiner, who did not respond to the confirmation in any way. Four months later, when the price of cotton had doubled, Loeb & Co. sought to enforce the contract. Is the contract enforceable?

12. American Sand & Gravel Inc. agreed to sell sand to Clark at a special discount if 20,000–25,000 tons were ordered. The discount price was 45¢ per ton, compared with the normal price of 55¢ per ton. Two years later, Clark orders, and receives, 1,600 tons of sand from American Sand & Gravel. Clark refuses to pay more than 45¢ per ton. American Sand & Gravel sues for the remaining 10¢ per ton. Decision?

13. In September 1973, Auburn Plastics submitted price quotations to CBS for the manufacture of eight cavity molds to be used in making parts for CBS's toys. Each quotation specified that the offer would not be binding unless accepted within fifteen days. Furthermore, CBS would be subject to an additional 30 percent charge for engineering services upon delivery of the molds. In December 1973 and January 1974, CBS sent detailed purchase orders to Auburn Plastics for cavity molds. The purchase order forms stated that CBS reserved the right to remove the molds from Auburn Plastics without an additional or "withdrawal" charge. Auburn Plastics acknowledged the purchase order and stated that the sale would be subject to all conditions contained in the price quotation. CBS paid Auburn for the molds, and Auburn began to fabricate toy parts from the molds for CBS. Later, Auburn announced a price increase, and CBS demanded delivery of the molds. Auburn refused to deliver the molds unless CBS paid the additional charge for engineering services. CBS claimed that the contract did not provide for a withdrawal charge. Who will prevail? Why?

14. Terminal Grain Corporation brought an action against Glen Freeman, a farmer, to recover damages for breach of an oral contract to deliver grain. According to the company, Freeman orally agreed to two sales of wheat to Terminal Grain of 4,000 bushels each at $1.65 a bushel and $1.71 a bushel, respectively. Dwayne Maher, merchandising manager of Terminal Grain, sent two written confirmations of the agreements to Freeman. Freeman never made any written objections to the confirmations. After the first transaction had occurred, the price of wheat rose to between $2.25 and $2.30 per bushel, and Freeman refused to deliver the remaining 4,000 bushels at the agreed-upon price. Freeman denies entering into any agreement to sell the second 4,000 bushels of wheat to Terminal Grain but admits that he received the two written confirmations sent by Maher. Decision?

15. The defendant, Gray Communications (http://www.graycommunications.com), desired to build a television tower. After a number of negotiation sessions conducted by telephone between the defendant and the plaintiff, Kline Iron, the parties allegedly reached an oral agreement under which the plaintiff would build a tower for the defendant for a total price of $1,485,368. A few days later, the plaintiff sent a written document, referred to as a proposal, for execution by the defendant. The proposal indicated that it had been prepared for immediate acceptance by the defendant and that prior to formal acceptance by the defendant it could be modified or withdrawn without notice. A few days later, without having executed the proposal, the defendant advised the plaintiff that a competitor had provided a lower bid for construction of the tower. The defendant requested that the plaintiff explain its higher bid price, which the plaintiff failed to do. The defendant then advised the plaintiff by letter that it would not be retained to construct the tower. The plaintiff then commenced suit, alleging breach of an oral contract, and asserting that the oral agreement was enforceable because the common law of contracts, not the UCC, governed the transaction and that under the common law a writing is not necessary to cover this type of transaction. Even if the transaction was subject to the UCC, the plaintiff alternatively argued, the contract was within the UCC "merchant's exception." Is the limitation of rights enforceable?

16. Dorton, as a representative for The Carpet Mart (http://www.carpet-mart.com/), purchased carpets from Collins & Aikman (http://www.collinsaikman.com/) that were supposedly manufactured of 100 percent Kodel polyester fiber but were, in fact, made of cheaper and inferior fibers. Dorton then brought suit for compensatory and punitive damages against Collins & Aikman for its fraud, deceit, and misrepresentation in the sale of the carpets. Collins & Aikman moved for a stay pending arbitration, claiming that Dorton was bound to an arbitration agreement printed on the reverse side of Collins & Aikman's printed sales acknowledgment form. A provision printed on the face of the acknowledgment form stated that its acceptance was "subject to all of the terms and conditions on the face and reverse side thereof, including arbitration, all of which are accepted by buyer." Holding that there existed no binding arbitration agreement between the parties, the district court denied the stay. Collins & Aikman appealed. Is the arbitration clause enforceable?

17. Thomson Printing Company is a buyer and seller of used machinery. On April 10, the president of the company, James Thomson, went to the surplus machinery department of B. F. Goodrich Company (http://www.bfgoodrichtires.com/bfgapp/index.pp) in Akron, Ohio, to examine some used equipment that was for sale. Thomson discussed the sale, including a price of $9,000, with Ingram Meyers, a Goodrich employee and agent. Four days later, on April 14, Thomson sent a purchase order to confirm the oral contract for purchase of the machinery and a partial payment of $1,000 to Goodrich in Akron. The purchase order contained Thomson Printing's name, address, and telephone number, as well as certain information about the purchase, but did not specifically mention Meyers or the surplus equipment department. Goodrich sent copies of the documents to a number of its divisions, but Meyers never learned of the confirmation until weeks later, by which time the equipment had been sold to another party. Is the oral contract enforceable? Explain.

http:// **Internet Exercise** Compare the provisions governing the formation of sales contracts under the United Nations Convention on Contracts for the International Sale of Goods (Vienna, 1980) with the provisions of Article 2 of the Uniform Commercial Code.

CHAPTER 20

Performance

The buyer needs a hundred eyes, the seller not one.

GEORGE HERVERT (1593–1633)

Learning Objectives

After reading this chapter you should be able to:

1. Explain the requirements of tender of delivery with respect to time, manner, and place of delivery.
2. Explain the perfect tender rule and the three limitations on it.
3. Explain when the buyer has the right to reject the goods and what obligations the buyer has upon rejection.
4. Explain what constitutes acceptance by the buyer and the buyer's right to revoke acceptance.
5. Identify and describe the excuses for nonperformance and the Uniform Commercial Code's provisions for protecting the parties' expectations of performance by the other party.

Performance is the process of discharging contractual obligations by carrying out those obligations according to a contract's terms. The basic obligation of the seller in a contract for the sale of goods is to transfer and deliver goods that conform to the terms of the contract. The basic obligation of the buyer is to accept and pay for conforming goods in accordance with the contract. In a lease, the basic obligation of the lessor is to transfer possession of the goods for the lease term and that of the lessee is to pay the agreed rent. A contract of sale also requires that each party not impair the other party's expectation of having the contract performed.

The obligations of the parties are determined by their contractual agreement. Thus, the contract of sale may expressly state, for example, whether the seller must deliver the goods before receiving payment of the price or whether the buyer must pay the price before receiving the goods. If the contract does not sufficiently cover the particulars of performance, these terms will be supplied by the Code, common law, course of dealings, usage of trade, and course of performance. (Article 2A provides only a few gap fillers.) In all events, both parties to the sales contract must perform their contractual obligations in good faith.

In this chapter, we will examine the performance obligations of the seller and the buyer as well as the contractual obligations that apply to both of them.

CPA PERFORMANCE BY THE SELLER

Unless the parties have agreed otherwise, tender (offer) of performance by one party is a condition to performance by the other party. Tender of conforming goods by the seller entitles him to acceptance of them by the buyer and to payment of the contractually agreed-upon price. Nonetheless, the terms of the contract may establish other rights for the parties. For example, if the seller has agreed to sell goods on sixty or ninety days' credit, he is required to perform his part of the contract by delivering the goods before the buyer performs.

Tender of delivery requires that the seller put and hold goods that conform to the contract at the buyer's disposition and that the seller give the buyer reasonable notification to enable her to take delivery. Tender must also be made at a reasonable time and be kept open for a reasonable period. For example, Jim agrees to sell Joan a stereo system composed of a CD player, a receiver, a tape deck, and two speakers. Each component is specified by manufacturer and model number, and delivery is to be at Jim's store. Jim obtains the ordered equipment in accordance with the contractual specifications and notifies Joan that she may pick up the system at her convenience. Jim has now tendered and thus has performed his obligations under the sales contract: he holds goods that conform to the contract, he has placed them at the buyer's disposition, and he has notified the buyer of their readiness.

CISG

As specified by the contract and the United Nations Convention on Contracts for the International Sale of Goods (CISG), the seller must deliver the goods, hand over any documents relating to them, and transfer the property in the goods.

TIME OF TENDER

Tender must be at a reasonable time, and the goods tendered must be kept available for the period reasonably necessary to enable the buyer to take possession of them. If the contract terms set no definite time for delivery, the seller is allowed a reasonable time after entering into the contract within which to tender the goods to the buyer. Likewise, the buyer has a reasonable time within which to accept delivery. What length of time is reasonable depends on the facts and circumstances of each case.

A contract may not be performed piecemeal or in installments unless the parties specifically so agree. Otherwise, all of the goods called for by a contract must be tendered in a single delivery, with payment due at the time of such tender.

CISG

If a date is fixed by or determinable from the contract, the seller must deliver the goods on that date; if no date is fixed, the seller must deliver the goods within a reasonable time after the conclusion of the contract.

PLACE OF TENDER

If the contract does not specify the place for delivery of the goods, the place for delivery is the seller's place of business or, if he has no place of business, his residence. If the contract is for the sale of identified goods that the parties know at the time of making the contract are not located either at the seller's place of business or residence, the location of the goods is then the place for delivery.

The parties frequently agree expressly on the place of tender, typically by using one of the various delivery terms. These terms specify whether the contract is a shipment or destination contract and determine where the seller must tender delivery of the goods.

CISG

Unless the seller is required to deliver the goods at any other particular place, his obligation to deliver consists of placing the goods at the buyer's disposal at the place where the seller had his place of business at the time of the conclusion of the contract. If the contract relates to specific goods and at the time of the conclusion of the contract the parties knew that the goods were at a particular place, the seller's obligation is to place the goods at the buyer's disposal at that place.

Shipment Contracts The delivery terms *F.O.B. place of shipment*, *F.A.S. seller's port*, *C.I.F.*, and *C. & F.* are all shipment contracts. Under a **shipment contract**, the seller is required or authorized to send the goods to the buyer, but the contract does not obligate her to deliver them at a particular destination. In these cases, the seller's tender of performance occurs at the point of shipment, provided the seller meets certain specified conditions designed to protect the interests of the absent buyer.

The initials **F.O.B.** and **F.A.S.** mean "free on board" and "free alongside," respectively. Under the Code, these are delivery terms, even though they are used only in connection with a stated price. A contract providing that the sale is **F.O.B. place of shipment** or **F.A.S. port of shipment** is a shipment contract. Under a **C.I.F.** ("cost, insurance, and freight") contract, in consideration for an agreed unit price for the goods, the seller pays all costs of transportation, insurance, and freight to the destination. Under a **C. & F.** contract, he will pay "cost and freight."

A seller under a shipment contract is required to (1) deliver the goods to a carrier; (2) make a contract for their transportation that is reasonable according to the nature of the goods and other circumstances; (3) obtain and promptly deliver or tender to the buyer any document necessary to enable the buyer to obtain possession of the goods from the carrier; and (4) promptly notify the buyer of the shipment.

CISG

If the seller is not bound to deliver the goods at any other particular place and if the contract of sale involves carriage of the goods, his obligation to deliver consists in handing the goods over to the first carrier for delivery to the buyer.

Destination Contracts The delivery terms *F.O.B. city of buyer*, *ex-ship*, and *no arrival, no sale* are destination contracts. Because a **destination contract** requires the seller to tender delivery of conforming goods at a specified destination, the seller must place the goods at the buyer's disposition and give the buyer reasonable notice to enable him to take delivery. In addition, if the destination contract involves documents of title, the seller must tender the necessary documents.

When the contract provides that the sale is **F.O.B. place of destination,** the seller must at his own expense and risk transport the goods to that place and there tender delivery of them to the buyer. For example, if the buyer is in Boston and the seller is in Chicago, a contract providing F.O.B. Boston is a destination contract under which the seller must tender the goods at the designated place in Boston at his own expense and risk. A contract that provides for delivery **ex-ship,** or "from the ship," is also a destination contract, requiring the seller to unload the goods from the carrier at a named destination. Finally, if the contract contains the terms **no arrival, no sale,** the title and risk of loss do not pass to the buyer until the seller makes a tender of the goods after they arrive at their destination.

Practical Advice

In your sales contracts clearly specify by use of the correct shipment term or specific language which party pays the shipping costs and where the seller must tender delivery of the goods.

Goods Held by Bailee When goods are in the possession of a bailee and are to be delivered without being moved, in most instances the seller may either tender to the buyer a document of title or obtain an acknowledgment by the bailee of the buyer's right to possess the goods. This acknowledgment permits the buyer to obtain the goods directly from the bailee.

For a summary of performance by the seller, see Figure 20-1 on page 371.

PERFECT TENDER RULE

The Code's **perfect tender rule** imposes on the seller the obligation to conform her tender of goods exactly to the terms of the contract. If either the tender of delivery or the goods fail in any respect to conform to the contract, the buyer may (1) reject the whole lot, (2) accept the whole lot, or (3) accept any commercial unit or units and reject the rest. (Article 2A.) A ***commercial unit*** means such a unit of goods that by commercial usage is a single unit and that, if divided, would be materially impaired in character or value. (Article 2A.)

Thus, a buyer may rightfully reject the delivery of 110 dozen shirts under an agreement calling for delivery of 100 dozen shirts. The size or extent of the breach does not affect the right to reject. The following case further illustrates the perfect tender rule.

CISG

The CISG does not follow the perfect tender rule. The buyer may declare the contract avoided only if the failure by the seller to perform any of his obligations under the contract or the CISG amounts to a **fundamental** breach of contract. A breach of contract committed by one of the parties is fundamental if it results in such detriment to the other party as substantially to deprive him of what he is entitled to expect under the contract, unless the party in breach did not foresee and a reasonable person would not have foreseen such a result.

Moulton Cavity & Mold Inc. v. Lyn-Flex Ind.

Supreme Court of Maine, 1979
396 A.2d 1024

FACTS Moulton Cavity & Mold Inc. agreed to manufacture twenty-six innersole molds to be purchased by Lyn-Flex. Moulton delivered the twenty-six molds to Lyn-Flex after Lyn-Flex allegedly approved the sample molds. However, Lyn-Flex rejected the molds, claiming that they did not satisfy the specifications exactly, and denied that it had ever approved the sample molds. Moulton then sued, contending that Lyn-Flex wrongfully rejected the molds. Lyn-Flex, arguing that the Code's perfect tender rule permitted its rejection of the imperfect molds, regardless of Moulton's substantial performance, appealed from a judgment entered by the trial court in favor of Moulton.

DECISION Judgment for Moulton reversed and a new trial ordered.

OPINION Delahanty, J. In *Smith, Fitzmaurice Co. v. Harris* [citation], a case decided under the common law, we recognized the then-settled rule that with respect to contracts for the sale of goods the buyer has the right to reject the seller's tender if in any way it fails to conform to the specifications of the contract. We held that "[t]he vendor has the duty to comply with his order in kind, quality and amount." [Citation.] Thus, in *Smith*, we ruled that a buyer who had contracted to purchase twelve dozen union suits could lawfully refuse a tender of sixteen dozen union suits. Various provisions of the Uniform Sales Act, enacted in Maine in 1923, codified the common-law approach. [Citation.] The so-called "perfect tender" rule came under considerable fire around the time the Uniform Commercial Code was drafted. No less an authority than Karl Llewellyn, recognized as the primum mobile of the Code's tender provisions, [citations], attacked the rule principally on the ground that it allowed a dishonest buyer to avoid an unfavorable contract on the basis of an insubstantial defect in the seller's tender. [Citation.] Although Llewellyn's views are represented in many Code sections governing tender, the basic tender provision, Section 2–601, represents a rejection of Llewellyn's approach and a continuation of the perfect tender policy developed by the common law and carried forward by the draftsmen of the Uniform Sales Act. [Citations.] Thus, Section 2–601 states that, with certain exceptions not here applicable, the buyer has the right to reject "if the goods or the tender of delivery fail *in any respect* to conform to the contract * * *" (emphasis supplied). Those few courts that have considered the question agree that the perfect tender rule has survived the enactment of the Code. [Citations.] We, too, are convinced of the soundness of this position.

INTERPRETATION If the seller does not perform his contractual obligations exactly, the buyer may rightfully reject the seller's performance.

CRITICAL THINKING QUESTION Do you agree with the Code's perfect tender rule? Explain.

Three basic conditions qualify the buyer's right to reject the goods upon the seller's failure to comply with the perfect tender rule: (1) agreement between the parties limiting the buyer's right to reject nonconforming goods, (2) cure by the seller, and (3) the existence of an installment contract. In addition, the perfect tender rule does not apply to a seller's breach of her obligation under a shipment contract to make a proper contract for transportation or to give proper notice of the shipment. A failure to perform either of these obligations is a ground for rejection only if material loss or delay results.

Agreement Between the Parties The parties may contractually agree to limit the operation of the perfect tender rule. For example, they may agree that the seller shall have the right to repair or replace any defective parts or goods. We will discuss these contractual limitations in Chapter 23.

Practical Advice

If you are the seller, consider using a contractual term to limit the operation of the perfect tender rule; if you are the buyer, carefully scrutinize such a limitation.

Cure by the Seller The Code recognizes two situations in which a seller may cure, or correct, a nonconforming tender of goods. This relaxation of the seller's obligation to make a perfect tender gives the seller an opportunity either to make a second delivery or to make a substitute tender. The first opportunity for cure occurs when the time for performance under the contract has not expired. The second opportunity for cure is available after the time for performance has expired but only if the seller had reasonable grounds to believe that the nonconforming tender would be acceptable to the buyer with or without a monetary adjustment.

Where the buyer refuses to accept a tender of goods that do not conform to the contract, the seller, by acting promptly and within the time allowed for performance, may make a proper tender or delivery of conforming goods and thereby cure the defective tender or performance. (Article 2A.) Upon notice of the buyer's rightful rejection, the seller must first give the buyer reasonable notice of her intention to cure the defect and must then make a proper tender according to the original contract. This rule gives the seller the full contractual period in which to perform but does not cause any harm to the buyer, who receives full performance within the time

Figure 20-1 *Tender of Performance by the Seller*

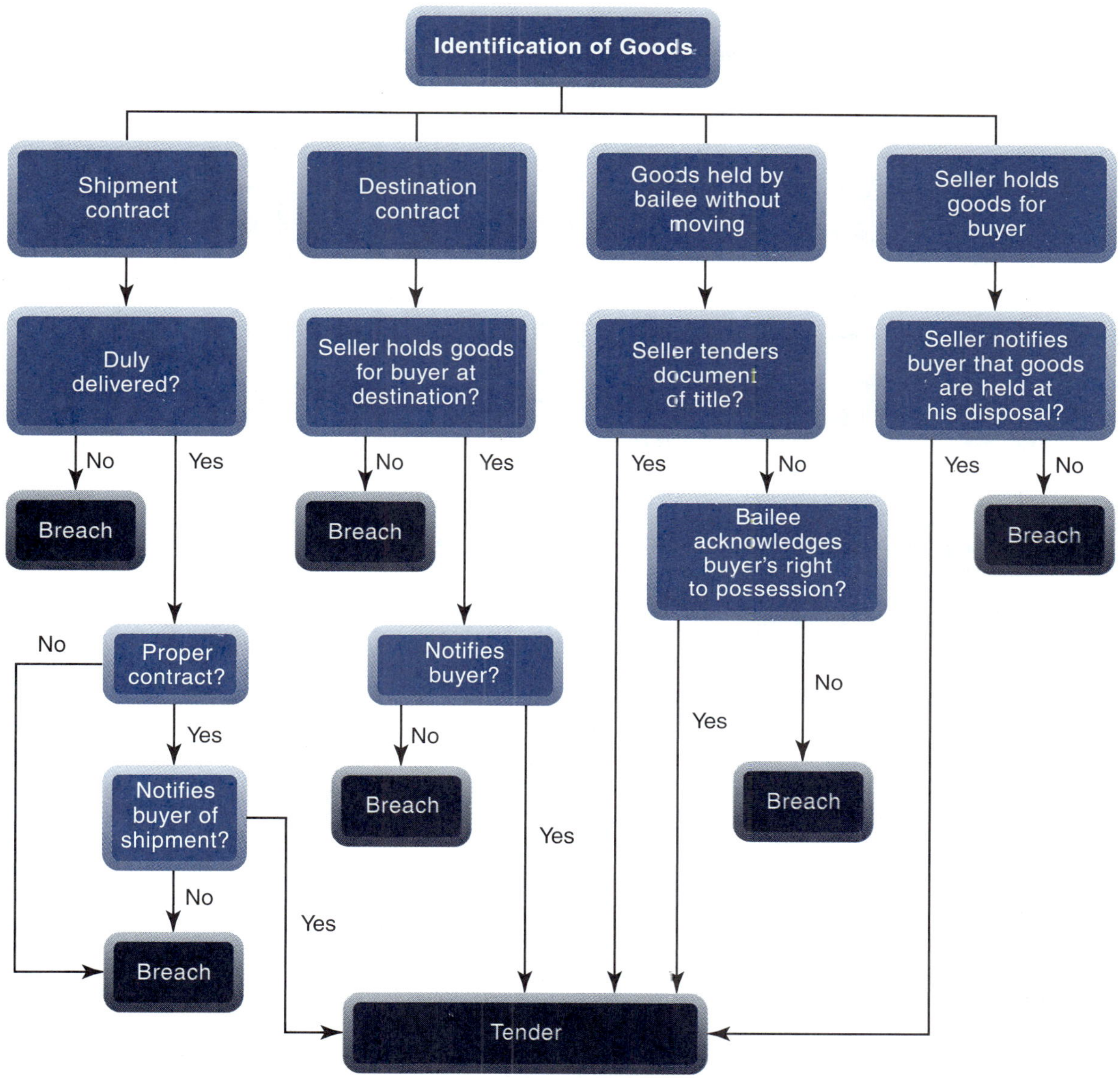

agreed to in the contract. For example, Neal is to deliver to Jessica twenty-five blue shirts and fifty white shirts by October 15. On October 1, Neal delivers twenty-nine blue shirts and forty-six white shirts, which Jessica rejects as not conforming to the contract. Jessica notifies Neal of her rejection and the reasons for it. Neal has until October 15 to cure the defect by making a perfect tender, provided he seasonably notifies Jessica of his intention to do so.

The Code also provides the seller an opportunity to cure a nonconforming tender that the seller had reasonable grounds to believe would be acceptable to the buyer with or without a money allowance. (Article 2A.) If, on the buyer's notice of rejection, the seller seasonably notifies the buyer of his intention to cure, the seller is permitted a reasonable time in which to substitute a conforming tender. For example, Tim orders from Noel a model 110X television to be delivered on January 20. The 110X is unavailable, but Noel can obtain a model 110, which is last year's model of the same television and which lists for 5 percent less than the 110X. On January 20, Noel delivers to Tim the 110 at a discount price of 10 percent less than the contract price for the 110X. Tim rejects the substituted television set. Noel, who promptly notifies Tim that she will obtain and deliver a model 110X, will have a reasonable time beyond the January 20 deadline in which to deliver the 110X television set to Tim, because under these facts she had reasonable grounds to believe the model 110 would be acceptable with the money allowance in Tim's favor.

> **Practical Advice**
>
> If you want to exercise the seller's right to cure, be sure to give the buyer timely notice of your intent to cure.

> **CISG**
>
> The seller may cure any deficiency in goods delivered before the date for delivery, provided that the exercise of this right does not cause the buyer unreasonable inconvenience or unreasonable expense. However, the buyer retains any right to claim damages as provided for in the CISG. If the seller does not perform on time, the buyer may fix an additional period of time of reasonable length for performance by the seller of his obligations. Unless the seller notifies the buyer that he will not perform within the period so fixed, the buyer may not, during that period, resort to any remedy for breach of contract. However, the buyer retains any right he may have to claim damages for delay in performance. If the seller does not deliver the goods within the additional period of time, the buyer may declare the contract avoided.
>
> The seller may, even after the date for delivery, cure a defective performance, if he can do so without unreasonable delay and without causing the buyer unreasonable inconvenience. However, the buyer retains any right to claim damages. If the seller notifies the buyer of his intent to cure and the buyer does not respond within a reasonable time, the seller may perform within the time indicated in the notice.

Installment Contracts Unless the parties have otherwise agreed, the buyer does not have to pay any part of the price of the goods until the seller has delivered or tendered to her the entire quantity specified in the contract. An **installment contract** represents an instance in which the parties have otherwise agreed. It expressly provides for delivery of the goods in separate lots or installments and usually provides for payment of the price in installments. If the contract is silent about payment, the Code provides that the seller may demand the price, if it can be apportioned, for each lot.

The buyer may reject any nonconforming installment if the nonconformity substantially impairs the value of that installment and cannot be cured. However, he cannot reject if the nonconforming installment substantially impairs the value of the installment but not the value of the entire contract if the seller gives adequate assurance of the installment's cure. (Article 2A.) On the other hand, whenever the nonconformity or default of one or more of the installments substantially impairs the value of the whole contract, the buyer can treat the breach as a breach of the whole contract. (Article 2A.)

> **CISG**
>
> When a contract calls for delivery of goods by installments, if the seller's failure to perform any of his obligations with respect to any installment constitutes a fundamental breach of contract with respect to that installment, the buyer may declare the contract avoided with respect to that installment. A buyer who declares the contract avoided with respect to any delivery may, at the same time, declare it avoided with respect to deliveries already made or to future deliveries if, by reason of their interdependence, those deliveries could not be used for the purpose contemplated by the parties at the time of the conclusion of the contract. If the seller's failure to perform any of his obligations with respect to any installment gives the buyer good grounds to conclude that a fundamental breach of contract will occur with respect to future installments, he may declare the contract avoided for the future, provided that he does so within a reasonable time.

CPA PERFORMANCE BY THE BUYER

A buyer is obliged to accept conforming goods and to pay for them according to the contract terms. (Article 2A.) Payment or tender of payment by the buyer, unless otherwise agreed, is a condition of the seller's duty to tender and to complete any delivery. The buyer is not obliged to accept a tender or delivery of goods that do not conform to the contract. Upon determining that the tender or delivery is nonconforming, the buyer has three choices. He may (1) reject all of the goods, (2) accept all of the goods, or (3) accept any commercial unit or units of the goods and reject the rest. (Article 2A.) The buyer must pay the contract rate for the commercial units he accepts.

> **CISG**
>
> The buyer must pay the price for the goods and take delivery of them as required by the contract and the CISG.

INSPECTION

Unless the parties agree otherwise, the buyer has a right to inspect the goods before payment or acceptance.

(Article 2A provides for the right to inspect before acceptance.) This **inspection** enables the buyer to determine whether the goods tendered or delivered conform to the contract. If the contract requires payment before acceptance (when, for example, the contract provides for shipment C.O.D., collect on delivery), payment must be made prior to inspection; however, such payment is not an acceptance of the goods and impairs neither the buyer's right to inspect nor any of her remedies.

The buyer, allowed a reasonable time to inspect the goods, may lose the right to reject or revoke acceptance of nonconforming goods by failing to inspect them within such time. Nevertheless, although the buyer must bear the expenses of inspection, she may recover them from the seller if the goods do not conform and are rightfully rejected. (Article 2A.)

Practical Advice

If you are the buyer, carefully inspect tendered goods before accepting them. If this is not feasible, inspect the goods as soon as possible.

CISG

The buyer is not bound to pay the price until he has had an opportunity to examine the goods, unless the parties have agreed otherwise. The buyer must examine the goods within as short a period of time as is practicable in the circumstances. Unless the buyer has a reasonable excuse, he loses the right to rely on a lack of conformity of the goods if he does not give notice to the seller of the nonconformity within a reasonable time after he has discovered it or ought to have discovered it.

REJECTION

Rejection is a manifestation by the buyer of her unwillingness to become owner of the goods. It must be made within a reasonable time after the goods have been tendered or delivered and is not effective unless the buyer reasonably notifies the seller. (Article 2A.)

Rejection of the goods may be rightful or wrongful, depending on whether the goods tendered or delivered conform to the contract. The buyer's rejection of nonconforming goods or tender is rightful under the perfect tender rule.

If the buyer refuses a tender of goods or rejects it as nonconforming without disclosing to the seller the nature of the defect, she may not assert such defect as an excuse for not accepting the goods or as a breach of contract by the seller if the defect is curable. (Article 2A.)

After the buyer has rejected the goods, the Code allows her to exercise no ownership of them. (Since the lessor retains title in a lease, this does not apply to leases.) If the buyer possesses the rejected goods but has no security interest in them, she is obliged to hold them with reasonable care for a time sufficient to permit the seller to remove them. (Article 2A.) The buyer who is not a merchant is under no further obligation with regard to goods rightfully rejected. (Article 2A.)

If the seller gives no instructions within a reasonable time after notification of rejection, the buyer may (1) store the goods for the seller's account, (2) reship them to the seller, or (3) resell them for the seller's account. Such action is not an acceptance or conversion of the goods. (Article 2A.) A *merchant* buyer of goods who has rightfully rejected them has additional duties: she is obligated to follow reasonable instructions from the seller regarding disposal of the goods in her possession or control when the seller has no agent or business at the place of rejection. (Article 2A.) If the merchant buyer receives no instructions from the seller within a reasonable time after giving notice of the rejection, and if the rejected goods are perishable or threaten to decline in value speedily, she is obligated to make reasonable efforts to sell them for the seller's account. (Article 2A.)

When the buyer sells the rejected goods, she is entitled to reimbursement for the reasonable expenses of caring for and selling them and to a reasonable selling commission not to exceed 10 percent of the gross proceeds. (Article 2A.)

Practical Advice

If you have rejected nonconforming goods, be sure to notify the seller in a timely manner and do not exercise ownership of the rejected goods.

CISG

If the goods do not conform with the contract and the nonconformity constitutes a fundamental breach of contract, the buyer may require delivery of substitute goods.

Furlong v. Alpha Chi Omega Sorority

Bowling Green County Municipal Court, 1993
73 Ohio Misc.2d 26, 657 N.E.2d 866

FACTS Alpha Chi Omega (AXO) **(http://www.alphachiomega.org)** entered into an oral contract with Furlong to buy 168 "custom-designed" sweaters for the Midnight Masquerade III. The purchase price of $3,612 was to be paid as follows: $2,000 down payment and $1,612 upon delivery. During phone conversations with Furlong, Emily, the AXO social chairperson, described the design to be imprinted on the sweater. She also specified the colors to be used in the lettering (hunter green on top of maroon outlined in navy blue) and the color of the mask design (hunter green). Furlong promised to have a third party imprint the sweaters as specified. Furlong later sent to Emily a sweater with maroon letters to show her the color. He then sent her a fax illustrating the sweater design with arrows indicating where each of the three colors was to appear. On the day before delivery was due, Argento, Furlong's supplier, requested design changes, which Furlong approved without the consent of AXO. These changes included deleting the navy blue outline, reducing the number of colors from three to two, changing the maroon lettering to red, and changing the color of the masks from hunter green to red. Upon delivery, AXO gave a check for the balance of the purchase price. Later that day, Emily inspected the sweaters and screamed her dismay at the design changes. AXO immediately stopped payment on the check. Amy, the president of AXO, phoned Furlong, stating that the sweaters were not what AXO had ordered. She gave the specifics as to why the sweaters were not as ordered and offered to return them. Furlong refused but offered to reduce the unit price of the sweaters if AXO agreed to accept them. AXO refused this offer. Furlong then filed suit against AXO for the unpaid portion of the sweaters' purchase price ($1,612) and AXO counterclaimed for return of the down payment ($2,000).

DECISION Judgment for AXO. The court ordered Furlong to pay $2,000 plus interest and costs and AXO to return the sweaters upon such payment.

OPINION Bachman, J. Furlong and Emily created an express warranty by * * * affirmation of fact (his initial phone calls); by sample (the maroon sweater); by description (the fax). This express warranty became part of the contract. Each of the three methods of showing the express warranty was not in conflict with the other two methods, and thus they are consistent and cumulative [U.C.C. § 2–317], and constitute the warranty.

The design was a "dickered" aspect of the individual bargain and went clearly to the essence of that bargain ([U.C.C. § 2–313]; Official Comment 1 to UCC 2–313). Thus, the express warranty was that the sweaters would be in accordance with the above design (including types of colors for the letters and the mask, and the number of colors for the same). Further, the express warranty became part of the contract.

* * *

Furlong's obligation as the seller was to transfer and deliver the goods in accordance with the contract. AXO's obligation was to accept and pay in accordance with that contract [U.C.C. § 2–301].

* * *

The sweaters did not conform to the contract (specifically, the express warranty in the contract). Thus (in the words of the statute), the sweaters did "fail in any respect to conform to the contract." Actually, the sweaters failed in at least five respects [U.C.C. § 2–601]. Further, not only did they "fail in any respect," they failed in a substantial respect. In either event, they were a nonconforming tender of goods [U.C.C. § 2–601].

* * *

AXO, as the buyer, had the right to inspect the boxes of sweaters before payment or acceptance [U.C.C. § 2–513]. AXO did so at a reasonable time and place, and in a reasonable manner, on the same day that Furlong had sent the sweaters and AXO had received them [U.C.C. § 2–513]. AXO's purpose of inspection had (in the words of the statute) "to do with the buyer's check-up on whether the seller's performance is in accordance with a contract previously made * * *." (Official Comment 9 to UCC 2–513.)

* * *

According to the statute, "if the goods *** fail in any respect to conform to the contract, the buyer may: (A) reject the whole * * * [.]" [U.C.C. § 2–601]. As concluded above, the sweaters were nonconforming goods. Therefore, Furlong breached the contract, and AXO had the right to reject the goods (sweaters).

* * *

One [section of the] statute provides: "Rejection of goods must be within a reasonable time after their delivery * * *. It is ineffective unless the buyer seasonably notifies the seller." [U.C.C. § 2–602(l)]. AXO did what this statute requires.

That statute further provides: "[I]f the buyer has before rejection taken physical possession of goods * * *, he is under a duty after rejection to hold them with reasonable care at the seller's disposition for a time sufficient to permit the seller to remove them[.]" [U.C.C. § 2–602(2)(b)] AXO had done this, too.

Another [section of the] statute provides: "The buyer's failure to state in connection with rejection a particular defect * * * precludes him from relying on the unstated defect to justify rejection or to establish breach[.]" [U.C.C. § 2–605(l).] AXO did enough to avoid the effect of this statute also.

* * *

AXO never had an acceptance of the sweaters (as the term "acceptance" is legally defined) [U.C.C. § 2–606]. That is, AXO never did any of the following (per the statute): (1) signified to Furlong that the sweaters were conforming or that AXO would take or retain the sweaters in spite of their non-conformity; (2) failed to make an effective rejection of the sweaters; (3) did any act inconsistent with Furlong's ownership. [U.C.C. § 2–606]

* * *

As concluded above, AXO rightfully rejected the sweaters, after having paid part of the purchase price: namely $2,000. * * *

INTERPRETATION If the goods fail in any respect to conform to the contract, the buyer may reject the whole lot.

ETHICAL QUESTION Did Furlong act in bad faith by not seeking AXO's consent to the changes? Explain.

CRITICAL THINKING QUESTION Does the court's decision remedy the situation in which the seller's breach left the sorority? Explain.

ACCEPTANCE

Acceptance of goods means a willingness by the buyer to become the owner of the goods tendered or delivered to her by the seller. Acceptance of the goods, which precludes any later rejection of them, includes overt acts or conduct that manifest such willingness. (Article 2A.) Such acts or conduct may include express words, the presumed intention of the buyer through her failure to act, or conduct of the buyer inconsistent with the seller's ownership of the goods. More specifically, acceptance occurs when the buyer, after a reasonable opportunity to inspect the goods (1) signifies to the seller that the goods conform to the contract, (2) signifies to the seller that she will take the goods or retain them in spite of their nonconformity to the contract, or (3) fails to make an effective rejection of the goods. (Article 2A.)

Acceptance of any part of a commercial unit is acceptance of the entire unit. (Article 2A.) The buyer must pay at the contract rate for any goods she accepts but may recover damages for any nonconformity of the goods, provided the buyer reasonably notifies the seller of any breach. (Article 2A, except for finance leases in some situations.) For example, Nancy agrees to deliver to Paul 500 lightbulbs, 100 watts each, for $300 and 1,000 lightbulbs, 60 watts each, for $500. Nancy delivers on time, but the shipment contains only 400 of the 100-watt bulbs and 750 of the 60-watt bulbs. If Paul accepts the shipment, he must pay Nancy $240 for the 100-watt bulbs accepted and $375 for the 60-watt bulbs accepted, less the amount of damages Nancy's nonconforming delivery caused him.

REVOCATION OF ACCEPTANCE

A buyer might accept defective goods either because it is difficult to discover the defect by inspection or because the buyer reasonably assumes that the seller will correct the defect. In either instance, the buyer may revoke his acceptance of the goods if the uncorrected defect substantially impairs the value of the goods to him. **Revocation of acceptance** gives the buyer the same rights and duties with respect to the goods as he would have acquired by rejecting them (Article 2A.)

More specifically, the buyer may revoke acceptance of goods that do not conform to the contract if the nonconformity *substantially* impairs the value of the goods to him, provided that his acceptance was (1) premised on the reasonable assumption that the seller would cure the nonconformity, and it was not seasonably cured or (2) made without discovery of the nonconformity, and such acceptance was reasonably induced by the difficulty of discovery before acceptance or by the seller's assurances. (Article 2A.)

Revocation of acceptance is not effective until notification is given to the seller. This must be done within a reasonable time after the buyer discovers or should have discovered the grounds for revocation and before the goods have undergone any substantial change not caused by their own defects. (Article 2A.)

The following case deals with the question of whether a party forfeits the right to revoke an acceptance by the continuing use of a good.

Practical Advice

If you have cause to revoke your acceptance of goods, be sure to notify the seller within a reasonable time after discovering the grounds for revocation.

In Re Stem

Alabama Supreme Court, 1990
571 So.2d 1112

FACTS On February 26, 1987, William Stem purchased a used BMW from Gary Braden for $6,600. Stem's primary purpose for buying the car was to use it to transport his child. Braden indicated to Stem that the car had not been wrecked and that it was in good condition. Stem thought the car had been driven only 70,000 miles. Less than a week after the purchase, Stem discovered a disconnected plug that, when plugged in, caused the oil warning light to turn on. When Stem then took his car to a mechanic, the mechanic discovered that the front end was that of a 1979 BMW and the rear end was that of a 1975 BMW. Further investigation revealed that the front half had been driven 170,000 miles. On March 10, 1987, Stem sent a letter informing Braden that he refused the automobile and that he intended to rescind the sale. Braden refused. Stem filed an action against Braden, seeking to rescind the sale, and the trial court awarded Stem the purchase price of the car, plus interest. The Court of Appeals reversed, holding that Stem had accepted the automobile by driving it for seven months and nearly 9,000 miles after sending the letter to Braden.

DECISION Decision of the Court of Appeals reversed and the case remanded.

OPINION Kennedy, J. Because there are numerous grounds for rescission of a contract, we do not agree that if Stem accepted the automobile then rescission necessarily was "not available," as the Court of Civil Appeals implies. That court, however, did address whether Stem revoked his acceptance of the automobile, which is the starting point for a proper analysis of this case.

* * *

The record would support a finding by the trial court that Stem revoked his acceptance of the automobile pursuant to [U.C.C.] § 2–608. The trial court could properly have determined that Stem's acceptance of the automobile had been reasonably induced by Braden's assurances. The record indicates that the vehicle had been previously involved in at least one accident, that the vehicle was composed of two welded together halves of other vehicles, that the speedometer had been disconnected for three and one-half months while Braden owned the car, that the vehicle had 100,000 more miles on its front half than Stem thought it had, and that the mileage on the back half was not known for certain. Although the trial court permissibly could have considered Stem's use of the car as evidence that its value was not substantially impaired, [citation], it was not compelled to do so. Accordingly, the trial court could have determined that the automobile's nonconformities substantially impaired its value to Stem. There is no substantial dispute either that Stem's revocation occurred within a reasonable time or that Stem properly notified Braden, and the trial court could have found that Stem revoked his acceptance within a reasonable time and that he met the notice requirements of [U.C.C.] § 2–608.

When Stem revoked his acceptance, he had the same rights and duties with regard to the automobile that he would have had had he rejected it. [U.C.C.] § 2–608(3). Section 2–602 addresses the manner and effect of rejection, and § 2–602(2)(a) provides that "after rejection any exercise of ownership by the buyer with respect to any commercial unit is wrongful as against the seller." Accordingly, although Stem revoked his acceptance, his continued use of the automobile was "wrongful" against Braden. There is no definition of "wrongful" as it is used in § 2–602(2)(a),* * * to explain the consequences of Stem's continued use of the vehicle.

* * *

Sections 2–602 and 2–606 through –608 are derived from the Uniform Commercial Code and, accordingly, many states have enacted similar provisions into statutory law. A review of the case law construing similar provisions indicates that the Court of Civil Appeals' treatment of the issue of Stem's use of the automobile only in terms of acceptance of the automobile is inappropriately simple. Many cases involve extensive use of automobiles and motor homes after revocation; the cases emphasize the practical consideration that an individual who buys an automobile or a motor home may very well be unable, without extraordinary financial difficulty, to tender the automobile or motor home and do without it until the litigation concerning it is completed. [Citations.] These courts * * * held that continued use after revocation was "wrongful" but did not constitute acceptance.

With uniformity, the courts have held that the "wrongful" use entitles the seller to prove the reasonable value of the buyer's use and to recover that amount as a setoff, and many courts have awarded setoffs in circumstances similar to those of the present case. [Citations.]

* * *

* * * Additionally, we note that if Stem had exercised any of his options available under Alabama's commercial code concerning storing or returning the vehicle, he would have been put in the position of doing without a vehicle for transporting his child, which was one of the primary purposes for which he bought the vehicle, until trial of this case or else he would have been required to purchase or lease an additional suitable vehicle. Under these circumstances Stem's continued use of the automobile was not an act of continued use that constituted an acceptance of ownership after revocation. [Citation.]

INTERPRETATION After rightfully revoking acceptance, the buyer may continue to use the goods if such use is reasonable, but this use may entitle the seller to a setoff in the amount of the value of the buyer's use.

CRITICAL THINKING QUESTION Do you agree with the requirements for revocation of acceptance? Explain.

OBLIGATION OF PAYMENT

The terms of the contract may expressly state the time and place at which the buyer is obligated to pay for the goods. If so, these terms are controlling. Thus, if the buyer has agreed to pay either the seller or a carrier for the goods in advance of delivery, his duty to pay is not conditional on performance or a tender of performance by the seller. Furthermore, when the sale is on credit, the buyer is not obligated to pay for the goods when he receives them. The credit provision in the contract will control the time of payment.

In the absence of agreement, payment is due at the time and place the buyer is to receive the goods, even though the place of shipment is the place of delivery. This rule is understandable in view of the right of the buyer, in the absence of agreement to the contrary, to inspect the goods before being obliged to pay for them. Tender of payment is sufficient when made by any means or in any manner current, such as a check, in the ordinary course of business, unless the seller demands cash and allows the buyer a reasonable time within which to obtain it.

For a summary of performance by the buyer, see Figure 20-2.

CISG

Unless the buyer is bound to pay the price at any other specific time, he must pay it when the seller places either the goods or documents controlling their disposition at the buyer's disposal in accordance with the contract and the CISG. The seller may make such payment a condition for handing over the goods or documents. If the buyer is not bound to pay the price at any other particular place, he must pay it to the seller (a) at the seller's place of business or (b) if the payment is to be made against the handing over of the goods or of documents, at the place where the handing over takes place.

Practical Advice

Specify in your sales contract the time and other terms of payment.

CPA OBLIGATIONS OF BOTH PARTIES

Contracts for the sale of goods necessarily involve risks concerning future events that may or may not occur. Though in some instances the parties explicitly allocate these risks, in most instances they do not. The Code contains three sections that allocate these risks when the parties fail to do so. Each provision, when applicable, relieves the parties from the obligation of full performance under the sales contract. (See also the Ethical Dilemma in this chapter.)

Related to the subject of whether the Code will excuse performance is the question of whether both parties will be able and willing to perform. In such instances, the Code allows the insecure party to seek reasonable assurance of the potentially defaulting party's willingness and ability to perform. In addition, if one of the parties clearly indicates an unwillingness or inability to perform, the Code protects the other party.

CASUALTY TO IDENTIFIED GOODS

If goods are destroyed before an offer to sell or to buy them is accepted, the offer is terminated by general contract law. But what if the goods are destroyed after the sales contract is formed? The rules for the passage of risk of loss, as discussed in Chapter 21, apply with one exception: if the contract is for goods that are **identified** when the contract was made and these goods are totally lost or damaged, without fault of either party, before the risk of

Figure 20-2 *Performance by the Buyer*

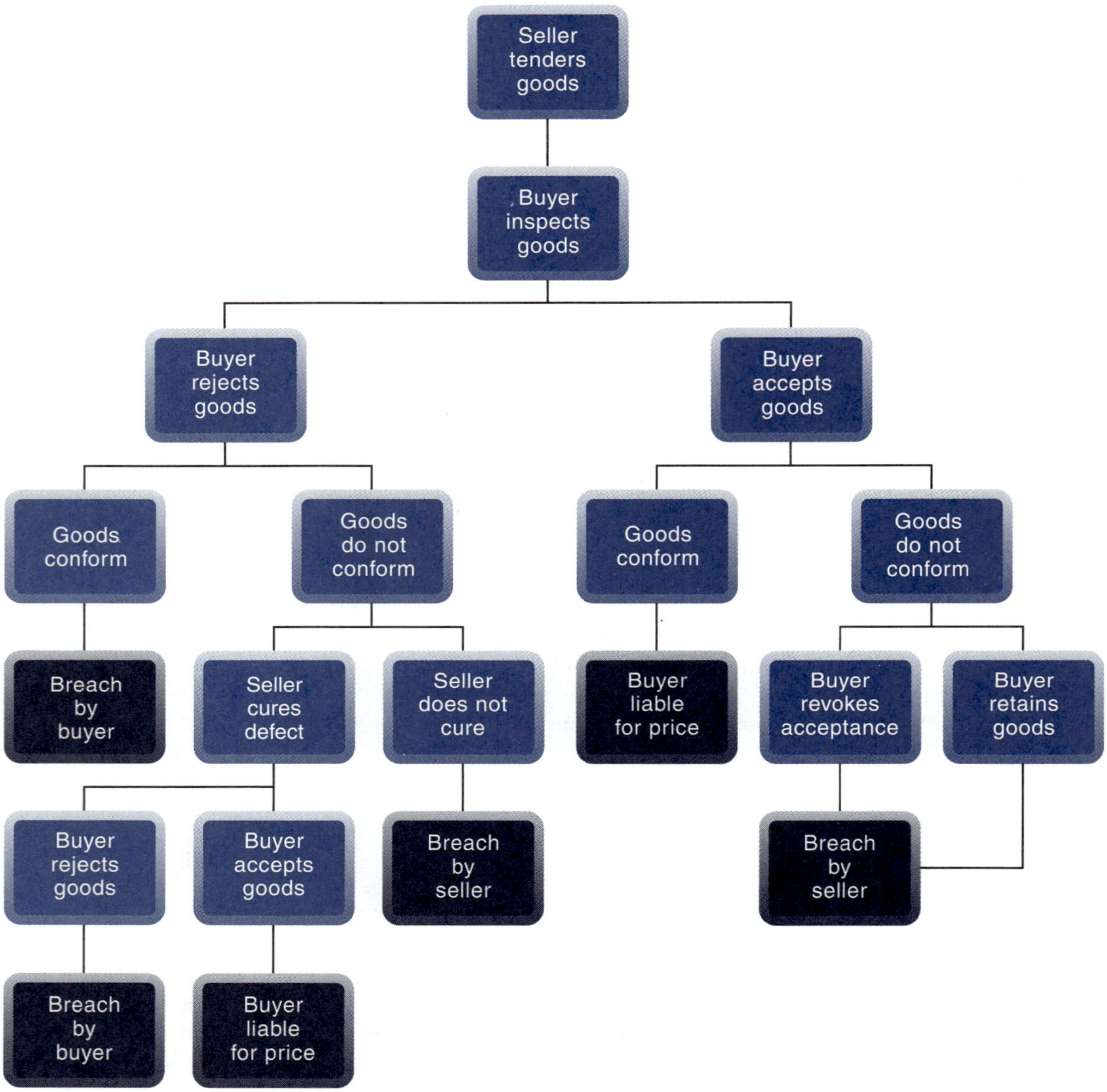

loss passes to the buyer, the contract is avoided. (Article 2A.) This means that each party is excused from his obligation to perform under the contract: the seller is no longer obligated to deliver, and the buyer need not pay the price. In the case of a partial destruction or deterioration of the goods, the buyer has the option to avoid the contract or to accept the goods with due allowance or deduction from the contract price sufficient to account for the deterioration or deficiency in quantity. (Article 2A, except in a finance lease that is not a consumer lease).

NONHAPPENING OF PRESUPPOSED CONDITION

Central to the Code's approach to impossibility of performance is the concept of **commercial impracticability**. Under this concept, the Code will excuse performance that, even though not actually or literally impossible, is commercially impracticable. This, however, requires more than mere hardship or increased cost of performance. For a party to be discharged, performance must be rendered impracticable as a result of an unforeseen supervening event not within the contemplation of the parties at the

Ethical Dilemma

Should a Buyer Refuse to Perform a Contract Because a Legal Product May Be Unsafe?

FACTS Carson and Olson are partners in a landscape and gardening business that operates out of three major locations and employs approximately thirty people. The business provides general lawn care predominately for residential homes; its services include grass cutting, fertilizing, and trimming of shrubbery. Carson and Olson also provide landscape design services.

One year ago, Carson and Olson entered into a two-year contract with Chem-Care, which manufactures chemical-based fertilizers effective in weed control. Because the contract was for a long term and because Carson and Olson have been excellent Chem-Care customers for the past fifteen years, they obtained an extremely favorable price of $40,000 for a two-year supply of Chem-Care fertilizers.

Now, however, due to publicity concerning health problems associated with certain chemical lawn treatments, the majority of Carson and Olson's customers have decided that they no longer want chemical lawn treatments. Concerned by the health hazards associated with chemical fertilizers, the customers insist upon natural fertilizers.

Chem-Care fertilizers have been approved by the government and do not violate any standards currently in place. Nevertheless, a congressional committee has begun studying approximately one hundred chemical treatments, including the fertilizers used by Chem-Care. The study will take at least a year to complete.

Carson wants to cancel the contract with Chem-Care. But Olson feels a sense of loyalty to Chem-Care and wants to honor the contract by trying to find new customers who would be willing to use the Chem-Care products.

Social, Policy, and Ethical Considerations

1. Should Carson and Olson attempt to invalidate the contract? Compare the social value of enforcing promises made with the good faith intention of being legally bound against the value of protecting the public from health or environmental threats.
2. Is it premature to characterize Chem-Care products as a threat to health or the environment?
3. Should the law excuse the performance of contracts that involve products that are under investigation for posing health or environmental problems?
4. As a practical matter, what should Carson and Olson do? Given the question as to the safety of Chem-Care products, does Olson's suggestion of getting new customers for Chem-Care products make sense from an ethical or a business standpoint?

time of contracting. Moreover, the nonoccurrence of the event must have been a "basic assumption" that both parties made when entering into the contract. (Article 2A.) See *Northern Corp. v. Chugach Electrical Association* in Chapter 17.

Increased production cost alone does not excuse performance by the seller, nor does a collapse of the market for the goods excuse the buyer. But a party to a contract for the sale of programs for a scheduled Super Bowl that is called off, for the sale of tin horns for export that become subject to embargo, or for the production of goods at a designated factory that becomes damaged or destroyed by fire would be excused from performance: in each case, an unforeseen supervening event has rendered performance impracticable.

Although the nonhappening of presupposed conditions may relieve the seller of her contractual duty, if the contingency affects only a part of the seller's capacity to perform, the seller must, to the extent of her remaining capacity, allocate delivery and production in a fair and reasonable manner among her customers. (Article 2A.)

Practical Advice

Specify in your contract which events will excuse the nonperformance of the contract, the basic assumptions of your contract, and which risks are assumed by each of the parties.

CISG

A party is not liable for a failure to perform any of his obligations if he proves that the failure was due to an impediment beyond his control and that he could not reasonably be expected to have taken the impediment into account at the time of contracting or to have avoided or overcome it or its consequences.

Substituted Performance

The Code provides that when neither party is at fault and the agreed-upon manner of delivering the goods becomes commercially impracticable—because of the failure of loading or unloading facilities or the unavailability of an agreed-upon type of carrier, for example—a substituted manner of performance, if commercially reasonable, must be tendered and accepted. (Article 2A.) When a practical alternative or substitute exists, the Code excuses neither seller nor buyer on the ground that delivery in the express manner provided in the contract is impossible.

Right to Adequate Assurance of Performance

A contract of sale also requires that each party not impair the other party's expectation of having the contract performed. Therefore, when reasonable grounds for insecurity arise regarding either party's performance, the other party may demand written assurance and suspend his own performance until he receives that assurance. The failure to provide adequate assurance of performance within a reasonable time, not exceeding thirty days, constitutes a repudiation of the contract. (Article 2A.)

CISG

A party may suspend the performance of his obligations if, after the conclusion of the contract, it becomes apparent that the other party will not perform a substantial part of his obligations. A party suspending performance must immediately notify the other party of the suspension and must continue with performance if the other party provides adequate assurance of his performance.

Right to Cooperation

When one party's cooperation is necessary to the agreed performance but is not timely forthcoming, the other party is excused with regard to any resulting delay in her own performance. The nonbreaching party either may proceed to perform in any reasonable manner or, if the time for her performance has occurred, may treat the other's failure to cooperate as a breach. In either event, the nonbreaching party has access to any other remedies the Code may provide, as discussed in Chapter 23.

Anticipatory Repudiation

Although a repudiation in itself is a clear indication by either party to a contract that he is unwilling or unable to perform his obligations under the contract, an **anticipatory repudiation** is a repudiation made *before* the time to perform occurs. It may occur by express communication or by the repudiating party's taking an action that makes performance impossible, such as selling unique goods to a third party. It also may result from the failure of a party to give timely assurance of performance after a justifiable demand. If an anticipatory repudiation substantially impairs the value of the contract, the aggrieved party may (1) await performance for a commercially reasonable time or (2) resort to any remedy for breach. In either case, he may suspend his own performance. (Article 2A.) The repudiating party may retract his anticipatory repudiation and thereby reinstate the contract unless the aggrieved party has canceled the contract, has materially changed his position, or has otherwise indicated that she considers the anticipatory repudiation final. (Article 2A.)

CISG

If prior to the date for performance of the contract it is clear that one of the parties will commit a fundamental breach of contract, the other party may declare the contract avoided.

Hessler v. Crystal Lake Chrysler-Plymouth, Inc.

Appellate Court of Illinois, Second District, 2003

788 N.E.2d 405, 273 Ill.Dec. 96, 50 U.C.C. Rep.Serv.2d 330

http://caselaw.lp.findlaw.com/scripts/getcase.pl?court=il&vol=app/2003/2020362&invol=3

FACTS In February 1997, Chrysler Corporation introduced a new promotional vehicle called the Plymouth Prowler but did not reveal whether it would manufacture any of the vehicles. Donald Hessler (the plaintiff), aware of the vehicle and of its uncertain production, contacted several dealerships to inquire about purchasing a Prowler. On February 5, 1997, plaintiff met with Gary Rosenberg, co-owner of Crystal Lake Chrysler-Plymouth, Inc. (defendant) and signed a "Retail Order for a Motor Vehicle" (Agreement). The Agreement, which was filled out primarily by Rosenberg, stated that the order was for a 1997, V6, two-door, purple Plymouth Prowler and provided "Customer to pay $5,000.00/100 over list price by manufacturer. Money refundable if can not [deliver] by 12/30/97. Dealer to keep car 2 weeks."

The order noted that plaintiff had deposited $5,000 for the car. The Agreement contained a box labeled "TO BE DELIVERED ON OR ABOUT." Inside the box was written "ASAP", which term Rosenberg stated is used in his business "in lieu of a stock number. Just line it up in order. As soon as you can get it done, do it." Rosenberg testified that Hessler was the first person to place an order for a Prowler and that Rosenberg was "pretty sure" that plaintiff's order was the first order on which he received a deposit. On May 11, 1997, Rosenberg and Hessler agreed that the information they had received was that the manufacturer's list price would be $39,000.

On May 23, 1997, Salvatore Palandri entered into a contract with defendant to purchase a 1997 Plymouth Prowler. His contract reflected a purchase price of "50,000 + tax + lic + doc" and a $10,000 deposit. It also stated that Palandri would receive the "first one delivered to [the] dealership."

Plaintiff testified that on August 11, 1997, Rosenberg informed plaintiff that no Prowlers would be delivered to the Midwest and that he would be returning plaintiff's check. Defendant, according to the plaintiff, nevertheless, stated that should defendant receive a vehicle, it would be plaintiff's. Defendant denies having stated this.

Plaintiff testified that he attended a Chrysler customer appreciation event at Great America on September 19 and spoke to a company representative about the Prowler. Two days later, the representative sent him a fax that contained a tentative list of dealers who were to receive Prowlers. Defendant's name was on the list. Plaintiff testified that he called Rosenberg on September 22 to notify him that his dealership was on a list of dealers due to receive Prowlers. Rosenberg informed plaintiff that he would not sell plaintiff a car because plaintiff had gone behind Rosenberg's back and that contacting Chrysler would cause Rosenberg problems. Rosenberg also stated that plaintiff was not the first person with whom he contracted to sell a Prowler. Plaintiff protested, and Rosenberg informed him that he would not sell plaintiff the car.

Beginning on September 23, 1997, plaintiff contacted thirty-eight Chrysler-Plymouth dealerships to inquire about purchasing a 1997 Prowler, but did not obtain one. On October 24, 1997, plaintiff attended a Prowler coming-out party at the Hard Rock Cafe and saw a purple Prowler in the parking lot with a sign in its window that had defendant's name written on it. On October 25, plaintiff went to defendant's showroom and saw a Prowler parked there. He found Rosenberg and informed him that he was there to pick up his car. Rosenberg stated that he was not going to sell plaintiff the car and that he did not want to do business with him. Later that day, plaintiff purchased a Prowler from another dealer for $77,706. On October 27, 1997, defendant sold the only Prowler it received in that year to Palandri for a total sale price of $54,859, including his $10,000 deposit.

On April 23, 1998, plaintiff sued defendant for breach of contract. The trial court entered judgment for plaintiff and awarded him $29,853 in damages. It concluded that defendant breached the Agreement and that plaintiff properly covered by purchasing a replacement vehicle for $29,853 more than the contract price. The trial court also concluded that defendant repudiated its contract in September and October of 1997 when Rosenberg told plaintiff that he would not sell him a car. It found plaintiff "ready, willing, and able to perform the contract." The court found that the price plaintiff paid for the car at another dealership was the best price he could receive for a Prowler after Rosenberg's refusal to sell to him a car.

DECISION The judgment of the trial court is affirmed.

OPINION Callum, J. Under the UCC, certain actions by a party to a contract may constitute an anticipatory repudiation of the contract if the actions are sufficiently clear manifestations of an intent not to perform under the contract. [UCC §] 2–610; [citation.]

* * *

Comment 1 to section 2–610 provides, in relevant part:

"Anticipatory repudiation centers upon an overt communication of intention or an action which renders performance impossible or demonstrates a clear determination not to continue with performance.

* * * When such a repudiation substantially impairs the value of the contract, the aggrieved party may at any time resort to his remedies for breach * * *." [UCC §] 2–610, Comment.

Comment 2 to section 2–610 provides, in relevant part:

"It is not necessary for repudiation that performance be made literally and utterly impossible. Repudiation can result from action which reasonably indicates a rejection of the continuing obligation." [UCC §] 2–610, Comment.

Comment 4 to section 2–610 provides, in relevant part:

"After repudiation, the aggrieved party may immediately resort to any remedy he chooses provided he moves in good faith (see Section 1–203)." [UCC §] 2–610, Comment.

* * *

Upon learning that defendant was on a tentative list to receive a Prowler, plaintiff testified that he called Rosenberg to relate the information and that Rosenberg responded that plaintiff was not the first person to contract to purchase a Prowler. Rosenberg also stated that he would not do business with plaintiff. Further, Rosenberg's testimony about this conversation corroborated plaintiff's, in that Rosenberg stated that he told plaintiff that the vehicle was already "committed." The trial court also heard both plaintiff and Rosenberg testify that, when plaintiff went to defendant's showroom on October 25 and informed Rosenberg that he was there to pick up his car, Rosenberg told plaintiff that he did not want to do business with him.

We conclude that the trial court did not err in finding that defendant's foregoing actions reasonably indicated to plaintiff that defendant would not deliver to him a Prowler under the Agreement. As we determined above, defendant contracted to deliver a Prowler to plaintiff as soon as possible. It was not against the manifest weight of the evidence for the trial court to find that defendant repudiated the Agreement when it repeatedly informed plaintiff that it would not deliver to him the first Prowler it received. Such actions made it sufficiently clear to plaintiff that defendant would not perform under the Agreement. [Citation.]

* * * With respect to plaintiff's actions, section 2–610(b) of the UCC provides that an aggrieved party may "resort to any remedy for breach" of the contract "even though he has notified the repudiating party that he would await the latter's performance." [UCC §] 2–610(b). One such remedy is to cover. [UCC §] 2–711(1)(a) (buyer may effect cover, upon seller's repudiation, whether or not buyer cancels the contract). The statute is clear that a buyer's willingness to proceed with performance under a contract does not excuse a repudiation. * * *

Defendant next asserts that, even if there was a repudiation in September or October of 1997, plaintiff did nothing to indicate that he thought this was the case. He took no self-help measures such as: terminating the contract; seeking to enjoin the sale to Palandri; requesting a retraction; or suspending his performance obligations. Again, we disagree. The UCC does not require a party to request assurances as a condition precedent to recovery. [Citation.]

For the foregoing reasons, we conclude that the trial court's finding of repudiation was not against the manifest weight of the evidence.

INTERPRETATION If an anticipatory repudiation substantially impairs the value of the contract, the injured party may await performance for a commercially reasonable time or resort to any remedy for breach.

CRITICAL THINKING QUESTION At what point should a buyer have a reasonable basis for believing the seller had repudiated? Explain.

CHAPTER SUMMARY

Performance by the Seller

Tender of Delivery the seller makes available to the buyer goods conforming to the contract and so notifies the buyer
- Buyer is obligated to accept conforming goods
- Seller is entitled to receive payment of the contract price

Time of Tender tender must be made at a reasonable time and kept open for a reasonable period of time

Place of Tender if none is specified, place for delivery is the seller's place of business or, if he has no such place, his residence
- *Shipment Contracts* seller is required to tender delivery of the goods to a carrier for delivery to buyer; shipment terms include F.O.B. place of shipment; F.A.S. port of shipment; C.I.F.; C. & F.
- *Destination Contracts* seller is required to tender delivery of the goods at a named destination; destination terms include F.O.B. place of destination; ex-ship; no arrival, no sale
- *Goods Held by Bailee* seller must either tender to the buyer a document of title or obtain an acknowledgment from the bailee

Perfect Tender Rule the seller's tender of performance must conform exactly to the contract, subject to the following qualifications:
- ***Agreement Between the Parties*** the parties may contractually limit the operation of the perfect tender rule
- ***Cure by the Seller*** when the time for performance under the contract has not expired or when the seller has shipped nonconforming goods in the belief that the nonconforming tender would be acceptable, a seller may cure or correct his nonconforming tender
- ***Installment Contracts*** when the contract calls for delivery of goods in separate lots, the buyer may reject a nonconforming installment if it substantially impairs the value of that installment and cannot be cured; but if nonconformity or default of one or more of the installments substantially impairs the value of the whole contract, the buyer can treat the breach as a breach of the whole contract

Performance by the Buyer

Inspection unless otherwise agreed, the buyer has a reasonable time in which to inspect the goods before payment or acceptance to determine whether they conform

Rejection buyer's manifestation of unwillingness to become the owner of the goods; must be made within a reasonable time after the goods have been tendered or delivered and gives the buyer the right to (1) reject all of the goods, (2) accept all of the goods, or (3) accept any commercial unit(s) and reject the rest

Acceptance buyer's express or implied manifestation of a willingness to become the owner of the goods

Revocation of Acceptance rescission of buyer's acceptance of the goods if nonconformity of the goods substantially impairs their value, provided that the acceptance was (1) premised on the assumption that the nonconformity would be cured by the seller and it was not, or (2) the nonconformity was an undiscovered hidden defect

Obligation of Payment in the absence of an agreement, payment is due at the time and place the buyer is to receive the goods

Obligations of Both Parties

Casualty to Identified Goods if the contract is for goods that were identified when the contract was made and those goods are totally lost or damaged without fault of either party and before the risk of loss has passed to the buyer, the contract is avoided

Nonhappening of Presupposed Condition the seller is excused from the duty of performance on the nonoccurrence of presupposed conditions that were a basic assumption of the contract, unless the seller has expressly assumed the risk

Substituted Performance when neither party is at fault and the agreed manner of delivery of goods becomes commercially impracticable, a substituted manner of performance must be tendered and accepted

Right to Adequate Assurance of Performance when reasonable grounds for insecurity arise regarding either party's performance, the other party may demand written assurance and suspend his own performance until he receives that assurance

Right to Cooperation if one party's required cooperation is untimely, the other party is excused from any resulting delay in her own performance

Anticipatory Repudiation if either party clearly indicates an unwillingness or inability to perform before the performance is due, the other party may await performance for a reasonable time or resort to any remedy for breach

QUESTIONS

1. Tammie contracted with Kristine to manufacture, sell, and deliver to Kristine and put in running order a certain machine. After Tammie set up the machine and put it in running order, Kristine found it unsatisfactory and notified Tammie that she rejected the machine. She continued to use it for three months but continually complained of its defective condition. At the end of the three months, she notified Tammie to come and get it. Has Kristine lost her right (a) to reject the machine? (b) to revoke acceptance of the machine?

2. Smith, having contracted to sell to Beyer thirty tons of described fertilizer, shipped to Beyer by carrier thirty tons of fertilizer that he stated conformed to the contract. Nothing was stated in the contract as to time of payment, but Smith demanded payment as a condition of handing over the fertilizer to Beyer. Beyer refused to pay unless he was given the opportunity to inspect the fertilizer. Who is correct? Explain.

3. Benny and Sheree entered into a contract for the sale of one hundred barrels of flour. No mention was made of any place of delivery. Thereafter, Sheree demanded that Benny deliver the flour at her place of business, and Benny demanded that Sheree come and take the flour from his place of business. Neither party acceded to the demand of the other. Has either one a right of action against the other?

4. Johnson, a manufacturer of air-conditioning units, made a written contract with Maxwell to sell to Maxwell forty units at a price of $200 each and to deliver them at a certain apartment building owned by Maxwell for installation by Maxwell. On the arrival of Johnson's truck for delivery at the apartment building, Maxwell examined the units on the truck, counted only thirty units, and asked the driver if that was the total delivery. The driver replied that it was as far as he knew. Maxwell told the driver that she would not accept delivery of the units. The next day, Johnson telephoned Maxwell and inquired why delivery was refused. Maxwell stated that the units on the truck were not what she ordered, that she ordered forty units, that only thirty were tendered, and that she was going to buy air-conditioning units elsewhere. In an action by Johnson against Maxwell for breach of contract, Maxwell defends on the ground that the tender of thirty units was improper, because the contract called for delivery of forty units. Is this a valid defense?

5. Edwin sells a sofa to Jack for $800. Edwin and Jack both know that the sofa is in Edwin's warehouse, located approximately ten miles from Jack's home. The contract does not specify the place of delivery, and Jack insists that the place of delivery is either his house or Edwin's store. Is Jack correct?

6. On November 4, Kim contracted to sell to Lynn five hundred sacks of flour at $4 each to be shipped in November to Lynn. On November 27, Kim shipped the flour. By December 5, when the car arrived, containing only 450 sacks, the market price of flour had fallen. The usual time required for shipment was five to twelve days. Lynn refused to accept delivery or to pay. Kim shipped 50 more sacks of flour, which arrived December 10. Lynn refused delivery. Kim resold the flour for $3 per sack. What are Kim's rights against Lynn?

7. Farley and Trudy entered into a written contract whereby Farley agreed to sell and Trudy agreed to buy 6,000 bushels of wheat at $3.75 per bushel, deliverable at the rate of 1,000 bushels a month commencing June 1, the price for each installment being payable ten days after delivery thereof. Though Farley delivered and received payment for the June installment, he defaulted by failing to deliver the July and August installments. By August 15, the market price of wheat had increased to $4 per bushel. Trudy thereupon entered into a contract with Albert to purchase 5,000 bushels of wheat at $4 per bushel deliverable over the ensuing four months. In late September, the market price of wheat started to decline and by December 1 was $3.25 per bushel. Explain whether Trudy would succeed in a legal action against Farley for breach of contract.

8. Bain ordered from Marcum a carload of lumber, which he intended to use in the construction of small boats for the U.S. Navy, pursuant to contract. The order specified that the lumber was to be free from knots, wormholes, and defects. The lumber was shipped, and immediately on receipt Bain looked into the door of the fully loaded car, ascertained that there was a full carload of lumber, and acknowledged to Marcum that the carload had been received. On the same day, Bain moved the car to his private siding and sent to Marcum full payment in accordance with the terms of the order.

   A day later, the car was moved to the work area and unloaded in the presence of the navy inspector, who refused to allow three-fourths of it to be used because of excessive knots and wormholes in the lumber. Bain then informed Marcum that he was rejecting the order and requested refund of the payment and directions on disposition of the lumber. Marcum replied that because Bain had accepted the order and unloaded it, he was not entitled to return of the purchase price. Who is correct? Explain.

CASE PROBLEMS

9. The plaintiff, a seller of milk, had for ten years bid on contracts to supply milk to the defendant school district, and had supplied milk to other school districts in the area. On June 15, 1987, the plaintiff contracted to supply the defendant's requirements of milk for the school year 1987/88, at a price of $.0759 per half-pint. The price of raw milk delivered from the farm had for years been controlled by the U.S. Department of Agriculture (http://www.usda.gov/). On June 15, 1987, the department's administrator for the New York/New New Jersey area had mandated a price for raw milk of $8.03 per hundredweight. By December 1987, the mandated price had been raised to $9.31 per hundredweight, an increase of nearly 20 percent. If required to complete deliveries at the contract price, the plaintiff would lose $7,350.55 on its contract with the defendant and would face similar losses on contracts with two other school districts. Is the plaintiff correct in its assertion (a) that its performance had become impracticable through unforeseen events, particularly unanticipated grain crop failures and the huge amounts of grain sold to Russia in mid-1987 and (b) that it is entitled to relief from performance?

10. In April of 1997, F. W. Lang Company (Lang) purchased an ice cream freezer and refrigeration compressor unit from Fleet for $2,160. Although the parties agreed to a written installment contract providing for an $850 down payment and eighteen installment payments, Lang made only one $200 payment upon receipt of the goods. One year later, Lang moved to a new location and took the equipment along without notifying Fleet. Then, in May or June of 1999, Lang disconnected the compressor from the freezer and used it to operate an air conditioner. Lang continued to use the compressor for that purpose until the sheriff seized the equipment and returned it to Fleet pursuant to a court order. Fleet then sold the equipment for $500 in what both parties conceded was a fair sale. Lang then brought an action charging that the equipment was defective and unusable for its intended purpose and sought to recover the down payment and expenses incurred in repairing the equipment. Fleet counterclaimed for the balance due under the installment contract less the proceeds from the sale. Who will prevail? Why?

11. Deborah McCullough bought a new car from Bill Swad Chrysler-Plymouth, Inc. The car was protected by both a limited warranty and an extended warranty. McCullough immediately encountered problems with the automobile's brakes, transmission, and air-conditioning and discovered a number of cosmetic defects as well. She returned the car to Swad for repairs, but Swad did not fix the brakes properly or perform any of the cosmetic work. Moreover, new problems appeared with respect to the car's steering mechanism. McCullough returned the car twice more for repairs, but on each occasion, old problems persisted and new ones emerged. After the engine abruptly shut off on a short trip away from home and the brakes again failed on a more extensive excursion, McCullough presented Swad with a list of thirty-two of the car's defects and demanded their correction. When Swad failed to remedy more than a few of the problems, McCullough wrote a letter to Swad calling for rescission of the purchase agreement and a refund of the purchase price and offering to return the car upon receipt of shipping instructions from Swad. Swad did not respond to the letter, and McCullough brought an action against Swad. She continued to operate the vehicle until the time of trial, some seventeen and one-half months (and 23,000 miles) later. Can McCullough rescind the agreement?

12. On March 17, Peckham bought a new car from Larsen Chevrolet for $6,400.85. During the first one and one-half months after the purchase, Peckham discovered that the car's hood was dented, its gas tank contained no baffles, its emergency brake was inoperable, the car did not have a jack or a spare tire, and neither the clock nor the speedometer worked. Larsen claimed that Peckham knew of the defects at the time of the purchase. Peckham, on the other hand, claimed that despite his repeated efforts, the defects were not repaired until June 11. Then, on July 15, the car's dashboard caught fire, leaving the car's interior damaged and the car itself inoperable. Peckham then returned to Larsen Chevrolet and told Larsen that Larsen had to repair the car at its own expense or that he, Peckham, would either rescind the contract or demand a new automobile. Peckham also claimed that at the end of their conversation, he notified Larsen Chevrolet that he was electing to rescind the contract and demanded the return of the purchase price. Larsen denied having received that oral notification. On October 12, Peckham sent a written notice of revocation of acceptance to Larsen. What are the rights of the parties?

13. Joc Oil bought a cargo of fuel oil for resale. The certificate from the foreign refinery stated the sulphur content of the oil was 0.5 percent. Joc Oil entered into a written contract with Con Ed (http://www.coned.com) for the sale of this oil. The contract specified a sulphur content of 0.5 percent. Joc Oil knew, however, that Con Ed was authorized to buy and burn oil of up to 1 percent sulphur content and that Con Ed often bought and mixed oils of varying contents to stay within this limit. The oil under contract was delivered to Con Ed, but independent testing revealed a sulphur content of 0.92 percent. Con Ed promptly rejected the nonconforming shipment. Joc Oil immediately offered to substitute a conforming shipment of oil, although the time for performance had expired after the first shipment of oil. Con Ed refused to accept the substituted shipment. Joc Oil sues Con Ed for breach of contract. Judgment?

14. The plaintiff, a German wine producer and exporter, contracted to ship 620 cases of wine to the defendant, a distributor in North Carolina. The contract was silent as to the

shipment destination. During the next several months, the defendant called repeatedly to find out the status of the shipment. Later, without notifying the defendant, the plaintiff delivered the wine to a shipping line in Rotterdam, destined for Wilmington, N.C. The ship and the wine were lost at sea en route to Wilmington. When the defendant refused to pay on the contract, the plaintiff sued. Decision?

15. Can-Key Industries, Inc., manufactured a turkey-hatching unit, which it sold to Industrial Leasing Corporation (ILC), which leased it to Rose-A-Linda Turkey Farms. ILC conditioned its obligation to pay on Rose-A-Linda's acceptance of the equipment. Rose-A-Linda indicated its dissatisfaction with the equipment, and ILC refused to perform its obligations under the contract. Can-Key then brought suit against ILC for breach of contract. It argued that Rose-A-Linda accepted the equipment, because it used it for fifteen months between March 1976 and May 1977. ILC countered that the equipment was unacceptable and asked that it be removed. It claimed that Can-Key refused and failed to instruct Rose-A-Linda to refrain from using the equipment. Therefore, ILC argued, Rose-A-Linda effectively rejected the turkey-hatching unit, relieving ILC of its contractual obligations. Who is correct? Explain.

16. Frederick Manufacturing Corp. (http://www.blount.com) ordered 500 dozen units of Import Traders' rubber pads for $2,580. The order indicated that the pads should be "as soft as possible." Import Traders delivered the rubber pads to Frederick Manufacturing on November 19. Frederick failed to inspect the goods upon delivery, even though the parties recognized that there might be a problem with the softness. Frederick finally complained about the nonconformity of the pads in April of the following year, when Import Traders requested the contract price for the goods. Can Import Traders recover the contract price from Frederick?

17. Neptune Research & Development, Inc. (the buyer) (http://www.nresearch.com), manufacturer of solar-operated valves used in scientific instruments, saw advertised in a trade journal a hole-drilling machine with a very high degree of accuracy, manufactured and sold by Teknics Industrial Systems, Inc. (the seller). Because the machine's specifications met the buyer's needs, the buyer contacted the seller in late March and ordered one of the machines to be delivered in mid-June. There was no "time-is-of-the-essence" clause in the contract.

Although the buyer made several calls to the seller throughout the month of June, the seller never delivered the machine and never gave the buyer any reasons for the nondelivery. By late August, the buyer desperately needed the machine. The buyer went to the seller's place of business to examine the machine and discovered that the still-unbuilt machine had been redesigned, omitting a particular feature that the buyer had wanted. Nonetheless, the buyer agreed to take the machine, and the seller promised that it would be ready on September 5. The seller also agreed to call the buyer on September 3 to give the buyer two days to arrange for transportation of the machine.

The seller failed to telephone the buyer on September 3 as agreed. On September 4 the buyer called the seller to find out the status of the machine and was told by the seller that "under no circumstances" could the seller have the machine ready by September 5. At this point, the buyer notified the seller that the order was canceled. One hour later, still on September 4, the seller called the buyer, retracted its earlier statement, and indicated that the machine would be ready by the agreed September 5 date. The buyer sued for the return of its $3,000 deposit. Should the buyer prevail? Explain.

http:// **Internet Exercise** Review the return policies of various sellers on the Internet.

CHAPTER 21

Transfer of Title and Risk of Loss

Aliud est possidere, aliud esse in possessione. *(It is one thing to possess; it is another to be in possession.)*

LEGAL MAXIM

Learning Objectives

After reading this chapter you should be able to:

1. Explain the relative importance of title under the common law and Article 2.
2. Explain when the seller has a right or power to transfer title and when the transfer is void or voidable.
3. Distinguish between a shipment contract and a destination contract and explain when title and risk of loss pass under each.
4. Identify and explain the rules covering (a) risk of loss in the absence of a breach and (b) risk of loss when there is a breach.
5. Explain how bulk transfers concern creditors and how the Uniform Commercial Code (UCC) attempts to regulate such transfers.

Historically, the principle of title governed nearly every aspect of the rights and duties of the buyer and seller arising from a sales contract. In an attempt to add greater precision and certainty to sales contracts, the UCC has abandoned the common law's reliance on title. Instead, the Code approaches each legal issue arising from a sales contract on its own merits and provides separate and specific rules to control various transactional situations. In this chapter, we will cover the Code's approach to the transfer of title and other property rights, the passage of risk of loss, and the transfer of goods sold in bulk.

CPA | TRANSFER OF TITLE

As previously stated, a sale of goods is defined as the transfer of title from the seller to the buyer for a consideration known as the price. Transfer of title is, therefore, fundamental to a sale of goods. Title, however, cannot pass under a contract for sale until existing goods have been identified as those to which the contract refers. Future goods (goods that are not both existing and identified) cannot constitute a present sale. If the buyer rejects the goods, whether justifiably or not, title revests to the seller.

In a lease, title does not pass. Instead, the lessee obtains the right to possess and use the goods for a period of time in return for consideration.

IDENTIFICATION

Identification is the designation of specific goods as goods to which the contract of sale refers. Identification may be made by either the seller or the buyer and may be made at any time and in any manner agreed upon by the parties. To illustrate, suppose Barringer contracts to purchase a particular Buick automobile from Stevenson's car lot. Identification occurs as soon as the parties enter the contract. If, however, Barringer agreed to purchase a television set from Stevenson, who has his storeroom filled with such televisions, identification will not occur until either Barringer or Stevenson selects a particular television to fulfill the contract. (Article 2A is similar.)

If the goods are **fungible** (the equivalent of any other unit), identification of a share of undivided goods occurs when the contract is entered into. Thus, if Barringer agreed to purchase 1,000 gallons of gasoline from Stevenson, who owns a 5,000 gallon tank of gasoline, identification occurs as soon as the contract is formed.

Security Interest The Code defines a **security interest** as an interest in personal property or fixtures that ensures payment or performance of an obligation. Any reservation by the seller of a title to goods *delivered* to the buyer is limited in effect to a reservation of a security interest. Security interests in goods are governed by Article 9 of the Code (discussed in Chapter 38).

Insurable Interest For a contract or policy of insurance to be valid, the insured must have an **insurable interest** in the subject matter. At common law, only a person with title or a **lien** (a legal claim of a creditor on property) could insure his interest in specific goods. The Code extends an insurable interest to a buyer's interest in goods that have been identified as goods to which the contract refers. (Article 2A.) This ***special property interest*** of the buyer, which arises upon identification, enables her to purchase insurance protection on goods that she does not presently own but will own upon delivery by the seller. The seller also has an insurable interest in the goods, as long as he has title to them or any security interest in them. In a lease, the lessor retains an insurable interest in the goods until an option to buy, if included in the lease, has been exercised by the lessee.

PASSAGE OF TITLE

Title passes when the parties *intend* it to pass, provided the goods are in existence and have been identified. When the parties have no explicit agreement as to transfer of title, the Code provides rules that determine when title passes to the buyer.

Physical Movement of the Goods When delivery is to be made by moving the goods, title passes at the time and place the seller completes his performance with reference to delivery of the goods. When and where delivery occurs depends on whether the contract is a shipment contract or a destination contract.

A **shipment contract** requires or authorizes the seller to send the goods to the buyer but does not require the seller to deliver them to a particular destination. Under a shipment contract, title passes to the buyer at the time and place the seller delivers the goods to the carrier for shipment to the buyer.

A **destination contract** requires the seller to deliver the goods to a particular destination. Under a destination contract, title passes to the buyer on tender of the goods at that destination. **Tender**, as discussed in Chapter 20, requires that the seller, at a reasonable time, (1) put and hold conforming goods at the buyer's disposition, (2) give notice to the buyer that the goods are available, and (3) keep the goods available for a reasonable period of time.

No Movement of the Goods When delivery is to be made without moving the goods, unless otherwise agreed, title passes (a) on delivery of a document of title, when the contract calls for delivery of such document (documents of title are documents that evidence a right to receive specified goods; they are discussed more fully in Chapter 49) or (b) at the time and place of contracting, if the goods at that time have been identified by either the seller or the buyer as the goods to which the contract refers and no documents are to be delivered. When the goods are not identified at the time of contracting, title passes when the goods are identified.

POWER TO TRANSFER TITLE

It is important to understand under what circumstances a seller has the right or **power to transfer title** to a buyer. If the seller is the rightful owner of goods or is authorized to sell the goods for the rightful owner, the seller has the ***right*** to transfer title. But when a seller possesses goods that he neither owns nor has authority to sell, the sale is not rightful. In some situations, however, unauthorized sellers may have the ***power*** to transfer good title to certain buyers. This section pertains to such sales by a person in possession of goods that he neither owns nor has authority to sell.

The rule of property law protecting existing ownership of goods is the starting point for any discussion of a sale of goods by a nonowner. One of the law's most basic tenets, expressly stated in the Code, is that a purchaser of goods obtains such title as his transferor had or had power to transfer. (Article 2A.) Likewise, the purchaser of a limited interest in goods acquires rights only to the extent of the interest that he purchased. By the same token, no one can transfer what he does not have. A purported sale by a thief or finder or ordinary bailee of goods does not transfer title to the purchaser.

The principal reason underlying the policy of the law in protecting existing ownership of goods is that a person should not be required to retain possession at all times of all the goods that he owns to maintain ownership of them. One valuable incident of the ownership of goods is the freedom of the owner to make a bailment of his goods as desired; the mere possession of goods by a bailee does not authorize the bailee to sell them.

Another legal policy conflicts, however, with the policy protecting existing ownership of goods; this latter protection, the protection of the good faith purchaser, is based on the importance in trade and commerce of ensuring the security of good faith transactions in goods. To encourage and make secure good faith acquisitions of goods, *bona fide* (good faith) purchasers for value must be protected under certain circumstances. A **good faith purchaser** is defined as one who acts honestly, gives value, and takes the goods without notice or knowledge of any defect in the title of the transferor.

Practical Advice

Be sure you give value and act honestly so as to obtain the protection the law grants a good faith purchaser.

Void and Voidable Title to Goods A **void title** is no title. A person claiming ownership of goods by an agreement that is void obtains no title to the goods. Thus, a thief or a finder of goods or a person who acquires goods from someone under physical duress or under guardianship has no title to them and can transfer none.

A **voidable title** is one acquired under circumstances that permit the former owner to rescind the transfer and revest herself with title, as in the case of mistake, common duress, undue influence, fraud in the inducement, misrepresentation, mistake, or sale by a person without contractual capacity (other than an individual under guardianship). In these situations, the buyer has acquired legal title to the goods, which may be divested by action of the seller. If, however, the buyer were to resell the goods to a good faith purchaser for value, before the seller has rescinded the transfer of title, the right of rescission in the seller is cut off, and the good faith purchaser acquires good title. The Code defines **good faith** as "honesty in fact in the conduct or transaction concerned" and value to include a consideration sufficient to support a simple contract.

The distinction between a void and voidable title is, therefore, extremely important in determining the rights of good faith purchasers of goods. The good faith purchaser always believes that she is buying the goods from the owner or from one with authority to sell. Otherwise, she would not be acting in good faith. In each situation, the party selling the goods appears to be the owner, whether his title is valid, void, or voidable. Given a case involving two innocent persons—the true owner who has done nothing wrong and the good faith purchaser who has done nothing wrong—the law will not disturb the legal title but will rule in favor of the one who has it. Thus, when A transfers possession of goods to B under such circumstances that B acquires no title or a void title, and B thereafter sells the goods to C, a good faith purchaser for value, B has nothing to transfer to C except possession. In a lawsuit between A and C involving the right to the goods, A will win because she has the legal title. (See Figure 21-1 for a diagram of void title.) C's only recourse is against B for breach of warranty of title, which we will discuss in Chapter 22. If, however, B acquired a voidable title from A and resold the goods to C, in a suit between A and C over the goods, C would win. In this case, B had title, though voidable, which she transferred to the good faith purchaser. The title thus acquired by C will be protected. The voidable title in B is title until it has been avoided, and, after transfer to a good faith purchaser, it may not be avoided. (See Figure 21-2 for a diagram of voidable title.) A's only recourse is against B for restitution or damages.

Figure 21-1
Void Title

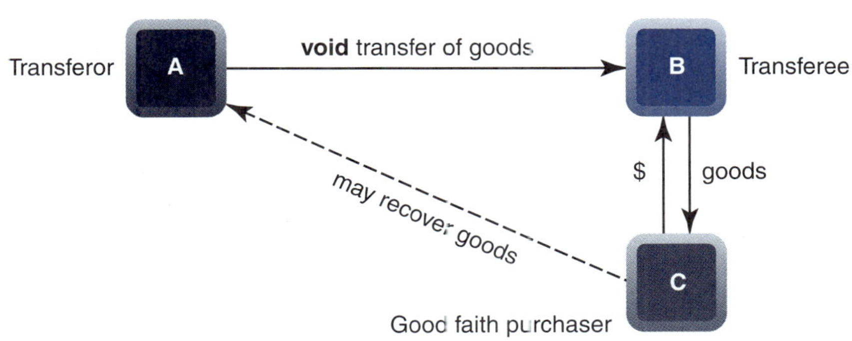

Figure 21-2
Voidable Title

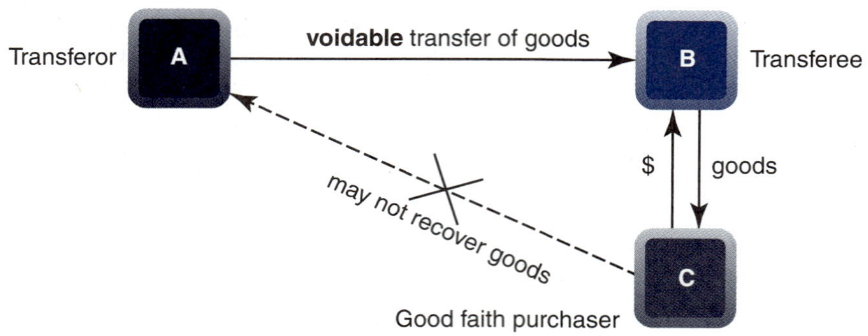

Robinson v. Durham

Alabama Court of Civil Appeals, 1988
537 So.2d 966

FACTS Mike Durham bought a used 1968 Chevrolet Camaro from Ronald and Wyman Robinson, owners of Friendly Discount Auto Sales. Unknown to either Durham or the Robinsons, the car had been stolen. In fact, when he first bought the car, Wyman Robinson had obtained tag receipts from what turned out to be the car thief and had subsequently registered the car in his name. Durham had received all prior documentation upon purchase of the car. However, the FBI seized the car from Durham and returned it to the original owner. Durham sued the Robinsons, alleging, among other things, breach of the warranty of title. The jury awarded Durham $5,200, the amount he had paid for the car. The Robinsons appealed.

DECISION Judgment for Durham.

OPINION Wright, J. Appellants assert that the grant of summary judgment was in error because there was "a scintilla of evidence, if not substantial evidence" from which the trial court could have concluded that appellants held good title "or at least voidable title" on the automobile, thereby conveying actual title to Durham at the time of the purchase.

Appellants' argument is without merit. It is unequivocable that "a person who has stolen goods of another cannot pass title thereto to another, whether such other knew, or did not know, that the goods were stolen." [Citations.] A thief gets only void title and without more cannot pass any title to a subsequent purchaser, even a good faith purchaser. [Citation.] It is undisputed that the automobile had been stolen. Therefore, at the time of purchase appellants obtained no title. In other words, the title was void. Appellants could not convey good title to Durham; therefore, the subsequent sale to Durham constituted a breach of warranty of good title.

Relying on § 2–403(1), [UCC], appellants contend that they at least acquired a voidable title when they purchased the automobile. Section 2–403 recognizes that a person with voidable title has power to transfer a good title to a good faith purchaser for value. Voidable title can only arise from a voluntary transfer, and the rightful owner must assent to the transfer. "A possessor of goods does not have voidable title unless the true owner has consented to the transfer of title to him." [Citation.] In this case the rightful owner did not consent or assent to the transfer of the automobile. Appellants obtained no title.

INTERPRETATION A void title is no title.

ETHICAL QUESTION Did either of the parties act unethically? Explain.

CRITICAL THINKING QUESTION Who should bear the loss between the Robinsons and Durham? Explain.

The Code has enlarged the common law voidable title doctrine by providing that a good faith purchaser for value obtains valid title from one possessing voidable title even if that person obtained voidable title by (1) fraud as to her identity; (2) exchange for a subsequently dishonored check; (3) an agreement that the transaction was to be a cash sale, and the sales price has not been paid; or (4) criminal fraud punishable as larceny. (Article 2A is similar.)

In addition, the Code has expanded the rights of good faith purchasers with respect to sales by ***minors***. Although the common law permitted a minor seller of goods to disaffirm the sale and to recover the goods from a third person who had purchased them in good faith from the party who had acquired the goods from the minor, the Code changed this rule by no longer permitting a minor seller to prevail over a good faith purchaser for value.

> **Practical Advice**
>
> A buyer should obtain a written express warranty that the seller has ownership of the property or the authority to transfer ownership.

Entrusting of Goods to a Merchant Frequently, an owner of goods entrusts (transfers possession of) goods to a bailee for resale, repair, or some other use. In some instances, the bailee violates this entrusting by selling the goods to a third party without the owner's permission or by keeping the proceeds of such a sale. Although the "true" owner has a right of recourse against the bailee for the value of the goods, what right, if any, should the true owner of the goods have against the third party? Once again, the law must balance the right of ownership against the rights of market transactions.

The Code protects buyers of goods in the ordinary course of business from merchants who deal in goods of that kind, when the owner has entrusted possession of the goods to the merchant. The Code defines **a buyer in the ordinary course of business** as a person who in good faith and without knowledge that the sale to him is in violation of the ownership rights or security interest of another buys the goods in the ordinary course of business from a person, other than a pawnbroker, in the business of selling goods of that kind. Because the merchant who deals in goods of that kind is cloaked with the appearance of ownership or apparent authority to sell, the Code seeks to protect the innocent third-party purchaser. Any such **entrusting** of possession bestows on the merchant the power to transfer all rights of the entruster to a buyer in the ordinary course of business. (Article 2A is similar.) For example, A brings his stereo for repair to B, who also sells both new and used stereo equipment. C purchases A's stereo from B in good faith and in the ordinary course of business. The Code protects the rights of C and defeats the rights of A, whose only recourse is against B.

The Code, however, does not go so far as to protect the buyer in the ordinary course of business from a merchant to whom the goods have been entrusted by a thief, a finder, or a completely unauthorized person. It merely grants the buyer in the ordinary course of business the rights of the entruster.

When a buyer of goods to whom title has passed leaves the seller in possession of the goods, the buyer has "entrusted the goods" to the seller. If that seller is a merchant and resells and delivers the goods to another buyer in the ordinary course of business, this second buyer acquires good title to the goods. Thus, Dennis sells certain goods to Sylvia, who pays the price but allows possession to remain with Dennis. Dennis thereafter sells the same goods to Karen, a buyer in the ordinary course of business. Karen takes delivery of the goods. Sylvia does not have any rights against Karen or to the goods. Sylvia's only remedy is against Dennis.

> **Practical Advice**
>
> Properly mark and identify goods you entrust to a merchant who is in the business of selling used goods of that type.

Heinrich v. Titus-Will Sales, Inc.

Court of Appeals of Washington, 1994
73 Wash.App. 147, 868 P.2d 169

FACTS In 1989, Michael Heinrich retained James Wilson to purchase a new Ford pickup truck for him. Wilson had held himself out as a dealer/broker, but unbeknownst to Heinrich, Wilson had lost his vehicle dealer license. Wilson negotiated with Titus-Will Ford Sales, Inc. (Titus-Will) to purchase the truck for Heinrich. Titus-Will had dealt with Wilson as a dealer before but also did not know that he had lost his dealer license. All payments for the truck went through Wilson, and the purchase order indicated that the truck was being sold to Wilson as a dealer for resale. Wilson agreed to deliver the truck to Heinrich at Titus-Will on Saturday, October 21, 1989. Wilson delivered to a clerk at Titus-Will a postdated check for the balance of the purchase price, which the clerk accepted, and in return delivered to Wilson a packet containing the keys to the truck, the owner's manual, an odometer disclosure statement, and the warranty card. The odometer statement showed that Wilson was the transferor and Titus-Will did not fill out the warranty card as the sale appeared to be dealer to dealer. Wilson's check, however, did not clear, and Titus-Will demanded the return of the truck. On November 6, Wilson picked up the truck from Heinrich, telling him he would have Titus-Will make certain repairs under the warranty, and returned the truck to Titus-Will. On November 9, 1989, Wilson admitted to Heinrich that he did not have funds to cover his check and that Titus-Will would not release the truck without payment. Heinrich then asked Titus-Will for the truck but was refused. Heinrich sued Titus-Will and Wilson, seeking return of the truck and damages for his loss of use. By pretrial arrangement, Heinrich regained possession of, but not clear title to, the truck. Heinrich also obtained a default order against Wilson. After a bench trial, the court awarded Heinrich title to the truck and $3,050 in damages for loss of its use. Titus-Will appeals.

DECISION Judgment affirmed.

OPINION Seinfeld, J.

The Entrustment Doctrine

[UCC] 2–403(2) and (3) contain the entrustment provisions of the Uniform Commercial Code (UCC).

* * *

To prevail under this statute, Heinrich must show 1) Titus-Will "entrusted" the truck to Wilson and, thus, empowered Wilson subsequently to transfer all rights of Titus-Will in the truck to Heinrich; 2) Wilson was a merchant dealing in automobiles; and 3) Heinrich bought the truck from Wilson as a "buyer in ordinary course of business." [Citations.]

Three general policies support [§]2–403(2), the UCC provision placing the risk of loss on the entruster. First, it protects the innocent buyer who, based on his observation of goods in the possession of a merchant of those goods, believes that the merchant has legal title to the goods and can, therefore, pass title in the goods to another. [Citation.] * * *

Secondly, the entrustment clause reflects the idea that the entruster is in a better position than the innocent buyer to protect against the risk that an intermediary merchant will not pay for or not deliver the goods. [Citations.]

Thirdly, the entrustment clause facilitates the flow of commerce by allowing purchasers to rely on a merchant's apparent legal right to sell the goods. [Citations.] Without the safeguards of the entrustment provision, a prudent buyer would have to delay the finalization of any sizeable sales transaction for the time necessary to research the merchant's ownership rights to the goods.

A. Entrusting The UCC * * * declares that "any delivery and any acquiescence in retention of possession" constitutes entrustment. 2–403(3). A person can entrust goods to a merchant by a variety of methods, such as consigning them, creating a bailment, taking a security interest in inventory, leaving them with the merchant after purchase, and delivering them for purposes of repair. [Citations.] A sale can also constitute an entrustment when some aspect of the transaction remains incomplete. [Citations.]

Titus-Will properly concedes that it entrusted the truck to Wilson. However, it argues Wilson was not a merchant and Heinrich was not a buyer in ordinary course. Further, Titus-Will contends that the timing of the entrusting deprived Wilson of the power to transfer its rights.

B. Merchant Titus-Will argues that Wilson was not a merchant because he had no inventory. However, it is not necessary to possess an inventory to fit within the broad statutory definition of merchant. Article 2 of the UCC defines (in part) "merchant" as "a person who deals in goods of the kind or otherwise by his occupation holds himself out as having knowledge or skill peculiar to the practices or goods involved in the transaction." 2–104(1). Wilson was a merchant who dealt in automobiles; he held himself out as a dealer in automobiles and appeared to be a dealer in automobiles. Both parties treated him as one. Titus-Will processed all the documents as it would for a dealer and understood that Wilson was buying the truck for resale.

Titus-Will also argues that Wilson was not a merchant because he did not have a vehicle dealer license. However, the UCC does not require proper state licensing for merchant status. 2–104(1), 2–403(2). * * *

C. Buyer in Ordinary Course There is also substantial evidence that Heinrich was a "buyer in ordinary course of business" although the trial court referred to him as a "good faith purchaser for value." A buyer in ordinary course of business is

> a person who in good faith and without knowledge that the sale to him is in violation of the ownership rights or security interest of a third party in the goods buys in ordinary course from a person in the business of selling goods of that kind[.] 1–201(9). "Buying" includes receiving goods * * * under a preexisting contract for sale." 1–201(9). Good faith is "honesty in fact in the conduct or transaction concerned." 1–201(19).

The amount of the consideration is significant as evidence of good faith. [Citation.] Heinrich gave substantial value for the truck, more than Wilson agreed to pay Titus-Will. Nor did Heinrich know or have a basis to believe that Wilson's sale and delivery of the truck to him violated Titus-Will's ownership or security interest rights. There was no showing that Heinrich acted other than in good faith. * * * Wilson's illegal and fraudulent activity does not taint Heinrich's status as a buyer under 2–403(2). * * *

D. Timing of Entrustment Titus-Will also argues that the UCC entrustment provisions should not apply because it entrusted the truck to Wilson *after* Heinrich had completely paid Wilson. This is an issue of first impression in this jurisdiction.

Before the completion of the Wilson-Heinrich sales transaction, Titus-Will entrusted Wilson not only with the truck, but also with the signed odometer disclosure statement, the owner's manual, the warranty card, and the keys. By doing so, Titus-Will clothed Wilson with additional indicia of ownership and with the apparent authority to transfer an ownership interest in the truck. It also enabled Wilson to complete the sales transaction. 2–401(2) ("Unless otherwise explicitly agreed title passes to the buyer at the time and place at which the seller completes his performance with reference to the physical delivery of the goods"). In addition, the entrustment allowed Wilson to continue to deceive Heinrich from October 21, 1989, the date of delivery of possession, to November 9, 1989, when Wilson finally admitted the truth. We believe that under these circumstances, application of the entrustment doctrine, 2–403(2), furthers the policy of protecting the buyer who relies on the merchant's apparent legal ability to sell goods in the merchant's possession.

The second rationale for the entrustment doctrine also supports its application here. Titus-Will, in the business of selling cars, was in a better position than Heinrich to protect itself against another dealer/broker who might fail to pay for the goods. It could have insured against the loss, and it could have adopted preventive procedures. * * *

The third rationale for the entrustment doctrine focuses on the flow of commerce. Here we consider the potential impact on commercial transactions of requiring purchasers to research their dealer/broker's legal title before accepting possession of the goods. Although the record contains no evidence on this issue, it seems obvious that this requirement would inevitably cause some delay. [Citation.]

Requiring the entruster to retain the burden of risk, even when the entrustment occurs after a third party purchaser gives value, supports the policies underlying the entrustment doctrine. * * *

INTERPRETATION A buyer in the ordinary course of business acquires good title when buying from a merchant seller who was entrusted with possession of the goods.

CRITICAL THINKING QUESTION Should Titus-Will be held responsible in this situation? Explain.

CPA RISK OF LOSS

Risk of loss, as the term is used in the law of sales, addresses the allocation of loss between seller and buyer when the goods have been damaged, destroyed, or lost without the fault of either the seller or the buyer. If the loss is placed on the buyer, he is under a duty to pay the price for the goods even though they were damaged or never received. If placed on the seller, she has no right to recover the purchase price from the buyer, although she does have a right to the return of the damaged goods.

CISG

Loss of or damage to the goods after the risk of loss has passed to the buyer does not discharge the buyer from his obligation to pay the purchase price.

In determining who has the risk of loss, the Code provides definite rules for specific situations—a sharp departure from the common law concept, which essentially determined risk of loss according to who had ownership of the goods and which depended on whether title had been transferred. The Code's transactional approach is necessarily detailed and for this reason is probably more understandable and meaningful than the common law's reliance on the abstract concept of title. The Code has adopted rules for determining the risk of loss in the absence of breach separate from those that apply where a breach of the sales contract has occurred.

Except in a finance lease, risk of loss is retained by the lessor and does not pass to the lessee. In a finance lease, risk of loss passes to the lessee as discussed later.

RISK OF LOSS WHERE THERE IS A BREACH

When one party breaches the contract, the Code places the risk of loss on that party, even though this allocation differs from the passage of risk of loss in the absence of a breach. Nevertheless, when the nonbreaching party is in control of the goods, the Code places the risk of loss on him to the extent of his insurance coverage.

Breach by the Seller If the seller ships to the buyer goods that do not conform to the contract, the risk of loss remains on the seller until the buyer has accepted the goods or until the seller has remedied the defect. (Article 2A.)

When the buyer has accepted nonconforming goods but thereafter by timely notice to the seller rightfully revokes his acceptance (discussed in Chapter 20), he may treat the risk of loss as resting from the beginning on the seller, to the extent of any deficiency in the buyer's effective insurance coverage. (Article 2A.) For example, Stuart delivers to Bernard nonconforming goods, which Bernard accepts. Subsequently, Bernard discovers a hidden defect in the goods and rightfully revokes his prior acceptance. If the goods are destroyed through no fault of either party, and Bernard has insured the goods for 60 percent of their fair market value of $10,000, then the insurance company will cover $6,000 of the loss and Stuart will cover the remainder, or $4,000. Had the buyer's insurance coverage been $10,000, Stuart would not bear any of the loss.

Breach by the Buyer When conforming goods have been identified to a contract that the buyer repudiates or breaches before risk of loss has passed to him, the seller may treat the risk of loss as resting on the buyer "for a commercially reasonable time" to the extent of any deficiency in the seller's effective insurance coverage. (Article 2A.) For example, Susan agrees to sell 40,000 pounds of plastic resin to Bella, F.O.B. Bella's factory, delivery by March 1. On February 1, Bella wrongfully repudiates the contract by telephoning Susan and telling her that she does not want the resin. Susan immediately seeks another buyer, but before she is able to locate one, and within a commercially reasonable time, the resin is destroyed by a fire through no fault of Susan's. The fair market value of the resin is $35,000. Because Susan's insurance covers only $15,000 of the loss, Bella is liable for $20,000.

RISK OF LOSS IN ABSENCE OF A BREACH

When there is no breach, the parties may allocate the risk of loss by agreement. Where there is no breach and the parties have not otherwise agreed, the Code places the risk of loss, for the most part, on the party who is more likely to have greater control over the goods, is more likely to insure the goods, or is better able to prevent the loss of the goods.

Agreement of the Parties The parties, by agreement, not only may shift the allocation of risk of loss but also may divide the risk between them. Such agreement is controlling. Thus, for example, the parties may agree that a seller shall retain the risk of loss even though the buyer is in possession of the goods or has title to them. Furthermore, the agreement may provide that the buyer bears 60 percent of the risk and that the seller bears 40 percent.

Practical Advice

Specify in your contract of sale how risk of loss should be allocated.

Trial Sales Some sales are made with the understanding that the buyer can return the goods even though they conform to the contract. These trial sales permit the buyer to try the goods for a period of time to determine if she wishes either to keep them or to try to resell them. The Code recognizes two types of trial sales—a sale on approval and a sale or return—and provides a test for distinguishing between them: unless otherwise agreed, if the goods are delivered primarily for the buyer's use, the transaction is a sale on approval; if they are delivered primarily for resale by the buyer, it is a sale or return.

In a **sale on approval**, possession of, but not title to, the goods is transferred to the buyer for a stated period of time. If no time is stated, the buyer may use the goods for a reasonable time to determine whether she wishes to accept them. Both title and risk of loss remain with the *seller* until the buyer "approves," or accepts, the goods. Until acceptance by the buyer, the sale is a bailment with an option to purchase.

Although use of the goods consistent with the purpose of approval by the buyer is not acceptance, the buyer's failure to notify the seller within a reasonable time of her election to return the goods *is* an acceptance. The buyer also may manifest approval by exercising any dominion or control over the goods inconsistent with the seller's ownership. On approval, title and risk of loss pass to the buyer, who then becomes liable to the seller for the purchase price of the goods. If, however, the buyer then decides to return the goods and so notifies the seller, the return is at the seller's risk and expense.

In a **sale or return**, the goods are sold and delivered to the buyer with an option to return them to the seller. The risk of loss is on the *buyer*, who has title until she revests it in the seller by returning the goods. The return of the goods is at the buyer's risk and expense.

A **consignment** is a delivery of possession of personal property to an agent for sale by the agent. Under the Code, a sale on consignment is regarded as a sale or return. Therefore, the creditors of the consignee (the agent who receives the merchandise for sale) prevail over the consignor and may obtain possession of the consigned goods, provided the consignee maintains a place of business where he deals in goods of the kind involved under a name other than the name of the consignor. Nevertheless, the consignor will prevail if she (a) complies with applicable state law requiring a consignor's interest to be evidenced by a sign, (b) establishes that the consignee is generally known by his creditors to be substantially engaged in selling the goods of others, or (c) complies with the filing provisions of Article 9 (Secured Transactions).

Contracts Involving Carriers Sales contracts frequently contain terms indicating the agreement of the parties as to delivery by a carrier. These terms identify the contract as a shipment contract or as a destination contract and, by implication, indicate the time at which the risk of loss passes. If the contract does not require the seller to deliver the goods to a particular destination but merely to the common carrier (a **shipment contract**), risk of loss passes to the buyer when the seller delivers the goods to the carrier. If the seller is required to deliver them to a particular destination (a **destination contract**), risk of loss passes to the buyer at destination when the goods are tendered to the buyer. (Article 2A.)

Practical Advice

Select the shipment term that passes the risk of loss when you desire it to pass.

CISG

If the sales contract involves the carriage of the goods and the seller is not obligated to hand them over at a particular destination, the risk of loss passes to the buyer when the goods are handed over to the first carrier. If the contract requires the seller to deliver the goods to a carrier at a particular destination, the risk of loss passes when the goods are handed over to the carrier at that place.

The following case deals with the question of when the risk of loss passes between parties whose sales contract contains no specific provision or any delivery term. The case demonstrates that if the contract is not clearly a destination contract or a shipment contract, the law assumes that it is a shipment contract.

Windows, Inc. v. Jordan Panel Systems Corp.

United States Court of Appeals, Second Circuit, 1999
177 F.3d 114
http://laws.findlaw.com/2nd/987603.html

FACTS Jordan Panel Systems, Inc (Jordan) ordered custom-made windows from Windows, Inc (Windows). The purchase contract provided that the windows were to be shipped properly packaged for cross country motor freight transit and "delivered to New York City." Windows constructed the windows according to Jordan's specifications and arranged to have them shipped to Jordan by a common carrier, Consolidated Freightways Corp. ("Consolidated"). Windows delivered them to Consolidated intact and properly packaged. During the course of shipment, however, the goods sustained extensive damage. Much of the glass was broken and many of the window frames were gouged and twisted. Jordan's president signed a delivery receipt noting that approximately two-thirds of the shipment was damaged due to "load shift." Jordan made a claim with Consolidated for damages it had sustained and also ordered a new shipment from Windows, which was delivered without incident. Jordan did not pay for either shipment of windows, and Windows brought suit. Jordan cross-claimed for incidental and consequential damages resulting from the damaged shipment. The parties resolved the claim by Windows, and the only issue that remains is Jordan's counter-claim. The district court granted Windows' motion for summary judgment on this matter. Jordan brings this appeal.

DECISION Judgment affirmed in favor of Windows.

OPINION Leval, J. Jordan seeks to recover incidental and consequential damages pursuant to [U.C.C.] § 2–715. Under that provision, Jordan's entitlement to recover incidental and consequential damages depends on whether those damages "result[ed] from the seller's breach." A destination contract is covered by [U.C.C.] § 2–503(3); it arises where "the seller is required to deliver at a particular destination." In contrast, a shipment contract arises where "the seller is required * * * to send the goods to the buyer and the contract does not require him to deliver them at a particular destination." [U.C.C.] § 2–504. Under a shipment contract, the seller must "put the goods in the possession of such a carrier and make such a contract for their transportation as may be reasonable having regard to the nature of the goods and other circumstances of the case." [U.C.C.] § 2–504(a). * * *

Where the terms of an agreement are ambiguous, there is a strong presumption under the U.C.C. favoring shipment contracts.

Unless the parties "expressly specify" that the contract requires the seller to deliver to a particular destination, the contract is generally construed as one for shipment. [Citations.]

Jordan's confirmation of its purchase order, by letter to Windows dated September 22, 1993, provided, "All windows to be shipped properly crated/packaged/boxed suitable for cross country motor freight transit and delivered to New York City." We conclude that this was a shipment contract rather than a destination contract. To overcome the presumption favoring shipment contracts, the parties must have explicitly agreed to impose on Windows the obligation to effect delivery at a particular destination. The language of this contract does not do so. Nor did Jordan use any commonly recognized industry term indicating that a seller is obligated to deliver the goods to the buyer's specified destination.

Under the terms of its contract, Windows thus satisfied its obligations to Jordan when it put the goods, properly packaged, into the possession of the carrier for shipment. Upon Windows' proper delivery to the carrier, Jordan assumed the risk of loss, and cannot recover incidental or consequential damages from the seller caused by the carrier's negligence.

This allocation of risk is confirmed by the terms of [U.C.C.] § 2–509(1)(a), entitled "Risk of Loss in the Absence of Breach." It provides that where the contract "does not require [the seller] to deliver [the goods] at a particular destination, the risk of loss passes to the buyer when the goods are duly delivered to the carrier." [U.C.C.] § 2–509(1)(a). As noted earlier, Jordan does not contest the court's finding that Windows duly delivered conforming goods to the carrier. Accordingly, as Windows had already fulfilled its contractual obligations at the time the goods were damaged and Jordan had assumed the risk of loss, there was no "seller's breach" as is required for a buyer to claim incidental and consequential damages under [U.C.C.] § 2–715.

INTERPRETATION Unless specifically designated as a destination contract, a sales contract that involves shipment by a carrier is a shipment contract.

ETHICAL QUESTION Did the court fairly decide this case? Explain

CRITICAL THINKING QUESTION What factors should be taken into consideration in deciding whether a contract is a shipment or a destination contract? Explain.

Goods in Possession of Bailee In some sales, the goods, at the time the contract is made, are held by a bailee and are to be delivered without being moved. For instance, a seller may contract with a buyer to sell grain that is located in a grain elevator and that the buyer intends to leave in the same elevator. In such situations, the time at which the risk of loss passes to the buyer depends on the document of title involved—or, as the case may be, on whether the transaction involves such a document at all (1) if a negotiable document of title (discussed in Chapter 49) is involved, the risk of loss passes when the buyer *receives* the document; (2) if a nonnegotiable document of title is involved, the risk passes when the document is *tendered* to the buyer; (3) if no documents of title are employed, it passes either (a) when the seller *tenders* to the buyer written directions to the bailee to deliver the goods to the buyer or (b) when the bailee acknowledges the buyer's right to possession of the goods. (Article 2A.)

In situations 2 and 3a, if the buyer seasonably objects, the risk of loss remains upon the seller until the buyer has had a reasonable time to present the document or direction to the bailee.

CISG

If the buyer is bound to take over the goods at a place other than the seller's place of business, the risk of loss passes when the buyer is aware of the fact that the goods are placed at her disposal at that location.

All Other Sales If the buyer possesses the goods when the contract is formed, risk of loss passes to the buyer at that time. (Article 2A.)

All other sales not involving breach are covered by the Code's catchall provision, which applies to those instances in which the buyer picks up the goods at the seller's place of business or those in which the seller delivers the goods using her own transportation. In these cases, risk of loss depends on whether the seller is a merchant. If the seller is a ***merchant***, risk of loss passes to the buyer on the buyer's receipt of the goods. If the seller is ***not a merchant***, it passes on tender of the goods from the seller to the buyer. (Article 2A.) The policy behind this rule is that so long as the merchant seller is making delivery at her place of business or with her own vehicle, she continues to control the goods and can be expected to insure them. The buyer, on the other hand, has no control over the goods and is not likely to have insurance on them.

Suppose Ted goes to Jack's furniture store, selects a particular set of dining room furniture, and pays Jack the agreed price of $800 on Jack's agreement to stain the set a darker color and to deliver it. Jack stains the furniture and notifies Ted that he will deliver it the next day. That night, the furniture is accidentally destroyed by fire. Ted can recover the $800 payment from Jack. The risk of loss is on the seller, Jack, because he is a merchant and the goods were not received by Ted but were only tendered to him.

On the other hand, suppose Debra, an accountant, having moved to a different city, contracts to sell her household furniture to Dwight for $3,000 by a written agreement signed by Dwight. Though she notifies Dwight that the furniture is available for Dwight to pick up, he delays picking it up for several days; in the interim, the furniture is stolen from Debra's residence through no fault of Debra's. Debra may recover the $3,000 purchase price from Dwight. The risk of loss is on the buyer, Dwight, because, as the seller, Debra, is not a merchant, tender is sufficient to transfer the risk of loss.

CISG

If the sales contract does not involve the carriage of the goods, the risk of loss passes to the buyer when he takes over the goods, or, if the buyer does not take over the goods in due time, from the time when the goods are placed at his disposal.

Martin v. Melland's Inc.

Supreme Court of North Dakota, 1979
283 N.W.2d 76

FACTS Martin entered into a written agreement with Melland's, Inc., a farm implement dealer, to purchase a truck and attached haystack mover. According to the contract, Martin was to trade in his old truck and haystack mover unit, to mail or bring the certificate of title to the old unit to Melland's within a week, and to retain the use and possession of the old unit until Melland's had the new one ready. The contract contained no provision allocating the risk of loss of the trade-in unit. After Martin mailed the certificate to Melland's, but while he still had possession of the trade-in unit itself, the unit was destroyed by fire. Martin then sued to compel Melland's to bear the loss of the trade-in, claiming that title had passed to Melland's before the destruction of the old unit. The district court dismissed the cause of action, and Martin appealed.

DECISION Judgment for Melland's Inc. affirmed.

OPINION Erickstad, C. J. Thus the concept of title under the U.C.C. is of decreased importance. * * * No longer is the question of title of any importance in determining whether a buyer or seller bears the risk of loss.

* * *

Thus, the question of this case is not answered by a determination of the location of title, but by the risk of loss provisions in [U.C.C. § 2–509]. Before addressing the risk of loss question in conjunction with [U.C.C. § 2–509], it is necessary to determine the posture of the parties with regard to the trade-in unit, i.e., who is the buyer and the seller and how are the responsibilities allocated. It is clear that a barter or trade-in is considered a sale and is therefore subject to the Uniform Commercial Code. [Citations.] It is also clear that the party who owns the trade-in is considered the seller. [U.C.C. § 2–304], provides that the "price can be made payable in money or otherwise. If it is payable in whole or in part in goods each party is a seller of the goods which he is to transfer." [Citations.]

Martin argues that he had already sold the trade-in unit to Melland's and, although he retained possession, he did so in the capacity of a bailee (apparently pursuant to [U.C.C. § 2–509(2)]). White and Summers in their hornbook on the Uniform Commercial Code argue that the seller who retains possession should not be considered a bailee within Section 2–509.

* * *

The courts that have addressed this issue have agreed with White and Summers. [Citations.]

It is undisputed that the contract did not require or authorize shipment by carrier pursuant to Section [2–509(1)]; therefore, the residue section, subsection 3, is applicable:

> In any case not within subsection 1 or 2, the risk of loss passes to the buyer on his receipt of the goods if the seller is a merchant; otherwise the risk passes to the buyer on tender of delivery.

Martin admits that he is not a merchant; therefore, it is necessary to determine if Martin tendered delivery of the trade-in unit to Melland's.

* * *

It is clear that the trade-in unit was not tendered to Melland's in this case. The parties agreed that Martin would keep the old unit "until they had the new one ready."

* * *

We hold that Martin did not tender delivery of the trade-in truck and haystack mover to Melland's pursuant to [U.C.C. § 2–509]; consequently, Martin must bear the loss.

INTERPRETATION In a sale involving a nonmerchant seller, the risk of loss stays with the seller until the goods are tendered to the buyer.

ETHICAL QUESTION Did the court fairly decide this case? Explain.

CRITICAL THINKING QUESTION When should risk of loss pass in this type of situation? Explain.

See Figure 21-3 for an illustration of risk of loss in the absence of breach. See also the following Ethical Dilemma.

CPA BULK SALES

A sale of goods in bulk occurs when a merchant sells all or a major portion of his inventory at once. Creditors have an

Ethical Dilemma

Who Should Bear the Loss?

FACTS Stratton Corporation, a regional pharmaceutical company located in Smithville, has embarked on a policy that encourages its employees to become computer literate. Accordingly, it has made a deal with BMI, a computer manufacturer, to have computers available for purchase by Stratton's employees at considerable savings from the standard retail price. The computers, which Stratton purchases in bulk, are delivered to the home office in Smithville.

The state in which Smithville is located imposes a 7 percent sales tax on any sale that takes place in the state. For state tax purposes, the place of sale is the point of delivery. To help reduce the costs to its employees, Stratton has arranged for its personnel to pick up their purchased computers at its Somerton office, located about 25 miles from Smithville in a neighboring state that does not impose a sales tax.

Arthur Johnson, a Stratton employee, took advantage of the offer and purchased a computer through Stratton on December 1, 1992. The computer arrived in Smithville on December 18, 1992, and was immediately placed on a Stratton pickup truck for transfer to Somerton. Johnson, however, wanting the computer home by Christmas, suggested that he put the unit in his car and deliver it to Somerton himself, where he would immediately pick it up. Stratton, seeing a chance to save time and money, agreed to the suggestion.

On December 19, 1992, in a heavy snowfall, Johnson left Smithville with the computer bound for Somerton. As he turned onto the highway, the snowfall became a whiteout. Hearing on his car radio that blizzard conditions had already made the roads into Somerton impassable, Johnson brought the computer to his home, planning to hold it there until he could deliver it to Somerton. On the night of December 21, 1992, when snow still blocked the Somerton roads, the Johnson home and many of its furnishings were destroyed by fire. Unfortunately, Johnson had no fire insurance at the time. The computer was among the items that were destroyed. Stratton refused to accept the loss on the computer and demanded that Johnson pay for it in full. Johnson refuses.

SOCIAL, POLICY, AND ETHICAL CONSIDERATIONS

1. From a legal standpoint, who must bear the risk of loss for the computer? From an ethical standpoint, who should bear the loss?
2. What social responsibility did Stratton violate in setting up the computer delivery scheme? Did it have a legitimate reason for implementing the plan?
3. Do cost savings ever give a business the right to violate a social or ethical responsibility?
4. Are there any similarities between Stratton's actions in this case and a company's decision to close one of its plants?

Figure 21-3 *Passage of Risk of Loss in Absence of Breach*

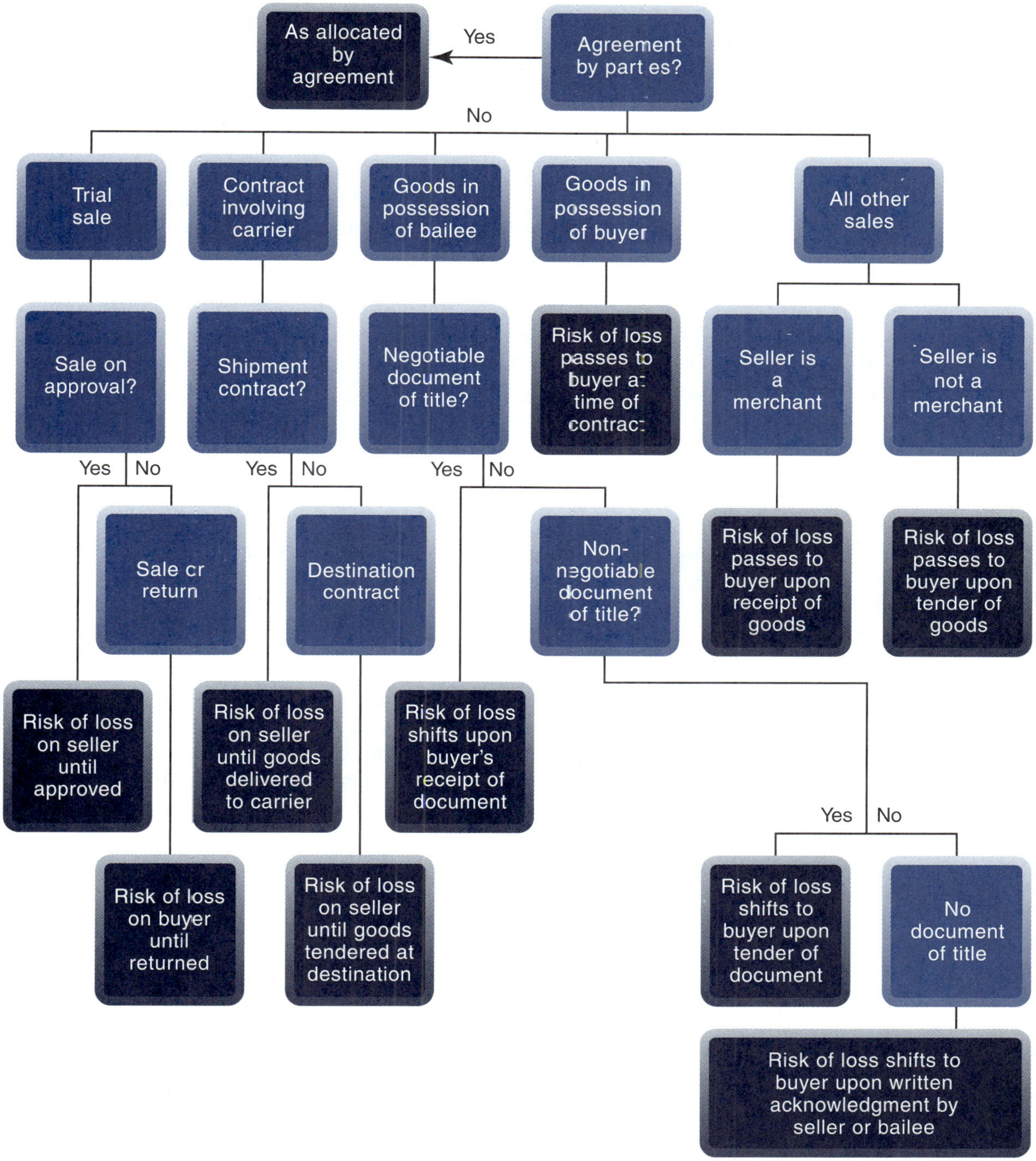

obvious interest in such a bulk disposal of merchandise made not in the ordinary course of business, for a debtor may secretly liquidate all or a major part of his tangible assets by a bulk sale and conceal or divert the proceeds of the sale without paying his creditors. The central purpose of bulk sales law is to deter two common forms of commercial fraud. These occur (a) when the merchant, owing debts, sells out his stock in trade to a friend for a low price, pays his creditors less than he owes them, and hopes to come back into the business "through the back door" sometime in the future; and (b) when the merchant, owing debts, sells out his stock in trade to anyone for any price, pockets the proceeds, and disappears without paying his creditors.

Article 6 of the Code, which applies to such sales, defines a **bulk transfer** as "any transfer in bulk and not in the ordinary course of the transferor's business of a major part of the materials, supplies, merchandise, or other inventory." The transfer of a substantial part of equipment is a bulk transfer only if made in connection with a bulk transfer of inventory. Those subject to Article 6 of the Code are merchants whose principal business is the sale of merchandise from stock, including those who manufacture what they sell.

The Code provides that a bulk transfer of assets is ineffective against any creditor of the transferor, unless the transfer meets certain Article 6 requirements designed to give the creditor notice of the bulk transfer. Should the transferor fail to comply with these requirements, the goods in the possession of the transferee continue to be subject to the claims of the transferor's unpaid creditors.

In 1988, the National Conference of Commissioners on Uniform State Laws and the American Law Institute jointly issued a recommendation stating "that changes in the business and legal contexts in which sales are conducted have made regulation of bulk sales unnecessary." They therefore recommended the repeal of Article 6 or, for those states that felt the need to continue the regulation of bulk sales, the adoption of a revised Article 6 designed to afford better protection to creditors while minimizing the obstacles to good faith transactions. More than two-thirds of the states have repealed Article 6; only a few states have adopted Revised Article 6.

CHAPTER SUMMARY

Transfer of Title

Identification designation of specific goods as goods to which the contract of sale refers
- ***Security Interest*** an interest in personal property or fixtures that ensures payment or performance of an obligation
- ***Insurable Interest*** buyer obtains an insurable interest and specific remedies in the goods by the identification of existing goods as goods to which the contract of sale refers

Passage of Title title passes when the parties intend it to pass; when the parties do not specifically agree, the Code provides rules to determine when title passes
- ***Physical Movement of the Goods*** when delivery is to be made by moving the goods, title passes at the time and place where the seller completes his performance with reference to delivery
- ***No Movement of the Goods***

Power to Transfer Title the purchaser of goods obtains such title because his transferor either has or had the power to transfer; however, to encourage and make secure good faith acquisitions of goods, it is necessary to protect certain third parties under certain circumstances
- ***Void Title*** no title can be transferred
- ***Voidable Title*** the good faith purchaser acquires good title
- ***Entrusting of Goods to a Merchant*** buyers in the ordinary course of business acquire good title when buying from merchants

Risk of Loss

Definition allocation of loss between seller and buyer when the goods have been damaged, destroyed, or lost without the fault of either party

Risk of Loss Where There Is a Breach
- ***Breach by the Seller*** if the seller ships to the buyer goods that do not conform to the contract, the risk of loss remains on the seller until the buyer has accepted the goods or until the seller has remedied the defect
- ***Breach by the Buyer*** the seller may treat the risk of loss as resting on the buyer for a commercially reasonable time to the extent of any deficiency in the seller's effective insurance coverage

Risk of Loss in Absence of a Breach

- ***Agreement of the Parties*** the parties may by agreement allocate the risk of loss
- ***Trial Sales*** unless otherwise agreed, if the goods are delivered primarily for the buyer's use, the transaction is a sale on approval (risk of loss remains with the seller until "approval" or acceptance of the goods by the buyer); if they are delivered primarily for resale by the buyer, it is a sale or return (the risk of loss is on the buyer until she returns the goods)
- ***Contracts Involving Carriers*** in shipment contracts, the seller bears the risk of loss and expense until the goods are delivered to the carrier for shipment; in destination contracts, the seller bears the risk of loss and expense until tender of the goods at a particular destination
- ***Goods in Possession of Bailee***
- ***All Other Sales*** for merchant seller, risk of loss passes to buyer on the buyer's receipt of the goods; for nonmerchant seller, risk of loss passes to buyer upon tender of goods

Bulk Sales

Definition a transfer, not in the ordinary course of the transferor's business, of a major part of inventory

Requirements of Article 6 transfer is ineffective against any creditor of the transferor, unless certain requirements are met

QUESTIONS

1. Stein, a mechanic, and Beal, a life insurance agent, entered into a written contract for the sale of Stein's tractor to Beal for $2,800 cash. It was agreed that Stein would tune the motor on the tractor. Stein fulfilled this obligation and on the night of July 1 telephoned Beal that the tractor was ready to be picked up on Beal's making payment. Beal responded, "I'll be there in the morning with the money." On the next morning, however, Beal was approached by an insurance prospect and decided to get the tractor at a later date. On the night of July 2, the tractor was destroyed by fire of unknown origin. Neither Stein nor Beal had any fire insurance. Who must bear the loss?

2. Regan received a letter from Chase, the material portion of which stated, "Chase hereby places an order with you for fifty cases of Red Top Tomatoes. Ship them C.O.D." As soon as he received the letter, Regan shipped the tomatoes to Chase. While en route, the railroad car carrying the tomatoes was wrecked. When Chase refused to pay for the tomatoes, Regan started an action to recover the purchase price. Chase defended on the ground that because the shipment was C.O.D., neither title to the tomatoes nor risk of loss passed until their delivery to Chase. Who has title? Who has the risk of loss? Explain.

3. On May 10, the Adair Company, acting through Brown, entered into a contract with Clark for the installation of a milking machine at Clark's farm. Following the enumeration of the articles to be furnished, together with the price of each article, the written contract provided: "This machinery is subject to thirty days' free trial and is to be installed about June 1." Within thirty days after installation, all the purchased machinery, except for a double utility unit, was destroyed by fire through no fault of Clark's. The Adair Company sued Clark to recover the value of the articles destroyed. Explain who bears the risk of loss.

4. Brown contracted to buy sixty cases of Lovely Brand canned corn from Smith, a Toledo seller, at a contract price of $600. Based on the contract, Smith selected and set aside sixty cases of Lovely Brand canned corn and tagged them "For Brown." The contract required Smith to ship the corn to Brown via T Railroad, F.O.B. Toledo. Before Smith delivered the corn to the railroad, the sixty cases were stolen from Smith's warehouse.
   a. Who is liable for the loss of the sixty cases of corn, Brown or Smith?
   b. Suppose Smith had delivered the corn to the railroad in Toledo. After the corn was loaded on a freight car but before the train left the yard, the car was broken open and its contents, including the corn, were stolen. Who is liable for the loss, Brown or Smith?
   c. Would your answer in Question 4(b) be the same if this contract were F.O.B. Brown's warehouse, and all other facts remained the same?

5. Farber owned a quantity of corn that was stored in a corncrib located on Farber's farm. On March 12, Farber wrote a letter to Barber stating that he would sell to Barber all of the corn in this crib, which he estimated at between 900 and 1,000 bushels, for $3.60 per bushel. Barber received this letter on March 13, and on the same day immediately wrote

and mailed a letter to Farber stating that he would buy the corn. The corncrib and contents were accidentally destroyed by a fire that broke out about 3 a.m. on March 14. What are the rights of the parties? What difference, if any, in result would there be if Farber were a merchant?

6. Franco, a New York dealer, purchased twenty-five barrels of specially graded and packed apples from a producer at Hood River, Oregon. He afterward resold the apples to Harris under a contract that specified an agreed price on delivery at Harris's place of business in New York. The apples were shipped to Franco from Oregon but, through no fault of either Franco or Harris, were totally destroyed before reaching New York. Does any liability rest on Franco?

7. Smith was approached by a man who introduced himself as Brown of Brown & Co. Smith, who did not know Brown, asked Dun & Bradstreet for a credit report on Brown. He thereupon sold Brown some expensive gems and billed Brown & Co. "Brown" turned out to be a clever jewel thief, who later sold the gems to Brown & Co. for valuable consideration. Brown & Co. was unaware of "Brown's" transaction with Smith. Can Smith successfully sue Brown & Co. for either the return of the gems or the price as billed to Brown & Co.?

8. Charlotte, the owner of a new Cadillac automobile, agreed to loan the car to Ellen for the month of February while she (Charlotte) went to Florida for a winter vacation. It was understood that Ellen, who was a small-town Cadillac dealer, would merely place Charlotte's car in her showroom for exhibition and sales promotion purposes. While Charlotte was away, Ellen sold the car to Bob. When Charlotte returned from Florida, she sued to recover the car from Bob. Who has title to the automobile? Explain.

9. Steven offered to sell his used automobile to Benito for $2,600 cash. Benito agreed to buy the car, gave Steven a check for $2,600, and drove away in the car. The next day, Benito sold the car for $3,000 to José, a good faith purchaser. The bank returned Benito's $2,600 check to Steven because of insufficient funds in Benito's account. Steven brings an action against José to recover the automobile. What is the judgment?

10. Justin told Jennifer he wished to buy Jennifer's automobile. He drove the car for about ten minutes, returned to Jennifer, stated he wanted to take the automobile to show it to his wife, and then left with the automobile and never returned. Justin sold the automobile in another state to Thomas and gave him a bill of sale. Can Jennifer recover the automobile from Thomas? Explain.

11. On February 7, Pillsbury purchased 8,000 bushels of wheat from Landis. The wheat was being stored at the Greensville Grain Company. Pillsbury also intended to store the wheat with Greensville. On February 10, the wheat was destroyed. Landis demands payment for the wheat from Pillsbury. Who prevails? Who has title? Who has the risk of loss? Explain.

12. Johnson, who owns a hardware store, was indebted to Hutchinson, one of his suppliers. Johnson sold his business to Lockhart, one of Johnson's previous competitors. Lockhart combined the inventory from Johnson's store with his own and moved the combined inventory to a new, larger store. Hutchinson claims that Lockhart must pay Johnson's debt because the sale of the business had been made without complying with the requirements of the bulk sales law. Discuss whether Lockhart is obligated to pay Hutchinson's debt to Johnson.

13. A seller had manufactured 40,000 pounds of plastic resin pellets specially for a buyer, who agreed to accept them at the rate of 1,000 pounds per day upon his issuance of shipping instructions. Despite numerous requests by the seller, the buyer issued no such instructions. On August 18, the seller, after warehousing the goods for forty days, demanded by letter that the buyer issue instructions. The buyer agreed to issue them beginning August 20, but never did. On September 22, a fire destroyed the seller's plant containing the goods, which were not covered by insurance. Who bears the risk of loss? Why?

14. McCoy, an Oklahoma cattle dealer, orally agreed with Chandler, a Texas cattle broker, to ship cattle to a New Mexico feedlot for delivery to Chandler. The agreement was for six lots of cattle valued at $119,000. After McCoy delivered the cattle, he presented invoices to Chandler that described the cattle and set forth the sales price. McCoy then demanded payment, which Chandler refused. Unknown to McCoy, Chandler had obtained a loan from First National Bank and had pledged the subject cattle as collateral. The bank had no knowledge of any interest that McCoy may have had in the cattle. McCoy sued to recover the cattle. The bank counterclaimed that it had a perfected security interest in the cattle that was superior to any interest of McCoy's. Who has title to the cattle? Explain.

CASE PROBLEMS

15. Porter, the owner of a collection of artworks, had a number of art transactions with Harold Von Maker, who used, among other names, that of Peter Wertz. Porter permitted Von Maker to temporarily have a painting by Maurice Utrillo, *Chateau de Lion-sur-Mer*, to hang in his home until he decided whether to purchase it. A few months later, Porter sought the return of the Utrillo painting but was unable to reach Von Maker. Porter subsequently discovered that he was not dealing with the "real" Peter Wertz but with Harold Von Maker, a man with an extensive criminal

record, including a conviction for defrauding the Chase Manhattan Bank. When Porter finally reached him, Von Maker claimed the Utrillo was on consignment with a client. Von Maker then agreed in writing either to return the painting to Porter within ninety days or to make compensation for it. At the time he entered this agreement, Von Maker had already sold the painting. He had used the real Peter Wertz, a delicatessen employee and acquaintance, to effect the sale of the Utrillo to Feigen for $20,000. Feigen, an art dealer, then sold the painting to Brenner, and it is now somewhere in Venezuela. Can Porter recover possession of either the Utrillo or its value? Explain.

16. Home Indemnity, an insurance company, paid one of its insureds after the theft of his car. The car reappeared in another state and was sold to Michael Schrier for $4,300 by a used car dealer. The dealer promised to give Mr. Schrier a certificate of title. One month later, the car was seized by the police on behalf of Home Indemnity. Explain who is entitled to possession of the car.

17. Fred Lane, who sells boats, motors, and trailers, sold a boat, motor, and trailer to John Willis in exchange for a check for $6,285.00. The check was not honored when Lane attempted to use the funds. Willis subsequently left the boat, motor, and trailer with John Garrett, who sold the items to Jimmy Honeycutt for $2,500.00. Honeycutt was surprised at how inexpensive the boat was, considering its quality. He did not know where Garrett got the boat, but he had dealt with Garrett before and described him as a "sly businessman." Garrett did not sell boats; normally, he sold fishing tackle and provisions. Honeycutt also received a forged certificate for the boat, on which he had observed Garrett forge the purported owner's signature. Can Lane compel Honeycutt to return the boat, motor, and trailer? Explain.

18. Mike Moses purchased a mobile home, including installation, from Gary Newman. Newman delivered the home to Moses's lot. Upon inspection of the home, Moses's fiancée found a broken window and water pipe. Moses also had not received keys to the front door. Before Newman corrected these problems, a windstorm destroyed the home. Who bears the risk for the loss of the home? Why?

19. United Road Machinery Company, a dealer in heavy road equipment (including truck scales supplied by Thurman Scale Company), received a telephone call on July 21 from James Durham, an officer of Consolidated Coal Company, seeking to acquire truck scales for his coal mining operation. United and Consolidated entered into a twenty-four-month lease-purchase agreement. United then notified Thurman that Consolidated would take possession of the scales directly. United paid for the scales and Consolidated took possession of them, but the latter never signed and returned the contract papers forwarded to it by United. Consolidated also never made any of the rental payments ($608/month) due under the lease. On September 20, Consolidated, through its officer Durham, sold the scales to Kentucky Mobile Homes for $8,500. Kentucky's president, Ethard Jasper, checked the county records prior to the purchase and found no lien or encumbrance on the title; likewise, he denied knowledge of the dispute between Consolidated and United. On September 22, Kentucky sold the scales to Clyde Jasper, individually, for $8,500. His search also failed to disclose any lien on the title to the scales, and he denied knowledge of the dispute between Consolidated and United. Can United recover the scales from Jasper? Explain.

20. Harrison, a men's clothing retailer located in Westport, Connecticut, ordered merchandise from Ninth Street East, Ltd., a Los Angeles-based clothing manufacturer. Ninth Street delivered the merchandise to Denver-Chicago Trucking Company (Denver) in Los Angeles and then sent four invoices to Harrison that bore the notation "F.O.B. Los Angeles." Denver subsequently transferred the merchandise to a connecting carrier, Old Colony Transportation Company, for final delivery to Harrison's Westport store. When Old Colony tried to deliver the merchandise, Harrison's wife asked the truck driver to deliver the boxes inside the store, but the driver refused. The dispute remained unresolved, and the truck departed with Old Colony still in possession of the goods. By letter, Harrison then notified Ninth Street of the nondelivery, but Ninth Street was unable to locate the shipment. Ninth Street then sought to recover the contract purchase price from Harrison. Harrison refused, contending that risk of loss remained with Ninth Street because of its refusal to deliver the merchandise to Harrison's place of business. Discuss whether the risk of loss passed from Ninth Street to Harrison.

http:// **Internet Exercise** Look at several retail Websites and determine who has the risk of loss if the goods ordered are damaged or lost in transit to the buyer.

CHAPTER 22

Product Liability: Warranties and Strict Liability

The explosion of [product liability] lawsuits—and the cost of insuring against them—is forcing managers to react. Some have pulled goods off the market. Other responses: raising prices, redesigning products, educating customers, and finding new ways of settling claims.

MICHAEL BRODY, IN *FORTUNE*

Learning Objectives

After reading this chapter you should be able to:

1. Identify and describe the types of warranties.
2. List and explain the various defenses that may be successfully raised to a warranty action.
3. Describe the elements of an action based on strict liability in tort.
4. List and explain the obstacles to an action based on strict liability in tort.
5. Compare strict liability in tort with the implied warranty of merchantability.

In this chapter, we will consider the liability of manufacturers and sellers of goods to buyers, users, consumers, and bystanders for damages caused by defective products. The rapidly expanding development of case law has established product liability as a distinct field of law that combines and enforces rules and principles of contracts, sales, negligence, strict liability, and statutory law.

One reason for the expansion of such liability has been the modern method of distributing goods. Today, retailers serve principally as a conduit of goods that are prepackaged in sealed containers and that are widely advertised by the manufacturer or distributor. This has hastened the extension of product liability coverage to include manufacturers and other parties within the chain of distribution. The extension of product liability to manufacturers, however, has not noticeably lessened the liability of a seller to his immediate purchaser. Rather, it has broadened the base of liability through the development and application of new principles of law.

Currently, the entire area of product liability has attracted a great deal of public attention. The cost of maintaining product liability insurance has skyrocketed, causing great concern in the business community. In response to the clamor over this insurance crisis, more than forty states have revised their tort law to make successful product liability lawsuits more difficult to bring.

Practical Advice

Thoroughly test your products prior to releasing them into the channels of distribution to ensure that they are safe and properly designed. In addition, include all necessary warnings and instructions and be sure that they are clear and conspicuous.

The liability of manufacturers and sellers of goods for a defective product, or for its failure to perform adequately, may be based on one or more of the following: (1) negligence, (2) misrepresentation, (3) violation of statutory duty, (4) warranty, and (5) strict liability in tort. We covered the first three of these causes of actions in Chapters 8 and 11. In this chapter, we will explore the last two.

http:// Consumer Product Safety Commission: http://www.cpsc.gov/
Consumers Union: http://www.consumersunion.org

WARRANTIES

A **warranty** creates a duty on the part of the seller to ensure that the goods he sells will conform to certain qualities, characteristics, or conditions. A seller, however, is not required to warrant the goods; and, in general, he may, by appropriate words, disclaim (exclude) or modify a particular warranty or even all warranties.

In bringing a warranty action, the buyer must prove that (1) a warranty existed, (2) the warranty has been breached, (3) the breach of the warranty proximately caused the loss suffered, and (4) notice of the breach of warranty was given to the seller. The seller has the burden of proving defenses based on the buyer's conduct. If the seller breaches his warranty, the buyer may reject or revoke acceptance of the goods. Moreover, whether the goods have been accepted or rejected, the buyer may recover a judgment against the seller for damages. Harm for which damages are recoverable includes personal injury, damage to property, and economic loss. Economic loss most commonly involves damages for loss of bargain and consequential damages for lost profits. (Damages for breach of warranty are discussed in detail in the next chapter.) In this section, we will examine the various types of warranties, as well as the obstacles to a cause of action for breach of warranty.

CPA TYPES OF WARRANTIES

A warranty may arise out of the mere existence of a sale (a warranty of title), out of any affirmation of fact or promise made by the seller to the buyer (an express warranty), or out of the circumstances under which the sale is made (an implied warranty). In a contract for the sale of goods, it is possible to have both express and implied warranties, as well as a warranty of title. All warranties are construed as consistent with each other and cumulative, unless such construction is unreasonable.

Article 2A carries over the warranty provisions of Article 2 with relatively minor revision to reflect differences in style, leasing terminology, or leasing practices. The creation of express warranties and, except for finance leases, the imposition of the implied warranties of merchantability and fitness for a particular purpose are virtually identical to their Article 2 analogues. Article 2 and Article 2A diverge somewhat in their treatment of the warranties of title and infringement as well as in their provisions for the exclusion and modification of warranties

WARRANTY OF TITLE

Under the Code's **warranty of title**, the seller implicitly warrants (1) that the title conveyed is good and its transfer rightful and (2) that the goods are subject to no security interest or other lien (a claim on property by another for payment of debt) of which the buyer did not know at the time of contracting. In a lease, title does not transfer to the lessee. Accordingly, Article 2A's analogous provision protects the lessee's right to possession and use of the goods from the claims of other parties arising from an act or omission of the lessor.

Let us assume that Steven acquires goods from Nancy in a transaction that is void and then sells the goods to Rachel. Nancy brings an action against Rachel and recovers the goods. Steven has breached the warranty of title because he did not have good title to the goods and, therefore, his transfer of the goods to Rachel was not rightful. Accordingly, Steven is liable to Rachel for damages.

The Code does not label the warranty of title an implied warranty, even though it arises out of the sale and not out of any particular words or conduct. Instead, the Code has a separate disclaimer provision for warranty of title; thus, the Code's general disclaimer provision for implied warranties does not apply.

EXPRESS WARRANTIES

An **express warranty** is an explicit undertaking by the seller with respect to the quality, description, condition, or performability of the goods. The undertaking may consist of an affirmation of fact or a promise that relates to the goods, a description of the goods, or a sample or model of the goods. In each of these instances, in order for an express warranty to be created, the undertaking must become or be made part of the basis of the bargain. It is not necessary, however, that the seller have a specific intention to make a warranty or use formal words such as "warrant" or "guarantee." Moreover, it is not necessary that, in order to be liable for breach of express warranty, a seller know of the falsity of a statement she makes; the seller may be acting in good faith. For example, if John mistakenly asserts to Sam that a rope will easily support 300 pounds and Sam is injured when the rope breaks while supporting only 200 pounds, John is liable for breach of an express warranty.

Creation A seller can create an express warranty either orally or in writing. One way in which the seller may create such a warranty is by an ***affirmation of fact*** or a ***promise*** that relates to the goods. (Article 2A.) For example, a statement made by a seller that an automobile will get 42 miles to the gallon of gasoline or that a camera has automatic focus is an express warranty.

The Code further provides that an affirmation of the ***value*** of the goods or a statement purporting merely to be the seller's ***opinion*** or recommendation of the goods does not create a warranty. (Article 2A.) Such statements are not factual and do not deceive the ordinary buyer, who accepts them merely as opinions or as *puffery* (sales talk). A statement of value, however, may be an express warranty where the seller states the price at which the goods were purchased from a former owner, or where she gives market figures relating to sales of similar goods. These are affirmations of facts. They are statements of events, not mere opinions; and the seller is liable for breach of warranty if they are untrue. Also, although a statement of opinion by the seller is not ordinarily a warranty, the seller who is an expert and who gives an opinion as such may be liable for breach of warranty.

Practical Advice

Make only those affirmations of fact or promises about the goods being sold that you wish to stand behind. Moreover, recognize that advertising claims and the statements made by salespeople can give rise to express warranties.

A seller also can create an express warranty by the use of a ***description*** of the goods that becomes a part of the basis of the bargain. (Article 2A.) Under such a warranty, the seller expressly warrants that the goods shall conform to the description. Examples include statements regarding a particular brand or type of goods, technical specifications, and blueprints.

The use of a ***sample*** or model is another means of creating an express warranty. (Article 2A.) When a sample or model is a part of the basis of the bargain, the seller expressly warrants that the entire lot of goods sold shall conform to the sample or model. A sample is a good that is actually drawn from the bulk of goods that is the subject matter of the sale. By comparison, a model is offered for inspection when the subject matter is not at hand; it is not drawn from the bulk.

CISG

The seller must deliver goods that conform to the quality and description required by the contract. In addition, the goods must possess the qualities of any sample or model used by the seller.

Basis of Bargain The Code does not require that the affirmations, promises, descriptions, samples, or models the seller makes or uses be relied on by the buyer but only that they constitute a part of the **basis of the bargain**. In other words, if they are part of the buyer's assumption underlying the sale, reliance by the buyer is presumed. Some courts merely require that the buyer know of the affirmation or promise for it to be presumed to be part of the basis of the bargain, while others require some showing of reliance. See the case that follows.

Felley v. Singleton

Appellate Court of Illinois, Second District, 1999
302 Ill.App.3d 248, 705 N.E.2d 930, 235 Ill.Dec. 747
http://caselaw.findlaw.com/scripts/getcase.pl?court=IL&vol=app\1999\2980043&invol=3

FACTS Plaintiff, Brian Felley, purchased a used 1991 Ford Taurus from the defendants, Thomas and Cheryl Singleton, for $5,800. The car had 126,000 miles on it. After test driving the car, the plaintiff discussed the condition of the car with the defendants who informed the plaintiff that the only thing known to be wrong with the car was that it had a noise in the right rear and that a grommet (a connector having to do with a strut) was bad or missing. Thomas further acknowledged that he told the plaintiff that the car was in good condition. Nevertheless, the plaintiff soon began experiencing problems with the car. On the second day that he owned the car, the plaintiff noticed a problem with the clutch. Over the next few days, the clutch problem worsened to the point where the plaintiff was unable to shift the gears no matter how far he pushed in the clutch pedal. The plaintiff presented an invoice showing that he paid $942.76 for the removal and repair of the car's clutch. The plaintiff further testified that the car developed serious brake problems within the first month that he owned it. The plaintiff presented two invoices for work he had done on the car's brakes totaling approximately $1,500. The plaintiff brought this case asserting that the defendants breached their express warranty. The trial court entered judgment for the plaintiff and the defendants brought this appeal.

DECISION Judgment for plaintiff affirmed.

OPINION Bowman, J. The question before the Court is whether the representations made constituted an Express Warranty * * *, or whether the auto was sold "as is" and representations made were mere "puffing."

The court notes that a substantial amount of money was paid for the car, and this is one of the factor[s] which would cause the buyer to reasonably rely on affirmations that the automobile was in good mechanical shape. It makes little sense to pay thousands of dollars, and then expect to immediately sink substantial money into repair.

In this case immediate problems were experienced with the brakes and clutch. These were not minor problems, but affected the very drivability of the car, and were directly related to the mechanical condition.

* * *

Applying the rational[e] of the *Weng* case [a prior Illinois Appellate case], for the sellers here to represent that the car was in "good mechanical shape or condition", having experience[d] "no brake problems", were affirmations of fact that became the basis of the bargain, and which created an Express Warranty.

"Having shown that Defendant's [*sic*] are liable for damages due to Breach of Warranty, the paid repair bills are the appropriate measure of damages."

* * *

Section 2–313 of the Uniform Commercial Code (Code) governs the formation of express warranties by affirmation in the context of a sale of goods such as a used car. Section 2–313 provides, in relevant part:

"(1) Express warranties by the seller are created as follows:

(a) Any affirmation of fact or promise made by the seller to the buyer which relates to the goods and becomes part of the basis of the bargain creates an express warranty that the goods shall conform to the affirmation or promise.

* * *

(2) It is not necessary to the creation of an express warranty that the seller use formal words such as 'warrant' or 'guarantee' or that he have a specific intention to make a warranty, but an affirmation merely of the value of the goods or a statement purporting to be merely the seller's opinion or commendation of the goods does not create a warranty."

* * *

In defendants' view, their statements to plaintiff cannot fairly be viewed as entering into the bargain. Defendants assert that they are not automobile dealers or mechanics with specialized knowledge of the brake and clutch systems of the car and therefore their statements were merely expressions of a vendor's opinion that did not constitute an express warranty.

Weng involved the sale of a 10-year-old used car for $800. The car had 96,000 miles on it. When the buyers attempted to drive the car home, it failed to operate properly. An inspection at an automobile dealership revealed that the car was unsafe to drive and needed repairs costing about $1,500. The seller had told the buyers that the car was "'mechanically sound,' 'in good condition,' 'a good reliable car,' 'a good car,' and had 'no problems.'" *Weng*, [citation.] The trial court ruled that such representations could not become part of the basis of the bargain unless the buyer relied on them and that no one could reasonably rely on such statements with respect to such a car.

In *Weng*, the Appellate Court, Third District, disagreed and reversed the trial court on the ground that its ruling was against the manifest weight of the evidence. The appellate court determined that the representations made by the sellers were affirmations of fact that created an express warranty. The court stated that affirmations of fact made during a bargaining process regarding the sale of goods are presumed to be part of the basis of the bargain unless clear affirmative proof to the contrary is shown; that a showing of reliance on the affirmations by the buyer is not necessary for the creation of an express warranty; and that the seller has the burden to establish by clear affirmative proof that the affirmations did not become part of the basis of the bargain. [Citation.] The court also stated that the seller may be held accountable for breach of warranty where affirmations are a basis of the bargain and the goods fail to conform to the affirmations. [Citation.]

* * * We agree with the *Weng* court that, in the context of a used car sale, representations by the seller such as the car is "in good mechanical condition" are presumed to be affirmations of fact that become part of the basis of the bargain.

Because they are presumed to be part of the basis of the bargain, such representations constitute express warranties, regardless of the buyer's reliance on them, unless the seller shows by clear affirmative proof that the representations did not become part of the basis of the bargain.

In this case, it is undisputed that plaintiff asked defendants about the car's mechanical condition and that defendants responded that the car was in good mechanical condition. Under the foregoing principles, defendants' representations are presumed to be affirmations of fact that became a part of the basis of the bargain.

* * *

INTERPRETATION Affirmations of fact made during the bargaining process regarding a sale of goods are presumed to be part of the basis of the bargain and thus constitute express warranties.

CRITICAL THINKING QUESTION Is it good policy to make non-commercial sellers of used cars liable for express warranties?

Like statements in advertisements or catalogs, statements or promises made by the seller to the buyer prior to the sale may be express warranties, as they may form a part of the basis of the bargain. In addition, under the Code, statements or promises made by the seller subsequent to the making of the contract of sale may become express warranties even though no new consideration is given. (Article 2A)

IMPLIED WARRANTIES

An implied warranty, unlike an express warranty, is not found in the language of the sales contract or in a specific affirmation or promise by the seller. Instead, it exists by operation of law. An **implied warranty** arises out of the circumstances under which the parties enter into their contract and depends on factors such as the type of contract or sale entered into, the seller's merchant or nonmerchant status, the conduct of the parties, and the applicability of other statutes.

Merchantability Under the Code, a ***merchant seller*** makes an implied warranty of the merchantability of goods that are of the kind in which he deals. The implied warranty of **merchantability** provides that the goods are reasonably fit for the *ordinary* purposes for which they are used, pass without objection in the trade under the contract description, and are of fair, average quality. (Article 2A.)

Practical Advice

Because the warranty of merchantability applies only to merchant sellers, when purchasing goods from a nonmerchant seller, attempt to obtain a written express warranty that the goods will be, at a minimum, of average quality and fit for ordinary purposes.

Fitness for Particular Purpose Unlike the warranty of merchantability, the implied warranty of fitness for a particular purpose applies to ***any*** seller, whether he is a merchant or not. The implied warranty of ***fitness for a particular purpose*** arises if at the time of contracting the seller had reason to know the buyer's particular purpose and to know that the buyer was relying on the seller's skill and judgment to select suitable goods. (Article 2A.)

CISG

The seller must deliver goods, unless otherwise agreed, that are fit for the purposes for which goods of the same description would ordinarily be used.

The implied warranty of fitness for a particular purpose does not require any specific statement by the seller. Rather, it requires only that the seller know that the buyer, in selecting a product for her specific purpose, is relying on the seller's expertise. The buyer need not specifically inform the seller of her particular purpose; it is sufficient if the seller has reason to know it. On the other hand, the implied warranty of fitness for a particular purpose would not arise in a situation where the buyer insists on a particular product and the seller simply conveys it to her.

In contrast to the implied warranty of merchantability, the implied warranty of fitness for a particular purpose pertains to a specific purpose for, rather than the ordinary purpose of, the goods. A particular purpose may be a specific use or may relate to a special situation in which the buyer intends to use the goods. Thus, if the seller has reason to know that the buyer is purchasing a pair of shoes for mountain climbing and that the buyer is relying on the seller's judgment to furnish suitable shoes for this purpose, a sale of shoes suitable only for ordinary walking purposes would be a breach of this implied warranty. Likewise, if a buyer indicates to a seller that she needs a stamping machine to stamp 10,000 packages in an eight-hour period and that she relies upon the seller to select an appropriate machine, the seller, by selecting a machine, impliedly warrants that the machine selected will stamp 10,000 packages in an eight-hour period.

CISG

The seller must deliver goods, unless otherwise agreed, that are fit for any particular purpose expressly or impliedly made known to the seller by the buyer, except when the buyer did not rely on the seller's skill and judgment when it was unreasonable for the buyer to rely on the seller.

Frequently, as in the case that follows, a seller's conduct may involve both the implied warranty of merchantability *and* the implied warranty of fitness for a particular purpose.

In Re L. B. Trucking, Inc.

United States Bankruptcy Court, 1994
163 BR 709, 23 UCC Rep. Serv.2d 1093

FACTS Dudley B. Durham, Jr., and his wife, Barbara Durham, owned and operated a trucking company, L. B. Trucking, Inc., and a farm, Double-D Farms, Inc. In April 1983, Dudley Durham met with Richard Thomas of Southern States Cooperative **(http://www.southernstates-coop.com)**—which is in the business of supplying various agricultural supplies to farmers—about arranging for the application of herbicides to the Durhams' fields.

At a subsequent meeting in early May, Durham met with Thomas to complete credit arrangements and to arrange the application of herbicides. Durham told Thomas, "I want it done the cheapest way, the best way it can be done." Thomas responded, "Will do." Thomas then outlined with some specificity the chemicals he proposed to use on the Durhams' fields. The plan included the use of a water-based carrier that was recommended by local experts, rather than a more expensive nitrogen solution. Durham had no experience or expertise on herbicidal chemicals and relied on Thomas's briefing on the various herbicide mixtures in choosing which ones to apply.

When the herbicides were actually to be applied, Southern States herbicide applicator, Gilbert McClements, received from Mr. Thomas instructions concerning which chemicals to apply and would mix the chemicals each day prior to spraying. Apparently, though, Mr. McClements used a nitrogen solution to prepare the herbicides and did not make extensive prespraying inspections of the grass and weeds in the fields to be sprayed. When Durham noticed a significant number of weeds and grasses had survived the herbicidal treatment, he promptly notified Southern States. Southern States attempted to remedy the problem, but the harvest was dismal and far below the county average.

In 1983, the Durhams and both their businesses filed for bankruptcy. Southern States brought a claim against the consolidated bankruptcy estate to collect payment for the herbicides as well as application and other services provided. The trustee of the estate asserted counterclaims against Southern States for negligence and breach of warranties in the application of herbicides that caused severe damage to the Durhams' 1983 crop.

DECISION Judgment for the trustee.

OPINION Balick, J.

1. Express Warranty An express warranty may be created by a seller through: (1) any affirmation of fact or promise to the buyer relating to the goods which becomes the basis of the bargain so that the goods conform to the affirmation or promise; (2) any description of the goods which is made part of the basis of the bargain so that the whole of the goods conform to the sample of model. U.C.C. § 2–313(1)(a)–(c). The question of whether an express warranty has been made in a particular transaction is for the trier of fact. [Citation.] In the case at bar, there are no written express warranties claimed, but instead, oral statements made principally by the Middletown store manager, Thomas, to Durham which the Trustee contends were, express warranties.

The relevant testimony concerning Thomas' statements to Durham reveal several oral express warranties concerning the herbicides and their application which Southern States plainly breached. First, Thomas stated that water would be the carrier for the herbicides, especially since Durham wanted the job done inexpensively. In its application, Southern States used the nitrogen solution regardless of the University of Delaware recommendations dissuading its use and despite the fact that it is more expensive than using water as a carrier. Southern States' reference to the common trade usage of nitrogen in 1983 is inapposite in an action for breach of express warranty because it is the affirmation or promise—not the custom or trade usage—which becomes the standard against which a breach is determined. In addition, Thomas' statements were more than "seller's talk" or puffing in that they were product specific and not overly broad or vague. Second, Thomas also made statements regarding the effectiveness of the herbicides in removing weeds and grass so as to promote successful no-till farming. The purchase of herbicides is characteristically the subject of express warranties because the buyer of the product cannot determine its effectiveness prior to use and evaluate its effectiveness in a given situation. Here, Thomas' statements in early May of 1983 were part of the basis of the bargain upon which Durham relied when purchasing the herbicides. Beyond this, Thomas had superior knowledge about the herbicides as opposed to Durham who had little or none. Consequently, Thomas' selection of herbicidal recipes combined with his statements as to their effectiveness amounted to an express warranty that the respective mixtures would do the job adequately. * * * [Citations.] Accordingly, the court finds that Southern States breached its express warranty to Durham and, thus, is liable for the Durham's crop damage. * * *

2. Implied Warranties There are two theories of recovery for breach of implied warranty under the Delaware UCC: breach of implied warranty of merchantability under U.C.C. § 2–314 and breach of implied warranty of fitness for a particular purpose under U.C.C. § 2–315. * * *

Turning first to the implied warranty of merchantability, there are five elements which the claimant must establish: (1) that a merchant sold goods, (2) which were not merchantable at the time of sale, (3) proximately causing by the defective nature of the goods, (4) injury and damages to the claimant or his property, and (5) notice to the seller of the injury. [Citation.] As to the element requiring the seller to be a merchant, there is no doubt that Southern States was a merchant. * * *

Addressing the second element concerning whether the herbicides were "merchantable," the goods must pass without objection in the trade under the contract description *and* be fit for the ordinary purposes for which it was intended, U.C.C. 2–314(2)(a) and (c). The facts show that Southern States sprayed (and in some instances resprayed) the various Durham farm tracts with herbicidal and other chemicals in order to increase the crop yields. Nevertheless, the farms' respective crop yields did not improve, but rather fell dramatically as the result of the chemical applications. Specifically, the herbicidal recipes were unfit for the ordinary purpose for which they were intended to be used, chemical agents that would kill weeds without damaging the primary crops. [Citation.] The chemicals did not operate for their ordinary purpose which was to promote no-till farming which is why Durham purchased them in the first place.

As for proximate cause and damages, the court finds that these elements have been met. * * *

Finally, the notice requirement for a breach of implied warranty of merchantability cause of action was plainly met. Durham notified Southern States as soon as he suspected that the herbicides were failing to work just a few weeks after their application. * * *

Southern States also breached the implied warranty that the herbicides were fit for their particular purpose. * * *

The breach of this warranty is the one most apparent on the facts. As indicated earlier, Durham relied on Thomas' skill and judgment in selecting suitable herbicides to conduct no-till farming on his farms. The chemicals were mixed by Southern States' herbicide applicator, McClements, before each job based on a formula or recipe provided by Thomas or some other Southern States official. The herbicides did not effectively do their job of keeping the fields clear of weeds and the crops died. Though thoroughly familiar with till farming, Durham had no experience with the no-till farming method and, therefore, was not a "sophisticated purchaser" who might have been able to recognize mistakes made by Southern States' personnel. As a result, the herbicides' failure to do their intended task coupled with Durham's reliance on Southern States' judgment and skill in formulating, mixing, and applying the herbicidal chemicals breached the implied warranty of fitness. [Citations.] Accordingly, Southern States is found to be liable under U.C.C. § 2–315.

INTERPRETATION In a contract for a sale of goods, it is possible to breach multiple warranties.

ETHICAL QUESTION Did any of the parties act unethically? Explain.

CRITICAL THINKING QUESTION Did the court correctly decide this case? Explain.

CPA OBSTACLES TO WARRANTY ACTIONS

A number of technical obstacles, which vary considerably from jurisdiction to jurisdiction, limit the effectiveness of warranty as a basis for recovery. These include disclaimers of warranties, limitations or modifications of warranties, privity, notice of breach, and the conduct of the plaintiff.

DISCLAIMER OF WARRANTIES

To be effective, a **disclaimer** (negation of warranty) must be positive, explicit, unequivocal, and conspicuous. The

Code calls for a reasonable construction of words or conduct to disclaim or limit warranties. (Article 2A.)

Express Exclusions In general, a seller cannot provide an **express warranty** and then disclaim it. A seller can, however, avoid making an express warranty by carefully refraining from making any promise or affirmation of fact relating to the goods, by refraining from making a description of the goods, or by refraining from using a sample or model in a sale. (Article 2A.) Oral warranties made before the execution of a written agreement containing an express disclaimer are subject to the parol evidence rule, however. Thus, as discussed in Chapter 15, if the parties intend the written contract to be the final and *complete* statement of the agreement between them, parol evidence of a warranty that *contradicts* the terms of the written contract is inadmissible.

> **Practical Advice**
>
> Recognize that once you make an express warranty, it is very difficult to disclaim the warranty.

A **warranty of title** may be excluded only by specific language or by certain circumstances, including a judicial sale or sales by sheriffs, executors, or foreclosing lienors. (Article 2A.) In the latter cases, the seller is clearly offering to sell only such right or title as he or a third person might have in the goods, because it is apparent that the goods are not the property of the person selling them.

To exclude or to modify an **implied warranty of merchantability**, the language of disclaimer or modification must mention *merchantability* and, in the case of a writing, must be *conspicuous*. Article 2A requires that a disclaimer of an implied warranty of merchantability mention merchantability, be in writing, and be conspicuous.

To exclude or to modify an **implied warranty of fitness for the particular purpose** of the buyer, the disclaimer must also be in *writing* and *conspicuous*. (Article 2A.)

All implied warranties, unless the circumstances indicate otherwise, are excluded by expressions like *"as is"* or *"with all faults"* or by other language plainly calling the buyer's attention to the exclusion of warranties. (Article 2A.) Most courts require the "as is" clause to be conspicuous. Implied warranties may also be excluded by course of dealing, course of performance, or usage of trade. (Article 2A.)

> **Practical Advice**
>
> If you want to disclaim the implied warranties, be sure to use large, conspicuous type; use the appropriate language; and place the disclaimer on the first page of the agreement.

The courts will invalidate disclaimers they consider unconscionable. The Code, as discussed in Chapter 19, permits a court to limit the application of any contract or contractual provision that it finds unconscionable. (Article 2A.)

Womco, Inc. v. Navistar International Corporation

Court of Appeals of Texas, Twelfth District, Tyler, 2002

84 S.W.3d 272, 48 U.C.C. Rep.Serv.2d 130

http://www.law.com/jsp/decisionstate.jsp?id=1022954269840

FACTS In 1993, Womco, Inc. ("Womco") purchased thirty 1993 International model 9300 tractor trucks manufactured by Navistar through Price, a dealer. Also, in 1993, C. L. Hall ("Hall") purchased sixteen 1994 International model 9300 tractor trucks also manufactured by Navistar through Mahaney, another dealer. Almost immediately after the trucks were put into service, Appellants each had problems with their respective trucks' engines overheating. As the problems occurred, Appellants took their trucks, which were still covered under warranty, to their respective dealerships for diagnoses and repairs related to the overheating problem. Although repeated attempts were made, the dealership's mechanics were unable to correct the problem. Subsequently it was discovered that the trucks radiators were unusually small and were insufficient to cool the engine.

Womco and Hall filed suit against Navistar, Price, and Mahaney. The defendants filed a motion for summary judgment based on their affirmative defenses of disclaimer of warranty. The trial court granted the defendants' motion. Womco and Hall appealed.

DECISION Summary judgment regarding claims for breach of warranty is reversed and remanded.

OPINION Griffith, J. It is undisputed that Appellants' breach of implied warranty claims as to nine [of the] trucks are not barred by [the statute of] limitations. However, * * * Appellees contend that such implied warranties were disclaimed. The Texas Uniform Commercial Code allows sellers to disclaim both the implied warranty of merchantability as well as the implied warranty of fitness for particular purpose. [UCC] § 2–316(b), [citation]. In order to disclaim an implied warranty of merchantability in a sales transaction, the disclaimer must mention the word "merchantability." The disclaimer may be oral or written, but if in writing, the disclaimer must be conspicuous. [Citation]; [UCC] § 2–316(b). To disclaim an implied warranty of fitness for a particular purpose, the disclaimer must be in writing and must be conspicuous. [UCC] § 2–316(b); [citation]. Whether a particular disclaimer is conspicuous is a question of law to be determined by the court. [Citation]. A term or clause is conspicuous if it is written so that a reasonable person against whom it is to operate ought to have noticed it. [UCC] § 1–201(10); [citation]. Language is "conspicuous" if it is in larger type or other contrasting font or color. [Citation]. Conspicuousness is not required if the buyer has actual knowledge of the disclaimer. [Citation].

* * *

Further, Appellants argue that Appellees were required to offer proof of the context of the purported disclaimers, contending that in order for a disclaimer of an implied warranty to be effective, the plaintiffs must have had an opportunity to examine it prior to consummation of the contract for sale. [Citation]. * * * In *Dickenson* [citation], the court held that a disclaimer of an express warranty was ineffective where the buyer was not given the opportunity to read the warranty or warranties made until after the contract is signed. Although the instant case concerns a converse situation to *Dickenson*, the rationale applied by the *Dickenson* court is helpful. One of the underlying purposes of [UCC] section 2–316 is to protect a buyer from surprise by permitting the exclusion of implied warranties. [UCC] § 2–316, comment 1. We fail to see how section [UCC] 2–316 can fulfill such a purpose unless a disclaimer is required to be communicated to the buyer before the contract of sale has been completed, unless the buyer afterward agrees to the disclaimer as a modification of the contract. [Citations.]

In support of their motion for summary judgment, Appellees offered six disclaimers, all of which were deposition exhibits. None of these six disclaimers is probative as to the issue of whether the disclaimer was communicated prior to the completion of the contract of sale. * * *

* * *

Accordingly, the trial court's order granting summary judgment is reversed as to Appellants' claims for breach of warranty filed less than four years after the delivery of the truck upon which the claim is based, and is remanded to the trial court for further proceedings.

INTERPRETATION A disclaimer is required to be communicated to the buyer before the contract of sale has been completed, unless the buyer afterward agrees to the disclaimer as a modification of the contract.

CRITICAL THINKING QUESTION What should be required to properly disclaim the implied warranties?

Buyer's Examination or Refusal to Examine If the buyer inspects the goods before entering into the contract, **implied warranties** do not apply to defects that are apparent on examination. Moreover, there is no implied warranty on defects that an examination ought to have revealed, not only when the buyer has examined the goods as fully as desired, but also when the buyer has refused to examine the goods. (Article 2A)

Practical Advice

If you are a seller, offer the buyer an opportunity to examine the goods to avoid an implied warranty for any defects that should be detected upon inspection. If you are a buyer and are offered an opportunity to examine the goods, make sure that you make a reasonable inspection of the goods.

CISG

If at the time of entering into the sales contract, the buyer knew or could not have been unaware of the lack of conformity, the seller is not liable for the warranty of particular purpose, ordinary purpose, or sale by sample or model.

Federal Legislation Relating to Warranties of Consumer Goods To protect purchasers of consumer goods (defined as "tangible personal property normally used for personal, family or household purposes"), Congress enacted the **Magnuson-Moss Warranty Act**. The purpose of the act is to prevent deception and to make sure that consumer purchasers are adequately informed about warranties. Some courts have applied the act to leases.

The Federal Trade Commission administers and enforces the act. The commission's guidelines for the type of consumer product warranty information a seller must supply are aimed at providing the consumer with clear and useful information. More significantly, the act provides that a seller who makes a written warranty cannot disclaim any implied warranty. For a complete discussion of the act, see Chapter 45.

http:// Magnuson-Moss Federal Warranty Act: http:// www4.law.cornell.edu/uscode/15/45.html
Federal Trade Commission: http://www.ftc.gov/

Practical Advice

If you are a seller of consumer goods and wish to disclaim the implied warranties, make sure that you do not provide any written express warranties.

LIMITATION OR MODIFICATION OF WARRANTIES

The Code permits a seller to ***limit*** or ***modify*** the buyer's remedies for breach of warranty. One important exception to this right is the prohibition against a seller's "unconscionable" limitations or exclusions of consequential damages. (Article 2A.) Specifically, the "[l]imitation of consequential damages for injury to the person in the case of consumer goods is prima facie unconscionable. . . ." In some cases, a seller may seek to impose time limits within which the warranty is effective. Except when such clauses result in unconscionability, the Code permits them; it does not, however, permit any attempt to shorten the time period for filing an action for personal injury to less than one year.

PRIVITY OF CONTRACT

Because of the close association between warranties and contracts, a principle of law in the nineteenth century established that a plaintiff could not recover for breach of warranty unless he was in a contractual relationship with the defendant. This relationship is known as **privity** of contract.

Under this rule, a warranty by seller Ingrid to buyer Sylvester, who resells the goods to purchaser Lyle under a similar warranty, gives Lyle no rights against Ingrid. There is no privity of contract between Ingrid and Lyle. In the event of breach of warranty, Lyle may recover only from his seller, Sylvester, who in turn may recover from Ingrid.

Horizontal privity determines who benefits from a warranty and who may therefore sue for its breach. Horizontal privity pertains to noncontracting parties who are injured by the defective goods; this group would include users, consumers, and bystanders who are not the contracting purchaser.

The Code relaxes the requirement of horizontal privity of contract by permitting recovery on a seller's warranty, at a minimum, to members of the buyer's family or household or to a guest in his home. The Code provides three alternative sections from which the states may select. Alternative A, the least comprehensive and most widely adopted alternative, provides that a seller's warranty, whether express or implied, extends to any natural person who is in the family or household of the buyer or who is a guest in his home, if it is reasonable to expect that such person may use, consume, or be affected by the goods, and who is injured in person by breach of the warranty. Alternative B extends Alternative A to "any natural person who may reasonably be expected to use, consume, or be affected by the goods." Alternative C further expands the coverage of the section to any person, not just natural persons, and to property damage as well as personal injury. (A natural person would not include artificial entities such as corporations, for example.) A seller, however, may not exclude or limit the operation of this section for injury to a person. Article 2A provides the same alternatives with slight modifications.

Nonetheless, the Code was not intended to establish outer boundaries for third-party recovery for injuries caused by defective goods. Rather, it sets a minimum standard that the states may expand through case law. Most states have judicially accepted the Code's invitation to relax the requirements of horizontal privity and, for all practical purposes, have *eliminated* horizontal privity in warranty cases.

Vertical privity, in determining who is liable for breach of warranty, pertains to remote sellers within the chain of distribution, such as manufacturers and wholesalers, with whom the consumer purchaser has not entered into a contract. Although the Code adopts a neutral position regarding vertical privity, the courts in most states have *eliminated* the requirement of vertical privity in warranty actions.

NOTICE OF BREACH OF WARRANTY

When a buyer has accepted a tender of goods that are not as warranted by the seller, she is required to notify the seller of any breach of warranty, express or implied, as well as any other breach, within a reasonable time after she has discovered or should have discovered it. If the buyer fails to notify the seller of any breach within a

CONCEPT REVIEW

Warranties

Type of Warranty	How Created	What Is Warranted	How Disclaimed
Title (Article 2) Use and Possession (Article 2A)	• Seller contracts to sell goods	• Good title • Rightful transfer • Not subject to lien	• Specific language • Circumstances giving buyer reason to know that seller does not claim title
Express (Articles 2 and 2A)	• Affirmation of fact • Promise • Description • Sample or model	• Conform to affirmation • Conform to promise • Conform to description • Conform to sample or model	• Specific language (extremely difficult)
Merchantability (Articles 2 and 2A)	• Merchant sells goods	• Fit for ordinary purposes • Adequately contained, packaged, and labeled	• Must mention "merchantability" • If in writing must be conspicuous/ In lease must be in writing and conspicuous • As-is sale • Buyer examination • Course of dealing, course of performance, usage of trade
Fitness for a Particular Purpose (Articles 2 and 2A)	• Seller knows buyer is relying upon seller to select goods suitable to buyer's particular purpose	• Fit for particular purpose	• No buzzwords necessary • Must be in writing and conspicuous • As-is sale • Buyer examination • Course of dealing, course of performance, usage of trade

reasonable time, she is barred from any remedy against the seller. (Article 2A.) In determining whether notice was provided in a reasonable period of time, commercial standards apply to a merchant buyer while different standards apply to a retail consumer, so as not to deprive a good faith consumer of her remedy.

PLAINTIFF'S CONDUCT

Because of the development of warranty liability in the law of sales and contracts, **contributory negligence** of the buyer is no defense to an action against the seller for breach of warranty. Comparative negligence statutes do apply, however, to warranty actions in some states. (Comparative negligence is discussed later in this chapter.)

If the buyer discovers a defect in the goods that may cause injury and nevertheless proceeds to make use of them, he will not be permitted to recover damages from the seller for loss or injuries caused by such use. This is not contributory negligence but **voluntary assumption** of a known risk.

STRICT LIABILITY IN TORT

The most recent and far-reaching development in the field of product liability is that of strict liability in tort. All but a very few states have now accepted the concept, which is embodied in **Section 402A** of the Restatement (Second) of Torts. A new Restatement of the Law (Third) Torts: Products Liability was promulgated. It is far more comprehensive than the second Restatement in dealing with the liability of commercial sellers and distributors of goods for harm caused by their products. (We will discuss this revision more fully later in this chapter).

Section 402A imposes **strict liability in tort** on merchant sellers both for personal injuries and for property damage that result from selling a product in a ***defective condition, unreasonably dangerous*** to the user or consumer. Section 402A applies even though "the seller has exercised all possible care in the preparation and sale of his product." Thus, negligence is not the basis of liability in strict liability cases. The essential distinction between the two doctrines is that actions in strict liability do not require the plaintiff to prove that the injury-producing defect resulted from any specific act of negligence of the seller. Strict liability actions focus on the *product*, not on the *conduct* of the manufacturer. Courts in strict liability cases are interested in the fact that a product defect arose—not in *how* it arose. Thus, even an "innocent" manufacturer—one who has not been negligent—may be liable if his product turns out to contain a defect that injures a consumer. Although liability for personal injuries caused by a defective condition that makes goods unreasonably dangerous is usually associated with sales of such goods, this type of liability also exists with respect to ***leases*** and ***bailments*** of defective goods.

http:// American Law Institute: http://www.ali.org/

CPA REQUIREMENTS OF STRICT LIABILITY IN TORT

Section 402A imposes strict liability in tort if (1) the defendant was engaged in the business of selling a product such as the defective one; (2) the defendant sold the product in a defective condition; (3) the defective condition made the product unreasonably dangerous to the user or consumer or to his property; (4) the defect in the product existed when it left the defendant's hands; (5) the plaintiff sustained physical harm or property damage by using or consuming the product; and (6) the defective condition was the proximate cause of the injury or damage.

This liability is imposed by law as a matter of public policy and does not depend on contract, either express or implied. Nor does it require reliance by the injured user or consumer on any statements made by the manufacturer or seller. It is not limited to persons in a buyer-seller relationship; thus, neither vertical nor horizontal privity is required. No notice of the defect is required to have been given by the injured user or consumer. The liability, furthermore, generally is not subject to disclaimer, exclusion, or modification by contractual agreement. Rather, it is solely in tort and arises out of the common law. It is not governed by the provisions of the Uniform Commercial Code. The majority of courts considering the question, however, have held that Section 402A imposes liability only for injury to person and damage to property, not for commercial loss (such as loss of bargain or profits), which is recoverable in an action for breach of warranty.

MERCHANT SELLERS

Section 402A imposes liability only upon a person who is in the *business* of selling the product involved. It does not apply to an occasional seller, such as a person who trades in his used car or who sells his lawn mower to a neighbor. In this respect, the section is similar to the implied warranty of merchantability, which applies only to sales by a merchant of goods that are of the type in which he deals. A growing number of jurisdictions recognize the applicability of strict liability in tort even to merchant-sellers of *used* goods.

DEFECTIVE CONDITION

In an action to recover damages under the rule of strict liability in tort, though the plaintiff must prove a defective condition in the product, she is not required to prove how or why or in what manner the product became defective. The plaintiff must, however, show that at the time she was injured, the condition of the product was not substantially changed from the condition in which the manufacturer or seller sold it. In general, defects may arise through faulty manufacturing, through faulty product design, or through inadequate warnings, labeling, packaging, or instructions.

Manufacturing Defect A **manufacturing defect** occurs when the product is not properly made; that is, it fails to meet its own manufacturing specifications. For instance, suppose a chair is manufactured with legs designed to be attached by four screws and glue. If the chair was produced without the appropriate screws, this would constitute a manufacturing defect.

Design Defect A product contains a **design defect** when, despite its being produced as specified, the product is dangerous or hazardous because its design is inadequate. Design defects can result from a number of causes, including poor engineering, poor choice of materials, and poor packaging. An example of a design defect that received great notoriety was the fuel tank assembly of the Ford Pinto. A number of courts found the car to be inadequately designed because the fuel tank had been placed too close to its rear axle, causing the tank to rupture when the car was hit from behind.

Section 402A provides no guidance in determining which injury-producing designs should give rise to strict liability and which should not. Consequently, the courts have adopted widely varying approaches in applying 402A to defective design cases. Nevertheless, virtually none of the courts has upheld a judgment in a strict liability case in which the defendant demonstrated that the **"state of the art"** was such that the manufacturer (1) neither knew nor could have known of a product hazard or (2) if he knew of the product hazard, could have designed a safer product given existing technology. Thus, almost all courts evaluate the design of a product on the basis of the dangers that the manufacturer could have known at the time he produced the product.

Failure to Warn A seller is under a duty to provide adequate warning of a product's possible danger, to provide appropriate directions for its safe use, and to package the product safely. Warnings do not, however, always protect sellers from liability. A seller who could have designed or manufactured a product in a safe yet cost-effective manner, but who instead chooses to produce the product cheaply and to provide a warning of the product's hazards, cannot escape liability simply by the warning. Warnings usually will avoid liability only if no cost-effective designs or manufacturing processes are available to reduce a risk of injury.

> **Practical Advice**
>
> Warn consumers of your products of any significant danger, such as toxicity or flammability.

The duty to give a warning arises from a foreseeable danger of physical harm that could result from the normal or probable use of the product and from the likelihood that, unless warned, the user or consumer would not ordinarily be aware of such danger or hazard.

Dunne v. Wal-Mart Stores, Inc.

Court of Appeal of Louisiana, First Circuit, 1996
679 So.2d1034

FACTS Plaintiff's children purchased an Aero Cycle exercise bike for their mother to use in a weight loss program. The Aero Cycle bike was manufactured by DP and purchased from Wal-Mart **(http://www.walmart.com)**. The second time the plaintiff, Judy Dunne, used the bike (the first time she had used it, she used it only for a few seconds), she pedaled for three or four rotations. The rear support strut failed and the bike collapsed under plaintiff. At the time of the accident, plaintiff weighed between 450 and 500 pounds. She fell off the bike backwards, struck her head on a nearby metal file cabinet, and was knocked unconscious. When plaintiff regained consciousness, her mouth was bleeding and her neck, left shoulder, arm, leg, knee, and ankle were injured.

Plaintiff was treated by a physician on the day of the accident. She was diagnosed as having a cervical strain and multiple contusions. She was also seen by her regular family physician with complaints of pain, dizziness, numbness, and sensitivity to light.

Plaintiff filed suit against Wal-Mart and DP. At the time of the trial, plaintiff still had complaints of neck pain and tingling, numbness and spasms in her left arm and hand, with slight swelling and muscle spasms in her right hand. Following trial on the merits, the trial court found that plaintiff failed to carry her burden of proving that the product was unreasonably dangerous because the use of the bike by someone weighing 500 pounds was not a reasonably anticipated use of the product. From this judgment, plaintiff appeals.

DECISION Judgment reversed and rendered.

OPINION Whipple, J. On appeal, plaintiff contends that the trial court was manifestly erroneous in its finding that use of the Aero Cycle by an obese person like plaintiff was not a reasonably anticipated use of the product. We agree.

The Louisiana Products Liability Act (LPLA) * * * sets forth the threshold elements which must be proven by a claimant [in a product liability cause of action], providing as follows:

> A. The manufacturer of a product shall be liable to a claimant for damage proximately caused by a characteristic of the product that renders the product unreasonably dangerous when such damage arose from a reasonably anticipated use of the product by the claimant or another person or entity.

A "reasonably anticipated use" means a use or handling of a product that the product's manufacturer should reasonably expect of an ordinary person in the same or similar circumstances. [Citation.] This definition is narrower in scope than its pre-LPLA counterpart, "normal use," which included "all reasonable foreseeable uses and misuses of the product." [Citation.] Under the current definition contained in the LPLA, a manufacturer is not responsible for accounting for every conceivable foreseeable use of a product. [Citation.]

The trial court, * * * concluded that "the use of this exercise bike by a woman of 500 pounds was not reasonably anticipated by [DP]." The trial court also cited the testimony of Mr. David Newton, the Consumer Affairs Manager for DP. Newton testified that DP manufactured the Aero Cycle to withstand use by adults weighing up to 250 pounds, as this encompasses greater than 98.5 percent of the United States adult population. Further, Newton stated that DP adheres to the American Society for Testing and Materials (ASTM) standards and that all DP products are tested and required to meet ASTM standards. He opined that because a prototype of the Aero Cycle was tested to a load of 440 pounds for five minutes without any resulting deflection * * *, a maximum load capacity warning was not required by the ASTM standards.

Initially, we note that DP is not automatically absolved of liability because it complied with the ASTM standards in not placing a maximum load capacity warning on the Aero Cycle. The ASTM standards, while relevant factors to be considered, are not determinative of the issue of liability. [Citation.]

More importantly, our review of the trial court's reasons for judgment convinces us that the trial court committed legal error * * * . Instead of considering whether plaintiff was engaged in a "reasonably anticipated use," the trial court considered whether plaintiff was a "reasonably anticipated user." In rejecting plaintiff's claim, the trial court [stated] that a manufacturer should not reasonably expect that an ordinary consumer will use a soft drink bottle for a hammer, attempt to drive an automobile across water or pour perfume on a candle to scent it. However, unlike these illustrations, there was no misuse of the product by plaintiff in this case. In fact, the record demonstrates that plaintiff used the product in a manner wholly consistent with its intended use. The Aero Cycle exercise bike was designed and marketed by DP primarily for use by overweight individuals. Plaintiff, an overweight person, was the type of consumer targeted by DP. The mere fact that plaintiff was considerably overweight does not place her in a category of persons for whom DP has no responsibility.

* * *

It is undisputed that there was no maximum weight limit warning accompanying the Aero Cycle. The issue for our consideration at this point is whether * * * DP was required to warn. * * * In this case, according to David Newton, the Aero Cycle was not designed for use by individuals weighing over 250 pounds. The cover of the owner's manual contains other safety information and warnings and it was entirely feasible for DP to have included a statement or warning that the product should not be used by persons weighing over 250 pounds. Plaintiff had no reason to know that the Aero Cycle would not sustain her weight as she previously had used a similar exercise bike for several years without incident. Therefore, in light of DP's admission that the Aero Cycle was only intended to have a limited use, we find that plaintiff proved that DP failed to exercise reasonable care by failing to place a limited use warning on the Aero Cycle.

[T]here are two circumstances when the manufacturer does not have a duty to warn. A warning is not required when the danger would be obvious to an ordinary reasonable user of the product or when a claimant already knows or should know of the danger. [Citation.] Here, there is absolutely no evidence contained in the record that the danger was obvious or that plaintiff knew or should have known of the danger.

INTERPRETATION The duty to give a warning arises from a foreseeable danger of physical harm that could result from the normal or probable use of the product and from the likelihood that, unless warned, the user or consumer would not ordinarily be aware of such danger or hazard.

CRITICAL THINKING QUESTION Under what circumstances should a seller warn of dangers from the product? Explain.

UNREASONABLY DANGEROUS

Section 402A liability applies only if the defective product is unreasonably dangerous to the user or consumer. An **unreasonably dangerous** product is one that contains a danger beyond that which would be contemplated by the ordinary consumer who purchases it with common knowledge of its characteristics. Thus, Comment i to Section 402A describes the difference between reasonable and unreasonable dangers: "good whiskey is not unreasonably dangerous merely because it will make some people drunk, and is especially dangerous to alcoholics; but bad whiskey, containing a dangerous amount of fuel oil, is unreasonably dangerous. Good tobacco is not unreasonably dangerous merely because the effects of smoking may be harmful; but tobacco containing something like marijuana may be unreasonably dangerous. Good butter is not unreasonably dangerous merely because, if such be the case, it deposits cholesterol in the arteries and leads to heart attacks; but bad butter, contaminated with poisonous fish oil, is unreasonably dangerous." Most courts have left the question of reasonable consumer expectations to the jury.

Greene v. Boddie-Noell Enterprises, Inc.

United States District Court, W.D. Virginia, 1997
966 F.Supp. 416

FACTS The plaintiff, Katherine Greene, contends that she was badly burned by hot coffee purchased from the drive-through window of a Hardees fast food restaurant **(http://www.hardeesrestaurants.com)**, when the coffee spilled on her after it had been handed to her by the driver of the vehicle. Greene's boyfriend, Blevins, purchased the coffee and some food and handed the food and beverages to Greene. The food was on a plate, and the beverages were in cups. Greene placed the plate on her lap and held a cup in each hand. According to Greene, the Styrofoam coffee cup was comfortable to hold, and had a lid on the top, although she did not notice whether the lid was fully attached.

Blevins drove out of the restaurant parking lot, and over a "bad dip" at the point at which the lot meets the road. When the front tires of the car went slowly across the dip, the coffee "splashed out" on Greene, burning her legs through her clothes. Blevins remembers Greene exclaiming, "The lid came off." As soon as the coffee burned her, Greene threw the food and drink to the floor of the car, and in the process stepped on the coffee cup. When the cup was later retrieved from the floor of the car, the bottom of the cup was damaged, and the lid was at least partially off of the top of the cup.

After Greene was burned by the coffee, Blevins drove her to the emergency room of a local hospital, where she was treated. She missed eleven days of work and suffered permanent scarring to her thighs.

The defendant restaurant operator moved for summary judgment on the ground that the plaintiff cannot show a prima facie case of liability.

DECISION Summary judgment granted in favor of defendant.

OPINION Jones, J. Both Greene and Blevins testified that they had heard of the "McDonalds' coffee case" prior to this incident and Greene testified that while she was not a coffee drinker, she had been aware that if coffee spilled on her, it would burn her. After the accident, Greene gave a recorded statement to a representative of the defendant in which she stated, "I know the lid wasn't on there good. It came off too easy."

[Court's footnote: On August 17, 1994, a state court jury in Albuquerque, New Mexico, awarded 81-year old Stella Liebeck $160,000 in compensatory damages and $2.7 million in punitive damages, after she was burned by coffee purchased from a drive-through window at a McDonalds restaurant. The trial judge later reduced the punitive damages to $480,000, and the parties settled the case before an appeal. According to news reports, Mrs. Liebeck contended that for taste reasons McDonalds served coffee about 20 degrees hotter than other fast food restaurants, and in spite of numerous complaints, had made a conscious decision not to warn customers of the possibility of serious burns. The jury's verdict received world-wide attention. See Andrea Gerlin, "A Matter of Degree: How a Jury Decided That One Coffee Spill Is Worth $2.9 Million," *The Wall Street Journal*]

* * *

To prove a case of liability in Virginia, a plaintiff must show that a product had a defect which rendered it unreasonably dangerous for ordinary or foreseeable use. [Citation.] In order to meet this burden, a plaintiff must offer proof that the product violated a prevailing safety standard, whether the standard comes from business, government or reasonable consumer expectation. [Citation.]

Here the plaintiff has offered no such proof. There is no evidence that either the heat of the coffee or the security of the coffee cup lid violated any applicable standard. Do other fast food restaurants serve coffee at a lower temperature, or with lids which will prevent spills even when passing over an obstruction in the road? Do customers expect cooler coffee, which may be less tasty, or cups which may be more secure, but harder to unfasten?

In fact, the plaintiff testified that she knew, and therefore expected, that the coffee would be hot enough to burn her if it spilled. While she also expressed the opinion that the cup lid was too loose, that testimony does not substitute for evidence of a generally applicable standard or consumer expectation, since "[the plaintiff's] subjective expectations are insufficient to establish what degree of protection * * * society expects from [the product]." [Citation.]

The plaintiff argues that the mere fact that she was burned shows that the product was dangerously defective, either by being too hot or by having a lid which came off unexpectedly. But it is settled in Virginia that the happening of an accident is not sufficient proof of liability, even in products cases. [Citation.] This is not like the case of a foreign substance being found in a soft drink bottle, where a presumption of negligence arises. [Citation.]

To be merchantable, a product need not be foolproof, or perfect. As one noted treatise has expressed, "[i]t is the lawyer's challenging job to define the term 'merchantability' in [the] case in some objective way so that the court or jury can make a determination whether that standard has been breached." [Citation.]

In the present case, there has been no showing that a reasonable seller of coffee would not conclude that the beverage must be sold hot enough to be palatable to consumers, even though it is hot enough to burn other parts of the body. A reasonable seller might also conclude that patrons desire coffee lids which prevent spillage in ordinary handling, but are not tight enough to avert a spill under other circumstances, such as when driving over a bump. It was the plaintiff's obligation to demonstrate that she had proof that the defendant breached a recognizable standard, and that such proof is sufficient to justify a verdict in her favor at trial. She has not done so, and accordingly the motion for summary judgment must be granted.

INTERPRETATION Strict liability in tort only applies if the defective product is unreasonably dangerous to the user or consumer.

CRITICAL THINKING QUESTION Do you agree with the court's decision? Explain.

CPA OBSTACLES TO RECOVERY

Few of the obstacles to recovery in warranty cases present serious problems to plaintiffs in strict liability actions brought pursuant to Section 402A because this section was drafted largely to avoid such obstacles.

DISCLAIMERS AND NOTICE

Comment m to Section 402A provides that the basis of strict liability rests solely in tort and therefore is not subject to contractual defenses. The comment specifically states that strict product liability is not governed by the Code, that it is not affected by contractual limitations or disclaimers, and that it is not subject to any requirement that notice be given to the seller by the injured party within a reasonable time. Nevertheless, most courts have *allowed* clear and specific disclaimers of Section 402A liability in *commercial* transactions between merchants of relatively equal economic power.

PRIVITY

With respect to horizontal privity, the strict liability in tort of manufacturers and other sellers extends not only to buyers, users, and consumers, but also to injured bystanders.

In terms of vertical privity, strict liability in tort imposes liability on any seller who is engaged in the business of selling the product, including a wholesaler or distributor as well as the manufacturer and retailer. The rule of strict liability in tort also applies to the manufacturer of a defective component that is used in a larger product if the manufacturer of the finished product has made no essential change in the component.

PLAINTIFF'S CONDUCT

Many product liability defenses relate to the conduct of the plaintiff. The claim common to all of them is that the plaintiff's improper conduct so contributed to the plaintiff's injury that it would be unfair to blame the product or its seller.

Contributory Negligence **Contributory negligence** is conduct on the part of the plaintiff (1) that falls below the standard to which he should conform for his own protection and (2) that is the legal cause of the plaintiff's harm. Because strict liability is designed to assess liability without fault, Section 402A rejects contributory negligence as a defense. Thus, a seller cannot defend a strict liability lawsuit on the basis of a plaintiff's negligent failure to discover a defect or to guard against its possibility. But, as discussed later, contributory negligence in the form of an assumption of the risk can bar recovery under Section 402A.

Comparative Negligence Under **comparative negligence,** the court apportions damages between the parties in proportion to the degree of fault or negligence it finds against them. Despite Section 402A's bar of contributory negligence in strict liability cases, most courts apply comparative negligence to strict liability cases. (Some courts use the term *comparative responsibility* rather than *comparative negligence*.) There are two basic types of comparative negligence or comparative responsibility. One is pure comparative responsibility, which simply reduces the plaintiff's recovery in proportion to her fault, whatever that may be. Thus, the recovery of a plaintiff found to be 80 percent at fault in causing an accident in which she suffered a $100,000 loss would be limited to 20 percent of her damages, or $20,000. Under the other type of negligence, modified comparative responsibility, the plaintiff

Ethical Dilemma

When Should a Company Order a Product Recall?

FACTS Walter Jones was feeding his five-month-old daughter Millie plums from a jar of Winkler baby food when she suddenly began to choke on a piece of aluminum foil that had come from the jar. Walter rushed her to the hospital, where more foil was found in her stomach. Although the amount of aluminum found was not in itself deadly, Millie was nauseous for several hours, and her parents had trouble getting her to eat for many days thereafter.

Walter sued Winkler. A number of similar incidents involving Winkler products had occurred at about the same time. Although the incidents covered a wide geographic area, their total number was not great, and the FDA decided not to require a recall of the baby food. Winkler faced two choices: (1) to do nothing and settle the cases as they arose or (2) to recall all jars of the same lot to protect other children from the possibility of ingesting foreign substances.

SOCIAL, POLICY, AND ETHICAL CONSIDERATIONS

1. What are the social and ethical issues Winkler must consider in choosing its course of action? Should the fact that none of the incidents had been fatal affect the company's decision? What should Winkler do?
2. Would the first option be good for business? Who eventually bears the cost of the lawsuits or recalls? Who should bear the cost?
3. What actions should be taken by the baby's parents? Do they have any social responsibility in this case to seek publicity sufficient to warn others?

recovers according to the general principles of comparative responsibility *unless* she is more than 50 percent responsible for her injuries, in which case she recovers nothing. The majority of comparative negligence states follows the modified comparative responsibility approach.

Voluntary Assumption of the Risk Assumption of risk is a defense in an action based on strict liability in tort. Basically, **assumption of the risk** is the plaintiff's express or implied consent to encounter a known danger. Thus, a person who drives an automobile after realizing that the brakes are not working and an employee who attempts to remove a foreign object from a high-speed roller press without shutting off the power have assumed the risk of their own injuries.

To establish such a defense, the defendant must show that (1) the plaintiff actually knew and appreciated the particular risk or danger the defect created; (2) the plaintiff voluntarily encountered the risk while realizing the danger; and (3) the plaintiff's decision to encounter the known risk was unreasonable.

Misuse or Abuse of the Product Closely connected to voluntary assumption of the risk is the valid defense of misuse or abuse of the product by the injured party. **Misuse** or **abuse** occurs when the injured party knows, or should know, that he is using the product in a manner the seller did not contemplate. The major difference between misuse or abuse and assumption of the risk is that the former includes actions that the injured party does not know to be dangerous, whereas the latter does not include such conduct. Instances of such misuse or abuse include standing on a rocking chair to change a light bulb or using a lawn mower to trim hedges. The courts, however, have significantly limited this defense by requiring that the misuse or abuse not be foreseeable by the seller. If a use is foreseeable, then the seller must take measures to guard against it.

SUBSEQUENT ALTERATION

Section 402A provides that liability exists only if the product reaches "the user or consumer without substantial change in the condition in which it is sold." Accordingly, most, but not all, courts would not hold a manufacturer liable for a faulty carburetor if a car dealer had removed the part and made significant changes in it before reinstalling it in an automobile.

STATUTE OF REPOSE

A number of lawsuits have been brought against manufacturers many years after a product was first sold. In response, many states have adopted statutes of repose. These enactments limit the period—typically between six and twelve years—for which a manufacturer is liable for injury caused by a defective product. After the statutory time period has elapsed, a manufacturer ceases to be liable for such harm. See the Ethical Dilemma "When Should a Company Order a Product Recall?" and the Managerial Insight "A. H. Robins: What Went Wrong?".

LIMITATIONS ON DAMAGES

More than half of the states have limited the punitive damages that a plaintiff can collect in a product liability lawsuit. They have done this by a number of means including:

1. Placing caps on the amount of damages that can be awarded—with caps ranging from $50,000 to $5,000,000;
2. Providing for the state to receive all or a portion of any punitive damages awarded with the state's share ranging from 35 percent to 100 percent in order to reduce the plaintiff's incentive to bring products liability suits;
3. Providing for bifurcated trials; i.e., separate hearings to determine liability and punitive damages;
4. Increasing the plaintiff's burden of proof for recovery of punitive damages with most states adopting the "clear and convincing" evidence standard; and
5. Requiring proportionality between compensatory and punitive damages by specifying an acceptable ratio between the two types of damages.

See the following Concept Review.

RESTATEMENT (THIRD) OF TORTS: PRODUCTS LIABILITY

The recently promulgated Restatement (Third) of Torts: Products Liability makes some significant changes in product liability. It is likely that the adoption of the new Restatement by the states will be a slow process, and in the meantime the great majority of states will continue to follow Section 402A of the Second Restatement of Torts.

The new Restatement expands Section 402A into an entire treatise of its own, comprising more than twenty sections. The Restatement (Third) does not use the term "strict liability" but instead defines separate liability standards for each type of defect. The new Restatement continues to cover anyone engaged in the business of selling or distributing a defective product if the defect causes harm to persons or property. Its major provision (Section 2)

CONCEPT REVIEW

Product Liability

	Merchantability*	Strict Liability in Tort (§ 402A)
Condition of Goods Creating Liability	Not fit for ordinary purposes	Defective condition, unreasonably dangerous
Type of Transaction	Sales and leases; some courts apply to bailments of goods	Sales, leases, and bailments of goods
Disclaimer	Must mention "merchantability." If in writing, must be conspicuous. Must not be unconscionable. Sales subject to Magnuson-Moss Act.	Not possible in consumer transactions; may be permitted in commercial transactions
Notice to Seller	Required within reasonable time	Not required
Causation	Required	Required
Who May Sue	In some states, buyer and the buyer's family or guests in home; in other states, any person who may be expected to use, consume, or be affected by goods	Any user or consumer of product; also, in most states, any bystander
Compensable Harms	Personal injury, property damage, economic loss	Personal injury, property damage
Who May Be Sued	Seller or lessor who is a merchant with respect to the goods sold	Seller who is engaged in business of selling such a product

*The warranty of fitness for a particular purpose differs from the warranty of merchantability in the following respects: (1) the condition that triggers liability is the failure of the goods to perform according to the particular purpose described in the warranty, and (2) a disclaimer need not mention "fitness for a particular purpose."

A.H. Robins: What Went Wrong?

Until the 1970s, A. H. Robins of Richmond, Virginia, operated as a relatively small, essentially family-run company with a fairly wholesome image. Nearly a decade later, however, the company's name rang sourly in the public ear.

For years, the pharmaceutical firm had been headed by E. Claiborne Robins, Sr., its chairman, and his son, E. Claiborne Robins, Jr., its chief executive officer. Both men were well respected in Richmond, and the elder Robins was known as a generous man who donated millions to educational and other concerns. Initially, A. H. Robins made such popular products as Robitussin cough medicine, Chap Stick lip balm, and Sergeant's flea and tick collars. Then the company decided to get into the birth-control business, and there its troubles began.

With the sexual revolution of the Sixties and the advent of the birth-control pill, corporate America sensed profits to be made from any new form of birth-control—potentially large profits. But the trick was to find a safe, easy-to-use, acceptable product.

At the prestigious Johns Hopkins Hospital in Baltimore in the late 1960s, Dr. Hugh J. Davis, director of the hospital's birth-control clinic, was testing a new intrauterine device, known as the Dalkon Shield. The plastic, nickel-sized, crablike instrument was inserted into a woman's uterus as a way to prevent pregnancy. No one knew why or how IUDs worked.

In February 1970, Davis reported in the *American Journal of Obstetrics and Gynecology* that the pregnancy rate for his Dalkon Shield was 1.1 percent, a rate similar to or lower than that of the birth-control pill. He did not disclose, however, that he was part owner of the small Dalkon Corporation that made the new IUD.

A few months later, A. H. Robins took notice of the Dalkon Shield at a physicians' conference in Pennsylvania. By June of that year, the firm had acquired the rights to the device and had hired Davis on as a consultant. Within two weeks of the Dalkon Shield's purchase, A. H. Robins began to hear of problems. One of its own officials cited potential difficulties with the device's tail, which, unlike the tails of other IUDs, consisted of hundreds of tiny filaments enclosed in a nylon shield that was open at one end. The tail's exposed threads could potentially attract bacteria and thus cause infection.

Still, A. H. Robins rushed the Dalkon Shield into production. The company made a few design changes but conducted no more research on the device. Nor did the Food and Drug Administration require the company to get approval for the device before introducing it, since the Dalkon Shield was classified as a medical device, not a drug.

Within six months of buying the Dalkon Shield, A. H. Robins launched a major marketing campaign. Thousands of reprints of Davis's study that included his 1.1 percent pregnancy rate were distributed across the country. Less than a year later, the Dalkon Shield had captured 60 percent of the IUD market in the United States.

Sales mounted, and the money rolled in. By February 1971, however, the company had received two reports of women developing pelvic inflammatory disease, a painful infection that can lead to sterility. Soon, more adverse evidence surfaced. New reports suggested that the pregnancy rate for the Dalkon Shield ran as high as 4.3 percent. Another study suggested that as many as 1 in 14 Dalkon Shield wearers suffered from infections. But that wasn't the only danger. While some Dalkon Shield wearers were hospitalized for infection, others were admitted for perforated uteruses or, if they happened to be pregnant, for ectopic pregnancies, for septic (or infected) abortions, or for premature labor and delivery. Some became sterile. Some died. By 1973, A. H. Robins had evidence that six women wearing the Dalkon Shield had died from septic abortions—yet it did little.

Nor did the Food and Drug Administration (FDA) respond quickly. Not until June of 1973 did the FDA write A. H. Robins to tell the company that it should stop selling the Dalkon Shield because of safety questions. Two days later, A. H. Robins voluntarily withdrew the device from the U.S. market, yet the company waited nearly another year before banning international sales of the Dalkon Shield.

By early 1974, A. H. Robins faced another threat: lawsuits from injured women. The company, however, fought back fiercely, often playing hardball with women who pressed their claims, questioning them vociferously about their sex lives and suggesting that their own behavior had led to any problems that they might be having. Until 1979, the company was able to settle many cases out of court for an average of $11,000 each.

But then things began to unravel for A. H. Robins. In 1979, a Denver jury decided against the company, awarding an injured woman more than $6.8 million, most of it in punitive damages.

By 1984, the company had paid out $314 million in some 8,300 lawsuits. It still faced 3,800 additional lawsuits, and women were filing new suits every day. Pressure was beginning to mount. Then, in February of that year, Judge Miles Lord of the U. S. District Court in Minneapolis, exasperated by the number of Dalkon Shield lawsuits that he had presided over, made national news when he summoned three top A. H. Robins executives, including CEO E. Claiborne Robins, Jr., to his courtroom and lashed out at the officers, condemning them for their hard-heartedness and begging them to take action to protect the women who still wore the Dalkon Shield.

Obviously, the company had to do something. So, by October, A. H. Robins launched a major advertising campaign to tell women that it would pay for the removal of their Dalkon Shields. But it did not issue a recall.

Then it asked the U.S. District Court in Richmond, Virginia, to set one national trial as part of a class action suit to determine whether punitive damages should be awarded to claimants and, if so, how much. The company also moved to establish a reserve fund of $615 million to pay for pending and future claims. The fund was the biggest ever to be set aside to settle liability claims for a medical device. Unfortunately, the company underestimated the Dalkon Shield's costs.

By August 1985, A. H. Robins was in deep trouble. The company and its insurer, Aetna Life and Casualty Co., had lost $530 million in 9,500 lawsuits, and they were facing 5,200 more cases. Meanwhile, 400 new cases were being filed each month. In addition, the company had been forced to stare down a shareholders' lawsuit, which it settled for $6.9 million. With nowhere else to go, A. H. Robins filed for bankruptcy.

The end had come. But how could things have gone so terribly wrong? How could a company such as A. H. Robins have miscalculated so badly?

Despite evidence of the Dalkon Shield's risks, the company, according to its critics, did not act quickly or responsibly to warn physicians and women of the danger. In fact, A. H. Robins, these critics say, attempted to slide over the problem. Moreover, to date the company has never issued a recall of the Dalkon Shield and has always said publicly that the device was neither defective nor unreasonably dangerous.

defines a product as defective "when, at the time of sale or distribution, it contains a manufacturing defect, is defective in design, or is defective because of inadequate instructions or warnings." Thus, Section 2 explicitly recognizes the three types of product defects discussed in this chapter: manufacturing defects, design defects, and failure to warn.

MANUFACTURING DEFECTS

Section 2(a) provides that "A product . . . contains a manufacturing defect when the product departs from its intended design even though all possible care was exercised in the preparation and marketing of the product." Therefore, sellers and distributors of products remain strictly liable for manufacturing defects, although a plaintiff may seek to recover based upon allegations and proof of negligent manufacture. In actions against the manufacturer, the plaintiff ordinarily must prove that the defect existed in the product when it left the manufacturer.

DESIGN DEFECT

Section 2(b) states: "A product . . . is defective in design when the foreseeable risks of harm posed by the product could have been reduced or avoided by the adoption of a reasonable alternative design by the seller or other distributor, or a predecessor in the commercial chain of distribution, and the omission of the reasonable alternative design renders the product not reasonably safe." This rule pulls back from a strict liability standard and imposes a negligence-like standard by requiring that the defect be reasonably foreseeable and that it could have been avoided by a reasonable alternative design. The Comments explain that this standard involves resolving "whether a reasonable alternative design would, at a reasonable cost, have reduced the foreseeable risk of harm posed by the product and, if so, whether the omission of the alternative design by the seller . . . rendered the product not reasonably safe." The burden rests upon the plaintiff to demonstrate the existence of a reasonable alternative safer design that would have reduced the foreseeable risks of harm. However, consumer expectations do not constitute an independent standard for judging the defectiveness of product designs.

FAILURE TO WARN

Section 2(c) provides: "A product . . . is defective because of inadequate instructions or warnings when the foreseeable risks of harm posed by the product could have been reduced or avoided by the provision of reasonable instructions or warnings by the seller or other distributor, or a predecessor in the commercial chain of distribution and the omission of the instructions or warnings renders the product not reasonably safe." Commercial product sellers must provide reasonable instructions and warnings about risks of injury associated with their products. The omission of warnings sufficient to allow informed decisions by reasonably foreseeable users or consumers renders the product not reasonably safe at time of sale. A seller, however, is under a duty to warn only if he knew or should have known of the risks involved. Moreover, warning about risks is effective only if an alternative design to avoid the risk cannot reasonably be implemented. Whenever safer products can be reasonably designed at a reasonable cost, adoption of the safer design is required rather than using a warning or instructions.

CHAPTER SUMMARY

Warranties

Types of Warranties

Definition of Warranty an obligation of the seller to the buyer (or lessor to lessee) concerning title, quality, characteristics, or condition of goods

Warranty of Title the obligation of a seller to convey the right of ownership without any lien (in a lease the warranty protects the lessee's right to possess and use the goods)

Express Warranty an affirmation of fact or promise about the goods or a description, including a sample, of the goods, which becomes part of the basis of the bargain

Implied Warranty a contractual obligation, arising out of certain circumstances of the sale or lease, imposed by operation of law and not found in the language of the sales or lease contract

- *Merchantability* warranty by a merchant seller that the goods are reasonably fit for the ordinary purpose for which they are manufactured or sold, pass without objection in the trade under the contract description, and are of fair, average quality
- *Fitness for Particular Purpose* warranty by any seller that goods are reasonably fit for a particular purpose if, at the time of contracting, the seller had reason to know the buyer's particular purpose and that the buyer was relying on the seller's skill and judgment to furnish suitable goods

Obstacles to Warranty Actions

Disclaimer of Warranties a negation of a warranty

- *Express Warranty* usually not possible to disclaim
- *Warranty of Title* may be excluded or modified by specific language or by certain circumstances, including judicial sale or a sale by a sheriff, executor, or foreclosing lienor
- *Implied Warranty of Merchantability* the disclaimer must mention "merchantability" and, in the case of a writing, must be conspicuous (in a lease the disclaimer must be in writing and conspicuous)
- *Implied Warranty of Fitness for a Particular Purpose* the disclaimer must be in writing and conspicuous
- *Other Disclaimers of Implied Warranties* the implied warranties of merchantability and fitness for a particular purpose may also be disclaimed (1) by expressions like "as is," "with all faults," or other similar language; (2) by course of dealing, course of performance, or usage of trade; or (3) as to defects an examination ought to have revealed where the buyer has examined the goods or where the buyer has refused to examine the goods
- *Federal Legislation Relating to Warranties of Consumer Goods* the Magnuson-Moss Warranty Act protects purchasers of consumer goods by providing that warranty information be clear and useful and that a seller who makes a written warranty cannot disclaim any implied warranty

Limitation or Modification of Warranties permitted as long as it is not unconscionable

Privity of Contract a contractual relationship between parties that was necessary at common law to maintain a lawsuit

- *Horizontal Privity* doctrine determining who benefits from a warranty and who therefore may bring a cause of action; the Code provides three alternatives
- *Vertical Privity* doctrine determining who in the chain of distribution is liable for a breach of warranty; the Code has not adopted a position on this

Notice of Breach if the buyer fails to notify the seller of any breach within a reasonable time, she is barred from any remedy against the seller

Plaintiff's Conduct
- *Contributory Negligence* is not a defense
- *Voluntary Assumption of the Risk* is a defense

Strict Liability in Tort

Nature

General Rule imposes tort liability on merchant sellers for both personal injuries and property damage for selling a product in a defective condition unreasonably dangerous to the user or consumer

Defective Condition
- *Manufacturing Defect* by failing to meet its own manufacturing specifications, the product is not properly made
- *Design Defect* the product, though made as designed, is dangerous because the design is inadequate
- *Failure to Warn* failure to provide adequate warning of possible danger or to provide appropriate directions for use of a product

Unreasonably Dangerous contains a danger beyond that which would be contemplated by the ordinary consumer

Obstacles to Recovery

Contractual Defenses defenses such as privity, disclaimers, and notice generally do not apply to tort liability

Plaintiff's Conduct
- *Contributory Negligence* not a defense in the majority of states
- *Comparative Negligence* most states have applied the rule of comparative negligence to strict liability in tort
- *Voluntary Assumption of the Risk* is a defense
- *Misuse or Abuse of the Product* is a defense

Subsequent Alteration liability exists only if the product reaches the user or consumer without substantial change in the condition in which it is sold

Statute of Repose limits the time period for which a manufacturer is liable for injury caused by its product

Limitations on Damages many states have limited the punitive damages that a plaintiff can collect in a product liability lawsuit

Restatement (Third) of Torts: Products Liability

General Rule one engaged in the business of selling products who sells a defective product is subject to liability for harm to persons or property caused by the defect

Defective Conditions
- *Manufacturing Defect* a seller is held to strict liability when the product departs from its intended design
- *Design Defect* a product is defective when the foreseeable risks of harm posed by the product could have been reduced or avoided by the adoption of a reasonable alternative design
- *Failure to Warn* a product is defective because of inadequate instructions or warnings when the foreseeable risks of harm posed by the product could have been reduced or avoided by the provision of reasonable instructions or warnings

QUESTIONS

1. At the start of the social season, Aunt Lavinia purchased a hula skirt in Sadie's dress shop. The salesperson told her, "This superior garment will do things for a person." Aunt Lavinia's houseguest, her niece, Florabelle, asked and obtained her aunt's permission to wear the skirt to a masquerade ball. In the midst of the festivity, where there was much dancing, drinking, and smoking, the long skirt brushed against a glimmering cigarette butt. Unknown to Aunt Lavinia and Florabelle, its wearer, the garment was made of a fine unwoven fiber that is highly flammable. It burst into flames, and Florabelle suffered severe burns. Aunt Lavinia notified Sadie of the accident and of Florabelle's intention to recover from Sadie. Can Florabelle recover damages from Sadie, the proprietor of the dress shop, and Exotic Clothes, Inc., the manufacturer from which Sadie purchased the skirt? Explain.

2. The Talent Company, manufacturer of a widely advertised and expensive perfume, sold a quantity of this product to Young, a retail druggist. Dorothy and Bird visited the store of Young, and Dorothy, desiring to make a gift to Bird, purchased a bottle of this perfume from Young, asking for it by its trade name. Young wrapped up the bottle and handed it directly to Bird. The perfume contained a foreign chemical that upon the first use of the perfume by Bird severely burned her face and caused a permanent facial disfigurement. What are the rights of Bird, if any, against Dorothy, Young, and the Talent Company?

3. John Doe purchased a bottle of "Bleach-All," a well-known brand, from Roe's combination service station and grocery store. When John used the "Bleach-All," his clothes severely deteriorated due to an error in mixing the chemicals during the detergent's manufacture. John brings an action against Roe to recover damages. Explain whether John will be successful in his lawsuit.

4. A route salesperson for Ideal Milk Company delivered a half-gallon glass jug of milk to Allen's home. The next day, when Allen grasped the milk container by its neck to take it out of his refrigerator, it shattered in his hand and caused serious injury. Allen paid Ideal on a monthly basis for the regular delivery of milk. Ideal's milk bottles each contained the legend "Property of Ideal—to be returned," and the route salesman would pick up the empty bottles when he delivered milk. Can Allen recover damages from Ideal Milk Company? Why?

5. While Butler and his wife, Wanda, were browsing through Sloan's used car lot, Butler told Sloan that he was looking for a safe but cheap family car. Sloan said, "That old Cadillac hearse ain't hurt at all, and I'll sell it to you for $2,950." Butler said, "I'll have to take your word for it because I don't know a thing about cars." Butler asked Sloan whether he would guarantee the car, and Sloan replied, "I don't guarantee used cars." Then Sloan added, "But I have checked that Caddy over, and it will run another 10,000 miles without needing any repairs." Butler replied, "It has to because I won't have an extra dime for any repairs." Butler made a down payment of $400 and signed a printed form contract, furnished by Sloan, that contained a provision: "Seller does not warrant the condition or performance of any used automobile."

   As Butler drove the car out of Sloan's lot, the left rear wheel fell off and Butler lost control of the vehicle. It veered over an embankment, causing serious injuries to Wanda. What is Sloan's liability to Butler and Wanda?

6. John purchased for cash a Revenge automobile manufactured by Japanese Motors, Ltd., from an authorized franchised dealer in the United States. The dealer told John that the car had a "twenty-four month 24,000-mile warranty." Two days after John accepted delivery of the car, he received an eighty-page manual in fine print that stated, among other things, on page 72:

   > The warranties herein are expressly in lieu of any other express or implied warranty, including any implied warranty of merchantability or fitness, and of any other obligation on the part of the company or the selling dealer.
   >
   > Japanese Motors, Ltd., and the selling dealer warrant to the owner each part of this vehicle to be free under use and service from defects in material and workmanship for a period of twenty-four months from the date of original retail delivery of first use or until it has been driven for 24,000 miles, whichever first occurs.

   Within nine months after the purchase, John was forced to return the car for repairs to the dealer on thirty different occasions; and the car has been in the dealer's custody for more than seventy days during these nine months. The dealer has been forced to make major repairs to the engine, transmission, and steering assembly. The car is now in the custody of the dealer for further major repairs, and John has demanded that it keep the car and refund his entire purchase price. The dealer has refused on the ground that it has not breached its contract and is willing to continue repairing the car during the remainder of the "twenty-four/twenty-four" period. What are the rights and liabilities of the dealer and John?

7. Fred Lyon of New York, while on vacation in California, rented a new model Home Run automobile from Hart's Drive-A-Car. The car was manufactured by the Ange Motor Company and was purchased by Hart's from Jammer, Inc., an automobile importer. Lyon was driving the car on a street in San Jose when, due to a defect in the steering mechanism, it suddenly became impossible to steer. The speed of the car at the time was thirty miles per hour, but before Lyon could bring it to a stop, the car jumped a low curb and struck Peter Wolf, who was standing on the sidewalk, breaking both of his legs and causing other injuries. What rights does Wolf have against (a) Hart's Drive-A-Car, (b) Ange Motor Company, (c) Jammer, and (d) Lyon?

8. The plaintiff brings this cause of action against a manufacturer for the loss of his leg below the hip. The leg was lost when caught in the gears of a screw auger machine sold and installed by the defendant. Shortly before the accident, the plaintiff's co-employees had removed a covering panel from the machine by use of sledgehammers and crowbars in order to do repair work. When finished with their repairs, they replaced the panel with a single piece of cardboard instead of restoring the equipment to its original condition. The plaintiff stepped on the cardboard in the course of his work and fell, catching his leg in the moving parts. Explain what causes of action the plaintiff may have against the defendant and what defenses the defendant could raise.

9. The plaintiff, while driving a pickup manufactured by the defendant, was struck in the rear by another motor vehicle. Upon impact, the plaintiff's head was jarred backward against the rear window of the cab, causing the plaintiff serious injury. The pickup was not equipped with a headrest, and none was required at the time. Should the plaintiff prevail on a cause of action based upon strict liability in tort? Why? Why not?

10. The plaintiff, while dining at the defendant's restaurant, ordered a chicken pot pie. While she was eating, she swallowed a sliver of chicken bone, which became lodged in her throat, causing her serious injury. The plaintiff brings a cause of action. Should she prevail? Why?

11. Salem Supply Co. sells new and used gardening equipment. Ben Buyer purchased a slightly used riding lawn mower for $1,500. The price was considerably less than that of comparable used mowers. The sale was clearly indicated to be "as is." Two weeks after Ben purchased the mower, the police arrived at his house with Owen Owner, the true owner of the lawn mower, which was stolen from his yard, and reclaimed the mower. What recourse, if any, does Ben have?

12. Seigel, a seventy-three-year-old man, was injured at one of Giant Food's retail food stores (http://www.giantfood.com) when a bottle of Coca-Cola (http://www.coca-cola.com) exploded as he was placing a six-pack of Coke into his shopping cart. The explosion caused him to lose his balance and fall, with injuries resulting. Has Giant breached its implied warranty of merchantability to Seigel? Why?

13. Guarino and two others (plaintiffs) died of gas asphyxiation and five others were injured when they entered a sewer tunnel without masks to answer the cries for help of their crew leader, Rooney. Rooney had left the sewer shaft and entered the tunnel to fix a water leakage problem. Having corrected the problem, Rooney was returning to the shaft when he apparently was overcome by gas because of a defect in his oxygen mask, which was manufactured by Mine Safety Appliance Company (defendant). The plaintiffs brought this action against the defendant for breach of warranty, and the defendant raised the defense of the plaintiffs' voluntary assumption of the risk. Explain who will prevail.

CASE PROBLEMS

14. Green Seed Company packaged, labeled, and marketed a quality tomato seed known as "Green's Pink Shipper" for commercial sale. Brown Seed Store, a retailer, purchased the seed from Green Seed and then sold it to Guy Jones, an individual engaged in the business of growing tomato seedlings for sale to commercial tomato growers. Williams purchased the seedlings from Jones and then transplanted and raised them in accordance with accepted farming methods. The plants, however, produced not the promised "Pink Shipper" tomatoes but an inferior variety that spoiled in the field. Williams then brought an action against Green Seed for $900, claiming that his crop damage had been caused by Green Seed's breach of an express warranty. Green Seed argued in defense that its warranty did not extend to remote purchasers and that the company did not receive notice of the claimed breach of warranty. Who will prevail? Why?

15. Shell Oil Company (http://www.shell.com) leased to Flying Tiger Line a gasoline tank truck with a movable ladder for refueling certain types of aircraft. Under the terms of the lease, Flying Tiger was to maintain the equipment in safe operating order, but Shell was obligated to make most of the repairs at Flying Tiger's request. Four years after the lease was entered, Shell, at Flying Tiger's request, replaced the original ladder with a new one built by an undisclosed manufacturer. Both Flying Tiger and Shell inspected the new ladder. Two years later, however, Price, an aircraft mechanic employed by Flying Tiger, was seriously injured when the ladder's legs split while he was climbing onto an airplane wing. What are Price's rights against Shell and Flying Tiger?

16. Mobley purchased from Century Dodge a car described in the contract as new. The contract also contained a disclaimer of all warranties, express or implied. Subsequently, Mobley discovered that the car had, in fact, been involved in an accident. He then sued Century Dodge to recover damages, claiming the dealer had breached its express warranty that the car was new. Century Dodge argues that it had adequately disclaimed all warranties. Decision?

17. On August 22, O'Neil purchased a used diesel tractor-trailer combination from International Harvester. O'Neil claimed that International Harvester's salesman had told him that the truck had recently been overhauled and that it would be suitable for hauling logs in the mountains. The

written installment contract signed by the parties provided that the truck was sold "AS IS WITHOUT WARRANTY OF ANY CHARACTER express or implied." O'Neil admitted that he had read the disclaimer clause but claimed that he understood it to mean that the tractor-trailer would be in the condition that International Harvester's salesman had promised.

O'Neil paid the $1,700 down payment, but he failed to make any of the monthly payments. He claimed that he refused to pay because his employee had many problems with the truck when he took it to the mountains. Delays resulting from those problems, O'Neil argued, had caused him to lose his permit to cut firewood and, therefore, the accompanying business. An International Harvester representative agreed to pay for one-half of the cost of certain repairs, but the several attempts made to fix the truck were unsuccessful. O'Neil then tried to return the truck and to rescind the sale, but International Harvester refused to cooperate. Decision?

18. Mrs. Embs went into Stamper's Cash Market to buy soft drinks for her children. She had removed five bottles from an upright soft drink cooler, placed them in a carton, and turned to move away from the display when a bottle of Seven-Up (http://www.7up.com) in a carton at her feet exploded, cutting her leg. Apparently, several other bottles had exploded that same week. Stamper's Cash Market received its entire stock of Seven-Up from Arnold Lee Vice, the area distributor. Vice in turn received his entire stock of Seven-Up from Pepsi-Cola Bottling Co. Can Mrs. Embs recover damages from (a) Stamper, (b) Vice, or (c) Pepsi-Cola Bottling? Why?

19. Catania wished to paint the exterior of his house. He went to Brown, a local paint store owner, and asked him to recommend a paint for the job. Catania told Brown that the exterior walls were stucco and in a chalky, powdery condition. Brown suggested Pierce's shingle and shake paint. Brown then instructed Catania how to mix the paint and how to use a wire brush to prepare the surface. Five months later, the paint began to peel, flake, and blister. Catania brings an action against Brown. Decision?

20. Robinson, a truck driver for a moving company, decided to buy a used truck from the company. Branch, the owner, told Robinson that the truck was being repaired and that Robinson should wait and inspect the truck before signing the contract. Robinson, who had driven the truck before, felt that inspection was unnecessary. Again, Branch suggested Robinson wait to inspect the truck, and again Robinson declined. Branch then told Robinson he was buying the truck "as is." Robinson then signed the contract. After the truck broke down four times, Robinson sued. Will Robinson be successful? What defenses can Branch raise?

21. Perfect Products manufactures balloons, which are then bought and resold by wholesale novelty distributors. Mego Corp. manufactures a doll called "Bubble Yum Baby." A balloon is inserted in the doll's mouth with a mouthpiece, and the doll's arm is pumped to inflate the balloon, simulating the blowing of a bubble. Mego Corp. used Perfect Products balloons in the dolls, bought through independent distributors. The plaintiff's infant daughter died after swallowing a balloon removed from the doll. Is Perfect Products liable to plaintiff under a theory of strict liability? Explain.

22. Patient was injured when the footrest of an adjustable X-ray table collapsed, causing Patient to fall to the floor. G.E. manufactured the X-ray table and the footrest. At trial, evidence was introduced that G.E. had manufactured for several years another footrest model complete with safety latches. However, there was no evidence that the footrest involved was manufactured defectively. The action is based on a theory of strict liability. Who wins? Why?

23. Vlases, a coal miner who had always raised small flocks of chickens, spent two years building a new two-story chicken coop large enough to house 4,000 chickens. After its completion, he purchased 2,200 one-day-old chicks from Montgomery Ward for the purpose of producing eggs for sale. He had selected them from Ward's catalog, which stated that these chicks, hybrid Leghorns, were noted for their excellent egg production. Vlases had equipped the coop with brand-new machinery and had taken further hygiene precautions for the chicks' health. Almost one month later, Vlases noticed that their feathers were beginning to fall off. A veterinarian's examination revealed signs of drug intoxication and hemorrhagic disease in a few of the chicks. Eight months later, it was determined that the chicks were suffering from visceral and avian leukosis, or bird cancer, which reduced their egg-bearing capacity to zero. Avian leukosis may be transmitted either genetically or by unsanitary conditions. Subsequently, the disease infected the entire flock. Vlases then brought suit against Montgomery Ward for its breach of the implied warranties of merchantability and of fitness for a particular purpose. Ward claimed that there was no way to detect the disease in the one-day-old chicks, nor was there medication available to prevent this disease from occurring. Is Montgomery Ward liable under a warranty and/or strict liability cause of action? Explain.

24. Heckman, an employee of Clark Equipment Company, severely injured his left hand when he caught it in a power press that he was operating at work. The press was manufactured by Federal Press Company and sold to Clark eight years ago. It could be operated either by hand controls that required the use of both hands away from the point of operation or by an optional foot pedal. When the foot pedal was used without a guard, nothing remained to keep the operator's hands from the point of operation. Federal Press did not provide safety appliances unless the customer requested them, but when it delivered the press to Clark with the optional pedal, it suggested that Clark install a guard. The press had a similar warning embossed on it. Clark did, in fact, purchase a guard for $100, but it was not mounted on the machine at the time of the injury; nor was it believed to be an effective safety device.

Heckman argued that one type of guard, if installed, would have made the press safe in 95 percent of its customary uses. Federal, in turn, argued that the furnishing of guards was not customary in the industry; that the machine's many uses made it impracticable to design and install any one guard as standard equipment; that Clark's failure to obey Federal's warning was a superseding cause of the injury; and that state regulations placed responsibility for the safe operation of presses on employers and employees. The jury awarded Heckman $750,000, and Federal appealed. Decision?

25. For sixteen years, the late Mrs. Dorothy Mae Palmer was married to Mr. Schultz, an insulator who worked with asbestos products. Mrs. Palmer was not exposed to asbestos dust in a factory setting; rather, she was exposed when Mr. Schultz brought his work clothes home to be washed. Mrs. Palmer died of mesothelioma in 1986. This product liability suit was brought by Mrs. Palmer's daughters, Suzan Rohrbaugh, Barbara Ann Clay, and Debra Mae Ambler, to recover for the alleged wrongful death of their mother. The daughters claim that Mrs. Palmer's mesothelioma was the result of exposure to asbestos-containing products manufactured by Owens-Corning. The daughters claim that the asbestos products were defective and unreasonably dangerous and that Owens-Corning was negligent in failing to warn of the dangers associated with their products. The trial jury found in favor of Mrs. Palmer's daughters and awarded them damages in the amount of $450,000. Owens-Corning asserted that instructions given to the jury indicated that the manufacturer was obligated to warn Mrs. Palmer of the dangers of their products and appealed on the basis of incorrect instructions given to the jury. Decision?

26. A gasoline-powered lawn mower, which had been used earlier to cut grass, was left unattended next to a water heater which had been manufactured by Sears. Expert testimony was presented to demonstrate that vapors from the mower's gas tank accumulated under the water heater and resulted in an explosion. Three-year-old Shawn Toups was injured as a result. Evidence was also presented negating any claim that Shawn had been handling the gasoline can located nearby or the lawn mower. He was not burned on the soles of his feet or the palms of his hands, and, similarly, the gas can remained in an upright position even after the explosion. Is Sears liable to the Toups in strict product liability? Explain.

27. Between 1942 and her death in 1984, Rose Cipollone smoked between one and two packs of cigarettes a day. Upon her death in 1984 from lung cancer, Rose's husband, Antonio Cipollone, filed suit against Liggett Group, Inc., Lorillard, Inc, and Philip Morris, Inc. three of the leading firms in the tobacco industry, for the wrongful death of his wife. Many theories of liability and defenses were asserted in this decidedly complex and protracted litigation.

One theory of liability claimed by Mr. Cipollone was breach of express warranty. It is uncontested that all three manufacturers ran multimedia ad campaigns that contained affirmations, promises, or innuendos that smoking cigarettes was safe. For example, ads for Chesterfield cigarettes boasted that a medical specialist could find no adverse health effects in subjects after six months of smoking. Chesterfields were also advertised as being manufactured with "electronic miracle" technology that made them "better and safer for you." Another ad stated that Chesterfield ingredients were tested and approved by scientists from leading universities. Another brand, L&M, publicly touted the "miracle tip" filter, claiming it was "just what the doctor ordered."

At trial, the defendant tobacco companies were not permitted to try to prove that Mrs. Cipollone disbelieved or placed no reliance on the advertisements and their safety assurances. Did the defendants breach an express warranty to the plaintiff? Explain.

28. Trans-Aire International, Inc. (TAI) converts ordinary automotive vans into recreational vehicles. TAI had been installing carpet and ceiling fabrics in the converted vans with an adhesive made by the 3M Company. Unfortunately, during the hot summer months, the 3M adhesive would often fail to hold the carpet and fabrics in place.

TAI contacted Northern Adhesive Company (Northern), seeking a "suitable" product to replace the 3M adhesive. Northern sent samples of several adhesives, commenting that hopefully one or more "might be applicable." Northern also informed TAI that one of the samples, Adhesive 7448, was a "match" for the 3M adhesive. After testing all the samples under cool plant conditions, TAI's chief engineer determined that Adhesive 7448 was better than the 3M adhesive. When TAI's president asked if the new adhesive should be tested under summerlike conditions, the chief engineer responded that it was unnecessary to do so. The president then asked if Adhesive 7448 came with any warranties. A Northern representative stated that there were no warranties, except that the orders shipped would be identical to the sample.

After converting more than 500 vans using Adhesive 7448, TAI became aware that high summer temperatures were causing the new adhesive to fail. Should TAI prevail against Northern in a suit claiming breach of an implied warranty of fitness for a particular purpose and breach of an implied warranty of merchantability, as well as breach of express warranty? Explain.

http:// **Internet Exercise** Find and review information about product liability reform. Also determine what warranties are provided by several retailers on the Internet.

CHAPTER 23

Sales Remedies

Remedies . . . shall be liberally administered to the end that the aggrieved party may be put in as good a position as if the other party had fully performed.

UNIFORM COMMERCIAL CODE

Learning Objectives

After reading this chapter you should be able to:

1. Identify and explain the goods-oriented remedies of the seller and the buyer.
2. Identify and explain the obligation-oriented remedies of the seller and the buyer.
3. Identify and explain the money-oriented damages of the seller and the buyer.
4. Identify and explain the "specific performance" remedies of the seller and the buyer.
5. Describe the basic types of contractual provisions affecting remedies and the limitations that the Code imposes upon those provisions.

A contract for the sale of goods may be completely performed at one time or may be performed in stages, according to the parties' agreement. At any stage, one of the parties may repudiate the contract, may become insolvent, or may breach the contract by failing to perform her obligations under it. In a sales contract, breach may consist of the seller's delivering defective goods, too few goods, the wrong goods, or no goods. The buyer may breach by not accepting conforming goods or by failing to pay for conforming goods that she has accepted. Breach may occur when the goods are in the possession of the seller, in the possession of a bailee of the buyer, in transit to the buyer, or in the possession of the buyer.

Remedies, therefore, need to address not only the type of breach of contract but also the situation with respect to the goods. Consequently, the Code provides separate and distinct remedies for the seller and for the buyer, each specifically keyed to the type of breach and the situation of the goods.

Practical Advice

Consider including in your contracts a provision for (a) the recovery of attorneys' fees in the event of breach of contract and (b) the arbitration of contract disputes.

In all events, the purpose of the Code is to put the aggrieved party in a position as good as the one she would have been in had the other party fully performed. To accomplish this purpose, the Code has provided that the courts should liberally administer its remedies. Moreover, damages do not have to be "calculable with mathematical precision"; they simply must be proved with "whatever definiteness and accuracy the facts permit, but no more." The purpose of remedies under the Code is compensation; therefore, punitive damages are generally not available.

Finally, the Code has rejected the doctrine of election of remedies. Essentially, the Code provides that remedies for breach are cumulative. Whether one remedy bars another depends entirely on the facts of the individual case.

> **CISG**
>
> Damages for breach of contract by one party consist of the loss, including loss of profit, suffered by the other party as a consequence of the breach. Such damages may not exceed the loss which the party in breach foresaw or should have foreseen at the time of the conclusion of the contract as a possible consequence of the breach of contract. The aggrieved party must take such measures as are reasonable in the circumstances to mitigate the loss, including loss of profit, resulting from the breach. If he fails to take such measures, the party in breach may claim a reduction in the damages in the amount by which the loss should have been mitigated.

CPA

REMEDIES OF THE SELLER

A **buyer's default** in performing any of his contractual obligations deprives the seller of the rights for which he bargained. Such default may consist of any of the following acts: wrongfully rejecting the goods, wrongfully revoking acceptance of the goods, failing to make a payment due on or before delivery, or repudiating (indicating an intention not to perform) the contract in whole or in part. (Article 2A.) The Code catalogs the seller's remedies for each of these defaults. (Article 2A has a comparable set of remedies for the lessor.) These remedies allow the seller to (1) withhold delivery of the goods, (2) stop delivery of the goods by a carrier or other bailee, (3) identify to the contract conforming goods not already identified, (4) resell the goods and recover damages, (5) recover damages for nonacceptance of the goods or repudiation of the contract, (6) recover the price, (7) recover incidental damages, (8) cancel the contract, and (9) reclaim the goods on the buyer's insolvency.

Under Article 2A, a lessor also may recover compensation for any loss of or damage to the lessor's residual interest in the goods caused by the lessee's default.

It is useful to note that the first three and the ninth remedies indexed above are ***goods oriented***—that is, they relate to the seller's exercising control over the goods. The fourth through seventh remedies are ***money oriented*** because they provide the seller with the opportunity to recover monetary damages. The eighth remedy is ***obligation oriented*** because it allows the seller to avoid his obligation under the contract.

Moreover, if the seller delivers goods on credit and the buyer fails to pay the price when due, the seller's sole remedy, unless the buyer is insolvent, is to sue for the unpaid price. If, however, the buyer received the goods on credit while insolvent, the seller may be able to reclaim the goods. The Code defines insolvency to include both its equity meaning and its bankruptcy meaning. The **equity** meaning of **insolvency** is the inability to pay debts in the ordinary course of business or as they become due. The **bankruptcy** meaning of **insolvency** is that total liabilities exceed the total value of all assets.

As noted, the Code's remedies are cumulative. Thus, by way of example, an aggrieved seller may (1) identify goods to the contract, *and* (2) withhold delivery, *and* (3) resell or recover damages for nonacceptance or recover the price, *and* (4) recover incidental damages, *and* (5) cancel the contract.

> **CISG**
>
> If the buyer fails to perform any of his obligations, the seller may (1) require the buyer to pay the price or (2) fix an additional period of time of reasonable length for the buyer to perform his obligations. Unless the buyer notifies the seller that he will not perform within the period so fixed, the seller may not, during that period, resort to any remedy for breach of contract. Moreover, if the buyer's breach is fundamental or the buyer fails to perform within the additional time granted by the seller, the seller may avoid the contract. In addition to these remedies, the seller also has the right to damages.

TO WITHHOLD DELIVERY OF THE GOODS

A seller may withhold delivery of goods to a buyer who has wrongfully rejected or revoked acceptance of the goods, who has failed to make a payment due on or before delivery, or who has repudiated the contract. (Article 2A.) This right is essentially that of a seller to withhold or discontinue performance of her side of the contract because of the buyer's breach.

When the contract calls for installments, any breach of an installment that impairs the value of the *whole* contract will permit the seller to withhold the entire undelivered balance of the goods. In addition, on discovery of the buyer's insolvency, the seller may refuse to deliver the goods except for cash, including payment for all goods previously delivered under the contract. (Article 2A.)

TO STOP DELIVERY OF THE GOODS

An extension of the right to withhold delivery is the right of an aggrieved seller **to stop delivery** of goods in transit to the buyer or in the possession of a bailee. A seller who discovers that the buyer is insolvent may stop any delivery. If the buyer is not insolvent but repudiates or otherwise breaches the contract, the seller may stop carload, truckload, planeload, or larger shipments. (Article 2A.) To stop delivery, the seller must notify the carrier or other bailee soon enough for the bailee to prevent delivery of the goods. After this notification, the carrier or bailee must hold and deliver the goods according to the directions of the seller, who is liable to the carrier or bailee for any charges or damages incurred. If a negotiable document of title has been issued for the goods, the bailee need not obey a notification until surrender of the document.

TO IDENTIFY GOODS TO THE CONTRACT

On a breach of the contract by the buyer, the seller may proceed to identify to the contract conforming goods in her possession or control that were not so identified at the time she learned of the breach. (Article 2A.) This enables the seller to exercise the remedy of resale of goods (discussed below). Furthermore, the seller may resell any unfinished goods that have been demonstrably intended to fulfill the particular contract. The seller may either complete the manufacture of unfinished goods and identify them to the contract or cease their manufacture and resell the unfinished goods for scrap or salvage value. (Article 2A.) In so deciding, the seller must exercise reasonable commercial judgment to minimize her loss.

TO RESELL THE GOODS AND RECOVER DAMAGES

Under the same circumstances that permit the seller to withhold delivery of goods to the buyer (i.e., wrongful rejection or revocation, repudiation, or failure to make timely payment), the seller may **resell the goods** concerned or the undelivered balance of the goods. If the resale is made in good faith and in a commercially reasonable manner, the seller may recover from the buyer the difference between the contract price and the resale price, plus any incidental damages (discussed below), less expenses saved because of the buyer's breach. For example, Floyd agrees to sell goods to Beverly for a contract price of $8,000 due on delivery. Beverly repudiates the contract and refuses to pay Floyd anything. Floyd resells the goods in strict compliance with the Code for $6,000, incurring incidental damages for sales commissions of $500 but saving $200 in transportation costs. Floyd would recover from Beverly the difference between the contract price ($8,000) and the resale price ($6,000), plus incidental damages ($500), minus expenses saved ($200), which equals $2,300.

In a lease, the comparable recovery is the ***difference*** between the ***present values*** of the ***old rent*** due under the original lease and the ***new rent*** due under the new lease. More specifically, the lessor may recover (1) the accrued and unpaid rent as of the date of commencement of the new lease; (2) the present value as of that date of total rent for the then remaining term of the original lease ***minus*** the present value, as of the same date, of the rent under the new lease applicable to a comparable time period; *and* (3) any incidental damages, *less* expenses saved because of the lessee's breach.

The resale may be a public or private sale, and the goods may be sold as a unit or in parcels. When the resale is a private sale, the seller must give the buyer reasonable notice of his intention to resell. When the resale is at a public sale (such as an auction), it must be made at a usual place or market for public sale if one is reasonably available. The seller must give the buyer reasonable notice of the time and place of the resale, unless the goods are perishable or threaten to decline in value speedily. In addition, the seller may be a purchaser of the goods at the public sale. In choosing between a public and private sale, the seller must observe relevant trade practices and usages and take into account the character of the goods.

The seller is not accountable to the buyer for any profit made on any resale of the goods. (Article 2A.) Moreover, a good faith purchaser at a resale takes the goods free of any rights of the original buyer, even if the seller has failed to comply with one or more of the requirements of the Code in making the resale. (Article 2A.)

Failure to act in good faith and in a commercially reasonable manner deprives the seller of this remedy and relegates him to the remedy of recovering damages for nonacceptance or repudiation (discussed next). (Article 2A.)

CISG

If the contract is avoided and the seller has resold the goods in a reasonable manner and within a reasonable time after avoidance, he may recover the difference between the contract price and the resale price. In addition, he may recover consequential damages.

TO RECOVER DAMAGES FOR NONACCEPTANCE OR REPUDIATION

In the event of the buyer's wrongful rejection or revocation, repudiation, or failure to make timely payment, the seller may recover damages from the buyer equal to the **market price differential**, or the difference between the unpaid contract price and the market price at the time and place of tender of the goods, plus incidental damages, less expenses saved because of the buyer's breach. This remedy is an alternative to the remedy of reselling the goods.

In a lease the comparable recovery is the ***difference*** between the ***present values*** of the ***old rent*** due under the original lease and the ***market rent***.

For example, Joyce in Seattle agrees to sell goods to Maynard in Chicago for $20,000 F.O.B. Chicago, delivery on June 15. Maynard wrongfully rejects the goods. The market price would be ascertained as of June 15 in Chicago because F.O.B. Chicago is a destination contract in which the place of tender would be Chicago. The market price of the goods on June 15 in Chicago is $15,000. Joyce, who incurred $1,000 in incidental expenses while saving $500 in expenses, would recover from Maynard the difference between the contract price ($20,000) and the market price ($15,000), plus incidental damages ($1,000), minus expenses saved ($500), which equals $5,500.

If the difference between the contract price and the market price will not place the seller in as good a position as performance would have, then the measure of damages is the **profit**, including reasonable overhead, that the seller would have realized from full performance by the buyer, plus any incidental damages, less expenses the seller saved because of the buyer's breach. For example, Green, an automobile dealer, enters into a contract to sell a large, fuel-inefficient luxury car to Holland for $32,000. The price of gasoline increases 20 percent, and Holland repudiates. The market value of the car is still $32,000, but because Green cannot sell as many cars as he can obtain, Green's sales volume has decreased by one as a result of Holland's breach. Therefore, Green would be permitted to recover the profits he lost on the sale to Holland (computed as the contract price, minus what the car costs Green, plus an allocation of overhead), plus any incidental damages. The following case further explains the computation of lost profits.

Article 2A has a comparable provision, except the profit is reduced to its present value since the lessor would have received it over the term of the lease.

Practical Advice

Carefully consider whether you are better off reselling the goods or seeking damages for nonacceptance or repudiation.

CISG

If the contract is avoided and the seller has not made a resale, he may recover the difference between the contract price and the current price at the time of avoidance and at the place where delivery of goods should have been made. In addition, he may recover consequential damages.

Kenco Homes, Inc. v. Williams

Court of Appeals of Washington, Division Two, 1999

94 Wn.App. 219, 972 P.2d 125

http://caselaw.lp.findlaw.com/scripts/getcase.pl?court=wa&vol=209071&invol=o01

FACTS Kenco buys mobile homes from the factory and sells them to the consumer. Sometimes, it contracts to sell a home that the factory has not yet built. It has a virtually unlimited supply of product. On September 27, 1994, Kenco Homes, Inc., and Dale E. and Debi A. Williams, husband and wife, signed a written contract by which Kenco agreed to sell a mobile home to the Williams that Kenco had not yet ordered from the factory. The contract called for a price of $39,400, with $500 down.

The contract contained two pertinent conditions. First, the contract would be enforceable only if Williams could obtain financing. Second, the contract would be enforceable only if Williams later approved a bid for site improvements. Financing was to cover the cost of the mobile home and the cost of the land on which the mobile home would be placed. The contract provided for damages. It stated, "I [Williams] understand that you [Kenco] shall have all the rights of a seller upon breach of contract under the Uniform Commercial Code, except the right to seek and collect 'liquidated damages' under Section 2–718." The contract provided for reasonable attorney's fees. In early October, Williams accepted Kenco's bid for site improvements. As a result, the parties (a) formed a second contract and (b) fulfilled the first contract's site-improvement-approval condition. Also in early October, Williams received preliminary approval on the needed financing.

Subsequently, Williams gave Kenco a $600 check so Kenco could order an appraisal of the land on which the mobile home would be located. Before Kenco could act, however, Williams stopped payment on the check and repudiated the entire transaction. His reason was that he "had found a better deal elsewhere." When Williams repudiated, Kenco had not yet ordered the mobile home from the factory. After Williams repudiated, Kenco simply did not place the order. As a result, Kenco's only out-of-pocket expense was a minor amount of office overhead. On November 1, 1994, Kenco sued Williams for lost profits.

The trial court found that Williams had breached the contract, causing Kenco to lose profits in the amount of $11,133—$6,720 on the mobile home, and $4,413 on the site improvements. Moreover, the trial court held that Kenco was entitled to damages, but ruled that Kenco would be adequately compensated by retaining Williams' $500 down payment. The trial court declared that Williams was the prevailing party; and that Williams should receive reasonable attorney's fees in the amount of $1,800. Kenco appealed, claiming the trial court used an incorrect measure of damages.

DECISION Reversed with directions to enter an amended judgment awarding Kenco its lost profit of $11,133 and reasonable attorneys' fees incurred at trial and on appeal.

OPINION Morgan, J. Under the Uniform Commercial Code (UCC), a nonbreaching seller may recover "damages for non-acceptance" from a breaching buyer. [U.C.C. § 2–703(e)] The measure of such damages is as follows: (1) * * * the measure of damages for non-acceptance or repudiation by the buyer is the difference between the market price at the time and place for tender and the unpaid contract price together with any incidental damages provided in this Article ([U.C.C. §] 2–710), but less expenses saved in consequence of the buyer's breach. (2) If the measure of damages provided in subsection (1) is inadequate to put the seller in as good a position as performance would have done then the measure of damages is the profit (including reasonable overhead) which the seller would have made from full performance by the buyer, together with any incidental damages provided in this Article ([U.C.C. §] 2–710), due allowance for costs reasonably incurred and due credit for payments or proceeds of resale. [U.C.C. §] 2–708. * * * [T]he statute's purpose is to put the nonbreaching seller in the position that he or she would have occupied if the breaching buyer had fully performed (or, in alternative terms, to give the nonbreaching seller the benefit of his or her bargain). [U.C.C. §] 1–106(1). A party claiming damages under subsection (2) bears the burden of showing that an award of damages under subsection (1) would be inadequate. [Citation.] In general, the adequacy of damages under subsection (1) depends on whether the nonbreaching seller has a readily available market on which he or she can resell the goods that the breaching buyer should have taken. [Citation.] When a buyer breaches before either side has begun to perform, the amount needed to give the seller the benefit of his or her bargain is the difference between the contract price and the seller's expected cost of performance. Using market price, this difference can, in turn, be subdivided into two smaller differences: (a) the difference between the contract price and the market price, and (b) the difference between the market price and the seller's expected cost of performance. So long as a nonbreaching seller can reasonably resell the breached goods on the open market, he or she can recover the difference between contract price and market price by invoking subsection (1), and the difference between market price and his or her expected cost of performance by reselling the breached goods on the open market. Thus, he or she is made whole by subsection (1), and subsection (1) damages should be deemed "adequate." But if a nonbreaching seller cannot reasonably resell the breached goods on the open market, he or she cannot recover, merely by invoking subsection (1), the difference between market price and his or her expected cost of performance. Hence, he or she is not made whole by subsection (1); subsection (1) damages are "inadequate to put the seller in as good a position as performance would have done;" and subsection (2) comes into play.

The cases illustrate at least three specific situations in which a nonbreaching seller cannot reasonably resell on the open market. In the first, the seller never comes into possession of the breached goods; although he or she plans to acquire such goods before the buyer's breach, he or she rightfully elects not to acquire them after the buyer's breach. [Citation.] In the second, the seller possesses some or all of the breached goods, but they are of such an odd or peculiar nature that the seller lacks a post- breach market on which to sell them; they are, for example, unfinished, obsolete, or highly specialized. [Citations.] In the third situation, the seller again possesses some or all of the breached goods, but because the market is already oversupplied with such goods (i.e., the available supply exceeds demand), he or she cannot resell the breached goods without displacing another sale. [Citations.] [Court's footnote: In passing, we observe that this lost volume situation can be described in several ways. Focusing on the breached unit, one can say that due to a market in which supply exceeds demand, the lost volume seller cannot resell the breached unit without sacrificing an additional sale. Focusing on the additional unit, one can say that but for the buyer's breach, the lost volume seller would have made an additional sale. Focusing on both units, one can say that but for the buyer's breach, the lost volume seller would have sold both units. Each statement is equivalent to the others.] Frequently, these sellers are labeled "jobber," "components seller," and "lost volume seller," respectively [, citation]; in our view, however, such labels confuse more than clarify.

* * * In this case, Kenco did not order the breached goods before Williams repudiated. After Williams repudiated, Kenco was not required to order the breached goods from the factory [U.C.C. §§ 2–703, 2–704(2)]; it rightfully elected not to do so; and it could not resell the breached goods on the open market. Here, then, "the measure of damages provided in subsection (1) is inadequate to put [Kenco] in as good a position as [Williams'] performance would have done;" [U.C.C. § 2–708] subsection (2) states the applicable measure of damages; and Kenco is entitled to its lost profit of $11,133.

The second issue is whether Kenco is entitled to reasonable attorneys fees. The parties' contract provided that the prevailing party would be entitled to such fees. Kenco is the prevailing party. * * *

INTERPRETATION When the market price-contract price measure of damages does not put the seller in as good a position as performance would have done, then a non-breaching seller is entitled to damages, which include the unrealized profit from the sale.

ETHICAL QUESTION Did either party act unethically? Explain.

CRITICAL THINKING QUESTION Do you agree with the Code's measure of damages for the "lost volume seller?" Explain.

TO RECOVER THE PRICE

The Code permits the seller **to recover the price** plus incidental damages in three situations: (1) when the buyer has accepted the goods; (2) when conforming goods have been lost or damaged after the risk of loss has passed to the buyer; and (3) where the goods have been identified to the contract and there is no ready market available for their resale at a reasonable price. For example, Kelly, in accordance with her agreement with Sally, prints 10,000 letterheads and envelopes with Sally's name and address on them. Sally wrongfully rejects the stationery, and Kelly is unable to resell it at a reasonable price. Kelly is entitled to recover the price plus incidental damages from Sally.

Article 2A has a similar provision except that the lessor is entitled to (1) accrued and unpaid rent as of the date of the judgment, (2) the present value as of the judgment date of the rent for the then remaining lease term, *and* (3) incidental damages *less* expenses saved.

A seller who sues for the price must hold for the buyer any goods that have been identified to the contract and are still in her control. (Article 2A.) If resale becomes possible, the seller may resell the goods at any time before the collection of the judgment, and the net proceeds of such resale must be credited to the buyer. Payment of the judgment entitles the buyer to any goods not resold. In a lease, payment of the judgment entitles the lessee to the use and possession of the goods for the remaining lease term.

CISG

The seller may require the buyer to pay the price, take delivery, or perform her other obligations, unless the seller has resorted to a remedy that is inconsistent with this requirement.

TO RECOVER INCIDENTAL DAMAGES

In addition to recovering damages for the difference between the contract price and the resale price, recovering damages for nonacceptance or repudiation, or recovering the price, the seller also may recover in the same action her incidental damages in order to recoup expenses she reasonably incurred as a result of the buyer's breach. The Code defines a **seller's incidental damages** to include any commercially reasonable charges, expenses, or commissions incurred in stopping delivery; in the transportation, care, and custody of goods after the buyer's breach; in connection with return or resale of the goods; or otherwise resulting from the breach. Article 2A has an analogous definition.

Practical Advice

As an aggrieved seller, maintain good records regarding incidental damages you incurred.

TO CANCEL THE CONTRACT

When the buyer wrongfully rejects or revokes acceptance of the goods, fails to make a payment due on or before delivery, or repudiates the contract in whole or in part, the seller may cancel the part of the contract that concerns the goods directly affected. If the breach is of an installment contract and it substantially impairs the whole contract, the seller may cancel the entire contract. (Article 2A.)

The Code defines **cancellation** as one party's putting an end to the contract because of a breach by the other. (Article 2A.) The obligation of the canceling party for any future performance under the contract is discharged,

CONCEPT REVIEW

Remedies of the Seller

Buyer's Breach	Seller's Remedies: Obligation Oriented	Goods Oriented[1]	Money Oriented[2]
Buyer wrongfully rejects goods	Cancel	• Withhold delivery of goods • Stop delivery of goods in transit • Identify conforming goods to the contract	• Resell and recover damages • Recover difference between unpaid contract and market prices or lost profits • Recover price
Buyer wrongfully revokes acceptance	Cancel	• Withhold delivery of goods • Stop delivery of goods in transit • Identify conforming goods to the contract	• Resell and recover damages • Recover difference between unpaid contract and market prices or lost profits • Recover price
Buyer fails to make payment	Cancel	• Withhold delivery of goods • Stop delivery of goods in transit • Identify conforming goods to the contract • Reclaim goods upon buyer's insolvency	• Resell and recover damages • Recover difference between unpaid contract and market prices or lost profits • Recover price
Buyer repudiates	Cancel	• Withhold delivery of goods • Stop delivery of goods in transit • Identify conforming goods to the contract	• Resell and recover damages • Recover difference between unpaid contract and market prices or lost profits • Recover price

[1] In a lease, the lessor has the right to recover possession of the goods upon default by the lessee.
[2] In a lease, the lessor's recovery of damages for future rent payments is reduced to their present value.

although he retains any remedy for breach of the whole contract or for any unperformed balance. (Article 2A.) Thus, if the seller has the right to cancel, he may recover damages for breach without having to tender any further performance.

CISG

The seller may declare the contract avoided if (1) the buyer commits a fundamental breach or (2) the buyer does not, within the additional period of time fixed by the seller, perform his obligation to pay the price or take delivery of the goods. Avoidance of the contract releases both parties from their obligations under it, subject to any damages that may be due. Avoidance does not affect any provision of the contract for the settlement of disputes or any other provision of the contract governing the rights and obligations of the parties consequent upon the avoidance of the contract.

TO RECLAIM THE GOODS UPON THE BUYER'S INSOLVENCY

In addition to the right of an unpaid seller to withhold and stop delivery of the goods, he may reclaim them from an insolvent buyer by demand made to the buyer within ten days after the buyer has received the goods. However, if the buyer has committed fraud by misrepresenting her solvency to the seller in writing within three months prior to delivery of the goods, the ten-day limitation does not apply.

The seller's right to reclaim the goods is subject to the rights of a buyer in the ordinary course of business or to the rights of any other good faith purchaser. In addition, a seller who successfully reclaims goods from an insolvent buyer is excluded from all other remedies with respect to those goods.

A lessor retains title to the goods and therefore has the right to recover possession of them upon default by the lessee.

Practical Advice

If you wish to exercise the seller's rights of reclamation of goods sold, you will need to act quickly.

CPA REMEDIES OF THE BUYER

Basically, a **seller** may **default** in one of three different ways: she may repudiate, fail to deliver the goods without repudiation, or deliver or tender goods that do not conform to the contract. (Article 2A.) The Code provides remedies for each of these breaches. Some remedies are available for all three types of breaches, whereas others are not. Moreover, the availability of some remedies depends on the buyer's actions. For example, if the seller tenders nonconforming goods, the buyer may reject or accept them. If the buyer rejects them, he can choose from a number of remedies. On the other hand, if the buyer accepts the nonconforming goods and does not justifiably revoke his acceptance, he limits himself to recovering damages.

When the seller fails to make delivery or repudiates, or when the buyer rightfully rejects or justifiably revokes acceptance, the buyer may, with respect to any goods involved, or with respect to the whole if the breach goes to the whole contract, (1) cancel *and* (2) recover payments made. In addition, the buyer may (3) "cover" and obtain damages, *or* (4) recover damages for nondelivery. When the seller fails to deliver or repudiates, the buyer, when appropriate, may also (5) recover identified goods if the seller is insolvent, *or* (6) "replevy" the goods, *or* (7) obtain specific performance. Moreover, on rightful rejection or justifiable revocation of acceptance, the buyer (8) has a security interest in the goods. When the buyer has accepted goods and notified the seller of their nonconformity, the buyer may (9) recover damages for breach of warranty. Finally, in addition to the remedies listed above, the buyer may, when appropriate, (10) recover incidental damages *and* (11) recover consequential damages. Article 2A provides for essentially the same remedies for the lessee.

We might observe that the first remedy cataloged above is ***obligation oriented***; the second through fourth and ninth through eleventh are ***money oriented***; and the fifth through eighth are ***goods oriented***.

The buyer may deduct from the price due any damages resulting from any breach of contract by the seller. The buyer must, however, give notice to the seller of her intention to withhold such damages from payment of the price due. (Article 2A.)

CISG

If the seller fails to perform any of his obligations, the buyer may (1) require the seller to perform his contractual obligations or (2) fix an additional period of time of reasonable length for performance by the seller of his obligations. Unless the seller notifies the buyer that he will not perform within the period so fixed, the buyer may not, during that period, resort to any remedy for breach of contract. Moreover, if the seller's breach is fundamental or the seller fails to perform within the additional time granted by the buyer, the buyer may avoid the contract. In addition to these remedies, the buyer also has the right to damages. If the goods do not conform with the contract, the buyer may reduce the price in the same proportion as the value that the goods actually delivered had at the time of the delivery bears to the value that conforming goods would have had at that time.

TO CANCEL THE CONTRACT

When the seller fails to make delivery or repudiates the contract or when the buyer rightfully rejects or justifiably revokes acceptance of goods tendered or delivered to him, the buyer may cancel the contract with respect to any goods involved; and, if the breach by the seller concerns the whole contract, the buyer may cancel the entire contract. (Article 2A). The buyer, who must give the seller notice of his cancellation, is excused from further performance or tender on his part. (Article 2A.)

CISG

The buyer may declare the contract avoided if the seller (1) commits a fundamental breach or (2) does not, within the additional period of time fixed by the buyer, deliver the goods. Avoidance of the contract releases both parties from their obligations under it, subject to any damages that may be due. Avoidance does not affect any provision of the contract for the settlement of disputes or any other provision of the contract governing the rights and obligations of the parties consequent upon the avoidance of the contract.

TO RECOVER PAYMENTS MADE

The buyer, on the seller's breach, may also recover as much of the price as he has paid. For example, Jonas and Sheila enter into a contract for a sale of goods for a contract price of $3,000, and Sheila, the buyer, has made a down payment of $600. Jonas delivers nonconforming goods to Sheila, who rightfully rejects them. Sheila may cancel the contract and recover the $600 plus whatever other damages she can prove. Under Article 2A, the lessee may recover so much of the rent and security as has been paid and is just under the circumstances.

To Cover

On the seller's breach, the buyer may protect herself by obtaining cover. **Cover** means that the buyer may in good faith and without unreasonable delay proceed to purchase needed goods or make a contract to purchase such goods in substitution for those due under the contract from the seller. In a lease, the lessee may purchase or lease substitute goods.

On making a reasonable contract of cover, the buyer may recover from the seller the difference between the cost of cover and the contract price, plus any incidental and consequential damages (discussed below), *less* expenses saved because of the seller's breach. For example, Phillip, whose factory is in Oakland, agrees to sell goods to Edith, in Atlanta, for $22,000 F.O.B. Oakland. Phillip fails to deliver, and Edith covers by purchasing substitute goods for $25,000, incurring $700 in sales commissions. Edith suffers no other damages as a consequence of Phillip's breach. Shipping costs from Oakland to Atlanta for the goods are $1,300. Edith would recover the difference between the cost of cover ($25,000) and the contract price ($22,000), plus incidental damages ($700 in sales commissions), plus consequential damages ($0 in this example), minus expenses saved (the $1,300 in shipping costs that Edith need not pay under the contract of cover), which equals $2,400.

In a lease, the comparable recovery is the ***difference*** between the ***present values*** of the ***new rent*** due under the new lease and the ***old rent*** due under the original lease.

The buyer is not required to obtain cover, and his failure to do so does not bar him from any other remedy the Code provides. (Article 2A.) The buyer may not, however, recover consequential damages that he could have prevented by cover. (Article 2A.)

CISG

If the contract is avoided and the buyer has bought goods in replacement in a reasonable manner and within a reasonable time after avoidance, he may recover the difference between the contract price and the price paid in the substitute transaction. In addition, he may recover consequential damages.

Bigelow-Sanford, Inc. v. Gunny Corp.

United States Court of Appeals, Fifth Circuit, 1981
649 F.2d 1060

FACTS The plaintiff, Bigelow-Sanford, Inc. **(http://www.arcat.com/arcatcos/cos30/arc30935.cfm)** contracted with the defendant, Gunny Corp., for the purchase of 100,000 linear yards of jute at $.64 per yard. Gunny delivered 22,228 linear yards in January 1979. The February and March deliveries required under the contract were not made, and eight rolls (each roll containing 66.7 linear yards) were delivered in April. With 72,265 linear yards ultimately undelivered, Gunny told Bigelow-Sanford that no more would be delivered. In mid-March, Bigelow-Sanford turned to the jute spot market to replace the balance of the order at a price of $1.21 per linear yard. As several other companies had also defaulted on their jute contracts with Bigelow-Sanford, the plaintiff purchased a total of 164,503 linear yards on the spot market. The plaintiff sued the defendant to recover losses sustained as a result of the breach of contract. Gunny appealed from a judgment in favor of Bigelow-Sanford.

DECISION Judgment for Bigelow-Sanford affirmed.

OPINION Kravitch, J. Gunny contends that appellee's [Bigelow-Sanford's] alleged cover purchases should not have been used to measure damages in that they were not made in substitution for the contract purchases, were not made seasonably or in good faith and were not shown to be due to Gunny's breach. [W]e disagree. Again, we quote UCC § 2–711 providing in part for cover damages where the seller fails to make delivery or repudiates the contract: * * *

> (a) "cover" and have damages under the next section as to all the goods affected whether or not they have been identified to the contract; or (b) recover damages for nondelivery as provided in this Article (2–713).

UCC § 2–712 defines cover:

(1) After a breach within the preceding section the buyer may "cover" by making in good faith and without unreasonable delay any reasonable purchase of or contract to purchase goods in substitution for those due from the seller.
(2) The buyer may recover from the seller as damages the difference between the cost of cover and the contract price together with any incidental or consequential damages as hereinafter defined (2–715), but less expenses saved in consequence of the seller's breach.
(3) Failure of the buyer to effect cover within this section does not bar him from any other remedy.

In addition, the purchaser may recover under 2–713:

(1) Subject to the provisions of this Article with respect to proof of market price (2–723), the measure of damages for nondelivery or repudiation by the seller is the difference between the market price at the time when the buyer learned of the breach and the contract price together with any incidental and consequential damages provided in this Article (2–715), but less expenses saved in consequence of the seller's breach.
(2) Market price is to be determined as of the place for tender or, in cases of rejection after arrival or revocation of acceptance, as of the place of arrival.

Most importantly, "whether a plaintiff has made his cover purchases in a reasonable manner poses a classic jury issue." [Citation.] The district court thus acted properly in submitting the question of cover damages to the jury, which found that Gunny had breached, appellee had covered, and had done so in good faith without unreasonable delay by making reasonable purchases, and was therefore entitled to damages under § 2–712. Gunny argues Bigelow is not entitled to such damages on the ground that it failed to make cover purchases without undue delay and that the jury should not have been permitted to average the cost of Bigelow's spot market purchases totalling 164,503 linear yards in order to arrive at the cost of cover for the 72,265 linear yards Gunny failed to deliver. Both arguments fail. Gunny notified Bigelow in February that no more jute would be forthcoming. Bigelow made its first spot market purchases in mid-March. Given that it is within the jury's province to decide the reasonableness of the manner in which cover purchases were made, we believe the jury could reasonably decide such purchases, made one month after the date the jury assigned to Gunny's breach, were made without undue delay. The same is true with respect to Gunny's second argument: Bigelow's spot market purchases were made to replace several vendors' shipments. Bigelow did not specifically allocate the spot market replacements to individual vendors' accounts, however, nor was there a requirement that they do so. The jury's method of averaging such costs and assigning them to Gunny in proportion to the amount of jute if [*sic*] failed to deliver would, therefore, seem not only fair but well within the jury's permissible bounds.

Gunny also argues that the court erroneously charged the jury regarding damages under both §§ 2–712 and 2–713. We disagree. Whether Bigelow covered was a question of fact submitted to the jury. In the event that it had not, alternative damages were available to Bigelow under § 2–713. [Citation.] The jury found that Bigelow had covered and awarded damages under § 2–712; § 2–713 then became irrelevant. Since either was applicable until that time, the court's charge as to both sections was not error.

INTERPRETATION If the buyer makes substitute purchases in good faith and without unreasonable delay, he may recover as damages the difference between the cost of cover and the contract price plus any incidental damages, but minus any expenses he saved because of the seller's breach.

CRITICAL THINKING QUESTION Do you agree with the remedy of cover? Explain.

TO RECOVER DAMAGES FOR NONDELIVERY OR REPUDIATION

If the seller repudiates the contract or fails to deliver the goods, or if the buyer rightfully rejects or justifiably revokes acceptance of the goods, the buyer is entitled to recover damages from the seller equal to the difference between the market price at the time the buyer learned of the breach and the contract price, together with incidental and consequential damages, less expenses saved because of the seller's breach. This remedy is a complete alternative to the remedy of cover and is available only to the extent the buyer has not covered. As previously indicated, the buyer who elects this remedy may not recover consequential damages that she could have avoided by cover.

In a lease, the comparable recovery is the ***difference*** between the ***present values*** of the ***market rent*** and the ***old rent*** due under the original lease.

The market price is to be determined as of the place for tender or, in the event that the buyer has rightfully rejected the goods or has justifiably revoked his acceptance of them, as of the place of arrival. For example, Janet, in Boston, agrees to sell goods to Laura, in Denver, for $7,000 C.O.D., with delivery by November 15. Janet fails to deliver. As a consequence, Laura suffers incidental damages of $1,500 and consequential damages of $1,000.

In the case of nondelivery or repudiation, market price is determined as of the place of tender. Because C.O.D. is a shipment contract, the place of tender would be the seller's city. Therefore, the market price must be the market price in Boston, the seller's city, on November 15, when Laura learned of the breach. At this time and place, the market price is $8,000. Laura would recover the difference between the market price ($8,000) and the contract price ($7,000), plus incidental damages ($1,500), plus consequential damages ($1,000), less expenses saved ($0 in this example), which equals $3,500.

In the example above, if Janet had instead delivered nonconforming goods that Laura rejected, the market price would be determined at Denver, Laura's place of business; if Janet had repudiated the contract on November 1, instead of November 15, then the market price would be determined as of November 1.

In a lease, market rent is to be determined as of the place for tender or, in cases of rejection after arrival or revocation of acceptance, as of the place of arrival.

Practical Advice

Carefully consider whether you are better off covering or seeking damages for nondelivery or repudiation.

CISG

If the contract is avoided and the buyer has not made a replacement purchase, he may recover the difference between the contract price and the current price at the time of avoidance and at the place where delivery of the goods should have been made. In addition, he may recover consequential damages.

To Recover Identified Goods on the Seller's Insolvency

When existing goods are identified to the contract of sale, the buyer acquires a ***special property interest*** in the goods. This interest exists even if the goods are nonconforming and the buyer therefore has the right to return or reject them. Either the buyer or the seller may identify the goods to the contract.

The Code gives the buyer a right, which does not exist at common law, to recover from an insolvent seller the goods in which the buyer has a special property interest and for which he has paid part or all of the price. This right exists where the seller, who is in possession or control of the goods, becomes insolvent within ten days after receiving the first installment of the price. To exercise it, the buyer must tender to the seller any unpaid portion of the price. If the special property interest exists by reason of an identification made by the buyer, he may recover the goods only if they conform to the contract for sale. (Article 2A.)

To Sue for Replevin

Replevin is an action at law to recover from a defendant's possession specific goods that are being unlawfully withheld from the plaintiff. When the seller has repudiated or breached the contract, the buyer may maintain against the seller an action for replevin for goods that have been identified to the contract if the buyer after a reasonable effort is unable to obtain cover for such goods. (Article 2A.) Article 2 also provides the buyer with the right to replevin if the goods have been shipped under reservation of a security interest in the seller and satisfaction of this security interest has been made or tendered.

To Sue for Specific Performance

Specific performance is an equitable remedy compelling the party in breach to perform the contract according to its terms. At common law, specific performance is available only if legal remedies are inadequate. For example, when the contract is for the purchase of a unique item, such as a work of art, a famous racehorse, or an heirloom, money damages may not be an adequate remedy. In such a case, a court of equity has the discretion to order the seller specifically to deliver to the buyer, on payment of the price, the goods described in the contract.

The Code not only has continued the availability of specific performance but also has sought to promote a more liberal attitude toward its use. Accordingly, it does not expressly require that the remedy at law be inadequate. Instead, the Code states that specific performance may be granted "where the goods are unique or in other proper circumstances." (Article 2A.)

CISG

The buyer may require the seller to perform his contractual obligations. If the goods do not conform to the contract and the nonconformity constitutes a fundamental breach of contract, the buyer may require delivery of substitute goods. If the goods do not conform to the contract, the buyer may require the seller to remedy the lack of conformity by repair, unless this is unreasonable under the circumstances. Nevertheless, a court is not bound to enter a judgment for specific performance unless a court would do so under its own law with respect to similar contracts of sale not governed by the CISG.

To Enforce a Security Interest in the Goods

A buyer who has rightfully rejected or justifiably revoked acceptance of goods that remain in her possession or control has a security interest in these goods for any payments made on their price and for any expenses reasonably incurred in their inspection, receipt, transportation, care, and custody. The buyer may hold such goods and resell them in the same manner as an aggrieved seller may resell goods. (Article 2A.) In the event of resale, the buyer is accountable to the seller for any amount of the net proceeds of the resale that exceeds the amount of her security interest. (Article 2A.)

To Recover Damages for Breach in Regard to Accepted Goods

When the buyer has accepted nonconforming goods and has timely notified the seller of the breach of contract, the buyer is entitled to recover from the seller the damages resulting in the ordinary course of events from the seller's breach as determined in any reasonable manner. (Article 2A.) When appropriate, incidental and consequential damages also may be recovered. Nonconformity includes breaches of warranty as well as any failure of the seller to perform according to her obligations under the contract. Thus, even if a seller cures a nonconforming tender, the buyer may recover under this section for any injury suffered because the original tender was nonconforming.

In the event of breach of warranty, the measure of damages is the difference at the time and place of acceptance between the value of the goods that have been accepted and the value that the goods would have had if they had been as warranted, unless special circumstances show proximate damages of a different amount. Article 2A has a comparable provision, except the recovery is for the ***present value*** of the difference between the value of the use of the goods accepted and the value if they had been as warranted for the lease term.

The contract price of the goods does not figure in this computation because the buyer is entitled to the benefit of his bargain, which is to receive goods that are as warranted. For example, Eleanor agrees to sell goods to Timothy for $1,000. Although the value of the goods accepted by Timothy is $800, if they had been as warranted, their value would have been $1,200. Timothy's damages for breach of warranty are $400, which he may deduct from any unpaid balance due on the purchase price upon notice to Eleanor of his intention to do so. (Article 2A.)

To Recover Incidental Damages

In addition to remedies such as covering, recovering damages for nondelivery or repudiation, or recovering damages for breach in regard to accepted goods, including breach of warranty, the buyer may recover incidental damages. A **buyer's incidental damages** provide reimbursement for the buyer who incurs reasonable expenses in handling rightfully rejected goods or in effecting cover. The buyer's incidental damages resulting from the seller's breach include expenses reasonably incurred in inspection, receipt, transportation, and care and custody of goods rightfully rejected; any commercially reasonable charges, expenses, or commissions in connection with obtaining cover; and any other reasonable expense connected to the delay or other breach. Article 2A has an analogous definition. For example, the buyer of a racehorse who justifiably revokes acceptance because the horse does not conform to the contract will be allowed to recover as incidental damages the cost of caring for the horse from the date the horse was delivered until the buyer returns it to the seller.

> **Practical Advice**
>
> As an aggrieved buyer, maintain good records regarding incidental damages you incurred.

To Recover Consequential Damages

In many cases, the remedies discussed above will not fully compensate the aggrieved buyer for her losses. For example, nonconforming goods that are accepted may in some way damage or destroy the buyer's warehouse and its contents, or undelivered goods may have been the subject of a lucrative contract of resale, the profits from which are now lost. The Code responds to this problem by providing the buyer with the opportunity to recover **consequential damages** resulting from the seller's breach, including (1) any loss resulting from the buyer's requirements and needs of which the seller at the time of contracting had reason to know and which the buyer could not reasonably prevent by cover or otherwise and (2) injury to person or property proximately resulting from any breach of warranty. (Article 2A.)

> **Practical Advice**
>
> As the buyer, be sure to inform the other party to the contract of any "particular needs" beyond the ordinary course of events that could result from a breach of contract.

CONCEPT REVIEW

Remedies of the Buyer

Seller's Breach	Buyer's Remedies: Obligation Oriented	Buyer's Remedies: Goods Oriented	Buyer's Remedies: Money Oriented*
Buyer rightfully rejects goods	Cancel	• Have a security interest	• Recover payments made • Cover and recover damages • Recover damages for nondelivery
Buyer justifiably revokes acceptance	Cancel	• Have a security interest	• Recover payments made • Cover and recover damages • Recover damages for nondelivery
Seller fails to deliver	Cancel	• Recover identified goods if seller is insolvent • Replevy goods • Obtain specific performance	• Recover payments made • Cover and recover damages • Recover damages for nondelivery
Seller repudiates	Cancel	• Recover identified goods if seller is insolvent • Replevy goods • Obtain specific performance	• Recover payments made • Cover and recover damages • Recover damages for nondelivery
Buyer accepts nonconforming goods			• Recover damages for breach of warranty

*In a lease, the lessee's recovery of damages for future rent payments is reduced to their present value.

With respect to the first type of consequential damages, *particular* needs of the buyer usually must be made known to the seller, whereas *general* needs usually need not be. In the case of a buyer who is in the business of reselling goods, resale is one requirement of which the seller has reason to know. For example, Supreme Machine Co., a manufacturer, contracts to sell Allied Sales, Inc., a dealer in used machinery, a used machine that Allied plans to resell. After Supreme repudiates and Allied is unable to obtain a similar machine elsewhere, Allied's damages include the net profit that it would have made on resale of the machine. A buyer may not, however, recover consequential damages he could have prevented by cover. (Article 2A.) For instance, Supreme Machine Co. contracts to sell Capitol Manufacturing Co. a used machine for $10,000 to be delivered at Capitol's factory by June 1. Supreme repudiates the contract on May 1. By reasonable efforts, Capitol could buy a similar machine from United Machinery Inc. for $11,000 in time for a June 1 delivery. Capitol fails to do so, losing a $5,000 profit that it would have made from the resale of the machine. Though it can recover $1,000 from Supreme, Capitol's damages do not include the loss of the $5,000 profit.

An example of the second type of consequential damage would be as follows: Federal Machine Co. sells a machine to Southern Manufacturing Co., warranting its suitability for Southern's purpose. However, the machine is not suitable for Southern's purpose and causes $10,000 in damage to Southern's property and $15,000 in personal injuries. Southern can recover the $25,000 in consequential damages in addition to any other loss suffered.

Practical Advice

If you are the seller, consider including a contractual provision for the limitation or exclusion of consequential damages. If you are the buyer, avoid such limitations.

CPA CONTRACTUAL PROVISIONS AFFECTING REMEDIES

Within specified limits, the Code permits the parties to a sales contract to modify, exclude, or limit by agreement the remedies or damages that will be available for breach of that contract. Two basic types of contractual provisions affect remedies: (1) liquidation or limitation of damages and (2) modification or limitation of remedy.

LIQUIDATION OR LIMITATION OF DAMAGES

The parties may provide for liquidated damages in their contract by specifying the amount or measure of damages that either party may recover in the event of a breach by the other. The amount of such damages must be reasonable in light of the anticipated or actual loss resulting from a breach, the difficulties of proof of loss, and the inconvenience or lack of feasibility of otherwise obtaining an adequate remedy. A contract provision that fixes unreasonably large liquidated damages is void as a penalty. By comparison, an unreasonably small amount might be stricken on the grounds of unconscionability.

To illustrate, Sterling Cabinetry Company contracts to build and install shelves and cabinets for an office building being constructed by Baron Construction Company. The contract price is $120,000, and the contract provides that Sterling would be liable for $100 per day for every day's delay beyond the completion date specified in the contract. The stipulated sum of $100 per day is reasonable and commensurate with the anticipated loss. Therefore, it is enforceable as liquidated damages. If, instead, the sum stipulated had been $5,000 per day, it would be unreasonably large and would, therefore, be void as a penalty.

Article 2A authorizes liquidated damages payable by either party for default, or any other act or omission. The amount of, or formula for, liquidated damages must be reasonable in light of the then anticipated harm caused by default or other act or omission.

Practical Advice

Both parties should consider including a contractual provision for reasonable liquidated damages, especially where damages will be difficult to prove.

Coastal Leasing Corporation v. T-Bar S Corporation

Court of Appeals of North Carolina, 1998
128 N.C.App. 379, 496 S.E.2d 795
http://www.aoc.state.nc.us/www/public/coa/opinions/1998/970382-1.htm

FACTS The plaintiff, Coastal Leasing Corporation (Coastal) **(http://www.coastalleasing.com)**, entered into a lease agreement with the defendant, T-Bar S Corporation (T-Bar), in May 1992, whereby Coastal agreed to lease certain cash register equipment to T-Bar. Under the lease, T-Bar agreed to monthly rental payments of $289.13 each for a total of forty-eight months. Defendants George and Sharon Talbott were the officers of T-Bar and personally guaranteed payment. After making eighteen of the monthly payments, the Talbotts and T-Bar defaulted on the lease. On February 28, 1994, Coastal mailed a certified letter to the Talbotts and T-Bar advising them that the lease was in default and, pursuant to the terms of the lease, Coastal was accelerating the remaining payments due under the lease. Coastal further advised the Talbotts and T-Bar that if the entire amount due of $8,841.06 was not received within seven days, Coastal would seek to recover the balance due plus interest and reasonable attorneys' fees, as well as possession of the equipment.

On March 10, Coastal mailed a certified letter and "Notice of Public Sale of Repossessed Leased Equipment" to the Talbotts and T-Bar at the same address. This letter advised the Talbotts and T-Bar that Coastal had taken possession of the equipment and was conducting a public sale pursuant to the terms of the lease. Although the date on the notice of sale stated that the sale was to be held on March 23, the sale was actually scheduled to be held on March 25. This letter and notice of sale were returned to Coastal "unclaimed" on March 29.

Coastal conducted a public sale of the equipment on March 25, and no one appeared on behalf of the Talbotts or T-Bar. There being no other bidders, Coastal purchased the equipment at the sale for $2,000.00. On October 4, 1994, Coastal leased some of the same equipment to another company at a rate calculated to be $212.67 for thirty-six months. Coastal then filed this action seeking to recover the balance due under the lease, minus the net proceeds from the public sale, plus interest and reasonable attorneys' fees. The Talbotts filed an answer and counterclaim. Coastal then filed a motion for summary judgment against the Talbotts. After a hearing, the trial court entered summary judgment in favor of Coastal on its complaint and the Talbotts' counterclaims and entered judgment against the Talbotts for the sum of $7,223.56 plus interest and attorneys' fees of $1,083.54. The Talbotts appealed.

DECISION Judgment affirmed.

OPINION Walker, J. * * * Since both parties agree that the transaction at issue in this case is not a security interest, but rather is a lease, Article 2A controls.

* * *

In their appeal, appellants contend that the trial court erred by granting summary judgment in favor of plaintiff because there exists a genuine issue of material fact as to whether: (1) the liquidated damages clause contained in Paragraph 13 of the lease is reasonable in light of the then anticipated harm caused by default; * * *.

As to appellants' first contention, the official commentary to Article 2A states that "in recognition of the diversity of the transactions to be governed [and] the sophistication of many of the parties to these transactions * * *, freedom of contract has been preserved." [U.C.C. §] 2A–102 Official Comment. Also, under general contract principles, when the parties to a transaction deal with each other at arms length and without the exercise by one of the parties of superior bargaining power, the parties will be bound by their agreement. [Citation.]

Article 2A recognizes that "[m]any leasing transactions are predicated on the parties' ability to agree to an appropriate amount of damages or formula for damages in the event of default or other act or omission." [U.C.C. §] 2A–504 Official Comment. [U.C.C. §] 2A–504 states, in pertinent part:

> (1) Damages payable by either party for default, or any other act or omission * * * may be liquidated in the lease agreement but only at an amount or by a formula that is reasonable in light of the then anticipated harm caused by the default or other act or omission.

This liquidated damages provision is more flexible than that provided by its statutory analogue under Article 2, [U.C.C. §] 2–718. The Article 2 liquidated damages section provides, in pertinent part:

> (1) Damages for breach by either party may be liquidated in the agreement but only at an amount which is reasonable in the light of the anticipated or actual harm caused by the breach, the difficulties of proof of loss, and the inconvenience or nonfeasibility of otherwise obtaining an adequate remedy. A term fixing unreasonably large liquidated damages is void as a penalty.

[U.C.C. §] 2–718(1). A review of these statutes reveals two major differences.

First, the drafters of Article 2A chose not to incorporate the two tests which are required by Article 2, i.e., the difficulties of proof of loss and the inconvenience or nonfeasibility of otherwise obtaining an adequate remedy. In fact, the official commentary to [U.C.C. §] 2A–504 states that since "[t]he ability to liquidate damages is critical to modern leasing practice * * * [and] given the parties' freedom to contract at common law, the policy behind retaining these two additional requirements here was thought to be outweighed." [Citation.]

Secondly, the drafters of Article 2A recognized that in order to further promote freedom of contract, it was necessary to delete the last sentence of [U.C.C. §] 2–718(1), which provided that unreasonably large liquidated damages provisions were void as a penalty. As such, the parties to a lease transaction are free to negotiate the amount of liquidated damages, restrained only by the rule of reasonableness.

"The basic test of the reasonableness of an agreement liquidating damages is whether the stipulated amount or amount produced by the stipulated formula represents a reasonable forecast of the probable loss." [Citation.] However, "no court should strike down a reasonable liquidated damage agreement based on foresight that has proved on hindsight to have contained an inaccurate estimation of the probable loss * * *." *Id.* And, "the fact that there is a difference between the actual loss, as determined at or about the time of the default, and the anticipated loss or stipulated amount or formula, as stipulated at the time the lease contract was entered into * * *," does not necessarily mean that the liquidated damage agreement is unreasonable. *Id.* This is so because "[t]he value of a lessor's interest in leased equipment depends upon 'the physical condition of the equipment and the market conditions at that time.'" [Citation.] Further, in determining whether a liquidated damages clause is reasonable:

> [A] court should keep in mind that the clause was negotiated by the parties, who are familiar with the circumstances and practices with respect to the type of transaction involved, and the clause carries with it a consensual apportionment of the risks of the agreement that a court should be slow to overturn. [Citation.]

In this case, Paragraph 13 of the lease (the liquidated damages clause) reads as follows:

> 13. REMEDIES. If an event of default shall occur, Lessor may, at its option, at any time (a) declare the entire amount of unpaid rental for the balance of the term of this lease immediately due and payable, whereupon Lessee shall become obligated to pay to Lessor forthwith the total amount of the said rental for the balance of the said term, and (b) without demand or legal process, enter into the premises where the equipment may be found and take possession of and remove the Equipment, without liability for suit, action or other proceeding, and all rights of Lessee in the Equipment so removed shall terminate absolutely. Lessee hereby waives notice of, or hearing with respect to, such retaking. Lessor may at its option, use, ship, store, repair or lease all Equipment so removed and sell or otherwise

dispose of any such Equipment at a private or public sale. In the event Lessor takes possession of the Equipment, Lessor shall give Lessee credit for any sums received by Lessor from the sale or rental of the Equipment after deduction of the expenses of sale or rental and Lessor's residual interest in the Equipment. * * * Lessor and Lessee acknowledge the difficulty in establishing a value for the unexpired lease term and owing to such difficulty agree that the provisions of this paragraph represent an agreed measure of damages and are not to be deemed a forfeiture or penalty. * * *

After a careful review, we conclude the liquidated damages clause is a reasonable estimation of the then anticipated damages in the event of default because it protects plaintiff's expectation interest. The liquidated damages clause places plaintiff in the position it would have occupied had the lease been fully performed by allowing it to accelerate the balance of the lease payments and repossess the equipment. Therefore, since there is no evidence that plaintiff exercised a superior bargaining position in the negotiation of the liquidated damages clause, no genuine issue of material fact exists as to its reasonableness, and the trial court did not err by enforcing its provisions.

INTERPRETATION Article 2A, which governs leases, allows the parties to liquidate damages as long as the negotiated amount is reasonable in light of the anticipated loss.

CRITICAL THINKING QUESTION Do you agree with the decision by the drafters of Article 2A to omit Article 2's requirements of difficulty of proof and inconvenience or nonfeasibility of otherwise obtaining an adequate remedy? Explain.

Modification or Limitation of Remedy by Agreement

The contract between the seller and buyer may expressly provide for remedies in addition to or instead of those provided in the Code and may limit or change the measure of damages recoverable in the event of breach. (Article 2A.) For instance, the contract may validly limit the buyer's remedy to a return of the goods and a refund of the price, or to the replacement of nonconforming goods or parts.

A contractual remedy is optional, however, unless the parties expressly agree that it is to be exclusive of other remedies, in which event it becomes the sole remedy. (Article 2A.) Moreover, when circumstances cause an exclusive or limited remedy to fail in its essential purpose, the parties may resort to the remedies provided by the Code. (Article 2A.)

The contract may expressly limit or exclude consequential damages unless such limitation or exclusion would be unconscionable. Limitation of consequential damages for personal injuries resulting from breach of warranty in the sale of consumer goods is ***prima facie*** unconscionable, whereas limitation of such damages for commercial loss is not. (Article 2A.) For example, Ace Motors, Inc. sells a pickup truck to Brenda, a consumer. The contract of sale excludes liability for all consequential damages. The next day, the truck explodes, causing serious personal injury to Brenda. Brenda would recover for her personal injuries unless Ace could prove that the exclusion of consequential damages was not unconscionable.

Bishop Logging Company v. John Deere Industrial Equipment Co.

Court of Appeals of South Carolina, 1995
317 S.C. 520, 455 S.E.2d 183

FACTS Bishop Logging Company is a large, family-owned logging contractor formed in 1980 in the low country of South Carolina. Bishop Logging has traditionally harvested pine timber. However, in 1988 Bishop Logging began investigating the feasibility of a fully mechanized hardwood swamp logging operation when its main customer, Stone Container Corporation, decided to expand hardwood production. In anticipating an increased demand for hardwood in conjunction with the operation of a new paper machine, Stone Container requested that

Bishop Logging harvest and supply hardwood for processing at its mill. In South Carolina, most suitable hardwood is located deep in the swamplands. Because of the high accident risk in the swamp, Bishop Logging did not want to harvest hardwood by the conventional method of manual felling of trees. Because Bishop Logging had already been successful in its totally mechanized pine logging operation, it began a search for improved methods of hardwood swamp logging centered on mechanizing the process in order to reduce labor, minimize personal injury and insurance costs, and improve efficiency and productivity.

Bishop Logging ultimately purchased several pieces of John Deere equipment to make up the system. The gross sales price of the machinery was $608,899. All the equipment came with a written John Deere "New Equipment Warranty," whereby John Deere agreed only to repair or replace the equipment during the warranty period and did not warrant the suitability of the equipment. In the "New Equipment Warranty," John Deere expressly provided: (1) John Deere would repair or replace parts that were defective in material or workmanship; (2) a disclaimer of any express warranties or implied warranties of merchantability or fitness for a particular purpose; (3) an exclusion of all incidental or consequential damages; and (4) no authority for the dealer to make any representations, promises, modifications, or limitations of John Deere's written warranty. Hoping to sell more equipment if the Bishop Logging system was successful, however, John Deere agreed to assume part of the risk of the new enterprise by extending its standard equipment warranties notwithstanding the unusual use and modifications to the equipment.

Soon after being placed in operation in the swamp, the machinery began to experience numerous mechanical problems. John Deere made more than $110,000 in warranty repairs on the equipment. However, Bishop Logging contended the swamp logging system failed to operate as represented by John Deere and, as a result, it suffered a substantial financial loss. The jury returned a verdict for Bishop Logging against John Deere and awarded Bishop Logging $1,000,000 in actual damages.

John Deere appealed, claiming that the court erred in allowing Bishop Logging to receive lost profits and consequential damages for breach of express warranty because it effectively disclaimed express and implied warranties other than those contained in the John Deere "New Equipment Warranty," and those warranty provisions limited Bishop Logging's remedies for breach of the warranty to repair or replacement of defective parts, and explicitly excluded liability for consequential damages. Bishop Logging, on the other hand, maintained the exclusive remedy as limited failed its essential purpose, thus entitling it to other remedies available under the Code, including consequential damages.

DECISION Judgment of trial court affirmed in part and reversed in part.

OPINION Cureton, J. Under the South Carolina Uniform Commercial Code (UCC), it is clear that the parties to a contract may establish exclusive, limited written warranties and limitation of damages as a remedy for breach thereof. [UCC] § 2–719. Section 2–719(1) of the Code provides that the agreement may limit the buyer's remedies to repair or replacement of nonconforming goods or parts, and if such remedy is expressly agreed to be exclusive, it is the sole remedy. Section 2–719(3) states that consequential damages may be limited or excluded unless the limitation or exclusion is unconscionable.

Despite the exclusive remedy provisions in § 2–719, in certain circumstances a party may nonetheless be entitled to the general remedies of the UCC. Section 2–719(2) states that when circumstances cause an exclusive remedy to "fail of its essential purpose, remedy may be had as provided in this Act." The official comments under § 2–719 further provide that "under subsection (2), where an apparently fair and reasonable clause because of circumstances fails in its purpose or operates to deprive either party of the substantial value of the bargain, it must give way to the general remedy provisions of this Article." [UCC] § 2–719, comment 1.

The purpose of the exclusive remedy of replacement or repair of defective parts from John Deere's viewpoint was to give it an opportunity to make the equipment conform with the contract while limiting the risks to which it was subject by excluding direct and consequential damages that might otherwise arise. From Bishop Logging's perspective, it was to insure that the equipment would be operable in the swamp application and if the equipment did not function properly, to insure John Deere would cure any defects within a reasonable time after they were discovered. Where a seller is given a reasonable chance to correct defects and the equipment still fails to function properly, the buyer is deprived of the benefits of the limited remedy and it therefore fails of its essential purpose. [Citation.] In such circumstances, § 2–719(2) permits the buyer to pursue the other remedies provided by the UCC if the defect substantially affects the value of the buyer's bargain. [UCC] § 2–719, comment 1; [citation].

* * *

The evidence at trial was clearly sufficient for the jury to determine that John Deere did not effectively perform its obligation to repair the equipment properly and within a reasonable time, and as a result, Bishop Logging was deprived of the substantial value of the equipment it contracted for. We therefore affirm the jury's verdict on the warranty claim implicitly finding that the limited warranty failed in its essential purpose so as to deprive Bishop

Logging of the substantial value of the bargain, and, as a consequence, gave Bishop Logging the right to pursue other remedies provided by the UCC.

Notwithstanding Bishop Logging's ability to recover direct damages for breach of the warranty on the equipment due to the failure of its essential purposes, John Deere argues that the limitation of consequential damages expressed in the warranty has independent significance and should be effective to disclaim such damages under the facts of this case unless to do so would be unconscionable. * * *

* * *

* * * [T]he parties in the present case assumed that any mechanical problems in the equipment could be corrected. In the context of the commercial nature of the transaction, John Deere's agent knew the equipment would be used in the swamp application and knew that regular, certain repair was promised and expected in order that all of the equipment could be used for its purpose. In negotiating the sale, John Deere's agent assured Bishop Logging that "those units would function properly in [the swamp] environment," and that he would have "at [his] beck and call * * * factory support to make sure that the equipment functioned properly." Therefore, we must interpret the exclusion of consequential damages in light of this premise of "certainty of repair" which underlies the entire contract. The parties obviously agreed to exclude consequential damages in the event that John Deere performed its obligation to repair or replace defects. However, Bishop Logging could reasonably have expected to recover consequential damages when, as here, the defects were never adequately corrected and the limited remedy proved ineffectual.

The failure of the limited remedy in this case materially altered the balance of risk set by the parties in the agreement. Therefore, we conclude that the court was correct in disregarding the other limitations and exclusions on John Deere's warranties, and allowing the full array of remedies provided by the UCC, including recovery of consequential damages and incidental losses under [UCC] §§ 2–714 and 2–715.

Section 2–714 sets forth the normal measure of direct damages for breach of warranty. The formula for calculating direct damages is the value of the goods as warranted less the value of the goods as accepted. [Citation.] In addition to the recovery of direct damages, § 2–714(3) also provides for the recovery of incidental and consequential damages. Incidental damages resulting from the sellers' breach include expenses reasonably incurred in inspection, receipt, transportation, and care and custody of goods rightfully rejected as well as expenses incident to effecting cover. See [UCC] § 2–715(1). Consequential damages include:

(a) any loss resulting from general or particular requirements and needs of which the seller at the time of contracting had reason to know and which could not reasonably be prevented by cover or otherwise; and
(b) injury to person or property proximately resulting from any breach of warranty.

See [UCC] § 2–715(2). Profits lost as a result of the breach are recoverable under this section as consequential damages. In [citation] the court indicated that consequential damages could also include additional operating expenses caused by the breach. The burden of proving the extent of loss incurred by way of consequential damages is on the buyer. [UCC] § 2–715, comment 4.

In the present case, the losses suffered by Bishop Logging were primarily lost anticipated profits. There was no personal injury and there was no injury to other property owned by Bishop Logging. According to Bishop Logging's expert witness who was hired to make a study of the economic loss in this case, the total financial loss to Bishop Logging was either $540,921 or $723,323 for the three year estimated life of the equipment. The difference depended upon the price Bishop Logging received per cord of wood logged by it. The one million dollar actual damage award recovered by Bishop Logging, however, was not only for lost profits from not meeting expected production schedules, but also other unspecified damages which the jury awarded. Although mathematical precision is not required in the proof of loss, we believe the jury's actual damage award lacked relation to the testimony in the record offered to establish damages and apparently included impermissible, noneconomic damages. To that extent, the actual damage award is reduced to the maximum total of economic damages claimed by Bishop Logging, $723,323.

INTERPRETATION Where circumstances cause an exclusive or limited remedy to fail in its essential purpose, the aggrieved party may resort to the remedies provided by the Code.

ETHICAL QUESTION Did either part act unethically? Explain.

CRITICAL THINKING QUESTION Do you agree with the Code's policy that parties to a sales contract must accept the legal consequence that there must be "at least a fair quantum of remedy" for breach of contractual obligations? Explain.

CONSUMER insight

Warranty of Title: Who Pays Attorneys' Fees When a Dispute Arises?

When Mr. De La Hoya walked into Slim's Gun Shop in California, he wanted only to purchase a gun. Unfortunately, he got more than he bargained for.

Because Slim's Gun Shop advertised itself as a licensed dealer, Mr. De La Hoya figured he had nothing to worry about. So he picked out a handgun and paid his money.

The particular gun that Mr. De La Hoya chose, however, had been purchased earlier from a third party. The owner of Slim's Gun Shop believed all to be fine with the gun. After all, he had filed the necessary federal and state reports, both when he purchased the gun and when he sold it to Mr. De La Hoya.

A short time later, Mr. De La Hoya went target shooting with his new handgun. But after his practice session began, a police officer walked up and asked Mr. De La Hoya about the weapon. Upon tracing the gun's serial number, the officer found out that the weapon had been reported stolen. Mr. De La Hoya was promptly arrested.

To escape criminal charges, Mr. De La Hoya was forced to hire a lawyer. Once his name was cleared, he sued the owner of Slim's Gun Shop, intent on receiving damages for a breach of warranty of title. In the end, the trial court awarded Mr. De La Hoya $949, which included $140 for the confiscated handgun and $800 for his attorneys' fees. Slim's Gun Shop appealed.

The dispute came down to whether the gun shop should pay Mr. De La Hoya's attorneys' fees. In cases involving a breach of contract, the law allows only damages that both contracting parties can anticipate at the time they make their agreement. Slim's Gun Shop argued that no one could have foreseen that Mr. De La Hoya would be arrested for possession of a stolen gun. No one had even known that the gun was stolen.

The California Court of Appeal, however, found for Mr. De La Hoya. The court reasoned that the owner of Slim's Gun Shop could have anticipated that if Mr. De La Hoya were questioned about the handgun and the gun happened to be stolen, Mr. De La Hoya might find himself in deep trouble.

Under a breach of warranty of title, Mr. De La Hoya also had a strong case, the court wrote. In so opining, the court pointed to California's Uniform Commercial Code, Section 3312, which reads: "The detriment caused by the breach of warranty of the title of personal property sold is deemed to be the value thereof to the buyer, when he is deprived of its possession, together with any costs which he has become liable to pay in an action brought for the property by the true owner."

Thus, although Mr. De La Hoya faced arrest for possessing stolen property, he did not have to pay for his release. That fell to Slim's Gun Shop, which had violated Mr. De La Hoya's warranty of title, even if it had done so unwittingly.

Chapter Summary

Remedies of the Seller

Buyer's Default the seller's remedies are triggered by the buyer's action in wrongfully rejecting or revoking acceptance of the goods, in failing to make payment due on or before delivery, or in repudiating the contract

To Withhold Delivery

To Stop Delivery if the buyer is insolvent (one who is unable to pay his debts as they become due or one whose total liabilities exceed his total assets), the seller may stop any delivery; if the buyer repudiates or otherwise breaches, the seller may stop carload, truckload, planeload, or larger shipments.

To Identify Goods

To Resell the Goods the seller may resell the goods concerned or the undelivered balance of the goods and recover the difference between the contract price and the resale price, together with any incidental damages, less expenses saved

- *Type of Resale* may be public or private
- *Manner of Resale* must be made in good faith and in a commercially reasonable manner

To Recover Damages for Nonacceptance or Repudiation

- *Market Price Differential* the seller may recover damages from the buyer measured by the difference between the unpaid contract price and the market price at the time and place of tender of the goods, plus incidental damages, less expenses saved

- *Lost Profit* in the alternative, the seller may recover the lost profit, including reasonable overhead, plus incidental damages, less expenses saved

To Recover the Price the seller may recover the price:
- when the buyer has accepted the goods
- when the goods have been lost or damaged after the risk of loss has passed to the buyer
- when the goods have been identified to the contract and there is no ready market available for their resale

To Recover Incidental Damages incidental damages include any commercially reasonable charges, expenses, or commissions directly resulting from the breach

To Cancel the Contract

To Reclaim the Goods upon the Buyer's Insolvency an unpaid seller may reclaim goods from an insolvent buyer under certain circumstances

Remedies of the Buyer

Seller's Default the buyer's remedies arise when the seller fails to make delivery or repudiates the contract or when the buyer rightfully rejects or justifiably revokes acceptance of goods tendered or delivered

To Cancel the Contract

To Recover Payments Made

To Cover the buyer may obtain cover by proceeding in good faith and without unreasonable delay to purchase substitute goods; the buyer may recover the difference between the cost of cover and the contract price, plus any incidental and consequential damages, less expenses saved

To Recover Damages for Nondelivery or Repudiation the buyer may recover the difference between the market price at the time the buyer learned of the breach and the contract price, plus any incidental and consequential damages, but less expenses saved

To Recover Identified Goods on the Seller's Insolvency for which he has paid all or part of the price

To Sue for Replevin the buyer may recover goods identified to the contract if (1) the buyer is unable to obtain cover or (2) the goods have been shipped under reservation of a security interest in the seller

To Sue for Specific Performance the buyer may obtain specific performance when the goods are unique or in other proper circumstances

To Enforce a Security Interest a buyer who has rightfully rejected or justifiably revoked acceptance of goods that remain in her possession has a security interest in these goods for any payments made on their price and for any expenses reasonably incurred

To Recover Damages for Breach in Regard to Accepted Goods the buyer may recover damages resulting in the ordinary course of events from the seller's breach; in the case of breach of warranty, such recovery is the difference between the value the goods would have had if they had been as warranted and the value of the nonconforming goods that have been accepted

To Recover Incidental Damages the buyer may recover incidental damages, which include any commercially reasonable expenses connected with the delay or other breach

To Recover Consequential Damages the buyer may recover consequential damages resulting from the seller's breach, including (1) any loss resulting from the buyer's requirements and needs of which the seller at the time of contracting had reason to know and which the buyer could not reasonably prevent by cover or otherwise, and (2) injury to person or property proximately resulting from any breach of warranty

Contractual Provisions Affecting Remedies

Liquidation or Limitation of Damages the parties may specify the amount or measure of damages that may be recovered in the event of a breach if the amount is reasonable

Modification or Limitation of Remedy by Agreement the contract between the parties may expressly provide for remedies in addition to those in the Code, or it may limit or change the measure of damages recoverable for breach

QUESTIONS

1. Mae contracted to sell 1,000 bushels of wheat to Lloyd at $4 per bushel. Just before Mae was to deliver the wheat, Lloyd notified her that he would not receive or accept the wheat. Mae sold the wheat for $3.60 per bushel, the market price, and later sued Lloyd for the difference of $400. Lloyd claims he was not notified by Mae of the resale and hence is not liable. Is Lloyd correct? Why?
2. On December 15, Judy wrote a letter to David stating that she would sell to David all of the mine-run coal that David might need to buy during the next calendar year for use at David's factory, delivered at the factory at a price of $40 per ton. David immediately replied by letter to Judy stating that he accepted the offer, that he would purchase all of his mine-run coal from Judy, and that he would need 200 tons of coal during the first week in January. During the months of January, February, and March, Judy delivered to David a total of 700 tons of coal, for which David made payment to Judy at the rate of $40 per ton. On April 10, David ordered 200 tons of mine-run coal from Judy, who replied to David on April 11 that she could not supply David with any more coal except at a price of $48 per ton delivered. David thereafter purchased elsewhere at the market price, namely $48 per ton, all of his factory's requirements of mine-run coal for the remainder of the year, amounting to a total of 2,000 tons of coal. Can David now recover damages from Judy at the rate of $8 per ton for the coal thus purchased, amounting to $16,000?
3. On January 10, Betty, of Emanon, Missouri, visited the showrooms of the Forte Piano Company in St. Louis and selected a piano. A sales memorandum of the transaction signed both by Betty and by the salesman of the Forte Piano Company read as follows: "Sold to Betty one new Andover piano, factory number 46832, price $3,300, to be shipped to the buyer at Emanon, Missouri, freight prepaid, before February 1. Prior to shipment, seller will stain the case a darker color in accordance with buyer's directions and will make the tone more brilliant." On January 15, Betty repudiated the contract by letter to the Forte Piano Company. The company subsequently stained the case, made the tone more brilliant, and offered to ship the piano to Betty on January 26. Betty persisted in her refusal to accept the piano. The Forte Piano Company sued Betty to recover the contract price. To what remedy, if any, is Forte entitled?
4. Sims contracted in writing to sell Blake 100 electric motors at a price of $100 each, freight prepaid to Blake's warehouse. By the contract of sale, Sims expressly warranted that each motor would develop twenty-five brake horsepower. The contract provided that the motors would be delivered in lots of twenty-five per week beginning January 2 and that Blake should pay for each lot of twenty-five motors as delivered, but that Blake was to have right of inspection on delivery. Immediately on delivery of the first lot of twenty-five motors on January 2, Blake forwarded Sims a check for $2,500, but on testing each of the twenty-five motors, Blake determined that none of them would develop more than fifteen brake horsepower. State all of the remedies available to Blake.
5. Henry and Mary entered into a written contract whereby Henry agreed to sell and Mary agreed to buy a certain automobile for $3,500. Henry drove the car to Mary's residence and properly parked it on the street in front of Mary's house, where he tendered it to Mary and requested payment of the price. Mary refused to take the car or pay the price. Henry informed Mary that he would hold her to the contract; but before Henry had time to enter the car and drive it away, a fire truck, answering a fire alarm and traveling at a high speed, crashed into the car and demolished it. Henry brings an action against Mary to recover the price of the car. Who is entitled to judgment? Would there be any difference in result if Henry were a dealer in automobiles?
6. Jane sells and delivers to Gerald on June 1 certain goods and receives from Gerald at the time of delivery Gerald's

check in the amount of $900 for the goods. The following day, Gerald is petitioned into bankruptcy; and Gerald's bank dishonors the check. On June 5, Jane serves notice on Gerald and the trustee in bankruptcy that she reclaims the goods. The trustee is in possession of the goods and refuses to deliver them to Jane. What are the rights of the parties?

7. The ABC Company, located in Chicago, contracted to sell a carload of television sets to Dodd in St. Louis, Missouri, on sixty days' credit. ABC Company shipped the carload to Dodd. On arrival of the car at St. Louis, Dodd paid the freight charges and reshipped the car to Hines of Little Rock, Arkansas, to whom he had previously contracted to sell the television sets. While the car was in transit to Little Rock, Dodd went bankrupt. ABC Company was informed of this at once and immediately telegraphed XYZ Railroad Company to withhold delivery of the television sets. What should the XYZ Railroad Company do?

8. Robert in Chicago entered into a contract to sell certain machines to Terry in New York. The machines were to be manufactured by Robert and shipped F.O.B. Chicago not later than March 25. On March 24, when Robert was about to ship the machines, he received a telegram from Terry wrongfully repudiating the contract. The machines cannot readily be resold for a reasonable price because they are a special kind used only in Terry's manufacturing processes. Robert sues Terry to recover the agreed price of the machines. What are the rights of the parties?

9. Calvin purchased a log home construction kit, manufactured by Boone Homes, Inc., from an authorized Boone dealer. The sales contract stated that Boone would repair or replace defective materials and that this was the exclusive remedy available against Boone. The dealer assembled the house, which was defective in a number of respects. The knotholes in the logs caused the walls and ceiling to leak. A support beam was too small and therefore cracked, causing the floor to crack also. These defects could not be completely cured by repair. Should Calvin prevail in a lawsuit against Boone for breach of warranty to recover damages for the loss in value?

10. Margaret contracted to buy a particular model Rolls-Royce from Paragon Motors, Inc. Only 100 of these models are built each year. She paid a $3,000 deposit on the car but Paragon sold the car to Gluck. What remedy, if any, does Margaret have against Paragon?

CASE PROBLEMS

11. Technical Textile agreed by written contract to manufacture and sell 20,000 pounds of yarn to Jagger Brothers (http://www.jaggeryarn.com) at a price of $2.15 per pound. After Technical had manufactured, delivered, and been paid for 3,723 pounds of yarn, Jagger Brothers by letter informed Technical that it was repudiating the contract and that it would refuse any further yarn deliveries. On August 12, the date of the letter, the market price of yarn was $1.90 per pound. Technical was awarded $4,069.25 in damages by the trial court, an amount equal to 16,277 times the difference between the contract price ($2.15) and the market price ($1.90) of the yarn on the repudiation date. Is this the appropriate method to calculate damages in this case?

12. Sherman Burrus, a job printer, purchased a printing press from the Itek Corporation for a price of $7,006.08. Before making the purchase, Burrus was assured by an Itek salesperson, Mr. Nessel, that the press was appropriate for the type of printing Burrus was doing. Burrus encountered problems in operating the press almost continuously from the time he received it. Burrus, his employees, and Itek representatives spent many hours in an unsuccessful attempt to get the press to operate properly. Burrus requested that the press be replaced, but Itek refused. Burrus then brought an action against Itek for (1) damages for breach of the implied warranty of merchantability and (2) consequential damages for losses resulting from the press's defective operation. Burrus was able to prove that the actual value of the press was $1,167 and, because of the defective press, that his output decreased and he sustained a great loss of paper. Itek contends that consequential damages are not recoverable in this case since Burrus elected to keep the press and continued to use it. How much should Burrus recover in damages for breach of warranty? Is he entitled to consequential damages?

13. A farmer made a contract in April to sell a grain dealer 40,000 bushels of corn to be delivered in October. On June 3, the farmer unequivocably informed the grain dealer that he was not going to plant any corn, that he would not fulfill the contract, and that if the buyer had commitments to resell the corn he should make other arrangements. The grain dealer waited in vain until October for performance of the repudiated contract. Then he bought corn at a greatly increased price on the market in order to fulfill commitments to his purchasers. To what damages, if any, is the grain dealer entitled ? Explain.

14. Through information provided by S-2 Yachts, Inc., the plaintiff, Barr, located a yacht to his liking at the Crow's Nest marina and yacht sales company. When Barr asked the price, he was told that, although the yacht normally sold for $102,000, Crow's Nest was willing to sell this particular one for only $80,000 in order to make room for a new model from the manufacturer, S-2 Yachts, Inc. Barr was assured that the yacht in question came with full manufacturer's warranties. Barr asked if the yacht was new and if anything was wrong with it. Crow's Nest told him that nothing was wrong with the yacht and that there were only twenty hours of use on the engines.

Once the yacht had been delivered and Barr had taken it for a test run, he noticed several problems associated with saltwater damage, such as rusted screws, a rusted stove, and faulty electrical wiring. Barr was assured that Crow's Nest would pay for these repairs. However, as was later discovered, the yacht was in such a damaged condition that Barr experienced great personal hazard the two times that he used the boat. Examination by a marine expert revealed clearly that the boat had been sunk in salt water prior to Barr's purchase. The engines were severely damaged, and there was significant structural and equipment damage as well. According to the expert, not only was the yacht not new, it was worth at most only a half of the new value of $102,000. What should Barr be able to recover from S-2 Yachts and Crow's Nest?

15. Lee Oldsmobile sells Rolls-Royce (http://www.rolls-roycemotorcars.com) automobiles. Mrs. Kaiden sent Lee a $25,000 deposit on a $135,500 1999 Rolls-Royce. Although Lee informed Mrs. Kaiden that the car would be delivered in November, the order form did not indicate the delivery date and contained a disclaimer for delay or failure to deliver due to circumstances beyond the dealer's control. On November 21, Mrs. Kaiden purchased another car from another dealer and canceled her car from Lee. When Lee attempted to deliver a Rolls-Royce to Mrs. Kaiden on November 29, Mrs. Kaiden refused to accept delivery. Lee later sold the car for $130,495.00. Mrs. Kaiden sued Lee for her $25,000 deposit plus interest. Lee counterclaims, based on the terms of the contract, for liquidated damages of $25,000 (the amount of the deposit) as a result of Mrs. Kaiden's breach of contract. What are the rights of the parties?

16. Servebest contracted to sell Emessee 200,000 pounds of 50 percent lean beef trimmings for $105,000. Upon a substantial fall in the market price, Emessee refused to pay the contract price and informed Servebest that the contract was canceled. Servebest sues Emessee for breach of contract including (a) damages for the difference between the contract price and the resale price of the trimmings and (b) incidental damages. Discuss.

17. Mrs. French was the highest bidder on eight antique guns at an auction held by Sotheby & Company. When Sotheby's billed Mrs. French $24,886.27 for the guns, she refused to pay. Is Sotheby's entitled to collect the price of the guns from Mrs. French?

18. Teledyne Industries, Inc, (http://www.alleghenytechnologies.com/index.asp) entered into a contract with Teradyne, Inc, (http://www.teradyne.com) to purchase a T-347A transistor test system for the list and fair market price of $98,400 less a discount of $984. After the system was packed for shipment, Teledyne canceled the order, offering to purchase a Field Effects Transistor System for $65,000. Teradyne refused the offer and sold the T-347A to another purchaser pursuant to an order that was on hand prior to the cancellation. Can Teradyne recover from Teledyne for lost profits resulting from the breach of contract? Explain.

19. Wilson Trading Corp. agreed to sell David Ferguson a specified quantity of yarn for use in making sweaters. The written contract provided that notice of defects, to be effective, had to be received by Wilson before knitting or within ten days of receipt of the yarn. When the knitted sweaters were washed, the color of the yarn "shaded" (i.e., variations in color from piece to piece appeared). David Ferguson immediately notified Wilson of the problem and refused to pay for the yarn, claiming that the defect made the sweaters unmarketable. Wilson brought suit against Ferguson for the contract price. What result?

20. Daniel Martin and John Duke contracted with J & S Distributors, Inc. to purchase a KIS Magnum Speed printer for $17,000. The parties agreed that Martin and Duke would send one-half of the money as a deposit and would pay the balance upon delivery. When the machine arrived five days late, Martin and Duke refused to accept it, stating that the company had purchased a substitute machine elsewhere. Martin and Duke requested the return of its deposit but J & S refused. Martin and Duke sued Jeff Sheffer and J & S for breach of contract, fraud, and breach of good faith. The defendants counter-claimed for full performance of the contract pursuant to a clause in the contract which provides: "In the event of non-payment of the balance of the purchase price reflected herein on due date and in the manner recorded or on such extended date which may be caused by late delivery on the part of [the seller], the Customer shall be liable for: (1) immediate payment of the full balance recorded herein; and (2) payment of interest at the rate of 12 percent per annum calculated on the balance due, when due, together with any attorney's fees, collection charges and other necessary expenses incurred by [the seller]." What are the rights of the parties?

http:// **Internet Exercise** Compare the remedies of the seller and buyer under the United Nations Convention on Contracts for the International Sale of Goods with their remedies under Article 2 of the Uniform Commercial Code.

PART V

NEGOTIABLE INSTRUMENTS

Uniform Commercial Code, Article 3
http://www.law.cornell.edu/ucc/3/overview.html

Uniform Commercial Code, Article 4
http://www.law.cornell.edu/ucc/4/overview.html

Federal Reserve System
http://www.federalreserve.gov/

Federal Deposit Insurance Corporation
http://www.fdic.gov/

Bank for International Settlements
http://www.bis.org/

Federal Trade Commission
http://www.ftc.gov

Washington Bar Association ("Signing Documents")
http://www.wsba.org/public/default.htm

U.S. Government Pamphlet ("Get the Facts on Saving and Investing")
http://www.pueblo.gsa.gov/money.htm

Utah Attorney General ("Checking Accounts—Pitfalls to Avoid"; "Co-maker, Co-signer, or Guarantor")
http://www.dfi.state.ut.us/ConsTips.htm

National Check Fraud Center
http://www.ckfraud.org/

Virginia Attorney General ("Checking Account Scams")
http://www.oag.state.va.us/Protecting/Consumer%20Fraud/default.htm

CHAPTER 24

Form and Content

Money is not, properly speaking, one of the subjects of commerce; but only the instrument which men have agreed upon to facilitate the exchange of one commodity for another. It is none of the wheels of trade: It is the oil which renders the motion of the wheels more smooth and easy.

DAVID HUME (1711–1776), IN *OF MONEY*

Learning Objectives

After reading this chapter you should be able to:

1. Describe the concept and importance of negotiability.
2. Identify and describe the types of negotiable instruments involving an order to pay.
3. Identify and describe the types of negotiable instruments involving a promise to pay.
4. List and explain the formal requirements that an instrument must meet to be negotiable.
5. Explain the effect on negotiability of an instrument's (1) being undated, antedated, or postdated, (2) lack of completion, and (3) ambiguity.

In July 1990, the American Law Institute and the National Conference of Commissioners on Uniform Laws approved a Revised Article 3 to the UCC. Named "Negotiable Instruments," the new Article, now adopted by nearly all of the states (only Massachusetts, New York, Rhode Island, South Carolina, and Utah have not adopted Revised Article 3), maintains the basic scope and content of prior Article 3 (Commercial Paper). This part of the text will discuss Revised Article 3 but will also point out the major changes from prior Article 3. Revised Article 3 is presented in Appendix B.

Negotiable instruments, also referred to simply as **instruments,** include drafts, checks, promissory notes, and certificates of deposit. These instruments are crucial to the sale of goods and services as well as to the financing of most businesses. The use of negotiable instruments has increased to such an extent that payments made with these instruments, with checks in particular, are now many times greater than payments made with cash. In fact, currency now is used primarily for smaller transactions. Accordingly, the vital importance of negotiable instruments as a method of payment cannot be overstated.

Modern business could not be conducted without the use of negotiable instruments. A tremendous number of transactions involve the writing of one or more checks. Drafts, of which checks are a specialized form, provide an important monetary and credit function in the business world, both inside and outside the banking system. Promissory notes serve an essential business purpose, not only in areas of high finance, but also at the level of the consumer and small businessperson as well. In recent years, individuals have increasingly used certificates of deposit instead of savings accounts.

CPA NEGOTIABILITY

Negotiability is a legal concept that makes written instruments freely transferable and therefore a readily accepted form of payment in substitution for money.

DEVELOPMENT OF LAW OF NEGOTIABLE INSTRUMENTS

The starting point for an understanding of negotiable instruments is recognizing that four or five centuries ago in England a contract right to the payment of money was not assignable because a contractual promise ran to the promisee. The fact that performance could be rendered only to him constituted a hardship for the owner of the right because it prevented him from selling or disposing of it. Eventually, however, the law permitted recovery upon an assignment by the assignee against the obligor.

An innocent assignee bringing an action against the obligor was subject to all defenses available to the obligor. Such an action would result in the same outcome whether it was brought by the assignee or assignor. Thus, a contract right became assignable but not very marketable because merchants had little interest in buying into a possible lawsuit. This remains the *law of assignments*: *The assignee stands in the shoes of his assignor*. For a discussion of assignments, see Chapter 16.

With the flourishing of trade and commerce, it became essential to develop a more effective means of exchanging contractual rights for money. For example, a merchant who sold goods for cash might use the cash to buy more goods for resale. If he were to make a sale on credit in exchange for a promise to pay money, why should he not be permitted to sell that promise to someone else for cash with which to carry on his business? One difficulty was that the buyer of the goods gave the seller only a promise to pay money to him. The seller was the only person to whom performance or payment was promised. If, however, the seller obtained from the buyer a promise in writing to pay money to anyone in possession (a *bearer*) of the writing (the *paper* or *instrument*) or to anyone the seller (or *payee* in this case) designated, then the duty of performance would run directly to the holder (the bearer of the paper or to the person to whom the payee ordered payment to be made). This is one of the essential distinctions between negotiable and nonnegotiable instruments. Although a negotiable instrument has other formal requirements, this particular one eliminates the limitations of a promise to pay money only to a named promisee.

Moreover, if the promise to pay were not subject to all of the defenses available against the assignor, a transferee would not only be more willing to acquire the promise but also would pay more for it. Accordingly, the law of negotiable instruments developed the concept of the ***holder in due course***, whereby certain good faith transferees who gave value acquired the right to be paid, free of most of the defenses to which an assignee would be subject. By reason of this doctrine, a transferee of a negotiable instrument could *acquire* greater rights than his transferor, whereas an assignee would acquire *only* the rights of his assignor. With these basic innovations, negotiable instruments enabled merchants to sell their contractual rights more readily and thereby keep their capital working.

ASSIGNMENT COMPARED WITH NEGOTIATION

Negotiability invests negotiable instruments with a high degree of marketability and commercial utility. It allows negotiable instruments to be freely transferable and enforceable by a person with the rights of a holder in due course against any person obligated on the instrument, subject only to a limited number of defenses. To illustrate, assume that George sells and delivers goods to Elaine for $50,000 on sixty days' credit and that, a few days later, George assigns this account to Marsha. Unless Elaine is duly notified of this assignment, she may safely pay the $50,000 to George on the due date without incurring any liability to Marsha, the assignee. Assume next that the goods were defective and that Elaine, accordingly, has a defense against George to the extent of $20,000. Assume also that Marsha duly notified Elaine of the assignment. The result is that Marsha can recover only $30,000, not $50,000, from Elaine because Elaine's defense against George is equally available against George's assignee, Marsha. In other words, an assignee of contractual rights merely "steps into the shoes" of her assignor and, hence, acquires only the same rights as her assignor—and no more.

Assume, instead, that upon the sale by George to Elaine, Elaine executes and delivers her negotiable note to George for $50,000, payable to George's order in sixty days, and that, a short time later, George duly negotiates (transfers) the note to Marsha. In the first place, Marsha is not required to notify Elaine that she has acquired the note from George, because one who issues a negotiable instrument is held to know that the instrument may be negotiated and is generally obligated to pay the holder of the instrument, whoever that may be. In the second place, Elaine's defense is not available against Marsha if Marsha acquired the note in good faith and for value and had no knowledge of Elaine's defense against George and took it without reason to question its authenticity. Marsha, therefore, is entitled to hold Elaine for the full face amount of the note at

Figure 24-1
Order to Pay: Draft or Check

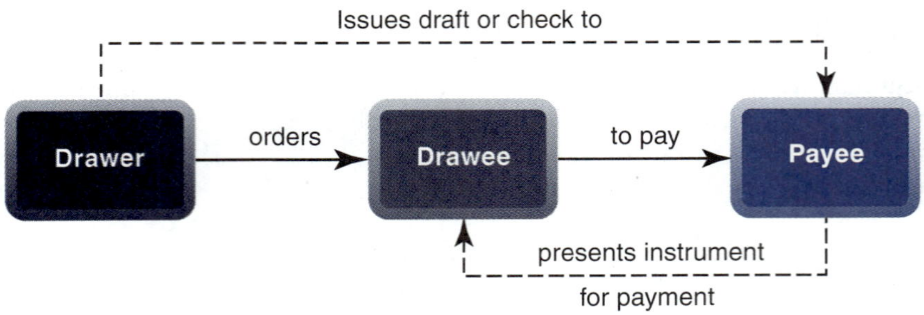

maturity, namely, $50,000. In other words, Marsha, by the negotiation of the negotiable note to her, acquired rights greater than those George had, because, by keeping the note, George could have recovered only $30,000 on it because Elaine successfully could have asserted her defense in the amount of $20,000 against him.

To have the full benefit of negotiability, negotiable instruments not only must meet the requirements of negotiability but also must be acquired by a holder in due course. This chapter discusses the formal requirements instruments must satisfy to be negotiable. Chapter 25 deals with the manner in which a negotiable instrument must be negotiated to preserve its advantages. Chapter 26 covers the requisites and rights of a holder in due course. Finally, Chapter 27 examines the liability of all the parties to a negotiable instrument.

CPA Types of Negotiable Instruments

There are four types of negotiable instruments: drafts, checks, notes, and certificates of deposit. The first two contain *orders* or directions to pay money; the last two involve *promises* to pay money.

Drafts

A draft involves three parties, each in a distinct capacity. One party, the drawer, orders a second party, the drawee, to pay a fixed amount of money to a third party, the payee (see Figure 24-1 for a three-party instrument). The drawee is ordinarily a person or entity who either is in possession of money belonging to the drawer or owes money to him. A sample draft is reproduced in Figure 24-2. The same party may appear in more than one capacity; for instance, the drawer may also be the payee.

Drafts may be either "time" or "sight." A *time draft* is one payable at a specified future date, whereas a *sight draft* is payable on demand (that is, immediately upon presentation to the drawee).

Checks

A **check** is a specialized form of draft, namely, an order to pay money drawn on a bank and payable on demand (that is, upon the payee's request for payment). Once again, there are parties involved in three distinct capacities: the drawer, who orders the drawee, a bank, to pay the payee on **demand** (see Figure 24-3 for a check). Checks are by far the most widely used form of negotiable instruments. Each year more than ten billion checks are written in the United States for a total of more than five trillion dollars.

A *cashier's check* is a check drawn by a bank upon itself to the order of a named payee.

Notes

A **promissory note** is an instrument involving two parties in two capacities. One party, the **maker**, promises to pay a second party, the payee, a stated sum of money, either on demand or at a stated future date (see Figure 24-4 for

Figure 24-2
Draft

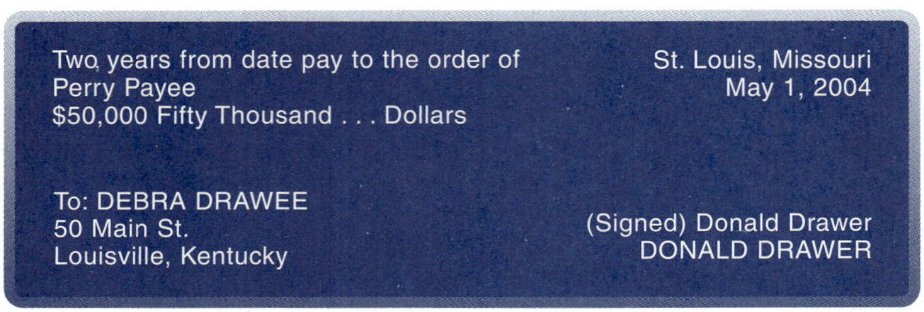
Two years from date pay to the order of
Perry Payee
$50,000 Fifty Thousand . . . Dollars

St. Louis, Missouri
May 1, 2004

To: DEBRA DRAWEE
50 Main St.
Louisville, Kentucky

(Signed) Donald Drawer
DONALD DRAWER

Figure 24-3
Check

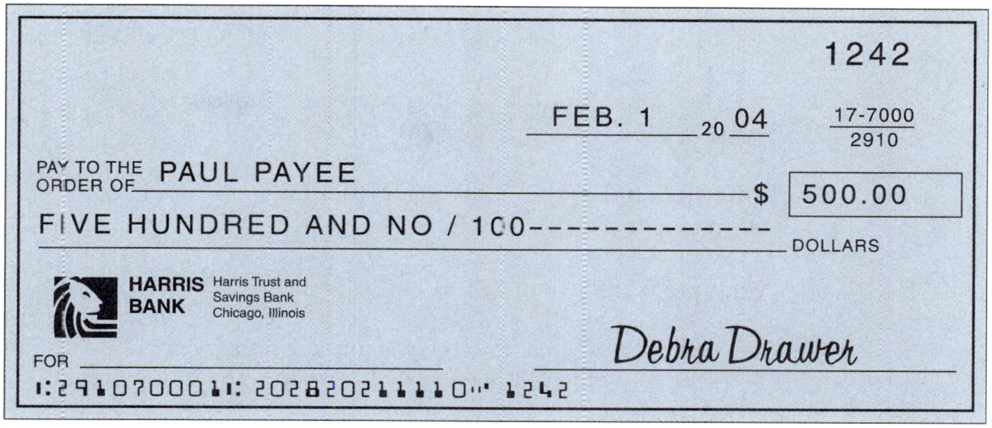

a two-party promise to pay). The note may range from a simple "I promise to pay $X to the order of Y" form to more complex legal instruments such as installment notes, collateral notes, mortgage notes, and judgment notes. Figure 24-5 is a note payable at a definite time—six months from the date of April 7, 2004—and hence is referred to as a *time note*. A note payable upon the request or demand of the payee or holder is a *demand note*.

Certificates of Deposit

A certificate of deposit, or CD, as it is frequently called, is a specialized form of *promise* to pay money given by a *bank*. A **certificate of deposit** is a written acknowledgment by a bank of the receipt of money that it promises to repay. The issuing party, the *maker*, which is always a bank, promises to pay a second party, the payee, who is named in the CD (see Figure 24-6 for a sample certificate of deposit).

Formal Requirements of Negotiable Instruments

CPA

To perform its function in the business community effectively, a negotiable instrument must be able to pass freely from person to person. The fact that ***negotiability*** is wholly a matter of form makes such freedom possible. The instrument must contain within its "four corners" all the information required to determine whether it is negotiable. No reference to any other source is permitted. For this reason, a negotiable instrument is called a "courier without luggage." In addition, indorsements *cannot* create or destroy negotiability.

In order to be negotiable, the *instrument* must

1. be in writing,
2. be signed,
3. contain a promise or order to pay,

Figure 24-4
Promise to Pay: Promissory Note or Certificate of Deposit

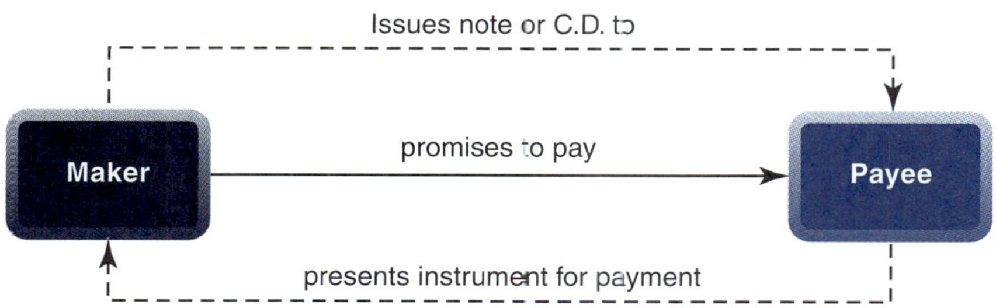

Figure 24-5
Note

$10,000	Albany, N.Y.	April 7, 2004

Six months from date I promise to pay to the order of Pat Payee ten thousand dollars.

(Signed) Matthew Maker

Figure 24-6
Certificate of Deposit

NEGOTIABLE CERTIFICATE OF DEPOSIT

The Mountain Bank
No. 13900 Mountain, N.Y. June 1, 2004

THIS CERTIFIES THAT THERE HAS BEEN DEPOSITED
with the undersigned the sum of $200,000.00

Two hundred thousand . . . . Dollars

Payable to the order of Pablo Payee on December 1, 2006, with interest only to maturity at the rate of Seven percent (7%) per annum upon surrender of this certificate properly indorsed.

The Mountain Bank
By (Signature) Malcolm Maker, Vice President
Authorized Signature

4. be unconditional,
5. be for a fixed amount,
6. be for money,
7. contain no other undertaking or instruction,
8. be payable on demand or at a definite time, and
9. be payable to order or to bearer.

If these requirements are not met, the undertaking is not negotiable (nor is it a negotiable instrument or simply an instrument), and the rights of the parties are governed by the law of contract (assignment).

Practical Advice

To increase the value of an undertaking, make sure that any document memorializing it qualifies as a negotiable instrument.

Practical Advice

Consider selecting a state that has adopted Revised Article 3 as the governing law for your instruments.

Yin v. Society National Bank Indiana

Court of Appeals of Indiana, 1996
665 N.E.2d 58

FACTS On January 2, 1991, plaintiff, Society National Bank (Society), agreed in a promissory note to lend U.S.A. Diversified Products, Inc. (USAD) up to $2,000,000.00 in the form of an operating line of credit. Paul Davis (Davis) signed the note both personally and as the president of USAD. Defendant, Sam Yin (Yin), who jointly owns USAD with Davis, also personally signed the note. Defendant, Sophia Kung (Kung), who at that time was married to Yin, also signed the note personally. During negotiations regarding the note, Society directly dealt only with Davis. Once negotiations were finalized, Davis took the note, obtained Yin's and Kung's signatures, and returned it to Society. The outstanding balance was to be paid on April 30, 1992.

Some time prior to the end of April 1992, Davis told Society that a sixty-day extension of the original payment date was needed. Society agreed to the extension. Davis represented that he would obtain Yin's and Kung's signatures as he had for the 1991 document. However, Yin's and Kung's signatures were forged on the extension document.

As a result of USAD's default on the line of credit, Society filed a complaint against USAD, Davis, Yin, and Kung. The trial court granted summary judgment in favor of Society and against Yin and Kung in the amount of $2,160,331.73 including interest and attorney fees and expenses.

DECISION Reversed and remanded.

OPINION Chezem, J. B. Is this line of credit a negotiable instrument?

[Article 3] appl[ies] only to negotiable instruments. [Citation.] Non-negotiable agreements are governed by Indiana common law. [Citations.] Yin and Kung challenge the trial court's finding that their agreement for a line of credit is a negotiable instrument. * * * We hold that it is not.

In determining the negotiability of an agreement, we apply the law in effect at the time of the execution of the agreement. [Prior Article 3.]

* * *

Yin and Kung assert that their line of credit meets neither the sum certain [fixed amount under Revised Article 3] nor the unconditional requirement. * * *

Other courts have faced the issue or a situation quite similar to it and held that such an agreement is not a negotiable instrument. For example, in [Citation] the Fifth Circuit agreed with a district court's opinion that "[t]he note in this case does not contain an obligation to pay a 'sum certain,' but rather 'the sum of TWO MILLION AND NO/100 DOLLARS ($2,000,000) or so much thereof as may be advanced. * * *'." [Citation.] The Fifth Circuit reasoned that the language employed by the note failed to disclose the exact amount to be repaid. [Citation.] That is, the amount advanced to the parties could not be determined with certainty absent an inquiry to other documents. Accordingly, the note did not facially demand payment of a sum certain [fixed amount], and hence was not negotiable. [Citations.]

The parties do not seriously dispute that the agreement in the present case is a line of credit upon which USAD could make draws of varying amounts. Indeed, the face of the note contains a notation regarding "draws." We note that although USAD did make various draws upon the line of credit, it was under no obligation to make any draws whatsoever. In fact, if USAD had never drawn upon the line of credit, it would have owed nothing when the agreement matured. The principal would have been zero. This is noteworthy because it illustrates an important feature of the line of credit: in order to ascertain the principal owed, one must look beyond the agreement itself. A current history of USAD's draws would also be necessary in order to calculate the amount USAD owed. Because of the potentially variable principal which results from such an arrangement, the line of credit contains no sum certain [nor fixed amount]. In addition, USAD's ability to make draws up to two million dollars was not unfettered. It was dependent upon the sufficiency of USAD's accounts receivable. That is, if USAD sold the accounts receivable (Society's security), then Society "in all likelihood * * * would put a hold on any further draws." Society conditioned USAD's access to the line of credit by tracking the company's collateral. Lacking an unconditional promise to pay a sum certain, the line of credit falls outside the definition of a negotiable instrument. Thus, in addressing the parties' other issues regarding the line of credit, we apply Indiana common law.

* * *

Because the change must be a material and binding one, we cannot agree with Yin's and Kung's assertion that the forged extension note serves to discharge them from the potential liability they incurred upon signing the original 1991 agreement. They cannot be bound by a document (here, the extension note) which does not bear their signatures. In addition, by signing the 1991 note which contained a consent to future extensions provision, they explicitly gave prior consent to an extension. [Citation.] Accordingly, the extension note has no effect on their liability.

INTERPRETATION An instrument must contain within its "four corners" all the information required to determine whether it is negotiable.

CRITICAL THINKING QUESTION Should negotiability be a matter of form? Explain.

WRITING

The requirement that the instrument be in **writing** is broadly construed. Printing, typewriting, handwriting, or any other tangible expression is sufficient to satisfy the requirement. Most negotiable instruments, of course, are written on paper, but this is not required. In one instance, a check was reportedly written on a coconut.

SIGNED

A note or certificate of deposit must be signed by the maker; a draft or check must be signed by the drawer. As in the case of a writing, extreme latitude is granted in determining what constitutes a **signature**, which is any symbol a party executes or adopts with the intent to validate a writing. Moreover, it may consist of any word or mark used in place of a written signature, such as initials, an X, or a thumbprint. It may be a trade name or an assumed name. Even the location of the signature on the document is unimportant. Normally, a maker or drawer signs in the lower right-hand corner of the instrument, but this is not required. Negotiable instruments are frequently signed by an agent for her principal. For a discussion of the appropriate way in which an agent should sign a negotiable instrument, see Chapter 27.

http:// Washington Bar Association ("Signing Documents"): http://www.wsba.org/public/default.htm

PROMISE OR ORDER TO PAY

A negotiable instrument must contain either a promise to pay money, in the case of a note or certificate of deposit, or an order to pay, in the case of a draft or check.

Promise to Pay A **promise to pay** is an undertaking and must be more than the mere acknowledgment or recognition of an existing obligation or debt. The so-called due bill or IOU is not a promise but merely an acknowledgment of indebtedness. Accordingly, an instrument reciting "due Adam Brown $100" or "IOU, Adam Brown, $100" is not negotiable because it does not contain a promise to pay.

Order to Pay An **order to pay** is an instruction to pay. It must be more than an authorization or request and must identify with reasonable certainty the person to be paid. The usual way to express an order is by use of the word *pay*: "*Pay* to the order of John Jones" or "*Pay* bearer." The addition of words of courtesy, such as *please pay* or *kindly pay*, will not destroy the negotiability. Nonetheless, caution should be exercised in employing words that modify the prototypically correct "*pay*." For example, the use of the words "I wish you would pay" has been held to destroy the negotiability of an instrument and to render its transfer a contractual assignment.

UNCONDITIONAL

The requirement that the promise or order be unconditional is to prevent the inclusion of any term that could reduce the promisor's obligation to pay. Conditions limiting a promise would diminish the payment and credit functions of negotiable instruments by necessitating costly and time-consuming investigations to determine the degree of risk such conditions imposed. Moreover, if the holder (transferee) had to take an instrument subject to certain conditions, her risk factor would be substantial, and this would lead to limited transferability. Substitutes for money must be capable of rapid circulation at a minimum risk.

A promise or order to pay is **unconditional** if it is absolute and not subject to any contingencies or qualifications. Thus, an instrument would not be negotiable if it stated that "ABC Corp. promises to pay $100,000 to the order of Johnson provided the helicopter sold meets all contractual specifications." On the other hand, suppose that upon delivering an instrument that provided, "ABC Corp. promises to pay $100,000 to the order of Johnson," Meeker, the president of ABC, stated that the money would be paid only if the helicopter met all contractual specifications. The instrument would be negotiable because negotiability is determined solely by examining the instrument itself and is not affected by matters beyond the instrument's face.

A promise or order is unconditional unless it states: (a) that there is an express condition to payment, (b) that the promise or order is subject to or governed by another writing, or (c) that rights or obligations concerning the order or promise are stated in another writing. A mere reference to another writing, however, does not make the promise or order conditional.

An instrument is not made conditional by the fact that it is subject to implied or constructive conditions; the condition must be expressed to destroy negotiability. Implications of law or fact are not to be considered in deciding whether an instrument is negotiable. Thus, a statement in an instrument that it is given for an executory promise does *not* imply that the instrument is conditioned upon performance of that promise.

Reference to Other Agreements The restriction against **reference to another agreement** is to enable any person to determine the right to payment provided by the instrument without having to look beyond its four corners. If such right is made subject to the terms of another agreement, the instrument is nonnegotiable.

A distinction is to be made between a mere recital of the *existence* of a separate agreement (this does not destroy negotiability) and a recital that makes the instrument *subject* to the terms of another agreement (this does destroy negotiability).

A statement in a note such as "This note is given in partial payment for a color TV set to be delivered two weeks from date in accordance with a contract of this date between the payee and the maker," does not impair negotiability. It merely describes the consideration and the transaction giving rise to the note. It does not place any restriction or condition on the maker's obligation to pay. The promise is not made subject to any other agreement.

The following is an example of added words that *would* impair negotiability: "This note is subject to all terms of said contract." Such words make the promise to pay conditional upon the adequate performance of the television set in accordance with the terms of the contract and thus render the instrument nonnegotiable.

The Particular Fund Doctrine Revised Article 3 eliminates the **particular fund doctrine** by providing that a promise or order is *not* made conditional because payment is to be made only out of a particular fund.

Under prior Article 3, an order or promise to pay only out of a particular fund was conditional and destroyed negotiability because payment depended on the existence and sufficiency of the particular fund. On the other hand, a promise or order to pay that merely indicated a particular fund out of which reimbursement was to be made or a particular account to be debited with the amount did not impair negotiability because the promise or order relied on the drawer's or maker's general credit and the notation charging a particular account was merely a bookkeeping entry to be followed after payment.

FIXED AMOUNT

The purpose of the requirement of a **fixed amount** in money is to enable the person entitled to enforce the instrument to determine from the instrument itself the amount that he is entitled to receive.

The requirement that payment be of a "fixed amount" must be considered from the point of view of the person entitled to enforce the instrument, not the maker or drawer. (Prior Article 3 used the term "sum certain," which means fundamentally the same as "fixed amount.") The holder must be assured of a determinable minimum payment, although provisions of the instrument may increase the recovery under certain circumstances. Revised Article 3, however, applies the fixed amount requirement only to the *principal*. Thus, the fixed amount portion does not apply to interest or to the charges, such as collection fees or attorneys' fees.

Moreover, negotiability of an instrument is not affected by the inclusion or omission of a stated rate of interest. If the instrument does not state a rate of interest, it is payable without interest. If the instrument states that it is payable "with interest" but does not specify a rate, the judgment rate of interest applies.

Most significantly, Revised Article 3 provides that "Interest may be stated in an instrument as a fixed or variable amount of money or it may be expressed as a fixed or variable rate or rates." Moreover, determination of the rate of interest "may require reference to information not contained in the instrument." Variable rate mortgages, therefore, may be negotiable; this result is consistent with the rule that the fixed amount requirement applies only to the principal.

Under prior Article 3, both principal and interest had to be determined from the face of the instrument. Thus, courts held that variable interest rate provisions destroyed negotiability because the interest rate was tied to a published index external to the instrument.

A sum payable is a fixed amount even though it is payable in installments or payable with a fixed discount, if paid before maturity, or with a fixed addition, if paid after maturity. This is because it is always possible to use the instrument itself to compute the amount due at any given time.

MONEY

The term **money** means a medium of exchange authorized or adopted by a sovereign government as part of its currency. Consequently, even though local custom may make gold or diamonds a medium of exchange, an instrument payable in such commodities would be nonnegotiable because of the lack of governmental sanction of such media as legal tender. On the other hand, an instrument paying a fixed amount in British pounds, Brazilian real, Japanese yen, or other foreign currency is negotiable.

NO OTHER UNDERTAKING OR INSTRUCTION

A negotiable instrument must contain a promise or order to pay money, but it may not "state any other undertaking or instruction by the person promising or ordering payment to do any act in addition to the payment of money." Accordingly, an instrument containing an order or promise to do an act in addition to or in lieu of the payment of money is not negotiable. For example, a promise to pay $100 "and a ton of coal" would be nonnegotiable.

The Code sets out a list of terms and provisions that may be included in instruments without adversely affecting negotiability. Among these are (1) an undertaking or power to give, maintain, or protect collateral in order to secure payment, (2) an authorization or power to confess judgment (written authority by the debtor to allow the holder to enter judgment against the debtor in favor of the holder) on the instrument, (3) an authorization or power to sell or dispose of collateral upon default, and (4) a waiver of the benefit of any law intended for the advantage or protection of the obligor. It is important to note that the Code does not render any of these terms legal or effective; it merely provides that their inclusion will not affect negotiability.

Practical Advice

To preserve the negotiability of an investment, avoid including any undertaking beyond the promise or order to pay.

PAYABLE ON DEMAND OR AT A DEFINITE TIME

A negotiable instrument must "be payable on demand or at a definite time." This requirement, like the other formal requirements of negotiability, is designed to promote certainty in determining the present value of a negotiable instrument.

Demand "Payable upon demand" means that the money owed under the instrument must be paid upon the holder's request. **Demand paper** always has been considered sufficiently certain as to time of payment to satisfy the requirements of negotiability because it is the person entitled to enforce the instrument who makes the demand and who thus sets the time for payment. Any instrument in which no time for payment is stated—a check, for example—is payable on demand. An instrument also qualifies as being payable on demand if it is payable at sight or on presentment.

NationsBank of Virginia, N.A. v. Barnes

Virginia Circuit Court, 1994
33 Va.Cir. 184, 24 UCC.Rep.Serv.2d 782

FACTS In 1991, Ad Barnes and Elaine Barnes (Barnes) executed a promissory note for $200,000 to Sovran Bank, N.A. (Sovran). The note was executed on a standard form and a box marked payable "on demand" was checked. There was no set time for repayment, only a provision requiring monthly payments of interest. NationsBank of Virginia, N.A. (NationsBank) **(http://www.bankofamerica.com/)** became the successor by merger to Sovran and is now the holder of this note. By a letter dated February 17, 1993, NationsBank made a demand for payment on the note. Barnes did not make payment and NationsBank brought this action to recover payment. NationsBank filed a motion for partial summary judgment on the issue of liability. Barnes argued that NationsBank must make a showing of good faith before it may demand payment on the note.

DECISION Decision for NationsBank.

OPINION Horne, J. The factual question still in dispute concerning the 1991 Note is whether it is a demand note. Plaintiff argues that the language of the note is unambiguous and is clearly a demand note. Defendants argue that the detailed enumeration of events constituting default is inconsistent with a demand note. Thus, a standard of good faith must be applied before a demand for accelerated repayment can be made.

[UCC] § 1–203 establishes a general duty of good faith in every contract governed by the Commercial Code. Under any contract providing for accelerated payment at will, § 1–208 states that the option is to be exercised only in the good faith belief that the prospect of payment or performance is impaired. However, the Official Comment to this section indicates that it is not applicable to a demand instrument.

[UCC Revised § 3–108(a)] states that a note is payable "on demand" if it says it is payable on demand or states no time for payment. In this case, the 1991 * * * Note is a standard form with different forms of repayment set out on the first page. The box marked payable "on demand" has been checked in this instance. There is no time set for repayment, only a provision requiring monthly payments of interest.

It is the court's opinion that the 1991 Note is unambiguous and is clearly a demand note. Thus, Plaintiff is under no obligation to show good faith before requesting payment on the note. Since demand has been made by Plaintiff, Defendants are liable. Thus, Plaintiff is entitled to summary judgment on the issue of liability under the 1991 Note.

INTERPRETATION An instrument payable on demand must be paid upon the holder's request.

ETHICAL QUESTION Did NationsBank act in good faith? Explain.

CRITICAL THINKING QUESTION Do you agree with the court's decision? Explain.

Definite Time Instruments payable at a definite time are called **time paper.** A promise or order is payable at a definite time if it is payable:

1. at a fixed date or dates,
2. at a definite period of time after sight or acceptance, or
3. at a time readily ascertainable at the time the promise or order is issued.

An instrument is payable at a definite time if it is payable "on or before" a stated date. The person entitled to enforce the instrument is thus assured that she will have her money by the maturity date at the latest, although she may receive it sooner. This right of anticipation enables the obligor, at his option, to pay before the stated maturity date (*prepayment*) and thereby stop the further accrual of interest or, if interest rates have gone down, to refinance at a lower rate of interest. Nevertheless, it constitutes sufficient certainty so as not to impair negotiability.

Frequently, instruments are made payable at a fixed period after a stated date. For example, the instrument may be made payable "thirty days after date." This means it is payable thirty days after the date of issuance, which is recited on the instrument. Such an instrument is payable at a definite time, for its exact maturity date can be determined by simple math.

An undated instrument payable "thirty days after date" is not payable at a definite time, as the date of payment cannot be determined from its face. It is therefore nonnegotiable until it is completed.

An instrument that by its terms is otherwise payable only upon an act or event whose time of occurrence is uncertain is *not* payable at a definite time. An example would be a note providing for payment to the order "when X dies." However, as previously stated, a time that is readily ascertainable at the time the promise or order is issued is a definite time. This changes prior Article 3 and seemingly would permit a note reading "payable on the day of the next presidential election." As long as the scheduled event is certain to happen, Revised Article 3 appears to be satisfied.

The clause "at a fixed period after sight" is frequently used in drafts. Because a fixed period after sight means a fixed period after acceptance, a simple mathematical calculation makes the maturity date certain; and the instrument is, therefore, negotiable.

An instrument payable at a fixed time subject to *acceleration* by the holder also satisfies the requirement of being payable at a definite time. Indeed, such an instrument would seem to have a more certain maturity date than a demand instrument because it at least states a definite maturity date. In addition, the acceleration may be contingent upon the happening of some act or event.

Finally, a provision in an instrument granting the *holder* an option to extend the maturity of the instrument for a definite or indefinite period does not impair its negotiability. Nor does a provision permitting the *obligor* of an instrument to extend the maturity date to a further *definite* time. For example, a provision in a note, payable one year from date, that the maker may extend the maturity date six months does not impair negotiability. If the obligor is given an option to extend the maturity of the instrument for an *indefinite* period, however, his promise is illusory; and there is no certainty regarding time of payment. Such an instrument is nonnegotiable. If the obligor's right to extend is limited to a definite time, the extension clause is no more indefinite than an acceleration clause with a time limitation.

In addition, extension may be made automatic upon or after a specified act or event, provided a definite time limit is stated. An example of such an extension clause is, "I promise to pay to the order of John Doe the sum of $2,000 on December 1, 2004, but it is agreed that if the crop of sections 25 and 26 of Twp. 145 is below eight bushels per acre for the 2004 season, this note shall be extended for one year."

At a Definite Time and on Demand If the instrument, payable at a fixed date, *also* provides that it is payable on demand made before the fixed date, it is still a negotiable instrument. Revised Article 3 provides that the instrument is payable on demand until the fixed date and, if demand is not made prior to the specified date, becomes payable at a definite time on the fixed date.

PAYABLE TO ORDER OR TO BEARER

A negotiable instrument must contain words indicating that the maker or drawer intends that it may pass into the hands of someone other than the payee. Although the "magic" words of negotiability typically are **payable to order or to bearer**, other clearly equivalent words also may fulfill this requirement. The use of synonyms, however, only invites trouble. Moreover, as noted above, indorsements cannot create or destroy negotiability, which must be determined from the "face" of the instrument. Words of negotiability must be present when the instrument is issued or first comes into possession of a holder.

Revised Article 3 provides that a *check* that meets all requirements of being a negotiable instrument except that it is not payable to bearer or order is nevertheless a negotiable instrument. This rule does *not* apply to instruments other than checks and does not exist under prior Article 3.

Payable to Order An instrument is **payable to order** if it is payable (a) to the order of an identified person or (b) to an identified person or order. If an instrument is payable to bearer, it cannot be payable to order; an instrument that is ambiguous as to this point is payable to bearer. Prior Article 3 provided that use of the word "assigns" met the requirement of words of negotiability; Revised Article 3, however, does not so provide.

Moreover, in every instance the person to whose order the instrument is payable must be designated with reasonable certainty. Within this limitation a broad range of payees is possible, including an individual, two or more payees, an office, an estate, a trust or fund, a partnership or unincorporated association, and a corporation.

This requirement should not be confused with the requirement that the instrument contain an order or promise to pay. An order to pay is an instruction to a third party to pay the instrument as drawn. The word "order" in terms of an "order instrument," on the other hand, pertains to the transferability of the instrument rather than to instructions directing a specific party to pay.

A writing, other than a *check*, that names a specified person without indicating that it is payable to order—for example, "Pay to Justin Matthew"—is not payable to order or to bearer. Such a writing is not a negotiable instrument and is not covered by Article 3. On the other hand, a check that meets all of the requirements of a negotiable instrument, except that it does not provide the words of negotiability, is still a negotiable instrument and falls within the purview of Article 3. Thus, a check "payable to Justin Matthew" is a negotiable check.

Cooperative Centrale Raiffeisen-Boerenleenbank B.A. v. Bailey

United States District Court, Central District of California, 1989
710 F.Supp. 737

FACTS William Bailey, M.D., executed a promissory note to California Dreamstreet, a joint venture that solicited investments in cattle breeding operations. California Dreamstreet subsequently sold the note to Cooperative Centrale Raiffeisen-Boerenleenbank B.A. (Bank).

The wording on the promissory note was unusual. In pertinent part it read: "DR. WILLIAM BAILEY * * * hereby promises to pay to the order to CALIFORNIA DREAMSTREET * * * the sum of Three Hundred Twenty-Nine Thousand Eight Hundred ($329,800) Dollars."

Dr. Bailey contended that the atypical wording "pay to the order to" rendered the note nonnegotiable, and refused to pay the Bank. The Bank, asserting that the note was negotiable, sued for payment.

DECISION Judgment for the Bank.

OPINION Rea, J. [The parties] agree that the sole issue is whether the unusual language in the note obliging Bailey to "pay to the order to California Dreamstreet" renders the note nonnegotiable.

Whether an instrument is negotiable is a question of law to be determined solely from the face of the instrument, without reference to the intent of the parties. [Citation.] To be negotiable, an instrument must "be payable to order or bearer." Code § 3–104(1)(d). "Payable to order" is further defined by Code § 3–110(1), as follows:

> (1) An instrument is payable to order when by its terms it is payable to the order * * * of any person therein specified with reasonable certainty, or to him or his order, or when it is conspicuously designated on its face as "exchange" or the like and names a payee.

It is well established that a promissory note is nonnegotiable if it states only "payable to (payee)," rather than "payable to the order of [payee]." [Citations.] Bailey claims that the instant note, which states "pay to the order to [payee]," falls between these two alternatives and should therefore be deemed nonnegotiable.

The authorities are unhelpful. There is apparently no case on record in which a variance this small from the language of the Code has been called into question. Both parties direct the Court's attention to Official UCC Comment 5 to Code § 3–104, which states:

> 5. This Article omits the original Section 10, which provided that the instrument need not follow the language of the act if it "clearly indicates an intention to conform" to it. The provision has served no useful purpose, and it has been an encouragement to bad drafting and to liberality in holding questionable paper to be negotiable. The omission is not intended to mean that the instrument must follow the language of this section, or that one term may not be recognized as clearly the equivalent of another, as in the case of "I undertake" instead of "I promise," or "Pay to holder" instead of

"Pay to bearer." It does mean that either the language of the section or a clear equivalent must be found, and that in doubtful cases the decision should be against negotiability.

In the Court's opinion, the Comment fails to persuasively support either party's position. Rules of grammar belie the Bank's argument that the preposition "to" is an apt substitute for "of" since the resulting sentence, read literally, is not just ambiguous but incomplete. On the other hand, the Comment expressly disavows Bailey's argument that the Code drafters intended to set forth certain "magic words," the absence of which precludes negotiability.

What does emerge from the Comment is the need for certainty in determining negotiability. Though sensitive to this goal and to the potentially harsh result of such a finding, the court does not find the instant facts to present the kind of "doubtful" case which should be resolved against negotiability. In this context, the phrase "pay to the order to" can plausibly be construed only to mean "pay to the order of." While other explanations are possible, none are realistic. To hold otherwise would, in this court's opinion, set an overly technical standard that could unexpectedly frustrate legitimate expectations of negotiability in commercial transactions.

INTERPRETATION An instrument is payable to order if it is payable to the order of an identified entity.

CRITICAL THINKING QUESTION Do you agree with the court's decision? Explain.

Payable to Bearer The UCC states that an instrument fulfills the requirements of being **payable to bearer** if it (1) states it is payable to bearer or the order of bearer, (2) does not state a payee, or (3) states it is payable to "cash" or to the order of "cash." An instrument made payable both to order and to bearer, that is, "pay to the order of Mildred Courts or bearer," is payable to bearer.

An instrument that does not state a payee is payable to bearer. Thus, if a drawer leaves blank the "pay to order of" line of a check or the maker of a notes writes "pay to ____________," the instrument is a negotiable bearer instrument.

TERMS AND OMISSIONS AND THEIR EFFECT ON NEGOTIABILITY

The negotiability of an instrument may be questioned because of an omission of certain provisions or because of ambiguity. Problems may also arise in connection with the interpretation of an instrument, whether or not negotiability is called into question. Accordingly, the Code contains rules of construction that apply to every instrument.

Dating of the Instrument The negotiability of an instrument is not affected by the fact that it is antedated or postdated. If the instrument is undated, its date is the date of its issuance. If it is unissued, its date is the date it first comes into the possession of a holder.

Incomplete Instruments Occasionally, a party will sign a paper that clearly is intended to become an instrument but that, either by intention or through oversight, is incomplete because of the omission of a necessary element such as a promise or order, a designated payee, an amount payable, or a time for payment. The Code provides that such an instrument is not negotiable until completed.

If, for example, an undated instrument is delivered on November 1, 2004, payable "thirty days after date," the payee has implied authority to fill in "November 1, 2004." Until he does so, however, the instrument is not negotiable because it is not payable at a definite time. If the payee completes the instrument by inserting an erroneous date, the rules as to material alteration, covered in Chapter 27, apply.

Ambiguous Instruments Rather than commit the parties to the use of parol evidence to establish the interpretation of an instrument, Revised Article 3 establishes rules to resolve common ambiguities. This promotes negotiability by providing added certainty to the holder.

Where it is doubtful whether the instrument is a draft or note, the holder may treat it as either and present it for payment to the drawee or the person signing it. For example, an instrument reading

To X: On demand, I promise to pay $500 to the order of Y.

Signed, Z

may be presented for payment to X as a draft or to Z as a note.

An instrument naming no drawee but stating

On demand, pay $500 to the order of Y.

Signed, Z

although in the form of a draft, may be treated as a note and presented to Z for payment.

If a printed form of note or draft is used and the party signing it inserts handwritten or typewritten language that is inconsistent with the printed words, the handwritten

THE LAW AND YOU

State Bar Associations

Louisiana:
http://www.lsba.org/Public_Resoources/consumer_brochures.html ("Truth in Savings")

State Attorney Generals

Massachusetts: http://www.ago.state.ma.us ("Check Cashier Report"; "Consumer Protection Regulations-Non-Bank Owned ATMs")

New Hampshire: http://doj.nh.gov/consumer/brochures.html ("Bank Savings Accounts"; "Debit (ATM) Cards")

Tennessee: http://www.state.tn.us/consumer/brochure.html ("Credit and ATM Cards")

Texas: http://www.oag.state.tx.us/ ("ATM, Debit, and Credit Cards")

Utah: http://www.consumer.utah.gov/dcp/education/index.html ("Checking Accounts—Pitfalls to Avoid"; "Co-maker, Co-signer, or Guarantor")

Virginia:
http://www.oag.state.va.us/Protecting/Consumer%20Fraud/default.htm ("Checking Account Scams")

U.S. Government

http://www.pueblo.gsa.gov/money.htm ("Get the Facts on Saving and Investing")

words control the typewritten and the printed words, and the typewritten words control the printed words.

If the amount payable is set forth on the face of the instrument in both figures and words and the amounts differ, the words control the figures. It is presumed that the maker or drawer would be more careful with words. If the words are ambiguous, however, then the figures control.

CHAPTER SUMMARY

Negotiability

Rule invests instruments with a high degree of marketability and commercial utility by conferring upon certain good faith transferees immunity from most defenses to the instrument

Formal Requirements negotiability is wholly a matter of form, and all the requirements for negotiability must be met within the "four corners" of the instrument

Types of Negotiable Instruments

Orders to Pay
- *Drafts* a draft involves three parties: the drawer orders the drawee to pay a fixed amount of money to the payee
- *Checks* a specialized form of draft that is drawn on a bank and payable on demand; the drawer orders the drawee (bank) to pay the payee on demand (upon the request of the holder)

Promises to Pay
- *Notes* a written promise by a maker (issuer) to pay a payee
- *Certificates of Deposit* a specialized form of note that is given by a bank or thrift association

Formal Requirements of Negotiable Instruments

Writing any reduction to tangible form is sufficient

Signature any symbol executed or adopted by a party with the intention to validate a writing

Promise or Order to Pay
- ***Promise to Pay*** an undertaking to pay, which must be more than a mere acknowledgment or recognition of an existing debt
- ***Order to Pay*** instruction to pay

Unconditional an absolute promise to pay that is not subject to any contingencies
- ***Reference to Other Agreements*** does not destroy negotiability unless the recital makes the instrument subject to or governed by the terms of another agreement
- ***The Particular Fund Doctrine*** an order or promise to pay only out of a particular fund is no longer conditional and does not destroy negotiability

Fixed Amount the holder must be assured of a determinable minimum principal payment, although provisions in the instrument may increase the amount of recovery under certain circumstances

Money legal tender authorized or adopted by a sovereign government as part of its currency

No Other Promise or Order a promise or order to do an act in addition to the payment of money destroys negotiability

Payable on Demand or at a Definite Time an instrument is demand paper if it must be paid upon request: an instrument is time paper if it is payable at a definite time

Payable to Order or to Bearer a negotiable instrument must contain words indicating that the maker or drawer intends that it pass into the hands of someone other than the payee
- ***Payable to Order*** payable to the "order of" (or other words that mean the same) a named person or anyone designated by that person
- ***Payable to Bearer*** payable to the holder of the instrument; includes instruments (1) payable to bearer or the order of bearer, (2) that do not specify a payee, or (3) payable to "cash" or to order of "cash"

QUESTIONS

1. State whether the following provisions impair or preclude negotiability, the instrument in each instance being otherwise in proper form. Answer each statement with either "Negotiable" or "Nonnegotiable" and explain why.
   a. A note for $2,000 payable in twenty monthly installments of $100 each that provides the following: "In case of death of maker, all payments not due at date of death are canceled."
   b. A note stating, "This note is secured by a mortgage of even date herewith on personal property located at 351 Maple Street, Smithton, Illinois."
   c. A certificate of deposit reciting, "June 6, 2004, John Jones has deposited in the Citizens Bank of Emanon, Illinois, Two Thousand Dollars, to the credit of himself, payable upon the return of this instrument properly indorsed, with interest at the rate of 6 percent per annum from date of issue upon ninety days' written notice. (Signed) Jill Crystal, President. Citizens Bank of Emanon."
   d. An instrument reciting, "IOU, Mark Noble, $1,000.00."
   e. A note stating, "In accordance with our contract of December 13, 2003, I promise to pay to the order of Sam Stone $100 on March 13, 2004."
   f. A draft drawn by Brown on the Acme Publishing Company for $500, payable to the order of the Sixth National Bank of Erehwon, directing the bank to "Charge this draft to my royalty account."
   g. A note executed by Pierre Janvier, a resident of Chicago, for $2,000, payable in Swiss francs.
   h. An undated note for $1,000 payable "six months after date."
   i. A note for $500 payable to the order of Ray Rodes six months after the death of Albert Olds.

j. A note of $500 payable to the assigns of Levi Lee.
k. A check made payable "to Ketisha Johnson."

2. State whether the following provisions in a note impair or preclude negotiability, the instrument in each instance being otherwise in proper form. Answer each statement with either "Negotiable" or "Nonnegotiable" and explain why.
   a. A note signed by Henry Brown in the trade name of the Quality Store.
   b. A note for $450, payable to the order of TV Products Company, "If, but only if, the color television set for which this note is given proves entirely satisfactory to me."
   c. A note executed by Adams, Burton, and Cady Company, a partnership, for $1,000, payable to the order of Davis, payable only out of the assets of the partnership.
   d. A note promising to pay $500 to the order of Leigh and to deliver ten tons of coal to Leigh.
   e. A note for $10,000 executed by Eaton payable to the order of the First National Bank of Emanon, in which Eaton promises to give additional collateral if the bank deems itself insecure and demands additional security.
   f. A note reading, "I promise to pay to the order of Richard Roe $2,000 on January 31, 2005, but it is agreed that if the crop of Blackacre falls below ten bushels per acre for the 2004 season, this note shall be extended indefinitely."
   g. A note payable to the order of Ray Rogers fifty years from date but providing that payment shall be accelerated by the death of Silas Hughes to a point of time four months after his death.
   h. A note for $4,000 calling for payments of installments of $250 each and stating, "In the event any installment hereof is not paid when due, this note shall immediately become due at the holder's option."
   i. An instrument dated September 17, 2004, in the handwriting of John Henry Brown, which reads in full: "Sixty days after date, I, John Henry Brown, promise to pay to the order of William Jones $500."
   j. A note reciting, "I promise to pay Ray Reed $100 on December 24, 2004."

3. On March 10, Tolliver Tolles, also known as Thomas Towle, delivered to Alonzo Craig and Abigail Craig the following instrument, written by him in pencil:

   For value received, I, Thomas Towle, promise to pay to the order of Alonzo Craig or Abigail Craig One Thousand Seventy-Five ($1,000.75) Dollars six months after my mother, Alma Tolles, dies with interest at the rate of 9 percent from date to maturity and after maturity at the rate of 9¾ percent. I hereby waive the benefit of all laws exempting real or personal property from levy or sale.

   Is this instrument negotiable? Explain.

4. Henry Hughes, who operates a department store, executed the following instrument:

   $2,600 Chicago, March 5, 2004

   On July 1, 2005, I promise to pay Daniel Dalziel, or order, the sum of Twenty-Six Hundred Dollars for the privilege of one framed advertising sign, size 24 × 36 inches, at one end of each of two hundred sixty motor coaches of the New Omnibus Company for a term of three months from May 15, 2005.

   Henry Hughes

   Is this instrument negotiable? Explain.

5. Pablo agreed to lend Marco $500. Thereupon Marco made and delivered his note for $500 payable to Pablo or order "ten days after my marriage." Shortly thereafter Marco was married. Is the instrument negotiable? Explain.

6. For the balance due on the purchase of a tractor, Henry Brown executed and delivered to Jane Jones his promissory note containing the following language:

   January 1, 2004, I promise to pay to the order of Jane Jones the sum of $7,000 to be paid only out of my checking account at the XYZ National Bank of Pinckard, Illinois, in two installments of $3,500 each, payable on May 1, 2004, and on July 1, 2004, provided that if I fail to pay the first installment on the due date, the entire sum shall become immediately due.

   (Signed) Henry Brown

   Is the note negotiable? Explain.

7. Sam Sharpe executed and delivered to Don Dole the following instrument:

   Knoxville, Tennessee

   May 29, 2004

   Thirty days after date I promise to pay Don Dole or order Five Thousand Dollars. The holder of this instrument shall have the election to require the assignment and delivery to him of my 100 shares of Brookside Iron Works Corporation stock in lieu of the payment of Five Thousand Dollars in money.

   (Signed) Sam Sharpe

   Is this instrument negotiable? Explain.

8. Explain whether the following instrument is negotiable.

   March 1, 2004

   One month from date, I, James Jimson, hereby promise to pay Edmund Edwards: Six thousand, Seven hundred Fifty ($6,750.00) dollars, plus 8¾% interest. Payment for cutting machines to be delivered on March 15, 2004.

   James Jimson

CASE PROBLEMS

9. Broadway Management Corporation obtained a judgment against Briggs. The note on which the judgment was based reads in part: "Ninety Days after date, I, we, or either of us, promise to pay to the order of Three Thousand Four Hundred Ninety Eight and 45/100———Dollars." (The underlined words and symbols were typed in; the remainder was printed.) There are no blanks on the face of the instrument, any unused space having been filled in with hyphens. The note contains clauses permitting acceleration in the event the holder deems itself insecure and authorizes judgment "if this note is not paid at any stated or accelerated maturity." Explain whether the note is negotiable order paper.

10. Sandra and Thomas McGuire entered into a purchase-and-sale agreement for "Becca's Boutique" with Pascal and Rebecca Tursi. The agreement provided that the McGuires would buy the store for $75,000, with a down payment of $10,000 and the balance of $65,000 to be paid at closing on October 5, 2002. The settlement clause stated that the sale was contingent upon the McGuires obtaining a Small Business Administration loan of $65,000. On September 4, 2002, Mrs. McGuire signed a promissory note in which the McGuires promised to pay to the order of the Tursis and the Green Mountain Inn the sum of $65,000. The note specified that interest payments of $541.66 would become due and payable on the fifth days of October, November, and December 2002. The entire balance of the note, with interest, would become due and payable at the option of the holder if any installment of interest was not paid according to that schedule.

    The Tursis had for several months been negotiating with Parker Perry for the purchase of the Green Mountain Inn (http://www.greenmountaininn.com/) in Stowe, Vermont. On September 7, 2002, the Tursis delivered to Perry a $65,000 promissory note payable to the order of Green Mountain Inn, Inc. This note was secured by transfer to the Green Mountain Inn of the McGuires' note to the Tursis. Subsequently, Mrs. McGuire learned that her Small Business Administration (http://www.sba.gov/) loan had been disapproved. On December 5, 2002, the Tursis defaulted on their promissory note to the Green Mountain Inn. On June 11, 2003, PP, Inc., formerly Green Mountain Inn, Inc., brought an action against the McGuires to recover on the note held as security for the Tursis' promissory note. Discuss whether the instrument is negotiable.

11. On September 2, 1999, Levine executed a mortgage bond under which she promised to pay the Mykoffs a preexisting obligation of $54,000. On October 14, 2002, the Mykoffs transferred the mortgage to Bankers Trust Co. (http://www.db.com), indorsing the instrument with the words "Pay to the Order of Bankers Trust Company Without Recourse." The Lincoln First Bank, N.A. (http://www.chase.com), brought this action asserting that the Mykoffs' mortgage is a nonnegotiable instrument because it is not payable to order or bearer; thus it is subject to Lincoln's defense that the mortgage was not supported by consideration because an antecedent debt is not consideration. Is the instrument payable to order or bearer? Discuss.

12. Horne executed a $100,000 note in favor of R. C. Clark. On the back of the instrument was a restriction stating that the note could not be transferred, pledged, or otherwise assigned without Horne's written consent. As part of the same transaction between Horne and Clark, Horne gave Clark a separate letter authorizing Clark to pledge the note as collateral for a loan of $50,000 that Clark intended to secure from First State Bank. Clark did secure the loan and pledged the note, which was accompanied by Horne's letter authorizing Clark to use the note as collateral. First State contacted Horne and verified the agreement between Horne and Clark as to using the note as collateral. Clark defaulted on the loan. When First Bank later attempted to collect on the note, Horne refused to pay, arguing that the note was not negotiable as it could not be transferred without obtaining Horne's written consent. This suit was instituted. Is the instrument negotiable? Explain.

13. Holly Hill Acres, Ltd., executed and delivered a promissory note and a purchase money mortgage to Rogers and Blythe. The note provided that it was secured by a mortgage on certain real estate and that the terms of that mortgage "are by this reference made a part hereof." Rogers and Blythe then assigned the note to Charter Bank, and the bank sought to foreclose on the note and mortgage. Holly Hill Acres refused to pay, claiming that it was defrauded by Rogers and Blythe. Is the note a negotiable instrument? Why?

http:// **Internet Exercise** Find the modifications of UCC Article 3 your state has adopted. (If your state is not available, choose another state.)

CHAPTER 25

Transfer

A negotiable instrument is a courier without luggage.

ANONYMOUS

Learning Objectives

After reading this chapter you should be able to:

1. Distinguish among (a) transfer, (b) negotiation, and (c) assignment.
2. Identify and explain what is necessary to become a holder of an instrument.
3. Explain the imposter rule and the fictitious payee rule.
4. Distinguish among a blank indorsement, a special indorsement, a qualified indorsement, and an unqualified indorsement.
5. Explain which types of restrictive indorsements are effective and ineffective.

The primary advantage of negotiable instruments is their ease of transferability. Nonetheless, although both negotiable instruments and nonnegotiable undertakings are transferable by assignment, only negotiable instruments can result in the transferee becoming a holder. This distinction is highly significant. If the transferee of a negotiable instrument is entitled to payment by the terms of the instrument, he is a holder of the instrument. Only holders may be holders in due course and thus may be entitled to greater rights in the instrument than the transferor may have possessed. These rights, discussed in the next chapter, are the reason why negotiable instruments move freely in the marketplace. This chapter discusses the methods by which negotiable instruments may be transferred.

CPA NEGOTIATION

A **holder** is broadly defined in Section 1–201(20) as "a person who is in possession of . . . an instrument . . . drawn, issued, or indorsed to him or his order or to bearer or in blank." **Negotiation** is the transfer of possession, whether voluntary or involuntary, by a person other than the issuer of a negotiable instrument in such a manner that the transferee becomes a holder. An instrument is transferred when a person other than its issuer delivers it for the purpose of giving the recipient the right to enforce the instrument. Accordingly, to qualify as a holder a person must have possession of an instrument that runs to him. Thus, there are two ways in which a person can be a holder: (1) the instrument has been issued to that person, or (2) the instrument has been transferred to that person by negotiation.

Figure 25-1
Bearer Paper

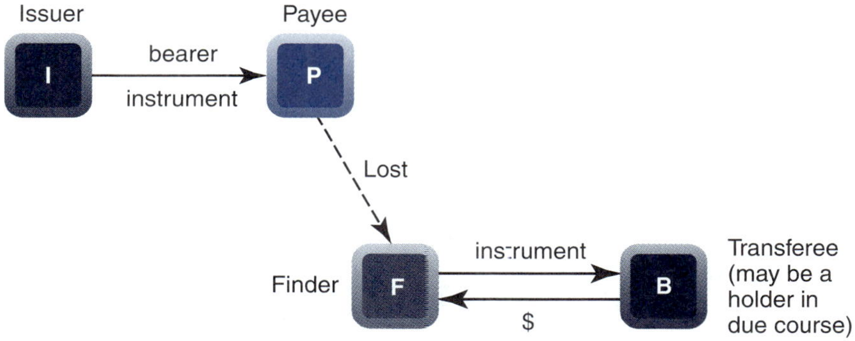

The transfer of a nonnegotiable promise or order operates as an assignment, as does the transfer of a negotiable instrument by a means that does not render the transferee a holder. As discussed in Chapter 16, an **assignment** is the voluntary transfer to a third party of the rights arising from a contract.

Whether a transfer is by *assignment* or by *negotiation*, the transferee acquires the rights the transferor had. The transfer need not be for value: if the instrument is transferred as a gift, the donee acquires all the rights of the donor. If the transferor was a holder in due course, the transferee acquires the rights of a holder in due course, which rights he in turn may transfer. This rule, sometimes referred to as the **shelter rule**, existed at common law and still exists under the UCC. The shelter rule is discussed more fully in Chapter 26.

The requirements for negotiation depend on whether the instrument is bearer paper or order paper.

NEGOTIATION OF BEARER PAPER

If an instrument is payable to bearer, it may be negotiated by transfer of possession alone. Because bearer paper (an instrument payable to bearer) runs to whoever is in possession of it, a finder or a thief of bearer paper would be a holder even though he did not receive possession by voluntary transfer. For example, P loses an instrument payable to bearer that I had issued to her. F finds it and sells and delivers it to B, who thus receives it by negotiation and is a holder. F also qualified as a holder because he was in possession of bearer paper. As a holder, F had the power to negotiate the instrument, and B, the transferee, may be a holder in due course if he meets the Code's requirements for such a holder (discussed in Chapter 26). See Figure 25-1 for an illustration of this example. Because a bearer instrument is transferred by mere *possession*, it is comparable to cash.

NEGOTIATION OF ORDER PAPER

If the instrument is order paper (an instrument payable to order), both (a) transfer of its *possession* and (b) its *indorsement* (signature) by the appropriate parties are necessary for the transferee to become a holder. Figure 25-2 compares the negotiation of bearer and order paper.

Any transfer for *value* of an instrument not payable to bearer gives the transferee the specifically enforceable right to have the unqualified indorsement of the transferor, unless the parties agree otherwise. The parties may agree that the transfer is to be an assignment rather than a negotiation, in which case no indorsement is required. Absent such agreement, the courts presume that negotiation was intended where value is given. When a transfer is not for value, the transaction is normally noncommercial; thus, the courts do not presume the intent to negotiate.

Figure 25-2
Negotiation of Bearer and Order Paper

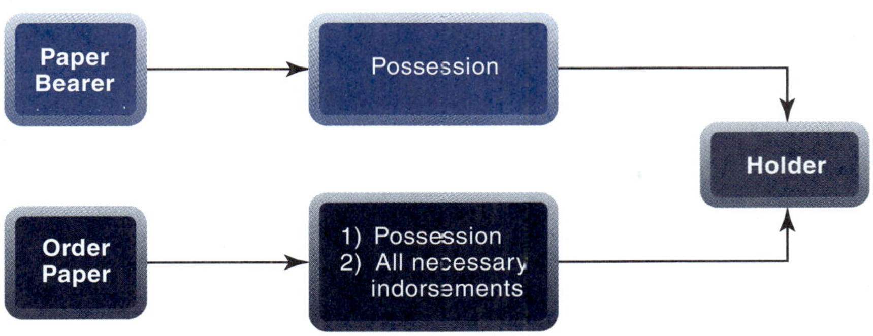

Until the necessary indorsement has been supplied, the transferee has nothing more than the contract rights of an assignee. Negotiation takes effect only when a proper indorsement is made, at which time the transferee becomes a holder of the instrument.

If a customer deposits a check or other instrument for collection without properly indorsing the item, the depository bank becomes a holder when it accepts the item for deposit if the depositor is a holder. It no longer needs to supply the customer's indorsement.

The Hyatt Corporation v. Palm Beach National Bank

Court of Appeal of Florida, Third District, 2003
840 So.2d 300, 49 U.C.C. Rep.Serv.2d 1039
http://www.3dca.flcourts.org/3d02-1276.pdf

FACTS Hyatt Corporation (appellant/defendant) hired Skyscraper Building Maintenance, LLC, to perform maintenance work for various Hyatt hotels in South Florida. Skyscraper entered into a loan agreement with J&D Financial Corporation under which Hyatt was to make checks payable for maintenance services to Skyscraper and J&D. Of the many checks issued by Hyatt to Skyscraper and J&D, two were negotiated by the bank but indorsed only by Skyscraper. They were made payable as follows:

1. Check No. 1-78671 for $22,531 payable to:
   J&D Financial Corp. Skyscraper Building Maint
   P.O. Box 610250
   North Miami, Florida 33261-0250
2. Check No. 1-75723 for $21,107 payable to:
   Skyscraper Building Maint
   J&D Financial Corp.
   P.O. Box 610250
   North Miami, Florida 33261-0250

Only Skyscraper indorsed these two checks. The bank cashed the checks. All the proceeds from the checks went to Skyscraper.

J&D filed a complaint against Skyscraper, Hyatt and the Palm Beach National Bank (bank). J&D sought damages against Skyscraper under the loan agreement and separately against Hyatt and the bank for negotiation of the two checks. The bank, Hyatt and J&D all moved for summary judgment on the issue of whether the bank properly negotiated the checks. It was uncontested that the bank had a duty to negotiate the checks only on proper indorsement, and if it did not, it would be liable.

The bank argued that the checks were payable to J&D and Skyscraper alternatively, and thus the bank could properly negotiate the checks based upon the indorsement of either of the two payees. The bank further argued that the checks were drafted ambiguously as to whether they were payable alternatively or jointly, and thus the checks would be construed as a matter of law to be payable alternatively.

Hyatt's position was that the checks were not ambiguous, were payable jointly and not alternatively, and thus the checks could only be negotiated by indorsement of both of the payees. J&D similarly argued that the checks were payable jointly. The trial court granted summary judgment for the bank. Hyatt and J&D appealed.

DECISION The trial court's grant of the summary judgment is affirmed.

OPINION Levy, J. The issue on appeal is whether or not a check payable to

J&D Financial Corporation
Skyscraper Building Maintenance

(stacked payees) is payable jointly to both payees requiring the indorsement of both, or whether it is ambiguous regarding whether the check was drafted payable alternatively, so that the bank could negotiate the check when it was indorsed by only one of the two payees.

In 1990, Article 3 of the UCC was revised. * * * Revised UCC Section 3-110(d) * * * states, "If an instrument payable to two or more persons is ambiguous as to whether it is payable to the persons alternatively, the instrument is payable to the persons alternatively." * * *

Turning to our jurisdiction, Florida has adopted the statutory revision to UCC 3-110, * * *.

* * *

The issue under review has not reached Florida's appellate courts. However, * * * trial courts in Florida have addressed this issue in *Bijlani v. Nationsbank of Florida, N.A.*, [citation] * * *. We find the reasoning in [*Bijlani*] to be persuasive.

In *Bijlani*, the appellee paid a check which did not have Bijlani's indorsement. The check was made payable to

Bay Village Inc. Michael Bijlani & Ron Delo & Assoc
5411 Grenada Blvd
Coral Gables, FL 33133

The trial court granted the bank's motion for summary judgment, stating that "The multiple payee designation on the check is ambiguous as to whether it is payable to 'Bay Village Inc.' 'Michael Bijlani * * * .' jointly or alternatively." Holding that the bank was not liable, the trial court noted that the predecessor statute "provided that if an ambiguity existed as to whether multiple payees were intended as joint or alternative payees, they were deemed joint payees," while the amended statute applicable to this case "reverses the prior rule." [Citation.]

* * *

Although Florida appellate courts have not yet considered the issue at hand, other courts in the country have. [Citations.]

For example, a case which has addressed this particular issue with almost identical facts to those before us is *Allied Capital Partners, L.L.P. v. Bank One, Texas, N.A.*, [citation]. In *Allied*, the checks were made payable to:

Complete Design
Allied Capital Partners, LLP.
2340 E. Trinity Mills St. 300
Carrollton, Texas 75006

The debtor indorsed the checks and deposited them into a corporate bank account. The factor then sued the bank for conversion for payment on the debtor's indorsement.

On appeal from the adverse summary judgment, the factor cited pre-revision law. The Texas appellate court affirmed the summary judgment, stating:

> While it does appear that former [Article 3] would have required the checks in this case to be payable to and negotiable only by all of the payees listed, this is no longer the case * * * . [Citation]. Under these facts, the court found that the check was unambiguous.

We conclude that based on the 1990 amendment to the Uniform Commercial Code, when a check lists two payees without the use of the word "and" or "or", the nature of the payee is ambiguous as to whether they are alternative payees or joint payees. Therefore, the UCC amendment prevails and they are to be treated as alternative payees, thus requiring only one of the payees' signatures. Consequently, the bank could negotiate the check when it was indorsed by only one of the two payees, thereby escaping liability.

INTERPRETATION The listing of multiple payees on a check rendered the check ambiguous as to whether alternate or joint payees were intended by drawer and entitled the bank to treat the check as payable alternatively upon valid indorsement by one payee.

CRITICAL THINKING QUESTION How would you decide this case? Explain.

The Impostor Rule Negotiation of an order instrument requires a valid indorsement by the person to whose order the instrument is payable. The impostor rule governing unauthorized signatures is an exception to this general rule. Usually, the impostor rule comes into play in situations involving a confidence man who impersonates a respected citizen and who deceives a third party into delivering a negotiable instrument to the impostor in the name of the respected citizen. For instance, John Doe, falsely representing himself as Richard Roe, a prominent citizen, induces Ray Davis to loan him $10,000. Davis draws a check payable to the order of Richard Roe and delivers it to Doe, who then forges Roe's name to the check and presents it to the drawee for payment. The drawee pays it. Subsequently, Davis, the drawer, denies the drawee's right of reimbursement on the ground that the drawee did not pay in accordance with his order: Davis ordered payment to Roe or to Roe's order. Roe did not order payment to anyone; therefore, the drawee would not acquire a right of reimbursement against Davis. The general rule governing unauthorized signatures supports this argument in favor of the drawer.

Nevertheless, the indorsement of the impostor (Doe) or of any other person in the name of the named payee is *effective* as the indorsement of the payee if the impostor has induced the maker or drawer (Davis) to issue the instrument to him or his confederate using the name of the payee (Roe). It is as if the named payee had indorsed the instrument. The reason for this rule is that the drawer or maker is to blame for failing to detect the impersonation by the impostor. Thus, in the above example, the drawee would be able to debit the drawer's account. Moreover, Revised Article 3 expands the impostor rule by extending its coverage to include an impostor who is impersonating an agent. Thus, if an impostor impersonates Jones and induces the drawer to draw a check to the order of Jones, the impostor can negotiate the check. Moreover, under the Revision, if an impostor impersonates Jones, the president of Jones Corporation, and the check is to the order of Jones Corporation, the impostor can negotiate the check.

If the person paying the instrument fails to exercise ordinary care, the issuer may recover from the payor to the extent the payor's negligence contributed to the loss. If the issuer is also negligent, comparative negligence would apply.

The Fictitious Payee Rule The rule just discussed also applies when a person who does not intend the payee to have an interest in the instrument signs as or on behalf of a maker or drawer. In such a situation, any person's indorsement in the name of the named payee is *effective* if the person identified as the payee is a fictitious person. For instance, Palmer gives Albrecht, her employee, authority to write checks in order to pay Palmer's debts. Albrecht writes a check for $2,000 to Foushee, a fictitious payee, which Albrecht takes and indorses in Foushee's name to Albrecht. Albrecht cashes the check at Palmer's bank, which can debit Palmer's account because Albrecht's signature in Foushee's name is effective against Palmer. Palmer should bear the risk of her unscrupulous employees.

In a similar situation also involving a disloyal employee, a drawer's employee falsely tells the drawer that money is owed to Leon, and the drawer writes a check payable to the order of Leon and hands it to the agent for delivery to him. The agent forges Leon's name to the check and obtains payment from the drawee bank. The drawer then denies the bank's claim to reimbursement upon the grounds that the bank did not comply with her order; that the drawer had ordered payment to Leon or order; that the drawee did not make payment either to Leon or as ordered by him, inasmuch as the forgery of Leon's signature is wholly inoperative; and that the drawee paid in accordance with the scheme of the faithless agent and not in compliance with the drawer's order. Under the Code, an employer has liability on the instrument when one of its employees, who is entrusted with responsibility with respect to such an instrument, makes a fraudulent indorsement if (1) the instrument is payable to the employer and the employee forges the indorsement of the employer or (2) the instrument is issued by the employer and the employee forges the indorsement of the person identified as the payee. The example above falls under the second part of the rule just stated. Accordingly, the employee's indorsement is effective as that of the unintended payee, and the drawee bank will be able to debit the drawer's (employer's) account. See "Details of $1 Million Embezzlement Case Emerge" in the Managerial Insight.

This rule also applies to a situation (number 1 of the paragraph above) not involving a fictitious payee: a fraudulent indorsement made by an employee entrusted with responsibility with respect to an instrument payable to the employer. For example, an employee, whose job involves posting amounts of checks payable to her employer, steals some of the checks and forges her employer's indorsement. The indorsement is effective as the employer's indorsement because the employee's duties included processing checks for bookkeeping purposes.

This section provides, however, that the employer may recover from the drawee bank to the extent the loss resulted from the bank's failure to exercise ordinary care. If the employer is also negligent, a rule of comparative negligence applies.

Practical Advice

Make sure that the payee of all your instruments are the appropriate parties and are being paid the appropriate amount.

Shearson Lehman Brothers, Inc. v. Wasatch Bank

United States District Court, D. Utah, C.D., 1992
788 F.Supp. 1184

FACTS Stanley A. Erb became a vice president of the Shearson Lehman Brothers, Inc. **(http://www.lehman.com/)** branch office in Provo, Utah, in 1987. That year, Erb was contacted by McKay Matthews, the controller for the Orem, Utah, based WordPerfect Corporation **(http://www.corel.com/)** and its sister corporation, Utah Softcopy. At Matthews's request, Erb established and managed three separate investment accounts at Shearson. The accounts were for the benefit of the WordPerfect and Utah Softcopy corporations, and one account was for the WordPerfect principals, Allen

Ashton, Bruce Bastian, and Willard Peterson. In March 1987, Erb personally accepted from Matthews a check drawn by Utah Softcopy for $460,150.23 and payable to the order of "ABP Investments." At that time, there was no ABP investment account at Shearson, although the WordPerfect principals maintained accounts elsewhere in that name. Erb accepted the check, but rather than deposit it in one of the three authorized accounts, Erb opened a new account at Shearson in the name of "ABP Investments," apparently by forging the signature of Bruce Bastian on the new account documents. Over the next eleven months, Erb induced Shearson to draft thirty-seven checks on the ABP Investment account, payable to ABP Investments, by submitting falsified payment requests to Shearson's cashier. The checks were mailed to an Orem post office box unknown to WordPerfect and its principals. Erb would obtain the checks and indorse them in the name of ABP Investments. He took the checks to Wasatch Bank for deposit into his personal account. Wasatch accepted the deposits and later allowed Erb to withdraw $504,295.30, the entire amount, from the account. Shearson discovered Erb's activities after Erb had left Shearson in 1989. Shearson settled with WordPerfect and its principals and was assigned all their legal rights.

Shearson brought suit against Wasatch. Wasatch moved for summary judgment, claiming under the "fictitious payee" rule that it was not liable.

DECISION Summary judgment for Wasatch.

OPINION Anderson, J.

I. Whether Shearson's claims are barred by the "Fictitious Payee" Defense of U.C.C. 3–405(1)(c). Wasatch acknowledges that, "[a]s a general rule, 'forged indorsements are ineffective to pass title or to authorize a drawee to pay.'" [Citations.] Consequently, when a collecting bank makes payment over a forged indorsement, it is generally liable for the amount paid. [Citations.]

Under this general rule, Wasatch clearly would be liable as the party that accepted checks over forged indorsements. Wasatch attempts to avoid such liability, however, by invoking what is known as the "fictitious payee" defense. The defense is an exception to the general rule that a party accepting or paying an instrument over a forged indorsement ultimately will be liable for the loss and is set forth in section 3–405 of the Uniform Commercial Code:

* * *

The policy underlying section 3–405 is thus to place the risk of loss of forgery on the party in the best position to avoid or insure against such loss. [Citations.]

As indicated, by the language of section 3–405(1)(c), if the defense applies to the facts of a given transaction, the result is to render the forged signature effective to transfer good title as if no forgery had occurred. [Citations.] * * *

For the defense to apply, an employee or agent of the drawer must "supply" the name of the payee to the drawer, and the faithless employee must intend that the payee have no interest in the instrument. Utah Code Ann. § 3–405(1)(c) (1990). Although the defense commonly has been referred to as the "fictitious payee" defense, the payee named on the check need not be a fictitious person or entity. "It is immaterial whether a person with the name of the payee actually exists or whether the name is in fact a wholly fictitious name." [Citations.] Moreover, courts applying the defense have liberally construed the term "supply." "An employee 'supplies' the name of the payee if he 'starts the wheels of normal business procedure in motion to produce a check for a nonauthorized transaction.'" [Citations.] * * *

Thus Wasatch argues that the fictitious payee defense of section 3–405(1)(c) applies to the undisputed facts of the present case. Erb, an employee of the drawer of the check, "supplied" the name of the payee within the meaning of the statute and obviously intended that the named payee have no interest in the checks. He then procured the checks and fraudulently indorsed them for deposit into his account at Wasatch. Wasatch accordingly argues that the effect of Erb's actions was to validate the forged indorsements and to allow good title to pass to Wasatch thereby extinguishing Wasatch's liability for the transaction.

* * *

II. Conclusion. The "fictitious payee" defense as articulated in section 3–405(1)(c) of the Uniform Commercial Code operates under the facts of the present case to shield the collecting bank, Wasatch, from liability resulting from Erb's misconduct while in Shearson's employ. Erb deliberately induced the issuance of checks by Shearson. The payee named on those checks was never intended by Erb to take an interest in the checks. In such circumstances the mandate of the Code is clear—the drawer shall bear the loss resulting from the misdeeds of its employee. Wasatch's conduct in the relevant transactions raises serious questions about whether the bank discharged its duty to act in a commercially reasonable manner. Nevertheless, no fact has been alleged which would support the inference that Wasatch acted in bad faith so as to preclude the operation of the fictitious payee defense.

INTERPRETATION An indorsement by any person in the name of the named payee is effective if an agent of the drawer supplied the name of the payee and intended the payee to have no interest in the instrument.

CRITICAL THINKING QUESTION Do you agree with the "fictitious payee" rule? When would you apply it? Explain.

NEGOTIATIONS SUBJECT TO RESCISSION

A negotiation conforming to the requirements discussed above is effective to transfer the instrument even if it is

1. made by an infant, a corporation exceeding its powers, or a person without capacity; or
2. obtained by fraud, duress, or mistake; or
3. made in breach of a duty or as part of an illegal transaction.

Thus, a negotiation is valid even though the transaction in which it occurs is voidable or even void. In all of these instances, the transferor loses all rights in the instrument until he regains possession of it. His right to do so, determined by state law, is valid against the immediate transferee and all subsequent holders, but not against a subsequent holder in due course or a person paying the instrument in good faith and without notice.

CPA INDORSEMENTS

An **indorsement** is "a signature, other than that of a signer as maker, drawer, or acceptor, that alone or accompanied by other words is made on an instrument for the purpose of (i) negotiating the instrument, (ii) restricting payment of the instrument, or (iii) incurring the indorser's liability on the instrument, but regardless of the intent of the signer, a signature and its accompanying words is an indorsement unless the accompanying words, terms of the instrument, place of the signature, or other circumstances unambiguously indicate that the signature was made for a purpose other than indorsement."

An indorsement may be complex or simple. It may be dated and may indicate where it is made, but neither date nor place is required to be shown. The simplest type is merely the signature of the indorser. Because the indorser undertakes certain obligations, as explained later, an indorsement consisting of merely a signature may be said to be the shortest contract known to the law. A forged or otherwise unauthorized signature necessary to negotiation is inoperative and thus breaks the chain of title to the instrument.

The type of indorsement used in first negotiating an instrument affects its subsequent negotiation. Every indorsement is (1) either blank or special, (2) either restrictive or nonrestrictive, and (3) either qualified or unqualified. These categories are not mutually exclusive. Indeed, each indorsement may be placed within three of these six categories because all indorsements disclose three things: (1) the method to be employed in making subsequent negotiations (this depends upon whether the indorsement is blank or special); (2) the kind of interest that is being transferred (this depends upon whether the indorsement is restrictive or nonrestrictive); and (3) the liability of the indorser (this depends on whether the indorsement is qualified or unqualified). For instance, an indorser who merely signs her name on the back of an instrument is making a blank, nonrestrictive, unqualified indorsement.

Revised Article 3 identifies an additional type of indorsement—an anomalous indorsement. An anomalous indorsement is "an indorsement made by a person that is not the holder of the instrument." The only effect of an anomalous indorsement is to make the signer liable on the instrument as an indorser. Such an indorsement does not affect the manner in which the instrument may be negotiated.

The effectiveness of an indorsement as well as the rights of the transferee and transferor depend on whether the indorsement meets certain formal requirements. This section will cover the different kinds of indorsements and the formal requirements of each.

Practical Advice

It is exceedingly important that you indorse your indorsements in the appropriate manner and at the appropriate time.

BLANK INDORSEMENTS

A **blank indorsement**, which specifies no indorsee, may consist solely of the signature of the indorser or an authorized agent. Such an indorsement converts order paper into bearer paper and leaves bearer paper as bearer paper. Thus, an instrument indorsed in blank may be negotiated by delivery alone without further indorsement. Hence, the holder should treat it with the same care as cash. See *Palmer & Ray Dental Supply of Abilene, Inc. v. First National Bank* later in this chapter.

Practical Advice

Blank indorsements present a major risk and should be used judiciously.

SPECIAL INDORSEMENTS

A **special indorsement** specifically identifies the person to whom or to whose order the instrument is to be payable. Thus, if Peter, the payee of a note, indorses it "Pay to the order of Andrea," or even "Pay Andrea," the indorsement is special because it names the transferee. Words of negotiability— "pay to order or bearer"—are *not* required in an indorsement. Thus, an indorsement reading "Pay Edward"

Details of $1 Million Embezzlement Case Emerge

RALEIGH: A glimpse into how an obscure accountant allegedly embezzled more than $1 million from Carolina Power & Light Co. is emerging as prosecutors prepare to seek an indictment against him.

Authorities now say they think Tony Creech stole $1.08 million since 1987 by tricking the utility into issuing checks to vendors that didn't exist or to which he owed money.

So far investigators have tracked down only $28,000, a house in Cary and three high-priced cars to show for Creech's alleged eight-year spree. But police and utility auditors are still looking.

"It's an incredibly complex investigation," CP&L spokesman Rick White said. "It's not going to be over as soon as I thought it would be. It's an extensive, methodical process. They're pulling one string at a time."

Creech, 46, remains in the Wake County Jail, where he has been held since his arrest June 15, and has not entered a plea. His bail has been raised to a $500,000 secured bond, and his assets have been frozen.

Six charges of obtaining property by false pretenses have been added to 15 counts of embezzlement against Creech.

Wake County Assistant District Attorney Susan Spurlin will ask a county grand jury July 10 to indict Creech on those charges, which account for $1,083,174.38 in CP&L money.

Creech, a mid-level accountant in the utility's downtown Raleigh office, was arrested after CP&L auditors and security officers began checking irregularities in the books several weeks ago. Just how they think Creech stole the money has remained a mystery until now.

In part, that's because they still don't know the size of the alleged swindle and are making sure it doesn't happen again.

"That's why we're still reluctant to say a whole lot," CP&L's White said. "They haven't had a chance to talk with everybody they have to talk to yet. They hope to finally do that this week."

But prosecutor Spurlin has disclosed in court some of the case against Creech, who was one of about 140 employees in the accounting department.

She said Creech embezzled the money two ways, using his position to submit bogus check requests for payments to vendors.

In one scheme, Creech set up an account at Wachovia Bank for a phony company, she said. When CP&L paid the non-existent firm, Creech simply transferred the money into his personal Wachovia account, she said.

That's how he funneled about $500,000 into a single fake firm, called G&C Associates, Spurlin said.

In the other, more complicated, method, Spurlin said, Creech had CP&L issue checks to real people who were also vendors, and he used that money to pay his own debts to them.

Investigators are trying to determine whether any of the companies knew those checks were not a legitimate way for Creech to pay them.

Spurlin said that anyone who took CP&L's checks to pay Creech's debts, knowing that he wasn't entitled to that money, could be prosecuted as a co-conspirator.

Creech allegedly funneled money through eight vendor accounts, using real and phony firms. Spurlin would not identify the vendors.

White said CP&L regularly pays 3,000 to 4,000 vendors, covering an array of services: janitors, security, temporary workers, supplies and equipment and vehicles, for example.

Most of the money Creech is accused of embezzling was taken during a two-month stretch more than a year ago, although the thefts began in 1987, according to the charges.

One warrant that suggests Creech embezzled nearly a quarter million dollars on one day in 1987 is misleading. Police and utility officials now say that amount was taken over several months that year.

CP&L is bonded for such losses, so rate-payers won't bear the cost.

"We feel very much like a victim," White said.

Meanwhile, investigators discovered that last week Creech's mother had withdrawn $53,000 from his personal checking account, using the power of attorney he granted her.

Investigators found $28,000 of that money, and it was seized and is being held by the court pending a review. The rest hasn't been accounted for.

Creech's mother, Ellen Smith Mitchell of Goldsboro, declined to discuss her son's case Tuesday. Spurlin said she didn't break the law by withdrawing the money.

After her son was arrested, Mitchell posted a $50,000 cash bond for his release. Creech was awaiting final arrangements to surrender his passport, but the judge raised the bail Thursday.

If Creech comes up with the $500,000 bond, he will have to submit to an alcohol abuse assessment and seek any treatment that is recommended, according to the court's conditions.

Cary police have arrested Creech twice in the past 14 months on charges of driving while intoxicated in his 1990 Corvette.

Creech claimed he was indigent after CP&L fired him in early June and applied for a court-appointed attorney, saying he had only $12,000 in the bank. His request was denied, and he has hired Raleigh attorney Philip Redwine.

By Craig Jarvis.
From *The Raleigh News & Observer*. Reprinted with permission of the Associated Press.

is interpreted as meaning "Pay to the order of Edward." Any further negotiation of the instrument would require Edward's indorsement.

Moreover, a holder of an instrument with a blank indorsement may protect himself by converting the blank indorsement to a special indorsement by writing over the signature of the indorser words identifying the person to whom the instrument is payable. For example, on the back of a negotiable instrument appears the blank indorsement "Sally Seller." Harry Holder, who receives the instrument from Seller, may convert this bearer instrument into order paper by inserting above Seller's signature "Pay Harry Holder" or other similar words.

State of New Mexico v. Herrera

Court of Appeals of New Mexico, 2001

130 N.M. 85, 18 P.3d 326, *cert. denied*, 130 N.M. 153, 20 P.3d 810

FACTS Defendant Joshua Herrera testified that he found a purse in a dumpster near San Pedro and Kathryn Streets in Albuquerque. Herrera took the purse to a friend's house. Either Herrera or his friend called the owner of the purse and the owner retrieved it. Herrera testified that after the purse was returned to the owner, he returned to the dumpster where he found a check and some other items. Herrera claimed that he did not know if the check or any of the other items belonged to the owner of the purse, as he did not remember the purse owner's name at that time.

The check Herrera found was written out to "Cash," and he thought this meant that he "could get money for [the] check." Herrera explained that when he presented the check to the teller at a credit union to cash it, the teller instructed him to put his name on the payee line next to "Cash." Herrera followed the teller's instructions and added "to Joshua Herrera" next to the word "Cash" on the payee line of the check. Herrera also indorsed the check.

The trial court ruled that "Defendant altered a writing purporting to [have] legal efficacy with intent to [defraud], [and] those acts constitute a crime of forgery."

Herrera argues on appeal that his acts fail to meet the elements of forgery because (1) he signed his own name and not another's; (2) he did not alter the genuineness of the check; (3) the legislature did not intend the concept of alteration to include the addition of a genuine signature to a genuine check; and (4) he did not alter the check because he did not change the legal efficacy of the check.

DECISION The trial court's denial of defendant's motion to dismiss is reversed because the defendant did not alter the legal efficacy of the instrument.

OPINION Wechsler, J. Section 30–16–10(A) [of the penal code] defines forgery as "falsely making or altering any signature to, or any part of, any writing purporting to have any legal efficacy with intent to injure or defraud." Section 30–16–10(B) defines forgery as the transfer of a forged document. Under Section 30–16–10(A), the State must prove that the defendant made a false document, a false signature, a false indorsement or "changed a genuine [document] so that its effect was different from the original" with an intent to deceive or cheat another. [Citation.] Under Section 30-16-10(B) the State must prove that the defendant gave or delivered a document to a victim with the intent to injure, deceive or cheat the victim or another, knowing that the document (1) was a false document; (2) contained a false signature; (3) had a false indorsement; or (4) was changed so that its effect was different from the original. [Citation.]

Defendant did not make a false signature or offer a false indorsement. Thus, a plain reading of the statute and the jury instructions indicates that under the facts of this case, Defendant could only have committed forgery by changing the legal effect of the check. [Citation.] * * * Therefore, whether Defendant changed the legal effect of the check is the dispositive question in this case. Defendant argues that the act of adding his name to the payee line next to the word "Cash" failed to alter the legal effect of the check. We look to the Uniform Commercial Code to determine whether Defendant is correct.

When a negotiable instrument is made payable to "Cash," it is a bearer instrument. [UCC] § 3–109(a)(3). A bearer instrument refers to an instrument that is payable to anyone possessing the instrument and is negotiable by transfer alone. [UCC] § 3–109(a)(1).

In contrast, an instrument payable to an identified person is considered an order instrument. [UCC] § 3–109(b).

An order instrument requires the indorsement of the identified person before it can be negotiated. [UCC] § 3–201(b). The legal effect of an order instrument is different from a bearer instrument because each type of instrument has different negotiability requirements:

> Whether an instrument is an order instrument or a bearer instrument is important in determining how an instrument is negotiated. If the instrument is payable to bearer, it can be negotiated by delivery alone. If it is payable to the order of an identified person it cannot be negotiated without the indorsement of that person. [Citations.]

At the time Defendant presented the check to the credit union teller, he possessed a bearer instrument because the check was written out to "Cash." At the direction of the teller, however, Defendant added the words "to Joshua Herrera" to the payee line after the word "Cash." By doing so, Defendant added a specific payee to what was otherwise a bearer instrument. We analyze whether Defendant changed the legal effect of the check by adding his name on the payee line of the check.

The concepts of bearer and order are mutually exclusive. [UCC] § 3–109(b) states that "[a] promise or order that is not payable to bearer is payable to order if it is payable * * * to the order of an identified person." An instrument payable to bearer cannot be payable to order. [Citation.]

As a result, under the definitions in the Uniform Commercial Code, the check in this case could not have been both a bearer and an order instrument. Defendant could have changed the legal effect of the bearer instrument he possessed by adding his name only if the instrument ceased to have bearer effect. We believe that it did not.

The Official Comment to [UCC] § 3–109 is instructive in this regard. The Comment addresses situations in which an instrument contains terms indicating that it is both payable to bearer and payable to order. The Comment states that when an instrument is payable both to bearer and order, the instrument states contradictory terms, but that it is nonetheless a bearer instrument. The Comment explains that

> an instrument that purports to be payable both to order and bearer states contradictory terms. A transferee of the instrument should be able to rely on the bearer term and acquire rights as a holder without obtaining the indorsement of the identified payee. [Citations.]

We discern from the Comment that the addition of an identified payee to a check that is otherwise a bearer instrument is insufficient to transform the legal effect of the check because it is still a bearer instrument and a transferee of the check is able to rely on the bearer term. [UCC] § 3–109 Official Cmt. 2.

We do not view the fact that Defendant wrote "to Joshua Herrera" and not "or Joshua Herrera" as significant. The Official Comment to [UCC] § 3–109 uses the word "or" in its example of an instrument containing bearer and order terms. [UCC] § 3–109 Official Comment 2. In determining the legal status of a negotiable instrument, the significant words are those that represent either bearer or order terms.

The words "Cash" and "Bearer" have distinct legal meanings. Their presence upon the face of an instrument signifies the particular legal status of that instrument; namely, that the instrument is payable to anyone bearing it. [UCC] § 3–201(b). Similarly, the presence of an identified payee such as "Joshua Herrera" on the face of an instrument signifies that the instrument is payable only to Joshua Herrera.

In this circumstance, with the check payable "to the order of Cash to Joshua Herrera," one who received it could reasonably be confused because it contains both bearer and order instructions. The Uniform Commercial Code resolves such confusion by making the bearer term prevail. [UCC] § 3–109 Official Cmt. 2. We do not view the conjunction "to" in this case as sufficient to avoid confusion from the conflicting terms so as to preclude application of the principles of the commentary.

Indeed, under specific circumstances, a bearer instrument can be transformed to an order instrument. [UCC] § 3–109(c) provides that when a bearer instrument is specially indorsed, it can be transformed to an order instrument. A special indorsement is one that "identifies a person to whom it makes the instrument payable." [UCC] § 3–205(a). Defendant's indorsement in this case included only his name and did not include language making the check payable to an identified person. [UCC] § 3–205(c). Thus, the indorsement was not a special indorsement and was not sufficient to transform the legal effect of the check from bearer to order. Instead, because Defendant's indorsement included only his signature, the indorsement qualified as an indorsement in blank. [UCC] § 3–205(b). Section 3–205(b) states that when an instrument is indorsed in blank, "the instrument" becomes payable to bearer and may be negotiated by transfer of possession alone." Consequently, Defendant's indorsement did not change the legal effect of the check from a bearer instrument into an order instrument under [UCC] § 3–109.

Because Defendant did not change the legal effect of the check when he added his name to the payee line or when he indorsed it, Defendant did not commit the crime of forgery.

* * *

INTERPRETATION A bearer instrument is an instrument that is payable to anyone in possession of the instrument.

ETHICAL QUESTION Is it unethical for Herrera to cash a check he knows is not intended for him? Explain.

CRITICAL THINKING QUESTION Should courts protect the writers of bearer checks from situations like this? Explain.

RESTRICTIVE INDORSEMENTS

As the term implies, a **restrictive indorsement** attempts to restrict the rights of the indorsee in some fashion. It limits the purpose for which the proceeds of the instrument can be applied. The Code discusses four types of indorsements as restrictive: conditional indorsements, indorsements prohibiting further transfer, indorsements for deposit or collection, and indorsements in trust. Only the last two are effective. An **unrestrictive indorsement**, in contrast, does not attempt to restrict the rights of the indorsee.

Indorsements for Deposit or Collection The most frequently used form of restrictive indorsement is that designed to place the instrument in the banking system for deposit or collection. Indorsements of this type, collectively referred to as "collection indorsements," include "for collection," "for deposit," and "pay any bank." Such an indorsement *effectively limits* further negotiation to those consistent with its limitation and binds (1) all nonbanking persons, (2) a depository bank that purchases the instrument or takes it for collection, and (3) a payor bank that is also the depository bank or that takes the instrument for immediate payment over the counter from a person other than a collecting bank. Thus, a collection indorsement binds all parties except an intermediary bank (discussed in Chapter 28) or a payor bank that is not also the depository bank. Compare the following two cases.

Practical Advice

Indorsements "for deposit only" protect you as the indorser and should be used whenever necessary.

Palmer & Ray Dental Supply of Abilene, Inc. v. First National Bank

Court of Civil Appeals of Texas, 1972
477 S.W.2d 954

FACTS Mrs. Wilson was employed as the office manager of Palmer & Ray Dental Supply of Abilene, Inc. Soon after an auditor discovered a discrepancy in the company's inventory, Mrs. Wilson confessed to cashing thirty-five checks that she was supposed to deposit on behalf of the company. Palmer & Ray Dental Supply used a rubber stamp to indorse checks. The stamp listed the company's name and address but did not read "for deposit only." Mrs. Wilson was authorized by the company's president, James Ray, to indorse checks with this stamp. All checks were cashed at First National Bank. Palmer & Ray Dental Supply claimed that First National converted the company's funds by giving Mrs. Wilson cash instead of depositing the checks into the company's bank account. Summary judgment was granted in favor of First National, and Palmer & Ray appealed.

DECISION Judgment for First National Bank affirmed.

OPINION Walter, J. Article 3–204, Tex. Uniform Commercial Code, * * * , defines a blank indorsement as one that specifies no particular indorsee and may consist of a mere signature. Article 3–205 of the UCC defines a restrictive indorsement to include one that uses the words "for deposit." Section 1–201(43), UCC, defines an unauthorized signature or indorsement as one made without actual implied or apparent authority and includes a forgery.

The summary judgment proof establishes that each of the checks has affixed thereto the blank rubber stamp indorsement of the appellant [Palmer & Ray]. We hold that such blank indorsement constitutes an authorized indorsement. When the Bank delivered cash to Mrs. Wilson instead of depositing the proceeds from the checks to appellant's account, the Bank [acted in accordance with the blank indorsement and therefore] was not guilty of conversion. [Citation.]

INTERPRETATION A blank indorsement may be negotiated by delivery alone and does not restrict proceeds of the instrument to the depositor's account.

ETHICAL QUESTION Did First National Bank or Palmer & Ray act inappropriately? Explain.

CRITICAL THINKING QUESTION When should you use a blank indorsement? Explain.

State of Qatar v. First American Bank of Virginia

United States District Court, E.D. Va., 1995
885 F.Supp. 849, 27 U.C.C. Rep.Serv.2d 168

FACTS From 1986 to 1992, Bassam Salous defrauded his employer, the state of Qatar, by drawing checks on Qatar's account to pay false or duplicate invoices that he himself had created. He then deposited the checks into his personal account at First American Bank of Virginia (First American). At the time they were deposited, the checks bore the forged indorsement of the named payee, followed by the stamped restriction "for deposit only." Qatar has sued First American for conversion.

DECISION Judgment for Qatar.

OPINION Ellis, J. It is now established that First American may be liable to Qatar for handling a check's proceeds in violation of a restrictive indorsement. [Citation.] Under § 3–205(c) of the pre-1993 Uniform Commercial Code ("UCC" or "Code") [Virginia adopted Revised Article 3 in 1993] restrictive indorsements are defined to "include the words 'for collection,' 'for deposit,' 'pay any bank,' or like terms signifying a purpose of deposit or collection." Thus, the UCC makes clear that the phrase "for deposit only" is, in fact, a restrictive indorsement. But the Code does not define "for deposit only" or specify what bank conduct would be inconsistent with that restriction. Nor does Virginia decisional law provide any guidance on this issue. As a result reference to decisional law from other jurisdictions is appropriate.

Not surprisingly, most courts confronted with this issue have held that the restriction "for deposit only," without additional specification or directive, instructs depositary banks to deposit the funds only into the payee's account. In addition, commentators on commercial law uniformly agree that the function of such a restriction is to ensure that the checks' proceeds be deposited into the payee's account.

This construction of "for deposit only" is commercially sensible and is adopted here. The clear purpose of the restriction is to avoid the hazards of indorsing a check in blank. Pursuant to former § 3–204(2), a check indorsed in blank "becomes payable to bearer." It is, essentially, cash. Thus, a payee who indorses her check in blank runs the risk of having the check stolen and freely negotiated before the check reaches its intended destination. To protect against this vulnerability, the payee can add the restriction "for deposit only" to the indorsement, and the depositary bank is required to handle the check in a manner consistent with that restriction. § 3–206(3). And in so adding the restriction, the payee's intent plainly is to direct that the funds be deposited into her own account, not simply that the funds be deposited into some account. [Citation.] Any other construction of the phrase "for deposit only" is illogical and without commercial justification or utility. Indeed, it is virtually impossible to imagine a scenario in which a payee cared that her check be deposited, but was indifferent with respect to the particular account to which the funds would be credited.

* * *

Finally, it is worth noting that the new revisions to the negotiable instruments provisions of the UCC, [Revised Article 3], support the result reached here. Although these revisions are inapplicable to this case, the commentary following § 3–206 states that the new subdivision dealing with "for deposit only" and like restrictions "continues previous law." § 3–206 comment 3. Shortly thereafter, the commentary provides an example in which a check bears the words "for deposit only" above the indorsement. In those circumstances, the commentary states, the depositary bank acts inconsistently with the restrictive indorsement where it deposits the check into an account other than that of the payee. Although the restriction in that example precedes the signature, whereas the restrictions on the checks at issue here follow the signature, this distinction is immaterial. The clear meaning of the restriction in both circumstances is that the funds should be placed into the payee's account.

Therefore, First American violated the restrictive indorsements in depositing into Bassam Salous' account checks made payable to others and restrictively indorsed "for deposit only." Pursuant to the holding in Qatar I, then, First American is liable to Qatar for conversion in the amount of the total face values of these checks.

INTERPRETATION A "for deposit only" restrictive indorsement effectively limits the depositary bank to handle the instrument in a manner consistent with the restriction.

ETHICAL QUESTION Who should bear the risk of loss in this case? Explain.

CRITICAL THINKING QUESTION Does the use of a "for deposit only" indorsement present any risks to the indorser or indorsee? Explain.

Indorsements in Trust Another common kind of restrictive indorsement is that in which the indorser creates a trust for the benefit of himself or others. If an instrument is indorsed "Pay Thelma in trust for Barbara," "Pay Thelma for Barbara," "Pay Thelma for account of Barbara," or "Pay Thelma as agent for Barbara," Thelma is a fiduciary, subject to liability for any breach of her obligation to Barbara. Trustees commonly and legitimately sell trust assets, and, consequently, a trustee has power to negotiate an instrument. The first taker under an indorsement to her in trust (in this case Thelma) is under a duty to pay or apply, in a manner consistent with the indorsement, all the funds she receives. Thelma's immediate transferee may safely pay Thelma for the instrument if he does not have *notice* of any breach of fiduciary duty. Subsequent indorsements or transferees are not bound by such indorsement *unless* they *know* that the trustee negotiated the instrument for her own benefit or otherwise in breach of her fiduciary duty.

Indorsements with Ineffective Restrictions A conditional indorsement is one by which the indorser makes the rights of the indorsee subject to the happening or nonhappening of a specified event. Suppose Marcin makes a note payable to Parker's order. Parker indorses it "Pay Rodriguez, but only if the good ship Jolly Jack arrives in Chicago harbor by November 15, 2005." If Marcin had used this language in the instrument itself, it would be nonnegotiable because her promise to pay must be unconditional to satisfy the formal requisites of negotiability. Revised Article 3 makes such indorsements ineffective by providing that an indorsement stating a condition to the right of a holder to receive payment does not affect the right of the indorsee to enforce the instrument.

An indorsement may by its express terms attempt to prohibit further transfer by stating "Pay [name] only" or language to similar effect. Such an indorsement, or any other purporting to prohibit further transfer, is designed to restrict the rights of the indorsee. To remove any doubt as to the effect of such a provision, the Code provides that *no* indorsement limiting payment to a particular person or otherwise prohibiting further transfer is effective. As a result, an indorsement that purports to *prohibit* further transfer of the instrument is given the same effect as an unrestricted indorsement.

Qualified and Unqualified Indorsements

Unqualified indorsers promise that they will pay the instrument according to its terms at the time of their indorsement to the holder or to any subsequent indorser who paid it. In short, an unqualified indorser guarantees payment of the instrument if certain conditions are met.

An indorser may disclaim liability on the contract of indorsement, but only if the indorsement so declares and the disclaimer is written on the instrument. The customary manner of disclaiming an indorser's liability is to add the words *without recourse*, either before or after her signature. A "without recourse" indorsement, called a **qualified indorsement**, does not, however, eliminate all of an indorser's liability. As discussed in Chapter 27, a qualified indorsement disclaims contract liability but does not

CONCEPT REVIEW

Indorsements

Indorsement	Type of Indorsement	Interest Transferred	Liability of Indorser
1. "John Doe"	Blank	Nonrestrictive	Unqualified
2. "Pay to Richard Roe, John Doe"	Special	Nonrestrictive	Unqualified
3. "Without recourse, John Doe"	Blank	Nonrestrictive	Qualified
4. "Pay to Richard Roe in trust for John Roe, without recourse, John Doe"	Special	Restrictive	Qualified
5. "For collection only, without recourse, John Doe"	Blank	Restrictive	Qualified
6. "Pay to XYZ Corp., on the condition that it delivers goods ordered this date, John Doe"	Special	Nonrestrictive (Revised Article 3)	Special

entirely remove the warranty liability of the indorser. A qualified indorsement and delivery is a negotiation and transfers legal title to the indorsee, but the indorser does not guarantee payment of the instrument. Furthermore, a qualified indorsement does not destroy negotiability or prevent further negotiation of the instrument. For example, assume that an attorney receives a check payable to her order in payment of a client's claim. She may indorse the check to the client without recourse, thereby disclaiming liability as a guarantor of payment of the check. The qualified indorsement plus delivery would transfer title to the client.

FORMAL REQUIREMENTS OF INDORSEMENTS

Place of Indorsement An indorsement must be written on the instrument or on a paper, called an **allonge**, affixed to the instrument. An allonge may be used even if the instrument contains sufficient space for the indorsement.

Customarily, indorsements are made on the back or reverse side of the instrument, starting at the top and continuing down. Under Federal Reserve Board guidelines, indorsements of checks must be in ink of an appropriate color, such as blue or black, and must be made within 1½ inches of the trailing (left) edge of the back of the check. The remaining space is reserved for bank indorsements. (See Figure 25-3 for the proper placement of indorsements.) Nevertheless, failure to comply with the guidelines does not destroy negotiability, and there are no penalties for violating the standard.

Occasionally, however, a signature may appear on an instrument in such a way that it is impossible to tell with certainty the nature of the liability the signer intended to undertake. In such an event, the Code specifies that the signer is to be treated as an indorser. In keeping with the rule that a transferee must be able to determine her rights from the face of the instrument, the person who signed in an ambiguous capacity may not introduce parol evidence to establish that she intended to be something other than an indorser.

Incorrect or Misspelled Indorsements If an instrument is payable to a payee or indorsee under a misspelled name or a name different from that of the holder, the holder may require the indorsement in the name stated or in the holder's correct name or both. Nevertheless, the person paying or taking the instrument for value may require the indorser to sign both names.

Figure 25-3
Placement of Indorsement

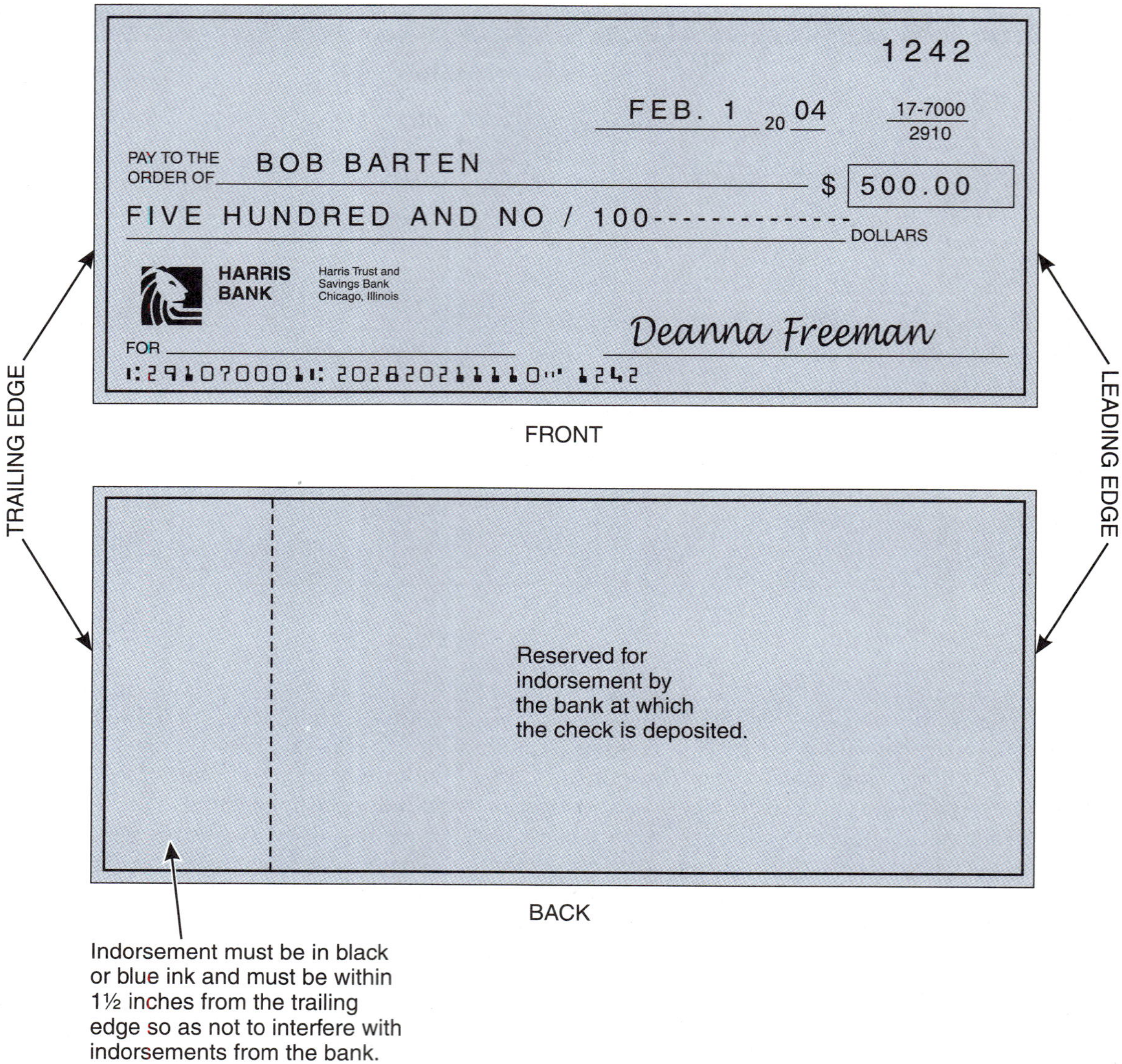

Chapter Summary

Negotiation

Holder possessor of an instrument with all necessary indorsements

Shelter Rule transferee gets rights of transferor

Negotiation of Bearer Paper transferred by mere possession

Negotiation of Order Paper transferred by possession and indorsement by all appropriate parties

- ***The Impostor Rule*** an indorsement of an impostor or of any other person in the name of the named payee is effective if the impostor has induced the maker or drawer to issue the instrument to him using the name of the payee

- *The Fictitious Payee Rule* an indorsement by any person in the name of the named payee is effective if an agent of the maker or drawer has supplied her with the name of the payee for fraudulent purposes

Negotiations Subject to Rescission negotiation is valid even though a transaction is void or voidable

Indorsement

Definition signature (on the instrument) of a payee, drawee, accommodation party, or holder

Blank Indorsement one specifying no indorsee and making the instrument bearer paper

Special Indorsement one identifying an indorsee to be paid and making the instrument order paper

Unrestrictive Indorsement one that does not attempt to restrict the rights of the indorsee

Restrictive Indorsement one attempting to limit the rights of the indorsee
- *Indorsements for Deposit or Collection* effectively limit further negotiation to those consistent with the indorsement
- *Indorsements in Trust* effectively require the indorsee to pay or apply all funds in accordance with the indorsement
- *Indorsements with Ineffective Restrictions* include conditional indorsements and indorsements attempting to prohibit further negotiation

Unqualified Indorsement one that imposes liability on the indorser

Qualified Indorsement without recourse, one that limits the indorser's liability

Formal Requirements of Negotiation
- *Place of Indorsement*
- *Incorrect or Misspelled Indorsement*

QUESTIONS

1. Roy Rand executed and delivered the following note to Sue Sims: "Chicago, Illinois, June 1, 2004; I promise to pay to Sue Sims or bearer, on or before July 1, 2004, the sum of $7,000. This note is given in consideration of Sims's transferring to the undersigned title to her 2000 Buick automobile. (signed) Roy Rand." Rand and Sims agreed that delivery of the car be deferred to July 1, 2004. On June 15, Sims sold and delivered the note, without indorsement, to Karl Kaye for $6,200. What rights, if any, has Kaye acquired?

2. Lavinia Lane received a check from Wilmore Enterprises, Inc., drawn on the Citizens Bank of Erehwon, in the sum of $10,000. Mrs. Lane indorsed the check "Mrs. Lavinia Lane for deposit only, Account of Lavinia Lane," placed it in a "Bank by Mail" envelope addressed to the First National Bank of Emanon, where she maintained a checking account, and placed the envelope over a tier of mailboxes in her apartment building along with other letters to be picked up by the postman the next day.

   Flora Fain stole the check, went to the Bank of Omaha, where Mrs. Lane was unknown, represented herself to be Lavinia Lane, and cashed the check. Has Bank of Omaha taken the check by negotiation? Why or why not?

3. What types of indorsements are the following?
   a. "Pay to Monsein without recourse."
   b. "Pay to Allinore for collection."
   c. "I hereby assign all my rights, title, and interest in this note to Fullilove in full."
   d. "Pay to the Southern Trust Company."
   e. "Pay to the order of the Farmers Bank of Nicholasville for deposit only."

   Indicate whether the indorsement is (1) blank or special, (2) restrictive or nonrestrictive, and (3) qualified or unqualified.

4. Explain whether each of the following transactions results in a valid negotiation:
   a. Arnold gives a negotiable check payable to bearer to Betsy without indorsing it.

b. Golden indorses a negotiable, promissory note payable to the order of Golden, "Pay to Chambers and Rambis, (signed) Golden."
c. Porter lost a negotiable check payable to his order. Kersey found it and indorsed the back of the check as follows: "Pay to Drexler, (signed) Kersey."
d. Thomas indorsed a negotiable promissory note payable to the order of Thomas, "(signed) Thomas," and delivered it to Sally. Sally then wrote above Thomas's signature, "Pay to Sally."

5. Alpha issues a negotiable check to Beta payable to the order of Beta in payment of an obligation Alpha owed Beta. Beta delivers the check to Gamma without indorsing it in exchange for 100 shares of General Motors stock owned by Gamma. How has Beta transferred the check? What rights, if any, does Gamma have against Beta?

6. Margarita executed and delivered to Poncho a negotiable promissory note payable to the order of Poncho as payment for 100 bushels of wheat Poncho had sold to Margarita. Poncho indorsed the note "Pay to Randy only, (signed) Poncho" and sold it to Randy. Randy then sold the note to Stephanie after indorsing it "Pay to Stephanie, (signed) Randy." What rights, if any, does Stephanie acquire in the instrument?

7. Simon Sharpe executed and delivered to Ben Bates a negotiable promissory note payable to the order of Ben Bates for $500. Bates indorsed the note, "Pay to Carl Cady upon his satisfactorily repairing the roof of my house, (signed) Ben Bates," and delivered it to Cady as a down payment on the contract price of the roofing job. Cady then indorsed the note and sold it to Timothy Tate for $450. What rights, if any, does Tate acquire in the promissory note?

8. Debbie Dean issued a check to Betty Brown payable to the order of Cathy Cain and Betty Brown. Betty indorsed the check, "Payable to Elizabeth East, (signed) Betty Brown." What rights, if any, does Elizabeth acquire in the check?

CASE PROBLEMS

9. Triplett attempted to arrange a $2,850,000 loan through Meyer Rabin and his Consumer's Investment Company (CIC). CIC issued a commitment letter conditioned on the payment of a $14,250 commitment fee and the personal guarantee of C. D. Wyche. Triplett sought an additional loan from E. S. Tubin to cover the commitment fee. Tubin agreed to provide the $14,250 if the money would be "safe" pending the closing of the $2,850,000 loan and if he would receive $4,500 for the use of his money. Triplett agreed, and Tubin purchased a $14,250 cashier's check payable to Melvin Rueckhaus, his attorney. Rueckhaus typed the following indorsement on the back of the check: "PAY TO THE ORDER—CONSUMERS INVESTMENT CO. and CHARLES D. WYCHE, SR. . . . "

    Rabin presented the check to Fair Park National Bank for immediate credit to CIC's account. Not knowing that Wyche's signature had been forged by Rabin, the bank complied, and Rabin subsequently depleted CIC's account. The loan was never closed, and the $14,250 was never returned to Tubin. Is Fair Park National Bank liable to Tubin? Discuss.

10. The drawer, Commercial Credit Corporation (Corporation), issued two checks payable to Rauch Motor Company. Rauch indorsed the checks in blank, deposited them to its account in University National Bank, and received a corresponding amount of money. The Bank stamped "pay any bank" on the checks and initiated collection. However, the checks were dishonored and returned to the Bank with the notation "payment stopped." Rauch, through subsequent deposits, repaid the bank. Later, to compromise a lawsuit, the Bank executed a special two-page indorsement of the two checks to Lamson. Lamson then sued the Corporation for the face value of the checks, plus interest. The Corporation contends that Lamson was not a holder of the checks because the indorsement was not in conformity with the UCC in that it was stapled to the checks. Is Lamson a holder? Why?

11. Edmund Jezemski, estranged and living apart from his wife, Paula, was administrator and sole heir-at-law of his deceased mother's estate, one asset of which was real estate in Philadelphia. Without Edmund's knowledge or consent, and with the assistance of John M. McAllister, an attorney, and Anthony DiBenedetto, a real estate broker, Paula arranged for a mortgage on the property through Philadelphia Title Insurance Company. Shortly before settlement, Paula represented to McAllister and DiBenedetto that her husband would be unable to attend the closing on the mortgage. She appeared at McAllister's office in advance of the closing accompanied by a man whom she introduced to McAllister and DiBenedetto as her husband. She and this man, in the presence of McAllister and DiBenedetto, executed a deed conveying the property from the estate to her husband and herself as tenants by the entireties and also executed the mortgage. McAllister and DiBenedetto were witnesses. Thereafter, McAllister, DiBenedetto, and Paula met at the office of the Title Company on the closing date, produced the signed deed and mortgage, and Paula obtained from Title Company its check for the mortgage loan proceeds of $15,640.82, payable to the order of Edmund Jezemski and Paula Jezemski individually and to Edmund as administrator.

    Paula cashed the check, bearing the purported indorsements of all the payees, at Penns Grove National Bank and Trust Company. Edmund received none of the proceeds, either individually or as administrator. His purported indorsements were forgeries. In the collection process, the check was presented to and paid by the drawee bank, Fidelity-Philadelphia Trust Company, and charged against the drawer Title Company's account. Upon discovery of the existence of the mortgage, Edmund brought an action that resulted in the setting aside of the deed and mortgage and the repayment of the amount advanced by the mortgagee. Title Company then sued the drawee bank (Fidelity) to recover the amount of the check, $15,640.82. Is the indorsement effective? Explain.

12. Cole was supervisor of the shipping department of Machine Mfg. Inc. In February, Cole found herself in need of funds and, at the end of that month, submitted to Ames, the treasurer of the corporation, a payroll listing that showed as an employee, among others, "Ben Day," to whom was allegedly owed $800 for services rendered during February. Actually, there was no employee named Day. Relying upon the word of Cole, Ames drew and delivered to her a series of corporate payroll checks, drawn upon the corporate account in the Capital Bank, one of which was made payable to the order of "Ben Day" for $800. Cole took the check, indorsed on its back "Ben Day," cashed it at the Capital Bank, and pocketed the proceeds. She repeated the same procedure at the end of March, April, and May. In mid-June, Machine Mfg. Inc. learned of Cole's fraudulent conduct, fired her, and brought an appropriate action against Capital Bank, seeking a judgment for $3,200. Is Cole's signature effective against Machine Mfg. Inc.? Explain.

13. While assistant treasurer of Travco Corporation, Frank Mitchell caused two checks, each payable to a fictitious company, to be drawn on Travco's account with Brown City Savings Bank. In each case, Mitchell indorsed the check in his own name and then cashed it at Citizens Federal Savings & Loan Association of Port Huron. Both checks were cleared through normal banking channels and charged against Travco's account with Brown City. Travco subsequently discovered the embezzlement, and after its demand for reimbursement was denied, it brought this suit against Citizens. Is the indorsement effective? Explain.

14. Arthur and Lucy Casarez contracted with Blas Garcia, who purported to be a representative of the Albuquerque Fence Company, for the construction of a new home. Blas introduced the Casarezes to Cecil Garcia, who agreed to make a loan to them to be used as a down payment on the project. Cecil then obtained a loan from Rio Grande Valley Bank in the form of a $25,000 cashier's check payable to himself, which he indorsed over to Lucy Casarez. Lucy indorsed the check with the words "Pay to the order of Albuquerque Fence Company, Lucy N. Casarez" and delivered it to Blas Garcia. Claiming he was following Cecil's instructions, Blas indorsed the check with the words "Alb. Fence Co." and gave the check to Cecil. Cecil signed his own name under "Alb. Fence Co." and presented the check to the bank in exchange for $25,000. The Casarezes soon learned that Blas and Cecil Garcia had never been in any way affiliated with or employed by the Albuquerque Fence Company. Explain whether the unauthorized signatures of Blas and Cecil Garcia invalidate the special indorsement to Albuquerque Fence Company.

15. J. R. Simplot, Inc. (d/b/a Simplot Soilbuilders) (http://www.simplot.com/) held a security interest in Richard L. Knight's 1996 crops. To protect this security interest, Simplot sent a "SECURITY INTEREST NOTICE" to all potential purchasers of Knight's crops. This notice informed the buyers of Simplot's security interest and requested: "If you purchase or are involved in the sale of these farm products, please include Simplot Soilbuilders on all drafts issued to [Knight]." In 1996 Knight sold crops to George DeRuyter & Sons Dairy, which paid for the crops with a check in the amount of $32,916.79. George DeRuyter & Sons Dairy made the check payable to the order of "Rick Knight-Simplot Soil Builders." Knight indorsed his name and forged the indorsement of Simplot Soilbuilders, and deposited the check into his account at Yakima Federal. Knight also sold crops to Connell Grain Growers in 1996. Connell Grain Growers paid for the crops with two checks, one in the amount of $22,494.73 and the other in the amount of $2,573.99. Connell Grain Growers made both checks payable to the order of "Rick Knight Simplot Soil Builders". Knight indorsed his name and forged the indorsement of Simplot Soilbuilders, and deposited both checks into his account at Yakima Federal.

Simplot Soilbuilders, George DeRuyter & Sons Dairy, and Connell Grain Growers did not maintain accounts at Yakima Federal, and the bank did not have a signature card for any of these businesses. Explain whether the instrument was properly indorsed.

http:// **Internet Exercise** Compare the provisions governing transfer and negotiation contained in the United Nations Convention on International Bills of Exchange and International Promissory Notes with those of Article 3 of the Uniform Commercial Code.

Chapter 26

Holder in Due Course

One might properly ask who gave the FTC [Federal Trade Commission] authority to help tear down one of the pillars of commercial law [the HDC doctrine in consumer credit transactions]. It is odd that its federal dismantling occurred not through federal legislation, but through regulations of an administrative agency.

WHITE & SUMMERS, *UNIFORM COMMERCIAL CODE* (4TH ED.), PAGE 530

Learning Objectives

After reading this chapter you should be able to:

1. Identify and explain the requirements for becoming a holder in due course.
2. Explain the shelter rule and when a payee can have the rights of a holder in due course.
3. Identify, define, and explain the real defenses.
4. Define and explain personal defenses.
5. Explain the limitations the Federal Trade Commission imposes on the rights of a holder in due course.

The unique and most significant aspect of negotiability is the concept of the holder in due course. While a mere holder acquires a negotiable instrument subject to all claims and defenses to it, a holder in due course, *except* in *consumer* credit transactions, takes the instrument free of all claims of other parties and free of all defenses to the instrument except for a very limited number. The law has conferred this preferred position upon the holder in due course in order to encourage the free transferability of negotiable instruments by minimizing the risks assumed by an innocent purchaser of the instrument. The transferee of a negotiable instrument wants payment for it; he does not want to be subject to any dispute between the obligor and the obligee (generally the original payee). This chapter discusses the requirements of becoming a holder in due course and the benefits conferred upon a holder in due course.

CPA Requirements of a Holder in Due Course

To acquire the preferential rights of a holder in due course, a person either must meet the requirements of the Code or must "inherit" these rights under the shelter rule (discussed later in this chapter). To satisfy the requirements of the Code, a transferee must

1. be a holder of a negotiable instrument;
2. take it for value;
3. take it in good faith; and
4. take it without notice
   a. that it is overdue or has been dishonored, or
   b. that the instrument contains an unauthorized signature or an alteration, or
   c. that any person has any defense against or claim to it; and

5. take it without reason to question its authenticity due to apparent evidence of forgery, alteration, incompleteness, or other irregularity.

Figure 26-1 illustrates the various requirements of becoming a holder in due course and the consequence of meeting or not meeting these requirements.

HOLDER

To become a **holder** in due course, the transferee must first be a holder. A holder, as discussed in Chapter 25, is a person who is in possession of a negotiable instrument that is "payable to bearer or, in the case of an instrument payable to an identified person, if the identified person is in possession." In other words, a holder is a person who has both possession of an instrument and all indorsements necessary to it. Whether the holder is the owner of the instrument or not, he may transfer it, negotiate it, enforce payment of it (subject to valid claims and defenses), or, with certain exceptions, discharge it.

The following factual situation, illustrated in Figure 26-2, defines the significance of being a holder. Poe indorsed her paycheck in blank and cashed it at a hardware store where she was a well-known customer. Shortly thereafter, a burglar stole the check from the hardware store. The owner of the hardware store immediately notified Poe's employer, who gave the drawee bank a stop payment order (an order not to pay the instrument). The burglar indorsed the check in a false name and transferred it to a grocer who took it in good faith and for value. The check was dishonored (not paid)

Figure 26-1
Rights of Tranferees

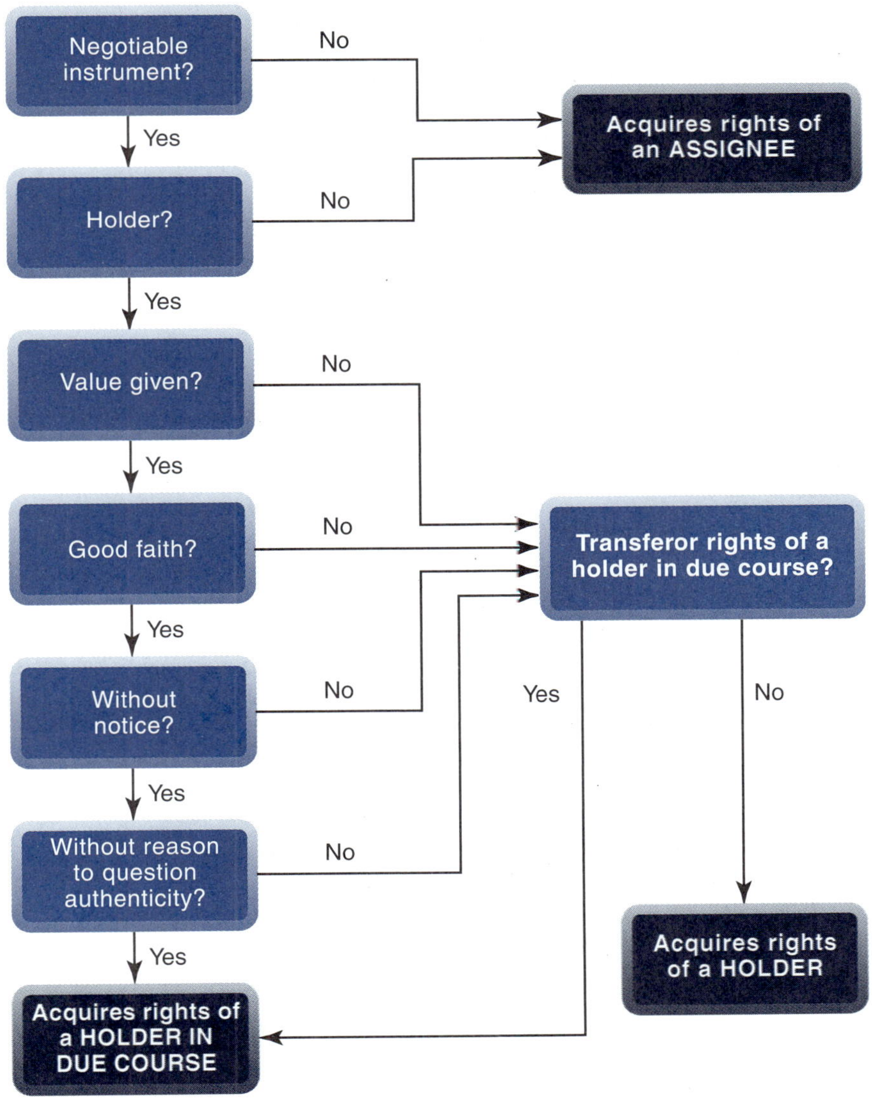

Figure 26-2
Stolen Bearer Paper

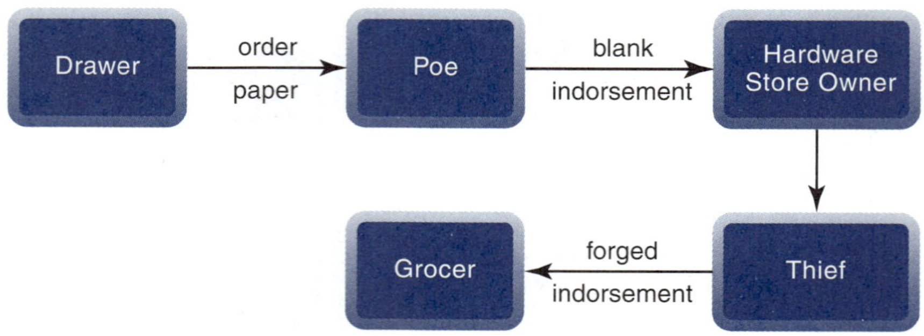

Grocer is a holder in due course because he
(1) Was a holder of a negotiable instrument,
(2) Gave value,
(3) Took in good faith,
(4) Took without notice, and
(5) Took without reason to question its authenticity.

when presented to the drawee bank. The paycheck became bearer paper when Poe indorsed it in blank. It retained this character in the hands of the owner of the hardware store, in the hands of the burglar, and in the hands of the grocer, who became a holder in due course even though he had received it from a thief who had indorsed it with a false name. Because an indorsement is not necessary to the negotiation of bearer paper, the fact that the indorsement was forged was immaterial. The thief was a "holder" of the check and could negotiate an instrument "whether or not he is the owner." Accordingly, one who, like the grocer, takes from a holder for value, in good faith, without notice, and without reason to question its authenticity, becomes a holder in due course. Furthermore, in the absence of a real defense, discussed later in this chapter, the grocer would be entitled to payment from the drawer.

This rule does not apply to a stolen order instrument. In the above example, assume that the thief had stolen the paycheck from Poe prior to indorsement. The thief then forged Poe's signature and transferred the check to the grocer, who again took it in good faith, for value, without notice, and without reason to question its authenticity. Negotiation of an order instrument requires a valid indorsement by the person to whose order the instrument is payable, in this case Poe. A forged indorsement is not valid. Consequently, the grocer had not taken the instrument with all necessary indorsements, and, therefore, he could not be a holder or a holder in due course. The grocer's only recourse would be to collect the amount of the check from the thief. Figure 26-3 illustrates this example.

In addition, certain other persons are entitled to enforce an instrument even though the person is not the owner of the instrument or is in wrongful possession of the instrument. These other persons entitled to enforce an instrument include a nonholder in possession of the instrument who has the rights of a holder, and a person not in possession of the instrument who is entitled to enforce the instrument pursuant to special situations, such as when the instrument has been lost, destroyed, or stolen or when the instrument has been paid or accepted by mistake and the payor or acceptor has recovered the money or revoked acceptance

Figure 26-3
Stolen Order Paper

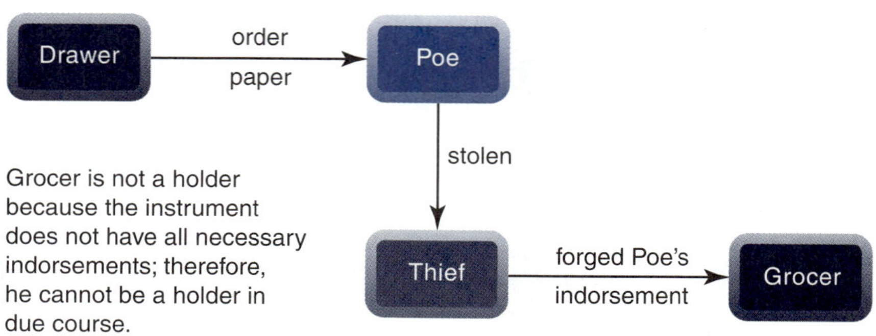

Turman v. Ward's Home Improvement, Inc.

Virginia Circuit Court, 1995
26 U.C.C. Rep.Serv.2d 175

FACTS On February 23, 1993, Turman executed a deed of trust note for $107,500 payable to Ward's Home Improvement, Inc. (Ward's). The note was in consideration of a contract for Ward's to build a house on Turman's property. On the same day, Ward's executed an assignment of the note to Robert Pomerantz for which Pomerantz paid Ward's $95,000. Although the document uses the word "assignment," no notation or indorsement was made on the note itself. Subsequently, Ward's failed to complete the house, and to do so would require the expenditure of an additional $42,000. The commissioner in this case found that Pomerantz was a holder in due course and awarded payment to Pomerantz. Turman appealed.

DECISION Judgment reversed and remanded.

OPINION Haley, J. This matter comes before the court upon Turman's exception to the finding of the Commissioner that Pomerantz was a holder in due course immune from defenses Turman might raise against Ward.

* * *

[Revised] Code § 3–201(b) states that " * * * if an instrument is payable to an identified person, negotiation requires * * * its indorsement by the holder." [Citation.] An assignment is not an indorsement. [Revised] Code § 3–204(a). Accordingly such a transfer is not a negotiation. [Citations.] And the transferee is not a holder. [Citations.]

An assignment does, however, vest " * * * in the transferee any right of the transferor to enforce the instrument * * * (under [Revised] Code § 3–301) * * * "[Revised] Code § 3–203(b). The transferee's rights are derivative of the transferor's. Accordingly, and pursuant to [Revised] Code § 3–305(a)(2), a maker may assert a defense " * * * that would be available if the person entitled to enforce the instrument were enforcing a right to payment under a simple contract." In short, the assignee of a negotiable instrument is subject to defenses the maker can raise against the original payee/assignor. [Citation.] And such a defense is failure of consideration. [Citations.] [Revised] Code § 3–303(b). " * * * If an instrument is issued for a promise of performance, the issuer has a defense to the extent performance of the promise is due and the promise has not been performed * * * "

In light of the foregoing the above noted exception to the Commissioner's Report is sustained and the court holds Pomerantz is not a holder in due course and is subject to the defenses to payment of the $107,500.00 note that Turman could raise against Ward.

This cause is remanded to the Commissioner for such proceedings as he or the parties deem appropriate in consequence of the court's ruling.

INTERPRETATION A holder is a person who has both possession of an instrument and all indorsements necessary to it.

CRITICAL THINKING QUESTION Does the UCC overemphasize formality in its requirements for transferring a negotiable instrument? Explain.

VALUE

The law requires a holder in due course to give value. An obvious case of the failure to do so is when the holder makes a gift of the instrument to a third person.

The concept of value in the law of negotiable instruments is not the same as that of consideration under the law of contracts. **Value**, for purposes of negotiable instruments, is defined as (1) the actual *performing* of the agreed promise (executory promises are excluded because they have not been performed); (2) the acquiring of a security interest or other lien in the instrument other than a judicial lien; (3) the taking of the instrument in payment of or as security for an antecedent debt; (4) the giving of a negotiable instrument; and (5) the giving of an irrevocable obligation to a third party.

Executory Promise An executory promise, though clearly valid consideration to support a contract, is *not* the giving of value to support holder in due course status because such a promise has yet to be performed. A purchaser of a note or draft who has not yet given value may rescind the transaction if she learns of a defense to the instrument. A person who has given value, however, cannot do this; to recover value, she needs the protection accorded a holder in due course.

For example, Mike executes and delivers a $1,000 note payable to the order of Pat, who negotiates it to Henry, who promises to pay Pat for it a month later. During the month, Henry learns that Mike has a defense against Pat. Henry can rescind the agreement with Pat and return or tender the note back to her. Because this makes him whole, Henry has no need to cut off Mike's defense. Assume, on the other hand, that Henry has paid Pat for the note before he learns of Mike's defense. Because he may be unable to recover his money from Pat, Henry needs holder in due course protection, which permits him to recover on the instrument from Mike.

A holder therefore takes an instrument for value to the extent that the agreed promise of performance has been performed provided the performance was given prior to the holder's learning of any defense or claim to the instrument. Assume that in the previous example, Henry had agreed to pay Pat $900 for the note. If Henry had paid Pat $600, he could be a holder in due course to the extent of $666.67 (600/900 × $1,000), and if a defense were available, it would be valid against him only to the extent of the balance. When Henry paid the $300 balance to Pat, he would become a holder in due course as to the full $1,000 face value of the note, provided payment was made prior to Henry's discovery of Mike's defense. If he made the $300 payment after discovering the defense or claim, Henry would be a holder in due course only to the extent of $666.67. A holder in due course, to give value, need pay only the amount he agreed to pay, not the face amount of the instrument.

The Code provides an exception to the executory promise rule in two situations: (1) the giving of a negotiable instrument and (2) the making of an irrevocable obligation to a third party.

Korzenik v. Supreme Radio, Inc.

Supreme Judicial Court of Massachusetts, 1964
347 Mass. 309, 197 N.E.2d 702

FACTS Supreme Radio, Inc., issued to Southern New England Distributing Corporation (Southern) two notes worth $1,900. The two notes and others, all of a total face value of about $15,000, were transferred to Korzenik, an attorney, by his client Southern "as a retainer for services to be performed" by Korzenik. Although Korzenik was unaware of the fact, Southern had obtained the notes by fraud. Southern retained Korzenik on October 25 in connection with certain antitrust litigation, and the notes were transferred on October 31. The value of the services Korzenik performed during that time is unclear. Korzenik brought this action against Supreme Radio to recover $1,900 on the notes.

DECISION Judgment for Supreme Radio affirmed.

OPINION Whittemore, J. Decisive of the case, as the Appellate Division held, is the correct ruling that the plaintiffs are not holders in due course under * * * § 3–302; they have not shown to what extent they took for value under § 3–303. That section provides: "A holder takes the instrument for value (a) to the extent that the agreed consideration has been performed or that he acquires a security interest in or a lien on the instrument otherwise than by legal process; * * * .

Under clause (a) of § 3–303 the "agreed consideration" was the performance of legal services. It is often said that a lawyer is "retained" when he is engaged to perform services, and we hold that the judge spoke of "retainer" in this sense. The phrase that the judge used, "retainer for services" shows his meaning as does the finding as to services already performed by Korzenik at the time of the assignments. Even if the retainer had been only a fee to insure the attorney's availability to perform future services [citation], there is no basis in the record for determining the value of this commitment for one week.

The [Official] Comment to § 3–303 points out that in this article "value is divorced from consideration" and that except as provided in paragraph (c) "[a]n executory promise to give value is not * * * value. * * * The underlying reason for policy is that when the purchaser learns of a defense * * * he is not required to enforce the instrument, but is free to rescind the transaction for breach of the transferor's warranty."

§ 3–307(3), provides: "After it is shown that a defense exists a person claiming the rights of a holder in due course has the burden of establishing that he or some person under whom he claims is in all respects a holder in due course." The defense of fraud having been established, this section puts the burden on the plaintiffs. The plaintiffs have failed to show "the extent * * * [to which] the agreed consideration * * * [had] been performed."

INTERPRETATION A holder takes an instrument for value to the extent that the agreed consideration has been given, provided the consideration was given prior to the holder's learning of any defense or claim to the instrument.

CRITICAL THINKING QUESTION Should executory promises be considered value for holder in due course purposes? Explain.

Security Interest When an instrument is given as security for an obligation, the lender is regarded as having given value to the extent of his security interest. For example, Pedro is the holder of a $1,000 note payable to his order, executed by Monica, and due in twelve months. Pedro uses the note as security for a $700 loan made to him by Larry. Larry has advanced $700; therefore, he has met the requirement of value to the extent of $700.

Likewise, a *bank* gives value when a depositor is allowed to withdraw funds against a deposited item. The provisional or temporary crediting of a depositor's account (discussed in Chapter 28) is not sufficient. If a number of checks have been deposited, and some but not all of the funds have been withdrawn, the Code traces the deposit by following the "FIFO" or "first-in, first-out" method of accounting.

Antecedent Debt Under general contract law, an antecedent debt (a preexisting obligation) is not consideration. Under the Code, however, a holder gives value when she takes an instrument in payment of or as security for an antecedent debt. Thus, Martha makes and delivers a note for $1,000 to the order of Penny, who indorses the instrument and delivers it to Howard in payment of an outstanding debt of $970 that she owes him. Howard has given value.

GOOD FAITH

Revised Article 3 defines **good faith** as "honesty in fact and the observance of reasonable commercial standards of fair dealing." Thus, Revised Article 3 adopts a definition of good faith that has both a subjective and objective component. The subjective component ("honesty in fact") measures good faith by what the purchaser knows or believes. The objective component ("the observance of reasonable commercial standards of fair dealing") is comparable to the definition of good faith applicable to *merchants* under Article 2 in that it includes the requirement of the observance of reasonable commercial standards of fairness. Buying an instrument at a discounted price does not demonstrate lack of good faith.

Any Kind Checks Cashed, Inc. v. Talcott

Court of Appeal of Florida, Fourth District, 2002
830 So.2d 160, 48 U.C.C. Rep.Serv.2d 800
http://www.4dca.org/Oct2002/10-09-02/4D01-2114.pdf

FACTS In the mid-1990's, D. J. Rivera, a "financial advisor," sold John G. Talcott, Jr., a ninety-three-year-old retiree, an investment for "somewhere in the amount of $75,000." The investment produced no returns.

On December 7, 1999, Salvatore Guarino, a cohort of Rivera, established check cashing privileges at Any Kind Checks Cashed, Inc. ("Any Kind") by filling out a customer card. The card included his social security number and identification by driver's license. On the card, Guarino listed himself as a broker. That day, he cashed a $450 check without incident.

On January 10, 2000, Rivera telephoned Talcott and talked him into sending him a check for $10,000 made out to Guarino, which was to be used for travel expenses to obtain a return on the original $75,000 investment. Talcott understood that Guarino was Rivera's partner. Rivera received the check on January 11. On that same morning Rivera spoke to Talcott and stated that the $10,000 was more than what was needed for travel. He said that $5,700 would meet the travel costs. Talcott called his bank and stopped payment on the $10,000 check.

In spite of what Rivera told Talcott, Guarino appeared at Any Kind's Stuart, Florida, office on January 11 and presented the $10,000 check to Nancy Michael. She was a supervisor with the company with the authority to approve checks over $2,000. Guarino showed Michael his driver's license and the Federal Express envelope from Talcott in which he received the check. She asked him the purpose of the check, and he told her that he was a broker and that the maker of the check had sent it as an investment. She was unable to contact the maker of the check by telephone. Based on her experience, Michael believed the check was good. The Federal Express envelope was "very crucial" to her decision, because it indicated that the maker of the check had sent it to the payee trying to cash the check. After deducting the 5% check cashing fee, Michael cashed the check and gave Guarino $9,500.

On January 15, 2000, Rivera called Talcott and asked about the $5,700, again promising to send him a return on his investment. The same day, Talcott sent a check for $5,700. He assumed that Rivera knew that he had stopped payment on the $10,000 check. On January 17, 2000, Guarino went into the Stuart branch of the Any Kind store and presented the $5,700 check to the teller, Joanne Kochakian. He showed her the Federal Express envelope in which the check had come. Company policy required a supervisor to approve a check over $2,000. Kochakian noticed that Michael had previously approved the $10,000 check. She called Michael, who was working at another location, and told her about Guarino's check. Any Kind had no written procedures that a supervisor was required to follow in deciding which checks over $2,000 to cash. Michael had the discretionary "decision-making power as a supervisor to decide whether or not the check [was] any good." She relied on "instinct and judgment" in deciding what inquiry to make before cashing a check.

Michael instructed the cashier not to cash the check until she contacted the maker, Talcott, to obtain approval. On her first attempt, Kochakian received no answer. On the second call, Talcott approved cashing the $5,700 check. There was no discussion of the $10,000 check. Any Kind cashed the second check for Guarino, from which it deducted a 3% fee.

On January 19, Rivera called Talcott to warn him that Guarino was a cheat and a thief. Talcott immediately called his bank and stopped payment on the $5,700 check. Talcott's daughter called Any Kind and told it of the stop payment on the $5,700 check. There was no dispute at trial that Guarino and Rivera had pulled a scam on Talcott to get him to issue the checks.

Any Kind filed a two-count complaint against Guarino and Talcott, claiming that it was a holder in due course. Talcott's defense was that Any Kind was not a holder in due course and that his obligation on the checks was nullified because of Guarino's illegal acts.

The trial court entered final judgment in favor of Any Kind for only the $5,700 check. On the $10,000 check, the judge found for Talcott. The court held that the check cashing store was not a holder in due course, because the procedures it followed with the $10,000 check did not comport with reasonable commercial standards of fair dealing. The court found that the circumstances surrounding the cashing of the $10,000 check were sufficient to put Any Kind on notice of potential defenses and/or infirmities.

DECISION Judgment of the trial court affirmed.

OPINION Gross, J. Using the terminology of the Uniform Commercial Code, Talcott was the maker or "drawer" of the check, the person who signed the draft "as a person ordering payment." [UCC § 3–103(3)(a)] By Federal Expressing the check to Guarino, Talcott issued the check to him. See [UCC § 3–105(a)] (defining "issue" as "the first delivery of an instrument by the maker or drawer * * * for the purpose of giving rights on the instrument to any person"). Guarino indorsed the check and cashed it with Any Kind. See [UCC § 3–204(a)] (defining "indorsement"). Any Kind immediately made the funds available to Guarino, less its fee. Talcott stopped payment on the check with his bank, so the check was returned to Any Kind. See [UCC § 4–403(a)] (regarding a customer's right to stop payment).

When Guarino negotiated the check with Any Kind, it became a holder of the check, making it a "person entitled to enforce" the instrument. See [UCC §§ 3–201 (a), –203(b), –301(a). As the drawer of the check dishonored by his bank, Talcott's obligation was to pay the draft to a person entitled to enforce the draft "according to its terms at the time it was issued. * * *" [UCC § 3–414(a)].

Unless Any Kind is a holder in due course, its right to enforce Talcott's obligation to pay the draft is subject to (1) all defenses Talcott could raise "if the person entitled to enforce the instrument were enforcing a right to payment under a simple contract," and (2) a claim of "recoupment" Talcott could raise against Guarino. [UCC § 3–305 (a) & (b)]. Because Talcott was fraudulently induced to issue the checks, this case turns on Any Kind's entitlement to holder in due course status.

A "holder in due course" is a holder who takes an instrument without "apparent evidence of forgery or alteration" for value, in good faith, and without notice of certain claims and defenses. See [UCC § 3–302(a)]. As the party claiming that it was a holder in due course, Any Kind had the burden to prove that status by a preponderance of the evidence. [Citations.]

The question for this court is whether the trial court erred in finding that Any Kind was not a holder in due course of the $10,000 check based on the findings of fact made at trial, keeping in mind that Any Kind bore the burden of proof. That question turns on whether Any Kind acted "in good faith" within the meaning of [UCC] Section [3–302(a)(2)(ii)].

The good faith requirement of the holder in due course doctrine "has been the source of an ancient and continuing dispute." [Citation.] On the one hand, should the courts apply a so-called objective test, and ask whether a reasonably prudent person, behaving the way the alleged holder in due course behaved, would have been acting in good faith? Or should the courts instead apply a subjective test and examine the person's actual behavior, however stupid and irrespective of the reaction a reasonably prudent person would have had in the same circumstance? The legal establishment has steered a crooked course through this debate. [Citations.]

Prior to 1992, [UCC] Section 1–201 (19), defined "good faith" as "honesty in fact in the conduct of the transaction concerned." Florida courts interpreted this definition as creating a subjective test. [Citation.] * * * In another case, Judge Schwartz wrote that the "Florida version of the holder in due course provision of the U.C.C. does seem to protect the objectively stupid so long as he is subjectively pure of heart." [Citation.]

Application of [old UCC's] "honesty in fact" standard to Any Kind's conduct in this case would clothe it with holder in due course status. It is undisputed that Any Kind's employees were pure of heart, that they acted without knowledge of Guarino's wrongdoing.

However, in 1992, the legislature adopted a new definition of "good faith" that applies to the [UCC] Section 3–302 definition of a holder in due course: "'good faith' means honesty in fact and the observance of reasonable commercial standards of fair dealing." [Citation.] To the old, subjective good faith, "honesty in fact" standard, the legislature added an objective component—the "pure heart of the holder must now be accompanied by reasoning that assures conduct comporting with reasonable commercial standards of fair dealing." [Citation.] No longer may a holder of an instrument act with "a pure heart and an empty head and still obtain holder in due course status." [Citation.]

Comment 4 to Section 3–103, Florida Statutes Annotated, attempts to shed light on how to interpret the new standard:

> Although fair dealing is a broad term that must be defined in context, it is clear that it is concerned with the fairness of conduct rather than the care with which an act is performed. Failure to exercise ordinary care in conducting a transaction is an entirely different concept than failure to deal fairly in conducting the transaction.

The Code does not define the term "fair dealing." * * *

Application of holder in due course status is the law's value judgment that certain holders are worthy of protection from certain types of claims. For example, it has been argued that application of the old subjective standard facilitated the transfer of checks in the stream of commerce; arguably one would be "more willing to accept the checks if * * * she knows * * * she can be a holder in due course of that instrument and take it free of defenses that might have existed between the buyer and the seller in the underlying transaction." [Citation.] In applying the new standard, "fairness" should be measured by taking a global view of the underlying transaction and all of its participants. A holder "must act in a way that is fair according to commercial standards that are themselves reasonable." [Citation.]

To apply the law requiring "good faith" under Section 3–302 (a), we adopt the analysis set forth by the Supreme Court of Maine:

> The factfinder must * * * determine, first, whether the conduct of the holder comported with industry or "commercial" standards applicable to the transaction and, second, whether those standards were reasonable standards intended to result in fair dealing. Each of those determinations must be made in the context of the specific transaction at hand. If the factfinder's conclusion on each point is "yes," the holder will be determined to have acted in good faith even if, in the individual transaction at issue, the result appears unreasonable. Thus a holder may be accorded holder in due course status where it acts pursuant to those reasonable commercial standards of fair dealing—even if it is negligent—but may lose that status, even where it complies with commercial standards, if those standards are not reasonably related to achieving fair dealing. [Citation.]

There was no evidence at trial concerning the check cashing industry's commercial standards. Even assuming that Any Kind's procedures for checks over $2,000 met the industry's gold standard, we hold that in this case the procedures followed were not reasonably related to achieve fair dealing with respect to the $10,000 check, taking into consideration all of the participants in the transaction, Talcott, Guarino, and Any Kind.

* * *

Check cashing businesses occupy a special niche in the financial industry. They are part of the "alternative financial services" or "fringe banking" sector, a part of the market that "has become a major source of traditional banking services for low-income and working poor consumers, residents of minority neighborhoods, and people with blemished credit histories." [Citations.]

Check cashing stores are often in locations where traditional banks fear to tread. * * *

In such areas, the typical check presented for cashing is not a large one—a paycheck, child support, social security, or public assistance check. [The Florida check cashing statute] contemplates that such checks will be presented at check cashing outlets; it limits the fee charged for the payment of "any kind of state public assistance or federal social security benefits payable to the bearer."

Attractions of check cashing outlets are convenience and speed. * * * Unlike banks, check cashing stores cannot place a hold on a check before releasing funds. The Florida * * * Code requires payment to be made "immediately in currency for every payment instrument received by a person engaging in the activities of a check casher." [Citation.] The statute and administrative rules also contemplate that a check cashing business will engage in various types of "verification" of a check. [Citation.]

Against this backdrop, we cannot say that the trial court erred in finding that the $10,000 check was a red flag. The $10,000 personal check was not the typical check cashed at a check cashing outlet. The size of the check, in the context of the check cashing business, was a proper factor to consider under the objective standard of good faith in deciding whether Any Kind was a holder in due course. [Citation.]

Guarino was not the typical customer of a check cashing outlet. As the trial judge observed, because of the 5% fee charged, it is unusual for a small businessman such as a broker to conduct business through a check cashing store instead of through a traditional bank. Guarino did not have a history with Any Kind of cashing checks of similar size without incident. The need for speed in a business transaction is usually less acute than for someone cashing a paycheck or welfare check to pay for life's necessities. The need for speed in cashing a large business check is consistent with a drawer who, for whatever reason, might stop payment. Fair dealing in this case required that the $10,000 check be approached with a degree of caution.

If a drawer has a right to stop payment of a check, and a traditional bank usually places a hold on uncollected funds after a payee deposits a check into an account, then the legal dispute after a stop payment will usually be between the drawer of the check and the payee, the two parties that had the dealings leading to the payment. Thus, where a check is cashed at a bank or savings and loan, the law will often place the loss on the wrongdoer in the underlying transaction. This is a desirable goal.

Where a check cashing store releases funds immediately, the holder in due course doctrine steps in, frequently putting the loss on a wronged maker, in furtherance of the policy that facilitating the transfer of checks benefits the economy. In this case, the policy reasons behind easy negotiability do not outweigh the reasons for caution. Very loose application of the objective component of "good faith" would make check cashing outlets the easy refuge of scam artists who want to take the money and run. The concept of "fair dealing" includes not being an easy, safe harbor for the dishonest.

To affirm the trial court is not to wreak havoc with the check cashing industry. Verification with the maker of a check will *not* be necessary to preserve holder in due course status in the vast majority of cases arising from check cashing outlets. This was neither the typical customer, nor the typical transaction of a check cashing outlet.

* * *

The legislature's addition of an objective standard of conduct may well have the effect of "slowing the 'wheels of commerce' " in some transactions. [Citation.] However, by adopting changes to the "good faith" standard in the holder in due course doctrine, the legislature "necessarily must have concluded that the addition of the objective requirement to the definition of 'good faith' serves an important goal. The paramount necessity of unquestioned negotiability has given way, at least in part, to the desire for reasonable commercial fairness in negotiable transactions." [Citation.] In this case, reasonable commercial fairness required Any Kind to approach the $10,000 check with some caution and to verify it with the maker if it wanted to preserve its holder in due course status.

INTERPRETATION Reasonable commercial standards of fair dealing mandated that Any Kind approach the $10,000 check with reasonable caution and to verify the check with the maker.

CRITICAL THINKING QUESTION Do you agree with the position taken by Revised Article 3? Explain.

LACK OF NOTICE

To become a holder in due course, a holder must also take the instrument without notice that it is (1) overdue, (2) dishonored, (3) forged or altered, or (4) subject to any claim or defense. Notice of any of these matters should alert the purchaser that she may be buying a lawsuit and, consequently, may not be accorded the favored position of a holder in due course. The Code defines *notice* as follows: "A person has 'notice' of a fact when (a) he has actual knowledge of it; or (b) he has received a notice or notification of it; or (c) from all the facts and circumstances known to him at the time in question, he has reason to know that it exists." Whereas the first two clauses of this definition impose a wholly subjective standard, the last clause provides a partially objective one: the presence of suspicious circumstances does not adversely affect the purchaser, unless he has reason to recognize them as suspicious. Because the applicable standard is "actual notice," "notice received," or "reason to know," constructive notice through public filing or recording is not of itself sufficient notice to prevent a person from being a holder in due course.

To be effective, notice must be received at a time and in a manner that the recipient will have a reasonable opportunity to act on it.

Notice an Instrument Is Overdue To be a holder in due course, the purchaser must take the instrument without notice that it is overdue. This requirement is based on the idea that overdue paper conveys a suspicion that something is wrong. ***Time paper*** is due on its stated due date if the stated date is a business day or, if not, on the next business day. It "becomes overdue on the day after the due date." Thus, if an instrument is payable on July 1, a purchaser cannot become a holder in due course by buying it on July 2, provided that July 1 was a business day. In addition, in the case of an installment note or of several notes issued as part of the same transaction with successive specified maturity dates, the purchaser has notice that an instrument is overdue if he has reason to know that any part of the principal amount is overdue or that there is an uncured default in payment of another instrument of the same series.

Demand paper is overdue for purposes of preventing a purchaser from becoming a holder in due course if the purchaser has notice that she is taking the instrument on a day after demand has been made or after it has been outstanding for an unreasonably long time. The Code provides that for checks, a reasonable time is ninety days after its date. For all other demand instruments, the reasonable period of time varies, depending on the facts of the particular case. Thus, the particular situation, business custom, and other relevant factors must be considered in determining whether an instrument is overdue: no hard-and-fast rules are possible.

Acceleration clauses have caused problems. If an instrument's maturity date has been accelerated, the instrument becomes overdue on the day after the accelerated due date even though the holder may be unaware that it is past due.

Notice an Instrument Has Been Dishonored **Dishonor** is the refusal to pay or accept an instrument when it becomes due. If a transferee has notice that an instrument has been dishonored, he cannot become a holder in due course. For example, a person who takes a check stamped "NSF" (not sufficient funds) or "no account" has notice of dishonor and will not be a holder in due course.

Notice of a Claim or Defense A purchaser of an instrument cannot become a holder in due course if he purchases it with notice of "any claim to the instrument described in Section 3–306" or "a defense or claim in recoupment described in Section 3–305(a)." A **defense** protects a person from liability on an instrument, whereas a **claim** to an instrument asserts ownership to it.

Claims covered by Section 3–306 include "not only claims to ownership but also any other claim of a property or possessory right. It includes the claim to a lien or the claim of a person in rightful possession of an instrument who was wrongfully deprived of possession." Claims to instruments may be made against thieves, finders, or possessors with void or voidable title. In many instances, both a defense and claim will be involved. For example, Donna is fraudulently induced to issue a check to Pablo. Donna has a claim to ownership of the instrument as well as a defense to Pablo's demand for payment.

Section 3–305(a), which is more fully discussed later in this chapter, provides that personal defenses are valid against a holder, while real defenses are effective against both holders and holders in due course. In addition, a person without the rights of a holder in due course is subject to an obligor's claim in recoupment "against the original payee of the instrument if the claim arose from the transaction that gave rise to the instrument." For example, Buyer gives Seller a negotiable note in exchange for Seller's promise to deliver certain goods. Seller delivers nonconforming goods that Buyer elects to accept. Buyer has a cause of action under Article 2 for breach of warranty under the contract, which a "claim may be asserted against Seller as a counterclaim or as a claim in recoupment to reduce the amount owing on the note. It is not relevant whether Seller knew or had notice that Buyer had the warranty claim."

Buying an instrument at a discount or for a price less than face value does not mean that the buyer had notice of any defense or claim against the instrument. Nonetheless, a court may construe an unusually large discount as notice of a claim or defense.

WITHOUT REASON TO QUESTION ITS AUTHENTICITY

Under prior Article 3, a purchaser had notice of a claim or defense if the instrument was so incomplete, contained such visible evidence of forgery or alteration, or was otherwise so irregular as to call into question its validity. Courts differed greatly as to how irregular an instrument had to be for a holder to have notice. Revised Article 3 provides that a party may become a holder in due course only if the instrument issued or negotiated to the holder "does not bear such apparent evidence of forgery or alteration or is not otherwise so irregular or incomplete as to

Ethical Dilemma

What Responsibility Does a Holder Have in Negotiating Commerical Paper?

FACTS Marcus Moore and David Arnold are subcontractors specializing in the installation of electrical wiring for commercial office space. They have incorporated their business as Moore & Arnold, Inc. Over the last two years, their business has been extremely slow. Recently, they obtained an offer to install wiring for a general contractor, Barnes & Sons, which was in charge of renovating an office to be occupied by three major tenants. The job was substantial and would pay $35,000.

Marcus and David disagreed on whether to accept the job. Marcus was concerned with the business reputation of Barnes & Sons. For years, the business had been reputably operated by Tom Barnes, the original owner, but when his son, John, assumed control of operations, problems began. The partnership was recently sued for negligence in connection with a major construction project in a mall. It is well known that John is a gambler, and the business has gained the reputation of being slow to pay creditors.

Marcus and David finally decided to accept the job. Upon their completing the work, John Barnes handed Marcus a negotiable promissory note drawn by John Major, one of three different names Barnes & Sons has been trading under during the last year. The note was payable to Moore & Arnold, Inc., one month from date.

Marcus is instinctively nervous about accepting the note. He is aware of the cash flow problems and the litigation pending against Barnes & Sons and has become increasingly suspicious because of the different trade names the contractor uses. David, who is more trusting, wants to accept the note and negotiate it to Wire Ways, Inc., one of their major suppliers of electrical wiring. Marcus wants to demand cash and, if Barnes refuses, to refer the account to a collection agency.

Social, Policy, and Ethical Considerations

1. Would it be ethical for Marcus and David to accept the note and negotiate it to Wire Ways, Inc.? Why?
2. What ethical responsibilities does one have to review the business reputations of prospective clients or customers and to refuse to do business with disreputable persons?
3. What risks did Moore & Arnold, Inc., assume in accepting the business? Was the risk limited to the failure to obtain payment?
4. Could Marcus and David have structured the business transaction in any way to insulate Moore & Arnold, Inc. from the risks it assumed?

call into question its authenticity." According to the comments to this section, the term "authenticity" clarifies the idea that the irregularity or incompleteness must indicate that the instrument may not be what it purports to be. The Revision takes the position that persons who purchase such instruments do so at their own peril and should not be protected against defenses of the obligor or claims of prior owners. In addition, the Revision takes the position that it makes no difference if the holder does not have notice of such irregularity or incompleteness; it depends only on whether the instrument's defect is apparent and whether the taker should have reason to know of the problem.

CPA Holder in Due Course Status

A holder who meets the requirements discussed in the previous section obtains the preferred position of holder in due course status. This section discusses whether a payee may become a holder in due course. It also addresses the rights of a transferee from a holder in due course under the shelter rule. Finally, it identifies those special circumstances that prevent a transferee from acquiring holder in due course status.

A Payee May Be a Holder in Due Course

A payee may be a holder in due course. This does not mean that a payee automatically is a holder in due course but that he *may* be one if he satisfies the requirements for such status. For example, if a seller delivers goods to a buyer and accepts a current check in payment, the seller will be a holder in due course if he acted in good faith and had no notice of defenses or claims and no reason to question its authenticity. The most common example is where the transaction involves three parties, and the defense involves the parties other than the payee. For example, after purchasing goods from Punky, Robin fraudulently obtains a check from Clem payable to the order of Punky and forwards it to Punky. Punky takes it for value and without any knowledge that Robin had defrauded Clem into issuing the check. In such a case, the payee, Punky, is a holder in due course and takes the instrument free and clear of Clem's defense of fraud in the inducement.

Gentner and Company, Inc. v. Wells Fargo Bank

Court of Appeal, Second District, Division 4, California, 1999
76 Cal.App.4th 1165, 90 Cal.Rptr.2d 904
http://freecaselaw.com/ca/B128574.htm

FACTS L & M Home Health Corporation ("L & M") had a checking account with Wells Fargo Bank **(http://wellsfargo.com/)**. L & M engaged Gentner and Company, Inc. ("Gentner") to provide consulting services, and paid Gentner for services rendered with a check drawn on its Wells Fargo account in the amount of $60,000, dated September 23, 1996. Eleven days later, on October 4, 1996, L & M orally instructed Wells Fargo to stop payment on the check. Eleven days after that, on October 15, 1996, Gentner presented the L & M check to Wells Fargo for payment. On the same date the teller issued a cashier's check, payable to Gentner, in the amount of $60,000. On November 5, 1996, Wells Fargo placed a "stop payment order" on the cashier's check. On January 15, 1997, Gentner deposited the cashier's check at another bank, but it was not honored and was returned stamped "Payment Stopped."

Gentner brought suit against Wells Fargo for wrongful dishonor of the cashier's check. The trial court ruled in favor of Gentner, finding that Gentner was a holder in due course of the cashier's check. Wells Fargo appealed.

DECISION Judgment affirmed.

OPINION Curry, J. On appeal, the parties dispute whether Gentner was a holder in due course of the cashier's check. The attributes of a holder in due course are set forth in section 3–302, which requires that it take the instrument "(A) for value, (B) in good faith, (C) without notice that the instrument is overdue or has been dishonored or that there is an uncured default with respect to payment of another instrument issued as part of the same series, (D) without notice that the instrument contains an unauthorized signature or has been altered, (E) without notice of any claim to the instrument described in Section 3–306, and (F) without notice that any party has a defense or claim in recoupment described in subdivision (a) of Section 3–305." [Citation.] In addition, a party can be a holder in due course only if the instrument "when issued or negotiated to the holder" did not "bear such apparent evidence of forgery or alteration or [wa]s not otherwise so irregular or incomplete as to call into question its authenticity."

It is true, as Wells Fargo asserts, that "value" has a different definition than the more familiar contractual term "consideration." Under Section 3–303, "[a]n instrument is issued or transferred for value" if: "(1) The instrument is issued or transferred for a promise of performance, to the extent the promise has been performed. (2) The transferee acquires a security interest or other lien in the instrument other than a lien obtained by judicial proceeding. (3) The instrument is issued or transferred as payment of, or as security for, an antecedent claim against any person, whether or not the claim is due. (4) The instrument is issued or transferred in exchange for a negotiable instrument. (5) The instrument is issued or transferred in exchange for the incurring of an irrevocable obligation to a third party by the person taking the instrument." [Citation.] As can be seen, the most significant differences are that "value" can include past performance or "antecedent claims," something which is not generally true of contractual consideration, and a promise to perform in the future—the most typical form of contractual consideration—constitutes "value" only to the extent it has already been performed. For purposes of the Commercial Code, "[i]f an instrument is issued for value * * *, the instrument is also issued for consideration." [Citation.]

The reason achieving the status of a holder in due course is important can be understood by reference to Section 3–305, which sets forth the recognized defenses to an obligation to pay an "instrument" such as a check. The only defenses available against a holder in due course are listed in Section 3–305, subdivision (a)(1), and include "infancy" of the obligor, "duress," lack of legal capacity, illegality of the transaction which "nullifies the obligation," fraud "that induced the obligor to sign the instrument with neither knowledge nor reasonable opportunity to learn of its character or its essential terms," and discharge of the obligor by bankruptcy. When the instrument is not in the hands of a holder in due course, the obligor can raise: all defenses set forth in any other "section of this division"; any defense "that would be available if the person entitled to enforce the instrument were enforcing a right to payment under a simple contract"; or "[a] claim in recoupment" which the obligor has against the original payee of the instrument "if the claim arose from the transaction that gave rise to the instrument. * * *" [Citation.]

Wells Fargo contends that the holder-in-due-course doctrine does not apply because the cashier's check was purchased by Gentner for payment to itself rather than by another party for payment to Gentner. Logically, one would think that must be so and that Gentner's status as the payee of the cashier's check would preclude it from claiming holder-in-due-course status. (See Uniform Commercial Code com. 4 ["In the typical case the holder in due course is not the payee of the instrument. Rather, the holder in due course is an immediate or remote transferee of the payee."].) However, as the commentators make clear, under the Commercial Code's definition of "holder in due course," "[t]he payee of an instrument can be a holder in due course" even though "use of the holder-in-due-course doctrine by the payee of an instrument is not the normal situation," and only "in a small percentage of cases" would it be "appropriate to allow the payee of an instrument to assert rights as a holder in due course." As we read the statutory definition, nothing in it precludes a payee from being a holder in due course—if it can somehow meet the requirements of good faith and complete lack of knowledge about any potential defenses held by the drawer or maker of the instrument. Because it is extremely unlikely that the original payee will be able to establish such complete ignorance under normal circumstances, the advantages of holder-in-due course status will apply to a payee only "in a small percentage of cases. * * * "

The older version of Section 3–305—the section which lays out the defenses available against holders in due course and others—created confusion because it stated that a holder in due course took the instrument free from "[a]ll defenses of any party to the instrument with whom the holder has not dealt. * * * " It is hard to imagine how an original payee, who always in some sense "deals" with the drawee, could ever claim holder-in-due-course status if that provision meant what it aid. The comment to revised Section 3–305, which eliminated the puzzling phrase, concedes that "[t]he meaning of this language was not at all clear and if read literally could have produced the wrong result."

The situation of a bank accepting a customer's check and giving the payee a cashier's check in return appears to fall within one of those small percentage of cases which presents an opportunity for the payee to establish holder-in-due-course status. Gentner, the payee of the cashier's check, was acting in complete good faith and had no knowledge of any potential defenses held by Wells Fargo as drawer of the instrument. Specifically it did not know, and had no reason to know, that the L & M check which it submitted to Wells Fargo was subject to a stop notice and was, from Wells Fargo's perspective, worthless since the funds could not be recovered from the customer's account.

* * *

INTERPRETATION A payee may be a holder in due course.

CRITICAL THINKING QUESTION Under what circumstances, if any, should a payee be permitted to be a holder in due course?

THE SHELTER RULE

Through operation of the **shelter rule**, the transferee of an instrument acquires the *same* rights in the instrument as the transferor had. Therefore, even a holder who does not comply fully with the requirements for being a holder in due course nevertheless acquires all the rights of a holder in due course if some previous holder of the instrument had been a holder in due course. For example, Prosser induces Mundheim, by fraud in the inducement, to make a note payable to her order and then negotiates it to Henn, a holder in due course. After the note is overdue, Henn gives it to Corbin, who has notice of the fraud. Corbin is not a holder in due course, because he took the instrument when overdue, did not pay value, and had notice of Mundheim's defense. Nonetheless, through the operation of the shelter rule, Corbin acquires Henn's rights as a holder in due course, and Mundheim cannot successfully assert his defense against Corbin. The purpose of the shelter provision is not to benefit the transferee but to assure the holder in due course of a free market for the negotiable instrument he acquires.

The shelter rule, however, provides that a transferee who has himself been a party to any fraud or illegality affecting the instrument cannot subsequently acquire the rights of a holder in due course. For example, Parker induces Miles, by fraud in the inducement, to make an instrument payable to the order of Parker, who subsequently negotiates the instrument to Henson, a holder in due course. If Parker later reacquires it from Henson, Parker will not succeed to Henson's rights as a holder in due course and will remain subject to the defense of fraud.

Practical Advice

If a negotiable instrument is transferred to you and you will not satisfy the requirements of a holder in due course, make sure that your transferor has the rights of a holder in due course.

Triffin v. Cigna Insurance Co.

Superior Court of New Jersey, Appellate Division, 1997
297 N.J.Super. 199, 687 A.2d 1045
http://lawlibrary.rutgers.edu/decisions/appellate/a4000-95.opn.html

FACTS The defendant, James Mills, received a draft in the amount of $484.12, dated July 7, 1993, from one of Cigna's **(http://www.cigna.com/)** constituent companies, Atlantic Employers Insurance Co. (Atlantic). The draft had been issued for workers' compensation benefits. Mills falsely indicated to Atlantic that he had not received the draft due to a change in his address and requested that payment be stopped and a new draft issued by defendant. Atlantic complied and stopped payment on the initial draft. Mills nevertheless negotiated the initial draft to Sun's Market (Sun), before the stop payment notation was placed on the draft. Sun was a holder in due course. Atlantic's bank dishonored the draft in accordance with its customer's direction, stamped it "Stop Payment," and returned the draft to Sun. There is no question that had Sun Corp. at that point pressed its claim against the insurer as the issuer of the instrument, Sun Corp. would have been entitled to a judgment because of its status as a holder in due course.

Thereafter, plaintiff, who is in the business of purchasing dishonored instruments, obtained Sun's interests in this instrument and proceeded with this lawsuit. Plaintiff does not contend that he is a holder in due course of the instrument by virtue of it being negotiated to him for value, in good faith, without notice of dishonor, under the former holder in due course statute, (UCC § 3–302), nor under the present statute: 3–302a(2). The trial court issued summary judgment in favor of Atlantic and Sun appeals.

DECISION Reversed and remanded.

OPINION Dreier, J. There exists a second method by which one may become a holder in due course. The shelter provisions of former UCC (§ 3–201), which was in effect when plaintiff obtained his assignment of this instrument, state clearly that "[t]ransfer of an instrument vests in the transferee such rights as the transferor has therein * * *." Official Comment 3 to that section sets to rest any question of whether this section applies to the transfer by assignment of the rights of a holder in due course. The Comment reads: "A holder in due course may transfer his rights as such * * *. [The] policy is to assure the holder in due course a free market for the paper, * * *." Example (a) following this comment could have been drawn from this case, but is even stronger because it adds an element of fraud and posits a gratuitous transfer rather than a purchase, as in our case:

> (a) A [Mills] induces M [Cigna] by fraud to make an instrument payable to A. A negotiates it to B [Sun Corp.], who takes as a holder in due course. After the instrument is overdue B gives it to C [plaintiff], who has notice of the fraud. C succeeds to B's rights as a holder in due course, cutting off the defense.

If the 1995 amendments are to be given retroactive effect, the law governing the rights of a transferee who merely has accepted the transfer of the instrument is now found in Revised UCC [§ 3–203]. It restates the principle of the former Official Comment 3, example (a), as substantive law.

* * *

The Uniform Commercial Code Comment 2 to this [Revised] section similarly states:

> Under subsection (b) a holder in due course that transfers an instrument transfers those rights as a holder in due course to the purchaser. The policy is to assure the holder in due course a free market for the instrument.

* * *

These sections could not be clearer. Plaintiff received by [negotiation] the right of a holder in due course to this instrument, which apparently had been presented and then dishonored because of defendant's stop payment order.

* * *

INTERPRETATION Through operation of the shelter rule, the transferee of an instrument acquires the same rights in the instrument as the transferor had.

CRITICAL THINKING QUESTION Do you agree with the shelter rule? Explain.

CPA THE PREFERRED POSITION OF A HOLDER IN DUE COURSE

In a *nonconsumer transaction*, a holder in due course takes the instrument (1) free from all *claims* on the part of any person and (2) free from all *defenses* of any party with whom he has not dealt, except for a limited number of defenses that are available against anyone, including a holder in due course. Such defenses that are available against all parties are referred to as **real defenses.** In contrast, defenses that may not be asserted against a holder in due course are referred to as **personal**, or **contractual**, defenses.

REAL DEFENSES

The real defenses available against *all* holders, including holders in due course, are

1. infancy, to the extent that it is a defense to a simple contract
2. any other incapacity, duress, or illegality of the transaction that renders the obligation void
3. fraud in the execution
4. discharge in insolvency proceedings
5. any other discharge of which the holder has notice when he takes the instrument
6. unauthorized signature and
7. fraudulent alteration

Infancy All states have a firmly entrenched public policy of protecting minors from persons who might take advantage of them through contractual dealings. The Code does not state when minority is available as a defense or the conditions under which it may be asserted. Rather, it provides that minority (infancy) is a defense available against a holder in due course to the extent that it is a defense to a contract under the laws of the state involved. See Chapter 14.

Void Obligations When the obligation on an instrument originates in such a way that it is *void* or null under the law of the state involved, the Code authorizes the use of this defense against a holder in due course. This follows from the idea that when the party was never obligated, it is unreasonable to permit an event over which she has no control—negotiation to a holder in due course—to convert a nullity into a valid claim against her.

Incapacity, duress, and the illegality of a transaction are defenses that may render the obligation of a party either voidable or void, depending on the law of the state involved as applied to the facts of a given transaction. To the extent the obligation is rendered void (because of duress by physical force, because the party is a person under guardianship, or, in some cases, because the contract is illegal), the defense may be asserted against a holder in due course. To the extent it is voidable, which is generally the case, the defense (other than minority, as discussed previously) is not effective against a holder in due course.

Federal Deposit Insurance Corporation v. Meyer

United States District Court, District of Columbia, 1991
755 F.Supp. 10

FACTS Certain partners of the Finley Kumble law firm signed promissory notes that secured loans made to the law firm by the National Bank of Washington (NBW). When Finley Kumble subsequently declared bankruptcy and defaulted on the loans, NBW filed suit to collect on the notes. Then NBW itself became insolvent, and the Federal Deposit Insurance Corporation (FDIC) **(http://www.fdic.gov/)** was appointed as receiver. The FDIC moved for summary judgment against each defendant on the grounds that Section 1823(e) the Federal Deposit Insurance Act (FDIA) of 1950 places the FDIC in the position of a holder in due course and thus bars all personal defenses against FDIC claims as a matter of law. Twenty of the Finley partners opposed the motion, claiming that they signed the notes under the threat that their wages and standing in the firm would decrease if they refused to sign. Such a threat constituted economic duress, which, they contended, is not a personal defense but a real one. They argued that the FDIA does not bar real defenses.

DECISION Summary judgment granted in favor of FDIC.

OPINION Pratt, J. The Finley Partners argue that the FDIC's motion for summary judgment should be denied because their defense of economic duress survives the effects of § 1823(e). They concede that § 1823(e) operates to place the FDIC in the position of a holder in due course, making promissory notes free of personal defenses. They argue, however, that § 1823(e) does not extinguish real defenses set forth in the Uniform Commercial Code ("UCC") and that their economic duress defense constitutes such a real defense.

Defendants are correct that § 1823(e) bars personal defenses but not real defenses. * * * As the Supreme Court explained in *Langley v. FDIC*, a real defense renders an instrument entirely void, leaving no interest that could be " 'diminish[ed] or defeat[ed].' " [Citations.] In contrast, personal defenses render a note voidable but not void. * * *

Thus, if the Finley Partners' economic duress constitutes a real defense, then their promissory notes were void from the beginning. * * * On the other hand, if the Finley Partners' economic duress defense is a personal defense, then the FDIC received voidable title to the promissory notes from the NBW, which [defense would be cut off by the FDIC] * * * .

The main legal question, then, is whether economic duress is a personal defense that rendered NBW's title to the promissory notes voidable, or a real defense that rendered its title entirely void. The Finley Partners suggest that duress of any nature constitutes a real defense, citing UCC § 3–305(2)(b) and several cases from outside of the District of Columbia. A careful reading of the UCC and its Official Commentary reveals that it does not make such a blanket classification.

First, § 3–305(2)(b) provides that holders in due course take free of all defenses except for "(b) such other incapacity, or duress, or illegality of the transaction, as renders the obligation of the party a nullity." The words "such" and "as" indicate that the section is not stating that any type of duress renders an obligation to be nullity. Rather, it suggests that only those types of duress that are so severe as to render it a nullity stand as exceptions to the rule that holders in due course take free of defenses.

Of course, the question left open is what type of duress is severe enough to render it a nullity. Neither UCC § 3–305(2)(b) nor the Official Comment attempt to establish a rule governing which types of duress render a transaction void as opposed to merely voidable. Instead, Official Comment 6 declares that "[a]ll such matters are therefore left to the local law."

* * *

Duress takes two forms. In one, a person physically compels conduct that appears to be a manifestation of assent by a party who has no intention of engaging in that conduct. The result of this type of duress is that the conduct is not effective to create a contract ([Restatement] § 174). In the other, a person makes an improper threat that induces a party who has no reasonable alternative to manifesting his assent. The result of this type of duress is that the contract that is created is voidable by the victim (§ 175). [Citation.]

* * *

The Finley Partners do not allege that they were physically compelled to sign the promissory notes in question. They themselves labeled their defense as "economic" duress, and the substance of their allegations are that they signed the notes because of the threat that their wages and standing in the firm would decrease if they refused. Such economic duress does not reach the level of physical compulsion capable of rendering a transaction entirely void. Thus, NBW held at least voidable title to the promissory notes when the FDIC took over as Receiver. * * * Thus, defendants' economic duress defense is not valid against the FDIC.

INTERPRETATION Where the obligation of an instrument is void, the Code authorizes the use of this real defense against a holder in due course.

CRITICAL THINKING QUESTION What other defenses, if any, should be real defenses? Explain.

Fraud in the Execution Fraud in the execution of the instrument renders the instrument void and therefore is a defense valid against a holder in due course. The Code describes this type of fraud as misrepresentation that induced the party to sign the instrument with neither knowledge nor reasonable opportunity to learn of its character or its essential terms. For example, Frances is asked to sign a receipt and does so without realizing or having the opportunity of learning that her signature is going on a promissory note cleverly concealed under the receipt. Because her signature has been obtained by fraud in the execution, Frances would have a valid defense against a holder in due course.

Discharge in Insolvency Proceedings If a party's obligation on an instrument is discharged in a proceeding for bankruptcy or for any other insolvency, he has a valid defense in any action brought against him on the instrument, including one brought by a holder in due course. Thus, a debtor, whose obligation on a negotiable instrument is discharged in an insolvency proceeding, is relieved of payment, even to a holder in due course.

Discharge of Which the Holder Has Notice Any holder, including a holder in due course, takes the instrument subject to *any* discharge of which she has notice at the time of taking. If only some, but not all, of the parties to the instrument have been discharged, the purchaser can still become a holder in due course. The discharged parties, however, have a real defense against a holder in due course who has notice of their discharge. For example, Harris, who is in possession of a negotiable instrument, strikes out the indorsement of Jones. The instrument is subsequently negotiated to Stephen, a holder in due course, against whom Jones has a real defense.

Unauthorized Signature A person's signature on an instrument is unauthorized when it is made without express, implied, or apparent authority. Because he has not made a contract, a person whose signature is unauthorized or forged cannot be held liable on the instrument in the absence of estoppel or ratification, even if the instrument is negotiated to a holder in due course. Similarly, if Joan's signature were forged on the back of an instrument, Joan could not be held as an indorser, because she has not made a contract. Thus, any unauthorized signature is totally invalid as that of the person whose name is signed unless she ratifies it or is precluded from denying it; the unauthorized signature operates only as the signature of the unauthorized signer.

A person may be ***estopped*** or prevented from asserting a defense because his conduct in the matter has caused reliance by a third party to his loss or damage. Suppose Neal's son forges Neal's name to a check, which the drawee bank cashes. When the returned check reaches Neal, he learns of the forgery. Rather than subject his son to trouble, possibly including criminal prosecution, Neal says nothing. Thereafter, Neal's son continues to forge checks and to cash them at the drawee bank. Although the bank may be suspicious of the signature, the fact that Neal has not complained may induce it to believe that the signatures are proper. When he finally seeks to compel the bank to recredit his account for all the forged checks, Neal will not succeed: his conduct has estopped him from denying that his son had authority to sign his name.

A party is similarly precluded from denying the validity of his signature if his ***negligence*** substantially contributes to the making of the unauthorized signature. The most obvious case is that of a drawer who uses a mechanized or other automatic signing device and is negligent in safeguarding it. In such an instance, the drawer would not be permitted to assert an unauthorized signature as a defense against a holder in due course.

An unauthorized signature may be ***ratified*** and thereby become valid so far as its effect as a signature. Thus, Kathy forges Laura's indorsement on a promissory note and negotiates it to Allison. Laura subsequently ratifies Kathy's act. As a result, Kathy is no longer liable to Allison on the note, although Laura is. Nonetheless, Laura's ratification does *not* relieve Kathy from civil liability to Laura; nor does it in any way affect Kathy's criminal liability for the forgery.

Fraudulent Alteration An alteration is (1) an unauthorized change that modifies the obligation of any party to the instrument or (2) an unauthorized addition or change to an incomplete instrument concerning the obligation of a party.

An alteration that is fraudulently made discharges a party whose obligation is affected by the alteration except where that party assents or is precluded by his own negligence from raising the defense. All other alterations do not discharge any party, and the instrument may be enforced according to its original terms. Thus, if an instrument has been nonfraudulently altered, it may be enforced, but only to the extent of its original tenor (that is, according to its initially written terms). See Figure 26-4 illustrating the effects of alterations.

A discharge under the Code for fraudulent alteration, however, is not effective against a holder in due course who took the instrument without notice of the alteration. Such a subsequent holder in due course may always enforce the instrument according to its original terms and, in the case of an incomplete instrument, may enforce it as completed. (Under the Code a person taking the instrument for value, in good faith, and without notice of the alteration is accorded the same protection as a holder in due course). The following examples demonstrate the operation of these rules (Figure 26-5 illustrates these examples).

1. M executes and delivers a note to P for $2,000, which P subsequently indorses and transfers to A for $1,900. A intentionally and skillfully changes the figure on the note to $20,000 and then negotiates it to B, who takes it, in good faith, without notice of any wrongdoing and without reason to question its authenticity, for $19,000. B is a holder in due course and, therefore, can collect the original amount of the note ($2,000) from M or P and the full amount ($20,000) from A, less any amount paid by the other parties.
2. Assume the facts in (1), except that B is not a holder in due course. M and P are both discharged by A's fraudulent alteration. B's only recourse is against A for the full amount ($20,000).
3. M issues his blank check to P, who is to complete it when the exact amount is determined. Though the

Figure 26-4
Effects of Alterations

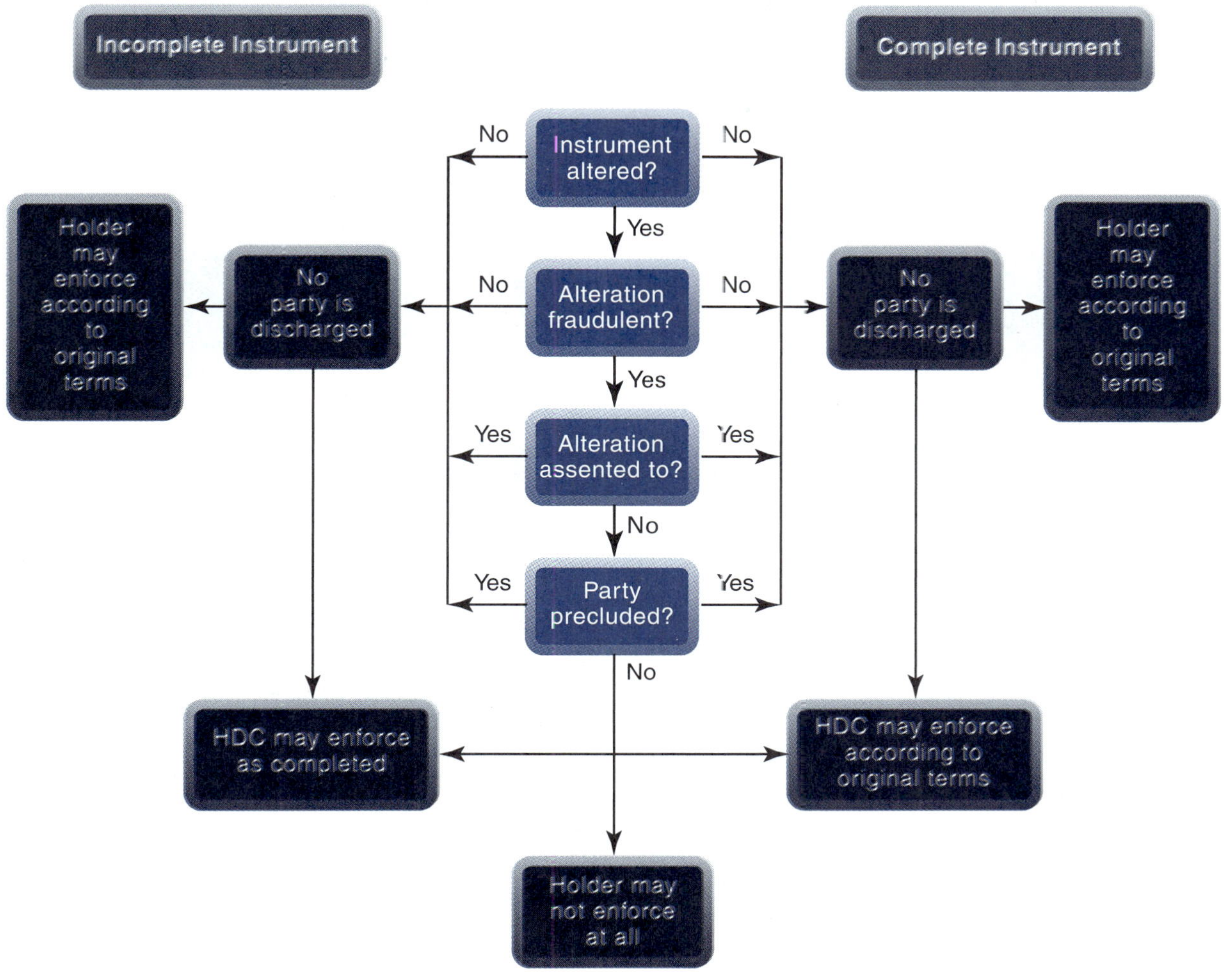

correct amount is set at $2,000, P fraudulently fills in $4,000 and then negotiates the check to T. If T is a holder in due course, she can collect the amount as completed ($4,000) from either M or P. If T is not a holder in due course, however, she has no recourse against M but may recover the full amount ($4,000) from P.

4. Assume the facts in (3), except that P filled in the $4,000 amount in good faith. No party is discharged from liability on the instrument because the alteration was not fraudulent. If T is not a holder in due course, M is liable for the correct amount ($2,000). If T is a holder in due course, T is entitled to receive $4,000 from M because she can enforce an incomplete instrument as completed. Whether or not T is a holder in due course, T may recover $4,000 from P.

PERSONAL DEFENSES

Defenses to an instrument may arise in many ways, either when the instrument is issued or later. In general, the numerous defenses to liability on a negotiable instrument, which are similar to those that may be raised in an action for breach of contract, are available against any holder of the instrument unless she has the rights of a holder in due course. Among the personal defenses are (1) lack of consideration; (2) failure of consideration; (3) breach of contract; (4) fraud in the inducement; (5) illegality that does not render the transaction void; (6) duress, undue influence, mistake, misrepresentation, or incapacity that does not render the transaction void; (7) setoff or counterclaim; (8) discharge of which the holder in due course does not have notice; (9) nondelivery of an instrument,

Figure 26-5
Alteration

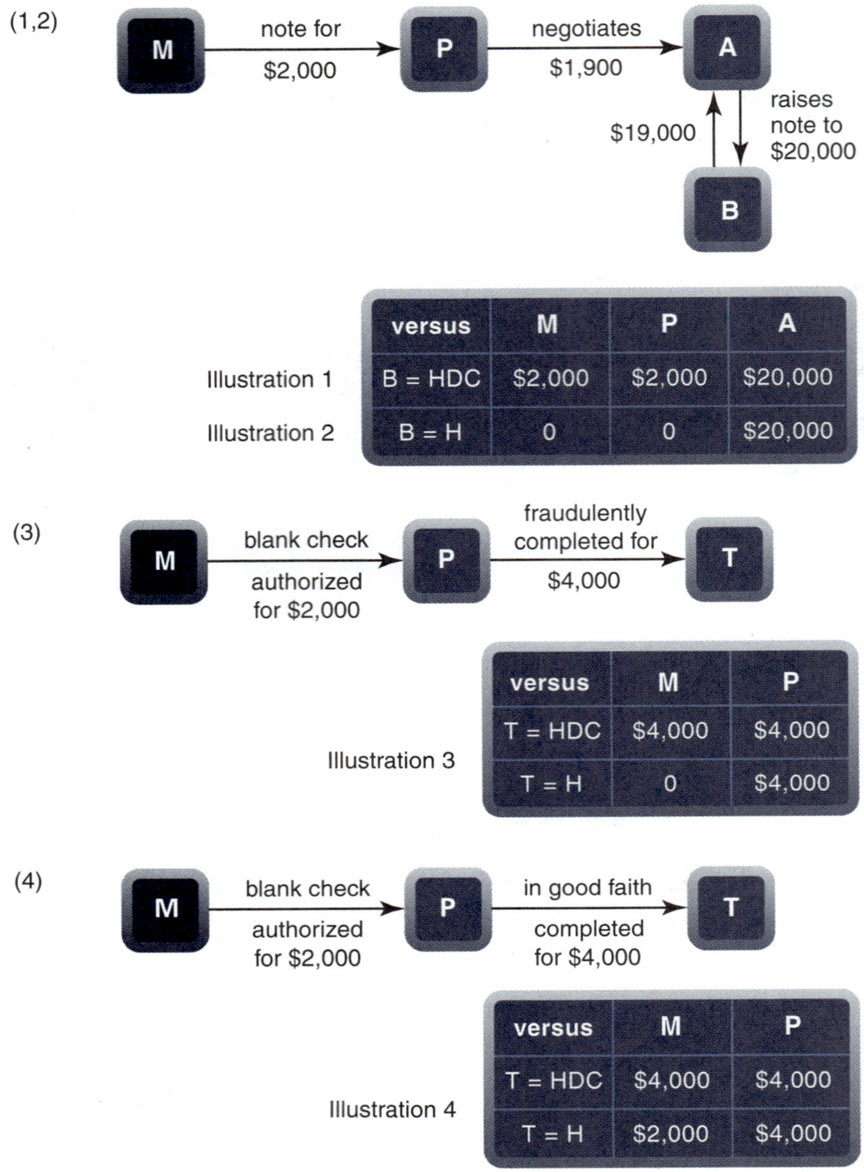

	versus	M	P	A
Illustration 1	B = HDC	$2,000	$2,000	$20,000
Illustration 2	B = H	0	0	$20,000

Illustration 3

versus	M	P
T = HDC	$4,000	$4,000
T = H	0	$4,000

Illustration 4

versus	M	P
T = HDC	$4,000	$4,000
T = H	$2,000	$4,000

whether complete or incomplete; (10) unauthorized completion of an incomplete instrument; (11) payment without obtaining surrender of the instrument; (12) theft of a bearer instrument or of an instrument payable to him; and (13) lack of authority of a corporate officer, agent, or partner as to the particular instrument, where such officer, agent, or partner had general authority to issue negotiable paper for his principal or firm.

These situations are the most common examples, but others exist. Indeed, the Code does not attempt to detail defenses that may be cut off. It is content to state that a holder in due course takes the instrument free and clear of all claims and defenses, except those listed as real defenses. See Figure 26-6 depicting the availability of defenses against holders and holders in due course.

Practical Advice

When taking a negotiable instrument, make sure that you satisfy the requirements for becoming holder in due course.

Figure 26-6
Availability of Defenses against Holders and Holders in Due Course

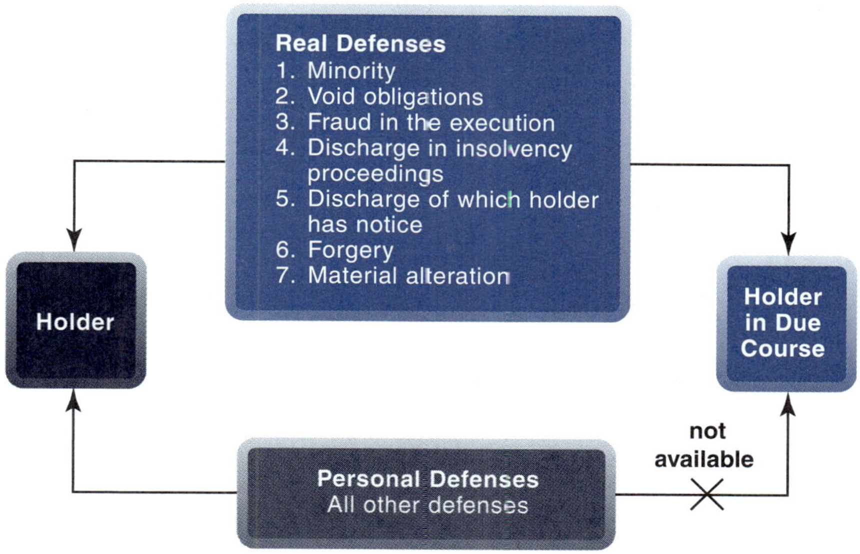

CPA | LIMITATIONS UPON HOLDER IN DUE COURSE RIGHTS

The preferential position enjoyed by a holder in due course has been severely limited by a Federal Trade Commission rule restricting the rights of a holder in due course of an instrument concerning a debt arising out of a ***consumer credit contract***, which includes negotiable instruments. The rule, entitled "Preservation of Consumers' Claims and Defenses," applies to sellers and lessors of consumer goods, which are goods for personal, household, or family use. It also applies to lenders who advance money to finance a consumer's purchase of consumer goods or services. The rule is intended to prevent consumer purchase transactions from being financed in such a manner that the purchaser is legally obligated to make full payment of the price to a third party, even though the dealer from whom she bought the goods committed fraud or the goods were defective. Such obligations arise when a purchaser executes and delivers to a seller a negotiable instrument that the seller negotiates to a holder in due course. The buyer's defense that the goods were defective or that the seller committed fraud, although valid against the seller, is not valid against the holder in due course. See Figure 26-7 illustrating the rights of holders in due course under the FTC rule.

To correct this situation, the Federal Trade Commission rule preserves claims and defenses of consumer buyers and borrowers against holders in due course. The rule states that no seller or creditor can take or receive a consumer credit contract unless the contract contains the conspicuous provision shown below:

> NOTICE: ANY HOLDER OF THIS CONSUMER CREDIT CONTRACT IS SUBJECT TO ALL CLAIMS AND DEFENSES WHICH THE DEBTOR COULD ASSERT AGAINST THE SELLER OF THE GOODS OR SERVICES OBTAINED PURSUANT HERETO OR WITH THE PROCEEDS HEREOF. RECOVERY HEREUNDER BY THE DEBTOR SHALL NOT EXCEED AMOUNTS PAID BY THE DEBTOR HEREUNDER.

The purpose of this notice is to inform any holder in due course of a paper or negotiable instrument that he takes the instrument subject to all claims and defenses that the buyer could assert against the seller. The effect of the rule is to place the holder in due course in the position of an assignee.

Practical Advice

As a consumer, make sure that any negotiable instrument you give in a consumer credit transaction contains the notation required by the FTC. As a transferee of negotiable instruments arising from a consumer credit transaction, recognize that you are subject to all defenses.

Figure 26-7
Rights of Holder in Due Course under FTC Rule

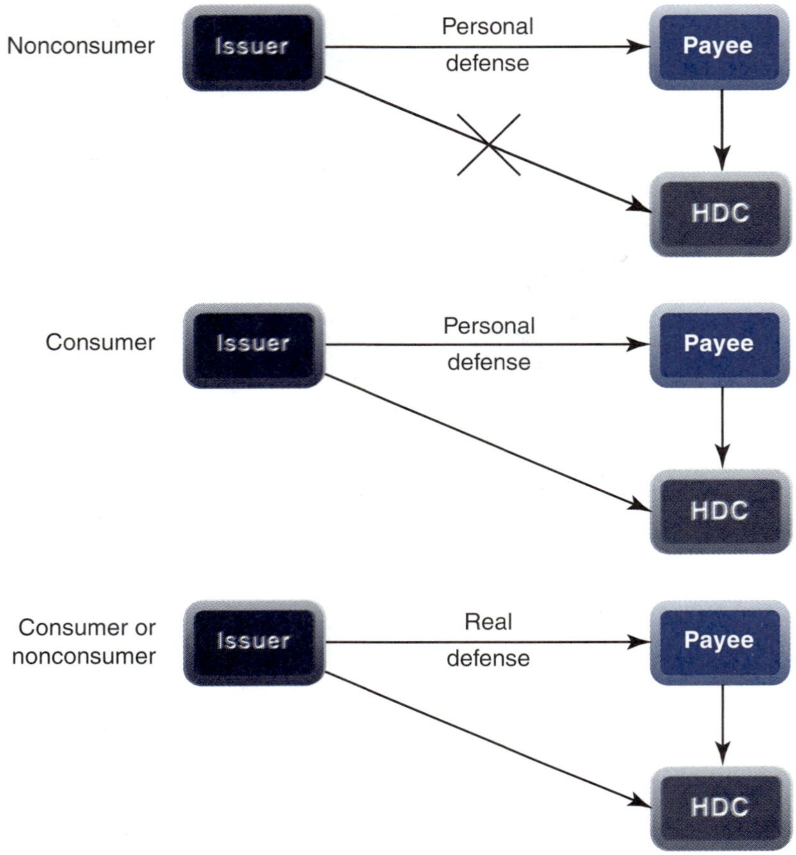

CHAPTER SUMMARY

Requirements of a Holder in Due Course

Holder a person who has both possession of an instrument and all indorsements necessary to it

Value differs from contractual consideration and consists of any of the following:
- the timely performance of legal consideration (which excludes executory promises);
- the acquisition of a security interest in or a lien on the instrument;
- taking the instrument in payment of or as security for an antecedent debt;
- the giving of a negotiable instrument; or
- the giving of an irrevocable commitment to a third party

Good Faith honesty in fact and the observance of reasonable commercial standards of fair dealing

Lack of Notice
- *Notice an Instrument Is Overdue* time paper is overdue after its stated date; demand paper is overdue after demand has been made or after it has been outstanding for an unreasonable period of time
- *Notice an Instrument Has Been Dishonored* dishonor is the refusal to pay or accept an instrument when it becomes due
- *Notice of Claim or Defense* a defense protects a person from liability while a claim is an assertion of ownership

Without Reason to Question Its Authenticity instrument cannot bear such apparent evidence of forgery or alteration or otherwise be so irregular or incomplete as to call into question its authenticity

Holder in Due Course Status

A Payee May Be a Holder in Due Course the payee's rights as a holder in due course are limited to defenses of persons with whom he has not dealt

The Shelter Rule the transferee of an instrument acquires the same rights that the transferor had in the instrument

The Preferred Position of a Holder in Due Course

Real Defenses real defenses are available against all holders, including holders in due course; such defenses are as follows:
- *Infancy*
- *Void Obligations*
- *Fraud in the Execution*
- *Discharge in Insolvency Proceedings*
- *Discharge of Which the Holder Has Notice*
- *Unauthorized Signature*
- *Fraudulent Alteration*

Personal Defenses all other defenses that might be asserted in the case of any action for breach of contract

Limitations on Rights of Holder in Due Course the preferential position of a holder in due course has been severely limited by a Federal Trade Commission rule that applies to consumer credit contracts; under which a transferee of consumer credit contracts cannot take as a holder in due course

QUESTIONS

1. Marcus issues a negotiable promissory note payable to the order of Parish for the amount of $3,000. Parish raises the amount to $13,000 and negotiates it to Hilda for $12,000.
   a. If Hilda is a holder in due course, how much can she recover from Marcus? How much from Parish? If Marcus's negligence substantially contributed to the making of the alteration, how much can Hilda recover from Marcus and Parish, respectively?
   b. If Hilda is not a holder in due course, how much can she recover from Marcus? How much from Parish? If Marcus's negligence substantially contributed to the making of the alteration, how much can Hilda recover from Marcus and Parish, respectively?

2. On December 2, 2004, Miles executed and delivered to Proctor a negotiable promissory note for $1,000, payable to Proctor or order, due March 2, 2005, with interest at 14 percent from maturity, in partial payment of a printing press. On January 3, 2005, Proctor, in need of ready cash, indorsed and sold the note to Hughes for $800. Hughes paid $600 in cash to Proctor on January 3 and agreed to pay the balance of $200 one week later, namely, on January 10. On January 6, Hughes learned that Miles claimed a breach of warranty by Proctor and, for this reason, intended to refuse to pay the note when it matured. On January 10, Hughes paid Proctor $200, in conformity with their agreement of January 3. Following Miles's refusal to pay the note on March 2, 2005, Hughes sues Miles for $1,000. Is Hughes a holder in due course? If so, for what amount?

3. Thornton fraudulently represented to Daye that he would obtain for her a new car to be used in Daye's business for $7,800 from Pennek Motor Company. Daye thereupon executed her personal check for $7,800 payable to the order of Pennek Motor Company and delivered the check to Thornton, who immediately delivered it to the motor company in payment of his own prior indebtedness. The motor company had no knowledge of the representations made by Thornton to Daye. Pennek Motor Company now brings an action on the check against Daye, who defends on the ground of failure of consideration. Is Pennek subject to this defense? Explain.

4. Adams, who reads with difficulty, arranged to borrow $200 from Bell. Bell prepared a note, which Adams read laboriously. As Adams was about to sign it, Bell diverted Adams's attention and substituted the following paper, which was identical to the note Adams had read except that the amounts were different:

   On June 1, 2004, I promise to pay Ben Bell or order Two Thousand Dollars with interest from date at 16 percent. This note is secured by certificate No. 13 for 100 shares of stock of Brookside Mills, Inc.

   Adams did not detect the substitution, signed as maker, handed the note and stock certificate to Bell, and received from Bell $200. Bell indorsed and sold the paper to Fore, a holder in due course, who paid him $1,800. Fore presented the note at maturity to Adams, who refused to pay. What are Fore's rights, if any, against Adams?

5. On January 2, 2004, Martin, seventeen years of age, as a result of Dealer's fraudulent misrepresentation, bought a used motorboat to use in his fishing business for $2,000 from Dealer, signed an installment contract for $1,500, and gave Dealer the following instrument as down payment:

   Dated:________2004

   I promise to pay to the order of Dealer, six months after date, the sum of $500 without interest. This is given as a down payment on an installment contract for a motorboat.

   (signed) Martin

   Dealer, on July 1, sold his business to Henry and included this note in the transaction. Dealer indorsed the note in blank and handed it to Henry, who left the note in his office safe. On July 10, Sharpie, an employee of Henry, without authority, stole the note and sold it to Bert for $300, indorsing the note "Sharpie." At the time, in Bert's presence, Sharpie filled in the date on the note as February 2, 2004. Bert demanded payment from Martin, who refused to pay.

   What are Bert's rights against Martin?

6. McLaughlin borrowed $1,000 from Adler, who, apprehensive about McLaughlin's ability to pay, demanded security. McLaughlin indorsed and delivered to Adler a negotiable promissory note executed by Topping for $1,200 payable to McLaughlin's order in twelve equal monthly installments. The note did not contain an acceleration clause, but it recited that the consideration for the note was McLaughlin's promise to paint and shingle Topping's barn. At the time McLaughlin transferred the note to Adler, the first installment was overdue and unpaid. Adler was unaware that the installment had not been paid. Topping did not pay any of the installments on the note. When the last installment became due, Adler presented the note to Topping for payment. Topping refused upon the ground that McLaughlin had not painted or reshingled her barn.

   What are Adler's rights, if any, against Topping on the note?

7. McEnolly purchased a refrigerator for his home from Perrault Appliance Store for $700. McEnolly paid $200 in cash and signed an installment contract for $500, which in its entirety stated:

   January 15, 2004

   I promise to pay to the order of Perrault Appliance Store the sum of $500 in ten equal monthly installments.

   (signed) McEnolly

   Perrault negotiated the installment contract to Hughes, who took the instrument for value, in good faith, without notice of any claim or defense of any party, and without question of the instrument's authenticity. After McEnolly had paid two installments, the refrigerator ceased operating, and McEnolly wishes to recover his down payment and first two monthly payments and to discontinue further payments. What outcome?

8. Adams, by fraudulent representations, induced Barton to purchase 100 shares of the capital stock of the Evermore Oil Company. The shares were worthless. Barton executed and delivered to Adams a negotiable promissory note for $5,000, dated May 5, in full payment for the shares, due six months after date. On May 20, Adams indorsed and sold the note to Cooper for $4,800. On October 21, Barton, having learned that Cooper now held the note, notified Cooper of the fraud and stated he would not pay the note. On December 1, Cooper negotiated the note to Davis who, while not a party, had full knowledge of the fraud perpetrated on Barton. Upon refusal of Barton to pay the note, Davis sues Barton for $5,000. Is Davis a holder in due course or, if not, does he have the rights of a holder in due course? Explain.

9. Donna gives Peter a check for $5,000 in return for a personal computer. The check is dated December 2. Peter transfers the check for value to Howard on December 14, and Howard deposits it in his bank on December 20. In the meantime, Donna has discovered that the personal computer is not what was promised and has stopped payment on the check. If Peter and Howard disappear, may the bank recover from Donna notwithstanding her defense of failure of consideration? What will be the bank's cause of action?

CASE PROBLEMS

10. Eldon's Super Fresh Stores, Inc., is a corporation engaged in the retail grocery business. William Drexler was the attorney for and the corporate secretary of Eldon's and was also the personal attorney of Eldon Prinzing, the corporation's president and sole shareholder. From January 1998 through January 1999, Drexler maintained an active stock trading account in his name with Merrill Lynch (http://www.ml.com/). Eldon's had no such account. On August 12, 1998, Drexler purchased 100 shares of Clark Oil & Refining Company stock through his Merrill Lynch stockbroker. He paid for the stock with a check drawn by Eldon's, made payable to Merrill Lynch and signed by Prinzing. On August 15, 1998, Merrill Lynch accepted the check as payment for Drexler's stock purchase. There was no communication between Eldon's and Merrill Lynch until November 1999, fifteen months after the issuance of the check. At that time, Eldon's asked Merrill Lynch about the whereabouts of the stock certificate and asserted a claim to its ownership. Does Merrill Lynch qualify as a holder in due course? Why?

11. Consolidated Business Forms leased a Phillips business computer from Benchmark. Benchmark subsequently transferred the lease and promissory note to Exchange International Leasing Corporation. Consolidated stopped making rental payments when the computer malfunctioned, and Exchange International brought this suit to recover the payments due on the promissory note. Consolidated defends on the grounds that Benchmark prevented its agent, Mr. Spohn, from examining the contents of the agreement between the two companies and further represented that the computer would be removed with a complete refund if it failed to operate properly. Is Exchange subject to Consolidated's defense?

12. Litton decided to purchase photocopiers to use in its offices. Angelo Buquicchio, a Royal (a division of Litton) salesman, recommended that Litton lease the machines from Regent. Regent was a company totally independent of Litton and had agreed to give Buquicchio "service fees" or, more appropriately, bribes. Regent borrowed money from Bankers Trust (http://www.bankerstrust.com/) to finance purchases and transferred the Litton leases as security. A clause in the leases permitted transfer and provided that the transferee's rights would be independent of any claims or offsets of Litton as against Regent. Litton defaulted on the obligations, and Litton argues that Regent's bribery of Royal's employee rendered Litton's obligations a nullity and a defense against the banks as holders in due course. Explain whether Litton is correct in its assertion.

13. Walter Duester purchased a John Deere (http://www.deere.com/en_US/deerecom/usa_canada.html) combine from St. Paul Equipment. John Deere Co. was the lender and secured party under the agreement. The combine was pledged as collateral. Duester defaulted on his debt, and the manager of St. Paul, Hansen, was instructed to repossess the combine. Hansen went to Duester's farm to accomplish this. Duester told him that he had received some payments for custom combining and would immediately purchase a cashier's check to pay the John Deere debt. Hansen followed Duester to the defendant, Boelus State Bank. Hansen remained outside, and Duester returned in a few minutes with a cashier's check in the amount of the balance of his indebtedness payable to John Deere. The check had been signed by an authorized bank employee. When John Deere, however, presented the check to the bank for payment shortly thereafter, the bank refused to pay, claiming that Duester acquired the cashier's check by theft. Is John Deere subject to this defense? Why?

14. Turman executed a deed of trust note for $107,500.00 payable to Ward's Home Improvement, Inc. The note was consideration for a contract by which Ward was to construct a home on property by Turman, and the note was secured by a deed of trust on that property. Later that day, Ward executed a separate written assignment of the note to Pomerantz. This document specifically uses the word "assigns." Ward did not endorse the note to Pomerantz or otherwise write upon the note. Ward received $95,000.00 for the assignment from Pomerantz. Ward failed to complete the house and to do so will require the expenditure of an additional $42,000.00. Is Pomerantz a holder in due course of the $107,500.00 note? Explain.

15. Stephens delivered 184 bushels of corn to Aubrey, for which he was to receive $478.23. Aubrey issued a check with $478.23 typewritten in numbers, and on the line customarily used to express the amount in words appeared "$100478 and 23 cts" imprinted in red with a check-writing machine. Before Stephens cashed the check, someone crudely typed "100" in front of the typewritten $478.23. When Stephens presented this check to the State Bank of Salem, Anderson, the manager, questioned Stephens. Anderson knew that Stephens had just declared bankruptcy and was not accustomed to making such large deposits. Stephens told Anderson he had bought and sold a large quantity of corn at a great profit. Anderson accepted the explanation, applied the monies to nine promissory notes, an installment payment, and accrued interest owed by Stephens. Stephens also received $2,000 in cash, with the balance deposited in his checking account.

Later that day, Anderson reexamined the check and discovered the suspicious appearance of the typewriting. He then contacted Aubrey, who said a check in that amount was suspicious, whereupon Anderson froze the transaction. When Aubrey stopped payment on the check, the bank sustained a $28,193.91 loss because Stephens could not be located. The bank then sued Aubrey for the loss. Explain who should bear the risk of loss.

http:// **Internet Exercise** Find information about the FTC's rule governing holders in due course.

Chapter 27

Liability of Parties

The truth shall be thy warrant . . .

Sir Walter Raleigh (1552–1618)

Learning Objectives

After reading this chapter you should be able to:

1. Explain contractual liability, warranty liability, and liability of conversion.
2. Explain the liability of makers, acceptors, drawers, drawees, indorsers, and accommodation parties.
3. Identify and discuss the condition precedents to the liability of secondary parties.
4. Explain the methods by which liability on an instrument may be terminated.
5. Compare the warranties on transfer with the warranties on presentment.

The preceding chapters discussed the requirements of negotiability, the transfer of negotiable instruments, and the preferred position of a holder in due course. When parties issue negotiable instruments, they do so with the expectation that they, either directly or indirectly, satisfy their obligation under the instrument. Likewise, when a person accepts, indorses, or transfers an instrument, he incurs liability for the instrument under certain circumstances. This chapter examines the liability of parties arising out of negotiable instruments and the ways in which liability may be terminated.

Two types of potential liability are associated with negotiable instruments: contractual liability and warranty liability. The law imposes **contractual liability** on those who *sign*, or have a representative agent sign, a negotiable instrument. Because some parties to a negotiable instrument never sign it, they never assume contractual liability.

Warranty liability, on the other hand, is not based on signature; thus, it may be imposed on both signers and nonsigners. **Warranty liability** applies (1) to persons who transfer an instrument and (2) to persons who obtain payment or acceptance of an instrument.

CONTRACTUAL LIABILITY

All parties whose signatures appear on a negotiable instrument incur certain contractual obligations, unless they disclaim liability. The *maker* of a promissory note and the *acceptor* of a draft assume primary, or unconditional, liability, subject to valid claims and defenses, to pay according to the terms of the instrument at the time they sign it or as completed according to the rules for incomplete instruments, discussed in Chapter 26. **Primary liability** means that a party is legally obligated to pay without the holder's having to resort first to another party. *Indorsers* of all instruments incur secondary, or conditional, liability if the instrument is not paid.

Secondary liability means that a party is legally obligated to pay only after another party, who is expected to pay, fails to do so. The liability of drawers of drafts and checks is also conditional because it is generally contingent upon the drawee's dishonor of the instrument. A *drawee* has ***no*** liability on the instrument until he *accepts* it.

An **accommodation party** signs the instrument to lend her credit to another party to the instrument and is a direct beneficiary of the value received. The liability of an accommodation party, who generally signs as a co-maker, or anomalous indorser, is determined by the capacity in which she signs. If the accommodation party signs as a maker, she incurs primary liability; if she signs as an anomalous indorser, she incurs secondary liability.

CPA SIGNATURE

The word **signature**, as discussed in Chapter 24, is broadly defined to include any name, word, or mark, whether handwritten, typed, printed, or in any other form, made with the intention of authenticating an instrument. The signature may be made by the individual herself or on her behalf by the individual's authorized agent.

AUTHORIZED SIGNATURES

Authorized agents often execute negotiable instruments on behalf of their principals. The agent is not liable if she is authorized to execute the instrument and does so properly (e.g., "Prince, principal, by Adams, agent"). If these two conditions are met, then only the principal is liable on the instrument. (For a comprehensive discussion of the principal-agent relationship, see Chapters 29 and 30.)

Occasionally, however, the agent, although fully authorized, uses an inappropriate form of signature that may mislead holders or prospective holders as to the identity of the obligor. Although incorrect signatures by agents assume many forms, they can be conveniently sorted into three groups. In each of these instances the intention of the original parties to the instrument is that the principal is to be liable on the instrument and the agent is not.

The first type occurs when an agent signs only his own name to an instrument, neither indicating that he is signing in a representative capacity nor stating the name of the principal. For example, Adams, the agent of Prince, makes a note on behalf of Prince but signs it "Adams." The signature does not indicate that Adams has signed in a representative capacity or that he has made the instrument on behalf of Prince. The second type of incorrect form occurs when an authorized agent indicates that he is signing in a representative capacity but does not disclose the name of his principal. For example, Adams, executing an instrument on behalf of Prince, merely signs it "Adams, agent." The third type of inappropriate signature occurs when an agent reveals both her name and her principal's name, but does not indicate that she has signed in a representative capacity. For example, Adams, signing an instrument on behalf of Prince, signs it "Adams, Prince."

In all three situations, the agent is liable on the instrument only to a holder in due course without notice that Adams was not intended to be liable. Because contract and agency law determine Prince's liability on the instrument, Prince is liable to all holders. Under Revised Article 3, if a representative (an agent) signs his name as the drawer of a *check* without indicating his representative status and the check is payable from an account of the represented person (the principal) who is identified on the check, the representative is not liable on the check if he is an authorized agent. Some courts reached this result under prior Article 3.

> **Practical Advice**
>
> If you are acting as an agent for another party, make sure that you properly sign any negotiable instrument by indicating your representative capacity and the identity of the principal. If you do that, you will avoid potential liability.

Cohen v. Disner

California Court of Appeal, 1995
36 Cal.App.4th 855, 42 Cal.Rptr.2d 782, 27 UCC Rep.Serv.2d 540

FACTS Attorney Eliot Disner tendered a check for $100,100 to Sidney and Lynne Cohen. In drawing the check, Disner was serving as an intermediary for his clients, Irvin and Dorothea Kipnes, who owed the money to the Cohens as part of a settlement agreement. The Kipneses had given Disner checks totaling $100,100, which he had deposited into his professional corporation's client trust account. After confirming with the Kipneses' bank that their account held sufficient funds, Disner wrote and delivered a trust account check for $100,100 to the

Cohens' attorney, with this note: "Please find $100,100 in settlement (partial) of *Cohen v. Kipnes*, et al[.] Per our agreement, delivery to you constitutes timely delivery to your clients." Also typed on the check was a notation identifying the underlying lawsuit.

Without Disner's knowledge, the Kipneses stopped payment on their checks, leaving insufficient funds in the trust account to cover the check to the Cohens. The trust account check therefore was not paid due to insufficient funds; the Kipneses declared bankruptcy; and the Cohens served Disner and his professional corporation (jointly, Disner) with demand for payment. The Cohens sought the amount written on the check plus a $500 statutory penalty. The trial court entered summary judgment for Disner, reasoning he is not liable on the check because he was a mere conduit or agent for transferring money from the Kipneses to the Cohens. The Cohens appeal from the judgment.

DECISION Judgment affirmed.

OPINION Ortega, J. [California] Civil Code § 1719, subdivision (a) provides in part that any person who draws a check that is dishonored due to insufficient funds shall be liable to the payee for the amount owing upon the check and treble damages of at least $100, not to exceed $500.

* * *

The Cohens do not appeal that Disner was a mere conduit or agent for transferring funds. They contend his representative status and motivations for transferring the funds are irrelevant. According to the Cohens, § 1719 imposes strict liability against the [drawer] of a check drawn on an account lacking sufficient funds.

Their contention of strict liability is based on legislative omission. While the UCC permits the [drawer] of a dishonored check to prove that he signed in a representative capacity and that the holder in due course took the check with notice of the representative's lack of liability (UCC, § 3–402, subd. (b)(2), sometimes hereinafter referred to as the "representative capacity" defense), § 1719 does not mention this defense.

* * *

The UCC recognizes the complexity of commercial transactions beyond the few good faith disputes mentioned in § 1719. For example, as against a holder in due course, the UCC permits the [drawer] to assert defenses of infancy, duress, lack of legal capacity, illegality of the contract, fraud in the inducement, or discharge in bankruptcy proceedings. (UCC, § 3–305, subd. (a).) If we were to accept the Cohens' position that § 1719 is a strict liability statute (with the sole exception of the stop payment defense), we would create a conflict with the pre-existing law of negotiable instruments. * * *

Nothing in § 1719 affirmatively supports the Cohens' contention that the "representative capacity" and other UCC defenses were written out of § 1719. On the contrary, the express language of subdivision (a) compels us to the opposite conclusion.

* * *

By acknowledging there must be an enforceable obligation to pay, § 1719 echoes the UCC, which precludes recovery where the payee has no "right to enforce the obligation of a party to pay an instrument." (UCC, § 3–305, subd. (a).) If the [drawer] has no enforceable obligation to pay a dishonored check, there is no amount "owing upon that check" under the plain language of § 1719.

* * *

We reject the Cohens' assertion in their reply brief that the "representative capacity" defense is inapplicable here because the conditions of UCC § 3–402, subdivision (c) have not been met. That subdivision provides: "If a representative signs the name of the representative as drawer of a check without indication of the representative status and the check is payable from an account of the representative person who is identified on the check, the signer is not liable on the check if the signature is an authorized signature of the represented person."

According to the official code comment on that subdivision: "Subdivision (c) is directed at the check cases. It states that if the check identifies the represented person, the agent who signs on the signature line does not have to indicate agency status. Virtually all checks used today are in personalized form which identify the person on whose account the check is drawn. In this case, nobody is deceived into thinking that the person signing the check is meant to be liable. * * * " [Citation.]

As we understand it, the Cohens' assertion is that because UCC § 3–402, subdivision (b)(2)'s "representative capacity" defense is "subject to" subdivision (c), Disner may not be relieved of liability unless he fulfills the requirements of the subdivision (c) defense. We do not read subdivisions (b)(2) and (c) in that restrictive manner. In our view, any finding of liability under UCC § 3–402, subdivision (b)(2) is subject to subdivision (c)'s additional exception that the representative is not liable if he signed his name on a personalized check identifying the account of the represented person. Subdivision (c) expands rather than contracts the representative's defenses.

We conclude that § 1719, by its clear and unambiguous language, permits the [drawer] of a dishonored check to prove he has no enforceable obligation to pay the check.

INTERPRETATION When a holder has notice that the drawer's signature is in the capacity of an agent, the drawer is not personally liable on the instrument.

CRITICAL THINKING QUESTION When should an agent be liable on an instrument that she signs?

UNAUTHORIZED SIGNATURES

Unauthorized signatures include both forgeries and signatures made by an agent without authority. Though generally not binding on the person whose name appears on the instrument, the unauthorized signature is binding upon the unauthorized signer, whether her own name appears on the instrument or not, to any person who in good faith pays or gives value for the instrument. Thus, if Adams, without authority, signed Prince's name to an instrument, Adams, not Prince, would be liable on the instrument. The rule, therefore, is an exception to the principle that only those whose names appear on a negotiable instrument can be liable on it.

Ratification of Unauthorized Signature An unauthorized signature may be *ratified* by the person whose name appears on the instrument. Although the ratification may relieve the actual signer from liability on the instrument, it does not itself affect any rights the person ratifying the signature may have against the actual signer.

Negligence Contributing to Forged Signature Any person who by his negligence substantially contributes to the making of a forged signature may not assert the lack of authority as a defense against a holder in due course or a person who in good faith pays the instrument or takes it for value or for collection. Nevertheless, if the person asserting the preclusion also fails to exercise reasonable care, Revised Article 3 adopts a comparative negligence standard.

Practical Advice

Exercise diligence to guard against forged signatures on your negotiable instruments.

CPA LIABILITY OF PRIMARY PARTIES

There is a primary party on every note: the *maker*. The maker's commitment is unconditional. No one, however, is unconditionally liable on a draft or check as issued. A *drawee* is *not* liable on the instrument unless he accepts it. If, however, the drawee accepts the draft, after which he is known as the *acceptor*, the drawee becomes primarily liable on the instrument. **Acceptance** or, in the case of a check, certification is the drawee's signed promise to pay a draft as presented. Presentment (that is, a demand for payment) is not a condition to the holder's right to recover from parties with primary liability.

MAKERS

The **maker** of a note is obligated to pay the instrument according to its terms at the time of issuance or, if the instrument is incomplete, according to its terms when completed, as discussed in Chapter 26. The obligation of the maker is owed to a person entitled to enforce the instrument or to an indorser who paid the instrument.

Primary liability also applies to issuers of cashier's checks and to issuers of drafts drawn on the drawer (that is, where the issuer is both the drawee and the drawer).

ACCEPTORS

A drawee has no liability on the instrument until she accepts it, at which time the drawee becomes an **acceptor** and, like the maker, primarily liable. The acceptor becomes liable on the draft according to its terms at the time of acceptance or as completed according to the rules for incomplete instruments as discussed in Chapter 26. Nevertheless, if the acceptor does not state the amount accepted and the amount of the draft is later raised, a subsequent holder in due course can enforce the instrument against the acceptor according to the terms at the time the holder in due course took possession. Thus, an acceptor should always indicate on the instrument the amount that it is accepting. The acceptor owes the obligation to pay a person entitled to enforce the instrument or to the drawer or an indorser who paid the draft under drawer's or indorser's liability.

An acceptance must be written on the draft. Having met this requirement, it may take many forms. It may be printed on the face of the draft, ready for the drawee's signature. It may consist of a rubber stamp, with the signature of the drawee added. It may be the drawee's signature, preceded by a word or phrase such as "Accepted," "Certified," or "Good." It may consist of nothing more than the drawee's signature. Normally, but by no means necessarily, an acceptance is written vertically across the face of the draft. It must not, however, contain any words indicating an intent to refuse to honor the draft. Furthermore, no writing separate from the draft and no oral statement or conduct of the drawee will convert the drawee into an acceptor.

Checks, when accepted, are said to be certified. **Certification** is a special type of acceptance consisting of the drawee bank's promise to pay the check when subsequently presented for payment.

The drawee bank has no obligation to certify a check, and its refusal to certify does not constitute dishonor of the instrument. If the drawee refuses to accept or pay the instrument, he may be liable to the drawer for breach of contract.

CPA LIABILITY OF SECONDARY PARTIES

Parties with secondary (conditional) liability do not unconditionally promise to pay the instrument; rather, they engage to pay the instrument if the party expected to pay does not do so. The drawer is liable if the drawee dishonors the instrument. Indorsers (including the payee if he indorses) of an instrument are also conditionally liable; their liability is subject to the conditions of dishonor and notice of dishonor. If an instrument is *not* paid by the party expected to pay and the conditions precedent to the liability of a secondary party are satisfied, a secondary party is liable unless he has disclaimed liability or possesses a valid defense to the instrument.

DRAWERS

A drawer of a draft orders the drawee to pay the instrument and does not expect to pay the draft personally. The drawer is obligated to pay the draft only if the drawee fails to pay the instrument. The drawer of an *unaccepted draft* is obligated to pay the instrument upon its dishonor according to its terms at the time it was issued or, in the case of an incomplete instrument, according to the rules discussed in Chapter 26. Under Revised Article 3, the drawer's liability is contingent only upon dishonor and does not require notice of dishonor. The drawer's obligation on an unaccepted draft is owed to a person entitled to enforce the instrument or to an indorser who paid the instrument under indorser's liability.

If the draft has been accepted and the acceptor is not a bank, the obligation of the drawer to pay the instrument is then contingent upon both dishonor of the instrument and notice of dishonor; the drawer's liability in this instance is equivalent to that of an indorser.

Davis v. Watson Brothers Plumbing, Inc.

Court of Civil Appeals of Texas, Dallas, 1981
615 S.W.2d 844

FACTS Arnett Lee presented a $152.38 check for cashing to the plaintiff, liquor store operator Troy Davis. After Davis gave Lee the cash, Lee requested a bottle of scotch and a six-pack of beer. As Davis turned to fill the order, a thief stole $110.00 of the $152.38. Lee immediately contacted the defendant-drawer of the check, Watson Brothers Plumbing, Inc., and notified them of the loss. The defendant then issued another check for $152.38 and stopped payment on the first check held by Davis. Davis brought this action against the defendant for the full face amount of the check.

DECISION Judgment for Davis for $152.38.

OPINION Akin, J. "Holder" is defined in *Tex. Bus. & Com. Code Ann.* [UCC] § 1.201(20) as: "[A] person *who is in possession* of a document of title or *an instrument* or an investment security drawn, issued or indorsed to him or to his order or to bearer or *in blank*." Under the undisputed facts, Lee, the payee indorsed the check in blank to plaintiff, who is now in possession of the check. Thus, as a matter of law, plaintiff is a "holder" under the code [U.C.C.] § 3.413(2), [Revised § 3–414(b)] which sets forth the rights of a holder, [and] provides, in pertinent part, that: "The drawer engages that upon dishonor of the draft * * * *he will pay the amount of the draft to the holder* or to any indorser who takes it up." Thus, the defendant is liable to the holder of the dishonored check unless the defendant has raised a valid defense against the holder.

The rights of a holder not in due course are subject to the defenses specified in § 3.306, [Revised § 3–3051] which provides:

> Unless he has the rights of a holder in due course any person takes the instrument subject to
>
> (1) all valid claims to it on the part of any person; and
>
> (2) all defenses of any party which would be available in an action on a simple contract; and
>
> (3) *the defenses of want or failure of consideration*, nonperformance of any condition precedent, nondelivery, or delivery for a special purpose (Section 3.408); and
>
> (4) the defense that he or a person through whom he holds the instrument acquired it by theft, or that payment or satisfaction to such holder would be inconsistent with

the terms of a restrictive indorsement. *The claim of any third person to the instrument is not otherwise available as a defense to any party liable thereon unless the third person himself defends the action for such party.*

Defendant here asserts that it may raise want or failure of consideration in the transaction between *plaintiff and Lee*, its payee, as a defense to plaintiff's enforcement of the instrument against it. We disagree.

[UCC] § 3.408 [Revised §§ 3–303(b), 3–305] provides, in pertinent part that: "Want or failure of consideration is a defense against any person not having the rights of a holder in due course * * *." The comments to § 3.408 provide that: "'Consideration' to what the obligor has received for his obligation, and is important only on the question of whether his obligation can be enforced against him." Thus, any holder can enforce the obligation of a draft against the drawer regardless of whether the holder gave anything in consideration for the draft to his indorser. The drawer can assert as a defense to enforcement of the draft want or failure of consideration only to the extent such defense lies against the payee of the draft. Thus, the fact that a holder remote to the drawer's transaction with the payee did not give full consideration for the draft is not a defense available to the drawer. [Citation.]

This is true because the drawer's sole obligation on the check is to pay it according to its tenor. Consequently, the fact that the transfer of the check by the payee to the transferee is without consideration is immaterial to the drawer's obligation and is not a defense available to the drawer against the holder. A similar conclusion was reached in [citation]. In that case the court held that a defendant maker was not the proper party to raise as a defense that the transfer of the note to the holder was void. Consequently, that court concluded that the maker could not assert the defense that the equitable ownership of the instrument was in someone other than the holder-plaintiff.

The rationale of this, and other decisions, reaching the same conclusion, is that the maker or drawer of an instrument admittedly owes the money and he should not be permitted to bring into the controversy equities of parties with which he has no connection. [Citation.] Furthermore, if the drawer or maker is permitted to assert the defense of another party such as the payee, the judgment on that issue would not be binding on the third party claimant who is not a party to the suit. [Citation.]

Because defendant here may not assert want or failure of consideration in the transaction between plaintiff and Lee, and because defendant has asserted no other defense against plaintiff, plaintiff is entitled to recover the full face value of the check under § 3–413(b) [Revised § 3–414] of the Texas Uniform Commercial Code.

INTERPRETATION The drawer's liability is contingent upon dishonor of the instrument.

CRITICAL THINKING QUESTION Should the drawer be permitted to raise defenses of other parties to the instrument? Explain.

INDORSERS

An indorser promises that, upon dishonor of the instrument *and* notice of dishonor, she will pay the instrument according to the terms of the instrument at the time it was indorsed or, if an incomplete instrument when indorsed, according to its terms when completed, as discussed in Chapter 26. Once again, this obligation is owed to a person entitled to enforce the instrument or to a subsequent indorser who paid the instrument under indorser's liability.

EFFECT OF ACCEPTANCE

When a *draft* is accepted by a *bank*, the drawer and all prior indorsers are discharged. The liability of indorsers subsequent to certification is not affected. When the bank accepts a draft, it should withhold from the drawer's account funds sufficient to pay the instrument. Because the bank is primarily liable on its acceptance and has the funds, whereas the drawer does not, the discharge is reasonable.

DISCLAIMER OF LIABILITY BY SECONDARY PARTIES

Both drawers and indorsers *may* disclaim their normal conditional liability by drawing or indorsing an instrument "*without recourse.*" However, drawers of *checks* may not disclaim contractual liability. The use of the qualifying words *without recourse* is understood to place purchasers on notice that they may not rely on the credit of the person using this language. A person drawing or indorsing an instrument in this manner does not incur the normal contractual liability of a drawer or indorser to pay the instrument, but he may nonetheless be liable for breach of warranty.

Practical Advice

If you take an instrument from another party, make sure that she unqualifiedly indorses the instrument to add her liability to it.

CONDITIONS PRECEDENT TO LIABILITY

A *condition precedent* is an event or events that must occur before liability arises. The condition precedent to the liability of the drawer of an *unaccepted* draft is dishonor. Conditions precedent to the liability of any indorser or the drawer of an *accepted* draft by a nonbank are dishonor and notice of dishonor. If the conditions to secondary liability are not met, a party's conditional obligation on the instrument is discharged, unless the conditions are excused.

Dishonor Dishonor generally involves the refusal to pay an instrument when it is presented. **Presentment** is a demand made by or on behalf of a person entitled to enforce the instrument for (1) *payment* by the drawee or other party obligated to pay the instrument or (2) *acceptance* by the drawee of a draft. The return of any instrument for lack of necessary indorsements or for failure of the presentment to comply with the terms of the instrument, however, is not a dishonor.

What constitutes dishonor varies depending on the type of instrument and whether presentment is required.

1. *Notes*: A *demand note* is dishonored if the maker does not pay it on the day of presentment. If the note is payable at a *definite time* and (1) the terms of the note require presentment or (2) the note is payable at or through a bank, the note is dishonored if it is not paid on the date it is presented or its due date, whichever is later. All *other time notes* need not be presented and are dishonored if they are not paid on their due dates. Nevertheless, because makers are primarily liable on their notes, their liability is not affected by failure of proper presentment.
2. *Drafts*: An *unaccepted draft* (other than a check, discussed below) that is payable on *demand* is dishonored if presentment is made and it is not paid on the date presented. A *time draft* presented for *payment* is due on the due date or presentment date, whichever is later. A *time draft* presented for *acceptance* prior to its due date is dishonored if it is not accepted on the day presented. Refusal to *accept a demand instrument* is not a dishonor, although acceptance may be requested. Of course, if an instrument is payable at a certain time period after acceptance or sight, a refusal to accept the draft on the day presented is a dishonor.

   An *accepted demand draft* is dishonored if the acceptor (who is primarily liable on the instrument) does not pay it on the day presented for payment. An *accepted time draft* is dishonored if it is not paid on the due date for payment or on the presentment date, whichever is later.

   Drawers, with the exception of drafts accepted by a bank, are not discharged from liability by a delay in presentment. Once an instrument has been properly presented and dishonored, a drawer becomes liable to pay the instrument. As previously indicated, drawers and prior indorsers are discharged from liability when a draft is accepted by a bank.
3. *Checks*: If a *check* is presented for payment directly to the payor/drawee bank for immediate payment, a refusal to pay the check on the day presented constitutes dishonor. In the more common situation of a check being presented through the normal collection process, a check is dishonored if the payor bank makes timely return of the check, sends timely notice of dishonor or nonpayment, or becomes accountable for the amount of the check (until that payment has been made, the check is dishonored). As more fully explained in Chapter 28, under Article 4 a bank in most instances has a midnight deadline (before midnight of the next banking day) in which to decide whether to honor or dishonor an instrument. Thus, depending on the number of banks involved in the collection process, the time for dishonor can vary greatly.

Delay in presentment discharges an *indorser* only if the instrument is a check and it is not presented for payment or given to a depositary bank for collection within thirty days after the day the indorsement was made. The same rule does not apply, however, to a drawer. If a person entitled to enforce a check fails to present a check within thirty days after its date, the drawer will be discharged only if the delay deprives the drawer of funds because of the suspension of payments by the drawee bank such as would result from a bank failure. This discharge is quite unlikely because of federal bank insurance but would be available where an account is not fully insured because it exceeds $100,000 or because the account doesn't qualify for deposit insurance.

> **Practical Advice**
>
> Make sure that you timely and properly present any negotiable instrument that you possess for acceptance or payment.

Notice of Dishonor The obligation of an indorser of any instrument and of a drawer of a draft accepted by a nonbank is not enforceable unless the indorser or drawer is given notice of dishonor or the notice is otherwise excused. Thus, lack of proper notice discharges the liability of an indorser; for this purpose a drawer of a draft accepted by a party other than a bank is treated as an indorser. Notice of dishonor is *not* required to retain the liability of drawers of unaccepted drafts. In addition, as previously mentioned, a drawer is discharged when a draft is accepted by a *bank*. In short, a drawer's liability is *usually* not contingent upon receiving notice of dishonor, whereas an indorser's liability is.

Notice of dishonor is normally given by the holder or by an indorser who has received notice. For example, Michael makes a note payable to the order of Phyllis; Phyllis indorses it to Arthur; Arthur indorses it to Bambi; and Bambi indorses it to Henry, the last holder. Henry presents it to Michael within a reasonable time, but Michael refuses to pay. Henry may give notice of dishonor to all secondary parties: Phyllis, Arthur, and Bambi. If he is satisfied that Bambi will pay him or if he does not know how to contact Phyllis or Arthur, he may notify only Bambi, who then must see to it that Arthur or Phyllis is notified, or she will have no recourse. Bambi may notify either or both. If she notifies Arthur only, Arthur will have to see to it that Phyllis is notified, or Arthur will have no recourse. When properly given, notice benefits all parties who have rights on the instrument against the party notified. Thus, Henry's notification to Phyllis operates as notice to Phyllis by both Arthur and Bambi. Likewise, if Henry notifies only Bambi and Bambi notifies Arthur and Phyllis, then Henry has the benefit of Bambi's notification of Arthur and Phyllis. Nonetheless, it would be advisable for Henry to give notice to all prior parties because Bambi may be insolvent and thus may not bother to notify Arthur or Phyllis.

If, in the above example, Henry were to notify Phyllis alone, Arthur and Bambi would be discharged. Because she has no claim against Arthur or Bambi, who indorsed after she did, Phyllis would have no ground for complaint. It cannot matter to Phyllis that she is compelled to pay Henry rather than Arthur. Therefore, subsequent parties are permitted to skip intermediate indorsers if they want to discharge them and are willing to look solely to prior indorsers for recourse.

Any necessary notice must be given by a *bank* before midnight on the *next* banking day following the banking day on which it receives notice of dishonor. Any *nonbank* with respect to an instrument taken for collection must give notice within thirty days following the day on which it received notice. In all other situations, notice of dishonor must be within thirty days following the day on which dishonor occurred. For instance, Donna draws a check on Youngstown Bank payable to the order of Pablo; Pablo indorses it to Andrea; Andrea deposits it to her account in Second Chicago National Bank; Second Chicago National Bank properly presents it to Youngstown Bank, the drawee; and Youngstown dishonors it because the drawer, Donna, has insufficient funds on deposit to cover it. Youngstown has until midnight of the following day to notify Second Chicago National, Andrea or Pablo, of the dishonor. Second Chicago National then has until midnight on the day after receipt of notice of dishonor to notify Andrea or Pablo. That is, if Second Chicago National received the notice of dishonor on Monday, it would have until midnight on Tuesday to notify Andrea or Pablo. If it failed to notify Andrea, it could not charge the item back to her. Andrea, in turn, has thirty days after receipt of notice of dishonor to notify Pablo. Donna, a drawer of an unaccepted draft, is not discharged from liability for failure to receive notice of dishonor.

Frequently, notice of dishonor is given by returning the unpaid instrument with an attached stamp, ticket, or memorandum stating that the item was not paid and requesting that the recipient make good on it. But because the purpose of notice is to give knowledge of dishonor and to inform the secondary party that he may be held liable on the instrument, any kind of notice that informs the recipient of potential liability is sufficient. No formal requisites are imposed—notice may be given by any commercially reasonable means, including oral, written, or electronic communication. An oral notice, while sufficient, is inadvisable because it may be difficult to prove. Notice of dishonor must reasonably identify the instrument.

Practical Advice

Upon dishonor of any instrument that you have presented for payment or acceptance, give proper notice, wherever possible, to all prior parties.

Presentment and Notice of Dishonor Excused The Code excuses *presentment* for payment or acceptance if (1) the person entitled to enforce the instrument cannot with reasonable diligence present the instrument; (2) the maker or acceptor of the instrument has repudiated the obligation to pay, is dead, or is in insolvency proceedings; (3) the terms of the instrument do not require presentment to hold the indorsers or drawer liable; (4) the drawer or indorser has waived the right of presentment; (5) the drawer instructed the drawee not to pay or accept the draft; or (6) the drawee was not obligated to the drawer to pay the draft.

Notice of dishonor is excused if the terms of the instrument do not require notice to hold the party liable or if notice has been waived by the party whose obligation is being enforced. Moreover, a waiver of presentment is also a waiver of notice of dishonor. Finally, delay in giving notice of dishonor is excused if the delay is caused by circumstances beyond the control of the person giving notice and that person exercised reasonable diligence in giving notice after the cause of the delay ceased to exist.

LIABILITY OF CONVERSION

Conversion is a *tort* by which a person becomes liable in damages because of his wrongful control over the personal property of another. The law applicable to conversion of personal property applies to instruments. An instrument is so converted if the instrument "is taken by transfer, other than by negotiation, from a person *not* entitled to enforce the instrument or a bank makes or obtains payment with respect to the instrument for a person *not* entitled to enforce the instrument or receive payment." (Section 3–420(a).) Examples of conversion thus would include a drawee bank that pays an instrument containing a forged indorsement or a bank that pays an instrument containing only one of two required indorsements.

CPA TERMINATION OF LIABILITY

Eventually, every commercial transaction must end, terminating the potential liabilities of the parties to the instrument. The Code specifies the various methods by and extent to which the liability of *any* party, primary or secondary, is discharged. It also specifies when the liability of all parties is discharged. No discharge of a party is effective against a subsequent holder in due course, however, unless she has notice of the discharge when taking the instrument. In addition, discharge of liability is not always final; liability under certain circumstances (e.g., coming into possession of a subsequent holder in due course) can be revived.

PAYMENT

The most obvious and common way for a party to discharge liability on an instrument is to pay a party entitled to enforce the instrument. An instrument is paid to the extent that payment is made by or for a person obligated to pay the instrument and to a person entitled to enforce the instrument. Subject to three exceptions, such payment results in a discharge even though it is made with knowledge of another person's claim to the instrument, unless such other person either supplies adequate indemnity or obtains an injunction in a proceeding to which the holder is made a party.

Practical Advice

The person making payment should take possession of the instrument or have it canceled—marked "paid" or "canceled"—so that it cannot pass to a subsequent holder in due course against whom his discharge would be effective.

TENDER OF PAYMENT

Any party liable on an instrument who makes proper tender of full payment to a person entitled to enforce the instrument when or after payment is due is discharged from liability for interest after the due date. If the party's tender is refused, she is not discharged from liability for the face amount of the instrument or for any interest accrued until the time of tender. Moreover, if an instrument requires presentment and the obligor is ready and

CONCEPT REVIEW

Contractual Liability

Party	Instrument	Liability	Conditions
Maker	Note	Unconditional	None
Acceptor	Draft	Unconditional	None
Drawer	Unaccepted draft	Conditional	Dishonor
	Draft accepted by a nonbank	Conditional	Dishonor and notice
	Cashier's check	Unconditional	None
	Draft drawn on drawer	Unconditional	None
	Draft accepted by a bank	None	
	Draft (not check) drawn without recourse	None	
Indorser	Note or draft	Conditional	Dishonor and notice
	Draft subsequently accepted by a bank	None	
	Note or draft indorsed without recourse	None	
Drawee	Draft	None	

able to pay the instrument when it is due at the place of payment specified in the instrument, such readiness is the equivalent of tender.

Occasionally a person entitled to enforce an instrument will refuse a tender of payment for reasons known only to himself. It may be that he believes his rights exceed the amount of the tender or that he desires to enforce payment against another party. In any event, his refusal of the tender wholly discharges to the extent of the amount of tender every party who has a right of recourse against the party making tender.

CANCELLATION AND RENUNCIATION

The Code provides that a person entitled to enforce an instrument may discharge the liability of any party to an instrument by an intentional voluntary act, such as by canceling the instrument or the signature of the party or parties to be discharged, by mutilating or destroying the instrument, by obliterating a signature, or by adding words indicating a discharge. A party entitled to enforce an instrument may also renounce his rights by a writing, signed and delivered, promising not to sue or otherwise renouncing rights against the party. Like other discharges, however, a written renunciation is of no effect against a subsequent holder in due course who takes without knowledge of the renunciation.

Cancellation or renunciation is effective even without consideration.

LIABILITY BASED ON WARRANTY

Article 3 imposes two types of implied warranties: (1) transferor's warranties and (2) presenter's warranties. Although these warranties are effective whether the transferor or presenter signs the instrument or not, the extension of the transferor's warranty to subsequent holders does depend on whether one or the other has indorsed the instrument. Like other warranties, these may be disclaimed by agreement between immediate parties. In the case of an indorser, his disclaimer of transfer warranties and presentment warranties must appear in the indorsement itself and be effective, except with respect to checks. Such disclaimers must be specific, such as "without warranty." The use of "without recourse" will only disclaim contract liability, not warranty liability.

CPA WARRANTIES ON TRANSFER

Any person who transfers an instrument, whether by negotiation or assignment, and receives consideration makes certain **transferor's warranties**. Any consideration sufficient to support a contract will support transfer warranties. If transfer is by delivery alone, warranties on transfer run only to the immediate transferee. If the transfer is made by indorsement, whether qualified or unqualified, the transfer warranty runs to "any subsequent transferee." Transfer means that the delivery of possession is voluntary. The warranties of the transferor are as follows.

ENTITLEMENT TO ENFORCE

The first warranty that the Code imposes on a transferor is that the transferor is a person entitled to enforce the instrument. This warranty "is in effect a warranty that there are no unauthorized or missing indorsements that prevent the transferor from making the transferee a person entitled to enforce the instrument." The following example illustrates this rule. Mitchell makes a note payable to the order of Penelope. A thief steals the note from Penelope, forges Penelope's indorsement, and sells the instrument to Aaron. Aaron is not entitled to enforce the instrument because the break in the indorsement chain prevents him from being a holder. If Aaron transfers the instrument to Judith for consideration, Judith can hold Aaron liable for breach of warranty. The warranty action is important to Judith because it enables her to hold Aaron liable, even if Aaron indorsed the note "without recourse."

AUTHENTIC AND AUTHORIZED SIGNATURES

The second warranty imposed by the Code is that all signatures are authentic and authorized. In the example presented above, this warranty would also be breached. If, however, the signature of a maker, drawer, drawee, acceptor, or indorser not in the chain of title is unauthorized, there is a breach of this warranty but no breach of the warranty of entitlement to enforce.

NO ALTERATION

The third warranty is the warranty against alteration. Suppose that Maureen makes a note payable to the order of the payee in the amount of $100. The payee, without authority, alters the note so that it appears to be drawn for $1,000 and negotiates the instrument to Lois, who buys it without knowledge of the alteration. Lois, indorsing "without recourse," negotiates the instrument to Kyle for consideration. Kyle presents the instrument to Maureen, who refuses to pay more than $100 on it. Kyle can collect the difference from Lois, for although her qualified indorsement saves Lois from liability to Kyle on the indorsement contract, she is liable to him for breach of warranty. If Lois had not qualified her indorsement, Kyle would be able to recover against her on the basis of either warranty or the indorsement contract.

NO DEFENSES

The fourth transferor's warranty imposed by the Code is that the instrument is not subject to a defense or claim in recoupment of any party. A claim in recoupment, as discussed in Chapter 26, is a counterclaim that arose from the transaction that gave rise to the instrument. Suppose that Madeline, a minor and a resident of a state where minors' contracts for nonnecessaries are voidable, makes a note payable to bearer in payment of a motorcycle. Pierce, the first holder, negotiates it to Iola by mere delivery. Iola indorses it and negotiates it to Justin, who unqualifiedly indorses it to Hector. All negotiations are made for consideration. Because of Madeline's minority (a real defense), Hector cannot recover upon the instrument against Iola. Hector therefore recovers against Justin or Iola on either the breach of warranty that no valid defenses exist to the instrument or the indorsement contract. Justin, if he is forced to pay Hector, can in turn recover against Iola on either a breach of warranty or the indorsement contract. Justin, however, cannot recover against Pierce. Pierce is not liable to Justin as an indorser because he did not indorse the instrument. Although Pierce, as a transferor, warrants that there are no defenses good against him, this warranty extends only to his immediate transferee, Iola. Therefore, Justin cannot hold Pierce liable. Iola, however, can recover from Pierce on either warranty or contract.

NO KNOWLEDGE OF INSOLVENCY

Any person who transfers a negotiable instrument warrants that he has no knowledge of any insolvency proceedings instituted with respect to the maker, acceptor, or drawer of an unaccepted instrument. Insolvency proceedings include bankruptcy and "any assignment for the benefit of creditors or other proceedings intended to liquidate or rehabilitate the estate of the person involved." Thus, if Marcia makes a note payable to bearer, and the first holder, Taylor, negotiates it for consideration without indorsement to Ursula, who then negotiates it for consideration by qualified indorsement to Valerie, both Taylor and Ursula warrant that they do not know that Marcia is in bankruptcy. Valerie could not hold Taylor liable for breach of warranty, however, because Taylor's warranty runs only in favor of her immediate transferee, Ursula, because Taylor transferred the instrument without indorsement. If Valerie could hold Ursula liable on her warranty, Ursula could thereupon hold Taylor, her immediate transferor, liable. Figure 27-1 summarizes liabilities on transfer.

CPA WARRANTIES ON PRESENTMENT

Any party who pays or accepts an instrument must do so in strict compliance with the orders that instrument contains. For example, the payment or acceptance must be made to a person entitled to receive payment or acceptance, the amount paid or accepted must be the correct amount, and the instrument must be genuine and unaltered. If the payment or acceptance is incorrect, the payor or acceptor potentially will incur a loss. In the case of a note, a maker who pays the wrong person will not be discharged from his obligation to pay the correct person. If the maker pays too much, the excess comes out of his pocket. If a drawee pays the wrong person, he generally cannot charge the drawer's account; if the drawee pays too much, he generally cannot charge the drawer's account for the excess. Indorsers who pay an instrument may make similar incorrect payments.

After paying or accepting an instrument to the wrong person, for the wrong amount, or in some other incorrect way, does the person who incorrectly paid or accepted have any recourse against the person who received the payment or acceptance? The Code addresses this critical question by providing that "if an instrument has been paid or accepted by mistake . . . the person paying or accepting may, to the extent permitted by the law governing mistake and restitution, (i) recover the payment from the person to whom or for whose benefit payment was made or (ii) in the case of acceptance, may revoke the acceptance." Nevertheless, this payment or acceptance is *final* and may not be asserted against a person who took the instrument in good faith and for value or who in good faith changed position in reliance on the payment or acceptance, unless there has been a breach of the implied **warranties on presentment**. What warranties are given by presenters depend upon who is

Figure 27-1
Liability on Transfer

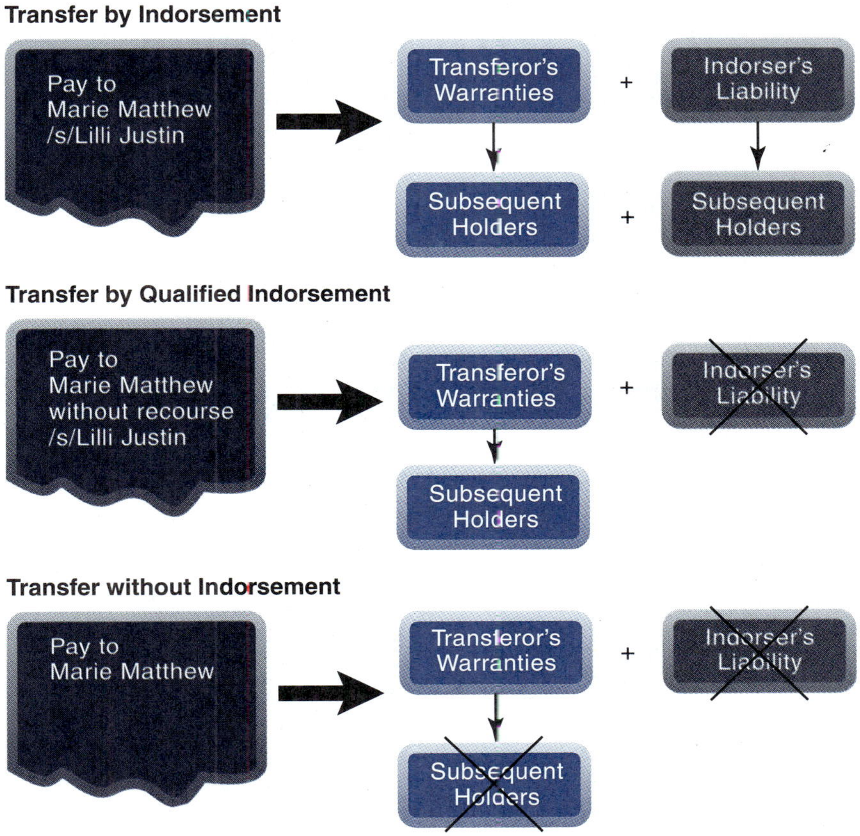

the payor or acceptor. The greatest protection is given to drawees of unaccepted drafts, while all other payors receive significantly less protection.

DRAWEES OF UNACCEPTED DRAFTS

A drawee of an unaccepted draft (including uncertified checks), who pays or accepts in good faith, receives a presentment warranty from the person obtaining payment or acceptance and from all prior transferors of the draft. These parties warrant to the drawee making payment or accepting the draft in good faith that: (1) the warrantor is a person entitled to enforce the draft, (2) the draft has not been altered, and (3) the warrantor has no knowledge that the drawer's signature is unauthorized.

Entitled to Enforce Presenters of unaccepted checks give the same warranty of entitlement to enforce to persons who pay or accept as is granted to transferees under the transferor's warranty. Thus, the presenter warrants that she is a person entitled to enforce the instrument. As explained above, this warranty extends to the genuineness and completeness of the indorser's signatures but not to the signature of the drawer or maker. It is "in effect a warranty that there are no unauthorized or missing indorsements."

For example, if Donnese draws a check to Peter or order, and Peter's indorsement is forged, the bank does not follow Donnese's order in paying such an item and therefore cannot charge her account (except in the impostor or fictitious payee situations discussed in Chapter 25). The bank, however, can recover for breach of the presenter's warranty of entitlement to enforce the instrument from the person who obtained payment of the check from the bank. Although it should know the signatures of its own customers, the bank should not be expected to know the signatures of payees or other indorsers of checks; the bank, therefore, should not have to bear this loss.

Travelers Indemnity Co. v. Stedman

U.S. District Court, Eastern District of Pennsylvania, 1995
895 F.Supp. 742, 27 UCC Rep.Serv.2d 1347

FACTS In November 1988, the plaintiff, Travelers Indemnity Co. (http://www.travelers.com), issued a comprehensive crime insurance policy to the American Lung Association (ALA) **(http://www.lungusa.org/)**, insuring the ALA against financial losses due to employee fraud or dishonesty. Shortly thereafter, in October of 1989, the ALA hired the defendant, Nancy Stedman, as the Director of Bureau Affairs. In this capacity, Stedman embezzled $129,624.23 of ALA funds by writing seventeen checks against the ALA's account with Merrill, Lynch, Pierce, Fenner & Smith (Merrill Lynch). Stedman deposited six of these checks into her personal checking account with the other defendant, Main Line Federal Savings Bank (Main Line). The checks were subsequently presented to and honored by Merrill Lynch. These checks bore two forged drawer's signatures and at least one forged indorsement. To recover its losses in paying the ALA's insurance claim, Travelers sued Stedman, Main Line, and Merrill Lynch. Merrill Lynch subsequently advanced a claim for indemnity and for breach of presentment warranties against Main Line. Main Line seeks judgment on the pleadings or partial summary judgment on Merrill Lynch's claims.

DECISION Judgment for Main Line.

OPINION Reed, J. B. Liability, or loss allocation, under the Uniform Commercial Code ("UCC") for honoring negotiable instruments containing forged or unauthorized signatures is governed by whether the forgery at issue is that of a [drawer's] signature or of the indorsement of a payee or holder. [Citations.] Generally, a drawee bank is strictly liable to its customer, the drawer, for payment over either a forged [drawer's] signature or a forged indorsement. [Citation.] * * * Moreover, when a drawee bank honors an instrument bearing a forged [drawer's] signature, that payment is final in favor of a holder in due course or one who has in good faith changed his position in reliance on the payment. UCC § 3–418. As a result, where the only forgery is of the signature of the [drawer] and not of the indorsement, the negligence of a holder in taking the forged instrument will not allow a drawee bank to shift liability to a prior collecting or depositary bank, unless such negligence amounts to a lack of good faith, or unless the payee bank returns the instrument or sends notice of dishonor within the limited time provided by § 4–301 of the UCC. [Citation.] But where the only forged signature is an indorsement, the drawee normally may pass liability back through the collection chain to the depositary or collecting bank, or to the forger herself if she is available, by a claim for breach of presentment warranties. [Citation.]

Regrettably, the drafters of the UCC failed to address the allocation of liability for honoring instruments containing *both* a forged [drawer's] signature and a forged indorsement, so called "double forgeries." [Citation.] Nor have the state courts of Pennsylvania addressed this issue. Based on a thorough examination of the rationales behind the allocation of liability in "single forgery" cases, however, the Court of Appeals for the Fifth Circuit concluded that double forgeries should be treated as though only containing forged [drawer's] signatures. [Citations.] * * * Therefore, this court concludes that under Pennsylvania's adoption of the UCC, checks containing both a forged [drawer's] signature and a forged indorsement should be treated, for loss allocation purposes, as though bearing only a forged [drawer's] signature.

* * *

The final count of the crossclaim by Merrill Lynch is a claim for an alleged breach of presentment warranties under [UCC] § 3–417. As the court illustrated above, the loss allocation rules of the UCC permit a payee bank to shift liability to a depositary bank via a claim for breach of presentment warranties if, and only if, the checks at issue contain only forged indorsements. Should the checks in fact also bear forged [drawer's] signatures, then a depositary or collecting bank is immunized from liability for having honored such checks unless the depositary or collecting bank failed to meet the requirements of the final payment rule codified in [UCC] § 3–418. [Citation.] Moreover, checks bearing dual forgeries are treated as though containing only forged [drawer's] signatures. Thus, because it is uncontested that all Group Two checks bear forged [drawer's] signatures, liability for honoring these checks may only be assessed under the loss allocation rules relevant to checks bearing only forged [drawer's] signatures. In other words, Merrill Lynch is precluded by the operation of law from asserting a claim for breach of presentment warranties under the loss allocation scheme of the UCC.

INTERPRETATION The presentment warranties extend to the genuineness of the indorser's signatures but not to the signature of the drawer.

CRITICAL THINKING QUESTION Should the warranties for negotiable instruments treat the forgeries of drawers' signatures differently from those of indorsers? Explain.

No Alteration Presenters also give a warranty of no alteration. For example, if Dolores makes a check payable to Porter's order in the amount of $30, and the amount is fraudulently raised to $30,000, the drawee bank cannot charge to the drawer's account the $30,000 it pays out on the check. The drawee bank can charge the drawer's account only $30, because that is all the drawer ordered it to pay. Nonetheless, because the presenter's warranty of no alteration has been breached, the drawee bank can collect the difference from all warrantors.

Genuineness of Drawer's Signature Presenters lastly warrant that they have no knowledge that the signature of the drawer is unauthorized. Thus, unless the presenter has knowledge that the drawer's signature is unauthorized, the drawee bears the risk that the drawer's signature is unauthorized.

Figure 27-2 summarizes liabilities based on warranty.

ALL OTHER PAYORS

In all instances other than a drawee of an unaccepted draft or uncertified check, the only presentment warranty that is given is that the warrantor is a person entitled to enforce the instrument or is authorized to obtain payment on behalf of the person entitled to enforce the instrument. This warranty is given by the person obtaining payment and prior transferors and applies to the presentment of notes and accepted drafts for the benefit of any party obliged to pay the instrument, including an indorser. It also applies to presentment of dishonored drafts if made to the drawer or an indorser.

The warranties of no alteration and authenticity of the drawer's signature are not given to all other payors. These warranties are not necessary for makers and drawers as they should know their own signatures and the terms of their instruments. Similarly, indorsers have already warranted the authenticity of signatures and that the instrument was not altered. Finally, acceptors should know the terms of the instrument when they accepted it; moreover, they did receive the full presentment warranties when they as drawees accepted the draft upon presentment.

Figure 27-2
Liability Based on Warranty

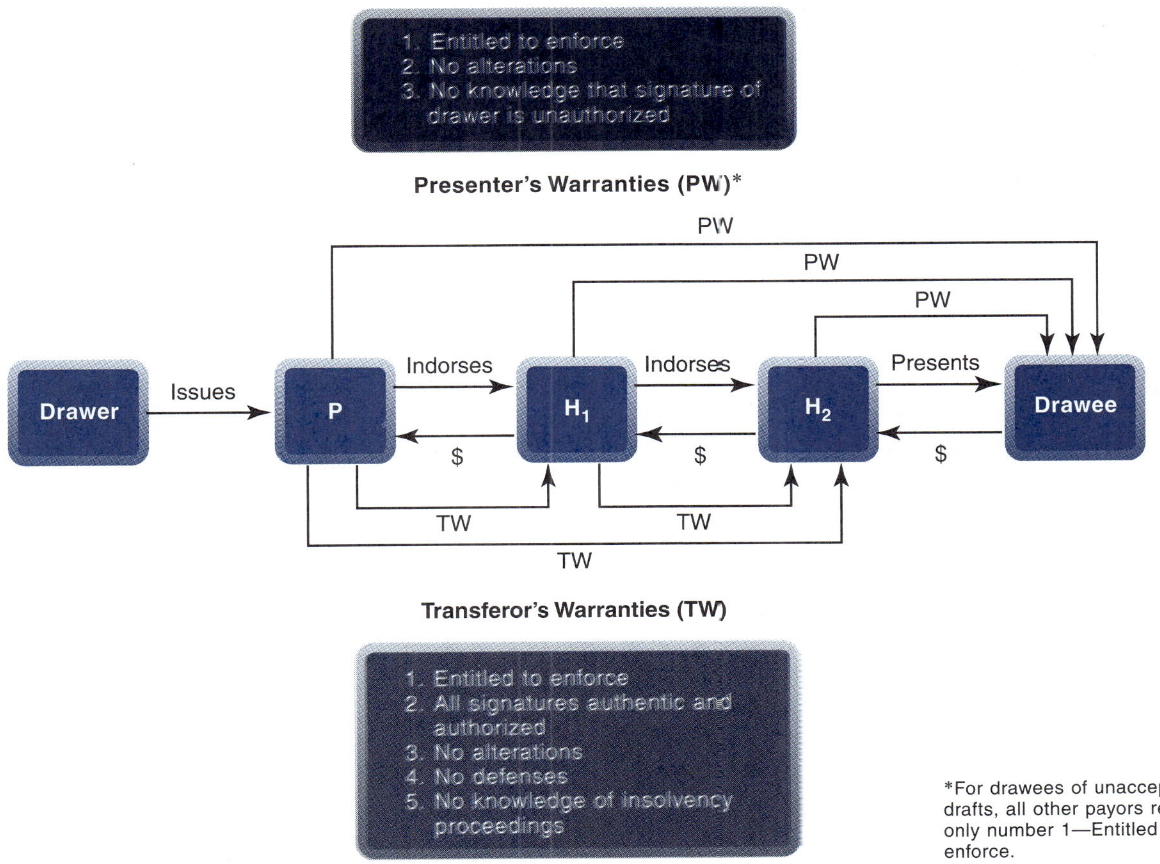

*For drawees of unaccepted drafts, all other payors receive only number 1—Entitled to enforce.

Ethical Dilemma

Who Gets to Pass the Buck on a Forged Indorsement?

FACTS Tom West goes to Libertyville Currency Exchange to cash a check for $3,525. The check belongs to West's friend, John Reston, who accompanies him. The check is a certified check drawn on NationsBank and made payable to the order of "Piscitello Enterprises, Inc." and indorsed on the reverse side by "Joe Piscitello."

Because West often transacts business at the currency exchange, the clerk, Rita Bosworth, recognizes him as soon as he walks in. West indorses the check and hands it to Bosworth, who dispenses the cash. West immediately turns to Reston, giving him some money.

Later, Libertyville Currency Exchange deposits the check with First National Bank, which eventually files a claim against the currency exchange because the indorsement "Joe Piscitello" has been forged. The currency exchange pays the claim, then brings an action against West.

During the trial, Bosworth testifies that she saw Reston hand some money back to West when the two men turned away from her. West vehemently denies this. He says that he received no money in exchange for helping Reston.

Libertyville Currency Exchange claims that West breached his warranty of good title under the transferor's warranty by obtaining payment for a check on which the payee's indorsement was forged. West, on the other hand, argues that he signed the check to lend his name to another party and that he is thus an accommodation party. He maintains that he is not liable to Libertyville Currency Exchange because NationsBank did not give him timely notice that the signature on the check was forged and also because the Currency Exchange paid the check, thus releasing him from liability as an accommodation indorser.

Social, Policy, and Ethical Considerations

1. How could the bank have prevented this problem? Is a clerk responsible for knowing exactly who is cashing a check and who gave value for it? What steps, if any, could Rita Bosworth have taken to verify the check's indorsements?
2. Did Tom West have a responsibility to ensure that his friend's check was legitimate? Should he have inquired about the indorsement?
3. What issues relating to the transfer of a negotiable instrument are involved here? What liability does the bank face? What liability does Tom West face? What warranties apply to each party?

Chapter Summary

Contractual Liability

General Principles

Liability on the Instrument no person has contractual liability on an instrument unless her signature appears on it

Signature a signature may be made by the individual herself or by her authorized agent
- *Authorized Signatures* an agent who executes a negotiable instrument on behalf of his principal is not liable if the instrument is executed properly and as authorized
- *Unauthorized Signatures* include forgeries and signatures made by an agent without proper power; are generally not binding on the person whose name appears on the instrument but are binding on the unauthorized signer

Liability of Primary Parties

Primary Liability absolute obligation to pay a negotiable instrument

Makers the maker guarantees that he will pay the note according to its original terms

Acceptors a drawee has no liability on the instrument until she accepts it; the drawee then becomes primarily liable
- *Acceptance* a drawee's signed engagement to honor the instrument
- *Certification* acceptance of a check by a bank

Liability of Secondary Parties

Secondary (Conditional) Liability obligation to pay a negotiable instrument that is subject to conditions precedent

Indorsers and Drawers if the instrument is not paid by a primary party and if the conditions precedent to the liability of secondary parties are satisfied, indorsers and drawers are secondarily (conditionally) liable unless they have disclaimed their liability or have a valid defense to the instrument

Effect of Acceptance when a draft is accepted by a bank, the drawer and all prior indorsers are discharged from contractual liability

Disclaimer by Secondary Parties a drawer (except of a check) or indorser may disclaim liability by a qualified drawing or indorsing ("without recourse")

Conditions Precedent to Liability
- *Drawer* liability is generally contingent only upon dishonor and does not require notice
- *Indorser* liability is contingent upon dishonor and notice of dishonor

Liability of Conversion

Tort Liability conversion occurs (1) when a drawee refuses to return a draft that was presented for acceptance, (2) when any person refuses to return an instrument after he dishonors it, or (3) when an instrument is paid on a forged indorsement

Termination of Liability

Effect of Discharge potential liability of parties to the instrument is terminated

Discharge
- *Performance*
- *Tender of Payment* for interest, costs, and attorneys' fees
- *Cancellation*
- *Renunciation*

Liability Based on Warranty

Warranties on Transfer

Parties
- *Warrantor* any person who transfers an instrument and receives consideration makes certain transferor's warranties
- *Beneficiary* if the transfer is by delivery, the warranties run only to the immediate transferee; if the transfer is by indorsement, the warranties run to any subsequent holder who takes the instrument in good faith

Warranties
- *Entitled to Enforce*
- *All Signatures Are Authentic and Authorized*
- *No Alteration*
- *No Defenses*
- *No Knowledge of Insolvency*

Warranties on Presentment

Parties
- *Warrantors* all people who obtain payment or acceptance of an instrument as well as all prior transferors give the presenter's warranties
- *Beneficiary* the presenter's warranties run to any person who in good faith pays or accepts an instrument

Warranties
- *Entitled to Enforce*
- *No Alteration*
- *No Knowledge That Drawer's Signature Is Unauthorized*

QUESTIONS

1. $800.00 Smalltown, Illinois
November 15, 2005
The undersigned promises to pay to the order of John Doe, Nine Hundred Dollars with interest from date of note. Payment to be made in five monthly installments of One Hundred Eighty Dollars, plus accrued interest beginning on December 1, 2005. In the event of default in the payment of any installment or interest on installment date, the holder of this instrument may declare the entire obligation due and owing and proceed forthwith to collect the balance due on this instrument.

(signed) Acton, agent

On December 18, no payment having been made on the note, Doe indorsed and delivered the instrument to Todd to secure a preexisting debt in the amount of $800.

On January 18, 2006, Todd brought an action against Acton and Phi Corporation, Acton's principal, to collect the full amount of the instrument with interest. Acton defended on the basis that he signed the instrument in a representative capacity and that Doe had failed to deliver the consideration for which the instrument had been issued. Phi Corporation defended on the basis that it did not sign the instrument and that its name does not appear on the instrument.

For what amount, if any, are Acton and Phi Corporation liable?

2. While employed as a night watchman at the place of business of A. B. Cate Trucking Company, Fred Fain observed that the office safe had been left unlocked. It contained fifty payroll checks, which were ready for distribution to employees two days later. The checks had all been signed by the sole proprietor, Cate. Fain removed five of these checks and two blank checks that were also in the safe. Fain forged the indorsements of the payees on the five payroll checks and cashed them at local supermarkets. He then filled out one of the blank checks, making himself payee, and forged Cate's signature as drawer. After cashing that check at a supermarket, Fain departed by airplane to Jamaica. The six checks were promptly presented for payment to the drawee bank, the Bank of Emanon, which paid each one. Shortly thereafter, Cate learned about the missing payroll checks and forgeries and demanded that the Bank of Emanon credit his account with the amount of the six checks.

Must the Bank comply with Cate's demand? What are the Bank's rights, if any, against the supermarkets? You may assume that the supermarkets cashed all of the checks in good faith.

3. A negotiable promissory note executed and delivered by B to C passed in due course to and was indorsed in blank by C, D, E, and F. G, the present holder, strikes out D's indorsement. What is the liability of D on her indorsement?

4. On June 15, 1998, Joanne, for consideration, executed a negotiable promissory note for $10,000, payable to Robert on or before June 15, 2004. Joanne subsequently suffered financial reverses. In January of 2004, Robert, on two occasions, told Joanne that he knew she was having a difficult time, that he, Robert, did not need the money, and that the debt should be considered completely canceled with no other act or payment being required. These conversations were witnessed by three persons, including Larry. On March 15, 2004, Robert changed his mind and indorsed the note for value to Larry. The note was not paid by June 15, 2004, and Larry sued Joanne for the amount of the note. Joanne defended on the ground that Robert had canceled the debt and renounced all rights against Joanne and that Larry had notice of this fact. Has the debt been properly canceled? Explain.

5. Tate and Fitch were longtime friends. Tate was a man of considerable means; Fitch had encountered financial difficulties. To bolster his failing business, Fitch desired to borrow $6,000 from Farmers Bank of Erehwon. To accomplish this, he persuaded Tate to aid him in the making of a promissory note by which it would appear that Tate had the responsibility of maker, but with Fitch's agreeing to pay the instrument when due. Accordingly, they executed the following instrument:

December 1, 2004

Thirty days after date and for value received, I promise to pay to the order of Frank Fitch the sum of $6,000.

/s/ Timothy Tate

On the back of the note, Fitch indorsed, "Pay to the order of Farmers Bank of Erehwon /s/ Frank Fitch" and delivered it to the bank in exchange for $6,000.

a. When the note was not paid at maturity, may the bank, without first demanding payment by Fitch, recover in an action on the note against Tate?
b. If Tate voluntarily pays the note to the bank, may he then recover on the note against Fitch, who appears as an indorser?

6. Alpha orally appointed Omega as his agent to find and purchase for him a 1930 Dodge automobile in good condition,

and Omega located such a car. Its owner, Roe, agreed to sell and deliver the car on January 10, 2004, for $9,000. To evidence the purchase price, Omega mailed to Roe the following instrument:

$9,000.00 December 1, 2003

We promise to pay to the order of bearer Nine Thousand Dollars with interest from date of this instrument on or before January 10, 2004. This note is given in consideration of John Roe's transferring title to and possession of his 1930 Dodge automobile.

(Signed) Omega, agent

Smith stole the note from Roe's mailbox, indorsed Roe's name on the note, and promptly discounted it with Sunset Bank for $8,700. Not having received the note, Roe sold the car to a third party. On January 10, 2004, the bank, having discovered all the facts, demanded payment of the note from Alpha and Omega. Both refused payment.

a. What are Sunset Bank's rights with regard to Omega?
b. What are Sunset Bank's rights with regard to Roe and Smith?

7. In payment of the purchase price of a used motorboat that had been fraudulently misrepresented, Young signed and delivered to Armstrong his negotiable note in the amount of $2,000 due October 1, with Selby as an accommodation co-maker. Young intended to use the boat for his fishing business. Armstrong indorsed the note in blank preparatory to discounting it. Tillman stole the note from Armstrong and delivered it to McGowan on July 1 in payment of a past-due debt in the amount of $600 that he owed to McGowan, with McGowan making up the difference by giving Tillman his check for $800 and an oral promise to pay Tillman an additional $600 on October 1.

When McGowan demanded payment of the note on December 1, both Young and Selby refused to pay the note because the note had not been presented for payment on its due date and because Armstrong had fraudulently misrepresented the motorboat for which the note had been executed.

What are McGowan's rights, if any, against Young, Selby, Tillman, and Armstrong, respectively?

8. On July 1, Anderson sold D'Aveni, a jeweler, a necklace containing imitation gems, which Anderson fraudulently represented to be diamonds. In payment for the necklace, D'Aveni executed and delivered to Anderson her promissory note for $25,000 dated July 1 and payable on December 1 to Anderson's order with interest at 12 percent per annum.

The note was thereafter successively indorsed in blank and delivered by Anderson to Bylinski, by Bylinski to Conrad, and by Conrad to Shearson, who became a holder in due course on August 10. On November 1, D'Aveni discovered Anderson's fraud and immediately notified Anderson, Bylinski, Conrad, and Shearson that she would not pay the note when it became due. Bylinski, a friend of Shearson, requested that Shearson release him from liability on the note, and Shearson, as a favor to Bylinski and for no other consideration, struck out Bylinski's indorsement.

On November 15, Shearson, who was solvent and had no creditors, indorsed the note to the order of Frederick, his father, and delivered it to Frederick as a gift. At the same time, Shearson told Frederick of D'Aveni's statement that D'Aveni would not pay the note when it became due. Frederick presented the note to D'Aveni for payment on December 1, but D'Aveni refused to pay. Thereafter, Frederick gave due notice of dishonor to Anderson, Bylinski, and Conrad.

What are Frederick's rights, if any, against Anderson, Bylinski, Conrad, and D'Aveni on the note?

9. Saul sold goods to Bruce, warranting that the goods were of a specified quality. The goods were not of the quality warranted, however, and Saul knew this at the time of the sale. Bruce drew and delivered a check payable to Saul and drawn on Third National Bank in the amount of the purchase price. Bruce subsequently discovered the goods were faulty and stopped payment on the check. Can Saul recover payment from Bruce? Why?

CASE PROBLEMS

10. R & A Concrete Contractors, Inc., executed a promissory note that identifies both R & A Concrete and Grover Roberts as its makers. On the reverse side of the note, the following appears: "X John Ament Sec. & Treas." National Bank of Georgia, the payee, now sues both R & A Concrete and Ament on the note. What rights does National Bank have against R&A and Ament?

11. On August 10, 2001, Theta Electronic Laboratories, Inc. executed a promissory note to George and Marguerite Thomson. Three other individuals, Gerald Exten, Emil O'Neil, and James Hane, and their wives also indorsed the note. The Thomsons then transferred the note to Hane on November 26, 2002. Although a default occurred at this time, it was not until April 2003, eighteen months later, that Hane gave notice of the dishonor and made a demand for payment on the Extens as indorsers. Are the Extens liable under their indorser's liability?

http:// **Internet Exercise** Find information discussing the liability of drawers, drawees, makers and indorsers.

CHAPTER 28

Bank Deposits, Collections, and Funds Transfers

Money is a poor man's credit card.

MARSHALL MCLUHAN, QUOTED IN *MACLEAN'S*, JUNE 1971

Learning Objectives

After reading this chapter you should be able to:

1. Identify and explain the various stages of and parties to the collection of a check.
2. Identify and explain the duties of collecting banks.
3. Explain the relationship between a payor bank and its customers.
4. Define a consumer electronic fund transfer, identify the various types of electronic fund transfers, and outline the major provisions of the Electronic Funds Transfer Act.
5. Explain wholesale fund transfers and discuss how they operate.

In today's society, most goods and services are bought and sold without a physical transfer of "money." Credit cards, charge accounts, and various deferred payment plans have made cash sales increasingly rare. But even credit sales must ultimately be settled—when they are, payment is usually made by check rather than with cash. If the parties to a sales transaction happen to have accounts at the same bank, a transfer of credit is easily accomplished. In the vast majority of cases, however, the parties do business at different banks. Then the buyer's check must journey from the seller-payee's bank (the depositary bank), where the check is deposited by the seller for credit to his account, to the buyer-drawer's bank (the payor bank) for payment. In this collection process, the check frequently passes through one or more other banks (intermediary banks), each of which must accurately record its passing, before it may be collected. Our banking system has developed a network to handle the collection of checks and other instruments.

In recent years, the amount of payment made by electronic funds transfers has increased at an astounding rate. The dollar volume of commercial payments made by wire transfer far exceeds the dollar amount made by checks or credit cards. In addition, electronic funds transfers have become exceedingly popular with consumers. Consumer electronic funds transfers are covered by the federal Electronic Funds Transfer Act; nonconsumer (wholesale) electronic transfers are covered by Article 4A of the Uniform Commercial Code.

This chapter will cover both the bank deposit-collection system and electronic funds *transfers*.

BANK DEPOSITS AND COLLECTIONS

Article 4 of the UCC, entitled "Bank Deposits and Collections," provides the principal rules governing the bank collection process. As items in the bank collection process are essentially those covered by Article 3, "Commercial Paper," and to a lesser extent by Article 8,

"Investment Securities," these Articles often apply to a bank collection problem. In addition, Articles 3 and 4 are supplemented and, at times, preempted by federal law: the Expedited Funds Availability Act and its implementing Federal Reserve Regulation (Regulation CC). This section will cover the collection of an item through the banking system and the relationship between the payor bank and its customer.

http:// Article 3: http://www.law.cornell.edu/ucc/4/overview.html
Federal Reserve System: http://www.federalreserve.gov

CPA COLLECTION OF ITEMS

When a person deposits a check in his bank (the **depositary bank**), the bank credits the individual's account by the amount of the check. This initial crediting is **provisional.** Normally, a bank does not permit a customer to draw funds against a provisional credit; by permitting its customer to thus draw, the bank will have given *value* and, provided it meets the other requirements, will be a holder in due course. Under the customer's contract with his bank, the bank is obligated to make a reasonable effort to obtain payment of all checks deposited for collection. When the amount of the check has been collected from the payor bank (the drawee), the credit becomes a **final credit.**

The Competitive Equality Banking Act has expedited the availability of funds by establishing maximum time periods for which a bank may hold (and thereby deny a customer access to the funds represented by) various types of instruments. Under the Act, (1) cash deposits, wire transfers, government checks, the first $100 of a day's check deposits, cashier's checks, and checks deposited in one branch of a depositary institution and drawn on the same or another branch of the same institution must clear by the next business day; (2) local checks must clear within one intervening business day; and (3) nonlocal checks must clear in no more than four intervening business days.

If the payor bank (the drawee bank) does not pay the check for some reason, such as a stop payment order or insufficient funds in the drawer's account, the depositary bank reverses the provisional credit to the account, debits his account for that amount, and returns the check to him with a statement of the reason for nonpayment. If, in the meantime, the customer has been permitted to draw against the provisional credit, the bank may recover the payment from him.

In some cases, the bank involved is both the depositary bank and the payor bank. In most cases, however, the depositary and payor banks are different, in which event the bank collection aspects of Article 4 come into play. When the depositary and payor banks differ, it is necessary for the item to pass from one to the other, either directly through a clearinghouse or through one or more **intermediary banks** (banks, other than the depositary or payor bank, that are involved in the collection process, such as one of the twelve Federal Reserve Banks), as illustrated in Figure 28-1. A **clearinghouse** is an association, composed of banks or other payors, whose members settle accounts with each other on a daily basis. Each member of the clearinghouse forwards all deposited checks drawn on other members and receives from the clearinghouse all checks drawn on it. Balances are adjusted and settled each day.

COLLECTING BANKS

A **collecting bank** is any bank, other than the payor bank, handling an item for payment. In the usual situation, when the depositary and payor banks are different, the depositary bank gives a provisional credit to its customer, transfers the item to the next bank in the chain, and receives a provisional credit or "settlement" from it; the process repeats until the item reaches the payor bank, which gives a provisional settlement to its transferor. When the item is paid, all the provisional settlements given by the respective banks in the chain become final, and the particular transaction has been completed. Because this procedure simplifies bookkeeping by necessitating only one entry if the item is paid, no adjustment is necessary on the books of any of the banks involved.

If, however, the payor bank does not pay the check, it returns the item, and each intermediary or collecting bank reverses the provisional settlement or credit it previously gave to its forwarding bank. Ultimately, the depositary bank will charge (remove the provisional credit from) the account of the customer who deposited the item. The customer must then seek recovery from the indorsers or the drawer.

A collecting bank is an **agent** or subagent of the owner of the item until the settlement becomes final. Unless otherwise provided, any credit given for the item initially is provisional. Once settled, the agency relationship changes to one of ***debtor-creditor***. The effect of this agency rule is that the risk of loss remains with the owner and that any chargebacks go to her, not to the collecting bank.

All collecting banks have certain responsibilities and duties in collecting checks and other items. These will now be discussed.

Duty of Care A collecting bank must exercise ordinary care in handling an item transferred to it for collection. The steps it takes in presenting an item or sending it for presentment are of particular importance. It must act within a reasonable time after receipt of the item and must choose a reasonable method of forwarding the item for presentment. It also is responsible for using care in routing and in selecting intermediary banks or other agents.

Figure 28-1
Bank Collections

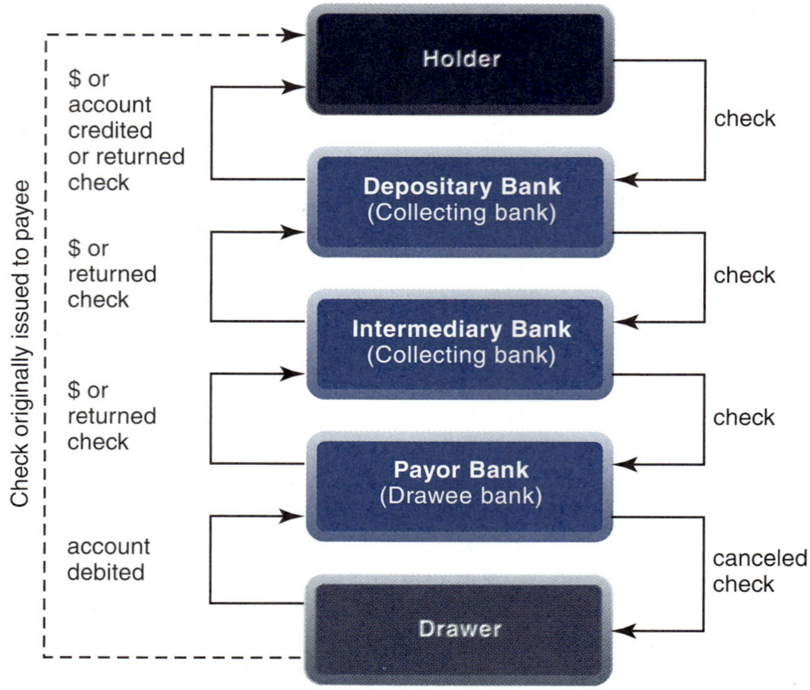

Honeycutt v. Honeycutt

Court of Special Appeals of Maryland, 2002
150 Md.App. 604, 822 A.2d 551
http://caselaw.lp.findlaw.com/data2/marylandstatecases/cosa/2003/68s02.pdf

FACTS Ron Honeycutt was the president, treasurer, and sole stockholder of Sheldon, Inc., which trades as Sheldon's Lounge (Sheldon), a bar located in Baltimore City. Christine Honeycutt was, at one time, Ron Honeycutt's wife and held the position of vice-president and secretary of Sheldon. On July 1, 1984, Ron Honeycutt and Christine Honeycutt opened a business checking account with Maryland National Bank, now Bank of America (Bank), in the name of Sheldon's Lounge. At that time, Ron Honeycutt and Christine Honeycutt executed a signature card for the account, which read, in pertinent part:

> In consideration of the opening of this account and the maintenance thereof by Maryland National Bank (hereinafter "Bank"), the signer(s) (hereinafter "depositor") by the signature(s) subscribed below agree(s) to the Rules and Regulations of Contract provided to depositor herewith. Bank is authorized to recognize and rely upon any of the signature(s) below on checks, drafts and orders for the payment of money, the withdrawals of funds, or the transaction of any business to this account. Depositor acknowledges receipt of a copy of the Rules and Regulations governing this account.

On the signature card, Ron Honeycutt and Christine Honeycutt checked off the box requiring only one signature to transact any business on the account. Ron Honeycutt and Christine Honeycutt were the only authorized signatories on the account.

Ron Honeycutt died February 10, 2000. On February 15, 2000, Christine Honeycutt withdrew funds in the amount of $13,066.48 from Sheldon's account. At the time of withdrawal, an employee of the Bank retrieved and reviewed the signature card on file with the Bank in order to verify Christine Honeycutt's authority to direct and conduct transactions on Sheldon's account. The Bank did not inquire as to Christine Honeycutt's status with respect to Sheldon, nor did they inquire of anyone at Sheldon as to her status. At the time, the Bank was unaware that Ron Honeycutt had died. According to the signature card on file at the Bank at the time Christine Honeycutt withdrew the funds, she was an authorized signatory on the account.

On March 13, 2000, Sheldon commenced an action against Christine Honeycutt and the Bank. Sheldon asserted claims for conversion, breach of contract, and negligence against the Bank for permitting the allegedly unauthorized withdrawal. On May 22, 2001, the Bank filed a motion for summary judgment arguing that at the time Christine Honeycutt withdrew funds from Sheldon's account, she was an authorized signatory on the account and, therefore, the Bank committed no legal wrong when it permitted the withdrawal. The circuit court granted the Bank's motion for summary judgment. Sheldon appealed.

DECISION The summary judgment of the circuit court is affirmed.

OPINION Thieme, J. Sheldon argues that the Bank breached its duty of care "by failing to make an adequate inquiry as to the authority of Christine Honeycutt to conduct banking on behalf of the business." We disagree.

"A bank and its customers enjoy a debtor/creditor relationship in which the rights and liabilities of each are contractual." [Citations.] "Implicit in the contract [between the bank and customer] is the duty of the bank to use ordinary care in disbursing the depositor's funds." [Citations.] * * *

A signature card may constitute a contract between a bank and its customer. [Citation.] "The signature card constituted the contract between the parties and, subject to the statutory schemes, regulates their rights and duties." [Citations.]

* * *

Here, Ron and Christine Honeycutt, on July 1, 1984, opened a business checking account in the name of Sheldon's Lounge with the Bank's predecessor. On that same day, Ron and Christine Honeycutt executed a signature card and checked off the box requiring only one signature to transact any business on the account. * * *, the signature card created a contractual obligation on the part of the Bank to pay the depositor's funds only as authorized by the signature card. The plain language of the signature card established that both Ron and Christine Honeycutt were authorized signatories able to transact business on Sheldon's account. Moreover, the signature card expressly and unambiguously provided that the Bank is authorized to recognize and rely upon either of Ron or Christine Honeycutt's signatures on checks, drafts and orders for the payment of money, the withdrawal of funds, or the transaction of any business to Sheldon's account.

When Christine Honeycutt withdrew funds from Sheldon's account, we find, the Bank did not breach any standard of care owed to appellants. The Bank exercised reasonable care when it inspected the signature card on file for Sheldon's account and verified that Christine Honeycutt was an authorized signatory on the account. Moreover, we are persuaded that no further inquiry was required as the Bank was legally entitled to release the funds to Christine Honeycutt based upon the express authority created by the signature card. Thus, because there was no genuine dispute as to any material fact, i.e., that the 1984 signature card was the authoritative document on file with the Bank, we find that the lower court was correct to conclude, as a matter of law, that the signature card controlled the transaction and was correct to enter summary judgment in favor of appellee.

* * *

INTERPRETATION A bank and its customers enjoy a debtor/creditor relationship in which the rights and liabilities of each are contractual.

CRITICAL THINKING QUESTION Do you agree with the court's decision? Explain.

Duty to Act Timely Closely related to the collecting bank's duty of care is its duty to act in a timely manner. A collecting bank acts timely in any event if it takes proper action, such as forwarding or presenting an item before the "midnight deadline" following its receipt of the item, notice, or payment. If the bank adheres to this standard, the timeliness of its action cannot be challenged; should it, however, take a reasonably longer time, the bank bears the burden of proof in establishing timeliness. The **midnight deadline** is the midnight of the banking day following the banking day on which the bank received the item or notice. Thus, if a bank receives a check on Monday, it must take proper action by midnight on the next banking day, or Tuesday. A banking day means the part of a day on which a bank is open to the public for carrying on substantially all of its banking functions.

The midnight deadline presents a problem because it takes time to process an item through a bank—whether it be the depositary, intermediary, or payor bank. If a day's transactions are to be completed without overtime work, the bank must either close early or fix an earlier cutoff time for the day's work. Accordingly, the Code provides that for the purpose of allowing time to process items, prove balances, and make the bookkeeping entries necessary to determine its position for the day, a bank may fix an afternoon hour of 2:00 P.M. or later as a cutoff point for handling money and items and for making entries on its books. Items received after the cutoff hour fixed as the close of the banking day are considered to have been received at the opening of the next banking day, and the time for taking action and for determining the bank's midnight deadline begins to run from that point.

Recognizing that everyone involved will be greatly inconvenienced if an item is not paid, the Code provides that unless otherwise instructed, a collecting bank in a good faith effort to secure payment may, in the case of a specific item drawn on a payor other than a bank, waive, modify, or extend the time limits, but not in excess of two additional banking days. This extension may be made without the approval of the parties involved and without discharging drawers or indorsers. This section does not apply to checks and other drafts drawn on a bank. The Code also authorizes delay when communications or computer facilities are interrupted as a result of blizzard, flood, hurricane, or other disaster; the suspension of payments by another bank; war; emergency conditions; failure of equipment; or other circumstances beyond the bank's control. Nevertheless, such delay will be excused only if the bank exercises such diligence as the circumstances require.

Indorsements An item restrictively indorsed with words such as "pay any bank" is locked into the bank collection system, and only a bank may acquire the rights of a holder. When forwarding an item for collection, a bank normally indorses the item "pay any bank," regardless of the type of indorsement, if any, that the item carried at the time of receipt. This serves to protect the collecting bank by making it impossible for the item to stray from regular collection channels.

If the item had no indorsement when the depositary bank received it, the bank nonetheless becomes a holder of the item at the time it takes possession of the item for collection if the customer was a holder at the time of delivery to the bank and, if the bank satisfies the other requirements of a holder in due course, it will become a holder in due course in its own right. In return, the bank warrants to the collecting banks, the payor, and the drawer that it has paid the amount of the item to the customer or deposited that amount to the customer's account. This rule speeds up the collection process by eliminating the necessity of returning checks for indorsement when the depositary bank knows they came from its customers.

Warranties Customers and collecting banks give substantially the same warranties as those given by parties under Article 3 upon presentment and transfer, which were discussed in Chapter 27. In addition, under Article 4, customers and collecting banks may give encoding warranties. Each customer or collecting bank who transfers an item and receives a settlement or other consideration warrants to his transferee and any subsequent collecting bank that (1) the person is entitled to enforce the item; (2) all signatures are authentic and authorized; (3) the item has not been altered; (4) he is not subject to any defense or claim in recoupment; and (5) he has no knowledge of any insolvency proceeding involving the maker or acceptor or the drawer of an unaccepted draft. Moreover, each customer or collecting bank who obtains payment or acceptance from a drawee on a draft as well as each prior transferor warrants to the drawee who pays or accepts the draft in good faith that (1) she is a person entitled to enforce the draft; (2) the item has not been altered; and (3) she has no knowledge that the signature of the drawer is unauthorized.

Processing of checks is now done by Magnetic Ink Character Recognition (MICR). When a check is deposited, the depositary bank magnetically encodes the check with the amount of the check (all checks are preencoded with the drawer's account number and the designation of the drawee bank), after which the processing occurs automatically, without further human involvement. Despite its efficiency, the magnetic encoding of checks has created several problems. The first is the problem a bank encounters when paying a postdated instrument prior to its date. The Revision changes prior law by providing that the drawee may debit the drawer's account, unless the drawer timely informs the drawee that the check is postdated. A second difficulty arises when a depositing bank or its customer who encodes her own checks miscodes a check. Revised Article 4 provides that such an encoder warrants to any subsequent collecting bank and to the payor that information on a check is properly encoded. If the encoding is done by the customer, the depositary bank also makes the warranty.

Final Payment The provisional settlements made in the collection chain are all directed toward final payment of the item by the payor bank. From this turnaround point in the collection process, the proceeds of the item begin their return flow, and provisional settlements become final. For example, a customer of the California Country State Bank may deposit a check drawn on the State of Maine Country National Bank. The check may then take a course such as follows: from the California Country State Bank to a correspondent bank in San Francisco, to the Federal Reserve Bank of San Francisco, to the Federal Reserve Bank of Boston, to the payor bank. Provisional settlements are made at each step. When the payor finally pays the item, the proceeds begin to flow back over the same course.

The critical question, then, is the point at which the payor has *paid* the item, because this not only commences the payment process but also affects questions of priority between the payment of an item and actions such as the filing of a stop payment order against it. Under the Code, **final payment** occurs when the payor bank first does any of the following: (1) pays an item in cash; (2) settles an item and does not have the right to revoke the settlement through statute, clearinghouse rule, or agreement; or (3) makes a provisional settlement and does not revoke it within the time and in the manner permitted by statute, clearinghouse rule, or agreement.

PAYOR BANKS

The **payor** or drawee **bank**, under its contract of deposit with the drawer, agrees to pay to the payee or his order a check issued by the drawer, provided that the order is not countermanded, and that there are sufficient funds in the drawer's account.

The tremendous increase in volume of bank collections has necessitated deferred posting procedures, whereby items are sorted and proved on the day of receipt but are not posted to customers' accounts or returned until the next banking day. The UCC not only approves such procedures but establishes specific standards to govern their application to the actions of payor banks.

When a payor bank that is not also a depositary bank receives a demand item other than for immediate payment over the counter, it must either return the item or give its transferor a provisional settlement before midnight of the banking day on which the item is received. Otherwise, the bank becomes liable to its transferor for the amount of the item, unless it has a valid defense, such as breach of a presentment warranty.

If the payor bank gives the provisional settlement as required, it has until the midnight deadline to return the item or, if the item is held for protest or is otherwise unavailable for return, to send written notice of dishonor or nonpayment. After doing this, the bank is entitled to revoke the settlement and recover any payment it has made. Should it fail to return the item or send notice before its midnight deadline, the payor bank will be accountable for the amount of the item unless it has a valid defense for its inaction.

There are innumerable reasons for a bank to dishonor an item and return it or send notice. The following situations are the most common: the drawer or maker may have no account or may have funds insufficient to cover the item; a signature on the item may be forged; or the drawer or maker may have stopped payment on the item.

RELATIONSHIP BETWEEN PAYOR BANK AND ITS CUSTOMER

CPA

The relationship between a payor bank and its checking account customer is primarily the product of their contractual arrangement. Although the parties have relatively broad latitude in establishing the terms of their agreement and in altering the provisions of the Code, a bank may not validly (1) disclaim responsibility for its lack of good faith, (2) disclaim responsibility for its failure to exercise ordinary care, or (3) limit its damages for a breach comprising such lack or failure. The parties may by agreement, however, determine the standards by which the bank's responsibility is to be measured, if these standards are not clearly unreasonable.

PAYMENT OF AN ITEM

A payor owes a duty to its customer, the drawer, to pay checks properly drawn by him on an account having funds sufficient to cover the items. A check or draft, however, is not an assignment of the drawer's funds that are in the drawee's possession. Moreover, as discussed in Chapter 27, the drawee is not liable on a check until it accepts the item. Therefore, the *holder* of a check has no right to require the drawee bank to pay it, whether the drawer's account contains sufficient funds or not. But if a payor bank improperly refuses payment when presented with an item, it will incur a liability to the *customer* from whose account the item should have been paid. If the customer has adequate funds on deposit, and there is no other valid basis for the refusal to pay, the bank is liable to its customer for damages proximately caused by the *wrongful dishonor*. Liability is limited to actual damages proved and may include damages for arrest, prosecution, or other consequential damages.

When a payor bank receives an item properly payable from a customer's account but the funds in the account are insufficient to pay it, the bank may (1) dishonor the item and return it or (2) pay the item and charge its customer's account, even though the actions create an overdraft. The item authorizes or directs the bank to make the payment and hence carries with it an enforceable implied promise to reimburse the bank. Further, the customer may be liable to pay the bank a service charge for its handling of the overdraft or to pay interest on the amount of the overdraft. A customer, however, is not liable for an overdraft if the customer did not sign the item or benefit from the proceeds of the item.

A payor bank is under no obligation to its customer to pay an uncertified check that is more than six months old. This rule reflects the usual banking practice of consulting a depositor before paying a "stale" item (one more than six months old) on her account. The bank is not required to dishonor such an item, however; and if the bank makes payment in good faith, it may charge the amount of the item to its customer's account.

Practical Advice

Be sure to present checks you hold before they become stale.

STOP PAYMENT ORDERS

A check drawn on a bank is an order to pay a sum of money and an authorization to charge the amount to the drawer's account. The customer, or any person authorized to draw on the account, may countermand this order, however, by means of a **stop payment order**. If the order does not come too late, the bank is bound by it. If the bank inadvertently pays a check over a valid stop order, it is *prima facie* liable to the customer, but only to the extent of the customer's loss resulting from the payment. The burden of establishing the fact and amount of loss is on the customer.

To be effective, a stop payment order must be received in time to provide the bank a reasonable opportunity to act on it. An oral stop order is binding on the bank for only fourteen calendar days. If the customer confirms an oral stop order in writing within the fourteen-day period, the order is effective for six months and may be renewed in writing for additional six-month periods.

Practical Advice

If you wish to stop payment on a check, contact your bank as soon as possible, and confirm in writing an oral stop payment order within fourteen days.

The fact that a drawer has filed a stop payment order does not automatically relieve her of liability. If the bank honors the stop payment order and returns the check, the holder may bring an action against the drawer. If the holder qualifies as a holder in due course, personal defenses that the drawer might have to such an action would be of no avail.

Leibling, P.C. v. Mellon PSFS (NJ) National Association

Superior Court of New Jersey, Law Division, Special Civil Part, Camden County, 1998
710 A.2d 1067, 311 N.J.Super. 651, 35 UCC Per.Serv.2d 590

FACTS Mr. Scott D. Liebling, P.C. (hereinafter "Plaintiff") is an attorney at law. Plaintiff maintains an attorney trust account ("Account") at Mellon Bank (NJ) National Association ("Mellon") **(http://www.mellon.com/)**. Mellon uses a computerized system to process checks for payment.

Plaintiff represented the defendant, Fredy Winda Ramos ("Ramos") in a personal injury action which resulted in a settlement. On May 19, 1995, plaintiff issued Check No. 1031 in the amount of $8,483.06 to Ramos, representing her net proceeds from the settlement. Mellon honored that check on May 26, 1995. On May 24, 1995, plaintiff mistakenly issued another check, Check No. 1043, to Ramos in the same amount of $8,483.06. Realizing his error, Plaintiff called Ramos in Puerto Rico and advised her that Check No. 1043 had been issued by mistake and instructed her to destroy the check. Plaintiff then called Mellon and ordered an oral stop payment on the check.

On December 21, 1996, some nineteen months after plaintiff issued Check No. 1043, Ramos cashed the check in Puerto Rico.

Plaintiff filed this complaint against both Ramos and Mellon. Ramos defaulted. Plaintiff's complaint against Mellon alleges breach of duty of good faith, negligence, breach of fiduciary duty, payment of a stale check, and breach of contract as a result of Mellon's honoring the second check.

DECISION Judgment for Mellon: the bank's conduct was fair and in accordance with reasonable commercial standards.

OPINION Rand, J. It is important to consider the relevant New Jersey statute sections before discussing what actions constitute "good faith." Under [UCC] 4–403(b):

> [a] stop payment order is effective for six months, but it lapses after 14 calendar days if the original order was oral and was not confirmed in writing within that period. A stop payment order may be renewed for additional six-month periods by a writing given to the bank within a period during which the stop-payment order is effective.

In addition, [UCC] 4–404 states:

> A bank is under no obligation to a customer having a checking account to pay a check, other than a certified check, which is presented more than six months after its date, but it may charge its customer's account for a payment made thereafter in good faith.

Thus, the issue in the present case turns on whether Mellon acted in good faith when it honored plaintiff's check. Good faith under N.J. Uniform Commercial Code has been defined in [UCC] 3–103(a)(4) as "honesty in fact and the observance of reasonable commercial standards of fair dealing." Since there is no New Jersey case law directly on point, it is necessary to consider alternate sources. One law review article [citation] addressed the present issue. Specifically, the article explained that "Article 4 of the Uniform Commercial Code imposes on all banks the responsibility to act in good faith and to exercise ordinary care. The drafters of the Code chose not to provide an explicit definition of 'ordinary' care, stating only that the term is to be used 'with its normal tort meaning and not in any special sense relating to bank collections'." [Citation.]

* * *

In addition, the Third Circuit case of *Hartford* * * * [citation] appears to be analogous to the present issue. In *Hartford*, an insurance company brought a subrogation action against a payor bank to recover on an altered check that the bank had paid. On April 17, 1984, the plaintiff placed a written stop-payment order on a certain check, and under applicable state law the stop payment order was good for six months. On December 26, 1984, two months after the stop payment order had expired, the bank honored the check. Before concluding that the payor bank had acted in good faith, the court analyzed the definition of "good faith." The court stated that "[UCC] § 1–201 defines good faith as 'honesty in fact.' This definition must be viewed subjectively; a finding of bad faith must be predicated on a showing of dishonesty. Likewise, mere negligence does not preclude a finding of good faith." [Citation.] In holding that the bank had acted in good faith, the court stated:

> [a]s a result of the expiration of the order, [the bank] cannot be said to have the actual knowledge that would deny it the status of a good faith payor * * * The obligations which a bank incurs as a result of its customer's imposing a stop order on a check do not continue in perpetuity. * * * [The bank] was neither negligent nor reckless and certainly cannot be said to have been subjectively dishonest. * * * A finding of bad faith requires actual knowledge on the part of the payor. An objective inquiry into what the circumstances should have revealed to [the bank] is simply not germane to the analysis.
> [Citation.]

* * *

In contrast, plaintiff's argument centers on the proposition that the bank's duty of good faith required it to inquire or consult with plaintiff before honoring a stale check that had a previous oral stop payment order on it. * * *

However, in the Uniform Commercial Code Treatise, Mr. Hawkland stated that * * * "[t]he duty [of inquiry] is inconsistent with the provisions of subsection 4–403(2) on the expiration of the 'effectiveness' of stop orders. Such a duty is hardly practical today." Moreover: "[t]o require that a payor bank check the date of every check received via the collection process would unreasonably increase the cost of processing every check written today."

* * *

The Commercial Code was initially adopted in November, 1961 in New Jersey. In 1990, Articles III and IV of the Code were substantially revised relating to, among other thing, bank deposits and collections to become effective on June 1, 1995. The court is satisfied as pointed out by the defendant that those Amendments were enacted in order to address the effect of automated systems utilized by banks with the substantial increase in check usage after the original enactment of the Code. The Official Code Comment to the 1995 Amendments for § [UCC] 4–101, states as follows:

> 1. The great number of checks handled by banks and the country-wide nature of the bank collection process require uniformity in the law of bank collections. There is needed a uniform statement of the principal rules of the bank collection process with ample provision for flexibility to meet the needs of the large volume handled and the changing needs and conditions that are bound to come with the years. The Article meets that need.
> 2. * * * An important goal of the 1990 revision of Article 4 is to promote the efficiency of the check collection process by making the provisions of Article 4 more compatible with the needs of an automated system and, by doing so, increase the speed and lower the cost of check collection for those who write and receive checks. * * *
>
> [Citation.]

* * *

Thus, in determining whether the defendant bank in the present action acted in good faith, the above cited material must be analyzed and applied. First, it appears clear that the Uniform Commercial Code acknowledges that computerized check processing systems are common and accepted banking procedures in the United States. [Citation.] Therefore, it can not be said that defendant bank acted in bad faith by using a computerized system when it honored plaintiff's "stale" check. Furthermore, it appears that the test for good faith is a subjective test. Thus, based on all of the foregoing material, as long as the defendant bank used an adequate computer system for processing checks (here there is no proof to the contrary), it appears to have acted in good faith even though it did not consult the Plaintiff before it honored the "stale" check that had an expired oral stop-payment order on it. As stated in *Hartford, supra*, the obligation of a bank to stop payment on a check does not continue in perpetuity once the stop payment order expires.

The bank's conduct was fair and in accordance with reasonable commercial standards. Accordingly, it appears that the defendant bank is not liable and should prevail. A finding of no liability is entered for the defendant bank.

INTERPRETATION It is the responsibility of the banking customer either to regain possession of the mistakenly issued check or to renew the stop payment order in writing every six months for as long as the risk of payment exists.

CRITICAL THINKING QUESTION Do you think that banks should be required to offer a permanent stop payment option? Explain.

Bank's Right to Subrogation on Improper Payment

If a payor bank pays an item over a stop payment order, after an account has been closed, or otherwise in violation of its contract with the drawer or maker, the payor bank is subrogated to (obtains) the rights of (1) any holder in due course on the item against the drawer or maker; (2) the payee or any other holder against the drawer or maker; and (3) the drawer or maker against the payee or any other holder. For instance, over the drawer's stop payment order, a bank pays a check presented to the bank by a holder in due course. The drawer's defense is that the check was obtained by fraud in the inducement. The drawee bank is subrogated to the rights of the holder in due course, who would not be subject to the drawer's personal defense, and thus can debit the drawer's account. The same would be true if the presenter were the payee, against whom the drawer did not have a valid defense.

Seigel v. Merrill Lynch, Pierce, Fenner & Smith, Inc.

District of Columbia Court of Appeals, 2000

745 A.2d 301

FACTS In early 1997, the plaintiff, Walter Seigel, a Maryland resident, traveled to Atlantic City, New Jersey to gamble. While there, he wrote a number of checks to various casinos in order to gamble. The checks were drawn on Seigel's cash management account with the defendant, which was established through Merrill Lynch's **(http://www.ml.com/)** District of Columbia offices. There were sufficient funds in the account to cover all the checks. Seigel eventually gambled away all of the money he had received for the checks. Upon returning to Maryland, Seigel discussed the status of the outstanding checks with Merrill Lynch, informing his broker of the gambling nature of the transactions and his desire to avoid realizing the losses. Merrill Lynch informed Seigel that it was possible to escape paying the checks by placing a stop payment order and closing out his cash management account. Seigel took this advice and instructed Merrill Lynch to close his account, liquidate the assets, and not to honor any checks drawn on the account. Merrill Lynch agreed and confirmed Seigel's instructions. Many of the checks were subsequently dishonored and are not now at issue. However, Merrill Lynch accidentally paid several of the checks totaling $143,000, despite the stop payment order and the account closure. Merrill Lynch then debited Seigel's margin account to cover the payments.

Seigel brought suit in the District of Columbia against Merrill Lynch, demanding a return of the $143,000 plus interest. Merill Lynch was granted a summary judgment. Seigel appealed.

DECISION Judgment affirmed.

OPINION Steadman, J. We begin with an examination of the statutory scheme relating to stop payment orders, because we believe these provisions are determinative of this appeal. The relevant sections are found in the Uniform Commercial Code * * * §§ 4–403 and 4–407.

The basic right of the depositor to stop payment on any item drawn on the depositor's account is set forth in section 4–403(a). However, liability on the bank for payment over a stop payment order is far from automatic. On the contrary, section 4–403(c) provides: "The burden of establishing the fact and amount of loss resulting from the payment of an item contrary to a stop-payment order or order to close an account is on the customer."

This provision, which places the burden on the customer to show actual loss, is reinforced by the extensive rights of subrogation given to the payor bank by section 4–407. Under that section, as to the drawer or maker (that is, the depositor), the bank is subrogated both to the rights of "any holder in due course on the item" and to the rights of "the payee or any other holder of the item against the drawer or maker either on the item or under the transaction out of which the item arose." As a leading authority on the Uniform Commercial Code has noted, this section "contemplates that the bank will use its subrogation rights primarily to defend against a suit by the customer to recover payment." [Citation.]

As applied to the facts here, then, Seigel is required to bear the burden of establishing that he in fact suffered a loss as a result of the payment of the checks. In assessing whether any such loss was actually incurred, Merrill Lynch must be treated as the subrogee of any rights of the casino payees against Seigel. As the payee of a dishonored check, the casino would have a prima facie right to recover its amount from Seigel as drawer, 3–414(b), and the burden would be on Seigel to establish any defense he might assert on the instrument. 3–308(b); [Citation.] Seigel asserts two such defenses: duress and illegality. We turn to an examination of those defenses.

* * *

The entirety of appellant's duress argument emanates from a single sentence in his affidavit: "For years I have had [a] gambling problem." If not ambiguous, the statement is conclusory. Unlike the gambler in [citation], appellant fails to produce any evidence in the record, specific or otherwise, regarding his problem and its relation to any unconscionable duress in the transactions at issue. [Citation] (describing an abusive and bizarre "marathon gambling session," that included unsolicited credit increases from the casino, the existence of an alleged psychological disorder and defendant's concomitant use of pain killers, during which the defendant lost $285,000 in little over two days). * * * We therefore conclude that Seigel's assertion that the checks would be unenforceable in New Jersey fails.

Seigel also invokes the fact that these checks were given in order to obtain chips with which to gamble, and cites us in particular to D.C. Code * * * [which] provides that:

> A thing in action, judgment, mortgage, or other security or conveyance made and executed by a person in which any part of the consideration is for money or other valuable things won by playing at any game whatsoever, or by betting on the sides or hands of persons who play, or for the reimbursement or payment of any money knowingly lent or advanced for the purpose, or lent or advanced at the time and place of the play or bet, to a person so playing or betting or who, during the play, so plays or bets, is void.

In substance, Seigel claims that this statute would serve as a defense if the casinos were to seek to enforce the checks in the first instance in a District of Columbia court, and therefore this same statute requires that he be entitled to affirmatively recover from Merrill Lynch the amount of the checks in a District of Columbia court, regardless of the checks' enforceability elsewhere.

We may assume for present purposes that this statute would prevent direct enforcement of the checks in the District of Columbia, a somewhat dubious proposition in itself given the validity of the checks where made. But that is not this case. Rather, the question is whether under the relevant provisions of the Uniform Commercial Code, Seigel has met his burden of proof to establish actual loss. We think he has not.

As already indicated, even if payment had been stopped, the casinos could have enforced the checks in New Jersey, where the transaction was entered into. Merrill Lynch therefore, under the Code scheme, conceptually has the same right. Furthermore, even if there were a problem in asserting jurisdiction over Seigel in New Jersey, Maryland would have provided an appropriate forum for enforcing the checks. The highest Maryland court has squarely held that because there is no longer a strong public policy against gambling per se, * * * and that therefore Maryland courts will enforce gambling debts if legally incurred in a foreign jurisdiction. [Citation.] Accordingly the casinos, and hence derivatively Merrill Lynch, could enforce the checks directly against Seigel in the state of his residence—Maryland.

* * *

We conclude that Seigel failed to establish that he ultimately suffered any actual loss as a result of the payment of the checks by Merrill Lynch. * * *

INTERPRETATION The drawer is required to bear the burden of establishing that he in fact suffered a loss as a result of the payment of a check over a stop payment order.

CRITICAL THINKING QUESTION What rule should be established for liability of a bank making a payment over a stop payment order?

DISCLOSURE REQUIREMENTS

In 1992, Congress enacted the Truth in Savings Act, which requires all depositary institutions (including commercial banks, savings and loan associations, savings banks, and credit unions) to disclose in great detail to consumers the terms and conditions of their deposit accounts. The stated purpose of the Act is to allow consumers to make informed decisions regarding deposit accounts by mandating standardized disclosure of rates of interest and fees in order to facilitate meaningful comparison of different deposit products.

More specifically, the Act provides that the disclosures must be made in a clear and conspicuous writing and must be given to the consumer when an account is opened or service is provided. These disclosures must include the following: (1) the annual percentage yield (APY) and the percentage rate; (2) how variable rates are calculated and when the rates may be changed; (3) balance information (including how the balance is calculated); (4) when and how interest is calculated and credited; (5) the amount of fees that may be charged and how they are calculated; and (6) any limitation on the number or amount of withdrawals or deposits. In addition, the Act requires the depositary institution to disclose the following information with periodic statements it sends to its customers: (1) the APY earned; (2) any fees debited during the covered period; (3) the dollar amount of the interest earned during the covered period; and (4) the dates of the covered period.

CUSTOMER'S DEATH OR INCOMPETENCE

The general rule is that death or incompetence revokes all agency agreements. Furthermore, adjudication of incompetency by a court is regarded as notice to the world of that fact. Actual notice is not required. The Code modifies these stringent rules in several ways with respect to bank deposits and collections.

First, if either a payor or collecting bank does not know that a customer has been adjudicated incompetent, the existence of such incompetence at the time an item is issued or its collection undertaken does not impair either bank's authority to accept, pay, or collect the item or to account for proceeds of its collection. The bank may pay the item without incurring any liability.

Second, neither death nor adjudication of incompetence of a customer revokes a payor or collecting bank's authority to accept, pay, or collect an item until the bank knows of the condition and has a reasonable opportunity to act on this knowledge.

Finally, even though a bank knows of the death of its customer, it may for ten days after the date of his death pay or certify checks drawn by the customer unless a person claiming an interest in the account, such as an heir, executor, or administrator, orders the bank to stop making such payments.

CUSTOMER'S DUTIES

The Code imposes certain affirmative duties on bank customers and fixes time limits within which they must assert their rights. The duties arise and the time starts to run from the point at which the bank either sends or makes available to its customer a statement of account showing payment of items against the account. The statement of account will suffice provided it describes by item the number of the item, the amount, and the date of payment. The customer must exercise reasonable promptness in examining the bank statement or the items to discover whether any payment was unauthorized due to an *unauthorized signature* on or any *alteration* of an item. Because he is not presumed to know the signatures of payees or indorsers, this duty of prompt and careful examination applies only to alterations and the customer's own signature, both of which he should be able to detect immediately. If the customer discovers an unauthorized signature or an alteration, he must notify the bank promptly. A failure to fulfill these duties of prompt examination and notice precludes the customer from asserting against the bank his unauthorized signature or any alteration if the bank establishes that it suffered a loss by reason of such failure.

Furthermore, the customer will lose his rights in a potentially more serious situation. Occasionally, a forger, possibly an employee who has access to the employer's checkbook, carries out a series of transactions involving the account of the same individual. He may forge one or more checks each month until finally detected. The bank, noticing nothing suspicious, might pay one or more of the customer's checks bearing the false signatures before the customer detects the forgery, months or even years later. The Code deals with these situations by stating that once the statement and items become available to him, the customer must examine them within a reasonable period, which in no event may exceed thirty calendar days and which may, under certain circumstances, be less and notify the bank. Any instruments containing alterations or unauthorized signatures by the same wrongdoer that the bank pays during that period will be the bank's responsibility, but any instruments paid thereafter but before the customer notifies the bank may not be asserted against it. This rule is based on the concept that the loss involved is directly traceable to the customer's negligence and that, as a result, he should stand the loss.

These rules depend, however, on the bank's exercising ordinary care in paying the items involved. If it does not and that failure by the bank substantially contributed to the loss, the loss will be allocated between the bank and the customer based on their comparative negligence. But whether the bank exercised due care or not, the customer must in all events report any alteration or his unauthorized signature within one year from the time the statement or items are made available to him or be barred from asserting them against the bank. Any *unauthorized indorsement* must be asserted within three years under the Article's general Statute of Limitations provisions.

Practical Advice

Promptly review your monthly bank statement to ensure that all checks and transactions were issued by you or your authorized agent and are for the correct amount.

Consistent with modern automated methods for processing checks, Articles 3 and 4 provide that "ordinary care" does not require a bank to examine every check if the failure to do so does not vary unreasonably from general banking usage.

Practical Advice

Promptly and carefully review all electronic fund activities to ensure that they are accurate, and if they are not, notify your financial institution immediately.

http:// National Check Fraud Center: http://www.ckfraud.org/

Mansi v. Gaines

Supreme Court, Appellate Division, Second Department, N.Y. 1995
216 A.D.2d 536, 628 N.Y.S.2D 804

FACTS Plaintiff, Mary Mansi, claims that twenty-one checks on her account contain forgeries but were paid by the defendant bank, Sterling National Bank **(http://www.sterlingbancorp.com/)**. Three of the twenty-one checks were disallowed because the plaintiff could not find them or they were found to have been drawn on another bank. The remaining eighteen checks bore signatures which, according to the plaintiff's handwriting expert, were apparently "written by another person who attempted to simulate her signature" and thus were not considered obvious forgeries.

Sterling National Bank moved for summary judgment on the remaining eighteen checks, acknowledging that while it did honor those eighteen checks, nine of them were returned to the plaintiff more than one year prior to this action. The defendant asserts that the plaintiff's claims on the remaining nine checks are barred due to her failure to examine her monthly bank statements.

DECISION Summary judgment granted in favor of defendant Sterling National Bank.

OPINION Memorandum by the court. The plaintiff * * * failed to identify a specific transaction in which the allegedly fraudulent power of attorney was used. Although the evidence in the record indicated that the appellant honored 18 checks which may have been forged, liability with respect to nine of those checks was barred by UCC 4–406(4) [Revised 4–406(f)] since the plaintiff did not report the alleged fraud within one year after those checks and the bank statements with respect thereto were made available to her [citations].

With respect to the remaining nine checks, liability was barred by UCC 4–406(2)(b) [Revised 4–406(d)(2)] since it was established that the plaintiff failed to exercise reasonable care to examine her bank statements and the plaintiff failed to submit any evidence that the appellant failed to exercise ordinary care in paying the items [Citation].

INTERPRETATION A bank customer must exercise reasonable promptness in examining account statements and canceled checks to detect unauthorized signatures or alterations.

CRITICAL THINKING QUESTION Do you agree with the court's decision? Explain.

ELECTRONIC FUNDS TRANSFER

As previously mentioned, the use of negotiable instruments for payment has transformed the United States into a virtually cashless society. The advent and technological advances of computers make it likely that in the foreseeable future electronic funds transfer systems (EFTS) will bring about a society that is virtually checkless as well. Financial institutions seek to substitute EFTS for checks for two principal reasons. The first is to eliminate the ever-increasing paperwork involved in processing the billions of checks issued annually. The second is to eliminate the "float" that a drawer of a check currently enjoys by maintaining the use of his funds during the processing period between the time at which he issues the check and final payment.

An **electronic funds transfer** (EFT) has been defined as "any transfer of funds, other than a transaction originated by check, draft, or similar paper instrument, which is initiated through an electronic terminal, telephonic instrument, or computer or magnetic tape so as to order, instruct or authorize a financial institution to debit or credit an account." For example, with an EFT, William in New York would be able to pay a debt he owes to Yvette in Illinois by entering into his computer an order to his bank to pay Yvette. The drawee bank would then instantly debit William's account and transfer the credit to Yvette's bank, where Yvette's account would immediately be credited in that amount. The entire transaction would be completed in minutes.

Although EFTs are still in their formative stages, their use has generated considerable confusion concerning the legal rights of customers and financial institutions. Congress provided a partial solution to these legal issues in 1978 by enacting the Electronic Fund Transfer Act (EFTA), discussed later. But significant and numerous legal problems remain. In an attempt to resolve some of these questions, the Permanent Editorial Board of the Uniform Commercial Code has promulgated Article 4A—Fund Transfer.

http:// Article 4—Fund Transfer: http://www.law.cornell.edu/ucc/4A/overview.html

CPA TYPES OF ELECTRONIC FUNDS TRANSFER

Although a number of new EFTs are likely to appear in the coming years, five main types of EFTs are currently in use: (1) automated teller machines, (2) point-of-sale systems, (3) direct deposit and withdrawal of funds, (4) pay-by-phone systems, and (5) wholesale wire transfers.

AUTOMATED TELLER MACHINES

Now available throughout the country, automated teller machines (ATMs) permit customers to conduct various transactions with their bank through the use of electronic terminals. After activating an ATM with a plastic identification card and a personal identification number, or PIN, a customer can deposit and withdraw funds from her account, transfer funds between accounts, obtain cash advances, and make payments on loan accounts. (See Consumer Insight, "Thwarting ATM Fraud.")

POINT-OF-SALE SYSTEMS

Computerized point-of-sale (POS) systems permit consumers to transfer funds from their bank accounts to a merchant automatically. The POS machines, located within the merchant's store and activated by the consumer's identification card and code, instantaneously debit the consumer's account and credit the merchant's account.

DIRECT DEPOSITS AND WITHDRAWALS

Another type of EFT involves deposits, authorized in advance by a customer, that are made directly to the customer's account through an electronic terminal. Examples include direct payroll deposits, deposits of Social Security payments, and deposits of pension payments. Conversely, automatic withdrawals are preauthorized electronic funds transfers from the customer's account for regular payments to some party other than the financial institution at which

Ethical Dilemma

Can Embezzlement Ever Be a Loan?

FACTS Susan Jennings was the head cashier for Pears, a highly respected discount store located in the heart of Chicago. Her job included distributing funds to each cashier, periodically collecting any large amounts from them, making a collection at the end of each shift, and depositing the previous day's receipts each morning. When a cashier brought money to Susan, the cashier would count the money and Susan would check it. At the end of each day, Susan would make out a deposit slip for the amount of cash and checks received, giving a copy of the slip to the accounting department for proper book entry. She would indorse each check with a company stamp marked "For Deposit Only."

On December 1, 1992, Alvin Troop, a new cashier, finished his shift and brought his money tray to Susan. While counting his receipts, he had noticed a check for $120 that had been made out without a payee. Alvin brought the check to Susan's attention. Matching his receipts to the cash register tape, Susan found that Alvin was exactly $120 over. Susan told him not to worry and said that she would fill in the store's name when she made the next deposit and would reconcile the receipts to the tape.

On December 2, 1992, Susan deposited the previous day's receipts in Pears's account in the First Sandy Hill Bank of Chicago, but decided to borrow $120 for her Christmas shopping. Short of cash and wanting to take advantage of a special sale, she intended to make up the difference on December 5, 1992, which was a payday. She filled her name in on the blank check, which also was drawn on the First Sandy Hill Bank, and the bank cashed it. Three days later, she replaced the money. No one knew what she had done until the customer who had written the check received his bank statement and demanded that the bank credit his account for the amount of the check that showed Susan as the payee.

Social, Policy, and Ethical Considerations

1. Were Susan's actions unethical or illegal? Explain. Would Susan's using the money for essential items, such as food or medicine, change your answer?
2. What should Susan have done?
3. What responsibility does the First Sandy Hill Bank have to its customers? In general, are banking procedures and standards established for the benefit of the bank or for that of the public?
4. If the bank teller had any idea that Susan had done something wrong, does the fact that he may have followed banking rules relieve him of any ethical responsibility?

the funds are deposited. Automatic withdrawals to pay insurance premiums, utility bills, or automobile loan payments are common examples of this type of EFT.

Pay-by-Phone Systems

Recently, some financial institutions have instituted a service that permits customers to pay bills by telephoning the bank's computer system and directing a transfer of funds to a designated third party. This service also permits customers to transfer funds between accounts.

Wholesale Electronic Funds Transfers

Wholesale electronic funds transfers, commonly called wholesale wire transfers, involve the movement of funds between financial institutions, between financial institutions and businesses, and between businesses. More than $1 trillion is transferred this way each business day over the two major transfer systems—the Federal Reserve wire transfer network system (Fedwire) and the New York Clearing House Interbank Payment System (CHIPS). In addition, a number of private wholesale wire systems exist among the large banks. Limited aspects of wholesale wire transfers are governed by uniform rules promulgated by the Federal Reserve, CHIPS, and the National Automated Clearing House Association.

CPA Consumer Funds Transfers

In 1978, Congress determined that the use of electronic systems to transfer funds provided the potential for substantial benefits to consumers. Existing consumer protection legislation failed to account for the unique characteristics of such systems, however, leaving the rights and obligations of consumers and financial institutions undefined. Accordingly, Congress enacted Title IX of the Consumer Protection Act, called the **Electronic Funds Transfer Act** (EFTA), to "provide a basic framework establishing the rights, liabilities, and responsibilities of participants in electronic fund transfers" with primary emphasis on "the provision of individual consumer rights." Because the EFTA deals exclusively with the protection of *consumers*, it does not govern electronic transfers between financial institutions, between financial institutions and businesses, and between businesses. The

Thwarting ATM Fraud

What is the easiest way to rob a bank these days? Head for your local ATM, or automatic teller machine. With nearly 90,000 machines open virtually round the clock nationwide, ATMs offer thieves a wide new frontier.

Thieves Get Sophisticated

These days, you still may find yourself held up by some robber who pulls a gun and demands your ATM withdrawal, but other thieves have gotten much more sophisticated. Often, ATM robbers will use binoculars or video cameras to record your finger movements as you enter your personal identification number at an ATM. Then they'll match your PIN with your account number on the ATM receipt that you perhaps carelessly threw away. If they encounter a problem, they'll even call you at home, posing as bank officials seeking to verify your PIN. You should know, however, that banks never do this sort of thing.

To reduce street crime around ATMs, banks have begun installing the machines in well-lighted public places such as 24-hour grocery stores and shopping malls. They have also teamed up with city officials in such places as Chicago and Los Angeles to install bank machines in police stations.

Malls Become Targets

Such measures, however, haven't stopped more cunning ATM robbers. One group, for example, carried out the most sophisticated heist so far in Manchester, Connecticut, in April and May 1993. That spring, operators approached mall officials at the Buckland Hills Mall about installing an ATM. Before a contract could be signed, the thieves rolled in a temporary-looking machine, which they left in the mall for two weeks, during which time shoppers who slipped in their cards and entered their PINs received an apologetic message saying that the machine was out of service. Often, a "repairman" stood by, ostensibly waiting to fix the machine. Even to mall employees, the ATM looked legitimate. Yet the machine, which rested on wheels, could have been carted away at any moment. Finally, two men dressed in uniforms, came on Mother's Day and did just that. Then, using the stolen PIN and account numbers that the machine had recorded, the robbers made fake cash cards, traveled to midtown Manhattan, and went on a banking spree that netted them $50,000 in one day.

Banks Held Liable

Fraud like this is costing banks plenty. According to ABC News, banks lost over $2 billion to ATM fraud in 2001.

One problem that banks face is that thieves like those in Connecticut can now buy used ATMs for as little as $6,000. Another is that customers often carelessly toss their ATM cards, PINs, or account receipts around. Many times, in fact, customers fall victim to friends or relatives who "borrow" their cards to make withdrawals.

Moreover, under the Electronic Funds Transfer Act, customers can limit their liability for unauthorized withdrawals. If, as a customer, you lose your card or it is stolen, you have two days to notify the bank from the time that you discover the problem. By acting quickly, you reduce your liability to no more than $50; if you wait four days, however, your liability shoots up to $500.

If you discover an unauthorized withdrawal on your monthly statement, you have sixty days from the postmark on the statement's envelope to report the problem. Again, your liability will be limited to $50. If you become the victim of a criminal who makes a fake ATM card for your account, you face no liability. Whatever the circumstance, the burden of proof rests with the bank. If your bank refuses to reimburse you in a timely manner, you can sue.

Precautions to Consider

Today, ATMs account for more than 7 billion transactions each year in the United States, and that number is growing. Increasingly, banks are using ATMs to sell everything from American Express traveler's checks to home equity loans. The list keeps expanding. And if you travel, some ATMs in foreign countries will even allow you to link up with your local bank, withdraw money from your account, and receive it in the local coin. To thwart would-be robbers, then, you may want to remember these important safety tips:

- Keep your ATM card and your PIN in separate places.
- Better yet, memorize your PIN, and never give it out to anyone.
- If you must keep a record of your PIN, put it in your safe deposit box at your bank.
- Never write your PIN on your ATM card or keep your PIN in your wallet.
- Avoid using the first part of your social security number, your driver's license number, your telephone number, or your birthday for your PIN.
- Don't leave your ATM card lying around the house for someone else to pick up.
- Keep all your ATM withdrawal receipts rather than tossing them away.
- Take someone with you to the cash machine and watch out for people who are loitering nearby.
- Head for ATMs in well-lighted, protected locations, such as grocery stores or malls.
- Never let a stranger into an ATM area with you, and get in and out quickly.
- Try to use ATMs during the day and have your card ready before you approach the machine.
- Conceal your finger movements from view as you enter your PIN.
- Opt for drive-through ATMs and keep your car windows and doors locked, except for the driver's side.
- Put your money away as soon as you get it and count it later.
- Finally, regularly compare your monthly statements with your ATM receipts.

act is similar in many respects to the Fair Credit Billing Act (see Chapter 45), which applies to credit card transactions. The Electronic Funds Transfer Act is administered by the Board of Governors of the Federal Reserve System, which is mandated to prescribe regulations to carry out the purposes of the act. Pursuant to this congressional mandate, the Federal Reserve has issued Regulation E.

DISCLOSURE

The EFTA is primarily a disclosure statute and as such requires that the terms and conditions of electronic funds transfers involving a consumer's account be disclosed in readily understandable language at the time the consumer contracts for such services. Included among the required disclosures are the consumer's liability for unauthorized transfers, the kinds of EFTs allowed, the charges for transfers or for the right to make transfers, the consumer's right to stop payment of preauthorized EFTs, the consumer's right to receive documentation of EFTs, rules concerning disclosure of information to third parties, procedures for correcting account errors, and the financial institution's liability to the consumer under the Act.

DOCUMENTATION AND PERIODIC STATEMENTS

The Act requires the financial institution to provide the consumer with written documentation of each transfer made from an electronic terminal at the time of transfer—a receipt. The receipt must clearly state the amount involved, the date, the type of transfer, the identity of the account(s) involved, the identity of any third party involved, and the location of the terminal involved.

In addition, the financial institution must provide each consumer with a periodic statement for each account of the consumer that may be accessed by means of an EFT. The statement must describe the amount, date, and location for each transfer; the fee, if any, to be charged for the transaction; and an address and phone number for questions and information.

PREAUTHORIZED TRANSFERS

A preauthorized transfer *from* a consumer's account must be authorized in advance by the consumer in *writing*, and a copy of the authorization must be provided to the consumer when the transfer is made. Up to three business days before the scheduled date of the transfer, a consumer may stop payment of a preauthorized EFT by notifying the financial institution orally or in writing, although the financial institution may require the consumer to provide written confirmation of an oral notification within fourteen days.

ERROR RESOLUTION

The consumer has sixty days after the financial institution sends a periodic statement in which to notify the institution of any errors appearing on that statement. The financial institution is required to investigate alleged errors and report its findings within ten business days. If the financial institution needs more than ten days to investigate, it may take up to forty-five days, provided it recredits the consumer's account for the amount alleged to be in error. If it determines that an error did occur, it must properly correct the error. Failure to investigate in good faith makes the financial institution liable to the consumer for treble damages (that is, three times the amount of provable damages).

CONSUMER LIABILITY

A consumer's liability for an unauthorized electronic funds transfer is limited to a maximum of $50 if the consumer notifies the financial institution within two days after he learns of the loss or theft. If the consumer does not report the loss or theft within two days, he is liable for losses up to $500. If the consumer fails to report the unauthorized use within sixty days of transmittal of a periodic statement, he is liable for losses resulting from any unauthorized EFT that appeared on the statement if the financial institution can show that the loss would not have occurred had the consumer reported the loss within sixty days.

> **Practical Advice**
>
> Promptly and carefully review all electronic fund activities to ensure that they are accurate, and if they are not, notify your financial institution immediately.

LIABILITY OF FINANCIAL INSTITUTION

A financial institution is liable to a consumer for all damages proximately caused by its failure to make an EFT in accordance with the terms and conditions of an account, in the correct amount, or in a timely manner when properly instructed to do so by the consumer. There are, however, exceptions to such liability. The financial institution will not be liable if

1. the consumer's account has insufficient funds through no fault of the financial institution,

2. the funds are subject to legal process,
3. the transfer would exceed an established credit limit,
4. an electronic terminal has insufficient cash, or
5. circumstances beyond the financial institution's control prevent the transfer.

The financial institution is also liable for failure to stop payment of a preauthorized transfer from a consumer's account when instructed to do so in accordance with the terms and conditions of the account.

CPA WHOLESALE FUNDS TRANSFERS

Article 4A, Funds Transfers, is designed to provide a statutory framework for a payment system that is not covered by existing Articles of the Uniform Commercial Code or by the Electronic Funds Transfer Act. The typical wholesale wire transfer involves sophisticated parties who desire great speed in transferring large sums of money. Article 4A has been universally adopted by the states and territories.

Article 4A provides that the parties to a funds transfer generally may by agreement vary their rights and obligations. Moreover, funds-transfer system rules governing banks that use the system may be effective even if such rules conflict with Article 4A. Rights and obligations under Article 4A can also be changed by Federal Reserve regulations and operating circulars of Federal Reserve Banks.

SCOPE OF ARTICLE

Article 4A, which covers wholesale funds transfers, defines a funds transfer as a "series of transactions, beginning with the originator's payment order, made for the purpose of making payment to the beneficiary of the order. The term includes any payment order issued by the originator's bank or an intermediary bank intended to carry out the originator's payment order. A funds transfer is completed by acceptance by the beneficiary's bank of a payment order for the benefit of the beneficiary of the originator's payment order." The Article, therefore, covers the transfers of credit that move from an originator to a beneficiary through the banking system. If any step in the process is governed by the Electronic Funds Transfer Act, however, the entire transaction is excluded from the Article's coverage.

The following examples illustrate the coverage of the Article.

1. Johnson Co. instructs its bank, First National Bank (FNB), to pay $2 million to West Co., also a customer of FNB. FNB executes the payment order by crediting West's account with $2 million and notifying West that the credit has been made and is available.
2. Assume the same facts as those in the first example, except that West's bank is Central Bank (CB). FNB will execute the payment order of Johnson Co. by issuing to CB its own payment order instructing CB to credit the account of West.
3. Assume the facts presented in the second example with the added fact that FNB does not have a correspondent relationship with CB. In this instance, FNB will have to issue its payment order to Northern Bank (NB), a bank that does have a correspondent relationship with CB, and NB will then issue its payment order to CB.

Payment Order A **payment order** is a sender's instruction to a receiving bank to pay, or to cause another bank to pay, a fixed or determinable amount of money to a beneficiary. The instruction may be communicated orally, electronically, or in writing. To be a payment order, the instruction must

1. contain no condition to payment other than the time of payment;
2. be sent to a receiving bank that is to be reimbursed either by debiting an account of the sender or by otherwise receiving payment from the sender; and
3. be transmitted by the sender directly to the receiving bank or indirectly through an agent, a funds-transfer system, or a communication system.

The payment order is issued when sent and, if more than one payment is to be made, each payment represents a separate payment order. In the examples above, there is one payment order in the first example (from Johnson Co.), two in the second example (from Johnson Co. and from FNB), and three in the third example (from Johnson Co., from FNB, and from Northern Bank).

Parties The **originator** is either the sender of the payment order or, in a series of payment orders, the sender of the first payment order. A **sender** is the party who gives an instruction to the **receiving bank**, or the bank to which the sender's instruction is addressed. The receiving bank may be the **originator's bank**, an intermediary bank, or the beneficiary's bank. The originator's bank is either the bank that receives the original payment order or the originator if the originator is a bank. The **beneficiary's bank**, the last bank in the chain of a funds transfer, is the bank instructed in the payment order to credit the beneficiary's account. The **beneficiary** is the person to be paid by the beneficiary bank. An **intermediary bank** is any receiving bank, other than the originator's bank or the beneficiary's bank, that receives the payment order. Thus, in the above examples,

CONCEPT REVIEW

Parties to a Funds Transfer

	Example 1	Example 2	Example 3
Originator	Johnson Co.	Johnson Co.	Johnson Co.
Sender(s)	Johnson Co.	Johnson Co. FNB	Johnson Co. FNB NB
Receiving Bank(s)	FNB	FNB CB	FNB CB NB
Originator's Bank	FNB	FNB	FNB
Beneficiary's Bank	FNB	CB	CB
Beneficiary	West	West	West
Intermediary Bank	—	—	NB

1. Johnson Co. is the *originator* in all three examples;
2. Johnson Co. is a *sender* in all three examples, FNB is a sender in examples 2 and 3, and NB is a sender in example 3;
3. FNB is the *receiving bank* of Johnson Co.'s payment order in all three examples; in example 2, CB is the receiving bank of FNB's payment order; and, in example 3, CB is the receiving bank of NB's payment order and NB is the receiving bank of FNB's payment order;
4. FNB is the *originator's bank* in all three examples;
5. FNB is the *beneficiary's bank* in example 1; CB is the beneficiary's bank in examples 2 and 3;
6. West is the *beneficiary* in all three examples;
7. NB is an intermediary bank in example 3.

In some instances, the originator and the beneficiary may be the same party. For example, a corporation may wish to transfer funds from one account to another account that is in the same or a different bank.

Excluded Transactions As previously mentioned, if any part of a funds transfer is governed by the Electronic Fund Transfer Act, the transfer is excluded from Article 4A coverage. In addition, Article 4A covers only credit transactions; it therefore excludes debit transactions. If the person making the payment gives the instruction, the transfer is a credit transfer. If, however, the person receiving the payment gives the instruction, the transfer is a debit transfer. For example, a seller of goods obtains authority from the purchaser to debit the purchaser's account after the seller ships the goods. Article 4A does not cover this transaction because the instructions to make payment issue from the beneficiary (the seller), not from the party whose account is to be debited (the purchaser). See Figure 28-2 for an example of credit transaction.

ACCEPTANCE

Rights and obligations arise as a result of a receiving bank's acceptance of a payment order. The effect of acceptance depends on whether the payment order was issued to the beneficiary's bank or to a receiving bank other than the beneficiary's bank.

If a receiving bank is not the beneficiary's bank, the receiving bank does not subject itself to any liability until it accepts the instrument. Acceptance by a receiving bank other than the beneficiary's bank occurs when the receiving bank executes the sender's order. Such execution occurs when the receiving bank "issues a payment order intended to carry out" the sender's payment order. When the receiving bank executes the sender's payment order, the bank is entitled to payment from the sender and can debit the sender's account.

The beneficiary's bank may accept an order in any of three ways, and acceptance occurs at the earliest of these

Figure 28-2 *Credit Transaction*

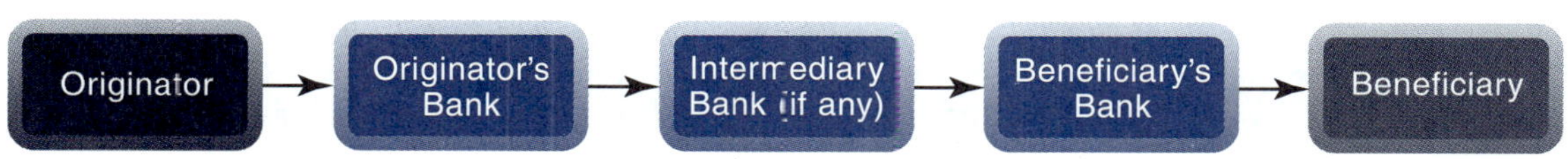

events: (1) when the bank (a) pays the beneficiary or (b) notifies the beneficiary that the bank has received the order or has credited the beneficiary's account with the funds; (2) when the bank receives payment of the sender's order; or (3) the opening of the next funds-transfer business day of the bank after the payment date of the order if the order was not rejected and funds are available for payment.

If a beneficiary's bank accepts a payment order, the bank is obliged to pay the beneficiary the amount of the order. The bank's acceptance of the payment order does not, however, create any obligation to either the sender or the originator.

ERRONEOUS EXECUTION OF PAYMENT ORDERS

If a receiving bank mistakenly executes a payment order for an amount greater than the amount authorized, the bank is entitled to payment only in the amount of the sender's correct order. To the extent allowed by the law governing mistake and restitution, the receiving bank may then recover from the beneficiary of the erroneous order the amount in excess of the authorized amount. If the wrong beneficiary is paid, however, the bank that issued the erroneous payment order is entitled to payment neither from its sender nor from prior senders and has the burden of recovering the payment from the improper beneficiary.

UNAUTHORIZED PAYMENT ORDERS

If a bank wishing to prevent unauthorized transactions establishes commercially reasonable security measures, to which a customer agrees, and the bank properly follows the process it has established, the customer must pay an order even if it was unauthorized. The customer, however, can avoid liability by showing that the unauthorized order was not caused directly or indirectly by (1) a person with access to confidential security information who was acting for the customer or (2) a person who obtained such information from a source controlled by the customer.

CHAPTER SUMMARY

Bank Deposits and Collections

Collection of Items

Depositary Bank the bank in which the payee or holder deposits a check for credit

Provisional Credit tentative credit for the deposit of an instrument until final credit is given

Final Credit payment of the instrument by the payor bank; if the payor bank (drawee) does not pay the check, the depositary bank reverses the provisional credit

Intermediary Bank a bank, other than the depositary or payor bank, involved in the collection process

Collecting Bank any bank (other than the payor bank) handling the item for payment

- *Agency* a collecting bank is an agent or subagent of the owner of the check until the settlement becomes final
- *Duty of Care* a collecting bank must exercise ordinary care in handling an item
- *Duty to Act Timely* a collecting bank acts timely if it takes proper action before its midnight deadline (midnight of the next banking day)
- *Indorsements* if an item is restrictively indorsed "for deposit only," only a bank may be a holder
- *Warranties* customers and collecting banks give warranties on transfer, presentment, and encoding
- *Final Payment* occurs when the payor bank does any of the following, whichever happens first: (1) pays an item in cash; (2) settles and does not have the right to revoke the settlement; or (3) makes a provisional settlement and does not properly revoke it

Payor Bank under its contract with the drawer, the payor or drawee bank agrees to pay to the payee or his order checks that are issued by the drawer, provided the order is not countermanded by a stop payment order and provided there are sufficient funds in the drawer's account

Relationship Between Payor Bank and Its Customers

Contractual Relationship the relationship between a payor bank and its checking account customer is primarily the product of their contractual arrangement

Payment of an Item when a payor receives an item for which the funds in the account are insufficient, the bank may either dishonor the item and return it or pay the item and charge the customer's account even though an overdraft is created

Stop Payment Orders an oral stop payment order (a command from a drawer to a drawee not to pay an instrument) is binding, for fourteen calendar days; a written order is effective for six months and may be renewed in writing

Bank's Right to Subrogation on Improper Payment if a payor bank pays an item over a stop payment order or otherwise in violation of its contract, the payor bank is subrogated to (obtains) the rights of (1) any holder in due course on the item against the drawer or maker; (2) the payee or any holder against the drawer or maker and (3) the drawer or maker against the payee or any other holder

Disclosure Requirement all depositary institutions must disclose in great detail to their consumers the terms and conditions of their deposit account

Customer's Death or Incompetence a bank may pay an item if it does not know of the customer's incompetency or death

Customer's Duties the customer must examine bank statements and items carefully and promptly to discover any unauthorized signatures or alterations

Electronic Funds Transfer

Types of Electronic Transfer

Definition any transfer of funds, other than a transaction originated by check, draft, or similar paper instrument, which is initiated through an electronic terminal, telephonic instrument, or computer or magnetic tape so as to order, instruct, or authorize a financial institution to debit or credit an account

Purpose to eliminate the paperwork involved in processing checks and the "float" available to a drawer of a check

Types of Electronic Funds Transfers
- *Automated Teller Machines*
- *Point-of-Sale Systems*
- *Direct Deposits and Withdrawals*
- *Pay-by-Phone Systems*
- *Wholesale Electronic Funds Transfers*

Consumer Funds Transfers

Electronic Funds Transfer Act provides a basic framework establishing the rights, liabilities, and responsibilities of participants in consumer electronic funds transfers

Financial Institution Responsibility liable to a consumer for all damage proximately caused by its failure to properly handle an EFT transaction

Article 4A—Funds Transfers

Scope
- *Wholesale Funds Transfers* the movement of funds through the banking system; excludes all transactions governed by the Electronic Funds Transfer Act
- *Payment Order* an instruction of a sender to a receiving bank to pay, or to cause another bank to pay, a fixed amount of money to a beneficiary
- *Parties* include originator, sender, receiving bank, originator's bank, beneficiary's bank, beneficiary, and intermediary banks

Acceptance rights and obligations that arise as a result of a receiving bank's acceptance of a payment order

QUESTIONS

1. On December 9, Jane Jones writes a check for $500 payable to Ralph Rodgers in payment for goods to be received later in the month. Before the close of business on the ninth, Jane notifies the bank by telephone to stop payment on the check. On Monday, December 19, Ralph gives the check to Bill Briggs for value and without notice. On the twentieth, Bill deposits the check in his account at Bank A. On the twenty-first, Bank A sends the check to its correspondent, Bank B. On the twenty-second, Bank B presents the check through the clearinghouse to Bank C. On the twenty-third, Bank C presents the check to Bank P, the payor bank. On Wednesday, December 28, the payor bank makes payment of the check final. Is Jane Jones' stop payment order effective against the payor bank? Explain.

2. Howard Harrison, a longtime customer of Western Bank, operates a small department store, Harrison's Store. Because his store has few experienced employees, Harrison frequently travels throughout the United States on buying trips, although he also runs the financial operations of the business. On one of his buying trips, Harrison purchased a gross of sport shirts from Well-Made Shirt Company and paid for the transaction with a check on his store account with Western Bank in the amount of $1,000. Adams, an employee of Well-Made who deposits its checks in Security Bank, sloppily raised the amount of the check to $10,000 and indorsed the check, "Pay to the order of Adams from Pension Plan Benefits, Well-Made Shirt Company by Adams." He cashed the check and cannot be found. Western Bank processed the check, paid it, and sent it to Harrison's Store with the monthly statement. After briefly examining the statement, Harrison left on another buying trip for three weeks.
   a. Assuming the bank acted in good faith and the alteration is not discovered and reported to the bank until an audit conducted thirteen months after the statement was received by Harrison's Store, who must bear the loss on the raised check?
   b. Assume that Harrison, who was unable to examine his statement promptly because of his buying trips, left instructions with the bank to carefully examine and to notify him of any item over $5,000 to be charged to his account; assume further that the bank nevertheless paid the item in his absence. Who bears the loss if the alteration is discovered one month after the statement was received by Harrison's Store? If the alteration is discovered thirteen months later?

3. Tom Jones owed Bank of Cleveland $10,000 on a note due November 17, with 1 percent interest due the bank for each day delinquent in payment. Jones issued a $10,000 check to Bank of Cleveland and deposited it in the night vault the evening of November 17. Several days later, he received a letter saying he owed one day's interest on the payment because of a one-day delinquency in payment. Jones refused because he said he had put the payment in the vault on November 17. Who is correct? Why?

4. Assume that Davis draws a check on Dallas Bank, payable to the order of Perkins; that Perkins indorses it to Cooper; that Cooper deposits it to her account in Houston Bank; that Houston Bank presents it to Dallas Bank, the drawee; and that Dallas Bank dishonors it because of insufficient funds. Houston Bank receives notification of the dishonor on Monday but, because of an interruption of communication facilities, fails to notify Cooper until Wednesday. What will be the result?

5. Jones, a food wholesaler whose company has an account with City Bank in New York City, is traveling in California on business. He finds a particularly attractive offer and decides to buy a carload of oranges for delivery in New York. He gives Saltin, the seller, his company's check for $25,000 to pay for the purchase. Saltin deposits the check, with others he received that day, with his bank, the Carrboro Bank. Carrboro Bank sends the check to Downs Bank in Los Angeles, which in turn deposits it with the Los Angeles Federal Reserve Bank (L.A. Fed). The L.A. Fed sends the check, with others, to the New York Federal Reserve Bank (N.Y. Fed), which forwards the check to City Bank, Jones's bank, for collection.

a. Is City Bank a depositary bank? A collecting bank? A payor bank?
b. Is Carrboro a depositary bank? A collecting bank?
c. Is the N.Y. Fed. an intermediary bank?
d. Is Downs Bank a collecting bank?

Explain your answers in each part.

6. On April 1, Moore gave Pipkin a check properly drawn by Moore on Zebra Bank for $500 in payment of a painting to be framed and delivered the next day. Pipkin immediately indorsed the check and gave it to Yeager Bank as payment in full of his indebtedness to the bank on a note he previously had signed. Yeager Bank canceled the note and returned it to Pipkin.

On April 2, upon learning that the painting had been destroyed in a fire at Pipkin's studio, Moore promptly went to Zebra Bank, signed a printed form of stop payment order, and gave it to the cashier. Zebra Bank refused payment on the check upon proper presentment by Yeager Bank.

a. What are the rights of Yeager Bank against Zebra Bank?
b. What are the rights of Yeager Bank against Moore?
c. Assuming that Zebra Bank inadvertently paid the amount of the check to Yeager Bank and debited Moore's account, what are the rights of Moore against Zebra Bank?

7. As payment in advance for services to be performed, Acton signed and delivered the following instrument:

December 1, 2003

LAST NATIONAL BANK
MONEYVILLE, STATE X

Pay to the order of Olaf Owen $1,500.00 ________Fifteen Hundred Dollars________ For services to be performed by Olaf Owen starting on December 6, 2003.

(signed) Arthur Acton

Owen requested and received Last National Bank's certification of the check even though Acton had only $900 on deposit. Owen indorsed the check in blank and delivered it to Dan Doty in payment of a preexisting debt.

When Owen failed to appear for work, Acton issued a written stop payment order ordering the bank not to pay the check. Doty presented the check to Last National Bank for payment. The bank refused payment.

What are the bank's rights and liabilities relating to the transactions described?

8. Jones drew a check for $1,000 on The First Bank and mailed it to the payee, Thrift, Inc. Caldwell stole the check from Thrift, Inc., chemically erased the name of the payee, and inserted the name of Henderson as payee. Caldwell also increased the amount of the check to $10,000 and, by using the name of Henderson, negotiated the check to Willis. Willis then took the check to The First Bank, obtained its certification on the check, and negotiated the check to Griffin, who deposited the check in The Second National Bank for collection. The Second National forwarded the check to the Detroit Trust Company for collection from The First Bank, which honored the check. Griffin exhausted her account in the Second National Bank, and the account was closed. Shortly thereafter, The First Bank learned that it had paid an altered check.

What are the rights of each of the parties?

9. On July 21, Boehmer, a customer of Birmingham Trust, secured a loan from that bank for the principal sum of $5,500 in order to purchase a boat allegedly being built for him by A. C. Manufacturing Company, Inc. After Boehmer signed a promissory note, Birmingham Trust issued a cashier's check to Boehmer and A. C. Manufacturing Company as payees. The check was given to Boehmer, who then forged A. C. Manufacturing Company's indorsement and deposited the check in his own account at Central Bank. Central Bank credited Boehmer's account and then placed the legend "P.I.G.," meaning "Prior Indorsements Guaranteed," on the check. The check was presented to and paid by Birmingham Trust on July 22. When the loan became delinquent in March of the following year, Birmingham Trust contacted A. C. Manufacturing Company to learn the location of the boat. They were informed that it had never been purchased, and they soon after learned that Boehmer had died on January 24 of that year. Can Birmingham Trust obtain reimbursement from Central Bank under Central's warranty of prior indorsements? Explain.

10. Jason, who has extremely poor vision, went to an ATM to withdraw $200 on February 1. Joshua saw that Jason was having great difficulty reading the computer screen and offered to help. Joshua obtained Jason's personal identification number and secretly exchanged one of his old credit cards for Jason's ATM card. Between February 1 and February 15, Joshua withdrew $1,600 from Jason's account. On February 15, Jason discovered that his ATM card was missing and immediately notified his bank. The bank closed Jason's ATM account on February 16, by which time Joshua had withdrawn another $150. What is Jason's liability, if any, for the unauthorized use of his account?

11. Advanced Alloys, Inc., issued a check in the amount of $2,500 to Sergeant Steel Corporation. The check was presented for payment fourteen months later to the Chase Manhattan Bank, which made payment on the check and charged Advanced Alloys's account. Can Advanced Alloys recover the payment made on the check? Why?

CASE PROBLEMS

12. Laboratory Management deposited into its account at Pulaski Bank a check issued by Fairway Farms in the amount of $150,000. The date of deposit was February 5. Pulaski, the depositary bank, initiated the collection process immediately by forwarding the check to Worthen Bank on the sixth. Worthen sent the check on for collection to M Bank Dallas, and M Bank Dallas, still on February 6, delivered the check to M Bank Fort Worth. That same day, M Bank Fort Worth delivered the check to the Fort Worth Clearinghouse. Because TAB/West Side, the drawee/payor bank, was not a clearinghouse member, it had to rely on TAB/Fort Worth for further transmittal of the check. TASI, a processing center used by both TAB/Fort Worth and TAB/West Side, received the check on the sixth and processed it as a reject item because of insufficient funds. On the seventh, TAB/West Side determined to return the check unpaid. TASI gave M Bank Dallas telephone notice of the return on February 7, but physically misrouted the check. Because of this, M Bank Dallas did not physically receive the check until February 19. However, M Bank notified Worthen telephonically on the fifteenth of the dishonor and return of the check. Worthen received the check on the twenty-first and notified Pulaski by telephone on the twenty-second. Pulaski actually received the check from Worthen on the twenty-third. On February 22 and 23, Laboratory Management's checking account with Pulaski was $46,000. Pulaski did not freeze the account because it considered the return to be too late. The Laboratory Management account was finally frozen on April 30, when it had a balance of $1,400. Pulaski brings this suit against TAB/Fort Worth, Tab/Dallas, and TASI, alleging their notice of dishonor was not timely relayed to Pulaski. Explain whether Pulaski is correct in its assertion.

13. On November 22, a $25,000 check drawn on the First National Bank of Nevada was deposited with Lincoln First Bank-Central (http://www.chase.com). Lincoln forwarded the check to Nevada via Hartford National Bank and Trust Company and Wells Fargo Bank (http://wellsfargo.com/). Nevada received the check on Friday, December 10, and discovered that it was drawn on insufficient funds. That same day, Nevada informed Wells Fargo by telephone that the check had been dishonored. On Monday, December 13, Nevada mailed the check to Wells Fargo, which received it on Friday, December 17. Upon receiving the check, Wells Fargo promptly wired notice of the dishonor to Hartford and mailed the check to Hartford. Hartford received the check on December 21 and mailed it to Lincoln, which received it on December 27. Lincoln refused to accept the check, claiming that the notice of dishonor had arrived too late. Wells Fargo, which eventually ended up with the check and the $25,000 loss, brought an action to reverse the $25,000 credit it had given to Hartford in the course of handling the check. Decision?

14. On Tuesday, June 11, Siniscalchi issued a $200 check on the drawee, Valley Bank. On Saturday morning, June 15, the check was cashed. This transaction, as well as others taking place on that Saturday morning, was not recorded or processed through the bank's bookkeeping system until Monday, June 17. On that date, Siniscalchi arrived at the bank at 9:00 A.M. and asked to place a stop payment order on the check. A bank employee checked the bank records, which at that time indicated the instrument had not cleared the bank. At 9:45 A.M., she gave him a printed notice confirming his request to stop payment. May Siniscalchi recover the $200 paid on the check? Explain.

15. Tally held a savings account with American Security Bank (http://www.asbank.com/). On seven occasions, Tally's personal secretary, who received his bank statements and had custody of his passbook, forged Tally's name on withdrawal slips that she then presented to the bank. The secretary obtained $52,825 in this manner. She confessed this to Tally after avoiding detection for several years. Can Tally recover the funds from American Security Bank? The bank moved for partial summary judgment. Decision?

16. Morvarid Kashanchi and her sister, Firoyeh Paydar, held a savings account with Texas Commerce Medical Bank. An unauthorized withdrawal of $4,900 from the account was allegedly made by means of a telephone conversation between some other unidentified individual and a bank employee. Paydar learned of the transfer of funds when she received her bank statement and notified the bank that the withdrawal was unauthorized. The bank, however, declined to recredit the account for the $4,900 transfer. Kashanchi brought an action against the bank, claiming that the bank had violated the Electronic Fund Transfer Act. The bank defended by arguing that the Act did not apply. Does the Electronic Fund Transfer Act govern the transaction? Explain.

17. On September 22, 1986, New York City Shoes (NYCS) issued a check in the amount of $100,000 to the Maxwell Shoe Company (Maxwell). The check was drawn on one of NYCS's accounts at Pennsylvania Fidelity Bank (http://www.fidelitybk.com/). Maxwell deposited the check in its account at the First National Bank of Boston (Boston), which credited Maxwell's account with the face amount of the check and then processed the check through the Federal Reserve system. Checks presently are processed by Magnetic Ink Character Recognition (MICR). Under this procedure, each bank check is preprinted with magnetic characters along the lower left-hand edge. These characters designate the bank upon which the check is drawn and the account number of the drawer. When a check is presented to another bank (the depositary bank), that bank adds additional magnetic encoding, at the lower right-hand side of the check, specifying the amount of the check. From there, the check goes through the bank clearing system to the bank on which the check is drawn (the payor bank) and is charged against the drawer's account without further human intervention.

In this case, Boston properly encoded NYCS's check, but NYCS's account contained insufficient funds; consequently, Fidelity returned the check to Boston. Boston did not charge Maxwell's account because of the check's uncollectibility but instead represented the check to Fidelity. To the bottom of the check, Boston attached a "tape skirt," on which it reencoded the check so that it could be processed through the Federal Reserve system. Boston's encoder made an error, however, and encoded the amount of the check as $10,000, rather than $100,000. The computers that processed the check did not detect the error. When the check arrived at Fidelity on October 3, 1986, it was charged against NYCS's account in the amount of $10,000. Boston, which became aware of the error only after that sum was forwarded to it, then made demand on Fidelity for $90,000. Fidelity replied that it was unable to honor the request because NYCS's account was insufficient to cover it.

Boston filed suit against Fidelity for the $90,000, arguing that Fidelity was liable under the "final payment" rule of the UCC, which provides that "[a]n item is finally paid by a payor bank when the bank . . . has completed the process of posting the item to the indicated account of the drawer, maker or other person to be charged therewith. . . . Upon a final payment . . . the payor bank shall be accountable for the amount of the item."

Boston argued that Fidelity did post the check against NYCS's account on October 3, 1986, and therefore, under the Code, was accountable to Boston for the amount of the check. Boston further argued that it was irrelevant that the check was encoded in the wrong amount, since it was undisputed that Fidelity "completed the process of posting the item to the indicated account of the drawer" on October 3, 1986. Fidelity countered that for purposes of the Code, the "amount of the item" for which the payor bank must account should be the encoded amount of the check rather than its actual face amount. Decide this case.

18. Between October 1990, and January, 1992, Great Lakes Higher Education Corp. (Great Lakes) (http://www.glhec.org/), a not-for-profit student loan servicer, issued 224 student loan checks totaling $273,152.88. The checks were drawn against Great Lakes's account at First Wisconsin National Bank of Milwaukee (First Wisconsin). Each of the 224 checks were presented to Austin Bank of Chicago (Austin) without indorsement of the named payee. Austin Bank accepted each check for purposes of collection and without delay forwarded each check to First Wisconsin for that purpose. First Wisconsin paid Austin Bank the face amount of each check even though the indorsement signature of the payee was not on any of the checks. Has Austin Bank breached its warranty to First Wisconsin and Great Lakes due to the absence of proper indorsements? Explain.

http:// **Internet Exercise** Find and review information about (a) electronic banking, (b) the Federal Reserve System, and (c) the Federal Deposit Insurance Company.

PART VI

AGENCY

The American Law Institute
http://www.ali.org/

Law About Agency
http://www.law.cornell.edu/topics/agency.html

Convention on Agency in the International Sale of Goods
http://www.unidroit.org/english/conventions/c-ag.htm

Florida Bar Association ("Florida Powers of Attorney")
http://www.flabar.org/newflabar/consumerservices/General.Pam/

Nevada Bar Association ("Power of Attorney Forms")
http://www.nvbar.org/Publications/Publications_Pamphlets/Power_of_Attorney_Forms.htm

Uniform Statutory Form Power of Attorney Act
http://www.law.upenn.edu/bll/ulc/fnact99/1980s/usfpaa88.htm

CHAPTER 29

Relationship of Principal and Agent

Practically all of the world's business involves agents and in most important transactions, an agent on each side.

WARREN SEABEY, IN *HANDBOOK ON THE LAW OF AGENCY*

Learning Objectives

After reading this chapter you should be able to:

1. Distinguish among the following relationships: (a) agency, (b) employment, and (c) independent contractor.
2. Explain the requirements for creating an agency relationship.
3. List and explain the duties owed by an agent to her principal.
4. List and explain the duties owed by a principal to his agent.
5. Identify the ways in which an agency relationship may be terminated.

By using agents, one person (the principal) may enter into any number of business transactions as though he had carried them out personally, thus multiplying and expanding his business activities. The law of agency, like the law of contracts, is basic to almost every other branch of business law.

Practically every type of contract or business transaction can be created or conducted through an agent. Therefore, the place and importance of agency in the practical conduct and operation of business cannot be overemphasized, particularly in the case of partnerships, corporations, and other business associations. Partnership is founded on the agency of the partners. Each partner is an agent of the partnership and as such has the authority to represent and bind the partnership in all usual transactions of the partnership. Corporations, in turn, must act through the agency of their officers and employees. Limited liability companies act through the actions of their members, managers, or both. Thus, practically and legally, agency is an essential part of partnerships, corporations, and other business associations. In addition, sole proprietors also may employ agents in the operations of their businesses. Business, therefore, is largely conducted by agents or representatives, not by the owners themselves.

Although some overlap occurs, the law of agency divides broadly into two main parts: the internal and the external. An agent functions as an agent by dealing with third persons, thereby establishing legal relationships between her principal and those third persons. These relationships are the external part of agency law, which we will discuss in the next chapter. In this chapter, we will consider the nature and function of agency, as well as other topics concerning the internal part of the law of agency.

Agency is primarily governed by state common law. An orderly presentation of this law is found in the Restatement (Second) of the Law of Agency published by the American Law Institute (ALI). Regarded as a valuable authoritative reference work, the Restatement is extensively cited and quoted in reported judicial opinions and by legal scholars. The ALI is in the process of adopting a third Restatement of Agency.

CPA NATURE OF AGENCY

Agency is a *consensual* relationship between two persons, the **principal** and the **agent**, through which the agent is authorized to act for and on behalf of the principal. An agent is, therefore, one who represents another, the principal, in business dealings with a third person; and the operation of agency therefore involves three persons: the principal, the agent, and a third person. In dealings with a third person, the agent acts for and in the name and place of the principal, who, along with the third person, is a party to the transaction, which is usually contractual. The result of the agent's functioning is exactly the same as if the principal had dealt directly with the third person. However, if the existence and identity of the principal are disclosed, the agent acts not as a party but simply as an intermediary.

Within the scope of the authority granted to her by her principal, the agent may negotiate the terms of contracts with others and bind her principal to such contracts. Moreover, the negligence of an agent who is an employee in conducting the business of her principal exposes the principal to tort liability for injury and loss suffered by third persons.

SCOPE OF AGENCY PURPOSES

As a general rule, a person may do through an agent whatever business activity he may accomplish personally. Conversely, whatever he cannot legally do, he cannot authorize another to do for him. In addition, a person may not appoint an agent to perform acts that are so personal that their performance may not be delegated to another, as in the case of a contract for personal services.

OTHER LEGAL RELATIONSHIPS

Two other legal relationships overlap with agency: employer-employee and principal-independent contractor. In the **employment relationship**, the employer has the right to control the physical conduct of the employee. In contrast, a person who engages an **independent contractor** to do a specific job does not have the right to control the conduct and activities of the independent contractor in the performance of his contract. The latter simply contracts to do a job and is free to choose the method and manner in which to perform it. For example, a full-time chauffeur is an employee, whereas a taxicab driver hired to carry a person to the airport is an independent contractor engaged by the passenger.

All employees are agents, even those employees not authorized to contract on behalf of the employer or otherwise to conduct business with third parties. Thus, an assembly-line worker in a factory is an agent of the company employing her.

Although all employees are agents, not all agents are employees. Agents who are not employees are independent contractors. For instance, an attorney retained to handle a particular transaction would be an independent contractor-agent for that particular transaction. Finally, not all independent contractors are agents. For example, the taxicab driver in the example above is not an agent. Likewise, if Pam hires Bill to build a stone wall around her property, Bill is an independent contractor who is not an agent.

The distinction between employee and independent contractor has a number of important legal consequences. For example, as we will discuss in the next chapter, a principal is liable for the torts an employee commits within the scope of her employment but ordinarily is not liable for torts committed by an independent contractor. The following case further explains the differences between an employee and an independent contractor.

Practical Advice

When appointing an agent, consider structuring the relationship as a principal and independent contractor.

Jaeger v. Western Rivers Fly Fisher

United States District Court, District of Utah, 1994
855 F.Supp. 1217

FACTS Western Rivers Fly Fisher (Western) **(http://www.wrflyfisher.com)** operates under license of the U.S. Forest Service **(http://www.fs.fed.us)** as an "outfitter," a corporation in the business of arranging fishing expeditions on the Green River. The defendant, Michael D. Petragallo, is licensed by the Forest Service as a guide to conduct fishing expeditions but cannot do so by himself, because the Forest Service licenses only outfitters to float patrons down the

Green River. Western and several other licensed outfitters contact Petragallo to guide clients on fishing trips. Because the Forest Service licenses only outfitters to sponsor fishing expeditions, every guide must display on the boat and vehicle he uses the insignia of the outfitter sponsoring the particular trip. Petragallo may agree or refuse to take individuals Western refers to him, and Western does not restrict him from guiding expeditions for other outfitters. Western pays Petragallo a certain sum per fishing trip and does not make any deductions from his compensation. The Internal Revenue Service has determined that, for tax purposes, Western is properly treating guides it hires as independent contractors. Petragallo's responsibilities include transporting patrons to the Green River, using his own boat for fishing trips, providing food and overnight needs for patrons, assisting patrons in fly fishing, and transporting them from the river to their vehicles.

Robert McMaster contacted Western and arranged for a fishing trip for himself and two others. The plaintiff, Jaeger, was a member of McMaster's fishing party. McMaster paid Western, which set the price for the trip, planned the itinerary for the McMaster party, rented fishing rods to them, and arranged for Petragallo to be their guide. When Petragallo met the McMaster party, he answered affirmatively when the plaintiff asked him if he worked for Western. Petragallo provided his own vehicle and boat and supplied the food, equipment, and gasoline for the trip. Both the vehicle and the boat had signs bearing Western's identification and logo. While driving the McMaster party back to town at the conclusion of the fishing trip, Petragallo lost control of his vehicle, injuring the plaintiff. The plaintiff brought suit against Western, Petragallo, and others. Western moved for summary judgment, arguing that, because Petragallo is an independent contractor and was never its employee, it is not liable, as a matter of law, for Petragallo's acts in causing the plaintiff's injuries.

DECISION Motion for summary judgment denied.

OPINION Sam, J. Plaintiff * * * argues Petragallo was Western's employee, and, thus, Western is liable for Petragallo's actions under the doctrine of *respondeat superior*. Western contends Petragallo is an independent contractor for whose conduct Western is not liable. [Citations.] * * * (generally, employer who hires independent contractor is not liable for independent contractor's negligence to third party).

The Utah Supreme Court distinguished between an employee and an independent contractor * * * :

> [a]n employee is one who is hired and paid a salary, a wage, or at a fixed rate, to perform, the employer's work as directed by the employer and who is subject to a comparatively high degree of control in performing those duties. In contrast, an independent contractor is one who is engaged to do some particular project or piece of work, usually for a set total sum, who may do the job in his own way, subject to only minimal restrictions or controls and is responsible only for its satisfactory completion.
>
> [Citations.] Factors a court may consider in determining the nature of the relationship include:
>
> (1) whatever covenants or agreements exist concerning the right of direction and control over the employee, whether express or implied; (2) the right to hire and fire; (3) the method of payment, i.e., whether in wages or fees, as compared to payment for a complete job or project; and (4) the furnishing of the equipment.

[Citations.] The court has placed varying significance upon the factor of control. [Court's footnote: * * * ("While the elements of control by the employer and the intent of the parties are the most important ones, none of the factors separately is controlling. It is from consideration of all of them together that determination is to be made whether the relationship is in essence that of employer-employee or of independent contractor.")]

The Utah Supreme Court has identified differences between employment and independent contractor relationships. For example, in [citation], a truck driver was found to be an employee because the truck he operated was registered in a corporate name and had a corporate sign on it, he had to obtain approval from a corporate supervisor before driving a load, he was obligated to haul loads as instructed and check in with a dispatcher at various times en route, he was directed as to how many miles per month the truck should be operated, and he was required to drive five miles per hour under the speed limit. In [citation], a dry wall applicator had employee status because he was "shown what services were to be performed, not allowed to commence work on his first appearance, directed where to stack the dry wall and to use care in protecting the floor, furnished a protective covering and a ladder and paid at an hourly rate." [Citation.]

In contrast, in [citation], the Utah Supreme Court affirmed a ruling by the Industrial Commission that the plaintiff was an independent contractor. The court noted the plaintiff had an oral agreement with the defendant to install roof shingles periodically on homes the defendant was constructing. The plaintiff billed the defendant monthly, and the defendant made no withholding deductions from the plaintiff's compensation. The plaintiff supplied his own tools, used his discretion in establishing his own work schedule, and worked on any house he chose, whether being built by the defendant or others. [Citation.] Despite the fact that the defendant supplied the plaintiff with shingles and nails and directed the plaintiff in the manner and timing of the installation, the court concluded the defendant did not maintain sufficient supervision or control over the plaintiff for the plaintiff to be considered an employee. [Citation.] Rather, the plaintiff was an independent contractor. [Citations.]

In the instant case, the record reveals Western: advertises fishing expeditions, sets the prices, and collects a deposit from patrons; may suggest fishing areas to patrons; may create an itinerary; engages guides such as Petragallo to conduct a particular trip for a set amount without withholding taxes; sets a meeting time and place for Petragallo and patrons; provides signs for Petragallo's vehicle and boat in compliance with Forest Service regulations; and may rent fishing rods and clothing to patrons. Western also holds the license under which Petragallo and other river guides must operate, pursuant to Forest Service requirements.

Once Western sets up a fishing trip and engages Petragallo for a certain sum as a guide, Petragallo: buys food for himself and patrons for the fishing trip, may provide transportation to and from the river, uses his own vehicle and boat, supplies his own fishing equipment, and uses his expertise in floating patrons to fishing areas and assisting them in fly fishing.

The court cannot say these facts, relative to whether Petragallo is Western's employee or an independent contractor, point to a single conclusion only. On the one hand, the facts suggest Petragallo is an independent contractor. Western engages Petragallo to guide particular fishing trips, for a set sum, allowing him to conduct the trips in his own discretion. Petragallo may even choose to refuse to guide patrons Western has referred to him. Western's actions appear to involve setting up the parameters of a fishing trip and place "only minimal restrictions or controls" upon Petragallo. [Citation.] Also, Western and Petragallo seem to operate as if Petragallo were an independent contractor, as Western has the right to hire Petragallo or any other available guide as it sees fit, pays him per trip, expects him to furnish his own equipment, and treats him as an independent contractor for tax purposes. Moreover, although Petragallo must operate under Western's license, as required by the Forest Service, Western does not control through its license the manner in which Petragallo conducts fishing trips. Apparently, once Western sets up a fishing trip and engages Petragallo as a guide, it relies upon and expects Petragallo to use his own discretion in doing everything else to ensure patrons have an enjoyable experience, including using his own expertise, vehicle, boat, and equipment. [Citation.] Finally, because Forest Service licensing regulations prohibit an individual river guide from conducting tours unless sponsored by an outfitter, it may be argued that, if Petragallo is subject to any control, it is by the Forest Service, not Western.

However, on the other hand, the facts may indicate Petragallo is an employee. It is actually a judgment call as to how much control Western has over Petragallo through its advertising and arranging of fishing expeditions. Although Petragallo may refuse to guide patrons, Western apparently contacts Petragallo only after it has planned the fishing trip, without involving him, and may provide him with a set itinerary. Also, Forest Service licensing regulations place Western in a position of having the ultimate right to control Petragallo's work as, without solicitations from Western and other outfitters, Petragallo would be prohibited completely from conducting fishing expeditions.

In applying the above factors and standards, the court concludes a determination of the nature of Petragallo's relationship with Western is a factual issue inappropriate for summary judgment. Accordingly, the court denies Western's motion for summary judgment on this issue.

INTERPRETATION Factors relevant to determining whether an employment relationship exists include (1) the principal's right to control the agent, (2) the right to hire and fire, (3) the method of payment, and (4) the furnishing of equipment.

CRITICAL THINKING QUESTION Do you agree that this case requires further fact finding? Explain.

In addition, under numerous federal and state statutes, the obligations of a principal apply only to agents who are employees. These statutes cover such matters as labor relations, employment discrimination, disability, employee safety, workers' compensation, social security, minimum wage, and unemployment compensation. We will discuss these and other statutory enactments affecting the employment relationship in Chapter 42.

CPA CREATION OF AGENCY

Agency is a consensual relationship that the principal and agent may form by contract or agreement. The Restatement defines an agency relationship as "the fiduciary relation which results from the manifestation of consent by one person [the principal] to another [the agent] that the other shall act on his behalf and subject to his control, and consent by the other so to act." The

Restatement further provides that "[a]n agency relation exists only if there has been a manifestation by the principal to the agent that the agent may act on his account, and consent by the agent so to act." Thus, whether an agency relationship has been created is determined by an *objective* test. If the principal requests another to act for him with respect to a matter and indicates that the other is to act without further communication, and the other consents to act, the relation of principal and agent exists. For example, Paula writes to Austin, a factor whose business is purchasing goods for others, telling him to select described goods and ship them at once to Paula. Before answering Paula's letter, Austin does as directed, charging the goods to Paula. He is authorized to do this because an agency relationship exists between Paula and Austin.

The principal has the right to control the conduct of the agent with respect to the matters entrusted to the agent. The principal's right to control continues throughout the duration of the agency relationship.

The relationship of principal and agent is consensual and not necessarily contractual; therefore, it may exist without consideration. An agency created without consideration is a **gratuitous agency**. For example, Patti asks her friend Andrew to return for credit goods recently purchased from a store. If Andrew consents, a gratuitous agency has been created. The power of a gratuitous agent to affect the principal's relationships with third persons is the same as that of a paid agent, and his liabilities to and rights against third persons are the same as well. Nonetheless, agency by contract, the most usual method of creating the relationship, must satisfy all of the requirements of a contract.

In some circumstances a person is held liable as a principal, even though no actual agency has been created. Called **agency by estoppel**, apparent agency or ostensible agency, this liability arises when (1) a person (P) intentionally or negligently causes a belief that another person (A) has authority to act on P's behalf, (2) a third person (T) reasonably and in good faith relies on the appearances created by P, and (3) T changes her position in reliance on A's apparent authority. When these requirements are met, P is liable to T for the loss T suffered by changing her position.

Miller v. McDonald's Corporation

Court of Appeals of Oregon, 1997
150 Or.App. 274, 945 P.2d 1107

FACTS Joni Miller seeks damages from defendant McDonald's Corporation **(http://www.mcdonalds.com)** for injuries that she suffered when she bit into a heart-shaped sapphire stone while eating a Big Mac sandwich that she had purchased at a McDonald's restaurant in Tigard. McDonald's claims it is not liable because the 3K Corporation owns the restaurant. 3K owned and operated the restaurant under a License Agreement with McDonald's that required 3K to operate in a manner consistent with the "McDonald's System." This system includes proprietary rights in trademarks, "designs and color schemes" for restaurant buildings and signs, and specifications for certain food products as well as other business practices and policies. 3K, as the licensee, agreed to adopt and exclusively use the business practices of McDonald's. Despite these detailed instructions, the Agreement provided that 3K was not an agent of McDonald's for any purpose. Rather, it was an independent contractor and was responsible for all obligations and liabilities, including claims based on injury, illness, or death directly or indirectly resulting from the operation of the restaurant.

Miller was under the assumption that McDonald's owned, controlled, and managed the restaurant because its appearance and menu were similar to that of other McDonald's restaurants. In short, Miller testified, she went to the Tigard McDonald's because she relied on defendant's reputation and because she wanted to obtain the same quality of service, standard of care in food preparation, and general attention to detail that she had previously enjoyed at other McDonald's restaurants.

The trial court granted summary judgment to McDonald's on the ground that it did not own or operate the restaurant; rather, the owner and operator was a nonparty, 3K Restaurants, that held a franchise from McDonald's. Miller appeals.

DECISION Reversed and remanded.

OPINION Warren, J. Under these facts, 3K would be directly liable for any injuries that plaintiff suffered as a result of the restaurant's negligence. The issue on summary judgment is whether there is evidence that would permit a jury to find defendant vicariously liable for those injuries because of its relationship with 3K. Plaintiff asserts two theories of vicarious liability, actual agency and apparent agency. We hold that there is sufficient evidence to raise a jury issue under both theories. We first discuss actual agency.

The kind of actual agency relationship that would make defendant vicariously liable for 3K's negligence requires that defendant have the right to control the method by which 3K performed its obligations under the Agreement. The common context for that test is a normal master-servant (or employer-employee) relationship. [Citations.] The relationship between two business entities is not precisely an employment relationship, but the Oregon Supreme Court, in common with most if not all other courts that have considered the issue, has applied the right to control test for vicarious liability in that context as well. [Citation.] We therefore apply that test to this case.

* * *

A number of other courts have applied the right to control test to a franchise relationship. The Delaware Supreme Court, in [citation], stated the test as it applies to that context:

> If, in practical effect, the franchise agreement goes beyond the stage of setting standards, and allocates to the franchisor the right to exercise control over the daily operations of the franchise, an agency relationship exists. [Citation.]

* * *

* * * [W]e believe that a jury could find that defendant retained sufficient control over 3K's daily operations that an actual agency relationship existed. The Agreement did not simply set standards that 3K had to meet. Rather, it required 3K to use the precise methods that defendant established, both in the Agreement and in the detailed manuals that the Agreement incorporated. Those methods included the ways in which 3K was to handle and prepare food. Defendant enforced the use of those methods by regularly sending inspectors and by its retained power to cancel the Agreement. That evidence would support a finding that defendant had the right to control the way in which 3K performed at least food handling and preparation. In her complaint, plaintiff alleges that 3K's deficiencies in those functions resulted in the sapphire being in the Big Mac and thereby caused her injuries. * * *

Plaintiff next asserts that defendant is vicariously liable for 3K's alleged negligence because 3K was defendant's apparent agent. The relevant standard is in Restatement (Second) of Agency, § 267, which we adopted in [citation]:

> One who represents that another is his servant or other agent and thereby causes a third person justifiably to rely upon the care or skill of such apparent agent is subject to liability to the third person for harm caused by the lack of care or skill of the one appearing to be a servant or other agent as if he were such. [Citation.]

We have not applied § 267 to a franchisor/franchisee situation, but courts in a number of other jurisdictions have done so in ways that we find instructive. In most cases the courts have found that there was a jury issue of apparent agency. The crucial issues are whether the putative principal held the third party out as an agent and whether the plaintiff relied on that holding out.

* * *

In this case * * * there is an issue of fact about whether defendant held 3K out as its agent. Everything about the appearance and operation of the Tigard McDonald's identified it with defendant and with the common image for all McDonald's restaurants that defendant has worked to create through national advertising, common signs and uniforms, common menus, common appearance, and common standards. The possible existence of a sign identifying 3K as the operator does not alter the conclusion that there is an issue of apparent agency for the jury. There are issues of fact of whether that sign was sufficiently visible to the public, in light of plaintiff's apparent failure to see it, and of whether one sign by itself is sufficient to remove the impression that defendant created through all of the other indicia of its control that it, and 3K under the requirements that defendant imposed, presented to the public.

Defendant does not seriously dispute that a jury could find that it held 3K out as its agent. Rather, it argues that there is insufficient evidence that plaintiff justifiably relied on that holding out. It argues that it is not sufficient for her to prove that she went to the Tigard McDonald's because it was a McDonald's restaurant. Rather, she also had to prove that she went to it because she believed that McDonald's Corporation operated both it and the other McDonald's restaurants that she had previously patronized. * * *

* * *

* * * [I]n this case plaintiff testified that she relied on the general reputation of McDonald's in patronizing the Tigard restaurant and in her expectation of the quality of the food and service that she would receive. Especially in light of defendant's efforts to create a public perception of a common McDonald's system at all McDonald's restaurants, whoever operated them, a jury could find that plaintiff's reliance was objectively reasonable. The trial court erred in granting summary judgment on the apparent agency theory.

INTERPRETATION If a franchisor exercises sufficient control over its franchisee's operations, actual agency and/or apparent agency can exist and cause the franchisor to be held vicariously liable as a principal for the acts of the franchisee even if their written agreement provides that no agency relationship exists.

CRITICAL THINKING QUESTION Do you agree that a franchise relationship should under certain circumstances be treated as an agency relationship? Explain.

FORMALITIES

As a general rule, a contract of agency requires no particular formality; and usually the contract either may be oral or may be inferred from the conduct of the principal. In some cases, however, the contract must be in writing. For example, the appointment of an agent for a period of more than a year comes within the one-year clause of the statute of frauds and thus must be in writing. In some states, the authority of an agent to sell land must be set down in a writing signed by the principal. Some states have "equal dignity" statutes providing that a principal must grant his agent in a written instrument the authority to enter into any contract required to be in writing. See Chapter 48 for a discussion of state and federal legislation giving electronic records and signatures the legal effect of traditional writings and signatures.

A **power of attorney** is a written instrument that evidences the formal appointment of an agent who is known as an attorney in fact. Under a power of attorney, a principal may, for example, appoint an agent not only to execute a contract for the sale of the principal's real estate but also to execute the deed conveying title to the real estate to the third party. A number of states have created an optional statutory short form power of attorney based on the Uniform Statutory Form Power of Attorney Act.

http://
Uniform Statutory Form Power of Attorney Act:
http://www.law.upenn.edu/bll/ulc/fnact99/1980s/usfpaa88.htm
Florida: http://www.flabar.org/newflabar/consumer services/General.Pam/ ("Florida Powers of Attorney")
Nevada: http://www.nvbar.org/Publications/Publications_Pamphlets/Power_of_Attorney_Forms.htm ("Power of Attorney Forms")

CAPACITY

The capacity to be a principal, and thus to act through an agent, depends on the **capacity of the principal** to do the act. For example, contracts entered into by a minor or an incompetent not under a guardianship are voidable. Consequently, the appointment of an agent by a minor or an incompetent not under a guardianship and any resulting contracts are voidable, regardless of the agent's contractual capacity. The capacity of a business association to be a principal is determined by the law governing that business association.

Almost all of the states have adopted the Uniform Durable Power of Attorney Statute providing for a durable power of attorney under which an agent's power survives or is triggered by the principal's loss of mental competence. A **durable power of attorney** is a written instrument that expresses the principal's intention that the agent's authority will not be affected by the principal's subsequent incapacity or that the agent's authority will become effective upon the principal's subsequent incapacity.

On the other hand, because the act of the agent is considered the act of the principal, the incapacity of an agent to bind himself by contract does not disqualify him from making a contract that is binding on the principal. Thus, any person, including individuals, corporations, partnerships, and other associations, has the capacity to be an agent. The agent's liability, however, depends upon the agent's capacity to contract. Therefore, although the contract of agency may be voidable, an authorized contract between the principal and the third person who dealt with the agent is valid. An "electronic agent" is a computer program or other automated means used independently to initiate an action or respond to electronic records or performances in whole or in part without review or action by an individual. Electronic agents are not persons and, therefore, are not considered agents. See Chapter 48 for a discussion of the legal effect given to electronic agents.

CPA DUTIES OF AGENT TO PRINCIPAL

Because the principal-agent relationship is ordinarily created by contract, the duties of the agent to the principal are determined primarily by the provisions of the contract. In addition to these contractual duties, the agent is subject to various other duties imposed by law, unless the parties agree otherwise. Normally, a principal bases the selection of an agent on the agent's ability, skill, and integrity. Moreover, the principal not only authorizes and empowers the agent to bind him on contracts with third persons but also often places the agent in possession of his money and other property. As a result, the agent is in a position to injure the principal, either through negligence or dishonesty. Accordingly, an agent, as a fiduciary (a person in a position of trust and confidence), owes her principal the duties of obedience, diligence, and loyalty; the duty to inform; and the duty to provide an accounting. Moreover, an agent is liable for any loss she causes to the principal through her breach of these duties.

A gratuitous agent is subject to the same duty of loyalty that is imposed upon a paid agent and is equally liable to the principal for the harm he causes by his careless performance. Although the lack of consideration usually places a gratuitous agent under no duty to perform for the principal, such an agent may be liable to the principal for failing to perform a promise on which the principal has relied.

> **Practical Advice**
>
> Recognize that even if you agree to serve as an agent without compensation, you owe a fiduciary duty to the principal and are liable to her for your negligence.

DUTY OF OBEDIENCE

The **duty of obedience** requires the agent to act in the principal's affairs only as authorized by the principal and to obey all reasonable instructions and directions of the principal. Except where the instructions are ambiguous, an agent is liable to the principal for unauthorized acts that are the result of the agent's misinterpretation of the principal's directions. An agent is not, however, under a duty to follow orders to perform illegal or unethical acts, such as misrepresenting the quality of his principal's goods or those of a competitor. The agent may be subject to liability to her principal for breach of the duty of obedience (1) if she entered into an unauthorized contract for which her principal is now liable; (2) if she has improperly delegated her authority; or (3) if she has committed a tort for which the principal is now liable. Thus, an agent who sells on credit in violation of his principal's explicit instructions has breached the duty of obedience and is liable to the principal for any amounts the purchaser does not pay. Moreover, an agent who breaches her duty of obedience loses her right to compensation.

DUTY OF DILIGENCE

A paid agent must act with reasonable care and skill in performing the work for which he is employed. He must also exercise any special skill that he may have. An agent who does not exercise the required care and skill is liable to his principal for any resulting loss. For example, Peg appoints Alvin as her agent to sell goods in markets where the highest price can be obtained. Although he could have obtained a higher price in a nearby market by carefully obtaining information, Alvin sells goods in a glutted market and obtains a low price. Consequently, he is liable to Peg for breach of the duty of diligence.

DUTY TO INFORM

An agent must use reasonable efforts to provide the principal with information that is relevant to the affairs entrusted to her and that, as the agent knows or should know, the principal would desire to have. The rule of agency providing that notice to an agent is notice to her principal makes this duty essential. Examples of information that an agent is under a duty to communicate may include the following: a customer of the principal has become insolvent; a debtor of the principal has become insolvent; a partner of a firm with which the principal has previously dealt, and with which the principal or agent is about to deal, has withdrawn from the firm; or property that the principal has authorized the agent to sell at a specified price can be sold at a higher price.

DUTY TO ACCOUNT

The agent is under a duty to maintain and to provide to the principal a true and complete account of money or other property that the agent has received or expended on the principal's behalf. An agent must also keep the principal's property separate from his own.

FIDUCIARY DUTY

A **fiduciary duty**, arising out of a relationship of trust and confidence, is one of *utmost loyalty and good faith*. An agent owes a fiduciary duty imposed by law to his principal as does an employee to his employer. An agent who violates his fiduciary duty is liable to his principal for breach of contract, in tort for losses caused, and in restitution for profits he made or property received in breach of the fiduciary duty. Moreover, he loses the right to compensation. The principal may avoid a transaction in which the agent breached his fiduciary duty, even though the principal suffered no loss. A breach of fiduciary duty may also constitute just cause for discharge of the agent.

Although the fiduciary duty is not limited to the following situations, they occur most frequently.

Conflicts of Interest An agent must act solely in the interest of his principal, not in his own interest or in the interest of another. In addition, an agent may not represent his principal in any transaction in which the agent has a personal interest. Nor may the agent act on behalf of adverse parties to a transaction without both principals' approval to the dual agency. An agent may take a position that conflicts with the interest of his principal only if the principal, with full knowledge of all of the facts, consents. For example, A, an agent of P who desires to purchase land, agrees with C, who represents B, a seller of land, that A and C will endeavor to effect a transaction between their principals and will pool their commissions. A and C have committed a breach of fiduciary duty to P and B.

Self-Dealing The courts closely scrutinize transactions between an agent and her principal. The agent may not deal at arm's length with her principal. The agent thus owes her principal a duty of full disclosure regarding all relevant facts that affect the transaction. Moreover, the transaction must be fair. Thus, Penny employs Albert to purchase for her a site suitable for a shopping center. Albert owns such a site and sells it to Penny at the fair market value but does not disclose to Penny that he had owned the land. Penny may rescind the transaction. The agent's loyalty must be undivided, and he must devote his actions exclusively to the representation and promotion of his principal's interests.

Duty Not to Compete An agent cannot compete with his current principal or act on behalf of a competitor. After the agency terminates without breach by the agent, however, unless otherwise agreed, the agent may compete with his former principal. The courts will enforce by injunction a contractual agreement by the agent not to compete after termination (see Chapter 13) if the restriction is reasonable as to time and place and necessary to protect the principal's legitimate interest. Moreover, as discussed in Chapter 48, contracts not to compete may be subject to different standards for Internet companies and their employees.

Confidential Information An agent may not use or disclose confidential information obtained in the course of the agency for her own benefit or contrary to the interest of her principal. Confidential information is information that, if disclosed, would harm the principal's business or that has value because it is not generally known. Confidential information includes unique business methods, trade secrets, business plans, and customer lists. An agent may, however, reveal confidential information that the principal is committing, or is about to commit, a crime.

Once the agency terminates, unless otherwise agreed, the agent may not use or disclose to third persons confidential information. The agent may, however, use the skills, knowledge, and general information she acquired during the agency relationship.

Duty to Account for Financial Benefits Unless otherwise agreed, an agent must account to the principal for any financial benefit she receives as a direct result of transactions conducted on behalf of the principal. Such benefits would include bribes, kickbacks, and gifts. Moreover, an agent may not make a secret profit from any transaction subject to the agency. All such profits belong to the principal, to whom the agent must account. Thus, if an agent, authorized to sell certain property of her principal for $1,000 sells it for $1,500, she may not secretly pocket the additional $500.

Practical Advice

If you are the principal, consider obtaining from your agents a reasonable covenant that they will not compete with you after the agency terminates.

Practical Advice

Do not agree to become an agent if you are not willing or able to fulfill all of the duties an agent owes unless your agency contract clearly relieves you of those duties you find unacceptable.

Detroit Lions, Inc. v. Argovitz

United States District Court, Eastern District of Michigan, 1984

580 F.Supp. 542

FACTS Jerry Argovitz was employed as an agent of Billy Sims **(http://www.heisman.com/years/1978.html)**, a professional football player. Early in 1983, Argovitz informed Sims that he was awaiting the approval of his application for a United States Football League franchise in Houston. Sims was unaware, however, of Argovitz's extensive ownership interest in the new Houston Gamblers **(http://www.geocities.com/Colosseum/Field/8520/gamblers.htm)** organization. Meanwhile, during the spring of 1983, Argovitz continued contract negotiations on behalf of Sims with the Detroit Lions **(http://www.detroitlions.com)** of the National Football League. By June 22, Argovitz and the Lions were very close to an agreement, although Argovitz represented to Sims that the negotiations were not proceeding well. Argovitz then sought an offer for Sims's services from the Gamblers.

The Gamblers offered Sims a $3.5 million, five-year deal. Argovitz told Sims that he thought the Lions would match this figure; however, he did not seek a final offer from the Lions and then presented the terms of both packages to Sims. Sims, convinced that the Lions were not negotiating in good faith, signed with the Gamblers on July 1, 1983. On December 16, 1983, Sims signed a second contract with the Lions. The Lions and Sims brought an action against Argovitz, seeking to invalidate Sims's contract with the Gamblers on the ground that Argovitz breached his fiduciary duty when negotiating the contract with the Gamblers.

DECISION Judgment for the Lions and Sims rescinding the Gamblers' contract with Sims.

OPINION DeMascio, J. The relationship between a principal and agent is fiduciary in nature, and as such imposes a duty of loyalty, good faith, and fair and honest dealing on the agent. [Citation.]

A fiduciary relationship arises not only from a formal principal-agent relationship, but also from informal relationships of trust and confidence. [Citations.]

In light of the express agency agreement, and the relationship between Sims and Argovitz, Argovitz clearly owed Sims the fiduciary duties of an agent at all times relevant to this lawsuit.

An agent's duty of loyalty requires that he not have a personal stake that conflicts with the principal's interest in a transaction in which he represents his principal. As stated in [citation]:

> (T)he principal is entitled to the best efforts and unbiased judgment of his agent. * * * (T)he law denies the right of an agent to assume any relationship that is antagonistic to his duty to his principal, and it has many times been held that the agent cannot be both buyer and seller at the same time nor connect his own interests with property involved in his dealings as an agent for another.

A fiduciary violates the prohibition against self-dealing not only by dealing with himself on his principal's behalf, but also by dealing on his principal's behalf with a third party in which he has an interest, such as a partnership in which he is a member. * * *

Where an agent has an interest adverse to that of his principal in a transaction in which he purports to act on behalf of his principal, the transaction is voidable by the principal unless the agent disclosed all material facts within the agent's knowledge that might affect the principal's judgment. [Citation.]

The mere fact that the contract is fair to the principal does not deny the principal the right to rescind the contract when it was negotiated by an agent in violation of the prohibition against self-dealing. * * *

Once it has been shown that an agent had an interest in a transaction involving his principal antagonistic to the principal's interest, fraud on the part of the agent is presumed. The burden of proof then rests upon the agent to show that his principal had full knowledge, not only of the fact that the agent was interested, but also of every material fact known to the agent which might affect the principal and that having such knowledge, the principal freely consented to the transaction.

It is not sufficient for the agent merely to inform the principal that he has an interest that conflicts with the principal's interest. Rather, he must inform the principal "of all facts that come to his knowledge that are or may be material or which might affect his principal's rights or interests or influence the action he takes." [Citation.]

Argovitz clearly had a personal interest in signing Sims with the Gamblers that was adverse to Sims's interest—he had an ownership interest in the Gamblers and thus would profit if the Gamblers were profitable, and would incur substantial personal liabilities should the Gamblers not be financially successful. Since this showing has been made, fraud on Argovitz's part is presumed, and the Gamblers' contract must be rescinded unless Argovitz has shown by a preponderance of the evidence that he informed Sims of every material fact that might have influenced Sims's decision whether or not to sign the Gamblers' contract.

We conclude that Argovitz has failed to show by a preponderance of the evidence either: 1) that he informed Sims of the [material] facts, or 2) that these facts would not have influenced Sims's decision whether to sign the Gamblers' contract. * * *

As a court sitting in equity, we conclude that rescission is the appropriate remedy. We are dismayed by Argovitz's egregious conduct. The careless fashion in which Argovitz went about ascertaining the highest price for Sims's service convinces us of the wisdom of the maxim: no man can faithfully serve two masters whose interests are in conflict.

INTERPRETATION An agent's fiduciary duty precludes the agent from acting in his own interest or in the interests of another if such action would conflict with his principal's interests.

ETHICAL QUESTION Did Argovitz act unethically? Explain.

CRITICAL THINKING QUESTION What is the appropriate relief in this situation? Explain.

CPA DUTIES OF PRINCIPAL TO AGENT

Although, in terms of the rights and duties arising out of the agency relationship, the duties of the agent receive more emphasis than those of the principal, an agent nonetheless has certain rights against the principal, both under the contract and by the operation of law. Connected to these rights are certain duties, based in contract and tort law, which the principal owes to the agent. For a summary of the primary duties in the principal-agent relationship, see Figure 29-1.

CONTRACTUAL DUTIES

The contractual duties owed by a principal to an agent are the duties of compensation, reimbursement, and indemnification; each may be excluded or modified by agreement between the principal and agent. Although a gratuitous agent is not owed a duty of compensation, she is entitled to reimbursement and indemnification.

Depending on the particular case, the principal must furnish either the agent's means of employment or the opportunity for work. For example, a principal who employs an agent to sell his goods must supply the agent with conforming goods. It is also the duty of the principal not to terminate the agency wrongfully.

Compensation A principal has a duty to compensate her agent unless the agent has agreed to serve gratuitously. If the agreement does not specify a definite compensation, a principal is under a duty to pay the reasonable value of authorized services the agent has performed. An agent loses the right to compensation by (1) breaching the duty of obedience, (2) breaching the duty of loyalty, or (3) willfully and deliberately breaching the agency contract. Furthermore, an agent whose compensation is dependent upon her accomplishing a specific result is entitled to the agreed compensation only if she achieves the result in the time specified or in a reasonable time, if no time is stated. A common example is a listing agreement between a seller and a real estate broker providing for a commission to the broker if he finds a buyer ready, willing, and able to buy the property on the terms specified in the agreement.

> **Practical Advice**
>
> Specify the compensation to be paid the agent; if none is to be paid, clearly state that the agency is intended to be gratuitous.

Figure 29-1
Duties of Principal and Agent

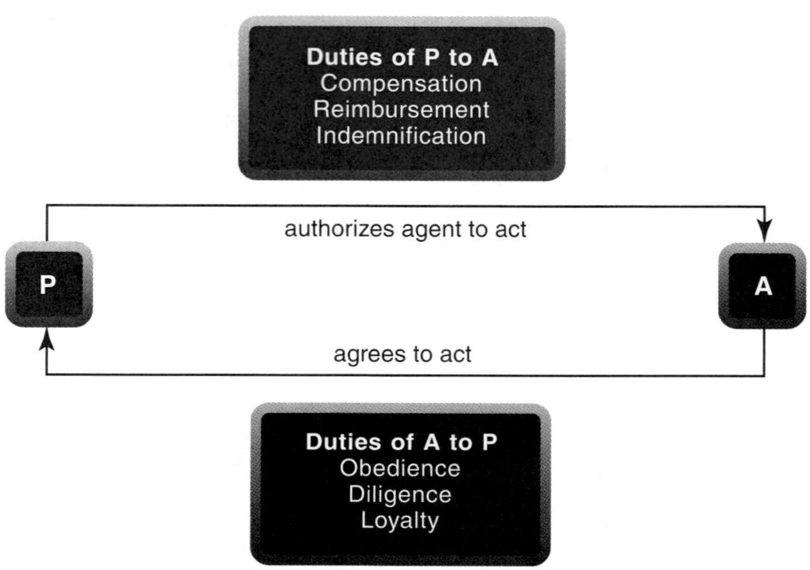

Holzman v. Fiola Blum, Inc.

Court of Special Appeals of Maryland, 1999
125 Md. App. 602, 726 A.2d 818
http://www.courts.state.md.us/opinions/cosa/1999/570s98.pdf

FACTS Allen Bruce Holzman and his wife, Terry Lee Holzman (the "Holzmans" or the "Sellers"), were the owners of an exclusive, three-story, eight-bedroom, brick house located on several acres of land in Baltimore County, Maryland. On January 23, 1996, they met with Hope Berman, a real estate agent associated with Fiola Blum, Inc., to discuss the possibility of selling the property. During that visit, they executed a Listing Agreement (the "Agreement") for the residence, which was effective for a six-month term. The Property was initially listed for sale on January 23, 1996, at a price of $1.95 million. Later, the price was reduced to $1,650,000.

Under the Agreement, the Broker's commission was to be calculated in the following way: six percent of the first $300,000 of the selling price, five percent of the second $300,000, and four percent of the balance. The Agreement, a standard form "Exclusive Right to Sell Listing Contract," provided that the owner would pay the fee if the broker produced a customer to purchase the property at a price agreeable to the seller. The broker must produce the customer while the agreement is in force and the sale must take place within six months of the termination of the agreement. The exception to this was if the property was sold by any other licensed real estate broker following the expiration of the agreement.

On July 19, 1996, the Agreement was extended until September 30, 1996. On August 9, 1996, the Holzmans received a letter of intent from Gil Stern and his wife, Ellen (the "Sterns"), offering $600,000 for the Property. On August 12, 1996, Heros Noravian and his wife, Dr. Emma Zargarian (the "Noravians"), submitted a letter of intent, offering a purchase price of $715,000 and a deposit of $10,000.

On August 20, 1996, while the Holzmans "were still in negotiation with the Noravians," the Broker presented the Holzmans with a revised offer from the Sterns in the amount of $850,000. Nevertheless, the Holzmans entered into a contract with the Noravians on August 25, 1996. The record does not reflect why the Holzmans proceeded with the Noravian contract after they learned of the increased offer from the Sterns. After the Holzmans executed the Noravian contract, they decided to pursue the Sterns' offer, relying on the advice of counsel. Accordingly, on August 26, 1996, just one day after signing the Noravian contract, the Holzmans canceled it. On the advice of their attorney, the Holzmans included a default provision in the Noravian contract which provided that, in the event of a breach by the Sellers, the Buyers' sole remedy would be a refund of their deposit.

Thereafter, on October 16, 1996, the Holzmans executed a contract of sale with the Sterns (the "Stern contract"). It contained a provision to pay the real estate commission to Blum and Long & Foster, the Sterns' real estate agent, calculated in accordance with the terms of the Agreement. Consequently, the commission due under the Stern contract was to be divided evenly between Blum and Long & Foster.

On November 7, 1996, Blum filed a complaint in the circuit court, claiming that the Holzmans defaulted on the Noravian contract and owed the Broker the real estate commission. Because there was no cooperating agent for the Noravian contract, any commission due under the Agreement would have been payable solely to Blum.

The trial court determined that the Agreement was unambiguous, and that it obligated the Holzmans to pay the fee because they entered into a written agreement to sell the Property during the term of the Agreement. The trial court ordered that judgment be entered in favor of Blum against Holzman in the amount of $37,600, plus attorney's fees.

On February 12, 1998, two days after trial, the Holzmans and the Sterns settled on the Property. As a result, Blum received a commission of $21,500. Accordingly, the Holzmans filed a revisory motion, asking the court to reduce the first judgment ($37,600) by the amount of the commission that Blum actually recovered. In its opposition, the Broker contended that it was entitled to two commissions. The trial court ruled that the original judgment should be reduced by the $21,500 that had been paid as commission for the sale of this property. Blum appealed.

DECISION Judgment affirmed.

OPINION Hollander, J. Maryland law requires that we give legal effect to the unambiguous provisions of a contract. [Citations.]

Our primary concern in interpreting a contract is to effectuate the parties' intention. [Citations.] If the terms of the contract are clear, we presume "the parties intended what they expressed, even if the expression differs from the parties' intentions at the time they created the contract." [Citations.] Of particular significance here, we may not "rewrite the terms of the contract or draw a new one * * * merely to avoid hardship or because one party has become dissatisfied with its provisions." [Citations.]

The trial court determined that the Agreement was unambiguous, and that it obligated the Holzmans to pay the fee because they entered into a written agreement to sell the Property during the term of the Agreement. * * * In our view, the trial court was legally correct. The terms of the Agreement and the provisions of the Noravian contract refute appellants' argument that settlement was a condition precedent to the Broker's contractual right to a commission. [Citation.]

* * *

Appellants claim that appellee breached its fiduciary duty to them because, when the Sellers sought to cancel the Noravian contract of sale, the Broker failed to advise them that the Agreement obligated them to pay the commission, even if the sale was not consummated, or that they would expose themselves to liability for more than one commission if they sold the Property to another party. * * *

A broker "is bound to act in good faith and to make disclosures of matters that are material and might affect the action of his employer in the premises." [Citations.] Moreover, if a broker breaches his or her fiduciary duty, acts in bad faith, or in another opprobrious manner, he or she may forfeit the right to compensation. [Citation.]

It is certainly unfortunate that the Broker did not opt to remind the Holzmans of the terms of the Agreement, with which the Broker undoubtedly had far more familiarity. Nevertheless, under the circumstances of this case, we perceive no breach by appellee of its fiduciary duty to appellants.

The Agreement clearly addressed the terms and conditions under which appellants would owe the Broker a fee, and appellee had no legal duty to remind appellants of the terms of the Agreement that appellants had signed. To the contrary, the Holzmans had a duty to ascertain their obligations under the Agreement.

One is under a duty to learn the contents of a contract before signing it; if, in the absence of fraud, duress, undue influence, and the like he fails to do so, he is presumed to know the contents, signs at his peril, suffers the consequences of his negligence, and is estopped to deny his obligation under the contract.

* * *

It is also noteworthy that there is no contention that appellee induced appellants to default on the Noravian contract. To the contrary, the evidence suggests that the Holzmans never endeavored to discuss with the Broker their intention to cancel the Noravian contract. Nonetheless, they knew enough to seek the advice of their counsel.

* * *

We are amply satisfied that the evidence shows neither fraud in the procurement of the Agreement, nor deception preventing appellants from reading its provisions. As a consequence, we find no merit to appellants' claims that appellee breached its fiduciary duty.

* * *

Because appellee based its claim for a commission on the basis of appellants' execution of the Noravian contract, pursuant to subparagraph (1) of the commission clause, the Agreement did not entitle the Broker also to recover based on the Stern contract, for which the Broker relied on subparagraph (3) of the commission clause. Accordingly, we are satisfied that the trial court properly reduced the judgment by the amount of the commission appellee received from the subsequent sale of the Property to the Sterns.

ETHICAL QUESTION Should Blum have pointed out to the Holzmans the ramifications of canceling the contract?

CRITICAL THINKING QUESTION Does an agent's fiduciary duty apply to the contact between the principal and agent?

Reimbursement A principal is under a duty to reimburse his agent for authorized payments the agent makes on the principal's behalf and for authorized expenses the agent incurs. For example, an agent who reasonably and properly pays a fire insurance premium for the protection of her principal's property is entitled to reimbursement for the payment.

Indemnification The principal is under a duty to indemnify the agent for losses the agent incurred or suffered while acting as directed by the principal in a transaction that is not illegal or not known by the agent to be wrongful. To ***indemnify*** is to make good or pay a loss. Suppose that Perry, the principal, has in his possession goods belonging to Margot. Perry directs Alma, his agent, to sell these goods. Alma, believing Perry to be the owner, sells the goods to Turner. Margot then sues Alma for the conversion of her goods and recovers a judgment, which Alma pays to Margot. Alma is entitled to payment from Perry for her loss, including the amount she reasonably expended in defense of the lawsuit brought by Margot.

TORT DUTIES

A principal owes to any agent the same duties under tort law that the principal owes to all parties. Moreover, a principal is under a duty to disclose to an agent those risks of which the principal knows or should know, if the principal should realize that the agent is unaware of such risks in the agency. For instance, in directing his agent to collect rent from a tenant who is known to have assaulted rent collectors, a principal has a duty to warn the agent of this risk.

When the agent is an employee, the principal owes the agent additional duties. Among these is the duty to provide the employee with reasonably safe conditions of employment and to warn the employee of any unreasonable risk involved in the employment. A negligent employer is also liable to his employees for injury caused by the negligence of other employees and of other agents doing work for him. We will discuss the tort duties owed by an employer to an employee more fully in Chapter 42.

CPA TERMINATION OF AGENCY

Because the authority of an agent is based on the consent of the principal, the agency is terminated when such consent is withdrawn or otherwise ceases to exist. On termination of the agency, the agent's actual authority ends, and she is not entitled to compensation for services subsequently rendered, although her fiduciary duties may continue. As discussed in Chapter 30, in some situations apparent authority also terminates, whereas in others, apparent authority continues until a third party has knowledge or notice of the termination of agency. Termination may take place by the acts of the parties or by operation of law.

ACTS OF THE PARTIES

Termination by the acts of the parties may occur by the provisions of the original agreement, by the subsequent acts of both principal and agent, or by the subsequent act of either one.

Lapse of Time Authority conferred upon an agent for a specified time terminates when that period expires. If no time is specified, authority terminates at the end of a reasonable period. For example, Palmer authorizes Avery to sell a tract of land for him. After ten years pass without communication between Palmer and Avery, Avery purports to sell the tract. But his authorization has terminated due to lapse of time.

Fulfillment of Purpose The authority of an agent to perform a specific act or to accomplish a particular result terminates when the agent performs the act or accomplishes the result. Thus, if Porter authorizes Alford to sell or lease Porter's land, Alford's authority terminates when he leases the land to Taft, and he may not thereafter sell or lease the land without new authorization.

Mutual Agreement of the Parties The agency relationship is created by agreement and may be terminated at any time by mutual agreement of the principal and the agent.

Revocation of Authority A principal may revoke an agent's authority at any time by giving notice to the agent. But if such revocation constitutes a breach of contract by the principal, the agent may recover damages from the principal. Nonetheless, when the agent has seriously breached the agency contract, has willfully disobeyed, or has violated the fiduciary duty, the principal is not liable for revocation. In addition, if the agency is gratuitous, the principal ordinarily may revoke it without liability to the agent.

Renunciation by the Agent The agent also has the power to end the agency by notice to the principal that she renounces the authority given her by the principal. If the agency is gratuitous, the agent ordinarily may renounce it without liability to the principal. However, if the parties have contracted for the agency to continue for a specified time, an unjustified renunciation prior to the expiration of that time is a breach of contract.

OPERATION OF LAW

By the operation of law, the occurrence of certain events will automatically terminate an agency relationship. These events either make it impossible for the agent to perform or unlikely that the principal would want the agent to act. As a matter of law, the occurrence of any of the following events ordinarily terminates agency.

Bankruptcy Bankruptcy is a federal court proceeding to afford relief to financially troubled debtors. The filing of a petition in bankruptcy, which initiates the proceedings, usually terminates all the debtor's existing agency relationships. Bankruptcy is discussed in Chapter 39.

Death Because the authority given to an agent by a principal is strictly personal, the agent's death terminates the agent's actual authority. The death of the principal also terminates the authority of the agent. For example, Polk employs Allison to sell Polk's line of goods under a contract

Ethical Dilemma

Is Medicaid Designed to Protect Inheritances?

FACTS Mrs. Singer is a seventy-eight-year-old widow. Although she remains somewhat active and lives in her own apartment, her physical and mental abilities are declining. She fell recently and needs assistance with bathing and some routine chores.

Mrs. Singer has two children, a son, Steven, who lives within fifteen minutes of her home, and a daughter, Kate, who lives a great distance away. While Mrs. Singer sees Kate only once a year, she remains in close contact with Steven, who does her grocery shopping, takes her to the doctor, and provides transportation, thereby enabling Mrs. Singer to maintain some social life.

Steven has become increasingly concerned about his mother's declining condition and is unsure how much longer she can remain in her apartment. Steven has consulted his lawyer, who suggested that Mrs. Singer give Steven a durable power of attorney authorizing Steven to manage most of her financial affairs. It would also give Steven the power to transfer Mrs. Singer's assets to himself so that Mrs. Singer will qualify for Medicaid should she need to enter a nursing home. Steven's lawyer explained that in order to qualify for Medicaid, Mrs. Singer must meet asset and income limits that are quite low.

Mrs. Singer has substantial assets. She has a portfolio of investments in stocks, bonds, and certificates of deposit worth more than $700,000. The durable power of attorney would enable Steven to strip Mrs. Singer of her assets within the time frame necessary to allow the declining Mrs. Singer to qualify for Medicaid.

Mrs. Singer has agreed to execute the power. But Kate objects to the plan. She does not get along with Steven, does not trust his judgment, and is concerned that he will not properly share his mother's assets.

Social, Policy, and Ethical Considerations

1. Is it ethical for Steven to execute the power of attorney in an effort to enable his mother to qualify for Medicaid?
2. Should Medicaid be available only to those with low income and few assets? Could a national health care plan provide a solution?
3. What role, if any, should private insurance play in providing a safety net against the catastrophic costs of nursing home care?
4. What questions of family ethics does a plan such as Steven's raise?

that specifies Allison's commission and the one-year period for which the employment is to continue. Unbeknownst to Allison, Polk dies; Allison no longer has authority to sell Polk's goods. The Uniform Durable Power of Attorney Act allows the holder of *any* power of attorney, durable or otherwise, to exercise it on the death of the principal, if its exercise is in good faith and without knowledge of the principal's death.

Incapacity Incapacity of the principal that occurs after the formation of the agency terminates the agent's authority. Likewise, the subsequent incapacity of an agent to perform the acts authorized by the principal terminates the agent's authority. If an agent is appointed under a durable power of attorney, the authority of an agent survives, or is triggered by, the incapacity of the principal. Moreover, the Uniform Durable Power of Attorney Act allows the holder of a power that is *not* durable to exercise it on the incapacity of the principal, if its exercise is in good faith and without knowledge of the principal's incapacity.

Practical Advice

A durable power of attorney is useful in families, allowing adult children to become the agents of their elderly or ill parents.

Change in Circumstances The authority of an agent is terminated by notice or knowledge of a change in the value of the subject matter or of a change in business conditions from which the agent should reasonably infer that the principal would not wish the agent to exercise the authority given him. For example, Patricia authorizes Aaron to sell her eighty acres of farmland for $800 per acre. Subsequently, oil is discovered on nearby land, and Patricia's land greatly increases in value. Because Aaron knows of this, whereas Patricia does not, Aaron's authority to sell the land is terminated.

Loss or Destruction of the Subject Matter When a specific subject matter to which an agent's authority relates becomes lost or is destroyed, such authority is thereby terminated. This corresponds to the rule stating that loss or destruction of the subject matter of an offer terminates the offer. For example, Pauline authorizes Abraham to make a contract for the sale of Pauline's residence. The next week, the residence burns completely, as Abraham is aware. Abraham's authority is terminated.

Disloyalty of Agent If an agent, without the knowledge of her principal, acquires interests adverse to those of the principal or otherwise breaches her duty of loyalty to the principal, her authority to act on behalf of the principal is terminated. Thus, Parker employs Agnes, a realtor, to sell Parker's land. Unknown to Parker, Agnes has been authorized by Trent to purchase this land from Parker. Agnes is not authorized to sell the land to Trent.

Change in Law A change in the law that takes effect after the employment of the agent may make the performance of an authorized act illegal or criminal. Such a change terminates the authority of the agent. Thus, Paul directs his agent, Allan, to ship young elm trees from State X to State Y. In order to control elm disease, State X establishes a quarantine on the shipment of elm trees to any other state, and any such shipment is punishable by fine. Allan's authority to ship the elm trees is terminated.

Outbreak of War When the outbreak of war places the principal and agent in the position of alien enemies, the authority of the agent is terminated because its exercise is illegal.

IRREVOCABLE AGENCIES

In the foregoing discussion of the various ways in which the authority of an agent may be terminated, the agency relationship was assumed to be the ordinary one in which the agent has no security interest in the power conferred on him by the principal. When the **agency** is **coupled with an interest** of the agent in the subject matter, as, for example, when the agent has advanced funds on behalf of the principal and his power to act is given as security for the loan, the principal may not revoke the authority of the agent. (This relationship is also referred to as a "power given as security.") In addition, neither the incapacity nor the bankruptcy of the principal will terminate the authority or power of the agent in such a situation. Not even the death of the principal will terminate the agency, unless the duty for which the security was given terminates with her death. An agency coupled with an interest is terminated by an event that discharges the obligation secured by it. Thus, in the example above, when the principal repays the loan, the agency coupled with an interest is terminated.

CHAPTER SUMMARY

Nature of Agency

Definition of Agency relationship authorizing one party (the agent) to act for and on behalf of the other party (the principal)

Scope of Agency Purposes whatever business activity a person may accomplish personally, he generally may do through an agent

Other Legal Relationships
- *Employment Relationship* one in which the employer has the right to control the physical conduct of the employee
- *Independent Contractor* a person who contracts with another to do a particular job and who is not subject to the control of the other

Creation of Agency

Formalities though agency is a consensual relationship that may be formed by contract or agreement between the principal and agent, agency may exist without consideration
- *Requirements* no particular formality is usually required in a contract of agency, although appointments of agents for a period of more than one year must be in writing
- *Power of Attorney* written, formal appointment of an agent

Capacity
- *Principal* if the principal is a minor or an incompetent not under a guardianship, his appointment of another to act as an agent is voidable
- *Agent* any person may act as an agent as the act of the agent is considered the act of the principal

Duties of Agent to Principal

Duty of Obedience an agent must act in the principal's affairs only as authorized by the principal and must obey all reasonable instructions and directions

Duty of Diligence an agent must act with reasonable care and skill in performing the work for which he is employed

Duty to Inform an agent must use reasonable efforts to give the principal information relevant to the affairs entrusted to her

Duty to Account an agent must maintain and provide the principal with a true and complete account of money or other property that the agent has received or expended on behalf of the principal

Fiduciary Duty an agent owes a duty of utmost loyalty and good faith to the principal
- *Conflicts of Interest*
- *Self-Dealing*
- *Duty Not to Compete*
- *Confidential Information*
- *Duty to Account for Financial Benefits*

Duties of Principal to Agent

Contractual Duties
- ***Compensation*** a principal must compensate the agent as specified in the contract or for the reasonable value of the services provided if no amount is specified
- ***Reimbursement*** the principal must pay back to the agent authorized payments the agent has made on the principal's behalf
- ***Indemnification*** the principal must pay the agent for losses the agent incurred while acting as directed by the principal

Tort Duties include the duty to provide an employee with reasonably safe conditions of employment and to warn the employee of any unreasonable risk involved in the employment

Termination of Agency

Acts of the Parties
- *Lapse of Time*
- *Fulfillment of Purpose*
- *Mutual Agreement of the Parties*
- *Revocation of Authority*
- *Renunciation by the Agent*

Operation of Law
- *Bankruptcy* of the principal usually terminates all of the principal's agency relationships; if the credit of the agent is important to the agency relationship, the relationship will be terminated by the bankruptcy of the agent
- *Death* of either the principal or the agent
- *Incapacity* of either the principal or the agent
- *Change in Circumstances*
- *Loss or Destruction of the Subject Matter*
- *Disloyalty of Agent*
- *Change in Law*
- *Outbreak of War*

Irrevocable Agency an agency coupled with an interest is irrevocable and occurs when the agent has a security interest in the subject matter of the agency

QUESTIONS

1. Parker, the owner of certain unimproved real estate in Chicago, employed Adams, a real estate agent, to sell the property for a price of $25,000 or more and agreed to pay Adams a commission of 6 percent for making a sale. Adams negotiated with Turner, who was interested in the property and willing to pay as much as $28,000 for it. Adams made an agreement with Turner that if Adams could obtain Parker's signature to a contract to sell the property to Turner for $25,000, Turner would pay Adams a bonus of $1,000. Adams prepared and Parker and Turner signed a contract for the sale of the property to Turner for $25,000. Turner refuses to pay Adams the $1,000 as promised. Parker refuses to pay Adams the 6 percent commission. In an action by Adams against Parker and Turner, what is the judgment?

2. Perry employed Alice to sell a parcel of real estate at a fixed price without knowledge that David had previously employed Alice to purchase the same property for him. Perry gave Alice no discretion as to price or terms, and Alice entered into a contract of sale with David on the exact terms authorized by Perry. After accepting a partial payment, Perry discovered that Alice was employed by David and brought an action to rescind. David resisted on the ground that Perry had suffered no damage because Alice had been given no discretion and the sale was made on the exact basis authorized by Perry. Discuss whether Perry will prevail.

3. Packer owned and operated a fruit cannery in Southton, Illinois. He stored a substantial amount of finished canned goods in a warehouse in East St. Louis, Illinois, owned and operated by Alden, in order to have goods readily available for the St. Louis market. On March 1, he had 10,000 cans of peaches and 5,000 cans of apples in storage with Alden. On the day named, he borrowed $5,000 from Alden, giving Alden his promissory note for this amount due June 1, together with a letter authorizing Alden, in the event the note was not paid at maturity, to sell any or all of his goods in storage, pay the indebtedness, and account to him for any surplus. Packer died on June 2 without having paid the note. On June 8, Alden told Taylor, a wholesale food distributor, that he had for sale, as agent of the owner, 10,000 cans of peaches and 5,000 cans of apples. Taylor said he would take the peaches and would decide later about the apples. A contract for the sale of 10,000 cans of peaches for $6,000 was thereupon signed "Alden, agent for Packer, seller; Taylor, buyer." Both Alden and Taylor knew of the death of Packer. Delivery of the peaches and payment were made on June 10. On June 11, Alden and Taylor signed a similar contract covering the 5,000 cans of apples, delivery and payment to be made June 30. On June 23, Packer's executor, having learned of these contracts, wrote Alden and Taylor stating that Alden had no authority to make the contracts, demanding that Taylor return the peaches, and directing Alden not to deliver the apples. Discuss the correctness of the contentions of Packer's executor.

4. Green, a licensed real estate broker in Illinois, and Jones, also an Illinois resident, while both in New York, signed a contract whereby Green agreed to endeavor to find a buyer for certain Illinois real estate owned by Jones, who agreed to pay Green a commission of $10,000 in the event of a sale. Green found a buyer, a resident of New York, to whom the land was sold. Thereafter, Jones refused to pay the commission, and Green commenced an action in Illinois to recover it. Jones defended on the sole ground that the brokerage contract was unenforceable because Green was not a licensed real estate broker in New York. Relevant provisions of the applicable New York statute forbid any person from holding himself out or acting temporarily as a real estate broker or salesperson without first procuring a license. A violation is declared to be a misdemeanor, and the commission of a single prohibited act is a violation for which the statute provides a penalty. For whom should judgment be rendered?

5. Palmer made a valid contract with Ames under which Ames was to sell Palmer's goods on commission from January 1 to June 30. Ames made satisfactory sales up to May 15 and was about to close an unusually large order when Palmer suddenly and without notice revoked Ames's authority to sell. Can Ames continue to sell Palmer's goods during the unexpired term of her contract?

6. Piedmont Electric Co. gave a list of delinquent accounts to Alexander, an employee, with instructions to discontinue electric service to delinquent customers. Among those listed was Todd Hatchery, which was then in the process of hatching chickens in a large, electrically heated incubator. Todd Hatchery told Alexander that it did not consider its account delinquent, but Alexander nevertheless cut the wires leading to the hatchery. Subsequently, Todd Hatchery recovered a judgment of $5,000 in an action brought against Alexander for the loss resulting from the interruption of the incubation process. Alexander has paid the judgment and brings a cause of action against Piedmont Electric Co. What may he recover? Explain.

7. In October 2001, Black, the owner of the Grand Opera House, and Harvey entered into a written agreement to lease the opera house to Harvey for five years at a rental of $30,000 a year. Harvey engaged Day as manager of the theater at a salary of $175 per week plus 10 percent of the profits. One of Day's duties was to determine the amounts of money taken in each night and, after deducting expenses, to divide the profits between Harvey and the manager of the particular attraction playing at the theater. In September 2006, Day went to Black and offered to rent the opera house from Black at a rental of $37,500 per year, whereupon Black entered into a lease with Day for five years at this figure. When Harvey learned of and objected to this transaction, Day offered to assign the lease to him for $60,000 per year. Harvey refused and brought an appropriate action against Day. Should Harvey recover? If so, on what basis and to what relief is he entitled?

8. Timothy retains Cynthia, an attorney, to bring a lawsuit upon a valid claim against Vincent. Recently enacted legislation has shortened the statute of limitations for this type of legal action. Cynthia fails to make herself aware of this new statute. Consequently, she files the complaint after the statute of limitations has run. As a result, the lawsuit is dismissed. What rights, if any, does Timothy have against Cynthia?

9. Wilson engages Ruth to sell Wilson's antique walnut chest to Harold for $2,500. The next day, Ruth learns that Sandy is willing to pay $3,000 for Wilson's chest. Ruth nevertheless sells the chest to Harold. Wilson then discovers these facts. What are Wilson's rights, if any, against Ruth?

10. Morris is a salesperson for Acme, Inc., a manufacturer of household appliances. Morris receives a commission on all sales made and no further compensation. He drives his own automobile, pays his own expenses, and calls on whom he pleases. While driving to make a call on a potential customer, Morris negligently collides with Hudson. Hudson sues Acme and Morris. Who should be held liable?

CASE PROBLEMS

11. Sierra Pacific Industries (http://www.sierrapacificind.com) purchased various areas of timber and six other pieces of real property, including a ten-acre parcel on which five duplexes and two single-family units were located. Sierra Pacific requested the assistance of Joseph Carter, a licensed real estate broker, in selling the nontimberland properties. It commissioned him to sell the property for an asking price of $85,000, of which Sierra Pacific would receive $80,000 and Carter would receive $5,000 as a commission. Unable to find a prospective buyer, Carter finally sold the property to his daughter and son-in-law for $85,000 and retained the $5,000 commission without informing Sierra Pacific of his relationship to the buyers. After learning of these facts, Sierra Pacific brought this action for fraud against Carter. To what relief, if any, is Sierra Pacific entitled?

12. Murphy, while a guest at a motel operated by the Betsy-Len Motor Hotel Corporation, sustained injuries from a fall allegedly caused by negligence in maintaining the premises. At that time, Betsy-Len was under a license agreement with Holiday Inns, Inc. (http://www.ichotelsgroup.com/h/d/hi/home). The license contained provisions permitting Holiday Inns to regulate the architectural style of the buildings as well as the type and style of the furnishings and equipment. The contract, however, did not grant Holiday Inns the power to control the day-to-day operations of Betsy-Len's motel, to fix customer rates, or to demand a share of the profits. Betsy-Len could hire and fire its employees, determine wages and working conditions, supervise the employee work routine, and discipline its employees. In return, Betsy-Len used the trade name "Holiday Inns" and paid a fee for use of the license and Holiday Inns' national advertising. Murphy sued Holiday Inns, claiming Betsy-Len was its agent. Is Murphy correct?

13. Hunter Farms contracted with Petrolia Grain & Feed Company, a Canadian company, to purchase a large supply of the farm herbicide Sencor from Petrolia for resale. Petrolia learned from the U.S. Customs Service (http://www.customs.gov) that the import duty for the Sencor would be 5 percent but that the final rate could be determined only upon an inspection of the Sencor at the time of importation. Petrolia forwarded this information to Hunter. Meanwhile, Hunter employed F. W. Myers & Company, an import broker, to assist in moving the herbicide through customs. When customs later determined that certain chemicals in the herbicide, not listed on its label, would increase the customs duty from $30,000 to $128,000, Myers paid the additional amount under protest and turned to Hunter for indemnification. Hunter refused to pay Myers, claiming that Myers breached its duty of care as an import broker in failing to inform Hunter that the 5 percent duty rate was subject to increase. Myers brought an action against Hunter, arguing that it was not employed to give advice to Hunter on matters of importation. Explain whether Myers had the duty to inform Hunter.

14. Tube Art was involved in moving a reader board sign to a new location. Tube Art's service manager and another employee went to the proposed site and took photographs and measurements. Later, a Tube Art employee laid out the exact size and location for the excavation by marking a four-by-four square on the asphalt surface with yellow paint. The dimensions of the hole, including its depth of six feet, were indicated with spray paint inside the square. After the layout was painted on the asphalt, Tube Art engaged a backhoe operator, Richard F. Redford, to dig the hole. Redford began digging in the early evening hours at the location designated by Tube Art. At approximately 9:30 P.M., the bucket of Redford's backhoe struck a small natural gas pipeline. After examining the pipe and finding no indication of a break or leak, he concluded that the line was not in use and left the site. Shortly before 2:00 A.M. on the following day, an explosion and fire occurred in the building serviced by that gas pipeline. As a result, two people in the building were killed, and most of its contents were destroyed. Massey and his associates, as tenants of the building, brought an action against Tube Art and Richard Redford for the total destruction of their property. Will the plaintiffs prevail? Explain.

15. Brian Hanson sustained a paralyzing injury while playing in a lacrosse match between Ohio State University (http://www.osu.edu) and Ashland University (http://www.ashland.edu). Hanson had interceded in a fight between one of his teammates and an Ashland player, William Kynast.

Hanson grabbed Kynast in a bear hug, but Kynast threw Hanson off his back. Hanson's head struck the ground, resulting in serious injuries. An ambulance was summoned, and after several delays, Hanson was transported to a local hospital where he underwent surgery. Doctors determined that Hanson suffered a compression fracture of his sixth spinal vertebrae. Hanson, now an incomplete quadriplegic, subsequently filed suit against William Kynast and Ashland University, maintaining that because Kynast was acting as the agent of Ashland, the university was therefore liable for Kynast's alleged wrongful acts under the doctrine of *respondeat superior*. Is Hanson correct?

16. Tony Wilson was a member of Troop 392 of the Boy Scouts of America (BSA) (http://www.scouting.org) and of the St. Louis Area Council (Council) (http://www.stlbsa.org). Tony went on a trip with the troop to Fort Leonard Wood, Missouri (http://www.ftleonardwood.com). Five adult volunteer leaders accompanied the troop. The troop stayed in a building, which had thirty-foot aluminum pipes stacked next to it. At approximately 10:00 p.m., Tony and other scouts were outside the building, and the leaders were inside. Tony and two other scouts picked up a pipe and raised it so that it came into contact with 7200-volt power lines that ran over the building. All three scouts were electrocuted, and Tony died.

    His parents brought a suit for wrongful death against the Council, claiming that the volunteer leaders were agents or servants of the Council and that it was vicariously liable for their negligence. The Council filed a motion for summary judgment, arguing as follows: the BSA chartered local councils in certain areas, and councils in turn granted charters to local sponsors such as schools, churches, or civic organizations. Local councils did not administer the scouting program for the sponsor, did not select volunteers, did not prescribe training for volunteers, and did not direct or control the activities of troops. Troops were not required to get permission from local councils before participating in an activity. Is the Council liable for the wrongful death of Tony? Explain.

17. Harvey Hilgendorf was a licensed real estate broker acting as the agent of the Hagues in the sale of eighty acres of farmland. The Hagues, however, terminated Hilgendorf's agency before the expiration of the listing contract when they encountered financial difficulties and decided to liquidate their entire holdings of land at one time. Hilgendorf brought this action for breach of the listing contract. The Hagues maintain that Hilgendorf's duty of loyalty required him to give up the listing contract. Are the Hagues correct in their assertion?

http://

Internet Exercise Find information about, and examples of, ordinary and durable powers of attorney.

Chapter 30

Relationship with Third Parties

Qui facit per alium facit per se. *(He who acts through another, acts himself.)*

Legal Maxim

Learning Objectives

After reading this chapter you should be able to:

1. Distinguish among actual express authority, actual implied authority, and apparent authority.
2. Explain the contractual liability of the principal, agent, and third party when the principal is (a) disclosed, (b) partially disclosed, and (c) undisclosed.
3. Explain how apparent authority is terminated and distinguish between actual and constructive notice.
4. Describe the tort liability of a principal for the (a) authorized acts of agents, (b) authorized acts of employees, and (c) unauthorized acts of independent contractors.
5. Explain the criminal liability of a principal for the acts of agents.

The purpose of an agency relationship is to allow the principal to extend his business activities by authorizing agents to enter into contracts with third persons on his behalf. Accordingly, it is important that the law balance the competing interests of principals and third persons. The principal wants to be liable only for those contracts he actually authorizes the agent to make for him. The third party, on the other hand, wishes the principal bound on all contracts that the agent negotiates on the principal's behalf. As we will discuss in this chapter, the law has adopted an intermediate outcome: the principal and the third party are bound to those contracts the principal actually authorizes plus those the principal has apparently authorized.

While pursuing the principal's business, an agent may tortiously injure third parties, who then may seek to hold the principal personally liable. Under what circumstances should the principal be held liable? Similar questions arise concerning a principal's criminal liability for an agent's violation of the criminal law. The law of agency has established rules to determine when the principal is liable for the torts and crimes his agents commit. We will discuss these rules in this chapter.

Finally, what liability to the third party should the agent incur and what rights should she acquire against the third party? Usually, the agent has no liability for, or rights under, contracts made on behalf of a principal. As we will discuss in this chapter, however, in some situations the agent has contractually created obligations or rights or both.

RELATIONSHIP OF PRINCIPAL AND THIRD PERSONS

In this section, we will first consider the contract liability of the principal; then we will examine the principal's potential tort liability.

CPA CONTRACT LIABILITY OF THE PRINCIPAL

The **power** of an agent is his ability to change the legal status of his principal. An agent who has either actual or apparent authority has the power to bind his principal. Thus, whenever an agent, acting within his authority, makes a contract for his principal, he creates new rights or liabilities for his principal and thus changes his principal's legal status. This power of an agent to act for his principal in business transactions is the basis of agency.

A principal's contract liability also depends on whether she is disclosed, partially disclosed, or undisclosed. The principal is a **disclosed principal** if at the time of a transaction conducted by an agent, the other party has notice that the agent is acting for a principal and also has notice of the principal's identity. The principal is a **partially disclosed principal** if at the time of the transaction conducted by the agent, the other party has notice that the agent is or may be acting for a principal but has no notice of the principal's identity. (Some courts refer to the partially disclosed principal as an "unidentified principal.") An example is an auctioneer who sells on behalf of a seller who is not identified: the seller is a partially disclosed principal since it is understood that the auctioneer acts as an agent. The principal is an **undisclosed principal** if the other party has no notice that the agent is acting for a principal. See Figures 30-1, 30-2, and 30-3, which explain the contract liability of disclosed principals, partially disclosed principals, and undisclosed principals.

Figure 30-1
Contract Liability of Disclosed Principal

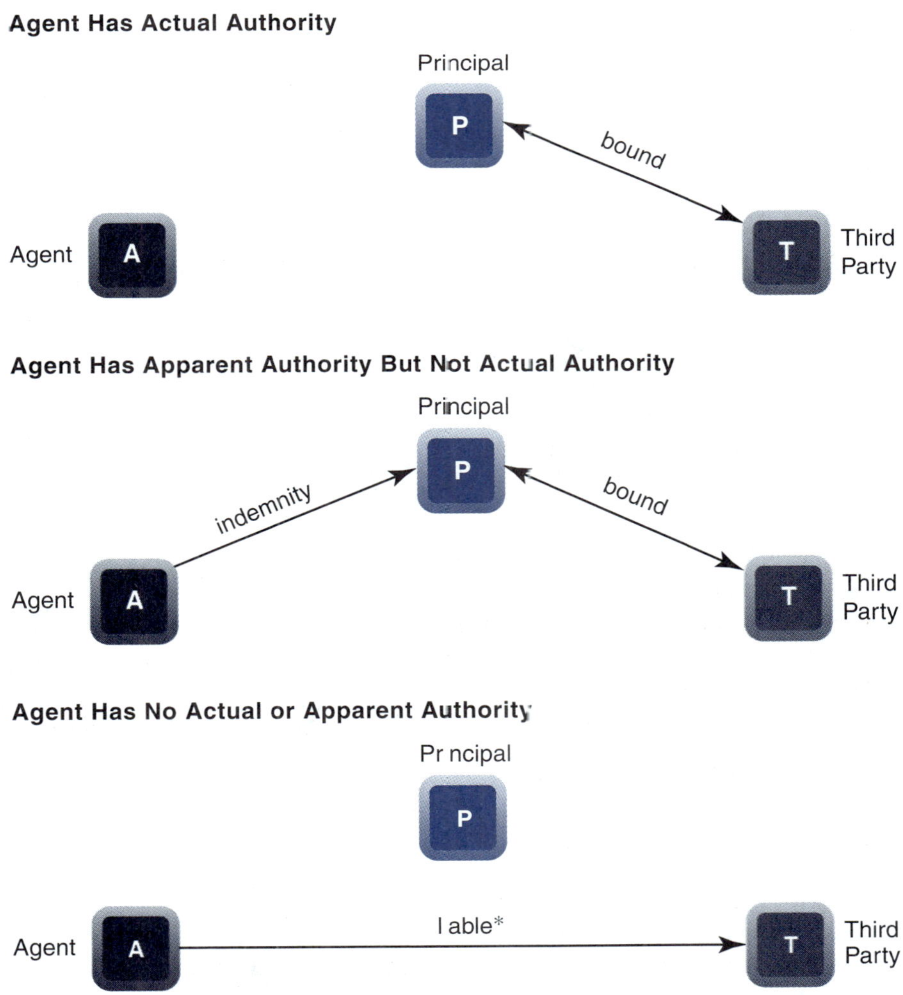

*Agent is liable for breach of implied warranty of authority or misrepresentation, as discussed later in this chapter.

Figure 30-2
Contract Liability of Partially Disclosed Principal

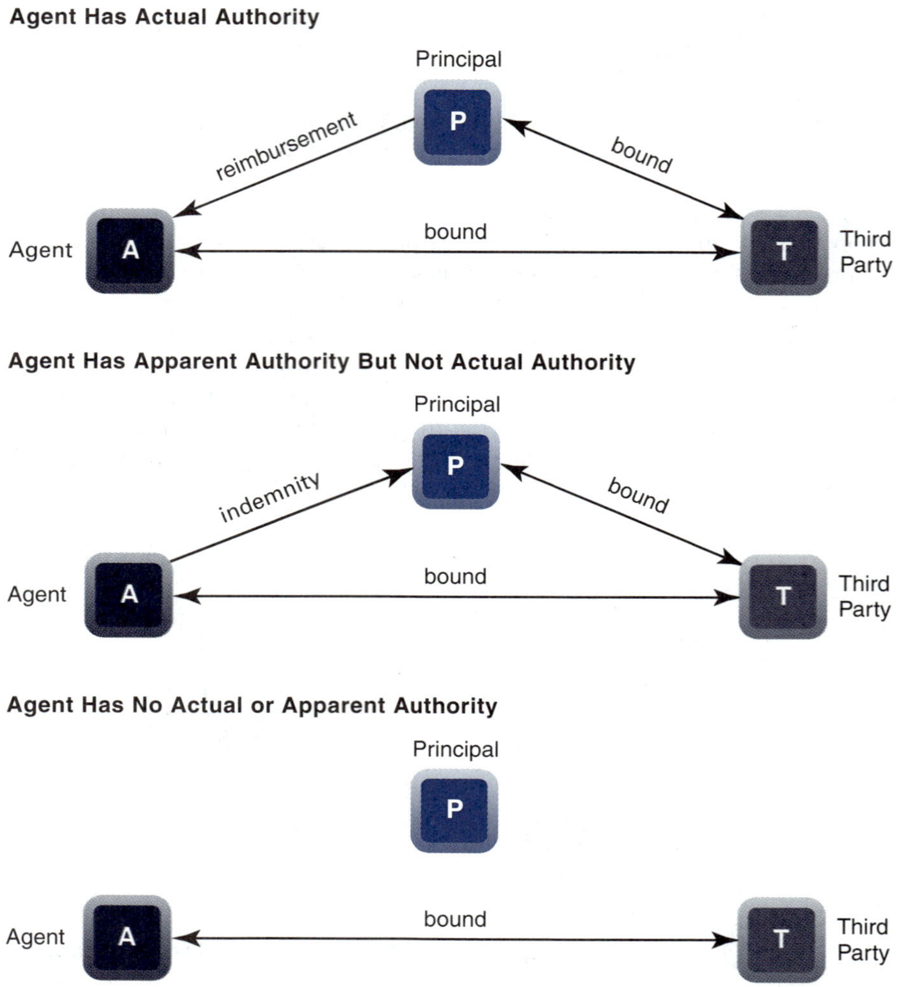

TYPES OF AUTHORITY

Authority is of two basic types: actual and apparent. **Actual authority** exists when the principal gives actual consent to the agent. Such authority may be either express or implied. In either case, it is binding and gives the agent both the power and the right to create or to affect the principal's legal relations with third persons. Where the principal is undisclosed, an agent acting with actual authority in making a contract will contractually bind the principal and the third party unless the terms of the contract exclude the principal from being a party or unless her existence is fraudulently concealed from the third party.

Apparent authority is based on acts or conduct of the principal that lead a third person to believe that the agent, or supposed agent, has actual authority, on which belief the third person justifiably relies. This manifestation, which confers upon the agent the power to create a legal relationship between the principal and a third party, may consist of words or actions of the principal as well as other facts and circumstances that induce the third person reasonably to rely on the existence of an agency relationship.

> **Practical Advice**
>
> As a principal, be careful how you hold out your employees and agents because you may create apparent authority in them.

Actual Express Authority The **express authority** of an agent, found in the spoken or written words the principal communicates to the agent, is actual authority stated in language directing or instructing the agent to do something specific. Thus, if Lee, orally or in writing, requests his agent, Anita, to sell his automobile for $6,500, Anita's authority to sell the car for this sum is actual and express. Actual express authority does not depend on the third party having knowledge of the statements made by the principal to the agent.

Figure 30-3
Contract Liability of Undisclosed Principal

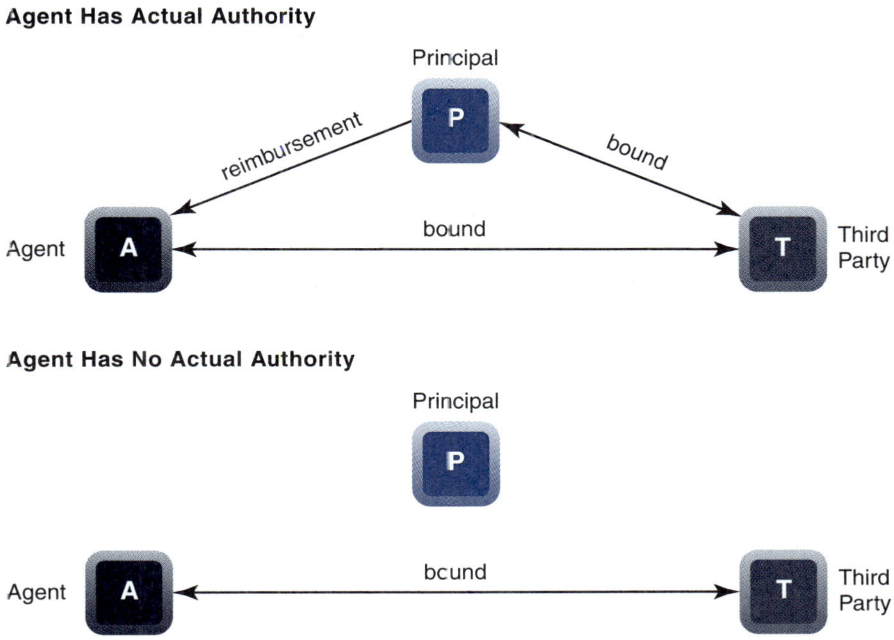

> **Practical Advice**
>
> As a principal, clearly and specifically communicate to your agents the extent of their actual authority. As a third party, be sure to check with the principal when there is any doubt as to the actual authority of an agent; this is a more certain approach than relying upon the possibility that you will be able to prove that the agent had apparent authority.

Actual Implied Authority **Implied authority** is not found in express or explicit words of the principal but is inferred from words or conduct that the principal manifests to the agent, who has implied authority to do what she reasonably infers the principal desires her to do, in light of the principal's manifestations to her and all other facts she knows or should know. Implied authority may arise from customs and usages of the principal's business. In addition, the authority granted to an agent to accomplish a particular purpose necessarily includes the authority to employ the means reasonably required to accomplish it. For example, Helen authorizes Clyde to manage her eighty-two-unit apartment complex but says nothing about expenses. In order to manage the building, Clyde must employ a janitor, purchase fuel for heating, and arrange for ordinary maintenance. Even though Helen has not expressly granted him the authority to incur such expenses, Clyde may infer the authority to incur them from the express authority to manage the building because such expenses are necessary to proper management.

Unless otherwise agreed, the authority to make a contract is inferred from the authority to conduct a transaction, if the making of such a contract is incidental to the transaction, usually accompanies such a transaction, or is reasonably necessary to accomplish it. Thus, Paragon, Inc., appoints Astor as the general manager of Paragon's manufacturing business. Astor's authority is interpreted as including the authority to make contracts for the employment of necessary employees. On the other hand, suppose Paige employs Arthur, a real estate broker, to find a purchaser for her residence at a stated price. Arthur has no authority to contract for its sale.

Unless otherwise agreed, general authority to manage or operate a business for a principal confers on an agent the implied authority (1) to buy and sell property for the principal; (2) to make contracts that are incidental or reasonably necessary to such business; (3) to acquire equipment and supplies; (4) to make repairs; (5) to employ, supervise, and discharge employees; (6) to receive payments due the principal and to pay debts due from the principal; and (7) to direct the ordinary operations of the business.

Apparent Authority Apparent authority is power arising from the conduct or words of a disclosed or partially disclosed principal that, when manifested to third persons, reasonably induce them to rely upon the assumption that actual authority exists. Apparent authority confers upon the agent, or supposed agent, the power to bind the disclosed or partially disclosed principal in contracts with

MANAGERIAL insight

Undisclosed Principal Working Through Agents Assembles Home for Famous Mouse, Duck, and Friends

One of the most ambitious, successful land purchases ever made by agents for an undisclosed principal took place in Orange County, Florida, in 1964 and 1965. In just eighteen months, buyers working for a mysterious developer assembled a piece of land twice the size of Manhattan. Rumors regarding the developer's identity were rampant as agents bought up cattle ranches and road frontage, scrub woods and swampland. When the agents were finished, they had acquired about 27,400 acres at an average reported price per acre of $185, for a total expenditure of somewhat more than $5 million.

The mystery ended in 1965. Walt Disney Productions announced its intention to build Disney World, an amusement park and resort, on 2,500 acres within the large tract. Disney World would be modeled on Disneyland Park, which had opened in 1955 in Anaheim, California. But Disney World would dwarf the 289 acres at Disneyland.

Disney's announcement set off the biggest wave of land speculation Florida had seen in fifty years. David Nusbickel, an Orlando real estate broker, worked with Disney's attorneys to help buy land. Several years after Disney's announcement of its purchase had set off a buying frenzy, Nusbickel said of the land speculators, "These guys, who obviously know their business, don't even blink when you quote them a price of $75,000 to $150,000 for an acre of property that maybe went for $3,000 a few years back." *BusinessWeek* estimated that between 1965 and 1971 more than $200 million in property changed hands-confirming the wisdom of Disney's secret buying.

Walt Disney World, as the project became known, opened on October 1, 1971. While still under construction, it was called by *Newsweek* the world's largest nongovernmental construction project. Despite occupying 2,500 acres of land, however, phase one of Walt Disney World took up slightly less than one-tenth of the total parcel Disney had assembled. Why had Disney directed its agents to buy so much land?

In Anaheim, hotels and restaurants had sprung up on the perimeter of Disneyland. The value of room and food revenues, which far exceeded the park's revenues, went to the owners and operators of the hotels and restaurants, not to Disney. And having developed without a plan, the hotels, restaurants, and stores gave the impression of clutter. Walt Disney's response: "It is necessary to control the environment. We learned this at Disneyland." Accordingly, Walt and his brother, Roy, decided to take their plan for Walt Disney World one step further. Not only would the company put restaurants, hotels, and golf courses inside the park, it would also buy enough land to develop housing—thus, the huge land purchase.

Said Roy Disney, who ran the financial side of the company, "I think we will make a lot more on the land than we ever will on the park. The development of this 20,000 acres can give us a future. And we will keep that future right in our own company."

Sources: *Newsweek*, 29 November 1965, 82; and 19 April 1971, 103–4; *Time*, 18 October 1971, 52–53; and *BusinessWeek*, 11 September 1971, 80.

third persons and prevents the principal from denying the existence of actual authority. Thus, when authority is apparent but not actual, the disclosed or partially disclosed principal is nonetheless bound by the act of the agent. By exceeding his actual authority, however, the agent violates his duty of obedience and is liable to the principal for any loss the principal suffers as a result of the agent's acting beyond his actual authority. See Figures 30-1 and 30-2.

Common ways in which apparent authority may arise include the following:

1. When a principal appoints an agent to a position in an organization, third parties may reasonably believe that the agent has the authority to do those acts customary of a person in such a position. (Apparent authority for agents of various business associations is discussed in Part 7 of this text.)
2. If a principal has given an agent general authority to engage in a transaction, subsequently imposed limitations or restrictions will not affect the agent's apparent authority to engage in that transaction until third parties are notified of the restrictions.
3. The principal's assent to prior similar transactions between the agent and a third party may create a basis for the third party reasonably to believe that the agent has apparent authority.
4. The agent shows the third party a document, such as a power of attorney, from the principal authorizing the agent to enter into such a transaction.
5. As discussed further later, after many terminations of authority, an agent has lingering apparent authority until the third party has actual knowledge or receives notice of the termination.

For example, Peter writes a letter to Alice authorizing her to sell his automobile and sends a copy of the letter to Thomas, a prospective purchaser. On the following day, Peter writes a letter to Alice revoking the authority to sell the car but does not send a copy of the second letter to Thomas, who is not otherwise informed of the revocation. Although Alice has no actual authority to sell the car, she continues to have apparent authority with respect to Thomas. Or suppose that Arlene, in the presence of Polly, tells Thad that Arlene is Polly's agent to buy lumber. Although this statement is not true, Polly does not deny it, as she easily could. Thad, in reliance upon the statement, ships lumber to Polly on Arlene's order. Polly is obligated to pay for the lumber because Arlene had apparent authority to act on Polly's behalf. Arlene's apparent authority exists only with respect to Thad. If Arlene were to give David an order for a shipment of lumber to Polly, David would not be able to hold Polly liable. Arlene would have had neither actual authority nor, as to David, apparent authority.

Because apparent authority is the power resulting from acts that appear to the third party to be authorized by the principal, no apparent authority can exist where the principal is undisclosed. See Figure 30-3. Nor can apparent authority exist where the third party *knows* that the agent has no actual authority.

Schoenberger v. Chicago Transit Authority

Appellate Court of Illinois, First District, First Division, 1980
84 Ill.App.3d 1132, 39 Ill.Dec. 941, 405 N.E.2d 1076

FACTS Schoenberger applied for and interviewed concerning a position with the Chicago Transit Authority (C.T.A.) **(http://www.transitchicago.com)**. He met several times with Frank ZuChristian, who was in charge of recruiting for the C.T.A. Data Center. At the third of these meetings, ZuChristian informed Schoenberger that he wanted to employ him at a salary of $19,800 and that he was making a recommendation to that effect. When the formal offer was made by the Placement Department, however, the salary was stated at $19,300. Schoenberger did not accept the offer immediately but instead called ZuChristian for an explanation of the salary difference. After making inquiries, ZuChristian informed Schoenberger that a clerical error had been made and that it would take some time to correct. He urged Schoenberger to accept the job at $19,300 and said that he would see that the $500 was made up to him at one of the salary reviews in the following year. When the increase was not given, Schoenberger resigned and filed this suit to recover damages. The trial court ruled in favor of C.T.A., and Schoenberger appealed.

DECISION Judgment for Chicago Transit Authority affirmed.

OPINION Campbell, J. The main question before us is whether ZuChristian, acting as an agent of the C.T.A., orally contracted with Schoenberger for $500 in compensation in addition to his $19,300 salary. The authority of an agent may only come from the principal and it is therefore necessary to trace the source of an agent's authority to some word or act of the alleged principal. [Citations.] The authority to bind a principal will not be presumed, but rather, the person alleging authority must prove its source unless the act of the agent has been ratified. [Citations.] Moreover, the authority must be founded upon some word or act of the principal, not on the acts or words of the agent. [Citations.]

* * * Both Hagan and Bonner, ZuChristian's superiors, testified that ZuChristian had no actual authority to either make an offer of a specific salary to Schoenberger or to make any promise of additional compensation. Furthermore, ZuChristian's testimony corroborated the testimony that he lacked the authority to make formal offers. From this evidence, it is clear that the trial court properly determined that ZuChristian lacked the actual authority to bind the C.T.A. for the additional $500 in compensation to Schoenberger.

Nor can it be said that the C.T.A. clothed ZuChristian with the apparent authority to make Schoenberger a promise of compensation over and above that formally offered by the Placement Department. The general rule to consider in determining whether an agent is acting within the apparent authority of his principal was stated in [citation] in this way:

> Apparent authority in an agent in such authority as the principal knowingly permits the agent to assume or which he holds his agent out as possessing—it is such authority as a reasonably prudent man, exercising diligence and discretion, in view of the principal's conduct, would naturally suppose the agent to possess.

* * *

Here, Schoenberger's initial contact with the C.T.A. was with the Placement Department where he filled out an application and had his first interview. There is no evidence that the C.T.A. did anything to permit ZuChristian to assume authority nor did they do anything to hold him out as having the authority to hire and set salaries. ZuChristian was not at a management level in the C.T.A. nor did his job title of Principal Communications Analyst suggest otherwise. The mere fact that he was allowed to interview prospective employees does not establish that the C.T.A. held him out as possessing the authority to hire employees or set salaries. Moreover, ZuChristian did inform Schoenberger that the formal offer of employment would be made by the Placement Department.

INTERPRETATION In order for an agent to bind a principal, she must have either actual authority or apparent authority, either of which must come from the conduct or words of the principal.

CRITICAL THINKING QUESTION Do you agree with the court's decision? Explain.

DELEGATION OF AUTHORITY

Because the appointment of an agent reflects the principal's confidence in the agent's personal skill, integrity, and other qualifications, the agent ordinarily has no power to delegate her authority to a subagent.

In certain situations, however, it is clear that the principal intended to permit the agent to delegate her granted authority. Such an intention may be gathered from the express authorization of the principal, the character of the business, the usages of trade, or the prior conduct of the parties. For example, if a check is deposited in a bank for collection at a distant place, the bank is impliedly authorized to employ another bank at the place of payment. Similarly, subagency is necessarily involved whenever a corporation is the agent because corporations may act only through their agents.

If an agent is authorized to appoint or select other persons, called **subagents**, to perform or to assist in the performance of the agent's duties, the acts of the subagent are as binding on the principal as those of the agent. The subagent, an agent of both the principal and the agent, owes a fiduciary duty to both. For example, P contracts with A, a real estate broker (agent), to sell P's house. P knows that A employs salespersons to show houses to prospective purchasers and to make representations about the property. The salespersons are A's employees and P's subagents.

If no authority exists to delegate the agent's authority, but the agent does so nevertheless, the acts of the subagent do not impose on the principal any obligations or liability to third persons. Likewise, the principal acquires no rights against such third persons.

EFFECT OF TERMINATION OF AGENCY ON AUTHORITY

When an agency terminates, the agent's *actual authority* ceases. When the termination is by the death or incapacity of the principal or agent, the agent's *apparent authority* also expires. Notice of such termination to third persons is *not* required. Thus, in a case when Thomas, a tenant of the principal, Perry, paid rent to Perry's agent, Augustus, in ignorance of Perry's death, and Augustus failed to account for the payment, Thomas is liable to Perry's estate for payment of the amount of the rent. The same holds where the performance of an authorized transaction becomes impossible, such as when the subject matter of the transaction is destroyed or the transaction is made illegal. The bankruptcy of the principal terminates without notice the power of an agent to affect the principal's property, which has passed to the bankruptcy trustee.

In other cases, apparent authority continues until the third party has actual knowledge or receives actual notice, if the third party is one (1) with whom the agent had previously dealt on credit, (2) to whom the agent has been specially accredited, or (3) with whom the agent has begun to deal, as the principal should know. **Actual notice** requires a communication, either oral or written, to the third party. All other third parties as to whom there was apparent authority must have actual knowledge or be given **constructive notice**, through publication, for example, in a newspaper of general circulation in the area where the agency is regularly carried on. See Figure 30-4 illustrating the effect of termination of agency on apparent authority.

To illustrate: Alfred is the general agent of Pace, who carries on business in Chicago. Carol knows of the agency, but has never dealt with Alfred. Daphne sells goods on credit to Alfred, as the agent of Pace. Pace revokes Alfred's authority and publishes a statement to that effect in a newspaper of general circulation published in Chicago. Carol does not see the statement and deals with Alfred in reliance upon the former agency. Daphne, who also does not see the statement and who has no knowledge of the revocation, sells more goods to Alfred, as the agent of Pace. Pace has given sufficient notice of revocation as to Carol, and, therefore, Alfred's apparent authority has terminated with respect to Carol. On the other hand, Pace has not given sufficient notice of revocation as to Daphne, and Pace is bound to Daphne by the contract of sale Alfred made on Pace's behalf.

Figure 30-4
Termination of Apparent Authority

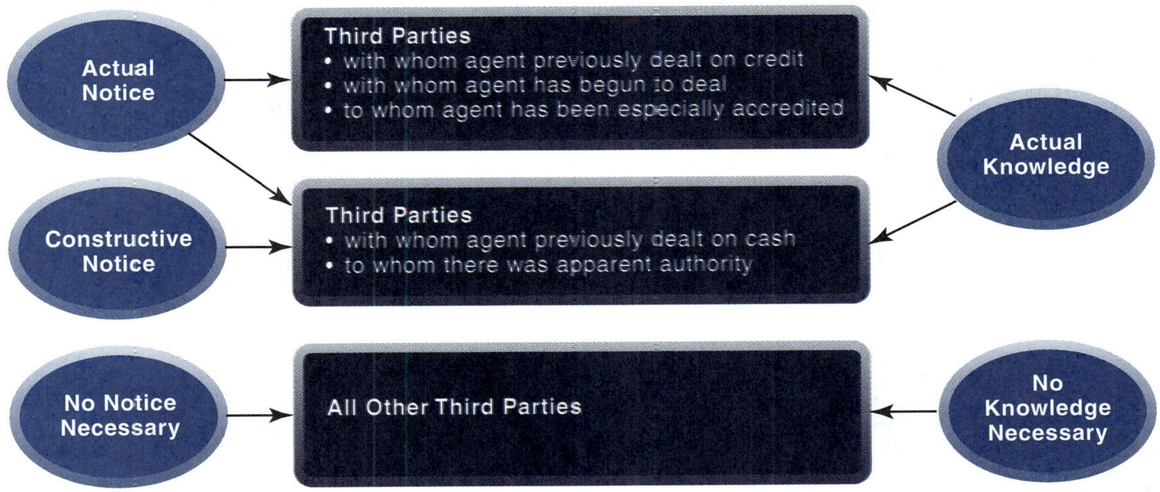

Zukaitis v. Aetna Casualty and Surety Co.

Supreme Court of Nebraska, 1975
195 Neb. 59, 236 N.W.2d 819

FACTS Raymond Zukaitis was a physician practicing medicine in Douglas County, Nebraska. Aetna **(http://www.aetna.com/index1.htm)** issued a policy of professional liability insurance to Zukaitis through its agent, the Ed Larsen Insurance Agency. The policy covered the period from August 31, 1969, through August of the following year. On August 7, 1971, Dr. Zukaitis received a written notification of a claim for malpractice that had occurred on September 27, 1969. Dr. Zukaitis notified the Ed Larsen Insurance Agency immediately and forwarded the written claim to it. The claim was then mistakenly referred to St. Paul Fire and Marine Insurance Company **(http://www.stpaul.com/wwwstpaul)**, the company that currently insured Dr. Zukaitis. Apparently without notice to Dr. Zukaitis, the agency contract between Larsen and Aetna had been canceled on August 1, 1970, and St. Paul had replaced Aetna as the insurance carrier. However, when St. Paul discovered it was not the carrier on the date of the alleged wrongdoing, it notified Aetna and withdrew from Dr. Zukaitis's defense. Aetna also refused to represent Dr. Zukaitis, contending that it was relieved of its obligation to Dr. Zukaitis because he had not notified Aetna immediately of the claim. Dr. Zukaitis then secured his own attorney to defend against the malpractice claim and brought this action against Aetna to recover attorneys' fees and other expenses incurred in the defense. The trial court found for Aetna, and Dr. Zukaitis appealed.

DECISION Judgment for Aetna reversed and remanded.

OPINION Blue, J. Ordinarily notice to a soliciting agent who countersigns and issues policies of insurance is notice to the insurance company. [Citations.] This is also true even if the agent forwards the notice to the wrong company. * * *

* * *

The question then is whether this is true after the agency contract between the insurance company and the agent has been terminated as it was in this case. To answer this, it is necessary to refer to the general law of agency.

The rule is that a revocation [by agreement of the principal and agent] of the agent's authority does not become effective as between the principal and third persons until they receive [actual] notice of the termination. [Citations.]

Here, Dr. Zukaitis did what most reasonable persons would do in this situation; he notified the agent who sold him the policy. There is no evidence that notice of the termination was sent to him or that he knew the agency contract had been canceled.

"When the insurer terminates the agency contract, it is its duty to notify third persons, such as the insureds with whom the agent dealt, and inform them of such termination. If it does not so notify and such third persons or insureds deal with the agent without notice or knowledge of the termination, and in reliance on the apparently continuing authority of the agent, the insurer is bound by the acts of the former agent." [Citation.]

"The principle of the carrying over of the authority of an agent after termination with respect to third persons having no notice or knowledge thereof has been applied so as to bind the insurer when the third person dealt with the apparent agent by contracting with him, or by forwarding or delivering to him suit papers and proofs of loss." [Citation.]

INTERPRETATION A revocation of an agent's authority does not bind third parties until they receive notice of the revocation.

ETHICAL QUESTION Did Aetna attempt to take unfair advantage of an honest mistake? Explain.

CRITICAL THINKING QUESTION What policy reasons support requiring actual notice to be given to certain third parties? Explain.

Practical Advice

As principal, be sure to give the appropriate notice to third parties whenever an agency relationship terminates.

RATIFICATION

Ratification is the confirmation or affirmance by one person of a prior unauthorized act performed by another who is, or who purports to be, his agent. The ratification of such act or contract binds the principal and the third party as if the agent or purported agent had been acting with actual authority initially. Once made, a valid ratification is irrevocable.

Requirements of Ratification Ratification may relate to acts that have exceeded the authority granted to an agent, as well as to acts that a person without any authority performs on behalf of an alleged principal. For the act to be ratified, however, the actor must have indicated to the third person that he was acting on a principal's behalf. There can be no ratification by an undisclosed principal.

To effect a ratification, the principal, with knowledge of all material facts concerning the transaction, must show an intent to ratify the entire act or contract. The principal does not need to communicate this intent either to the purported agent or to the third person. It may be manifested by express language or implied from conduct of the principal, such as accepting or retaining the benefits of a transaction. Thus, if Amanda, without authority, contracts in Penelope's name for the purchase of goods from Tate on credit, and Penelope, having learned of Amanda's unauthorized act, accepts the goods from Tate, she thereby impliedly ratifies the contract and is bound on it. If formalities are required for the authorization of an act, the same formalities apply to a ratification of that act.

To be effective, ratification must occur before the third person gives notice of his withdrawal to the principal or agent. If the affirmance of a transaction occurs when the situation has so materially changed that it would be inequitable to subject the third party to liability, the third party may elect to avoid liability. For example, Alex has no authority, but, purporting to act for Penny, he contracts to sell Penny's house to Taylor. The next day, the house burns down. Penny then affirms the sale. Taylor is not bound. Moreover, the power to ratify would be terminated by the third party's death or loss of capacity and by the lapse of a reasonable time.

Finally, for ratification to be effective, the purported principal must have been in existence when the act was done. For example, a promoter of a corporation not yet in existence may enter into contracts on behalf of the corporation. However, in the majority of states, these acts cannot be ratified by the corporation because it did not exist when the contracts were made. Instead, the corporation may ***adopt*** the contract. Adoption differs from ratification because it is not retroactive and does release the promoter from liability. See Chapter 34.

If a principal's lack of capacity entitles her to avoid transactions, the principal may also avoid any ratification made when under the incapacity. The principal may, however, ratify a contract that is voidable because of the principal's incapacity when the incapacity no longer exists. Thus, after she reaches majority, a principal may ratify an unauthorized contract made on her behalf while she was a minor. She may also avoid any ratification made prior to attaining majority.

Practical Advice

As a principal, recognize that if you accept the benefits of an unauthorized contract with full knowledge, under the doctrine of ratification, you will be obliged to fulfill the contract's burdens.

Effect of Ratification Ratification is equivalent to prior authority, which means that the effect of ratification is substantially the same as if the agent or purported agent had been actually authorized when he performed the act. The respective rights, duties, and remedies of the principal and the third party are the same as if the agent had originally possessed actual authority. Both the principal and the agent are in a position the same as the one they would have been in had the principal actually authorized the act originally. The agent is entitled to her due compensation. Moreover, she is freed from liability to the principal for acting as his agent without authority or for exceeding her authority, as the case may be. Between the agent and the third party, the agent is released from any liability she may have to the third party by reason of having induced the third party to enter into the contract without the principal's authority.

FUNDAMENTAL RULES OF CONTRACTUAL LIABILITY

The following rules summarize the contractual relations between the principal and the third party:

1. A disclosed principal and the third party are contractually bound if the agent acts within her *actual* or *apparent* authority in making the contract. See Figure 30-1.
2. A partially disclosed principal and the third party are contractually bound if the agent acts within her *actual* or *apparent* authority in making the contract. See Figure 30-2.
3. An undisclosed principal and the third party are contractually bound if the agent acts within her *actual* authority in making the contract unless (a) the terms of the contract exclude the principal or (b) his existence is fraudulently concealed. See Figure 30-3.
4. No principal is contractually bound to a third party if the agent acts *without* any authority, unless a disclosed or partially disclosed principal ratifies the contract.

> **Practical Advice**
>
> As a principal, carefully consider the extent to which you want your agent to disclose your existence and identity.

CPA TORT LIABILITY OF THE PRINCIPAL

In addition to being contractually liable to third persons, a principal may be liable in tort to third persons because of the acts of her agent. Tort liability may arise directly or indirectly (vicariously) from authorized or unauthorized acts of an agent. Also, a principal is liable for the unauthorized torts an agent commits in connection with a transaction that the purported principal, with full knowledge of the tort, subsequently ratifies. Cases involving unauthorized but ratified torts are extremely rare. Of course, in all of these situations, the wrongdoing agent is personally liable to the injured person because the agent committed the tort. See Figure 30-5 explaining the tort liability of the principal.

DIRECT LIABILITY OF PRINCIPAL

A principal is liable for his *own* tortious conduct involving the use of agents. Such liability may arise in two primary ways. First, a principal is directly liable in damages for harm resulting from his directing an agent to commit a tort. Second, the principal is directly liable if he fails to exercise care in employing competent agents.

Authorized Acts of Agent A principal who authorizes his agent to commit a tortious act concerning the property or person of another is liable for the injury or loss that person sustains. The authorized act is that of the principal. Thus, if Phillip directs his agent, Anthony, to enter Clark's land and cut timber, which neither Phillip nor Anthony has any right to do, the cutting of the timber is a trespass, and Phillip is liable to Clark. Or suppose Phillip instructs his agent, Anthony, to make certain representations as to Phillip's property that Anthony is authorized to sell. Phillip knows these representations are false, but Anthony does not. Such representations by Anthony to Dryden, who buys the property in reliance on them, constitute a deceit for which Phillip is liable to Dryden.

Unauthorized Acts of Agent A principal who conducts activities through an employee or other agent is liable for harm resulting from the principal's negligence or recklessness in hiring, instructing, supervising, or controlling the employee or other agent. The liability of a principal under this provision—called *negligent hiring*—arises when the principal does not exercise proper care in selecting an agent for the job to be done. For example, if Patricia lends to her employee, Art, a company car with which to run a business errand, knowing that Art is incapable of driving the vehicle, Patricia would be liable for her own negligence to anyone injured by Art's unsafe driving. The negligent hiring doctrine has also been used to impose liability on a principal for intentional torts committed by an agent against customers of the principal or members of the public, when the principal either knew or should have known that the agent was violent or aggressive.

Figure 30-5
Tort Liability

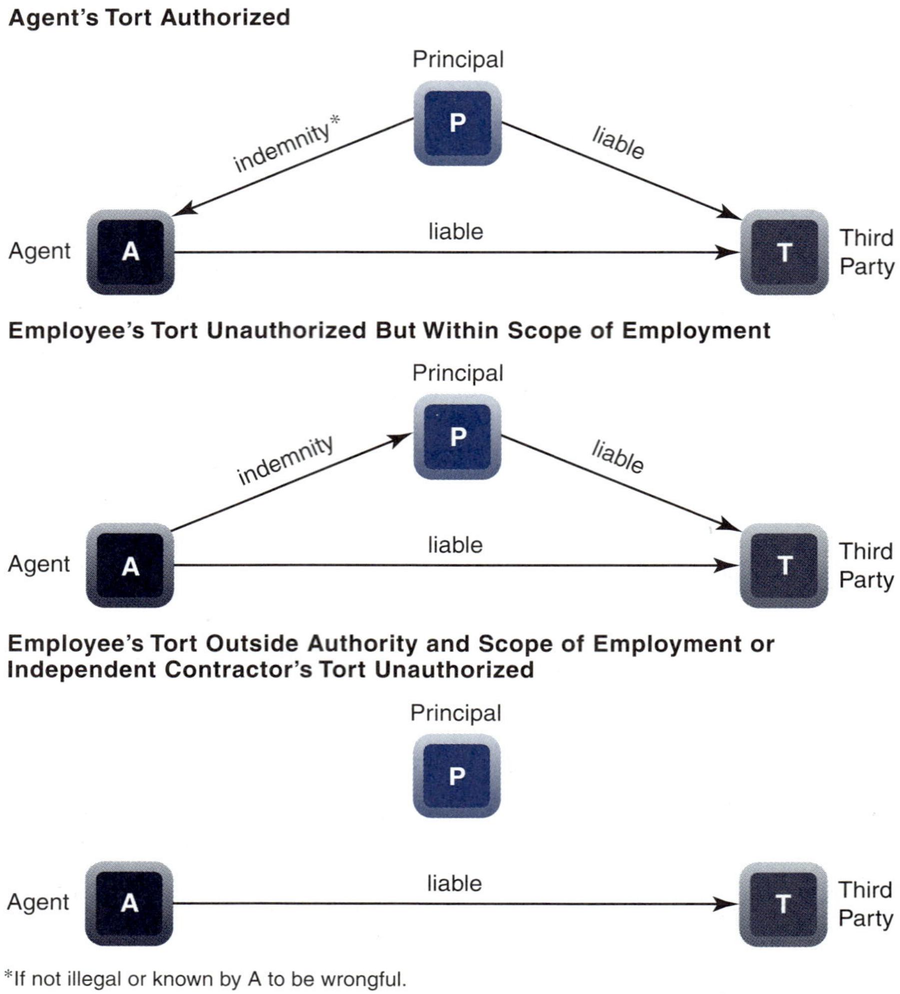

Connes v. Molalla Transport System, Inc.

Supreme Court of Colorado, 1992
831 P.2d 1316

FACTS Terry Taylor was an employee of Molalla Transport. In hiring Taylor, Molalla followed its standard hiring procedure, which includes a personal interview with each applicant and requires the applicant to fill out an extensive job application form and to produce a current driver's license and a certificate from a medical examiner. Molalla also contacts prior employers and other references about the applicant's qualifications and conducts an investigation of the applicant's driving record in the state where the applicant obtained the driver's license. Although applicants are asked whether they have been convicted of a crime, Molalla does not conduct an independent investigation to determine whether or not an applicant has ever been convicted. Approximately three months after Taylor began working for Molalla, he was assigned to transport freight from Kansas to Oregon. While traveling through Colorado, Taylor left the highway and drove by a hotel where Grace Connes was working as a night clerk. Observing that Connes was alone in the lobby, Taylor pulled his truck into the parking lot and entered the lobby. Once inside, Taylor sexually assaulted Connes at knifepoint. Although Taylor denied any prior criminal convictions on his application and during his interview, police and court records obtained since these events show that Taylor had been convicted of three felonies in

Colorado and had been issued three citations for lewd conduct and another citation for simple assault in Seattle, Washington.

Connes sued Molalla on the theory of negligent hiring, claiming that Molalla knew or should have known that Taylor would come into contact with members of the public, that Molalla had a duty to hire and retain high-quality employees so as not to endanger members of the public, and that Molalla had breached its duty by failing to investigate fully and adequately Taylor's criminal background. The district court granted Molalla's motion for summary judgment. The Court of Appeals upheld the lower court's ruling, holding that Molalla had no legal duty to investigate the nonvehicular criminal record of its driver prior to hiring him as an employee. Connes appealed.

DECISION Judgment affirmed.

OPINION Quinn, J. The tort of negligent hiring is based on the principle that a person conducting an activity through employees is subject to liability for harm resulting from negligent conduct "in the employment of improper persons or instrumentalities in work involving risk of harm to others." Restatement (Second) of Agency § 213(b). This principle of liability is not based on the rule of agency but rather on the law of torts. In [citation], the New Jersey Supreme Court offered the following distinction between the tort of negligent hiring and the agency doctrine of vicarious liability based on the rule of *respondeat superior*:

> Thus, the tort of negligent hiring addresses the risk created by exposing members of the public to a potentially dangerous individual, while the doctrine of *respondeat superior* is based on the theory that the employee is the agent or is acting for the employer. Therefore the scope of employment limitation on liability which is part of the *respondeat superior* doctrine is not implicit in the wrong of negligent hiring.

Accordingly, the negligent hiring theory has been used to impose liability in cases where the employee commits an intentional tort, an action almost invariably outside the scope of employment, against the customer of a particular employer or other member of the public, where the employer either knew or should have known that the employee was violent or aggressive, or that the employee might engage in injurious conduct toward third persons.

Several jurisdictions, in addition to New Jersey, have recognized the tort of negligent hiring, * * * and we now join those jurisdictions in formally recognizing this cause of action.

In recognizing the tort of negligent hiring, we emphasize that an employer is not an insurer for violent acts committed by an employee against a third person. On the contrary, liability is predicated on the employer's hiring of a person under circumstances antecedently giving the employer reason to believe that the person, by reason of some attribute of character or prior conduct, would create an undue risk of harm to others in carrying out his or her employment responsibilities. See Restatement (Second) of Agency § 213, comment d. The scope of the employer's duty in exercising reasonable care in a hiring decision will depend largely on the anticipated degree of contact which the employee will have with other persons in performing his or her employment duties.

Where the employment calls for minimum contact between the employee and other persons, there may be no reason for an employer to conduct any investigation of the applicant's background beyond obtaining past employment information and personal data during the initial interview. [Citation.] * * *

* * *

We endorse the proposition that where an employer hires a person for a job requiring frequent contact with members of the public, or involving close contact with particular persons as a result of a special relationship between such persons and the employer, the employer's duty of reasonable care is not satisfied by a mere review of personal data disclosed by the applicant on a job application form or during a personal interview. However, in the absence of circumstances antecedently giving the employer reason to believe that the job applicant, by reason of some attribute of character or prior conduct, would constitute an undue risk of harm to members of the public with whom the applicant will be in frequent contact or to particular persons standing in a special relationship to the employer and with whom the applicant will have close contact, we decline to impose upon the employer his duty to obtain and review official records of an applicant's criminal history. To impose such a requirement would mean that an employer would be obligated to seek out and evaluate official police and perhaps court records from every jurisdiction in which a job applicant had any significant contact. We have serious doubts whether such a task could be effectively achieved. * * * Accordingly, in the absence of circumstances antecedently giving the employer reason to believe that a job applicant, by reason of some attribute of character or prior conduct, would constitute an undue risk of harm to members of the public with whom the applicant will be in frequent contact or to particular persons who stand in a special relationship to the employer and with whom the applicant will be in close contact, the employer's duty of reasonable care does not extend to searching for and reviewing official records of a job applicant's criminal history.

In the instant case, we agree with the court of appeals' determination that Molalla had no duty to conduct an independent investigation into Taylor's non-vehicular criminal background before hiring him as a long-haul driver.

Molalla had no reason to foresee that its hiring of Taylor under the circumstances of this case would create a risk that Taylor would sexually assault or otherwise endanger a member of the public by engaging in violent conduct. To be sure, Molalla had a duty to use reasonable care in hiring a safe driver who would not create a danger to the public in carrying out the duties of the job. Far from requiring frequent contact with members of the public or involving close contact with persons having a special relationship with the employer, Taylor's duties were restricted to the hauling of freight on interstate highways and, as such, involved only incidental contact with third persons having no special relationship to Molalla or to Taylor. After checking on Taylor's driving record and contacting some of his references, Molalla had no reason to believe that Taylor would not be a safe driver or a dependable employee. In addition, Molalla specifically instructed its drivers to stay on the interstate highways and, except for an emergency, to stop only in order to service the truck and to eat and to sleep. It further directed its drivers to sleep in the sleeping compartment behind the driver's seat of the truck at rest areas or truck stops located along the interstate highway system. Furthermore, Molalla required Taylor to fill out a job application and to submit to a personal interview. Taylor stated on the application form and at the interview that he had never been convicted of a crime. Nothing in the hiring process gave Molalla reason to foresee that Taylor would pose an unreasonable risk of harm to members of the public with whom he might have incidental contact during the performance of his duties. * * *

We accordingly hold that Molalla, in hiring Taylor as a long-haul truck driver, had no legal duty to conduct an independent investigation into Taylor's non-vehicular criminal background in order to protect a member of the public, such as Connes, from a sexual assault committed by Taylor in the course of making a long-haul trip over the interstate highway system.

INTERPRETATION An employer's liability for negligent hiring is based on the employer's hiring a person under circumstances antecedently giving the employer reason to believe that the person would create an undue risk of harm to others in carrying out his employment duties.

ETHICAL QUESTION Was the court's decision fair? Explain.

CRITICAL THINKING QUESTION When should a prospective employer be required to check the criminal record of a job applicant? Explain.

VICARIOUS LIABILITY OF PRINCIPAL FOR UNAUTHORIZED ACTS OF AGENT

The ***vicarious liability*** of a principal for unauthorized torts by an agent depends primarily on whether the agent is an employee or not. An employee is an agent whose physical conduct in the performance of services for the principal-employer is controlled by the principal or subject to the principal's right to control. By comparison, an agent whose physical conduct is not controlled by, or subject to the control of, the principal is not an employee but an independent contractor. The general rule is that a principal is not liable for physical harm caused by the tortious conduct of an agent who is an independent contractor if the principal did not intend or authorize the result or the manner of performance. Conversely, a principal is liable for an unauthorized tort committed by an employee in the course of his employment.

On the other hand, the liability of a principal whose agent makes an unauthorized yet tortious ***misrepresentation*** does not depend upon whether the agent is an employee. Rather, the principal is liable for loss caused to another who relies upon a tortious representation made by an agent (whether an employee or an independent contractor) if the representation is *apparently* authorized. For example, Pillsbury engages Adams as an agent to sell some land. While negotiating with Trent, Adams states that a stream running through the property has not overflowed its banks during the past ten years. Adams knows that this is untrue. In reliance upon this false statement, Trent purchases the land. Pillsbury is liable to Trent for fraudulent misrepresentation.

Respondeat Superior

An employer may be liable for an unauthorized tort committed by his employee, even one that is in flagrant disobedience of his instructions, if the employee committed the tort in the course of her employment. This form of employer liability without fault is based on the doctrine of ***respondeat superior***, or "let the superior respond." It does not matter how carefully the employer selected the employee if, in fact, the latter tortiously injures a third person while engaged in the employer's business. Under the Restatement, even an *undisclosed* principal employer is liable for the torts his employee commits within the scope of employment.

The doctrine of *respondeat superior* is fundamental to the operation of tort law in the United States. The rationale of this doctrine is that a person who conducts his business activities through the use of employees should be liable for the employees' tortious conduct in carrying out

Ethical Dilemma

When Should an Agent's Power to Bind His Principal Terminate?

FACTS Tim Banks was an employee of Golden Harvest Florists International (GHFI). GHFI operated a wholesale florist business on the East Coast and also maintained a small chain of retail shops in the Washington, D.C.-Baltimore area. Tim, whose responsibilities included buying large quantities of fresh cut flowers from various greenhouses along the East Coast, had established an excellent rapport with all of his suppliers and was well respected throughout the entire industry.

Because of his good reputation, Tim was shocked to discover on April 1, 1993, that he had been released by GHFI. This notice came after five years of faithful service to the company. Though the company would not tell Tim why he had been fired, Tim learned that GHFI felt threatened by his reputation and was worried that he was becoming better known and more important than the company itself.

GHFI did not, moreover, notify any of Tim's suppliers of his release until January 1, 1994. The company was worried that notice might undermine the suppliers' confidence in the company and could possibly cause prices to rise. Meanwhile, deciding to begin his own business, Tim continued to purchase flowers from the same greenhouses. He was able to pay his supply bills from April through November of 1993, but, when his funds were low in December, he charged the flowers to GHFI. GHFI refused to pay, and the greenhouses have filed suit against Tim and GHFI.

Social, Policy, and Ethical Considerations

1. Who is legally responsible for the bills? Who is ethically responsible?
2. What is the social policy behind the requirement of notice prior to termination of a principal-agent relationship?
3. Does Tim have a responsibility to the greenhouses to notify them of the source of his funds, as long as the bill is paid?

those activities. The employer is more likely to insure against liability and is more likely to have the assets to satisfy a tort judgment than the employee. Moreover, *respondeat superior* creates an economic incentive for employers to exercise care in choosing, training, supervising, and insuring employees.

The liability of the principal under *respondeat superior* is vicarious or derivative and depends on proof of wrongdoing by the employee in the course of his employment. Frequently, both principal and employee are defendants in the same suit. If the employee is not held liable, the principal is not liable either, because the employer's liability is based upon the employee's tortious conduct. A principal who is held liable for her employee's tort has a right of ***indemnification*** against the employee, which is the right to be reimbursed for the amount that she was required to pay as a result of the employee's wrongful act. Frequently, however, an employee is not able to reimburse his employer, and the principal must bear the brunt of the liability.

The wrongful act of the employee must be connected with his employment and within its scope if the principal is to be held liable for resulting injuries or damage to third persons. For example, Hal, delivering gasoline for Martha, lights his pipe and negligently throws the blazing match into a pool of gasoline that has dripped on the ground during the delivery. The gasoline ignites, burning Arnold's filling station. Martha is subject to liability for the resulting harm because the negligence of the employee who delivered the gasoline relates directly to the manner in which he handled the goods in his custody. But if a chauffeur, while driving his employer's car on an errand for his employer, suddenly decides to shoot his pistol at pedestrians on the sidewalk, the employer would not be liable to the pedestrians. This willful and intentional misconduct is not related to the performance of the services for which the chauffeur was employed.

The same rule applies to an employee's tortious conduct that is unrelated to his employment. If Page employs Edward to deliver merchandise to Page's customers in a given city, and while driving a delivery truck to or from a place of delivery Edward negligently causes the truck to hit and injure Fred, Page is liable to Fred for injuries sustained. But if, after making the scheduled deliveries, Edward drives the truck to a neighboring city to visit a friend and while so doing negligently causes the truck to hit and injure Debra, Page is not liable. In the latter case, Edward is said to be on a "frolic of his own." By using the truck to accomplish his own purposes, not those of his employer, he has deviated from the purpose of his employment.

Rubin v. Yellow Cab Company

Appellate Court of Illinois, First District, Fifth Division, 1987
154 Ill.App.3d 336, 107 Ill.Dec. 450, 507 N.E.2d 114

FACTS Rubin, the plaintiff, was driving on one of the city's streets when he inadvertently obstructed the path of a taxicab, causing the cab to come into contact with his vehicle. Angered by the plaintiff's sudden blocking of his traffic lane, the defendant taxi driver exited his cab, approached Rubin, and struck him about the head and shoulders with a metal pipe. Rubin filed suit against the cab driver to recover for bodily injuries resulting from the altercation. He also sued the Yellow Cab Company (Yellow Cab) **(http://www.yellowcabchicago.com/index.htm)**, asserting that the company was vicariously liable under the doctrine of *respondeat superior*. The trial court ruled in favor of Yellow Cab, and the plaintiff appealed.

DECISION Judgment for Yellow Cab affirmed.

OPINION Lorenz, J. We initially consider whether the subject complaint states a cause of action under the doctrine of *respondeat superior*.

It is well established that an employer may be held liable for the negligent, willful, malicious or criminal acts of its employees where such acts are committed in the course of employment and in furtherance of the business of the employer. [Citation.] However, where the acts complained of are committed solely for the benefit of the employee, the employer will not be held liable to an injured third party. [Citation.]

Plaintiff in the instant case maintains that his fourth amended complaint alleges sufficient facts to show that Ball committed the battery within the course and scope of his duties as a cab driver. According to plaintiff, Ball's acts were designed to further the business purposes of Yellow Cab by virtue of the fact that they: (1) fulfilled his obligation to investigate and report any accidents damaging property owned by Yellow Cab; (2) were performed pursuant to his obligation to protect property owned by Yellow Cab; and (3) were meant to prevent plaintiff and others from delaying his progress to obtain fares. We disagree.

First, the complaint in question contains no allegation that plaintiff was interfering with Ball's investigation or attempt to report the accident or, for that matter, that Ball was even attempting to investigate or report the incident at the time he struck plaintiff with the pipe. Rather, the subject complaint merely states that Ball got out of his cab, walked over to plaintiff and proceeded to hit him over the head with a pipe. This act patently has no relation to the business of driving a cab. In view of their duties, cab drivers are not expected to strike individuals on the street with metal pipes. Second, the battery could have no relation to Yellow Cab's interest in protecting its property since the contact between the two vehicles had already occurred. Lastly, the battery could not have prevented plaintiff from delaying Ball's progress to the airport to obtain passengers as a delay had already occurred before Ball got out of his cab to strike plaintiff.

While we accept the principles stated in the cases primarily relied on by plaintiff, their factual inappositeness makes their application improper in the resolution of the instant case. [Citations], all present situations in which bartenders or bouncers endeavored to maintain order or protect the property of their employers. The nature of a bartender's or bouncer's job makes the use of force during the course of his employment highly probable. A cab driver, on the other hand, is basically relegated to transporting individuals from one destination to another and, as such, it is unlikely that he will undertake to attack a person that is neither a passenger nor is connected with the cab company. * * *

As Ball's assault of plaintiff was clearly not an act undertaken to further Yellow Cab's business but rather one propelled singularly by anger and frustration, the trial court properly dismissed Count IX of plaintiff's fourth amended complaint for failure to state a cause of action under the doctrine of *respondeat superior*.

INTERPRETATION Under *respondeat superior*, an employer's liability for torts extends only to torts committed within the scope of employment.

CRITICAL THINKING QUESTION Do you agree that the taxi driver's conduct was outside his employment duties? If so, should it exonerate the employer from liability? Explain.

Torts of Independent Contractor An **independent contractor** is not the employee of the person for whom he is performing work or rendering services. Hence, the doctrine of *respondeat superior* generally does not apply to torts committed by an independent contractor. For example, Parnell authorizes Bob, his broker, to sell land for him. Parnell, Teresa, and Bob meet in Teresa's office; and Bob arranges the sale to Teresa. While Bob is preparing a deed for Parnell to sign, he negligently knocks over an inkstand and ruins a valuable rug belonging to Teresa. Bob, *not* Parnell, is liable to Teresa.

Nonetheless, the principal may be *directly* liable if she fails to exercise reasonable care in selecting an independent contractor. For example, Melanie employs Gordon, whom she knows to be an alcoholic, as an independent contractor to repair her roof. Gordon attempts the repairs while heavily intoxicated and negligently drops a fifty-pound bundle of shingles upon Eric, a pedestrian walking on the sidewalk. Both Gordon and Melanie are liable to Eric.

Moreover, under some circumstances, a principal will be *vicariously* liable for torts committed by a carefully selected independent contractor. Certain duties imposed by law are nondelegable, and a person may not escape the consequences of their nonperformance by having entrusted them to an independent contractor. For example, a landowner who permits an independent contractor to maintain a dangerous condition on his premises, such as an excavation that is neither surrounded by a guardrail nor lit at night and that adjoins a public sidewalk, is liable to a member of the public who is injured by falling into the excavation.

A principal is also vicariously liable for an independent contractor's negligent conduct in carrying on an ultrahazardous activity, such as using fire or high explosives. Finally, a principal is vicariously liable if an independent contractor negligently conducts an inherently dangerous activity, such as excavating a public road, demolishing a building, or spraying crops.

> **Practical Advice**
>
> As a principal, consider hiring an independent contractor to limit your potential tort liability.

CPA Criminal Liability of the Principal

A principal is liable for the **authorized criminal acts** of his agents only if the principal directed, participated in, or approved of the acts. For example, if an agent, at his principal's direction or with his principal's knowledge, fixes prices with the principal's competitors, both the agent and the principal have criminally violated the antitrust laws. Otherwise, a principal ordinarily is not liable for the unauthorized criminal acts of his agents. One of the elements of a crime is mental fault, and this element is absent, so far as the principal's criminal responsibility is concerned, when the principal did not authorize the agent's act.

An employer may, nevertheless, be subject to a criminal penalty for the unauthorized act of an advisory or managerial employee acting in the scope of her employment. Moreover, an employer may be criminally liable under liability without fault statutes for certain **unauthorized criminal acts** of an employee, whether the employee is managerial or not. These statutes are usually regulatory and do not require mental fault. For example, many states have statutes that punish "every person who by himself or his employee or agent sells anything at short weight," or "whoever sells liquor to a minor and any sale by an employee shall be deemed the act of the employer as well." Another example is a statute prohibiting the sale of unwholesome or adulterated food. See Chapter 6 for a more detailed discussion of this topic.

RELATIONSHIP OF AGENT AND THIRD PERSONS

The function of an agent is to assist in the conduct of the principal's business by carrying out his orders. Generally, the agent acquires no rights against third parties and likewise incurs no liabilities to them. There are, however, several exceptions to this proposition. In certain instances, an agent may become personally liable to the third party for contracts she made on behalf of her principal. Occasionally, the agent also may acquire rights against the third party. In addition, an agent who commits a tort is personally liable to the injured third party. In this section, we will cover these circumstances involving the personal liability of an agent, as well as those in which an agent may acquire rights against third persons.

CPA Contract Liability of the Agent

The agent normally is not a party to the contract he makes with a third person on behalf of a disclosed principal. An agent who exceeds his actual and apparent authority may, however, be personally liable to the third party. In addition, an agent acting for a disclosed principal may become liable if he expressly assumes liability on the contract. When an agent enters into a contract on behalf of a partially disclosed principal or an undisclosed principal, the agent becomes personally liable to the third party on the contract. Furthermore, an agent who knowingly enters into a contract on behalf of a nonexistent or incompetent principal is personally liable to the third party on that contract.

DISCLOSED PRINCIPAL

When transacting business with an agent who is acting for an identified principal, a third person is on notice that the agent is not personally undertaking to perform the contract but is simply negotiating on behalf of her principal. The resulting contract, if within the agent's actual authority, is between the third person and the principal. The agent ordinarily incurs no liability on the contract to either party. (See Figure 30-1.) This is also true of unauthorized contracts that are subsequently ratified by the principal. However, if the agent has apparent authority but no actual authority, the agent has no liability to the third party but is liable to the principal for any loss the agent has caused by exceeding his actual authority.

> **Practical Advice**
>
> When signing contracts as an agent, be sure to indicate clearly your representative capacity.

Unauthorized Contracts If an agent exceeds his actual and apparent authority, the principal is not bound. The fact that the principal is not bound does not, however, make the agent a party to the contract. The agent's liability, if any, arises from express or implied representations about his authority that he makes to the third party. For example, an agent may ***expressly warrant*** that he has authority by stating that he has authority and that he will be personally liable to the third party if he does not in fact have the authority to bind his principal.

Moreover, a person who undertakes to make a contract on behalf of another gives an ***implied warranty*** that he is in fact authorized to make the contract on behalf of the party whom he purports to represent. If the agent does not have authority to bind the principal, the agent is liable to the third party for damages unless the principal ratifies the contract or unless the third party knew that the agent was unauthorized. No implied warranty exists, however, if the contract expressly provides that the agent shall not be responsible for any lack of authority or if the agent, acting in good faith, discloses to the third person all of the facts upon which his authority rests. For example, agent Larson has received an ambiguous letter of instruction from his principal, Dan. Larson shows it to Carol, stating that it represents all of the authority that he has to act, and both Larson and Carol rely upon its sufficiency. In this case, Larson has made to Carol no implied or express warranty of his authority.

If a purported agent ***misrepresents*** to a third person that he has authority to make a contract on behalf of a principal whom he has no power to bind, he is liable in a tort action to the third person for the loss she sustained in reliance upon the misrepresentation. However, if the third party knows that the representation is false, the agent is not liable.

> **Practical Advice**
>
> As an agent, consider disclaiming liability for any lack of authority; as a third party, consider obtaining from the agent an express warranty of authority.

Agent Assumes Liability An agent may agree to become liable on a contract between the principal and the third party by (1) making the contract in her own name, (2) co-making the contract with the principal, or (3) guaranteeing that the principal will perform the contract between the third party and the principal. In all of these situations, the agent's liability is separate unless the parties agree otherwise. Therefore, the third party may sue the agent separately without joining the principal and may obtain a judgment against either the principal or the agent, or both. If the principal satisfies the judgment, the agent is discharged. If the agent pays the judgment, he usually will have a right of reimbursement from the principal. This right is based upon the principles of suretyship, discussed in Chapter 38.

PARTIALLY DISCLOSED PRINCIPAL

An agent, as we discussed previously, acts for a partially disclosed principal (or unidentified principal) if the third party has notice that the agent is acting for a principal but has no notice of the principal's identity. Using a partially disclosed principal may be helpful when, for example, the third party might inflate the price of property he is selling if he knew the identity of the principal. Partial disclosure may also occur inadvertently, when the agent fails through neglect to inform the third party of the principal's identity.

Unless otherwise agreed, an agent making a contract for a **partially disclosed principal** is a party to the contract. For example, Ashley writes to Terrence offering to sell a rare painting on behalf of its owner, who wishes to remain unknown. Terrence accepts. Ashley is a party to the contract.

Whether the particular transaction is authorized or not, an agent for a partially disclosed principal is liable on the contract to the third party. (See Figure 30-2.) If the agent is actually authorized to make the contract, both the agent and the partially disclosed principal are liable. In any event, the agent is separately liable, and the third party may sue her individually, without joining the principal, and the agent or the principal may obtain a judgment against either or both. If the principal satisfies the judgment, the agent is discharged. If the agent pays the judgment, he has the right to be reimbursed by the principal.

UNDISCLOSED PRINCIPAL

An agent acts for an undisclosed principal when she appears to be acting on her own behalf and the third person with whom she is dealing has no knowledge that she is acting as an agent. The principal has instructed the agent to conceal not only the principal's identity but also the agency relationship. Such concealment can also occur if the agent simply neglects to disclose the existence and identity of her principal. Thus, the third person is dealing with the agent as though the agent were a principal.

The agent is personally liable upon a contract she enters into with a third person on behalf of an **undisclosed principal**, unless the third person, after discovering the existence and identity of the principal, elects to hold the principal to the contract. (See Figure 30-3.) The reason for the agent's liability is that the third person has relied upon the agent individually and has accepted the agent's personal undertaking to perform the contract. Obviously, when the principal is undisclosed, the third person does not know of the interest of anyone in the contract other than that of himself and the agent.

After learning the identity of the undisclosed principal, the third person may hold either the principal or the agent to performance of the contract, but not both; and his choice, once made, binds him irrevocably. However, to avoid the risk that evidence at trial may fail to establish the agency relationship, the third person may bring suit against both the principal and agent. In most states, this act of bringing suit and proceeding to trial against both is not an election, but, before the entry of any judgment, the third person is compelled to make an election because he is not entitled to a judgment against both. A judgment against the agent by a third party who knows the identity of the previously undisclosed principal discharges the principal's liability to the third party but leaves her liable to the agent, who would have the right to be reimbursed by the principal. If the third party obtains a judgment against the agent before learning the identity of the principal, the principal is not discharged. Finally, the agent is discharged from liability if the third party obtains a judgment against the principal. (Some states have recently rejected the election rule, holding that a third party's rights against the principal are additional and not alternative to the third party's rights against the agent.)

Redi-Floors, Inc. v. Sonenberg Co.

Court of Appeals of Georgia, 2002
254 Ga.App. 615, 563 S.E.2d 505

FACTS Sonenberg managed Westchester Manor Apartments through its on-site property manager, Judith. Manor Associates Limited Partnership, whose general partner is Westchester Manor, Ltd., owned the complex. The entry sign to the property did not reveal the owner's name but did disclose that Sonenberg managed the property.

Judith contacted Redi-Floors and requested a proposal for installing carpet in several of the units. In preparing the proposal, Redi-Floors confirmed that Sonenberg was the managing company and that Judith was its on-site property manager. Judith and her assistant orally ordered the carpet, and Redi-Floors installed the carpet. Redi-Floors sent invoices to the complex and received checks from "Westchester Manor Apartments." Believing Sonenberg owned the complex, Redi-Floors did not learn of the true owner's identity until a dispute arose after the work was complete concerning the payment of some of its later invoices.

To recover on the outstanding invoices, Redi-Floors sued Sonenberg, Manor Associates Limited Partnership, and Westchester Manor, Ltd. At trial Sonenberg admitted that it had no evidence that it informed Redi-Floors of the owner's identity. Nevertheless, the court directed a verdict in Sonenberg's favor on the ground that evidence showed that Redi-Floors was aware that Sonenberg was only acting as agent. The court entered a verdict exceeding $20,000 in favor of Redi-Floors and against the owner and its general partner. Redi-Floors appealed, contending that the directed verdict was error.

DECISION Judgment reversed and case remanded.

OPINION Blackburn, C. J. An agent who makes a contract without identifying his principal becomes personally liable on the contract. [Citations.] If the agent wishes to avoid personal liability, "the duty is on him to disclose his agency, and not on the party with whom he deals to discover it." [Citations.] The agent's disclosure of a trade name and the plaintiff's awareness of that name are not necessarily sufficient so as to protect the agent from liability. [Citations.] The disclosure of an agency is not complete for the purpose of relieving the agent from personal liability unless it embraces the name of the principal." [Citations.] This is generally a question for the jury. [Citations.]

* * * Here, at least some evidence showed that Sonenberg never disclosed the name of Manor Associates Limited Partnership to Redi-Floors. Accordingly, the trial court erred in entering a directed verdict in favor of Sonenberg.

* * * [T]his error by the trial court is not harmless, and it requires us to remand this case to enable Redi-Floors to elect which defendant it wishes to pursue. Georgia case law makes clear that Redi-Floor's obtaining of a judgment against Manor Associates, after the trial court removed Sonenberg as a party against which Redi-Floor could elect to secure a judgment, did not constitute an election on Redi-Floor's part. * * *

* * *

With respect to an undisclosed principal, the rule in Georgia is that if the buyer "is in fact merely an agent and acts with the authority of an undisclosed principal, either he or such principal may be held liable at the election of the opposite party; but the contractual liability of such agent and principal is not joint, and, after an election to proceed against one, the other cannot be held." [Citation.]

* * * Thus, while it is true that a judgment against both the agent and the principal cannot stand, it is the plaintiff who is entitled to elect against which of the defendants, principal or agent, to take the judgment. The erroneous direction of a verdict to one of the defendants does not constitute an election by the plaintiff. A different result would obtain, had the direction of the verdict been proper.

* * * Here, Manor Associates became the sole remaining defendant by operation of law rather than the election of the plaintiff.

* * * This Court has held that it is the plaintiff who must elect which defendant is to be dismissed and against which defendant the judgment would be entered. In the present case the trial court's erroneous granting of a directed verdict deprived the plaintiff of its right to elect which defendant it would proceed against. This Court should vacate the judgment and remand the case to the trial court where Redi-Floors must make an election as to which defendant it will proceed against. Redi-Floors can obtain a judgment against only one of the defendants. If it elects to proceed against Sonenberg, a new trial will be necessary, but not if it elects to enforce its judgment against Manor Associates.

INTERPRETATION To avoid personal liability on a contract, an agent must disclose both that she is acting as an agent and the identity of her principal.

ETHICAL QUESTION Is it fair that Sonenberg should be held personally liable to Redi-Floors? Explain.

CRITICAL THINKING QUESTION Should it be legally permissible for an agent not to disclose the existence and identity of his principal? Explain.

NONEXISTENT OR INCOMPETENT PRINCIPAL

A person who purports to act as agent for a principal whom both the agent and the third party know to be nonexistent or wholly incompetent is personally liable on a contract entered into with a third person on behalf of such a principal. An agent who makes a contract for a disclosed principal whose contracts are voidable for lack of contractual capacity is not liable to the third party, with two exceptions: (1) if the agent warrants or represents that the principal has capacity or (2) if the agent has reason to know both of the principal's lack of capacity and of the third party's ignorance of that incapacity.

CPA TORT LIABILITY OF THE AGENT

An agent is personally liable for his tortious acts that injure third persons, whether such acts are authorized by the principal or not and whether the principal may also be liable or not. For example, an agent is personally liable if he converts the goods of a third person to his principal's use. An agent is also liable for making representations that he knows to be fraudulent to a third person who in reliance sustains a loss.

CPA Rights of the Agent Against Third Person

Though an agent for an **undisclosed principal** or a **partially disclosed principal** may maintain in her own name an action against a third person for breach of contract, an agent who makes a contract with a third person on behalf of a **disclosed principal** usually has no right of action against the third person for breach of contract; for the agent is not a party to the contract. An agent for a disclosed principal may sue on the contract, however, if it provides that the agent is a party to the contract.

Chapter Summary

Principal and Third Persons

Contract Liability of Principal

Types of Principals
- *Disclosed Principal* principal whose existence and identity are known
- *Partially Disclosed Principal* principal whose existence is known but whose identity is not known
- *Undisclosed Principal* principal whose existence and identity are not known

Authority power of an agent to change the legal status of the principal
- *Actual Authority* power conferred upon the agent by actual consent given by the principal
- *Actual Express Authority* actual authority derived from written or spoken words of the principal
- *Actual Implied Authority* actual authority inferred from words or conduct manifested to the agent by the principal
- *Apparent Authority* power conferred upon the agent by acts or conduct of the principal that reasonably lead a third party to believe that the agent has such power

Delegation of Authority is usually not permitted unless expressly or impliedly authorized by the principal; if the agent is authorized to appoint other subagents, the acts of these subagents are as binding on the principal as those of the agent

Effect of Termination of Agency on Authority ends actual authority
- *Termination by Operation of Law* apparent authority also ends without notice to third parties
- *Termination by Act of Parties* apparent authority ends when third parties have actual knowledge or when appropriate notice is given to third parties; actual notice must be given to third parties with whom the agent had previously dealt on credit, has been specially accredited, or has begun to deal; all other third parties as to whom there was apparent authority need only be given constructive notice

Ratification affirmation by one person of a prior unauthorized act that another has done as her agent or as her purported agent

Fundamental Rules of Contractual Liability
- *Disclosed Principal* contractually bound with the third party if the agent acts within her actual or apparent authority in making the contract
- *Partially Disclosed Principal* contractually bound with the third party if the agent acts within her actual or apparent authority in making the contract
- *Undisclosed Principal* contractually bound with the third party if the agent acts within her actual authority in making the contract

Tort Liability of Principal

Direct Liability of Principal a principal is liable for his own tortious conduct involving the use of agents
- ***Authorized Acts of Agent*** a principal is liable for torts she authorizes another to commit
- ***Unauthorized Acts of Agent*** a principal is liable for failing to exercise care in employing agents whose unauthorized acts cause harm

Vicarious Liability of Principal for Unauthorized Acts of Agent
- **Respondeat Superior** an employer is liable for unauthorized torts committed by an employee in the course of his employment
- ***Independent Contractor*** a principal is usually not liable for the unauthorized torts of an independent contractor

Criminal Liability of Principal

Authorized Acts the principal is liable if he directed, participated in, or approved the acts of his agents

Unauthorized Acts the principal may be liable either for a criminal act of a managerial person or under liability without fault statutes

Agents and Third Persons

Contract Liability of Agent

Disclosed Principals the agent is not normally a party to the contract she makes with a third person if she is authorized or if the principal ratifies an unauthorized contract
- ***Unauthorized Contracts*** if an agent exceeds her actual and apparent authority, the principal is not bound but the agent may be liable for breach of warranty or for misrepresentation
- ***Agent Assumes Liability*** an agent may agree to become liable on a contract between the principal and the third party

Partially Disclosed Principal an agent who acts for a partially disclosed principal is a party to the contract with the third party unless otherwise agreed

Undisclosed Principal an agent who acts for an undisclosed principal is personally liable on the contract to the third party

Nonexistent or Incompetent Principal a person who purports to act as agent for a principal whom both the agent and the third party know to be nonexistent or wholly incompetent is personally liable on a contract entered into with a third person on behalf of such a principal

Tort Liability of Agent

Authorized Acts the agent is liable to the third party for his own torts

Unauthorized Acts the agent is liable to the third party for his own torts

Rights of Agents

Disclosed Principal the agent usually has no rights against the third party

Partially Disclosed Principal the agent may enforce the contract against the third party

Undisclosed Principal the agent may enforce the contract against the third party

QUESTIONS

1. Alice was Peter's traveling salesperson and was authorized to collect accounts. Before the agreed termination of the agency, Peter wrongfully discharged Alice. Alice then called on Tom, an old customer, and collected an account from Tom. She also called on Laura, a new prospect, as Peter's agent, secured a large order, collected the price of the order,

sent the order to Peter, and disappeared with the collections. Peter delivered the goods to Laura per the order.

a. What will be the result if Peter sues Tom for his account?
b. What will be the result if Peter sues Laura for the agreed price of the goods?

2. Paula instructed Alvin, her agent, to purchase a quantity of hides. Alvin ordered the hides from Ted in his own (Alvin's) name and delivered the hides to Paula. Ted, learning later that Paula was the principal, sends the bill to Paula, who refuses to pay Ted. Ted sues Paula and Alvin. What are Ted's rights against Paula and Alvin?

3. Stan sold goods to Bill in good faith, believing him to be a principal. Bill in fact was acting as agent for Nancy and within the scope of his authority. The goods were charged to Bill, and, on his refusal to pay, Stan sued Bill for the purchase price. While this action was pending, Stan learned of Bill's relationship with Nancy. Nevertheless, thirty days after learning of that relationship, Stan obtained judgment against Bill and had an execution issued that was never satisfied. Three months after the judgment was made, Stan sued Nancy for the purchase price of the goods. Is Nancy liable? Explain.

4. Green Grocery Company employed Jones as its manager and gave her authority to purchase supplies and goods for resale. Jones had conducted business for several years with Brown Distributing Company, although her purchases had been limited to groceries. Jones contacted Brown Distributing Company and had it deliver a color television set to her house. She told Brown Company that the set was to be used in promotional advertising to increase Green Grocery Company's business. The advertising did not develop, and Jones disappeared from the area, taking the television set with her. Brown Company now seeks to recover the purchase price of the set from Green Company. Will Brown prevail? Explain.

5. Stone was the agent authorized to sell stock of the Turner Company at $10 per share and was authorized in case of sale to fill in the blanks in the certificates with the name of the purchaser, the number of shares, and the date of sale. He sold 100 shares to Barrie, and without the knowledge or consent of the company and without reporting to the company, he indorsed the back of the certificate as follows:

> It is hereby agreed that Turner Company shall, at the end of three years after the date, repurchase the stock at $11 per share on thirty days' notice. Turner Company, by Stone.

After three years, demand was made on Turner Company to repurchase. The company refused the demand and repudiated the agreement on the ground that the agent had no authority to make the agreement for repurchase. Is Turner Company liable to Barrie? Explain.

6. Helper, a delivery boy for Gunn, delivered two heavy packages of groceries to Reed's porch. As instructed by Gunn, Helper rang the bell to let Reed know the groceries had arrived. Mrs. Reed came to the door and asked Helper if he would deliver the groceries into the kitchen because the bags were heavy. Helper did so, and on leaving he observed Mrs. Reed having difficulty in moving a cabinet in the dining room. He undertook to assist her, but being more interested in watching Mrs. Reed than in noting the course of the cabinet, he failed to observe a small, valuable antique table, which he smashed into with the cabinet and totally destroyed. Does Reed have a cause of action against Gunn for the value of the destroyed antique?

7. Driver picked up Friend to accompany him on an out-of-town delivery for his employer, Speedy Service. A "No Riders" sign was prominently displayed on the windshield of the truck, and Driver violated specific instructions of his employer by permitting an unauthorized person to ride in the vehicle. While discussing a planned fishing trip with Friend, Driver ran a red light and collided with an automobile driven by Motorist. Both Friend and Motorist were injured. Is Speedy Service liable to either Friend or Motorist for the injuries they sustained?

8. Cook's Department Store advertises that it maintains a barber shop in its store and that the shop is managed by Hunter, a Cook's employee. Actually, Hunter is not an employee of the store but merely rents space in the store. While shaving Jordan in the barber shop, Hunter negligently puts a deep gash, requiring ten stitches, into one of Jordan's ears. Should Jordan be entitled to collect damages from Cook's Department Store?

9. The following contract was executed on August 22:

> Ray agrees to sell and Shaw, the representative of Todd and acting on his behalf, agrees to buy 10,000 pounds of 0.32 × 15/8 stainless steel strip type 410.
>
> (signed) Ray
>
> (signed) Shaw

On August 26 Ray informs Shaw and Todd that the contract was in reality signed by him as agent for Upson. What are the rights of Ray, Shaw, Todd, and Upson in the event of a breach of the contract?

10. Harris, owner of certain land known as Red Bank, mailed a letter to Byron, a real estate broker in City X, stating, "I have been thinking of selling Red Bank. I have never met you, but a friend has advised me that you are an industrious and honest real estate broker. I therefore employ you to find a purchaser for Red Bank at a price of $35,000." Ten days after receiving the letter, Byron mailed the following reply to Harris: "Acting pursuant to your recent letter requesting me to find a purchaser for Red Bank, this is to advise that I have sold the property to Sims for $35,000. I enclose your copy of the contract of sale signed by Sims. Your name was signed to the contract by me as your agent." Is Harris obligated to convey Red Bank to Sims?

CASE PROBLEMS

11. While crossing a public highway in the city, Joel was struck by a horse-drawn cart driven by Morison's agent. The agent was traveling between Burton Crescent Mews and Finchley on his employer's business and was not supposed to go into the city at all. Apparently, the agent was on a detour to visit a friend when the accident occurred. Joel brought this action against Morison for the injuries he sustained as a result of the agent's negligence. Morison argues that he is not liable for his agent's negligence because the agent had strayed from his assigned path. Who is correct?

12. Serges is the owner of a retail meat marketing business. His managing agent borrowed $3,500 from David, on Serges's behalf, for use in Serges's business. Serges paid $200 on the alleged loan and on several other occasions told David that the full balance owed would eventually be paid. He then disclaimed liability on the debt, asserting that he had not authorized his agent to enter into the loan agreement. Should David succeed in an action to collect on the loan?

13. Sherwood negligently ran into the rear of Austen's car, which was stopped at a stoplight. As a result, Austen received bodily injuries and her car was damaged. Sherwood, arts editor for the *Mississippi Press Register* was en route from a concert he had covered for the newspaper. When the accident occurred, he was on his way to spend the night at a friend's house. Austen sued Sherwood and—under the doctrine of *respondeat superior*—Sherwood's employer, the *Mississippi Press Register*. Who is liable? Explain.

14. Aretta J. Parkinson owned a 200-acre farm. Prior to her death on December 23, Parkinson deeded a one-eighth undivided interest in the farm to each of her eight children as tenants in common. On January 15 of the following year, one of the daughters, Roma Funk, approached Barbara Bradshaw about selling the Parkinson farm. They orally agreed to a selling price of $33,000. After this meeting, Funk contacted Bryant Hansen, a real estate broker, to assist her in completing the transaction. Hansen prepared an earnest money agreement that was signed by the Bradshaws but by none of the Parkinson children. Hansen also prepared warranty deeds, which were signed by three of the children. Several of the children subsequently refused to convey their interests in the farm to the Bradshaws. Explain whether the Bradshaws can get specific performance of the oral contract of sale, due to the defendants' ratification of the oral contract by their knowledge of and failure to repudiate it.

15. Chris Zulliger was a chef at the Plaza Restaurant in the Snowbird Ski Resort (http://www.snowbird.com) in Utah. The restaurant is located at the base of a mountain. As a chef for the Plaza, Zulliger was instructed by his supervisor and the restaurant manager to make periodic trips to inspect the Mid-Gad Restaurant, which was located halfway up the mountain. Because skiing helped its employees to get to work, Snowbird preferred that its employees know how to ski and gave them ski passes as part of their compensation. Prior to beginning work at the Plaza on December 5, 1985, Zulliger went skiing. The restaurant manager asked Zulliger to stop at the Mid-Gad before beginning work that day, and Zulliger stopped at the Mid-Gad during his first run and inspected the kitchen. He then skied four runs before heading down the mountain to begin work. On the last run, Zulliger decided to take a route often taken by Snowbird employees. About midway down, Zulliger decided to jump off a crest on the side of an intermediate run. Because of the drop, a skier above the crest cannot see if there are skiers below, and Zulliger ran into Margaret Clover, who was below the crest. The jump was well known to Snowbird; the resort's ski patrol often instructed people not to jump, and there was a sign instructing skiers to take it slow at that point. Clover sued Zulliger and, under the doctrine of respondeat superior, Snowbird, claiming that Zulliger had been acting within the scope of his employment. Who is liable? Explain.

16. Van D. Costas, Inc. (Costas), entered into a contract to remodel the entrance of the Magic Moment Restaurant owned by Seascape Restaurants, Inc. Rosenberg, part owner and president of Seascape, signed the contract on a line under which was typed "Jeff Rosenberg, The Magic Moment." When a dispute arose over the performance and payment of the contract, Costas brought suit against Rosenberg for breach of contract. Rosenberg contended that he had no personal liability for the contract and that only Seascape, the owner of the restaurant, was liable. Costas claimed that Rosenberg signed for an undisclosed principal and, therefore, was individually liable. Is Rosenberg liable on the contract? Explain.

17. Virginia and her husband Ronnie Hulbert were involved in an accident in Mobile County when their automobile collided with another automobile driven by Dr. Murray's nanny. The nanny's regular duties of employment included housekeeping, supervising the children, and taking the children places that they needed to go. At the time of the collision, the nanny was driving her own car and was following Dr. Murray and her family to Florida from Louisiana to accompany Dr. Murray's family on their vacation. One of Dr. Murray's daughters was in the automobile driven by the nanny. Virginia Hulbert sued Dr. Murray under the doctrine of *respondeat superior*, alleging that the nanny was acting within the scope of her employment when the automobile accident occurred. Should she be able to recover from Dr. Murray? Explain.

http:// **Internet Exercise** Find information about "software agents" on the World Wide Web.

PART VII

BUSINESS ASSOCIATIONS

Uniform Unincorporated Nonprofit Association Act
http://www.law.upenn.edu/bll/ulc/ulc_frame.htm

Revised Uniform Partnership Act
http://www.law.upenn.edu/bll/ulc/ulc_frame.htm

Revised Uniform Limited Partnership Act
http://www.law.upenn.edu/bll/ulc/ulc_frame.htm

Uniform Limited Liability Company Act
http://www.law.upenn.edu/bll/ulc/ulc_frame.htm

State Incorporation Statutes
http://www.law.cornell.edu/topics/state_statutes.html#corporations

Center for Non-Profit Corporations
http://www.njnonprofits.org/index2.html

National Council of Nonprofit Associations
http://www.ncna.org/

Business Roundtable on Corporate Governance
http://www.brtable.org/issue.cfm/2

Corporate Governance
http://www.corpgov.net/

Corporate Governance OECD
http://www.oecd.org/daf/corporate-affairs/

CHAPTER 31

Formation and Dissolution of General Partnerships

Except for marriage, it is hard to think of a voluntary legal relationship that is more intimate or complex, in human terms, than the normal partnership whose members work constantly together.

ALAN BROMBERG, IN *CRANE AND BROMBERG ON PARTNERSHIP*

Learning Objectives

After reading this chapter you should be able to:

1. Identify the various types of business associations and explain the factors relevant to deciding which form to use.
2. Distinguish between a legal entity and a legal aggregate and identify those purposes for which a partnership is treated as a legal entity and those purposes for which it is treated as a legal aggregate.
3. Distinguish between a partner's rights in specific partnership property and a partner's interest in the partnership.
4. Identify the causes of dissolution of a partnership and the conditions under which partners have the right to continue the partnership after dissolution.
5. Explain the effect of dissolution on the authority and liability of the partners and the order in which the assets of a partnership are distributed to creditors and partners.

A business enterprise may be operated or conducted as a sole proprietorship, an unincorporated business association (such as a general partnership, a limited partnership, or a limited liability company), or a corporation. The choice of the most appropriate form cannot be determined in a general way but depends on the particular circumstances of the owners. We will begin this chapter with a brief overview of the various types of business associations and the factors relevant to deciding which form to use. The rest of this chapter and the next chapter will examine general partnerships. Chapter 33 will cover other types of unincorporated business associations. Chapters 34 through 37 will address corporations.

CHOOSING A BUSINESS ASSOCIATION

The owners of an enterprise determine the form of business unit they wish to use based upon their specific circumstances. There are more than 24 million business entities in the United States with annual receipts of more than $20 trillion. Corporations today outnumber unincorporated business associations (general partnerships, joint ventures, limited partnerships, and limited liability companies) by two-and-one-half to one and generate greater revenues by about ten to one. See Figure 31-1 for

Figure 31-1
Business Entities

Type of Entity	Total Number (1,000)	Total Revenue (1,000)	Average Revenue Per Entity	Percent of Total Businesses	Percent of Total Revenue
Sole Proprietorships	17,905	1,020,957,284	57,021	72%	5%
Partnerships	1,339	1,829,568,091	1,366,369	5%	8%
Limited Liability Companies	719	344,751,557	479,488	3%	2%
Corporations	5,045	17,636,561,349	3,495,850	20%	85%
Totals	25,008	20,831,838,281	833,007	100%	100%

Source: *http://www.BizStats.com,* accessed September 2, 2003.

the number and size of business entities. Nevertheless, unincorporated business associations are common in a number of areas. General partnerships, for example, are used frequently in finance, insurance, accounting, real estate, law, and other service-related fields. Joint ventures have enjoyed popularity among major corporations planning to engage in cooperative research; in the exploitation of land and mineral rights; in the development, promotion, and sale of patents, trade names, and copyrights; and in manufacturing operations in foreign countries. Limited partnerships have been widely used for enterprises such as real estate investment and development, motion picture and theater productions, oil and gas ventures, and equipment leasing. In the last few years the states have authorized the formation of limited liability companies. This form of business organization will probably appeal to a number of businesses including real estate ventures, high technology enterprises, businesses where transactions involve foreign investors, professional organizations, corporate joint ventures, start-up businesses, and venture capital projects.

First to be discussed are the most important factors to consider in choosing a form of business association. Then how the various forms of business associations differ with respect to these factors will be explained.

Practical Advice

You should give considerable thought to choosing the best form of business association for you and your co-owners.

CPA FACTORS AFFECTING CHOICE

In choosing the form in which to conduct business the owners should consider a number of factors, including ease of formation, federal and state income tax laws, external liability, management and control, transferability of ownership interests, and continuity. The relative importance of each factor will vary with the specific needs and objectives of the owners.

EASE OF FORMATION

Business associations differ as to the formalities and expenses of formation. Some can be created with no formality, while others require the filing of documents with the state.

TAXATION

Some business associations are not considered to be separate taxable entities and taxation is on a "pass-through" basis. In these cases, the income of the business is conclusively presumed to have been distributed to the owners, who must pay taxes on that income. Losses receive comparable treatment and can be used to offset some of the owners' income. In contrast, some business forms, most significantly corporations, are considered separate tax entities and are directly taxed. When such an entity distributes income to the owners, that income is currently separately taxed to the recipients. Thus, these funds are currently taxed twice: once to the entity and once to the owners. Unincorporated business entities can elect whether or not to be taxed as a separate entity. All businesses that have publicly traded ownership interests must be taxed as a corporation.

http:// Internal Revenue Service: http://www.irs.gov/

EXTERNAL LIABILITY

External liability arises in a variety of ways, but the crucial and most commonly occurring are tort and contract liability. Owners of some business forms have unlimited liability for all of the obligations of the business. Thus, if the business does not have sufficient funds to pay its debts, each and every owner has personal liability to the creditors for the full amount of the debts. In brief, owners of interests in businesses with unlimited liability place their entire estate at risk. In some types of entities, the owners have unlimited liability for some but not all of the entity's obligations. Finally, in some types of business associations, the owners enjoy limited liability, which means their liability is limited to the extent of their capital contribution. It should be noted, however, that creditors often require that the owners of small businesses guarantee personally loans made to the businesses. Moreover, an owner of any type of business does not have limited liability for his own tortious conduct; the person is liable as an individual tortfeasor.

MANAGEMENT AND CONTROL

In some entities, the owners can fully share in the control of the business. In other types of business associations, the owners are restricted as to their right to take part in control.

TRANSFERABILITY

An ownership interest in a business consists of a financial interest, which is the right to share in the profits of the business, and a management interest, which is the right to participate in control of the business. In some types of business associations, the owners may freely transfer their financial interest but may not transfer their management interest without the consent of all of the other owners. In other types of business associations, the entire ownership interest is freely transferable.

CONTINUITY

Some business associations have low continuity, which means that the death, bankruptcy, or withdrawal of an owner results in the dissolution of the association. Other types have high continuity and are not affected by the death, bankruptcy, or withdrawal of owners.

CPA FORMS OF BUSINESS ASSOCIATIONS

This section contains a brief description of the various types of business associations and how they differ with respect to the factors just discussed. In addition, general partnerships, limited partnerships, limited liability companies, limited liability partnerships, and corporations will be more extensively discussed in this part of the book.

SOLE PROPRIETORSHIP

A **sole proprietorship** is an unincorporated business consisting of one person who owns and completely controls the business. It is formed without any formality, and no documents need be filed. Moreover, if one person conducts a business and does not file with the state to form an LLC or corporation, a sole proprietorship will result by default. A sole proprietorship is not a separate taxable entity and only the sole proprietor is taxed. Sole proprietors have unlimited liability for the sole proprietorship's debts. The sole proprietor's interest in the business is freely transferable. The death of a sole proprietor dissolves the sole proprietorship.

GENERAL PARTNERSHIP

A **general partnership** is an unincorporated business association consisting of two or more persons who co-own a business for profit. It is formed without any formality and no documents need be filed. Thus, if two or more people conduct a business and do not file with the state to form another type of business organization, a general partnership will result by default. A partnership may elect not to be a separate taxable entity, in which case only the partners are taxed. Partners have unlimited liability for the partnership's debts. Each partner has an equal right to control of the partnership. Partners may assign their financial interest in the partnership, but the assignee may become a member of the partnership only if all of the members consent. The death, bankruptcy, or withdrawal of a partner dissolves a partnership.

JOINT VENTURE

A **joint venture** is an unincorporated business association composed of persons who combine their property, money, efforts, skill, and knowledge for the purpose of carrying out a particular business enterprise for profit. Usually, although not necessarily, it is of short duration. A joint venture, therefore, differs from a partnership, which is formed to carry on a business over a considerable or indefinite period of time. Nonetheless, except for a few differences, the law of partnerships generally governs a joint venture. An example of a joint venture is a securities underwriting syndicate or a syndicate formed to acquire a certain tract of land for subdivision and resale. Other common examples involve joint research conducted by corporations, the exploitation of mineral rights, and manufacturing operations in foreign countries.

LIMITED PARTNERSHIP

A **limited partnership** is an unincorporated business association consisting of at least one general partner and at least one limited partner. It is formed by filing a certificate of limited partnership with the state. A limited partnership may elect not to be a separate taxable entity, in which case only the partners are taxed. Publicly traded limited partnerships, however, are subject to corporate income taxation. General partners have unlimited liability for the partnership's debts; limited partners have limited liability. Each general partner has an equal right to control of the partnership; limited partners have no right to participate in control. Partners may assign their financial interest in the partnership, but the assignee may become a limited partner only if all of the members consent. The death, bankruptcy, or withdrawal of a general partner dissolves a limited partnership; the limited partners have neither the right nor the power to dissolve the limited partnership.

LIMITED LIABILITY COMPANY

A **limited liability company** (LLC) is an unincorporated business association that provides limited liability to all of its owners (members) and permits all of its members to participate in management of the business. It may elect not to be a separate taxable entity, in which case only the members are taxed. As noted previously, publicly traded LLCs are subject to corporate income taxation. If an LLC has only one member, then it will be taxed as a sole proprietorship, unless separate entity tax treatment is elected. Thus, the LLC provides many of the advantages of a general partnership plus limited liability for all its members. Its benefits outweigh those of a limited partnership in that all members of an LLC not only enjoy limited liability but also may participate in management and control of the business. In most states members may assign their financial interest in the LLC, but the assignee may become a member of the LLC only if all of the members consent or the LLC's operating agreement provides otherwise. In some states the death, bankruptcy, or withdrawal of a member dissolves an LLC; in others they do not. Every state has adopted an LLC statute.

LIMITED LIABILITY PARTNERSHIP

A registered **limited liability partnership** (LLP) is a general partnership that, by making the statutorily required filing, limits the liability of its partners for some or all of the partnership's obligations. To become an LLP, a general partnership must file with the state an application containing specified information. All of the states have enacted LLP statutes. Except for the filing requirements and the partners' liability shield, the law governing LLPs is identical to the law governing general partnerships.

LIMITED LIABILITY LIMITED PARTNERSHIP

A **limited liability limited partnership** (LLLP) is a limited partnership in which the liability of the general partners has been limited to the same extent as in an LLP. A growing number of states authorize LLLPs, enabling the general partners in an LLLP to obtain the same degree of liability limitation that general partners can achieve in LLPs. Where available, a limited partnership may register as an LLLP without having to form a new organization, as would be the case in converting to an LLC.

CORPORATION

A **corporation** is a legal entity separate and distinct from its owners. It is formed by filing its articles of incorporation with the state. A corporation is taxed as a separate entity, and shareholders are taxed on corporate earnings that are distributed to them. (Some corporations are eligible to elect to be taxed as Subchapter S corporations, which results in only the shareholders being taxed.) The shareholders have limited liability for the corporation's obligations. The board of directors elected by the shareholders manages the corporation. Shares in a corporation are freely transferable. The death, bankruptcy, or withdrawal of a shareholder does not dissolve the corporation.

BUSINESS TRUSTS

The **business trust**, sometimes called a Massachusetts trust, was devised to avoid the burdens of corporate regulation, particularly the formerly widespread prohibition denying to corporations the power to own and deal in real estate. The business trust is used today primarily for asset securitization ventures in which income-generating assets, such as mortgages, are pooled in a trust. Like an ordinary trust between natural persons, a business trust may be created by a voluntary agreement without any authorization or consent of the state. A business trust has three distinguishing characteristics: (1) the trust estate is devoted to the conduct of a business; (2) by the terms of the agreement, each beneficiary is entitled to a certificate evidencing his ownership of a beneficial interest in the trust, which he is free to sell or otherwise transfer; and (3) the trustees have the exclusive right to manage and control the business free from

Concept Review

General Partnership, Limited Partnership, Limited Liability Company, and Corporation

	General Partnership	Limited Partnership	Limited Liability Company	Corporation
Transferability	Financial interest may be assigned; membership requires consent of all partners	Financial interest may be assigned, and assignee may become limited partner if all partners consent	Financial interest may be assigned; membership requires consent of all members	Freely transferable unless shareholders agree otherwise
Liability	Partners have unlimited liability*	General partners have unlimited liability⁺; Limited partners have limited liability	All members have limited liability	Shareholders have limited liability
Control	By all partners	By general partners, not limited partners	By all members	By board of directors elected by shareholders
Continuity	RUPA: Usually unaffected by death, bankruptcy, or withdrawal of partner; UPA: Dissolved by death, bankruptcy, or withdrawal of partner	Dissolved by death, bankruptcy, or withdrawal of general partner; Unaffected by death, bankruptcy, or withdrawal of limited partner	In many states death, bankruptcy, or withdrawal of member does *not* dissolve LLC	Unaffected by death, bankruptcy, or withdrawal of shareholder
Taxation	May elect that only partners are taxed	May elect that only partners are taxed	May elect that only members are taxed	Corporation taxed unless Subchapter S applies; shareholders taxed

*In an LLP, the partners' liability is limited for some or all of the partnership's obligations.
⁺In an LLLP, the partners' liability is limited for some or all of the partnership's obligations.

control of the beneficiaries. If the third condition is not met, the trust may fail; for the beneficiaries, by participating in control, would become personally liable as partners for the obligations of the business.

The trustees are personally liable for the debts of the business unless, in entering into contractual relations with others, it is expressly stated or definitely understood between the parties that the obligation is incurred solely upon the responsibility of the trust estate. To escape personal liability on the contractual obligations of the business, the trustee must obtain the agreement or consent of the other contracting party to look solely to the assets of the trust. The personal liability of the trustees for their own torts or the torts of their agents and servants employed in the operation of the business stands on a different footing. Although this liability cannot be avoided, the risk involved may be reduced substantially or eliminated altogether by insurance. In most jurisdictions, the beneficiaries of a business trust have no liability for obligations of the business trust.

FORMATION OF GENERAL PARTNERSHIPS

The form of business association known as partnership can be traced to ancient Babylonia, classical Greece, and the Roman Empire. It was also used in Europe and England during the Middle Ages. Eventually the English common law recognized partnerships. In the nineteenth century, partnerships were widely used in England and the United States, and the common law of partnership developed considerably during this period. Partnerships are important in that they allow individuals with different expertise, backgrounds, resources, and interests to form a more competitive enterprise by combining their various skills. This part of the chapter will cover the nature of general partnerships and how they are formed. It should be recalled that except for the filing requirements and the partners' liability shield, the law governing LLPs is identical to the law governing general partnerships.

THE LAW AND YOU

State Bar Associations

Illinois: http://www.illinoislawyerfinder.com/publicinfo/home.html ("Starting a Business")

Maine: http://www.mainebar.org/lawyer_pamphlets.asp (legal information pamphlets) ("Organizing a Business")

Maryland: http://www.msba.org/public/brochure.htm ("Entering a Franchise Agreement")

Minnesota: http://www.mnbar.org/consumer.htm ("Business Organization")

New Hampshire: http://www.nhbar.org/?area/15.html ("Small Businesses in New Hampshire")

Oregon: http://www.osbar.org/public/legalinfo/business.html ("How to Start a Business in Oregon"; "Should I Incorporate?")

Wisconsin: http://www.wisbar.org/asp/titles.asp ("Answering Your Questions About Starting a Business")

State Attorney Generals

Arkansas: http://www.ag.state.ar.us/index_high.htm ("Consumer Guide to Buying a Franchise")

Illinois: http://www.ag.state.il.us/consumer/consumer/htm ("Franchises in Illinois")

New Hampshire: http://www.state.nh.us/nhdoj/Consumer/brochures.html ("Franchising & Business Opportunities")

U.S. Government

Consumer Information Center http://www.pueblo.gsa.gov/specpubs.htm#SB ("Facts About Starting a Small Business")

http://www.pueblo.gsa.gov/other/o-smbuss.htm ("Running a Small Business"; "Small Business Handbook")

Small Business Administration http://www.sba.gov/library/pubs.html ("Small Business Management Series")

CPA NATURE OF PARTNERSHIP

In 1914, the National Conference of Commissioners on Uniform State Laws promulgated the Uniform Partnership Act (UPA). Since then it has been adopted in all states (except Louisiana), as well as by the District of Columbia, the Virgin Islands, and Guam. (The UPA is reprinted in Appendix C.)

In August 1986, the UPA Revision Subcommittee of the Committee on Partnerships and Unincorporated Business Organizations of the American Bar Association's Section of Corporation, Banking and Business Law and the National Conference of Commissioners on Uniform State Laws decided to undertake a complete revision of the Uniform Partnership Act. The revision was approved in August 1992 and was amended in 1993, 1994, 1996, and 1997. At least thirty-one states have adopted the Revised Act. (Selected provisions of the RUPA are reprinted in Appendix D.) This chapter will discuss the Revised Uniform Partnership Act (RUPA). Where the RUPA has made significant changes, the original 1914 UPA will also be discussed. The chapter summary reflects the RUPA.

Though fairly comprehensive, the RUPA and UPA do not cover all legal issues concerning partnerships. Accordingly, both the RUPA and the UPA provide that unless displaced by particular provisions of this Act, the principles of law and equity supplement this Act.

http:// Revised Uniform Partnership Act: http://www.law.upenn.edu/bll/ulc/ulc_frame.htm

DEFINITION

The RUPA defines a **partnership** as "an association of two or more persons to carry on as co-owners a business for profit." The RUPA broadly defines "person" to include individuals, partnerships, corporations, joint ventures, business trusts, estates, trusts, and any other legal or commercial entity." The comments indicate that this definition would include a limited liability company. Moreover, a business includes every trade, occupation, and profession.

ENTITY THEORY

A **legal entity** is a unit capable of possessing legal rights and of being subject to legal duties. A legal entity may acquire, own, and dispose of property. It may enter into contracts, commit wrongs, sue, and be sued. For example, each business corporation is a legal entity having a legal existence separate from that of its shareholders.

A partnership was regarded by the common law as a **legal aggregate**, a group of individuals having no legal existence apart from that of its members. The Revised Act has greatly increased the extent to which partnerships are treated as entities. It applies aggregate treatment to very few aspects of partnerships, the most significant of which is that partners still have unlimited liability for the partnership's obligations. The UPA treats partnerships as legal entities for some purposes and as aggregates for others.

Partnership as a Legal Entity The RUPA states: "A partnership is an entity distinct from its partners." The Revised Act embraces the entity treatment of partnerships, particularly in matters concerning title to partnership property, legal actions by and against the partnership, and continuity of existence. Examples of entity treatment include: (1) The assets of the firm are treated as those of the business and are considered to be distinct from the individual assets of the members. (2) A partner is accountable as a fiduciary to the partnership. (3) Every partner is considered an agent of the partnership. (4) A partnership may sue and be sued in the name of the partnership.

Partnership as a Legal Aggregate The Revised Act has retained the aggregate characteristic of a partner's unlimited liability for partnership obligations, unless the partnership has filed a statement of qualification to become a limited liability partnership (LLP). Thus, if Meg and Mike enter into a partnership that becomes insolvent, as does Meg, Mike is fully liable for the partnership's debts. Likewise, although a partner's interest in the partnership may be assigned, the assignee does not become a partner without the consent of all the partners. Moreover, a partner's dissociation results in dissolution, although only in limited circumstances.

Under the UPA, because a partnership is considered an aggregate for some purposes, it can neither sue nor be sued in the firm name unless a statute specifically allows such an action. In addition, a partnership generally lacks continuity of existence: whenever any partner ceases to be associated with the partnership, it is dissolved.

CPA Formation of a Partnership

The RUPA provides that the association of two or more persons to carry on as co-owners a business for profit forms a partnership, whether or not the parties intend to form a partnership. The formation of a partnership is relatively simple and may be done consciously or unconsciously. A partnership may result from an oral or written agreement between the parties, from an informal arrangement, or from the conduct of the parties, who become partners by associating themselves in a business as co-owners. Consequently, if two or more individuals share the control and profits of a business, the law may deem them partners without regard to how they themselves characterize their relationship. Thus, associates frequently discover, to their chagrin, that they have inadvertently formed a partnership and have thereby subjected themselves to the duties and liabilities of partners. The legal existence of the relationship depends merely upon the parties' explicit or implicit agreement and their association in business as co-owners.

> **Practical Advice**
>
> Be careful that you do not unwittingly enter into a partnership: doing so will greatly increase your risk of personal liability.

Partnership Agreement

The RUPA defines a "partnership agreement" as "the agreement, whether written, oral, or implied, among the partners concerning the partnership, including amendments to the partnership agreement." This definition does not include other agreements between some or all of the partners, such as a lease or a loan agreement.

Except as otherwise provided by the RUPA, the partnership agreement governs relations among the partners and between the partners and the partnership. Thus, the RUPA gives almost total freedom to the partners to provide whatever provisions they agree upon in their partnership agreement. In essence, RUPA is primarily a set of "default rules" that apply only when the partnership agreement does not address the issue. Nevertheless, the RUPA makes some duties mandatory; these cannot be waived or varied by the partnership agreement.

To render their understanding more clear, definite, and complete, partners are advised, though not usually required, to put their partnership agreement in writing. A partnership agreement can provide almost any conceivable arrangement of capital investment, control sharing, and profit distribution that the partners desire. Unless the agreement provides otherwise, the partners may amend it only by unanimous consent. Any partnership agreement should include

1. the firm name and the identity of the partners;
2. the nature and scope of the partnership business;
3. the duration of the partnership;
4. the capital contributions of each partner;

5. the division of profits and sharing of losses;
6. the managerial duties of each partner;
7. a provision for salaries, if desired;
8. restrictions, if any, upon the authority of particular partners to bind the firm;
9. any desired variations from the partnership statute's default provisions governing dissolution; and
10. a statement of the method or formula for determining the value of a partner's interest in the partnership.

Statute of Frauds Because the statute of frauds does not apply expressly to a contract for the formation of a partnership, usually no writing is required to create the relationship. A contract to form a partnership to continue for a period longer than one year is within the statute, however, as is a contract for the transfer of an interest in real estate to or by a partnership; consequently, both of these contracts require a writing in order to be enforceable.

Firm Name In the interest of acquiring and retaining goodwill, a partnership should have a firm name. Although the name selected by the partners may not be identical or deceptively similar to the name of any other existing business concern, it may be the name of the partners or of any one of them; or the partners may decide to operate the business under a fictitious or assumed name, such as "Peachtree Restaurant," "Globe Theater," or "Paradise Laundry." A partnership may not use a name that would be likely to indicate to the public that it is a corporation. Nearly all of the states have enacted statutes that require any person or persons conducting business under an assumed or fictitious name to file in a designated public office a certificate setting forth the name under which the business is conducted and the real names and addresses of all persons conducting the business as partners or proprietors.

Practical Advice

Partners should have a comprehensive written partnership agreement: doing so brings about a clearer and more reliable understanding of their respective rights and obligations in their relations as partners.

TESTS OF PARTNERSHIP EXISTENCE

Partnerships can be formed without the slightest formality. Consequently, it is important that the law establish a test for determining whether or not a partnership has been formed. Two situations most often require this determination. The most common involves a creditor who has dealt only with one person but who wishes to hold another liable as well by asserting that the two were partners. Less frequently, a person seeks to share profits earned and property held by another by claiming that they are partners.

As previously mentioned, the RUPA provides the operative rule for formation of a partnership: an association of two or more persons to carry on as co-owners a business for profit. Thus, three components are essential to the existence of a partnership: (1) an association of two or more persons, (2) conducting a business for profit, (3) which they co-own.

Association A partnership must consist of two or more persons who have agreed to become partners. Any natural person having full *capacity* may enter into a partnership. A corporation is defined as a "person" by the RUPA and is, therefore, legally capable of entering into a partnership in those states whose incorporation statutes authorize a corporation to do so. Furthermore, as previously noted, a partnership, joint venture, business trust, estate, trust, and any other legal or commercial entity may be a member of a partnership.

Business for Profit The RUPA provides that co-ownership does not in itself establish a partnership, even if the co-owners share profits made by the use of the property. For a partnership to exist, there must be co-ownership of a business. Thus, passive co-ownership of property by itself, as distinguished from the carrying on of a business, does not establish a partnership. Moreover, to be a partnership, the business carried on by the association of two or more persons must be "for profit." This requirement excludes unincorporated nonprofit organizations from being partnerships. State common law and statutes govern such unincorporated nonprofit organizations. These laws, however, generally do not address the issues facing nonprofit associations in a systematic or integrated fashion. Consequently, in 1996, the National Conference of Commissioners on Uniform State Laws promulgated a Uniform Unincorporated Nonprofit Association Act to reform the common law concerning unincorporated nonprofit associations in a limited number of major issues, including ownership of property, authority to sue and be sued, and the contract and tort liability of officers and members of the association. At least ten states have adopted the act.

http:// Uniform Unincorporated Nonprofit Association Act: http://www.law.upenn.edu/bll/ulc/ulc_frame.htm

Nor does a partnership exist where persons associate for mutual financial gain on a temporary or limited basis involving a single transaction or a few isolated transactions: such persons are not engaged in the continuous series of commercial activities necessary to constitute a business. Co-ownership of the means or instrumentality of accomplishing a single business transaction or a limited series of transactions may result in a joint venture but not in a general partnership.

For example, Katherine and Edith have joint ownership of shares of the capital stock of a corporation, have a joint bank account, and have inherited or purchased real estate as joint tenants or tenants in common. They share the dividends paid on the stock, the interest on the bank account, and the net proceeds from the sale or lease of the real estate. Nevertheless, Katherine and Edith are not partners. Although they are co-owners and share profits, they are not engaged in carrying on a business; hence, no partnership exists. On the other hand, if Katherine and Edith continuously bought and sold real estate over a period of time and conducted a business of trading in real estate, a partnership relation would exist between them, regardless of whether they considered themselves partners or not.

To illustrate further: Alec, Laura, and Shirley each inherit an undivided one-third interest in a hotel and, instead of selling the property, decide by an informal agreement to continue operating the hotel. The operation of a hotel is a business; as co-owners of a hotel business, Alec, Laura, and Shirley are partners and are subject to all of the rights, duties, and incidents arising from the partnership relation.

Co-ownership Although the co-ownership of *property* used in a business is a condition neither necessary nor sufficient for the existence of a partnership, the co-ownership of a *business* is essential. In identifying business co-ownership, the two most important factors are the sharing of profits and the right to manage and control the business.

A person who receives a share of the ***profits*** from a business is presumed to be a partner in the business. This means that persons who share profits are deemed to be partners unless they can prove otherwise. The RUPA, however, provides that the existence of a partnership relation shall not be presumed where such profits were received in payment

1. of a debt, by installments or otherwise;
2. for services as an independent contractor or of wages or other compensation to an employee;
3. of rent;
4. of an annuity or other retirement or health benefit to a beneficiary, representative, or designee of a deceased or retired partner;
5. of interest or other charge on a loan, even if the amount of payment varies with the profits of the business; or
6. for the sale of the goodwill of a business or other property by installments or otherwise.

These transactions do not give rise to a presumption that the party is a partner because the law assumes that the creditor, employee, landlord, or other recipient of such profits is unlikely to be a co-owner. It is possible, nonetheless, to establish that such a person is a partner by proof of other facts and circumstances, such as the sharing of control.

The sharing of *gross returns*, in contrast to profits, does *not* of itself establish a partnership. This is so whether or not the persons sharing the gross returns have a joint or common right or interest in property from which the returns are derived. Thus, two brokers who share commissions are not necessarily partners, or even presumed to be. Similarly, an author who receives royalties (a share of gross receipts from the sales of a book) is not a partner with her publisher.

By itself, evidence as to participation in the *management* or ***control*** of a business is not conclusive proof of a partnership relation, but it is persuasive. Limited voice in the management and control of a business may be accorded to an employee, a landlord, or a creditor. On the other hand, an actual partner may choose to take no active part in the affairs of the firm and may, by agreement with his copartners, forgo all right to exercise any control over the ordinary affairs of the business. In any event, the right to participate in control is an important factor considered by the courts in conjunction with other factors, particularly with profit sharing.

Figure 31-2 illustrates the tests for determining whether a partnership exists, as does the following case.

Practical Advice

If you receive a share of a partnership's profits in a capacity other than a partner, be sure to document your actual relationship and refrain from exercising such control that would be considered that of a partner or from holding yourself out as a partner.

Figure 31-2
Tests for Existence of a Partnership

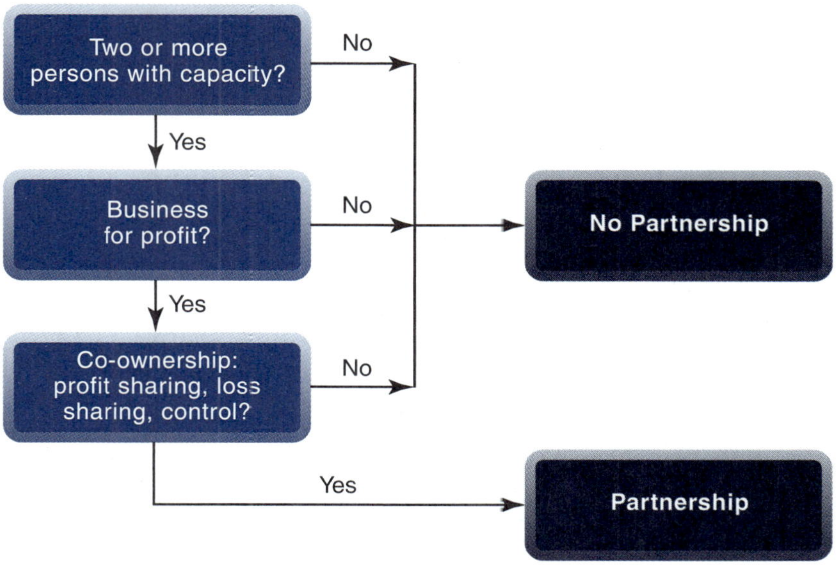

Chaiken v. Employment Security Commission

Superior Court of Delaware, 1971
274 A.2d 707

FACTS Chaiken entered into separate but nearly identical agreements with Strazella and Spitzer to operate a barber shop. Under the terms of the "partnership" agreements, Chaiken would provide barber chairs, supplies, and licenses, while the other two would provide tools of the trade. The agreements also stated that gross returns from the partnership were to be divided on a percentage basis among the three men and that Chaiken would decide all matters of partnership policy. Finally, the agreements stated hours of work and holidays for Strazella and Spitzer and required Chaiken to hold and distribute all receipts. The Delaware Employment Security Commission (Commission), however, determined that Strazella and Spitzer were not partners of Chaiken but rather were his employees. The Commission then brought this action to assess unemployment compensation contributions against Chaiken for the two barbers. Chaiken contended that they were not employees but partners pursuant to written partnership agreements. As their partner, rather than their employer, Chaiken would not be liable for unemployment compensation contributions.

DECISION Judgment for the Commission.

OPINION Storey, J. Chaiken contends that he and his "partners":

(1) properly registered the partnership name and names of partners in the Prothonotary's [head clerk's] office, in accordance with [citation],
(2) properly filed federal partnership information returns and paid federal taxes quarterly on an estimated basis, and
(3) duly executed partnership agreements.

Of the three factors, the last is most important. * * *

The mere existence of an agreement labeled "partnership" agreement and the characterization of signatories as "partners" does not conclusively prove the existence of a partnership. Rather, the intention of the parties, as explained by the wording of the agreement, is paramount. [Citation.]

A partnership is defined as an association of two or more persons to carry on as co-owners a business for profit. [Citation.] As co-owners of a business, partners have an equal right in the decision-making process. [Citation.] But this right may be abrogated by agreement of the parties without destroying the partnership concept, provided other partnership elements are present. [Citation.]

Thus, while paragraph four reserves for Chaiken all right to determine partnership policy, it is not standing alone, fatal to the partnership concept. Co-owners should also contribute valuable consideration for the creation of the business. Under paragraph two, however, Chaiken provides the barber chair (and implicitly the barber shop itself), mirror, licenses and linen, while the other partners merely provide their tools and labor—nothing more than any barber-employee would furnish. Standing alone, however, mere contribution of work and skill can be valuable consideration for a partnership agreement. [Citations.]

Partnership interests may be assignable, although it is not a violation of partnership law to prohibit assignment in a partnership agreement. [Citation.] Therefore, paragraph five on assignment of partnership interests does not violate the partnership concept. On the other hand, distribution of partnership assets to the partners upon dissolution is only allowed after all partnership liabilities are satisfied. [Citation.] But paragraph two of the agreement, in stating the ground rules for dissolution, makes no declaration that the partnership assets will be utilized to pay partnership expenses before reversion to their original owners. This deficiency militates against a finding in favor of partnership intent since it is assumed Chaiken would have inserted such provision had he thought his lesser partners would accept such liability. Partners do accept such liability, employees do not.

Most importantly, co-owners carry on "a business for profit." The phrase has been interpreted to mean that partners share in the profits and the losses of the business. The intent to divide the profits is an indispensable requisite of partnership. [Citation.] Paragraph three of the agreement declares that each partner shall share in the income of the business. There is no sharing of the profits and as the agreement is drafted, there are no profits. Merely sharing the gross returns does not establish a partnership. [Citation.] Nor is the sharing of profits prima facie evidence of a partnership where the profits received are in payment of wages. [Citation.]

The failure to share profits, therefore, is fatal to the partnership concept here.

Evaluating Chaiken's agreement in the light of the elements implicit in a partnership, no partnership intent can be found. The absence of the important right of decision-making or the important duty to share liabilities upon dissolution individually may not be fatal to a partnership. But when both are absent, coupled with the absence of profit sharing, they become strong factors in discrediting the partnership argument. * * *

In addition, the total circumstances of the case taken together indicate the employer-employee relationship between Chaiken and his barbers. The agreement set forth the hours of work and days off—unusual subjects for partnership agreements. The barbers brought into the relationship only the equipment required of all barber shop operators. * * * Furthermore, Chaiken conducted all transactions with suppliers, and purchased licenses, insurance, and the lease for the business property in his own name.

INTERPRETATION Two important tests for the existence of a partnership are (1) the sharing of profits (not gross receipts) by the partners and (2) participation by the partners in control of the business.

CRITICAL THINKING QUESTION Do you agree with the test for the existence of a partnership?

PARTNERSHIP CAPITAL AND PROPERTY

The total money and property that the partners contribute and dedicate to use in the enterprise is the **partnership capital**. Partnership capital represents the partners' equity in the partnership. No minimum amount of capitalization is necessary before a partnership may commence business.

Partnership property is property acquired by a partnership. Property acquired by the partnership is conclusively deemed to be partnership property. Property becomes partnership property if acquired in the name of the partnership, which includes a transfer to (1) the partnership in its name or (2) one or more partners in their capacity as partners in the partnership, if the name of the partnership is indicated in the instrument transferring title to the property. Property also may be partnership property even if it is not acquired in the name of the partnership. Property is partnership property if acquired in the name of one or more of the partners with an indication in the instrument transferring title of either (1) their capacity as partners or (2) of the existence of a partnership, even if the name of the partnership is not indicated.

Even if the instrument transferring title to one or more of the partners does not indicate their capacity as a partner or the existence of a partnership, the property nevertheless may be partnership property. Ultimately, the partners' intention controls whether property belongs to the partnership or to one or more of the partners in their individual capacities. The RUPA sets forth two rebuttable presumptions that apply when the partners have failed to express their intent. First, property purchased with partnership funds is presumed to be partnership property, without regard to the name in which title is held. The presumption applies not only when partnership cash or property is used for payment but also when partnership credit is used to obtain financing.

Second, property acquired in the name of one or more of the partners, without an indication of their capacity as partners and without use of partnership funds or credit, is presumed to be the partners' separate property, even if used for partnership purposes. In this last case it is presumed that only the *use* of the property is contributed to the partnership.

As discussed later, who owns the property—an individual partner or the partnership—determines (1) who gets it upon dissolution of the partnership, (2) who shares in any loss or gain upon its sale, (3) who shares in income from it, and (4) who may sell it or transfer it by will.

A question may arise regarding whether property that was owned by a partner before formation of the partnership and was used in the partnership business is a capital contribution and hence an asset of the partnership. For example, a partner who owns a store building may contribute to the partnership the use of the building but not the building itself. The building is, therefore, not partnership property, and the amount of capital contributed by this partner is the reasonable value of the rental of the building.

The fact that legal title to property remains unchanged is not conclusive evidence that such property has not become a partnership asset. The intent of the partners controls the question of who owns the property. Without an express agreement, an intention to consider property as partnership property may be inferred from any of the following facts: (1) the property was improved with partnership funds; (2) the property was carried on the books of the partnership as an asset; (3) taxes, liens, or expenses, such as insurance or repairs, were paid by the partnership; (4) income or proceeds of the property were treated as partnership funds; or (5) the partners declared or admitted the property to be partnership property.

Practical Advice

Make clear by a written agreement whether property previously owned by one partner but used by the partnership belongs to the partnership or to the partner.

Thomas v. Lloyd

Missouri Court of Appeals, Southern District, Division One, 2000
17 S.W.3d 177
http://caselaw.findlaw.com/scripts/getcase.pl?court=mo&vol=/appeals/052000/&invol=29051600_2000

FACTS In February 1989, Plaintiff, Mary Dean Thomas, met Defendant, Eubert Gayle Lloyd, Jr., in Mobile, Alabama, while she was traveling. Their chance meeting quickly blossomed into a romantic relationship. When Plaintiff returned to her home in Maryland, Defendant accompanied her and they began living together. Initially, Defendant told Plaintiff he worked for a major oil company, had been outside the country for the past three years, was independently wealthy, and was not married. As Plaintiff later learned, none of these statements was true. In truth, Defendant had recently been released from prison. He had multiple criminal convictions, including convictions for counterfeiting and stealing. In addition, Defendant's assets at the time were no more than $2,000, and he was legally married to Patricia Lloyd. Prior to Plaintiff's discovering that Defendant was not single, the parties were "married" on July 10, 1989 in Canada. Due to the circumstances this marriage was void.

Plaintiff and Defendant resided in Plaintiff's home in Maryland from late February 1989 through October 1990. During that period, Defendant made repairs and renovations to Plaintiff's house. In October 1990, Plaintiff sold her home and the parties moved to Missouri. After looking at several farm properties, they bought a 600-acre farm in Crawford County, Missouri, for $150,000. The deed was dated March 8, 1991. The deed named Plaintiff, a single person, and Defendant, a single person, as joint tenants with right of survivorship. The $150,000 purchase price was paid with a $100,000 cash down payment and a $50,000 promissory note that called for 120 monthly installments of $633.38.

After buying the farm, Plaintiff and Defendant bought cattle and farm machinery, and then began operating a cattle business on the property. The parties also made improvements to the farm, including remodeling an old farmhouse in which they lived. In June 1992, they began construction on a 4,200 square-foot house. Later, the house was expanded to 6,500 square feet. By the time of trial, Plaintiff's expenditures for labor and materials on the home exceeded $201,000.

A progressive deterioration in the parties' relationship led to the filing of this lawsuit in October 1995. The trial court found that the subject real estate was not a partnership asset and ordered it be sold at public auction and the net sale proceeds to be distributed ninety-eight percent to Plaintiff and two percent to Defendant. The Defendant appealed the trial court's refusal to classify farm real estate as a partnership asset.

DECISION The judgment of the trial court is affirmed.

OPINION Shrum, J. "The true method of determining whether, as between partners themselves, land standing in the names of individuals is to be treated as partnership property is to ascertain from the conduct of the parties and their course of dealing, the understanding and intention of the partners themselves, which, when ascertained, unquestionably should control." [Citations.] Whether real estate titled in the names of individual partners is partnership property is a question of fact and the burden of proof is on the one alleging that the ownership does not accord with the legal title. [Citation.]

In attempting to demonstrate that the parties intended for the real estate to be a partnership asset, Defendant points to the joint ownership of the farm and the fact that the parties operated the partnership cattle business on the farm as evidence that the two understood and intended for the farm to be a partnership asset. His reliance on those facts is misplaced, however. A joint purchase of real estate by two individuals does not, in and of itself, prove the land is a partnership asset. [Citation.] On the contrary, when land is conveyed to partnership members without any statement in the deed that the grantees hold the land as property of the firm, there is a presumption that title is in the individual grantees. [Citation.] Moreover, "[e]vidence that the land is used by the firm is of itself insufficient to rebut the presumption." [Citation.] The mere use of land by a partnership does little to show the land is owned by the partnership. [Citation.] Standing alone, evidence of partnership usage does not compel a finding that the land is a partnership asset. [Citations.]

Defendant points to evidence that some real estate taxes and promissory note payments for the farm came from partnership funds. He argues such evidence indicates the parties intended the farm to be a partnership asset. We agree that such evidence is a factor to be considered, but it is not determinative of the issue, especially, when, as here, the partnership payment evidence is viewed in context. For instance, none of the $100,000 downpayment for the farm came from partnership funds. Instead, it all came from Plaintiff's separate funds. Plaintiff was never reimbursed by either the partnership or Defendant for her downpayment. Of eighty-four monthly farm note payments, only three were paid from the parties' joint account. Seventy-seven of the monthly farm note payments, a total of $48,770.26, were paid from Plaintiff's separate funds. Plaintiff also spent $201,927.87 of her separate money to build a new house on the farm. None of the house construction costs came from partnership funds. Of the seven years' worth of state and county real estate taxes that had been paid on the farm property, only one year was paid out of partnership funds. On the whole, the evidence is that Plaintiff invested over $350,000 of her own funds in this farm while less than $2,400 of partnership funds were used to pay the farm note and real estate taxes. Such minimal partnership expenditures is more indicative of the tendency of people—particularly in family or quasi-family businesses—to intermingle personal and partnership affairs, than it is an indication of the parties' intent to include the farm as a partnership asset. [Citation.]

Other evidence from which the parties' intent can be gleaned includes the following: (A) Plaintiff and Defendant signed as individuals on the $50,000 purchase money note and deed of trust securing the same, without a recital of partnership status; (B) neither party filed a partnership income tax return; (C) Plaintiff filed income tax returns as an individual; (D) Defendant never filed an income tax return after the farm was purchased; (E) Plaintiff wrote checks on her individual account for materials and labor for farm improvements; and (F) Plaintiff repeatedly testified she never intended nor agreed to a partnership with Defendant. We find these circumstances sufficient to support the implicit finding and judgment of the trial court that a partnership agreement did not exist regarding the land and it was not a partnership asset. The trial court did not commit reversible error when it failed to include the farm as a partnership asset.

INTERPRETATION Whether property is partnership property depends on the intent of the parties as indicated by factors such as their express agreement; the use of the property in the partnership business; the listing of the property as an asset on the partnership's books; the improvement of the property with partnership assets; and the payment by the partnership of taxes, insurance, and other expenses of property ownership.

CRITICAL THINKING QUESTION What factors did the court use to determine whether the properties were partnership assets?

RIGHTS IN SPECIFIC PARTNERSHIP PROPERTY

In adopting the entity theory, the Revised Act abolishes the UPA's concept of tenants in partnership: partnership property is owned by the partnership entity and not by the individual partners. Moreover, RUPA provides, "A partner is not a co-owner of partnership property and has no interest in partnership property which can be transferred, either voluntarily or involuntarily." A partner may use or possess partnership property only on behalf of the partnership.

Under the UPA a partner's ownership interest in any specific item of partnership property is that of a tenant in partnership. The UPA's tenancy in partnership reaches a similar entity result to the RUPA but states that result in aggregate terms. This type of ownership, which exists only in a partnership, has the following principal characteristics:

1. Each partner has a right equal to that of his copartners to possess partnership property for partnership purposes, but he has no right to possess it for any other purpose without his copartners' consent.
2. A partner may not make an individual assignment of his right in specific partnership property.
3. A partner's interest in specific partnership property is not subject to attachment or execution by his individual creditors. It is subject to attachment or execution only on a claim against the partnership.
4. Upon the death of a partner, his right in specific partnership property vests in the surviving partner or partners. Upon the death of the last surviving partner, his right in such property vests in his legal representative.

PARTNER'S INTEREST IN THE PARTNERSHIP

Each partner has an **interest in the partnership**, which is defined as "all of a partner's interests in the partnership, including the partner's transferable interest and all management and other rights." A **partner's transferable interest** is a more limited concept; it is the partner's share of the profits and losses of the partnership and the partner's right to receive distributions. This interest is personal property. A partner's transferable interest is discussed here; a partner's management and other rights are discussed in the next chapter.

Assignability A partner may voluntarily transfer, in whole or in part, his transferable interest in the partnership. The transfer does not by itself cause the partner's dissociation or a dissolution and winding up of the partnership business. (Dissolution is discussed later in this chapter.) The transferee, however, is not entitled to (1) participate in the management or conduct of the partnership business, (2) require access to any information concerning partnership transactions, or (3) inspect or copy the partnership books or records. She is merely entitled to receive, in accordance with the terms of the assignment, any distributions to which the assigning partner would have been entitled under the partnership agreement before dissolution. After dissolution, the transferee is entitled to receive the net amount that would have been distributed to the transferring partner upon the winding up of the business. Moreover, the assignee may apply for a court-ordered dissolution. The assigning partner remains a partner with all of a partner's other rights and duties other than the transferred interest in distributions.

However, the other partners by a unanimous vote may expel a partner who has transferred substantially all of his transferable partnership interest, other than as security for a loan. The partner may be expelled, however, upon foreclosure of the security interest.

The partners may agree among themselves to restrict the right to transfer their partnership interests.

Creditors' Rights A partner's transferable interest (the right to distributions from the partnership and the right to seek court-ordered dissolution of the partnership) is subject to the claims of that partner's creditors, who may obtain a **charging order** (a type of judicial lien) against the partner's transferable interest. On application by a judgment creditor of a partner, a court may charge the transferable interest of the partner to satisfy the judgment. A charging order is also available to the judgment creditor of a *transferee* of a partnership interest. The court may appoint a receiver of the debtor's share of the distributions due or to become due. The court may order a foreclosure of the interest subject to the charging order at any time. The purchaser at the foreclosure sale has the rights of a transferee. At any time before foreclosure, an interest charged may be redeemed by (1) the partner who is the judgment debtor; (2) other partners with non-partnership property; or (3) other partners with partnership property but only with the consent of all of the remaining partners.

Neither the judgment creditor, the receiver, nor the purchaser at foreclosure becomes a partner, and thus none is entitled to participate in the partnership's management or to have access to information. Furthermore, neither the charging order nor its sale upon foreclosure causes dissolution, though the other partners may dissolve the partnership or redeem the charged interest. Moreover, a partner may be expelled by a unanimous vote of the other partners upon foreclosure of a judicial lien charging a partner's interest.

Concept Review

Partnership Property Compared with Partner's Interest

	Partnership Property		
	RUPA	UPA	Partner's Interest
Definition	A partner is *not* a co-owner of partnership property	Tenant in partnership	Share of profits and surplus
Possession	For partnership purposes, not individual ones	For partnership purposes, not individual ones	Intangible, personal property right
Assignability	Partner has *no* interest in partnership property which can be transferred	If all other partners assign their rights in the property	Assignee does not become a partner
Attachment	Only for a claim against the partnership	Only for a claim against the partnership	By a charging order
Inheritance	Partner has *no* interest in partnership property which can be transferred	Goes to surviving partner(s)	Passes to the personal representative of deceased partner

DISSOCIATION AND DISSOLUTION OF GENERAL PARTNERSHIPS UNDER RUPA

Dissociation occurs when a partner ceases to be associated in carrying on of the business. "Dissolution" refers to those situations when the Revised Act requires a partnership to wind up and terminate. A dissociation of a partner results in dissolution only in limited circumstances. In many instances, dissociation will result merely in a buyout of the withdrawing partner's interest rather than a winding up of the partnership. When dissociation or other cause results in dissolution, the partnership is *not terminated* but continues until the winding up of its affairs is complete. During winding up, unfinished business is completed, receivables are collected, payments are made to creditors, and the remaining assets are distributed to the partners. Termination occurs when the process is finished.

CPA Dissociation

Dissociation occurs when a partner ceases to be associated in carrying on of the business. A number of events that were considered causes of dissociation or dissolution under the common law are no longer considered so under the RUPA. For example, the assignment of a partner's interest, a creditor's charging order on a partner's interest, and an accounting are not considered a dissociation or dissolution.

A partner has the *power* to dissociate at any time, rightfully or wrongfully, by expressing an intent to withdraw. A partner does not, however, always have the *right* to dissociate. A partner who wrongfully dissociates is liable to the partnership for damages caused by the dissociation. In addition, if the wrongful dissociation results in the dissolution of the partnership, the wrongfully dissociating partner is not entitled to participate in winding up the business.

Wrongful Dissociations

A partner's dissociation is wrongful if it breaches an express provision of the partnership agreement. In addition, dissociation is wrongful in a *term partnership* if before the expiration of the term or the completion of the undertaking (1) the partner voluntarily withdraws by express will unless the withdrawal follows within 90 days after another partner's dissociation by death, bankruptcy, or wrongful dissociation; (2) the partner is expelled for misconduct by judicial determination; (3) the partner becomes a debtor in bankruptcy; or (4) the partner is an entity (other than a trust or estate) and is expelled or otherwise dissociated because its dissolution or termination was willful. A **"term partnership"** is a partnership for a specific term or particular undertaking. The partnership agreement may eliminate or expand the dissociations that are wrongful or modify the effects of wrongful dissociation, except for the power of a court to expel a partner for misconduct.

RIGHTFUL DISSOCIATIONS

The RUPA provides that a partner's dissociation is wrongful only if it results from one of the events just discussed. All other dissociations are rightful including (1) the death of partner in *any* partnership, (2) the withdrawal of a partner in a *partnership at will*, (3) in *any* partnership an event occurs that was agreed to in the partnership agreement as causing dissociation, and (4) in *any* partnership a court determines that a partner has become incapable of performing the partner's duties under the partnership agreement. The RUPA defines a **"partnership at will"** as a partnership in which the partners have not agreed to remain partners until the expiration of a definite term or the completion of a particular undertaking.

EFFECT OF DISSOCIATION

Upon a partner's dissociation the partner's right to participate in the management and conduct of the partnership business terminates. If, however, the dissociation results in a dissolution and winding up of the business, all of the partners who have not wrongfully dissociated may participate in winding up the business. The duty not to compete terminates upon dissociation, and the dissociated partner may immediately engage in a competitive business, without any further consent The partner's other fiduciary duties and duty of care continue only with regard to matters arising and events occurring before the partner's dissociation, unless the partner participates in winding up the partnership's business. For example, a partner who leaves a partnership providing consulting services may immediately compete with the firm for new clients, but must exercise care in completing current transactions with clients and must account to the firm for any fees received from the old clients on account of those transactions.

CPA DISSOLUTION

In accordance with the Revised Act's emphasis on the entity treatment of partnerships, only a limited subset of dissociations requires the dissolution of a partnership. In addition, some events other than dissociation can bring about the dissolution of a partnership under RUPA. The following sections discuss the causes and effects of dissolution.

CAUSES OF DISSOLUTION

The basic rule under the RUPA is that a partnership is dissolved and its business must be wound up only if one of the events listed in Section 801 occur. The events causing dissolution may be brought about by (1) an act of the partners (i.e., some dissociations), (2) operation of law, or (3) court order. The provisions of Section 801 that involve an act of the parties are default provisions: the partners may by agreement modify or eliminate these grounds. The partners may *not* vary or eliminate the grounds for dissolution based on operation of law or court order.

Dissolution by Act of the Partners These causes of dissolution comprise a subset of dissociations. In a ***partnership at will***, a partner's giving notice of intent to withdraw will result in dissolution of a partnership. Thus, any member of a partnership at will has the right to force a liquidation of the partnership. (The death or bankruptcy of a partner does *not* dissolve a partnership at will.)

The Revised Act provides for three ways in which a ***term partnership*** will be dissolved. No partner by herself has the power to dissolve a term partnership.

1. The term of the partnership expires or the undertaking is complete. It should be noted that if the partners continue a term partnership after the expiration of the term or completion of the undertaking, the partnership will be treated as a partnership at will.
2. All of the partners expressly agree to dissolve. This reflects the principle that the partners can unanimously amend the partnership agreement.
3. A partner's dissociation caused by a partner's death or incapacity, bankruptcy or similar financial impairment, or wrongful dissociation will bring on a dissolution if within 90 days after dissociation at least half of the remaining partners express their will to wind up the partnership business. Thus, if a term partnership has eight partners and one of the partners wrongfully dissociates before the end of the term, the partnership will be dissolved only if four of the remaining seven partners vote in favor of liquidation.

In ***all partnerships*** dissolution occurs upon the happening of an event that was specified in the partnership agreement as resulting in dissolution. The partners may, however, agree to continue the business.

Dissolution by Operation of Law A partnership is dissolved by operation of law if an event occurs that makes it unlawful to continue all or substantially all of the partnership's business. For example, a law prohibiting the production and sale of alcoholic beverages would dissolve a partnership formed to manufacture liquor. A cure of such illegality within 90 days after notice to the partnership of the event is effective retroactively. The partnership agreement cannot vary the requirement that an uncured illegal business must be dissolved and liquidated.

Dissolution by Court Order On application by a *partner*, a court may order dissolution on grounds of another partner's misconduct or upon a finding that (1) the economic purpose of the partnership is likely to be unreasonably frustrated; (2) another partner has engaged in conduct relating to the partnership business that makes it not reasonably practicable to carry on the business in partnership with that partner; or (3) it is not otherwise reasonably practicable to carry on the partnership business in conformity with the partnership agreement. On application of a ***transferee*** of a partner's transferable interest or a purchaser at foreclosure of a charging order, a court may order dissolution if it determines that it is equitable to wind up the partnership business (1) at any time in a partnership at will or (2) after the term of a term partnership has expired. The partners may *not* by agreement vary or eliminate the court's power to wind up a partnership.

Horizon/CMS Healthcare Corporation v. Southern Oaks Health Care, Inc.

Court of Appeal of Florida, Fifth District, 1999
732 So.2d 1156, *review denied*, 744 So.2d 454

FACTS Horizon is a large, publicly traded provider of both nursing homes and management for nursing homes. It wanted to expand into Osceola County, Florida, in 1993. Southern Oaks was already operating in Osceola County; it owned the Southern Oaks Health Care Center and had a Certificate of Need issued by the Florida Agency for Health Care Administration for a new 120-bed facility in Kissimmee. Horizon and Southern Oaks decided to form a partnership to own the proposed Kissimmee facility, which was ultimately named Royal Oaks, and agreed that Horizon would manage both the Southern Oaks facility and the new Royal Oaks facility. To that end, Southern Oaks and Horizon entered into several twenty-year partnership and management contracts in 1993.

In 1996, Southern Oaks filed suit alleging that Horizon breached its obligations under two different partnership agreements and that Horizon had breached several management contracts. The court ordered that the partnerships be dissolved, finding that they were incapable of continuing to operate in business together. Because it was dissolving the partnerships, the court ruled that, "there is no entitlement to future damages." In its appeal, Southern Oaks asserts that because Horizon unilaterally and wrongfully sought dissolution of the partnerships, Southern Oaks should receive a damage award for the loss of the partnerships' seventeen remaining years' worth of future profits.

DECISION Dissolution affirmed and damages request denied.

OPINION Goshorn, J. * * * First, the trial court's finding that the parties are incapable of continuing to operate in business together is a finding of "irreconcilable differences," a permissible reason for dissolving the partnerships under the express terms of the partnership agreements. Thus, dissolution was not "wrongful," assuming there can be "wrongful" dissolutions, and Southern Oaks was not entitled to damages for lost future profits. Additionally, the partnership contracts also permit dissolution by "judicial decree." Although neither party cites this provision, it appears that pursuant thereto, the parties agreed that dissolution would be proper if done by a trial court for whatever reason the court found sufficient to warrant dissolution.

Second, even assuming the partnership was dissolved for a reason not provided for in the partnership agreements, damages were properly denied. Under RUPA, it is clear that wrongful dissociation triggers liability for lost future profits. See § 602(3) ("A partner who wrongfully dissociates is liable to the partnership and to the other partners for damages caused by the dissociation. The liability is in addition to any other obligation of the partner to the partnership or to the other partners."). However, RUPA does not contain a similar provision for dissolution; RUPA does not refer to the dissolutions as rightful or wrongful. Section 801, "Events causing dissolution and winding up of partnership business," outlines the events causing dissolution without any provision for liability for damages. Under subsection 801(5), the statute recognizes judicial dissolution:

> A partnership is dissolved, and its business must be wound up, only upon the occurrence of any of the following events:
>
> * * *

(5) On application by a partner, a judicial determination that:

(a) The economic purpose of the partnership is likely to be unreasonably frustrated;

(b) Another partner has engaged in conduct relating to the partnership business which makes it not reasonably practicable to carry on the business in partnership with such partner; or

(c) It is not otherwise reasonably practicable to carry on the partnership business in conformity with the partnership agreement; * * *.

Paragraph (5)(c) provides the basis for the trial court's dissolution in this case. While "reasonably practicable" is not defined in RUPA, the term is broad enough to encompass the inability of partners to continue working together, which is what the court found.

Certainly the law predating RUPA allowed for recovery of lost profits upon the wrongful dissolution of a partnership. [Citations.] However, RUPA brought significant changes to partnership law, among which was the adoption of the term "dissociation." Although the term is undefined in RUPA, dissociation appears to have taken the place of "dissolution" as that word was used pre-RUPA. [Citation.] "Dissolution" under RUPA has a different meaning, although the term is undefined in RUPA. [Citation.] It follows that the pre-RUPA cases providing for future damages upon wrongful dissolution are no longer applicable to a partnership dissolution. In other words a "wrongful dissolution" referred to in the pre-RUPA case law is now, under RUPA, known as "wrongful dissociation." Simply stated, under section 602, only when a partner dissociates and the dissociation is wrongful can the remaining partners sue for damages. [Court's footnote: Dissociation is not a condition precedent to dissolution under RUPA. * * * ("Most dissolution events are dissociations. On the other hand, it is not necessary to have a dissociation to cause a dissolution and winding up.").] * * *

Southern Oaks' attempt to bring the instant dissolution under the statute applicable to dissociation is rejected. The trial court ordered dissolution of the partnership, not the dissociation of Horizon for wrongful conduct. There no longer appears to be "wrongful" dissolution—either dissolution is provided for by contract or statute or the dissolution was improper and the dissolution order should be reversed. In the instant case, because the dissolution either came within the terms of the partnership agreements or paragraph 801(5)(c) (judicial dissolution where it is not reasonably practicable to carry on the partnership business), Southern Oaks' claim for lost future profits is without merit.

INTERPRETATION A court-ordered dissolution for good cause is not wrongful and does not entitle either party to damages from the other.

CRITICAL THINKING QUESTION Should the courts have placed blame on Horizon for breaching the partnership agreements and management contracts?

EFFECTS OF DISSOLUTION

A partnership continues after dissolution only for the purpose of winding up its business. The partnership is terminated when the winding up of its business is completed. The remaining partners have the right, however, to continue the business after dissolution if *all* of the partners, including any dissociating partner other than a wrongfully dissociating partner, waive the right to have the partnership's business wound up and the partnership terminated. In that event the partnership resumes carrying on its business as if dissolution had not occurred.

Authority Upon dissolution, the *actual authority* of a partner to act for the partnership terminates, except so far as is appropriate to wind up partnership business. Actual authority to wind up includes the authority to complete existing contracts, to collect debts, to sell partnership assets, and to pay partnership obligations. A person winding up a partnership's business also has the authority to preserve the partnership business or property as a going concern for a reasonable time, bring and defend legal actions, settle and close the partnership's business, distribute the assets of the partnership pursuant to the RUPA, settle disputes by mediation or arbitration, and perform other necessary acts.

With respect to apparent authority, the partnership is bound in a transaction not appropriate for winding up only if the partner's act would have bound the partnership before dissolution and the other party to the transaction did not have notice of the dissolution. A person has notice of a fact if the person (1) knows of it, (2) has received a notification of it, or (3) has reason to know it exists from all of the facts known to the person at the time in question. Moreover, RUPA provides that, after an event of dissolution, any partner who has not wrongfully dissociated may file a statement of dissolution on behalf of the partnership and that 90 days after the filing of the statement of dissolution nonpartners are deemed to have notice of the dissolution and the corresponding limitation on the authority of all partners. Thus, after 90 days the statement of dissolution operates as constructive notice conclusively limiting the apparent authority of partners to transactions that are appropriate for winding up the business.

> **Practical Advice**
>
> Be sure to give the appropriate notice to third parties whenever a partnership dissolves.

Liability Dissolution does not in itself discharge the existing liability of any partner. Partners are liable to the other partners for their share of partnership liabilities incurred after dissolution. That includes not only obligations that are appropriate for winding up the business, but also obligations that are inappropriate but within the partner's apparent authority. A partner, however, who, with knowledge of the dissolution nevertheless incurs a liability binding on the partnership by an act that is not appropriate for winding up the partnership business, is liable to the partnership for any damage caused to the partnership by the liability.

WINDING UP

Whenever a dissolved partnership is not to be continued, the partnership must be liquidated. The process of liquidation, called **winding up**, involves completing unfinished business, collecting debts, taking inventory, reducing assets to cash, auditing the partnership books, paying creditors, and distributing the remaining assets to the partners. During this period, the fiduciary duties of the partners continue in effect except the duty not to compete.

Participation in Winding Up After dissolution, a partner who has not wrongfully dissociated may participate in winding up the partnership's business. On application of any partner, partner's legal representative, or transferee, the court may order judicial supervision of the winding up if good cause is shown. Any partner winding up the partnership is entitled to reasonable compensation for services rendered in the winding up.

Distribution of Assets After all the partnership assets have been collected and reduced to cash, they are distributed to creditors and the partners. When the partnership has been profitable, the order of distribution is not critical; however, when liabilities exceed assets, the order of distribution has great importance. In winding up a partnership's business, the "assets" of the partnership include all required contributions of partners.

The RUPA provides that the partnership must apply its assets first to discharge the obligations of partners who are creditors on *parity* with other creditors, subject to any other laws, such as fraudulent conveyance laws and voidable transfers under the Bankruptcy Act. Second, any surplus must be applied to pay a liquidating distribution equal to the net amount distributable to partners in accordance with their right to distributions. (This does not distinguish between amounts owing to partners for return of capital and amounts owing to partners for profits.) The partnership agreement may vary the RUPA's rules for distributing the surplus among the partners. For example, it may distinguish between capital and operating losses, as the original UPA does.

Each partner is entitled to a settlement of all partnership accounts upon winding up. In settling accounts among the partners, profits and losses that result from the liquidation of the partnership assets must be credited and charged to the partners' accounts according to their respective shares of profits and losses. Then, the partnership must make a final liquidating distribution to those partners with a positive account balance in an amount equal to any excess of the credits over the charges in the partner's account. Any partner with a negative account balance must contribute to the partnership an amount equal to any excess of the charges over the credits in the partner's account. (In an LLP a partner is *not* required to contribute for any partnership obligations for which that partner is not personally liable under the LLP statute's shield.)

Partners share proportionately in the shortfall caused by partners who fail to contribute their proportionate share. The partnership may enforce a partner's obligation to contribute. A partner is entitled to recover from the other partners any contributions in excess of that partner's share of the partnership's liabilities. After the settlement of accounts, each partner must contribute, in the proportion in which the partner shares partnership losses, the amount necessary to satisfy partnership obligations that were not known at the time of the settlement. The estate of a deceased partner is liable for the partner's obligation to contribute to the partnership.

Marshaling of Assets The Revised Act abolishes the marshalling of assets doctrine—which segregates and considers separately the assets and liabilities of the partnership and the respective assets and liabilities of the individual partners—and the dual priority rule. (These are discussed later in this chapter.) Under RUPA, like the UPA, **partnership creditors** are entitled to be satisfied first out of partnership assets. Unlike the UPA, the Revised Act provides that unsatisfied partnership creditors may recover any deficiency out of the individually owned assets of the partners on equal footing with the **partners' creditors**.

CPA DISSOCIATION WITHOUT DISSOLUTION

As already mentioned, the RUPA uses the term "dissociation," instead of the UPA term "dissolution," to denote the change in the relationship caused by a partner's ceasing to be associated in carrying on of the business. Under the RUPA, a dissociation of a partner results in dissolution only in limited circumstances, discussed above. Thus, in many instances, dissociation will result merely in a buyout of the withdrawing partner's interest rather than a winding up of the partnership.

NON-DISSOLVING DISSOCIATIONS

In a ***partnership at will***, a partner will be dissociated from the partnership without dissolution upon specified causes, including that partner's death, bankruptcy, incapacity; the expulsion of that partner; or, in the case of an entity-partner, its termination. (As covered earlier, a partnership at will is *dissolved* upon notice of a partner's intent to withdraw.)

In a ***term partnership***, if within 90 days after any specified causes of dissolution occurs, fewer than half of the remaining partners express their will to wind up the partnership business, then the partnership will not dissolve. These causes include the following: a partner's dissociation by death, bankruptcy, incapacity; the distribution by a trust-partner of its entire partnership interest; the termination of an entity-partner; or a partner's wrongful dissociation. (A wrongful dissociation includes a partner's voluntary withdrawal in violation of the partnership agreement and the judicial expulsion of a partner.)

With three exceptions, the partners may by agreement modify or eliminate any of the grounds for dissolution. The three exceptions are carrying on an illegal business, a court ordered dissolution on application of a partner, and a court ordered dissolution on application of a transferee of a partner's interest. Moreover, at any time after the dissolution of a partnership and before the winding up of its business is completed, all of the partners, including any dissociating partner other than a wrongfully dissociating partner, may waive the right to have the partnership's business wound up and the partnership terminated. In that event, the partnership resumes carrying on its business as if dissolution had never occurred.

CONTINUATION AFTER DISSOCIATION

If a partner is dissociated from a partnership without resulting in dissolution, the remaining partners have the right to continue the business. Creditors of the partnership remain creditors of the continued partnership. Moreover, the dissociated partner remains liable for partnership obligations incurred before dissociation.

The partnership must purchase the dissociated partner's interest in the partnership. The partnership agreement can vary these rights. The buyout price of a dissociated partner's interest is the amount that would have been distributable to the dissociating partner in a winding up of the partnership if, on the date of dissociation, the assets of the partnership were sold at a price equal to the greater of liquidation value or going concern value without the dissociated partner. The partnership must offset against the buyout price all other amounts owing from the dissociated partner to the partnership, including damages for wrongful dissociation. These rules, however, are merely default rules, and the partnership agreement may specify the method or formula for determining the buyout price and all of the other terms and conditions of the buyout right.

A partner in a term partnership who wrongfully dissociates before the expiration of a definite term or the completion of a particular undertaking is not entitled to payment of any portion of the buyout price until the expiration of the term or completion of the undertaking, unless the partner establishes to the satisfaction of the court that earlier payment will not cause undue hardship to the business of the partnership.

A partnership must indemnify a dissociated partner whose interest is being purchased against all partnership liabilities, whether incurred before or after the dissociation, except liabilities incurred by an act of the dissociated partner after dissociation that binds the partnership, as discussed later.

> **Practical Advice**
>
> Consider whether to include a provision in your partnership agreement specifying a method for valuing each partner's interest in the partnership.

Creel v. Lilly

Court of Appeals of Maryland, 1999

354 Md.77, 729 A.2d 385

http://www.findlaw.com/11stategov/md/1999md.html

FACTS During the summer of 1993, Joseph Creel began a retail business selling NASCAR racing memorabilia. His business was originally located in a section of his wife Anne's florist shop, but after about a year and a half he decided to raise capital from partners so that he could expand and move into his own space. On September 20, 1994, Mr. Creel entered into a partnership agreement—prepared without the assistance of counsel—with Arnold Lilly and Roy Altizer to form a general partnership called "Joe's Racing." The partnership agreement covered such matters as the partnership's purpose, location, and operations, and stated the following regarding termination of the business:

> 7. TERMINATION
> (a) That, at the termination of this partnership a full and accurate inventory shall be prepared, and the assets, liabilities, and income, both in gross and net, shall be ascertained: the remaining debts or profits will be distributed according to the percentages shown above in the 6(e).
>
> * * *
>
> (d) Upon the death or illness of a partner, his share will go to his estate. If his estate wishes to sell his interest, they must offer it to the remaining partners first.

The three-man partnership operated a retail store in the St. Charles Towne Center Mall in Waldorf, Maryland, for almost nine months when Mr. Creel died on June 14, 1995. Mrs. Creel was appointed personal representative of his estate. The lease on the store premises occupied by the partnership expired on August 31, 1995, and on that date, Lilly conducted an inventory of all merchandise in the store. Based on that inventory, an accountant computed the value of the partnership business. Subsequently, Lilly and Altizer ceased doing business as Joe's Racing and began doing business together under the name "Good Ole Boys Racing."

The trial court accepted the valuation prepared by Lilly and Altizer's accountant. Rejecting Mrs. Creel's assertions that Mr. Lilly and Mr. Altizer were obligated to liquidate the partnership assets in order to wind up the partnership, the court declared that the estate was entitled to a total of $21,631. The Court of Special Appeals affirmed the judgment of the trial court finding that under UPA "winding up" does not always mean "liquidate;" therefore, Joe's Racing had no duty to sell off all of its assets in a liquidation sale. Mrs. Creel appealed.

DECISION Judgment affirmed.

OPINION Chasanow, J. While the death of a partner automatically dissolves the partnership unless there is an agreement stating otherwise, the partnership is not terminated until the winding-up process is complete. [Citation.] See also [RUPA]. Winding up is generally defined as "getting in the assets, settling with [the] debtors and creditors, and appropriating the amount of profit or loss [to the partners]." [Citation.] * * *

Historically, under many courts and commentators' interpretation of UPA, when a partner died and the partnership automatically dissolved because there was no consent by the estate to continue the business nor was there a written agreement allowing for continuation, the estate had the right to compel liquidation of the partnership assets. [Citation.] Reducing all of the partnership assets to cash through a liquidation was seen as the only way to obtain the true value of the business. [Citation.] However, while winding up has often traditionally been regarded as synonymous with liquidation, this "fire sale" of assets has been viewed by many courts and commentators as a harsh and destructive measure. Consequently, to avoid the drastic result of a forced liquidation, many courts have adopted judicial alternatives to this potentially harmful measure. [Citation.]

Over time, the UPA rule requiring automatic dissolution of the partnership upon the death of a partner, in the absence of consent by the estate to continue the business or an agreement providing for continuation, with the possible result of a forced sale of all partnership assets was viewed as outmoded by many jurisdictions including Maryland. The development and adoption of RUPA by the National Conference of Commissioners on Uniform State Laws (NCCUSL) mitigated this harsh UPA provision of automatic dissolution and compelled liquidation.

RUPA's underlying philosophy differs radically from UPA's, thus laying the foundation for many of its innovative measures. RUPA adopts the "entity" theory of partnership as opposed to the "aggregate" theory that the UPA espouses. [Citation.] Under the aggregate theory, a partnership is characterized by the collection of its individual members, with the result being that if one of the partners dies or withdraws, the partnership ceases to exist. [Citation.] On the other hand, RUPA's entity theory allows for the partnership to continue even with the departure of a member because it views the partnership as "an entity distinct from its partners." [RUPA Section] 201.

This adoption of the entity theory, which permits continuity of the partnership upon changes in partner identity, allows for several significant changes in RUPA. Of particular importance to the instant case is that under RUPA "a partnership no longer automatically dissolves due to a change in its membership, but rather the existing partnership may be continued if the remaining partners elect to buy out the dissociating partner." [Citation.] [Court's footnote: RUPA uses the term "dissociation" rather than dissolution. "Dissociation" is viewed as having a less significant impact on the partnership than dissolution, which is in line with RUPA's entity theory of partnership of continuing the business whenever possible.] In contrast to UPA, RUPA's "buy-out" option does not have to be expressly included in a written partnership agreement in order for it to be exercised; however, the surviving partners must still actively choose to exercise the option, as "continuation is not automatic as with a corporation." [Citation.] This major RUPA innovation therefore delineates two possible paths for a partnership to follow when a partner dies or withdraws: "[o]ne leads to the winding up and termination of the partnership and the other to continuation of the partnership and purchase of the departing partner's share." [Citation.] Critically, under RUPA the estate of the deceased partner no longer has to consent in order for the business to be continued nor does the estate have the right to compel liquidation.

* * *

* * * In adopting RUPA, the Maryland legislature was clearly seeking to eliminate some of UPA's harsh provisions, such as the automatic dissolution of a viable partnership upon the death of a partner and the subsequent right of the estate of the deceased partner to compel liquidation. In essence, the NCCUSL drafted RUPA to reflect the emerging trends in partnership law. RUPA is intended as a flexible, modern alternative to the more rigid UPA and its provisions are consistent with the reasonable expectations of commercial parties in today's business world.

* * *

In applying the law * * * to the facts of this case, we want to clarify that while UPA is the governing act [for this case], our holding is also consistent with RUPA and its underlying policies. The legislature's recent adoption of RUPA indicates that it views with disfavor the compelled liquidation of businesses and that it has elected to follow the trend in partnership law to allow the continuation of business without disruption, in either the original or successor form, if the surviving partners choose to do so through buying out the deceased partner's share.

In this appeal, however, we would arrive at the same holding regardless of whether UPA or RUPA governs. Although our holding departs from the general UPA rule that the representative of the deceased partner's estate has a right to demand liquidation of the partnership, * * * our position of "no forced sale" hardly represents a radical departure from traditional partnership law. The cases, * * * many of which arose early in UPA's existence, illustrate the lengths other courts have gone to in order to avoid a compelled liquidation and adopt an alternative method for ascertaining the true value of a partnership. * * *

* * * Unless there is consent to continue the business or an agreement providing for continuation, upon the death of a partner the accurate value of the partnership must be ascertained as of the date of dissolution and the proportionate share paid to the deceased partner's estate, no matter if we are dealing with a subsequent new partnership or a continuation of the original business. If a compelled liquidation of all partnership assets is seen as the only way to arrive at its true value, then property from the original partnership will have to be sold whether the present business is a continuation or a successor business; regardless, the potential harm of such a "fire sale" affects both equally. * * *

* * * We reiterate that both UPA and RUPA only apply when there is either no partnership agreement governing the partnership's affairs, the agreement is silent on a particular point, or the agreement contains provisions contrary to law.

* * *

In this case, the winding-up method outlined in [paragraph] 7(a) was followed exactly by the surviving partners: a full and accurate inventory was prepared on August 31, 1995; this information was given to an accountant, who ascertained the assets, liabilities, and income of the partnership; and finally, the remaining debt or profit was distributed according to the percentages listed in 6(e).

* * *

Thus, when we look to the intention of the parties as reflected in 7(a) of the partnership agreement, the trial judge could conclude that the partners did not anticipate that a "fire sale" of the partnership assets would be necessary to ascertain the true value of Joe's Racing. Paragraph 7(a) details the preferred winding-up procedure to be followed, to include an inventory, valuation, and distribution of debt or profit to the partners.

Moreover, paragraph 7(d), which discusses what happens to a partner's share of the business upon his death, also makes no mention of a sale or liquidation as being essential in order to determine the deceased partner's proportionate interest of the partnership. * * *

* * *

We find it is sound public policy to permit a partnership to continue either under the same name or as a successor partnership without all of the assets being liquidated. Liquidation can be a harmful and destructive measure, especially to a small business like Joe's Racing, and is often unnecessary to determining the true value of the partnership. * * *

INTERPRETATION Unless otherwise provided by the partnership agreement, the value of a deceased partner's interest may be determined, where appropriate, without liquidation of the partnership assets.

ETHICAL QUESTION Did any of the parties act unethically? Explain.

CRITICAL THINKING QUESTION Do you agree with the court's decision? Explain.

DISSOCIATED PARTNER'S POWER TO BIND THE PARTNERSHIP

A dissociated partner has no actual authority to act for the partnership. With respect to apparent authority, the RUPA provides that for two years after a partner dissociates without resulting in a dissolution of the partnership business, the partnership is bound by an act of the dissociated partner which would have bound the partnership before dissociation but *only if* at the time of entering into the transaction the other party:

1. reasonably believed that the dissociated partner was then a partner;
2. did not have notice of the partner's dissociation; *and*
3. is not deemed to have had constructive notice from a filed statement of dissociation.

A dissociated partner is liable to the partnership for any damage caused to the partnership arising from an obligation improperly incurred by the dissociated partner after dissociation for which the partnership is liable. The dissociated partner is also personally liable to the third party for the unauthorized obligation.

A person has "notice" of a fact if he knows or has reason to know it exists from all the facts that are known to him or he has received a notification of it. The RUPA provides that 90 days after a statement of dissociation is filed, nonpartners are deemed to have constructive notice of the dissociation, thereby conclusively terminating a dissociated partner's apparent authority. Thus, under the RUPA a partnership should notify all known creditors of a partner's dissociation and file a statement of dissociation, which will conclusively limit a dissociated partner's continuing agency power to 90 days after filing. Conversely, third parties dealing with a partnership should check for partnership filings at least every 90 days.

DISSOCIATED PARTNER'S LIABILITY TO THIRD PERSONS

A partner's dissociation does not of itself discharge the partner's liability for a partnership obligation incurred before dissociation. A dissociated partner is not liable for a partnership obligation incurred more than two years after dissociation. For partnership obligations incurred within two years after a partner dissociates without resulting in a dissolution of the partnership business, a dissociated partner is liable for a partnership obligation if at the time of entering into the transaction the other party: (1) reasonably believed that the dissociated partner was then a partner; (2) did not have notice of the partner's dissociation; and (3) is not deemed to have had constructive notice from a filed statement of dissociation.

By agreement with the partnership creditor and the partners continuing the business, a dissociated partner may be released from liability for a partnership obligation. Moreover, a dissociated partner is released from liability for a partnership obligation if a partnership creditor, with notice of the partner's dissociation but without the partner's consent, agrees to a material alteration in the nature or time of payment of a partnership obligation.

DISSOLUTION OF GENERAL PARTNERSHIPS UNDER UPA

The extinguishment of a partnership consists of three stages: (1) dissolution, (2) winding up or liquidation, and (3) termination. Dissolution occurs when the partners cease to carry on the business together. Upon dissolution, the partnership is not terminated but continues until the winding up of its affairs is complete. During winding up, unfinished business is completed, receivables are collected, payments are made to creditors, and the remaining assets are distributed to the partners. Termination occurs when the process is finished.

CPA DISSOLUTION

The Uniform Partnership Act defines dissolution as the change in the relation of the partners caused by any partner's ceasing to be associated in the carrying on, as distinguished from the winding up, of the business. The following sections discuss the causes and effects of dissolution.

CONCEPT REVIEW

Dissociation and Dissolution under RUPA

Cause	Effects			
	Partnership at Will		Term Partnership	
	Dissociation	Dissolution	Dissociation	Dissolution
Acts of Partners				
Assignment of partner's interest				
Accounting				
Withdrawal	•	•	•	*
Bankruptcy	•		•	*
Incapacity	•		•	*
Death	•		•	*
Expulsion of partner	•		•	
Expiration of term				•
Event specified in partnership agreement	•	•	•	•
Unanimous agreement to dissolve	•	•	•	•
Operation of Law				
Illegality		•		•
Court Order				
Judicial expulsion of partner	•		•	*
Judicial determination of partner's incapability to perform partnership duties	•		•	*
Judicial determination of economic frustration or impracticability		•		•
Application by transferee of partner's interest if equitable		•		•

*Dissolution will occur if, within 90 days after dissociation, at least half the remaining partners express their will to wind up the partnership business.

CAUSES OF DISSOLUTION

Dissolution may be brought about by (1) an act of the partners, (2) operation of law, or (3) court order. A number of events that were considered causes of dissolution under the common law are no longer considered so under the UPA. For example, the assignment of a partner's interest, a creditor's charging order (judicial lien) on a partner's interest, and an accounting no longer trigger dissolution.

Dissolution by Act of the Partners Because a partnership is a personal relationship, a partner always has the power to dissolve it by his actions, but whether he has the right to do so is determined by the partnership agreement. A partner who has withdrawn from the partnership in violation of the partnership agreement is liable to the remaining partners for damages resulting from the ***wrongful dissolution***.

A partnership is ***rightfully dissolved***, that is, dissolved in such a manner that the partner's or partners' act does not violate the partnership agreement (1) when all of those partners who have not assigned their interests or permitted their interests to be charged expressly agree to dissolve the partnership; (2) when the time period provided in the agreement has ended or the purpose for

Ethical Dilemma

What Duty of Disclosure Is Owed to Incoming Partners?

FACTS James Edwards was just appointed managing partner of the northeastern division of Banks & Borre, a prestigious national CPA firm operating as a partnership. The position is an excellent one, and James is the youngest partner ever to have served as a regional managing partner. However, although Banks & Borre is a well-established firm, it recently has been subject to several sizable lawsuits that allege the firm's misconduct in services it provided to several banks and certain tax shelters.

Robert Smith, the national manager, has given James clear guidelines on management strategy for the northeast division. Smith has emphasized the importance of expanding the client base in light of the pending lawsuits. A principal strategy is to expand through acquisition of smaller firms. Because of his position as manager of the northeastern division, James receives both a salary and a percentage of new client revenues.

Jones, Jones, & Frank is a medium-sized CPA firm that provides auditing, tax, and management advisory services to a variety of clients. Brothers Ken Jones and Richard Jones began the practice twenty-five years ago. Donald Frank began as an employee but was brought into the partnership in its fifth year.

Jones, Jones, & Frank has been considering the possibility of merging its practice with that of a larger firm. Ken and Richard are in their late fifties and no longer want managerial responsibilities. Nevertheless, they wish to remain active in the practice.

James Edwards initiated discussions with Jones, Jones, & Frank regarding the possibility of a merger. James indicated that he could arrange attractive compensation packages for the partners of the smaller firm. Ken, Richard, and Donald have inquired about the lawsuits pending against Banks & Borre. Not having been involved in the services that gave rise to the lawsuits, James does not know most of the details. He does know, however, that concern about the litigation could destroy all prospects for the merger. James reassures Ken, Richard, and Donald that he does not know much about the lawsuits but is under the impression that they are not significant.

Social, Policy, and Ethical Considerations

1. Should James make a point of acquainting himself with the details of the litigation? Were his preliminary statements about the lawsuits justifiable?
2. Is it ethical for Banks & Borre to recruit new partners and to institute a policy that encourages mergers, given the pending litigation?
3. If a merger takes place, could Ken, Richard, and Donald be held liable for any judgments arising from the litigation?
4. How might a CPA firm insulate its partners from personal liability?
5. What actions should Jones, Jones, & Frank take to investigate Banks & Borre before proceeding with the merger?

which the partnership was formed has been accomplished; (3) when a partner withdraws from a partnership at will, that is, a partnership with no definite term or specific undertaking; or (4) when a partner is expelled in accordance with a power to expel conferred by the partnership agreement.

Dissolution by Operation of Law A partnership is dissolved by operation of law upon (1) the death of a partner, (2) the bankruptcy of a partner or of the partnership, or (3) the subsequent illegality of the partnership, which includes any event that makes it unlawful for the partnership business to be carried on or for the members to carry on the business in partnership form.

Dissolution by Court Order Upon application by or for a partner, a court will order a dissolution if it finds that (1) a partner has been adjudicated mentally incompetent or suffers some other incapacity that prevents him from functioning as a partner; (2) a partner has engaged in conduct prejudicial to the business, has willfully or persistently breached the partnership agreement, or has conducted himself so that it is impracticable to carry on business; (3) the business can be carried on only at a loss; or (4) other circumstances render a dissolution equitable. An assignee of a partner's interest or a partner's personal creditor who has obtained a charging order against the partner's interest is entitled to dissolution by court decree. If the partnership is not at will, however, the partnership will not be dissolved until the term or particular undertaking specified in the partnership agreement is complete.

Effects of Dissolution

On dissolution, the partnership is not terminated but continues until the winding up of its affairs is complete. Moreover, dissolution does not discharge the existing liability of any partner, though it does restrict her authority to act for the partnership.

Upon dissolution, the *actual authority* of a partner to act for the partnership terminates, except so far as may be necessary to wind up partnership affairs. Actual authority to wind up includes the authority to complete existing contracts, to collect debts, to sell partnership assets, and to pay partnership obligations.

Although actual authority terminates upon dissolution, *apparent authority* continues to bind the partnership for acts within the scope of the partnership business unless the third party is given notice of the dissolution. A third party who extended credit to the partnership before dissolution may hold the partnership liable for any transaction that would have bound the partnership had dissolution not occurred, unless the third party had knowledge or actual notice of the dissolution. ***Actual notice*** requires a verbal statement to the third party or actual delivery of a written statement. On the other hand, a third party who knew of or had dealt with the partnership but who had not extended credit to it before its dissolution can hold the partnership liable unless he had knowledge, actual notice, or constructive notice of the dissolution. ***Constructive notice*** consists of advertising a notice of dissolution in a newspaper of general circulation in the places at which the partnership regularly conducted its business. No notice need be given to third parties who had no knowledge of the partnership before its dissolution.

CPA WINDING UP

Whenever a dissolved partnership is not to be continued, the partnership must be liquidated. The process of liquidation, called ***winding up***, involves completing unfinished business, collecting debts, taking inventory, reducing assets to cash, auditing the partnership books, paying creditors, and distributing the remaining assets to the partners. During this period, the fiduciary duties of the partners continue in effect.

THE RIGHT TO WIND UP

Upon dissolution any partner who has not wrongfully dissolved the partnership or been rightfully expelled according to the terms of the partnership agreement has the right to insist on the winding up of the partnership unless the partnership agreement provides otherwise. Unless otherwise agreed, all nonbankrupt partners who have not wrongfully dissolved the partnership have the right to wind up the partnership affairs.

DISTRIBUTION OF ASSETS

After all the partnership assets have been collected and reduced to cash, they are distributed to creditors and the partners. When the partnership has been profitable, the order of distribution is not critical; however, when liabilities exceed assets, the order of distribution has great importance.

The UPA sets forth the rules for settling accounts between the parties after dissolution. It states that the liabilities of a partnership are to be paid out of partnership assets in the following order: (1) amounts owing to nonpartner creditors, (2) amounts owing to partners other than for capital and profits (loans or advances), (3) amounts owing to partners for capital, and (4) amounts owing to partners for profits. The partners may by agreement among themselves change the internal priorities of distribution (numbers 2, 3, and 4) but not the preferred position of third parties (number 1). The UPA defines partnership assets to include all partnership property as well as the contributions necessary for the payment of all partnership liabilities, which consist of numbers 1, 2, and 3.

In addition, the UPA provides that, in the absence of any contrary agreement, each partner shall share equally in the profits and surplus remaining after all liabilities (numbers 1, 2, and 3) are satisfied and must contribute toward the partnership's losses, capital or otherwise, according to his share in the profits. Thus, the proportion in which the partners bear losses depends not on their relative capital contributions but on their agreement. If no specific agreement exists, the partners bear losses in the same proportion in which they share profits.

If the partnership is insolvent, the partners individually must contribute their respective share of the losses to pay the creditors. Furthermore, if one or more of the partners is insolvent or bankrupt or is out of the jurisdiction and refuses to contribute, the other partners must contribute the additional amount necessary to pay the firm's liabilities in the relative proportions in which they share the profits. Any partner who pays an amount in excess of his proper share of the losses has a right of contribution against the partners who have not paid their share.

MARSHALING OF ASSETS

The doctrine of marshaling of assets applies only where a court of equity is administering the assets of a partnership and of its members. ***Marshaling of assets*** means segregating and considering separately the assets and liabilities of the partnership and the respective assets and liabilities of the individual partners. Partnership creditors are entitled to be satisfied first out of partnership assets and may recover any deficiency out of the individually owned assets of the partners. This right is subordinate, however, to the rights of nonpartnership creditors to those assets. Conversely, the nonpartnership creditors have first claim to the individually owned assets of their respective debtors, whereas their claims to partnership assets are subordinate to the claims of partnership creditors. This approach is called the "dual priority" rule.

Finally, the assets of an insolvent partner are distributed in the following order: (1) debts and liabilities owing to her nonpartnership creditors, (2) debts and liabilities owing to partnership creditors, and (3) contributions owing to other partners who have paid more than their respective share of the firm's liabilities to partnership creditors.

This rule, however, is no longer followed if the partnership is a debtor under the Bankruptcy Code. In a proceeding under the federal bankruptcy law, a trustee is appointed to administer the estate of the debtor. If the partnership property is insufficient to pay all the claims against the partnership, the statute directs the trustee to seek recovery of the deficiency first from the general partners who are not bankrupt. The trustee may then seek recovery against the estates of bankrupt partners on the same basis as other creditors of the bankrupt partner. This provision, although contrary to the UPA's doctrine of marshaling of assets, governs whenever a bankruptcy court is administering partnership assets.

CPA Continuation After Dissolution

Dissolution produces one of two outcomes: either the partnership is liquidated or the remaining partners continue the partnership. Whereas liquidation sacrifices the value of a going concern, continuation of the partnership after dissolution avoids this loss. The UPA, nonetheless, gives each partner the right to have the partnership liquidated except in a few instances where the remaining partners have the right to continue the partnership.

Right to Continue Partnership

After dissolution, the remaining partners have the right to continue the partnership when (1) the partnership has been dissolved in contravention of the partnership agreement, (2) a partner has been expelled in accordance with the partnership agreement, or (3) all the partners agree to continue the business. Nevertheless, the noncontinuing partner, or his legal representative, has a right to an account of his interest against the person or partnership continuing the business as of the date of dissolution, unless otherwise agreed. Moreover, when a partner dies or retires and the surviving partners continue the business, the retired partner or the legal representative of the deceased partner is entitled to be paid the value of his interest as of the date of the dissolution as an ordinary creditor of the partnership. In addition, he is entitled to receive interest on this amount or, at his option, in lieu of interest, the profits of the business attributable to the use of his right in the property of the dissolved partnership. His rights are subordinate, however, to those of creditors of the dissolved partnership.

Continuation After Wrongful Dissolution A partner who causes dissolution by wrongfully withdrawing cannot force the liquidation of the firm. The aggrieved partners may either liquidate the firm and recover damages for the breach of the partnership agreement or continue the partnership by buying out the withdrawing partner, who is entitled to realize his interest in the partnership less the amount of the damages that the other partners have sustained because of his breach. The withdrawing partner's interest is computed without considering the goodwill of the business. In addition, the remaining partners may use the capital contributions of the wrongdoing partner for the unexpired period of the partnership agreement. They must, however, indemnify the former partner against all present and future partnership liabilities.

Continuation After Expulsion A partner expelled pursuant to the partnership agreement cannot force the liquidation of the partnership. He is entitled only (1) to be discharged from all partnership liabilities either by payment or by a novation with the creditors and (2) to receive in cash the net amount due him from the partnership.

Continuation Agreement of the Partners By far the best and most reliable tool for preserving a partnership business after dissolution is through a continuation agreement. Frequently used to ensure continuity in the event of a partner's death or retirement, continuation agreements permit remaining partners to keep partnership property, carry on partnership business, and specify settlements for outgoing partners.

Rights of Creditors

Any change in membership dissolves a partnership and forms a new one, despite the fact that the new combination may include a majority of the old partners. The creditors of the old partnership may pursue their claims against the new partnership and also may proceed to hold all of the members of the dissolved partnership personally liable. If a withdrawing partner has made arrangements with those who continue the business whereby they assume and pay all debts and obligations of the firm, the partner is still liable to creditors whose claims arose before the dissolution. If compelled to pay such debts, the withdrawing partner nonetheless has a right of indemnity against her former partners, who agreed to pay the debts but failed to do so.

A retiring partner may be discharged from his existing liabilities by entering into a ***novation*** with the continuing partners and the creditors. A creditor must agree to a novation, although his consent may be inferred from his course of dealing with the partnership after dissolution. Whether such dealings with a continuing partnership constitute an implied novation is a factual question of intent.

A withdrawing partner may protect herself against liability upon contracts the firm enters subsequent to her withdrawal by giving notice that she is no longer a member of the firm. Otherwise, she will be liable for debts thus incurred to creditors who had no notice or knowledge of the partner's withdrawal. Persons who had extended credit to the partnership prior to its dissolution must receive actual notice, whereas constructive notice by newspaper publication will suffice for those who knew of the partnership but had not extended credit to it before its dissolution.

CHAPTER SUMMARY

Formation of General Partnerships

Nature

Definition of Partnership an association of two or more persons to carry on as co-owners a business for profit

Entity Theory
- *Partnership as Legal Entity* an organization having a legal existence separate from that of its members; the RUPA considers a partnership a legal entity for nearly all purposes
- *Partnership as Legal Aggregate* a group of individuals not having a legal existence separate from that of its members; the RUPA considers a partnership a legal aggregate for few purposes

Types of Partnerships
- *Term Partnership* partnership for a specific term or particular undertaking
- *Partnership at Will* partnership in which the partners have not agreed to remain partners until the expiration of a definite term or the completion of a particular undertaking

Formation

Partnership Agreement it is preferable, although not usually required, that the partners enter into a written partnership agreement

Tests of Partnership Existence the formation of a partnership requires all of the following:
- *Association* two or more persons with legal capacity who agree to become partners
- *Business for Profit*
- *Co-ownership* includes sharing of profits and control of the business

Partnership Capital total money and property contributed by the partners for use by the partnership

Partnership Property sum of all of the partnership's assets, including all property acquired by the partnership

Partner's Interest in Partnership includes the partner's transferable interest and all management and other rights
- *Partner's Transferable Interest* the partner's share of the profits and losses of the partnership and the partner's right to receive distributions
- *Assignability* a partner may sell or assign his transferable interest in the partnership; the new owner becomes entitled to the assigning partner's right to receive distributions but does not become a partner
- *Creditor's Rights* a partner's transferable interest is subject to the claims of creditors, who may obtain a charging order (judicial lien) against the partner's transferable interest

Dissociation and Dissolution of General Partnerships Under RUPA

Dissociation

Definition of Dissociation change in the relation of partners caused by any partner's ceasing to be associated in carrying on of the business

Wrongful Dissociation a dissociation that breaches an express provision of the partnership agreement or in a term partnership if before the expiration of the term or the completion of the undertaking (1) the partner voluntarily withdraws by express will, (2) the partner is judicially expelled for misconduct, (3) the partner becomes a debtor in bankruptcy, or (4) the partner is an entity (other than a trust or estate) and is expelled or otherwise dissociated because its dissolution or termination was willful

Rightful Dissociation all other dissociations are rightful including the death of a partner in any partnership and the withdrawal of a partner in a *partnership at will*

Effect of Dissociation terminates dissociating partner's right to participate in the management of the partnership business and duties to partnership

Dissolution

Causes of Dissolution
- ***Dissolution by Act of the Partners*** **partnership at will**: withdrawal of a partner; **term partnership**: (1) the term ends, (2) all partners expressly agree to dissolve, or (3) a partner's dissociation is caused by a partner's death or incapacity, bankruptcy or similar financial impairment, or wrongful dissociation if within 90 days after dissociation at least half of the remaining partners express their will to wind up the partnership business; **any partnership**: an event occurs that was specified in the partnership agreement as resulting in dissolution
- ***Dissolution by Operation of Law*** a partnership is dissolved by operation of law upon the subsequent illegality of the partnership business
- ***Dissolution by Court Order*** a court will order dissolution of a partnership under certain conditions

Effects of Dissolution upon dissolution a partnership is not terminated but continues until the winding up is completed
- ***Authority*** a partner's actual authority to act for the partnership terminates, except so far as may be appropriate to wind up partnership affairs; apparent authority continues unless notice of the dissolution is given to a third party
- ***Existing Liability*** dissolution does not in itself discharge the existing liability of any partner; partners are liable to the other partners for their share of partnership liabilities incurred after dissolution

Winding Up completing unfinished business, collecting debts, and distributing assets to creditors and partners; also called liquidation
- ***Winding Up Required*** A dissolved partnership must be wound up and terminated when the winding up of its business is completed unless *all* of the partners, including any rightfully dissociating partner, waive the right to have the partnership's business wound up and the partnership terminated
- ***Participation in Winding Up*** any partner who has not wrongfully dissociated may participate in winding up the partnership's business
- ***Distribution of Assets*** the assets of the partnership include all required contributions of partners; the liabilities of a partnership are to be paid out of partnership assets in the following order: (1) amounts owing to nonpartner and partner creditors and (2) amounts owing to partners on their partners' accounts

- *Partnership Creditors* are entitled to be first satisfied out of partnership assets
- *Nonpartnership Creditors* share on equal footing with unsatisfied partnership creditors in the individually owned assets of their respective debtor-partners

Dissociation Without Dissolution

Non-Dissolving Dissociations

- *Partnership at Will* a partner's death, bankruptcy, or incapacity, the expulsion of a partner, or the termination of an entity-partner results in a dissociation of that partner but does not result in a dissolution
- *Term Partnership* if within 90 days after any of following causes of dissolution occurs, fewer than half of the remaining partners express their will to wind up the partnership business, then the partnership will *not* dissolve: a partner's dissociation by death, bankruptcy or incapacity, the distribution by a trust-partner of its entire partnership interest, the termination of an entity-partner, or a partner's wrongful dissociation

Continuation After Dissociation the remaining partners have the right to continue the partnership with a mandatory buyout of the dissociating partner; the creditors of the partnership have claims against the continued partnership

Dissociated Partner's Power to Bind the Partnership a dissociated partner's actual authority to act for the partnership terminates; apparent authority continues for two years unless notice of the dissolution is given to a third party

Dissociated Partner's Liability to Third Persons a partner's dissociation does not of itself discharge the partner's liability for a partnership obligation incurred before dissociation; a dissociated partner is liable for a partnership obligation incurred within two years after a partner dissociates unless notice of the dissolution is given to a third party

QUESTIONS

1. Lynn and Jack jointly own shares of stock of a corporation, have a joint bank account, and have purchased and own as tenants in common a piece of real estate. They share equally the dividends paid on the stock, the interest on the bank account, and the rent from the real estate. Without Lynn's knowledge, Jack makes a trip to inspect the real estate and on his way runs over Samuel. Samuel sues Lynn and Jack for his personal injuries, joining Lynn as defendant on the theory that Lynn was Jack's partner. Is Lynn liable as a partner of Jack?

2. James and Suzanne engaged in the grocery business as partners. In one year they earned considerable money, and at the end of the year they invested a part of the profits in oil land, taking title to the land in their names as tenants in common. The investment was fortunate, for oil was discovered near the land, and its value increased many times. Is the oil land partnership property? Why?

3. Sheila owned an old roadside building, which she believed could be easily converted into an antique shop. She talked to her friend Barbara, an antique fancier, and they executed the following written agreement:

   a. Sheila would supply the building, all utilities, and $10,000 capital for purchasing antiques.
   b. Barbara would supply $3,000 for purchasing antiques, Sheila to repay her when the business terminated.
   c. Barbara would manage the shop, make all purchases, and receive a salary of $100 per week plus 5 percent of the gross receipts.
   d. Fifty percent of the net profits would go into the purchase of new stock. The balance of the net profits would go to Sheila.
   e. The business would operate under the name "Roadside Antiques."

   Business went poorly, and after one year a debt of $4,000 is owed to Old Fashioned, Inc., the principal supplier of antiques purchased by Barbara in the name of Roadside Antiques. Old Fashioned sues Roadside Antiques, and Sheila and Barbara as partners. Decision?

4. Clark, who owned a vacant lot, and Bird, who was engaged in building houses, entered into an oral agreement by which Bird was to erect a house on the lot. Upon the sale of the house and lot, Bird was to have his money first. Clark was

then to have the agreed value of the lot, and the profits were to be equally divided. Did a partnership exist?

5. Grant, Arthur, and David formed a partnership for the purpose of betting on boxing matches. Grant and Arthur would become friendly with various boxers and offer them bribes to lose certain bouts. David would then place large bets, using money contributed by all three, and would collect the winnings. After David had accumulated a large sum of money, Grant and Arthur demanded their share, but David refused to make any split. Can Grant and Arthur compel David to account for the profits of the partnership? Why?

6. Teresa, Peter, and Walker were partners under a written agreement made in January that the partnership should continue for ten years. During the same year, Walker, being indebted to Smith, sold and conveyed his interest in the partnership to Smith. Teresa and Peter paid Smith $5,000 as Walker's share of the profits for that year but refused Smith permission to inspect the books or to come into the managing office of the partnership. Smith brings an action setting forth the above facts and asks for an account of partnership transactions and an order to inspect the books and to participate in the management of the partnership business.
   a. Does Walker's action dissolve the partnership?
   b. To what is Smith entitled with respect to (1) partnership profits, (2) inspection of partnership books, (3) an account of partnership transactions, and (4) participation in the partnership management?

7. Horn's Crane Service furnished supplies and services under a written contract to a partnership engaged in operating a quarry and rock-crushing business. Horn brought this action against Prior and Cook, the individual members of the partnership, to recover a personal judgment against them for the partnership's liability under that contract. Horn has not sued the partnership itself, nor does he claim that the partnership property is insufficient to satisfy its debts. What result? Explain.

8. Cutler worked as a bartender for Bowen until they orally agreed that Bowen would have the authority and responsibility for the entire active management and operation of the tavern business known as the Havana Club. Each was to receive $100 per week plus half of the net profits. The business continued under this arrangement for four years until the building was taken over by the Salt Lake City Redevelopment Agency. The agency paid $10,000 to Bowen as compensation for disruption. The business, however, was terminated after Bowen and Cutler failed to find a new, suitable location. Cutler, alleging a partnership with Bowen, then brought this action against him to recover one-half of the $10,000. Bowen contends that he is entitled to the entire $10,000 because he was the sole owner of the business and that Cutler was merely his employee. Cutler argues that although Bowen owned the physical assets of the business, she, as a partner in the business, is entitled to one-half of the compensation that was paid for the business's goodwill and going-concern value. Who is correct? Explain.

9. In 1993, Gauldin and Corn entered into a partnership for the purpose of raising cattle and hogs. The two men were to share equally all costs, labor, losses, and profits. The business was started on land owned initially by Corn's parents but later acquired by Corn and his wife. No rent was ever requested or paid for use of the land. Partnership funds were used to bulldoze and clear the land, to repair and build fences, and to seed and fertilize the land. In 1997, at a cost of $2,487.50, a machine shed was built on the land. In 2002, a Cargill unit was built on the land at a cost of $8,000. When the partnership dissolved in 2003, Gauldin paid Corn $7,500 for the "removable" assets; however, the two had no agreement regarding the distribution of the barn and the Cargill unit. Is Gauldin entitled to one-half of the value of the two buildings? Explain.

10. Simmons, Hoffman, and Murray were partners doing business under the firm name of Simmons & Co. The firm borrowed money from a bank and gave the bank the firm's note for the loan. In addition, each partner guaranteed the note individually. The firm became insolvent, and a receiver was appointed. The bank claims that it has a right to file its claim as a firm debt and also that it has a right to participate in the distribution of the assets of the individual partners before partnership creditors receive any payment from such assets.
   a. Explain the principle involved in this case.
   b. Is the bank correct?

11. Lauren, Matthew, and Susan form a partnership, Lauren contributing $10,000; Matthew $5,000; and Susan her time and skill. Nothing is said regarding the division of profits. The firm later dissolves. No distributions to partners have been made since the partnership was formed. The partnership sells its assets for a loss of $9,000. After payment of all firm debts, $6,000 is left. Lauren claims that she is entitled to the entire $6,000. Matthew contends that the distribution should be $4,000 to Lauren and $2,000 to Matthew. Susan claims the $6,000 should be divided equally among the partners. Who is correct? Explain.

12. Martin, Mark, and Marvin formed a retail clothing partnership named M Clothiers and conducted a business for many years, buying most of their clothing from Hill, a wholesaler. On January 15, Marvin retired from the business, but Martin and Mark decided to continue it. As part of the retirement agreement, Martin and Mark agreed in writing with Marvin that Marvin would not be responsible for any of the partnership debts, either past or future. On January 15 the partnership published a notice of Marvin's retirement in a newspaper of general circulation where the partnership carried on its business.

    Before January 15, Hill was a creditor of M Clothiers to the extent of $10,000, and on January 30, he extended additional credit of $5,000. Hill was not advised and did not in fact know of Marvin's retirement and the change of the partnership. On January 30, Ray, a competitor of Hill, extended credit for the first time to M Clothiers in the amount of $3,000. Ray also was not advised and did not in fact know of Marvin's retirement and the change of the partnership.

On February 1, Martin and Mark departed for parts unknown, leaving no partnership assets with which to pay the described debts. What is Marvin's liability, if any, (a) to Hill and (b) to Ray?

13. Ben, Dan, and Lilli were partners sharing profits in proportions of one-fourth, one-third, and five-twelfths, respectively. Their business failed, and the firm was dissolved. At the time of dissolution, no financial adjustments between the partners were necessary with reference to their respective partners' accounts, but the firm's liabilities to creditors exceeded its assets by $24,000. Without contributing any amount toward the payment of the liabilities, Dan moved to a destination unknown. Ben and Lilli are financially responsible. How much must each contribute?

14. Ames, Bell, and Cole were equal partners in the ABC Construction Company. Their written partnership agreement provided that the partnership would dissolve upon the death of any partner. Cole died on June 30, and his widow, Cora Cole, qualified as executor of his will. Ames and Bell wound up the business of the partnership and on December 31 they completed the sale of all of the partnership's assets. After paying all partnership debts, they distributed the balance equally among themselves and Mrs. Cole as executor.

Subsequently, Mrs. Cole learned that Ames and Bell had made and withdrawn a net profit of $20,000 from July 1 to December 31. The profit was made through new contracts using the partnership name and assets. Ames and Bell had concealed such contracts and profit from Mrs. Cole, and she learned about them from other sources. Immediately after acquiring this information, Mrs. Cole made demand upon Ames and Bell for one-third of the profit of $20,000. They rejected her demand. What are the rights and remedies, if any, of Cora Cole as executor?

15. The articles of partnership of the firm of Wilson and Company provide

> William Smith to contribute $50,000; to receive interest thereon at 13 percent per annum and to devote such time as he may be able to give; to receive 30 percent of the profits.
>
> John Jones to contribute $50,000; to receive interest on same at 13 percent per annum; to give all of his time to the business and to receive 30 percent of the profits.
>
> Henry Wilson to contribute all of his time to the business and to receive 20 percent of the profits.
>
> James Brown to contribute all of his time to the business and to receive 20 percent of the profits.

There is no provision for sharing losses. After six years of operation, the firm is dissolved and wound up. No distributions to partners have been made since the partnership was formed. The partnership assets are sold for $400,000 with a loss of $198,000. Liabilities to creditors total $420,000. What are the rights and liabilities of the respective parties?

16. Adam, Stanley, and Rosalind formed a partnership in State X to distribute beer and wine. Their agreement provided that the partnership would continue until December 31, 2006. Which of the following events would cause the ABC partnership to dissolve? If so, when would the partnership be dissolved?

a. Rosalind assigns her interest in the partnership to Mary on April 1, 2004.
b. Stanley dies on June 1, 2006.
c. Adam withdraws from the partnership on September 15, 2005.
d. A creditor of Stanley obtains a charging order against Stanley's interest on October 9, 2003.
e. In 2004, the legislature of State X enacts a statute making the sale or distribution of alcoholic beverages illegal.
f. Stanley has a formal accounting of partnership affairs on September 19, 2005.

CASE PROBLEMS

17. In 1985, Donald Petersen joined his father, William Petersen, in a chicken hatchery business William had previously operated as a sole proprietorship. When the partnership was formed, William contributed the assets of the proprietorship, which included cash, equipment, and inventory having a total value of $41,000. Donald contributed nothing. From 1985 until his death in 2003, Donald took over the operation of the hatchery. This suit was brought on behalf of Donald's estate when William refused to distribute any of the partnership assets to the estate. William contended that the total value of the partnership property at the time of Donald's death was $18,572. He claimed the full amount on the theory that he was entitled to the return of his capital investment of $41,000 before Donald's estate could recover anything. Explain whether William is correct in his contention.

18. Davis and Shipman founded a partnership in 1998 under the name of Shipman & Davis Lumber Company. On September 20, 2002, the partnership was dissolved by written agreement. Notice of the dissolution was published in a newspaper of general circulation in Merced County, where the business was conducted. No actual notice of dissolution was given to firms that had previously extended credit to the partnership. By the dissolution agreement, Shipman, who was to continue the business, was to pay all of the partnership's debts. He continued the business as a sole proprietorship for a short time until he formed a successor corporation, Shipman Lumber Servaes Co. After the partnership's dissolution, two firms that had previously done business with the partnership extended credit to Shipman for certain repair work and merchandise. The partnership also had a balance due to Valley Company for prior purchases. In 2003, two checks were drawn by Shipman Lumber Servaes Co. and accepted by Valley as partial payment on this debt. Credit Bureaus of Merced County, as assignee of these three accounts, sued the partnership as well as Shipman and Davis individually. Does the dissolution of the partnership relieve Davis of personal liability for the accounts? Explain.

19. In August 2002, Victoria Air Conditioning, Inc. (VAC), entered into a subcontract for insulation services with Southwest Texas Mechanical Insulation Company (SWT), a partnership composed of Charlie Jupe and Tommy Nabors. In February 2003, Jupe and Nabors dissolved the partnership, but VAC did not receive notice of the dissolution at that time. Sometime later, insulation was removed from Nabors's premises to Jupe's possession and Jupe continued the insulation project with VAC. From then on, Nabors had no more involvement with SWT. One month later, Nabors informed VAC's project manager, Von Behrenfeld, that Nabors was no longer associated with SWT, had formed his own insulation company, and was interested in bidding on new jobs. Subsequently, SWT failed to perform the subcontract and Jupe could not be found. VAC brought suit for breach of contract against SWT, Jupe, and Nabors. Nabors claims that several letters and change orders introduced by both parties show that VAC knew of the dissolution and impliedly agreed to discharge Nabors from liability. These documents indicated that VAC had dealt with Jupe, but had not dealt with Nabors, after the dissolution. VAC denies that the course of dealings between VAC and Jupe was the type from which an agreement to discharge Nabors could be inferred. Who is correct? Explain.

http:// Internet Exercise Find and review information about the selection of a form of business organization.

CHAPTER 32

Operation of General Partnerships

Joint adventurers, like copartners, owe to one another, while the enterprise continues, the duty of the finest loyalty.
BENJAMIN CARDOZO, U.S. SUPREME COURT JUSTICE

Learning Objectives

After reading this chapter you should be able to:

1. Identify and explain the duties owed by a partner to her copartners.
2. Identify and describe the rights of partners.
3. Explain the contract liability of a partnership and the partners.
4. Explain the tort liability of a partnership and the partners.
5. Distinguish between the liability of incoming partner for debts arising before his admission and those arising after admission.

The operation and management of a partnership involves interactions among the partners as well as their interactions with third persons. This chapter will consider both of these relationships. The first part of the chapter focuses on the rights and duties of the partners among themselves and to the partnership, which are determined by the partnership agreement, the partnership statute, and the common law. The second part of the chapter focuses on the relations among the partnership, the partners and third persons who deal with the partnership. These relations are governed by the laws of agency, contracts, and torts as well as by the partnership statute.

RELATIONSHIPS AMONG PARTNERS

When parties enter into a partnership, the law imposes certain obligations upon them and also grants them specific rights. Except as otherwise provided by the RUPA, the partnership agreement governs relations among the partners and between the partners and the partnership. Thus, the RUPA gives almost total freedom to the partners to provide whatever provisions they agree upon in their partnership agreement. Nevertheless, the RUPA makes some duties mandatory; these cannot be waived or varied by the partnership agreement.

> **Practical Advice**
>
> When forming a partnership, carefully consider which, if any, duties you wish to vary by agreement.

CPA DUTIES AMONG PARTNERS

The principal legal duties imposed upon partners in their relations with one another are (1) the fiduciary duty (the duty of loyalty), (2) the duty of obedience, and (3) the duty of care. In addition, each partner has a duty to inform his copartners and a duty to account to the partnership. (These additional duties are discussed later, in a section covering the rights of partners.) All of these duties correspond precisely with those duties owed by an agent to his principal and reflect the fact that much of the law of partnership is the law of agency.

FIDUCIARY DUTY

The extent of the fiduciary duty or duty of loyalty has been most eloquently expressed by the often-quoted words of Judge (later Justice) Cardozo:

> Joint adventurers, like copartners, owe to one another, while the enterprise continues, the duty of the *finest loyalty*. Many forms of conduct permissible in a workaday world for those acting at arm's length, are forbidden to those bound by fiduciary ties. A trustee is held to something stricter than the morals of the market place. *Not honesty alone, but the punctilio of an honor the most sensitive, is then the standard of behavior*. As to this there has developed a tradition that is unbending and inveterate. Uncompromising rigidity has been the attitude of courts of equity when petitioned to undermine the rule of undivided loyalty by the "disintegrating erosion" of particular exceptions. Only thus has the level of conduct for fiduciaries been kept at a level higher than that trodden by the crowd. It will not consciously be lowered by any judgment of this court. *Meinhard v. Salmon*, 249 N.Y. 458, 459, 164 N.E. 545, 546 (1928) [emphasis added]

The RUPA's provision regarding the fiduciary duty is both comprehensive and exclusive. The comment to this provision explains: "In that regard, it is structurally different from the UPA which touches only sparingly on a partner's duty of loyalty and leaves any further development of the fiduciary duties of partners to the common law of agency." The RUPA completely and exclusively states the components of the duty of loyalty by specifying that a partner has a duty not to appropriate partnership benefits without the consent of her partners, to refrain from self dealing, and to refrain from competing with the partnership. More specifically, the RUPA provides that a partner's duty of loyalty to the partnership and the other partners is limited to the following:

1. to account to the partnership and hold as trustee for it any property, profit, or benefit derived by the partner in the conduct and winding up of the partnership business or derived from a use by the partner of partnership property, including the appropriation of a partnership opportunity;
2. to refrain from dealing with the partnership in the conduct or winding up of the partnership business as, or on behalf of, a party having an interest adverse to the partnership; and
3. to refrain from competing with the partnership in the conduct of the partnership business before the dissolution of the partnership.

In addition, the Revised Act provides that a partner does not violate the duty of loyalty merely because the partner's conduct furthers the partner's own interest.

For example, a partner committed a breach of fiduciary duty when he retained a secret discount on purchases of petroleum that he obtained through acquisition of a bulk plant, and the partnership was entitled to the entire amount of the discount.

Within the demands of the fiduciary duty, a partner cannot acquire for herself a partnership asset or opportunity without the consent of all the partners. Thus, a partner may not renew a partnership lease in her name alone. A partner cannot, without the permission of her partners, engage in any other business within the scope of the partnership enterprise. Should she participate in a competing or similar business, the disloyal partner not only must surrender any profit she has acquired from such business but must compensate the existing partnership for any damage it may have suffered as a result of the competition. A partner, however, may enter into any business neither in competition with nor within the scope of the partnership's business. For example, a partner in a law firm may, without violating her fiduciary duty, act as an executor or administrator of an estate. Furthermore, she need not account for her fees where it cannot be shown that her service in this other capacity impaired her duty to the partnership (e.g., by monopolizing her attention).

The fiduciary duty does not extend to the formation of the partnership, when, according to the comments to RUPA, the parties are really negotiating at arm's length. The duty not to compete terminates upon dissociation, and the dissociated partner may immediately engage in a competitive business, without any further consent. The partner's other fiduciary duties continue only with regard to matters arising and events occurring before the partner's dissociation, unless the partner participates in winding up the partnership's business. Thus, upon a partner's dissociation, a partner may appropriate to his own benefit any *new* business opportunity coming to his attention after dissociation, even if the partnership continues, and a partner may deal with the partnership as an adversary with respect to *new* matters or events. A dissociated partner is not, however, free to use confidential partnership information after dissociation.

The Revised Act imposes a duty of good faith and fair dealing when a partner discharges duties to the partnership and the other partners under the RUPA or under the partnership agreement and exercises any rights. The comments state:

> The obligation of good faith and fair dealing is a contract concept, imposed on the partners because of the consensual nature of a partnership. . . . It is not characterized, in RUPA, as a fiduciary duty arising out of the partners' special relationship. Nor is it a separate and independent obligation. It is an ancillary obligation that applies whenever a partner discharges a duty or exercises a right under the partnership agreement or the Act.

The partnership agreement may not eliminate the duty of loyalty or the obligation of good faith and fair dealing. However, the partnership agreement may identify specific types or categories of activities that do not violate the duty of loyalty, if not clearly unreasonable. In addition, the other partners may consent to a specific act or transaction that otherwise violates the duty of loyalty, if there has been full disclosure of all material facts regarding the act or transaction as well as the partner's conflict of interest. Similarly, the partnership agreement may prescribe the standards by which the performance of the obligation of good faith and fair dealing is to be measured, if the standards are not manifestly unreasonable.

The fiduciary duty under the UPA differs in some respects from that of the RUPA. First, the partner's fiduciary duty under the UPA applies to the formation of the partnership. Second, it applies to the winding up of the partnership. The UPA states that every partner must account to the partnership for any benefit he receives and must hold as trustee for it any profits he derives without the consent of the other partners from any transaction connected with the formation, conduct, or liquidation of the partnership or from any use he makes of its property. A partner may not prefer himself over the firm, nor may he even deal at arm's length with his partners, to whom his duty is one of undivided and continuous loyalty. The fiduciary duty also applies to the purchase of a partner's interest from another partner. Each partner owes the highest duty of honesty and fair dealing to the other partners, including the obligation to disclose fully and accurately all material facts.

The next case illustrates how rigorously the courts enforce the fiduciary duty.

Practical Advice

As a partner, be sure to make full disclosure of all material facts regarding the partnership and your relationship to your partners.

Clement v. Clement

Supreme Court of Pennsylvania, 1970
436 Pa. 466, 260 A.2d, 728

FACTS Charles and L. W. Clement were brothers who had formed a partnership lasting forty years. In 1964, Charles discovered that his brother, who was the brighter of the two and who kept the partnership's books, had made several substantial personal investments with funds improperly withdrawn from the partnership. He then brought an action in equity seeking dissolution of the partnership, appointment of a receiver, and an accounting. The chancellor of the court of equity issued a decree in favor of Charles, but the court *en banc* reversed his decision. Charles appealed.

DECISION Order of the court *en banc* reversed and case remanded.

OPINION Roberts, J. We disagree with the court *en banc's* statement of the applicable law and therefore reverse. Our theory is simple. There is a fiduciary relationship between partners. Where such a relationship exists, actual fraud need not be shown. There was ample evidence of self-dealing and diversion of partnership assets on the part of L. W.—more than enough to sustain the chancellor's conclusion that several substantial investments made by L. W. over the years were bankrolled with funds improperly withdrawn from the partnership. * * * In all this we are strongly motivated by the fact that the chancellor saw and heard the various witnesses for exhausting periods of time and was in a much better position than we could ever hope to be to taste the flavor of the testimony.

[U.P.A.] § 21 very simply and unambiguously provides that partners owe a fiduciary duty one to another. [Citation.] One should not have to deal with his partner as though he were the opposite party in an arms-length transaction. One should be allowed to trust his partner, to expect that he is pursuing a common goal and not working at cross-purposes. * * *

It would be unduly harsh to require that one must prove fraud before he can recover for a partner's derelictions.

Where one partner has so dealt with the partnership as to raise the probability of wrongdoing it ought to be his responsibility to negate that inference. It has been held that "where a partner fails to keep a record of partnership transactions, and is unable to account for them, every presumption will be made against him." [Citation.] Likewise, where a partner commingles partnership funds with his own assets, he ought to have to shoulder the task of demonstrating the probity of his conduct.

In the instant case, L. W. dealt loosely with partnership funds. At various times he made substantial investments in his own name. He was totally unable to explain where he got the funds to make these investments. The court *en banc* held that Charles had no claim on the fruits of these investments because he could not trace the money that was invested therein dollar for dollar from the partnership. Charles should not have had this burden. He did show that his brother diverted substantial sums from the partnership funds under his control. The inference that these funds provided L. W. with the wherewithal to make his investments was a perfectly reasonable one for the chancellor to make and his decision should have been allowed to stand.

INTERPRETATION Partners are held to a fiduciary duty in their dealings with each other, which includes the obligation to disclose accurately to their partners all material facts.

ETHICAL QUESTION Did L. W. act unethically? Explain.

CRITICAL THINKING QUESTION Do you agree that L. W. should have the burden of showing where he obtained the funds he had invested? Explain.

DUTY OF OBEDIENCE

A partner owes his partners a duty to act in obedience to the partnership agreement and to any business decisions properly made by the partnership. Any partner who violates this duty is liable individually to his partners for any resulting loss. For example, a partner who, in violation of a specific agreement not to extend credit to relatives, advances money from partnership funds and sells goods on credit to an insolvent relative, would be held personally liable to his partners for the unpaid debt.

DUTY OF CARE

Whereas under the fiduciary duty a partner "is held to something stricter than the morals of the market place," he is held to something less than the skill of the marketplace. Each partner owes the partnership a duty of faithful service to the best of his ability. Nonetheless, he need not possess the degree of knowledge and skill of an ordinary paid agent. Under the Revised Act a partner's duty of care to the partnership and the other partners in the conduct and winding up of the partnership business is limited to refraining from engaging in grossly negligent or reckless conduct, intentional misconduct, or a knowing violation of law. For example, a partner assigned to keep the partnership books uses an overly complicated bookkeeping system and consequently produces numerous mistakes. Because these errors result simply from poor judgment, not an intent to defraud, and are not intended to and do not operate to the personal advantage of the negligent bookkeeping partner, she is *not* liable to her copartners for any resulting loss. The duty of care may not be eliminated entirely by agreement, but the standard may be reasonably reduced. The standard may be increased by agreement to one of ordinary care or an even higher standard of care.

CPA RIGHTS AMONG PARTNERS

The law provides partners with certain rights, which include (1) their right to use and possess partnership property for partnership purposes, (2) their transferable interest in the partnership, (3) their right to share in distributions (part of their transferable interest), (4) their right to participate in management, (5) their right to choose associates, and (6) their enforcement rights. The first two rights were discussed in Chapter 31. The four remaining rights among partners are discussed in this section.

RIGHT TO SHARE IN DISTRIBUTIONS

A **distribution** is a transfer of money or other partnership property from the partnership to a partner in the partner's capacity as a partner. Distributions include a division of profits, a return of capital contributions, a repayment of a loan or advance made by a partner to the partnership, and a payment made to compensate a partner for services rendered to the partnership. The RUPA's rules regarding distribution are subject to contrary agreement of the partners. A partner has no right to receive, and may not be required to accept, a distribution in kind. The RUPA provides that each partner is deemed to have an account that

Ethical Dilemma

When Is an Opportunity a Partnership Opportunity?

FACTS Ted Johnson is a real estate manager and investor. Nearly twenty years ago, Ted embarked on a partnership with Karla Jones to improve and operate an office building in New Haven, Connecticut. The building and land are owned by James Jason. James gave Ted and Karla a twenty-year lease. At the end of twenty years, the lease would terminate and the property would revert to James. Pursuant to their partnership agreement, Ted and Karla each provided 50 percent of the capital for improvements of the office space and received 50 percent of allocable net profits.

Ted has successfully managed the building and during the past twenty years has accumulated some additional capital. Six months before the twenty-year lease was scheduled to expire, he and James had dinner together. Indicating how pleased he had been with Ted's management skills, James offered to lease the property for another twenty-year term and mentioned the idea of knocking down the present structure and building a small mall. In light of the recent building of luxury condominiums and exclusive restaurants in the neighborhood, the development of a mall appeared to be a sound idea.

Though he no longer needed Karla's capital for the project, Ted suspected that Karla would be interested in participating in the mall development. However, it was not clear whether James made the offer to renew the lease solely to Ted or to the partnership. Because Karla had not been invited to dinner and her name had never been mentioned, Ted believed that the offer was made solely to him.

Social, Policy, and Ethical Considerations

1. Does Ted have an ethical responsibility to inform Karla of the opportunity to renew the lease?
2. Does it matter that the renewal offer for the long-term lease was initially raised in a dinner conversation between Ted and James?
3. Should Ted be free to sever relations with Karla with regard to the property? Consider that Ted has managed the property and no longer needs Karla's capital. What competing social values does his dilemma involve?

is credited with the partner's contributions and share of the partnership profits and charged with distributions to the partner and the partner's share of partnership losses.

Right to Share in Profits Because a partnership is an association to carry on a business for profit, each partner is entitled, unless otherwise agreed, to a share of the profits. Absent an agreement to the contrary, however, a partner does not have a right to receive a current distribution of the profits credited to his account, the timing of the distribution of profits being a matter arising in the ordinary course of business to be decided by majority vote of the partners. In the absence of an agreement regarding the division of profits, the partners share the profits *equally*, regardless of the ratio of their financial contributions or the degree of their participation in management. Thus, under this default rule, partners share profits per capita and not in proportion to their capital contributions.

Conversely, each partner is chargeable with a share of any losses the partnership sustains. A partner, however, is not obligated to contribute to partnership losses before his withdrawal or the liquidation of the partnership, unless the partners agree otherwise. The partners bear losses in a proportion *identical* to that in which they share profits. The partnership agreement may, however, validly provide for bearing losses in a proportion different from that in which profits are shared.

For example, Alice, Betty, and Carol form a partnership, with Alice contributing $10,000; Betty, $20,000; and Carol, $30,000. They could agree that Alice would receive 20 percent of the profits and assume 30 percent of the losses; that Betty would receive 30 percent of the profits and assume 50 percent of the losses; and that Carol would receive 50 percent of the profits and assume 20 percent of the losses. If their agreement is silent as to the sharing of profits and losses, however, each would have an equal one-third share of both profits and losses.

Right to Return of Capital Absent an agreement to the contrary, a partner does not have a right to receive a distribution of the capital contributions in his account before his withdrawal or the liquidation of the partnership.

Under the UPA after all the partnership's creditors have been paid, each partner is entitled to repayment of his capital contribution during the winding up of the firm. Unless otherwise agreed, a partner is not entitled to interest on his capital contribution; however, a delay in the return of his capital contribution entitles the partner to interest at the legal rate from the date when it should have been repaid.

Right to Repayment of Advances A partner who makes an advance beyond his agreed capital contribution is entitled to reimbursement from the partnership. An advance is treated as a loan to the partnership that accrues interest. In addition, the partnership must reimburse a partner for payments made and indemnify a partner for liabilities incurred by the partner in the ordinary course of the business of the partnership or for the protection of the partnership business or property. Under the Revised Act a loan from a partner to the partnership is treated the same as loans of a person not a partner, subject to other applicable law, such as fraudulent transfer law, the law of avoidable preferences under the Bankruptcy Act, and general debtor-creditor law.

Under the UPA a partner's claim as a creditor of the firm, though subordinate to the claims of nonpartner creditors, is superior to the partners' rights to the return of capital.

Practical Advice

If, as a partner, you advance money to your partnership, make it clear by a written agreement signed by all of the partners that your advance is to be treated as a loan, not as additional capital.

Right to Compensation The RUPA provides that, unless otherwise agreed, no partner is entitled to payment for services performed for the partnership. Even a partner who works disproportionately harder than the others to conduct the business is entitled to no salary but only to his share of the profits. A partner may, however, by agreement among all of the partners, receive a salary. Moreover, a partner is entitled to reasonable compensation for services rendered in winding up the business of the partnership.

Practical Advice

If, as a partner, you expect to be compensated for services you render to the partnership, make that understanding clear by a written agreement signed by all of the partners.

RIGHT TO PARTICIPATE IN MANAGEMENT

Each of the partners, unless otherwise agreed, has *equal* rights in the management and conduct of the partnership business. The majority governs the actions and decisions of the partnership with respect to matters in the ordinary course of partnership business. *All* the partners must consent to any act outside the ordinary course of partnership business and to any amendment of the partnership agreement. In their partnership agreement, the partners may provide for unequal voting rights. For example, Jones, Smith, and Williams form a partnership, agreeing that Jones will have two votes, Smith four votes, and Williams five votes. Large partnerships commonly concentrate most or all management authority in a committee of a few partners or even in just one partner. Classes of partners with different management rights also may be created. This practice is common in accounting and law firms, which may have two classes (e.g., junior and senior partners) or three classes (e.g., junior, senior, and managing partners).

RIGHT TO CHOOSE ASSOCIATES

No partner may be forced to accept as a partner any person of whom she does not approve. This is partly because of the fiduciary relationship between the partners and partly because each partner has a right to take part in the management of the business, to handle the partnership's assets for partnership purposes, and to act as an agent of the partnership. An ill-chosen partner, through negligence, poor judgment, or dishonesty, may bring financial loss or ruin to her copartners. Because of this danger and because of the close relationship among the members, partnerships must necessarily be founded on mutual trust and confidence. All this finds expression in the term ***delectus personae*** (literally, "choice of the person"), which indicates the right one has to choose her partners. This principle is embodied in the RUPA, which provides: "A person may become a partner only with the consent of ***all*** of the partners" [emphasis added.] It is because of *delectus personae* that a purchaser (assignee) of a partner's interest does not become a partner and is not entitled to participate in management. The partnership agreement may provide, however, for admission of a new partner by a less-than-unanimous vote.

Practical Advice

Consider whether your partnership agreement should permit the admission of partners by a less-than-unanimous vote, recognizing that by doing so you forfeit veto power over new members of the partnership.

ENFORCEMENT RIGHTS

As discussed, the partnership relationship creates a number of duties and rights among partners. Accordingly, partnership law provides partners and the partnership with the means to enforce these rights and duties.

Right to Information and Inspection of the Books The RUPA provides that if a partnership maintains books and records, they must be kept at its chief executive office. A partnership must provide partners access to its books and records to inspect and copy them during ordinary business hours. Former partners are given a similar right, although limited to the books and records pertaining to the period during which they were partners. A duly authorized agent on behalf of a partner may also exercise this right. A partnership may impose a reasonable charge, covering the costs of labor and material, for copies of documents furnished. The partnership agreement may not unreasonably restrict a partner's right of access to partnership books and records.

Each partner and the partnership must affirmatively disclose to a partner, *without demand*, any information concerning the partnership's business and affairs reasonably required for the proper exercise of the partner's rights and duties under the partnership agreement or the Act. (In addition, under some circumstances, a disclosure duty may arise from the obligation of good faith and fair dealing.) Moreover, *on demand*, each partner and the partnership must furnish to a partner any other information concerning the partnership's business and affairs, except to the extent the demand or the information demanded is unreasonable or otherwise improper under the circumstances. The rights to receive and demand information extend also to the legal representative of a deceased partner. They may, however, be waived or varied by agreement of the partners.

Legal Action Under RUPA a partner may maintain a direct suit against the partnership or another partner for legal or equitable relief, with or without an accounting as to partnership business, to enforce the partner's rights under the partnership agreement and the Revised Act. Thus, under the RUPA, an accounting is not a prerequisite to the availability of the other remedies a partner may have against the partnership or the other partners. Since general partners are not passive investors, the RUPA does not authorize derivative actions. Reflecting the entity theory of partnership, the RUPA provides that the partnership itself may maintain an action against a partner for any breach of the partnership agreement or for the violation of any duty owed to the partnership, such as a breach of fiduciary duty.

The UPA grants to each partner the right to an account whenever (1) his copartners wrongfully exclude him from the partnership business or possession of its property, (2) the partnership agreement so provides, (3) a partner makes a profit in violation of his fiduciary duty, or (4) other circumstances render it just and reasonable. If a partner does not receive or is dissatisfied with a requested account, she may bring an enforcement action, called an *accounting*. Designed to produce and evaluate all testimony relevant to the various claims of the partners, an accounting is an equitable proceeding for a comprehensive and effective settlement of partnership affairs.

RELATIONSHIP BETWEEN PARTNERS AND THIRD PARTIES

In the course of transacting business, the partnership and the partners also may acquire rights over and incur duties to third parties. For example, under the law of ***agency***, a principal is liable upon contracts that his duly authorized agents make on his behalf and is liable in tort for the wrongful acts his employees commit in the course of their employment. Because much of the law of partnership is the law of agency, most problems arising between partners and third persons require the application of principles of agency law. The RUPA makes this relationship explicit by stating that that "[e]ach partner is an agent of the partnership for the purpose of its business." In addition, the RUPA provides that unless displaced by particular provisions of the RUPA, the principles of law and equity supplement the RUPA. The law of agency is discussed in Chapters 29 and 30.

When a partnership becomes liable to a third party, each partner has **unlimited personal liability** for that partnership obligation.

CPA CONTRACTS OF PARTNERSHIP

The act of every partner binds the partnership to transactions within the scope of the partnership business unless the partner does not have actual or apparent authority to so act. If the partnership is bound, then each general partner has unlimited, personal liability for that partnership obligation unless the partnership is an LLP and the LLP statute shields contract obligations. See Figure 32-1 for a depiction of the contract liability of partnerships. Under the Revised Act, the partners are jointly and severally liable for all contract obligations of the partnership. **Joint and several liability** means that all of the partners may be sued jointly in one action or that separate actions, leading to separate judgments, may be maintained against each of them. Judgments obtained are enforceable, however, against only property of the defendant or defendants named in the suit; and payment of

Figure 32-1
Contract Liability

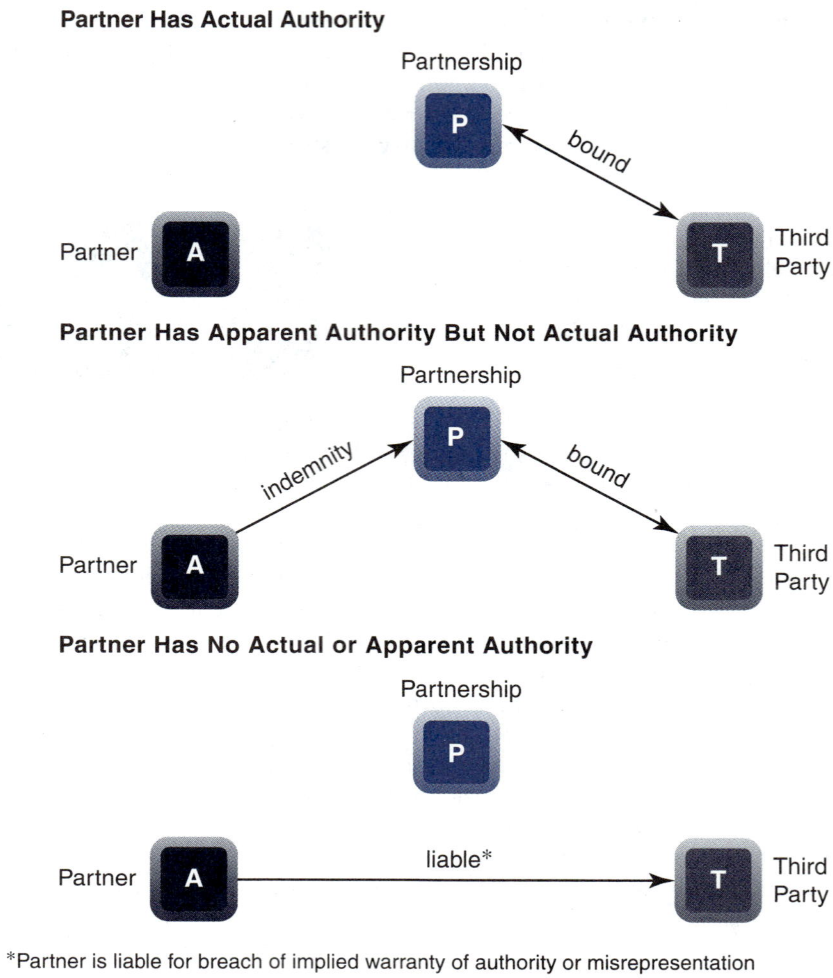

any one of the judgments satisfies all of them. The Revised Act, in keeping with its entity treatment of partnerships, requires the judgment creditor to exhaust the partnership's assets before enforcing a judgment against the separate assets of a partner.

The UPA provides that partners are jointly liable on all debts and contract obligations of the partnership. Under ***joint liability***, a creditor must bring suit against all of the partners as a group, and the judgment must be against all of the obligors. Therefore, any suit in contract against the partners must name all of them as defendants.

AUTHORITY TO BIND PARTNERSHIP

A partner may bind the partnership by her act if (1) she has actual authority, express or implied, to perform the act or (2) she has apparent authority to perform the act. If the act is not apparently for carrying on in the ordinary course the partnership business, then the partnership is bound only where the partner has actual authority. In such a case, the third person dealing with the partner assumes the risk that such actual authority exists. Ratification is discussed in Chapter 30.

Actual Express Authority

The **actual express authority** of partners may be written or oral; it may be specifically set forth in the partnership agreement or in an additional agreement between the partners. In addition, it may arise from decisions made by a majority of the partners regarding ordinary matters connected with the partnership business.

A partner who does not have actual authority from *all* of her partners may not bind the partnership by any act that does not apparently carry on in the ordinary course the partnership business. Acts outside the ordinary course of the partnership business would include the following: (1) execution of contracts of guaranty or suretyship in the firm name, (2) sale of partnership property not held for sale in the usual course of business, and (3) payment of an individual partner's debts out of partnership assets.

The Revised Act also authorizes the optional, central filing of a statement of partnership authority specifying the names of the partners authorized to execute instruments transferring real property held in the name of the partnership. A statement may also limit the authority of a partner or partners to transfer real property. In addition, a statement may grant extraordinary authority to some or all the partners, or limit their ordinary authority, to enter into transactions on behalf of the partnership. A filed statement is effective for up to five years.

The UPA provides that the following acts do ***not*** bind the partnership unless authorized by ***all*** of the partners: (1) assignment of partnership property for the benefit of its creditors; (2) disposal of the goodwill of the business; (3) any act which would make it impossible to carry on the ordinary business of the partnership; (4) confession of a judgment; or (5) submission of a partnership claim or liability to arbitration or reference.

Actual Implied Authority **Actual implied authority** is neither expressly granted nor expressly denied but is reasonably deduced from the nature of the partnership, the terms of the partnership agreement, or the relations of the partners. For example, a partner has implied authority to hire and fire employees whose services are necessary to carry on the partnership business. In addition, a partner has implied authority to purchase property necessary for the business, to receive performance of obligations due to the partnership, and to bring legal actions to enforce claims of the partnership.

Apparent Authority **Apparent authority** (which may or may not be actual) is authority that a third person, in view of the circumstances, the conduct of the parties, and a lack of knowledge or notification to the contrary, may reasonably believe to exist. The RUPA provides

> Each partner is an agent of the partnership for the purpose of its business. An act of a partner, including the execution of an instrument in the partnership name, for apparently carrying on in the ordinary course the partnership business or business of the kind carried on by the partnership binds the partnership, unless the partner had no authority to act for the partnership in the particular matter and the person with whom the partner was dealing knew or had received a notification that the partner lacked authority.

This provision characterizes a partner as a general managerial agent having both actual and apparent authority within the scope of the firm's ordinary business. For example, a partner has apparent authority to indorse checks and notes, to make representations and warranties in selling goods, and to enter into contracts for advertising. A third person, however, may not rely upon apparent authority in any situation where he already knows, or has received notification, that the partner does not have actual authority. A person knows a fact if the person has actual knowledge of it. A person receives a notification when the notification comes to the person's attention or is duly delivered at the person's place of business or at any other place held out by the person as a place for receiving communications.

RNR Investments Limited Partnership v. Peoples First Community Bank

Court of Appeal of Florida, First District, 2002
812 So.2d 561

FACTS RNR Investments (RNR) is a Florida limited partnership formed to purchase vacant land in Destin, Florida, and to construct a house on the land for resale. Bernard Roeger was RNR's general partner and Heinz Rapp, Claus North, and S. E. Waltz, Inc., were limited partners. The limited partnership agreement provided for various restrictions on the authority of the general partner: (a) paragraph 4.1 required the general partner to prepare a budget covering the cost of acquisition and construction of the project ("Approved Budget"); (b) paragraph 4.3 restricted the general partner's ability to borrow or spend partnership funds if not specifically provided for in the Approved Budget; and (c) paragraph 2.2(b) limited the general partner's ability to exceed any line item in the Approved Budget by more than 10% or the total budget by more than 5%.

In June 1998, RNR, through its general partner, entered into a construction loan agreement, note and mortgage in the principal amount of $990,000 with Peoples First Community Bank (Bank). From June 25, 1998, through March 13, 2000, the bank disbursed the aggregate sum of $952,699. All draws were approved by an architect, who certified that the work had progressed as indicated and that the quality of the work was in accordance with the construction contract. No representative of RNR objected to any draw of funds.

RNR defaulted under the terms of the note and mortgage by failing to make payments due in July 2000 and all monthly payments due after that. The Bank filed a complaint seeking foreclosure. RNR defended by alleging that the Bank had failed to review the limitations on the general partner's authority in RNR's limited partnership agreement. RNR asserted that the Bank had negligently failed to investigate and to realize that the general partner had no authority to execute notes, a mortgage and a construction loan agreement. Stephen E. Waltz alleged that the limited partners understood and orally agreed that the general partner would seek financing in the approximate amount of $650,000. RNR also asserted that a copy of the limited partnership agreement was maintained at its offices. However, the record contained no copy of an Approved Budget of the partnership or any evidence that would show that a copy of RNR's partnership agreement or any partnership budget was given to the Bank or that any notice of the general partner's restricted authority was provided to the Bank.

The trial court entered a summary judgment of foreclosure in favor of the Bank. RNR appealed.

DECISION Summary judgment is affirmed.

OPINION Van Nortwick, J. Although the agency concept of apparent authority was applied to partnerships under the common law, [citation], in Florida the extent to which the partnership is bound by the acts of a partner acting within the apparent authority is now governed by statute. Section 301(1), [citation], a part of the Florida Revised Uniform Partnership Act (FRUPA), provides:

> Each partner is an agent of the partnership for the purpose of its business. An act of a partner, including the execution of an instrument in the partnership name, for apparently carrying on in the ordinary scope of partnership business or business of the kind carried on by the partnership, in the geographic area in which the partnership operates, binds the partnership unless the partner had no authority to act for the partnership in the particular manner and the person with whom the partner was dealing knew or had received notification that the partner lacked authority.

[Court's footnote: RNR mistakenly argues that section 301(1) has no application to a limited partnership because that section is part of the Florida Revised Uniform Partnership Act, not the Florida Revised Uniform Limited Partnership Act [FRUPA]. Section 620.186 (comparable to Revised Uniform Limited Partnership Act section 1105), however, provides, as follows: "In any case not provided for in this act, the provisions of the Uniform Partnership Act or the Revised Uniform Partnership Act of 1995, as applicable, and the rules of law and equity shall govern.]

Thus, even if a general partner's actual authority is restricted by the terms of the partnership agreement, the general partner possesses the apparent authority to bind the partnership in the ordinary course of partnership business or in the business of the kind carried on by the partnership, unless the third party "knew or had received a notification that the partner lacked authority." [Citation.] "Knowledge" and "notice" under FRUPA are defined in section 102. That section provides that "[a] person knows a fact if the person has actual knowledge of the fact." [Citation.] Further, a third party has notice of a fact if that party "(a) knows of the fact; (b) has received notification of the fact; or (c) has reason to know the fact exists from all other facts known to the person at the time in question." Section 102(2). Finally, under [FRUPA] section 303 a partnership may file a statement of partnership authority setting forth any restrictions in a general partner's authority.

* * *

"Absent actual knowledge, third parties have no duty to inspect the partnership agreement or inquire otherwise to ascertain the extent of a partner's actual authority in the ordinary course of business * * * even if they have some reason to question it." [Citation.] The apparent authority provisions of section 301(1) reflect a policy by the drafters that "the risk of loss from partner misconduct more appropriately belongs on the partnership than on third parties who do not knowingly participate in or take advantage of the misconduct. * * *" [Citation.]

Under section 301(1), the determination of whether a partner is acting with authority to bind the partnership involves a two-step analysis. The first step is to determine whether the partner purporting to bind the partnership apparently is carrying on the partnership business in the usual way or a business of the kind carried on by the partnership. An affirmative answer on this step ends the inquiry, unless it is shown that the person with whom the partner is dealing actually knew or had received a notification that the partner lacked authority. [Citation.] Here, it is undisputed that, in entering into the loan, the general partner was carrying on the business of RNR in the usual way. The dispositive question in this appeal is whether there are issues of material fact as to whether the Bank had actual knowledge or notice of restrictions on the general partner's authority.

RNR argues that, as a result of the restrictions on the general partner's authority in the partnership agreement, the Bank had constructive knowledge of the restrictions and was obligated to inquire as to the general partner's specific authority to bind RNR in the construction loan. We cannot agree. Under section 301, the Bank could rely on the general partner's apparent authority, unless it had actual knowledge or notice of restrictions on that authority. While the RNR partners may have agreed upon restrictions that would limit the general partner to borrowing no more than $650,000 on behalf of the partnership, RNR does not contend and nothing before us would show that the Bank had actual knowledge or notice of any restrictions on the general partner's authority. Here, the partnership could have protected itself by filing a statement pursuant to section 303 or by providing notice to the Bank of the specific restrictions on the authority of the general partner.

INTERPRETATION A general partner has the apparent authority to bind the partnership in the ordinary course of partnership business or in the business of the kind carried on by the partnership, unless the third party knew or had received a notification that the partner lacked authority.

CRITICAL THINKING QUESTION Do you agree with the RUPA policy that "the risk of loss from partner misconduct more appropriately belongs on the partnership than on third parties who do not knowingly participate in or take advantage of the misconduct"? Explain.

PARTNERSHIP BY ESTOPPEL

Partnership by estoppel imposes partnership duties and liabilities upon a nonpartner who has either represented himself or consented to be represented as a partner. It extends to a third person to whom such a representation is made and who justifiably relies upon the representation.

For example, Marks and Saunders are partners doing business as Marks and Company. Marks introduces Patterson to Taylor, describing Patterson as a member of the partnership. Patterson verbally confirms the statement made by Marks. Believing that Patterson is a member of the partnership and relying upon Patterson's good credit standing, Taylor sells goods on credit to Marks and Company. In an action by Taylor against Marks, Saunders, and Patterson as partners to recover the price of the goods, Patterson is liable although he is not a partner in Marks and Company. Taylor had justifiably relied upon the representation that Patterson was a partner in Marks and Company, to which Patterson actually consented. If, however, Taylor had known at the time of the sale that Patterson was not a partner, his reliance on the representation would not have been justified; and Patterson would not be liable.

Except where the representation of membership in a partnership has been made publicly, no person is entitled to rely upon a representation of partnership unless it is made directly to him. For example, Patterson falsely tells Dillon that he is a member of the partnership Marks and Company. Dillon casually relays this statement to Taylor, who in reliance sells goods on credit to Marks and Company. Taylor cannot hold Patterson liable, as he was not justified in relying on the representation made privately by Patterson to Dillon, which Patterson did not consent to have repeated to Taylor.

Where Patterson, however, knowingly consents to his name appearing publicly in the firm name or in a list of partners, or to be used in public announcements or advertisements in a manner which indicates that he is a partner in the firm, Patterson is liable to any member of the public who relies on the purported partnership, whether or not Patterson is aware of being held out as a partner to such person.

CPA TORTS AND CRIMES OF PARTNERSHIP

As discussed in Chapter 30, under the doctrine of *respondeat superior* a partnership, like any employer, may be liable for an unauthorized tort committed by its employee if the employee committed the tort in the course of his employment. With respect to *partner's* conduct, the RUPA provides that a partnership is liable for the loss or injury any partner causes by any wrongful act or omission, or other actionable conduct, while acting within the ordinary course of the partnership business or with the authority of the partnership. See Figure 32-2 for the tort liability of partnerships.

Tort liability of the partnership may include not only the negligence of the partners but also trespass, fraud, defamation, and breach of fiduciary duty, so long as the tort is committed in the course of partnership business. Moreover, though the fact that a tort is intentional does not necessarily remove it from the course of business, it is a factor to be considered. The Revised Act makes the partnership liable for no-fault torts by the addition of the phrase, "or other actionable conduct." A partnership is also liable if a partner in the course of the partnership's business or while acting with authority of the partnership breaches a trust by receiving money or property of a person not a partner, and the partner misapplies the money or property.

If the partnership is liable, each partner has **unlimited, personal liability** for the partnership obligation unless the partnership is an LLP. The liability of partners for a tort or breach of trust committed by any partner or by an employee of the firm in the course of partnership business is joint and several. As mentioned earlier, the Revised Act

Figure 32-2
Tort Liability

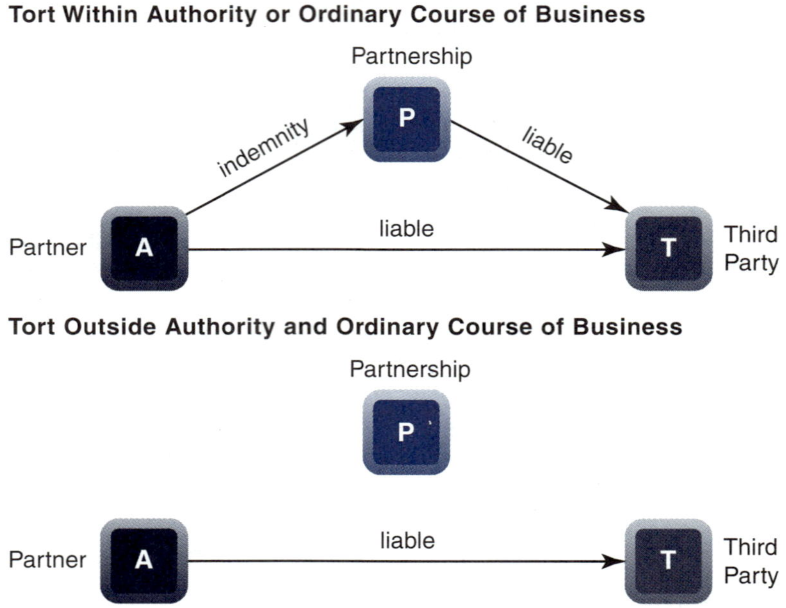

requires the judgment creditor to exhaust the partnership's assets before enforcing a judgment against the separate assets of a partner.

The partner who commits the tort or breach of trust is directly liable to the third party and must also *indemnify* the partnership for any damages it pays to the third party.

A partner is not criminally liable for the crimes of her partners unless she authorized or participated in them. Nor is a partnership criminally liable for the crimes of individual partners or employees unless a statute imposes vicarious liability. Even under such a statute, a partnership usually is liable only in those states that have adopted the entity theory or if the statute itself expressly imposes liability upon partnerships. Otherwise, the vicarious liability statute renders the partners liable as individuals.

Husted v. McCloud

Supreme Court of Indiana, 1983
450 N.E.2d 491

FACTS Herman McCloud retained the firm of Husted and Husted, a partnership consisting of Selwyn and Edgar Husted, to act as attorneys for his mother's estate. After the estate was closed, an additional estate tax liability of $18,006.73 was assessed by the IRS. Edgar falsely represented to McCloud that the precise amount of this liability was unknown and then induced McCloud to issue a check for $18,800 to a fictitious Husted and Husted trust account. Edgar indicated that he would pay the tax liability out of this sum and keep the remainder as his fee. Instead, he converted all of McCloud's funds to his own use, convincing local bank officials to issue a check from another estate for the McCloud estate tax liability. When Edgar's illegal conduct was subsequently discovered, the IRS canceled the satisfaction of the McCloud estate tax liability and reassessed the additional tax due with additional interest, which McCloud then paid. Edgar Husted was sentenced to prison, and McCloud brought an action against the partnership of Husted and Husted, seeking compensatory and punitive damages. The trial court awarded compensatory and punitive damages against Edgar Husted and the partnership. The Court of Appeals affirmed the decision.

DECISION Punitive damages awarded against Edgar Husted and the partnership set aside.

OPINION Pivarnik, J. The public interest in punishing Husted and in deterring him from such misconduct was fully satisfied by the sentence Husted received. Accordingly, punitive damages are inappropriate. [Citation.] * * *

The trial court relied upon the provisions of Indiana's Uniform Partnership Act, [citation], when it entered judgment against the partnership for both punitive and compensatory damages. The trial court particularly relied upon the following sections of the Uniform Partnership Act, which state:

> [§] 13. Partnership bound by partner's wrongful act. Where, by any wrongful act or omission of any partner acting in the ordinary course of the business of the partnership or with the authority of his copartners, loss or injury is caused to any person, not being a partner in the partnership, or any penalty is incurred, the partnership is liable therefore to the same extent as the partner so acting or omitting to act.
>
> [§] 14. Partnership bound by partner's breach of trust. The partnership is bound to make good the loss:
>
> (a) Where one partner acting within the scope of his apparent authority receives money or property of a third person and misapplies it; and
>
> (b) Where the partnership in the course of its business receives money or property of a third person and the money or property so received is misapplied by any partner while it is in the custody of the partnership.

The trial court and the Court of Appeals determined that § 13 required that the partnership be liable to the same extent as Edgar Husted for any civil penalty imposed in this case.

The partnership claims that Edgar's criminal acts were not within the ordinary course of partnership business. Furthermore, the partnership claims that it never had possession of the certain funds converted and therefore the partnership cannot be held liable for Edgar's acts with respect to said funds. There were two partners in the partnership law firm, Edgar Husted and Selwyn Husted, Edgar's father. McCloud clearly was a client of the partnership since McCloud dealt with both Selwyn and Edgar on his estate case. In fact, Selwyn was the partner who first brought McCloud's case into the partnership's office. Edgar was acting within the ordinary course of the partnership's business and with apparent authority since Edgar's request for and acceptance of money from McCloud to pay McCloud's estate tax liability was well within the work parameters of an attorney properly handling a decedent's estate. We therefore find that even though fraud and conversion of a client's funds are not part of the ordinary course of a law partnership's business, the trial court correctly found pursuant to § 14 that the partnership was responsible for partner Edgar in taking money entrusted to him and misapplying it. We also find that the trial court was justified in finding that McCloud's money was in the partnership's possession when it was in Edgar's possession since Edgar deviated from McCloud's plan and converted the money to his own use only after he received it in the ordinary course of the partnership's business. Accordingly, the trial court did not err by holding the partnership responsible to McCloud for compensatory damages.

Whether Appellant partnership is liable for punitive damages, however, is another story. Husted & Husted argues that the cases decided under § 13 or its counterpart in other jurisdictions as well as the earlier cases decided under the common law of agency and partnership have generally held that where a partnership is sued for a partner's intentional tort, the partnership's liability turns on whether the purpose or effect of the tortious act was to benefit the partnership's business or whether the tort was so removed from the ordinary course of that business that it could not be considered within the implicit authorization of the copartners. * * *

We accept Appellant's contention that § 13 is the only section by which punitive damages can be imposed against a partnership since § 14 merely limits a partnership's liability to restitution. We further agree with Appellant partnership that the rationale behind punitive damages in Indiana prohibits awarding such damages against an individual who is personally innocent of any wrongdoing. Punitive damages are not intended to compensate a plaintiff but rather are intended to punish the wrongdoer and thereby deter others from engaging in similar conduct in the future. [Citations.] Accordingly, we now hold that the trial court erred by adjudging the innocent partners in this case responsible for punitive damages.

INTERPRETATION A partnership is liable in *compensatory* damages for the injury or loss caused by the wrongful act of any partner in the course of the partnership business.

ETHICAL QUESTION Did Selwyn Husted act ethically? Explain.

CRITICAL THINKING QUESTION Under what circumstances, if any, should the partnership of Husted and Husted have been held liable for punitive damages? Explain.

CPA NOTICE TO A PARTNER

A partner's knowledge, notice, or receipt of a notification of a fact relating to the partnership is effective immediately as knowledge by, notice to, or receipt of a notification by the partnership, except in the case of a fraud on the partnership committed by or with the consent of that partner. A person has notice of a fact if the person (1) knows of it, (2) has received a notification of it, or (3) has reason to know it exists from all of the facts known to the person at the time in question.

CPA LIABILITY OF INCOMING PARTNER

A person admitted as a partner into an existing partnership is *not* personally liable for any partnership obligations incurred before the person's admission as a partner. This means that the liability of an incoming partner for **antecedent debts** and obligations of the firm is limited to his capital contribution. This restriction does not apply, of course, to **subsequent debts** (obligations arising after his admission into the partnership), for which obligations his liability is *unlimited*. For example, Nash is admitted to Higgins, Cooke, and White Co., a partnership. Nash's capital contribution is $7,500, which she paid in cash upon her admission to the partnership. A year later, when liabilities of the firm exceed its assets by $40,000, the partnership is dissolved. Porter had lent the firm $15,000 eight months before Nash was admitted; Skinner lent the firm $20,000 two months after Nash was admitted. Nash has no liability to Porter except to the extent of her capital contribution, but she is *personally* liable to Skinner.

In an LLP, an incoming partner does not have personal liability for antecedent *and* those subsequent debts that are shielded by that state's LLP statute.

Conklin Farm v. Leibowitz

Supreme Court of New Jersey, 1995

140 N.J. 417, 658 A.2d 1257

http://lawlibrary.rutgers.edu/courts/supreme/a-99-94.opn.html

FACTS In December 1986, Paula Hertzberg, Elliot Leibowitz, and Joel Leibowitz formed a general partnership, LongView Estates (LongView), to acquire from plaintiff Conklin Farm (Conklin) approximately 100 acres of land in the Township of Montville. Paula Hertzberg owned forty percent of LongView; Elliot and Joel Leibowitz owned thirty percent each. They intended to build a residential condominium complex on the property.

On the same day that the partners formed the partnership, it executed a promissory note in favor of Conklin for $9 million. The three LongView partners signed the note as partners and also guaranteed the note personally. The note represented a portion of the purchase price for the land and was secured by a mortgage on the land.

On March 15, 1990, Joel Leibowitz assigned his thirty percent interest in LongView to his wife, defendant Doris Leibowitz, who agreed to be bound by all the terms and conditions of the partnership agreement. Seventeen months later, Doris assigned the interest back to her husband. During those seventeen months, the entire principal of the Conklin note of $9 million was outstanding, and interest accrued at an annual rate of nine percent.

LongView's condominium project failed, and LongView defaulted on the Conklin note. In March 1991, LongView filed a petition for bankruptcy. Eventually, Paula Hertzberg, Elliot Leibowitz, and Joel Leibowitz filed for personal bankruptcy protection, and all three were discharged of any personal liability on the Conklin note.

Conklin sued Doris Leibowitz in November 1991, claiming that she was personally liable for $547,000: thirty percent of the interest on the Conklin note that accrued during the seventeen months during which she had held her husband's partnership interest, plus interest since then and costs. Conklin asserted that, although the principal of the note was preexisting debt, the interest that accrued while Doris Leibowitz had been a partner was new debt. Doris Leibowitz filed a motion for summary judgment arguing that as an incoming partner she was not personally liable for LongView's preexisting debt, including interest. The trial court held that the interest was part of the preexisting debt, not new debt. Holding that Doris Leibowitz was thus not personally liable for the interest, the court granted her motion for summary judgment. Conklin appealed and the Appellate Division reversed, ruling that the interest on preexisting debt is new debt. Doris Leibowitz appealed.

DECISION The judgment of the Appellate Division is reversed.

OPINION Garibaldi, J. We find that the plain language of section 17 of New Jersey's Uniform Partnership Law and its legislative history compel the conclusion that Doris Leibowitz, as an incoming partner, is liable for debt to Conklin only to the extent of her interest in partnership assets. Under [section 15(b) of New Jersey's Uniform Partnership Law] each partner is personally liable for the debts and obligations of a partnership. [Section 17 of New Jersey's Uniform Partnership Law] defines the liability of new partners entering an existing partnership. That statute provides:

> A person admitted as a partner into an existing partnership is liable for all the obligations of the partnership arising before his admission as though he had been a partner when such obligations were incurred, *except that this liability shall be satisfied only out of partnership property*. (Emphasis added).

Under this statute, although the original partners are personally liable for preexisting debt, the incoming partner's liability for preexisting debt is limited to partnership property.

* * * One of the primary goals of the Uniform Partnership Act, and of the New Jersey Legislature in adopting it, was to define the rights of creditors. The rule at common law was that an incoming partner was not liable at all for preexisting debt, and that the entry of the new partner terminated the old partnership and created a new one. [Citation.] As a result, creditors of the new partnership had priority over creditors of the old partnership, even though the partners were operating the same business with the same assets.

* * *

Thus, section 17 of the Uniform Partnership Act struck a compromise: It made incoming partners personally liable for preexisting debts, but only to the extent of their investment in the partnership. * * *

* * *

The Conklin note was executed by the partnership prior to Doris Leibowitz's having any interest in LongView. She did not sign or guarantee payment of that note. Thus, the issue appears resolved by the clear language of [section 17 of New Jersey's Uniform Partnership Law]: Because the note was a preexisting debt, and because Doris Leibowitz was an incoming partner, she is not personally liable for the debt. The parties agree that the principal of the note was preexisting debt. However, while Doris Leibowitz argues that the interest that accrued while she was a partner was part of that preexisting debt, Conklin argues that it was new debt that arose each month as it became due. Thus, according to Conklin, Doris Leibowitz is personally liable for the interest that accrued while she was a partner. We disagree.

* * *

Conklin argues, however, that interest is new debt that "arises" at the time it becomes due, rather than at the time that the borrower assumes the original debt. The Appellate Division agreed and, based on that characterization of interest as new debt, held that [section 17 of New Jersey's Uniform Partnership Law] did not apply and that Doris Leibowitz was personally liable for the interest that had accrued while she had been a partner.

* * *

Conklin argues that just as a rent obligation arises for current use of property, an interest obligation arises for current use of principal. The Appellate Division described the analogy as a "sound approach," and agreed that "interest is current rent for money and also should be treated as new debt." [Citation.] We disagree, and we find the rent analogy faulty.

Contractual interest is created by the contract, and is therefore inseparable from the contractual debt. In [citation], we described contractual interest as "an integral part of the debt itself." Indeed, contractual interest does not exist absent provision for it in the debt-creating instrument. As the Appellate Division has noted, "Interest is no part of a debt unless so stipulated in the contract." [Citation.] The interest obligation cannot be a separate debt from the principal obligation because, independent of the contract establishing the principal obligation, there is no obligation to pay interest.

That the interest is not an independent or "new" debt is reflected in the method Conklin used to calculate the claimed liability: Conklin referred to the promissory note executed prior to Doris Leibowitz's admission as a partner. Conklin referred to the preexisting note because no other source exists to define the interest obligation. Conklin's own claim demonstrates that interest is part of the contractual debt, and that the obligation to pay interest on a loan *arises*, if at all, at the time that the parties execute the note or other debt instrument.

* * *

Because there is no obligation to pay interest independent of the promissory note, Conklin's rent analogy fails. Since the obligation to pay interest arises only as a result of the original loan instrument, interest, unlike rent, cannot be "new" debt. * * *

* * *

Moreover, there is no prejudice to Conklin in the fact that it may look to only the original partners for payment of the preexisting debt and interest. In executing the note, Conklin considered the personal credit of only Paula Hertzberg, Elliot Leibowitz, and Joel Leibowitz, all of whom guaranteed the loan. Conklin did not rely on the personal credit of Doris Leibowitz. When lenders loan money, they rely on the financial statements of the general partners, and not of some future, unknown general partner. Furthermore, lenders can protect themselves by providing in the promissory note that if new partners enter the partnership, the partnership will terminate, and the note will be accelerated unless the new partner agrees to sign or guarantee the note.

We find that contractual interest is not new debt. It is not a separate and distinct obligation, but is an integral part of the debt itself. [Citation.] Accordingly, LongView's obligation to pay interest arose when it executed the Conklin note, before Doris Leibowitz became a partner. Hence, the interest on the note was preexisting debt under [section 17 of New Jersey's Uniform Partnership Law], and Doris Leibowitz is not personally liable for its payment.

INTERPRETATION A new partner is not personally liable for preexisting debt including interest on a preexisting note, even though the interest accrues after the partner's admission.

CRITICAL THINKING QUESTION Do you agree with the court's decision? Explain.

Chapter Summary

Relationships Among Partners

Duties Among Partners

Fiduciary Duty duty of utmost loyalty, fairness, and good faith owed by partners to each other and to the partnership; includes duty not to appropriate partnership opportunities, not to compete, not to have conflicts of interest, and not to reveal confidential information

Duty of Obedience duty to act in accordance with the partnership agreement and any business decisions properly made by the partners

Duty of Care duty owed by partners to manage the partnership affairs without gross negligence, reckless conduct, intentional misconduct, or knowing violation of law

Rights Among Partners

Rights in Partnership Property partners have the right to use and possess partnership property for partnership purposes

Transferable Interest in Partnership partner's right to share in profits and surplus; may be transferred

Distributions transfer of partnership property from the partnership to a partner
- *Profits* each partner is entitled to an equal share of the profits unless otherwise agreed
- *Capital* a partner does not have a right to receive a distribution of the capital contributions in his account before his withdrawal or the liquidation of the partnership
- *Advances* if a partner makes an advance (loan) to the firm, he is entitled to repayment of the advance plus interest
- *Compensation* unless otherwise agreed, no partner is entitled to payment for services rendered to the partnership

Management each partner has equal rights in management of the partnership unless otherwise agreed

Choice of Associates under the doctrine of *delectus personae*, no person can become a member of a partnership without the consent of all of the partners

Enforcement Rights
- *Information* each partner has the right (1) *without demand*, to any information concerning the partnership and reasonably required for the proper exercise of the partner's rights and duties and (2) *on demand*, to any other information concerning the partnership

- *Legal Actions* a partner may maintain a direct suit against the partnership or another partner for legal or equitable relief to enforce the partner's rights; the partnership itself may maintain an action against a partner for any breach of the partnership agreement or for the violation of any duty owed to the partnership

Relationship Between Partners and Third Parties

Contracts

Partners' Liability
- *Personal Liability* if the partnership is contractually bound, each partner has joint and several, unlimited personal liability
- *Joint and Several Liability* a creditor may sue the partners jointly as a group or separately as individuals

Authority to Bind Partnership a partner who has actual authority (express or implied) or apparent authority may bind the partnership
- *Actual Express Authority* authority set forth in the partnership agreement, in additional agreements among the partners, or in decisions made by a majority of the partners regarding the ordinary business of the partnership
- *Actual Implied Authority* authority that is reasonably deduced from the nature of the partnership, the terms of the partnership agreement, or the relations of the partners
- *Apparent Authority* an act of a partner for apparently carrying on in the ordinary course the partnership business or business of the kind carried on by the partnership binds the partnership, so long as that third person has no knowledge or notice of the lack of actual authority

Partnership by Estoppel imposes partnership duties and liabilities on a nonpartner who has either represented himself or consented to be represented as a partner

Torts and Crimes

Torts the partnership is liable for loss or injury caused by any wrongful act or omission or other actionable conduct of any partner while acting within the ordinary course of the business or with the authority of her copartners

Breach of Trust the partnership is liable if a partner in the course of the partnership's business or while acting with authority of the partnership breaches a trust by misapplying money or property entrusted by a third person

Joint and Several Liability the partners are jointly and severally liable for a tort or breach of trust committed by any partner or by an employee of the firm in the course of partnership business

Crimes a partner is not criminally liable for the crimes of her partners unless she authorized or participated in them

Notice to a Partner

Binds Partnership a partnership is bound by a partner's knowledge, notice, or receipt of a notification of a fact relating to the partnership

Notice a person has notice of a fact if the person (1) knows of it, (2) has received a notification of it, or (3) has reason to know it exists from all of the facts known to the person at the time in question

Liability of Incoming Partner

Antecedent Debts the liability of an incoming partner for antecedent debts of the partnership is limited to her capital contribution

Subsequent Debts the liability of an incoming partner for subsequent debts of the partnership is unlimited

QUESTIONS

1. Albert, Betty, and Carol own and operate the Roy Lumber Company. Each contributed one-third of the capital, and they share equally in the profits and losses. Their partnership agreement provides that two partners must authorize all purchases over $500 in advance and that only Albert is authorized to draw checks. Unknown to Albert or Carol, Betty purchases on the firm's account a $2,500 diamond bracelet and a $5,000 forklift and orders $2,000 worth of logs, all from Doug, who operates a jewelry store and is engaged in various activities connected with the lumber business. Before Betty made these purchases, Albert told Doug that Betty is not the log buyer. Albert refuses to pay Doug for Betty's purchases. Doug calls at the mill to collect, and Albert again refuses to pay him. Doug calls Albert an unprintable name, and Albert then punches Doug in the nose, knocking him out. While Doug is lying unconscious on the ground, an employee of Roy Lumber Company negligently drops a log on Doug's leg, breaking three bones. The firm and the three partners are completely solvent.

   What are the rights of Doug against Roy Lumber Company, Albert, Betty, and Carol?

2. Paula, Fred, and Stephanie agree that Paula and Fred will form and conduct a partnership business and that Stephanie will become a partner in two years. Stephanie agrees to lend the firm $5,000 and take 10 percent of the profits in lieu of interest. Without Stephanie's knowledge, Paula and Fred tell Harold that Stephanie is a partner, and Harold, relying on Stephanie's sound financial status, gives the firm credit. The firm later becomes insolvent, and Harold seeks to hold Stephanie liable as a partner. Should Harold succeed?

3. Anita and Duncan had been partners for many years in a mercantile business. Their relationship deteriorated to the point where Anita threatened to bring an action for an accounting and dissolution of the firm. Duncan then offered to buy Anita's interest in the partnership for $25,000. Anita refused the offer and told Duncan that she would take no less than $36,000. A short time later, James approached Duncan and informed him he had inside information that a proposed street change would greatly benefit the business and that he, James, would buy the entire business for $100,000 or buy a one-half interest for $50,000. Duncan made a final offer of $35,000 to Anita for her interest. Anita accepted this offer, and the transaction was completed. Duncan then sold the one-half interest to James for $50,000. Several months later, Anita learned for the first time of the transaction between Duncan and James.

   What rights, if any, does Anita have against Duncan?

4. Anthony and Karen were partners doing business as the Petite Garment Company. Leroy owned a dye plant that did much of the processing for the company. Anthony and Karen decided to offer Leroy an interest in their company, in consideration for which Leroy would contribute his dye plant to the partnership. Leroy accepted the offer and was duly admitted as a partner. At the time he was admitted as a partner, Leroy did not know that the partnership was on the verge of insolvency. About three months after Leroy was admitted to the partnership, a textile firm obtained a judgment against the partnership in the amount of $50,000. This debt represented an unpaid balance that had existed before Leroy was admitted as a partner.

   The textile firm brought an action to subject the partnership property, including the dye plant, to the satisfaction of its judgment. The complaint also requested that, in the event the judgment was unsatisfied by sale of the partnership property, Leroy's home be sold and the proceeds applied to the balance of the judgment. Anthony and Karen own nothing but their interest in the partnership property.

   What should be the result (a) with regard to the dye plant and (b) with regard to Leroy's home?

5. Jones and Ray formed a partnership on January 1, known as JR Construction Co., to engage in the construction business, each partner owning a one-half interest. On February 10, while conducting partnership business, Jones negligently injured Ware, who brought an action against Jones, Ray, and JR Construction Co. and obtained judgment for $25,000 against them on March 1. On April 15, Muir joined the partnership by contributing $10,000 cash, and by agreement each partner was entitled to a one-third interest. In July, the partners agreed to purchase new construction equipment for the partnership, and Muir was authorized to obtain a loan from XYZ Bank in the partnership name for $20,000 to finance the purchase. On July 10, Muir signed a $20,000 note on behalf of the partnership, and the equipment was purchased. In November, the partnership was in financial difficulty, its total assets amounting to $5,000. The note was in default, with a balance of $15,000 owing to XYZ Bank. Muir has substantial resources, while Jones and Ray each individually have assets of $2,000.

   What is the extent of Muir's personal liability and the personal liability of Jones and Ray as to (a) the judgment obtained by Ware and (b) the debt owing to XYZ Bank?

6. ABCD Company is a general partnership organized under the UPA. It consists of Dianne, Greg, Knox, and Laura, whose capital contributions were as follows: Dianne = $5,000, Greg = $7,500, Knox = $10,000, and Laura = $5,000. The partnership agreement provided that the partnership would continue for three years and that no withdrawals of capital were to be made without the consent of all the partners. The agreement also provided that all advances would be entitled to interest at 10 percent per year. Six months after the partnership was formed, Dianne advanced $10,000 to the partnership. At the end of the first year, net profits totaled $11,000 before any moneys had been distributed to partners. How should the $11,000 be allocated to Dianne, Greg, Knox, and Laura? Explain.

7. Adams, a consulting engineer, entered into a partnership with three others for the practice of their profession. The

only written partnership agreement is a brief document specifying that Adams is entitled to 55 percent of the profits and the others to 15 percent each. The venture is a total failure. Creditors are pressing for payment, and some have filed suit. The partners cannot agree on a course of action.

How many of the partners must agree to achieve each of the following objectives?

a. To add Jones, also an engineer, as a partner, Jones being willing to contribute a substantial amount of new capital.
b. To sell a vacant lot held in the partnership name, which had been acquired as a future office site for the partnership.
c. To move the partnership's offices to less expensive quarters.
d. To demand a formal accounting.
e. To dissolve the partnership.
f. To agree to submit certain disputed claims to arbitration, which Adams believes will prove less expensive than litigation.
g. To sell all of the partnership's personal property, Adams having what he believes to be a good offer for the property from a newly formed engineering firm.
h. To alter the respective interests of the parties in the profits and losses by decreasing Adams's share to 40 percent and increasing the others' shares accordingly.
i. To assign all the partnership's assets to a bank in trust for the benefit of creditors, hoping to work out satisfactory arrangements without filing for bankruptcy.

8. Charles and Jack orally agreed to become partners in a small tool and die business. Charles, who had experience in tool and die work, was to operate the business. Jack was to take no active part but was to contribute the entire $50,000 capitalization. Charles worked ten hours a day at the plant, for which he was paid nothing. Nevertheless, despite Charles's best efforts, the business failed. The $50,000 capital was depleted, and the partnership owed $50,000 in debts. Prior to the failure of the partnership business, Jack became personally insolvent; consequently, the creditors of the partnership collected the entire $50,000 indebtedness from Charles, who was forced to sell his home and farm to satisfy the indebtedness. Jack later regained his financial responsibility, and Charles brought an appropriate action against Jack for (a) one-half of the $50,000 he had paid to partnership creditors and (b) one-half of $18,000, the reasonable value of Charles's services during the operation of the partnership. Who will prevail and why?

9. Glenn refuses an invitation to become a partner of Dorothy and Cynthia in a retail grocery business. Nevertheless, Dorothy inserts an advertisement in the local newspaper representing Glenn as their partner. Glenn takes no steps to deny the existence of a partnership between them. Ron, who extended credit to the firm, seeks to hold Glenn liable as a partner. Is Glenn liable? Explain.

10. Hanover leased a portion of his farm to Brown and Black, doing business as the Colorite Hatchery. Brown went upon the premises to remove certain chicken sheds that he and Black had placed there for hatchery purposes. Thinking that Brown intended to remove certain other sheds, which were Hanover's property, Hanover accosted Brown, who willfully struck Hanover and knocked him down. Brown then ran to the Colorite truck, which he had previously loaded with chicken coops, and drove back to the hatchery. On the way, he picked up George, who was hitchhiking to the city to look for a job. Brown was driving at seventy miles an hour down the highway. At an open intersection with another highway, Brown in his hurry ran a stop sign, striking another vehicle. The collision caused severe injuries to George. Immediately thereafter, the partnership was dissolved, and Brown was insolvent. Hanover and George each bring separate actions against Black as copartner for the alleged tort committed by Brown against each. What judgments as to each?

CASE PROBLEMS

11. Phillips and Harris are partners in a used car business. Under their oral partnership, each has an equal voice in the conduct and management of the business. Because of their irregular business hours, the two further agreed that they could use any partnership vehicle as desired. This use includes transportation to and from work, even though the vehicles are for sale at all times. While driving a partnership vehicle home from the used car lot, Harris negligently hit a car driven by Cook, who brought this action against Harris and Phillips individually and as copartners for his injuries. Who is liable?

12. Stroud and Freeman are general partners in Stroud's Food Center, a grocery store. Nothing in the articles of partnership restricts the power or authority of either partner to act in respect to the ordinary and legitimate business of the Food Center. In late 1955, however, Stroud informed National Biscuit that he would not be personally responsible for any more bread sold to the partnership. Then, in February 1956, at the request of Freeman, National Biscuit sold and delivered more bread to the Food Center. Explain whether National Biscuit will be able to recover the value of the bread delivered to the Food Center from Stroud and the partnership.

13. Hodge and Voeller, the managing partner of the Pay-Out Drive-In Theatre, signed a contract for the sale of a small parcel of land belonging to the partnership. Except for the last twenty feet, which was necessary for the theatre's driveway, the parcel was not used in theatre operations. The agreement stated that it was between Hodge and the partnership, with Voeller signing for the partnership. Voeller

claims that he told Hodge before signing that a plat plan would have to be approved by the other partners before the sale. Hodge denies this and sues for specific performance, claiming that Voeller had actual and apparent authority to bind the partnership. The partners argue that Voeller had no such authority and that Hodge knew this. Who is correct? Explain.

14. L. G. and S. L. Patel, husband and wife, owned and operated the City Center Motel in Eureka. On April 16, 1986, Rajeshkumar, the son of L. G. and S. L., formed a partnership with his parents and became owner of 35 percent of the City Center Motel. The partnership agreement required that Rajeshkumar approve any sale of the motel. Record title to the motel was not changed, however, to reflect his interest. On April 21, L. G. and S. L. listed their motel for sale with a real estate broker. On May 2, P. V. and Kirit Patel made an offer on the motel, which L. G. and S. L. accepted. Neither the broker nor the purchasers knew of the son's interest in the motel. When L. G. and S. L. notified Rajeshkumar of their plans, to their surprise, he refused to sell his 35 percent of the motel. On May 4, L. G. and S. L. notified P. V. and Kirit that they wished to withdraw their acceptance. They offered to pay $10,000 in damages and to give the purchasers a right of first refusal for five years. Rather than accept the offer, on May 29, P. V. and Kirit filed an action for specific performance and incidental damages. L. G., S. L., and Rajeshkumar responded that the contract could not lawfully be enforced. Discuss who will prevail and why.

http:// **Internet Exercise** Examine sites that discuss and explain the duties of fiduciaries.

CHAPTER 33

Limited Partnerships and Limited Liability Companies

A limited partner is not liable for the obligations of a limited partnership.
REVISED UNIFORM LIMITED PARTNERSHIP ACT

A member is not personally liable for a debt, obligation, or liability of the [limited liability] company.
UNIFORM LIMITED LIABILITY COMPANY ACT

Learning Objectives

After reading this chapter you should be able to:

1. Distinguish between a general partnership and a limited partnership.
2. Identify those activities in which a limited partner may engage without forfeiting limited liability.
3. Distinguish between a limited partnership and a limited liability company.
4. Distinguish between a member-managed limited liability company and a manager-managed limited liability company.
5. Distinguish between a limited liability partnership and a limited liability limited partnership.

In this chapter, we will consider other types of unincorporated business associations: limited partnerships, limited liability companies, limited liability partnerships, and limited liability limited partnerships. These organizations have developed to meet special business and investment needs. Each has characteristics that make it appropriate for certain purposes.

CPA LIMITED PARTNERSHIPS

The limited partnership has proved to be an attractive vehicle for a variety of investments because of its tax advantages and the limited liability it confers upon the limited partners. Unlike general partnerships, limited partnerships are statutory creations. Before 1976, the governing statute in all states except Louisiana was the Uniform Limited Partnership Act (ULPA), which was promulgated in 1916. In 1976, the National Conference of Commissioners on Uniform State Laws promulgated the Revised Uniform Limited Partnership Act (RULPA). In 1985, the National Conference revised the RULPA; the resulting 1985 Act is substantially similar to the 1976 RULPA and does not alter its underlying philosophy or thrust. All states except Louisiana have adopted either the 1976 Act or the 1985 Act with more than three times as many states adopting the 1985 version than the 1976 version.

In 2001 the National Conference of Commissioners on Uniform State Laws promulgated a new revision of the 1985 Revised Uniform Limited Partnership Act (ReRULPA). The new Act has been drafted to reflect that limited liability partnerships and limited liability companies can meet many of the needs formerly met by limited partnerships. Accordingly, the ReRULPA adopts as default rules provisions that strongly favor current management and treat limited partners as passive investors with little control over or right to exit the limited partnership. To date, one state has adopted it.

In this chapter, we will discuss the 1985 RULPA. The ULPA, the 1976 RULPA, and the 1985 RULPA are supplemented by the Uniform Partnership Act, which applies to limited partnerships in any case for which the Limited Partnership Act does not provide. (The ReRULPA is a stand-alone statute and is not linked the Uniform Partnership Act.) For a concise comparison of general and limited partnerships, see the first Concept Review in Chapter 31.

In addition, limited partnership interests are almost always considered to be securities, and their sale is therefore subject to state and federal regulation, as we will discuss in Chapter 40.

http:// 2001 Revision of Revised Uniform Limited Partnership Act: http://www.nccusl.org/nccusl/Annual_Meeting_2001/LMDTPART01AM.pdf

DEFINITION

A **limited partnership** is a partnership formed by two or more persons under the laws of a state and that has one or more general partners and one or more limited partners. A *person* includes a natural person, a partnership, a limited partnership, a trust, an estate, an association, or a corporation. Such a partnership differs from a general partnership in several respects, three of which are fundamental:

1. a statute providing for the formation of limited partnerships must be in effect.
2. the limited partnership must substantially comply with the requirements of that statute.
3. the liability of a limited partner for partnership debts or obligations is limited to the extent of the capital he has contributed or has agreed to contribute.

FORMATION

Although the **formation** of a *general* partnership requires no special procedures, the formation of a *limited* partnership requires substantial compliance with the limited partnership statute. Failure to comply may result in the limited partners not obtaining limited liability.

Filing of Certificate The RULPA provides that two or more persons desiring to form a limited partnership shall file in the office of the secretary of state of the state in which the limited partnership has its principal office a signed certificate of limited partnership. The certificate must include the following information: (1) the name of the limited partnership; (2) the address of its office and the name and address of the agent for service of process; (3) the name and the business address of each general partner; (4) the latest date upon which the limited partnership is to dissolve; and (5) any other matters the general partners decide to include in the certificate.

The certificate of limited partnership must be amended if a new general partner is admitted, a partner withdraws, or a general partner becomes aware that any statement in the certificate was or has become false. In addition, the certificate may be amended at any time for any other purpose the general partners deem proper. As discussed later, false statements in a certificate or amendment that cause loss to third parties who rely on the statements may result in liability for the general partners.

Name Including the surname of a limited partner in the partnership name is prohibited unless it is also the surname of a general partner or unless the business had been carried on under that name before the admission of that limited partner. A limited partner who knowingly permits his name to be used in violation of this provision is liable to any creditor who did not know that he was a limited partner. The RULPA also prohibits a partnership name that is the same as, or deceptively similar to, that of any corporation or other limited partnership. Finally, the name of the limited partnership must contain, unabbreviated, the words "limited partnership."

Contributions The contribution of a partner may be cash, property, services rendered, a promissory note, or an obligation to contribute cash or property or to perform services. A promise by a limited partner to contribute to the limited partnership is not enforceable unless it is in a signed writing. Should a partner fail to make a required capital contribution described in a signed writing, the limited partnership may hold her liable to contribute the cash value of the stated contribution.

Defective Formation A limited partnership is formed when a certificate of limited partnership that substantially complies with the statutory requirements is filed. Therefore, if no certificate is filed or if the certificate filed does not substantially meet the statutory requirements, the formation is defective. In either case, the limited liability of limited partners is jeopardized. The RULPA provides that a person who has contributed to the capital of a business (an "equity participant"), believing erroneously and in good faith that he has become a limited partner in a limited partnership, is not liable as a general partner, provided that on ascertaining the mistake he either (1) withdraws from the business and renounces *future* profits or (2) files a certificate or an amendment curing the defect. However, the equity participant will be liable to any third party who transacted business with the enterprise before the withdrawal or amendment and who in good faith believed that the equity participant was a general partner at the time of the transaction.

The 1985 Act does not require that the limited partners be named in the certificate. This greatly reduces the risk that an inadvertent omission of such information will expose a limited partner to liability.

Practical Advice

To obtain limited liability as a limited partner, make sure that the limited partnership has been properly organized.

Foreign Limited Partnerships A limited partnership is considered "foreign" in any state other than the one in which it was formed. The laws of the state in which a foreign limited partnership is organized govern its organization, its internal affairs, and the liability of its limited partners. In addition, the RULPA requires all foreign limited partnerships to register with the secretary of state before transacting any business in a state. Any foreign limited partnership transacting business without so registering may not bring enforcement actions in the state's courts until it registers, although it may defend itself in the state's courts.

RIGHTS

Because limited partnerships are organized pursuant to statute, the rights of the parties are usually set forth in the articles of limited partnership and in the limited partnership agreement. Unless otherwise agreed or provided in the act, a general partner of a limited partnership has all the rights and powers of a partner in a partnership without limited partners. A general partner may also be a limited partner and thereby may also share in profits, losses, and distributions as a limited partner.

Practical Advice

When forming a limited partnership, carefully specify the rights and duties of the general and limited partners but be sure to adhere to the statutory limitations on the powers of limited partners.

Control The general partners of a limited partnership have almost exclusive control and management of the limited partnership. A limited partner, on the other hand, may not share in this management or control; if he does, he may forfeit his limited liability. A limited partner who participates in the control of the business is liable only to those persons who transact business with the limited partnership reasonably believing, based upon the limited partner's conduct, that the limited partner is a general partner.

Moreover, both versions of the RULPA provide a "safe harbor" by enumerating certain activities, any or all of which a limited partner may perform without being deemed to have participated in control of the business. They include (1) being a contractor for, or an agent or employee of, the limited partnership or a general partner; (2) consulting with and advising a general partner with respect to the business of the limited partnership; (3) acting as surety for the limited partnership; (4) approving or disapproving an amendment to the partnership agreement; and (5) voting on various fundamental changes in the limited partnership.

Practical Advice

As a limited partner, exercise care not to take part in the control of the limited partnership beyond that which is legally permitted.

Alzado v. Blinder, Robinson & Company, Inc.

Supreme Court of Colorado, 1988

752 P.2d 544

FACTS In 1979, Lyle Alzado and two business associates formed Combat Promotions, Inc., to promote an eight-round exhibition boxing match in Denver, Colorado, between Alzado and Muhammad Ali. Ali agreed to participate on the condition that prior to the match he would receive an irrevocable letter of credit guaranteeing payment of $250,000. Combat Promotions persuaded Blinder, Robinson & Company, Inc. (B-R), to put up the $250,000 letter of credit. B-R, however, insisted on several conditions. First, B-R required the formation of a limited partnership, Combat Associates, with B-R as limited partner and Combat Promotions as general partner. Second, B-R required that the partnership agreement provide that the letter of credit be paid off as a partnership expense. Finally, B-R required Alzado's personal secured guarantee to reimburse B-R for any losses it might suffer. In a separate transaction Alzado signed an agreement with Combat Associates stating that he would be paid $100,000 for the match but subordinating that right to payment for expenses of the promotion.

B-R used its office as a ticket outlet, gave two parties to promote the exhibition match, and gave several promotional TV interviews. Nonetheless, few tickets were sold and the exhibition boxing match was a financial disaster. After Ali collected on the letter of credit as he was entitled to do, Combat Associates could pay B-R only $65,000, and paid nothing to Alzado or other creditors. B-R then sued Alzado for $185,000 in damages. Alzado counterclaimed, alleging that B-R should be deemed a general partner of Combat Associates and therefore liable to Alzado for $100,000. The jury awarded Alzado $92,500. B-R appealed, and the Colorado Court of Appeals reversed. Alzado then appealed to the Colorado Supreme Court.

DECISION Judgment of the Court of Appeals for Blinder, Robinson & Co., Inc., reversing the trial court's award to Alzado, affirmed.

OPINION Kirshbaum, J. Alzado next contends that the Court of Appeals erred in concluding that Blinder-Robinson's conduct in promoting the match did not constitute sufficient control of Combat Associates to justify the conclusion that the company must be deemed a general rather than a limited partner. We disagree.

A limited partner may become liable to partnership creditors as a general partner if the limited partner assumes control of partnership business. [Citations]; *see also* [RULPA] § 303, which provides that a limited partner does not participate in the control of partnership business solely by doing one or more of the following:

> (a) Being a contractor for or an agent or employee of the limited partnership or of a general partner;
> (b) Being an officer, director, or shareholder of a corporate general partner;
> (c) Consulting with and advising a general partner with respect to the business of the limited partnership;

* * *

Early determinations regarding whether a limited partner's conduct constituted control of partnership business were largely fact-specific and did not attempt to state general standards for determining what acts evidence such control. [Citation.] More recent decisions construing section 7 of the Uniform Limited Partnership Act [predecessor to Section 303 of the RULPA] have also failed to provide definitive interpretations of what constitutes "control." [Citation.] One commentator has attributed this lack of definitive interpretation to the limited amount of litigation in this area and the tendency of courts to deal with section 7 control issues on an *ad hoc* basis. [Citation.] Any determination of whether a limited partner's conduct amounts to control over the business affairs of the partnership must be determined by consideration of several factors, including the purpose of the partnership, the administrative activities undertaken, the manner in which the entity actually functioned, and the nature and frequency of the limited partner's purported activities.

A judgment notwithstanding the verdict may be entered only if, when viewing the evidence in the light most favorable to the party against whom the motion is directed, reasonable persons could not reach the same conclusion as the jury. [Citations.] The record here reflects that Blinder-Robinson used its Denver office as a ticket outlet, gave two parties to promote the exhibition match and provided a meeting room for many of Combat Associates' meetings. Blinder personally appeared on a television talk show and gave television interviews to promote the match. Blinder-Robinson made no investment, accounting or other financial decisions for the partnership; all such fiscal decisions were made by officers or employees of Combat Promotions, Inc., the general partner. The evidence established at most that Blinder-Robinson engaged in a few promotional activities. It does not establish that it took part in the management or control of the business affairs of the partnership. Accordingly, we agree with the Court of Appeals that the trial court erred in denying Blinder-Robinson's motion for judgment notwithstanding the verdict with respect to Alzado's first counterclaim.

* * *

Alzado finally asserts that Blinder-Robinson fostered the appearance of being in control of Combat Associates, that such actions rendered Blinder-Robinson liable as a general partner and that this conduct allowed third parties to believe that Blinder-Robinson was in fact a general partner. The evidence does not support this argument. Certainly, as Vice President of Combat Promotions, Inc., the general partner of Combat Associates, Alzado had no misconception concerning the function and role of Blinder-Robinson as a limited partner only. The Court of Appeals concluded that the evidence failed to establish that Blinder-Robinson exercised control over the business affairs of Combat Associates. We agree with that conclusion.

INTERPRETATION The RULPA permits limited partners to carry on certain specified activities without losing their limited liability.

CRITICAL THINKING QUESTION Do you agree that limited partners should forfeit their limited liability because they take part in control of the limited partnership? Explain.

Voting Rights The partnership agreement may grant to all or a specified group of general or limited partners the right to vote on any matter. If, however, the agreement grants limited partners voting powers beyond the act's safe harbor provisions, a court may hold that the limited partners have participated in control of the business. The RULPA does not require that limited partners have the right to vote on matters as a class separate from the general partners, although the partnership agreement may provide such a right.

Choice of Associates After the formation of a limited partnership, the admission of additional limited partners requires the written consent of all partners, unless the partnership agreement provides otherwise. Regarding additional general partners, the written partnership agreement determines the procedure for authorizing their admission. The written consent of all partners is required only if the partnership agreement fails to deal with this issue.

Withdrawal A general partner may withdraw from a limited partnership at any time by giving written notice to the other partners. If the withdrawal violates the partnership agreement, the limited partnership may recover damages from the withdrawing general partner. A limited partner may withdraw as provided in the limited partnership certificate or, under the 1985 Act, the written partnership agreement. If the certificate (or written partnership agreement, under the 1985 Act) does not specify when a limited partner may withdraw or a definite time for the limited partnership's dissolution, a limited partner may withdraw upon giving at least six months' prior written notice to each general partner. Upon withdrawal, a withdrawing partner is entitled to receive any distribution to which she is entitled under the partnership agreement, subject to the amount restrictions discussed below. The partner is also entitled to receive the fair value of her interest in the limited partnership as of the date of withdrawal, based upon her right to share in distributions from the limited partnership, if the partnership agreement does not provide otherwise.

Assignment of Partnership Interest A partnership interest is a partner's share of the profits and losses of a limited partnership and the right to receive distributions of partnership assets. A partnership interest is personal property. Unless the partnership agreement provides otherwise, a partner may assign his partnership interest. An assignment does not dissolve the limited partnership. The assignee does not become a partner and may not exercise any rights of a partner: the assignment entitles the assignee only to receive, to the extent of the assignment, the assigning partner's share of distributions. However, an assignee of a partnership interest, including an assignee of a general partner, may become a *limited* partner if all the other partners consent or if the assigning partner, having such power provided to her in the certificate (or in the partnership agreement, under the 1985 Act), grants the assignee this right. Except as otherwise provided in the partnership agreement, a partner ceases to be a partner upon assignment of all his partnership interest.

A creditor of a partner may obtain a charging order against a partner's interest in the partnership. To the extent of the charging order, the creditor has the rights of an assignee of the partnership interest.

Profit and Loss Sharing The profits and losses are allocated among the partners as provided in the partnership agreement. If the partnership agreement makes no such provision in writing, the profits and losses are allocated on the basis of the value of the contributions each partner has actually made. Nonetheless, limited partners are usually not liable for losses beyond their capital contribution. The 1985 Act requires the agreement for sharing profits and losses to be in writing.

Distributions The partners share **distributions** of cash or other assets of the limited partnership as provided in writing in the partnership agreement. The RULPA allows partners to share in distributions in a proportion different from that in which they share profits. If the partnership agreement does not allocate distributions in writing, they are made on the basis of the contributions each partner actually made. A partner who becomes entitled to a distribution has the status of a creditor with respect to that distribution. A partner may not receive a distribution from a limited partnership unless its postdistribution assets would be sufficient to pay all of its liabilities other than liabilities to partners on account of their partnership interests.

Loans Both general and limited partners may be secured or unsecured creditors of the partnership with rights the same as those of a person who is not a partner, subject to applicable state and federal bankruptcy and fraudulent conveyance statutes.

Information The partnership must continuously maintain within the state an office at which basic organizational and financial records are kept. Each partner has the right to inspect and copy any of the partnership records.

Derivative Actions A limited partner has the right to bring an action on behalf of a limited partnership to recover a judgment in its favor if the general partners having authority to bring the action have refused to do so.

DUTIES AND LIABILITIES

The duties and liabilities of general partners in a limited partnership are quite different from those of a limited partner. A general partner is subject to all the duties and restrictions of a partner in a partnership without limited partners, whereas a limited partner is subject to few, if any, duties and enjoys limited liability.

Duties A *general partner* of a limited partnership has a *fiduciary* relationship to her general and limited partners. This fiduciary duty of the general partner is extremely important to the limited partners because of their circumscribed roles in the control and management of the business enterprise. Conversely, it remains unclear whether a limited partner owes a fiduciary duty to his general partners or to the limited partnership itself. The very limited judicial authority on this question seems to indicate that the limited partner does not.

The RULPA does not distinguish between the duty of care owed by a general partner to a general partnership and that owed by a general partner to a limited partnership. Thus, a general partner owes her partners a duty not to be culpably negligent, as such negligence was discussed in Chapter 32. As in the next case, however, some courts have imposed upon general partners a higher duty of care toward *limited partners*. On the other hand, a limited partner owes no duty of care to a limited partnership as long as she remains a limited partner.

Wyler v. Feuer

California Court of Appeal, Second District, Division 2, 1978
85 Cal.App.3d 392, 149 Cal.Rptr. 626

FACTS Feuer and Martin, associated as Feuer and Martin Productions, Inc. (FMPI), had been successful producers of Broadway musical comedies. Their first motion picture, *Cabaret*, received eight Academy Awards (**http://www.oscars.org/**) in 1973. In 1972, FMPI bought the motion picture and television rights to Simone Berteaut's best-selling book about her life with her half-sister Edith Piaf. To finance a movie based on this novel, FMPI sought a substantial private investment from Wyler. In July 1973, Wyler signed a final limited partnership agreement with FMPI. The agreement stated that Wyler would provide, interest free, 100 percent financing for the proposed $1.6 million project in return for a certain portion of the profits, not to exceed 50 percent. In addition, FMPI would obtain $850,000 in production financing by September 30, 1973. The contract specifically provided that FMPI's failure to raise this amount by September 30, 1973, "shall not be deemed a breach of this agreement" and that Wyler's sole remedy would be a reduction in the producer's fee.

A year after its release in 1974, the motion picture proved less than an overwhelming success—costing $1.5 million and taking in total receipts of only $478,000. From the receipts, Wyler received $313,500 for his investment. FMPI had failed to obtain an amount even close to the required $850,000 for production financing. Wyler then sued Feuer, Martin, and FMPI for mismanagement of the limited partnership business and to recover his $1.5 million as damages. The trial court found in favor of Feuer, Martin, and FMPI.

DECISION Judgment for Feuer, Martin, and FMPI affirmed.

OPINION Fleming, J. In a limited partnership, the limited partner restricts his liability to the amount of his capital investment. In return, the limited partner surrenders the right to manage and control the partnership business. The general partner owes to the limited partner a duty of reasonable care in his management of the business. But the general partner may not be held liable to the limited partner for mistakes made or losses incurred in the good faith exercise of reasonable business judgment.

Here, Wyler proved only that the motion picture did not make money, was not sought after by distributors, and did not live up to its producer's expectations. He failed to show that Feuer and Martin's decisions and efforts breached the standards of good faith and reasonableness. Therefore, he cannot recover damages from Feuer and Martin for an investment that simply turned sour.

INTERPRETATION A general partner is not liable for business losses if he or she conducts the business prudently and in good faith.

ETHICAL QUESTION Did the general partners act ethically? Explain.

CRITICAL THINKING QUESTION What standard of care should the general partners owe to the limited partners? Explain.

Liabilities One of the most appealing features of a limited partnership is the limited personal liability it offers to limited partners. **Limited liability** means that a limited partner who has paid her contribution has no further liability to the limited partnership or its creditors. Thus, if a limited partner buys a 25 percent share of a limited partnership for $50,000 and does not forfeit limited liability, her liability is limited to the $50,000 contributed, even if the partnership suffers losses of $500,000.

This protection is subject to three conditions discussed earlier: (1) that the partnership has substantially complied in good faith with the requirement that a certificate of limited partnership be filed; (2) that the surname of the limited partner does not appear in the partnership name; and (3) that the limited partner does not take part in control of the business. In addition, if the certificate contains a false statement, anyone who suffers loss by reliance on that statement may hold liable any party to the certificate who knew the statement to be false when the certificate was executed. As long as the limited partner abides by these conditions, his liability for any and all obligations of the partnership is limited to his capital contribution.

At the same time, the general partners of a limited partnership have unlimited external liability, unless the limited partnership is a limited liability limited partnership (LLLP), discussed later in this chapter. Also, any general partner who knew or should have known that the limited partnership certificate contained a false statement is liable to anyone who suffers loss by reliance on that false statement. Moreover, a general partner who knows or should know that a statement has become false, but who does not amend the certificate within a reasonable time, is liable as well. Accordingly, it has become a common practice for limited partnerships to be formed with a corporation or other limited liability entity as the sole general partner.

Any partner to whom any part of her contribution has been returned without violation of the partnership agreement or of the limited partnership act is liable for one year to the limited partnership, to the extent necessary to pay creditors who extended credit during the period the partnership held the contribution. In contrast, any partner to whom any part of her contribution was returned in violation of the partnership agreement or the limited partnership act is liable to the limited partnership for six years for the amount of the contribution wrongfully returned.

> **Practical Advice**
>
> Consider using a corporation as the sole general partner; then no natural person will be subject to unlimited, personal liability.

DISSOLUTION

As with a general partnership, extinguishing a limited partnership involves three steps: (1) dissolution, (2) winding up or liquidation, and (3) termination. The causes of dissolution and the priorities in distributing the assets, however, differ somewhat from those in a general partnership.

Causes In a limited partnership, the limited partners have no right or power to dissolve the partnership, except by court decree. The death or bankruptcy of a limited partner does *not* dissolve the partnership. The RULPA specifies the events that will trigger a dissolution, after which the partnership affairs must be liquidated: (1) the expiration of the time period specified in the certificate; (2) the happening of events specified in writing in the partnership agreement; (3) the unanimous written consent of all the partners; (4) the withdrawal of a general partner, unless either (a) there is at least one other general partner and the written provisions of the partnership agreement permit the remaining general partners to continue the business or (b) within 90 days all partners agree in writing to continue the business; or (5) a decree of judicial dissolution, which may be granted whenever it is not reasonably practicable to carry on the business in conformity with the partnership agreement. A general partner's withdrawal includes his retirement, the assignment of all his general partnership interest, removal, bankruptcy, death, and adjudication of incompetency. A certificate of cancellation must be filed when the limited partnership dissolves and winding up commences.

Winding Up Unless otherwise provided in the partnership agreement, the general partners who have not wrongfully dissolved the limited partnership may wind up its affairs. The limited partners may wind up the limited partnership if the general partners all have wrongfully dissolved the partnership. But, by showing cause, any partner, his legal representative, or his assignee may obtain a winding up by the court.

Distribution of Assets The priorities in distributing the assets of a limited partnership are as follows:

1. to creditors, including partners who are creditors except with respect to liabilities for distributions;
2. to partners and ex-partners in satisfaction of liabilities for unpaid distributions;
3. to partners for the return of their contributions, except as otherwise agreed; and
4. to partners for their partnership interests in the proportions in which they share in distributions, except as otherwise agreed.

CONCEPT REVIEW

Comparison of General and Limited Partners

	General Partner	Limited Partner
Control	Has all the rights and powers of a partner in a partnership without limited partners	Has no right to take part in management or control
Liability	Unlimited	Limited, unless partner takes part in control or partner's name is used
Agency	Is an agent of the partnership	Is not an agent of the partnership
Fiduciary Duty	Yes	No
Duty of Care	Yes	No

General and limited partners rank equally unless the partnership agreement provides otherwise.

CPA | LIMITED LIABILITY COMPANIES

A limited liability company (LLC) is another form of unincorporated business association. Prior to 1990, only two states had statutes permitting LLCs. Now all states have enacted LLC statutes, and many have been amended several times. Until 1995, there was no uniform statute on which states might base their LLC legislation, and only eight states have adopted the Uniform Limited Liability Company Act (ULLCA), which was amended in 1996. Therefore, the enabling legislation varies from state to state. Nevertheless, the LLC statutes generally share certain characteristics.

A **limited liability company** is a noncorporate business organization that provides limited liability to *all* of its owners (members) and permits all of its members to participate in management of the business. It may elect not to be a separate taxable entity, in which case only the members are taxed. (Publicly traded LLCs, however, are subject to corporate income taxation.) If an LLC has only one member, it will be taxed as a sole proprietorship, unless separate entity tax treatment is elected. Thus, the LLC provides many of the advantages of a general partnership plus limited liability for all its members. Its benefits outweigh those of a limited partnership in that all members of an LLC not only enjoy limited liability but also may participate in management and control of the business. See the first Concept Review in Chapter 31. LLCs have become the most popular and widely used unincorporated business form that provides limited liability for its members. Ownership interests in a limited liability company may be considered to be securities, especially interests in those LLCs operated by managers. If a particular LLC interest is considered a security, its sale would be subject to state and federal securities regulation, as discussed in Chapter 40.

http:// Uniform Limited Liability Company Act:
http://www.law.upenn.edu/bll/ulc/ulc_frame.htm

FORMATION

The **formation** of a limited liability company requires substantial compliance with a state's limited liability company statute. All of the states permit an LLC to have only one member. Once formed, an LLC is a separate legal entity that is distinct from its members, who are normally not liable for its debts and obligations. An LLC can contract in its own name and is generally empowered to carry on any lawful business purpose, although some statutes restrict the permissible activities of LLCs.

Filing The LLC statutes generally require the central filing of articles of organization in a designated state office. The states vary regarding the information they require the articles to include. Most states do not limit the duration of LLCs, and in most states, LLCs must file annual reports with the state.

Name LLC statutes generally require the name of the LLC to include the words "limited liability company" or the abbreviation "LLC." A number of states also permit the use of the name "limited company" and the abbreviation "LC."

Contribution The contribution of a member to a limited liability company may be cash, property, services rendered, a promissory note, or other obligation to contribute cash, property, or to perform services. Members are liable to the LLC for failing to make an agreed contribution.

Operating Agreement The members of an LLC adopt an ***operating agreement***, which is the basic contract governing the affairs of a limited liability company and stating the various rights and duties of the members. LLC statutes generally do not require the operating agreement to be in writing, although some statutes permit modification of certain statutory rules to be only by written provision in an operating agreement.

Foreign Limited Liability Companies A limited liability company is considered "foreign" in any state other than that in which it was formed. LLC statutes typically provide that the laws of the state in which a foreign LLC is organized govern its organization, its internal affairs, and the liability of its members and managers. Foreign limited liability companies must register with the secretary of state before transacting any business in a state. Any foreign limited liability company transacting business without so registering may not bring enforcement actions in the state's courts until it registers, although it may defend itself in the state's courts.

Practical Advice

To obtain limited liability as a member of a limited liability company, make sure that the LLC has been properly organized.

RIGHTS OF MEMBERS

A member has no property interest in property owned by the LLC. On the other hand, a member does have an interest in the LLC, which is personal property. A member's interest in the LLC includes two components:

1. the *financial interest*, which is the right to distributions, and
2. the *management interest*, which consists of all other rights granted to a member by the LLC operating agreement and the LLC statute. The management interest typically includes the right to manage, vote, obtain information, and bring enforcement actions.

Profit and Loss Sharing The LLC's operating agreement determines how the partners allocate the profits and losses. If the LLC's operating agreement makes no such provision, the profits and losses are typically allocated on the basis of the value of the members' contributions. The ULLCA's default rule follows the partnership model and assumes that profits will be divided equally.

Distributions The members share distributions of cash or other assets of a limited liability company as provided in the operating agreement. If the LLC's operating agreement does not allocate distributions, they are typically made on the basis of the contributions each member made.

Withdrawal Most statutes permit a member to withdraw and demand payment of her interest upon giving the notice specified in the statute or the LLC's operating agreement. Some of the statutes permit the operating agreement to deny members the right to withdraw from the LLC.

Management Most LLC statutes provide that, in the absence of a contrary agreement, each member has equal rights in the management of the LLC. All LLC statutes permit LLCs to be managed by one or more managers who may, but need not, be members. In a member-managed LLC, the members have actual and apparent authority to bind the LLC. In a manager-managed LLC, the managers have this authority, while the members have no actual or apparent authority to bind the manager-managed LLC.

Taghipour v. Jerez

Supreme Court of Utah, 2002
2002 UT 74, 52 P.3d 1252

FACTS Namvar Taghipour, Danesh Rahemi, and Edgar Jerez ("Jerez") formed a limited liability company (the "LLC"), on August 30, 1994, to purchase and develop a parcel of real estate. The LLC's articles of organization designated Jerez as the LLC's manager. In addition, the operating agreement between the members of the LLC provided: "No loans may be contracted on behalf of the [LLC] * * * unless authorized by a resolution of the members."

On August 31, 1994, the LLC acquired the intended real estate. Then, on January 10, 1997, Jerez, without the knowledge of the LLC's other members, entered into a loan agreement on behalf of the LLC with Mt. Olympus. According to the loan agreement, Mt. Olympus lent the LLC $25,000 and, as security for the loan, Jerez executed and delivered a trust deed encumbering the LLC's real estate property. Mt. Olympus then dispensed $20,000 to Jerez and retained the $5,000 balance to cover various fees. In making the loan, Mt. Olympus did not investigate Jerez's authority to enter into the loan agreement beyond determining that Jerez was the manager of the LLC.

Jerez absconded with the $20,000. The LLC never made payments on the loan, since it was unaware of the loan, and consequently defaulted. Mt. Olympus then foreclosed on the LLC's property giving notice of the default and pending foreclosure sale to only Jerez.

On June 18, 1999, Namvar Taghipour, Danesh Rahemi, and the LLC (collectively, "Taghipour") filed suit against Mt. Olympus and Jerez seeking that the loan agreement and the foreclosure be declared invalid because Jerez lacked the authority to bind the LLC. Mt. Olympus moved to dismiss asserting that the loan agreement documents are valid and binding on the LLC since they were signed by the LLC's manager. Utah Code section 48–2b–127(2) pertinently provides:

> Instruments and documents providing for the acquisition, mortgage, or disposition of property of the limited liability company shall be valid and binding upon the limited liability company if they are executed by one or more managers of a limited liability company having a manager or managers or if they are executed by one or more members of a limited liability company in which management has been retained by the members.

The trial court granted Mt. Olympus' motion to dismiss. Taghipour appealed to the Utah Court of Appeals. Taghipour argued that the trial court failed to consider Utah Code section 48–2b–125(2)(b), which provides that a manager's authority to bind a limited liability company can be limited by the operating agreement.

The Utah Court of Appeals affirmed the trial court, concluding that the plain language of section 48–2b–127(2) provided no limitation on a manager's authority to execute certain documents and bind a limited liability company. Further, the court of appeals concluded that this specific statute prevailed over the general statute, section 48–2b–125(2)(b), and that the loan documents executed by Jerez were therefore binding on the LLC. Taghipour petitioned the Supreme Court of Utah for certiorari, which was granted.

DECISION Judgment is affirmed.

OPINION Russon, J. To determine whether the loan agreement in this case is valid and binding on the LLC, it must first be determined whether this case is governed by section 48–2b–127(2), which makes certain kinds of documents binding on a limited liability company when executed by a manager, or section 48–2b–125(2)(b), which provides that a manager's authority to bind a limited liability company can be limited or eliminated by an operating agreement.

When two statutory provisions purport to cover the same subject, the legislature's intent must be considered in determining which provision applies. [Citation.] To determine that intent, our rules of statutory construction provide that "when two statutory provisions conflict in their operation, the provision more specific in application governs over the more general provision." [Citations.]

* * *

Section 48–2b–127(2) is the more specific statute because it applies only to documents explicitly enumerated in the statute, i.e., the section expressly addresses "instruments and documents" that provide "for the acquisition, mortgage, or disposition of property of the limited liability company." [Citations.] Thus, this section is tailored precisely to address the documents and instruments Jerez executed, e.g., the trust deed and trust deed note. * * * Conversely, section 48–2b–125(2)(b) is more general because it addresses every situation in which a manager can bind a limited liability company.

* * *

Moreover, if we were to hold that section 48–2b–125(2)(b) is the more specific provision, we would essentially render section 48–2b–127(2) "superfluous and inoperative," [citation], because section 48–2b–127(2) would simply restate section 48–2b–125(2)(b) and would therefore be subsumed by section 48–2b–125(2)(b). Accordingly, the court of appeals correctly concluded that section 48–2b–127(2) is more specific, and therefore, the applicable statute in this case.

Section 48–2b–127(2) must be applied to the facts of this case to determine whether the documents are valid and bind the LLC. * * * According to this section, the documents are binding if they are covered by the statute and if executed by a manager. There are no other requirements for such documents to be binding on a limited liability company.

In this case * * * Jerez was designated as the LLC's manager in the articles of organization. Jerez, acting in his capacity as manager, executed loan agreement documents, e.g., the trust deed and trust deed note, on behalf of the LLC that are specifically covered by the above statute. [Citation.] As such, these documents are valid and binding on the LLC under section 48–2b–127(2). Therefore, the court of appeals correctly concluded that the LLC was bound by the loan agreement and, consequently, that Mt. Olympus was not liable to Taghipour for Jerez's actions.

INTERPRETATION In a manager-managed LLC, the managers have actual and apparent authority to bind the LLC.

CRITICAL THINKING QUESTION Given this provision of Utah's LLC statute, is there any way that the members of the LLC could have protected themselves?

Voting Most of the LLC statutes specify the voting rights of members, subject to a contrary provision in an LLC's operating agreement. In about half the states the default rule for voting follows a partnership approach (each member has equal voting rights) while the other states take a corporate approach (voting is based on the financial interests of members). Typically, members have the right to vote on proposals to (1) adopt or amend the operating agreement, (2) admit any person as a member, (3) sell all or substantially all of the LLC's assets prior to dissolution, and (4) merge the LLC with another LLC.

Derivative Actions A member has the right to bring an action on behalf of a limited liability company to recover a judgment in its favor if the managers or members with authority to bring the action have refused to do so.

Assignment of LLC Interest Unless otherwise provided in the LLC's operating agreement, a member may assign his financial interest in the LLC. An assignment does not dissolve the LLC. The assignment entitles the assignee to receive, to the extent of the assignment, only the assigning member's share of distributions. A judgment creditor of a member may obtain a charging order against the member's financial interest in the LLC.

The assignee does not become a member and may not exercise any rights of a member. However, an assignee of a financial interest in an LLC may acquire the other rights by being admitted as a member of the company by all the remaining members. (Some states allow admission by majority vote.) In most states this unanimous acceptance rule is now a default rule, and the operating agreement may eliminate or modify it. For example, the ULLCA provides, "A transferee of a [financial] interest may become a member of a limited liability company if and to the extent that the transferor gives the transferee the right in accordance with authority described in the operating agreement or all other members consent."

PB Real Estate, Inc. v. DEM II Properties

Appellate Court of Connecticut, 1998

50 Conn.App. 741, 719 A.2d 73

FACTS After obtaining a deficiency judgment resulting from a mortgage foreclosure against the defendants, Edward J. Botwick, David J. Kurzawa and DEM II Properties, the plaintiff, PB Real Estate, Inc., applied for a charging order directed to Botwick & Kurzawa, LLC , a limited liability company (LLC) engaged in the practice of law. The plaintiff was attempting to satisfy the judgment from any payments owed to the individual defendants, each of whom owns one half of the LLC. The trial court granted the application and directed the LLC to pay to the plaintiff "present and future shares of any and all distributions, credits, drawings, or payments due to the defendant[s] * * * until the judgment is satisfied in full. * * *" The order also directed the LLC to furnish to the plaintiff a copy of the LLC agreement and other financial information.

The plaintiff applied for a turnover order, claiming that the LLC had not fully complied with the charging order because the 1996 profit and loss statement indicated that a portion of the item designated on the statement as "legal staff" expense appeared to have been paid to the defendants, contrary to the directive in the charging order that all distributions should be paid to the plaintiff. The trial court found that, since the date of the charging order, the LLC had paid approximately $28,000 to each of two defendants. The trial court rejected the defendants' claim that those payments were merely compensation for their services to the LLC as lawyers and were similar to the wages paid to other employees of the firm. The payments to the defendants were not shown in the "salary" column of the business record where payments to employees of the law firm are recorded but were listed separately under their initials. The 1996 tax returns of the individual defendants indicated that they received little or no wages, but they reported significant earnings from self-employment. The trial court concluded that the payments made by the law firm to the defendants were "distributions" that were subject to the charging order and granted the application for a turnover order. The LLC appeals from that order, contending that several provisions of the Connecticut Limited Liability Company Act preclude the conclusion that the challenged payments were distributions.

DECISION The judgment issuing the turnover order is affirmed.

OPINION Shea, J. The Connecticut Limited Liability Company Act, [citation], was adopted in 1993 and is generally similar to the model act promulgated in 1995 by the Uniform Laws Commissioners. "The allure of the limited liability company is its unique ability to bring together in a single business organization the best features of all other business forms—properly structured, its owners obtain both a corporate-styled liability shield and the pass-through tax benefits of a partnership." Unif. Limited Liability Company Act, prefatory note, [citation]. The central issue in this appeal is the extent to which that liability shield protects the interest of a member of a limited liability company against a judgment creditor when the basis for the judgment is an obligation unrelated to the activities of the company. Under the circumstances of this case, we conclude that it raises no barrier to the satisfaction of such a judgment from the member's interest in the company.

The LLC claims that the trial court incorrectly failed to limit the turnover order to the "rights of an assignee of the member's limited liability company interest," as provided by [citation], in defining the rights of a judgment creditor. That statute provides that, "[t]o the extent so charged, the judgment creditor has only the rights of an assignee of the member's limited liability company interest." The phrase, "[l]imited liability company membership interest," is defined by [citation] to mean "a member's share of the profits and losses of the limited liability company and a member's right to receive distributions of the limited liability company's assets, unless otherwise provided in the operating agreement." The operating agreement for the LLC provides that "all distributions * * * shall be made at such time as determined by the Manager," who consists solely of the two owners. They maintain that they have authorized no distributions, and therefore, the court's finding that the $28,000 each of them has received was a distribution is contrary to [citation], which provides in part that "[a] member is entitled to receive distributions * * * from a limited liability company to the extent and at the times or upon the happening of the events specified in the operating agreement or at the times determined by the members or managers pursuant to section 34–142."

It defies common sense for the defendants, who jointly comprise the "Manager," to contend that the payments they made to themselves from the assets of their LLC do not constitute distributions, simply because they never voted to order such distributions. The operating agreement requires that distributions "shall be made at such time as determined by the Manager," but does not specify any formal procedure for authorizing distributions. General Statutes § 34–142(a) require "the affirmative vote, approval or consent of * * * more than one-half by number of the managers" to decide matters connected with the LLC, but these are alternatives. The defendants can hardly deny that they approved or consented to the payments they received from the LLC, which they own and control. Neither § 34–142(a) nor General Statutes § 34–158, which authorizes distributions "at the times determined by the members or managers pursuant to section 34–142," raises any barrier to the finding of the court that the payments to the defendants constituted distributions subject to the charging order they have disregarded.

INTERPRETATION A judgment creditor of a member may obtain a charging order against the member's financial interest in the LLC, which entitles the creditor to receive the member's share of distributions.

CRITICAL THINKING QUESTION If the LLC's books and the members' tax returns had characterized the payments as wages, would the outcome of the case change? Explain.

DUTIES

As with general partnerships and limited partnerships, the duties of care and loyalty also apply to LLCs. In a number of states, the LLC statute expressly imposes these duties. In other states, the common law imposes these duties. Who has these duties in a limited liability company depends on whether the LLC is a manager-managed LLC (analogous to a limited partnership) or a member-managed LLC (analogous to a partnership).

Manager-Managed LLCs Most LLC statutes impose upon the managers of an LLC a duty of care. In some states, this is a duty to refrain from grossly negligent, reckless, or intentional conduct; in other states, it is a duty to act as a prudent person would in similar circumstances. Managers also have a fiduciary duty, although the statutes vary in how they specify that duty. Usually, members of manager-managed LLCs have no duties to the LLC or its members by reason of being a member.

Member-Managed LLCs Members of member-managed LLCs have the same duties of care and loyalty that managers have in manager-managed LLCs.

CONCEPT REVIEW

Comparison of Member-Managed and Manager-Managed LLCs

	Member of Member-Managed LLC Manager of Manager-Managed LLC	Member of Manager-Managed LLC
Control	Full	None
Liability	Limited	Limited
Agency	Is an agent of the LLC	Is not an agent of the LLC
Fiduciary Duty	Yes	No
Duty of Care	Yes	No

Practical Advice

Recognize that your rights and duties as a member of a limited liability company depend on whether the LLC is member-managed or manager-managed.

LIABILITIES

One of the most appealing features of a limited liability company is the limited personal liability it offers to all of its members and managers. Statutes typically provide that no member or manager of a limited liability company shall be obligated personally for any debt, obligation, or liability of the limited liability company solely by reason of being a member or acting as a manager of the limited liability company. The limitation on liability, however, will not affect the liability of a member or manager who committed the wrongful act giving rise to the liability. A member or manager is also personally liable for any LLC obligations guaranteed by the member or manager.

As mentioned earlier, a member who fails to make an agreed contribution is liable to the limited liability company for the deficiency. Moreover, under the great majority of statutes, any member who receives a return of her contribution in violation of the LLC's operating agreement or the limited liability company act is liable to the limited liability company for the amount of the contribution wrongfully returned. Under a few of the statutes, even members who receive a return of their capital contribution without violating the LLC agreement or the limited liability company act remain liable to the limited liability company for a specified time to the extent necessary to pay creditors.

DISSOLUTION

Limited liability company statutes generally provide that an LLC will automatically dissolve upon

1. the expiring of the LLC's agreed duration or the happening of any of the events specified in the articles,
2. the written consent of all the members, or
3. a decree of judicial dissolution.

Dissociation **Dissociation** means that a member has ceased to be associated with the company and includes voluntary withdrawal, death, incompetence, expulsion, or bankruptcy. Initially, many LLC statutes required an LLC to be dissolved upon the dissociation of a member. Most statutes permitted the nondissociating members by unanimous consent to continue the LLC after a member dissociates. Some allowed continuation by majority vote. Although some states still retain these provisions, a number of states and the amended ULLCA have eliminated a member's dissociation as a mandatory cause of dissolution.

Distribution of Assets Most statutes provide default rules for distributing the assets of a limited liability company as follows:

1. to creditors, including members and managers who are creditors, except with respect to liabilities for distributions;
2. to members and former members in satisfaction of liabilities for unpaid distributions, except as otherwise agreed;
3. to members for the return of their contributions, except as otherwise agreed; and
4. to members for their limited liability company interests in the proportions in which members share in distributions, except as otherwise agreed.

OTHER UNINCORPORATED BUSINESS ASSOCIATIONS

CPA

LIMITED LIABILITY PARTNERSHIPS

All of the states have enacted statutes enabling the formation of limited liability partnerships (LLPs). Until 1996 there was no uniform LLP statute, so the enabling statutes varied from state to state. In 1996 the Revised Uniform Partnership Act (RUPA) was amended to add provisions enabling general partnerships to elect to become limited liability partnerships, and a number of states have adopted this version of the RUPA. A registered **limited liability partnership** is a general partnership that, by making the statutorily required filing, limits the liability of its partners for some or all of the partnership's obligations.

Formalities To become an LLP, a general partnership must file with the secretary of state an application containing specified information. The RUPA requires the partnership to file a statement of qualification. Most of the statutes require only a majority of the partners to authorize registration as an LLP; others require unanimous approval. Some statutes require renewal of registrations annually; other statutes require periodic reports; and a few require no renewal. The RUPA requires filing annual reports. Some statutes require a new filing after any change in membership of the partnership, but a few of the statutes do not. The RUPA does not.

Designation All statutes require LLPs to designate themselves as such. Most statutes require the name of the LLP to include the words "limited liability partnership" or "registered limited liability partnership," or the abbreviation "LLP" or "RLLP." Most statutes provide that the laws of the jurisdiction under which a foreign LLP is registered shall govern its organization, internal affairs, and the liability and authority of its partners. Many, but not all, of the statutes require a foreign LLP to register or obtain a certificate of authenticity. The RUPA requires a foreign LLP to qualify and file annual reports.

Liability Limitation LLP statutes have taken three different approaches to limiting the liability of partners for the partnership's obligations. The earliest statutes limited liability only for negligent acts; they retain unlimited liability for all other obligations. The next generation of statutes extended limited liability to any partnership tort or contract obligation that arose from negligence, malpractice, wrongful acts, or misconduct committed by any partner, employee, or agent of the partnership. Unlimited liability remained for ordinary contract obligations, such as those owed to suppliers, lenders, and landlords. The first two generations of LLP statutes are called "partial shield" statutes. Many of the more recent statutes, including the RUPA, have provided limited liability for all debts and obligations of the partnership. These statutes are called "full shield" statutes. Many states have now adopted full shield statutes although some states still provide only a partial shield.

The statutes, however, generally provide that the limitation on liability will not affect the liability of (1) a partner who committed the wrongful act giving rise to the liability and (2) a partner who supervised the partner, employee, or agent of the partnership who committed the wrongful act. A partner is also personally liable for any partnership obligations guaranteed by the partner. The statutes also provide that the limitations on liability will apply only to claims that arise while the partnership was a registered limited liability partnership. Accordingly, partners would have unlimited liability for obligations that arose either before registration or after registration lapses.

Although limited liability company statutes provide greater protection against liability than most LLP statutes, the LLP form has attracted some businesses, especially professional firms. One advantage of the LLP is that an existing general partnership may become an LLP without forming a new organization or negotiating a new operating agreement.

Practical Advice

Professionals should consider registering their partnerships as limited liability partnerships or organizing their firms as LLPs.

LIMITED LIABILITY LIMITED PARTNERSHIPS

A **limited liability limited partnership (LLLP)** is a limited partnership in which the liability of the general partners has been limited to the same extent as in an LLP. A growing number of states allow limited partnerships to become limited liability limited partnerships. A few states have statutes expressly providing for LLLPs. In other states, by operation of the provision in the RULPA that a general partner in a limited partnership has the liabilities of a general partner in a general partnership, the LLP statute may provide limited liability to general partners in a limited partnership that registers as an LLLP under the LLP statute. When authorized, the general partners in an LLLP will obtain the same degree of liability limitation that general partners can achieve in LLPs. When

CONCEPT REVIEW

Liability Limitations in LLPs

LLP Statutes	Limited Liability	Unlimited Liability
First Generation	Negligent acts	• All other obligations • Wrongful partner • Supervising partner
Second Generation	Tort and contract obligations arising from wrongful acts	• All other obligations • Wrongful partner • Supervising partner
Third Generation	All obligations	• Wrongful partner • Supervising partner

available, a limited partnership may register as an LLLP without having to form a new organization, as would be the case in converting to an LLC.

The new revision of the RULPA promulgated in 2001 provides that a limited liability limited partnership "means a limited partnership whose certificate of limited partnership states that the limited partnership is a limited liability limited partnership." The revision provides a full shield for general partners in limited liability limited partnerships: "An obligation of a limited partnership incurred while the limited partnership is a limited liability limited partnership, whether arising in contract, tort, or otherwise, is solely the obligation of the limited partnership. A general partner is not personally liable . . . for such an obligation solely by reason of being or acting as a general partner."

CHAPTER SUMMARY

Limited Partnership

Definition of a Limited Partnership a partnership formed by two or more persons under the laws of a state and having one or more general partners and one or more limited partners

Formation a limited partnership can be formed only by substantial compliance with a state limited partnership statute

- *Filing of Certificate* two or more persons must file a signed certificate of limited partnership
- *Name* inclusion of a limited partner's surname in the partnership name in most instances will result in the loss of the limited partner's limited liability
- *Contributions* may be cash, property, services, or a promise to contribute cash, property, or services
- *Defective Formation* if no certificate is filed or if the one filed does not substantially meet the statutory requirements, the formation is defective and the limited liability of the limited partners is jeopardized
- *Foreign Limited Partnerships* a limited partnership is considered "foreign" in any state other than that in which it was formed

Rights a general partner in a limited partnership has all the rights and powers of a partner in a general partnership

- *Control* the general partners have almost exclusive control and management of the limited partnership; a limited partner who participates in the control of the limited partnership may lose limited liability
- *Voting Rights* the partnership agreement may grant to all or a specified group of general or limited partners the right to vote on any matter

- *Choice of Associates* no person may be added as a general partner or a limited partner without the consent of all partners
- *Withdrawal* a general partner may withdraw from a limited partnership at any time by giving written notice to the other partners; a limited partner may withdraw as provided in the limited partnership certificate
- *Assignment of Partnership Interest* unless otherwise provided in the partnership agreement, a partner may assign his partnership interest; an assignee may become a limited partner if all other partners consent
- *Profit and Loss Sharing* profits and losses are allocated among the partners as provided in the partnership agreement; if the partnership agreement has no such provision, then profits and losses are allocated on the basis of the contributions each partner actually made
- *Distributions* the partners share distributions of cash or other assets of a limited partnership as provided in the partnership agreement
- *Loans* both general and limited partners may be secured or unsecured creditors of the partnership
- *Information* each partner has the right to inspect and copy the partnership records
- *Derivative Actions* a limited partner may sue on behalf of a limited partnership if the general partners refuse to bring the action

Duties and Liabilities

- *Duties* general partners owe a duty of care and loyalty (fiduciary duty) to the general partners, the limited partners, and the limited partnership; limited partners do not
- *Liabilities* the general partners have unlimited liability; the limited partners have limited liability (liability for partnership obligations only to the extent of the capital that the limited partner contributed or agreed to contribute)

Dissolution

- *Causes* the limited partners have neither the right nor the power to dissolve the partnership, except by decree of the court. The following events trigger a dissolution: (1) the expiration of the time period; (2) the withdrawal of a general partner, unless all partners agree to continue the business; or (3) a decree of judicial dissolution
- *Winding Up* unless otherwise provided in the partnership agreement, the general partners who have not wrongfully dissolved the partnership may wind up its affairs
- *Distribution of Assets* the priorities for distribution are as follows: (1) creditors, including partners who are creditors; (2) partners and ex-partners in satisfaction of liabilities for unpaid distributions; (3) partners for the return of contributions, except as otherwise agreed; and (4) partners for their partnership interests in the proportions in which they share in distributions, except as otherwise agreed

Limited Liability Company

Definition a limited liability company is a noncorporate business organization that provides limited liability to all of its owners (members) and permits all of its members to participate in management of the business

Formation the formation of a limited liability company requires substantial compliance with a state's limited liability company statute

- *Filing* the LLC statutes generally require the central filing of articles of organization in a designated state office
- *Name* LLC statutes generally require the name of the LLC to include the words "limited liability company" or the abbreviation "LLC"
- *Contribution* the contribution of a member to a limited liability company may be cash, property, services rendered, a promissory note, or other obligation to contribute cash or property, or to perform services

- ***Operating Agreement*** is the basic contract governing the affairs of a limited liability company and stating the various rights and duties of the members
- ***Foreign Limited Liability Companies*** a limited liability company is considered "foreign" in any state other than that in which it was formed

Rights of Members a member's interest in the LLC includes the financial interest (the right to distributions) and the management interest (which consists of all other rights granted to a member by the LLC operating agreement and the LLC statute)

- ***Profit and Loss Sharing*** the LLC's operating agreement determines how the partners allocate the profits and losses; if the LLC's operating agreement makes no such provision, the profits and losses are typically allocated on the basis of the value of the members' contributions
- ***Distributions*** the members share distributions of cash or other assets of a limited liability company as provided in the operating agreement; if the LLC's operating agreement does not allocate distributions, they are typically made on the basis of the contributions each member made
- ***Withdrawal*** a member may withdraw and demand payment of her interest upon giving the notice specified in the statute or the LLC's operating agreement
- ***Management*** in the absence of a contrary agreement, each member has equal rights in the management of the LLC; but LLCs may be managed by one or more managers who may be members
- ***Voting*** LLC statutes usually specify the voting rights of members, subject to a contrary provision in an LLC's operating agreement
- ***Derivative Actions*** a member has the right to bring an action on behalf of a limited liability company to recover a judgment in its favor if the managers or members with authority to bring the action have refused to do so
- ***Assignment of LLC Interest*** unless otherwise provided in the LLC's operating agreement, a member may assign his financial interest in the LLC; an assignee of a financial interest in an LLC may acquire the other rights by being admitted as a member of the company if all the remaining members consent or the operating agreement so provides

Duties

- ***Manager-managed LLCs*** the managers of manager-managed LLCs have a duty of care and loyalty; usually, members of a manager-managed LLC have no duties to the LLC or its members by reason of being a member
- ***Member-managed LLCs*** members of member-managed LLCs have the same duties of care and loyalty that managers have in manager-managed LLCs

Liabilities no member or manager of a limited liability company is obligated personally for any debt, obligation, or liability of the limited liability company solely by reason of being a member or acting as a manager of the limited liability company

Dissolution an LLC will automatically dissolve upon (1) in some states the dissociation of a member, (2) the expiration of the LLC's agreed duration or the happening of any of the events specified in the articles, (3) the written consent of all the members, or (4) a decree of judicial dissolution

- ***Dissociation*** means that a member has ceased to be associated with the company and includes voluntary withdrawal, death, incompetence, expulsion, or bankruptcy
- ***Distribution of Assets*** the default rules for distributing the assets of a limited liability company are (1) to creditors, including members and managers who are creditors, except with respect to liabilities for distributions; (2) to members and former members in satisfaction of liabilities for unpaid distributions, except as otherwise agreed; (3) to members for the return of their contributions, except as otherwise agreed; and (4) to members for their limited liability company interests in the proportions in which members share in distributions, except as otherwise agreed

Other Unincorporated Business Associations

Limited Liability Partnership is a general partnership that, by making the statutorily required filing, limits the liability of its partners for some or all of the partnership's obligations

- *Formalities* most statutes require only a majority of the partners to authorize registration as an LLP; others require unanimous approval
- *Designation* the name of the LLP must include the words "limited liability partnership" or "registered limited liability partnership," or the abbreviation "LLP"
- *Liability Limitation* some statutes limit liability only for negligent acts; others limit liability to any partnership tort or contract obligation that arose from negligence, malpractice, wrongful acts, or misconduct committed by any partner, employee, or agent of the partnership; many provide limited liability for all debts and obligations of the partnership

Limited Liability Limited Partnership is a limited partnership in which the liability of the general partners has been limited to the same extent as in an LLP

QUESTIONS

1. John Palmer and Henry Morrison formed the limited partnership of Palmer & Morrison for the management of the Huntington Hotel. The limited partnership agreement provided that Palmer would contribute $40,000 and be a general partner and that Morrison would contribute $30,000 and be a limited partner. Palmer was to manage the dining and cocktail rooms, and Morrison was to manage the rest of the hotel. Nanette, a popular French singer who knew nothing of the limited partnership affairs, appeared for four weeks in the Blue Room at the hotel and was not paid her fee of $8,000. Subsequently, the limited partnership became insolvent. Nanette sued Palmer and Morrison for $8,000.
   a. For how much, if anything, are Palmer and Morrison liable?
   b. If Palmer and Morrison had formed a limited liability limited partnership, for how much, if anything, would Palmer and Morrison be liable?
   c. If Palmer and Morrison had formed a limited liability company with each as members, for how much, if anything, would Palmer and Morrison be liable?
   d. If Palmer and Morrison had formed a limited liability partnership with each as general partners, for how much, if anything, would Palmer and Morrison be liable?

2. A limited partnership was formed consisting of Webster as the general partner and Stevens and Stewart as the limited partners. The limited partnership was organized in strict compliance with the limited partnership statute. Stevens was employed by the partnership as a purchasing agent. Stewart personally guaranteed a loan made to the partnership. Both Stevens and Stewart consulted with Webster about partnership business, voted on a change in the nature of the partnership business, and disapproved an amendment to the partnership agreement proposed by Webster. The partnership experienced serious financial difficulties, and its creditors seek to hold Webster, Stevens, and Stewart personally liable for the debts of the partnership. Who, if any, is personally liable?

3. Fox, Dodge, and Gilbey agreed to become limited partners in Palatine Ventures, a limited partnership. The certificate of limited partnership stated that each would contribute $20,000. Fox's contribution consisted entirely of cash; Dodge contributed $12,000 in cash and gave the partnership her promissory note for $8,000; and Gilbey's contribution was his promise to perform 500 hours of legal services for the partnership
   a. What liability, if any, do Fox, Dodge, and Gilbey have to the partnership by way of capital contribution?
   b. If Palatine Ventures had been formed as a limited liability company with Fox, Dodge, and Gilbey as members, what liability, if any, would Fox, Dodge, and Gilbey have to the LLC by way of capital contribution?

4. Madison and Tilson agree to form a limited partnership with Madison as general partner and Tilson as the limited partner, each to contribute $12,500 as capital. No papers are ever filed, and after ten months the enterprise fails with liabilities exceeding assets by $30,000. Creditors of the partnership seek to hold Madison and Tilson personally liable for the $30,000. Explain whether the creditors will prevail.

5. Kraft is a limited partner of Johnson Enterprises, a limited partnership. As provided in the limited partnership agreement, Kraft decided to leave the partnership and demanded that her capital contribution of $20,000 be returned. At this time, the partnership assets were $150,000 and liabilities to all creditors totaled $140,000. The partnership returned to Kraft her capital contribution of $20,000.
   a. What liability, if any, does Kraft have to the creditors of Johnson Enterprises?

b. If Johnson Enterprises had been formed as a limited liability company, what liability, if any, would Kraft have to the creditors of Johnson Enterprises?

6. Gordon is the only limited partner in Bushmill Ventures, a limited partnership whose general partners are Daniels and McKenna. Gordon contributed $10,000 for his limited partnership interest and loaned the partnership $7,500. Daniels and McKenna each contributed $5,000 by way of capital. After a year, the partnership is dissolved, at which time it owes $12,500 to its only creditor, Dickel, and has assets of $30,000.
   a. How should these assets be distributed?
   b. If Bushmill Ventures had been formed as a limited liability company with Gordon, Daniels, and McKenna as members, how should these assets be distributed?

7. Albert, Betty, and Carol own and operate the Roy Lumber Company, a limited liability partnership. Each contributed one-third of the capital, and they share equally in the profits and losses. Their LLP agreement provides that all purchases over $500 must be authorized in advance by two partners and that only Albert is authorized to draw checks. Unknown to Albert or Carol, Betty purchases on the firm's account a $2,500 diamond bracelet and a $5,000 forklift and orders $2,000 worth of logs, all from Doug, who operates a jewelry store and is engaged in various activities connected with the lumber business. Before Betty made these purchases, Albert told Doug that Betty is not the log buyer. Albert refuses to pay Doug for Betty's purchases. Doug calls at the mill to collect, and Albert again refuses to pay him. Doug calls Albert an unprintable name, and Albert then punches Doug in the nose, knocking him out. While Doug is lying unconscious on the ground, an employee of Roy Lumber Company negligently drops a log on Doug's leg, breaking three bones. The firm and the three partners are completely solvent.

   What are the rights of Doug against Roy Lumber Company, Albert, Betty, and Carol?

CASE PROBLEMS

8. Dr. Vidricksen contributed $25,000 to become a limited partner in a Chevrolet car agency business with Thom, the general partner. Articles of limited partnership were drawn up, but no effort was made to comply with the state's statutory requirement of recording the certificate of limited partnership. In March, Vidricksen learned that, because of the failure to file, he might not have formed a limited partnership. At this time, the business developed financial difficulties and went into bankruptcy on September 11. Eight days later, Vidricksen filed a renunciation of the business's profits. Is Dr. Vidricksen a general partner?

9. Weil organized Diversified Properties as a limited partnership with varying degrees of ownership in several apartment complexes and other real estate located in Maryland. The parties signed a formal written agreement in July, and the partnership was properly registered in the District of Columbia. Weil was the only general partner and managed the partnership's affairs until May 1 of the following year. At that time, the partnership encountered cash flow problems; and, to help matters, Weil gave up both his office and his salary. At a partnership meeting held the following week, two third parties, Rubenstein and Tempchin, were selected by the limited partners to manage the partnership properties on a commission basis in accordance with a proposal that Weil had advanced earlier. Weil began working for another real estate company as a vice president, but he remained a general partner of Diversified Properties. Creditors of the partnership, therefore, turned to him with demands for payment of the partnership debts that had not been met. Weil claims that after he surrendered his office and his salary, he remained as the general partner but that his directions were ignored. He also claims that the limited partners at various times gave direct orders to Rubenstein and Tempchin as to how to manage the partnership's affairs. Explain whether the limited partners should be declared general partners.

10. Dale Fullerton was chairman of the board of Envirosearch and the sole stockholder in Westover Hills Management. James Anderson was president of AGFC. Fullerton and Anderson agreed to form a limited partnership to purchase certain property from WYORCO, a joint venture of which Fullerton was a member. The parties intended to form a limited partnership with Westover Hills Management as the sole general partner and AGFC and Envirosearch as limited partners. The certificate filed with the Wyoming secretary of state, however, listed all three companies as both general and limited partners of Westover Hills Ltd. Anderson and Fullerton later became aware of this error and filed an amended certificate of limited partnership, which correctly named Envirosearch and AGFC as limited partners only. Subsequently Westover Hills Ltd. became insolvent. What is the potential liability of Envirosearch and AGFC to creditors of the limited partnership?

http:// **Internet Exercise** Find and review information about (a) limited partnerships and (b) limited liability companies.

Chapter 34

Nature and Formation of Corporations

A corporation is an artificial being, invisible, intangible, and existing only in contemplation of law.

CHIEF JUSTICE JOHN MARSHALL, 1819

Learning Objectives

After reading this chapter you should be able to:

1. Identify the principal attributes and classifications of corporations.
2. Explain how a corporation is formed and the role, liability, and duties of promoters.
3. Distinguish between the statutory and common law approaches to defective formation of a corporation.
4. Explain how the doctrine of piercing the corporate veil applies to closely held corporations and parent-subsidiary corporations.
5. Identify the sources of corporate powers and explain the legal consequences of a corporation's exceeding its powers.

A corporation is an entity created by law that exists separately and distinctly from the individuals whose contributions of initiative, property, and control enable it to function. The corporation is the dominant form of business organization in the United States, accounting for 85 percent of the gross revenues of all business entities. Five million domestic corporations are currently doing business in the United States, with annual revenues and assets approaching 20 trillion dollars. See Figure 31-1 in Chapter 31. Approximately 50 percent of American adults own stock directly or indirectly through institutional investors such as mutual funds, pension funds, banks, and insurance companies. Corporations have achieved this dominance because their attributes of limited liability, free transferability of shares, and continuity have attracted great numbers of widespread investors. Moreover, the centralized management of corporations has facilitated the development of large organizations that employ great quantities of invested capital, thereby taking advantage of economies of scale.

Use of the corporation as an instrument of commercial enterprise has made possible the vast concentrations of wealth and capital that have largely transformed this country's economy from an agrarian to an industrial one. Due to its size, power, and impact, the business corporation is a key institution not only in the American economy but also in the world power structure.

In 1946, a committee of the American Bar Association, after careful study and research, submitted a draft of a Model Business Corporation Act (MBCA). The Model Act has been amended frequently since then. Its provisions do not become law until a state enacts them, but the influence of the act has been widespread: a majority of the states adopted it in whole or in part.

In 1984, the Revised Model Business Corporation Act (RMBCA) was promulgated. More than half of the states have adopted it in whole or in part. The Revised Act, as amended, will be used throughout the chapters on corporations in this text and will be referred to as the Revised Act or the RMBCA. Appendix E contains selected provisions of the RMBCA, as amended.

http:// State incorporation statutes: http://www.law.cornell.edu/topics/state_statutes.html#corporations

NATURE OF CORPORATIONS

A corporation is a **creature of the state**: it may be formed only by substantial compliance with a state incorporation statute. To understand corporations, it is helpful to examine the various types of corporations and their common attributes. We will discuss both of these topics in this section.

CPA CORPORATE ATTRIBUTES

These are the principal attributes of a corporation: (1) it is a legal entity; (2) it provides limited liability to its shareholders; (3) its shares of stock are freely transferable; (4) its existence may be perpetual; (5) its management is centralized; and it is considered, for some purposes, (6) a person and (7) a citizen. See the first Concept Review in Chapter 31.

LEGAL ENTITY

A corporation is a **legal entity** separate from its shareholders, with rights and liabilities entirely distinct from theirs. It may sue or be sued by, as well as contract with, any other party, including any one of its shareholders. A transfer of stock in the corporation from one individual to another has no effect on the legal existence of the corporation. Title to corporate property belongs not to the shareholders but to the corporation. Even where a single individual owns all of the stock of the corporation, the shareholder and the corporation have distinct existences.

LIMITED LIABILITY

A corporation is a legal entity and is therefore liable out of its own assets for its debts. Generally, the shareholders have **limited liability** for the corporation's debts—their liability does not extend beyond the amount of their investment—although later in this chapter we will discuss certain circumstances under which a shareholder may be personally liable. The limitation on liability, however, will not affect the liability of a shareholder who committed the wrongful act giving rise to the liability. A shareholder is also personally liable for any corporate obligations guaranteed by the shareholder.

FREE TRANSFERABILITY OF CORPORATE SHARES

In the absence of contractual restrictions, shares in a corporation may be freely transferred by sale, gift, or pledge. The ability to transfer shares is a valuable right and may enhance their market value. Article 8 of the Uniform Commercial Code, Investment Securities, governs transfers of shares of stock.

PERPETUAL EXISTENCE

A corporation has **perpetual existence** unless otherwise stated in its articles of incorporation. Consequently, the death, withdrawal, or addition of a shareholder, director, or officer does not terminate its existence. A corporation's existence will terminate upon its dissolution or merger into another business.

CENTRALIZED MANAGEMENT

The shareholders of a corporation elect a board of directors that manages the business affairs of the corporation. The board must then appoint officers to run the day-to-day operations of the business. Because neither the directors nor the officers (collectively referred to as "management") need be shareholders, it is entirely possible, and in large corporations quite typical, for the ownership of the corporation to be separate from its management. We will discuss the management structure of corporations in Chapter 36.

AS A PERSON

Whether a corporation is a "person" within the meaning of a constitution or statute is a matter of construction based on the intent of the lawmakers in using the word. For example, a corporation is considered a person within the provisions in the Fifth and Fourteenth Amendments to the U.S. Constitution that no "person" shall be "deprived of life, liberty, or property, without due process of law" and in the Fourteenth Amendment provision that no state shall "deny to any person within its jurisdiction the equal protection of the laws." A corporation also enjoys the right of a person to be secure against unreasonable searches and seizures, as provided for in the Fourth Amendment. On the other hand, a corporation is not considered to be a person within the Fifth Amendment clause that protects a "person" against self-incrimination.

As a Citizen

A corporation is considered a citizen for some purposes but not for others. For instance, a corporation is not a citizen as the term is used in the Fourteenth Amendment, which provides, "No state shall make or enforce any law which shall abridge the privileges or immunities of citizens of the United States."

A corporation is, however, regarded as a citizen of the state of its incorporation and of the state in which it has its principal office for the purpose of determining whether diversity of citizenship exists between the parties to a lawsuit, so as to provide a basis for federal court jurisdiction.

CPA Classification of Corporations

Corporations may be classified as public or private, profit or nonprofit, domestic or foreign, publicly held or closely held, subchapter S, and professional. As you will see, these classifications are not mutually exclusive. For example, a corporation may be a closely held, professional, private, profit, domestic corporation.

Public or Private

A **public corporation** is one that is created to administer a unit of local civil government, such as a county, city, town, village, school district, or park district, or one created by the United States to conduct public business, such as the Tennessee Valley Authority or the Federal Deposit Insurance Corporation. A public corporation is usually created by specific legislation, which determines the corporation's purpose and powers. Many public corporations are also referred to as municipal corporations.

A **private corporation** is founded by and composed of private persons for private purposes and has no governmental duties. A private corporation may be for profit or nonprofit.

Profit or Nonprofit

A **profit corporation** is one founded for the purpose of operating a business for profit from which payments are made to the corporation's shareholders in the form of dividends.

Although a **nonprofit** (or not-for-profit) **corporation** may make a profit, the profit may not be distributed to its members, directors, or officers but must be used exclusively for the charitable, educational, or scientific purpose for which the corporation was organized. Most states have special incorporation statutes governing nonprofit corporations, most of which are patterned after the Model Nonprofit Corporation Act.

http://

Center for Non-Profit Corporations: http://www.njnonprofits.org/index2.html
National Association of Non-Profit Associations: http://www.ncna.org/

Domestic or Foreign

A corporation is a **domestic corporation** in the state in which it is incorporated. It is a **foreign corporation** in every other state or jurisdiction. A corporation may not do business, except for acts in interstate commerce, in a state other than the state of its incorporation without the permission and authorization of the other state. Every state, however, provides for the issuance of certificates of authority, which allow foreign corporations to do business within its borders, and for the taxation of such foreign businesses. Obtaining a certificate (or "qualifying") usually involves filing certain information with the secretary of state, paying prescribed fees, and designating a resident agent. Conduct typically requiring a certificate of authority includes maintaining an office to conduct local intrastate business, selling personal property not in interstate commerce, entering into contracts relating to local business or sales, and owning or using real estate for general corporate purposes. A single agreement or isolated transaction within a state does not constitute doing business.

A foreign corporation that transacts business without having first qualified may be subject to a number of penalties. Most statutes provide that an unlicensed foreign corporation doing business in the state shall not be entitled to maintain a suit in a state court until it has obtained a certificate of authority. However, the failure to obtain a certificate of authority to transact business in the state does not impair the validity of a contract entered into by the corporation and does not prevent it from defending any action or proceeding brought against it in the state. In addition, many states impose fines on corporations that do not obtain certificates, and a few states also impose fines on the corporation's officers and directors, as well as holding them personally liable on contracts made within the state.

MANAGERIAL insight

Why Delaware?

If you owned a business and wanted to operate it as a corporation, in what state would you incorporate? Wouldn't you choose your home state?

Then why are the following companies incorporated in Delaware, even though their headquarters are elsewhere?

- McDonald's (Oak Brook, Illinois)
- Wal-Mart (Bentonville, Arkansas)
- Microsoft (Redmond, Washington)
- Ford (Dearborn, Michigan)

Since World War I, Delaware has been the favorite state of incorporation, and many Fortune 500 companies are its citizens. (Many actually reincorporated there.) This situation did not come about by accident. Corporations are chartered by the states, not by the federal government, and laws of incorporation vary significantly from state to state. New Jersey, for example, was the favorite domicile of large corporations early in the twentieth century, but later fell behind Delaware, partly because it failed to update its corporation laws often enough.

Delaware purposely has made itself attractive to corporations, and the reason is money. Franchise taxes paid by Delaware corporations are a very significant source of income for that small state. The preamble to the 1963 revision of the Delaware General Corporation Law plainly acknowledges this fact:

> The favorable climate which the State of Delaware has traditionally provided for corporations has been a leading source of revenue for the State; . . . the General Assembly of the State of Delaware declares it to be the public policy of the State to maintain a favorable business climate and to encourage corporations to make Delaware their domicile. . . .

Delaware has long offered an incorporation law that favors management. And over the years Delaware's General Assembly has revised and amended the Delaware General Corporation Law to keep it attractive to corporate managements. (Remember that laws of incorporation also should protect the rights of shareholders and creditors.) In addition, the Delaware law is considered to be both clear and up to date.

Delaware's courts, which have been characterized as "a judiciary of corporate specialists," are another significant attraction. Delaware judges have created a large body of case law that is "well-settled law with unique predictability" and that allows corporations to be flexible in their operations.

Specifically, a few of the advantages of Delaware incorporation are as follows:

- incorporating is quick and easy;
- fees and taxes are moderate;
- the only specification the state sets for purposes of incorporation is that they be lawful;
- there is no minimum capital requirement, and shares may be issued for cash, property, or services;
- provisions allow a single incorporator and a single director;
- directors have no residence requirements, and directors' and shareholders' meetings expressly may be held outside of Delaware;
- directors and officers are indemnified more liberally than in other states;
- the charter may limit or eliminate the personal liability of directors to the corporation or its shareholders;
- there are restrictions on shareholders' derivative actions;
- voting trusts are authorized; and
- there are broad provisions for mergers and consolidations.

Today, other states share many of Delaware's favorable provisions, but none has had so many for so long. And Delaware's great body of legal precedents has helped to give the state a head start that is hard to overcome.

Sources: William L. Cary and Melvin Aron Eisenberg, *Cases and Materials on Corporations*, 7th ed., 1988, 125–132; Alfred F. Conard, Robert L. Knauss, and Stanley Siegel, *Enterprise Organization*, 1987, 527; Harry G. Henn and John R. Alexander, *Laws of Corporations*, 1983, 186–201; and Detlev F. Vagts, *Basic Corporation Law*, 1989, 77.

Tiller Construction Corp. v. Nadler

Court of Appeals of Maryland, 1994
334 Md. 1, 637 A.2d 1183

FACTS Ronald Nadler was a resident of Maryland and the chief executive officer of Glenmar Cinestate, Inc., a Maryland corporation, as well as its principal, if not only, stockholder. Glenmar leased certain space in the Westridge Square Shopping Center, located in Frederick, Maryland, and in Cranberry Mall, located in Westminster, Maryland. Tiller Construction Corporation and Nadler entered into two contracts for the construction of movie theaters at these locations, one calling for Tiller to do "the work" for Nadler at Westridge for $637,000, and the other for Tiller to do "the work" for Nadler at Cranberry for $688,800. Ronald Nadler requested that Tiller send all bills to Glenmar, the lessee at both shopping malls, but agreed to be personally liable to Tiller for the payment of both contracts.

At the time of the suit, there was a net balance due for the Cranberry project in the amount of $229,799.46, and on the Westridge project for the sum of $264,273.85, which Nadler refused to pay, even though he had approved all work and the work had been performed in a timely, good, and workmanlike manner. Tiller Construction Corporation sued Ronald Nadler and Glenmar Cinestate, Inc., for breach of contract in the amounts due under the Cranberry and Westridge contracts.

Nadler submitted a motion to dismiss based on § 7–301 of Maryland's business corporation statute. This section prohibits foreign corporations that conduct intrastate business in Maryland but fail to register or qualify under Maryland law from maintaining a suit in Maryland courts. Nadler asserted that Tiller was a New York corporation that has never qualified to transact business in the state of Maryland. Tiller conceded that the corporation had not qualified to do business in Maryland but argued that Tiller was not required to qualify because its activities did not constitute, in the contemplation of the statute, doing business in the state as Tiller just had occasional business in Maryland. Nadler countered by asserting that the two separate contracts to build movie theaters, each "in excess of one-half million dollars," involved the employment of a substantial number of subcontractors (most of whom were Maryland subcontractors), the maintaining of a supervisor on each job, and the opening of Maryland bank accounts. The trial court granted Nadler's motion to dismiss.

DECISION Judgment affirmed.

OPINION Orth, Jr., J. In *Snavely, Inc. v. Wheeler*, the Court of Special Appeals * * * made a thorough analysis of the principles that have been applied to determine when a foreign corporation is doing intrastate business in Maryland. Judge Bell concluded:

> The appellate decisions of this State make clear that "a foreign corporation is doing business within a state when it transacts some substantial part of its ordinary business therein." [Citations.]
>
> * * *
>
> [Citation.] "Where," however,
>
> the corporation does not engage in significant business activity in Maryland, § 7–301 has been interpreted to permit a corporation to maintain an action in the courts of this State even though it has neither registered nor qualified. [Citation.]
>
> * * *
>
> Mere solicitation, even if accompanied by activities directly related to the solicitation, including interstate delivery of the goods into the state, is not sufficient to constitute "doing business"; however, solicitation, accompanied by the shipment of goods and an extensive set of activities or management functions in the state, is. [Citations.]
>
> * * *
>
> Whether the acts engaged in by the foreign corporation are sufficient to constitute "doing business" must be determined from the facts of each case, with particular emphasis on the nature and extent of the business and activities occurring in the forum state. [Citations.]
>
> Among the factors to be considered are: (1) whether the foreign corporation pays state taxes; (2) whether it maintains property, an office, telephone listings, employees, agents, inventory, research and development facilities, advertising and bank accounts in the state; (3) whether it makes contracts in the state; and (4) whether its management functions in the state are pervasive. [Citation.]

* * *

The [trial] judge recognized that the burden of proving that an unqualified foreign corporation is doing business in this State is upon the party presenting that defense, * * * [citation]. He observed that Maryland's foreign corporation law

> is not unique to the State of Maryland. It is done all over the United States. Frankly, [Maryland's provisions] I think [are] based on the Model Business Corporation Act, * * * so there is nothing really unique about Maryland's statutes, either.

* * *

The trial judge looked at the facts in the light of the factors designated in *Snavely*, which may be considered in determining whether Tiller was doing business in Maryland, as he found those facts to be from the evidence before him. As to taxes:

> To the extent that there were contracts made with local suppliers, that sales taxes were paid in this State.
>
> [All] inventory was, in fact, local. According to Mr. Tiller, it was all bought locally and paid for locally, and the tax paid locally as well.

As to an office and telephones:

> While there was no office maintained here, there was a motel room leased for a considerable period of time. There was presence of the corporation for up to five months. There was, while no, as I said, formal office,

there was a sign on the job site and telephones listed in information.

As to management functions and bank accounts:

> There was no substantial advertising in the State, although there was, in fact, a bank account that was maintained in the State. There were, in fact, fairly pervasive management functions in terms of these two projects. That, in fact, was what the general contractor was engaged to do.

As to the amount of Tiller's business which was conducted in Maryland:

> The fact of the matter is that for the five-month period or so that Tiller Construction was on the job in Maryland, the value of the projects in question was far better than 50 percent of its income during that period of time based on the testimony given yesterday.

Mr. Tiller indicated that these two projects alone were in excess of $1 million. He mentioned a project in Detroit and another in New York State. Whatever it was, it was a substantial part, whatever the exact percentage, of the revenues of the corporation in that time frame.

The judge rejected Tiller's notion that "there must be a continuing course of conduct, and that coming in and even doing all these things is not sufficient to cause the corporation to be found to be doing business for purposes of having to qualify." The judge declared:

> What we have here, essentially, is a builder coming in from a foreign jurisdiction to basically construct two projects of some substance over a five-month period, all aspects of the project. They contract for services, as defense counsel points out, to buy supplies here, to manage, to basically set up shop here, whether or not you have a desk and chair or office, but basically to do all the operations in this case.

INTERPRETATION A foreign corporation must obtain a certificate of authority in every state in which it conducts intrastate business.

ETHICAL QUESTION Is the court's decision fair to all the parties? Explain.

CRITICAL THINKING QUESTION Do you agree with the test for doing business within a state? Explain.

PUBLICLY HELD OR CLOSELY HELD

A **publicly held corporation** is one whose shares are owned by a large number of people and are widely traded. There is no accepted minimum number of shareholders, but any corporation required to register under the federal Securities and Exchange Act of 1934 is considered to be publicly held. In addition, corporations that have issued securities subject to a registered public distribution under the federal Securities Act of 1933 are also usually considered publicly held. (The federal securities laws are discussed in Chapter 40.)

A **closely held corporation** (or close corporation) is one whose outstanding shares of stock are held by a small number of persons, frequently relatives or friends. In most closely held corporations, the shareholders are active in the management and control of the business. Accordingly, the shareholders, concerned about the identities of their fellow shareholders, frequently restrict the transfer of shares in order to prevent "outsiders" from obtaining the stock. Although a vast majority of corporations in the United States are closely held, they account for only a small fraction of corporate revenues and assets.

In most states, closely held corporations are subject to the general incorporation statute that governs all corporations. The Revised Act includes a number of liberalizing provisions for closely held corporations. In addition, about twenty states have enacted special legislation to accommodate the needs of closely held corporations, and a Statutory Close Corporation Supplement to the Model and Revised Acts was promulgated.

The Supplement applies only to an eligible corporation (one having fewer than fifty shareholders) that elects statutory close corporation status. A corporation may voluntarily terminate statutory close corporation status. We will discuss other provisions of the Supplement in this and other chapters.

In 1991 the Revised Act was amended to authorize shareholders in closely held corporations to adopt unanimous shareholders' agreements that depart from the statutory norms by altering (1) the governance of the corporation, (2) the allocation of the economic return from the business, and (3) other aspects of the relationship among shareholders, directors, and the corporation. Such a shareholder agreement is valid for ten years unless the agreement provides otherwise but terminates automatically if the corporation's shares become publicly traded. Moreover, shareholder agreements bind only the shareholders and the corporation; they do not bind the state, creditors, or other third parties. These provisions will be discussed in this and other chapters.

> **Practical Advice**
>
> If you take a minority interest in a closely held corporation, attempt to provide adequate protection for your rights in the corporation's charter and bylaws as well as in shareholder agreements.

SUBCHAPTER S CORPORATION

Subchapter S of the Internal Revenue Code permits a **corporation** meeting specified requirements to elect to be taxed essentially as though it were a partnership. (Approximately one-half of all corporations in the United States are subchapter S corporations.) Under subchapter S, a corporation's income is taxed only once at the individual shareholder level. The requirements for a corporation to elect subchapter S treatment are (1) it must be a domestic corporation; (2) it must have no more than 75 shareholders; (3) each shareholder must be an individual, not a business entity; (4) no shareholder may be a nonresident alien; and (5) it may have only one class of stock, although classes of common stock differing only in voting rights are permitted.

PROFESSIONAL CORPORATIONS

All of the states have **professional** association or **corporation** statutes that permit duly licensed professionals to practice in the corporate form. Some statutes apply to all professions licensed to practice within the state, whereas others apply only to specified professions. There is a Model Professional Corporation Supplement to the MBCA.

FORMATION OF A CORPORATION

The formation of a corporation under a general incorporation statute requires action by various groups, individuals, and state officials.

CPA ORGANIZING THE CORPORATION

The procedure to organize a corporation begins with the promotion of the proposed corporation by its organizers, also known as promoters, who procure offers by interested persons, known as subscribers, to buy stock in the corporation, once created, and who also prepare the necessary incorporation papers. The incorporators then execute the articles of incorporation and file them with the secretary of state, who issues the charter or certificate of incorporation. Finally, the parties hold an organizational meeting.

PROMOTERS

A **promoter** is a person who takes the preliminary steps to organize a corporation. The promoter arranges for the capital and financing of the corporation; assembles the necessary assets, equipment, licenses, personnel, leases, and services; and attends to the actual legal formation of the corporation. On incorporation, the promoter's organizational task is finished.

Promoters' Contracts In addition to procuring subscriptions and preparing the incorporation papers, promoters often enter into contracts in anticipation of the creation of the corporation. The contracts may be ordinary agreements necessary for the eventual operation of the business, such as leases, purchase orders, employment contracts, sales contracts, or franchises. If the promoter executes these contracts in her own name and there is no further action, the promoter is liable on such contracts; the corporation, when created, is not liable. Moreover, a preincorporation contract made by a promoter in the name of the corporation and on its behalf does not bind the corporation. Before its formation, a corporation has no capacity to enter into contracts or to employ agents or representatives. After its formation, it is not liable at common law on any prior contract, even one made in its name, unless it adopts the contract expressly, impliedly, or by knowingly accepting benefits under it.

A promoter who enters into a preincorporation contract in the name of the corporation usually remains liable on that contract even if the corporation adopts it. This liability results from the rule of agency law stating that a principal, in order to be able to ratify a contract, must be in existence when the contract is made. A promoter will be relieved of liability, however, if the contract itself provides that adoption shall terminate the promoter's liability or if the promoter, the third party, and the corporation enter into a novation substituting the corporation for the promoter.

Figure 34-1 summarizes the liability of the promoter and the corporation for preincorporation contracts made in the corporation's name.

Figure 34-1
Promoters' Preincorporation Contracts Made in Corporation's Name

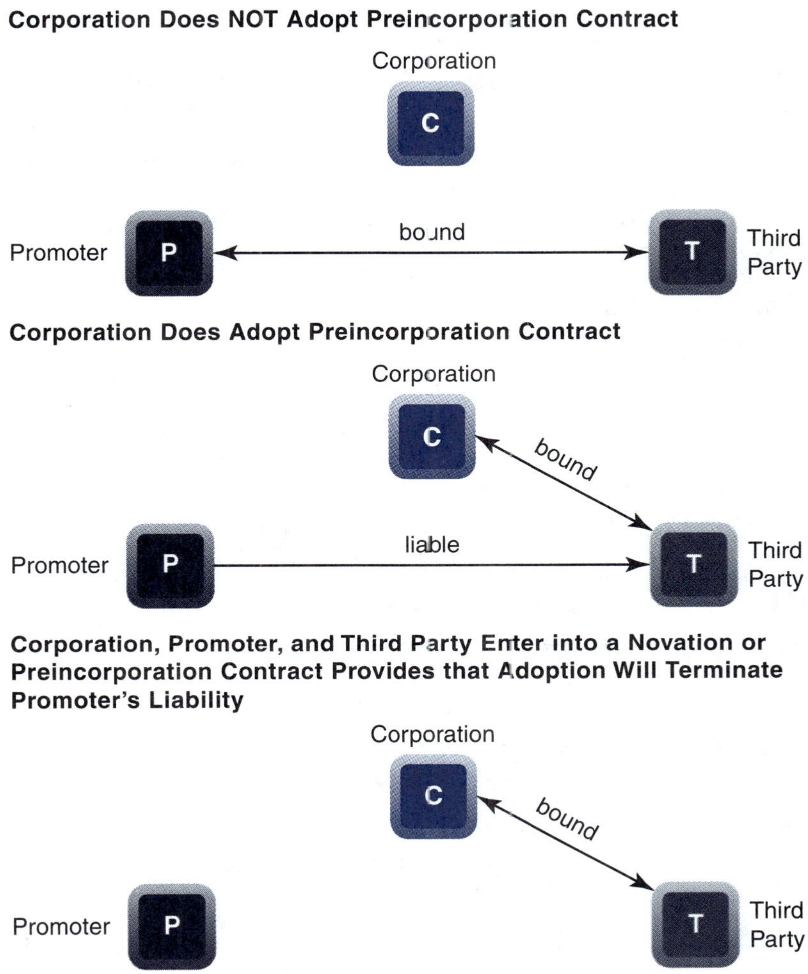

Coopers & Lybrand v. Fox

Colorado Court of Appeals, Division IV, 1988
758 P.2d 683

FACTS Fox met with a representative of Coopers & Lybrand (C&L) **(http://www.pwcglobal.com)**, a national accounting firm, to obtain accounting services. Fox informed C&L that he was acting on behalf of a corporation he was in the process of forming, to be called "G. Fox and Partners, Inc." C&L accepted the engagement with the knowledge that the corporation was not yet in existence. C&L completed the assignment and billed Fox for a reasonable fee of $10,827. When neither Fox nor G. Fox and Partners, Inc., paid, C&L sued Fox for breach of express and implied contracts based on a theory of promoter liability. Fox insisted that he was acting as an agent for the future corporation. The trial court ruled for Fox after determining that there was no agreement that would obligate Fox individually to pay the fee. C&L appealed.

DECISION Judgment for Coopers & Lybrand.

OPINION Kelly, C. J. As a preliminary matter, we reject Fox's argument that he was acting only as an agent for the future corporation. One cannot act as the agent of a nonexistent principal. [Citation.]

On the contrary, the uncontroverted facts place Fox squarely within the definition of a promoter. A promoter is one who, alone or with others, undertakes to form a corporation and to procure for it the rights, instrumentalities, and capital to enable it to conduct business. [Citations.]

When Fox first approached Coopers, he was in the process of forming G. Fox and Partners, Inc. He engaged Coopers' services for the future corporation's benefit. In addition, though not dispositive on the issue of his status as a promoter, Fox became the president, a director, and the principal shareholder of the corporation, which he funded, only nominally, with a $100 contribution. Under these circumstances, Fox cannot deny his role as a promoter.

Coopers asserts that the trial court erred in finding that Fox was under no obligation to pay Coopers' fee in the absence of an agreement that he would be personally liable. We agree.

As a general rule, promoters are personally liable for the contracts they make, though made on behalf of a corporation to be formed. [Citation.] The well-recognized exception to the general rule of promoter liability is that if the contracting party knows the corporation is not in existence but nevertheless agrees to look solely to the corporation and not to the promoter for payment, then the promoter incurs no personal liability. [Citations.] In the absence of an express agreement, the existence of an agreement to release the promoter from liability may be shown by circumstances making it reasonably certain that the parties intended to and did enter into the agreement. [Citations.]

Here, the trial court found there was no agreement, either express or implied, regarding Fox's liability. Thus, in the absence of an agreement releasing him from liability, Fox is liable.

INTERPRETATION A promoter is personally liable for the contracts he makes on behalf of a future corporation unless there is an agreement releasing him from liability.

CRITICAL THINKING QUESTION Do you agree that a promoter should be liable when the corporation adopts a preincorporation contract? Explain.

Practical Advice

As a promoter, obtain the agreement of the third party that the corporation's adoption of a preincorporation contract will terminate your liability; as a third party, carefully consider whether you should agree to such a provision.

Promoters' Fiduciary Duty The promoters of a corporation have a fiduciary relationship among themselves as well as with the corporation, its subscribers, and its initial shareholders. This duty requires good faith, fair dealing, and full disclosure to an independent board of directors. If an independent board has not been elected, full disclosure must be made to all shareholders. Accordingly, the promoters are under a duty to account for any secret profit they realize. Failure to disclose may also violate federal or state securities laws.

SUBSCRIBERS

A **subscriber** is a person who agrees to purchase stock in a corporation. A **preincorporation subscription** is an offer to purchase capital stock in a corporation yet to be formed. Courts traditionally have viewed such subscriptions in one of two ways. The majority regards a subscription as a continuing offer to purchase stock from a nonexisting entity incapable of accepting the offer until it exists. Under this view, a subscription may be revoked at any time prior to its acceptance. By comparison, a minority of jurisdictions treat a subscription as a contract among the various subscribers, making the subscription irrevocable except with all of the subscribers' consent. Modern incorporation statutes have adopted an intermediate position. For example, the Revised Act provides that a preincorporation subscription is irrevocable for six months, unless the subscription agreement provides a different period or all of the subscribers consent to the revocation. If the corporation accepts the subscription during the period of irrevocability, the subscription becomes a contract binding on both the subscriber and the corporation.

Practical Advice

As a preincorporation subscriber, consider how long you are willing to have your subscription be irrevocable.

A **postincorporation subscription** is a subscription agreement entered into after incorporation. It is treated as a contract between the subscriber and the corporation. Unlike preincorporation subscriptions, the subscriber may withdraw her offer to enter into a postincorporation subscription any time before the corporation accepts it. She cannot, however, withdraw the offer after the corporation has accepted it as the acceptance forms a contract.

CPA FORMALITIES OF INCORPORATION

Although the procedure involved in organizing a corporation varies somewhat from state to state, typically the incorporators execute and deliver articles of incorporation to the secretary of state or to another designated official. The Revised Act provides that after incorporation, the board of directors named in the articles of incorporation shall hold an organizational meeting for the purpose of adopting bylaws, appointing officers, and carrying on any other business brought before the meeting. After completion of these organizational details, the corporation's business and affairs are managed by its board of directors and by its officers.

SELECTION OF NAME

Most general incorporation laws require that the name contain a word or words that clearly designate the organization as a corporation, such as *corporation, company, incorporated, limited, Corp., Co., Inc.,* or *Ltd.* A corporate name must be distinguishable from the name of any domestic corporation or any foreign corporation authorized to do business within the state.

INCORPORATORS

The **incorporators** are the persons who sign the articles of incorporation filed in the state of incorporation with the secretary of state. Although they perform a necessary function, in many states their services as incorporators are perfunctory and short-lived, ending with the organizational meeting following incorporation. Furthermore, modern statutes have greatly relaxed the qualifications of incorporators and have also reduced the number required. The Revised Act and almost all states provide that only one person need act as the incorporator, though more may do so. The Revised Act and most states permit artificial entities to serve as incorporators. For example, the Revised Act defines a "person" to include individuals and entities, with an entity defined to include domestic and foreign corporations, not-for-profit corporations, profit and not-for-profit unincorporated associations, business trusts, estates, partnerships, and trusts.

ARTICLES OF INCORPORATION

The **articles of incorporation** or charter is generally a rather simple document that under the Revised Act must include the name of the corporation, the number of authorized shares, the street address of the registered office and the name of the registered agent, and the name and address of each incorporator. The Revised Act also permits the charter to include optional information such as the identities of the corporation's initial directors; corporate purposes; management of internal affairs; powers of the corporation; par value of shares; and any provision required or permitted to be set forth in the bylaws. Some optional provisions may be elected *only* in the charter including cumulative voting, supermajority voting requirements, preemptive rights, and limitations on the personal liability of directors for breach of their duty of care.

To form a corporation, the charter, once drawn up, must be executed and filed with the secretary of state. The charter then becomes the basic governing document of the corporation, so long as its provisions are consistent with state and federal law. Figure 34-2 shows a sample charter.

ORGANIZATIONAL MEETING

As previously mentioned, the Revised Act requires that an **organizational meeting** be held to adopt the new corporation's bylaws, appoint officers, and carry on any other business brought before it. If the articles do not name the corporation's initial directors; the incorporators hold the organizational meeting to elect directors, and either the incorporators or the directors then complete the organization of the corporation.

BYLAWS

The **bylaws** are the rules and regulations that govern the internal management of a corporation. Because bylaws are necessary to the organization of the corporation, their adoption is one of the first items of business at the organizational meeting held promptly after incorporation. The bylaws may contain any provision for managing the business and regulating the affairs of the corporation that is not inconsistent with law or the articles of incorporation. Under the Revised Act, the shareholders may amend or repeal the bylaws, which, in contrast to the certificate of incorporation embodying the articles of incorporation, do not have to be publicly filed. In addition, the board of directors may amend or repeal the bylaws, unless the articles of incorporation or other sections of the RMBCA reserve that power exclusively to the shareholders in whole or in part.

The Statutory Close Corporation Supplement permits close corporations to avoid adopting bylaws by including, either in a shareholder agreement or in the articles of incorporation, all the information necessary to corporate bylaws.

Figure 34-2 *Sample Articles of Incorporation*

ARTICLES OF INCORPORATION OF [CORPORATE NAME]

The undersigned, acting as incorporator(s) of a corporation under the ________ Business Corporation Act, adopt(s) the following Articles of Incorporation for such corporation:

First: The name of the corporation is ____________________

Second: The period of its duration is ____________________

Third: The purpose or purposes for which the corporation is organized are ____________________

Fourth: The aggregate number of shares which the corporation shall have authority to issue is ____________________

Fifth: Provisions granting preemptive rights are ____________________

Sixth: Provisions for the regulation of the internal affairs of the corporation are ____________________

Seventh: The address of the initial registered office of the corporation is ____________________ and the name of its initial registered agent at such address is ____________________

Eighth: The number of directors constituting the initial board of directors of the corporation is ________, and the names and addresses of the persons who are to serve as directors until the first annual meeting of shareholders or until their successors are elected and shall qualify are

Name	Address
____________________	____________________
____________________	____________________
____________________	____________________

Ninth: The name and address of each incorporator is

Name	Address
____________________	____________________
____________________	____________________
____________________	____________________

Dated________________, 20______.

____

____

____

Source: Reprinted from *Corporations*, 3ed, by Henn & Alexander, copyright 1983 with permission of Thomson West.

Practical Advice

When you have the choice of placing a provision in either the charter or the bylaws, carefully consider the advantages and disadvantages of each. You may prefer the charter for provisions that protect your interests because charter provisions prevail over bylaws provisions and are more difficult to amend.

RECOGNITION OR DISREGARD OF CORPORATENESS

Business associates choose to incorporate to obtain one or more of the corporate attributes, primarily limited liability

CONCEPT REVIEW

Comparison of Charter and Bylaws

	Charter	Bylaws
Filing	Publicly	Not publicly
Amendment	Requires board and shareholder approval	Requires only board approval
Availability	Must include certain mandatory provisions; may include optional provisions, although some optional provisions may be elected only in the charter	Must include certain provisions unless they are included in the charter
Validity	May include any provision not inconsistent with law	May include any provision not inconsistent with law and the charter

and perpetual existence. Because a corporation is a creature of the state, such attributes are recognized when the enterprise complies with the state's requirements for incorporation. Although the formal procedures are relatively simple, errors or omissions sometimes occur. In some cases the mistakes may be trivial, such as incorrectly stating an incorporator's address in the charter; in other instances the error may be more significant, such as a complete failure to file the articles of incorporation. The consequences of procedural noncompliance depend on the seriousness of the error. Conversely, even when a corporation has been formed in strict compliance with the incorporation statute, a court may disregard the corporateness of the enterprise if justice requires.

CPA DEFECTIVE INCORPORATION

Although modern corporation statutes have greatly simplified incorporation procedures, defective incorporations do occur. The possible consequences of a defective incorporation include the following: (1) the state brings an action against the association for involuntary dissolution; (2) the associates are held personally liable to a third party; (3) the association asserts that it is not liable on an obligation; or (4) a third party asserts that it is not liable to the association. Corporate statutes addressing this issue have taken an approach considerably different from that of the common law.

COMMON LAW APPROACH

Under the common law, a defectively formed corporation was, under certain circumstances, accorded corporate attributes. The courts developed a set of doctrines granting corporateness to *de jure* (of right) corporations, *de facto* (of fact) corporations, and corporations by estoppel but denying corporateness to corporations that were too defectively formed.

Corporation *de jure* A **corporation *de jure*** is one that has been formed in substantial compliance with the incorporation statute and the required organizational procedure. Once a *de jure* corporation is formed, its existence may not be challenged by anyone, even the state in a direct proceeding for this purpose.

Corporation *de facto* Although it fails to comply in some way with the incorporation statute and, hence, is not *de jure*, a **corporation *de facto*** is nevertheless recognized for most purposes as a corporation. A failure to form a *de jure* corporation may result in the formation of a *de facto* corporation if the following requirements are met: (1) the existence of a general corporation statute, (2) a bona fide attempt to comply with that law in organizing a corporation under the statute, and (3) the actual exercise of corporate power by conducting business in the belief that a corporation has been formed. The existence of a *de facto* corporation can be challenged only by the state in an action of *quo warranto* ("by what right").

Corporation by Estoppel The doctrine of **corporation by estoppel** is distinct from that of corporation *de facto*. Estoppel does not create a corporation. It operates only to prevent a person or persons under the facts and circumstances of a particular case from questioning a corporation's existence or its capacity to act or to own property. Corporation by estoppel requires a holding out by a purported corporation or its associates and reliance by a third party. In addition, application of the doctrine depends on equitable considerations. A person who has dealt with a defectively organized corporation may be precluded or estopped from denying its corporate existence if the necessary elements of holding out and reliance are present. The doctrine can be applied not only to third parties but also to the purported corporation and to the associates who held themselves out as a corporation.

Defective Corporation If the associates who purported to form a corporation fail to comply with the requirements of the incorporation statute to such an extent that neither a *de jure* nor a *de facto* corporation is formed and the circumstances do not justify applying the corporation by estoppel doctrine, the courts generally deny the associates the benefits of incorporation. Some or all of the associates are then held unlimitedly liable for the obligations of the business.

Statutory Approach

In contrast to the common law approach to defective incorporation, which is cumbersome in both theory and application, incorporation statutes now address the issue more simply. All states provide that corporate existence begins either upon the filing of the articles of incorporation or their acceptance by the secretary of state. Moreover, under the Revised Act (**RMBCA**) and most state statutes, the filing or acceptance of the articles of incorporation by the secretary of state is conclusive proof that the incorporators have satisfied all conditions precedent to incorporation, except in a proceeding brought by the state. This applies even if the articles of incorporation contain mistakes or omissions.

With respect to the attribute of limited liability, the original Model Act (**MBCA**) and a few states provide that all persons who assume to act as a corporation without authority to do so shall have joint and several unlimited liability for all debts and liabilities incurred or arising as a result of their so acting. The Revised Act, however, imposes liability *only* on persons who purport to act as or on behalf of a corporation, knowing that there was no incorporation.

Consider two illustrations: First, Smith had been shown executed articles of incorporation some months before he invested in the corporation and became an officer and director. He was also told by the corporation's attorney that the articles had been filed; however, because of confusion in the attorney's office, they had not in fact been filed. Under the Revised Act and many court decisions, Smith would not be held liable for the obligations of the defective corporation. Second, knowing that no corporation has been formed because no attempt has been made to file articles of incorporation, Jones represents that a corporation exists and enters into a contract in the corporate name. Jones would be held liable for the obligations of the defective corporation under the Model Act, the Revised Act, and most court decisions involving similar situations.

Practical Advice

To obtain limited liability as a shareholder in a corporation, make sure that the corporation has been properly organized.

Harris v. Looney

Court of Appeals of Arkansas, 1993

43 Ark.App. 127, 862 S.W.2d 282

FACTS On February 1, 1988, Robert L. Harris sold his business and its assets to J & R Construction. Joe Alexander, one of three J & R incorporators, signed the contract on behalf of J & R Construction with Harris. On the same day, the incorporators (Joe Alexander, Avanell Looney, and Rita Alexander) signed the articles of incorporation for J & R Construction, but they were not filed with the secretary of state's office until February 3, 1988. In 1991, J & R Construction defaulted on its contract and promissory note, and Harris sued the three incorporators of J & R Construction for the corporation's debt of $49,696.21. Joe Alexander and Avanell Looney stated that they were both present at the signing. Harris testified, however, that only he, his wife, and Joe Alexander were present when the contract was signed and that he does not remember Avanell Looney being present. Kathryn Harris testified that Alexander and Looney were not present when the contract was signed. The trial court held that Joe Alexander was personally liable for the debt because he was the contracting party who dealt on behalf of the corporation. The court refused to hold Avanell Looney or Rita Alexander liable because neither of them had acted for or on behalf of the corporation. Harris appealed.

DECISION Judgment affirmed.

OPINION Pittman, J. In 1987, the Arkansas General Assembly passed Act 958 which adopted the Arkansas

Business Corporation Act. Section 204 of this Act, Ark. Code Ann. § 4–27–204, concerns liability for pre-incorporation transactions and is identical to Section 2.04 of the Revised Model Business Corporation Act. It states: "All persons purporting to act as or on behalf of a corporation, knowing there was no incorporation under this Act, are jointly and severally liable for all liabilities created while so acting." The official comment to § 2.04 of the Revised Model Business Corporation Act explains:

> Earlier versions of the Model Act, and the statutes of many states, have long provided that corporate existence begins only with the acceptance of articles of incorporation by the secretary of state. Many states also have statutes that provide expressly that those who prematurely act as or on behalf of a corporation are personally liable on all transactions entered into or liabilities incurred before incorporation. A review of recent case law indicates, however, that even in states with such statutes courts have continued to rely on common law concepts of *de facto* corporations, *de jure* corporations, and corporations by estoppel that provide uncertain protection against liability for preincorporation transactions. These cases caused a review of the underlying policies represented in earlier versions of the Model Act and the adoption of a slightly more flexible or relaxed standard.
>
> Incorporation under modern statutes is so simple and inexpensive that a strong argument may be made that nothing short of filing articles of incorporation should create the privilege of limited liability. A number of situations have arisen, however, in which the protection of limited liability arguably should be recognized even though the simple incorporation process established by modern statutes has not been completed.
>
> * * *
>
> * * * [I]t seemed appropriate to impose liability only on persons who act as or on behalf of corporations "knowing" that no corporation exists. Analogous protection has long been accorded under the uniform limited partnership acts to limited partners who contribute capital to a partnership in the erroneous belief that a limited partnership certificate has been filed. UNIFORM LIMITED PARTNERSHIP ACT § 12 (1916); REVISED UNIFORM LIMITED PARTNERSHIP ACT § 3.04 (1976). Persons protected under § 3.04 of the latter are persons who "erroneously but in good faith" believe that a limited partnership certificate has been filed. The language of section 2.04 has essentially the same meaning.
>
> While no special provision is made in section 2.04, the section does not foreclose the possibility that persons who urge defendants to execute contracts in the corporate name knowing that no steps to incorporate have been taken may be estopped to impose personal liability on individual defendants. This estoppel may be based on the inequity perceived when persons, unwilling or reluctant to enter into a commitment under their own name, are persuaded to use the name of a nonexistent corporation, and then are sought to be held personally liable under section 2.04 by the party advocating that form of execution. By contrast, persons who knowingly participate in a business under a corporate name are jointly and severally liable on "corporate" obligations under section 2.04 and may not argue that plaintiffs are "estopped" from holding them personally liable because all transactions were conducted on a corporate basis.
>
> Model Business Corporation Act Ann. § 2.04 official cmt. at 130. 2–33 (3d ed. 1992).

In passing this Act, the Arkansas General Assembly adopted a heightened standard for imposing personal liability for transactions entered into before incorporation. The Act requires that, in order to find liability under § 4–27–204, there must be a finding that the persons sought to be charged acted as or on behalf of the corporation and knew there was no incorporation under the Act.

The evidence showed that the contract to purchase appellant's business and the promissory note were signed only by Joe Alexander on behalf of the corporation. The only evidence introduced to support appellant's allegation that appellees were acting on behalf of the corporation was Joe Alexander's and Avanell Looney's statements that they were present when the contract with appellant was signed; however, these statements were disputed by appellant and his wife. Appellant testified that he, his wife, Kathryn Harris, and Joe Alexander were present when the documents were signed to purchase his business and he did not remember appellee Avanell Looney being present. Kathryn Harris testified that appellees were not present when the contract was signed.

The trial court denied appellant judgment against appellees because he found appellees had not acted for or on behalf of J & R Construction as required by § 4–27–204. The findings of fact of a trial judge sitting as the factfinder will not be disturbed on appeal unless the findings are clearly erroneous or clearly against the preponderance of the evidence, giving due regard to the opportunity of the trial court to assess the credibility of the witnesses. [Citation.] From our review of the records, we cannot say that the trial court's finding in this case is clearly against the preponderance of the evidence, and we find no error in the court's refusal to award appellant judgment against appellees.

INTERPRETATION The Revised Act imposes liability on all persons who purport to act as or on behalf of a corporation if they knew there was no incorporation.

ETHICAL QUESTION Was the court's decision fair to all of the parties? Explain.

CRITICAL THINKING QUESTION With which approach to recognition of corporate attributes do you agree: that taken by the MBCA or by the RMBCA? Explain.

CPA PIERCING THE CORPORATE VEIL

If substantial compliance with the incorporation statute results in a *de jure* or *de facto* corporation, the general rule is that the courts will recognize corporateness and its attendant attributes—including limited liability. Nonetheless, the courts will disregard the corporate entity when it is used to defeat public convenience, commit a wrongdoing, protect fraud, or circumvent the law. Reaching behind a corporate shield to prevent individuals from insulating themselves against personal accountability and the consequences of their wrongdoing is known as **piercing the corporate veil.** When they deem it necessary, courts will pierce the corporate veil to remedy wrongdoing. They have done so most frequently with closely held corporations and with parent-subsidiary relationships. Piercing the corporate veil is the exception, and in most cases courts uphold the separateness of the corporation.

CLOSELY HELD CORPORATIONS

The joint and active management by all the shareholders of closely held corporations frequently results in a tendency to forgo corporate formalities, such as holding meetings of the board and shareholders, while the small size of close corporations often renders certain creditors unable to fully satisfy their claims against the corporation. Such frustrated creditors will likely ask the court to disregard the organization's corporateness and to impose personal liability for the corporate obligations on the shareholders. Courts have responded by piercing the corporate veil when the shareholders (1) have not conducted the business on a corporate basis, (2) have not provided an adequate financial basis for the business, or (3) have used the corporation to defraud. Conducting the business on a corporate basis involves separately maintaining the corporation's and the shareholders' funds, maintaining separate financial records, holding regular directors' meetings, and generally observing corporate formalities. Adequate capitalization requires that the shareholders invest capital or purchase liability insurance sufficient to meet the reasonably anticipated requirements of the enterprise.

Practical Advice

If you form a closely held corporation, be sure to adhere to the required corporate formalities and adequately capitalize the corporation.

The Revised Act validates unanimous shareholder agreements by which the shareholders may relax traditional corporate formalities. The Revised Act further provides that the existence or performance of an agreement authorized by the Act "shall not be grounds for imposing personal liability on any shareholder for the acts or the debts of the corporation even if the agreement or its performance treats the corporation as if it were a partnership or results in failure to observe the corporate formalities otherwise applicable to the matters governed by the agreement." Thus, this provision narrows the grounds for imposing personal liability on shareholders for the liabilities of a corporation for acts or omissions authorized by a valid shareholder agreement.

The Statutory Close Corporation Supplement validates a number of arrangements that allow the shareholders to relax traditional corporate formalities. The Supplement is intended to prevent the shareholders in a statutory close corporation from being held individually liable for the debts and torts of the business merely because the corporation does not follow the traditional corporate model. Although courts may still pierce the corporate veil of a statutory close corporation if the same circumstances would justify imposing personal liability on the shareholders of a general business corporation, the Supplement simply prevents a court from piercing the corporate veil just because the corporation is a statutory close corporation.

PARENT-SUBSIDIARY

A corporation wishing to risk only a portion of its assets in a particular enterprise may choose to form a subsidiary corporation. A **subsidiary corporation** is one in which another corporation, the **parent corporation,** owns at least a majority of the shares and over which the parent corporation therefore has control. Courts may pierce the corporate veil and hold the parent liable for the debts of its subsidiary if (1) both corporations are not adequately capitalized, *or* (2) the formalities of separate corporate procedures are not observed, *or* (3) each corporation is not held out to the public as a separate enterprise, *or* (4) the funds of the two corporations are commingled, *or* (5) the parent corporation completely dominates the subsidiary only to advance the parent's own interests. So long as a parent-subsidiary duo avoids these pitfalls, the courts generally will recognize the subsidiary as a separate entity, even if the parent owns all the subsidiary's stock and the two corporations share facilities, employees, directors, and officers.

National Hotel Associates v. O. Ahlborg & Sons, Inc.

Supreme Court of Rhode Island, 2003
827 A.2d 646
http://caselaw.lp.findlaw.com/data2/rhodeislandstatecases/2003/01-145.pdf

FACTS In 1983, the plaintiff, National Hotel Associates (NHA) sought to renovate the National Hotel, a large Victorian-style hotel overlooking Old Harbor on Block Island, Rhode Island. Richard Ahlborg (Richard), aware that he was one of several contractors competing for the job, proposed that NHA use nonunion labor through an O. Ahlborg & Sons, Inc. (O. Ahlborg) nonunion entity, Construction Services, Inc. (CSI), to reduce the overall cost of the project. At that time, Richard, CSI's sole stockholder, assured NHA that he personally would rectify any problems with the work of CSI. Barry Evans (Evans), one of NHA's principals, testified that Richard described CSI as a "Siamese twin" of O. Ahlborg's and that CSI operated out of the same offices and shared the same computer facilities, personnel, vehicles, and equipment. Evans further testified that Richard convinced him that NHA "should have no concern about the project being carried out by CSI" because both Richard and the entire O. Ahlborg organization "would back up CSI from start to middle to the end." The record also indicates that Richard repeatedly boasted that "he was CSI" and he "was O. Ahlborg." When asked why he would deploy O. Ahlborg's resources to a project belonging to CSI—a different company—Richard responded, "Because I am both companies." Evans testified that in the face of these promises and Richard's many representations, NHA entered into a contract with CSI.

The renovation work on the National Hotel began in the fall of 1983, but by early December, CSI's cash flow problems led to construction delays. Consequently, O. Ahlborg extended a $400,000 line of credit to the struggling corporation. Later, when CSI's inability to perform further delayed construction, Richard and O. Ahlborg assumed control over the project; CSI's construction manager was fired and was replaced by an O. Ahlborg project manager. The evidence submitted at trial demonstrated that despite its undercapitalization, CSI continued operations with the financial backing of O. Ahlborg. However, CSI never reimbursed O. Ahlborg for the $400,000 cash infusion. In total, approximately $360,000 of the $400,000 advanced by O. Ahlborg was directly attributable to the project. Richard openly admitted that without O. Ahlborg's financial assistance, CSI would have been unable to proceed with the construction. Anthony D. Lee, a certified public accountant specializing in the construction industry, reviewed CSI's financial operating history, work in progress, and cash flow requirements and testified that CSI was undercapitalized during each year from 1982 through 1986 and was, at all relevant times since its inception in 1981, insolvent.

In 1984, CSI commenced arbitration proceedings against NHA in an effort to collect approximately $500,000 on O. Ahlborg's behalf. This claim centered on defendants' contention that NHA owed money for work performed on the project. Richard later admitted that he and O. Ahlborg were the real parties in interest in this arbitration. The evidence disclosed that O. Ahlborg financed the entire arbitration proceeding, including costs for expert witnesses and attorneys' fees. NHA counterclaimed and sought recovery for CSI's nonconforming, defective, and untimely performance of the work. On May 7, 1986, the arbitration panel awarded NHA $230,687.20 in damages based upon construction delays and defective work and denied all claims asserted by CSI. On June 19, 1986, a judgment confirming the arbitration award was entered in the Superior Court, and on September 3, 1986, an execution was returned unsatisfied. NHA filed this action against O. Ahlborg and Richard, seeking to impose liability on both defendants for the full amount of the judgment because CSI was a sham entity and a mere instrumentality of O. Ahlborg The trial justice found in favor of the defendants, and NHA appealed.

DECISION The judgment is vacated and the case is remanded.

OPINION Goldberg, J. * * * [T]he trial justice correctly observed that if two corporations are affiliated through common stock ownership, each will be considered a separate and independent entity "unless the totality of the circumstances surrounding their relationship indicates that one of the corporations 'is so organized and controlled, and its affairs are so conducted, as to make it merely an instrumentality, agency, conduit, or adjunct of [the other].' " [Citation.] The criteria for piercing the corporate veil to impose liability on non-corporate defendants vary with the particular circumstances of each case. [Citation.] However, "when the facts of a particular case render it unjust and inequitable to consider the subject corporation a separate entity" we will not hesitate to disregard the corporate form and treat the defendant as an individual who is personally liable for the debts of the disregarded corporation. [Citation.] Thus, in circumstances in which there is such a unity of interest and ownership between the corporation and its owner or parent corporation such that their separate identities and personalities no longer exist we have held that "adherence to the principle of their separate existence would, under the circumstances, result in injustice." [Citation.] In those situations the corporate form is disregarded and liability is determined by justice and fairness.

In evaluating the degree of separateness between two corporations, we look to the totality of the circumstances and examine such factors as stock ownership, capitalization, dual office holding and directorships, financial support or dependence, a lack of substantial business contracts independent from the other corporation and a domination of finances, policies and practices. [Citation.] Having reviewed the evidence in the record in this case, this Court is of the opinion that a finding that CSI was operated as an instrumentality of O. Ahlborg is amply demonstrated and that liability for CSI's judgment debt should rest with O. Ahlborg.

* * *

* * * The evidence disclosed that although defendants scrupulously adhered to the usual corporate formalities, thus endeavoring to preserve the corporate protections afforded by law, CSI wound up an empty shell, unable to pay this judgment because its assets were dissipated for the benefit of Richard and O. Ahlborg. Accordingly, we are of the opinion that CSI was dominated and controlled by Richard as an alter ego of O. Ahlborg, all to the detriment of NHA, its victim and judgment creditor.

In her decision, the trial justice failed to consider the totality of the evidentiary circumstances that support a finding that O. Ahlborg is responsible for the corporate debt of CSI. The evidence that Richard Ahlborg dominated the affairs of each entity was overwhelming; not only did he declare, whenever it was expedient to do so, that he was CSI and he was O. Ahlborg, he unhesitatingly deployed the resources of one corporation in favor of the other whenever the circumstances warranted, including steering NHA to CSI, financing the undercapitalized CSI, completing its contract with NHA, and attempting to collect CSI's indebtedness on O. Ahlborg's behalf by financing a meritless arbitration followed by a clandestine war of hide the assets.

We are satisfied that the trial justice erroneously limited her analysis to the period of CSI's inception and based her refusal to pierce the corporate veil in large part on CSI's allegiance to the corporate formalities. The trial justice overlooked the defendants' conduct during the relevant time period, when Richard—the sole stockholder of CSI and president and sole stockholder of O. Ahlborg—was operating both entities as his personal fiefdoms. The trial justice concluded that CSI was incorporated to engage in and "in fact, did engage in a business [that was] different from O. Ahlborg," the performance of small-scale projects. However, the evidence established that with respect to this project, and at other critical points in CSI's history, Richard dominated the affairs of all three entities—CSI, O. Ahlborg and CPC—to an extraordinary degree. The plaintiff testified that Richard made sweeping representations that CSI was a nonunion arm of O. Ahlborg that could perform the work at a cheaper price but, if it became necessary, the project would be completed by O. Ahlborg with O. Ahlborg's resources. We are satisfied that the trial justice misconceived the import of this evidence. CSI, as alleged by plaintiff, was wholly owned by Richard and operated as an alter ego of O. Ahlborg, the larger, more established corporation.

The plaintiff presented evidence, through Evans, that Richard described CSI as a "Siamese twin" of O. Ahlborg, that "CSI was O. Ahlborg," and he promised NHA that O. Ahlborg would complete the project if CSI was unable to do so. We conclude that these personal promises, although found by the trial justice to be unenforceable as a promise to pay the debt of another, are relevant factors in deciding whether the corporate form should be disregarded. It is undisputed that Richard promised to complete the project with O. Ahlborg's resources if it became necessary and honored that promise when CSI stumbled. In this circumstance, as plaintiff argued, O. Ahlborg ignored the corporate distinctions and disregarded CSI's corporate separateness at every stage: during the bidding and negotiations; with respect to the financing, when it "loaned" CSI $400,000 to remain afloat; during construction when O. Ahlborg's employees, equipment and expertise were employed to complete the work, and finally, during the arbitration, by bankrolling a proceeding that clearly was intended to recoup O. Ahlborg's cash disbursements to CSI.

We are not persuaded that O. Ahlborg's allegiance to separate corporate records and accounts shields it from liability. As plaintiff has alleged, this is really corporate "bells and whistles" designed as a smokescreen for unfair manipulation of the corporate enterprise in furtherance of defendants' interests. [Citation.]

Additionally, the evidence that CSI was undercapitalized from its inception and was insolvent for this entire period, including when it was retained by NHA, was overlooked by the trial justice, who focused her analysis on CSI's initial capitalization and found that CSI adequately was capitalized at its inception. However, plaintiff presented evidence that without the infusion of $400,000 in cash from O. Ahlborg, CSI's very existence was threatened. * * * The evidence disclosed that CSI was unable to qualify for a $20,000 bank loan and that Richard was forced to personally borrow even more money to keep CSI afloat. Richard's indebtedness was repaid by CSI, at his direction, after the arbitration award was issued. Further, no effort was made to collect CSI's $400,000 indebtedness to O. Ahlborg, either before or after CSI's assets were transferred to CPC. This evidence demonstrates undercapitalization and is damning proof that CSI was operated as a shell corporation for defendants' benefit. [Citation.]

Thus, as Richard so often proclaimed, at least for financial operations, O. Ahlborg was CSI. Accordingly, the corporate form that otherwise would shield O. Ahlborg from liability is unavailing and O. Ahlborg is liable for CSI's judgment debt.

INTERPRETATION Courts may pierce the corporate veil and hold the parent liable for the debts of its subsidiary if both corporations are not adequately capitalized or the parent corporation completely dominates the subsidiary.

ETHICAL QUESTION Was Richard's conduct unethical?

CRITICAL THINKING QUESTION Are the standards for piercing the corporate veil sufficiently definite and predictable? Explain.

CORPORATE POWERS

Because a corporation derives its existence and all of its powers from its state of incorporation, it possesses only those powers that the state has conferred on it. Corporate powers consist of those expressly set forth in the incorporation statute unless limited by the articles of incorporation.

CPA SOURCES OF CORPORATE POWERS

STATUTORY POWERS

Typical of the general corporate powers granted by incorporation statutes are those provided by the Revised Act, which include the following: (1) to have perpetual succession; (2) to sue and be sued in the corporate name; (3) to acquire and dispose of property, including shares or other interests in, or obligations of, any other entity; (4) to make contracts, borrow money, and secure any corporate obligations; (5) to lend money; (6) to be a promoter, partner, member, associate, or manager of any partnership, joint venture, trust, or other entity; (7) to conduct business within or without the state of incorporation; (8) to establish pension plans, profit sharing plans, share option plans, and other employee benefit plans; and (9) to make charitable donations. In most states this list is not exclusive. Moreover, the Revised Act also grants to all corporations the same powers individuals have to do all things necessary or convenient to carry out their business and affairs.

PURPOSES

All state incorporation statutes provide that a corporation may be formed for any lawful purpose. The Revised Act permits a corporation's articles of incorporation to state a more limited purpose. Many state statutes, but not the RMBCA, require that the articles of incorporation specify the corporation's purposes although they usually permit a general statement that the corporation is formed to engage in any lawful purpose.

CPA *ULTRA VIRES* ACTS

Because a corporation has authority to act only within its powers, any corporate action or contract that exceeds these powers is ***ultra vires***. The doctrine of *ultra vires* is less significant today because modern statutes permit incorporation for any lawful purpose and most articles of incorporation do not limit corporate powers. As a consequence, far fewer acts are *ultra vires*.

EFFECT OF *ULTRA VIRES* ACTS

Traditionally, *ultra vires* contracts were unenforceable as null and void. Under the modern approach, courts allow the *ultra vires* defense when the contract is wholly executory on both sides. A corporation having received full performance from the other party to the contract is not permitted to escape liability by a plea of *ultra vires*. Conversely, the other party may not use the defense of *ultra vires* against a corporation suing for breach of a contract that has been fully performed on its side. Almost all statutes, including the Revised

Act, have abolished the defense of *ultra vires* in an action by or against a corporation. These statutes do not, however, validate illegal corporate actions.

REMEDIES FOR *ULTRA VIRES* ACTS

Although *ultra vires* under modern statutes may no longer be used as a shield against liability, corporate activities that are *ultra vires* may be redressed in any of three ways, as provided by the Revised Act:

1. in a proceeding by a shareholder against the corporation to enjoin the act, if equitable and if all affected persons are parties to the proceeding, the court may award damages for loss suffered by the corporation or another party because of the enjoining of the unauthorized act;
2. in a proceeding by the corporation, or a shareholder derivatively (in a representative capacity), against the incumbent or former directors or officers for exceeding their authority; or
3. in a proceeding by the attorney general of the state of incorporation to dissolve the corporation or to enjoin it from the transaction of unauthorized business.

CPA LIABILITY FOR TORTS AND CRIMES

A corporation is liable for the torts its agents commit in the course of their employment. The doctrine of *ultra vires*, even in those jurisdictions where it is permitted as a defense, does not apply to wrongdoing by the corporation. Rather, the doctrine of *respondeat superior* imposes full liability on a corporation for such agent and employee torts. For example, Robert, a truck driver employed by the Webster Corporation, while on a business errand negligently runs over Pamela, a pedestrian. Both Robert and the Webster Corporation are liable to Pamela in her action to recover damages for the injuries she sustained. A corporation may also be found liable for fraud, false imprisonment, malicious prosecution, libel, and other torts; but some states hold the corporation liable for *punitive* damages only if it authorized or ratified the agent's act.

Historically, corporations were not held criminally liable because, under the traditional view, a corporation could not possess the criminal intent requisite for committing a crime. The dramatic growth in size and importance of corporations has changed this view. Under the modern approach, a corporation may be liable for violating statutes imposing liability without fault. In addition, a corporation may be liable for an offense perpetrated by a high corporate officer or by its board of directors. Punishment of a corporation for crimes is necessarily by fine, not imprisonment.

CHAPTER SUMMARY

Nature of Corporations

Corporate Attributes

Creature of the State a corporation may be formed only by substantial compliance with a state incorporation statute

Legal Entity a corporation is an entity apart from its shareholders, with entirely distinct rights and liabilities

Limited Liability a shareholder's liability is limited to the amount invested in the business enterprise

Free Transferability of Corporate Shares unless otherwise specified in the charter

Perpetual Existence unless the charter provides otherwise

Centralized Management shareholders of a corporation elect the board of directors to manage its business affairs; the board appoints officers to run the day-to-day operations of the business

As a Person a corporation is considered a person for some but not all purposes

As a Citizen a corporation is considered a citizen for some but not all purposes

Classification of Corporations

Public or Private
- *Public Corporation* one created to administer a unit of local civil government or one created by the United States to conduct public business
- *Private Corporation* one founded by and composed of private persons for private purposes; has no governmental duties

Profit or Nonprofit
- *Profit Corporation* one founded to operate a business for profit
- *Nonprofit Corporation* one whose profits must be used exclusively for charitable, educational, or scientific purposes

Domestic or Foreign
- *Domestic Corporation* one created under the laws of a given state
- *Foreign Corporation* one created under the laws of any other state or jurisdiction; it must obtain a certificate of authority from each state in which it does intrastate business

Publicly Held or Closely Held
- *Publicly Held* corporation whose shares are owned by a large number of people and are widely traded
- *Closely Held* corporation that is owned by few shareholders and whose shares are not actively traded

Subchapter S Corporation eligible corporation electing to be taxed as a partnership under the Internal Revenue Code

Professional Corporation corporate form under which duly licensed individuals may practice their professions

Formation of a Corporation

Organizing the Corporation

Promoter person who takes the preliminary steps to organize a corporation
- *Promoters' Contracts* promoters remain liable on preincorporation contracts made in the name of the corporation unless the contract provides otherwise or unless a novation is effected
- *Promoters' Fiduciary Duty* promoters owe a fiduciary duty among themselves and to the corporation, its subscribers, and its initial shareholders

Subscribers persons who agree to purchase stock in a corporation
- *Preincorporation Subscription* an offer to purchase capital stock in a corporation yet to be formed which under many incorporation statutes is irrevocable for a specified time period
- *Postincorporation Subscription* a subscription agreement entered into after incorporation; an offer to enter into such a subscription is revocable any time before the corporation accepts it

Formalities of Incorporation

Selection of Name the name must clearly designate the entity as a corporation

Incorporators the persons who sign the articles of incorporation

Articles of Incorporation the charter or basic organizational document of a corporation

Organizational Meeting the first meeting, held to adopt the bylaws and appoint officers

Bylaws rules governing a corporation's internal management

Recognition or Disregard of Corporateness

Defective Incorporation

Common Law Approach
- ***Corporation* de jure** one formed in substantial compliance with the incorporation statute and having all corporate attributes
- ***Corporation* de facto** one not formed in compliance with the statute but recognized for most purposes as a corporation
- ***Corporation by Estoppel*** prevents a person from raising the question of a corporation's existence
- ***Defective Corporation*** the associates are denied the benefits of incorporation

Statutory Approach the filing or acceptance of the articles of incorporation is generally conclusive proof of proper incorporation
- ***RMBCA*** liability is imposed only on persons who act on behalf of a defectively formed corporation knowing that there was no incorporation
- ***MBCA*** unlimited personal liability is imposed on all persons who act on behalf of a defectively formed corporation

Piercing the Corporate Veil

General Rule the courts may disregard the corporate entity when it is used to defeat public convenience, commit a wrongdoing, protect fraud, or circumvent the law

Application most frequently applied to
- *Closely Held Corporations*
- *Parent-Subsidiary Corporations*

Corporate Powers

Sources of Corporate Powers

Statutory Powers typically include perpetual existence, right to hold property in the corporate name, and all powers necessary or convenient to effect the corporation's purposes

Purposes a corporation may be formed for any lawful purposes unless its articles of incorporation state a more limited purpose

Ultra Vires Acts

Definition of *Ultra Vires* Acts any action or contract that goes beyond a corporation's express and implied powers

Effect of *Ultra Vires* Acts under RMBCA, *ultra vires* acts and conveyances are not invalid

Remedies for *Ultra Vires* Acts the RMBCA provides three possible remedies

Liability for Torts and Crimes

Torts under the doctrine of *respondeat superior*, a corporation is liable for torts committed by its employees within the course of their employment

Crime a corporation may be criminally liable for violations of statutes imposing liability without fault or for an offense perpetrated by a high corporate officer or its board of directors

QUESTIONS

1. After part of the shares of a proposed corporation had been successfully subscribed, one of the promoters hired a carpenter to repair a building that was intended to be conveyed to the proposed corporation. The promoters subsequently secured subscriptions to the balance of the shares and completed the organization, but the corporation, finding the building to be unsuitable for its purposes, declined to use the building or to pay the carpenter. The carpenter brought suit against the corporation and the promoter for the amount that the promoter agreed would be paid to him. Who, if anyone, is liable?

2. C. A. Nimocks was a promoter engaged in organizing the Times Printing Company. On September 12, on behalf of the proposed corporation, he made a written contract with McArthur for her services as comptroller for a one-year period beginning October 1. The Times Printing Company was incorporated October 16, and on that date McArthur commenced her duties as comptroller. Neither the board of directors nor any officer took formal action on her employment, but all the shareholders, directors, and officers knew of the contract made by Nimocks. On December 1, McArthur was discharged without cause.
   a. Has she a cause of action against the Times Printing Company?
   b. Has she a cause of action against Nimocks?

3. Todd and Elaine obtained an option on a building that was used for manufacturing pianos. They acted as the promoters for a corporation and turned the building over to the new corporation for $500,000 worth of stock. In truth, their option on the building called for a purchase price of only $300,000. The other shareholders desire to have $200,000 of the common stock canceled. Can they succeed in this action?

4. Wayne signed a subscription agreement for ten shares of stock, having a value of $100 per share, of the proposed ABC Company. Two weeks later, the company was incorporated. A certificate was duly tendered to Wayne, but he refused to accept it. He was notified of all shareholders' meetings, but he never attended. A dividend check was sent to him, but he returned it. ABC Company brings a legal action against Wayne to recover $1,000. He defends on the ground that his subscription agreement was an unaccepted offer, that he had done nothing to ratify it, and that he was therefore not liable on it. Is he correct? Explain.

5. Julian, Cornelia, and Sheila petitioned for a corporate charter for the purpose of conducting a retail shoe business. They complied with all the statutory provisions except having their charter recorded. This was simply an oversight on their part, and they felt that they had fully complied with the law. They operated the business for three years, after which time it became insolvent. The creditors desire to hold the members personally and individually liable. May they do so?

6. Arthur, Barbara, Carl, and Debra decided to form a corporation for bottling and selling apple cider. Arthur, Barbara, and Carl were to operate the business, while Debra was to supply the necessary capital but was to have no voice in the management. They went to Jane, a lawyer, who agreed to organize a corporation for them under the name A-B-C Inc., and paid her funds sufficient to accomplish the incorporation. Jane promised that the corporation would definitely be formed by May 3. On April 27, Arthur telephoned Jane to inquire how the incorporation was progressing, and Jane said she had drafted the articles of incorporation and would send them to the secretary of state that very day. She assured Arthur that incorporation would occur before May 3.

   Relying on Jane's assurance, Arthur, with the approval of Barbara and Carl, on May 4 entered into a written contract with Grower for his entire apple crop. The contract was executed by Arthur on behalf of "A-B-C Inc." Grower delivered the apples as agreed. Unknown to Arthur, Barbara, Carl, Debra, or Grower, the articles of incorporation were never filed, through Jane's negligence. The business subsequently failed.

   What are Grower's rights, if any, against Arthur, Barbara, Carl, and Debra as individuals?

7. The Pyro Corporation has outstanding 20,000 shares of common stock, of which 19,000 are owned by Peter B. Arson; 500 shares are owned by Elizabeth Arson, his wife; and 500 shares are owned by Joseph Q. Arson, his brother. These three individuals are the officers and directors of the corporation. The Pyro Corporation obtained a $250,000 fire insurance policy to cover a certain building it owned. Thereafter, Peter B. Arson set fire to the building, and it was totally destroyed. Can the corporation recover from the fire insurance company on the $250,000 fire insurance policy? Why?

8. A corporation is formed for the purpose of manufacturing, buying, selling, and dealing in drugs, chemicals, and similar products. The corporation, under authority of its board of directors, contracted to purchase the land and building it occupied as a factory and store. Collins, a shareholder, sues in equity to restrain the corporation from completing the contract, claiming that as the certificate of incorporation contained no provision authorizing the corporation to purchase real estate, the contract was *ultra vires*. Can Collins prevent the contract from being executed?

9. Amalgamated Corporation, organized under the laws of State S, sends traveling salespersons into State M to solicit orders, which are accepted only at the home office of Amalgamated Corporation in State S. Riley, a resident of State M, places an order that is accepted by Amalgamated Corporation in State S. The Corporation Act of State M provides that "no foreign corporation transacting business in this state without a certificate of authority shall be permitted to maintain an action in any court of this state until such corporation shall have obtained a certificate of authority." Riley fails to pay for the goods, and when Amalgamated Corporation sues Riley in a court of State M, Riley defends on the ground that Amalgamated Corporation does not possess a certificate of authority from State M. Result?

CASE PROBLEMS

10. Dr. North, a surgeon practicing in Georgia, engaged an Arizona professional corporation consisting of twenty lawyers to represent him in a dispute with a Georgia hospital. West, a member of the law firm, flew to Atlanta and hired local counsel with Dr. North's approval. West represented Dr. North in two hearings before the hospital and in one court proceeding, as well as negotiating a compromise between Dr. North and the hospital. The total bill for the law firm's travel costs and professional services was $21,000, but Dr. North refused to pay $6,000 of it. The law firm brought an action against Dr. North for the balance owed. Dr. North argued that the action should be dismissed because the law firm failed to register as a foreign corporation in accordance with the Georgia Corporation Statute. Will the law firm be prevented from collecting on the contract? Explain.

11. An Arkansas statute provides that if any foreign corporation authorized to do business in the state should remove to the federal court any suit brought against it by an Arkansas citizen or initiate any suit in the federal court against a local citizen, without the consent of the other party, Arkansas's secretary of state should revoke all authority of the corporation to do business in the state. The Burke Construction Company, a Missouri corporation authorized to do business in Arkansas, has brought a suit in federal court and has also removed to a federal court a state suit brought against it. Burke now seeks to enjoin the secretary of state from revoking its authority to do business in Arkansas, contending that the Arkansas statute is unconstitutional. Should the injunction be issued? Explain.

12. Little Switzerland Brewing Company was incorporated on January 28. On February 18, Ellison and Oxley were made directors of the company after they purchased some stock. Then, on September 25, Ellison and Oxley signed stock subscription agreements to purchase 5,000 shares each. Under the agreement, they both issued a note that indicated that they would pay for the stock "at their discretion." Two years later in March, the board of directors passed a resolution canceling the stock subscription agreements of Ellison and Oxley. The creditors of Little Switzerland brought suit against Ellison and Oxley to recover the money owed under the subscription agreements. Are Ellison and Oxley liable? Why?

13. Oahe Enterprises was formed by the efforts of Emmick, who acted as a promoter and contributed shares of Colonial Manors, Inc. (CM) stock in exchange for stock in Oahe. The CM stock had been valued by CM's directors for internal stock option purposes at $19 per share. However, one month prior to Emmick's incorporation of Oahe Enterprises, CM's board reduced the stock value to $9.50 per share. Although Emmick knew of this reduction before the meeting to form Oahe Enterprises, he did not disclose this information to the Morrises, the other shareholders of the new corporation. Can Oahe Enterprises recover the shortfall?

14. In April, Cranson was asked to invest in a new business corporation that was about to be created. He agreed to purchase stock and to become an officer and director. After his attorney advised him that the corporation had been formed under the laws of Maryland, Cranson paid for and received a stock certificate evidencing his ownership of shares. The business of the new venture was conducted as if it were a corporation. Cranson was elected president, and he conducted all of his corporate actions, including those with IBM (http://www.ibm.com), as an officer of the corporation. At no time did he assume any personal obligation or pledge his individual credit to IBM. As a result of an oversight of the attorney, of which Cranson was unaware, the certificate of incorporation, which had been signed and acknowledged prior to May 1, was not filed until November 24. Between May 1 and November 8, the "corporation" purchased eight computers from IBM. The corporation made only partial payment. Can IBM hold Cranson personally liable for the $4,333.40 balance due? Explain.

15. On September 14, 2000, Healthwin-Midtown Convalescent Hospital, Inc. (Healthwin) was incorporated in California for the purpose of operating a health care facility. From that date until November 30, 2003, it participated as a provider of services under the federal Medicare Act and received periodic payments from the United States Department of Health, Education and Welfare (http://www.hhs.gov/). Undisputed audits revealed that a series of overpayments had been made to Healthwin in the total amount of $30,481.00. The United States brought an action to recover this sum from the defendants, Healthwin and Israel Zide. Zide was a member of the board of directors of the Healthwin corporation, the administrator of its health care facility, its president, and owner of 50 percent of its stock. Only Zide could sign the corporation's checks without prior approval of another corporate officer. In addition, Zide had a 50 percent interest in a partnership that owned both the realty in which Healthwin's health care facility was located and the furnishings used at that facility. The corporation was initially undercapitalized, and its liabilities continued to exceed its assets substantially. Zide exercised control over Healthwin, causing its finances to become inextricably intertwined both with his personal finances and with his other business holdings. The United States contends that the corporate veil should be pierced and that Zide should be held personally liable for the Medicare overpayments made to Healthwin. Is the United States correct in its assertion? Why?

16. MPL Leasing Corporation is a California corporation that provides financing plans to dealers of Saxon Business Products. MPL invited Jay Johnson, a Saxon dealer in Alabama, to attend a sales seminar in Atlanta. MPL and Johnson entered into an agreement under which Johnson was to lease Saxon copiers with an option to buy. MPL

shipped the equipment into Alabama and filed a financing statement with the secretary of state. When Johnson became delinquent with his payments to MPL, MPL brought an action against Johnson in an Alabama court. Johnson moved to dismiss the action, claiming that MPL was not qualified to conduct business in Alabama and was thus barred from enforcing its contract with Johnson in an Alabama court. Is Johnson correct?

17. Berger was planning to produce a fashion show in Las Vegas. In April Berger entered into a written licensing agreement with CBS Films, Inc., a wholly owned subsidiary of CBS (http://www.cbs.com), for presentation of the show. The next year, Stewart Cowley decided to produce a fashion show similar to Berger's and entered into a contract with CBS. CBS broadcast Cowley's show, but not Berger's. Berger brought this action against CBS to recover damages for breach of his contract with CBS Films. Berger claimed that CBS was liable because CBS Films was its instrumentality or *alter ego*, and that the court should disregard the parent-subsidiary form. In support of this claim, Berger showed that CBS Films's directors were employees of CBS, that CBS's organizational chart included CBS Films, and that all lines of employee authority from CBS Films passed through CBS employees to the CBS chairman of the board. CBS, in turn, argued that Berger had failed to justify piercing the corporate veil and disregarding the corporate identity of CBS Films to hold CBS liable. Decision?

18. Frank McAnarney and Joseph Lemon entered into an agreement to promote a corporation to engage in the manufacture of farm implements. Before the corporation was organized, McAnarney and Lemon solicited subscriptions to the stock of the corporation and presented a written agreement for the subscribers to sign. The agreement provided that the subscribers would pay $100 per share for stock in the corporation in consideration of McAnarney and Lemon's agreement to organize the corporation and advance the preincorporation expenses. Thomas Jordan signed the agreement, making application for 100 shares of stock. After the articles of incorporation had been filed with the Secretary of State but before the charter was issued to the corporation, Jordan died. The administrator of Jordan's estate notified McAnarney and Lemon that the estate would not honor Jordan's subscription.

After the formation of the corporation, Franklin Adams signed a subscription agreement making application for 100 shares of stock. Before the corporation accepted the subscription, Adams informed the corporation that he was canceling it.

a. Can the corporation enforce Jordan's stock subscription against Jordan's estate?
b. Can the corporation enforce Adams's stock subscription?

19. Green & Freedman Baking Company (Green & Freedman) was a family-owned Massachusetts corporation formed in 1934 that produced and sold baked goods. The terms of a collective bargaining agreement required Green & Freedman Baking Company to make periodic payments on behalf of its unionized drivers to the New England Teamsters and Baking Industry Health Benefits and Insurance Fund (Health Fund) (http://www.teamstersjc10.com/medical.html). After experiencing financial difficulties, Green & Freedman ceased to make the agreed-upon contributions and on January 15, 1993, transferred all remaining assets to a successor entity named Boston Bakers, Inc. (Boston Bakers). Boston Bakers operated essentially the same business as Green & Freedman until its demise in 1995. The Health Fund sued Green & Freedman, Boston Bakers, and the two corporations' principals, Richard Elman and Stanley Elman to recover the payments owed by Green & Freedman with interest, costs, and penalties. Both corporate defendants conceded liability for the delinquent contributions owed by Green & Freedman to the Health Fund. The suit against the Elmans was based on piercing the corporate veil with respect to Green & Freedman and Boston Bakers. The Elmans, however, denied they were personally liable for these corporate debts. Are the Elmans liable? Explain.

http:// **Internet Exercise** Find samples of (a) articles of incorporation and (b) corporate bylaws.

CHAPTER 35

Financial Structure of Corporations

Corporation. An ingenious device for obtaining individual profit without individual responsibility.

AMBROSE BIERCE, *THE DEVIL'S DICTIONARY*, 1881–1906

Learning Objectives

After reading this chapter you should be able to:

1. Distinguish between equity and debt securities.
2. Identify and describe the principal kinds of debt securities.
3. Identify and describe the principal kinds of equity securities.
4. Explain what type and amount of consideration a corporation may validly receive for the shares it issues.
5. Explain the legal restrictions imposed upon dividends and other distributions.

Capital is necessary for any business to function. Two of the principal sources for corporate financing involve debt and equity investment securities. Although equity securities represent an ownership interest in the corporation and include both common and preferred stock, corporations finance most of their continued operations through debt securities. Debt securities, which include notes and bonds, do not represent an ownership interest in the corporation; rather, they create a debtor-creditor relationship between the corporation and the bondholder. The third principal way in which a corporation may meet its financial needs is through retained earnings.

All states have statutes regulating the issuance and sale of corporate shares and other securities. Popularly known as **Blue Sky Laws,** these statutes typically contain provisions prohibiting fraud in the sale of securities. In addition, a number of states require the registration of securities, and some states also regulate brokers, dealers, and others who engage in the securities business.

In 1933, Congress passed the first federal statute for the regulation of securities offered for sale and sold through the use of the mails or otherwise in interstate commerce. The statute requires a corporation to disclose certain information about a proposed security in a registration statement and in its ***prospectus*** (an offer a corporation makes to interest people in buying securities). Although the SEC does not examine the merits of the proposed security and although registration does not guarantee the accuracy of the facts presented in the registration statement or prospectus, the law does prohibit false and misleading statements under penalty of fine or imprisonment or both.

Under certain conditions, a corporation may receive an exemption from the requirement of registration under the

Blue Sky Laws of most states and the Securities Act of 1933. If no exemption is available, a corporation offering for sale or selling its shares of stock or other securities, as well as any person selling such securities, is subject to court injunction, possible criminal prosecution, and civil liability in damages to the persons to whom securities are sold in violation of the regulatory statute. A discussion of federal regulation of securities appears in Chapter 40.

An investor has the right to transfer her investment securities by sale, gift, or pledge. The right to transfer is a valuable one, and easy transferability augments the value and marketability of investment securities. The availability of a ready market for any security affords liquidity and makes the security both attractive to investors and useful as collateral. The Uniform Commercial Code, Article 8, Investment Securities, contains the statutory rules applicable to transfers of investment securities; these rules are similar to those in Article 3, which concern negotiable instruments. In 1994 a revision to Article 8 was promulgated, which has now been adopted by all of the states. The federal securities laws also regulate several aspects of the transfer of investment securities, as discussed in Chapter 40.

In this chapter, we will discuss debt and equity securities as well as the payment of dividends and other distributions to shareholders.

DEBT SECURITIES

Corporations frequently find it advantageous to use debt as a source of funds. **Debt securities** (also called **bonds**) generally involve the corporation's promise to repay the principal amount of a loan at a stated time and to pay interest, usually at a fixed rate, while the debt is outstanding. In addition to bonds, a corporation may finance its operations through other forms of debt, such as credit extended by its suppliers and short-term commercial paper. Some states, but not the Revised Act, permit articles of incorporation to confer voting rights on debt security holders; a few states allow other shareholder rights to be conferred on bondholders.

Practical Advice

Carefully consider the ratio between debt and equity financing, recognizing that this ratio varies considerably with the type and life cycle of a corporation.

CPA AUTHORITY TO ISSUE DEBT SECURITIES

The Revised Act provides that every corporation has the power to borrow money and to issue its notes, bonds, and other obligations. The board of directors may issue bonds without the authorization or consent of the shareholders.

CPA TYPES OF DEBT SECURITIES

Depending on their characteristics, debt securities can be classified into various types, each offering numerous variants and combinations. A corporation typically issues debt securities under an **indenture** or debt agreement, which specifies in great detail the terms of the loan.

Metropolitan Life Insurance Company v. RJR Nabisco, Inc.

United States District Court, S.D. New York, 1989
716 F.Supp. 1504

FACTS On October 20, 1988, F. Ross Johnson, then the CEO of RJR Nabisco (RJR) **(http://www.nabisco.com)**, proposed a $17 billion leveraged buyout (LBO) of RJR's shareholders at $75 dollars per share. (An LBO occurs when a group of investors, usually including the company's management, buy the company with little equity and significant new debt. The debt typically is financed through mortgages or high-risk/high-yield bonds, known as "junk bonds." A portion of this debt normally is secured by the company's assets. After the transaction is complete, some of these assets usually are sold to reduce the debt.) Within a few days, the investment group led by Johnson, the Kohlberg Kravis Roberts & Co. (KKR) **(http://www.kkr.com)** investment firm, and others began a bidding war. On December 1, 1988, an RJR committee recommended that RJR accept KKR's proposal of a $24 billion LBO at $109 per share. Metropolitan Life Insurance Co. (MetLife) **(http://www.metlife.com)**, a life insurance company with $88 billion in assets and $49 billion in debt securities holdings, owned $340,542,000 in principal amount of RJR Nabisco bonds purchased between July 1975 and July 1988. These bonds bore interest rates from 8 to 10.25 percent. Jefferson-Pilot Life Insurance Co. **(http://www.jpfinancial.com)**, with $3 billion in assets, of which $1.5 billion was in debt securities, owned $9.34 million in principal of RJR bonds purchased between June 1978 and June 1988.

MetLife and Jefferson-Pilot (plaintiffs) argued that RJR had an implied duty of good faith and fair dealing not to incur the debt involved in the LBO. They asserted that RJR consistently had reassured its bondholders that it had a "mandate" from its board of directors to maintain RJR's preferred credit rating. The plaintiffs alleged that RJR's actions drastically impaired the value of their bond holdings, in effect misappropriated the value of those bonds to finance the LBO, and distributed the windfall to the company's shareholders. They declared that these actions constituted a breach of the implied duty and betrayed the fundamental basis of their bargain with RJR. The plaintiffs alleged that they unfairly suffered a multimillion dollar loss in the value of their bonds and that, therefore, RJR should redeem their bonds.

RJR defended the LBO by pointing to express provisions in the bond indentures that permitted mergers and the assumption of additional debt. These provisions, RJR pointed out, were known to the market and to the plaintiffs, who were sophisticated investors who freely bought the bonds and who were equally free to sell them at any time. RJR argued that no legal grounds supported the existence of an implied duty.

DECISION Judgment for RJR.

OPINION Walter, J. The bonds implicated by this suit are governed by long, detailed indentures, which in turn are governed by New York contract law. No one disputes that the holders of public bond issues, like plaintiffs here, often enter the market after the indentures have been negotiated and memorialized. Thus, those indentures are often not the product of face-to-face negotiations between the ultimate holders and the issuing company. What remains equally true, however, is that underwriters ordinarily negotiate the terms of the indentures with the issuers. Since the underwriters must then sell or place the bonds, they necessarily negotiate in part with the interests of the buyers in mind. Moreover, these indentures were not secret agreements foisted upon unwitting participants in the bond market. No successive holder is required to accept or to continue to hold the bonds, governed by their accompanying indentures; indeed, plaintiffs readily admit that they could have sold their bonds right up until the announcement of the LBO. [Citation.] Instead, sophisticated investors like plaintiffs are well aware of the indenture terms and, presumably, review them carefully before lending hundreds of millions of dollars to any company.

Indeed, the prospectuses for the indentures contain a statement relevant to this action:

> The Indenture contains no restrictions on the creation of unsecured short-term debt by [RJR Nabisco] or its subsidiaries, no restriction on the creation of unsecured Funded Debt by [RJR Nabisco] or its subsidiaries which are not Restricted Subsidiaries, and no restriction on the payment of dividends by [RJR Nabisco].

Further, as plaintiffs themselves note, the contracts at issue "[do] not impose debt limits, since debt is assumed to be used for productive purposes." [Citation.]

* * *

The indentures at issue clearly address the eventuality of a merger. They impose certain related restrictions not at issue in this suit, but no restriction that would prevent the recent RJR Nabisco merger transaction. * * *

* * *

In contracts like bond indentures, "an implied covenant * * * derives its substance directly from the language of the Indenture, and 'cannot give the holders of Debentures any rights inconsistent with those set out in the Indenture.' *[Where] plaintiffs' contractual rights [have not been] violated, there can have been no breach of an implied covenant.*" [Citation.].

* * *

The appropriate analysis, then, is first to examine the indentures to determine "the fruits of the agreement" between the parties, and then to decide whether those "fruits" have been spoiled—which is to say, whether plaintiffs' contractual rights have been violated by defendants.

* * *

A review of the parties' submissions and the indentures themselves satisfies the Court that the substantive "fruits" guaranteed by those contracts and relevant to the present motions include the periodic and regular payment of interest and the eventual repayment of principal. * * *

It is not necessary to decide that indentures like those at issue could never support a finding of additional benefits under different circumstances with different parties. Rather, for present purposes, it is sufficient to conclude what obligation is not covered, either explicitly or implicitly, by these contracts held by these plaintiffs. Accordingly, this Court holds that the "fruits" of these indentures do not include an implied restrictive covenant that would prevent the incurrence of new debt to facilitate the recent LBO. To hold otherwise would permit these plaintiffs to straightjacket the company in order to guarantee their investment. These plaintiffs do not invoke an implied covenant of good faith to protect a legitimate, mutually contemplated benefit of the indentures; rather, they seek to have this Court create an additional benefit for which they did not bargain.

* * *

The sort of unbounded and one-sided elasticity urged by plaintiffs would interfere with and destabilize the market. And this Court, like the parties to these contracts, cannot ignore or disavow the marketplace in which the contract is performed. Nor can it ignore the expectations of that market—expectations, for instance, that the terms of an indenture will be upheld, and that a court will not, sua sponte, add new substantive terms to that indenture as it sees fit. The Court has no reason to believe that the market, in evaluating bonds such as those at issue here, did not discount for the possibility that any company, even one the size of RJR Nabisco, might engage in an LBO heavily financed by debt. That the bonds did not lose any of their value until the October 20, 1988 announcement of a possible RJR Nabisco LBO only suggests that the market had theretofore evaluated the risks of such a transaction as slight.

INTERPRETATION Bond indentures are highly detailed contracts specifying the terms of the underlying loan. The courts will not imply any duties that are inconsistent with the terms of such a contract.

ETHICAL QUESTION Is the court's decision fair to the bondholders? Explain.

CRITICAL THINKING QUESTION Do you agree with the court's reluctance to imply an implied duty of good faith and fair dealing? Explain.

UNSECURED BONDS

Unsecured bonds, usually called **debentures**, have only the obligation of the corporation behind them. Debenture holders are thus unsecured creditors and rank equally with other general creditors. To protect the unsecured bondholders, indentures frequently impose limitations on the corporation's borrowing, its payment of dividends, and its redemption and reacquisition of its own shares. An indenture may also require a corporation to maintain specified minimum reserves.

SECURED BONDS

A secured creditor is one whose claim is not only enforceable against the general assets of the corporation but is also a lien on specific property. Thus, **secured** or mortgage **bonds** provide the security of specific corporate property in addition to the general obligation of the corporation. After resorting to the specified security, the holder of secured bonds becomes a general creditor for any unsatisfied amount of the debt.

INCOME BONDS

Traditionally, debt securities bear a fixed interest rate that is payable without regard to the financial condition of the corporation. **Income bonds**, on the other hand, condition the payment of interest to some extent on corporate earnings. **Participating bonds** call for a stated percentage of return regardless of earnings, with additional payments dependent on earnings.

CONVERTIBLE BONDS

Usually at the option of the holder, **convertible bonds** may be exchanged, in a specified ratio, for other securities of the corporation. For example, a convertible bond may provide that the bondholder shall have the right for a specified time to exchange each bond for twenty shares of common stock.

CALLABLE BONDS

Callable bonds are bonds subject to a redemption provision that permits the corporation to redeem or call (pay off) all or part of the issue before maturity at a specified redemption price.

Practical Advice

If you purchase callable bonds, recognize that if interest rates decline, the corporation is likely to exercise its redemption privilege.

EQUITY SECURITIES

An **equity security** is a source of capital creating an ownership interest in the corporation. The holders of equity securities, as owners of the corporation, occupy a position financially riskier than that of creditors; and changes in the corporation's fortunes and general economic conditions have a greater effect on shareholders than on any other class of investor.

CONSUMER insight

Bond Ratings: What Do They Tell Us? Who Makes Them?

"Triple-A," "investment grade," and "junk" are familiar terms to those who invest in bonds. All three terms refer to a central concern of investors: what is the probability that the issuer of bonds will repay the principal at maturity and make scheduled interest payments on time? Put another way, what is the risk of default?

A high rating is supposed to reflect a high probability of repayment. The greater this probability, the less risk to the investor. Conversely, lower rated bonds are judged to be riskier. Generally, safer bonds have a lower yield, riskier bonds a higher yield. Investors taking greater risks demand a higher return.

Independent rating agencies analyze the companies and municipalities that issue bonds and assign ratings to reflect the creditworthiness of the issuer. The best-known agencies in the United States are Standard & Poor's and Moody's Investor Service. Standard & Poor's bond ratings, from highest to lowest, are AAA, AA, A; BBB, BB, B; CCC, CC, C; and D (in payment default). Moody's ratings are comparable: Aaa, Aa, A; Baa, Ba, B; and Caa, Ca, C. Moody's does not give a D.

"Investment grade" refers to the top four ratings, denoting bonds that are relatively safe investments for individuals and institutions. In contrast, "junk bonds" (generally anything rated below the top four ratings) are low-rated, risky, and high-yielding. Junk bonds were a favorite financing vehicle for leveraged buyouts during the 1980s. The bonds attracted buyers hungry for yield and not very concerned about safety. However, they put a huge debt burden on the issuing companies—some of which went into highly publicized bankruptcies.

The relationship of risk to return in the bond markets can be checked in the financial pages of a newspaper such as *The Wall Street Journal*. For example, on a day when bonds of an AAA-rated company, with a maturity date in the year 2023, were priced to yield 6.569 percent, bonds of a BB+-rated company, with a maturity date in 2013, were priced to yield 8.619 percent.

The quality of a particular bond can change over time as business conditions change for the issuer. For this reason, bond ratings have a subjective component. Analysts look not only at an issuing company's financial statements but also at trends in the industry-and adjust their ratings accordingly. For example, a *New York Times* article described the efforts of big bank holding companies such as Chase Manhattan Corp., Citicorp, and Chemical Banking Corp. to raise their ratings. Formerly rated as high as AAA in the 1970s, these banks had seen their ratings decline to BBB by the early 1990s through a succession of woes; new competition from Wall Street and from banks abroad, then losses on loans to Latin American countries, followed by bad real estate loans in the United States. Structural changes in the banking industry have made high ratings much harder to obtain. The *Times* quoted a Moody's official: "Most institutions think, 'If we get our financial ratios back to where they were when we were double-A, we will be double-A again.' That is not going to happen. The bar is getting higher."

Raising its rating can save a company money when it issues new bonds: with a higher rating the company pays a lower interest rate, resulting in savings that can directly affect the bottom line. For example, one of the big banks in the *Times* story, with a stated goal of raising its rating from triple-B to double-A, figured that the upgrade could increase its annual earnings by at least $150 million.

If a rating tells us how risky a bond is, then what, if anything, does it not tell us?

Bond ratings relate to bond issuers, not investors. Thus, the ratings do not say whether a particular bond is an appropriate investment for a particular buyer. And ratings do not forecast the movement of interest rates, movement that causes bond prices to rise or fall.

In other words, bond ratings are only a tool for investors, not a substitute for good judgment.

Sources: "Big Banks' Goal: Higher Ratings," *New York Times*, 8 June 1993, C1; "Bond Market Data Bank 10/6/93," *The Wall Street Journal*, 7 October 1993, C21; *Moody's Bond Record*, 3; and *Understanding Wall Street*, 3d ed., 131.

Though a proportionate proprietary interest in a corporate enterprise can be described in terms of the **shares** a person owns, shares do not in any way vest their owner with title to any of the corporation's property. However, shares do confer on their owner a threefold interest in the corporation: (1) the right to participate in control, (2) the right to participate in the earnings of the corporation, and (3) the right to participate in the residual assets of the corporation on dissolution. The shareholder's interest is usually represented by a certificate of ownership and is recorded by the corporation.

CPA Issuance of Shares

The state of incorporation regulates the issuance of shares by determining the type of shares that may be issued, the kinds and amount of consideration for which shares may be issued, and the rights of shareholders to purchase a proportionate part of additionally issued shares. Moreover, the federal government and each state in which the shares are issued or sold regulate the issuance and sale of shares.

AUTHORITY TO ISSUE

The initial amount of shares to be issued is determined by the promoters or incorporators and is generally governed by practical business considerations and financial needs. A corporation is limited, however, to selling only the amount of shares that has been authorized in its articles of incorporation. Unauthorized shares of stock that are purportedly issued by a corporation are void. The rights of parties entitled to these over-issued shares are governed by Article 8 of the Uniform Commercial Code, which provides that the corporation must either obtain an identical security, if one is reasonably available, for the person entitled to the security or pay that person the price he (or the last purchaser for value) paid for it, with interest.

Once the amount of shares that the corporation is authorized to issue has been established and specified in the charter, it cannot be increased or decreased without amendment to the charter. Consequently, articles of incorporation commonly specify more shares than are to be issued immediately.

Practical Advice

When drafting the articles of incorporation, you should authorize shares in addition to those that are to be immediately issued unless the state-imposed fees based on the number of authorized shares is prohibitive.

PREEMPTIVE RIGHTS

A shareholder's proportionate interest in a corporation can be changed by either a disproportionate issuance of additional shares or a disproportionate reacquisition of outstanding shares. Management is subject to fiduciary duties in both types of transactions. Moreover, when a corporation issues additional shares, a shareholder may have the **preemptive right** to purchase a proportionate part of the new issue. Preemptive rights are used far more frequently in closely held corporations than in publicly traded corporations, possibly because, without such rights, a shareholder may be unable to prevent a dilution of his ownership interest in the corporation. For example, Leonard owns 200 shares of stock of the Fordham Company, which has a total of 1,000 shares outstanding. The company decides to increase its capital stock by issuing 1,000 additional shares of stock. If Leonard has preemptive rights, he and every other shareholder will be offered one share of the newly issued stock for every share they own. If he accepts the offer and buys the stock, he will have 400 shares of a total of 2,000 outstanding, and his relative interest in the corporation will be unchanged. Without preemptive rights, however, he would have only 200 out of the 2,000 shares outstanding; instead of owning 20 percent of the stock, he would own 10 percent.

At common law, shareholders have preemptive rights to the issuance of additionally authorized shares. Such rights do not apply, however, to the reissue of previously issued shares, shares issued for noncash consideration, or shares issued in connection with a merger or consolidation. The jurisdictions are divided over whether preemptive rights apply to the issuance of unissued shares that were originally authorized.

Modern statutes expressly authorize articles of incorporation to deny or limit preemptive rights. In some states, preemptive rights exist unless denied by the charter ("opt-out"); in others, they do not exist unless the charter so provides ("opt-in"). The Revised Act adopts the latter approach: shareholders have no preemptive rights unless the charter provides for them. If the charter simply states that the corporation elects to have preemptive rights, the shareholders have a preemptive right to acquire proportional amounts of the corporation's unissued shares but have no such right with respect to (1) shares issued as compensation to directors, officers, and employees; (2) shares issued within six months of incorporation; and (3) shares issued for consideration other than money. In addition, holders of nonvoting preferred stock have no preemptive rights with respect to any class of shares; and holders of voting common shares have no preemptive rights with respect to preferred stock unless the preferred stock is convertible into common stock. The articles of incorporation may expressly modify any one or all of these limitations.

Practical Advice

To protect your ownership share from dilution, when organizing a close corporation you should consider including in the charter a carefully drafted provision for preemptive rights. You should recognize, however, that preemptive rights will protect you only if you can afford to purchase a proportionate part of a new issue of shares.

AMOUNT OF CONSIDERATION FOR SHARES

The board of directors usually determines the price for which the corporation will issue shares, although the charter may reserve this power to the shareholders. Shares are deemed fully paid and nonassessable when the corporation receives the consideration for which the board of directors authorized their issuance. The amount of consideration depends on the kind of shares being issued.

Par Value Stock Par value shares may be issued for any amount, not less than par, set by the board of directors or shareholders. The par value of stock must be stated in the articles of incorporation. The consideration received constitutes *stated capital* to the extent of the par value of the shares; any consideration in excess of par value constitutes *capital surplus*. It is common practice to authorize *low* or *nominal* par shares, such as $1 per share, and issue these shares at a considerably higher price, thereby providing ample capital surplus. By doing so, the company, in some jurisdictions, obtains greater flexibility in declaring subsequent distributions to shareholders.

The Revised Act, the 1980 amendments to the MBCA, and at least twenty-eight states have eliminated the concepts of par value, stated capital, and capital surplus. Under these acts, all shares may be issued for such consideration as authorized by the board of directors or, if the charter so provides, the shareholders. A corporation may, however, elect to issue shares with par value.

No Par Value Stock Shares without par value may be issued for any amount set by the board of directors or shareholders. Under incorporation statutes recognizing par value, stated capital, and capital surplus, the entire consideration a corporation receives for such stock constitutes *stated capital* unless the board of directors allocates a portion of the consideration to capital surplus. The directors are free to allocate any or all of the consideration received, unless the no par stock has a liquidation preference. In that event, only the consideration in excess of the amount of liquidation preference may be allocated to capital surplus. No par shares provide the directors great latitude in establishing capital surplus, which can, in some jurisdictions, provide greater flexibility in terms of subsequent distributions to shareholders.

Practical Advice

Because a number of states grant more favorable tax treatment to par value stock, often it is more cost effective to issue low par value stock: this approach provides nearly the same flexibility of no par stock but with lower taxes.

Treasury Stock **Treasury stock** refers to shares that a corporation buys back after it has issued them. Treasury shares are issued but not outstanding, in contrast to shares owned by shareholders, which are deemed issued and outstanding. A corporation may sell treasury shares for any amount the board of directors determines, even if the shares have a par value that is more than the sale price. Treasury shares do not provide voting rights or preemptive rights. In addition, no dividend is paid on treasury stock.

The Revised Act carries forward the 1980 amendments to the MBCA, which eliminated the concept of treasury shares. Under the Revised Act, all shares reacquired by a corporation are authorized but unissued shares, unless the articles of incorporation prohibit reissue, in which event the authorized shares are reduced by the number of shares reacquired.

Figure 35-1 illustrates the categorization of authorized shares.

PAYMENT FOR SHARES

Payment for shares involves two major issues. First, what type of consideration may the corporation validly accept in payment for shares? Second, who shall determine the value to be placed upon the consideration the corporation receives in payment for shares?

Type of Consideration The definition of consideration for the issuance of capital stock is somewhat more limited than the definition of consideration under contract law. In about twenty-five states, cash, property, and services actually rendered to the corporation are generally acceptable as valid consideration, whereas promissory notes and promises regarding the performance of future services are not. Some states permit shares to be issued for preincorporation services; other states do not.

The Revised Act greatly liberalized these rules by specifically validating for the issuance of shares consideration consisting of any tangible or intangible property or benefit to the corporation, including cash, services performed, contracts for future services, and promissory notes.

Valuation of Consideration Determining the value to be placed on the consideration that stock purchasers will exchange for shares is the responsibility of the directors. Many jurisdictions hold that this valuation is a matter of opinion and that, in the absence of fraud in the transaction, the judgment of the board of directors as to the value of the consideration the corporation receives for shares shall be conclusive. For example, assume that the directors of Elite Corporation authorize the issuance of 2,000 shares of common stock for $5 per share to Kramer for property the directors purportedly value at $10,000. The valuation, however, is fraudulent; and the property is actually worth only $5,000. Kramer is liable to Elite Corporation and its creditors for $5,000. If, on the other hand, the directors had made the valuation without fraud and in good faith, Kramer would not be liable, even though the property is actually worth less than $10,000.

Figure 35-1
Issuance of Shares

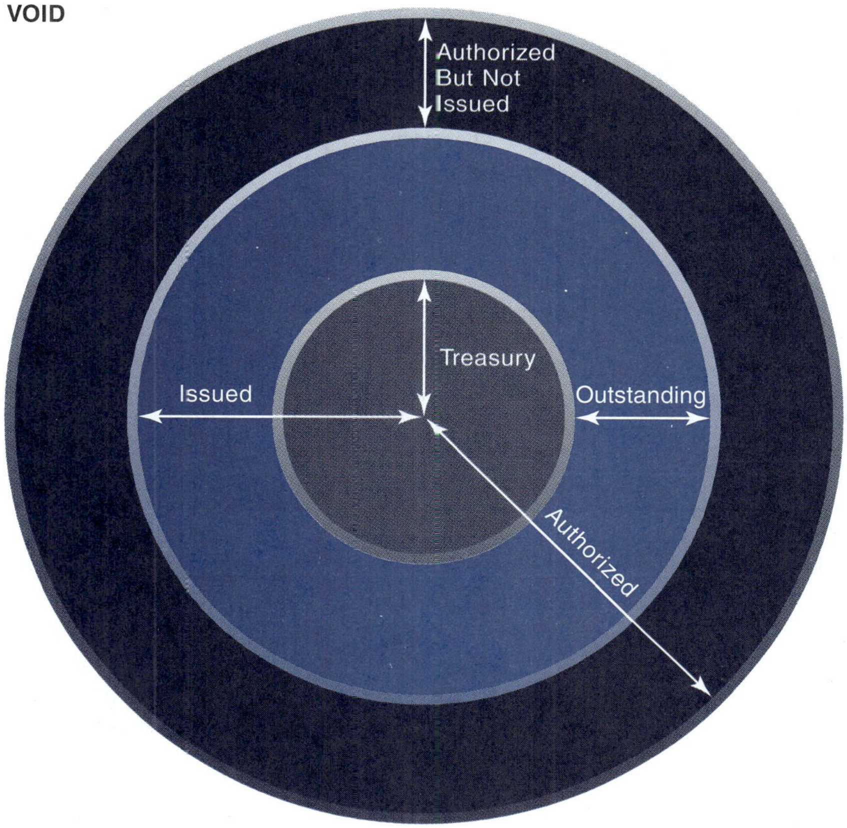

Under the Revised Act, the directors simply determine whether the consideration received (or to be received) for shares is *adequate*. Their determination is "conclusive insofar as the adequacy of consideration for the issuance of shares relates to whether the shares are validly issued, fully paid, and nonassessable." Under the Revised Act, the articles of incorporation may reserve to the shareholders the powers granted to the board regarding the issuance of shares.

> **Practical Advice**
>
> To protect the value of your shares from dilution, when organizing a close corporation you should consider including in the charter a carefully drafted provision reserving to the shareholders the power to determine the value of consideration received for the issuance of additional shares.

LIABILITY FOR SHARES

A purchaser of shares has no liability to the corporation or its creditors with respect to shares except to pay the corporation either the consideration for which the shares were authorized to be issued or the consideration specified in the preincorporation stock subscription. When the corporation receives that consideration, the shares are fully paid and nonassessable. A transferee who acquires shares in good faith and without knowledge or notice that the full consideration had not been paid is not personally liable to the corporation or its creditors for the unpaid portion of the consideration.

CPA CLASSES OF SHARES

Corporations are generally authorized by statute to issue different classes of stock, which may vary with respect to their rights to dividends, their voting rights, and their right to share in the assets of the corporation on liquidation. The usual stock classifications are common and preferred shares. Although the Revised Act has eliminated the terms *preferred* and *common*, it permits the issuance of shares with different preferences, limitations, and relative rights. The Revised Act, however, explicitly requires a corporation's charter to authorize "(1) one or more classes of shares that together have unlimited voting rights, and (2) one or more classes of shares (which may be the same class or classes as those with voting rights) that together are entitled to receive the net assets of the corporation upon dissolution." In most states, however, even nonvoting shares may vote on certain mergers, share exchanges, and other fundamental changes that affect that class of shares as a class. See Chapter 37.

COMMON STOCK

Common stock does not have any special contract rights or preferences. Frequently the only class of stock outstanding, it generally represents the greatest proportion of the corporation's capital structure and bears the greatest risk of loss should the enterprise fail.

PREFERRED STOCK

Stock generally is considered **preferred stock** if it has contractual rights superior to those of common stock with regard to dividends, assets on liquidation, or both. Other special rights or privileges generally do not remove stock from the common stock classification. The articles of incorporation must provide for the contractual rights and preferences of an issue of preferred stock.

Dividend Preferences Though the holders of an issue of preferred stock with a **dividend preference** will receive full dividends before any dividend may be paid to holders of common stock, no dividend is payable on any class of stock, common or preferred, unless the board of directors has declared such dividend.

Preferred stock may provide that dividends are cumulative, noncumulative, or cumulative to the extent earned. For ***cumulative*** dividends, if the board does not declare regular dividends on the preferred stock, such omitted dividends cumulate, and no dividend may be declared on the common stock until all dividend arrearages on the preferred stock are declared and paid. If noncumulative, regular dividends do not cumulate on the board's failure to declare them, and all rights to a dividend for the period omitted are gone forever. Accordingly, ***noncumulative*** stock has priority over common stock only in the fiscal period during which a dividend on common stock is declared. Unless the charter expressly makes the dividends on preferred stock noncumulative, the courts generally hold them to be cumulative. ***Cumulative-to-the-extent-earned*** shares cumulate unpaid dividends only to the extent funds were legally available to pay such dividends during that fiscal period.

Preferred stock also may be participating, although generally it is not. **Participating preferred** shares are entitled to their original dividend, and after the common shares receive a specified amount, the participating preferred share with the common in any additional dividends. The nature and extent of such participation on a specified basis with the common stock must be stated in the articles of incorporation. For example, a class of participating preferred stock could be entitled to share at the same rate with the common stock in any additional distribution of earnings for a given year after provision has been made for payment of the prior preferred dividend and for payment of dividends on the common stock at a rate equal to the fixed rate of the preferred.

Liquidation Preferences After a corporation has been dissolved, its assets liquidated, and the claims of its creditors satisfied, the remaining assets are distributed *pro rata* among the shareholders according to their priority as provided in the articles of incorporation. If a class of stock with a dividend preference does not expressly provide for a preference of any kind on dissolution and liquidation, its holders share pro rata with the common shareholders.

When the articles provide a **liquidation preference**, preferred stock has priority over common to the extent the articles state. In addition, if specified, preferred shares may participate beyond the liquidation preference in a stated ratio with other classes of shares. Such shares are said to be participating preferred with reference to liquidation. Preferred shares not so specified do not participate beyond the liquidation preference.

> **Practical Advice**
>
> When organizing a corporation, consider issuing common stock to the original shareholders and preferred stock to subsequent investors.

STOCK OPTIONS

A corporation may issue **stock options** entitling their holders to purchase from the corporation shares of a specified class or classes. A ***stock warrant*** is a type of stock option that typically has a longer term and is freely transferable. A ***stock right*** is a short-term warrant. The board of directors determines the terms upon which stock rights, options, or warrants are issued; their form and content; and the consideration for which the shares are to be issued. One use of stock options and warrants is in incentive compensation plans for directors, officers, and employees. Another is to assist a corporation in raising capital by making one class of securities more attractive by including in it the right to purchase shares in another class.

CONCEPT REVIEW

Debt and Equity Securities

	Debt	Equity: Common	Equity: Preferred
Ownership Interest	No	Yes	Yes
Obligation to Repay Principal	Yes	No	No
Fixed Maturity	Yes	No	No
Obligation to Pay Income	Yes	No	No
Preference on Income	Yes	No	Yes
Preference on Liquidation	Yes	No	Yes
Voting Rights	Some states	Yes, unless denied	Yes, unless denied
Redeemable	Yes	In some states	Yes
Convertible	Yes	In some states	Yes

DIVIDENDS AND OTHER DISTRIBUTIONS

The board of directors, at its discretion, determines the time and amount in which to declare distributions and dividends. The corporation's working capital requirements, shareholder expectations, tax consequences, and other factors influence the board in forming distribution policy.

TYPES OF DIVIDENDS AND OTHER DISTRIBUTIONS

CPA

The Revised Act defines a **distribution** as "a direct or indirect transfer of money or other property (except its own shares) or incurrence of indebtedness by a corporation to or for the benefit of its shareholders with respect to any of its shares. A distribution may be in the form of a declaration or payment of a dividend; a purchase, redemption, or other acquisition of shares; a distribution of indebtedness; or otherwise." A stock or share dividend is a ratable distribution of additional shares of the corporation's capital stock to its shareholders. In a stock split, the corporation simply breaks each of the issued and outstanding shares into a larger number of shares, each representing a proportionately smaller interest in the corporation. Neither a stock dividend nor a stock split is a distribution.

The Revised Act validates in close corporations unanimous shareholder agreements by which the shareholders may relax traditional corporate formalities. This provision of the Act, for example, expressly authorizes shareholder agreements that permit making distributions not in proportion to share ownership.

CASH DIVIDENDS

The most customary type of dividend is a cash dividend, declared and paid at regular intervals from legally available funds. These dividends may vary in amount, depending on the policy of the board of directors and the earnings of the enterprise.

PROPERTY DIVIDENDS

Although dividends are almost always paid in cash, shareholders occasionally have received a property dividend, a distribution of earnings in the form of property. On one occasion, a distillery declared and paid a dividend in bonded whiskey.

LIQUIDATING DIVIDENDS

Although dividends ordinarily are identified with the distribution of profits, a distribution of capital assets to shareholders is referred to as a **liquidating dividend** in some jurisdictions. Incorporation statutes usually require that the shareholder be informed when a distribution is a liquidating dividend.

REDEMPTION OF SHARES

Redemption is the corporation's repurchase of its own shares, usually at its own option. Though the Model Act and the statutes of many states permit preferred shares to be redeemed, they do not allow the redemption of common stock; in contrast, the Revised Act does not prohibit redeemable common stock. The power of redemption must be expressly provided for in the articles of incorporation.

ACQUISITION OF SHARES

A corporation may acquire its own shares. As stated previously, such shares, unless canceled, are referred to as treasury shares. Under the Revised Act, such shares are considered authorized but unissued. As with redemption, the acquisition of shares constitutes a distribution to shareholders and has an effect similar to that of a dividend.

CPA LEGAL RESTRICTIONS ON DIVIDENDS AND OTHER DISTRIBUTIONS

A number of **legal restrictions** limit the amount of **distributions** the board of directors may declare. All states have statutes restricting the funds that are legally available for dividends and other distributions of corporate assets. In many instances, contractual restrictions imposed by lenders provide even more stringent limitations on the declaration of dividends and distributions.

States restrict the payment of dividends and other distributions to protect creditors. All states impose a **"cash flow test,"** the *equity insolvency test*, which prohibits the payment of any dividend or other distribution when the corporation either is insolvent or would become so through the payment of the dividend or distribution. **Insolvency** indicates the inability of a corporation to pay its debts as they become due in the usual course of business. In addition, each state imposes further restrictions on what funds are legally available to pay dividends and other distributions. These additional restrictions, called the **balance sheet test**, are based on the corporation's assets or balance sheet, whereas the equity insolvency test is based on the corporation's cash flow.

DEFINITIONS

The legal, asset-based restrictions on the payment of dividends or other distributions involve the concepts of earned surplus, surplus, net assets, stated capital, and capital surplus. See Figure 35-2, which displays the key concepts in the legal restrictions on distributions.

Earned surplus consists of the corporation's undistributed net profits, income, gains, and losses, computed from its date of incorporation.

Surplus is the amount by which the net assets of a corporation exceed its stated capital.

Net assets equal the amount by which the total assets of a corporation exceed its total debts.

Stated capital is the sum of the consideration the corporation has received for its issued stock (except that part of the consideration properly allocated to capital surplus), including any amount transferred to stated capital when

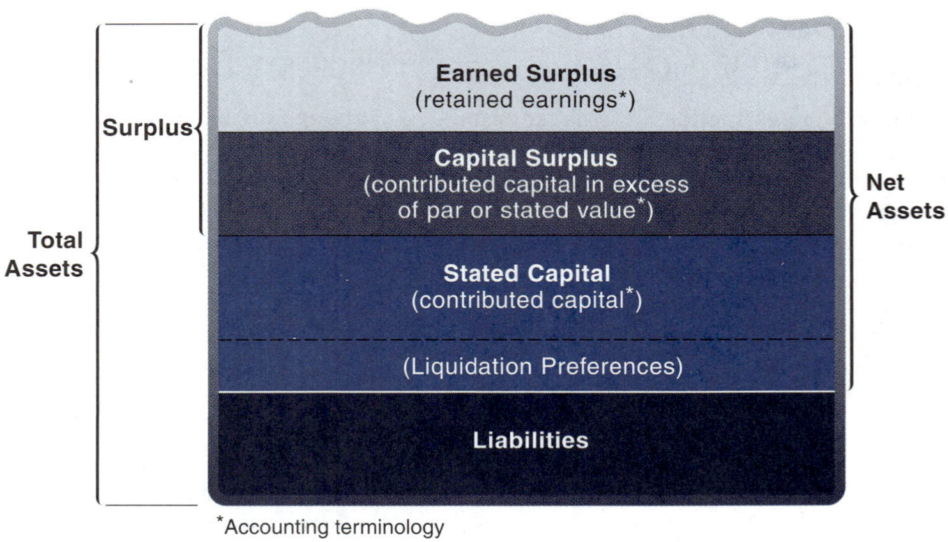

Figure 35-2
Key Concepts in Legal Restrictions Upon Distributions

stock dividends are declared. In the case of par value shares, the amount of stated capital is the total par value of all the issued shares. In the case of no par stock, it is the consideration the corporation has received for all the no par shares it has issued, except that amount allocated in a manner permitted by law, to an account designated as capital surplus or paid-in surplus.

Capital surplus means the entire surplus of a corporation other than its earned surplus. It may result from an allocation of part of the consideration received for no par shares, from any consideration in excess of par value received for par shares, or from a higher reappraisal of certain corporate assets.

LEGAL RESTRICTIONS ON CASH DIVIDENDS

Each state imposes an equity insolvency test on the payment of dividends. The states differ as to the asset-based or balance sheet test they apply. Some apply the earned surplus test and others use the surplus test. The Revised Act adopts a net asset test.

Earned Surplus Test Unreserved and unrestricted earned surplus is available for dividends in all jurisdictions. Many states permit dividends to be paid only from earned surplus; corporations in these jurisdictions may not pay dividends out of capital surplus or stated capital. In addition, dividends may not be paid if the corporation is or would be rendered insolvent in the equity sense by the payment. The MBCA used this test until 1980.

Surplus Test A number of less-restrictive states permit dividends to be paid out of any surplus—earned or capital. Some of these states express a surplus test by prohibiting dividends that impair stated capital. Moreover, dividends may not be paid if the corporation is or would be rendered insolvent in the equity sense by the payment.

Net Assets Test The MBCA, as amended in 1980, and the Revised Act have adopted a net asset test that permits a corporation to pay dividends unless its total assets after such payment would be less than the sum of its total liabilities and the maximum amount that then would be payable for all outstanding shares having preferential rights in liquidation.

LEGAL RESTRICTIONS ON LIQUIDATING DISTRIBUTIONS

Even those states that do not permit cash dividends to be paid from capital surplus usually will permit distributions, or dividends, in partial liquidation from that source. Prior to 1980, the Model Act had such a provision. A distribution paid out of such surplus returns to the shareholders part of their investment.

No such distribution may be made, however, when the corporation is insolvent or would become insolvent by the distribution. Distributions from capital surplus are also restricted to protect the liquidation preference and cumulative dividend arrearages of preferred shareholders. Unless provided for in the articles of incorporation, a liquidating dividend must be authorized not only by the board of directors but also by the affirmative vote of the holders of a majority of the outstanding shares of stock of each class.

Because the Revised Act does not distinguish between cash and liquidating dividends, it therefore imposes the same limitations upon both.

LEGAL RESTRICTIONS ON REDEMPTION AND ACQUISITION OF SHARES

To protect creditors and holders of other classes of shares, most states have statutory restrictions on redemption. A corporation may not redeem or purchase its redeemable shares when insolvent or when such redemption or purchase would render it insolvent or would reduce its net assets below the aggregate amount payable on shares having prior or equal rights to the corporation's assets upon involuntary dissolution.

A corporation may purchase its own shares only out of earned surplus or, if the articles of incorporation permit or if the shareholders approve, out of capital surplus. As with redemption, the corporation may make no purchase of shares when it is insolvent or when such purchase would make it insolvent.

The Revised Act permits a corporation to purchase, redeem, or otherwise acquire its own shares unless (1) the corporation's total assets after the distribution would be less than the sum of its total liabilities and the maximum amount that then would be payable for all outstanding shares having preferential rights in liquidation or (2) the corporation would be unable to pay its debts as they become due in the usual course of its business.

Additional restrictions may apply to a corporation's acquisition of its own shares. In close corporations, for example, courts may scrutinize acquisitions for compliance with the good faith and fair dealing requirements of the fiduciary duty. See *Donahue v. Rodd Electrotype Co., Inc.* in Chapter 36.

Klang v. Smith's Food & Drug Centers, Inc.

Supreme Court of Delaware, 1997

702 A.2d 150

FACTS Smith's Food & Drug Centers, Inc. ("SFD") **(http://www.hoovers.com/co/capsule/0/0,2163,11360,00.html)**, is a Delaware corporation that owns and operates a chain of supermarkets in the Southwestern United States. Jeffrey P. Smith, SFD's chief executive officer, and his family hold common and preferred stock constituting 62.1 percent voting control of SFD. The plaintiff and the class he purports to represent are holders of common stock in SFD. On January 29, 1996, SFD entered into a merger agreement with the Yucaipa Companies **(http://www.hoovers.com/co/capsule/3/0,2163,40153,00.html)** that would involve a recapitalization of SFD and the repurchase by SFD of up to 50 percent of its common stock. SFD was also to repurchase 3 million shares of preferred stock from Jeffrey Smith and his family. SFD hired the investment firm of Houlihan Lokey Howard & Zukin ("Houlihan") **(http://www.hlhz.com)** to examine the transactions, and it rendered a favorable solvency opinion. On May 17, 1996, in reliance on the Houlihan opinion, SFD's board determined that there existed sufficient surplus to consummate the transactions. On May 23, 1996, SFD's stockholders voted to approve the transactions, which closed on that day. The self-tender offer was oversubscribed, so SFD repurchased fully 50 percent of its shares at the offering price of $36 per share.

The plaintiff brought this purported class action alleging that the corporation's repurchase of shares violated the statutory prohibition against the impairment of capital. The Court of Chancery found for SFD. The plaintiff appealed.

DECISION The judgment of the Court of Chancery is affirmed.

OPINION Veasey, C. J. A corporation may not repurchase its shares if, in so doing, it would cause an impairment of capital, unless expressly authorized by Section 160. [Citation.] A repurchase impairs capital if the funds used in the repurchase exceed the amount of the corporation's "surplus," defined by Section 154 to mean the excess of net assets over the par value of the corporation's issued stock. [Citation.]

Plaintiff asked the Court of Chancery to rescind the transactions in question as violative of Section 160. As we understand it, plaintiff's position breaks down into two analytically distinct arguments. First, he contends that SFD's balance sheets constitute conclusive evidence of capital impairment. He argues that the negative net worth that appeared on SFD's books following the repurchase compels us to find a violation of Section 160. Second, he suggests that even allowing the Board to "go behind the balance sheet" to calculate surplus does not save the transactions from violating Section 160. In connection with this claim, he attacks the SFD Board's off-balance-sheet method of calculating surplus on the theory that it does not adequately take into account all of SFD's assets and liabilities. * * * We hold that each of these claims is without merit.

* * *

Plaintiff advances an erroneous interpretation of Section 160. We understand that the books of a corporation do not necessarily reflect the current values of its assets and liabilities. Among other factors, unrealized appreciation or depreciation can render book numbers inaccurate. It is unrealistic to hold that a corporation is bound by its balance sheets for purposes of determining compliance with Section 160. Accordingly, we adhere to the principles of [citation] allowing corporations to revalue properly its assets and liabilities to show a surplus and thus conform to the statute.

It is helpful to recall the purpose behind Section 160. The General Assembly enacted the statute to prevent boards from draining corporations of assets to the detriment of creditors and the long-term health of the corporation. [Citation.] That a corporation has not yet realized or reflected on its balance sheet the appreciation of assets is irrelevant to this concern. Regardless of what a balance sheet that has not been updated may show, an actual, though unrealized, appreciation reflects real economic value that the corporation may borrow against or that creditors may claim or levy upon. Allowing corporations to revalue assets and liabilities to reflect current realities complies with the statute and serves well the policies behind this statute.

* * *

On May 17, 1996, Houlihan released its solvency opinion to the SFD Board, expressing its judgment that the merger and self-tender offer would not impair SFD's capital. Houlihan reached this conclusion by comparing SFD's "Total Invested Capital" of $1.8 billion—a figure Houlihan arrived at by valuing SFD's assets under the "market multiple" approach—with SFD's long-term debt of $1.46 billion. This comparison yielded an approximation of SFD's "concluded equity value" equal to $346 million, a figure clearly in excess of the outstanding par value of SFD's stock. Thus, Houlihan concluded, the transactions would not violate Section 160.

* * *

The record contains, in the form of the Houlihan opinion, substantial evidence that the transactions complied with Section 160. Plaintiff has provided no reason to distrust Houlihan's analysis. In cases alleging impairment of capital under Section 160, the trial court may defer to the board's measurement of surplus unless a plaintiff can show that the directors "failed to fulfill their duty to evaluate the assets on the basis of acceptable data and by standards which they are entitled to believe reasonably reflect present values." [Citation.] In the absence of bad faith or fraud on the part of the board, courts will not "substitute [our] concepts of wisdom for that of the directors." [Citation.] Here, plaintiff does not argue that the SFD Board acted in bad faith. Nor has he met his burden of showing that the methods and data that underlay the board's analysis are unreliable or that its determination of surplus is so far off the mark as to constitute actual or constructive fraud.

INTERPRETATION A corporation may repurchase stock only out of surplus but it may revalue its assets and liabilities from book value if the revaluation is done in good faith, on the basis of acceptable data, and by methods that reasonably reflect present values.

ETHICAL QUESTION Was it fair for SFD to repurchase the preferred stock from its controlling shareholders? Explain.

CRITICAL THINKING QUESTION How independent can an investment firm be that is hired by the controlling shareholders of the corporation? Explain.

CPA DECLARATION AND PAYMENT OF DISTRIBUTIONS

The board of directors of a corporation declares dividends and other distributions, and this power may not be delegated. If the charter clearly and expressly provides for mandatory dividends, however, the board must comply with the provision. Nonetheless, such provisions are extremely infrequent, and shareholders cannot assume this power in any other way, although it is in their power to elect a new board. Moreover, the board cannot discriminate in its declaration of dividends among shareholders of the same class.

SHAREHOLDERS' RIGHT TO COMPEL A DIVIDEND

If the directors fail to declare a dividend, a shareholder may bring a suit in equity against them and the corporation to seek a mandatory injunction requiring the directors to declare a dividend. However, courts of equity are reluctant to order an injunction of this kind, for such a judgment involves substituting the court's business judgment for that of the directors elected by the shareholders. With respect to the directors' discretion regarding the declaration of dividends, a preferred shareholder having prior rights with respect to dividends is in the same position as the holder of common shares.

Dodge v. Ford Motor Co.

Supreme Court of Michigan, 1919
204 Mich. 459, 170 N.W. 668

FACTS Ford Motor Company **(http://www.ford.com/)** had made large profits for several years. Henry Ford **(http://www.hfmgv.org/exhibits/hf)**, Ford's president and the dominant figure on its board of directors, declared that although it had paid special dividends in the past, Ford would not, as a matter of policy, pay any special dividends in the future but instead would reinvest the profits in the proposed expansion of the company. At the conclusion of Ford's most prosperous year, John and Horace Dodge, minority shareholders in Ford, brought this action against Ford's directors to compel the declaration of dividends and to enjoin the expansion of the business. The Dodges complained that the reinvestment of the profits was not in the best interests of Ford and its shareholders and that it was an arbitrary action of the directors. The trial court entered a decree requiring the directors to declare and pay a dividend of $19,275,385.96.

DECISION That part of the decree fixing and determining the specific amount to be distributed to stockholders affirmed; decree reversed in other respects.

OPINION Ostrander, J. The case for plaintiffs must rest upon the claim, and the proof in support of it, that the proposed expansion of the business of the corporation involving the further use of profits as capital, ought to be enjoined because inimical to the best interests of the company and its shareholders, and upon the further claim that in any event the withholding of the special dividend asked for by plaintiffs is arbitrary action of the directors requiring judicial interference.

The rule which will govern courts in deciding these questions is not in dispute. * * * In [citation], it is stated:

> Profits earned by a corporation may be divided among its shareholders; but it is not a violation of the charter if they are allowed to accumulate and remain invested in the company's business. The managing agents of a corporation are impliedly invested with a discretionary power with regard to the time and manner of distributing its profits. They may apply profits in payment of floating or funded debts, or in development of the company's business; and so long as they do not abuse their discretionary powers, or violate the company's charter, the courts cannot interfere.
>
> But it is clear that the agents of a corporation, and even the majority, cannot arbitrarily withhold profits earned by the company, or apply them to any use which is not authorized by the company's charter. The nominal capital of a company does not necessarily limit the scope of its operations; a corporation may borrow money for the purpose of enlarging its business, and in many instances it may use profits for the same purpose. * * *

When plaintiffs made their complaint and demand for further dividends the Ford Motor Company had concluded its most prosperous year of business. The demand for its cars at the price of the preceding year continued. It could make and could market in the year beginning August 1, 1916, more than 500,000 cars. Sales of parts and repairs would necessarily increase. The cost of materials was likely to advance, and perhaps the price of labor, but it reasonably might have expected a profit for the year of upwards of $60,000,000. It had assets of more than $132,000,000, a surplus of almost $112,000,000, and its cash on hand and municipal bonds were nearly $54,000,000. Its total liabilities, including capital stock, were a little over $20,000,000. It had declared no special dividend during the business year except the October, 1915, dividend. It had been the practice under similar circumstances, to declare larger dividends. Considering only these facts, a refusal to declare and pay further dividends appears to be not an exercise of discretion on the part of the directors, but an arbitrary refusal to do what the circumstances required to be done. * * *

It is the contention of plaintiffs that the apparent effect of the plan is intended to be the continued and continuing effect of it and that it is deliberately proposed, not of record and not by official corporate declaration, but nevertheless proposed, to continue the corporation henceforth as a semi-eleemosynary institution and not as a business institution. In support of this contention they point to the attitude and to the expressions of Mr. Henry Ford.

Mr. Henry Ford is the dominant force in the business of the Ford Motor Company. No plan of operations could be adopted unless he consented, and no board of directors can be elected whom he does not favor. One of the directors of the company has no stock. One share was assigned to him to qualify him for the position, but it is not claimed that he owns it. A business, one of the largest in the world, and one of the most profitable, has been built up. It employs many men, at good pay.

"My ambition," said Mr. Ford, "is to employ still more men, to spread the benefits of this industrial system to the greatest possible number, to help them build up their lives and their homes. To do this we are putting the greatest share of our profits back in the business." * * *

The record, and especially the testimony of Mr. Ford, convinces that he has to some extent the attitude towards shareholders of one who has dispensed and distributed to them large gains and that they should be content to take what he chooses to give. His testimony creates the impression, also, that he thinks the Ford Motor Company has made too much money; has had too large profits, and that although large profits might still be earned, a sharing of them with the public, by reducing the price of the output of the company, ought to be undertaken. We have no doubt that certain sentiments, philanthropic and altruistic, creditable to Mr. Ford, had large influence in determining the policy to be pursued by the Ford Motor Company—the policy which has been herein referred to. * * *

These cases, after all, like all others in which the subject is treated, turn finally upon the point, the question, whether it appears that the directors were not acting for the best interest of the corporation. * * * The difference between an incidental humanitarian expenditure of corporate funds for the benefit of the employees, like the building of a hospital for their use and the employment of agencies for the betterment of their condition, and a general purpose and plan to benefit mankind at the expense of others, is obvious. * * * A business corporation is organized and carried on primarily for the profit of the stockholders. The powers of the directors are to be employed for that end. The discretion of directors is to be exercised in the choice of means to attain that end and does not extend to a change in the end itself, to the reduction of profits or to the nondistribution of profits among stockholders in order to devote them to other purposes. * * *

INTERPRETATION The right of shareholders to receive a share of the corporation's profits may not be arbitrarily withheld by the directors.

ETHICAL QUESTION Was the court's decision fair to all of the parties? Explain.

CRITICAL THINKING QUESTION Under what circumstances should a court override a decision by the board of directors not to declare a dividend? Explain.

EFFECT OF DECLARATION

Once lawfully and properly declared, a cash dividend is considered a debt the corporation owes to the shareholders. It follows from this debtor-creditor relationship that, once declared, a declaration of a cash dividend cannot be rescinded without the shareholders' consent; a stock dividend, however, may be revoked unless actually distributed.

CPA LIABILITY FOR IMPROPER DIVIDENDS AND DISTRIBUTIONS

The Revised Act imposes personal liability on the directors of a corporation who vote for or assent to the declaration of a dividend or other distribution of corporate assets contrary to the incorporation statute or the articles of incorporation. Directors generally are liable either to the corporation or to the corporation's creditors. The Revised Act expressly provides that the directors who vote for or assent to an illegal dividend or distribution are liable to the corporation. The damages equal the amount of the dividend or distribution in excess of the amount that the corporation lawfully may have paid.

A director is not liable if she acted in accordance with the relevant standard of conduct: in good faith, with reasonable care, and in a manner she reasonably believed to be in the best interests of the corporation. (This standard of conduct is discussed in the next chapter.) In discharging this duty, a director is entitled to rely in good faith on financial statements presented by the corporation's officers, public accountants, or finance committee. Such statements must be prepared on the basis of "accounting practices and principles that are reasonable in the circumstances or on a fair valuation or other method that is reasonable in the circumstances." According to the Comments to the Revised Act, generally accepted accounting principles are always reasonable in the circumstances; other accounting principles may be acceptable under a general standard of reasonableness.

A shareholder's obligation to repay an illegally declared dividend depends on a variety of factors, which may include the faith, good or bad, in which the shareholder accepted the dividend, his knowledge of the facts, the solvency or insolvency of the corporation, and, in some instances, special statutory provisions. The existence of statutory liability on the part of directors does not relieve shareholders from the duty to make repayment.

A shareholder who receives illegal dividends with knowledge of their unlawful character is under a duty to refund them to the corporation. When the corporation is insolvent, the shareholder may not retain even a dividend received in good faith. However, when an unsuspecting shareholder receives an illegal dividend from a solvent corporation, the majority rule is that the corporation cannot compel a refund.

CONCEPT REVIEW

Liability for Improper Distributions

	Corporation Solvent	Corporation Insolvent
Nonbreaching Director	No	No
Breaching Director	Yes	Yes
Knowing Shareholder	Yes	Yes
Innocent Shareholder	No	Yes

CHAPTER SUMMARY

Debt Securities

Authority to Issue Debt Securities

Definitions
- *Debt Security* source of capital creating no ownership interest and involving the corporation's promise to repay funds lent to it
- *Bond* a debt security

Rule each corporation has the power to issue debt securities as determined by the board of directors

Types of Debt Securities

Unsecured Bonds called debentures, have only the obligation of the corporation behind them

Secured Bonds are claims against a corporation's general assets and a lien on specific property

Income Bonds condition to some extent the payment of interest on corporate earnings

Participating Bonds call for a stated percentage of return regardless of earnings, with additional payments dependent upon earnings

Convertible Bonds may be exchanged for other securities

Callable Bond bonds subject to redemption

Equity Securities

Issuance of Shares

Definitions
- *Equity Security* source of capital creating an ownership interest in the corporation
- *Share* a proportionate ownership interest in a corporation
- *Treasury Stock* shares reacquired by a corporation

Authority to Issue only those shares authorized in the articles of incorporation may be issued

Preemptive Rights right to purchase a *pro rata* share of new stock offerings

Amount of Consideration for Shares shares are deemed fully paid and nonassessable when a corporation receives the consideration for which the board of directors authorized the issuance of the shares, which in the case of par value stock must be at least par

Payment for Newly Issued Shares may be cash, property, and services actually rendered, as determined by the board of directors; under the Revised Act, promises to contribute cash, property, or services are also permitted

Classes of Shares

Common Stock stock not having any special contract rights

Preferred Stock stock having contractual rights superior to those of common stock
- *Dividend Preferences* must receive full dividends before any dividend may be paid on common stock
- *Liquidation Preferences* priority over common stock in corporate assets upon liquidation

Stock Options contractual right to purchase stock from a corporation

Dividends and Other Distributions

Types of Dividends and Other Distributions

Distributions transfers of property by a corporation to any of its shareholders with respect to its shares; become debts of the corporation if and when declared by the board

Cash Dividends the most common type of distribution

Property Dividends distribution in form of property

Stock Dividends a ratable distribution of additional shares of stock

Stock Splits each of the outstanding shares is broken into a larger number of shares

Liquidating Dividends a distribution of capital assets to shareholders

Redemption of Shares a corporation's exercise of the right to repurchase its own shares

Acquisition of Shares a corporation's repurchase of its own shares

Legal Restrictions on Dividends and Other Distributions

Legal Restrictions on Cash Dividends dividends may be paid only if the cash flow and applicable balance sheet tests are satisfied

- *Cash Flow Test* a corporation must not be or become insolvent (unable to pay its debts as they become due in the usual course of business)
- *Balance Sheet Test* varies among the states and includes the earned surplus test (available in all states), the surplus test, and the net assets test (used by the Model and Revised Acts)

Legal Restrictions on Liquidating Distributions states usually permit distribution in partial liquidation from capital surplus unless the company is insolvent

Legal Restrictions on Redemptions of Shares in most states, a corporation may not redeem shares when insolvent or when such redemption would render it insolvent

Legal Restrictions on Acquisition of Shares restrictions similar to those on cash dividends usually apply

Declaration and Payment of Distributions

Shareholders' Right to Compel a Dividend the declaration of dividends is within the discretion of the board of directors and only rarely will a court substitute its business judgment for that of the board

Effect of Declaration once properly declared, a cash dividend is considered a debt the corporation owes to the shareholders

Liability for Improper Dividends and Distributions

Directors the directors who assent to an improper dividend are liable for the unlawful amount of the dividend

Shareholder a shareholder must return illegal dividends if he knew of the illegality, if the dividend resulted from his fraud, or if the corporation is insolvent

Questions

1. Olympic National Agencies was organized with an authorized capitalization of preferred stock and common stock. The articles of incorporation provided for a 7 percent annual dividend for the preferred stock. The articles further stated that the preferred stock would be given priority interests in the corporation's assets up to the par value of the stock. After some years, the shareholders voted to dissolve Olympic. Olympic's assets greatly exceeded its liabilities. The liquidating trustee petitioned the court for instructions on the respective rights of the shareholders in the assets of the corporation upon dissolution. The court ordered the trustee to distribute the corporate assets remaining after the preference of the preferred stock is satisfied to the common and preferred stockholders on a *pro rata* basis. Was the court correct in rendering this decision? Explain.

2. XYZ Corporation was duly organized on July 10. Its certificate of incorporation provides for a total authorized capital of $100,000, consisting of 1,000 shares of common stock with a par value of $100 per share. The corporation issues for cash a total of fifty certificates, numbered 1 to 50 inclusive, representing various amounts of shares in the names of various individuals. The shares were all paid for in advance, so the certificates are all dated and mailed on the same day. The fifty certificates of stock represent a total of 1,050 shares. Certificate 49 for thirty shares was issued to Jane Smith. Certificate 50 for twenty-five shares was issued to William Jones. Is there any question concerning the validity of any of the stock thus issued? What are the rights of Smith and Jones?

3. Doris subscribed for 200 shares of 12 percent cumulative, participating, redeemable, convertible, preferred shares of the Ritz Hotel Company with a par value of $100 per share. The subscription agreement provided that she was to receive a bonus of one share of common stock of $100 par value for each share of preferred stock. Doris fully paid her subscription agreement of $20,000 and received the 200 shares of preferred and the bonus stock of 200 shares of the par value common. The Ritz Hotel company later becomes insolvent. Ronald, the receiver of the corporation, brings suit for $20,000, the par value of the common stock. What judgment?

4. Hyperion Company has an authorized capital stock of 1,000 shares with a par value of $100 per share, of which 900 shares, all fully paid, are outstanding. Having an ample surplus, Hyperion Company purchases from its shareholders 100 shares at par. Subsequently, Hyperion, needing additional working capital, issues the 200 shares in question to Alexander at $80 per share. Two years later, Hyperion Company is forced into bankruptcy. How much, if any, may the trustee in bankruptcy recover from Alexander?

5. For five years, Henry and James had been engaged as partners in building houses. They owned the equipment necessary to conduct the business and had an excellent reputation. In March, Joyce, who previously had been in the same kind of business, proposed that Henry, James, and Joyce form a corporation for the purpose of constructing medium-priced houses. They engaged attorney Portia, who did all the work required and caused the business to be incorporated under the name of Libra Corp.

   The certificate of incorporation authorized one hundred shares of $100 par value stock. At the organizational meeting of the incorporators, Henry, James, and Joyce were elected directors, and Libra Corp. issued a total of sixty-five shares of its stock. Henry and James each received twenty shares in consideration for transferring to Libra Corp. the equipment and goodwill of their partnership, which had a combined value of more than $4,000. Joyce received twenty shares as an inducement to work for Libra Corp. in the future, and Portia received five shares as compensation for the legal services she rendered in forming Libra Corp.

   Later that year, Libra Corp. had a number of financial setbacks and in December ceased operations. What rights, if any, does Libra Corp. have against Henry, James, Joyce, and Portia in connection with the original issuance of its shares?

6. Paul Bunyan is the owner of noncumulative 8 percent preferred stock in the Broadview Corporation, which had no earnings or profits in 2001. In 2002, the corporation had large profits and a surplus from which it might properly have declared dividends. However, the directors refused to do so, using the surplus instead to purchase goods necessary for the corporation's expanding business. The corporation earned a small profit in 2003. The directors at the end of 2003 declared a 10 percent dividend on the common stock and an 8 percent dividend on the preferred stock without paying preferred dividends for 2002.
   a. Is Bunyan entitled to dividends for 2001? For 2002?
   b. Is Bunyan entitled to a dividend of 10 percent rather than 8 percent in 2003?

7. Alpha Corporation has outstanding 400 shares of $100 par value common stock, which has been issued and sold at $105 per share for a total of $42,000. Alpha is incorporated in State X, which has adopted the earned surplus test for all distributions. At a time when the assets of the corporation amount to $65,000 and the liabilities to creditors total $10,000, the directors learn that Rachel, who holds 100 of the 400 shares of stock, is planning to sell her shares on the open market for $10,500. Believing that this will not be in the best interest of the corporation, the directors enter into an agreement with Rachel to buy the shares for $10,500. About six months later, when the assets of the corporation have decreased to $50,000 and its liabilities, not including

its liability to Rachel, have increased to $20,000, the directors use $10,000 to pay a dividend to all of the shareholders. The corporation later becomes insolvent.

a. Does Rachel have any liability to the corporation or its creditors in connection with the corporation's reacquisition of the 100 shares?
b. Was the payment of the $10,000 dividend proper?

8. Almega Corporation, organized under the laws of State S, has outstanding 20,000 shares of $100 par value nonvoting preferred stock calling for noncumulative dividends of $5 per year; 10,000 shares of voting preferred stock of par $50 value, calling for cumulative dividends of $2.50 per year; and 10,000 shares of no par common stock. State S has adopted the earned surplus test for all distributions. As of the end of 1998, the corporation had no earned surplus. In 1999, the corporation had net earnings of $170,000; in 2000, $135,000; in 2001, $60,000; in 2002, $210,000; and in 2003, $120,000. The board of directors passed over all dividends during the four years from 1999 to 2002, as the company needed working capital for expansion purposes. In 2003, however, the directors declared a dividend of $5 per share on the noncumulative preferred shares, a dividend of $12.50 per share on the cumulative preferred shares, and a dividend of $30 per share on the common stock. The board submitted its declaration to the voting shareholders, and they ratified it. Before the dividends were paid, Payne, the record holder of 500 shares of the noncumulative preferred stock, brought an appropriate action to restrain any payment to the cumulative preferred or common shareholders until the company paid a full dividend for the period from 1999 to 2003. Decision? What is the maximum lawful dividend that may be paid to the owner of each share of common stock?

9. Sayre learned that Adams, Boone, and Chase were planning to form a corporation for the purpose of manufacturing and marketing a line of novelties to wholesale outlets. Sayre had patented a self-locking gas tank cap but lacked the financial backing to market it profitably. He negotiated with Adams, Boone, and Chase, who agreed to purchase the patent rights for $5,000 in cash and 200 shares of $100 par value preferred stock in a corporation to be formed.

The corporation was formed and Sayre's stock issued to him, but the corporation has refused to make the cash payment. It has also refused to declare dividends, although the business has been very profitable because of Sayre's patent and has a substantial earned surplus with a large cash balance on hand. It is selling the remainder of the originally authorized issue of preferred shares, ignoring Sayre's demand to purchase a proportionate number of these shares. What are Sayre's rights, if any?

CASE PROBLEMS

10. Wood, the receiver of Stanton Oil Company, sued Stanton's shareholders to recover dividends paid to them for three years, claiming that at the time these dividends were declared, Stanton was in fact insolvent. Wood did not allege that the present creditors were also creditors when the dividends were paid. Were the dividends wrongfully paid? Explain.

11. International Distributing Export Company (IDE) was organized as a corporation on September 7, 1996, under the laws of New York and commenced business on November 1, 1996. IDE formerly had existed as an individual proprietorship. On October 31, 1996, the newly organized corporation had liabilities of $64,084. Its only assets, in the sum of $33,042, were those of the former sole proprietorship. The corporation, however, set up an asset on its balance sheet in the amount of $32,000 for goodwill. As a result of this entry, IDE had a surplus at the end of each of its fiscal years from 1997 until 2002. Cano, a shareholder, received $7,144 in dividends from IDE during the period from 1998 to 2003. May Fried, the trustee in bankruptcy of IDE, recover the amount of these dividends from Cano on the basis that they had been paid when IDE was insolvent or when its capital was impaired?

http:// **Internet Exercise** Using the Securities and Exchange Commission's EDGAR database, find the Annual Report (Form 10-K) and, if necessary, the proxy statement (DEF 14A) of three companies of interest and determine, with respect to their common stock (a) on which exchanges it is listed, (b) earnings for the most recent quarter, (c) annual dividends, and (d) the high and low price for the stock over the previous 52-week period.

Chapter 36

Management Structure of Corporations

The director is really a watch-dog, and the watch-dog has no right, without the knowledge of his master, to take a sop from a possible wolf.

Chief Justice Timothy Bowen, 1892

Learning Objectives

After reading this chapter you should be able to:

1. Compare the actual governance of closely held corporations, the actual governance of publicly held corporations, and the statutory model of corporate governance.
2. Explain the role of shareholders in the management of a corporation.
3. Explain the role of the board of directors in the management of a corporation.
4. Explain the role of officers in the management of a corporation.
5. Explain management's duties of loyalty, obedience, and diligence.

The corporate management structure, as required by state incorporation statutes, is pyramidal. At the base of the pyramid are the ***shareholders***, who are the residual owners of the corporation. Basic to their role in controlling the corporation is the right to elect representatives to manage the ordinary business matters of the corporation and the right to approve all extraordinary matters.

The ***board of directors***, as the shareholders' elected representatives, are delegated the power to manage the business of the corporation. Directors exercise dominion and control over the corporation, hold positions of trust and confidence, and determine questions of operating policy. Because they are not expected to devote their full time to the corporation's affairs, directors have broad authority to delegate power to agents and to officers, who hold their offices at the will of the board. These ***officers***, in turn, hire and fire all necessary operating personnel and run the day-to-day affairs of the corporation. The pyramid structure of corporate management under the statutory model is illustrated in Figure 36-1.

CORPORATE GOVERNANCE

The statutory model of corporate management, although required by most states, accurately describes the actual governance of only a few corporations. The great majority of corporations are closely held: they have a small number of stockholders and no ready market for their shares, and most of the shareholders actively participate in the management of the business. Typically, the shareholders of a closely held corporation are also its directors and officers. Figure 36-2 depicts the actual management structure of a typical closely held corporation.

Although the statutory model and the actual governance of closely held corporations diverge, in most states closely held corporations must adhere to the general corporate statutory model. One of the greatest burdens conventional general business corporation statutes impose on closely held corporations is a set of rigid corporate formalities. Although these formalities may be necessary and desirable in publicly held corporations having separate management and ownership, in a closely held corporation, where the owners are usually the managers, many of these formalities are unnecessary and meaningless. Consequently, shareholders in closely held corporations tend to disregard the formalities, sometimes forfeiting their limited liability as a result. In response to this problem, the 1969 amendments to the Model Business Corporation Act (MBCA), which were carried over to the Revised Act, included several liberalizing provisions for closely held corporations. Moreover, about twenty states have enacted special legislation to accommodate the needs of closely held corporations. These statutes vary considerably, but they are all optional and must be specifically elected by eligible corporations. Eligibility is generally based on the corporation's having fewer than a specified number of shareholders. These special close corporation statutes permit operation without a board of directors and authorize broad use of shareholder agreements, including their use in place of bylaws. Some prohibit courts from denying limited liability simply because an electing corporation engages in informal conduct.

As noted in Chapter 34, a Statutory Close Corporation Supplement (the Supplement) to the Model and Revised Acts has been promulgated. The Supplement relaxes most of the nonessential corporate formalities. It permits operation without a board of directors, authorizes broad use of shareholder agreements (including their use in place of bylaws), makes annual meetings optional, and authorizes one person to execute documents in more than one capacity. Most important, it prevents courts from denying limited liability simply because the corporation is a statutory close corporation. The general incorporation statute applies to closely held corporations except to the extent that it is inconsistent with the Supplement.

The Revised Act was amended to authorize shareholders in closely held corporations to adopt unanimous shareholders' agreements that depart from the statutory norms. This section of the Act requires that the agreement be set forth either (a) in the articles of incorporation or bylaws and approved by all persons who are shareholders at the time of the agreement or (b) in a written agreement that is signed by all persons who are shareholders at the time of the agreement and is made known to the corporation. The section *specifically* validates a number of provisions including those: (1) eliminating or restricting the powers of the board of directors; (2) establishing who shall be directors or officers; (3) specifying how directors or officers will be selected or removed; (4) governing the exercise or division of voting power by or between the shareholders and directors; (5) permitting the use of weighted voting rights or director proxies; and (6) transferring the authority of the board of directors to one or more shareholders or other persons. The section also *generally* authorizes any provision that governs the exercise of the corporate powers or the management of the business and affairs of the corporation or the relationship among the shareholders, the directors and the corporation, or among any of them, so long as it is not contrary to public policy. There are limits, however, and a shareholder agreement that provides that the directors of the corporation have no duties of care or loyalty to the corporation or the shareholders would be beyond the authorization of the section. To the extent that an agreement authorized by this section limits the discretion or powers of the board of directors, it relieves the directors of liability while imposing that liability upon the person or persons in whom such discretion or powers are vested.

In sharp contrast is the large, publicly held corporation with a vast market for its shares. These shares typically are widely dispersed, and very few are owned by management. Approximately one-half are held by institutional investors (such as insurance companies, pension funds, mutual funds, and university endowments). The remaining shares are owned directly by individual investors. Whereas the great majority of institutional investors exercise their right to vote their shares, most individual investors do not. Nonetheless, virtually all shareholders who vote for the directors do so through the use of a proxy—an authorization by a shareholder to an agent (usually the chief executive officer of the corporation) to vote his shares. The majority of shareholders who return their proxies vote as management advises. As a result, the nominating committee of the board of directors actually determines the board's membership. Figure 36-3 illustrates the actual management structure of a typical large, publicly held corporation.

Thus, the 500 to 1,000 large, publicly held corporations—which own the great bulk of the industrial wealth of the United States—are controlled by a small group of corporate officers. This great concentration of the control over wealth, and the power that results from it, raises social, policy, and ethical issues concerning the governance of these corporations and the accountability of their management. The actions (or inactions) of these powerful corporations greatly affect the national economy, employment policies, the health and safety of the workplace and the environment, the quality of products, and the effects of overseas operations. Accordingly, the accountability of management is a critical issue.

Figure 36-1
Management Structure of Corporations: The Statutory Model

Figure 36-2
Management Structure of Typical Closely Held Corporation

Figure 36-3
Management Structure of Typical Publicly Held Corporation

In response to the business scandals involving companies such as Enron, WorldCom, Global Crossing, and Arthur Andersen, in 2002 Congress passed the Sarbanes-Oxley Act, which is discussed more fully in Chapter 40, Securities Regulation. The legislation seeks to prevent these types of scandals by increasing corporate responsibility; adding new financial disclosure requirements; creating new criminal offenses; increasing the penalties of existing federal crimes; and creating a powerful new five-person Accounting Oversight Board with authority to review and discipline auditors. Several provisions of the Act impose governance requirements on publicly held corporations and will be discussed in this chapter.

The structure and governance of corporations must adhere to incorporation statute requirements. Therefore, in this chapter we will discuss the rights, duties, and liabilities of shareholders, directors, and officers under these statutes.

http://
Business Roundtable on Corporate Governance: http://www.brtable.org/issue.cfm/2
Corporate Governance: http://www.corpgov.net/
Corporate Governance OECD: http://www.oecd.org/daf/corporate-affairs/

ROLE OF SHAREHOLDERS

The role of the shareholders in managing the corporation is generally restricted to the election of directors, the approval of certain extraordinary matters, the approval of corporate transactions that are void or voidable unless ratified, and the right to bring suits to enforce these rights.

CPA VOTING RIGHTS OF SHAREHOLDERS

The shareholder's right to vote is fundamental to the concept of the corporation and its management structure. In most states today, a shareholder is entitled to one vote for each share of stock that she owns, unless the articles of incorporation provide otherwise; the articles may provide for more or less than one vote for any share. In addition, incorporation statutes generally permit the issuance of one or more classes of nonvoting stock, as long as at least one class of shares has voting rights.

SHAREHOLDER MEETINGS

Shareholders may exercise their voting rights at both annual and special **shareholder meetings**. Under the Revised Act, ***annual meetings*** are required and must be held at a time fixed by the corporation's bylaws. If the annual shareholder meeting is not held within the earlier of six months after the end of the corporation's fiscal year or fifteen months after its last annual meeting, any shareholder may petition and obtain a court order requiring that a meeting be held. By comparison, the Close Corporation Supplement provides that no annual meeting of shareholders need be held unless a shareholder makes a written request at least thirty days in advance of the date specified for the meeting. The date may be established in the articles of incorporation, in the bylaws, or in a shareholder agreement.

Special meetings may be called by the board of directors, by holders of at least 10 percent of the shares, or by other persons authorized to do so in the articles of incorporation.

Written notice stating the date, time, and place of the meeting and, in the case of a special meeting, the purposes for which it is called must be given in advance. Notice, however, may be waived in writing by any shareholder entitled to notice.

A number of states permit shareholders to conduct business without a meeting if all the shareholders consent in writing to the action taken. Some states have further relaxed the formalities of shareholder action by permitting shareholders to act without a meeting with the written consent of only the number of shares required to act on the matter.

QUORUM AND VOTING

A **quorum** of shares must be presented at the meeting, either in person or by proxy. Unissued shares and treasury stock may not be voted or counted in determining whether a quorum exists. Decisions made at the meeting will have no effect if a quorum is not present. Once a quorum is present at a meeting, it is deemed present for the rest of the meeting, even if shareholders withdraw in an effort to break it. Unless the articles of incorporation otherwise provide, a majority of shares entitled to vote constitutes a quorum. In most states and under the Model Act, a quorum may not consist of less than one-third of the shares entitled to vote; the Revised Act and some states do not contain a statutory minimum for a quorum. Because state statutes do not impose an upper limit upon a quorum, it may be set higher than a majority and may even require all the outstanding shares.

Most states require shareholder actions to be approved by a majority of the shares represented at the meeting and entitled to vote if a quorum exists. The Revised Act and some states, however, provide a different rule: if a quorum exists, a shareholder action (other than the election of directors) is approved if the votes cast for the action exceed the votes cast against it. Moreover, virtually all states permit the articles of incorporation to increase the percentage of shares required to take any action that is subject to shareholder approval. A provision that increases the voting requirements is commonly called a "supermajority provision." Close corporations frequently have used supermajority shareholder voting requirements to protect minority shareholders from oppression by the majority. Recently, some publicly held corporations have used them to defend against hostile takeover bids as well.

> **Practical Advice**
>
> If you are forming a close corporation and will hold a minority interest in it, consider including in the charter supermajority quorum and voting provisions for shareholder decisions to ensure that you will have veto power over specified managerial issues.

ELECTION OF DIRECTORS

The shareholders elect directors each year at the annual shareholders' meeting. Most states provide that when a corporation's board consists of nine or more directors, the charter or bylaws may provide for a ***classification*** of directors, that is, a division into two or three classes to be as nearly equal in number as possible and to serve for staggered terms. If the directors are divided into two classes, the members of each class are elected once a year in alternate years for a two-year term; if divided into three classes, they are elected for three-year terms. This permits one-half of the board to be elected every two years or one-third to be elected every three years, thus providing continuity in the board's membership. Moreover, given two or more classes of shares and the authorization for such an action in the articles of incorporation, each class may elect a specified number of directors.

Straight Voting Normally, each shareholder has one vote for each share owned, and under the Revised Act and many state statutes, directors are elected by a *plurality* of the votes. In other states directors are elected by a *majority* of the votes. The charter may increase the percentage of shares required for the election of directors.

Cumulative Voting In certain states shareholders electing directors have the right of cumulative voting. In most states, and under the Revised Act, cumulative voting is permissive, not mandatory. **Cumulative voting** entitles shareholders to multiply the number of votes they are entitled to cast by the number of directors for whom they are entitled to vote and to cast the product for a single candidate or distribute the product among two or more candidates. Cumulative voting permits a minority shareholder or a group of minority shareholders acting together to obtain minority representation on the board if they own a certain minimum number of shares. In the absence of cumulative voting, the holder or holders of 51 percent of the voting shares can elect all of the members of the board.

The formula for determining how many shares a minority shareholder with cumulative voting rights must own, or have proxies to vote, in order to secure representation on the board is as follows:

$$X = \frac{ac}{b+1} + 1$$

where

a = number of shares voting
b = number of directors to be elected
c = number of directors desired to be elected
X = number of shares necessary to elect the number of directors desired to be elected.

For example, Gray Corporation has two shareholders, Stephanie with sixty-four shares and Thomas with thirty-six shares. The board of directors of Gray Corporation consists of three directors. Under "straight" or noncumulative voting, Stephanie could cast sixty-four votes for each of her three candidates, and Thomas could cast thirty-six votes for his three candidates. As a result, all three of Stephanie's candidates would be elected. On the other hand, if cumulative voting were in force, Thomas could elect one director:

$$X = \frac{ac}{b+1} + 1$$

$$X = \frac{100(1)}{3+1} + 1 = 26 \text{ Shares}$$

Because Thomas has the right to vote more than twenty-six shares, he would be able to elect one director. Stephanie, of course, with her sixty-four shares, could elect the remaining two directors.

Practical Advice

If you are forming a close corporation and will hold a minority interest in it, consider including in the charter a provision for cumulative voting to ensure you a position on the board of directors.

REMOVAL OF DIRECTORS

By a majority vote, shareholders may remove any director or the entire board of directors, with or without cause, in a meeting called for that purpose. In the case of a corporation having cumulative voting, however, removal of a director requires sufficient votes to prevent his election. We will discuss the removal of directors more fully later in this chapter.

APPROVAL OF FUNDAMENTAL CHANGES

The board of directors manages the ordinary business affairs of the corporation. Extraordinary matters involving fundamental changes in the corporation require shareholder approval; such matters include amendments to the articles of incorporation, a sale or lease of all or substantially all of the corporate assets not in the regular course of business, most mergers, consolidations, compulsory share exchanges, and dissolution. We will discuss fundamental changes in Chapter 37.

CONCENTRATIONS OF VOTING POWER

Certain devices enable groups of shareholders to combine their voting power for purposes such as obtaining or maintaining control or maximizing the impact of cumulative voting. The most important methods of concentrating voting power are proxies, voting trusts, and shareholder agreements.

Proxies A shareholder may vote either in person or by written proxy. As we mentioned earlier, a **proxy** is a shareholder's authorization to an agent to vote his shares at a particular meeting or on a particular question. Generally, proxies must be in writing to be effective; and statutes typically limit the duration of proxies to no more than eleven months, unless the proxy specifically provides otherwise. Some states limit all proxy appointments to a period of eleven months. Because a proxy is the appointment of an agent, it is revocable, as all agencies are, unless conspicuously stated to be irrevocable and coupled with an interest, such as shares held as collateral. The solicitation of proxies by publicly held corporations is also regulated by the Securities Exchange Act of 1934, as we will discuss in Chapter 40.

Voting Trusts Voting trusts, which are devices designed to concentrate corporate control in one or more persons, have been used in both publicly held and closely held corporations. A voting trust is a device by which one or more shareholders separate the voting rights of their shares from the ownership of them. Under a voting trust, one or more shareholders confer on a trustee the right to vote or otherwise act for them by signing an agreement setting out the provisions of the trust and transferring their shares to the trustee. In most states, voting trusts are permitted by statute but are usually limited in duration to ten years.

Shareholder Voting Agreements In most jurisdictions, shareholders may agree in writing to vote in a specified manner for the election or removal of directors or on any matter subject to shareholder approval. Unlike voting trusts, **shareholder voting agreements** are not limited in duration. Shareholder agreements are used frequently in closely held corporations, especially in conjunction with restrictions on the transfer of shares, in order to provide each shareholder with greater control and *delectus personae* (the right to choose those who will become shareholders).

Practical Advice

If you are forming a close corporation and will hold a minority interest in it, consider using a detailed shareholder agreement to provide fair treatment for all of the shareholders.

Galler v. Galler

Supreme Court of Illinois, 1964
32 Ill.2d 16, 203 N.E.2d 577

FACTS In 1927, two brothers, Benjamin and Isadore Galler, incorporated the Galler Drug Co., a wholesale drug business that they had operated as equal partners since 1919. The company continued to grow, and in 1955 the two brothers and their wives, Emma and Rose Galler, entered into a written shareholder agreement to leave the corporation in equal control of each family after the death of either brother. Specifically, the agreement provided that the corporation should continue to provide income for the support and maintenance of their immediate families and that the parties should vote for directors so as to give the estate and heirs of a deceased shareholder the same representation as before.

Benjamin died in 1957, and shortly thereafter his widow, Emma, requested that Isadore, the surviving brother, comply with the terms of the agreement. When he refused and proposed that certain changes be made in the agreement, Emma brought this action seeking specific performance of the agreement. Isadore and his wife, Rose, defended on the ground that the shareholder agreement was against public policy and the state's corporation law. The trial court entered a decree of specific performance in favor of Emma. On appeal, the decree was reversed.

DECISION Judgment of appellate court reversed.

OPINION Underwood, J. At this juncture it should be emphasized that we deal here with a so-called close corporation. Various attempts at definition of the close corporation have been made. [Citation.] For our purposes, a close corporation is one in which the stock is held in a few hands, or in a few families, and wherein it is not at all, or only rarely, dealt in by buying or selling. [Citation.] Moreover, it should be recognized that shareholder agreements similar to that in question here are often, as a practical consideration, quite necessary for the protection of those financially interested in the close corporation. While the shareholder of a public-issue corporation may readily sell his shares on the open market should management fail to use, in his opinion, sound business judgment, his counterpart of the close corporation often has a large total of his entire capital invested in the business and has no ready market for his shares should he desire to sell. He feels, understandably, that he is more than a mere investor and that his voice should be heard concerning all corporate activity. Without a shareholder agreement, specifically enforceable by the courts, insuring him a modicum of control, a large minority shareholder might find himself at the mercy of an oppressive or unknowledgeable majority. Moreover, as in the case at bar, the shareholders of a close corporation are often also the directors and officers thereof. With substantial shareholding interests abiding in each member of the board of directors, it is often quite impossible to secure, as in the large public-issue corporation, independent board judgment, free from personal motivations concerning corporate policy. For these and other reasons too voluminous to enumerate here, often the only sound basis for protection is afforded by a lengthy, detailed shareholder agreement securing the rights and obligations of all concerned.

* * *

* * * While limiting voting trusts in 1947 to a maximum duration of 10 years, the legislature has indicated no similar policy regarding straight voting agreements although these have been common since prior to 1870. In view of the history of decisions of this court generally upholding, in the absence of fraud or prejudice to minority interests or public policy, the right of stockholders to agree among themselves as to the manner in which their stock will be voted, we do not regard the period of time within which this agreement may remain effective as rendering the agreement unenforceable.

The clause that provides for the election of certain persons to specified offices for a period of years likewise does not require invalidation. * * *

We turn next to a consideration of the effect of the stated purpose of the agreement upon its validity. The pertinent provision is: "The said Benjamin A. Galler and Isadore A. Galler desire to provide income for the support and maintenance of their immediate families." Obviously, there is no evil inherent in a contract entered into for the reason that the persons originating the terms desired to so arrange their property as to provide post-death support for those dependent upon them. Nor does the fact that the subject property is corporate stock alter the situation so long as there exists no detriment to minority stock interests, creditors or other public injury.

* * *

The terms of the dividend agreement require a minimum annual dividend of $50,000, but this duty is limited by the subsequent provision that it shall be operative only so long as an earned surplus of $500,000 is maintained. It may be noted that in 1958, the year prior to commencement of this litigation, the corporation's net earnings after taxes amounted to $202,759 while its earned surplus was $1,543,270 and this was increased in 1958 to $1,680,079 while earnings were $172,964. The minimum earned surplus requirement is designed for the protection of the corporation and its creditors, and we take no exception to the contractual dividend requirements as thus restricted. [Citation.]

The salary continuation agreement is a common feature, in one form or another, of corporate executive employment. It requires that the widow should receive a total benefit, payable monthly over a five-year period, aggregating twice the amount paid her deceased husband in one year. This requirement was likewise limited for the protection of the corporation by being contingent upon the payments being income tax-deductible by the corporation. The charge made in those cases which have considered the validity of payment to the widow of an officer and shareholder in a corporation is that a gift of its property by a noncharitable corporation is in violation of the rights of its shareholders and *ultra vires*. Since there are no shareholders here other than the parties to the contract, this objection is not here applicable, and its effect, as limited, upon the corporation is not so prejudicial as to require its invalidation.

INTERPRETATION Written shareholder agreements are an important means of enabling minority shareholders in a close corporation to maintain *delectus personae* and control as well as otherwise protecting their interest in the corporation.

ETHICAL QUESTION Did the court decide this case fairly? Explain.

CRITICAL THINKING QUESTION What limitations, if any, should the law impose upon the types of provisions that may be included in a shareholder agreement in a close corporation? Explain.

RESTRICTIONS ON TRANSFER OF SHARES

In the absence of a specific agreement, shares of stock are freely transferable. Although free transferability of shares is usually considered an advantage of the corporate form, in some situations the shareholders may prefer to restrict the transfer of shares. In closely held corporations, for example, stock transfer restrictions are used to control who may become shareholders, thereby achieving the corporate equivalent of *delectus personae* (choice of the

CONCEPT REVIEW

Concentrations of Voting Power

	Proxy	Voting Trust	Shareholder Agreement
Definition	Authorization of an agent to vote shares	Conferral of voting rights on trustee	Agreement among shareholders on voting of shares
Formalities	Signed writing delivered to corporation	Signed writing delivered to corporation	Signed writing
Duration	Eleven months, unless otherwise agreed	Ten years; may be extended	No limit
Revocability	Yes, unless coupled with an interest	No	Only by unanimous agreement
Prevalence	Publicly held	Publicly and closely held	Closely held

person). They are also used to maintain statutory close corporation status by restricting the number of persons who may become shareholders. In publicly held corporations, restrictions on the transfer of shares are used to preserve exemptions under state and federal securities laws. (These are discussed in Chapter 40.)

Most incorporation statutes have no provisions governing share transfer restrictions. The common law validates such restrictions if they are adopted for a lawful purpose and do not unreasonably restrain or prohibit transferability. In addition, the Uniform Commercial Code provides that an otherwise valid share transfer restriction is ineffective against a person without actual knowledge of it unless the restriction is conspicuously noted on the share certificate.

The Revised Act and the statutes of several states permit the articles of incorporation, bylaws, or a shareholder agreement to impose transfer restrictions but require that the restriction be noted conspicuously on the stock certificate. The Revised Act authorizes restrictions for any reasonable purpose, including maintaining statutory close corporation status and preserving exemptions under federal and state securities law.

Practical Advice

To achieve *delectus personae* (choice of person) when organizing a close corporation, you should consider including in the charter a carefully drafted provision restricting the transfer of shares. If you do so, be sure to note such share transfer restriction on the share certificates.

CPA ENFORCEMENT RIGHTS OF SHAREHOLDERS

To protect a shareholder's interests in the corporation, the law provides shareholders with certain enforcement rights. These include the right to obtain information, the right to sue the corporation directly or to sue on the corporation's behalf, and the right to dissent.

RIGHT TO INSPECT BOOKS AND RECORDS

Most states have enacted statutory provisions granting shareholders the right to inspect, for a *proper purpose*, books and records in person or through an agent and to copy parts of them. The right generally covers all records relevant to the shareholder's legitimate interest. The Revised Act provides that every shareholder is entitled to examine *specified* corporate records upon prior written request if the demand is made in good faith, for a proper purpose, and during regular business hours at the corporation's principal office. Many states, however, limit this right to shareholders who own a minimum number of shares or to those who have been shareholders for a minimum period of time. For example, the Model Act requires that a shareholder either must own 5 percent of the outstanding shares or must have owned his shares for at least six months (though a court may order an inspection even when neither condition is met).

A ***proper purpose*** for inspection is one that is reasonably relevant to that shareholder's interest in the corporation. Proper purposes include determining the financial condition of the corporation, the value of shares, the existence of mismanagement, or the names of other shareholders in order to communicate with them about corporate affairs. The right of inspection is subject to abuse and will be denied a shareholder who is seeking proprietary information for an improper purpose. Examples of improper purposes include obtaining information for use by a competing company or obtaining a list of shareholders in order to offer it for sale.

Compaq Computer Corp. v. Horton

Supreme Court of Delaware, 1993

631 A.2d 1

FACTS Charles E. Horton has beneficially owned 112 shares of common stock in Compaq Computer Corporation (Compaq) **(http://h18000.www1.hp.com)** continuously since December 6, 1990. On July 22, 1991, Horton and seventy-eight other parties sued Compaq, fifteen of its advisers, and certain management personnel, alleging that Compaq and its codefendants violated the Texas Security Act and the Texas Deceptive Trade Practices Consumer Protection Act as well as committing fraud and breaching their fiduciary duty. All these claims arise from the contention that Compaq misled the public regarding the true value of its stock at a time when members of management were selling their own shares.

On September 22, 1992, Horton delivered a letter demanding to inspect Compaq's stock ledger and related information for the period from October 1, 1990, to June 30, 1991. The demand letter stated that the purpose of the request was to enable Horton to communicate with other Compaq shareholders to inform them of the pending shareholders' suit and to ascertain whether any of them would desire to become associated with that suit or bring similar actions against Compaq and assume a *pro rata* share of the litigation expenses. On September 30, 1992, Compaq refused the demand, stating that the purpose described in the letter was not a "proper purpose" under Section 220(b) of the General Corporation Law of the state of Delaware.

Horton brought suit and the trial court concluded that the plaintiff's desire to contact other stockholders and solicit their involvement in the litigation was a purpose reasonably related to his interest as a stockholder. Accordingly, the trial court ordered Compaq to permit Horton to inspect and copy the stockholder lists and related stockholder information requested in his demand letter. Compaq appealed.

DECISION Judgment affirmed.

OPINION Moore, J. * * * [Section] 220(b) * * * provides in pertinent part:

> Any stockholder * * * shall, upon written demand under oath stating the purpose thereof, have the right during the usual hours for business to inspect for any proper purpose the corporation's stock ledger. * * * A proper purpose shall mean a purpose reasonably related to such person's interest as a stockholder. [Citation.]

Under Section 220, when a stockholder complies with the statutory requirements as to form and manner of making a demand, then the corporation bears the burden of proving that the demand is for an improper purpose. [Citation]. If there is any doubt, it must be resolved in favor of the statutory right of the stockholder to have an inspection. [Citation.]

Horton contends that this purpose is not only proper, but was earlier approved in *State ex rel. Foster v. Standard Oil Co. of Kansas* [citation]. The holding in *Standard Oil* has been interpreted by a number of authoritative treatises for the proposition Horton advances—that shareholders may inspect stocklists for the purpose of communicating with fellow shareholders, not only about pending litigation, but to solicit their interest in joining it. [Citations.] * * *

Essentially, Horton alleges that it is in the interests of Compaq's shareholders to know that acts of mismanagement and fraud are continuing and cannot be overlooked. Thus, it is assumed that the resultant filing of a large number of individual damage claims might well discourage further acts of misconduct by the defendants. In this specific context, the antidotal effect of the Texas litigation may indeed serve a purpose reasonably related to Horton's current interest as a Compaq stockholder.

We recognize that even though a purpose may be reasonably related to one's interest as a stockholder, it cannot be adverse to the interests of the corporation. [Citations.] In this respect, it becomes clear that a stockholder's right to inspect and copy a stockholder list is not absolute. Rather, it is a qualified right depending on the facts presented. [Citation.]

Horton's ultimate objective, to solicit additional parties to the Texas litigation, may impose substantial expenses upon the company. Compaq argues, therefore, that such a purpose is per se improper as adverse to the interests of the corporation. Significantly, however, Compaq conceded at oral argument that it could cite no authority in support of its proposition that the purpose behind a demand must benefit the defendant corporation.

Horton, as a current stockholder of Compaq, has nothing to gain by harming the legitimate interests of the company. Moreover, as he argues, the prospect of the Texas litigation poses no legitimate threat to Compaq's interests. The Texas litigation is already pending with seventy-nine plaintiffs. The inclusion of more plaintiffs will not substantially increase Compaq's costs of defending the action. The real risk to Compaq is that any additional plaintiffs, who may join the suit, potentially increase the damage award against the company. Yet, insofar as law and policy require corporations and their agents to answer for the breaches of their duties to shareholders, Compaq has no legitimate interest in avoiding the payment of compensatory damages which it, its management or advisors may owe to those who own the enterprise. [Citation.] Thus, common sense and public policy dictate that a proper purpose may be stated in these circumstances, notwithstanding the lack of a direct benefit flowing to the corporation.

Equally important is the fact that if damages are assessed against Compaq in the Texas litigation, the company is entitled to seek indemnification from its co-defendant managers and advisors or to pursue its own claims against them. The availability of this diminishes the possibility that Compaq will suffer any harm at all. It is well settled that the mere prospect of harm to a corporate defendant is insufficient to deny relief under Section 220. [Citation.] * * * Accordingly, we are satisfied that the purpose for which Horton seeks to inspect the stock ledger and related materials is not adverse to the legitimate interests of the company.

This conclusion does not suggest that Compaq's burden of showing an improper purpose is impossible to bear. Previous cases provide valuable examples of the degree to which a stated purpose is so indefinite, doubtful, uncertain or vexatious as to warrant denial of the right of inspection. In [citation], the trial court held that instituting annoying or harassing litigation against the corporation was an improper purpose. In [citation], the court ruled improper the stockholder's plan to use a stocklist in furtherance of a scheme to bring pressure on a third corporation. In [citation], it was recognized that obtaining a list for purposes of selling the stockholders' names was also improper. Finally, in [citation], the Court stated that neither conducting a "fishing expedition" nor satisfying idle curiosity were proper purposes to justify inspection. On the whole, a fair reading of these cases leads to the conclusion that where the person making demand is acting in bad faith or for reasons wholly unrelated to his or her role as a stockholder, access to the ledger will be denied. That simply is not the case here.

Horton seeks in good faith to solicit the support of other similarly situated Compaq stockholders, not only to seek monetary redress for their individual economic injuries, but also to prevent further acts of fraud or mismanagement from disrupting the fair market value of Compaq's stock. * * *

First, in [citation], the Chancellor held that a stockholder's desire to contact other stockholders for the purpose of encouraging them to dissent from a merger and seek their appraisal rights was proper. [Citation] is analogous to this case insofar as both claimants seek to solicit other stockholders to bring actions against the corporation which may ultimately protect the value of its stock. Second, in [citation], this Court upheld a stockholder's right to inspect the ledger for the purposes of investigating allegedly improper transactions or mismanagement. [Citation] is similar to this case because Horton also seeks to curb managerial fraud and mismanagement.

We find, therefore, that Compaq's arguments simply fail to meet the burden imposed on it by law to show that Horton acts from an improper purpose. First, Compaq's contention that Horton's demand is not connected to his status as a stockholder is unsubstantiated. Horton's demand is connected to his status as a stockholder because he seeks to bring an end to injuries sustained, past and present, that directly, and adversely, affect his stock ownership. Second, Compaq's complaint that Horton seeks an historical stocklist is inconsequential. Many cases recognize a stockholder's right to investigate past acts of mismanagement. Furthermore, Section 220(b) expressly grants the right to inspect not only a corporation's list of present stockholders, but also the stock ledger. Third, Compaq's accusation that Horton only seeks inspection for his personal gain is immaterial. So long as Horton establishes a single proper purpose related to his role as a stockholder, all other purposes are irrelevant. [Citation.]

Finally, Compaq's contention that Horton's purpose is contrary to the best interests of the corporation and its current stockholders is both speculative and specious. Any harm that may accrue to the corporation as a result of releasing the list is too remote and uncertain to warrant denial of the stockholder's statutory right to inspection. If anything, the corporation and its stockholders, as well as public policy, will best be served by exposure of the fraud, if that is the case, and restoration of the stock to a value set by a properly informed market.

INTERPRETATION Upon demand, a stockholder has the right to inspect for a proper purpose the corporation's books and records. A proper purpose means a purpose reasonably related to that shareholder's interest in the corporation.

CRITICAL THINKING QUESTION Can a proper purpose ever be adverse to the corporation's interests? Explain.

SHAREHOLDER SUITS

The ultimate recourse of a shareholder, short of selling his shares, is to bring suit against or on behalf of the corporation. Shareholder suits are essentially of two kinds: direct suits and derivative suits.

Direct Suits A shareholder may bring a **direct suit** to enforce a claim that she has *against* the corporation, based on her ownership of shares. Any recovery in a direct suit goes to the shareholder plaintiff. Examples of direct suits include shareholder actions to compel payment of dividends properly declared, to enforce the right to inspect corporate records, to enforce the right to vote, to protect preemptive rights, and to compel dissolution. A *class suit* is a direct suit in which one or more shareholders purport to act as a representative for a class of shareholders in order to recover for injuries to the entire class. Such a suit is a direct suit because the representative claims that all similarly situated shareholders were injured by an act that did not injure the corporation.

Derivative Suits A **derivative suit** is a cause of action brought by one or more shareholders *on behalf of* the corporation to enforce a right belonging to it. Shareholders may bring such an action when the board of directors refuses to so act on the corporation's behalf. Recovery usually goes to the corporation's treasury, so that all shareholders can benefit proportionately. Examples of derivative suits are actions to recover damages from management for an *ultra vires* act, to recover damages for a managerial breach of duty, and to recover improper dividends. In such situations, the board of directors may well be hesitant to bring suit against the corporation's officers or directors. Consequently, a shareholder derivative suit is the only recourse.

In most states, a shareholder must have owned his shares at the time the transaction complained of occurred in order to bring a derivative suit. In addition, under the Revised Act and some state statutes, the shareholder must first make demand on the board of directors to enforce the corporate right. In a number of states, demand is excused in limited situations.

Figure 36-4 compares direct and derivative suits.

Figure 36-4 *Shareholder Suits*

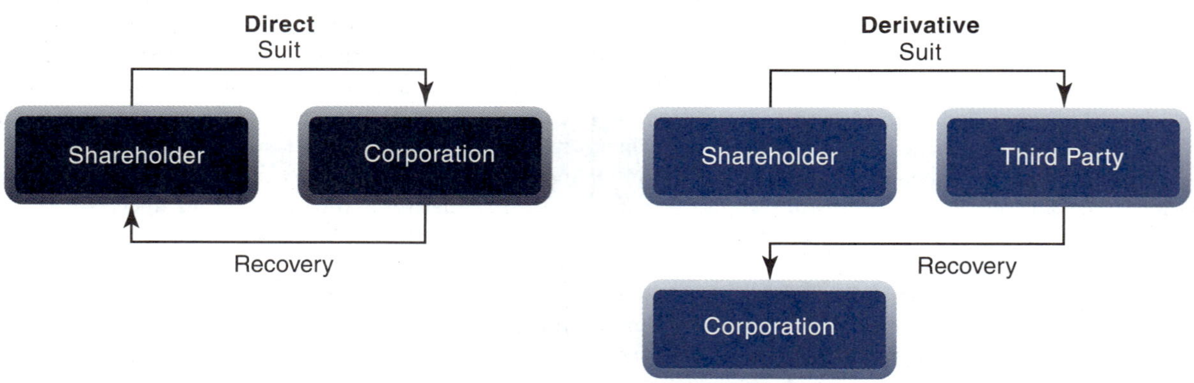

Direct Suit
1. Compel payment of properly declared dividends
2. Enforce right to inspect corporate records
3. Protect preemptive rights
4. Compel dissolution
5. Enjoin an *ultra vires* act

Derivative Suit
1. Recover damages from management for breach of duty
2. Recover improper dividend
3. Enjoin wrongful issuance of shares
4. Recover damages from third party
5. Recover damages from management for *ultra vires* act

Strougo v. Bassini

United States Court of Appeals, Second Circuit, 2002
282 F.3d 162
http://caselaw.lp.findlaw.com/cgi-bin/getcase.pl?court=2nd&navby=case&no=009303

FACTS Strougo is a shareholder of the Brazilian Equity Fund, Inc. (the "Fund"), a non-diversified, publicly traded, closed-end investment company incorporated under the laws of Maryland. As a "closed-end" fund, it has a fixed number of outstanding shares, so that investors who wish to acquire shares in the Fund ordinarily must purchase them from a shareholder rather than, as in open-end funds, directly from the Fund itself. Shares in closed-end funds are traded in the same manner as are other shares of corporate stock. Shares in the Fund are listed and traded on the New York Stock Exchange. The number of outstanding shares in the Fund are "fixed" because it does not change on a daily basis as it would were the Fund open-end, in which case the number of outstanding shares would change each time an investor invested new money in the fund, causing issuance of new shares, and each time a shareholder divested and thereby redeemed shares.

Although closed-end funds do not sell their shares to the public in the ordinary course of their business, there are methods available to them to raise new capital after their initial public offering. One such device is a "rights offering," by which a fund offers shareholders the opportunity to purchase newly issued shares. Rights so offered may be transferable, allowing the current shareholder to sell them in the open market, or non-transferable, requiring the current shareholder to use them herself or lose their value when the rights expire.

On June 6, 1996, the Fund announced that it would issue one non-transferable "right" per outstanding share to every shareholder, and that every three rights would enable the shareholder to purchase one new share in the Fund. The subscription price per share was set at ninety percent of the lesser of (1) the average of the last reported sales price of a share of the Fund's common stock on the New York Stock Exchange on August 16, 1996, the date on which the rights expired, and the four business days preceding, and (2) the per-share net asset value at the close of business on August 16.

At the close of business on August 16, 1996, the last day of the rights offering, the closing market price for the Fund's shares was $12.38, and the Fund's per-share net asset value was $17.24. The Fund's shareholders purchased 70.3 percent of the new shares available at a subscription price set at $11.09 per share, ninety percent of the average closing price for the Fund on that and the preceding four days. Through the rights offering, the Fund raised $20.6 million in new capital.

On May 16, 1997, the plaintiff brought this class action against the Fund's directors, senior officers, and investment advisor. The plaintiff asserted that this sort of rights offering is coercive because it penalized shareholders who did not participate. The introduction of new shares at a discount diluted the value of old shares. Because the rights could not be sold on the open market, a shareholder could avoid a consequent reduction in the value of his or her net equity position in the Fund only by purchasing new shares at the discounted price. This put pressure on every shareholder to "pony up" and purchase more shares, enabling the Fund to raise new capital and thereby increase its asset holdings. Such purchases would, in turn, have tended to increase the management fee paid to defendant BEA Associates, the Fund's investment advisor, because that fee is based on the Fund's total assets.

The plaintiff's complaint included three direct class-action claims on behalf of all shareholders. It alleges that the defendants, by approving the rights offering, breached their duties of loyalty and care at common law. It asserted that these breaches of duty resulted in four kinds of injury to shareholders: (1) loss of share value resulting from the underwriting and other transaction costs associated with the rights offering; (2) downward pressure on share prices resulting from the supply of new shares; (3) downward pressure on share prices resulting from the offering of shares at a discount; and (4) injury resulting from coercion, in that "shareholders were forced to either invest additional monies in the Fund or suffer a substantial dilution."

The district court dismissed the direct claims on the ground that the injuries alleged "applied to the shareholders as a whole" and entered judgment for the defendants. The plaintiff appealed.

DECISION The judgment of the district court is vacated, and the case is remanded for further proceedings.

OPINION Sack, J. *Waller v. Waller*, [citation], remains the leading Maryland case on shareholder standing. There, a shareholder brought a direct action against * * * a corporation's sales manager alleging that he and others had caused injury to the shareholder through the improvident discharge of employees, diversion of customers to competitors, choice of detrimental pricing policies, embezzlement of corporate funds, and disruption of corporate governance activities. [Citation.] In ruling that the plaintiff's claims could not be brought in a direct shareholder suit, the Maryland Court of Appeals observed:

> It is a general rule that an action at law to recover damages for an injury to a corporation can be brought only in the name of the corporation itself acting through its directors, and not by an individual stockholder, though the injury may incidentally result in diminishing or destroying the value of the stock. The reason for this rule is that the cause of action for injury to the property of a corporation or for impairment or destruction of its business is in the corporation, and such injury, although it may diminish the value of the capital stock, is not primarily or necessarily a damage to the stockholder, and hence the stockholder's derivative right can be asserted only through the corporation.

[Citation.] The Court of Appeals further explained:

> The rule is advantageous not only because it avoids a multiplicity of suits by the various stockholders, but also because any damages so recovered will be available for the payment of debts of the corporation, and, if any surplus remains, for distribution to the stockholders in proportion to the number of shares held by each.

[Citation.] Thus, *Waller* noted that a direct action for injuries shared by the corporation may inequitably displace the claims of creditors and thereby subvert the creditors' priority. * * *

Waller, in holding that a corporation and not its shareholders may recover for "injury to [its] property * * * or * * * impairment or destruction of its business," does not elaborate on the meaning of "property" or "business" for these purposes. It does hold, however, that these terms include not only the corporation's funds and inventory, but also its relationships with employees and customers and its internal processes for decision-making. [Citation.] More recently, the Maryland Court of Appeals held that injury to the corporation's business or property also occurs when officers and directors waste funds on perquisites, salaries, and bonuses, or make imprudent investments. [Citation.] * * * These Maryland cases indicate * * * that ill-advised investments by a corporation, even if paid for with the corporation's shares, may constitute an impairment or destruction of the corporation's business.

In deciding whether a shareholder may bring a direct suit, the question the Maryland courts ask is not whether the shareholder suffered injury; if a corporation is injured those who own the corporation are injured too. The inquiry, instead, is whether the shareholders' injury is "distinct" from that suffered by the corporation. [Citation.]

* * *

Thus, under Maryland law, when the shareholders of a corporation suffer an injury that is distinct from that of the corporation, the shareholders may bring direct suit for redress of that injury; there is shareholder standing. When the corporation is injured and the injury to its shareholders derives from that injury, however, only the corporation may bring suit; there is no shareholder standing. The shareholder may, at most, sue derivatively, seeking in effect to require the corporation to pursue a lawsuit to compensate for the injury to the corporation, and thereby ultimately redress the injury to the shareholders.

* * * To sue directly under Maryland law, a shareholder must allege an injury distinct from an injury to the corporation, not from that of other shareholders.

* * *

Applying Maryland's law of shareholder standing to the plaintiff's four alleged injuries, we conclude that one that he alleges does not support direct claims under Maryland law. The remaining alleged injuries, however—describing the set of harms arising from the alleged coercion—do.

The plaintiff alleges a loss in share value resulting from the "substantial underwriting and other transactional costs associated with the Rights Offering." * * * Underwriter fees, advisory fees, and other transaction costs incurred by a corporation decrease share price primarily because they deplete the corporation's assets, precisely the type of injury to the corporation that can be redressed under Maryland law only through a suit brought on behalf of the corporation. [Citation.]

The plaintiff's remaining alleged injuries can be read to describe the set of harms resulting from the coercive nature of the rights offering. The particular harm allegedly suffered by an individual shareholder as a result of the coercion depends on whether or not that shareholder participated in the rights offering. For example, when read in the light most favorable to the plaintiff, the alleged injury of "substantial downward pressure on the price of the Fund's shares" resulting from the issuance of new shares describes the reduction in the net equity value of the shares owned by non-participating shareholders. [Citation.] Similarly, the alleged injury from the downward pressure on share prices resulting from the setting of the "exercise price of the rights * * * at a steep discount from the pre-rights offering net asset value" can be read to refer to the involuntary dilution in equity value suffered by the non-participating shareholders. [Citation.]

* * *

* * * On the other hand, participating shareholders may have suffered harm in the form of transaction costs in liquidating other assets to purchase the new shares, and the impairment of their right to dispose of their assets as they prefer if they purchased new shares to avoid dilution.

* * *

Thus, in the case of both the participating and non-participating shareholders, it would appear that the alleged injuries were to the shareholders alone and not to the Fund. These harms therefore constitute "distinct" injuries supporting direct shareholder claims under Maryland law. The corporation cannot bring the action seeking compensation for these injuries because they were suffered by its shareholders, not itself.

INTERPRETATION A class action is a direct suit *against* the corporation and seeks recovery for the shareholders as individuals. A derivative suit is brought by shareholders *on behalf of* the corporation and seeks recovery for the corporation so that all shareholders benefit proportionately.

CRITICAL THINKING QUESTION When should derivative suits be permitted? Explain.

SHAREHOLDER'S RIGHT TO DISSENT

A shareholder has the right to dissent from certain corporate actions that require shareholder approval. These actions include most mergers, consolidations, compulsory share exchanges, and a sale or exchange of all or substantially all the assets of the corporation not in the usual and regular course of business. We will discuss the shareholder's right to dissent in Chapter 37.

ROLE OF DIRECTORS AND OFFICERS

Management of a corporation is vested by statute in its board of directors, which determines general corporate policy and appoints officers to execute that policy and to administer the day-to-day operations of the corporation. Both the directors and officers of the corporation owe certain duties to the corporate entity as well as to the corporation's shareholders and are liable for breaching these duties.

In the following sections we will discuss the roles of corporate directors and officers. In some instances, controlling shareholders (those who own a number of shares sufficient to allow them effective control over the corporation) are held to the same duties as directors and officers, which we will discuss later in this chapter. Moreover, in close corporations, many courts impose upon *all* the shareholders a fiduciary duty similar to that imposed upon partners.

Donahue v. Rodd Electrotype Co., Inc.

Massachusetts Supreme Court, 1975
367 Mass. 578, 328 N.E.2d 505

FACTS Euphemia Donahue was a minority stockholder in the Rodd Electrotype Company of New England, Inc. Rodd Electrotype was, by definition, a close corporation. Members of the Rodd and Donahue families were the sole owners of the corporate stock, and no ready market for the shares existed. Moreover, the Rodds effectively controlled the corporation through their control of the chief management positions and their ownership of the majority of the stock. When Harry Rodd, a director, officer, and controlling stockholder of Rodd Electrotype, retired from the business, Rodd Electrotype purchased his shares in the corporation for $36,000. Donahue, who was not offered an equal opportunity to sell her shares to the corporation, brought an action against Rodd Electrotype, Harry Rodd, and the present directors of the corporation, claiming that the defendants breached their fiduciary duty to her in causing the corporation to purchase the shares of Harry Rodd. She sought rescission of the purchase and repayment by Harry Rodd to Rodd Electrotype of the purchase price of the shares plus interest. The trial court dismissed the case, and the appellate court affirmed.

DECISION Judgment reversed and relief granted to the plaintiff.

OPINION Tauro, C. J. We deem a close corporation to be typified by: (1) a small number of stockholders; (2) no ready market for the corporate stock; and (3) substantial majority stockholder participation in the management, direction and operations of the corporation.

As thus defined, the close corporation bears striking resemblance to a partnership. Commentators and courts have noted that the close corporation is often little more than an "incorporated" or "chartered" partnership. * * *

Just as in a partnership, the relationship among the stockholders must be one of trust, confidence and absolute loyalty if the enterprise is to succeed. Close corporations with substantial assets and with more numerous stockholders are no different from smaller close corporations in this regard. All participants rely on the fidelity and abilities of those stockholders who hold office. Disloyalty and self-seeking conduct on the part of any stockholder will engender bickering, corporate stalemates, and perhaps, efforts to achieve dissolution. * * *

* * *

Although the corporate form provides * * * advantages for the stockholders (limited liability, perpetuity, and so forth), it also supplies an opportunity for the majority stockholders to oppress or disadvantage minority stockholders. The minority is vulnerable to a variety of oppressive devices, termed "freeze-outs," which the majority may employ. [Citation.] An authoritative study of such "freeze-outs" enumerates some of the possibilities: "The squeezers [those who employ the freeze-out techniques] may refuse to declare dividends; they may drain off the corporation's earnings in the form of exorbitant salaries and bonuses to the majority shareholder officers and perhaps to their relatives, or in the form of high rent by the corporation for property leased from majority shareholders * * *; they may deprive minority shareholders of corporate offices and of employment by the company; they may cause the corporation to sell its assets at an inadequate price to the majority shareholders. * * *" [Citation.] In particular, the power of the board of directors, controlled by the majority, to declare or withhold dividends and to deny the minority employment is easily converted to a device to disadvantage minority stockholders. * * *

* * *

The minority can, of course, initiate suit against the majority and their directors. Self-serving conduct by directors is proscribed by the director's fiduciary obligation to the corporation. [Citation.] However, in practice, the plaintiff will find difficulty in challenging dividend or employment policies. Such policies are considered to be within the judgment of the directors. This court has said: "The courts prefer not to interfere * * * with the sound financial management of the corporation by its directors, but declare as a general rule that the declaration of dividends rests within the sound discretion of the directors, refusing to interfere with their determination unless a plain abuse of discretion is made to appear." * * *

Thus, when these types of "freeze-outs" are attempted by the majority stockholders, the minority stockholders, cut off from all corporation-related revenues, must either suffer their losses or seek a buyer for their shares. Many minority stockholders will be unwilling or unable to wait for an alteration in majority policy. Typically, the minority stockholder in a close corporation has a substantial percentage of his personal assets invested in the corporation. [Citation.] The stockholder may have anticipated that his salary from his position with the corporation would be his livelihood. Thus, he cannot afford to wait passively. He must liquidate his investment in the close corporation in order to reinvest the funds in income-producing enterprises.

At this point, the true plight of the minority stockholder in a close corporation becomes manifest. He cannot easily reclaim his capital. In a large public corporation, the oppressed or dissident minority stockholder could sell his stock in order to extricate some of his invested capital. By definition, this market is not available for shares in the close corporation. In a partnership, a partner who feels abused by his fellow partners may cause dissolution by his "express will * * * at any time" [citation] and recover his share of partnership assets and accumulated profits. * * * To secure dissolution of the ordinary close corporation subject to [citation], the stockholder, in the absence of corporate deadlock, must own at least fifty per cent of the shares (citation] or have the advantage of a favorable provision in the articles of organization [citation]. The minority stockholder, by definition lacking fifty per cent of the corporate shares, can never "authorize" the corporation to file a petition for dissolution under [citation], by his own vote. He will seldom have at his disposal the requisite favorable provision in the articles of organization.

Thus, in a close corporation, the minority stockholders may be trapped in a disadvantageous situation. No outsider would knowingly assume the position of the disadvantaged minority. The outsider would have the same difficulties. To cut losses the minority stockholder may be compelled to deal with the majority. This is the capstone of the majority plan. Majority "freeze-out" schemes which withhold dividends are designed to compel the minority to relinquish stock at inadequate prices. * * * When the minority stockholder agrees to sell out at less than fair value, the majority has won.

Because of the fundamental resemblance of the close corporation to the partnership, the trust and confidence which are essential to this scale and manner of enterprise, and the inherent danger to minority interests in the close corporation, we hold that stockholders in the close corporation owe one another substantially the same fiduciary duty in the operation of the enterprise that partners owe to one another. In our previous decisions, we have defined the standard of duty owed by partners to one another as the "utmost good faith and loyalty." [Citations.] Stockholders in close corporations must discharge their management and stockholder responsibilities in conformity with this strict good faith standard. They may not act out of avarice, expediency or self-interest in derogation of their duty of loyalty to the other stockholders and to the corporation.

We contrast this strict good faith standard with the somewhat less stringent standard of fiduciary duty to which directors and stockholders of all corporations must adhere in the discharge of their corporate responsibilities. Corporate directors are held to a good faith and inherent fairness standard of conduct [citation] and are not "permitted to serve two masters whose interests are antagonistic." [Citation] "Their paramount duty is to the corporation, and their personal pecuniary interests are subordinate to that duty." [Citation.]

The more rigorous duty of partners and participants in a joint adventure, here extended to stockholders in a close corporation, was described by then Chief Judge Cardozo of the New York Court of Appeals in [citation]: "Joint adventurers, like copartners, owe to one another, while the enterprise continues, the duty of the finest loyalty. Many forms of conduct permissible in a workaday world for those acting at arm's length, are forbidden to those bound by fiduciary ties. * * * Not honesty alone, but the punctilio of an honor the most sensitive, is then the standard of behavior."

* * *

Under settled Massachusetts law, a domestic corporation, unless forbidden by statute, has the power to purchase its own shares. When the corporation reacquiring its own stock is a close corporation, the purchase is subject to the additional requirement, in the light of our holding in this opinion, that the stockholders, who, as directors or controlling stockholders, caused the corporation to enter into the stock purchase agreement, must have acted with the utmost good faith and loyalty to the other stockholders.

To meet this test, if the stockholder whose shares were purchased was a member of the controlling group, the controlling stockholders must cause the corporation to offer each stockholder an equal opportunity to sell a ratable number of his shares to the corporation at an identical price.* * *

The benefits conferred by the purchase are twofold: (1) provision of a market for shares; (2) access to corporate assets for personal use. By definition, there is no ready market for shares of a close corporation. The purchase creates a market for shares which previously had been unmarketable. It transforms a previously illiquid investment into a liquid one. If the close corporation purchases shares only from a member of the controlling group, the controlling stockholder can convert his shares into cash at a time when none of the other stockholders can. Consistent with its strict fiduciary duty, the controlling group may not utilize its control of the corporation to establish an exclusive market in previously unmarketable shares from which the minority stockholders are excluded. * * *

The purchase also distributes corporate assets to the stockholder whose shares were purchased. Unless an equal opportunity is given to all stockholders, the purchase of shares from a member of the controlling group operates as a preferential distribution of assets. In exchange for his shares, he receives a percentage of the contributed capital and accumulated profits of the enterprise. The funds he so receives are available for his personal use. The other stockholders benefit from no such access to corporate property and cannot withdraw their shares of the corporate profits and capital in this manner unless the controlling group acquiesces. Although the purchase price for the controlling stockholder's shares may seem fair to the corporation and other stockholders under the tests established in the prior case law, the controlling stockholder whose stock has been purchased has still received a relative advantage over his fellow stockholders, inconsistent with his strict fiduciary duty—an opportunity to turn corporate funds to personal use.

The rule of equal opportunity in stock purchases by close corporations provides equal access to these benefits for all stockholders. We hold that, in any case in which the controlling stockholders have exercised their power over the corporation to deny the minority such equal opportunity, the minority shall be entitled to appropriate relief. * * *

* * *

On its face, then, the purchase of Harry Rodd's shares by the corporation is a breach of the duty which the controlling stockholders, the Rodds, owed to the minority stockholders, the plaintiff and her son. The purchase distributed a portion of the corporate assets to Harry Rodd, a member of the controlling group, in exchange for his shares. The plaintiff and her son were not offered an equal opportunity to sell their shares to the corporation. In fact, their efforts to obtain an equal opportunity were rebuffed by the corporate representative. As the trial judge found, they did not, in any manner, ratify the transaction with Harry Rodd.

INTERPRETATION Recognizing the strong resemblance of a close corporation to a partnership, some courts impose upon all shareholders in a close corporation substantially the same fiduciary duty that partners owe each other.

ETHICAL QUESTION Did the defendant act unethically? Explain.

CRITICAL THINKING QUESTION Should close corporation law be separate and distinct from general corporation law? Explain.

FUNCTION OF THE BOARD OF DIRECTORS

Although the shareholders elect them to manage the corporation, the directors are neither trustees nor agents of the shareholders or the corporation. They are, however, fiduciaries who must perform their duties in good faith, in the best interests of the corporation, and with due care.

> **Practical Advice**
>
> Do not agree to serve on a corporate board of directors unless you have sufficient time and energy to meet the requirements of the position.

The Revised Act and the statutes of many states provide that "[a]ll corporate powers shall be exercised by or under the authority of, and the business and affairs of the corporation managed under the direction of, its board of directors, subject to any limitation set forth in the articles of incorporation." In some corporations, the board members are all actively involved in the management of the business. In these cases, the corporate powers are exercised by the board of directors. On the other hand, in publicly held corporations, a majority of board members often are not actively involved in management. Here, the corporate powers are exercised *under* the authority of the board, which formulates major management policy and monitors management's performance but does not involve itself in day-to-day management.

In publicly held corporations, the directors who are also officers or employees of the corporation are ***inside directors***, while the directors who are not officers or employees are ***outside directors***. Outside directors who have no business contacts with the corporation are ***unaffiliated directors***; outside directors having business contacts—such as investment bankers, lawyers, or suppliers—are ***affiliated directors***. Historically, the boards of many publicly held corporations consisted mainly or entirely of inside directors. During the past two decades, however, the number and influence of outside directors have increased substantially, and now boards of the great majority of publicly held corporations consist primarily of outside directors.

The Sarbanes-Oxley Act confers on the audit committee of every publicly held corporation direct responsibility for the appointment, compensation, and oversight of the work of the public accounting firm employed by the company to perform audit services. Moreover, the public accounting firm must report directly to the audit committee. The Act requires that the company provide appropriate funding for the audit committee to compensate the auditors, independent counsel, and other advisers. The audit committee is responsible for resolving disagreements between management and the auditor regarding the company's financial reporting. Each member of the audit committee must be independent.

In those states with special close corporation statutes, electing corporations can operate without a board of directors. Moreover, under the Revised Act, as originally enacted, a corporation having fifty or fewer shareholders may dispense with or limit the authority of a board of directors by designating in its articles of incorporation those who will perform some or all of the duties of a board. The Revised Act as amended permits *any* corporation to dispense with a board of directors by a written agreement executed by all of the shareholders.

> **Practical Advice**
>
> To achieve greater flexibility, when organizing a close corporation you should consider including in the charter a provision eliminating the board of directors and assigning the board's duties to designated shareholders.

Under incorporation statutes the board has the responsibility for determining corporate policy in a number of areas, including (1) selecting and removing officers, (2) determining the corporation's capital structure, (3) initiating fundamental changes, (4) declaring dividends, and (5) setting management compensation.

SELECTION AND REMOVAL OF OFFICERS

In most states, the board of directors is responsible for choosing the corporation's officers and may remove any officer at any time. Officers are corporate agents who are delegated their responsibilities by the board of directors.

CAPITAL STRUCTURE

The board of directors determines the capital structure and financial policy of the corporation. For example, the board of directors has the power (1) to fix the selling price of newly issued shares, unless the articles of incorporation reserve to the shareholders the power to do so; (2) to determine the value of the consideration the corporation will receive in payment for the shares it issues; (3) to borrow money, issue notes, bonds, and other obligations, and secure any of the corporation's obligations; and (4) to sell, lease, or exchange assets of the corporation in the *usual* and *regular* course of business.

FUNDAMENTAL CHANGES

The board of directors has the power to amend or repeal the bylaws, unless the articles of incorporation reserve this power exclusively to the shareholders. In a few states directors may not repeal or amend bylaws adopted by the shareholders. In addition, the board initiates certain actions that require shareholder approval. For instance, the board initiates proceedings to amend the articles of incorporation; to effect a merger, consolidation, compulsory share exchange, or the sale or lease of all or substantially all of the assets of the corporation *other* than in the usual and regular course of business; and to dissolve the corporation.

DIVIDENDS

The board of directors declares the amount and type of dividends, subject to restrictions in the state incorporation statute; the articles of incorporation; and corporate loan and preferred stock agreements. The board also may purchase, redeem, or otherwise acquire shares of the corporation's equity securities.

MANAGEMENT COMPENSATION

The board of directors usually determines the compensation of officers. In addition, a number of states allow the board to fix the compensation of its members.

CPA ELECTION AND TENURE OF DIRECTORS

The incorporation statute, the articles of incorporation, and the bylaws determine the qualifications necessary to those who would be directors of the corporation. They also determine election procedures for and the number, tenure, and compensation of directors. Only individuals may serve as directors.

ELECTION, NUMBER, AND TENURE OF DIRECTORS

The initial board of directors generally is named in the articles of incorporation and serves until the first meeting of the shareholders at which directors are elected. Thereafter, directors are elected at annual meetings of the shareholders and hold office for one year unless their terms are staggered. However, if the shares represented at a meeting in person or by proxy are insufficient to constitute a quorum or if the shareholders are deadlocked and unable to elect a new board, the incumbent directors continue in office as "holdover" directors until their successors are duly elected and qualified. Though state statutes traditionally required each corporation to have three or more directors, most states permit the board to consist of one or more members. Moreover, the number of directors may be increased or decreased, within statutory limits, by amendment to the bylaws or charter.

VACANCIES AND REMOVAL OF DIRECTORS

The Revised Act provides that a vacancy in the board may be filled either by the shareholders or by the affirmative vote of a majority of the remaining directors, even if they should constitute less than a quorum of the board. The term of a director elected to fill a vacancy expires at the next shareholders' meeting at which directors are elected.

Some states have no statutory provision for the removal of directors, although a common law rule permits removal for cause by action of the shareholders. The Revised Act and an increasing number of other statutes permit the shareholders to remove one or more directors or the entire board, with or without cause, at a special meeting called for that purpose, subject to cumulative voting rights, if applicable. However, the Revised Act also permits the articles of incorporation to provide that directors may be removed only for cause.

COMPENSATION OF DIRECTORS

Traditionally, directors did not receive salaries for their directorial services, although they commonly received a fee or honorarium for their attendance at meetings. The Revised Act and many incorporation statutes now specifically authorize the board of directors to fix the compensation of directors, unless a contrary provision exists in the articles of incorporation or bylaws.

Under the Sarbanes-Oxley Act, if a publicly held company is required to issue an accounting restatement due to a material violation of securities law, the chief executive officer and the chief financial officer must forfeit certain bonuses and compensation received, as well as any profit realized from the sale of the company's securities, during the 12-month period following the original issuance of the noncomplying financial document.

CPA EXERCISE OF DIRECTORS' FUNCTIONS

Though they are powerless to bind the corporation when acting individually, directors do have this power when acting as a board. The board may act only through a meeting of the directors or through written consent signed by all of the directors, if such consent without a directors' meeting is authorized by the incorporation statute and is not contrary to the charter or bylaws.

Meetings are either held at a regular time and place fixed in the bylaws or called at special times. Notice of meetings must be given as prescribed in the bylaws. A director's attendance at any meeting is a waiver of such notice, unless the director attends only to object to the holding of the meeting or to the transaction of business at it and does not vote for or assent to action taken at the meeting. Waiver of notice also may be given in a signed writing. Most modern statutes provide that meetings of the board may be held either in or outside of the state of incorporation.

QUORUM AND VOTING

A majority of the board members constitutes a quorum (the minimum number of members that must be present at a meeting in order to transact business). Although most states do not permit a quorum to be set at less than a majority, the Revised Act and some states allow the articles of incorporation or the bylaws to authorize a quorum consisting of as few as one-third of a board's members. In contrast, however, in all states the articles of incorporation or bylaws may require a number greater than a simple majority. If a quorum is present at any meeting, the act of a majority of the directors in attendance is the act of the board, unless the articles of incorporation or bylaws require the act of a greater number.

Closely held corporations sometimes use supermajority or unanimous quorum requirements. In addition, they may require a supermajority or unanimous vote of the board for some or all matters.

> **Practical Advice**
>
> If you are forming a close corporation and will hold a minority interest in it, consider including in the charter supermajority quorum and voting provisions for voting by the board of directors to ensure that you will have control over specified managerial issues.

By requiring a quorum to be present when "a vote is taken," the Revised Act makes it clear that the board may act only when a quorum is present. This rule is in contrast to the rule governing shareholder meetings: recall that once a quorum of shareholders is obtained, it cannot be broken by the withdrawal of shareholders. Many state statutes, however, do not have this provision. In any event, directors may not vote by proxy, although most states permit directors to participate in meetings through teleconference.

A director present at a board meeting at which action on any corporate matter is taken is deemed to have assented to such action unless, in addition to dissenting or abstaining from it, he (1) has his dissent or abstention entered in the minutes of the meeting, (2) files his written dissent or abstention to such action with the presiding officer before the meeting adjourns, or (3) delivers his written dissent or abstention to the corporation immediately after adjournment.

ACTION TAKEN WITHOUT A MEETING

The Revised Act and most states provide that unless the articles of incorporation or bylaws provide otherwise, any action the statute requires or permits to be taken at a meeting of the board may be taken without a meeting if consent in writing is signed by all of the directors.

DELEGATION OF BOARD POWERS

Unless otherwise provided by the articles of incorporation or the bylaws, the board of directors may, by majority vote of the full board, appoint one or more committees, all of whose members must be directors. Many state statutes permit committees only if the charter expressly authorizes their formation. The Revised Act and the statutes of many states require that a committee consist of at least two directors, although some statutes permit a committee to have as few as one member. Committees may exercise all the authority of the board, except with regard to certain matters specified in the incorporation statute, such as declaring dividends and other distributions, filling vacancies on the board or on any of its committees, amending the bylaws, recommending fundamental changes to the shareholders, approving a merger or charter amendment not requiring shareholder approval, and authorizing the sale or reacquisition of stock. Delegating authority to a committee does not relieve any board member of his duties to the corporation. Commonly used committees include executive committees, audit committees (to recommend and oversee independent public accountants), compensation committees, finance committees, nominating committees, and investment committees.

DIRECTORS' INSPECTION RIGHTS

So that they can perform their duties competently and fully, directors have the right to inspect corporate books and records. This right is considerably broader than a shareholder's right to inspect.

CPA OFFICERS

The board of directors appoints the officers of a corporation to hold the offices provided for in the bylaws, which set forth the respective duties of each officer. Statutes generally require as a minimum that the officers consist of a president; one or more vice presidents, as prescribed by the bylaws; a secretary; and a treasurer. With the exception that the same person may not hold the office of president and secretary at the same time, a person may hold more than one office.

The Revised Act and other modern statutes permit every corporation to designate whatever officers it wants. Although the Act specifies no particular number of officers, one of them must be delegated responsibility to prepare the minutes of directors' and shareholders' meetings and to authenticate corporate records. The Revised Act permits the same individual to hold *all* of the offices of a corporation.

SELECTION AND REMOVAL OF OFFICERS

Most state statutes provide that officers be appointed by the board of directors and that they serve at the pleasure of the board. Accordingly, the board may remove officers with or without cause. Of course, if the officer has an employment contract that is valid for a specified time period, removing the officer without cause before the contract expires would constitute a breach of the employment contract. The board also determines the compensation of officers.

ROLE OF OFFICERS

The officers are, like the directors, fiduciaries to the corporation. On the other hand, unlike the directors, they are agents of the corporation. The roles of officers are set forth in the corporate bylaws.

AUTHORITY OF OFFICERS

The Revised Act provides that each officer has the authority provided in the bylaws or prescribed by the board of directors, to the extent that such prescribed authority is consistent with the bylaws. Like that of other agents, the authority of an officer to bind the corporation may be (1) actual express, (2) actual implied, or (3) apparent.

Actual Express Authority **Actual express authority** results from the corporation's manifesting to the officer its assent that the officer should act on the corporation's behalf. Actual express authority arises from the incorporation statute, the articles of incorporation, the bylaws, and resolutions of the board of directors. The latter provide the principal source of actual express authority. The Revised Act further provides that the board of directors may authorize an officer to prescribe the duties of other officers. This provision empowers officers to delegate authority to subordinates.

Actual Implied Authority Officers, as agents of the corporation, have **actual implied authority** to do what is reasonably necessary to perform their actual, delegated authority. In addition, a common question is whether officers possess implied authority merely by virtue of their positions. The courts have been cautious in granting such implied or inherent authority. However, any act requiring board approval, such as issuing stock, is clearly beyond the implied authority of any officer.

Apparent Authority **Apparent authority** arises from acts of the corporation that lead third parties to believe reasonably and in good faith that an officer has the required authority. Apparent authority might arise when a third party relies on the fact that an officer has exercised the same authority in the past with the consent of the board of directors.

Ratification A corporation may ratify the unauthorized acts of its officers. Equivalent to the corporation's having granted the officer prior authority, **ratification** relates back to the original transaction and may be either express or implied from the corporation's acceptance of the contract's benefits with full knowledge of the facts.

Practical Advice

When signing contracts in your capacity as an officer for a corporation, be sure to indicate your representative status.

CPA DUTIES OF DIRECTORS AND OFFICERS

Generally, directors and officers owe the duties of obedience, diligence, and loyalty to the corporation. These duties are for the most part judicially imposed. By imposing liability upon directors and officers for specific acts, state and federal statutes supplement the common law, which nonetheless remains the most significant source of duties.

A corporation may not recover damages from its directors and officers for losses resulting from their poor business judgments or honest mistakes of judgment. Directors and officers are not duty bound to ensure business success. They are required only to be obedient, reasonably diligent, and completely loyal. In 1999 an amendment to the Revised Act was adopted refining the act's standards of conduct and liability for directors.

DUTY OF OBEDIENCE

Directors and officers must act within their respective authority. For any loss the corporation suffers because of their unauthorized acts, they are held absolutely liable in some jurisdictions; in others, they are held liable only if they exceeded their authority intentionally or negligently.

DUTY OF DILIGENCE

In discharging their duties, directors and officers must exercise ordinary care and prudence. Some states interpret this standard to mean that directors and officers must exercise "the same degree of care and prudence that [those] promoted by self-interest generally exercise in their own affairs." The great majority of states, as well as the Revised Act, however, hold that the test requires a director or officer to discharge corporate duties (1) in good faith; (2) with the care an ordinarily prudent person in a like position would exercise under similar circumstances; and (3) in a manner the director or officer reasonably believes to be in the best interests of the corporation. A director or officer whose performance of her duties complies with these requirements is not liable for any action she takes as a director or officer or for any failure to act.

So long as the directors and officers act in good faith and with due care, the courts will not substitute their judgment for that of the board or officer—the so-called business judgment rule. Directors and officers will nevertheless be held liable for bad faith or negligent conduct. Moreover, they may be liable for failing to act. In one instance, a bank director, who in the five and one-half years that he had been on the board had never attended a board meeting or examined the institution's books and records, was held liable for losses resulting from the unsupervised acts of the president and cashier, who had made various improper loans and had permitted large overdrafts.

In 1999 an amendment to the Revised Act was adopted refining the Act's standards of conduct and liability for directors. It substituted a different duty of care standard for point 2 above: When becoming informed in connection with their decision-making function or devoting attention to their oversight function, directors shall discharge their duties with the care that a person in a like position would reasonably believe appropriate under similar circumstances. While some aspects of a director's role will be performed individually, such as preparing for meetings, this reformulation explicitly recognizes that directors perform most of their functions as a unit.

Reliance on Others Directors and officers are permitted to entrust important work to others, and if they have selected employees with care, they are not personally liable for the negligent acts or willful wrongs of those selected. However, a reasonable amount of supervision is required; and an officer or director who knew or should have known or suspected that an employee was incurring losses through carelessness, theft, or embezzlement will be held liable for such losses.

A director also may rely in good faith on information provided him by officers and employees of the corporation; legal counsel, public accountants, or other persons as to matters the director reasonably believes are within the person's professional or expert competence; and a committee of the board of directors of which the director is not a member if the director reasonably believes the committee merits confidence. A director is not acting in good faith if he has knowledge concerning the matter in question that makes reliance unwarranted. The 1999 amendments to the Revised Act added a provision entitling a director to rely on the *performance* of board functions properly delegated by the board to officers, employees, or a committee of the board of directors of which the director is not a member unless the director has knowledge that makes reliance unwarranted.

An officer is also entitled to rely upon this information, but this right may, in many circumstances, be more limited than a director's because of the officer's greater familiarity with the affairs of the corporation.

Business Judgment Rule Directors and officers are continuously called on to make decisions that require balancing benefits and risks to the corporation. Although hindsight may reveal that some of these decisions were not the best, the **business judgment rule** precludes imposing liability on the directors or officers for honest mistakes of judgment. To later benefit from the business judgment rule, a director or officer must make an informed decision, in good faith without any conflict of interests, and have a rational basis for believing it was in the corporation's best interests. (With respect to *directors*, the 1999 amendments to the Revised Act added a new provision codifying much of the business judgment rule and providing guidance as to its application.) Moreover, where this standard of conduct has not been met, the director's action (or inaction) must be shown to be the proximate cause of damage to the corporation.

Hasty or ill-advised action also can render directors liable. In a recent case, the Supreme Court of Delaware held directors liable for approving the terms of a cash-out merger. The court found that the directors did not adequately inform themselves of the company's intrinsic value and were grossly negligent in approving the terms of the merger upon two hours' consideration and without prior notice.

Brehm v. Eisner

Supreme Court of Delaware, 2000

746 A.2d 244

http://caselaw.lp.findlaw.com/data2/delawarestatecases/469-1998.pdf

FACTS On October 1, 1995, Disney **(http://disney.go.com)** hired as its president Michael S. Ovitz, who was a long time friend of Disney Chairman and CEO Michael Eisner. At the time, Ovitz was an important talent broker in Hollywood. Although he lacked experience managing a diversified public company, other companies with entertainment operations had been interested in hiring him for high-level executive positions. The employment agreement approved by the board of directors then in office (Old Board) had an initial term of five years and required that Ovitz "devote his full time and best efforts exclusively to the Company," with exceptions for volunteer work, service on the board of another company, and managing his passive investments. In return, Disney agreed to give Ovitz a base salary of $1 million per year, a discretionary bonus, and two sets of stock options (the "A" options and the "B" options) that collectively would enable Ovitz to purchase 5 million shares of Disney common stock. The "A" options were scheduled to vest in three annual increments of 1 million shares each, beginning at the end of the third full year of employment and continuing for the following two years. The agreement specifically provided that the "A" options would vest immediately if Disney granted Ovitz a non-fault termination of the employment agreement. The "B" options, consisting of 2 million shares, were scheduled to vest annually starting the year after the last "A" option would vest and were conditioned on Ovitz and Disney first having agreed to extend his employment beyond the five-year term of the employment agreement. In addition, Ovitz would forfeit the "B" options if his initial employment term of five years ended prematurely for any reason, even if from a non-fault termination.

The employment agreement provided three ways for Ovitz' employment to end. He might serve his five years and Disney might decide against offering him a new contract. If so, Disney would owe Ovitz a $10 million termination payment. Before the end of the initial term, Disney could terminate Ovitz for "good cause" only if Ovitz committed gross negligence or malfeasance, or if Ovitz resigned voluntarily. Disney would owe Ovitz no additional compensation if it terminated him for "good cause." Termination without cause (non-fault termination) would entitle Ovitz to the present value of his salary payments remaining under the agreement, a $10 million severance payment, an additional $7.5 million for each fiscal year remaining under the agreement, and the immediate vesting of the first 3 million stock options (the "A" Options).

Soon after Ovitz began work, problems surfaced and the situation continued to deteriorate during the first year of his employment. The deteriorating situation led Ovitz to begin seeking alternative employment and expressing his desire to leave the Company. On December 11, 1996, Eisner and Ovitz agreed to arrange for Ovitz to leave Disney on the non-fault basis provided for in the 1995 employment agreement. The board of directors then in office (New Board) approved this by authorizing a "non-fault termination" agreement with cash payments to Ovitz of almost $39 million and the immediate vesting of 3 million stock options with a value of $101 million.

Shareholders brought a derivative suit alleging that: (a) the Old Board had breached its fiduciary duty in approving an extravagant and wasteful employment agreement and (b) the New Board had breached its fiduciary duty in agreeing to an extravagant and wasteful "non-fault" termination of the Ovitz employment agreement. The plaintiffs alleged that the Old Board had failed properly to inform itself about the total costs and incentives of the Ovitz employment agreement, especially the severance package, and failed to realize that the contract gave Ovitz an incentive to find a way to exit the Company via a non-fault termination as soon as possible because doing so would permit him to earn more than he could by fulfilling his contract. They alleged that the corporate compensation expert, Graef Crystal, who had advised Old Board in connection with its decision to approve the Ovitz employment agreement, stated two years later that the Old Board failed to consider the incentives and the total cost of the severance provisions. The defendants moved to dismiss, and the Court of Chancery granted the motion. The shareholders appealed.

DECISION Dismissal affirmed in part, reversed in part, and remanded.

OPINION Veasey, C. J. This is potentially a very troubling case on the merits. On the one hand, it appears from the Complaint that: (a) the compensation and termination payout for Ovitz were exceedingly lucrative, if not luxurious, compared to Ovitz' value to the Company; and (b) the processes of the boards of directors in dealing with the approval and termination of the Ovitz Employment Agreement were casual, if not sloppy and perfunctory. [T]he processes of the Old Board and the New Board were hardly paradigms of good corporate governance practices. Moreover, the sheer size of the payout to Ovitz, as alleged, pushes the envelope of judicial respect for the business judgment of directors in making compensation decisions. Therefore, both as to the processes of the two Boards and the waste test, this is a close case.

* * *

This is a case about whether there should be personal liability of the directors of a Delaware corporation to the corporation for lack of due care in the decisionmaking process and for waste of corporate assets This case is not about the failure of the directors to establish and carry out ideal corporate governance practices

All good corporate governance practices include compliance with statutory law and case law establishing fiduciary duties. But the law of corporate fiduciary duties and remedies for violation of those duties are distinct from the aspirational goals of ideal corporate governance practices. Aspirational ideals of good corporate governance practices for boards of directors that go beyond the minimal legal requirements of the corporation law are highly desirable, often tend to benefit stockholders, sometimes reduce litigation and can usually help directors avoid liability. But they are not required by the corporation law and do not define standards of liability. [Citation.]

The inquiry here is not whether we would disdain the composition, behavior and decisions of Disney's Old Board or New Board as alleged in the Complaint if we were Disney stockholders. In the absence of a legislative mandate, [citation], that determination is not for the courts. That decision is for the stockholders to make in voting for directors, urging other stockholders to reform or oust the board, or in making individual buy-sell decisions involving Disney securities. The sole issue that this Court must determine is whether the particularized facts alleged in this Complaint provide a reason to believe that the conduct of the Old Board in 1995 and the New Board in 1996 constituted a violation of their fiduciary duties.

Plaintiffs claim that the Court of Chancery erred when it concluded that a board of directors is "not required to be informed of every fact, but rather is required to be reasonably informed." [Citation.] Applying that conclusion, the Court of Chancery held that the Complaint did not create a reasonable doubt that the Old Board had satisfied the requisite informational component when it approved the Ovitz contract in 1995. [Citation.] In effect, Plaintiffs argue that being "reasonably informed" is too lax a standard to satisfy Delaware's legal test for the informational component of board decisions. They contend that the Disney directors on the Old Board did not avail themselves of all material information reasonably available in approving Ovitz' 1995 contract, and thereby violated their fiduciary duty of care. [Citation.]

The "reasonably informed" language used by the Court of Chancery here may have been a shorthand attempt to paraphrase the Delaware jurisprudence that, in making business decisions, directors must consider all material information reasonably available, and that the directors' process is actionable only if grossly negligent. [Citation.] The question is whether the trial court's formulation is consistent with our objective test of reasonableness, the test of materiality and concepts of gross negligence. We agree with the Court of Chancery that the standard for judging the informational component of the directors' decisionmaking does not mean that the Board must be informed of every fact. The Board is responsible for considering only material facts that are reasonably available, not those that are immaterial or out of the Board's reasonable reach. [Citation.]

Certainly in this case the economic exposure of the corporation to the payout scenarios of the Ovitz contract was material, particularly given its large size, for purposes of the directors' decision making process. [Court's footnote: The term "material" is used in this context to mean relevant and of a magnitude to be important to directors in carrying out their fiduciary duty of care in decisionmaking.] And those dollar exposure numbers were reasonably available because the logical inference from plaintiffs' allegations is that Crystal or the New Board could have calculated the numbers. Thus, the objective tests of reasonable availability and materiality were satisfied by this Complaint. But that is not the end of the inquiry for liability purposes.

* * *

* * * The Complaint, fairly construed, admits that the directors were advised by Crystal as an expert and that they relied on his expertise. Accordingly, the question here is whether the directors are to be "fully protected" (i.e., not held liable) on the basis that they relied in good faith on a qualified expert [citation]. * * *

* * * Plaintiffs must rebut the presumption that the directors properly exercised their business judgment, including their good faith reliance on Crystal's expertise. * * *

* * * [T]he Complaint must allege particularized facts (not conclusions) that, if proved, would show, for example,

that: (a) the directors did not in fact rely on the expert; (b) their reliance was not in good faith; (c) they did not reasonably believe that the expert's advice was within the expert's professional competence; (d) the expert was not selected with reasonable care by or on behalf of the corporation, and the faulty selection process was attributable to the directors; (e) the subject matter (in this case the cost calculation) that was material and reasonably available was so obvious that the board's failure to consider it was grossly negligent regardless of the expert's advice or lack of advice; or (f) that the decision of the Board was so unconscionable as to constitute waste or fraud. This Complaint includes no particular allegations of this nature, and therefore it was subject to dismissal as drafted.

* * *

We conclude that * * * the Complaint * * * as drafted, fails to create a reasonable doubt that the Old Board's decision in approving the Ovitz Employment Agreement was protected by the business judgment rule. * * *

Plaintiffs allege not only that the Old Board committed a procedural due care violation in the process of approving the Ovitz 1995 Employment Agreement but also that the Board committed a "substantive due care" violation constituting waste. They contend that the Court of Chancery erred in holding that the Complaint failed to set forth particularized facts creating a reasonable doubt that the directors' decision to enter into the Ovitz Employment Agreement was a product of the proper exercise of business judgment.

Plaintiffs' principal theory is that the 1995 Ovitz Employment Agreement was a "wasteful transaction for Disney *ab initio*" because it was structured to "incentivize" Ovitz to seek an early non-fault termination. The Court of Chancery correctly dismissed this theory as failing to meet the stringent requirements of the waste test, i.e., "an exchange that is so one sided that no business person of ordinary, sound judgment could conclude that the corporation has received adequate consideration." Moreover, the Court concluded that a board's decision on executive compensation is entitled to great deference. It is the essence of business judgment for a board to determine if "a 'particular individual warrant[s] large amounts of money, whether in the form of current salary or severance provisions.' " [Citation.]

* * *

* * * Irrationality is the outer limit of the business judgment rule. Irrationality may be the functional equivalent of the waste test or it may tend to show that the decision is not made in good faith, which is a key ingredient of the business judgment rule. [Court's footnote: The business judgment rule has been well formulated by *Aronson* and other cases. ("It is a presumption that in making a business decision the directors * * * acted on an informed basis, in good faith and in the honest belief that the action taken was in the best interests of the corporation."). Thus, directors' decisions will be respected by courts unless the directors are interested or lack independence relative to the decision, do not act in good faith, act in a manner that cannot be attributed to a rational business purpose or reach their decision by a grossly negligent process that includes the failure to consider all material facts reasonably available.]

The plaintiffs contend in this Court that Ovitz resigned or committed acts of gross negligence or malfeasance that constituted grounds to terminate him for cause. In either event, they argue that the Company had no obligation to Ovitz and that the directors wasted the Company's assets by causing it to make an unnecessary and enormous payout of cash and stock options when it permitted Ovitz to terminate his employment on a "non-fault" basis. We have concluded, however, that the Complaint currently before us does not set forth particularized facts that he resigned or unarguably breached his Employment Agreement.

* * *

Construed most favorably to plaintiffs, the facts in the Complaint (disregarding conclusory allegations) show that Ovitz' performance as president was disappointing at best, that Eisner admitted it had been a mistake to hire him, that Ovitz lacked commitment to the Company, that he performed services for his old company, and that he negotiated for other jobs (some very lucrative) while being required under the contract to devote his full time and energy to Disney.

All this shows is that the Board had arguable grounds to fire Ovitz for cause. But what is alleged is only an argument—perhaps a good one—that Ovitz' conduct constituted gross negligence or malfeasance. * * *

The Complaint, in sum, contends that the Board committed waste by agreeing to the very lucrative payout to Ovitz under the non-fault termination provision because it had no obligation to him, thus taking the Board's decision outside the protection of the business judgment rule. Construed most favorably to plaintiffs, the Complaint contends that, by reason of the New Board's available arguments of resignation and good cause, it had the leverage to negotiate Ovitz down to a more reasonable payout than that guaranteed by his Employment Agreement. But the Complaint fails on its face to meet the waste test because it does not allege with particularity facts tending to show that no reasonable business person would have made the decision that the New Board made under these circumstances.

We agree with the conclusion of the Court of Chancery:

> The Board made a business decision to grant Ovitz a Non-Fault Termination. Plaintiffs may disagree with the Board's judgment as to how this matter should have been handled. But where, as here, there is no reasonable doubt as to the disinterest of or absence of fraud by the

Board, mere disagreement cannot serve as grounds for imposing liability based on alleged breaches of fiduciary duty and waste. * * *

To rule otherwise would invite courts to become super-directors, measuring matters of degree in business decisionmaking and executive compensation. Such a rule would run counter to the foundation of our jurisprudence.

* * *

One can understand why Disney stockholders would be upset with such an extraordinarily lucrative compensation agreement and termination payout awarded a company president who served for only a little over a year and who underperformed to the extent alleged. That said, there is a very large—though not insurmountable—burden on stockholders who believe they should pursue the remedy of a derivative suit instead of selling their stock or seeking to reform or oust these directors from office.

INTERPRETATION In exercising their duties, all corporate directors must act in good faith, in the corporation's best interests, and on an informed basis with due care.

ETHICAL QUESTION Did Eisner, Ovitz, or the boards of directors act unethically? Explain.

CRITICAL THINKING QUESTION Do you agree with the court's decision in this case? Explain.

DUTY OF LOYALTY

The officers and directors of a corporation owe a duty of loyalty (a ***fiduciary duty***) to the corporation and to its shareholders. The essence of a fiduciary duty is the subordination of self-interest to the interest of the person or persons to whom the duty is owing. It requires officers and directors to be constantly loyal to the corporation, which they both serve and control.

An officer or director is required to disclose fully to the corporation any financial interest he may have in any contract or transaction to which the corporation is a party. (This is a corollary to the rule that forbids fiduciaries from making secret profits.) His business conduct must be insulated from self-interest, and he may not advance his personal interest at the corporation's expense. Moreover, an officer or director may not represent conflicting interests; her duty is one of strict allegiance to the corporation.

The remedy for breach of fiduciary duty is a suit in equity by the corporation, or more often a derivative suit instituted by a shareholder, to require the fiduciary to pay to the corporation the profits she obtained through the breach. It need not be shown that the corporation could otherwise have made the profits that the fiduciary realized. The object of the rule is to discourage breaches of duty by taking from the fiduciary all of the profits she has made. Though the enforcement of the rule may result in a windfall to the corporation, this is incidental to the rule's deterrent objective. Whenever a director or officer breaches his fiduciary duty, he forfeits his right to compensation during the period he engaged in the breach.

Conflict of Interests A contract or other transaction between an officer or a director and the corporation inherently involves a conflict of interest. Contracts between officers and the corporation are covered under the law of agency. (See Chapter 29.) Early on, the common law viewed all director-corporation transactions as automatically void or voidable but eventually recognized that this rule was unreasonable because it would prevent directors from entering into contracts beneficial to the corporation. Now, therefore, if such a contract is honest and fair, the courts will uphold it. In the case of contracts between corporations having an interlocking directorate (corporations whose boards of directors share one or more members), the courts subject the contracts to scrutiny and will set them aside unless the transaction is shown to have been entirely fair and entered in good faith.

Most states and the original version of the Revised Act address these related problems by providing that such transactions are neither void nor voidable if, after full disclosure, they are approved by either the board of disinterested directors or the shareholders or if they are fair and reasonable to the corporation.

The Revised Act was amended in 1988 to adopt a more specific approach to a director's conflict-of-interest transactions. The Revised Act establishes more clearly prescribed safe harbors to validate conflict-of-interest transactions. The Revised Act provides two alternative safe harbors, each of which is available before or after the transaction: approval by "qualified" (disinterested) directors or approval by the shareholders. In either case, the interested director must make full disclosure to the approving group. If neither of these safe harbor provisions is satisfied, then the transaction is subject to appropriate judicial action unless the transaction is fair to the corporation.

Loans to Directors and Officers The Model Act and some states permit a corporation to lend money to its *directors* only with its shareholders' authorization for each loan. The statutes in most states permit such loans either on a general or limited basis. The Revised Act initially permitted such loans if each particular loan was approved (1) by a majority of disinterested shareholders or (2) by the board of directors after determining that the loan would benefit the corporation; however, the 1988 amendments to the Revised Act deleted this section, subjecting loans to directors to the procedure that applies to directors' conflicting-interest transactions.

The Sarbanes-Oxley Act prohibits any publicly held corporation from making personal loans to its directors or its executive officers. The Act provides certain limited exceptions to this prohibition.

Corporate Opportunity Directors and officers may not usurp any corporate opportunity that in all fairness should belong to the corporation. A corporate opportunity is one in which the corporation has a right, property interest, or expectancy; whether such an opportunity exists depends on the facts and circumstances of each case. A corporate opportunity should be promptly offered to the corporation, which, in turn, should promptly accept or reject it. Rejection may be based on one or more of several factors, such as the corporation's lack of interest in the opportunity, its financial inability to acquire the opportunity, legal restrictions on its ability to accept the opportunity, or a third party's unwillingness to deal with the corporation.

Klinicki v. Lundgren

Supreme Court of Oregon, 1985
298 Or. 662, 695 P.2d 906

FACTS Klinicki and Lundgren, both furloughed Pan Am **(http://www.flypanam.com)** pilots stationed in West Germany, decided to start their own charter airline company. They therefore formed Berlinair, Inc., a closely held Oregon corporation. Lundgren was president and a director in charge of developing the business. Klinicki was vice president and a director in charge of operations and maintenance. Klinicki, Lundgren, and Lelco, Inc. (Lundgren's family business), each owned one third of the stock. Klinicki and Lundgren, as representatives of Berlinair, met with BFR, a consortium of Berlin travel agents, to negotiate a lucrative air transportation contract. When Lundgren learned of the likelihood of actually obtaining the BFR contract, he formed his own solely owned company, Air Berlin Charter Company (ABC); and, though he continued to negotiate for the BFR contract, he did so on behalf of ABC, not Berlinair. Eventually BFR awarded the contract to ABC. Klinicki commenced a derivative action on behalf of Berlinair and a suit against Lundgren individually for usurping a corporate opportunity of Berlinair. The trial court found that ABC, acting through Lundgren, had indeed usurped such an opportunity. Additionally, the trial court determined that Lundgren had breached the fiduciary duties of good faith, fair dealing, and full disclosure he owed to Klinicki and to Berlinair. The Court of Appeals affirmed the trial court opinion. ABC through Lundgren appealed, claiming that Berlinair was not financially able to undertake the BFR contract and that, therefore, no usurpation of corporate opportunity could occur.

DECISION Judgment for Klinicki affirmed.

OPINION Jones, J. There is no dispute that the corporate opportunity doctrine precludes corporate fiduciaries from diverting to themselves business opportunities in which the corporation has an expectancy, property interest or right, or which in fairness should otherwise belong to the corporation. [Citation.] The doctrine follows from a corporate fiduciary's duty of undivided loyalty to the corporation. ABC agrees that, unless Berlinair's financial inability to undertake the contract makes a difference, the BFR contract was a corporate opportunity of Berlinair.

* * *

Where a director or principal senior executive of a close corporation wishes to take personal advantage of a "corporate opportunity," * * * the director or principal senior executive must comply strictly with the following procedure:

(1) The director or principal senior executive must promptly offer the opportunity and disclose all material facts known regarding the opportunity to the disinterested directors or, if there is no disinterested director, to the disinterested shareholders. If the director or principal senior executive learns of other material facts after such disclosure, the director or principal senior executive must disclose these additional facts in a like manner before personally taking the opportunity.

(2) The director or principal senior executive may take advantage of the corporate opportunity only after full disclosure and only if the opportunity is rejected by a majority of the disinterested directors or, if there are no disinterested directors, by a majority of the disinterested shareholders. If, after full disclosure, the disinterested

directors or shareholders unreasonably fail to reject the offer, the interested director or principal senior executive may proceed to take the opportunity if he can prove the taking was otherwise "fair" to the corporation. Full disclosure to the appropriate corporate body is, however, an absolute condition precedent to the validity of any forthcoming rejection as well as to the availability to the director or principal senior executive of the defense of fairness.

(3) An appropriation of a corporate opportunity may be ratified by rejection of the opportunity by a majority of disinterested directors or a majority of disinterested shareholders, after full disclosure subject to the same rules as set out above for prior offer, disclosure and rejection. Where a director or principal senior executive of a close corporation appropriates a corporate opportunity without first fully disclosing the opportunity and offering it to the corporation, absent ratification, that director or principal senior executive holds the opportunity in trust for the corporation.

Applying these rules to the facts in this case, we conclude:

(1) Lundgren, as director and principal executive officer of Berlinair, owed a fiduciary duty to Berlinair.
(2) The BFR contract was a "corporate opportunity" of Berlinair.
(3) Lundgren formed ABC for the purpose of usurping the opportunity presented to Berlinair by the BFR contract.
(4) Lundgren did not offer Berlinair the BFR contract.
(5) Lundgren did not attempt to obtain the consent of Berlinair to his taking of the BFR corporate opportunity.
(6) Lundgren did not fully disclose to Berlinair his intent to appropriate the opportunity for himself and ABC.
(7) Berlinair never rejected the opportunity presented by the BFR contract.
(8) Berlinair never ratified the appropriation of the BFR contract.
(9) Lundgren, acting for ABC, misappropriated the BFR contract.

Because of the above, the defendant may not now contend that Berlinair did not have the financial ability to successfully pursue the BFR contract.

INTERPRETATION Corporate directors and officers may not usurp any opportunity in which the corporation has a right, property interest, or expectancy that in all fairness should belong to the corporation.

ETHICAL QUESTION Did the defendant act unethically? Explain.

CRITICAL THINKING QUESTION What should be the test for determining when an opportunity belongs to the corporation? Explain.

Transactions in Shares The issuance of shares at favorable prices to management by excluding other shareholders normally will constitute a violation of the fiduciary duty. So might the issuance of shares to a director at a fair price if the purpose of the issuance is to perpetuate corporate control rather than to raise capital or to serve some other corporate interest. Officers and directors have access to inside advance information, unavailable to the public, that may affect the future market value of the corporation's shares. Federal statutes have attempted to deal with this trading advantage by prohibiting officers and directors from purchasing or selling shares of their corporation's stock without adequately disclosing all material facts in their possession that may affect the stock's actual or potential value. We will discuss these matters more fully in Chapter 40.

Although state law has inconsistently imposed liability on officers and directors for secret, profitable use of inside information, the trend is toward holding them liable for breach of fiduciary duty to shareholders from whom they purchase stock without disclosing facts that give the stock added potential value. They are also held liable to the corporation for profits they realize on a sale of the stock when undisclosed conditions of the corporation make a substantial decline in value practically inevitable.

Duty Not to Compete As fiduciaries, directors and officers owe to the corporation the duty of undivided loyalty, which means that they may not compete with the corporation. A director or officer who breaches his fiduciary duty by competing with the corporation is liable for damages caused to the corporation. Although directors and officers may engage in their own business interests, courts will closely scrutinize any interest that competes with the corporation's business. Moreover, an officer or director may not use corporate personnel, facilities, or funds for her own benefit or disclose trade secrets of the corporation to others.

INDEMNIFICATION OF DIRECTORS AND OFFICERS

Directors and officers incur personal liability for breaching any of the duties they owe to the corporation and its shareholders. Under many modern incorporation statutes,

Ethical Dilemma

Whom Does a Director Represent? What Are a Director's Duties?

FACTS Maulington's, a large, publicly held food processing company, is run by an old, dictatorial CEO, who is also chairman of the board—a board packed with inside directors and retired chief executive officers of other businesses. Industry analysts regard Maulington's as stodgy and unimaginative in its use of capital. Yet its profits are dependable, it pays a decent dividend, and its stock is widely held by conservative investors. In the city where the company has its headquarters, it is regarded as a good corporate citizen. Many community organizations depend on its charitable contributions.

Upon the unexpected death of a director, the remaining directors nominate a forty-year-old doctor and children's health advocate, Peter Maxwell-Deane, who has wide community connections but little business experience. The directors reason that the board could use some youth, at least for appearances. Dr. Maxwell-Deane is duly elected to the board. He knows the visibility will help his career. He also hopes to influence the company to donate to his favorite children's health projects.

After his election, Dr. Maxwell-Deane is approached by Carola Campbell, a woman he knows from his charitable work and whom, in fact, he once dated for several months. Campbell is the granddaughter of the company's founder, owns 1 percent of the company's shares, and is feuding with the current CEO. She says that the CEO has held Maulington's back, thereby hurting its share price, and that she thinks he should have retired long ago. She tells Maxwell-Deane that the board's compensation committee has improperly given stock options to the current CEO and other inside directors. Campbell, who has no friends on the board, appeals to Maxwell-Deane for help. Specifically, she asks him to sound out other outside directors to see if they also find the stock option deals fishy. Finally, she tells him that she is thinking about requesting a list of shareholders from the board so that she can communicate directly with other shareholders about the management of the corporation. She wonders whether, if she has any trouble obtaining the list, Maxwell-Deane will help her.

Social, Policy, and Ethical Considerations

1. Does Dr. Maxwell-Deane, as a director, represent Carola Campbell? Should he quietly sound out the other directors as she asks? What risks would he run by doing so?
2. Does Maxwell-Deane have a duty to disclose to the board his previous relationship with Campbell? What details, if any, of his conversation with her should he report to the board?
3. What duty does Maxwell-Deane have to follow up on Campbell's allegation that stock options were improperly awarded to the CEO and other inside directors?
4. What should Maxwell-Deane do?

a corporation may indemnify a director or officer for liability incurred if he acted in good faith and in a manner he reasonably believed to be in the best interests of the corporation, so long as he has not been judged negligent or liable for misconduct. The Revised Act provides for mandatory indemnification of directors and officers for reasonable expenses they incur in the wholly successful defense of any proceeding brought against them because they are or were directors or officers. These provisions, however, may be limited by the articles of incorporation. In addition, a corporation may purchase insurance to indemnify officers and directors for liability arising out of their corporate activities, including liabilities against which the corporation is not empowered to indemnify directly.

> **Practical Advice**
>
> Before agreeing to serve on a corporate board of directors, make sure that the company has sufficient director's liability insurance and determine what the policy covers.

Liability Limitation Statutes

At least forty states have enacted legislation limiting the liability of directors. Most of these states, including Delaware, have authorized corporations—with shareholder approval—to limit or eliminate the liability of directors for some breaches of duty. A few states permit shareholders to limit the liability of officers. The Delaware statute provides that the articles of incorporation may contain a provision eliminating or limiting the personal liability of a director to the corporation or its stockholders for monetary damages for breach of directorial duty, provided that such provision does not eliminate or limit the liability of a director (1) for any breach of the director's duty of loyalty to the corporation or its stockholders, (2) for acts or omissions lacking good faith or involving intentional misconduct or a knowing violation of law, (3) for liability for unlawful dividend payments or redemptions, or (4) for any transaction from which the director derived an improper personal benefit.

A handful of states have directly eliminated personal liability for money damages, subject to certain exceptions. For example, under the Indiana statute, a director is liable only if she has breached or failed to perform her duties in compliance with the statutory standard of care and the breach or failure to perform constitutes willful misconduct or recklessness. A third approach, taken by some states, limits the amount of money damages that may be assessed against a director or officer.

The Revised Act authorizes the articles of incorporation to include a provision eliminating or limiting—with certain exceptions—the liability of a director to the corporation or its shareholders for any action he takes, or fails to take, as a director. The exceptions, for which his liability would not be affected, are (1) the amount of any financial benefit the director receives to which he is not entitled, such as a bribe, kickback, or profits from a usurped corporate opportunity; (2) an intentional infliction of harm on the corporation or the shareholders; (3) liability under Section 8.33 for unlawful distributions; and (4) an intentional violation of the criminal law.

CHAPTER SUMMARY

Role of Shareholders

Voting Rights of Shareholders

Management Structure of Corporations see Figures 36–1, 2, and 3 for illustrations of the statutory model of corporate governance, the structure of the typical closely held corporation, and the structure of the typical publicly held corporation

Shareholder Meetings shareholders may exercise their voting rights at both annual and special shareholder meetings

Quorum minimum number necessary to be present at a meeting in order to transact business

Election of Directors the shareholders elect the board at the annual meeting of the corporation
- *Straight Voting* directors are elected by a plurality of votes
- *Cumulative Voting* entitles shareholders to multiply the number of votes they are entitled to cast by the number of directors for whom they are entitled to vote and to cast the product for a single candidate or to distribute the product among two or more candidates

Removal of Directors the shareholders may by majority vote remove directors with or without cause, subject to cumulative voting rights

Approval of Fundamental Changes shareholder approval is required for charter amendments, most acquisitions, and dissolution

Concentrations of Voting Power
- *Proxy* authorization to vote another's shares at a shareholder meeting
- *Voting Trust* transfer of corporate shares' voting rights to a trustee
- *Shareholder Voting Agreement* used to provide shareholders with greater control over the election and removal of directors and other matters

Restrictions on Transfer of Shares must be reasonable and conspicuously noted on stock certificate

Enforcement Rights of Shareholders

Right to Inspect Books and Records if the demand is made in good faith and for a proper purpose

Shareholder Suits
- *Direct Suits* brought by a shareholder or a class of shareholders against the corporation based upon the ownership of shares
- *Derivative Suits* brought by a shareholder on behalf of the corporation to enforce a right belonging to the corporation

Shareholder's Right to Dissent a shareholder has the right to dissent from certain corporate actions that require shareholder approval

Role of Directors and Officers

Function of the Board of Directors

Selection and Removal of Officers

Capital Structure

Fundamental Changes the directors have the power to make, amend, or repeal the bylaws, unless this power is exclusively reserved to the shareholders

Dividends directors declare the amount and type of dividends

Management Compensation

Vacancies in the Board may be filled by the vote of a majority of the remaining directors

Exercise of Directors' Functions

Meeting directors have the power to bind the corporation only when acting as a board

Action Taken Without a Meeting permitted if a consent in writing is signed by all of the directors

Delegation of Board Powers committees may be appointed to perform some but not all of the board's functions

Directors' Inspection Rights directors have the right to inspect corporate books and records

Officers

Role of Officers officers are agents of the corporation

Authority of Officers
- *Actual Express Authority* arises from the incorporation statute, the charter, the bylaws, and resolutions of the directors
- *Actual Implied Authority* authority to do what is reasonably necessary to perform actual authority
- *Apparent Authority* acts of the principal that lead a third party to believe reasonably and in good faith that an officer has the required authority
- *Ratification* a corporation may ratify the unauthorized acts of its officers

Duties of Directors and Officers

Duty of Obedience must act within respective authority

Duty of Diligence must exercise ordinary care and prudence

Duty of Loyalty requires undeviating loyalty to the corporation

Business Judgment Rule precludes imposing liability on directors and officers for honest mistakes in judgment if they act with due care, in good faith, and in a manner reasonably believed to be in the best interests of the corporation

Indemnification a corporation may indemnify a director or officer for liability incurred if he acted in good faith and was not adjudged negligent or liable for misconduct

Liability Limitation Statutes many states now authorize corporations—with shareholder approval—to limit or eliminate the liability of directors for some breaches of duty

QUESTIONS

1. Brown, the president and director of a corporation engaged in owning and operating a chain of motels, was advised, on what seemed to be good authority, that a superhighway was to be constructed through the town of X, which would be a most desirable location for a motel. Brown presented these facts to the board of directors of the motel corporation and recommended that the corporation build a motel in the town of X at the location described. The board of directors agreed, and the new motel was constructed. However, the superhighway plans were changed after the motel was constructed, and the highway was never built. Later, a packinghouse was built on property adjoining the motel, and as a result the corporation sustained a considerable loss. The shareholders brought an appropriate action against Brown, charging that his proposal had caused the corporation a substantial loss. What is the result?

2. A, B, C, D, and E constituted the board of directors of the X Corporation. While D and E were out of town, A, B, and C held a special meeting of the board. Just as the meeting began, C became ill. He then gave a proxy to A and went home. A resolution was then adopted directing and authorizing the X Corporation's purchase of an adjoining piece of land owned by S as a site for an additional factory building. A and B voted for the resolution, and A, as C's proxy, cast C's vote in favor of the resolution. The X Corporation then made a contract with S for the purchase of the land. After the return of D and E, another special meeting of the board was held with all five directors present. A resolution was then unanimously adopted to cancel the contract with S. May S recover damages from X Corporation for breach of contract?

3. Bernard Koch was president of United Corporation, a closely held corporation. Koch, James Trent, and Henry Phillips made up the three-person board of directors. At a meeting of the board, Trent was elected president, replacing Koch. At the same meeting, Trent attempted to have the salary of the president increased. He was unable to obtain board approval of the increase because although Phillips voted for the increase, Koch voted against it. Trent was disqualified from voting by the charter. As a result, the directors, by a two-to-one vote, amended the bylaws to provide for the appointment of an executive committee composed of three reputable businesspersons to pass upon and fix all matters of salary for employees of the corporation. Subsequently, the executive committee, consisting of Jane Jones, James Black, and William Johnson, increased the salary of the president. Will Koch succeed in an appropriate action against the corporation, Trent, and Phillips to enjoin them from paying compensation to the president above that fixed by the board of directors? Explain.

4. Zenith Steel Company operates a prosperous business. In January, its president, Roe, who is also a director, was voted a \$100,000 bonus by the board of directors for valuable services he provided to the company during the previous year. Roe received an annual salary of \$85,000 from the company. Black, Inc., a minority shareholder in Zenith Steel Company, brings an appropriate action to enjoin the payment by the company of the \$100,000 bonus. Explain whether Black will succeed in its attempt.

5. a. Smith, a director of the Sample Corporation, sells a piece of vacant land to the Sample Corporation for \$50,000. The land cost him \$20,000.

   b. Jones, a shareholder of the Sample Corporation, sells a used truck to the Sample Corporation for \$8,400, although the truck is worth \$6,000.

   Raphael, a minority shareholder of the Sample Corporation, claims that these sales are void and should be annulled. Is he correct? Why?

6. X Corporation manufactures machine tools. Its two principal competitors are Y Corporation and Z Corporation. The five directors of X Corporation are Black, White, Brown, Green, and Crimson. At a duly called meeting of the board of directors of X Corporation in January, all five directors were present. A contract for the purchase of \$1 million worth of steel from the D Company, of which Black, White, and Brown are directors, was discussed and approved by a unanimous vote. There was a lengthy discussion about entering into negotiations for the purchase of Q Corporation, which allegedly was about to be sold for around \$15 million. By a three-to-two vote, it was decided not to open such negotiations.

   Three months later, Green purchased Q Corporation for \$15 million. Shortly thereafter, a new board of directors for X Corporation took office. X Corporation now brings actions to rescind its contract with D Company and to compel Green to assign to X Corporation his contract for the purchase of Q Corporation. Decisions as to each action?

7. Gore had been the owner of 1 percent of the outstanding shares of the Webster Company, a corporation since its organization ten years ago. Ratliff, the president of the company, was the owner of 70 percent of the outstanding shares. Ratliff used the shareholders' list to submit to the shareholders an offer of \$50 per share for their stock. Gore, on receiving the offer, called Ratliff and told him that the offer was inadequate and advised that she was willing to offer \$60 per share and for that purpose demanded a shareholders' list. Ratliff knew that Gore was willing and able to supply the funds necessary to purchase the stock, but he nevertheless refused to supply the list to Gore. Further, he did not offer to transmit Gore's offer to the shareholders of record. Gore then brought an action to compel the corporation to make the shareholders' list available to her. Will Gore be able to obtain a copy of the shareholders' list? Why?

8. Mitchell, Nelson, Olsen, and Parker, experts in manufacturing baubles, each owned fifteen of one hundred authorized shares of Baubles, Inc., a corporation of State X that does not permit cumulative voting. On July 7, 1996, the corporation sold forty shares to Quentin, an investor, for $1,500,000, which it used to purchase a factory building. On July 8, 1996, Mitchell, Nelson, Olsen, and Parker contracted as follows:

   All parties will act jointly in exercising voting rights as shareholders. In the event of a failure to agree, the question shall be submitted to George Yost, whose decision shall be binding upon all parties.

   Until a meeting of shareholders on April 17, 2003, when a dispute arose, all parties to the contract had voted consistently and regularly for Nelson, Olsen, and Parker as directors. At that meeting, Yost considered the dispute and decided and directed that Mitchell, Nelson, Olsen, and Parker vote their shares for the latter three as directors. Nelson, Olsen, and Parker so voted. Mitchell and Quentin voted for themselves and Olsen as directors.
   a. Is the contract of July 8, 1996, valid, and, if so, what is its effect?
   b. Who were elected directors of Baubles, Inc., at the meeting of its shareholders on April 17, 2003?

9. Acme Corporation's articles of incorporation require cumulative voting for the election of its directors. The board of directors of Acme Corporation consists of nine directors, each elected annually.
   a. Peter owns 24 percent of the outstanding shares of Acme Corporation. How many directors can he elect with his votes?
   b. If Acme Corporation were to classify its board into three classes, each consisting of three directors elected every three years, how many directors would Peter be able to elect?

CASE PROBLEMS

10. Neese, trustee in bankruptcy for First Trust Company, brings a suit against the directors of the company for losses the company sustained as a result of the directors' failure to use due care and diligence in the discharge of their duties. The specific acts of negligence alleged are (1) failure to give as much time and attention to the affairs of the company as its business interests required; (2) abdication of their control of the corporation by turning the entire management of the corporation over to its president, Brown; (3) failure to keep informed as to the affairs, condition, and management of the corporation; (4) taking no action to direct or control the corporation's affairs; (5) permitting large, open, unsecured loans to affiliated but financially unsound companies that were owned and controlled by Brown; (6) failure to examine financial reports that would have shown illegal diversions and waste of the corporation's funds; and (7) failure to supervise properly the corporation's officers and directors. Which, if any, of these allegations can constitute a breach of the duty of diligence?

11. Minority shareholders of Midwest Technical Institute Development Corporation, a closed-end investment company owning assets consisting principally of securities of companies in technological fields, brought a shareholder derivative suit against officers and directors of Midwest, seeking to recover on Midwest's behalf the profits the officers and directors realized through dealings in stock held in Midwest's portfolio in breach of their fiduciary duty. Approximately three years after commencement of the action, a new corporation, Midtex, was organized to acquire Midwest's assets. May the shareholders now add Midtex as a party defendant to their suit? Why?

12. Litton, an officer and the dominant shareholder of Dixie Splint Coal Company, transferred the company's remaining assets to himself when the company came to the verge of bankruptcy. The transfer allegedly was in satisfaction of an accrued salary claim that Litton had not enforced until the company came into financial difficulty. May the trustee in bankruptcy have Litton's claim disallowed?

13. Riffe, while serving as an officer of Wilshire Oil Company (http://www.hoovers.com/co/capsule/9/0,2163,11639,00.html), received a secret commission for work he did on behalf of a competing corporation. Can Wilshire Oil recover these secret profits and, in addition, recover the compensation Wilshire Oil paid to Riffe during the period that he acted on behalf of the competitor? Explain.

14. Muller, a shareholder of SCM, brought an action against SCM over his unsuccessful negotiations to purchase some of SCM's assets overseas. He then formed a shareholder committee to challenge the position of SCM's management in that suit. In order to conduct a proxy battle for management control at the next election of directors, the committee sought to obtain the list of shareholders who would be eligible to vote. At the time, however, no member of the committee had owned stock in SCM for the six-month period required to gain access to such information. Then Lopez, a former SCM executive and a shareholder for more than one year, joined the committee and demanded to be allowed to inspect the minutes of SCM shareholder proceedings and to gain access to the current shareholder list. His stated reason for making the demand was to solicit proxies in support of the committee's nominees for positions as directors. Lopez brought this action after SCM rejected his demand. Will Lopez succeed?

15. A bylaw of Betma Corporation provides that no shareholder can sell his shares unless he first offers them for sale to the corporation or its directors. The bylaw also states that this restriction shall be printed or stamped upon each stock certificate and shall bind all present or future owners or holders. Betma Corporation did not comply with this latter provision. Shaw, having knowledge of the bylaw restriction, nevertheless purchased twenty shares of the corporation's stock from Rice, without having Rice first offer them for sale to the corporation or its directors. When Betma Corporation refused to effectuate a transfer of the shares to her, Shaw sued to compel a transfer and the issuance of a new certificate to her. What is the result?

16. Pritchard & Baird was a reinsurance broker. A reinsurance broker arranges contracts between insurance companies so that companies that have sold large policies may sell participations in these policies to other companies in order to share the risks. Pritchard & Baird was controlled for many years by Charles Pritchard, who died in December 1973. Prior to his death, he brought his two sons, Charles, Jr. and William, into the business. The pair assumed an increasingly dominant role in the affairs of the business during the elder Charles's later years. Starting in 1970, Charles, Jr. and William began to withdraw from the corporate account ever-increasing sums that were designated as "loans" on the balance sheet. These "loans," however, represented a significant misappropriation of funds belonging to the corporation's clients. By late 1975, Charles, Jr. and William had plunged the corporation into hopeless bankruptcy. A total of $12,333,514.47 in "loans" had accumulated by October of that year. Mrs. Lillian Pritchard, the widow of the elder Charles, was a member of the corporation's board of directors until her resignation on December 3, 1975, the day before the corporation filed for bankruptcy. Francis, as trustee in the bankruptcy proceeding, brought suit against United Jersey Bank, the administrator of the estate of Charles, Sr. He also charged that Lillian Pritchard, as a director of the corporation, was personally liable for the misappropriated funds on the basis of negligence in discharging her duties as director. Is Francis correct?

17. Donald J. Richardson, Grove L. Cook, and Wayne Weaver were stockholders of Major Oil. They brought a direct action, individually and on behalf of all other stockholders of Major, against certain directors and other officers of the corporation. The complaint stated twelve causes of action. The first eight causes alleged some misappropriation of Major's assets by the defendants and sought to require the defendants to return the assets to Major. Three of the remaining four causes alleged breaches of fiduciary duty implicit in those fraudulent acts and sought compensatory or punitive damages for the injury that resulted. The final cause sought the appointment of a receiver. Richardson, Cook, and Weaver moved for an order certifying the suit as a class action. Decision?

http:// **Internet Exercise** Using the Security and Exchange Commission's EDGAR database, find the annual report (Form 10-K) and, if necessary, the proxy statement (DEF 14A) of three companies of interest and determine (a) the number of inside and outside directors, (b) what committees the board of directors has established, (c) the compensation for the three highest paid officers (including the value of stock options), and (d) whether any person owns more than 5 percent of the outstanding shares of common stock.

CHAPTER 37

Fundamental Changes of Corporations

The minority, in other words, should have the right to say to the majority, "we recognize your right to restructure the enterprise, provided you are willing to buy us out at a fair price if we object, so that we are not forced to participate in an enterprise other than the one we contemplated at the outset of our mutual association."

M. EISENBERG, IN *THE STRUCTURE OF THE CORPORATION*, 1976

Learning Objectives

After reading this chapter you should be able to:

1. Explain the procedure for amending the charter and list which amendments give rise to the appraisal remedy.
2. Identify which combinations do not require shareholder approval and which give dissenting shareholders an appraisal remedy.
3. Distinguish between a tender offer and a compulsory share exchange.
4. Compare and contrast a cash-out combination and a management buyout.
5. Identify the ways by which voluntary and involuntary dissolution may occur.

Certain extraordinary changes affect a corporation so fundamentally that they fall outside the authority of the board of directors and require shareholder approval. Such fundamental changes include charter amendments, mergers, consolidations, compulsory share exchanges, dissolution, and the sale or lease of all or substantially all of the corporation's assets (other than those in the regular course of business), all of which alter the corporation's basic structure. Although each of these actions is authorized by state incorporation statutes that impose specific procedural requirements, they are also subject to equitable limitations imposed by the courts. In 1999 substantial revisions were made to the Revised Act's treatment of fundamental changes.

As shareholder approval for fundamental changes usually does not need to be unanimous, such changes frequently will be approved despite opposition by minority shareholders. Shareholder approval means a majority (or some other specified fraction) of *all* votes *entitled* to be cast, rather than a majority (or other fraction) of votes represented at a shareholders' meeting at which a quorum is present. (The 1999 amendments to the Revised Act significantly changed the voting rule: fundamental changes need be approved by only a majority of the shares present at a meeting at which a quorum is present.) In some instances, minority shareholders have the right to dissent and to recover the fair value of their shares if they follow the prescribed procedure for doing so. This right is called the appraisal remedy. We will discuss the legal aspects of fundamental changes in this chapter.

CPA CHARTER AMENDMENTS

Shareholders do not have a vested property right resulting from any provision in the articles of incorporation. Accordingly, the corporate charter may be amended by following proper procedures. The amended articles of incorporation, however, may contain only those provisions that might lawfully be contained in the articles of incorporation at the time of the amendment.

APPROVAL BY DIRECTORS AND SHAREHOLDERS

Under the Revised Act and most statutes, the typical **procedure** for amending the articles of incorporation requires the board of directors to adopt a resolution setting forth the proposed amendment, which must then be approved by a majority vote of the shareholders entitled to vote, although some older statutes require a two-thirds shareholder vote. In some states shareholders may approve charter amendments without a prior board of directors' resolution. After the shareholders approve the amendment, the corporation executes articles of amendment and delivers them to the secretary of state for filing. The amendment does not affect the existing rights of nonshareholders.

Under the Revised Act, *dissenting shareholders* receive the appraisal remedy *only* if an amendment materially and adversely affects their rights by (1) altering or abolishing a preferential right of the shares; (2) creating, altering, or abolishing a right involving the redemption of the shares; (3) altering or abolishing a preemptive right of the holder of such shares; (4) excluding or limiting a shareholder's right to vote on any matter or to cumulate his votes; or (5) reducing to a fraction of a share the number of shares a shareholder owns, if the fractional share is to be acquired for cash. The 1999 amendments to the Revised Act eliminate the appraisal remedy for virtually all charter amendments.

Under the Revised Act, the shareholder approval required for an amendment depends upon the nature of the amendment. An amendment that would give rise to dissenters' rights must be approved by a majority of all votes entitled to be cast on the amendment, unless the act or the charter requires a greater vote. All other amendments must be approved by a majority of all votes cast on the amendment, unless the act or the charter requires a greater vote.

> **Practical Advice**
>
> If you are forming a close corporation and will hold a minority interest in it, consider including in the charter supermajority quorum and voting provisions for charter amendments to ensure that you will have veto power.

APPROVAL BY DIRECTORS

The Revised Act permits the board of directors to adopt certain amendments without shareholder action, unless the articles of incorporation provide otherwise. These amendments include (1) extending the duration of a corporation that was incorporated when limited duration was required by law, (2) changing each issued and unissued authorized share of an outstanding class into a greater number of whole shares if the corporation has only one class of shares, and (3) making minor name changes.

CPA COMBINATIONS

Acquiring all or substantially all of the assets of another corporation or corporations may be both desirable and profitable for a corporation. To accomplish this, the corporation may (1) purchase or lease other corporations' assets, (2) purchase a controlling stock interest in other corporations, (3) merge with other corporations, or (4) consolidate with other corporations. A few states and the 1999 amendments to the Revised Act contain provisions authorizing a corporation to merge into another type of business organization, such as a limited partnership, limited liability company, or a limited liability partnership.

Any method of combination that involves issuing shares, proxy solicitations, or tender offers may be subject to federal securities regulation, as we will discuss in Chapter 40. Moreover, when a combination may have a detrimental effect on competition, federal antitrust laws, as discussed in Chapter 43, may apply.

PURCHASE OR LEASE OF ALL OR SUBSTANTIALLY ALL OF THE ASSETS

When one corporation purchases or leases all or substantially all of the assets of another corporation, the legal personality of neither corporation changes. The purchaser or lessee corporation simply acquires ownership or control of additional physical assets. The selling or lessor corporation, in exchange for its physical properties, receives cash, other property, or a stipulated rental. Each corporation continues its separate existence, having altered only the form or extent of its assets.

Generally, a corporation that purchases the assets of another corporation does not assume the other's liabilities unless (1) the purchaser expressly or impliedly agrees to assume the seller's liabilities; (2) the transaction amounts to a consolidation or merger of the two corporations; (3) the purchaser is a mere continuation of the seller; or (4) the sale is for the fraudulent purpose of avoiding the seller's liabilities. Some courts, as the next case illustrates, recognize a fifth exception (called the "product line" exception), which imposes strict tort liability upon the purchaser for defects in products manufactured and distributed by the seller corporation when the purchaser corporation continues the product line.

Practical Advice

Recognize that under some circumstances courts will treat the purchase of all the assets of a corporation as a *de facto* merger and make the purchaser liable for the debts of the seller.

Ray v. Alad Corporation

Supreme Court of California, 1977
19 Cal.3d 22, 136 Cal.Rptr. 574, 560 P.2d 3

FACTS On March 24, 1969, Ray fell from a defective ladder while working for his employer. Ray brought suit in strict tort liability against the Alad Corporation (Alad II), which neither manufactured nor sold the ladder to Ray's employer. Prior to the accident, Alad II succeeded to the business of the ladder's manufacturer, the now-dissolved "Alad Corporation" (Alad I), through a purchase of Alad I's assets for an adequate cash consideration. Alad II acquired Alad I's plant, equipment, inventory, trade name, and goodwill and continued to manufacture the same line of ladders under the "Alad" name, using the same equipment, designs, and personnel. In addition, Alad II solicited through the same sales representatives with no outward indication of any change in the ownership of the business. The parties had no agreement, however, concerning Alad II's assumption of Alad I's tort liabilities. Ray appealed from a judgment for Alad II.

DECISION Judgment reversed.

OPINION Wright, J. Our discussion of the law starts with the rule ordinarily applied to the determination of whether a corporation purchasing the principal assets of another corporation assumes the other's liabilities. As typically formulated the rule states that the purchaser does not assume the seller's liabilities unless (1) there is an express or implied agreement of assumption, (2) the transaction amounts to a consolidation or merger of the two corporations, (3) the purchasing corporation is a mere continuation of the seller, or (4) the transfer of assets to the purchaser is for the fraudulent purpose of escaping liability for the seller's debts. [Citations.]

If this rule were determinative of Alad II's liability to plaintiff it would require us to affirm the summary judgment. None of the rule's four stated grounds for imposing liability on the purchasing corporation is present here. There was no express or implied agreement to assume liability for injury from defective products previously manufactured by Alad I. Nor is there any indication or contention that the transaction was prompted by any fraudulent purpose of escaping liability for Alad I's debts.

With respect to the second stated ground for liability, the purchase of Alad I's assets did not amount to a consolidation or merger. * * *

* * *

We therefore conclude that the general rule governing succession to liabilities does not require Alad II to respond to plaintiff's claim. * * * We must decide whether the policies underlying strict tort liability for defective products call for a special exception to the rule that would otherwise insulate the present defendant from plaintiff's claim. [Citations.]

The purpose of the rule of strict tort liability "is to insure that the costs of injuries resulting from defective products are borne by the manufacturers that put such products on the market rather than by the injured persons who are powerless to protect themselves." [Citation.] However, the rule "does not rest on the analysis of the financial strength or bargaining power of the parties to the particular action. It rests, rather, on the proposition that '[t]he cost of an injury and the loss of time or health may be an overwhelming misfortune to the person injured, and a needless one, for the risk of injury can be insured by the manufacturer and distributed among the public as a cost of doing business.' [Citations.]" Thus, "the paramount policy to be promoted by the rule is the protection of otherwise defenseless victims of manufacturing defects and the *spreading throughout society* of the cost of compensating them." (Italics added.) [Citation.] Justification for imposing strict liability upon a *successor* to a manufacturer under the circumstances here presented rests upon (1) the virtual destruction of the plaintiff's remedies against the original manufacturer caused by the successor's acquisition of the business, (2) the successor's ability to assume the original manufacturer's risk-spreading rule, and (3) the fairness of requiring the successor to assume a responsibility for defective products that was a burden necessarily attached to the original manufacturer's good will being enjoyed by the successor in the continued operation of the business. We turn to a consideration of each of these aspects in the context of the present case.

We must assume for purposes of the present proceeding that plaintiff was injured as a result of defects in a ladder manufactured by Alad I and therefore could assert strict tort liability against Alad I under the rule of [citation]. However, the practical value of this right of recovery against the original manufacturer was vitiated by the purchase of Alad I's tangible assets, trade name and good will on behalf of Alad II and the dissolution of Alad I within two months thereafter in accordance with the purchase agreement. The injury giving rise to plaintiff's claim against Alad I did not occur until more than six months after the filing of the dissolution certificate declaring that Alad I's "known debts and liabilities have been actually paid" and its "known assets have been distributed to its shareholders." This distribution of assets was perfectly proper as there was no requirement that provision be made for claims such as plaintiff's that had not yet come into existence. Thus, even if plaintiff could obtain a judgment on his claim against the dissolved and assetless Alad I he would face formidable and probably insuperable obstacles in attempting to obtain satisfaction of the judgment from former stockholders or directors. [Citations.]

* * *

While depriving plaintiff of redress against the ladder's manufacturer, Alad I, the transaction by which Alad II acquired Alad I's name and operating assets had the further effect of transferring to Alad II the resources that had previously been available to Alad I for meeting its responsibilities to persons injured by defects in ladders it had produced. These resources included not only the physical plant, the manufacturing equipment, and the inventories of raw material, work in process, and finished goods, but also the know-how available through the records of manufacturing designs, the continued employment of the factory personnel, and the consulting services of Alad I's general manager. With these facilities and sources of information, Alad II had virtually the same capacity as Alad I to estimate the risks of claims for injuries from defects in previously manufactured ladders for purposes of obtaining insurance coverage or planning self-insurance. [Citation.] * * *

Finally, the imposition upon Alad II of liability for injuries from Alad I's defective products is fair and equitable in view of Alad II's acquisition of Alad I's trade name, good will, and customer lists, its continuing to produce the same line of ladders, and its holding itself out to potential customers as the same enterprise. * * *

We therefore conclude that a party which acquires a manufacturing business and continues the output of its line of products under the circumstances here presented assumes strict tort liability for defects in units of the same product line previously manufactured and distributed by the entity from which the business was acquired. * * *

INTERPRETATION If a purchaser of all of a corporation's assets continues the seller's product line, some courts impose upon the purchaser strict tort liability for defects in products previously manufactured by the seller corporation.

CRITICAL THINKING QUESTION What are the policy arguments supporting and opposing the court's approach in this case? Explain.

Regular Course of Business If the sale or lease of all or substantially all of its assets is in the selling or lessor corporation's usual and regular course of business, approval by its board of directors is required but shareholder authorization is not. In addition, a mortgage or pledge of any or all of a corporation's property and assets—whether in the usual or regular course of business or not—also requires only the approval of the board of directors. The Revised Act considers a transfer of any or all of a corporation's assets to a wholly owned subsidiary to be a sale in the regular course of business.

Other Than in Regular Course of Business Shareholder approval is necessary only for a sale or lease of all or substantially all of a corporation's assets that is not in the usual and regular course of business. (The 1999 amendments to the Revised Act adopt an objective test for determining when shareholder approval is required.) The selling corporation, by liquidating its assets, or the lessor corporation, by placing its physical assets beyond its control, has significantly changed its position and perhaps its ability to carry on the type of business contemplated by its charter. For this reason, such a sale or lease must be approved not only by action of the directors but also by the affirmative vote of the holders of a majority of the corporation's shares entitled to be cast at a shareholders' meeting called for this purpose. In most states, dissenting shareholders of the selling corporation are given an appraisal remedy.

PURCHASE OF SHARES

An alternative to the purchase of another corporation's assets is the purchase of its stock. When one corporation acquires all of, or a controlling interest in, the stock of another corporation, the legal existence of neither corporation changes. The acquiring corporation acts through its board of directors, while the corporation that becomes a subsidiary does not act at all, because the decision to sell stock is made by the individual shareholders, not by the corporation itself. The capital structure of the subsidiary remains unchanged, and that of the parent is usually not altered unless financing the acquisition requires a change in capital. Because formal approval is required of neither corporation's shareholders, there is no appraisal remedy (see Figure 37-1).

Sale of Control When one or a few shareholders own a controlling interest, the shareholder(s) may privately negotiate a sale of such interest, although the courts require that these transactions be made with due care. The controlling shareholders must make a reasonable investigation so as not to transfer control to purchasers who wrongfully plan to steal or "loot" the corporation's assets or to act against its best interests. In addition, purchasers frequently are willing to pay a premium for a block of shares that conveys control. Although historically some courts have required that this so-called control premium inure to the benefit of the corporation, today virtually all courts permit the controlling shareholders to retain the full amount of the control premium.

Tender Offer When one or a few shareholders do not hold a controlling interest, the acquisition of a corporation through the purchase of shares may take the form of a tender offer. A **tender offer** is a general invitation to all shareholders of a target company to tender their shares for sale at a specified price. The offer may be for all of the target company's shares or for just a controlling interest. Tender offers for publicly held companies, which are subject to federal securities regulation, will be discussed in Chapter 40.

COMPULSORY SHARE EXCHANGE

The Revised Act and some states provide different procedures when a corporation acquires shares through a **compulsory share exchange**, a transaction by which the corporation becomes the owner of all the outstanding shares of one or more classes of shares of another corporation by an exchange that is compulsory on all owners of the acquired shares. The corporation may acquire the shares with its or any other corporation's shares, obligations, or other securities, or with cash or other property. For example, if A Corporation acquires all of B Corporation's outstanding shares through a compulsory exchange, B becomes a wholly owned subsidiary of A. A compulsory share exchange does not affect the separate existence of the corporate parties to the transaction. Although their results are similar to those of mergers, as discussed below, compulsory share exchanges are used instead of mergers when it is desirable that the acquired corporation remain in existence, as, for example, in the formation of holding company systems for insurance companies and banks.

A compulsory share exchange requires approval from the board of directors of each corporation and from the shareholders of the corporation whose shares are being acquired. Each class of shares included in the exchange must vote separately. The shareholders of the corporation acquiring the shares need not approve the transaction. After the shareholders adopt and approve the compulsory share exchange plan, it is binding on all who hold shares of the class to be acquired. Dissenting shareholders of the corporation whose shares are acquired are given an appraisal remedy.

MERGER

A **merger** of two or more corporations is the combination of all of their assets. One of the corporations, known as the ***surviving corporation***, receives title to all the

Figure 37-1
Purchase of Shares

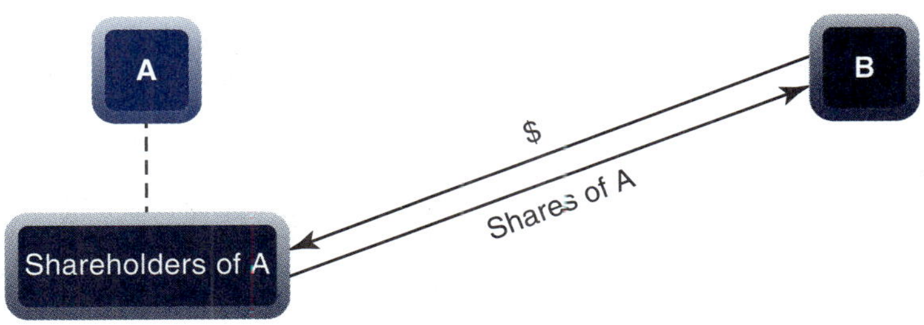

assets. The other party or parties to the merger, known as the ***merged corporation*** or corporations, is merged into the surviving corporation and ceases to exist as a separate entity. Thus, if A Corporation and B Corporation combine into the A Corporation, A is the surviving corporation and B the merged corporation. Under the Revised Act and most statutes, the shareholders of the merged corporation may receive stock or other securities issued by the surviving corporation or other consideration *including cash*, as provided in the merger agreement. Moreover, the surviving corporation assumes all debts and other liabilities of the merged corporation.

A merger requires the approval of each corporation's board of directors, as well as the affirmative vote of each corporation's holders of a majority of the shares entitled to vote. Dissenting shareholders of each corporation have an appraisal remedy. Many states and the 1999 amendments to the Revised Act permit the vote of the shareholders of the surviving corporation to be eliminated when a merger increases the number of outstanding shares by no more than twenty percent.

In a **short-form merger**, however, a corporation that owns a statutorily specified percent of the outstanding shares of each class of a subsidiary may merge the subsidiary into itself without approval by the shareholders of either corporation. The Revised Act and many states specify 90 percent. The parent's 90 percent ownership precludes the need to seek direct approval either from the shareholders or from the subsidiary's board of directors. All that is required is a resolution by the board of directors of the parent corporation.

Whereas the dissenting shareholders of the subsidiary have the right to obtain payment from the parent for their shares, the shareholders of the parent do not have this appraisal remedy, because the transaction has not materially changed their rights. Instead of indirectly owning 90 percent of the subsidiary's assets, the parent now directly owns 100 percent of the same assets.

CONSOLIDATION

A **consolidation** of two or more corporations is a combination of all of their assets, the title to which is taken by a newly created corporation known as the ***consolidated corporation***. Each constituent corporation ceases to exist, and all of its debts and liabilities are assumed by the new corporation. The shareholders of each constituent corporation receive stock or other securities, not necessarily of the same class, issued to them by the new corporation, or other consideration provided in the plan of consolidation. A consolidation requires the approval of each corporation's board of directors, as well as the affirmative vote of each corporation's holders of a majority of the shares entitled to vote. Dissenting shareholders have an appraisal remedy. The Revised Act, however, has deleted all references to consolidations, because in modern corporate practice, ensuring the survival of one corporation is almost always advantageous.

GOING PRIVATE TRANSACTIONS

Corporate combinations are sometimes used to take a publicly held corporation private to eliminate minority interests, to reduce the burdens of certain provisions of the federal securities laws, or both. One method of going private is for the corporation or its majority shareholder to acquire the corporation's shares through purchases on the open market or through a tender offer for the shares. Other methods include a cash-out combination (a merger or a sale of assets) with a corporation controlled by the majority shareholder. If the majority shareholder is a corporation, it may arrange a cash-out combination with itself or, if it owns enough shares, may use a short-form merger. In recent years, a new type of going private transaction—a management buyout—has become much more frequent. In this section, we will examine cash-out combinations and management buyouts.

Cash-out Combinations Cash-out combinations are used to eliminate minority shareholders by forcing them to accept cash or property for their shares. A cash-out combination often follows the acquisition, by a person, group, or company, of a large interest in a target company (T) through a tender offer. The tender offeror (TO) then seeks to eliminate all other shareholders, thereby achieving complete control of T. To do so, TO might form a new corporation (Corporation N) and take 100 percent of its stock. TO then arranges a cash-out merger of T into N, with all the shareholders of T, other than TO, to receive cash for their shares. Because TO owns all the stock of N and a controlling interest in T, the shareholders of both companies will approve the merger. Alternatively, TO could purchase for cash or notes the assets of T, leaving the minority shareholders with only an interest in the proceeds of the sale. The use of cash-out combinations has raised questions concerning both their purpose and their fairness to minority shareholders. Some states require that cash-out combinations have a valid business purpose and that they be fair to all concerned. Fairness, in this context, includes both fair dealing (which involves the procedural aspects of the transaction) and fair price (which involves the financial considerations of the merger). Other states require only that the transaction be fair.

Alpert v. 28 Williams St. Corp.

New York Court of Appeals, 1984
63 N.Y.2d 557, 483 N.Y.S.2d 667, 473 N.E.2d 19

FACTS 79 Realty Corporation owned a valuable seventeen-story office building in Manhattan. The plaintiffs in this action held 26 percent of the outstanding shares of 79 Realty Corporation. The defendants formed a limited partnership, Madison 28 Associates, to buy the building. This limited partnership created 28 Williams Street Corporation to act as the nominal purchaser. The defendants planned to achieve the purchase by means of a "two-step" merger in which Madison Associates would buy control of the majority shares of Realty Corporation and then merge Realty Corporation with Williams Street, "freezing out" the minority shareholders of Realty Corporation through a cash buyout. All shareholders of Realty Corporation were sent a statement of intent explaining the details of the proposed merger. Soon after the merger was approved, and in accordance with the merger plan, Realty Corporation, the surviving corporation, was dissolved, and title to the building passed to Madison Associates. The plaintiffs brought an action for equitable relief in the form of rescission of the merger. The trial court found for 28 Williams Street Corporation, and the appellate court affirmed.

DECISION Judgment for 28 Williams Street Corporation affirmed.

OPINION Cooke, C. J. In New York, two or more domestic corporations are authorized to "merge into a single corporation which shall be one of the constituent corporations," known as the "surviving corporation" [citation]. The statute does not delineate substantive justifications for mergers, but only requires compliance with certain procedures: the adoption by the boards of each corporation of a plan of merger setting forth, among other things, the terms and conditions of the merger; a statement of any changes in the certificate of incorporation of the surviving corporation; the submission of the plan to a vote of shareholders pursuant to notice to all shareholders; and adoption of the plan by a vote of two thirds of the shareholders entitled to vote on it [citation].

Generally, the remedy of a shareholder dissenting from a merger and the offered "cash-out" price is to obtain the fair value of his or her stock through an appraisal proceeding [citation]. This protects the minority shareholder from being forced to sell at unfair values imposed by those dominating the corporation while allowing the majority to proceed with its desired merger [citations]. The pursuit of an appraisal proceeding generally constitutes the dissenting stockholder's exclusive remedy [citations]. An exception exists, however, when the merger is unlawful or fraudulent as to that shareholder, in which event an action for equitable relief is authorized [citations]. Thus, technical compliance with the Business Corporation Law's requirements alone will not necessarily exempt a merger from further judicial review.

* * *

* * * In reviewing a freeze-out merger, the essence of the judicial inquiry is to determine whether the transaction, viewed as a whole, was "fair" as to all concerned. This concept has two principal components: the majority shareholders must have followed "a course of fair dealing toward minority holders" * * * and they must also have offered a fair price for the minority's stock. * * *

* * *

Fair dealing is also concerned with the procedural fairness of the transaction, such as its timing, initiation, structure, financing, development, disclosure to the independent directors and shareholders, and how the necessary approvals were obtained. * * * Basically, the courts must look for complete and candid disclosure of all the material facts and circumstances of the proposed merger known to the majority of directors, including their dual roles and events leading up to the merger proposal. * * *

In determining whether there was a fair price, the court need not ascertain the precise "fair value" of the shares as it would be determined in an appraisal proceeding. It should be noted, however, that the factors used in an appraisal proceeding are relevant here. * * * This would include but would not be limited to net asset value, book value, earnings, market value, and investment value. * * *

In the context of a freeze-out merger, variant treatment of the minority shareholders—i.e., causing their removal—will be justified when related to the advancement of a general corporate interest. The benefit need not be great, but it must be for the corporation. For example, if the sole purpose of the merger is reduction of the number of profit sharers—in contrast to increasing the corporation's capital or profits, or improving its management structure—there will exist no "independent corporate interest" [citation]. All of these purposes ultimately seek to increase the individual wealth of the remaining shareholders. What distinguishes a proper corporate purpose from an improper one is that, with the former, removal of the minority shareholders furthers the objective of conferring some general gain upon the corporation. Only then will the fiduciary duty of good and prudent management of the corporation serve to override the concurrent duty to treat all shareholders fairly [citation]. * * *

In sum, in entertaining an equitable action to review a freeze-out merger, a court should view the transaction as a whole to determine whether it was tainted with fraud, illegality, or self-dealing, whether the minority shareholders were dealt with fairly, and whether there exists any independent corporate purpose for the merger.

* * *

Without passing on all of the business purposes cited by [the trial court] as underlying the merger, it is sufficient to note that at least one justified the exclusion of plaintiffs' interests: attracting additional capital to effect needed repairs of the building. There is proof that there was a good-faith belief that additional, outside capital was required. Moreover, this record supports the conclusion that this capital would not have been available through the merger had not plaintiffs' interest in the corporation been eliminated. Thus, the approval of the merger, which would extinguish plaintiffs' stock, was supported by a bona fide business purpose to advance this general corporate interest of obtaining increased capital.

INTERPRETATION In a cash-out merger, the directors and majority shareholders have a fiduciary duty to treat all shareholders fairly, the merger must have an independent business purpose, and the transaction must be conducted without fraud and illegality.

CRITICAL THINKING QUESTION When, if ever, should cash-out mergers be permitted? Explain.

Management Buyout A management buyout is a transaction by which existing management increases its ownership of a corporation while eliminating the entity's public shareholders. The typical procedure is as follows. The management of an existing company (Corporation A) forms a new corporation (Corporation B), in which the management owns some of the stock and institutional investors own the rest. Corporation B issues bonds to institutional investors to raise cash, with which it purchases the assets or stock of Corporation A. The assets of Corporation A are used as security for the bonds issued by Corporation B. Because of the extensive use of borrowed funds, a management buyout is commonly called a ***leveraged buyout*** (LBO). The result of this transaction is twofold: the public shareholders of Corporation A no longer have any proprietary interest in the assets of Corporation A, and management's equity interest in Corporation B is greater than its interest was in Corporation A.

A critical issue is a management buyout's fairness to the shareholders of Corporation A. The transaction inherently presents a potential conflict of interest for those in management, who owe a fiduciary duty to represent the interests of the shareholders of Corporation A. As substantial shareholders of Corporation B, however, those in management have a personal and probably adverse financial interest in the transaction.

DISSENTING SHAREHOLDERS

The shareholder's right to dissent, a statutory right to obtain payment for shares, is accorded to shareholders who object to certain fundamental changes in the corporation.

Transactions Giving Rise to Dissenters' Rights Most states grant dissenters' rights to (1) dissenting shareholders of a corporation selling or leasing all or substantially all of its property or assets not in the usual or regular course of business; (2) dissenting shareholders of each corporation that is a party to a merger, except in short-form mergers, when only the dissenting shareholders of the subsidiary have dissenters' rights; and (3) dissenting shareholders of each corporation that is a party to a consolidation. In addition to the first and second fundamental changes, the Revised Act also provides a right to dissent to (1) any plan of compulsory share exchange in which the corporation will be the one acquired; (2) any amendment to the articles of incorporation that materially and adversely affects the dissenter's rights with respect to shares; and (3) any other corporate action taken pursuant to a shareholder vote with respect to which the articles of incorporation, the bylaws, or a resolution of the board of directors provides that shareholders shall have a right to dissent and obtain payment for their shares.

Many states, however, have a stock market exception to the appraisal remedy. Under these statutes, the right to dissent does not exist if an established market, such as the New York Stock Exchange, exists for the shares. The Revised Act does not contain this exception, but the 1999 amendments to the Revised Act have added it.

Procedure The corporation must notify the shareholders of the existence of dissenters' rights before taking the vote on the corporate action. A shareholder who dissents and strictly complies with the provisions of the statute is entitled to receive the fair value of his shares. However, unless he makes written demand within the prescribed time period, he is not entitled to payment for his shares.

Appraisal Remedy A dissenting shareholder who complies with all applicable requirements is entitled to an **appraisal remedy**, which is the corporation's payment of the fair value of the shares, plus accrued interest. The **fair value** is that value immediately preceding the corporate action to which the dissenter objects, excluding any appreciation or depreciation that occurs in anticipation of such corporate action, unless such exclusion would be inequitable. The next case explains how fair value is determined.

Practical Advice

If you wish to dissent and obtain your appraisal remedy, be sure to follow all of the required procedures and do so in a timely manner.

In Re Valuation of Common Stock of McLoon Oil Co.

Supreme Judicial Court of Maine, 1989
565 A.2d 997

FACTS McLoon, Morse Bros., and T-M Oil Companies were closely held companies entirely owned by members of the Pescosolido family, under the leadership of Carl Pescosolido, Sr. His sons, Carl, Jr. and Richard, each held shares in McLoon, Morse Bros., and T-M. Together, their shares constituted 50 percent of the McLoon and Morse Bros. common stock and 14.3 percent of the T-M common stock. In December 1975, Carl, Sr. proposed to merge all of the family-held companies into Lido Inc., over which he would exercise sole voting control. Carl, Jr. and Richard (the dissenters) objected to the proposed merger. On December 6, 1976, the parties executed a merger agreement in which the dissenters expressly preserved their statutory appraisal rights. On December 15, 1976, the dissenters individually wrote to each of the three Maine companies and requested payment for their shares. Lido responded by offering each dissenter $128,685.55 for his combined interests in all three companies. Both dissenters rejected that offer.

On April 1, 1977, the dissenters filed a suit for valuation of their stock in all three companies. Ten years later, on May 22, 1987, the court appointed a referee to determine all the issues in the case, including the stock value. The referee held eight days of hearings. The dissenters offered two expert appraisal witnesses, who testified to the value of the real estate owned by the three companies and the companies' net asset value. One of Lido's expert witnesses countered by presenting a discounted cash analysis for T-M and McLoon and a net asset valuation for Morse Bros. The other expert for Lido testified about hypothetical returns on investments in comparable business properties. In his report, the referee weighed the discounted cash analysis and the net asset analysis for T-M and McLoon—75 percent and 25 percent, respectively—and accepted fully the net asset valuation of Morse Bros. The referee held that the fair value of each dissenter's stock was his proportionate share of the full value of each company, as determined from the expert testimony. Lido objected to the report, contending that the referee should discount the full value of each company because of the minority status and lack of marketability of the dissenters' stock. The court accepted the referee's report in full, ordering Lido to pay each dissenter $334,925 with 8 percent simple interest from December 6, 1976. Lido appealed.

DECISION Judgment affirmed.

OPINION McKusick, C. J. Ten years ago in the *Libby* case we ruled that a stock's fair value under section 909 could appropriately be determined by weighing three factors—the stock's market price, the company's net asset value, and the company's investment value—with the weight to be accorded each factor depending on its reliability as an indicator of fair value. [Citation.] We recognized that the reliability of each factor will vary with the particular facts and circumstances of each case, so that "[t]he weighing of these interdependent elements of fair value is more akin to an artistic composition than to a scientific process. A judicial determination of fair value cannot be computed according to any precise mathematical formula." [Citation.] However, the court should in each case consider all three elements of fair value, even if only to find one or more of them unreliable in the circumstances. [Citation.]

* * *

The appraisal remedy has deep roots in equity. The traditional rule through much of the 19th century was that any corporate transaction that changed the rights of common shareholders required unanimous consent. The appraisal remedy for dissenting shareholders evolved as it became clear that unanimous consent was inconsistent with the growth and development of large business enterprises. By the bargain struck in enacting an appraisal statute, the shareholder who disapproves of a proposed merger or other major corporate change gives up his right of veto in exchange for the right to be bought out—not at market value, but at "fair value." [Citations.] Methods used in valuing stock for tax, probate, ERISA, and like purposes in which market value is of the essence are inapposite to the determination of the fair value owed to dissenting shareholders. [Citation.] ("The purpose of applying these discount variables is to determine the investment value or fair market value of a minority interest in the context of a hypothetical sale between a willing seller and buyer, a situation that does not exist in the dissenting shareholder situation.") In the statutory appraisal proceeding, the involuntary change of ownership caused by a merger requires as a matter of fairness that a dissenting shareholder be compensated for the loss of his proportionate interest in the business as an entity. The valuation focus under the appraisal statute is not the stock as a commodity, but rather the stock only as it represents a proportionate part of the enterprise as a whole. The question for the court becomes simple and direct: What is the best price a single buyer could reasonably be expected to pay for the firm as an entirety? The court then prorates that value for the whole firm equally among all shares of its common stock. The result is that all of those shares have the same fair value.

* * *

In the case at bar the referee explicitly held that discounting the value of the dissenters' stock because they chose to dissent from the merger and to exercise their appraisal rights would be inconsistent with the concept of fair value under the appraisal statute. Relying on testimony by Lido's own expert that no market exists for the stock, the referee found that market price has no reliability in the calculus of fair value in this case and accorded no weight to any market price factor. As a matter of law, the dissenters are entitled to their proportionate share of each Maine company at its full fair value.

INTERPRETATION In determining the fair value of shares in a close corporation for the appraisal remedy, the court should prorate among the shares the highest price a single buyer would reasonably pay for the whole enterprise.

CRITICAL THINKING QUESTION Do you agree that fair value is not the same as market value? Explain.

A shareholder who has a right to obtain payment for her shares does not have the right to attack the validity of the corporate action that gives rise to the right to obtain payment or to have the action set aside or rescinded, except when the corporate action is unlawful or fraudulent with regard to the complaining shareholders or to the corporation. When the corporate action is not unlawful or fraudulent, the appraisal remedy is usually exclusive, and the shareholder may not challenge the action. Some states, however, make the appraisal remedy exclusive in all cases; others, in contrast, make it nonexclusive in all cases.

Cohen v. Mirage Resorts, Inc.

Supreme Court of Nevada, 2003
62 P.3d 720; petition for rehearing denied 2003
http://caselaw.lp.findlaw.com/scripts/getcase.pl?court=nv&vol=119NevAdvOpNo1&invol=2

FACTS Harvey Cohen was a minority shareholder in the Boardwalk, a small, publicly held casino on Las Vegas Boulevard, "The Strip." The Boardwalk had 1,200 feet of Strip frontage located between the Bellagio and the Monte Carlo, large casinos in which the Mirage Resorts had an interest. Mirage also owned twenty-three acres of land adjacent to the Boardwalk. Mirage wished to acquire the Boardwalk as well as three parcels of land surrounding the Boardwalk. The three parcels were either owned by entities connected with the Boardwalk's majority shareholders and directors or were subject to options to purchase in favor of the Boardwalk. Mirage sought to negate the Boardwalk's options and acquire the adjacent properties for purposes of expansion.

Mirage made an offer to acquire the Boardwalk's shares through a merger with a Mirage subsidiary, Acquisition. Prior to or contemporaneous with the merger, Mirage acquired the surrounding parcels. On May 27, 1998, the Boardwalk convened a special shareholder meeting to consider the offer. A majority of the shareholders approved the merger, and it was consummated. Cohen and other members of the class tendered their shares without challenging the merger's validity or claiming statutory dissenters' rights.

A little over a year after the consumation of the merger, Cohen filed a suit for damages, alleging breach of fiduciary duty and/or loyalty by the Boardwalk's majority shareholders, board of directors, and financial advisors. Cohen asserts Mirage conspired with the Boardwalk's majority shareholders and directors to purchase the Boardwalk at an artificially low price by offering special transactions to majority shareholders and/or members of the Boardwalk's board of directors. Cohen claims that Mirage bought land or rights owned or controlled by majority shareholders or directors in properties around or involving the Boardwalk at inflated prices. Cohen contends that these shareholders and directors then agreed to approve or recommend the merger for an amount per share that was less than the fair value of the Boardwalk's stock. Finally, Cohen asserts that the directors mismanaged the Boardwalk, causing decreased profits, and that they or majority shareholders usurped corporate opportunities.

Respondents moved to dismiss, arguing that, even assuming the truth of the allegations, Cohen had no standing to sue for breach of fiduciary duty because he failed to exercise his statutory rights to dissent to the merger and tendered his shares. Respondents further asserted that the statutory right to dissent is the exclusive method for a dissenting shareholder to challenge the value of a merged corporation's stock. Respondents also contended that because Cohen and the class were no longer shareholders, they could not bring derivative claims for lost profits and usurpation of corporate opportunities.

Cohen contended, however, that the complaint asserted that the merger was approved unlawfully or as a result of wrongful conduct and therefore the time frames set forth for an appraisal proceeding did not apply. Cohen claimed that if the merger was accomplished through wrongful conduct, then he had the right to seek monetary damages, including any difference in value between the merger price and the fair value of his stock. Because he was seeking monetary damages arising from an allegedly invalid merger, Cohen contended the claims were individual and not derivative in nature and the motion to dismiss should be denied.

The district court granted respondents' motion to dismiss. Cohen then appealed.

DECISION The order is affirmed as to the derivative causes of action; it is reversed as to the allegations of misconduct affecting the validity of the merger.

OPINION Becker, J. This case involves the rights of dissenting shareholders to challenge the validity of corporate mergers, issues of first impression in the State of Nevada. Under Nevada law, a corporate merger must be approved by a majority of the corporation's shareholders. The existing shareholders then substitute their stock ownership in the old corporation for stock ownership in the new merged corporation. [Citation.] Shareholders who oppose the merger are not forced to become stockholders in the new corporation. Instead, the statutes give such shareholders three choices: (1) accept the terms of the merger and exchange their existing shares for new shares; (2) dissent from the merger, compelling the merged corporation to purchase their shares pursuant to a judicial appraisal proceeding; and/or (3) challenge the validity of the merger based on unlawful or wrongful conduct committed during the merger process. [Citation.] The procedures that govern dissenters' rights are set forth in NRS 92A.300-92A.500.

The provisions of NRS 92A.300-92A.500 * * * are patterned after, or are identical to, the provisions of the 1984 Model Business Corporation Act ("Model Act"). [Citation.] In turn, the Model Act is based upon case law from Delaware and New York. [Citation.] The Model Act and Nevada's statutes are designed to facilitate business mergers, while protecting minority shareholders from being unfairly impacted by the majority shareholders' decision to approve a merger. [Citation.]

At common law, merger approval required the unanimous vote of the shareholders. [Citations.] Before the enactment of dissenters' rights statutes, minority shareholders might block a merger simply because they disagreed with the majority's view that the merger was advisable. [Citation.] Dissenters' rights statutes do away with the common-law need for unanimous consent to the merger. [Citations.] Mergers are approved by a majority vote of the shareholders, and the Model Act limits the ability of minority shareholders to challenge a merger. Under the Model Act, minority shareholders are no longer able to enjoin a merger simply because they disagree with the majority's decision. [Citation.] Instead, minority shareholders are limited to dissenting to the merger and seeking an independent evaluation of the fair value of their stock. [Citation.]

However, the states and the Model Act also recognize two circumstances when minority shareholders should be able to challenge the merger process. [Citation.] A merger may be challenged if it is unlawful, that is, procedurally deficient. For example, it may have been approved in a manner inconsistent with the articles of incorporation or there may have been irregularities in the voting process. [Citation.] In addition, minority shareholders may seek to stop a merger if fraud or material misrepresentation affected the shareholder vote on the merger; that is, the shareholders approved the merger based upon materially incorrect information. [Citation.] Under either theory, minority shareholders may bring suit to enjoin or rescind the merger or to recover monetary damages attributable to the loss of their shareholder interest caused by an invalid merger. They may also allege that the merger was accomplished through the wrongful conduct of majority shareholders, directors, or officers of the corporation and attempt to hold those individuals liable for monetary damages under theories of breach of fiduciary duty or loyalty. [Citation.]

Challenges to the validity of a merger based on fraud usually encompass either or both of the following: (1) lack of fair dealing or (2) lack of fair price. [Citation.] Both involve corporate directors' general duties to make independent, fully informed decisions when recommending a merger and to fully disclose material information to the shareholders before a vote is taken on a proposed merger. [Citation.] They also can involve allegations that majority shareholders breached their limited fiduciary duties to minority shareholders. [Citation.]

Lack of fair dealing involves allegations that the board of directors did not make an independent, informed decision to recommend approval of the merger, [citation] or that the majority shareholders approved the merger at the expense of the minority shareholders. [Citation.] Cases involving fair dealing frequently contain claims that directors, officers, or majority shareholders had conflicts of interest or were improperly compensated or influenced in return for their approval of the merger and that the shareholders lacked material information regarding the merger when they voted for it. [Citation.] These cases also frequently involve the timing of the merger, merger negotiations, how the merger was structured, and the approval process. [Citation.]

Lack of fair price may involve similar allegations plus claims that the price per share was deliberately undervalued, but it can also include negligent conduct. [Citation.] For example, the directors may have hired incompetent or inexperienced persons to determine if the merger price was fair or to evaluate the fair value of the corporation's stock. [Citation.]

Statutes that limit a minority shareholder's right of dissent to an appraisal proceeding are known as exclusivity provisions. [Citation.] Most states have some type of exclusivity provision in their corporate law. [Citation.] Like Nevada's provisions, they provide that, absent unlawful procedures or fraud, a minority shareholder has only two options when confronted with a merger. The minority shareholder may dissent from the merger and seek an independent valuation or tender his or her shares and accept the merger price for the stock. [Citations.] * * *

A dissenting shareholder who wishes to attack the validity of the merger or seek monetary damages based upon improper actions during the merger process must allege wrongful conduct that goes to the approval of the merger. [Citation.] * * * In addition, the term "fraudulent," as used in the Model Act, has not been limited to the elements of common-law fraud; it encompasses a variety of acts involving breach of fiduciary duties imposed upon corporate officers, directors, or majority shareholders. [Citation.] * * *

* * *

Finally, dissenting shareholders may forfeit even their appraisal remedies if they fail to comply with the time lines for exercising their dissenters' rights. [Citation.] * * *

Cohen concedes that he and the other class members failed to exercise their dissenters' rights under the statutes. Therefore, they are not entitled to maintain a court action based solely on a theory that the price paid for their shares pursuant to the merger was less than the fair value of the shares. Cohen argues, however, that he is still entitled to seek damages if the merger was based upon fraud or misrepresentation. If he is successful in proving that the merger was the result of wrongful conduct, his monetary damages may include the difference, if any, between the merger price and the fair value of the shares. Cohen asserts that the time line for seeking the appraisal remedy does not apply to claims for monetary damages arising from an improper merger. We agree.

* * * Once shareholders prove that the merger was wrongfully accomplished, they may * * * receive compensatory and punitive damages, including the ability to litigate the value of the merged corporation's stock. [Citation.] Thus, the mere fact that Cohen's complaint alleges that his stock was worth more than the amount he received under the merger does not constitute grounds for dismissing it under [Nevada's exclusivity provision] so long as the complaint also contains allegations that the merger was approved through unlawful or fraudulent conduct. [Citations.]

* * *

Shareholders who vote in favor of the merger generally have no standing to contest the validity of the merger. [Citations.] * * * Misinformed shareholders [, however,] retain their right to challenge the merger regardless of their vote on the merger and a tender of their shares. [Citation.]

* * *

Under the general rule set forth in *Bershad,* [citation], Cohen lacks standing to challenge the Boardwalk merger more than a year after he tendered his shares of stock. However, as noted in [citation], the general doctrine does not apply when the unlawful or wrongful conduct affecting the merger's validity was unknown to the stockholders until after they approved the merger and/or tendered their shares of stock. In such cases, the former shareholders may still bring a cause of action for damages resulting from an invalid merger. [Citation.] *Bershad* only applies to informed shareholders. [Citation.]

Former shareholders, however, cannot simply seek more money for their stock. They must assert and prove in an equitable action that the merger was improper. [Citation.]

If this is proven, then they are entitled to any monetary damages they are able to prove were proximately caused by the improper merger. [Citation.] Moreover, damages are not limited to the surviving corporation. They may also be levied against the individuals whose wrongful conduct led to the approval of the merger or the unfair stock evaluation. [Citation.]

* * *

* * * Because a derivative claim is brought on behalf of the corporation, a former shareholder does not have standing to assert a derivative claim. [Citations.] A former shareholder does, however, have standing to seek relief for direct injuries that are independent of any injury suffered by the corporation. [Citation.]

A claim brought by a dissenting shareholder that questions the validity of a merger as a result of wrongful conduct on the part of majority shareholders or directors is properly classified as an individual or direct claim. The shareholder has lost unique personal property—his or her interest in a specific corporation. [Citations.] Therefore, if the complaint alleges damages resulting from an improper merger, it should not be dismissed as a derivative claim. [Citations.] On the other hand, if it seeks damages for wrongful conduct that caused harm to the corporation, it is derivative and should be dismissed. [Citation.] * * *

* * *

We further conclude that the district court was correct in dismissing all of the derivative claims in the complaint, but erred in not permitting Cohen to amend the complaint to clarify that he was seeking rescission of the merger and/or monetary damages based upon the invalidity of the merger.

INTERPRETATION A shareholder who has a right to obtain payment for her shares does not have the right to attack the validity of the corporate action that gives rise to the right to obtain payment or to have the action set aside or rescinded, except when the corporate action is unlawful or fraudulent with regard to the complaining shareholders or to the corporation.

ETHICAL QUESTION Did the defendants act unethically? Explain.

CRITICAL THINKING QUESTION Do you agree with the court's decision? Explain.

CPA DISSOLUTION

Although a corporation may have perpetual existence, its life may be terminated in a number of ways. Incorporation statutes usually provide for both voluntary and involuntary dissolution. Dissolution itself does not terminate the corporation's existence but does require that the corporation wind up its affairs and liquidate its assets.

VOLUNTARY DISSOLUTION

A board of directors may effect a **voluntary dissolution** by a resolution approved by the affirmative vote of the holders of a majority of the corporation's shares entitled to vote at a shareholders' meeting duly called for this purpose. Although shareholders who object to dissolution usually have no right to dissent and recover the fair value of their shares, the Revised Act grants dissenters' rights in connection with a sale or exchange of all or substantially all of a corporation's assets not made in the usual or regular course of business, including a sale in dissolution. However, the act excludes such rights in sales by court order and in sales for cash on terms requiring that all or substantially all of the net proceeds be distributed to the shareholders within one year. In addition, in many states dissolution without action by the directors may be effected by unanimous consent of the shareholders.

The Revised Act authorizes shareholders in closely held corporations to adopt unanimous shareholders' agreements requiring dissolution of the corporation at the request of one or more shareholders or upon the occurrence of a specified event or contingency.

The Statutory Close Corporation Supplement gives shareholders who elect such a right in the articles of incorporation the power to dissolve the corporation. Unless the charter specifies otherwise, an amendment to include, modify, or delete a power to dissolve must be approved by all of the shareholders. The power to dissolve may be conferred upon any shareholder or holders of a specified number or percentage of shares of any class and may be exercised at will or upon the occurrence of a specified event or contingency.

Practical Advice

To achieve increased protection, when organizing a close corporation you should consider including in the charter a provision giving each shareholder the power to dissolve the corporation.

INVOLUNTARY DISSOLUTION

A corporation may be involuntarily dissolved by administrative dissolution or by judicial dissolution.

Ethical Dilemma

What Rights Do Minority Shareholders Have?

FACTS Frank, James, and Thomas were fraternity brothers who graduated from college in the same year. Shortly after graduation they began a private security company incorporated as Secure, Inc. The company specialized in providing systems and personnel keyed to improving retail loss prevention efforts. The company also offered electronic theft detection systems for both homes and businesses.

When the company was formed, Frank put up the majority of the capital and became a 60 percent shareholder. James and Thomas had gone through college on scholarships and had little capital to invest. They received minority interests of 20 percent each.

The business became successful. Frank was excellent at customer and personnel relations, accounting, and routine business management. James and Thomas, however, were the real brains behind the business. They developed innovative techniques and systems that were highly attractive to customers. Their innovations attracted attention in the business community, and the company was the focus of a feature article in a major newspaper.

Safety First, Inc., has made an offer that would merge Secure, Inc., into Safety First, Inc. Frank wants to accept the merger proposal, but James and Thomas are adamantly opposed. They believe that in the long run they will make considerably more money if they operate the business independently for at least five to ten more years before considering selling out. The initial intention of Secure, Inc., was to enable the three shareholders to operate an independent business. James and Thomas do not want their technology and systems sold to another company.

Social, Policy, and Ethical Considerations

1. What moral or fiduciary obligation does Frank have to James and Thomas? What obligations do James and Thomas have to Frank?
2. To what extent should initial expectations as to business goals and operations continue to bind business associates morally? To what extent should associates spell out their expectations in advance?
3. What types of legal remedies, if any, are necessary when business associates no longer agree on fundamental business plans? To what extent should the law intervene in private management disputes among members of closely held businesses?
4. If Frank pays James and Thomas the fair value of their shares and proceeds with a merger, will this provide sufficient compensation to James and Thomas? Who owns the technological advances?

Administrative Dissolution The secretary of state may commence an administrative proceeding to dissolve a corporation if (1) the corporation does not pay within sixty days after they are due any franchise taxes or penalties; (2) the corporation does not deliver its annual report to the secretary of state within sixty days after it is due; (3) the corporation is without a registered agent or registered office in the state for sixty days or more; (4) the corporation does not notify the secretary of state within sixty days that it has changed its registered agent or registered office, that its registered agent has resigned, or that it has discontinued its registered office; or (5) the corporation's period of duration stated in its articles of incorporation expires.

Judicial Dissolution The state, a shareholder, or a creditor may bring a proceeding for judicial dissolution. A court may dissolve a corporation in a proceeding brought by the attorney general if it is proved that the corporation obtained its charter through fraud or has continued to exceed or abuse the authority conferred upon it by law.

A court may dissolve a corporation in a proceeding brought by a shareholder if it is established that (1) the directors are deadlocked in the management of the corporate affairs, the shareholders are unable to break the deadlock, and the corporation is threatened with or is suffering irreparable injury; (2) the acts of the directors or those in control of the corporation are illegal, oppressive, or fraudulent; (3) the corporate assets are being misapplied or wasted; or (4) the shareholders are deadlocked and have failed to elect directors for at least two consecutive annual meetings.

A creditor may bring a court action to dissolve a corporation on showing that the corporation has become unable to pay its debts and obligations as they mature in the regular course of its business and that either (1) the creditor has reduced his claim to a judgment and an execution issued on it has been returned unsatisfied or (2) the corporation has admitted in writing that the claim of the creditor is due and owing.

Cooke v. Fresh Express Foods Corporation, Inc.

Court of Appeals of Oregon, 2000
169 Or. App. 101, 7 P.3d 717
http://caselaw.lp.findlaw.com/scripts/getcase.pl?court=or&vol=A101185&invol=1

FACTS Terry J. Cooke (plaintiff) is the former husband of defendant, Joni Quicker (Joni); defendant Allen John Quicker (John) is Joni's father. In the early 1980s John and Joni began a business distributing fresh produce. Terry soon left his job and began working with John and Joni full time. The business was originally a partnership, with John having a half interest and Joni and Terry together having the other half interest. The business grew throughout the 1980s. In June 1990 John, Joni, and Terry incorporated the business as Fresh Express Foods Corporation, Inc. (Fresh Express). John received 50 percent of the stock, and Joni and Terry each received 25 percent. John was the president of the corporation, Joni was the vice-president, and plaintiff was the secretary and treasurer. They also constituted the three members of the board of directors.

Fresh Express was the primary source of income for all three parties. Part of that income came from their salaries, but substantial additional amounts came as loans that the corporation made to them for various purposes, including paying their individual taxes on their portions of the corporation's retained earnings. Because Fresh Express elected to be a subchapter S corporation, which for tax purposes does not pay taxes itself but passes its income through to its shareholders, plaintiff and defendants were liable for taxes on those retained earnings whether or not the corporation actually distributed them. Without the loans, they would have had no corporate money to pay the taxes on that corporate income.

Joni and Terry separated at about the time of the incorporation. The tension between them increased significantly beginning in June 1993 when, after starting a relationship with a Fresh Express employee, Terry filed for dissolution of the marriage.

Terry managed the company's delivery system, which included supervising the operation of its trucks. In December 1993, while Terry was on vacation, John discovered a notice on Terry's desk from the Public Utilities Commission (PUC) that showed deficiencies resulting in a fine of $6,000 and additional penalties of $4,000. Terry had not paid those amounts, and that failure threatened Fresh Express with the loss of its PUC authority to operate. When Terry returned from vacation, John, acting as president of the company, gave him a written notice of termination that included the statement that "Fresh Express Foods Corporation has suffered monetary loss associated with [your] position and this constitutes a Breach of Fiduciary Responsibility to the Corporation." It did not refer to a threatened loss of PUC operating authority. After the termination, Terry received his unpaid wages and two weeks' severance pay. Before the termination, the corporation distributed money to all of its shareholders that it treated as shareholder loans. It continued to make those distributions to John and Joni, but it did not make them to Terry after his termination. Although Terry remained a corporate officer and director for almost two years, he was never again informed of or consulted about corporate business.

The court entered a judgment dissolving Terry's and Joni's marriage in August 1994, awarding Joni approximately $27,000. Because the corporation had never issued any stock certificates, Joni was unable to use Terry's ownership interest in the corporation to satisfy the court judgment. In order to provide Joni a stock certificate to garnish, John called a directors' meeting for November 2, 1995, for the purpose of electing officers. At the meeting John and Joni first reelected John as president and Joni as vice-president; then they also elected Joni as secretary and treasurer. Terry abstained from all three votes. A few days later Joni issued a stock certificate to Terry. Instead of sending the certificate to Terry, she immediately delivered it to the sheriff under a writ of garnishment on her judgment against Terry.

In September 1996, John and Joni called a special shareholders' meeting, at which they reduced the number of directors to two, over Terry's dissenting vote, and elected John and Joni to those positions. During an informal discussion, Terry asked John's attorney if the company intended to pay the considerable amount of money it owed to him. After consulting with John, the attorney responded that John had decided not to make any more distributions to shareholders at that time. After the shareholders' meeting ended and Terry left the room at their request, John and Joni held a directors' meeting at which they first removed Terry "from all of his positions as an officer, employee and agent of the corporation." John and Joni then agreed, despite the attorney's statement to Terry, to distribute the corporation's entire accumulated adjustment account to the shareholders by using it to reduce the outstanding shareholder loans. Finally, they agreed to purchase automobiles for John and Joni and to increase John's salary from $54,000 per year to $120,000.

Terry brought suit against the corporation, John, and Joni. The trial court found that John would not have terminated Joni for a comparable error. It concluded that the purpose for firing Terry was to exclude him from participating in the corporate business or receiving any benefits from the corporation. The court found that the reason for the exclusion was the breakdown of the marriage and the animosities that followed. The trial court found that the defendants had acted oppressively toward the plaintiff in the management and control of defendant Fresh Express. As a remedy, the court ordered the defendants to purchase the plaintiff's interest in Fresh Express at a price set by the court. The defendants appealed.

DECISION Judgment for the plaintiff affirmed.

OPINION Armstrong, J. Plaintiff argues that these actions together constituted a course of oppressive conduct and that defendants breached their fiduciary duties to him by freezing him out of all participation in the corporation and depriving him of all of the benefits of being a stockholder. ORS 60.661(2)(b) provides that a court may dissolve a corporation when the directors or those in control "have acted, are acting or will act in a manner that is illegal, oppressive, or fraudulent[.]" Although there is not, and probably cannot be, a definitive definition of oppressive conduct under the statute, at least in a closely held corporation conduct that violates the majority's fiduciary duties to the minority is likely to be oppressive. [Citations.] Cases that discuss either oppressive conduct or the majority's fiduciary duties are, thus, relevant to this question.

A number of cases make it clear that when

> the majority shareholders of a closely held corporation use their control over the corporation to their own advantage and exclude the minority from the benefits of participating in the corporation, [in the absence of] a legitimate business purpose, the actions constitute a breach of their fiduciary duties of loyalty, good faith and fair dealing.

[Citation.] A finding that the majority shareholders have engaged in oppressive conduct under ORS 60.661 permits the court either to order a dissolution of the corporation or to award lesser appropriate relief, including requiring the majority to buy out the minority's interest at a price that the court fixes. [Citation.] Because many things can constitute oppressive conduct or a breach of fiduciary duties, what matters is not so much matching the specific facts of one case to those of another but examining the pattern and intent of the majority and the effect on the minority of those specific facts. [Citation.]

The facts of this case show a classic squeeze-out. * * * Defendants withheld dividends and other benefits from plaintiff while preserving benefits for themselves.

> * * * [W]ithholding dividends can be especially devastating in an S corporation as all corporate income is passed through to the shareholders for tax purposes and shareholders are required to pay taxes on that income, but if no dividends are declared, the shareholders will have no cash from the enterprise with which to pay those taxes.

[Citation.] * * * In addition, the "abrupt removal of a minority shareholder from positions of employment and management can be a devastatingly effective squeeze-out technique." [Citation.] Finally, majority shareholders may siphon off corporate wealth by causing a corporation to pay the majority shareholders excessively high compensation, not only in salaries but in generous expense accounts and other fringe benefits. * * *

The existence of one or more of these characteristic signs of oppression does not necessarily mean that the majority has acted oppressively within the meaning of ORS 60.661(2)(b). Courts give significant deference to the majority's judgment in the business decisions that it makes, at least if the decisions appear to be genuine business decisions. * * * The court must evaluate the majority's actions, keeping in mind that, even if some actions may be individually justifiable, the actions in total may show a pattern of oppression that requires the court to provide a remedy to the minority.

The background of this case is a corporation that consisted of a father, a daughter, and a son-in-law and that came into existence at the very time that the marriage between the daughter and son-in-law began to dissolve. The events that we have described can best be understood as steps in a pattern whose ultimate goal was to eliminate plaintiff from all participation in what John and Joni saw as a family business. As plaintiff suggests in his brief, after firing him as an employee they tried also to fire him as a shareholder. That, however, is not as easy to achieve.

Although there were some previous signs of tension, the first action that might fit into a pattern of oppression was John's termination of plaintiff's employment with the company. Plaintiff does not challenge the dismissal as a matter of employment law. However, it is unusual for a close corporation to terminate the employment of a 25-percent shareholder and corporate director for a mistake of the sort that John described, particularly in the absence of evidence of previous problems and accompanying warnings. The written notice of termination appears to be more an attempt to create a paper justification for the termination than a statement of the actual reasons. After the termination, defendants excluded plaintiff from all involvement in the corporation and its business and all participation in its profits, things that relate to his continuing status as a shareholder and a director, not to his terminated status as an employee. Those actions suggest that the purpose of the termination was not to remove an unsatisfactory employee but, rather, to exclude plaintiff from participation in the corporation.

Defendants nominally recognized plaintiff's continuing status after his termination only when they had to follow corporate forms in order to benefit themselves at his expense. The sole purpose for the directors' meeting in November 1995 was to produce a stock certificate that Joni could garnish * * *

Finally, in September 1996 defendants acted to ensure that they would permanently receive all benefits of the corporation. They began by replacing plaintiff as a director and reducing the number of directors to two. Although that was not necessarily improper in itself, their first actions as the sole directors of Fresh Express showed their purpose to exclude plaintiff from any share in the corporation other than his tax liabilities. They first removed plaintiff from any office or agency with the corporation and then took a number of actions to direct all corporate income to themselves. Despite having told plaintiff that there would be no corporate distributions, defendants distributed the entire retained earnings through a paper transaction that ensured that the corporate books would show no source for making any cash distribution to plaintiff. They then more than doubled John's salary, with the result that he received his income from the corporation as an expense that would reduce its profits rather than as a distribution of profits. Finally, they had the corporation pay for their recently purchased automobiles, again adding to the corporation's expenses and reducing its profits for their benefit.

* * *

In summary, we conclude that defendants consistently acted to further their individual interests, not the interests of the corporation, and without regard to their fiduciary duties to plaintiff. They did so either knowing or intending that their actions would harm plaintiff, among other ways by excluding him from any benefits of his ownership of one quarter of the corporate stock. They thereby violated their fiduciary duties to him and engaged in oppressive conduct.

Under ORS 60.661, the trial court had the authority to choose a remedy for defendants' actions; we agree with it that requiring defendants to purchase plaintiff's shares is the preferable option. A purchase will disentangle the parties' affairs while keeping the corporation a going concern; dissolution would not benefit anyone, and plaintiff did not seek it at trial. Defendants, however, raise some issues concerning the court's determination of the price that defendants must pay.

Plaintiff presented extensive testimony from an expert appraiser concerning the value of plaintiff's shares in the context of a judicial remedy for oppressive conduct. In doing so, the appraiser determined the value of the company as a profitable going business, made certain adjustments for excessive expenses, and determined plaintiff's one-quarter share of the total. The expert then added plaintiff's unpaid wages since his termination as a way of reflecting the benefits that he did not receive after that date. The only directly contradictory evidence that defendants presented came from the company's accountant, who calculated plaintiff's proportionate share of its liquidation value. In this case, however, the issue is the fair value of plaintiff's shares in a profitable going concern, which is not necessarily tied to the company's liquidation value; that evidence, thus, has limited relevance. The court ordered defendants to purchase plaintiff's shares at the price that the expert recommended.

* * * [B]ecause defendants must purchase plaintiff's shares as a remedy for their misconduct, and the price for plaintiff's shares is therefore based on their fair value rather than their fair market value, either a minority or marketability discount would be inappropriate. [Citation.]

INTERPRETATION A court may dissolve a corporation in a proceeding brought by a shareholder if it is established that the acts of the directors are oppressive.

ETHICAL QUESTION Did the directors act unethically? Explain.

CRITICAL THINKING QUESTION Do you agree with the court's decision in this case? Explain.

LIQUIDATION

As we mentioned earlier, dissolution requires that the corporation devote itself to winding up its affairs and liquidating its assets. After dissolution, the corporation must cease carrying on its business except as is necessary to wind up. When a corporation is dissolved, its assets are liquidated and used first to pay the expenses of liquidation and its creditors according to their respective contract or lien rights. Any remainder is proportionately distributed to shareholders according to their respective contract rights; stock with a liquidation preference has priority over common stock. The board of directors, who serve as trustees, carries out voluntary liquidation; a court-appointed receiver may conduct involuntary liquidation.

CONCEPT REVIEW

Fundamental Changes Under Pre-1999 RMBCA

Change	Board of Director Resolution Required	Shareholder Approval Required	Shareholders' Appraisal Remedy Available
A amends its articles of incorporation	A: Yes	A: Yes	A: No, unless amendment materially and adversely affects rights of shares
B sells its assets in usual and regular course of business to A	B: Yes	B: No	B: No
B sells its assets not in usual and regular course of business to A	B: Yes	B: Yes	B: Yes
A voluntarily purchases shares of B	A: Yes B: No	A: No B: No, individual shareholders decide	A: No B: No
A acquires shares of B through a compulsory exchange	A: Yes B: Yes	A: No B: Yes	A: No B: Yes
A and B merge	A: Yes B: Yes	A: Yes B: Yes	A: Yes B: Yes
A merges its 90 percent subsidiary B into A	A: Yes B: No	A: No B: No	A: No B: Yes
A and B consolidate	A: Yes B: Yes	A: Yes B: Yes	A: Yes B: Yes
A voluntarily dissolves	A: Yes	A: Yes	A: No (usually)

PROTECTION OF CREDITORS

The statutory provisions governing dissolution and liquidation usually prescribe procedures to safeguard the interests of the corporation's creditors. Such procedures typically include the required mailing of notice to known creditors, a general publication of notice, and the preservation of claims against the corporation.

CHAPTER SUMMARY

Charter Amendments

Authority to Amend statutes permit charters to be amended

Procedure the board of directors adopts a resolution, which must be approved by a majority vote of the shareholders

Combinations

Purchase or Lease of All or Substantially All of the Assets results in no change in the legal personality of either corporation

- ***Regular Course of Business*** approval by the selling corporation's board of directors is required, but shareholder authorization is not

- *Other Than in Regular Course of Business* approval by the board of directors and shareholders of the selling corporation is required

Purchase of Shares a transaction by which one corporation acquires all of, or a controlling interest in, the stock of another corporation; no change occurs in the legal existence of either corporation and no formal shareholder approval of either corporation is required

Compulsory Share Exchange a transaction by which a corporation becomes the owner of all of the outstanding shares of one or more classes of stock of another corporation by an exchange that is compulsory on all owners of the acquired shares; the board of directors of each corporation and the shareholders of the corporation whose shares are being acquired must approve

Merger the combination of the assets of two or more corporations into one of the corporations
- *Procedure* requires approval by the board of directors and shareholders of each corporation
- *Short-Form Merger* a corporation that owns at least 90 percent of the outstanding shares of a subsidiary may merge the subsidiary into itself without approval by the shareholders of either corporation
- *Effect* the surviving corporation receives title to all of the assets of the merged corporation and assumes all of its liabilities; the merged corporation ceases to exist

Consolidation the combination of two or more corporations into a new corporation
- *Procedure* requires approval of the board of directors and shareholders of each corporation
- *Effect* each constituent corporation ceases to exist; the new corporation assumes all of their debts and liabilities

Going Private Transactions a combination that makes a publicly held corporation a private one; includes cash-out combinations and management buyouts

Dissenting Shareholder one who opposes a fundamental change and has the right to receive the fair value of her shares
- *Availability* dissenters' rights arise in (1) mergers, (2) consolidations, (3) sales or leases of all or substantially all of the assets of a corporation not in the regular course of business, (4) compulsory share exchanges, and (5) amendments that materially and adversely affect the rights of shares
- *Appraisal Remedy* the right of a dissenter to receive the fair value of his shares (the value of shares immediately before the corporate action to which the dissenter objects takes place, excluding any appreciation or depreciation in anticipation of such corporate action unless such exclusion would be inequitable)

Dissolution

Voluntary Dissolution may be brought about by a resolution of the board of directors that is approved by the shareholders

Involuntary Dissolution may occur by administrative or judicial action taken (1) by the attorney general, (2) by shareholders under certain circumstances, and (3) by a creditor on a showing that the corporation has become unable to pay its debts and obligations as they mature in the regular course of its business

Liquidation when a corporation is dissolved, its assets are liquidated and used first to pay its liquidation expenses and its creditors according to their respective contract or lien rights; any remainder is proportionately distributed to shareholders according to their respective contract rights

QUESTIONS

1. The stock in Hotel Management, Inc., a hotel management corporation, was divided equally between two families. For several years the two families had been unable to agree on or cooperate in the management of the corporation. As a result, no meeting of shareholders or directors had been held for five years. There had been no withdrawal of profits for five years, and last year the hotel operated at a loss. Although the corporation was not insolvent, such a state was imminent because the business was poorly managed and its properties were in need of repair. As a result, the owners of half the stock brought an action in equity for dissolution of the corporation. Will they succeed? Explain.

2. a. When may a corporation sell, lease, exchange, mortgage, or pledge all or substantially all of its assets in the usual and regular course of its business?
   b. When may a corporation sell, lease, exchange, mortgage, or pledge all or substantially all of its assets other than in the usual and regular course of its business?
   c. What are the rights of a shareholder who dissents from a proposed sale or exchange of all or substantially all of the assets of a corporation other than in the usual and regular course of its business?

3. Cutler Company was duly merged into Stone Company. Yetta, a shareholder of the former Cutler Company, having paid only one-half of her subscription, is now sued by Stone Company for the balance of the subscription. Yetta, who took no part in the merger proceedings, denies liability on the ground that, inasmuch as Cutler Company no longer exists, all her rights and obligations in connection with Cutler Company have been terminated. Explain whether she is correct.

4. Smith, while in the course of his employment with the Bee Corporation, negligently ran the company's truck into Williams, injuring him severely. Subsequently, the Bee Corporation and the Sea Corporation consolidated, forming the SeaBee Corporation. Williams filed suit against the SeaBee Corporation for damages, and the SeaBee Corporation argued the defense that the injuries Williams sustained were not caused by any of SeaBee's employees, that SeaBee was not even in existence at the time of the injury, and that the SeaBee Corporation was therefore not liable. What decision?

5. Johnson Company, a corporation organized under the laws of State X, after proper authorization by the shareholders, sold its entire assets to Samson Company, also a State X corporation. Ellen, an unpaid creditor of Johnson Company, sues Samson Company on her claim. Is Sampson liable? Explain.

6. Zenith Steel Company operates a prosperous business. The board of directors voted to spend $20 million of the company's surplus funds to purchase a majority of the stock of two other companies—Green Insurance Company and Blue Trust Company. Green Insurance Company is a thriving business whose stock is an excellent investment at the price at which it will be sold to Zenith Steel Company. The principal reasons for Zenith's purchase of Green Insurance stock are to invest surplus funds and to diversify its business. Blue Trust Company owns a controlling interest in Zenith Steel Company. The Blue Trust Company is subject to special governmental controls. The main purpose for Zenith's purchase of Blue Trust Company stock is to enable the present management and directors of Zenith Steel Company to continue their management of the company. Jones, a minority shareholder in Zenith Steel Company, brings an appropriate action to enjoin the purchase by Zenith Steel Company of the stock of either Green Insurance Company or of Blue Trust Company. What is the decision as to each purchase?

7. Mildred, Deborah, and Bob each own one third of the stock of Nova Corporation. On Friday, Mildred received an offer to merge Nova into Buyer Corporation. Mildred, who agreed to call a shareholders' meeting to discuss the offer on the following Tuesday, telephoned Deborah and Bob and informed them of the offer and the scheduled meeting. Deborah agreed to attend. Bob was unable to attend because he was leaving on a trip on Saturday and asked if the three of them could meet Friday night to discuss the offer. Mildred and Deborah agreed. The three shareholders met informally Friday night and agreed to accept the offer only if they received preferred stock of Buyer Corporation for their shares. Bob then left on his trip. On Tuesday, at the time and place appointed by Mildred, Mildred and Deborah convened the shareholders' meeting. After discussion, they concluded that the preferred stock payment limitation was unwise and passed a formal resolution to accept Buyer Corporation's offer without any such condition. Bob files suit to enjoin Mildred, Deborah, and the Nova Corporation from implementing this resolution. Explain whether the injunction should be issued.

CASE PROBLEMS

8. Tretter alleged that his exposure over the years to asbestos products manufactured by Philip Carey Manufacturing Corporation caused him to contract asbestosis. Tretter brought an action against Rapid American Corporation, which was the surviving corporation of a merger between Philip Carey and Rapid American. Rapid American denied liability, claiming that immediately after the merger it had transferred its asbestos operations to a newly formed subsidiary corporation. Can Rapid avoid liability by such transfer? Explain.

9. Wilcox, chief executive officer and chairman of the board of directors, owned 60 percent of the shares of Sterling Corporation. When the market price of Sterling's shares was $22 per share, Wilcox sold all of his shares in Sterling to Conrad for $29 per share. The minority shareholders of Sterling brought suit against Wilcox to demand a portion of the amount Wilcox received in excess of the market price. What is the result?

10. All Steel Pipe and Tube is a closely held corporation engaged in the business of selling steel pipes and tubes. Leo and Scott Callier are its two equal shareholders. Scott is Leo's uncle. Leo is one of the company's two directors and is president of the corporation. Scott is the general manager. Scott's father and Leo's grandfather, Felix, is the other director. Over the years, Scott and Leo have had differences of opinion about various aspects of the operation of the business. However, despite the deterioration of their relationship, the company has flourished. When negotiations aimed at the redemption of Scott's shares by Leo began, the parties could not reach an agreement. The discussion then turned to voluntary dissolution and liquidation of the corporation, but still no agreement could be reached. Finally, Leo fired Scott and began to wind down All Steel's business and to form a new corporation, Callier Steel Pipe and Tube. Leo then brought an action seeking a dissolution and liquidation of All Steel. Should the court order dissolution? Explain.

11. The shareholders of Endicott Johnson who had dissented from a proposed merger of Endicott with McDonough Corporation brought a proceeding to fix the fair value of their stock. At issue was the proper weight to be given the market price of the stock in fixing its fair value. The shareholders argued that the market value should not be considered because McDonough controlled 70 percent of Endicott's stock and the stock had been delisted from the New York Stock Exchange. Are the shareholders correct?

12. In early 1984, Royal Dutch Petroleum Company (Royal Dutch) (http://www.shell.com/royal-en/), through various subsidiaries, controlled approximately 70 percent of the outstanding common shares of Shell Oil Co. (Shell) (http://www.countonshell.com). On January 24, 1984, Royal Dutch announced its intention to merge Shell into SPNV Holdings, Inc. (Holdings), which is now Shell Petroleum, Inc., by offering the minority shareholders $55 per share. Shell's board of directors, however, rejected the offer as inadequate. Royal Dutch then withdrew the merger proposal and initiated a tender offer at $58 per share. As a result of the tender offer, Holdings' ownership interest increased to 94.6 percent of Shell's outstanding stock. Holdings then initiated a short-form merger. Under the terms of the merger, Shell's minority stockholders were to receive $58 per share. However, if before July 1, 1985, a shareholder waived his right to seek an appraisal, he would receive an extra $2 per share. In conjunction with the short-form merger, Holdings distributed several documents to the minority, including a document entitled "Certain Information About Shell" (CIAS).

The CIAS included a table of discounted future net cash flows (DCF) for Shell's oil and gas reserves. However, due to a computer programming error, the DCF failed to account for the cash flows from approximately 295 million barrel equivalents of U.S. proved oil and gas reserves. Shell's failure to include the reserves in its calculations resulted in an understatement of its discounted future net cash flows of approximately $993 million to $1.1 billion or $3.00 to $3.45 per share. Moreover, as a result of the error, Shell stated in the CIAS that there had been a slight decline in the value of its oil and gas reserves from 1984 to 1985. When properly calculated, the value of the reserves had actually increased over that time period.

Shell's minority shareholders sued in the Court of Chancery, asserting that the error in the DCF along with other alleged disclosure violations constituted a breach of Holdings' fiduciary "duty of candor." Was the error in the DCF material and misleading?

http:// **Internet Exercise** Find your state's incorporation statute and determine what kinds of fundamental changes it recognizes. (If your state's incorporation statute is not available, choose that of another state.)

PART VIII

DEBTOR AND CREDITOR RELATIONS

California Attorney General ("Credit")
http://www.dca.ca.gov/r_r/conspub1.htm

Florida Bar Association ("Applying for Credit"; "Debtors' Rights in Florida")
http://www.flabar.org/newflabar/consumerservices/General/Consumer.Pam/

Illinois Bar Association ("Buying on Time")
http://www.illinoislawyerfinder.com/publicinfo/home.html

Iowa Attorney General ("Debt Collection")
http://www.state.ia.us/government/ag/consumer/consumer_tips.html

Missouri Bar Association ("Buying on Time")
http://www.mobar.org/pamphlets/broindex.htm

North Carolina Bar Association ("Buying on Time")
http://www.ncbar.org

Ohio Bar Association ("Ohio's Credit Laws")
http://www.ohiobar.org/conres/pamphlets

Oregon Bar Association ("Debtor's Rights"; "Liens")
http://www.osbar.org/public/legalinfo/bankruptcy.html

South Dakota Bar Association ("Credit and Debt Policy")
http://www.sdbar.org/public/consumers/default.htm

Wisconsin Bar Association
http://www.legalexplorer.com/consumer/consumer.asp

Bankruptcy Code
http://www4.law.cornell.edu/uscode/11/

American Bankruptcy Institute
http://www.abiworld.org/

Georgetown University: Bankruptcy Law
http://www.ll.georgetown.edu/topics/bankruptcy.cfm

U.S. Government Pamphlet ("Managing Your Debts: How to Regain Financial Health")
http://www.pueblo.gsa.gov/cic_text/money/managing-debt/mangdebt.htm

U.S. Government Pamphlet ("Bankruptcy")
http://www.pueblo.gsa.gov/other/o-money.htm

Connecticut Attorney General ("Bankruptcy: Is It Right for You?")
http://www.cslib.org/attygenl/mainlinks/tabindex3.htm

Illinois Attorney General ("Things You Should Know About Bankruptcy")
http://www.ag.state.il.us/consumer/consume.htm

Maine Attorney General ("Consumer Rights and a Bankrupt Business")
http://www.maine.gov/index.php?r=clgds=chap23

Pennsylvania Attorney General ("Bankruptcy and You—What If I Do File?")
http://www.attorneygeneral.gov/pei/brochures/index.cfm

CHAPTER 38

Secured Transactions and Suretyship

Neither a borrower nor a lender be: For loan oft loses both itself and friend, And borrowing dulls the edge of husbandry.

WILLIAM SHAKESPEARE, *HAMLET*

Learning Objectives

After reading this chapter you should be able to:

1. Name and define the various types of collateral.
2. Explain the purposes, methods, and requirements of attachment and perfection.
3. Discuss the priorities among the various parties who may have competing interests in collateral and the rights and remedies of the parties to a security agreement after default by the debtor.
4. Explain the requirements for the formation of a suretyship relationship.
5. Explain the rights of a creditor against a surety and the rights of a surety, including those of a cosurety.

Shakespeare's well-known lines in *Hamlet* reflect an earlier view of debt, for today borrowed funds are both essential and honorable under our economic system. In fact, the absence of loans would severely restrict the availability of goods and services and would greatly limit the quantities consumers would be able to purchase.

The public policy and social issues created by today's enormous use of debt center on certain tenets, among which are the following:

1. The means by which debt is created and transferred should be as simple and as inexpensive as possible.
2. The risks to lenders should be minimized.
3. Lenders should have a way to collect unpaid debts.

A lender typically incurs two basic collection risks: the borrower could be unwilling to repay the loan even though he is able to, or the borrower could prove to be unable to repay the loan. In addition to the remedies dealing with the first of these risks, the law has developed several devices to maximize the likelihood of repayment. These devices, which we will discuss in this chapter, include consensual security interests (also called secured transactions) and suretyships.

In addition, debtors of all sorts—wage earners, sole proprietorships, partnerships, and corporations—sometimes accumulate debts far in excess of their assets or suffer financial reverses that make it impossible for them to meet their obligations. In such an event, it is an important policy of the law to treat all creditors fairly and equitably and to provide the debtor with relief from these debts so that he may continue to contribute to society. These are the two basic purposes of the federal bankruptcy law, which we will briefly discuss in this chapter and more fully in Chapter 39.

SECURED TRANSACTIONS IN PERSONAL PROPERTY

An obligation or debt can exist without security if the creditor deems adequate the integrity, reputation, and net worth of the debtor. Often, however, businesses or individuals cannot obtain credit without giving adequate security, or, in some cases, even if the borrower can obtain an unsecured loan, he can negotiate more favorable terms by giving security.

Transactions involving security in personal property are governed by Article 9 of the Uniform Commercial Code (UCC). This chapter will cover Revised Article 9, which became effective in all the states on July 1, 2001. The article provides a simple and unified structure within which a tremendous variety of secured financing transactions can take place with less cost and with greater certainty than was possible before the article's enactment. Moreover, the article's flexibility and simplified formalities allow new forms of secured financing to fit comfortably under its provisions. In addition, the new article recognizes and provides coverage for electronic commerce.

http:// UCC Article 9: http://www.law.cornell.edu/ucc/9/overview.html

CPA ESSENTIALS OF SECURED TRANSACTIONS

Article 9 governs a secured transaction in personal property in which the debtor *consents* to provide a security interest in personal property to secure the payment of a debt. A security interest in property cannot exist apart from the debt it secures, and discharging the debt in any manner terminates the security interest in the property. Article 9 also applies to the *sales* of certain types of collateral (accounts, chattel paper, payment intangibles, and promissory notes.) Article 9 does *not* apply to nonconsensual security interests that arise by operation of law, such as mechanics' or landlords' liens, although it does cover nonpossessory statutory agricultural liens.

A common type of consensual secured transaction covered by Article 9 occurs when a person wanting to buy goods has neither the cash nor a sufficient credit standing to obtain the goods on open credit, and the seller, to secure payment of all or part of the price, obtains a security interest in the goods. Alternatively, the buyer may borrow the purchase price from a third party and pay the seller in cash. The third-party lender may then take a security interest in the goods to secure repayment of the loan.

Every consensual secured transaction involves a debtor, a secured party, collateral, a security agreement, and a security interest. Some Article 9 definitions follow:

- A **security interest** is "an interest in personal property or fixtures which secures payment or performance of an obligation."
- A **security agreement** is an agreement that creates or provides for a security interest.
- **Collateral** is the property subject to a security interest or agricultural lien.
- A **secured party** is the person in whose favor a security interest in the collateral is created or provided for under a security agreement. The definition of a secured party includes lenders, credit sellers, consignors, purchasers of certain types of collateral (accounts, chattel paper, payment intangibles, or promissory notes), and other specified persons.
- A **debtor** is a person (1) having an interest in the collateral other than a security interest or lien, whether or not the person is an obligor (2) a seller of accounts, chattel paper, payment intangibles, or promissory notes; or (3) a consignee.
- An **obligor** is a person who, with respect to an obligation secured by a security interest in or an agricultural lien on the collateral, owes payment or other performance, has provided property other than the collateral to secure payment or performance, or is otherwise accountable for payment or performance.
- A **secondary obligor** is usually a guarantor or surety of the debt.
- A **purchase money security interest** (PMSI) is created in goods when a seller retains a security interest in the goods sold on credit by a security agreement. Similarly, a third-party lender who advances funds to enable the debtor to purchase goods has a purchase money security interest in goods if she has a security agreement and the debtor in fact uses the funds to purchase the goods.

In most secured transactions, the debtor is an obligor with respect to the obligation secured by the security interest. Thus, a security interest is created when an automobile dealer sells and delivers a car to an individual (the *debtor*) under a retail installment contract (a *security agreement*) that provides that the dealer (the *secured party*) obtains a *security interest* (a *purchase money security interest*) in the car (the *collateral*) until the price is paid. See Figure 38-1 for the fundamental rights of the secured party and the debtor.

Figure 38-1
Fundamental Rights of Secured Party and Debtor

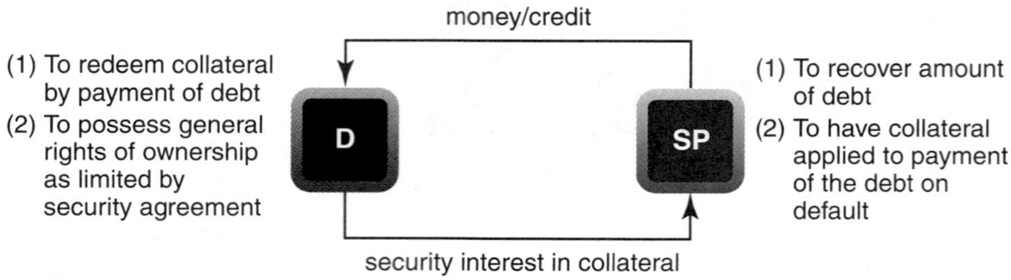

CLASSIFICATION OF COLLATERAL

CPA

Although most of the provisions of Article 9 apply to all kinds of personal property, some provisions state special rules that apply only to particular kinds of collateral. Under the Code, collateral is classified according to its nature and its use. The classifications according to nature are (a) goods, (b) indispensable paper, and (c) intangibles.

GOODS

Goods are all things that are movable when a security interest attaches and include fixtures, standing timber to be cut, the unborn young of animals, crops grown, growing, or to be grown, and manufactured homes. The new act also includes computer programs embedded in goods if the software becomes part of the goods. (When software maintains its separate state it is considered a general intangible.) Goods are further classified according to their use. Goods are subdivided into (1) consumer goods, (2) farm products, (3) inventory, (4) equipment, (5) fixtures, and (6) accessions. Depending on its primary use or purpose, the same item of goods may fall into different classifications. For example, a refrigerator purchased by a physician to store medicines in his office is classified as equipment, but the same refrigerator would be classified as consumer goods if the physician purchased it for home use. In the hands of a refrigerator dealer or manufacturer, the refrigerator would be classified as inventory. If goods are used for multiple purposes, such as by a physician in both his office and his home, their classification is dependent upon their predominant use.

Consumer Goods Goods used or bought for use primarily for personal, family, or household purposes are **consumer goods**.

Farm Products The Code defines **farm products** as "goods, other than standing timber, which are part of a farming operation and which are crops grown, growing or to be grown, including crops produced on trees, vines, and bushes and aquatic goods. . . ." In addition, farm products also include livestock, born or unborn, including aquatic goods such as fish raised on a fish farm as well as supplies used or produced in a farming operation. Thus, farm products would include wheat growing on the farmer's land; the farmer's pigs, cows, and hens; and the hens' eggs. When such products become the possessions of a person not engaged in farming operations, they cease to be farm products.

Inventory The term **inventory** includes nonfarm product goods (1) held for sale, lease, or to be furnished under a service contract or (2) consist of raw materials, work in process, or materials used or consumed in a business. Thus, a retailer's or a wholesaler's merchandise, as well as a manufacturer's raw materials, are inventory.

Equipment Goods not included in the definition of inventory, farm products, or consumer goods are classified as **equipment**. This category is broad enough to include a lawyer's library, a physician's office furniture, or machinery in a factory.

Fixtures Goods and personal property that have become so related to particular *real property* that an interest in them arises under real estate law are called **fixtures**. Thus, state law other than the Code determines whether and when goods become fixtures. In general terms, fixtures are goods so firmly affixed to real estate that they are considered part of such real estate. Examples are furnaces, central air-conditioning units, and plumbing fixtures. See Chapter 49 for a further discussion of fixtures. A security interest in fixtures may arise under Article 9, and, under certain circumstances, a perfected security interest in fixtures will have priority over a conflicting security interest or mortgage in the real property to which the goods are attached.

Accession Goods installed in or firmly affixed to *personal property* are **accessions** if the identity of the original goods is not lost. Thus, a new engine placed in an old car automobile is an accession.

INDISPENSABLE PAPER

Four kinds of collateral involve rights evidenced by **indispensable paper:** (1) chattel paper, (2) instruments, (3) documents, and (4) investment property.

Chattel Paper **Chattel paper** is a record or records that evidence both a monetary obligation and a security interest in or a lease of specific goods. A **record** is information inscribed on a tangible medium (written on paper) or is stored in an electronic or other medium and is retrievable in perceivable form (electronically stored). Thus chattel paper can be either tangible chattel paper or electronic chattel paper.

For example, Dealer sells goods on credit to Buyer who uses the goods as equipment. Dealer retains a purchase money security interest in the goods. Dealer then borrows against (or sells) the security agreement of Buyer along with Dealer's security interest in the collateral. The collateral provided by Dealer to his lender in this type of transaction (consisting of the security agreement and the security interest) is chattel paper.

Instruments The definition of an **instrument** includes negotiable instruments (drafts, checks, promissory notes, and certificate of deposits) as well as any other any writing that evidences a right to payment of money that is transferable by delivery with any necessary indorsement or assignment and that is not of itself a security agreement or lease. Negotiable instruments are covered in Chapters 24–28. An instrument does not include an investment property, a letter of credit, or writings evidencing a right to payment from a credit or charge card.

Documents The term **document** includes documents of title, such as bills of lading and warehouse receipts, which may be either negotiable or nonnegotiable. A document of title is negotiable if by its terms the goods it covers are deliverable to bearer or to the order of a named person. Any other document is nonnegotiable. Documents of title are covered in Chapter 49.

Investment Property The term **investment property** means an investment security, such as stocks and bonds, as well as securities accounts, commodity contracts, and commodity accounts. A ***certificated security*** is an investment security that is represented by a paper certificate. An ***uncertificated security*** is not represented by a paper certificate but is recognized on the books or records of the corporation. A ***security entitlement*** refers to the rights and property interest of a person who holds securities or other financial assets through a securities intermediary such as a bank, broker, or clearinghouse, which in the ordinary course of business maintains security accounts for others. A security entitlement thus includes both the rights against the securities intermediary and an interest in the property held by the securities intermediary.

INTANGIBLES

The Code also recognizes two kinds of collateral that are neither goods nor indispensable paper, namely, accounts and general intangibles. These types of **intangible** collateral are not evidenced by any indispensable paper, such as a stock certificate or a negotiable bill of lading.

Accounts The term **account** includes the right to monetary payment, whether or not such right has been earned by performance, for (1) goods sold, leased, licensed, or otherwise disposed of or (2) services rendered. Accounts include credit card receivables and health-care-insurance receivables. An example of an account is a business's accounts receivable.

General Intangibles The term **general intangibles** applies to any personal property *other than* goods, accounts, chattel paper, commercial tort claims, deposit accounts, documents, instruments, investment property, letter-of-credit rights, money, and oil, gas and other minerals before extraction. Included in the definition are software, goodwill, literary rights, and interests in patents, trademarks, and copyrights to the extent they are not regulated by federal statute. Also included is a payment intangible, which is a general intangible under which the account debtor's principal obligation is the payment of money.

OTHER KINDS OF COLLATERAL

Proceeds include whatever is received upon the sale, lease, license exchange, or other disposition of collateral; whatever is collected on, or distributed on account of, collateral; or other rights arising out of collateral. For example, an automobile dealer grants a security interest in its inventory to the automobile manufacturer that sold the inventory. When the dealer sells a car to Henry and receives from Henry a used car and the remainder of the purchase price in a monetary payment, the used car and the money are both proceeds from the sale of the new car. Unless otherwise agreed, a security agreement gives the secured party (the manufacturer in this example) rights to proceeds.

Additional types of collateral include timber to be cut, minerals, motor vehicles, mobile goods (goods used in more than one jurisdiction), and money. Revised Article 9 also adds the following kinds of collateral: commercial tort claim, letter-of-credit rights, and **deposit accounts** (a demand, savings, time, or similar account maintained with a bank). In consumer transactions, however, deposit accounts may not be taken as *original* collateral.

CPA Attachment

Attachment is the Code's term to describe the creation of a security interest that is enforceable against the *debtor*. Attachment is also a prerequisite to rendering a security interest enforceable against third parties, though in some instances attachment in itself is sufficient to create such enforceability. Perfection, which provides the greatest enforceability against third parties who assert competing interests in the collateral, is discussed below.

Until a security interest "attaches," it is *ineffective* against the debtor. Under the Code, the security interest created by a security agreement attaches to the described collateral once the following events have occurred:

1. the secured party has given value;
2. the debtor has acquired rights in the collateral or has the power to transfer such rights to a secured party; and
3. the debtor and secured party have an agreement, which in most instances must be authenticated by the debtor although in some cases alternative evidence, such as possession by the secured party pursuant to agreement, will suffice.

The parties may, however, by explicit agreement postpone the time of attachment.

Value

The term **value** is broadly defined and includes consideration under contract law, a binding commitment to extend credit, and an antecedent debt. For example, Buyer purchases equipment from Seller on credit. When Buyer fails to make timely payment, Seller and Buyer enter into a security agreement that grants Seller a security interest in the equipment. By entering the agreement, Seller has given value, even though he relies upon an antecedent debt—the original transfer of goods to Buyer—instead of providing new consideration. Moreover, Seller is not limited to acquiring a security interest in the equipment he sold to Buyer but also may obtain a security interest in other personal property of Buyer.

Debtor's Rights in Collateral

The elusive concept of the debtor's rights in collateral is not specifically defined by the Code. As a general rule, the debtor is deemed to have **rights in collateral** that he owns or is in possession of as well as in those items that he is in the process of acquiring from the seller. For example, if Adrien borrows money from Richard and grants him a security interest in corporate stock that she owns, then Adrien had rights in the collateral before entering into the secured transaction. Likewise, if Sally sells goods to Benjamin on credit and he provides Sally a security interest in the goods, Benjamin will acquire rights in the collateral upon identification of the goods to the contract. In addition, the Revised Code added the words "or the power to transfer rights in the collateral to a secured party." The comments to this section state "[h]owever, in accordance with basic personal property conveyancing principles, the baseline rule is that a security interest attaches only to whatever rights a debtor may have, broad or limited as those rights may be."

Security Agreement

A security interest cannot attach unless an agreement (contract) between the debtor and creditor creates or provides the creditor with a security interest in the debtor's collateral. With certain exceptions (discussed below), the agreement must (1) be authenticated by the debtor and (2) contain a reasonable description of the collateral. In addition, if the collateral is timber to be cut, the agreement must contain a reasonable description of the land concerned. A description of personal or real property is sufficient if it reasonably identifies what is described. A description of personal property may identify the collateral by specific listing, category, or in most cases, a type of collateral defined in the Code (e.g., inventory or farm equipment). The description, however, may not be a super generic description, such as "all my personal property."

The Code provides the parties with a great deal of freedom to draft the security agreement, although this freedom is limited by good faith, diligence, reasonableness, and care. Moreover, security agreements frequently contain a provision for acceleration at the secured party's option of all payments upon the default in any payment by the debtor, the debtor's bankruptcy or insolvency, or the debtor's failure to meet other requirements of the agreement. Sometimes security agreements require the debtor to furnish additional collateral if the secured party becomes insecure about the prospects of future payments.

Authenticating Record In most instances there must be a record of the security agreement authenticated by the debtor. Authentication can occur in one of two ways. First, the debtor can sign a written security agreement. A writing can include any printing, typewriting, or other intentional reduction to tangible form. To sign includes any symbol executed or adopted by a party with the present intention to authenticate a writing. Second, in recognition of e-commerce and electronic security agreements, Revised Article 9 provides that a debtor can authenticate a security agreement by executing or otherwise adopting a symbol, or by encrypting or similarly processing a record in whole or in part, with the present intent of the authenticating party to adopt or accept the record. As already mentioned, a record means information (1) on a tangible medium or (2) that is stored in an *electronic* or other medium and is retrievable in perceivable form. "Examples of current technologies commercially used to communicate or store information include, but are not limited to, magnetic media, optical discs, digital voice messaging systems, electronic mail, audio tapes, and photographic media, as well as paper. 'Record' is an inclusive term that includes all of these methods. . . ." It does not, however, include any oral or other communication that is not stored or preserved.

Authenticating Record Not Required Under the Code a record of a security agreement is not mandated in some situations. A record of a security agreement is not required when some types of collateral are pledged or in the possession of the secured party pursuant to an agreement. This rule applies to a security interest in negotiable documents, goods, instruments, money, and tangible chattel paper. A pledge is the delivery of personal property to a creditor as security for the payment of a debt. A **pledge** requires that the secured party (the pledgee) and the debtor agree to the pledge of the collateral and that the collateral be *delivered* to the pledgee. Other situations in which a secured party does not need a record authenticated by the debtor include (1) The collateral is a certificated security in registered form that has been delivered to the secured party. (2) The collateral is a deposit account, electronic chattel paper, investment property, or letter-of-credit rights; the secured party has control over the collateral. Control is discussed later.

The following case illustrates how a security interest attaches when an agreement grants, creates, or provides a creditor a security interest in a debtor's collateral.

New West Fruit Corporation v. Coastal Berry Corporation

California Court of Appeal, Sixth District, 1991
1 Cal.App.4th 92, 1 Cal.Rptr.2d 664

FACTS New West Fruit Corporation (New West) and Coastal Berry Corporation are both brokers of fresh strawberries. In the second half of 1984, New West's predecessor, Monc's Consolidated Produce, Inc., loaned money and strawberry plants to a group of strawberry growers known as Cooperativa La Paz (La Paz). In September 1984, Monc's and La Paz signed a "Sales and Marketing Agreement" to allow Monc's the exclusive right to market the strawberries grown by La Paz during the 1984–85 season. The agreement did not mention the advances of money or plants, but did give Monc's a security interest in all crops and proceeds on specified property in the 1984–85 season. The financing statement was properly signed and filed. Monc's closed down in January 1985, and its assets were assigned to New West. In April, New West learned that La Paz had agreed to market its 1985 crop through Coastal Berry. New West immediately arranged a meeting to advise the Coastal Berry officers of its contract with the growers. New West requested that Coastal Berry either pay New West the amounts owed by the growers or allow New West to market the berries to recover the money. Coastal Berry did not respond.

After Coastal Berry began marketing the berries, New West sent letters demanding payment of the proceeds. In August 1985, New West filed suit against Coastal Berry, La Paz, the individual growers, and a berry freezing company that had accepted some of the berries. All the defendants except Coastal Berry settled with New West before trial. An outstanding claim of more than $14,000 remained.

At trial, New West asserted that its security interest was valid and that it had duly notified Coastal Berry both through the financing statement on file and through the letters it had sent to Coastal Berry directly. Coastal Berry claimed that the security agreement was not effective because it did not specifically identify the debt (money and plants) being secured.

DECISION Judgment for New West.

OPINION Capaccioli, J. The rules governing secured transactions are embodied in [Article] 9 of the California Uniform Commercial Code [citation]. These sections apply to any transaction, regardless of its form, which is intended to create a security interest in personal property or fixtures, including goods. (§ 9–102, subd. (1)(a).) "Security interest" is defined by section 1–201, subdivision (37)(a), as "an interest in personal property or fixtures which secures payment or performance of an obligation."

A security interest becomes enforceable against the debtor when three conditions are met: (1) the debtor has signed a security agreement containing a description of the collateral and, when the security interest is in crops, a description of the land concerned; (2) value has been given; and (3) the debtor has rights in the collateral. (§ 9–203.) The filing of a financing statement perfects the security interest, thereby giving notice to and assuring priority over interested third parties. (§ 9–302.)

There is no dispute that the second and third conditions of section 9–203 were met in this case. Our focus is instead on the first requirement, in determining whether the document Matias Rosales signed on behalf of Cooperativa La Paz was a "security agreement." Coastal Berry argues that the Sales and Marketing Agreement was not a valid security agreement because it failed to describe the advances to the growers and their obligation to repay them.

A security agreement is simply defined by section 9–105, subdivision (1)(l), as "an agreement which creates or provides for a security interest." With specified exceptions, a security agreement is "effective according to its terms between the parties, against purchasers of the collateral and against creditors." (§ 9–201.) Section 9–102 does not limit the scope of secured obligations to pledges or loans of money, but can apply to any security interest created by contract. (§ 9–102, subd. (2))

[Article] 9 does not specifically require delineation of the debt owed to the secured party. Instead, the creation of a valid security interest turns on "whether the parties intended the transaction to have effect as a security." (Cal.Code Comm to § 9–102.) * * *

"Briefly stated, under section 9–201 alone the parties to a commercial security agreement can effectively secure the payment or performance of any past, present, or future legally enforceable obligation of the debtor to the creditor, and can do so with any of the debtor's existing or subsequently acquired personal property. Section 9–201 thus generally validates future advance and all obligations clauses against both debtors and third parties. Those agreements not meeting the formalities required by section 9–203 and those agreements running afoul of the common-law policing doctrines are the only commercially important exceptions." [Citations.]

Section 9–204, subdivision (3) further validates grants of security interests where, as in this case, the collateral secures "all obligations" or future advances: "Obligations covered by a security agreement may include future advances or other value whether or not the advances or value are [*sic*] given pursuant to commitment."

These provisions of the Commercial Code make it clear that to be enforceable, a security agreement need not specify the value of the loan or recite the debtor's obligation to repay it. As long as the formalities of section 9–203 have been met, any payment or performance obligation covered by the security agreement may be secured. [Citation.] The pivotal question, therefore, is whether the challenged obligation is covered by the security agreement. This question can be answered only be ascertaining the intent of the parties to the transaction.

* * *

* * * In summary, although the Sales and Marketing Agreement was, in the trial court's words, "not terribly artfully drafted," we agree with the court below that it was adequate to convey the parties' intent to grant Monc's a security interest in the strawberries and the proceeds thereof. Furthermore, when considered together with the circumstances of its execution—including the financing statement, the past relationship between Monc's and the growers, and general practice in the strawberry production industry—this document should be read to encompass the growers' obligation to repay loans made by Monc's to assist them in financing production of their strawberry crop.

INTERPRETATION A security interest must (1) be in writing, unless the secured party has possession of the collateral; (2) be signed by the debtor; and (3) contain a reasonable description of the collateral.

ETHICAL QUESTION Did the court fairly decide this case? Explain.

CRITICAL THINKING QUESTION What should the law require a security agreement to contain? Explain.

Consumer Goods Federal regulation prohibits a credit seller or lender from obtaining a consumer's grant of a nonpossessory security interest in household goods. This rule does not apply to purchase money security interests or to pledges. Rather, it prevents a lender or seller from obtaining a nonpurchase money security interest covering the consumer's household goods, which are defined to include clothing, furniture, appliances, kitchenware, personal effects, wedding rings, one radio, and one television. (These hard-to-sell items are also referred to as "junk" collateral.) The definition of household goods specifically excludes works of art, other electronic entertainment equipment, antiques, and jewelry.

After-Acquired Property "[A] security agreement may create or provide for a security interest in after-acquired collateral." **After-acquired property** is property that the debtor presently does not own or have rights to but may acquire at some time. For example, an after-acquired property clause in a security agreement may include all present and subsequently acquired inventory, accounts, or equipment of the debtor. This clause would provide the secured party with a valid security interest not only in the typewriter, desk, and file cabinet that the debtor currently owns, but also in a personal computer she purchases later. Article 9 therefore accepts the concept of a "continuing general lien," or a *floating lien*, though the Code limits the operation of an after-acquired property clause against consumers by providing that no such interest can be claimed as additional security in consumer goods, except accessions, if the goods are acquired more than ten days after the secured party gives value.

Future Advances The obligations covered by a security agreement may include **future advances**. Frequently, a debtor obtains a line of credit from a creditor for advances to be made at some later time. For instance, a manufacturer may provide a retailer with a $60,000 line of credit, only $20,000 of which the retailer initially uses. Nevertheless, the manufacturer and the retailer may enter a security agreement granting to the manufacturer a security interest in the retailer's inventory that covers not only the initial $20,000 advance but also any future advances.

CPA PERFECTION

To be effective against third parties who assert competing interests in the collateral (including other creditors of the debtor, the debtor's trustee in bankruptcy, and transferees of the debtor), the security interest must be perfected. **Perfection** of a security interest occurs when it has attached *and* when all the applicable steps required for perfection have been satisfied. If these steps precede attachment, the security interest is perfected at the time it attaches. Once a security interest becomes perfected, it "may still be or become subordinate to other interests . . . [h]owever, in general, after perfection the secured party is protected against creditors and transferees of the debtor and, in particular, against any representative of creditors in insolvency proceedings instituted by or against the debtor." Thus, in most instances a perfected secured party will prevail over a subsequent perfected security interest, a subsequent lien creditor or a representative or creditors (e.g., a trustee in bankruptcy), and subsequent buyers of the collateral.

Depending on the type of collateral, a security interest may be perfected:

1. by the secured party filing a financing statement in the designated public office;
2. by the secured party taking or retaining possession of the collateral;
3. automatically, on the attachment of the security interest;
4. temporarily, for a period specified by the Code; or
5. by the secured party taking control of the collateral.

A security interest or agricultural lien is perfected continuously if it is originally perfected by one method and is later perfected by another if there is no intermediate period when it was unperfected.

Many states have adopted certificate of title statutes for automobiles, trailers, mobile homes, boats, and farm tractors. A **certificate of title** is an official representation of ownership. In these states, Article 9's filing requirements do not apply to perfecting a security interest in such collateral except when the collateral is inventory held by a dealer for sale. See the Concept Review on page 782 for an overview of the requisites for attachment and perfection.

> **Practical Advice**
>
> As a creditor, make sure that you properly perfect any security interest that you acquire.

FILING A FINANCING STATEMENT

Filing a financing statement is the most common method of perfecting a security interest under Article 9. Filing is *required* to perfect a security interest in general intangibles and accounts except for assignments of isolated accounts. Filing *may* be used to perfect a security interest in any other kind of collateral, with the general *exception* of deposit accounts, letter-of-credit rights, and money. A financing statement may be filed before or after the security interest attaches. The form of the **financing statement**, which is filed to give public notice of the security interest, may vary from state to state.

What to File The Revised Act continues to adopt a system of "notice filing": it indicates merely that a person may have a security interest in the collateral. It also authorizes and encourages filing financing statements electronically. Though it need not be highly detailed, the financing statement must include the name of the debtor, the name of the secured party or a representative of the secured party, and an indication of the collateral covered by the financing statement. If the financing statement substantially complies with these requirements, minor errors that do not seriously mislead will not render the financing statement ineffective. Significantly, the Revised Act no longer requires the debtor's signature on the financing statement in order to facilitate ***paperless or electronic*** filing. Since a signature is not required, the Revised Act attempts to deter unauthorized filings by imposing statutory damages of $500 in addition to damages for any loss caused.

Financing statements are indexed under the debtor's name so it is particularly important that the financing statement provide the debtor's name. The Code provides rules for what names must appear for registered organizations (such as corporations, limited partnerships, and limited liability companies), trusts, and other organizations. If the organization does not have a name, the names of the partners, members, associates or other persons comprising the debtor are the names used. A financing statement that includes only the trade name is insufficient. A financing statement that does not comply with these requirements is considered to be seriously misleading.

The description of the collateral is sufficient if it meets the requirements for a security agreement discussed above or it indicates that the financing statement covers all assets or all personal property. Thus, the use of super generic descriptions is permitted in financing statements but is *not* permitted in security agreements. In ***real-property-related filings*** (collateral involving fixtures, timber to be cut, or minerals to be extracted), a description of the real property must be included sufficient to reasonably identify the real property.

Figure 38-2 shows a sample financing statement.

Duration of Filing A financing statement is generally effective for five years from the date of filing. A ***continuation statement*** filed by the secured party within six months prior to expiration will extend the effectiveness of the filing for another five years. If the financing statement lapses, the security interest is no longer perfected unless it is perfected by another method.

In many states, security interests in motor vehicles and other specified collateral must be perfected by making a notation on the certificate of title rather than by filing a financing statement. Nevertheless, as previously indicated, certificate of title laws do not apply if a dealer holds the collateral as inventory for sale.

Place of Filing Except for real-estate-related collateral, financing statements must be filed in a central location designated by the state. With respect to real-estate-related collateral, the financing statement is to be filed in the office designated for the filing or recording of mortgages on the related real property, which is usually local. If the debtor is an individual, the financing statement is to be filed in the state of the individual's principal residence; for a registered organization, the place of filing is the state where the debtor is organized.

Subsequent Change of Debtor's Location After a secured party has properly filed a financing statement, the debtor may change the place of his residence or business or the location or use of the collateral and thus render the information in the filing incorrect. A change in the use of the collateral or a move within the state (intrastate) does not impair the effectiveness of the original filing. If the debtor moves to another state after the initial filing, the security interest remains perfected until the earliest of (a) the time the security interest would have terminated in the state in which perfection occurred; (b) four months after the debtor moved to the new state; or (3) the expiration of one year after the debtor transfers the collateral to a person in another state who becomes the debtor.

POSSESSION

Possession by the secured party perfects a security interest in goods (e.g., those in the possession of pawnbrokers), instruments, money, negotiable documents, or tangible chattel paper. Moreover, a secured party may perfect a security interest in a certificated security by taking delivery of it. Possession is *not* available, however, as a means of perfecting a security interest in accounts, commercial tort claims, deposit accounts, other types of investment property, letter-of-credit rights, or oil, gas, and other minerals before extraction.

A pledge, which is a possessory security interest, is the delivery of personal property to a creditor or to a third party acting as an agent or bailee for the creditor as security for the payment of a debt. No pledge occurs where the debtor retains possession of the collateral. In making a pledge, the debtor is not legally required to sign a written security agreement; an oral agreement granting the secured party a security interest is sufficient. In any situation not involving a pledge, however, the Code requires an authenticated record of the security agreement.

One type of pledge is the **field warehouse**. This common arrangement for financing inventory allows the debtor access to the pledged goods and provides the secured party with control over the pledged property at the same time. In this arrangement, a professional warehouseman generally establishes a warehouse on the debtor's premises—usually by enclosing a portion of those premises and posting appropriate signs—to store the debtor's unsold inventory. The warehouseman then typically issues nonnegotiable receipts for the goods to the secured party, who may then authorize the warehouseman

Figure 38-2 *Sample Financing Statement*

UCC FINANCING STATEMENT

FOLLOW INSTRUCTIONS (front and back) CAREFULLY

A. NAME & PHONE OF CONTACT AT FILER [optional]

B. SEND ACKNOWLEDGMENT TO: (Name and Address)

THE ABOVE SPACE IS FOR FILING OFFICE USE ONLY

1. DEBTOR'S EXACT FULL LEGAL NAME - insert only one debtor name (1a or 1b) - do not abbreviate or combine names

1a. ORGANIZATION'S NAME			
OR 1b. INDIVIDUAL'S LAST NAME	FIRST NAME	MIDDLE NAME	SUFFIX
1c. MAILING ADDRESS	CITY	STATE / POSTAL CODE	COUNTRY
1d. TAX ID #: SSN OR EIN / ADD'L INFO RE ORGANIZATION DEBTOR / 1e. TYPE OF ORGANIZATION	1f. JURISDICTION OF ORGANIZATION	1g. ORGANIZATIONAL ID #, if any	NONE

2. ADDITIONAL DEBTOR'S EXACT FULL LEGAL NAME - insert only one debtor name (2a or 2b) - do not abbreviate or combine names

2a. ORGANIZATION'S NAME			
OR 2b. INDIVIDUAL'S LAST NAME	FIRST NAME	MIDDLE NAME	SUFFIX
2c. MAILING ADDRESS	CITY	STATE / POSTAL CODE	COUNTRY
2d. TAX ID #: SSN OR EIN / ADD'L INFO RE ORGANIZATION DEBTOR / 2e. TYPE OF ORGANIZATION	2f. JURISDICTION OF ORGANIZATION	2g. ORGANIZATIONAL ID #, if any	NONE

3. SECURED PARTY'S NAME (or NAME of TOTAL ASSIGNEE of ASSIGNOR S/P) - insert only one secured party name (3a or 3b)

3a. ORGANIZATION'S NAME			
OR 3b. INDIVIDUAL'S LAST NAME	FIRST NAME	MIDDLE NAME	SUFFIX
3c. MAILING ADDRESS	CITY	STATE / POSTAL CODE	COUNTRY

4. This FINANCING STATEMENT covers the following collateral:

5. ALTERNATIVE DESIGNATION [if applicable]: ☐ LESSEE/LESSOR ☐ CONSIGNEE/CONSIGNOR ☐ BAILEE/BAILOR ☐ SELLER/BUYER ☐ AG. LIEN ☐ NON-UCC FILING

6. ☐ This FINANCING STATEMENT is to be filed [for record] (or recorded) in the REAL ESTATE RECORDS. Attach Addendum [if applicable]

7. Check to REQUEST SEARCH REPORT(S) on Debtor(s) [ADDITIONAL FEE] [optional] ☐ All Debtors ☐ Debtor 1 ☐ Debtor 2

8. OPTIONAL FILER REFERENCE DATA

FILING OFFICE COPY — NATIONAL UCC FINANCING STATEMENT (FORM UCC1) (REV. 07/29/98)

CONCEPT REVIEW

Requisites for Enforceability of Security Interests

Attachment	Perfection
A. Value given by secured party	A. Secured party files a financing statement
B. Debtor has rights in collateral	B. Secured party takes possession
C. Agreement	C. Automatically
1. record authenticated by debtor (except for most pledges)	D. Temporarily, or
2. providing a security interest	E. Control
3. in described collateral	

to release a portion of the goods to the debtor as the goods are sold, at a specified quantity per week, or at any rate on which the parties agree. Thus, the secured party legally possesses the goods while allowing the debtor easy access to her inventory.

Practical Advice

Field warehousing is a useful way for a creditor to perfect her security interest while providing the debtor with easy access to his inventory.

AUTOMATIC PERFECTION

In some situations, a security interest is automatically perfected on attachment. The most important situation to which **automatic perfection** applies is a purchase money security interest in consumer goods. A partial or isolated assignment of accounts that transfers a less-than-significant portion of the assignor's outstanding accounts is also automatically perfected.

A purchase money security interest in consumer goods, with the exception of motor vehicles, is perfected automatically upon attachment; filing a financing statement is unnecessary. For example, Doris purchases a refrigerator from Carol on credit for Doris's personal, family, or household use. Doris takes possession of the refrigerator and then grants Carol a security interest in the refrigerator pursuant to a written security agreement. Upon Doris's granting Carol the security interest, Carol's security interest attaches and is automatically perfected. The same would be true if Doris purchased the refrigerator for cash but borrowed the money from Logan, to whom Doris granted a security interest in the refrigerator pursuant to a written security agreement. Logan's security interest would attach and would be automatically perfected when she received the security agreement from Doris. Nevertheless, because an automatically perfected PMSI in consumer goods protects the secured party less fully than a filed PMSI, secured parties frequently file a financing statement rather than rely solely on automatic perfection.

Kimbrell's of Sanford, Inc. v. KPS, Inc.

Court of Appeals of North Carolina, 1994
113 N.C.App. 830, 440 S.E.2d 329

FACTS The defendant, Burns, purchased a VCR at Kimbrell's of Sanford. At the time of sale, Burns signed a purchase money security agreement with Kimbrell's. However, Kimbrell's did not file a financing statement to perfect its purchase money security interest. Burns immediately pawned the VCR to KPS, Inc. After Burns defaulted on the security agreement, Kimbrell's filed suit in small claims court to recover the VCR. The magistrate entered judgment denying recovery. On appeal to the district court, the judgment was affirmed. Kimbrell's appeals.

DECISION Judgment reversed.

OPINION McCrodden, J. Plaintiff offers one argument raising the issue of whether it was entitled to recover from defendant pawn shop a VCR plaintiff had sold to defendant Burns under a purchase money security agreement. * * *

Plaintiff argues that the judgment denying it recovery of the VCR contravened Article 9 of the Uniform Commercial Code, [citation.] We agree.

At the time defendant Burns purchased the VCR from plaintiff, he signed a purchase money security agreement, thereby granting plaintiff a purchase money security interest in the VCR. [UCC] § 9–107. Since a VCR is a consumer good, [UCC] § 9–109(1), plaintiff did not have to file a financing statement in order to perfect its purchase money security interest in the VCR. [UCC] § 9–302(1)(d). Defendant Burns failed to make any further payments for the VCR and defaulted on the security agreement. Therefore, plaintiff was entitled to recover possession of the VCR when it filed its action in small claims court. [UCC] §§ 9–501, 9–503. Accordingly, we hold that the trial court erred in dismissing plaintiff's claim to recover possession of the VCR.

INTERPRETATION A purchase money security interest in consumer goods, with the exception of motor vehicles, is perfected automatically on attachment.

CRITICAL THINKING QUESTION When, if ever, should the law make a security interest automatically perfected? Explain.

TEMPORARY PERFECTION

Security interests in certain types of collateral are automatically, but only temporarily, perfected. The Code provides that a security interest in a certificated security, negotiable document, or instrument is perfected upon attachment for a period of twenty days. This provision, however, is applicable only to the extent that the security interest arises for new value given under an authenticated security agreement. A perfected security interest in a certificated security or an instrument also remains perfected for twenty days if the secured party delivers the security certificate or instrument to the debtor for the purpose of (a) sale or exchange or (b) presentation, collection, enforcement, renewal, or registration of transfer. After the temporary period expires, the security interest becomes unperfected unless it is perfected by other means.

PERFECTION BY CONTROL

A security interest in investment property, deposit accounts (not including consumer deposit accounts), electronic chattel paper, and letter-of-credit rights may be perfected by control of the collateral. A security interest in deposit accounts and letter-of-credit rights may be perfected *only* by control. What constitutes control varies with the type of collateral involved. For example, control of a commercial deposit account (e.g., a checking account) is acquired if (1) the secured party is the bank with which the checking account is maintained or (2) the debtor, secured party, and bank agree in an authenticated record that the bank will comply with the secured party's instructions. The rules for control for other collateral are somewhat different as provided in the following sections: investment property, electronic chattel paper, and letter-of-credit rights.

CPA PRIORITIES AMONG COMPETING INTERESTS

As previously noted, a security interest must be perfected to be most effective against the debtor's other creditors, her trustee in bankruptcy, and her transferees. Nonetheless, perfection of a security interest does *not* provide the secured party with a **priority** over *all* third parties with an interest in the collateral. On the other hand, even an unperfected but attached security interest has priority over a limited number of third parties and is enforceable against the debtor. Article 9 establishes a complex set of rules that determine the relative priorities among these parties.

AGAINST UNSECURED CREDITORS

Once a security interest *attaches*, it has priority over claims of other creditors who do not have a security interest or a lien. This priority does not depend upon perfection. If a security interest does not attach, the creditor is merely an unsecured or general creditor of the debtor.

AGAINST OTHER SECURED CREDITORS

The rights of a secured creditor against other secured creditors depend upon the security interests perfected, when they are perfected, and the type of collateral. Notwithstanding the rules of priority, a secured party entitled to priority may subordinate her interest to that of another secured creditor. The parties may do this by agreement, and nothing need be filed.

Perfected Versus Unperfected A creditor with a perfected security interest or agricultural lien has superior rights in the collateral than a creditor with an unperfected

CONCEPT REVIEW

Methods of Perfecting Security Interests

	Applicable Method of Perfection				
Collateral	Filing	Possession	Automatic	Temporary (for 20 days)	Control
Goods					
Consumer goods	•	•	PMSI		
Farm products	•	•			
Inventory	•	•			
Equipment	•	•			
Fixtures	•	•			
Indispensable Paper					
Chattel paper	•	Tangible			Electronic
Instruments	•	•		•	
Documents	Negotiable	Negotiable		Negotiable	
Investment property	•	Certificated		Certificated	•
Intangibles					
Accounts	•		Isolated Assignment		
General intangibles	•				
Deposit Accounts					Commercial
Letter-of-Credit Accounts					•
Money		•			

security interest or agricultural lien, whether or not the unperfected security interest has attached.

Perfected Versus Perfected Two parties each having a perfected security interest or agricultural lien rank according to priority in *time of filing* or *perfection*. This general rule is stated in the Code, which provides:

> Conflicting perfected security interests and agricultural liens rank according to priority in time of filing or perfection. Priority dates from the earlier of the time a filing covering the collateral is first made or the security interest or agricultural lien is first perfected, if there is no period thereafter when there is neither filing nor perfection.

This rule favors filing, because it can occur prior to attachment and thus grant priority from a time that may precede perfection. Generally, the original time for filing or perfection of a security interest in collateral is also the time of filing or perfection for a security interest in proceeds from that collateral.

Practical Advice

If perfecting by filing, file your financing statement as soon as possible.

Practical Advice

Before accepting personal property as collateral, check the public records to ensure that there are no prior filings against that property.

For example, Debter Store and Leynder Bank enter into a loan agreement (assume there is no binding commitment to extend credit) under the terms of which Leynder agrees to lend $5,000 on the security of Debter's existing store equipment. A security agreement is executed and a financing statement is filed, but no funds are advanced. One week later, Debter enters into a loan agreement with Reserve Bank, and Reserve agrees to lend $5,000 on the security of the same store equipment. The funds are advanced, a security agreement is executed, and a financing statement is filed. One week later, Leynder Bank advances the agreed sum of $5,000. Debter Store defaults on both loans. Between Leynder Bank and Reserve Bank, Leynder has priority because priority among security interests perfected by filing is determined by the order in which they were filed. Reserve Bank should have checked the financing statements on file. Had it done so, it would have discovered that Leynder Bank claimed a security interest in the equipment. Conversely, after filing its financing statement, with no prior secured party of record, Leynder had no need to check the files before advancing funds to Debter Store in accordance with its loan commitment.

To further illustrate, assume that Marc grants a security interest in a Chagall painting to Miro Bank and that the bank advances funds to Marc in accordance with the loan agreement. A financing statement is filed. Later, Marc wants more money and goes to Brague, an art dealer, who advances funds to Marc upon a pledge of the painting. Marc defaults on both loans. Between Miro and Brague, Miro has priority because its financing statement was filed before Brague's perfection by possession. By checking the financing statement on file, Brague would have discovered that Miro had a prior security interest in the painting.

There are several exceptions to the general rules just discussed:

1. A ***purchase money security interest in noninventory goods*** (except livestock) takes priority over a conflicting security interest if the purchase money security interest is perfected when the debtor receives possession of the collateral *or* within twenty days of receiving possession. Thus, the secured party has a twenty-day grace period in which to perfect.

   For example, Dawkins Manufacturing Co. enters into a loan contract with Larkin Bank, which loans money to Dawkins on the security (as provided in the security agreement) of Dawkins's existing and future equipment and files a financing statement stating that the collateral is "all equipment presently owned and subsequently acquired" by Dawkins. At a later date, Dawkins buys new equipment from Parker Supply Co., paying 25 percent of the purchase price, with Parker retaining a security interest (as provided in the security agreement) in the equipment to secure the remaining balance. If Parker files a financing statement within ten days of Dawkins's obtaining possession of the equipment, Parker's purchase money security interest in the new equipment purchased from Parker has priority over Larkin's interest. If, however, Parker files one day beyond the statutory grace period, Parker's interest is subordinate to Larkin's.
2. A ***purchase money security interest in inventory*** has priority over earlier-filed security interests in inventory if the following requirements are met. The purchase money security holder must (a) perfect his interest in the inventory at the time the debtor receives the inventory; (b) send an authenticated notification to the holder of a conflicting security interest; (c) the holder of the conflicting security interest receives the notification within five years before the debtor receives possession of the inventory; and (d) the notification states that person sending the notification has or will acquire a PMSI in inventory of the debtor and describes the inventory.

   For example, Dodger Store and Lyons Bank enter into a loan agreement in which Lyons agrees to finance Dodger's entire inventory of stoves, refrigerators, and other kitchen appliances. A security agreement is executed and a financing statement is filed, and Lyons advances funds to Dodger. Subsequently, Dodger enters into an agreement under which Rodger Stove Co. will supply Dodger with stoves, retaining a purchase money security interest in this inventory. Rodger will have priority as to the inventory it supplies to Dodger provided that Rodger files a financing statement by the time Dodger receives the goods and notifies Lyons that it is going to engage in this purchase money financing of the described stoves. If Rodger fails either to give the required notice or to file timely a financing statement, Lyons will have priority over Rodger as to the stoves Rodger supplies to Dodger. As noted, the Code adopts a system of notice filing, and secured parties who fail to check the financing statements on file proceed at their peril.
3. A ***security interest perfected by control*** in deposit accounts, letter-of-credit rights, or investment property has priority over a conflicting perfected security interest held by a secured party who does not have control. If both conflicting security interests are perfected by control, they rank according to priority in time of obtaining control.

Unperfected Versus Unperfected If neither security interest or agricultural lien is perfected, then the first to attach has priority. If neither attaches, both of the creditors are general, unsecured creditors.

AGAINST BUYERS

A security interest or agricultural lien continues even in collateral that is sold, leased, licensed, exchanged, or otherwise disposed of unless the secured party authorizes the sale. Thus, following a sale, lease, license, exchange, or other disposition of collateral, a secured party who did not authorize the transaction does not have to file a new financing statement to continue her perfected interest. The security interest also attaches to any identifiable proceeds from the sale, including proceeds in consumer deposit accounts.

In many instances, however, buyers of collateral sold without the secured party's authorization take it free of an

unperfected security interest. A buyer of goods, tangible chattel paper, documents, instruments, or certificated securities who gives value and receives delivery of the collateral without knowledge of the security interest *before* it is perfected takes free of the security interest. Similarly, a buyer of accounts, electronic chattel paper, general intangibles, or investment property other than certificated securities takes free of a security interest if the buyer gives value without knowledge of the security interest and *before* it is perfected. Thus, with respect to all of these types of collateral, an unperfected security interest prevails over a buyer who does *not* give value or has *knowledge* of the security interest.

In addition, in some instances, purchasers take the collateral free of a ***perfected*** security interest. The most significant of these instances are discussed here.

Buyers in the Ordinary Course of Business **A buyer in the ordinary course of business** takes collateral (other than farm products) free of any security interest created by ***the buyer's*** seller, even if the security interest is perfected and the buyer *knows* of its existence. A buyer in the ordinary course of business is a person who, without knowledge that a sale will violate a security interest of a third party, buys in good faith from a person in the business of selling goods of that kind. Thus, this rule applies primarily to purchasers of inventory. For example, a consumer who purchases a sofa from a furniture dealer and the dealer who purchases the sofa from another dealer are both buyers in the ordinary course of business. On the other hand, a person who purchases a sofa from a dentist who used the sofa in his waiting room or from an individual who used the sofa in his home is not a buyer in the ordinary course of business.

To illustrate further, a person who in the ordinary course of business buys an automobile from an automobile dealership will take free and clear of a security interest created by the dealer from whom she purchased the car. That same buyer in the ordinary course of business will not, however, take clear of a security interest created by any person who owned the automobile prior to the dealer.

Buyers of Farm Products Buyers in the ordinary course of business of farm products, although not protected by the Code, may be protected by the Federal Food Security Act. This Act defines a buyer in the ordinary course of business as "a person who, in the ordinary course of business, buys farm products from a person engaged in farming operations who is in the business of selling farm products." The Act provides that such a buyer shall take free of most security interests created by the seller, even if the security interest is perfected and the buyer knows of its existence.

Buyers of Consumer Goods In the case of consumer goods, a buyer who buys without knowledge of a security interest, for value, and primarily for personal, family, or household purposes takes the goods free of any purchase money security interest *automatically* perfected but takes the goods subject to a security interest perfected by filing. For example, Ann purchases on credit a refrigerator from Sean for use in her home and grants Sean a security interest in the refrigerator. Sean does not file a financing statement but has a security interest perfected by attachment. Ann subsequently sells the refrigerator to her neighbor, Juwan, for use in his home. Juwan does not know of Sean's security interest and therefore takes the refrigerator free of that interest. If Sean had filed a financing statement, however, his security interest would continue in the collateral, even in Juwan's hands.

Buyers of Other Collateral To the extent provided by UCC Articles 3, 7, and 8, a secured party who has a perfected security interest in a negotiable instrument, a negotiable document of title, or a security has a *subordinate* interest to a purchaser of (1) the instrument who has the rights of a holder in due course, (2) the document of title to whom it has been duly negotiated, or (3) the security who is a protected purchaser. In addition, in certain instances a secured party who has a perfected security interest in chattel paper also may have subordinate rights to a purchaser of such collateral.

AGAINST LIEN CREDITORS

A **lien creditor** is a creditor who has acquired a lien in the property by judicial decree ("attachment garnishment, or the like"), an assignee for the benefit of creditors, a receiver in equity, or a trustee in bankruptcy. (A **trustee in bankruptcy** is a representative of an estate in bankruptcy who is responsible for collecting, liquidating, and distributing the debtor's assets.) Whereas a ***perfected*** security interest or agricultural lien has priority over lien creditors who acquire their liens after perfection, an ***unperfected*** security interest or agricultural lien is subordinate to the rights of one who becomes a lien creditor before (1) its perfection or (2) a financing statement covering the collateral is filed and (a) the debtor has authenticated a properly drawn security agreement, (b) if the collateral is a certificated security, the certificate has been delivered to the secured party, or (c) if the collateral is an uncertificated security, it is in possession of the secured party. If a secured party files with respect to a *purchase money security interest* within twenty days after the debtor receives possession of the collateral, however, the secured party takes priority over the rights of a lien creditor that arise between the time the security interest attaches and the time of filing. Nonetheless, a lien securing claims arising from services or materials furnished in the ordinary course of a person's business with respect to goods (an artisan's or mechanic's lien) has priority over a security interest in the goods unless the lien is created by a statute that expressly provides otherwise.

AGAINST TRUSTEE IN BANKRUPTCY

The Bankruptcy Act empowers a trustee in bankruptcy to invalidate secured claims in certain instances. It also imposes some limitations on the rights of secured parties. This section will examine the power of a trustee in bankruptcy to (a) take priority over an unperfected security interest and (b) avoid preferential transfers.

Priority over Unperfected Security Interest A trustee in bankruptcy may invalidate any security interest that is voidable by a creditor who obtained a judicial lien on the date the bankruptcy petition was filed. Under the Code and the Bankruptcy Act, the trustee, as a hypothetical ***lien creditor***, has priority over a creditor whose security interest was not perfected when the bankruptcy petition was filed. A creditor with a purchase money security interest who files within the statutory grace period of twenty days after the debtor receives the collateral will defeat the trustee, even if the bankruptcy petition is filed before the creditor perfects and after the security interest is created. For example, David borrowed $5,000 from Cynthia on September 1 and gave her a security interest in the equipment he purchased with the borrowed funds. On October 3, before Cynthia perfected her security interest, David filed for bankruptcy. The trustee in bankruptcy can invalidate Cynthia's security interest because it was unperfected when the bankruptcy petition was filed. If, however, David had filed for bankruptcy on September 8 and Cynthia had perfected the security interest within the statutory grace period of twenty days, Cynthia would prevail.

Avoidance of Preferential Transfers The Bankruptcy Act provides that a trustee in bankruptcy may invalidate any transfer of property—including the granting of a security interest—from the debtor, provided that the transfer (1) was to or for the benefit of a creditor; (2) was made on account of an antecedent debt; (3) was made when the debtor was insolvent; (4) was made on the date of or within ninety days before the filing of the bankruptcy petition or, if made to an insider, was made within one year before the date of the filing; and (5) enabled the transferee to receive more than he would have received in bankruptcy. (An insider includes a relative or general partner of a debtor, as well as a partnership in which the debtor is a general partner or a corporation of which the debtor is a director, officer, or person in control.) In determining whether the debtor is insolvent, the Act establishes a rebuttable presumption of insolvency for the ninety days prior to the filing of the bankruptcy petition. To avoid a transfer to an insider that occurred more than one year before bankruptcy, the trustee must prove that the debtor was insolvent when the transfer was made. If a security interest is invalidated as a preferential transfer, the creditor may still make a claim for the unpaid debt, but the creditor's claim is unsecured.

To illustrate the operation of this rule, consider the following. On May 1, Debra bought and received merchandise from Stuart and gave him a security interest in the goods for the unpaid price of $20,000. On June 5, Stuart filed a financing statement. On August 1, Debra filed a petition for bankruptcy. The trustee in bankruptcy may avoid the perfected security interest as a preferential transfer because (1) the transfer of the perfected security interest on June 5 was to benefit a creditor (Stuart); (2) the transfer was on account of an antecedent debt (the $20,000 owed from the sale of the merchandise); (3) the debtor was insolvent at the time (the Act presumes that the debtor is insolvent for the ninety days preceding the date the bankruptcy petition was filed—August 1); (4) the transfer was made within ninety days of bankruptcy (June 5 is less than ninety days before August 1); and (5) the transfer enabled the creditor to receive more than he would have received in bankruptcy (Stuart would have a secured claim on which he would recover more than he would on an unsecured claim).

Nevertheless, not all transfers made within ninety days of bankruptcy are voidable. The Bankruptcy Code makes exceptions for certain prebankruptcy transfers. If the creditor gives the debtor new value that the debtor uses to acquire property in which he grants the creditor a security interest, the resulting purchase money security interest is not voidable if the creditor perfects it within twenty days after the debtor receives possession of the property. For example, if within ninety days of the filing of the petition, the debtor purchases a refrigerator on credit and grants the seller or lender a purchase money security interest in the refrigerator, the transfer of that interest is not voidable if the secured party perfects within twenty days after the debtor receives possession of the property.

CPA DEFAULT

Because the Code does not define or specify what constitutes default, general contract law or the agreement between the parties will determine when a default occurs.

CONCEPT REVIEW

Priorities

Versus	Unsecured Creditor	Creditor with Unperfected Security Interests	Creditor with Perfected Security Interest	Creditor with Perfected Purchase Money Security Interest
Unsecured creditor	=	↑	↑	↑
Creditor with unperfected security interest	←	first to attach	↑	↑
Creditor with perfected purchase money security interest—noninventory	←	←	first to file or perfect	↑ if PMSI perfected within grace period
Creditor with perfected purchase money security interest—inventory	←	←	first to file or perfect	↑ if PMSI gives notice and perfects by time debtor gets possession
Buyer in ordinary course of business	←	←	← if created by immediate seller	←
Consumer buyer of consumer goods	←	←	↑	← if not filed
Lien creditor (including trustee in bankruptcy)	←	←	first in time	first in time but PMSI has grace period
Trustee in bankruptcy—voidable preferences	←	←	↑ if secured party perfects within grace period	↑ if PMSI perfects within grace period

After default, the security agreement and the applicable provisions of the Code govern the rights and remedies of the parties. In general, the secured party may reduce his claim to judgment, foreclose, or otherwise enforce the claim, security interest, or agricultural lien by any available judicial procedure. If the collateral consists of documents, the secured party may proceed against the documents or the goods they cover. These rights and remedies of the creditor are cumulative.

Practical Advice

Provide in your security agreement which events place the debtor in default and what remedies the creditor will have in the event of default.

Unless the debtor has waived his rights in the collateral after default, he has a right of **redemption** (to free the collateral of the security interest by fulfilling all obligations securing the collateral and paying reasonable expenses and attorney's fees) at any time before the secured party has collected the collateral, has disposed of the collateral, has entered a contract to dispose of it, or has discharged the obligation by accepting the collateral.

REPOSSESSION

Unless the parties have agreed otherwise, the secured party may take possession of the collateral on default. If it can be done without a breach of the peace, such taking may occur without judicial process. The Code leaves the term *breach of the peace* for the courts to define. Some states have defined such a breach to require either the use of violence or the threat of violence while others require merely an entry without consent. Most states require permission for entry to a residence or garage. On the other hand, the courts do permit the repossession of motor vehicles from driveways or streets. Some courts, however, do not permit a creditor to repossess if the debtor has orally protested the repossession.

After default, instead of removing the collateral, the secured party may render it unusable and leave it on the debtor's premises until disposing of it. It also may be done without judicial process if accomplished without a breach of peace.

Chrysler Credit Corporation v. Koontz

Appellate Court of Illinois, 1996
214 Ill.Dec. 726, 661 N.E.2d 1171

FACTS Defendant James Koontz agreed to purchase a 1988 Plymouth Sundance from Chrysler Credit Corporation ("Chrysler") in exchange for 60 payments of $185.92. Koontz defaulted in early 1991, and Chrysler notified Koontz that, unless he made the payments, it would repossess the vehicle. Koontz responded by notifying Chrysler that he would make every effort to make up missed payments, that he did not want the car repossessed, and that Chrysler was not to enter his private property to repossess the vehicle. On the night of April 21, 1991, Chrysler sent the M & M Agency to repossess the vehicle.

Koontz, dressed only in his underwear, came outside and yelled, "Don't take it!" The repossessor ignored him and took the car anyway. Koontz did not physically challenge or threaten the repossessor. Chrysler sold the car and filed a complaint to recover the balance remaining on the loan. Koontz defended on the ground that Chrysler breached the peace in repossessing the car and thus was not entitled to a deficiency judgment. The trial court entered judgment for Chrysler, and Koontz appealed.

DECISION Judgment affirmed.

OPINION Maag, J. Koontz raises only a single issue on appeal. He contends that the trial court erred in finding that Chrysler's repossession did not breach the peace because there was evidence that Koontz made an unequivocal oral protest to the repossession of his vehicle at the time of repossession. Koontz argues that when the vehicle was taken despite his protest, "Don't take it," a breach of the peace occurred, citing *Dixon v. Ford Motor Credit Co.* (1979), [citation.] In *Dixon*, the court . . . stated that "[w]hen a creditor repossesses in disregard of the debtor's unequivocal oral protest, the repossession may be found to be in breach of the peace." [Citation.]

Chrysler contends that Koontz's oral protest did not breach the peace because "none of the elements of violence indicated in the decisions cited by the Defendant exists (sic) in this case." Chrysler argues by implication that without an element of violence there can be no breach of the peace. Chrysler also argues that if we find that an oral protest without an element of violence constitutes a breach of the peace, then we would be narrowing the self-help repossession statute to the point that it would be useless to a secured creditor.

We recognize that the self-help repossession statute extends a conditional self-help privilege to secured parties; however, we must apply the statute in a way that reduces the risk to the public associated with extrajudicial conflict resolution. It is apparent that the self-help remedy is efficient for secured creditors and results in reduced costs for both creditors and debtors. Efficiency and reduced litigation costs are desirable. Still, a debtor's private property interests and society's interest in tranquility must also be protected.

Because self-help repossession is statutory, we look to the language of section 9–503 [Revised 9-609] to establish the parameters of the remedy that the statute offers to secured parties who seek to repossess collateral without judicial process. The statute provides in pertinent part: "Unless otherwise agreed a secured party has on default the right to take possession of the collateral. In taking possession a secured party may proceed without judicial process if this can be done without breach of the peace or may proceed by action." [The Revised Act provides "A secured party may proceed [against the collateral] * * * without judicial process, if it proceeds without breach of the peace." Revised 9-609 (b)]. The key to whether a self-help repossession is permissible depends on whether the peace has been or is likely to be breached.

Section 9–503 [Revised 9-609] does not define breach of the peace, and the phrase "breach of the peace" has never had a precise meaning in relation to specific conduct. The phrase has been construed on several occasions. In *Cantwell v. State of Connecticut* (1940), [citation], the [United States Supreme] court stated: "The offense known as breach of the public peace embraces a great variety of conduct destroying or menacing public order and tranquility. It includes not only violent acts but acts and words likely to produce violence in others." * * * The Restatement (Second) of Torts § 116, provides that "[a] breach of the peace is a public offense done by violence, or by one causing or likely to cause an immediate disturbance of public order." Threats and epithets directed at another may or may not constitute a breach of the peace, depending upon the likelihood that a disturbance will follow.

We therefore conclude that the term "breach of the peace" connotes conduct which incites or is likely to incite immediate public turbulence, or which leads to or is likely to lead to an immediate loss of public order and tranquility. Violent conduct is not a necessary element. The probability of violence at the time of or immediately prior to the repossession is sufficient. We now turn to Koontz's contention that Chrysler's repossession and the events at the time of and immediately prior to the repossession breached the peace.

After a thorough examination of the record, we find no abuse of discretion on the part of the trial court in ruling that Chrysler's repossession did not breach the peace. Whether a given act provokes a breach of the peace depends upon the accompanying circumstances of each particular case. In this case, Koontz testified that he only yelled, "Don't take it," and that the repossessor made no verbal or physical response. He also testified that although he was close enough to the repossessor to run over and get into a fight, he elected not to because he was in his underwear.

Furthermore, there was no evidence in the record that Koontz implied violence at the time of or immediately prior to the repossession by holding a weapon, clenching a fist, or even vehemently arguing toe-to-toe with the repossessor so that a reasonable repossessor would understand that violence was likely to ensue if he continued with the vehicle repossession. We think that the evidence, viewed as a whole, could lead a reasonable fact finder to determine that the circumstances of the repossession did not amount to a breach of the peace.

We note that to rule otherwise would be to invite the ridiculous situation whereby a debtor could avoid a deficiency judgment by merely stepping out of his house and yelling once at a nonreponsive repossessor. Such a narrow definition of the conduct necessary to breach the peace would, we think, render the self-help repossession statute useless. Therefore, we reject Koontz's invitation to define "an unequivocal oral protest," without more, as a breach of the peace.

Koontz also argues that Chrysler breached the peace by repossessing the vehicle under circumstances which would constitute a Class C misdemeanor, criminal trespass to real property, * * * Koontz testified that he notified Chrysler prior to the date of the repossession that Chrysler did not have permission to enter onto his real property. Criminal trespass occurs when some person "enters upon the land * * * of another, after receiving, prior to such entry, notice from the owner or occupant that such entry is forbidden * * * ." [Citation.] * * *

This is an issue of first impression in Illinois, so we turn to other jurisdictions for guidance. A review of the law in other jurisdictions reveals that in general, a mere trespass, standing alone, does not automatically constitute a breach of the peace. [Citations.] It is generally held that "simply going upon the private driveway of the debtor and taking possession of secured collateral, without more, does not constitute a breach of the peace." [Citations.]

In making this analysis, certain principles are clear and must be considered. When the collateral is located inside a fence or is otherwise enclosed, the secured creditor's privilege is considerably abridged. [Citation.] The creditor's privilege is most severely restricted when repossession can only be accomplished by the actual breaking or destruction of barriers designed to exclude trespassers. [Citations.] * * *

In this case, Koontz testified that he notified Chrysler prior to the repossession that it was not permitted to enter onto his property. He also testified that he pulled his vehicle into his front yard so that he could see it by the light of the front porch. This testimony was uncontroverted. There was no testimony, however, that Chrysler entered through any barricade or did anything other than simply enter onto the property and drive the car away. Viewing this evidence in the light most favorable to the prevailing party, we believe that Chrysler's entry upon the private real property of Koontz and taking possession of the secured collateral, without more, did not constitute a breach of the peace. Chrysler enjoyed a limited privilege to enter Koontz's property for the sole and exclusive purpose of effecting the repossession. So long as the entry was limited in purpose (repossession), and so long as no gates, barricades, doors, enclosures, buildings, or chains were breached or cut, no breach of the peace occurred by virtue of the entry onto his property.

* * *

INTERPRETATION A secured party may take possession of the collateral on default without judicial process if it can be done without a breach of the peace.

ETHICAL QUESTION Did the court fairly decide this case? Explain.

CRITICAL THINKING QUESTION Why is it important for creditors to have the right to repossess? Explain.

SALE OF COLLATERAL

The secured party may sell, lease, license, or otherwise dispose of any collateral in its existing condition at the time of default or following any commercially reasonable preparation or processing. A secured party's disposition of the collateral after default (1) transfers to a transferee for value all of the debtor's rights in the collateral, (2) discharges the security interest under which the disposition occurred, and (3) discharges any subordinate security interests and liens.

The collateral may be disposed of at *public* sale (auction) or *private* sale, so long as all aspects of the disposition, including its method, manner, time, place, and other terms, are "commercially reasonable." The secured party may buy at a public sale and at a private sale if the collateral is customarily sold in a recognized market or is the subject of widely distributed standard price quotations.

THE LAW AND YOU

State Bar Associations

Florida: http://www.flabar.org/newflabar/consumerservices/General/Consumer.Pam/ ("Applying for Credit", "Debtors' Rights in Florida")

Illinois: http://www.illinoislawyerfinder.com/publicinfo/home.html ("Buying on Time")

Missouri: http://www.mobar.org/pamphlets/broindex.htm (Public information brochures) ("Buying on Time")

North Carolina: http://www.ncbar.org/ ("Buying on Time")

Ohio: http://www.ohiobar.org/conres/pamphlets/ ("Ohio's Credit Laws")

Oregon: http://www.osbar.org/public/legalinfo/bankruptcy.html ("Debtor's Rights"; "Liens")

South Dakota: http://www.sdbar.org/ public/consumers/default.htm ("Credit and Debt Policy")

Texas: http://www.texasbar.com

Utah: http://www.utahbar.org/public/useful_information.html

Washington: http://www.wsba.org/public/default.htm

Wisconsin: http://www.legalexplorer.com/consumer/consumer.asp

State Attorney Generals

California: http://www.dca.ca.gov/r_r/ conspub1.htm ("Credit")

Iowa: http://www.state.ia.us/government/ag/consumer/consumer_tips.html ("Debt Collection")

The collateral, if it is commercially reasonable, may be disposed of by one or more contracts or as a unit or in parcels. The Code favors private sales since they generally garner a higher price for the collateral. The fact that the secured party could have received a greater amount is not of itself sufficient to establish that the sale was not made in a commercially reasonable manner. Unless the collateral is perishable or threatens to decline speedily in value or is of a type customarily sold on a recognized market, the secured party must send a reasonable authenticated notification of disposition to the debtor, any secondary obligor (surety or guarantor) and, except in the case of consumer goods, other parties who have sent an authenticated notice of a claim or any secured party or lienholder who has filed a financing statement at least 10 days before the notification date.

The Code provides that the proceeds from the sale of the collateral are to be applied in the following order:

1. paying the reasonable expenses of retaking and disposing of the collateral,
2. paying the debt owed to the secured party,
3. paying any subordinate interests in the collateral, and
4. paying a secured party that is a consignor.

The debtor is entitled to any *surplus* and is liable for any *deficiency*, except in the case of a sale of accounts, chattel paper, payment intangibles, or promissory notes where he is neither entitled nor liable unless the security agreement so provides. If the goods are consumer goods, the secured party must give the debtor an explanation of how the surplus or deficiency was calculated.

ACCEPTANCE OF COLLATERAL

Acceptance of collateral (strict foreclosure) is a way for a secured party to acquire the debtor's interests without the need for a sale or other disposition. The secured party may, after default and repossession if the debtor consents in a record authenticated after default, keep the collateral in full or partial satisfaction of the obligation. In addition, the secured party may accept the collateral in *full* satisfaction of the obligation if she sends an unconditional proposal to the debtor to accept the collateral in full satisfaction of the obligation and she does not receive a notice of objection authenticated by the debtor within twenty days. If there is an objection, however, the secured party must dispose of the collateral as provided in the Code. Silence is not consent to a *partial* satisfaction of the obligation. The debtor's consent, however, will not permit the secured party to accept the collateral in satisfaction of the obligation if a person holding a junior interest (secured party or lienholder) lodges a proper objection to the proposal.

In the case of *consumer goods*, if the debtor has paid 60 percent or more of the obligation, the secured party who has taken possession of the collateral must dispose of it by sale within ninety days after repossession unless the

Ethical Dilemma

What Price Is "Reasonable" in Terms of Reposession?

FACTS On credit, Jill Carr purchased a $1,000 television set at Ryko Appliance Store. The store's credit policy required Jill to give Ryko a security interest in the television set to secure her payment of the purchase price. Though she did not clearly comprehend the repossession procedures, Jill basically understood the terms; and she signed the credit slip and the security agreement on the reverse side.

Set at $40 per month, Jill's payments to Ryko were to extend for three years. Jill made the first six payments without a problem, but then, beset with large medical bills, she defaulted on the seventh payment. Her payments up to that point had reduced her principal balance by $180. Ryko exercised its option to repossess the set.

Ryko's standard operating procedure was to offer repossessed sets at a special sale, to take the best price offered, and to make arrangements for the defaulting customer to pay any deficiency between the resale price and the balance due on the original selling price. But Marge Glass, the store manager, saw Jill's set and realized that it was just the type her husband wanted. She also knew that if she paid even a minimal price for the set, Ryko would eventually get the rest of the money from Jill. Thus, Marge paid Ryko $100 for the set and the store proceeded to make arrangements to collect the balance from Jill. Marge stated that $100 was the highest price anyone would have offered for the set and that her actions were, therefore, commercially reasonable.

Social, Policy, and Ethical Considerations

1. Is a store responsible for ensuring a customer's understanding of the nature and consequences of a sales transaction? Why? Why not?
2. Did Marge and Ryko act ethically or legally? Explain. In what ways would Jill's full understanding of the repossession process change your answer?
3. What ethical or social implications does Article 9 of the Uniform Commercial Code have in this situation?

debtor and all secondary obligors have agreed in a record authenticated after default to a longer period of time. Additionally, with a consumer debt, the secured party may not accept collateral in *partial* satisfaction of the obligation it secures.

The acceptance of collateral in full or partial satisfaction discharges the obligation to the extent consented to by the debtor, transfers all of the debtor's rights to the secured party, and terminates all subordinate interests in the collateral.

SURETYSHIP

In many business transactions involving the extension of credit, the creditor will require that someone in addition to the debtor promise to fulfill the obligation. This promisor generally is known as a surety. In a contract involving a minor, a surety commonly acts as a party with full contractual capacity who can be held responsible for the obligations arising from the contract. Sureties are often used in addition to security to further reduce the risks involved in the extension of credit and are used instead of security interests when security is unavailable or when the use of a secured transaction is too expensive or inconvenient. Employers frequently use sureties to protect against losses caused by employees' embezzlement, and property owners use sureties to bond the performance of contracts for the construction of commercial buildings. Similarly, statutes commonly require that contracts for work to be done for governmental entities have the added protection of a surety. Premiums for compensated sureties exceed $1 billion annually in the United States.

CPA Nature and Formation

A surety promises to answer for the payment of a debt or the performance of a duty owed to one person (called the ***creditor***) by another (the ***principal debtor***) on the principal debtor's *failure* to make payment or otherwise to perform the obligation. Thus, the suretyship relationship involves three parties—the principal debtor, the creditor, and the surety—and three contractual obligations, as illustrated by Figure 38-3. Two or more persons bound for the same debt of a principal debtor are **cosureties.**

The creditor's rights against the principal debtor are determined by the contract between them. The creditor also may take action on any collateral that the creditor or the surety holds to secure the principal debtor's performance. In addition, the creditor may proceed against the surety if the principal debtor defaults. If the surety is an **absolute surety**, the creditor may hold the surety liable as

Figure 38-3
Suretyship Relationship

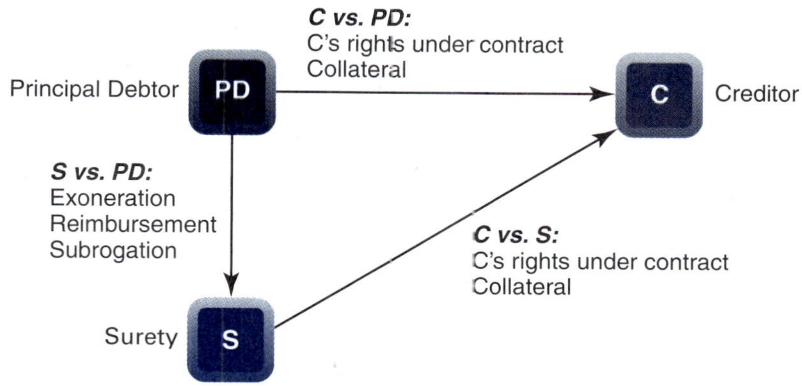

soon as the principal debtor defaults. The creditor need not proceed first against the principal debtor. In contrast, a surety who is a conditional guarantor of collection is liable only when the creditor exhausts his legal remedies against the principal debtor. Thus, a **conditional guarantor of collection** is liable if the creditor first obtains, but is unable to collect, a judgment against the principal debtor.

A surety who is required to pay the creditor is entitled to be exonerated (relieved of liability) and reimbursed by the principal debtor. In addition, the surety is subrogated to (assumes) the rights of the creditor and has a right to contribution from cosureties (see Figure 38-3). The rights of sureties will be discussed more fully later in this chapter.

Although in theory a distinction exists between a surety and a guarantor, the two terms are almost synonymous in common usage. Strictly speaking, a surety is bound with the principal debtor as a primary obligor, usually, although not necessarily, on the same instrument, whereas the guarantor is separately or collaterally bound to pay if the principal debtor does not. For convenience, and because the rights and duties of a surety and a guarantor are almost indistinguishable, the term surety will be used to include both of these terms.

TYPES OF SURETIES

A suretyship arrangement is frequently used by creditors seeking to reduce the risk of default by their debtors. For example, Philco Developers, a closely held corporation, applies to Caldwell Bank, a lending institution, for a loan. After scrutinizing Philco's assets and financial prospects, the lender refuses to extend credit unless Simpson, Philco's sole shareholder, promises to repay the loan if Philco does not. Simpson agrees, and Caldwell Bank makes the loan. Simpson's undertaking is that of a surety. Similarly, Philco Developers wishes to purchase goods on credit from Bird Enterprises, the seller, who agrees to extend credit only if Philco Developers obtains an acceptable surety. Simpson agrees to pay Bird Enterprises for the goods if Philco Developers does not. Simpson is a surety. In each of these examples, the surety's promise gives the creditor recourse for payment against two persons—the principal debtor and the surety—instead of one, thereby reducing the creditor's risk of loss.

Another common suretyship relation arises when an owner of property subject to a mortgage sells the property to a purchaser who ***assumes the mortgage***. Although by assuming the obligation, the purchaser becomes the principal debtor and therefore personally obligated to pay the seller's debt to the lender, the seller nevertheless remains liable to the lender and is a surety on the obligation the purchaser has assumed (see Figure 38-4). However, a purchaser who does *not* assume the mortgage, but simply takes the property subject to the mortgage is *not* personally liable for the mortgage; nor is he a surety for the mortgage obligation. In this case, the purchaser's potential loss is limited to the value of the property, for although the mortgagee creditor may foreclose against the property, she may not hold the purchaser personally liable for the debt.

> **Practical Advice**
>
> If you sell your house and the purchaser assumes the mortgage, recognize that you are a surety and are liable to the lender if the purchaser defaults on the mortgage.

In addition to the more general kinds of sureties, there are numerous specialized kinds of suretyship, the most important of which are (1) fidelity, (2) performance, (3) official, and (4) judicial. A surety undertakes a ***fidelity bond*** to protect an employer against employee dishonesty. ***Performance bonds*** guarantee the performance of the terms and conditions of a contract. These bonds are used frequently in the construction industry to protect an

Figure 38-4
Assumption of Mortgage

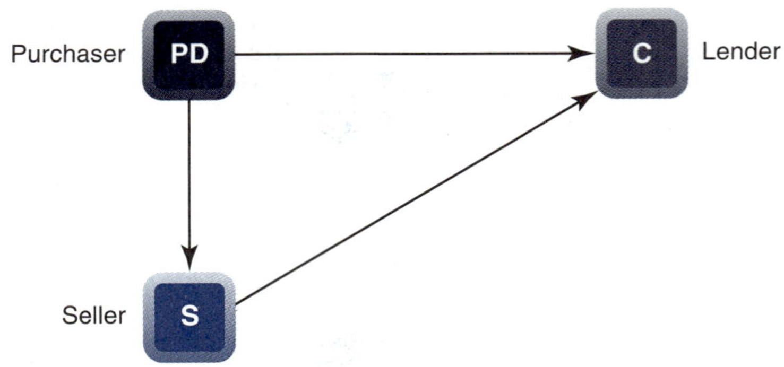

owner from losses that may result from a contractor's failure to perform a building contract. ***Official bonds*** arise from statutes requiring public officers to furnish bonds for the faithful performance of their duties. Such bonds obligate a surety for all losses an officer causes through negligence or through nonperformance of her duties. ***Judicial bonds***, provided on behalf of a party to a judicial proceeding, cover losses caused by delay or by the deprivation of the use of property resulting from the institution of the action. In criminal proceedings, the purpose of a judicial bond, called a bail bond, is to ensure the appearance of the defendant in court.

FORMATION

The suretyship relationship is contractual and must satisfy all of the usual elements of a contract. No particular words are required to constitute a contract of suretyship or guaranty.

As we discussed in Chapter 15, under the ***statute of frauds***, the contractual promise of a surety to the creditor must be in writing to be enforceable. This requirement, which applies only to collateral promises, is subject to the exception known as the *main purpose doctrine*. Under this doctrine, if the leading object, or main purpose, of the promisor (surety) is to obtain an economic benefit that he did not previously enjoy, the promise is *not* within the statute of frauds.

The promise of a surety is *not* binding without ***consideration***. Because the surety generally makes her promise to induce the creditor to confer a benefit on the principal debtor, the consideration that supports the principal debtor's promise usually supports the surety's promise as well. Thus, if Constance lends money to Philip on Sally's promise to act as a surety, Constance's extension of credit is the consideration to support not only Philip's promise to repay the loan but also Sally's suretyship undertaking. However, a surety's promise made *after* the principal debtor's receipt of the creditor's consideration must be supported by new consideration. Accordingly, if Constance has already sold goods on credit to Philip, a subsequent guaranty by Sally will not be binding unless new consideration is given.

> **Practical Advice**
>
> If you seek the additional security of a surety, obtain the surety's promise in writing. If you have already lent money to a debtor and then obtain a surety, new consideration must be given to the surety to make the promise binding.

CPA RIGHTS OF SURETY

A surety whose principal debtor defaults has certain rights against the principal debtor, third parties, and cosureties. These rights include (1) exoneration, (2) reimbursement, (3) subrogation, and (4) contribution. As discussed above, a surety or absolute guarantor has *no* right to compel the creditor to collect from the principal debtor or to take action on collateral provided by the principal debtor. Nor is the creditor required to give the surety notice of the principal debtor's default unless the contract of suretyship provides otherwise. A conditional guarantor of collection, on the other hand, has no liability until the creditor exhausts his legal remedies of collection against the principal debtor.

EXONERATION

The ordinary expectation in a suretyship relation is that the principal debtor will perform the obligation and the surety will not be required to perform. Therefore, the surety has the right to require that her principal debtor pay the creditor when the obligation is due. This right of the surety against the principal debtor, called the right of **exoneration**, is enforceable at equity. If the principal debtor fails to pay the creditor when the debt is due, the surety may obtain a decree ordering the principal debtor to pay the creditor. However, this remedy in no way affects the creditor's right to proceed against the surety.

A surety also has a right of exoneration against his cosureties. When the principal debtor's obligation becomes due, each surety owes every other cosurety the duty to pay her proportionate share of the principal debtor's obligation to the creditor. Accordingly, a surety may bring an action in equity to obtain an order requiring his cosureties to pay their share of the debt.

REIMBURSEMENT

When, on the default of the principal debtor, a surety pays the creditor, the surety has the right of **reimbursement** (repayment) against the principal debtor. This right arises, however, only when the surety actually has made payment and then applies only to the extent of the payment. Thus, a surety who advantageously negotiates a defaulted obligation and settles it at a compromise figure less than the original sum may recover from the principal debtor only the sum the surety actually paid, not the sum before negotiation.

SUBROGATION

On payment of the principal debtor's *entire* obligation, the surety "steps into the shoes" of the creditor. Called **subrogation**, this confers on the surety all the rights the creditor has against or through the principal debtor. These include the creditor's rights

1. against the principal debtor, including the creditor's priorities in a bankruptcy proceeding;
2. in security of the principal debtor;
3. against third parties such as comakers, who also are obligated on the principal debtor's obligation; and
4. against cosureties.

CONTRIBUTION

Up to the amount of each surety's undertaking, cosureties are *jointly* and *severally* liable for the principal debtor's default. The creditor may proceed against any or all of the cosureties and collect from any of them the amount that that surety has agreed to guarantee, up to and including the entire amount of the principal debtor's obligation.

A surety who pays her principal debtor's obligation may require the cosureties to pay to her their proportionate shares of the obligation she paid. This right of **contribution** arises when a surety has paid more than her proportionate share of a debt, even though the cosureties originally were unaware of each other or were bound on separate instruments. They need be sureties only for the same principal debtor and the same obligation. The contractual agreement among the cosureties determines the right and extent of contribution for each. If no such agreement exists, sureties obligated for equal amounts share equally; when they are obligated for varying amounts, the proportion of the debt that each surety must contribute is determined by proration according to each surety's undertaking. For example, if X, Y, and Z are cosureties for PD to C in the amounts of $5,000, $10,000, and $15,000, respectively, which totals $30,000, then X's share of the total is one sixth ($5,000/$30,000), Y's share is one third ($10,000/$30,000), and Z's share is one half ($15,000/$30,000).

CPA DEFENSES OF SURETY AND PRINCIPAL DEBTOR

The obligations the principal debtor and the surety owe to the creditor arise out of contracts. Accordingly, the usual contractual defenses apply, such as those that result from (1) the nonexistence of the principal debtor's obligation, (2) a discharge of the principal debtor's obligation, (3) a modification of the principal debtor's contract, or (4) a variation of the surety's risk. Some of these defenses are available only to the principal debtor, some only to the surety, and others to both parties (see Figure 38-5).

PERSONAL DEFENSES OF PRINCIPAL DEBTOR

The defenses available *only* to a principal debtor are known as the **personal defenses of the principal debtor**. For example, ***incapacity*** due to infancy or mental incompetency may serve as a defense for the principal debtor but *not* for the surety. If, however, the principal debtor disaffirms the contract *and* returns the consideration he received from the creditor, the surety is discharged from his liability. A discharge of the principal debtor's obligation in bankruptcy, by comparison, does not discharge the surety's liability to the creditor on that obligation. In addition, the surety may not use as a setoff any claim that the principal debtor has against the creditor.

PERSONAL DEFENSES OF SURETY

Those defenses that only the surety may assert are called **personal defenses of the surety**. The surety may use, as a defense, his own ***incapacity***, noncompliance with the ***statute of frauds***, or the absence of mutual assent or consideration to support his obligation. ***Fraud*** or ***duress*** practiced by the creditor on the surety is also a defense.

Figure 38-5 *Defenses of Surety and Principal Debtor*

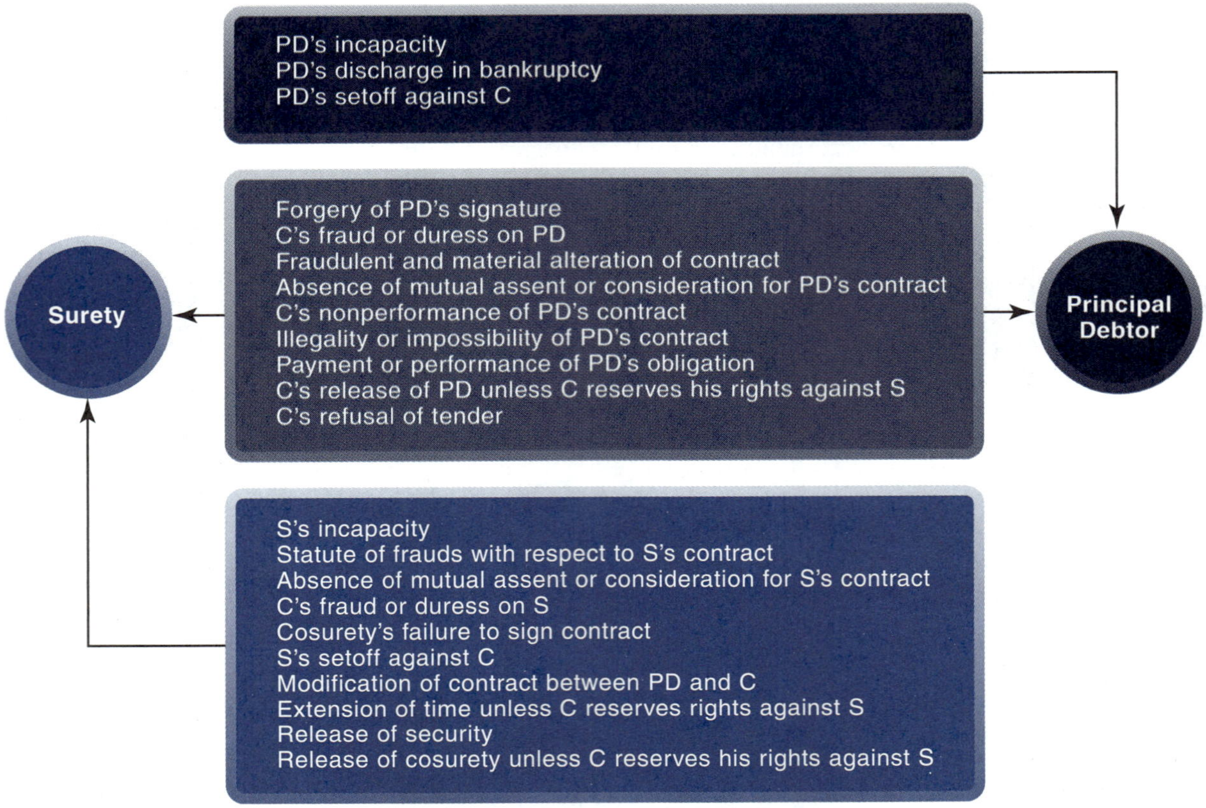

Although, as a general rule, the creditor's nondisclosure of material facts to the surety is not fraud, there are two important exceptions. If a prospective surety requests information, the creditor must disclose it; the concealment of material facts will constitute fraud. Second, a creditor who knows, or who should know, that a surety is being deceived is under a duty to disclose this information; nondisclosure is considered fraud upon the surety. Fraud on the part of the principal debtor may *not* be asserted against the creditor if the creditor is unaware of such fraud. Similarly, duress exerted by the principal debtor on the surety is not a defense against the creditor.

American Manufacturing Mutual Insurance Company v. Tison Hog Market, Inc.

United States Court of Appeals, Eleventh Circuit., 1999

182 F.3d 1284, *cert. denied*, 531 U.S. 819, 121 S.Ct. 59, 148 L.Ed.2d 26 (2000)

http://www.law.emory.edu/11circuit/aug99/98-8506.man.html

FACTS Every livestock dealer must execute and maintain a reasonable bond to secure the performance of its obligations. Thurston Paulk, d/b/a Paulk Livestock Company ("Paulk Livestock"), and Coffee County Stockyard, Incorporated ("Coffee County Livestock"), both livestock dealers, applied to plaintiff American Manufacturing Mutual Insurance Company ("American") to serve as a surety and issue bonds for them to meet their legal requirements. The applications for both bonds contained agreements to indemnify American for any losses that it might incur as a result of their issuance. The principal *debtor* on the first bond was

Thurston Paulk, d/b/a Paulk Livestock. The application was signed by Thurston Paulk in his role as the sole proprietor of Paulk Livestock. The indemnification agreement contained the purported signatures of Thurston Paulk and Betty Paulk. The principal *debtor* on the second bond was Coffee County Livestock. This application contained the signature of Thurston Paulk in his role as president of Coffee County Livestock and contained the purported signatures of Thurston Paulk, Betty Paulk, and Ashley Paulk.

After the bonds were issued, Paulk Livestock and Coffee County Livestock purchased numerous hogs from defendants Tison Hog Market, Inc.; Gainesville Livestock Market, Inc.; Townsend Livestock Market; South Carolina Farm Bureau Marketing Association; and Georgia Farm Bureau Marketing Association, Inc. **(http://www.gfb.org)**. When the defendant hog sellers did not receive payment for the hogs, they made claims against American on the surety bonds for the purchase money that they were owed. American conducted an investigation and learned that the bonds' indemnification agreements contained forged signatures of Ashley Paulk and Betty Paulk. American claimed that it would not have issued the bonds had it known that Betty and Ashley Paulk had not agreed to indemnify it, and it declared the bonds rescinded and returned all the premiums.

American then brought an action seeking a declaratory judgment relieving it from liability to the defendants on the ground that the bonds were void under Georgia insurance law due to the fraudulent and material misrepresentations of the bonds' principals. American argued that the principals had forged the signatures of Betty and Ashley Paulk on the indemnification agreements. The district court granted American's motion for summary judgment.

DECISION Summary judgment vacated and remanded for trial.

OPINION Cox, J. The ultimate issue presented by this appeal is whether a surety in Georgia is liable on its bond to creditors when the principal fraudulently induces the surety to issue the bond. The defendants argue that American is still liable on the bonds under general surety law because fraud committed by a principal alone in inducing a surety to issue a surety bond does not release the surety from liability. * * *

* * *

It is well established under the common law of suretyship that "fraud or misrepresentation practiced by the principal alone on the surety, without any knowledge or participation on the part of the creditor or obligee, in inducing the surety to enter into the suretyship contract will not affect the liability of the surety." [Citations.] From a practical standpoint, this common law treatment of a principal's fraud is the only one that makes sense. A creditor does business with a principal in reliance upon the existence of a bond. The bond provides security for the creditor because normally the creditor would have no way of knowing whether the principal is insolvent or otherwise an unreliable party with which to engage in business. [Citation.] If the creditor's ability to recover on a bond was dependent on the accuracy of the principal's representations to the surety, then the value of the bond to the creditor would be greatly lessened because the creditor would have no way of knowing what representations were made in the procurement of the bond. More importantly for the case at bar, this common law approach * * * enables a livestock seller to deal freely with livestock dealers knowing that the required bond will protect them in the event of a default even if the principal hid facts from the surety when obtaining the bond.

* * *

Instead of applying * * * insurance law, however, the district court should have applied Georgia surety law. The surety bonds in this case are surety contracts that are not governed exclusively by the insurance law of Georgia. * * *

The Georgia Code contains an entirely separate title that applies to suretyship contracts. [Citation.] The chapter defines a contract of suretyship as one "whereby a person obligates himself to pay the debt of another in consideration of a benefit flowing to the surety * * * ." [Citation.] This is the commonly understood definition of a surety relationship and describes the situation that we have in the case at bar. The Georgia Code does not contain a statement as to the effect of a principal's fraud on a surety's liability to the creditor. Georgia courts, however, have applied the common law and held that a surety is still liable to a creditor even if the principal commits fraud so long as the creditor does not participate in the fraud. [Citation.] * * *

Applying the common law to the case at bar, there is no evidence that the defendants participated in any fraud. The fraud was committed solely by the principals. Under these circumstances, American is not relieved of liability on the bonds.

INTERPRETATION Fraud on the part of the principal debtor does not relieve the surety of its liability to the creditor on a surety bond if the creditor is unaware of such fraud.

ETHICAL QUESTION Is the court's decision fair to the surety? Explain.

CRITICAL THINKING QUESTION Should the fraud of the principal debtor relieve the surety of its obligation on the surety bond? Explain.

A surety is not liable if an intended cosurety, as named in the contract instrument, does not sign. A surety may ***set off*** his claims against a solvent creditor. Against an insolvent creditor, the surety may use his claim only if the principal debtor is also insolvent.

If a principal debtor and a creditor enter into a binding ***modification*** of their contract, a surety who does not assent to such modification may be discharged. The courts vary in their approach to modifications made without the surety's assent. An uncompensated surety (an ***accommodation surety***) is more likely to be discharged for any material modification, even one that does not prejudice his rights. In contrast, when contemplating the discharge of a compensated surety, a number of courts require the alteration to be both material and prejudicial to the surety's interests.

Modifications possibly leading to a surety's discharge include valid and binding extensions of the time of payment *unless* the creditor expressly reserves his rights against the surety. An extension of time with reservation is construed only as an agreement by the creditor not to sue the principal debtor for the period of the extension. Accordingly, the surety's rights of exoneration, reimbursement, and subrogation are not postponed. Thus, the surety's risk is not changed and he is not discharged.

If the creditor releases or impairs the value of the security, the surety is discharged to the extent of the value of the security released or impaired. Similarly, if the creditor releases a cosurety, the other cosureties are discharged to the extent of the released surety's contributive share. If the creditor reserves his rights against the remaining cosureties, however, the release is considered a promise not to sue. As a result, the remaining cosureties are not discharged.

DEFENSES OF BOTH SURETY AND PRINCIPAL DEBTOR

A number of defenses are available to both the surety and the principal debtor. If the principal debtor's signature on an instrument is ***forged*** or if the creditor has exerted ***fraud*** or ***duress*** on the principal debtor, neither the principal debtor nor the surety is liable. Likewise, if the creditor has fraudulently and ***materially altered*** the contract instrument, both the principal debtor and the surety are discharged.

The absence of mutual assent or consideration to support the principal debtor's obligation is a defense for both the principal debtor and the surety. In addition, both may assert as defenses the ***illegality*** and the ***impossibility*** of performance of the principal debtor's contract.

Payment or ***performance*** of the principal debtor's obligation discharges both the principal debtor and the surety. If the principal debtor owes several debts to the creditor and makes a payment to the creditor without specifying the debt to which the payment should apply, the creditor is free to apply it to any one of them. For example, Pam owes Charles two debts, one for $5,000 and another for $10,000. Susan is a surety on the $10,000 debt. Pam sends Charles a payment in the amount of $3,500. If Pam directs Charles to apply the payment to the $10,000 debt, Charles must do so. Otherwise, Charles may, if he pleases, apply the payment to the $5,000 debt.

If the creditor ***releases*** the principal debtor, the surety is also discharged unless the surety consents to the release of the principal debtor. If the creditor reserves his rights against the surety, however, the surety is not discharged. Such a release with reservation is construed as a promise not to sue, which leaves the surety's rights against the principal debtor unimpaired. Therefore, the surety is not discharged.

The creditor's refusal to accept ***tender*** of payment or performance by either the principal debtor or the surety completely discharges the surety. However, the creditor's refusal to accept a tender of payment by the principal debtor does not discharge the principal debtor. Rather, such refusal stops further accrual of interest on the debt and deprives the creditor of court costs on a subsequent suit by him to recover the amount due.

CHAPTER SUMMARY

Secured Transactions in Personal Property

Essentials of Secured Transactions

Definition of Secured Transaction an agreement by which one party obtains a security interest in the personal property of another to secure the payment of a debt

- *Debtor* person who has an interest in the collateral other than a security interest; typically the person obligated on the debt secured by the security interest
- *Secured Party* person in whose favor a security interest in the collateral is created or provided for under the security agreement

- ***Collateral*** property subject to a security interest
- ***Security Agreement*** agreement that creates or provides for a security interest
- ***Security Interest*** right in personal property that secures payment or performance of an obligation
- ***Purchase Money Security Interest*** security interest in goods purchased; interest is retained either by the seller of the goods or by a lender who advances the purchase price

Fundamental Rights of Debtor
- to redeem collateral by payment of the debt
- to possess general rights of ownership

Fundamental Rights of Secured Party
- to recover amount of debt
- to have collateral applied to payment of debt upon default

Classification of Collateral

Goods things that are movable when a security interest attaches
- ***Consumer Goods*** goods bought or used primarily for personal, family, or household purposes
- ***Farm Products*** goods that are part of a farming operation including crops, livestock, or supplies used or produced in farming
- ***Inventory*** includes non-farm product goods (1) held for sale, lease, or to be furnished under a service contract, or (2) consists of raw materials, work in process, or materials used or consumed in a business
- ***Equipment*** goods not included in the definition of consumer goods, inventory, or farm products
- ***Fixtures*** goods that are so related to real property that they are considered part of the real estate
- ***Accession*** goods installed in or firmly affixed to personal property

Indispensable Paper
- ***Chattel Paper*** tangible or electronic record that evidences both a debt and a security interest in specific goods
- ***Instruments*** negotiable instruments or any other writing that evidences a right to payment of money that is transferable by delivery with any necessary indorsement
- ***Documents*** documents of title
- ***Investment Property*** investment security (stocks and bonds), security accounts, commodity contracts, and commodity accounts

Intangibles
- ***Account*** right to payment for (1) goods sold, leased, licensed, or otherwise disposed of or (2) services rendered
- ***General Intangibles*** catchall category of collateral not otherwise covered; includes software, goodwill, literary rights, and interests in patents, trademarks, and copyrights

Other Kinds of Collateral
- ***Proceeds*** whatever is received upon sale, lease, license, exchange, or other disposition of collateral; the secured party, unless the security agreement states otherwise, has rights to the proceeds
- ***Deposit Accounts*** a demand, savings, time, or similar account maintained with a bank

Attachment

Definition security interest that is enforceable against the debtor

Value consideration under contract law, a binding commitment to extend credit, or an antecedent debt

Debtor's Rights in Collateral a debtor is deemed to have rights in personal property the debtor owns, possesses, is in the process of acquiring, or has the power to transfer rights to a secured party

Security Agreement agreement between debtor and creditor creating a security interest: must be in a record authenticated by the debtor, unless, in the case of most types of collateral, the secured party has possession of the collateral, and must contain a reasonable description of the collateral
- *Authenticity Record*
- *Consumer Goods* federal regulation prohibits a credit seller or lender from obtaining a consumer's grant of a nonpossessory security interest in household goods
- *After-Acquired Property* a security agreement may cover property the debtor may acquire in the future
- *Future Advances* a security agreement may include future advances

Perfection

Definition attachment plus any steps required for perfection

Effect enforceable against most third parties

Methods of Perfecting

Filing a Financing Statement may be used for all collateral except deposit accounts, letter-of-credit rights, and money
- *Financing Statement* document filed to provide notice of a security interest
- *Duration of Filing* filing is effective for five years but may be continued by filing a continuation statement
- *Place of Filing* statements, except for real-estate-related collateral, must be filed in a central location designated by the state.
- *Subsequent Change of Debtor's Location*

Possession by the secured party (a pledge); may be used for goods, instruments, money, negotiable documents, tangible chattel paper, or certificated securities

Automatic Perfection perfection upon attachment; applies to a purchase money security interest in consumer goods and isolated assignments of accounts

Temporary Perfection a security interest in certificated securities, instruments, and negotiable documents is automatically perfected for twenty days

Control may be used to perfect a security interest in electronic chattel paper, investment property, non-consumer deposit accounts, and letter-of-credit rights

Priorities among Competing Interests

See the Concept Review, Priorities, on page 788 for a summary of the priority rules

Default

Repossession of Collateral the secured party may take possession of the collateral on default without judicial process if it can be done without a breach of the peace

Sale of Collateral the secured party may sell, lease, license or otherwise dispose of any collateral

Acceptance of Collateral the secured party, unless the debtor objects, may retain the collateral in full or partial satisfaction of the obligation (with the exception of the compulsory disposition of some consumer goods)

Suretyship

Nature and Formation

Definition of Surety a person who promises to answer for the payment of a debt or the performance of a duty owed to the creditor by the principal debtor, upon the principal debtor's failure to perform.
- *Principal Debtor* the party primarily liable on the obligation
- *Cosurety* each of two or more sureties who are liable for the same debt of the principal debtor
- *Absolute Surety* surety liable to a creditor immediately upon the default of a principal debtor
- *Conditional Guarantor of Collection* surety liable to a creditor only after the creditor has exhausted the legal remedies against the principal debtor

Types of Sureties
- *Party Assuming a Mortgage*
- *Fidelity Bonds*
- *Performance Bonds*
- *Official Bonds*
- *Judicial Bonds*

Formation the promise of the surety must satisfy all the elements of a contract and must also be in writing

Rights of Surety

Exoneration the right of a surety to be relieved of his obligation to the creditor by having the principal debtor perform the obligation

Reimbursement the right of a surety who has paid the creditor to be repaid by the principal debtor

Subrogation the right of a surety who has paid the creditor to assume all the rights the creditor has against the principal debtor

Contribution the right to payment from each cosurety of his proportionate share of the amount paid to the creditor

Defenses of Surety and Principal Debtor

Personal Defenses of Principal Debtor defenses available only to the principal debtor, including her incapacity, discharge in bankruptcy, and setoff

Personal Defenses of Surety defenses available only to the surety, including her own incapacity, the statute of frauds, contract defenses to her suretyship undertaking, setoff, modification of the contract between the creditor and the principal debtor, and the creditor's release of security or a cosurety

Defenses of Both Surety and Principal Debtor include contract defenses to the contract between the creditor and the principal debtor

QUESTIONS

1. Victor sells to Bonnie a refrigerator for $600 payable in monthly installments of $30 for twenty months. Bonnie signs a security agreement granting Victor a security interest in the refrigerator. The refrigerator is installed in the kitchen of Bonnie's apartment. There is no filing of any financing statement. Assume that after Bonnie has made the first three monthly payments:
   a. Bonnie moves from her apartment and sells the refrigerator in place to the new occupant for $350 cash. What are the rights of Victor?
   b. Bonnie is adjudicated bankrupt, and her trustee in bankruptcy claims the refrigerator. What are the rights of the parties?

2. On January 2, Burt asked Logan to loan him money "against my diamond ring." Logan agreed to do so. To guard against intervening liens, Logan received permission to file a financing statement, and Burt and Logan signed a security agreement giving Logan an interest in the ring. Burt also signed a financing statement that Logan properly filed on January 3. On January 4, Burt borrowed money from Tillo, pledging his ring to secure the debt. Tillo took possession of the ring and paid Burt the money on the same day. The next day, January 5, Logan loaned Burt the money under the assumption that Burt still had the ring. Who has priority, Logan or Tillo? Explain.

3. Joanna takes a security interest in the equipment in Jason Store and files a financing statement claiming "equipment and all after-acquired equipment." Berkeley later sells Jason Store a cash register, taking a security interest in the register and (a) files nine days after Jason receives the register, or (b) files twenty-five days after Jason receives the register. If Jason fails to pay both Joanna and Berkeley and they foreclose their security interests, who has priority on the cash register? What would occur if Jason Store were a consumer who purchased goods for personal use?

4. Finley Motor Company sells an automobile to Sara and retains a security interest in it. The automobile is insured, and Finley is named beneficiary. Three days after the automobile is totally destroyed in an accident, Sara files a petition in bankruptcy. As between Finley and Sara's trustee in bankruptcy, who is entitled to the insurance proceeds?

5. On September 5, Wanda, a widow who occasionally teaches piano and organ in her home, purchased an electric organ from Murphy's music store for $4,800, trading in her old organ for $1,200, promising in writing to pay the balance at $120 per month, and granting to Murphy a security interest in the property in terms consistent with and incorporating provisions of the UCC. A financing statement covering the transaction was also properly filled out and signed, and Murphy properly filed it. After Wanda failed to make the December or January payments, Murphy went to her home to collect the payments or take the organ. Finding no one home and the door unlocked, he went in and took the organ. Two hours later, Tia, a third party and the present occupant of the house, who had purchased the organ for her own use, stormed into Murphy's store, demanding the return of the organ. She showed Murphy a bill of sale from Wanda to her, dated December 15, that listed the organ and other furnishings in the house.
   a. What are the rights of Murphy, Tia, and Wanda?
   b. Would your answer change if Murphy had not filed a financing statement? Why?
   c. Would your answer change if the organ had been principally used to give lessons?

6. On May 1, Lincoln lends Donaldson $20,000 and receives from Donaldson his agreement to pay this amount in two years and takes a security interest in the machinery and equipment in Donaldson's factory. A proper financing statement is filed with respect to the security agreement. On August 1, upon Lincoln's request, Donaldson executes an addendum to the security agreement covering after-acquired machinery and equipment in Donaldson's factory. A second financing statement covering the addendum is filed. In September, Donaldson acquires $5,000 worth of new equipment from Thompson, which Donaldson installs in his factory. In December, Carter, a judgment creditor of Donaldson, causes an attachment to issue against the new equipment. What are the rights of Lincoln, Donaldson, Carter, and Thompson? What can the parties do to best protect themselves?

7. Anita bought a television set from Bertrum for her personal use. Bertrum, who was out of security agreement forms, showed Anita a form he had executed with Nathan, another consumer. Anita and Bertrum orally agreed to the terms of the form. Anita subsequently defaults on payment, and Bertrum seeks to repossess the television. Decision? Would the result differ if Bertrum had filed a financing statement? What if Anita subsequently sent Bertrum an e-mail that met all the requirements of an effective security agreement?

8. Aaron bought a television set for personal use from Penny. Aaron properly signed a security agreement and paid Penny $25 down, as their agreement required. Penny did not file, and subsequently Aaron sells the television for $300 to Clark, his neighbor, for use in Clark's hotel lobby.
   a. When Aaron fails to make the January and February payments, may Penny repossess the television from Clark?
   b. What if, instead of Aaron's selling the television set to Clark, a judgment creditor levied (sought possession) on the television? Who would prevail?
   c. What if Clark intended to use the television set in his home? Who would prevail?

9. Jones bought a used car from the A–Herts Car Rental System, which regularly sold its used equipment at the end of its fiscal year. First National Bank of Roxboro had

previously obtained a perfected security interest in the car based upon its financing of A–Herts's automobiles. Upon A–Herts's failure to pay, First National is seeking to repossess the car from Jones. Does First National have an enforceable security interest in the car against Jones? Explain.

10. Allen, Barker, and Cooper are cosureties on a $750,000 loan by Durham National Bank to Kingston Manufacturing Co., Inc. The maximum liability of the sureties is as follows: Allen—$750,000, Barker—$300,000, and Cooper—$150,000. If Kingston defaults on the entire $750,000 loan, what are the liabilities of Allen, Barker, and Cooper?

11. Peter Diamond owed Carter $500,000 secured by a first mortgage on Diamond's plant and land. Stephens was a surety on this obligation in the amount of $250,000. After Diamond defaulted on the debt, Carter demanded and received payment of $250,000 from Stephens. Carter then foreclosed upon the mortgage and sold the property for $375,000. What rights, if any, does Stephens have in the proceeds from the sale of the property?

12. Paula Daniels purchased an automobile from Carey on credit. At the time of the sale, Scott agreed to be a surety for Paula, who is sixteen years old. The automobile's odometer stated 52,000 miles, but Carey had turned it back from 72,000 miles. Paula refuses to make any payments due on the car. Carey proceeds against Paula and Scott. What defenses, if any, are available to (a) Paula and (b) Scott?

13. Stafford Surety Co. agreed to act as the conditional guarantor of collection on a debt owed by Preston Decker to Cole. Stafford was paid a premium by Preston to serve as surety. Preston defaults on the obligation. What are Cole's rights against Stafford Surety Co.?

14. Campbell loaned Perry Dixon $7,000, which was secured by a possessory security interest in stock owned by Perry. The stock had a market value of $4,000. In addition, Campbell insisted that Perry obtain a surety. For a premium, Sutton Surety Co. agreed to act as a surety for the full amount of the loan. Prior to the due date of the loan, Perry convinced Campbell to return the stock because its value had increased and he wished to sell it to realize the gain. Campbell released the stock and Perry subsequently defaulted. Is Sutton released from his liability? Explain.

15. Pamela Darden owed Clark $5,000 on an unsecured loan. On May 1, Pamela approached Clark for an additional loan of $3,000. Clark agreed to make the loan only if Pamela could obtain a surety. On May 5, Simpson agreed to be a surety on the $3,000 loan, which was granted that day. Both loans were due on October 1. On June 15, Pamela sent $1,000 to Clark but did not provide any instructions.
a. What are Clark's rights?
b. What are Simpson's rights?

16. Patrick Dillon applied for a $10,000 loan from Carlton Savings & Loan. Carlton required him to obtain a surety. Patrick approached Sinclair Surety Co., which insisted that Patrick provide it with a financial statement. Patrick did so, but the statement was materially false. In reliance upon the financial statement and in return for a premium, Sinclair agreed to act as surety. Upon Sinclair's commitment to act as surety, Carlton loaned Patrick the $10,000. After one payment of $400, Patrick defaulted. He then filed a voluntary petition in bankruptcy. Does Sinclair have any valid defense against Carlton?

17. On June 1, Smith contracted with Martin, d/b/a Martin Publishing Company, to distribute Martin's newspapers and to account for the proceeds. As part of the contract, Smith agreed to furnish Martin a bond in the amount of $10,000 guaranteeing the payment of the proceeds. At the time the contract was executed and the credit extended, the bond was not furnished, and no mention was made as to the prospective sureties. On July 1, Smith signed the bond with Black and Blue signing as sureties. The bond recited the awarding of the contract for distribution of the newspapers as consideration for the bond.

On December 1, there was due from Smith to Martin the sum of $3,600 under the distributor's contract. Demand for payment was made, but Smith failed to make payment. As a result, Martin brought an appropriate action against Black and Blue to recover the $3,600. What result?

18. Diggitt Construction Company was the low bidder on a well-digging job for the Village of Drytown. On April 15, Diggitt signed a contract with Drytown for the job at a price of $40,000. At the same time, pursuant to the notice of bidding, Diggitt prevailed upon Ace Surety Company to execute a performance bond indemnifying Drytown on the contract. On May 1, after Diggitt had put in three days on the job, the president of the company refigured his bid and realized that if his company were to complete the job it would lose $10,000. Accordingly, Diggitt notified Drytown that it was canceling the contract, effective immediately. What are the rights and duties of Ace Surety Company?

CASE PROBLEMS

19. Standridge purchased a Chevrolet automobile from Billy Deavers, an agent of Walker Motor Company. According to the sales contract, the balance due after the trade-in allowance was $282.50, to be paid in twelve weekly installments. Standridge claims that he was unable to make the second payment and that Billy Deavers orally agreed that he could make two payments the next week. The day after the double payment was due, Standridge still had not

paid. That day Ronnie Deavers, Billy's brother, went to Standridge's place of employment to repossess the car. Rather than consenting to the repossession, Standridge drove the car to the Walker Motor Company's place of business and tendered the overdue payments. The Deavers refused to accept the late payment and instead demanded the entire unpaid balance. Standridge could not pay it. The Deavers then blocked in Standridge's car with another car and told him he could just "walk his home." Standridge brought suit, seeking damages for the Deavers's wrongful repossession of his car. The Deavers deny that they granted Standridge permission to make a double payment, that Standridge tendered the double payment, and that they rejected it. They claim that he made no payment and that, therefore, they were entitled to repossess the car. Discuss whether the car was properly repossessed.

20. National Cash Register Company (NCR), a manufacturer of cash registers, entered into a sales contract for a cash register with Edmund Carroll. On November 18, Firestone and Company made a loan to Carroll, who conveyed certain property to Firestone as collateral under a security agreement. The property outlined in the security agreement included "[a]ll contents of luncheonette including equipment such as . . ." twenty-five different listed items, ". . . together with all property and articles now, and which may hereafter be, used . . . with, [or] added . . . to . . . any of the foregoing described property." A similarly detailed description of the property conveyed as collateral appeared in Firestone's financing statement, but the financing statement made no mention of property to be acquired thereafter, and neither document made a specific reference to a cash register. NCR delivered the cash register to Carroll in Canton between November 19 and November 25 and filed a financing statement with the town clerk of Canton on December 20 and with the Secretary of State on December 21. Carroll subsequently defaulted both on the contract with NCR and on the security agreement with Firestone. Firestone took possession of the cash register and sold it at auction. Discuss whether Firestone has a security interest in the cash register.

21. National Acceptance Company loaned Ultra Precision Industries $692,000, and to secure repayment of the loan, Ultra executed a chattel mortgage security agreement on National's behalf on March 7, 2000. National perfected the security interest by timely filing a financing statement. Although the security interest covered specifically described equipment of Ultra, both the security agreement and the financing statement contained an after-acquired property clause that did not refer to any specific equipment.

Later in 2000 and in 2001, Ultra placed three separate orders for machines from Wolf Machinery Company. In each case it was agreed that after the machines had been shipped to Ultra and installed, Ultra would be given an opportunity to test them in operation for a reasonable period. If the machines passed inspection, Wolf would then provide financing that was satisfactory to Ultra. In all three cases, financing was arranged with Community Bank (Bank) and accepted, and a security interest was given in the machines. Furthermore, in each case a security agreement was entered into, and a financing statement was then filed by the secured parties within ten days. Ultra became bankrupt on October 7, 2002. National claimed that its security interest in the after-acquired machines should take priority over those of Wolf and Bank because their interests were not perfected by timely filed financing statements. Discuss who has priority in the disputed collateral.

22. Elizabeth Tilleraas received three student loans totaling $3,500 under the Federal Insured Student Loan Program (FISLP) of the Higher Education Act of 1965. These loans were secured by three promissory notes executed in favor of Dakota National Bank & Trust Co., Fargo, North Dakota. Under the terms of these student loans, periodic payments were required beginning twelve months after Tilleraas ceased to carry at least one-half of a full-time academic workload at an eligible institution. Her student status terminated on January 28, 1991, and the first installment payment thus became due January 28, 1992. She never made any payment on any of her loans. Under the provisions of the FISLP, the United States assured the lender bank repayment in event of any failure to pay by the borrower. The first payment due on the loans was in "default" on July 27, 1992, 180 days after the failure to make the first installment payment. On December 17, 1993, Dakota National Bank & Trust sent notice of its election under the provisions of the loan to accelerate the maturity of the note. The bank demanded payment in full by December 27, 1993. It then filed FISLP insurance claims against the United States on May 6, 1994, and assigned the three Tilleraas notes to the United States on May 10, 1994. The government, in turn, paid the bank's claim in full on July 5, 1994. On June 4, 2000, the government filed suit against Tilleraas. Discuss whether the United States will prevail.

http:// Internet Exercise Find and examine (a) some surety and fidelity companies, and (b) the federal Small Business Administration's surety bond guarantee program.

Chapter 39

Bankruptcy

Always pay; for first or last you must pay your entire debt.

Ralph Waldo Emerson, 1841

Learning Objectives

After reading this chapter you should be able to:

1. Explain (a) the requirements for voluntary and involuntary bankruptcy cases, (b) the priorities of creditors' claims, (c) the debtor's exemptions, and (d) the debts that are not dischargeable in bankruptcy.
2. Explain the duties of a trustee and his rights (a) as a lien creditor, (b) to avoid preferential transfers, (c) to avoid fraudulent transfers, and (d) to avoid statutory liens.
3. Explain the procedure followed in distributing the debtor's estate under Chapter 7.
4. Compare the adjustment of debt proceedings under Chapters 11, 12, and 13.
5. Identify and define the nonbankruptcy compromises between debtors and creditors.

A debt is an obligation to pay money owed by a debtor to a creditor. Debts are created daily by countless purchasers of goods at the consumer level; by retailers of goods in buying merchandise from a manufacturer, wholesaler, or distributor; by borrowers of funds from various lending institutions; and through the issuance and sale of debentures, corporate mortgage bonds, and other types of debt securities. Multitudes of business transactions are entered into daily on a credit basis. Commercial activity would be greatly restricted if credit were not readily obtainable or if needed funds were unavailable for lending.

Fortunately, most debts are paid when due, thus justifying the extension of credit and encouraging its continuation. Although defaults may create credit and collection problems, normally the total amount in default represents a very small percentage of the total amount of outstanding indebtedness. Nevertheless, both individuals and corporations encounter financial crises and business misfortune. An accumulation of debts that exceeds total assets may confront an individual as well as a business. Or these debtors might have assets in excess of total indebtedness but in such noncash form that they are unable to pay their debts as they mature. For both businesses and individuals, relief from pressing debt and from the threat of impending lawsuits by creditors is frequently necessary for economic survival.

The conflict between creditor rights and debtor relief has engendered various solutions, such as compromises requiring installment payments to creditors over a period of time during which they agree to withhold legal action. Other voluntary methods include compositions and assignments of assets by a debtor to a trustee or assignee for the benefit of creditors. In addition, creditors sometimes file equity receiverships or insolvency proceedings in a state court, according to statute. Nonetheless, the most adaptable and frequently used method of debtor relief—one that also affords protection to creditors—is a proceeding in a federal court under federal bankruptcy law.

FEDERAL BANKRUPTCY LAW

Bankruptcy legislation serves a dual purpose: (1) to bring about a quick, *equitable distribution* of the debtor's property among her creditors and (2) to *discharge* the debtor from her debts, enabling the debtor to rehabilitate herself and to start afresh. Other purposes are to provide uniform treatment of similarly situated creditors, to preserve existing business relations, and to stabilize commercial usages.

The U.S. Bankruptcy Code consists of eight chapters: seven odd-numbered chapters and one even-numbered chapter. Chapters 7, 9, 11, 12, and 13 provide five different types of proceedings; Chapters 1, 3, and 5 apply to those five proceedings unless otherwise specified. ***Straight***, or ordinary, ***bankruptcy*** (Chapter 7) provides for the liquidation of the debtor's property, whereas the other proceedings provide for the ***reorganization*** and adjustment of the debtor's debts and, in the case of a business debtor, the continuance of the debtor's business. In reorganization cases, the creditors usually look to the debtor's future earnings, whereas in liquidation cases, the creditors look to the debtor's property at the commencement of the bankruptcy proceeding. Chapters 7, 11, 12, and 13 have provisions governing transfer of a case under that chapter to another chapter.

Chapter 7 applies to all debtors, with the exception of railroads, insurance companies, banks, savings and loan associations, homestead associations, licensed small business investment companies, and credit unions. Moreover, Chapter 7 has special provisions for liquidating the estates of stockbrokers and commodity brokers. (Approximately 70 percent of bankruptcies are filed under Chapter 7.) Railroads and any person who may be a debtor under Chapter 7 (except a stockbroker or a commodity broker) may be debtors under Chapter 11. (Less than 1 percent of bankruptcies are filed under Chapter 11.) Chapter 9 applies only to municipalities that are generally authorized to be debtors under that chapter, that are insolvent, and that desire to effect plans to adjust their debts. Chapter 12 applies to individuals, or individuals and their spouses, engaged in farming if 50 percent of their gross income is from farming, their aggregate debts do not exceed $1.5 million, and at least 80 percent of their debts arise from farming operations. (Less than one tenth of 1 percent of bankruptcies are filed under Chapter 12.) Corporations or partnerships may also qualify for Chapter 12. Chapter 13 applies to individuals with regular income who owe liquidated unsecured debts of less than $290,525 and secured debts of less than $871,550. (Approximately 29 percent of bankruptcies are filed under Chapter 13.)

The 1994 amendments to the Bankruptcy Act require that every three years, beginning in 1998, the U.S. Judicial Conference adjust for inflation the dollar amounts of the following provisions: eligibility for Chapter 13, requirements for filing involuntary cases, priorities, exemptions, and exceptions to discharge.

http://
Bankruptcy Code: http://www4.law.cornell.edu/uscode/11/
American Bankruptcy Institute: http://www.abiworld.org/
Georgetown University: Bankruptcy Law:
http//:www.ll.georgetown.edu/topics/bankruptcy.cfm

The Bankruptcy Code grants to U.S. District Courts original and exclusive jurisdiction over all bankruptcy cases and original, but not exclusive, jurisdiction over civil proceedings arising under bankruptcy cases. The district court must, however, abstain from related matters that, except for their relationship to bankruptcy, could not have been brought in a federal court. The district court in which a bankruptcy case is commenced has exclusive jurisdiction over all of the debtor's property. In addition, within each federal district court is established a bankruptcy court staffed by bankruptcy judges. Bankruptcy courts are authorized to hear certain matters specified by the Bankruptcy Code and to enter appropriate orders and judgments subject to review by the district court or, when established, by a panel of three bankruptcy judges. The federal circuit court of appeals has jurisdiction over appeals from the district court or panel. In all other matters, unless the parties agree otherwise, only the district court may issue a final order or judgment based upon proposed findings of fact and conclusions of law submitted to the court by the bankruptcy judge.

CASE ADMINISTRATION—CHAPTER 3

CPA

Chapter 3 of the Bankruptcy Code contains provisions dealing with the commencement of a case in bankruptcy, the meetings of creditors, the officers who administer the case, and the officers' administrative powers.

COMMENCEMENT OF THE CASE

The filing of a voluntary or involuntary petition begins the jurisdiction of the bankruptcy court and the operation of the bankruptcy laws.

Voluntary Petitions More than 99 percent of all bankruptcy petitions are filed voluntarily. Any person eligible to be a debtor under a given bankruptcy proceeding may file a **voluntary petition** under that chapter, and need *not* be insolvent to do so. The commencement of a voluntary case constitutes an automatic ***order for relief***. The petition must include a list of all creditors (secured and unsecured), a list of all property the debtor owns, a list of property that the debtor claims is exempt, and a statement of the debtor's affairs.

Involuntary Petitions An **involuntary petition** in bankruptcy may be filed only under Chapter 7 (liquidation) or Chapter 11 (reorganization). It may be filed (1) by three or more creditors who have unsecured claims that total $11,625 or more or (2) if the debtor has fewer than twelve creditors, by one or more creditors whose total unsecured claims equal $11,625 or more. An involuntary petition may not be filed against a farmer or against a banking, insurance, or nonprofit corporation.

If the debtor does not contest the involuntary petition, the court will enter an order for relief against the debtor. However, if the debtor opposes the petition, the court may enter an order of relief only (1) if the debtor is generally not paying his debts as they become due or (2) if, within 120 days before the filing of the petition, a custodian or receiver took possession of substantially all of the debtor's property to enforce a lien against that property.

DISMISSAL

The court may dismiss a Chapter 7 case for cause after notice and a hearing. In 1984, Congress amended the Bankruptcy Code to deal with abuses of Chapter 7 by consumer debtors who had the ability to pay their debts. The amendment empowers the court on its own motion, after notice and a hearing, to dismiss a case filed by an individual debtor whose debts are primarily consumer debts if the court finds that granting relief would be a substantial abuse of the provisions of Chapter 7.

Under Chapter 11, the court may dismiss a case for cause after notice and a hearing. Under Chapters 12 and 13, the debtor has an absolute right to have his case dismissed. Under these chapters, if a motion to dismiss is filed by an interested party other than the debtor, the court may dismiss the case only for cause after notice and a hearing.

AUTOMATIC STAYS

The filing of a voluntary or involuntary petition operates as a stay against (that is, it prevents) attempts by creditors to begin or continue to recover claims against the debtor, to enforce judgments against the debtor, or to create or enforce liens against property of the debtor. This stay applies to both secured and unsecured creditors, although a secured creditor may petition the court to terminate the stay as to her security on showing that she lacks adequate protection in the secured property. An automatic stay ends when the bankruptcy case is closed or dismissed or when the debtor receives a discharge.

Practical Advice

If you file a bankruptcy petition, you are protected from creditors' pursuing their claims against you except through the bankruptcy proceeding; this may be advantageous in that it requires all claims to be heard in one court at one time.

TRUSTEES

A **trustee** is the representative of an estate and has the capacity to sue and be sued on behalf of the estate. In proceedings under Chapter 7, trustees are selected by a vote of the creditors. The 1994 amendments allow the creditors to elect a trustee in a Chapter 11 proceeding if the court orders the appointment of a trustee for cause. In Chapters 12 and 13 the trustee is appointed. Responsible, under Chapter 7, for collecting, liquidating, and distributing the debtor's estate, the trustee has, among others, the following duties and powers: (1) collecting the property of the estate; (2) challenging certain transfers of property of the estate; (3) using, selling, or leasing property of the estate; (4) depositing or investing money of the estate; (5) employing attorneys, accountants, appraisers, or auctioneers; (6) assuming or rejecting any executory contract or unexpired lease of the debtor; (7) objecting to creditors' claims that are improper; and (8) opposing, if advisable, the debtor's discharge. Trustees under Chapters 11, 12, and 13 perform some but not all of the duties of a Chapter 7 trustee.

MEETINGS OF CREDITORS

Within a reasonable time after relief is ordered, a meeting of creditors must be held. Although the court may not attend this meeting, the debtor must appear and submit to an examination of his financial situation by the creditors and the trustee. In a proceeding under Chapter 7, qualified creditors at this meeting elect a permanent trustee.

CREDITORS, THE DEBTOR, AND THE ESTATE—CPA CHAPTER 5

CREDITORS

The Bankruptcy Code defines a **creditor** as any entity having a claim against the debtor that arose at the time of or before the order for relief. A **claim** is a right to payment.

Proofs of Claim Creditors who wish to participate in the distribution of the debtor's estate may file a proof of claim. If a creditor does not do so in a timely manner, the debtor or trustee may file a proof of such claim. By doing this the debtor may prevent a claim from becoming nondischargeable. Filed claims are allowed unless a party who has an interest objects. If an objection is made, the court determines, after a hearing, the amount and validity of the claim. The court will not allow any claim that (1) is unenforceable against the debtor or her property, (2) is for unmatured interest, (3) may be offset against a debt owing the debtor, or (4) is for insider or attorney services in excess of the reasonable value of such services. An **insider** includes a relative or general partner of a debtor, as well as a partnership in which the debtor is a general partner or a corporation of which the debtor is a director, officer, or person in control.

Practical Advice

If you are a debtor in a bankruptcy proceeding, file a proof of claim for any creditor who does not file on her own. Such a filing may enable you to receive a discharge from that claim.

Secured Claims An allowed claim of a creditor who has a lien on property of the estate is a **secured claim** to the extent of the value of the creditor's interest in the property. The creditor's claim is **unsecured** to the extent of the difference between the value of his secured interest and the allowed amount of his claim. Thus, if Alice has an allowed claim of $5,000 against the estate of debtor Bart and has a security interest in property of the estate that is valued at $3,000, Alice has a secured claim in the amount of $3,000 and an unsecured claim for $2,000.

Priority of Claims After secured claims have been satisfied, the remaining assets are distributed among creditors with unsecured claims. Certain classes of unsecured claims, however, have a *priority*, which means that they must be paid in full before any distribution is made to claims of lesser rank. Each claimant within a priority class shares *pro rata* if the assets are insufficient to satisfy all claims in that class. The claims having a priority and the order of their priority are as follows:

1. ***Expenses of administration*** of the debtor's estate, including the filing fees paid by creditors in involuntary cases, the expenses of creditors in recovering concealed assets for the benefit of the bankrupt's estate, the trustee's necessary expenses, and reasonable compensation to receivers, trustees, and their attorneys, as allowed by the court;
2. Unsecured claims in an involuntary case arising in the ordinary course of the debtor's business after the commencement of the case but before the earlier of either the appointment of the trustee or the entering of the order for relief (such claimants are referred to as *"gap" creditors*);
3. Allowed, unsecured claims up to $4,650 for ***wages, salaries,*** or ***commissions*** earned within ninety days before the filing of the petition or before the date on which the debtor's business ceases, whichever comes first;
4. Allowed, unsecured claims for contributions to ***employee benefit plans*** arising from services rendered within 180 days before the filing of the petition or the cessation of the debtor's business, whichever occurs first, but limited to $4,650 multiplied by the number of employees covered by the plan, less the aggregate amount paid to such employees under number 3 above;
5. Allowed, unsecured claims up to $4,650 for ***grain*** or ***fish producers*** against a storage facility;
6. Allowed, unsecured claims up to $2,100 for ***consumer deposits***; that is, moneys deposited in connection with the purchase, lease, or rental of property or the purchase of services for personal, family, or household use;
7. ***Alimony*** and ***support*** of a child or spouse;
8. Specified income, property, employment, or excise ***taxes owed to governmental units.***

After creditors with secured claims and creditors with claims having a priority have been satisfied, creditors with allowed, unsecured claims share proportionately in any remaining assets.

Subordination of Claims A subordination agreement is enforceable under the Bankruptcy Code to the same extent that it is enforceable under nonbankruptcy law. In addition to statutory and contract priorities, the bankruptcy court itself can, at its discretion in proper cases, apply equitable priorities. The court accomplishes this through the doctrine of subordination of claims, whereby, assuming two claims of equal statutory priority, the court declares that one claim must be paid in full before the other claim can be paid anything. Bankruptcy courts apply subordination when allowing a claim in full, such as the inflated salary claims of officers in a closely held corporation, would be unfair and inequitable to other creditors. In such cases, the court does not disallow the claim but merely orders that it be paid after all other claims are paid in full. For example, the court may subordinate the claim of a parent corporation against its bankrupt subsidiary to the claims of the subsidiary's other creditors if the parent has so mismanaged the subsidiary to the detriment of its innocent creditors that this unconscionable conduct precludes the parent from seeking the court's aid.

DEBTORS

As previously indicated, the purpose of the Bankruptcy Code is to bring about an equitable distribution of the debtor's assets and to provide him a discharge. Accordingly, the Code explicitly subjects the debtor to specified duties, while exempting some of his property and discharging most of his debts.

Debtor's Duties Under the Bankruptcy Code, the debtor must file a list of creditors, a schedule of assets and liabilities, and a statement of her financial affairs. In any case in which a trustee is serving, the debtor must cooperate with the trustee and surrender to the trustee all property of the estate and all records relating to such property.

Debtor's Exemptions The Bankruptcy Code exempts specified property of an individual debtor from bankruptcy proceedings, including the following: (1) up to \$17,425 in equity in property used as a residence or burial plot; (2) up to \$2,775 in equity in one motor vehicle; (3) up to \$450 for any particular item of household furnishings, household goods, wearing apparel, appliances, books, animals, crops, or musical instruments that are primarily for personal, family, or household use with an aggregate limitation of \$9,300; (4) up to \$1,150 in jewelry; (5) any property up to \$925 plus up to \$8,725 of any unused amount of the first exemption; (6) up to \$1,750 in implements, professional books, or tools of the debtor's trade; (7) unmatured life insurance contracts owned by the debtor, other than a credit life insurance contract; (8) professionally prescribed health aids; (9) social security, veteran's, and disability benefits; (10) unemployment compensation; (11) alimony and support payments, including child support; (12) payments from pension, profit-sharing, and annuity plans; and (13) payments from an award under a crime victim's reparation law, a wrongful death award, and up to \$17,425, not including compensation for pain and suffering or for actual pecuniary loss, from a personal injury award. In addition, the debtor may avoid judicial liens on any exempt property and nonpossessory, nonpurchase money security interests on household goods, tools of the trade, and professionally prescribed health aids.

The debtor has the option of using either the exemptions provided by the Bankruptcy Code or those available under state law. Nevertheless, a state may, by specific legislative action, limit its citizens to the exemptions provided by state law. More than two thirds of the states have enacted such legislation.

> **Practical Advice**
>
> If you intend to enter bankruptcy, determine what property is exempt from the debtor's estate in your state and take appropriate action.

Discharge Discharge relieves the debtor from liability for all his dischargeable debts. A discharge of a debt voids any judgment obtained at any time concerning that debt and operates as an injunction against the commencement or continuation of any action to recover it.

No private employer may terminate the employment of, or discriminate with respect to employment against, an individual who is or has been a debtor under the Bankruptcy Code solely because such debtor (1) is or has been such a debtor; (2) has been insolvent before the commencement of a case or during the case; or (3) has not paid a debt that is dischargeable in a case under the Bankruptcy Code.

An agreement between a debtor and a creditor permitting the creditor to enforce a discharged debt is enforceable to the extent state law permits but only if (1) the agreement was made before the discharge has been granted; (2) the agreement contains a clear and conspicuous statement that advises the debtor that the agreement may be rescinded; (3) the agreement has been filed with the court, accompanied, if applicable, by a declaration or an affidavit of the attorney who represented the debtor during the course of negotiating the agreement, which states that such agreement represents a fully informed and voluntary agreement by the debtor and imposes no undue hardship on her; (4) the debtor has not rescinded the agreement at any time prior to discharge or within sixty days after the agreement is filed with the court, whichever occurs later; (5) the court has informed a debtor who is an individual that he is not required to enter into such an agreement and has explained the legal effect of the agreement; and (6) in a case concerning an individual who was not represented by an attorney during the course of negotiating the agreement, the court has approved such agreement as imposing no undue hardship on the debtor and being in her best interests.

The Bankruptcy Code provides that certain debts of an individual are ***not dischargeable*** in bankruptcy. This provision applies to individuals receiving discharges under Chapters 7, 11, 12, and, as discussed later in this chapter, the "hardship discharge" provision of Chapter 13. The nondischargeable debts are

1. Certain taxes and customs duties
2. Legal liabilities resulting from obtaining money or property by false pretenses or false representations
3. Legal liability for willful and malicious injuries to the person or property of another
4. Alimony and support of a spouse or a child
5. Debts not scheduled, unless the creditor knew of the bankruptcy
6. Debts the debtor created by fraud or embezzlement while acting in a fiduciary capacity
7. Student loans unless the debt would impose undue hardship
8. Debts that were or could have been listed in a previous bankruptcy in which the debtor waived or was denied a discharge
9. Consumer debts for luxury goods or services in excess of $1,150 per creditor if incurred by an individual debtor on or within sixty days before the order for relief
10. Cash advances aggregating more than $1,150 obtained by an individual debtor under an open-ended credit plan within sixty days before the order for relief
11. Liability for a court judgment based upon the debtor's operation of a motor vehicle while legally intoxicated
12. Fines, penalties, or forfeitures owed to a governmental entity
13. Certain debts incurred for violations of securities fraud law. (This provision was added by the Sarbanes-Oxley Act.)

In Chapter 13 cases, usually the only debts not discharged are the above numbered debts: 4, 7, 11, and 12.

The following illustrates the operation of discharge. Donaldson files a petition in bankruptcy. Donaldson owes Anders $1,500, Boynton $2,500, and Conroy $3,000. Assume that Anders's claim is not dischargeable in bankruptcy, while Boynton's and Conroy's are. Anders receives $180 from the liquidation of Donaldson's bankruptcy estate, Boynton receives $300, and Conroy receives $360. If Donaldson receives a bankruptcy discharge, Boynton and Conroy will be precluded from pursuing Donaldson for the remainder of their claims ($2,200 and $2,640 respectively). Anders, on the other hand, because his debt is not dischargeable, may pursue Donaldson for the remaining $1,320, subject to the applicable statute of limitations. If Donaldson does not receive a discharge, Anders, Boynton, and Conroy may all pursue Donaldson for the unpaid portions of their claims.

THE ESTATE

The commencement of a bankruptcy case creates an **estate** consisting of all legal and equitable interests of the debtor in nonexempt property at that time. The estate also includes property that the debtor acquires, within 180 days after the filing of the petition, by inheritance, by a property settlement, by divorce decree, or as a beneficiary of a life insurance policy. In addition, the estate includes proceeds, rents, and profits from property of the estate and any interest in property that the estate acquires after the case commences. Finally, the estate includes property that the trustee recovers under her powers (1) as a lien creditor, (2) to avoid voidable preferences, (3) to avoid fraudulent transfers, and (4) to avoid statutory liens. Although the estate does not include earnings from services an individual debtor performs after the case commences, it does include, in a Chapter 12 or 13 case, wages the debtor earns and property she acquires after the case commences.

Trustee as Lien Creditor When the case commences, the trustee gains the rights and powers of any creditor with a judicial lien against the debtor that is returned unsatisfied, whether such a creditor exists or not. Obtained by a judgment, a levy, or some other legal or equitable process, a **judicial lien** is a charge or interest in property to secure payment of a debt or performance of an obligation. The trustee is made an ideal creditor possessing every right and power conferred by the law of the state on its most favored creditor who has acquired a lien by legal or equitable proceedings. Because the trustee assumes the rights and powers of a purely hypothetical lien creditor, she need not locate an actual existing lien creditor.

Thus, under the Uniform Commercial Code and the Bankruptcy Code, the trustee, as a hypothetical lien creditor, has priority over a creditor with a security interest that was not perfected when the bankruptcy petition was filed. A creditor with a purchase money security interest who files within the grace period allowed under state law, which in most states is twenty days after the debtor receives the collateral, however, will defeat the trustee, even if the petition is gap-filed before the creditor perfects and after the security interest is created. For example,

Donald borrows $5,000 from Cathy on September 1 and gives her a security interest in the equipment he purchases with the borrowed funds. On October 3, before Cathy perfects her security interest, Donald files for bankruptcy. The trustee in bankruptcy can invalidate Cathy's security interest because it was unperfected when the bankruptcy petition was filed. Cathy would be able to assert a claim as an unsecured creditor. If, however, Donald had filed for bankruptcy on September 18 and Cathy had perfected the security interest on September 19, Cathy would prevail because she perfected her purchase money security interest within twenty days after Donald received the equipment.

Voidable Preferences The Bankruptcy Code invalidates certain preferential transfers from the debtor to favored creditors before the date of bankruptcy. A creditor who has received a transfer invalidated as preferential may still make a claim for the unpaid debt, but the property he received under the preferential transfer becomes a part of the debtor's estate to be shared by all creditors. The trustee may recover any *transfer* of the debtor's property (1) to or for the benefit of a creditor; (2) for or on account of an antecedent debt the debtor owed before the transfer was made; (3) made while the debtor was insolvent; (4) made on or within ninety days before the date of the filing of the petition; or, if the creditor was an "insider" (as defined earlier), within one year of the date of the filing of the petition; and (5) that enables such creditor to receive more than he would have received under Chapter 7.

A transfer is any means, direct or indirect, voluntary or involuntary, of disposing of property or an interest in property, including the retention of title as a security interest. The Bankruptcy Code presumes that the debtor has been insolvent on and during the ninety days immediately preceding the date of the filing of the petition. **Insolvency** is a financial condition such that the sum of one's debts exceeds the sum of all one's property at fair valuation.

For example, on March 3, David borrows $15,000 from Carla, promising to repay the loan on April 3. David repays Carla on April 3. Then, on June 1, David files a petition in bankruptcy. His assets are sufficient to pay general creditors only $.40 on the dollar. David's repayment of the loan is a voidable preference, which the trustee may recover from Carla. The transfer (repayment) on April 3 (1) was to a creditor (Carla); (2) was on account of an antecedent debt (the $15,000 loan made on March 3); (3) was made while the debtor was insolvent (the debtor is presumed insolvent for the ninety days preceding the filing of the bankruptcy petition—June 1); (4) was made within ninety days of bankruptcy (April 3 is less than ninety days before June 1); and (5) enabled the creditor to receive more than she would have received under Chapter 7 (Carla received $15,000; she would have received 0.40 × $15,000 = $6,000 in bankruptcy). After returning the property to the trustee, Carla would have an unsecured claim of $15,000 against David's estate in bankruptcy, for which she would receive $6,000.

Consider another example. On May 1, Debra buys and receives merchandise from Stuart and gives him a security interest in the goods for the unpaid price of $20,000. On May 25, Stuart files a financing statement. On August 1, Debra files a petition for bankruptcy. The trustee in bankruptcy may avoid the perfected security interest as a preferential transfer. The transfer of the perfected security interest on May 25 (1) was to benefit a creditor (Stuart); (2) the transfer was on account of an antecedent debt (the $20,000 owed from the sale of the merchandise); (3) the debtor was insolvent at the time (the debtor's insolvency is presumed for the ninety days preceding the filing of the bankruptcy petition—August 1); (4) the transfer was made within ninety days of bankruptcy (May 25 is less than ninety days before August 1); and (5) the transfer enabled the creditor to receive more than he would have received in bankruptcy (on his secured claim, Stuart would recover more than he would on an unsecured claim).

Nevertheless, not all transfers made within ninety days of bankruptcy are voidable. The Bankruptcy Code makes exceptions for certain pre-bankruptcy transfers, including

1. ***Exchanges for new value.*** If, for example, within ninety days before the petition is filed, the debtor purchases an automobile for $9,000, this transfer of property (i.e., the $9,000) is not voidable because it was not made for an antecedent debt but as a substantially contemporaneous exchange for new value.
2. ***Enabling security interests.*** If the creditor gives the debtor new value that the debtor uses to acquire property in which he grants the creditor a security interest, the security interest is not voidable if the creditor perfects it within twenty days after the debtor receives possession of the property. For example, if within ninety days of the filing of the petition, the debtor purchases a refrigerator on credit and grants the seller or lender a security interest in the refrigerator, the transfer of that interest is not voidable if the secured party perfects within twenty days after the debtor receives possession of the property.
3. ***Payments in ordinary course.*** The trustee may not avoid a transfer (1) in payment of a debt incurred in the ordinary course of business or financial affairs of the debtor and the transferee, (2) made in the ordinary course of business or financial affairs of the debtor and transferee, and (3) made according to ordinary business terms.

4. ***Consumer debts.*** This exception provides that if the debtor is an individual whose debts are primarily consumer debts, the trustee may not avoid any transfer of property valued at less than $600.
5. ***Alimony and support.*** This exception, added in 1994, provides that the trustee may not avoid any transfer that is a *bona fide* payment of a debt for alimony, maintenance, or support made to a spouse, former spouse, or a child of the debtor.

Fraudulent Transfers The trustee may avoid **fraudulent transfers** made on or within one year before the date of the filing of the petition. One type of fraudulent transfer consists of the debtor's transferring property with the actual intent to hinder, delay, or defraud any of her creditors. Another consists of the debtor's transferring property for less than a reasonably equivalent consideration when she is insolvent or when the transfer would make her so. For example, Carol, who is in debt, transfers title to her house to Wallace, her father, without any payment by Wallace to Carol and with the understanding that when the house is no longer in danger of seizure by creditors, Wallace will reconvey it to Carol. Carol's transfer of the house is a fraudulent transfer. A 1998 amendment to the Bankruptcy Code provides that a transfer of a charitable contribution to a qualified religious or charitable entity or organization will not be considered a fraudulent transfer if the amount of that contribution does not exceed 15 percent of the gross annual income of the debtor for the year in which the transfer is made. Transfers that exceed 15 percent are protected if they are "consistent with the practices of the debtor in making charitable contributions."

Statutory Liens A **statutory lien** arises solely by force of a statute and does not include a security interest or judicial lien. The trustee may avoid a statutory lien on property of the debtor if the lien (1) first becomes effective when the debtor becomes insolvent, (2) is not perfected or enforceable against a *bona fide* purchaser on the date the petition was filed, or (3) is for rent.

CPA LIQUIDATION—CHAPTER 7

To accomplish its dual goals of distributing the debtor's property fairly and providing the debtor with a fresh start, the Bankruptcy Code has established two approaches: liquidation and adjustment of debts. Chapter 7 uses liquidation, whereas Chapters 11, 12, and 13, discussed later, use the adjustment of debts. Liquidation involves terminating the business of the debtor, distributing his nonexempt assets, and, usually, discharging all his dischargeable debts.

PROCEEDINGS

Proceedings under Chapter 7 apply to all debtors except railroads, insurance companies, banks, savings and loan associations, homestead associations, and credit unions. A petition commencing a case under Chapter 7 may be either voluntary or involuntary. After the order for relief, an interim trustee is appointed, who serves until the creditors select a permanent trustee. If the creditors do not elect a trustee, the interim trustee becomes the permanent trustee. Under Chapter 7, the trustee collects and reduces to money the property of the estate; accounts for all property received; investigates the financial affairs of the debtor; examines and, if appropriate, challenges proofs of claims; opposes, if advisable, the discharge of the debtor; and makes a final report of the administration of the estate.

The creditors also may elect a committee of not fewer than three and not more than eleven unsecured creditors to consult with the trustee, to make recommendations to him, and to submit questions to the court.

DISTRIBUTION OF THE ESTATE

After the trustee has collected all the assets of the debtor's estate, she distributes them to the creditors (and, if any assets remain, to the debtor) in the following order:

1. Secured creditors, on their security interests;
2. Creditors entitled to a priority, in the order provided;
3. Unsecured creditors who filed their claims on time (or tardily, if they did not have notice or actual knowledge of the bankruptcy);
4. Unsecured creditors who filed their claims late;
5. Claims for fines and multiple, exemplary, or punitive damages;
6. Interest at the legal rate from the date of the filing of the petition, to all of the above claimants; and
7. Whatever property remains, to the debtor.

Claims of the same rank are paid proportionately. For example, Donley has filed a petition for a Chapter 7 proceeding. The total value of Donley's estate after paying the expenses of administration is $25,000. Evans, who is owed $15,000, has a security interest in property valued at $10,000. Fishel has an unsecured claim of $6,000, which is entitled to a priority of $2,000. The United States has a claim for income taxes of $4,000. Green has an unsecured claim of $9,000 that was filed on time. Hiller has an unsecured claim of $12,000 that was filed on time. Jerdee has a claim of $8,000 that was filed late. The distribution would be as follows: (1) Evans receives $11,500; (2) Fishel receives $3,200; (3) the United States receives $4,000; (4) Green receives $2,700; (5) Hiller receives $3,600; and (6) Jerdee receives $0.

Let us analyze this distribution: Evans receives $10,000 as a secured creditor and has an unsecured claim of $5,000. Fishel receives $2,000 on the portion of his claim entitled to a priority and has an unsecured claim of $4,000. The United States has a priority of $4,000. After paying $10,000 to Evans, $2,000 to Fishel, and $4,000 to the United States, there remains $9,000 ($25,000 – $10,000 – $2,000 – $4,000) to be distributed *pro rata* to unsecured creditors who filed on time. Their claims total $30,000 (Evans = $5,000, Fishel = $4,000, Green = $9,000, and Hiller = $12,000). Therefore, each will receive $9,000/$30,000, or $0.30 on the dollar. Accordingly, Evans receives an additional $1,500, Fishel receives an additional $1,200, Green receives $2,700, and Hiller receives $3,600. Because the assets were insufficient to pay all unsecured claimants who filed on time, Jerdee, who filed tardily, receives nothing. However, if Jerdee's claim were filed late because Donley had failed to schedule the claim, Donley's debt to Jerdee would not be discharged unless Jerdee knew or had notice of the bankruptcy.

Figure 39-1 summarizes the collection and distribution of the debtor's estate.

DISCHARGE

A **discharge** under Chapter 7 relieves the debtor of all debts that arose before the date of the order for relief, except for those debts that are not dischargeable. After distribution of the estate, the court will grant the debtor a discharge unless the debtor (1) is not an individual (partnerships and corporations may not receive a discharge under Chapter 7); (2) has destroyed, falsified, concealed, or failed to keep records and books of account; (3) has knowingly and fraudulently made a false oath or account, presented or used a false claim, or given or received bribes; (4) has transferred, removed, destroyed, or concealed any of his property with intent to hinder, delay, or defraud his creditors within twelve months before the filing of the bankruptcy petition; (5) has within six years before the bankruptcy been granted a discharge under Chapter 7 or 11; (6) has refused to obey any lawful order of the court or to answer any question approved by the court; (7) has failed to explain satisfactorily any losses of assets or any deficiency of assets to meet his liabilities; or (8) has executed a written waiver of discharge approved by the court. A debtor also will be denied a discharge under Chapter 7 if she received a discharge under Chapter 12 or 13 within the past six years, unless payments under that chapter's plan totaled at least (1) 100 percent of the allowed unsecured claims or (2) 70 percent of such claims and the plan was the debtor's best effort.

On request of the trustee or a creditor and after notice and a hearing, the court may revoke within one year a discharge the debtor obtained through fraud.

Figure 39-1 *Collection and Distribution of the Debtor's Estate*

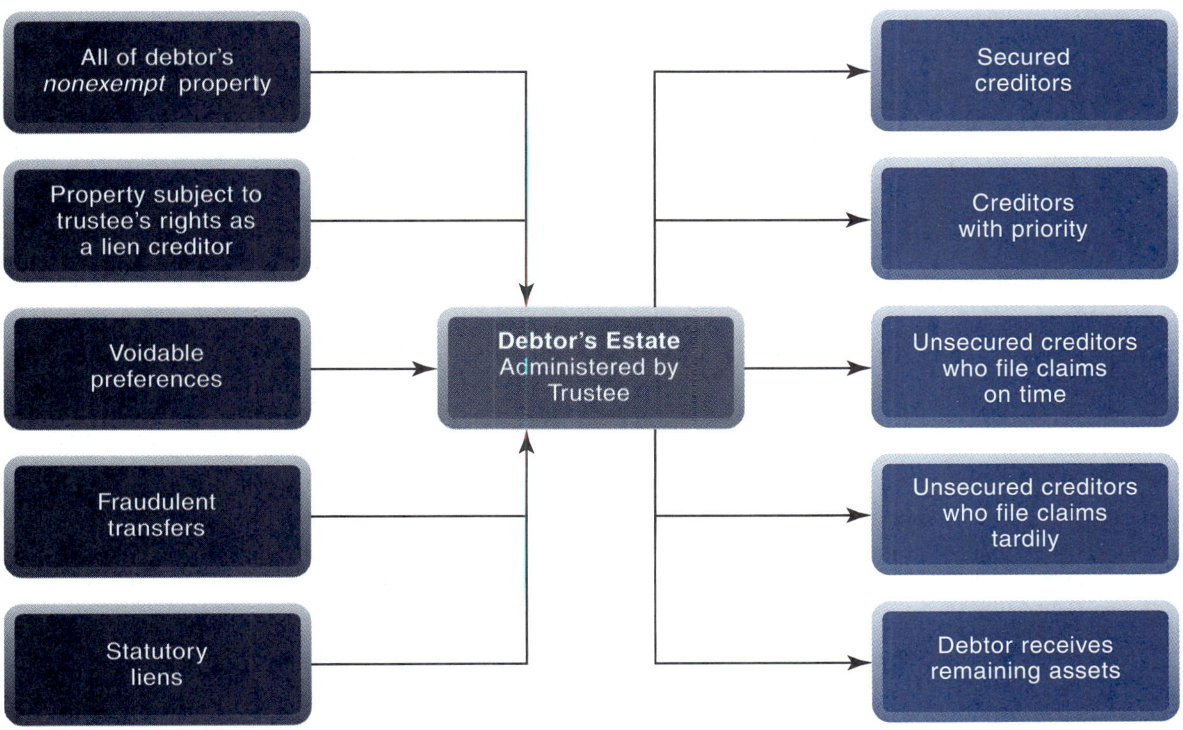

Archer v. Warner

Supreme Court of the United States, 2003
538 U.S. 314, 123 S.Ct. 1462, 155 L.Ed.2d 454
http://caselaw.lp.findlaw.com/cgi-bin/getcase.pl?court=US&navby=case&vol=000&invol=01-1418

FACTS In late 1991, Leonard and Arlene Warner bought the Warner Manufacturing Company for $250,000. About six months later they sold the company to Elliott and Carol Archer for $610,000. A few months after that the Archers sued the Warners in a North Carolina state court for fraud connected with the sale. In May 1995, the parties settled the lawsuit. The settlement agreement specified that the Warners would pay the Archers "$300,000.00 less legal and accounting expenses" "as compensation for emotional distress/personal injury type damages." It added that the Archers would "execute releases to any and all claims * * * arising out of this litigation, except as to amounts set forth in [the] Settlement Agreement." The Warners paid the Archers $200,000 and executed a promissory note for the remaining $100,000. The Archers executed releases "discharging" the Warners "from any and every right, claim, or demand" that the Archers "now have or might otherwise hereafter have against" them, "excepting only obligations under" the promissory note and related instruments. The releases, signed by all parties, added that the parties did not "admit any liability or wrongdoing," that the settlement was "the compromise of disputed claims, and that payment [was] not to be construed as an admission of liability." A few days later the Archers voluntarily dismissed the state-court lawsuit with prejudice.

In November 1995, the Warners failed to make the first payment on the $100,000 promissory note. The Archers sued for the payment in state court. The Warners filed for bankruptcy. The Bankruptcy Court ordered liquidation under Chapter 7 of the Bankruptcy Code. The Archers brought the present claim, asking the Bankruptcy Court to find the $100,000 debt nondischargeable and to order the Warners to pay the $100,000. Leonard Warner agreed to a consent order holding his debt nondischargeable. Arlene Warner contested nondischargeability. The Archers argued that Arlene Warner's promissory note debt was nondischargeable because it was for "money * * * obtained by * * * fraud" as provided by Section 523 the Bankruptcy Code.

The Bankruptcy Court, finding the promissory note debt dischargeable, denied the Archers' claim. The District Court affirmed the Bankruptcy Court. The Court of Appeals for the Fourth Circuit, dividing two to one, affirmed the District Court. The majority reasoned that the new debt was not for money obtained by fraud, but rather it was for money promised in a settlement contract. Thus, the debt was dischargeable in bankruptcy.

The U.S Supreme Court granted the Archers' petition for certiorari because different Circuits have come to different conclusions about this matter.

DECISION The Court of Appeals' judgment is reversed, and the case is remanded.

OPINION Breyer, J. The Bankruptcy Code [Section 523(a)(2)(A)] provides that a debt shall not be dischargeable in bankruptcy "to the extent" it is "for money * * * obtained by * * * false pretenses, a false representation, or actual fraud." [Citation.] Can this language cover a debt embodied in a settlement agreement that settled a creditor's earlier claim "for money * * * obtained by * * * fraud"? In our view, the statute can cover such a debt, and we reverse a lower court judgment to the contrary.

This case arises out of circumstances that we outline as follows: (1) *A* sues *B* seeking money that (*A* says) *B* obtained through fraud; (2) the parties settle the lawsuit and release related claims; (3) the settlement agreement does not resolve the issue of fraud, but provides that *B* will pay *A* a fixed sum; (4) *B* does not pay the fixed sum; (5) *B* enters bankruptcy; and (6) *A* claims that *B's* obligation to pay the fixed settlement sum is nondischargeable because, like the original debt, it is for "money * * * obtained by * * * fraud."

We agree with the Court of Appeals * * * that "the settlement agreement and promissory note here, coupled with the broad language of the release, completely addressed and released each and every underlying state law claim." [Citation.] That agreement left only one relevant debt: a debt for money promised in the settlement agreement itself. To recognize that fact, however, does not end our inquiry. We must decide whether that same debt can *also* amount to a debt for *money obtained by fraud*, within the terms of the nondischargeability statute. Given this Court's precedent, we believe that it can.

Brown v. Felsen, [citation], governs the outcome here. The circumstances there were the following: (1) Brown sued Felsen in state court seeking money that (Brown said) Felsen had obtained through fraud; (2) the state court entered a consent decree embodying a stipulation providing that Felsen would pay Brown a certain amount; (3) neither the decree nor the stipulation indicated the payment was for fraud; (4) Felsen did not pay; (5) Felsen entered bankruptcy; and (6) Brown asked the Bankruptcy Court to look behind the decree and stipulation and to hold that the debt was nondischargeable because it was a debt for money obtained by fraud. [Citation.]

The lower courts had held against Brown. They pointed out that the relevant debt was for money owed pursuant to a consent judgment; they noted that the relevant judgment-related documents did not refer to fraud; they added that the doctrine of res judicata prevented the Bankruptcy Court from looking behind those documents to uncover the nature of the claim that had led to their creation; and they consequently concluded that the relevant debt could not be characterized as one for money obtained by fraud. [Citation.]

This Court unanimously rejected the lower court's reasoning. The Court conceded that the state law of claim preclusion would bar Brown from making any claim " ' based on the same cause of action' " that Brown had brought in state court. [Citation.] Indeed, this aspect of res judicata would prevent Brown from litigating "all grounds for * * * recovery" previously available to Brown, whether or not Brown had previously "asserted" those grounds in the prior state court "proceeding." [Citation.] But all this, the Court held, was beside the point. Claim preclusion did not prevent the Bankruptcy Court from looking beyond the record of the state-court proceeding and the documents that terminated that proceeding (the stipulation and consent judgement) in order to decide whether the debt at issue (namely, the debt embodied in the consent decree and stipulation) was a debt for money obtained by fraud. [Citation.]

As a matter of logic, *Brown's* holding means that the Fourth Circuit's novation theory cannot be right. The reduction of Brown's state-court fraud claim to a stipulation (embodied in a consent decree) worked the same kind of novation as the "novation" at issue here. * * * Yet, in *Brown*, this Court held that the Bankruptcy Court should look behind that stipulation to determine whether it reflected settlement of a valid claim for fraud. If the Fourth Circuit's view were correct—if reducing a fraud claim to settlement definitively changed the nature of the debt for dischargeability purposes—the nature of the debt in *Brown* would have changed similarly, thereby rendering the debt dischargeable. This Court's instruction that the Bankruptcy Court could "weigh all the evidence," [citation], would have been pointless. There would have been nothing for the Bankruptcy Court to examine.

Moreover, the Court's language in *Brown* strongly favors the Archers' position here. The Court said that "the mere fact that a conscientious creditor has previously reduced his claim to judgment should not bar further inquiry into the true nature of the debt." [Citation.] If we substitute the word "settlement" for the word "judgment," the Court's statement describes this case.

Finally, the Court's basic reasoning in *Brown* applies here. The Court pointed out that the Bankruptcy Code's nondischargeability provision had originally covered "only 'judgments' sounding in fraud." [Citation.] Congress later changed the language so that it covered all such " ' liabilities.' " [Citation.] This change indicated that "Congress intended the fullest possible inquiry" to ensure that "all debts arising out of" fraud are "excepted from discharge," no matter what their form. [Citation.] Congress also intended to allow the relevant determination (whether a debt arises out of fraud) to take place in bankruptcy court, not to force it to occur earlier in state court at a time when nondischargeability concerns "are not directly in issue and neither party has a full incentive to litigate them." *Brown*, [citation].

The only difference we can find between *Brown* and the present case consists of the fact that the relevant debt here is embodied in a settlement, not in a stipulation and consent judgment. But we do not see how that difference could prove determinative. The dischargeability provision applies to all debts that "arise out of" fraud. [Citations.] A debt embodied in the settlement of a fraud case "arises" no less "out of" the underlying fraud than a debt embodied in a stipulation and consent decree. * * *

* * *

We conclude that the Archers' settlement agreement and releases may have worked a kind of novation, but that fact does not bar the Archers from showing that the settlement debt arose out of "false pretences, a false representation, or actual fraud," and consequently is nondischargeable, § 523(a)(2)(A) [of the Bankruptcy Act].

INTERPRETATION The Bankruptcy Code prevents the discharge of all liability arising from fraud, including a settlement agreement for a claim of fraud.

ETHICAL QUESTION Was the Court's decision fair to all of the parties affected by this case? Explain.

CRITICAL THINKING QUESTION What are the policy arguments supporting and opposing the Court's decision in this case? Explain.

CPA REORGANIZATION—CHAPTER 11

Reorganization is the process of correcting or eliminating the factors that caused the distress of a business enterprise and thereby preserving both the enterprise and its value as a going concern. Chapter 11 of the Bankruptcy Code governs reorganization of eligible debtors—including partnerships, corporations, and individuals—and permits the restructuring of their finances. A number of large corporations have made use of Chapter 11, including WorldCom, Enron, Kmart, Texaco, A. H. Robins, Johns Manville, Allied Stores, and Global Crossing. The main objective of a reorganization proceeding is to develop and carry out a fair, equitable, and feasible plan of reorganization. After a plan has been prepared and filed, a hearing held before the court determines whether or not it will be confirmed.

PROCEEDINGS

Any person who may be a debtor under Chapter 7 (except a stockbroker or a commodity broker) and railroads may be debtors under Chapter 11. Petitions may be voluntary or involuntary. See *In Re Johns Manville Corporation* later in this chapter.

The 1994 amendments permit small businesses to elect to be subject to streamlined procedures designed to expedite the administration of Chapter 11. The amendments define *small business* to include persons engaged in commercial or business activities whose aggregate, noncontingent, liquidated debts do not exceed $2 million.

As soon as possible after the order for relief, a committee of unsecured creditors (usually those who hold the seven largest unsecured claims against the debtor) is appointed. In addition, the court may order the appointment of additional committees of creditors or of equity security holders, if necessary, to ensure adequate representation. The committee may, with the court's approval, employ attorneys, accountants, and other agents to represent or perform services for the committee. The committee should consult with the debtor or trustee concerning the administration of the case and may investigate the debtor's affairs and participate in formulating a reorganization plan.

The debtor remains in possession and management of the property of the estate unless the court orders the appointment of a trustee, who may then operate the debtor's business. The court orders the appointment of a trustee only for cause (including fraud, dishonesty, incompetence, or gross mismanagement of the debtor's affairs) or if the appointment is in the interests of creditors or equity security holders. The 1994 amendments allow the creditors to elect the trustee.

The duties of a trustee in a case under Chapter 11 include the following: (1) to be accountable for all property received; (2) to examine proofs of claims; (3) to furnish information to all parties with an interest; (4) to provide the court and taxing authorities with financial reports of the debtor's business operations; (5) to make a final report and account of the administration of the estate; (6) to investigate the debtor's financial condition and to determine whether continuing the debtor's business is desirable; and (7) to file a plan or to file a report on why there will be no plan or to recommend either dismissal of the case or its conversion to Chapter 7.

At any time before confirming a plan, the court may terminate the trustee's appointment and restore the debtor to possession and management of the estate property and the operation of the debtor's business. When a trustee has not been appointed, the debtor in possession performs many of the functions and duties of a trustee, with the principal exception of (self-) investigation.

The Bankruptcy Amendments Act of 1984 added a new provision dealing with the rejection of union-drafted collective bargaining agreements. It provides that subsequent to filing and prior to seeking such rejection, the trustee or debtor-in-possession must propose the necessary labor contract modifications that will enable the debtor to reorganize and that will also provide for the fair and equitable treatment of all parties concerned. The provision also requires that good faith meetings to reach a mutually satisfactory agreement be held between management and the union. It authorizes the court to approve rejection of the collective bargaining agreement only if the court finds that the proposal for rejection was made in accordance with these conditions, that the union refused the proposal without good cause, and that the balance of equities clearly favors rejection.

PLAN OF REORGANIZATION

The debtor may file a plan at any time and has the exclusive right to file a plan during the 120 days after the order for relief, unless a trustee has been appointed. Then other parties in interest, including the trustee, if one has been appointed, or a creditors' committee, may file a plan. On request of an interested party and after notice and a hearing, the court may reduce or increase the 120-day or 180-day periods.

A plan of reorganization must divide creditors' claims and shareholders' interests into classes, specify how each class will be treated, deal with claims within each class equally, and provide adequate means for implementing

Ethical Dilemma

For a Company Contemplating Bankruptcy, When Is Disclosure the Best Policy?

FACTS Doris Williams is a senior executive for Foundation Insurance Corporation, a publicly held insurance company that issues a broad range of policies. Early in January, Williams was appointed to serve on a management team composed of herself and four other executive officers. The team reviews and finalizes recommendations for establishing loss reserves, recommendations regarding dividend payments to shareholders, and proposals for press releases.

For the past few years, Foundation has experienced increasingly alarming financial difficulties. Ten years ago, in order to compete with alternative investments, the company developed many innovative life insurance products to provide both traditional insurance and an attractive savings vehicle for the insured. However, to meet the high interest payments on these new insurance products, management invested in risky real estate ventures that promised—but often failed to deliver-high returns. Foundation's property and casualty lines also experienced increased losses due to poor actuarial decisions and an unexpected rise in workers' compensation claims.

Toward the end of the first quarter, during the management team's review of dividend payments, Williams recommended slashing dividend payments, bolstering loss reserves, and publicly disclosing the company's growing financial problems. The four other committee members disagreed. They feared that the public would panic and that the effect on the market would be disastrous. They wanted more time to attempt to turn the business around. Williams went along with the committee for the first and second quarters. By the third quarter, however, the committee could no longer avoid recommending an unprecedented reduction in dividends and a dramatic increase in reserves. By the end of the year, the company, having become insolvent, filed for bankruptcy protection. The current management team now wishes to reorganize the company.

Social, Policy, and Ethical Considerations

1. Was it ethical for Williams to acquiesce with regard to the first and second quarters? Consider the interests of the consumer/policyholder, the company, the shareholders, and the members of the committee. Was there merit to the committee's request for more time to remedy the company's problems?
2. Should bankrupt insurers be treated differently from other bankrupt corporations? What role, if any, should government play in insuring insurance companies?
3. Should the old management team be allowed to retain control of Foundation? Why? Why not?

the plan. After a plan has been filed, the plan and a written disclosure statement approved by the court as containing adequate information must be transmitted to each holder of a claim before seeking acceptance or rejection of the plan. Adequate information is that which would enable a hypothetical reasonable investor to make an informed judgment about the plan.

Acceptance of Plan

Each class of claims and interests has the opportunity to accept or reject the proposed plan. To be accepted by a ***class of claims***, a plan must be accepted by creditors that hold at least two thirds in amount and more than one half in number of the allowed claims of such class that actually voted on the plan. Acceptance of a plan by a ***class of interests***, such as shareholders, requires acceptance by holders of at least two thirds in amount of the allowed interests of such class that actually voted on the plan.

A class that is not impaired under a plan is deemed to have accepted the plan. Basically, a class is not impaired if the plan leaves unaltered the legal, equitable, and contractual rights to which the holder of such claim or interest is entitled. However, a class that will receive no distribution under a plan is automatically deemed not to have accepted the plan.

Confirmation of Plan

The court must confirm a plan before it is binding on any parties, and a court will confirm only a plan that meets all the requirements of the Bankruptcy Code. The following requirements are the most important:

1. The plan must have been proposed in good faith.
2. The court must find that confirmation of the plan is feasible and not likely to be followed by the debtor's liquidation or by its need for further financial reorganization.

3. Certain classes of creditors must have their allowed claims paid in full in cash immediately or, in some instances, on a deferred basis.
4. The plan must be accepted by at least one class of claims, and with respect to each class, each holder must either accept the plan or receive not less than the amount he would have received under Chapter 7. In addition, each class must accept the plan or be unimpaired by it. Nonetheless, under certain circumstances, the court may confirm a plan that is not accepted by all impaired classes by determining that the plan does not discriminate unfairly and that it is fair and equitable. Under these circumstances, a class of claims or interests may, despite its objections, be subjected to the provisions of a plan.

EFFECT OF CONFIRMATION

After its confirmation, the plan governs the debtor's performance obligations. The plan binds the debtor and any creditor, equity security holder, or general partner of the debtor. After the entry of a final decree closing the proceedings, the debtor is discharged from all of its debts and liabilities that arose before the date the plan was confirmed, except as otherwise provided in the plan, the order of confirmation, or the Bankruptcy Code. Unlike Chapter 7, partnerships and corporations may receive a discharge under Chapter 11 unless the plan calls for the liquidation of the business entity's property and termination of its business. The confirmation of a plan does not discharge an *individual* debtor from debts that are not dischargeable.

In Re Johns Manville Corporation

United States Bankruptcy Court, Southern District of New York, 1984
36 B.R. 727, *appeal denied*, 39 B.R. 234

FACTS Johns Manville Corporation **(http://www.jm.com)** and its affiliated companies (Manville) were highly successful industrial enterprises among the nation's Fortune 500. As of August 26, 1982, Manville had some 16,000 asbestos-related health suits pending against it because of its longtime use of products containing this deadly substance. The number of lawsuits was expected to multiply over the next two or three decades as individuals who had been exposed to asbestos began to develop asbestos-related diseases. Moreover, the insurance industry had generally disclaimed any liability to Manville on policies written for this purpose. Therefore, as a result of this mammoth economic burden, Manville filed for protection under Chapter 11 of the Bankruptcy Code on August 26, 1982. Four separate motions to dismiss Manville's petition were lodged before the court.

DECISION Motions to dismiss the Manville petition denied.

OPINION Lifland, Bkrtcy. J. Preliminarily, it must be stated that there is no question that Manville is eligible to be a debtor under the Code's statutory requirements.* * *

* * *

Moreover, it should also be noted that [no] * * * provision relating to voluntary petitions by companies contains any insolvency requirement. * * *

* * *

Accordingly, it is abundantly clear that Manville has met all of the threshold eligibility requirements for filing a voluntary petition under the Code. This Court will now turn to the issue of whether any of the movants have demonstrated sufficient "cause" * * * to warrant the dismissal of Manville's petition.

* * *

A "principal goal" of the Bankruptcy Code is to provide "open access" to the "bankruptcy process." [Citation.] The rationale behind this "open access" policy is to provide access to bankruptcy relief which is as "open" as "access to the credit economy." [Citation.] Thus, Congress intended that "there, should be no legal barrier to voluntary petitions." [Citation.] Another major goal of the Code, that of "rehabilitation of debtors," requires that relief for debtors must be "timely." [Citation.] * * *

Accordingly, the drafters of the Code envisioned that a financially beleaguered debtor with real debt and real creditors should not be required to wait until the economic situation is beyond repair in order to file a reorganization petition. The "Congressional purpose" in enacting the Code was to encourage resort to the bankruptcy process. [Citation.] This philosophy not only comports with the elimination of an insolvency requirement, but also is a corollary of the key aim of Chapter 11 of the Code, that of avoidance of liquidation. The drafters of the Code announced this goal, declaring that reorganization is more efficient than liquidation because "assets that are used for production in the industry for which they were designed are more valuable than those same assets sold for scrap." [Citation.] Moreover, reorganization also fosters the goals of preservation of jobs in the threatened entity. [Citation.]

In the instant case, not only would liquidation be wasteful and inefficient in destroying the utility of valuable assets of the companies as well as jobs, but, more importantly, liquidation would preclude just compensation of some present asbestos victims and all future asbestos claimants. This unassailable reality represents all the more reason for this Court to adhere to this basic potential liquidation avoidance aim of Chapter 11 and deny the motions to dismiss. Manville must not be required to wait until its economic picture has deteriorated beyond salvation to file for reorganization.

* * *

In [this case] it is undeniable that there has been no sham or hoax perpetrated on the Court in that Manville is a real business with real creditors in pressing need of economic reorganization. Indeed, the Asbestos Committee has belied its own contention that Manville has no debt and no real creditors by quantifying a benchmark settlement demand approaching one billion dollars for compensation of approximately 15,500 prepetition asbestos claimants, during the course of negotiations pitched toward achieving a consensual plan. This huge asserted liability does not even take into account the estimated 6,000 new asbestos health claims which have arisen in only the first 16 months since the filing date. The number of post-filing claims increases each day as "future claims back into the present." * * *

Moreover, asbestos related property damage claims present another substantial contingent and unliquidated liability. Prior to the filing date, various schools initiated litigation seeking compensatory and punitive damages from * * * Manville for their unknowing use of asbestos-containing products in ceilings, walls, structural members, piping, ductwork and boilers in school buildings. * * *

* * *

Accordingly, it is clear that Manville's liability for compensatory, if not punitive, damages to school authorities is not hypothetical, but real and massive debt. A range of $500 million to $1.4 billion is the total projected amount of Manville's real debt to the school creditors.

In addition, claims of $425 million of liquidated commercial debt have been filed in this proceeding. The filing also triggered the acceleration of more than $275 million in unsecured public and institutional debt which had not been due prior to the filing. Upon a dismissal of this petition, Manville may be liable in the amount of all of the above-described real debts, plus interest. Manville's present holdings of cash and liquid assets would be insufficient to pay these obligations and, as noted above, its insurance carriers have repeatedly expressed the unwillingness to contribute to the payment of this debt. Thus, upon dismissal, Manville would become a target for economic dismemberment, liquidation, and chaos, which would benefit no one except the few winners of the race to the courthouse. The economic reality of Manville's highly precarious financial position due to massive debt sustains its eligibility and candidacy for reorganization.

In short, there was justification for Manville to elect a course contemplating a viable court-supervised rehabilitation of the real debt owed by Manville to its real creditors. Manville's filing did not in the appropriate sense abuse the jurisdiction of this Court and it is indeed, like the debtor in (citation), a "once viable business supporting employees and unsecured creditors (which) has more recently been burdened with judgments (and suits) that threaten to put it out of existence." * * * [Citation.] Thus, its petition must be sustained.

INTERPRETATION The main objective of a Chapter 11 proceeding is to effect a reorganization of the debtor so as to preserve the enterprise and its value as a going concern.

ETHICAL QUESTION Did Johns Manville Corporation act unethically? Explain.

CRITICAL THINKING QUESTION Do you agree with the court's decision? Explain.

CPA Adjustments of Debts of a Family Farmer—Chapter 12

In 1986, Congress amended the Bankruptcy Act by adding Chapter 12, which provides for the adjustment of the debts of a family farmer with regular annual income. Family farmers are defined as individuals, or individuals and their spouses, who are engaged in farming and who receive 50 percent of their gross income from farming. Their aggregate debts may not exceed $1.5 million, and at least 80 percent of those debts must arise from the farming operation. A corporation or partnership may also qualify as a family farmer if, in addition to meeting the requirements just mentioned, one family holds 50 percent of the stock or equity, and more than 80 percent of the assets of the corporation or partnership are related to the farming operation.

Chapter 12 has a "sunset" provision: it will expire on January 1, 2004 unless Congress reenacts it. The purpose of Chapter 12 is to provide a proceeding for family farmers who do not qualify for Chapter 13 and who find Chapter 11 proceedings overly burdensome. The provisions of Chapter 12 are based on and are substantially the same as those of Chapter 13.

Adjustment of Debts of Individuals—Chapter 13

CPA

Chapter 13 of the Bankruptcy Code permits an individual debtor to file a repayment plan that, if confirmed by the court, will discharge him from almost all of his debts upon completion of the payments under the plan.

Proceedings

Chapter 13 provides a procedure for the adjustment of debts of an individual with regular income who owes liquidated, unsecured debts of less than $290,525 and secured debts of less than $871,550. Sole proprietorships that meet these debt limitations are also eligible; partnerships and corporations are not. Only a voluntary petition may initiate a case under Chapter 13, and a trustee is appointed in every Chapter 13 case. Property of the estate in Chapter 13 includes wages the debtor earned and property she acquired after the Chapter 13 filing.

The Plan

The debtor files the plan and may modify it at any time before confirmation. The plan must meet three requirements:

1. It must require the debtor to submit all or any portion of her future earnings or income, as is necessary for the execution of the plan, to the trustee's supervision and control.
2. It must provide for full payment on a deferred basis of all claims entitled to a priority unless a holder of a claim agrees to a different treatment of such claim.
3. If the plan classifies claims, it must provide the same treatment for each claim in the same class.

In addition, the plan may modify the rights of unsecured creditors and the rights of secured creditors, except those secured only by a security interest in the debtor's principal residence. The plan may not provide for payments over a period longer than three years, unless the court approves, for cause, a longer period not to exceed five years.

Confirmation

To be confirmed by the court, the plan must meet certain requirements. First, the plan must comply with applicable law and be proposed in good faith. Second, the value of the property to be distributed to unsecured creditors must not be less than the amount they would receive under Chapter 7. Third, either the secured creditors must accept the plan, the plan must provide that the debtor will surrender the collateral to the secured creditors, or the plan must permit the secured creditors to retain their security interests and the value of the property to be distributed to them is not less than the allowed amount of their claim. Fourth, the debtor must be able to make all payments and comply with the plan. Fifth, if the trustee or the holder of an unsecured claim objects to the plan's confirmation, then the plan must either provide for payment in full of that claim or provide that all of the debtor's disposable income for three years be applied to payments under the plan. For purposes of this provision, *disposable income* means income received by the debtor that is not reasonably necessary for the maintenance or support of the debtor or a dependent of the debtor or, if the debtor is engaged in business, for the payment of expenditures necessary for continuing, preserving, and operating the business.

Associates Commercial Corporation v. Rash

Supreme Court of the United States, 1997

520 U.S. 953, 117 S. Ct. 1879, 138 L.Ed.2d 148

http://supct.law.cornell.edu/supct/html/96-454.ZD.html

FACTS In 1989, Elray Rash purchased for $73,700 a Kenworth tractor truck for use in his freight-hauling business. Rash made a down payment on the truck, agreed to pay the seller the remainder in 60 monthly installments, and pledged the truck as collateral on the unpaid balance. The seller assigned the loan, and its lien on the truck, to Associates Commercial Corporation (ACC). In March 1992, Elray and Jean Rash filed a joint petition and a repayment plan under Chapter 13 of the Bankruptcy Code. At the time of the bankruptcy filing, the balance owed to ACC on the truck loan was $41,171. The Rashes' Chapter 13 plan invoked the "cram down" power. It proposed that the Rashes retain the truck for use in the freight-hauling business and pay ACC, over 58 months, an amount equal to the present value of the truck. That value, the Rashes' petition alleged, was $28,500. ACC objected to the plan and asked the Bankruptcy Court to lift the automatic stay so ACC could repossess the truck. ACC also filed a proof of claim alleging that its claim was fully secured in the amount of $41,171. The Rashes filed an objection to ACC's claim.

At an evidentiary hearing held to resolve the dispute, ACC maintained that the proper valuation was the price the Rashes would have to pay to purchase a like vehicle (the replacement-value standard), estimated to be $41,000. The Rashes, however, maintained that the proper valuation was the net amount ACC would realize upon foreclosure and sale of the collateral (the foreclosure-value standard), estimated to be $31,875. The Bankruptcy Court adopted the Rashes' valuation figure and approved the plan. The District Court and the Fifth Circuit affirmed.

DECISION Judgment reversed and remanded.

OPINION Ginsburg, J. To qualify for confirmation under Chapter 13, the Rashes' plan had to satisfy the requirements set forth in § 1325(a) of the Code. The Rashes' treatment of ACC's secured claim, in particular, is governed by subsection (a)(5). Under this provision, a plan's proposed treatment of secured claims can be confirmed if one of three conditions is satisfied: the secured creditor accepts the plan, the debtor surrenders the property securing the claim to the creditor, or the debtor invokes the so-called "cram down" power. Under the cram down option, the debtor is permitted to keep the property over the objection of the creditor; the creditor retains the lien securing the claim, and the debtor is required to provide the creditor with payments, over the life of the plan, that will total the present value of the allowed secured claim, i.e., the present value of the collateral. The value of the allowed secured claim is governed by § 506(a) of the Code.

* * *

Courts of Appeals have adopted three different standards for valuing a security interest in a bankruptcy proceeding when the debtor invokes the cram down power to retain the collateral over the creditor's objection. In contrast to the Fifth Circuit's foreclosure-value standard, a number of Circuits have followed a replacement-value approach. [Citation.] Other courts have settled on the midpoint between foreclosure value and replacement value.

The Bankruptcy Code provision central to the resolution of this case is § 506(a), which states:

> "An allowed claim of a creditor secured by a lien on property in which the estate has an interest * * * is a secured claim to the extent of the value of such creditor's interest in the estate's interest in such property, * * * and is an unsecured claim to the extent that the value of such creditor's interest * * * is less than the amount of such allowed claim. Such value shall be determined in light of the purpose of the valuation and of the proposed disposition or use of such property. * * * ." [Citation.]

* * *

We do not find in the § 506(a) first sentence words—"the creditor's interest in the estate's interest in such property"—the foreclosure-value meaning advanced by the Fifth Circuit. Even read in isolation, the phrase imparts no valuation standard: A direction simply to consider the "value of such creditor's interest" does not expressly reveal how that interest is to be valued.

Reading the first sentence of § 506(a) as a whole, we are satisfied that the phrase the Fifth Circuit considered key is not an instruction to equate a "creditor's interest" with the net value a creditor could realize through a foreclosure sale. The first sentence, in its entirety, tells us that a secured creditor's claim is to be divided into secured and unsecured portions, with the secured portion of the claim limited to the value of the collateral. [Citation.] To separate the secured from the unsecured portion of a claim, a court must compare the creditor's claim to the value of "such property," i.e., the collateral. * * * The full first sentence of § 506(a), in short, tells a court what it must evaluate, but it does not say more; it is not enlightening on how to value collateral.

The second sentence of § 506(a) does speak to the how question. "Such value," that sentence provides, "shall be determined in light of the purpose of the valuation and of the proposed disposition or use of such property." § 506(a). By deriving a foreclosure-value standard from § 506(a)'s first sentence, the Fifth Circuit rendered inconsequential the sentence that expressly addresses how "value shall be determined."

As we comprehend § 506(a), the "proposed disposition or use" of the collateral is of paramount importance to the valuation question. If a secured creditor does not accept a debtor's Chapter 13 plan, the debtor has two options for handling allowed secured claims: surrender the collateral to the creditor; or, under the cram down option, keep the collateral over the creditor's objection and provide the creditor, over the life of the plan, with the equivalent of the present value of the collateral. The "disposition or use" of the collateral thus turns on the alternative the debtor chooses—in one case the collateral will be surrendered to the creditor, and in the other, the collateral will be retained and used by the debtor. Applying a foreclosure-value standard when the cram down option is invoked attributes no significance to the different consequences of the debtor's choice to surrender the property or retain it. A replacement-value standard, on the other hand, distinguishes retention from surrender and renders meaningful the key words "disposition or use."

Tying valuation to the actual "disposition or use" of the property points away from a foreclosure-value standard when a Chapter 13 debtor, invoking cram down power, retains and uses the property. Under that option, foreclosure is averted by the debtor's choice and over the creditor's objection. From the creditor's perspective as well as the debtor's, surrender and retention are not equivalent acts.

When a debtor surrenders the property, a creditor obtains it immediately, and is free to sell it and reinvest the proceeds. We recall here that ACC sought that very advantage. [Citation.] If a debtor keeps the property and continues to use it, the creditor obtains at once neither the property nor its value and is exposed to double risks: The debtor may again default and the property may deteriorate from extended use. * * *

Of prime significance, the replacement-value standard accurately gauges the debtors "use" of the property. It values "the creditor's interest in the collateral in light of the proposed [repayment plan] reality: no foreclosure sale and economic benefit for the debtor derived from the collateral equal to * * * its [replacement] value." [Citation.] The debtor in this case elected to use the collateral to generate an income stream. That actual use, rather than a foreclosure sale that will not take place, is the proper guide under a prescription hinged to the property's "disposition or use."

* * *

Nor are we persuaded that the split-the-difference approach adopted by the Seventh Circuit provides the appropriate solution. [Citation.] Whatever the attractiveness of a standard that picks the midpoint between foreclosure and replacement values, there is no warrant for it in the Code. Section 506(a) calls for the value the property possesses in light of the "disposition or use" in fact "proposed," not the various dispositions or uses that might have been proposed. * * *

In sum, under § 506(a), the value of property retained because the debtor has exercised the § 1325(a)(5)(B) "cram down" option is the cost the debtor would incur to obtain a like asset for the same "proposed * * * use."

INTERPRETATION When a Chapter 13 plan proposes to retain the collateral for use in the debtor's trade or business over a creditor's objection under the cram down provisions, the value of the collateral is the price a willing buyer in the debtor's trade, business, or situation would pay to obtain like property from a willing seller.

ETHICAL QUESTION Is the Court's decision fair to all of the parties? Explain.

CRITICAL THINKING QUESTION Which of the three approaches taken by the Courts of Appeal do you prefer? Explain.

EFFECT OF CONFIRMATION

The provisions of a confirmed plan bind the debtor and all of her creditors. The confirmation of a plan vests in the debtor all property of the estate free and clear of any creditor's claim or interest for which the plan provides, except as otherwise provided in the plan or in the order confirming the plan. A plan may be modified after confirmation at the request of the debtor, the trustee, or a holder of an unsecured claim.

DISCHARGE

After a debtor completes all payments under the plan, the court will grant him a discharge of all debts for which the plan provides, except the nondischargeable debts for alimony, maintenance, support, most student loans, liability for driving while intoxicated, governmental fines, and certain long-term obligations on which payments extend beyond the term of the plan. This discharge is considerably more extensive than that granted under Chapter 7. Moreover, though a debtor who receives a discharge under Chapter 7 cannot obtain another discharge under that chapter for six years, a debtor discharged under Chapter 13 is not subject to that limitation if payments under the plan totaled at least (1) 100 percent of unsecured claims or (2) 70 percent of such claims and the plan was the debtor's best effort.

Even if the debtor fails to make all payments, the court may, after a hearing, grant a "hardship discharge" if the debtor's failure is due to circumstances for which the debtor is not justly accountable, the value of property actually distributed is not less than what the creditors would have received under Chapter 7, and modification of the plan is not practicable. This discharge is subject, however, to the same exceptions for nondischargeable debts as a discharge under Chapter 7.

CONCEPT REVIEW

Comparison of Bankruptcy Proceedings

	Chapter 7	Chapter 11	Chapter 12	Chapter 13
Objective	Liquidation	Reorganization	Adjustment	Adjustment
Eligible Debtors	Most debtors	Most debtors, including railroads	Family farmer who meets certain debt limitations	Individual with regular income who meets certain debt limitations
Type of Petition	Voluntary or involuntary	Voluntary or involuntary	Voluntary	Voluntary
Trustee	Usually selected by creditors; otherwise appointed	Only if court orders appointment for cause; creditors then may select trustee	Appointed	Appointed

CREDITORS' RIGHTS AND DEBTORS' RELIEF OUTSIDE OF BANKRUPTCY

The rights and remedies of debtors and creditors outside of bankruptcy are governed mainly by state law. Because of the expense and notoriety associated with bankruptcy, resolving claims outside of a bankruptcy proceeding is often in the best interests of both debtor and creditor. Accordingly, bankruptcy is usually considered a last resort.

Outside of bankruptcy, the rights and remedies of creditors are varied. In the first part of this section, we will examine the basic right of *all* creditors to pursue their overdue claims to judgment and to satisfy that judgment out of property belonging to the debtor. (Other rights and remedies are discussed elsewhere in this book.) The second part of this section will describe the various forms of nonbankruptcy compromises that provide relief to debtors who have become overextended and who are unable to pay all of their creditors.

CPA CREDITORS' RIGHTS

When a debtor fails to pay a debt, the creditor may file suit to collect it. The goal is to obtain a judgment against the debtor and to collect on that judgment.

PREJUDGMENT REMEDIES

Because litigation takes time, a creditor attempting to collect on a claim through the judicial process almost always experiences delay in obtaining judgment. To prevent the debtor from meanwhile disposing of his assets, the creditor may use, when available, certain prejudgment remedies. The most important of these is **attachment**, the process of seizing property, through a judicial order, and bringing the property into the court's custody to secure satisfaction of the judgment ultimately to be entered in the action. Most states limit attachment to specified grounds and provide the debtor an opportunity for a hearing before a judge prior to the issuance of a writ of execution. In addition, the plaintiff generally must post a bond to compensate the defendant for loss should the plaintiff not prevail in the cause of action.

Similar in purpose is the remedy of prejudgment **garnishment**, which is a statutory proceeding directed at a third person who owes a debt to the debtor or who has property belonging to the debtor. Garnishment is most commonly used against the debtor's employer and the bank in which the debtor has a savings or checking account. Garnished property remains in the hands of the third party pending the outcome of the suit.

POSTJUDGMENT REMEDIES

If the debtor still has not paid the claim, the creditor may proceed to trial and try to obtain a court judgment against the debtor. Although necessary, obtaining a judgment is, nevertheless, only the first step. If the debtor does not voluntarily pay the judgment, the creditor will have to take additional steps to collect on it. These steps are called postjudgment remedies.

First, the judgment creditor will have the court clerk issue a **writ of execution** demanding payment of the

THE LAW AND YOU

State Bar Associations

Illinois: http://www.illinoislawyerfinder.com/publicinfo/home.html ("Bankruptcy")

Maine: http://www.mainebar.org/lawyer_pamphlets.asp (legal information pamphlets) ("Some Basic Facts About Bankruptcy")

Maryland: http://www.msba.org/public/brochure.htm ("Should I File for Bankruptcy?")

Minnesota: http://www.mnfindalawyer.com/comsumer-faq.htm ("Bankruptcy: Frequently Asked Questions")

Missouri: http://www.mobar.org/pamphletsbroindex.htm (brochures on legal topics) ("Bankruptcy")

Nevada: http://www.nvbar.org/Publications/Publications_Pamphlets/Bankruptcy_Pamphlet.htm ("Bankruptcy")

New Hampshire: http://www.nhbar.org/?area/15.html ("Should I Declare Bankruptcy?")

New Jersey: http://www.hg.org/cgi-bin/redir.cgi?url=http://www.njsba.com/ ("Bankruptcy")

North Carolina: http://www.ncbar.org/ ("Filing for Bankruptcy")

Oklahoma: http://www.okbar.org/publicinfo/brochures/ ("Is Bankruptcy the Answer?")

Oregon: http://www.osbar.org/public/legalinfo/specinfo.html ("Bankruptcy and Credit")

South Dakota: http://www.sdbar.org/public/Default.htm ("Bankruptcy")

Tennessee: http://www.tba.org/LawBytes/LawBytes.html ("Bankruptcy")

Washington: http://www.wsba.org/public/default.htm ("Bankruptcy")

Wisconsin: http://www.wisbar.org/asp/titles.asp ("Bankruptcy")

State Attorney Generals

Connecticut: http://www.cslib.org/attygenl/mainlinks/tabindex3.htm ("Bankruptcy: Is It Right for You?")

Illinois: http://www.ag.state.il.us/consumer/consume/htm ("Things You Should Know About Bankruptcy")

Maine: http://www.maine.gov/portal/living/consumer_protection.html ("Consumer Rights and a Bankrupt Business")

Pennsylvania: http://www.attorneygeneral.gov/ppd/bcp/brochures.htm ("Bankruptcy and You—Is It the Right Choice?")

U.S. Government

Consumer Information Center: http://www.pueblo.gsa.gov/cic_text/money/managing-debt/mangdebt.htm ("Managing Your Debts: How to Regain Financial Health")

http://www.pueblo.gsa.gov/specpubs.htm#MM ("Bankruptcy")

judgment, which is served by the sheriff upon the defendant debtor. Upon return of the writ "unsatisfied," the judgment creditor may post bond or other security and order a levy on and sale of specified nonexempt property belonging to the defendant debtor, which is then seized by the sheriff, advertised for sale, and sold at public sale under the writ of execution.

The writ of execution is limited to nonexempt property of the debtor. All states restrict creditors from recourse to certain property, the type and amount of which varies greatly from state to state.

If the proceeds of the sale do not produce funds sufficient to pay the judgment, the creditor may institute a ***supplementary proceeding*** in an attempt to locate money or other property belonging to the defendant. She may also proceed by ***garnishment*** against the debtor's employer or against a bank in which the debtor has an account.

CPA DEBTORS' RELIEF

The rights of creditors and the debtor's need for relief involve inherent conflicts arising from the following: (1) the right of diligent creditors to pursue their claims to judgment and to satisfy their judgments by sale of property of the debtor; (2) the right of unsecured creditors who have refrained from suing the debtor; and (3) the social policy of giving relief to a debtor who has contracted debts beyond his ability to pay and who therefore may carry a lifetime burden. Various forms of nonbankruptcy compromises have been developed to resolve these conflicts.

COMPOSITIONS

A common law or nonstatutory **composition** is an ordinary contract or agreement between the debtor and her creditors under which the creditors receive a proportional part of their claims and the debtor is discharged from the balance of the claims. As a contract, it requires contractual formalities. For example, debtor D, owing debts of $5,000 to A, $2,000 to B, and $1,000 to C, offers to settle these claims by paying a total of $4,000 to A, B, and C. If A, B, and C accept the offer, a composition results, with A receiving $2,500, B $1,000, and C $500. The consideration for the promise of A to forgive the balance of his claim consists of the promises of B and C to forgive the balance of their claims. By avoiding a conflict among themselves to obtain the debtor's limited assets, all the creditors benefit.

We should note, however, that the debtor in a composition is discharged from liability only on the claims of those creditors who voluntarily consent to the composition. If, in this illustration, C had refused to accept the offer of composition and had refused to take the $500, he could attempt to collect his full $1,000 claim. Likewise, if D owed additional debts to X, Y, and Z, these creditors would not be bound by the agreement between D and A, B, and C. Another disadvantage of the composition is the fact that any creditor can attach the debtor's assets during the bargaining period that usually precedes the execution of the composition agreement. For instance, once D had advised A, B, and C that he was offering to compose the claims, any one of the creditors could seize D's property.

ASSIGNMENTS FOR BENEFIT OF CREDITORS

A common law or nonstatutory **assignment for the benefit of creditors**, or a general assignment, as it is sometimes called, is a debtor's voluntary transfer of some or all of her property to a trustee, who applies the property to the payment of all the debtor's debts. For instance, debtor D transfers title to her property to trustee T, who converts the property into money and pays it to all of the creditors on a *pro rata* basis.

The advantage of the assignment over the composition is that it prevents the debtor's assets from being attached or executed and halts diligent creditors in their race to attach. On the other hand, though the common law assignment does not require the creditors' consent, the trustee's payment of part of the claims does not discharge the debtor from the balance of them. Thus, in the previous example, even after T pays A $2,500, B $1,000, and C $500 (and makes appropriate payments to all other creditors), A, B, and C and the other creditors may still attempt to collect the balance of their claims.

STATUTORY ASSIGNMENTS

Because assignments benefit creditors by protecting the debtor's assets from attachment, many statutory enactments have endeavored to combine the idea of the assignment with a corresponding benefit that would discharge the debtor from the balance of his debts. However, because the United States Constitution prohibits a state from impairing a contractual obligation between private citizens, it is impossible for a state to force all creditors to discharge a debtor on a *pro rata* distribution of assets, although, as previously discussed, the federal government does have such power and exercises it in the Bankruptcy Code. Accordingly, the states generally have enacted assignment statutes permitting the debtor to obtain voluntary releases of the balance of claims from creditors who accept partial payments, thus combining the advantages of common law compositions and assignments.

EQUITY RECEIVERSHIPS

One of the oldest remedies in equity is the court's appointment of a receiver, a disinterested person who collects and preserves the debtor's assets and income and disposes of them at the court's direction. The court may instruct the receiver (1) to liquidate the assets by public or private sale; (2) to operate the business as a going concern temporarily; or (3) to conserve the assets until final disposition of the matter before the court.

A receiver will be appointed on the petition (1) of a secured creditor seeking foreclosure of his security; (2) of a judgment creditor who has exhausted legal remedies to satisfy the judgment; or (3) of a shareholder of a corporate debtor whose assets will likely be dissipated by fraud or mismanagement. The receiver is always appointed at the discretion of the court. Insolvency, in the equity sense of the debtor's inability to pay her debts as they mature, is one of the factors the court considers in appointing a receiver.

CHAPTER SUMMARY

Federal Bankruptcy Law

Case Administration—Chapter 3

Commencement of the Case the filing of a voluntary or involuntary petition begins jurisdiction of the bankruptcy court
- ***Voluntary Petitions*** available to any debtor even if solvent
- ***Involuntary Petitions*** may be filed only under Chapter 7 or Chapter 11 if the debtor is generally not paying his debts as they become due

Dismissal the court may dismiss a case for cause after notice and a hearing; under Chapters 12 and 13, the debtor has an absolute right to have his case dismissed

Automatic Stay prevents attempts by creditors to recover claims against the debtor

Trustee responsible for collecting, liquidating, and distributing the debtor's estate

Meeting of Creditors debtor must appear and submit to an examination of her financial situation

Creditors, the Debtor, and the Estate—Chapter 5

Creditor any entity that has a claim against the debtor
- ***Claim*** a right to payment
- ***Secured Claim*** claim with a lien on property of the debtor
- ***Unsecured Claim*** portion of a claim that exceeds the value of any property securing that claim
- ***Priority of Claim*** the right of certain claims to be paid before claims of lesser rank

Debtors
- ***Debtor's Duties*** the debtor must file specified information, cooperate with the trustee, and surrender all property of the estate
- ***Debtor's Exemptions*** determined by state or federal law, depending upon the state
- ***Discharge*** relief from liability for all debts except those the Bankruptcy Code specifies as not dischargeable

The Estate all legal and equitable interests of a debtor in nonexempt property
- ***Trustee as Lien Creditor*** trustee gains the rights and powers of a creditor with a judicial lien (an interest in property, obtained by court action, to secure payment of a debt)
- ***Voidable Preferences Bankruptcy Code*** invalidates certain preferential transfers made before the date of bankruptcy from the debtor to favored creditors
- ***Fraudulent Transfers*** trustee may avoid fraudulent transfers made on or within one year before the date of bankruptcy
- ***Statutory Liens*** trustee may avoid statutory liens that first become effective on insolvency, are not perfected at commencement of the case, or are for rent

Liquidation—Chapter 7

Purpose to distribute equitably the debtor's nonexempt assets and usually to discharge all dischargeable debts of the debtor

Proceedings apply to most debtors

Distribution of the Estate in the following order: (1) secured creditors, (2) creditors entitled to a priority, (3) unsecured creditors, and (4) the debtor

Discharge granted by the court unless the debtor has committed an offense under the Bankruptcy Code or has received a discharge within six years

Reorganization—Chapter 11

Purpose to preserve a distressed entity and its value as a going concern

Proceedings debtor usually remains in possession of the property of the estate

Acceptance of Plan requires a specified proportion of creditors to approve the plan

Confirmation of Plan requires (1) good faith, (2) feasibility, (3) cash payments to certain creditors, and usually (4) acceptance by creditors

Effect of Confirmation binds the debtor and creditors and discharges the debtor

Adjustment of Debts of a Family Farmer—Chapter 12

Purpose to permit a family farmer to file a repayment plan that will discharge him from most debts

Proceedings available to a farmer who receives at least 50 percent of his income from farming and who meets certain debt limitations

Confirmation of Plan same as a Chapter 13 proceeding

Discharge after a debtor completes all payments under the plan

Adjustment of Debts of Individuals—Chapter 13

Purpose to permit an individual debtor to file a repayment plan that will discharge her from most debts

Confirmation of Plan requires (1) that it be made in good faith, (2) that the value of property distributed to creditors not be less than the amount that would be paid them under Chapter 7, (3) that secured creditors accept the plan, and (4) that the debtor be able to make all payments and comply with the plan

Discharge after a debtor completes all payments under the plan

Creditors' Rights and Debtors' Relief Outside Bankruptcy

Creditors' Right

Prejudgment Remedies include attachment and garnishment

Postjudgment Remedies include writ of execution and garnishment

Debtors' Relief

Compositions agreement between debtor and two or more of her creditors that each will take a portion of his claim as full payment

Assignment for Benefit of Creditors voluntary transfer by the debtor of some or all of his property to a trustee, who applies the property to the payment of all the debtor's debts

Statutory Assignment provides a voluntary release of balance of claims from creditors who accept partial payments made by the trustee for the debtor

Equity Receivership receiver is a disinterested person appointed by the court to collect and preserve the debtor's assets and income and to dispose of them at the direction of the court

QUESTIONS

1. a. Benson goes into bankruptcy. His estate has no assets. Are Benson's taxes discharged by the proceedings? Why or why not?
   b. Benson obtains property from Anderson on credit by representing that he is solvent when in fact he knows he is insolvent. Is Benson's debt to Anderson discharged by Benson's discharge in bankruptcy?

2. Bradley goes into bankruptcy owing $5,000 as wages to his four employees. There is enough in his estate to pay all costs of administration and enough to pay his employees, but nothing will be left for general creditors. Do the employees take all the estate? If so, under what conditions? If the general creditors received nothing at all, would these debts be discharged?

3. Jessica sold goods to Stacy for $2,500 and retained a security interest in them. Three months later, Stacy filed a petition in bankruptcy under Chapter 7. At this time, Stacy still owed Jessica $2,000 for the purchase price of the goods, whose value was $1,500.
   a. May the trustee invalidate Jessica's security interest? If so, under what provision?
   b. If the security interest is invalidated, what is Jessica's status in the bankruptcy proceeding?
   c. If the security interest is not invalidated, what is Jessica's status in the bankruptcy proceeding?

4. A debtor went through bankruptcy and received his discharge. Which of the following debts were completely discharged, and which remain as future debts against him?
   a. A claim of $900 for wages earned within three months immediately prior to bankruptcy.
   b. A judgment of $3,000 against the debtor for breach of contract.
   c. Sales taxes of $1,800.
   d. $1,000 in past alimony and support money owed to his divorced wife for herself and their child.
   e. A judgment of $4,000 for injuries received because of the debtor's negligent operation of an automobile.

5. Rosinoff and his wife, who were business partners, entered bankruptcy. A creditor, Baldwin, objected to their discharge in bankruptcy on the grounds that
   a. the partners had obtained credit from Baldwin on the basis of a false financial statement;
   b. the partners had failed to keep books of account and records from which their financial condition could be determined; and
   c. Rosinoff had falsely sworn that he had taken $70 from the partnership account when he had actually taken $700.

   Were the debtors entitled to a discharge?

6. X Corporation is a debtor in a reorganization proceeding under Chapter 11 of the Bankruptcy Code. By fair and proper valuation, its assets are worth $100,000. The indebtedness of the corporation is $105,000, and it has outstanding preferred stock of par value of $20,000 and common stock of par value of $75,000. The plan of reorganization submitted by the trustees would eliminate the common shareholders and give bonds of the face amount of $5,000 to the creditors and common stock in the ratio of 84 percent to the creditors and 16 percent to the preferred shareholders. Should this plan be confirmed?

7. Alex is a wage earner with a regular income. He has unsecured debts of $42,000 and secured debts owing to Betty, Connie, David, and Eunice totaling $120,000. Eunice's debt is secured only by a mortgage on Alex's house. Alex files a petition under Chapter 13 and a plan providing payment as follows: (a) 60 percent of all taxes owed, (b) 35 percent of all unsecured debts, and (c) $100,000 in total to Betty, Connie, David, and Eunice. Should the court confirm the plan? If not, how must the plan be modified or what other conditions must be satisfied?

8. John Bunker has assets of $130,000 and liabilities of $185,000 owed to nine creditors. Nonetheless, his cash flow is positive and he is making payment on all of his obligations as they become due. I. M. Flintheart, who is owed $22,000 by Bunker, files an involuntary petition in bankruptcy against Bunker. Bunker contests the petition. What will be the result? Explain.

9. Karen has filed a petition for a Chapter 7 proceeding. The total value of Karen's estate is $35,000. Ben, who is owed $18,000, has a security interest in property valued at $12,000. Lauren has an unsecured claim of $9,000, which is entitled to a priority of $2,000. The United States has a claim for income taxes of $7,000. Steve has an unsecured claim of $10,000 that was filed on time. Sarah has an unsecured claim of $17,000 that was filed on time. Wally has a claim of $14,000 that he filed late, even though Wally was aware of the bankruptcy proceedings. What should each of the creditors receive in a distribution under Chapter 7?

CASE PROBLEMS

10. Landmark at Plaza Park, Ltd., filed a plan of reorganization under Chapter 11 of the Bankruptcy Code. Landmark is a limited partnership whose only substantial asset is a 200-unit garden apartment complex. City Federal holds the first mortgage on the property in the face amount of $2,250,000. The mortgage bears an interest rate of 9.5 percent and is due and payable on October 1, 2006.

    Landmark has proposed a plan of reorganization under which the property now in possession of City Federal would be returned. Landmark will then deliver a nonrecourse note, payable in three years, in the face amount of $2,705,820.31 to City Federal in substitution of all of the partnership's existing liabilities. On the sixteenth month through the thirty-sixth month after the effective date of the plan, Landmark will make monthly interest payments at a rate of 12.5 percent computed on a property value of $2,260,000. Finally, the note will be secured by the existing mortgage. Landmark's theory is that the note will be paid off at the end of thirty-six months by a combination of refinancing and accumulation of cash from the project. The key is Landmark's proposal to obtain a new first mortgage in three years in the face amount of $2,400,000.

City Federal is a first mortgagee without recourse that has been collecting rents pursuant to a rent assignment agreement since the default on the mortgage eleven months ago. City Federal is impaired by the plan and has rejected it. May it complete its foreclosure action? Explain.

11. Freelin Conn filed a voluntary petition under Chapter 7 of the Bankruptcy Code on September 30, 2000. Conn listed BancOhio National Bank as having a claim incurred in October of 1999 in the amount of $4,000 secured by a 1998 Oldsmobile Omega. The car is listed as having a market value of $3,500. During the period from June 30, 2000, to September 30, 2000, Conn made three payments totaling $439.17 to BancOhio. The net payoff balance on the installment loan was $4,015.91 on September 30, the date on which the bankruptcy petition was filed. May the trustee in bankruptcy set aside those three payments as voidable preferences? Explain.

12. On March 6, the debtor negotiated a loan with Interfirst Bank of Dallas (the Bank) and signed a promissory note for the purchase of a BMW from Howard Thornton Ford for his daughter. The daughter picked up the car on March 8, but the Bank did not perfect the purchase money security interest until March 19, which was within the twenty-day limit for perfecting a purchase money security interest under Texas law. On May 23, the debtor filed a bankruptcy petition, and on August 25, the Bank repossessed the daughter's BMW. The bankruptcy trustee sought recovery of the BMW as an asset of the estate, arguing that the transfer of the collateral (the BMW) to the Bank was a voidable preference under the Bankruptcy Code because the Bank's security interest in the car was not perfected within the ten-day grace period then required by the Bankruptcy Code. Should the trustee succeed? Why?

13. Yolanda Christophe filed her Chapter 13 petition on April 19. Her scheduled debts consist of $11,100 of secured debt, $9,300 owed on an unsecured student loan, and $6,960 of other unsecured debt. Christophe asserts that the student loan is nondischargeable and that assertion has not been questioned. Christophe's proposed amended Chapter 13 plan calls for fifty-six monthly payments of $440 a month. The questioned provision in that plan is the division of the unsecured creditors into two classes. Under Christophe's proposed plan, the general unsecured creditors would receive 32 percent and the separately classified student loan creditor would receive 100 percent. Should this plan be confirmed?

14. On December 17, 1986, ZZZZ Best Co., Inc., (the debtor) borrowed $7 million from Union Bank (the bank) (http://www.uboc.com). On July 8, 1987, the debtor filed a voluntary petition for bankruptcy under Chapter 7. During the preceding ninety days, the debtor had made interest payments of $100,000 to the bank on the loan. Wolas, appointed trustee of the debtor's estate, filed a complaint against the bank to recover those payments as a voidable preference. The bankruptcy court held that the payments were not voidable because they came within the ordinary course of business exception. This exception provides that the trustee may not avoid a transfer that was (a) in payment of a debt incurred by the debtor in the ordinary course of business or financial affairs of the debtor and the transferee; (b) made in the ordinary course of business or financial affairs of the debtor and the transferee; and (c) made according to ordinary business terms. Wolas maintains that the exception applies only to short-term, not long-term, debt. Is Wolas correct? Explain.

15. A landlord owned several residential properties in and around Hoboken, New Jersey, one of which was subject to a local rent control ordinance. In 1989, the Hoboken Rent Control Administrator determined that the landlord had been charging rents above the levels permitted by the ordinance and ordered him to refund the wrongfully collected rents to the affected tenants. The landlord did not comply with the order. The landlord subsequently filed for relief under Chapter 7 of the Bankruptcy Code, seeking to discharge his debts. The tenants filed an adversary proceeding against the landlord in the Bankruptcy Court, arguing that the debt owed to them arose from rent payments obtained by "actual fraud" and that the debt was therefore nondischargeable under § 523(a)(2)(A) of the Bankruptcy Code. They also sought treble damages and attorney's fees and costs pursuant to the New Jersey Consumer Fraud Act. The Bankruptcy Court ruled in favor of the tenants, finding that the landlord had committed "actual fraud" within the meaning of § 523(a)(2)(A) and that his conduct violated the New Jersey law. The court therefore awarded the tenants treble damages totaling $94,147.50. Does the Bankruptcy Code bar the discharge of treble damages awarded on account of the debtor's fraud? Explain.

http:// **Internet Exercise** Using the American Bankruptcy Institute's site, find for the most recent year (a) the total number of bankruptcy filings, (b) the number of nonbusiness filings according to chapter of the Bankruptcy Code, and (c) the number of business filings.

Part IX

Regulation of Business

Securities and Exchange Commission
http://www.sec.gov

State Enactments of the Uniform Securities Act
http://www.law.cornell.edu/uniform/vol7.html#secur

Patent and Trademark Office
http://www.uspto.gov/

Copyright Office
http://lcweb.loc.gov/copyright/

Equal Employment Opportunity Commission
http://www.eeoc.gov/

Occupational Safety and Health Administration
http://www.osha.gov/

Federal Trade Commission, Antitrust/Competition Division
http://www.ftc.gov/ftc/antitrust.htm

Department of Justice Antitrust Division
http://www.usdoj.gov/atr/index.html

American Institute of Certified Public Accountants (AICPA)
http://www.aicpa.org/

Financial Accounting Standards Board (FASB)
http://accounting.rutgers.edu/raw/fasb

Consumer Product Safety Commission
http://www.cpsc.gov/

Food and Drug Administration
http://www.fda.gov/

Environmental Protection Agency
http://www.epa.gov/

State Environmental Protection Agencies
http://www.epa.gov/epapages/statelocal/envrolst.htm

United Nations
http://www.unsystem.org/

European Union
http://europa.eu.int/index-en.htm

Chapter 40

Securities Regulation

The merchandise of securities is really traffic in the economic and social welfare of our people. Such traffic demands the utmost good and fair dealing on the part of those engaged in it. If the country is to flourish, capital must be invested in the enterprise.

Franklin D. Roosevelt

Learning Objectives

After reading this chapter you should be able to:

1. Explain the disclosure requirements of the 1993 Act including which securities and transactions are exempt from these disclosure requirements.
2. Explain the potential civil liabilities under the 1933 Act.
3. List which provisions of the 1934 Act apply only to publicly held companies and which apply to all companies.
4. Explain the disclosure requirements of the 1934 Act.
5. Explain the potential civil liabilities under the 1934 Act.

The primary purpose of federal securities regulation is to prevent fraudulent practices in the sale of securities and thereby to foster public confidence in the securities market. Federal securities law consists principally of two statutes: the Securities Act of 1933, which focuses on the issuance of securities, and the Securities Exchange Act of 1934, which deals mainly with trading in issued securities. These "secondary" transactions greatly exceed in number and dollar value the original offerings by issuers.

Both statutes are administered by the Securities and Exchange Commission (SEC), an independent, quasi-judicial agency consisting of five commissioners. In 1996 Congress enacted legislation requiring the SEC, when making rules under either of the securities statutes, to consider, in addition to the protection of investors, whether its action will promote efficiency, competition, and capital formation. The SEC has the power to seek civil injunctions in a federal district court against violation of the statutes, to recommend that the Justice Department bring criminal prosecutions, and to issue orders censuring, suspending, or expelling broker-dealers, investment advisers, and investment companies. The Securities Enforcement Remedies and Penny Stock Reform Act of 1990 granted the SEC the power to issue cease-and-desist orders and to impose administrative, civil penalties up to $600,000. Congress enacted the Private Securities Litigation Reform Act of 1995 (Reform Act) to amend both the 1933 Act and the 1934 Act. One of its provisions grants authority to the SEC to bring civil actions for specified violations of the 1934 Act against aiders and abettors (those who knowingly provide substantial assistance to a person who violates the statute).

The Reform Act sought to prevent abuses in private securities fraud lawsuits. To prevent certain state private securities class action lawsuits alleging fraud from being used to frustrate the objectives of the Reform Act, Congress enacted The Securities Litigation Uniform Standards Act of 1998. The act sets national standards for securities class action lawsuits involving nationally traded securities while it preserves the appropriate enforcement powers of state securities regulators but does not change the current treatment of individual lawsuits. The act amends both the 1933 Act and the 1934 Act by prohibiting any private class action suit in state or federal court by any private party based upon state statutory or common law alleging (1) an untrue statement or omission in connection with the purchase or sale of a covered security or (2) that the defendant used any manipulative or deceptive device in connection with such a transaction.

In response to the business scandals involving companies such as Enron, WorldCom, Global Crossing, and Arthur Andersen in 2002, Congress passed the Sarbanes-Oxley Act, which amends the securities acts in a number of significant respects. The act allows the SEC to add civil penalties to a disgorgement fund for the benefit of victims of violations of the 1933 Act or the 1934 Act. Other provisions of the act are discussed later in this chapter.

The 1933 Act has two basic objectives: (1) to provide investors with material information concerning securities offered for sale to the public and (2) to prohibit misrepresentation, deceit, and other fraudulent acts and unfair practices in the sale of securities generally, whether they are required to be registered or not.

The 1934 Act extends protection to investors trading in securities that are already issued and outstanding. The 1934 Act also imposes disclosure requirements on publicly held corporations and regulates tender offers and proxy solicitations.

Effective October 6, 1995, the SEC provided interpretative guidance for the use of electronic media for the delivery of information required by the federal securities laws. The SEC defined *electronic media* to include audiotapes, videotapes, facsimiles, CD-ROM, electronic mail, bulletin boards, Internet Websites, and computer networks. Basically, electronic delivery must provide notice, access, and evidence of delivery comparable to that provided by paper delivery.

The SEC has established the EDGAR (Electronic Data Gathering, Analysis, and Retrieval) computer system, which performs automated collection, validation, indexing, acceptance, and dissemination of reports required to be filed with the SEC. Its primary purpose is to increase the efficiency and fairness of the securities market for the benefit of investors, corporations, and the economy by speeding up the receipt, acceptance, dissemination, and analysis of corporate information filed with the SEC. After a phase-in period, the SEC now requires all public domestic companies to make their filings on EDGAR, except filings exempted for hardship. EDGAR filings are posted at the SEC's Web site twenty-four hours after the date of filing.

In addition to the federal laws regulating the sale of securities, each state has its own laws regulating such sales within its borders. Commonly called Blue Sky Laws, these statutes all have provisions prohibiting fraud in the sale of securities. In addition, most states require the registration of securities and regulate brokers and dealers.

Any person who sells securities must comply with the federal securities laws as well as with the securities laws of each state in which he intends to offer his securities. However, in 1996 Congress enacted the National Securities Markets Improvements Act, which preempted state regulation of many offerings of securities. Because state securities laws vary greatly, we will discuss only the 1933 Act and the 1934 Act in this chapter.

http:// Securities and Exchange Commission: http://www.sec.gov
State enactments of the Uniform Securities Act: http://www.law.cornell.edu/uniform/vol7.html#secur

THE SECURITIES ACT OF 1933

The 1933 Act, also called the "Truth in Securities Act," requires that a registration statement be filed with the SEC and that it become effective before any securities may be offered for sale to the public, unless either the transaction in which the securities are offered or the securities themselves are exempt from registration. The purpose of registration is to disclose financial and other information about the issuer and those who control it, so that potential investors may consider the merits of the securities. The 1933 Act also requires that potential investors be furnished with a ***prospectus*** (a document offering the securities for sale to interested buyers) containing the important data set forth in the registration statement. The 1933 Act prohibits fraud in *all* sales of securities involving interstate commerce or the mails, even if the securities are exempt from the 1933 Act's registration and disclosure requirements. Civil and criminal liability may be imposed for violations of the 1933 Act.

The National Securities Markets Improvements Act of 1996 broadly authorized the SEC to issue regulations or rules exempting any person, security, or transaction from any of the provisions of the 1933 Act or the SEC's rules promulgated under that act. This authorization extends so far as such exemption is necessary or appropriate in the public interest and is consistent with the protection of investors.

http:// Securities Act of 1933: http://www4.law.cornell.edu/uscode/15/ch2A.html
http://www.law.uc.edu/CCL/33Act/index.html

CPA

DEFINITION OF A SECURITY

The 1933 Act defines the term **security** to include any note, stock, bond, debenture, evidence of indebtedness, preorganization certificate or subscription, investment contract, voting-trust certificate, fractional undivided interest in oil, gas, or other mineral rights, or, in general, any interest or instrument commonly known as a security. This definition broadly includes the many types of instruments that fall within the ordinary concept of a security. Furthermore, the courts generally have interpreted the statutory definition to include nontraditional forms of investments. The Supreme Court, more specifically, employs a two-tier analysis to identify securities. Under this analysis, the Court will presumptively treat as a security a financial instrument designated as a note, stock, bond, or other instrument specifically named in the act.

On the other hand, if a financial transaction lacks the traditional characteristics of an instrument specifically named in the act, the Court has used a three-part test, derived from *Securities and Exchange Commission v. W. J. Howey Co.*, to determine whether that financial transaction constitutes an investment contract and thus a security. Under the *Howey* test, a financial instrument or transaction constitutes an **investment contract** if it involves (1) an investment in a common venture (2) premised on a reasonable expectation of profit (3) to be derived from the entrepreneurial or managerial efforts of others. In certain circumstances, investments in limited partnership interests, citrus groves, whiskey warehouse receipts, real estate condominiums, cattle, franchises, and pyramid schemes have been held to be securities under this test.

Practical Advice

Because securities are so broadly defined, if you plan to sell any type of financial investment, be sure to obtain legal counsel to assist you in complying with the requirements of the securities laws.

Reves v. Ernst & Young

Supreme Court of the United States, 1990
494 U.S. 56, 110 S.Ct. 945, 108 L.Ed.2d 47
http://laws.findlaw.com/US/494/56.html

FACTS In order to raise money to support its business, the Farmer's Cooperative of Arkansas and Oklahoma (the Co-Op) sold promissory notes payable on demand by the holder. The notes were uncollateralized and uninsured, but they paid a variable interest rate, adjusted monthly. In offering the notes to members and nonmembers as part of an "Investment Program," the Co-Op advertised the notes in newsletters by stating, "YOUR CO-OP has more than $11,000,000 in assets to stand behind your investments. The investment is not Federal [sic] insured but is * * * Safe * * * Secure and available when you need it." In 1984, the Co-Op filed for bankruptcy. At that time, 1,600 people held notes worth a total of $10 million. A class of holders (plaintiffs) filed suit against Arthur Young & Co. (Young), the firm that audited the Co-Op's financial statements (and the predecessor to Ernst & Young) **(http://www.ey.com/global/content.nsf/International/Home)**. The plaintiffs alleged that Young intentionally failed to follow generally accepted accounting principles in its audit and that it did so in an effort to inflate the Co-Op's assets and net worth. Specifically, the plaintiffs claimed that Young overvalued the Co-Op's gasohol plant, a major asset, and that if Young had treated the plant properly in its audit, they would not have purchased the demand notes. On these grounds, the plaintiffs argued that Young had violated the antifraud provisions of the Securities Exchange Act of 1934.

The plaintiffs won at trial and were awarded $6.1 million. On appeal, Young argued that the demand notes were not securities under the 1934 Act. The Court of Appeals reversed, and the plaintiffs appealed.

DECISION Judgment of the Court of Appeals reversed and remanded.

OPINION Marshall, J. This case requires us to decide whether the note issued by the Co-Op is a "security" within the meaning of the 1934 Act. * * *

The fundamental purpose undergirding the Securities Acts is "to eliminate serious abuses in a largely unregulated securities market." [Citation.] In defining the scope of the market that it wished to regulate, Congress painted with a broad brush. It recognized the virtually limitless scope of human ingenuity, especially in the creation of "countless and variable schemes devised by those who seek the use of the money of others on the promise of profits," *SEC v. W. J. Howey Co.*, [citation], and determined that the best way to achieve its goal of protecting investors was "to define the 'term security' in sufficiently broad and general terms so as to include within that definition the many types of instruments that in our commercial world fall within the ordinary concept of a security." [Citation.] Congress therefore did not attempt precisely to cabin the scope of the Securities Acts. [Court's footnote: We have consistently held that "[t]he definition of a security in § 3(a)(10) of the 1934 Act, is virtually identical [to the 1933 Act's definition] and, for present purposes, the coverage of the two Acts may be considered the same." [Citation.] We reaffirm that principle here.] Rather, it enacted a definition of "security" sufficiently broad to encompass virtually any instrument that might be sold as an investment.

Congress did not, however, "intend to provide a broad federal remedy for all fraud." [Citation.] Accordingly, "[t]he task has fallen to the Securities and Exchange Commission (SEC), the body charged with administering the Securities Acts, and ultimately to the federal courts to decide which of the myriad financial transactions in our society come within the coverage of these statutes." [Citation.] In discharging our duty, we are not bound by legal formalisms, but instead take account of the economics of the transaction under investigation. [Citation.] Congress' purpose in enacting the securities laws was to regulate *investments*, in whatever form they are made and by whatever name they are called.

* * *

* * * While common stock is the quintessence of a security, [citation], and investors therefore justifiably assume that a sale of stock is covered by the Securities Acts, the same simply cannot be said of notes, which are used in a variety of settings, not all of which involve investments. Thus, the phrase "any note" should not be interpreted to mean literally "any note," but must be understood against the backdrop of what Congress was attempting to accomplish in enacting the Securities Acts.

* * *

* * * First, we examine the transaction to assess the motivations that would prompt a reasonable seller and buyer to enter into it. If the seller's purpose is to raise money for the general use of a business enterprise or to finance substantial investments and the buyer is interested primarily in the profit the note is expected to generate, the instrument is likely to be a "security." If the note is exchanged to facilitate the purchase and sale of a minor asset or consumer good, to correct for the seller's cash-flow difficulties, or to advance some other commercial or consumer purpose, on the other hand, the note is less sensibly described as a "security." [Citation.] Second, we examine the "plan of distribution" of the instrument, [citation], to determine whether it is an instrument in which there is "common trading for speculation or investment," [citation]. Third, we examine the reasonable expectations of the investing public: The Court will consider instruments to be "securities" on the basis of such public expectations, even where an economic analysis of the circumstances of the particular transaction might suggest that the instruments are not "securities" as used in that transaction. [Citations.] Finally, we examine whether some factor such as the existence of another regulatory scheme significantly reduces the risk of the instrument, thereby rendering application of the Securities Acts unnecessary. [Citation.]

* * *

Applying [this] approach to this case, we have little difficulty in concluding that the notes at issue here are "securities." * * * The Co-Op sold the notes in an effort to raise capital for its general business operations, and purchasers bought them in order to earn a profit in the form of interest. Indeed, one of the primary inducements offered purchasers was an interest rate constantly revised to keep it slightly above the rate paid by local banks and savings and loans. From both sides, then, the transaction is most naturally conceived as an investment in a business enterprise rather than as a purely commercial or consumer transaction.

As to the plan of distribution, the Co-Op offered the notes over an extended period to its 23,000 members, as well as to nonmembers, and more than 1,600 people held notes when the Co-Op filed for bankruptcy. To be sure, the notes were not traded on an exchange. They were, however, offered and sold to a broad segment of the public, and that is all we have held to be necessary to establish the requisite "common trading" in an instrument. [Citations.]

The third factor—the public's reasonable perceptions—also supports a finding that the notes in this case are "securities." We have consistently identified the fundamental essence of a "security" to be its character as an "investment." [Citation.] * * * The advertisements for the notes here characterized them as "investments," [citation] * * * and there were no countervailing factors that would have led a reasonable person to question this characterization. In these circumstances, it would be reasonable for a prospective purchaser to take the Co-Op at its word.

Finally, we find no risk-reducing factor to suggest that these instruments are not in fact securities. The notes are uncollateralized and uninsured. Moreover, * * * the notes here would escape federal regulation entirely if the Acts were held not to apply.

INTERPRETATION In determining whether a financial transaction is a security, the courts examine the economic realities of the transaction.

CRITICAL THINKING QUESTION How would you define a security? Explain.

CPA REGISTRATION OF SECURITIES

The 1933 Act prohibits the offer or sale of any security through the use of the mails or any means of interstate commerce unless a registration statement for that security is in effect or the issuer secures an exemption from registration. The purpose of registration is to adequately and accurately disclose financial and other information on which investors may judge the merits of securities. However, registration does not insure investors against loss—the SEC does not judge the financial merits of any security. Moreover, the SEC does not guarantee the accuracy of the information presented in the registration statement.

> **Practical Advice**
>
> When deciding whether to invest in a publicly offered security, keep in mind that the SEC does not pass on the merits of the securities nor does it guarantee the accuracy of the statements made in the registration statement or prospectus.

DISCLOSURE REQUIREMENTS

In general, registration calls for disclosure of information such as (1) a description of the registrant's properties, business, and competition, (2) a description of the significant provisions of the security to be offered for sale and its relationship to the registrant's other capital securities, (3) information about the management of the registrant, and (4) financial statements certified by independent public accountants. In 1992, the SEC imposed new disclosure requirements regarding compensation paid to senior executives and directors. The registration statement must be signed by the issuer, its chief executive officer, its chief financial officer, its chief accounting officer, and a majority of its board of directors.

A registration statement and prospectus become public immediately on filing with the SEC. The effective date of a registration statement is the twentieth day after filing, although the commission, at its discretion, may advance the effective date or require an amendment to the filing, which will begin a new twenty-day period.

Before the filing of the registration statement, it is unlawful to sell, offer to sell, or offer to buy the securities; after the filing, the issuer still may not lawfully sell the securities until the effective date. Nevertheless, before filing, the issuer may give notice that it proposes to make a public offer. Furthermore, after the filing but before the statement's effective date, the issuer may *offer* the securities (1) orally; (2) by certain summaries of the information in the registration statement, as permitted by SEC rules; (3) by a "tombstone advertisement" that identifies the security, its price, and by whom orders will be executed; or (4) by a preliminary prospectus, called a "red herring," which may contain substantially the same information as a final prospectus but which must have a legend in red ink stating that the registration statement has not become effective. After the effective date, the issuer may make sales, provided the purchaser has received a final prospectus. See Figure 40-1 for what sales activities are permissible during the stages of registration.

In 1998 the SEC issued a rule requiring issuers to write and design the cover page, summary, and risk factors section of their prospectuses in plain English. In these sections, issuers must use short sentences; definite, concrete, every-day language; tabular presentation of complex information; no legal or business jargon; and no multiple negatives. Issuers also must design these sections to make

Figure 40-1 *Permissible Sales Activities*

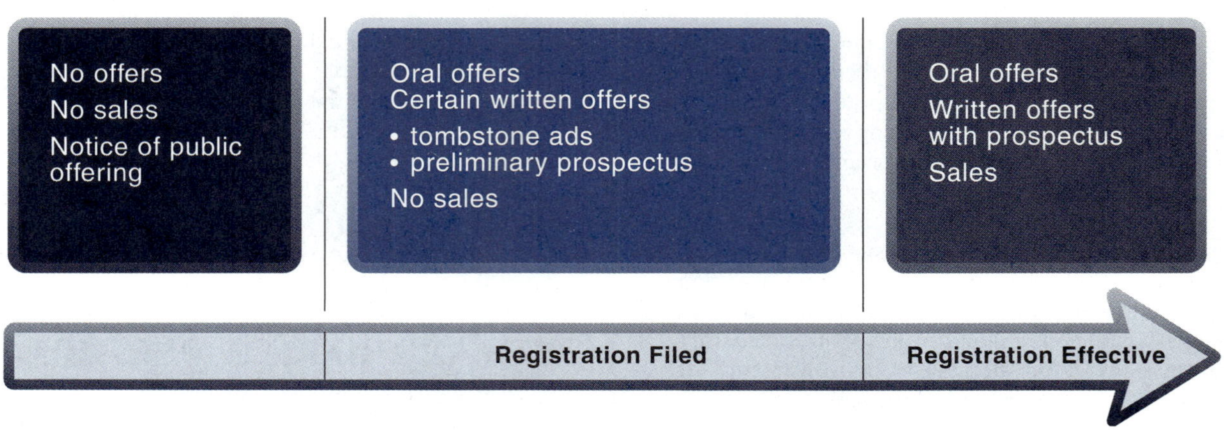

them inviting to the reader and free from legalese and repetition that blur important information.

INTEGRATED DISCLOSURE

The disclosure system under the 1933 Act developed independently of that required by the 1934 Act, which we will discuss later in this chapter. As a result, issuers subject to both statutes were compelled to provide duplicative or overlapping disclosure. Then, in 1982, the SEC, in an effort to reduce or eliminate unnecessary duplication of corporate reporting, adopted an integrated system that provides for three levels of disclosure, depending on the issuer's reporting history and market following. All issuers may use the detailed form described previously. Corporations that have reported continuously under the 1934 Act for at least three years are permitted to disclose less detailed information in the 1933 Act registration statement and to incorporate some information by reference to reports filed under the 1934 Act. Those corporations that have filed continuously under the 1934 Act for at least one year and that have a minimum market value of publicly held voting and nonvoting stock of $75 million are permitted to disclose even less detail in the 1933 Act registration and to incorporate even more information by reference to 1934 Act reports.

In 1992, the SEC issued new rules establishing an integrated registration and reporting system for small business issuers. These rules are intended to facilitate access to the public financial markets for start-up and developing companies and to reduce costs for small business issuers wishing to have their securities traded in public markets. The rules define a small business issuer as a noninvestment company whose annual revenues total less than $25 million and whose voting and nonvoting common stock has a market value of less than $25 million.

http:// 1933 Act registration forms: http://www.law.uc.edu/CCL/33forms/index.html

SHELF REGISTRATIONS

Shelf registrations permit certain qualified issuers to register securities that are to be offered and sold "off the shelf" on a delayed or continuous basis in the future. The information in the original registration must be kept accurate and current and the issuer must reasonably expect that the securities will be sold within two years of the effective date of the registration. Only companies eligible to use the shortest form of registration qualify for shelf registrations.

CPA EXEMPT SECURITIES

The 1933 Act exempts a number of specific securities (called exempt securities) from its registration requirements. Because these exemptions apply to the securities themselves, they also may be resold without registration.

SHORT-TERM COMMERCIAL PAPER

The act exempts any note, draft, or bankers' acceptance (a draft accepted by a bank), issued for working capital, that has a maturity of not more than nine months when issued. This exemption is not available, however, if the proceeds are to be used for permanent purposes, such as the acquisition of a plant, or if the paper is of a type not ordinarily purchased by the general public.

OTHER EXEMPT SECURITIES

The 1933 Act also exempts the following kinds of securities from registration: (1) securities issued or guaranteed by domestic governmental organizations, such as municipal bonds; (2) securities of domestic banks and savings and loan associations; (3) securities of nonprofit charitable organizations; (4) certain securities issued by federally regulated common carriers; and (5) insurance policies and annuity contracts issued by state-regulated insurance companies.

CPA EXEMPT TRANSACTIONS FOR ISSUERS

In addition to exempting specific types of securities, the 1933 Act also exempts *issuers* from the registration requirements for certain kinds of transactions. These **exempt transactions** include (1) private placements (Rule 506), (2) limited offers not exceeding $5 million (Rule 505), (3) limited offers not exceeding $1 million (Rule 504), and (4) limited offers solely to accredited investors (Section 4(6)). Except for some issuances under Rule 504, these registration exemptions apply only to the transaction in which the securities are issued; therefore, any resale must be made by registration, unless the resale qualifies as an exempt transaction.

In addition, the 1933 Act identifies a number of securities exemptions that are in effect transaction exemptions. These include intrastate issues, exchanges between an issuer and its security holders, and reorganization securities issued and exchanged with court or other governmental approval. Moreover, the Bankruptcy Act exempts securities issued by a debtor if they are offered under a reorganization plan in exchange for a claim or interest in the debtor. These exemptions apply only to the original issuance, and resales may be made only by registration, unless the resale qualifies as an exempt transaction.

Another transaction exemption is Regulation A, which permits an issuer to sell a limited amount of securities in an unregistered public offering, if certain conditions are met. Unlike other transaction exemptions, Regulation A places no restrictions upon the resale of securities issued pursuant to it.

Figure 40-2 illustrates registration and exemptions from registration under the 1933 Act.

Practical Advice

If you plan to issue securities, carefully explore the possibility of using a transaction that is exempt from registration.

LIMITED OFFERS

The 1933 Act exempts, or authorizes the SEC to exempt, transactions that do not require the protection of registration because they either involve a small amount of money or are made in a limited manner. Promulgated in 1982 to simplify and clarify the transaction exemptions relating to small issues and small issuers, **Regulation** D contains three separate exemptions (Rules 504, 505, and 506), each involving limited offers. Section 4(6), also aimed at small issues, is a companion section to the exemptions under Regulation D.

Securities sold pursuant to these exemptions (with the exception of some sold pursuant to Rule 504) are considered **restricted securities** and may be resold only by registration or in another transaction exempt from registration. An issuer who uses these exemptions must take reasonable care to prevent nonexempt, unregistered resales of restricted securities. Reasonable care includes, but is not limited to, the following: (a) making a reasonable inquiry to determine whether the purchaser is acquiring the securities for herself or for other persons; (b) providing written disclosure, prior to the sale to each purchaser, that the securities have not been registered and therefore cannot be resold unless they are registered or unless an exemption from registration is available; and (c) placing a legend on the securities certificate stating that the securities have not been registered and that they are restricted securities.

http:// Regulation D: http://www.law.uc.edu/CCL/33ActRls/regD.html

Private Placements The most important transaction exemption for issuers is the so-called private placement provision of the act, which exempts "transactions by an issuer not involving any public offering." SEC **Rule 506** establishes a nonexclusive safe harbor for limited offers and sales without regard to the dollar amount of the

Figure 40-2 *Registration and Exemptions under the 1933 Act*

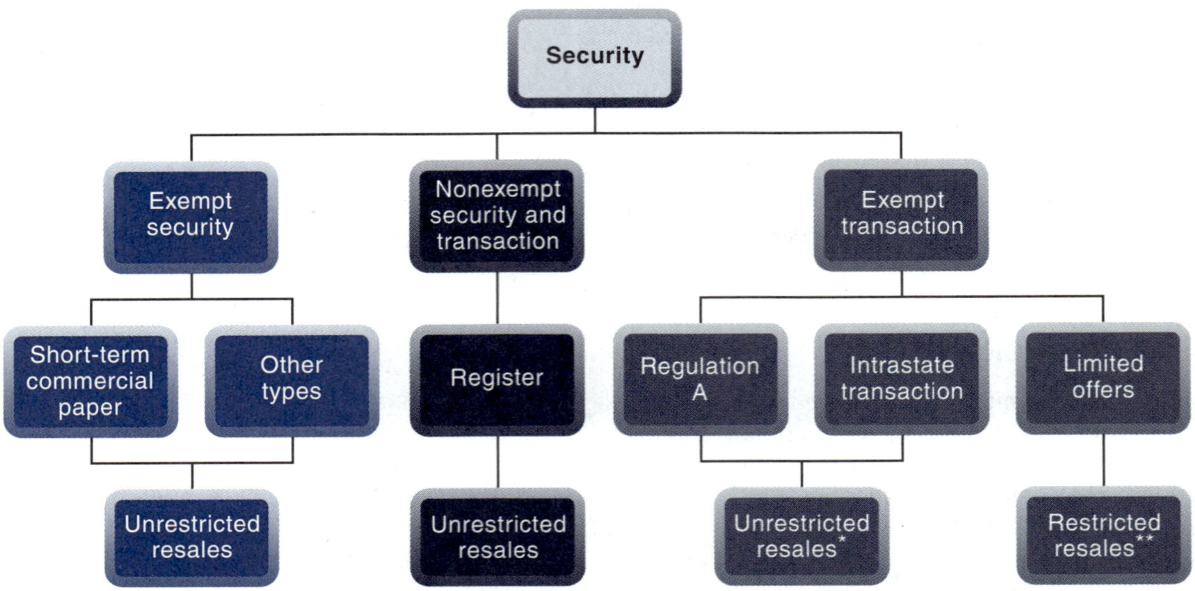

* Under intrastate exemption, resales to nonresidents may only be made nine months after the last sale in the initial issuance.
** Except some issuances under Rule 504.

offering. Satisfying the rule assures the exemption, but there is no presumption that the exemption is unavailable for transactions that do not comply with the rule.

Securities sold under this exemption are restricted securities and may be resold only by registration or in a transaction exempt from registration. General advertising or solicitation is not permitted. The issue may be purchased by an unlimited number of "accredited investors" and by no more than thirty-five other purchasers. ***Accredited investors*** include banks, insurance companies, investment companies, executive officers or directors of the issuer, savings and loan associations, registered broker-dealers, certain employee benefit plans with total assets in excess of $5 million, any person whose net worth exceeds $1 million, and any person whose income exceeded $200,000 in each of the two preceding years and who reasonably expects an income in excess of $200,000 in the current year. If the sale involves any nonaccredited investors, the issuer must, before the sale, give such purchasers specified material information about the issuer, its business, and the securities being offered. If all the purchasers are accredited investors, such disclosure is not mandatory. The issuer must reasonably believe that each purchaser who is not an accredited investor has sufficient knowledge and experience in financial and business matters to evaluate the merits and risks of the investment or has the services of a representative who possesses such knowledge and experience. The issuer must notify the SEC of sales made under the exemption and must take precautions against nonexempt, unregistered resales.

Limited Offers Not Exceeding $5 Million SEC ***Rule 505*** exempts from registration those offerings by noninvestment company issuers that do not exceed $5 million over twelve months. Securities sold under this exemption are restricted securities and may be resold only by registration or in a transaction exempt from registration. General advertising or general solicitation is not permitted. The issue may be purchased by an unlimited number of accredited investors and by no more than thirty-five other purchasers. If the sale involves any nonaccredited investors, the issuer must, before the sale, give them specified material information about the issuer, its business, and the securities being offered; otherwise, such disclosure is not required. Unlike the issuer under Rule 506, however, the issuer under Rule 505 is not required to believe reasonably that each nonaccredited investor, either alone or with his representative, has sufficient knowledge and experience in financial matters to be capable of evaluating the investment's merits and risks. As under Rule 506, the issuer must take precautions against nonexempt, unregistered resales and must notify the SEC of sales made under the exemption.

Limited Offers Not Exceeding $1 Million As amended in 1999, SEC ***Rule 504*** provides private, noninvestment company issuers with an exemption from registration for small issues not exceeding $1 million within twelve months. (Issuers required to report under the 1934 Act and investment companies may not use Rule 504.) The issuer is to notify the SEC of sales under the rule, which permits sales to an unlimited number of investors and does not require the issuer to furnish any information to them.

If the issuance meets certain conditions, Rule 504 permits general solicitations, and acquired shares are freely transferable. The conditions are that the issuance is either (1) registered under state law requiring public filing and delivery of a disclosure document to investors before sale or (2) exempted under state law permitting general solicitation and advertising so long as sales are made only to accredited investors.

If the issuance does not meet these conditions, general solicitation and advertising are not permitted. Moreover, the securities issued are restricted, and the issuer must take precautions against nonexempt, unregistered resales.

Limited Offers Solely to Accredited Investors In 1980, Congress added ***Section 4(6)***, which provides an exemption for offers and sales, not in excess of $5 million, made by an issuer solely to accredited investors. General advertising or public solicitation is not permitted. As with Rules 505 and 506, an unlimited number of accredited investors may purchase the issue; however, Section 4(6) allows no unaccredited investors to purchase. No information is required to be furnished to the purchasers. Securities sold under this exemption are restricted securities and may be resold only by registration or in a transaction exempt from registration. The issuer must notify the SEC of sales made under the exemption and must take precautions against nonexempt, unregistered resales.

REGULATION A

As amended in 1992, Regulation A permits an issuer to offer up to $5 million of securities in any twelve-month period without registering them, provided that the issuer files an offering statement with the SEC's regional office prior to the sale of the securities. An offering circular must also be provided to offerees and purchasers. The issuer may make offers upon filing the offering statement but may make sales only after the SEC has qualified it. (Issuers required to report under the 1934 Act and investment companies may not use Regulation A.) Regulation A filings are less detailed and time consuming than full registration statements, and the required financial statements are simpler and need not be audited unless the issuer has audited financial statements prepared for other purposes. Issuers now may use an optional, simplified question-and-answer disclosure document.

Regulation A sets no restrictions regarding the number or qualifications of investors who may purchase securities under its provisions. Furthermore, securities sold under Regulation A may be resold freely after they are issued.

http:// Regulation A: http://www.law.uc.edu/CCL/33ActRls/regA.html

INTRASTATE ISSUES

The 1933 Act also exempts from registration any security that is a part of an issue offered and sold only to persons who live in a single state where the issuer of such security is resident and doing business. This exemption is intended to apply to local issues representing local financing carried out by local persons through local investments. The exemption does not apply if any offeree, who need not become a purchaser, is not a resident of the state in which the issuer is resident.

Rule 147, promulgated by the SEC, provides a nonexclusive safe harbor for securing the intrastate exemption. Although satisfying the rule assures the exemption, the exemption is not presumed to be unavailable for transactions that do not comply with the rule. Rule 147 requires that (1) the issuer be incorporated or organized in the state in which the issuance occurs; (2) the issuer be doing business principally in that state, meaning that the issuer must derive 80 percent of its gross revenues from that state, 80 percent of its assets must be located in that state, and it must use 80 percent of the net proceeds from the issue in that state; (3) all of the offerees and purchasers be residents of that state; (4) no resales to nonresidents be made during the period of sale and for nine months after the last sale; and (5) the issuer take precautions against interstate distributions. Such precautions include (a) placing on the security certificate a legend stating that the securities have not been registered and that resales can be made only to residents of the state and (b) obtaining a written statement of residence from each purchaser.

CPA EXEMPT TRANSACTIONS FOR NON-ISSUERS

The 1933 Act requires registration for ***any*** sale by any person (including non-issuers) of any nonexempt security, unless a statutory exemption can be found for the transaction. The act, however, provides a transaction exemption for any person other than an issuer, underwriter, or dealer. In addition, the act exempts most transactions by dealers and brokers. These three provisions exempt from the registration requirements of the 1933 Act most secondary transactions; that is, the numerous resales that occur on an exchange or in the over-the-counter market. Nevertheless, these exemptions do not extend to some situations involving resales by non-issuers, in particular to (1) resales of restricted securities acquired under Regulation D (Rules 506, 505, or 504) or Section 4(6) and (2) sales of restricted or nonrestricted securities by affiliates. Such sales must be made pursuant to registration, Rule 144, or Regulation A, subject to the limited exception provided some issuances under Rule 504. An **affiliate** is a person who controls, is controlled by, or is under common control with the issuer. **Control** is the direct or indirect possession of the power to direct the management and policies of a person through ownership of securities, by contract, or otherwise.

Practical Advice

If you acquire restricted securities, do not resell them until you register them—which is rarely feasible—or you comply with an exemption for non-issuers.

RULE 144

Rule 144 of the SEC sets forth conditions that, if met by an affiliate or by any person selling restricted securities, exempt her from registering such securities. The rule requires that there be adequate current public information about the issuer, that the person selling under the rule have owned the securities for at least one year, that she sell them only in limited amounts in unsolicited brokers' transactions, and that notice of the sale be provided to the SEC. A person who is not an affiliate of the issuer when the restricted securities are sold and who has owned the securities for at least two years, however, may sell them in unlimited amounts and is not subject to any of the other requirements of Rule 144. Sales by an affiliate are subject to Rule 144 whether the securities are restricted or nonrestricted; however, compliance with the one-year holding period is not required when an affiliate sells nonrestricted securities.

REGULATION A

Regulation A, in addition to providing issuers an exemption from registration for securities up to $5 million, also provides an exemption for non-issuers. The regulation places a $1.5 million limit on the total amount of securities

CONCEPT REVIEW

Exempt Transactions for Issuers Under the 1933 Act

Exemption	Price Limitation	Information Required	Limitations on Purchasers	Resales
Regulation A	$5 million	Offering circular	None	Unrestricted
Intrastate Rule 147	None	None	Intrastate only	Only to residents before 9 months
Rule 506	None	Material information to unaccredited purchasers	Unlimited accredited; 35 unaccredited	Restricted
Rule 505	$5 million	Material information to unaccredited purchasers	Unlimited accredited; 35 unaccredited	Restricted
Rule 504	$1 million	None	None	Restricted*
Section 4(6)	$5 million	None	Only accredited	Restricted

* Unrestricted if under state law the issuance is either (1) registered or (2) exempted with sales only to accredited investors.

sold by all non-issuers in any twelve-month period. Use of this exemption requires compliance with all of the conditions Regulation A imposes upon issuers, as discussed previously.

CPA LIABILITY

To implement its objectives of providing full disclosure and preventing fraud in the sale of securities, the 1933 Act imposes a number of sanctions for noncompliance with its requirements. These sanctions include administrative remedies by the SEC, civil liability to injured investors, and criminal penalties. In addition, the court may award attorneys' fees against any party who brings suit or asserts a defense without merit.

The Reform Act provides "forward-looking" statements (predictions) a "safe harbor" under the 1933 Act from civil liability that is based on an untrue statement of material fact or an omission of a material fact necessary to make the statement not misleading. The safe harbor applies only to issuers required to report under the 1934 Act. The safe harbor eliminates civil liability if a forward-looking statement is (1) immaterial, (2) made without actual knowledge that it was false or misleading, or (3) identified as a forward-looking statement and is accompanied by meaningful cautionary statements identifying important factors that could cause actual results to differ materially from those predicted. "Forward-looking" statements include projections of revenues, income, earnings per share, capital expenditures, dividends, or capital structure; management's plans and objectives for future operations; and statements of future economic performance. The safe harbor provision, however, does not cover statements made in connection with an initial public offering, a tender offer, a going private transaction, or offerings by a partnership or a limited liability company.

UNREGISTERED SALES

Section 12(a)(1) of the act imposes express civil liability for the sale of an unregistered security that is required to be registered, the sale of a registered security without delivery of a prospectus, the sale of a security by use of an outdated prospectus, or the offer of a sale before the filing of the registration statement. Liability is strict or absolute, because there are no defenses. The person who purchases a security sold in violation of this provision has the right to tender it back to the seller and recover the purchase price. If the purchaser no longer owns the security, he may recover monetary damages from the seller.

FALSE REGISTRATION STATEMENTS

When securities have been sold subject to a registration statement, Section 11 of the act imposes express liability on those who have included any untrue statement of a material fact in the registration statement or who have omitted any material fact from it. **Material** matters are those to which a reasonable investor would be substantially likely to attach importance in determining whether to purchase the security registered. Usually, proof of reliance upon the misstatement or omission is not required. The section imposes liability on (1) the issuer; (2) all persons who signed the registration statement, including the principal executive officer, principal financial officer, and principal accounting officer; (3) every person who was a director or partner; (4) every accountant, engineer, appraiser, or expert who prepared or certified any part of the registration statement; and (5) all underwriters. These persons are generally jointly and severally liable for the amount paid for the security, less either its value at the time of suit or the price for which it was sold, to any person who acquires the security without knowledge of the untruth or omission. A defendant is not liable for any or the entire amount otherwise recoverable under Section 11 that the defendant proves was caused by something other than the defective disclosure.

An expert is liable only for misstatements or omissions in the portion of the registration that she prepared or certified. Moreover, any defendant, other than the issuer (who has strict liability), may assert the defense of due diligence. The **due diligence defense** generally requires the defendant to show that he had reasonable grounds to believe and did believe that there were no untrue statements or material omissions. In some instances, due diligence requires a reasonable investigation to determine grounds for belief. The standard of reasonableness for such investigation and such grounds is that required of a prudent person in the management of his own property.

Escott v. BarChris Const. Corp.

United States District Court, Southern District of New York, 1968
283 F.Supp. 643

FACTS BarChris Construction Corporation sold shares of common stock to the public in December 1959. By early 1961, BarChris needed additional working capital and sold debentures to meet this need. A registration statement was filed with the SEC in March 1961, with amendments filed in May. By the time BarChris received the net proceeds of this sale, it was experiencing financial difficulties. Eventually BarChris filed for bankruptcy. Escott, a purchaser of the debentures, brought suit under the Securities Act of 1933 against BarChris, the underwriters, the company's auditors (Peat, Marwick, Mitchell & Co.) **(http://www.kpmg.com)**, and the persons who signed the registration, alleging that the registration statement contained materially false statements and material omissions. The defendants denied the falsity of the statements and their materiality. Furthermore, all of the defendants, except BarChris, claimed that they individually had exercised due diligence in connection with the statement so as to be free from liability under the statute.

DECISION Judgment for Escott granted.

OPINION McLean, J. It is a prerequisite to liability under Section 11 of the Act that the fact which is falsely stated in a registration statement, or the fact that is omitted when it should have been stated to avoid misleading, be "material." The regulations of the Securities and Exchange Commission pertaining to the registration of securities define the word as follows:

> The term "material," when used to qualify a requirement for the furnishing of information as to any subject, limits the information required to those matters as to which an average prudent investor ought reasonably to be informed before purchasing the security registered.

* * *

The average prudent investor is not concerned with minor inaccuracies or with errors as to matters which are of no interest to him. The facts which tend to deter him from purchasing a security are facts which have an important bearing upon the nature or condition of the issuing corporation or its business.

Judged by this test, there is no doubt that many of the misstatements and omissions in this prospects were material. * * *

* * *

Section 11(b) of the Act provides that:

> * * * [N]o person, other than the issuer, shall be liable * * * who shall sustain the burden of proof—
>
> * * *
>
> (3) that (A) as regards any part of the registration statement not purporting to be made on the authority of an expert * * * he had, after reasonable investigation, reasonable ground to believe and did believe, at the time such part of the registration statement became effective, that the statements therein were true and that there was no omission to state a material fact required to be stated therein or necessary to make the statements therein not misleading; * * * and (C) as regards any part of the registration statement purporting to be made on the authority of an expert (other than himself) * * * he had no reasonable ground to believe and did not believe, at

the time such part of the registration statement became effective, that the statements therein were untrue or that there was an omission to state a material fact required to be stated therein or necessary to make the statements therein not misleading * * *

Section 11(c) defines "reasonable investigation" as follows:

In determining, for the purposes of paragraph (3) of subsection (b) of this section, what constitutes reasonable investigation and reasonable ground for belief, the standard of reasonableness shall be that required of a prudent man in the management of his own property.

Every defendant, except BarChris itself, to whom, as the issuer, these defenses are not available, and except Peat, Marwick, whose position rests on a different statutory provision, has pleaded these affirmative defenses. Each claims that (1) as to the part of the registration statement purporting to be made on the authority of an expert (which, for convenience, I shall refer to as the "expertised portion"), he had no reasonable ground to believe and did not believe that there were any untrue statements or material omissions, and (2) as to the other parts of the registration statement, he made a reasonable investigation, as a result of which he had reasonable ground to believe and did believe that the registration statement was true and that no material fact was omitted. As to each defendant, the question is whether he has sustained the burden of proving these defenses. Surprising enough, there is little or no judicial authority on this question. No decisions directly in point under Section 11 have been found.

Before considering the evidence, a preliminary matter should be disposed of. The defendants do not agree among themselves as to who the "experts" were or as to the parts of the registration statement which were expertised.

* * *

* * * Neither the lawyer for the company nor the lawyer for the underwriters is an expert within the meaning of Section 11. The only expert, in the statutory sense, was Peat, Marwick, and the only parts of the registration statement which purported to be made upon the authority of an expert were the portions which purported to be made on Peat, Marwick's authority.

[The court found that none of the defendants had sustained the burden of proving the due diligence defense.]

INTERPRETATION The 1933 Act imposes liability for material misstatements and omissions in a registration statement on the issuer, the directors, certain officers, experts, and the underwriters. These parties, except the issuer, may avoid liability by proving that they exercised due diligence in executing their duties with respect to the registration process.

CRITICAL THINKING QUESTION Do you agree with the court's decision? Explain.

ANTIFRAUD PROVISIONS

The 1933 Act also contains two antifraud provisions: Section 12(a)(2) and Section 17(a). In addition, Rule 10b–5 of the 1934 Act applies to the issuance or sale of all securities, even those exempted by the 1933 Act. Rule 10b–5 is discussed later in this chapter.

Section 12(a)(2) imposes express liability on any person who offers or sells a security by means of a prospectus or oral communication that contains an untrue statement of material fact or omits a material fact. This liability extends only to the immediate purchaser, provided she did not know of the untruth or omission. The seller may avoid liability by proving that he did not know, and in the exercise of reasonable care could not have known, of the untrue statement or omission. The seller is liable to the purchaser for the amount paid on tender of the security. If the purchaser no longer owns the security, she may recover damages from the seller. A defendant is not liable for any or the entire amount otherwise recoverable under Section 12(a)(2) that the defendant proves was caused by something other than the defective disclosure.

Section 17(a) makes it unlawful for any person in the offer or sale of any securities, whether registered or not, to do any of the following when using any means of transportation or communication in interstate commerce or the mails: (1) employ any device, scheme, or artifice to defraud; (2) obtain money or property by means of any untrue statement of a material fact or any statement that omits a material fact, without which the information is misleading; or (3) engage in any transaction, practice, or course of business that operates or would operate as a fraud or deceit upon the purchaser. There is considerable doubt whether the courts may imply a private right of action for persons injured by violations of this section. The Supreme Court has reserved this question, and most lower courts have denied the existence of a private remedy. The SEC may, however, bring enforcement actions under Section 17(a).

CRIMINAL SANCTIONS

The 1933 Act imposes **criminal sanctions** on any person who willfully violates any of the provisions of the act or the rules and regulations promulgated by the SEC pursuant to the act. Conviction may carry a fine of not more than $10,000 or imprisonment of not more than five years, or both.

The registration and liability provisions of the 1933 Act are summarized in Figure 40-3.

THE SECURITIES EXCHANGE ACT OF 1934

The Securities Exchange Act of 1934 deals mainly with the secondary distribution (resale) of securities. The 1934 Act's definition of a security is substantially the same as that of the 1933 Act. The 1934 Act seeks to ensure fair and orderly securities markets by establishing rules for market operations and by prohibiting fraudulent and manipulative practices. It protects holders of all securities listed on national exchanges, as well as holders of equity securities of companies traded over the counter whose corporate assets exceed $10 million and whose equity securities include a class with 500 or more shareholders. Companies must register such securities and are subject to the 1934 Act's periodic reporting requirements, short-swing profits provision, tender offer provisions, and proxy solicitation provisions, as well as the internal control and recordkeeping requirements of the Foreign Corrupt Practices Act. In addition, issuers of securities, whether registered under the 1934 Act or not, must comply with the antifraud and antibribery provisions of the Act. Figure 40-4 illustrates the applicability of the 1934 Act's provisions to different types of issuers.

The National Securities Markets Improvements Act of 1996 broadly authorized the SEC to issue regulations, rules, or orders exempting any person, security, or transaction from any of the provisions of the 1934 Act or the SEC's rules promulgated under that Act. This authorization extends so far as such exemption is necessary or appropriate in the public interest and is consistent with the protection of investors. This exemptive authority does not, however, extend to the regulation of government securities broker-dealers.

http:// Securities Exchange Act of 1934: http://www4.law.cornell.edu/uscode/15/ch2B.html
http://www.law.uc.edu/CCL/34Act/index.html

Figure 40-3 *Registration and Liability Provisions of the 1933 Act*

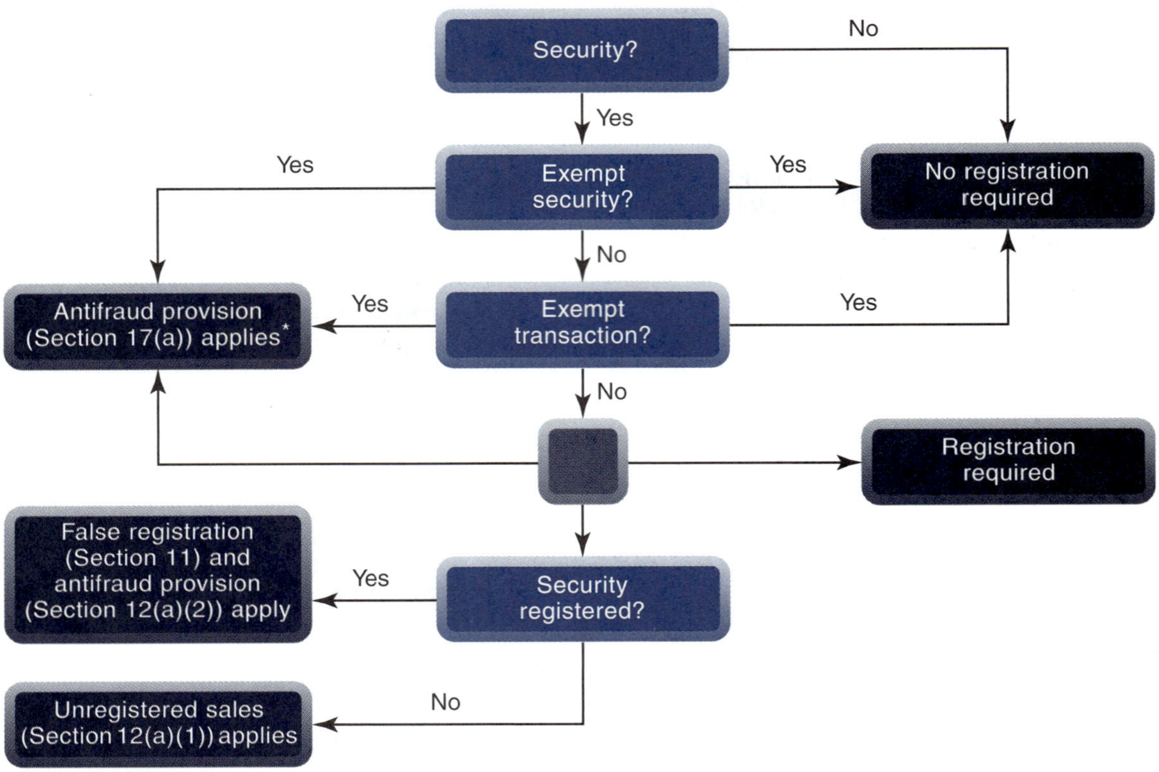

*Section 12(a)(2) *may* apply to some of these issuances.

Figure 40-4 *Applicability of the 1934 Act*

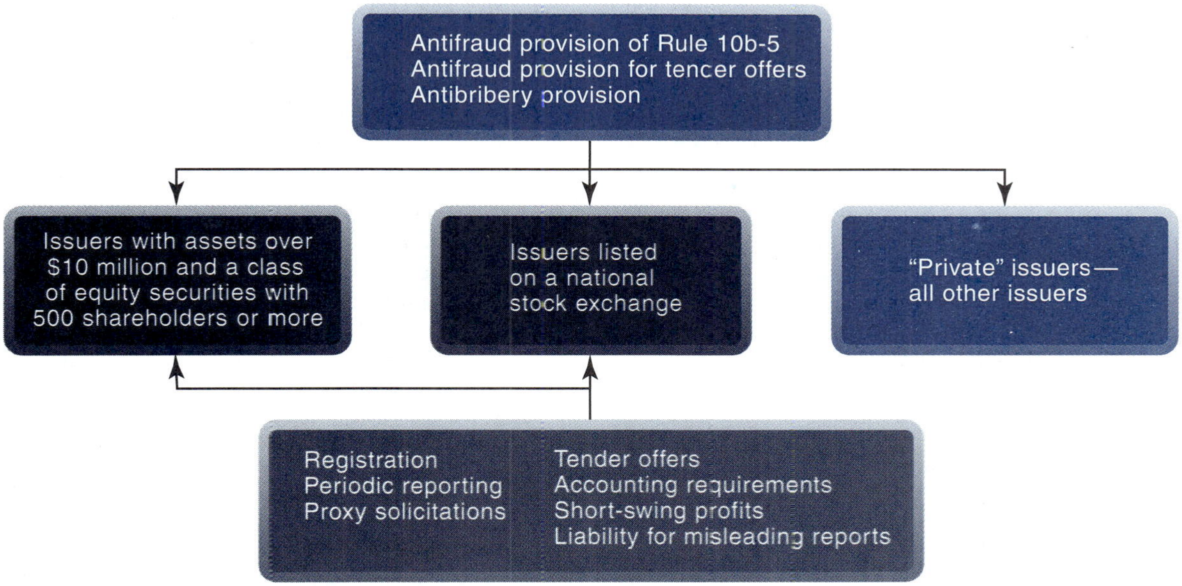

CPA DISCLOSURE

The 1934 Act imposes significant disclosure requirements upon reporting companies. These include the filing of securities registrations, periodic reports, disclosure statements for proxy solicitations, and disclosure statements for tender offers, as well as complying with the accounting requirements imposed by the Foreign Corrupt Practices Act. As part of its integrated registration and reporting system for small business issuers, in 1992 the SEC developed a new series of forms for qualifying issuers to use for registration and periodic reporting under the 1934 Act. Also in 1992, the SEC required disclosure of the compensation paid to senior executives and directors in registration statements, periodic reports, and proxy statements. Effective in 2000, a plain English summary term sheet is required in all tender offers, mergers, and going private transactions.

http:// Forms prescribed under the Securities Exchange Act of 1934: http://www.law.uc.edu/CCL/34forms/index.html

REGISTRATION REQUIREMENTS FOR SECURITIES

The 1934 Act requires all regulated publicly held companies to register with the SEC. These one-time registrations apply to an entire class of securities. Thus, they differ from registrations under the Securities Act of 1933, which relate only to the securities involved in a specific offering. Registration requires disclosure of information such as the organization, financial structure, and nature of the business; the terms, positions, rights, and privileges of the different classes of outstanding securities; the names of the directors, officers, and underwriters and of each security holder owning more than 10 percent of any class of nonexempt equity security; bonus and profit-sharing arrangements; and balance sheets and profit-and-loss statements for the three preceding fiscal years.

PERIODIC REPORTING REQUIREMENTS

Following registration, an issuer must file specified annual and periodic reports to update the information contained in the original registration. The SEC has adopted rules under the Sarbanes-Oxley Act requiring an issuer's chief executive and chief financial officers to *certify* the financial and other information contained in the issuer's annual and quarterly reports. Moreover, the act requires that each periodic report shall be *accompanied* by a written statement by the chief executive officer and chief financial officer of the issuer certifying that the periodic report fully complies with the requirements of the 1934 Act and that information contained in the periodic report fairly presents, in all material respects, the financial condition and results of operations of the issuer. A CEO or CFO who certifies while *knowing* that the report does not comport with the act is subject to a fine of not more than $1 million or imprisonment of not more than 10 years, or both. A CEO or CFO who *willfully* certifies a statement knowing it does not comport with the act shall be fined not more than $5 million or imprisoned not more than 20 years, or both.

The Sarbanes-Oxley Act requires that issuers disclose in plain English to the public on a rapid and current basis such additional information concerning material changes in the financial condition or operations of the issuer as the SEC determines is necessary or useful for the protection of investors and in the public interest.

The 1934 Act also requires that each director, officer, and any person who owns more than 10 percent of a registered equity security file reports with the SEC for any month in which changes in his ownership of such equity securities have occurred. Previously, such transactions were required to be reported within ten days after the close of that month. The Sarbanes-Oxley Act now requires that these reports be filed before the end of the second business day following the day on which the transaction was executed unless the SEC establishes a different deadline. The act also requires that these filings be made electronically on EDGAR, that the SEC make them publicly available on its Internet site, and that the issuer make them available on its corporate Web site, if it maintains one.

Practical Advice

If you are a director, officer, or own more than 10 percent of a registered security, be sure to report to the SEC any sales or purchases you make of the company's equity securities.

PROXY SOLICITATIONS

A **proxy** is a writing signed by a shareholder authorizing a named person to vote his shares of stock at a specified shareholders' meeting. To ensure that shareholders have adequate information upon which to vote, the 1934 Act regulates the proxy solicitation process. The act makes it unlawful for any person to solicit any proxy concerning any registered security "in contravention of such rules and regulations as the Commission may prescribe." ***Solicitation*** includes any request for a proxy, any request not to execute a proxy, or any request to revoke a proxy. The SEC has issued comprehensive and detailed rules prescribing the solicitation process and the disclosure of information about the issuer.

http:// Proxy solicitation rules: http://www.law.uc.edu/CCL/34ActRls/reg14A.html

Proxy Statements The 1934 Act prohibits solicitation of a proxy unless each person solicited has been furnished with a written **proxy statement** containing specified information. An issuer making solicitations must furnish security holders with a proxy statement describing all material facts concerning the matters being submitted to their vote, together with a proxy form on which the security holders can indicate their approval or disapproval of each proposal to be presented. Even a company that does not solicit proxies from its shareholders but submits a matter to their vote must provide them with information substantially equivalent to that which would appear in a proxy statement. With few exceptions, the issuer must file preliminary copies of a proxy statement and proxy form with the SEC at least ten days prior to the first date on which the forms are to be sent. In addition, in an election of directors, solicitations of proxies by a person other than the issuer are subject to similar disclosure requirements. The issuer in such an election also must include an annual report with the proxy statement.

Shareholder Proposals When management makes a solicitation, any security holder entitled to vote has the opportunity to communicate with other security holders. On written request, the corporation must mail the communication at the security holder's expense or, at its option, promptly furnish to that security holder a current list of security holders.

If an eligible security holder entitled to vote submits a timely and appropriate proposal for action at a forthcoming meeting, management must include the proposal in its proxy statement along with a brief statement explaining the shareholder's reasons for making the proposal. Management may omit a proposal if, among other things, (1) under state law it is not a proper subject for shareholder action, (2) it would require the company to violate any law, (3) it is beyond the issuer's power or authority to accomplish, (4) it relates to the conduct of the issuer's ordinary business operations, or (5) it relates to an election to office.

TENDER OFFERS

A **tender offer** is a general invitation to a company's shareholders to purchase their shares at a specified price for a specified time. In 1968, Congress enacted the Williams Act, which amended the 1934 Act to extend reporting and disclosure requirements to tender offers and other block acquisitions. The purpose of the Williams Act is to provide public shareholders with full disclosure by both the bidder and the target company so that the shareholders may make an informed decision.

http:// Tender offer rules: http://www.law.uc.edu/CCL/34ActRls/reg14D.html

Disclosure Requirements The 1934 Act imposes **disclosure requirements** in three situations: (1) when a person or group acquires more than 5 percent of a class of voting securities registered under the 1934 Act, (2) when a person makes a tender offer for more than 5 percent of a class of registered equity securities, or (3) when the issuer makes an offer to repurchase its own registered shares. Although different rules govern each situation, the disclosure required is substantially the same. The acquiring entity must file with the SEC a statement containing (1) the acquisitor's background; (2) the source of the funds it will use to acquire the securities; (3) the purpose of the acquisition, including any plans to liquidate the company or to make major changes in the corporate structure; (4) the number of shares the acquisitor owns; (5) the terms of the transaction; and (6) any relevant contracts, arrangements, or understandings. This disclosure is also required of anyone soliciting shareholders to accept or reject a tender offer. A copy of the statement must be furnished to each offeree and sent to the issuer.

The target company has ten days in which to respond to the bidder's tender offer by (1) recommending acceptance or rejection, (2) expressing no opinion and remaining neutral, or (3) stating that it is unable to take a position. The target company's response must include the reasons for the position it takes.

Required Practices A tender offer either by a third party or by the issuer is subject to the following rules: the initial tender offer must be kept open for at least twenty business days and for at least ten days after any change in terms. Shareholders who tender their shares may withdraw them at any time during the offering period. The tender offer must be open to all holders of the class of shares subject to the offer. All shares tendered must be purchased for the same price; thus, if an offering price is increased, both those who have tendered and those who have yet to tender will receive the benefit of the increase. A tender offeror who offers to purchase fewer than all of the outstanding securities of the target must accept, on a *pro rata* basis, securities tendered during the offer. During the tender offer, the bidder may buy shares of the target only through that tender offer. Effective in 2000, in a tender offer for all outstanding shares of a class, a tender offeror may provide a subsequent offering period of three to twenty days after completion of a tender offer, during which security holders can tender shares without withdrawal rights.

Defensive Tactics When confronted by an uninvited takeover bid—or by a potential, uninvited bid—management of the target company may decide either to oppose the bid or to seek to prevent it. The defensive tactics management employs to prevent or defend against undesired tender offers have developed (and are still evolving) into a highly ingenious, and metaphorically named, set of maneuvers, some of which require considerable planning—and some of which are of questionable legality.

State Regulation More than forty states have enacted statutes regulating tender offers. Although they vary greatly, most of these statutes tend to protect the target company from an unwanted tender offer. Some empower the state to review the merits of the offer or the adequacy of disclosure. Many impose waiting periods before the tender offer becomes effective. The state statutes generally require disclosures more detailed than those the Williams Act requires, and many of them exempt tender offers supported by the target company's management. A number of states have adopted fair price statutes, which require the acquisitor to pay to all shareholders the highest price paid to any shareholder. Some states have enacted business combination statutes prohibiting transactions with an acquisitor for a specified period after a change in control, unless disinterested shareholders approve.

FOREIGN CORRUPT PRACTICES ACT

In 1977, Congress enacted the Foreign Corrupt Practices Act (FCPA) as an amendment to the 1934 Act. Amended in 1988, the FCPA imposes internal control requirements on companies with securities registered under the 1934 Act and prohibits all domestic concerns from bribing foreign governmental or political officials (an activity we will discuss later in this chapter). The accounting requirements of the FCPA reflect the ideas that accurate recordkeeping is essential to managerial responsibility and that investors should be able to rely on the financial reports they receive. Accordingly, the accounting requirements were enacted (1) to ensure that an issuer's books accurately reflect financial transactions, (2) to protect the integrity of independent audits of financial statements, and (3) to promote the reliability of financial information required by the 1934 Act.

CPA LIABILITY

To implement its objectives, the 1934 Act imposes sanctions for noncompliance with its disclosure and antifraud requirements. These sanctions include civil liability to injured investors and issuers, civil penalties, and criminal penalties.

The Reform Act contains several provisions that affect civil liability under the 1934 Act. First, the Reform Act imposes on a plaintiff in any private action under the 1934 Act the burden of proving that the defendant's alleged violation of the 1934 Act caused the loss for

CONCEPT REVIEW

Disclosure under the 1934 Act

	Initial Registration	Periodic Reporting	Insider Reporting	Proxy Statement	Tender Offer
Registrant	Issuer if regulated, publicly held company	Issuer if regulated, publicly held company	Statutory insiders (directors, officers, and principal stockholders)	Issuer and other persons soliciting proxies	5 percent stockholder, tender offeror, or issuer
Information	Nature of business; Financial structure; Directors and executive officers; Financial statements	Annual, quarterly, or current report updating information in initial registration	Initial statement of beneficial ownership of equity securities; Changes in beneficial ownership	Details of solicitation; Legal terms of proxy; Annual report (if directors to be elected)	Identity and background; Terms of transaction; Source of funds; Intentions
Filing Date	Within 120 days after becoming a reporting company	Annual: within 90 days after year's end; Quarterly: within 45 days after quarter's end; Current: within 15 days after any material change	Within 10 days of becoming a statutory insider; Within 2 days after a change in ownership takes place	10 days before final proxy statement is distributed	5 percent stockholder: within 10 days after acquiring more than 5 percent of a class of registered securities Tender offeror: before tender offer is made Issuer: before offer to repurchase
Purpose of Disclosure	Adequate and accurate disclosure of material facts regarding securities listed on a national exchange or traded publicly over the counter	Update information contained in initial registration	Prevent unfair use of information that may have been obtained by a statutory insider	Full disclosure of material information; Facilitation of shareholder proposals	Adequate and accurate disclosure of material facts; Opportunity to reach uncoerced decision

which the plaintiff seeks to recover damages. Second, the Reform Act imposes a limit on the amount of damages a plaintiff can recover in any private action under the 1934 Act based on a material misstatement or omission in which she seeks to establish damages by reference to the market price of a security. The plaintiff may not recover damage in excess of the difference between the purchase or sale price she paid or received for the security and the mean trading price of that security during the ninety-day period beginning on the date when the information correcting the misstatement or omission is disseminated to the market. Third, the Reform Act provides a "safe harbor" under the 1934 Act from civil liability based on an untrue statement of material fact or an omission of a material fact necessary to make the statement not misleading. The safe harbor applies to issuers required to report under the 1934 Act and who make "forward-looking" statements (predictions) if the statements meet specified requirements. The requirements of the safe harbor and the transactions to which it does not apply were discussed earlier in this chapter.

MISLEADING STATEMENTS IN REPORTS

Section 18 imposes express civil liability upon any person who makes or causes to be made any false or misleading statement with respect to any material fact in any application, report, document, or registration filed with the SEC under the 1934 Act. Any person who purchased or sold a security in reliance upon such a false or misleading statement without knowing that it was false or misleading may recover under this section. A person is not liable, however, if she proves that she acted in good faith and had no knowledge that such statement was false or misleading. The court may award attorneys' fees against either the plaintiff or the defendant.

SHORT-SWING PROFITS

Section 16(b) of the 1934 Act imposes express liability upon insiders—directors, officers, and any person owning more than 10 percent of the stock of a corporation listed on a national stock exchange or registered with the SEC—for all profits resulting from their "short-swing" trading in such stock. If any insider sells such stock within six months from the date of its purchase or purchases such stock within six months from the date of a sale of the stock, the corporation is entitled to recover any and all profit the insider realizes from these transactions. The "profit" recoverable is calculated by matching the highest sale price against the lowest purchase price within the relevant six-month period. Losses cannot be offset against profits. Suit to recover such profit may be brought by the issuer or by the owner of any security of the issuer in the name and on behalf of the issuer if the issuer fails or refuses to bring such suit within sixty days of the owner's request.

ANTIFRAUD PROVISION

Section 10(b) of the 1934 Act and SEC ***Rule 10b–5*** make it unlawful for any person using the mails or facilities of interstate commerce in connection with the purchase or sale of any security (1) to employ any device, scheme, or artifice to defraud; (2) to make any untrue statement of a material fact; (3) to omit to state a material fact without which the information is misleading; or (4) to engage in any act, practice, or course of business that operates or would operate as a fraud or deceit upon any person.

Rule 10b–5 applies to any purchase or sale of ***any*** security, whether it is registered under the 1934 Act or not, whether it is publicly traded or closely held, whether it is listed on an exchange or sold over the counter, or whether it is part of an initial issuance or a secondary distribution. There are ***no*** exemptions. The implied liability under Rule 10b–5 applies to purchaser as well as seller misconduct and allows both defrauded sellers and buyers to recover.

Requisites of Rule 10b–5 Recovery of damages under Rule 10b–5 requires proof of (1) a misstatement or omission (2) that is material, (3) made with *scienter*, and (4) relied upon (5) in connection with the purchase or sale of a security. This rule differs from common law fraud in that Rule 10b–5 imposes an affirmative duty of disclosure. A misstatement or omission is ***material*** if there is a substantial likelihood that a reasonable investor would consider it important in deciding whether to purchase or sell the security. Examples of material facts include substantial changes in dividends or earnings, significant misstatements of asset value, and the fact that the issuer is about to become a target of a tender offer. In an action for damages under Rule 10b–5, it must be shown that the violation was committed with **scienter**, or intentional misconduct. Negligence is not sufficient. Although the Supreme Court has not yet decided whether reckless conduct is sufficient to satisfy the requirement of *scienter*, the vast majority of circuit and district courts have held recklessness to be sufficient. Reliance upon the misstatement or omission is required, although in some circumstances it may be satisfied by the presumption of reliance upon the market place.

Remedies for Rule 10b–5 violations include rescission, damages, and injunctions. The courts, however, are divided over the measure of damages to impose.

Insider Trading Rule 10b–5 applies to sales or purchases of securities made by an "insider" who possesses material information that is not available to the general public. An insider who fails to disclose such information before trading on it will be liable under Rule 10b–5 unless he waits for the information to become public. Under new SEC Rule 10b5–1, a purchase or sale of an issuer's security is based on material nonpublic information about that security or issuer if the person making the purchase or sale was *aware* of the information when the person entered into the transaction. **Insiders**, for the purpose of Rule 10b–5, include directors, officers, employees, and agents of the security issuer, as well as those with whom the issuer has entrusted information solely for corporate purposes, such as underwriters, accountants, lawyers, and consultants. In some instances, the rule also precludes persons who receive material, nonpublic information from insiders—tippees—from trading on that information. A tippee is under a duty not to trade on inside information from an insider who has breached his fiduciary duty to the shareholders by disclosing the information to the tippee, who knows or should know that such a breach has occurred. (See Figure 40-5, which illustrates which parties are forbidden to trade on inside information.) In the case that follows, the U.S. Supreme Court upholds the misappropriation theory as an additional and complementary basis for imposing liability for insider trading. Under this theory, a person who trades in securities for personal profit using confidential information misappropriated in breach of a fiduciary duty to the source of the information may be held liable for insider trading under Rule 10b–5. This liability applies even though the source of information is not the issuer of the securities that were traded. New SEC Rule 10b5–2 adopts

Figure 40-5 *Parties Forbidden to Trade on Inside Information*

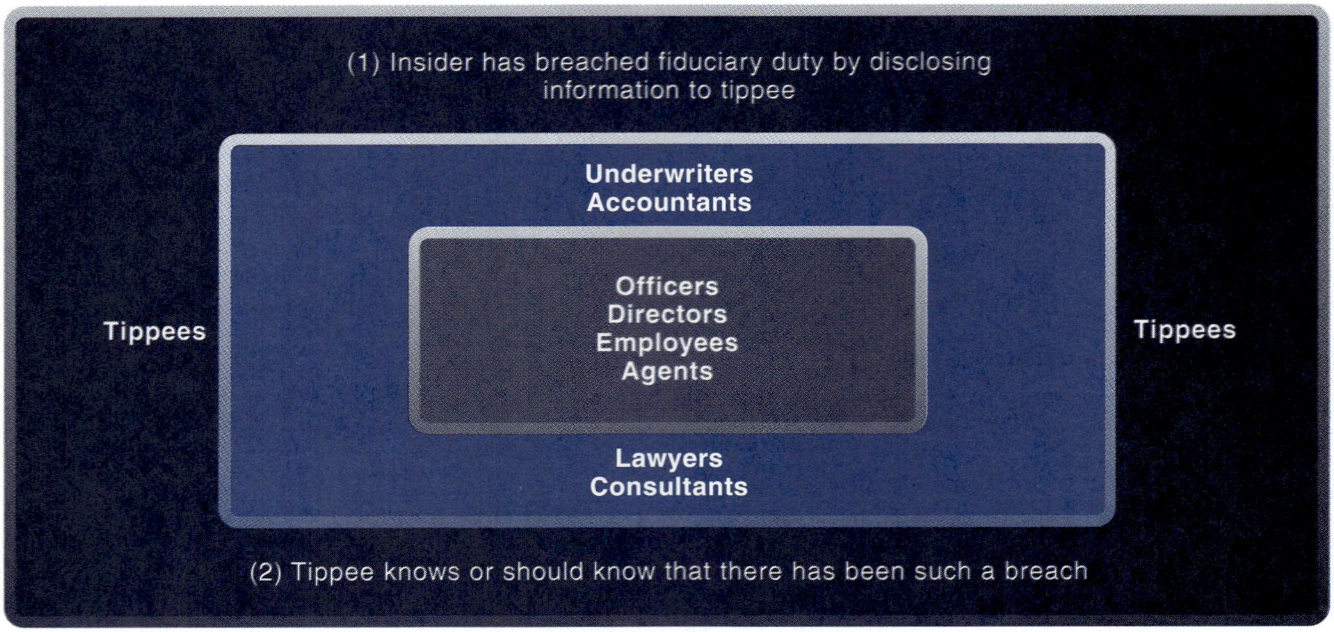

the misappropriation theory of liability: A violation of Section 10(b) includes the purchase or sale of a security of an issuer on the basis of material nonpublic information about that security or issuer in breach of trust or confidence that is owed to the issuer, the shareholders of that issuer, or *any other person who is the source of the material nonpublic information*. Under new SEC Rule 10b5–2, a person has a duty of trust or confidence for purposes of the misappropriation theory of liability when (1) a person agrees to maintain information in confidence; (2) two people have a history, pattern, or practice of sharing confidences such that the recipient of the information knows or reasonably should know that the person communicating the material nonpublic information expects that the recipient will maintain its confidentiality; *or* (3) a person receives or obtains material nonpublic information from his or her spouse, parent, child, or sibling.

Under new SEC Regulation FD, regulated issuers who disclose material nonpublic information to specified persons (primarily securities market professionals such as analysts and mutual fund managers) must make public disclosure of that information. If the selective disclosure was intentional or reckless, the issuer must make public disclosure simultaneously; for a nonintentional disclosure, the issuer must make public disclosure promptly, usually within 24 hours. With a few exceptions, Regulation FD does not apply to disclosures made in connection with securities offering registered under the 1933 Act. The SEC can enforce this rule by bringing an administrative action seeking a cease-and-desist order or a civil action seeking an injunction and/or civil money penalties.

Although both Section 16(b) and Rule 10b–5 address the problem of insider trading and both may apply to the same transaction, they differ in several respects. First, Section 16(b) applies only to transactions involving registered equity securities; Rule 10b–5 applies to all securities. Second, the definition of insider under Rule 10b–5 extends beyond directors, officers, and owners of more than 10 percent of a company's stock, whereas the definition under Section 16(b) does not. Third, Section 16(b) does not require that the insider possess material, nonpublic information; liability is strict. Rule 10b–5 applies to insider trading only when such information is not disclosed. Fourth, Section 16(b) applies only to transactions occurring within six months of each other; Rule 10b–5 has no such limitation. Fifth, under Rule 10b–5, injured investors may recover damages on their own behalf; under Section 16(b), although shareholders may bring suit, any recovery is on behalf of the corporation.

United States v. O'Hagan

Supreme Court of the United States, 1997

521 U.S. 642, 117 S.Ct. 2199, 138 L.Ed.2d 724

http://laws.findlaw.com/US/000/96-842.html

FACTS James Herman O'Hagan was a partner in the law firm of Dorsey & Whitney **(http://www.dorsey.com/)** in Minneapolis, Minnesota. In July 1988, Grand Metropolitan PLC (Grand Met), a company based in London, England, retained Dorsey & Whitney to represent Grand Met regarding a potential tender offer for the common stock of the Pillsbury Company **(http://www.pillsbury.com)**, headquartered in Minneapolis. Both Grand Met and Dorsey & Whitney took precautions to protect the confidentiality of Grand Met's tender offer plans. O'Hagan did no work on the Grand Met project. On August 18, 1988, O'Hagan began purchasing call options for Pillsbury stock. Each option gave him the right to purchase 100 shares of Pillsbury stock by a specified date in September 1988. Later in August and in September, O'Hagan made additional purchases of Pillsbury call options. By the end of September, he owned 2,500 unexpired Pillsbury options, apparently more than any other individual investor. O'Hagan also purchased, in September 1988, some 5,000 shares of Pillsbury common stock, at a price just under $39 per share. When Grand Met announced its tender offer in October, the price of Pillsbury stock rose to nearly $60 per share. O'Hagan then sold his Pillsbury call options and common stock, making a profit of more than $4.3 million.

The Securities and Exchange Commission initiated an investigation into O'Hagan's transactions, culminating in an indictment alleging that O'Hagan defrauded his law firm and its client, Grand Met, by using for his own trading purposes material, nonpublic information regarding Grand Met's planned tender offer in violation of § 10(b) of the Securities Exchange Act of 1934 and SEC Rule l0b–5. A jury convicted O'Hagan and he was sentenced to a 41-month term of imprisonment. A divided panel of the Court of Appeals for the Eighth Circuit reversed O'Hagan's conviction, holding that liability under § 10(b) and Rule l0b–5 may not be grounded on the "misappropriation theory" of securities fraud on which the prosecution relied.

DECISION Judgment of the Court of Appeals for the Eighth Circuit is reversed and remanded.

OPINION Ginsburg, J. Under the "traditional" or "classical theory" of insider trading liability, § 10(b) and Rule l0b–5 are violated when a corporate insider trades in the securities of his corporation on the basis of material, nonpublic information. Trading on such information qualifies as a "deceptive device" under § 10(b), we have affirmed, because "a relationship of trust and confidence [exists] between the shareholders of a corporation and those insiders who have obtained confidential information by reason of their position with that corporation." [Citation.] That relationship, we recognized, "gives rise to a duty to disclose [or to abstain from trading] because of the 'necessity of preventing a corporate insider from * * * tak[ing] unfair advantage of * * * uninformed * * * stockholders.'" [Citation.] The classical theory applies not only to officers, directors, and other permanent insiders of a corporation, but also to attorneys, accountants, consultants, and others who temporarily become fiduciaries of a corporation. [Citation.]

The "misappropriation theory" holds that a person commits fraud "in connection with" a securities transaction, and thereby violates § 10(b) and Rule l0b–5, when he misappropriates confidential information for securities trading purposes, in breach of a duty owed to the source of the information. [Citation.] Under this theory, a fiduciary's undisclosed, self-serving use of a principal's information to purchase or sell securities, in breach of a duty of loyalty and confidentiality, defrauds the principal of the exclusive use of that information. In lieu of premising liability on a fiduciary relationship between company insider and purchaser or seller of the company's stock, the misappropriation theory premises liability on a fiduciary-turned-trader's deception of those who entrusted him with access to confidential information.

The two theories are complementary, each addressing efforts to capitalize on nonpublic information through the purchase or sale of securities. The classical theory targets a corporate insider's breach of duty to shareholders with whom the insider transacts; the misappropriation theory outlaws trading on the basis of nonpublic information by a corporate "outsider" in breach of a duty owed not to a trading party, but to the source of the information. The misappropriation theory is thus designed to "protec[t] the integrity of the securities markets against abuses by 'outsiders' to a corporation who have access to confidential information that will affect th[e] corporation's security price when revealed, but who owe no fiduciary or other duty to that corporation's shareholders." [Citation.]

In this case, the indictment alleged that O'Hagan, in breach of a duty of trust and confidence he owed to his law firm, Dorsey & Whitney, and to its client, Grand Met, traded on the basis of nonpublic information regarding Grand Met's planned tender offer for Pillsbury common stock. This conduct, the Government charged, constituted a fraudulent device in connection with the purchase and sale of securities. [Court's footnote: The Government could not have prosecuted O'Hagan under the classical theory, for O'Hagan was not an "insider" of Pillsbury, the corporation in whose stock he traded. * * *]

We agree with the Government that misappropriation, as just defined, satisfies § 10(b)'s requirement that chargeable conduct involve a "deceptive device or contrivance" used "in connection with" the purchase or sale of securities. We observe, first, that misappropriators, as the Government describes them, deal in deception. A fiduciary who "[pretends] loyalty to the principal while secretly converting the principal's information for personal gain," [citation], "dupes" or defrauds the principal. [Citation.]

* * *

* * * Because the deception essential to the misappropriation theory involves feigning fidelity to the source of information, if the fiduciary discloses to the source that he plans to trade on the nonpublic information, there is no "deceptive device" and thus no § 10(b) violation—although the fiduciary-turned-trader may remain liable under state law for breach of a duty of loyalty.

We turn next to the § 10(b) requirement that the misappropriator's deceptive use of information be "in connection with the purchase or sale of [a] security." This element is satisfied because the fiduciary's fraud is consummated, not when the fiduciary gains the confidential information, but when, without disclosure to his principal, he uses the information to purchase or sell securities. The securities transaction and the breach of duty thus coincide. This is so even though the person or entity defrauded is not the other party to the trade, but is, instead, the source of the nonpublic information. [Citation.] A misappropriator who trades on the basis of material, nonpublic information, in short, gains his advantageous market position through deception; he deceives the source of the information and simultaneously harms members of the investing public. [Citation.]

* * *

The misappropriation theory comports with § 10(b)'s language, which requires deception "in connection with the purchase or sale of any security," not deception of an identifiable purchaser or seller. The theory is also well-tuned to an animating purpose of the Exchange Act: to insure honest securities markets and thereby promote investor confidence. [Citation.] Although informational disparity is inevitable in the securities markets, investors likely would hesitate to venture their capital in a market where trading based on misappropriated nonpublic information is unchecked by law. An investor's informational disadvantage vis-a-vis a misappropriator with material, nonpublic information stems from contrivance, not luck; it is a disadvantage that cannot be overcome with research or skill. [Citation.]

In sum, considering the inhibiting impact on market participation of trading on misappropriated information, and the congressional purposes underlying § 10(b), it makes scant sense to hold a lawyer like O'Hagan a §10(b) violator if he works for a law firm representing the target of a tender offer, but not if he works for a law firm representing the bidder. The text of the statute requires no such result. The misappropriation at issue here was properly made the subject of a § 10(b) charge because it meets the statutory requirement that there be "deceptive" conduct "in connection with" securities transactions.

INTERPRETATION A person who trades in securities for personal profit using confidential information misappropriated in breach of a fiduciary duty to the source of the information may be held liable for insider trading under Rule l0b–5.

ETHICAL QUESTION Did the defendant act unethically? Explain.

CRITICAL THINKING QUESTION What are the arguments for and against the misappropriation theory? With which position do you agree? Explain.

EXPRESS INSIDER TRADING LIABILITY

Section 20A imposes express civil liability upon any person who violates the act by purchasing or selling a security while in possession of material, nonpublic information. Any person who contemporaneously sold or purchased securities of the same class as those improperly traded may bring a private action against the trader to recover damages for the violation. The total amount of damages may not exceed the profit gained or loss avoided by the violation, diminished by any amount the violator disgorges to the SEC pursuant to a court order. The action must be brought within five years after the date of the last transaction that is the subject of the violation. Tippers are jointly and severally liable with tippees who commit a violation by trading on the inside information.

CIVIL PENALTIES FOR INSIDER TRADING

In addition to the remedies discussed above, the SEC is authorized to bring an action in a U.S. district court to

Ethical Dilemma

What Information May a Corporate Employee Disclose?

FACTS Sam Thompson is the director of tax research in the tax department of Anna Louise, Inc., a publicly traded clothing manufacturer. Formed by James and Anna Louise around the turn of the century, the corporation has been managed ever since by family members, who still own a controlling interest.

While studying certain tax matters in connection with a highly sensitive marketing project, Sam learned that an international company had offered to purchase a controlling interest in Anna Louise. Later, while he was having lunch with Mike, his good friend and stockbroker, Mike began pressuring Sam for information about the offer. Mike is ambitious and is attempting to build a solid client base. He is a diligent worker, performs extensive research to support recommendations to clients, and socializes a great deal with the business community. Mike told Sam that he could tell something special was going on at Sam's office. Sam had been working overtime and for the past two weeks had been unable to meet Mike as usual on Friday evening for drinks after work.

Social, Policy, and Ethical Considerations

1. What are Sam's ethical responsibilities to his employer with regard to information he obtains at work? How should he respond to Mike's requests for information?
2. If Sam took Mike into his confidence, what ethical responsibilities would Mike have to Sam to keep the information to himself?
3. Does Mike have any duties of loyalty to Sam's employer?
4. As a practical matter, to what extent must one keep in confidence information obtained in one's employment? Is it "safe" for example, to discuss matters with one's closest friends or one's spouse?

have a civil penalty imposed upon any person who purchases or sells a security while in possession of material, nonpublic information. Liability also extends to any person who by communicating material, nonpublic information aids and abets another person in such a violation. Liability may also be imposed on any person who directly or indirectly controlled a person who ultimately committed a violation if the controlling person knew or recklessly disregarded the likelihood that the controlled person would commit a violation and consequently failed to take appropriate steps to prevent the transgression. Under this provision, law firms, accounting firms, issuers, financial printers, news media, and others must implement policies to prevent insider trading. The violating transaction must be on or through the facilities of a national securities exchange or from or through a broker or dealer. Purchases that are part of a public offering by an issuer of securities are not subject to this provision.

The civil penalty for a person who trades on inside information is determined by the court in light of the facts and circumstances but may not exceed three times the profit gained or loss avoided as a result of the unlawful purchase or sale. The maximum amount that may be imposed upon a controlling person is the greater of $1.2 million or three times the profit gained or loss avoided as a result of the controlled person's violation. If that violation consists of tipping inside information, the court measures the controller's liability by the profit gained or loss avoided by the person to whom the controlled person directed the tip. For the purpose of this provision, "profit gained" or "loss avoided" is "the difference between the purchase or sale price of the security and the value of that security as measured by the trading price of the security a reasonable period after public dissemination of the nonpublic information."

Civil penalties for insider trading are payable into the United States Treasury. The SEC is authorized to award bounties of up to 10 percent of a recovered penalty to informants who provided information leading to the imposition of the penalty. An action to recover a penalty must be brought within five years after the date of the purchase or sale.

Practical Advice

If you confidentially acquire any nonpublic information about a company, do not trade in that company's securities until that information has become public.

Misleading Proxy Statements

Any person who distributes a materially false or **misleading proxy statement** may be liable to a shareholder who relies upon the statement in purchasing or selling a security and consequently suffers a loss. In this context, a misstatement or omission is material if there is a substantial likelihood that a reasonable shareholder would consider it important in deciding how to vote. A number of courts have held that negligence is sufficient for an action under the proxy rule's antifraud provisions. In addition, when the proxy disclosure or filing requirement has been violated, a court may, if appropriate, enjoin a shareholder meeting or any action taken at that meeting. Other remedies are rescission, damages, and attorneys' fees.

FRAUDULENT TENDER OFFERS

Section 14(e) makes it unlawful for any person to make any untrue statement of material fact, to omit to state any material fact, or to engage in any fraudulent, deceptive, or manipulative practices in connection with any tender offer. This provision applies even if the target company is not subject to the 1934 Act's reporting requirements. Insider trading during a tender offer is prohibited by Rule 14e–3, which has been upheld by the U.S. Supreme Court in the *United States v. O'Hagan* case above.

Some courts have implied civil liability for violations of Section 14(e). Because of the small number of cases, however, the requirements for such an action are not entirely clear. A target company may seek an injunction, and a shareholder of the target may be able to recover damages or obtain rescission. The courts are likely to require *scienter*.

Schreiber v. Burlington Northern, Inc.

Supreme Court of the United States, 1985
472 U.S. 1, 105 S.Ct. 2458, 86 L.Ed.2d 1
http://laws.findlaw.com/US/472/1.html

FACTS On December 21, 1982, Burlington Northern, Inc. **(http://www.bnsf.com)**, made a hostile tender offer for El Paso Gas Co. **(http://www.epenergy.com)**, proposing to purchase 25.1 million El Paso shares at $24 per share. The shareholders of El Paso fully subscribed the offer by the December 30, 1982, deadline. Burlington refused to accept those tendered shares and instead announced the terms of a new and friendly takeover agreement on January 10, 1983. Under this agreement, Burlington withdrew the December tender offer and substituted a new tender offer for 21 million shares at $24 per share. More than 40 million shares were tendered in response to this offer. Thus, the new offer disadvantaged those shareholders who had tendered during the first offer, for those who retendered were subject to substantial proration and hence received a diminished payment. Barbara Schreiber, one of the disadvantaged shareholders, brought an action against Burlington, El Paso, and members of El Paso's board, claiming that Burlington's rescission of the first tender offer and substitution of the new one was a "manipulative" distortion of the market for El Paso stock, which is prohibited by Section 14(e) of the Securities Exchange Act. The District Court dismissed the suit for failure to state a claim, and the Court of Appeals affirmed.

DECISION Judgment of the Court of Appeals affirmed.

OPINION Burger, C. J. We are asked in this case to interpret § 14(e) of the Securities Exchange Act, [citation]. The starting point is the language of the statute. Section 14(e) provides:

> It shall be unlawful for any person to make any untrue statement of a material fact or omit to state any material fact necessary in order to make the statements made, in the light of the circumstances under which they are made, not misleading, or to engage in any fraudulent, deceptive or manipulative acts or practices, in connection with any tender offer or request or invitation for tenders, or any solicitation of security holders in opposition to or in favor of any such offer, request, or invitation. The Commission shall, for the purposes of this subsection, by rules and regulations define, and prescribe means reasonably designed to prevent, such acts and practices as are fraudulent, deceptive, or manipulative. [Citation.]

* * * Petitioner reads the phrase "fraudulent, deceptive or manipulative acts or practices" to include acts which, although fully disclosed, "artificially" affect the price of the takeover target's stock. Petitioner's interpretation relies on the belief that § 14(e) is directed at purposes broader than providing full and true information to investors.

Petitioner's reading of the term "manipulative" conflicts with the normal meaning of the term. We have held in the context of an alleged violation of § 10(b) of the Securities Exchange Act:

> Use of the word 'manipulative' is especially significant. It is and was virtually a term of art when used in connection with the securities markets. It connotes intentional or willful conduct *designed to deceive or defraud investors by controlling or artificially affecting the price of securities. Ernst & Ernst v. Hochfelder*, [see Chapter 44].

* * * The meaning the Court has given the term "manipulative" is consistent with the use of the term at common law, and with its traditional dictionary definition.

* * *

Our conclusion that "manipulative" acts under § 14(e) require misrepresentation or nondisclosure is buttressed by the purpose and legislative history of the provision. Section 14(e) was originally added to the Securities Exchange Act as part of the Williams Act, [citation]. "The purpose of the Williams Act is to insure that public shareholders who are confronted by a cash tender offer for their stock will not be required to respond without adequate information." [Citation.]

* * *

Section 14(e) adds a "broad antifraud prohibition," [citation], modeled on the antifraud provisions of § 10(b) of the Act and Rule 10b–5, [citation]. It supplements the more precise disclosure provisions found elsewhere in the Williams Act, while requiring disclosure more explicitly addressed to the tender offer context than that required by § 10(b).

* * * Nowhere in the legislative history is there the slightest suggestion that § 14(e) serves any purpose other than disclosure, or that the term "manipulative" should be read as an invitation to the courts to oversee the substantive fairness of tender offers; the quality of any offer is a matter for the marketplace.

To adopt the reading of the term "manipulative" urged by petitioner would not only be unwarranted in light of the legislative purpose but would be at odds with it. Inviting judges to read the term "manipulative" with their own sense of what constitutes "unfair" or "artificial" conduct would inject uncertainty into the tender offer process. An essential piece of information—whether the court would deem the fully disclosed actions of one side or the other to be "manipulative"—would not be available until after the tender offer had closed. This uncertainty would directly contradict the expressed Congressional desire to give investors full information.

Congress' consistent emphasis on disclosure persuades us that it intended takeover contests to be addressed to shareholders. In pursuit of this goal, Congress, consistent with the core mechanism of the Securities Exchange Act, created sweeping disclosure requirements and narrow substantive safeguards. The same Congress that placed such emphasis on shareholder choice would not at the same time have required judges to oversee tender offers for substantive fairness. It is even less likely that a Congress implementing that intention would express it only through the use of a single word placed in the middle of a provision otherwise devoted to disclosure.

We hold that the term "manipulative" as used in § 14(e) requires misrepresentation or nondisclosure. It connotes "conduct designed to deceive or defraud investors by controlling or artificially affecting the price of securities." *Ernst & Ernst v. Hochfelder* [see Chapter 44]. Without misrepresentation or nondisclosure 14(e) has not been violated.

Applying that definition to this case, we hold that the actions of respondents were not manipulative. The amended complaint fails to allege that the cancellation of the first tender offer was accompanied by any misrepresentation, nondisclosure or deception. The District Court correctly found, "All activity of the defendants that could have conceivably affected the price of El Paso shares was done openly." [Citation.]

INTERPRETATION Shareholders have a right to full and accurate disclosure of information from those making tender offers to them.

ETHICAL QUESTION Did the defendants act unethically? Explain.

CRITICAL THINKING QUESTION Do you agree with Court's interpretation of "manipulative"? Explain.

ANTIBRIBERY PROVISION OF FCPA

The Foreign Corrupt Practices Act (FCPA) makes it unlawful for any domestic concern or any of its officers, directors, employees, or agents to offer or give anything of value directly or indirectly to any foreign official, political party, or political official for the purpose of (1) influencing any act or decision of that person or party in his, or its, official capacity, (2) inducing an act or omission in violation of his, or its, lawful duty, or (3) inducing such person or party to use his, or its, influence to affect a decision of a foreign government in order to assist the domestic concern in obtaining or retaining business. An offer or promise to make a prohibited payment is a violation even if the offer is not accepted or the promise is not performed. The 1988 amendments to the act explicitly excluded routine governmental action not involving the official's discretion, such as obtaining permits or processing applications. They also added an affirmative defense for payments that are lawful under the written laws or regulations of the foreign officials' country.

CONCEPT REVIEW

Civil Liability under the 1933 and 1934 Acts

Provision	Conduct	Plaintiffs	Defendants	Standard of Culpability	Reliance Required	Type of Liability	Remedies
Section 12(a)(1) 1933 Act	Unregistered sale or sale without prospectus	Purchasers from a violator	Sellers in violation	Strict liability	No	Express	Rescission Damages
Section 11 1933 Act	Registration statement containing material misstatement or omission	Purchasers of registered security	Issuer Directors Signers Underwriters Experts	Strict liability for issuer; Negligence for others	No	Express	Damages Attorneys' fees
Section 12(a)(2) 1933 Act	Material misstatement or omission	Purchasers from a violator	Sellers in violation	Negligence	No	Express	Rescission Damages
Section 18 1934 Act	False or misleading statements in a document filed with SEC	Purchasers or sellers	Persons making filing in violation	Knowledge or bad faith	Yes	Express	Damages Attorneys' fees
Section 16(b) 1934 Act	Short-swing profit by insider	Issuer; Shareholder of issuer	Directors; Officers; 10 percent shareholders	Strict liability	No	Express	Damages
Rule 10b–5 1934 Act	Deception or material misstatement or omission	Purchasers or sellers	Purchasers or sellers in violation	*Scienter*	Yes	Implied	Rescission Damages Injunction
Section 20A 1934 Act	Insider trading	Contemporaneous purchasers or sellers	Inside traders	*Scienter*	No	Express	Damages
Section 14(a) 1934 Act	Materially false or misleading proxy solicitation	Shareholders	Persons making proxy solicitation in violation	Negligence (probably)	Probably	Implied	Rescission Damages Injunction Attorneys' fees
Section 14(e) 1934 Act	Tender offer with deception or manipulation or material misstatement or omission	Target company Shareholders of target	Persons making tender offer in violation	*Scienter* (probably)	Probably	Implied	Rescission Damages Injunction

Violations can result in fines of up to $2 million for companies; individuals may be fined a maximum of $100,000 or be imprisoned for up to five years, or both. Fines imposed upon individuals may not be paid directly or indirectly by the domestic concern on whose behalf they acted. In addition, civil penalties up to $11,000 may be imposed.

In 1997 the United States and thirty-three other nations signed the Organisation for Economic Co-operation and

Development Convention on Combating Bribery of Foreign Public Officials in International Business Transactions (OECD Convention). In 1998 Congress enacted the International Anti-Bribery and Fair Competition Act of 1998 to conform the FCPA to the Convention. The 1998 Act expands the FCPA to include (1) payments made to "secure any improper advantage" from foreign officials, (2) all foreign persons who commit an act in furtherance of a foreign bribe while in the United States, and (3) officials of public international organizations within the definition of a "foreign official." A public international organization is defined as either an organization designated by executive order pursuant to the International Organizations Immunities Act, or any other international organization designated by executive order of the president.

http:// OECD Convention: http://www.oecd.org/

CRIMINAL SANCTIONS

Section 32 of the 1934 Act imposes **criminal sanctions** on any person who willfully violates any provision of the act (except the antibribery provision) or the rules and regulations promulgated by the SEC pursuant to the act. As amended by the Sarbanes-Oxley Act, for individuals, conviction may carry a fine of not more than $5 million or imprisonment of not more than twenty years, or both, with one exception: a person who proves she had no knowledge of the rule or regulation is not subject to imprisonment. If the person, however, is not a natural person (for example, a corporation), a fine not exceeding $25 million may be imposed.

CHAPTER SUMMARY

Securities Act of 1933

Definition of a Security

Security includes any note, stock, bond, preorganization subscription, and investment contract

Investment Contract any investment of money or property made in expectation of receiving a financial return solely from the efforts of others

Registration of Securities

Disclosure Requirements disclosure of accurate material information required in all public offerings of nonexempt securities unless offering is an exempt transaction

Integrated Disclosure and Shelf Registrations permitted for certain qualified issuers

Exempt Securities

Definition securities not subject to the registration requirements of the 1933 Act

Types exempt securities include short-term commercial paper, municipal bonds, and certain insurance policies and annuity contracts

Exempt Transactions for Issuers

Definition issuance of securities not subject to the registration requirements of the 1933 Act

Types exempt transactions include limited offers under Regulation D and Section 4(6), Regulation A, and intrastate issues

Exempt Transactions for Non-Issuers

Definition resales by persons other than the issuer that are exempted from the registration requirements of the 1933 Act

Types exempt transactions include Rule 144 and Regulation A

Liability

Unregistered Sales Section 12(a)(1) imposes absolute civil liability; there are no defenses

False Registration Statements Section 11 imposes liability on the issuer, all persons who signed the statement, every director or partner, experts who prepared or certified any part of the statement, and all underwriters; defendants other than issuer may assert the defense of due diligence

Antifraud Provisions Section 12(a)(2) imposes liability upon the seller to the immediate purchaser, provided the purchaser did not know of the untruth or omission; but the seller is not liable if he did not know, and in the exercise of reasonable care could not have known, of the untrue statement or omission. Section 17(a) broadly prohibits fraud in the sale of securities

Criminal Sanctions willful violations are subject to a fine of not more than $10,000 and/or imprisonment of not more than five years

Securities Exchange Act of 1934

Disclosure

Registration and Periodic Reporting Requirements apply to all regulated, publicly held companies and include one-time registration as well as annual, quarterly, and monthly reports

Proxy Solicitations
- ***Definition of a Proxy*** a signed writing by a shareholder authorizing a named person to vote her stock at a specified meeting of shareholders
- ***Proxy Statements*** proxy disclosure statements are required when proxies are solicited or an issuer submits a matter to a shareholder vote

Tender Offers
- ***Definition of a Tender Offer*** a general invitation to shareholders to purchase their shares at a specified price for a specified time
- ***Disclosure Requirements*** a statement disclosing specified information must be filed with the SEC and furnished to each offeree

Foreign Corrupt Practices Act imposes internal control requirements on companies with securities registered under the 1934 Act

Liability

Misleading Statements in Reports Section 18 imposes civil liability for any false or misleading statement made in a registration or report filed with the SEC

Short-Swing Profits Section 16(b) imposes liability on certain insiders (directors, officers, and shareholders owning more than 10 percent of the stock of a corporation) for all profits made on sales and purchases within six months of each other, with any recovery going to the issuer

Antifraud Provision Rule 10b–5 makes it unlawful to (1) employ any device, scheme, or artifice to defraud; (2) make any untrue statement of a material fact; (3) omit to state a material fact; or (4) engage in any act that operates as a fraud
- ***Requisites of Rule 10b–5*** recovery requires (1) a misstatement or omission, (2) materiality, (3) *scienter* (intentional and knowing conduct), (4) reliance, and (5) connection with the purchase or sale of a security
- ***Insider Trading*** "insiders" are liable under Rule 10b–5 for failing to disclose material, nonpublic information before trading on the information

Express Insider Trading Liability is imposed on any person who sells or buys a security while in possession of inside information

Civil Penalties for Inside Trading may be imposed on inside traders in an amount up to three times the gains they made or losses they avoided

Misleading Proxy Statement any person who distributes a false or misleading proxy statement is liable to injured investors

Fraudulent Tender Offers Section 14(e) imposes civil liability for false and material statements or omissions or fraudulent, deceptive, or manipulative practices in connection with any tender offer

Antibribery Provision of FCPA prohibited bribery can result in fines and imprisonment

Criminal Sanctions individuals who willfully violate the 1934 Act are subject to a fine of not more than $5 million and/or imprisonment of not more than twenty years

QUESTIONS

1. Acme Realty, a real estate development company, is a limited partnership organized in Georgia. It is planning to develop a 200-acre parcel of land for a regional shopping center and needs to raise $1,250,000. As part of its financing, Acme plans to offer $1,250,000 worth of limited partnership interests to about 100 prospective investors in the southeastern United States. It anticipates that about forty to fifty private investors will purchase the limited partnership interests.
   a. Must Acme register this offering? Why or why not?
   b. If Acme must register but fails to do so, what are the legal consequences?

2. Bigelow Corporation has total assets of $850,000, sales of $1,350,000, and one class of common stock with 375 shareholders and a class of preferred stock with 250 shareholders, both of which are traded over the counter. Which provisions of the Securities Exchange Act of 1934 apply to Bigelow Corporation?

3. Capricorn, Inc., is planning to "go public" by offering its common stock, which previously had been owned by only three shareholders. The company intends to limit the number of purchasers to twenty-five persons resident in the state of its incorporation. All of Capricorn's business and all of its assets are located in its state of incorporation. Based on these facts, what exemptions from registration, if any, are available to Capricorn, and what conditions would each of these available exemptions impose on the terms of the offer?

4. The boards of directors of DuMont Corp. and Epsot, Inc., agreed to enter into a friendly merger, with DuMont Corp. to be the surviving entity. The stock of both corporations was listed on a national stock exchange. In connection with the merger, both corporations distributed to their shareholders proxy statements seeking approval of the proposed merger. The shareholders of both corporations voted to approve the merger. About three weeks after the merger was consummated, the price of DuMont stock fell from $25 to $13 as a result of the discovery that Epsot had entered into several unprofitable long-term contracts two months before the merger had been proposed. The contracts will result in substantial losses from Epsot's operations for at least the next four years. The existence and effect of these contracts, although known to both corporations at the time of the proposed merger, were not disclosed in the proxy statements of either corporation. Can the shareholders of DuMont recover in a suit against DuMont under the 1934 Act? Explain.

5. Farthing is a director and vice president of Garp, Inc., whose common stock is listed on the New York Stock Exchange. Farthing engaged in the following transactions in the same calendar year: on January 2, Farthing sold 500 shares at $30 per share; on January 15, she purchased 300 shares at $30 per share; on February 1, she purchased 200 shares at $45 per share; on March 1, she purchased 300 shares at $50 per share; on March 15, she sold 200 shares at $55 per share; and on April 1, she sold 100 shares at $40 per share. Howell brings suit on behalf of Garp, alleging that Farthing has violated the Securities Act of 1934. Farthing defends on the ground that she lost money on the transactions in question. Is Farthing liable? If so, under which provisions and for what amount of money?

6. Intercontinental Widgets, Inc., had applied for a patent for a new state-of-the-art widget that, if patented, would significantly increase the value of Intercontinental's shares. On September 1, the Patent Office notified Jackson, the attorney for Intercontinental, that the patent application had been approved. After informing Kingsley, the company's president, of the good news, Jackson called his broker and purchased 1,000 shares of Intercontinental at $18 per share. He also told his partner, Lucas, who immediately proceeded to purchase 500 shares at $19 per share. Lucas then called his brother-in-law, Mammon, and told him the news. On September 3, Mammon bought 4,000 shares at $21 per share. On September 4, Kingsley issued a press release that accurately reported that a patent had been granted to Intercontinental. On the next day, Intercontinental's stock soared to $38 per share. A class action suit is brought against Jackson, Lucas, Mammon, and Intercontinental for violations of Rule 10b–5. Who, if anyone, is liable?

7. Nova, Inc., sought to sell a new issue of common stock. It registered the issue with the SEC but included false information in both the registration statement and the prospectus. The issue was underwritten by Omega & Sons and was sold in its entirety by Periwinkle, Rameses, and Sheffield, Inc., a securities broker-dealer. Telford purchased 500 shares at $6 per share. Three months later, the falsity of the information contained in the prospectus was made public, and the price of the shares fell to $1 per share. The following week, Telford brought suit against Nova, Inc.; Omega & Sons; and Periwinkle, Rameses, and Sheffield, Inc., under the Securities Act of 1933.
   a. Who, if anyone, is liable under the 1933 Act? If liable, under which provisions?
   b. What defenses, if any, are available to the various defendants?

8. Tanaka, a director and officer of Deep Hole Oil Company, approached Romani for the purpose of buying 200 shares of Deep Hole Company stock owned by Romani. During the period of negotiations, Tanaka concealed his identity and did not disclose the fact that earlier in the day he had received a report of two rich oil strikes on the oil company's property. Romani sold his 200 shares to Tanaka for $10 per share. Taking into consideration the new strikes, the fair value of the stock was approximately $20 per share. Romani sues Tanaka to recover damages. Is Tanaka liable? If so, under which provisions and for what amount of money?

9. Venable Corporation has 750,000 shares of common stock outstanding, which are owned by 640 shareholders. The assets of Venable Corporation are valued at more than $10 million. In March, Underhill began purchasing shares of Venable's common stock in the open market. By April, he had acquired 40,000 shares at prices ranging from $12 to $14. Upon discovering Underhill's activities in late April, the directors of Venable had the corporation purchase the 40,000 shares from Underhill for $18 per share. Which provisions of the 1934 Act, if any, have been violated?

CASE PROBLEMS

10. Dirks was an officer of a New York broker-dealer firm who specialized in providing investment analysis of insurance company securities to institutional investors. On March 6, Dirks received information from Ronald Secrist, a former officer of Equity Funding of America. Secrist alleged that the assets of Equity Funding, a diversified corporation primarily engaged in selling life insurance and mutual funds, were vastly overstated as the result of fraudulent corporate practices. Dirks decided to investigate the allegations. He visited Equity Funding's headquarters in Los Angeles and interviewed several officers and employees of the corporation. The senior management denied any wrongdoing, but certain corporation employees corroborated the charges of fraud. Neither Dirks nor his firm owned or traded any Equity Funding stock, but throughout his investigation he openly discussed the information he had obtained with a number of clients and investors. Some of these persons sold their holdings of Equity Funding securities, including five investment advisers who liquidated holdings of more than $16 million.

    While Dirks was in Los Angeles, he was in touch regularly with William Blundell, *The Wall Street Journal's* (http://interactive.wsj.com/ushome.html) Los Angeles bureau chief. Dirks urged Blundell to write a story on the fraud allegations. Blundell did not believe, however, that such a massive fraud could go undetected and declined to write the story. He feared that publishing such damaging hearsay might be libelous.

    During the two-week period in which Dirks pursued his investigation and spread word of Secrist's charges, the price of Equity Funding stock fell from $26 per share to less than $15 per share. This led the New York Stock Exchange (http://www.nyse.com) to halt trading on March 27. Shortly thereafter, California insurance authorities impounded Equity Funding's records and uncovered evidence of the fraud. Only then did the Securities and Exchange Commission (SEC) file a complaint against Equity Funding.

    The SEC began an investigation into Dirks's role in the exposure of the fraud. After a hearing by an administrative law judge, the SEC found that Dirks had aided and abetted violations of Section 10(b) of the Securities Exchange Act of 1934 and SEC Rule 10b–5 by repeating the allegations of fraud to members of the investment community who later sold their Equity Funding stock. Has Dirks violated Section 10(b) and Rule 10b–5? Explain.

11. Texas Gulf Sulphur Company (TGS) was a corporation engaged in exploring for and mining certain minerals. A particular tract of Canadian land looked very promising as a source of desired minerals, and Texas Gulf drilled a test hole on November 8. Because the core sample of the hole contained minerals of amazing quality, Texas Gulf began to acquire surrounding tracts of land. Stevens, the president of Texas Gulf, instructed all on-site personnel to keep the find a secret. Because subsequent test drillings were performed, the amount of activity surrounding the drilling had resulted in rumors as to the size and quality of the find. To counteract these rumors, Stevens authorized a press release denying the validity of the rumors and describing them as excessively optimistic. The release was issued on April 12 of the following year, though drilling continued through April 15. In the meantime, several officers, directors, and employees had purchased or accepted options to purchase additional Texas Gulf stock on the basis of the information concerning the drilling. They also recommended similar purchases to outsiders without divulging the inside information to the public. At 10:00 a.m. on April 16, an accurate report on the find was finally released to the American financial press. The SEC brought this action against Texas

Gulf Sulphur and several of its officers, directors, and employees to enjoin conduct alleged to violate Section 10(b) of the Securities Act of 1934 and to compel rescission by the individual defendants of securities transactions assertedly conducted in violation of Rule 10b–5. Have any of the defendants violated Section 10(b)? Explain.

12. W. J. Howey Co. and Howey-in-the-Hills Service, Inc., were Florida corporations under direct common control and management. The Howey Company owned large tracts of citrus acreage in Florida. The service company cultivated, harvested, and marketed the crops. For several years, Howey Company offered one half of its planted acreage to the public to help it "finance additional development." Each prospective customer was offered both a land sales contract and a service contract with Howey-in-the-Hills after being told that it was not feasible to invest in the grove without a service arrangement. Upon payment of the purchase price, the land was conveyed by warranty deed. The service company was given full discretion over cultivating and marketing the crop. The purchaser had no right of entry to market the crop. The service company also was accountable only for an allocation of the net profits after the companies pooled the produce. The purchasers were predominantly nonresident businesspersons attracted by the expectation of substantial profits. Contending that this arrangement was an investment contract within the coverage of the Securities Act of 1933, the Securities and Exchange Commission brought an action against the two companies to restrain them from using the mails and instrumentalities of interstate commerce in the offer and sale of unregistered and nonexempt securities. Should the SEC succeed?

13. Prior to December 20, 2000, Basic Inc. was a publicly traded company engaged in the business of manufacturing chemical refractories for the steel industry. Beginning in September 1998, Combustion Engineering, Inc., and Basic began discussions concerning the possibility of a merger of the two companies. Nevertheless, during 1999 and 2000, Basic made three public statements denying that it was engaged in merger negotiations. On December 18, 2000, Basic asked the New York Stock Exchange to suspend trading in its shares and issued a statement saying that it had been "approached" by another company concerning a merger. On December 20, Basic publicly announced its approval of Combustion's offer for all its outstanding shares. The plaintiffs were former owners of Basic stock who sold their shares after Basic publicly denied that it was engaged in merger negotiation situations. The plaintiffs brought a class action suit against Basic and its directors, alleging that they had released false or misleading information in violation of Section 10(b) of the 1934 Act and in violation of Rule 10b–5. The plaintiffs claimed that they were injured by selling their shares at prices that were artificially depressed as a consequence of Basic's misleading public statements. The defendants claimed that the plaintiffs had not proven that they had, in fact, relied upon the misleading statements in selling their stock. Should the plaintiffs be able to recover?

http:// **Internet Exercise** Find the Securities and Exchange Commission Web site and learn about the agency's (a) structure, (b) functions, and (c) current activities.

Chapter 41

Intellectual Property

And he that invents a machine augments the power of a man and the well-being of mankind.

Henry Ward Beecher, 1870

Learning Objectives

After reading this chapter you should be able to:

1. Explain what trade secrets protect and how they may be infringed.
2. Distinguish among the various types of trade symbols.
3. Explain the extent to which trade names are protected.
4. Explain what copyrights protect and the remedies for infringement.
5. Explain what patents protect and the remedies for infringement.

Intellectual property is an economically significant type of intangible personal property that includes trade secrets, trade symbols, copyrights, and patents. These interests are protected from **infringement**, or unauthorized use, by others. Such protection is essential to the conduct of business. For example, a company would be far less willing to invest considerable resources in research and development if resulting discoveries, inventions, and processes were not protected by patents and by regulations safeguarding trade secrets. Similarly, a company would not be secure in devoting time and money to marketing its products and services without laws to defend its trade symbols and trade names. Moreover, without copyright protection, the publishing, entertainment, and computer software industries would be vulnerable to piracy, both by competitors and by the general public. In this chapter, we will discuss the law protecting (1) trade secrets; (2) trade symbols, including trademarks, service marks, certification marks, collective marks, and trade names; (3) copyrights; and (4) patents.

Trade Secrets

Every business has secret information. Such information may include customer lists or contracts with suppliers and customers; it may also consist of secret formulas, processes, and production methods that are vital to the successful operation of the business. A business may disclose a trade secret in confidence to an employee with the understanding that the employee will not, in turn, reveal the information. To the extent the owner of the information obtains a patent on it, it is no longer a trade secret but is protected by patent law. Some businesses, however, choose not to obtain a patent because it provides protection for only a limited time, whereas state trade secret law protects a trade secret as long as it is kept secret. Moreover, if the courts invalidate a patent, the information will have been disclosed to competitors without the owner of the information obtaining any benefit. The Uniform Trade Secrets Act, promulgated in 1979 and amended in 1985, has been adopted by more than forty states.

http:// Uniform Trade Secrets Act: http://www.law.upenn.edu/bll/ulc/fnact99/1980s/utsa85.pdf

DEFINITION

Basically, a **trade secret** is commercially valuable information that is guarded from disclosure and is not general knowledge. The Uniform Trade Secrets Act defines a trade secret as

> information, including a formula, pattern, compilation, program, device, method, technique, or process that:
>
> (i) derives independent economic value, actual or potential, from not being generally known to, and not being readily ascertainable by proper means by, other persons who can obtain economic value from its disclosure or use, and
>
> (ii) is the subject of efforts that are reasonable under the circumstances to maintain its secrecy.

A famous example of a trade secret is the formula for Coca-Cola.

MISAPPROPRIATION

Misappropriation of a trade secret is the wrongful use of a trade secret. A person misappropriates a trade secret of another (1) by knowingly acquiring it through improper means or (2) by disclosing or using it without consent, if his knowledge of the trade secret came under circumstances giving rise to a duty to maintain secrecy or came from a person who used improper means or who owed the owner of the trade secret a duty to maintain secrecy. Trade secrets are most frequently misappropriated in two ways: (1) an employee wrongfully uses or discloses such secrets or (2) a competitor wrongfully obtains them.

An employee is under a duty of loyalty to his employer, which, among other things, charges the employee not to disclose trade secrets to competitors. It is wrongful, in turn, for a competitor to obtain vital secret trade information from an employee through bribery or other means. Besides breaching the duty of loyalty, the faithless employee who divulges secret trade information also commits a tort. In the absence of a contract restriction, an employee is under no duty upon termination of her employment to refrain from working for a competitor of, or competing with, a former employer; but she may not use trade secrets or disclose them to third persons. The employee is entitled, however, to use the skill, knowledge, and general information she acquired during the previous employment relationship.

Another improper method of acquiring trade secrets is industrial espionage conducted through methods such as electronic surveillance or spying. Improper means of acquiring another person's trade secrets also include theft, bribery, fraud, unauthorized interception of communications, and inducement or knowing participation in a breach of confidence. In the broadest sense, discovering another's trade secrets by any means other than independent research or personal inspection of the publicly available finished product is improper unless the other party voluntarily discloses the secret or fails to take reasonable precautions to protect its secrecy.

Practical Advice

Before disclosing a trade secret to another, require that person to sign a nondisclosure agreement.

REMEDIES

Remedies for misappropriation of trade secrets are damages and, when appropriate, injunctive relief. Damages are awarded in the amount of either the pecuniary loss to the plaintiff caused by the misappropriation or the pecuniary gain to the defendant, whichever is greater. A court will grant an injunction to prevent a continuing or threatened misappropriation of a trade secret for as long as is necessary to protect the plaintiff from any harm attributable to the misappropriation and to deprive the defendant of any economic advantage attributable to the misappropriation.

Ed Nowogroski Insurance, Inc. v. Rucker

Supreme Court of Washington, 1999
137 Wash.2d 427, 971 P.2d 936
http://caselaw.lp.findlaw.com/scripts/getcase.pl?court=wa&vol=662240&invol=o01

FACTS Ed Nowogroski Insurance, Inc. (Nowogroski Inc.), owned by the Rupp family, sued its former employees, Michael Rucker, Darwin Rieck, and Jerry Kiser, for soliciting its clients using confidential information. The employees had worked for Nowogroski Inc. as insurance salesmen and servicers of insurance business. Nowogroski

Inc. also sued Potter, Leonard and Cahan, Inc., a rival insurance agency, for which employees Rucker, Rieck, and Kiser commenced work when they left their employment with Nowogroski Inc. Following a bench trial, the trial court found that the employees had misappropriated Nowogroski Inc.'s trade secrets by retaining and using confidential client lists and other information. However, the court did not award damages for one employee's solicitation of clients through the use of memorized client information.

Nowogroski Inc. appealed, arguing that the employees should be liable for misappropriation of a trade secret whether the information that constituted the protected information was written or memorized. The Washington Court of Appeals held that there was no legal distinction between written and memorized information under the Washington Uniform Trade Secrets Act and remanded for a recalculation of damages. The Supreme Court of Washington granted the employees and their new employer's petition for review.

DECISION Court of Appeals' decision affirmed.

OPINION Guy, C. J. As a general rule, an employee who has not signed an agreement not to compete is free, upon leaving employment, to engage in competitive employment. In so doing, the former employee may freely use general knowledge, skills, and experience acquired under his or her former employer. However, the former employee, even in the absence of an enforceable covenant not to compete, remains under a duty not to use or disclose, to the detriment of the former employer, trade secrets acquired in the course of previous employment. Where the former employee seeks to use the trade secrets of the former employer in order to obtain a competitive advantage, then competitive activity can be enjoined or result in an award of damages. [Citation.]

Once a common law concept, trade secret protection is now governed by statutes in most states, including Washington. [Citation.] Forty-one states and the District of Columbia have adopted the Uniform Trade Secrets Act. [Citation.] * * *. [Citations.] The Act codifies the basic principles of common law trade secret protection. [Citation.] A purpose of trade secrets law is to maintain and promote standards of commercial ethics and fair dealing in protecting those secrets. [Citation.]

The Uniform Trade Secrets Act defines trade secret as follows:

> "Trade secret" means information, including a * * * compilation * * * that:
>
> (a) Derives independent economic value, actual or potential, from not being generally known to, and not being readily ascertainable by proper means by, other persons who can obtain economic value from its disclosure or use; and
>
> (b) Is the subject of efforts that are reasonable under the circumstances to maintain its secrecy.
>
> [Citation.]

In determining whether information has "independent economic value" under the Uniform Trade Secrets Act, one of the key factors used by the courts is the effort and expense that was expended on developing the information. [Citation.] A plaintiff seeking damages for misappropriation of a trade secret under the Uniform Trade Secrets Act has the burden of proving that legally protectable secrets exist. [Citation.]

In this case, the trial court found that the insurance information, including the customer lists: (1) derived independent economic value from not being known or readily ascertainable by proper means by other persons who can obtain economic value from its disclosure or use, and (2) that the plaintiff's efforts to keep the customer files secret by educating its staff and by providing employment manuals and employment agreements had been reasonable.

The portion of the Act's definition of "misappropriation" which applies here proscribes the disclosure or use of a trade secret of another without express or implied consent by a person who, at the time of disclosure or use, knew or had reason to know his or her knowledge of the trade secret was acquired under circumstances giving rise to a duty to maintain its secrecy or limit its use. [Citation.]

The nature of the employment relationship imposes a duty on employees and former employees not to use or disclose the employer's trade secrets. [Citation.] The Petitioners in the present case do not argue that the trial court erred in concluding that they "misappropriated" a trade secret; rather, they argue that information in the memory of the employee about a customer list is not a trade secret.

A customer list is one of the types of information which can be a protected trade secret if it meets the criteria of the Trade Secrets Act. [Citations.]

Trade secret protection will not generally attach to customer lists where the information is readily ascertainable. [Citations.] If information is readily ascertainable from public sources such as trade directories or phone books, then customer lists will not be considered a trade secret and a prior employee, not subject to a noncompetition agreement, would be free to solicit business after leaving employment. [Citation.] * * *

Briefly expressed, whether a customer list is protected as a trade secret depends on three factual inquiries: (1) whether the list is a compilation of information; (2) whether it is valuable because unknown to others; and (3) whether the owner has made reasonable attempts to keep the information secret. There is no dispute in this case that the customer names, expiration dates, coverage information and related information is a compilation of information. The trial court found that the customer list and associated information derived independent economic value from not being known, or readily ascertainable by proper means, by other persons who can obtain economic value from its disclosure or use and that Nowogroski Inc. undertook reasonable steps to protect its secrecy.

The question before us is whether the fact that the customer information was in one of the employee's memory allows him to use with impunity the information which was otherwise a trade secret under our statute. We recognize a split of authority on this issue. * * *

* * *

While there is no reported case law on this issue in Washington subsequent to the adoption of the Uniform Trade Secrets Act, common law in Washington prior to the adoption of the Act holds that a former employee could not use confidential information of his or her former employer's customers to actively solicit their business. The fact that the former employee memorized the information, rather than taking it in a written form, made no difference. [Citation.] * * * In the absence of legislative intent to the contrary, prior common law which is not contradicted by the Uniform Trade Secrets Act should continue to guide courts in the interpretation of the Act. [Citation.] * * *

The Uniform Trade Secrets Act does not distinguish between written and memorized information. The Act does not require a plaintiff to prove actual theft or conversion of physical documents embodying the trade secret information to prove misappropriation. [Citations.] The Washington Uniform Trade Secrets Act defines a "trade secret" to include compilations of information which have certain characteristics without regard to the form that such information might take. The definition of "misappropriation" includes unauthorized "disclosure or use." [Citation.] As the Court of Appeals noted, two types of information mentioned in the Uniform Trade Secrets Act as examples of trade secrets include "method" and "technique;" these do not imply the requirement of written documents. [Citation.]

* * *

In the present case, the trial court's conclusion that only written confidential customer lists are protected conflicts with prior Washington law on trade secrets and essentially adds an element to the Uniform Trade Secret Act's definition of a trade secret. While the Act defines a trade secret as a compilation of information that derives independent economic value from not being generally known or readily ascertainable to others and subject to reasonable efforts to maintain secrecy, the trial court added the element that such information be taken or misappropriated while in some tangible form. If an employee was privy to a secret formula of a manufacturing company, which was valuable and kept secret, it should not cease to be a trade secret if an employee committed it to memory. [Citation.] While customer lists may or may not be trade secrets depending on the facts of the case, we conclude that trade secret protection does not depend on whether the list is taken in written form or memorized.

INTERPRETATION Although a former employee may use general knowledge, skills and experience acquired during the prior employment in competing with a former employer, the employee may not use or disclose trade secrets belonging to the former employer to actively solicit customers from a confidential customer list, whether written or memorized.

ETHICAL QUESTION Did any of the parties act unethically? Explain.

CRITICAL THINKING QUESTION What factors should be considered in determining whether a trade secret exists? Explain.

CRIMINAL PENALTIES

In 1996 Congress enacted the Economic Espionage Act of 1996 prohibiting the theft of trade secrets and providing criminal penalties for violations. (The statute does not provide any civil remedies.) The statute defines trade secrets to mean

> all forms and types of financial, business, scientific, technical, economic, or engineering information, including patterns, plans, compilations, program devices, formulas, designs, prototypes, methods, techniques, processes, procedures, programs, or codes, whether tangible or intangible, and whether or how stored, compiled, or memorialized physically, electronically, graphically, photographically, or in writing if (a) the owner thereof has taken reasonable measures to keep such information secret; and (b) the information derives independent economic value, actual or potential, from not being generally known to, and not being readily ascertainable through proper means by the public.

The act broadly defines theft to include all types of conversion of trade secrets including:

1. stealing, obtaining by fraud, or concealing such information;
2. without authorization copying, duplicating, sketching, drawing, photographing, downloading, uploading, photocopying, or mailing such information;
3. purchasing or possessing a trade secret with knowledge that it has been stolen.

The act punishes thefts of trade secrets, as well as attempts and conspiracies to steal secrets, with fines of up to $500,000, imprisonment for up to 10 years, or both. Organizations that violate the act are subject to fines of up to $5 million.

TRADE SYMBOLS

One of the earliest forms of unfair competition was the fraudulent marketing of one person's goods as those of another. Still common today, this unlawful practice is sometimes referred to as "passing off" or "palming off." Basically, "cashing in" fraudulently on the goodwill, good name, and reputation of a competitor and his products deceives the public and deprives honest businesses of trade. Section 43(a) of the Federal Trademark Act (the Lanham Act) prohibits businesses from using a false designation of origin in connection with any goods or services in interstate commerce. This section also prohibits a business from falsely describing or representing its own goods and services. In 1988, Congress amended this section to prohibit the misrepresentation of *another* person's goods, services, or commercial activities. As a result, Section 43(a) also forbids "reverse palming off," by which a producer misrepresents someone else's goods as his own. Accordingly, James would violate Section 43(a) by passing off his product as Sally's or by reverse passing off Sally's product as his. A violator of Section 43(a) is liable in a civil action to any person who is, or is likely to be, injured by the violation.

The Lanham Act also established federal registration of trade symbols and protection against misuse or infringement by injunctive relief and a right of action for damages against the infringer. An infringement involves passing off one's goods or services as those of the owner of the mark in a manner that deceives the public and constitutes unfair competition. Thus, trade symbol infringement law not only protects consumers from being misled by the use of infringing trade symbols but also protects producers from unfair practices by a competitor.

http:// Trademark Act: http://www4.law.cornell.edu/uscode/15/ch22.html#PC22

TYPES OF TRADE SYMBOLS

The Lanham Act recognizes four types of trade symbols or ***marks***. A **trademark** is a *distinctive* symbol, word, name, device, letter, number, design, picture, or combination in any arrangement that a person adopts or uses to identify the goods he manufactures or sells, as well as to distinguish them from those manufactured or sold by others. Examples of trademarks include Kodak, Xerox, and the rainbow apple logo on Apple computers. A trademark can also consist of goods' "trade dress," which is the appearance or image of goods as presented to prospective purchasers. Trade dress would include the distinctive but nonfunctional design of packaging labels, containers, and the product itself or its features. Examples include the Campbell Soup label and the shape of the Coca-Cola bottle. Internet domain names that are used to identify and distinguish the goods or services of one person from the goods or services of others and to indicate the source of the goods and services may be registered as a trademark. To qualify, an applicant must show that it offers services via the Internet and that it uses the Internet domain name as a source identifier.

Similar in function to the trademark, which identifies tangible goods and products, is a **service mark**, used to identify and distinguish the services of one person from those of others. For example, the titles, character names, and other distinctive elements of radio and television shows may be registered as service marks. Service marks may also consist of trade dress such as the décor or shape of buildings in which services are provided. Examples include the Fotomat kiosk and Howard Johnson's orange roof.

A **certification mark** is used on or in connection with goods or services to certify their regional or other origin, composition, mode of manufacture, quality, accuracy, or other characteristics, or that the work or labor in the goods or services was performed by members of a union or other organization. The marks "Good Housekeeping Seal of Approval" and "Underwriter's Laboratory" are examples of certification marks. The owner of the certification mark does not produce or provide the goods or services with which the mark is used.

A **collective mark** is a distinctive mark or symbol used to indicate either that the producer or provider belongs to a trade union, trade association, fraternal society, or other organization, or that members of a collective group produce the goods or services. Like the owner of a certification mark, the owner of a collective mark is not the producer or provider but rather is the group of which the producer or provider is a member. An example of a collective mark is the union mark that indicates a product's manufacture by a unionized company.

REGISTRATION

To be protected by the Lanham Act, a mark must be distinctive enough to identify clearly the origin of goods or services; it may not be immoral, deceptive, or scandalous. A trade symbol may satisfy the distinctiveness requirement in either of two ways. First, it may be *inherently distinctive* if prospective purchasers are likely to associate it with the product or service it designates because of the nature of the designation and the context in which it is used. Fanciful or arbitrary marks satisfy the distinctiveness requirement. In contrast, a descriptive or geographic designation is not inherently distinctive. Such a designation is one that is likely to be perceived by prospective purchasers as merely descriptive of the nature, qualities, or other characteristics of the goods or service with which it is used. Thus, the word *Apple* cannot be a trademark for apples, although it may be a trademark for computers.

Descriptive or geographic designations may, however, satisfy the distinctiveness requirement through the second method: acquiring distinctiveness through a "secondary meaning." A designation acquires a ***secondary meaning*** when a substantial number of prospective purchasers associate the designation with the product or service it identifies. The trademark office may accept as *prima facie* evidence of secondary meaning proof of substantially exclusive and continuous use of a mark for five years.

A ***generic designation*** is one that is understood by prospective purchasers to denominate the general category, type, or class of goods or services with which it is used. A user cannot acquire rights in a generic designation as a trade symbol. Moreover, a trade symbol will lose its eligibility for protection if prospective purchasers come to perceive a trade symbol primarily as a generic description for the category, type, or class of goods or services with which it is used. Under the Lanham Act, the test for when this has occurred is "the primary significance of the registered mark to the relevant public rather than purchaser motivation." Examples of marks that have lost protection because they became generic include "aspirin," "thermos," "escalator," and "cellophane."

Practical Advice

Guard against losing your trade symbols' distinctiveness by advertising the proper use of them, as the owners of Teflon, Kleenex, and Xerox have done.

Federal registration is denied to marks that are immoral, deceptive, or scandalous. Marks may not be registered if they disparage or falsely suggest a connection with persons, living or dead; institutions; beliefs; or national symbols. In addition, a trademark may not consist of the flag, coat of arms, or other insignia of the United States or of any state, municipality, or foreign nation. Moreover, a mark will not be registered if it so resembles a registered or previously used mark such that it would be likely to cause confusion, mistake, or deceit.

To obtain federal protection, which has a ten-year term with unlimited ten-year renewals, the mark must be registered with the Patent and Trademark Office. The registrant must either (1) have actually used the mark in commerce or (2) demonstrate a *bona fide* intent to use the mark in commerce and actually use it within six months.

Federal registration is not required to establish rights in a mark, nor is it required to begin using a mark. Registration, however, provides numerous advantages. It gives nationwide constructive notice of the mark to all later users. It permits the registrant to use the federal courts to enforce the mark and constitutes *prima facie* evidence of the registrant's exclusive right to use the mark. This right becomes incontestable, subject to certain specified limitations, after five years. Finally, registration provides the registrant with Customs Bureau protection against imports that threaten to infringe upon the mark. A U.S. trade symbol registration provides protection only in the United States. However, in 2002 Congress enacted legislation implementing the Madrid Protocol, a procedural agreement allowing U.S. trademark owners to file for registration in more than sixty-five member countries by filing a single application in English and paying a single fee.

Practical Advice

Give notice of your registered marks by displaying with the mark the words "Registered in U.S. Patent and Trademark Office" or the abbreviation "Reg. U.S. Pat. & Tm. Off." or the symbol ®.

To retain trademark protection, the owner of a mark must not abandon it by failing to make *bona fide* use of it in the ordinary course of trade. Abandonment occurs when an owner does not use a mark and no longer intends to use it. Three years of nonuse raises a presumption of abandonment, which the owner may rebut by proving her intent to resume use.

Anyone who claims rights in a mark may use the TM (trademark) or SM (service mark) designation, even if the mark is not registered. Only owners of registered marks may use the symbol ®.

http:// Patent and Trademark Office: http://www.uspto.gov/

Wal-Mart Stores, Inc. v. Samara Brothers, Inc.

Supreme Court of the United States, 2000

529 U.S. 205, 120 S.Ct. 1339, 146 L.Ed.2d 182

http://caselaw.findlaw.com/cgi-bin/getcase.pl?court=US&navby=case&vol=000&invol=99-150

FACTS Samara Brothers, Inc., designs and manufactures children's clothing. Its primary product is a line of spring/summer one-piece seersucker outfits decorated with appliqués of hearts, flowers, fruits, and the like. A number of chain stores, including JCPenney **(http://www2.jcpenney.com)**, sell this line of clothing under contract with Samara. Wal-Mart Stores, Inc. **(http://www.walmart.com)**, is one of the nation's best-known retailers, selling among other things children's clothing. In 1995, Wal-Mart contracted with one of its suppliers, Judy-Philippine, Inc., to manufacture a line of children's outfits for sale in the 1996 spring/summer season. Wal-Mart sent Judy-Philippine photographs of a number of garments from Samara's line, on which Judy-Philippine's garments were to be based; Judy-Philippine duly copied, with only minor modifications, sixteen of Samara's garments, many of which contained copyrighted elements. In 1996, Wal-Mart briskly sold the so-called knockoffs, generating more than $1.15 million in gross profits. Samara officials launched an investigation, which disclosed that Wal-Mart and several other major retailers—Kmart **(http://www.kmart.com)**, Caldor, Hills, and Goody's **(http://www.goodysonline.com)**—were selling the knockoffs of Samara's outfits produced by Judy-Philippine.

After sending cease and desist letters, Samara brought an action against Wal-Mart, Judy-Philippine, Kmart, Caldor, Hills, and Goody's for copyright infringement under federal law and infringement of unregistered trade dress under § 43(a) of the Lanham Act. All of the defendants except Wal-Mart settled before trial. After a week-long trial, the jury found in favor of Samara on all of its claims. The District Court awarded Samara damages, interest, costs, and fees totaling almost $1.6 million, together with injunctive relief. The Second Circuit affirmed, and the United States Supreme Court granted *certiorari.*

DECISION Judgment of Court of Appeals reversed and case remanded.

OPINION Scalia, J. The Lanham Act provides for the registration of trademarks, which it defines * * * to include "any word, name, symbol, or device, or any combination thereof [used or intended to be used] to identify and distinguish [a producer's] goods * * * from those manufactured or sold by others and to indicate the source of the goods * * *." [Citation.]. Registration of a mark under the Act, [citation], enables the owner to sue an infringer, [citation]; it also entitles the owner to a presumption that its mark is valid, [citation], and ordinarily renders the registered mark incontestable after five years of continuous use, [citation]. In addition to protecting registered marks, the Lanham Act, in § 43(a), gives a producer a cause of action for the use by any person of "any word, term, name, symbol, or device, or any combination thereof * * * which * * * is likely to cause confusion * * * as to the origin, sponsorship, or approval of his or her goods * * *." [Citation.] It is the latter provision that is at issue in this case.

The breadth of the definition of marks registrable [under the Act], and of the confusion producing elements recited as actionable by § 43(a), has been held to embrace not just word marks, such as "Nike," and symbol marks, such as Nike's "swoosh" symbol, but also "trade dress"—a category that originally included only the packaging, or "dressing," of a product, but in recent years has been expanded by many courts of appeals to encompass the design of a product. [Citations.] These courts have assumed, often without discussion, that trade dress constitutes a "symbol" or "device" for purposes of the relevant sections, and we conclude likewise. "Since human beings might use as a 'symbol' or 'device' almost anything at all that is capable of carrying meaning, this language, read literally, is not restrictive." [Citation.] This reading of [the registration provision of the Act] and § 43(a) is buttressed by a recently added subsection of § 43(a), § 43(a)(3), which refers specifically to "civil action[s] for trade dress infringement under this chapter for trade dress not registered on the principal register." [Citation.]

The text of § 43(a) provides little guidance as to the circumstances under which unregistered trade dress may be protected. It does require that a producer show that the allegedly infringing feature is not "functional," [citation], and is likely to cause confusion with the product for which protection is sought, [citation]. Nothing in § 43(a) explicitly requires a producer to show that its trade dress is distinctive, but courts have universally imposed that requirement, since without distinctiveness the trade dress would not "cause confusion * * * as to the origin, sponsorship, or approval of [the] goods," as the section requires.

Distinctiveness is, moreover, an explicit prerequisite for registration of trade dress * * *, and "the general principles qualifying a mark for registration * * * are for the most part applicable in determining whether an unregistered mark is entitled to protection under § 43(a)." [Citation.]

In evaluating the distinctiveness of a mark * * *, courts have held that a mark can be distinctive in one of two ways. First, a mark is inherently distinctive if "[its] intrinsic nature serves to identify a particular source." [Citation.] In the context of word marks, courts have applied the now classic test originally formulated by Judge Friendly, in which word marks that are "arbitrary" ("Camel" cigarettes), "fanciful" ("Kodak" film), or "suggestive" ("Tide" laundry detergent) are held to be inherently distinctive. [Citation.] Second, a mark has acquired distinctiveness, even if it is not inherently distinctive, if it has developed secondary meaning, which occurs when, "in the minds of the public, the primary significance of a [mark] is to identify the source of the product rather than the product itself." [Citation.]

The judicial differentiation between marks that are inherently distinctive and those that have developed secondary meaning has solid foundation in the statute itself. [The Act] requires that registration be granted to any trademark "by which the goods of the applicant may be distinguished from the goods of others"—subject to various limited exceptions. [Citation.] It also provides, again with limited exceptions, that "nothing in this chapter shall prevent the registration of a mark used by the applicant which has become distinctive of the applicant's goods in commerce"—that is, which is not inherently distinctive but has become so only through secondary meaning. [Citation.] Nothing in [the Act], however, demands the conclusion that every category of mark necessarily includes some marks "by which the goods of the applicant may be distinguished from the goods of others" without secondary meaning—that in every category some marks are inherently distinctive.

Indeed, with respect to at least one category of mark—colors—we have held that no mark can ever be inherently distinctive. * * * We held that a color could be protected as a trademark, but only upon a showing of secondary meaning. * * *

It seems to us that design, like color, is not inherently distinctive. The attribution of inherent distinctiveness to certain categories of word marks and product packaging derives from the fact that the very purpose of attaching a particular word to a product, or encasing it in a distinctive packaging, is most often to identify the source of the product. Although the words and packaging can serve subsidiary functions—a suggestive word mark (such as "Tide" for laundry detergent), for instance, may invoke positive connotations in the consumer's mind, and a garish form of packaging (such as Tide's squat, brightly decorated plastic bottles for its liquid laundry detergent) may attract an otherwise indifferent consumer's attention on a crowded store shelf—their predominant function remains source identification. Consumers are therefore predisposed to regard those symbols as indication of the producer, which is why such symbols "almost *automatically* tell a customer that they refer to a brand," [citation], and "immediately * * * signal a brand or a product 'source,'" [citation]. And where it is not reasonable to assume consumer predisposition to take an affixed word or packaging as indication of source—where, for example, the affixed word is descriptive of the product ("Tasty" bread) or of a geographic origin ("Georgia" peaches)—inherent distinctiveness will not be found. That is why the statute generally excludes, from those word marks that can be registered as inherently distinctive, words that are "merely descriptive" of the goods, [citation], or "primarily geographically descriptive of them," [citation]. In the case of product design, as in the case of color, we think consumer predisposition to equate the feature with the source does not exist. Consumers are aware of the reality that, almost invariably, even the most unusual of product designs—such as a cocktail shaker shaped like a penguin—is intended not to identify the source, but to render the product itself more useful or more appealing.

The fact that product design almost invariably serves purposes other than source identification not only renders inherent distinctiveness problematic; it also renders application of an inherent distinctiveness principle more harmful to other consumer interests. Consumers should not be deprived of the benefits of competition with regard to the utilitarian and esthetic purposes that product design ordinarily serves by a rule of law that facilitates plausible threats of suit against new entrants based upon alleged inherent distinctiveness. How easy it is to mount a plausible suit depends, of course, upon the clarity of the test for inherent distinctiveness, and where product design is concerned we have little confidence that a reasonably clear test can be devised. * * *

It is true, of course, that the person seeking to exclude new entrants would have to establish the nonfunctionality of the design feature, [citation]—a showing that may involve consideration of its esthetic appeal, [citation]. Competition is deterred, however, not merely by successful suit but by the plausible threat of successful suit, and given the unlikelihood of inherently source identifying design, the game of allowing suit based upon alleged inherent distinctiveness seems to us not worth the candle. That is especially so since the producer can ordinarily obtain protection for a design that is inherently source identifying (if any such exists), but that does not yet have secondary meaning, by securing a design patent or a copyright for the design—as, indeed, respondent did for certain elements of the designs in this case. The availability of these other protections greatly reduces any harm to the producer that might ensue from our conclusion that a product design cannot be protected under § 43(a) without a showing of secondary meaning.

* * *

* * * We believe, however, that the frequency and the difficulty of having to distinguish between product design and product packaging will be much less than the frequency and the difficulty of having to decide when a product design is inherently distinctive. To the extent there are close cases, we believe that courts should err on the side of caution and classify ambiguous trade dress as product design, thereby requiring secondary meaning. The very closeness will suggest the existence of relatively small utility in adopting an inherent distinctiveness principle, and relatively great consumer benefit in requiring a demonstration of secondary meaning.

* * *

We hold that, in an action for infringement of unregistered trade dress under § 43(a) of the Lanham Act, a product's design is distinctive, and therefore protectible, only upon a showing of secondary meaning.

INTERPRETATION Unregistered trade dress is protected in a § 43(a) action for infringement only upon a showing of secondary meaning for the product's design.

ETHICAL QUESTION Did any of the parties act unethically? Explain.

CRITICAL THINKING QUESTION Do you agree with the Court's decision? Explain.

INFRINGEMENT

Infringement of a mark occurs when a person without authorization uses an identical or substantially indistinguishable mark that is likely to cause confusion, to cause mistake, or to deceive. The intention to confuse purchasers is not required, nor is proof of actual confusion, although likelihood of confusion may be inferred from either. Infringement occurs if an appreciable number of ordinarily prudent purchasers are *likely* to be misled or confused as to the source of the goods or services. In deciding whether infringement has occurred, the courts consider various factors, including the strength of the mark, the intent of the unauthorized user, the degree of similarity between the two marks, the relation between the two products or services the marks identify, and the marketing channels through which the goods or services are purchased.

The Federal Trademark Dilution Act of 1995 amended the Lanham Act to protect famous marks from dilution of their distinctive quality. The term **dilution** means the lessening of the capacity of a famous mark to identify and distinguish goods or services even if (1) there is no competition between the owner of the famous mark and the other party using the mark or (2) the other party's use of the mark does not result in the likelihood of confusion, mistake, or deception. Examples of dilution would include DUPONT shoes, BUICK aspirin, and KODAK pianos. In determining whether a mark is distinctive and famous, a court may consider factors such as (1) the degree of inherent or acquired distinctiveness of the mark; (2) the degree of recognition of the mark; (3) the duration and extent of the use, advertising, and publicity of the mark; (4) the geographical extent of the trading area in which the mark is used; and (5) the channels of trade for the goods or services with which the mark is used. The amendment exempts fair use of a famous mark in comparative commercial advertising, noncommercial use of a mark, and mention of a famous mark in news reporting.

The Trademark Cyberpiracy Prevention Act of 1999 amended the Lanham Act to protect the owner of a trademark or service mark from any person who, with a bad faith intent to profit from the mark, registers, traffics in, or uses a domain name which, at the time of its registration, is (1) identical or confusingly similar to a distinctive mark or (2) dilutive of a famous mark. See Chapter 48 for further discussion of this statute.

REMEDIES

The Lanham Act provides several remedies for infringement: (1) injunctive relief, (2) an accounting for profits, (3) damages, (4) destruction of infringing articles, (5) attorneys' fees in exceptional cases, and (6) costs. In assessing profits, the plaintiff has only to prove the gross sales made by the defendant; the defendant, in contrast, must prove any costs to be deducted in determining profits. If the court finds that the amount of recovery based on profits is either inadequate or excessive, the court may, in its discretion, award an amount it determines to be just. In assessing damages, the court *may* award up to three times the actual damages, according to the circumstances of the case. When an infringement is knowing and intentional, the court *shall* award attorneys' fees plus the greater of treble profits or treble damages, unless there are extenuating circumstances. In an action under the Federal Trademark Dilution Act of 1995, the owner of the famous mark can obtain only injunctive relief unless the

MANAGERIAL insight

Licensed Trademarks Beset by Pirates, Counterfeiters, and Copycats

Before the information age with its high-speed global communications and internationally recognized corporate symbols, trademark law existed as a sleepy corner of intellectual property law. Today, however, things have changed.

Now, companies are much more ready to go to court to protect their registered trademarks. In fact, they often have too much to lose to do otherwise.

These days, a registered trademark can provide a company with an essential marketing tool: worldwide name recognition. In addition, a well-known trademark encourages brand loyalty, as well as offering an implicit guarantee of consistent product quality.

But a trademark can also present problems for a company. There is always the danger that an aggressive competitor will infringe upon the trademark, dilute its distinctive nature by improper use, or, worse still, transform it into a generic label, which spells legal death for a trademark in the United States.

How difficult is it, then, to fend off trademark assaults? Ask Rollerblade, Inc. The Minneapolis-based company was the first to market in-line skates, a product that since has captured the sports world. With its success, however, the company found itself struggling to maintain its hold on its trademark. Rollerblade, despite public misuse of the word, is a federally registered trademark and not, as the company notes, the specific name of a sport or the general name of a skate. Neither "rollerblading" nor "rollerblades" is an appropriate use of the term. Today, Rollerblade, Inc., must battle daily with the media, the public, and its competitors to keep its trademark from becoming a generic label.

As global competition intensifies, companies such as Rollerblade are also finding that they must protect their trademarks overseas. Rollerblade, for instance, markets its in-line skates in Europe, Australia, and Japan, among other places. Currently, though, neither Rollerblade nor any other company can turn to a single international law that would give it worldwide rights to a trademark, patent, or copyright. Rather, companies must work within each individual country to protect their rights. Increasingly, companies are reaping substantial profits from their trademarks, which is why they have turned to the courts for protection. Numerous companies, for example, are profiting from the hot new area of trademark licensing, which is especially lucrative when it comes to athletic sportswear. At the same time, companies are facing new challenges. They are being threatened as never before by cheap knockoffs and flagrant piracy. They are also being called on to deal with the popular culture's assimilation of corporate symbols.

Like everyone else, companies want to protect their good names. As a result, more and more of them are seeking trademark protection, sometimes with mixed results. A few noteworthy examples follow:

- Walt Disney, Inc., as well as many other companies, breathed a sigh of relief when Poland gave in to international pressure in 1994 and passed a strengthened copyright law that would subject violators to heavy fines and imprisonment. U.S. companies had been losing millions of dollars under Poland's lax policing of copyright piracy and trademark infringement, which had led to the marketing of such items as fake Mickey Mouse dolls and contraband Jurassic Park videos.
- Several companies, notably Warner-Lambert and American Home Products, have dragged the Perrigo corporation to court for its knockoff versions of over-the-counter drugstore items. Warner-Lambert is the manufacturer of Cool Mint Listerine mouthwash, so it didn't much like it when Perrigo took to describing its own mouthwash as "Blue Mint" antiseptic mouth rinse. Nor did American Home Products, which makes Advil, fancy Perrigo bottling up its own ibuprofen tablets in Advil-style packaging. To American Home Products' dismay, though, it lost its case.
- The Cousteau Society took offense when Clover-Stornetta Farms decked out a cow in diving gear and plastered her picture on a billboard to advertise its dairy. Clo the Cow, the dairy's advertising symbol, had turned up previously as Christopher Cowlumbus, with nary a complaint. But Jacques Cowsteau got a chillier reception. The real-life Cousteau and his environmental society filed a $1.2 million trademark infringement lawsuit, which was settled out of court.
- French champagne makers protested when Yves Saint Laurent decided to name his new perfume Champagne. In France, a product with such an appellation must come from the region of Champagne. Otherwise, the name represents a violation of French trademark law. Although French vintners won in court and Saint Laurent was forced to rename his perfume after himself, he did retain the perfume's specially crafted bottle, shaped like a champagne cork. He also will be allowed to market the perfume in the United States as Champagne, since the American and French legal systems don't follow the same rules.

person against whom the injunction is sought willfully intended to trade on the owner's reputation or to cause dilution of the famous mark. If willful intent is proven, the owner of the famous mark may also obtain the other remedies discussed.

Where a defendant has intentionally and knowingly used a counterfeit mark, the court may impose criminal sanctions; and goods bearing the counterfeit mark may be destroyed. A *counterfeit mark* means a spurious mark that is identical with, or substantially indistinguishable from, a registered mark. Criminal sanctions include a fine of up to $250,000 or imprisonment of up to five years, or both. For a repeat offense, the limits are $1 million and fifteen years, respectively. For an offender who is not an individual (a corporation, for example), the fine may be up to $1 million for a first offense and up to $5 million for a repeat offense.

TRADE NAMES

A **trade name** is any name used to identify a business, vocation, or occupation. Descriptive and generic words, and personal and generic names, although not proper trademarks, may become protected as trade names upon acquiring a special significance in the trade. A name acquires such significance, frequently referred to as a "secondary meaning," through its continuing and extended use in connection with specific goods or services, whereby the name's acquired meaning eclipses its primary meaning in the minds of many purchasers or users. Although they may not be federally registered under the Lanham Act, trade names are protected, and a person who palms off her goods or services under the trade name of another is liable in damages and also may be enjoined from doing so.

COPYRIGHTS

Copyright is a form of protection provided by the Federal Copyright Act to authors of original works, which include literary, musical, and dramatic works; pantomimes; choreographic works; pictorial, graphic, and sculptural works; motion picture and other audiovisual works; sound recordings; and architectural works. This listing is illustrative but not exhaustive; the act extends **copyright** protection to "original works of authorship in any tangible medium of expression, now known or later developed." Moreover, in 1980, the Copyright Act was amended to extend copyright protection to computer programs. Furthermore, the Semiconductor Chip Protection Act of 1984 extended protection for ten years to safeguard mask works embodied in a semiconductor chip product.

On March 1, 1989, the United States joined the Berne Convention, an international treaty protecting copyrighted works. In 1998 Congress enacted the Digital Millenium Copyright Act (DMCA), which amended the Copyright Act to implement the World Intellectual Property Organization (WIPO) Copyright Treaty and the WIPO Performances and Phonograms Treaty of 1996 by extending U.S. copyright protection to works required to be protected under these two treaties. The WIPO treaty called for adequate legal protection and effective legal remedies against the circumvention of effective technological measures that are used by copyright owners to prevent unauthorized exercise of their copyrights. The DMCA contains three principal anticircumvention provisions, which are discussed in Chapter 48.

In no case does the copyright protection for an original work of authorship protect also any idea, procedure, process, system, method of operation, concept, principle, or discovery, regardless of the form in which it is described, explained, illustrated, or embodied in such work. Copyright protection extends only to an *original expression* of an idea. For example, the idea of interfamily feuding cannot be copyrighted; but a particular expression of that idea in the form of a novel, drama, movie, or opera may be thus protected.

http://
Copyright Act: http://www4.law.cornell.edu/uscode/17/index.html
Berne Convention: http://www.law.cornell.edu/treaties/berne/overview.html
Copyright Office: http://www.copyright.gov

PROCEDURE

Copyright applications are filed with the Register of Copyrights in Washington, D.C. Although registration of the copyright is not required, because copyright protection begins automatically as soon as the work is fixed in a tangible medium, registration is advisable nonetheless, being a condition of the remedies of statutory damages and attorneys' fees for copyright infringement. When a work is published, it is advisable, though no longer required, to place a copyright notice on all publicly distributed copies, so as to notify users about the copyright claim. If proper notice appears on the published copies to which a defendant in a copyright infringement case had access, the defendant will be unable to mitigate actual or statutory damages by asserting a defense of innocent infringement.

Practical Advice

You should register your copyrights and place a copyright notice on all publicly distributed copies. Notice consists of three elements: (1) the symbol © or the word *Copyright* or the abbreviation *Copr.*; (2) the year of first publication of the work; and (3) the name of the owner of the copyright in the work.

RIGHTS

As amended in 1998 by the Sonny Bono Copyright Extension Act, in most instances, copyright protection lasts the duration of the author's life plus an additional seventy years. The Copyright Act gives the copyright owner the exclusive **right**, and the right to authorize others, to reproduce the copyrighted work, prepare derivative works based upon the copyrighted work, distribute copies or recordings of the copyrighted work, perform the work publicly, and display the work publicly.

These broad rights are subject, however, to several limitations, the most important of which are "compulsory licenses" and "fair use." ***Compulsory licenses*** permit certain limited uses of copyrighted material upon the payment of specified royalties and compliance with statutory conditions. The Copyright Act provides that the ***fair use*** of a copyrighted work for purposes such as criticism, comment, news reporting, teaching (including multiple copies for classroom use), scholarship, or research is not an infringement of copyright. In determining whether the use made of a work in any particular case is fair, the courts consider the following factors: (1) the purpose and character of the use, including whether such use is of a commercial nature or is for nonprofit educational purposes; (2) the nature of the copyrighted work; (3) the amount and substantiality of the portion used in relation to the copyrighted work as a whole; and (4) the effect of the use upon the potential market for or value of the copyrighted work.

OWNERSHIP

The author of a creative work owns the entire copyright. Although the actual creator of a work is usually the author, in two situations under the doctrine of ***works for hire***, she is not considered the author. First, if an employee prepares a work within the scope of her employment, her employer is considered the author of the work. Second, if a work is specially ordered or commissioned for certain purposes specified in the copyright statute and the parties expressly agree in writing that the work shall be considered a work for hire, the person commissioning the work is deemed to be the author. The kinds of works subject to becoming works for hire by commission include contributions to collective works; parts of motion pictures or other audiovisual works; translations; supplementary works such as prefaces, illustrations, or afterwords; compilations; instructional texts; and tests. In a work made for hire, the copyright lasts for a term of 95 years from the year of its first publication, or a term of 120 years from the year of its creation, whichever expires first.

The ownership of a copyright may be transferred in whole or in part by conveyance, will, or intestate succession. However, a transfer of copyright ownership, other than by operation of law, is not valid unless a note or memorandum chronicles the transfer in writing and is signed by the owner of the rights conveyed or by the owner's duly authorized agent. An author may terminate any transfer of copyright ownership, other than that of a work for hire, during the five-year period beginning thirty-five years after the transfer was granted.

Ownership of a copyright, or of any of the exclusive rights under a copyright, is distinct from the ownership of any material object that embodies the work. The transfer of ownership of any material object, including the copy or recording in which the work was first fixed, does not in itself convey any rights in the copyrighted work the object embodies; nor, in the absence of an agreement, does the transfer of copyright ownership or of any exclusive rights under a copyright convey property rights in any material object. Thus, the purchase of this textbook neither affects the publisher's copyright nor authorizes the purchaser to make and sell copies of the book, though the purchaser may rent, lend, or resell it. Were this a recorded text, however, the purchaser's latter rights would be somewhat more limited: in 1990, amendments to the Copyright Act prohibited the rental, lease, or commercial lending of sound recordings and computer programs unless authorized by the copyright owner.

New York Times Company, Inc. v. Tasini

Supreme Court of the United States, 2001
533 U.S. 483, 121 S.Ct. 2381, 150 L.Ed.2d 500
http://supct.law.cornell.edu/supct/htm /00-201.ZO.html

FACTS This copyright case concerns the rights of freelance authors and a presumptive privilege of their publishers. The litigation was initiated by six freelance authors and relates to articles they contributed to three print periodicals (the *New York Times*, *Newsday*, and *Time*). Under agreements with the periodicals' publishers, but without the freelancers' consent, two computer database companies (one of which was LEXIS/NEXIS) placed copies of the freelancers' articles—along with all other articles from the periodicals in which the freelancers' work appeared—into three databases. Whether written by a freelancer or staff member, each article is presented to, and retrievable by the user in isolation, clear of the context the original print publication presented. These computerized databases store information in a text-only format and contain articles from hundreds of journals (newspapers and periodicals) spanning many years. On most of these databases, each article appears as a separate, isolated "story"—without any visible link to the other stories originally published in the same newspaper or magazine edition.

The freelance authors' complaint alleged that their copyrights had been infringed by the inclusion of their articles in the databases. The publishers, in response, relied on the privilege of reproduction and distribution accorded them by § 201(c) of the Copyright Act, which provides:

> Copyright in each separate contribution to a collective work is distinct from copyright in the collective work as a whole, and vests initially in the author of the contribution. In the absence of an express transfer of the copyright or of any rights under it, the owner of copyright in the collective work is presumed to have acquired only the privilege of reproducing and distributing the contribution as part of that particular collective work, any revision of that collective work, and any later collective work in the same series.

Specifically, the publishers maintained that, as copyright owners of collective works (i.e., the original print publications), they had merely exercised "the privilege" § 201(c) accords them to "reproduce and distribute" the author's discretely copyrighted contribution.

The District Court granted summary judgment for the publishers, holding that § 201(c) shielded the database reproductions. The privilege conferred by § 201(c) is transferable, the court first concluded, and therefore could be conveyed from the original print publishers to the electronic publishers.

The authors appealed, and the Second Circuit reversed. The Court of Appeals granted summary judgment for the authors on the ground that the databases were not among the collective works covered by § 201(c), and specifically, were not "revisions" of the periodicals in which the articles first appeared.

DECISION Judgment of the Court of Appeals affirmed.

OPINION Ginsburg, J. Under the Copyright Act, as amended in 1976, "copyright protection subsists * * * in original works of authorship fixed in any tangible medium of expression * * * from which they can be perceived, reproduced, or otherwise communicated." [Citation] § 102(a). When, as in this case, a freelance author has contributed an article to a "collective work" such as a newspaper or magazine, see § 101 (defining "collective work"), the statute recognizes two distinct copyrighted works: "Copyright in *each separate contribution to a collective work is distinct from copyright in the collective work as a whole.* * * * " § 201(c) (emphasis added). Copyright in the separate contribution "vests initially in the author of the contribution" (here, the freelancer). *Ibid.* Copyright in the collective work vests in the collective author (here, the newspaper or magazine publisher) and extends only to the creative material contributed by that author, not to "the preexisting material employed in the work," § 103(b). [Citation.]

* * *

Section 201(c) both describes and circumscribes the "privilege" a publisher acquires regarding an author's contribution to a collective work:

> "In the absence of an express transfer of the copyright or of any rights under it, the owner of copyright in the collective work is presumed to have acquired *only* the privilege of reproducing and distributing the contribution as part of that particular collective work, any revision of that collective work, and any later collective work in the same series." (Emphasis added.)

A newspaper or magazine publisher is thus privileged to reproduce or distribute an article contributed by a freelance author, absent a contract otherwise providing, only "as part of" any (or all) of three categories of collective works: (a) "that collective work" to which the author contributed her work, (b) "any revision of that collective work," or (c) "any later collective work in the same series." In accord with Congress' prescription, a "publishing company could reprint a contribution from one issue in a later issue of its magazine, and could reprint an article from a 1980 edition of an encyclopedia in a 1990 revision of it; the publisher could not revise the contribution itself or include it in a new anthology or an entirely different magazine or other collective work." [Citation.]

Essentially, § 201(c) adjusts a publisher's copyright in its collective work to accommodate a freelancer's copyright in her contribution. If there is demand for a freelance article standing alone or in a new collection, the Copyright Act allows the freelancer to benefit from that demand; after authorizing initial publication, the freelancer may also sell the article to others. [Citations.] It would scarcely "preserve the author's copyright in a contribution" as contemplated by Congress, [citation], if a newspaper or magazine publisher were permitted to reproduce or distribute copies of the author's contribution in isolation or within new collective works. [Citation.]

* * *

In determining whether the Articles have been reproduced and distributed "as part of" a "revision" of the collective works in issue, we focus on the Articles as presented to, and perceptible by, the user of the Databases. [Citations.] In this case, the three Databases present articles to users clear of the context provided either by the original periodical editions or by any revision of those editions. The Databases first prompt users to search the universe of their contents: thousands or millions of files containing individual articles from thousands of collective works (*i.e.*, editions), either in one series (the *Times*, in NYTO) or in scores of series (the sundry titles in NEXIS and GPO). When the user conducts a search, each article appears as a separate item within the search result. In NEXIS and NYTO, an article appears to a user without the graphics, formatting, or other articles with which the article was initially published. In GPO, the article appears with the other materials published on the same page or pages, but without any material published on other pages of the original periodical. In either circumstance, we cannot see how the Database perceptibly reproduces and distributes the article "as part of " either the original edition or a "revision" of that edition.

One might view the articles as parts of a new compendium—namely, the entirety of works in the Database. In that compendium, each edition of each periodical represents only a miniscule fraction of the ever-expanding Database. The Database no more constitutes a "revision" of each constituent edition than a 400-page novel quoting a sonnet in passing would represent a "revision" of that poem. "Revision" denotes a new "version," and a version is, in this setting, a "distinct form of something regarded by its creators or others as one work." *Webster's Third New International Dictionary* 1944, 2545 (1976). The massive whole of the Database is not recognizable as a new version of its every small part.

Alternatively, one could view the Articles in the Databases "as part of" no larger work at all, but simply as individual articles presented individually. That each article bears marks of its origin in a particular periodical (less vivid marks in NEXIS and NYTO, more vivid marks in GPO) suggests the article was *previously* part of that periodical. But the markings do not mean the article is *currently* reproduced or distributed as part of the periodical. The Databases' reproduction and distribution of individual Articles—simply *as individual Articles*—would invade the core of the Authors' exclusive rights under § 106.

* * *

* * * [Court's footnote: Furthermore, it bears reminder here and throughout that these Publishers and all others can protect their interests by private contractual arrangement.]

* * *

We conclude that the Electronic Publishers infringed the Authors' copyrights by reproducing and distributing the Articles in a manner not authorized by the Authors and not privileged by § 201(c). We further conclude that the Print Publishers infringed the Authors' copyrights by authorizing the Electronic Publishers to place the Articles in the Databases and by aiding the Electronic Publishers in that endeavor.

INTERPRETATION Reproduction of freelance authors' magazine and newspaper articles in computer databases, without the authors' permission, infringes the authors' copyrights.

ETHICAL QUESTION Should an author be able to retain copyright protection even after allowing a publisher to publish his work? Explain.

CRITICAL THINKING QUESTION In the future, how can publishers protect themselves from the Court's decision?

INFRINGEMENT AND REMEDIES

Infringement occurs whenever somebody exercises, without authorization, the rights exclusively reserved for the copyright owner. Infringement need not be intentional. To prove infringement, the plaintiff must simply establish that he owns the copyright and that the defendant violated one or more of the plaintiff's exclusive rights under the copyright. Proof of infringement usually consists of showing that the allegedly infringing work is substantially similar to the copyrighted work and that the alleged infringer had access to the copyrighted work. The Digital Millenium Copyright Act of 1998 amended the Copyright Act to create limitations on the liability of online providers for copyright infringement when engaging in certain activities.

In order for the owner to sue for infringement, the copyright must be registered with the Copyright Office, unless the work is a Berne Convention work whose country of origin is not the United States. For an infringement occurring after registration, the following **remedies** are available: (1) injunction; (2) impoundment and possible destruction of infringing articles; (3) actual damages plus profits made by the infringer that are additional to those damages, *or* statutory damages of at least $750 but no more than $30,000 (though the ceiling may reach $150,000 if the infringement is willful), according to what the court determines to be just; (4) costs and, in the court's discretion, reasonable attorneys' fees to the prevailing party; or (5) criminal penalties of a fine of up to $10,000 or up to one year's imprisonment for willful infringement for purposes of commercial advantage or private financial gain. In 1997 Congress enacted the No Electronic Theft Act, increasing criminal penalties for certain copyright violations. Imprisonment for up to five

Ethical Dilemma

Who Holds the Copyright on Lecture Notes?

FACTS Tom Rigsby considers himself a young, aspiring entrepreneur. At twenty-three, he has already established a highly successful small business, Take Note, which provides students at the University of the Midwest with detailed class notes for approximately seventy-five university courses, covering subjects that range from business law to modern literature. For each of his note sets, Rigsby charges $35.

He also offers, for $25, an exam package that includes summary notes as well as exam questions that professors have used in the past, which many fraternities on campus already keep on file exclusively for their members.

To make a profit, Rigsby has concentrated on the university's more popular courses, which often pack up to 500 students into a single lecture hall. At present, he is grossing about $400,000 a year.

Most students who have used Rigsby's notes consider them to be of exceptionally high quality. Many believe that the notes have made the difference between an "A" and a "B" in their courses.

Rigsby received his degree from the University of the Midwest, where he graduated summa cum laude. Until recently, when he expanded his business, he based his Take Note packages either on notes he had taken while a regular student or on notes from classes he audited after he graduated. Now, he has hired two additional notetakers, both 4.0 students at the university. He pays them each a small salary plus royalties of 12 percent on every sale of their notes that he makes.

To the dismay of many professors at the university, though, Rigsby has never sought their permission to distribute notes of their classes. He doesn't see why he should. In fact, he believes that any question of copyright here should be answered in favor of the notetaker, not the professor. He acknowledges that in other states, businesses such as his pay royalties to professors, but he thinks such expenditures unnecessary.

Now, on behalf of the University of the Midwest and its professors, lawyers for the university have sued Rigsby for copyright infringement. He, in turn, has filed a countersuit, charging disparagement. Rigsby was planning to expand his business to three other midwestern states, but now he says the university has disrupted his business with false accusations.

SOCIAL, POLICY, AND ETHICAL CONSIDERATIONS

1. Who does hold the copyright in this case? Did Rigsby act ethically in not seeking the professors' permission? Should he be required to share a part of his profits as royalties with the professors whose classes are covered by his Take Note packages?
2. Are the students acting ethically in buying Rigsby's Take Note packages? Does using one of Rigsby's exam packages constitute cheating? Does employing someone else's notes or old exam questions to study for an exam differ from using someone else's notes or outline to write a term paper?
3. Is the University of the Midwest acting responsibly in scheduling such large classes? What responsibility does it have to protect students from an impersonal or inadequate education? Is the university acting responsibly toward its professors? How should the university protect a professor's intellectual work?

years (ten years for subsequent offenses) may be imposed for willful infringement if at least ten copies or phonorecords with a total retail value of more than $2,500 in a 180-day period are reproduced or distributed.

PATENTS

Through a **patent**, the federal government grants an inventor a monopolistic right to make, use, or sell an invention to the absolute exclusion of others for the period of the patent. The patent owner may also profit by selling the patent or by licensing others to use the patent on a royalty basis. However, the patent may not be renewed: upon expiration, the invention enters the "public domain," and anyone may then use it.

PATENTABILITY

The Patent Act specifies those inventions that may be patented as ***utility patents***: any new and useful process, machine, manufacture, or composition of matter or any new and useful improvement thereof. Thus, naturally occurring substances are not patentable, as the invention must be made or modified by humans. For example, the discovery of a bacterium with useful properties is not patentable, whereas the manufacture of a genetically engineered bacterium is. By the same token, laws of nature, principles, bookkeeping systems, fundamental truths, calculation methods, and ideas are not patentable. Accordingly, Einstein could not have patented his law that $E = mc^2$; nor could Newton have patented the law of gravity. Similarly, isolated computer programs are not

THE LAW AND YOU

State Bar Associations

Georgia: http://www.gabar.org/cps.asp?Header=CPS ("Patents, Trademarks, and Copyrights")

Minnesota: http://www.mnbar.findlawyer.com/consumer-faq.htm ("Patents, Trademarks, Copyrights")

Ohio: http://www.ohiobar.org/conres/pamphlets ("Intellectual Property Rights")

Oregon: http://www.osbar.org/public/legalinfo/business.html ("Patents, Trademarks, and Copyrights")

Tennessee: http://www.tba.org/LawBytes/T4.html ("What Is a Patent, Trademark, and Copyright?")

U.S. Government

Consumer Information Center:
http://www.pueblo.gsa.gov/smbuss.htm ("Copyright Basics")

http://www.pueblo.gsa.gov/specpubs.htm#SB (General Information Concerning Patents")

http://www.pueblo.gsa.gov/cic_text/smbuss/trademark/tradmark.txt ("Basic Facts about Registering a Trademark")

Patent and Trademark Office: http://www.uspto.gov/main/trademarks.htm ("Basic Facts about Trademarks")

Copyright Office: http://www.copyright.gov ("Copyright Basics"; "How to Register a Work")

Patent and Trademark Office: http://www.uspto.gov/web/patents/guides.htm ("General Information Concerning Patents")

patentable, although, as we mentioned above, they may be copyrighted.

To be patentable as a utility patent, the process, machine, manufacture, or composition of matter must meet three criteria: (1) novelty, (2) utility, and (3) nonobviousness.

In addition to utility patents, the Patent Act provides for plant patents and design patents. A ***plant patent*** protects the exclusive right to reproduce a new and distinctive variety of asexually producing plant. Plant patents require (1) novelty, (2) distinctiveness, and (3) nonobviousness. A ***design patent*** protects a new, original, ornamental design for an article of manufacture. Design patents require (1) novelty, (2) ornamentality, and (3) nonobviousness.

Utility and plant patents have a term that begins on the date of the patent's grant and ends twenty years from the date of application, subject to extensions for statutorily specified delays. Design patents have a term of fourteen years from the date of grant.

http:// Patent Act: http://www4.law.cornell.edu/uscode/35/

PROCEDURE

The United States Patent and Trademark Office issues a patent upon the basis of a patent application containing a specification, which describes how the invention works, and claims, which describe the features that make the invention patentable. The applicant must be the inventor. Before granting a patent, the Patent Office carefully and thoroughly examines the prior art and determines whether the submitted invention has novelty (does not conflict with a prior pending application or a previously issued patent) and utility, and is nonobvious. A patent application is confidential, and the Patent Office will not divulge its contents. This confidentiality ends, however, upon the granting of the patent. Unlike rights under a copyright, no monopoly rights arise until the Patent Office actually issues a patent. Therefore, anyone is free to make, use, and sell an invention for which a patent application is filed until the patent has been granted.

Congress recently amended the Patent Act to require the publication of certain utility and plant patent applications eighteen months after filing even if the patent has not yet been granted. This requirement applies only to those patent applications that are filed in other countries that require publication after eighteen months or under the Patent Cooperation Treaty. An applicant may obtain a reasonable royalty from a third party who between publication and issuance of the patent infringes it, provided the third party had actual notice of the published application.

An applicant whose application is rejected may apply for reexamination. If the application is again rejected, the applicant may appeal to the Patent and Trademark Office's Board of Appeals, and from there to the federal courts.

CONCEPT REVIEW

Intellectual Property

	Trade Secrets	Trade Symbols	Copyright	Patents
What Is Protected	Information	Mark	Work of authorship	Invention
Rights Protected	Use or sell	Use or sell	Reproduce, prepare derivative works, distribute, perform, or display	Make, use, or sell
Duration	Until disclosed	Until abandoned	Usually author's life plus 70 years	For utility and plant patents, 20 years from application; For design patents 14 years from grant
Federally Protected	No	Yes	Yes	Yes
Requirements for Protection	Valuable secret	Distinctive	Original and fixed	Novel, useful, and nonobvious

INFRINGEMENT

Anyone who, without permission, makes, uses, or sells a patented invention is a *direct infringer*, whereas a person who actively encourages another to make, use, offer to sell, or sell a patented invention without permission is an *indirect infringer*. A *contributory infringer* is one who knowingly sells, or offers to sell, a part or component of a patented invention, unless the component is a staple or commodity or is suitable for a substantial noninfringing use. Though good faith and ignorance are defenses to contributory infringement, they are not defenses to direct infringement. To recover damages, a patent owner must mark a patented article with the word "Patent" and the number of the patent or give actual notice to an infringer.

Practical Advice

Give notice of your patented articles by fixing on them the word patent or the abbreviation pat., together with the number of the patent.

REMEDIES

The remedies for infringement under the Patent Act are (1) injunctive relief; (2) damages adequate to compensate the plaintiff but "in no event less than a reasonable royalty for the use made of the invention by the infringer"; (3) treble damages, when appropriate; (4) attorneys' fees in exceptional cases, such as those that involve knowing infringement; and (5) costs.

CHAPTER SUMMARY

Trade Secrets

Definition of Trade Secret commercially valuable, secret information

Protection owner of a trade secret may obtain damages or injunctive relief when the secret is misappropriated (wrongfully used) by an employee or a competitor

Criminal Penalties federal law imposes penalties for the theft of trade secrets

Trade Symbols

Types of Trade Symbols
- ***Trademark*** distinctive symbol, word, or design on a good that is used to identify the manufacturer
- ***Service Mark*** distinctive symbol, word, or design that is used to identify a provider's services
- ***Certification Mark*** distinctive symbol, word, or design used with goods or services to certify specific characteristics
- ***Collective Mark*** distinctive symbol used to indicate membership in an organization

Registration to be registered and thus protected by the Lanham Act, a mark must be distinctive and not immoral, deceptive, or scandalous

Infringement occurs when a person without authorization uses a substantially indistinguishable mark that is likely to cause confusion, mistake, or deception

Remedies the Lanham Act provides the following remedies for infringement: injunctive relief, profits, damages, destruction of infringing articles, costs, and, in exceptional cases, attorneys' fees

Trade Names

Definition of Trade Name any name used to identify a business, vocation, or occupation

Protection may not be registered under the Lanham Act, but infringement is prohibited

Remedies damages and injunctions are available if infringement occurs

Copyrights

Definition of Copyright exclusive right, usually for the author's life plus seventy years, to original works of authorship

Procedure registration is not required but provides additional remedies for infringement

Rights copyright protection provides the exclusive right to (1) reproduce the copyrighted work, (2) prepare derivative works based on the work, (3) distribute copies of the work, and (4) perform or display the work publicly

Ownership the author of the copyrighted work is usually the owner of the copyright, which may be transferred in whole or in part

Infringement occurs when someone exercises the copyright owner's rights without authorization

Remedies if infringement occurs after registration, the following remedies are available: (1) injunction, (2) impoundment and possible destruction of infringing articles, (3) actual damages plus profits or statutory damages, (4) costs, and(5) criminal penalties

Patents

Definition of Patent the exclusive right to an invention for twenty years from the date of application for utility and plant patents; fourteen years from grant for design patents

Patentability to be patentable, the invention must be (1) novel, (2) useful, and (3) not obvious

Procedure patents are issued upon application to and after examination by the U.S. Patent and Trademark Office

Infringement occurs when anyone without permission makes, uses, or sells a patented invention

Remedies for infringement of a patent are (1) injunctive relief; (2) damages; (3) treble damages, when appropriate; (4) attorneys' fees; and (5) costs

QUESTIONS

1. Keller, a professor of legal studies at Rhodes University, is a diligent instructor. Late one night, while reading a newly published, copyrighted treatise of 1,800 pages written by Gilbert, he came across a three-page section discussing the subject matter he intended to cover in class the next day. Keller considered the treatment to be illuminating and therefore photocopied the three pages and distributed the copies to his class. One of Keller's students is a second cousin of Gilbert, the author of the treatise, and she showed Gilbert the copies. May Gilbert recover from Keller for copyright infringement? Explain.

2. Jennings conceived a secret process for the continuous freeze-drying of foodstuffs and related products and constructed a small pilot plant that practiced the process. However, Jennings lacked the financing necessary to develop the commercial potential of the process and, in hopes of obtaining a contract for its development and the payment of royalties, disclosed it in confidence to Merrick, a coffee manufacturer, who signed an agreement not to disclose it to anyone else. At the same time, Jennings signed an agreement not to disclose the process to any other person as long as Jennings and Merrick were considering a contract for its development. Upon Jennings's disclosure of the process, Merrick became extremely interested and offered to pay Jennings the sum of $1,750,000 if, upon further development, the process proved to be commercially feasible. While negotiations between Jennings and Merrick were in progress, Nelson, a competitor of Merrick, learned of the process and requested a disclosure from Jennings, who informed Nelson that the process could not be disclosed to anyone unless negotiations with Merrick were broken off. Nelson offered to pay Jennings $2,500,000 for the process, provided it met certain defined objective performance criteria. A contract was prepared and executed between Jennings and Nelson on this basis, without any prior disclosure of the process to Nelson. Upon the making of this contract, Jennings rejected Merrick's offer. The process was thereupon disclosed to Nelson, and demonstration runs of the pilot plant in the presence of Nelson representatives were conducted under varying conditions. After three weeks of observing experimental demonstrations, compiling data, and analyzing results, Nelson informed Jennings that the process did not meet the performance criteria in the contract and that for this reason Nelson was rejecting the process. Two years later, Nelson placed on the market freeze-dried coffee that resembled in color, appearance, and texture the product of Jennings's pilot plant. What are the rights of the parties?

3. Stella, a chemist, was employed by Johnson, a manufacturer, to work on a secret process for Johnson's product under an exclusive three-year contract. Johnson employed Dabney, a salesperson, on a week-to-week basis. Stella and Dabney resigned their employment with Johnson and accepted employment in their respective capacities with Washington, a rival manufacturer. Dabney began soliciting patronage from Johnson's former customers, whose names he had memorized. What are the rights of the parties in (a) a suit by Johnson to enjoin Stella from working for Washington and (b) a suit by Johnson to enjoin Dabney from soliciting Johnson's customers?

4. Conrad and Darby were competitors in the business of dehairing raw cashmere, the fleece of certain Asiatic goats. Dehairing is the process of separating the commercially valuable soft down from the matted mass of raw fleece, which contains long coarse guard hairs and other impurities. Machinery for this process is not readily available on the open market. Each company in the business designed and built its own machinery and kept the nature of its process secret. Conrad contracted with Lawton, owner of a small machine shop, to build and install new improved dehairing machinery of increased efficiency for which Conrad furnished designs, drawings, and instructions. Lawton, who knew that the machinery design was confidential, agreed that he would manufacture the machinery exclusively for Conrad and that he would not reproduce the machinery or any of its essential parts for anyone else. Darby purchased from Lawton a copy of the dehairing machinery that Conrad had specially designed. What are Conrad's rights, if any, against (a) Darby and (b) Lawton? Explain.

5. Sally, having filed locally an affidavit required under the assumed name statute, has been operating and advertising her exclusive toy store for twenty years in Centerville, Illinois. Her advertising has consisted of large signs on her premises reading "The Toy Mart." Bob, after operating a store in Chicago under the name of "The Chicago Toy Mart," relocated in Centerville, Illinois, and erected a large sign reading "TOY MART" with the word "Centerville" written underneath in substantially smaller letters. Thereafter, Sally's sales declined, and many of Sally's customers patronized Bob's store, thinking it to be a branch of Sally's business. What are the rights of the parties?

6. Ryan Corporation manufactures and sells a variety of household cleaning products in interstate commerce. On national television, Ryan falsely advertises that its laundry liquid is biodegradable. Has Ryan violated the Lanham Act?

7. Gibbons, Inc., and Marvin Corporation are manufacturers who sell a variety of household cleaning products in interstate commerce. On national television Gibbons states that its laundry liquid is biodegradable and that Marvin's is not. In fact, both products are biodegradable. Has Gibbons violated the Lanham Act?

8. George McCoy of Florida has been manufacturing and distributing a cheesecake for more than five years, labeling his product with a picture of a cheesecake, which serves as a background for a Florida bathing beauty and under which

is written the slogan, "McCoy All Spice Florida Cheese Cake." George McCoy has not registered his trademark. Subsequently, Leo McCoy of California begins manufacturing a similar product on the West Coast using a label similar in appearance to that of George McCoy, containing a picture of a Hollywood star and the words "McCoy's All Spice Cheese Cake." Leo McCoy begins marketing his products in the eastern United States, using labels with the word "Florida" added, as in George McCoy's label. Leo McCoy has registered his product under the Federal Trademark Act. To what relief, if any, is George McCoy entitled?

CASE PROBLEMS

9. Sony Corporation (http://www.sony.com/) manufactured and sold home video recorders, specifically Betamax videotape recorders (VTRs). Universal City Studios, Inc. (Universal) (http://www.universalstudios.com), owned the copyrights on some programs aired on commercially sponsored television. Individual Betamax owners frequently used the device to record some of Universal's copyrighted television programs for their own noncommercial use. Universal brought suit, claiming that the sale of the Betamax VTRs to the general public violated its rights under the Copyright Act. It sought no relief against any Betamax consumer. Instead, Universal sued Sony for contributory infringement of its copyrights, seeking money damages, an equitable accounting of profits, and an injunction against the manufacture and sale of Betamax VTRs. Explain whether Universal will prevail in its action.

10. The Coca-Cola Company (http://www.cocacola.com) manufactures a carbonated beverage, Coke, made from coca leaves and cola nuts. The Koke Company of America introduced into the beverage market a similar product named Koke. The Coca-Cola Company brought a trademark infringement action against Koke. Coca-Cola claimed unfair competition within the beverage business due to Koke's imitation of the Coca-Cola product and Koke's attempt to reap the benefit of consumer identification with the Coke name. Should Coca-Cola succeed? Why?

11. Vuitton (http://www.vuitton.com/), a French corporation, manufactures high-quality handbags, luggage, and accessories. Crown Handbags, a New York corporation, manufactures and distributes ladies' handbags. Vuitton handbags are sold exclusively in expensive department stores, and distribution is strictly controlled to maintain a certain retail selling price. The Vuitton bags bear a registered trademark and a distinctive design. Crown's handbags appear identical to the Vuitton bags but are of inferior quality. May Vuitton recover from Crown for manufacturing counterfeit handbags and selling them at a discount? Explain.

12. T.G.I. Friday's (http://www.tgifridays.com), a New York corporation and registered service mark, entered into an exclusive licensing agreement with Tiffany & Co. (http://www.tiffany.com) that allowed Tiffany to open a Friday's restaurant in Jackson, Mississippi. International Restaurant Group, operated by the owners of Tiffany, applied for a license to open a Friday's in Baton Rouge, Louisiana, but was refused. In Baton Rouge, International then opened a restaurant, called E.L. Saturday's, or Ever Lovin' Saturday's, which had the same type of menu and decor as Friday's. Friday's sues International for trademark infringement. Will Friday's prevail? Why?

13. As part of its business, Kinko's Graphics Corporation (Kinko's) (http://www.kinkos.com) copied excerpts from books, compiled them in "packets," and sold the packets to college students. Kinko's did this without permission from the owners of the copyrights to the books and without paying copyright fees or royalties. Kinko's has more than 200 stores nationwide and reported $15 million in assets and $3 million in profits for 1989. Basic Books, Harper & Row (http://www.harpercollins.com), John Wiley & Sons (http://www.wiley.com), and others (plaintiffs) sued Kinko's for violation of the Copyright Act of 1976. The plaintiffs owned copyrights to the works copied and sold by Kinko's and derived substantial income from royalties. They argued that Kinko's had infringed on their copyrights by copying excerpts from their books and selling the copies to college students for profit. Kinko's admitted that it had copied excerpts without permission and had sold them in packets to students, but it contended that its actions constituted a fair use of the works in question under the Copyright Act. What is the result? Explain.

14. In 1967, a Chicago brewer, Meister Brau, Inc., began making and selling a reduced-calorie, reduced-carbohydrate beer under the name "LITE." Late in 1968, that company filed applications to register "LITE" as a trademark in the United States Patent Office, which ultimately approved three registrations of labels containing the name "LITE" for "beer with no available carbohydrates." In 1972, Meister Brau sold its interest in the "LITE" trademarks and the accompanying goodwill to Miller Brewing Company (http://www.millerbrewing.com). Miller decided to expand its marketing of beer under the brand "LITE." It developed a modified recipe, which resulted in a beer lower in calories than Miller's regular beer but not without available carbohydrates. The label was revised, and one of the registrations was amended to show "LITE" printed rather than in script. In addition, Miller undertook an extensive advertising campaign. From 1973 through 1976, Miller expanded its annual sales of "LITE" from 50,000 barrels to 4,000,000 barrels and increased its annual advertising expenditures from $500,000 to more than $12,000,000.

Beginning in early 1975, a number of other brewers, including G. Heileman Brewing Company, introduced reduced calorie beers labeled or described as "light." In response, Miller began filing trademark infringement actions against competitors to enjoin the use of the word "light." Should Miller be granted the injunction? Explain.

15. B. C. Ziegler and Company (Ziegler) (http://www.bcziegler.com) was a securities company located in West Bend. It had established an internal procedure by which its customer lists were treated confidentially. This procedure included burning or shredding any paper to be disposed of that contained a customer name or information. Nonetheless, in late 1985, Ziegler delivered a number of boxes of unshredded scrap paper to Lynn's Waste Paper Company for disposal. One of Lynn's employees, Ehren, who had been in the securities business and had worked for two of Ziegler's competitors, noticed the information contained in the delivery from Ziegler and purchased six boxes of the Ziegler wastepaper for $16.75 from Lynn's. Shortly thereafter, Ehren and his daughter sorted through the information and ultimately obtained 11,600 envelopes of information on Ziegler's customers, including names, account summaries, and other information. Ehren sold this information to Thorson, a broker in competition with Ziegler. Thorson then sent a mailing to the Ziegler customers to solicit security sales for his firm and obtained an abnormally high response rate as a result. Ziegler, with the help of the West Bend Police Department, traced the dissemination of this information to Ehren and sought from the court a permanent injunction against Ehren using or disclosing the information regarding Ziegler's clients. What is the result?

16. Since the 1950s Qualitex Company has used a special shade of green-gold color on the pads that it makes and sells to dry cleaning firms for use on dry cleaning presses. In 1989 Jacobson Products (a Qualitex rival) began to sell its own press pads to dry cleaning firms, and it colored those pads a similar green-gold. In 1991 Qualitex registered the special green-gold color on press pads with the Patent and Trademark Office as a trademark. Qualitex sued Jacobson for trademark infringement. Jacobson argues that the Lanham Act does not permit registering "color alone" as a trademark. Explain whether a trademark violation has been committed.

http:// **Internet Exercise** Find information about the organization and procedures of (a) the United States Copyright Office and (b) the United States Patent and Trademark Office.

CHAPTER 42

Employment Law

I'm sticking to the union till the day I die.

FROM "UNION MAID," WRITTEN BY WOODY GUTHRIE, 1946

Learning Objectives

After reading this chapter you should be able to:

1. List and describe the major labor law statutes.
2. List and describe the major laws prohibiting employment discrimination.
3. Discuss the defenses available to employers under the various laws prohibiting discrimination in employment.
4. Explain the doctrine of employment at will and the laws protecting employee privacy.
5. Explain (a) the Occupational Safety and Health Administration (OSHA) and the Occupational Safety and Health Act, (b) workers' compensation, (c) unemployment compensation, (d) social security, (e) the Fair Labor Standards Act, (f) the Worker Adjustment and Retraining Notification Act, and (g) the Family and Medical Leave Act.

Though the common law originally governed the relationship between employer and employee in terms of tort and contract duties (rules that are a part of the law of agency, as discussed in Chapter 29—Relationship of Principal and Agent), this common law has been supplemented—and in some instances replaced—by statutory enactments, principally at the federal level. In fact, government regulation now affects the balance and working relationship between employers and employees in three principal areas. First, the general framework in which management and labor negotiate the terms of employment is regulated by federal statutes designed to promote both labor-management harmony and the welfare of society at large. Second, federal law has been enacted to prohibit employment discrimination based upon race, sex, religion, age, disability, or national origin. Finally, Congress, in response to the changing nature of American industry and the tremendous number of industrial accidents, has intervened by mandating that employers provide their employees with a safe and healthy work environment. Moreover, all of the states have adopted workers' compensation acts to provide compensation to employees injured during the course of employment.

In this chapter, we will focus on these three categories of government regulation of the employment relationship: (1) labor law, (2) employment discrimination law, and (3) employee protection.

LABOR LAW

Traditionally, **labor law** opposed concerted activities by workers (such as strikes, picketing, and refusals to deal) to obtain higher wages and better working conditions. At various times, such activities were found to constitute criminal conspiracy, tortious conduct, and violation of antitrust law. Eventually, public pressure in response to the adverse treatment accorded labor forced Congress to intervene.

NORRIS–LA GUARDIA ACT

Congress enacted the **Norris–La Guardia Act** in 1932 in response to growing criticism of the use of injunctions in peaceful labor disputes. The act withdrew from the federal courts the power to issue injunctions in nonviolent **labor disputes**, broadly defined to include any controversy concerning terms or conditions of employment or union representation, regardless of whether the parties stood in an employer-employee relationship or not. More significantly, the act declared it to be U.S. policy that labor was to have full freedom to form unions, without employer interference. Accordingly, the act prohibited the so-called "yellow dog" contracts through which employers coerced their employees into promising that they would not join a union.

http:// Norris–La Guardia Act: http://www4.law.cornell.edu/uscode/29/101.html

NATIONAL LABOR RELATIONS ACT

Enacted in 1935, the **National Labor Relations Act (NLRA)**, or the *Wagner Act*, marked the federal government's effort to support collective bargaining and unionization. The act provides that "the right to self-organization, to form, join or assist labor organizations, to bargain collectively through representatives of their own choosing, and to engage in concerted activities for the purpose of collective bargaining or other mutual aid or protection" is, for workers, a federally protected right. Thus, the act gave employees the right to union representation when negotiating employment terms with their employers.

Moreover, the act sought to enforce the collective bargaining right by prohibiting certain employer and union activities deemed to be **unfair labor practices**. For example, the act identifies the following activities as **unfair employer practices**: (1) to interfere with employees' rights to unionize and bargain collectively; (2) to dominate the union; (3) to discriminate against union members; (4) to discriminate against an employee who has filed charges or testified under the NLRA; and (5) to refuse to bargain in good faith with duly established employee representatives.

http:// National Labor Relations Act: http://www4.law.cornell.edu/uscode/29/151.html

Practical Advice

Treat all employees with appropriate respect and dignity.

LABOR-MANAGEMENT RELATIONS ACT

Following the passage of the National Labor Relations Act, the country underwent a tremendous increase in union membership and labor unrest. In response to this trend, Congress passed the **Labor-Management Relations Act** (the **LMRA**, or **Taft-Hartley Act**) in 1947. The act prohibits certain **unfair union practices** and separates the prosecutorial and adjudicative functions of the National Labor Relations Board (NLRB). More specifically, the act amended the NLRA by declaring the following seven union activities of the National Labor Relations Board (NLRB) to be ***unfair labor practices***: (1) coercing an employee to join a union, (2) causing an employer to discharge or discriminate against a nonunion employee, (3) refusing to bargain in good faith, (4) levying excessive or discriminatory dues or fees, (5) causing an employer to pay for work not performed ("featherbedding"), (6) picketing an employer to require it to recognize an uncertified union, and (7) engaging in secondary activities. A secondary activity is a boycott, strike, or picketing of an employer with whom a union has no labor dispute in order to persuade the employer to cease doing business with the company that is the target of the labor dispute. For example, assume that a union is engaged in a labor dispute with Anderson Company. To coerce Anderson into resolving the dispute in the union's favor, the union organizes a strike against Brooking Company, with which the union has no labor dispute. The union agrees to cease striking Brooking Company if Brooking agrees to cease doing business with Anderson. The strike against Brooking is a secondary activity prohibited as an unfair labor practice. See Figure 42-1 for a summary of union and employer unfair labor practices.

In addition to prohibiting unfair union practices, the act also fosters employer free speech by declaring that unions or employees wishing to identify an employer labor practice as unfair cannot use as proof any employer statement of opinion or argument that contains no threat of reprisal.

The LMRA also prohibits the closed shop but permits union shops, unless a state right-to-work law prohibits the latter. A **closed shop** contract requires the employer to hire only union members. A **union shop** contract permits the employer to hire nonunion members but requires the employee to become a union member within a specified time after gaining employment and to remain a member in good standing as a condition of employment. A **right-to-work law** is a state statute that prohibits union shop contracts. However, most states permit the existence of union shops.

Finally, the act reinstates the availability of civil injunctions in labor disputes if requested of the NLRB in order to prevent an unfair labor practice. The act also empowers

Figure 42-1 *Unfair Labor Practices*

Unfair Employer Practices	Unfair Union Practices
• Interfering with right to unionize • Refusing to bargain in good faith • Discriminating against union members • Dominating the union • Discriminating against an employee	• Coercing an employee to join the union • Refusing to bargain in good faith • Causing an employer to discriminate against a nonunion employee • Featherbedding • Picketing an employer to require recognition of an uncertified union • Engaging in secondary activity • Levying excessive or discriminatory dues

the President of the United States to obtain an injunction for an eighty-day cooling-off period for a strike that is likely to endanger the national health or safety.

http://
Labor-Management Relations Act: http://www4.law.cornell.edu/uscode/29/141.html
National Labor Relations Board: http://www.nlrb.gov/

LABOR-MANAGEMENT REPORTING AND DISCLOSURE ACT

The **Labor-Management Reporting and Disclosure Act**, also known as the ***Landrum-Griffin Act***, is aimed at eliminating corruption in labor unions. The act attempts to eradicate corruption through an elaborate reporting system and a union "bill of rights" designed to make unions more democratic. The latter provides union members with the right to nominate candidates for union offices, to vote in elections, to attend membership meetings, to participate in union business, to express themselves freely at union meetings and conventions, and to be accorded a full and fair hearing before the union takes any disciplinary action against them.

CPA EMPLOYMENT DISCRIMINATION LAW

A number of federal statutes prohibit discrimination in employment on the basis of race, sex, religion, national origin, age, and disability. The cornerstone of federal employment discrimination law is Title VII of the 1964 Civil Rights Act, but other statutes and regulations are significant as well, including the ***Civil Rights Act of 1991*** and the ***Americans with Disabilities Act of 1990***. In addition, most states have enacted similar laws prohibiting discrimination based on race, sex, religion, national origin, and disability. The Civil Rights Act of 1991 extended the coverage of both Title VII and the Americans with Disabilities Act to include United States citizens working for U.S.-owned or -controlled companies in foreign countries.

EQUAL PAY ACT

The **Equal Pay Act** prohibits an employer from discriminating between employees on the basis of *gender* by paying unequal wages for the same work. The act forbids an employer from paying wages at a rate less than the rate at which he pays wages to employees of the opposite sex for equal work at the same establishment. Most courts define *equal work* to mean "substantially equal" rather than identical. The burden of proof is on the claimant to make a *prima facie* showing that the employer pays unequal wages for work requiring equal skill, effort, and responsibility under similar working conditions. Once the employee has demonstrated that the employer pays unequal wages for *equal* work to members of the opposite sex, the burden shifts to the employer to prove that the pay differential is based on (1) a seniority system, (2) a merit system, (3) a system that measures earnings by quantity or quality of production, or (4) any factor except gender.

Remedies include awarding back pay, awarding liquidated damages (an additional amount equal to back pay), and enjoining the employer from further unlawful conduct. Though the Department of Labor is the federal agency designated by the statute to interpret and enforce the act, in 1979 these functions were transferred to the Equal Employment Opportunity Commission.

CIVIL RIGHTS ACT OF 1964

Title VII of the **Civil Rights Act of 1964** *prohibits* **employment discrimination** on the basis of race, color, gender, religion, or national origin in hiring, firing, compensating, promoting, training, and other employment-related processes. The definition of "religion" includes all aspects of religious observance and practice; the statute provides that an employer must make reasonable efforts to accommodate an employee's religious belief. The act applies to employers engaged in an industry affecting commerce and having fifteen or more employees.

http:// Civil Rights Act of 1964: http://www4.law.cornell.edu/uscode/42/1971.html

When Congress passed the ***Pregnancy Discrimination Act***, it extended the benefits of Title VII to pregnant women. Under the act, an employer cannot refuse to hire a pregnant woman, fire her, or force her to take maternity leave unless the employer can establish a *bona fide* occupational qualification defense (discussed later in this section). The act, which protects the job reinstatement rights of women returning from maternity leave, requires employers to treat pregnancy as they would a temporary disability.

The enforcement agency for Title VII is the **Equal Employment Opportunity Commission** (EEOC). The EEOC is empowered (1) to file legal actions in its own name or to intervene in actions filed by third parties; (2) to attempt to resolve alleged violations through informal means prior to bringing suit; (3) to investigate all charges of discrimination; and (4) to issue guidelines and regulations concerning enforcement policy. See Figure 42-2 for the number of charges filed with the EEOC in 2002.

http:// Equal Employment Opportunity Commission: http://www.eeoc.gov/

Practical Advice

Issue a strong company policy against all types of prohibited discrimination and ensure that all business decisions comply with your policy.

International Union, United Automobile, Aerospace and Agricultural Implement Workers of America, UAW v. Johnson Controls, Inc.

Supreme Court of the United States, 1991
499 U.S. 187, 11 S.Ct. 1196, 113 L.Ed.2d 158
http://supct.law.cornell.edu/supct/html/89-1215.ZS.html

FACTS In April 1984, petitioners filed a class action lawsuit challenging Johnson Controls' **(http://www.jci.com/)** fetal-protection policy as sex discrimination that violated Title VII of the Civil Rights Act of 1964. Among the individual plaintiffs were petitioners Mary Craig, who had chosen to be sterilized to avoid losing her job; Elsie Nason, a 50-year-old divorcee, who had suffered a loss in compensation when she was transferred out of a job that exposed her to lead; and Donald Penney, who had been denied a request for a leave of absence for the purpose of lowering his lead level because he intended to become a father.

DECISION Judgment for the petitioners.

OPINION Blackmun, J. The bias in Johnson Controls' policy is obvious. Fertile men, but not fertile women, are given a choice as to whether they wish to risk their reproductive health for a particular job. [T]he Civil Rights Act of 1964, [citation], prohibits sex-based classifications in terms and conditions of employment, in hiring and discharging decisions, and in other employment decisions that adversely affect an employee's status. Respondent's fetal-protection policy explicitly discriminates against women on the basis of their sex. The policy excludes women with childbearing capacity from lead-exposed jobs and so creates a facial classification based on gender.

* * *

We concluded above that Johnson Controls' policy is not neutral because it does not apply to the reproductive capacity of the company's male employees in the same way as it applies to that of the females. Moreover, the absence of a malevolent motive does not convert a facially discriminatory policy into a neutral policy with a discriminatory effect. Whether an employment practice involves disparate treatment through explicit facial discrimination does not depend on why the employer discriminates but rather on the explicit terms of the discrimination. * * *

In sum, Johnson Controls' policy "does not pass the simple test of whether the evidence shows 'treatment of a person in a manner which but for that person's sex would be different.'" [Citation.] We hold that Johnson Controls' fetal-protection policy is sex discrimination forbidden under Title VII unless respondent can establish that sex is a "bona fide occupational qualification."

Under Title VII, an employer may discriminate on the basis of "religion, sex, or national origin in those certain instances where religion, sex, or national origin is a bona fide occupational qualification reasonably necessary to the normal operation of that particular business or enterprise." * * *

* * *

Our case law, therefore, makes clear that the safety exception is limited to instances in which sex or pregnancy actually interferes with the employee's ability to perform the job. This approach is consistent with the language of the BFOQ provision itself, for it suggests that permissible distinctions based on sex must relate to ability to perform the duties of the job. Johnson Controls suggests, however, that we expand the exception to allow fetal-protection policies that mandate particular standards for pregnant or fertile women. We decline to do so. Such an expansion contradicts not only the language of the BFOQ and the narrowness of its exception but the plain language and history of the Pregnancy Discrimination Act.

The PDA's amendment to Title VII contains a BFOQ standard of its own: unless pregnant employees differ from others "in their ability or inability to work," they must be "treated the same" as other employees "for all employment-related purposes."

* * *

We conclude that the language of both the BFOQ provision and the PDA which amended it, as well as the legislative history and the case law, prohibit an employer from discriminating against a woman because of her capacity to become pregnant unless her reproductive potential prevents her from performing the duties of her job. * * *

We have no difficulty concluding that Johnson Controls cannot establish a BFOQ. Fertile women, as far as appears in the record, participate in the manufacture of batteries as efficiently as anyone else. Johnson Controls' professed moral and ethical concerns about the welfare of the next generation do not suffice to establish a BFOQ of female sterility. Decisions about the welfare of future children must be left to the parents who conceive, bear, support, and raise them rather than to the employers who hire those parents. Congress has mandated this choice through Title VII, as amended by the Pregnancy Discrimination Act.

INTERPRETATION Disparate treatment occurs when an employer uses a criterion such as race, color, gender, national origin, or religion, in making an employment decision.

CRITICAL THINKING QUESTION When should an employer be permitted to impose an occupational qualification? Explain.

Proving Discrimination Each of the following constitutes discriminatory conduct prohibited by the act:

1. **Disparate Treatment.** Such treatment occurs when an employer uses a prohibited criterion in making an employment decision. The Supreme Court has held that the plaintiff will have shown a *prima facie* case of discrimination if she (a) is within a protected class, (b) had applied for an open position, (c) was qualified for

Figure 42-2 *Charges Filed in 2002 with the EEOC*

Category	Number of Charges
Race	29,910
Sex	25,536
National Origin	9,046
Religion	2,572
Retaliation	20,814
Age	19,921
Disability	15,964
Equal Pay Act	1,256

Source: Equal Employment Opportunity Commission National Database, 2003, http://www.eeoc.gov/stats/charges.html.

the position, (d) was denied the job, and (e) the employer continued to try to fill the position from a pool of applicants with the complainant's qualifications. Once the plaintiff establishes a *prima facie* case, the burden shifts to the defendant to "articulate legitimate and nondiscriminatory reasons for the plaintiff's rejection." If the defendant so rebuts, the plaintiff then has the opportunity to demonstrate that the employer's stated reason was merely a pretext.

2. **Present Effects of Past Discrimination.** Such effects result when an employer engages in conduct that on its face is "neutral"—that is, nondiscriminatory—but that actually perpetuates past discriminatory practices. For example, it has been held illegal for a union that previously had limited its membership to whites to adopt a requirement that new members be related to or recommended by existing members.
3. **Disparate Impact.** This occurs when an employer adopts "neutral" rules that adversely affect a protected class and that are not justified as being necessary to the business. Despite the employee's proof of disparate impact, the employer may prevail if it can demonstrate that the challenged practice is "job related for the position in question and consistent with business necessity." Thus, all requirements that might have a disparate impact upon women, such as height and weight requirements, must be shown to be job related. Nevertheless, under the Civil Rights Act of 1991, even if the employer can demonstrate the business necessity of the questioned practice, the complainant will still prevail if she shows that a nondiscriminatory alternative practice exists.

Defenses The act provides three basic defenses: (1) a *bona fide* seniority or merit system; (2) a professionally developed ability test; and (3) a *bona fide* occupational qualification. The BFOQ defense does not apply to discrimination based on race. A fourth defense, business necessity, is available in a disparate impact case.

Desert Palace, Inc. v. Costa

Supreme Court of the United States, 2003

__ U.S. __, 123 S.Ct. 2148, 156 L.Ed.2d 84

http://www.supremecourtus.gov/opinions/02pdf/02-679.pdf

FACTS Petitioner/defendant Desert Palace, Inc., doing business as Caesar's Palace Hotel & Casino of Las Vegas, Nevada, employed respondent Catharina Costa as a warehouse worker and heavy equipment operator. Respondent was the only woman in this job and in her local Teamsters bargaining unit. Respondent experienced a number of problems with management and her co-workers that led to an escalating series of disciplinary sanctions, including informal rebukes, a denial of privileges, and suspension. Petitioner finally terminated respondent after she was involved in a physical confrontation in a warehouse elevator with fellow Teamsters member Herbert Gerber. Petitioner disciplined both employees because the facts surrounding the incident were in dispute, but Gerber, who had a clean disciplinary record, received only a five-day suspension.

Respondent subsequently filed this lawsuit against petitioner in the United States District Court for the District of Nevada, asserting claims of sex discrimination and sexual harassment under Title VII. The District Court dismissed the sexual harassment claim, but allowed the claim for sex discrimination to go to the jury. At trial, respondent presented evidence that (1) she was singled out for "intense 'stalking'" by one of her supervisors, (2) she received harsher discipline than men for the same conduct, (3) she was treated less favorably than men in the assignment of overtime, and (4) supervisors repeatedly "stacked" her disciplinary record and "frequently used or tolerated" sex-based slurs against her.

Based on this evidence, the District Court denied petitioner's motion for judgment as a matter of law, and submitted the case to the jury with instructions: First, that " '[t]he plaintiff has the burden of proving * * * by a preponderance of the evidence" that she "suffered adverse work conditions" and that her sex "was a motivating factor in any such work conditions imposed upon her.'" Second, the District Court gave the jury the following mixed-motive instruction:

> You have heard evidence that the defendant's treatment of the plaintiff was motivated by the plaintiff's sex and also by other lawful reasons. If you find that the plaintiff's sex was a motivating factor in the defendant's treatment of the plaintiff, the plaintiff is entitled to your verdict, even if you find that the defendant's conduct was also motivated by a lawful reason.
>
> However, if you find that the defendant's treatment of the plaintiff was motivated by both gender and lawful reasons, you must decide whether the plaintiff is

entitled to damages. The plaintiff is entitled to damages unless the defendant proves by a preponderance of the evidence that the defendant would have treated plaintiff similarly even if the plaintiff's gender had played no role in the employment decision.

The jury rendered a verdict for respondent, awarding backpay, compensatory damages, and punitive damages.

The Court of Appeals affirmed the District Court's judgment concluding that references to "direct evidence" had been "wholly abrogated" by the Civil Rights Act of 1991. Accordingly, the court concluded that a "plaintiff * * * may establish a violation through a preponderance of evidence (whether direct or circumstantial) that a protected characteristic played 'a motivating factor.'" Based on that standard, the Court of Appeals held that respondent's evidence was sufficient to warrant a mixed-motive instruction and that a reasonable jury could have found that respondent's sex was a "motivating factor in her treatment." The United States Supreme Court granted certiorari.

DECISION The judgment of the Court of Appeals is affirmed.

OPINION Thomas, J. The question before us in this case is whether a plaintiff must present direct evidence of discrimination in order to obtain a mixed-motive instruction under Title VII of the Civil Rights Act of 1964, as amended by the Civil Rights Act of 1991 (1991 Act). * * *

Since 1964, Title VII has made it an "unlawful employment practice for an employer * * * to discriminate against any individual * * *, *because of* such individual's race, color, religion, sex, or national origin." [Citation.] In *Price Waterhouse v. Hopkins*, [citation], the Court considered whether an employment decision is made "because of" sex in a "mixed-motive" case, *i.e.*, where both legitimate and illegitimate reasons motivated the decision. The Court concluded that, under [Title VII], an employer could "avoid a finding of liability * * * by proving that it would have made the same decision even if it had not allowed gender to play such a role." [Citation.] The Court was divided, however, over the predicate question of when the burden of proof may be shifted to an employer to prove the affirmative defense.

Justice Brennan, writing for a plurality of four Justices, would have held that "when a plaintiff * * * proves that her gender played a *motivating* part in an employment decision, the defendant may avoid a finding of liability only by proving by a preponderance of the evidence that it would have made the same decision even if it had not taken the plaintiff's gender into account." [Citation.] * * *

* * *

Two years after *Price Waterhouse,* Congress passed the 1991 Act "in large part [as] a response to a series of decisions of this Court interpreting the Civil Rights Acts of 1866 and 1964." [Citation.] In particular, §107 of the 1991 Act, which is at issue in this case, "respond[ed]" to *Price Waterhouse* by "setting forth standards applicable in 'mixed motive' cases" in two new statutory provisions. [Citation.] The first establishes an alternative for proving that an "unlawful employment practice" has occurred:

> Except as otherwise provided in this subchapter, an unlawful employment practice is established when the complaining party demonstrates that race, color, religion, sex, or national origin was a motivating factor for any employment practice, even though other factors also motivated the practice. [Citation.]

The second provides that, with respect to " 'a claim in which an individual proves a violation under [Title VII],' " the employer has a limited affirmative defense that does not absolve it of liability, but restricts the remedies available to a plaintiff. The available remedies include only declaratory relief, certain types of injunctive relief, and attorney's fees and costs. [Citation.] In order to avail itself of the affirmative defense, the employer must "demonstrat[e] that [it] would have taken the same action in the absence of the impermissible motivating factor." [Citation.]

Since the passage of the 1991 Act, the Courts of Appeals have divided over whether a plaintiff must prove by direct evidence that an impermissible consideration was a "motivating factor" in an adverse employment action. * * * a number of courts have held that direct evidence is required to establish * * *. [Citations.] In the decision below, however, the Ninth Circuit concluded otherwise. [Citation.]

* * *

This case provides us with the first opportunity to consider the effects of the 1991 Act on jury instructions in mixed-motive cases. Specifically, we must decide whether a plaintiff must present direct evidence of discrimination in order to obtain a mixed-motive instruction under [Title VII]. * * *

Our precedents make clear that the starting point for our analysis is the statutory text. [Citation.] And where, as here, the words of the statute are unambiguous, the " 'judicial inquiry is complete.' " [Citation.] [Title VII] unambiguously states that a plaintiff need only "demonstrat[e]" that an employer used a forbidden consideration with respect to "any employment practice." On its face, the statute does not mention, much less require, that a plaintiff make a heightened showing through direct evidence. * * *

Moreover, Congress explicitly defined the term "demonstrates" in the 1991 Act, leaving little doubt that no special evidentiary showing is required. Title VII defines the term " 'demonstrates' " as to "mee[t] the burdens of production and persuasion." [Citation.] If Congress intended the term "'demonstrates'" to require that the "burdens of production and persuasion" be met by direct evidence or some other heightened showing, it could have made that intent clear by including language to that effect * * *. Its failure to do so is significant, for Congress has been unequivocal when imposing heightened proof requirements in other circumstances * * *

In addition, Title VII's silence with respect to the type of evidence required in mixed-motive cases also suggests that we should not depart from the "[c]onventional rul[e] of civil litigation [that] generally appl[ies] in Title VII cases." [Citation.] * * * We have often acknowledged the utility of circumstantial evidence in discrimination cases. * * *

* * *

For the reasons stated above, we agree with the Court of Appeals that no heightened showing is required * * *.

* * *

In order to obtain an instruction under [Title VII], a plaintiff need only present sufficient evidence for a reasonable jury to conclude, by a preponderance of the evidence, that "race, color, religion, sex, or national origin was a motivating factor for any employment practice." Because direct evidence of discrimination is not required in mixed-motive cases, the Court of Appeals correctly concluded that the District Court did not abuse its discretion in giving a mixed-motive instruction to the jury.

INTERPRETATION A plaintiff does not need to present direct evidence of discrimination in order to prove discrimination under Title VII.

CRITICAL THINKING QUESTION Do you agree with the court's decision? Explain.

Remedies Remedies for violation of the act include enjoining the employer from engaging in the unlawful behavior, taking appropriate affirmative action, and reinstating employees to their rightful place (which may include promotion) and awarding them back pay from a date not more than two years prior to the filing of the charge with the EEOC. First promulgated by executive order, as discussed below, **affirmative action** generally means the active recruitment of minority applicants, although courts also have used the remedy to impose numerical hiring ratios (quotas) and hiring goals based on race and gender. In 1985, the EEOC defined affirmative action in employment as "actions appropriate to overcome the effects of past or present practices, policies, or other barriers to equal employment opportunity."

Prior to 1991, only victims of racial discrimination could recover compensatory and punitive damages from the courts. Today, however, under the Civil Rights Act of 1991, all victims of intentional discrimination based on race, gender, religion, national origin, or disability can recover compensatory and punitive damages, except in cases involving disparate impact. In cases not involving race, the act limits the amount of recoverable damages according to the number of persons the defendant employs. Companies with 15 to 100 employees are required to pay no more than $50,000; companies with 101 to 200 employees, no more than $100,000; those with 201 to 500 employees, no more than $200,000; and those with 501 or more employees, no more than $300,000. Either party may demand a jury trial. Victims of racial discrimination are still entitled to recover unlimited compensatory and punitive damages.

Reverse Discrimination A major controversy has arisen over the use of reverse discrimination in achieving affirmative action. In this context, reverse discrimination refers to affirmative action that directs an employer to remedy the underrepresentation of a given race or gender in a traditionally segregated job by considering an individual's race or gender when hiring or promoting. An example would be an employer who discriminates against white males in order to increase the proportion of females or racial minority members in a company's workforce.

Due to the absence of state action, challenges to affirmative action plans adopted by private employers—those that are not governmental units at the local, state, or federal level—are tested under Title VII of the Civil Rights Act of 1964, not under the Equal Protection Clause of the U.S. Constitution. In 1987, the U.S. Supreme Court, under a Title VII cause of action, upheld an employer's right to promote a female employee rather than a white male employee who had scored higher on a qualifying examination.

When a state or local government adopts an affirmative action plan that is challenged as constituting illegal reverse discrimination, the plan is subject to strict scrutiny under the ***Equal Protection Clause*** of the Fourteenth Amendment. Under the strict scrutiny test, the subject classification must (1) be justified by a compelling governmental interest and (2) be the least intrusive means available. (For a fuller discussion of the Equal Protection Clause and the standards of review, see Chapter 4.)

With regard to racial discrimination, the U.S. Supreme Court in 1989 held that the federal government has "unique remedial powers" far exceeding those of state and local governments and that federal programs enacted to address such discrimination "are subject to a different [and less burdensome] standard than such classifications prescribed by state and local governments." However, in 1995 the U.S. Supreme Court placed significant constraints upon the federal government's ability to create programs favoring minority-owned businesses over white-owned businesses and appeared to apply the same strict standard to federal programs as to those required of state and local governments. Following this decision, the EEOC issued a statement which provided that "affirmative action is lawful only when it is designed to respond to a demonstrated and serious imbalance in the workforce, is flexible, time-limited, applies only to qualified workers, and respects the rights of non-minorities and men."

> **Practical Advice**
>
> In attempting to promote equal opportunity, respect the rights of non-minority applicants and employees.

Sexual Harassment In 1980, the EEOC issued a definition of sexual harassment:

> Unwelcome sexual advances, requests for sexual favors, and other verbal or physical conduct of a sexual nature constitute sexual harassment when
>
> 1. submission to such conduct is made either explicitly or implicitly a term or condition of an individual's employment,
> 2. submission to or rejection of such conduct by an individual is used as the basis for employment decisions affecting such individual, or
> 3. such conduct has the purpose or effect of reasonably interfering with an individual's work performance or creating an intimidating, hostile or offensive working environment.

The courts, including the Supreme Court, have held that sexual harassment may constitute illegal sexual discrimination in violation of Title VII. Moreover, an employer will be held liable for sexual harassment committed by one of its employees if it does not take immediate action when it knows or should have known of the harassment. When the employee engaging in sexual harassment is an agent of the employer or holds a supervisory position over the victim, the employer may be liable without knowledge or reason to know.

In 1998, the U.S. Supreme Court concluded that sex discrimination consisting of same-sex harassment is actionable under Title VII.

> **Practical Advice**
>
> Issue a strong company policy against sexual harassment and thoroughly investigate any charge of a violation of such policy.

Faragher v. City of Boca Raton

Supreme Court of the United States, 1998

524 U.S. 775, 118 S.Ct. 2275, 141 L.Ed.2d 662

http://supct.law.cornell.edu/supct/html/97-282.ZS.html

FACTS Between 1985 and 1990, while attending college, petitioner Beth Ann Faragher worked as an ocean lifeguard for the Marine Safety Section of the Parks and Recreation Department of the City of Boca Raton, Florida (City) **(http://www.bocaraton.com/)**. During this period, Faragher's immediate supervisors were Bill Terry, David Silverman, and Robert Gordon. In June 1990, Faragher resigned.

In 1986, the City had adopted a sexual harassment policy. Although the City may actually have circulated the memo and statement to some employees, it failed to disseminate its policy among employees of the Marine Safety Section, with the result that Terry, Silverman, Gordon, and many lifeguards were unaware of it. From time to time over the course of Faragher's tenure at the Marine Safety Section, between four and six of the forty to fifty lifeguards were women. During that five-year period, Terry repeatedly touched the bodies of female employees without invitation and made crudely demeaning references to women and once commented disparagingly on Faragher's shape. During a job interview with a woman he hired as a lifeguard, Terry said that the female lifeguards had sex with their male counterparts and asked whether she would do the same.

Silverman behaved in similar ways. He once tackled Faragher and remarked that, but for a physical characteristic he found unattractive, he would readily have had sexual relations with her. Another time, he pantomimed an act of oral sex. Within earshot of the female lifeguards, Silverman made frequent, vulgar references to women and sexual matters, commented on the bodies of female lifeguards and beachgoers, and at least twice told female lifeguards that he would like to engage in sex with them.

Faragher did not complain to higher management about Terry or Silverman. Although she spoke of their behavior to Gordon, she did not regard these discussions as formal complaints to a supervisor but as conversations with a person she held in high esteem. Other female lifeguards had similarly informal talks with Gordon, but because Gordon did not feel that it was his place to do so, he did not report these complaints to Terry, his own supervisor, or to any other city official. In April 1990, however, two months before Faragher's resignation, Nancy Ewanchew, a former lifeguard, wrote to Richard Bender, the city's personnel director, complaining that Terry and Silverman had harassed her and other female lifeguards. The City found that Terry and Silverman had behaved improperly, reprimanded them, and required them to choose between a suspension without pay or the forfeiture of annual leave. On the basis of these findings, the district court concluded that the conduct of Terry and Silverman was discriminatory harassment sufficiently serious to alter the conditions of Faragher's employment and constitute an abusive working environment. The district court then ruled that there were three justifications for holding the City liable. First, the harassment was pervasive enough to support an inference that the City had "knowledge, or constructive knowledge" of it. Next, the City was liable under traditional agency principles because Terry and Silverman were acting as its agents. Finally, Gordon's knowledge of the harassment, combined with his inaction, "provides a further basis for imputing liability on [sic] the City." The Court of Appeals had "no trouble concluding that Terry's and Silverman's conduct * * * was severe and pervasive enough to create an objectively abusive work environment," but it overturned the district court's conclusion that the City was liable.

DECISION The judgment of the Court of Appeals is reversed, and the case is remanded for reinstatement of the judgment of the district court.

OPINION Souter, J. Thus, in *Meritor* we held that sexual harassment so "severe or pervasive" as to "'alter the conditions of [the victim's] employment and create an abusive working environment'" violates Title VII. [Citation.]

In thus holding that environmental claims are covered by the statute, we drew upon earlier cases recognizing liability for discriminatory harassment based on race and national origin, [citations], just as we have also followed the lead of such cases in attempting to define the severity of the offensive conditions necessary to constitute actionable sex discrimination under the statute. [Citations.]

So, in *Harris*, we explained that in order to be actionable under the statute, a sexually objectionable environment must be both objectively and subjectively offensive, one that a reasonable person would find hostile or abusive, and one that the victim in fact did perceive to be so. [Citation.] We directed courts to determine whether an environment is sufficiently hostile or abusive by "looking at all the circumstances," including the "frequency of the discriminatory conduct; its severity; whether it is physically threatening or humiliating, or a mere offensive utterance; and whether it unreasonably interferes with an employee's work performance." [Citation.] Most recently, we explained that Title VII does not prohibit "genuine but innocuous differences in the ways men and women routinely interact with members of the same sex and of the opposite sex." *Oncale*, [citation]. A recurring point in these opinions is that "simple teasing," [citation], offhand comments, and isolated incidents (unless extremely serious) will not amount to discriminatory changes in the "terms and conditions of employment."

These standards for judging hostility are sufficiently demanding to ensure that Title VII does not become a "general civility code." [Citation.] Properly applied, they will filter out complaints attacking "the ordinary tribulations of the workplace, such as the sporadic use of abusive language, gender-related jokes, and occasional teasing." [Citations.]

While indicating the substantive contours of the hostile environments forbidden by Title VII, our cases have established few definite rules for determining when an employer will be liable for a discriminatory environment that is otherwise actionably abusive. * * * There have, for example, been myriad cases in which District Courts and Courts of Appeals have held employers liable on account of actual knowledge by the employer, or high-echelon officials of an employer organization, of sufficiently harassing action by subordinates, which the employer or its informed officers have done nothing to stop. * * *

Nor was it exceptional that standards for binding the employer were not in issue in *Harris*, supra. In that case of discrimination by hostile environment, the individual charged with creating the abusive atmosphere was the president of the corporate employer, [citation], who was indisputably within that class of an employer organization's officials who may be treated as the organization's proxy. [Citations.]

Finally, there is nothing remarkable in the fact that claims against employers for discriminatory employment actions with tangible results, like hiring, firing, promotion, compensation, and work assignment, have resulted in employer liability once the discrimination was shown. [Citations.]

* * *

The soundness of the results in these cases (and their continuing vitality), in light of basic agency principles, was confirmed by this Court's only discussion to date of standards of employer liability, in *Meritor*, which involved a claim of discrimination by a supervisor's sexual harassment of a subordinate over an extended period. In affirming the Court of Appeals's holding that a hostile atmosphere resulting from sex discrimination is actionable under Title VII, we also anticipated proceedings on remand by holding agency principles relevant in assigning employer liability and by rejecting three *per se* rules of liability or immunity. * * *

We then proceeded to reject two limitations on employer liability, while establishing the rule that some limitation was intended. We held that neither the existence of a company grievance procedure nor the absence of actual notice of the harassment on the part of upper management would be dispositive of such a claim; while either might be relevant to the liability, neither would result automatically in employer immunity.

* * *

* * * [I]n implementing Title VII it makes sense to hold an employer vicariously liable for some tortious conduct of a supervisor made possible by abuse of his supervisory authority, and that the aided-by-agency-relation principle embodied in § 219(2)(d) of the Restatement provides an appropriate starting point for determining liability for the kind of harassment presented here.

* * *

There is certainly some authority for requiring active or affirmative, as distinct from passive or implicit, misuse of supervisory authority before liability may be imputed.

* * *

In order to accommodate the principle of vicarious liability for harm caused by misuse of supervisory authority, as well as Title VII's equally basic policies of encouraging forethought by employers and saving action by objecting employees, we adopt the following holding in this case and in *Burlington Industries, Inc. v. Ellerth,* [citation], also decided today. An employer is subject to vicarious liability to a victimized employee for an actionable hostile environment created by a supervisor with immediate (or successively higher) authority over the employee. When no tangible employment action is taken, a defending employer may raise an affirmative defense to liability or damages, subject to proof by a preponderance of the evidence, see [citation]. The defense comprises two necessary elements: (a) that the employer exercised reasonable care to prevent and correct promptly any sexually harassing behavior, and (b) that the plaintiff employee unreasonably failed to take advantage of any preventive or corrective opportunities provided by the employer or to avoid harm otherwise. While proof that an employer had promulgated an antiharassment policy with complaint procedure is not necessary in every instance as a matter of law, the need for a stated policy suitable to the employment circumstances may appropriately be addressed in any case when litigating the first element of the defense. And while proof that an employee failed to fulfill the corresponding obligation of reasonable care to avoid harm is not limited to showing an unreasonable failure to use any complaint procedure provided by the employer, a demonstration of such failure will normally suffice to satisfy the employer's burden under the second element of the defense. No affirmative defense is available, however, when the supervisor's harassment culminates in a tangible employment action, such as discharge, demotion, or undesirable reassignment. [Citation.]

Applying these rules here, we believe that the judgment of the Court of Appeals must be reversed. The District Court found that the degree of hostility in the work environment rose to the actionable level and was attributable to Silverman and Terry. It is undisputed that these supervisors "were granted virtually unchecked authority" over their subordinates, "directly controll[ing] and supervis[ing] all aspects of [Faragher's] day-to-day activities." [Citation.] It is also clear that Faragher and her colleagues were "completely isolated from the City's higher management." [Citation.] The City did not seek review of these findings.

While the City would have an opportunity to raise an affirmative defense if there were any serious prospect of its presenting one, it appears from the record that any such avenue is closed. The District Court found that the City had entirely failed to disseminate its policy against sexual harassment among the beach employees and that its officials made no attempt to keep track of the conduct of supervisors like Terry and Silverman. The record also makes clear that the City's policy did not include any assurance that the harassing supervisors could be bypassed in registering complaints. Under such circumstances, we hold as a matter of law that the City could not be found to have exercised reasonable care to prevent the supervisors' harassing conduct. Unlike the employer of a small workforce, who might expect that sufficient care to prevent tortious behavior could be exercised informally, those responsible for city operations could not reasonably have thought that precautions against hostile environments in any one of many departments in farflung locations could be effective without communicating some formal policy against harassment, with a sensible complaint procedure.

* * *

INTERPRETATION Employers may become liable for the sexual harassment committed by their agents despite lack of knowledge.

ETHICAL QUESTION Should Faragher be allowed to prevail against the city when she had made no formal complaint? Explain.

CRITICAL THINKING QUESTION Do you agree with the court's decision? Explain.

Comparable Worth Industrial statistics on salaries indicate that women earn approximately two thirds as much as men do. Because the Equal Pay Act only requires equal pay for equal work, it does not apply to different jobs even if they are comparable. Thus, that statute provides no remedy for women who have been systematically undervalued and underpaid in "traditional" occupations, such as secretary, teacher, or nurse. As a result, women have sought redress under Title VII by arguing that the failure to pay comparable worth is discrimination on the basis of gender. The concept of **comparable worth** provides that employers should measure the relative values of different jobs through a job evaluation rating system that is free of any potential gender bias. Theoretically, the consistent application of objective criteria (including factors such as skill, effort, working conditions, responsibility, and mental demands) across job categories will ensure fair payment for all employees. For example, if evaluation under such a system found the jobs of truck driver and nurse to be at the same level, workers in both jobs would receive the same pay.

In a 1981 case, the Supreme Court held that a claim of discriminatory undercompensation based on sex could be brought under Title VII, even when female plaintiffs were performing jobs different than those of their male counterparts. As the Court noted, however, the case involved a situation in which the defendant intentionally discriminated in wages; and the defendant, not the courts, had compared the jobs in terms of value. The Court also held that the four defenses available under the Equal Pay Act would apply to a Title VII claim. Since this decision, the concept of comparable worth has met with limited success in the courts. Nonetheless, more than a dozen states have adopted legislation requiring public and private employers to pay equally for comparable work.

EXECUTIVE ORDER

In 1965, President Johnson issued an **executive order** that prohibits discrimination by federal contractors on the basis of race, color, gender, religion, or national origin in employment on *any work* the contractor performs during the period of the federal contract. Federal contractors are also required to take affirmative action in recruiting. The Secretary of Labor, *Office of Federal Contract Compliance Programs (OFCCP)*, administers enforcement of the program.

The program applies to all contractors and all of their subcontractors in excess of $10,000 who enter into a federal contract to be performed in the United States. Compliance with the affirmative action requirement differs for construction and nonconstruction contractors. All *nonconstruction* contractors with fifty or more employees or with contracts for more than $50,000 must have a written affirmative action plan in order to be in compliance. The plan must include a workforce analysis; planned corrective action, if necessary, with specific goals and timetables; and procedures for auditing and reporting. The director of the OFCCP periodically issues goals and timetables for each segment of the construction industry in each region of the country. As a condition precedent to bidding on a federal contract, a contractor must agree to make a good faith effort to achieve current published goals.

AGE DISCRIMINATION IN EMPLOYMENT ACT OF 1967

The **Age Discrimination in Employment Act (ADEA)** prohibits discrimination on the basis of age in employment areas that include hiring, firing, and compensating. The act applies to private employers having twenty or more employees and to all governmental units, regardless of size. The act also prohibits mandatory retirement for most employees, no matter what their age, unless the retirement is justified by a suitable defense.

The major statutory defenses include (1) a *bona fide* occupational qualification, (2) a *bona fide* seniority system, and (3) any other reasonable action. Remedies include back pay, injunctive relief, affirmative action, and liquidated damages equal to the amount of the award for "willful" violations.

http:// Age Discrimination in Employment Act of 1967: http://www4.law.cornell.edu/uscode/29/621.html

DISABILITY LAW

The ***Rehabilitation Act of 1973*** attempts to assist the handicapped in obtaining rehabilitation training, access to public facilities, and employment. The act requires federal contractors and federal agencies to take affirmative action to hire qualified handicapped persons. It also prohibits discrimination on the basis of handicap in federal programs and programs receiving federal financial assistance.

A *handicapped person* is defined as an individual who (1) has a physical or mental impairment that substantially affects one or more of her major life activities, (2) has a history of major life activity impairment, *or* (3) is regarded as having such an impairment. Major life activities include functions such as caring for oneself, seeing, speaking, or walking. Alcohol and drug abuses are not considered handicapping conditions for the purposes of this statute.

The ***Americans with Disabilities Act (ADA) of 1990*** forbids an employer from discriminating against any person with a disability with regard to "hiring or discharge * * *, employee compensation, advancement, job training and other terms, conditions and privileges of employment." In addition, businesses must make special accommodations, such as installing wheelchair-accessible bathrooms, for workers and customers with disabilities unless the cost is unduly burdensome. An employer may use qualification standards, tests, or selection criteria that screen out workers with disabilities if these measures are job related and consistent with business necessity and if no reasonable accommodation is possible. Remedies for violation of the ADA are those generally allowed under Title VII and include injunctive relief, reinstatement, back pay, and, for intentional discrimination, compensatory and punitive damages (capped according to company size by the Civil Rights Act of 1991).

Practical Advice

Make reasonable accommodation for individuals with disabilities.

In addition, the ***Vietnam Veterans Readjustment Act*** of 1974 requires firms having $10,000 or more in federal contracts to engage in affirmative action for disabled veterans and Vietnam-era veterans.

http://

Rehabilitation Act of 1967: http://www4.law.cornell.edu/uscode/29/701.html

Americans with Disabilities Act: http://www.usdoj.gov/crt/ada/statute.html

Toyota Motor Manufacturing, Kentucky, Inc. v. Williams

Supreme Court of the United States, 2002
534 U.S. 184, 122 S.Ct. 681, 151 L.Ed.2d 615
http://laws.findlaw.com/us/000/00-1089.html

FACTS Respondent began working at petitioner's automobile manufacturing plant in Georgetown, Kentucky, in August 1990. She was soon placed on an engine fabrication assembly line, where her duties included work with pneumatic tools. Use of these tools eventually caused pain in her hands, wrists, and arms. She sought treatment at petitioner's in-house medical service, where she was diagnosed with bilateral carpal tunnel syndrome and bilateral tendinitis. Respondent consulted a personal physician who placed her on permanent work restrictions that precluded her from lifting more than 20 pounds or from "frequently lifting or carrying of objects weighing up to 10 pounds," engaging in "constant repetitive * * * flexion or extension of [her] wrists or elbows," performing "overhead work," or using "vibratory or pneumatic tools."

In light of these restrictions, for the next two years petitioner assigned respondent to various modified duty jobs. Nonetheless, respondent missed some work for medical leave, and eventually filed a claim under the Kentucky Workers' Compensation Act. The parties settled this claim, and respondent returned to work. She was unsatisfied by petitioner's efforts to accommodate her work restrictions, however, and responded by bringing an action in the United States District Court alleging that petitioner had violated the ADA by refusing to accommodate her disability. That suit was also settled, and as part of the settlement, respondent returned to work in December 1993.

Upon her return, petitioner placed respondent on a team in Quality Control Inspection Operations (QCIO). In this position, she visually inspected painted cars moving slowly down a conveyor. When respondent began working in QCIO, inspection team members were required to open and shut the doors, trunk, and hood of each passing car. Sometime during respondent's tenure, however, the position was modified to include only visual inspection with few or no manual tasks. This position also required team members to use their hands to wipe each painted car with a glove as it moved along a conveyor. The parties agree that respondent was physically capable of performing both of these jobs and that her performance was satisfactory.

During the fall of 1996, petitioner announced that it wanted QCIO employees to be able to rotate through all four of the QCIO processes. (Respondent had previously been on a team that did only two of the processes.) In part of the expanded job responsibilities, respondent was to apply a highlight oil to the hood, fender, doors, rear quarter panel, and trunk of passing cars at a rate of approximately one car per minute. Wiping the cars required respondent to hold her hands and arms up around shoulder height for several hours at a time.

A short while later, respondent began to experience pain in her neck and shoulders, and she again sought care at petitioner's in-house medical service, where she was diagnosed with an inflammation of the muscles and tendons around both of her shoulder blades and a condition that causes pain in the nerves that lead to the upper extremities. Respondent requested that petitioner accommodate her medical conditions by allowing her to return to doing only her original two jobs in QCIO, which respondent claimed she could still perform without difficulty.

The parties disagree about what happened next. According to respondent, petitioner refused her request and forced her to continue working in the shell body audit job, which caused her even greater physical injury. According to petitioner, respondent simply began missing work on a regular basis. Regardless, it is clear that on December 6, 1996, the last day respondent worked at petitioner's plant, she was placed under a no-work-of-any-kind restriction by her treating physicians. On January 27, 1997, respondent received a letter from petitioner that terminated her employment, citing her poor attendance record.

Respondent, claiming to be disabled because of her carpal tunnel syndrome and other related impairments, sued petitioner for failing to provide her with a reasonable accommodation as required by the ADA. The District Court granted summary judgment to petitioner, finding that respondent's impairments did not substantially limit any of her major life activities. The Court of Appeals reversed, finding that the impairments substantially limited respondent in the major life activity of performing manual tasks, and therefore granting partial summary judgment to respondent on the issue of whether she was disabled under the ADA.

DECISION Reversal of the Court of Appeals' judgment granting partial summary judgment to respondent and the case remanded for further proceedings consistent with this opinion.

OPINION O'Connor, J. The ADA requires covered entities, including private employers, to provide "reasonable accommodations to the known physical or mental limitations of an otherwise qualified individual with a disability who is an applicant or employee, unless such covered entity can demonstrate that the accommodation would impose an undue hardship." [Citation.] The Act defines a "qualified individual with a disability" as "an individual with a disability who, with or without reasonable accommodation, can perform the essential functions of the employment position that such individual holds or desires." [Citation.] In turn, a "disability" is:

> (A) a physical or mental impairment that substantially limits one or more of the major life activities of such individual;
> (B) a record of such an impairment; or
> (C) being regarded as having such an impairment."

* * *

To qualify as disabled, a claimant must further show that the limitation on the major life activity is "substantial." [Citation.] * * * According to the EEOC regulations, "substantially limited" means "unable to perform a major life activity that the average person in the general population can perform"; or "significantly restricted as to the condition, manner or duration under which an individual can perform a particular major life activity as compared to the condition, manner, or duration under which the average person in the general population can perform that same major life activity." [Citation.] In determining whether an individual is substantially limited in a major life activity, the regulations instruct that the following factors should be considered: "the nature and severity of the impairment; the duration or expected duration of the impairment; and the permanent or long-term impact, or the expected permanent or long-term impact of or resulting from the impairment." [Citation.]

The question presented by this case is whether the Sixth Circuit properly determined that respondent was disabled under * * * the ADA's disability definition at the time that she sought an accommodation from petitioner. [Citation.] * * *

Our consideration of this issue is guided first and foremost by the words of the disability definition itself. "Substantially" in the phrase "substantially limits" suggests "considerable" or "to a large degree." [Citations.] The word "substantial" thus clearly precludes impairments that interfere in only a minor way with the performance of manual tasks from qualifying as disabilities. [Citation.]

"Major" in the phrase "major life activities" means important. [Citation.] "Major life activities" thus refers to those activities that are of central importance to daily life. In order for performing manual tasks to fit into this category—a category that includes such basic abilities as walking, seeing, and hearing—the manual tasks in question must be central to daily life. If each of the tasks included in the major life activity of performing manual tasks does not independently qualify as a major life activity, then together they must do so.

That these terms need to be interpreted strictly to create a demanding standard for qualifying as disabled is confirmed by the first section of the ADA, which lays out the legislative findings and purposes that motivate the Act. [Citation.] When it enacted the ADA in 1990, Congress found that "some 43,000,000 Americans have one or more physical or mental disabilities." [Citation.] If Congress intended everyone with a physical impairment that precluded the performance of some isolated, unimportant, or particularly difficult manual task to qualify as disabled, the number of disabled Americans would surely have been much higher. [Citation.]

We therefore hold that to be substantially limited in performing manual tasks, an individual must have an impairment that prevents or severely restricts the individual from doing activities that are of central importance to most people's daily lives. The impairment's impact must also be permanent or long-term. [Citation.]

It is insufficient for individuals attempting to prove disability status under this test to merely submit evidence of a medical diagnosis of an impairment. Instead, the ADA requires those "claiming the Act's protection * * * to prove a disability by offering evidence that the extent of the limitation [caused by their impairment] in terms of their own experience * * * is substantial. [Citation.]" That the Act defines "disability" "with respect to an individual," [citation], makes clear that Congress intended the existence of a disability to be determined in such a case-by-case manner. [Citations.]

An individualized assessment of the effect of an impairment is particularly necessary when the impairment is one whose symptoms vary widely from person to person. Carpal tunnel syndrome, one of respondent's impairments, is just such a condition. While cases of severe carpal tunnel syndrome are characterized by muscle atrophy and extreme sensory deficits, mild cases generally do not have either of these effects and create only intermittent symptoms of numbness and tingling. [Citation.] Studies have further shown that, even without surgical treatment, one quarter of carpal tunnel cases resolve in one month, but that in 22 percent of cases, symptoms last for eight years or longer. [Citation.] * * * Given these large potential differences in the severity and duration of the effects of carpal tunnel syndrome, an individual's carpal tunnel syndrome diagnosis, on its own, does not indicate whether the individual has a disability within the meaning of the ADA.

* * *

While the Court of Appeals in this case addressed the different major life activity of performing manual tasks, its analysis circumvented [citation] by focusing on respondent's inability to perform manual tasks associated only with her job. This was error. When addressing the major life activity of performing manual tasks, the central inquiry must be whether the claimant is unable to perform the variety of tasks central to most people's daily lives, not whether the claimant is unable to perform the tasks associated with her specific job. Otherwise, * * * restriction[s] on claims of disability based on a substantial limitation in working will be rendered meaningless because an inability to perform a specific job always can be recast as an inability to perform a "class" of tasks associated with that specific job.

* * *

Even more critically, the manual tasks unique to any particular job are not necessarily important parts of most people's lives. As a result, occupation-specific tasks may have only limited relevance to the manual task inquiry. In this case, "repetitive work with hands and arms extended at or above shoulder levels for extended periods of time," the manual task on which the Court of Appeals relied, is not an important part of most people's daily lives. The court, therefore, should not have considered respondent's inability to do such manual work in her specialized assembly line job as sufficient proof that she was substantially limited in performing manual tasks.

At the same time, the Court of Appeals appears to have disregarded the very type of evidence that it should have focused upon. It treated as irrelevant "the fact that [respondent] can * * * tend to her personal hygiene [and] carry out personal or household chores." Yet household chores, bathing, and brushing one's teeth are among the types of manual tasks of central importance to people's daily lives, and should have been part of the assessment of whether respondent was substantially limited in performing manual tasks.

The District Court noted that at the time respondent sought an accommodation from petitioner, she admitted that she was able to do the manual tasks required by her original two jobs in QCIO. In addition, according to respondent's deposition testimony, even after her condition worsened, she could still brush her teeth, wash her face, bathe, tend her flower garden, fix breakfast, do laundry, and pick up around the house. The record also indicates that her medical conditions caused her to avoid sweeping, to quit dancing, to occasionally seek help dressing, and to reduce how often she plays with her children, gardens, and drives long distances. But these changes in her life did not amount to such severe restrictions in the activities that are of central importance to most people's daily lives that they establish a manual-task disability as a matter of law. On this record, it was therefore inappropriate for the Court of Appeals to grant partial summary judgment to respondent on the issue whether she was substantially limited in performing manual tasks, and its decision to do so must be reversed.

* * *

INTERPRETATION To be substantially limited in performing manual tasks, an individual must have an impairment that prevents or severely restricts the individual from doing activities that are of central importance to most people's daily lives. The impairment's impact must also be permanent or long term.

ETHICAL QUESTION Was the company ethical in its refusal to accommodate respondent? Explain.

CRITICAL THINKING QUESTION Should the specific tasks of the job be considered in determining disability?

CPA EMPLOYEE PROTECTION

Employees are accorded a number of job-related protections. These include a limited right not to be unfairly dismissed, a right to a safe and healthy workplace, compensation for injuries sustained in the workplace, and some financial security upon retirement or loss of employment. This section discusses (1) employee termination at will, (2) occupational safety and health, (3) employee privacy, (4) workers' compensation, (5) Social Security and unemployment insurance, (6) the Fair Labor Standards Act, (7) employee notice of termination or layoff, and (8) family and health leave.

EMPLOYEE TERMINATION AT WILL

Under the common law, a contract of employment for other than a definite term is terminable at will by either party. Accordingly, under the common law, employers may "dismiss their employees at will for good cause, for no cause or even for cause morally wrong, without being thereby guilty of legal wrong." In recent years, however, a growing number of judicial exceptions to the rule, based on implied contract, tort, and public policy, have developed. A number of federal and state statutes enacted in the last fifty years also limit the rule, which may in addition be restricted by contractual agreement between employer and employee. In particular, most collective bargaining agreements negotiated through union representatives contain a provision prohibiting dismissal "without cause."

Statutory Limitations Federal legislation has been passed that limits the employer's right to discharge. These statutes fall into three categories: (1) those protecting certain employees from discriminatory discharge, (2) those protecting certain employees in their exercise of statutory rights, and (3) those protecting certain employees from discharge without cause.

At the state level, statutes protect workers from discriminatory discharge for filing workers' compensation claims. Also, many state statutes parallel federal legislation. Some states have adopted statutes similar to the NLRA, and many states prohibit discrimination in employment on the basis of factors such as race, creed, nationality, gender, or age. In addition, some states have statutes prohibiting discharge or other punitive actions taken for the purpose of influencing voting or, in some states, political activity.

Judicial Limitations **Judicial limitations** on the employment-at-will doctrine have been based on contract law, tort law, and public policy. Cases founded in contract theory have relied on arguments maintaining, among other things, (1) that the dismissal was improper because the employee had detrimentally relied on the employer's promise of work for a reasonable time; (2) that the employment was not at will because of implied-in-fact promises of employment for a specific duration, which meant that the employer could not terminate the employee without just cause; (3) that the employment contract implied or expressly provided that the employee would not be dismissed so long as he satisfactorily performed his work; (4) that the employer had assured the employee that he would not be dismissed except for cause; or (5) that, upon entering into the employment contract, the employee gave consideration over and above the performance of services to support a promise of job security.

Courts have also created exceptions to the employment-at-will doctrine by imposing tort obligations on employers, most particularly with respect to the torts of intentional infliction of emotional distress and of interference with employment relations.

The most frequent basis for finding a discharge to be wrongful is that the discharge violates statutory or other established public policy. In general, these cases involve dismissal for (1) refusing to violate a statute, (2) exercising a statutory right, (3) performing a statutory obligation, or (4) reporting an alleged violation of a statute that is of public interest.

Hunger v. Grand Central Sanitation

Superior Court of Pennsylvania, 1996

670 A.2d 173

FACTS Mark Hunger was the safety director at Grand Central Sanitation (Grand Central). On September 7, 1991, Hunger "became aware" that hazardous materials consisting of blasting caps were being deposited into garbage containers at Shu-Deb, Inc. (Shu-Deb). Grand Central collected garbage from these containers and dumped it at a dump site. Hunger knew that Grand Central was not licensed to dispose of hazardous materials and believed that it would violate state and/or federal law if the company transported or disposed of hazardous materials. Hunger also became concerned about the safety of company employees from the danger of transporting blasting caps. On September 9, 1991, Hunger informed Grand Central's owner and vice president, Gary Perin, of the information he received about the blasting caps. On September 12, 1991, Hunger, accompanied by Pennsylvania state police and agents of the Federal Bureau of Alcohol, Tobacco, and Firearms, went to search the contents of Shu-Deb's containers. However, the garbage had already been collected, so Hunger and the police located the garbage truck that had collected the garbage and searched it. No hazardous materials were found in the truck. On October 4, 1991, Hunger was terminated because of the incident. Hunger sued for wrongful discharge. The trial court granted summary judgment to Grand Central and Hunger appealed.

DECISION Judgment affirmed.

OPINION Hester, J. Appellant first alleges that his wrongful discharge claim was dismissed improperly due to the public policy exception to the doctrine of at-will employment. We examine the applicable law:

In Pennsylvania, as a general rule, no common law cause of action exists against an employer for termination of an at-will employment relationship. [Citation.] Moreover, "exceptions to this rule have been recognized in only the most limited of circumstances, where discharges of at-will employees would threaten the clear mandates of public policy." [Citation.]

The public policy exception to the at-will doctrine was recognized by our Supreme Court in *Geary v. United States Steel Corp.*, [citation], a case remarkably similar to the one at bar. There, the plaintiff was a salesman for the defendant and criticized to company officials above his immediate supervisors the quality of the steel being produced. He was discharged even though the product later was determined to be substandard and withdrawn from the market. Geary alleged that his termination fell within a public policy exception to the at-will doctrine since he was acting in the interest of the safety of the general public.

While the Supreme Court recognized that a public policy exception may exist under appropriate conditions, it rejected plaintiff's argument that his allegations fell within its ambit on two grounds. First, the plaintiff was not obligated statutorily to report defective products. Second, on its face, the complaint offered the existence of a plausible reason for discharge in that the plaintiff had bypassed his immediate supervisors to make the complaint.

To state a public policy exception to the at-will-employment doctrine, the employee must point to a clear public policy articulated in the constitution, in legislation, an administrative regulation, or a judicial decision. [Citation.] Furthermore, the stated mandate of public policy, as articulated in the constitution, statute, or judicial decision, must be applicable directly to the employee and the employee's actions. It is not sufficient that the employer's actions toward the employee are unfair. [Citations.]

We have recognized a public policy exception only in extremely limited circumstances. If an employee is fired for performing a function that he is required to perform by law, an action for wrongful discharge on public policy grounds will be allowed. See e.g., [citation] (employee fired for reporting a nuclear safety violation that he was required to report under federal law); [citation] (employer fired an employee for serving on a jury; public policy was violated since people are required by law to serve on jury and since service on jury has constitutional implications).

A public policy exception to the at-will doctrine also will be found when the firing itself is a criminal activity * * *.

Herein, appellant notes that it is illegal to transport hazardous materials without a license. We agree. However, appellant admitted in his complaint that no blasting caps were discovered. Thus, appellees did not violate the law. If appellant had observed a deliberate violation of the law, reported it to proper authorities, and was fired, then the reasoning of [citation] may have been applicable. There is no indication that this occurred herein.

In this case, appellant's actions were premature. He provides no specifics about how he "became aware" that blasting caps were being dumped. He fails to indicate the capacity of the person who informed him of this, the nature of his investigation into substantiating the reliability of the information, and why it was necessary to inform state and federal law enforcement officials about the situation immediately.

Our disposition of this case may have been different if appellant discovered that his employer was deliberately transporting hazardous materials after being told of the situation. That is not what occurred, regardless of appellant's concern with the public safety. The source of appellant's "awareness" of the alleged illegal activities is completely unsubstantiated. Furthermore, his employer's criminal intent is not established. At most, one of the employer's customers allegedly was dumping illegal explosives.

* * *

INTERPRETATION Wrongful discharge exists only when an employer's termination of an employee violates public policy as evidenced in the Constitution, in legislation, in administrative regulation, or in judicial decision.

CRITICAL THINKING QUESTION Do you agree with the principle of termination at will? Explain.

CONCEPT REVIEW

Federal Employment Discrimination Laws

	Protected Characteristics	Prohibited Conduct	Defenses	Remedies
Equal Pay Act	Sex	Wages	Seniority Merit Quality or quantity measures Any factor other than sex	Back pay Injunction Liquidated damages Attorneys' fees
Title VII of Civil Rights Act	Race Color Sex Religion National origin	Terms, conditions or privileges of employment	Seniority Ability test BFOQ (except for race) Business necessity (disparate impact only)	Back pay Injunction Reinstatement Compensatory and punitive damages for intentional discrimination • unlimited for race • limited for all others Attorneys' fees
Age Discrimination in Employment Act	Age	Terms, conditions, or privileges of employment	Seniority BFOQ Any other reasonable act	Back pay Injunction Reinstatement Liquidated damages for willful violation Attorneys' fees
Americans with Disabilities Act	Disability	Terms, conditions, or privileges of employment	Undue hardship Job-related criteria and business necessity Risk to public health and safety	Back pay Injunction Reinstatement Compensatory and punitive damages for intentional discrimination (limited) Attorneys' fees

OCCUPATIONAL SAFETY AND HEALTH ACT

In 1970, Congress enacted the **Occupational Safety and Health Act** to ensure, as far as possible, a safe and healthful working environment for every worker. The act established the ***Occupational Safety and Health Administration (OSHA)*** to develop standards, conduct inspections, monitor compliance, and institute enforcement actions against those who are not in compliance.

Upon each employer who is engaged in a business affecting interstate commerce, the act imposes a general duty to provide a work environment that is "free from recognized hazards that are causing or likely to cause death or serious physical harm to his employees." In addition to this general duty, the employer must comply with specific OSHA-promulgated safety rules. The act also requires employees to comply with all OSHA rules and regulations. Finally, the act prohibits any employer from discharging or discriminating against an employee who exercises her rights under the act.

Enforcing the act generally involves OSHA inspections and citations of employers, as appropriate, for (1) breach of the general duty obligation, (2) breach of specific safety and health standards, or (3) failure to keep records, make reports, or post notices required by the act.

When a violation is discovered, the offending employer receives a written citation, a proposed penalty, and a date by which the employer must remedy the breach. Citations may be contested; in such cases, the Occupational Safety and Health Review Commission assigns administrative law judges to hold hearings. The commission, at its discretion, may grant review of an administrative law judge's decision; review is not a matter of right. If no such review occurs, the judge's decision becomes the commission's final order thirty days after receipt, and the aggrieved party may then appeal the order to the appropriate U.S. Circuit Court of Appeals.

Penalties for violations are both civil and criminal. In cases involving civil penalties, serious violations require that a penalty be proposed; in contrast, for nonserious violations, penalties are discretionary and rarely proposed. The act further empowers the secretary of labor to obtain temporary restraining orders in situations where regular OSHA procedures are insufficient to halt imminently hazardous or deadly business operations.

One stated purpose of the act is to encourage state participation in regulating safety and health. The act therefore permits a state to regulate the safety and health of the work environment within its borders, provided that OSHA approves the plan. The act sets minimum acceptable standards for the states to impose, but does not require that a state plan be identical to the OSHA guidelines. More than half of the states regulate health and safety in the workplace through state-promulgated plans.

http://

Occupational Safety and Health Act: http://www4.law.cornell.edu/uscode/29/651.html

Occupational Safety and Health Administration: http://www.osha.gov/

Practical Advice

Ensure your workers a safe and healthy work environment.

EMPLOYEE PRIVACY

Over the last decade, employee privacy has become a major issue. The fundamental right to privacy is a product of common law protection, discussed in Chapter 7. Thus, the tort of invasion of privacy safeguards employees from unwanted searches, electronic monitoring and other forms of surveillance, and disclosure of confidential records. The tort actually consists of four different torts: (1) unreasonable intrusion into the seclusion of another; (2) unreasonable public disclosure of private facts; (3) unreasonable publicity that places another in a false light; and (4) appropriation of a person's name or likeness. In addition, the federal government and some states have legislatively supplemented the common law in certain areas.

Drug and Alcohol Testing Although no federal legislation deals comprehensively with **drug and alcohol tests**, legislation in a number of states either prohibits such tests altogether or prescribes certain scientific and procedural standards for conducting them. In the absence of a state statute, *private* sector employees have little or no protection from such tests. The NLRB has held, however, that drug and alcohol testing in a union setting is a mandatory subject of collective bargaining.

In 1989, the U.S. Supreme Court ruled that the employer of a *public* sector employee whose position involved public health or safety or national security could subject the employee to a drug or alcohol test without either first obtaining a search warrant or having reasonable grounds to believe the individual had engaged in any wrongdoing. Based on Supreme Court and lower court decisions, it appears that a government employer may use (1) random or universal testing when the public health or safety or national security is involved and (2) selective drug testing when there is sufficient cause to believe an employee has a drug problem.

Lie Detector Tests The ***Federal Employee Polygraph Protection Act of 1988*** prohibits private employers from requiring employees or prospective employees to undergo a **lie detector test**, inquiring about the results of such a test, or using the results of such a test or the refusal to be tested as grounds for an adverse employment decision. The act exempts government employers and, in certain situations, Energy Department contractors or persons providing consulting services for federal intelligence agencies. In addition, security firms and manufacturers of controlled substances may use a polygraph to test prospective employees. Moreover, an employer, as part of an ongoing investigation of economic loss or injury to its business, may use a polygraph test. Nevertheless, the use of the test must meet the following requirements: (1) it must be designed to investigate a specific incident or activity, not to document a chronic problem; (2) the employee to be tested must have had access to the property that is the subject of the investigation; and (3) the employer must have reason to suspect the particular employee.

Employees and prospective employees tested under any of these exemptions cannot be terminated, disciplined, or denied employment solely as a result of the test. The act further provides that those subjected to a polygraph test (1) cannot be asked intrusive or degrading questions regarding topics such as their religious beliefs, opinions as to racial matters, political views, or sexual preferences or behaviors; (2) must be given the right to review all questions before the test and to terminate the test at any time; and (3) must receive a complete copy of the test results.

Practical Advice

Be careful to respect the privacy of employees.

Ethical Dilemma

What (Unwritten) Right to a Job Does an Employee Have?

FACTS Gary Johnson was a six-year employee of Simon Corporation, a manufacturer of small appliances. Gary worked part of the time on the production line, where he manufactured fruit juicers, and the rest of the time as a quality control inspector.

Two years ago, the line foreman, James Sullivan, Gary's good and long-standing friend, observed that Gary was intoxicated on the job. James warned his friend privately against drinking on the job. Two months later, James again noticed that Gary was intoxicated; again he warned Gary that such conduct could not be tolerated. Because of the recession, James was worried about causing his friend to lose his job and therefore remained silent. Finally, after another month passed and James again noticed that Gary was intoxicated, he reported the problem to his supervisor.

The company's employee handbook explained that alcohol and drugs were prohibited on the job and that all employees identified as drug or alcohol dependent were to attend an alcohol and drug dependence program. After talking to James, the supervisor informed Gary that he must attend the company's program. Gary refused to cooperate and was fired.

Simon Corporation had regularly rehired employees who had been fired for intoxication but who had subsequently overcome their addiction. Although the rehiring practice was not spelled out in the handbook, the corporation had consistently followed the unwritten policy for ten years. However, although Gary eventually overcame his addiction, the corporation refused to rehire him. Gary is now suing the company to rehire him, alleging that his original employment contract implied that he would be rehired if he demonstrated that he had overcome an addiction.

Social, Policy, and Ethical Considerations

1. Should James have waited so long before reporting the problem to his supervisor? Explain.
2. Does the nature of the product and the role of the employee affect the ethical considerations in such a decision? Assume, for example, that the juicer Gary produced would be potentially harmful if defective and consider, as well, his role in quality control.
3. How should a company handle alcohol and drug abuse among its employees?
4. Compare the goal of supporting recovering addicts with the need to ensure that the best employees are selected to perform a job.
5. How, if at all, should the state or federal government be involved in this type of situation?

Workers' Compensation

In order to provide speedier and more certain relief to injured employees, all states have adopted statutes providing for **workers' compensation**. (Several states, however, exempt specified employers from workers' compensation statutes.) These statutes create commissions or boards that determine whether an injured employee is entitled to receive compensation and, if so, how much. The basis of recovery under workers' compensation is strict liability: the employee does not have to prove that the employer was negligent. The common law defenses of contributory negligence, voluntary assumption of risk, and the fellow servant rule (which covers injury caused by the negligence of a fellow employee) are *not* available to employers in workers' compensation proceedings. Such defenses are *abolished*. The *only* requirement is that the employee be injured and that the injury arises out of and in the course of his employment. The amounts recoverable are fixed by statute for each type of injury and are lower than the amounts a court or jury would probably award in an action at common law. The courts, therefore, do not have jurisdiction over such cases, except to review decisions of the board or commission; even then, the courts may determine only whether such decisions are in accordance with the statute. If a third party, however, causes the injury, the employee may bring a tort action against that third party.

Early workers' compensation laws did not provide coverage for occupational disease, and most courts held that occupational injury did not include disease. Today, virtually all states provide general compensation coverage for occupational diseases, although the coverage varies greatly from state to state.

http://

Cornell Legal Information Institute: Workers Compensation: An Overview: http://wwwsecure.law.cornell.edu/topics/workers_compensation.html

U.S. Department of Labor: Employment Standards Administration Office of Workers' Compensation Programs: http://www.dol.gov/esa/owcp_org.htm

THE LAW AND YOU

State Bar Associations

Arizona: http://www.azbar.org/PublicResources/pubinfo.asp ("A Guide to Guardianships and Conservatorships")

Florida: http://www.flabar.org/newflabar/consumerservices/General/Consumer.Pam/ ("Sexual Harassment n the Workplace")

Louisiana: http://www.lsba.org/Public_Resources/consumer_brochures.html ("Rights of the Fired Employee")

Maine: http://www.mainebar.org/ (legal information pamphlets) ("Social Security Disability"; "Workers Compensation")

Maryland: http://www.msba.org/public/brochure.htm ("Employees Rights in the Workplace"; "Filing for Workers' Compensation")

Missouri: http://www.mobar.org/pamphlets/broindex.htm (brochures on legal topics) ("The ADA: Rules for the Workplace"; "Workers' Compensation")

New Hampshire: http://www.nhbar.org/?area/15.html ("Workers' Compensation"; "Employment Discrimination & Wrongful Termination")

Oregon: http://www.osbar.org/public/legalinfo/specinfo.html ("Employment and Public Benefits"; "Disabilities")

Tennessee: http://www.tba.org/LawBytes/LawBytes.html ("Employment")

Texas: http://www.texasbar.com/public/consumerinfo/helpfulinfo/pamphlets.asp ("Social Security")

U.S. Government

http://www.pueblo.gsa.gov/other/o-smbuss.htm ("Reporting & Disclosure Guide for Employee Benefit Plans")

http:// www.pueblo.gsa.gov/ ("Small Business Resource Guide 2003")

http://www.pueblo.gsa.gov/specpubs.htm#EM ("OSHA: Employee Workplace Rights")

http:// www.pueblo.gsa.gov/fedprogs.htm ("Social Security: Your Number and Card")

http://www.pueblo.gsa.gov/fedprogs.htm ("Americans with Disabilities Act: Questions Answered")

http://www.pueblo.gsa.gov/fedprogs.htm ("Guide to Disability Rights Laws")

http://www.pueblo.gsa.gov/specpubs.htm#FB ("Future of Social Security")

http://www.pueblo.gsa.gov/fedprogs.htm ("Social Security: Basic Facts")

http://www.pueblo.gsa.gov/fedprogs.htm ("Social Security: Understanding the Benefits")

http://www.pueblo.gsa.gov/specpubs.htm ("Social Security: What Every Woman Should Know")

SOCIAL SECURITY AND UNEMPLOYMENT INSURANCE

Social Security was enacted in 1935 in an attempt to provide limited retirement and death benefits to certain employees. Since then, the benefits have greatly increased, and the federal Social Security system, which has expanded to cover almost all employees, now contains four major benefit programs: (1) Old-Age and Survivors Insurance (OASI) (providing retirement and survivor benefits), (2) Disability Insurance (DI), (3) Hospitalization Insurance (Medicare), and (4) Supplemental Security Income (SSI).

The system is financed by contributions (taxes) paid by employers, employees, and self-employed individuals. Employees and employers pay matching contributions. It is the employer's responsibility to withhold the employee's contribution and to forward the full amount of the tax to the Internal Revenue Service. Employee-made contributions are not tax deductible by the employee, whereas those made by the employer are. Self-employed persons are also required to report their taxable income and to pay the Social Security tax.

The federal *unemployment insurance* system was initially created by Title IX of the Social Security Act of 1935. Subsequently, Title IX was supplemented by the Federal Unemployment Tax Act and by numerous other federal statutes. This complex system depends upon the cooperation of state and federal programs. Federal law provides the general guidelines, standards, and requirements, while the states administer the program through their own employment laws. The system is funded by employer taxes: federal taxes generally pay the program's administrative costs, and state contributions pay for the actual benefits.

The purpose of the Federal Unemployment Tax Act is to provide *unemployment compensation* to workers who have lost their jobs, usually through no fault of their own, and cannot find other employment. Payments, generally made weekly, are based on a particular state's formula.

http:// Social Security Administration: http://www.ssa.gov/

FAIR LABOR STANDARDS ACT

The **Fair Labor Standards Act (FLSA)** regulates the employment of child labor outside of agriculture. The act prohibits the employment of anyone under fourteen years of age in nonfarm work, except for newspaper deliverers and child actors. Fourteen- and fifteen-year-olds may work for a limited number of hours outside of school hours, under specific conditions, in certain *nonhazardous* occupations. Sixteen- and seventeen-year-olds may work in any *nonhazardous* job, while persons eighteen years old or older may work in *any* job, whether it is hazardous or not. The secretary of labor determines which occupations are considered hazardous.

In addition, the FLSA imposes wage and hour requirements upon covered employers. The act provides for a minimum hourly wage and overtime pay of time-and-a-half for hours worked in excess of forty hours per week. However, the FLSA exempts certain workers from both its minimum wage and overtime provisions; those excluded include professionals, managers, and outside salespersons.

http:// Fair Labor Standards Act: http://www4.law.cornell.edu/uscode/29/201.html

WORKER ADJUSTMENT AND RETRAINING NOTIFICATION ACT

The **Worker Adjustment and Retraining Notification Act (WARN)** requires an employer to provide sixty days' advance notice of a plant closing or mass layoff. A "plant closing" is defined as the permanent or temporary shutting down of a single site or units within a site if the shutdown results in fifty or more employees losing employment during any thirty-day period. A "mass layoff" is defined as a loss of employment during a thirty-day period either for 500 employees or for at least one-third of the employees at a given site, if that one-third equals or exceeds fifty employees. WARN requires that notification be given to specified state and local officials as well as to the affected employees or their union representatives. The act, which reduces the notification period with regard to failing companies and emergency situations, applies to employers with a total of 100 or more employees who in the aggregate work at least 2,000 hours per week, not including overtime.

http:// Worker Adjustment and Retraining Notification Act: http://www4.law.cornell.edu/uscode/29/2101.html

FAMILY AND MEDICAL LEAVE ACT OF 1993

The **Family and Medical Leave Act of 1993** requires employers with fifty or more employees and governments at the federal, state, and local levels to grant employees up to twelve weeks of leave during any twelve-month period for the birth of a child; adopting or gaining foster care of a child; or the care of a spouse, child, or parent who suffers from a serious health condition. The act defines a "serious health condition" as an "illness, injury, impairment or physical or mental condition" that involves inpatient medical care at a hospital, hospice, or residential care facility or continuing medical treatment by a health-care provider. Employees are eligible for such leave if they have been employed by their present employer for at least twelve months and have worked at least 1,250 hours for their employer during the twelve months preceding the leave request. The requested leave may be paid, unpaid, or a combination of both.

http:// Family and Medical Leave Act of 1993: http://www4.law.cornell.edu/uscode/29/2601.html

CHAPTER SUMMARY

Labor Law

Purpose to provide the general framework in which management and labor negotiate terms of employment

Norris–La Guardia Act established as U.S. policy the full freedom of labor to form labor unions without employer interference and withdrew from the federal courts the power to issue injunctions in nonviolent labor disputes (any controversy concerning terms or conditions of employment or union representation)

National Labor Relations Act
- *Right to Unionize* declares it a federally protected right of employees to unionize and to bargain collectively
- *Prohibits Unfair Employer Practices* the act identifies five unfair labor practices by an employer
- *National Labor Relations Board (NLRB)* created to administer these rights

Labor-Management Relations Act
- *Prohibits Unfair Union Practices* the act identifies seven unfair labor practices by a union
- *Prohibits Closed Shops* agreement that mandates that an employer can hire only union members
- *Allows Union Shops* an employer can hire nonunion members, but the employee must join the union

Labor-Management Reporting and Disclosure Act aimed at eliminating corruption in labor unions

Employment Discrimination Law

Equal Pay Act prohibits an employer from discriminating between employees on the basis of gender by paying unequal wages for the same work

Civil Rights Act of 1964 prohibits employment discrimination on the basis of race, color, gender, religion, or national origin
- *Equal Employment Opportunity Commission (EEOC)* enforcement agency for the act
- *Affirmative Action* the active recruitment of a designated group of applicants
- *Discrimination* prohibited by the act; includes (1) using proscribed criteria to produce disparate treatment, (2) engaging in nondiscriminatory conduct that perpetuates past discrimination, and (3) adopting neutral rules that have a disparate impact
- *Reverse Discrimination* affirmative action that directs an employer to consider an individual's race or gender when hiring or promoting for the purpose of remedying underrepresentation of that race or gender in traditionally segregated jobs
- *Sexual Harassment* is an illegal form of sexual discrimination that includes unwelcome sexual advances, requests for sexual favors, and other verbal or physical conduct of a sexual nature
- *Comparable Worth* equal pay for jobs that are of equal value to the employer

Executive Order prohibits discrimination by federal contractors on the basis of race, color, gender, religion, or national origin on any work the contractors perform during the period of the federal contract

Age Discrimination in Employment Act prohibits discrimination on the basis of age in hiring, firing, or compensating

Disability Law several federal acts, including the Americans with Disabilities Act, provide assistance to people with disabilities in obtaining rehabilitation training, access to public facilities, and employment

Employee Protection

Employee Termination at Will under the common law, a contract of employment for other than a definite term is terminable at will by either party
- *Statutory Limitations* have been enacted by the federal government and some states
- *Judicial Limitations* based on contract law, tort law, or public policy
- *Limitations Imposed by Union Contract*

Occupational Safety and Health Act enacted to ensure workers a safe and healthful work environment

Employee Privacy
- ***Drug and Alcohol Testing*** some states either prohibit such tests or prescribe certain scientific and procedural safeguards
- ***Lie Detector Tests*** federal statute prohibits private employers from requiring employees or prospective employees to take such tests

Workers' Compensation compensation awarded to an employee who is injured in the course of his or her employment

Social Security measures by which the government provides economic assistance to disabled or retired employees and their dependents

Unemployment Compensation compensation awarded to workers who have lost their jobs and cannot find other employment

Fair Labor Standards Act regulates the employment of child labor outside of agriculture

Worker Adjustment and Retraining Notification Act federal statute that requires an employer to provide sixty days' advance notice of a plant closing or mass layoff

Family and Medical Leave Act of 1993 requires some employers to grant employees leave for serious health conditions or certain other events

QUESTIONS

1. Gooddecade manufactures and sells automobile parts throughout the eastern part of the United States. Among its full-time employees are 220 fourteen- and fifteen-year-olds. These teenagers are employed throughout the company and are paid at an hourly wage rate of $3 per hour. Discuss the legality of this arrangement.

2. Janet, a twenty-year-old woman, applied for a position driving a truck for Federal Trucking, Inc. Janet, who is 5'4" tall and weighs 135 lbs. was denied the job because the company requires that all employees be at least 5'6" tall and weigh at least 150 lbs. Federal justifies this requirement on the basis that its drivers are frequently forced to move heavy loads in making pickups and deliveries. Janet brings a cause of action. Has Federal Trucking violated the Civil Rights Act? Explain.

3. N.I.S. promoted John, a forty-two-year-old employee, to a supervisor's position while passing over James, a fifty-eight-year-old employee. N.I.S. told James he was too old for the job and that it preferred a younger man. Discuss whether James will succeed if he brings a cause of action.

4. Anthony was employed as a forklift operator for Blackburn Construction Company. While on the job, he operated the forklift in a manner that was careless and in direct violation of Blackburn's procedural manual and, as a result, caused himself severe injury. Blackburn denies liability based on Anthony's (a) gross negligence, (b) disobedience of the procedural manual, and (c) written waiver of liability. Can Anthony recover for his injury? Explain.

5. Hazelwood School District is located in Sleepy Hollow Township. It is being sued by several teachers who applied for teaching positions with the school but were rejected. The plaintiffs, who are all African-Americans, produce the following evidence:
   a. 1.8 percent of the Hazelwood School District's teachers are African-Americans, whereas 15.4 percent of the teachers in Sleepy Hollow Township are African-Americans; and
   b. the hiring decisions by Hazelwood School District are based solely on subjective criteria.

   What decision should be made?

6. T. W. E., a large manufacturer, prohibited its employees from distributing union leaflets to other employees while on the company's property. Richard, an employee of T. W. E., disregarded the prohibition and passed out the leaflets before his work shift began. T. W. E. discharged Richard for his actions. Has T. W. E. committed an unfair labor practice?

7. Erwick was dismissed from her job at the C & T Steel Company because she was "an unsatisfactory employee." At the time, Erwick was active in an effort to organize a union at C & T. Is the dismissal valid?

8. Johnson, president of the First National Bank of A, believes that it is appropriate to employ only female tellers. Hence, First National refuses to employ Ken Baker as a teller but does offer him a maintenance position at the same salary.

Baker brings a cause of action against First National Bank. Is First National illegally discriminating based on gender? Why?

9. Section 103 of the Federal Public Works Employment Act of 1977 establishes the Minority Business Enterprise (MBE) program and requires that, absent a waiver by the Secretary of Commerce, 10 percent of all federal grants given by the Economic Development Administration be used to purchase services or supplies from businesses owned and controlled by U.S. citizens belonging to one of six minority groups: African-American, Spanish speaking, Oriental, Native American, Eskimo, and Aleut. White owners of businesses contend the act constitutes illegal reverse discrimination. Discuss.

CASE PROBLEMS

10. Worth H. Percivil, a mechanical engineer, was employed by General Motors (http://www.gm.com/flash_homepage/) for twenty-six years until he was discharged. At the time his employment was terminated, Percivil was head of GM's Mechanical Development Department. Percivil sued GM for wrongful discharge. He contends that he was discharged as a result of a conspiracy among his fellow executives to force him out of his employment because of his age, because he had legitimately complained about certain deceptive practices of GM, because he had refused to give the government false information although urged to do so by his superiors, and because he had, on the contrary, undertaken to correct certain alleged misrepresentations made to the government. General Motors claims that Percivil's employment was terminable at the will of GM for any reason and with or without cause, provided that the discharge was not prohibited by statute. Has Percivil been wrongly discharged? Why?

11. On May 26, the trial examiner issued his intermediate report finding that the respondent (Sailors' Union) had not engaged in unfair union practices under Section 8(b) in its dispute with Samsoc. With respect to the unfair labor practices, the complaint alleged that the respondent induced and encouraged employees of Moore Dry Dock Company to engage in a strike or concerted refusal in the course of their employment to perform services for Moore in connection with the conversion into a bulk gypsum carrier of the *S. S. Phopho*, a vessel owned by Samsoc, the object being to force Moore to cease doing business with Samsoc and thus force Samsoc to resolve its dispute with the respondent. Has an unfair labor practice been committed? Explain.

12. The United Steelworkers of America (http://www.uswa.org/) and Kaiser Aluminum (http://www.kaiseral.com) entered into a master collective bargaining agreement covering terms and conditions of employment at fifteen Kaiser plants. The agreement contained an affirmative action plan designed to eliminate conspicuous racial imbalances in Kaiser's then almost exclusively white craftwork forces. African-American craft-hiring goals were set for each Kaiser plant equal to the percentage of African-Americans in the respective local labor forces. To meet these goals, on-the-job training programs were established to teach unskilled production workers—African-Americans and whites—the skills necessary to become craftworkers. The plan reserved for African-American employees 50 percent of the openings in these newly created in-plant training programs.

Pursuant to the national agreement, Kaiser altered its craft-hiring practice in its Gramercy, Louisiana, plant by establishing a program to train its production workers to fill craft openings. Selection of craft trainees was made on the basis of seniority. At least 50 percent of the new trainees were to be African-American until the percentage of African-American skilled craftworkers in the Gramercy plant approximated the percentage of African-Americans in the local labor force. During this affirmative action plan's first year of operation, thirteen craft trainees (seven African-American, six white) were selected from Gramercy's production workforce. The most senior African-American selected had less seniority than several white production workers who were denied admission to the program. Does the affirmative action plan wrongfully discriminate against white employees and therefore violate the Civil Rights Act of 1964? Justify your decision.

13. At Whirlpool's (http://www.whirlpoolcorp.com/whr/) manufacturing plant in Ohio, overhead conveyors transported household appliance components throughout the plant. A wire mesh screen was positioned below the conveyors in order to catch falling components and debris. Maintenance employees frequently had to stand on the screens to clean them. Whirlpool began installing heavier wire because several employees had fallen partly through the old screens, and one had fallen completely through to the plant floor. At this time, the company warned workers to walk only on the frames beneath the wire but not on the wire itself. Before the heavier wire had been completely installed, a worker fell to his death through the old screen. A short time after this incident, Deemer and Cornwell, two plant employees, met with the plant safety director to discuss the mesh, to voice their concerns, and to obtain the name, address, and telephone number of the local Occupational Safety and Health Administration (OSHA) representative. The next day, the two employees refused to clean a portion of the old screen. They were then ordered to punch out for the remainder of the shift without pay and received written reprimands, which were placed in their employment files. Does Whirlpool's actions against Deemer and Cornwell constitute discrimination in violation of the Occupational Safety and Health Act? Explain.

14. The defendant, Berger Transfer and Storage (http://www.berger-transfer.com/), operated a national moving and transfer business employing approximately forty persons. In May and June, Local 705 of the International Brotherhood of Teamsters (http://www.teamster.org/) spoke with a number of Berger employees, obtaining twenty-eight cards signed in support of the union. The management of Berger, unwilling to work with the union, attempted to prevent it from representing Berger employees. The company first assigned all work to those with high seniority, in effect temporarily laying off low-seniority employees. The management then threatened to lay off permanently those with low seniority and threatened all employees with a total closedown of the plant. The management interrogated several employees about their union involvement and attempted to extract information about other employees' activities. When the union presented the company with the signed cards and recognition agreement, Berger refused to acknowledge the union's existence or its right to bargain on behalf of the employees. The union then called a strike, with employees picketing the Berger warehouse. During the picketing, the company threatened to terminate the picketers if they did not return to work. Later, one manager on two occasions recklessly drove a truck through the picket line, striking employees. Finally, the company contacted several of the employees and offered them the "grievance procedures and job security" the union would provide. The employees refused the offer. On June 15, the strike ended, with most of the picketers returning to work. Local 705 filed a complaint with the National Labor Relations Board, alleging that Berger had committed unfair labor practices in violation of the National Labor Relations Act. Will Local 705 succeed? Explain.

15. The City of Richmond, Virginia (the City) (http://www.ci.richmond.va.us/) adopted a Minority Business Utilization Plan requiring prime contractors awarded city construction contracts to subcontract at least 30 percent of the dollar amount of each contract to one or more Minority Business Enterprises (MBEs). The plan defined an MBE to include a business from anywhere in the country that is at least 51 percent owned and controlled by African-American, Spanish-speaking, Oriental, Native American, Eskimo, or Aleut citizens. Although the plan declared that it was "remedial" in nature, it was adopted after a public hearing at which no direct evidence was presented that the City had discriminated on the basis of race in letting contracts or that its prime contractors had discriminated against minority subcontractors. The evidence introduced in support of the plan included a statistical study indicating that, although the City's population was 50 percent African-American, less than 1 percent of its prime construction contracts had been awarded to minority businesses in recent years. Additional evidence showed that a variety of local contractors' trade associations had virtually no MBE members. J. A. Croson Co., the sole bidder on a city contract, was denied a waiver and lost its contract because of the plan. Is the plan unconstitutional under the Fourteenth Amendment's Equal Protection Clause? Why?

16. Burdine, a woman, was hired by the Texas Department of Housing & Community Affairs (http://www.tdhca.state.tx.us/) as a clerk in the Public Service Careers Division (PSC). The PSC provides training and employment opportunities for unskilled workers. At the time she was hired, Burdine already had several years' experience in employment training. She was soon promoted, and later, when her supervisor resigned, she performed additional duties that usually had been assigned to the supervisor. Burdine applied for the position of supervisor, but the position remained unfilled for six months, until a male employee from another division was brought in to fill it. Burdine alleges discrimination violating Title VII of the 1964 Civil Rights Act. The defendant, Texas Department of Community Affairs, responds that nondiscriminatory evaluation criteria were used to choose the new supervisor. In order to comply with Title VII, must the Texas Department of Community Affairs hire Burdine as supervisor if she and the male candidate are equally qualified? Explain.

17. Ms. Wise was fired from her job at the Mead Corporation (http://www.meadwestvaco.com/) after she was involved in a fight with a co-worker. On four other unrelated occasions, fights had occurred between male co-workers. Only one of the males was fired, but this was after his second fight, in which he seriously injured another employee. There is no dispute that Ms. Wise was qualified and performed her duties adequately. Ms. Wise successfully establishes a *prima facie* case of discrimination. However, the defendant, Mead Corporation, meets its burden to "articulate legitimate and nondiscriminatory reasons" for firing Ms. Wise. Can she prevail? Explain.

18. John Novosel was employed by Nationwide Insurance Company (http://www.nationwide.com/) from December 1966 until November 1981. Novosel had been a model employee and, at the time of discharge, was a district claims manager and a candidate for the position of division claims manager. In October 1981, Nationwide circulated a memorandum requesting the participation of all employees in an effort to lobby the Pennsylvania state legislature for the passage of a certain bill before the body. Novosel, who had privately indicated his disagreement with Nationwide's political views, refused to lend his support to the lobby, and his employment with Nationwide was terminated. Novosel brought two separate claims against Nationwide, arguing, first, that his discharge for refusing to lobby the state legislature on behalf of Nationwide constituted the tort of wrongful discharge in that it was arbitrary, malicious, and contrary to public policy. Novosel also contended that Nationwide breached an implied contract guaranteeing continued employment so long as his job performance was satisfactory. What decision as to each claim?

19. During the years prior to the passage of the Civil Rights Act of 1964, Duke Power (http://www.dukepower.com/) openly discriminated against African-Americans by allowing them to work only in the labor department of the plant's five departments. The highest paying job in the labor department

paid less than the lowest paying jobs in the other four "operating" departments in which only whites were employed. In 1955, the company began requiring a high school education for initial assignment to any department except labor. However, when Duke Power stopped restricting African-Americans to the labor department in 1965, it made completion of high school a prerequisite to transfer from labor to any other department. White employees hired before the high school education requirement was adopted continued to perform satisfactorily and to achieve promotions in the "operating" departments.

In 1965, the company also began requiring new employees in the departments other than labor to register satisfactory scores on two professionally prepared aptitude tests, in addition to having a high school education. In September 1965, Duke Power began to permit employees to qualify for transfer to another department from labor by passing two tests, neither of which was directed or intended to measure the ability to learn to perform a particular job or category of jobs. Griggs brought suit against Duke Power, claiming that the high school education and testing requirements were discriminatory and therefore prohibited by the Civil Rights Act of 1964. Is Griggs correct? Why?

20. Mechelle Vinson was an employee of Meritor Savings Bank for approximately four years. Beginning as a teller-trainee, she ultimately advanced to the position of assistant branch manager. Her promotions were based solely upon merit. Sidney Taylor, a vice president of the bank and manager of the branch office in which Vinson worked, was Vinson's supervisor throughout her employment with the bank. After the bank fired Vinson for her abusive use of sick leave, she brought an action against Taylor and the bank, alleging that during her employment she had "constantly been subjected to sexual harassment" by Taylor in violation of Title VII of the Civil Rights Act of 1964. At trial, Vinson stated that Taylor repeatedly demanded sexual favors from her, fondled her in front of other employees, and forcibly raped her on a number of occasions. Taylor and the bank categorically denied Vinson's allegations. Does the conduct constitute sexual harassment? Explain.

21. Plaintiff, Beth Lyons, a staff attorney for the Legal Aid Society (Legal Aid) brought suit against her employer, alleging that Legal Aid violated the Americans with Disabilities Act (ADA) and the Rehabilitation Act by failing to provide her with a parking space near her office. Plaintiff worked for defendant in its lower Manhattan office.

Lyon's disability was the result of being struck and nearly killed by an automobile. From the date of the accident (September 1987) until June 1993, Lyons was on disability leave from Legal Aid; she underwent multiple reconstructive surgeries and received "constant" physical therapy. Since the accident, Lyons has been able to walk only by using walking devices, including walkers, canes, and crutches. Since returning to work, Lyons has performed her job duties successfully. Nevertheless, her condition severely limits her ability to walk long distances either at one time or during the course of a day.

Before returning to work, Lyons asked Legal Aid to accommodate her disability by providing her a parking space near her office and the courts in which she would practice. She stated that this would be necessary because she is unable to take public transportation from her home in New Jersey to the Legal Aid office in Manhattan because such "commuting would require her to walk distances, climb stairs, and on occasion to remain standing for extended periods of time," thereby "overtax[ing] her limited physical capabilities." Lyons's physician advised Legal Aid by letter that such a parking space was "necessary to enable [Lyons] to return to work." Legal Aid informed Lyons that it would not pay for a parking space for her. Accordingly, Lyons has spent $300 to $520 a month, representing 15 percent to 26 percent of her monthly net salary, for a parking space adjacent to her office building. Are the accommodations requested by Lyons unreasonable? Why?

22. The Steamship Clerks Union has approximately 124 members, 80 of whom are classified as active. Members serve as steamship clerks who, during the loading and unloading of vessels in the port of Boston, check cargo against inventory lists provided by shippers and consignees. The work is not taxing; it requires little in the way of particular skills. On October 1, 1980, the Union formally adopted the membership sponsorship policy (the MSP), which provided that any applicant for membership in the Union (other than an injured longshoreman) had to be sponsored by an existing member for his application to be considered. The record reveals, without contradiction, that (1) the Union had no African-American or Hispanic members when it adopted the MSP; (2) blacks and Hispanics constituted from 8 percent to 27 percent of the relevant labor pool in the Boston area; (3) the Union welcomed at least thirty new members between 1980 and 1986 and then closed the membership rolls; (4) all "sponsored" applicants during this period and, hence, all the new members, were Caucasian; and (5) every recruit was related to (usually the son or brother of) a Union member. Does the MSP discriminate against African-Americans and Hispanics? Explain.

http:// **Internet Exercise** Find the Occupational Safety and Health Administration's home page and (a) explore "what's new," (b) determine what OSHA is doing about workplace violence, (c) examine the occupational injury and illness incidence rates, and (d) review the latest news releases.

CHAPTER 43

Antitrust

Monopolies are odious, contrary to the spirit of free government and the principles of commerce, and ought not to be suffered.

MARYLAND DECLARATION OF 1776

Learning Objectives

After reading this chapter you should be able to:

1. Describe and explain horizontal restraints of trade.
2. Describe and explain vertical restraints of trade.
3. Explain monopolization, attempts to monopolize, and conspiracies to monopolies and why they are illegal.
4. Explain the Clayton Act and its rules governing (a) tying contracts, (b) exclusive dealing, (c) horizontal mergers, (d) vertical mergers, and (e) conglomerate mergers.
5. Describe (a) the Robinson-Patman Act and the various defenses to it and (b) the Federal Trade Commission Act.

The economic community is best served in normal times by free competition in trade and industry. It is in the public interest that quality, price, and service in an open, competitive market for goods and services be determining factors in the business rivalry for the customer's dollar. Rather than compete, however, businesses would prefer to eliminate their competition and, consequently, to enjoy a position from which they could dictate both the price of their goods and the quantity they produce. Although eliminating competition by producing a better product is the proper goal of a business, some businesses effect this elimination through illegitimate means, such as fixing prices and allocating exclusive territories to certain competitors within an industry. The law of antitrust prohibits such activities and attempts to ensure free and fair competition in the marketplace.

The common law has traditionally favored competition and has held that agreements and contracts in restraint of trade are illegal and unenforceable. In addition, although several states enacted antitrust statutes during the 1800s, the latter half of the nineteenth century revealed concentrations of economic power in the form of "trusts" and "combinations" that were too powerful and widespread to be curbed effectively by state action. In 1890, this awesome and uncontrollable growth of power prompted Congress to enact the Sherman Antitrust Act, the first federal statute in this field. Since then, Congress has enacted other antitrust statutes, including the Clayton Act, the Robinson-Patman Act, and the Federal Trade Commission Act. These statutes prohibit anticompetitive practices and seek to prevent unreasonable concentrations of economic power that stifle or weaken competition.

SHERMAN ANTITRUST ACT

Section 1 of the Sherman Act prohibits contracts, combinations, and conspiracies that restrain trade, while Section 2 outlaws both monopolies and attempts to monopolize. Failure to comply with either section is a criminal violation and subjects the offender to fine or imprisonment or both. As amended by the 1990 Antitrust Amendments, the act subjects individual offenders to imprisonment of up to three years and fines of up to $350,000, while corporate offenders are subject to fines of up to $10,000,000 per violation. Moreover, the act empowers the federal district courts to issue injunctions restraining violations; and anyone injured by a violation is entitled to recover in a civil action **treble damages** (that is, three times the amount of the actual loss sustained). The U.S. Department of Justice and the Federal Trade Commission have the duty to institute appropriate enforcement proceedings other than treble damages actions.

The case the United States brought against Microsoft, Inc., may have a profound effect upon antitrust law. In June 2000, U.S. District Court Judge Thomas Penfield Jackson ordered the breakup of Microsoft for violating the Sherman Antitrust Act. The breakup order followed more than two years of litigation in which Microsoft was accused of illegally maintaining its monopoly over the personal computer operating system market and then attempting to extend it into the market for Internet browsers. The U.S. Court of Appeals upheld the district court's ruling that Microsoft used illegal conduct to retain its operating system monopoly, reversed the browser monopolization finding and the breakup order, and remanded the case to the district court to determine an appropriate remedy. After the appellate court decision, the Department of Justice and a number of states settled the case with Microsoft, although some states are contesting it. The settlement allows Microsoft to remain as one company but includes the following provisions: (a) Microsoft may not "retaliate against" a computer maker in any way, including raising prices or withholding technical support, for dealing with Microsoft's competitors; (b) Microsoft must establish and follow a schedule of fixed prices; (c) computer makers such as Dell, Gateway, and IBM will be allowed to install non-Microsoft products and "desktop shortcuts of any size or shape" on its computers; (d) Microsoft will reveal previously confidential programming interfaces that its products rely on to link to Windows code; and (e) Microsoft "shall not retaliate" against other companies because their products compete with other Microsoft applications.

Practical Advice

Be advised that a violation of the Sherman Antitrust Act carries both civil (including treble damages) and criminal penalties.

The Justice Department has expanded its enforcement policy regarding the Sherman Act to cover conduct by foreign companies that harms U.S. exports. Under this policy, the department examines conduct to determine whether it would violate the law if it occurred within borders of the United States. The department has indicated that it will focus primarily on boycotts and cartels that injure the export of U.S. products and services.

http://

Federal Trade Commission, Antitrust/Competition Division: http://www.ftc.gov/ftc/antitrust.htm
Department of Justice Antitrust Division: http://www.usdoj.gov/atr/index.html
United States v. Microsoft, Department of Justice information: http://www.usdoj.gov/atr/cases/ms_index.htm
Antitrust Policy: http://www.antitrust.org/
American Antitrust Institute: http://www.antitrustinstitute.org/
American Bar Association, Antitrust Section: http://www.abanet.org/antitrust/
Cornell Legal Information Institute: Antitrust: http://www.law.cornell.edu/topics/antitrust.html
Sherman Act: http://www4.law.cornell.edu/uscode/15/1.html

RESTRAINT OF TRADE

Section 1 of the Sherman Act provides that "[e]very contract, combination in the form of trust or otherwise, or conspiracy, in restraint of trade or commerce among the several states, or with foreign nations is hereby declared to be illegal." Because the section's language is so broad, identifying the elements that constitute a violation has been largely a product of judicial interpretation.

Standards As noted above, Section 1 prohibits every contract, combination, or conspiracy in restraint of trade. Taken literally, this prohibition would invalidate every unperformed contract. To avoid such an unrealistic application, the courts have interpreted this section to invalidate only *unreasonable* restraints of trade. This standard is known as the **rule of reason test**, a flexible standard under which the courts, in determining whether a challenged practice unreasonably restricts competition, consider a variety of factors, including the makeup of the relevant industry, the defendants' positions within that industry, the ability of the defendants' competitors to respond to the challenged practice, and the defendants' purpose in adopting the restraint. After reviewing the various factors, a court determines whether the challenged restraint unreasonably restricts competition.

By requiring the courts to balance the *anticompetitive* effects of every questioned restraint against its *procompetitive* effects, this standard placed a substantial burden upon the judicial system. The Supreme Court addressed this problem by declaring certain categories of restraints to be unreasonable by their very nature, that is, **illegal *per se***. Characterizing a type of restraint as *per se* illegal significantly affects the prosecution of an antitrust suit. In such a case, the plaintiff need only show that the type of restraint occurred; she need not prove that the restraint limited competition. The defendants, in turn, may not defend on the basis that the restraint is reasonable.

Furthermore, the court is not required to conduct extensive, and often difficult, economic analysis.

Over the last decade, a third, intermediate test has been frequently used when the *per se* approach is not appropriate for the situation but the challenged conduct has obvious anticompetitive effects. Under this "quick look" rule of reason analysis, the courts will apply an abbreviated rule of reason standard rather than using the extensive analysis required by a full-blown rule of reason test. However, as shown by the following case, the extensiveness of the legal analysis required under the quick look test will vary based upon the circumstances, details, and logic of the restraint being reviewed.

Practical Advice

Recognize that certain types of conduct, due to their pernicious effect on competition and their lack of any redeeming virtue, are conclusively presumed to be unreasonable and therefore are illegal *per se*..

California Dental Association v. Federal Trade Commission

Supreme Court of the United States, 1999

526 U.S. 756, 119 S.Ct. 1604, 143 L.Ed.2d 935

http://caselaw.lp.findlaw.com/cgi-bin/getcase.pl?court=US&navby=case&vol=000&invol=97-1625

FACTS The California Dental Association (CDA) **(http://www.cda.org)** is a voluntary nonprofit association of local dental societies to which some 19,000 dentists belong, about three quarters of those practicing in the state. The CDA lobbies on behalf of its members' interests, and conducts marketing and public relations campaigns for their benefit. The dentists who belong to the CDA through these associations agree to abide by a Code of Ethics (Code) **(http://www.cda.org/public/coe99.html)** including Section 10, which provides:

> "Although any dentist may advertise, no dentist shall advertise or solicit patients in any form of communication in a manner that is false or misleading in any material respect. In order to properly serve the public, dentists should represent themselves in a manner that contributes to the esteem of the public. Dentists should not misrepresent their training and competence in any way that would be false or misleading in any material respect."

Responsibility for enforcing the Code rests in the first instance with the local dental societies, to which applicants for CDA membership must submit copies of their own advertisements and those of their employers or referral services to assure compliance with the Code. The local societies also actively seek information about potential Code violations by CDA members. Applicants who refuse to withdraw or revise objectionable advertisements may be denied membership, and members are subject to censure, suspension, or expulsion from the CDA.

The Federal Trade Commission (Commission) brought a complaint against the CDA, alleging that it applied its guidelines so as to restrict truthful, nondeceptive advertising and therefore violated § 5 of the FTC Act. The Commission alleged that the CDA unreasonably restricted price advertising, particularly discounted fees, and advertising relating to the quality of dental services. An Administrative Law Judge (ALJ) found that, although there had been no proof that the CDA exerted market power, no such proof was required to establish an antitrust violation, since the CDA had unreasonably prevented members and potential members from using truthful, nondeceptive advertising, all to the detriment of both dentists and consumers of dental services. The Commission adopted the factual findings of the ALJ except for his conclusion that the CDA lacked market power and treated the CDA's restrictions on discount advertising as illegal *per se*. In the alternative, the Commission held the price advertising (as well as the nonprice) restrictions violate the Sherman and FTC Acts under an abbreviated (quick look) rule-of-reason analysis. The Court of Appeals thought it error for the Commission to have applied *per se* analysis to the price advertising restrictions but affirmed the Commission's applying the quick look rule-of-reason analysis designed for restraints that are not *per se* unlawful but are sufficiently anticompetitive on their face that they do not require a full-blown rule of reason inquiry. The Court of Appeals found the truncated rule-of-reason analysis appropriate because (1) the discount advertising, "amounted in practice to a fairly 'naked' restraint on price competition itself" and (2) the nonprice advertising restrictions, "are in effect a form of output limitation, as they restrict the supply of information about individual dentists' services." The Supreme Court granted *certiorari* to resolve a conflict among the Circuit Courts of Appeals over the occasions for abbreviated rule-of-reason analysis.

DECISION Judgment vacated and remanded.

OPINION Souter, J. The Court of Appeals treated as distinct questions the sufficiency of the analysis of anticompetitive effects and the substantiality of the evidence supporting the Commission's conclusions. Because we decide that the Court of Appeals erred when it held as a matter of law that quick-look analysis was appropriate (with the consequence that the Commission's abbreviated analysis and conclusion were sustainable), we do not reach the question of the substantiality of the evidence supporting the Commission's conclusion.

In [citation], we held that a "naked restraint on price and output requires some competitive justification even in the absence of a detailed market analysis." [Citation]. Elsewhere, we held that "no elaborate industry analysis is required to demonstrate the anticompetitive character of" horizontal agreements among competitors to refuse to discuss prices, [citation], or to withhold a particular desired service, [citation.] In each of these cases, which have formed the basis for what has come to be called abbreviated or "quick-look" analysis under the rule of reason, an observer with even a rudimentary understanding of economics could conclude that the arrangements in question would have an anticompetitive effect on customers and markets. * * * As in such cases, quick-look analysis carries the day when the great likelihood of anticompetitive effects can easily be ascertained. [Citations.]

The case before us, however, fails to present a situation in which the likelihood of anticompetitive effects is comparably obvious. Even on Justice Breyer's view that bars on truthful and verifiable price and quality advertising are *prima facie* anticompetitive, (opinion concurring in part and dissenting in part [which was joined by three other Justices]), and place the burden of procompetitive justification on those who agree to adopt them, the very issue at the threshold of this case is whether professional price and quality advertising is sufficiently verifiable in theory and in fact to fall within such a general rule. Ultimately our disagreement with Justice Breyer turns on our different responses to this issue. Whereas he accepts, as the Ninth Circuit seems to have done, that the restrictions here were like restrictions on advertisement of price and quality generally, * * * it seems to us that the CDA's advertising restrictions might plausibly be thought to have a net procompetitive effect, or possibly no effect at all on competition. The restrictions on both discount and nondiscount advertising are, at least on their face, designed to avoid false or deceptive advertising in a market characterized by striking disparities between the information available to the professional and the patient. [Citations.]

In a market for professional services, in which advertising is relatively rare and the comparability of service packages not easily established, the difficulty for customers or potential competitors to get and verify information about the price and availability of services magnifies the dangers to competition associated with misleading advertising. What is more, the quality of professional services tends to resist either calibration or monitoring by individual patients or clients, partly because of the specialized knowledge required to evaluate the services, and partly because of the difficulty in determining whether, and the degree to which, an outcome is attributable to the quality of services (like a poor job of tooth-filling) or to something else (like a very tough walnut). [Citations.] Patients' attachments to particular professionals, the rationality of which is difficult to assess, complicate the picture even further. [Citations.] The existence of such significant challenges to informed decisionmaking by the customer for professional services immediately suggests that advertising restrictions arguably protecting patients from misleading or irrelevant advertising call for more than cursory treatment as obviously comparable to classic horizontal agreements to limit output or price competition.

The explanation proffered by the Court of Appeals for the likely anticompetitive effect of the CDA's restrictions on discount advertising began with the unexceptionable statements that "price advertising is fundamental to price competition," [citation] and that "[r]estrictions on the ability to advertise prices normally make it more difficult for consumers to find a lower price and for dentists to compete on the basis of price," [citations.] The court then acknowledged that, according to the CDA, the restrictions nonetheless furthered the "legitimate, indeed procompetitive, goal of preventing false and misleading price advertising." [Citation]. The Court of Appeals might, at this juncture, have recognized that the restrictions at issue here are very far from a total ban on price or discount advertising, and might have considered the possibility that the particular restrictions on professional advertising could have different effects from those "normally" found in the commercial world, even to the point of promoting competition by reducing the occurrence of unverifiable and misleading across-the-board discount advertising. Instead, the Court of Appeals confined itself to the brief assertion that the "CDA's disclosure requirements appear to prohibit across-the-board discounts because it is simply infeasible to disclose all of the information that is required," [citation], followed by the observation that "the record provides no evidence that the rule has in fact led to increased disclosure and transparency of dental pricing," [citation.]

But these observations brush over the professional context and describe no anticompetitive effects. Assuming that the record in fact supports the conclusion that the CDA disclosure rules essentially bar advertisement of across-the-board discounts, it does not obviously follow that such a ban would have a net anticompetitive effect here.

* * *

The Court of Appeals was comparably tolerant in accepting the sufficiency of abbreviated rule-of-reason analysis as to the nonprice advertising restrictions. The court began with the argument that "[t]hese restrictions are in effect a form of output limitation, as they restrict the supply of information about individual dentists' services." [Citations.] Although this sentence does indeed appear as cited, it is puzzling, given that the relevant output for antitrust purposes here is presumably not information or advertising, but dental services themselves. The question is not whether the universe of possible advertisements has been limited (as assuredly it has), but whether the limitation on advertisements obviously tends to limit the total delivery of dental services. * * *

Although the Court of Appeals acknowledged the CDA's view that "claims about quality are inherently unverifiable and therefore misleading," [citation], it responded that this concern "does not justify banning all quality claims without regard to whether they are, in fact, false or misleading," [citation.] * * *

The point is not that the CDA's restrictions necessarily have the procompetitive effect claimed by the CDA; it is possible that banning quality claims might have no effect at all on competitiveness if, for example, many dentists made very much the same sort of claims. And it is also of course possible that the restrictions might in the final analysis be anticompetitive. The point, rather, is that the plausibility of competing claims about the effects of the professional advertising restrictions rules out the indulgently abbreviated review to which the Commission's order was treated. The obvious anticompetitive effect that triggers abbreviated analysis has not been shown.

* * *

Saying here that the Court of Appeals's conclusion at least required a more extended examination of the possible factual underpinnings than it received is not, of course, necessarily to call for the fullest market analysis. Although we have said that a challenge to a "naked restraint on price and output" need not be supported by "a detailed market analysis" in order to "requir[e] some competitive justification," [citation], it does not follow that every case attacking a less obviously anticompetitive restraint (like this one) is a candidate for plenary market examination. The truth is that our categories of analysis of anticompetitive effect are less fixed than terms like "*per se*," "quick look," and "rule of reason" tend to make them appear. We have recognized, for example, that "there is often no bright line separating *per se* from Rule of Reason analysis," since "considerable inquiry into market conditions" may be required before the application of any so-called "*per se*" condemnation is justified. * * * As the circumstances here demonstrate, there is generally no categorical line to be drawn between restraints that give rise to an intuitively obvious inference of anticompetitive effect and those that call for more detailed treatment. What is required, rather, is an enquiry meet for the case, looking to the circumstances, details, and logic of a restraint. The object is to see whether the experience of the market has been so clear, or necessarily will be, that a confident conclusion about the principal tendency of a restriction will follow from a quick (or at least quicker) look, in place of a more sedulous one. And of course what we see may vary over time, if rule-of-reason analyses in case after case reach identical conclusions. For now, at least, a less quick look was required for the initial assessment of the tendency of these professional advertising restrictions. * * *

INTERPRETATION Under Section 1 of the Sherman Act, the extensiveness of legal analysis employed will vary based upon the circumstances, details, and logic of the restraint being reviewed.

CRITICAL THINKING QUESTION Do you agree with the court's decision? Explain.

Horizontal and Vertical Restraints A trade restraint may be classified as either horizontal or vertical. A **horizontal restraint** involves collaboration among competitors at the same level in the chain of distribution. For example, an agreement among manufacturers, among wholesalers, or among retailers would be horizontal.

On the other hand, an agreement among parties who are not in direct competition at the same distribution level is a **vertical restraint**. Thus, an agreement between a manufacturer and a wholesaler is vertical. Although the distinction between horizontal and vertical restraints can become blurred, it often determines whether a restraint is illegal *per se* or should be judged by the rule of reason test. For instance, horizontal market allocations are illegal *per se*, whereas vertical market allocations are subject to the rule of reason test.

Concerted Action Section 1 does not prohibit ***unilateral*** conduct; rather, it forbids ***concerted*** action. Thus, one person or business by itself cannot violate the section. As the U.S. Supreme Court held in *Monsanto Co. v. Spray-Rite Service Corporation*, an organization has the "right to deal, or refuse to deal, with whomever it likes, as long as it does so independently." For example, if a manufacturer announces its resale prices in advance and refuses to deal with those who disagree with the pricing, there is no violation of Section 1 because the manufacturer has acted alone. On the other hand, if a manufacturer and its retailers together agree that the manufacturer will sell only to those retailers who agree to sell at a specified price, a violation of Section 1 may exist.

For purposes of the concerted action requirement, the courts view a firm and its employees as one entity. The same is also true for a corporation and its wholly owned subsidiaries; thus, the Sherman Act is not violated when a parent and its wholly owned subsidiary agree to a restraint in trade.

The concerted action requirement may be established by an express agreement. Not surprisingly, however, express agreements often are nonexistent, leaving the court to infer an interparty agreement from circumstantial evidence. Nonetheless, similar patterns of conduct among competitors, called **conscious parallelism**, are not sufficient in themselves to imply a conspiracy in violation of Section 1. Actual conspiracy requires an *additional* factor—such as complex actions that would benefit each competitor only if all of them acted—or indications of a traditional conspiracy—such as identical sealed bids from each competitor.

Joint ventures (discussed in Chapter 31) are a form of business association organized to carry out a particular business enterprise. Competitors frequently pool their resources in order to share costs and to eliminate wasteful redundancy. The validity under antitrust law of a joint venture generally depends on the competitors' primary purpose in forming it. A joint venture that was not formed to fix prices or divide markets will be judged under the rule of reason.

However, because uncertainty about the legality of joint ventures seemed to discourage their use for joint research and development, Congress passed the National Cooperative Research Act in order to facilitate such applications. The act provides that the courts must judge joint ventures in the research and development of new technology under the rule of reason test and that treble damages do *not* apply to ventures formed in violation of Section 1 if those forming the venture have notified the Justice Department and the FTC of their intent to form the joint venture.

http://

National Cooperative Research Act: http://www4.law.cornell.edu/uscode/15/4301.html
Department of Justice Antitrust Division and Federal Trade Commission, Joint Venture Guidelines: http://www.usdoj.gov/atr/public/guidelines/jointindex.htm

Price Fixing **Price fixing** is an agreement with the purpose or effect of inhibiting price competition; such agreements may, among other things, raise, depress, fix, peg, or stabilize prices. Price fixing is the primary and most serious example of a *per se* violation under the Sherman Act. All ***horizontal*** price-fixing agreements are illegal *per se*. This prohibition covers any agreement by which sellers establish *maximum* prices at which certain commodities or services are to be offered for sale, as well as those by which they set *minimum* prices. The law also prohibits sellers' agreements to change the prices of certain commodities or services simultaneously or to not advertise their prices.

The U.S. Supreme Court has condemned not only agreements among horizontal competitors that directly fix prices but also agreements that affect price indirectly. For example, in finding an agreement among beer wholesalers to eliminate interest-free short-term credit on sales to beer retailers to be illegal *per se*, the Court viewed the credit terms "as an inseparable part of price" and concluded that the agreement to eliminate interest-free short-term credit was equivalent to an agreement to eliminate discounts and, thus, was an agreement to fix prices.

Similarly, it is illegal *per se* for a seller to fix the price at which its purchasers must resell its product. This ***vertical*** form of price fixing—usually called "retail price maintenance"—is considered a *per se* violation of Section 1.

Despite its early and consistent condemnation of resale price maintenance agreements, the Supreme Court has found no Section 1 violation when a manufacturer who announces in advance that it will not sell to dealers who cut prices then terminates its dealers who have cut prices. Not surprisingly, courts sometimes have difficulty distinguishing between an illegal resale price maintenance agreement and a manufacturer's legal refusal to deal with a retailer who refuses to charge the manufacturer's dictated minimum price. More significantly, in the case that follows, the U.S. Supreme Court overruled a thirty-year-old precedent by holding that vertical maximum price fixing is not *per se* illegal but is to be judged by a rule of reason standard.

State Oil Company v. Khan

Supreme Court of the United States, 1997
522 U.S. 3, 118 S.Ct. 275, 139 L.Ed.2d 199
http://laws.findlaw.com/US/000/96-871.htm

FACTS Plaintiffs, Barkat U. Khan and his corporation (Khan), entered into an agreement with defendant, State Oil Company (State Oil), to lease and operate a gas station and convenience store owned by State Oil. The agreement provided that respondents would obtain the station's gasoline supply from State Oil at a price equal to a suggested retail price set by State Oil, less a margin of 3.25 cents per gallon. Under the agreement, respondents could charge any amount for gasoline sold to the station's customers, but if the price charged was higher than State Oil's suggested retail price, the excess was to be paid to State Oil. Khan could sell gasoline for less than State Oil's suggested retail price, but any such decrease would reduce its 3.25 cents-per-gallon margin.

About a year after Khan began operating the gas station, it fell behind in lease payments. State Oil then gave notice of its intent to terminate the agreement and commenced a state court proceeding to evict Khan. Khan sued State Oil in the U.S. district court, alleging in part that State Oil had engaged in price fixing in violation of Section 1 of the Sherman Act by preventing it from raising or lowering retail gas prices.

The district court found that the allegations in the complaint did not state a *per se* violation of the Sherman Act because they did not establish the sort of "manifestly anticompetitive implications or pernicious effect on competition" that would justify *per se* prohibition of State Oil's conduct. Subsequently, in ruling on cross-motions for summary judgment, the district court concluded that respondents had failed to demonstrate antitrust injury or harm to competition. Accordingly, the district court entered summary judgment for State Oil on Khan's Sherman Act claim.

The Court of Appeals for the Seventh Circuit reversed. The court first noted that the agreement between respondents and State Oil did indeed fix maximum gasoline prices by making it "worthless" for respondents to exceed the suggested retail prices. The court concluded that State Oil's pricing scheme was a *per se* antitrust violation under *Albrecht v. Herald Co.*

DECISION Reversed and remanded.

OPINION O'Connor, J. Although the Sherman Act, by its terms, prohibits every agreement "in restraint of trade," this Court has long recognized that Congress intended to outlaw only unreasonable restraints. [Citations.] As a consequence, most antitrust claims are analyzed under a "rule of reason," according to which the finder of fact must decide whether the questioned practice imposes an unreasonable restraint on competition, taking into account a variety of factors, including specific information about the relevant business, its condition before and after the restraint was imposed, and the restraint's history, nature, and effect. [Citations.]

Some types of restraints, however, have such predictable and pernicious anticompetitive effect, and such limited potential for procompetitive benefit, that they are deemed unlawful *per se*. [Citation.] *Per se* treatment is appropriate "[o]nce experience with a particular kind of restraint enables the Court to predict with confidence that the rule of reason will condemn it." [Citations.] Thus, we have expressed reluctance to adopt *per se* rules with regard to "restraints imposed in the context of business relationships where the economic impact of certain practices is not immediately obvious." [Citation.]

A review of this Court's decisions leading up to and beyond *Albrecht* is relevant to our assessment of the continuing validity of the *per se* rule established in *Albrecht*. * * * The Court [in *Albrecht*] acknowledged that "[m]aximum and minimum price fixing may have different consequences in many situations," but nonetheless condemned maximum price fixing for "substituting the perhaps erroneous judgment of a seller for the forces of the competitive market." [Citation.]

Albrecht was animated in part by the fear that vertical maximum price fixing could allow suppliers to discriminate against certain dealers, restrict the services that dealers could afford to offer customers, or disguise minimum price fixing schemes. * * *

* * *

We noted in [citation] that vertical restraints are generally more defensible than horizontal restraints. [Citation.] And we explained * * * that decisions such as [citation] "recognize the possibility that a vertical restraint imposed by a single manufacturer or wholesaler may stimulate interbrand competition even as it reduces intrabrand competition."

Thus, our reconsideration of *Albrecht's* continuing validity is informed by several of our decisions, as well as a considerable body of scholarship discussing the effects of vertical restraints. Our analysis is also guided by our general view that the primary purpose of the antitrust laws is to protect interbrand competition. [Citation.] "Low prices," we have explained, "benefit consumers regardless of how those prices are set, and so long as they are above predatory levels, they do not threaten competition." [Citation.] Our interpretation of the Sherman Act also incorporates the notion that condemnation of practices resulting in lower prices to consumers is "especially costly" because "cutting prices in order to increase business often is the very essence of competition." [Citation.]

So informed, we find it difficult to maintain that vertically-imposed maximum prices could harm consumers or competition to the extent necessary to justify their *per se* invalidation.

* * *

The *Albrecht* Court also expressed the concern that maximum prices may be set too low for dealers to offer consumers essential or desired services. [Citation.] But such conduct, by driving away customers, would seem likely to harm manufacturers as well as dealers and consumers, making it unlikely that a supplier would set such a price as a matter of business judgment. [Citations.] * * *

Finally, *Albrecht* reflected the Court's fear that maximum price fixing could be used to disguise arrangements to fix minimum prices [citation], which remain illegal *per se*. Although we have acknowledged the possibility that maximum pricing might mask minimum pricing, [citation], we believe that such conduct as with the other concerns articulated in Albrecht can be appropriately recognized and punished under the rule of reason. [Citation.]

* * *

After reconsidering *Albrecht's* rationale and the substantial criticism the decision has received, however, we conclude that there is insufficient economic justification for *per se* invalidation of vertical maximum price fixing. * * *

* * *

In overruling *Albrecht*, we of course do not hold that all vertical maximum price fixing is *per se* lawful. Instead, vertical maximum price fixing, like the majority of commercial arrangements subject to the antitrust laws, should be evaluated under the rule of reason. In our view, rule-of-reason analysis will effectively identify those situations in which vertical maximum price fixing amounts to anticompetitive conduct.

INTERPRETATION Maximum vertical price fixing is to be judged by a rule of reason standard.

CRITICAL THINKING QUESTION Do you agree with the Court's decision? Explain.

Market Allocations Direct price fixing is not the only way to control prices. Another method is through **market allocation**, whereby competitors agree not to compete with each other in specific markets, which may be defined by geographic area, customer type, or product class. All ***horizontal*** agreements to divide markets have been declared illegal *per se* because they grant to the firm remaining in the market a monopolistic control over price. Thus, if RAC and Sonny, both manufacturers of color televisions, agree that RAC shall have the exclusive right to sell color televisions in Illinois and Iowa and that Sonny shall have the exclusive right in Minnesota and Wisconsin, RAC and Sonny have committed a *per se* violation of Section 1 of the Sherman Act. Likewise, if RAC and Sonny agree that RAC shall have the exclusive right to sell color televisions to Sears and that Sonny shall sell exclusively to JCPenney or that RAC shall have exclusive rights to manufacture 20-inch color televisions and that Sonny shall manufacture 13-inch sets, they are also in *per se* violation of Section 1 of the Sherman Antitrust Act.

No longer illegal *per se*, ***vertical*** territorial and customer restrictions are now judged by the rule of reason. This change in approach results from the Supreme Court's decision in *Continental T.V., Inc. v. GTE Sylvania, Inc.*, (1977), which mandated the lower federal courts to balance the positive effect of vertical market restrictions on interbrand competition against the negative effects on intraband competition. Consequently, in some situations, vertical territorial restrictions will be found legitimate if, on balance, they do not inhibit competition in the relevant market.

In 1985, the U.S. Department of Justice issued a "market structure screen," under which the department will challenge no restraints by a firm having a less than 10 percent share of the relevant market or a "Vertical Restraint Index" (a measure of relative market share) indicating that neither collusion nor exclusion is possible. We will discuss the concept of relevant market later, in the section on monopolization.

Boycotts As we noted earlier, Section 1 of the Sherman Act applies not to unilateral action but only to agreements or combinations. Accordingly, a seller's refusal to deal with any particular buyer does not violate the act; and a manufacturer can thus refuse to sell to a retailer who persists in selling below the manufacturer's suggested retail price. On the other hand, when two or more firms agree not to deal with a third party, their agreement represents a ***concerted refusal to deal***, or a group **boycott**, which may violate Section 1 of the Sherman Act. Such a boycott may be clearly anticompetitive, eliminating competition or reducing market entry.

Some group boycotts are illegal *per se* while others are subject to the rule of reason. Group boycotts designed to eliminate a competitor or to force that competitor to meet a group standard are illegal *per se* if the group has market power. On the other hand, cooperative arrangements "designed to increase economic efficiency and render markets more, rather than less, competitive" are subject to the rule of reason. Finally, most courts hold that the *per se* rule of illegality for concerted refusals to deal extends only to horizontal boycotts, not to vertical refusals to deal. Most courts have held that a rule of reason test should govern all nonprice vertical restraints, including concerted refusals to deal.

Practical Advice

When attending trade association meetings or other conferences with competitors, be extremely careful not to discuss pricing, refusals to deal with certain customers, and territorial emphases.

Tying Arrangements A **tying arrangement** occurs when the seller of a product, service, or intangible (the "tying" product) conditions its sale on the buyer's purchasing a second product, service, or intangible (the "tied" product) from the seller. For example, imagine that Xerox, a major manufacturer of photocopying equipment, required all purchasers of its photocopiers also to purchase from Xerox all of the paper they would use with the copiers. Xerox would thereby tie the sale of its photocopier—the *tying* product—to the sale of paper—the *tied* product.

Because tying arrangements limit buyers' freedom of choice and may exclude competitors, the law closely scrutinizes such agreements. A tying arrangement exists when a seller exploits its economic power in one market to expand its empire into another market. When the seller has considerable economic power in the tying product and more than an insubstantial amount of interstate commerce is affected in the tied product, the tying arrangement will be *per se* illegal. Economic power may be demonstrated by showing that (1) the seller occupied a dominant position in the tying market; (2) the seller's product enjoys an advantage not shared by its competitors in the tying market; or (3) a substantial number of customers have accepted the tying arrangement, and the only explanation for their willingness to comply is the seller's economic power in the tying market. If the seller lacks economic power, the tying arrangement is judged by the rule of reason test.

See the Ethical Dilemma later in this chapter.

Eastman Kodak Co. v. Image Technical Services, Inc.

United States Supreme Court, 1992

504 U.S. 451, 112 S.Ct. 2072, 119 L.Ed.2d 265

http://supct.law.cornell.edu/supct/html/90-1029.25.ZD.html

FACTS Eastman Kodak Co. **(http://www.kodak.com/)** manufactures and sells photocopiers and micrographic equipment. Kodak also services the equipment and sells replacement parts. Image Technical Services, Inc., is a group of independent service organizations (ISOs) that in the early 1980s began servicing Kodak equipment. Kodak subsequently established policies of selling parts only to buyers of the Kodak equipment who used Kodak service or who repaired their own machines. As part of the same policy, Kodak sought to limit ISO access to other sources of Kodak parts (such as those manufactured by original equipment manufacturers—OEMs). Kodak made an agreement with the OEMs not to sell parts to ISOs and pressured individual equipment owners and independent parts distributors not to sell Kodak parts. Kodak succeeded in its intention to restrict ISOs from servicing Kodak machines. Some ISOs were forced out of business; others lost significant revenue. Customers were forced to switch to Kodak service, even if they preferred ISO service.

In 1987, the ISOs filed an action alleging that Kodak had unlawfully tied the sale of service to the sale of parts, in violation of Section 1 of the Sherman Act, and had unlawfully monopolized and attempted to monopolize the sale of service for Kodak machines, in violation of Section 2 of the Sherman Act. Kodak filed for summary judgment.

DECISION Summary judgment denied.

OPINION Blackmun, J. A tying arrangement is "an agreement by a party to sell one product but only on the condition that the buyer also purchases a different (or tied) product, or at least agrees that he will not purchase that product from any other supplier." [Citation.] Such an arrangement violates § 1 of the Sherman Act if the seller has "appreciable economic power" in the tying product market and if the arrangement affects a substantial volume of commerce in the tied market. [Citation.]

Kodak did not dispute that its arrangement affects a substantial volume of interstate commerce. It, however, did challenge whether its activities constituted a "tying arrangement" and whether Kodak exercised "appreciable economic power" in the tying market. We consider these issues in turn.

For the respondents [ISOs] to defeat a motion for summary judgment on their claim of a tying arrangement, a reasonable trier of fact must be able to find, first, that service and parts are two distinct products, and, second, that Kodak has tied the sale of the two products.

For service and parts to be considered two distinct products, there must be sufficient consumer demand so that it is efficient for a firm to provide service separately from parts. [Citation.] Evidence in the record indicates that service and parts have been sold separately in the past and still are sold separately to self-service equipment owners. Indeed, the development of the entire high-technology service industry is evidence of the efficiency of a separate market for service.

Kodak insists that because there is no demand for parts separate from service, there cannot be separate markets for service and parts. By that logic, we would be forced to conclude that there can never be separate markets, for example, for cameras and film, computers and software, or automobiles and tires. That is an assumption we are unwilling to make.

* * *

Having found sufficient evidence of a tying arrangement, we consider the other necessary feature of an illegal tying arrangement: appreciable economic power in the tying market. Market power is the power "to force a purchaser to do something that he would not do in a competitive market." [Citation.] It has been defined as "the ability of a single seller to raise price and restrict output." [Citations.] The existence of such power ordinarily is inferred from the seller's possession of a predominant share of the market. [Citations.]

Respondents contend that Kodak has more than sufficient power in the parts market to force unwanted purchases of the tied market, service. Respondents provide evidence that certain parts are available exclusively through Kodak. Respondents also assert that Kodak has control over the availability of parts it does not manufacture. According to respondents' evidence, Kodak has prohibited independent manufacturers from selling Kodak parts to ISOs, pressured Kodak equipment owners and independent parts distributors to deny ISOs the purchase of Kodak parts, and taken steps to restrict the availability of used machines.

Respondents also allege that Kodak's control over the parts market has excluded service competition, boosted service prices, and forced unwilling consumption of Kodak service. Respondents offer evidence that consumers have switched to Kodak service even though they preferred ISO service, that Kodak service was of higher price and lower quality than the preferred ISO service, and that ISOs were driven out of business by Kodak's policies. Under our prior precedents, this evidence would be sufficient to entitle respondents to a trial on their claim of market power.

Kodak counters that even if it concedes monopoly share of the relevant parts market, it cannot actually exercise the necessary market power for a Sherman Act violation. This is so, according to Kodak, because competition exists in the equipment market. Kodak argues that it could not have the ability to raise prices of service and parts above the level that would be charged in a competitive market because any increase in profits from a higher price in the aftermarkets at least would be offset by a corresponding loss in profits from lower equipment sales as consumers began purchasing equipment with more attractive service costs.

* * *

The extent to which one market prevents exploitation of another market depends on the extent to which consumers will change their consumption of one product in response to a price change in another, i.e., the "cross-elasticity of demand." See *du Pont*, [citations]. Kodak's proposed rule rests on a factual assumption about the cross-elasticity of demand in the equipment and aftermarkets: "If Kodak raised its parts or service prices above competitive levels, potential customers would simply stop buying Kodak equipment. Perhaps Kodak would be able to increase short-term profits through such a strategy, but at a devastating cost to its long-term interests." Kodak argues that the Court should accept, as a matter of law, this "basic economic realit[y]," that competition in the equipment market necessarily prevents market power in the aftermarkets.

We conclude * * * that Kodak has failed to demonstrate that respondents' inference of market power in the service and parts markets is unreasonable, and that, consequently, Kodak is entitled to summary judgment. It is clearly reasonable to infer that Kodak has market power to raise prices and drive out competition in the aftermarkets, since respondents offer direct evidence that Kodak did so. It is also plausible, as discussed above, to infer that Kodak chose to gain immediate profits by exerting that market power where locked-in customers, high information costs, and discriminatory pricing limited and perhaps eliminated any long-term loss. Viewing the evidence in the light most favorable to respondents, their allegations of market power "mak[e] * * * economic sense." [Citation.]

* * *

We need not decide whether Kodak's behavior has any procompetitive effects and, if so, whether they outweigh the anticompetitive effects. We note only that Kodak's service and parts policy is simply not one that appears always or almost always to enhance competition, and therefore to warrant a legal presumption without any evidence of its actual economic impact. In this case, when we weigh the risk of deterring procompetitive behavior by proceeding to trial against the risk that illegal behavior go unpunished, the balance tips against summary judgment. [Citations.]

* * * We therefore affirm the denial of summary judgment on respondents' § 1 claim.

Respondents also claim that they have presented genuine issues for trial as to whether Kodak has monopolized or attempted to monopolize the service and parts markets in violation of § 2 of the Sherman Act. "The offense of monopoly under § 2 of the Sherman Act has two elements: (1) the possession of monopoly power in the relevant market and (2) the willful acquisition or maintenance of that power as distinguished from growth or development as a consequence of a superior product, business acumen, or historic accident." [Citation.]

The existence of the first element, possession of monopoly power, is easily resolved. As has been noted, respondents have presented a triable claim that service and parts are separate markets, and that Kodak has the "power to control prices or exclude competition" in service and parts. *du Pont*, [citation]. Monopoly power under § 2 requires, of course, something greater than market power under § 1. [Citation.] Respondents' evidence that Kodak controls nearly 100% of the parts market and 80% to 95% of the service market, with no readily available substitutes, is, however, sufficient to survive summary judgment under the more stringent monopoly standard of § 2. [Citations.]

Kodak also contends that, as a matter of law, a single brand of a product or service can never be a relevant market under the Sherman Act. We disagree. The relevant market for antitrust purposes is determined by the choices available to Kodak equipment owners. [Citation.] Because service and parts for Kodak equipment are not interchangeable with other manufacturers' service and parts, the relevant market from the Kodak-equipment owner's perspective is composed of only those companies that service Kodak machines. See *du Pont*, [citation] (the "market is composed of products that have reasonable interchangeability"). This Court's prior cases support the proposition that in some instances one brand of a product can constitute a separate market. [Citations.]

The second element of a § 2 claim is the use of monopoly power "to foreclose competition, to gain a competitive advantage, or to destroy a competitor." [Citation.] If Kodak adopted its parts and service policies as part of a scheme of willful acquisition or maintenance of monopoly power, it will have violated § 2. [Citations.]

As recounted at length above, respondents have presented evidence that Kodak took exclusionary action to maintain its parts monopoly and used its control over parts to strengthen its monopoly share of the Kodak service market. Liability turns, then, on whether "valid business reasons" can explain Kodak's actions. [Citations.] * * *

* * *

In the end, of course, Kodak's arguments may prove to be correct. It may be that its parts, service, and equipment are components of one unified market, or that the equipment market does discipline the aftermarkets so that all three are priced competitively overall, or that any anticompetitive effects of Kodak's behavior are outweighed by its competitive effects. * * *

INTERPRETATION One who possesses sufficient economic power in one market will not be permitted to gain unfair advantage in a different or tied market.

CRITICAL THINKING QUESTION Do you think tying arrangements are anticompetitive?

MONOPOLIES

Economic analysis indicates that a monopolist will use its power to limit production and increase prices. Therefore, a monopolistic market will produce fewer goods than a competitive market would and will sell these goods at higher prices. Addressing the problem of monopolization, Section 2 of the Sherman Act prohibits monopolies and any attempts or conspiracies to monopolize. Thus, Section 2 prohibits both agreements among businesses and, unlike Section 1, unilateral conduct by one firm.

Monopolization Although the language of Section 2 ostensibly prohibits *all* monopolies, the courts have required that a firm not only must possess market power but also must have attained the monopoly power unfairly or abused that power, once attained. By itself, the possession of monopoly power is not considered a violation of Section 2 because a firm may have obtained such power through its skills in developing, marketing, and selling products—that is, through the very competitive conduct that the antitrust laws are designed to promote.

Because it is extremely rare to find an unregulated industry with only one firm, determining the presence of monopoly power involves defining the degree of market dominance that constitutes such power. **Monopoly power** is the ability to control price or to exclude competitors from the marketplace. In grappling with this

CONCEPT REVIEW

Restraints of Trade under Sherman Act

Type of Restraint	Standard: *Per Se* Illegal	Standard: Rule of Reason
Price Fixing	Horizontal Vertical (Minimum)	Vertical (Maximum)
Market Allocations	Horizontal	Vertical
Group Boycotts or Refusals to Deal	Horizontal Vertical (Minority)	Vertical (Majority)
Tying Arrangements	If seller has economic power in tying product and affects a substantial amount of interstate commerce in the tied product	If seller lacks economic power in tying product

question of power, the courts have developed a number of criteria; but the most common test is market share. A market share greater than 75 percent generally indicates monopoly power, while a share less than 50 percent does not. A share between 50 and 75 percent is, in itself, inconclusive.

Market share is a firm's fractional share of the total relevant product and geographic markets, but defining these relevant markets is often a difficult and subjective project for the courts. The relevant *product market*, as demonstrated in the following case, includes products that are substitutable for the firm's product on the basis of price, quality, and adaptability for other purposes. For example, although brick and wood siding are both used on building exteriors, it is unlikely they would be considered part of the same product market. On the other hand, Coca-Cola and Seven-Up are both soft drinks and would be considered part of the same product market.

United States v. E.I. du Pont de Nemours & Co.

United States Supreme Court, 1956

351 U.S. 377, 76 S.Ct. 994, 100 L.Ed. 1264

http://laws.findlaw.com/US/351/377.html

FACTS In 1923, du Pont **(http://www.dupont.com/)** was granted the exclusive right to make and sell cellophane in North America. In 1927, the company introduced a moistureproof brand of cellophane that was ideal for various wrapping needs. Although more expensive than most competing wrapping, it offered a desired combination of transparency, strength, and cost. Except for its permeability to gases, however, cellophane had no qualities that a number of competing materials did not possess as well. Cellophane sales increased dramatically, and by 1950, du Pont produced almost 75 percent of the cellophane sold in the United States. Nevertheless, sales of the material constituted less than 20 percent of the sales of "flexible packaging materials."

The United States brought this action, contending that by so dominating cellophane production, du Pont had monopolized a part of trade or commerce in violation of the Sherman Act. Du Pont argued that it had not monopolized because it did not have the power to control the price of cellophane or to exclude competitors from the market for flexible wrapping materials. The government took a direct appeal from a ruling in favor of du Pont.

DECISION Judgment for du Pont affirmed.

OPINION Reed, J. Our cases determine that a party has monopoly power if it has, over "any part of the trade or commerce among the several states," a power of controlling prices or unreasonably restricting competition. * * * If cellophane is the "market" that du Pont is found to dominate, it may be assumed it does have monopoly power over that "market." Monopoly power is the power to control prices or exclude competition. It seems apparent that du Pont's power to set the price of cellophane has been limited only by the competition afforded by other flexible packaging materials.

* * *

Determination of the competitive market for commodities depends on how different from one another are the offered commodities in character or use, how far buyers will go to substitute one commodity for another. * * * Whatever the market may be, we hold that control of price or competition establishes the existence of monopoly power under § 2. Section 2 requires the application of a reasonable approach in determining the existence of monopoly power just as surely as did § 1. This of course does not mean that there can be a reasonable monopoly. Our next step is to determine whether du Pont has monopoly power over cellophane: that is, power over its price in relation to or competition with other commodities. The charge was monopolization of cellophane. The defense, that cellophane was merely a part of the relevant market for flexible packaging materials.

* * *

But where there are market alternatives that buyers may readily use for their purposes, illegal monopoly does not exist merely because the product said to be monopolized differs from others. If it were not so, only physically identical products would be a part of the market. To accept the Government's argument, we would have to conclude that the manufacturers of plain as well as moistureproof cellophane were monopolists, and so with films such as Pliofilm, foil, glassine, polyethylene, and Saran, for each of these wrapping materials is distinguishable. These were all exhibits in the case. New wrappings appear, generally similar to cellophane: is each a monopoly? What is called for is an appraisal of the "cross-elasticity" of demand in the trade. * * * In considering what is the relevant market for determining the control of price and competition, no more definite rule can be declared than that commodities reasonably interchangeable by consumers for the same purposes make up that "part of the trade or commerce," monopolization of which may be illegal. As respects flexible packaging materials, the market geographically is nationwide.

* * *

An element for consideration as to cross-elasticity of demand between products is the responsiveness of the sales of one product to price changes of the other. If a slight decrease in the price of cellophane causes a considerable number of customers of other flexible wrappings to switch to cellophane, it would be an indication that a high cross-elasticity of demand exists between them; that the products compete in the same market. The court below held that the "[g]reat sensitivity of customers in the flexible packaging markets to price or quality changes" prevented du Pont from possessing monopoly control over price. The record sustains these findings.

We conclude that cellophane's interchangeability with the other materials mentioned suffices to make it a part of this flexible packaging material market.

* * *

[T]he trial court found that du Pont could not exclude competitors even from the manufacture of cellophane, an immaterial matter if the market is flexible packaging material. Nor can we say that du Pont's profits, while liberal (according to the Government 15.9% net after taxes on the 1937–1947 average), demonstrate the existence of a monopoly without proof of lack of comparable profits during those years in other prosperous industries. Cellophane was a leader, over 17%, in the flexible packaging materials market. There is no showing that du Pont's rate of return was greater or less than that of other producers of flexible packaging materials.

The "market" which one must study to determine when a producer has monopoly power will vary with the part of commerce under consideration. The tests are constant. That market is composed of products that have reasonable interchangeability for the purposes for which they are produced—prices, use and qualities considered. While the application of the tests remains uncertain, it seems to us that du Pont should not be found to monopolize cellophane when that product has the competition and interchangeability with other wrappings that this record shows.

INTERPRETATION The relevant product includes products that are substituted for the firm's product on the basis of price, quality, and adaptability.

ETHICAL QUESTION Did the Court fairly decide this case? Explain.

CRITICAL THINKING QUESTION What factors should be considered in deciding the interchangeability of products? Explain.

The relevant *geographic market* is the territory in which the firm sells its products or services. This may be at the local, regional, or national level. For instance, the relevant geographic market for the manufacture and sale of aluminum might be national, whereas that of a taxi company would be local. The scope of a geographic market depends on factors such as transportation costs, the type of product or service, and the location of competitors and customers.

If sufficient monopoly power has been proved, the law must then show that the firm has engaged in ***unfair***

Ethical Dilemma

When Is an Agreement Anticompetitive?

FACTS Robert Crane has been hired as a manager of Sandra Renee, Inc., a prosperous fashion design manufacturer. A maker of women's dresses, Sandra Renee specializes in formal gowns. An important and growing segment of its business consists of renting gowns to retail chains. Because high prices often deter consumers from purchasing formalwear, the design industry as a whole has been benefiting from formal gown rentals. Under its rental arrangement, Sandra Renee receives a percentage from each rental. The rental also provides increased exposure and advertising for Sandra Renee.

Robert was sent to a meeting of the Association of Fashion Design Manufacturers. At the meeting, representatives from throughout the industry discussed the advantages of rentals; two members raised the question of what action should be taken if a retailer sold one of the gowns. After a brief debate, the members agreed that gowns should no longer be provided to such retailers. The representatives also discussed the different pricing mechanisms their respective firms used in dealing with renting retailers. They generally agreed that a flat dollar fee plus a significant percentage of the rental fee was the best pricing scheme.

Robert grew concerned that this discussion was inappropriate. But because he was new to the association, he was uncertain what to do. He considered voicing his objection, leaving the meeting, or staying but remaining silent.

Social, Policy, and Ethical Considerations

1. Was Robert's sense of discomfort with the discussion justified? Explain.
2. What action should Robert have taken?
3. Whose interests were at stake at this meeting? How might such a meeting affect the public, Sandra Renee, and the company's competitors?
4. To what extent should employees be informed about the ethical and legal obligations of trade associations before attending meetings such as this?
5. What actions are open to an employee who disagrees with a company position that violates the law?

conduct. However, the courts have yet to agree on what constitutes such conduct. One judicial approach is to place upon a firm possessing monopoly power the burden of proving that it acquired such power passively or that the power was "thrust" upon it. An alternative view is that monopoly power, combined with conduct designed to exclude competitors, violates Section 1. A third approach requires monopoly power plus some type of predatory practice, such as pricing below marginal costs. For example, one case that adopted the third approach held that a firm does not violate Section 2 of the Sherman Act if it attained its market share (1) through research, technical innovation, or a superior product or (2) through ordinary marketing methods available to all. In a decision that appears to combine these approaches, the Supreme Court has held that "[i]f a firm has been attempting to exclude rivals on some basis other than efficiency, it is fair to characterize its behavior as predatory."

To date, however, the U.S. Supreme Court has yet to identify the exact conduct, beyond the mere possession of monopoly power, that violates Section 2. To do so, the Court must resolve the complex and conflicting market and business policies this most basic question of monopolies involves.

Attempts to Monopolize Section 2 also prohibits **attempts to monopolize**. As with monopolization, the courts have had difficulty developing a standard that distinguishes undesirable conduct likely to engender a monopoly from healthy, competitive conduct. The standard test applied by the courts requires proof of a specific intent to monopolize plus a dangerous probability of success; however, among other things, this test neither defines an "intent" nor offers a standard of power by which to measure "success." Recent cases suggest that the greater the measure of market power a firm acquires, the less flagrant must its conduct be to constitute an attempt. These cases, however, do not specify any threshold level of market power.

Conspiracies to Monopolize Section 2 also condemns conspiracies to monopolize. Few cases involve this offense alone, as any conspiracy to monopolize would also constitute, in violation of Section 1, a combination in restraint of trade.

CLAYTON ACT

In 1914, Congress strengthened the Sherman Act by adopting the Clayton Act, which was expressly designed "to supplement existing laws against unlawful restraints and monopolies." The Clayton Act provides only for civil actions, not for criminal penalties. Private parties may bring civil actions in federal court for treble damages and attorneys' fees. In addition, the Justice Department and the Federal Trade Commission are authorized to bring civil actions, including proceedings in equity, to prevent and restrict violations of the act.

The major provisions of the Clayton Act deal with price discrimination, tying contracts, exclusive dealing, and mergers. Section 2, which deals with price discrimination, was amended and rewritten by the Robinson-Patman Act, which we will discuss later in the chapter. The Clayton Act exempts labor, agricultural, and horticultural organizations from all antitrust laws.

http:// Clayton Act: http://www4.law.cornell.edu/uscode/15/12.html

TYING CONTRACTS AND EXCLUSIVE DEALING

Section 3 of the Clayton Act prohibits **tying arrangements** and exclusive dealing, selling, or leasing arrangements that prevent purchasers from dealing with the seller's competitors when such arrangements *may* substantially lessen competition or *tend* to create a monopoly. This section is intended to stifle fledgling anticompetitive practices before they grow into violations of Section 1 or 2 of the Sherman Act. Unlike the Sherman Act, however, Section 3 applies only to practices involving commodities, not to those that involve services, intangibles, or land.

Tying arrangements, which we discussed earlier, have been labeled by the Supreme Court as serving "hardly any purpose beyond the suppression of competition." Although the Court at one time indicated that the standards applied under the Sherman Act differed from those applied under the Clayton Act, recent lower court cases suggest that the same rules now govern both types of actions.

Exclusive dealing arrangements are agreements by which the seller or lessor of a product conditions the agreement upon the buyer's or lessee's promise not to deal in a competitor's goods. For example, a manufacturer of razors might require retailers wishing to sell its line of shaving equipment to agree not to carry competing merchandise. Such conduct, although treated more leniently than tying arrangements, violates Section 3 if it tends to create a monopoly or may substantially lessen competition. The courts treat exclusive dealing arrangements more leniently because such arrangements may bolster competition to the extent that they benefit buyers, and thus, indirectly, the ultimate consumers, by ensuring supplies, deterring price increases, and enabling long-term planning on the basis of known costs.

MERGERS

In the United States, corporate mergers have helped to reshape both corporate structure and our economic system. **Mergers** are horizontal, vertical, or conglomerate, depending on the relationship between the acquirer and the company acquired. A **horizontal merger** involves a company's acquisition of all or part of the stock or assets of a competing company. For example, if IBM were to acquire Apple, this would be a horizontal merger. A **vertical merger** is a company's acquisition of one of its customers or suppliers. A vertical merger is a *forward* merger if the acquiring company purchases a *customer*, such as the purchase of Revco Discount Drug Stores by Procter & Gamble. A vertical merger is a *backward* merger if the acquiring company purchases a *supplier*; for example, IBM's purchase of a microchip manufacturer. The third type of merger, the **conglomerate merger**, is a catchall category that covers all acquisitions not involving a competitor, customer, or supplier.

Section 7 of the Clayton Act prohibits a corporation from merging or acquiring another corporation's stock or assets when such an action would substantially lessen competition or would tend to create a monopoly. Currently, the law regarding horizontal, vertical, and conglomerate mergers is, particularly with respect to the last two, in a state of flux.

The principal objective of the antitrust law governing mergers is to maintain competition. Accordingly, the courts scrutinize the legality of horizontal mergers most carefully. Factors that affect this review include the market share of each of the merging firms, the degree of industry concentration, the number of firms in the industry, entry barriers, market trends, the vigor and strength of other competitors in the industry, the character and history of the merging firms, market demand, and the extent of industry price competition. The leading Supreme Court cases on horizontal mergers date from the 1960s and early 1970s. Since then, lower federal courts, the Department of Justice, and the FTC have emphasized antitrust's goal of promoting economic efficiency. Accordingly, while the Supreme Court cases remain the law of the land, recent lower court decisions reflect a greater willingness to tolerate industry concentrations. Nevertheless, the government continues to prosecute, and the courts continue to condemn, horizontal mergers that are likely to harm consumers.

Hospital Corp. of America v. FTC

U.S. Court of Appeals, Seventh Circuit, 1986
807 F.2d 1381

FACTS Hospital Corporation of America (HCA) **(http://www.hcahealthcare.com)**, the largest proprietary hospital chain in the United States, originally owned one hospital in the Chattanooga, Tennessee, area. Between 1981 and 1982, at a cost of $700 million, HCA acquired two hospital corporations, which also owned or managed hospitals in the Chattanooga area. After this acquisition, HCA owned or managed five of the eleven hospitals in the area. This acquisition also raised HCA's market share in the Chattanooga area from 14 percent to 26 percent. This made HCA the second largest provider of hospital services in a highly concentrated market where the four largest firms now had a collective market share of 91 percent, compared with a preacquisition share of 79 percent. After investigation, the Federal Trade Commission (FTC) ruled that the acquisitions by HCA violated § 7 of the Clayton Act. HCA appealed.

DECISION Judgment for the FTC affirmed.

OPINION Posner, J. The commission may have made its task harder (and opinion longer) than strictly necessary * * * by studiously avoiding reliance on any of the [U.S.] Supreme Court's Section 7 decisions from the 1960s except [citation], which took an explicitly economic approach to the interpretation of the statute. The other decisions in that decade * * * seemed, taken as a group, to establish the illegality of any nontrivial acquisition of a competitor, whether or not the acquisition was likely either to bring about or shore up collusive or oligopoly pricing. The elimination of a significant rival was thought by itself to infringe the complex of social and economic values conceived by a majority of the Court to inform the statutory words "may * * * substantially * * * lessen competition."

None of these decisions has been overruled. * * *

The most important developments that cast doubt on the continued vitality of such [1960s] cases as [citations] are found in other cases, where the Supreme Court, echoed by the lower courts, has said repeatedly that the economic concept of competition, rather than any desire to preserve rivals as such, is the lodestar that shall guide the contemporary application of the antitrust laws, not excluding the Clayton Act. * * * Applied to cases brought under Section 7, this principle requires the district court (in this case, the Commission) to make a judgment whether the challenged acquisition is likely to hurt consumers, as by making it easier for the firms in the market to collude, expressly or tacitly, and thereby force prices above or further above the competitive level. So it was prudent for the Commission, rather than resting on the very strict merger decisions of the 1960s, to inquire into the probability of harm to consumers. * * *

When an economic approach is taken in a Section 7 case, the ultimate issue is whether the challenged acquisition is likely to facilitate collusion. In this perspective the acquisition of a competitor has no economic significance in itself; the worry is that it may enable the acquiring firm to cooperate (or cooperate better) with other leading competitors on reducing or limiting output, thereby pushing up the market price. * * * There is plenty of evidence to support the Commission's prediction of adverse competitive effect in this case. * * *

The acquisitions reduced the number of competing hospitals in the Chattanooga market from 11 to 7. * * *

The reduction in the number of competitors is significant in assessing the competitive vitality of the Chattanooga hospital market. The fewer competitors there are in a market, the easier it is for them to coordinate their pricing without committing detectable violations of Section 1 of the Sherman Act, which forbids price fixing. This would not be very important if the four competitors eliminated by the acquisitions in this case had been insignificant, but they were not; they accounted in the aggregate for 12 percent of the sales of the market. As a result of the acquisitions, the four largest firms came to control virtually the whole market, and the problem of coordination was therefore reduced to one of coordination among these four.

Moreover, both the ability of the remaining firms to expand their output should the big four reduce their own output in order to raise the market price (and, by expanding, to offset the leading firms' restriction of their own output), and the ability of outsiders to come in and build completely new hospitals, are reduced by Tennessee's certificate-of-need law. Any addition to hospital capacity must be approved by a state agency.

* * *

In showing that the challenged acquisitions gave four firms control over an entire market so that they would have little reason to fear a competitive reaction if they raised prices above the competitive level, the Commission went far to justify its prediction of probable anticompetitive effects. Maybe it need have gone no further. [Citations.] But it did. First it pointed out that the demand for hospital services by patients and their doctors is highly inelastic under competitive conditions. This is not only because people place a high value on their safety and comfort and because many of their treatment decisions are made for them by their doctor, who doesn't pay their hospital bills; it is also because most hospital bills are paid largely by insurance companies or the federal government rather than by the patient. The less elastic the demand for a good or service is, the greater are the profits that providers can make by raising price through collusion. * * *

Second, there is a tradition, well documented in the Commission's opinion, of cooperation between competing hospitals in Chattanooga. * * * But a market in which competitors are unusually disposed to cooperate is a market prone to collusion. * * *

Third, hospitals are under great pressure from the federal government and the insurance companies to cut costs. One way of resisting this pressure is by presenting a united front in negotiations with the third-party payors * * *. The fewer the independent competitors in a hospital market, the easier they will find it, by presenting an unbroken phalanx of representations and requests, to frustrate efforts to control hospital costs. This too is a form of collusion that the antitrust laws seek to discourage * * *.

All these considerations, taken together, supported * * * the Commission's conclusion that the challenged acquisitions are likely to foster collusive practices, harmful to consumers, in the Chattanooga hospital market. Section 7 does not require proof that a merger or other acquisition has caused higher prices in the affected market. All that is necessary is that the merger create an appreciable danger of such consequences in the future. A predictive judgment, necessarily probabilistic and judgmental rather than demonstrable [citation].

INTERPRETATION A merger is illegal if it tends to create a monopoly or would substantially lessen competition.

ETHICAL QUESTION Did the Court fairly decide this case? Explain.

CRITICAL THINKING QUESTION Do you agree that the government sufficiently proved its case? Explain.

Though far less likely to challenge vertical mergers, the Justice Department and the FTC will attack vertical mergers that are likely to raise entry barriers in the industry or to bar other firms in the acquiring firm's industry from competitively significant customers or suppliers. Although the Supreme Court has not decided a vertical merger case since 1972, recent decisions indicate that at least some lower courts have been willing to condemn only those vertical mergers that clearly show anticompetitive effects.

Finally, conglomerate mergers have been challenged only (1) when one of the merging firms would be highly likely to enter the other firm's market or (2) when the merged company would be disproportionately large, compared with the largest competitors in its industry.

The Justice Department and the FTC have both indicated that they will be primarily concerned with horizontal mergers in highly or moderately concentrated industries and that they question the benefits of challenging vertical and conglomerate mergers. Both the Justice Department and the FTC have justified this policy on the basis that the latter two types of mergers are necessary to transfer assets to their most productive use and that any challenge to such mergers would impose costs on consumers without corresponding benefits.

Antitrust law, as currently applied, focuses on the size of the merged firm in relation to the relevant market, not on the resulting entity's absolute size. In 1992 (subsequently revised in 1997), the Justice Department and the Federal Trade Commission jointly issued new Horizontal Merger Guidelines to replace their earlier and separate guidelines. In doing so, the two agencies sought to prevent market power that results in "a transfer of wealth from buyers to sellers or a misallocation of resources." The guidelines are designed to provide an analytical framework to judge the impact of potential mergers:

> The process of assessing market concentration, potential adverse competitive effects, entry, efficiency and failure is a tool that allows the Agency to answer the ultimate inquiry in merger analysis: whether the merger is likely to create or enhance market power or to facilitate its exercise.

Moreover, the guidelines clearly indicate that neither agency will apply them mechanically.

The 1992 and 1997 guidelines, like their earlier counterparts, quantify market concentration through the Herfindahl-Hirschman Index (HHI) and measure a horizontal merger's impact on the index. This concentration index is calculated by summing the squares of the individual market shares of all firms in the market. An industry with only one firm would have an HHI of 10,000 (1002). With two firms of equal size, the index would be 5,000 (502 + 502); with five firms of equal size, the result would be 2,000 (202 + 202 + 202 + 202 + 202). The increase a merger would cause in the index is calculated by doubling the product of the merging firms' market shares. For example, the merger of two firms with market shares of 5 percent and 10 percent respectively would increase the index by 100 ($5 \times 10 \times 2 = 100$).

The guidelines use three categories of market concentration to analyze horizontal mergers and to determine the likelihood of governmental opposition, based on the increase the proposed merger would cause in the index. The three categories are classified according to the postmerger HHI. If the postmerger figure is below 1,000, the agencies are unlikely to challenge the merger without regard to the increase the merger would cause in the index. For postmerger HHIs between 1,000 and 1,800, the department will examine the increase in HHI due to the merger. Increases of less than 100 are unlikely to generate a challenge, but those greater than 100 raise significant competitive concerns that mandate an examination of other factors. When the postmerger HHI is above 1,800, an increase of more than 50 points also will raise significant competitive concerns and thus force an examination of other factors; furthermore, the department is likely to challenge any merger contributing an increase of more than 100, for such a merger is *presumed* to enhance market power.

In 1987, the National Association of Attorney Generals, composed of the attorneys general of the fifty states and five U.S. territories and protectorates, promulgated its own set of guidelines for horizontal mergers. Intended to apply to enforcement actions brought by the state attorneys general under federal and state antitrust statutes, the state guidelines place a greater emphasis on preventing transfers of wealth from consumers to producers than do the federal guidelines. Accordingly, the state attorneys general would be more likely to challenge certain mergers would the federal government.

http:// Herfindahl-Hirschman Index http://www.usdoj.gov/atr/public/guidelines/merger.txt

Practical Advice

When considering potential merger targets, make sure to take into consideration the Herfindahl-Hirschman Index and the impact of the merger on the Index.

ROBINSON-PATMAN ACT

Originally, Section 2 of the Clayton Act prohibited sellers only from differentially pricing their products in order to injure local or regional competitors. In 1936, in an attempt to limit the power of large purchasers, Congress amended Section 2 of the Clayton Act by adopting the Robinson-Patman Act, which further prohibits **price discrimination** in interstate commerce concerning commodities of like grade and quality. More specifically, the act prohibits buyers from inducing and sellers from granting discrimination in prices. In order to constitute a violation, the price discrimination must substantially lessen competition or tend to create a monopoly.

Under this act, a seller of goods may not grant discounts to buyers, including allowances for advertisements, counter displays, and samples, unless the seller offers the same discounts to all other purchasers on proportionately equal terms. The act also prohibits other types of discounts, rebates, and allowances and makes it unlawful to sell goods at unreasonably low prices for the purpose of destroying competition or eliminating a competitor. The act also makes it unlawful for a person knowingly to "induce or receive" an illegal discrimination in price, thus imposing liability on the buyer as well as the seller. Violation of the Robinson-Patman Act, with limited exceptions, is civil, not criminal, in nature. Price differentials may be justified by proof of either a cost savings to the seller or a good faith price reduction to meet a competitor's lawful price.

http:// Robinson-Patman Act: http://www4.law.cornell.edu/uscode/15/13.html

PRIMARY-LINE INJURY

In enacting Section 2 of the Clayton Act in 1914, Congress was concerned with sellers who sought to harm or eliminate their competitors through price discrimination. Injuries accruing to a seller's competitors are called **"primary-line" injuries**. Because the act forbids price discrimination only when such discrimination may substantially lessen competition or may tend to create a monopoly, the plaintiff in a Robinson-Patman primary-line injury case either must show that the defendant, with the intention of harming competition, has engaged in predatory pricing or must present a detailed market analysis that demonstrates how the defendant's price discrimination actually harmed competition. To prove predatory intent, a plaintiff may rely either on direct evidence of such intent or, more commonly, on inferences drawn from the defendant's conduct, such as below-cost or unprofitable pricing for a significant period of time. A predatory pricing scheme may also be challenged under the Sherman Act.

SECONDARY- AND TERTIARY-LINE INJURY

In amending Section 2 of the Clayton Act through the adoption of the Robinson-Patman Act, Congress was

THE LAW AND YOU

State Bar Associations

Kansas: http://www.accesskansas.org/ksag/contents/consumer/main.htm ("Consumer Protection & Antitrust Annual Reports")

U.S. Government

http://www.pueblo.gsa.gov/cic_text/misc/antitrust/antitrus.htm ("Antitrust Enforcement and the Consumer")

http://www.ftc.gov/bc/compguide/index.htm ("Promoting Competition, Protecting Consumers: A Plain English Guide to Antitrust Laws")

http://www.ftc.gov/bc/guidelin.htm ("FTC Guidelines")

http://www.usdoj.gov/05publications/05_3. html ("Antitrust Enforcement and the Consumer")

concerned primarily with small buyers, who were harmed by the discounts that sellers granted to large buyers. Injuries that accrue to some buyers because of the lower prices granted to others are called "secondary-line" injuries. To prove the required harm to competition, a plaintiff in a **secondary-line injury** case either must show substantial and sustained intramarket price differentials or must offer a detailed market analysis that demonstrates actual harm to competition. Because courts have been willing in secondary-line injury cases to infer harm to competition from a sustained and substantial price differential, proving a secondary-line injury is generally easier than proving a primary-line injury.

Tertiary-line injury occurs when the recipient of a favored price passes the benefits of the lower price on to the next level of distribution. Purchasers from other secondary-line sellers are injured in that they do not receive the benefits of the lower price; these purchasers may recover damages from the original discriminating seller.

COST JUSTIFICATION

If a seller can show that it costs less to sell a product to a particular buyer, the seller may lawfully pass along the cost savings. Section 2(a) provides that the Clayton Act does not "prevent differentials which make only due allowance for differences in the cost of manufacture, sale, or delivery resulting from the differing methods or quantities in which . . . commodities are . . . sold or delivered." For example, if Retailer A orders goods from Seller X by the carload, whereas Retailer B orders in small quantities, Seller X, who delivers F.O.B. buyer's warehouse, may pass along the transportation savings to Retailer A. Nonetheless, although it is possible to pass along transportation savings, passing along alleged savings in manufacturing or distribution is extremely difficult because calculating and proving such savings is a complex task. Therefore, sellers rarely rely upon the defense of cost justification.

MEETING COMPETITION

A seller may lower its price in a good faith attempt to meet competition. To illustrate:

1. Manufacturer X sells its motor oil to retail outlets for 65 cents per can. Manufacturer Y approaches A, one of Manufacturer X's customers, and offers to sell a comparable type of motor oil for 60 cents per can. Manufacturer X will be permitted to lower its price to A to 60 cents per can and need not lower its price to its other retail customers—B, C, and D. However, Manufacturer X may not lower its price to A to 55 cents unless it also offers this price to B, C, and D.
2. Manufacturer X will not be permitted to lower its price to A without also lowering its price to B, C, and D, in order to allow A to meet the lower price A's competitor, N, charges when selling Manufacturer Y's oil. The "meeting competition" defense is available only to meet the competition of the seller: the defense does not extend to a competitor's price to a specific, individual purchaser (see Figure 43-1).

A seller may beat its competitor's price, however, if it does not know the competitor's price, cannot reasonably determine the competitor's price, and acts reasonably in setting its own price.

Figure 43-1
Meeting Competition Defense

Illustration One

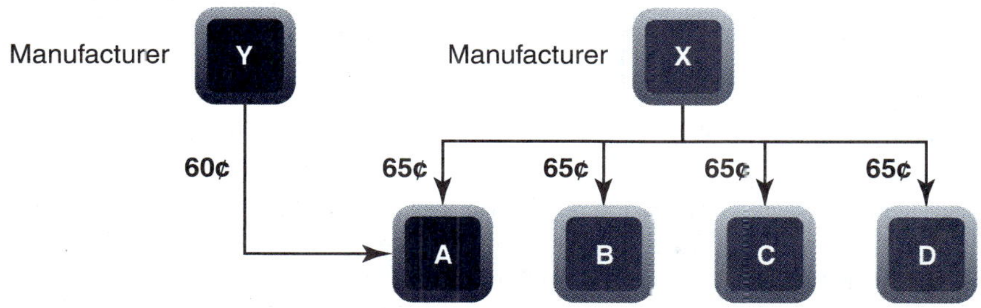

Result: Manufacturer **X** may lower its price to A to 60¢ without lowering its price to B, C, and D.

Illustration Two

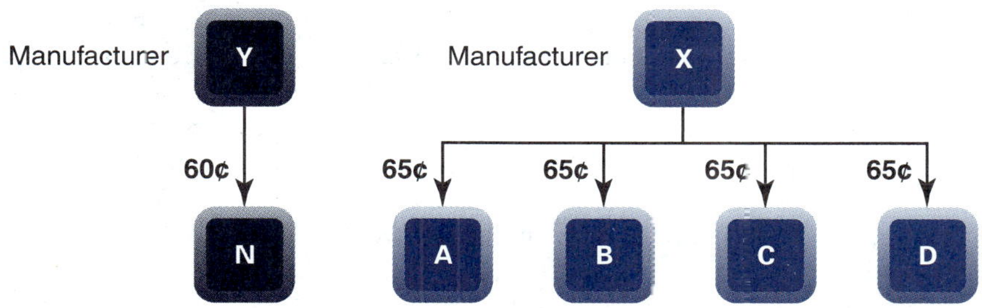

Result: Manufacturer **X** may *not* lower its price to A to 60¢ without lowering its price to B, C, and D.

FEDERAL TRADE COMMISSION ACT

In 1914, through the enactment of the **Federal Trade Commission Act**, Congress created the Federal Trade Commission (FTC), charged with preventing unfair methods of competition and unfair or deceptive acts or practices in commerce. To this end, the five-member commission is empowered to conduct appropriate investigations and hearings and to issue against violators cease and desist orders that are enforceable in the federal courts. The Supreme Court has commented on the breadth of the commission's power:

> The "unfair methods of competition," which are condemned by . . . the Act, are not confined to those that were illegal at common law or that were condemned by the Sherman Act. . . . It is also clear that the Federal Trade Commission Act was designed to supplement and bolster the Sherman Act and the Clayton Act . . . *to stop in their incipiency acts and practices which, when full blown, would violate those Acts.* (Emphasis added.)

Complaints may be instituted by the FTC, which, after a hearing, "has wide latitude for judgment and the courts will not interfere except where the remedy selected has no reasonable relation to the unlawful practices found to exist." Although the FTC most frequently enters a cease and desist order having the effect of an injunction, it may order other relief, such as affirmative disclosure, corrective advertising, and the granting of patent licenses on a reasonable royalty basis. Appeals may be taken from orders of the FTC to the United States Courts of Appeals, which have exclusive jurisdiction to enforce, set aside, or modify FTC orders.

In performing its duties, the FTC investigates not only possible violations of the antitrust laws but also unfair methods of competition. For a more detailed discussion of the FTC and its powers, see Chapter 45.

http:// Federal Trade Commission Act: http://www4.law.cornell.edu/uscode/15/41.html

CHAPTER SUMMARY

Sherman Antitrust Act

Restraint of Trade Section 1 prohibits contracts, combinations, and conspiracies that restrain trade
- ***Rule of Reason*** standard that balances the anticompetitive effects against the procompetitive effects of the restraint
- **Per Se *Violations*** conclusively presumed unreasonable and therefore illegal
- ***Quick Look Standard*** a modified or abbreviated rule of reason standard
- ***Horizontal Restraints*** agreements among competitors
- ***Vertical Restraints*** agreements among parties at different levels in the chain of distribution

Application of Section 1
- ***Price Fixing*** an agreement with the purpose or effect of inhibiting price competition; both horizontal and minimum vertical agreements are *per se* illegal, while maximum vertical price fixing is judged by the rule of reason
- ***Market Allocation*** division of markets by customer type, geography, or products; horizontal agreements are *per se* illegal, while vertical agreements are judged by the rule of reason standard
- ***Boycott*** agreement among competitors not to deal with a supplier or customer; *per se* illegal
- ***Tying Arrangement*** conditioning a sale of a desired product (tying product) on the buyer's purchasing a second product (tied product); *per se* illegal if the seller has considerable power in the tying product or affects a more than insubstantial amount of interstate commerce in the tied product

Monopolies Section 2 prohibits monopolization, attempts to monopolize, and conspiracies to monopolize
- ***Monopolization*** requires market power (ability to control or exclude others from the marketplace) plus either the unfair attainment of the power or the abuse of such power
- ***Attempt to Monopolize*** specific intent to monopolize, plus a dangerous probability of success
- ***Conspiracies to Monopolize***

Sanctions
- ***Treble Damages*** three times actual loss
- ***Criminal Penalties***

Clayton Act

Tying Arrangement prohibited if it tends to create a monopoly or may substantially lessen competition

Exclusive Dealing arrangement by which a party has sole right to a market; prohibited if it tends to create a monopoly or may substantially lessen competition

Merger prohibited if it tends to create a monopoly or may substantially lessen competition
- ***Horizontal Merger*** one company's acquisition of a competing company
- ***Vertical Merger*** a company's acquisition of one of its suppliers or customers
- ***Conglomerate Merger*** the acquisition of a company that is not a competitor, customer, or supplier

Sanctions treble damages

Robinson-Patman Act

Price Discrimination the act prohibits buyers from inducing or sellers from giving different prices to buyers of commodities of similar grade and quality

Injury plaintiff may prove injury to competitors of the seller (primary-line injury), to competitors of other buyers (secondary-line injury), or to purchasers from other secondary-line sellers (tertiary-line injury)

Defenses (1) cost justification, (2) meeting competition, and (3) functional discounts

Sanctions civil (treble damages); criminal in limited situations

Federal Trade Commission Act

Purpose to prevent unfair methods of competition and unfair or deceptive practices

Sanctions actions may be brought by the FTC, not by private individuals

QUESTIONS

1. Discuss the validity and effect of each of the following situations:
   a. A, B, and C, manufacturers of radios, orally agree that due to the disastrous, cutthroat competition in the market, they will establish a reasonable price to charge their purchasers.
   b. A, B, C, and D, newspaper publishers, agree not to charge their customers more than 30 cents per newspaper.
   c. A, a distiller of liquor, and B, A's retail distributor, agree that B should charge a price of $5 per bottle.

2. Discuss the validity of the following:
   a. A territorial allocation agreement between two manufacturers of the same type of products, whereby neither will sell its products in the area allocated to the other.
   b. An agreement between manufacturer and distributor not to sell a dealer a particular product or parts necessary for the product's repair.

3. Universal Video sells $40 million worth of video recording equipment in the United States. The total sales of such equipment in the United States is $100 million. One half of Universal's sales are to Giant Retailer, a company that possesses 50 percent of the retail market. Giant is presently seeking (1) to obtain an exclusive dealing arrangement with Universal or (2) to acquire Universal. Advise Giant as to the validity of its alternatives.

4. Z sells cameras to A, B, C, and D for $60 per camera. Y, one of Z's competitors, sells a comparable camera to A for $58.50. Z, in response to this competitive pressure from Y, lowers its price to A to $58.50. B, C, and D insist that Z lower its price to them to $58.50, but Z refuses. B, C, and D sue Z for unlawful price discrimination. Decision? Would your answer differ if Z reduced its price to A to $58?

5. Discount is a discount appliance chain store that continually sells goods at a price below manufacturers' suggested retail prices. A, B, and C, the three largest manufacturers of appliances, agree that unless Discount ceases its discount pricing, they will no longer sell to Discount. Discount refuses, and A, B, and C refuse to sell to Discount. Discount contends that A, B, and C are in violation of antitrust law. Explain whether Discount is correct.

6. Taylor Company produces 77 percent of the coal used in the United States. Coal provides 25 percent of the energy used in the United States. In a suit brought by the United States against Taylor for violation of the antitrust laws, what is the result?

7. Whirlpool Corporation (http://www.whirlpool.com/) manufactured vacuum cleaners under both its own name and under the Kenmore name. Oreck (http://www.oreck.com/) exclusively distributed the vacuum cleaners sold under the Whirlpool name. Sears, Roebuck & Co. (http://www.sears.com) exclusively distributed the Kenmore vacuum cleaners. Oreck alleged that its exclusive distributorship agreement with Whirlpool was not renewed because an unlawful conspiracy existed between Whirlpool and Sears. Oreck further contended that a *per se* rule was applicable because the agreement was (a) price fixing or (b) a group boycott, or both. Who should prevail? Why?

8. Indian Coffee of Pittsburgh, Pennsylvania, marketed vacuum-packed coffee under the Breakfast Cheer brand name in the Pittsburgh and Cleveland, Ohio, areas. Later in 1971, Folger Coffee (http://www.folgers.com/), a leading coffee seller, began selling coffee in Pittsburgh. In order to make inroads into the new territory, Folger sold its coffee at greatly reduced prices. At first, Indian Coffee met Folger's prices but could not continue operating at such a reduced price and was forced out of the market. Indian Coffee brings an antitrust action. Explain whether Folger has violated the Sherman Act.

9. Justin Manufacturing Company sells high-fashion clothing under the prestigious "Justin" label. The company has a

firm policy that it will not deal with any company that sells below its suggested retail price. Justin is informed by one of its customers, XYZ, that its competitor, Duplex, is selling the "Justin" line at a great discount. Justin now demands that Duplex comply with the agreement not to sell the "Justin" line below the suggested retail price. Discuss the implications of this situation.

10. Jay Corporation, the largest manufacturer of bicycles in the United States with 40 percent of the market, has recently entered into an agreement with Retail Bike, the largest retailer of bicycles in the United States with 37 percent of the market, under which Jay will furnish its bicycles only to Retail, and Retail will sell only Jay's bicycles. The government is now questioning this agreement. Discuss.

CASE PROBLEMS

11. Von's Grocery (http://www.safeway.com/corp_home.asp), a large retail grocery chain in Los Angeles, sought to acquire Shopping Bag Food Stores, a direct competitor. At the time of the proposed merger, Von's sales ranked third in the Los Angeles area and Shopping Bag's ranked sixth. Both chains were increasing their number of stores. The merger would have created the second largest grocery chain in Los Angeles, with total sales in excess of $170 million. Prior to the proposed merger, the number of owners operating single stores declined from 5,365 in 1950 to 3,590 by 1963. During this same period, the number of chains with two or more stores rose from 96 to 150. The United States brought suit against Von's to prevent the merger, claiming that the proposed merger violated Section 7 of the Clayton Act in that it could result in the substantial lessening of competition or could tend to create a monopoly. What should be the result?

12. Boise Cascade Corporation (http://www.bc.com/) is a wholesaler and retailer of office products. The Federal Trade Commission issued a complaint charging that Boise had violated the Robinson-Patman Act by receiving a wholesaler's discount from certain suppliers on products that Boise resold at retail, in competition with other retailers that could not obtain wholesale discounts. Has the Robinson-Patman Act been violated? Explain.

13. Zenith (http://www.zenith.com/), an American manufacturer of television sets, and National Union Electric Corporation (NUE), the successor company to an American television-manufacturing firm that had since withdrawn from the market, sued twenty-one Japanese-controlled corporations that manufactured or sold consumer electronic products (CEP), claiming that these petitioners/defendants, over a twenty-year period, had legally conspired to drive American firms from the American CEP market by engaging in a scheme to fix and maintain artificially high prices for television sets sold by the petitioners in Japan, while simultaneously maintaining low prices for sets exported to and sold in the United States. The respondents claimed that such activity was concerted action in violation of Section 1 of the Sherman Act. Is there a restraint of trade in this situation? Explain.

14. Great Atlantic and Pacific Tea Company (http://www.aptea.com/) desired to achieve cost savings by switching to the sale of "private label" milk. A&P asked Borden Company, its longtime supplier of "brand label" milk, to submit a bid to supply certain A&P private label dairy products. A&P was not satisfied with Borden's bid, however, so it solicited other offers. Bowman Dairy, a competitor of Borden's, submitted a lower bid. At this point, A&P contacted Borden and asked it to rebid on the private label contract. A&P included a warning that Borden would have to lower its original bid substantially in order to undercut Bowman's bid. Borden offered a bid that doubled A&P's potential annual cost savings. A&P accepted Borden's bid. The Federal Trade Commission then brought this action, charging that A&P had violated the Robinson-Patman Act by knowingly inducing or receiving illegal price discrimination from Borden. Discuss whether the FTC is correct in its allegations.

15. Clorox (http://www.clorox.com/) is the nation's leading manufacturer of household liquid bleach (accounting for 49 percent—$40,000,000—of sales annually) and is the only brand sold nationally. Clorox and its next largest competitor, Purex (http://www.dialcorp.com/brand/purex/), hold 65 percent of national sales; and the top four bleach manufacturers control 80 percent of sales. Because all bleach is chemically identical, Clorox spends more than $5,000,000 each year in advertising to attract and keep customers.

Procter & Gamble (http://www.pg.com/main.jhtml) is the dominant national manufacturer of household cleaning products, with yearly sales of $1.1 billion. As with bleach, advertising is vital in the household cleaning products industry. Procter & Gamble annually spends more than $127,000,000 in advertising and promotions. Procter & Gamble decided to diversify into the bleach business because its household cleaning products and bleach are both low-cost, high-turnover consumer goods, are dependent on mass advertising, and are sold to the same customers at the same stores by the same merchandising methods. Procter & Gamble decided to merge with Clorox, rather than start its own bleach division, in order to secure the dominant position in the bleach market immediately. Should the FTC take action against this merger, and, if so, what decision should it make?

16. The NCAA (http://www.ncaa.org/) adopted a plan for televising college football games in order to reduce the adverse effect of TV coverage on spectator attendance. The plan limited the total number of televised intercollegiate football games and the number of games any one school could televise. No member of the NCAA was permitted to sell any television rights except in accordance with the plan. As part of the plan, the NCAA had agreements with the American Broadcasting Company (ABC) (http://abc.go.com/) and the

Columbia Broadcasting System (CBS) (http://cbs.com/) to pay to each school at least a specified minimum price for televising football games. Several member universities now join to bring suit against the NCAA, claiming the new plan is a horizontal price fixing agreement and output limitation and as such is illegal per se. The NCAA counters that the existence of the product, college football, depends upon member compliance with restrictions and regulations. According to the NCAA, its restrictions, including the TV plan, have a procompetitive effect. Is the TV plan valid? Explain.

17. The National Society of Professional Engineers (Society) (http://www.nspe.org/) had an ethics rule that prohibited member engineers from disclosing or discussing price/fee information with customers until after the customer had hired a particular engineer. This rule against competitive bidding was designed to maintain high standards in the field of engineering. The Society felt that competitive pressure to offer engineering services at the lowest possible price would encourage engineers to design and specify inefficient, unsafe, and unnecessarily expensive structures and construction methods. According to the Society, awarding engineering contracts to the lowest bidder, regardless of quality, would be dangerous to the public health, safety, and welfare. The Society emphasizes that the rule is not an agreement to fix prices. Rather, it claims the rule was drafted by experienced, highly trained professional engineers to prevent public harm and is therefore reasonable. Does the rule unreasonably restrain trade and thus violate § 1 of the Sherman Act? Why?

18. In the early 1930s, intense price competition characterized both the retail and the wholesale oil markets. At times, prices in the wholesale market fell below the manufacturer's cost. One cause of the volatile situation was the supply of "distress gasoline" placed on the market by seventeen independent refiners. These independent refiners had no retail sales outlets and little storage capacity, so they were forced to sell their product at "distress prices." In spite of their unprofitable operations, they could not afford to shut down, for, if they did so, they would be apt to lose both their oil connections in the field and their regular customers.

In an attempt to remedy this problem, the major oil companies entered into an informal agreement whereby each selected as its "dancing partner" one or more independent refiners having distress gasoline. The major oil company would then assume responsibility for purchasing the independent's distress supply at the "fair going market price." As a result, the market price of oil rose in 1935 and 1936, and the spot market became stable. Have the companies engaged in horizontal price fixing in violation of the Sherman Act? Why?

19. As part of a corporate plan to stimulate sagging color television sales, GTE Sylvania began to phase out its wholesale distributors and began to sell its television sets directly to a smaller and more select group of franchised retailers. To this end, Sylvania limited the number of franchises granted for any given area and required each franchisee to sell Sylvania products only from the location or locations at which he was franchised. A franchise did not constitute an exclusive territory, and Sylvania retained sole discretion to increase the number of retailers in an area in light of the success or failure of existing retailers. The strategy apparently was successful, as Sylvania's national market share increased from less than 2 percent to 5 percent.

In the course of carrying out its plan, Sylvania franchised Young Brothers as a television retailer at a San Francisco location one mile from that of Continental T.V., Inc., one of Sylvania's most successful franchisees. A course of feuding began between Sylvania and Continental that reached a head when Continental requested permission to open a store in Sacramento, and Sylvania refused. Continental opened the Sacramento store anyway and began shipping merchandise there from its San Jose warehouse. Shortly thereafter, Sylvania terminated Continental's franchise. Is the franchise location restriction a *per se* violation of the Sherman Act? Explain.

20. Certified registered nurse anesthetists (CRNAs) compete with physician-anesthesiologists (MDAs) to provide anesthesia services. BCB Anesthesia Care, Ltd. (BCB) is owned by three CRNAs who, prior to July 29, 1991, were employed by Passavant Memorial Area Hospital Association (Passavant). Prior to July 29, 1991, Dr. Peter Roodhouse, a physician-anesthesiologist working as an independent contractor, provided anesthesia services at the hospital. On July 29, 1991, BCB entered into an agreement with Passavant to provide anesthesia services to Passavant's patients, billing the patients directly.

During the last five months of 1991, BCB and other staff physicians performed all but three anesthesia procedures at the hospital. However, BCB alleges that Dr. Roodhouse billed patients and third-party payers for services he did not perform, causing patients to complain about double billing and interfering with BCB's ability to collect payments. Dr. Roodhouse also derided BCB's billing practices to local physicians, causing them to believe that BCB billings were either too high or unethical. Beginning in April 1992, Dr. Roodhouse scheduled anesthesia services at the hospital so as to perform the majority of those services during that month. On May 20, 1992, Passavant terminated its contract with BCB. Subsequently, Passavant entered into an agreement with Dr. Roodhouse and raised the price it charged patients for anesthesia from $11 to $17 per unit.

Does this conduct constitute an illegal (a) conspiracy in restraint of trade, (b) tying agreement between Passavant and Dr. Roodhouse, (c) boycott of the nurse anesthetists, or (d) price fixing agreement? Explain.

http:// **Internet Exercise** At the home pages for the Federal Trade Commission and the Department of Justice, explore the business and consumer issues these two agencies are currently examining.

CHAPTER 44

Accountants' Legal Liability

It is not uncommon these days to hear expressions of grave concern within our [the accounting] profession about excessive competition, unrestrained solicitation, concentration and a general decline in intraprofessional courtesy. . . . These concerns have led some to worry that our professionalism is either dead or teetering on the brink of extinction.

WALLACE E. OLSON, "IS PROFESSIONALISM DEAD?"
THE JOURNAL OF ACCOUNTANCY, JULY 1978

Learning Objectives

After reading this chapter you should be able to:

1. Describe the contract liability of an accountant to her client.
2. Describe for what and to whom an accountant has tort liability.
3. Describe who owns the working papers an accountant generates and whether client information is privileged.
4. Discuss the potential civil and criminal liability of an accountant under the 1933 Securities Act.
5. Discuss the potential civil and criminal liability of an accountant under the 1934 Securities Act.

An accountant is subject to potential civil liability arising from the professional services he provides to his clients and third parties. This legal liability is imposed by both the common law at the state level and by federal securities laws. In addition, an accountant may violate federal and state criminal law through the performance of his professional activities. In this chapter, we will discuss accountants' legal liability under both state and federal law.

CPA COMMON LAW

An accountant's legal responsibility under state law may be based on (1) contract law, (2) tort law, or (3) criminal law. In addition, the common law gives accountants certain rights and privileges; in particular, the ownership of their working papers and, in some states, a limited accountant-client privilege.

CONTRACT LIABILITY

The employment contract between an accountant and client is subject to the general principles of contract law. All of the requirements of a common law contract must be present for the contract to be binding, including offer and acceptance, capacity, consideration, legality, and a writing if, as is often the case, the agreement falls within the one-year provision of the statute of frauds.

On entering into a binding contract (frequently referred to as an **engagement**), the accountant is bound to perform all **explicit duties** she agrees to provide under the contract. For example, if an accountant agrees to complete the audit of a client by October 15 so that the client may release its annual report on time, the accountant is under a contractual obligation to do so. Likewise, an accountant who contractually promises to conduct an audit to detect possible embezzlement is under a contractual obligation to provide for her client an expanded audit *beyond* generally accepted auditing standards (GAAS).

By entering into a contract, an accountant also **implicitly** agrees to perform the contract in a competent and professional manner. By agreeing to render professional services, an accountant is held to those standards that are generally accepted by the accounting profession, such as GAAS and generally accepted accounting principles (GAAP). Although accountants need not ensure the absolute accuracy of their work, they must exercise the care of a reasonably skilled professional.

Practical Advice

As an auditor, always exercise due diligence when auditing a client's financial statements. Moreover, be sure to issue the appropriate opinion.

An accountant who breaches his contract will incur liability not only to the client but also to certain third-party beneficiaries. As you will recall from Chapter 16, a **third-party beneficiary** is a noncontracting party whom the contracting parties *intend* to receive the *primary* benefit under the contract. For example, Otis Manufacturing Co. hires Adler, an accountant, to prepare a financial statement for Otis to use in obtaining a loan from Chemical Bank. Chemical Bank is a third-party beneficiary of the contract between Otis and Adler. Another example of a potential third party is an investor considering the purchase of part or all of a particular company. For a more detailed discussion of third-party beneficiaries, see Chapter 16.

Practical Advice

In your engagement letter clearly specify the terms of your contract and the parties for whom the financial statements are being prepared.

Following general contract principles, an accountant who *materially breaches* his contract will be entitled to no compensation. Thus, if an accountant does not perform an audit on time when time is of the essence, or completes only 60 percent of the audit, she has committed a material breach. On the other hand, an accountant who *substantially performs* her contractual duties is generally entitled to be compensated for the contractually agreed-upon fee, less any damages or loss her nonmaterial breach has caused the client. (See Chapter 18.)

http://
American Institute of Certified Public Accountants (AICPA): http://www.aicpa.org/
Financial Accounting Standards Board (FASB): http://accounting.rutgers.edu/raw/fasb
Governmental Accounting Standards Board (GASB): http://accounting.rutgers.edu/raw/gasb

TORT LIABILITY

In performing his professional services, an accountant may incur tort liability to his client or third parties for negligence or fraud. A **tort**, as we discussed in Chapter 7, is a private or civil wrong or injury, other than a breach of contract, for which the courts will provide a remedy in the form of an action for damages.

Negligence An accountant is **negligent** if she does not exercise the degree of care a reasonably competent accountant would exercise under the circumstances. For example, Arthur, an accountant, is engaged to audit the books of Zebra Corporation. During the audit, Olivia, an officer of Zebra Corporation, notifies Arthur that she suspects that Terrance, the company's treasurer, is engaged in a scheme to embezzle from the corporation. Previously informed that Olivia and Terrance are on bad terms, Arthur does not pursue the matter. Terrance is, in fact, engaged in a commonly used embezzlement scheme. Arthur is negligent for failing to conduct a reasonable investigation of the alleged defalcation. Nonetheless, as we mentioned earlier, an accountant is *not* liable for honest inaccuracies or errors of judgment, so long as she exercises reasonable care in performing her duties. Moreover, an accountant need *not guarantee* the accuracy of her reports, provided she acts in a reasonably competent and professional manner.

Most courts do not permit an accountant to raise the defense of the plaintiff's contributory (or comparative) negligence. Nevertheless, a few courts do permit such a defense despite the fact that they recognize "that professional malpractice actions pose peculiar problems and that the comparison of fault between a layperson and a professional should be approached with caution."

Historically, an accountant's liability for negligence extended only to the client and to third-party beneficiaries. Under this view, **privity** of contract was a requirement for a cause of action based on negligence. This approach was established by the landmark case of *Ultramares Corp. v. Touche.*

In recent years, a majority of the states have adopted a **foreseen users or foreseen class of users test**. This approach, which also has been adopted by the Restatement of Torts, expands the class of protected individuals to include those the accountant knew would use the work product *or* those who use the accountant's work for a purpose for which the accountant knew the work would be used. For instance,

Denise, an accountant, knows that her client will use a work product to try to obtain a bank loan from Nationsbank. Even if the client uses the audited financial statements to obtain a loan from a different bank, Denise would be liable to that second bank for any negligent misrepresentations in the financial statements. This class of protected individuals does not, however, include potential investors and the general public.

NorAm Investment Services, Inc. v. Stirtz Bernards Boyden Surdel & Larter, P.A.

Court of Appeals of Minnesota, 2000
611 N.W.2d 372
http://www.lawlibrary.state.mn.us/archive/capmo.html

FACTS Equisure, Inc., was required to file audited financial statements when it applied to have its stock listed on the American Stock Exchange (AmEx) **(http://www.amex.com)**. It retained an accounting firm, defendant Stirtz Bernards Boyden Surdel & Larter, P.A. (Stirtz) **(http://www.sbbsl.com)**. Stirtz issued a favorable interim audit report that Equisure used to gain listing on the stock exchange. Subsequently, Equisure retained Stirtz to audit the financial statements required for Equisure's Form 10 filing with the U.S. Securities and Exchange Commission (SEC) **(http://www.sec.gov/)**. Stirtz's auditor knew that the audit was for the SEC reports. Stirtz issued a "clean" audit opinion, which, with the audited financial statements, was included in Equisure's SEC filing and made available to the public.

Appellant NorAm Investment Services, Inc., also known as Equity Securities Trading Company, Inc. (NorAm), a securities broker, began lending margin credit to purchasers of Equisure stock. These purchasers advanced only a portion of the purchase price; NorAm extended credit (a margin loan) for the balance and held the stock as collateral for the loan, charging interest on the balance. When NorAm had loaned approximately $900,000 in margin credit, its president, Nathan Newman, reviewed Stirtz's audit report and the audited financial statements. Based on his review, NorAm extended over $1.6 million of additional margin credit for the purchase of Equisure shares.

When AmEx stopped trading Equisure stock due to allegations of insider trading and possible stock manipulation, the stock became worthless. NorAm was left without collateral for over $2.5 million in margin loans. Stirtz resigned as auditor of Equisure and warned that its audit report might be misleading and should no longer be relied upon. NorAm sued Stirtz for negligent misrepresentation and negligence. The district court granted Stirtz's motion for summary judgment, ruling that under the Restatement (Second) of Torts § 552, Stirtz was not liable to NorAm. NorAm appealed.

DECISION Judgment affirmed.

OPINION Harten, J. Is an accountant liable under Restatement (Second) of Torts § 552 for negligent misrepresentation to a securities broker who relied on the accountant's report to extend margin credit?

* * *

The Restatement (Second) of Torts § 552 sets out the criteria for accountants' liability to third parties who rely on the accountants' negligent audits.

(1) One who, in the course of his business, profession or employment, or in any other transaction in which he has a pecuniary interest, supplies false information for the guidance of others in their business transactions, is subject to liability for pecuniary loss caused to them by their justifiable reliance upon the information, if he fails to exercise reasonable care or competence in obtaining or communicating the information.

(2) * * * [T]he liability stated in Subsection (1) is limited to loss suffered

(a) by the person or one of a limited group of persons for whose benefit and guidance he intends to supply the information or knows that the recipient intends to supply it; and

(b) through reliance upon it in a transaction that he intends the information to influence or knows that the recipient so intends or in a substantially similar transaction. Minnesota has adopted the Restatement approach. [Citations.] [Court's footnote: The Restatement presents a middle ground between two other rules: the traditional foreseeability rule, extending accountants' liability to all foreseeable users of their work, and the privity rule, restricting accountants' liability to those with whom they are in privity. [Citation.]

Bonhiver [citation] held that an accounting firm owed a duty of care to an insurance broker because a "chain of reliance" linked the firm, the state insurance commissioner who the firm knew would rely on its work product, and the insurance broker within the class of persons who should be protected by the commissioner's reliance.

NorAm relies on *Bonhiver*, arguing that a similar chain links Stirtz, the SEC that Stirtz knew would rely on its work, and NorAm, which should be protected by the SEC's reliance. We disagree.

The chain of reliance here is several links longer than the chain in *Bonhiver*.

> It is not enough that the maker merely knows of the ever-present possibility of repetition to anyone, and the possibility of action in reliance upon it, on the part of anyone to whom it may be repeated.

Restatement (Second) of Torts § 552, cmt. h. Unlike the insurance broker in *Bonhiver*, NorAm as a broker extending margin credit is not clearly in the class that should be protected by the SEC's reliance. "If that liability is to be drawn somewhere short of foreseeability, it must be drawn on pragmatic grounds alone." [Citation.]

INTERPRETATION This case adopts the intermediate position of the Restatement of Torts.

ETHICAL QUESTION Did the court fairly decide this case? Explain.

CRITICAL THINKING QUESTION What is the appropriate test for determining an accountant's liability to third parties for negligence? Explain.

Some courts have extended liability to benefit an even broader group: reasonably foreseeable plaintiffs who are neither known to the accountant nor members of a class of intended recipients. A few states have adopted this test, which requires only that the accountant reasonably foresee that such an individual might use the financial statements. The rationale behind the foreseeability standard of the law of negligence is that a tortfeasor should be fully liable for all the reasonably foreseeable consequences of her conduct. See Figure 44-1 for the various tests applied to accountants' liability to third parties for negligent misrepresentation.

Fraud An accountant who commits a fraudulent act is liable to any person the accountant *should have* reasonably foreseen would be injured through justifiable reliance on the misrepresentation. The required elements of **fraud**, which were more fully discussed in Chapter 11, are (1) a false representation (2) of fact (3) that is material and (4) made with knowledge of its falsity and with the intention to deceive, (5) is justifiably relied on, and (6) causes injury to the plaintiff. An accountant who commits fraud may be held liable for *both* compensatory and punitive damages.

Figure 44-1 *Accoutant's Liability to Third Parties for Negligent Misrepresentation*

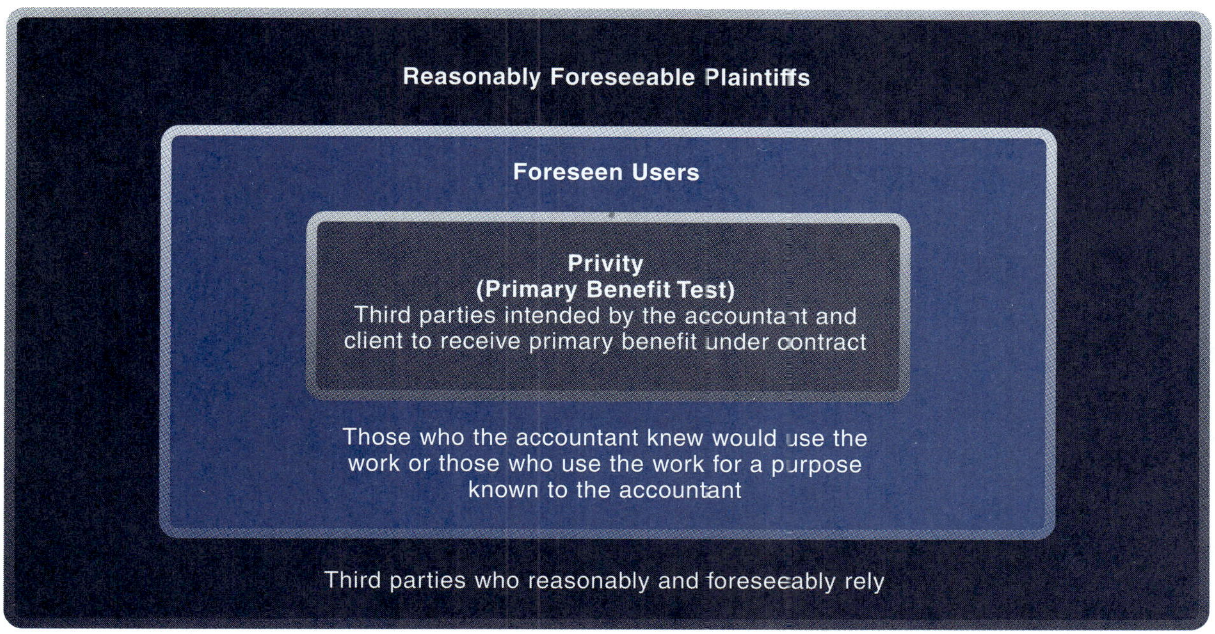

In recent years, accountants also have been subject to a number of civil lawsuits based on the Racketeering Influenced and Corrupt Organizations Act (RICO). For a discussion of this act, see Chapter 6.

CRIMINAL LIABILITY

An accountant's potential **criminal liability** in rendering professional services is based primarily on the federal law of securities regulation and taxation. Nonetheless, an accountant would violate state criminal law by knowingly and willfully certifying false documents, altering or tampering with accounting records, using false financial reports, giving false testimony under oath, or committing forgery.

Criminal sanctions may be imposed under the Internal Revenue Code for knowingly preparing false or fraudulent tax returns or documents used in connection with a tax return. Such liability also extends to willfully assisting or advising a client or others to prepare a false return. Penalties for tax fraud may be a fine not to exceed $100,000 ($500,000 for a corporation) or three years' imprisonment, or both.

CLIENT INFORMATION

In providing services for his client, an accountant necessarily obtains information concerning the client's business affairs. Two legal issues arise concerning this client information: (1) who owns the working papers the accountant generates and (2) whether the information is privileged.

Working Papers Audit **working papers** include an auditor's records of the procedures she followed, the tests she performed, the information she obtained, and the conclusions she reached in connection with an audit. All relevant information that pertains to the examination should be included in the working papers. Because an accountant is held to be the owner of his working papers, he need not surrender them to his client. Nevertheless, the accountant may not disclose the contents of these papers unless (1) the client consents or (2) a court orders the disclosure.

Accountant-Client Privilege The issue of confidentiality as it concerns accountant-client communication is important, for if such information is considered to be privileged, it may not be admitted into evidence over the objection of the person possessing the privilege. The question of a possible **accountant-client privilege** frequently arises in tax disputes, criminal prosecution, and civil litigation.

Neither the common law nor federal law recognizes a general privilege. Nevertheless, some states have adopted statutes granting some form of accountant-client privilege. Most of these statutes grant the privilege to the client, although a few extend the prerogative to the accountant. In addition, the IRS Restructuring and Reform Act of 1998 grants accountants authorized under federal law to practice before the IRS the privilege of confidentiality for tax advice given their client-taxpayers with respect to Internal Revenue Code matters. Regardless of whether the privilege exists or not, it is generally considered to be professionally unethical for an accountant to disclose confidential communications from a client unless the disclosure is in accordance with (1) American Institute of Certified Public Accountants (AICPA) or GAAS requirements, (2) a court order, or (3) the client's request.

CPA FEDERAL SECURITIES LAW

Accountants may be both civilly and criminally liable under provisions of the 1933 and 1934 Acts. (Chapter 40 contains a fuller discussion of the securities laws.) This liability is more extensive and has fewer limitations than liability under the common law. SEC regulations require that public accounting firms and their members not have, or commit to acquire, any direct or material indirect financial interest in their audit clients or their clients' parents, subsidiaries, or other affiliates. SEC regulation defines the term *member* to mean (1) all partners, shareholders, and other principals of the firm, (2) any professional employee involved in providing any professional service to the client, its parents, subsidiaries, or other affiliates, and (3) any professional employee having managerial responsibilities and located in the engagement office or other office of the firm which participates in a significant portion of the audit.

http:// Securities and Exchange Commission: http://www.sec.gov/

1933 ACT

Accountants are subject to express **civil liability** under Section 11 of the 1933 Act if the financial statements they prepare or certify for inclusion in a registration statement contain any untrue statement or omit any material fact. This liability extends to anyone who acquires the security without knowledge of the untruth or omission. Not only does such liability require no proof of privity between the accountant and the purchasers, but proof of reliance on the financial statements also is not usually required under Section 11. An accountant will not be liable, however, if he can prove "due diligence." The defense of ***due diligence*** requires that the accountant had, after reasonable investigation, reasonable grounds to believe and did believe, at the *time* the registration statement became *effective*, that the financial statements were true, complete, and accurate. The standard of reasonableness is that required of a prudent person in the management of his or her own property. Thus, Section 11 imposes liability on accountants for ***negligence*** in the conduct of an audit or in the presentation of information in the financial statements. In addition, an accountant is not liable for any or the entire amount otherwise recoverable under Section 11 that the defendant proves was caused by something other than the defective disclosure.

Moreover, an accountant who willfully violates this section may be held **criminally** liable for a fine of not more than $10,000 or imprisonment of not more than five years, or both.

http:// Securities Act of 1933: http://www4.law.cornell.edu/uscode/15/77a.html

1934 ACT

Civil Liability Section 18 of the 1934 Act imposes express ***civil*** liability on an accountant who makes or causes to be made any false or misleading statement about any material fact in any application, report, document, or registration filed with the SEC under the 1934 Act. Liability extends to any person who purchased or sold a security in reliance on that statement without knowing that it was false or misleading. An accountant is not liable, however, if she proves that she acted in good faith and had no knowledge that such statement was false or misleading. Thus, an accountant is not liable for false or misleading statements that result from good faith negligence.

Accountants may also be held ***civilly*** liable for violations of **Rule 10b–5**. Rule 10b–5, as discussed in Chapter 40, is extremely broad in that it applies to both oral and written misstatements or omissions of material fact and to *all* securities. An accountant may be liable for a violation of the rule to those who rely on the misstatement or omission of material fact when purchasing or selling a security. However, liability is imposed only if the accountant acted with ***scienter***, or intentional or knowing conduct. Therefore, accountants are not liable under Rule 10b–5 for mere negligence, although most courts have held that reckless disregard of the truth is sufficient. See Figure 44-2 for a summary of accountants' civil liability under the federal securities laws.

Practical Advice

Recognize that civil liability for accountants under the federal securities laws extends to a greater range of misconduct and third parties than under common law.

Ernst & Ernst v. Hochfelder

Supreme Court of the United States, 1976
425 U.S. 185, 96 S.Ct 1375, 47 L.Ed.2d 668
http://laws.findlaw.com/US/425/185.html

FACTS The defendant, Ernst & Ernst **(http://www.ey.com/)**, was an accounting firm. From 1946 through 1967, it was retained by First Securities Company of Chicago, a small brokerage firm and member of the Midwest Stock Exchange **(http://www.chx.com/)** and the National Association of Securities Dealers **(http://www.nasd.com/)**, to perform periodic audits of the firm's books and records. In connection with these audits, Ernst & Ernst prepared for filing with the Securities and Exchange Commission the annual reports required of First Securities under the 1934 Act. It also prepared First Securities's responses to the financial questionnaires of the Midwest Stock Exchange.

Hochfelder and others (plaintiffs) were customers of First Securities who invested in a fraudulent securities scheme perpetrated by Leston B. Nay, president of the firm and owner of 92 percent of its stock. This fraud came to light in 1968 when Nay committed suicide, leaving a note that described First Securities as bankrupt and the escrow accounts as "spurious." Plaintiffs subsequently filed this action for damages against Ernst & Ernst under § 10(b) of the 1934 Act. The complaint charged that Nay's escrow scheme violated § 10(b) and Commission Rule 10b–5 and that Ernst & Ernst had "aided and abetted" Nay's violations by its "failure" to conduct proper audits of First Securities. The plaintiffs' cause of action rested on a theory of negligent nonfeasance—that, by failing to use "appropriate auditing procedures" in its audits of First Securities, Ernst & Ernst had thereby failed to discover internal practices of the firm said to prevent an effective audit. The

District Court dismissed the action, but the Court of Appeals reversed and remanded.

DECISION Judgment of the Court of Appeals reversed.

OPINION Powell, J. Federal regulation of transactions in securities emerged as part of the aftermath of the market crash in 1929. The Securities Act of 1933 (1933 Act), [citation] was designed to provide investors with full disclosure of material information concerning public offerings of securities in commerce, to protect investors against fraud and, through the imposition of specified civil liabilities, to promote ethical standards of honesty and fair dealing. [Citation.] The 1934 Act was intended principally to protect investors against manipulation of stock prices through regulation of transactions upon securities exchanges and in over-the-counter markets, and to impose regular reporting requirements on companies whose stock is listed on national securities exchanges. [Citation.] * * *

Section 10 of the 1934 Act makes it "unlawful for any person * * * (b) [t]o use or employ, in connection with the purchase or sale of any security * * * any manipulative or deceptive device or contrivance in contravention of such rules and regulations as the Commission may prescribe as necessary or appropriate in the public interest or for the protection of investors." [Citation.] In 1942, acting pursuant to the power conferred by § 10(b), the Commission promulgated Rule 10b–5.

* * *

Although § 10(b) does not by its terms create an express civil remedy for its violation, and there is no indication that Congress, or the Commission when adopting Rule 10b–5, contemplated such a remedy, the existence of a private cause of action for violations of the statute and the Rule is now well established. [Citation.] During the 30-year period since a private cause of action was first implied under § 10(b) and Rule 10b–5, a substantial body of case law and commentary has developed as to its elements. Courts and commentators long have differed with regard to whether scienter is a necessary element of such a cause of action, or whether negligent conduct alone is sufficient.

* * *

Although the extensive legislative history of the 1934 Act is bereft of any explicit explanation of Congress' intent, we think the relevant portions of that history support our conclusion that § 10(b) was addressed to practices that involve some element of scienter and cannot be read to impose liability for negligent conduct alone.

* * *

We have addressed, to this point, primarily the language and history of § 10(b). The Commission contends, however, that subsections (b) and (c) of Rule 10b–5 are cast in language which—if standing alone—could encompass both intentional and negligent behavior. These subsections respectively provide that it is unlawful "[t]o make any untrue statement of a material fact or to omit to state a material fact necessary in order to make the statements made, in the light of the circumstances under which they were made, not misleading * * *" and "[t]o engage in any act, practice, or course of business which operates or would operate as a fraud or deceit upon any person * * *."

Viewed in isolation the language of subsection (b), and arguably that of subsection (c), could be read as proscribing, respectively, any type of material misstatement or omission, and any course of conduct, that has the effect of defrauding investors, whether the wrongdoing was intentional or not.

We note first such a reading cannot be harmonized with the administrative history of the Rule, a history making clear that when the Commission adopted the Rule it was intended to apply only to activities that involved scienter. More importantly, Rule 10b–5 was adopted pursuant to authority granted the Commission under § 10(b). The rulemaking power granted to an administrative agency charged with the administration of a federal statute is not the power to make law. Rather, it is "'the power to adopt regulations to carry into effect the will of Congress as expressed by the statute.'" [Citations.] * * * When a statute speaks so specifically in terms of manipulation and deception, and of implementing devices and contrivances the commonly understood terminology of intentional wrongdoing—and when its history reflects no more expansive intent, we are quite unwilling to extend the scope of the statute to negligent conduct.

INTERPRETATION Accountants are not liable under Rule 10b–5 for mere negligence.

CRITICAL THINKING QUESTION Do you agree with the Court's decision in this case? Explain.

Criminal Liability Those who willfully violate Section 18 or Rule 10b–5 also may be held ***criminally liable.*** As amended by the Sarbanes-Oxley Act, for an accountant, conviction may carry a fine of not more than $5 million or imprisonment for not more than twenty years, or both, while an accounting firm may be fined up to $25 million.

Sarbanes-Oxley Act In response to the business scandals involving companies such as Enron, WorldCom, Global Crossing, and the accounting firm of Arthur Andersen, in 2002 Congress passed the Sarbanes-Oxley Act, which amends the securities acts in a number of significant respects to protect investors by improving the accuracy

Figure 44-2 *Accountants' Liability under Federal Securities Law*

	Section 11 (1933 Act)	Section 18 (1934 Act)	Rule 10b-5 (1934 Act)
Conduct	Registration statement containing material misstatement or omission	False or misleading statements in a document filed with SEC	Deception or material misstatement or opinion
Fault	Negligence	Knowledge or bad faith	Scienter
Plaintiff's knowledge is a defense	Yes	Yes	Yes
Reliance required	No	Yes	Yes
Privity required	No	No	No

and reliability of corporate disclosures. The Act provides for the establishment of the five-member Public Company Accounting Oversight Board to oversee the audit of public companies in order to further the public interest in the preparation of informative, accurate, and independent audit reports for public companies. The SEC has oversight and enforcement authority over the Board. The duties of the Board include (1) registering public accounting firms that prepare audit reports for issuers; (2) overseeing the audit of public companies; (3) establishing audit report standards and rules; and (4) inspecting, investigating, and enforcing compliance on the part of registered public accounting firms and their associated persons. The Act directs the Board to establish or modify the auditing and related attestation standards, quality control standards, and ethics standards used by registered public accounting firms to prepare and issue audit reports.

In order to make auditors more independent from their clients, the Act prohibits accounting firms from performing eight specified non-audit services for audit clients, including bookkeeping or other services related to the accounting records or financial statements; financial information systems design and implementation, appraisal or valuation services; fairness opinions; management functions or human resources; and actuarial services. Accounting firms may perform other non-audit services not expressly forbidden by the Act if the company's audit committee grants prior approval and the approval by the audit committee is disclosed to investors in periodic reports. The lead audit partner having primary responsibility for the audit and the audit partner responsible for reviewing the audit must rotate at least every five years.

Auditors must report directly to the company's audit committee and make timely disclosure of accounting issues concerning (1) critical accounting policies and practices used in the audit; (2) alternative treatments and their ramifications within generally accepted accounting principles that have been discussed with management officials and the treatment preferred by the auditor; and (3) other material written communications between the auditor and management.

Audit Requirements The Private Securities Litigation Reform Act of 1995 (Reform Act) imposed a significant set of obligations upon independent public accountants who audit financial statements required by the 1934 Act. The Reform Act authorizes the SEC to adopt rules that modify or supplement the practices or procedures followed by auditors in the conduct of an audit. Moreover, the act requires auditors to establish procedures capable of detecting material illegal acts, identifying material-related party transactions, and evaluating whether there is a substantial doubt about the issuer's ability to continue as a going concern during the next fiscal year.

If the auditor becomes aware of information indicating an illegal act, it must determine whether an illegal act occurred and the illegal act's possible effect on the issuer's financial statements. Then the auditor must inform the issuer's management about any illegal activity and assure itself that the audit committee of the board of directors is adequately informed. If the auditor concludes that (1) the illegal act has a material effect on the issuer's financial statement; (2) neither senior management nor the board has taken timely and appropriate remedial action; *and* (3) the failure to take remedial action is reasonably expected to warrant departure from a standard auditor report or warrant resignation from the auditor's engagement, then the auditor promptly must report its conclusions to the issuer's board.

Within one day of receiving such report, the issuer must notify the SEC and furnish the auditor with a copy of that notice. If the auditor does not receive such notice, then the auditor must either resign or furnish the SEC with its report to the board. If the auditor resigns, it must furnish the SEC with a copy of its report.

The Reform Act provides that an auditor shall not be held liable in a private action for any finding, conclusion, or statement expressed in the report the Act requires the auditor to make to the SEC. The SEC can impose civil penalties against an auditor who willfully violates the Reform Act by failing to resign or to furnish a report to the SEC.

CHAPTER SUMMARY

Common Law

Contract Liability the employment contract between an accountant and her client is subject to the general principles of contract law
- *Explicit Duties* the accountant is bound to perform all the duties she expressly agrees to provide
- *Implicit Duties* the accountant impliedly agrees to perform the contract in a competent and professional manner
- *Beneficiaries* contract liability extends to the client/contracting party and to third-party beneficiaries (noncontracting parties intended by the contracting parties to receive the primary benefit under the contract)
- *Breach of Contract* general contract law principles apply

Tort Liability a tort is a private or civil wrong or injury other than a breach of contract
- *Negligence* an accountant is liable for failing to exercise the degree of care a reasonably competent accountant would exercise under the circumstances; most courts have extended an accountant's liability for negligence beyond the client and third-party beneficiaries to foreseen third parties
- *Fraud* an accountant who commits a fraudulent act is liable for both compensatory and punitive damages to any person whom he should have reasonably foreseen would be injured; a fraudulent act is a false representation of fact that is material, is made with knowledge of its falsity and with the intention to deceive, and is justifiably relied on

Criminal Liability state law imposes criminal liability on accountants for willfully certifying false documents, altering or tampering with accounting records, using false financial reports, giving false testimony, and committing forgery

Client Information
- *Working Papers* an accountant is considered the owner of his working papers but may not disclose their contents unless the client agrees or a court orders the disclosure
- *Accountant-Client Privilege* not recognized generally by the common law or federal law, although some states have adopted statutes granting some form of privilege, and accountants authorized to practice before the IRS have privilege for tax advice given their client-taxpayers with respect to Internal Revenue Code matters

Federal Securities Law

1933 Act
- *Civil Liability* Section 11 imposes express civil liability upon accountants if the financial statements they prepare or certify for a registration statement contain any untrue statement or omit any material fact, unless the accountant proves his due diligence defense, which requires that the accountant had, after reasonable investigation, reasonable grounds to believe and did believe that the financial statements were true, complete, and accurate

- *Criminal Liability* a willful violator of Section 11 is subject to fines of not more than $10,000 and/or imprisonment of not more than five years

1934 Act

- *Section 18* imposes express civil liability on an accountant who knowingly makes any false or misleading statement about any material fact in any report, document, or registration filed with the SEC
- *Rule 10b–5* an accountant is civilly liable under this rule if he acts with scienter in making oral or written misstatements or omissions of material fact in connection with the purchase or sale of a security
- *Criminal Liability* a willful violator of either Section 18 or Rule 10b–5 is subject to fines of not more than $5 million and/or imprisonment of not more than twenty years

Sarbanes-Oxley Act establishes a new regulatory body to oversee public company auditors, makes auditors more independent from their clients, and places direct responsibility for the audit relationship on audit committees

Audit Requirements auditors must establish procedures capable of detecting material illegal acts, identifying material-related party transactions, and evaluating whether there is a substantial doubt about the issuer's ability to continue as a going concern during the next fiscal year

QUESTIONS

1. Baldwin Corporation made a public offering of $25,000,000 of convertible debentures and registered the offering with the SEC. The registration statement contained financial statements certified by Adams and Allen, CPAs. The financial statements overstated Baldwin's net income and assets by 20 percent while understating the company's liability by 15 percent. Because Adams and Allen did not carefully follow GAAS, it failed to detect these inaccuracies, the discovery of which has caused the bond prices to drop from their original selling price of $1,000 per bond to $720. Can Conrad, who purchased $10,000 of the debentures, collect from Adams and Allen for his damages? Explain.

2. Ingram is a CPA employed by Jordan, Keller and Lane, CPAs, to audit Martin Enterprises, Inc., a fast-growing service firm that went public two years ago. The financial statements that Ingram audited were included in a proxy statement proposing a merger with several other firms. The proxy statement was filed with the SEC and included several inaccuracies. First, approximately $1 million, or more than 20 percent, of the previous year's "net sales originally reported" had proven nonexistent by the time the proxy statement was filed and had been written off on Martin's own books. This was not disclosed in the proxy statement, in violation of *Accounting Board Opinion Number 9*. Second, Martin's net sales for the current year were stated as $11,300,000, when in truth they were less than $10,500,000. Third, Martin's net profits for the current year were reported as $700,000, when in fact the firm had no earnings at all.
   a. What civil liability, if any, does Ingram have?
   b. What criminal liability, if any, does Ingram have?

3. Girard & Company, CPAs, audited the financial statements included in the annual report submitted by PMG Enterprises, Inc., to the SEC. The audit failed to detect numerous false and misleading statements contained in the financial statements.
   a. Investors who subsequently purchased PMG stock have brought suit against Girard under Section 18 of the 1934 Act. What defenses, if any, are available to Girard?
   b. The SEC has initiated criminal proceedings under the 1934 Act against Girard. What must be proven for Girard to be held criminally liable?

4. Dryden, a certified public accountant, audited the books of Elixir, Inc., and certified incorrect financial statements in a form that was filed with the SEC. Shortly thereafter, Elixir, Inc., went bankrupt. Investigation into the bankruptcy disclosed that through an intricate and clever embezzlement scheme, Kraft, the president of Elixir, had siphoned off substantial sums of money that now support Kraft in a luxurious lifestyle in South America. Investors who purchased shares of Elixir have brought suit against Dryden under Rule 10b–5. At trial, Dryden produces evidence that demonstrates that his failure to discover the embezzlement resulted merely from negligence on his part and that he had no knowledge of the fraudulent conduct. Is Dryden liable under the Securities Exchange Act of 1934? Why?

5. Johnson Enterprises, Inc., contracted with the accounting firm of P, A & E to perform an audit of Johnson. The accounting firm performed its duty in a nonnegligent, competent manner but failed to discover a novel embezzlement scheme perpetrated by Johnson's treasurer. Shortly

thereafter, Johnson's treasurer disappeared with $75,000 of the company's money. Johnson now refuses to pay P, A & E its $20,000 audit fee and is seeking to recover $75,000 from P, A & E.

a. What are the rights and liabilities of P, A & E and Johnson? Explain.
b. Would your answer to (a) differ if the scheme was a common embezzlement scheme that GAAS should have disclosed? Explain.

6. The accounting firm of T, W & S was engaged to perform an audit of Progate Manufacturing Company. During the course of its investigation, T, W & S discovered that the company had overvalued its inventory by carrying the inventory on the books at the previous year's prices, which were significantly higher than current prices. When T, W & S approached Progate's president, Lehman, about the improper valuation of inventory, Lehman became enraged and told T, W & S that unless the firm accepted the valuation, Progate would sue T, W & S. Although T, W & S knew that Progate's suit was frivolous and unfounded, it wished to avoid the negative publicity that would arise from any suit brought against it. Therefore, on the assumption that the overvaluation would not harm anybody, T, W & S accepted Progate's inflated valuation of inventory. Progate subsequently went bankrupt, and T, W & S is now being sued by (1) First National Bank, a bank that relied upon T, W & S's statement to loan money to Progate, and (2) Thomas, an investor who purchased 20 percent of Progate's stock after receiving T, W & S's statement. What are the rights and liabilities of First National Bank, Thomas, and T, W & S?

7. J, B & J, CPAs, has audited the Highcredit Corporation for the past five years. Recently, the SEC has commenced an investigation of Highcredit for possible violations of federal securities law. The SEC has subpoenaed all of J, B & J's working papers pertinent to the audit of Highcredit. Highcredit insists that J, B & J not turn over the documents to the SEC. What action should J, B & J take? Why?

8. On February 1, the Gazette Corporation hired Susan Sharp to conduct an audit of its books and to prepare financial statements for the corporation's annual meeting on July 1. Sharp made every reasonable attempt to comply with the deadline but could not finish the report on time due to delays in receiving needed information from Gazette. Gazette now refuses to pay Sharp for her audit and is threatening to bring a cause of action against Sharp. What course of action should Sharp pursue? Why?

CASE PROBLEMS

9. John P. Butler Accountancy Corporation agreed to audit the financial statements of Westside Mortgage, Inc., a mortgage company that arranged financing for real property, for the year ending December 31, 1998. On March 22, 1999, after completing the audit, Butler issued unqualified audited financial statements listing Westside's corporate net worth as $175,036. The primary asset on the balance sheet was a $100,000 note receivable that had, in reality, been rendered worthless in August 1997 when the trust deed on real property securing the note was wiped out by a prior foreclosure of a superior deed of trust. The note constituted 57 percent of Westside's net worth and was thus material to an accurate representation of Westside's financial position. In October 1999, International Mortgage Company (IMC) approached Westside for the purpose of buying and selling loans on the secondary market. IMC signed an agreement with Westside in December after reviewing Westside's audited financial statements. In June 2000, Westside issued a $475,293 promissory note to IMC, on which it ultimately defaulted. IMC brought an action against Westside, its owners, principals, and Butler. IMC alleged negligence and negligent misrepresentation against Butler in auditing and issuing without qualification the defective financial statements on which IMC relied in deciding to do business with Westside. Butler moved for summary judgment, claiming that it owed no duty of care to IMC, a third party who was not specifically known to Butler as an intended recipient of the audited financial statements. The trial court granted Butler's motion, and IMC appealed. Decision?

10. Osborne Computer Corporation manufactured the first portable personal computer for the mass market. Shipments began in 1981, and by fall 1982, sales of the company's sole product, the Osborne I, had reached $10 million per month. In late 1982, the company began planning for an early 1983 initial public offering of its stock. In order to obtain the financing it needed to meet its capital requirements until the offering, the company issued warrants to investors, in exchange for direct loans or letters of credit, to secure bank loans to the company. The warrants entitled their holders to purchase blocks of the company's stock at favorable prices that were expected to yield a sizable profit when the public offering took place. The company retained Arthur Young & Company (http://www.ey.com/), which issued unqualified or "clean" audit opinions on the company's 1981 and 1982 financial statements. Each opinion appeared on Arthur Young's letterhead and stated that (1) Arthur Young had examined the accompanying financial statements in accordance with the accounting profession's generally accepted auditing standards (GAAS); (2) the statements had been prepared in accordance with generally accepted accounting principles (GAAP); and (3) the statements "presented fairly" the company's financial position. The 1981 financial statement showed a net operating loss of approximately $1 million on sales of $6 million. The

1982 financial statement revealed a modest net operating profit of $69,000 on sales of more than $68 million. As the warrant transaction closed on April 8, 1983, the company's financial performance began to falter, and the company later filed for bankruptcy. Investors who had purchased Osborne stock and warrants (plaintiffs) brought suit against Arthur Young, claiming that they had made their investments in reliance on Arthur Young's unqualified audit. The plaintiffs presented evidence that Arthur Young's audit was not performed in accordance with GAAS and that, as a result, Osborne's financial statements had overstated the company's profits by $3 million. The plaintiffs also presented evidence that Arthur Young had discovered material weaknesses in the company's accounting controls but had failed to report these weaknesses to management. Should the defendant be held liable under the common law? Explain.

11. Arthur Young & Co., a firm of certified public accountants, was the independent auditor for Amerada Hess Corporation. During its review of Amerada's financial statements as required by federal securities laws, Young confirmed Amerada's statement of its contingent tax liabilities and prepared tax accrual work papers. These work papers, which pertained to Young's evaluation of Amerada's reserves for contingent tax liabilities, included discussions of questionable positions Amerada might have taken on its tax returns. The Internal Revenue Service initiated a criminal investigation of Amerada's tax returns when, during a routine audit, it discovered questionable payments made by Amerada from a "special disbursement account." The IRS summoned Young to make available all its information relating to Amerada, including the tax accrual work papers. Amerada instructed Young not to obey the summons. The IRS then brought an action against Young to enforce the administrative summons. Is Arthur Young entitled to any type of protection? Explain.

http:// **Internet Exercise** Find information about the structure and mission of the Financial Accounting Standards Board and examine its recent announcements and documents.

CHAPTER 45

Consumer Protection

Consumption is the sole end and purpose of production; and the interest of the producer ought to be attended to only so far as it may be necessary for promoting that of the consumer.

ADAM SMITH, *WEALTH OF NATIONS* (1776)

Learning Objectives

After reading this chapter you should be able to:

1. Describe the role of the Federal Trade Commission (FTC) and the major enforcement sanctions that it may use.
2. Describe the role and workings of the Consumer Product Safety Commission (CPSC).
3. Explain the principal provisions of the Magnuson-Moss Act and distinguish between a full and a limited warranty.
4. Describe what information a creditor must provide a consumer before the consumer incurs the obligation.
5. Outline the major remedies that are available to a creditor.

Consumer transactions have increased enormously since World War II, and today consumer debt amounts to more than $1 trillion. Although the definition varies, a consumer transaction generally involves goods, credit, services, or land acquired for personal, household, or family purposes. Historically, consumers were subject to the rule of *caveat emptor*—let the buyer beware. The law, however, has largely abandoned this principle and now offers greater protection to consumers. Most of this protection takes the form of statutory enactments at both the state and federal levels, and a wide variety of governmental agencies are charged with enforcing these statutes. This enforcement varies enormously. In some cases, only government agencies may exercise enforcement rights, through the imposition of criminal penalties, civil penalties, injunctions, and cease and desist orders. In other cases, in addition to government's enforcement rights, consumers may privately seek the rescission of contracts and damages for harm resulting from violations of consumer protection laws. Finally, under certain consumer protection statutes such as state "lemon laws," consumers alone may exercise enforcement rights. In this chapter, we will examine state and federal consumer protection agencies and consumer protection statutes.

STATE AND FEDERAL CONSUMER PROTECTION AGENCIES

Through the enactment of laws and regulations, legislatures and administrative bodies at the federal, state, and local levels all actively seek to shield consumers from an enormous range of harm. The most common abuses involving consumer transactions occur in the extension of credit, deceptive trade practices, unsafe products, and unfair pricing.

STATE AND LOCAL CONSUMER PROTECTION AGENCIES

The many consumer protection agencies at the state and local levels typically deal with fraudulent and deceptive trade practices and fraudulent sales practices, such as false statements about a product's value or quality. In most jurisdictions, consumer protection agencies also help to resolve consumer complaints about defective goods or poor service.

Most state attorney generals facilitate consumer protection by enforcing laws against consumer fraud through judicially imposed injunctions and restitution. In recent years, as the federal government's role in consumer protection has diminished in response to the deregulatory movement, the states have correspondingly expanded their role. The National Association of Attorneys General (NAAG) has been active in coordinating lawsuits among the states. Under NAAG's guidance, several states will often simultaneously file lawsuits against a company that has been engaging in fraudulent acts involving more than one state.

In some instances, however, states have not coordinated their efforts and have, instead, acted inconsistently with respect to consumer protection, especially in health and safety matters. This lack of coordination can present serious problems to companies that sell large numbers of products in interstate commerce.

http://
Consumer World: http://www.consumerworld.org/
Consumers Union: http://www.consumersunion.org/
Consumer Reports: http://www.consumerreports.org/

THE FEDERAL TRADE COMMISSION

At the federal level, the most significant consumer protection agency is the **Federal Trade Commission (FTC)**. Established in 1914, the FTC has two major functions: (1) under its mandate to prevent "unfair methods of competition in commerce," it is responsible for roughly half of the antitrust enforcement at the federal level (the FTC's role in antitrust enforcement was discussed in Chapter 43) and (2) under its mandate to prevent "unfair and deceptive" trade practices, it is responsible for stopping fraudulent sales techniques.

In addressing unfair and deceptive trade practices, the five-member commission (no more than three of whose members may be from the same political party) has the power to issue substantive "trade regulation rules" and to conduct appropriate investigations and hearings. Among the rules it has issued so far are those regulating used car sales, franchising and business opportunity ventures, funeral home services, and the issuance of consumer credit, as well as those requiring a "cooling-off" period for door-to-door sales (discussed later in this chapter).

In many instances, the agency, in considering a deceptive trade practice, may seek a cease and desist order rather than issue a substantive trade rule. A **cease and desist order** directs a party to stop a certain practice or face punishment such as a fine. In a typical situation, the FTC staff discovers a potentially deceptive practice, investigates the matter, files (if appropriate) a complaint against the alleged offender (usually referred to as the respondent), and, after a hearing in front of an administrative law judge (ALJ) to determine whether a violation of the law has occurred, obtains a cease and desist order if the ALJ finds that one is necessary. The respondent may appeal to the FTC commissioners to reverse or modify the order. Appeals from orders issued by the commissioners go to the U.S. Courts of Appeals, which have exclusive jurisdiction to enforce, set aside, or modify orders of the commission.

http://
Federal Trade Commission: http://www.ftc.gov/
Federal Trade Commission Act: http://www4.law.cornell.edu/uscode/15/41.html

Standards Though the FTC act does not define the words *unfair* or *deceptive*, the commission has issued three policy statements addressing the meaning of **unfairness** and has provided that an injury is unfair if it is substantial, not outweighed by any benefits to consumers or competition, and is one that consumers themselves could not reasonably have avoided. The standard, therefore, applies a cost-benefit analysis to the issue of unfairness.

The second policy statement deals with the meaning of **deception**—the basis of most FTC consumer protection actions—by providing that the commission will find deception in a misrepresentation, omission, or practice that is likely to mislead a consumer acting reasonably in the circumstances, to the consumer's detriment.

Deception may occur either through false representation or material omission. Examples of deceptive practices have included advertising that a certain product would save consumers 25 percent on their automotive motor oil, when the product simply replaced a quart of oil in the engine (which normally contains four quarts of oil) and was, in fact, more expensive than the oil it replaced; placing marbles in a bowl of vegetable soup in order to displace the vegetables from the bottom of the bowl and therefore make the soup look thicker; and claiming that one drug provided greater pain relief than another named drug, when evidence actually was insufficient to prove the claim to the medical community.

Deception can also occur through a failure to *disclose* important product information if such disclosure is necessary to correct a false and material expectation created in the consumer's mind by the product or by the circumstances of sale. For example, the FTC has insisted that the failure to disclose a product's country of origin constitutes a deceptive omission, based on the agency's view that consumers assume the United States to be the country of origin of a product that bears no other country's name.

The third policy statement issued by the commission involves **ad substantiation**. This policy requires that advertisers have a reasonable basis for their claims at the time they make such claims. Moreover, in determining the reasonableness of a claim, the commission places great weight on the cost and benefits of substantiation.

http://

FTC Unfairness Policy: http://www.ftc.gov/bcp/menu-ads.htm#policy
FTC Deception Policy: http://www.ftc.gov/bcp/menu-ads.htm#policy
FTC Ad Substantiation Policy: http://www.ftc.gov/bcp/menu-ads.htm#policy

Federal Trade Commission v. Pantron I Corporation

United States Court of Appeals, Ninth Circuit, 1994
33 F.3d 1088, *cert denied*, 514 U.S. 1083, 115 S.Ct. 1794, 131 L.Ed.2d 722 (1995)
http://www.ftc.gov/opa/1997/02/pantron.htm

FACTS Pantron I Corporation and Hal Z. Lederman market a product known as the Helsinki Formula **(http://www.headstartvitamins.com/Page3.html)**. This product supposedly arrests hair loss and stimulates hair regrowth in baldness sufferers. The formula consists of a conditioner and a shampoo, and it sells at a list price of $49.95 for a three-month supply. The ingredients which allegedly cause the advertised effects are polysorbate 60 and polysorbate 80. Pantron offers a full money-back guarantee for those who are not satisfied with the product.

The FTC challenged both Pantron's claims that the formula arrested hair loss and promoted growth of new hair as unfair and deceptive trade practices. The FTC presented a variety of evidence that tended to show that the Helsinki Formula had no effectiveness other than its placebo effect (achieving results due solely to belief that the product will work). The FTC introduced expert testimony of a dermatologist and two other experts who denied there was any scientific evidence that the Helsinki Formula would be in any way useful in treating hair loss. Finally, the FTC introduced evidence of two studies which had determined that polysorbate-based products were ineffective in stopping hair loss and promoting regrowth.

In response, Pantron introduced evidence that users of the Helsinki Formula were satisfied that it was effective. It offered testimony of 18 users who had experienced hair regrowth or a reduction in hair loss after using the formula. It also introduced evidence of a "consumer satisfaction survey" it had conducted. Pantron also introduced evidence that over half of its orders come from repeat purchasers, that it had received very few written complaints, and that very few of Pantron's customers (less than 3 percent) had redeemed the money-back guarantee.

Pantron finally introduced several clinical studies of its own, none performed in the United States or under U.S. standards for scientific studies. The evidence from these studies did show effectiveness, but the studies were not random, blind reviewed studies, and thus did not take into account the placebo effect.

The district court found that Pantron's representations were false, but that "[t]here is no evidence in the record to support a contention that the Helsinki Formula is wholly ineffective." The district court found that the studies and anecdotal evidence showed that the compound works for some people some of the time. Thus, it concluded that the FTC had failed to carry its burden of showing that Pantron made a false claim when it represented that the Helsinki Formula was effective.

However, the district court found "no scientifically valid evidence that polysorbate 60 is effective for treatment of hair loss or for inducing growth." Accordingly, it entered an injunction, which barred Pantron and Lederman from making any express or explicit representations that scientific evidence establishes that the Helsinki Formula "is effective in any way in the treatment of baldness or hair loss."

DECISION The judgment of the district court is reversed.

OPINION Reinhardt, J.

A.

The Federal Trade Commission brought this suit pursuant to sections 5(a) and 12 of the Federal Trade Commission Act, [Citation]. Section 5(a) of the Act declares unlawful "unfair or deceptive acts or practices in or affecting commerce" and empowers the Commission to prevent such acts or practices. [Citation.] Section 12 of the Act is specifically directed to false advertising. That section prohibits the dissemination of "any false advertisement" in order to induce the purchase of "food, drugs, devices, or cosmetics." * * *

In its own adjudications, the F.T.C. has to some extent clarified the legal standards which apply in section 12 cases. In *Cliffdale Associates* [citation], the Commission announced a three-part test for determining whether an advertisement is misleading and deceptive in violation of section 12. Under this test,

> the Commission will find an act or practice deceptive if, first, there is a representation, omission, or practice that, second, is likely to mislead consumers acting reasonably under the circumstances, and third, the representation, omission, or practice is material.

* * * [W]e believe that the general outlines of the *Cliffdale Associates* test set forth the appropriate general principles for determining whether advertising is deceptive. * * *

In this case, there is no question that Pantron represented that the Helsinki Formula was effective. * * * There is also no question that these claims are material. * * * Therefore, the only question before us is whether Pantron's representations regarding the product's effectiveness were likely to deceive or mislead consumers.

There are a number of ways in which a representation, omission, or practice can mislead consumers within the meaning of section 12. In particular, the Commission has identified two theories on which the government can and often does rely in section 12 cases involving objective product claims. First, the government can assert a so-called "falsity" theory. To prevail on such a theory, the government must "carry the burden of proving that the express or implied message conveyed by the ad is false." [Citation.] Alternatively, the government can rely on a so-called "reasonable basis" theory. To prevail on this theory, the government must "show that the advertiser lacked a reasonable basis for asserting that the message was true." * * *

Although the district court conducted both a "falsity" and a "reasonable basis" analysis, the F.T.C clearly and expressly abandoned the reasonable basis theory, both in the district court and in this court. [Court's footnote: This abandonment is puzzling, to say the least, because it is difficult to imagine how the Commission could fail to prevail on a reasonable basis theory. * * *] Accordingly, we discuss only the falsity theory.

B.

The district court concluded that the F.T.C. failed to carry its burden of proving that Pantron's efficacy representations were false. It held that "[t]o prevail on its charge that defendant has misrepresented the efficacy of the 'Helsinki Formula,' the F.T.C. must prove that the product is wholly ineffective; i.e., that it does not work at all." * * *

We hold that the district court erred in concluding that Pantron's representations regarding the Helsinki Formula's efficacy did not amount to false advertising. Although there was sufficient evidence in the record to support the district court's finding that use of the Helsinki Formula might arrest hair loss in some of the people some of the time, the overwhelming weight of the proof at trial made clear that any effectiveness is due solely to the product's placebo effect. * * * , [W]e conclude that a claim of product effectiveness is "false" for purposes of section 12 of the Federal Trade Commission Act if evidence developed under accepted standards of scientific research demonstrates that the product has no force beyond its placebo effect.

* * *

Yet Pantron did not present any evidence which rebutted the consensus of the medical community that polysorbate-based products such as the Helsinki Formula are inherently ineffective. All of the evidence of effectiveness adduced by Pantron can be explained by the placebo effect. * * *

None of Pantron's evidence of effectiveness takes the placebo effect into account. Pantron's evidence of consumer satisfaction is the most obviously flawed. The substantial placebo effect indicates that consumers simply cannot tell whether over-the-counter baldness cures are effective, inherently or otherwise. * * * Much of Pantron's "consumer satisfaction" evidence is suspect on other grounds as well. Pantron's so-called "consumer satisfaction survey" was conducted by its own sales staff "as we did our follow ups to offer additional product." No record of the questions was kept. In addition, Pantron's low refund rate may not represent satisfaction.

* * *

C.

* * *

However, neither scientific standards on the one hand, nor the broadest possible definition of "truth" on the other, can determine what constitutes a "false advertisement" under section 12 of the Federal Trade Commission Act. Indeed, a "false advertisement" need not even be "false"; it need only be "misleading in a material respect." [Citation.] We must read this definition of "false advertis[ing]" in light of the overriding purpose of the F.T.C. Act: "to protect the consumer from being misled by governing the conditions under which goods and services are advertised and sold to individual purchasers." [Citations.] The question we must face, then, is not whether Pantron's claims were "true" in some abstract epistemological sense, nor even whether they could conceivably be described as "true" in ordinary parlance.

Rather, we must determine whether or not efficacy representations based solely on the placebo effect are "misleading in a material respect," and hence prohibited as "false advertis[ing]" under the Act.

Taking account of these principles, we hold that the Federal Trade Commission is not required to prove that a product is "wholly ineffective" in order to carry its burden of showing that the seller's representations of product efficacy are "false." Where, as here, a product's effectiveness arises solely as a result of the placebo effect, a representation that the product is effective constitutes a "false advertisement" even though some consumers may experience positive results. In such circumstances, the efficacy claim "is 'misleading' because the [product] is not inherently effective, its results being attributable to the psychosomatic effect produced by the advertising and marketing of the [product]." * * *

* * *

The evidence before the district court made clear that there is no reason to believe that the Helsinki Formula is at all effective outside of its placebo effect. Accordingly, it was materially "misleading" under *Cliffdale Associates* for Pantron to represent that the Formula is effective in combatting male pattern baldness. * * *

* * * On remand, the district court shall modify its injunction to prohibit the company from making any representations that the Helsinki Formula is effective in arresting hair loss or promoting hair regrowth.

* * *

The F.T.C. argues that the district court erred in refusing to order Pantron or Lederman to pay restitution to consumers or disgorge their profits. Because the district court's refusal to award monetary equitable relief was based on the application of erroneous legal principles, we reverse. We conclude that an application of the correct legal principles requires the district court to order monetary relief in this case, especially in light of our conclusion, set forth in the previous Part, that the F.T.C. fully proved its falsity case.

* * *

INTERPRETATION The FTC is not required to prove that a product is "wholly ineffective" to carry its burden of showing that the seller's representations of product efficacy are "false."

CRITICAL THINKING QUESTION Do you agree with the court's decision? Explain.

REMEDIES

In addition to the remedies discussed above, the FTC has employed three other remedies: (1) affirmative disclosure, (2) corrective advertising, and (3) multiple product orders. **Affirmative disclosure**, a remedy frequently employed by the FTC, requires an offender to include in its advertisements certain information that will prevent the ads from being considered deceptive.

Corrective advertising goes beyond affirmative disclosure by requiring an advertiser who has made a deceptive claim to disclose in future advertisements that such prior claims were in fact untrue. The theory behind this requirement is that a previous deception's effects will continue until expressly corrected.

Multiple product orders require a deceptive advertiser to cease and desist from any future deception not only in regard to the product in question but also in regard to all products sold by the company. This remedy is particularly useful in dealing with companies that have repeatedly violated the law.

THE CONSUMER PRODUCT SAFETY COMMISSION

The **Consumer Product Safety Act (CPSA)** established an independent federal regulatory agency, the Consumer Product Safety Commission (CPSC). The purposes of the CPSA are (1) to protect the public against unreasonable risks of injury associated with consumer products, (2) to assist consumers in evaluating the comparative safety of consumer products, (3) to develop uniform safety standards for consumer products and to minimize conflicting state and local regulations, and (4) to promote research and investigation into the causes and prevention of product-related deaths, illnesses, and injuries.

Consisting of five commissioners, no more than three of whom can be from the same political party, the CPSC has authority to set safety standards for consumer products; to ban unsafe products; to issue administrative recall orders to compel repair, replacement, or refunds for products found to present substantial hazards; and to seek court orders requiring the recall of "imminently hazardous" products. In addition, Congress requires businesses under CPSC jurisdiction to notify the agency of any information indicating that their products contain defects that "could create" substantial product hazards. By triggering investigations that may lead to product recalls, these reports play a major role in the agency's regulatory activities.

The CPSC also enforces four statutes previously enforced by other agencies. These acts, commonly referred to as the "transferred acts," are the Federal Hazardous

Substances Act, the Flammable Fabrics Act, the Poison Prevention Packaging Act, and the Refrigerator Safety Act. When the CPSC can regulate a product under one of these specific acts, rather than under the more general CPSA, the agency is directed to do so unless it specifically finds that regulation under the CPSA is in the public interest. Thus, a large number of CPSC regulations, such as those for toys, children's flammable sleepwear, and hazard warnings on household chemical products, arise under the transferred acts rather than under the CPSA.

When first established, the CPSC promulgated a number of ***mandatory safety standards***; manufacturers either must follow these rules, which regulate product design, packaging, and warning labels, or face legal sanctions. To save time and money, the agency began to rely on industry to establish ***voluntary safety standards***—rules for which noncompliance does not violate the law—reserving mandatory standards for those instances in which voluntary standards proved inadequate. In 1981, Congress enacted legislation requiring the CPSC to rely on voluntary standards "whenever compliance with such voluntary standards would eliminate or adequately reduce the risk of injury addressed and there is substantial compliance with such voluntary standards." Although the 1981 amendments do not bar the CPSC from writing mandatory standards, the CPSC has promulgated few such standards since the law was amended.

http://
Consumer Product Safety Act: http://www4.law.cornell.edu/uscode/15/2051.html
Consumer Product Safety Commission: http://www.cpsc.gov/

OTHER FEDERAL CONSUMER PROTECTION AGENCIES

Among the many other federal agencies that play a major consumer protection role are the ***National Highway Traffic Safety Administration (NHTSA)*** and the ***Food and Drug Administration (FDA)***.

Established in 1966 to reduce the number of deaths and injuries resulting from highway crashes, the NHTSA has the authority to set motor vehicle safety standards that promote crash prevention and crashworthiness. Manufacturers are required to report possible safety defects, and the agency may seek a recall if it determines that a particular automobile model presents a sufficiently great hazard. The NHTSA is also authorized to provide grants-in-aid for state highway safety programs and to conduct research on improving highway safety. See *Motor Vehicle Mfrs. Ass'n v. State Farm Mutual Automobile Ins. Co.* in Chapter 5.

The Food and Drug Administration is the oldest federal consumer protection agency, dating back to 1906. The FDA enforces the Food, Drug and Cosmetic Act, enacted in 1938, which authorizes the agency to regulate "adulterated and misbranded" products. The agency uses two basic enforcement methods: it sets standards for products or requires their premarket approval. The products most often subject to premarket approval are drugs. Since 1976, the agency also has had the authority to subject medical devices such as pacemakers and intrauterine devices to premarket approval; it recently has been requiring a large and increasing number of such devices to undergo this approval process.

Although the FTC, CPSC, NHTSA, and FDA are perhaps the best-known federal consumer protection agencies, numerous others play important roles. For example, the U.S. Postal Service brings many cases every year to close down mail fraud operations and the Securities and Exchange Commission (SEC), as we discussed in Chapter 40, protects consumers against fraud in the sale of securities. In addition, many other agencies assist consumers with specific types of problems that fall within an agency's scope.

http://
National Highway Traffic Safety Administration: http://www.nhtsa.dot.gov/
Food and Drug Administration: http://www.fda.gov/
United States Postal Service: http://www.usps.gov/
Securities and Exchange Commission: http://www.sec.gov/

CONSUMER PURCHASES

When a consumer purchases a product or obtains a service, certain rights and obligations arise. (The extent to which these rights and obligations apply to all contracts was discussed more fully in Chapters 9 through 18; the extent to which they apply to a sale of goods under the Uniform Commercial Code was discussed in Chapters 19 through 23.) Although a number of consumer protection laws have been enacted in recent years, they still leave much of a consumer's rights and duties to state contract law. In particular, Article 2 of the Uniform Commercial Code provides the basic rules governing when a contract for the sale of goods is formed, what constitutes a breach of contract, and what rights an innocent party has against a party who commits a breach. Though many consumer protection laws add rights the UCC does not contain, they still use its tenets as building blocks. For example, many states have passed so-called "lemon laws" to provide additional contract cancellation rights to dissatisfied automobile purchasers.

FEDERAL WARRANTY PROTECTION

A **warranty** creates a duty on the seller's part to assure that the goods or services she sells will conform to certain qualities, characteristics, or conditions. A seller is not required, however, to warrant what she sells; and in general she may, by appropriate words, disclaim (exclude) or modify a particular warranty or all warranties. Because a seller's power to disclaim or modify is so flexible, consumer protection laws have been enacted to ensure that consumers understand the warranty protection provided them.

In 1974, to protect buyers and to prevent deception in selling, Congress enacted the ***Magnuson-Moss Warranty Act***, which requires sellers of consumer products to provide adequate information about warranties. The FTC administers and enforces the act, which provides for (1) disclosure in clear and understandable language of the warranty that is to be offered, (2) a description of the warranty as either "full" or "limited," (3) a prohibition against disclaiming implied warranties if a written warranty is given, and (4) an optional informal settlement mechanism.

The act applies to consumer products with ***written warranties***. A **consumer product** is any item of tangible personal property that is *normally* used for family, household, or personal use and that is distributed in commerce. The act does *not* protect commercial purchasers, partly because they are considered sufficiently knowledgeable, in terms of contracting, to protect themselves. Also, they are able to employ their own attorneys to protect themselves and, in the marketplace, can spread the cost of their injuries.

http:// Magnuson-Moss Warranty Act: http://www4.law.cornell.edu/uscode/15/45.html

Presale Disclosures The act contains **presale disclosure** provisions calculated to prevent confusion and deception and to enable purchasers to make educated product comparisons. A person making a warranty must, to the extent required by the rules of the Federal Trade Commission, fully and conspicuously disclose in simple and readily understood language the terms and conditions of such warranty. Separate rules apply to mail order, catalog, and door-to-door sales.

Labeling Requirements The act further divides written warranties into two categories—limited and full—either of which, for any product costing more than $10, must be designated on the written warranty itself. The purpose of this provision is to enable the consumer to make an initial comparison of the legal rights under certain warranties. Under a **warranty** designated as **full**, the warrantor must agree to repair the product, without charge, to conform with the warranty; no limitation may be placed on the duration of any implied warranty; the consumer must be given the option of a refund or replacement if repair is unsuccessful; and consequential damages may be excluded only if the warranty conspicuously indicates their exclusion. A limited warranty is any warranty not designated as full.

Limitations on Disclaimers Most significantly, the act provides that a *written* warranty, whether full or limited, may ***not disclaim any implied*** warranty. Specifically, a full warranty may not disclaim, modify, or limit any implied warranty; and a limited warranty may not disclaim or modify any implied warranty but may limit its duration to that of the written warranty, provided that the limitation is reasonable, conscionable, and conspicuously displayed. Some states, however, do not allow limitations in the duration of implied warranties.

Practical Advice

As a consumer, check to see if the product you are purchasing is covered by a full or limited warranty. If the warranty is limited, ascertain the coverage and terms of the warranty.

For example, GE sells consumer goods to Barry for $150 and provides a written warranty regarding the quality of the goods. GE must designate the warranty as full or limited, depending on the warranty's characteristics, and may not disclaim or modify any implied warranty. On the other hand, had GE not provided Barry with a written warranty, the Magnuson-Moss Warranty Act would not apply; and GE could disclaim any and all implied warranties (see Figure 45-1).

STATE "LEMON LAWS"

A number of state legislatures have enacted **lemon laws** that attempt to provide new car purchasers with rights that are similar to full warranties under the Magnuson-Moss Warranty Act. (Some states have broadened their laws to cover used cars; some also cover motorcycles.) There are many different lemon laws, but most define a *lemon* as a car that continues to have a defect that substantially impairs its use, value, or safety, even after the manufacturer has made reasonable attempts to correct the problem. If a consumer can prove that her car is a lemon, most lemon laws require the manufacturer either to replace the car or to refund its retail price, less an allowance for the consumer's use of the car. In addition, most lemon laws provide that the consumer may recover attorneys' fees and expenses if the case goes to litigation.

Figure 45-1
Magnuson-Moss Act

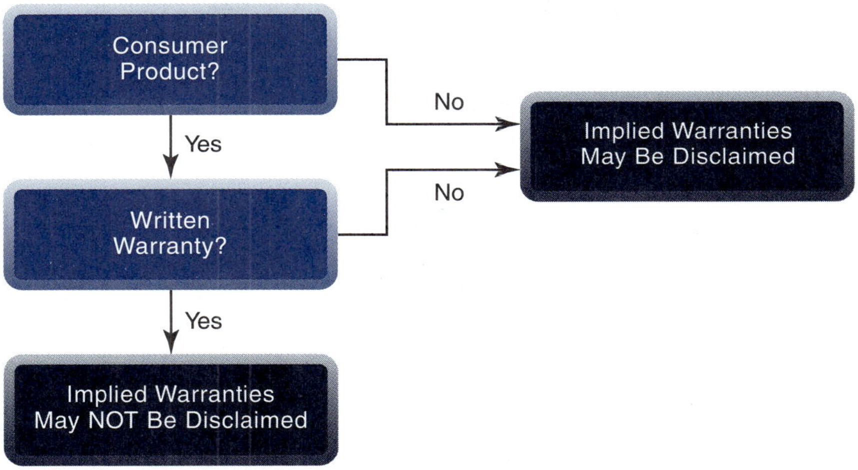

CONSUMER RIGHT OF RESCISSION

In most cases, a consumer is legally obligated once he has signed a contract. Many states, however, have statutes allowing a consumer a brief period—generally two or three days—during which he may rescind an otherwise binding credit obligation if the sale was solicited in his home. Moreover, the Federal Trade Commission has also set forth a trade regulation that applies to door-to-door sales, leases, or rentals of goods and services for $25 or more, whether the sale is for cash or on credit. The regulation permits a consumer to rescind a contract within *three days* of signing.

The right of **rescission** also exists under the ***Federal Consumer Credit Protection Act*** (discussed more fully in the next section), which allows a consumer three days during which he may withdraw from any credit obligation secured by a mortgage on his home, unless the extension of credit was made to acquire the dwelling. After the consumer rescinds, the creditor has twenty days to return any money or property he has received from the consumer.

The ***Interstate Land Sales Full Disclosure Act*** requires a developer of unimproved land to file a detailed statement of record containing specified information about specified subdivisions with the Department of Housing and Urban Development before offering the lots for sale or lease. The developer must provide a property report (a condensed version of the statement of record) to each prospective purchaser or lessee. The act provides that a purchaser or lessee may revoke any contract or agreement for sale or lease at her option within seven days of signing the contract, and that the contract must clearly provide this right. A purchaser or lessee who does not receive a property report before signing a contract may revoke the contract within two years from the date of signing.

http://
Consumer Credit Protection Act: http://www4.law.cornell.edu/uscode/15/1601.html
Interstate Land Sales Full Disclosure Act: http://www4.law.cornell.edu/uscode/15/1701.html

Practical Advice

As a consumer, recognize that in certain situations you have a period of time in which you may rescind your contract.

CONSUMER CREDIT TRANSACTIONS

In the absence of special regulation, consumer credit transactions are governed by the laws that regulate commercial transactions generally. A **consumer credit transaction** is customarily defined as any credit transaction involving goods, services, or land acquired for personal, household, or family purposes. The following examples illustrate consumer credit transactions: Atkins borrows $600 from a bank to pay a dentist bill or to take a vacation; Bevins buys a refrigerator for her home from a department store and agrees to pay the purchase price in twelve equal monthly installments; Carpenter has an oil company credit card with which he purchases gasoline and tires for his family car.

Regulation of consumer credit has increased considerably because of the dramatic expansion of consumer credit and the numerous abuses in credit transactions, including misleading credit disclosures, unfair marketing practices, and oppressive collection methods. In 1968, in response to concerns about consumer credit, Congress passed the ***Federal Consumer Credit Protection Act (FCCPA)***, which requires creditors to disclose finance charges (including interest and other charges) and credit

CONCEPT REVIEW

Consumer Rescission Rights

Law	Rescission Period	Door-to-Door Solicitation Required?	Credit or Cash
State "Cooling-Off" Laws	Varies	Yes	Varies
FTC Trade Regulation	Within 3 days of signing the contract	Yes	Both
Consumer Credit Protection Act (CCPA)	Within 3 days of signing the contract	No	Credit only
Interstate Land Sales Full Disclosure Act	Within 7 days of signing the contract	No	Both

extension charges, and sets limits on garnishment proceedings. Since 1968, Congress has added titles to this law. Also in 1968, the National Conference of Commissioners on Uniform State Laws (the group that drafted the Uniform Commercial Code) promulgated the ***Uniform Consumer Credit Code (UCCC)***, which consolidated into one recommended law the regulation of all consumer credit transactions—loans and purchases on credit. Although only a few states have adopted the UCCC, its impact on the development of consumer credit has extended well beyond their borders.

ACCESS TO THE MARKET

The ***Equal Credit Opportunity Act***, enacted by Congress in 1974 and revised several times since then, prohibits all businesses that regularly extend credit from discriminating against any credit applicant on the basis of gender, marital status, race, color, religion, national origin, or age. Under the act, a creditor must notify an applicant, within thirty days of receiving an application, of the action the creditor has taken and must give specific reasons for denying credit. Although several federal agencies administer and enforce the act, the FTC has overall enforcement authority. A credit applicant aggrieved by a violation of the act may recover actual and punitive damages, plus attorneys' fees.

http://

Uniform Consumer Credit Code: http://www.creditcode.gov.au

Equal Credit Opportunity Act: http://www4.law.cornell.edu/uscode/15/1691.html

DISCLOSURE REQUIREMENTS

Title One of the FCCPA, also known as the **Truth-in-Lending Act**, has superseded state disclosure requirements relating to credit terms for both consumer loans and credit sales under $25,000. The act does not cover credit transactions for business, commercial, or agricultural purposes. Creditors in every state not specifically exempted by the Federal Reserve Board must comply with federal disclosure standards.

Before a consumer formally incurs a contractual obligation for credit, both state and federal statutes require the creditor to present to the consumer a written statement containing certain information about contract terms. Generally, the required disclosure concerns the cost of credit, that is, interest or sales finance charges. An important requirement in the Truth-in-Lending Act is that sales finance and interest rates must be quoted in terms of an **APR** (*annual percentage rate*) and must be calculated on a uniform basis. Congress required disclosure of this information to encourage consumers to compare credit terms, to increase competition among financial institutions, and to facilitate economic stability. Enforcement and interpretation of the Truth-in-Lending Act was assigned to the Federal Reserve Board, which issued ***Regulation Z*** to carry out this responsibility.

Practical Advice

As a lender, make sure that you disclose the annual percentage rate (including all appropriate costs) and all other required information prior to closing the loan.

The ***Fair Credit and Charge Card Disclosure Act of 1988*** adds to the Truth-in-Lending Act a new section requiring all credit and charge card applications and solicitations to include extensive disclosures whose requirements depend on the type of card involved and whether the application or solicitation is by mail, telephone, or other means.

Credit Accounts Under the Truth-in-Lending Act a creditor must inform consumers who open revolving or open-end credit accounts about how the finance charge is computed and when it is charged, what other charges may be imposed, and whether the creditor retains or acquires a security interest. Moreover, the Federal Reserve Board in 2000 published a rule requiring marketing material to display clearly a table that shows the APR and other important information such as the annual fee. An **open-end credit** account is one that permits the debtor to enter into a series of credit transactions that he may pay off either in installments or in a lump sum. Examples of this type of credit include most department store credit cards, most gasoline credit cards, Visa cards, and MasterCards. With this type of credit, the creditor is also required to provide a statement of account for each billing period.

Closed-ended credit, in contrast, is credit extended for a specified time, during which the debtor generally makes periodic payments in an amount and at a time agreed upon in advance. Examples of this type of credit include most automobile financing agreements, most real estate mortgages, and numerous other major purchases. For nonrevolving or closed-ended credit accounts, the creditor must provide the consumer with information about the total amount financed; the cash price; the number, amount, and due date of installments; delinquency charges; and a description of the security, if any.

ARMs In 1987, the Federal Reserve Board amended Regulation Z to deal with variable or adjustable rate mortgages (ARMs). The *ARM disclosure rules* apply to any loan that is (1) a closed-ended consumer transaction, (2) secured by the consumer's principal residence, (3) longer than one year in duration, and (4) subject to interest rate variation. This coverage excludes open-ended lines of credit secured by the consumer's principal dwelling. The disclosures must be made when a creditor furnishes an application to a prospective borrower or before the creditor receives payment of a nonrefundable fee, whichever occurs first. The ARM disclosure rules require that the creditor provide the consumer with a consumer handbook on ARMs and a loan program disclosure statement covering the terms of each ARM that the creditor offers.

Home Equity Loans In recent years a popular method of consumer borrowing has been the home equity loan. In order to regulate the disclosures and advertising of these loans, in 1988 Congress enacted the ***Home Equity Loan Consumer Protection Act (HELCPA)***. HELCPA amends the Truth-in-Lending Act to require that lenders provide a disclosure statement and consumer pamphlet at (or, in some limited instances, within three days of) the time they provide an application to a prospective consumer borrower. HELCPA applies to all open-ended credit plans for consumer loans that are secured by the consumer's principal dwelling. Unlike other Truth-in-Lending statutes, HELCPA defines a principal dwelling to include second or vacation homes. The disclosure statement must include a statement that (1) a default on the loan may result in the consumer's loss of the dwelling; (2) some conditions must be met, such as a time by which the consumer must submit an application in order to obtain the specific terms; and (3) the creditor, under certain circumstances, may terminate the plan and accelerate the outstanding balance, prohibit further extension of credit, reduce the plan's credit limit, or impose fees upon the termination of the account. In addition, if the plan contains a fixed interest rate, the creditor must disclose each APR imposed. If the plan involves an ARM, it must include how the rate is computed, the manner in which rates will be changed, the initial rate and how it was determined, the maximum rate change that may occur in any one year, the maximum rate that can be charged under the plan, the earliest time at which the maximum interest can be reached, and an itemization of all fees the plan imposes. Regulation Z provides the consumer with the right to rescind such a plan until midnight of the third day following the opening of the plan, until delivery of a notice of the right to rescind, or until delivery of all material disclosures, whichever comes last.

Billing Errors In 1975, the ***Fair Credit Billing Act*** went into effect to relieve some of the problems and abuses associated with credit card billing errors. The act establishes procedures for the consumer to follow in making complaints about specified billing errors and requires the creditor to explain or correct such errors. Until it responds to the complaint, the creditor may not take any action to collect the disputed amount, restrict the use of an open-ended credit account because the disputed amount is unpaid, or report the disputed amount as delinquent.

http:// Fair Credit Billing Act: http://www4.law.cornell.edu/uscode/15/1666.html

Settlement Charges In 1974, Congress enacted the ***Real Estate Settlement Procedures Act (RESPA)*** to provide consumer home purchasers with greater and more timely information on the nature and costs of the settlement process and to protect them from unnecessarily high settlement charges. The act, which applies to all federally related mortgage loans, requires advance disclosure to home buyers and sellers of all settlement costs, including attorneys' fees, credit reports, title insurance, and, if relevant, an

THE LAW AND YOU

State Bar Associations

Alabama: http://www.alabar.org/ ("Consumer Finance or Buying on Time")

Arkansas: http://www.arkbar.com/publications/publication_public.html ("Consumer Law Handbook")

Florida: http://www.flabar.org/newflabar/consumerservices/General/Consumer.Pam/ ("Applying for Credit")

Illinois: http://www.illinioslawyerfinder.com/publicinfo/home.html ("Buying on Time")

Iowa: http://www.iowabar.org/pamphlet.nsf/$about!OpenAbout ("Consumer Guide to Iowa Law")

Louisiana: http://www.lsba.org/Public_Resources/consumer_brochures.html ("Fair Debt Collection Practices"; "Equal Credit Opportunity")

Missouri: http://www.mobar.org/pamphlet/broindex.htm (brochures on legal topics) ("Buying on Time")

Ohio: http://www.ohiobar.org/conres/pamphlets ("Ohio's Credit Laws")

Oregon: http://www.osbar.org/public/legalinfo.html ("Consumer Rights and Remedies")

South Carolina: http://www.scbar.org/Free_Publications/free_publications.htm ("Consumer Debts and the Law")

South Dakota: http://www.sdbar.org/public/Default.htm ("Consumer's Guide")

Tennessee: http://www.tba.org/LawBytes/LawBytes.html ("Consumer Information")

Texas: http://www.texasbar.com/public/consumerinfo/helpfulinfo/pamphlets.asp ("Consumer Issues"; "A Guide to the Texas Deceptive Trade Practices-Consumer Protection Act")

U.S. Government

http://www.pueblo.gsa.gov/specpubs.htm#MM ("At-Home Shopping Rights")

http://www.pueblo.gsa.gov/specpubs.htm#MM ("Getting What You Pay For: Weights & Measures Tips for Consumers")

http://www.pueblo.gsa.gov/cic_text/money/credit-card/credcard.htm ("Choosing & Using Credit Cards")

http://www.pueblo.gsa.gov/ (money) ("Consumer Handbook to Credit Protection Laws")

http://www.pueblo.gsa.gov/specpubs.htm#MM ("Credit and Divorce")

http://www.pueblo.gsa.gov/money.htm ("Fair Credit Reporting")

http://www.pueblo.gsa.gov/money.htm ("Fair Debt Collection")

http://www.pueblo.gsa.gov/specpubs.htm#MM ("Shop . . . The Card You Pick Can Save You Money")

http://www.pueblo.gsa.gov/specpubs.htm#MM ("What Savvy Consumers Need to Know About Debit Cards")

http://www.pueblo.gsa.gov/food.htm ("Can Your Kitchen Pass the Food Safety Test?")

http://www.pueblo.gsa.gov/ (food) ("Consumer's Guide to Fats")

http://www.pueblo.gsa.gov/food.htm ("Keep Your Food Safe")

http://www.pueblo.gsa.gov/specpubs.htm#FO ("Making Healthy Food Choices")

http://www.pueblo.gsa.gov/misc.htm ("2004 Consumer Action Handbook")

http://www.pueblo.gsa.gov/misc.htm ("Funerals: A Consumer Guide")

http://www.pueblo.gsa.gov/cic_text/money/swindlers/swindler.htm ("Swindlers Are Calling")

Federal Trade Commission: http://www.ftc.gov/bcp/menu-tmark.htm ("Advance-Fee Loan Scams Campaign"; "Are You a Target of . . . Telephone Scams?"; "Automatic Debit Scams"; "Border-Line Scams Are the Real Thing"; "Catch the Bandit in Your Mailbox"; "Easy Credit? Not So Fast. The Truth About Advance Fee Loan Scams"; "FTC Names Its Dirty Dozen: 12 Scams Most Likely to Arrive via Bulk Email"; "International Lottery Scams"; "Magazine Subscription Scams"; "Reloading Scams: Double Trouble for Consumers"; "Telemarketing Recovery Scams"; "Telemarketing Travel Fraud")

initial escrow account statement. Nearly all first mortgage loans fall within the scope of the act. RESPA, which is administered and enforced by the Secretary of Housing and Urban Development, prohibits kickbacks and referral fees and limits the amount home buyers must place in escrow accounts to ensure payment of real estate taxes and insurance. In 1990, the National Affordable Housing Act amended RESPA to require an annual analysis of escrow accounts.

http:// Real Estate Settlement Procedures Act: http://www4.law.cornell.edu/uscode/12/2601.html

CONTRACT TERMS

Consumer credit is marketed on a mass basis. Frequently, contract documents are printed forms containing blank spaces to accommodate the contractual details the creditor will normally negotiate at the time she extends credit. Standardization and uniformity of contract terms facilitate the transfer of the creditor's rights (in most situations, those of a seller) to a third party, usually a bank or finance company.

Almost all states impose statutory ceilings on the amount that creditors may charge for the extension of consumer credit. Statutes regulating rates also specify what other charges may be made. Most statutes require a creditor to permit the debtor to pay her obligation in full at any time before the maturity date of the final installment. If the interest charge for the loan period was computed in advance and added to the principal of the loan, a debtor who prepays in full is entitled to a refund of the unearned interest already paid.

In the past, certain purchases involving consumer goods were financed in such a way that a consumer was legally obligated to make full payment of the price to a third party, even though the dealer from whom she bought the goods had committed fraud or the goods were defective. This occurred when the purchaser executed and delivered to the seller a negotiable instrument (a promissory note, draft, or check), and the seller negotiated it to a holder in due course, who purchased the note for value, in good faith, and without notice that it was overdue or that it had any defenses or claims attached to it. Though valid against the seller, the buyer's defenses—that the goods were defective or that the seller had committed fraud—were not valid against a holder in due course of the note. To preserve the claims and defenses of consumer buyers and borrowers and to make such claims and defenses available against holders in due course, the FTC adopted a rule that limits the rights of a holder in due course of an instrument evidencing a debt that arises out of a *consumer credit contract*. The rule, which we discussed in Chapter 26, applies to sellers and lessors of goods.

A similar rule applies to credit card issuers under the ***Fair Credit Billing Act***. The act preserves a consumer's defense against the issuer (provided the consumer has made a good faith attempt to resolve the dispute with the seller), but only if (1) the seller is controlled by the card issuer or is under common control with the issuer, (2) the issuer has included the seller's promotional literature in the monthly billing statements sent to the card holder, or (3) the sale involves more than $50 and the consumer's billing address is in the same state as, or within one hundred miles of, the seller's place of business.

CONSUMER CREDIT CARD FRAUD

In 1984, Congress enacted the **Credit Card Fraud Act**, which closed many loopholes in prior law. The act prohibits the following practices: (1) possessing unauthorized cards, (2) counterfeiting or altering credit cards, (3) using account numbers alone, and (4) using cards obtained from a third party with his consent, even if the third party conspires to report the cards as stolen. It also imposes stiffer, criminal penalties for violation.

The FCCPA protects the *credit card holder* from loss by limiting to $50 the card holder's liability for another's unauthorized use of the holder's card. However, the card issuer may collect up to that amount for unauthorized use only if (1) the holder has accepted the card; (2) the issuer has furnished adequate notice of potential liability to the card holder; (3) the issuer has provided the card holder with a statement describing the means by which the holder may notify the card issuer of the loss or theft of the credit card; (4) the unauthorized use occurs before the card holder has notified the card issuer of the loss or theft; and (5) the card issuer has provided a method by which the person using the card can be identified as the person authorized to use the card.

http:// Credit Card Fraud Act: http://www4.law.cornell.edu/uscode/18/1029.html

FAIR REPORTAGE

Because creditors usually grant consumers credit only after investigating their creditworthiness, it is essential that the information on which creditors base such decisions is accurate and current. To this end, in 1970 Congress enacted the ***Fair Credit Reporting Act***, which applies to consumer reports used to secure employment, insurance, and credit. The act prohibits the inclusion of inaccurate or specified obsolete information in consumer reports and requires consumer reporting agencies to give consumers written advance notice before making an investigative report.

Practical Advice

The consumer may request information regarding the nature and substance of all information in the consumer reporting agency's files, the source of the information, and the names of all who received the consumer reports furnished for employment purposes within the preceding two years and for other purposes within the preceding six months.

If the consumer does not agree that the information in the file is accurate and complete, and so notifies the agency, the agency must then reinvestigate the matter within a reasonable time, unless the complaint is frivolous or irrelevant. If reinvestigation proves that the information is inaccurate, it must promptly be deleted. If the dispute remains unresolved after reinvestigation, the consumer may submit to the agency a brief statement setting forth the nature of the dispute, and this statement must be incorporated into the report.

In 1997, Congress amended the act to restrict the use of credit reports by employers. An employer must now notify a job applicant or current employee that a report may be used and must obtain the applicant's consent prior to requesting an individual's credit report from a credit bureau. In addition, prior to taking an adverse action (refusal to hire, reassignment or termination, or denying a promotion) against the applicant or employee, the employer must provide the individual with a "pre-adverse action disclosure," which must contain the credit report and a copy of the FTC's "A Summary of Your Rights Under the Fair Credit Reporting Act."

http:// Fair Credit Reporting Act: http://www4.law.cornell.edu/uscode/15/1681.html

Phillips v. Grendahl

United States Court of Appeals, Eighth Circuit, 2002
312 F.3d 357

FACTS Lavon Phillips became engaged to marry Sarah Grendahl and moved in with her. Sarah's mother, Mary, became suspicious that Phillips was not telling the truth about his past, particularly about whether he was an attorney and where he had worked. She also was confused about who his ex-wives and girlfriends were and where they lived. She did some preliminary investigation herself, but she felt that she was hampered by not being able to use a computer, so she contacted Kevin Fitzgerald, a family friend who worked for McDowell, a private investigation agency. She asked Fitzgerald to do a "background check" on Phillips.

Fitzgerald searched public records in Minnesota and Alabama, where Phillips had lived earlier and discovered one suit against Phillips for delinquent child support in Alabama, a suit to establish child support for two children in Minnesota, and one misdemeanor conviction for writing dishonored checks. Fitzgerald then supplied the social security information to Econ Control and asked for "Finder's Reports" on Phillips. Fitzgerald testified that he believed that Finder's Reports were not consumer reports and therefore that they were not subject to the Fair Credit Reporting Act.

Econ Control was in the business of furnishing credit reports, Finder's Reports, and credit scoring for credit grantors and for private investigators. William Porter, president of Econ Control, stated that he believed a "Finder's Report" could be obtained without authorization of the person who was the subject of the report because the Finder's Report contained no information on credit history or creditworthiness. Porter stated that a Credit Report, on the other hand, requires authorization from the subject. Robert McDowell, on behalf of McDowell Agency, had earlier signed an agreement with Econ Control stating that he would properly use all consumer reports.

Econ Control than obtained a consumer report from Computer Science Corporation on Phillips and passed it onto McDowell. Fitzgerald met with Mary Grendahl and gave her the results of his investigation, including the Finder's Report. Someone wrote on the copy of the Finder's Report on Phillips: "Credit inquiry report and Employment Trace."

Phillips learned that Sarah Grendahl's family had investigated his past when Laura Grendahl, Sarah's sister, telephoned Sarah about nine months after the investigation.

Each defendant has some familiarity with the fact that the law limits access to consumer credit reports. Mary Grendahl owns the Park Apartments in Minneapolis. The apartment business office obtains credit information on prospective tenants as part of its business. The office always obtains the tenant's written permission to obtain a credit report, "because it's necessary to have their signature to get a credit report," according to Mary Grendahl. Porter, the president of Econ Control, testified that he had read the section of the Fair Credit Reporting Act governing resale of credit information. Fitzgerald testified that sometime during his employment with McDowell, he had heard of the Fair Credit Reporting Act.

Phillips brought this suit against Mary Grendahl, McDowell Agency, and Econ Control, alleging, "Defendants willfully and maliciously obtained Plaintiff's credit report for impermissible and illegal purposes in violation of the Fair Credit Reporting Act * * *." Phillips and the defendants filed cross motions for summary judgment. The court entered summary judgment for the defendants.

DECISION Summary judgment on the issue of the Fair Credit and Reporting Act is reversed and remanded.

OPINION Gibson, J. The Fair Credit Reporting Act, [citation], prohibits the disclosure of consumer credit reports by consumer credit reporting agencies, except in response to the following kinds of requests: (1) court order or subpoena, [citation]; (2) request by governmental agencies involved in setting or enforcing child support awards, [citation]); (3) request authorized in writing by the consumer about whom the report is made, [citation]; or (4) request by a person whom the reporting agency has reason to believe intends to use the consumer report for one of a number of specific, permissible business reasons, [citation].

Phillips pursues two theories under the Fair Credit Reporting Act—that the defendants obtained a consumer report on him by use of false pretenses, [citation], and that they obtained a consumer report for an impermissible purpose, [citation]. * * *

* * *

The Fair Credit Reporting Act was amended in 1996 to add to section [citation] a provision that forbids using or obtaining a consumer report unless the report was obtained for a permitted purpose. [Citation]. Moreover, section [citation] received new language imposing civil liability * * * against natural persons for "obtaining a consumer report under false pretenses or knowingly without a permissible purpose." [Citation]. Thus, the civil liability provisions now explicitly cover the act of obtaining a consumer report without a permissible purpose, which formerly was included only by incorporating the criminal liability statute. * * *

* * *

We therefore will test Phillips's claim against each of the three defendants under sections [citation], for allegations of willful and negligent misuse or acquisition of a consumer report. Under both sections, Phillips must prove that there was a consumer report, that defendants used or obtained it, and that they did so without a permissible statutory purpose. He must also prove that the defendants acted with the specified level of culpability, which is willfulness under section [citation] and negligence under section [citation].

* * *

The first step in establishing liability under [FCRA] for obtaining a consumer report without a permissible purpose is to show that the document at issue was a "consumer report." The statutory definition is complex. [The FCRA] defines a consumer report as (1) any written, oral, or other communication of information (2) by a consumer reporting agency (3) bearing on a consumer's credit worthiness, credit standing, credit capacity, character, general reputation, personal characteristics, or mode of living (4) which is used or expected to be used or collected in whole or in part for the purpose of serving as a factor in establishing the consumer's eligibility for (A) credit or insurance to be used primarily for personal, family, or household purposes; (B) employment purposes; or (C) any other purposes authorized under section [citation]. * * *

In this case, there is no dispute that the Finder's Report was (1) a written communication (2) by a consumer reporting agency, Computer Science Corporation. The two issues in dispute pertaining to whether the Finder's Report is a consumer report are (3) whether it contained the sort of personal information that would bring it within the definition and (4) whether anyone "expected" the Finder's Report or the information in it to be used for one of the purposes listed in the definition or "collected" the information in it for that purpose.

A consumer report must contain information "bearing on a consumer's credit worthiness, credit standing, credit capacity, character, general reputation, personal characteristics, or mode of living." [Citation.] The District of Columbia Circuit observed that this element "does not seem very demanding," [citation], for "almost any information about consumers arguably bears on their personal characteristics or mode of living." [Citation.] The Finder's Report listed "Trade line Information," consisting of the names of several creditors with whom Phillips had credit accounts and the existence of a child support obligation, with dates for "last activity," but no other details such as amount of obligation or payment history. * * * The Finder's Report also lists Phillips's former employers, which also would bear on his mode of living by showing that he has been employed. We conclude that the Finder's Report contains the kind of personal information required by the definition of consumer report.

The second question, whether the putative consumer report or the information in it was "used or expected to be used" or "collected for" one of the listed purposes, such as use in a credit or employment decision, [citation], is more difficult. Three statutory ambiguities in this clause could affect what communications are covered by the clause: the statutory language does not specify who must do the using, collecting or expecting; whether those verbs describe a specific or habitual action; or whether those actions must be done with regard to "information" or with regard to the consumer report itself. McDowell Agency essentially argues the clause requires that either the credit agency prepared the

Finder's Report in the expectation that it would be used for a statutory purpose or that the requestors did so use it. McDowell Agency contends that the Finder's Report was too incomplete to enable anyone to base a credit decision on it, so neither the requestors nor the credit agency could have expected the report to be used in a credit decision. Phillips, on the other hand, focuses on the information in the report, rather than the report itself. He argues that some of the information was of a type habitually "used" by people within the credit industry for the purposes covered by the statute and that therefore no showing about anyone's actual intent with regard to the Finder's Report was necessary to make it a consumer report.

We need not choose among the competing interpretations of the clause urged by the parties, because we conclude that the Finder's Report fell within the "used, expected to be used, or collected" clause even under the interpretation urged by McDowell Agency. The record demonstrates that the Finder's Report, not just the information in it, was actually intended by the credit reporting agency that prepared it to be used for a statutory purpose. The sample Finder's Report supplied by Econ Control to McDowell Agency states: "FINDERS delivers skip-locate power in a cost effective, easy-to-use format. This remarkable product was designed by and for collections professionals who need timely debt-recovery support at an economical price." * * *

We next determine whether each of the defendants "obtained or used" the consumer report. There is no dispute that McDowell Agency and Econ Control obtained a consumer report, for each of them requested a Finder's Report.

Mary Grendahl, on the other hand, testified that she did not request the release of any credit information on Phillips. Mere passive receipt of the report would not be enough to satisfy the statutory element that she "use or obtain" a consumer report. [Citations.] However, Phillips argues that the phone machine message Grendahl left for Sarah is evidence that she asked Fitzgerald to obtain credit information: "Sarah, this is mom. I didn't directly do a credit report. I hired a PI and they have every right to do that." This evidence is ambiguous. On the one hand, it could mean that Grendahl hired a private investigator because she thought he was entitled to do a credit report. On the other hand, it could mean that she simply hired a private investigator who ordered a credit report on his own initiative, which she now understood he was entitled to do. Because this case was disposed of on summary judgment, we must resolve any ambiguities in the evidence in favor of Phillips. [Citation.] In this procedural posture, the ambiguous telephone message is sufficient to create a genuine issue of fact as to whether Mary Grendahl asked Fitzgerald to obtain a consumer report on Phillips.

* * *

The next inquiry is whether any of the defendants had a permissible statutory purpose for obtaining the consumer report. The only purpose for obtaining the report was to obtain information on Mary Grendahl's prospective son-in-law. Investigating a person because he wants to marry one's daughter is not a statutory consumer purpose * * *. Even if getting married can be characterized as a consumer transaction * * *, it was not Mary Grendahl, but her daughter, whom Phillips was engaged to marry. He had no business transaction pending with Mary Grendahl. There was no permissible purpose for obtaining or using a consumer report.

The element of culpability varies according to whether the cause arises under section 1681n generally, section 1681n(a), or section 1681o.

Section 1681n(a) provides civil liability for willful noncompliance with any requirement of the Fair Credit Reporting Act.

We must initially determine first, what state of mind amounts to willfulness and second, whether the defendant must willfully request the report or willfully violate a requirement of the Fair Credit Reporting Act. * * *

The statute's use of the word "willfully" imports the requirement that the defendant know his or her conduct is unlawful. [Citation.] * * *

* * *

We conclude * * * that willful noncompliance under section 1681n requires knowing and intentional commission of an act the defendant knows to violate the law.

Here, there is evidence that none of the three defendants believed their conduct to be covered by the Fair Credit Reporting Act. * * *

On the other hand, there is also evidence that each defendant had some experience in dealing with credit reports and either knew of the Fair Credit Reporting Act or at least knew that such reports can only be obtained legally under certain circumstances. This kind of experience can support an inference that the defendants knew that their actions were impermissible. * * * These facts are sufficient to create a genuine issue of material fact as to whether defendants acted knowingly and with conscious disregard for Phillips's legal rights.

Section 1681n(a)(1)(B) provides for statutory damages for obtaining a consumer report under false pretenses or knowingly without a permissible purpose, only in actions against natural persons. Our discussion of this section is therefore limited to the claim against Mary Grendahl. This section requires either false pretenses or knowing acquisition of a consumer report without a permissible purpose. Since either is sufficient, Phillips's evidence raising a fact issue as to whether Mary Grendahl knowingly obtained a consumer report on him with conscious disregard for his legal rights is also sufficient to make a submissible case under this section. We therefore need not reach the question of whether the statute's use of the term "false pretenses" requires intent to mislead.

Section 1681o provides a private cause of action for negligent failure to comply with the Fair Credit Reporting Act. Since Phillips has raised factual issues sufficient to require trial on whether defendants willfully violated his rights under the Act, it follows that he has also made a submissible case as to negligent violation of those same rights.

INTERPRETATION The Fair Credit Reporting Act limits the disclosure of consumer credit reports by consumer credit reporting agencies.

CRITICAL THINKING QUESTION Does the Fair Credit Reporting Act go too far in limiting the use of "consumer credit reports"?

CREDITORS' REMEDIES

A primary concern of creditors involves their rights should a debtor default or become late in payment. When the credit charge is precomputed, the creditor may impose a delinquency charge for late payments, subject to statutory limits for such charges. If, instead of being delinquent, the consumer defaults, the creditor may declare the entire balance of the debt immediately due and payable and may sue on the debt. The other courses of action that are open to the creditor depend on his security. Security provisions in consumer credit contracts may require a cosigner, an assignment of wages, a security interest in the goods sold, a security interest in other real or personal property of the debtor, and a confession of judgment clause (i.e., a clause by the defendant giving the plaintiff power to enter judgment against the defendant).

WAGE ASSIGNMENTS AND GARNISHMENT

Wage assignments are prohibited by some states. In most states and under the FCCPA, a limitation is imposed on the amount that may be deducted from an individual's wages during any pay period. In addition, the FCCPA prohibits an employer from discharging an employee solely because of a creditor's exercise of an assignment of wages in connection with any one debt.

Even where wage assignments are prohibited, the creditor may still reach a consumer's wages through garnishment. But garnishment is available only in a court proceeding to enforce the collection of a judgment. The FCCPA and state statutes contain exemption provisions that limit the amount of wages subject to garnishment.

SECURITY INTEREST

In the case of credit sales, the seller may retain a security interest in the goods sold. Many states impose restrictions on other security the creditor may obtain. Where the debt is secured by property as collateral, the creditor, on default by the debtor, may take possession of the property and, subject to the provisions of the Uniform Commercial Code, either retain it in full satisfaction of the debt or sell it and, if the proceeds are less than the outstanding debt, sue the debtor for the balance and obtain a deficiency judgment. The UCC provides that when a buyer of goods has paid 60 percent of the purchase price or 60 percent of a loan secured by consumer goods, the secured creditor may not retain the property in full satisfaction but must sell the goods and pay to the buyer that part of the sale proceeds in excess of the balance due. (We discussed secured transactions in Chapter 38.)

In addition, federal regulation prohibits a credit seller or lender from obtaining a consumer's grant of a nonpossessory security interest in household goods. Household goods include clothing, furniture, appliances, kitchenware, personal effects, one radio, and one television; such goods specifically exclude works of art, other electronic entertainment equipment, antiques, and jewelry. This rule, which does not apply to purchase money security interests or to pledges, prevents a lender or seller from obtaining a nonpurchase money security interest covering the consumer's household goods.

DEBT COLLECTION PRACTICES

In 1977, Congress enacted the *Fair Debt Collection Practices Act* to prevent debt collection agencies from employing abusive, deceptive, and unfair practices in the collection of consumer debts. The act, which is enforced by the Federal Trade Commission, does not apply to creditors

Ethical Dilemma

Should Some Be Protected from High-Pressure Sales?

FACTS Glen Thomas, a recent college graduate, was hired as a rental agent by New Vistas Condominiums, Inc., of Old Saybrook, Connecticut. Initially responsible for handling rentals on two apartment buildings, Glen was also assigned to an aggressive sales program for new time-share condominiums to be developed in Florida.

Under the new sales program, Glen was to be trained as a marketing specialist. His boss, Sabrina Cassey, explained that the marketing plan would target those between the ages of sixty and eighty. The condominiums would feature an attractive communal social program that would include swimming exercises, Friday night bingo games, and monthly movies. Also available, for additional fees, would be special services, such as food delivery, shopping, and domestic help.

In the following months, in marketing the new condominiums, New Vistas made particular efforts to interest those who had recently lost their spouses. The company devised a system for following obituaries and purchased lists that directed its marketing personnel to recent widows and widowers at certain income levels.

For the new condominiums, Sabrina's marketing team has concocted a presentation she terms "lethal." The program begins with a direct mailing. Thereafter, individuals are invited to a party and are promised free prizes. A movie is shown that features elderly people socializing around a pool, playing cards, and having intimate candlelight dinners. Wine and dessert are served afterward. Then, once the terms of the condominium purchase have been explained, New Vistas salespeople distribute contracts and pressure the attendees to sign the contracts before the distribution of gifts. At the meetings, Sabrina's job is to explain the condominiums; Glen's role is to get the contracts signed.

On the first night of the sales promotion, Glen meets Irving Sherman, who happens to be the father of a girl Glen dated in high school. Irving tells Glen that his wife has recently died, succumbing to a three-year battle with cancer. Glen knows that Irving has been through quite an ordeal; Irving himself had suffered from colon cancer several years earlier. When it comes time to press for signatures on the contracts, Glen becomes very uncomfortable and wants to leave.

Social, Policy, and Ethical Considerations

1. What should Glen do? Why? What alternative sales methods are available?
2. Is there anything ethically wrong with gearing sales to a special segment of the population? Should certain segments of the population be protected from high-powered sales programs?
3. Can the public ever be overprotected with regard to sales promotions? To what extent, if any, should individuals be limited in the nonfraudulent marketing of their products?

themselves. Rather, the act provides that any debt collector who communicates with a person other than the consumer for the purpose of acquiring information about the consumer's location may not state that the consumer owes any debt. Moreover, the act prohibits a number of abusive collection practices, including (1) communication with the consumer at unusual or inconvenient hours; (2) communication with the consumer if she is represented by an attorney; (3) harassing, oppressive, or abusive conduct, such as obscene language or threats of violence; (4) false, deceptive, or misleading representations or means of collection; and (5) unfair or unconscionable means to collect any debt.

The act requires a debt collector, within five days of the initial communication with a consumer, to provide the consumer with a written notice that includes (1) the amount of the debt; (2) the name of the current creditor; and (3) a statement informing the consumer that she can request verification of the alleged debt. The consumer may recover damages from the collection agency for violations of the act.

http:// Fair Debt Collection Practices Act: http://www4.law.cornell.edu/uscode/15/1692.html

Practical Advice

As a creditor carefully refrain from harassing or abusing a debtor and make sure that all contacts with the debtor strictly comply with all laws and regulations.

Miller v. McCalla, Raymer, Padrick, Cobb, Nichols, And Clark, L.L.C.

United States Court of Appeals, Seventh Circuit, 2000
214 F.3d 872
http://laws.findlaw.com/7th/993263.html

FACTS The plaintiff, Kevin Miller, bought a house in Atlanta in 1992 and took out a mortgage. He lived in the house until 1995, when he accepted a job in Chicago; from then on, he rented the house. He received a dunning (a demand for payment) letter from one of the defendant law firms on behalf of the mortgage company in 1997. By this time, the plaintiff was renting the property to strangers and thus was making a business use of the property. The plaintiff claimed that the defendants violated the Fair Debt Collection Practices Act by failing to state "the amount of the debt" in the dunning letter of which he complains. The defendants replied that they did state the amount and that the letter is outside the scope of the Act because they were trying to collect a business debt rather than a consumer debt. In response the plaintiff argued that the relevant time for determining the nature of the debt is when the debt first arises, not when collection efforts begin. The district court granted summary judgment for the defendants.

DECISION Judgment reversed and remanded.

OPINION Posner, C. J. The defendants [argue] that since the Act under which the plaintiff is suing * * * governs debt *collection*, the relevant time is when the attempt at collection is made. Oddly, there are no reported appellate decisions on the issue, though it was assumed in [citation] that the relevant time is when the loan is made, not when collection is attempted.

The language of the statute favors this interpretation. "Debt" is defined as "any obligation or alleged obligation of a consumer to pay money arising out of a transaction in which the money, property, insurance, or services which are the subject of the transaction are primarily for personal, family, or household purposes." [Citation.] The defendants don't deny that the plaintiff is a "consumer," even though he is in the "business" of renting his house (they can't deny this, because "the term 'consumer' means any natural person obligated or allegedly obligated to pay any debt," [citation]). And the antecedent of the first "which" in the clause "in which the money, property, insurance, or services which are the subject of the transaction are primarily for personal, family, or household purposes" is, as a matter of grammar anyway, the transaction out of which the obligation to repay arose, not the obligation itself; and that transaction was the purchase of a house for a personal use, namely living in it. Grammar needn't trump sense; the purpose of statutory interpretation is to make sense out of statutes not written by grammarians. But we cannot say that it is senseless to base the debt collector's obligation on the character of the debt when it arose rather than when it is to be collected. The original creditor is more likely to know whether the debt was personal or commercial at its incipience than either the creditor or the debt collector is to know what current use the debtor is making of the loan (in this case, the plaintiff is using the loan, in effect, to generate income from the house that secures the loan).

Against this the defendants argue that the plaintiff's interpretation creates a loophole. Suppose the plaintiff had bought the house to use as an office, and later converted it to personal use; on the plaintiff's interpretation of the Act the debt collector would not have to give him the statutory warnings. But this makes perfect sense. The Act regulates the debt collection tactics employed against personal borrowers on the theory that they are likely to be unsophisticated about debt collection and thus prey to unscrupulous collection methods. [Citations.] Businessmen don't need the warnings. A businessman who converts a business purchase to personal use does not by virtue of that conversion lose his commercial sophistication and so acquire a need for statutory protection. * * *

So the Act is applicable and we move to the question whether the defendants violated the statutory duty to state the amount of the loan. [Citation.] The dunning letter said that the "unpaid principal balance" of the loan was $178,844.65, but added that "this amount does not include accrued but unpaid interest, unpaid late charges, escrow advances or other charges for preservation and protection of the lender's interest in the property, as authorized by your loan agreement. The amount to reinstate or pay off your loan changes daily. You may call our office for complete reinstatement and payoff figures." An 800 number is given.

The statement does not comply with the Act (again we can find no case on the question). The unpaid principal balance is not the debt; it is only a part of the debt; the Act requires statement of the debt. The requirement is not satisfied by listing a phone number. It is notorious that trying to get through to an 800 number is often a vexing and protracted undertaking, and anyway, unless the call is recorded, to authorize debt collectors to comply orally would be an invitation to just the sort of fraudulent and coercive tactics in debt collection that the Act aimed (rightly or wrongly) to put an end to. It is no excuse that it was "impossible" for the defendants to comply when as in this case the amount of the debt changes daily. What would or might be impossible for the defendants to do would be to determine what the amount of the debt might be at some future date if for example the interest rate in the loan agreement was variable. What they certainly could do was to state the total amount due—interest and other charges as well as principal—on the date the dunning letter was sent. We think the statute required this.

In a previous case, in an effort to minimize litigation under the debt collection statute, we fashioned a "safe harbor" formula for complying with another provision of the statute. [Citation.] We think it useful to do the same thing for the "amount of debt" provision. We hold that the following statement satisfies the debt collector's duty to state the amount of the debt in cases like this where the amount varies from day to day: "As of the date of this letter, you owe $___ [the exact amount due]. Because of interest, late charges, and other charges that may vary from day to day, the amount due on the day you pay may be greater. Hence, if you pay the amount shown above, an adjustment may be necessary after we receive your check, in which event we will inform you before depositing the check for collection. For further information, write the undersigned or call 1-800- [phone number]." A debt collector who uses this form will not violate the "amount of the debt" provision, provided, of course, that the information he furnishes is accurate and he does not obscure it by adding confusing other information (or misinformation). [Citations.] Of course we do not hold that a debt collector must use this form of words to avoid violating the statute; but if he does, and (to repeat an essential qualification) does not add other words that confuse the message, he will as a matter of law have discharged his duty to state clearly the amount due. No reasonable person could conclude that the statement that we have drafted does not inform the debtor of the amount due. [Citation.]

* * *

INTERPRETATION In order to protect a consumer's right to verify a debt, a collection agency letter must contain the amount of the debt.

CRITICAL THINKING QUESTION Do you agree with the court's decision? Explain.

CHAPTER SUMMARY

Federal Trade Commission

Purpose to prevent unfair methods of competition and unfair or deceptive acts or practices

Standards
- ***Unfairness*** requires injury to be (1) substantial, (2) not outweighed by any countervailing benefit, and (3) unavoidable by reasonable consumer action
- ***Deception*** misrepresentation, omission, or practice that is likely to mislead the consumer acting reasonably in the circumstances
- ***Ad Substantiation*** requires advertisers to have a reasonable basis for their claims

Remedies
- ***Cease and Desist Order*** command to stop doing the act in question
- ***Affirmative Disclosure*** requires an advertiser to include certain information in its ad so that the ad is not deceptive
- ***Corrective Advertising*** requires an advertiser to disclose that previous ads were deceptive
- ***Multiple Product Order*** requires an advertiser to cease and desist from deceptive statements regarding all products it sells

Consumer Health and Safety

Consumer Product Safety Act federal statute enacted to
- *Protect Public Against Unsafe Products*
- *Assist Consumers in Evaluating Products*
- *Develop Uniform Safety Standards*
- *Promote Safety Research*

Other Federal Consumer Protection Agencies

Consumer Purchases

Federal Warranty Protection applies to sellers of consumer goods who give written warranties
- *Presale Disclosure* requires terms of warranty to be simple and readily understood and to be made available before the sale
- *Labeling Requirement* requires warrantor to inform consumers of their legal rights under a warranty (full or limited)
- *Disclaimer Limitation* prohibits a written warranty from disclaiming any implied warranty

State "Lemon Laws" state laws that attempt to provide new car purchasers with rights similar to full warranties under Magnuson-Moss

Consumer Right of Rescission in certain instances a consumer is granted a brief period of time during which she may rescind (cancel) an otherwise binding obligation

Consumer Credit Transactions

Definition any credit transaction involving goods, services, or land for personal, household, or family purposes

Access to the Market discrimination in extending credit on the basis of gender, marital status, race, color, religion, national origin, or age is prohibited

Disclosure Requirements (Truth-in-Lending Act) requires creditor to provide certain information about contract terms, including APR (annual percentage rate), to the consumer before he formally incurs the obligation

Contract Terms statutory and judicial limitations have been imposed on consumer obligations

Credit Card Fraud Act prohibits certain fraudulent practices and limits a card holder's liability for unauthorized use of a credit card to $50

Fair Credit Reporting consumer credit reports are prohibited from containing inaccurate or obsolete information

Creditors' Remedies

Wage Assignments and Garnishment most states limit the amount that may be deducted from an individual's wages through either assignment or garnishment

Security Interest seller may retain a security interest in goods sold or other collateral of the buyer, although some restrictions are imposed

Debt Collection Practices abusive, deceptive, and unfair practices by debt collectors in collecting consumer debts are prohibited by the Fair Debt Collection Practices Act

QUESTIONS

1. The FTC brings a deceptive trade practice action against Beneficial Finance Company (http://www.household.com/) based on Beneficial's use of its "instant tax refund" slogan. The FTC argues that Beneficial's advertising a tax refund loan or instant tax refund is deceptive in that the loan is not in any way connected with a tax refund but is merely Beneficial's everyday loan based on the applicant's creditworthiness. Is this an unfair or deceptive trade practice? Explain.

2. Brenda borrows $1,000 from Lincoln for one year, agreeing to pay Lincoln $200 in interest on the loan and to repay the loan in twelve monthly installments of $100. The contract that Lincoln provides and Brenda signs specifies that the APR is 20 percent. Does this contract violate the Federal Consumer Credit Protection Act (FCCPA)? Why?

3. A consumer entered into an agreement with Rent-It Corporation for the rental of a television set at a charge of $17 per week. The agreement also provides that if the renter chooses to rent the set for seventy-eight consecutive weeks, title will be transferred. The consumer now contends that the agreement is really a sales agreement, not a lease, and therefore is a credit sale subject to the Truth-in-Lending Act. Explain whether the consumer is correct.

4. Central Adjustment Bureau allegedly threatened Consumer with a lawsuit, service at his office, and attachment and sale of his property in order to collect a debt, although it did not intend to carry out the threat and did not have the authority to commence litigation. On some notices sent to Consumer, Central failed to disclose that it was attempting to collect a debt. In addition, Consumer contends that Central sent notices demanding payment that were purportedly from attorneys but were written, signed, and sent by Central. Has Central violated the Fair Debt Collection Act? Explain.

5. The Giant Development Company undertakes a massive real estate venture to sell 9,000 one-acre unimproved lots in Utah. The company advertises the project nationally. Arrington, a resident of New York, learns of the opportunity and requests information about the project. The company provides Arrington with a small advertising brochure that contains no information about the developer and the land. The brochure consists of vague descriptions of the joys of homeownership and nothing else. Arrington purchases a lot. Two weeks after entering into the agreement, Arrington wishes to rescind the contract. Will Arrington prevail?

6. Jane Jones, a married woman, applies for a credit card from Exxon but is refused credit. Jane is bewildered as to why she was turned down. What are her legal rights in this situation?

7. On a beautiful Saturday in October, Francie decides to take the twenty-mile ride from her home in New Jersey into New York City to do some shopping. Francie finds that Brown's Retail Sales, Inc., has a terrific sale on television sets and decides to surprise her husband with a new color TV. She purchases the set from Brown's on her American Express credit card for $450. When the set is delivered, Francie discovers that it does not work. Brown's refuses to repair or replace it or to credit Francie's charge account. Francie therefore refuses to pay American Express for the television. American Express brings a suit against Francie. Will American Express prevail? Why?

8. Frank finds Thomas's wallet, which contains many credit cards and Thomas's identification. By using Thomas's identification and Visa card, Frank goes on a shopping spree and runs up $5,000 in charges. Thomas does not discover that he has lost his wallet until the following day, when he promptly notifies his Visa bank. How much can Visa collect from Thomas?

9. Robert applies to Northern National Bank for a loan. Before granting the loan, Northern requests that Callis Credit Agency provide it with a credit report on Robert. Callis reports that three years previously, Robert had embezzled money from his employer. Based on this report, Northern rejects Robert's loan application.
   a. Robert demands to know why the loan was rejected, but Northern refuses to divulge the information, arguing that it is privileged. Is Robert entitled to the information?
   b. Assume that Robert obtains the information and alleges that it is inaccurate. What recourse does Robert have?

CASE PROBLEMS

10. Colgate-Palmolive Co. (http://www.colgate.com/) produced a television advertisement that dramatically demonstrated the effectiveness of its Rapid Shave shaving cream. The ad purported to show the shaving cream being used to shave sandpaper. But because actual sandpaper appeared on television to be regular colored paper, Colgate substituted a sheet of Plexiglas with sand sprinkled on it. The FTC brought an action against Colgate, claiming that Colgate's ad was deceptive. Colgate defended on the ground that the consumer was merely being shown a representation of the actual test. Explain whether Colgate has engaged in an unfair or deceptive trade practice.

11. In 1982, several manufacturers introduced into the American market a product known as all-terrain vehicles (ATVs). ATVs are motorized bikes that sit on three or four low-pressure balloon tires and are meant to be driven off

paved roads. Almost immediately, the Consumer Product Safety Commission began receiving reports of deaths and serious injuries. As the number of injuries and deaths increased, the CPSC began investigating ATV hazards. According to CPSC staff, children under the age of sixteen accounted for roughly half the deaths and injuries associated with this product. What type of rule, if any, may the CPSC issue for ATVs?

12. Sears (http://www.sears.com) formulated a plan to increase sales of its top-of-the-line Lady Kenmore brand dishwasher. Sears's plan sought to change the Lady Kenmore's image without reengineering or making any mechanical improvements in the dishwasher itself. To accomplish this, Sears undertook a four-year, $8 million advertising campaign that claimed that the Lady Kenmore completely eliminated the need to prerinse and prescrape dishes. As a result of this campaign, sales rose by more than 300 percent. The "no scraping, no prerinsing" claim was not true, however; and Sears had no reasonable basis for asserting the claim. In addition, the owner's manual that customers received after they purchased the dishwasher contradicted the claim.

After a thorough investigation, the Federal Trade Commission filed a complaint against Sears, alleging that the advertisements were false and misleading. The final FTC order required Sears to stop making the no scraping, no prerinsing claim. The order also prevented Sears from (1) making any "performance claims" for "major home appliances" without first possessing a reasonable basis consisting of substantiating tests or other evidence; (2) misrepresenting any test, survey, or demonstration regarding "major home appliances"; and (3) making any advertising statements not consistent with statements in postpurchase materials supplied to purchasers of "major home appliances." Sears contends the order is too broad, because it covers appliances other than dishwashers and includes "performance claims" as well. Explain whether Sears is correct.

13. Onondaga Bureau of Medical Economics (OBME), a collection agency for physicians, sent the plaintiff, Seabrook, a letter demanding payment for a $198 physicians' bill. In addition to demanding payment, the letter stated that the bureau's client could commence against Seabrook a legal action that could result in a garnishment of his wages. Does OBME's letter violate the Fair Debt Collection Practices Act in that it (a) does not give Seabrook the required notice or (b) threatened legal action against him?

14. William Thompson was denied credit based on an inaccurate credit report compiled by the San Antonio Retail Merchant's Association. The Association confused Thompson's credit history with that of another William Thompson and failed to use social security numbers to distinguish the two men. The second Mr. Thompson had a poor credit history. Thompson made numerous attempts to have the Association correct its mistake, but the error was never corrected. Has the Association violated the Fair Credit Reporting Act? Explain.

15. Thompson Medical Company (http://www.chattem.com/main.asp) manufactures and sells Aspercreme, a topical analgesic. Aspercreme is a pain reliever that contains no aspirin. Thompson's advertisements strongly suggest that Aspercreme is related to aspirin, however, by claiming that it provides "the strong relief of aspirin right where you hurt." Is Thompson's advertisement for Aspercreme false and misleading? Explain.

16. Mary Smith bought a car from Doug Chapman under an installment sales contract. Smith carried the insurance on the car, as required by the contract. Shortly after Smith purchased the car, it was wrecked in an accident. Smith's insurance company paid Chapman the installments still owed on the car, as well as Smith's equity in the car. Smith requested a new car from Chapman under an installment plan the same as the one under which she had purchased the first car. Chapman refused, claiming that the contract for the first car allowed him to retain the equity amount as security interest and that Smith understood this as a term of the contract. The provision relating to the security interest appeared on the back of the contract, although the Truth-in-Lending Act required it to be on the front side. The front side had a notice referring to provisions on the back side. Explain whether Chapman's contract violates the Truth-in-Lending Act.

17. The FTC ordered Warner-Lambert (http://www.pfizer.com) to cease and desist from advertising that its product, Listerine antiseptic mouthwash, prevents, cures, or alleviates the common cold and sore throats. The order further required Warner-Lambert to disclose in future advertisements that "[c]ontrary to prior advertising, Listerine will not help prevent colds or sore throats or lessen their severity." Warner-Lambert contended that even if its past advertising claims were false, the corrective advertising portion of the order exceeded the FTC's statutory power. The FTC claimed that corrective advertising was necessary in light of Warner-Lambert's 100 years of false claims and the resulting persistence of erroneous consumer beliefs. Explain whether the FTC is correct.

18. Lenvil Miller owed $2,501.61 to the Star Bank of Cincinnati. Star Bank referred collection of Miller's account to Payco-General American Credits, Inc. (Payco), a debt collection agency. Payco sent Miller a collection form. Across the top of the form was the caption, "DEMAND FOR PAYMENT," in large, red, boldface type. The middle of the page stated "THIS IS A DEMAND FOR IMMEDIATE FULL PAYMENT OF YOUR DEBT," also in large, red, boldface type. That statement was followed in bold by "YOUR SERIOUSLY PAST DUE ACCOUNT HAS BEEN GIVEN TO US FOR IMMEDIATE ACTION. YOU HAVE HAD AMPLE TIME TO PAY YOUR DEBT, BUT YOU HAVE NOT. IF THERE IS A VALID REASON, PHONE US AT [***] TODAY. IF NOT, PAY US—NOW." The word "NOW" covered the bottom third of the form. At the very bottom in the smallest type to appear on the form was the statement, "NOTICE: SEE REVERSE SIDE FOR

IMPORTANT INFORMATION." The notice was printed in white against a red background. On the reverse side were four paragraphs in gray ink. The last three paragraphs contained the validation notice required by the Fair Debt Collection Practices Act (FDCPA) to inform the consumer how to obtain verification of the debt.

Miller sued Payco on the ground that the validation notice did not comply with the FDCPA. Miller argued that even though the validation notice contained all the necessary information, it violated the FDCPA because it contradicted other parts of the collection letter, was overshadowed by the demands for payment, and was not effectively conveyed to the consumer. Discuss whether Payco has violated the FDCPA.

19. In 1990, Greg Henson sold his 1980 Chevrolet Camaro Z-28 to his brother, Jeff Henson. To purchase the car, Jeff secured a loan with Cosco Federal Credit Union (Cosco). Soon thereafter, the car was stolen and Jeff stopped making payments on his loan from Cosco. At the time, Cosco was unsure whether Greg retained an interest in the car so Cosco sued both Jeff and Greg for possession of the car. The trial court rendered a default judgment against Jeff and ruled that Greg had no longer any interest in the car. The court further entered a deficiency judgment against Jeff in the amount of $4,076. However, the clerk erroneously noted in the judgment docket that the money judgment had been rendered against Greg as well as against Jeff. However, the official record of judgments and orders correctly reflected that only Jeff was affected by the money judgment. Two credit agencies, CSC Credit Services (CSC) and Trans Union Corporation (Trans Union) (http://www.tuc.com/), relied on the state court judgment docket and indicated in Greg's credit report that he owed the money judgment. Greg and his wife, Mary Henson, allege that they then "contacted Trans [Union] twice, in writing, to correct this horrible injustice." When Trans Union did not respond, the Hensons brought this action alleging violations of the Federal Credit Reporting Act (FCRA). Should the Hensons prevail? Explain.

http:// **Internet Exercise** Learn about the consumer protection activities of (a) the Federal Trade Commission, (b) the Consumer Product Safety Commission, (c) the National Highway Safety Administration, (d) the Food and Drug Administration, and (e) the Federal Reserve.

CHAPTER 46

Environmental Law

Only within the moment of time represented by the present century has one species—man—acquired significant power to alter the nature of the world.

RACHEL CARSON, *SILENT SPRING*, 1962

Learning Objectives

After reading this chapter you should be able to:

1. Outline and explain the common law actions for environmental damage and the difficulties in prevailing in such actions.
2. Explain the major substantive provisions of the National Environmental Policy Act.
3. Explain the regulatory scheme of the Clean Air Act.
4. Explain the regulation of both point and nonpoint sources of pollution by the Clean Water Act.
5. Explain (a) the Federal Insecticide, Fungicide and Rodenticide Act, (b) the Toxic Substances Control Act, (c) the Resource Conservation and Recovery Act, (d) the Superfund, (e) the Montreal Protocol, and (f) the Kyoto Protocol.

As technology has advanced and people have become more urbanized, their effect on the environment has increased. Our air has become dirtier; our waters have become more polluted. While individuals and environmental groups have brought private actions against some polluters, the common law has proved unable to control environmental damage. Because of this inadequacy, the federal and state governments have enacted a variety of statutes designed to promote environmental concerns and prevent environmental harm. Although in recent years certain developed countries, such as the United States, have made significant progress in controlling pollutants, such is not the case worldwide. Moreover, even as we have enjoyed some success in controlling some pollutants, a new generation of environmental problems has arisen. In this chapter, we will discuss both common law causes of action for environmental damage and federal regulation of the environment.

COMMON LAW ACTIONS FOR ENVIRONMENTAL DAMAGE

Private tort actions may be used to recover for harm to the environment. For example, if Alice's land is polluted by the mill next door, Alice may sue the mill in tort for the damage to her land. In suing to recover for environmental damage, plaintiffs generally have relied on the theories of nuisance, trespass, and strict liability.

CPA NUISANCE

The term *nuisance* encompasses two distinct types of wrong: private nuisance and public nuisance. A private nuisance involves an interference with a person's use and enjoyment of his or her land; a public nuisance is an act that interferes with a public right.

PRIVATE NUISANCE

To establish a **private nuisance**, a plaintiff must show that the defendant has substantially and unreasonably interfered with the use and enjoyment of the plaintiff's land. In an action for damages, the plaintiff need not prove that the defendant's conduct was unreasonable, only that the interference was unreasonable. Thus, assuming all other requirements are met, the question in a private nuisance suit for damages is whether the defendant should pay for the harm it caused the plaintiff, even if the defendant's action was not unreasonable. For example, in one case, an electric utility using a coal-burning electric generator that employed the latest scientific methods for reducing emissions was held liable for the harm it caused its neighbor's alfalfa crops, even though the utility was performing the socially useful function of creating electric power.

Although a plaintiff need not prove the defendant's conduct is unreasonable to recover in a private nuisance action for damages, such reasonableness is an issue when the plaintiff sues for an injunction. In determining whether an injunction against a nuisance is appropriate, a court will "balance the equities" by considering a number of factors, including the gravity of the harm to the plaintiff, the social value of the defendant's activity that is causing the harm, the feasibility and costs of avoiding the harm, and the public interest, if any.

The need to balance the equities has meant that courts often deny injunctions when the defendant is engaged in a socially useful activity. Additionally, injunctions are frequently denied because the defendant successfully raises an equitable defense. Consequently, private nuisance actions have been of limited value in controlling environmental damage.

PUBLIC NUISANCE

To be treated as a **public nuisance**, an activity must somehow interfere with the health, safety, or comfort of the public. For example, the actions of an industrial plant in polluting a stream will be treated as a private nuisance if such actions inconvenience only the owners of land downstream but will be treated as a public nuisance if they kill the stream's marine life. Generally, only a public representative, such as the attorney general, may sue to stop a public nuisance. If, however, the nuisance inflicts upon an individual some unique harm that the general populace does not suffer, that individual may also sue to halt the nuisance. Out of concern about the economic impact of closing an industrial operation, public representatives frequently are unwilling to sue to abate a public nuisance. Consequently, because these representatives often will not, and private parties may not, sue, relatively few public nuisance actions have been brought against polluters.

CPA TRESPASS TO LAND

To establish **trespass to land**, a plaintiff must show an invasion that interferes with the plaintiff's right of exclusive possession of the property and that is the direct result of an action by the defendant. For example, entering or throwing trash on someone else's land without permission constitutes a trespass. Trespass differs from private nuisance in that trespass requires an interference with the plaintiff's possession of the land. Thus, sending smoke or gas onto another's property may constitute a private nuisance but does not constitute a trespass.

Trespass often is difficult to establish in actions for environmental damage, either because the plaintiff is not in possession of the property or because the injury does not stem from an invasion of the property. Trespass actions have thus been of limited benefit in halting environmental damage. For a more complete discussion of trespass, see Chapter 8.

CPA STRICT LIABILITY FOR ABNORMALLY DANGEROUS ACTIVITIES

Although they generally base tort liability on fault, the courts may hold **strictly liable**, that is, liable without fault, a person engaged in an abnormally dangerous activity. To establish such strict liability, a plaintiff must show that the defendant is carrying on an unduly dangerous activity in an inappropriate location and that the plaintiff has suffered damage because of this activity. For example, a person who operates an oil refinery in a densely populated area may be held strictly liable for any damage the refinery causes. The requirement that the activity engaged in be (1) ultrahazardous and (2) inappropriate for its locale has limited the number of strict liability actions brought against polluters.

CPA PROBLEMS COMMON TO PRIVATE CAUSES OF ACTION

In addition to the shortcomings of each tort theory discussed above, using a private cause of action to control environmental damage presents its own problems. The costs associated with private litigation (including the payment of one's own legal fees) are high, and although overall the environmental damage may be considerable, the extent of any particular injury may not warrant pursuing a private lawsuit. Furthermore, tort actions generally do not provide relief for aesthetic, as opposed to physical, injury. Additionally, in many tort actions a significant issue of causation arises. For example, if a landowner lives near several plants, each of which emits pollution and none of which, by itself, would cause the amount of damage the landowner's property has suffered, the landowner may have difficulty recovering from any of the plant owners. Finally, even if a private plaintiff is successful, his recovery may be limited to monetary damages, leaving the defendant free to continue to pollute.

FEDERAL REGULATION OF THE ENVIRONMENT

Because private causes of action have proved inadequate to recompense and prevent environmental damage, the federal, state, and some local governments have enacted statutes designed to protect the environment. In this chapter, we will consider some of the more important federal environmental laws. In addition, the Environmental Protection Agency (EPA) has encouraged companies to conduct voluntary environmental audits. One of the key issues surrounding such self-audits is whether these audits are discoverable by state or federal prosecutors.

http://
Environmental Protection Agency: http://www.epa.gov/
State Environmental Protection Agencies: http://www.epa.gov/epapages/statelocal/envrolst.htm

CPA THE NATIONAL ENVIRONMENTAL POLICY ACT

In 1969, Congress enacted the **National Environmental Policy Act (NEPA)** to establish environmental protection as a goal of federal policy. The NEPA's declaration of national environmental policy states:

> The Congress, recognizing the profound impact of man's activity on the interrelations of all components of the natural environment, particularly the profound influences of population growth, high-density urbanization, industrial expansion, resource exploitation, and new and expanding technological advances, and recognizing further the critical importance of restoring and maintaining environmental quality to the overall welfare and development of man, declares that it is the continuing policy of the Federal Government in cooperation with State and local governments . . . to use all practicable means and measures . . . in a manner calculated to foster and promote the general welfare, to create and maintain conditions under which man and nature can exist in productive harmony, and fulfill the social, economic and other requirements of present and future generations of Americans.

The NEPA has two major substantive sections, one creating the Council on Environmental Quality (CEQ) and the other requiring that each federal agency, when recommending or reporting on proposals for legislation or other major federal action, prepare an **environmental impact statement** (**EIS**) if the legislation or federal action will have a significant environmental effect.

http://
National Environmental Policy Act: http://www4.law.cornell.edu/uscode/42/4321.html
Council on Environmental Quality: http://www.whitehouse.gov/ceq/

THE COUNCIL ON ENVIRONMENTAL QUALITY

The **Council on Environmental Quality** (CEQ), a three-member advisory group, is not a separate administrative agency but rather is part of the Executive Office of the President; as such, it makes recommendations to the president on environmental matters and prepares annual reports on the condition of the environment. Although not expressly authorized to do so by statute, the CEQ, acting under a series of executive orders, has issued regulations regarding the content and preparation of environmental impact statements. The federal courts generally have deferred to these regulations.

ENVIRONMENTAL IMPACT STATEMENTS

Unlike most federal environmental statutes, the NEPA does not focus on a particular type of environmental damage or harmful substance but instead expresses the federal government's continuing concern with protection of the environment. The NEPA's promotion of environmental considerations is effected through the EIS requirement.

Procedure for Preparing an EIS When proposing legislation or considering a major federal action, the CEQ regulations require that a federal agency initially make an "environmental assessment," which is a short analysis of the need for an EIS. If the agency decides that no EIS is required, it must make this decision available to the public. If, on the other hand, the agency concludes that an EIS is required, the agency must engage in "scoping," which consists of consulting other relevant federal agencies and the public to determine the significant issues the EIS will address and the statement's appropriate scope. After scoping, the agency prepares a draft EIS, for which there is a comment period. After the comment period ends and revisions, if necessary, are made, a final EIS is published.

Scope of EIS Requirement The EIS requirement of the NEPA applies to a broad range of projects:

> [T]here is "Federal action" within the meaning of the statute not only when an agency proposes to build a facility itself, but also whenever an agency makes a decision which permits action by other parties which will affect the quality of the environment. NEPA's impact statement procedure has been held to apply where a federal agency approves a lease of land to private parties, grants licenses and permits to private parties, or approves and funds state highway projects. In each of these instances the federal agency took action affecting the environment in the sense that the agency made a decision which permitted some other party—private or governmental—to take action affecting the environment.

The NEPA's EIS requirement applies not only to a broad range of projects but also to a broad range of environmental effects. The NEPA has been held to apply not only to the natural environment but also to the urban environment.

The Act [NEPA] must be construed to include protection of the quality of life for city residents. Noise, traffic, overburdened mass transportation systems, crime, congestion and even availability of drugs all affect the urban "environment" and are surely results of the "profound influences of . . . high-density urbanization [and] industrial expansion." Although effects on health, including psychological health, are considered environmental effects under the NEPA, the Supreme Court has held that an effect is environmental only if it has a reasonably close causal relation to an impact on the physical environment.

Content of an EIS The NEPA requires that an EIS describe in detail the environmental impact of a proposed action, any adverse environmental effects that could not be avoided if the proposal were implemented, alternatives to the proposed action, the relationship between local short-term uses of the environment and the maintenance and enhancement of long-term productivity, and any irreversible and irretrievable commitments of resources the proposed action would involve if it were implemented. Impact statements provide a basis for evaluating the benefits of a proposed project in light of its environmental risks and for comparing its environmental risks with those of alternatives. The Supreme Court has held that a federal agency is required to consider only all *reasonable* alternatives in its EIS.

Nature of EIS Requirement Whether the NEPA was solely procedural or whether it had a substantive component was initially unclear. The Supreme Court resolved the issue by holding that the NEPA's requirements are primarily procedural and that the NEPA does not require that the relevant federal agency attempt to mitigate the adverse effects of a proposed federal action.

CPA THE CLEAN AIR ACT

Initially, the federal government's role in controlling air pollution was quite limited. The states had primary responsibility for air pollution control, and the federal government merely supervised their efforts and offered technical and financial assistance. When state efforts proved inadequate to alleviate the problem, Congress enacted the **Clean Air Act** Amendments of 1970, greatly expanding the federal role in antipollution efforts. Major revisions to the Clean Air Act were enacted in 1977 and 1990. The Act establishes two regulatory schemes, one for existing sources and one for new stationary sources. The states retain primary responsibility for regulating existing stationary sources and motor vehicles then in use (that is, in use when the Act, or its subsequently enacted amendments, took effect), while the federal government regulates new sources, new vehicles, and hazardous air pollutants.

Under the Act, the Environmental Protection Agency (EPA) may impose civil penalties of up to $25,000 per day of violation. Criminal penalties, which depend on the type of violation, vary greatly, providing for a maximum fine of $1 million per violation and/or fifteen years' imprisonment for a knowing violation that endangers a person. For repeat convictions, the Act doubles the maximum punishments.

http:// Clean Air Act: http://www4.law.cornell.edu/uscode/42/7401.html

EXISTING STATIONARY SOURCES AND MOTOR VEHICLES THEN IN USE

Because the states had not managed adequately to control air pollution, the 1970 amendments provided that, with respect to existing stationary sources and motor vehicles then in use, the federal government would set national air quality standards that the states would be primarily responsible for achieving.

National Ambient Air Quality Standards Under the act, the EPA administrator is required to establish **national ambient air quality standards (NAAQS)** for air pollutants that endanger the public health and welfare. The EPA administrator must establish "primary" standards to protect the public health, allowing for an adequate safety margin, and "secondary" standards to protect elements relating to the public welfare, such as animals, crops, and structures. The NAAQS for a particular pollutant specifies the concentration of that pollutant that will be allowed in the outside air over designated periods of time.

The EPA administrator established quality standards for seven major classes of pollutants—carbon monoxide, particulates, sulfur dioxide, nitrogen dioxide, hydrocarbons, ozone, and lead, although the hydrocarbon NAAQS was subsequently withdrawn as no longer being necessary. Recognizing that many areas would not meet the 1977 NAAQS deadline, Congress, in the 1977 amendments to the Act, extended the deadline to December 1982 and further provided that states demonstrating the impossibility of meeting the 1982 deadline "despite the implementation of all reasonably available measures" could obtain an extension until December 1987. In 1987, Congress extended the deadline for another eight months. The August 1988 deadline expired without extension, but the EPA has not vigorously enforced it.

The 1990 amendments sought to hasten attainment of the standards and provided that the EPA must establish new standards for major pollutants every five years. The amendments also imposed tighter standards with regard to ozone pollution, due to the lack of progress in this area.

Whitman v. American Trucking Associations, Inc.

Supreme Court of the United States, 2001

531 U.S. 457, 121 S.Ct. 903; 149 L.Ed.2d 1

http://laws.findlaw.com/us/000/99-1257.html

FACTS These cases present the following questions: (1) Whether § 109(b)(1) of the Clean Air Act (CAA) delegates legislative power to the Administrator of the Environmental Protection Agency (EPA) and (2) Whether the Administrator may consider the costs of implementation in setting national ambient air quality standards (NAAQS) under § 109(b)(1).

The Administrator of the EPA promulgates NAAQS for each air pollutant for which "air quality criteria" have been issued and must review (and revise if needed) the standard (and the criteria on which it is based) at five-year intervals. These cases arose when, on July 18, 1997, the Administrator revised the NAAQS for particulate matter (PM) and ozone. The American Trucking Associations, Inc., and its co-respondents challenged the new standards in the Court of Appeals for the District of Columbia Circuit.

The District of Columbia Circuit accepted some of the challenges and rejected others. It agreed with the respondents that § 109(b)(1) unconstitutionally delegated legislative power to the Administrator. The court thought, however, that the EPA could perhaps avoid the unconstitutional delegation by adopting a more restrictive construction of § 109(b)(1), so instead of declaring the section unconstitutional, the court remanded the NAAQS to the agency.

On the second issue that the Court of Appeals addressed, it unanimously rejected respondents' argument that the court should depart from prior cases that established the precedent that the EPA may not consider the cost of implementing a NAAQS in setting the initial standard.

DECISION The judgment of the Court of Appeals is affirmed in part and reversed in part, and the cases are remanded for reinterpretation that would avoid a supposed delegation of legislative power.

OPINION Scalia, J.

II

In *Lead Industries Assn., Inc. v. EPA*, [citation], the District of Columbia Circuit held that "economic considerations [may] play no part in the promulgation of ambient air quality standards under Section 109" of the CAA. In the present cases, the court adhered to that holding, [citation], as it had done on many other occasions. [Citations.] Respondents argue that these decisions are incorrect. We disagree; * * *.

Section 109(b)(1) instructs the EPA to set primary ambient air quality standards "the attainment and maintenance of which * * * are requisite to protect the public health" with "an adequate margin of safety." [Citation.] * * * The language, as one scholar has noted, "is absolute."

[Citation.] The EPA, "based on" the information about health effects contained in the technical "criteria" documents compiled under § 108(a)(2), [citation], is to identify the maximum airborne concentration of a pollutant that the public health can tolerate, decrease the concentration to provide an "adequate" margin of safety, and set the standard at that level. Nowhere are the costs of achieving such a standard made part of that initial calculation.

* * *

Even so, respondents argue, many more factors than air pollution affect public health. In particular, the economic cost of implementing a very stringent standard might produce health losses sufficient to offset the health gains achieved in cleaning the air—for example, by closing down whole industries and thereby impoverishing the workers and consumers dependent upon those industries. That is unquestionably true, and Congress was unquestionably aware of it. Thus, Congress had commissioned in the Air Quality Act of 1967 (1967 Act) "a detailed estimate of the cost of carrying out the provisions of this Act; a comprehensive study of the cost of program implementation by affected units of government; and a comprehensive study of the economic impact of air quality standards on the Nation's industries, communities, and other contributing sources of pollution." [Citation.] The 1970 Congress, armed with the results of this study, [citation], not only anticipated that compliance costs could injure the public health, but provided for that precise exigency. Section 110(f)(1) of the CAA permitted the Administrator to waive the compliance deadline for stationary sources if * * * sufficient control measures were simply unavailable and "the continued operation of such sources is *essential * * * to the public health* or welfare." [Citation.] Other provisions explicitly permitted or required economic costs to be taken into account in implementing the air quality standards. * * * We have therefore refused to find implicit in ambiguous sections of the CAA an authorization to consider costs that has elsewhere, and so often, been expressly granted. [Citation.]

* * *

* * * The text of § 109(b), interpreted in its statutory and historical context and with appreciation for its importance to the CAA as a whole, unambiguously bars cost considerations from the NAAQS-setting process, and thus ends the matter for us as well as the EPA. We therefore affirm the judgment of the Court of Appeals on this point.

III

Section 109(b)(1) of the CAA instructs the EPA to set "ambient air quality standards the attainment and maintenance of which in the judgment of the Administrator, based on [the] criteria and allowing an adequate margin of safety, are requisite to protect the public health." [Citation.] The Court of Appeals held that this section as interpreted by the Administrator did not provide an "intelligible principle" to guide the EPA's exercise of authority in setting NAAQS. "[The] EPA," it said, "lacked any determinate criteria for drawing lines. It has failed to state intelligibly how much is too much." [Citation.] The court hence found that the EPA's interpretation (but not the statute itself) violated the nondelegation doctrine. [Citation.] We disagree.

In a delegation challenge, the constitutional question is whether the statute has delegated legislative power to the agency. Article I, § 1, of the Constitution vests "all legislative Powers herein granted * * * in a Congress of the United States." This text permits no delegation of those powers, [citation], and so we repeatedly have said that when Congress confers decisionmaking authority upon agencies *Congress* must "lay down by legislative act an intelligible principle to which the person or body authorized to [act] is directed to conform." [Citation.] We have never suggested that an agency can cure an unlawful delegation of legislative power by adopting in its discretion a limiting construction of the statute. * * * Whether the statute delegates legislative power is a question for the courts, and an agency's voluntary self-denial has no bearing upon the answer.

We agree with the Solicitor General that the text of § 109(b)(1) of the CAA at a minimum requires that "for a discrete set of pollutants and based on published air quality criteria that reflect the latest scientific knowledge, [the] EPA must establish uniform national standards at a level that is requisite to protect public health from the adverse effects of the pollutant in the ambient air." Requisite, in turn, "means sufficient, but not more than necessary." These limits on the EPA's discretion are strikingly similar to the ones we approved in [citation]. * * *

The scope of discretion § 109(b)(1) allows is in fact well within the outer limits of our nondelegation precedents. In the history of the Court we have found the requisite "intelligible principle" lacking in only two statutes, one of which provided literally no guidance for the exercise of discretion, and the other of which conferred authority to regulate the entire economy on the basis of no more precise a standard than stimulating the economy by assuring "fair competition." * * *

It is true enough that the degree of agency discretion that is acceptable varies according to the scope of the power congressionally conferred. [Citation.] While Congress need not provide any direction to the EPA regarding the manner in which it is to define "country elevators," which are to be exempt from new-stationary-source regulations governing grain elevators, [citation], it must provide substantial guidance on setting air standards that affect the entire national economy. But even in sweeping regulatory schemes we have never demanded, as the Court of Appeals did here, that statutes provide a "determinate criterion" for saying "how much [of the regulated harm] is too much." * * * "[A] certain degree of discretion, and thus of lawmaking, inheres in most executive or judicial action." [Citation.] Section 109(b)(1) of the CAA, which to repeat we interpret as requiring the EPA to set air quality standards at the level that is "requisite"—that is, not lower or higher than is necessary—to protect the public health with an adequate margin of safety, fits comfortably within the scope of discretion permitted by our precedent.

We therefore reverse the judgment of the Court of Appeals remanding for reinterpretation that would avoid a supposed delegation of legislative power. * * *

* * *

INTERPRETATION Economic considerations play no part in the promulgation of ambient air quality standards; the degree of agency discretion that is acceptable varies according to the scope of the power congressionally conferred.

CRITICAL THINKING QUESTION Should cost be a factor in setting air quality standards?

State Implementation Plans Once the EPA promulgates a new NAAQS, each state must submit to the agency a **state implementation plan (SIP)** detailing how the state will implement and maintain the NAAQS within the state. If the state adopted the SIP after public hearings and the SIP meets certain statutory conditions, the EPA is required to approve it. Foremost among the statutory conditions is the requirement that under the SIP the state will attain primary standards as soon as practicable but in any case within three years after the EPA approves the SIP. If the EPA determines that under an SIP a state will not attain an NAAQS within the designated time and the state fails to make the necessary amendments, the EPA is authorized to make amendments that will be binding on the state.

Under the 1990 amendments, the EPA also must decide whether an SIP is complete. If it is not, the EPA may treat the plan as a nullity in whole or in part. If it is complete, the EPA must approve or disapprove the plan within a year. Once the EPA approves an SIP, the plan is regarded as both state and federal law, enforceable by either its state of implementation or the federal government.

Prevention of Significant Deterioration Areas Prior to the 1977 amendments, an issue arose as to whether air that was cleaner than required by an applicable NAAQS would be allowed to deteriorate to the NAAQS level. This issue was significant because much of the United States, particularly land in the Southwest, had air whose quality was higher than that required by applicable standards. Responding to this issue, Congress, in the 1977 amendments, established a policy to prevent the quality of such air from deteriorating. To effectuate this policy, Congress established rules for areas whose air quality was higher than the applicable NAAQS required it to be or for which information was insufficient to determine the air quality (so-called **prevention of significant deterioration [PSD] areas**). Because the rules classified an area on a pollutant-by-pollutant basis, a particular area might be a PSD area with respect to one pollutant and an area that had not met the applicable NAAQS with respect to another pollutant.

In PSD areas, only limited increases in air pollution are allowed. Before a major stationary source in a PSD area may be constructed or modified, the owner or operator of the source must receive a permit from the applicable state regulator. In order to receive a permit, the owner/operator must demonstrate that the source will not increase pollution beyond permitted levels and must show that the source will use the best control technology available.

Nonattainment Areas The 1977 and 1990 amendments also established special rules for areas that did not meet applicable NAAQSs, so-called **nonattainment areas.** Before a major stationary source may be constructed or modified in a nonattainment area, the owner/operator of the source must receive a permit from the applicable state regulator. In order to receive a permit, the owner/operator must show that the source will comply with the lowest achievable emission rate, which is the more stringent of either the most stringent emission limitation contained in any SIP or the most stringent emission limitation actually achieved. Additionally, total emissions from existing stationary sources and the proposed new or modified source together must be less than the total emissions allowed from existing sources at the time the permit is sought. Thus, to obtain a permit in a nonattainment area, an owner/operator must in some way reduce total emissions from all sources (existing and new/modified). Under the 1990 amendments, the reduction required varies with the severity of the area's nonattainment problem. One way to reduce total emissions from all sources is to pay the owner/operator of another source to reduce its emissions by either installing more advanced emission control technology or closing its source. Alternatively, an owner/operator may reduce its own total emissions by altering the mix of emission controls at its plant. Under the EPA's **bubble concept**, an entire plant is viewed as one source; consequently, the permit process applies only if total emissions from the plant increase. If, instead, the EPA treated each unit at a plant as a separate source, the owner/operator would be required to obtain a permit whenever it made a change to one unit. The bubble concept thus enables an owner/operator to bypass the permit process in some instances. Though environmental groups challenged the concept on this basis, in 1984 the Supreme Court upheld the bubble concept, finding the regulation to be a reasonable exercise of the EPA's discretion.

> **Practical Advice**
>
> When considering where to locate a facility that will emit pollution, carefully scrutinize pollution levels in those locations.

NEW SOURCE STANDARDS

The scheme of federal NAAQSs and state SIPs applies to existing stationary sources and to motor vehicles then in use. In contrast, the Clean Air Act authorizes the federal government to establish national emission standards for new stationary sources, hazardous air pollutants, and new vehicles.

New Stationary Sources The Act requires the EPA administrator to establish performance standards for stationary sources that are constructed or modified after the publication of applicable regulations. The standard of performance must "reflect the degree of emission limitation and percentage reduction achievable through application of the best technological system of continuous emission reduction which . . . has been adequately demonstrated." The standard governing new sources is more stringent than the standard governing existing sources; accordingly, it is, from industry's perspective, better to be considered an existing source than a new or modified one.

New Vehicles The Clean Air Act requires the EPA administrator to establish emission standards for **new** motor **vehicles** and new motor vehicle engines. The Act also requires the use of reformulated automotive fuels to reduce ozone and carbon monoxide pollution. The reformulated gasoline must contain more oxygen and less in terms of volatile organic compounds.

Hazardous Air Pollutants The Act authorizes the EPA administrator to establish national emission standards for **hazardous** or toxic **air pollutants**, defined as "air pollutant[s] . . . caus[ing], or contribut[ing] to, air pollution which may reasonably be anticipated to result in an increase in mortality or an increase in serious irreversible, or incapacitating reversible, illness." The standard must be set at a level that "provides an ample margin of safety to protect the public health."

Acid Rain The 1990 amendments attempt to halt environmental destruction caused by **acid rain**—precipitation that contains high levels of sulfuric or nitric acid. Because sulfur dioxide (which forms sulfuric acid in the atmosphere and comes back as acid rain) is primarily released into the atmosphere by electric utilities, the 1990 amendments regulate such utilities by allotting them emission allowances with regard to the amount of sulfur dioxide they may release into the atmosphere, based upon past emissions and fuel consumption. The amendments established an allowance schedule that should significantly reduce emissions of sulfur dioxide and nitrous oxides. The amendments also permit each utility to bank or sell its emission allowances.

CPA THE CLEAN WATER ACT

As with air pollution control, the primary responsibility for controlling water pollution fell initially to the states. When their efforts proved inadequate, Congress fundamentally revised the nation's water pollution laws in its 1972 amendments to the Federal Water Pollution Control Act (subsequently renamed the **Clean Water Act**). Substantially amended again in 1977, 1981, and 1987, the act attempts comprehensively to restore and maintain the chemical, physical, and biological integrity of the nation's waters.

The EPA may impose civil penalties of up to $25,000 per day for each violation. Maximum criminal penalties for knowing violations are $50,000 per day of violation and/or three years' imprisonment. For repeat convictions, the maximum punishments are doubled.

Like the Clean Air Act, the Clean Water Act establishes different schemes for existing sources and new sources. Additionally, the act provides different programs for point and nonpoint sources of pollution. A **point source** is "any discernible, confined and discrete conveyance . . . from which pollutants are or may be discharged." A **nonpoint source**, in contrast, is a land use that causes pollution, such as a pesticide runoff from farming operations.

The scope of the act is extremely broad, applying not only to all navigable waters in the United States but also to tributaries of navigable waters, interstate waters and their tributaries, the use of nonnavigable intrastate waters (if their misuse could affect interstate commerce), and freshwater wetlands.

http:// Clean Water Act: http://www4.law.cornell.edu/uscode/33/1251.html

POINT SOURCES

The act mandates that the EPA administrator establish effluent limitations for categories of existing point sources. An **effluent limitation** is a technology-based standard that limits the amount of a pollutant that a point source may discharge into a body of water. The act effectuates such limitations through the ***National Pollutant Discharge Elimination System (NPDES)***, a permit system.

Effluent Limitations Under the 1972 amendments, effluent limitations for existing point sources, other than publicly owned treatment works, required application of the best practicable control technology currently available (**BPT**) by 1977 and application of the best available technology economically achievable (**BAT**) by 1983. According to the EPA, BPT is "the average of the best existing performance by well-operated plants within each industrial category or subcategory," while BAT is "the very best control and treatment measures that have been or are capable of being achieved." Somewhat different standards apply to publicly owned treatment works.

The National Pollutant Discharge Elimination System

The National Pollutant Discharge Elimination System (NPDES), the permit system through which effluent limitations are to be achieved, requires that any person responsible for the discharge from a point source of a pollutant into U.S. waters must obtain a discharge permit from the EPA, the Army Corps of Engineers, or, in some circumstances, the relevant state. An NPDES permit incorporates the applicable effluent limitations and establishes a schedule for compliance. The holder of an NPDES permit is required to notify the appropriate authority if the holder will not meet its obligations under the permit. A discharge not in compliance with a permit is unlawful. With limited exceptions, new permits for existing facilities cannot be less stringent than current permits.

Practical Advice

If your plant will discharge effluents into a body of water, make sure that you obtain all necessary permits.

Arkansas v. Oklahoma

Supreme Court of the United States, 1992
503 U.S. 91, 112 S.Ct. 1046
http://laws.findlaw.com/US/503/91.html

FACTS The Clean Water Act provides for two water quality measures: effluent limitations, which are promulgated by the Environmental Protection Agency (EPA), and water quality standards, which are promulgated by the states. In order to discharge effluents into a navigable body of water, a point source must obtain a National Pollutant Discharge Elimination System (NPDES) permit from a relevant state or the EPA. The city of Fayetteville, Arkansas (**http://www.fayettevillear.com/**), received an EPA-issued NPDES permit for the discharge of sewage into a stream that ultimately reaches the Illinois River, twenty-two miles upstream from the Oklahoma (**http://www.state.ok.us/**) border. The EPA permit limited the effluent discharge to comply with Oklahoma water quality standards, but the EPA stated that those standards would be violated only if the discharge would cause an actual, detectable violation of Oklahoma standards. Oklahoma appealed the permit, arguing that the permit violated Oklahoma water quality standards, which allow no degradation of water quality. The Court of Appeals denied the permit, holding that the Act does not allow a permit where a proposed source would discharge effluent that would contribute to conditions currently constituting a violation of water quality standards and that the Illinois River was already degraded.

DECISION Decision of the Court of Appeals reversed.

OPINION Stevens, J. The parties have argued three analytically distinct questions concerning the interpretation of the Clean Water Act. First, does the Act require the EPA, in crafting and issuing a permit to a point source in one State, to apply the water quality standards of downstream States? Second, even if the Act does not require as much, does the Agency have the statutory authority to mandate such compliance? Third, does the Act provide, as the Court of Appeals held, that once a body of water fails to meet water quality standards no discharge that yields effluent that reach the degraded waters will be permitted?

In this case, it is neither necessary nor prudent for us to resolve the first of these questions. In issuing the Fayetteville permit, the EPA assumed it was obligated by both the Act and its own regulations to ensure that the

Fayetteville discharge would not violate Oklahoma's standards. As we discuss below, this assumption was permissible and reasonable and therefore there is no need for us to address whether the Act requires as much. * * * Our decision not to determine at this time the scope of the Agency's statutory obligations does not affect our resolution of the second question, which concerns the Agency's statutory authority. Even if the Clean Water Act itself does not require the Fayetteville discharge to comply with Oklahoma's water quality standards, the statute clearly does not limit the EPA's authority to mandate such compliance.

Since 1973, EPA regulations have provided that an NPDES permit shall not be issued "[w]hen the imposition of conditions cannot ensure compliance with the applicable water quality requirements of all affected States." [Citations.] Those regulations—relied upon by the EPA in the issuance of the Fayetteville permit—constitute a reasonable exercise of the Agency's statutory authority.

Congress has vested in the Administrator broad discretion to establish conditions for NPDES permits. Section 402(a)(2) provides that for EPA-issued permits "[t]he Administrator shall prescribe conditions for such permits to assure compliance with the requirements of [§ 402(a)(1)] and such other requirements as he deems appropriate." [Citation.]

Similarly, Congress preserved for the Administrator broad authority to oversee state permit programs:

* * *

The regulations relied on by the EPA were a perfectly reasonable exercise of the Agency's statutory discretion. The application of state water quality standards in the interstate context is wholly consistent with the Act's broad purpose, "to restore and maintain the chemical, physical, and biological integrity of the Nation's waters." [Citation.] Moreover, as noted above, [the Act] expressly identifies the achievement of state water quality standards as one of the Act's central objectives. The Agency's regulations conditioning NPDES permits are a well-tailored means of achieving this goal.

Notwithstanding this apparent reasonableness, Arkansas argues that our description in *Ouellette* of the role of affected States in the permit process and our characterization of the affected States' position as "subordinate," [citation], indicates that the EPA's application of the Oklahoma standards was error. We disagree. Our statement in *Ouellette* concerned only an affected State's input into the permit process; that input is clearly limited by the plain language of § 402(b). Limits on an affected State's direct participation in permitting decisions, however, do not in any way constrain the EPA's authority to require a point source to comply with downstream water quality standards.

* * *

Similarly, we agree with Arkansas that in the Clean Water Act Congress struck a careful balance among competing policies and interests, but do not find the EPA regulations concerning the application of downstream water quality standards at all incompatible with that balance. * * *

For these reasons, we find the EPA's requirement that the Fayetteville discharge comply with Oklahoma's water quality standards to be a reasonable exercise of the Agency's substantial statutory discretion. [Citation.]

The Court of Appeals construed the Clean Water Act to prohibit any discharge of effluent that would reach waters already in violation of existing water quality standards. We find nothing in the Act to support this reading.

INTERPRETATION The EPA has broad discretionary power in administering the Clean Water Act.

CRITICAL THINKING QUESTION Should the EPA have such broad discretion? Explain.

The 1977 Amendments Recognizing that the application deadlines it had set In the 1972 amendments would not be met, Congress extended and modified the deadlines in 1977. The 1977 amendments to the Clean Water Act divided pollutants into three categories—toxic, conventional, and nonconventional (any pollutants that are neither toxic nor conventional)—and established different deadlines and standards for each category. For toxic pollutants, the 1983 BAT deadline was extended to 1984; for nonconventional pollutants, this standard was to be achieved by 1984 or within three years after the effluent limitation was established, whichever was later. For conventional pollutants, a new standard, best conventional pollution control technology (**BCT**), was to be achieved.

NONPOINT SOURCE POLLUTION

Controlling nonpoint source pollution—such as agricultural and urban runoff—is inherently more difficult than controlling point source pollution.

> There is no effective way as yet, other than land use control, by which you can intercept that runoff and control it in a way that you do a point source. We have not yet developed technology to deal with that kind of a problem. We need to find ways to deal with it, because a great quantity of pollutants [are] discharged by runoff, not only from agriculture but from construction sites, from streets, from parking lots, and so on, and we have to be concerned with developing controls for them.

Although Congress tried to address the problem of nonpoint source pollution in the 1972 amendments, little effective control of nonsource pollution occurred before 1987. The 1987 amendments require states to identify state waters that will not meet the Act's requirements without the management of nonpoint sources of pollution and to institute "best management practices" to control such sources. The EPA must approve each state's management plan.

NEW SOURCE PERFORMANCE STANDARDS

The Act requires the EPA administrator to establish federal performance standards for new sources. A performance standard should "reflect the greatest degree of effluent reduction . . . achievable through application of the best available demonstrated control technology." The preferred standard for new sources is one "permitting no discharge of pollutants." Violation of a standard by an owner/operator of a new source is unlawful.

CPA HAZARDOUS SUBSTANCES

Technological advances have enabled human beings to produce numerous artificial substances, some of which have proven extremely hazardous to health. As the potential and actual harm from these latter substances became clear, Congress responded by enacting various substances-related statutes. In this section, we will consider some of the most important federal statutes governing hazardous substances: the Federal Insecticide, Fungicide and Rodenticide Act (FIFRA); the Toxic Substances Control Act (TSCA); the Resource Conservation and Recovery Act (RCRA); the Comprehensive Environmental Response, Compensation and Liability Act (CERCLA, or the Superfund); and the Superfund Amendments and Reauthorization Act of 1986 (SARA).

THE FEDERAL INSECTICIDE, FUNGICIDE AND RODENTICIDE ACT

The federal government began regulating pesticides in 1910 and greatly expanded its control over such substances in 1947 with the passage of the **Federal Insecticide, Fungicide and Rodenticide Act (FIFRA)**. Concern about pesticides increased dramatically after the publication in 1962 of *Silent Spring*, by Rachel Carson, and Congress has amended the FIFRA several times in the last forty years.

The FIFRA requires that a pesticide be registered with the EPA before any person in any state may distribute it. Such registration is legal only if the pesticide's composition warrants the claims its manufacturer proposes for it, the pesticide will perform its intended function without "unreasonable adverse effects on the environment," the pesticide generally will not cause unreasonably adverse environmental effects when used in accordance with widespread and commonly recognized practice, and the pesticide complies with FIFRA labeling requirements. The FIFRA defines "unreasonable adverse effects on the environment" as any unreasonable risk to humans or the environment, taking into account the economic, social, and environmental costs and benefits of the use of any pesticide. Thus, unlike many environmental statutes, the FIFRA expressly requires the EPA to consider the costs of the action it takes under the statute.

If a pesticide is registered and subsequent data reveal additional hazards, the EPA may cancel the registration after an administrative hearing. The 1988 amendments placed upon industry the cost of disposing of canceled pesticides. Cancellation proceedings typically take years, both because of the numerous stages of the administrative process and because of the required use of a scientific advisory committee. While the cancellation process is in progress, the pesticide may be manufactured and sold. If additional hazard is imminent, however, the product's registration may be suspended until the cancellation proceeding is completed. Once its registration has been suspended, the pesticide may not be manufactured or distributed.

Until recently, the FIFRA did not adequately address the problem of old pesticides that had been registered under earlier and less strict standards. Concerned that these pesticides did not meet current standards, Congress in 1988 amended the FIFRA to require the re-registration of pesticides registered before 1984. U.S. exports are not subject to most of the act's requirements, though an exported pesticide not registered under the FIFRA must bear a label stating "Not Registered for Use in the United States of America."

The EPA may impose civil penalties of up to $5,000 for each offense. Maximum criminal penalties for knowing violations are a $50,000 fine and/or one year imprisonment.

http:// Federal Insecticide, Fungicide and Rodenticide Act: http://www4.law.cornell.edu/uscode/7/136.html

THE TOXIC SUBSTANCES CONTROL ACT

Congress passed the **Toxic Substances Control Act (TSCA)** in 1976 in an effort to provide a comprehensive scheme for regulating toxic substances. The TSCA contains provisions on the manufacture of new chemicals, the testing of suspect chemicals, the regulation of chemicals that present an unreasonable risk of injury to health and the environment, and the inventorying of all chemicals.

Under the act, a manufacturer must notify the EPA before it manufactures a new chemical or makes a significant new use of an existing chemical. If the EPA administrator concludes that the information submitted is insufficient to permit a reasoned evaluation of the health and environmental effects of the chemical and the chemical may present an unreasonable risk of injury to health or the environment, the administrator may limit or prohibit the chemical's manufacture or distribution.

The Act authorizes the EPA to require the testing of any substance, whether existing or new, if (1) the manufacture or distribution of the substance may present an unreasonable risk of injury to health or the environment, (2) the data on the effects of the substance on health and the environment are insufficient, and (3) testing is necessary to develop such data.

Because of the many substances that might be subject to testing under the statutory standard, the TSCA mandates that the EPA establish a priority list for testing that contains no more than fifty substances at any time. This list is established by a committee whose members come from eight specified agencies.

Once the EPA determines, either through its testing program or through the premanufacturing notice process, that a substance "presents or will present an unreasonable risk of injury to health or the environment," the agency may restrict or prohibit use of the substance.

If the EPA administrator believes that a substance presents an imminent hazard, he is authorized to bring an action in federal district court for seizure of the substance or other appropriate relief. The statute defines an "imminently hazardous chemical substance or mixture" as one that presents an unreasonable risk of serious or widespread injury to health or the environment.

The TSCA requires the EPA to compile and keep current a list of each chemical substance manufactured or processed in the United States. The EPA's initial inventory of existing chemicals, completed in 1980, listed approximately 55,000 substances. A chemical not listed on the inventory is subject to premanufacture review, even if it was in fact previously manufactured. Although not explicitly required to do so by the TSCA, the EPA reviews the substances on the inventory to determine their safety.

The EPA may impose civil penalties of up to $20,000 per day for a violation of the TSCA. Maximum criminal penalties for knowing violations are $25,000 fines for each day of violation and/or one year imprisonment.

http:// Toxic Substances Control Act: http://www4.law.cornell.edu/uscode/15/2601.html

THE RESOURCE CONSERVATION AND RECOVERY ACT

In 1976, Congress enacted the **Resource Conservation and Recovery Act (RCRA)** to provide a comprehensive scheme for the treatment of solid waste, particularly hazardous waste. The statute provides that the states are primarily responsible for nonhazardous waste, and the EPA regulates all phases of hazardous waste—generation, transportation, and disposal. Under the act, the federal government must establish criteria for identifying hazardous waste, taking into account factors that include toxicity, persistence, degradability, flammability, and corrosiveness.

The act prescribes for generators (entities that produce hazardous waste) standards concerning recordkeeping, labeling, the use of appropriate containers, and reporting. The statute requires the EPA to establish a ***manifest system*** to be used by generators. A *manifest* is a form on which the generator must specify the quantity, composition, origin, routing, and destination of hazardous waste. On the manifest the generator also must certify that the volume and toxicity of the waste have been reduced to the greatest degree economically practicable and that the method of treatment, storage, and disposal minimizes the threat to health and the environment.

Transporters must maintain records and properly label the waste they transport. Furthermore, they must comply with manifests and may transport hazardous waste only to facilities that have an RCRA hazardous waste facility permit.

Owners/operators of hazardous waste treatment, storage, and disposal sites must maintain records and comply with generator manifests. Facilities for hazardous waste treatment, storage, and disposal must obtain an RCRA hazardous waste facility permit. To obtain a permit, a facility must comply with relevant EPA standards. Failure to comply may subject the owner/operator to civil or criminal penalties.

Practical Advice

Make sure that you maintain proper records, apply proper labels, and obtain all necessary permits for the generation, transportation, and disposal of all hazardous waste material.

The act authorizes the EPA administrator to sue in federal court for an injunction if the administrator has

Ethical Dilemma

Distant Concerns

FACTS In February 1990, an American chemical manufacturer gave the Environmental Protection Agency test results suggesting that one of the company's chemicals causes tumors and reproductive problems in laboratory mice. The chemical, known as R-11 [scientific name-2,3,4,5-Bis (2 butylene) tetrahydro-2 furaldehyde], repelled biting flies and was sold by its manufacturer to other companies that made and marketed insecticides for human use. Such insecticides included familiar national brands sold in drugstores and other retail outlets to families, anglers, boaters, hikers, and campers.

The U.S. makers of name-brand insecticides immediately stopped adding R-11 to their products, and they notified retailers to take products containing it off their shelves. (The maker of R-11 had already stopped shipping it to the insecticide manufacturers.) In early April 1990, the Canadian government banned the use of R-11 in Canada. In late April, the EPA issued a public warning to U.S. consumers not to use products containing the chemical. By the end of April, the EPA had not yet banned the chemical but was expected to do so any day. After the ban, retail stores would have just sixty days to get rid of any products containing R-11.

J. Randolph Ewing, a U.S. entrepreneur with trading partners in the Caribbean and South America, had contracted with a small manufacturer of insecticides for a shipment of mosquito and biting-fly repellent containing R-11. Ewing planned to sell the insecticide, through his trading partners, under a variety of his own labels. He took delivery in the United States April 1 and shipped about half of the insecticides out at once. He heard about the EPA waring in late April. Anticipating a ban, Ewing thought about what to do next. He had several thousand dollars invested in the insecticides. Should he ship the rest of the insecticides overseas immediately and not mention the EPA warning to his foreign trading partners? Should he tell his trading partners about the warning and offer to take the product back? Should he be concerned at all?

Social, Policy, and Ethical Considerations

1. What should Ewing do?
2. Would your advice to Ewing be any different if R-11 were already banned in the United States?
3. If a chemical is banned in the United States but not in certain foreign nations, should the U.S. government prohibit the manufacturer from making the chemical here and exporting it to countries where it's not banned? What about a U.S. company that manufactures a banned chemical offshore, for example, in joint venture with a foreign partner?
4. In answering Question 3, would you take a chemical-by-chemical approach? Or would you stand for or against an export ban based on the principle that what's not safe enough for Americans is not safe enough for others?
5. What, if any, would be the justifications for a double standard of safety for Americans and the rest of the world's citizens?

evidence that "the past or present handling, storage, treatment, transportation or disposal of any solid waste or hazardous waste may present an imminent and substantial endangerment to health or the environment." Moreover, the EPA may impose civil penalties of up to $25,000 per day of violation. Maximum criminal penalties for knowing violations are $50,000 for each day of violation and/or five years' imprisonment. When a knowing violation endangers a person, the maximum criminal penalty is a $1 million fine and/or fifteen years' imprisonment.

http:// The Resource Conservation and Recovery Act: http://www4.law.cornell.edu/uscode/42/6901.html

The Superfund

Although the RCRA regulates current and future generation, transportation, and disposal of hazardous waste, the Act provides only limited authority for the cleanup of abandoned or inactive hazardous waste sites. To fill this gap, Congress in 1980 enacted the **Comprehensive Environmental Response, Compensation, and Liability Act (CERCLA**, or the **Superfund)**. By 1986, the EPA, working under the Act, had spent $1.6 billion and had begun the cleanup of only eight sites. This record and other problems with the initial legislation prompted Congress to amend the CERCLA by enacting the Superfund Amendments and Reauthorization Act of 1986 (SARA). The EPA has cleaned up over 500 National Priorities List sites and has over 400 still under construction. Nevertheless, it is predicted that if Congress does not provide additional funds the Superfund will run out of money in the near future.

CERCLA requires the federal government to establish a National Contingency Plan (NCP) prescribing procedures and standards for responding to hazardous substance releases. The NCP specifies criteria for determining

THE LAW AND YOU

State Bar Associations

Illinois: http://www.ag.state.il.us/ ("Protecting Illinois Environment")

Massachusetts: http://www.massbar.org ("Environmental Consumer Information")

U.S. Government

http://www.ftc.gov/bcp/conline/edcams/eande/index.html ("Energy and Environment")

http://www.epa.gov/epahome/publications2.htm ("Air Quality Planning and Standards")

http://www.epa.gov/epahome/publications2.htm ("Indoor Air Quality")

http://www.epa.gov/epahome/publications2.htm ("Ozone Depletion")

http://www.epa.gov/epahome/publications2.htm ("Chemical Emergency Preparedness and Prevention")

http://www.epa.gov/epahome/publications2.htm ("Hazardous Waste Technology Innovations")

http://www.epa.gov/epahome/publications2.htm ("Oil Spill Program")

http://www.epa.gov/epahome/publications2.htm ("Solid Waste")

http://www.epa.gov/epahome/publications2.htm ("Superfund")

http://www.epa.gov/epahome/publications2.htm ("Office of Ground Water and Drinking Water")

http://www.epa.gov/epahome/publications2.htm ("Office of Wastewater Management")

http://www.epa.gov/epahome/publications2.htm ("Office of Wetlands, Oceans, and Watersheds")

the priority of sites to be cleaned. The plan also identifies, on at least an annual basis, the sites that most require immediate cleanup.

Under the act, the federal government has authority to take either removal or remedial actions in response to a release or threatened release of hazardous substances, as long as such removal or remedial actions are consistent with the NCP. Removal typically is an immediate response to control a specific release of a hazardous substance. Remedial actions, on the other hand, consist of efforts to prevent or reduce the release of hazardous substances; such actions are intended to be long-term solutions. The president may impose a civil penalty of up to $25,000 per day of violation; for repeat violations, the penalty may reach up to $75,000 per day of violation.

States and private parties also may engage in response actions, although such actions must meet certain conditions in order for the responder to recover its costs from either the governmental trust fund or the parties responsible under CERCLA for the release or threatened release of hazardous substances.

CERCLA establishes a trust fund to pay for hazardous waste removal and other remedial actions. The trust fund is financed in part by a surtax on businesses with annual incomes over $2 million, a tax on petroleum, and a tax on chemical feedstocks. An additional part of the trust fund comes from money recovered from persons responsible for the release of hazardous substances. These parties include the owners and operators of a hazardous waste disposal facility from which there has been a release, as well as any generator of hazardous wastes that were disposed of at that facility.

Because CERCLA initially imposed liability on all owners of contaminated property, some parties were held liable even though they had acquired the land either involuntarily or without knowledge of the hazardous wastes stored there. For example, after foreclosing on a mortgage of $335,000 and taking title to a piece of property, a bank was held liable for Superfund costs of more than $555,000. Responding to the inequity of such situations, Congress in SARA established a new defense to CERCLA liability for "innocent landowners." To qualify as an innocent landowner, one "must have undertaken, at the time of acquisition, all appropriate inquiry into the previous ownership and uses of the property consistent with good commercial or customary practice in an effort to minimize liability." In addition, under the Superfund Recycling Act of 1999, recyclers are exempt from liability to third parties, although they remain liable in suits brought by the federal or state governments.

In 2002, President Bush signed into law the Small Business Liability Relief and Brownfields Revitalization Act. The purpose of the Act is to promote the purchase, development, and use of brownfields, which are industrially

CONCEPT REVIEW

Major Federal Environmental Statutes

Act	Major Purpose	Maximum Civil Penalty	Maximum Criminal Penalty
National Environmental Policy Act (NEPA)	• Establish environmental protection as a major national goal • Mandate environmental impact statements be prepared prior to federal action having a significant environmental effect	None	None
Clean Air Act	• Control and reduce air pollution • Establish National Ambient Air Quality Standards	$32,500 per day of violation	$1,000,000 fine per violation and/or 15 years imprisonment*
Clean Water Act	• Protect against water pollution • Establish effluent limitations	$32,500 per day of violation	$50,000 per day of violation and/or 3 years imprisonment*
Federal Insecticide, Fungicide and Rodenticide Act (FIFRA)	• Regulate the sale and distribution of pesticides • Prevent pesticides having an unreasonably adverse effect on the environment	$6,500 per offense	$50,000 fine and/or 1 year imprisonment
Toxic Substances Control Act (TSCA)	• Regulate toxic substances • Prevent unreasonable risk of injury to health and the environment from toxic substances	$32,500 per day of violation	$25,000 fine per day of violation and/or 1 year imprisonment
Resource Conservation and Recovery Act (RCRA)	• Regulate the disposal of solid waste • Establish standards to protect human health and the environment from hazardous wastes	$32,500 per day of violation	$1,000,000 fine and/or 15 years imprisonment
Comprehensive Environmental Response, Compensation and Liability Act (CERCLA, or the Superfund) and Superfund Amendments and Reauthorization Act (SARA)	• Establish a national contingency plan for responding to releases of hazardous substances • Establish a trust fund to pay for removal of hazardous waste and other remedial actions	$32,500 per day of violation; $92,500 for repeat violations	None

*Doubled for repeat convictions.

polluted property that are not sufficiently contaminated to be classified as a priority by either the EPA or state environmental agencies. The Act attempts to accomplish this purpose by providing protection from liability under CERCLA to any purchaser of contaminated property, to owners and developers who clean up property under state voluntary cleanup programs, and to owners of property that have become contaminated by migrating pollutants.

http:// Comprehensive Environment Response, Compensation, and Liability Act: http://www.epa.gov/superfund/action/law/cercla.htm
Small Business Liability Relief and Brownfields Revitalization Act: http://www.epa.gov/swerosps/bf/sblrbra.htm

United States v. Bestfoods

Supreme Court of the United States, 1998
524 U.S. 51, 118 S.Ct. 1876, 141 L.Ed.2d 43
http://laws.findlaw.com/us/000/97-454.html

FACTS In 1957, Ott Chemical Co. (Ott I) began manufacturing chemicals at a plant near Muskegon, Michigan, and its intentional and unintentional dumping of hazardous substances significantly polluted the soil and ground water at the site. In 1965, CPC International Inc. (Bestfoods) **(http://www.bestfoods.com)**, incorporated a wholly owned subsidiary to buy Ott I's assets in exchange for CPC stock. The new company, Ott Chemical Co. (Ott II), continued chemical manufacturing at the site, and continued to pollute its surroundings. CPC kept the managers of Ott I, including its founder, president, and principal shareholder, Arnold Ott, on board as officers of Ott II. Arnold Ott and several other Ott II officers and directors were also given positions at CPC, and they performed duties for both corporations. In 1972, CPC sold Ott II to Story Chemical Company, which operated the Muskegon plant until its bankruptcy in 1977. Shortly thereafter, the Michigan Department of Natural Resources (MDNR) **(http://www.michigan.gov/dnr)** examined the site for environmental damage. It found the land littered with thousands of leaking and even exploding drums of waste, and the soil and water saturated with noxious chemicals. MDNR sought a buyer for the property who would be willing to contribute toward its cleanup, and after extensive negotiations, Aerojet-General Corp. arranged for transfer of the site from the Story bankruptcy trustee in 1977. Aerojet created a wholly owned California subsidiary, Cordova Chemical Company (Cordova/California), to purchase the property, and Cordova/California in turn created a wholly owned Michigan subsidiary, Cordova Chemical Company of Michigan (Cordova/Michigan), which manufactured chemicals at the site until 1986.

By 1981, the federal Environmental Protection Agency had undertaken to oversee the cleanup of the site, and its long-term remedial plan called for expenditures well into the tens of millions of dollars. To recover some of that money, the United States filed this action in 1989, naming five defendants as responsible parties: CPC, Aerojet, Cordova/California, Cordova/Michigan, and Arnold Ott. (By that time, Ott I and Ott II were defunct.) The District Court held a 15-day bench trial on the issue of liability. The trial focused on the issues of whether CPC and Aerojet, as the parent corporations of Ott II and the Cordova companies, had "owned or operated" the facility within the meaning of statute, and the court held them both to be operators Applying Michigan's veil-piercing law, the Court of Appeals decided that neither CPC nor Aerojet was liable for controlling the actions of its subsidiaries, since the parent and subsidiary corporations maintained separate personalities and the parents did not utilize the subsidiary corporate form to perpetrate fraud or subvert justice.

DECISION The judgment of the Court of Appeals is vacated, and the case is remanded with instructions to return it to the District Court for further proceedings consistent with this opinion.

OPINION Souter, J. The issue before us, under the Comprehensive Environmental Response, Compensation, and Liability Act of 1980 (CERCLA), is whether a parent corporation that actively participated in, and exercised control over, the operations of a subsidiary may, without more, be held liable as an operator of a polluting facility owned or operated by the subsidiary. We answer no, unless the corporate veil may be pierced. But a corporate parent that actively participated in, and exercised control over, the operations of the facility itself may be held directly liable in its own right as an operator of the facility.

In 1980, CERCLA was enacted in response to the serious environmental and health risks posed by industrial pollution. [Citation.] "As its name implies, CERCLA is a comprehensive statute that grants the President broad power to command government agencies and private parties to clean up hazardous waste sites." [Citation.] If it satisfies certain statutory conditions, the United States may, for instance, use the "Hazardous Substance Superfund" to finance cleanup efforts, [citation], which it may then replenish by suits brought under § 107 of the Act against, among others, "any person who at the time of disposal of any hazardous substance owned or operated any facility." [Citation.] So, those actually "responsible for any damage, environmental harm, or injury from chemical poisons [may be tagged with] the cost of their actions." * * *

* * *

It is a general principle of corporate law deeply "ingrained in our economic and legal systems" that a parent corporation (so-called because of control through ownership of another corporation's stock) is not liable for the acts of its subsidiaries. [Citations.] * * * The Government has indeed made no claim that a corporate parent is liable as an owner or an operator under § 107 simply because its subsidiary is subject to liability for owning or operating a polluting facility.

But there is an equally fundamental principle of corporate law, applicable to the parent-subsidiary relationship as well as generally, that the corporate veil may be pierced and the shareholder held liable for the corporation's conduct when, *inter alia*, the corporate form would otherwise be misused to accomplish certain wrongful purposes, most notably fraud, on the shareholder's behalf. [Citations.] Nothing in CERCLA purports to rewrite this well-settled rule, either. * * * The Court of Appeals was accordingly correct in holding that when (but only when) the corporate veil may be pierced, may a parent corporation be charged with derivative CERCLA liability for its subsidiary's actions.

If the act rested liability entirely on ownership of a polluting facility, this opinion might end here; but CERCLA liability may turn on operation as well as ownership, and nothing in the statute's terms bars a parent corporation from direct liability for its own actions in operating a facility owned by its subsidiary. As Justice (then-Professor) Douglas noted almost 70 years ago, derivative liability cases are to be distinguished from those in which "the alleged wrong can seemingly be traced to the parent through the conduit of its own personnel and management" and "the parent is directly a participant in the wrong complained of." [Citation.] In such instances, the parent is directly liable for its own actions. [Citation.] The fact that a corporate subsidiary happens to own a polluting facility operated by its parent does nothing, then, to displace the rule that the parent "corporation is [itself] responsible for the wrongs committed by its agents in the course of its business," [Citations.] It is this direct liability that is properly seen as being at issue here.

Under the plain language of the statute, any person who operates a polluting facility is directly liable for the costs of cleaning up the pollution. [Citation.] This is so regardless of whether that person is the facility's owner, the owner's parent corporation or business partner, or even a saboteur who sneaks into the facility at night to discharge its poisons out of malice. If any such act of operating a corporate subsidiary's facility is done on behalf of a parent corporation, the existence of the parent-subsidiary relationship under state corporate law is simply irrelevant to the issue of direct liability. [Citations.]

This much is easy to say; the difficulty comes in defining actions sufficient to constitute direct parental "operation." * * * So, under CERCLA, an operator is simply someone who directs the workings of, manages, or conducts the affairs of a facility. To sharpen the definition for purposes of CERCLA's concern with environmental contamination, an operator must manage, direct, or conduct operations specifically related to pollution, that is, operations having to do with the leakage or disposal of hazardous waste, or decisions about compliance with environmental regulations.

With this understanding, we are satisfied that the Court of Appeals correctly rejected the District Court's analysis of direct liability. But we also think that the appeals court erred in limiting direct liability under the statute to a parent's sole or joint venture operation, so as to eliminate any possible finding that CPC is liable as an operator on the facts of this case.

By emphasizing that "CPC is directly liable under section 107(a)(2) as an operator because CPC actively participated in and exerted significant control over Ott II's business and decision-making," [citation], the District Court applied the "actual control" test of whether the parent "actually operated the business of its subsidiary," [citation].

* * *

In imposing direct liability on these grounds, the District Court failed to recognize that "it is entirely appropriate for directors of a parent corporation to serve as directors of its subsidiary, and that fact alone may not serve to expose the parent corporation to liability for its subsidiary's acts." [Citations.]

This recognition that the corporate personalities remain distinct has its corollary in the "well established principle [of corporate law] that directors and officers holding positions with a parent and its subsidiary can and do 'change hats' to represent the two corporations separately, despite their common ownership." * * * The Government would have to show that, despite the general presumption to the contrary, the officers and directors were acting in their capacities as CPC officers and directors, and not as Ott II officers and directors, when they committed those acts. The District Court made no such enquiry here, however, disregarding entirely this time-honored common law rule.

* * *

We accordingly agree with the Court of Appeals that a participation and control test looking to the parent's supervision over the subsidiary, especially one that assumes that dual officers always act on behalf of the parent, cannot be used to identify operation of a facility resulting in direct parental liability. Nonetheless, a return to the ordinary meaning of the word "operate" in the organizational sense will indicate why we think that the Sixth Circuit stopped short when it confined its examples of direct parental operation to exclusive or joint ventures, and declined to find at least the possibility of direct operation by CPC in this case.

In our enquiry into the meaning Congress presumably had in mind when it used the verb "to operate," we recognized that the statute obviously meant something more than mere mechanical activation of pumps and valves, and must be read to contemplate "operation" as including the exercise of direction over the facility's activities. The Court of Appeals recognized this by indicating that a parent can be held directly liable when the parent operates the facility in the stead of its subsidiary or alongside the subsidiary in some sort of a joint venture. We anticipated a further possibility above, however, when we observed that a dual officer or director might depart so far from the norms of parental influence exercised through dual officeholding as to serve the parent, even when ostensibly acting on behalf of the subsidiary in operating the facility. Yet another possibility, suggested by the facts of this case, is that an agent of the parent with no hat to wear but the parent's hat might manage or direct activities at the facility.

Identifying such an occurrence calls for line drawing yet again, since the acts of direct operation that give rise to parental liability must necessarily be distinguished from the interference that stems from the normal relationship between parent and subsidiary. Again norms of corporate behavior (undisturbed by any CERCLA provision) are crucial reference points. * * * The critical question is whether, in degree and detail, actions directed to the facility by an agent of the parent alone are eccentric under accepted norms of parental oversight of a subsidiary's facility.

There is, in fact, some evidence that CPC engaged in just this type and degree of activity at the Muskegon plant. The District Court's opinion speaks of an agent of CPC alone who played a conspicuous part in dealing with the toxic risks emanating from the operation of the plant. G.R.D. Williams worked only for CPC; he was not an employee, officer, or director of Ott II, and thus, his actions were of necessity taken only on behalf of CPC. The District Court found that "CPC became directly involved in environmental and regulatory matters through the work of * * * Williams, CPC's governmental and environmental affairs director. Williams * * * became heavily involved in environmental issues at Ott II." He "actively participated in and exerted control over a variety of Ott II environmental matters," [citation] and he "issued directives regarding Ott II's responses to regulatory inquiries."

We think that these findings are enough to raise an issue of CPC's operation of the facility through Williams's actions, though we would draw no ultimate conclusion from these findings at this point.

INTERPRETATION Direct parental liability under CERCLA's operator provision is not limited to a corporate parent's sole or joint venture operation with subsidiary.

CRITICAL THINKING QUESTION Who should be responsible for the cleanup of these polluted sites? Explain.

CPA International Protection of the Ozone Layer

In 1987, the United States and twenty-three other countries entered into the **Montreal Protocol** on Substances that Deplete the Ozone Layer, a treaty designed to prevent pollution that harms the ozone layer. The treaty requires all signatories to reduce their production and consumption of all chemicals, in particular chlorofluorocarbons (CFCs, more commonly called freon), that deplete the ozone layer. Although having excessive ozone in the air we breathe can be hazardous, the ozone layer in the stratosphere helps to protect the earth from harmful ultraviolet radiation. By 1985, scientists believed that the release of CFCs into the atmosphere had caused a hole to develop in the ozone layer over Antarctica.

Chlorofluorocarbons, halocarbons, carbon dioxide, methane, and nitrous oxide are extremely potent "greenhouse gases," which trap heat and thereby warm the earth. Human activities, however, have increased the release of greenhouse gases, resulting in the serious threat of global warming. Scientists warn that the earth's temperature could rise by as much as 6.3 degrees over the next century due to global warming. If this occurs, the levels of the seas will rise and the climate will change over most of the earth, causing severe flooding and disruptions of agricultural production.

To combat this predicted climate change, 165 nations in 1992 negotiated a treaty at the UN Convention on Climate Change (FCCC) in Rio de Janeiro. The treaty's ultimate objective was to stabilize the "greenhouse gas concentration in the atmosphere at a level that would prevent dangerous anthropogenic [human-induced] interference with the climate system." More than 160 countries eventually ratified the treaty, which went into effect on March 21, 1994. The FCCC calls for all signatory countries to develop and update national inventories of all greenhouse gases not otherwise covered by the Montreal Protocol. The treaty, however, is voluntary and most nations, including the United States, will not meet its objectives. At a subsequent FCCC, held in Kyoto, Japan, in December 1997, the participating nations proposed the **Kyoto Protocol**, which is a set of binding emission targets for developed nations. Under this Protocol, the United States is by the years 2008–2012 to reduce its emissions of greenhouse gases (carbon dioxide, methane, nitrous oxide, and synthetic substitutes for CFCs) to a level 7 percent below 1990 emission standards. Japan agreed to reduce its level to 6 percent below 1990 levels, and the European Union agreed to a level 8 percent below 1990 emission levels. The United States has not yet ratified this treaty. However, in 2001, President George W. Bush stated that he does not support the Kyoto Treaty and saw no hope to salvage it. This followed a 95-0 vote in the Senate against its ratification.

http:// United Nations Environment Progamme: http://www.unep.org/

CHAPTER SUMMARY

Common Law Actions for Environmental Damage

Nuisance

Private Nuisance substantial and unreasonable interference with the use and enjoyment of a person's land

Public Nuisance interference with the health, safety, or comfort of the public

Other Common Law Actions

Trespass an invasion of land that interferes with the right of exclusive possession of the property

Strict Liability for Abnormally Dangerous Activities liability without fault for an individual who engages in an unduly dangerous activity in an inappropriate location

Federal Regulation of the Environment

National Environmental Policy Act (NEPA)

Purpose to establish environmental protection as a goal of federal policy

Council on Environmental Quality three-member advisory group in the Executive Office of the President that makes recommendations to the president on environmental matters

Environmental Impact Statement a detailed statement concerning the environmental impact of a proposed federal action

- *Scope* NEPA applies to a broad range of activities, including direct action by a federal agency as well as any action by a federal agency that permits action by other parties that will affect the quality of the environment
- *Content* the EIS must contain, among other items, a detailed statement of the environmental impact of the proposed action, any adverse environmental effects that cannot be avoided, and alternative proposals

Clean Air Act

Purpose to control and reduce air pollution

Existing Sources

- *National Ambient Air Quality Standards (NAAQSs)* the EPA administrator must establish NAAQSs for air pollutants that endanger the public health and welfare
- *State Implementation Plan* each state must submit a plan for each NAAQS detailing how the state will implement and maintain the standard

New Sources

- *New Stationary Sources* owner/operator must employ the best technological system of continuous emission reduction that has been adequately demonstrated
- *New Vehicles* extensive emission standards are established
- *Hazardous Air Pollutants* to protect the public health, the EPA administrator must establish for hazardous air pollutants standards that provide ample safety margins
- *Acid Rain* standards are established to protect against acid rain (precipitation that contains high levels of sulfuric or nitric acid)

Clean Water Act

Purpose protect against water pollution

Point Sources act establishes National Pollutant Discharge Elimination System (NPDES), a permit system, to control the amount of pollutants that may be discharged by a point source into U.S. waters

Nonpoint Sources act requires the states to use the best management practices to control water runoff from agricultural and urban areas

Hazardous Substances

FIFRA the Federal Insecticide, Fungicide and Rodenticide Act regulates the sale and distribution of pesticides

TSCA the Toxic Substances Control Act provides a comprehensive scheme for regulation of toxic substances

RCRA the Resource Conservation and Recovery Act provides a comprehensive scheme for treatment of solid waste, particularly hazardous waste

Superfund the Comprehensive Environmental Response, Compensation, and Liability Act (CERCLA) establishes (1) a National Contingency Plan for responding to releases of hazardous substances and (2) a trust fund to pay for removal and cleanup of hazardous waste

International Protection of the Ozone Layer

Montreal Protocol treaty by which countries agreed to cut production of chlorofluorocarbons (CFCs) by 50 percent

Kyoto Protocol resolution on greenhouse gases

QUESTIONS

1. Atlantic Cement operated a large cement plant. Neighboring landowners sued for damages and an injunction, claiming that their properties were injured by the dirt, smoke, and vibrations coming from the plant. The lower court found that the plant constituted a nuisance and granted temporary damages but refused to grant an injunction because the benefits of operating the plant outweighed the harm to the plaintiffs' properties. The landowners appealed. Does the plant constitute a nuisance? Should it be shut down?

2. Seindenberg and Hutchinson (the site owners) leased a four-acre tract of land (the Bluff Road site) to a chemical manufacturing corporation (COCC). While the lease initially was for the sole purpose of allowing COCC to store raw materials and finished products in a warehouse on the land, COCC later expanded its business to include the brokering and recycling of chemical waste generated by third parties. COCC's owners subsequently formed a new corporation, South Carolina Recycling and Disposal, Inc. (SCRDI), for the purpose of taking over COCC's waste-handling business. The site owners accepted rent from SCRDI. The waste stored at Bluff Road contained many chemical substances that federal law defines as hazardous. In 1980, the EPA concluded that the site was a major fire hazard. The federal government contracted with a third party to perform a partial cleanup of the site. South Carolina completed the cleanup. The federal government and South Carolina sued SCRDI, COCC, the site owners, and three third-party generators as responsible parties under the RCRA and CERCLA. Explain whether the United States and South Carolina will prevail.

3. The state of Y submits a plan under the Clean Air Act to attain national ambient air quality standards. Can the EPA administrator deny approval of the state plan because it is (a) less stringent or (b) more stringent than the agency believes is feasible? Explain.

CASE PROBLEMS

4. Kennecott Copper Corp. brings this challenge to an EPA order that rejected a portion of the state of Nevada's implementation plan dealing with the control of stationary sources of sulfur dioxide (SO_2). All of the SO_2 emissions come from a single source—the Kennecott copper smelter at McGill. The EPA based its decision on the belief that the Clean Air Act NAAQS must be met by continuous emission limitations to the maximum extent possible and that the Act permits the intermittent use of emission controls only when continuous controls are not economically feasible. Kennecott contends that the EPA must approve any state implementation plan that will attain and maintain an NAAQS within the statutory time period. Who will prevail? Why?

5. The EPA administrator issued an order suspending the registration of the pesticides heptachlor and chlordane under the FIFRA. Velsicol Chemical Corp. (http://www.velsicol.com/), the sole manufacturer of these pesticides, brings this action, contending that the evidence does not support the administrator's contention that the continued use of these chemicals poses an imminent hazard to human health. Velsicol and the U.S. Department of Agriculture (USDA) (http://www.usda.gov/) contend (1) that the EPA's laboratory tests on mice and rats do not "conclusively" show that either chemical is carcinogenic; (2) that mice are too prone to tumors to be reliable test subjects; and (3) that human exposure to these chemicals is insufficient to create a risk. Nonetheless, human epidemiology studies on both chemicals provide no basis for concluding that either pesticide is safe. The administrator based part of his claim on residues of these chemicals found in soil, air, and the aquatic ecosystem over long periods of time and on the presence of these chemicals in the human diet and human tissue. Does FIFRA apply in this situation? Explain.

6. The U.S. Department of the Interior (http://www.doi.gov/) filed an environmental impact statement with regard to its proposal to lease approximately eighty tracts of submerged land, primarily located off the coast of Louisiana, for oil and gas exploration. Adjacent to the proposed area is the greatest estuarine coastal marsh in the United States. This marsh provides rich nutrients for the Gulf of Mexico, the most productive fishing region of the country. The environmental impact statement (EIS) focused primarily on oil pollution and its negative environmental effect. Three conservation groups contend that the EIS is insufficient in that it does not properly discuss alternatives. The government contends that (a) it need only provide a detailed statement of the alternatives, not a discussion of their environmental impact, and (b) the only alternatives the NEPA requires it to discuss are those that can be adopted and implemented by the agency issuing the impact statement. Is the government correct in its contentions? Why?

7. Chemical Manufacturers Association (CMA) (http://es.epa.gov/techinfo/facts/cma/cma.htm) and four companies that manufacture chemicals challenged a test rule promulgated by the Environmental Protection Agency under the Toxic Substances Control Act, (TSCA). The plaintiffs asserted that the EPA must find that the existence of an unreasonable risk of injury to health is more probable than not before it may issue a test rule under the act. In response, the EPA claimed that it may issue a test rule under the TSCA if the agency determines that there is a substantial probability of an unreasonable risk of injury to health. The test rule required toxicological testing to determine the health effects of the chemical, 2-ethylhexanoic acid, and imposed on exporters of this chemical a duty to file certain notices with the EPA. What standard should be applied? Why?

8. National-Southwire Aluminum Company (NSA) owns and operates a plant that emits fluoride. In 1982, when its wet scrubbers were turned off as part of its regular maintenance program, NSA discovered no appreciable change in ambient fluoride levels. Because of the expense of operating the scrubbers and its belief that using the scrubbers did not significantly affect ambient fluoride levels, NSA desired to turn the scrubbers off permanently. Accordingly, NSA sought a determination from the EPA that turning off the scrubbers would not constitute a modification requiring the application of new source performance standards to the plant. Turning off the scrubbers would result in an increase of more than 1,100 tons per year of fluoride emissions with no decrease in the emission of any other pollutant. This increase was nearly 400 times the level the EPA had established as inconsequential. The EPA determined that turning off the scrubbers would constitute a "new source" modification. Accordingly, NSA was required either to leave the scrubbers on or to install new pollutant control equipment. Is the EPA correct in its assertion? Explain.

http:// **Internet Exercise** Find information about the U.S. Environmental Protection Agency, then choose a state and determine whether it has a state environmental protection agency and, if so, what its responsibilities are.

Chapter 47

International Business Law

Peace, commerce, and honest friendship with all nations, entangling alliances with none.

THOMAS JEFFERSON, 1801

Learning Objectives

After reading this chapter you should be able to:

1. Describe the purposes and major features of regional trade communities (especially the European Union and NAFTA) and the World Trade Organization (GATT).
2. Explain sovereign immunity, the act of state doctrine, expropriation, and confiscation.
3. Explain the legal controls imposed on the flow of trade, labor, and capital across national borders.
4. Explain the international dimensions of antitrust law, securities regulation, and the protection of intellectual property.
5. List and describe the forms in which a multinational enterprise may conduct its business in a foreign country.

Today every aspect of business, including business law, requires some understanding of international business practices. Since World War II, the global economy has become increasingly interconnected. Many U.S. corporations now have investments or manufacturing facilities in other countries; simultaneously, the number of foreign corporations with business operations in the United States has increased dramatically. Furthermore, whether a domestic corporation exports goods or not, it competes with imports from many other countries. For example, U.S. firms face competition from Japanese electronics and automobiles, French wines and fashions, German machinery, and Taiwanese textiles. In order to compete effectively, U.S. firms need to be aware of international business practices and developments.

Laws vary greatly from country to country: what one nation requires by law, another may forbid. To complicate matters, there is no single authority in international law that can compel countries to act. When the laws of two or more nations conflict, or when one party has violated an agreement and the other party wishes to enforce it or to recover damages, establishing who will adjudicate the matter, which laws will be applied, what remedies will be available, or where the matter should be decided often is very confusing. Nonetheless, given the growing impact of the global economy, a basic understanding of international business law is essential.

The International Environment

International law deals with the conduct and relations between nation-states and international organizations, as well as some of their relations with persons. Unlike domestic law, international law generally cannot be enforced. Consequently, international courts do not have compulsory jurisdiction, though they do have authority to resolve an international dispute if the parties to the dispute accept the court's jurisdiction over the matter. Furthermore, a sovereign nation that has adopted an international law will enforce that law to the same extent as all of its domestic laws. In this section, we will examine some of the sources and institutions of international law.

INTERNATIONAL COURT OF JUSTICE

The United Nations, which is probably the most famous international organization, has a judiciary branch called the **International Court of Justice (ICJ)**. The ICJ consists of fifteen judges, no two of whom may be from the same sovereign state, elected for nine-year terms by a majority of both the U.N. General Assembly and the U.N. Security Council. The usefulness of the ICJ is limited, however, because only nations (not private individuals or corporations) may be parties to an action before the court. Furthermore, the ICJ has contentious jurisdiction only over nation-parties who agree both to allow the ICJ to decide the case and to be bound by its decision. Moreover, because the ICJ cannot enforce its rulings, countries displeased with an ICJ decision may simply ignore it. Consequently, few nations submit their disputes to the ICJ.

The ICJ also has advisory jurisdiction if requested by a U.N. organ or specialized U.N. agency. Neither sovereign states nor individuals may request an advisory opinion. These opinions are nonbinding, and the U.N. agency requesting the opinion usually votes to decide whether to follow it.

http:// ABA Section on international law: **http://www.abanet.org/intlaw/**
United Nations: **http://www.unsystem.org/**
United Nations charter: **http://www.un.org/aboutun/charter**
International Court of Justice: **http://www.icj-cij.org/**

REGIONAL TRADE COMMUNITIES

Of much greater significance are international organizations, conferences, and treaties that focus on business and trade regulation. **Regional trade communities**, such as the European Union (EU), promote common trade policies among member nations. Other important regional trade communities include the Central American Common Market (CACM), the Caribbean Community Market (CARICOM), the Association of South East Asian Nations (ASEAN), the Andean Common Market (ANCOM), the Common Market for Eastern and Southern Africa (COMESA), the Asian Pacific Economic Cooperation (APEC), Mercado Comun del Cono Sur (Latin American Trading Group, MERCO-SUR), and the Economic Community of West African States (ECOWAS).

European Union (EU) The European Community (EC), the predecessor to the European Union, was formed in 1967 through a merger between the European Economic Community (better known as the Common Market), the European Coal and Steel Community, and the European Atomic Energy Community (Euratom). The EC worked to remove trade barriers among its member nations and to unify their economic policies. The EC had the power to make rules that bound member nations and that preempted its members' domestic laws.

In 1993 the Treaty on European Union (popularly called the Maastricht Treaty) took effect. It changed the name of the EC to the European Union and stated the Union's objectives to include (1) promoting economic and social progress by creating an area without internal borders and by establishing an economic and monetary union; (2) asserting its identity on the international scene by implementing a common foreign and security policy; (3) strengthening the protection of the rights and interests of citizens of its member states; and (4) developing close cooperation on justice and home affairs. The EU currently has fifteen full members: Austria, Belgium, Denmark, Finland, France, Germany, Greece, Ireland, Italy, Luxembourg, the Netherlands, Portugal, Spain, Sweden, and the United Kingdom. The EU is preparing for admitting ten eastern and southern European countries in 2004. Bulgaria and Romania expect to follow a few years later, and Turkey is also a candidate country. The EU has almost 400 million citizens.

http:// European Union: **http://europa.eu.int/index-en.htm**

NAFTA The North American Free Trade Agreement, which took effect in 1994, established a free trade area among the United States, Canada, and Mexico. Its objectives are to (1) eliminate trade barriers to the movement of goods and services across the borders, (2) promote conditions of fair competition in the free trade area, (3) increase investment opportunities in the area, and (4) provide adequate and effective enforcement of intellectual property rights. Over fifteen years, the treaty will gradually eliminate all tariffs between the three countries.

http:// NAFTA: **http://www.sice.oas.org/tradee.asp#NAFTA**

INTERNATIONAL TREATIES

A treaty is an agreement between or among independent nations. As we discussed in Chapter 1, the U.S. Constitution authorizes the President to enter into treaties with the advice and consent of the Senate "providing two-thirds of the Senators present concur." The U.S. Constitution provides that all valid treaties are "the law of the land," having the legal force of a federal statute.

Nations have entered into bilateral and multilateral treaties in order to facilitate and regulate trade and to protect their national interests. In addition, treaties have been used to serve as constitutions of international organizations, to establish general international law, to transfer territory, to settle disputes, to secure human rights, and to protect investments. The Treaty Section of the Office of Legal Affairs within the United Nations Secretariat is responsible for registering and publishing treaties and agreements among member nations. Since its inception in 1946, the U.N. Secretariat has registered and published more than 30,000 treaties that expressly or indirectly concern international business.

Probably the most important multilateral trade treaty is the General Agreement on Tariffs and Trade (GATT), which is now called the World Trade Organization (WTO) and has more than 140 members accounting for more than 95 percent of world trade. (Approximately thirty other countries are negotiating membership.) Its basic purpose is to facilitate the flow of trade by establishing agreements on potential trade barriers such as import quotas, customs, export regulations, antidumping restrictions (the prohibition against selling goods for less than their fair market value), subsidies, and import fees. Such agreements arise under GATT's ***most favored nation provision***, which states that all signatories must treat each other as favorably as they treat any other country. Thus, any privilege, immunity, or favor given to one country must be given to all. Nevertheless, nations may give preferential treatment to developing nations and may enter into free trade areas with one or more other nations. A free trade area permits countries to discriminate in favor of their free trade partners, provided that the agreement covers substantially all trade among the partners. A second important principle adopted by GATT is that the protection offered domestic industries should take the form of customs tariffs, rather than other, more trade-inhibiting measures.

The most recent set of accords, adopted in 1994, included agreements on such matters as agricultural products, textiles and clothing, technical barriers to trade, trade-related investment measures, customs valuation, subsidies and countervailing measures, trade in services, antidumping measures, and protection of intellectual property rights. It also created the Dispute Settlement Body and increased the scope of GATT's dispute resolution process.

http://

United Nations treaty collection: http://untreaty.un.org/
WTO: http://www.wto.org/
GATT: http://www2.law.cornell.edu/cgi-bin/foliocgi.exe/gatt?

JURISDICTION OVER ACTIONS OF FOREIGN GOVERNMENTS

In this section, we will focus on a sovereign nation's power—and the factors limiting that nation's power—to exercise jurisdiction over a foreign nation or to take over property owned by foreign citizens. More specifically, we will examine state immunities (the principle of sovereign immunity and the act of state doctrine) and the power of a state to take foreign investment property.

SOVEREIGN IMMUNITY

One of the oldest concepts in international law is that each nation has absolute and total authority over the events occurring within its territory. It has also been long recognized, however, that in order to maintain international relations and trade, a host country must refrain from imposing its laws on a foreign sovereign nation present within its borders. This absolute immunity from the courts of a host country is known as **sovereign immunity**. Originally, all acts of a foreign sovereign nation within a host country were considered immune from the host country's laws. In modern times, however, international law distinguishes between a foreign nation's public acts and its commercial ones. Only public acts, such as those concerning diplomatic activity, internal administration, or armed forces, will be granted sovereign immunity. By engaging in trade or commercial activities, a foreign nation subjects itself to the jurisdiction of its host country's courts with respect to any disputes that arise out of those commercial activities.

In 1976, Congress enacted the Foreign Sovereign Immunities Act in order to establish exactly the circumstances under which the United States would extend immunity to foreign nations. The act specifically provides that a foreign state shall be immune from neither federal nor state court jurisdiction if the suit is based upon (1) a commercial activity conducted in the United States by the foreign state, (2) an act that the foreign state performed in the United States in connection with a commercial activity it conducted elsewhere, or (3) a commercial activity performed outside the United States that nonetheless directly affects the United States. If an activity is one that a private party could normally carry on, it is commercial and a foreign government engaging in that activity is not immune. On the other hand, if the activity is one that only governments can undertake, it is noncommercial under the act. Examples of commercial activities include a contract by a foreign government to buy provisions or equipment for its armed forces; a foreign government's contract to construct or repair a government building;

and a foreign government's sale of a service or a product or its leasing of property, borrowing of money, or investing in a security of a U.S. corporation. Examples of public (noncommercial) activities to which sovereign immunity would extend include nationalizing a corporation, determining limitations upon the use of the foreign state's natural resources, and the granting of licenses to export a natural resource.

Saudi Arabia v. Nelson

Supreme Court of the United States, 1993
507 U.S. 349, 113 S.Ct. 1471, 123 L.Ed.2d 47
http://supct.law.cornell.edu:8080/supct/html/91-522.ZX1.html

FACTS The Kingdom of Saudi Arabia **(http://www.saudiembassy.net)** owns and operates King Faisal Specialist Hospital in Riyadh (Hospital) **(http://www.kfshrc.edu.sa/)**. The Hospital Corporation of America, Ltd. (HCA) **(http://www.columbia-hca.com)**, an independent corporation existing under the laws of the Cayman Islands, recruits Americans for employment at the Hospital under an agreement signed with Saudi Arabia in 1973. HCA placed an advertisement in a periodical seeking applicants for a monitoring systems engineer position at the Hospital. Scott Nelson saw the ad in September 1983 while he was in the United States. After interviewing for the position in Saudi Arabia, Nelson returned to the United States, where he signed an employment contract with the Hospital, satisfied personnel processing requirements, and attended an orientation session that HCA conducted for Hospital employees. In December 1983, Nelson went to Saudi Arabia and began work at the Hospital. In March 1984, he discovered safety defects in the Hospital's oxygen and nitrous oxide lines that posed fire hazards. Nelson repeatedly advised Hospital officials of the safety defects and reported the defects to a Saudi government commission. On September 27, 1984, the Saudi government arrested him. Agents transported Nelson to a jail cell, where they shackled, tortured, and beat him and kept him for four days without food. Government agents forced him to sign a statement written in Arabic, which language Nelson did not know. Two days later, government agents transferred Nelson to the Al Sijan Prison to await trial. Nelson was confined in an overcrowded cell infested with rats, where he had to fight other prisoners for food and from which he was taken only once a week for fresh air and exercise. Only after the personal request of a U.S. senator did the Saudi government release Nelson, thirty-nine days after his arrest. Seven days later, the Saudi government allowed him to leave the country.

In 1988, Nelson filed suit against Saudi Arabia in the U.S. District Court for the Southern District of Florida, seeking damages for personal injury. The district court dismissed the case for lack of subject-matter jurisdiction under the Foreign Sovereign Immunities Act of 1976. The Court of Appeals reversed, holding that under the act, a foreign state is not immune from the jurisdiction of U.S. courts in any case involving an action based upon a commercial activity carried on in the United States by the foreign state. It concluded that Nelson's recruitment and hiring were commercial activities of Saudi Arabia and the Hospital carried on in the United States.

DECISION Decision of the Court of Appeals reversed.

OPINION Souter, J. The Foreign Sovereign Immunities Act "provides the sole basis for obtaining a jurisdiction over a foreign state in the courts of this country." [Citation.] Under the Act, a foreign state is presumptively immune from the jurisdiction of United States courts; unless a specified exception applies, a federal court lacks subject-matter jurisdiction over a claim against a foreign state. [Citations.]

Only one such exception is said to apply here. The first clause of § 1605(a)(2) of the Act provides that a foreign state shall not be immune from the jurisdiction of United States courts in any case "in which the action is based upon a commercial activity carried on in the United States by the foreign state." The Act defines such activity as "commercial activity carried on by such state and having substantial contact with the United States," [citation], and provides that a commercial activity may be "either a regular course of commercial conduct or a particular commercial transaction or act," the "commercial character of [which] shall be determined by reference to" its "nature," rather than its "purpose." [Citation.]

* * *

We took up the task [of defining commercial activity for purposes of the Act] just last Term in [*Republic of Argentina v.] Weltover*, [citation], which involved Argentina's unilateral refinancing of bonds it has issued under a plan to stabilize its currency. Bondholders sued Argentina in federal court, asserting jurisdiction under the third clause of § 1605(a)(2). In the course of holding the refinancing to be a commercial activity for purposes of the Act, we observed that the statute "largely codifies the so-called 'restrictive' theory of foreign sovereign immunity first endorsed by the State Department in 1952." [Citation.] We accordingly held that the meaning of "commercial" for purposes of the Act must be the meaning congress understood the restrictive theory to require at the time it passed the statute. [Citation.]

Under the restrictive, as opposed to the "absolute," theory of foreign sovereign immunity, a state is immune from the jurisdiction of foreign courts as to its sovereign or public acts (jure imperii), but not as to those that are private or commercial in character (jure gestionis). [Citations.] We explained in Weltover, [citation], that a state engages in commercial activity under the restrictive theory where it exercises "only those powers that also be exercised by private citizens," as distinct from those "powers peculiar to sovereigns." Put differently, a foreign state engages in commercial activity for purposes of the restrictive theory only where it acts "in the manner of a private player within" the market. [Citation.]

We emphasized in *Weltover* that whether a state acts "in the manner of" a private party is a question of behavior, not motivation: "[B]ecause the Act provides that the commercial character of an act is to be determined by reference to its 'nature' rather than its 'purpose,' the question is not whether the foreign government is acting with a profit motive or instead with the aim of fulfilling uniquely sovereign objectives. Rather, the issue is whether the particular actions that the foreign state performs (whatever the motive behind them) are the type of actions by which a private party engages in 'trade and traffic or commerce.' " [Citation.] We did not ignore the difficulty of distinguishing " 'purpose' (i.e., the reason why the foreign state engages in the activity) from 'nature' (i.e., the outward form of the conduct that the foreign state performs or agrees to perform)," but recognized that the Act "unmistakably commands" us to observe the distinction. [Citation.] Because Argentina had merely dealt in the bond market in the manner of a private player, we held, its refinancing of the bonds qualified as a commercial activity for purposes of the Act despite the apparent governmental motivation. [Citation.]

Unlike Argentina's activities that we considered in *Weltover*, the intentional conduct alleged here (the Saudi Government's wrongful arrest, imprisonment, and torture of Nelson) could not qualify as commercial under the restrictive theory. The conduct boils down to abuse of the power of its police by the Saudi Government, and however monstrous such abuse undoubtedly may be, a foreign state's exercise of the power of its police has long been understood for purposes of the restrictive theory as peculiarly sovereign in nature. [Citations.] Exercise of the powers of police and penal officers is not the sort of action by which private parties can engage in commerce. "[S]uch acts as legislation, or the expulsion of an alien, or a denial of justice, cannot be performed by an individual acting in his own name. They can be performed only by the state acting as such." [Citation.]

INTERPRETATION Only lawsuits based on the commercial activities of a foreign state are subject to the jurisdiction of the state or federal courts in the United States.

CRITICAL THINKING QUESTION What are the public policy arguments supporting and opposing the Court's approach in this case? Explain.

ACT OF STATE DOCTRINE

The act of state doctrine provides that a nation's judicial branch should not question the validity of the actions a foreign government takes within that foreign sovereign's own borders. In 1897, the U.S. Supreme Court described the act of state doctrine in terms that remain valid today: "Every sovereign State is bound to respect the independence of every other sovereign State, and the courts of one country will not sit in judgment on the acts of the government of another done within its own territory."

In the United States, there are several possible exceptions to the act of state doctrine. Some courts hold (1) that a sovereign may waive its right to raise the act of state defense and (2) that the doctrine may be inapplicable to commercial activities of a foreign sovereign. In addition, by federal statute, courts will not apply the act of state doctrine to a claim to specific property located in the United States when such a claim is based on the assertion that a foreign state confiscated the property in violation of international law, unless the President of the United States determines that the doctrine should be applied to that particular case.

TAKING OF FOREIGN INVESTMENT PROPERTY

Investing in foreign states involves the risk that the host nation's government may take the investment property. An **expropriation** or nationalization occurs when a government seizes foreign-owned property or assets for a public purpose and pays the owner just compensation for what is taken. In contrast, **confiscation** occurs when a government offers no payment (or a highly inadequate payment) in exchange for seized property, or seizes it for a nonpublic purpose. Confiscations violate generally observed principles of international law, whereas expropriations do not. In either case, few remedies are available to injured parties.

The World Bank established the Multilateral Investment Guarantee Agency (MIGA) to encourage increased investment in developing nations. The MIGA Convention has been signed by more than 150 nations. It offers foreign investment risk insurance for noncommercial risks including deprivation of ownership or control by governmental actions, breach of contract by a government when there is no judicial recourse, and loss from military action or civil disturbance.

Practical Advice

If you invest in foreign states, consider obtaining expropriation insurance from a private insurer or from the Overseas Private Investment Corporation (OPIC), an agency of the U.S. government.

TRANSACTING BUSINESS ABROAD

Transacting business abroad may involve activities such as selling goods, information, or services; investing capital; or arranging for the movement of labor. Because these transactions may affect the national security, economy, foreign policy, and interests of both the exporting and importing countries, nations have imposed measures to restrict or encourage such transactions. In this section, we will examine the legal controls imposed upon the flow of trade, labor, and capital across national borders.

FLOW OF TRADE

Advances in modern technology, communication, transportation, and production methods have swelled the flow of goods across national boundaries. The governments within each country thereby face a dilemma. On the one hand, they wish to protect and stimulate domestic industry. On the other hand, they want to provide their citizens with the best quality goods at the lowest possible prices and to encourage exports from their own countries.

Governments have used a variety of trade barriers to protect domestic businesses. A frequently applied device is the **tariff**, which is a duty or tax imposed on goods moving into or out of a country. Tariffs raise the price of imported goods, prompting some consumers to purchase less expensive, domestically produced items. Governments can also use **nontariff barriers** to give local industries a competitive advantage. Examples of nontariff barriers include unilateral or bilateral import quotas, import bans, overly restrictive safety, health, or manufacturing standards, environmental laws, complicated and time-consuming customs procedures, and subsidies to local industry.

Dumping is the sale of exported goods from one country to another country at less than normal value. Under the WTO's Antidumping Code, "normal value" is the price that would be charged for the same or a similar product in the ordinary course of trade for domestic consumption in the exporting country. Dumping violates the GATT "if it causes or threatens material injury to an established industry in the territory of a contracting party or materially retards the establishment of a domestic industry."

Governments also control the flow of goods out of their countries by imposing quotas, tariffs, or total prohibitions. ***Export controls*** or restrictions usually result from important policy considerations, such as national defense, foreign policy, or the protection of scarce national resources. For example, the United States passed the Export Administration Act of 1979, which, as amended in 1985 and 1988, restricts the flow of technologically advanced goods and data from the United States to other countries. Nonetheless, in order to assist domestic businesses, countries generally encourage exports through the use of ***export incentives*** and ***export subsidies***.

Practical Advice

If you export goods, be sure to determine whether you must obtain an export license from the U.S. government and what import barriers, such as tariffs, you must satisfy in the countries to which you are sending the goods.

FLOW OF LABOR

The **flow of labor** across national borders generates policy questions concerning the employment needs of local workers. Each country has its own immigration policies and regulations. Almost all countries require that foreigners obtain valid passports before entering their borders; citizens, in turn, often must have passports in order to leave or reenter the country. In addition, a country may issue foreign citizens visas that permit them to enter the country for identified purposes or for specific periods of time. For example, the U.S. Immigration and Naturalization Service issues various types of visas to persons who are temporarily visiting the United States for pleasure or business, to persons who enter the United States to perform services that the unemployed in this country cannot

Ethical Dilemma

Who May Seek Economic Shelter Under U.S. Trade Law?

FACTS Stanlon, Inc., a U.S. manufacturer of educational computer software for children, has grown into a major employer in New England. Over the last eight years, Stanlon has developed programs on reading readiness and basic phonics aimed at preschool children. This innovative software, which recognizes the cultural diversity in America, sells for an average price of $150. Stanlon sells its products primarily through several subsidiary companies that retail children's educational toys. The retailers accept cash, checks, and major credit cards. They have no arrangements for installment sales. Over the past eight years, Stanlon, Inc., has enjoyed an excellent sales record.

Two years ago, Soeki, Ltd., a Japanese corporation, entered the market. Soeki sells substantially similar products for $75 per software package. In addition, the retail stores through which Soeki sells offer liberal credit terms, including installment sales. Soeki's stores are located in neighborhoods of various social and economic classes, and several are located near stores operated by Stanlon, whose retailers are located primarily in affluent neighborhoods.

Since Soeki entered the market, Stanlon's sales have plummeted. Now, having begun to lay off substantial numbers of workers, Stanlon has instituted a lawsuit against Soeki, Ltd., alleging that Soeki is selling its software at unprofitable prices in order to drive Stanlon from the market.

Social, Policy, and Ethical Considerations

1. Should a foreign corporation be free to sell goods at the lowest price possible? What is the social policy behind laws that prohibit foreign companies from selling below cost? What cost should be considered fair?
2. Is it in U.S. consumers' interest to encourage all competition from foreign enterprises?
3. How would your answers change if a foreign drug company were selling a medically valuable drug at a price significantly below that charged by its U.S. competitors?

perform, and to persons who are transferred to the United States by their employers.

Flow of Capital

Multinational businesses frequently need to transfer funds to, and receive money from, operations in other countries. Because there is no international currency, nations have sought to ease the ***flow of capital*** among themselves. In 1945, the International Monetary Fund (IMF) was established to facilitate the expansion and balanced growth of international trade, to assist in the elimination of foreign exchange restrictions that hamper such growth, and to shorten the duration and ease the disequilibrium in the international balance of payments between the members of the fund. Currently, more than 150 countries are members of the IMF.

Many nations have laws regulating foreign investment. Restrictions on the establishment of foreign investment tend to limit the amount of equity and the amount of control allowed to foreign investors. They may also restrict the way in which the investment is created, such as limiting or prohibiting investment by acquiring an existing locally owned business. Approximately 150 nations have signed the Convention on the Settlement of Investment Disputes Between States and Nationals of Other States. The Convention created the International Centre for the Settlement of Investment Disputes, which offers a form of arbitration for investment disputes between governments and foreign investors to promote increased flows of international investment.

Nations also have cooperated in forming international and regional banks to facilitate the flow of capital and trade. Such banks include the International Bank for Reconstruction and Development (part of the World Bank), the African Development Bank, the Asian Development Bank, the European Investment Bank, and the Inter-American Development Bank.

http://
International Monetary Fund: http://www.imf.org/
World Bank: http://www.worldbank.org/

International Contracts

The legal issues inherent in domestic commercial contracts also arise in **international contracts**. Moreover, additional issues, such as differences in language, customs, legal systems, and currency, are peculiar to international contracts. Such a contract should specify its official language and include definitions for all the significant legal terms used in it. In addition, it should specify the acceptable currency (or currencies) and payment method. The contract should include a choice of law clause designating what law will govern any breach or dispute regarding the contract, and a choice of forum clause designating whether the parties will resolve disputes through one nation's court system or through third-party arbitration. (The United Nations Committee on International Trade Law and the International Chamber of Commerce have promulgated arbitration rules that have won broad international acceptance.) Finally, the contract should include a *force majeure* (unavoidable superior force) clause apportioning the parties' liabilities and responsibilities in the event of an unforeseeable occurrence, such as a typhoon, tornado, flood, earthquake, war, or nuclear disaster.

The United Nations Commission on International Trade Law (UNCITRAL) was established by the U.N. General Assembly to further the progressive harmonization and unification of the law of international trade. The Commission is composed of thirty-six member states elected by the General Assembly and is structured to be representative of the world's various geographic regions and its principal economic and legal systems. One of its primary functions is to develop conventions, model laws, and rules that are acceptable worldwide. One example is the CISG (discussed below and in Chapters 19–23) and the arbitration rules mentioned above. Another is the UNCITRAL Model Law on Electronic Commerce, adopted in 1996, which is intended to facilitate the use of modern means of communications and storage of information. Legislation based on it has been adopted in more than ten nations and, in the United States, it has influenced the Uniform Electronic Transactions Act, adopted in 1999 by the National Conference of Commissioners on Uniform State Law. See Chapter 48.

Practical Advice

When you enter into international contracts, be sure that your contracts include provisions for payment, including acceptable currencies, choice of law, choice of forum, and *force majeure*.

CISG The United Nations Convention on Contracts for the International Sales of Goods (**CISG**), which has been ratified by the United States and about sixty other countries, governs all contracts for the international sales of goods between parties located in different nations that have ratified the CISG. Because treaties are federal law, the CISG supersedes the Uniform Commercial Code in any situation to which either could apply. The CISG includes provisions dealing with interpretation, trade usage, contract formation, obligations and remedies of sellers and buyers, and risk of loss. Parties to an international sales contract may, however, expressly exclude CISG governance from their contract. The CISG specifically excludes sales of (1) goods bought for personal, family, or household use; (2) ships or aircraft; and (3) electricity. In addition, it does not apply to contracts in which the primary obligation of the party furnishing the goods consists of supplying labor or services. The CISG is discussed in Chapters 19 through 23.

http:// CISG: http://www.cisg.law.pace.edu/

Letters of Credit International trade involves a number of risks not usually encountered in domestic trade, most notably governmental controls over the export or import of goods and currency. The most effective means of managing these risks—as well as the ordinary trade risks of nonperformance by seller and buyer—is the irrevocable documentary letter of credit. Most international letters of credit are governed by the Uniform Customs and Practices for Documentary Credits, a document drafted by commercial law experts from many countries and adopted by the International Chamber of Commerce. A **letter of credit** is a promise by a buyer's bank to pay the seller, provided certain conditions are met. The letter of credit transaction involves three or four different parties and three underlying contracts. To illustrate: a U.S. business wishes to sell computers to a Belgian company. The U.S. and Belgian firms enter into a sales agreement that includes details such as the number of computers, the features they will have, and the date they will be shipped. The buyer then enters into a second contract with a local bank, called an ***issuer***, committing the bank to pay the agreed price upon receiving specified documents. These documents normally include a bill of lading (proving that the seller has delivered the goods for shipment), a commercial invoice listing the purchase terms, proof of insurance, and a customs certificate indicating that customs officials have cleared the goods for export. The buyer's bank's commitment to pay is the irrevocable letter of credit. Typically, a ***correspondent*** or ***paying bank*** located in the seller's country makes payment to the seller. Here, the Belgian issuing bank arranges to pay the U.S. correspondent bank the agreed sum of money in exchange for the documents. The issuer then sends the U.S. computer firm the letter of credit. When the U.S. firm obtains all the necessary documents, it presents them to the U.S. correspondent bank, which verifies the documents, pays the computer company in U.S. dollars, and sends the documents to the Belgian issuing bank. Upon receiving the required documents, the issuing bank pays the correspondent bank and then presents the documents to the buyer. In our example, the Belgian buyer pays the issuing bank in Euros for the letter of credit when the buyer receives the specified documents from the bank.

http:// International Chamber of Commerce: http://www.iccwbo.org/

ANTITRUST LAWS

Section 1 of the Sherman Act provides that U.S. **antitrust laws** shall have a broad, extraterritorial reach. As we discussed in Chapter 43, contracts, combinations, or conspiracies that restrain trade with foreign nations, as well as among the domestic states, are deemed illegal. Therefore, agreements among competitors to increase the cost of imports, as well as arrangements to exclude imports from U.S. domestic markets in exchange for agreements not to compete in other countries, clearly violate U.S. antitrust laws. The antitrust provisions are also designed to protect U.S. exports when privately imposed restrictions seek to exclude U.S. competitors from foreign markets. Amendments to the Sherman Act and the Federal Trade Commission Act limit their application to unfair methods of competition that have a direct, substantial, and reasonably foreseeable effect on U.S. domestic commerce, U.S. import commerce, or U.S. export commerce.

United States v. Nippon Paper Industries Co., Ltd.

United States Court of Appeals, First Circuit, 1997
109 F.3d 1, *cert. denied*, 522 U.S. 1044, 118 S.Ct. 685, 139 L.Ed.2d 632 (1998)
http://www.law.emory.edu/1circuit/mar97/96-2001.01a.html

FACTS In 1995, a federal grand jury handed down an indictment naming as a defendant Nippon Paper Industries Co., Ltd. (NPI) **(http://www.hoovers.com/co/capsule/9/0,2163,52499,00.html)**, a Japanese manufacturer of facsimile paper. The indictment alleged that in 1990 NPI and certain unnamed coconspirators held a number of meetings in Japan, which culminated in an agreement to fix the price of thermal fax paper throughout North America. NPI and other manufacturers who were privy to the scheme purportedly accomplished their objective by selling the paper in Japan to unaffiliated trading houses on condition that the latter charge specified (inflated) prices for the paper when they resold it in North America. The trading houses then shipped and sold the paper to their subsidiaries in the United States who in turn sold it to U.S. consumers at swollen prices. The indictment further relates that to ensure the success of the venture, NPI monitored the paper trail and confirmed that the prices charged to end users were those that it had arranged. These activities, the indictment posits, had a substantial adverse effect on commerce in the United States and unreasonably restrained trade in violation of Section One of the Sherman Act. The district court, declaring that a criminal antitrust prosecution could not be based on wholly extraterritorial conduct, dismissed the indictment.

DECISION Reversed and remanded.

OPINION Selya, J. * * * [in] the Supreme Court's most recent exploration of the Sherman Act's extraterritorial reach, *Hartford Fire Ins. Co. v. California*, [citation], the Justices endorsed [citation]'s core holding, permitting civil antitrust claims under Section One to go forward despite the fact that the actions which allegedly violated Section One occurred entirely on British soil. * * * [T]he *Hartford Fire* Court deemed it "well established by now that the Sherman Act applies to foreign conduct that was meant to produce and did in fact produce some substantial effect in the United States." [Citation.] The conduct alleged, a London-based conspiracy to alter the American insurance market, met that benchmark. [Citation.]

* * *

Were this a civil case, our journey would be complete. But here the United States essays a criminal prosecution for solely extraterritorial conduct rather than a civil action. This is largely uncharted terrain; we are aware of no authority directly on point, and the parties have cited none.

Be that as it may, one datum sticks out like a sore thumb: in both criminal and civil cases, the claim that Section One applies extraterritorially is based on the same language in the same section of the same statute: "Every contract, combination in the form of trust or otherwise, or conspiracy, in restraint of trade or commerce among the several States, or with foreign nations, is declared to be illegal." [Citation.] Words may sometimes be chameleons, possessing different shades of meaning in different contexts, [citation], but common sense suggests that courts should interpret the same language in the same section of the same statute uniformly, regardless of whether the impetus for interpretation is criminal or civil.

Common sense is usually a good barometer of statutory meaning. Here, however, we need not rely on common sense alone; accepted canons of statutory construction point in the same direction. It is a fundamental interpretive principle that identical words or terms used in different parts of the same act are intended to have the same meaning. [Citation.] * * *

* * *

* * * The words of Section One have not changed since the *Hartford Fire* Court found that they clearly evince Congress' intent to apply the Sherman Act extraterritorially in civil actions, and it would be disingenuous for us to pretend that the words had lost their clarity simply because this is a criminal proceeding. Thus, unless some special circumstance obtains in this case, there is no principled way in which we can uphold the order of dismissal.

* * *

International comity is a doctrine that counsels voluntary forbearance when a sovereign which has a legitimate claim to jurisdiction concludes that a second sovereign also has a legitimate claim to jurisdiction under principles of international law. [Citation.] Comity is more an aspiration than a fixed rule, more a matter of grace than a matter of obligation. In all events, its growth in the antitrust sphere has been stunted by *Hartford Fire*, in which the Court suggested that comity concerns would operate to defeat the exercise of jurisdiction only in those few cases in which the law of the foreign sovereign required a defendant to act in a manner incompatible with the Sherman Act or in which full compliance with both statutory schemes was impossible. See *Hartford Fire*, [citations]. Accordingly, the *Hartford Fire* Court gave short shrift to the defendants' entreaty that the conduct leading to antitrust liability was perfectly legal in the United Kingdom. [Citation.]

In this case the defendant's comity-based argument is even more attenuated. The conduct with which NPI is charged is illegal under both Japanese and American laws, thereby alleviating any founded concern about NPI being whipsawed between separate sovereigns. And, moreover, to the extent that comity is informed by general principles of reasonableness, see Restatement (Third) of Foreign Relations Law § 403, the indictment lodged against NPI is well within the pale. In it, the government charges that the defendant orchestrated a conspiracy with the object of rigging prices in the United States. If the government can prove these charges, we see no tenable reason why principles of comity should shield NPI from prosecution. We live in an age of international commerce, where decisions reached in one corner of the world can reverberate around the globe in less time than it takes to tell the tale. Thus, a ruling in NPI's favor would create perverse incentives for those who would use nefarious means to influence markets in the United States, rewarding them for erecting as many territorial firewalls as possible between cause and effect.

INTERPRETATION Antitrust actions predicated on wholly foreign conduct which has an intended and substantial effect in the United States come within Section One's jurisdictional reach.

ETHICAL QUESTION Did Nippon act unethically? Explain.

CRITICAL THINKING QUESTION Do you agree with the court's decision? Explain.

SECURITIES REGULATION

The securities markets have become increasingly internationalized, thereby raising questions regarding which country's law governs a particular transaction in securities. (U.S. federal securities laws are discussed in Chapter 40.) Foreign issuers who issue securities in the United States must register them under the 1933 Act unless an exemption is available. Foreign issuers whose securities are sold in the secondary market in the United States must register under the 1934 Act unless the issuer is exempt. Some nonexempt foreign issuers may avoid registration under the 1934 Act by providing the SEC with copies of all information material to investors that they have made public in their home country. Regulation S provides a safe harbor from the 1933 Act registration requirements for offshore sales of equity securities of U.S. issuers. The antifraud provisions of the U.S. securities laws apply to securities sold by the use of any means or instrumentality of interstate commerce. In determining the extraterritorial application of these provisions, the courts have generally found jurisdiction where there is either *conduct* or *effects* in the United States relating to a violation of the federal securities laws.

SEC v. Berger

United States Court of Appeals for the Second Circuit, 2003
322 F.3d 187
http://laws.findlaw.com/2nd/016254v2.html

FACTS Defendant Michael W. Berger, along with two partners, formed an offshore investment company known as the Manhattan Investment Fund, Ltd. ("the Fund"), which was organized under the laws of the British Virgin Islands and commenced trading operations in 1996. The Fund was designed for foreign investors and tax-exempt domestic investors; its investment objective was to achieve capital appreciation by investing primarily in publicly traded securities. Berger is the Fund's only active director.

At the time the complaint was filed, the Fund had approximately 280 investors, only a small percentage having addresses in the United States. Manhattan Capital Management, Inc. ("MCM"), served as the investment advisor to the Fund and was paid an annual management fee of 1 percent of the Fund's net asset value as well as an incentive fee equal to 20 percent of the Fund's net gains. Berger was the sole officer of and shareholder in MCM, a Delaware corporation headquartered in New York. The Fund maintained a brokerage account at Financial Asset Management, Inc. ("FAM"), a broker-dealer located in Columbus, Ohio. FAM cleared all of its transactions through Bear Stearns Securities Corporation ("Bear Stearns"), which is located in New York City. The majority of the Fund's assets and securities were held in the Bear Stearns account.

Berger invested the Fund's assets in stocks on domestic securities exchanges, employing the risky strategy of "short selling." The strategy of short selling involves the "sale of a security that the seller does not own or has not contracted for at the time of sale, and that the seller must borrow to make delivery." This strategy is premised upon the belief that the investor will be able to buy the stock in the future for less money than the price at which he or she sold the stock. Berger chose this investment strategy because he believed that the stock market in general, and particularly technology stocks, were overvalued. Because the stocks he sold short continued to climb in value, however, the Fund suffered substantial losses. Using this strategy, the Fund suffered over $300 million in losses between 1996 and 2000. Rather than reporting these losses, Berger, working in New York, created fraudulent account statements that vastly overstated the market value of the Fund's holdings. These statements were forwarded from New York by Berger, acting on behalf of MCM, to Fund Administration Services (the "Fund Administrator") in Bermuda every month for thirty-nine months. Although the Fund Administrator also received accurate account statements directly from Bear Stearns, Berger instructed the Administrator to ignore the Bear Stearns statements, claiming that they did not fully and accurately reflect the Fund's entire portfolio. Accordingly, the Fund Administrator relied upon the fraudulent statements created by Berger in New York to calculate the net asset value of the Fund each month. These overstated calculations were reflected in the Fund's monthly account statements, which the Fund Administrator sent from Bermuda to investors, and in the Fund's annual financial statements, which were created at MCM's offices in New York and made available for potential investors to review. Berger also arranged for these false reports to be sent to the Fund's auditors, Deloitte & Touche, which issued unqualified opinions on the Fund as a result of these false statements.

In telephone calls to the Fund Administrator in January 2000, Berger revealed that he had made serious mistakes, that his calculations were based on misrepresentations, and that the Fund had suffered substantial losses. Then Berger sent a letter to all shareholders in the Fund, stating that "the financial statements of the Fund that have been distributed over the last several years have been inaccurate" and that "the Fund's actual net assets are substantially less than those previously reported."

Four days later the SEC brought a civil action against Berger, MCM, and the Fund, alleging violations of various provisions of the federal securities laws.

In August 2000, a criminal proceeding was commenced against Berger in the Southern District of New York, and on November 27, 2000, Berger pleaded guilty to securities fraud charges. During the plea allocution, Berger admitted to the relevant misconduct described above. When asked by the district court whether "some of these acts [were] committed by [him] here in New York or in [the Southern District], or were * * * caused to be committed by [him] in this district," Berger replied, "They were caused to be committed by me in this district, yes." On September 24, 2001, Berger filed a motion to withdraw his guilty plea, which the district court denied.

Based largely on the facts stipulated to by Berger under oath during his plea allocution, the SEC filed a motion for summary judgment in the civil case. In opposing the motion, Berger argued, among other things, that the district court lacked subject matter jurisdiction over the civil action because it involved extraterritorial conduct that did not directly result from acts occurring within the United States and that did not have an effect on U.S. residents or U.S. markets. After determining that it had jurisdiction, the court granted the SEC's motion for summary judgment, holding that "either through Berger's plea allocution or through other documentary and testimonial evidence, the SEC has offered sufficient evidence of Berger's liability." Immediately after Berger filed an appeal, but prior to his sentencing in the criminal matter, Berger fled the United States.

DECISION Summary judgment affirmed.

OPINION Cabranes, J. Although Title 15 of the United States Code, which sets forth the various statutes governing securities exchanges, is silent as to the extraterritorial application of these statutes, we have recognized that subject matter jurisdiction may extend to claims involving transnational securities frauds. [Citation.] To provide guidance on this topic, we have stated that, where "a court is confronted with transactions that on any view are predominantly foreign, it must seek to determine whether Congress would have wished the precious resources of United States courts and law enforcement agencies to be devoted to them rather than [to] leave the problem to foreign countries." [Citation.] In applying this standard, we have consistently looked at two factors: (1) whether the wrongful conduct occurred in the United States, and (2) whether the wrongful conduct had a substantial effect in the United States or upon United States citizens. [Citations.] In evaluating these two factors, we apply what are known respectively as the "conduct test" and the "effects test."

In considering the conduct test, we have held that jurisdiction exists only when "substantial acts in furtherance of the fraud were committed within the United States," [citation], and that the test is met whenever (1) "the defendant's activities in the United States were more than 'merely preparatory' to a securities fraud conducted elsewhere" and (2) the "activities or culpable failures to act within the United States 'directly caused' the claimed losses." [Citation.]

* * *

Applying this test, we hold that subject matter jurisdiction clearly exists over Berger's actions. As an initial matter, Berger's conduct was more than "merely preparatory": Berger admits that

> the following activities which materially related to the fraud took place in the United States: (1) creation of false financial information; (2) transmission of that false financial information overseas; [and] (3) approval of the resulting false financial statements prior [to] the statements being sent to investors.

[Citation.] In the words of [the trial judge],

> Berger prepared the fictitious financial statements in New York. These statements were then sent offshore to the Fund's administrators, and then calculations based on these statements were re-transmitted back into this country and abroad to prospective investors, current shareholders, and their agents.

[Citation.] Clearly, the fraudulent scheme was masterminded and implemented by Berger in the United States. [Citations.]

Even if his actions in the United States were more than "merely preparatory," Berger maintains that these actions are insufficient to confer jurisdiction on United States courts because the activity *directly* causing harm to investors occurred in Bermuda. * * *

* * *

* * * To the contrary, [citation] makes clear that we do not lack subject matter jurisdiction in this case simply because the financial statements that were disseminated to the Fund's investors were prepared in Bermuda. As we explained in [citation], were we to hold otherwise, the protection afforded by the securities laws could be circumvented simply by preparing such statements outside of the United States.

In sum, while operating entirely from New York, Berger executed a massive fraud upon hundreds of investors involving transactions on United States exchanges. Accordingly, the District Court properly determined that it had subject matter jurisdiction under the conduct test. We have no doubt that the effects of Berger's actions were felt substantially in the United States, but because jurisdiction clearly exists pursuant to the conduct test, we need not consider whether jurisdiction over the instant action might also be grounded on the effects test. [Citation.]

INTERPRETATION The U.S. securities laws apply extraterritorially when there is either conduct or effects in the United States relating to a violation of the federal securities laws.

ETHICAL QUESTION Did the defendant act unethically? Explain.

CRITICAL THINKING QUESTION What test should apply in determining the extraterritorial application of U.S. securities laws? Explain.

PROTECTION OF INTELLECTUAL PROPERTY

The U.S. laws protecting intellectual property (discussed in Chapter 41) do not apply to transactions in other countries. Generally, the owner of an intellectual property right must comply with each country's requirements to obtain from that country whatever protection is available. The requirements vary substantially from country to country, as does the degree of protection. The United States belongs to multinational treaties that try to coordinate the application of member nations' intellectual property laws. The principal treaties for patent protection are the Paris Convention for the Protection of Industrial Property and the Patent Cooperation Treaty. International treaties protecting trademarks are the Paris Convention, the Trademark Law Treaty, the Arrangement of Nice Concerning the International Classification of Goods and Services, and the Vienna Trademark Registration Treaty. In 2002 Congress enacted legislation implementing the Madrid Protocol, a procedural agreement allowing U.S. trademark owners to file for registration in any number of more than sixty-five member countries by filing a single application in English and paying a single fee. Copyrights are covered by the Universal Copyright Convention and the Berne Convention for the Protection of Literary and Artistic Works. The Trade-Related Aspects of Intellectual Property Rights (TRIPS) portion of the World Trade Organization Agreement covers the range of intellectual property. The World Intellectual Property Organization (WIPO), one of the specialized agencies of the United Nations, attempts to promote—through cooperation among nations—the protection of intellectual property throughout the world. WIPO administers twenty-one international treaties dealing with intellectual property protection and includes more than 175 nations as member states.

http://

TRIPS: http://www.wto.org/english/tratop_e/trips_e/trips_e.htm
World Intellectual Property Organization: http://www.wipo.org/eng/main.htm

FOREIGN CORRUPT PRACTICES ACT

In 1977, Congress enacted the **Foreign Corrupt Practices Act (FCPA)** prohibiting all domestic concerns from bribing foreign governmental or political officials. The FCPA makes it unlawful for any domestic concern or any of its officers, directors, employees, or agents to offer or give anything of value directly or indirectly to any foreign official, political party, or political official for the purpose of (1) influencing any act or decision of that person or party in his or its official capacity, (2) inducing an act or omission in violation of his or its lawful duty, or (3) inducing such person or party to use his or its influence to affect a decision of a foreign government in order to assist the domestic concern in obtaining or retaining business. An offer or promise to make a prohibited payment is a violation even if the offer is not accepted or the promise is not performed. The 1988 amendments to the FCPA explicitly excluded routine governmental actions not involving the discretion of the official, such as obtaining permits or processing applications. This exclusion does *not* cover any decision by a foreign official whether, or on what terms, to award new business or to continue business with a particular party. The amendments also added an affirmative defense for payments that are lawful under the written laws or regulations of the foreign official's country.

Violations can result in fines of up to $2 million for companies; individuals may be fined a maximum of $100,000 or imprisoned up to five years, or both. Fines imposed upon individuals may not be paid directly or indirectly by the domestic concern on whose behalf they acted. In addition, the courts may impose civil penalties of up to $11,000.

Practical Advice

Take care to instruct your employees and agents not to bribe foreign officials, political parties, or political officials. Moreover, train them to distinguish between bribes, which are prohibited, and nondiscretionary facilitating payments, which are permitted.

In 1997 the United States and thirty-three other nations signed the Organization for Economic Cooperation and Development Convention on Combating Bribery of Foreign Public Officials in International Business Transactions (OECD Convention). In 1998 Congress enacted the International Anti-Bribery and Fair Competition Act of 1998 to conform the FCPA to the Convention. The 1998 Act expands the FCPA to include (1) payments made to "secure any improper advantage" from foreign officials, (2) all foreign persons who commit an act in furtherance of a foreign bribe while in the United States, (3) officials of public international organizations within the definition of a "foreign official." A public international organization is defined as either an organization designated by executive order pursuant to the International Organizations Immunities Act or any other international organization designated by executive order of the president.

http:// OECD Convention: http://www.oecd.org/

EMPLOYMENT DISCRIMINATION

Title VII of the Civil Rights Act of 1964, the Americans with Disabilities Act, and the Age Discrimination in Employment Act, discussed in Chapter 42, apply to U.S. citizens employed abroad by U.S. employers or by foreign companies controlled by U.S. employers. Employers, however, are not required to comply with these employment discrimination laws if compliance would violate the law of the foreign country in which the workplace is located.

FORMS OF MULTINATIONAL ENTERPRISES

The term **multinational enterprise** (or **MNE**) refers to any business that engages in transactions involving the movement of goods, information, money, people, or services across national borders. Such an enterprise may conduct its business in any of several forms: through direct sales, foreign agents, distributorships, licensing, joint ventures, and wholly owned subsidiaries. A number of considerations determine which form of business organization would be best to use in conducting international transactions. These factors include financing, tax consequences, legal restrictions imposed by the host country, and the degree to which the multinational enterprise wishes to control the business.

DIRECT EXPORT SALES

Under a **direct export sale**, the seller contracts directly with the buyer in the other country. This is the simplest and least involved multinational enterprise.

FOREIGN AGENTS

An agency relationship often is used by multinational enterprises seeking limited involvement in an international market. The principal firm will appoint a local agent, who may be empowered to enter into contracts in the agent's country on the principal's behalf or who may be authorized only to solicit and take orders. The agent generally does not take title to the merchandise.

http:// Convention on Agency in the International Sale of Goods: http://www.unidroit.org/english/conventions/c-ag.htm

DISTRIBUTORSHIPS

A commonly used form of multinational enterprise is the **distributorship**, in which a producer of goods appoints a foreign distributor. Unlike an agent, a distributor takes title to the merchandise it receives; in other words, the distributor, not the producer, bears many of the risks connected with commercial sales. The distributorship format, however, is especially susceptible to antitrust violations. Therefore, both the producer and the distributor must take special care to ensure that the arrangement does not violate the antitrust laws of their respective governments.

LICENSING

A multinational enterprise wishing to exploit an intellectual property right, such as a patent, trademark, trade secret, or an unpatented but innovative production technology, may choose to sell a foreign company the right to use such property, rather than enter the foreign market itself. The sale of such rights, called **licensing**, is one of the major means by which technology and information are transferred among nations. Normally, the foreign firm will pay royalties in exchange for the information, technology, or patent. Franchising is a form of licensing in which the owner of intellectual property grants permission to a foreign business under carefully specified conditions.

JOINT VENTURES

In a **joint venture**, two or more independent businesses from different countries agree to coordinate their efforts to achieve a common result. The sharing of profits and liabilities, as well as the delegation of responsibilities, is fixed by contract. One advantage of the joint venture is that each company can be responsible for that which it does best. In order to promote local ownership of investments, several developing nations and regional groups have enacted legislation that prohibits foreign businesses from owning more than 49 percent of any business enterprise in those countries. In addition, each country may require that its citizens comprise the majority of an enterprise's management.

WHOLLY OWNED SUBSIDIARIES

By far, **wholly owned subsidiaries** require the most active participation by a parent firm. Nevertheless, creating a foreign wholly owned subsidiary corporation can offer a firm numerous advantages, most significantly the ability to retain authority and control over all phases of operation. This is especially attractive to businesses wishing to safeguard their technology.

Bulova Watch Company, Inc. v. K. Hattori & Co.

United States District Court, Eastern District of New York, 1981
508 F.Supp. 1322

FACTS The plaintiff, Bulova Watch Company **(http://www.bulova.com)**, was a New York corporation with its principal place of business in Flushing, New York. As both a manufacturer and seller of watches, Bulova claimed to have the largest direct sales marketing system in the watch business. The defendant, K. Hattori & Company (Hattori), incorporated under the laws of Japan with its principal office in Tokyo, was the parent company of the wholly owned subsidiary Seiko Corporation of America (SCA) **(http://www.seiko.co.jp/index.php?lang_is=eng)**, a New York corporation. SCA, in turn, owned all the stock of three "sub-subsidiaries"—namely, Seiko Time Corp., Pulsar Time, and SPD Precision Inc.—all of which were incorporated under New York law. While the United States was Hattori's largest market, accounting for more than $500 million in sales, Hattori distributed its products in more than one hundred countries, using wholly owned subsidiaries in ten of those countries. For the remaining countries, Hattori employed independent distributors who conducted their own marketing and advertising activities and maintained their own repair centers. Desiring to expand the markets of its U.S.-based wholly owned subsidiaries, Hattori masterminded certain advertising campaigns and began recruiting and hiring several high-level direct sales marketing personnel from the Bulova company. Bulova filed this action against Hattori, alleging unfair competition, disparagement, and conspiracy to raid the plaintiff's marketing personnel. The defendant moved to dismiss the case for lack of jurisdiction, claiming that the Japanese parent company, Hattori, was an entity distinct and separate from its American subsidiaries and therefore lacked sufficient control over the subsidiaries to satisfy jurisdictional requirements.

DECISION Motion to dismiss denied.

OPINION Weinstein, C. J. [The N.Y. statute] confers personal jurisdiction over unlicensed foreign corporations that are "doing business" in New York. [Citations.]

The definition of "doing business" has been variously stated, but the common denominator is that the corporation is operating within the state "not occasionally or casually, but with a fair measure of permanence and continuity." [Citations.]

It is no longer a matter of doubt that a foreign corporation can do business in New York through its employees, [citations].

Equally settled is the concept that a corporation may be amenable to New York personal jurisdiction when the systematic activities of a subsidiary in this state may fairly be attributed to the parent. [Citations.]

* * *

* * * By 1972 it was estimated that in a world that produced about $3,000 billion of goods and services a year, something like one-eighth of the output moved across international boundaries. [Citation.] In that same year the value of American investments abroad was $94 billion. [Citation.]

After the Second World War investment in the United States by foreign parent companies also expanded tremendously so that by the early 1970s non-United States corporations owned more than seven hundred "major manufacturing enterprises" in this country. [Citation.] Direct foreign investment, defined as ownership by foreign parents of at least ten percent of the equity of an American enterprise, was $3.4 billion at the start of the 1950s, $6.6 billion in 1959 and $26.5 billion by 1974. [Citation.] Total assets of foreign-owned affiliates in the United States in 1974 were $174.3 billion, of which more than one-fifth was Japanese-owned. [Citation.] These trends have accelerated.

The vehicles of this modern international economic growth were and are the multinational enterprises. Their size is often awesome: the annual sales of General Motors exceeded the gross national products of Switzerland, Pakistan, or South Africa. [Citation.]

* * * Aside from their magnitude, today's multinationals are unique in the way vast investments in myriad locations are made to serve the interests of a single organization. Large advantages lie in the possibility of making centralized management and investment decisions on the basis of the situations and opportunities prevailing in various host countries. [Citations.] Such an organization has the resources and scope to plan and to utilize worldwide markets and resources. [Citations.]

The profit motivation for international expansion is common to multinationals. [Citations.] Nevertheless, the means by which the multinational exercises control over its far-flung elements vary. The degree and nature of control may depend upon the nationality of the corporate parent. [Citations.] The formal structure of the parent's form of ownership also has control implications. Choice among the various corporate modes of entering a market, e.g., by means of licensing arrangement, joint venture, minority-, majority- or wholly-owned subsidiary, has very significant implications for the control exercised by the parent. [Citation.] Utilization of a wholly-owned marketing-based subsidiary is found where "the * * * retention of unambiguous control of foreign operations is critical to the firm's strategy." [Citation.] The decision of marketing-oriented firms to choose wholly owned subsidiaries means that they can exercise more control over their foreign operation in subtle, indirect ways as well as directly. [Citation.]

Another criterion that will determine the "corporate intimacy" joining a parent and its subsidiary, [citation], is the type and range of products being sold. Enterprises with narrow product lines tend to organize their operations on a highly integrated basis, linking production and marketing into tight strategic patterns. [Citation.] While Hattori manufactures a number of products, the overwhelming concern of its American marketing operation is with its timepieces—constituting ninety percent of its total production by value.

Thus sales subsidiaries tend to be under especially close control where a company produces a limited number of products. In such a case the company has

> a higher stake in the maintenance of quality standards, a higher sense of risk in sharing its technology with others, a higher need for a centralized marketing strategy * * *. The strategy of [these] firms, therefore, requires relatively tight controls.
>
> [Citation.]

Finally, a crucial factor in the degree of control over the subsidiary is the age of the subsidiary and the extent to which the subsidiary has been able to develop independently of its parent. * * *

An important question in assessing presence for jurisdictional purposes is whether a multinational has reached a state in its evolution when it can be said that its sales and marketing subsidiaries truly have a "life of their own." [Citation.] * * *

The expanding multinational generally traverses a number of stages. At first it exports its goods to markets abroad, next it establishes sales organizations abroad, then it may license the use of its patents, and finally it may establish foreign manufacturing facilities. At a later stage it may "multinationalize its management and, ultimately multinationalize the ownership of its stock." [Citation.] While many thousands of corporations are at the first, export stage, only a handful have developed into advanced multinational enterprises each of whose elements can be said to be significant in its own right.

After World War II, foreign companies gained familiarity with the United States market "by first exporting to this country; then, after achieving acceptance for their products, foreign firms set up manufacturing or assembly plants here." [Citation.] As these later stages were reached, the businesses established came to have lives of their own. The "monocentric" enterprise gradually gave way to a polycentric one, with more autonomy in the different elements. Wilkins detects three stages: in the first stage, the firm "reached out to sell or to obtain and in doing so felt the necessity or saw the opportunity to cross over domestic boundaries." [Citation.] The relationship was "monocentric" with the center of operations clearly in the parent's home country. The external activities in a monocentric relationship were "spokes on a wheel, with the parent company at the hub." [Citation.] In stage two, the functions of the branches broadened. There might, for example, be investment by the subsidiary in a plant for local production or the subsidiary might sell products in third-country markets. "What characterizes stage two is the presence of foreign units that have developed their own separate histories, and their own satellite activities." [Citation.] The final, third, stage is characteristic of the most advanced of these entities:

> It garbles any chart's attempt to delineate international trade and control lines. The parent company comes to have a number of foreign multifunctional centers, serving overlapping geographical areas with various products. Supply and market lines cross international boundaries in * * * chaotic confusion.* * *

[Citation.]

> Over time, certain foreign subsidiaries and affiliates have become full-fledged, fully integrated, multiprocess, multiproduct enterprises, with engineering, product planning and research staffs, with a continuity of employee, supplier, dealer, consumer and banking relationships, with their own prominent role in foreign industries, with their own dealings with foreign governments and with their own third-country investments.

[Citation.] At this final stage, complicated, many-faceted relationships have replaced simple bilateral connections. [Citation.]

* * *

It is apparent that Hattori's international activities, large as they may be in terms of sales figures and associated product lines, are essentially akin to Wilkins' stage one "monocentric" export model and not to the much more complex multinationals to which defendants point. What is involved here is a series of relatively young sales and marketing subsidiaries abroad, whose purpose is to market a single product—timepieces. There is no manufacturing or product research done by any of these subsidiaries. They do not seem to have developed third-country trade except for the purpose of selling Hattori's Japanese manufactured goods. Only very recently have they begun to make some investments in third countries, again to produce further outlets for Hattori's factories in Japan. The use of the wholly owned subsidiary form here reflects the desire for "unambiguous control" over sales and marketing subsidiaries to insure uniform quality and promotion of the product sold. [Citations.]

Hattori and its American subsidiaries do maintain some independence—about as much as the egg and vegetables in a western omelette. Just as, from a culinary point of view, we focus on the ultimate omelette and not its ingredients, so too, from a jurisdictional standpoint, it is the integrated international operation of Hattori affecting activities in New York that is the primary focus of our concern.

Although with time the Hattori subsidiaries might well evolve, along with their parent, into the later stages of multinational development, today Hattori is a highly effective export manufacturer and not a fully developed multinational. It is monocentric more than polycentric. Large and sophisticated as it may be, it is very much the hub of a wheel with many spokes. It is appropriate, therefore, to look to the center of the wheel in Japan when the spokes violate substantive rights in other countries.

* * *

A court might well find substantial unfairness were it to drag a foreign parent into court to defend itself against actions completely unrelated to the subsidiary corporation's purposive activities on behalf of its parent. The holding in this case is simply that while a subsidiary establishes and expands a parent's marketing position, then, so long as that activity is being conducted, and with respect to those activities furthering the parent's ends, the parent is doing business in New York. This is particularly true as to activities directly related to primary steps taken to ensure a place for its subsidiaries, as where action is taken to raid an established competitor's personnel in penetrating the American market.

INTERPRETATION Wholly owned subsidiaries are established by a parent company seeking to retain unambiguous control over the subsidiary's operation. Such control over a U.S. subsidiary may be sufficient to support jurisdiction by the U.S. courts over the parent.

ETHICAL QUESTION Was the court's decision fair to all of the parties? Explain.

CRITICAL THINKING QUESTION What factors should be relevant in deciding whether a company exercises sufficient control over a U.S. subsidiary to support U.S. jurisdiction over the parent? Explain.

CHAPTER SUMMARY

The International Environment

International Law includes law that deals with the conduct and relations of nation-states and international organizations as well as some of their relations with persons; such law is enforceable by the courts of a nation that has adopted the international law as domestic law

International Court of Justice judicial branch of the United Nations having voluntary jurisdiction over nations

Regional Trade Communities international organizations, conferences, and treaties focusing on business and trade regulations; the EU (European Union) is the most prominent of these

International Treaties agreements between or among independent nations, such as the General Agreement on Tariffs and Trade (GATT), now called the World Trade Organization

Jurisdiction over Actions of Foreign Governments

Sovereign Immunity foreign country's freedom from a host country's laws

Act of State Doctrine rule that a court should not question the validity of actions taken by a foreign government in its own country

Taking of Foreign Investment Property
- *Expropriation* governmental taking of foreign-owned property for a public purpose and with payment of just compensation
- *Confiscation* governmental taking of foreign-owned property without payment (or for a highly inadequate payment) or for a nonpublic purpose

Transacting Business Abroad

Flow of Trade controlled by trade barriers on imports and exports
- *Tariff* duty or tax imposed on goods moving into or out of a country
- *Nontariff Barriers* include quotas, bans, safety standards, and subsidies

Flow of Labor controlled through passport, visa, and immigration regulations

Flow of Capital International Monetary Fund facilitates the expansion and balanced growth of international trade, assists in eliminating foreign exchange restrictions, and smoothes the international balance of payments

International Contracts involve additional issues beyond those in domestic contracts, such as differences in language, legal systems, and currency
- *CISG* U.N. Convention on Contracts for the International Sales of Goods governs all contracts for international sales of goods between parties located in different nations that have ratified the CISG
- *Letter of Credit* bank's promise to pay the seller, provided certain conditions are met; used to manage the payment risks in international trade

Antitrust Laws of the United States apply to unfair methods of competition that have a direct, substantial, and reasonably foreseeable effect on the domestic, import, or export commerce of the United States

Securities Regulation foreign issuers who issue securities, or whose securities are sold in the secondary market in the United States, must register them unless an exemption is available; the antifraud provisions apply where there is either *conduct* or *effects* in the United States relating to a violation of the federal securities laws

Protection of Intellectual Property the owner of an intellectual property right must comply with each country's requirements to obtain from that country whatever protection is available

Foreign Corrupt Practices Act prohibits all U.S. companies from bribing foreign governmental or political officials

Employment Discrimination Title VII of the Civil Rights Act of 1964, the Americans with Disabilities Act, and the Age Discrimination in Employment Act apply to U.S. citizens employed in foreign countries by U.S.-owned or -controlled companies

Forms of Multinational Enterprises

Definition of Multinational Enterprise (MNE) any business that engages in transactions involving the movement of goods, information, money, people, or services across national borders

Forms of MNE the choice of form depends on a number of factors, including financing considerations, tax consequences, and degree of control
- *Direct Export Sales* seller contracts directly with the buyer in the other country
- *Foreign Agents* a local agent in the host country is used to provide limited involvement for an MNE
- *Distributorship* MNE sells to a foreign distributor who takes title to the merchandise
- *Licensing* MNE sells a foreign company the right to use technology or information
- *Joint Ventures* two independent businesses from different countries share profits, liabilities, and duties
- *Wholly Owned Subsidiary* enables an MNE to retain control and authority over all phases of operation

QUESTIONS

1. Three banks that are wholly owned by the Republic of Costa Rica had issued promissory notes, payable in U.S. dollars in New York City. The notes are now in default due solely to actions of the Costa Rican government, which had suspended all payments of external debt because of escalating economic problems. Efforts by Costa Rica to curb foreign debt payment difficulties conflicted with U.S. policy for debt resolution procedures as conducted under the auspices of the International Monetary Fund (http://www.imf.org). A syndicate of U.S. banks brought suit to recover on the promissory notes. The three Costa Rican banks assert the act of state doctrine as a defense. Should the doctrine apply? Explain.

2. Six U.S. manufacturers of broad-spectrum antibiotics derived a large percentage of their sales from overseas markets, including India, Iran, the Philippines, Spain, South Korea, Germany, Colombia, and Kuwait. The manufacturers agreed to a common plan of marketing, whereby territories were divided and prices for products were set. The plan members also agreed not to grant foreign producers licenses to the manufacturing technology of any of their "big money" drugs. May the above foreign countries recover treble damages for violation of the U.S. antitrust laws? Why?

3. After reading attractive brochures advertising a package tour of the Dominican Republic (http://www.dominicana-sun.com), a U.S. family decided to purchase tickets for the family vacation plan. The tour was a product of four different business entities, two domestic (U.S.) and two foreign. Sheraton Hotels & Inns, World Corporation (http://www.sheraton.com), was to provide food and lodging; Dominicana Airlines, wholly owned by the government of the Dominican Republic, which routinely flew into Miami International Airport and sold tickets within the United States, was to provide round-trip air transportation and "tourist cards" necessary for entry into the Dominican Republic; and two U.S. firms organized and sold the tour. Problems for the family began when their Dominicana flight landed in the Dominican Republic, and immigration officials denied them entry. Forced to leave, the family was shuttled first to Puerto Rico and then to Haiti, where they had to secure their own passage back to the United States at additional expense. The family brings suit for battery, false imprisonment, breach of warranty, and breach of contract against all four different business entities. Dominicana Airlines asserts the act of state doctrine as a defense. Explain whether this defense applies in this situation.

4. A privately owned business in a developing country determines that current computer technology could solve many of the problems faced by its country's private and public sectors. This business, however, lacks the capital resources necessary for research and development to acquire such computer technology, even if trained personnel were available. Furthermore, despite a sense of patriotism, the business concludes that its national government could not efficiently or effectively handle such a development project. What business forms are available to this business for acquiring sophisticated computer technology? What are the advantages and problems inherent in the various options?

5. King Faisal II of Iraq was killed on July 14, 1958, in the midst of a revolution in that country that led to the establishment of a republic subsequently recognized by the U.S. government. On July 19, 1958, the new republic issued a decree that all property of the former ruling dynasty, regardless of location, should be confiscated. Subsequently, the Republic of Iraq brought suit in the United States to obtain possession of money and stocks deposited in the deceased king's U.S. bank account in New York City. Explain whether Iraq will be able to collect the funds.

6. A business entity incorporated under the laws of one of the EU member nations contracts with the government of a developing nation to form a joint venture for the mining and refining of a scarce raw material used by several developed nations in the manufacture of highly sensitive weapons systems. The contract calls for the EU-based corporation to invest money and technology that will be used to build permanent refinery plants that will eventually revert to the developing nation. The developing nation also reserves the right to set quotas on sales of this scarce resource and to choose the destination of exports. Due to political conflicts, the developing nation refuses to allow any exports of the scarce material to the United States. This causes a sharp price increase in exports to the United States by other suppliers. The United States asserts antitrust violations against the EU-based corporation for the effects produced within the United States. Should the United States succeed? Explain.

CASE PROBLEMS

7. A Panamanian corporation lends money to a Turkish enterprise, which issues a promissory note. The loan contract specifies that payment on the interest and principal shall be made to the Chemical Bank of New York City (http://www.chase.com), where both parties maintain accounts. The loan contract contains no choice of law designation, but the Panamanian and Turkish companies have referred to the Chemical Bank in New York as their "legal address." As a result of a contractual performance dispute, the Turkish company suspends payments on the loan. The

Panamanian corporation then brings suit in the United States to recover the balance of the payments due. What possible options for choice of law apply?

8. New England Petroleum Corporation (NEPCO), a New York corporation, was in the business of selling fuel oil in the United States. PETCO, a refinery incorporated in the Bahamas, was a wholly owned subsidiary of NEPCO. In 1968, PETCO entered into a long-term contract to purchase crude oil from Chevron Oil Trading (COT) (http://www.chevron.com/), which held 50 percent of an oil concession in Libya. In 1973, Libya nationalized COT and several other foreign-owned oil concessions, thereby forcing COT to terminate its contract with PETCO. In order to secure needed oil supplies, PETCO entered into a new contract with National Oil Corporation (NOC) (http://www.hoovers.com/co/capsule/2/0,2163,55882,00.html), which was wholly owned by the Libyan government. This contract was at a substantially higher price than the original contract with COT. The following month, Libya declared an oil embargo on exports to the United States, the Netherlands, and the Bahamas. Accordingly, NOC canceled its contracts with PETCO. After oil prices rose dramatically, NOC accepted bids for new contracts to replace the ones inactivated by the embargo. NEPCO brought suit in a U.S. district court against the Libyan government and NOC, alleging breach of contract. Does the district court have jurisdiction? Explain.

9. Nigeria, experiencing an economic boom due to exports of high-grade oil, embarked on an infrastructure development plan. Accordingly, Nigeria entered into at least 109 contracts with 68 suppliers for the purchase of cement at a price of almost $1 billion. Among the contracting suppliers were four American corporations, including Texas Trading & Milling Corporation. Nigeria misjudged the cement market (having anticipated only a 20 percent fulfillment rate) and was forced to repudiate most of the contracts. Texas Trading & Milling Corporation and three other U.S. companies brought suit, alleging anticipatory breach of contract. Nigeria claimed immunity under the Foreign Sovereign Immunities Act of 1976. Is Nigeria's claim correct? Explain.

10. Prior to 1918, a Russian corporation had deposited sums of money with August Belmont, a private banker doing business in New York City. In 1918, the Soviet government nationalized the corporation and appropriated all of the corporation's property and assets, including the deposit account with Belmont. The deposit became the property of the Soviet government until 1933, when it was released and assigned to the U.S. government as part of an international compact between the United States and the Soviet Union. The purpose of this arrangement was to bring about a final settlement of the claims and counterclaims between the two countries. The United States brought an action to recover the deposit from Belmont. Belmont resists arguing that the act of nationalization by the Soviets was a confiscation prohibited by the Fifth Amendment to the U.S. Constitution and was also a violation of New York public policy. Explain who will prevail.

11. Lep Group PLC (Lep) is a London-based holding company with some fifty subsidiaries in thirty countries. Lep's "ordinary shares," the British equivalent of common stock, are registered in the United Kingdom, obligating the company to comply with United Kingdom securities laws. In 1988, to create a U.S. market for its ordinary shares, Lep deposited 12,842,850 of its approximately 136 million shares in an American depository, which in turn issued an American Depository Receipt (ADR) for each five ordinary shares of Lep deposited. Because these ADRs trade in the form of American Depository Shares (ADSs) on the National Association of Securities Dealers Automated Quotation System (NASDAQ) (http://www.nasdaq.com), Lep is subject to the reporting and disclosure requirements of United States securities law.

Itoba Limited is a wholly owned subsidiary of A.D.T. Limited (ADT). ADT is a transnational holding company based in Bermuda. Its shares are listed on the New York Stock Exchange and approximately 50 percent of its shareholders of record reside in the United States. ADT also is the corporate parent of A.D.T. Securities Systems, Inc. (http://www.adt.com), a Delaware-based firm and one of America's largest suppliers of security and protection services.

In mulling over expansion plans for A.D.T. Securities Systems, ADT considered the possible acquisition of one of A.D.T. Securities Systems's largest competitors in the U.S. security market, National Guardian. ADT already owned a small interest in that corporation through shares it held of Lep, the parent company of National Guardian. Because ownership of Lep would lead to control of National Guardian, ADT considered increasing its Lep holdings.

At the same time, Canadian Pacific (http://www.cpr.ca) was pondering a sizable investment in Lep, so Canadian Pacific and ADT agreed to explore a joint purchase of Lep. Canadian Pacific hired S.G. Warburg (http://www.ubswarburg.com/index.shtml), a London investment bank, to evaluate Lep's business operations. ADT also performed an in-house valuation of Lep. In December 1989, S.G. Warburg issued an extensive report assessing Lep's prospects. The analysis in this report was based on Lep's U.K. annual reports; the Form 20–F that Lep filed with the U.S. Securities and Exchange Commission for the year ended December 31, 1988; Lep's shareholder register; and broker reports. Shortly after the Warburg report was issued, Canadian Pacific abandoned the proposed joint venture. ADT's interest, on the other hand, did not diminish. ADT continued its examination of Lep, relying heavily on the Warburg report. To supplement its research, ADT obtained from Canadian Pacific a copy of Lep's Form 20-F for 1988.

Based on its own analyses and a review of the Warburg report, ADT decided to acquire Lep by making anonymous purchases on the market through Itoba. By November 1990, Itoba had acquired more than 37 million Lep ordinary shares for approximately $114 million, paid for by

ADT. Before ADT could complete its planned acquisition, however, Lep disclosed a series of business reversals that decimated its share value; Lep's stock price plummeted 97 percent and the value of Itoba's holdings in Lep declined by nearly $111 million. Lep wrote off approximately $522 million from its books for the fiscal year ended December 31, 1991.

Itoba sued Lep and its officers in a U.S. district court, asserting violations of the Securities Exchange Act of 1934. According to Itoba, Lep failed to disclose material matters in statements filed with the SEC. Specifically, Itoba alleged that Lep made high-risk investments and engaged in speculative business ventures without informing the investing public. Itoba claimed that had these matters been properly disclosed, it would not have purchased Lep's stock at artificially inflated prices. The defendants moved to dismiss Itoba's claims for lack of subject matter jurisdiction. Does the district court have jurisdiction? Explain.

http:// **Internet Exercise** Find information about (a) the United Nations, (b) the International Court of Justice, (c) GATT (WTO), (d) NAFTA, and (e) the European Union.

Chapter 48

CyberLaw

While the Internet and other information technologies are bringing enormous benefits to society, they also provide new opportunities for criminal behavior.

Attorney General Janet Reno (January 10, 2000)

Learning Objectives

After reading this chapter you should be able to:

1. Explain how the Internet has affected laws protecting intellectual property.
2. Explain the laws governing online contracting.
3. Explain the extent to which the law protects individuals (1) from private entities regarding the collection, use, and accuracy of personal identifiable information on the Internet and (2) from unwanted government intrusion through the Internet.
4. Explain what transactions in securities are permitted over the Internet.
5. List and explain examples of cybercrimes using computers as the instrument of the crime and examples of cybercrimes with computers as a target of the crime.

Technology and business have frequently outpaced the law. In today's business environment, the widening of this gap has accelerated with the rapid growth of e-commerce and communication on the Internet. (For example, between 1996 and 2000, the number of people online tripled.) The resulting legal vacuum has created considerable uncertainty in business transactions and numerous opportunities for abuse. In this chapter we will identify some of the types of legal and regulatory issues that have arisen or are likely to arise. We will also describe the extent to which the law has responded or is in the process of responding. This chapter will cover the following areas of the law that have been most significantly affected by e-commerce and the evolution of the Internet: defamation, intellectual property, contract and sales law, privacy, securities regulation, and cybercrime.

Defamation

As discussed in Chapter 7, the elements of a **defamation** action are (1) a false and defamatory statement concerning another person, (2) an unprivileged publication (communication) to a third party, (3) in some cases, depending on the status of the defendant, some degree of fault on her part in knowing or failing to ascertain the falsity of the statement, and (4) in some cases, proof of special harm caused by the publication. *Defamatory* means causing injury to a person's reputation by disgracing him and diminishing the respect in which he is held. An example is the publication of a false statement that a person had committed a crime or had committed an offensive act. The burden of proof in a defamation action is on the plaintiff to prove the falsity of the statement.

If the defamatory communication is handwritten, typewritten, printed, pictorial, or in any other medium with similar communicative power, such as a television or radio broadcast, it is designated as **libel**. If it is spoken or oral, it is designated as **slander**. To date, defamation via the Internet has been treated as libel, similar to the treatment of newspapers, radio, and television. In both libel and slander, a defamatory statement must be communicated to a person or persons other than the one who is defamed, a process referred to as its **publication**. Thus, if Maurice writes a defamatory letter about Pierre's character that he hands or mails to Pierre, this is not a publication because it is intended only for Pierre.

In response to a court decision holding an Internet service provider (**ISP**) liable for defamatory remarks posted on its online financial bulletin board, Congress enacted Section 230 of the **Communications Decency Act of 1996 (CDA)**. This provision grants ISPs immunity when publishing information originating from a third party. The language of Section 230 provides, in part, that "no provider . . . shall be treated as the publisher . . . of any information provided by another information content provider." A court has interpreted this provision of the CDA as immunizing an ISP that refused to remove or retract an allegedly defamatory posting made on its bulletin board. In *Zeran v. America Online, Inc. (AOL)*, which follows, the plaintiff sued AOL after his name and home phone number were posted on an AOL bulletin board with an assertion that he was selling T-shirts with tasteless slogans related to the Oklahoma City federal building bombing. The court ruled that CDA immunity extended to ISPs regardless of their classifications as either publishers or distributors.

Zeran v. America Online, Inc.

United States Court of Appeals, Fourth Circuit, 1997
129 F.3d 327
http://laws.findlaw.com/4th/971523p.html

FACTS On April 25, 1995, a notice appeared on the bulletin board of America Online (AOL) authored by an unknown person or persons identified only as "Ken ZZ03" and titled "Naughty Oklahoma T-Shirts." The notice advertised T-shirts with vulgar and offensive slogans related to the Oklahoma City bombing of the Alfred P. Murrah Federal Building. Readers were invited to call "Ken," Kenneth Zeran's first name, at Zeran's telephone number. This posting was made without Zeran's knowledge or authority, and it is undisputed that he has never been involved in any way with the sale of the advertised T-shirts. Indeed, Zeran had never subscribed to AOL's Internet services. Zeran was inundated with calls, most of which were derogatory and some of which included death threats and intimidation. Zeran contacted AOL that same day, and a representative assured him that the offending notice would be removed. As a matter of policy, however, AOL declined to post a retraction on its network. To his dismay, Zeran continued to be subjected to offensive and threatening telephone calls, approximately one call every two minutes. Unable to suspend or change his telephone number due to business necessity, Zeran was forced to tolerate the harassment and threats occasioned by the hoax. Zeran sued, arguing that AOL unreasonably delayed in removing defamatory messages posted by an unidentified third party, refused to post retractions of those messages, and subsequently failed to screen for similar postings. The district court granted judgment for AOL on the grounds that § 230 of the Communications Decency Act of 1996 (CDA) bars Zeran's claims. Zeran appealed.

DECISION Judgment for America Online affirmed.

OPINION Wilkinson, J. The relevant portion of § 230 states: "No provider or user of an interactive computer service shall be treated as the publisher or speaker of any information provided by another information content provider." [Citation.] By its plain language, § 230 creates a federal immunity to any cause of action that would make service providers liable for information originating with a third-party user of the service. Specifically, § 230 precludes courts from entertaining claims that would place a computer service provider in a publisher's role. Thus, lawsuits seeking to hold a service provider liable for its exercise of a publisher's traditional editorial functions—such as deciding whether to publish, withdraw, postpone, or alter content—are barred.

Zeran argues, however, that the § 230 immunity eliminates only publisher liability, leaving distributor liability intact. Publishers can be held liable for defamatory statements contained in their works even absent proof that they had specific knowledge of the statement's inclusion. [Citation.] According to Zeran, interactive computer service providers like AOL are normally considered instead to be distributors, like traditional news vendors or book sellers. Distributors cannot be held liable for defamatory statements contained in the materials they distribute unless it is proven at a minimum that they have actual knowledge of the defamatory statements upon which liability is predicated. [Citation.] Zeran contends that he provided AOL with sufficient notice of the defamatory statements appearing on the company's bulletin board. This notice is significant, says Zeran, because AOL could be held liable as a distributor only if it acquired knowledge of the defamatory statements' existence.

Because of the difference between these two forms of liability, Zeran contends that the term "distributor" carries a legally distinct meaning from the term "publisher." Accordingly, he asserts that Congress' use of only the term "publisher" in § 230 indicates a purpose to immunize service providers only from publisher liability. He argues that distributors are left unprotected by § 230 and, therefore, his suit should be permitted to proceed against AOL. We disagree. Assuming arguendo that Zeran has satisfied the requirements for imposition of distributor liability, this theory of liability is merely a subset, or a species, of publisher liability, and is therefore also foreclosed by § 230.

* * *

Zeran simply attaches too much importance to the presence of the distinct notice element in distributor liability. The simple fact of notice surely cannot transform one from an original publisher to a distributor in the eyes of the law. To the contrary, once a computer service provider receives notice of a potentially defamatory posting, it is thrust into the role of a traditional publisher. The computer service provider must decide whether to publish, edit, or withdraw the posting. In this respect, Zeran seeks to impose liability on AOL for assuming the * * * role for which § 230 specifically proscribes liability—the publisher role.

* * * If computer service providers were subject to distributor liability, they would face potential liability each time they receive notice of a potentially defamatory statement—from any party, concerning any message. Each notification would require a careful yet rapid investigation of the circumstances surrounding the posted information, a legal judgment concerning the information's defamatory character, and an on-the-spot editorial decision whether to risk liability by allowing the continued publication of that information. Although this might be feasible for the traditional print publisher, the sheer number of postings on interactive computer services would create an impossible burden in the Internet context. [Citation.] Because service providers would be subject to liability only for the publication of information, and not for its removal, they would have a natural incentive simply to remove messages upon notification, whether the contents were defamatory or not. [Citation.] Thus * * * liability upon notice has a chilling effect on the freedom of Internet speech.

Similarly, notice-based liability would deter service providers from regulating the dissemination of offensive material over their own services. Any efforts by a service provider to investigate and screen material posted on its service would only lead to notice of potentially defamatory material more frequently and thereby create a stronger basis for liability. Instead of subjecting themselves to further possible lawsuits, service providers would likely eschew any attempts at self-regulation.

* * * Section 230 represents the approach of Congress to a problem of national and international dimension. The Supreme Court underscored this point in *ACLU v. Reno*, finding that the Internet allows "tens of millions of people to communicate with one another * * * and to access vast amounts of information from around the world. [It] is 'a unique and wholly new medium of worldwide human communication.' " [Citation.] Application of the canon invoked by Zeran here would significantly lessen Congress' power, derived from the Commerce Clause, to act in a field whose international character is apparent. While Congress allowed for the enforcement of "any State law that is consistent with [§ 230]," [citation], it is equally plain that Congress' desire to promote unfettered speech on the Internet must supersede conflicting common law causes of action. Section 230(d)(3) continues: "No cause of action may be brought and no liability may be imposed under any State or local law that is inconsistent with this section." With respect to federal-state preemption, the Court has advised: "When Congress has 'unmistakably * * * ordained,' that its enactments alone are to regulate a part of commerce, state laws regulating that aspect of commerce must fall. The result is compelled whether Congress' command is explicitly stated in the statute's language or implicitly contained in its structure and purpose." [Citation.] Here, Congress' command is explicitly stated. Its exercise of its commerce power is clear and counteracts the caution counseled by the interpretive canon favoring retention of common law principles.

INTERPRETATION Under the Communications Decency Act of 1996, an interactive computer service provider cannot be held liable for content placed on its bulletin boards or chat rooms by another information content provider.

ETHICAL QUESTION Given the immediacy and severity of the Oklahoma City bombings, was America Online justified in its decision not to post a retraction on its Website?

CRITICAL THINKING QUESTION Do you agree with the court's decision or with Section 230 of the CDA? Explain.

The immunity granted by the CDA to ISPs has spawned a number of lawsuits urging ISPs to reveal the identities of subscribers who have posted allegedly defamatory statements. To date, ISPs have complied, generating additional litigation by angry ISP patrons attempting to keep their identities protected by asserting that their right to free speech is being compromised.

> **Practical Advice**
>
> If you are defamed by a posting on the Internet, you should immediately notify the ISP and request that it remove the defamatory statement and disclose who posted the statement so you can bring legal action against that entity.

Because Section 230 of the CDA grants immunity only to ISPs, there is the possibility that employers will be held liable for some online defamatory statements made by an employee. Section 577(2) of the Restatement of Torts provides that a person who intentionally and unreasonably fails to remove defamatory matter that she knows is exhibited on property in her possession or under her control is liable for its continued publication. Therefore, employers in control of e-forums, such as electronic bulletin boards and chat rooms, should act quickly to remove any defamatory statement brought to their attention. For example, the New Jersey Supreme Court left open the possibility that Continental Airlines could be liable for defamatory messages posted by its pilots on a frequently used company bulletin board accessible through the Internet.

Employers may also be held vicariously (indirectly) liable for defamatory e-mail messages sent by their employees. Because most e-mail messages are instantly copied to another computer or server when sent, these additional copies may satisfy the publication requirement for defamation. To illustrate: If employee Anthony writes an e-mail message defaming employee Betty and sends it only to Betty, Anthony could be held to have defamed Betty, who may also seek to hold her employer vicariously liable.

INTELLECTUAL PROPERTY

Intellectual property, which is covered in greater detail in Chapter 41, is the area of law most affected by the Internet. This is understandable because the Internet consists mainly of information, and the law of intellectual property protects ideas and/or their expression. In this section we will examine the Internet's impact on the law governing copyrights, trademarks, patents, and trade secrets.

COPYRIGHTS

Copyright is a form of protection provided by the Federal Copyright Act to authors of original works, which include literary, musical, and dramatic works; pantomimes; choreographic works; pictorial, graphic, and sculptural works; motion picture and other audiovisual works; sound recordings; and architectural works. This listing is illustrative but not exhaustive; the act extends **copyright** protection to "original works of authorship in any tangible medium of expression, now known or later developed." Moreover, the Copyright Act has been amended to extend copyright protection to computer programs. Nevertheless, copyright protection extends only to an *original expression* of an idea.

http://
Copyright Act: http://www4.law.cornell.edu/uscode/17/index.html
Berne Convention: http://www.law.cornell.edu/treaties/berne/overview.html
Copyright Office: http://lcweb.loc.gov/copyright/

The Internet's speed, wide accessibility, rapid growth, and ability to make exact duplicates of digital files have created copyright issues primarily relating to infringements of an author's *exclusive* right to reproduce his copyrighted works. For example, the Internet allows an individual to distribute illegally to millions of users, virtually without cost, a single computer program or other copyrighted work, by merely making it available on a single server and pointing others to that location. Congress has responded to some of the copyright issues raised by the Internet. In 1997 Congress enacted the **No Electronic Theft Act (NET Act)** to close a loophole in the Copyright Act, which permitted infringers to pirate copyrighted works willfully and knowingly, so long as they did not do so for profit. The NET Act amended federal copyright law to define "financial gain" to include the receipt of anything of value, including the receipt of other copyrighted works. The NET Act also clarified that when Internet users or any other individuals distribute copyrighted works broadly, even if they do not intend to profit personally, they have violated the Copyright Act. The act accomplished this by imposing penalties for willfully infringing a copyright (1) for purposes of commercial advantage or private financial gain or (2) by reproducing or distributing, including by electronic means, during any 180-day period, one or more copies of one or more copyrighted works with a total retail value of more than $1,000. It also extended the statute of limitations for criminal copyright infringement from three to five years. Moreover, it increased criminal penalties for certain copyright violations. Imprisonment for up to five years (ten years for subsequent offenses) may be imposed for willful infringement if at least ten copies with a total retail value of more than $2,500 in a 180-day period are reproduced or distributed.

http:// No Electronic Theft Act: http://www.gseis.ucla.edu/iclp/hr2265.html

In 1998 Congress enacted the **Digital Millennium Copyright Act (DMCA)**, which amended the Copyright Act to implement the World Intellectual Property Organization (WIPO) Copyright Treaty and the WIPO Performances and Phonograms Treaty of 1996. The WIPO treaty called for adequate legal protection and effective legal remedies against the circumvention of effective technological measures that are used by copyright owners to prevent unauthorized exercise of their copyrights. The DMCA contains three principal anticircumvention provisions. The first provision prohibits the act of circumventing a technological protection measure put in place by a copyright owner to control *access* to a copyrighted work. Under the DMCA, "to circumvent a technological measure" means "to descramble a scrambled work, to decrypt an encrypted work, or otherwise to avoid, bypass, remove, deactivate, or impair a technological measure, without the authority of the copyright owner." The second provision prohibits creating or making available technologies developed or advertised to defeat technological protections against unauthorized *access* to a copyrighted work. The third provision prohibits creating or making available technologies developed or advertised to defeat technological protections against unauthorized *copying* or other infringements of the exclusive rights of the copyright owner in a copyrighted work. Thus, the first two prohibitions deal with access controls while the third prohibition deals with copy controls. They make it illegal, for example, to create or distribute a computer program that can break the access or copy protection security code on an electronic book or a DVD movie. The act provides civil remedies including injunctions, damages (actual and statutory), attorneys' fees, and destruction of the offending device. It also imposes criminal penalties of fines or imprisonment or both. Eight major U.S. movie studios brought suit under the Digital Millennium Copyright Act against Eric Corley and his company, 2600 Enterprises, Inc., to enjoin them from posting software (called DeCSS), which the studios claimed enables users to decode digital versatile discs (DVDs). The court ruled in favor of the plaintiffs, holding that the defendants violated the DMCA provision making it illegal for anyone to provide to the public or traffic in a device that is designed to circumvent a measure controlling access to a copyright-protected work.

http:// Digital Millennium Copyright Act: http://thomas.loc.gov/cgi-bin/query/z?c105:H.R.2281.ENR:

The Digital Theft Deterrence and Copyright Damages Improvement Act of 1999 amended federal copyright law with respect to the statutory damages available for copyright infringement by increasing the minimum damages from $500 to $750 and the maximum damages from $20,000 to $30,000. It also increased from $100,000 to $150,000 the maximum additional damages a court may award for willful infringement.

http:// The Digital Theft Deterrence and Copyright Damages Improvement Act of 1999: http://thomas.loc.gov/cgi-bin/query/z?c106:H.R.3456.ENR:

Practical Advice

Be vigilant to protect your intellectual property.

Because an author has the exclusive right to reproduce and display his work, the posting of a copyrighted work or sending of an e-mail containing that work may constitute copyright infringement. It is virtually impossible to view or post anything on the Internet without making a copy of it, at least temporarily, in the computer's RAM (random access memory), on the computer's hard drive, or on a floppy disk. Courts have ruled that even a temporary copy of another person's work made in RAM constitutes copyright infringement. E-mails also fall within the scope of some of these decisions since any electronic transmission containing a copyrighted work may violate the author's exclusive right to distribute, perform, or display that work in public.

The music industry has been the most publicized entity to raise concerns about the electronic distribution of copyrighted works. The emergence of the **MP3** (Motion Pictures Experts Group—Layer 3 Compression) file format has provided millions of users the opportunity to download compact disc-quality music via the Internet. Because these exchanges are usually established between two computers through the World Wide Web, ISPs had become a prime target for liability. Depending on an ISP's intent, knowledge, or control of the infringing behavior of its users, courts have held the ISPs liable for direct, contributory, or vicarious infringement. In 1998, however, the enactment of the Digital Millennium Copyright Act essentially immunized ISPs from liability for third-party infringement. While ISPs have effectively been insulated from liability concerns related to MP3 downloads, the courts have not yet resolved conclusively whether the end user who downloads copyrighted material is liable for copyright infringement.

Websites dedicated to MP3 distribution have come under fire in federal courts. A number of recording companies and music publishers sued Napster, a Web-based company that offers a program that creates a user-driven database and search engine to facilitate MP3 downloads. The plaintiffs claim that Napster is contributorily and vicariously liable for copyright infringement by engaging in or assisting others in copying, downloading, uploading, transmitting, or distributing copyrighted music without the express permission of the copyright owners. In *A&M Records v. Napster* the U.S. Court of Appeals ordered Napster to disable access to any copyrighted materials posted on its system once the holders of the copyrights have provided notice to Napster of infringing songs on its system. It also ordered Napster to police its own system to find such songs.

The music industry also sued for copyright infringement a company (MP3.com) that allows users to download songs in MP3 format if they already own the compact disc (CD). The court found that the defendant had willfully infringed plaintiffs' copyrights and ordered damages in the amount of $53,400,000.

Hyperlinking enables Internet users to move quickly and easily from one Website to another. When a Website is linked to another, a user can click on highlighted text or a graphic, which triggers the page displayed to switch to the new "linked" page. Although most Website owners encourage links to their sites because it increases the number of hits, or visitors to their sites, others may not want additional links. Hyperlinking to a file without its owner's permission may violate his exclusive right to distribute, reproduce, or display that file in public.

Universal City Studios, Inc. v. Reimerdes

United States District Court, Southern District of New York, 2000

111 F.Supp. 2d 294

FACTS Motion picture studios distribute many of their copyrighted motion pictures for home use on digital versatile disks (DVDs), which contain copies of the motion pictures in digital form. They protect those motion pictures from copying by using an encryption system called Content Scramble System (CSS). CSS-protected motion pictures on DVDs may be viewed only on players and computer drives equipped with licensed technology that permits the devices to decrypt and play—but not copy—the films.

In late 1999, computer hackers devised a computer program called DeCSS that circumvents the CSS protection system and allows CSS-protected motion pictures to be copied and played on devices that lack the licensed decryption technology. Eric Corley and his company, 2600 Enterprises, Inc. (defendants), quickly posted DeCSS on their Internet Website, thus making it readily available. Eight major U.S. movie studios brought suit under the Digital Millennium Copyright Act (DMCA) to enjoin defendants from posting DeCSS and to prevent them from electronically "linking" their site to others that post DeCSS. Defendants responded with what they termed "electronic civil disobedience"—increasing their efforts to link their Website to a large number of others that continue to make DeCSS available.

DECISION Injunction in favor of the motion picture studios.

OPINION Kaplan, J. Defendants argue first that the DMCA should not be construed to reach their conduct, principally because the DMCA, so applied, could prevent those who wish to gain access to technologically protected copyrighted works in order to make fair—that is, non-infringing—use of them from doing so. They argue that those who would make fair use of technologically protected copyrighted works need means, such as DeCSS, of circumventing access control measures not for piracy, but to make lawful use of those works.

Technological access control measures have the capacity to prevent fair uses of copyrighted works as well as foul. Hence, there is a potential tension between the use of such access control measures and fair use. Defendants are not the first to recognize that possibility. As the DMCA made its way through the legislative process, Congress was preoccupied with precisely this issue. Proponents of strong restrictions on circumvention of access control measures argued that they were essential if copyright holders were to make their works available in digital form because digital works otherwise could be pirated too easily. Opponents contended that strong anti-circumvention measures would extend the copyright monopoly inappropriately and prevent many fair uses of copyrighted material.

Congress struck a balance. The compromise it reached, depending upon future technological and commercial developments, may or may not prove ideal. [Citation.] But the solution it enacted is clear. The potential tension to which (the) defendants point does not absolve them of liability under the statute. There is no serious question that defendants' posting of DeCSS violates the DMCA.

* * *

Plaintiffs seek also to enjoin defendants from "linking" their Website to other sites that make DeCSS available to users. Their request obviously stems in no small part from what defendants themselves have termed their act of "electronic civil disobedience"—their attempt to defeat the purpose of the preliminary injunction by (a) offering the practical equivalent of making DeCSS available on their own Website by electronically linking users to other sites still offering DeCSS, and (b) encouraging other sites that had not been enjoined to offer the program. The dispositive question is whether linking to another Website containing DeCSS constitutes "offering [DeCSS] to the public" or "providing or otherwise trafficking" in it within the meaning of the DMCA. * * *

* * *

The statute makes it unlawful to offer, provide or otherwise traffic in described technology. * * * In consequence, the anti-trafficking provision of the DMCA is implicated where one presents, holds out or makes a circumvention technology or device available, knowing its nature, for the purpose of allowing others to acquire it.

To the extent that defendants have linked to sites that automatically commence the process of downloading DeCSS upon a user being transferred by defendants' hyperlinks, there can be no serious question. Defendants are engaged in the functional equivalent of transferring the DeCSS code to the user themselves. Substantially the same is true of defendants' hyperlinks to web pages that display nothing more than the DeCSS code or present the user only with the choice of commencing a download of DeCSS and no other content. The only distinction is that the entity extending to the user the option of downloading the program is the transferee site rather than defendants, a distinction without a difference.

* * *

* * * The offense under the DMCA is offering, providing or otherwise trafficking in circumvention technology. An essential ingredient, as explained above, is a desire to bring about the dissemination. Hence, a strong requirement of that forbidden purpose is an essential prerequisite to any liability for linking.

Accordingly, there may be no injunction against, nor liability for, linking to a site containing circumvention technology, the offering of which is unlawful under the DMCA, absent clear and convincing evidence that those responsible for the link (a) know at the relevant time that the offending material is on the linked-to site, (b) know that it is circumvention technology that may not lawfully be offered, and (c) create or maintain the link for the purpose of disseminating that technology. Such a standard will limit the fear of liability on the part of Website operators. * * * And it will not subject Website operators to liability for linking to a site containing proscribed technology where the link exists for purposes other than dissemination of that technology.

In this case, plaintiffs have established by clear and convincing evidence that these defendants linked to sites posting DeCSS, knowing that it was a circumvention device. Indeed, they initially touted it as a way to get free movies, [citation], and they later maintained the links to promote the dissemination of the program in an effort to defeat effective judicial relief. They now know that dissemination of DeCSS violates the DMCA. An anti-linking injunction on these facts does no violence to the First Amendment. Nor should it chill the activities of Website operators dealing with different materials, as they may be held liable only on a compelling showing of deliberate evasion of the statute.

INTERPRETATION The anti-trafficking provision of the DMCA applies to the posting on a Website of computer code that circumvents measures that control access to copyrighted works in digital form as well as to linking to other Websites that post that code.

ETHICAL QUESTION Did the defendants act unethically by publishing DeCSS or by linking to other Websites? Explain.

CRITICAL THINKING QUESTION Do you agree with the court's decision? Explain.

Framing on the Internet occurs when the information from the linked Website is viewed from within the linking Website. This can be misleading because the user views the linked site's information bordered, or framed, by the linking site. Thus, it appears that the linking site is providing the information. In one landmark case, the *Washington Post* sued Total News for copyright and trademark infringement after Total News continued to frame the newspaper's articles giving the appearance that Total News was the source of the information. The parties settled the case, agreeing that Total News could continue linking to the plaintiffs' Websites but could not use framing technology. Total News had to show that the information was being provided by the *Washington Post*.

There are, however, valid defenses to accusations of copyright infringement. The copyright laws attempt to balance an author's rights to protect his work with the public's access to it. Accordingly, the Copyright Act provides that the ***fair use*** of a copyrighted work for purposes such as criticism, comment, news reporting, teaching (including multiple copies for classroom use), scholarship, or research is not an infringement of copyright. In determining whether the use made of a work in any particular case is fair, the courts consider the following factors:

(1) the purpose and character of the use, including whether such use is of a commercial nature or is for nonprofit educational purposes; (2) the nature of the copyrighted work; (3) the amount and substantiality of the portion used in relation to the copyrighted work as a whole; and (4) the effect of the use upon the potential market for or value of the copyrighted work. In past cases addressing new technologies, the U.S. Supreme Court has suggested that Congress, not the courts, must determine what constitutes fair use.

A&M Records, Inc., et al. v. Napster, Inc.

United States Court of Appeals, Ninth Circuit, 2001
239 F.3d 1004
http://caselaw.lp.findlaw.com/scripts/getcase.pl?navby=case&court=9th&no=00-16401

FACTS Napster, Inc. ("Napster"), facilitates the transmission of MP3 files (a digital format for the storage of audio recordings) between and among its users. Through a process commonly called "peer-to-peer" file sharing, Napster allows its users to: (1) make MP3 music files stored on individual computer hard drives available for copying by other Napster users; (2) search for MP3 music files stored on other users' computers; and (3) transfer exact copies of the contents of other users' MP3 files from one computer to another via the Internet. These functions are made possible by Napster's MusicShare software, available free of charge from Napster's Internet site, and Napster's network servers and server-side software. The plaintiffs include A&M Records **(http://www.amrecords.com/)**, Geffen Records, Sony Music Entertainment **(http://www.sonymusic.com/)**, MCA Records **(http://www.mcarecords.com/)**, Atlantic Recording Corporation **(http://www.atlantic-records.com/)**, Motown Record Company **(http://www.motown.com/)**, and Capitol Records **(http://hollywoodandvine.com/)**. The plaintiffs are engaged in the commercial recording, distribution, and sale of copyrighted musical compositions and sound recordings. The plaintiffs allege that Napster is a contributory and vicarious copyright infringer. On July 26, 2000, the district court granted plaintiffs' motion for a preliminary injunction. The injunction was slightly modified by written opinion on August 10, 2000. The district court preliminarily enjoined Napster "from engaging in, or facilitating others in copying, downloading, uploading, transmitting, or distributing plaintiffs' copyrighted musical compositions and sound recordings, protected by either federal or state law, without express permission of the rights owner." Napster was granted a temporary stay of the preliminary injunction pending resolution of this appeal.

DECISION Affirmed in part, reversed in part and remanded.

OPINION Beezer, J. Plaintiffs claim Napster users are engaged in the wholesale reproduction and distribution of copyrighted works, all constituting direct infringement. Secondary liability for copyright infringement does not exist in the absence of direct infringement by a third party. [Citation.] It follows that Napster does not facilitate infringement of the copyright laws in the absence of direct infringement by its users. The district court agreed. We note that the district court's conclusion that plaintiffs have presented a prima facie case of direct infringement by Napster users is not presently appealed by Napster.

A. Infringement

Plaintiffs must satisfy two requirements to present a prima facie case of direct infringement: (1) they must show ownership of the allegedly infringed material and (2) they must demonstrate that the alleged infringers violate at least one exclusive right granted to copyright holders under 17 U.S.C. § 106 [the federal copyright statute]. [Citation.] Plaintiffs have sufficiently demonstrated ownership. The record supports the district court's determination that "as much as eighty-seven percent of the files available on Napster may be copyrighted and more than seventy percent may be owned or administered by plaintiffs."

The district court further determined that plaintiffs' exclusive rights under § 106 were violated: "here the evidence establishes that a majority of Napster users use the service to download and upload copyrighted music. * * * And by doing that, it constitutes—the uses constitute direct infringement of plaintiffs' musical compositions, recordings." [Citation.] The district court also noted that "it is pretty much acknowledged * * * by Napster that this is infringement." We agree that plaintiffs have shown that Napster users infringe at least two of the copyright holders' exclusive rights: the rights of reproduction, [citation]; and distribution, [citation]. Napster users who upload file names to the search index for others to copy violate plaintiffs' distribution rights. Napster users who download files containing copyrighted music violate plaintiffs' reproduction rights.

Napster asserts an affirmative defense to the charge that its users directly infringe plaintiffs' copyrighted musical compositions and sound recordings.

B. Fair Use

Napster contends that its users do not directly infringe plaintiffs' copyrights because the users are engaged in fair use of the material. [Citation.] ("[T]he fair use of a copyrighted work * * * is not an infringement of copyright.") Napster identifies three specific alleged fair uses: sampling, where users make temporary copies of a work before purchasing; space-shifting, where users access a sound recording through the Napster system that they already own in audio CD format; and permissive distribution of recordings by both new and established artists.

The district court considered factors listed in 17 U.S.C. § 107, which guide a court's fair use determination. These factors are: (1) the purpose and character of the use; (2) the nature of the copyrighted work; (3) the "amount and substantiality of the portion used" in relation to the work as a whole; and (4) the effect of the use upon the potential market for the work or the value of the work. [Citation.] * * * The district court concluded that Napster users are not fair users. * * *

1. Purpose and Character of the Use

This factor focuses on whether the new work merely replaces the object of the original creation or instead adds a further purpose or different character. In other words, this factor asks "whether and to what extent the new work is 'transformative.'" *Campbell v. Acuff-Rose Music, Inc.*

The district court first concluded that downloading MP3 files does not transform the copyrighted work. [Citation.] This conclusion is supportable. Courts have been reluctant to find fair use when an original work is merely retransmitted in a different medium. * * *

This "purpose and character" element also requires the district court to determine whether the allegedly infringing use is commercial or noncommercial. [Citation.] A commercial use weighs against a finding of fair use but is not conclusive on the issue. The district court determined that Napster users engage in commercial use of the copyrighted materials largely because (1) "a host user sending a file cannot be said to engage in a personal use when distributing that file to an anonymous requester" and (2) "Napster users get for free something they would ordinarily have to buy." [Citation.] The district court's findings are not clearly erroneous. Direct economic benefit is not required to demonstrate a commercial use. Rather, repeated and exploitative copying of copyrighted works, even if the copies are not offered for sale, may constitute a commercial use. [Citations.] In the record before us, commercial use is demonstrated by a showing that repeated and exploitative unauthorized copies of copyrighted works were made to save the expense of purchasing authorized copies. * * *

We also note that the definition of a financially motivated transaction for the purposes of criminal copyright actions includes trading infringing copies of a work for other items, "including the receipt of other copyrighted works." See No Electronic Theft Act ("NET Act"), [citation] (defining "Financial Gain").

* * *

2. The Nature of the Use

Works that are creative in nature are "closer to the core of intended copyright protection" than are more fact-based works. [Citation]. The district court determined that plaintiffs' "copyrighted musical compositions and sound recordings are creative in nature * * * which cuts against a finding of fair use under the second factor." * * *

3. The Portion Used

"While 'wholesale copying does not preclude fair use per se,' copying an entire work 'militates against a finding of fair use.'" [Citation.] The district court determined that Napster users engage in "wholesale copying" of copyrighted work because file transfer necessarily "involves copying the entirety of the copyrighted work." * * *

4. Effect of Use on Market

"Fair use, when properly applied, is limited to copying by others which does not materially impair the marketability of the work which is copied." [Citation.] * * *

* * *

Addressing this factor, the district court concluded that Napster harms the market in "at least" two ways: it reduces audio CD sales among college students and it "raises barriers to plaintiffs' entry into the market for the digital downloading of music." * * *

5. Identified Uses

Napster maintains that its identified uses of sampling and space-shifting were wrongly excluded as fair uses by the district court.

a. Sampling

Napster contends that its users download MP3 files to "sample" the music in order to decide whether to purchase the recording. Napster argues that the district court: (1) erred in concluding that sampling is a commercial use because it conflated a noncommercial use with a personal use; (2) erred in determining that sampling adversely affects the market for plaintiffs' copyrighted music, a requirement if the use is noncommercial; and (3) erroneously concluded that sampling is not a fair use because it determined that samplers may also engage in other infringing activity. The district court determined that sampling remains a commercial use even if some users eventually purchase the music. We find no error in the district court's determination. * * *

* * *

Napster further argues that the district court erred in rejecting its evidence that the users' downloading of "samples" increases or tends to increase audio CD sales. The district court, however, correctly noted that "any potential enhancement of plaintiffs' sales * * * would not tip the fair use analysis conclusively in favor of defendant." * * *

b. Space-Shifting

Napster also maintains that space-shifting is a fair use. Space-shifting occurs when a Napster user downloads MP3 music files in order to listen to music he already owns on audio CD. Napster asserts that we have already held that space-shifting of musical compositions and sound recordings is a fair use. * * * We conclude that the district court did not err when it refused to apply the "shifting" analyses of *Sony* [video taping a television show for later viewing] and *Diamond* [copying a music file from the owner's hard drive to a portable MP3 player]. Both *Diamond* and *Sony* are inapposite because the methods of shifting in these cases did not also simultaneously involve distribution of the copyrighted material to the general public; the time or space-shifting of copyrighted material exposed the material only to the original user. * * *

* * *

IV

We first address plaintiffs' claim that Napster is liable for contributory copyright infringement. Traditionally, "one who, with knowledge of the infringing activity, induces, causes or materially contributes to the infringing conduct of another, may be held liable as a 'contributory' infringer." [Citations.] Put differently, liability exists if the defendant engages in "personal conduct that encourages or assists the infringement." [Citation.]

The district court determined that plaintiffs in all likelihood would establish Napster's liability as a contributory infringer. The district court did not err; Napster, by its conduct, knowingly encourages and assists the infringement of plaintiffs' copyrights.

A. Knowledge

Contributory liability requires that the secondary infringer "know or have reason to know" of direct infringement. [Citations.] The district court found that Napster had both actual and constructive knowledge that its users exchanged copyrighted music. The district court also concluded that the law does not require knowledge of "specific acts of infringement" and rejected Napster's contention that because the company cannot distinguish infringing from noninfringing files, it does not "know" of the direct infringement. * * *

* * *

B. Material Contribution

Under the facts as found by the district court, Napster materially contributes to the infringing activity. * * * [T]he district court concluded that "[w]ithout the support services defendant provides, Napster users could not find and download the music they want with the ease of which defendant boasts." [Citation.]

* * *

V

We turn to the question whether Napster engages in vicarious copyright infringement. Vicarious copyright liability is an "outgrowth" of respondeat superior. [Citation.] In the context of copyright law, vicarious liability extends beyond an employer/employee relationship to cases in which a defendant "has the right and ability to supervise the infringing activity and also has a direct financial interest in such activities." [Citations.]

* * *

A. Financial Benefit

The district court determined that plaintiffs had demonstrated they would likely succeed in establishing that Napster has a direct financial interest in the infringing activity. We agree. Financial benefit exists where the availability of infringing material "acts as a 'draw' for customers." [Citation.] Ample evidence supports the district court's finding that Napster's future revenue is directly dependent upon "increases in userbase." More users register with the Napster system as the "quality and quantity of available music increases." * * *

B. Supervision

The district court determined that Napster has the right and ability to supervise its users' conduct. We agree in part.

The ability to block infringers' access to a particular environment for any reason whatsoever is evidence of the right and ability to supervise. [Citations.] Here, plaintiffs have demonstrated that Napster retains the right to control access to its system. Napster has an express reservation of rights policy, stating on its website that it expressly reserves the "right to refuse service and terminate accounts in [its] discretion, including, but not limited to, if Napster believes that user conduct violates applicable law * * * or for any reason in Napster's sole discretion, with or without cause."

To escape imposition of vicarious liability, the reserved right to police must be exercised to its fullest extent. Turning a blind eye to detectable acts of infringement for the sake of profit gives rise to liability. [Citations.]

The district court correctly determined that Napster had the right and ability to police its system and failed to exercise that right to prevent the exchange of copyrighted material. The district court, however, failed to recognize that the boundaries of the premises that Napster "controls and patrols" are limited. [Citation.] Put differently, Napster's reserved "right and ability" to police is cabined by the system's current architecture. As shown by the record, the Napster system does not "read" the content of indexed files, other than to check that they are in the proper MP3 format.

Napster, however, has the ability to locate infringing material listed on its search indices, and the right to terminate users' access to the system. The file name indices, therefore, are within the "premises" that Napster has the ability to police. * * *

* * *

VII

The district court correctly recognized that a preliminary injunction against Napster's participation in copyright infringement is not only warranted but required. We believe, however, that the scope of the injunction needs modification in light of our opinion. Specifically, we reiterate that contributory liability may potentially be imposed only to the extent that Napster: (1) receives reasonable knowledge of specific infringing files with copyrighted musical compositions and sound recordings; (2) knows or should know that such files are available on the Napster system; and (3) fails to act to prevent viral distribution of the works. [Citation.] The mere existence of the Napster system, absent actual notice and Napster's demonstrated failure to remove the offending material, is insufficient to impose contributory liability. [Citation.]

Conversely, Napster may be vicariously liable when it fails to affirmatively use its ability to patrol its system and preclude access to potentially infringing files listed in its search index. Napster has both the ability to use its search function to identify infringing musical recordings and the right to bar participation of users who engage in the transmission of infringing files. The preliminary injunction which we stayed is overbroad because it places on Napster the entire burden of ensuring that no "copying, downloading, uploading, transmitting, or distributing" of plaintiffs' works occur on the system. As stated, we place the burden on plaintiffs to provide notice to Napster of copyrighted works and files containing such works available on the Napster system before Napster has the duty to disable access to the offending content. Napster, however, also bears the burden of policing the system within the limits of the system. Here, we recognize that this is not an exact science in that the files are user named. In crafting the injunction on remand, the district court should recognize that Napster's system does not currently appear to allow Napster access to users' MP3 files.

INTERPRETATION Napster is liable for contributory and vicarious infringement only to the extent that Napster is aware that such copyright works are available on its servers and has failed to prevent their free exchange.

CRITICAL THINKING QUESTION Should MP3 files be permitted to be shared free of charge?

TRADEMARKS

Like copyright law, federal law primarily governs trademark law. The Federal Trademark Act (the Lanham Act) recognizes four types of trade symbols or marks. A **trademark** is a *distinctive* mark, word, letter, number, design, picture, or combination in any arrangement that a person adopts or uses to identify the goods he manufactures or sells, as well as to distinguish them from those manufactured or sold by others. A **service mark** is used to identify and distinguish the services of one person from those of others. A **certification mark** is used on or in connection with goods or services to certify their regional or other origin, composition, mode of manufacture, quality, accuracy, or other characteristics or that the work or labor in the goods or services was performed by members of a union or other organization. A **collective mark** is a distinctive mark or symbol used to indicate either that the producer or provider belongs to a trade union, trade association, fraternal society, or other organization, or that members of a collective group produced the goods or services. To be protected by the Lanham Act, a mark must be distinctive enough to identify clearly the origin of goods or services; it may not be immoral, deceptive, or scandalous. Trademark infringement occurs when a person without authorization uses an identical or substantially indistinguishable mark that is likely to cause confusion, to cause mistake, or to deceive.

http:// Trademark Act: http://www.law.cornell.edu/topics/trademark.html

Trademark issues on the Internet first arose with **domain names**. A domain name is the technical name for a Website's electronic address on the Internet. The domain name constitutes one of the most important ways a user locates a Website. For example, www.unc.edu, www.sony.com, and www.pepsi.com are domain names. Until recently, registering a domain name was done on a first-come, first-served basis, which has brought about a practice called *cybersquatting*. **Cybersquatting** is the registering of domain names containing trademarks owned by others with the intent to sell the rights to the domain name to the companies that own the trademarks. In one notable example, an individual registered more than 200 domain names including crateandbarrel.com, ussteel.com, and deltaairlines.com.

In response to the increasing number of lawsuits brought against cybersquatters, in 1999 Congress amended the **Lanham Act** by passing the **Anticybersquatting Consumer Protection Act.** The act allows the owner of a mark to bring a civil suit against any person who, with a bad faith intent to profit from that mark, registers or uses a domain name, which, at the time of its registration (1) is identical or confusingly similar to a distinctive mark; (2) dilutes a famous mark; or (3) is a protected trademark, word, or name. The act specifies factors a court may consider in determining bad faith intent but prohibits such a determination if the defendant believed, with reasonable grounds, that the use of the domain name was fair or otherwise lawful. It authorizes a court to order cancellation of the domain name or its transfer to the owner of the mark. In addition to injunctive relief, it makes available remedies such as recovery of the defendant's profits, actual damages, attorneys' fees, and court costs. It also provides for statutory damages in an amount of at least $1,000 and up to $100,000 per domain name, as the court considers just. The act shields a registrar, registry, or other registration authority from liability for damages for the registration or maintenance of a domain name for another, unless there is a showing of bad faith intent to profit from such registration or maintenance of the domain name registration.

http:// Anticybersquatting Consumer Protection Act: http://www.gigalaw.com/library/anticybersquattingact-1999-11-29-p1.html

An alternative way for users to find Internet sites is by using search engines, each of which uses its own algorithm for searching through the Internet and arranging the order of the sites it reports. The operating mechanism of search engines has generated legal issues regarding the use of metatags. **Metatags** are essentially key words that Website designers and owners use to describe the contents of their sites. These words and phrases are embedded within the Website's pages and are not readily visible. Search engines, such as Yahoo! and Excite, use these metatags to create large indexes that are scanned for matches when users query a search engine to find Websites on specific subjects, such as "antique cars."

Legal controversy has arisen when one Website uses metatags that are actually trademarks of another company in order to divert traffic from the competitor's sites to its own site. For example, a user who searches for Brand X may wind up at Brand Y's Website because Brand Y uses on its Website Brand X's trademark as a "hidden" metatag. A number of courts have issued injunctions against this practice, including the case of *Playboy Enterprises, Inc. v. Calvin Designer Label* in which the defendant used "playboy" as a metatag for its site.

Another type of metatag litigation has involved the banner advertisements often displayed on the Websites of search engines in an attempt to attract a user to the advertiser's site. In a common but controversial Internet advertising practice known as **keying,** a search engine offers advertisers the ability to display specific banner ads whenever users enter selected search terms, including trademarks or metatags of a competitor's site. For example, Estée Lauder sued Excite for federal trademark infringement after users who typed in trademarked product names of Estée Lauder were presented with banner ads for The Fragrance Counter. So far, there are few court decisions in this area, so it remains uncertain whether search engines will be permitted to continue this practice.

PATENTS

Patents, unlike copyrights or trademarks, protect ideas and processes. Through a **patent,** the federal government grants an inventor a monopolistic right to make, use, or sell an invention to the absolute exclusion of others for the period of the patent. To be patentable as a utility patent, the process, machine, manufacture, or composition of matter must meet three criteria: (1) novelty, (2) utility, and (3) nonobviousness. Utility patents have a term that begins on the date of the patent's grant and ends twenty years from the date of application. The patent owner may also profit by licensing others to use the patent. The patent may not be renewed and, upon expiration, the invention enters the public domain, and anyone may then use it.

http:// Patent and Trademark Office: http://www.uspto.gov/

The explosion of business use of the Internet has necessitated new ways of doing business to adapt to the demands of e-commerce. A number of companies have sought patent protection for their new business methods. In the landmark case concerning the validity of patenting such business methods, *State Street Bank & Trust Co. v. Signature Financial Group, Inc.*, the court held as patentable a computerized financial system in which individual mutual funds' contributions to an investment portfolio are calculated daily. This decision paved the way for other Internet business patents such as a Lycos Internet search method, Priceline.com's Name-Your-Price Reverse Auctions, and Pitney Bowes's Internet postage delivery system.

TRADE SECRETS

A **trade secret** is commercially valuable information that is guarded from disclosure and is not general knowledge. The recipe for making Coca-Cola is an example of a famous trade secret. Generally, trade secrets are governed by state law, which provides civil remedies for misappropriation of them. Trade secrets are most frequently misappropriated in two ways: (1) an employee wrongfully uses or discloses such secrets or (2) a competitor wrongfully obtains them.

Unlike other areas of intellectual property law, the Internet explosion has created few issues for trade secret law. It has, however, facilitated the disclosure of trade secrets by disgruntled employees and the theft of trade secrets by competitors. In 1996 Congress enacted the Economic Espionage Act of 1996 prohibiting the theft of trade secrets and providing criminal penalties for violations; the statute does not provide any civil remedies. The act broadly defines theft to include all types of conversion of trade secrets including:

1. stealing, obtaining by fraud, or concealing such information;
2. without authorization copying, duplicating, sketching, drawing, photographing, *downloading*, *uploading*, photocopying, or mailing such information;
3. purchasing or possessing a trade secret with knowledge that it has been stolen.

The Act punishes theft of trade secrets, as well as attempts and conspiracies to steal secrets, with fines of up to $500,000, imprisonment for up to ten years, or both. Organizations that violate the act are subject to fines of up to $5 million.

http:// Uniform Trade Secrets Act: http://www.law.upenn.edu/bll/ulc/ulc_frame. htm

Practical Advice

Sometimes it is better to protect valuable information as a trade secret than file for patent protection because the patent may be very difficult to police.

CONTRACTS AND SALES

Contract law, as discussed in Part III of this book, provides a means of binding parties to an agreement. Contracts are primarily governed by state common law. The sale of personal property (covered in Part IV of this book) is a large part of commercial activity; Article 2 of the **Uniform Commercial Code** (the Code, or UCC) governs such sales in all states except Louisiana. A **sale** consists in the passing of title to goods from seller to buyer for a price. A contract for sale includes both a present sale of goods and a contract to sell goods at a future time.

http:// Uniform Commercial Code, Article 2: http://www.law.cornell.edu/ucc/2/overview.html
United Nations Commission on International Trade Law: http://www.uncitral.org/en-index.htm

As with other areas of law, contract law is lagging behind the technology of the Internet. Electronic consumer transactions on the Internet raise questions about contract enforceability, authenticity, bargaining power, and even the applicability of current UCC provisions. Moreover, questions have arisen whether the UCC, common law, or both apply to Internet business transactions and computer software purchases or licenses. Software transactions in particular are not included in the UCC's definition of a "good" or "sale." Many companies, nevertheless, have continued to follow UCC rules.

A number of cases involving "shrinkwrap licenses" raised the question of whether the UCC applied to software transactions. The term "shrinkwrap license" gets its name from retail software packages that are covered in plastic or cellophane "shrinkwrap" and contain licenses that purport to become effective as soon as the customer removes the shrinkwrap from the package. The term has also been applied to license agreement pages displayed when software is first installed onto a computer system. The question of whether a "shrinkwrap license" is an enforceable contract has not been resolved to date. Similar questions apply to clickwrap or click-through licenses. Today, software is frequently purchased and delivered over the Internet. Often before such a transaction is completed, the buyer must click, using her mouse, on a button that displays the terms of the agreement. Usually, the buyer must agree to those terms before the transaction is complete, thereby forming a contract with the company.

Practical Advice

Carefully read all terms of the contract when opening a software package or ordering on the Internet.

UCITA

With Internet transactions increasing dramatically in number and value and gaps in the UCC and common law becoming more apparent, in 1999 the National Conference of Commissioners on Uniform State Laws (NCCUSL) promulgated the Uniform Computer

Information Transactions Act (UCITA). UCITA, which was last revised in 2002, was developed to provide a comprehensive set of rules for computer information transactions. To date, it has been adopted by only two states.

http:// Uniform Computer Information Transactions Act: http://www.law.upenn.edu/bll/ulc/ucita/ucita200.htm

The UCITA defines a "computer information transaction" as "an agreement or the performance of it to create, modify, transfer, or license computer information or informational rights in computer information." This definition would include transfers of computer programs or multimedia products, software and multimedia development contracts, and contracts to obtain information for use in a program or multimedia product. UCITA also governs access contracts, which are contracts to enter the information system of another to obtain information or use that information system for specific purposes. UCITA also applies to support and service contracts. Thus, examples of computer information transactions include contracts to acquire software, online access services and content, books and databases on CD-ROM, and nontrivial software elements embedded in goods. UCITA would also apply to storage devices, such as disks and CDs that exist only to hold computer information. UCITA does *not* govern contracts or licenses for the traditional distribution of movies, books, magazines, or newspapers; it would, however, apply to online books, music, and databases. The parties' agreement to communicate in digital form does not bring a transaction within a computer information transaction. For example, a contract for an airline ticket is not a computer information transaction because the ticket may be represented in digital form. In this case, the subject matter of the contract is a service: air transportation.

UCITA adapts Article 2 and common law contract provisions to the special needs and nature of computer information transactions. UCITA includes provisions dealing with formation, unconscionability, good faith, interpretation, warranties, risk of loss, transfer of contractual rights, financing arrangements, performance, termination, and remedies. Most of these provisions are default rules that the parties may change.

One of the most frequently criticized provisions of the UCITA is its rule permitting **shrinkwrapped** and **clickable** contractual provisions to be disclosed *after* the consumer has paid for the software and opens the package. The UCITA permits a mass-marketed shrinkwrap license if (1) the purchaser had reason to know that more terms would be coming, (2) the purchaser is given a right to return the product if he objects to the terms, (3) the right of return is cost free, and (4) the license does not alter terms to which the parties had actually agreed. The delayed disclosure approach of UCITA applies to all terms, including *warranty disclaimers*, remedy limitations, and restrictions on transfer and use. Permitting the withholding of warranty information until after the sale conflicts with the approach of the Magnuson-Moss Warranty Act discussed in Chapter 45.

http:// Magnuson-Moss Warranty Act: http://www.ftc.gov/bcp/conline/pubs/buspubs/warranty.htm

ELECTRONIC RECORDS

One significant impediment to e-commerce has been the questionable enforceability of contracts entered into through electronic means such as the Internet or e-mail because of the writing requirements under contract and sales law (statute of frauds). In response, the **Uniform Electronic Transactions Act (UETA)** was promulgated by the NCCUSL in July 1999 and has been adopted by at least forty states and introduced in a number of others. UETA applies only to transactions between parties each of which has agreed to conduct transactions by electronic means. It gives full effect to electronic contracts, encouraging their widespread use, and develops a uniform legal framework for their implementation. UETA protects electronic signatures and contracts from being denied enforcement because of the statute of frauds. Section 7 of UETA accomplishes this by providing:

1. A record or signature may not be denied legal effect or enforceability solely because it is in electronic form.
2. A contract may not be denied legal effect or enforceability solely because an electronic record was used in its formation.
3. If a law requires a record to be in writing, an electronic record satisfies the law.
4. If a law requires a signature, an electronic signature satisfies the law.

Section 14 of UETA further validates contracts formed by machines functioning as electronic agents for parties to a transaction: "A contract may be formed by the interaction of electronic agents of the parties, even if no individual was aware of or reviewed the electronic agents' actions or the resulting terms and agreements." The act excludes from its coverage wills, codicils, and testamentary trusts as well as all Articles of the UCC except Articles 2 and 2A.

http:// Uniform Electronic Transactions Act: http://www.law.upenn.edu/bll/ulc/ulc_frame.htm

Congress in 2000 enacted the **Electronic Signatures in Global and National Commerce (E-Sign)**. The act, which uses language very similar to that of UETA, makes electronic records and signatures valid and enforceable across the United States for many types of transactions in or affecting interstate or foreign commerce. E-Sign does not generally preempt UETA. E-Sign does not require any person to agree to use or accept electronic records or electronic signatures The act defines transactions quite broadly to include the sale, lease, exchange, and licensing of personal property and services, as well as the sale, lease, exchange, or other disposition of any interest in real property. E-Sign defines an electronic record as "a contract or other record created, generated, sent, communicated, received, or stored by electronic means." It defines an electronic signature as "an electronic sound, symbol, or process, attached to or logically associated with a contract or other record and executed or adopted by a person with the intent to sign the record." Like UETA, E-Sign ensures that Internet and e-mail agreements will not be unenforceable because of the statute of frauds by providing that:

1. a signature, contract, or other record relating to such transaction may not be denied legal effect, validity, or enforceability solely because it is in electronic form; and
2. a contract relating to such transaction may not be denied legal effect, validity, or enforceability solely because an electronic signature or electronic record was used in its formation.

http:// Electronic Signatures in Global and National Commerce: http://www.law.nyu.edu/benklery/informationlaw/106%20H.R.%201714.html

To protect consumers, E-Sign provides that they must consent *electronically* to conducting transactions with electronic records after being informed of the types of hardware and software required. Prior to consent, consumers must also receive a "clear and conspicuous" statement informing consumers of their right to (1) have the record provided on paper or in nonelectronic form, (2) after consenting to electronic records, receive paper copies of the electronic record, and (3) withdraw consent to receiving electronic records.

Practical Advice

Recognize that your name on an e-mail or other electronic communication may be considered to be your signature.

As defined by E-Sign, an electronic agent is a computer program or other automated means used independently to initiate an action or respond to electronic records or performances in whole or in part without review or action by an individual at the time of the action or response. The Act validates contracts or other records relating to a transaction in or affecting interstate or foreign commerce formed by electronic agents so long as the action of each electronic agent is legally attributable to the person to be bound.

E-Sign specifically excludes certain transactions, including (1) wills, codicils, and testamentary trusts, (2) adoptions, divorces, and other matters of family law, and (3) the Uniform Commercial Code other than sales and leases of goods.

NONCOMPETE AGREEMENTS

As discussed in Chapter 13, employees' covenants not to compete (agreements to refrain from a particular trade, profession, or business) are enforceable if (1) the purpose of the restraint is to protect a property interest of the promisee and (2) the restraint is no more extensive than is reasonably necessary to protect that interest. The reasonableness of the restraint depends on the geographic area the restraint covers, the period for which it is to be effective, and the hardship it imposes on the employee and the public.

Due to the rapid evolution of business practices in the Internet industry, it has been argued that noncompete agreements for Internet company employees need their own rules. For instance, a period of time that is reasonable for a conventional company might be unreasonable for an Internet company. In *Earthweb, Inc. v. Schlack*, the courts were faced with this issue, and a U.S. Circuit Court of Appeals upheld a district court decision striking down a one-year noncompete agreement for an Internet employee because it found the time period to be too long given the "dynamic nature of [the Internet] industry." Emphasizing its point, the district court then concluded that "[w]hen measured against the IT industry in the Internet environment, a one-year hiatus from the workforce is several generations, if not an eternity." *National Business Services, Inc. v. Wright*, which was decided a year before *Earthweb*, addressed the geographic scope of an Internet noncompete agreement, upholding a one-year time restriction and a territorial clause that prevented the employee from taking another Internet-related job anywhere in the United States. The court stated, "Transactions involving the Internet, unlike traditional 'sales territory' cases, are not limited by state boundaries."

Practical Advice

Recognize that covenants not to compete may be subject to different standards for Internet companies and employees.

PRIVACY AND THE INTERNET

Technology has greatly increased the ability of online companies to collect, store, transfer, and analyze vast amounts of data about consumers who visit their Websites. The Internet's impact on privacy rights has generated considerable public awareness and consumer concern about online privacy. Internet privacy issues consist of two distinct branches: (1) protection from private entities regarding the collection, use, and accuracy of "personal identifiable information" on the Internet and (2) freedom from unwanted government intrusion through the Internet.

PROTECTION OF PERSONAL IDENTIFIABLE INFORMATION ON THE INTERNET

Most Internet users fear exploitation of their personal information including their names, phone numbers, home addresses, credit card information, banking information, and social security numbers. Although most attention is given to the involuntary means by which personal identifiable information is obtained, Internet users regularly provide such data voluntarily by filling out online purchases, registrations, applications, and surveys. Even when a person voluntarily provides the information, most companies do not clearly indicate how that data will be used.

The public, academics, and regulators consider the involuntary collection of personal information even more troubling. One method of data capture is with "cookies," whereby a text file is placed on a user's computer hard drive by the Website visited. That file contains information about the user that the Website automatically retrieves and updates each time the user makes subsequent visits. Thus, over time, the Website compiles information about the user's preferences and personal data. In addition, the user's "clickstream" tracks the user as he clicks on pages within the Website and records where the user goes before and after surfing a specific Website. Gradually, the clickstream builds a map of where the user has been and where he is likely to go.

Whether voluntarily or involuntarily, almost all Internet sites collect personal identifiable information. Typically, companies use the data to build a "profile" of their users. These profiles are then frequently sold to advertising companies that focus marketing based on each user's preferences. The companies contend that consumers benefit from the targeted marketing that presents them with goods and services in which they are likely to be interested. Many users view such information as their private property and object to its misappropriation.

> **Practical Advice**
>
> Consider that whatever information you put out on the Internet may not remain private.

Privacy and Intrusion by Private Parties The U.S. Constitution does not protect a person's right to privacy with respect to intrusions by private parties. Instead, privacy rights regulating the conduct of private parties are derived from tort law. As discussed in Chapter 7, the invasion of a person's right to privacy actually consists of four distinct torts: (1) appropriation of a person's name or likeness, (2) unreasonable intrusion on the seclusion of another, (3) unreasonable public disclosure of private facts, or (4) unreasonable publicity that places another in a false light in the public eye. However, traditional privacy torts offer little protection for a person whose privacy has been compromised on the Internet.

With increasing public and political pressure to address the dearth of available remedies for online privacy invasions, the Federal Trade Commission has recommended that Congress enact legislation that would establish a basic level of privacy protection for consumer-oriented Websites. Under the proposal, consumer-oriented Websites that collect personal identifying information from or about consumers online would be required to comply with four widely accepted fair information practices:

1. **Notice** Websites would be required to provide consumers clear and conspicuous notice of their information practices, including what information they collect, how they collect it, whether they disclose the information to other entities, and whether other entities are collecting information through the site.
2. **Choice** Websites would be required to offer consumers choice as to how their personal identifying information is used beyond the use for which the information was provided, such as completing a purchase.
3. **Access** Websites would be required to offer consumers reasonable access to the information the Websites have collected about them, including a reasonable opportunity to review information and to correct inaccuracies.
4. **Security** Websites would be required to take reasonable steps to protect the security of information they collect from consumers.

http:// FTC Privacy Initiatives: http://www.ftc.gov/privacy/

Protecting Children The Communications Decency Act (CDA) of 1996 was Congress's attempt to protect children from pornography on the Internet. The Act made it a crime to send "obscene or indecent" content to anyone under eighteen years of age. However, in the case of *Reno v. ACLU*, the Supreme Court struck down much of the CDA.

In 1988, at the behest of the FTC, Congress enacted the **Children's Online Privacy Protection Act (COPPA)** to protect the privacy of young children and their parents. The purpose of the act, which became effective in April 2000, is to protect children under thirteen from commercial Websites that collect, store, and distribute their personal data. Much like general Websites, those targeting children offered little notice or protection of personal data. In fact, some sites used questionable means to obtain such information from children.

COPPA applies to a Website or online service directed to children as well as to the operator of any Website or online service that has actual knowledge that it is collecting personal information from a child. COPPA protects children by requiring the operator of the Website (1) to post notice on the Website of what information the operator collects from children, how the operator uses such information, and the operator's disclosure practices for such information and (2) to obtain verifiable parental consent for the collection, use, or disclosure of personal information from children.

http:// Children's Online Privacy Protection Act: http://www.cdt.org/legislation/105th/privacy/coppa.html

In 2000 Congress passed the **Children's Internet Protection Act** (CIPA). This Act requires all federally funded schools and libraries to have some type of filter or blocking technology on all of their computers with Internet access. These filters must block images that constitute obscenity or child pornography and to prevent minors from obtaining access to material that is harmful to them.

United States v. American Library Association

Supreme Court of the United States, 2003
__ U.S. ___, 123 S.Ct. 2297, 156 L.Ed.2d 221

FACTS To help public libraries provide their patrons with Internet access, Congress offers two forms of federal assistance to libraries. First, the E-rate program established by the Telecommunications Act of 1996 entitles qualifying libraries to buy Internet access at a discount. In the year ending June 30, 2002, libraries received $58.5 million in such discounts. Second, the government makes grants to state library administrative agencies (1) to electronically link libraries with educational, social, or information services; (2) to assist libraries in accessing information through electronic networks; and (3) to pay costs for libraries to acquire or share computer systems and telecommunications technologies. In fiscal year 2002, Congress appropriated more than $149 million for these purposes. These programs have succeeded greatly in bringing Internet access to public libraries; by 2000, 95 percent of the Nation's libraries provided public Internet access.

By connecting to the Internet, public libraries provide patrons with a vast amount of valuable information. But there is also an enormous amount of pornography on the Internet, much of which is easily obtained. The accessibility of this material has created serious problems for libraries, which have found that patrons of all ages, including minors, regularly search for online pornography. Some patrons also expose others to pornographic images by leaving them displayed on Internet terminals or printed at library printers.

Upon discovering these problems, Congress became concerned that its programs were facilitating access to illegal and harmful pornography. But Congress also learned that filtering software that blocks access to pornographic Websites could provide a reasonably effective way to prevent such uses of library resources. But a filter set to block pornography may sometimes block other sites that present neither obscene nor pornographic material, but that nevertheless trigger the filter. To minimize this problem, a library can set its software to prevent the blocking of material that falls into categories like "Education," "History," and "Medical." A library may also add or delete specific sites from a blocking category, and anyone can ask companies that furnish filtering software to unblock particular sites.

Responding to this information, Congress enacted the Children's Internet Protection Act (CIPA). It provides that a library may not receive financial assistance unless it has "a policy of Internet safety for minors that includes the operation of a technology protection measure * * * that protects against access" by all persons to "visual depictions" that constitute "obscen[ity]" or "child pornography," and that protects against access by minors to "visual depictions" that are "harmful to minors."

A group of libraries, library associations, library patrons, and Web site publishers, including the American Library Association (ALA) and the Multnomah County Public Library in Portland, Oregon, (Multnomah) sued the United States challenging the constitutionality of CIPA's filtering provisions. A three-judge District Court ruled that CIPA was facially unconstitutional and enjoined the relevant agencies and officials from withholding federal assistance for failure to comply with CIPA. The District Court held that Congress had exceeded its authority under the Spending Clause, U.S. Const., Art. I, §8, cl. 1, because, in the court's view, "any public library that complies with CIPA's conditions will necessarily violate the First Amendment." The court held that the filtering software contemplated by CIPA was a content-based restriction on access to a public forum, and was therefore subject to strict scrutiny. Applying this standard, the District Court held that, although the Government has a compelling interest "in preventing the dissemination of obscenity, child pornography, or, in the case of minors, material harmful to minors," the use of software filters is not narrowly tailored to further those interests. The case was subsequently appealed to the United States Supreme Court.

DECISION The judgment of the district court is reversed.

OPINION Rehnquist, C. J. Congress has wide latitude to attach conditions to the receipt of federal assistance in order to further its policy objectives. [Citation]. But Congress may not "induce" the recipient "to engage in activities that would themselves be unconstitutional." [Citation]. To determine whether libraries would violate the First Amendment by employing the filtering software that CIPA requires, we must first examine the role of libraries in our society.

Public libraries pursue the worthy missions of facilitating learning and cultural enrichment. Appellee ALA's Library Bill of Rights states that libraries should provide "[b]ooks and other * * * resources * * * for the interest, information, and enlightenment of all people of the community the library serves." [Citation]. To fulfill their traditional missions, public libraries must have broad discretion to decide what material to provide to their patrons. Although they seek to provide a wide array of information, their goal has never been to provide "universal coverage." [Citation]. Instead, public libraries seek to provide materials "that would be of the greatest direct benefit or interest to the community." * * *

We have held in two analogous contexts that the government has broad discretion to make content-based judgments in deciding what private speech to make available to the public. In *Arkansas Ed. Television Comm'n v. Forbes*, [citation], we held that public forum principles do not generally apply to a public television station's editorial judgments regarding the private speech it presents to its viewers. * * * Recognizing a broad right of public access "would [also] risk implicating the courts in judgments that should be left to the exercise of journalistic discretion." [Citation.]

Similarly, in *National Endowment for Arts v. Finley*, [citation], we upheld an art funding program that required the National Endowment for the Arts (NEA) to use content-based criteria in making funding decisions. We explained that "[a]ny content-based considerations that may be taken into account in the grant-making process are a consequence of the nature of arts funding." [Citation.] In particular, "[t]he very assumption of the NEA is that grants will be awarded according to the 'artistic worth of competing applicants,' and absolute neutrality is simply inconceivable." * * *

The principles underlying *Forbes* and *Finley* also apply to a public library's exercise of judgment in selecting the material it provides to its patrons. * * * Public library staffs necessarily consider content in making collection decisions and enjoy broad discretion in making them.

The public forum principles on which the District Court relied, [citation], are out of place in the context of this case. Internet access in public libraries is neither a "traditional" nor a "designated" public forum. [Citation.] * * *

Nor does Internet access in a public library satisfy our definition of a "designated public forum." To create such a forum, the government must make an affirmative choice to open up its property for use as a public forum. * * *

The situation here is very different. A public library does not acquire Internet terminals in order to create a public forum for Web publishers to express themselves, any more than it collects books in order to provide a public forum for the authors of books to speak. It provides Internet access, not to "encourage a diversity of views from private speakers," [citation], but for the same reasons it offers other library resources: to facilitate research, learning, and recreational pursuits by furnishing materials of requisite and appropriate quality. * * * As Congress recognized, "[t]he Internet is simply another method for making information available in a school or library." [Citation.] It is "no more than a technological extension of the book stack." [Citation.]

The District Court disagreed because, whereas a library reviews and affirmatively chooses to acquire every book in its collection, it does not review every Web site that it makes available. [Citation.] Based on this distinction, the court reasoned that a public library enjoys less discretion in deciding which Internet materials to make available than in making book selections. [Citation.] We do not find this distinction constitutionally relevant. A library's failure to make quality-based judgments about all the material it furnishes from the Web does not somehow taint the judgments it does make. A library's need to exercise judgment in making collection decisions depends on its traditional role in identifying suitable and worthwhile material; it is no less entitled to play that role when it collects material from the Internet than when it collects material from any other source. Most libraries already exclude pornography from their print collections because they deem it inappropriate for inclusion. We do not subject these decisions to heightened scrutiny; it would make little sense to treat libraries' judgments to block online pornography any differently, when these judgments are made for just the same reason.

Moreover, because of the vast quantity of material on the Internet and the rapid pace at which it changes, libraries cannot possibly segregate, item by item, all the Internet material that is appropriate for inclusion from all that is not. While a library could limit its Internet collection to just those sites it found worthwhile, it could do so only at the cost of excluding an enormous amount of valuable information that it lacks the capacity to review. Given that tradeoff, it is entirely reasonable for public libraries to reject that approach and instead exclude certain categories of content, without making individualized judgments that everything they do make available has requisite and appropriate quality.

Like the District Court, the dissents fault the tendency of filtering software to "overblock"—that is, to erroneously block access to constitutionally protected speech that falls outside the categories that software users intend to block. [Citation.] Due to the software's limitations, "[m]any erroneously blocked [Web] pages contain content that is completely innocuous for both adults and minors, and that no rational person could conclude matches the filtering companies' category definitions, such as 'pornography' or 'sex.'" [Citation.] Assuming that such erroneous blocking presents constitutional difficulties, any such concerns are dispelled by the ease with which patrons may have the filtering software disabled. When a patron encounters a blocked site, he need only ask a librarian to unblock it or (at least in the case of adults) disable the filter. As the District Court found, libraries have the capacity to permanently unblock any erroneously blocked site * * *. With respect to adults, CIPA also expressly authorizes library officials to "disable" a filter altogether "to enable access for bona fide research or other lawful purposes." * * *

* * *

Justice Stevens asserts the premise that "[a] federal statute penalizing a library for failing to install filtering software on every one of its Internet-accessible computers would unquestionably violate [the First] Amendment." [Citation.] But—assuming again that public libraries have First Amendment rights—CIPA does not "penalize" libraries that choose not to install such software, or deny them the right to provide their patrons with unfiltered Internet access. Rather, CIPA simply reflects Congress' decision not to subsidize their doing so. To the extent that libraries wish to offer unfiltered access, they are free to do so without federal assistance. "'A refusal to fund protected activity, without more, cannot be equated with the imposition of a 'penalty' on that activity.'" [Citation.] "'[A] legislature's decision not to subsidize the exercise of a fundamental right does not infringe the right.'" [Citation.]

* * *

Because public libraries' use of Internet filtering software does not violate their patrons' First Amendment rights, CIPA does not induce libraries to violate the Constitution, and is a valid exercise of Congress' spending power. Nor does CIPA impose an unconstitutional condition on public libraries.

INTERPRETATION The requirement that libraries receiving federal funding place Internet filters designed to block access to pornography on all of its computers does not violate the First Amendment.

CRITICAL THINKING QUESTION Do you think the Court was correct? What other alternatives exist to protect minors from Internet pornography?

FREEDOM FROM UNWANTED GOVERNMENT INTRUSION

Like private companies "profiling" users on the Internet, the government can track individuals' cyberspace movements and tap into their e-mail and bulletin board postings. For many, this poses an even greater threat to their privacy and autonomy. However, unlike private companies' activities, the U.S. Constitution protects an individual's privacy from intrusion by the government. Even with this Constitutional protection, the U.S. Supreme Court has recognized areas in which governmental agencies can monitor a person's communications—even from his own home.

The government's access to the Internet, e-mail, and other emerging communication technologies—in particular, the government's crime-fighting tool, "Carnivore"—has raised serious privacy concerns. Carnivore is the name given to the FBI's e-mail reviewing software program. The Carnivore system is attached to an Internet service provider's network and searches through all its customers' electronic messages (including e-mail, Web addresses, and instant messages) looking for the messages of a person suspected of a crime.

EMPLOYEE PRIVACY INTRUSIONS BY EMPLOYERS

The Internet and more advanced computer networks now allow an employer to monitor all her employees' e-mail, computer files, and Internet activities from a single central computer. For example, an employer can discover whether an employee has visited a specific Website and the number of times he has done so. In addition, using readily available commercial software, an employer can know which files an employee has downloaded, which chat rooms he has visited, what Internet e-mail he has received, and where he stored that data on his work computer's hard drive. Moreover, technology permits an employer to count the number of key strokes an employee makes in an hour.

Employers seek to monitor employees' computer activities for a variety of reasons: security concerns, employee efficiency and productivity, misuse of company resources for personal purposes, and uncovering wrongdoing. Because of the *respondeat superior* doctrine (discussed in Chapter 30), employers clearly have an interest in limiting their liability for employee misconduct via the Internet or e-mail, including sexual harassment, defamation, copyright infringement, and discrimination. The actions of private employers are not governed by the U.S Constitution, and, as the next case indicates, a company's examination of messages posted by its employees through its own e-mail system does not tortiously invade the employees' privacy. Legislation has been introduced in Congress prohibiting an employer from electronically monitoring an employee's wire communication, oral communication, electronic communication, or computer usage unless the employer has provided prior notice to the employee.

Smyth v. The Pillsbury Company

United States District Court, Eastern District of Pennsylvania, 1996
914 F.Supp. 97

FACTS The Pillsbury Company (defendant) maintained an electronic mail communication system ("e-mail") in order to promote internal corporate communications among its employees. Defendant repeatedly assured its employees, including the plaintiff, Michael Smyth, an at-will employee, that all e-mail communications would remain confidential and privileged. The defendant also assured its employees, including plaintiff, that e-mail communications could not be intercepted and used by the defendant against its employees as grounds for termination or reprimand. In October 1994, Michael Smyth received certain e-mail communications from his supervisor over the company's e-mail system on his computer at home. In reliance on the defendant's assurances regarding its e-mail system, Smyth responded and exchanged e-mails with his supervisor. At some later date, contrary to the assurances of confidentiality made by the company, Pillsbury, acting through its agents and employees, intercepted Smyth's private e-mail messages made in October 1994. On January 17, 1995, Pillsbury notified Smyth that it was terminating his employment effective February 1, 1995, for transmitting what it deemed to be inappropriate and unprofessional comments over the company's e-mail system. The defendant alleged that the e-mails concerned sales management and contained threats to "kill the backstabbing bastards" and referred to the planned Holiday party as the "Jim Jones Koolaid affair." The plaintiff sued claiming that he had been wrongfully discharged from his position with the defendant. The defendant moved for dismissal for failure to state a claim upon which relief can be granted.

DECISION The defendant's motion to dismiss granted.

OPINION Weiner, J. As a general rule, Pennsylvania law does not provide a common law cause of action for the wrongful discharge of an at-will employee such as plaintiff. *Borse v. Piece Goods Shop, Inc.*, [citation]. * * *

However, in the most limited of circumstances, exceptions have been recognized where discharge of an at-will employee threatens or violates a clear mandate of public policy. * * *

* * *

Plaintiff claims that his termination was in violation of "public policy which precludes an employer from terminating an employee in violation of the employee's right to privacy as embodied in Pennsylvania common law." * * *

The Court of Appeals in *Borse* observed that one of the torts which Pennsylvania recognizes as encompassing an action for invasion of privacy is the tort of "intrusion upon seclusion." As noted by the Court of Appeals, the Restatement (Second) of Torts defines the tort as follows:

> One who intentionally intrudes, physically or otherwise, upon the solitude or seclusion of another or his private affairs or concerns, is subject to liability to the

other for invasion of his privacy, if the intrusion would be highly offensive to a reasonable person.

[Citation.] Liability only attaches when the "intrusion is substantial and would be highly offensive to the 'ordinary reasonable person.'" [Citation.] Although the Court of Appeals in *Borse* observed that "the Pennsylvania courts have not had occasion to consider whether a discharge related to an employer's tortious invasion of an employee's privacy violates public policy," the Court of Appeals predicted that in any claim where the employee claimed that his discharge related to an invasion of his privacy "the Pennsylvania Supreme Court would examine the facts and circumstances surrounding the alleged invasion of privacy. If the court determined that the discharge was related to a substantial and highly offensive invasion of the employee's privacy, [the Court of Appeals] believe that it would conclude that the discharge violated public policy." [Citation.]

* * *

Applying the Restatement definition of the tort of intrusion upon seclusion to the facts and circumstances of the case [before us], we find that plaintiff has failed to state a claim upon which relief can be granted. In the first instance, unlike urinalysis and personal property searches, we do not find a reasonable expectation of privacy in e-mail communications voluntarily made by an employee to his supervisor over the company e-mail system notwithstanding any assurances that such communications would not be intercepted by management. Once plaintiff communicated the alleged unprofessional comments to a second person (his supervisor) over an e-mail system which was apparently utilized by the entire company, any reasonable expectation of privacy was lost. Significantly, the defendant did not require plaintiff, as in the case of an urinalysis or personal property search, to disclose any personal information about himself. Rather, plaintiff voluntarily communicated the alleged unprofessional comments over the company e-mail system. We find no privacy interests in such communications.

In the second instance, even if we found that an employee had a reasonable expectation of privacy in the contents of his e-mail communications over the company e-mail system, we do not find that a reasonable person would consider the defendant's interception of these communications to be a substantial and highly offensive invasion of his privacy. Again, we note that by intercepting such communications, the company is not, as in the case of urinalysis or personal property searches, requiring the employee to disclose any personal information about himself or invading the employee's person or personal effects. Moreover, the company's interest in preventing inappropriate and unprofessional comments or even illegal activity over its e-mail system outweighs any privacy interest the employee may have in those comments.

In sum, we find that the defendant's actions did not tortuously invade the plaintiff's privacy and, therefore, did not violate public policy. As a result, the motion to dismiss is granted.

INTERPRETATION A company's examination of messages posted by its employees through its own e-mail system does not tortuously invade the employees' privacy and, therefore, a discharge of an at-will employee based on that examination does not violate public policy.

ETHICAL QUESTION Did Pillsbury act unethically when it failed to keep its assurance to its employees that e-mail communications would not be intercepted and used by Pillsbury against its employees as grounds for termination or reprimand? Explain.

CRITICAL THINKING QUESTION When should a company be permitted to examine the e-mail of its employees? Explain.

SECURITIES REGULATION

As discussed in Chapter 40, a **security** is defined broadly to generally include stocks, bonds, notes, certificates of interest, and investment contracts. Federal and state laws regulate securities, although state laws vary widely. The federal laws affecting securities are designed to encourage market transactions while (1) ensuring that individual investors receive full disclosure of material facts and (2) protecting them from fraudulent activities.

The **Securities Act of 1933** and the Securities Exchange Act of 1934 are the basis for federal law. The Securities Exchange Commission (SEC), created by the 1934 Act, is a quasi-judicial agency responsible for promulgating securities regulations and monitoring market compliance. The 1933 Act, also called the "Truth in Securities Act," prohibits the offer or sale of any security through the use of the mails or any means of interstate commerce unless a registration statement for that security is in effect or the issuer secures an exemption from registration. The purpose of registration is to adequately and accurately disclose financial and other information on which investors may judge the merits of securities. The 1933 act prohibits fraud in *all* sales of securities involving interstate commerce or the mails, even if the securities are exempt from the 1933 Act's registration and disclosure requirements. Civil and criminal liability may be imposed for violations of the 1933 Act.

The **Securities Exchange Act of 1934** deals mainly with the secondary distribution (resale) of securities. The 1934 Act seeks to ensure fair and orderly securities markets by establishing rules for market operations and by prohibiting fraudulent and manipulative practices. It protects holders of all securities listed on national exchanges, as well as holders of equity securities of companies traded over the counter whose corporate assets exceed $10 million and whose equity securities include a class with 500 or more shareholders. Companies must register such securities and are subject to the 1934 Act's periodic reporting requirements, short-swing profits provision, tender offer provisions, and proxy solicitation provisions. In addition, issuers of securities, whether registered under the 1934 Act or not, must comply with the antifraud and antibribery provisions of the act.

The SEC has recognized the impact of recent technological changes on securities markets:

> Advances in computers and electronic media technology are enabling companies to disseminate information to more people at a faster and more cost-effective rate than traditional distribution methods, which have been largely paper based. . . . Until recently, online use of corporate information was generally limited to large corporations and institutional investors. The dramatic growth in personal computer ownership, however, is enabling many small investors to access online corporate information just as readily as institutions. Access to information through electronic means permits small investors to communicate quickly and efficiently with companies as well as with each other. Use of electronic media also enhances the efficiency of the securities markets by allowing for the rapid dissemination of information to investors and financial markets in a more cost-efficient, widespread, and equitable manner than traditional paper-based methods.

To realize the benefits of electronic technology, the SEC has provided interpretative guidance for the use of electronic media for the delivery of information required by the federal securities laws. The SEC defined *electronic media* to include audiotapes, videotapes, facsimiles, CD-ROM, electronic mail, bulletin boards, Internet Websites, and computer networks. Basically, electronic delivery must provide notice, access, and evidence of delivery comparable to that provided by paper delivery. In addition, the SEC established the **EDGAR (Electronic Data Gathering, Analysis, and Retrieval)** computer system, which performs automated collection, validation, indexing, acceptance, and dissemination of reports required to be filed with the SEC. Its primary purpose is to increase the efficiency and fairness of the securities market for the benefit of investors, corporations, and the economy by speeding up the receipt, acceptance, dissemination, and analysis of corporate information filed with the SEC. After a phase-in period, the SEC now requires all public domestic companies to make their filings on EDGAR, except filings exempted for hardship. EDGAR filings are posted at the SEC's Website twenty-four hours after the date of filing.

http://

Securities Act of 1933: http://www4.law.cornell.edu/uscode/15/ch2A.html
http://www.law.uc.edu/CCL/33Act/index.html

Securities Exchange Act of 1934: http://www4.law.cornell.edu/uscode/15/ch2B.html
http://www.law.uc.edu/CCL/34Act/index.html

PERMITTED SECURITIES ACTIVITIES OVER THE INTERNET

The rapid spread of the Internet into the sale of securities can be explained by simple economics: unmatched speed, accessibility, and affordability. In addition, Internet access continues to expand with increasing numbers of potential investors. Not only has online trading increased, but also the Internet has changed the way many investors conduct investment research. Moreover, some issuers are raising capital online by Internet direct public offerings (DPO), which are made without a professional underwriter. It is estimated that several hundred DPOs may have been offered.

For public offerings registered under the 1933 Act, the Internet has provided a new means to disclose certain required documents such as a prospectus. The SEC, however, requires electronic delivery to provide notice, access, and evidence of delivery comparable to that provided by paper delivery. Thus, electronic disclosure via a company's Internet Website would not satisfy the delivery requirements under the 1933 Act unless the investor has given prior consent to receive electronic delivery via that Website or the investor has actually accessed the document on the Website.

For some companies, the registration costs of a public offering under the 1933 Act are prohibitive. However, federal law provides certain exemptions, and the Internet has made these exemptions more accessible. Regulation A permits an issuer to offer up to $5 million of securities in any twelve-month period without registering them, provided that the issuer files an offering statement with the SEC's regional office prior to the sale of the securities. An offering circular must also be provided to offerees and purchasers. Regulation A sets no restrictions regarding the number or qualifications of investors who may purchase securities under its provisions and permits advertising and general solicitations. In 1995, relying on

Regulation A, Spring Street Brewing Company became the first to use the Internet to issue securities.

Private offerings under Regulation D are also exempt from registration under the 1933 Act. General advertising or solicitation, however, is not permitted, and the securities may be purchased by an unlimited number of "accredited investors" and by no more than thirty-five other purchasers. For exempt private offerings, the use of the Internet poses difficult general solicitation issues. Unless there are methods to restrict access solely to investors qualified to participate in a private offering, an online offering under these exemptions likely would violate the general solicitation restrictions. The SEC has issued letters to clarify how these offerings can be conducted online without violating the general solicitation restrictions. For example, the IPONet received SEC approval for posting notice of an Internet-based, private offering in a password-protected page of its Website accessible only to members who had previously qualified as accredited investors.

http://

Regulation A: http://www.law.uc.edu/CCL/33ActRls/regA.html

Regulation D: http://www.law.uc.edu/CCL/33ActRls/regD.html

FRAUDULENT USE OF THE INTERNET

Offsetting the benefits of the Internet's speed and accessibility is its anonymity, which enables and protects fraudulent activity. In addition, the Internet confers credibility on information: People tend to believe statements seen on the Internet. Consequently, the Internet facilitates fraud by providing access to large numbers of people with little time, effort, or monetary investment. As a result, the Internet has expanded the possibilities for securities fraud and created additional challenges for recovery of money defrauded. The SEC is responding to attempts to use the Internet to perpetrate securities fraud through an evolving program of education, surveillance, and litigation.

Fraudulent statements made through the Internet are typically intended to (1) sell worthless or overvalued securities to the public or (2) manipulate the price of securities traded in the secondary market. One example of the first type of Internet securities fraud is perpetrated by creating Websites that appear to be legitimate company Websites but are really nonexistent businesses. After receiving payment for these securities, the promoters abscond with the proceeds. An example of the second type of securities fraud is the "pump and dump." First, the defrauder enters an Internet chat room under an assumed name and encourages those online to purchase X Company's stock immediately. This is the pump. Then, while the stock price is artificially inflated, the defrauder sells his stock for a healthy profit. This is the dump.

> **Practical Advice**
>
> Be suspicious of any information about the value of a company obtained from a website or chat room.

CYBERCRIME

Defining "cybercrime" or "computer crime" is elusive. For many, cybercrime is any crime committed or facilitated by a computer, such as murder for hire over the Internet. But for others, cybercrime describes a new genre of crime that typically is associated with expert computer "hackers," that is, persons who gain unauthorized access to a computer. However, most agree that computer crimes are best categorized, at least for purposes of prosecution, based on whether the computer was the target or the instrument of the crime.

Not surprisingly, the proliferation of personal computers and Internet accessibility has fueled a rise in cybercrime. A recent cybercrime study found that more than half of the corporations responding reported unauthorized access to their computers. Of those, 66 percent claimed losses of more than $50,000 and 18 percent in excess of $1 million. Furthermore, studies show that financial institutions have been especially hard hit by computer hackers and online fraud. Even larger is the number of cybercrime-related losses that go unreported because the attack was never detected or fears that "hacking" reports might alarm investors or customers.

Examples of cybercrimes using computers as the **instrument** of the crime include the distribution of child pornography, money laundering, illegal gambling, copyright infringement, illegal communication of trade secrets, and fraud involving credit cards, e-commerce, and securities. Cybercrime with a computer as a **target** of the crime attacks a computer's confidentiality, integrity, or availability; examples include theft or destruction of proprietary information, vandalism, denial of service, Website defacing and interference, and implanting malicious code. This type of crime targets the computer system, generally to acquire information stored on that computer system, to control the target system without authorization or payment, or to alter the integrity of data or interfere with the availability of the computer or server. As examples, a hacker might gain access to a hotel reservation system to steal credit card numbers or might seek private information about another individual to extort money or obtain commercial advantage.

In the category of attacks known as "denial of service," the objective is to disable the target system without necessarily gaining access to it. For example, a common denial of service crime occurs when an Internet service provider's central computer, or server, is intentionally flooded with e-mails ("mail bombing"), which "bring it down," or freeze it. As a result, customers using the ISP cannot gain access to the Internet and are thus denied service. Website defacing involves hackers who illegally substitute their own graphics or language for what is usually seen on a particular site. In addition, hackers may use access to a Website as a vehicle to hack farther into a company's computer system where they can steal sensitive passwords, alter its Websites, copy credit card numbers, plant damaging programs, and create "back doors," which would allow the hacker to reenter the system at a later date. Finally, hackers plant malicious code, such as viruses, worms, logic bombs, or Trojan horses, which infect a computer and cause damage to it before the user realizes that it has been infected. A notable example is the "I Love You" computer virus that attacked 45 million computer users worldwide and caused an estimated $2.6 billion in losses.

Every state now has laws targeting cybercriminals. Originally passed in 1984 and amended in 1986, 1994, and 1996, the Computer Fraud and Abuse Act protects a broad range of computers that facilitate interstate and international commerce and communications. The Act makes it a crime with respect to any computer that is used in interstate commerce or communications (1) to access or damage it, without authorization, (2) to access it with the intent to commit fraud, (3) to traffic in passwords for it, and (4) to threaten to cause damage to it with the intent to extort money or anything of value. Furthermore, depending on the details of the crime, cybercriminals may also be prosecuted under other federal laws, such as copyright, mail fraud, or wire fraud laws.

http://

Department of Justice Computer Crime: http://www.usdoj.gov/criminal/cybercrime/compcrime.html
National Security Institute: http://www.nsi.org/ (Federal legislation) http://nsi.org/Library/Compsec/computerlaw/statelaws.html (State legislation)

CHAPTER SUMMARY

Defamation

Definition a false communication that injures a person's reputation

Communications Decency Act of 1996 grants Internet service providers immunity from liability for defamation when publishing information originating from a third party

Intellectual Property

Copyrights exclusive right to original works of authorship, including computer programs
- *No Electronic Theft Act (NET Act)* amended federal copyright law to prohibit willful infringement even if not for personal profit
- *Digital Millennium Copyright Act (DMCA)* prohibits circumventing, as well as creating or trafficking in devices that circumvent, a technological protection measure put in place by a copyright owner to control access to or copying of a copyrighted work

Trademarks or trade symbols include trademarks, service marks, certification marks, and collective marks
- *Lanham Act* protects marks that are distinctive and not immoral, deceptive, or scandalous
- *Anticybersquatting Consumer Protection Act* protects the owner of a mark against any person who, with a bad faith intent to profit from that mark, registers or uses a domain name which, at the time of its registration (1) is identical or confusingly similar to a distinctive mark, (2) dilutes a famous mark, or (3) is a protected trademark, word, or name

Patents utility patents protect the exclusive right to an invention for twenty years from the date of application if the invention is novel, useful, and not obvious; patent protection has been granted for some Internet business methods

Trade Secrets commercially valuable, secret information; the federal Economic Espionage Act prohibits the theft of trade secrets (including downloading or uploading such information) and provides criminal penalties for violations

Contracts and Sales

Governing Law contracts are primarily governed by state common law; Article 2 of the Uniform Commercial Code (UCC) governs the sale of goods

Uniform Computer Information Transaction Act (UCITA) applies to agreements to create, modify, transfer, or license computer information or informational rights in computer information

- *Transfer Contracts* UCITA applies to transfers of computer programs or multimedia products, software, and multimedia development contracts
- *Access Contracts* UCITA applies to contracts to enter the information system of another to obtain information or use that information system for specific purposes

Electronic Records include contracts or transactions entered into online or by e-mail

- *The Uniform Electronic Transactions Act (UETA)* state law that gives full effect to electronic contracts and signatures
- *The Electronic Signatures in Global and National Commerce (E-Sign)* federal law that makes electronic records and signatures valid and enforceable across the United States for many types of transactions in or affecting interstate or foreign commerce

Noncompete Agreements by employees are enforceable if (1) the purpose of the restraint is to protect a property interest of the employer and (2) the restraint is no more extensive than is reasonably necessary to protect that interest; in determining the reasonableness of restraint, courts considers the rapid evolution of business practices in the Internet industry

Privacy and the Internet

Protection of Personal Identifiable Information on the Internet almost all Internet sites collect personal identifiable information on their users

- *Privacy and Intrusion by Private Parties* currently an individual is accorded very limited rights with regard to online privacy invasions
- *Protecting Children* COPPA protects children under thirteen from commercial websites that collect, store, and distribute their personal data; CIPA requires all federally funded schools and libraries to block Internet access to obscenity or child pornography

Freedom from Unwanted Government Intrusion the U.S. Constitution protects an individual's privacy from intrusion by the government.

Employee Privacy Intrusions by Employers the actions of private employers are not governed by the U.S. Constitution with regard to the individual's privacy

Securities Regulation

Definition of a Security generally includes stocks, bonds, notes, certificates of interest, and investment contracts

- *Regulation of Securities Issuances* the Securities Act of 1933 requires disclosure of accurate material information in all public offerings of nonexempt securities unless the offering is an exempt transaction and prohibits fraud in all issuances of securities
- *Regulation of Secondary Distributions* the Securities Exchange Act of 1934 requires regulated, publicly held companies to register their securities and subjects them to the Act's periodic reporting requirements, short-swing profits provision, tender offer provisions, and proxy solicitation provisions; issuers of securities, whether registered under the 1934 Act or not, must comply with the antifraud and antibribery provisions of the Act
- *Electronic Media* the SEC permits the use of electronic media for the delivery of information required by the federal securities laws if the media provide notice, access, and evidence of delivery comparable to that provided by paper delivery
- *EDGAR (Electronic Data Gathering, Analysis, and Retrieval)* SEC's computer system that performs automated collection, validation, indexing, acceptance, and dissemination of reports required to be filed with the SEC

Permitted Securities Activities over the Internet

- ***Registered Public Offerings*** disclosure of certain documents required by the 1933 Act may be made over the Internet so long as electronic delivery to provide notice, access, and evidence of delivery is comparable to that provided by paper delivery
- ***Regulation A*** permits an issuer to offer up to $5 million of securities in any twelve-month period without registering them if the issuer files an offering statement with the SEC's regional office prior to the sale of the securities and provides an offering circular to offerees and purchasers; Regulation A has been used to issue securities over the Internet
- ***Private Offerings Under Regulation D*** are exempt from registration under the 1933 Act but general advertising or solicitation is not permitted and the securities may be purchased by an unlimited number of accredited investors and by no more than thirty-five other purchasers; the SEC has approved posting notice of an Internet-based, private offering in a password-protected page of a Website accessible only to members who had previously qualified as accredited investors

Fraudulent Use of the Internet the Internet has expanded the possibilities for securities fraud and created additional challenges for recovery of money defrauded; the SEC is responding through an evolving program of education, surveillance, and litigation

Cybercrime

Definition any crime committed or facilitated by a computer, including crimes using computers as instruments of the crime and crimes with computers as targets of the crime

Laws every state as well as the federal government has enacted laws targeting cybercriminals

QUESTIONS

1. LOA is an Internet service provider located in Virginia. Freeman is the creator and operator of defendants AAF Marketing and AAF Industries (collectively AAF). LOA alleges that Freeman and AAF improperly sent unauthorized bulk e-mail advertisements ("spam") to LOA subscribers. Specifically, LOA alleges that Freeman sent over 60 million e-mail messages over the course of 10 months, many of which contained the letters "loa.com" in their headers; that he continued to send unauthorized bulk e-mail after he was notified in writing by LOA to cease and desist these activities; that his activities caused LOA to spend technical resources and staff time to "defend" its computer system and its membership against this spam; and that Freeman's messages damaged LOA's goodwill among its members and generated more than 50,000 member complaints. Discuss whether LOA will prevail in an action against AAF.

2. Murphy is currently employed within the Foreign Bureau of Information Services component of the CIA. He has access to a government computer system owned and operated by the CIA and access to the Internet. An examination of the company's firewall logs revealed that a number of Websites were repeatedly accessed at Murphy's workstation. The sites were characterized by a systems manager as not "necessarily for business purposes." On orders from his supervisors, the systems manager copied the contents of Murphy's workstation hard drive for investigators to review and then discovered that Murphy had downloaded files containing child pornography. Murphy argues that the systems manager's search was in violation of the Fourth Amendment because it was conducted without a warrant or other lawful justification. Should the CIA be permitted to continue its investigation into Murphy's conduct? Why?

3. Corcoran was the system operator of a bulletin board Service (BBS) called "The Front Line" and was known as "Dirty Scum." Corcoran knew the BBS contained a directory with the file names of approximately 20 Sega Genesis game programs, including Jurassic Park and Sonic Spinball. These files were available for download by her BBS users. Sega claimed that Corcoran is liable for contributory copyright infringement because Corcoran knew that her BBS users were making copies of Sega games and Corcoran encouraged them to do so. Corcoran argued that uploading and downloading of Sega files was fair use. Is Sega entitled to prevent this use by Corcoran?

4. James developed a Website for some students who made a ten-minute film in their film production class. Included on the Website was a one-minute theatrical trailer that included a sound clip from the "Imperial March" by John

Williams. The sound clip contained more than 10 percent of the musical composition. The site was created for a Web design class in which James was enrolled, and his professor has told him to take down the trailer until he receives permission from the record label to use the music. James believes such a permission is not needed because he owns a copy of the "Imperial March." James contends that this use of the sound clip falls within "fair use" because the trailer was created for educational purposes. Who is correct?

5. SportsShoes4All.com sells many types of shoes, including sneakers, skates, and rollerblades. The company has a wide selection of running shoes by many top-brand manufacturers, including Nike. To increase business, SportsShoes4All.com includes a metatag in its index.html file that includes the keyword "nike." When a search for "Nike" on Yahoo! or Excite takes place, SportsShoes4All.com is listed as a possible site. Is SportsShoes4All.com guilty of dilution of Nike's trademark?

6. Steve is in search of a CD for his younger sister's birthday. After browsing online, he decides the best price for the CD can be found at LowestPricedCDEver.com. LowestPricedCDEver.com does not accept returns or refunds—all sales are final. Steve makes his selection and uses his virtual "shopping cart" to check out. While the CD cover and price are displayed in the shopping cart, no mention of the purchasing contract (including hyperlinks) is shown. Upon entering his credit card information, Steve presses the "Submit" button and his browser is taken back to LowestPricedCDEver.com's homepage. One week later the CD arrives, and Steve's sister has changed her taste in music. Can Steve return the gift?

7. Emily was a Java programmer employed with Sun Microsystems in Palo Alto, California. Upon beginning employment, Emily signed a contract which included a noncompete clause that prevented her from taking another Java programming position with any of five companies Sun listed as "direct competitors" within three months of terminating her employment. Later that year Emily resigned and two months later accepted a position with Hewlett-Packard (HP) in Houston, Texas. HP was listed in Emily's contract as a "direct competitor," but she argues that due to the significant geographic distance between both jobs, the contract is not enforceable. Explain whether the contract is enforceable.

8. Joel picked names out of a local telephone book and then hacked into a consumer credit–reporting agency to learn more about those people. Using this information, he then ordered fraudulent credit cards and made purchases on these cards. What was the result?

9. Felipe began working with a small engineering firm in 1998. In 2000, the firm decided to go public, allowing Felipe to take advantage of more than $100,000 in stock options per his employment contract. Later that year, Felipe entered a Yahoo! financial chat room and posted a bogus financial report detailing a proposed merger between his engineering firm and a publicly traded textiles firm. The fake report caused the engineering firm's stock price to rise 36 percent, at which point Felipe sold his shares. What are the consequences of Felipe's actions?

http:// **Internet Exercise** Find information about (a) intellectual property and the Internet, (b) privacy on the Internet, and (c) cybercrime.

PART X

PROPERTY

Insurance Information Institute
http://www.iii.org/

AM Best Insurance Rating Service
http://www.ambest.com/

Standard & Poor's Rating Services Insurance Ratings Publications
http://www.insure.com/ratings/sandp.cfm/

McCarran-Ferguson Act
http://www4.law.cornell.edu/uscode/15/1011.html

Pennsylvania Insurance Fraud Prevention Authority
http://www.helpstopfraud.org

U.S. Government ("What You Should Know about Buying Life Insurance")
http://www.pueblo.gsa.gov/money.htm

U.S. Government ("HUD Home Buying Guide")
http://www.pueblo.gsa.gov/housing.htm

U.S. Government ("How to Buy a Home with a Low Down Payment")
http://www.pueblo.gsa.gov/housing.htm

U.S. Government ("Selling a Home")
http://www.pueblo.gsa.gov/specpubs

CHAPTER 49

Introduction to Property, Property Insurance, Bailments, and Documents of Title

Property and law are born together, and die together. Before laws were made there was no property; take away laws, and property ceases.

JEREMY BENTHAM, ENGLISH JURIST AND PHILOSOPHER (1748–1832)

Learning Objectives

After reading this chapter you should be able to:

1. Define (a) tangible and intangible property, (b) real and personal property, and (c) a fixture.
2. Explain (a) the ways to transfer title to personal property, (b) the three elements of a valid gift, and (c) the difference in the law's treatment of abandoned property, lost property, and mislaid property.
3. With respect to property insurance, explain (a) the different types of fires, (b) co-insurance clauses, (c) other insurance clauses, (d) insurable interest, (e) valued and open policies, and (f) the defenses of misrepresentation, breach of warranty, concealment, waiver, and estoppel.
4. Define the essential elements of a bailment and describe the rights and duties of the bailor and bailee.
5. (a) Explain what a document of title is and (b) identify and describe the various types of documents of title.

In our democratic and free enterprise society, the importance of the concept of property is second only to that of the idea of liberty. Although many of our rules of property stem directly from English law, in the United States property occupies a unique status because of the protection expressly granted it by the U.S. Constitution and by most state constitutions as well. The Fifth Amendment to the federal Constitution provides that "No person shall be . . . deprived of life, liberty, or property, without due process of law; nor shall private property be taken for public use, without just compensation." The Fourteenth Amendment contains a similar requirement: "No State shall . . . deprive any person of life, liberty, or property, without due process of law." Under the police power, however, this protection afforded to property owners is subject to regulation for the public good.

In the first part of this chapter, we will provide a general introduction to the law governing real and personal property. The second part of this chapter deals specifically with personal property; the third part covers property insurance. The fourth part of the chapter covers bailments, and the last part discusses documents of title.

INTRODUCTION TO PROPERTY AND PERSONAL PROPERTY

Property is a legally protected interest or group of interests. It is valuable only because our law provides that certain consequences follow from the ownership of it. The right to use property, to sell it, and to control to whom it shall pass on the death of the owner are all included within the term *property*. Thus, a person who speaks of "owning property" may have one of two separate ideas in mind: (1) the *physical thing itself*, as when a homeowner says, "I just bought a piece of property in Oakland," meaning complete ownership of a physically identifiable parcel of land, or (2) a *right or interest* in a physical object (for example, with respect to land, a tenant under a lease has a property interest in the leased land, although he does not own the land).

CPA KINDS OF PROPERTY

Property may be classified as (1) tangible or intangible and (2) real or personal, but these classifications are not mutually exclusive.

TANGIBLE AND INTANGIBLE

A forty-acre farm, a chair, and a household pet are tangible property. Each of these *physical* objects embodies the group of rights or interests known as "title" to or "ownership" of **tangible property**. **Intangible property**, in contrast, does not exist in a physical form. For example, the rights represented by a stock certificate, a promissory note, and a deed granting Jones a right-of-way over Smith's land are intangible property. Each represents certain rights that defy reduction to physical possession but have a legal reality in that the courts will protect them.

The same item may be the object of both tangible and intangible property rights. Suppose Ann purchases a book published by Brown & Sons. On the first page is the statement "Copyright 2004 by Brown & Sons." Ann owns the volume she has purchased. She has the right to exclusive physical possession and use of that particular copy. It is a tangible piece of property of which she is the owner. Brown & Sons, however, has the exclusive right to publish copies of the book, a right granted the publisher by the copyright laws. The courts will protect this intangible property of Brown & Sons, as well as Ann's right to her particular volume.

REAL AND PERSONAL

The most significant practical distinction between types of property is the classification into real and personal property. To define this distinction simply, land and all interests in it are **real property** (also called ***realty***), and every other thing or interest identified as property is **personal property** (also called ***chattel***). This easy description encompasses most property, with the exception of certain physical objects that are personal property under most circumstances but that may, because of their attachment to land or their use in connection with land, become a form of real property called fixtures.

FIXTURES

As we noted above, a **fixture** is an article or piece of property that was formerly treated as personal property but has been attached in such a manner to land or a building that it is now designated as real property even though it retains its original identity. The intent of the parties to convert the property to real property from personal property is usually shown by the permanent manner of affixation or the adaptation of the affixed object to the property. For example, building materials are clearly personal property; but when worked into a building as its construction progresses, such materials become real property, as buildings are a part of the land they occupy. Thus, clay in its natural state is, of course, real property; when made into bricks, it becomes personal property; and if the bricks are then built into the wall of a house, the "clay" once again becomes real property.

Although doing so may be difficult, determining whether various items are personal property or real property may be the only way to settle certain conflicting ownership claims. Unless otherwise provided by agreement, personal property remains the property of the person who placed it on the real estate. On the other hand, property that has been affixed so as to become a fixture (an actual part of the real estate) becomes the property of the real estate owner.

In determining whether personal property has become a fixture, the intention of the parties, as expressed in their agreement, will control the settlement of conflicting claims. In the absence of an agreement, the following factors are relevant in determining whether any particular item is a fixture:

1. the physical relationship of the item to the land or building;
2. the intention of the person who attached the item to the land or building;

CONCEPT REVIEW

Kinds of Property

	Personal	Real
Tangible	Goods	Land Buildings Fixtures
Intangible	Negotiable instruments Stock certificates Contract rights Copyrights Patents	Leases Easements Mortgages

3. the purpose the item serves in relation to the land or building and in relation to the person who brought it there; and
4. the interest of that person in the land or building at the time of the item's attachment.

Although physical attachment is significant, a more important test is whether the item can be removed without causing material injury to the land or building on the land. If it *cannot* be so removed, the item is generally held to have become part of the realty.

Practical Advice

Specify in your contracts for the sale of real estate which fixtures stay with the property and which fixtures may be removed by the seller.

By comparison, the test of purpose or use applies only if the item (1) is affixed to the realty in some way but (2) can be removed without material injury to the realty. In such a situation, if the use or purpose of the item is peculiar to a particular owner or occupant of the premises, the courts will tend to let him remove the item when he leaves. Accordingly, in the law of landlord and tenant, the tenant may remove *trade fixtures* (that is, items used in connection with a trade but not intended to become part of the realty), provided that she can accomplish this without material injury to the realty. On the other hand, doors may be removed without injury to the structure; yet, because they are necessary to the ordinary use of the building and are not peculiar to the use of the occupant, they are considered to be fixtures and thus part of the real property.

Practical Advice

When placing on real property a permanently affixed structure, such as a billboard, provide in your agreement with the owner of the land terms specifying who owns the structure and whether you have the right to remove it upon termination of the lease.

New England Telephone and Telegraph Co. v. City of Franklin

Supreme Court of New Hampshire, 1996
141 N.H. 449, 685 A.2d 913
http://caselaw.findlaw.com/scripts/getcase.pl?court=NH&vol=9611\netel&invol=1

FACTS The plaintiffs, New England Telephone and Telegraph Company (NET) **(http://www.verizon.com/)**, Merrimack County Telephone Company (MCT) **(http://www.mcttelecom.com/)**, and Contoocook Valley Telephone Company (CVT) **(http://www.prexar.com/)**, are public utilities providing telecommunications services in New Hampshire. The plaintiffs commenced separate actions for abatement of real estate taxes against the City of Franklin and fifteen other municipalities. NET disputed the defendants' treatment of its communications equipment as real estate, thereby challenging their authority to tax its equipment. The communications equipment at issue involves two basic categories: (1) distribution plant, which includes telephone poles, wires, and underground conduits and (2) central office equipment, consisting of frames, switches, and other power equipment. The superior court granted the plaintiffs' motion for summary judgment.

In support of the summary judgment motion, the plaintiffs submitted affidavits setting forth the following facts. All of the plaintiffs' poles, wires, and underground conduits located in the municipalities are placed either on public rights of way or on private property owned by third parties. Approximately 90 percent of the poles are located on public rights of way pursuant to licenses issued by the State or the municipalities. The remaining ten percent of the poles are placed on private property either by consent of the property owner or pursuant to an easement. The poles, wires, and underground conduits are installed in a manner that permits and facilitates their removal and relocation. Consequently, removal of that equipment is neither complicated nor time consuming, and does not harm the underlying land or change its usefulness. The plaintiffs remove and relocate their poles, wires, and underground conduits at the request of the State or the applicable private landowner or municipality. In obtaining the licenses, consents, or easements for their poles, wires, and underground conduits, the plaintiffs insist on maintaining ownership of that equipment and refuse any requests to make the equipment a permanent part of the realty. The plaintiffs' central office equipment, most of which is located in buildings owned by the plaintiffs, is both portable and designed to permit removal and relocation. The plaintiffs' practice and policy is to move pieces of central office equipment among buildings in response to changes in technology or system use. Although certain frames are bolted to the buildings, their removal is achieved without affecting the usefulness of the buildings or the frames themselves. When the plaintiffs ultimately vacate a building used as a central office, they remove all of their equipment and merely transfer the building "as a shell." The vacated building, though devoid of central office equipment, retains utility for other commercial or professional uses. The defendants did not dispute the specific facts set forth by the plaintiffs.

DECISION Judgment affirmed.

OPINION Horton, J. Accordingly, if the items of communications equipment "are real estate * * *, they are taxable unless exempted by some other provision." [Citation.]

The defendants primarily argue that the superior court erred by refusing to characterize the communications equipment as fixtures and, therefore, by failing to treat the equipment as realty. "A chattel loses its character as personalty and becomes a fixture and part of the realty when there exists an actual or constructive annexation to the realty with the intention of making it a permanent accession to the freehold, and an appropriation or adaptation to the use or purpose of that part of the realty with which it is connected." [Citation.] A mixed question of law and fact, [citation] whether an item of property is properly classified as either personalty or a fixture turns on several factors, including: the item's nature and use; the intent of the party making the annexation; the degree and extent to which the item is specially adapted to the realty; the degree and extent of the item's annexation to the realty; and the relationship between the realty's owner and the person claiming the item. [Citations.] * * *

In this case, the items of communications equipment did not constitute fixtures. Each of the relevant factors supports the superior court's holding that the property remained personalty. The poles, wires, and central office equipment, though placed in the ground or bolted to the buildings, were readily removable and transportable without affecting the utility of the underlying land, the buildings, or the equipment itself. Because removal of the equipment would not render the land or buildings "incomplete and unfit for use," and because the equipment could be "equally useful and adapted for general use elsewhere," the communications equipment did not constitute fixtures. [Citations.] In addition, the very nature of telephone poles and wires, as well as their use by the plaintiffs in connection with integrated telecommunications systems, belies the proposition that the equipment became a permanent and essential part of the underlying realty so as to pass by conveyance with it. [Citation.] Furthermore, the statute governing the licensing of telephone poles and wires on public ways specifically provides for their removal on ten days' notice and therefore establishes, as a matter of law, their impermanence. [Citation.] Finally, the defendants never challenged the plaintiffs' asserted intent to maintain the communications equipment as personalty.

The defendants' other arguments on the fixtures issue are not persuasive. First, the defendants' evidence concerning the installation, durability, and longevity of the distribution equipment failed to raise a genuine issue of material fact regarding the status of the property under our law of fixtures in light of the defendants' failure to contradict the specific facts in the plaintiffs' affidavits. [Citations.] Similarly, the defendants' conclusory assertions concerning the "permanent" nature of the communications equipment did not satisfy their burden in opposing the summary judgment motion. [Citation.] * * *

INTERPRETATION A fixture is personal property so firmly attached to real property that an interest in it arises under real property.

ETHICAL QUESTION Did the court fairly decide this case? Explain.

CRITICAL THINKING QUESTION When should personal property become a fixture? What criteria should be used in the determination? Explain.

CPA TRANSFER OF TITLE TO PERSONAL PROPERTY

The transfer of title to real property typically is a formal affair. In contrast, title to personal property may be acquired and transferred with relative ease and little formality. Such facility with regard to the transfer of personal property is essential within a society whose trade and industry are based principally on transactions in personal property. In a free economy, stocks, bonds, merchandise, and intellectual property must be sold with minimal delay. It is only natural that the law will reflect these needs.

Accordingly, the law concerning personal property has been largely codified. The Uniform Commercial Code includes the law of sales of goods (Article 2), as well as the law governing the transfer and negotiation of negotiable instruments (Article 3) and of investment securities (Article 8). Nonetheless, the Code does not cover a number of issues (addressed here) involving the ownership and transfer of title to personal property. In addition, personal property may be, and often is, acquired by producing the item, rather than by selling or transferring it.

BY SALE

By definition, a **sale** of *tangible* personal property (goods) is a transfer of title to specified existing goods for a consideration known as the price. Title passes when the parties intend it to pass, and transfer of possession is not required for a transfer of title. For a discussion of transfer of title, see Chapter 21.

Sales of *intangible* personal property also involve the transfer of title. Many of these sales also are governed by UCC provisions, while some, such as sales of copyrights and patents, are governed by specialized federal legislation.

BY GIFT

A **gift** is a transfer of title to property from one person to another without consideration. This lack of consideration is the basic distinction between a gift and a sale. Because a gift involves no consideration or compensation, it must be completed by delivery of the gift to be effective. A gratuitous promise to make a gift is not binding. In addition, there must be intent on the part of the maker (the **donor**) of the gift to make a present transfer, and there must be acceptance by the recipient (the **donee**) of the gift.

Delivery Delivery is essential to a valid gift. The term *delivery* has a very special meaning that includes, but is not limited to, the manual transfer of the item to the donee. A donor may effect an irrevocable delivery by, for example, turning an item over to a third person with instructions to give it to the donee. Frequently, an item, because of its size, location, or intangibility, is incapable of immediate manual delivery. In such cases, an irrevocable gift may be effected through the delivery of something that symbolizes dominion over the item. This is referred to as **constructive delivery**. For example, if Joanne declares that she gives an antique desk and all its contents to Barry and hands Barry the key to the desk, in many states a valid gift has been made.

Practical Advice

As a donee of a gift, attempt to receive actual or constructive delivery of the item as quickly as possible.

Intent The law also provides clearly that the donor must intend to make a gift of the property. Thus, if Jack leaves a packet of stocks and bonds with Joan, her acquiring good title to them depends on whether Jack intended to make a gift of them or simply intended to place them in Joan's hands for safekeeping. A voluntary, uncompensated delivery made with the intent to give the recipient title constitutes a gift when the donee accepts the delivery. If these conditions are met, the donor has no further claim to the property.

Gifts, therefore, cannot be conditional. There is, however, one major exception to this rule: an engagement gift given in anticipation of marriage. If the marriage does not take place, the donor usually can recover the gift unless the donor broke the engagement without justification. But the courts will not apply the exception when a marriage is called off due to the death of one of the engaged parties.

Acceptance The final requirement of a valid gift is acceptance by the donee. In most instances, of course, the donee will accept the gift gratefully. Accordingly, the law usually presumes that the donee has accepted. But certain circumstances may render acceptance objectionable, such as when a gift would impose a burden upon the donee. In such cases, the law will not require the recipient to accept an unwanted gift. For example, a donee may prudently reject a gift of an elephant or a wrecked car in need of extensive repairs.

O'Fallon v. O'Fallon

Supreme Court of Arkansas, 2000
341 Ark. 138, 14 S.W.3d 506
http://caselaw.lp.findlaw.com/scripts/getcase.pl?court=ar&vol=supreme/2000a/20000420/99-806&invol=2

FACTS Barney Laron O'Fallon died intestate (without a will) on May 3, 1997, and was survived by three children. His oldest son, William Martin O'Fallon, was appointed administrator of the estate and, pursuant to the probate court's order, proceeded to collect the assets of the estate. One of those assets was a 1996 Chevrolet Camaro automobile that had been purchased by the decedent two weeks prior to his death and delivered to his seventeen-year-old son, Ronnie O'Fallon. After the administrator of the estate took possession of the vehicle, Ronnie O'Fallon filed a motion in the probate court for return of the property. He alleged that the "vehicle was intended to be a gift to [him] and from and after the purchase of the vehicle the Decedent never had possession of same." The administrator denied that the decedent had made a gift of the 1996 Chevrolet Camaro to Ronnie O'Fallon. After a hearing, the probate court found "by clear and convincing evidence" that the vehicle was a gift from the decedent to Ronnie. Subsequently, the Arkansas Supreme Court reversed and remanded because the probate court was without jurisdiction to adjudicate Ronnie O'Fallon's claim to the car as an alleged donee of a gift made prior to the decedent's death and held that the appropriate jurisdiction for the matter was chancery court. Ronnie O'Fallon then asked the chancery court to enter judgment based upon the record of the probate court, where the matter had been fully tried before the same judge. The chancellor granted the motion, finding that the 1996 Chevrolet Camaro purchased by the decedent prior to his death was a gift to Ronnie O'Fallon. From that order, the administrator again appealed.

DECISION Judgment affirmed.

OPINION Imber, J. For his first point on appeal, the administrator challenges the chancellor's finding that the decedent made an *inter vivos* gift of the vehicle to Ronnie O'Fallon. Our law determining a valid *inter vivos* gift is clear and well established. We have stated that a valid *inter vivos* gift is effective when the following requirements are proven by clear and convincing evidence: (1) the donor was of sound mind; (2) an actual delivery of the property took place; (3) the donor clearly intended to make an immediate, present, and final gift; (4) the donor unconditionally released all future dominion and control over the property; and (5) the donee accepted the gift. [Citation.]

In the case at hand, it is undisputed on appeal that the donor, Barney O'Fallon, was of sound mind, that there was actual delivery, and that the donee, Ronnie O'Fallon, accepted the car. The administrator's argument focuses instead on the evidence that pertains to the other two requirements for a valid *inter vivos* gift; that is, whether Barney O'Fallon intended to make the automobile a gift and whether he relinquished dominion and control over the automobile.

The administrator first points out that Barney O'Fallon retained title to the automobile. We have held, however, that the intent of the donor can negate the fact that actual title was not transferred. [Citation.] Here, Ronnie O'Fallon's mother, Linda Ngar, testified that Barney O'Fallon told her he "was going to buy" the car for Ronnie O'Fallon. Later, he told her that he "had bought" the car for Ronnie. Similar testimony was elicited from Mike Gorman, a loan officer with the Potlatch Credit Union where Barney O'Fallon applied for a loan to purchase the automobile. According to Mr. Gorman, Mr. O'Fallon told him that he was buying the car for his son who was getting ready to go to college. It should be noted that Ronnie O'Fallon was a minor at the time of the alleged gift and, therefore, could not acquire title to the automobile. [Citation.] With regard to the fact that Barney O'Fallon insured the vehicle in his name and listed himself as the only driver, Mr. O'Fallon's insurance agent, Sammy Mullis, testified that the children of a named insured may be covered as occasional drivers. Mr. Mullis further confirmed that parents do not always list their children as drivers on the family's car insurance policy because the premium would be significantly higher.

The record reflects additional evidence regarding Mr. O'Fallon's intent to make a gift and to relinquish all dominion and control over the automobile. Ms. Ngar testified that she drove Barney O'Fallon to Warren, where he picked up the 1996 Chevrolet Camaro from the dealership. He then drove it to Gillett, where Ronnie lived with his mother. After Ronnie got home from school, Mr. O'Fallon delivered the car and one set of car keys to Ronnie and gave the other set of keys to Ms. Ngar. According to Ms. Ngar, Mr. O'Fallon did not retain a set of keys to the car. Ronnie then drove his father back to his home in Arkansas City and returned to Gillett that same day in the 1996 Chevrolet Camaro. Ronnie testified that the keys and paperwork on the car were given to him by his father and that the car stayed with him in Gillett. Furthermore, Ronnie stated that his father may have driven the car one other time prior to his death "because of his truck [being] in a bad position, like blocking the driveway or something, to go to the store." * * *

INTERPRETATION Intent and relinquishment of control are necessary for an effective gift.

CRITICAL THINKING QUESTION When should the making of a gift be considered complete? Explain.

Classification Gifts may be either *inter vivos* or *causa mortis*. An *inter vivos* gift is a gift made by a donor during her lifetime. A gift *causa mortis* is a gift made by a donor in contemplation of her imminent death. A gift *causa mortis* is a conditional gift, contingent upon (1) the donor's death as she anticipated, (2) the donor's not revoking the gift prior to her death, and (3) the donee's surviving the donor.

BY WILL OR DESCENT

Title to personal property frequently is acquired by inheritance from a person who dies, either with or without a will. We will discuss this method of acquiring title in Chapter 52.

BY ACCESSION

Many of the practical problems surrounding the right to title to personal property stem from its principal characteristic—movability. The phrase "title by accession" denotes one general solution to the movability problem. **Accession**, in its strict sense, means the right of the owner of property to any increase in it, whether natural or human-made. For example, the owner of a cow acquires title by accession to any calves born to that cow.

BY CONFUSION

The basic problem of confusion is somewhat similar to problems involving title by accession. **Confusion** arises when identical goods belonging to different people become so *commingled* (mixed) that the owners cannot identify their own property. For example, Hereford cattle belonging to Benton become mixed with Hereford cattle belonging to Armstrong, and neither can specifically identify his herd as a result; or grain owned by Courts is combined inseparably with similar grain owned by Reichel. Confusion may result from accident, mistake, willful act, or agreement of the parties. If the goods can be apportioned, each owner who can prove his proportion of the whole is entitled to receive his share. If, however, the confusion results from the willful and wrongful act of one of the parties, he will lose his entire interest if unable to prove his share. Frequently, problems arise not because the owners cannot prove their original interests but because there is not enough left to distribute a full share to each. In such cases, if the confusion was due to mistake, accident, or agreement, each owner will bear the loss in proportion to his share. If the confusion resulted from an intentional and unauthorized act, the wrongdoer will first bear any loss.

BY POSSESSION

Sometimes a person may acquire title to movable personal property by taking possession of it. If the property has been intentionally **abandoned** (intentionally disposed of), a finder is entitled to the property. Moreover, under the general rule, a *finder* is entitled to **lost** (unintentionally left) **property** against everyone except the true *owner*. Suppose Zenner, the owner of an apartment complex, leases a kitchenette apartment to Terrell. One night, Waters, Terrell's mother-in-law, is invited to sleep in the convertible bed in the living room. In the course of preparing the bed, Waters finds an emerald ring caught on the springs under the mattress. She turns the ring over to the police, but diligent inquiry fails to ascertain the true owner. As the finder, Waters will be entitled to the ring.

A different rule applies when the lost property is in the ground. Here, the owner of the land has a claim superior to that of the finder. For example, Josephs employs Kasarda to excavate a lateral sewer. Kasarda uncovers ancient Native American artifacts. Josephs, not Kasarda, has the superior claim.

A further exception to the rule gives the finder first claim against all but the true owner. If property is intentionally placed somewhere by the owner, who then unintentionally leaves it, it becomes **mislaid property**. Most courts hold that if property has been mislaid, not lost, then the owner of the premises, not the finder, has first claim if the true owner is not discovered. This doctrine is frequently invoked in cases involving items found in restaurants or on trains, buses, or airplanes.

Another category of property is the **treasure trove**, which consists of coins or currency concealed by the owner. To be classified as treasure trove, the property must have been hidden or concealed for such a length of time that the owner is probably dead or undiscoverable. Treasure trove belongs to the finder as against all but the true owner.

Many states now have statutes that provide a means of vesting title to lost property in the finder where a prescribed search for the owner proves fruitless.

PROPERTY INSURANCE

Insurance covers a vast range of contracts, each of which distributes risk among a large number of members (the insureds) through an insurance company (the insurer). **Insurance** is a contractual undertaking by the insurer to pay a sum of money or give something of value to the insured or a beneficiary upon the happening of a contingency or fortuitous event that is beyond the control of the contracting parties.

Insurance coverage of one form or another affects every commercial activity. Through insurance, a business can safeguard its tangible assets against almost any form of damage or destruction, whether resulting from natural causes or from the accidental or improper actions of people. Insurance may also protect a business from tort liability, including assertions involving strict liability, negligence, or the intentional acts of its representatives. A business may procure credit insurance to guard against losses from poor credit risks and fidelity bonds to secure it against losses incurred through employee defalcations. If a business hires a famous pianist, it may insure the latter's hands; if it decides to present an outdoor concert, it may insure against the possibility of rain. A business may purchase life insurance on its key executives to reimburse it for financial losses arising from their deaths, or it may purchase such life insurance payable to the families of executives as part of their compensation. An additional, increasingly important use of insurance is to carry out pension commitments arising from agreements with employees. Nonetheless, the remaining sections of this chapter will focus on the insurance of property.

The McCarran-Ferguson Act, enacted by Congress in 1945, left insurance regulation to the states. Statutes in each state regulate domestic insurance companies and establish standards for foreign (out-of-state) insurance companies wishing to do business within the state. Most state legislation relates to the incorporation, licensing, supervision, and liquidation of insurers and to the licensing and supervision of agents and brokers.

Because the insurance relationship arises from a contract of insurance between the insurer and the insured, the law of insurance is a branch of contract law. For this reason, the doctrines of offer and acceptance, consideration, and other rules applicable to contracts in general are equally applicable to insurance contracts. Beyond that, however, insurance law, like the law of sales, bailments, negotiable instruments, or other specialized types of contracts, contains numerous modifications of fundamental contract law, which we will examine in the following sections.

http://
Insurance Information Institute: http://www.iii.org/
AM Best Insurance Rating Service: http://www.ambest.com/
Standard & Poor's Rating Services Insurance Ratings Publications: http://www.insure.com/ratings/sandp.cfm/
McCarran-Ferguson Act: http://www4.law.cornell.edu/uscode/15/1011.html

CPA FIRE AND PROPERTY INSURANCE

Fire and property insurance protects the owner (or another person with an insurable interest, such as a secured creditor or mortgagee) of real or personal property against loss resulting from damage to or destruction of the property by fire and certain related perils. Most fire insurance policies also cover damage caused by lightning, explosion, earthquake, water, wind, rain, collision, and riot.

Fire insurance policies are standardized in the United States, either by statute or by order of the state insurance departments, but their coverage is frequently enlarged through an "endorsement" or "rider" to include other perils or to benefit the insured in ways the provisions in the standard form do not. These policies normally are written for periods of one or three years.

For a general discussion of insurance fraud, see the Consumer Insight later in this chapter.

Practical Advice

Maintain, off the premises, a detailed inventory of your insured property in case you must file a claim for loss.

THE LAW AND YOU

State Attorney Generals

Massachusetts: http://www.ago.state.ma.us ("Buying Life Insurance and Annuities in Massachusetts")

Oregon: http://www.doj.state.or.us/FinFraud/Info2.htm ("Insurance")

Tennessee: http://www.state.tn.us/consumer/brochure.html ("Insurance")

U.S. Government

U.S. Government: http://www.pueblo.gsa.gov/money.htm ("What You Should Know About Buying Life Insurance")

TYPES OF FIRE

Fire insurance policies usually are held to cover damage from "hostile" fires, but they do not cover losses caused by "friendly" fires. A **friendly fire** is one contained in its intended location (for instance, a fire in a fireplace, furnace, or stove). A **hostile fire** is any other fire—all fires outside their intended or usual locales. Thus, a friendly fire becomes hostile if it escapes from its usual confines.

A standard insurance policy therefore will not cover heat or soot damage to a fireplace resulting from its continual use or damage done to personal property accidentally thrown into a stove. Damages caused by smoke, soot, water, and heat from a hostile fire are covered by the standard fire insurance policy, whereas such damages caused by a friendly fire generally are not. Moreover, most policies do not cover recovery for business interruption, unless they contain endorsements specifically covering such loss.

CO-INSURANCE CLAUSES

An arrangement common in property insurance, **co-insurance** is a means of sharing the risk between insurer and insured. For example, under the typical 80 percent co-insurance clause, the insured may recover the full amount of loss, not to exceed the face amount of the policy, provided the policy is for an amount not less than 80 percent of the property's insurable value. If the policy is for less than 80 percent, the insured recovers that proportion of the loss that the amount of the policy bears, up to 80 percent of the insurable value. The formula for recovery is as follows:

$$\text{Recovery} = \frac{\text{Face Value of Policy}}{\text{Fair Market Value of Property} \times \text{Co-insurance \%}} \times \text{Loss}$$

Thus, if the co-insurance percentage is 80 percent, the value of the property is \$100,000, and the policy is for \$80,000 or more, the insured is fully protected against loss not to exceed the policy amount. If the policy amount is less than 80 percent of the property value, however, the insured receives only the proportion of the loss amount as determined in the formula above. Thus, in the above example, if the fire policy was for \$60,000 and the property was 50 percent destroyed, the loss would be \$50,000, of which the insurer would pay \$37,500, which is \$60,000/(\$100,000 × 80%) of \$50,000. On a total loss, the recovery could not, of course, exceed the face amount of the policy. Some states do not favor co-insurance clauses and strictly construe the applicable statute against their validity. In addition, property insurance is not held to be co-insurance unless the policy specifically so provides.

Practical Advice

When purchasing property insurance, determine whether there is a co-insurance clause and, if so, what the co-insurance percentage is.

OTHER INSURANCE CLAUSES

Recovery under property insurance policies typically is also limited by **other insurance clauses**, which generally require that liability be distributed *pro rata* among the various insurers. For example, Alexander insures his \$120,000 building with Hamilton Insurance Co. for \$60,000 and Jefferson Insurance Co. for \$90,000. Alexander's building is partially destroyed by fire, causing Alexander \$20,000 in damages. Alexander will collect two-fifths (\$60,000/\$150,000) of his damages from Hamilton (\$8,000) and three-fifths (\$90,000/\$150,000) from Jefferson (\$12,000).

TYPES OF POLICIES

Property insurance may be either a **valued policy** or an open policy. A valued policy is one providing for the full value of the property, upon which value the insured and the insurer specifically agree at the time the policy is issued. Should total loss occur, the insurer must pay this amount, not the actual or fair market value of the property. By comparison, no agreement in an **open policy** specifies the property's value; instead, the insurer pays the fair market value of the property calculated immediately prior to its loss. Thus, if Latrisha insures her building for $650,000 and at the time of its loss the property is valued at $600,000, under an open policy Latrisha would recover $600,000, while under a valued policy she would recover $650,000. If she insured the building for $700,000, and it was valued at that amount just prior to being blown apart by a tornado, under both types of policies Latrisha would recover $700,000. Insurance of property under a marine policy (insurance covering marine vessels and cargo) is generally considered to be valued, whereas nonmarine property insurance is presumed to be unvalued or open.

CPA NATURE OF INSURANCE CONTRACTS

The basic principles of ***contract*** law apply to insurance policies. Furthermore, because insurance companies engage in a large volume of business over wide areas, they tend to standardize their policies. In some states, standardization is required by statute. This usually means that the insured must accept a given policy or do without the desired insurance.

OFFER AND ACCEPTANCE

No matter how many stories tell of insurance agents aggressively soliciting would-be insureds to take out policies, the applicant usually makes the offer, and the contract is created when the insurance company accepts that offer. The company may condition its acceptance—upon payment of the premium, for instance. It also may write a policy that differs from the application, thereby making a counteroffer that the applicant may or may not choose to accept.

In fire and casualty insurance, agents often have authority to make the insurance effective immediately, when needed, by means of a **binder**. Should a loss occur before the company actually issues a policy, the binder will be effective on the same terms and conditions the policy would have had if it had been issued.

In general, insurance contracts have not been held to be subject to the statute of frauds; thus, courts have held oral contracts for insurance to be enforceable. As a practical matter, however, oral contracts for insurance are very infrequent.

INSURABLE INTEREST

The concept of insurable interest has been developed over many years, primarily to eliminate gambling and to lessen the moral hazard. If a person could obtain an enforceable fire insurance policy on property that he did not own or in which he had no interest, he would be in a position to profit unfairly by the destruction of such property. An **insurable interest** is a relationship a person has with respect to certain property such that the happening of a possible, specific, damage-causing contingency would result in direct loss or injury to her. The purpose of insurance is protection against the risk of loss that would result from such a happening, not the realization of gain or profit.

Whether sole or concurrent, ownership obviously creates an insurable interest in property. Moreover, a right deriving from a contract concerning the property also gives rise to an insurable interest. For instance, shareholders in a closely held corporation have been held to have an insurable interest in the corporation's property to the extent of their interest. Likewise, lessees of property have insurable interests, as do holders of security interests, such as mortgagees or sellers with a purchase money security interest. Most courts have gone beyond the requirement of a legally recognized interest and apply a factual expectancy test. Under this test, the determinative question is whether the insured will obtain a benefit from the continued existence of the property or suffer a loss from its destruction. Thus, an individual who buys and insures a stolen automobile without knowledge that the automobile is stolen has an insurable interest in the automobile.

The insurable interest must exist at the time the property *loss* occurs, although some courts speak in terms of having the insurable interest at the time of insuring *and* at the time of loss. Property insurance policies are freely assignable after, but not before, a loss occurs.

Practical Advice

When purchasing property insurance, make sure you have an insurable interest in the property and terminate the policy once you cease to have an insurable interest.

CONSUMER insight

Insurance Fraud, Supposedly the Victimless Crime—Who Pays? Who Cares?

Here's a little quiz. Which of the following do you think are examples of insurance fraud? Who, if anyone, should be punished?

- A show horse, insured for several hundred thousand dollars, turns out to be a loser on the show-jumping circuit. The horse costs a lot to feed and train, and its selling price would be far less than the amount for which it's currently insured. The owner hires a hit man to electrocute the horse, a death that resembles death from colic. The owner collects the insurance and pays the hit man.
- A bus rear-ends another vehicle in heavy city traffic. Several people standing on the sidewalk see the accident and jump onto the bus. They then claim to have been injured in the accident and get cooperative doctors to diagnose accident-related injuries.
- Several apartment managers, having the power to pick contractors to repair fire- and accident-related damage to their buildings, charge their chosen contractors 10 percent kickbacks for being awarded repair jobs. The contractors, in turn, jack up their charges to cover the cost of the kickbacks.
- An insurance company calculates the pay of an independent insurance adjuster as a percentage of each claim she evaluates. The adjuster persuades policyholders to inflate their claims so that she—and they—can collect more money. She also bribes employees of the insurance company to approve the claims.
- Auto owners in states X and Y insure their cars in nearby state Z, which has lower auto insurance rates. The cars, of course, are kept at the owners' residences in states X and Y and are driven almost exclusively in those states.
- A beachside restaurant goes up in flames one night at the end of summer. No one can prove arson, but the owner has been floundering in cash flow problems.

Now consider one more scenario: Your apartment is broken into, and the thief takes your leather jacket, camera, two bikes, sound system, and about 200 tapes, CDs, and DVDs. You have renter's insurance. You're relieved that you can replace the jacket and music, but the bikes make you stop and think. You're a bike nut. You know your two bikes won't get you more than $750 from the insurance company, but with $1,800 you could buy the racing bike of your dreams. What do you tell the insurance company on your claim form?

Insurance fraud is a huge problem in the United States (and a growing problem in Europe). Fraudulent claims may total as much as $100 billion a year in the United States. Part of the problem is that people use a double standard to judge insurance fraud. We think it's outrageous when a ring of crooks sets small fires in shops (after bribing the owners), makes inflated claims, bribes insurance brokers and adjusters as part of the scheme, and pockets millions. But, ironically, many of us can't see the harm in padding our own claims just a little when we lose property by theft or fire. After all, some faraway, faceless company is the one who pays.

Wrong. We all pay. Ten cents of every dollar spent to purchase property and casualty insurance goes toward covering the cost of fraud. According to one U.S. insurer, fraud is second only to tax evasion in the list of largest economic crimes. Or, as expressed slightly differently by a British insurance investigator, "Insurance fraud is second only to tax fraud as a socially acceptable crime."

Insurers in the United States have stepped up their fight against claims made for staged accidents, padded body shop repair bills, faked bodily injury reports, cars falsely reported stolen, and actual auto theft. Insurers are pressing the battle on two fronts: public opinion and criminal investigation. Of the two, insurance companies believe that public opinion will make the bigger difference—*if* attitudes really can be changed. In an interesting comparison, one insurer notes that drunk driving, considered a trivial offense just a decade ago, is now the target of laws that are increasingly tough *and* increasingly apt to be enforced, as a result of the public campaign waged by Mothers Against Drunk Driving and similar grassroots groups.

Behavioral tip-offs—a person's eagerness for a quick settlement, use of a post office box or hotel as an address, or insistence on pursuing a claim in person rather than by mail or over the phone—lead insurers to investigate claims for fraud. They likewise become suspicious when a surprisingly large number of people submit medical bills from the same doctor or clinic.

However, insurance companies would very much like to win the hearts and minds of the public in fighting insurance fraud—first, so that ordinary law-abiding citizens resist the temptation to cheat (one poll reports that 23 percent of Americans think it's OK to pad a claim) and, second, to encourage the honest majority to report those who do cheat. For example, one insurer advises its policyholders to do the following to fight fraud:

- If you're in an accident, report it to the police. If you witness an accident, report it. Your report can help to determine whether or not a claim is legitimate.
- When you've been in an accident, call your insurer immediately. Obtain a police report and get the other driver's name, address, and license number and his car's registration number. Write down what happened while your memory is fresh.
- Call the police and your insurance company if someone tells you about a doctor or lawyer who will help you to falsify or inflate a claim. Do the same if a body shop says it can inflate its estimate for you.
- Pay attention when you're car shopping: don't buy a car that you suspect may be stolen. You should look at the vehicle identification number to see whether it appears to have been changed. Other red flags: a new paint job, remade keys, and a lack of title or registration.
- Make yourself heard with your state legislators. Ask them to support antifraud legislation and regulations.
- If you suspect fraud, report it. One organization you can call is the National Insurance Crime Bureau. Its toll-free hot line is 1-800-835-6422.

PREMIUMS

Premiums are the consideration paid for an insurance policy. Property insurance policies are written only for periods lasting a few years at most. Long, continued liability on this type of policy is the exception rather than the rule. State law regulates the rates that may be charged for fire and various kinds of casualty insurance. The regulatory authorities are under a duty to require that the companies' rates be reasonable, not unfairly discriminatory, and neither excessively high nor inordinately low.

DEFENSES OF THE INSURER

An insurer may assert the ordinary defenses available to any contract. In addition, the terms of the insurance contract may provide specific defenses, such as the subject matter of the policy, types of perils covered, amount of coverage and period of coverage. Moreover, the insurer may assert the closely related defenses of misrepresentation, breach of warranty, and concealment.

Misrepresentation A representation is a statement made by or on behalf of an applicant for insurance to induce an insurer to enter into a contract. The representation is not a part of the insurance contract, but if the application containing the representation is incorporated by reference into the contract, the representation becomes a warranty. For a **misrepresentation** to have legal consequences, it must be material, the insurer must have relied on it as an inducement to enter into the contract, and it must either have been substantially false when the insured made it or have become so, to the insured's knowledge, before the contract was created. The principal remedy of the insurer on discovery of the material misrepresentation is rescission of the contract. To rescind the contract, the insurer must tender to the insured all premiums that have been paid, unless the misrepresentation was fraudulent. To be effective, rescission must be made as soon as possible after discovery of the misrepresentation.

http:// Pennsylvania Insurance Fraud Prevention Authority: http://www.helpstopfraud.org

Breach of Warranty Warranties are of great importance in insurance contracts because they operate as conditions that must exist before the contract is effective or before the insurer's promise to pay is enforceable. If such is the case, the insurer does not merely have a defense against payment of the policy but can void the policy.

Failure of the condition to exist or to occur relieves the insurer from any obligation to perform its promise. Broadly speaking, a condition is simply an event whose happening or failure to happen either precedes the existence of a legal relationship or terminates one previously existing. Conditions are either precedent or subsequent. For example, payment of the premium is a condition precedent to the enforcement of the insurer's promise, as is the happening of the insured event. A condition subsequent is an operative event the happening of which terminates an existing, matured legal obligation. A provision in a policy to the effect that the insured shall not be liable unless suit is brought within twelve months from the date on which the loss occurs is an example of a condition subsequent.

To be a warranty, the provision must be expressly included in the insurance contract or clearly incorporated by reference. Usually, the policy statements that the insurer considers to be express warranties are characterized by words such as *warrant, on condition that, provided that*, or words of similar import. Other statements important to the risk assumed, such as the address of a building in a case where personal property at a particular location is insured against fire, are sometimes held to be informal warranties.

Generally, it is becoming more difficult for an insurer to avoid liability on a policy when an insured breaches a warranty. For example, a number of states now require a breach to be material before the insurer may avoid liability.

Concealment **Concealment** is the failure of an applicant for insurance to disclose material facts that the insurer does not know. The nondisclosure normally must be fraudulent as well as material to invalidate the policy; the applicant must have had reason to believe the fact was material; and its disclosure must have affected the insurer's acceptance of the risk.

WAIVER AND ESTOPPEL

In certain instances, an insurer who normally would be entitled to deny liability under a policy because of a misrepresentation, breach of condition, or concealment is "estopped" from taking advantage of the defense or else is said to have "waived" the right to rely on it because of other facts.

The terms *waiver* and *estoppel* are used interchangeably, although by definition they are not synonymous. As generally defined, **waiver** is the intentional relinquishment of a known right; and **estoppel** means that a person is prevented by his own conduct from asserting a position inconsistent with such conduct, on which another person has justifiably relied.

Because a corporation such as an insurance company can act only through agents, situations involving waiver invariably are based on an agent's conduct. The higher the agent's position in the company's organization, the more likely his conduct is to bind the company, as an agent acting within the scope of his authority binds his principal. Insureds have the right to rely on representations made by the insurer's employees, and when such representations reasonably induce or cause the insured to change her position or prevent her from causing a condition to occur, the insurer may not assert as a defense the condition's failure to occur, whether the term applied to her situation be waiver or estoppel. Companies have tried with little success to limit the authority of local selling agents to bind the company through waiver or estoppel.

TERMINATION

Most insurance contracts are performed according to their terms, and due ***performance*** terminates the insurer's obligation. Normally, the insurer pays the principal sum due and the contract is thereby performed and discharged.

Cancellation by mutual consent is another way of terminating an insurance contract. Cancellation by the insurer alone means that the insurer remains liable, according to the terms of the policy, until such time as the cancellation is effective. To cancel a policy, the insurer must tender the unearned portion of the premium to the insured.

BAILMENTS AND DOCUMENTS OF TITLE

CPA BAILMENTS

A **bailment** is the relationship created when one person (the **bailor**) transfers the possession of personal property by delivery, without transfer of title, to another (the **bailee**) for the accomplishment of a certain purpose, after which the bailee is to return the property to the bailor or dispose of it according to the bailor's directions. One of the most common occurrences in everyday life, bailments are of great commercial importance. Bailments include the transportation, storage, repair, and rental of goods, which together involve billions of dollars in transactions each year. The following are common examples of bailments: keeping a car in a public garage; leaving a car, a watch, or any other article to be repaired; renting a car or truck; checking a hat or coat at a theater or restaurant; leaving clothes to be laundered; delivering jewelry, stocks, bonds, or other valuables to secure the payment of a debt; storing goods in a warehouse; and shipping goods by public or private transportation.

The benefit of a bailment may, by its terms, accrue solely to the bailor, solely to the bailee, or to both parties. A bailment may be with or without compensation. On these bases, bailments are classified as follows:

1. ***Bailments for the bailor's sole benefit*** include the gratuitous custody of personal property and the gratuitous services that involve custody of personal property, such as repairs or transportation. For example, if Sherry stores, repairs, or transports Tim's goods without compensation, this is a bailment for the sole benefit of the bailor, Tim.
2. ***Bailments for the bailee's sole benefit*** are usually limited to the gratuitous loan of personal property for use by the bailee, as where Tim, without compensation, lends his car, lawn mower, or book to Sherry for her use.
3. ***Bailments for the mutual benefit of both parties*** include ordinary commercial bailments, such as the delivery of goods to a person for repair, jewels to a pawnbroker, or an automobile to a parking lot attendant.

ESSENTIAL ELEMENTS OF A BAILMENT

The basic elements of a bailment are (1) the delivery of possession from a bailor to a bailee; (2) the delivery of personal property, not real property; (3) possession without ownership by the bailee for a determinable period; and (4) an absolute duty on the bailee to return the property to the bailor or to dispose of it according to the bailor's directions.

In most cases, two simple elements determine the existence of a bailment: (1) a separation of ownership and possession of the property (possession without ownership) and (2) a duty on the party in possession to redeliver the identical property to the owner or to dispose of it according to the owner's directions. Since a bailment need not be a contract, consideration is not required. A bailment may be created by operation of law from the facts of a particular situation; thus, a bailment may be ***implied*** or ***constructive***.

Delivery of Possession Possession by a bailee involves (1) the bailee's power to control the personal property and (2) either the bailee's intention to control the property or her awareness that the rightful possessor has given up physical control of it. Thus, for example, when a restaurant customer hangs his hat or coat on a hook furnished for that purpose, the hat or coat is within an area under the restaurant owner's physical control. But the restaurant owner is not a bailee of the hat or coat unless he clearly signifies an intention to exercise control over the hat or coat. On the other hand, when a clerk in a store helps a customer to remove his coat in order to try on a new one, the owner of the store usually is held to have become a bailee of the old coat through the clerk, her employee. Here, the clerk has signified an intention to control the coat by taking it from the customer, and a bailment results.

Personal Property The bailment relationship can exist only with respect to personal property. The delivery of possession of real property by the owner to another is covered by real property law. Bailed property need not be tangible. Intangible property, such as the rights represented by promissory notes, corporate bonds, shares of stock, documents of title, and life insurance policies that are evidenced by written instruments and are thus capable of delivery, may be and frequently are the subject matter of bailments.

Possession for a Determinable Time To establish a bailment relationship, the person receiving possession must be under a duty to return the personal property and must not obtain title to it. If the identical property transferred is to be returned, even in an altered form, the transaction is a bailment; however, if other property of equal value or the money value of the original property may be returned, a transfer of title has occurred, and the transaction is a sale.

Restoration of Possession to the Bailor The bailee is legally obligated to restore the property to the bailor's possession when the bailment period ends. Normally, the bailee is required to return the identical goods bailed, although their condition may be changed because of the work that the bailee was required to perform on them. An exception to this rule concerns **fungible goods**, such as grain, which, for all practical purposes, consist of particles that are the equivalent of every other particle and are expected to be mingled with other like goods during a bailment. Given such goods, a bailee obviously cannot be required to return the identical goods bailed. His obligation is simply to return goods of the same quality and quantity.

A bailee has a duty to return the property to the right person. Her mistake in delivering property to the wrong person does not excuse her, even when the bailor's negligence induces the mistake. A bailee who, through mistake or intention, *misdelivers* the property to a third person who has no right to its possession is guilty of conversion and is liable to the bailor.

RIGHTS AND DUTIES OF BAILOR AND BAILEE

The bailment relationship creates rights and duties on the part of the bailor and the bailee. The bailee is under a duty to exercise due care for the safety of the property and to return it to the right person; conversely, the bailee has the exclusive right to possess the property for the term of the bailment. In addition, depending on the nature of the transaction, a bailee may have the right to limit his liability, as well as to receive compensation and reimbursement of expenses. The bailor, in turn, has certain duties with respect to the condition of the bailed goods.

Bailee's Duty to Exercise Due Care The bailee must exercise due care not to permit injury to or destruction of the property by the bailee or by third parties. The degree of care depends on the nature of the bailment relationship and the character of the property. In the context of a **commercial bailment**, from which the parties derive a mutual benefit, the law requires the bailee to exercise the care that a reasonably prudent person would exercise under the same circumstances. When the bailment benefits the bailee alone (Tim's borrowing Michael's truck without payment would be an example), the law requires more-than-reasonable care of the bailee. On the other hand, where the bailee accepts the property for the bailor's sole benefit, the law requires a lesser degree of care. Nevertheless, the amount of care required to satisfy any of the standards will vary with the character of the property.

When the property is lost, damaged, or destroyed while in the bailee's possession, it is often impossible for the bailor to obtain enough information to show that the loss or damage was due to the bailee's failure to exercise required care. The law aids the bailor in this respect by *presuming* that the bailee was at fault. The bailor is merely required to show that certain property was delivered by way of bailment and that the bailee either has failed to return it or has returned it in a damaged condition. The burden is then on the bailee to prove that he exercised the degree of care required.

Hadfield v. Gilchrist

Court of Appeals of South Carolina, 2000
343 S.C. 88, 538 S.E.2d 268
http://caselaw.lp.findlaw.com/scripts/getcase.pl?court=sc&vol=20001115165132.CEDE8&invol=1

FACTS Sam Gilchrist owns a motor vehicle towing service and maintains a storage facility for the retention of the towed vehicles. Gilchrist operates under a license issued by the city of Charleston.

Mark Hadfield, a medical student at Medical University of South Carolina (MUSC), went to retrieve his 1988 Lincoln Continental from the parking spot where his wife parked the vehicle. The parking spot, located near MUSC, was on private property owned by Allen Saffer. Hadfield's wife parked the vehicle on Saffer's property without Saffer's permission. The vehicle was not in the parking spot when Hadfield arrived because Saffer had called Gilchrist to have the vehicle removed.

Gilchrist towed Hadfield's car to his storage facility. Gilchrist maintained a chain link fence around the storage area and had an employee on the lot around the clock. The employees' duties included periodically leaving the office to check on the storage area, which was some distance away from the office.

Hadfield called to retrieve his vehicle but was informed he would have to wait until the next morning and pay towing and storage fees. Upon Hadfield's arrival to pick up his car the following morning, he discovered the vehicle had been extensively vandalized. The vandals stole the radio/compact disc player, smashed windows, and pulled many electrical wires out of the dashboard. The vehicle depended heavily upon computers and never functioned properly after the incident. The vandals entered the storage area by cutting a hole in the fence. They vandalized between six and eight vehicles on the lot that night.

Hadfield's attempts to persuade Gilchrist to pay for the damages were futile. Hadfield secured estimates for the damage to the automobile at $4,021.43. After more than sixty days elapsed, Hadfield sold the vehicle for $1,000. The magistrate found Gilchrist liable for the damages as a bailee and entered judgment in favor of Hadfield for $4,035. Gilchrist appealed to the Circuit Court, which affirmed the decision of the magistrate.

DECISION The decision of the magistrate is affirmed.

OPINION Anderson, J.

I. Bailments

A bailment is created by the delivery of personal property by one person to another in trust for a specific purpose, pursuant to an express or implied contract to fulfill that trust. [Citations.]

Bailments are generally classified as being for (1) the sole benefit of the bailor; (2) the sole benefit of the bailee; or (3) the mutual benefit of both. [Citation.] Bailments which benefit only one of the parties, the first and second classifications, are often described as gratuitous. [Citation.]

A. Gratuitous Bailment

"A gratuitous bailment is, by definition, one in which the transfer of possession or use of the bailed property is without compensation." [Citation.] For instance, a gratuitous bailment arises if the bailment is undertaken as a personal favor or is involuntary. [Citations.]

A "gratuitous bailee" acts without expectation of reward or compensation. [Citation.] To show the bailment was for the sole benefit of the bailor, the bailee must establish that it was not expecting compensation. * * *

B. Bailment for Mutual Benefit

By contrast, a bailment for the mutual benefit of the parties arises when one party takes the personal property of another into his or her care or custody in exchange for payment or other benefit. [Citations.]

C. Constructive Bailment

Although a bailment is ordinarily created by the agreement of the parties, the agreement of the parties may be implied or constructive, and the bailment may arise by operation of law. [Citation.] Such a constructive bailment arises when one person has lawfully acquired possession of another's personal property, other than by virtue of a bailment contract, and holds it under such circumstances that the law imposes on the recipient of the property the obligation to keep it safely and redeliver it to the owner. [Citations.] A constructive bailment may occur even in the absence of the voluntary delivery and acceptance of the property which is usually necessary to create a bailment relationship.

Gilchrist argues he towed the vehicle pursuant to the Charleston Municipal Ordinances, and the ordinances are for the sole benefit of the vehicle owners. Accordingly, he contends, the relationship created is a gratuitous bailment. We disagree. * * *

Clearly, the [applicable Charleston] ordinances provide for the payment to the city or its agent, the towing service, for the costs of towing and storage. Gilchrist charged Hadfield towing and storage fees.

The vehicle owned by Hadfield was plucked by Gilchrist from the private property of Saffer. Gilchrist acted pursuant to and by virtue of the licensing authority under the city ordinance. Quintessentially, the factual scenario encapsulated in this case is a paradigm of a "constructive bailment." We conclude a constructive bailment, for the mutual benefit of Hadfield and Gilchrist, was created.

II. Bailment Action/Nature of Theory

Although contractual in nature, and involving the conveyance of personal property, an action for breach of the duty of care by a bailor sounds in tort. [Citations.] Concomitantly, after finding a bailment for mutual benefit exists in this case, we must determine whether Hadfield is entitled to damages, relying on the application of tort principles rather than contract principles.

III. Bailee's Degree of Care/Burden of Proof

The degree of care required of a bailee for mutual benefit is defined as ordinary care, or due care, or the degree of care which would be exercised by a person of ordinary care in the protection of his own property. [Citations.]

In a bailment action alleging a breach of the duty of care, the bailor is entitled to be compensated for all losses that are the natural consequence and proximate result of the bailee's negligence. [Citation.] * * * The Supreme Court, in [citation], discussed a bailee's liability under a bailment for mutual benefit:

> Under the decided cases in this State, liability of a bailee under a bailment for mutual benefit arises upon a showing that (1) the goods were delivered to the bailee in good condition, (2) they were lost or returned in a damaged condition, and (3) the loss or damage to the goods was due to the failure of the bailee to exercise ordinary care in the safekeeping of the property. The burden of proof in such cases, in the first instance, rests upon the bailor to make out a prima face case. This has been done when the bailor proves that he delivered the goods to the bailee in good condition and their loss or return in a damaged condition. When the bailor has so proven, the burden is then shifted to the bailee to show that he has used ordinary care in the storage and safekeeping of the property. [Citations.]

[Citation.]

* * *

Hadfield testified before the magistrate regarding the "nice" condition of the vehicle prior to being towed, and the damage to his vehicle, and the other vehicles on the lot. In addition, he introduced photographs depicting the damage. Thus, Hadfield made out his *prima facie* case * * *. The burden then shifted to Gilchrist to show that he used ordinary care in protecting the vehicle while in his care.

Gilchrist impounded the cars in a storage lot surrounded by a chain link fence. There was an individual on the clock at all times. The person on duty spent time in the office and only visited the storage lot to check on it. The vandal cut a hole in the fence and broke into six to eight cars on the night in question. The fact the guard was not on duty at the impound lot and, considering the only other security for the vehicles was the chain link fence, the magistrate and Circuit Court judge could have concluded Gilchrist failed to exercise ordinary care. * * *

INTERPRETATION A bailment for mutual benefit confers a responsibility upon the bailee to exercise due care in protection of the property.

ETHICAL QUESTION Was Gilchrist negligent in its care of the automobiles on his lot?

CRITICAL THINKING QUESTION Would Hadfield have taken any better care of his car if it had been parked in his driveway at home? Why is Gilchrist held to a higher standard of care?

Bailee's Absolute Liability to Return Property As we discussed earlier, the bailee is free from liability if she exercised the degree of care required of her under the particular bailment while the property was within her control. This general rule has certain important exceptions that impose an absolute duty on the bailee to return the property undamaged to the proper person.

When the bailee has an obligation by express agreement with the bailor or by custom to insure the property against certain risks but fails to do so, and the property is destroyed or damaged through such risks, she is liable for the damage or nondelivery, even if she has exercised due care.

When the bailee uses the bailed property in a manner not authorized by the bailor or by the character of the bailment, and during the course of such use the property is damaged or destroyed, without fault on the bailee's part, the bailee is nonetheless absolutely (strictly) liable for the damage or destruction. The wrongful use by the bailee automatically terminates her lawful possession: she becomes a trespasser as to the property and, as such, is absolutely liable for whatever harm befalls it.

Practical Advice

As a bailee, exercise appropriate care to protect the safety of the property and to return it to its true owner.

Bailee's Right to Limit Liability Certain bailees—namely common carriers, public warehousers, and innkeepers—may limit their liability for breach of their duties to the bailor only as provided by statute. Other bailees, however, may vary their duties and liabilities by contract with the bailor. When liability may be limited by contract, the law requires that any such limitation be properly brought to the bailor's attention before he bails the property. This is especially true in the case of "professional bailees," such as repair garages, who make it their business to act as bailees and who deal with the public on a uniform, rather than on an individual, basis. Thus, a variation or limitation in writing, contained, for example, in a claim check or stub given to the bailor or posted on the walls of the bailee's place of business, ordinarily will *not* bind the bailor unless the bailee (a) draws the bailor's attention to the writing, (b) informs the bailor that it contains a limitation or variation of liability, and (c) the limitation is not the result of unequal bargaining power. Some states do not permit professional bailees (who commonly include warehousers, garagers, and parking lot owners) to disclaim liability for their own negligence.

> **Practical Advice**
>
> When dealing with bailees, be alert as to whether they are attempting to limit their liability, and if they are, carefully consider whether you are comfortable with the limitations.

Bailee's Right to Compensation A bailee who by express or implied agreement undertakes to perform work on or render services in connection with the bailed goods is entitled to reasonable compensation for those services or that work. In most cases, the agreement between bailor and bailee fixes the amount of compensation and provides how it shall be paid. In the absence of a contrary agreement, the compensation is payable when the bailee completes the work or performs the services. If, after such completion or performance but before the redelivery of the goods to the bailor, the goods are lost or damaged through no fault of the bailee, the bailee is still entitled to compensation for his work and services.

> **Practical Advice**
>
> If you are a bailee, specify in your contract what your compensation will be.

Most bailees who are entitled to compensation for work and services performed in connection with bailed goods acquire a possessory lien on the goods to secure the payment of such compensation. In most jurisdictions, the bailee has a statutory right to obtain a judicial foreclosure of his lien and a sale of the goods. Many statutes also provide that the bailee does not lose his lien on redelivery of the goods to the bailor, as was the case at common law. Instead, the lien will continue for a specified period after redelivery, if the bailee timely records with the proper authorities an instrument claiming such a lien.

Bailor's Duties In a bailment for the sole benefit of the bailee, the bailor warrants that she is unaware of any defects in the bailed property. In all other instances, the bailor has a duty to warn the bailee of all defects she knows of or should have discovered upon a reasonable inspection of the bailed property. A number of courts have extended strict liability in tort and the implied warranties under Article 2 of the UCC to leases and bailments. Article 2A imposes implied warranties on the lease of goods.

SPECIAL TYPES OF BAILMENTS

Although the general principles that apply to all bailees govern pledgees, warehousers, and safe deposit companies, certain special features about the transactions in which they respectively engage subject them to extraordinary duties of care and liability. Innkeepers and common carriers may also be said to be *extraordinary* bailees, whereas all other bailees are *ordinary* bailees. This distinction is based on the character and extent of the liability of these two classes of bailees for the loss of or injury to bailed goods. As we have seen, an **ordinary bailee** is liable only for the loss or injury that results from his failure to exercise ordinary or reasonable care. The liability of the **extraordinary bailee**, on the other hand, is, in general, *absolute*. Just as an insurer, in general, becomes automatically liable to the insured on the happening of the hazard insured against, regardless of the cause, the extraordinary bailee becomes liable to the bailor for any loss or injury to the goods, regardless of the cause and without regard to the question of his care or negligence. Thus, he insures the safety of the goods.

Pledges A **pledge** is a bailment for security in which the owner gives possession of her personal property to another (the secured party) to secure a debt or the performance of some obligation. The secured party does not have title to the property involved but merely a possessory security interest. Pledges of most types of personal property for security purposes are governed by Article 9 of the Uniform Commercial Code, which we

CONCEPT REVIEW

Duties in a Bailment

Type of Bailment	Bailee's Duty of Care	Bailor's Duty
For sole benefit of bailor	Slight care	To warn of defects of which she knew or should have known
For sole benefit of bailee	Utmost care	To warn of known defects
For mutual benefit	Ordinary care	To warn of defects of which she knew or should have known

discussed in Chapter 38. In most respects, the secured party's duties and liabilities are the same as those of a bailee for compensation.

Warehousing A **warehouser** is a bailee who, for compensation, receives goods to be stored in a warehouse. Under the common law, his duties and liabilities were identical to those of the ordinary bailee for compensation. Today, because a strong public interest affects their activities, warehousers are subject to extensive state and federal regulation. Warehousers must also be distinguished from ordinary bailees in that the receipts they issue for storage have acquired a special status in commerce. Regarded as documents of title, these receipts are governed by Article 7 of the Uniform Commercial Code. (We will discuss documents of title later in this chapter.)

Safe Deposit Boxes A majority of states hold that a person who rents a safe deposit box from a bank enters into a bailment relationship. As this constitutes a bailment for the parties' mutual benefit, the bailee bank owes the customer the duty to act with ordinary due care and is liable only if negligent.

Carriers of Goods In the broadest sense, anyone who transports goods from one place to another, either gratuitously or for compensation, is a **carrier**. Carriers are classified primarily as common carriers and private carriers. A **common carrier** offers its services and facilities to the public on terms and under circumstances indicating that the offering is made to all persons. Stated somewhat differently, the criteria that define common carriers are as follows: (1) the carriage must be part of its business; (2) the carriage must be for remuneration; and (3) the carrier must represent to the general public that it is willing to serve the public in the transportation of property. Common carriers of goods include railroad, steamship, aircraft, public trucking, and pipeline companies. In contrast, a **private** or **contract carrier** is one who carries the goods of another on isolated occasions or who serves a limited number of customers under individual contracts without offering the same or similar contracts to the public at large.

The person who delivers goods to a carrier for shipment is known as the **consignor** or shipper. The person to whom the carrier is to deliver the goods is known as the **consignee**. The instrument containing the terms of the contract of transportation, which the carrier issues to the shipper, is called a ***bill of lading*** (discussed later in this chapter).

A common carrier is under a duty to serve the public to the limits of its capacity and, within those limits, to accept for carriage goods of the kind that it normally transports. A private carrier, by comparison, has no duty to accept goods for carriage, except where it agrees by contract to do so. Whether common or private, the carrier is under an absolute duty to deliver the goods to the person to whom the shipper has consigned them.

A private carrier, in the absence of special contract terms, is liable as a bailee for the goods it undertakes to carry. The liability of a common carrier, on the other hand, approaches that of an insurer of the safety of the goods, except when loss or damage is caused by an act of God, an act of a public enemy, the acts or fault of the shipper, the inherent nature of or a defect in the goods, or an act of public authority. The carrier, however, is permitted, through its contract with the shipper, to limit its liability, provided the carrier gives the shipper notice of this limitation and the opportunity to declare a higher value for the goods.

Innkeepers At common law, **innkeepers** (today better known as hotel and motel owners or operators) are held to the same ***strict*** or ***absolute liability*** for their guests' belongings as are common carriers for the goods they carry. This rule of strict liability applies only to those who furnish lodging to the public for compensation as a regular business and extends only to the belongings of lodgers who are guests. Today, in almost all jurisdictions, case law and statute have substantially modified the innkeeper's strict liability under common law.

CPA DOCUMENTS OF TITLE

A **document of title** is a warehouse receipt, bill of lading, or other document evidencing a right to receive, hold, and dispose of the document *and* the goods it covers. To be a document of title, a document must be issued by or addressed to a bailee and must cover goods in the bailee's possession that are either identified or are fungible portions of an identified mass.

Briefly, a document of title symbolizes ownership of the goods it describes. Because of the document's legal characteristics, its ownership is equivalent to the ownership or control of the goods it represents, without the necessity of actual or physical possession of the goods. Likewise, its transfer transfers the ownership or control of the goods without necessitating the physical transfer of the goods themselves. For these reasons, documents of title are a convenient means of handling the billions of dollars' worth of goods that are transported by carriers or are stored with warehousers. Documents of title also facilitate the transfer of title to goods and the creation of a security interest in goods. Article 7 of the UCC governs documents of title.

http:// UCC Article 7: http://www.law.cornell.edu/ucc/7/overview.html

TYPES OF DOCUMENTS OF TITLE

Warehouse Receipts A warehouse receipt is a receipt issued by a person engaged in the business of storing goods for hire. A warehouser is liable for damages for loss or injury to the goods caused by his failure to exercise such care in regard to them as a reasonably careful person would exercise under the circumstances. The warehouser must deliver the goods to the person entitled to receive them under the terms of the warehouse receipt. Though a warehouser may limit his liability through a provision in the warehouse receipt fixing a specific maximum liability per article or item or unit of weight, this limitation does not apply when a warehouser converts goods to his own use.

> **Practical Advice**
>
> When dealing with warehousers, be alert as to whether they are attempting to limit their liability, and if they are, carefully consider whether you are comfortable with the limitations.

To enforce the payment of her charges and necessary expenses in connection with keeping and handling the goods, a warehouser has a lien on the goods that enables her to sell them at public or private sale after notice and to apply the net proceeds of the sale to the amount of her charges. The Code, moreover, provides the warehouser a definite procedure for enforcing her lien against the goods stored and in her possession.

Bills of Lading A **bill of lading** is a document issued by a carrier on receipt of goods for *transportation*. It serves a threefold function: (1) as a receipt for the goods, (2) as evidence of the contract of carriage, and (3) as a document of title. A bill of lading is negotiable if, by its terms, the goods are deliverable to bearer or to the order of a named person. Any other document is nonnegotiable.

Under the Code, bills of lading may be issued not only by common carriers but also by contract carriers, freight forwarders, or any person engaged in the business of transporting or forwarding goods.

The carrier must deliver the goods to the person entitled to receive them under the terms of the bill of lading. Common carriers are extraordinary bailees under the law and are subject to greater liability than are ordinary bailees, such as warehousers.

The Code allows a carrier to limit its liability by contract in all cases where its rates depend on the value of the goods and the carrier allows the shipper an opportunity to declare a higher value. The limitation does not apply, however, when the carrier converts goods to its own use.

> **Practical Advice**
>
> When dealing with common carriers, be alert as to whether they are attempting to limit their liability, and if they are, carefully consider whether you are comfortable with the limitations.

On goods in its possession that are covered by a bill of lading, the carrier has a lien for the charges and expenses necessary for its preservation of such goods. Against a purchaser for value of a negotiable bill of lading, this lien is limited to charges stated in the bill or in the applicable published tariff or, if no charges are so stated, to a reasonable charge.

The carrier may enforce its lien by public or private sale of the goods after notice to all persons known by the carrier to claim an interest in them. The sale must be on terms that are "commercially reasonable," and the carrier must conduct it in a "commercially reasonable manner."

A purchaser in good faith of goods sold to enforce the lien takes free of any rights of persons against whom the lien was valid, even if the enforcement of the lien does not comply with Code requirements. This rule applies both to carrier's and to warehouser's liens.

Ethical Dilemma

Who Is Responsible for the Operation of Rental Property?

FACTS Bobby Jones, a schoolteacher from a suburb of Atlanta, rents a fourteen-foot aluminum boat for the three-day Memorial Day weekend from Riverside Canoe and Boat Rentals on the Chattahoochee River. The manager of boat rentals gives Jones general instructions concerning the use of the craft and provides him with a booklet entitled "Boating Safety Rules." The manager also follows the routine procedure of examining the fuel line of the boat and starting the motor to ensure its serviceability.

On Memorial Day, while Jones is operating the boat on the Chattahoochee River, the motor stalls, forcing Jones to row the boat back to shore. Later that same day, Jones takes six minor children out in the boat to give them a ride on the river. Jones has been drinking beer nonstop since 8 A.M., and at the time of the afternoon boat ride his blood alcohol level is 0.22 percent. Jones recklessly moves into the swift current and heads toward a concrete dam and spillway. When he finally tries to reverse course, the motor stalls again, the boat is swept over the dam, and all of the children drown. Improbably, Jones lives.

SOCIAL, POLICY, AND ETHICAL CONSIDERATIONS

1. Could the boat rental company (and manager) have done more to prevent the accident that resulted in the children's deaths? Should the manager have done more?
2. Much rental property, including boats, cars, and power tools such as mowers and saws, is either potentially or inherently dangerous. What is the responsibility of the owner of such equipment to the renter of it? What, if anything, is the responsibility of the renter to the owner? Should the owner be held strictly liable for the renter's accidents with the property, regardless of fault? Why or why not? Who do you think was at fault in this accident?
3. Jones's neighbors, the Corcorans and Duvals, are the parents of four of the drowned children. Together, in their anger, they consult a lawyer to explore the idea of suing either Jones or Riverside Canoe and Boat Rentals, or both. What cause might their lawyer try to make against Jones? Against Riverside Canoe and Boat Rentals? Do you think they should sue? Why or why not?
4. Are some items of equipment so dangerous that state legislatures should pass laws forbidding their rental? If so, what items?

NEGOTIABILITY OF DOCUMENTS OF TITLE

The concept of negotiability has long been established in law. It is important not only in connection with documents of title but also in connection with commercial paper and investment securities, topics treated in other chapters of this book.

The Code provides that a warehouse receipt, bill of lading, or other document of title is negotiable if, by its terms, the goods are to be delivered to bearer or to the order of a named person or where, in overseas trade, the document runs to a named person or assigns. Any other document is nonnegotiable.

A nonnegotiable document, such as a straight bill of lading or a warehouse receipt under which the goods are deliverable only to a person named in the bill, not to the order of any person or to bearer, may be transferred by assignment but may not be negotiated. Only a negotiable document or instrument may be negotiated.

DUE NEGOTIATION

The Code sets forth the manner in which a negotiable document of title may be negotiated and the requirements of due negotiation. An order negotiable document of title running to the order of a named person is negotiated by her indorsement and delivery. After such indorsement in blank or to bearer, the document may be negotiated by delivery alone. A special indorsement, by which the document is indorsed over to a specified person, requires the indorsement of the special indorsee as well as delivery to accomplish a further negotiation.

Due negotiation, a term peculiar to Article 7, requires not only that the purchaser of the negotiable document take it in good faith, without notice of any adverse claim or defense, and pay value, but also that she take it in the regular course of business or financing, not in settlement or payment of a money obligation (in essence, a holder by due negotiation). Thus, a transfer for value of a negotiable document of title to a nonbanker or to a person not in business, such as a college professor or student, would not be a due negotiation.

Due negotiation creates new rights in the holder of the document. The transferee does not stand in the shoes of his transferor; in other words, the defects and defenses available against the transferor are not available against the new holder. Newly created by the negotiation, his rights are free of such defects and defenses. This enables bankers and businesspersons to extend credit on documents of title without concern about possible adverse claims or the rights of third parties.

The rights of a holder of a negotiable document of title to whom it has been duly negotiated include (1) title to the document; (2) title to the goods; (3) all rights accruing under the law of agency or estoppel, including rights to goods delivered to the bailee after the document was issued; and (4) the issuer's direct obligation to hold or deliver the goods according to the document's terms.

WARRANTIES

A person, other than a collecting bank or other intermediary, who either negotiates or transfers a document of title for value incurs certain warranty obligations, unless otherwise agreed. Such transferor warrants to her immediate purchaser (1) that the document is genuine, (2) that she had no knowledge of any fact that would impair its validity or worth, and (3) that her negotiation or transfer is rightful and fully effective with respect to the title to the document and the goods it represents.

INEFFECTIVE DOCUMENTS OF TITLE

In order for a person to obtain title to goods through the negotiation of a document to him, the goods must have been delivered to the document's issuer by their owner or by either one to whom the owner has delivered the goods or one whom the owner has entrusted with actual or apparent authority to ship, store, or sell them. A warehouser or carrier, however, may deliver goods according to the terms of the document that it has issued or otherwise dispose of the goods as provided in the Code without incurring liability, even if the document did not represent title to the goods. The warehouser or carrier need only have acted in good faith and complied with reasonable commercial standards in both the receipt and delivery or other disposition of the goods. Such a bailee has no liability even though the person from whom the bailee received the goods had no authority to obtain the issuance of the document or to dispose of the goods, and the person to whom it delivered the goods had no authority to receive them.

Thus, a carrier or warehouser who receives goods from a thief or finder and later delivers them to a person to whom the thief or finder ordered them to be delivered is not liable to the true owner of the goods. Even a sale of the goods by the carrier or warehouser to enforce a lien for transportation or storage charges and expenses would not subject it to liability.

CHAPTER SUMMARY

Introduction to Property and Personal Property

Kinds of Property

Definition interest, or group of interests, that is legally protected

Tangible Property physical objects

Intangible Property property that does not exist in a physical form

Real Property land and interests in land

Personal Property all property that is not real property

Fixture personal property so firmly attached to real property that an interest in it arises under real property law

Transfer of Title to Personal Property

Sale transfer of property for consideration (price)

Gift transfer of property without consideration

- *Delivery* includes both manual transfer of the item and constructive delivery (delivery of something that symbolizes control over the item)
- *Intent*
- *Acceptance*
- *Classification*

Will right to property acquired upon death of the owner

Accession right of a property owner to any increase in such property

Confusion intermixing of goods belonging to two or more owners such that they can identify their individual property only as part of a mass of like goods
- If due to mistake, accident, or agreement, loss shared proportionately
- If caused by an intentional or unauthorized act, wrongdoer bears loss

Possession a person may acquire title by taking possession of property
- *Abandoned Property* intentionally disposed of by the owner; the finder is entitled to the property
- *Lost Property* unintentionally left by the owner; the finder is generally entitled to the property
- *Mislaid Property* intentionally placed by the owner but unintentionally left; the owner of the premises is generally entitled to the property
- *Treasure Trove* coins or currency concealed by the owner for such a length of time that the owner is probably dead or undiscoverable; the finder is entitled to the property

Property Insurance

Fire and Property Insurance

General Definition of Insurance contractual arrangement that distributes risk of loss among a large number of members (the insureds) through an insurance company (the insurer)

Coverage of fire and property insurance provides protection against loss due to fire or related perils

Types of Fire
- *Friendly Fire* fire contained in its intended location
- *Hostile Fire* any fire outside its intended or usual location

Co-insurance insurance in which a person insures property for less than its full or stated value and agrees to share the risk of loss

Other Insurance Clauses if multiple insurers are involved, liability is distributed pro rata

Types of Policies
- *Valued Policy* covers full value of property as agreed upon by the parties at the time the policy is issued
- *Open Policy* covers fair market value of property as calculated immediately prior to the loss

Nature of Insurance Contracts

General Contract Law basic principles of contract law apply

Insurable Interest a financial interest or a factual expectancy in someone's property that justifies insuring the property; the interest must exist at the time the property loss occurs

Premiums amount to be paid for an insurance policy

Defenses of the Insurer
- *Misrepresentation* false representation of a material fact made by the insured that is justifiably relied upon by the insurer; enables the insurer to rescind the contract within a specified time
- *Breach of Warranty* the failure of a required condition; generally an insurer may avoid liability for a breach of warranty only if the breach is material
- *Concealment* fraudulent failure of an applicant for insurance to disclose material facts that the insurer does not know; allows the insurer to rescind the contract
- *Waiver* an insurer intentionally relinquishes the right to deny liability
- *Estoppel* an insurer is prevented by its own conduct from asserting a defense

Termination an insurance contract may be terminated by due performance or cancellation

Bailments and Documents of Title

Bailments

Definition the temporary transfer of personal property by one party (the bailor) to another (the bailee)

Classification of Bailments
- *For the Bailor's Sole Benefit*
- *For the Bailee's Sole Benefit*
- *For Mutual Benefit* includes ordinary commercial bailments

Essential Elements
- *Delivery of Possession*
- *Personal Property*
- *Possession, but Not Ownership, for a Determinable Time*
- *Restoration of Possession to the Bailor*

Rights and Duties
- *Bailee's Duty to Exercise Due Care* the bailee must exercise reasonable care to protect the safety of the property and to return it to the proper person
- *Bailee's Absolute Liability* occurs when (1) the parties so agree; (2) the custom of the industry requires the bailee to insure the property against the risk in question, but he fails to do so; or (3) the bailee uses the bailed property in an unauthorized manner
- *Bailee's Right to Limit Liability* certain bailees are not permitted to limit their liability for breach of their duties, except as provided by statute
- *Bailee's Right to Compensation* entitled to reasonable compensation for work or services performed on the bailed goods
- *Bailor's Duties* in bailment for sole benefit of bailee, the bailor warrants that she is unaware of any defects; in all other bailments, the bailor has a duty to warn of all known defects and all defects she should discover upon a reasonable inspection

Special Types
- *Pledge* security interest by possession
- *Warehouser* storer of goods for compensation; warehouser must exercise reasonable care to protect the safety of the stored goods and to deliver them to the proper person
- *Carrier of Goods* transporter of goods; a common carrier is an extraordinary bailee, and a private carrier is an ordinary bailee
- *Innkeeper* hotel or motel operator; is an extraordinary bailee except as limited by statute or case law

Documents of Title

Definition an instrument evidencing ownership of the document and the goods it covers

Types
- *Warehouse Receipt* receipt issued by person storing goods
- *Bill of Lading* document issued to the shipper by the carrier (1) as a receipt for the goods, (2) as evidence of their carriage contract, and (3) as a document of title

Negotiability a document of title is negotiable if, by its terms, the goods are to be delivered to bearer or to the order of a named person

Due Negotiation transfer of a negotiable document in the regular course of business to a holder, who takes in good faith, for value, and without notice of any defense or claim

Warranties a person who negotiates or transfers a document of title for value, other than a collecting bank or other intermediary, incurs certain warranty obligations unless otherwise agreed

Ineffective Documents in order for a person to obtain title to goods by negotiation of a document, the goods must have been delivered to the issuer of the document by their owner or by one to whom the owner has entrusted actual or apparent authority

QUESTIONS

1. In January, Roger Burke loaned his favorite nephew, Jimmy White, his valuable Picasso painting. Knowing that Jimmy would celebrate his twenty-first birthday on May 15, Burke sent a letter to Jimmy on April 14 stating:

   Dear Jimmy,
   Tomorrow I leave on my annual trip to Europe, and I want to make you a fitting birthday gift, which I do by sending you my enclosed promissory note. Also I want you to keep the Picasso that I loaned you last January, and you may now consider it yours. Happy birthday!

   Affectionately,
   /s/ Uncle Roger

   The negotiable promissory note for $5,000 sent with the letter was signed by Roger Burke, payable to Jimmy White or bearer, and dated May 15. On May 21, Burke was killed in an automobile accident while motoring in France.

   First Bank was appointed administrator of Burke's estate. Jimmy presented the note to the administrator and demanded payment, which was refused. Jimmy brought an action against First Bank as administrator, seeking recovery on the note. The administrator in turn brought an action against Jimmy, seeking the return of the Picasso.
   a. What decision in the action on the note?
   b. What decision in the action to recover the painting?

2. Several years ago, Pierce purchased a tract of land on which stood an old, vacant house. Recently, Pierce employed Fried, a carpenter, to repair and remodel the house. While Fried was tearing out a partition to enlarge one of the rooms, he found a metal box hidden in the wall. After breaking open the box and discovering that it contained $2,000 in gold and silver coins and old-style bills, Fried took the box and its contents to Pierce and told her where he had found it. When Fried handed the box and the money over to Pierce, he said, "If you do not find the owner, I claim the money." Pierce placed the money in an envelope and deposited it in her safe deposit box, where it presently remains. No one has ever claimed the money, but Pierce refuses to give it to Fried.

   Will Fried be able to recover the money from Pierce? Why?

3. Gable, the owner of a lumber company, was cutting trees over the boundary line between his property and property owned by Lane. Although he realized he had crossed onto Lane's property, Gable continued to cut trees of the same kind as those he had cut on his own land. While on Lane's property, he found a diamond ring on the ground, which he took home. All of the timber Gable cut that day was commingled.

   What are Lane's rights, if any (a) in the timber and (b) in the ring?

4. Decide each of the following problems.
   a. A chimney sweep found a jewel and took it to a goldsmith, whose apprentice removed the stone and refused to return it. The chimney sweep sues the goldsmith.
   b. One of several boys walking along a railroad track found an old stocking. All started playing with it until it burst in the hands of its discoverer, revealing several hundred dollars. The original discoverer claims all of the money; the other boys claim it should be divided equally.
   c. A traveling salesperson leaving a store notices a parcel of bank notes on the floor. He picks them up and gives them to the owner of the store to keep for the true

owner. After three years, they have not been reclaimed, and the salesperson sues the storekeeper.

d. Frank is hired to clean the swimming pool at the country club. He finds a diamond ring on the bottom of the pool. The true owner cannot be found. The country club sues Frank for possession of the ring.

e. A customer found a pocketbook lying on a barber's table. He gave it to the barber to hold for the true owner, who failed to appear. The customer sues the barber.

5. Jones had 50 crates of oranges equally divided between grades A, B, and C, grade A being the highest quality and C being the lowest. Smith had 1,000 crates of oranges, about 90 percent of which were grade A, but some of which were grades B and C, the exact percentage of each being unknown. Smith willfully mixed Jones's crates with his own so that it was impossible to identify any particular crate. Jones seized the whole lot. Smith demanded 900 crates of grade A and 50 crates each of grades B and C. Jones refused to give them up unless Smith could identify particular crates. This Smith could not do. Smith brought an action against Jones to recover what he demanded or its value. Judgment for whom, and why?

6. Barnes, the owner and operator of Blackacre, decided to cease farming operations and liquidate his holdings. Barnes sold fifty head of yearling Merino sheep to Billing and then sold Blackacre to Clifton. He executed and delivered to Billing a bill of sale for the sheep and was paid for them. It was understood that Billing would send a truck for the sheep within a few days. At the same time, Barnes executed a warranty deed conveying Blackacre to Clifton. Clifton took possession of the farm and brought along one hundred head of his yearling Merino sheep and turned them into the pasture, not knowing the sheep Barnes sold Billing were still in the pasture. After the sheep were mixed, it was impossible to identify the fifty head belonging to Billing. Explain whether Billing will recover the fifty head of sheep from Clifton.

7. Susan permitted Kevin to take her very old grandfather clock on the basis of Kevin's representations that he was skilled at repairing such clocks and restoring them to their original condition and could do the job for $60. The clock had been badly damaged for years. Kevin immediately sold the clock to Fixit Shop for $30. Fixit Shop was in the business of repairing a large variety of items and also sold used articles. Three months later, Susan was in the Fixit Shop and clearly identified a grandfather clock Fixit Shop had for sale as the one she had given Kevin to repair. Fixit Shop had replaced more than half of the moving parts by having exact duplicates custom-made; the clock's exterior had been restored by a skilled cabinetmaker; and the clock's face had been replaced by a duplicate. All materials belonged to Fixit Shop, and its employees accomplished the work. Fixit Shop asserts it bought the clock in the normal course of business from Kevin, who represented that it belonged to him. The fair market value of the clock in its damaged condition was $30, and the value of repairs made is $220.

Susan sued Fixit Shop for return of the clock. Fixit Shop defended that it then had title to the clock and, in the alternative, that Susan must pay the value of the repairs if she is entitled to regain possession. Who will prevail? Why?

8. Hyer rented a vacant lot from Bateman for a filling station under an oral agreement and placed on it a lightly constructed building bolted to a concrete slab and storage tanks laid on the ground in a shallow excavation. Later, Hyer prepared a lease providing that he might remove the equipment at the termination of the lease. This lease was not executed, having been rejected by Bateman because of a renewal clause it contained, but several years later another lease was prepared, which both Hyer and Bateman did sign. This lease did not mention removal of the equipment. At the termination of this lease, Hyer removed the equipment, and Bateman brought an action to recover possession of the equipment. What judgment?

9. Elvers sold a parcel of real estate, describing it by its legal description and making no mention of any improvements or fixtures on it. The land had upon it a residence, a barn, a rail fence, a stack of hay, some growing corn, and a windmill. The residence had a mirror built into the west wall of the living room and a heating system consisting of a furnace, steam pipes, and coils. In the house were chairs, beds, tables, and other furniture. On the house was a lightning rod. In the basement were screens for the windows. Which of these things passed by the deed and which did not?

10. John Swan rented a safety deposit box at the Tenth Citizens Bank of Emanon, State of X. On December 17, 1997, Swan went to the bank with stock certificates to place in the safety deposit box. After he was admitted to the vault and had placed the stock certificates in the box, Swan found lying on the floor of the vault a $5,000 negotiable bearer bond issued by the State of Wisconsin with coupons attached, due June 30, 2003. Swan picked up the bond and, observing that it did not carry the name of the owner, left the vault and went to the office of the president of the bank. He told the president what had occurred and delivered the bond to the president only after obtaining his promise that, should the owner not call for the bond or become known to the bank by June 30, 1998, the bank would redeliver the bond to Swan. On July 1, 1998, Swan learned that the owner of the bond had not called for it, nor was his identity known to the bank. Swan then asked that the bond be returned to him. The bank refused, stating that it would continue to hold the bond until the owner claimed it. Explain whether Swan will prevail in his action to recover possession of the bond.

11. Lile, an insurance broker who handled all insurance for Tempo Co., purchased a fire policy from Insurance Company insuring Tempo Co.'s factory against fire in the amount of $150,000. Before the policy was delivered to Tempo and while it was still in Lile's hands, Tempo advised Lile to cancel the policy. Prior to cancellation, however, Tempo suffered a loss. Tempo now makes a claim against

Insurance Company on the policy. The premium had been billed to Lile but was unpaid at the time of loss. In an action by Tempo Co. against Insurance Company, what judgment?

12. On July 15, Adler purchased in Chicago a Buick sedan, intending to drive it that day to St. Louis, Missouri. He telephoned a friend, Maruchek, who was in the insurance business, and told him that he wanted liability insurance on the automobile, limited in amount to $50,000 for injuries to one person and to $100,000 for any one accident. Maruchek took the order and told Adler over the telephone that he was covered and that his policy would be written by the Young Insurance Company. Later that same day and before Maruchek had informed the Young Insurance Company of Adler's application, Adler negligently operated the automobile and seriously injured Brown, who brings suit against Adler. Is Adler covered by liability insurance?

13. Graham owns a building having a fair market value of $120,000. She takes out a fire insurance policy from the Bentley Insurance Company for $72,000; the policy contains an 80 percent co-insurance clause. The building is damaged by fire to the extent of $48,000. How much insurance is Graham entitled to collect?

14. Phil was the owner of a herd of twenty highly bred dairy cows. He was a prosperous farmer, but his health was very poor. On the advice of his doctor, Phil decided to winter in Arizona. Before he left, he made an agreement with Freya under which Freya was to keep the cows on Freya's farm through the winter, be paid the sum of $800 by Phil, and return to Phil the twenty cows at the close of the winter. For reasons that Freya thought made good farming sense, Freya sold six of the cows and replaced them with six other cows. After winter was over, Phil returned from Arizona. Is Freya liable for conversion of the original six cows? Why?

15. Hines stored her furniture, including a grand piano, in Arnett's warehouse. Needing more space, Arnett stored Hines's piano in Butler's warehouse next door. As a result of a fire, which occurred without any fault of Arnett or Butler, both warehouses and their contents were destroyed. Is Arnett liable to Hines for the value of her piano and furniture? Explain.

16. Curtis rented a safe deposit box from Reliable Safe Deposit Company, in which he deposited valuable securities and $4,000 in cash. Later, after opening the box and discovering $1,000 missing, Curtis brought an action against Reliable. At the trial, the company showed that its customary procedure was as follows: that there were two keys for each box furnished to each renter; that if a key was lost, the lock was changed; that new keys were provided for each lock each time a box was rented; that there were two clerks in charge of the vault; and that one of the clerks was always present to open the box. Reliable Safe Deposit Company also proved that two keys were given to Curtis at the time he rented his box; that his box could not be opened without the use of one of the keys in his possession; and that the company had issued no other keys to Curtis's box. Explain whether Reliable is obligated to pay Curtis for the missing $1,000.

17. A, B, and C each stored 5,000 bushels of yellow corn in the same bin in X's warehouse. X wrongfully sold 10,000 bushels of this corn to Y. A contends that inasmuch as his 5,000 bushels of corn were placed in the bin first, the remaining 5,000 bushels belong to him. What are the rights of the parties?

18. a. On April 1, Mary Rich, at the solicitation of Super Fur Company, delivered a $3,000 mink coat to the company at its place of business for storage in its vaults until November 1. On the same day, she paid the company its customary charge of $20 for such storage. After Mary left the store, the general manager of the company, on finding that its storage vaults were already filled to capacity, delivered Mary's coat to Swift Trucking Company for shipment to Fur Storage Company. En route, the truck in which Mary's coat was being transported was badly damaged by fire caused by the driver's negligence, and Mary's coat was totally destroyed. Is Super Fur Company liable to Mary for the value of her coat? Why?
    b. Would your answer be the same if Mary's coat had been safely delivered to Fur Storage Company and had been stolen from the company's storage vaults without negligence on its part? Why?

19. Rich, a club member, left his golf clubs with Bogan, the pro at the Happy Hours Country Club, to be refinished at Bogan's pro shop. The refinisher employed by Bogan suddenly left town, taking Rich's clubs with him. The refinisher had previously been above suspicion, although Bogan had never checked on the man's character references. A valuable sand wedge that Bogan had borrowed from another member, Smith, for his own use in an important tournament was also stolen by the refinisher, as well as several pairs of golf shoes that Bogan had checked for members without charge as an accommodation. The club members concerned each made claims against Bogan for their losses. Can (a) Rich, (b) Smith, and (c) the other members compel Bogan to make good their respective losses?

20. Donna drove an automobile into Terry's garage and requested him to make repairs for which the charge would be $125. Donna, however, never returned to get the automobile. Two months later, Carla saw the automobile in Terry's garage and claimed it as her own, asserting that it had been stolen from her. Terry told Carla that she could have the automobile if she paid for the repairs and storage. One week later, Molly appeared and proved that the automobile was hers, that it had been stolen from her, and that neither Donna nor Carla had any rights in it. Discuss whether Terry is liable for conversion of the automobile.

21. On June 1 Cain delivered his 1994 automobile to Barr, the operator of a repair shop, for necessary repairs. Barr put the car in his lot on Main Street. The lot, which is fenced on all sides except along Main Street, holds one hundred

cars and is unguarded at night, although the police make periodic checks. The lot is well lighted. The cars do not have the keys in them when left out overnight. At some time during the night of June 4, the hood, starter, alternator, and gearshift were stolen from Cain's car. The car remained on the lot, and during the evening of June 5, the transmission was stolen from the car. The cost to replace the parts stolen in the first theft was $900 and in the second theft $800. Did Barr exercise due care in taking care of the automobile?

22. Seton in Phoenix, according to a contract with Rider in New York, ships to Rider goods conforming to the contract and takes from the carrier a shipper's order bill of lading that Seton indorses in blank and forwards by mail to Clemson, his agent in New York, with instructions to deliver the bill of lading to Rider on receipt of payment of the price for the goods. Forest, a thief, steals the bill of lading from Clemson and transfers it for value to Pace, a bona fide purchaser. Before the goods arrive in New York, Rider is petitioned into bankruptcy. What are the rights of the parties?

CASE PROBLEMS

23. Scarola purchased an automobile for value and without knowledge that it was stolen. After he insured the car with Insurance Company of North America (INA) (http://www.cigna.com/), the car was stolen once again. When INA refused to reimburse Scarola for the loss, contending that he did not have an insurable interest in the car, Scarola brought an action. Did Scarola have an insurable interest in the automobile? Why?

24. In 1999, Butler purchased a 1967 Austin-Healy for $3,500. He received an Arizona certificate of title and was unaware that the vehicle had been stolen previously. Two years later, Tucson police seized the automobile and returned it to its lawful owner. Butler was insured against loss of the vehicle by Farmers Insurance Company of Arizona (http://www.farmersinsurance.com/). When Farmers Insurance denied his claim for benefits, Butler brought suit. Farmers Insurance based its refusal to reimburse Butler upon lack of insurable interest. Both parties moved for summary judgment. Decision?

25. Sears (http://www.sears.com) had sold to and installed in the Seven Palms Motor Inn a number of furnishings, including drapes and bedspreads, in connection with the construction of a motel on land Seven Palms owned. Sears did not receive payment in full for the materials and labor and brought suit to recover $8,357.49, with interest, and to establish a mechanic's lien on the motel and land for the unpaid portion of the furnishings. Seven Palms asserted that neither the drapes nor bedspreads were fixtures and that, thus, Sears could not obtain a mechanic's lien on them. Explain whether the drapes and bedspreads are fixtures.

26. While in the examination booth in the safety deposit vault of Old Orchard Bank, Brenice Paset found $6,235 in currency in the seat of a chair that was partially under the table. She notified the bank officials and turned the money over to them. They told her that they would try to locate the owner but that, if they failed to locate the owner within one year, she, Brenice, could have the money. The bank then sent a notice to all of its safety deposit box customers asking if they had lost some property. Though it received no response within a year, the bank still refused to turn over the money, contending that it had to hold the money for the true owner. A state statute governed the rights to lost property. Brenice sought to establish herself as the owner of the money by her compliance with the requirements of the state statute. The bank argued that the money was mislaid and that therefore the statute was not applicable. How should the money be classified? Should the statute govern this situation?

27. David E. Ross, his two brothers, and their families operated and owned the entire stock of five businesses. Ross had three children: Rod, David II, and Betsy. David II and Betsy were not involved in the operation of the companies, but Rod began working for one of the firms, Equitable Life and Casualty Insurance Company, in 1996. Between 1998 and 2002, the elder Ross informed a number of persons of his desire to reward Rod for his work with Equitable Life by giving him stock in addition to the stock he would inherit. He subsequently executed several stock transfers to Rod, representing shares in various family businesses, which were reflected by appropriate entries on the corporate books. Certificates were issued in Rod's name and placed in an envelope identified with the name Rod Ross, but they were kept with the other family stock certificates in an office safe to which Rod did not have access. In all, one-fourth of the stock holdings of David E. Ross were transferred to Rod in this manner. This fact is consistent with the elder Ross's expressed intention that Rod should ultimately receive a total of one-half of the stock upon his father's death. David E. died in April 2002. His will divided the estate equally among the three children and made no reference to prior gifts of stock to Rod. David II and Betsy brought an action contesting the validity of the stock transfers. Are the *inter vivos* gifts of the stock valid? Explain.

28. Mrs. Laval was a patient of Dr. Leopold, a practicing psychiatrist. Dr. Leopold shared an office with two associates practicing in the same field. No receptionist or other employee attended the office. Mrs. Laval placed her coat in the clothes closet in the office reception room. Later, when she returned to retrieve the coat to leave, she found it missing. Is Dr. Leopold liable to Mrs. Laval for the value of her coat? Explain.

29. Mr. Sewall left his car in a parking lot owned by Fitz-Inn Auto Parks, Inc. The lot was approximately 100 by 200 feet in size and had a chain link fence along the rear boundary to separate the lot from a facility of the Massachusetts Bay Transportation Authority. Although the normal entrance and exit were located at the front of the lot, it was also possible to leave by way of small side streets on either side of the lot. Upon entering the lot, the driver would pay the attendant on duty a fee of twenty-five cents to park. The attendant's duties were limited to collecting money from patrons and directing them to parking spaces. Ordinarily, the attendant remained on duty until 11:00 A.M., after which time the lot was left unattended. Furthermore, a patron could remove his car from the lot at any time without interference by any employee of the parking lot.

On the morning of April 15, Sewall entered the lot, paid the twenty-five cent fee, parked his car in a space designated by the attendant, locked it, and took the keys with him. This was a routine he had followed for several years. When he returned to the unattended lot that evening, however, he found that his car was gone, apparently having been stolen by an unidentified third person. Is Fitz-Inn, the owner of the lot, liable for the value of the car? Why?

30. Mrs. Mieske delivered thirty-two 50-foot reels of developed movie film to the Bartell Drug Company to be spliced together into four reels for viewing convenience. She placed the films, which contained irreplaceable pictures of her family's activities over a period of years, into the order in which they were to be spliced and then delivered them to the manager of Bartell. The manager placed a film processing packet on the bag of films and gave Mrs. Mieske a receipt that stated, "We assume no responsibility beyond retail cost of film unless otherwise agreed to in writing." Although the disclaimer was not discussed, Mrs. Mieske's parting words to the store manager were, "Don't lose these. They are my life."

Bartell sent the film to its processing agent, GAF Corporation, which intended to send them to another processing lab for splicing. While at the GAF laboratory, however, the film was accidentally placed in the garbage dumpster and was never recovered. Upon learning of the loss of their film, the Mieskes brought action to recover damages from Bartell and GAF. The defendants argued that their liability was limited to the cost of the unexposed film. Are GAF or Bartell liable to the Mieskes? If so, for how much?

http:// **Internet Exercise** Find information about (a) business insurance, (b) homeowner's insurance, and (c) the ten largest home insurers and their market shares.

CHAPTER 50

Interests in Real Property

Aedificare in tuo proprio solo non licet quod alteri noceat. *To build upon your land what may injure another is not lawful.*
LEGAL MAXIM

Learning Objectives

After reading this chapter you should be able to:

1. Identify and explain the freehold interests: (a) fee simple, (b) qualified fee, (c) life estate, (d) remainder interest, and (e) reversionary interest.
2. Distinguish between a vested and contingent remainder.
3. Explain the primary rights and obligations of landlords and tenants.
4. Identify and explain the various forms of concurrent ownership of real property.
5. Identify and describe the various ways in which an easement may be created.

Interests in real property may be divided into possessory and nonpossessory interests. Possessory interests in real property, called estates, are classified, according to the quantity, nature, and extent of the rights they involve, into two major categories: freehold estates (those existing for an indefinite time or for the life of a person) and estates less than freehold (those that exist for a predetermined time), called leasehold estates. Both freehold estates and leasehold estates are regarded as possessory interests in property. In addition, there are several nonpossessory interests in property, including easements and *profits à prendre*. In addition, a person may have a privilege or license to go on property for a certain purpose. The ownership of interests in property may be held by one individual or concurrently by two or more persons, each of whom is entitled to an undivided interest in the entire property. We will consider all of these topics in this chapter.

CPA FREEHOLD ESTATES

As we just mentioned, a **freehold estate** is a right of ownership of real property for an indefinite time (fee estate) or for the life of a person (life estate). Of all the estates in real property, the most valuable are usually those present estates that combine the enjoyment of immediate possession with ownership at least for life. These estates are either some form of fee estates or estates for life. In addition, either type of estate may be created without immediate right to possession; such an estate is known as a future interest.

FEE ESTATES

Fee estates include the right to immediate possession for an indefinite time and the right to transfer the interest by deed or will. Fee estates include both fee simple and qualified fee estates.

Fee Simple Estate **Fee simple** means that the property is owned absolutely and can be sold or passed on at will. The absolute rights to transfer ownership and to transmit such ownership through inheritance are basic characteristics of a fee simple estate. Fee simple is the most extensive and comprehensive estate in land; all other estates are derived from it.

A fee simple is created by any words that indicate an intent to convey absolute ownership. "To B in fee simple" will accomplish the purpose, as will "to B forever." The general presumption is that a conveyance is intended to convey full and absolute title in the absence of a clear intent to the contrary. The grantor must possess, or have the right to transfer, a fee simple interest in order to transfer such an interest.

Qualified or Base Fee Estate It is possible to convey or will property to a person to enjoy absolutely, *subject* to its being taken away at a later date should a certain event occur. The estate thus created is known as a **qualified fee**, base fee, conditional fee, or fee simple defeasible. For example, Abe may provide in his will that his daughter is to have his house and lot in "fee simple forever so long as she does not use it to sell alcoholic beverages, in which case the house shall revert to Abe's estate." If his daughter dies without using the house to sell alcoholic beverages, the property is transferred to her heirs as if she had owned it absolutely. However, if she uses the house to sell alcoholic beverages, the daughter would lose her title to the land; and it would revert to Abe's heirs.

The holder of a qualified fee interest may transfer the property by deed or will, and the property will pass by intestate succession. All transferees, however, take the property subject to the initial condition imposed upon the interest.

Life Estates

A **life estate** is an ownership right in property for the life of a designated individual; a **remainder** is the ownership estate that takes effect when the prior life estate terminates. For example, a grant or a devise (grant by will) "to Alex for life" creates in Alex an estate that terminates on his death. Such a provision may stand alone, in which case the property will revert to the grantor and his heirs; or, as is more likely, the provision will be followed by a subsequent grant to another party, such as "to Alex for life and then to Mario and his heirs." Alex is the *life tenant*, and Mario generally is described as the *remainderman*. Alex's life, however, need not be the measure of his life estate, as where an estate is granted "to Alex for the life of Bob." On Bob's death, Alex's interest terminates; if Alex dies before Bob, Alex's interest passes to his heirs or as he directs in his will for the remainder of Bob's life.

No particular words are necessary to create a life estate, as long as the words chosen clearly reflect the grantor's intent. Life estates arise most frequently in connection with the creation of trusts, which we will discuss in Chapter 52.

Generally, a life tenant may make reasonable use of the property as long as he does not commit "waste." Any act or omission that permanently injures the realty or unreasonably changes its characteristics or value constitutes waste. For example, the failure to repair a building, the unreasonable cutting of timber, or the neglect of an adequate conservation policy may subject the life tenant to an action by the remainderman to recover damages for waste.

A conveyance by the life tenant passes only her interest. The life tenant and the remainderman may, however, join in a conveyance to pass the entire fee to the property, or the life tenant may terminate her interest by conveying it to the remainderman.

> **Practical Advice**
>
> The use of a life estate with a remainder is a useful way of providing income to one person with the ability to control the distribution of the corpus upon the termination of the life estate.

Future Interests

Not all interests in property carry the right to immediate possession, even though the right and title to the interest are absolute. Thus, where property is conveyed or devised by will "to A during his life and then to B and her heirs," B has a definite, existing *interest* in the property, but she is not entitled to immediate *possession*. This right and similar rights, generically referred to as future interests, are of two principal types: reversions and remainders.

Reversions If Anderson conveys property "to Benson for life" and makes no disposition of the remainder of the estate, Anderson holds the **reversion**—the grantor's right to the property on the death of the life tenant. Thus, Anderson would regain ownership to the property when Benson dies. However, because Anderson has only to await the termination of his grantee's estate before he regains ownership, a reversion in Anderson is also created if he conveys property "to Caldwell for ten years." Reversions may be transferred by deed or will and pass by intestate succession.

A conditional reversionary interest, a **possibility of reverter** exists when property may return to the grantor or his successor in interest because an event on which a fee simple estate was to terminate has occurred. This potential reversion is present in the grant of a base or qualified fee, previously discussed in this chapter. Thus, Karlene has a possibility of reverter if she dedicates property to a public use "so long as it is used as a park" and indicates that if it is not so used, it will revert to her heirs. If, in one hundred years, the city ceases to use the property for a park, Karlene's heirs will be entitled to the property. A possibility of a reverter may pass by will or intestate succession. In some states, it may be transferred by deed.

Remainders A remainder, as we discussed earlier, is an estate in property that, like a reversion, will take effect in possession, if at all, on the termination of a prior estate created by the *same instrument*. Unlike a reversion, a remainder is held by a person other than the grantor or his successors. A grant from Gwen "to Lew for his life and then to Robert and his heirs" creates a remainder in Robert. On the termination of the life estate, Robert will be entitled to possession as remainderman, taking his title not from Lew but from the original grantor, Gwen.

A **vested remainder** is one in which the only contingency to possession by the remainderman is the termination of all preceding estates created by the transferor. When Richard has a remainder in fee, subject only to a life estate in Laura, the only obstacle to the right of immediate possession by Robert or his heirs is Laura's life. Laura's death is sufficient and necessary to place Robert in possession. The law considers this unconditional or vested remainder as a fixed, *present* interest to be enjoyed in the future.

By comparison, a **contingent remainder** is one in which the right to possession is dependent or conditional on the happening of some event *in addition* to the termination of the preceding estates. The contingent remainder may be conditioned on the existence of someone yet to be born or on the happening of an event that may never occur. A provision in a will "to David for life and then to his children, but if he has no children then to Julie" creates contingent remainders both as to the children and as to Julie. Transferable by deed in most states, a contingent remainder is also inheritable, unless limited to termination prior to the death of the remainderman.

CPA LEASEHOLD ESTATES

A lease is both a contract and a grant of an estate in land. It is a contract by which the owner of the land, the **landlord**, grants to another, the **tenant**, an exclusive right to use and possess the land for a definite or ascertainable period or term. The possessory term thus granted is an estate in land called a **leasehold estate**. The landlord retains an interest, or a *reversion*, in the property. A leasehold estate has two principal characteristics: it continues for a definite or ascertainable term and carries with it the tenant's obligation to pay rent to the landlord. Thus, if Linda, the owner of a house and lot, rents both to Ted for a year, Linda, of course, still holds title to the property; but she has sold to Ted the right to occupy it. Ted's right to occupy the property is superior to that of Linda, and as long as Ted occupies the property according to the terms of the lease contract, he has, as a practical matter, exclusive possession against all the world as though he were the actual owner.

The law of leasehold estates has changed considerably over the last few decades. Traditionally, the common law viewed a leasehold estate less as a contract than as a conveyance of the use of land. Today, the landlord-tenant relationship is primarily viewed as a contract and therefore subject to the contract doctrines of unconscionability, implied warranties, and constructive conditions.

Moreover, numerous ordinances and statutes, such as the Uniform Residential Landlord and Tenant Act enacted by at least twenty states, now protect tenants' rights, thereby further modifying the landlord-tenant relationship. The Uniform Act, which was promulgated by the Commission on Uniform State Laws, provides a comprehensive system for regulating the relationship between landlord and tenant under rental agreements for residential purposes. The act does not apply to rental agreements made for commercial, industrial, agricultural or any purpose other than residential.

The act contains detailed requirements regarding the (1) obligations of the landlord, including maintenance of the premises, restrictions on security deposits, methods for providing notices to tenants, and prohibited provisions in rental agreements; (2) rights of the landlord to collect rent, to evict, to enter, and to terminate the lease; (3) obligations of the tenant to pay rent and comply with rules; and (4) rights of the tenant to possess the premises, to terminate the lease, to receive essential services, and to avoid unlawful eviction. Finally, the act provides remedies for noncompliance by either the landlord or tenant.

CREATION AND DURATION

Because leaseholds are created by contract, the usual requirements for contract formation therefore apply. In most jurisdictions, leases for a term longer than a statutorily specified period, generally fixed at either one or three years, must be in writing. A few states require that all leases be in writing.

CONCEPT REVIEW

Freehold Estates

Interest	Complementary Estate	Duration	Transfer by Deed	Transfer by Will or Intestacy
Fee Simple	None	Perpetual	Yes	Yes
Qualified Fee	Possibility of reverter	Until contingency occurs	Yes	Yes
Life Estate	Reversion or remainder	Life of indicated person	Yes	No, unless measuring life is not life tenant's
Reversion	Life estate	Perpetual	Yes	Yes
Possibility of Reverter	Qualified fee	Perpetual if contingency occurs	In some states	Yes
Vested Remainder	Life estate	Perpetual	Yes	Yes
Contingent Remainder	Life estate	Perpetual if contingency occurs	In most states	Yes, unless it is limited such that it terminates before the death of the remainderman

Definite Term A lease for a **definite term** automatically expires at the end of the term. Such a lease is frequently termed an ***estate for years***, even though the duration may be one year or less. No notice to terminate is required.

Periodic Tenancy A **periodic tenancy** is a lease of indefinite duration that continues for successive periods unless terminated by notice to the other party. For example, a lease "to Ted from month to month" or "from year to year" creates a periodic tenancy. Periodic tenancies arise frequently by implication. For example, Laura leases to Ted without stating any term in the lease. This creates a tenancy at will. If Ted pays rent to Laura at the beginning of each month and Laura accepts such payments, most courts would hold that the tenancy at will has been transformed into a tenancy from month to month.

Either party may terminate a periodic tenancy at the expiration of any one period, but only on adequate notice to the other party. If the lease contains no specific agreement, the common law requires six months' notice in tenancies from year to year. However, in most jurisdictions, this period has been shortened by statute to periods ranging between thirty and ninety days in duration. In periodic tenancies involving periods of less than one year, the notice required at common law is one full period in advance; but, again, this may be subject to statutory regulation.

Tenancy at Will A lease containing a provision that either party may terminate at any time creates a **tenancy at will**. A lease that does not specify a duration also creates a tenancy at will. At common law, such tenancies were terminable without any prior notice, but many jurisdictions now have statutes requiring a period of notice before termination, usually thirty days.

Tenancy at Sufferance A **tenancy at sufferance** arises when a tenant fails to vacate the premises when the lease expires and thereby becomes a holdover tenant. Under the common law, the landlord may elect either to dispossess such tenant or to hold her for another term. Until the landlord makes this election, a tenancy at sufferance exists.

> **Practical Advice**
>
> When entering into a lease, specify the duration of the lease and any optional periods of extension.

TRANSFER OF INTERESTS

Both the tenant's possessory interest in the leasehold and the landlord's reversionary interest in the property may be freely transferred in the absence of contractual or statutory prohibition. This general rule is subject to one major exception: the tenancy at will. Any attempt by either party to transfer her interest is usually considered an expression of the intent to terminate the tenancy.

Transfers by Landlord After conveying the leasehold interest, a landlord is left with a reversionary interest in the property plus the right to rent and other benefits acquired under the lease. The landlord may transfer either or both of these interests. The party to whom the reversion is transferred takes the property subject to the tenant's leasehold interest, if the transferee has actual *or* constructive notice of the lease. For example, Linda leases Whiteacre to Tina for five years, and Tina records the lease with the register of deeds. Linda then sells Whiteacre to Arthur. Tina's lease is still valid and enforceable against Arthur, whose right to possession of Whiteacre begins only after the lease expires.

Transfers by Tenant A tenant may dispose of his interest either by (1) assignment or (2) sublease, and in the absence of a lease provision to the contrary the tenant may do both. As a result, most standard leases expressly require the landlord's consent to an assignment or subletting of the premises. However, under the majority view, a covenant against assignment of a lease does not prohibit the tenant from subleasing the premises; conversely, a prohibition against subleasing does not restrict the right to assign the lease.

A tenant who transfers all interest in a leasehold (consequently forfeiting her reversionary rights) has made an **assignment.** The tenant's agreement to pay rent and certain other contractual **covenants** (express promises) pass to and obligate the assignee of the lease as long as the assignee remains in possession of the leasehold estate. Although the assignee is thus bound to pay rent, the original tenant is not relieved of her contractual obligation to do so. If the assignee fails to pay the stipulated rent, the original tenant will have to pay, though she will have a right to be reimbursed by the assignee. Thus, after an assignment of a tenant's interest, both the original tenant and the assignee are liable to the landlord for failure to pay rent.

A **sublease** differs from an assignment in that the tenant transfers less than all her rights in the lease and thereby retains a reversion in the leasehold. For example, T is a tenant under a lease from L that is to terminate on December 31, 2003. If T leases the premises to SL for a shorter period than that covered by her own lease, say, until November 30, 2003, T, in transferring less than her whole interest in the lease, has subleased the premises.

The legal effects of a sublease are entirely different from those of an assignment. In a sublease, the sublessee, SL in the example above, has no obligation to T's landlord, L. SL's obligations run solely to T, the original tenant; and T is not relieved of any of her obligations under the lease. Thus, L has no right of action against T's sublessee, SL, under any covenants contained in the original lease between him and T, because that lease has not been assigned to SL. T, of course, remains liable to L for the rent and for all other covenants in the original lease.

Practical Advice

As the landlord, clearly specify in the lease whether it may be assigned or sublet and, if so, whether your written consent is required.

Figure 50-1
Assignment Compared with Sublease

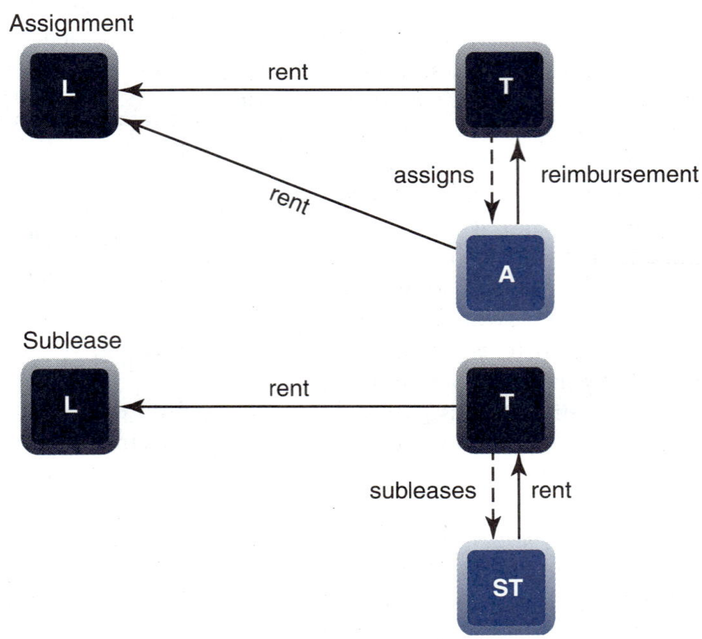

TENANT'S OBLIGATIONS

Although the leasehold estate carries with it only an implied obligation on the part of the tenant to pay reasonable rent, the lease contract almost always contains an express promise or covenant by the tenant to pay rent in specified amounts at specified times. In the absence of a covenant specifying the rent amount and payment times, the rent will be a *reasonable* amount *payable only at the end of the term.*

Most leases provide that if the tenant breaches any of the covenants in the lease, the landlord may declare the lease at an end and regain possession of the premises. The tenant's express undertaking to pay rent thus becomes one of the covenants on which this provision can operate. If a lease contains no such provision, at common law, the tenant's failure to pay rent when due gives the landlord only the right to recover a judgment for the amount of such rent; it does not give him the right to oust the tenant from the premises. In most jurisdictions, however, statutory changes to the common law rule allow the landlord to dispossess the tenant for nonpayment of rent, even if the lease does not provide the landlord with such a right.

Unless the lease specifically provides otherwise, a tenant is under no duty to make any repairs to the leased premises. He is not obliged to repair or restore substantial or extraordinary damage occurring without his fault, nor to repair damage caused by ordinary wear and tear. However, the tenant is obliged to use the premises so that no substantial injury is caused them. The law imposes this duty; it need not be expressly stated in the lease. For example, a tenant who overloads an electrical connection and consequently shorts out a wiring system is liable to the landlord.

Destruction of the Premises When the tenant leases land together with a building, and the building is destroyed by fire or some other chance event, the common law does not relieve him of his obligation to pay rent or permit him to terminate the lease. Most states, however, have statutorily modified the rule to exclude tenants who occupy only a portion of a building and who have no interest in the building as a whole, such as apartment tenants. Most leases contain clauses covering the accidental destruction of the premises.

Eviction When the tenant breaches a covenant in her lease, such as the covenant to pay rent, and the landlord evicts or removes the tenant from the premises according to a specific lease provision or under a statute authorizing him to do so, the lease is terminated. Because breaching the covenant to pay rent does not injure the premises and because the landlord's action in evicting the tenant terminates the lease, the evicted tenant normally is not liable to the landlord for any future rent installments. Most long-term leases, however, contain a survival clause providing that the tenant's eviction for nonpayment of rent will not relieve her of liability for damages equal to the difference between the rent specified in the lease and the rent the landlord is able to obtain when reletting the premises.

Unlike authorized eviction, the landlord's wrongful eviction of the tenant terminates the tenant's obligations under the lease. Moreover, as discussed later, the landlord is liable for breach of the tenant's right of quiet enjoyment.

Abandonment If the tenant wrongfully abandons the premises before the lease term expires and the landlord reenters the premises or relets them to another, a majority of the courts hold that the tenant's obligation to pay rent terminates after such reentry. ("Reenter" in this case means to occupy the premises.) The landlord who desires to hold the tenant to his obligation to pay rent must either leave the premises vacant or have another "survival clause" in the lease that covers this situation.

LANDLORD'S OBLIGATIONS

Under the Fair Housing Act, a landlord cannot discriminate against a tenant with regard to race, color, gender, religion, national origin, or familial status (except under the housing for older persons exception). Nevertheless, unless the lease contains specific provisions, the landlord, under the common law, has few obligations to her tenant. Under the majority rule (the American rule), at the beginning of the lease, the landlord has only to give the tenant the right to possession. In a minority of states (the English rule), she has to give actual possession.

Quiet Enjoyment The landlord may not interfere with the tenant's right to physical possession, use, and enjoyment of the premises. Rather, the landlord is bound to provide the tenant with quiet and peaceful enjoyment, a duty known as the landlord's covenant of **quiet enjoyment**. The landlord breaches this covenant, which arises by implication, whenever he wrongfully evicts the tenant. The law also regards the landlord as having breached this covenant if someone having better title to the property than the landlord evicts the tenant. The landlord is not responsible, however, for the wrongful acts of third parties unless they are done with his assent and under his direction.

Eviction need not be actual. Under the doctrine of **constructive eviction**, a failure by the landlord in any of her obligations under the lease that causes a substantial and lasting injury to the tenant's beneficial enjoyment of the premises is regarded as being, in effect, an eviction of the tenant. Under such circumstances, the courts permit the tenant to abandon the premises and terminate the lease. However, in order to claim that a constructive eviction occurred, the tenant must abandon possession within a reasonable time.

Home Rentals Corp. v. Curtis.

Appellate Court of Illinois, Fifth District, 1992
236 Ill.App.3d 994, 602 N.E.2d 859, 176 Ill. Dec. 913

FACTS In February 1989, Home Rentals agreed to rent a single-family residence to Chris Curtis, Ed Domaracki, Mike Fraser, and Carson Flugstad (tenants), all of whom were students at Southern Illinois University **(http://www.siu.edu/)**. The terms of the written lease stated that the lease was to commence on August 17, 1989, and to expire on August 13, 1990. The tenants were to receive the premises in "good order and repair," rent was to be $740 per month, and a $500 deposit was required. The tenants initially paid $1,980 to cover the deposit and advance rent for the last two months of the lease. Although the house was fine when the tenants signed the lease in February, when they arrived on August 15, it was not. The electricity had not yet been turned on. Roaches had overrun the rooms, and the kitchen was so filthy and so infested by bugs that food could not be stored there. The carpet smelled, and one could see outside through holes in the wall. The bathrooms were unsanitary, no toilets worked, one of the bathtubs did not drain, and an open sewage drain emptied bathroom wastewater onto the basement floor. The tenants notified Home Rentals on the 16th that the place was uninhabitable because of the filth and roaches. Home Rentals responded that the tenants should just clean the place up and that it would reimburse them. Accordingly, the tenants attempted to clean the house, but the roach problem continued even after professional extermination, and Home Rentals did nothing about the plumbing. The tenants were never able to stay in the house. On August 21, the tenants finally sought housing elsewhere. They advised Home Rentals that they would not be living in the house, returned the keys, and reported the condition of the house to the city of Carbondale's Code Enforcement Division. The city notified Home Rentals on August 25, 1989, that it had found numerous city code violations and warned the corporation that the house would be posted "occupancy prohibited" unless all violations were corrected within 72 hours. By August 28, 1989, eleven days after the tenants' lease was to have commenced, Home Rentals had finally remedied all the violations. The city withdrew its threat, but Home Rentals did not rent the house to anyone else. Instead, it sued the tenants for breach of the lease and claimed $6,900 for all twelve months under the lease, less the deposit. The tenants denied the allegations and raised as affirmative defenses breach of the implied warranty of habitability and constructive eviction. Based on the latter theory, they asserted a counterclaim seeking the return of the $500 deposit and the $1,480 they had paid in advance rent. The trial court found for the tenants in the amount of $1,980, and Home Rentals appealed.

DECISION Judgment for the tenants affirmed.

OPINION Harrison, J. A constructive eviction occurs when a landlord has done "something of a grave and permanent character with the intention of depriving the tenant of enjoyment of the premises." [Citation.] Because persons are presumed to intend the natural and probable consequences of their acts, constructive eviction does not require a finding that the landlord had the express intention to compel a tenant to leave the demised premises or to deprive him of their beneficial enjoyment. All that is necessary is that the landlord committed acts or omissions which rendered the leased premises useless to the tenant or deprived the tenant of the possession and enjoyment of the premises, in whole or part, making it necessary for the tenant to move. * * *

At oral argument, counsel for Home Rentals asserted that defendants did what they did simply because "the premises did not meet their expectations." The inference, of course, was that defendants were overly particular and that their expectations were unrealistic. It is scarcely unreasonable, however, for tenants paying $740 per month to expect flushing toilets, sewage-free basements, and kitchens that are not overrun with roaches. These are things that Home Rentals failed to provide. What Home Rentals did provide was a house that was clearly and unquestionably unfit for people to live in. As a result, defendants had no alternative but to vacate the premises.

Home Rentals correctly points out that a tenant may not abandon premises under the theory of constructive eviction without first affording the lessor a reasonable opportunity to correct the defects in the property [citation], but such an opportunity existed here. Home Rentals' president, Henry Fisher, admitted that he actually inspected the premises as early as August 13. * * *

Considering the magnitude of the problems, four days was opportunity enough for Home Rentals to act. Constructive eviction has been found in analogous circumstances where an even shorter period was involved. [Citation.] We note, moreover, that there is no indication that giving Home Rentals additional time would have made any difference. In the four days before defendants left, the only action the company took at all was to send someone out to spray for bugs, which did not work, and to dispatch a man with a plunger. In the end, it was only because of the intervention by the City of Carbondale that Home Rentals implemented the necessary remedial measures.

INTERPRETATION If a landlord's failure to meet any of his obligations under a lease causes a substantial and lasting injury to the tenant's beneficial enjoyment of the premises, that failure, in effect, is a constructive and wrongful eviction of the tenant.

ETHICAL QUESTION Did Home Rentals act unethically? Explain.

CRITICAL THINKING QUESTION Did the court correctly decide this case? Explain.

Fitness for Use Because the lease's primary value to the tenant is land, the landlord, under the common law, is under no obligation to provide or maintain the premises in a livable condition or to make them fit for any purpose, unless the lease specifically so provides. Most courts, however, have abandoned this rule in residential leases, instead imposing an **implied warranty of habitability** that requires leased premises to be habitable, that is, fit for ordinary residential purposes. These courts also have held that the covenant to pay rent is conditioned on the landlord's performance of this warranty. Courts reaching these results have emphasized that the tenant's interest is in a place to live, not merely in land.

A number of states have statutes requiring landlords to keep residential premises fit for occupation. Zoning ordinances, health and safety regulations, and building and housing codes also may impose certain duties on the landlord.

Tucker v. Hayford

Court of Appeals of Washington, Division Three, 2003
75 P.3d 980
http://search.mrsc.org/nxt/gateway.dll?f=templates&fn=courts.htm$vid=courts:court

FACTS Robert Hayford bought a lot and mobile home in Kennewick, Washington, from Mike Kirby in 1994. The water to the home was supplied by a well, which was tested on December 8, 1993. On March 15, 1994, the Benton Franklin District Health Department wrote to Mr. Kirby that: (1) the nitrate level of the well water was 8.8 mg/L; (2) the well was free of bacterial contamination; (3) the sanitary seal was improperly installed and maintained; and (4) chemicals were stored within 100 feet of the well. And "to protect and improve" the water system, the health department recommended that: (1) the sanitary seal be properly installed; and (2) the chemicals be stored at least 100 feet from the well. The health department also recommended that the well be tested yearly.

Mr. Hayford leased the home to Don and Shalee Tucker in October of 1998. The Tuckers asked if the well water was drinkable. Mr. Hayford said it was as long as a "Brita" filter was used. He said that the nitrates were a bit high.

The Tuckers signed a written residential lease prepared by Mr. Hayford. They ultimately extended the tenancy through August 1, 2000. The Tucker family, including their four children, all became ill. The family's pediatric nurse practitioner suggested that they test their well water. The test, dated March 28, 2000, showed bacteria in the water. The Tuckers told Mr. Hayford. He had the well repaired and that solved the problem.

The Tuckers, nevertheless, moved out of the home on May 15, 2000. They sued Mr. Hayford for damages for personal injury arising from contaminated water. Mr. Hayford moved for summary judgment. The trial court granted the motion.

DECISION The trial court's summary judgment order is reversed.

OPINION Sweeney, J. The Tuckers sued for damages based on their contract (obligation to perform major maintenance and repair, and covenant of quiet enjoyment); violation of the Landlord-Tenant Act; and negligent misrepresentation as to the water quality. We evaluate the viability of each claim.

* * *

CONTRACT CLAIMS

Obligations Imposed by This Contract. * * * The tenant may recover for personal injuries caused by the landlord's breach of a repair covenant only if the unrepaired defect created an unreasonable risk of harm to the tenant. The *Restatement (Second) of Torts* § 357 (1965) provides that the lessor of land is liable if (a) the lessor has contracted to keep the land in repair; (b) the disrepair creates an unreasonable risk that performance of the lessor's agreement would have prevented; and (c) the lessor fails to exercise reasonable care in performing the agreement. [Citation.] The contract defines the extent of the duty when a landlord's duty arises out of a covenant.

Both the trial court and Mr. Hayford, here on appeal, rely on our decision in *Brown* for the proposition that the landlord must have notice of the "defect" before he is subject to liability. * * * We do not read our decision in *Brown* so broadly.

In *Brown* the landlord had notice of the tenant's problem (a high door sill). The holding in *Brown* turned on the nature of the claimed defect, not notice. * * * The court ultimately held that the landlord would not be liable under the contract's safety provision because the door sill was not then unreasonably unsafe. *Brown* did * * * adopt portions of the *Restatement of Torts* which are relevant to the claims here:

> The lessor's duty to repair * * * is not contractual but is a tort duty based on the fact that *the contract gives the lessor ability to make the repairs and control over them.* * * * *Unless* the contract stipulates that the *lessor shall inspect the premises to ascertain the need of repairs*, a contract to keep the *interior* in safe condition subjects the lessor to liability if, but *only if, reasonable care is not exercised after the lessee has given him notice of the need of repairs.*

[Citations.]

Notice then under this provision of the *Restatement* becomes an issue when the particular condition under consideration is *inside* the residence where the landlord has no right to enter. But that is not the case here. The source of water here was an outside well, which the landlord had physical access to. Actual notice is not then required.

Here the lease includes (1) an express covenant of quiet enjoyment and (2) requires that the lessor maintain and repair the leased premises.

So the factual question is the usual threshold question where the claim has been dismissed on motion—whether the condition of this well interfered with their quiet enjoyment of the home, or whether the well required "major maintenance" as spelled out in the lease agreement.

Quiet Enjoyment. No Washington case directly addresses the impact of drinking water on one's quiet enjoyment of his home. Washington does, however, recognize the relationship of water and habitability. In [citation] the court held that without water, a property is uninhabitable. [Citation.] * * * Other jurisdictions have also held that a property without potable water is uninhabitable.

It is well settled that unsafe drinking water renders a home uninhabitable. And that by definition interferes with the quiet enjoyment of the home. The Tuckers have made out an actionable claim for breach of the covenant of quiet enjoyment if we look at the evidence in the light most favorable to the Tuckers.

Major Maintenance and Repair. A health inspector recommended that this well be tested at least annually for bacteria. The question then is whether a reasonable person knew or in the exercise of ordinary care should have known that this well should have been tested annually—as part of the major maintenance of this home. Again, the evidence, viewed in a light most favorable to the Tuckers, includes high nitrate levels together with a recommendation for yearly bacteria testing. That is a sufficient showing to support a breach of the major maintenance and repair covenant of this lease, if proved.

DUTIES AT COMMON LAW

Traditional Common Law Landlord Liability. Common law landlord liability requires a showing: "(1) latent or hidden defects in the leasehold (2) that existed at the commencement of the leasehold (3) of which the landlord had actual knowledge (4) and of which the landlord failed to inform the tenant." [Citation.] The landlord need not discover obscure defects or dangers, nor does the law impose any duty to repair defective conditions. [Citation.] A "landlord is liable only for failing to inform the tenant of known dangers which are not likely to be discovered by the tenant." [Citation.]

The Tuckers moved into this home in 1998. The well was last tested in 1993. It was not tested again until after the Tuckers tested it in 2000. But this was after the Tuckers got sick. It had not then been tested for the five years prior to the Tuckers' moving in despite a recommendation by the health department that it be tested annually. This well was not then maintained at the time the property was leased to the Tuckers. And the condition of the water was certainly hidden or latent as to the Tuckers. Mr. Hayford did not warn the Tuckers. Mr. Hayford was aware of the report that required the annual testing. The Tuckers have then raised an issue of fact—whether Mr. Hayford knew or should have known of this latent defect.

* * *

Implied Warranty of Habitability. A landlord is subject to liability for physical harm caused to the tenant and others upon the leased property with the consent of the tenant or his subtenant by a dangerous condition existing before or arising after the tenant has taken possession, if he has failed to exercise reasonable care to repair the condition and the existence of the condition is in violation of:

(1) an *implied duty of habitability*; or
(2) *a duty created by a statute* or administrative regulation.

Restatement (Second) of Property § 17.6 (1977).

* * *

RESIDENTIAL LANDLORD-TENANT ACT
* * * The Uniform Residential Landlord and Tenant Act (Uniform Landlord-Tenant Act) was drafted by the National Conference of Commissions on Uniform State Laws in 1972. [Citation.] While Washington made "substantial changes" to the Uniform Landlord-Tenant Act when it adopted its own Landlord-Tenant Act, our state's version still reflects a "strong [Uniform Landlord-Tenant Act] influence." [Citation.] * * * The purpose of the Uniform Landlord-Tenant Act was twofold: " 'simplify, clarify, modernize and revise' " landlord and tenant law, and to " '*encourage landlords to maintain and improve the quality of housing*.' " [Citation.]

Washington's Landlord-Tenant Act. The Landlord-Tenant Act requires the landlord to "keep the premises fit for human habitation" and to particularly maintain the premises in substantial compliance with health or safety codes for the benefit of the tenant. [Citation.] It requires the landlord to make repairs, except in the case of normal wear and tear, "necessary to put and keep the premises in as good condition as it by law or rental agreement should have been, at the commencement of the tenancy." [Citation.]

It lists the landlord's obligations. [Citation.] And it lists the tenant's remedies: (1) terminate the rental agreement; (2) "[b]ring an action in an appropriate court, or at arbitration if so agreed, for any remedy provided under this chapter or *otherwise provided by law*;" or (3) pursue the other remedies available under the Landlord-Tenant Act. [Citation.]

* * * We conclude that the Washington Residential Landlord-Tenant Act of 1973 provides a cause of action for the injury sustained here.

INTERPRETATION Most states impose an implied warranty of habitability that requires leased premises to be fit for ordinary residential purposes.

CRITICAL THINKING QUESTION When should the law require that premises be habitable? Explain.

Repair Under the common law, unless there is a specific provision in the lease or a statutory duty to do so, the landlord has *no* obligation to **repair** or restore the premises. The landlord does, however, have a duty to maintain, repair, and keep in safe condition those parts of the premises that remain under her control. For example, an apartment house owner who controls the building's stairways, elevators, lobbies, and other common areas is liable for keeping them maintained and repaired and is responsible for injuries that occur because of her failure to do so. With respect to apartment buildings, the courts presume that any portion of the premises that is not specifically leased to the tenants remains under the landlord's control. Thus, in such cases, the landlord is liable for making external repairs, including repairs to the roof. The courts have further expanded the "common areas" rule to individual rental unit equipment that is connected to a central system, such as central heating and air conditioning, hot water, and plumbing and electrical systems. For a discussion of a landlord's duties and tort liabilities to a tenant in common areas, see the section on duties of possessors in Chapter 8.

Although at common law the landlord is under no duty to repair, restore, or keep the premises in a livable condition, she may and often does assume those duties in the lease. However, her breach of such obligations under a lease does not entitle a tenant to abandon the premises and refuse to pay rent. Unless the lease specifically provides the tenant this right, the common law allows him only an action for damages. As mentioned above, a number of states now have statutes that require the landlord to keep residential premises fit for occupancy and accordingly have imposed upon the landlord a duty to repair those items.

Landlord's Liability for Injury Caused by Third Parties

Chapter 7 discusses the duties and tort liabilities of a landlord to a tenant for defects in common areas and for the failure to disclose hidden defects in the rented premises of which the landlord knew or should have known. Under the common law, a landlord also was liable if he did not exercise reasonable care in repairing such defects. Today, by statute or judicial decision, many states require landlords to maintain leased premises in good repair and hold them liable for a negligent failure to do so.

Some states hold landlords liable for injuries their tenants and others suffer as a result of the foreseeable criminal conduct of third parties. Although landlords cannot insure their tenants' safety, courts have held landlords liable for failure "to take minimal precautions to protect members of the public from the reasonably foreseeable criminal acts of third persons."

Practical Advice

In your written lease, attempt to provide for the landlord's duty to repair, the landlord's liability to third parties, and the landlord's obligation to maintain the premises in habitable condition.

CPA CONCURRENT OWNERSHIP

As we mentioned in Chapter 49, property may be owned by one individual or by two or more persons concurrently. Two or more persons who hold title concurrently generally are known as **co-tenants**. Each is entitled to an undivided interest in the entire property, and neither has a claim to any specific part of it. Each may have an equal undivided interest, or one may have a larger undivided share than the other.

The two major types of concurrent ownership are joint tenancy and tenancy in common. Both provide an undivided interest in the whole, the right of both tenants to possession, and the right of either to sell his interest during life and thus terminate the original relationship. Other forms of concurrent ownership of real estate are tenancy by the entireties, community property, condominiums, and cooperatives.

TENANCY IN COMMON

Under a **tenancy in common**, the most frequently used form of concurrent ownership, each co-owner has both an undivided interest in the property and the right to possession, but none claims any specific portion of the property. Tenants in common need not have acquired their interests at the same time or by the same instrument, and their interests may differ as to duration and scope. Because there is no right of survivorship, the interests of tenants in common may be devised by will or pass by intestate succession. By statute in all states, a transfer of title to two or more persons is presumed to create a tenancy in common.

Partition is a physical division of the property that changes undivided interests into smaller, individually owned parcels. The size of the individual parcels is based upon the size of the owners' prior shares of the undivided interest. If physical division of the property (e.g., a house) is not practicable, the property will be sold and the proceeds will be divided.

JOINT TENANCY

The most significant feature of joint tenancy is the right of *survivorship*. On the death of a joint tenant, title to the entire property passes by operation of law to the survivor or survivors. Neither the heirs of the deceased joint tenant nor his general creditors have a claim to his interest after his death, and a joint tenant cannot transfer his interest by executing a will. Any joint tenant may sever the joint tenancy, however, by conveying or mortgaging his interest to a third party. Further, the interest of either co-tenant is subject to levy and sale on execution. To *sever* a joint tenancy is to forfeit the right of survivorship: following severance, the tenancy becomes a tenancy in common among the remaining joint tenants and the transferee.

To sustain a **joint tenancy**, the common law requires the presence of what are known as the **four unities** of time, title, interest, and possession. The unity of time means that all the tenants' interests must take effect at the same time; the unity of title means that all the tenants must acquire title by the same instrument; the unity of interest means that the tenants' interests must be identical in duration and scope; and the unity of possession means that the tenants have identical rights of possession and enjoyment. The absence of any unity will prevent the creation of a joint tenancy. The presence of the fourth unity and any two of the others, however, will result in the creation of a tenancy in common, because the only unity required of a tenancy in common is the unity of possession.

Practical Advice

If you jointly hold property with another, specify the type of joint ownership.

James v. Taylor

Court of Appeals of Arkansas, Division III, 1998
62 Ark.App. 130, 969 S.W.2d 672
http://caselaw.lp.findlaw.com/scripts/getcase.pl?court=ar&vol=1998a/980520/ca971404&invol=2

FACTS On January 14, 1993 Eura Mae Redmon deeded land to her daughter, Melba Taylor, and two sons, W. C. Sewell and Billy Sewell, "jointly and severally, and unto their heirs, assigns and successors forever," with the grantor retaining a life estate. W. C. Sewell died on November 18, 1993, and Billy Sewell died on May 11, 1995. Mrs. Redmon died on February 17, 1997. Melba Taylor then sought a declaration that her mother had intended to convey the property to the grantees as joint tenants, thereby making her, by virtue of her brothers' deaths, sole owner of the property. Descendants of W. C. and Billy Sewell (appellants) opposed the complaint on the ground that the deed created a tenancy in common among the grantees. The case went to trial, and the chancellor found that Mrs. Redmon intended to convey the property to her children as joint tenants with the right of survivorship. Thus the chancellor granted title to the property to Melba Taylor. This appeal followed.

DECISION Judgment reversed and remanded.

OPINION Pittman, J. Appellants and appellee agree that the term "jointly and severally" as used to describe an estate in property is ambiguous. * * * Appellants contend that, under Arkansas law, a deed to two or more persons presumptively creates a tenancy in common unless the deed expressly creates a joint tenancy. They cite Ark. Code Ann. § 18–12–603, which reads as follows: "Every interest in real estate granted or devised to two (2) or more persons, other than executors and trustees as such, shall be in tenancy in common unless expressly declared in the grant or devise to be a joint tenancy." According to appellants, the very existence of an ambiguity within the deed means that, under the statute, a tenancy in common has been created. Appellee, on the other hand, points to the well-established rule that, when faced with an ambiguity in a deed, the trial court may determine the intent of the grantor by looking to extraneous circumstances to decide what was really intended by the language in the deed. [Citations.] Because, appellee argues, the chancellor in this case had strong evidence before him that Mrs. Redmon intended to create a joint tenancy in her children, his finding should not be overturned unless clearly erroneous. [Citations.]

The extrinsic evidence considered by the chancellor in this case weighs in favor of appellee. That evidence consisted of appellee's testimony that her mother had informed her attorney that she wanted the deed drafted so that, if one of her children died, the property would belong to the other two children, and so on; that shortly after the death of W. C. Sewell, Mrs. Redmon executed a new will leaving her property to Billy Sewell and appellee and leaving nothing to W. C.'s children; that Mrs. Redmon had set up bank accounts payable upon her death to her children, and, after W. C. and Billy died, deleted their names leaving the name of the surviving child; and that Mrs. Redmon was upset before her death upon learning that there was a problem with the deed. However, we hold that the considerations expressed in Ark. Code Ann. § 18–12–603 override the rule of construction urged by appellee.

Section 18–12–603 is a statute like one of many throughout the country. At common law, joint tenancy was favored and, where possible, that estate was held to exist. [Citation.] However, in Arkansas, and in many other states, statutes have been adopted which presumptively construe an instrument to create a tenancy in common rather than a joint tenancy. [Citations.] These statutes do not prohibit joint tenancies but merely provide for a construction against a joint tenancy if the intention to create it is not clear. [Citations.] A statute such as section 18–12–603 is not an expression of a public policy against joint tenancies but is merely a choice by the legislature of a rule of construction that selects one of two possible interpretations of a provision otherwise ambiguous. [Citation.]

Ordinarily, a statute such as section 18–12–603 does not require the actual use of the words "joint tenancy." [Citation.] * * * Survivorship is the distinctive characteristic of a joint tenancy. [Citation.] Where, from the four corners of an instrument, a court can interpret the intention of the grantor or testator as creating a survivorship estate, the court will deem the estate to be a joint tenancy with the right of survivorship. [Citations.]

Nothing appears from the four corners of the deed in this case to indicate Mrs. Redmon's intent to convey a survivorship interest, unless that intention is to be found in the term "jointly and severally." Appellants do not cite, nor have we discovered through our own research, any Arkansas case in which a grant of ownership was made to two or more parties "jointly and severally." As the chancellor noted below, "jointly and severally" are words of tort, not property. They have no meaning in the world of estates. In the context of an ownership interest, such a term is a legal anomaly; several ownership is, by definition, a denial of joint ownership. [Citation.] However, two cases from other jurisdictions are persuasive. In [citation], the court interpreted a will that had devised property to two devisees "jointly and severally." The court held that, in light of a statute similar to ours, no joint tenancy was created. * * *

In [citation], property was deeded to two grantees "jointly." The Missouri court, relying on a statute virtually identical to ours, held that a joint tenancy was not created by the use of such language. * * *

If use of the word "jointly" is not sufficient to create a joint tenancy, the term "jointly and severally," with its elusive connotation, cannot do so either. * * *

Appellee argues that, given the deed's ambiguity, our focus should be on the intent of the grantor as gleaned not only from the instrument itself but from the extrinsic evidence presented at trial. However, evidence of the grantor's intention cannot prevail over the statute. To allow that would be to render section 18–12–603 meaningless.

INTERPRETATION A deed to two or more persons presumptively creates a tenancy in common unless the deed expressly creates a joint tenancy.

CRITICAL THINKING QUESTION Do you agree with court's application of the statute in this case? Explain.

TENANCY BY THE ENTIRETIES

Tenancy by the entireties, recognized in some, but not all states, is created only by a conveyance to a husband and wife. It is distinguished from joint tenancy by the inability of either spouse to convey separately his or her interest during life and thus destroy the right of survivorship. Likewise, creditors cannot attach the interest of either spouse. By the nature of the tenancy, divorce would terminate the relationship, and partition would then be available as a method of creating separate interests in the property.

COMMUNITY PROPERTY

In Arizona, California, Idaho, Louisiana, Nevada, New Mexico, Puerto Rico, Texas, Washington, and Wisconsin, under the **community property** system, one-half of any property acquired by either the husband or the wife belongs to each spouse. In most instances, the only property that belongs separately to either spouse is any property acquired before the marriage or acquired subsequent to it by gift or inheritance. On the death of either spouse, one-half of the community property belongs outright to the survivor, and the interest of the deceased spouse in the other half may go to the heirs of the decedent or as directed by will.

CONDOMINIUMS

Condominiums embody a form of concurrent ownership now common in the United States. All states have enacted statutes authorizing this form of ownership. The purchaser of a condominium acquires separate ownership to the unit and becomes a tenant in common with respect to its common facilities, such as the land on which the project is built, recreational facilities, hallways, parking areas, and spaces between the units. A condominium association, funded by assessments levied on each unit, maintains the common elements. The transfer of a condominium conveys both the separate ownership of the unit and the share in the common elements.

COOPERATIVES

Cooperatives involve an indirect form of common ownership. A cooperative, usually a corporation, purchases or constructs dwelling units and then leases the units to its shareholders as tenants, who acquire the right to use and occupy their units.

CPA NONPOSSESSORY INTERESTS

Although a nonpossessory interest in land entitles the holder to use the land or to take something from it, the interest does not give him the right to possess the land. Nonpossessory interests include easements, ***profits à prendre***, and licenses.

DEFINITION OF EASEMENTS

An **easement** is a *limited right* to use another's land in a specific manner that is created by the acts of the parties or by operation of law and that has all the attributes of an estate in the land itself. For example, a typical easement exists when Liz sells part of her land to Bill and expressly provides in the same document or in a separate one that Bill, as the adjoining landowner, shall have a right-of-way over a strip of Liz's remaining parcel of land. Bill's land is said to be the **dominant** parcel (land whose owner has rights in other land), and Liz's land, which is subject to the easement, is the **servient** parcel. Easements may, of course, exist for many different uses, as, for example, the right to run a ditch across another's land, to lay pipe under the surface, to erect power lines, or, in the case of adjacent buildings, to use a stairway or a common or "party" wall.

TYPES OF EASEMENTS

Easements fall into two classes: easements appurtenant and easements in gross. **Appurtenant easements** are by far the more common, and, as the name indicates, the rights and duties they create pertain to the land itself, not to the

CONCEPT REVIEW

Rights of Concurrent Owners

	Undivided Interest	Right to Possession	Right to Sell	Right to Mortgage	Levy by Creditors	Right to Will	Right of Survivorship
Joint Tenancy	Yes	Yes	Yes	Yes	Yes	No	Yes
Tenancy in Common	Yes	Yes	Yes	Yes	Yes	Yes	No
Tenancy by Entireties	Yes	Yes	No	No	No	No	Yes

individuals who have created such easements. Therefore, the easement usually stays with the land when it is sold. For example, continuing with the illustration of Liz and Bill above, if Liz sells her servient parcel to Kyle, who has actual notice of the easement for the benefit of Bill's land or constructive notice through a local recording act, Kyle takes the parcel subject to the easement. Likewise, if Bill sells his dominant parcel to Daniel, the deed from Bill to Daniel does not need to refer specifically to the easement in order to give to Daniel, as the dominant parcel's new owner, the right to use the right-of-way over the servient parcel.

The second type of easement is an **easement in gross**, which is personal to the particular individual who receives the right. In effect, it amounts to little more than an irrevocable personal right to use another's land.

Borton v. Forest Hills Country Club

Missouri Court of Appeals, Eastern District, Division Five, 1996
926 S.W.2d 232

FACTS Plaintiffs, Gene and Deborah Borton, owners of a home which was adjacent to golf course, brought nuisance action against country club seeking injunctive relief and money damages based on golf balls which were hit onto their property. The defendant, Forest Hills Country Club **(http://courseguide.golfweb.com/ocdata.cgi/detail?gwid=09070)**, filed a counterclaim seeking declaration of easement allowing members to enter the plaintiff's property to retrieve errant golf balls.

The developer of defendant's golf course began to sell lots for residential use adjacent to the golf course in 1963. The developer filed and recorded a set of deed restrictions on all the residential lots adjacent to the golf course. Paragraph 11 of these deed restrictions recites:

> All owners and occupants of any lot in the Forest Hills Club Estates Subdivision shall extend to one person, in a group of members or guests playing a normal game of golf on the Forest Hills Golf and Country Club, or their caddy, the courtesy of allowing such person or caddy the privilege of retrieving any and all errant golf balls which may have landed or remained on any lot in the subdivision. However, care shall be exercised in the retrieving of such golf ball to prevent damage to any lawn, flowers, shrubbery, or other improvement on the lot.

Plaintiffs purchased a residence adjacent to the fairway on the eleventh hole on defendant's golf course in March 1994. The general warranty deed to plaintiffs provided that the property was subject to the set of deed restrictions and covenants. Because of the proximity of the tee boxes on the eleventh hole to plaintiffs' home, thousands of errant golf balls have been hit onto plaintiffs' property since they purchased their residence.

The trial court granted summary judgment in favor of defendant on plaintiff's claim and its counterclaim. Plaintiff appeals.

DECISION Affirmed in part and reversed and remanded in part.

OPINION Ahrens, J. Plaintiffs concede that paragraph 11 of the deed restriction gives defendant and its members some right with respect to retrieving errant golf balls. Plaintiffs argue, however, that the right created in paragraph 11 is simply a license. Defendant contends it has an easement over the Bortons' property, either by express grant via paragraph 11 in the deed restriction or by prescription.

Both a license and easement give the grantee the right to go onto the grantor's property for a limited use.

[Citations.] A license is a personal right and as such, may be revoked at the will of the licensor. [Citation.] An easement, by contrast, gives the grantee an interest in the property of the grantor and thus runs with the land and is binding upon successive landowners. [Citations.]

In the instant case, since the original developer of the property properly recorded and filed the deed restrictions, those restrictions created property interests that run with the land and are binding on successive landowners. [Citations.] Thus, plaintiffs do not have the power to revoke or modify the rights granted to defendant in paragraph 11 of the deed restrictions. Therefore, the deed restrictions in paragraph 11 are in the nature of an easement in favor of defendant and its members to retrieve errant golf balls hit onto plaintiffs' property during a normal game of golf.

* * *

Since the terms of paragraph 11 are binding upon the parties and run with the land, we hold that defendant was granted an express easement by paragraph 11 of the deed restrictions.

* * *

Plaintiffs may recover * * * if they can demonstrate that defendant's current use of the easement constitutes a greater burden to their land than what was contemplated or intended. [Citations.] The defendant did not address plaintiffs' [claims] in its cross motion for summary judgment, and did not submit summary judgment facts to demonstrate that there is no material issue of fact in dispute as to this issue. Thus, the trial court's dismissal of plaintiffs' [claim] was premature and must be reversed.

INTERPRETATION Most easements give the grantee an interest in property of the grantor and run with the land and are binding upon successive landowners.

CRITICAL THINKING QUESTION Should the plaintiff be able to get out of the deed restriction? Explain.

CREATION OF EASEMENTS

The most common way to create an easement is by *express grant* or reservation. For example, when Amy sells part of her land to Robert, she may, in the same deed, expressly grant him an easement over her remaining property.

Easements by *implication* arise whenever an owner of adjacent properties establishes an *apparent* and *permanent* use in the nature of an easement and then conveys one of the properties without mention of any easement. An easement may also arise by *necessity*: if Andrew conveys part of his land to Sharon, and the part conveyed to Sharon is so situated that she would have no access to it except across Andrew's remaining land, the law implies a grant by Andrew to Sharon of an easement by necessity across his remaining land.

Finally, an easement may arise by *prescription* in most states if certain required conditions are met. To obtain an easement by prescription, a person must use a portion of land owned by another in a way (1) that is adverse to the rightful owner's use, (2) that is open and generally known, and (3) that continues, uninterrupted, for a specific period that varies from state to state. The claimant acquires no easement by prescription, however, if given the owner's permission to use the land.

Practical Advice

Be sure to have any easement you obtain put in writing and properly file it with the recorder of deeds.

PROFITS À PRENDRE

Coming from the French, the phrase ***profit à prendre*** means the right to remove the produce from another's land. An example would be the grant by B to A, an adjoining landowner, of the right to remove coal, fish, or timber from B's land or to graze his cattle on B's land. Like an easement, a *profit à prendre* may arise by prescription, but if it comes about through an act of the parties, it must be created with all the formalities accorded the grant of an estate in real property. Unless the right is clearly designated as exclusive, the owner of the land is entitled to exercise it as well. Unlike A in the example above, even those who do not own adjacent land may hold the right to take profits. Thus, C may have a right to remove crushed gravel from B's acreage even though C lives in another part of the county.

LICENSES

A **license**, which is created by a contract granting permission to use an owner's land, does not create an interest in the property. A license is usually exercised only at the will of the owner and subject to revocation by him at any time. For example, if Adams tells Ebone she may cut across Adams's land to pick hickory nuts, Ebone has nothing but a license subject to revocation at any time. Nonetheless, should Ebone, on the basis of that license, expend funds to exercise the right, the courts may prevent Adams from revoking the license simply because penalizing Ebone

THE LAW AND YOU

State Bar Associations

California: http://www.dca.ca.gov/r_r/index.html ("A Guide to Residential Tenants' and Landlords' Rights and Responsibilities")

Colorado: http://www.cobar.org/ ("Joint Tenancy")

Illinois: http://www.iillinioslawyerfinder.com/publicinfo/home.html ("Landlord-Tenant")

Iowa: http://www.iowabar.org/pamphlet.nsf/$about!OpenAbout ("Joint Tenancy")

Louisiana: http://www.lsba.org/PublicResources/consumer_brochures.html ("Community Property: What Is Mine? What Is Yours?")

Maine: http://www.mainebar.org/ (legal information pamphlets) ("Landlord Tenant Law")

Maryland: http://www.msba.org/public/brochure.htm ("Rights of Landlords and Tenants")

Missouri: http://www.mobar.org/pamphlet/broindex.htm (public information brochures) ("Your Rights as a Tenant")

Montana: http://www.montanabar.org/ ("Renting a House or an Apartment")

New Hampshire: http://www.nhbar.org/?area/15.html ("Condominium Law in New Hampshire")

New York: http://www.nysba.org/ ("Rights of Residential Owners and Tenants")

North Carolina: http://www.ncbar.org/ ("Landlords Maintenance and Repair Duties")

Oklahoma: http://www.okbar.org/publicinfo/brochures/ ("What Are Your Rights as a Landlord?"; "What Are Your Rights and Duties as a Tenant?"; "When Do You Need Joint Tenancy?")

Oregon: http://www.osbar.org/public/legallinks.html ("Tenants and Landlords"—15 brochures)

South Dakota: http://www.sdbar.org/public/pamphlets/pamphlets.htm ("Joint Tenancy")

Tennessee: http://www.tba.org/LawBytes/LawBytes.html ("Home Ownership and Rental")

Washington: http://www.wsba.org/public/default.htm ("Landlord-Tenant")

Wisconsin: http://www.wisbar.org/asp/ titles.asp ("Landlord/Tenant"; "Marriage/ Marital Property")

State Attorney Generals

Arkansas: http://www.ag.state.ar.us/ ("What You Should Know About Landlord/Tenant Rights")

California: http://www.dca.ca.gov/r_r/conspub1.htm ("Tenants, Landlords, and Homeowners Associations")

Florida: http://myfloridalegal.com ("Florida's Landlord/ Tenant Law")

Illinois: http://www.ag.state.il.us/consumer/consume.htm ("Landlord & Tenant Rights and Laws")

Kansas: http://www.ink.org/public/ksag/contents/consumer/main.htm ("Landlord and Tenant Rights and Obligations")

Kentucky: http://www.law.state.ky.us/cp/resource.htm ("Rental Housing")

Maine: http://www.maine.gov/ag/index.php?r=clg ("The Maine Attorney General's Consumer Law Guide")

Massachusetts: http://www.ago.state.ma.us ("Tenants Rights")

Minnesota: http://www.ag.state.mn.us/consumer/default.shtml ("Housing")

New Hampshire: http://doj.nh.gov/consumer/brochures.html ("Condominiums and Timeshares"; "Renting, Security Deposits and Evictions"; "Rental Referral Agencies")

New York: http://www.consumer.state.ny.us/ ("Rent Smarts")

North Dakota: http://www.ag.state.nd.us/ ("Tenant's Rights")

South Dakota: http://www.state.sd.us/attorney/office/divisions/consumer ("Landlord Tenant Disputes")

Texas: http://www.oag.state.tx.us/ ("Tenant Rights")

Washington: http://www.atg.wa.gov/consumer ("Landlord/Tenant")

would be unfair, given the circumstances. In such a case, Ebone's interest would be, in practice, indistinguishable from an easement.

A common example of a license is a theatre ticket or the use of a hotel room. No interest is acquired in the premises; there is simply a right of use for a given length of time, subject to good behavior. No formality is required to create a license; a shopkeeper licenses persons to enter his establishment merely by being open for business.

CHAPTER SUMMARY

Freehold Estates

Fee Estates right to immediate possession of real property for an indefinite time
- *Fee Simple* absolute ownership of property
- *Qualified Fee* ownership subject to its being taken away upon the happening of an event

Life Estates ownership right in property for the life of a designated person, while remainder is the ownership estate that takes effect when the prior estate terminates

Future Interests
- *Reversion* grantor's right to property upon termination of another estate
- *Remainders* are of two kinds: vested remainders (unconditional remainder that is a fixed, present interest to be enjoyed in the future) and contingent remainders (remainder interest conditional upon the happening of an event in addition to the termination of the preceding estate)

Leasehold Estates

Lease both (1) a contract for use and possession of land and (2) a grant of an estate in land
- *Landlord* owner of land who grants a leasehold interest to another while retaining a reversionary interest in the property
- *Tenant* possessor of the leasehold interest in the land

Duration of Leases
- *Definite Term* lease that automatically expires at the end of the term
- *Periodic Tenancy* lease consisting of specific terms that continue in indefinite succession
- *Tenancy at Will* lease that is terminable at any time
- *Tenancy at Sufferance* possession of real property without a lease

Transfer of Tenant's Interest
- *Assignment* transfer of all of the tenant's interest in the leasehold
- *Sublease* transfer of less than all of the tenant's interest in the leasehold

Tenant's Obligations the tenant has an obligation to pay a specified rent at specified times or, if none is specified, to pay a reasonable amount at the end of the term
- *Destruction of the Premises* under the common law, if the premises are destroyed, the tenant is not relieved of his obligation to pay rent and cannot terminate the lease
- *Eviction* if the tenant breaches one of the covenants of her lease, the landlord may terminate the lease and evict (remove) her from the premises
- *Abandonment* if the tenant abandons property and the landlord reenters or relets it, the tenant's obligation to pay rent terminates

Landlord's Obligations
- *Quiet Enjoyment* the right of the tenant to have physical possession of the premises free of landlord interference
- *Fitness for Use* most courts impose for residential leases an implied warranty of habitability that the leased premises are fit for ordinary residential purposes
- *Repair* unless there is a statute or a specific provision in the lease, the landlord has no duty to repair or restore the premises

Concurrent Ownership

Tenancy in Common co-ownership in which each tenant holds an undivided interest with no right of survivorship

Joint Tenancy co-ownership with the right of survivorship; requires the presence of the four unities (time, title, interest, and possession)

Tenancy by the Entireties co-ownership by spouses in which neither may convey his or her interest during life

Community Property spouses' rights in property acquired by the other during their marriage

Condominium separate ownership of an individual unit with tenancy in common with respect to common areas

Cooperative the corporate owner of the property leases units to its shareholders as tenants

Nonpossessory Interest

Easement limited right to use the land of another in a specified manner
- ***Appurtenant*** rights and duties created by the easement pertain to and run with the land of the owner of the easement (dominant parcel) and the land subject to the easement (servient parcel)
- ***In Gross*** rights and duties created by the easement are personal to the individual who received the right
- ***Creation of Easements*** easements may be created by (1) express grant or reservation, (2) implied grant or reservation, (3) necessity, and (4) prescription (adverse use)

Profits à Prendre right to remove produce from the land of another

Licenses permission to use the land of another

QUESTIONS

1. Kirkland conveyed a farm to Sandler to have and to hold for and during his life and on Sandler's death to Rubin. Some years thereafter, oil was discovered in the vicinity. Sandler thereupon made an oil and gas lease, and the oil company set up its machinery to begin drilling operations. Rubin then filed suit to enjoin the operations. Assuming an injunction to be the proper form of remedy, what decision?

2. Smith owned Blackacre in fee simple absolute. In section 3 of a properly executed will, Smith devised Blackacre as follows: "I devise my farm Blackacre to my son Darwin so long as it is used as a farm." Sections 5 and 6 of the will made gifts to persons other than Darwin. The last clause of Smith's will provided: "All the remainder of my real and personal property not disposed of heretofore in this will, I devise and bequeath to Stanford University."

   Smith died in 2003, survived by her son Darwin. Smith's estate has been administered. Darwin has been offered $100,000 for Blackacre if he can convey title to it in fee simple. What interests in Blackacre were created by Smith's will?

3. Panessi leased to Barnes, for a term of ten years beginning May 1, certain premises located at 527–529 Main Street in Cleveland. The premises were improved with a three-story building, the first floor being occupied by stores and the upper stories by apartments. On May 1 of the following year, Barnes leased one of the apartments to Clinton for one year. On July 5, a fire destroyed the second and third floors of the building. The first floor was not burned but was rendered unusable. Neither the lease from Panessi to Barnes nor the lease from Barnes to Clinton contained any provision regarding loss by fire. Discuss the liability of Barnes and Clinton to continue to pay rent.

4. Ames leased an apartment to Boor for $200 a month, payable the last day of each month. The term of the written lease was from January 1, 2002, through April 30, 2003. On March 15, 2002, Boor moved out, telling Ames that he disliked all the other tenants. Ames replied, "Well, you're no prize as a tenant; I can probably get more rent from someone more agreeable." Ames and Boor then had a minor physical altercation in which neither was injured. Boor sent the apartment keys to Ames by mail. Ames wrote Boor, "It will be my pleasure to hold you for every penny you owe me. I am renting the apartment on your behalf to Clay until April 30, 2003, at $175 a month." Boor had paid his rent through February 28, 2002. Clay entered the premises on April 1, 2002. How much rent, if any, may Ames recover from Boor?

5. Jay signed a two-year lease containing a clause that expressly prohibited subletting. After six months, Jay asked the landlord for permission to sublet the apartment for one year. The landlord refused. This angered Jay, and he immediately assigned his right under the lease to Kay. Kay was a distinguished gentleman, and Jay knew that everyone would consider him a desirable tenant. Is Jay's assignment of his lease to Kay valid?

6. In 1994, Roy Martin and his wife, Alice; their son, Hiram; and Hiram's wife, Myrna, acquired title to a 240-acre farm. The deed ran to Roy Martin and Alice Martin, the father and mother, as joint tenants with the right of survivorship, and to Hiram Martin and Myrna Martin, the son and his wife, as joint tenants with the right of survivorship. Alice Martin died in 1999, and in 2002, Roy Martin married Agnes Martin. By his will, Roy Martin bequeathed and devised his entire estate to Agnes Martin. When Roy Martin died in 2004, Hiram and Myrna Martin assumed complete control of the farm. State the interest in the farm, if any, of Agnes, Hiram, and Myrna Martin on the death of Roy Martin.

7. In her will, Teressa granted a life estate to Amos in certain real estate, with remainder to Brenda and Clive in joint tenancy. All the rest of Teressa's estate was left to Hillman College. While going to Teressa's funeral, the car in which Amos, Brenda, and Clive were riding was wrecked. Brenda was killed, Clive died a few minutes later, and Amos died on his way to the hospital. Who is entitled to the real estate in question?

8. Otis Olson, the owner of two adjoining city lots, A and B, built a house on each. He laid a drainpipe from lot B across lot A to the main sewer pipe under the alley beyond lot A. Olson then sold and conveyed lot A to Fred Ford. The deed, which made no mention of the drainpipe, was promptly recorded. Ford had no actual knowledge or notice of the drainpipe, although it would have been apparent to anyone inspecting the premises because it was only partially buried. Later, Olson sold and conveyed lot B to Luke Lane. This deed also made no reference to the drainpipe and was promptly recorded. A few weeks later, Ford discovered the drainpipe across lot A and removed it. Did he have the right to do so?

9. At the time of his marriage to Ann, Robert owned several parcels of real estate in joint tenancy with his brother, Sam. During his marriage, Robert purchased a house and put the title in his name and his wife's name as joint tenants, not as tenants in common. Robert died; within a month of his death, Smith obtained a judgment against Robert's estate. What are the relative rights of Sam, Smith, and Ann?

CASE PROBLEMS

10. In 1976, Ogle owned two adjoining lots numbered 6 and 7 fronting at the north on a city street. In that year, she laid out and built a concrete driveway along and two feet in front of what she erroneously believed to be the west boundary of lot 7. Ogle used the driveway for access to buildings situated at the southern end of both lots. Later in the same year, she conveyed lot 7 to Dale, and thereafter in the same year, she conveyed lot 6 to Pace. Neither deed made any reference to the driveway, and after the conveyance, Dale used it exclusively for access to lot 7. In 2004, a survey by Pace established that the driveway overlapped 6 inches on lot 6, and he brought an appropriate action to establish his lawful ownership of the strip on which the driveway approaches, to enjoin its use by Dale, and to require Dale to remove the overlap. Will Pace prevail? Why?

11. Temco, Inc., conveyed to the Wynns certain property adjoining an apartment complex being developed by Sonnett Realty Company. Although nothing to this effect was contained in the deed, the sales contract gave the purchaser of the property use of the apartment's swimming pool. Temco's sales agent also emphasized that use of the pool would be a desirable feature in the event that the Wynns decided to sell the property.

Seven years later, the Bunns contracted to buy the property from the Wynns through the latter's agent, Sonnett Realty. Although both the Wynns and Sonnett Realty's agent told the Bunns that use of the apartment's pool went with the purchased property, neither the contract nor the deed subsequently conveyed to the Bunns so provided. When the Bunns requested pool passes from Temco and Offutt, the company that owned the apartments, their request was refused. Discuss whether the Bunns have a right to use the apartment's pool.

12. In 1960, a deed for land in Pitt County, North Carolina, was executed and delivered by Joel and Louisa Tyson "unto M. H. Jackson and wife Maggie Jackson, for and during the term of their natural lives and after their death to the children of the said M. H. Jackson and Maggie Jackson that shall be born to their intermarriage as shall survive them to them and their heirs and assigns in fee simple forever." Thelma Jackson Vester, a daughter of M. H. and Maggie Jackson, died in 2002, survived by three children. M. H. Jackson, who survived his wife, Maggie Jackson, died in 2003, survived by four sons. The children of Thelma Jackson Vester brought this action against M. P. Jackson, a son of and executor of the will of M. H. Jackson. The children of Vester contended that through their deceased mother they were entitled to a one-fifth interest in the land conveyed by the deed of 1960. The executor contended that the deed conveyed a contingent remainder and that only those children who survived the parents took an interest in the land. Discuss the contentions of both of the parties.

13. Robert and Majorie Wake owned land that they used as both a cattle ranch and a farm. Each spring and autumn, the Wakes would drive their cattle from the ranch portion of the operation across an access road on the farmland to Butler Springs, which was also on the farmland.

In December 1979, the Wakes sold the farm to Jesse and Maud Hess but retained for themselves a right-of-way over the farm access road and the right to use Butler Springs for watering their livestock. In 1986, the Hesses sold the farm to the Johnsons, granting them uninterrupted possession of the property "excepting only that permissive use of the premises" owned by the Wakes.

The Wakes continued to use the access road and Butler Springs until 1987, when they sold their ranch and granted the new owners "their rights to the water of Butler Springs," but they said nothing about the access road. The ranch was subsequently sold several times, and all the owners used the access road and watering hole. In 2001, the Nelsons purchased the ranch. Shortly thereafter, the Johnsons notified the Nelsons that they had revoked the Nelsons' right to use the access road and Butler Springs. In 2002, the Johnsons closed the access road by locking the gates across the road. The Nelsons brought this action, claiming easements to both the access road and Butler Springs. The trial court ruled in favor of the Nelsons, and the Johnsons appealed. Does an easement in favor of the Nelsons exist? Why?

14. Clayton and Margie Gulledge owned a house at 532 Somerset Place, N.W. (the Somerset property) as tenants by the entirety. They had three children: Bernis Gulledge, Johnsie Walker, and Marion Watkins. When Margie Gulledge died in 1970, Clayton became the sole owner of the Somerset property. The following year, Clayton remarried, but the marriage was unsuccessful. To avoid a possible loss of the Somerset property, Bernis forwarded Clayton funds to satisfy the second wife's financial demands. In exchange, Clayton conveyed the property to Bernis and himself as joint tenants. In 1988, Clayton conveyed his interest in the Somerset property to his daughter, Marion Watkins. In 1991, Clayton died. Bernis died in 1993 and Johnsie Walker died in 1994. In these proceedings, Marion Watkins claims to be a tenant in common with the estate of Bernis Gulledge. The estate claims that when Clayton died, Watkin's interest was extinguished and Bernis became the sole owner of the Somerset property. Who is correct? Why?

15. By separate leases, Javins and a few others rented an apartment at the Clifton Terrace apartment complex. When they defaulted on their rent payments, the landlord, First National Realty, brought an action to evict them. The tenants admitted to the default but defended on the ground that the landlord had failed to maintain the premises in compliance with the Washington, D.C., Housing Code. They alleged that approximately 1,500 violations of this code had arisen since the term of their lease began. Discuss the merits of this case.

http:// **Internet Exercise** Find and explore information about the rights of residential tenants.

CHAPTER 51

Transfer and Control of Real Property

The right of property has not made poverty, but it has powerfully contributed to make wealth.
J.R. MCCULLOCH, *PRINCIPLES OF POLITICAL ECONOMY*

Learning Objectives

After reading this chapter you should be able to:

1. Explain (a) the essential elements of a contract of sale of an interest in real property, (b) the meaning and importance of marketable title, and (c) the concept of implied warranty of habitability.
2. Describe the fundamental requirements of a valid deed and distinguish among warranty, special warranty, and quitclaim deeds.
3. (a) Describe the elements of a secured transaction, (b) distinguish between a mortgage and a deed, and (c) distinguish between an assumption of a mortgage and buying subject to a mortgage.
4. Define and give examples of (a) adverse possession, (b) a variance, (c) a nonconforming use, and (d) eminent domain.
5. Describe the nature and types of restrictive covenants.

The law has always been extremely cautious about the transfer of title to real estate. Personal property may, for the most part, be passed easily and informally from owner to owner, but real property can be transferred only through compliance with a variety of formalities.

Title to land may be transferred in three principal ways: (1) by deed, (2) by will or by the law of descent on the death of the owner, and (3) by open, continuous, and adverse possession by a nonowner for a statutorily prescribed period of time. In this chapter, we will discuss the first and third methods of transfer; we will cover the second method in Chapter 52.

In addition to the legal restrictions placed on the transfer of real property, a number of other controls apply to the use of privately owned property. Governmental units impose some of these, including zoning and the taking of property by eminent domain. Private parties through restrictive covenants impose others. We will consider these three controls in the second part of this chapter.

TRANSFER OF REAL PROPERTY

The transfer of real property occurs most commonly by deed. Such transfers usually involve a contract for the sale of the land, the subsequent delivery of the deed, and the payment of the agreed-upon consideration. The transfer of real estate by deed, however, does not require consideration to be valid; it may be made as a gift. In most cases, the real estate purchaser must borrow part of the purchase price, using the real property as security. An unusual and far less common method of transferring title, adverse possession, requires no contract, deed, or other formality.

CPA CONTRACT OF SALE

As indicated in the chapters on general contracts, general contract law governs the sale of real property. In addition, the Fair Housing Act (Title VIII of the Civil Rights Act, as amended) prohibits discrimination in the real estate market on the basis of race, color, religion, gender, national origin, disability, or familial status. The act exempts the sale or rental of a single-family house owned by a private individual who owns fewer than four houses, provided that the owner does not use a broker or discriminatory advertising. Nevertheless, these exemptions do not apply to discrimination based on race or color; in the sale or rental of property, the act prohibits all discrimination based on these factors.

http:// Law and You Nevada: http://www.nvbar.org/Pamphlets.htm ("Real Estate Escrows and Title Insurance")

FORMATION

Because an oral agreement for the sale of an interest in land is not enforceable under the statute of frauds, the buyer and seller not only must reduce the agreement to writing but must have it signed by the other party in order to be able to enforce the agreement against that party. The simplest agreement should contain (1) the names and addresses of the parties, (2) a description of the property to be conveyed, (3) the time for the conveyance (called the *closing*), (4) the type of deed to be given, and (5) the price and manner of payment. To avoid dispute and to ensure adequately both parties' rights, a properly drawn contract for the sale of land will cover many other points as well.

MARKETABLE TITLE

The law of conveyancing firmly establishes that a contract for the sale of land carries with it an *implied* obligation on the part of the seller to transfer marketable title. **Marketable title** means that the title is free from (1) encumbrances (such as mortgages, easements, liens, leases, and restrictive covenants); (2) defects in the chain of title appearing in the land records (such as a prior recorded conveyance of the same property by the seller); and (3) events that deprive the seller of title, such as adverse possession or eminent domain. The obligation to convey marketable title is significant: if the title search reveals any defect not *specifically* excepted in the contract, the seller has materially breached the contract. The buyer's remedies for breach include specific performance with a price reduction, rescission and restitution, or damages for loss of bargain.

Practical Advice

Before title to the property passes, the buyer should ensure that she is receiving good title by having the title searched.

A title search involves examining prior transfers of and encumbrances to the property. Such an examination does not, however, guarantee rightful ownership; consequently, most buyers purchase title insurance as well. Issued in the amount of the purchase price of the property, ***title insurance*** indemnifies the owner against any loss due to defects in the title to the property or due to liens or encumbrances, except for those the policy identifies as existing when the policy was issued. Such policies also may be issued to protect the interests of mortgagees or tenants of property.

Practical Advice

As a buyer, obtain title insurance on the property to be purchased to insure against loss from defective title.

IMPLIED WARRANTY OF HABITABILITY

Because the obligation to transfer marketable title covers only the title to the property conveyed, such an obligation does not apply to the quality of any improvements to the land. The traditional common law rule is *caveat emptor*—let the buyer beware. Under this rigid maxim, the buyer must thoroughly inspect the property before the sale is completed, as any undiscovered defect would not be the seller's responsibility. The seller is liable only for any misrepresentations or express warranties he may have made about the property.

A majority of states have relaxed the harshness of the common law in sales made by one who builds and then sells residential dwellings. In such a sale, the builder-seller *impliedly* warrants a newly constructed house to be free of latent defects, that is, those defects not apparent upon a reasonable inspection of the house at the time of sale. In some states, this implied warranty of habitability benefits only the original purchaser; other states have extended it to subsequent purchasers for a reasonable period of time. In addition, many jurisdictions now require *all* sellers to disclose hidden defects that materially affect the property's value if reasonable examination would not reveal such defects. (See Chapter 11 for a discussion of misrepresentation.)

Practical Advice

As a buyer, carefully inspect any dwelling prior to purchasing it. Also seek to have the seller expressly warrant the dwelling's condition and habitability.

VonHoldt v. Barba & Barba Construction, Inc.

Supreme Court of Illinois, 1997

175 Ill.2d 426, 677 N.E.2d 836, 222 Ill.Dec. 302

http://www.state.il.us/court/Opinions/SupremeCourt/1997/January/Opinions/HTML/80342.txt

FACTS In August 1982, defendant, Barba & Barba Construction, Inc., constructed a multilevel addition to a single-family house in Glenview, Illinois **(http://www.glenview. il.us/)**. Before the addition, the residence consisted of approximately 2,300 square feet. After the addition, the house consisted of approximately 3,200 square feet. More than eleven years later, on November 5, 1993, plaintiff, John W. VonHoldt, purchased the house.

Shortly after taking occupancy, plaintiff noticed a deflection of the wood flooring at the partition wall separating the master bedroom from an adjoining bathroom. This deflection created a depression in the floor plane. Plaintiff maintained that, due to the thickness of the carpet, the depression was nearly concealed. An investigation revealed that the addition had not been constructed in accordance with the architectural plans approved by the Village of Glenview or the Glenview Building Code. This variance resulted in excessive stress on the floor joists and inadequate support for a portion of the roof and ceiling causing a greater than expected floor deflection.

The plaintiff brought the present action against defendant alleging that defendant breached an implied warranty of habitability. The trial judge dismissed plaintiff's complaint for failure to state a cause of action. Plaintiff appealed and the appellate court affirmed.

DECISION Judgment affirmed due to the fact that plaintiff's action was barred by the ten-year statute of repose.

OPINION Miller, J. On appeal to this court, plaintiff contends that the appellate court erred in rejecting his claim of breach of an implied warranty of habitability. Plaintiff asks us to extend the implied warranty of habitability to a cause of action by a subsequent purchaser for damages against a builder constructing a later addition to a house. Defendant argues that the protection of the implied warranty of habitability should be limited to actions against builder-vendors and that plaintiff's action, if any exists, is time-barred. For the reasons expressed below, we find that the implied warranty of habitability extends to cases brought by subsequent purchasers involving subsequent additions to homes.

The implied warranty of habitability is a judicially created doctrine designed to avoid the unjust results of caveat emptor and the doctrine of merger. [Citation.] Initially, Illinois courts applied the doctrine to the sale of new homes to protect innocent purchasers who did not possess the ability to determine whether the house they purchased contained latent defects. [Citation.]

* * * [T]he owner needs this protection because he is making a major investment, in many instances the largest single investment of his life. [Citation.] Additionally, the owner usually relies on the integrity and skill of the builder, who is in the business of building houses. [Citation.] Finally, the owner has a right to expect to receive a house that is reasonably fit for use as a residence. [Citation.]

* * * Illinois courts have [subsequently] defined and extended the circumstances under which claims based on an implied warranty of habitability can be recognized. [Citation.] (builder-vendor need not be mass producer, just one engaged in the business of building such that the sale is of a commercial nature); [citation.] (house built upon foundation of an old house still qualified as a "new" home); [citation.] (doctrine applies to person who erected a house manufactured by another company and built on the plaintiff's land); [citation.] (latent defect in common land can affect habitability); [citation.] (innocent purchaser could bring an action against a subcontractor when he had no recourse to the builder-vendor and he had sustained a loss in his home due to a latent defect); [citation.] (doctrine applies against developer-seller of new condominium unit).

Plaintiff claims that the implied warranty of habitability should now be extended to include actions against a builder brought by a subsequent purchaser for latent defects in a later addition to a home. In [citation], this court held that the defendants were not subject to the implied warranty of habitability for a condominium-conversion project. The court held that the doctrine of implied warranty of habitability did not apply because the refurbishing and renovation of the project had not been significant. [Citation.] In the present case, the builder made a major addition to an existing home. We now hold that, when a builder makes a significant addition to a previously built home, an action for damages resulting from latent defects affecting habitability exists under the doctrine of implied warranty of habitability.

An owner claiming that latent defects exist in a major addition to a structure, should be provided the same protection for the addition as that given to the [original] owners * * *. In both cases, the owner of the house usually has little knowledge regarding the construction. The purchaser of both a completed home and an addition places the same trust in the builder that the structure being erected is suitable for living. Further, the ordinary buyer is not in a position to discover hidden defects in a structure even through the exercise of ordinary and reasonable care.

We must next determine whether the plaintiff can bring this action even though he is a subsequent purchaser. In [citation], this court extended the implied warranty of habitability to subsequent purchasers of a new home, finding that there was no need for privity of contract because the warranty of habitability exists independently of the contract for sale. Because the doctrine of implied warranty of habitability has been extended to actions by subsequent purchasers of new homes, we can see no reason why the doctrine should not be extended to actions by subsequent purchasers of a home for latent defects in a significant addition to the home made prior to the time of sale.

* * *

For the foregoing reasons, we hold that actions for damages from latent defects in the construction of a significant structural addition to an existing residence can be brought against the builder by subsequent purchasers under the doctrine of implied warranty of habitability. However, because here the action was time-barred * * * plaintiff's complaint was properly dismissed.

INTERPRETATION The implied warranty of habitability applies to a subsequent purchase against a builder who makes a significant addition to a previously built home.

CRITICAL THINKING QUESTION Under what conditions should the implied warranty of habitability apply? Explain.

CPA DEEDS

A **deed** is a formal document transferring any interest in land upon delivery and acceptance. The party who transfers property by a deed is called the **grantor**; the transferee of the property is the **grantee**.

TYPES OF DEEDS

The rights a deed conveys depend on the type of deed used. Deeds are of three basic types: warranty, special warranty, and quitclaim.

Warranty Deed By a **warranty deed** (also called a general warranty deed), the grantor promises the grantee that the grantor has a valid title to the property. In addition, under a warranty deed, the grantor, either expressly or implicitly, obliges herself to make the grantee whole for any damage the grantee suffers should the grantor's title prove defective. A warranty deed includes certain promises or covenants, the most usual of which are *title*, *against encumbrances*, *quiet enjoyment*, and *warranty*. These various covenants constitute an assurance that the grantee will have undisturbed possession of the land and will, in turn, be able to transfer it without adverse claims of third parties. A phrase common in a warranty deed is "convey and warrant," although in a number of states the phrase "grant, bargain, and sell" is used, together with the seller's covenant (appearing later in the deed) that she will "warrant and defend the title."

Special Warranty Deed Whereas a warranty deed contains a general warranty of title, a **special warranty deed** warrants only that the title has not been impaired, encumbered, or made defective because of any act or omission *of the grantor*. The grantor merely warrants the title so far as it concerns his acts or omissions. He does *not* warrant title as to the acts or omissions of others.

Quitclaim Deed By a **quitclaim deed**, the grantor, in effect, says no more than "I make no promise as to what interest I do have in this land, but whatever it is, I convey it to you." A quitclaim deed usually provides that the grantor "conveys and quitclaims" or more simply "quitclaims all interest" in the property. Quitclaim deeds are used most frequently in transfers requiring persons who appear to have an interest in land to release their interest.

> **Practical Advice**
>
> As a buyer, have the seller grant a general warranty deed that specifically provides for the seller's liability if the title is defective.

FORMAL REQUIREMENTS

As we noted previously, any transfer of an interest in land that is of more than a limited duration falls within the statute of frauds and must therefore be in writing. Almost every deed, whatever the type, contains substantially similar wording.

Often, the deed will first describe the land. The description must be sufficiently clear to permit identification of the property conveyed. After describing the property, the deed usually will proceed to describe the quantity of estate conveyed to the grantee. Deeds generally end with the grantor's signature, a seal, and an acknowledgment before a notary public or other official authorized to verify the authenticity of documents.

DELIVERY OF DEEDS

A deed does not transfer title to land until it is delivered. **Delivery**, or an *intent* that the deed is to take effect, is evidenced by the acts or statements of the grantor. Physical transfer of the deed is usually the best evidence of this intent, but it is not necessary. Frequently, in a transfer known as an **escrow**, a grantor will turn a deed over to a third party (the escrow agent) to hold until the grantee performs certain conditions. When the grantee so performs, the escrow agent must give her the deed.

RECORDATION

In almost all states, recording a deed is not necessary to pass title from grantor to grantee. Unless the grantee has the deed recorded, however, a subsequent good faith purchaser for value of the property will acquire title superior to that of the grantee. **Recordation** consists of delivering a duly executed and acknowledged deed to the recorder's office in the county where the property is located. There, a copy of the instrument is inserted in the current deed book and indexed.

In some states, called *notice* states, unrecorded instruments are invalid against any subsequent purchaser without notice. In *notice-race* states, an unrecorded deed is invalid against any subsequent purchaser without notice of who recorded first. Finally, in a few states, called *race* states, an unrecorded deed is invalid against any deed recorded before it.

> **Practical Advice**
>
> Promptly record your deed with the recorder of deeds; if possible, do this before or simultaneously with the seller's receipt of the purchase price.

CPA | SECURED TRANSACTIONS

As we discussed in Chapter 38, a **secured transaction** essentially involves two elements: (1) a debt or obligation to pay money and (2) the creditor's interest in specific property that secures performance of the obligation. A security interest in property cannot exist apart from the debt it secures: discharging the debt in any manner terminates the interest. Transactions involving the use of real estate as security for a debt are subject to real estate law, which consists of statutes and rules developed through common law interpretations of mortgages and trust deeds. In these cases, the real estate itself is used to secure the obligation, which is evidenced by a note and by either a mortgage or deed of trust. The debtor is referred to as the **mortgagor**; the creditor is the **mortgagee**. The Uniform Commercial Code does *not* apply to real estate mortgages or deeds of trust.

FORM OF MORTGAGES

A **mortgage** is a security interest in land. The instrument that embodies a mortgage must meet all the requirements for such a document: it must be in writing, it must contain an adequate description of the property, and it must be executed and delivered. Nearly identical to a mortgage, a **deed of trust** contains one major difference: under a deed of trust, the property is conveyed not to the creditor as security but to a third person, who acts as trustee for the benefit of the creditor. The deed of trust creates rights almost the same as those created by a mortgage. In some states, it is customary to use a deed of trust in lieu of the ordinary form of mortgage.

As with all interests in realty, the mortgage or deed of trust should be promptly recorded to protect the mortgagee's rights against third persons who acquire an interest in the mortgaged property without knowledge of the mortgage.

RIGHTS AND DUTIES

The rights and duties of the parties to a mortgage may depend on whether it is considered to create a lien or to transfer legal title to the mortgagee. Most states have adopted the ***lien*** theory. The mortgagor retains title and, even in the absence of any stipulation in the mortgage, is entitled to possession of the premises to the exclusion of the mortgagee, even if the mortgagor defaults. Only through foreclosure (sale) or through the court appointment of a receiver can the right of possession be taken from the mortgagor. Other states have adopted the common law ***title*** theory, which gives the mortgagee the right of ownership and possession. In most cases, as a practical matter, the mortgagor retains possession simply because the mortgagee does not care about possession unless the mortgagor defaults.

Even though the mortgagor generally is entitled to possession and to many of the advantages of unrestricted ownership, he has a responsibility to deal with the property in a manner that will not impair the security. In most instances, *waste* (impairment of the security) results from the mortgagor's failure to prevent the actual or threatened actions of third parties against the land. For example, the debtor's failure to pay taxes or to discharge a prior lien may seriously impair the mortgagee's security. In such cases, the courts usually permit the mortgagee to pay the obligation and add it to his claim against the mortgagor.

The mortgagor may relieve his property from a mortgage lien by paying the debt that the mortgage secures. Characteristic of a mortgage, this right of **redemption** can be defeated only by operation of law. The right to redeem carries with it the obligation to pay the debt, and payment in full, with interest, is prerequisite to redemption. See Figure 51-1 for the fundamental rights of the mortgagor and mortgagee.

TRANSFER OF THE INTERESTS UNDER THE MORTGAGE

The interests of the original mortgagor and mortgagee can be transferred, and the rights and obligations of their assignees will depend primarily on (1) the agreement of the parties to the assignment and (2) the legal rules protecting the interest of one who is party to the mortgage but not to the transfer.

If the mortgagor conveys the land, the purchaser is *not* personally liable for the mortgage debt unless she expressly **assumes the mortgage.** If she assumes the mortgage, she is personally obligated to pay the debt the mortgagor owes to the mortgagee. Furthermore, the mortgagee can also hold the mortgagor on his promise to pay. In contrast, a transfer of mortgaged property **"subject to" the mortgage** does *not* personally obligate the transferee to pay the mortgage debt. In such a case, the transferee's risk of loss is limited to the property.

A mortgagee has the right to assign the mortgage to another person without the mortgagor's consent.

> **Practical Advice**
>
> An assignee of a mortgage is well advised to obtain the assignment in a writing duly executed by the mortgagee and to record it promptly with the proper public official. This will protect her rights against persons who subsequently acquire an interest in the mortgaged property without knowledge of the assignment.

FORECLOSURE

The right to foreclose usually arises upon default by the mortgagor. **Foreclosure** is an action through which the mortgage holder takes the property from the mortgagor, ends the mortgagor's rights in the property, and sells the property to pay the mortgage debt. If the proceeds are not sufficient to satisfy the debt in full, the debtor-mortgagor remains liable for paying the balance. Generally, the mortgagee will obtain a *deficiency judgment* for any unsatisfied balance of the debt and may proceed to enforce the payment of this amount out of the mortgagor's other assets. The mortgagor's default by nonperformance of other promises in the mortgage also may give the mortgagee the right to foreclose. For example, a mortgage may provide that the mortgagor's failure to pay taxes is a default that permits foreclosure. Mortgages also commonly provide that default in the payment of an installment makes the entire unpaid balance of the debt

Figure 51-1
Fundamental Rights of Mortgagor and Mortgagee

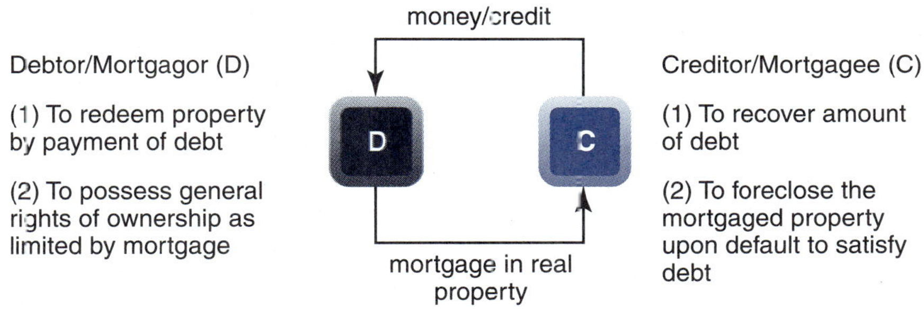

immediately due and payable, permitting foreclosure for the entire amount.

http://
Law and You Maryland: http://www.msba.org/public/brochure.htm ("Foreclosure Proceedings in Maryland")
Oregon: http://www.osbar.org/public/legalinfo/realestate.html ("Foreclosure on Real Property")

CPA ADVERSE POSSESSION

It is possible, although very rare, that title to land may be transferred involuntarily, without any deed or other formality, through adverse possession. In most states, a person who openly and continuously occupies the land of another for a statutorily prescribed period, typically twenty years, will gain title to the land by **adverse possession.** The **possession** must be actual. Courts have held that living on land, farming it, building on it, or maintaining structures on it is sufficient to constitute possession. However, the possession must be adverse. In other words, any act of dominion by the true owner, such as her entry on the land or assertion of ownership, will stop the period from running. Once broken, the statutory period would have to begin again, from the point at which the owner interrupted it.

By statute, some jurisdictions have established shorter periods of adverse possession when possession exists in conjunction with some other claim, such as the payment of taxes for seven years and an apparent claim of title, even if it is not valid.

Practical Advice

If you own real property, inspect it on a regular basis and exercise control over it in order to prevent any person from obtaining adverse possession.

PUBLIC AND PRIVATE CONTROLS

In exercising its police power for the benefit of the community, the state can and does place controls on the use of privately owned land. Furthermore, the state does not compensate the owner for loss or damage he sustains because of such legitimate controls. The enforcement of zoning laws, which is a proper exercise of the police power, is not a taking of property but a regulation of its use. The taking of private property for a public use or purpose under the state's power of eminent domain is not, however, an exercise of police power, and the owners of the property so taken are entitled to be paid its fair and reasonable value. In addition, by means of restrictive covenants, which we will also consider in this section, the use of privately owned property may be privately controlled.

CPA ZONING

Zoning is the principal method of public control over land use. The validity of zoning is rooted in the police power of the state, the inherent power of government to provide for the public health, safety, morals, and welfare. Police power can be used only to regulate private property, never to "take" it. It is firmly established that regulation having no reasonable relation to public health, safety, morals, or welfare is unconstitutional as a denial of due process of law.

ENABLING ACTS AND ZONING ORDINANCES

The power to zone generally is delegated to local city and village authorities by statutes known as enabling statutes. A typical enabling statute grants municipalities the following powers: (1) to regulate and limit the height and bulk of buildings to be erected; (2) to establish, regulate, and limit the building or setback lines on or along any street, trafficway, drive, or parkway; (3) to regulate and limit the intensity of the use of lot areas and to regulate and determine the area of open spaces within and around buildings; (4) to classify, regulate, and restrict the location of trades and industries and the location of buildings designated for specified industrial, business, residential, and other uses; (5) to divide the entire municipality into districts of such number, shape, area, and class (or classes) as may be deemed best suited to carry out the purposes of the statute; and (6) to set standards to which buildings or structures must conform.

Under these powers, the local authorities may enact zoning ordinances, consisting of a map and its accompanying descriptive text. The map divides the municipality into districts designated principally as industrial, commercial, or residential, with possible subclassifications. A well-drafted zoning ordinance will carefully define the uses permitted in each area. A special use (also called a conditional use or special exception) is a use authorized by the zoning ordinance but only upon specific approval by the zoning authorities on a case-by-case basis. Special uses include churches, schools, hospitals, homes for the disabled, and cemeteries.

Practical Advice

Prior to buying or developing real property make sure that your plans conform with all zoning ordinances and private restrictive covenants.

VARIANCE

Enabling statutes permit zoning authorities to grant variances when application of a zoning ordinance to specific property would cause its owner "particular hardship" unique or peculiar to the property. A **variance** permits a deviation from the zoning ordinance. Special circumstances applicable to particular property might include its unusual shape, topography, size, location, or surroundings. A variance is not available, however, if the hardship is caused by conditions general to the neighborhood or by the actions of the property owner. It must affirmatively appear that the property as presently zoned cannot yield a reasonable return on the owner's investment.

NONCONFORMING USES

A zoning ordinance may not immediately terminate a lawful use that existed before the ordinance was enacted. Rather, this **nonconforming use** must be permitted to continue for at least a reasonable time. Most ordinances provide that a nonconforming use may be terminated (1) when the use is discontinued, (2) when a nonconforming structure is destroyed or substantially damaged, or (3) when a nonconforming structure has been permitted to exist for the period of its useful life, as fixed by municipal authorities.

JUDICIAL REVIEW OF ZONING

Although the zoning process traditionally is considered as legislative, it is subject to judicial review on several grounds, including the following: (1) that the resulting zoning ordinance is invalid, (2) that the ordinance has been applied unreasonably, and (3) that the ordinance amounts to a confiscation, or taking, of property. For example, a zoning ordinance may be invalid as a whole either because it bears no reasonable relation to public health, safety, morals, or welfare or because it involves the exercise of powers that the enabling act has not granted to the municipality.

SUBDIVISION MASTER PLANS

Most states have legislation enabling local authorities to require municipality approval of every land subdivision plat. These enabling statutes provide penalties for failure to secure such approval when required by local ordinance. Some statutes make it a criminal offense to sell lots by reference to unrecorded plats and provide that such plats may not be recorded unless approved by the local planning board. Other statutes provide that building permits will not be issued unless the plat is approved and recorded.

CPA EMINENT DOMAIN

The power to take private property for public use, known as the power of **eminent domain,** is recognized as one of the inherent powers of government both in the U.S. Constitution and in state constitutions. Nevertheless, this power is carefully circumscribed and controlled. The Fifth Amendment to the federal Constitution provides, "[N]or shall private property be taken for public use without just compensation," and the constitutions of the states contain similar or identical provisions. Consequently, constitutional provisions directly prohibit the taking of private property without just compensation and implicitly prohibit the taking of private property for other than public use. Moreover, both federal and state constitutions entitle to due process of law the individual from whom property is to be taken.

Tahoe-Sierra Preservation Council, Inc. v. Tahoe Regional Planning Agency

Supreme Court of the United States, 2002
535 U.S. 302, 122 S.Ct. 1465, 152 L.Ed.2d 517
http://a257.g.akamaitech.net/7/257/2422/23apr20021030/www.supremecourtus.gov/opinions/01pdf/00-1167.pdf

FACTS The states of California and Nevada established the Tahoe Regional Planning Agency (TRPA) (Respondent) to study the impact of development on Lake Tahoe. The TRPA imposed two moratoria beginning in 1981, totaling 32 months, on development in the Lake Tahoe Basin while formulating a comprehensive land-use plan for the area. In 1984 the TRPA adopted a new and comprehensive land-use plan.

Petitioners/plaintiffs, real estate owners impacted by the moratoria and an association representing area landowners, filed suits claiming that TRPA's actions constituted a taking of their property without just compensation. The District Court held that the moratoria did constitute a taking because TRPA temporarily deprived petitioners of all economically viable use of their land. On appeal, the Court of Appeals for the Ninth Circuit held that because the regulations had only a temporary impact, no categorical taking had occurred. The Supreme Court granted *certiorari*.

DECISION Two moratoria on residential development did not constitute *per se* takings requiring compensation under Fifth Amendment.

OPINION Stevens, J. The question presented is whether a moratorium on development imposed during the process of devising a comprehensive land-use plan constitutes a *per se* taking of property requiring compensation under the Takings Clause of the United States Constitution. * * *

* * *

Petitioners * * * contend that the mere enactment of a temporary regulation that, while in effect, denies a property owner all viable economic use of her property gives rise to an unqualified constitutional obligation to compensate her for the value of its use during that period. Hence, they "face an uphill battle," [citation], that is made especially steep by their desire for a categorical rule requiring compensation whenever the government imposes such a moratorium on development. Under their proposed rule, there is no need to evaluate the landowners' investment-backed expectations, the actual impact of the regulation on any individual, the importance of the public interest served by the regulation, or the reasons for imposing the temporary restriction. For petitioners, it is enough that a regulation imposes a temporary deprivation—no matter how brief—of all economically viable use to trigger a *per se* rule that a taking has occurred. Petitioners assert that our opinions in *First English* and *Lucas* have already endorsed their view, and that it is a logical application of the principle that the Takings Clause was "designed to bar Government from forcing some people alone to bear burdens which, in all fairness and justice, should be borne by the public as a whole." [Citation].

We shall first explain why our cases do not support their proposed categorical rule—indeed, fairly read, they implicitly reject it. * * * In our view the answer to the abstract question whether a temporary moratorium effects a taking is neither "yes, always" nor "no, never"; the answer depends upon the particular circumstances of the case. Resisting "the temptation to adopt what amount to *per se* rules in either direction," [citation], we conclude that the circumstances in this case are best analyzed within the *Penn Central* framework.

The text of the Fifth Amendment itself provides a basis for drawing a distinction between physical takings and regulatory takings. Its plain language requires the payment of compensation whenever the government acquires private property for a public purpose, whether the acquisition is the result of a condemnation proceeding or a physical appropriation. But the Constitution contains no comparable reference to regulations that prohibit a property owner from making certain uses of her private property. Our jurisprudence involving condemnations and physical takings is as old as the Republic and, for the most part, involves the straightforward application of *per se* rules. Our regulatory takings jurisprudence, in contrast, is of more recent vintage and is characterized by "essentially ad hoc, factual inquiries," *Penn Central*, [citation], designed to allow "careful examination and weighing of all the relevant circumstances." [Citation].

When the government physically takes possession of an interest in property for some public purpose, it has a categorical duty to compensate the former owner, [citation], regardless of whether the interest that is taken constitutes an entire parcel or merely a part thereof. Thus, compensation is mandated when a leasehold is taken and the government occupies the property for its own purposes, even though that use is temporary. [Citations]. Similarly, when the government appropriates part of a rooftop in order to provide cable TV access for apartment tenants, [citation]; or when its planes use private airspace to approach a government airport, [citation], it is required to pay for that share no matter how small. But a government regulation that merely prohibits landlords from evicting tenants unwilling to pay a higher rent, [citation]; that bans certain private uses of a portion of an owner's property, [citations]; or that forbids the private use of certain airspace, [citation], does not constitute a categorical taking. "The first category of cases requires courts to apply a clear rule; the second necessarily entails complex factual assessments of the purposes and economic effects of government actions." [Citations].

This longstanding distinction between acquisitions of property for public use, on the one hand, and regulations prohibiting private uses, on the other, makes it inappropriate to treat cases involving physical takings as controlling precedents for the evaluation of a claim that there has been a "regulatory taking," and vice versa. * * * Land-use regulations are ubiquitous and most of them impact property values in some tangential way—often in completely unanticipated ways. Treating them all as *per se* takings would transform government regulation into a luxury few governments could afford. By contrast, physical appropriations are relatively rare, easily identified, and usually represent a greater affront to individual property rights. "This case does not present the 'classic taking' in which the government directly appropriates private property for its own use," [citation]; instead the interference with property rights "arises from some public program adjusting the benefits and burdens of economic life to promote the common good," *Penn Central*, [citation].

Perhaps recognizing this fundamental distinction, petitioners wisely do not place all their emphasis on analogies to physical takings cases. Instead, they rely principally on our decision in *Lucas v. South Carolina Coastal Council*, [citation]—a regulatory takings case that, nevertheless, applied a categorical rule—to argue that the *Penn Central* framework is inapplicable here. * * *

* * *

The categorical rule that we applied in *Lucas* states that compensation is required when a regulation deprives an owner of "all economically beneficial uses" of his land. [Citation]. Under that rule, a statute that "wholly eliminated the value" of *Lucas'* fee simple title clearly qualified as a taking. But our holding was limited to "the extraordinary circumstance when *no* productive or economically beneficial use of land is permitted." [Citation.] The emphasis on the word "no" in the text of the opinion was, in effect, reiterated in a footnote explaining that the categorical rule would not apply if the diminution in value were 95% instead of 100%. [Citation.] Anything less than a "complete elimination of value," or a "total loss," the Court acknowledged, would require the kind of analysis applied in *Penn Central. Lucas*, [citation].

Certainly, our holding that the permanent "obliteration of the value" of a fee simple estate constitutes a categorical taking does not answer the question whether a regulation prohibiting any economic use of land for a 32-month period has the same legal effect. * * * The starting point for the court's analysis should have been to ask whether there was a total taking of the entire parcel; if not, then *Penn Central* was the proper framework.

An interest in real property is defined by the metes and bounds that describe its geographic dimensions and the term of years that describes the temporal aspect of the owner's interest. See Restatement of Property §§ 7–9. Both dimensions must be considered if the interest is to be viewed in its entirety. Hence, a permanent deprivation of the owner's use of the entire area is a taking of "the parcel as a whole," whereas a temporary restriction that merely causes a diminution in value is not. Logically, a fee simple estate cannot be rendered valueless by a temporary prohibition on economic use, because the property will recover value as soon as the prohibition is lifted. [Citation].

Neither *Lucas*, * * * nor any of our other regulatory takings cases compels us to accept petitioners' categorical submission. In fact, these cases make clear that the categorical rule in *Lucas* was carved out for the "extraordinary case" in which a regulation permanently deprives property of all value; the default rule remains that, in the regulatory taking context, we require a more fact specific inquiry. * * *

* * *

In rejecting petitioners' *per se* rule, we do not hold that the temporary nature of a land-use restriction precludes finding that it effects a taking; we simply recognize that it should not be given exclusive significance one way or the other.

A narrower rule that excluded the normal delays associated with processing permits, or that covered only delays of more than a year, would certainly have a less severe impact on prevailing practices, but it would still impose serious financial constraints on the planning process. Unlike the "extraordinary circumstance" in which the government deprives a property owner of all economic use, *Lucas*, [citation], moratoria like [the ones in this case] are used widely among land-use planners to preserve the status quo while formulating a more permanent development strategy. In fact, the consensus in the planning community appears to be that moratoria, or "interim development controls" as they are often called, are an essential tool of successful development. * * *

* * *

It may well be true that any moratorium that lasts for more than one year should be viewed with special skepticism. But given the fact that the District Court found that the 32 months required by TRPA to formulate the 1984 Regional Plan was not unreasonable, we could not possibly conclude that every delay of over one year is constitutionally unacceptable. Formulating a general rule of this kind is a suitable task for state legislatures. In our view, the duration of the restriction is one of the important factors that a court must consider in the appraisal of a regulatory takings claim, but with respect to that factor as with respect to other factors, the "temptation to adopt what amount to *per se* rules in either direction must be resisted." * * *

INTERPRETATION The prohibition against a state taking private property without paying the owner just compensation applies *per se* to regulatory takings that deny all economically beneficial or productive use of the land but temporary moratoria on residential development do *not* constitute *per se* takings.

CRITICAL THINKING QUESTION Do you agree with the Court's decision? Explain.

Ethical Dilemma

Where Should Cities House the Disadvantaged?

FACTS Susan Kate is a member of the city council in Wissahicken City. The Clinton Living Center, Inc., has just applied for a special use permit to allow the center to lease a building to use as a group house for the emotionally ill. The home will provide supervised group living quarters for individuals who have suffered from a wide range of emotional problems, including depression, anxiety, substance abuse, and sexual disorders. A small percentage of the proposed occupants will be criminal offenders embarking on the rehabilitative phase of their sentencing, with the ultimate goal of reentering the community. Many of the members will attend school and other job training programs under supervision during the day.

The Wissahicken zoning ordinance requires that a special permit be obtained annually for hospitals for the insane, the mentally retarded, alcoholics, or drug addicts and for penal or correctional institutions. The building the Center wishes to lease is in an R-3 zone that expressly permits apartment houses, multiple dwellings, hospitals, or nursing homes, but excludes penal institutions and homes for the insane, the mentally retarded, alcoholics, or drug addicts. In addition, the building is not far from an upper middle-class neighborhood consisting of single-family homes. The home would be across the street from a junior high school.

Public hearings have been held, and there is widespread community opposition to the proposed lease. Susan Kate, a new and politically ambitious member of the city council, must cast the deciding vote as to whether the special permit should be issued.

Social, Policy, and Ethical Considerations

1. What are the goals of zoning classifications?
2. Is there any justification for requiring a special permit under the circumstances? What are the community's concerns? Are these concerns justified?
3. What is the social policy behind placing rehabilitative group homes in the heart of a thriving community rather than in an isolated neighborhood?
4. Should a permit be refused for the purpose of preserving property values? Consider the concerns of a sixty-year-old couple who are close to retirement, who have modest cash savings, and who have always planned to sell their house in their mid-sixties and move to an apartment. Consider also the concerns of a young, newly married couple in search of affordable housing in a stable, established neighborhood.
5. Would your answers change if the special permit request were for a meeting home for homosexuals or for a group home for the profoundly retarded?

Public Use

As noted, there is an implicit constitutional prohibition against taking private property for other than public use. Most states interpret **public use** to mean "public advantage." Thus, the power of eminent domain may be delegated to railroad and public utility companies. Because it enables such companies to offer continued and improved service to the public, the reasonable exercise of such power is upheld as a public advantage. As society grows more complex, other public purposes become legitimate grounds for exercising the power of eminent domain. One such use is in the area of urban renewal. Most states have legislation permitting the establishment of housing authorities with the power to condemn slum, blighted, and vacant areas and to finance, construct, and maintain housing projects. Some states have recently gone further by allowing private companies to exercise the power of eminent domain, provided the use is primarily for the public benefit, including the alleviation of unemployment or economic decay within the community.

Just Compensation

When the power of eminent domain is exercised, the owners of the property taken must receive **just compensation.** The measure of compensation is the fair market value of the property as of the time of taking. The compensation goes to holders of vested interests in the condemned property.

For an overview of eminent domain see Figure 51-2.

CPA Private Restrictions on Land Use

Owners of real property may impose private restrictions, called **restrictive covenants** (or negative covenants), on the use of land. Historically, two types of private restrictions

Figure 51-2
Eminent Domain

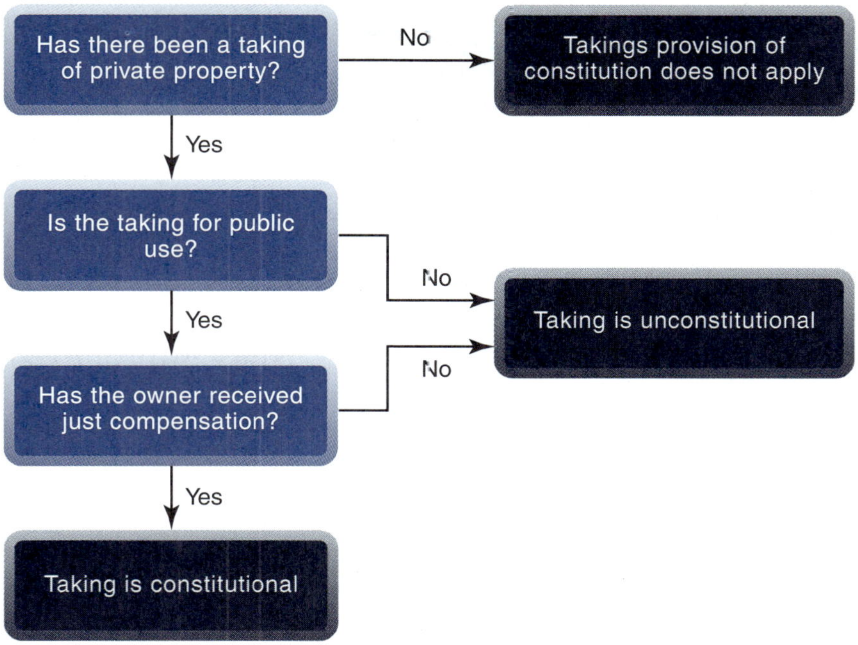

developed—real covenants and equitable servitudes. The two had different, although overlapping, requirements. Today, equitable servitudes have nearly replaced real covenants. Accordingly, this section will cover only equitable servitudes, which we will identify by the more general term *restrictive covenant.*

REQUIREMENTS FOR COVENANTS RUNNING WITH THE LAND

If certain conditions are satisfied, a restrictive covenant will bind not only the original parties to it but also remote parties who subsequently acquire the property. A restrictive covenant that binds remote parties is said to "run with the land." To run with the land, the covenant must involve promises that are enforceable under the law of contracts. Accordingly, a majority of courts hold that restrictive covenants must be in writing. The parties who agree to the restrictive covenant must intend that the covenant bind their successors. Moreover, the covenant must "touch and concern" the land, affecting its use, utility, or value. Finally, a restrictive covenant will bind only those successors who have had actual or constructive notice of the covenant.

RESTRICTIVE COVENANTS IN SUBDIVISIONS

Restrictive covenants are widely used in subdivisions. The owners of lots are subject to restrictive covenants that, if actually brought to the attention of subsequent purchasers or recorded by original deed or by means of a recorded plat or separate agreement, bind purchasers of lots in the subdivision as though the restrictions had actually been inserted in their own deeds. If the entire subdivision has been subjected to a general building plan designed to benefit all of the lots, any lot owner in the subdivision has the right to enforce the restriction against a purchaser whose title descends from a common grantor. If a restriction is clearly intended to benefit an entire tract, the covenant will be enforced against a subsequent purchaser of one of the lots in the tract if (1) the restriction was apparently intended to benefit the purchaser of any lot in the tract and (2) the restriction appears somewhere in the chain of title to which the lot is subject.

Subdivisions may involve many types of restrictive covenants. The more common ones limit the use of property to residential purposes, restrict the area of the lot on which a structure can be built, or provide for a special type of architecture. Frequently, a subdivider will specify a minimum size for each house in an attempt to maintain structural unity in a neighborhood.

Restrictive covenants are construed strictly against the party asserting their applicability.

TERMINATION OF RESTRICTIVE COVENANTS

A restrictive covenant may end by the terms of the original agreement. For example, the developer of a subdivision may provide that the restrictive covenant will terminate after thirty-five years unless a specified majority of the property owners reaffirm the covenant. In addition, a

THE LAW AND YOU

State Bar Associations

Florida: http://www.flabar.org/newflabar/consumerservices/General/Consumer.Pam/ ("Buying a Condominium"; "Buying a Home")

Georgia: http://www.gabar.org/ ("Buying a Home")

Illinois: http://www.illinioslawyerfinder.com/publicinfo.html ("Buying a Home")

Iowa: http://www.iowabar.org/pamphlet.nsf/$about!OpenAbout ("Sound Steps in Purchasing a Home")

Maine: http://www.mainebar.org/ (legal information pamphlets) ("Buying and Selling Real Estate")

Maryland: http://www.msba.org/public/brochure.htm ("Buying a Home")

Minnesota: http://www.mnbar.org/consumer.htm ("Buying a Home"; "Buying Real Property")

Mississippi: http://www.msbar.org/ ("You and Your Home")

Missouri: http://www.mobar.org/pamphlets/broindex.htm (brochures on legal topics) ("Buying a Home")

New York: http://www.nysba.org/Template.cfm?Section=Public_Resources ("Buying and Selling Real Estate" [English and Spanish]; "The Attorney's Role in Buying or Selling a House")

North Carolina: http://www.ncbar.org ("Buying a Home")

Oklahoma: http://www.okbar.org/publicinfo/brochures/ ("Thinking of Buying a Home?")

Oregon: http://www.osbar.org/public/legalinfo/html ("Real Estate")

South Dakota: http://www.sdbar.org/public/Default.htm ("Buying a Home")

Washington: http://www.wsba.org/public/default.htm ("Real Estate")

Wisconsin: http://www.wisbar.org/asp/ titles.asp ("Buying/Selling Real Estate") http://www.wisbar.org/pubres/bytes.html (audio) ("Real Estate")

State Attorney Generals

Maine: http://www.maine.gov/ag/?r=protection ("The Maine Attorney General's Consumer Law Guide")

Minnesota: http://www.ag.state.mn.us/default/consumer.shtml ("Housing")

Tennessee: http://www.state.tn.us/consumer/brochure.html ("Home"; "Real Estate & Estate Planning")

U.S. Government

http://www.pueblo.gsa.gov/housing.htm ("HUD Home Buying Guide")

http://www.pueblo.gsa.gov/housing.htm ("How to Buy a Home with a Low Down Payment")

http://www.pueblo.gsa.gov/specpubs ("Buying Your Home: Settlement Costs and Helpful Information")

http://www.pueblo.gsa.gov/housing.htm ("100 Questions and Answers About Buying a Home")

http://www.pueblo.gsa.gov/housing.htm ("Looking for the Best Mortgage—Shop, Compare, Negotiate")

http://www.pueblo.gsa.gov/specpubs ("Selling a Home")

court will not enforce a restrictive covenant if changed circumstances make enforcement inequitable and oppressive. Evidence of changed conditions may be found either within the tract covered by the original covenant or within the area adjacent to or surrounding the tract.

VALIDITY OF RESTRICTIVE COVENANTS

Although restrictions on land use have never been popular in the law, the courts will enforce a restriction that apparently will operate to the general benefit of the owners of all the land the restriction will affect. The usual method of enforcing such agreements is by injunction to restrain a violation.

The law for many years, however, has held that under the Fourteenth Amendment to the Constitution, a state or municipality cannot impose racial restrictions by statute or ordinance. In 1947, in holding that state courts, as an arm of state government, cannot enforce private racial restrictive covenants, the Supreme Court effectively invalidated such covenants.

Corner v. Mills
Court of Appeals of Indiana, 1995
650 N.E.2d 712

FACTS Christiana Acres is a subdivision consisting of thirty-two lots in Elkhart, Indiana **(http://www.elkhartindiana.org/)**. The tract was divided in 1937 by then owners Perry and Florence Shupert. Between 1939 and 1941, four lots were sold without restrictions. In 1942, one of the lots was sold with several restrictions, including a residential use restriction, a sideline and setback provision, a minimum lot size to build restriction, a prohibition of noxious or offensive activities, a racial restriction (prohibiting occupancy by non-whites), a restriction against temporary residential structures, and a minimum building size and cost restriction. Between 1942 and 1946, two of the lots were sold; one with the above restrictions and one without. In 1946, the tract was recorded without any restrictions by all of the owners. At the time, all of the owners were using their lots for residential purposes. Subsequently, thirteen lots were sold. These lots all had restrictions, although they did not all have identical restrictions. All but one had a residential use restriction.

The plaintiffs own lots in the subdivision that are located near a commercialized thoroughfare. They believed that their property would be more valuable if used for commercial purposes and filed a complaint seeking declaratory relief to have the restrictive covenants on their property lifted. The defendants, who are also residents of the subdivision, filed a counterclaim seeking enforcement of the covenants. The trial court found the racial covenants unenforceable but upheld the residential use restrictions on Christiana Acres.

DECISION Judgment affirmed.

OPINION Hoffman, J. Restrictive covenants which restrict use of land based on race are unconstitutional. [Citation.] Thus, indisputably, the racial restriction contained in the deeds are invalid. However, as the defendants point out, restrictive covenants are express contracts between a grantor and a grantee. [Citation.] Accordingly, as in other contracts, illegal covenants may be removed if to do so will not affect the intent or symmetry of the remaining covenants. [Citation.]

Racial restrictions aside, it is evident that the other residential covenants seek to independently ensure the residential quality of Christiana Acres They do this by setting forth very specific set-back and minimum value requirements, by prohibiting certain commercial and trade behavior, and by imposing restrictions against certain temporary residential structures. As the trial court noted in its findings, severing the illegal racial covenants only destroys a small portion of the covenants' intent. It does not affect the prevailing and apparent intent to have Christiana Acres remain residential. Consequently, the trial court did not err in redacting the illegal covenants while allowing the others to remain intact

Plaintiffs next contend the trial court erred in finding a general scheme or plan of residential development to exist in Christiana Acres. In support of their argument, plaintiffs argue that some of the covenants are ambiguous, and point out that many of the deeds are not identical in their restrictions, that some properties do not have restrictions on them at all, and that several lots were conveyed without restrictions before the plat was recorded.

However, the lack of uniformity in restrictions in a subdivision does not conclusively prove the nonexistence of a general plan or scheme for residential development. [Citation.] Nor does the fact that some of the lots contain no restrictions, that a few lots were conveyed before the plat was recorded, or that the recorded plat itself contains no restrictions, conclusively show the nonexistence of such a plan. [Citations.]

Instead, in determining whether a general scheme or plan of development exists, the pertinent focus is on whether the circumstances and facts of the case, including the language of the deeds and the grantors' actions, reveal an intent by them to create such a plan or scheme. [Citation.]

* * *

In 1946, the plat was recorded. At that time, all owners maintained their properties strictly for residential use. Also, each property owner joined in the recording. In doing so, it is reasonable to infer that the owners all intended to combine in their efforts to develop Christiana Acres as a residential neighborhood. By making Christiana Acres exclusively residential, it is also inferable that the common grantors wished to enhance the value of their lots to the benefit of all others in the subdivision.

At present, every owner can trace their properties to this common source beginning in 1946. Moreover, a review of the deeds in aggregate reveals unmistakable intent to place residential restrictions on the properties and the subdivision as a whole. [Citation.] After the initial recording, although not identical, lots were consistently transferred with various residential restrictions. * * *

Next, plaintiffs complain that because there has been significant commercial development [next to Christiana Acres] in recent years, the continued residential nature of

Christiana Acres is no longer feasible. The facts, however, indicate a conclusion to the contrary.

It is only where the use of the property and the surrounding area has so radically changed from what was originally envisioned making the covenants no longer sustainable, that they will be lifted as unenforceable [Citation.] In this analysis, the equities must be viewed to determine if they favor dismantling the neighborhood restrictions.

Plaintiffs' unilateral speculation that their properties are worth more if developed commercially is insufficient by itself to nullify the otherwise valid covenants for residential use. [Citation.] * * *

INTERPRETATION Illegal covenants can be removed from an agreement, provided it will not affect the intent or symmetry of the remaining covenants.

ETHICAL QUESTION Did the court fairly decide this case? Explain.

CRITICAL THINKING QUESTION What limits should the law place on the extent and duration of private restrictive covenants? Explain.

Chapter Summary

Transfer of Real Property

Contract of Sale

Formation a contract to transfer any interest in land must be in writing to be enforceable

Marketable Title the seller must transfer marketable title, which is a title free from any defects or encumbrances

Quality of Improvements
- *Common Law Rule* under *caveat emptor* ("let the buyer beware"), the seller is not liable for any undiscovered defects
- *Implied Warranty of Habitability* in a number of states, the builder-seller of a dwelling impliedly warrants that a newly constructed house is free from latent defects

Deeds

Definition a formal document transferring any type of interest in land

Types
- *Warranty Deed* the grantor (seller) promises the grantee (buyer) that she has valid title to the property without defect
- *Special Warranty Deed* the seller promises that he has not impaired the title
- *Quitclaim Deed* the seller transfers whatever interest she has in the property

Requirements the deed must (1) be written, (2) contain certain words of conveyance and a description of the property, (3) end with the signature of the grantor, a seal, and an acknowledgment before a notary public, and (4) be delivered

Delivery intent that the deed take effect, as evidenced by acts or statements of the grantor

Recordation required to protect the buyer's interest against third parties; consists of delivery of a duly executed and acknowledged deed to the appropriate recorder's office

Secured Transactions

Elements a secured transaction involves (1) a debt or obligation to pay money, (2) an interest of the creditor in specific property that secures performance, and (3) the debtor's right to redeem the property (remove the security interest) by paying the debt

Mortgage interest in land created by a written document that provides security to the mortgagee (secured party) for payment of the mortgagor's debt

Deed of Trust an interest in real property that is conveyed to a third person as trustee for the benefit of the creditor

Transfer
- ***Assumes the Mortgage*** the purchaser of mortgaged property becomes personally liable to pay the debt
- ***Subject to the Mortgage*** purchaser is not personally liable to pay the debt, but the property remains subject to the mortgage

Foreclosure upon default, sale of the mortgaged property to satisfy the debt

Adverse Possession

Definition acquisition of title to land by open, continuous, and adverse occupancy for a statutorily prescribed period

Possession must be actual and without intervening dominion by true owner

Public and Private Controls

Zoning

Definition principal method of public control over private land use, involves regulation of land but may not constitute a taking of the property

Authority the power to zone is generally delegated to local authorities by statutes known as enabling acts

Variance a use differing from that provided in the zoning ordinance and granted in order to avoid undue hardship

Nonconforming Use a use not in accordance with, but existing prior to, a zoning ordinance; permitted to continue for at least a reasonable time

Judicial Review zoning ordinances may be reviewed to determine if they are invalid or a confiscation of property

Eminent Domain

Definition the power of a government to take (buy) private land for public use

Public Use public advantage

Just Compensation the owner of the property taken by eminent domain must be paid the fair market value of the property

Restrictive Covenants

Definition private restrictions on property contained in a conveyance

Covenants Running with the Land covenants that bind not only the original parties but also subsequent owners of the property

Covenants in Subdivision bind purchasers of lots in the subdivision as if the restrictions had been inserted in their own deeds

QUESTIONS

1. A was the father of B, C, and D and the owner of Redacre, Blackacre, and Greenacre.

   A made and executed a warranty deed conveying Redacre to B. The deed provided that "this deed shall become effective only on the death of the grantor." A retained possession of the deed and died, leaving the deed in his safe deposit box.

   A made and executed a warranty deed conveying Blackacre to C. This deed also provided that "this deed shall become effective only on the death of the grantor."

A delivered the deed to C. After A died, C recorded the deed.

A made and executed a warranty deed conveying Greenacre to D. A delivered the deed to X with specific instructions to deliver the deed to D on A's death. X duly delivered the deed to D when A died.

a. What is the interest of B in Redacre, if any?
b. What is the interest of C in Blackacre, if any?
c. What is the interest of D in Greenacre, if any?

2. Arkin, the owner of Redacre, executed a real estate mortgage to the Shawnee Bank and Trust Company for $10,000. After the mortgage was executed and recorded, Arkin constructed a dwelling on the premises and planted a corn crop. After Arkin defaulted in the payment of the mortgage debt, the bank proceeded to foreclose the mortgage. At the time of the foreclosure sale, the corn crop was mature and unharvested. Arkin contends (a) that the value of the dwelling should be credited to him and (b) that he is entitled to the corn crop. Explain whether Arkin is correct.

3. Robert and Stanley held legal title of record to adjacent tracts of land, each consisting of acres. Stanley fenced his acres in 1978, placing his east fence fifteen feet onto Robert's property. Thereafter, he was in possession of this fifteen-foot strip of land and kept it fenced and cultivated continuously until he sold his tract of land to Nathan on March 1, 1984. Nathan took possession under deed from Stanley, and continued possession and cultivation of the fifteen-foot strip until May 27, 2003, when Robert, having on several occasions strenuously objected to Nathan's possession, brought suit against Nathan for trespass. Explain whether Nathan has gained title by adverse possession.

4. Marcia executed a mortgage of Blackacre to secure her indebtedness to Ajax Savings and Loan Association in the amount of $25,000. Later, Marcia sold Blackacre to Morton. The deed contained the following provision: "This deed is subject to the mortgage executed by the Grantor herein to Ajax Savings and Loan Association."

The sale price of Blackacre to Morton was $50,000. Morton paid $25,000 in cash, deducting the $25,000 mortgage debt from the purchase price. On default in the payment of the mortgage debt, Ajax brings an action against Marcia and Morton to recover a judgment for the amount of the mortgage debt and to foreclose the mortgage. Can Ajax recover from Marcia and Morton? Explain.

5. On January 1, 2001, Davis and Hershey owned Blackacre as tenants in common. On July 1, 2001, Davis made a written contract to sell Blackacre to Dibbert for $25,000. Pursuant to this contract, Dibbert paid Davis $25,000 on August 1, 2002, and Davis executed and delivered to Dibbert a warranty deed to Blackacre. On May 1, 2003, Hershey quitclaimed his interest in Blackacre to Davis. Dibbert brings an action against Davis for breach of warranty of title. What judgment?

6. John Doe, for valuable consideration, agreed to convey to Richard Roe eighty acres of land. He delivered a deed, the material portions of which read:

"I, John Doe, grant and convey to Richard Roe eighty acres of land [land description]: To have and to hold unto Richard Roe, his heirs, and assigns forever.

"I, John Doe, covenant to warrant and defend the premises hereby conveyed against all persons claiming the same or any part thereof by or through me."

Thereafter, Roe conveyed "all my right, title, and interest" in the eighty acres to Paul Poe. It develops that Doe had no title to the land when he conveyed it to Roe. Subsequently, Doe inherited an undivided one-half interest in the property.

What rights, if any, does Poe have against Doe and Roe?

7. In adjoining locations along one side of a single suburban village block, Barker operated a retail bakery; Davidson, a drugstore; Farrell, a food store; Gibson, a gift shop; and Harper, a hardware store. As the population grew, the business section developed at the other end of the village, and the establishments of Barker, Davidson, Farrell, Gibson, and Harper were surrounded for at least a mile in each direction solely by residences. A zoning ordinance with the usual provisions was adopted by the village, and the area including the five stores was declared to be a "residential district for single-family dwellings." Thereafter, Barker tore down the frame building that housed the bakery and began to construct a modern brick bakery. Davidson found her business increasing to such an extent that she began to build an addition on the drugstore to extend it to the rear alley. Farrell's building was destroyed by fire, and he started to reconstruct it to restore it to its former condition. Gibson changed the gift shop into a sporting goods store and after six months of operation decided to go back into the gift shop business. Harper sold his hardware store to Hempstead.

The village building commission brings an action under the zoning ordinance to enjoin the construction work of Barker, Davidson, and Farrell and to enjoin the carrying on of any business by Gibson and Hempstead. Assume the ordinance is valid. What result?

8. Alda and Mattingly are residents of Unit I of Chimney Hills Subdivision. The lots owned by Alda and Mattingly are subject to the following restrictive covenant: "Lots shall be for single-family residence purposes only." Alda intends to convert her carport into a beauty shop, and Mattingly brings suit against Alda to enjoin her from doing so. Alda argues that the covenant restricts only the type of building that can be constructed, not the incidental use to which residential structures are put. Will Alda be able to operate a beauty shop on the property? Why?

CASE PROBLEMS

9. The City of Boston (http://www.cityofboston.gov) sought to condemn land in fee simple for use in constructing an entrance to an underground terminal for a subway. The owners of the land contend that no more than surface and subsurface easements are necessary for the terminal entrance and seek to retain air rights above 36 feet. The city argues that any building using this airspace would require structural supports that would interfere with the city's plan for the terminal. The city concedes that the properties around the condemned property could be assembled and structures could be designed to span over the condemned property, in which case the air rights would be quite valuable. Can the city condemn the property?

10. For seven years, Desford Potts had owned a six-acre tract of land within the corporate limits of the city of Franklin. The tract contained a livestock barn in which Potts stored lumber and other building materials. Bricks were also stored in stacks four or five feet high outside and behind the barn. Franklin passed a zoning ordinance by virtue of which Potts's lot was classified as residential property. Soon afterward, Potts moved some saw logs onto his back lot, and the city complained that Potts's use of his property for storage of building materials was a "nonconforming use." Potts then brought an action to enjoin interference by the city of Franklin. Explain whether Potts will prevail.

11. In May 1991, Fred Parramore executed four deeds, each conveying a life estate in his land to him and his wife and a remainder interest in one-fourth of his land to each of his four children: Alney, Eudell, Bernice, and Iris. Although Fred executed and acknowledged the four deeds as part of his plan to distribute his estate at his death, he did not deliver them to his children at this time. Instead, he placed the deeds with his will in a safe deposit box and instructed the children to pick up their deeds at his death. Fred later conveyed Alney's deed to Alney, thereby vesting Alney's interest in that parcel, but Eudell, Bernice, and Iris's deeds were never handed over to them during Fred's lifetime. Fred, however, acted as if the land was beyond his control, and on one occasion told a prospective buyer that the land had already been deeded away. When Fred died in November 2002, Alney brought this action, claiming that the deeds to Eudell, Bernice, and Iris were ineffective because they had never been handed over during Fred's lifetime. Accordingly, Alney argued the remaining land should pass in equal shares to each of the four children under the residuary clause of Fred's will. Who will prevail? Why?

12. The Gerwitz family resides on a piece of land known as Lot #24 of the Belleville tract, which they acquired by deed in 1983. Shortly thereafter, the Gerwitzes began to use the adjacent vacant Lot #25. At various times they planted grass seed, flowers, and shrubs on the land and used it for picnics and cookouts. In 2003, Gelsomin acquired Lot #25 and constructed a foundation on it so that he could place a house there. The Gerwitzes then brought this action to stop him, claiming title to Lot #25 by adverse possession. Discuss whether the Gerwitzes have obtained title by adverse possession.

13. Leo owned a one-story, one-family dwelling in a single-family residential zoning district in Detroit (http://www.ci.detroit.mi.us/). He attempted to sell the house with its adjoining lot for $38,500. Houses in the neighborhood generally sold for $20,000 to $25,000. Immediately to the west of Leo's property was a gasoline service station. In addition, Leo's property was located on a corner frequented with heavy traffic. After he received no offers from residence-use buyers during the period of more than a year that the property was listed and offered for sale, Leo applied to the board of zoning appeals for a variance to permit the use of the property as a dental and medical clinic and to use the side yard for off-street parking. The variance would be subject to certain conditions, including the preservation of the building's exterior as that of a one-family dwelling. Puritan-Greenfield Improvement Association, a nonprofit corporation, filed a complaint against Leo's variance request. Discuss whether the variance should be granted.

14. The Glendale Church purchased a twenty-one-acre parcel of land in a canyon along the banks of Mill Creek in Angeles National Forest (http://www.r5.fs.fed.us/angeles/). The church used the 12 flat acres next to the stream to operate a campground for disabled children. This area had a number of improved buildings located on it. In July, a forest fire destroyed all ground cover upstream from the church's campground, and a subsequent flood destroyed all the buildings. In response, the county of Los Angeles enacted an interim ordinance that temporarily prohibited the church from constructing new buildings. Is the church entitled to compensation for a temporary taking of its property? Why?

15. Robert V. Gross owned certain land on which he proposed to construct an eighty-three-unit apartment house. The land, however, was subject to a restriction imposed by a 1957 deed to a predecessor in title that provided that no part of the premises could be used for business purposes other than raising, growing, and selling live bait, fishing tackle, and sporting goods. Explain whether the restriction prohibits the construction and operation of an apartment house.

16. Sam and Eleanor Gaito purchased a home from Howard Frank Auman, Jr., in the spring of 2001. Auman had completed the construction of the house in November 1996. In the interim, three different parties had lived in the house for brief periods, but Auman had retained ownership. The last tenants, the Ashleys, experienced difficulties with the home's air-conditioning system. Repairs were attempted, but no effort was made to change the capacity of the air-conditioning unit.

When the Gaitos moved into the house in June 2001 they too had problems with the air-conditioning. The system created only a ten-degree difference between the outside and inside temperatures. The Gaitos complained to Auman on a number of occasions, but extensive repairs failed to correct the cooling problem. In May 2004, the Gaitos brought an action against Auman, alleging that the purchase price of the home included central air-conditioning and that Auman had breached the implied warranty of habitability. At trial, an expert in the field of heating and air-conditioning testified that a 4-ton air-conditioning system, rather than the 3.5-ton system originally installed, was appropriate for the Gaitos's house. The jury returned a verdict in favor of the Gaitos in the amount of $3,655. Explain whether this decision is correct.

17. Playtime Theaters and Sea-First Properties purchased two theaters in Renton, Washington, with the intention of exhibiting adult films. About the same time, they filed suit seeking injunctive relief and a declaratory judgment that the First and Fourteenth Amendments were violated by a city of Renton ordinance that prohibits adult motion picture theaters from locating within 1,000 feet of any residential zone, single- or multiple-family dwelling, church, park, or school. Does the city have the right to enforce such an ordinance? Explain.

http:// **Internet Exercise** Find and compare the rates among mortgage providers on (a) thirty-year mortgages, (b) fifteen-year mortgages, and (c) adjustable rate mortgages.

CHAPTER 52

Trusts and Wills

It was said . . . many years ago that the parents of the trust were fraud and fear and that the court of conscience was its nurse.
GEORGE T. BOGERT, *TRUSTS* (6TH ED., 1987)

Learning Objectives

After reading this chapter you should be able to:

1. Describe and explain the following types of trusts: (a) express, (b) testamentary, (c) *inter vivos*, (d) charitable, (e) spendthrift, (f) totten, (g) implied, (h) constructive, and (i) resulting.
2. Describe the powers and duties of a trustee.
3. Explain the formal requirements for making a valid will and the various ways in which a will may be revoked.
4. Define the following types of wills: (a) nuncupative, (b) holographic, and (c) soldiers' and sailors'.
5. Describe intestate succession and the administration of decedents' estates.

In previous chapters, we have seen that real and personal property may be transferred in a number of ways, including by sale and by gift. Another important way in which a person may convey property or allow others to use or benefit from it is through trusts and wills. Trusts may take effect during the transferor's lifetime, or, when used in a will, they may become effective upon his death. Wills enable individuals to control the transfer of their property at their death. Upon a person's death, his or her property must pass to someone, and individuals are well advised to decide how their property should be distributed. Except for the limitations of dower and curtesy, the law permits individuals to make such distributions by sale, gift, trust, and will. If, however, an individual dies without a will—that is, intestate—state law prescribes who shall be entitled to the property that the individual owned at death. In this chapter, we will examine trusts and wills, as well as the manner in which property descends when a person dies intestate.

TRUSTS

A **trust** is a *fiduciary relationship* in which one or more persons hold legal title to property while its use, enjoyment, and benefit (equitable title) belong to another. Allowed to serve any purpose that is not against the law or public policy, a trust may be created by agreement of the parties, by a grant in a will, or by a court decree. However fashioned, the relationship is known as a trust. The party creating the trust is the **creator** or **settlor**, the party holding the legal title to the property is the trustee of the trust, and the person who receives the benefit of the trust is the **beneficiary** (see Figure 52-1).

CPA TYPES OF TRUSTS

Although there are many varieties, all trusts fall into one of two major groups: express or implied. The implied

Figure 52-1
Trusts

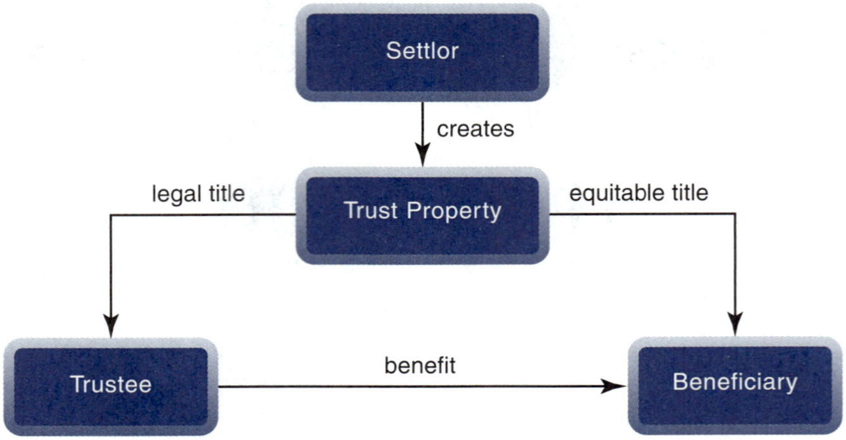

trusts, which are imposed upon property by court order, are categorized as either "constructive" or "resulting" trusts.

EXPRESS TRUSTS

The **express trust** is, as the name indicates, a trust established by voluntary action and is represented either by a written document or, under some conditions, by an oral statement or conduct of the settlor. In a majority of jurisdictions, an express trust of real property must be in writing to meet the requirements of the statute of frauds.

No particular words are necessary to create a trust, provided that the settlor's intent to establish a trust is unmistakable. Determining whether a settlor really intended to create a trust is not always easy. Sometimes, in connection with a gift, a settlor will use words of request or recommendation that imply or express hope that the gift should or will be used for a particular purpose. Thus, instead of leaving property "to X for the benefit and use of Y," a settlor may leave property to X "in full confidence and with hope that he will care for Y." Such a **precatory** (wishful) expression may be so definite as to impose a trust upon the property for Y's benefit. Whether the expression will create a trust or will constitute nothing more than a gratuitous wish depends on whether the court believes from all the facts that the settlor genuinely intended a trust.

Testamentary Trust Trusts employed in wills are known as **testamentary trusts** because they become effective after the settlor's death.

Inter Vivos* Trust** A trust established during the settlor's lifetime is referred to as an ***inter vivos, or "between-the-living," trust.

> **Practical Advice**
>
> As your estate grows, you should determine whether tax or other legal considerations make it beneficial to use a trust as a vehicle to distribute your assets.

Charitable Trusts Almost any trust that has for its purpose the improvement of the whole or a class of humankind is a **charitable trust**, unless it is so vague that it cannot be enforced. Gifts for public museums, for park maintenance, and for the dissemination of a particular political doctrine or religious belief have been upheld as charitable.

Spendthrift Trusts A settlor who believes that a beneficiary cannot be trusted to preserve even the limited rights granted her as beneficiary may provide in the trust instrument that the beneficiary cannot, by assignment or otherwise, impair her rights to receive principal or income and that creditors of the beneficiary cannot attach the fund or the income. Such a trust is called a **spendthrift trust**. Spendthrift provisions are valid in most states. However, once the beneficiary actually receives income from the trust, creditors may seize it or the beneficiary may use it as she pleases.

Totten Trusts A **totten trust** or savings account trust involves a joint bank account opened by the trust settlor. For example, Sally deposits a sum of money into a savings account in the name of "Sally, in trust for Justin." Sally may make additional deposits into the account and may withdraw money from it whenever she pleases. Because the settlor may revoke a totten trust by withdrawing the funds or by changing the form of the account, such a trust is tentative. Usually the transfer of ownership becomes complete only on the depositor's death.

IMPLIED TRUSTS

In some cases, the courts, in the absence of any expressed intent to create a trust, will impose a trust on property because the parties' acts appear to warrant such a construction. An **implied trust** owes its existence to the law.

Constructive Trusts A **constructive trust** results when a court imposes a trust on property to rectify fraud or to prevent unjust enrichment. A court will establish a constructive trust when a confidential relationship has been abused or where actual fraud or duress constitutes an equitable ground for creating the trust. The mere existence of a confidential relationship prohibits the trustee from seeking any personal benefit during the course of the relationship. For example, a director of a corporation who takes advantage of a "corporate opportunity" or who makes an undisclosed profit in a transaction with the corporation will be treated as a trustee for the corporation with respect to the property or profits he has acquired. Likewise, a trustee under an express trust who permits a lease held by the trust to expire and then acquires a new lease of the property in his individual capacity will be required to hold the new lease in a confidential trust for the beneficiary.

In Re Estate of Welch

Court of Appeals of Iowa, 1995
534 N.W.2d 109

FACTS George Welch, a wealthy man, died on April 25, 1991, and was survived by his second wife, Dorothy Welch, and his daughter by his first marriage, Patricia Fisher. At the time George and Dorothy were married, George was in very poor health and he relied on Dorothy to care for him. During the eight months George and Dorothy were married, George became isolated from his family and his health deteriorated. Prior to his death, George transferred the bulk of his assets to Dorothy. Dorothy assisted in the transfer of George's assets and often completed checks and other papers for George's signature. George also made a new will that named Dorothy as his sole beneficiary. Patricia was the sole beneficiary of his prior will. Through the transfers of assets and the new will, Dorothy received $570,000, about 60 percent of George's estate. Patricia sought to set aside the will and the transfers based on undue influence. The will contest was submitted to the jury, which found undue influence and set aside the will. However, the trial court, which considered the transfers of assets, did not find undue influence and refused to create a constructive trust over the assets. Patricia appealed the trial court's ruling.

DECISION Judgment reversed and remanded.

OPINION Cady, J. A constructive trust is a remedial device by which the holder of legal title is held to be a trustee for the benefit of another who in good conscience is entitled to the beneficial interest. [Citation.] It is an equitable doctrine applied for purposes of restitution, to prevent unjust enrichment. [Citation.]

Constructive trusts fall into three categories: "(1) those arising from actual fraud; (2) those arising from constructive fraud (appropriation of property by fiduciaries or others in confidential relationships); and (3) those based on equitable principles other than fraud." [Citation.] Other circumstances supporting imposition of equitable principles include bad faith, duress, coercion, undue influence, abuse of confidence, or any form of unconscionable conduct or questionable means by which one obtains the legal right to property which they should not in equity and good conscience hold. [Citations.] * * *

Patricia seeks imposition of a constructive trust on two alternative bases. First she asserts a constructive trust should be created because a confidential relationship existed between Dorothy and George, and Dorothy abused this relationship. Second, she claims even if a confidential relationship did not exist, a constructive trust should be established on the basis that Dorothy unduly influenced George.

Undue influence is unfair persuasion of a party who is under the domination of the person exercising the persuasion or who by virtue of the relation between them is justified in assuming that the person will not act in a manner inconsistent with his or her welfare. [Citation.] The ultimate question is whether the result was produced by means that seriously impaired the free and competent exercise of judgment. [Citation.] There are four elements necessary to sustain a finding of undue influence. They are: (1) the grantor's susceptibility to undue influence; (2) opportunity to exercise such influence and effect the wrongful purpose; (3) disposition to influence unduly for the purpose of procuring an improper favor; and (4) a result clearly the effect of undue influence. [Citation.]

On our review of the record, we find it unnecessary to determine the existence of a confidential relationship or to determine the effect of the prenuptial agreement. We find clear and convincing evidence that Dorothy acted unconscionably by exercising undue influence over George in order to gain title to his property. Under the circumstances of this case, allowing Dorothy to retain the property gained in this manner would be inequitable.

George was in very poor health at the time of his marriage to Dorothy in August 1990. He suffered a crippling heart attack in 1988 and was told by doctors he would only live a few more years. After the heart attack, George was not permitted to drive and could not live alone. There was evidence that the damage to his heart might have affected the flow of blood to his brain. George suffered from severe depression and was suicidal. He was also an alcoholic.

Dorothy was a friend of George and his previous wife, Betty. Betty died in May 1988. Within a few days after Betty's death, Dorothy told George she had always loved him and wanted to marry him. She later threatened to commit suicide if George did not marry her. George asked other women to marry him before he married Dorothy. He was lonely and desperately looking for companionship.

After George and Dorothy married, George became isolated from his family and medical assistance. He stopped seeing his cardiologist and psychiatrist. His physical and medical condition deteriorated. There was medical testimony that George was very vulnerable and susceptible to undue influence during the last year of his life. He was dependent upon Dorothy for transportation, to remind him to take his medicine, for care when he had angina attacks, and for emotional support.

Dorothy was aware of George's wealth and knew George had a limited time to live due to his heart condition. * * * The transfer of assets into joint tenancy began shortly after the marriage and continued until shortly before George's death. Dorothy even removed George's name from their joint bank account within a month before his death.

When George died she had all the locks changed on the house and allegedly informed Patricia of George's death by stating the money was put in joint accounts, the wills were changed, and your father has died. We do not share the trial court's view that the various financial arrangements between George and Dorothy were normal transactions between a husband and wife.

We conclude that a fair and pragmatic review of all the evidence clearly shows undue influence. Dorothy positioned herself as a dominant influence over George during the last months of his life. At the same time, George became particularly susceptible to being influenced due to his advancing age, impending death, deteriorating physical condition, and unstable emotional health. Furthermore, the manner in which George and Dorothy conducted their business, and even Dorothy's actions after George died, reveal a pattern of unfair persuasion or influence. George was isolated from family, friends, and complete medical care. The efforts to transfer his property were rushed and the transactions were done at unusual times. Upon our review of all the facts and circumstances, we find: George was susceptible; Dorothy had an opportunity to exercise undue influence, as well as the disposition to wrongfully influence George for the purpose of obtaining money and assets; and the assets she received resulted from the undue influence.

INTERPRETATION A court may impose a constructive trust to prevent the unjust enrichment of a person who has abused a confidential relationship with another.

CRITICAL THINKING QUESTION When should a court impose a constructive trust? Explain.

Resulting Trusts A **resulting trust** serves to effect the inferred or presumed *intent* of parties who have inadequately expressed their actual wishes. A resulting trust does not depend on contract or agreement but on presumed intent, as evidenced by the parties' acts. Because a resulting trust is created by implication and operation of law, it need not be evidenced in writing. The most common example of a resulting trust is the case of Joel, who pays the purchase price for property and takes title in Ellen's name. Here, the courts presume that the parties intended Ellen to hold the property for Joel's benefit, and Ellen will be treated as a trustee.

CPA CREATION OF TRUSTS

Each trust has (1) a creator or settlor, (2) a "corpus" or trust property, (3) a trustee, and (4) a beneficiary. As we mentioned before, no particular words are necessary to create a trust, provided that the settlor's intent to establish a trust is unmistakable. Consideration is not essential to an enforceable trust.

SETTLOR

Any person legally capable of making a contract may create a trust. But if a settlor's conveyance would be voidable or void because of infancy, incompetency, or some other reason, the settlor's declaration of trust is also voidable or void.

SUBJECT MATTER

One major requirement of a trust is that the trust corpus or *res* must consist of property that is definite and specific. A trust cannot be effective immediately for property not yet in existence or yet to be acquired.

TRUSTEE

Anyone legally capable of holding title to and dealing with property may be a trustee. The lack of a trustee, however, will not destroy a trust. The court will appoint an individual or institution to act as trustee if the settlor neglects to appoint one, if the named trustee does not qualify, or if the named trustee declines to serve.

Duties of the Trustee A trustee has three primary **duties:** (1) to carry out the purposes of the trust, (2) to administer the trust prudently and carefully, and (3) to exercise a high degree of loyalty toward the beneficiary.

Ordinarily, no special skills are required of a trustee, who is required simply to act with the same degree of care that a ***prudent person*** would use to carry out his or her personal affairs. The trustee has a duty to make the trust property productive and thus to invest it in income-producing assets. Given the myriad circumstances of any particular case, what constitutes the care of a "prudent person" is, of course, not easy to generalize.

The duty of loyalty arises from the fiduciary character of the relationship between the trustee and the beneficiary. In all his dealings with the trust property, the beneficiary, and third parties, the trustee must act exclusively in the beneficiary's interest.

In the Matter of the Estate of Rowe

Supreme Court, Appellate Division, Third Department, New York, 2000
274 A.D.2d 87, 712 N.Y.S.2d 662
http://www.nycourts.com/scripts/csearch.exe/DecisionRSLT?&CR=In_20the_20Matter_20of_20the_20Estate_20of_20ROWE&CT=&JUDGE=&crt=3&SRCH=dec&NL=10&SL=1&DFrom=&DTo=&RNF=1&RNL=2&FILE=3701

FACTS The petitioner, Wilber National Bank **(http://www.wilberbank.com/)**, was appointed trustee of a charitable trust created under the will of Frances E. Rowe (decedent). The trust was funded solely by 30,000 shares of International Business Machines (IBM) **(http://www.ibm.com/)** common stock, which was trading for approximately $113 per share at the time of decedent's death in April 1989 and approximately $117 per share when the trust was funded in September 1989. Under the terms of the trust, the petitioner was required to make annual distributions to qualified charities of 8 percent of the estate trust assets, or $270,300; at the end of fifteen years, the balance remaining in the trust, if any, was payable to the respondents, who are the decedent's nieces, or their children.

In August 1994, the respondents made a demand that the petitioner file an intermediate accounting, claiming that the petitioner's failure to diversify the trust assets had resulted in a decline in yield and forced sales of trust principal, thereby threatening the assets of the trust. In December 1994, the Surrogate's Court required the petitioner to prepare an intermediate accounting. The petitioner filed its accounting and then commenced this proceeding for a judicial settlement. The respondents objected to the accounting upon the grounds that the petitioner's failure to diversify the trust was imprudent in that it violated the petitioner's own policy requiring diversification, the policy of the Comptroller of Currency, and regulations of the Federal Reserve Bank.

Because the value of the stock had dropped from the time the trust was funded, the Petitioner Trust Committee felt that it would be imprudent to diversify immediately, but gave its approval to a plan of diversifying at a later time when the stock had reached a higher price. In the meantime, the petitioner generated some income by selling various call options, and several small sales and in-kind distributions were made of IBM stock in order to fulfill the annual payout requirements. The first move toward diversification came in February 1991, when the petitioner sold 5,000 shares of IBM stock at $125 per share and an additional 2,959 shares at $136 per share. As of the close of the accounting period on December 31, 1994, the petitioner still held 19,393 shares of IBM stock valued at $74 per share. Over the course of the accounting period, the market value of the trust assets had dropped from $3,521,250 to $1,853,937.

In August 1997, the Surrogate's Court rendered its decision that, from the period September 8, 1989 to December 31, 1994, the petitioner had been negligent, that it had violated its own policy manual and that it should have diversified most of the trust's holdings in IBM in January 1990.

The Surrogate's Court ordered the petitioner to refund its commissions to the trust and directed that the petitioner pay damages of $496,259, together with $133,990 in interest, for a total of $630,249. The petitioner appealed.

DECISION Judgment affirmed.

OPINION Mercure, J. The evidence adduced at the July 1996 trial of the proceeding to settle petitioner's intermediate account showed that petitioner's own written policy required diversification of the trust assets. At the time of the original funding of the trust in 1989, petitioner's Trust Policy Manual provided:

> [I]t is the [Trust] Committee's recommendation that where practicable, the Investment staff follow a balanced and diversified approach in the management of those funds. Any trust accounts not conforming to this principle must be brought to the Committee's attention with supporting data as to the reason for these exceptions.

The policy became even more specific in 1994, then providing:

> [I]t is the Committee's recommendation that the Investment staff adhere to the principles of the "Prudent Investor" rule by using modern portfolio theory and following a balanced and diversified approach in the management of those funds. Any trust accounts not conforming to these principles must be brought to the Committee's attention with supporting data as to the reason for these exceptions. Exceptions to diversification may be made when an agency customer or the trust instrument specifically permits, or where large capital gains would be incurred, or when the cost basis of the property has the potential to be written up in the near future.

Further, the 1994 policy advised that existing holdings exceeding 10% of a portfolio should be trimmed down over a period of time, supported by several research houses and reviewed annually by petitioner's Trust Committee (hereinafter the Committee).

* * *

During petitioner's administration of the trust, New York followed the "prudent person rule" of investment which provided:

> A fiduciary holding funds for investment may invest the same in the kinds and classes of securities described in the succeeding subparagraphs, provided that investment is made only in such securities as would be acquired by prudent [persons] of discretion and intelligence in such matters who are seeking a reasonable income and the preservation of their capital [Citation.]

To determine whether the prudent person standard has been violated, the court should engage in "a balanced and perceptive analysis of [the trustee's] consideration and action in the light of the history of each individual investment, viewed at the time of its action or its omission to act" [citations]. All of the facts and circumstances of the case must be examined to determine whether a concentration of a particular stock in an estate's portfolio violates the prudent person standard [citation]. Further, each individual investment decision should be examined in relation to the entire portfolio as an entity [citation], and a trustee can be found to have been imprudent for losses resulting from negligent inattentiveness, inaction or indifference [citation].

At trial, the generalized testimony of Herbert Simmerly, who was petitioner's vice-president and trust officer and a supervisor of the trust, Benjamin Nesbitt, petitioner's senior vice-president and senior trust officer, and investment officers Lynda Peet and Erica Decker was directly contradicted by the testimony of respondent's expert, Loren Ross. Significantly, Ross expressed the strong opinion that petitioner had acted imprudently in failing to diversify the trust's assets immediately upon receipt of the IBM stock, in furtherance of its initial goal of creating a diversified portfolio of fixed income oriented assets and equity or growth assets. According to Ross, both the 15-year duration of the trust and the 8% annual payout requirement made the investment in IBM stock particularly inappropriate. First, IBM's dividends of less than $5 per share fell far short of satisfying the "extremely heavy burden" of having to pay out "an unvarying $270,300 a year" to charities, thereby requiring that capital be depleted to supplement the shortfall. Second, the extreme volatility and overall downward trend of IBM stock during this period and the fact that IBM itself was undergoing an "extremely stressful time" made it unsuitable for fulfilling the trust's investment goals. Moreover, Ross stated that petitioner's tactic of waiting for the IBM stock to rise was based on "wishful hoping" and that any hesitancy on the part of petitioner to sell the IBM stock below acquisition costs was a "cosmetic kind of consideration." Finally, Ross testified that the use of call options increased the risk of the portfolio.

In addition to Ross's testimony describing petitioner's decision to delay diversification as unwise and unreasonably risky, the evidence reveals that petitioner failed to follow its own internal protocol during the administration of the trust up to the time of the intermediate accounting, that petitioner failed to conduct more than routine reviews of the IBM stock and that the target prices set for the trust's IBM stock were department-wide positions affecting many accounts, giving no particular consideration to the unique needs of this particular trust [citation]. Finally, we note that neither adverse tax consequences nor any provision of the trust instrument restricted petitioner's freedom to sell the IBM stock and diversify the trust's investments. * * *

* * *

INTERPRETATION A trustee is under a duty to manage trust assets with prudence and care and to act exclusively in the beneficiary's interest.

ETHICAL QUESTION Did the court fairly decide this case? Explain.

CRITICAL THINKING QUESTION What criteria should a court apply in scrutinizing the trustee's use, disposition, and distribution of the trust's assets? Explain.

Powers of the Trustee The **powers** of a trustee are determined by (1) the authority granted him by the settlor in the instrument creating the trust and (2) the rules of law in the jurisdiction in which the trust is established. State laws affecting the powers of trustees have their greatest impact on the investments a trustee may make with trust funds. Most states prescribe a prudent investor rule. Some, however, still follow the historical test, which prescribes a list of types of securities qualified for trust investment. In some jurisdictions, this list is permissive; in others, it is mandatory. If the list is permissive, the trustee may invest in securities of types not listed, though he carries the burden of showing that he made a prudent choice. The trust instrument itself may give the trustee wide discretion as to investments, in which case the trustee need not adhere to the list deemed advisable under the statute.

Practical Advice

When creating a trust, carefully consider which powers you grant to your trustee in the trust instrument.

Allocation of Principal and Income Trusts often settle a life estate in the trust corpus on one beneficiary and a remainder interest on another beneficiary. For example, on his death, Bill leaves his property to a trustee who is instructed to pay the income from the property to Bill's widow during her life and to distribute the property to his children when she dies. In an instance such as this, the trustee must distribute the principal to one party (the remainderman) and the income to another (the life tenant or income beneficiary). The trustee must also allocate receipts and charge expenses between the income beneficiary and the remainderman. If the trust agreement does not specify how the funds should be allocated, the trustee is provided statutory guidance, embodied in most states in the **Uniform Principal and Income Act**. A trustee who fails to comply with the trust agreement or the statute is personally liable for any loss.

The general rule in allocating benefits and burdens between income beneficiaries and remaindermen is that ordinary or current receipts and expenses are chargeable to the income beneficiary, whereas extraordinary receipts and expense are allocated to the remainderman. (The Concept Review below illustrates these four types of allocations.) Ordinary income is money paid for the use of trust property and any gain or profit from such use, while either property received as a substitute for or a change in the form of the original trust property is trust principal.

BENEFICIARY

There are very few restrictions on who (or what) may be a beneficiary. Charitable uses are a common purpose of trusts, and if the settlor's object does not outrage public policy or morals, the courts will uphold almost any purpose that happens to strike a settlor's fancy.

A person named as a trust beneficiary may accept or reject the trust. In the absence of restrictive provisions in the trust instrument, such as a spendthrift clause, a beneficiary's interest may be reached by his creditors, or the beneficiary may sell or dispose of his interest. Upon death, if the beneficiary held more than a life estate in the trust, the beneficiary's interest, unless disposed of by his will, passes to his heirs or personal representatives.

CPA TERMINATION OF A TRUST

Unless the settlor reserves a power of revocation, the general rule is that a trust, once validly created, is irrevocable. If so reserved, the trust may be terminated at the settlor's discretion.

Normally, the instrument creating a trust establishes the date on which the trust will terminate. The instrument may specify a period of years for which the trust is to last, or the settlor may provide that the trust shall continue during the life of a named individual. The death of the trustee or beneficiary does not terminate the trust if neither of their lives is the measure of the trust's duration.

Though a court will usually decree a trust terminated if the beneficiary acquires legal title to the trust assets, courts will not order the termination of a trust simply because all of the beneficiaries petition the court to do so.

CONCEPT REVIEW

Allocation of Principal and Income

	Receipts	Expenses
Ordinary—Income Beneficiary	Rents Royalties Cash dividends (regular and extraordinary) Interest	Interest payments Insurance Ordinary taxes Ordinary repairs Depreciation
Extraordinary—Remainderman	Stock dividends Stock splits Proceeds from sale or exchange of corpus Settlement of claims for injury to corpus	Extraordinary repairs Long-term improvements Principal amortization Costs incurred in the sale or purchase of corpus Business losses

The purposes the settlor set forth in the trust instrument, not the beneficiaries' wishes, will govern the court's actions.

If the same beneficiary holds both the equitable and legal title, the ***merger doctrine*** applies and the beneficiary holds the property outright. In order for a trust to exist, the trustee and beneficiary must be different persons.

DECEDENT'S ESTATES

The assets (the estate) of a person who dies leaving a valid will are to be distributed according to the directions contained in the will. A will is also called a **testament**; the maker of a will is called a testator; and gifts made in a will are called devises or bequests. If a person dies without leaving a will, her property will pass to her heirs and next of kin in the proportions provided in the applicable state statute. This is known as **intestate** (dying-without-a-will) succession. If a person dies without a will and leaves no heirs or next of kin, her property *escheats* (reverts) to the state. Nonetheless, not all of the decedent's property will pass through the probate estate (the distribution of a decedent's estate to her successors). Certain property will pass through arrangements unaffected by distribution. For instance, the decedent's life insurance policy or pension plan will pass to the beneficiary of the policy or plan, property the decedent jointly owned with a right of survivorship will pass to the survivor, and property subject to a trust will be governed by the trust instrument.

CPA WILLS

A **will** is a written instrument, executed according to statutorily dictated formalities, whereby a person makes a disposition of his property, which is to take effect after his death. One major characteristic of a will sets it apart from other transactions such as deeds and contracts: a will is revocable at any time during life. There is no such thing as an irrevocable will. A will takes effect only on the death of the testator.

Practical Advice

All adults should have a will that disposes of their assets in accordance with their wishes.

MENTAL CAPACITY

In order to make a valid will, the testator must have both the "power" and the "capacity" to do so. In addition, the requisite testamentary intent must also be present.

Testamentary Capacity and Power The state grants the power to make a will to persons of a class whose members are believed generally able to handle their affairs without regard to personal limitations. Thus, in most states, children under a certain age cannot make valid wills.

The capacity to make a will refers to the measures by which the courts determine whether a particular person belonging to the class generally granted the power to make wills is, in fact, mentally fit enough to do so. A person who is capable of understanding the nature and extent of her property, appreciating the natural objects of her bounty, and formulating an orderly plan of disposition has mental capacity sufficient to make a will.

In the Matter of the Guardianship and Conservatorship of Lanning

Supreme Court of South Dakota, 1997
565 N.W.2d 794, 1997 S.D. 81
http://www.sdbar.org/opinions/1997/July/1997_081.htm

FACTS Ursula Lanning had twelve children from two marriages. Ten children were born of her first marriage to John Cathey, but one child predeceased her. She has two children from her current marriage to Edward Lanning. In January 1996, at the time of the hearing for guardianship and conservatorship, Mrs. Lanning was eighty-seven years old. She lived with her husband in a mobile home. Neither of the Lannings was in good health; Mrs. Lanning was recovering from colon cancer surgery, and Mr. Lanning was suffering from congestive heart failure. A housekeeper was paid to come in forty hours a week to see to the daily needs of the couple. The Lannings' daughter, Sherry, lived nearby.

Mrs. Lanning and her first husband raised sheep on their ranch in Montana. Upon his death, each of the Cathey children inherited a share of the ranch from their father's estate. Mrs. Lanning eventually gifted the widow's share she received to the children of her second marriage.

Edward Lanning owned a ranch in Montana where the couple lived until ill-health forced them to move to South Dakota to be near their daughter. The Lannings received royalties for oil on the property in Montana, and at the time of the hearing in this matter, the value of their combined assets was in the neighborhood of $2 million.

In 1984, Mrs. Lanning had executed a will leaving the bulk of her estate to the Lanning children. In 1993, due to the size of their assets and upon the advice of their accountant, the Lannings began estate tax planning. Edward Lanning gifted property to his wife in an attempt to equalize their estates for federal estate tax purposes. The property was placed into trust. Testimony at hearing indicated that the Lannings were aware that Edward Lanning could have placed restrictions on Mrs. Lanning's right to convey the property to the children of her first marriage, but no such restrictions were imposed. Nonetheless, Mrs. Lanning's 1984 will and the 1994 trust contained identical dispositive provisions: upon Mrs. Lanning's death, each Cathey child would receive $1,000, and the rest of the estate would be divided equally between the two Lanning children.

In November 1995, Danny Lanning petitioned for temporary guardianship of his mother. Pioneer Bank & Trust **(http://www.pbtok.com/)**, which had been the Lannings' bank for some forty years, was named as temporary conservator of Mrs. Lanning's estate. In January 1996, during the pendency of the proceedings for appointment of a permanent guardian and conservator, Mrs. Lanning executed a new will which was a 180-degree reversal of her former will. The new will gave each of the Lanning children $1,000, and gave the remainder of her $1 million estate in equal shares to the Cathey children.

Following its appointment as permanent conservator, Pioneer Bank moved to revoke the January 1996 will. In April 1996, Mrs. Lanning had a third attorney prepare a new will; this provided that all of Mrs. Lanning's children would get an equal share of the estate. Following a hearing, the trial court determined that the January and April 1996 wills were invalid. The Cathey children appeal.

DECISION Affirmed.

OPINION Gilbertson, J. Under our law, anyone over the age of 18 years who is of sound mind may make a will. [Citation.] We have defined "sound mind" for purposes of testamentary capacity as follows:

> One has a sound mind, for the purposes of making a will, if, without prompting, he is able "to comprehend the nature and extent of his property, the persons who are the natural objects of his bounty and the disposition that he desires to make of such property." [Citation.] Soundness of mind, for the purpose of executing a will, does not mean "that degree of intellectual vigor which one has in youth or that is usually enjoyed by one in perfect health." [Citation.] Mere physical weakness is not determinative of the soundness of mind, [citation], and it is not necessary that a person desiring to make a will "should have sufficient capacity to make contracts and do business generally nor to engage in complex and intricate business matters." [Citation.]

Testamentary capacity cannot be determined based on a single moment in time, but rather is based on consideration of the condition of the testator's mind over a reasonable length of time before and after the making of the will. [Citation.]

Our review of the record supports the trial court's finding that Mrs. Lanning did not know the natural objects of her bounty. She could not, without prompting, name all 12 of the children born to her. The first time she was asked, by her own attorney at a January 19, 1996 hearing, Mrs. Lanning testified she thought she had six children born of the Cathey marriage. The second time she testified, four months later, she named 11 of her 12 children (seven of whom apparently were in attendance at the hearing). However, the transcripts indicate that following a discussion the morning of trial, one of the Cathey children had provided Mrs. Lanning with a written list of the children, which Mrs. Lanning took to the stand with her.

Mrs. Lanning also was unable to understand the nature and extent of her property. When asked about her assets, Mrs. Lanning testified she was "not right on top of this" and did not know "what everything is and where it's at." * * * The attorney testified that, in 1993, Mrs. Lanning was assertive in expressing her estate planning desires, but after watching her testimony at the 1996 hearing, he testified that she appeared to be vague and that he would be "on inquiry" as to her competence if she now came to him to change her estate plan.

Mrs. Lanning's testimony regarding her disposition of property was conflicting. She testified she wanted to change her plan to be "fair" to all her children "alike," which is the general effect of the plan in her petition. Nevertheless, when asked if the petition disposed of her property as she wanted, she stated she hadn't made a decision on the disposal of her property yet. When presented with a copy of the 1994 trust agreement, she could not identify it or figure out what it did.

INTERPRETATION A person who is capable of understanding the nature and extent of her property, appreciating the natural objects of her bounty, and formulating an orderly plan of disposition has mental capacity sufficient to make a will.

ETHICAL QUESTION Did the court fairly decide this case? Explain.

CRITICAL THINKING QUESTION Do you agree with the court's definition of mental capacity to make a will? Explain.

Conduct Invalidating a Will Any document appearing to be a will that reflects an intent other than the testator's is not a valid will. This is the basis for the rule that a will that transmits property as a result of duress, undue influence, or fraud is no will at all.

For there to be undue influence, there must be improper pressure directed specifically to the act of making the will. The charge of undue influence most frequently arises when a testator leaves his property to one who is not a blood relative, such as a friend who took care of the testator in his last illness or during his last years. If the evidence demonstrates that the beneficiary under the will was in close contact with the testator and that the will ignores the natural objects of the testator's bounty, a suggestion of undue influence exists. The charge of fraud can also be used to invalidate a will. See In re Estate of Welch earlier in the chapter.

FORMAL REQUIREMENTS OF A WILL

By statute in all jurisdictions, a will must comply with certain formalities to be valid. Such formalities are necessary not only to indicate that the testator understood what she was doing but also to help prevent fraud.

Writing A basic requirement for a valid will is that it be in writing. The writing may be informal, as long as it substantially meets the basic statutory formalities. Pencil, ink, and photocopy are equally valid media, and valid wills have been made on scratch paper and on an envelope.

It is also valid to incorporate into a will by reference another document that in itself is not a will because it was improperly executed. To incorporate a memorandum into a will by reference, the following four conditions must exist: (1) the memorandum must be in writing; (2) it must be in existence when the will is executed; (3) it must be adequately described in the will; and (4) it must be described in the will as being in existence.

Signature The testator (or someone else in the testator's name in the presence of the testator and at the direction of the testator) must sign her will; the signature verifies that the will has been executed. Most statutes require the signature to be at the end of the will. Even in jurisdictions that do not so specify, an ending signature will preclude the charge that the portions of the will that follow the signature were written after its execution and are therefore invalid.

Attestation With the exception of a few isolated types of wills (noted later in this chapter) that are valid in a limited number of jurisdictions, a written will must be attested, or certified, by witnesses. The number and qualifications of witnesses and the manner of attestation generally are determined by statute. Usually, two or three witnesses are required.

Witnesses serve to acknowledge that the testator did execute the will and that she had the required intent and capacity. It is important that the testator sign first in the presence of all the witnesses; each witness should then sign in the testator's presence and in the presence of the other witnesses.

The most common restriction on a person's ability to act as a witness is that a witness must not have any interest under the will. At least two types of statute express this requirement. One type disqualifies a witness who is also a beneficiary under the will. The other voids the bequest or devise to the interested witness, thus making him a disinterested, and thereby qualified, witness.

REVOCATION OF A WILL

By definition, a will is revocable by the testator. Under certain circumstances, a will may be revoked by operation of law. Nevertheless, certain formalities are still necessary to effect a ***revocation***. Most jurisdictions specify by statute the methods by which a will may be revoked. The three generally accepted methods for revoking a will are as follows.

Destruction or Alteration Tearing, burning, or otherwise destroying a will is a strong sign that the testator intended to revoke it, and, unless such destruction is proven to be inadvertent, it is an effective way of revoking a will. In some states, partial revocation may be accomplished by erasing or obliterating part of the will. But substituted or additional bequests inserted between the written or printed lines of a will are not effective without reexecution and reattestation.

Golini v. Bolton

Court of Appeals of South Carolina, 1997
326 S.C. 333, 482 S.E.2d 784

FACTS Willie Mae Arant executed her Last Will and Testament on August 5, 1992, in her home with two witnesses present. The original will could not be found after Arant's death, so a copy of the will was filed and admitted in Calhoun County Probate Court. The will left the bulk of the estate to Melvin Bolton, Arant's nephew, and Kent Sutcliffe, Arant's grandson. Mary Lou Golini, Arant's only surviving daughter, filed suit challenging the probate of the will on the ground that because the original will could not be found, it had been destroyed with the intent to revoke.

The probate court found Arant's will had not been revoked because it was returned to her attorney's office after it was executed and it was lost sometime after that. Furthermore, the probate court found Arant thought she had the original in her possession but did not. The probate court found that Arant always indicated where her will was located and copies of her will were found in those locations after her death. Golini appealed to circuit court. The circuit court affirmed the probate court.

DECISION Judgment affirmed.

OPINION Howard, J. All parties agree Arant properly executed her will. The dispute arises over what happened to the original will after its execution. Golini claims the evidence proves Arant was the last person to have possession of her will because the will was executed in Arant's home and the witnesses to the will testified they left the will with Arant after it was executed. Bolton claims, and the lower courts agreed, the evidence tended to show the last verifiable location of the will was in Arant's attorney's office, and therefore, the presumption of animo revocandi [intent to revoke] did not apply.

* * *

"A will or any part thereof is revoked * * * by being burned, torn, canceled, obliterated, or destroyed, with the intent and for the purpose of revoking it by the testator or by another person in his presence and by his direction." [Citation.] Revocation by an act or by a subsequent instrument must be accompanied by an intention to revoke, and, without the intention, revocation does not take place. [Citation.]

Generally, contestants of a will have the burden of establishing revocation. [Citation.] However, when the testator takes possession of his will and it cannot be found at his death, the law presumes that the testator destroyed the will *animo revocandi* [with intent to revoke]. [Citations.]

"This is merely a presumption of fact and may be rebutted by showing by the evidence that the will existed at the time of his death, was lost subsequent thereto, or had been destroyed by another without authority to do so." [Citation.]

If the testator was known to have her last will in her possession or had ready access to it, and it cannot be found on her death, it is presumed, rebuttably, that she destroyed it and thereby revoked it. * * * [T]he evidence to rebut the presumption most be clear and convincing. * * *

From a review of the record, this court finds evidence which reasonably supports the factual findings of the probate court including the fact Arant was not in possession of her will. Both witnesses to the will's execution testified they were the only ones present when Arant signed her will and Arant had possession of the will when they left her home. Arant told the witnesses to the will she intended to have the will taken to her attorney's office.

Attorney Thomas Culclasure drafted two wills for Arant. He prepared the first will, which also excluded Golini, in 1988. He prepared the second will in 1992 after Arant's daughter, Sally, died. The second will Culclasure drafted was picked up from his office. After it was executed, Culclasure testified the will was returned to his office. However, Culclasure said he "can only assume that the original made it back" to his office because he had a copy of the executed will. Culclasure stated "I did not give her the original will, nor did I receive the original will back, personally."

Culclasure maintained a card file for all wills he drafted in his practice. The card for Arant states that Arant signed her will August 5, 1992, and that "Mrs. Arant has the original." This handwritten notation was written by Culclasure's secretary. Culclasure's practice was to put any original wills he kept in his lock-box at the bank. He searched the lock-box and all his office files but was unable to locate Arant's original will. Culclasure did not know who may have picked up the will from his office but he thought the will had been given to someone.

Kent Sutcliffe, Arant's grandson, testified Arant kept her important papers in a little chest and that she kept a sealed envelope in there which he thought contained her will. Sutcliffe's stepmother, Beth, testified Arant was a very organized person and kept her important papers in a little desk in her dining room. * * * After Arant's death, Bolton retrieved the two sealed envelopes from the two locations and took them to the probate court judge to have them opened. Only then did he discover the envelopes contained copies of Arant's will but neither contained the original. Bolton also checked Arant's personal lock-box at the bank but the original will was not there.

"Proof that a testator, whose will cannot be found after his death, entertained a kindly or loving feeling toward the beneficiaries under the will carries weight and tends toward the conclusion of nonrevocation of the will by the testator." [Citations.] Numerous witnesses testified as to the love and affection that existed between Arant and Bolton and Bolton's daily visits with Arant as well as his cooking her meals and running her errands. Even Golini testified Bolton was "like a son" to Arant. Before she died, Arant gave Bolton her Power of Attorney.

Numerous witnesses also testified that Arant and Golini did not get along and that Arant stated on numerous occasions she intended to leave Golini out of her will. * * *

INTERPRETATION Revocation of a will must be accompanied by an intention to revoke it.

CRITICAL THINKING QUESTION What criteria should be considered in determining whether a lost will was revoked? Explain.

Subsequent Will The execution of a second will does not in itself constitute a revocation of an earlier will. The first will is revoked to the extent that the second will is inconsistent with the first. The most certain manner of revocation is through the execution of a later will containing a declaration that all former wills are revoked. In some, but not all, jurisdictions, a testator may revoke a will by a written declaration to this effect in a subsequent document, such as a letter, even if that document does not meet the formal requirements of a will.

Practical Advice

If you wish to revoke a previous will (1) make sure that your new will indicates that it revokes all prior wills, (2) destroy or cancel all prior wills, and (3) make sure that your witnesses and others know that you have intentionally revoked all prior wills.

Codicils A codicil is an addition to or a revision of a will, generally by a separate instrument, that expressly refers to the will and that, in effect, incorporates the will by reference. Codicils must by executed with all the formal requirements of a will.

Practical Advice

If you wish to alter your will, you will need to either execute a codicil or a new will. In either case you need to comply with all the requirements of a new will.

Operation of Law A *marriage* generally revokes a will executed before the marriage. *Divorce*, on the other hand, generally does not revoke a provision in the will of one party for the benefit of the other.

The *birth* of a child after a will's execution may revoke the will, at least as far as that child is concerned, if the testator apparently has omitted a provision for the child. In some jurisdictions, the subsequent birth of a child will not revoke the will, if the child's omission from it is not apparently intentional; however, the share to which the child is entitled is equal to the share he would have received if the testator had died without a will.

Renunciation by the Surviving Spouse Statutes generally provide a surviving spouse the right to renounce a will and describe the method by which the spouse may do so. Such statutory provisions enable the spouse to decide which method of taking—under the will or under intestate succession—would be most advantageous.

> **Practical Advice**
>
> Store your will in a safe place and make sure that others know where it is kept. In addition, place an inventory of your assets where you store your will.

SPECIAL TYPES OF WILLS

There are many special types of wills, including nuncupative wills, holographic wills, soldiers' and sailors' wills, and living wills.

Noncupative Wills A nuncupative will is an unwritten oral declaration made before witnesses. In the few jurisdictions that authorize them, such declarations usually may be made only by a testator in his last illness. Under most statutes permitting nuncupative wills, only limited amounts of personal property may be passed by such wills.

Holographic Wills In approximately one-half of the jurisdictions, a will entirely in the handwriting of the testator is a valid testamentary document even if the will is *not* witnessed. Such an instrument, referred to as a holographic will, must comply strictly with the statutory requirements for such wills.

Soldiers' and Sailors' Wills For soldiers on active duty and sailors at sea, most statutes relax the formal requirements for a will and permit a testamentary disposition to be valid regardless of the informality of the document. In most jurisdictions, however, such a will cannot pass title to real estate.

Living Wills Almost all states have adopted statutes that permit an individual to execute a living will. A living will is a document by which an individual states that she does not wish to receive extraordinary medical treatment in order to preserve her life. Through such a will, which must comply with applicable statutory requirements, the individual rejects the use of life-prolonging procedures that artificially delay the dying process and asks to be allowed to die naturally should she contract an incurable illness or suffer an incurable injury. See the Ethical Dilemma on the next page.

> **Practical Advice**
>
> You should prepare a living will that specifically states your wishes concerning extraordinary medical treatment to preserve your life.

CPA INTESTATE SUCCESSION

Property not effectively disposed of before death or by will passes in accordance with the law of intestate succession. The rules set forth in statutes for determining, in cases involving intestacy, to whom the decedent's property shall be distributed not only ensure an orderly transfer of title to property but also purport to effect what probably would be the decedent's wishes. However, even if its requirements run contrary to the clear intention of the decedent, the intestacy statute will still govern the distribution.

The rules of descent vary widely from state to state, but as a general rule and except for the specific statutory rights of the widow, the intestate property passes in equal shares to each child of the decedent living at the time of his death, with the share of any child who dies before the decedent to be divided equally among that child's children. For example, if A dies intestate, leaving a widow and children, his widow generally will receive one-third of his real estate and personal property, and the remainder will pass to his children in the manner stated above. If his wife does not survive A, his entire estate passes to their children. If A dies and leaves two surviving children, B and C, and two grandchildren, D1 and D2, the children of a predeceased child D, the estate will go one third to B, one third to C, and one sixth each to D1 and D2, the grandchildren, who divide equally their parent's one third share. This result is described legally by the statement that *lineal* descendants of predeceased children take property ***per stirpes***, or by representation of their parent. If A had executed a will, he may have provided that all his lineal descendants, regardless of generation, would share equally. In that case, A's estate would be divided into four equal parts, and his descendants would be said to take the property ***per capita*** (see Figure 52-2).

Ethical Dilemma

When Should Life Support Cease?

FACTS Marge Hilton, an inhalation therapist at Lankard Hospital, was recently assigned to a unit that has been treating Leslie Andrews. Andrews, a single, twenty-eight-year-old woman, was in a car accident two weeks ago and remains in a coma. All of her nutrition and hydration must be administered through a gastrostomy tube. Andrews, who was a dental assistant, has no known relatives, no medical insurance, and no significant assets.

Her medical condition offers no hope for recovery. Andrews does not have a living will, and the only evidence concerning whether she would wish to have life-sustaining efforts continued is a casual statement, related to Lankard's administration by two of her friends, that she "would not want to live like that." She had said this after the three attended a movie in which a young female character had been comatose for many years.

When Hilton was performing inhalation therapy for Leslie, she observed Andrews groan. She brought this to the attention of two physicians. The doctors explained that this did not indicate Andrews was showing signs of recovery or was regaining consciousness. The doctors did state that the patient may be experiencing discomfort, but reassured Hilton that properly administered medication should take care of any pain.

Social, Policy, and Ethical Considerations

1. Under what circumstances should life-sustaining mechanisms be removed? Who should make the decision?
2. How would your answer change if Leslie were discovered to be six months pregnant?
3. If attending physicians must make the decision, should they be subject to civil or criminal liability arising out of their actions?

If only the widow and relatives other than children survive the decedent, a larger share usually is allotted the widow. She may receive all the decedent's personal property and one-half his real estate or, in some states, his entire estate.

At common law, property could not lineally ascend; parents of an intestate decedent did not share in his estate. Today, in many states, if a decedent has no lineal descendants or a surviving spouse, the statute provides that parents are the next to share.

Most statutes make some provision for brothers and sisters in the event that no spouse, parents, or children survive the decedent. Brothers and sisters, together with nieces, nephews, aunts, and uncles, are termed *collateral* heirs. Beyond these limits, most statutes provide that, if there are no survivors in the named classes, the property shall be distributed equally among the next of kin in equal degree.

The common law did not consider a *stepchild* as an heir or next of kin, that is, as one to whom property

Figure 52-2
Per Stirpes *and* Per Capita

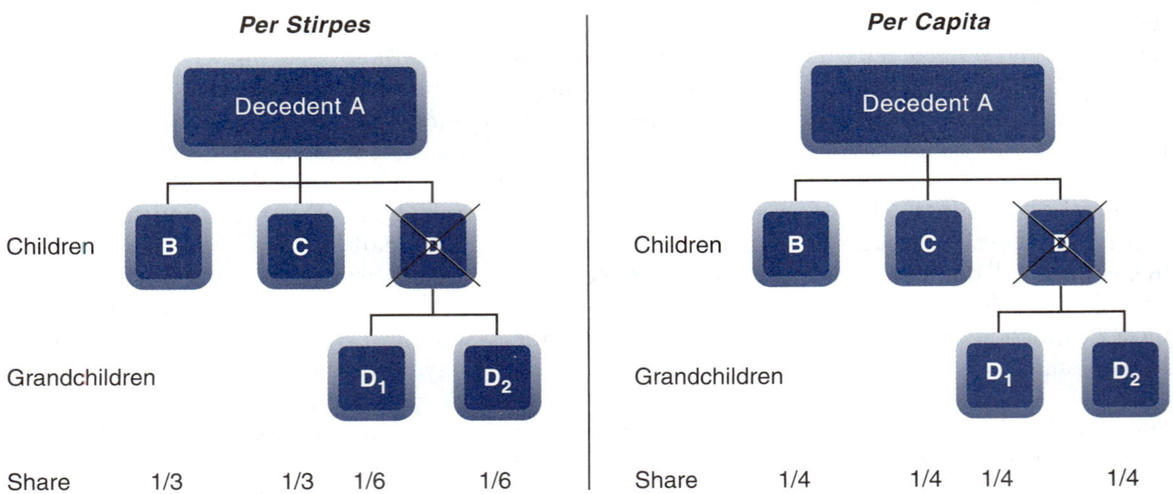

THE LAW AND YOU

State Bar Associations

Alabama: http://www.alabar.org/ ("Last Will and Testament")

Arizona: http://www.azbar.org/PublicResources/pubinfo.asp ("The Truth About Living Trusts"; "A Guide to Understanding Wills")

Arkansas: http://www.arkbar.com/publications/publication_public.html ("Handbook for Personal Representatives")

Colorado: http://www.cobar.org/ ("Estate Planning"; "Living Trusts"; "Probate in Colorado"; "So Now You Are a Personal Representative"; "So Now You Are a Trustee"; "What to Do When Someone Dies"; "Wills in Colorado")

Florida: http://www.flabar.org/newflabar/consumerservices/General/Consumer.Pam/ ("Do You Have a Will?" (also available in Spanish); "Probate in Florida")

Georgia: http://www.gabar.org/cps. asp?Header=cps ("Wills")

Illinois: http://www.illinoislawyerfinder.com/publicinfo/pamphlets.asp ("Living Trusts")

Iowa: http://www.iowabar.org/pamphlet.nsf/$about!OpenAbout ("Do You Need a Will?"; "Estate Planning"; "Executor's Handbook")

Louisiana: http://www.lsba.org/Public_Resources/consumer_brochures.html ("Do I Need a Will?")

Maine: http://www.mainebar.org/ (legal information pamphlets) ("Making a Will"; "Probate: What I Should Know?")

Maryland: http://www.msba.org/public/brochure.htm ("Wills and Estates")

Minnesota: http://www.mnbar.org/consumer.htm ("Wills in Minnesota")

Mississippi: http://www.msbar.org/law_you_can_use.htm ("Where There's a Will There's a Way")

Missouri: http://www.mobar.org/pamphlet/broindex/htm (public information brochures) ("Probate Law Resource Guide")

Montana: http://www.montanabar.org/forthepublic/index.htm ("Estate Planning"; "Living Trust Scams")

New York: http://www.nysba.org/ ("Living Wills and Health Care Proxies"; "Why You Need a Will"; [English and Spanish])

North Carolina: http://www.ncbar.org/public/pamphlets/pamphlets_index.asp ("Living Wills and Health Care Powers of Attorney"; "Making Your Will")

Ohio: http://www.ohiobar.org/conres/pamphlets/ ("Administering an Estate Without a Will"; "Living Wills and Health Care Powers of Attorney"; "Probate"; "Wills")

Oklahoma: http://www.okbar.org/publicinfo/brochures/ ("Do You Need a Will?"; "Is Probate Needed?")

Oregon: http://www.osbar.org/legallinks.html ("Wills"; "Estates and Elder Law")

Pennsylvania: http://www.pabar.org/generalpublic.shtml ("Why a Will Can't Wait")

Rhode Island: http://www.ribar.com/public/default.asp ("Probate—What to Do About It.")

South Dakota: http://www.sdbar.org/public/Default.htm ("Your Will"; "Living Trust"; "Probate")

Tennessee: http://www.tba.org/LawBytes/LawBytes.html ("Wills, Estates, Living Will, Long-Term Care")

Texas: http://www.texasbar.com/public/consumerinfo/helpfulinfo/pamphlets.asp ("To Will or Not to Will"; "Administering an Estate and Probate"; "Directives to Physicians [Living Wills]"; "Independent Executor Rights and Duties"; "Trusts")

Utah: http://www.utahbar.org/public/useful_information.html ("Wills and Probate"; "Estate Planning")

Washington: http //www.wsba.org/public/consumer/default.htm ("Probate"; "Revocable Living Trusts"; "Trusts"; "Wills")

Wisconsin: http://www.legalexplorer.com/resources/booksearch.asp ("Probate"; "Revocable Living Trusts")

State Attorney Generals

Arizona: http://www.attorney_general.state.az.us/consumer/help.html ("Living Trust Scam")

Arkansas: http://www.ag.state.ar.us/ ("Living Trust Tip Sheet")

Colorado: http://www.ago.state.co.us/CONSPROT.stm ("Living Trust Scams")

Minnesota: http://www.ag.state.mn.us/ ("Senior Center")

South Dakota: http://www.state.sd.us/attorney/seniors/default.asp ("Senior Citizens")

Tennessee: http://www.state.tn.us/consumer/brochure.html ("Real Estate & Estate Planning")

U.S. Government

"Being an Executor" http://www.pueblo.gsa.gov/specpubs.htm#mm

"Making a Will" http://www.pueblo.gsa.gov/money.htm

"Planning Your Estate" http://www.pueblo.gsa.gov/money.htm

would descend by operation of law; and this rule prevails today. Legally *adopted* children are, however, recognized as lawful heirs of their adoptive parents.

These generalities should be accepted as such; few fields of the law of property are so strictly a matter of statute, and the rights of heirs cannot reasonably be predicted without a knowledge of the exact terms of the applicable statute.

CPA ADMINISTRATION OF ESTATES

The rules and procedures controlling the management of a decedent's estate are statutory and therefore vary somewhat from state to state. In all jurisdictions, the estate is managed and finally disbursed under the supervision of a court. The procedure of managing the distribution of decedents' estates is referred to as probate, and the court that supervises the procedure is often designated the **probate** court.

The first legal step after death is usually to determine whether the deceased left a will. If a will exists, the testator has likely named her **executor** in it. If there is no will or if there is a will that fails to name an executor, the court will, on petition, appoint an **administrator**. The closest adult relative who is a resident of the state is entitled to this appointment.

Once approved or appointed by the court, the **executor** or **administrator** holds title to all the personal property of the deceased and is accountable to her creditors and beneficiaries. The estate is his responsibility.

If there is a will, the witnesses must prove it before the court by testifying to the signing of the will by all signatories and by confirming the mental condition of the testator at the time she executed the will. If the witnesses are dead, proof of their handwriting is necessary. If satisfied that the will is proved, the court will enter a formal decree admitting the will to probate.

Soon after the admission of the will to probate, the decedent's personal representative—the executor or administrator—must file an inventory of the estate. The personal representative will then begin his duties of collecting the assets, paying the debts, and disbursing the remainder. The executor or administrator occupies a *fiduciary* position not unlike that of a trustee, and his responsibility for investing proceeds and otherwise managing the estate is just as demanding.

The administration of every estate involves probate expenses, as well as fees to be paid to the executor or administrator and to the attorney who handles the estate. In addition, taxes are imposed at death by both the federal and state governments. The federal government imposes an *estate tax* on the transfer of property at death, whereas most state governments impose an *inheritance tax* on the privilege of an heir or beneficiary to receive the property. These taxes are separate from the basic income tax that the estate must pay on income received during estate administration.

CHAPTER SUMMARY

Trusts

Definition a fiduciary relationship in which legal title to property is held by one or more parties (the trustee) for the use, enjoyment, and benefit of another (the beneficiary)

Express Trust a trust established by voluntary action; usually in writing, although it may be oral

- ***Testamentary Trust*** a trust employed in a will; becomes effective after the settler's death.
- **Inter Vivos *Trust*** a trust established during the settlor's lifetime
- ***Charitable Trust*** a trust that has as its purpose the benefit of humankind
- ***Spendthrift Trust*** a trust designed to remove the trust estate from the beneficiary's control and from liability for his individual debts
- ***Totten Trust*** a tentative trust consisting of a joint bank account opened by the settlor (creator of the trust)

Implied Trust a trust created by operation of law

- ***Constructive Trust*** an implied trust imposed to rectify fraud or to prevent unjust enrichment
- ***Resulting Trust*** an implied trust imposed to fulfill the presumed intent of the settlor

Trustee anyone legally capable of holding title to and dealing with property may be a trustee

- *Duties* the three primary duties of a trustee are to (1) carry out the purposes of the trust, (2) act prudently, and (3) act with utmost loyalty
- *Powers* generally established by the trust instrument and state law
- *Allocation of Principal and Income* see the Concept Review

Termination the general rule is that the trust is irrevocable unless a power of revocation is reserved in the trust instrument

Wills

Definition a will (or testament) is a written instrument, executed with the formalities required by statute, whereby a person makes a disposition of his property to take effect after his death

Mental Capacity
- *Testamentary Capacity* for a will to be valid the testator must be sufficiently competent to intend the document to be her will
- *Conduct Invalidating a Will* a will that is the product of duress, undue influence, or fraud is invalid and of no effect

Formal Requirements a will must be (1) in writing, (2) signed, and (3) attested to by witnesses

Revocation a will is revocable by the testator and under certain circumstances may be revoked by operation of law
- *Destruction or Alteration* revokes a will
- *Subsequent Will* revokes prior wills to the extent they are inconsistent
- *Codicil* an addition to or revision of a will executed with all the formalities of a will
- *Marriage* generally revokes a will executed before the marriage
- *Birth of a Child* may revoke a will at least as far as that child is concerned
- *Renunciation by Surviving Spouse* surviving spouse may elect to take under laws of descent

Special Types of Wills generally binding only in specific situations and may have limitations upon their use

Intestate Succession

Intestate person who dies without a valid will

Course of Descent each state prescribes rules for the passage of property not governed by a valid will; as a general rule, the property passes in equal shares to each child after the widow's statutory or dower rights have been settled

Administration of Estates

Probate the court's supervision of the management and distribution of the estate

Executor or Administrator a person who is responsible for collecting the assets, paying the debts, and disbursing the remainder according to the will or interstate statute
- *Executor* the person named in the will and appointed by the court to administer the will
- *Administrator* a person appointed by the court to administer the estate when there is no will or when the person named in the will fails to qualify

QUESTIONS

1. State whether or not a trust is created in each of the following situations:
   a. A declares herself trustee of "the bulk of my securities" in trust for B.
   b. A, the owner of Blackacre, purports to convey to B in trust for C "a small part" of Blackacre.
   c. A orders B, a stockbroker, to buy 2,000 shares of American Steel or any part thereof at $20 per share. After the broker has bought 500 shares but before A knows whether any shares have been bought for him, A declares himself trustee for C of such shares of American Steel as B has bought.
   d. A owns ten bonds. He declares himself trustee for B of such five of the bonds as B may select at any time within a month.
   e. A deposits $1,000 in a savings bank. He declares himself trustee of the deposit in trust to pay B $500 out of the deposit, reserving the power to withdraw from the deposit any amounts not in excess of $500.

2. Testator gives property to Timothy in trust for Barney's benefit, providing that Barney cannot anticipate the income by assignment or pledge. Barney borrows money from Linda, assigning his future income under the trust for a stated period. Can Linda obtain any judicial relief to prevent Barney from collecting this income?

3. Collins was trustee for Indolent under the will of Indolent's father. Indolent, a middle-aged doctor, gave little concern to the management of the trust fund, contenting himself with receiving the income paid to him by the trustee. Among the assets of the trust were 100 shares of ABC Corporation and 100 shares of XYZ Corporation. About two years before the termination of the trust, Collins purchased the ABC stock from the trust at a fair price and after a full explanation to Indolent. At the same time but without saying anything to Indolent, he purchased the XYZ stock at a price higher than its current market value. At the termination of the trust, both stocks had advanced in market value well beyond the prices paid by Collins, and Indolent demanded that Collins either account for this advance in the value of both stocks or replace the stocks. What are Indolent's rights?

4. On September 1, 1990, Joe Brown gave $35,000 to his wife, Mary, with which to buy real property. They orally agreed that title to the real property should be taken in the name of Mary Brown but that she should hold the property in trust for Joe Brown. There were two witnesses to the oral agreement, both of whom are still living. Mary purchased the property on September 2, and a deed to it with Mary Brown as the grantee was delivered.

   Mary died on October 5, 2000, without a will. The real property is now worth $100,000. Joe Brown is claiming the property as the beneficiary of a trust. Mary's children are claiming that the property belongs to Mary's estate and have pleaded the statute of limitations and the statute of frauds as defenses to Joe's claim. There is no evidence to prove whether Mary would or would not have conveyed the property to Joe during her lifetime if she had been requested to do so. What are Joe's ownership rights to this particular real property?

5. On March 10, 2000, John Carver executed his will, which was witnessed by William Hobson and Sam Witt. By his will, Carver devised his farm, Stonecrest, to his nephew, Roy White. The residue of his estate was given to his sister, Florence Carver.

   A codicil to his will executed April 15, 2000, provided that $5,000 be given to Carver's niece, Mary Jordan, and $5,000 to Wanda White, Roy White's wife. The codicil was witnessed by Roy White and Harold Brown. John Carver died September 1, 2000, and the will and codicil were admitted to probate. How should Carver's estate be distributed?

6. Edwin Fuller, a bachelor, prepared his will in his office. The will, which contained no residuary clause, provided that one-third of his estate would go to his nephew, Tom Fuller, one-third to the city of Emanon to be used for park improvements, and one-third to his brother, Kurt.

   He signed the will in his office and then went to the office of his nephew, Tom Fuller, who signed the will as a witness at Edwin's request. No other persons were available in Tom's office, so Edwin then went to the bank, where Frank Cash, the cashier, also signed as a witness at Edwin's request. In each instance, Edwin stated that he had signed the document but did not state that it was his will.

   Edwin returned to his office and placed the will in his safe. Subsequently, Edwin died, survived by Kurt, his only heir-at-law. How should the estate be distributed?

7. Arnold executed a one-page will in which he devised his farm to Burton. Later, after a quarrel with Burton, Arnold wrote the words "I hereby cancel and revoke this will /s/Arnold" in the margin of the will but did not destroy the will. Arnold then executed a deed to the farm, naming Connie as grantee, and placed the deed and will in his safe. Shortly afterward, Arnold married Donna, with whom he had one child, Ernest. Arnold died some time later, and the deed and will were found in his safe. Burton, Connie, and Ernest claim the farm, and Donna claims dower. Discuss the validity of each claim.

8. John Walker, a widower, made a will containing the following provisions:

   "I give and bequeath my piano to my daughter Nancy. I give and bequeath to my daughter Jennifer the sum of $1,000. I give and bequeath to my son John the sum of $1,000 to be paid out of my account at the Tenth National Bank in the city of Erehwon. All the rest and residue of my estate I give to Nancy, Jennifer, and John, share and share alike."

After the will was executed, Walker sold his piano for $2,300 and deposited the proceeds in the Citizens Bank of Erehwon. He withdrew the money he had on deposit in the Tenth National Bank and purchased a new automobile.

When Walker died, he had no debts. The account in the Citizens Bank of Erehwon had a balance of $2,300, which constituted his entire net estate after all administration expenses were paid. How should Walker's estate be distributed?

9. The validly executed will of John Dane contained the following provision: "I give and devise to my daughter, Mary, Redacre for and during her natural life and, at her death, the remainder to go to Wilmore College." The will also provided that the residue of his estate should go to Wilmore College. Thereafter, Dane sold Redacre and then added a validly executed codicil to his will, "Due to the fact that I have sold Redacre, which I previously gave to my daughter, Mary, I now give and devise Blackacre to Mary in place and instead of Redacre."

Another clause of the codicil provided: "I give my one-half interest in the oil business that I own in common with William Steele to my son, Henry." Subsequently, Dane acquired all of the interest in the oil business from his partner, Steele, and, at the time of his death, Dane owned the entire oil business. The will and codicil have been admitted to probate.

a. What interest, if any, does Mary acquire in Blackacre?
b. What interest, if any, does Henry acquire in the oil business?

10. Leonard Wolfe was killed in an automobile accident while driving his 1994 Toyota Camry. The car was rendered a total loss, and Wolfe's insurance carrier paid his estate $7,550 for damage to the vehicle. Under the terms of Wolfe's will, any car owned at his death was to be given to his brother, David. Wolfe's daughter, Carol, however, brought an action, claiming that the gift of the car to David was adeemed by its total destruction and that she, as the residuary legatee under the will, was entitled to the insurance proceeds. Who is entitled to the insurance proceeds?

11. In April 1997, Grace Peterson, a spinster then aged seventy-four, asked Chester Gustafson, a Minneapolis attorney, to draw a will for her. Gustafson, who had also probated Peterson's sister's estate, drew this first will and six subsequent wills and codicils free of charge because he claimed that she had no money to pay for his services. Over the five-year period during which Gustafson redrew Peterson's will, an increasing amount of property was devised to Gustafson's children, until, finally, the seventh will so devised Peterson's entire estate. Peterson, however, hardly knew the children except from several chance encounters ten years before. She died on February 1, 2002, without ever having changed the seventh will, and Gustafson, who was named as executor, now seeks to have the will admitted to probate. Discuss whether the seventh will should be probated.

CASE PROBLEMS

12. By his last will and testament, Henry Nussbaum made a residual bequest and devise of his estate to his niece, Jane Blair, as trustee, in trust for the education of his grandchildren. If the trust could not be fulfilled, the residue was to revert to the plaintiff, Dorothy Witmer. After Nussbaum died in 1991, the plaintiff contended that the trustee had breached her fiduciary duty by failing to invest the trust corpus. A considerable portion of the trust funds were held in a checking account from 1993 to 2002. The trustee claimed that the will failed to specify when and what investments were to be made and, hence, such matters were left to her good-faith discretion. She also explained the large checking account balances by the fact that college for the grandchild, Janice, "was talked about through high school." Decision?

13. Rodney Sharp was a fifty-six-year-old dairy farmer whose education did not go beyond the eighth grade. Upon the death of his wife of thirty-two years, Sharp developed a very close relationship with Jean Kosmalski, a schoolteacher sixteen years his junior. Sharp eventually proposed to Kosmalski, but when she refused, he continued to make gifts to her in hope of changing her mind. He also gave her access to his bank account, from which she withdrew substantial amounts of money; made a will naming her as sole beneficiary; and executed a deed naming her as a joint owner of his farm. Then, in September 2001, Sharp transferred his remaining joint interest in the farm to Kosmalski. In February 2003, Kosmalski ordered Sharp to move out of his home and to vacate the farm. She then took possession of both, leaving Sharp with assets of $300. Discuss whether a constructive trust should be imposed on the property transferred to Kosmalski.

14. John Hobelsberger lived alone on his farm near Kranzburg, South Dakota. A grandniece, Phyllis Raml, and her husband, Ralph, lived on and operated a farm about two miles away. Hobelsberger and the Ramls had a friendly and cordial relationship. The Ramls visited him rather frequently and largely cared for him during his later years. Hobelsberger was hospitalized on October 23, 2003, and his condition was diagnosed as intermittent cerebral insufficiency. During his hospitalization, he requested that the Ramls send an attorney to see him about the preparation of a will. Thomas Green, an attorney, interviewed the testator on or about November 10 and prepared a will in compliance with his instructions.

Hobelsberger was transferred to a nursing home on November 19. On November 22, Green and a secretary went to the nursing home and witnessed his signing of the will. Hobelsberger was then eighty years old. He subscribed the will with a mark because he was having trouble with his hands. Hobelsberger died on July 19, 2004, survived by twenty-seven nieces and nephews and seven grandnieces and grandnephews. The will, after providing for the payment of debts and funeral expenses, left Hobelsberger's entire estate to Phyllis Raml. Nine of the nieces and nephews contested the will, claiming lack of testamentary capacity, undue influence by the Ramls, and improper execution. The county court admitted the will to probate, the circuit court affirmed, and the contestants appealed. Decision?

15. Mamie Henry, a widow, died on October 18. She had no children but was survived by several nieces and nephews. At first no will was found, and Joe Barksdale, a nephew, was appointed administrator of Mrs. Henry's estate. Later, Rita Pendergrass produced a copy of a will allegedly made by Mrs. Henry. The will left all of Mrs. Henry's property to Mrs. Pendergrass and appointed her as executrix. When Mrs. Pendergrass sought to have the will admitted to probate, Joe Barksdale and Olen Barksdale filed a contest on the grounds that the purported will was never duly executed, or, if executed, was destroyed by Mrs. Henry prior to her death. Should the will be probated? Explain.

16. George Washington Croom died testate. In his will Croom left various bequests of real and personal property to his children and a grandchild. In Item Eight of his will Croom stated "I leave nothing whatsoever to my daughter Kathryn Elizabeth Turner, and my son Ernest Edward Croom." At his death, Croom also left three optional share certificates in Carolina Savings & Loan Association issued to George W. Croom or Kimberly Joyce Croom, the deceased's minor daughter. Each of these certificates had attached to it an "Agreement Concerning Stock in Carolina Savings and Loan Association" which purported to create a joint account with a right of survivorship. Two of these agreements were signed by George Croom only and the third agreement was not signed at all. None of these certificates were specifically devised by Croom's will and the will contained no residuary clause. Who is entitled to share in these assets?

http:// **Internet Exercise** Find the last will and testament of three celebrities.

APPENDICES

Appendix A

The Constitution of the United States of America

We the People of the United States, in Order to form a more perfect Union, establish Justice, insure domestic Tranquility, provide for the common defense, promote the general Welfare, and secure the Blessings of Liberty to ourselves and our Posterity, do ordain and establish this Constitution for the United States of America.

ARTICLE I

Section 1

All legislative Powers herein granted shall be vested in a Congress of the United States, which shall consist of a Senate and House of Representatives.

Section 2

The House of Representatives shall be composed of Members chosen every second Year by the People of the several States, and the Electors in each State shall have the Qualifications requisite for Electors of the most numerous Branch of the State Legislature.

No Person shall be a Representative who shall not have attained to the Age of twenty five Years, and been seven Years a Citizen of the United States, and who shall not, when elected, be an Inhabitant of that State in which he shall be chosen.

Representatives and direct Taxes shall be apportioned among the several States which may be included within this Union, according to their respective Numbers, which shall be determined by adding to the whole Number of free Persons, including those bound to Service for a Term of Years, and excluding Indians not taxed, three fifths of all other Persons. The actual Enumeration shall be made within three Years after the first Meeting of the Congress of the United States, and within every subsequent Term of ten Years, in such Manner as they shall by Law direct. The number of Representatives shall not exceed one for every thirty Thousand, but each State shall have at Least one Representative; and until such enumeration shall be made, the State of New Hampshire shall be entitled to chuse three, Massachusetts eight, Rhode Island and Providence Plantations one, Connecticut five, New-York six, New Jersey four, Pennsylvania eight, Delaware one, Maryland six, Virginia ten, North Carolina five, South Carolina five, and Georgia three.When vacancies happen in the Representation from any State, the Executive Authority thereof shall issue Writs of Election to fill such vacancies.

The House of Representatives shall chuse their Speaker and other Officers; and shall have the sole Power of Impeachment.

Section 3

The Senate of the United States shall be composed of two Senators from each State, chosen by the Legislature thereof, for six Years; and each Senator shall have one Vote.

Immediately after they shall be assembled in Consequence of the first Election, they shall be divided as equally as may be into three Classes. The Seats of the Senators of the first Class shall be vacated at the Expiration of the second Year, of the second Class at the Expiration of the fourth Year, and of the third Class at the Expiration of the sixth Year, so that one third may be chosen every second Year; and if Vacancies happen by Resignation or otherwise, during the Recess of the Legislature of any State, the Executive thereof may make temporary Appointments until the next Meeting of the Legislature, which shall then fill such Vacancies.

No Person shall be a Senator who shall not have attained to the Age of thirty Years, and been nine Years a Citizen of the United States, and who shall not, when elected, be an Inhabitant of that State for which he shall be chosen.

The Vice President of the United States shall be President of the Senate, but shall have no Vote, unless they be equally divided.

The Senate shall chuse their other Officers, and also a President pro tempore, in the Absence of the Vice President, or when he shall exercise the Office of President of the United States.

The Senate shall have the sole power to try all Impeachments. When sitting for that Purpose, they shall be an Oath or Affirmation. When the President of the United States is tried, the Chief Justice shall preside: And no Person shall be convicted without the Concurrence of two thirds of the Members present.

Judgment in Cases of Impeachment shall not extend further than to removal from Office, and disqualification to hold and enjoy any Office of honor, Trust or Profit under the United States: but the Party convicted shall nevertheless be liable and subject to Indictment, Trial, Judgment and Punishment, according to Law.

Section 4

The Times, Places and Manner of holding Elections for Senators and Representatives, shall be prescribed in each State by the Legislature thereof: but the Congress may at any time by Law make or alter such Regulations, except as to the Places of chusing Senators.

The Congress shall assemble at least once in every Year, and such Meeting shall be on the first Monday in December, unless they shall by Law appoint a different Day.

Section 5

Each House shall be the Judge of the Elections, Returns and Qualifications of its own Members, and a Majority of each shall constitute a Quorum to do Business; but a smaller Number may adjourn from day to day, and may be authorized to compel the Attendance of absent Members, in such Manner, and under such Penalties as each House may provide.

Each House may determine the Rules of its Proceedings, punish its Members for disorderly Behaviour, and, with the Concurrence of two thirds, expel a Member.

Each House shall keep a Journal of its Proceedings, and from time to time publish the same, excepting such Parts as may in their Judgment require Secrecy; and the Yeas and Nays of the Members of either House on any question shall, at the Desire of one fifth of those Present, be entered on the Journal.

Neither House, during the Session of Congress, shall, without the Consent of the other, adjourn for more than three days, nor to any other Place than that in which the two Houses shall be sitting.

Section 6

The Senators and Representatives shall receive a Compensation for their Services, to be ascertained by Law, and paid out of the Treasury of the United States. They shall in all Cases, except Treason, Felony and Breach of the Peace, be privileged from Arrest and Breach of the Peace, be privileged from Arrest during their Attendance at the Session of their respective Houses, and in going to and returning from the same; and for any Speech or Debate in either House, they shall not be questioned in any other Place.

No Senator or Representative shall, during the Time for which he was elected, be appointed to any civil Office under the Authority of the United States, which shall have been created, or the Emoluments whereof shall have been encreased during such time; and no Person holding any Office under the United States, shall be a Member of either House during his Continuance in Office.

Section 7

All Bills for raising Revenue shall originate in the House of Representatives; but the Senate may propose or concur with Amendments as on other Bills.

Every Bill which shall have passed the House of Representatives and the Senate, shall, before it become a Law, be presented to the President of the United States; If he approve he shall sign it, but if not he shall return it, with his Objections to that House in which it shall have originated, who shall enter the Objections at large on their Journal, and proceed to reconsider it. If after such Reconsideration two thirds of that House shall agree to pass the Bill, it shall be sent, together with the Objections, to the other House, by which it shall likewise be reconsidered, and if approved by two thirds of that House, it shall become a Law. But in all such Cases the Votes of both Houses shall be determined by Yeas and Nays, and the Names of the Persons voting for and against the Bill shall be entered on the Journal of each House respectively. If any Bill shall not be returned by the President within ten Days (Sundays excepted) after it shall have been presented to him, the Same shall be a Law, in like Manner as if he had signed it, unless the Congress by their Adjournment prevent its Return, in which Case it shall not be a Law.

Every Order, Resolution, or Vote to which the Concurrence of the Senate and House of Representatives may be necessary (except on a question of Adjournment) shall be presented to the President of the United States; and before the Same shall take Effect, shall be approved by him, or being disapproved by him, shall be repassed by two thirds of the Senate and House of Representatives, according to the Rules and Limitations prescribed in the Case of a Bill.

Section 8

The Congress shall have Power to lay and collect Taxes, Duties, Imposts and Excises, to pay the Debts and provide for the common Defense and general Welfare of the United States; but all Duties, Imposts and Excises shall be uniform throughout the United States;

To borrow Money on the credit of the United States;

To regulate Commerce with foreign Nations, and among the several States, and with the Indian Tribes;

To establish an uniform Rule of Naturalization, and uniform Laws on the subject of Bankruptcies throughout the United States;

To coin Money, regulate the Value thereof, and of foreign Coin, and fix the Standard of Weights and Measures;

To provide for the Punishment of counterfeiting the Securities and current Coin of the United States;

To establish Post Offices and post Roads;

To promote the Progress of Science and useful Arts, by securing for limited Times to Authors and Inventors the exclusive Right to their respective Writings and Discoveries;

To constitute Tribunals inferior to the supreme Court;

To define and punish Piracies and Felonies committed on the high Seas, and Offenses against the Law of Nations;

To declare War, grant Letters of Marque and Reprisal, and make Rules concerning Captures on Land and Water;

To raise and support Armies, but no Appropriation of Money to that Use shall be for a longer Term than two Years;

To provide and maintain a Navy;

To make Rules for the Government and Regulation of the land and naval Forces;

To provide for calling forth the Militia to execute the Laws of the Union, suppress Insurrections and repel Invasions;

To provide for organizing, arming, and disciplining, the Militia, and for governing such Part of them as may be employed in the Service of the United States, reserving to the States respectively, the Appointment of the Officers, and the Authority of training the Militia according to the discipline described by Congress;

To exercise exclusive Legislation in all Cases whatsoever, over such District (not exceeding ten Miles square) as may, by Cession of particular States, and the Acceptance of Congress, become the Seat of the Government of the United States, and to exercise like Authority over all Places purchased by the Consent of the Legislature of the State in which the Same shall be, for the Erection of Forts, Magazines, Arsenals, dock-Yards, and other needful Buildings;—And

To make all Laws which shall be necessary and proper for carrying into Execution the foregoing Powers, and all other Powers vested by this Constitution in the Government of the United States, or in any Department or Officer thereof.

Section 9

The Migration or Importation of such Persons as any of the States now existing shall think proper to admit, shall not be prohibited by the Congress prior to the Year one thousand eight hundred and eight, but a Tax of Duty may be imposed on such Importation, not exceeding ten dollars for each Person.

The Privilege of the Writ of Habeas Corpus shall not be suspended, unless when in Cases of Rebellion or Invasion the public Safety may require it.

No Bill of Attainder or ex post facto Law shall be passed.

No Capitation, or other direct, Tax shall be laid, unless in Proportion to the Census or Enumeration herein before directed to be taken.

No Tax or Duty shall be laid on Articles exported from any State.

No Preference shall be given by any Regulation of Commerce or Revenue to the Ports of one State over those of another; nor shall Vessels bound to, or from, one State, be obliged to enter, clear, or pay Duties in another.

No Money shall be drawn from the Treasury, but in Consequence of Appropriations made by Laws; and a regular Statement and Account of the Receipts and Expenditures of all public Money shall be published from time to time.

No Title of Nobility shall be granted by the United States: And no Person holding any Office of Profit or Trust under them, shall, without the Consent of the Congress, accept of any present, Emolument, Office, or Title, of any kind whatever, from any King, Prince, or foreign State.

Section 10

No State shall enter into any Treaty, Alliance, or Confederation; grant Letters of Marque and Reprisal; coin Money; emit Bills of Credit; make any Thing but gold and silver Coin a Tender in Payment of Debts; pass any Bill of Attainder, ex post facto Law, or Law impairing the Obligation of Contracts, or grant any Title of Nobility.

No State shall, without the Consent of the Congress, lay any Imposts or Duties on Imports or Exports, except what may be absolutely necessary for executing its inspection Laws: and the net Produce of all Duties and Imposts, laid by any State on Imports or Exports, shall be for the Use of the Treasury of the United States; and all such Laws shall be subject to the Revision and Controul of the Congress.

No State shall, without the Consent of Congress, lay any Duty of Tonnage, keep Troops, or Ships of War in time of Peace, enter into any Agreement or Compact with another State, or with a foreign Power, or engage in War, unless actually invaded, or in such imminent Danger as will not admit of delay.

ARTICLE II

Section 1

The executive Power shall be vested in a President of the United States of America. He shall hold his Office during the Term of four Years, and, together with the Vice President, chosen for the same Term, be elected, as follows:

Each State shall appoint, in such Manner as the Legislature thereof may direct, a Number of Electors, equal to the whole Number of Senators and Representatives to which the State may be entitled in the Congress: but no Senator or Representative, or Person holding an Office of Trust or Profit under the United States, shall be appointed an Elector.

The Electors shall meet in their respective States, and vote by Ballot for two Persons, of whom one at least shall not be an Inhabitant of the same State with themselves. And they shall make a list of all the Persons voted for, and of the Number of Votes for each; which List they shall sign and certify, and transmit sealed to the Seat of the Government of the United States, directed to the President of the Senate. The President of the Senate shall, in the presence of the Senate and House of Representatives, open all the Certificates, and the Votes shall be counted. The Person having the greatest Number of Votes shall be the President, if such Number be a Majority of the whole Number of Electors appointed; and if there be more than one who have such Majority, and have an equal Number of Votes, then the House of Representatives shall immediately chuse by Ballot one of them for President; and if no Person have a Majority, then from the five highest on the List the said House shall in like Manner chuse the President. But in chusing the President, the Votes shall be taken by States, the Representation from each State having one Vote; A quorum for this Purpose shall consist of a Member or Members from two thirds of the States, and a Majority of all the States shall be necessary to a Choice. In every Case, after the Choice of the President, the Person having the Greatest Number of Votes of the Electors shall be the Vice President. But if there should remain two or more who have equal Votes, the Senate shall chuse from them by Ballot the Vice President.

The Congress may determine the Time of Chusing the Electors, and the Day on which they shall give their Votes; which Day shall be the same throughout the United States.

No Person except a natural born Citizen, or a Citizen of the United States, at the time of the Adoption of this Constitution, shall be eligible to the Office of President; neither shall any Person be eligible to that Office who shall not have attained to the Age of thirty five Years, and been fourteen Years a Resident within the United States.

In Case of the Removal of the President from Office, or of his Death, Resignation, or Inability to discharge the Powers and Duties of the said Office, the Same shall devolve on the Vice President, and the Congress may by Law provide for the Case of Removal, Death, Resignation or Inability, both of the President and Vice President, declaring what Officer shall then act as President, and such Officer shall act accordingly, until the Disability be removed, or a President shall be elected.

The President shall, at stated Times, receive for his Services, a Compensation, which shall neither be encreased nor diminished during the Period for which he shall have been elected, and he shall not receive within that Period any other Emolument from the United States, or any of them.

Before he enter on the Execution of his Office, he shall take the following Oath or Affirmation:—"I do solemnly swear (or affirm) that I will faithfully execute the Office of President of the United States, and will to the best of my Ability, preserve, protect and defend the Constitution of the United States."

Section 2

The President shall be Commander in Chief of the Army and Navy of the United States, and of the Militia of the several States, when called into the actual Service of the United States; he may require the Opinion, in writing, of the principal Officer in each of the executive Departments, upon any Subject relating to the Duties of their respective Offices, and he shall have Power to grant Reprieves and Pardons for Offences against the United States, except in Cases of Impeachment.

He shall have Power, by and with the Advice and Consent of the Senate, to make Treaties, providing two thirds of the Senators present concur; and he shall nominate, and by and with the Advice and Consent of the Senate, shall appoint Ambassadors, other public Ministers and Consuls, Judges of the supreme Court, and all other Officers of the United States, whose Appointments are not herein otherwise provided for, and which shall be established by Law: but the Congress may by Law vest the Appointment of such inferior Officers, as they think proper, in the President alone, in the Courts of Law, or in the Heads of Departments.

The President shall have Power to fill up all Vacancies that may happen during the Recess of the Senate, by granting Commissions which shall expire at the End of their next Session.

Section 3

He shall from time to time give to the Congress Information of the State of the Union, and recommend to their Consideration such Measures as he shall judge necessary and expedient; he may, on extraordinary Occasions, convene both Houses, or either of them, and in Case of Disagreement between them, with Respect to the Time of Adjournment, he may adjourn them to such Time as he shall think proper, he shall receive Ambassadors and other public Ministers; he shall take Care that the Laws be faithfully executed, and shall Commission all the Offices of the United States.

Section 4

The President, Vice President and all civil Officers of the United States, shall be removed from Office on Impeachment for, and Conviction of, Treason, Bribery, or other high Crimes and Misdemeanors.

ARTICLE III

Section 1

The judicial Power of the United States, shall be vested in one supreme Court, and in such inferior Courts as the Congress may from time to time ordain and establish. The Judges, both of the supreme and inferior Courts, shall hold their Offices during good Behaviour, and shall, at Times, receive for their Services, a Compensation, which shall not be diminished during their Continuance in Office.

Section 2

The judicial Power shall extend to all Cases, in Law and Equity, arising under this Constitution, the Laws of the United States, and Treaties made, or which shall be made, under their Authority;—to all Cases affecting Ambassadors, other public Ministers and Consuls;—to all Cases of admiralty and maritime Jurisdiction;—to Controversies to which the United States shall be a Party;—to controversies between two or more States;—between a State and Citizens of another State;—between Citizens of different States;—between Citizens of the same State claiming Lands under Grants of different States; and between a State, or the Citizens thereof, and foreign States, Citizens or Subjects.

In all Cases affecting Ambassadors, other public Ministers and Consuls, and those in which a State shall be Party, the supreme Court shall have original Jurisdiction. In all the other Cases before mentioned, the supreme Court shall have appellate Jurisdiction, both as to Law and Fact, with such Exceptions, and under such Regulations as the Congress shall make.

The Trial of all Crimes, except in Cases of Impeachment, shall be by Jury; and such Trial shall be held in the State where the said Crimes shall have been committed; but when not committed within any State, the Trial shall be at such Place or Places as the Congress may by Law have directed.

Section 3

Treason against the United States, shall consist only in levying War against them, or in adhering to their Enemies, giving them Aid and Comfort. No Person shall be convicted of Treason unless on the Testimony of two Witnesses to the same overt Act, or on Confession in open Court.

The Congress shall have Power to declare the Punishment of Treason, but no Attainder of Treason shall work Corruption of Blood, or Forfeiture except during the Life of the Person attainted.

ARTICLE IV

Section 1

Full Faith and Credit shall be given in each State to the public Acts, Records, and judicial Proceedings of every other State. And the Congress may by general Laws prescribe the Manner in which such Arts, Records and Proceedings shall be proved, and the Effect thereof.

Section 2

The Citizens of each State shall be entitled to all Privileges and Immunities of Citizens in the several States.

A Person charged in any State with Treason, Felony, or other Crime, who shall flee from Justice, and be found in another State, shall on Demand of the executive Authority of the State from which he fled, be delivered up, to be removed to the State having Jurisdiction of the Crime.

No Person held to Service or Labour in one State, under the Laws thereof, escaping into another, shall, in Consequence of any Law or Regulation therein, be discharged from such Service or Labour, but shall be delivered up on Claim of the Party to whom such Service or Labour may be due.

Section 3

New States may be admitted by the Congress into this Union; but no new State shall be formed or erected within the Jurisdiction of any other State; nor any State be formed by the Junction of two or more States, or Parts of States, without the Consent of the Legislatures of the States concerned as well as the Congress.

The Congress shall have Power to dispose of and make all needful Rules and Regulations respecting the Territory or other Property belonging to the United States; and nothing in this Constitution shall be so construed as to Prejudice any Claims of the United States, or of any particular State.

Section 4

The United States shall guarantee to every State in this Union a Republican Form of Government, and shall protect each of them against Invasion; and on Application of the Legislature, or of the Executive (when the Legislature cannot be convened) against domestic Violence.

ARTICLE V

The Congress, whenever two thirds of both Houses shall deem it necessary, shall propose Amendments to this Constitution, or, on the Application of the Legislatures of two thirds of the several States, shall call a Convention for proposing Amendments, which, in either Case, shall be valid to all Intents and Purposes, as Part of this Constitution, when ratified by the Legislatures of three fourths of the several States, or by Conventions in three fourths thereof, as the one or the other Mode of Ratification may be proposed by the Congress; Provided that no Amendment which may be made prior to the Year One thousand eight hundred and eight shall in any Manner affect the first and fourth Clauses in the Ninth Section of the first Article; and that no State, without its Consent, shall be deprived of its equal Suffrage in the Senate.

ARTICLE VI

All Debts contracted and Engagements entered into, before the Adoption of this Constitution, shall be as valid against the United States under this Constitution, as under the Confederation.

This Constitution, and the Laws of the United States which shall be made in Pursuance thereof; and all Treaties made, or which shall be made, under the Authority of the United States, shall be the supreme Law of the Land; and the Judges in every State shall be bound thereby, any Thing in the Constitution or Laws of any State to the Contrary notwithstanding.

The Senators and Representatives before mentioned, and the Members of the several State Legislatures, and all executive and judicial Officers, both of the United States and of the Several States, shall be bound by Oath or Affirmation, to support this Constitution; but no religious Test shall ever be required as a Qualification to any Office or public Trust under the United States.

ARTICLE VII

The Ratification of the Conventions of nine States, shall be sufficient for the Establishment of this Constitution between the States so ratifying the Same.

Amendment I [1791]

Congress shall make no law respecting an establishment of religion, or prohibiting the free exercise thereof; or abridging the freedom of speech, or the press; or the right of the people peaceably to assemble, and to petition the Government for a redress of grievances.

Amendment II [1791]

A well regulated Militia, being necessary to the security for a free State, the right of the people to keep and bear Arms, shall not be infringed.

Amendment III [1791]

No Soldier shall, in time of peace be quartered in any house, without the consent of the Owner, nor in time of war, but in a manner to be prescribed by law.

Amendment IV [1791]

The right of the people to be secure in their persons, houses, papers, and effects, against unreasonable searches and seizures, shall not be violated, and no Warrants shall issue, but upon probable cause, supported by Oath or Affirmation, and particularly describing the place to be searched, and the persons or things to be seized.

Amendment V [1791]
No person shall be held to answer for a capital, or otherwise infamous crime, unless on a presentment or indictment of a Grand Jury, except in cases arising in the land or naval forces, or in the Militia, when in actual service in time of War or public danger; nor shall any person be subject for the same offense to be twice put in jeopardy of life or limb; nor shall be compelled in any criminal case to be a witness against himself, nor be deprived of life, liberty, or property, without due process of law; nor shall private property be taken for public use, without just compensation.

Amendment VI [1791]
In all criminal prosecutions, the accused shall enjoy the right to a speedy and public trial, by an impartial jury of the State and district wherein the crime shall have been committed, which district shall have been previously ascertained by law, and to be informed of the nature and cause of the accusation; to be confronted with the Witnesses against him; to have compulsory process for obtaining witnesses in his favor, and to have the Assistance of counsel for his defense.

Amendment VII [1791]
In suits at common law, where the value in controversy shall exceed twenty dollars, the right of trial by jury shall be preserved, and no fact tried by a jury, shall be otherwise re-examined in any Court of the United States, than according to the rules of the common law.

Amendment VIII [1791]
Excessive bail shall not be required, no excessive fines imposed, nor cruel and unusual punishments inflicted.

Amendment IX [1791]
The enumeration in the Constitution, of certain rights, shall not be construed to deny or disparage others retained by the people.

Amendment X [1791]
The powers not delegated to the United States by the Constitution, nor prohibited by it to the States, are reserved to the States respectively, or to the people.

Amendment XI [1798]
The judicial power of the United States shall not be construed to extend to any suit in law or equity, commenced or prosecuted against one of the United States by Citizens of another State, or by Citizens or Subjects of any Foreign State.

Amendment XII [1804]
The Electors shall meet in their respective states and vote by ballot for President and Vice-President, one of whom, at least, shall not be an inhabitant of the same state with themselves; they shall name in their ballots the person voted for as President, and in distinct ballots the person voted for as Vice-President, and they shall make distinct lists of all persons voted for as President, and of all persons voted for as Vice-President, and of the number of votes for each, which lists they shall sign and certify, and transmit sealed to the seat of the government of the United States, directed to the President of the Senate;—The President of the Senate shall, in the presence of the Senate and House of Representatives, open all the certificates and the votes shall then be counted;—The person having the greatest number of votes for President, shall be the President, if such a number be a majority of the whole number of Electors appointed; and if no person have such majority, then from the persons having the highest numbers not exceeding three on the list of those voted for as President, the House of Representatives shall choose immediately, by ballot, the President. But in choosing the President, the votes shall be taken by states, the representation from each state having one vote; a quorum for this purpose shall consist of a member or members from two-thirds of the states, and a majority of all the states shall be necessary to a choice. And if the House of Representatives shall not choose a President whenever the right of choice shall devolve upon them, before the fourth day of March next following, then the Vice-President shall act as President, as in the case of the death or other constitutional disability of the President. The person having the greatest number of votes as Vice-President, shall be the Vice-President, if such number be a majority of the whole number of Electors appointed, and if no person have a majority, then from the two highest numbers on the list, the Senate shall choose the Vice-President; a quorum for the purpose shall consist of two-thirds of the whole number of Senators, and a majority of the whole number shall be necessary to a choice. But no person constitutionally ineligible to the office of President shall be eligible to that of the Vice-President of the United States.

Amendment XIII [1865]

Section 1
Neither slavery nor involuntary servitude, except as a punishment for crime whereof the party shall have been duly convicted, shall exist within the United States, or any place subject to their jurisdiction.

Section 2
Congress shall have power to enforce this article by appropriate legislation.

Amendment XIV [1868]

Section 1
All persons born or naturalized in the United States, and subject to the jurisdiction thereof, are citizens of the United States and of the State wherein they reside. No State shall make or enforce any law which shall abridge the privileges or immunities of citizens of the United States; nor shall any State deprive any person of life, liberty, or property, without due process of law; nor deny to any person within its jurisdiction the equal protection of the laws.

Section 2
Representatives shall be appointed among the several States according to their respective numbers, counting the whole number of persons in each State, excluding Indians not taxed. But when the right to vote at any election for the choice of electors for President and Vice President of the United States, Representatives in Congress, the Executive and Judicial officers of a State, or the members of the Legislature thereof, is denied to any of the male inhabitants of such State, being twenty-one years of age, and citizens of the United States, or in any way abridged, except for participation in rebellion, or other crime, the basis of representation therein shall be reduced in the proportion which the number of such male citizens shall bear the whole number of male citizens twenty-one years of age in such State.

Section 3
No person shall be a Senator or Representative in Congress, or elector of President and Vice President, or hold any office, civil or military, under the United States, or under any State, who, having previously taken an oath, as a member of Congress, or as an officer of the United States, or as a member of any State legislature, or as an executive or judicial officer of any State, to support the Constitution of the United States, shall have engaged in insurrection or rebellion against the same, or given aid or comfort to the enemies thereof. But Congress may by a vote of two-thirds of each House, remove such disability.

Section 4
The validity of the public debt of the United States, authorized by law, including debts incurred for payment of pensions and bounties for services in suppressing insurrection or rebellion, shall not be questioned. But neither the United States nor any State shall assume or pay

any debt or obligation incurred in aid of insurrection of rebellion against the United States, or any claim for the loss or emancipation of any slave; but all such debts, obligations and claims shall be held illegal and void.

Section 5
The Congress shall have power to enforce, by appropriate legislation, the provisions of this article.

Amendment XV [1870]

Section 1
The right of citizens of the United States to vote shall not be denied or abridged by the United States or by any State on account of race, color, or previous condition of servitude.

Section 2
The Congress shall have power to enforce this article by appropriate legislation.

Amendment XVI [1913]

The Congress shall have power to lay and collect taxes on incomes, from whatever source derived, without apportionment among the several States, and without regard to any census or enumeration.

Amendment XVII [1913]

The Senate of the United States shall be composed of two Senators from each State, elected by the people thereof, for six years; and each Senator shall have one vote. The electors in each State shall have the qualifications requisite for electors of the most numerous branch of the State legislatures.

When vacancies happen in the representation of any State in the Senate, the executive authority of each State shall issue writs of election to fill such vacancies; Provided, That the legislature of any State may empower the executive thereof to make temporary appointments until the people fill the vacancies by election as the legislature may direct.

This amendment shall not be construed as to affect the election or term of any Senator chosen before it becomes valid as part of the Constitution.

Amendment XVIII [1919]

Section 1
After one year from the ratification of this article the manufacture, sale, or transportation of intoxicating liquors within, the importation thereof into, or the exportation thereof from the United States and all territory subject to the jurisdiction thereof for beverage purposes is hereby prohibited.

Section 2
The Congress and the several States shall have concurrent power to enforce this article by appropriate legislation.

Section 3
This article shall be inoperative unless it shall have been ratified as an amendment to the Constitution by the legislatures of the several States, as provided in the Constitution, within seven years from the date of the submission hereof to the States by the Congress.

Amendment XIX [1920]

The right of citizens of the United States to vote shall not be denied or abridged by the United States or by any State on account of sex.

Congress shall have power to enforce this article by appropriate legislation.

Amendment XX [1933]

Section 1
The terms of the President and Vice President shall end at noon on the 20th day of January, and the terms of Senators and Representatives at noon on the 3d day of January, of the years in which such terms would have ended if this article had not been ratified; and the terms of their successors shall then begin.

Section 2
The Congress shall assemble at least once in every year, and such meeting shall begin at noon on the 3d day of January, unless they shall by law appoint a different day.

Section 3
If, at the time fixed for the beginning of the term of the President, the President elect shall have died, the Vice President elect shall become President. If a President shall not have been chosen before the time fixed for the beginning of his term, or if the President elect shall have failed to qualify, then the Vice President elect shall act as President until a President shall have qualified; and the Congress may by law provide for the case wherein neither a President elect nor a Vice President elect shall have qualified, declaring who shall then act as President, or the manner in which one who is to act shall be selected, and such person shall act accordingly until a President or Vice President shall have qualified.

Section 4
The Congress may by law provide for the case of the death of any of the persons from whom the House of Representatives may choose a President whenever the right of choice shall have devolved upon them, and for the case of the death of any of the persons from whom the Senate may choose a Vice President whenever the right of choice shall have devolved upon them.

Section 5
Sections 1 and 2 shall take effect on the 15th day of October following the ratification of this article.

Section 6
This article shall be inoperative unless it shall have been ratified as an amendment to the Constitution by the legislatures of three-fourths of the several States within seven years from the date of its submission.

Amendment XXI [1933]

Section 1
The eighteenth article of amendment to the Constitution of the United States is hereby repealed.

Section 2
The transportation or importation into any State, Territory, or possession of the United States for delivery or use therein of intoxicating liquors, in violation of the laws thereof, is hereby prohibited.

Section 3
This article shall be inoperative unless it shall have been ratified as an amendment to the Constitution by conventions in the several States, as provided in the Constitution, within seven years from the date of the submission hereof to the States by the Congress.

Amendment XXII [1951]

Section 1
No person shall be elected to the office of the President more than twice, and no person who has held the office of President, or acted as President, for more than two years of a term to which some other person was elected President shall be elected to the office of the President more than once. But this Article shall not apply to any person holding the office of President when this Article was proposed by the Congress, and shall not prevent any person who may be holding the office of President, or acting as President, during the term within which this Article becomes operative from holding the office of President, or acting as President during the remainder of such term.

Section 2
This article shall be inoperative unless it shall have been ratified as an amendment to the Constitution by the legislatures of three-fourths of the several States within seven years from the date of its submission to the States by the Congress.

Amendment XXIII [1961]
Section 1
The District constituting the seat of Government of the United States shall appoint in such manner as the Congress may direct:

A number of electors of President and Vice President equal to the whole number of Senators and Representatives in Congress to which the District would be entitled if it were a State, but in no event more than the least populous State; they shall be in addition to those appointed by the States, but they shall be considered, for the purposes of the election of President and Vice President, to be electors appointed by a State; and they shall meet in the District and perform such duties as provided by the twelfth article of amendment.

Section 2
The Congress shall have power to enforce this article by appropriate legislation.

Amendment XXIV [1964]
Section 1
The right of citizens of the United States to vote in any primary or other election for President or Vice President, for electors for President or Vice President or for Senator or Representative in Congress, shall not be denied or abridged by the United States or any State by reason of failure to pay any poll tax or other tax.

Section 2
The Congress shall have power to enforce this article by appropriate legislation.

Amendment XXV [1967]
Section 1
In case of the removal of the President from office or of his death or resignation, the Vice President shall become President.

Section 2
Whenever there is a vacancy in the office of the Vice President, the President shall nominate a Vice President who shall take office upon confirmation by a majority vote of both Houses of Congress.

Section 3
Whenever the President transmits to the President pro tempore of the Senate and the Speaker of the House of Representatives his written declaration that he is unable to discharge the powers and duties of his office, and until he transmits to them a written declaration to the contrary, such powers and duties shall be discharged by the Vice President as Acting President.

Section 4
Whenever the Vice President and a majority of either the principal officers of the executive departments or of such other body as Congress may by law provide, transmit to the President pro tempore of the Senate and the Speaker of the House of Representatives their written declaration that the President is unable to discharge the powers and duties of his office, the Vice President shall immediately assume the powers and duties of the office as Acting President.

Thereafter, when the President transmits to the President pro tempore of the Senate and the Speaker of the House of Representatives his written declaration that no inability exists, he shall resume the powers and duties of his office unless the Vice President and a majority of either the principal officers of the executive department or of such other body as Congress may by law provide, transmit within four days to the President pro tempore of the Senate and the Speaker of the House of Representatives their written declaration that the President is unable to discharge the powers and duties of his office. Thereupon Congress shall decide the issue, assembling within forty-eight hours for that purpose if not in session. If the Congress, within twenty-one days after receipt of the latter written declaration, or, if Congress is not in session, within twenty-one days after Congress is required to assemble, determines by two-thirds vote of both Houses that the President is unable to discharge the powers and duties of his office, the Vice President shall continue to discharge the same as Acting President; otherwise, the President shall resume the powers and duties of his office.

Amendment XXVI [1971]
Section 1
The right of citizens of the United States, who are eighteen years of age or older, to vote shall not be denied or abridged by the United States or by any State on account of age.

Section 2
The Congress shall have power to enforce this article by appropriate legislation.

Amendment XXVII [1992]
No law, varying the compensation for the services of the Senators and Representatives, shall take effect, until an election of Representatives shall have intervened.

APPENDIX B

UNIFORM COMMERCIAL CODE (SELECTED PROVISIONS)

The Code consists of the following Articles:

1. General Provisions
2. Sales

2A. Leases

3. Commercial Paper
4. Bank Deposits and Collections

4A. Funds Transfers

5. Letters of Credit
6. Bulk Transfers
7. Warehouse Receipts, Bills of Lading and Other Documents of Title
8. Investment Securities
9. Secured Transactions: Sales of Accounts, Contract Rights and Chattel Paper
10. Effective Date and Repealer
11. Effective Date and Transition Provisions

ARTICLE 1: GENERAL PROVISIONS

Part 1—Short Title, Construction, Application and Subject Matter of the Act

§ 1–101. Short Title.
This Act shall be known and may be cited as Uniform Commercial Code.

§ 1–102. Purposes; Rules of Construction; Variation by Agreement.
(1) This Act shall be liberally construed and applied to promote its underlying purposes and policies.
(2) Underlying purposes and policies of this Act are
(a) to simplify, clarify and modernize the law governing commercial transactions;
(b) to permit the continued expansion of commercial practices through custom, usage and agreement of the parties;
(c) to make uniform the law among the various jurisdictions.
(3) The effect of provisions of this Act may be varied by agreement, except as otherwise provided in this Act and except that the obligations of good faith, diligence, reasonableness and care prescribed by this Act may not be disclaimed by agreement but the parties may by agreement determine the standards by which the performance of such obligations is to be measured if such standards are not manifestly unreasonable.
(4) The presence in certain provisions of this Act of the words "unless otherwise agreed" or words of similar import does not imply that the effect of other provisions may not be varied by agreement under subsection (3).
(5) In this Act unless the context otherwise requires
(a) words in the singular number include the plural, and in the plural include the singular;
(b) words of the masculine gender include the feminine and the neuter, and when the sense so indicates words of the neuter gender may refer to any gender.

§ 1–103. Supplementary General Principles of Law Applicable.
Unless displaced by the particular provisions of this Act, the principles of law and equity, including the law merchant and the law relative to capacity to contract, principal and agent, estoppel, fraud, misrepresentation, duress, coercion, mistake, bankruptcy, or other validating or invalidating cause shall supplement its provisions.

§ 1–104. Construction Against Implicit Repeal.
This Act being a general act intended as a unified coverage of its subject matter, no part of it shall be deemed to be impliedly repealed by subsequent legislation if such construction can reasonably be avoided.

§ 1–105. Territorial Application of the Act; Parties' Power to Choose Applicable Law.
(1) Except as provided hereafter in this section, when a transaction bears a reasonable relation to this state and also to another state or nation the parties may agree that the law either of this state or of such other state or nation shall govern their rights and duties. Failing such agreement this Act applies to transactions bearing an appropriate relation to this state.
(2) Where one of the following provisions of this Act specifies the applicable law, that provision governs and a contrary agreement is effective only to the extent permitted by the law (including the conflict of laws rules) so specified:
Rights of creditors against sold goods. Section 2–402.
Applicability of the Article on Bank Deposits and Collections. Section 4–102.
Bulk transfers subject to the Article on Bulk Transfers. Section 6–102.
Applicability of the Article on Investment Securities. Section 8–106.
Perfection provisions of the Article on Secured Transactions. Section 9–103.

§ 1–106. Remedies to Be Liberally Administered.
(1) The remedies provided by this Act shall be liberally administered to the end that the aggrieved party may be put in as good a position as if the other party had fully performed but neither consequential or special nor penal damages may be had except as specifically provided in this Act or by other rule of law.

*Copyright © 2004 by The American Law Institute and the National Conference of Commissioners on Uniform State Laws. Reproduced with the permission of the Permanent Editorial Board for the Uniform Commercial Code. All rights reserved.

(2) Any right or obligation declared by this Act is enforceable by action unless the provision declaring it specifies a different and limited effect.

§ 1–107. Waiver or Renunciation of Claim or Right After Breach.
Any claim or right arising out of an alleged breach can be discharged in whole or in part without consideration by a written waiver or renunciation signed and delivered by the aggrieved party.

§ 1–108. Severability.
If any provision or clause of this Act or application thereof to any person or circumstances is held invalid, such invalidity shall not affect other provisions or applications of the Act which can be given effect without the invalid provision or application, and to this end the provisions of this Act are declared to be severable.

§ 1–109. Section Captions.
Section captions are parts of this Act.

Part 2—General Definitions and Principles of Interpretation
§ 1–201. General Definitions.
Subject to additional definitions contained in the subsequent Articles of this Act which are applicable to specific Articles or Parts thereof, and unless the context otherwise requires, in this Act:
(1) "Action" in the sense of a judicial proceeding includes recoupment, counterclaim, set-off, suit in equity and any other proceedings in which rights are determined.
(2) "Aggrieved party" means a party entitled to resort to a remedy.
(3) "Agreement" means the bargain of the parties in fact as found in their language or by implication from other circumstances including course of dealing or usage of trade or course of performance as provided in this Act (Sections 1–205 and 2–208). Whether an agreement has legal consequences is determined by the provisions of this Act, if applicable; otherwise by the law of contracts (Section 1–103). (Compare "Contract".)
(4) "Bank" means any person engaged in the business of banking.
(5) "Bearer" means the person in possession of an instrument, document of title, or certificated security payable to bearer or indorsed in blank.
(6) "Bill of lading" means a document evidencing the receipt of goods for shipment issued by a person engaged in the business of transporting or forwarding goods, and includes an airbill. "Airbill" means a document serving for air transportation as a bill of lading does for marine or rail transportation, and includes an air consignment note or air waybill.
(7) "Branch" includes a separately incorporated foreign branch of a bank.
(8) "Burden of establishing" a fact means the burden of persuading the triers of fact that the existence of the fact is more probable than its non-existence.
(9) "Buyer in ordinary course of business" means a person who in good faith and without knowledge that the sale to him is in violation of the ownership rights or security interest of a third party in the goods buys in ordinary course from a person in the business of selling goods of that kind but does not include a pawnbroker. All persons who sell minerals or the like (including oil and gas) at wellhead or minehead shall be deemed to be persons in the business of selling goods of that kind. "Buying" may be for cash or by exchange of other property or on secured or unsecured credit and includes receiving goods or documents of title under a pre-existing contract for sale but does not include a transfer in bulk or as security for or in total or partial satisfaction of a money debt.
(10) "Conspicuous": A term or clause is conspicuous when it is so written that a reasonable person against whom it is to operate ought to have noticed it. A printed heading in capitals (as: NON-NEGOTIABLE BILL OF LADING) is conspicuous. Language in the body of a form is "conspicuous" if it is in larger or other contrasting type or color. But in a telegram any stated term is "conspicuous". Whether a term or clause is "conspicuous" or not is for decision by the court.
(11) "Contract" means the total legal obligation which results from the parties' agreement as affected by this Act and any other applicable rules of law. (Compare "Agreement".)
(12) "Creditor" includes a general creditor, a secured creditor, a lien creditor and any representative of creditors, including an assignee for the benefit of creditors, a trustee in bankruptcy, a receiver in equity and an executor or administrator of an insolvent debtor's or assignor's estate.
(13) "Defendant" includes a person in the position of defendant in a cross-action or counterclaim.
(14) "Delivery" with respect to instruments, documents of title, chattel paper, or certificated securities means voluntary transfer of possession.
(15) "Document of title" includes bill of lading, dock warrant, dock receipt, warehouse receipt or order for the delivery of goods, and also any other document which in the regular course of business or financing is treated as adequately evidencing that the person in possession of it is entitled to receive, hold and dispose of the document and the goods it covers. To be a document of title a document must purport to be issued by or addressed to a bailee and purport to cover goods in the bailee's possession which are either identified or are fungible portions of an identified mass.
(16) "Fault" means wrongful act, omission or breach.
(17) "Fungible" with respect to goods or securities means goods or securities of which any unit is, by nature or usage of trade, the equivalent of any other like unit. Goods which are not fungible shall be deemed fungible for the purposes of this Act to the extent that under a particular agreement or document unlike units are treated as equivalents.
(18) "Genuine" means free of forgery or counterfeiting.
(19) "Good faith" means honesty in fact in the conduct or transaction concerned.
(20) "Holder" means a person who is in possession of a document of title or an instrument or a certificated investment security drawn, issued, or indorsed to him or his order or to bearer or in blank.
(21) To "honor" is to pay or to accept and pay, or where a credit so engages to purchase or discount a draft complying with the terms of the credit.
(22) "Insolvency proceedings" includes any assignment for the benefit of creditors or other proceedings intended to liquidate or rehabilitate the estate of the person involved.
(23) A person is "insolvent" who either has ceased to pay his debts in the ordinary course of business or cannot pay his debts as they become due or is insolvent within the meaning of the federal bankruptcy law.
(24) "Money" means a medium of exchange authorized or adopted by a domestic or foreign government as a part of its currency.
(25) A person has "notice" of a fact when
- (a) he has actual knowledge of it; or
- (b) he has received a notice or notification of it; or
- (c) from all the facts and circumstances known to him at the time in question he has reason to know that it exists.

A person "knows" or has "knowledge" of a fact when he has actual knowledge of it. "Discover" or "learn" or a word or phrase of similar import refers to knowledge rather than to reason to know. The time and circumstances under which a notice or notification may cease to be effective are not determined by this Act.
(26) A person "notifies" or "gives" a notice or notification to another by taking such steps as may be reasonably required to inform the other in ordinary course whether or not such other actually comes to know of it. A person "receives" a notice or notification when
- (a) it comes to his attention; or
- (b) it is duly delivered at the place of business through which the contract was made or at any other place held out by him as the place for receipt of such communications.

(27) Notice, knowledge or a notice or notification received by an organization is effective for a particular transaction from the time when it is

brought to the attention of the individual conducting that transaction, and in any event from the time when it would have been brought to his attention if the organization had exercised due diligence. An organization exercises due diligence if it maintains reasonable routines for communicating significant information to the person conducting the transaction and there is reasonable compliance with the routines. Due diligence does not require an individual acting for the organization to communicate information unless such communication is part of his regular duties or unless he has reason to know of the transaction and that the transaction would be materially affected by the information.

(28) "Organization" includes a corporation, government or governmental subdivision or agency, business trust, estate, trust, partnership or association, two or more persons having a joint or common interest, or any other legal or commercial entity.

(29) "Party", as distinct from "third party", means a person who has engaged in a transaction or made an agreement within this Act.

(30) "Person" includes an individual or an organization (See Section 1–102).

(31) "Presumption" or "presumed" means that the trier of fact must find the existence of the fact presumed unless and until evidence is introduced which would support a finding of its non-existence.

(32) "Purchase" includes taking by sale, discount, negotiation, mortgage, pledge, lien, or re-issue, gift or any other voluntary transaction creating an interest in property.

(33) "Purchaser" means a person who takes by purchase.

(34) "Remedy" means any remedial right to which an aggrieved party is entitled with or without resort to a tribunal.

(35) "Representative" includes an agent, an officer of a corporation or association, and a trustee, executor or administrator of an estate, or any other person empowered to act for another.

(36) "Rights" includes remedies.

(37) "Security interest" means an interest in personal property or fixtures which secures payment or performance of an obligation. The retention or reservation of title by a seller of goods notwithstanding shipment or delivery to the buyer (Section 2–401) is limited in effect to a reservation of a "security interest". The term also includes any interest of a buyer of accounts or chattel paper which is subject to Article 9. The special property interest of a buyer of goods on identification of such goods to a contract for sale under Section 2–401 is not a "security interest", but a buyer may also acquire a "security interest" by complying with Article 9. Unless a lease or consignment is intended as security, reservation of title thereunder is not a "security interest" but a consignment is in any event subject to the provisions on consignment sales (Section 2–326). Whether a lease is intended as security is to be determined by the facts of each case; however, (a) the inclusion of an option to purchase does not of itself make the lease one intended for security, and (b) an agreement that upon compliance with the terms of the lease the leasee shall become or has the option to become the owner of the property for no additional consideration or for a nominal consideration does make the lease one intended for security.

(38) "Send" in connection with any writing or notice means to deposit in the mail or delivery for transmission by any other usual means of communication with postage or cost of transmission provided for and properly addressed and in the case of an instrument to an address specified thereon or otherwise agreed, or if there be none to any address reasonable under the circumstances. The receipt of any writing or notice within the time at which it would have arrived if properly sent has the effect of a proper sending.

(39) "Signed" includes any symbol executed or adopted by a party with present intention to authenticate a writing.

(40) "Surety" includes guarantor.

(41) "Telegram" includes a message transmitted by radio, teletype, cable, any mechanical method of transmission, or the like.

(42) "Term" means that portion of an agreement which relates to a particular matter.

(43) "Unauthorized" signature or indorsement means one made without actual, implied or apparent authority and includes a forgery.

(44) "Value". Except as otherwise provided with respect to negotiable instruments and bank collections (Sections 3–303, 4–208 and 4–209) a person gives "value" for rights if he acquires them

(a) in return for a binding commitment to extend credit or for the extension of immediately available credit whether or not drawn upon or whether or not a chargeback is provided for in the event of difficulties in collection; or

(b) as security for or in total or partial satisfaction of a pre-existing claim; or

(c) by accepting delivery pursuant to a pre-existing contract for purchase; or

(d) generally, in return for any consideration sufficient to support a simple contract.

(45) "Warehouse receipt" means a receipt issued by a person engaged in the business of storing goods for hire.

(46) "Written" or "writing" includes printing, typewriting or any other intentional reduction to tangible form. Amended in 1962, 1972 and 1977.

§ 1–202. Prima Facie Evidence by Third Party Documents.

A document in due form purporting to be a bill of lading, policy or certificate of insurance, official weigher's or inspector's certificate, consular invoice, or any other document authorized or required by the contract to be issued by a third party shall be prima facie evidence of its own authenticity and genuineness and of the facts stated in the document by the third party.

§ 1–203. Obligation of Good Faith.

Every contract or duty within this Act imposes an obligation of good faith in its performance or enforcement.

§ 1–204. Time; Reasonable Time; "Seasonably".

(1) Whenever this Act requires any action to be taken within a reasonable time, any time which is not manifestly unreasonable may be fixed by agreement.

(2) What is a reasonable time for taking any action depends on the nature, purpose and circumstances of such action.

(3) An action is taken "seasonably" when it is taken at or within the time agreed or if no time is agreed at or within a reasonable time.

§ 1–205. Course of Dealing and Usage of Trade.

(1) A course of dealing is a sequence of previous conduct between the parties to a particular transaction which is fairly to be regarded as establishing a common basis of understanding for interpreting their expressions and other conduct.

(2) A usage of trade is any practice or method of dealing having such regularity of observance in a place, vocation or trade as to justify an expectation that it will be observed with respect to the transaction in question. The existence and scope of such a usage are to be proved as facts. If it is established that such a usage is embodied in a written trade code or similar writing the interpretation of the writing is for the court.

(3) A course of dealing between parties and any usage of trade in the vocation or trade in which they are engaged or of which they are or should be aware give particular meaning to and supplement or qualify terms of an agreement.

(4) The express terms of an agreement and an applicable course of dealing or usage of trade shall be construed wherever reasonable as consistent with each other, but when such construction is unreasonable express terms control both course of dealing and usage of trade and course of dealing controls usage of trade.

(5) An applicable usage of trade in the place where any part of performance is to occur shall be used in interpreting the agreement as to that part of the performance.
(6) Evidence of a relevant usage of trade offered by one party is not admissible unless and until he has given the other party such notice as the court finds sufficient to prevent unfair surprise to the latter.

§ 1–206. Statute of Frauds for Kinds of Personal Property Not Otherwise Covered.
(1) Except in the cases described in subsection (2) of this section a contract for the sale of personal property is not enforceable by way of action or defense beyond five thousand dollars in amount or value of remedy unless there is some writing which indicates that a contract for sale has been made between the parties at a defined or stated price, reasonably identifies the subject matter, and is signed by the party against whom enforcement is sought or by his authorized agent.
(2) Subsection (1) of this section does not apply to contracts for the sale of goods (Section 2–201) nor of securities (Section 8–319) nor to security agreements (Section 9–203).

§ 1–207. Performance or Acceptance Under Reservation of Rights.
A party who with explicit reservation of rights performs or promises performance or assents to performance in a manner demanded or offered by the other party does not thereby prejudice the rights reserved. Such words as "without prejudice", "under protest" or the like are sufficient.

§ 1–208. Option to Accelerate at Will.
A term providing that one party or his successor in interest may accelerate payment or performance or require collateral or additional collateral "at will" or "when he deems himself insecure" or in words of similar import shall be construed to mean that he shall have power to do so only if he in good faith believes that the prospect of payment or performance is impaired. The burden of establishing lack of good faith is on the party against whom the power has been exercised.

§ 1–209. Subordinated Obligations.
An obligation may be issued as subordinated to payment of another obligation of the person obligated, or a creditor may subordinate his right to payment of an obligation by agreement with either the person obligated or another creditor of the person obligated. Such a subordination does not create a security interest as against either the common debtor or a subordinated creditor. This section shall be construed as declaring the law as it existed prior to the enactment of this section and not as modifying it. Added 1966.

Note: *This new section is proposed as an optional provision to make it clear that a subordination agreement does not create a security interest unless so intended.*

ARTICLE 2: SALES

Part 1—Short Title, Construction and Subject Matter
§ 2–101. Short Title.
This Article shall be known and may be cited as Uniform Commercial Code—Sales.

§ 2–102. Scope; Certain Security and Other Transactions Excluded From This Article.
Unless the context otherwise requires, this Article applies to transactions in goods; it does not apply to any transaction which although in the form of an unconditional contract to sell or present sale is intended to operate only as a security transaction nor does this Article impair or repeal any statute regulating sales to consumers, farmers or other specified classes of buyers.

§ 2–103. Definitions and Index of Definitions.
(1) In this Article unless the context otherwise requires
(a) "Buyer" means a person who buys or contracts to buy goods.
(b) "Good faith" in the case of a merchant means honesty in fact and the observance of reasonable commercial standards of fair dealing in the trade.
(c) "Receipt" of goods means taking physical possession of them.
(d) "Seller" means a person who sells or contracts to sell goods.
(2) Other definitions applying to this Article or to specified Parts thereof, and the sections in which they appear are:
"Acceptance". Section 2–606.
"Banker's credit". Section 2–325.
"Between merchants". Section 2–104.
"Cancellation". Section 2–106(4).
"Commercial unit". Section 2–105.
"Confirmed credit". Section 2–325.
"Conforming to contract". Section 2–106.
"Contract for sale". Section 2–106.
"Cover". Section 2–712.
"Entrusting". Section 2–403.
"Financing agency". Section 2–104.
"Future goods". Section 2–105.
"Goods". Section 2–105.
"Identification". Section 2–501.
"Installment contract". Section 2–612.
"Letter of Credit". Section 2–325.
"Lot". Section 2–105.
"Merchant". Section 2–104.
"Overseas". Section 2–323.
"Person in position of seller". Section 2–707.
"Present sale". Section 2–106.
"Sale". Section 2–106.
"Sale on approval". Section 2–326.
"Sale or return". Section 2–326.
"Termination". Section 2–106.
(3) The following definitions in other Articles apply to this Article:
"Check". Section 3–104.
"Consignee". Section 7–102.
"Consignor". Section 7–102.
"Consumer goods". Section 9–109.
"Dishonor". Section 3–507. "Draft". Section 3–104.
(4) In addition Article 1 contains general definitions and principles of construction and interpretation applicable throughout this Article.

§ 2–104. Definitions: "Merchant"; "Between Merchants"; "Financing Agency".
(1) "Merchant" means a person who deals in goods of the kind or otherwise by his occupation holds himself out as having knowledge or skill peculiar to the practices or goods involved in the transaction or to whom such knowledge or skill may be attributed by his employment of an agent or broker or other intermediary who by his occupation holds himself out as having such knowledge or skill.
(2) "Financing agency" means a bank, finance company or other person who in the ordinary course of business makes advances against goods or documents of title or who by arrangement with either the seller or the buyer intervenes in ordinary course to make or collect payment due or claimed under the contract for sale, as by purchasing or paying the seller's draft or making advances against it or by merely taking it for collection whether or not documents of title accompany the draft. "Financing agency" includes also a bank or other person who similarly intervenes between persons who are in the position of seller and buyer in respect to the goods (Section 2–707).
(3) "Between merchants" means in any transaction with respect to which both parties are chargeable with the knowledge or skill of merchants.

§ 2–105. Definitions: Transferability; "Goods"; "Future" Goods; "Lot"; "Commercial Unit".

(1) "Goods" means all things (including specially manufactured goods) which are movable at the time of identification to the contract for sale other than the money in which the price is to be paid, investment securities (Article 8) and things in action. "Goods" also includes the unborn young of animals and growing crops and other identified things attached to realty as described in the section on goods to be severed from realty (Section 2–107).

(2) Goods must be both existing and identified before any interest in them can pass. Goods which are not both existing and identified are "future" goods. A purported present sale of future goods or of any interest therein operates as a contract to sell.

(3) There may be a sale of a part interest in existing identified goods.

(4) An undivided share in an identified bulk of fungible goods is sufficiently identified to be sold although the quantity of the bulk is not determined. Any agreed proportion of such a bulk or any quantity thereof agreed upon by number, weight or other measure may to the extent of the seller's interest in the bulk be sold to the buyer who then becomes an owner in common.

(5) "Lot" means a parcel or a single article which is the subject matter of a separate sale or delivery, whether or not it is sufficient to perform the contract.

(6) "Commercial unit" means such a unit of goods as by commercial usage is a single whole for purposes of sale and division of which materially impairs its character or value on the market or in use. A commercial unit may be a single article (as a machine) or a set of articles (as a suite of furniture or an assortment of sizes) or a quantity (as a bale, gross, or carload) or any other unit treated in use or in the relevant market as a single whole.

§ 2–106. Definitions: "Contract"; "Agreement"; "Contract for Sale"; "Sale"; "Present Sale"; "Conforming" to Contract; "Termination"; "Cancellation".

(1) In this Article unless the context otherwise requires "contract" and "agreement" are limited to those relating to the present or future sale of goods. "Contract for sale" includes both a present sale of goods and a contract to sell goods at a future time. A "sale" consists in the passing of title from the seller to the buyer for a price (Section 2–401). A "present sale" means a sale which is accomplished by the making of the contract.

(2) Goods or conduct including any part of a performance are "conforming" or conform to the contract when they are in accordance with the obligations under the contract.

(3) "Termination" occurs when either party pursuant to a power created by agreement or law puts an end to the contract otherwise than for its breach. On "termination" all obligations which are still executory on both sides are discharged but any right based on prior breach or performance survives.

(4) "Cancellation" occurs when either party puts an end to the contract for breach by the other and its effect is the same as that of "termination" except that the cancelling party also retains any remedy for breach of the whole contract or any unperformed balance.

§ 2–107. Goods to Be Severed From Realty: Recording.

(1) A contract for the sale of minerals or the like (including oil and gas) or a structure or its materials to be removed from realty is a contract for the sale of goods within this Article if they are to be severed by the seller but until severance a purported present sale thereof which is not effective as a transfer of an interest in land is effective only as a contract to sell.

(2) A contract for the sale apart from the land of growing crops or other things attached to realty and capable of severance without material harm thereto but not described in subsection (1) or of timber to be cut is a contract for the sale of goods within this Article whether the subject matter is to be severed by the buyer or by the seller even though it forms part of the realty at the time of contracting, and the parties can by identification effect a present sale before severance.

(3) The provisions of this section are subject to any third party rights provided by the law relating to realty records, and the contract for sale may be executed and recorded as a document transferring an interest in land and shall then constitute notice to third parties of the buyer's rights under the contract for sale.

Part 2—Form, Formation and Readjustment of Contract

§ 2–201. Formal Requirements; Statute of Frauds.

(1) Except as otherwise provided in this section a contract for the sale of goods for the price of $500 or more is not enforceable by way of action or defense unless there is some writing sufficient to indicate that a contract for sale has been made between the parties and signed by the party against whom enforcement is sought or by his authorized agent or broker. A writing is not insufficient because it omits or incorrectly states a term agreed upon but the contract is not enforceable under this paragraph beyond the quantity of goods shown in such writing.

(2) Between merchants if within a reasonable time a writing in confirmation of the contract and sufficient against the sender is received and the party receiving it has reason to know its contents, it satisfies the requirements of subsection (1) against such party unless written notice of objection to its contents is given within ten days after it is received.

(3) A contract which does not satisfy the requirements of subsection (1) but which is valid in other respects is enforceable

(a) if the goods are to be specially manufactured for the buyer and are not suitable for sale to others in the ordinary course of the seller's business and the seller, before notice of repudiation is received and under circumstances which reasonably indicate that the goods are for the buyer, has made either a substantial beginning of their manufacture or commitments for their procurement; or

(b) if the party against whom enforcement is sought admits in his pleading, testimony or otherwise in court that a contract for sale was made, but the contract is not enforceable under this provision beyond the quantity of goods admitted; or

(c) with respect to goods for which payment has been made and accepted or which have been received and accepted (Sec. 2–606).

§ 2–202. Final Written Expression: Parol or Extrinsic Evidence.

Terms with respect to which the confirmatory memoranda of the parties agree or which are otherwise set forth in a writing intended by the parties as a final expression of their agreement with respect to such terms as are included therein may not be contradicted by evidence of any prior agreement or of a contemporaneous oral agreement but may be explained or supplemented

(a) by course of dealing or usage of trade (Section 1–205) or by course of performance (Section 2–208); and

(b) by evidence of consistent additional terms unless the court finds the writing to have been intended also as a complete and exclusive statement of the terms of the agreement.

§ 2–203. Seals Inoperative.

The affixing of a seal to a writing evidencing a contract for sale or an offer to buy or sell goods does not constitute the writing a sealed instrument and the law with respect to sealed instruments does not apply to such a contract or offer.

§ 2–204. Formation in General.

(1) A contract for sale of goods may be made in any manner sufficient to show agreement, including conduct by both parties which recognizes the existence of such a contract.

(2) An agreement sufficient to constitute a contract for sale may be found even though the moment of its making is undetermined.

(3) Even though one or more terms are left open a contract for sale does not fail for indefiniteness if the parties have intended to make a contract and there is a reasonably certain basis for giving an appropriate remedy.

§ 2–205. Firm Offers.

An offer by a merchant to buy or sell goods in a signed writing which by its terms gives assurance that it will be held open is not revocable, for lack of consideration, during the time stated or if no time is stated for reasonable time, but in no event may such period of irrevocability exceed three months; but any such term of assurance on a form supplied by the offeree must be separately signed by the offeror.

§ 2–206. Offer and Acceptance in Formation of Contract.

(1) Unless other unambiguously indicated by the language or circumstances

(a) an offer to make a contract shall be construed as inviting acceptance in any manner and by any medium reasonable in the circumstances;

(b) an order or other offer to buy goods for prompt or current shipment shall be construed as inviting acceptance either by a prompt promise to ship or by the prompt or current shipment of conforming or nonconforming goods, but such a shipment of non-conforming goods does not constitute an acceptance if the seller seasonably notifies the buyer that the shipment is offered only as an accommodation to the buyer.

(2) Where the beginning of a requested performance is a reasonable mode of acceptance an offeror who is not notified of acceptance within a reasonable time may treat the offer as having lapsed before acceptance.

§ 2–207. Additional Terms in Acceptance or Confirmation.

(1) A definite and seasonable expression of acceptance or a written confirmation which is sent within a reasonable time operates as an acceptance even though it states terms additional to or different from those offered or agreed upon, unless acceptance is expressly made conditional on assent to the additional or different terms.

(2) The additional terms are to be construed as proposals for addition to the contract. Between merchants such terms become part of the contract unless:

(a) the offer expressly limits acceptance to the terms of the offer;

(b) they materially alter it; or

(c) notification of objection to them has already been given or is given within a reasonable time after notice of them is received.

(3) Conduct by both parties which recognizes the existence of a contract is sufficient to establish a contract for sale although the writings of the parties do not otherwise establish a contract. In such case the terms of the particular contract consist of those terms on which the writings of the parties agree, together with any supplementary terms incorporated under any other provisions of this Act.

§ 2–208. Course of Performance or Practical Construction.

(1) Where the contract for sale involves repeated occasions for performance by either party with knowledge of the nature of the performance and opportunity for objection to it by the other, any course of performance accepted or acquiesced in without objection shall be relevant to determine the meaning of the agreement.

(2) The express terms of the agreement and any such course of performance, as well as any course of dealing and usage of trade, shall be construed whenever reasonable as consistent with each other; but when such construction is unreasonable, express terms shall control course of performance and course of performance shall control both course of dealing and usage of trade (Section 1–205).

(3) Subject to the provisions of the next section on modification and waiver, such course of performance shall be relevant to show a waiver or modification of any term inconsistent with such course of performance.

§ 2–209. Modification, Rescission and Waiver.

(1) An agreement modifying a contract within this Article needs no consideration to be binding.

(2) A signed agreement which excludes modification or rescission except by a signed writing cannot be otherwise modified or rescinded, but except as between merchants such a requirement on a form supplied by the merchant must be separately signed by the other party.

(3) The requirements of the statute of frauds section of this Article (Section 2–201) must be satisfied if the contract as modified is within its provisions.

(4) Although an attempt at modification or rescission does not satisfy the requirements of subsection (2) or (3) it can operate as a waiver.

(5) A party who has made a waiver affecting an executory portion of the contract may retract the waiver by reasonable notification received by the other party that strict performance will be required of any term waived, unless the retraction would be unjust in view of a material change of position in reliance on the waiver.

§ 2–210. Delegation of Performance; Assignment of Rights.

(1) A party may perform his duty through a delegate unless otherwise agreed or unless the other party has a substantial interest in having his original promisor perform or control the acts required by the contract. No delegation of performance relieves the party delegating of any duty to perform or any liability for breach.

(2) Unless otherwise agreed all rights of either seller or buyer can be assigned except where the assignment would materially change the duty of the other party, or increase materially the burden or risk imposed on him by his contract, or impair materially his chance of obtaining return performance. A right to damages for breach of the whole contract or a right arising out of the assignor's due performance of his entire obligation can be assigned despite agreement otherwise.

(3) Unless the circumstances indicate the contrary a prohibition of assignment of "the contract" is to be construed as barring only the delegation to the assignee of the assignor's performance.

(4) An assignment of "the contract" or of "all my rights under the contract" or an assignment in similar general terms is an assignment of rights and unless the language or the circumstances (as in an assignment for security) indicate the contrary, it is a delegation of performance of the duties of the assignor and its acceptance by the assignee constitutes a promise by him to perform those duties. This promise is enforceable by either the assignor or the other party to the original contract.

(5) The other party may treat any assignment which delegates performance as creating reasonable grounds for insecurity and may without prejudice to his rights against the assignor demand assurances from the assignee (Section 2–609).

Part 3—General Obligation and Construction of Contract

§ 2–301. General Obligations of Parties.

The obligation of the seller is to transfer and deliver and that of the buyer is to accept and pay in accordance with the contract.

§ 2–302. Unconscionable Contract or Clause.

(1) If the court as a matter of law finds the contract or any clause of the contract to have been unconscionable at the time it was made the court may refuse to enforce the contract, or it may enforce the remainder of the contract without the unconscionable clause, or it may so limit the application of any unconscionable clause as to avoid any unconscionable result.

(2) When it is claimed or appears to the court that the contract or any clause thereof may be unconscionable the parties shall be afforded a reasonable opportunity to present evidence as to its commercial setting, purpose and effect to aid the court in making the determination.

§ 2–303. Allocation or Division of Risks.

Where this Article allocates a risk or a burden as between the parties "unless otherwise agreed", the agreement may not only shift the allocation, but may also divide the risk or burden.

§ 2–304. Price Payable in Money, Goods, Realty, or Otherwise.
(1) The price can be made payable in money or otherwise. If it is payable in whole or in part in goods each party is a seller of the goods which he is to transfer.
(2) Even though all or part of the price is payable in an interest in realty the transfer of the goods and the seller's obligations with reference to them are subject to this Article, but not the transfer of the interest in realty or the transferor's obligations in connection therewith.

§ 2–305. Open Price Term.
(1) The parties if they so intend can conclude a contract for sale even though the price is not settled. In such a case the price is a reasonable price at the time for delivery if
(a) nothing is said as to price; or
(b) the price is left to be agreed by the parties and they fail to agree; or
(c) the price is to be fixed in terms of some agreed market or other standard as set or recorded by a third person or agency and it is not so set or recorded.
(2) A price to be fixed by the seller or by the buyer means a price for him to fix in good faith.
(3) When a price left to be fixed otherwise than by agreement of the parties fails to be fixed through fault of one party the other may at his option treat the contract as cancelled or himself fix a reasonable price.
(4) Where, however, the parties intend not to be bound unless the price be fixed or agreed and it is not fixed or agreed there is no contract. In such a case the buyer must return any goods already received or if unable so to do must pay their reasonable value at the time of delivery and the seller must return any portion of the price paid on account.

§ 2–306. Output, Requirements and Exclusive Dealings.
(1) A term which measures the quantity by the output of the seller or the requirements of the buyer means such actual output or requirements as may occur in good faith, except that no quantity unreasonably disproportionate to any stated estimate or in the absence of a stated estimate to any normal or otherwise comparable prior output or requirements may be tendered or demanded.
(2) A lawful agreement by either the seller or the buyer for exclusive dealing in the kind of goods concerned imposes unless otherwise agreed an obligation by the seller to use best efforts to supply the goods and by the buyer to use best efforts to promote their sale.

§ 2–307. Delivery in Single Lot or Several Lots.
Unless otherwise agreed all goods called for by a contract for sale must be tendered in a single delivery and payment is due only on such tender but where the circumstances give either party the right to make or demand delivery in lots the price if it can be apportioned may be demanded for each lot.

§ 2–308. Absence of Specified Place for Delivery.
Unless otherwise agreed
(a) the place for delivery of goods is the seller's place of business or if he has none his residence; but
(b) in a contract for sale of identified goods which to the knowledge of the parties at the time of contracting are in some other place, that place is the place for their delivery; and
(c) documents of title may be delivered through customary banking channels.

§ 2–309. Absence of Specific Time Provisions; Notice of Termination.
(1) The time for shipment or delivery or any other action under a contract if not provided in this Article or agreed upon shall be a reasonable time.
(2) Where the contract provides for successive performances but is indefinite in duration it is valid for a reasonable time but unless otherwise agreed may be terminated at any time by either party.
(3) Termination of a contract by one party except on the happening of an agreed event requires that reasonable notification be received by the other party and an agreement dispensing with notification is invalid if its operation would be unconscionable.

§ 2–310. Open Time for Payment or Running of Credit; Authority to Ship Under Reservation.
Unless otherwise agreed
(a) payment is due at the time and place at which the buyer is to receive the goods even though the place of shipment is the place of delivery; and
(b) if the seller is authorized to send the goods he may ship them under reservation, and may tender the documents of title, but the buyer may inspect the goods after their arrival before payment is due unless such inspection is inconsistent with the terms of the contract (Section 2–513); and
(c) if delivery is authorized and made by way of documents of title otherwise than by subsection (b) then payment is due at the time and place at which the buyer is to receive the documents regardless of where the goods are to be received; and
(d) where the seller is required or authorized to ship the goods on credit the credit period runs from the time of shipment but post-dating the invoice or delaying its dispatch will correspondingly delay the starting of the credit period.

§ 2–311. Options and Cooperation Respecting Performance.
(1) An agreement for sale which is otherwise sufficiently definite (subsection (3) of Section 2–204) to be a contract is not made invalid by the fact that it leaves particulars of performance to be specified by one of the parties. Any such specification must be made in good faith and within limits set by commercial reasonableness.
(2) Unless otherwise agreed specifications relating to assortment of the goods are at the buyer's option and except as otherwise provided in subsections (1)(c) and (3) of Section 2–319 specifications or arrangements relating to shipment are at the seller's option.
(3) Where such specification would materially affect the other party's performance but is not seasonably made or where one party's cooperation is necessary to the agreed performance of the other but is not seasonably forthcoming, the other party in addition to all other remedies
(a) is excused for any resulting delay in his own performance; and
(b) may also either proceed to perform in any reasonable manner or after the time for a material part of his own performance treat the failure to specify or to cooperate as a breach by failure to deliver or accept the goods.

§ 2–312. Warranty of Title and Against Infringement; Buyer's Obligation Against Infringement.
(1) Subject to subsection (2) there is in a contract for sale a warranty by the seller that
(a) the title conveyed shall be good, and its transfer rightful; and
(b) the goods shall be delivered free from any security interest or other lien or encumbrance of which the buyer at the time of contracting has no knowledge.
(2) A warranty under subsection (1) will be excluded or modified only by specific language or by circumstances which give the buyer reason to know that the person selling does not claim title in himself or that he is purporting to sell only such right or title as he or a third person may have.
(3) Unless otherwise agreed a seller who is a merchant regularly dealing in goods of the kind warrants that the goods shall be delivered free of the rightful claim of any third person by way of infringement or the like but a buyer who furnishes specifications to the seller must hold the seller harmless against any such claim which arises out of compliance with the specifications.

§ 2–313. Express Warranties by Affirmation, Promise, Description, Sample.

(1) Express warranties by the seller are created as follows:

(a) Any affirmation of fact or promise made by the seller to the buyer which relates to the goods and becomes part of the basis of the bargain creates an express warranty that the goods shall conform to the affirmation or promise.

(b) Any description of the goods which is made part of the basis of the bargain creates an express warranty that the goods shall conform to the description.

(c) Any sample or model which is made part of the basis of the bargain creates an express warranty that the whole of the goods shall conform to the sample or model.

(2) It is not necessary to the creation of an express warranty that the seller use formal words such as "warrant" or "guarantee" or that he have a specific intention to make a warranty, but an affirmation merely of the value of the goods or a statement purporting to be merely the seller's opinion or commendation of the goods does not create a warranty.

§ 2–314. Implied Warranty: Merchantability; Usage of Trade.

(1) Unless excluded or modified (Section 2–316), a warranty that the goods shall be merchantable is implied in a contract for their sale if the seller is a merchant with respect to goods of that kind. Under this section the serving for value of food or drink to be consumed either on the premises or elsewhere is a sale.

(2) Goods to be merchantable must be at least such as

(a) pass without objection in the trade under the contract description; and

(b) in the case of fungible goods, are of fair average quality within the description; and

(c) are fit for the ordinary purpose for which such goods are used; and

(d) run, within the variations permitted by the agreement, of even kind, quality and quantity within each unit and among all units involved; and

(e) are adequately contained, packaged, and labeled as the agreement may require; and

(f) conform to the promises or affirmations of fact made on the container or label if any.

(3) Unless excluded or modified (Section 2–316) other implied warranties may arise from course of dealing or usage of trade.

§ 2–315. Implied Warranty: Fitness for Particular Purpose.

Where the seller at the time of contracting has reason to know any particular purpose for which the goods are required and that the buyer is relying on the seller's skill or judgment to select or furnish suitable goods, there is unless excluded or modified under the next section an implied warranty that the goods shall be fit for such purpose.

§ 2–316. Exclusion or Modification of Warranties.

(1) Words or conduct relevant to the creation of an express warranty and words or conduct tending to negate or limit warranty shall be construed wherever reasonable as consistent with each other, but subject to the provisions of this Article on parol or extrinsic evidence (Section 2–202) negation or limitation is inoperative to the extent that such construction is unreasonable.

(2) Subject to subsection (3), to exclude or modify the implied warranty of merchantability or any part of it the language must mention merchantability and in case of a writing must be conspicuous, and to exclude or modify any implied warranty of fitness the exclusion must be by a writing and conspicuous. Language to exclude all implied warranties of fitness is sufficient if it states, for example, that "There are no warranties which extend beyond the description on the face hereof."

(3) Notwithstanding subsection (2)

(a) unless the circumstances indicate otherwise, all implied warranties are excluded by expressions like "as is", "with all faults" or other language which in common understanding calls the buyer's attention to the exclusion of warranties and makes plain that there is no implied warranty; and

(b) when the buyer before entering into the contract has examined the goods or the sample or model as fully as he desired or has refused to examine the goods there is no implied warranty with regard to defects which an examination ought in the circumstances to have revealed to him; and

(c) an implied warranty can also be excluded or modified by course of dealing or course of performance or usage of trade.

(4) Remedies for breach of warranty can be limited in accordance with the provisions of this Article on liquidation or limitation of damages and on contractual modification of remedy (Sections 2–718 and 2–719).

§ 2–317. Cumulation and Conflict of Warranties Express or Implied.

Warranties whether express or implied shall be construed as consistent with each other and as cumulative, but if such construction is unreasonable the intention of the parties shall determine which warranty is dominant. In ascertaining that intention the following rules apply:

(a) Exact or technical specifications displace an inconsistent sample or model or general language of description.

(b) A sample from an existing bulk displaces inconsistent general language of description.

(c) Express warranties displace inconsistent implied warranties other than an implied warranty of fitness for a particular purpose.

§ 2–318. Third Party Beneficiaries of Warranties Express or Implied.

Note: *If this Act is introduced in the Congress of the United States this section should be omitted. (States to select one alternative.)*

Alternative A A seller's warranty whether express or implied extends to any natural person who is in the family or household of his buyer or who is a guest in his home if it is reasonable to expect that such person may use, consume or be affected by the goods and who is injured in person by breach of the warranty. A seller may not exclude or limit the operation of this section.

Alternative B A seller's warranty whether express or implied extends to any natural person who may reasonably be expected to use, consume or be affected by the goods and who is injured in person by breach of the warranty. A seller may not exclude or limit the operation of this section.

Alternative C A seller's warranty whether express or implied extends to any person who may reasonably be expected to use, consume or be affected by the goods and who is injured by breach of the warranty. A seller may not exclude or limit the operation of this section with respect to injury to the person of an individual to whom the warranty extends.

§ 2–319. F.O.B. and F.A.S. Terms.

(1) Unless otherwise agreed the term F.O.B. (which means "free on board") at a named place, even though used only in connection with the stated price, is a delivery term under which

(a) when the term is F.O.B. the place of shipment, the seller must at that place ship the goods in the manner provided in this Article (Section 2–504) and bear the expense and risk of putting them into the possession of the carrier; or

(b) when the term is F.O.B. the place of destination, the seller must at his own expense and risk transport the goods to that place and there tender delivery of them in the manner provided in this Article (Section 2–503);

(c) when under either (a) or (b) the term is also F.O.B. vessel, car or other vehicle, the seller must in addition at his own expense and risk load the goods on board. If the term is F.O.B. vessel the buyer must name the vessel and in an appropriate case the seller must comply with the provisions of this Article on the form of bill of lading (Section 2–323).

(2) Unless otherwise agreed the term F.A.S. vessel (which means "free alongside") at a named port, even though used only in connection with the stated price, is a delivery term under which the seller must

(a) at his own expense and risk deliver the goods alongside the vessel in the manner usual in that port or on a dock designated and provided by the buyer; and

(b) obtain and tender a receipt for the goods in exchange for which the carrier is under a duty to issue a bill of lading.

(3) Unless otherwise agreed in any case falling within subsection (1)(a) or (c) or subsection (2) the buyer must seasonably give any needed instructions for making delivery, including when the term is F.A.S. or F.O.B. the loading berth of the vessel and in an appropriate case its name and sailing date. The seller may treat the failure of needed instructions as a failure of cooperation under this Article (Section 2–311). He may also at his option move the goods in any reasonable manner preparatory to delivery or shipment.

(4) Under the term F.O.B. vessel or F.A.S. unless otherwise agreed the buyer must make payment against tender of the required documents and the seller may not tender nor the buyer demand delivery of the goods in substitution for the documents.

§ 2–320. C.I.F. and C. & F. Terms.

(1) The term C.I.F. means that the price includes in a lump sum the cost of the goods and the insurance and freight to the named destination. The term C. & F. or C.F. means that the price so includes cost and freight to the named destination.

(2) Unless otherwise agreed and even though used only in connection with the stated price and destination, the term C.I.F. destination or its equivalent requires the seller at his own expense and risk to

(a) put the goods into the possession of a carrier at the port for shipment and obtain a negotiable bill or bills of lading covering the entire transportation to the named destination; and

(b) load the goods and obtain a receipt from the carrier (which may be contained in the bill of lading) showing that the freight has been paid or provided for; and

(c) obtain a policy or certificate of insurance, including any war risk insurance, of a kind and on terms then current at the port of shipment in the usual amount, in the currency of the contract, shown to cover the same goods covered by the bill of lading and providing for payment of loss to the order of the buyer or for the account of whom it may concern; but the seller may add to the price the amount of premium for any such war risk insurance; and

(d) prepare an invoice of the goods and procure any other documents required to effect shipment or to comply with the contract; and

(e) forward and tender with commercial promptness all the documents in due form and with any indorsement necessary to perfect the buyer's rights.

(3) Unless otherwise agreed the term C. & F. or its equivalent has the same effect and imposes upon the seller the same obligations and risks as a C.I.F. term except the obligation as to insurance.

(4) Under the term C.I.F. or C. & F. unless otherwise agreed the buyer must make payment against tender of the required documents and the seller may not tender nor the buyer demand delivery of the goods in substitution for the documents.

§ 2–321. C.I.F. or C. & F.: "Net Landed Weights"; "Payment on Arrival"; Warranty of Condition on Arrival.

Under a contract containing a term C.I.F. or C. & F.

(1) Where the price is based on or is to be adjusted according to "net landed weights", "delivered weights", "out turn" quantity or quality or the like, unless otherwise agreed the seller must reasonably estimate the price. The payment due on tender of the documents called for by the contract is the amount so estimated, but after final adjustment of the price a settlement must be made with commercial promptness.

(2) An agreement described in subsection (1) or any warranty of quality or condition of the goods on arrival places upon the seller the risk of ordinary deterioration, shrinkage and the like in transportation but has no effect on the place or time of identification to the contract for sale or delivery or on the passing of the risk of loss.

(3) Unless otherwise agreed where the contract provides for payment on or after arrival of the goods the seller must before payment allow such preliminary inspection as is feasible; but if the goods are lost delivery of the documents and payment are due when the goods should have arrived.

§ 2–322. Delivery "Ex-Ship".

(1) Unless otherwise agreed a term for delivery of goods "ex-ship" (which means from the carrying vessel) or in equivalent language is not restricted to a particular ship and requires delivery from a ship which has reached a place at the named port of destination where goods of the kind are usually discharged.

(2) Under such a term unless otherwise agreed

(a) the seller must discharge all liens arising out of the carriage and furnish the buyer with a direction which puts the carrier under a duty to deliver the goods; and

(b) the risk of loss does not pass to the buyer until the goods leave the ship's tackle or are otherwise properly unloaded.

§ 2–323. Form of Bill of Lading Required in Overseas Shipment; "Overseas".

(1) Where the contract contemplates overseas shipment and contains a term C.I.F. or C. & F. or F.O.B. vessel, the seller unless otherwise agreed must obtain a negotiable bill of lading stating that the goods have been loaded on board or, in the case of a term C.I.F. or C. & F., received for shipment.

(2) Where in a case within subsection (1) a bill of lading has been issued in a set of parts, unless otherwise agreed if the documents are not to be sent from abroad the buyer may demand tender of the full set; otherwise only one part of the bill of lading need be tendered. Even if the agreement expressly requires a full set

(a) due tender of a single part is acceptable within the provisions of this Article on cure of improper delivery (subsection (1) of Section 2–508); and

(b) even though the full set is demanded, if the documents are sent from abroad the person tendering an incomplete set may nevertheless require payment upon furnishing an indemnity which the buyer in good faith deems adequate.

(3) A shipment by water or by air or a contract contemplating such shipment is "overseas" insofar as by usage of trade or agreement it is subject to the commercial, financing or shipping practices characteristic of international deep water commerce.

§ 2–324. "No Arrival, No Sale" Term.

Under a term "no arrival, no sale" or terms of like meaning, unless otherwise agreed,

(a) the seller must properly ship conforming goods and if they arrive by any means he must tender them on arrival but he assumes no obligation that the goods will arrive unless he has caused the non-arrival; and

(b) where without fault of the seller the goods are in part lost or have so deteriorated as no longer to conform to the contract or arrive after the contract time, the buyer may proceed as if there had been casualty to identified goods (Section 2–613).

§ 2–325. "Letter of Credit" Term; "Confirmed Credit".

(1) Failure of the buyer seasonably to furnish an agreed letter of credit is a breach of the contract for sale.

(2) The delivery to seller of a proper letter of credit suspends the buyer's obligation to pay. If the letter of credit is dishonored, the seller may on seasonable notification to the buyer require payment directly from him.

(3) Unless otherwise agreed the term "letter of credit" or "banker's credit" in a contract for sale means an irrevocable credit issued by a financing agency of good repute and, where the shipment is overseas, of good international repute. The term "confirmed credit" means that the credit must also carry the direct obligation of such an agency which does business in the seller's financial market.

§ 2–326. Sale on Approval and Sale or Return; Consignment Sales and Rights of Creditors.

(1) Unless otherwise agreed, if delivered goods may be returned by the buyer even though they conform to the contract, the transaction is

(a) a "sale on approval" if the goods are delivered primarily for use, and

(b) a "sale or return" if the goods are delivered primarily for resale.

(2) Except as provided in subsection (3), goods held on approval are not subject to the claims of the buyer's creditors until acceptance; goods held on sale or return are subject to such claims while in the buyer's possession.

(3) Where goods are delivered to a person for sale and such person maintains a place of business at which he deals in goods of the kind involved, under a name other than the name of the person making delivery, then with respect to claims of creditors of the person conducting the business the goods are deemed to be on sale or return. The provisions of this subsection are applicable even though an agreement purports to reserve title to the person making delivery until payment or resale or uses such words as "on consignment" or "on memorandum". However, this subsection is not applicable if the person making delivery

(a) complies with an applicable law providing for a consignor's interest or the like to be evidenced by a sign, or

(b) establishes that the person conducting the business is generally known by his creditors to be substantially engaged in selling the goods of others, or

(c) complies with the filing provisions of the Article on Secured Transactions (Article 9).

(4) Any "or return" term of a contract for sale is to be treated as a separate contract for sale within the statute of frauds section of this Article (Section 2–201) and as contradicting the sale aspect of the contract within the provisions of this Article on parol or extrinsic evidence (Section 2–202).

§ 2–327. Special Incidents of Sale on Approval and Sale or Return.

(1) Under a sale on approval unless otherwise agreed

(a) although the goods are identified to the contract the risk of loss and the title do not pass to the buyer until acceptance; and

(b) use of the goods consistent with the purpose of trial is not acceptance but failure seasonably to notify the seller of election to return the goods is acceptance, and if the goods conform to the contract acceptance of any part is acceptance of the whole; and

(c) after due notification of election to return, the return is at the seller's risk and expense but a merchant buyer must follow any reasonable instructions.

(2) Under a sale or return unless otherwise agreed

(a) the option to return extends to the whole or any commercial unit of the goods while in substantially their original condition, but must be exercised seasonably; and

(b) the return is at the buyer's risk and expense.

§ 2–328. Sale by Auction.

(1) In a sale by auction if goods are put up in lots each lot is the subject of a separate sale.

(2) A sale by auction is complete when the auctioneer so announces by the fall of the hammer or in other customary manner. Where a bid is made while the hammer is falling in acceptance of a prior bid the auctioneer may in his discretion reopen the bidding or declare the goods sold under the bid on which the hammer was falling.

(3) Such a sale is with reserve unless the goods are in explicit terms put up without reserve. In an auction with reserve the auctioneer may withdraw the goods at any time until he announces completion of the sale. In an auction without reserve, after the auctioneer calls for bids on an article or lot, that article or lot cannot be withdrawn unless no bid is made within a reasonable time. In either case a bidder may retract his bid until the auctioneer's announcement of completion of the sale, but a bidder's retraction does not revive any previous bid.

(4) If the auctioneer knowingly receives a bid on the seller's behalf or the seller makes or procures such a bid, and notice has not been given that liberty for such bidding is reserved, the buyer may at his option avoid the sale or take the goods at the price of the last good faith bid prior to the completion of the sale. This subsection shall not apply to any bid at a forced sale.

Part 4—Title, Creditors and Good Faith Purchasers

§ 2–401. Passing of Title; Reservation for Security; Limited Application of This Section.

Each provision of this Article with regard to the rights, obligations and remedies of the seller, the buyer, purchasers or other third parties applies irrespective of title to the goods except where the provision refers to such title. Insofar as situations are not covered by the other provisions of this Article and matters concerning title became material the following rules apply:

(1) Title to goods cannot pass under a contract for sale prior to their identification to the contract (Section 2–501), and unless otherwise explicitly agreed the buyer acquires by their identification a special property as limited by this Act. Any retention or reservation by the seller of the title (property) in goods shipped or delivered to the buyer is limited in effect to a reservation of a security interest. Subject to these provisions and to the provisions of the Article on Secured Transactions (Article 9), title to goods passes from the seller to the buyer in any manner and on any conditions explicitly agreed on by the parties.

(2) Unless otherwise explicitly agreed title passes to the buyer at the time and place at which the seller completes his performance with reference to the physical delivery of the goods, despite any reservation of a security interest and even though a document of title is to be delivered at a different time or place; and in particular and despite any reservation of a security interest by the bill of lading

(a) if the contract requires or authorizes the seller to send the goods to the buyer but does not require him to deliver them at destination, title passes to the buyer at the time and place of shipment; but

(b) if the contract requires delivery at destination, title passes on tender there.

(3) Unless otherwise explicitly agreed where delivery is to be made without moving the goods,

(a) if the seller is to deliver a document of title, title passes at the time when and the place where he delivers such documents; or

(b) if the goods are at the time of contracting already identified and no documents are to be delivered, title passes at the time and place of contracting.

(4) A rejection or other refusal by the buyer to receive or retain the goods, whether or not justified, or a justified revocation of acceptance revests title to the goods in the seller. Such revesting occurs by operation of law and is not a "sale".

§ 2–402. Rights of Seller's Creditors Against Sold Goods.

(1) Except as provided in subsections (2) and (3), rights of unsecured creditors of the seller with respect to goods which have been identified to a contract for sale are subject to the buyer's rights to recover the goods under this Article (Sections 2–502 and 2–716).

(2) A creditor of the seller may treat a sale or an identification of goods to a contract for sale as void if as against him a retention of possession by the seller is fraudulent under any rule of law of the state where the goods are situated, except that retention of possession in good faith and current course of trade by a merchant-seller for a commercially reasonable time after a sale or identification is not fraudulent.

(3) Nothing in this Article shall be deemed to impair the rights of creditors of the seller

(a) under the provisions of the Article on Secured Transactions (Article 9); or

(b) where identification to the contract or delivery is made not in current course of trade but in satisfaction of or as security for a pre-existing claim for money, security or the like and is made under circumstances which under any rule of law of the state where the goods are situated would apart from this Article constitute the transaction a fraudulent transfer or voidable preference.

§ 2–403. Power to Transfer; Good Faith Purchase of Goods; "Entrusting".

(1) A purchaser of goods acquires all title which his transferor had or had power to transfer except that a purchaser of a limited interest acquires rights only to the extent of the interest purchased. A person with voidable title has power to transfer a good title to a good faith purchaser for value. When goods have been delivered under a transaction of purchase the purchaser has such power even though

(a) the transferor was deceived as to the identity of the purchaser, or

(b) the delivery was in exchange for a check which is later dishonored, or

(c) it was agreed that the transaction was to be a "cash sale", or

(d) the delivery was procured through fraud punishable as larcenous under the criminal law.

(2) Any entrusting of possession of goods to a merchant who deals in goods of that kind gives him power to transfer all rights of the entruster to a buyer in ordinary course of business.

(3) "Entrusting" includes any delivery and any acquiescence in retention of possession regardless of any condition expressed between the parties to the delivery or acquiescence and regardless of whether the procurement of the entrusting or the possessor's disposition of the goods have been such as to be larcenous under the criminal law.

(4) The rights of other purchasers of goods and of lien creditors are governed by the Articles on Secured Transactions (Article 9), Bulk Transfers (Article 6) and Documents of Title (Article 7).

Part 5—Performance

§ 2–501. Insurable Interest in Goods; Manner of Identification of Goods.

(1) The buyer obtains a special property and an insurable interest in goods by identification of existing goods as goods to which the contract refers even though the goods so identified are nonconforming and he has an option to return or reject them. Such identification can be made at any time and in any manner explicitly agreed to by the parties. In the absence of explicit agreement identification occurs

(a) when the contract is made if it is for the sale of goods already existing and identified;

(b) if the contract is for the sale of future goods other than those described in paragraph (c), when goods are shipped, marked or otherwise designated by the seller as goods to which the contract refers;

(c) when the crops are planted or otherwise become growing crops or the young are conceived if the contract is for the sale of unborn young to be born within twelve months after contracting or for the sale of crops to be harvested within twelve months or the next normal harvest season after contracting whichever is longer.

(2) The seller retains an insurable interest in goods so long as title to or any security interest in the goods remains in him and where the identification is by the seller alone he may until default or insolvency or notification to the buyer that the identification is final substitute other goods for those identified.

(3) Nothing in this section impairs any insurable interest recognized under any other statute or rule of law.

§ 2–502. Buyer's Right to Goods on Seller's Insolvency.

(1) Subject to subsection (2) and even though the goods have not been shipped a buyer who has paid a part or all of the price of goods in which he has a special property under the provisions of the immediately preceding section may on making and keeping good a tender of any unpaid portion of their price recover them from the seller if the seller becomes insolvent within ten days after receipt of the first installment on their price.

(2) If the identification creating his special property has been made by the buyer he acquires the right to recover the goods only if they conform to the contract for sale.

§ 2–503. Manner of Seller's Tender of Delivery.

(1) Tender of delivery requires that the seller put and hold conforming goods at the buyer's disposition and give the buyer any notification reasonably necessary to enable him to take delivery. The manner, time and place for tender are determined by the agreement and this Article, and in particular

(a) tender must be at a reasonable hour, and if it is of goods they must be kept available for the period reasonably necessary to enable the buyer to take possession; but

(b) unless otherwise agreed the buyer must furnish facilities reasonably suited to the receipt of the goods.

(2) Where the case is within the next section respecting shipment tender requires that the seller comply with its provisions.

(3) Where the seller is required to deliver at a particular destination tender requires that he comply with subsection (1) and also in any appropriate case tender documents as described in subsections (4) and (5) of this section.

(4) Where goods are in the possession of a bailee and are to be delivered without being moved

(a) tender requires that the seller either tender a negotiable document of title covering such goods or procure acknowledgment by the bailee of the buyer's right to possession of the goods; but

(b) tender to the buyer of a non-negotiable document of title or of a written direction to the bailee to deliver is sufficient tender unless the buyer seasonably objects, and receipt by the bailee of notification of the buyer's rights fixes those rights as against the bailee and all third persons; but risk of loss of the goods and of any failure by the bailee to honor the non-negotiable document of title or to obey the direction remains on the seller until the buyer has had a reasonable time to present the document or direction, and a refusal by the bailee to honor the document or to obey the direction defeats the tender.

(5) Where the contract requires the seller to deliver documents

(a) he must tender all such documents in correct form, except as provided in this Article with respect to bills of lading in a set (subsection (2) of Section 2–323); and

(b) tender through customary banking channels is sufficient and dishonor of a draft accompanying the documents constitutes non-acceptance or rejection.

§ 2–504. Shipment by Seller.

Where the seller is required or authorized to send the goods to the buyer and the contract does not require him to deliver them at a particular destination, then unless otherwise agreed he must

(a) put the goods in the possession of such a carrier and make such a contract for their transportation as may be reasonable having regard to the nature of the goods and other circumstances of the case; and

(b) obtain and promptly deliver or tender in due form any document necessary to enable the buyer to obtain possession of the goods or otherwise required by the agreement or by usage of trade; and

(c) promptly notify the buyer of the shipment.

Failure to notify the buyer under paragraph (c) or to make a proper contract under paragraph (a) is a ground for rejection only if material delay or loss ensues.

§ 2–505. Seller's Shipment Under Reservation.

(1) Where the seller has identified goods to the contract by or before shipment:

(a) his procurement of a negotiable bill of lading to his own order or otherwise reserves in him a security interest in the goods. His procurement of the bill to the order of a financing agency or of the buyer indicates in addition only the seller's expectation of transferring that interest to the person named.

(b) a non-negotiable bill of lading to himself or his nominee reserves possession of the goods as security but except in a case of conditional delivery (subsection (2) of Section 2–507) a non-negotiable bill of lading naming the buyer as consignee reserves no security interest even though the seller retains possession of the bill of lading.

(2) When shipment by the seller with reservation of a security interest is in violation of the contract for sale it constitutes an improper contract for transportation within the preceding section but impairs neither the rights given to the buyer by shipment and identification of the goods to the contract nor the seller's powers as a holder of a negotiable document.

§ 2–506. Rights of Financing Agency.

(1) A financing agency by paying or purchasing for value a draft which relates to a shipment of goods acquires to the extent of the payment or purchase and in addition to its own rights under the draft and any document of title securing it any rights of the shipper in the goods including the right to stop delivery and the shipper's right to have the draft honored by the buyer.

(2) The right to reimbursement of a financing agency which has in good faith honored or purchased the draft under commitment to or authority from the buyer is not impaired by subsequent discovery of defects with reference to any relevant document which was apparently regular on its face.

§ 2–507. Effect of Seller's Tender; Delivery on Condition.

(1) Tender of delivery is a condition to the buyer's duty to accept the goods and, unless otherwise agreed, to his duty to pay for them. Tender entitles the seller to acceptance of the goods and to payment according to the contract.

(2) Where payment is due and demanded on the delivery to the buyer of goods or documents of title, his right as against the seller to retain or dispose of them is conditional upon his making the payment due.

§ 2–508. Cure by Seller of Improper Tender or Delivery; Replacement.

(1) Where any tender or delivery by the seller is rejected because non-conforming and the time for performance has not yet expired, the seller may seasonably notify the buyer of his intention to cure and may then within the contract time make a conforming delivery.

(2) Where the buyer rejects a non-conforming tender which the seller had reasonable grounds to believe would be acceptable with or without money allowance the seller may if he seasonably notifies the buyer have a further reasonable time to substitute a conforming tender.

§ 2–509. Risk of Loss in the Absence of Breach.

(1) Where the contract requires or authorizes the seller to ship the goods by carrier

(a) if it does not require him to deliver them at a particular destination, the risk of loss passes to the buyer when the goods are duly delivered to the carrier even though the shipment is under reservation (Section 2–505); but

(b) if it does require him to deliver them at a particular destination and the goods are there duly tendered while in the possession of the carrier, the risk of loss passes to the buyer when the goods are there duly so tendered as to enable the buyer to take delivery.

(2) Where the goods are held by a bailee to be delivered without being moved, the risk of loss passes to the buyer

(a) on his receipt of a negotiable document of title covering the goods; or

(b) on acknowledgment by the bailee of the buyer's right to possession of the goods; or

(c) after his receipt of a non-negotiable document of title or other written direction to deliver, as provided in subsection (4)(b) of Section 2–503.

(3) In any case not within subsection (1) or (2), the risk of loss passes to the buyer on his receipt of the goods if the seller is a merchant; otherwise, the risk passes to the buyer on tender of delivery.

(4) The provisions of this section are subject to contrary agreement of the parties and to the provisions of this Article on sale on approval (Section 2–327) and on effect of breach on risk of loss (Section 2–510).

§ 2–510. Effect of Breach on Risk of Loss.

(1) Where a tender or delivery of goods so fails to conform to the contract as to give a right of rejection the risk of their loss remains on the seller until cure or acceptance.

(2) Where the buyer rightfully revokes acceptance he may to the extent of any deficiency in his effective insurance coverage treat the risk of loss as having rested on the seller from the beginning.

(3) Where the buyer as to conforming goods already identified to the contract for sale repudiates or is otherwise in breach before risk of their loss has passed to him, the seller may to the extent of any deficiency in his effective insurance coverage treat the risk of loss as resting on the buyer for a commercially reasonable time.

§ 2–511. Tender of Payment by Buyer; Payment by Check.

(1) Unless otherwise agreed tender of payment is a condition to the seller's duty to tender and complete any delivery.

(2) Tender of payment is sufficient when made by any means or in any manner current in the ordinary course of business unless the seller demands payment in legal tender and gives any extension of time reasonably necessary to procure it.

(3) Subject to the provisions of this Act on the effect of an instrument on an obligation (Section 3–802), payment by check is conditional and is defeated as between the parties by dishonor of the check on due presentment.

§ 2–512. Payment by Buyer Before Inspection.

(1) Where the contract requires payment before inspection non-conformity of the goods does not excuse the buyer from so making payment unless

(a) the non-conformity appears without inspection; or

(b) despite tender of the required documents the circumstances would justify injunction against honor under the provisions of this Act (Section 5–114).

(2) Payment pursuant to subsection (1) does not constitute an acceptance of goods or impair the buyer's right to inspect or any of his remedies.

§ 2–513. Buyer's Right to Inspection of Goods.

(1) Unless otherwise agreed and subject to subsection (3), where goods are tendered or delivered or identified to the contract for sale, the buyer has a right before payment or acceptance to inspect them at any reasonable place and time and in any reasonable manner. When the seller is required or authorized to send the goods to the buyer, the inspection may be after their arrival.

(2) Expenses of inspection must be borne by the buyer but may be recovered from the seller if the goods do not conform and are rejected.

(3) Unless otherwise agreed and subject to the provisions of this Article on C.I.F. contracts (subsection (3) of Section 2–321), the buyer is not entitled to inspect the goods before payment of the price when the contract provides

(a) for delivery "C.O.D." or on other like terms; or

(b) for payment against documents of title, except where such payment is due only after the goods are to become available for inspection.

(4) A place or method of inspection fixed by the parties is presumed to be exclusive but unless otherwise expressly agreed it does not postpone identification or shift the place for delivery or for passing the risk of loss. If compliance becomes impossible, inspection shall be as provided in this section unless the place or method fixed was clearly intended as an indispensable condition failure of which avoids the contract.

§ 2–514. When Documents Deliverable on Acceptance; When on Payment.

Unless otherwise agreed documents against which a draft is drawn are to be delivered to the drawee on acceptance of the draft if it is payable more than three days after presentment; otherwise, only on payment.

§ 2–515. Preserving Evidence of Goods in Dispute.

In furtherance of the adjustment of any claim or dispute

(a) either party on reasonable notification to the other and for the purpose of ascertaining the facts and preserving evidence has the right to inspect, test and sample the goods including such of them as may be in the possession or control of the other; and

(b) the parties may agree to a third party inspection or survey to determine the conformity or condition of the goods and may agree that the findings shall be binding upon them in any subsequent litigation or adjustment.

Part 6—Breach, Repudiation and Excuse

§ 2–601. Buyer's Rights on Improper Delivery.

Subject to the provisions of this Article on breach in installment contracts (Section 2–612) and unless otherwise agreed under the sections on contractual limitations of remedy (Sections 2–718 and 2–719), if the goods or the tender of delivery fail in any respect to conform to the contract, the buyer may

(a) reject the whole; or

(b) accept the whole; or

(c) accept any commercial unit or units and reject the rest.

§ 2–602. Manner and Effect of Rightful Rejection.

(1) Rejection of goods must be within a reasonable time after their delivery or tender. It is ineffective unless the buyer seasonably notifies the seller.

(2) Subject to the provisions of the two following sections on rejected goods (Sections 2–603 and 2–604),

(a) after rejection any exercise of ownership by the buyer with respect to any commercial unit is wrongful as against the seller; and

(b) if the buyer has before rejection taken physical possession of goods in which he does not have a security interest under the provisions of this Article (subsection (3) of Section 2–711), he is under a duty after rejection to hold them with reasonable care at the seller's disposition for a time sufficient to permit the seller to remove them; but

(c) the buyer has no further obligations with regard to goods rightfully rejected.

(3) The seller's rights with respect to goods wrongfully rejected are governed by the provisions of this Article on seller's remedies in general (Section 2–703).

§ 2–603. Merchant Buyer's Duties as to Rightfully Rejected Goods.

(1) Subject to any security interest in the buyer (subsection (3) of Section 2–711), when the seller has no agent or place of business at the market of rejection a merchant buyer is under a duty after rejection of goods in his possession or control to follow any reasonable instructions received from the seller with respect to the goods and in the absence of such instructions to make reasonable efforts to sell them for the seller's account if they are perishable or threaten to decline in value speedily. Instructions are not reasonable if on demand indemnity for expenses is not forthcoming.

(2) When the buyer sells goods under subsection (1), he is entitled to reimbursement from the seller or out of the proceeds for reasonable expenses of caring for and selling them, and if the expenses include no selling commission then to such commission as is usual in the trade or if there is none to a reasonable sum not exceeding ten per cent on the gross proceeds.

(3) In complying with this section the buyer is held only to good faith and good faith conduct hereunder is neither acceptance nor conversion nor the basis of an action for damages.

§ 2–604. Buyer's Options as to Salvage of Rightfully Rejected Goods.

Subject to the provisions of the immediately preceding section on perishables if the seller gives no instructions within a reasonable time after notification of rejection the buyer may store the rejected goods for the seller's account or reship them to him or resell them for the seller's account with reimbursement as provided in the preceding section. Such action is not acceptance or conversion.

§ 2–605. Waiver of Buyer's Objections by Failure to Particularize.

(1) The buyer's failure to state in connection with rejection a particular defect which is ascertainable by reasonable inspection precludes him from relying on the unstated defect to justify rejection or to establish breach

(a) where the seller could have cured it if stated seasonably; or

(b) between merchants when the seller has after rejection made a request in writing for a full and final written statement of all defects on which the buyer proposes to rely.

(2) Payment against documents made without reservation of rights precludes recovery of the payment for defects apparent on the face of the documents.

§ 2–606. What Constitutes Acceptance of Goods.

(1) Acceptance of goods occurs when the buyer

(a) after a reasonable opportunity to inspect the goods signifies to the seller that the goods are conforming or that he will take or retain them in spite of their nonconformity; or

(b) fails to make an effective rejection (subsection (1) of Section 2–602), but such acceptance does not occur until the buyer has had a reasonable opportunity to inspect them; or

(c) does any act inconsistent with the seller's ownership; but if such act is wrongful as against the seller it is an acceptance only if ratified by him.

(2) Acceptance of a part of any commercial unit is acceptance of that entire unit.

§ 2–607. Effect of Acceptance; Notice of Breach; Burden of Establishing Breach After Acceptance; Notice of Claim or Litigation to Person Answerable Over.

(1) The buyer must pay at the contract rate for any goods accepted.

(2) Acceptance of goods by the buyer precludes rejection of the goods accepted and if made with knowledge of a non-conformity cannot be revoked because of it unless the acceptance was on the reasonable assumption that the non-conformity would be seasonably cured but acceptance does not of itself impair any other remedy provided by this Article for non-conformity.

(3) Where a tender has been accepted

(a) the buyer must within a reasonable time after he discovers or should have discovered any breach notify the seller of breach or be barred from any remedy; and

(b) if the claim is one for infringement or the like (subsection (3) of Section 2–312) and the buyer is sued as a result of such a breach he must so notify the seller within a reasonable time after he receives notice of the litigation or be barred from any remedy over for liability established by the litigation.

(4) The burden is on the buyer to establish any breach with respect to the goods accepted.

(5) Where the buyer is sued for breach of a warranty or other obligation for which his seller is answerable over

(a) he may give his seller written notice of the litigation. If the notice states that the seller may come in and defend and that if the seller does not do so he will be bound in any action against him by his buyer by any determination of fact common to the two litigations, then unless the seller after seasonable receipt of the notice does come in and defend he is so bound.

(b) if the claim is one for infringement or the like (subsection (3) of Section 2–312) the original seller may demand in writing that his buyer turn over to him control of the litigation including settlement or else be barred from any remedy over and if he also agrees to bear all expense and to satisfy any adverse judgment, then unless the buyer after seasonable receipt of the demand does turn over control the buyer is so barred.

(6) The provisions of subsections (3), (4) and (5) apply to any obligation of a buyer to hold the seller harmless against infringement or the like (subsection (3) of Section 2–312).

§ 2–608. Revocation of Acceptance in Whole or in Part.

(1) The buyer may revoke his acceptance of a lot or commercial unit whose non-conformity substantially impairs its value to him if he has accepted it

(a) on the reasonable assumption that its non-conformity would be cured and it has not been seasonably cured; or

(b) without discovery of such non-conformity if his acceptance was reasonably induced either by the difficulty of discovery before acceptance or by the seller's assurances.

(2) Revocation of acceptance must occur within a reasonable time after the buyer discovers or should have discovered the ground for it and before any substantial change in condition of the goods which is not caused by their own defects. It is not effective until the buyer notifies the seller of it.

(3) A buyer who so revokes has the same rights and duties with regard to the goods involved as if he had rejected them.

§ 2–609. Right to Adequate Assurance of Performance.

(1) A contract for sale imposes an obligation on each party that the other's expectation of receiving due performance will not be impaired. When reasonable grounds for insecurity arise with respect to the performance of either party the other may in writing demand adequate assurance of due performance and until he receives such assurance may if commercially reasonable suspend any performance for which he has not already received the agreed return.

(2) Between merchants the reasonableness of grounds for insecurity and the adequacy of any assurance offered shall be determined according to commercial standards.

(3) Acceptance of any improper delivery or payment does not prejudice the aggrieved party's right to demand adequate assurance of future performance.

(4) After receipt of a justified demand failure to provide within a reasonable time not exceeding thirty days such assurance of due performance as is adequate under the circumstances of the particular case is a repudiation of the contract.

§ 2–610. Anticipatory Repudiation.

When either party repudiates the contract with respect to a performance not yet due the loss of which will substantially impair the value of the contract to the other, the aggrieved party may

(a) for a commercially reasonable time await performance by the repudiating party; or

(b) resort to any remedy for breach (Section 2–703 or Section 2–711), even though he has notified the repudiating party that he would await the latter's performance and has urged retraction; and

(c) in either case suspend his own performance or proceed in accordance with the provisions of this Article on the seller's right to identify goods to the contract notwithstanding breach or to salvage unfinished goods (Section 2–704).

§ 2–611. Retraction of Anticipatory Repudiation.

(1) Until the repudiating party's next performance is due he can retract his repudiation unless the aggrieved party has since the repudiation cancelled or materially changed his position or otherwise indicated that he considers the repudiation final.

(2) Retraction may be by any method which clearly indicates to the aggrieved party that the repudiating party intends to perform, but must include any assurance justifiably demanded under the provisions of this Article (Section 2–609).

(3) Retraction reinstates the repudiating party's rights under the contract with due excuse and allowance to the aggrieved party for any delay occasioned by the repudiation.

§ 2–612. "Installment Contract"; Breach.

(1) An "installment contract" is one which requires or authorizes the delivery of goods in separate lots to be separately accepted, even though the contract contains a clause "each delivery is a separate contract" or its equivalent.

(2) The buyer may reject any installment which is non-conforming if the non-conformity substantially impairs the value of that installment and cannot be cured or if the non-conformity is a defect in the required documents; but if the non-conformity does not fall within subsection (3) and the seller gives adequate assurance of its cure the buyer must accept that installment.

(3) Whenever non-conformity or default with respect to one or more installments substantially impairs the value of the whole contract there is a breach of the whole. But the aggrieved party reinstates the contract if he accepts a non-conforming installment without seasonably notifying of cancellation or if he brings an action with respect only to past installments or demands performance as to future installments.

§ 2–613. Casualty to Identified Goods.

Where the contract requires for its performance goods identified when the contract is made, and the goods suffer casualty without fault of either party before the risk of loss passes to the buyer, or in a proper case under a "no arrival, no sale" term (Section 2–324) then

(a) if the loss is total the contract is avoided; and

(b) if the loss is partial or the goods have so deteriorated as no longer to conform to the contract the buyer may nevertheless demand inspection and at his option either treat the contract as avoided or accept the goods with due allowance from the contract price for the deterioration or the deficiency in quantity but without further right against the seller.

§ 2–614. Substituted Performance.

(1) Where without fault of either party the agreed berthing, loading, or unloading facilities fail or an agreed type of carrier becomes unavailable or the agreed manner of delivery otherwise becomes commercially impracticable but a commercially reasonable substitute is available, such substitute performance must be tendered and accepted.

(2) If the agreed means or manner of payment fails because of domestic or foreign governmental regulation, the seller may withhold or stop delivery unless the buyer provides a means or manner of payment which is commercially a substantial equivalent. If delivery has already been taken, payment by the means or in the manner provided by the regulation discharges the buyer's obligation unless the regulation is discriminatory, oppressive or predatory.

§ 2–615. Excuse by Failure of Presupposed Conditions.

Except so far as a seller may have assumed a greater obligation and subject to the preceding section on substituted performance:

(a) Delay in delivery or non-delivery in whole or in part by a seller who complies with paragraphs (b) and (c) is not a breach of his duty under a contract for sale if performance as agreed has been made impracticable by the occurrence of a contingency the non-occurrence of which was a basic assumption on which the contract was made or by compliance in good faith with any applicable foreign or domestic governmental regulation or order whether or not it later proves to be invalid.
(b) Where the causes mentioned in paragraph (a) affect only a part of the seller's capacity to perform, he must allocate production and deliveries among his customers but may at his option include regular customers not then under contract as well as his own requirements for further manufacture. He may so allocate in any manner which is fair and reasonable.
(c) The seller must notify the buyer seasonably that there will be delay or non-delivery and, when allocation is required under paragraph (b), of the estimated quota thus made available for the buyer.

§ 2–616. Procedure on Notice Claiming Excuse.
(1) Where the buyer receives notification of a material or indefinite delay or an allocation justified under the preceding section he may by written notification to the seller as to any delivery concerned, and where the prospective deficiency substantially impairs the value of the whole contract under the provisions of this Article relating to breach of installment contracts (Section 2–612), then also as to the whole,
(a) terminate and thereby discharge any unexecuted portion of the contract; or
(b) modify the contract by agreeing to take his available quota in substitution.
(2) If after receipt of such notification from the seller the buyer fails so to modify the contract within a reasonable time not exceeding thirty days the contract lapses with respect to any deliveries affected.
(3) The provisions of this section may not be negated by agreement except in so far as the seller has assumed a greater obligation under the preceding section.

Part 7—Remedies
§ 2–701. Remedies for Breach of Collateral Contracts Not Impaired.
Remedies for breach of any obligation or promise collateral or ancillary to a contract for sale are not impaired by the provisions of this Article.

§ 2–702. Seller's Remedies on Discovery of Buyer's Insolvency.
(1) Where the seller discovers the buyer to be insolvent he may refuse delivery except for cash including payment for all goods theretofore delivered under the contract, and stop delivery under this Article (Section 2–705).
(2) Where the seller discovers that the buyer has received goods on credit while insolvent he may reclaim the goods upon demand made within ten days after the receipt, but if misrepresentation of solvency has been made to the particular seller in writing within three months before delivery the ten day limitation does not apply. Except as provided in this subsection the seller may not base a right to reclaim goods on the buyer's fraudulent or innocent misrepresentation of solvency or of intent to pay.
(3) The seller's right to reclaim under subsection (2) is subject to the rights of a buyer in ordinary course or other good faith purchaser under this Article (Section 2–403). Successful reclamation of goods excludes all other remedies with respect to them.

§ 2–703. Seller's Remedies in General.
Where the buyer wrongfully rejects or revokes acceptance of goods or fails to make a payment due on or before delivery or repudiates with respect to a part or the whole, then with respect to any goods directly affected and, if the breach is of the whole contract (Section 2–612), then also with respect to the whole undelivered balance, the aggrieved seller may
(a) withhold delivery of such goods;
(b) stop delivery by any bailee as hereafter provided (Section 2–705);
(c) proceed under the next section respecting goods still unidentified to the contract;
(d) resell and recover damages as hereafter provided (Section 2–706);
(e) recover damages for non-acceptance (Section 2–708) or in a proper case the price (Section 2–709);
(f) cancel.

§ 2–704. Seller's Right to Identify Goods to the Contract Notwithstanding Breach or to Salvage Unfinished Goods.
(1) An aggrieved seller under the preceding section may
(a) identify to the contract conforming goods not already identified if at the time he learned of the breach they are in his possession or control;
(b) treat as the subject of resale goods which have demonstrably been intended for the particular contract even though those goods are unfinished.
(2) Where the goods are unfinished an aggrieved seller may in the exercise of reasonable commercial judgment for the purposes of avoiding loss and of effective realization either complete the manufacture and wholly identify the goods to the contract or cease manufacture and resell for scrap or salvage value or proceed in any other reasonable manner.

§ 2–705. Seller's Stoppage of Delivery in Transit or Otherwise.
(1) The seller may stop delivery of goods in the possession of a carrier or other bailee when he discovers the buyer to be insolvent (Section 2–702) and may stop delivery of carload, truckload, planeload or larger shipments of express or freight when the buyer repudiates or fails to make a payment due before delivery or if for any other reason the seller has a right to withhold or reclaim the goods.
(2) As against such buyer the seller may stop delivery until
(a) receipt of the goods by the buyer; or
(b) acknowledgment to the buyer by any bailee of the goods except a carrier that the bailee holds the goods for the buyer; or
(c) such acknowledgment to the buyer by a carrier by reshipment or as warehouseman; or
(d) negotiation to the buyer of any negotiable document of title covering the goods.
(3) **(a)** To stop delivery the seller must so notify as to enable the bailee by reasonable diligence to prevent delivery of the goods.
(b) After such notification the bailee must hold and deliver the goods according to the directions of the seller but the seller is liable to the bailee for any ensuing charges or damages.
(c) If a negotiable document of title has been issued for goods the bailee is not obliged to obey a notification to stop until surrender of the document.
(d) A carrier who has issued a non-negotiable bill of lading is not obliged to obey a notification to stop received from a person other than the consignor.

§ 2–706. Seller's Resale Including Contract for Resale.
(1) Under the conditions stated in Section 2–703 on seller's remedies, the seller may resell the goods concerned or the undelivered balance thereof. Where the resale is made in good faith and in a commercially reasonable manner the seller may recover the difference between the resale price and the contract price together with any incidental damages allowed under the provisions of this Article (Section 2–710), but less expenses saved in consequence of the buyer's breach.
(2) Except as otherwise provided in subsection (3) or unless otherwise agreed resale may be at public or private sale including sale by way of one or more contracts to sell or of identification to an existing contract of the seller. Sale may be as a unit or in parcels and at any time and place and on any terms but every aspect of the sale including the method, manner, time, place and terms must be commercially reasonable. The resale must be reasonably identified as referring to the broken contract,

but it is not necessary that the goods be in existence or that any or all of them have been identified to the contract before the breach.
(3) Where the resale is at private sale the seller must give the buyer reasonable notification of his intention to resell.
(4) Where the resale is at public sale
(a) only identified goods can be sold except where there is a recognized market for a public sale of futures in goods of the kind; and
(b) it must be made at a usual place or market for public sale if one is reasonably available and except in the case of goods which are perishable or threaten to decline in value speedily the seller must give the buyer reasonable notice of the time and place of the resale; and
(c) if the goods are not to be within the view of those attending the sale the notification of sale must state the place where the goods are located and provide for their reasonable inspection by prospective bidders; and
(d) the seller may buy.
(5) A purchaser who buys in good faith at a resale takes the goods free of any rights of the original buyer even though the seller fails to comply with one or more of the requirements of this section.
(6) The seller is not accountable to the buyer for any profit made on any resale. A person in the position of a seller (Section 2–707) or a buyer who has rightfully rejected or justifiably revoked acceptance must account for any excess over the amount of his security interest, as hereinafter defined (subsection (3) of Section 2–711).

§ 2–707. "Person in the Position of a Seller".
(1) A "person in the position of a seller" includes as against a principal an agent who has paid or become responsible for the price of goods on behalf of his principal or anyone who otherwise holds a security interest or other right in goods similar to that of a seller.
(2) A person in the position of a seller may as provided in this Article withhold or stop delivery (Section 2–705) and resell (Section 2–706) and recover incidental damages (Section 2–710).

§ 2–708. Seller's Damages for Non-Acceptance or Repudiation.
(1) Subject to subsection (2) and to the provisions of this Article with respect to proof of market price (Section 2–723), the measure of damages for non-acceptance or repudiation by the buyer is the difference between the market price at the time and place for tender and the unpaid contract price together with any incidental damages provided in this Article (Section 2–710), but less expenses saved in consequence of the buyer's breach.
(2) If the measure of damages provided in subsection (1) is inadequate to put the seller in as good a position as performance would have done then the measure of damages is the profit (including reasonable overhead) which the seller would have made from full performance by the buyer, together with any incidental damages provided in this Article (Section 2–710), due allowance for costs reasonably incurred and due credit for payments or proceeds of resale.

§ 2–709. Action for the Price.
(1) When the buyer fails to pay the price as it becomes due the seller may recover, together with any incidental damages under the next section, the price
(a) of goods accepted or of conforming goods lost or damaged within a commercially reasonable time after risk of their loss has passed to the buyer; and
(b) of goods identified to the contract if the seller is unable after reasonable effort to resell them at a reasonable price or the circumstances reasonably indicate that such effort will be unavailing.
(2) Where the seller sues for the price he must hold for the buyer any goods which have been identified to the contract and are still in his control except that if resale becomes possible he may resell them at any time prior to the collection of the judgment. The net proceeds of any such resale must be credited to the buyer and payment of the judgment entitles him to any goods not resold.
(3) After the buyer has wrongfully rejected or revoked acceptance of the goods or has failed to make a payment due or has repudiated (Section 2–610), a seller who is held not entitled to the price under this section shall nevertheless be awarded damages for non-acceptance under the preceding section.

§ 2–710. Seller's Incidental Damages.
Incidental damages to an aggrieved seller include any commercially reasonable charges, expenses or commissions incurred in stopping delivery, in the transportation, care and custody of goods after the buyer's breach, in connection with return or resale of the goods or otherwise resulting from the breach.

§ 2–711. Buyer's Remedies in General; Buyer's Security Interest in Rejected Goods.
(1) Where the seller fails to make delivery or repudiates or the buyer rightfully rejects or justifiably revokes acceptance then with respect to any goods involved, and with respect to the whole if the breach goes to the whole contract (Section 2–612), the buyer may cancel and whether or not he has done so may in addition to recovering so much of the price as has been paid
(a) "cover" and have damages under the next section as to all the goods affected whether or not they have been identified to the contract; or
(b) recover damages for non-delivery as provided in this Article (Section 2–713).
(2) Where the seller fails to deliver or repudiates the buyer may also
(a) if the goods have been identified recover them as provided in this Article (Section 2–502); or
(b) in a proper case obtain specific performance or replevy the goods as provided in this Article (Section 2–716).
(3) On rightful rejection or justifiable revocation of acceptance a buyer has a security interest in goods in his possession or control for any payments made on their price and any expenses reasonably incurred in their inspection, receipt, transportation, care and custody and may hold such goods and resell them in like manner as an aggrieved seller (Section 2–706).

§ 2–712. "Cover"; Buyer's Procurement of Substitute Goods.
(1) After a breach within the preceding section the buyer may "cover" by making in good faith and without unreasonable delay any reasonable purchase of or contract to purchase goods in substitution for those due from the seller.
(2) The buyer may recover from the seller as damages the difference between the cost of cover and the contract price together with any incidental or consequential damages as hereinafter defined (Section 2–715), but less expenses saved in consequence of the seller's breach.
(3) Failure of the buyer to effect cover within this section does not bar him from any other remedy.

§ 2–713. Buyer's Damages for Non-Delivery or Repudiation.
(1) Subject to provisions of this Article with respect to the proof of market price (Section 2–723), the measure of damages for non-delivery or repudiation by the seller is the difference between the market price at the time when the buyer learned of the breach and the contract price together with any incidental and consequential damages provided in this Article (Section 2–715), but less expenses saved in consequence of the seller's breach.
(2) Market price is to be determined as of the place for tender or, in cases of rejection after arrival or revocation of acceptance, as of the place of arrival.

§ 2–714. Buyer's Damages for Breach in Regard to Accepted Goods.
(1) Where the buyer has accepted goods and given notification (subsection (3) of Section 2–607) he may recover as damages for any non-conformity of tender the loss resulting in the ordinary course of events from the seller's breach as determined in any manner which is reasonable.

(2) The measure of damages for breach of warranty is the difference at the time and place of acceptance between the value of the goods accepted and the value they would have had if they had been as warranted, unless special circumstances show proximate damages of a different amount.
(3) In a proper case any incidental and consequential damages under the next section may be recovered.

§ 2–715. Buyer's Incidental and Consequential Damages.
(1) Incidental damages resulting from the seller's breach include expenses reasonably incurred in inspection, receipt, transportation and care and custody of goods rightfully rejected, any commercially reasonable charges, expenses or commissions in connection with effecting cover and any other reasonable expense incident to the delay or other breach.
(2) Consequential damages resulting from the seller's breach include
(a) any loss resulting from general or particular requirements and needs of which the seller at the time of contracting had reason to know and which could not reasonably be prevented by cover or otherwise; and
(b) injury to person or property proximately resulting from any breach of warranty.

§ 2–716. Buyer's Right to Specific Performance or Replevin.
(1) Specific performance may be decreed where the goods are unique or in other proper circumstances.
(2) The decree for specific performance may include such terms and conditions as to payment of the price, damages, or other relief as the court may deem just.
(3) The buyer has a right of replevin for goods identified to the contract if after reasonable effort he is unable to effect cover for such goods or the circumstances reasonably indicate that such effort will be unavailing or if the goods have been shipped under reservation and satisfaction of the security interest in them has been made or tendered.

§ 2–717. Deduction of Damages From the Price.
The buyer on notifying the seller of his intention to do so may deduct all or any part of the damages resulting from any breach of the contract from any part of the price still due under the same contract.

§ 2–718. Liquidation or Limitation of Damages; Deposits.
(1) Damages for breach by either party may be liquidated in the agreement but only at an amount which is reasonable in the light of the anticipated or actual harm caused by the breach, the difficulties of proof of loss, and the inconvenience or nonfeasibility of otherwise obtaining an adequate remedy. A term fixing unreasonably large liquidated damages is void as a penalty.
(2) Where the seller justifiably withholds delivery of goods because of the buyer's breach, the buyer is entitled to restitution of any amount by which the sum of his payments exceeds
(a) the amount to which the seller is entitled by virtue of terms liquidating the seller's damages in accordance with subsection (1), or
(b) in the absence of such terms, twenty per cent of the value of the total performance for which the buyer is obligated under the contract or $500, whichever is smaller.
(3) The buyer's right to restitution under subsection (2) is subject to offset to the extent that the seller establishes
(a) a right to recover damages under the provisions of this Article other than subsection (1), and
(b) the amount or value of any benefits received by the buyer directly or indirectly by reason of the contract.
(4) Where a seller has received payment in goods their reasonable value or the proceeds of their resale shall be treated as payments for the purposes of subsection (2); but if the seller has notice of the buyer's breach before reselling goods received in part performance, his resale is subject to the conditions laid down in this Article on resale by an aggrieved seller (Section 2–706).

§ 2–719. Contractual Modification or Limitation of Remedy.
(1) Subject to the provisions of subsection (2) and (3) of this section and of the preceding section on liquidation and limitation of damages,
(a) the agreement may provide for remedies in addition to or in substitution for those provided in this Article and may limit or alter the measure of damages recoverable under this Article, as by limiting the buyer's remedies to return of the goods and repayment of the price or to repair and replacement of non-conforming goods or parts; and
(b) resort to a remedy as provided is optional unless the remedy is expressly agreed to be exclusive, in which case it is the sole remedy.
(2) Where circumstances cause an exclusive or limited remedy to fail of its essential purpose, remedy may be had as provided in this Act.
(3) Consequential damages may be limited or excluded unless the limitation or exclusion is unconscionable. Limitation of consequential damages for injury to the person in the case of consumer goods is prima facie unconscionable but limitation of damages where the loss is commercial is not.

§ 2–720. Effect of "Cancellation" or "Rescission" on Claims for Antecedent Breach.
Unless the contrary intention clearly appears, expressions of "cancellation" or "rescission" of the contract or the like shall not be construed as a renunciation or discharge of any claim in damages for an antecedent breach.

§ 2–721. Remedies for Fraud.
Remedies for material misrepresentation or fraud include all remedies available under this Article for non-fraudulent breach. Neither rescission or a claim for rescission of the contract for sale nor rejection or return of the goods shall bar or be deemed inconsistent with a claim for damages or other remedy.

§ 2–722. Who Can Sue Third Parties for Injury to Goods.
Where a third party so deals with goods which have been identified to a contract for sale as to cause actionable injury to a party to that contract
(a) a right of action against the third party is in either party to the contract for sale who has title to or a security interest or a special property or an insurable interest in the goods; and if the goods have been destroyed or converted a right of action is also in the party who either bore the risk of loss under the contract for sale or has since the injury assumed that risk as against the other;
(b) if at the time of the injury the party plaintiff did not bear the risk of loss as against the other party to the contract for sale and there is no arrangement between them for disposition of the recovery, his suit or settlement is subject to his own interest, as a fiduciary for the other party to the contract;
(c) either party may with the consent of the other sue for the benefit of whom it may concern.

§ 2–723. Proof of Market Price: Time and Place
(1) If an action based on anticipatory repudiation comes to trial before the time for performance with respect to some or all of the goods, any damages based on market price (Section 2–708 or Section 2–713) shall be determined according to the price of such goods prevailing at the time when the aggrieved party learned of the repudiation.
(2) If evidence of a price prevailing at the times or places described in this Article is not readily available the price prevailing within any reasonable time before or after the time described or at any other place which in commercial judgment or under usage of trade would serve as a reasonable substitute for the one described may be used, making any proper allowance for the cost of transporting the goods to or from such other place.
(3) Evidence of a relevant price prevailing at a time or place other than the one described in this Article offered by one party is not admissible

unless and until he has given the other party such notice as the court finds sufficient to prevent unfair surprise.

§ 2–724. Admissibility of Market Quotations.
Whenever the prevailing price or value of any goods regularly bought and sold in any established commodity market is in issue, reports in official publications or trade journals or in newspapers or periodicals of general circulation published as the reports of such market shall be admissible in evidence. The circumstances of the preparation of such a report may be shown to affect its weight but not its admissibility.

§ 2–725. Statute of Limitations in Contracts for Sale.
(1) An action for breach of any contract for sale must be commenced within four years after the cause of action has accrued. By the original agreement the parties may reduce the period of limitation to not less than one year but may not extend it.
(2) A cause of action occurs when the breach occurs, regardless of the aggrieved party's lack of knowledge of the breach. A breach of warranty occurs when tender of delivery is made, except that where a warranty explicitly extends to future performance of the goods and discovery of the breach must await the time of such performance the cause of action accrues when the breach is or should have been discovered.
(3) Where an action commenced within the time limited by subsection (1) is so terminated as to leave available a remedy by another action for the same breach such other action may be commenced after the expiration of the time limited and within six months after the termination of the first action unless the termination resulted from voluntary discontinuance or from dismissal for failure or neglect to prosecute.
(4) This section does not alter the law on tolling of the statute of limitations nor does it apply to causes of action which have accrued before this Act becomes effective.

ARTICLE 2A: LEASES

Part 1—General Provisions
§ 2A–101. Short Title.
This Article shall be known and may be cited as the Uniform Commercial Code—Leases.

§ 2A–102. Scope.
This Article applies to any transaction, regardless of form, that creates a lease.

§ 2A–103. Definitions and Index of Definitions.
(1) In this Article unless the context otherwise requires:
(a) "Buyer in ordinary course of business" means a person who in good faith and without knowledge that the sale to him [or her] is in violation of the ownership rights or security interest or leasehold interest of a third party in the goods buys in ordinary course from a person in the business of selling goods of that kind but does not include a pawnbroker. "Buying" may be for cash or by exchange of other property or on secured or unsecured credit and includes receiving goods or documents of title under a pre-existing contract for sale but does not include a transfer in bulk or as security for or in total or partial satisfaction of a money debt.
(b) "Cancellation" occurs when either party puts an end to the lease contract for default by the other party.
(c) "Commercial unit" means such a unit of goods as by commercial usage is a single whole for purposes of lease and division of which materially impairs its character or value on the market or in use. A commercial unit may be a single article, as a machine, or a set of articles, as a suite of furniture or a line of machinery, or a quantity, as a gross or carload, or any other unit treated in use or in the relevant market as a single whole.
(d) "Conforming" goods or performance under a lease contract means goods or performance that are in accordance with the obligations under the lease contract.
(e) "Consumer lease" means a lease that a lessor regularly engaged in the business of leasing or selling makes to a lessee who is an individual and who takes under the lease primarily for a personal, family, or household purpose [, if the total payments to be made under the lease contract, excluding payments for options to renew or buy, do not exceed $________].
(f) "Fault" means wrongful act, omission, breach, or default.
(g) "Finance lease" means a lease with respect to which:
(i) the lessor does not select, manufacture, or supply the goods;
(ii) the lessor acquires the goods or the right to possession and use of the goods in connection with the lease; and
(iii) one of the following occurs:
(A) the lessee receives a copy of the contract by which the lessor acquired the goods or the right to possession and use of the goods before signing the lease contract;
(B) the lessee's approval of the contract by which the lessor acquired the goods or the right to possession and use of the goods is a condition to effectiveness of the lease contract;
(C) the lessee, before signing the lease contract, receives an accurate and complete statement designating the promises and warranties, and any disclaimers of warranties, limitations or modifications of remedies, or liquidated damages, including those of a third party, such as the manufacturer of the goods, provided to the lessor by the person supplying the goods in connection with or as part of the contract by which the lessor acquired the goods or the right to possession and use of the goods; or
(D) if the lease is not a consumer lease, the lessor, before the lessee signs the lease contract, informs the lessee in writing (a) of the identity of the person supplying the goods to the lessor, unless the lessee has selected that person and directed the lessor to acquire the goods or the right to possession and use of the goods from that person, (b) that the lessee is entitled under this Article to the promises and warranties, including those of any third party, provided to the lessor by the person supplying the goods in connection with or as part of the contract by which the lessor acquired the goods or the right to possession and use of the goods, and (c) that the lessee may communicate with the person supplying the goods to the lessor and receive an accurate and complete statement of those promises and warranties, including any disclaimers and limitations of them or of remedies.
(h) "Goods" means all things that are movable at the time of identification to the lease contract, or are fixtures (Section 2A–309), but the term does not include money, documents, instruments, accounts, chattel paper, general intangibles, or minerals or the like, including oil and gas, before extraction. The term also includes the unborn young of animals.
(i) "Installment lease contract" means a lease contract that authorizes or requires the delivery of goods in separate lots to be separately accepted, even though the lease contract contains a clause "each delivery is a separate lease" or its equivalent.
(j) "Lease" means a transfer of the right to possession and use of goods for a term in return for consideration, but a sale, including a sale on approval or a sale or return, or retention or creation of a security interest is not a lease. Unless the context clearly indicates otherwise, the term includes a sublease.
(k) "Lease agreement" means the bargain, with respect to the lease, of the lessor and the lessee in fact as found in their language or by implication from other circumstances including course of dealing or usage of trade or course of performance as provided in this Article. Unless the context clearly indicates otherwise, the term includes a sublease agreement.

(l) "Lease contract" means the total legal obligation that results from the lease agreement as affected by this Article and any other applicable rules of law. Unless the context clearly indicates otherwise, the term includes a sublease contract.

(m) "Leasehold interest" means the interest of the lessor or the lessee under a lease contract.

(n) "Lessee" means a person who acquires the right to possession and use of goods under a lease. Unless the context clearly indicates otherwise, the term includes a sublessee.

(o) "Lessee in ordinary course of business" means a person who in good faith and without knowledge that the lease to him [or her] is in violation of the ownership rights or security interest or leasehold interest of a third party in the goods, leases in ordinary course from a person in the business of selling or leasing goods of that kind but does not include a pawnbroker. "Leasing" may be for cash or by exchange of other property or on secured or unsecured credit and includes receiving goods or documents of title under a pre-existing lease contract but does not include a transfer in bulk or as security for or in total or partial satisfaction of a money debt.

(p) "Lessor" means a person who transfers the right to possession and use of goods under a lease. Unless the context clearly indicates otherwise, the term includes a sublessor.

(q) "Lessor's residual interest" means the lessor's interest in the goods after expiration, termination, or cancellation of the lease contract.

(r) "Lien" means a charge against or interest in goods to secure payment of a debt or performance of an obligation, but the term does not include a security interest.

(s) "Lot" means a parcel or a single article that is the subject matter of a separate lease or delivery, whether or not it is sufficient to perform the lease contract.

(t) "Merchant lessee" means a lessee that is a merchant with respect to goods of the kind subject to the lease.

(u) "Present value" means the amount as of a date certain of one or more sums payable in the future, discounted to the date certain. The discount is determined by the interest rate specified by the parties if the rate was not manifestly unreasonable at the time the transaction was entered into; otherwise, the discount is determined by a commercially reasonable rate that takes into account the facts and circumstances of each case at the time the transaction was entered into.

(v) "Purchase" includes taking by sale, lease, mortgage, security interest, pledge, gift, or any other voluntary transaction creating an interest in goods.

(w) "Sublease" means a lease of goods the right to possession and use of which was acquired by the lessor as a lessee under an existing lease.

(x) "Supplier" means a person from whom a lessor buys or leases goods to be leased under a finance lease.

(y) "Supply contract" means a contract under which a lessor buys or leases goods to be leased.

(z) "Termination" occurs when either party pursuant to a power created by agreement or law puts an end to the lease contract otherwise than for default.

(2) Other definitions applying to this Article and the sections in which they appear are:

"Accessions". Section 2A–310(1).
"Construction mortgage". Section 2A–309(1)(d).
"Encumbrance". Section 2A–309(1)(e).
"Fixtures". Section 2A–309(1)(a).
"Fixture filing". Section 2A–309(1)(b).
"Purchase money lease". Section 2A–309(1)(c).

(3) The following definitions in other Articles apply to this Article:

"Account". Section 9–106.
"Between merchants". Section 2–104(3).
"Buyer". Section 2–103(1)(a).
"Chattel paper". Section 9–105(1)(b).
"Consumer goods". Section 9–109(1).
"Document". Section 9–105(1)(f).
"Entrusting". Section 2–403(3).
"General intangibles". Section 9–106.
"Good faith". Section 2–103(1)(b).
"Instrument". Section 9–105(1)(i).
"Merchant". Section 2–104(1).
"Mortgage". Sect 9–105(1)(j).
"Pursuant to commitment". Section 9–105(1)(k).
"Receipt". Section 2–103(1)(c).
"Sale". Section 2–106(1).
"Sale on approval". Section 2–326.
"Sale or return" Section 2–326.
"Seller". Section 2–103(1)(d).

(4) In addition Article 1 contains general definitions and principles of construction and interpretation applicable throughout this Article.

As amended in 1990.

§ 2A–104. Leases Subject to Other Law.

(1) A lease, although subject to this Article, is also subject to any applicable:

(a) certificate of title statute of this State: (list any certificate of title statutes covering automobiles, trailers, mobile homes, boats, farm tractors, and the like);

(b) certificate of title statute of another jurisdiction (Section 2A–105); or

(c) consumer protection statute of this State, or final consumer protection decision of a court of this State existing on the effective date of this Article.

(2) In case of conflict between this Article, other than Sections 2A–105, 2A–304(3), and 2A–305(3), and a statute or decision referred to in subsection (1), the statute or decision controls.

(3) Failure to comply with an applicable law has only the effect specified therein.

As amended in 1990.

§ 2A–108. Unconscionability.

(1) If the court as a matter of law finds a lease contract or any clause of a lease contract to have been unconscionable at the time it was made the court may refuse to enforce the lease contract, or it may enforce the remainder of the lease contract without the unconscionable clause, or it may so limit the application of any unconscionable clause as to avoid any unconscionable result.

(2) With respect to a consumer lease, if the court as a matter of law finds that a lease contract or any clause of a lease contract has been induced by unconscionable conduct or that unconscionable conduct has occurred in the collection of a claim arising from a lease contract, the court may grant appropriate relief.

(3) Before making a finding of unconscionability under subsection (1) or (2), the court, on its own motion or that of a party, shall afford the parties a reasonable opportunity to present evidence as to the setting, purpose, and effect of the lease contract or clause thereof, or of the conduct.

(4) In an action in which the lessee claims unconscionability with respect to a consumer lease:

(a) If the court finds unconscionability under subsection (1) or (2), the court shall award reasonable attorney's fees to the lessee.

(b) If the court does not find unconscionability and the lessee claiming unconscionability has brought or maintained an action he [or she] knew to be groundless, the court shall award reasonable attorney's fees to the party against whom the claim is made.

(c) In determining attorney's fees, the amount of the recovery on behalf of the claimant under subsections (1) and (2) is not controlling.

Part 2—Formation and Construction of Lease Contract

§ 2A–201. Statute of Frauds.

(1) A lease contract is not enforceable by way of action or defense unless:

(a) the total payments to be made under the lease contract, excluding payments for options to renew or buy, are less than $1,000; or

(b) there is a writing, signed by the party against whom enforcement is sought or by that party's authorized agent, sufficient to indicate that a lease contract has been made between the parties and to describe the goods leased and the lease term.

(2) Any description of leased goods or of the lease term is sufficient and satisfies subsection (1)(b), whether or not it is specific, if it reasonably identifies what is described.

(3) A writing is not insufficient because it omits or incorrectly states a term agreed upon, but the lease contract is not enforceable under subsection (1)(b) beyond the lease term and the quantity of goods shown in the writing.

(4) A lease contract that does not satisfy the requirements of subsection (1), but which is valid in other respects, is enforceable:

(a) if the goods are to be specially manufactured or obtained for the lessee and are not suitable for lease or sale to others in the ordinary course of the lessor's business, and the lessor, before notice of repudiation is received and under circumstances that reasonably indicate that the goods are for the lessee, has made either a substantial beginning of their manufacture or commitments for their procurement;

(b) if the party against whom enforcement is sought admits in that party's pleading, testimony or otherwise in court that a lease contract was made, but the lease contract is not enforceable under this provision beyond the quantity of goods admitted; or

(c) with respect to goods that have been received and accepted by the lessee.

(5) The lease term under a lease contract referred to in subsection (4) is:

(a) if there is a writing signed by the party against whom enforcement is sought or by that party's authorized agent specifying the lease term, the term so specified;

(b) if the party against whom enforcement is sought admits in that party's pleading, testimony, or otherwise in court a lease term, the term so admitted; or

(c) a reasonable lease term.

§ 2A–202. Final Written Expression: Parol or Extrinsic Evidence.

Terms with respect to which the confirmatory memoranda of the parties agree or which are otherwise set forth in a writing intended by the parties as a final expression of their agreement with respect to such terms as are included therein may not be contradicted by evidence of any prior agreement or of a contemporaneous oral agreement but may be explained or supplemented:

(a) by course of dealing or usage of trade or by course of performance; and

(b) by evidence of consistent additional terms unless the court finds the writing to have been intended also as a complete and exclusive statement of the terms of the agreement.

§ 2A–204. Formation in General.

(1) A lease contract may be made in any manner sufficient to show agreement, including conduct by both parties which recognizes the existence of a lease contract.

(2) An agreement sufficient to constitute a lease contract may be found although the moment of its making is undetermined.

(3) Although one or more terms are left open, a lease contract does not fail for indefiniteness if the parties have intended to make a lease contract and there is a reasonably certain basis for giving an appropriate remedy.

§ 2A–205. Firm Offers.

An offer by a merchant to lease goods to or from another person in a signed writing that by its terms gives assurance it will be held open is not revocable, for lack of consideration, during the time stated or, if no time is stated, for a reasonable time, but in no event may the period of irrevocability exceed 3 months. Any such term of assurance on a form supplied by the offeree must be separately signed by the offeror.

§ 2A–206. Offer and Acceptance in Formation of Lease Contract.

(1) Unless otherwise unambiguously indicated by the language or circumstances, an offer to make a lease contract must be construed as inviting acceptance in any manner and by any medium reasonable in the circumstances.

(2) If the beginning of a requested performance is a reasonable mode of acceptance, an offeror who is not notified of acceptance within a reasonable time may treat the offer as having lapsed before acceptance.

§ 2A–207. Course of Performance or Practical Construction.

(1) If a lease contract involves repeated occasions for performance by either party with knowledge of the nature of the performance and opportunity for objection to it by the other, any course of performance accepted or acquiesced in without objection is relevant to determine the meaning of the lease agreement.

(2) The express terms of a lease agreement and any course of performance, as well as any course of dealing and usage of trade, must be construed whenever reasonable as consistent with each other; but if that construction is unreasonable, express terms control course of performance, course of performance controls both course of dealing and usage of trade, and course of dealing controls usage of trade.

(3) Subject to the provisions of Section 2A–208 on modification and waiver, course of performance is relevant to show a waiver or modification of any term inconsistent with the course of performance.

§ 2A–208. Modification, Rescission and Waiver.

(1) An agreement modifying a lease contract needs no consideration to be binding.

(2) A signed lease agreement that excludes modification or rescission except by a signed writing may not be otherwise modified or rescinded, but, except as between merchants, such a requirement on a form supplied by a merchant must be separately signed by the other party.

(3) Although an attempt at modification or rescission does not satisfy the requirements of subsection (2), it may operate as a waiver.

(4) A party who has made a waiver affecting an executory portion of a lease contract may retract the waiver by reasonable notification received by the other party that strict performance will be required of any term waived, unless the retraction would be unjust in view of a material change of position in reliance on the waiver.

§ 2A–209. Lessee Under Finance Lease as Beneficiary of Supply Contract.

(1) The benefit of a supplier's promises to the lessor under the supply contract and of all warranties, whether express or implied, including those of any third party provided in connection with or as part of the supply contract, extends to the lessee to the extent of the lessee's leasehold interest under a finance lease related to the supply contract, but is subject to the terms of the warranty and of the supply contract and all defenses or claims arising therefrom.

(2) The extension of the benefit of a supplier's promises and of warranties to the lessee (Section 2A–209(1)) does not: (i) modify the rights and obligations of the parties to the supply contract, whether arising therefrom or otherwise, or (ii) impose any duty or liability under the supply contract on the lessee.

(3) Any modification or rescission of the supply contract by the supplier and the lessor is effective between the supplier and the lessee unless, before the modification or rescission, the supplier has received notice that the lessee has entered into a finance lease related to the supply contract. If the modification or rescission is effective between the supplier and the lessee, the lessor is deemed to have assumed, in addition to the obligations of the lessor to the lessee under the lease contract, promises of the supplier to the lessor and warranties that were so modified or rescinded as they existed and were available to the lessee before modification or rescission.

(4) In addition to the extension of the benefit of the supplier's promises and of warranties to the lessee under subsection (1), the lessee retains all rights that the lessee may have against the supplier which arise from an agreement between the lessee and the supplier or under other law.

As amended in 1990.

§ 2A–210. Express Warranties.

(1) Express warranties by the lessor are created as follows:

(a) Any affirmation of fact or promise made by the lessor to the lessee which relates to the goods and becomes part of the basis of the bargain creates an express warranty that the goods will conform to the affirmation or promise.

(b) Any description of the goods which is made part of the basis of the bargain creates an express warranty that the goods will conform to the description.

(c) Any sample or model that is made part of the basis of the bargain creates an express warranty that the whole of the goods will conform to the sample or model.

(2) It is not necessary to the creation of an express warranty that the lessor use formal words, such as "warrant" or "guarantee," or that the lessor have a specific intention to make a warranty, but an affirmation merely of the value of the goods or a statement purporting to be merely the lessor's opinion or commendation of the goods does not create a warranty.

§ 2A–211. Warranties Against Interference and Against Infringement; Lessee's Obligation Against Infringement.

(1) There is in a lease contract a warranty that for the lease term no person holds a claim to or interest in the goods that arose from an act or omission of the lessor, other than a claim by way of infringement or the like, which will interfere with the lessee's enjoyment of its leasehold interest.

(2) Except in a finance lease there is in a lease contract by a lessor who is a merchant regularly dealing in goods of the kind a warranty that the goods are delivered free of the rightful claim of any person by way of infringement or the like.

(3) A lessee who furnishes specifications to a lessor or a supplier shall hold the lessor and the supplier harmless against any claim by way of infringement or the like that arises out of compliance with the specifications.

§ 2A–212. Implied Warranty of Merchantability.

(1) Except in a finance lease, a warranty that the goods will be merchantable is implied in a lease contract if the lessor is a merchant with respect to goods of that kind.

(2) Goods to be merchantable must be at least such as

(a) pass without objection in the trade under the description in the lease agreement;

(b) in the case of fungible goods, are of fair average quality within the description;

(c) are fit for the ordinary purposes for which goods of that type are used;

(d) run, within the variation permitted by the lease agreement, of even kind, quality, and quantity within each unit and among all units involved;

(e) are adequately contained, packaged, and labeled as the lease agreement may require; and

(f) conform to any promises or affirmations of fact made on the container or label.

(3) Other implied warranties may arise from course of dealing or usage of trade.

§ 2A–213. Implied Warranty of Fitness for Particular Purpose.

Except in a finance lease, if the lessor at the time the lease contract is made has reason to know of any particular purpose for which the goods are required and that the lessee is relying on the lessor's skill or judgment to select or furnish suitable goods, there is in the lease contract an implied warranty that the goods will be fit for that purpose.

§ 2A–214. Exclusion or Modification of Warranties.

(1) Words or conduct relevant to the creation of an express warranty and words or conduct tending to negate or limit a warranty must be construed wherever reasonable as consistent with each other; but, subject to the provisions of Section 2A–202 on parol or extrinsic evidence, negation or limitation is inoperative to the extent that the construction is unreasonable.

(2) Subject to subsection (3), to exclude or modify the implied warranty of merchantability or any part of it the language must mention "merchantability", be by a writing, and be conspicuous. Subject to subsection (3), to exclude or modify any implied warranty of fitness the exclusion must be by a writing and be conspicuous. Language to exclude all implied warranties of fitness is sufficient if it is in writing, is conspicuous and states, for example, "There is no warranty that the goods will be fit for a particular purpose".

(3) Notwithstanding subsection (2), but subject to subsection (4),

(a) unless the circumstances indicate otherwise, all implied warranties are excluded by expressions like "as is," or "with all faults," or by other language that in common understanding calls the lessee's attention to the exclusion of warranties and makes plain that there is no implied warranty, if in writing and conspicuous;

(b) if the lessee before entering into the lease contract has examined the goods or the sample or model as fully as desired or has refused to examine the goods, there is no implied warranty with regard to defects that an examination ought in the circumstances to have revealed; and

(c) an implied warranty may also be excluded or modified by course of dealing, course of performance, or usage of trade.

(4) To exclude or modify a warranty against interference or against infringement (Section 2A–211) or any part of it, the language must be specific, be by a writing, and be conspicuous, unless the circumstances, including course of performance, course of dealing, or usage of trade, give the lessee reason to know that the goods are being leased subject to a claim or interest of any person.

§ 2A–215. Cumulation and Conflict of Warranties Express or Implied.

Warranties, whether express or implied, must be construed as consistent with each other and as cumulative, but if that construction is unreasonable, the intention of the parties determines which warranty is dominant. In ascertaining that intention the following rules apply:

(a) Exact or technical specifications displace an inconsistent sample or model or general language of description.

(b) A sample from an existing bulk displaces inconsistent general language of description.

(c) Express warranties displace inconsistent implied warranties other than an implied warranty of fitness for a particular purpose.

§ 2A–216. Third-Party Beneficiaries of Express and Implied Warranties.

Alternative A A warranty to or for the benefit of a lessee under this Article, whether express or implied, extends to any natural person who is in the family or household of the lessee or who is a guest in the lessee's home if it is reasonable to expect that such person may use, consume, or be affected by the goods and who is injured in person by breach of the warranty. This section does not displace principles of law and equity that extend a warranty to or for the benefit of a lessee to other persons. The operation of this section may not be excluded, modified, or limited, but an exclusion, modification, or limitation of the warranty, including any with respect to rights and remedies, effective against the lessee is also effective against any beneficiary designated under this section.

Alternative B A warranty to or for the benefit of a lessee under this Article, whether express or implied, extends to any natural person who may reasonably be expected to use, consume, or be affected by the goods and who is injured in person by breach of the warranty. This section does not displace principles of law and equity that extend a warranty to or for the benefit of a lessee to other persons. The operation of this section may not be excluded, modified, or limited, but an exclusion, modification, or limitation of the warranty, including any with respect to rights and remedies, effective against the lessee is also effective against the beneficiary designated under this section.

Alternative C A warranty to or for the benefit of a lessee under this Article, whether express or implied, extends to any person who may reasonably be expected to use, consume, or be affected by the goods and who is injured by breach of the warranty. The operation of this section may not be excluded, modified, or limited with respect to injury to the person of an individual to whom the warranty extends, but an exclusion, modification, or limitation of the warranty, in-cluding any with respect to rights and remedies, effective against the lessee is also effective against the beneficiary designated under this section.

§ 2A–219. Risk of Loss.

(1) Except in the case of a finance lease, risk of loss is retained by the lessor and does not pass to the lessee. In the case of a finance lease, risk of loss passes to the lessee.

(2) Subject to the provisions of this Article on the effect of default on risk of loss (Section 2A–220), if risk of loss is to pass to the lessee and the time of passage is not stated, the following rules apply:

(a) If the lease contract requires or authorizes the goods to be shipped by carrier

(i) and it does not require delivery at a particular destination, the risk of loss passes to the lessee when the goods are duly delivered to the carrier; but

(ii) if it does require delivery at a particular destination and the goods are there duly tendered while in the possession of the carrier, the risk of loss passes to the lessee when the goods are there duly so tendered as to enable the lessee to take delivery.

(b) If the goods are held by a bailee to be delivered without being moved, the risk of loss passes to the lessee on acknowledgment by the bailee of the lessee's right to possession of the goods.

(c) In any case not within subsection (a) or (b), the risk of loss passes to the lessee on the lessee's receipt of the goods if the lessor, or, in the case of a finance lease, the supplier, is a merchant; otherwise the risk passes to the lessee on tender of delivery.

Part 3—Effect of Lease Contract

§ 2A–302. Title to and Possession of Goods.

Except as otherwise provided in this Article, each provision of this Article applies whether the lessor or a third party has title to the goods, and whether the lessor, the lessee, or a third party has possession of the goods, notwithstanding any statute or rule of law that possession or the absence of possession is fraudulent.

§ 2A–303. Alienability of Party's Interest Under Lease Contract or of Lessor's Residual Interest in Goods; Delegation of Performance; Transfer of Rights.

(1) As used in this section, "creation of a security interest" includes the sale of a lease contract that is subject to Article 9, Secured Transactions, by reason of Section 9–102(1)(b).

(2) Except as provided in subsections (3) and (4), a provision in a lease agreement which (i) prohibits the voluntary or involuntary transfer, including a transfer by sale, sublease, creation or enforcement of a security interest, or attachment, levy, or other judicial process, of an interest of a party under the lease contract or of the lessor's residual interest in the goods, or (ii) makes such a transfer an event of default, gives rise to the rights and remedies provided in subsection (5), but a transfer that is prohibited or is an event of default under the lease agreement is otherwise effective.

(3) A provision in a lease agreement which (i) prohibits the creation or enforcement of a security interest in an interest of a party under the lease contract or in the lessor's residual interest in the goods, or (ii) makes such a transfer an event of default, is not enforceable unless, and then only to the extent that, there is an actual transfer by the lessee of the lessee's right of possession or use of the goods in violation of the provision or an actual delegation of a material performance of either party to the lease contract in violation of the provision. Neither the granting nor the enforcement of a security interest in (i) the lessor's interest under the lease contract or (ii) the lessor's residual interest in the goods is a transfer that materially impairs the prospect of obtaining return performance by, materially changes the duty of, or materially increases the burden or risk imposed on, the lessee within the purview of subsection (5) unless, and then only to the extent that, there is an actual delegation of a material performance of the lessor.

(4) A provision in a lease agreement which (i) prohibits a transfer of a right to damages for default with respect to the whole lease contract or of a right to payment arising out of the transferor's due performance of the transferor's entire obligation, or (ii) makes such a transfer an event of default, is not enforceable, and such a transfer is not a transfer that materially impairs the prospect of obtaining return performance by, materially changes the duty of, or materially increases the burden or risk imposed on, the other party to the lease contract within the purview of subsection

(5) Subject to subsections (3) and (4):

(a) if a transfer is made which is made an event of default under a lease agreement, the party to the lease contract not making the transfer, unless that party waives the default or otherwise agrees, has the rights and remedies described in Section 2A–501(2);

(b) if paragraph (a) is not applicable and if a transfer is made that (i) is prohibited under a lease agreement or (ii) materially impairs the prospect of obtaining return performance by, materially changes the duty of, or materially increases the burden or risk imposed on, the other party to the lease contract, unless the party not making the transfer agrees at any time to the transfer in the lease contract or otherwise, then, except as limited by contract, (i) the transferor is liable to the party not making the transfer for damages caused by the transfer to the extent that the damages could not reasonably be prevented by the party not making the transfer and (ii) a court having jurisdiction may grant other appropriate relief, including cancellation of the lease contract or an injunction against the transfer.

(6) A transfer of "the lease" or of "all my rights under the lease", or a transfer in similar general terms, is a transfer of rights and, unless the language or the circumstances, as in a transfer for security, indicate the contrary, the transfer is a delegation of duties by the transferor to the transferee. Acceptance by the transferee constitutes a promise by the transferee to perform those duties. The promise is enforceable by either the transferor or the other party to the lease contract.

(7) Unless otherwise agreed by the lessor and the lessee, a delegation of performance does not relieve the transferor as against the other party of any duty to perform or of any liability for default.

(8) In a consumer lease, to prohibit the transfer of an interest of a party under the lease contract or to make a transfer an event of default, the language must be specific, by a writing, and conspicuous.

As amended in 1990.

§ 2A–304. Subsequent Lease of Goods by Lessor.

(1) Subject to Section 2A–303, a subsequent lessee from a lessor of goods under an existing lease contract obtains, to the extent of the leasehold interest transferred, the leasehold interest in the goods that the lessor had or had power to transfer, and except as provided in subsection (2) and Section 2A–527(4), takes subject to the existing lease contract. A lessor with voidable title has power to transfer a good leasehold interest to a good faith subsequent lessee for value, but only to the extent set forth in the preceding sentence. If goods have been delivered under a transaction of purchase, the lessor has that power even though:

(a) the lessor's transferor was deceived as to the identity of the lessor;

(b) the delivery was in exchange for a check which is later dishonored;

(c) it was agreed that the transaction was to be a "cash sale"; or

(d) the delivery was procured through fraud punishable as larcenous under the criminal law.

(2) A subsequent lessee in the ordinary course of business from a lessor who is a merchant dealing in goods of that kind to whom the goods were entrusted by the existing lessee of that lessor before the interest of the subsequent lessee became enforceable against that lessor obtains, to the extent of the leasehold interest transferred, all of that lessor's and the existing lessee's rights to the goods, and takes free of the existing lease contract.

(3) A subsequent lessee from the lessor of goods that are subject to an existing lease contract and are covered by a certificate of title issued under a statute of this State or of another jurisdiction takes no greater rights than those provided both by this section and by the certificate of title statute.

As amended in 1990.

§ 2A–307. Priority of Liens Arising by Attachment or Levy on, Security Interests in, and Other Claims to Goods.

(1) Except as otherwise provided in Section 2A–306, a creditor of a lessee takes subject to the lease contract.

(2) Except as otherwise provided in subsections (3) and (4) and in Sections 2A–306 and 2A–308, a creditor of a lessor takes subject to the lease contract unless:

(a) the creditor holds a lien that attached to the goods before the lease contract became enforceable:

(b) the creditor holds a security interest in the goods and the lessee did not give value and receive delivery of the goods without knowledge of the security interest; or

(c) the creditor holds a security interest in the goods which was perfected (Section 9–303) before the lease contract became enforceable.

(3) A lessee in the ordinary course of business takes the leasehold interest free of a security interest in the goods created by the lessor even though the security interest is perfected (Section 9–303) and the lessee knows of its existence.

(4) A lessee other than a lessee in the ordinary course of business takes the leasehold interest free of a security interest to the extent that it secures future advances made after the secured party acquires knowledge of the lease or more than 45 days after the lease contract becomes enforceable, whichever first occurs, unless the future advances are made pursuant to a commitment entered into without knowledge of the lease and before the expiration of the 45-day period.

As amended in 1990.

§ 2A–308. Special Rights of Creditors.

(1) A creditor of a lessor in possession of goods subject to a lease contract may treat the lease contract as void if as against the creditor retention of possession by the lessor is fraudulent under any statute or rule of law, but retention of possession in good faith and current course of trade by the lessor for a commercially reasonable time after the lease contract becomes enforceable is not fraudulent.

(2) Nothing in this Article impairs the rights of creditors of a lessor if the lease contract (a) becomes enforceable, not in current course of trade but in satisfaction of or as security for a pre-existing claim for money, security, or the like, and (b) is made under circumstances which under any statute or rule of law apart from this Article would constitute the transaction a fraudulent transfer or voidable preference.

(3) A creditor of a seller may treat a sale or an identification of goods to a contract for sale as void if as against the creditor retention of possession by the seller is fraudulent under any statute or rule of law, but retention of possession of the goods pursuant to a lease contract entered into by the seller as lessee and the buyer as lessor in connection with the sale or identification of the goods is not fraudulent if the buyer bought for value and in good faith.

Part 4—Performance of Lease Contract: Repudiated, Substituted and Excused

§ 2A–407. Irrevocable Promises: Finance Leases.

(1) In the case of a finance lease that is not a consumer lease the lessee's promises under the lease contract become irrevocable and independent upon the lessee's acceptance of the goods.

(2) A promise that has become irrevocable and independent under subsection (1):

(a) is effective and enforceable between the parties, and by or against third parties including assignees of the parties; and

(b) is not subject to cancellation, termination, modification, repudiation, excuse, or substitution without the consent of the party to whom the promise runs.

(3) This section does not affect the validity under any other law of a covenant in any lease contract making the lessee's promises irrevocable and independent upon the lessee's acceptance of the goods.

As amended in 1990.

Part 5—Default

A. In General

§ 2A–503. Modification or Impairment of Rights and Remedies.

(1) Except as otherwise provided in this Article, the lease agreement may include rights and remedies for default in addition to or in substitution for those provided in this Article and may limit or alter the measure of damages recoverable under this Article.

(2) Resort to a remedy provided under this Article or in the lease agreement is optional unless the remedy is expressly agreed to be exclusive If circumstances cause an exclusive or limited remedy to fail of its essential purpose, or provision for an exclusive remedy is unconscionable. remedy may be had as provided in this Article.

(3) Consequential damages may be liquidated under Section 2A–504, or may otherwise be limited, altered, or excluded unless the limitation, alteration, or exclusion is unconscionable. Limitation, alteration, or exclusion of consequential damages for injury to the person in the case of consumer goods is prima facie unconscionable but limitation, alteration, or exclusion of damages where the loss is commercial is not prima facie unconscionable.

(4) Rights and remedies on default by the lessor or the lessee with respect to any obligation or promise collateral or ancillary to the lease contract are not impaired by this Article.

As amended in 1990.

§ 2A–504. Liquidation of Damages.

(1) Damages payable by either party for default, or any other act or omission, including indemnity for loss or diminution of anticipated tax benefits or loss or damage to lessor's residual interest, may be liquidated in the lease agreement but only at an amount or by a formula that is reasonable in light of the then anticipated harm caused by the default or other act or omission.

(2) If the lease agreement provides for liquidation of damages, and such provision does not comply with subsection (1), or such provision is an exclusive or limited remedy that circumstances cause to fail of its essential purpose, remedy may be had as provided in this Article.
(3) If the lessor justifiably withholds or stops delivery of goods because of the lessee's default or insolvency (Section 2A–525 or 2A–526), the lessee is entitled to restitution of any amount by which the sum of his [or her] payments exceeds:

(a) the amount to which the lessor is entitled by virtue of terms liquidating the lessor's damages in accordance with subsection (1); or
(b) in the absence of those terms, 20 percent of the then present value of the total rent the lessee was obligated to pay for the balance of the lease term, or, in the case of a consumer lease, the lesser of such amount or $500.

(4) A lessee's right to restitution under subsection (3) is subject to offset to the extent the lessor establishes:

(a) a right to recover damages under the provisions of this Article other than subsection (1); and
(b) the amount or value of any benefits received by the lessee directly or indirectly by reason of the lease contract.

§ 2A–507. Proof of Market Rent: Time and Place.

(1) Damages based on market rent (Section 2A–519 or 2A–528) are determined according to the rent for the use of the goods concerned for a lease term identical to the remaining lease term of the original lease agreement and prevailing at the times specified in Sections 2A–519 and 2A–528.
(2) If evidence of rent for the use of the goods concerned for a lease term identical to the remaining lease term of the original lease agreement and prevailing at the times or places described in this Article is not readily available, the rent prevailing within any reasonable time before or after the time described or at any other place or for a different lease term which in commercial judgment or under usage of trade would serve as a reasonable substitute for the one described may be used, making any proper allowance for the difference, including the cost of transporting the goods to or from the other place.
(3) Evidence of a relevant rent prevailing at a time or place or for a lease term other than the one described in this Article offered by one party is not admissible unless and until he [or she] has given the other party notice the court finds sufficient to prevent unfair surprise.
(4) If the prevailing rent or value of any goods regularly leased in any established market is in issue, reports in official publications or trade journals or in newspapers or periodicals of general circulation published as the reports of that market are admissible in evidence. The circumstances of the preparation of the report may be shown to affect its weight but not its admissibility.

As amended in 1990.

B. Default by Lessor

§ 2A–508. Lessee's Remedies.

(1) If a lessor fails to deliver the goods in conformity to the lease contract (Section 2A–509) or repudiates the lease contract (Section 2A–402), or a lessee rightfully rejects the goods (Section 2A–509) or justifiably revokes acceptance of the goods (Section 2A–517), then with respect to any goods involved, and with respect to all of the goods if under an installment lease contract the value of the whole lease contract is substantially impaired (Section 2A–510), the lessor is in default under the lease contract and the lessee may:

(a) cancel the lease contract (Section 2A–505(1));
(b) recover so much of the rent and security as has been paid and is just under the circumstances;
(c) cover and recover damages as to all goods affected whether or not they have been identified to the lease contract (Sections 2A–518 and 2A–520), or recover damages for nondelivery (Sections 2A–519 and 2A–520);
(d) exercise any other rights or pursue any other remedies provided in the lease contract.

(2) If a lessor fails to deliver the goods in conformity to the lease contract or repudiates the lease contract, the lessee may also:

(a) if the goods have been identified, recover them (Section 2A–522); or
(b) in a proper case, obtain specific performance or replevy the goods (Section 2A–521).

(3) If a lessor is otherwise in default under a lease contract, the lessee may exercise the rights and pursue the remedies provided in the lease contract, which may include a right to cancel the lease, and in Section 2A–519(3).
(4) If a lessor has breached a warranty, whether express or implied, the lessee may recover damages (Section 2A–519(4)).
(5) On rightful rejection or justifiable revocation of acceptance, a lessee has a security interest in goods in the lessee's possession or control for any rent and security that has been paid and any expenses reasonably incurred in their inspection, receipt, transportation, and care and custody and may hold those goods and dispose of them in good faith and in a commercially reasonable manner, subject to Section 2A–527(5).
(6) Subject to the provisions of Section 2A–407, a lessee, on notifying the lessor of the lessee's intention to do so, may deduct all or any part of the damages resulting from any default under the lease contract from any part of the rent still due under the same lease contract.

As amended in 1990.

§ 2A–509. Lessee's Rights on Improper Delivery; Rightful Rejection.

(1) Subject to the provisions of Section 2A–510 on default in installment lease contracts, if the goods or the tender or delivery fail in any respect to conform to the lease contract, the lessee may reject or accept the goods or accept any commercial unit or units and reject the rest of the goods.
(2) Rejection of goods is ineffective unless it is within a reasonable time after tender or delivery of the goods and the lessee seasonably notifies the lessor.

§ 2A–510. Installment Lease Contracts: Rejection and Default.

(1) Under an installment lease contract a lessee may reject any delivery that is nonconforming if the nonconformity substantially impairs the value of that delivery and cannot be cured or the nonconformity is a defect in the required documents; but if the nonconformity does not fall within subsection (2) and the lessor or the supplier gives adequate assurance of its cure, the lessee must accept that delivery.
(2) Whenever nonconformity or default with respect to one or more deliveries substantially impairs the value of the installment lease contract as a whole there is a default with respect to the whole. But, the aggrieved party reinstates the installment lease contract as a whole if the aggrieved party accepts a nonconforming delivery without seasonably notifying of cancellation or brings an action with respect only to past deliveries or demands performance as to future deliveries.

§ 2A–511. Merchant Lessee's Duties as to Rightfully Rejected Goods.

(1) Subject to any security interest of a lessee (Section 2A–508(5)), if a lessor or a supplier has no agent or place of business at the market of rejection, a merchant lessee, after rejection of goods in his [or her] possession or control, shall follow any reasonable instructions received from the lessor or the supplier with respect to the goods. In the absence of those instructions, a merchant lessee shall make reasonable efforts to sell, lease, or otherwise dispose of the goods for the lessor's account if they threaten to decline in value speedily. Instructions are not reasonable if on demand indemnity for expenses is not forthcoming.
(2) If a merchant lessee (subsection (1)) or any other lessee (Section 2A–512) disposes of goods, he [or she] is entitled to reimbursement either from the lessor or the supplier or out of the proceeds for reasonable expenses of caring for and disposing of the goods and, if the expenses include no disposition commission, to such commission as is usual in the trade, or if there is none, to a reasonable sum not exceeding 10 percent of the gross proceeds.

(3) In complying with this section or Section 2A–512, the lessee is held only to good faith. Good faith conduct hereunder is neither acceptance or conversion nor the basis of an action for damages.
(4) A purchaser who purchases in good faith from a lessee pursuant to this section or Section 2A–512 takes the goods free of any rights of the lessor and the supplier even though the lessee fails to comply with one or more of the requirements of this Article.

§ 2A–512. Lessee's Duties as to Rightfully Rejected Goods.
(1) Except as otherwise provided with respect to goods that threaten to decline in value speedily (Section 2A–511) and subject to any security interest of a lessee (Section 2A–508(5)):

(a) the lessee, after rejection of goods in the lessee's possession, shall hold them with reasonable care at the lessor's or the supplier's disposition for a reasonable time after the lessee's seasonable notification of rejection;
(b) if the lessor or the supplier gives no instructions within a reasonable time after notification of rejection, the lessee may store the rejected goods for the lessor's or the supplier's account or ship them to the lessor or the supplier or dispose of them for the lessor's or the supplier's account with reimbursement in the manner provided in Section 2A–511; but
(c) the lessee has no further obligations with regard to goods rightfully rejected.

(2) Action by the lessee pursuant to subsection (1) is not acceptance or conversion.

§ 2A–513. Cure by Lessor of Improper Tender or Delivery; Replacement.
(1) If any tender or delivery by the lessor or the supplier is rejected because nonconforming and the time for performance has not yet expired, the lessor or the supplier may seasonably notify the lessee of the lessor's or the supplier's intention to cure and may then make a conforming delivery within the time provided in the lease contract.
(2) If the lessee rejects a nonconforming tender that the lessor or the supplier had reasonable grounds to believe would be acceptable with or without money allowance, the lessor or the supplier may have a further reasonable time to substitute a conforming tender if he [or she] seasonably notifies the lessee.

§ 2A–515. Acceptance of Goods.
(1) Acceptance of goods occurs after the lessee has had a reasonable opportunity to inspect the goods and

(a) the lessee signifies or acts with respect to the goods in a manner that signifies to the lessor or the supplier that the goods are conforming or that the lessee will take or retain them in spite of their nonconformity; or
(b) the lessee fails to make an effective rejection of the goods (Section 2A–509(2)).

(2) Acceptance of a part of any commercial unit is acceptance of that entire unit.

§ 2A–517. Revocation of Acceptance of Goods.
(1) A lessee may revoke acceptance of a lot or commercial unit whose nonconformity substantially impairs its value to the lessee if the lessee has accepted it:

(a) except in the case of a finance lease, on the reasonable assumption that its nonconformity would be cured and it has not been seasonably cured; or
(b) without discovery of the nonconformity if the lessee's acceptance was reasonably induced either by the lessor's assurances or, except in the case of a finance lease, by the difficulty of discovery before acceptance.

(2) Except in the case of a finance lease that is not a consumer lease, a lessee may revoke acceptance of a lot or commercial unit if the lessor defaults under the lease contract and the default substantially impairs the value of that lot or commercial unit to the lessee.
(3) If the lease agreement so provides, the lessee may revoke acceptance of a lot or commercial unit because of other defaults by the lessor.
(4) Revocation of acceptance must occur within a reasonable time after the lessee discovers or should have discovered the ground for it and before any substantial change in condition of the goods which is not caused by the nonconformity. Revocation is not effective until the lessee notifies the lessor.
(5) A lessee who so revokes has the same rights and duties with regard to the goods involved as if the lessee had rejected them.
As amended in 1990.

§ 2A–518. Cover; Substitute Goods.
(1) After a default by a lessor under the lease contract of the type described in Section 2A–508(1), or, if agreed, after other default by the lessor, the lessee may cover by making any purchase or lease of or contract to purchase or lease goods in substitution for those due from the lessor.
(2) Except as otherwise provided with respect to damages liquidated in the lease agreement (Section 2A–504) or otherwise determined pursuant to agreement of the parties (Sections 1–102(3) and 2A–503), if a lessee's cover is by a lease agreement substantially similar to the original lease agreement and the new lease agreement is made in good faith and in a commercially reasonable manner, the lessee may recover from the lessor as damages (i) the present value, as of the date of the commencement of the term of the new lease agreement, of the rent under the new lease agreement applicable to that period of the new lease term which is comparable to the then remaining term of the original lease agreement minus the present value as of the same date of the total rent for the then remaining lease term of the original lease agreement, and (ii) any incidental or consequential damages, less expenses saved in consequence of the lessor's default.
(3) If a lessee's cover is by lease agreement that for any reason does not qualify for treatment under subsection (2), or is by purchase or otherwise, the lessee may recover from the lessor as if the lessee had elected not to cover and Section 2A–519 governs.
As amended in 1990.

§ 2A–519. Lessee's Damages for Non-delivery, Repudiation, Default, and Breach of Warranty in Regard to Accepted Goods.
(1) Except as otherwise provided with respect to damages liquidated in the lease agreement (Section 2A–504) or otherwise determined pursuant to agreement of the parties (Sections 1–102(3) and 2A–503), if a lessee elects not to cover or a lessee elects to cover and the cover is by lease agreement that for any reason does not qualify for treatment under Section 2A–518(2), or is by purchase or otherwise, the measure of damages for non-delivery or repudiation by the lessor or for rejection or revocation of acceptance by the lessee is the present value, as of the date of the default, of the then market rent minus the present value as of the same date of the original rent, computed for the remaining lease term of the original lease agreement, together with incidental and consequential damages, less expenses saved in consequence of the lessor's default.
(2) Market rent is to be determined as of the place for tender or, in cases of rejection after arrival or revocation of acceptance, as of the place of arrival.
(3) Except as otherwise agreed, if the lessee has accepted goods and given notification (Section 2A–516(3)), the measure of damages for non-conforming tender or delivery or other default by a lessor is the loss resulting in the ordinary course of events from the lessor's default as determined in any manner that is reasonable together with incidental and consequential damages, less expenses saved in consequence of the lessor's default.
(4) Except as otherwise agreed, the measure of damages for breach of warranty is the present value at the time and place of acceptance of the difference between the value of the use of the goods accepted and the

value if they had been as warranted for the lease term, unless special circumstances show proximate damages of a different amount, together with incidental and consequential damages, less expenses saved in consequence of the lessor's default or breach of warranty.

As amended in 1990.

§ 2A–520. Lessee's Incidental and Consequential Damages.

(1) Incidental damages resulting from a lessor's default include expenses reasonably incurred in inspection, receipt, transportation, and care and custody of goods rightfully rejected or goods the acceptance of which is justifiably revoked, any commercially reasonable charges, expenses or commissions in connection with effecting cover, and any other reasonable expense incident to the default.

(2) Consequential damages resulting from a lessor's default include:

(a) any loss resulting from general or particular requirements and needs of which the lessor at the time of contracting had reason to know and which could not reasonably be prevented by cover or otherwise; and

(b) injury to person or property proximately resulting from any breach of warranty.

§ 2A–521. Lessee's Right to Specific Performance or Replevin.

(1) Specific performance may be decreed if the goods are unique or in other proper circumstances.

(2) A decree for specific performance may include any terms and conditions as to payment of the rent, damages, or other relief that the court deems just.

(3) A lessee has a right of replevin, detinue, sequestration, claim and delivery, or the like for goods identified to the lease contract if after reasonable effort the lessee is unable to effect cover for those goods or the circumstances reasonably indicate that the effort will be unavailing.

§ 2A–522. Lessee's Right to Goods on Lessor's Insolvency.

(1) Subject to subsection (2) and even though the goods have not been shipped, a lessee who has paid a part or all of the rent and security for goods identified to a lease contract (Section 2A–217) on making and keeping good a tender of any unpaid portion of the rent and security due under the lease contract may recover the goods identified from the lessor if the lessor becomes insolvent within 10 days after receipt of the first installment of rent and security.

(2) A lessee acquires the right to recover goods identified to a lease contract only if they conform to the lease contract.

C. Default by Lessee

§ 2A–523. Lessor's Remedies.

(1) If a lessee wrongfully rejects or revokes acceptance of goods or fails to make a payment when due or repudiates with respect to a part or the whole, then, with respect to any goods involved, and with respect to all of the goods if under an installment lease contract the value of the whole lease contract is substantially impaired (Section 2A–510), the lessee is in default under the lease contract and the lessor may:

(a) cancel the lease contract (Section 2A–505(1));

(b) proceed respecting goods not identified to the lease contract (Section 2A–524);

(c) withhold delivery of the goods and take possession of goods previously delivered (Section 2A–525);

(d) stop delivery of the goods by any bailee (Section 2A–526);

(e) dispose of the goods and recover damages (Section 2A–527), or retain the goods and recover damages (Section 2A–528), or in a proper case recover rent (Section 2A–529);

(f) exercise any other rights or pursue any other remedies provided in the lease contract.

(2) If a lessor does not fully exercise a right or obtain a remedy to which the lessor is entitled under subsection (1), the lessor may recover the loss resulting in the ordinary course of events from the lessee's default as determined in any reasonable manner, together with incidental damages, less expenses saved in consequence of the lessee's default.

(3) If a lessee is otherwise in default under a lease contract, the lessor may exercise the rights and pursue the remedies provided in the lease contract, which may include a right to cancel the lease. In addition, unless otherwise provided in the lease contract:

(a) if the default substantially impairs the value of the lease contract to the lessor, the lessor may exercise the rights and pursue the remedies provided in subsections (1) or (2); or

(b) if the default does not substantially impair the value of the lease contract to the lessor, the lessor may recover as provided in subsection (2).

As amended in 1990.

§ 2A–524. Lessor's Right to Identify Goods to Lease Contract.

(1) After default by the lessee under the lease contract of the type described in Section 2A–523(1) or 2A–523(3)(a) or, if agreed, after other default by the lessee, the lessor may:

(a) identify to the lease contract conforming goods not already identified if at the time the lessor learned of the default they were in the lessor's or the supplier's possession or control; and

(b) dispose of goods (Section 2A–527(1)) that demonstrably have been intended for the particular lease contract even though those goods are unfinished.

(2) If the goods are unfinished, in the exercise of reasonable commercial judgment for the purposes of avoiding loss and of effective realization, an aggrieved lessor or the supplier may either complete manufacture and wholly identify the goods to the lease contract or cease manufacture and lease, sell, or otherwise dispose of the goods for scrap or salvage value or proceed in any other reasonable manner.

As amended in 1990.

§ 2A–525. Lessor's Right to Possession of Goods.

(1) If a lessor discovers the lessee to be insolvent, the lessor may refuse to deliver the goods.

(2) After a default by the lessee under the lease contract of the type described in Section 2A–523(1) or 2A–523(3)(a) or, if agreed, after other default by the lessee, the lessor has the right to take possession of the goods. If the lease contract so provides, the lessor may require the lessee to assemble the goods and make them available to the lessor at a place to be designated by the lessor which is reasonably convenient to both parties. Without removal, the lessor may render unusable any goods employed in trade or business, and may dispose of goods on the lessee's premises (Section 2A–527).

(3) The lessor may proceed under subsection (2) without judicial process if it can be done without breach of the peace or the lessor may proceed by action.

As amended in 1990.

§ 2A–526. Lessor's Stoppage of Delivery in Transit or Otherwise.

(1) A lessor may stop delivery of goods in the possession of a carrier or other bailee if the lessor discovers the lessee to be insolvent and may stop delivery of carload, truckload, planeload, or larger shipments of express or freight if the lessee repudiates or fails to make a payment due before delivery, whether for rent, security or otherwise under the lease contract, or for any other reason the lessor has a right to withhold or take possession of the goods.

(2) In pursuing its remedies under subsection (1), the lessor may stop delivery until

(a) receipt of the goods by the lessee;

(b) acknowledgment to the lessee by any bailee of the goods, except a carrier, that the bailee holds the goods for the lessee; or

(c) such an acknowledgment to the lessee by a carrier via reshipment or as warehouseman.

(3) (a) To stop delivery, a lessor shall so notify as to enable the bailee by reasonable diligence to prevent delivery of the goods.

(b) After notification, the bailee shall hold and deliver the goods according to the directions of the lessor, but the lessor is liable to the bailee for any ensuing charges or damages.

(c) A carrier who has issued a nonnegotiable bill of lading is not obliged to obey a notification to stop received from a person other than the consignor.

§ 2A–527. Lessor's Rights to Dispose of Goods.

(1) After a default by a lessee under the lease contract of the type described in Section 2A–523(1) or 2A–523(3)(a) or after the lessor refuses to deliver or takes possession of goods (Section 2A–525 or 2A–526), or, if agreed, after other default by a lessee, the lessor may dispose of the goods concerned or the undelivered balance thereof by lease, sale, or otherwise.

(2) Except as otherwise provided with respect to damages liquidated in the lease agreement (Section 2A–504) or otherwise determined pursuant to agreement of the parties (Sections 1–102(3) and 2A–503), if the disposition is by lease agreement substantially similar to the original lease agreement and the new lease agreement is made in good faith and in a commercially reasonable manner, the lessor may recover from the lessee as damages (i) accrued and unpaid rent as of the date of the commencement of the term of the new lease agreement, (ii) the present value, as of the same date, of the total rent for the then remaining lease term of the original lease agreement minus the present value, as of the same date, of the rent under the new lease agreement applicable to that period of the new lease term which is comparable to the then remaining term of the original lease agreement, and (iii) any incidental damages allowed under Section 2A–530, less expenses saved in consequence of the lessee's default.

(3) If the lessor's disposition is by lease agreement that for any reason does not qualify for treatment under subsection (2), or is by sale or otherwise, the lessor may recover from the lessee as if the lessor had elected not to dispose of the goods and Section 2A–528 governs.

(4) A subsequent buyer or lessee who buys or leases from the lessor in good faith for value as a result of a disposition under this section takes the goods free of the original lease contract and any rights of the original lessee even though the lessor fails to comply with one or more of the requirements of this Article.

(5) The lessor is not accountable to the lessee for any profit made on any disposition. A lessee who has rightfully rejected or justifiably revoked acceptance shall account to the lessor for any excess over the amount of the lessee's security interest (Section 2A–508(5)).

As amended in 1990.

§ 2A–528. Lessor's Damages for Non-acceptance, Failure to Pay, Repudiation, or Other Default.

(1) Except as otherwise provided with respect to damages liquidated in the lease agreement (Section 2A–504) or otherwise determined pursuant to agreement of the parties (Sections 1–102(3) and 2A–503), if a lessor elects to retain the goods or a lessor elects to dispose of the goods and the disposition is by lease agreement that for any reason does not qualify for treatment under Section 2A–527(2), or is by sale or otherwise, the lessor may recover from the lessee as damages for a default of the type described in Section 2A–523(1) or 2A–523(3)(a), or, if agreed, for other default of the lessee, (i) accrued and unpaid rent as of the date of default if the lessee has never taken possession of the goods, or, if the lessee has taken possession of the goods, as of the date the lessor repossesses the goods or an earlier date on which the lessee makes a tender of the goods to the lessor, (ii) the present value as of the date determined under clause (i) of the total rent for the then remaining lease term of the original lease agreement minus the present value as of the same date of the market rent at the place where the goods are located computed for the same lease term, and (iii) any incidental damages allowed under Section 2A–530, less expenses saved in consequence of the lessee's default.

(2) If the measure of damages provided in subsection (1) is inadequate to put a lessor in as good a position as performance would have, the measure of damages is the present value of the profit, including reasonable overhead, the lessor would have made from full performance by the lessee, together with any incidental damages allowed under Section 2A–530, due allowance for costs reasonably incurred and due credit for payments or proceeds of disposition.

As amended in 1990.

§ 2A–529. Lessor's Action for the Rent.

(1) After default by the lessee under the lease contract of the type described in Section 2A–523(1) or 2A–523(3)(a) or, if agreed, after other default by the lessee, if the lessor complies with subsection (2), the lessor may recover from the lessee as damages:

(a) for goods accepted by the lessee and not repossessed by or tendered to the lessor, and for conforming goods lost or damaged within a commercially reasonable time after risk of loss passes to the lessee (Section 2A–219), (i) accrued and unpaid rent as of the date of entry of judgment in favor of the lessor, (ii) the present value as of the same date of the rent for the then remaining lease term of the lease agreement, and (iii) any incidental damages allowed under Section 2A–530, less expenses saved in consequence of the lessee's default; and

(b) for goods identified to the lease contract if the lessor is unable after reasonable effort to dispose of them at a reasonable price or the circumstances reasonably indicate that effort will be unavailing, (i) accrued and unpaid rent as of the date of entry of judgment in favor of the lessor, (ii) the present value as of the same date of the rent for the then remaining lease term of the lease agreement, and (iii) any incidental damages allowed under Section 2A–530, less expenses saved in consequence of the lessee's default.

(2) Except as provided in subsection (3), the lessor shall hold for the lessee for the remaining lease term of the lease agreement any goods that have been identified to the lease contract and are in the lessor's control.

(3) The lessor may dispose of the goods at any time before collection of the judgment for damages obtained pursuant to subsection (1). If the disposition is before the end of the remaining lease term of the lease agreement, the lessor's recovery against the lessee for damages is governed by Section 2A–527 or Section 2A–528, and the lessor will cause an appropriate credit to be provided against a judgment for damages to the extent that the amount of the judgment exceeds the recovery available pursuant to Section 2A–527 or 2A–528.

(4) Payment of the judgment for damages obtained pursuant to subsection (1) entitles the lessee to the use and possession of the goods not then disposed of for the remaining lease term of and in accordance with the lease agreement.

(5) After default by the lessee under the lease contract of the type described in Section 2A–523(1) or Section 2A–523(3)(a) or, if agreed, after other default by the lessee, a lessor who is held not entitled to rent under this section must nevertheless be awarded damages for non-acceptance under Section 2A–527 or Section 2A–528.

As amended in 1990.

§ 2A–530. Lessor's Incidental Damages.

Incidental damages to an aggrieved lessor include any commercially reasonable charges, expenses, or commissions incurred in stopping delivery, in the transportation, care and custody of goods after the lessee's default, in connection with return or disposition of the goods, or otherwise resulting from the default.

ARTICLE 3: NEGOTIABLE INSTRUMENTS

Part 1—General Provisions and Definitions

§ 3–101. Short Title.

This Article may be cited as Uniform Commercial Code—Negotiable Instruments.

§ 3–102. Subject Matter.

(a) This Article applies to negotiable instruments. It does not apply to money or to payment orders governed by Article 4A. A negotiable instrument that is also a certificated security under Section 8–102(1)(a) is subject to Article 8 and to this Article.

(b) In the event of conflict between the provisions of this Article and those of Article 4, Article 8, or Article 9, the provisions of Article 4, Article 8 and Article 9 prevail over those of this Article.

(c) Regulations of the Board of Governors of the Federal Reserve System and operating circulars of the Federal Reserve Banks supersede any inconsistent provision of this Article to the extent of the inconsistency.

§ 3–103. Definitions.

(a) In this Article:

(1) "Acceptor" means a drawee that has accepted a draft.

(2) "Drawee" means a person ordered in a draft to make payment.

(3) "Drawer" means a person that signs a draft as a person ordering payment.

(4) "Good faith" means honesty in fact and the observance of reasonable commercial standards of fair dealing.

(5) "Maker" means a person that signs a note as promisor of payment.

(6) "Order" means a written instruction to pay money signed by the person giving the instruction. The instruction may be addressed to any person, including the person giving the instruction, or to one or more persons jointly or in the alternative but not in succession. An authorization to pay is not an order unless the person authorized to pay is also instructed to pay.

(7) "Ordinary care" in the case of a person engaged in business means observance of reasonable commercial standards, prevailing in the area in which that person is located, with respect to the business in which that person is engaged. In the case of a bank that takes an instrument for processing for collection or payment by automated means, reasonable commercial standards do not require the bank to examine the instrument if the failure to examine does not violate the bank's prescribed procedures and the bank's procedures do not vary unreasonably from general banking usage not disapproved by this Article or Article 4.

(8) "Party" means party to an instrument.

(9) "Promise" means a written undertaking to pay money signed by the person undertaking to pay. An acknowledgment of an obligation by the obligor is not a promise unless the obligor also undertakes to pay the obligation.

(10) "Prove" with respect to a fact means to meet the burden of establishing the fact (Section 1–201(8)).

(11) "Remitter" means a person that purchases an instrument from its issuer if the instrument is payable to an identified person other than the purchaser.

(b) Other definitions applying to this Article and the sections in which they appear are:

"Acceptance" Section 3–409.
"Accommodated party" Section 3–419.
"Accommodation indorsement" Section 3–205.
"Accommodation party" Section 3–419.
"Alteration" Section 3–407.
"Blank indorsement" Section 3–205.
"Cashier's check" Section 3–104.
"Certificate of deposit" Section 3–104.
"Certified check" Section 3–409.
"Check" Section 3–104.
"Consideration" Section 3–303.
"Draft" Section 3–104.
"Fiduciary" Section 3–307.
"Guarantor" Section 3–417.
"Holder in due course" Section 3–302.
"Incomplete instrument" Section 3–115.
"Indorsement" Section 3–204.
"Indorser" Section 3–204.
"Instrument" Section 3–104.
"Issue" Section 3–105.
"Issuer" Section 3–105.
"Negotiable instrument" Section 3–104.
"Negotiation" Section 3–201.
"Note" Section 3–104.
"Payable at a definite time" Section 3–108.
"Payable on demand" Section 3–108.
"Payable to bearer" Section 3–109.
"Payable to order" Section 3–110.
"Payment" Section 3–603.
"Person entitled to enforce" Section 3–301.
"Presentment" Section 3–501.
"Reacquisition" Section 3–207.
"Represented person" Section 3–307.
"Special indorsement" Section 3–205.
"Teller's check" Section 3–104.
"Traveler's check" Section 3–104.
"Value" Section 3–303.

(c) The following definitions in other Articles apply to this Article:

"Bank" Section 4–105.
"Banking day" Section 4–104.
"Clearing house" Section 4–104.
"Collecting bank" Section 4–105.
"Customer" Section 4–104.
"Depositary bank" Section 4–105.
"Documentary draft" Section 4–104.
"Intermediary bank" Section 4–105.
"Item" Section 4–104.
"Midnight deadline" Section 4–104.
"Payor bank" Section 4–105.
"Suspends payments" Section 4–104.

(d) In addition, Article 1 contains general definitions and principles of construction and interpretation applicable throughout this Article.

§ 3–104. Negotiable Instrument.

(a) "Negotiable instrument" means an unconditional promise or order to pay a fixed amount of money, with or without interest or other charges described in the promise or order, if it:

(1) is payable to bearer or to order at the time it is issued or first comes into possession of a holder;

(2) is payable on demand or at a definite time; and

(3) does not state any other undertaking or instruction by the person promising or ordering payment to do any act in addition to the payment of money except that the promise or order may contain (i) an undertaking or power to give, maintain, or protect collateral to secure payment, (ii) an authorization or power to the holder to confess judgment or realize on or dispose of collateral, or (iii) a waiver of the benefit of any law intended for the advantage or protection of any obligor.

(b) "Instrument" means negotiable instrument.

(c) An order that meets all of the requirements of subsection (a) except subparagraph (1) and otherwise falls within the definition of "check" in subsection (f) is a negotiable instrument and a check.

(d) Notwithstanding subsection (a), a promise or order other than a check is not an instrument if, at the time it is issued or first comes into possession of a holder, it contains a conspicuous statement, however expressed, indicating that the writing is not an instrument governed by this Article.

(e) An instrument is a "note" if it is a promise, and is a "draft" if it is an order. If an instrument falls within the definition of both "note" and "draft," the person entitled to enforce the instrument may treat it as either.
(f) "Check" means (i) a draft, other than a documentary draft, payable on demand and drawn on a bank or (ii) a cashier's check or teller's check. An instrument may be a check even though it is described on its face by another term such as "money order."
(g) "Cashier's check" means a draft with respect to which the drawer and drawee are the same bank or branches of the same bank.
(h) "Teller's check" means a draft drawn by a bank (i) on another bank, or (ii) payable at or through a bank.
(i) "Traveler's check" means an instrument that (i) is payable on demand, (ii) is drawn on or payable at or through a bank, (iii) is designated by the term "traveler's check" or by a substantially similar term, and (iv) requires, as a condition to payment, a countersignature by a person whose specimen signature appears on the instrument.
(j) "Certificate of deposit" means an instrument containing an acknowledgment by a bank that a sum of money has been received by the bank, and a promise by the bank to repay the sum of money. A certificate of deposit is a note of the bank.

§ 3–105. Issue of Instrument.
(a) "Issue" means the first delivery of an instrument by the maker or drawer, whether to a holder or nonholder, for the purpose of giving rights on the instrument to any person.
(b) An unissued instrument, or an unissued incomplete instrument (Section 3–115) that is completed, is binding on the maker or drawer, but nonissuance is a defense. An instrument that is conditionally issued or is issued for a special purpose is binding on the maker or drawer, but failure of the condition or special purpose to be fulfilled is a defense.
(c) "Issuer" applies to issued and unissued instruments and means any person that signs an instrument as maker or drawer.

§ 3–106. Unconditional Promise or Order.
(a) Except as provided in subsections (b) and (c), for the purposes of Section 3–104(a), a promise or order is unconditional unless it states (i) an express condition to payment or (ii) that the promise or order is subject to or governed by another writing, or that rights or obligations with respect to the promise or order are stated in another writing; however, a mere reference to another writing does not make the promise or order conditional.
(b) A promise or order is not made conditional (i) by a reference to another writing for a statement of rights with respect to collateral, prepayment, or acceleration, or (ii) because payment is limited to resort to a particular fund or source.
(c) If a promise or order requires, as a condition to payment, a countersignature by a person whose specimen signature appears on the promise or order, the condition does not make the promise or order conditional for the purposes of Section 3–104(a). If the person whose specimen signature appears on an instrument fails to countersign the instrument, the failure to countersign is a defense to the obligation of the issuer, but the failure does not prevent a transferee of the instrument from becoming a holder of the instrument.
(d) If a promise or order at the time it is issued or first comes into possession of a holder contains a statement, required by applicable statutory or administrative law, to the effect that the rights of a holder or transferee are subject to claims or defenses that the issuer could assert against the original payee, the promise or order is not thereby made conditional for the purposes of Section 3–104(a), but there cannot be a holder in due course of the promise or order.

§ 3–107. Instrument Payable in Foreign Money.
Unless the instrument otherwise provides, an instrument that states the amount payable in foreign money may be paid in the foreign money or in an equivalent amount in dollars calculated by using the current bank-offered spot rate at the place of payment for the purchase of dollars on the day on which the instrument is paid.

§ 3–108. Payable on Demand or at a Definite Time.
(a) A promise or order is "payable on demand" if (i) it states that it is payable on demand or at sight, or otherwise indicates that it is payable at the will of the holder, or (ii) it does not state any time of payment.
(b) A promise or order is "payable at a definite time" if it is payable on elapse of a definite period of time after sight or acceptance or at a fixed date or dates or at a time or times readily ascertainable at the time the promise or order is issued, subject to rights of (i) prepayment, (ii) acceleration, or (iii) extension at the option of the holder or (iv) extension to a further definite time at the option of the maker or acceptor or automatically upon or after a specified act or event.
(c) If an instrument, payable at a fixed date, is also payable upon demand made before the fixed date, the instrument is payable on demand until the fixed date and, if demand for payment is not made before that date, becomes payable at a definite time on the fixed date.

§ 3–109. Payable to Bearer or to Order.
(a) A promise or order is payable to bearer if it:
> **(1)** states that it is payable to bearer or to the order of bearer or otherwise indicates that the person in possession of the promise or order is entitled to payment,
> **(2)** does not state a payee, or
> **(3)** states that it is payable to or to the order of cash or otherwise indicates that it is not payable to an identified person.

(b) A promise or order that is not payable to bearer is payable to order if it is payable (i) to the order of an identified person or (ii) to an identified person or order. A promise or order that is payable to order is payable to the identified person.
(c) An instrument payable to bearer may become payable to an identified person if it is specially indorsed as stated in Section 3–205(a). An instrument payable to an identified person may become payable to bearer if it is indorsed in blank as stated in Section 3–205(b).

§ 3–110. Identification of Person to Whom Instrument Is Payable.
(a) A person to whom an instrument is payable is determined by the intent of the person, whether or not authorized, signing as, or in the name or behalf of, the maker or drawer. The instrument is payable to the person intended by the signer even if that person is identified in the instrument by a name or other identification that is not that of the intended person. If more than one person signs in the name or behalf of the maker or drawer and all the signers do not intend the same person as payee, the instrument is payable to any person intended by one or more of the signers.
(b) If the signature of the maker or drawer of an instrument is made by automated means such as a check-writing machine, the payee of the instrument is determined by the intent of the person who supplied the name or identification of the payee, whether or not authorized to do so.
(c) A person to whom an instrument is payable may be identified in any way including by name, identifying number, office, or account number. For the purpose of determining the holder of an instrument, the following rules apply:
> **(1)** If an instrument is payable to an account and the account is identified only by number, the instrument is payable to the person to whom the account is payable. If an instrument is payable to an account identified by number and by the name of a person, the instrument is payable to the named person, whether or not that person is the owner of the account identified by number.
> **(2)** If an instrument is payable to:

(i) a trust, estate, or a person described as trustee or representative of a trust or estate, the instrument is payable to the trustee, the representative, or a successor of either, whether or not the beneficiary or estate is also named;
(ii) a person described as agent or similar representative of a named or identified person, the instrument is payable either to the represented person, the representative, or a successor of the representative;
(iii) a fund or organization that is not a legal entity, the instrument is payable to a representative of the members of the fund or organization; or
(iv) an office or to a person described as holding an office, the instrument is payable to the named person, the incumbent of the office, or a successor to the incumbent.

(d) If an instrument is payable to two or more persons alternatively, it is payable to any of them and may be negotiated, discharged, or enforced by any of them in possession of the instrument. If an instrument is payable to two or more persons not alternatively, it is payable to all of them and may be negotiated, discharged, or enforced only by all of them. If an instrument payable to two or more persons is ambiguous as to whether it is payable to the persons alternatively, the instrument is payable to the persons alternatively.

§ 3–111. Place of Payment.
Except as otherwise provided for items in Article 4, an instrument is payable at the place of payment stated in the instrument. If no place of payment is stated, an instrument is payable at the address of the drawee or maker stated in the instrument. If no address is stated, the place of payment is the place of business of the drawee or maker. If a drawee or maker has more than one place of business, the place of payment is any place of business of the drawee or maker chosen by the person entitled to enforce the instrument. If the drawee or maker has no place of business, the place of payment is the residence of the drawee or maker.

§ 3–112. Interest.
(a) Unless otherwise provided in the instrument, (i) an instrument is not payable with interest, and (ii) interest on an interest-bearing instrument is payable from the date of the instrument.
(b) Interest may be stated in an instrument as a fixed or variable amount of money or it may be expressed as a fixed or variable rate or rates. The amount or rate of interest may be stated or described in the instrument in any manner and may require reference to information not contained in the instrument. If an instrument provides for interest but the amount of interest payable cannot be ascertained from the description, interest is payable at the judgment rate in effect at the place of payment of the instrument and at the time interest first accrues.

§ 3–113. Date of Instrument.
(a) An instrument may be antedated or postdated. The date stated determines the time of payment if the instrument is payable at a fixed period after date. Except as provided in Section 4–401(3), an instrument payable on demand is not payable before the date of the instrument.
(b) If an instrument is undated, its date is the date of its issue or, in the case of an unissued instrument, the date it first comes into possession of a holder.

§ 3–114. Contradictory Terms of Instrument.
If an instrument contains contradictory terms, typewritten terms prevail over printed terms, handwritten terms prevail over both, and words prevail over numbers.

§ 3–115. Incomplete Instrument.
(a) "Incomplete instrument" means a signed writing, whether or not issued by the signer, the contents of which show at the time of signing that it is incomplete but that the signer intended it to be completed by the addition of words or numbers.
(b) Subject to subsection (c), if an incomplete instrument is an instrument under Section 3–104, it may be enforced (i) according to its terms if it is not completed, or (ii) according to its terms as augmented by completion. If an incomplete instrument is not an instrument under Section 3–104 but, after completion, the requirements of Section 3–104 are met, the instrument may be enforced according to its terms as augmented by completion.
(c) If words or numbers are added to an incomplete instrument without authority of the signer, there is an alteration of the incomplete instrument governed by Section 3–407.
(d) The burden of establishing that words or numbers were added to an incomplete instrument without authority of the signer is on the person asserting the lack of authority.

§ 3–116. Joint and Several Liability; Contribution.
(a) Except as otherwise provided in the instrument, two or more persons who have the same liability on an instrument as makers, drawers, acceptors, indorsers who are indorsing joint payees, or anomalous indorsers, are jointly and severally liable in the capacity in which they sign.
(b) Except as provided in Section 3–417(e) or by agreement of the affected parties, a party with joint and several liability that pays the instrument is entitled to receive from any party with the same joint and several liability contribution in accordance with applicable law.
(c) Discharge of one party with joint and several liability by a person entitled to enforce the instrument does not affect the right under subsection (b) of a party with the same joint and several liability to receive contribution from the party discharged.

§ 3–117. Other Agreements Affecting an Instrument.
Subject to applicable law regarding exclusion of proof of contemporaneous or prior agreements, the obligation of a party to an instrument to pay the instrument may be modified, supplemented, or nullified by a separate agreement of the obligor and a person entitled to enforce the instrument if the instrument is issued or the obligation is incurred in reliance on the agreement or as part of the same transaction giving rise to the agreement. To the extent an obligation is modified, supplemented, or nullified by an agreement under this section, the agreement is a defense to the obligation.

§ 3–118. Statute of Limitations.
(a) Except as provided in subsection (e), an action to enforce the obligation of a party to pay a note payable at a definite time must be commenced within six years after the payment date or dates stated in the note or, if a payment date is accelerated, within six years after the accelerated payment date.
(b) Except as provided in subsection (d) or (e), if demand for payment is made to the maker of a note payable on demand, an action to enforce the obligation of a party to pay the note must be commenced within six years after the demand. If no demand for payment is made to the maker, an action to enforce the note is barred if neither principal nor interest on the note has been paid for a continuous period of 10 years.
(c) Except as provided in subsection (d), an action to enforce the obligation of a party to an unaccepted draft to pay the draft must be commenced within six years after dishonor of the draft or 10 years after the date of the draft, whichever period expires first.
(d) An action to enforce the obligation of the acceptor of a certified check or the issuer of a teller's check, cashier's check, or traveler's check must be commenced within six years after demand for payment is made to the acceptor or issuer, as the case may be.
(e) An action to enforce the obligation of a party to a certificate of deposit to pay the instrument must be commenced within six years after demand for payment is made to the maker, but if the instrument states a maturity date and the maker is not required to pay before that date, the six-year period begins when a demand for payment is in effect and the maturity date has passed.

(f) This subsection applies to an action to enforce the obligation of a party to pay an accepted draft, other than a certified check. If the obligation of the acceptor is payable at a definite time, the action must be commenced within six years after the payment date or dates stated in the draft or acceptance. If the obligation of the acceptor is payable on demand, the action must be commenced within six years after the date of the acceptance.
(g) Unless governed by other law regarding claims for indemnity or contribution, an action (i) for conversion of an instrument, for money had and received, or like action based on conversion, (ii) for breach of warranty, or (iii) to enforce an obligation, duty, or right arising under this Article and not governed by this section must be commenced within three years after the cause of action accrues.

§ 3–119. Notice of Right to Defend Action.
In an action for breach of an obligation for which a third person is answerable over pursuant to this Article or Article 4, the defendant may give the third person written notice of the litigation, and the person notified may then give similar notice to any other person who is answerable over. If the notice states (i) that the person notified may come in and defend and (ii) that failure to do so will bind the person notified in an action later brought by the person giving the notice as to any determination of fact common to the two litigations, the person notified is so bound unless after seasonable receipt of the notice the person notified does come in and defend.

Part 2—Negotiation, Transfer and Indorsement
§ 3–201. Negotiation.
(a) "Negotiation" means a transfer of possession, whether voluntary or involuntary, of an instrument to a person who thereby becomes its holder if possession is obtained from a person other than the issuer of the instrument.
(b) Except for a negotiation by a remitter, if an instrument is payable to an identified person, negotiation requires transfer of possession of the instrument and its indorsement by the holder. If an instrument is payable to bearer, it may be negotiated by transfer of possession alone.

§ 3–202. Negotiation Subject to Rescission.
(a) Negotiation is effective even if obtained (i) from an infant, a corporation exceeding its powers, or a person without capacity, or (ii) by fraud, duress, or mistake, or in breach of duty or as part of an illegal transaction.
(b) To the extent permitted by law, negotiation may be rescinded or may be subject to other remedies, but those remedies may not be asserted against a subsequent holder in due course or a person paying the instrument in good faith and without knowledge of facts that are a basis for rescission or other remedy.

§ 3–203. Rights Acquired by Transfer.
(a) An instrument is transferred when it is delivered by a person other than its issuer for the purpose of giving to the person receiving delivery the right to enforce the instrument.
(b) Transfer of an instrument, regardless of whether the transfer is a negotiation, vests in the transferee any right of the transferor to enforce the instrument, including any right as a holder in due course, but the transferee cannot acquire rights of a holder in due course by a transfer, directly or indirectly, from a holder in due course if the purchaser engaged in fraud or illegality affecting the instrument.
(c) Unless otherwise agreed, if an instrument is transferred for value and the transferee does not become a holder because of lack of indorsement by the transferor, the transferee has a specifically enforceable right to the unqualified indorsement of the transferor, but negotiation of the instrument does not occur until the indorsement is made.
(d) If a transferor purports to transfer less than the entire instrument, negotiation of the instrument does not occur. The transferee obtains no rights under this Article and has only the rights of a partial assignee.

§ 3–204. Indorsement.
(a) "Indorsement" means a signature, other than that of a maker, drawer, or acceptor, that alone or accompanied by other words, is made on an instrument for the purpose of (i) negotiating the instrument, (ii) restricting payment of the instrument, or (iii) incurring indorser's liability on the instrument, but regardless of the intent of the signer, a signature and its accompanying words is an indorsement unless the accompanying words, the terms of the instrument, the place of the signature, or other circumstances unambiguously indicate that the signature was made for a purpose other than indorsement. For the purpose of determining whether a signature is made on an instrument, a paper affixed to the instrument is a part of the instrument.
(b) "Indorser" means a person who makes an indorsement.
(c) For the purpose of determining whether the transferee of an instrument is a holder, an indorsement that transfers a security interest in the instrument is effective as an unqualified indorsement of the instrument.
(d) If an instrument is payable to a holder under a name that is not the name of the holder, indorsement may be made by the holder in the name stated in the instrument or in the holder's name or both, but signature in both names may be required by a person paying or taking the instrument for value or collection.

§ 3–205. Special Indorsement; Blank Indorsement; Anomalous Indorsement.
(a) If an indorsement is made by the holder of an instrument, whether payable to an identified person or payable to bearer, and the indorsement identifies a person to whom it makes the instrument payable, it is a "special indorsement." When specially indorsed, an instrument becomes payable to the identified person and may be negotiated only by the indorsement of that person. The principles stated in Section 3–110 apply to special indorsements.
(b) If an indorsement is made by the holder of an instrument and it is not a special indorsement, it is a "blank indorsement." When indorsed in blank, an instrument becomes payable to bearer and may be negotiated by transfer of possession alone until specially indorsed.
(c) The holder may convert a blank indorsement that consists only of a signature into a special indorsement by writing, above the signature of the indorser, words identifying the person to whom the instrument is made payable.
(d) "Anomalous indorsement" means an indorsement made by a person that is not the holder of the instrument. An anomalous indorsement does not affect the manner in which the instrument may be negotiated.

§ 3–206. Restrictive Indorsement.
(a) An indorsement limiting payment to a particular person or otherwise prohibiting further transfer or negotiation of the instrument is not effective to prevent further transfer or negotiation of the instrument.
(b) An indorsement stating a condition to the right of the indorsee to receive payment does not affect the right of the indorsee to enforce the instrument. A person paying the instrument or taking it for value or collection may disregard the condition, and the rights and liabilities of that person are not affected by whether the condition has been fulfilled.
(c) The following rules apply to an instrument bearing an indorsement (i) described in Section 4–201(2), or (ii) in blank or to a particular bank using the words "for deposit," "for collection," or other words indicating a purpose of having the instrument collected for the indorser or for a particular account:

(1) A person, other than a bank, that purchases the instrument when so indorsed converts the instrument unless the proceeds of the instrument are received by the indorser or are applied consistently with the indorsement.

(2) A depositary bank that purchases the instrument or takes it for collection when so indorsed converts the instrument unless the proceeds of the instrument are received by the indorser or applied consistently with the indorsement.

(3) A payor bank that is also the depositary bank or that takes the instrument for immediate payment over the counter from a person other than a collecting bank converts the instrument unless the proceeds of the instrument are received by the indorser or applied consistently with the indorsement.

(4) Except as otherwise provided in paragraph (3), a payor bank or intermediary bank may disregard the indorsement and is not liable if the proceeds of the instrument are not received by the indorser or applied consistently with the indorsement.

(d) Except for an indorsement covered by subsection (c), the following rules apply to an instrument bearing an indorsement using words to the effect that payment is to be made to the indorsee as agent, trustee, or other fiduciary for the benefit of the indorser or another person.

(1) Unless there is notice of breach of fiduciary duty as provided in Section 3–307, a person that purchases the instrument from the indorsee or takes the instrument from the indorsee for collection or payment may pay the proceeds of payment or the value given for the instrument to the indorsee without regard to whether the indorsee violates a fiduciary duty to the indorser.

(2) A later transferee of the instrument or person that pays the instrument is neither given notice nor otherwise affected by the restriction in the indorsement unless the transferee or payor knows that the fiduciary dealt with the instrument or its proceeds in breach of fiduciary duty.

(e) Purchase of an instrument bearing an indorsement to which this section applies does not prevent the purchaser from becoming a holder in due course of the instrument unless the purchaser is a converter under subsection (c).

(f) In an action to enforce the obligation of a party to pay the instrument, the obligor has a defense if payment would violate an indorsement to which this section applies and the payment is not permitted by this section.

§ 3–207. Reacquisition.

Reacquisition of an instrument occurs if it is transferred, by negotiation or otherwise, to a former holder. A former holder that reacquires the instrument may cancel indorsements made after the reacquirer first became a holder of the instrument. If the cancellation causes the instrument to be payable to the reacquirer or to bearer, the reacquirer may negotiate the instrument. An indorser whose indorsement is canceled is discharged, and the discharge is effective against any later holder.

Part 3—Enforcement of Instruments

§ 3–301. Person Entitled to Enforce Instrument.

"Person entitled to enforce" an instrument means (i) the holder of the instrument, (ii) a nonholder in possession of the instrument who has the rights of a holder, or (iii) a person not in possession of the instrument who is entitled to enforce the instrument pursuant to Section 3–309. A person may be a person entitled to enforce the instrument even though the person is not the owner of the instrument or is in wrongful possession of the instrument.

§ 3–302. Holder in Due Course.

(a) Subject to subsection (c) and Section 3–106(d), "holder in due course" means the holder of an instrument if:

(1) the instrument when issued or negotiated to the holder does not bear such apparent evidence of forgery or alteration or is not otherwise so irregular or incomplete as to call into question its authenticity, and

(2) the holder took the instrument (i) for value, (ii) in good faith, (iii) without notice that the instrument is overdue or has been dishonored or that there is an uncured default with respect to payment of another instrument issued as part of the same series, (iv) without notice that the instrument contains an unauthorized signature or has been altered, (v) without notice of any claim to the instrument stated in Section 3–306, and (vi) without notice that any party to the instrument has any defense or claim in recoupment stated in Section 3–305(a).

(b) Notice of discharge of a party to the instrument, other than discharge in an insolvency proceeding, is not notice of a defense under subsection (a), but discharge is effective against a person who became a holder in due course with notice of the discharge. Public filing or recording of a document does not of itself constitute notice of a defense, claim in recoupment, or claim to the instrument.

(c) Except to the extent a transferor or predecessor in interest has rights as a holder in due course, a person does not acquire rights of a holder in due course of an instrument taken (i) by legal process or by purchase at an execution, bankruptcy, or creditor's sale or similar proceeding, (ii) by purchase as part of a bulk transaction not in ordinary course of business of the transferor, or (iii) as the successor in interest to an estate or other organization.

(d) If, under Section 3–303(a)(1), the promise of performance that is the consideration for an instrument has been partially performed, the holder may assert rights as a holder in due course of the instrument only to the fraction of the amount payable under the instrument equal to the value of the partial performance divided by the value of the promised performance.

(e) If (i) the person entitled to enforce an instrument has only a security interest in the instrument and (ii) the person obliged to pay the instrument has a defense, claim in recoupment or claim to the instrument that may be asserted against the person who granted the security interest, the person entitled to enforce the instrument may assert rights as a holder in due course only to an amount payable under the instrument which, at the time of enforcement of the instrument, does not exceed the amount of the unpaid obligation secured.

(f) To be effective, notice must be received at such time and in such manner as to give a reasonable opportunity to act on it.

(g) This section is subject to any law limiting status as a holder in due course in particular classes of transactions.

§ 3–303. Value and Consideration.

(a) An instrument is issued or transferred for value if:

(1) the instrument is issued or transferred for a promise of performance, to the extent the promise has been performed;

(2) the transferee acquires a security interest or other lien in the instrument other than a lien obtained by judicial proceedings;

(3) the instrument is issued or transferred as payment of, or as security for, an existing obligation of any person, whether or not the obligation is due;

(4) the instrument is issued or transferred in exchange for a negotiable instrument; or

(5) the instrument is issued or transferred in exchange for the incurring of an irrevocable obligation to a third party by the person taking the instrument.

(b) "Consideration" means any consideration sufficient to support a simple contract. The drawer or maker of an instrument has a defense if the instrument is issued without consideration. If an instrument is issued for a promise of performance, the drawer or maker has a defense to the extent performance of the promise is due and the promise has not been performed. If an instrument is issued for value as stated in subsection (a), the instrument is also issued for consideration.

§ 3–304. Overdue Instrument.

(a) An instrument payable on demand becomes overdue at the earliest of the following times:

(1) on the day after the day demand for payment is duly made;

(2) if the instrument is a check, 90 days after its date; or

(3) if the instrument is not a check, when the instrument has been outstanding for a period of time after its date which is unreasonably long under the circumstances of the particular case in light of the nature of the instrument and trade usage.

(b) With respect to an instrument payable at a definite time the following rules apply: (1) If the principal is payable in installments and a due date has not been accelerated, the instrument becomes overdue upon default under the instrument for nonpayment of an installment, and the instrument remains overdue until the default is cured. (2) If the principal is not payable in installments and the due date has not been accelerated, the instrument becomes overdue on the day after the due date. (3) If a due date with respect to principal has been accelerated, the instrument becomes overdue on the day after the accelerated due date.

(c) Unless the due date of principal has been accelerated, an instrument does not become overdue if there is default in payment of interest but no default in payment of principal.

§ 3–305. Defenses and Claims in Recoupment.

(a) Except as stated in subsection (b), the right to enforce the obligation of a party to pay the instrument is subject to the following:

(1) A defense of the obligor based on (i) infancy of the obligor to the extent it is a defense to a simple contract, (ii) duress, lack of legal capacity, or illegality of the transaction that nullifies the obligation of the obligor, (iii) fraud that induced the obligor to sign the instrument with neither knowledge nor reasonable opportunity to learn of its character or its essential terms, or (iv) discharge of the obligor in insolvency proceedings.

(2) A defense of the obligor stated in another section of this Article or a defense of the obligor that would be available if the person entitled to enforce the instrument were enforcing a right to payment under a simple contract.

(3) A claim in recoupment of the obligor against the original payee of the instrument if the claim arose from the transaction that gave rise to the instrument. The claim of the obligor may be asserted against a transferee of the instrument only to reduce the amount owing on the instrument at the time the action is brought.

(b) The right of a holder in due course to enforce the obligation of a party to pay the instrument is subject to defenses of the obligor stated in subsection (a)(1), but is not subject to defenses of the obligor stated in subsection (a)(2) or claims in recoupment stated in subsection (a)(3) against a person other than the holder.

(c) Except as stated in subsection (d), in an action to enforce the obligation of a party to pay the instrument, the obligor may not assert against the person entitled to enforce the instrument a defense, claim in recoupment, or claim to the instrument (Section 3–306) of another person, but the other person's claim to the instrument may be asserted by the obligor if the other person is joined in the action and personally asserts the claim against the person entitled to enforce the instrument. An obligor is not obliged to pay the instrument if the person seeking enforcement of the instrument does not have rights of a holder in due course and the obligor proves that the instrument is a lost or stolen instrument.

(d) In an action to enforce the obligation of an accommodation party to pay an instrument, the accommodation party may assert against the person entitled to enforce the instrument any defense or claim in recoupment under subsection (a) that the accommodated party could assert against the person entitled to enforce the instrument, except the defenses of discharge in insolvency proceedings, infancy, or lack of legal capacity.

§ 3–306. Claims to an Instrument.

A person taking an instrument, other than a person having rights of a holder in due course, is subject to a claim of a property or possessory right in the instrument or its proceeds, including a claim to rescind a negotiation and to recover the instrument or its proceeds. A person having rights of a holder in due course takes free of the claim to the instrument.

§ 3–307. Notice of Breach of Fiduciary Duty.

(a) This section applies if (i) an instrument is taken from a fiduciary for payment or collection or for value, (ii) the taker has knowledge of the fiduciary status of the fiduciary, and (iii) the represented person makes a claim to the instrument or its proceeds on the basis that the transaction of the fiduciary is a breach of fiduciary duty. Notice of breach of fiduciary duty by the fiduciary is notice of the claim of the represented person. "Fiduciary" means an agent, trustee, partner, corporation officer or director, or other representative owing a fiduciary duty with respect to the instrument. "Represented person" means the principal, beneficiary, partnership, corporation, or other person to whom the duty is owed.

(b) If the instrument is payable to the fiduciary, as such, or to the represented person, the taker has notice of the breach of fiduciary duty if the instrument is (i) taken in payment of or as security for a debt known by the taker to be the personal debt of the fiduciary, (ii) taken in a transaction known by the taker to be for the personal benefit of the fiduciary, or (iii) deposited to an account other than an account of the fiduciary, as such, or an account of the represented person.

(c) If the instrument is made or drawn by the fiduciary, as such, payable to the fiduciary personally, the taker does not have notice of the breach of fiduciary duty unless the taker knows of the breach of fiduciary duty.

(d) If the instrument is made or drawn by or on behalf of the represented person to the taker as payee, the taker has notice of the breach of fiduciary duty if the instrument is (i) taken in payment of or as security for a debt known by the taker to be the personal debt of the fiduciary, (ii) taken in a transaction known by the taker to be for the personal benefit of the fiduciary, or (iii) deposited to an account other than an account of the fiduciary, as such, or an account of the represented person.

§ 3–308. Proof of Signatures and Status as Holder in Due Course.

(a) In an action with respect to an instrument, the authenticity of, and authority to make, each signature on the instrument is admitted unless specifically denied in the pleadings. If the validity of a signature is denied in the pleadings, the burden of establishing validity is on the person claiming validity, but the signature is presumed to be authentic and authorized unless the action is to enforce the liability of the purported signer and the signer is dead or incompetent at the time of trial of the issue of validity of the signature. If an action to enforce the instrument is brought against a person as the undisclosed principal of a person who signed the instrument as a party to the instrument, the plaintiff has the burden of establishing that the defendant is liable on the instrument as a represented person pursuant to Section 3–402(a).

(b) If the validity of signatures is admitted or proved and there is compliance with subsection (a), a plaintiff producing the instrument is entitled to payment if the plaintiff proves entitlement to enforce the instrument under Section 3–301, unless the defendant proves a defense or claim in recoupment. If a defense or claim in recoupment is proved, the right to payment of the plaintiff is subject to the defense or claim except to the extent the plaintiff proves that the plaintiff has rights of a holder in due course which are not subject to the defense or claim.

§ 3–309. Enforcement of Lost, Destroyed, or Stolen Instrument.

(a) A person not in possession of an instrument is entitled to enforce the instrument if (i) that person was in rightful possession of the instrument and entitled to enforce it when loss of possession occurred, (ii) the loss of possession was not the result of a voluntary transfer by that person or a lawful seizure, and (iii) that person cannot reasonably obtain possession of the instrument because the instrument was destroyed, its whereabouts cannot be determined, or it is in the wrongful possession of an unknown person or a person that cannot be found or is not amenable to service of process.

(b) A person seeking enforcement of an instrument pursuant to subsection (a) must prove the terms of the instrument and the person's right to enforce the instrument. If that proof is made, Section 3–308 applies to the case as though the person seeking enforcement had produced the instrument. The court may not enter judgment in favor of the person seeking enforcement unless it finds that the person required to pay the instrument is adequately protected against loss that might occur by reason of a claim by another person to enforce the instrument. Adequate protection may be provided by any reasonable means.

§ 3–310. Effect of Instrument on Obligation for Which Taken.
(a) Unless otherwise agreed, if a certified check, cashier's check, or teller's check is taken for an obligation, the obligation is discharged to the same extent discharge would result if an amount of money equal to the amount of the instrument were taken in payment of the obligation. Discharge of the obligation does not affect any liability that the obligor may have as an indorser of the instrument.
(b) Unless otherwise agreed and except as provided in subsection (a), if a note or an uncertified check is taken for an obligation, the obligation is suspended to the same extent the obligation would be discharged if an amount of money equal to the amount of the instrument were taken.

(1) In the case of an uncertified check, suspension of the obligation continues until dishonor of the check or until it is paid or certified. Payment or certification of the check results in discharge of the obligation to the extent of the amount of the check.

(2) In the case of a note, suspension of the obligation continues until dishonor of the note or until it is paid. Payment of the note results in discharge of the obligation to the extent of the payment.

(3) If the check or note is dishonored and the obligee of the obligation for which the instrument was taken has possession of the instrument, the obligee may enforce either the instrument or the obligation. In the case of an instrument of a third person which is negotiated to the obligee by the obligor, discharge of the obligor on the instrument also discharges the obligation.

(4) If the person entitled to enforce the instrument taken for an obligation is a person other than the obligee, the obligee may not enforce the obligation to the extent the obligation is suspended. If the obligee is the person entitled to enforce the instrument but no longer has possession of it because it was lost, stolen, or destroyed, the obligation may not be enforced to the extent of the amount payable on the instrument, and to that extent the obligee's rights against the obligor are limited to enforcement of the instrument.

(c) If an instrument other than one described in subsection (a) or (b) is taken for an obligation, the effect is (i) that stated in subsection (a) if the instrument is one on which a bank is liable as maker or acceptor, or (ii) that stated in subsection (b) in any other case.

§ 3–311. Accord and Satisfaction by Use of Instrument.
(a) This section applies if a person against whom a claim is asserted proves that (i) that person in good faith tendered an instrument to the claimant as full satisfaction of the claim, (ii) the amount of the claim was unliquidated or subject to a bona fide dispute, and (iii) the claimant obtained payment of the instrument.
(b) Unless subsection (c) applies, the claim is discharged if the person against whom the claim is asserted proves that the instrument or an accompanying written communication contained a conspicuous statement to the effect that the instrument was tendered as full satisfaction of the claim.
(c) Subject to subsection (d), a claim is not discharged under subsection (b) if the claimant is an organization and proves that within a reasonable time before the tender, the claimant sent a conspicuous statement to the person against whom the claim is asserted that communications concerning disputed debts, including an instrument tendered as full satisfaction of a debt, are to be sent to a designated person, office or place, and the instrument or accompanying communication was not received by that designated person, office, or place.
(d) Notwithstanding subsection (c), a claim is discharged under subsection (b) if the person against whom the claim is asserted proves that within a reasonable time before collection of the instrument was initiated, an agent of the claimant having direct responsibility with respect to the disputed obligation knew that the instrument was tendered in full satisfaction of the claim, or received the instrument and any accompanying written communication.

Part 4—Liability of Parties
§ 3–401. Signature.
(a) A person is not liable on an instrument unless (i) the person signed the instrument, or (ii) the person is represented by an agent or representative who signed the instrument and the signature is binding on the represented person under Section 3–402.
(b) A signature may be made (i) manually or by means of a device or machine, and (ii) by the use of any name, including any trade or assumed name, or by any word, mark, or symbol executed or adopted by a person with present intention to authenticate a writing.

§ 3–402. Signature by Representative.
(a) If a person acting, or purporting to act, as a representative signs an instrument by signing either the name of the represented person or the name of the signer, the represented person is bound by the signature to the same extent the represented person would be bound if the signature were on a simple contract. If the represented person is bound, the signature of the representative is the "authorized signature of the represented person" and the represented person is liable on the instrument, whether or not identified in the instrument.
(b) If a representative signs the name of the representative to an instrument and that signature is an authorized signature of the represented person, the following rules apply:

(1) If the form of the signature shows unambiguously that the signature is made on behalf of the represented person who is identified in the instrument, the representative is not liable on the instrument.

(2) Subject to subsection (c), if (i) the form of the signature does not show unambiguously that the signature is made in a representative capacity or (ii) the represented person is not identified in the instrument, the representative is liable on the instrument to a holder in due course that took the instrument without notice that the representative was not intended to be liable on the instrument. With respect to any other person, the representative is liable on the instrument unless the representative proves that the original parties to the instrument did not intend the representative to be liable on the instrument.

(c) If a representative signs the name of the representative as drawer of a check without indication of the representative status and the check is payable from an account of the represented person who is identified on the check, the signer is not liable on the check if the signature is an authorized signature of the represented person.

§ 3–403. Unauthorized Signature.
(a) Except as otherwise provided in this Article, an unauthorized signature is ineffective except as the signature of the unauthorized signer in favor of a person who in good faith pays the instrument or takes it for value. An unauthorized signature may be ratified for all purposes of this Article.
(b) If the signature of more than one person is required to constitute the authorized signature of an organization, the signature of the organization is unauthorized if one of the required signatures is missing.
(c) The civil or criminal liability of a person who makes an unauthorized signature is not affected by any provision of this Article that makes the unauthorized signature effective for the purposes of this Article.

§ 3–404. Impostors; Fictitious Payees.

(a) If an impostor by use of the mails or otherwise induces the maker or drawer of an instrument to issue the instrument to the impostor, or to a person acting in concert with the impostor, by impersonating the payee of the instrument or a person authorized to act for the payee, an indorsement of the instrument by any person in the name of the payee is effective as the indorsement of the payee in favor of any person that in good faith pays the instrument or takes it for value or for collection.

(b) If (i) a person whose intent determines to whom an instrument is payable (Section 3–110(a) or (b)) does not intend the person identified as payee to have any interest in the instrument, or (ii) the person identified as payee of the instrument is a fictitious person, the following rules apply until the instrument is negotiated by special indorsement:

(1) Any person in possession of the instrument is its holder.

(2) An indorsement by any person in the name of the payee stated in the instrument is effective as the indorsement of the payee in favor of any person that in good faith pays the instrument or takes it for value or for collection.

(c) Under subsection (a) or (b) an indorsement is made in the name of a payee if (i) it is made in a name substantially similar to that of the payee or (ii) the instrument, whether or not indorsed, is deposited in a depositary bank to an account in a name substantially similar to that of the payee.

(d) With respect to an instrument to which subsection (a) or (b) applies, if a person paying the instrument or taking it for value or for collection fails to exercise ordinary care in paying or taking the instrument and that failure substantially contributes to loss resulting from payment of the instrument, the person bearing the loss may recover from the person failing to exercise ordinary care to the extent the failure to exercise ordinary care contributed to the loss.

§ 3–405. Employer Responsibility for Fraudulent Indorsement by Employee.

(a) This section applies to fraudulent indorsements of instruments with respect to which an employer has entrusted an employee with responsibility as part of the employee's duties. The following definitions apply to this section:

(1) "Employee" includes, in addition to an employee of an employer, an independent contractor and employee of an independent contractor retained by the employer.

(2) "Fraudulent indorsement" means (i) in the case of an instrument payable to the employer, a forged indorsement purporting to be that of the employer, or (ii) in the case of an instrument with respect to which the employer is drawer or maker, a forged indorsement purporting to be that of the person identified as payee.

(3) "Responsibility" with respect to instruments means authority (i) to sign or indorse instruments on behalf of the employer, (ii) to process instruments received by the employer for bookkeeping purposes, for deposit to an account, or for other disposition, (iii) to prepare or process instruments for issue in the name of the employer, (iv) to supply information determining the names or addresses of payees of instruments to be issued in the name of the employer, (v) to control the disposition of instruments to be issued in the name of the employer, or (vi) to otherwise act with respect to instruments in a responsible capacity. "Responsibility" does not include the assignment of duties that merely allow an employee to have access to instruments or blank or incomplete instrument forms that are being stored or transported or are part of incoming or outgoing mail, or similar access.

(b) For the purpose of determining the rights and liabilities of a person who, in good faith, pays an instrument or takes it for value or for collection, if an employee entrusted with responsibility with respect to the instrument or a person acting in concert with the employee makes a fraudulent indorsement to the instrument, the indorsement is effective as the indorsement of the person to whom the instrument is payable if it is made in the name of that person. If the person paying the instrument or taking it for value or for collection fails to exercise ordinary care in paying or taking the instrument and that failure substantially contributes to loss resulting from the fraud, the person bearing the loss may recover from the person failing to exercise ordinary care to the extent the failure to exercise ordinary care contributed to the loss.

(c) Under subsection (b) an indorsement is made in the name of the person to whom an instrument is payable if (i) it is made in a name substantially similar to the name of that person or (ii) the instrument, whether or not indorsed, is deposited in a depositary bank to an account in a name substantially similar to the name of that person.

§ 3–406. Negligence Contributing to Forged Signature or Alteration of Instrument.

(a) A person whose failure to exercise ordinary care substantially contributes to an alteration of an instrument or to the making of a forged signature on an instrument is precluded from asserting the alteration or the forgery against a person that, in good faith, pays the instrument or takes it for value.

(b) If the person asserting the preclusion fails to exercise ordinary care in paying or taking the instrument and that failure substantially contributes to loss, the loss is allocated between the person precluded and the person asserting the preclusion according to the extent to which the failure of each to exercise ordinary care contributed to the loss.

(c) Under subsection (a) the burden of proving failure to exercise ordinary care is on the person asserting the preclusion. Under subsection **(d)** the burden of proving failure to exercise ordinary care is on the person precluded.

§ 3–407. Alteration.

(a) "Alteration" means (i) an unauthorized change in an instrument that purports to modify in any respect the obligation of a party to the instrument, or (ii) an unauthorized addition of words or numbers or other change to an incomplete instrument relating to the obligation of any party to the instrument.

(b) Except as provided in subsection (c), an alteration fraudulently made by the holder discharges any party to whose obligation the alteration applies unless that party assents or is precluded from asserting the alteration. No other alteration discharges any party, and the instrument may be enforced according to its original terms.

(c) If an instrument that has been fraudulently altered is acquired by a person having rights of a holder in due course, it may be enforced by that person according to its original terms. If an incomplete instrument is completed and is then acquired by a person having rights of a holder in due course, it may be enforced by that person as completed, whether or not the completion is a fraudulent alteration.

Drawee Not Liable on Unaccepted Draft.

A check or other draft does not of itself operate as an assignment of funds in the hands of the drawee available for its payment, and the drawee is not liable on the instrument until the drawee accepts it.

§ 3–409. Acceptance of Draft; Certified Check.

(a) "Acceptance" means the drawee's signed agreement to pay a draft as presented. It must be written on the draft and may consist of the drawee's signature alone. Acceptance may be made at any time and becomes effective when notification pursuant to instructions is given or the accepted draft is delivered for the purpose of giving rights on the acceptance to any person.

(b) A draft may be accepted although it has not been signed by the drawer, is otherwise incomplete, is overdue, or has been dishonored.

(c) If a draft is payable at a fixed period after sight and the acceptor fails to date the acceptance, the holder may complete the acceptance by supplying a date in good faith.

(d) "Certified check" means a check accepted by the bank on which it is drawn. Acceptance may be made as stated in subsection (a) or by a writing on the check which indicates that the check is certified. The drawee of a check has no obligation to certify the check, and refusal to certify is not dishonor of the check.

§ 3–410. Acceptance Varying Draft.

(a) If the terms of a drawee's acceptance vary from the terms of the draft as presented, the holder may refuse the acceptance and treat the draft as dishonored. In that case, the drawee may cancel the acceptance.
(b) The terms of a draft are not varied by an acceptance to pay at a particular bank or place in the United States, unless the acceptance states that the draft is to be paid only at that bank or place.
(c) If the holder assents to an acceptance varying the terms of a draft, the obligation of each drawer and indorser that does not expressly assent to the acceptance is discharged.

§ 3–411. Refusal to Pay Cashier's Checks, Teller's Checks, and Certified Checks.

(a) In this section, "obligated bank" means the acceptor of a certified check or the issuer of a cashier's check or teller's check bought from the issuer.
(b) If the obligated bank wrongfully (i) refuses to pay a cashier's check or certified check, (ii) stops payment of a teller's check, or (iii) refuses to pay a dishonored teller's check, the person asserting the right to enforce the check is entitled to compensation for expenses and loss of interest resulting from the nonpayment and may recover consequential damages if the obligated bank refused to pay after receiving notice of particular circumstances giving rise to the damages.
(c) Expenses or consequential damages under subsection (b) are not recoverable if the refusal of the obligated bank to pay occurs because (i) the bank suspends payments, (ii) the obligated bank is asserting a claim or defense of the bank that it has reasonable grounds to believe is available against the person entitled to enforce the instrument, (iii) the obligated bank has a reasonable doubt whether the person demanding payment is the person entitled to enforce the instrument, or (iv) payment is prohibited by law.

§ 3–412. Obligation of Maker.

A maker of a note is obliged to pay the note (i) according to its terms at the time it was issued or, if not issued, at the time it first came into possession of a holder, or (ii) if the maker signed an incomplete instrument, according to its terms when completed as stated in Sections 3–115 and 3–407. The obligation is owed to a person entitled to enforce the note or to an indorser that paid the note pursuant to Section 3–415.

§ 3–413. Obligation of Acceptor.

(a) An acceptor of a draft is obliged to pay the draft (i) according to its terms at the time it was accepted, even though the acceptance states that the draft is payable "as originally drawn" or equivalent terms, (ii) if the acceptance varies the terms of the draft, according to the terms of the draft as varied, or (iii) if the acceptance is of a draft that is an incomplete instrument, according to its terms when completed as stated in Sections 3–115 and 3–407. The obligation is owed to a person entitled to enforce the draft or to the drawer or an indorser that paid the draft pursuant to Section 3–414 or 3–415.
(b) If the certification of a check or other acceptance of a draft states the amount certified or accepted, the obligation of the acceptor is that amount. If (i) the certification or acceptance does not state an amount, (ii) the instrument is subsequently altered by raising its amount, and (iii) the instrument is then negotiated to a holder in due course, the obligation of the acceptor is the amount of the instrument at the time it was negotiated to the holder in due course.

§ 3–414. Obligation of Drawer.

(a) If an unaccepted draft is dishonored, the drawer is obliged to pay the draft (i) according to its terms at the time it was issued or, if not issued, at the time it first came into possession of a holder, or (ii) if the drawer signed an incomplete instrument, according to its terms when completed as stated in Sections 3–115 and 3–407. The obligation is owed to a person entitled to enforce the draft or to an indorser that paid the draft pursuant to Section 3–415.
(b) If a draft is accepted by a bank and the acceptor dishonors the draft, the drawer has no obligation to pay the draft because of the dishonor, regardless of when or by whom acceptance was obtained.
(c) If a draft is accepted and the acceptor is not a bank, the obligation of the drawer to pay the draft if the draft is dishonored by the acceptor is the same as the obligation of an indorser stated in Section 3–415(a) and (c).
(d) Words in a draft indicating that the draft is drawn without recourse are effective to disclaim all liability of the drawer to pay the draft if the draft is not a check or a teller's check, but they are not effective to disclaim the obligation stated in subsection (a) if the draft is a check or a teller's check.
(e) If (i) a check is not presented for payment or given to a depositary bank for collection within 30 days after its date, (ii) the drawee suspends payments after expiration of the 30-day period without paying the check, and (iii) because of the suspension of payments the drawer is deprived of funds maintained with the drawee to cover payment of the check, the drawer to the extent deprived of funds may discharge its obligation to pay the check by assigning to the person entitled to enforce the check the rights of the drawer against the drawee with respect to the funds.

§ 3–415. Obligation of Indorser.

(a) Subject to subsections (b), (c) and (d) and to Section 3–419(d), if an instrument is dishonored, an indorser is obliged to pay the amount due on the instrument (i) according to the terms of the instrument at the time it was indorsed, or (ii) if the indorser indorsed an incomplete instrument, according to its terms when completed as stated in Sections 3–115 and 3–407. The obligation of the indorser is owed to a person entitled to enforce the instrument or to a subsequent indorser that paid the instrument pursuant to this section.
(b) If an indorsement states that it is made "without recourse" or otherwise disclaims liability of the indorser, the indorser is not liable under subsection (a) to pay the instrument.
(c) If notice of dishonor of an instrument is required by Section 3–503 and notice of dishonor complying with that section is not given to an indorser, the liability of the indorser under subsection (a) is discharged.
(d) If a draft is accepted by a bank after an indorsement was made and the acceptor dishonors the draft, the indorser is not liable under subsection (a) to pay the instrument.
(e) If an indorser of a check is liable under subsection (a) and the check is not presented for payment, or given to a depositary bank for collection, within 30 days after the day the indorsement was made, the liability of the indorser under subsection (a) is discharged.

§ 3–416. Transfer Warranties.

(a) A person that transfers an instrument for consideration warrants to the transferee and, if the transfer is by indorsement, to any subsequent transferee that:

(1) the warrantor is a person entitled to enforce the instrument,
(2) all signatures on the instrument are authentic and authorized,
(3) the instrument has not been altered,
(4) the instrument is not subject to a defense or claim in recoupment stated in Section 3–305(a) of any party that can be asserted against the warrantor, and
(5) the warrantor has no knowledge of any insolvency proceeding commenced with respect to the maker or acceptor or, in the case of an unaccepted draft, the drawer.

(b) A person to whom the warranties under subsection (a) are made and who took the instrument in good faith may recover from the warrantor as damages for breach of warranty an amount equal to the loss suffered as a result of the breach, but not more than the amount of the instrument plus expenses and loss of interest incurred as a result of the breach.
(c) The warranties stated in subsection (a) cannot be disclaimed with respect to checks. Unless notice of a claim for breach of warranty is given to the warrantor within 30 days after the claimant has reason to know of the breach and the identity of the warrantor, the warrantor is discharged to the extent of any loss caused by the delay in giving notice of the claim.
(d) A cause of action for breach of warranty under this section accrues when the claimant has reason to know of the breach.

§ 3–417. Presentment Warranties.

(a) If an unaccepted draft is presented to the drawee for payment or acceptance and the drawee pays or accepts the draft, (i) the person obtaining payment or acceptance, at the time of presentment, and (ii) a previous transferor of the draft, at the time of transfer, warrant to the drawee making payment or accepting the draft in good faith that:

(1) the warrantor is or was, at the time the warrantor transferred the draft, a person entitled to enforce the draft or authorized to obtain payment or acceptance of the draft on behalf of a person entitled to enforce the draft;

(2) the draft has not been altered; and

(3) the warrantor has no knowledge that the signature of the purported drawer of the draft is unauthorized.

(b) A drawee making payment may recover from any warrantor damages for breach of warranty equal to the amount paid by the drawee less the amount the drawee received or is entitled to receive from the drawer because of payment of the draft. In addition the drawee is entitled to compensation for expenses and loss of interest resulting from the breach. The right of the drawee to recover damages under this subsection is not affected by any failure of the drawee to exercise ordinary care in making payment. If the drawee accepts the draft (i) breach of warranty is a defense to the obligation of the acceptor, and (ii) if the acceptor makes payment with respect to the draft, the acceptor is entitled to recover from any warrantor for breach of warranty the amounts stated in the first two sentences of this subsection.
(c) If a drawee asserts a claim for breach of warranty under subsection (a) based on an unauthorized indorsement of the draft or an alteration of the draft, the warrantor may defend by proving that the indorsement is effective under Section 3–404 or 3–405 or the drawer is precluded under Section 3–406 or 4–406 from asserting against the drawee the unauthorized indorsement or alteration.
(d) This subsection applies if (i) a dishonored draft is presented for payment to the drawer or an indorser or (ii) any other instrument is presented for payment to a party obliged to pay the instrument, and payment is received. The person obtaining payment and a prior transferor of the instrument warrant to the person making payment in good faith that the warrantor is or was, at the time the warrantor transferred the instrument, a person entitled to enforce the instrument or authorized to obtain payment on behalf of a person entitled to enforce the instrument. The person making payment may recover from any warrantor for breach of warranty an amount equal to the amount paid plus expenses and loss of interest resulting from the breach.
(e) The warranties stated in subsections (a) and (d) cannot be disclaimed with respect to checks. Unless notice of a claim for breach of warranty is given to the warrantor within 30 days after the claimant has reason to know of the breach and the identity of the warrantor, the warrantor is discharged to the extent of any loss caused by the delay in giving notice of the claim.
(f) A cause of action for breach of warranty under this section accrues when the claimant has reason to know of the breach.

§ 3–418. Payment or Acceptance by Mistake.

(a) Except as provided in subsection (c), if the drawee of a draft pays or accepts the draft and the drawee acted on the mistaken belief that (i) payment of the draft had not been stopped under Section 4–403, (ii) the signature of the purported drawer of the draft was authorized, or (iii) the balance in the drawer's account with the drawee represented available funds, the drawee may recover the amount paid from the person to whom or for whose benefit payment was made or, in the case of acceptance, may revoke the acceptance. Rights of the drawee under this subsection are not affected by failure of the drawee to exercise ordinary care in paying or accepting the draft.
(b) Except as provided in subsection (c), if an instrument has been paid or accepted by mistake and the case is not covered by subsection (a), the person paying or accepting may recover the amount paid or revoke acceptance to the extent allowed by the law governing mistake and restitution.
(c) The remedies provided by subsection (a) or (b) may not be asserted against a person who took the instrument in good faith and for value. This subsection does not limit remedies provided by Section 3–417 for breach of warranty.

§ 3–419. Instruments Signed for Accommodation.

(a) If an instrument is issued for value given for the benefit of a party to the instrument ("accommodated party") and another party to the instrument ("accommodation party") signs the instrument for the purpose of incurring liability on the instrument without being a direct beneficiary of the value given for the instrument, the instrument is signed by the accommodation party "for accommodation."
(b) An accommodation party may sign the instrument as maker, drawer, acceptor, or indorser and, subject to subsection (d), is obliged to pay the instrument in the capacity in which the accommodation party signs. The obligation of an accommodation party may be enforced notwithstanding any statute of frauds and regardless of whether the accommodation party receives consideration for the accommodation.
(c) A person signing an instrument is presumed to be an accommodation party and there is notice that the instrument is signed for accommodation if the signature is an anomalous indorsement or is accompanied by words indicating that the signer is acting as surety or guarantor with respect to the obligation of another party to the instrument. Except as provided in Section 3–606, the obligation of an accommodation party to pay the instrument is not affected by the fact that the person enforcing the obligation had notice when the instrument was taken by that person that the accommodation party signed the instrument for accommodation.
(d) If the signature of a party to an instrument is accompanied by words indicating unambiguously that the party is guaranteeing collection rather than payment of the obligation of another party to the instrument, the signer is obliged to pay the amount due on the instrument to a person entitled to enforce the instrument only if (i) execution of judgment against the other party has been returned unsatisfied, (ii) the other party is insolvent or in an insolvency proceeding, (iii) the other party cannot be served with process, or (iv) it is otherwise apparent that payment cannot be obtained from the party whose obligation is guaranteed.
(e) An accommodation party that pays the instrument is entitled to reimbursement from the accommodated party and is entitled to enforce the instrument against the accommodated party. An accommodated party that pays the instrument has no right of recourse against, and is not entitled to contribution from, an accommodation party.

§ 3–420. Conversion of Instrument.

(a) The law applicable to conversion of personal property applies to instruments. An instrument is also converted if the instrument lacks an indorsement necessary for negotiation and it is purchased or taken for collection or the drawee takes the instrument and makes

payment to a person not entitled to receive payment. An action for conversion of an instrument may not be brought by (i) the maker, drawer, or acceptor of the instrument or (ii) a payee or indorsee who did not receive delivery of the instrument either directly or through delivery to an agent or a co-payee.
(b) In an action under subsection (a), the measure of liability is presumed to be the amount payable on the instrument, but recovery may not exceed the amount of the plaintiff's interest in the instrument.
(c) A representative, other than a depositary bank, that has in good faith dealt with an instrument or its proceeds on behalf of one who was not the person entitled to enforce the instrument is not liable in conversion to that person beyond the amount of any proceeds that it has not paid out.

Part 5—Dishonor

§ 3-501. Presentment.

(a) "Presentment" means a demand (i) to pay an instrument made to the maker, drawee, or acceptor or, in the case of a note or accepted draft payable at a bank, to the bank, or (ii) to accept a draft made to the drawee, by a person entitled to enforce the instrument.
(b) Subject to Article 4, agreement of the parties, clearing house rules and the like,

(1) presentment may be made at the place of payment of the instrument and must be made at the place of payment if the instrument is payable at a bank in the United States; may be made by any commercially reasonable means, including an oral, written, or electronic communication; is effective when the demand for payment or acceptance is received by the person to whom presentment is made; is effective if made to any one of two or more makers, acceptors, drawees or other payors; and
(2) without dishonoring the instrument, the party to whom presentment is made may (i) treat presentment as occurring on the next business day after the day of presentment if the party to whom presentment is made has established a cut-off hour not earlier than 2 p.m. for the receipt and processing of instruments presented for payment or acceptance and presentment is made after the cut-off hour, (ii) require exhibition of the instrument, (iii) require reasonable identification of the person making presentment and evidence of authority to make it if made on behalf of another person, (iv) require a signed receipt on the instrument for any payment made or surrender of the instrument if full payment is made, (v) return the instrument for lack of a necessary indorsement, or (vi) refuse payment or acceptance for failure of the presentment to comply with the terms of the instrument, an agreement of the parties, or other law or applicable rule.

§ 3-502. Dishonor.

(a) Dishonor of a note is governed by the following rules:

(1) If the note is payable on demand, the note is dishonored if presentment is duly made and the note is not paid on the day of presentment.
(2) If the note is not payable on demand and is payable at or through a bank or the terms of the note require presentment, the note is dishonored if presentment is duly made and the note is not paid on the day it becomes payable or the day of presentment, whichever is later.
(3) If the note is not payable on demand and subparagraph (2) does not apply, the note is dishonored if it is not paid on the day it becomes payable.

(b) Dishonor of an unaccepted draft other than a documentary draft is governed by the following rules:

(1) If a check is presented for payment otherwise than for immediate payment over the counter, the check is dishonored if the payor bank makes timely return of the check or sends timely notice of dishonor or nonpayment under Section 4–301 or 4–302, or becomes accountable for the amount of the check under Section 4–302.
(2) If the draft is payable on demand and subparagraph (1) does not apply, the draft is dishonored if presentment for payment is duly made and the draft is not paid on the day of presentment.
(3) If the draft is payable on a date stated in the draft, the draft is dishonored if (i) presentment for payment is duly made and payment is not made on the day the draft becomes payable or the day of presentment, whichever is later, or (ii) presentment for acceptance is duly made before the day the draft becomes payable and the draft is not accepted on the day of presentment.
(4) If the draft is payable on elapse of a period of time after sight or acceptance, the draft is dishonored if presentment for acceptance is duly made and the draft is not accepted on the day of presentment.

(c) Dishonor of an unaccepted documentary draft occurs according to the rules stated in subparagraphs (2), (3), and (4) of subsection (b) except that payment or acceptance may be delayed without dishonor until no later than the close of the third business day of the drawee following the day on which payment or acceptance is required by those subparagraphs.
(d) Dishonor of an accepted draft is governed by the following rules:

(1) If the draft is payable on demand, the draft is dishonored if presentment for payment is duly made and the draft is not paid on the day of presentment.
(2) If the draft is not payable on demand, the draft is dishonored if presentment for payment is duly made and payment is not made on the day it becomes payable or the day of presentment, whichever is later.

(e) In any case in which presentment is otherwise required for dishonor under this section and presentment is excused under Section 3–504, dishonor occurs without presentment if the instrument is not duly accepted or paid.
(f) If a draft is dishonored because timely acceptance of the draft was not made and the person entitled to demand acceptance consents to a late acceptance, from the time of acceptance the draft is treated as never having been dishonored.

§ 3-503. Notice of Dishonor.

(a) The obligation of an indorser stated in Section 3–415(a) and the obligation of a drawer stated in Section 3–414(c) may not be enforced unless (i) the indorser or drawer is given notice of dishonor of the instrument complying with this section or (ii) notice of dishonor is excused under Section 3–504(c).
(b) Notice of dishonor may be given by any person; may be given by any commercially reasonable means including an oral, written, or electronic communication; is sufficient if it reasonably identifies the instrument and indicates that the instrument has been dishonored or has not been paid or accepted. Return of an instrument given to a bank for collection is a sufficient notice of dishonor.
(c) Subject to Section 3–504(d), with respect to an instrument taken for collection by a collecting bank, notice of dishonor must be given (i) by the bank before midnight of the next banking day following the banking day on which the bank receives notice of dishonor of the instrument, and (ii) by any other person within 30 days following the day on which the person receives notice of dishonor. With respect to any other instrument, notice of dishonor must be given within 30 days following the day on which dishonor occurs.

§ 3-504. Excused Presentment and Notice of Dishonor.

(a) Presentment for payment or acceptance of an instrument is excused if (i) the person entitled to present the instrument cannot with reasonable diligence make presentment, (ii) the maker or acceptor has repudiated an obligation to pay the instrument or is dead or in insolvency proceedings, (iii) by the terms of the instrument presentment is not necessary to enforce the obligation of indorsers or the drawer, or (iv) the drawer or indorser whose obligation is being enforced waived presentment or otherwise had no reason to expect or right to require that the instrument be paid or accepted.

(b) Presentment for payment or acceptance of a draft is also excused if the drawer instructed the drawee not to pay or accept the draft or the drawee was not obligated to the drawer to pay the draft.

(c) Notice of dishonor is excused if (i) by the terms of the instrument notice of dishonor is not necessary to enforce the obligation of a party to pay the instrument, or (ii) the party whose obligation is being enforced waived notice of dishonor. A waiver of presentment is also a waiver of notice of dishonor.

(d) Delay in giving notice of dishonor is excused if the delay was caused by circumstances beyond the control of the person giving the notice and the person giving the notice exercised reasonable diligence after the cause of the delay ceased to operate.

§ 3–505. Evidence of Dishonor.

(a) The following are admissible as evidence and create a presumption of dishonor and of any notice of dishonor stated:

(1) a document regular in form as provided in subsection (b) which purports to be a protest;

(2) a purported stamp or writing of the drawee, payor bank, or presenting bank on or accompanying the instrument stating that acceptance or payment has been refused unless reasons for the refusal are stated and the reasons are not consistent with dishonor;

(3) a book or record of the drawee, payor bank, or collecting bank, kept in the usual course of business which shows dishonor, even if there is no evidence of who made the entry.

(b) A protest is a certificate of dishonor made by a United States consul or vice consul, or a notary public or other person authorized to administer oaths by the law of the place where dishonor occurs. It may be made upon information satisfactory to that person. The protest must identify the instrument and certify either that presentment has been made or, if not made, the reason why it was not made, and that the instrument has been dishonored by nonacceptance or nonpayment. The protest may also certify that notice of dishonor has been given to some or all parties.

Part 6—Discharge and Payment

§ 3–601. Discharge and Effect of Discharge.

(a) The obligation of a party to pay the instrument is discharged as stated in this Article or by an act or agreement with the party which would discharge an obligation to pay money under a simple contract.

(b) Discharge of the obligation of a party is not effective against a person acquiring rights of a holder in due course of the instrument without notice of the discharge.

§ 3–602. Payment.

(a) Subject to subsection (b), an instrument is paid to the extent payment is made (i) by or on behalf of a party obliged to pay the instrument, and (ii) to a person entitled to enforce the instrument. To the extent of the payment, the obligation of the party obliged to pay the instrument is discharged even though payment is made with knowledge of a claim to the instrument under Section 3–306 by another person.

(b) The obligation of a party to pay the instrument is not discharged under subsection (a) if:

(1) a claim to the instrument under Section 3–306 is enforceable against the party receiving payment and (i) payment is made with knowledge by the payor that payment is prohibited by injunction or similar process of a court of competent jurisdiction, or (ii) in the case of an instrument other than a cashier's check, teller's check, or certified check, the party making payment accepted, from the person having a claim to the instrument, indemnity against loss resulting from refusal to pay the person entitled to enforce the instrument, or

(2) the person making payment knows that the instrument is a stolen instrument and pays a person that it knows is in wrongful possession of the instrument.

§ 3–603. Tender of Payment.

(a) If tender of payment of an obligation of a party to an instrument is made to a person entitled to enforce the obligation, the effect of tender is governed by principles of law applicable to tender of payment of an obligation under a simple contract.

(b) If tender of payment of an obligation to pay the instrument is made to a person entitled to enforce the instrument and the tender is refused, there is discharge, to the extent of the amount of the tender, of the obligation of an indorser or accommodation party having a right of recourse against the obligor making the tender.

(c) If tender of payment of an amount due on an instrument is made by or on behalf of the obligor to the person entitled to enforce the instrument, the obligation of the obligor to pay interest after the due date on the amount tendered is discharged. If presentment is required with respect to an instrument and the obligor is able and ready to pay on the due date at every place of payment stated in the instrument, the obligor is deemed to have made tender of payment on the due date to the person entitled to enforce the instrument.

§ 3–604. Discharge by Cancellation or Renunciation.

(a) A person entitled to enforce an instrument may, with or without consideration, discharge the obligation of a party to pay the instrument (i) by an intentional voluntary act such as surrender of the instrument to the party, destruction, mutilation, or cancellation of the instrument, cancellation or striking out of the party's signature, or the addition of words to the instrument indicating discharge, or (ii) by agreeing not to sue or otherwise renouncing rights against the party by a signed writing.

(b) Cancellation or striking out of an indorsement pursuant to subsection (a) does not affect the status and rights of a party derived from the indorsement.

§ 3–605. Discharge of Indorsers and Accommodation Parties.

(a) For the purposes of this section, the term "indorser" includes a drawer having the obligation stated in Section 3–414(c).

(b) Discharge of the obligation of a party to the instrument under Section 3–605 does not discharge the obligation of an indorser or accommodation party having a right of recourse against the discharged party.

(c) If a person entitled to enforce an instrument agrees, with or without consideration, to a material modification of the obligation of a party to the instrument, including an extension of the due date, there is discharge of the obligation of an indorser or accommodation party having a right of recourse against the person whose obligation is modified to the extent the modification causes loss to the indorser or accommodation party with respect to the right of recourse. The indorser or accommodation party is deemed to have suffered loss as a result of the modification equal to the amount of the right of recourse unless the person enforcing the instrument proves that no loss was caused by the modification or that the loss caused by the modification was less than the amount of the right of recourse.

(d) If the obligation of a party to an instrument is secured by an interest in collateral and impairment of the value of the interest is caused by a person entitled to enforce the instrument, there is discharge of the obligation of an indorser or accommodation party having a right of recourse against the obligor to the extent of the impairment. The value of an interest in collateral is impaired to the extent (i) the value of the interest is reduced to an amount less than the amount of the right of recourse of the party asserting discharge, or (ii) the reduction in value of the interest causes an increase in the amount by which the amount of the right of recourse exceeds the value of the interest. The burden of proving impairment is on the party asserting discharge.

(e) If the obligation of a party to an instrument is secured by an interest in collateral not provided by an accommodation party and the value of the interest is impaired by a person entitled to enforce the instrument, the obligation of any party who is jointly and severally liable with respect to the secured obligation is discharged to the extent the impairment causes the party asserting discharge to pay more than that party would have been obliged to pay, taking into account rights of contribution, if impairment had not occurred. If the party asserting discharge is an accommodation party not entitled to discharge under subsection (d), the party is deemed to have a right to contribution based on joint and several liability rather than a right to reimbursement. The burden of proving impairment is on the party asserting discharge.
(f) Under subsection (d) or (e) causation of impairment includes (i) failure to obtain or maintain perfection or recordation of the interest in collateral, (ii) release of collateral without substitution of collateral of equal value, (iii) failure to perform a duty to preserve the value of collateral owed, under Article 9 or other law, to a debtor or surety or other person secondarily liable, or (iv) failure to comply with applicable law in disposing of collateral.
(g) An accommodation party is not discharged under subsection (c) or (d) unless the person agreeing to the modification or causing the impairment knows of the accommodation or has notice under Section 3–419(c) that the instrument was signed for accommodation. There is no discharge of any party under subsection (c), (d), or (e) if (i) the party asserting discharge consents to the event or conduct that is the basis of the discharge, or (ii) the instrument or a separate agreement of the party provides for waiver of discharge under this section either specifically or by general language indicating that parties to the instrument waive defenses based on suretyship or impairment of collateral.

ARTICLE 4: BANK DEPOSITS AND COLLECTIONS

Part 1—General Provisions and Definitions

§ 4–101. Short Title.
This Article shall be known and may be cited as Uniform Commercial Code—Bank Deposits and Collections.

§ 4–102. Applicability.
(1) To the extent that items within this Article are also within the scope of Articles 3 and 8, they are subject to the provisions of those Articles. In the event of conflict the provisions of this Article govern those of Article 3 but the provisions of Article 8 govern those of this Article.
(2) The liability of a bank for action or non-action with respect to any item handled by it for purposes of presentment, payment or collection is governed by the law of the place where the bank is located. In the case of action or non-action by or at a branch or separate office of a bank, its liability is governed by the law of the place where the branch or separate office is located.

§ 4–103. Variation by Agreement; Measure of Damages; Certain Action Constituting Ordinary Care.
(1) The effect of the provisions of this Article may be varied by agreement except that no agreement can disclaim a bank's responsibility for its own lack of good faith or failure to exercise ordinary care or can limit the measure of damages for such lack or failure; but the parties may by agreement determine the standards by which such responsibility is to be measured if such standards are not manifestly unreasonable.
(2) Federal Reserve regulations and operating letters, clearing house rules, and the like, have the effect of agreements under subsection (1), whether or not specifically assented to by all parties interested in items handled.
(3) Action or non-action approved by this Article or pursuant to Federal Reserve regulations or operating letters constitutes the exercise of ordinary care and, in the absence of special instructions, action or non-action consistent with clearing house rules and the like or with a general banking usage not disapproved by this Article, prima facie constitutes the exercise of ordinary care.
(4) The specification or approval of certain procedures by this Article does not constitute disapproval of other procedures which may be reasonable under the circumstances.
(5) The measure of damages for failure to exercise ordinary care in handling an item is the amount of the item reduced by an amount which could not have been realized by the use of ordinary care, and where there is bad faith it includes other damages, if any, suffered by the party as a proximate consequence.

§ 4–104. Definitions and Index of Definitions.
(1) In this Article unless the context otherwise requires
- **(a)** "Account" means any account with a bank and includes a checking, time, interest or savings account;
- **(b)** "Afternoon" means the period of a day between noon and midnight;
- **(c)** "Banking day" means that part of any day on which a bank is open to the public for carrying on substantially all of its banking functions;
- **(d)** "Clearing house" means any association of banks or other payors regularly clearing items;
- **(e)** "Customer" means any person having an account with a bank or for whom a bank has agreed to collect items and includes a bank carrying an account with another bank;
- **(f)** "Documentary draft" means any negotiable or non-negotiable draft with accompanying documents, securities or other papers to be delivered against honor of the draft;
- **(g)** "Item" means any instrument for the payment of money even though it is not negotiable but does not include money;
- **(h)** "Midnight deadline" with respect to a bank is midnight on its next banking day following the banking day on which it receives the relevant item or notice or from which the time for taking action commences to run, whichever is later;
- **(i)** "Properly payable" includes the availability of funds for payment at the time of decision to pay or dishonor;
- **(j)** "Settle" means to pay in cash, by clearing house settlement, in a charge or credit or by remittance, or otherwise as instructed. A settlement may be either provisional or final;
- **(k)** "Suspends payments" with respect to a bank means that it has been closed by order of the supervisory authorities, that a public officer has been appointed to take it over or that it ceases or refuses to make payments in the ordinary course of business.

(2) Other definitions applying to this Article and the sections in which they appear are:
"Collecting bank" Section 4–105.
"Depositary bank" Section 4–105.
"Intermediary bank" Section 4–105.
"Payor bank" Section 4–105.
"Presenting bank" Section 4–105.
"Remitting bank" Section 4–105.

(3) The following definitions in other Articles apply to this Article:
"Acceptance" Section 3–410.
"Certificate of deposit" Section 3–104.
"Certification" Section 3–411.
"Check" Section 3–104.
"Draft" Section 3–104.
"Holder in due course" Section 3–302.
"Notice of dishonor" Section 3–508.
"Presentment" Section 3–504.
"Protest" Section 3–509.
"Secondary party" Section 3–102.

(4) In addition Article 1 contains general definitions and principles of construction and interpretation applicable throughout this Article.

§ 4–105. "Depositary Bank"; "Intermediary Bank"; "Collecting Bank"; "Payor Bank"; "Presenting Bank"; "Remitting Bank".
In this Article unless the context otherwise requires:
(a) "Depositary bank" means the first bank to which an item is transferred for collection even though it is also the payor bank;
(b) "Payor bank" means a bank by which an item is payable as drawn or accepted;
(c) "Intermediary bank" means any bank to which an item is transferred in course of collection except the depositary or payor bank;
(d) "Collecting bank" means any bank handling the item for collection except the payor bank;
(e) "Presenting bank" means any bank presenting an item except a payor bank;
(f) "Remitting bank" means any payor or intermediary bank remitting for an item.

§ 4–106. Separate Office of a Bank.
A branch or separate office of a bank [maintaining its own deposit ledgers] is a separate bank for the purpose of computing the time within which and determining the place at or to which action may be taken or notices or orders shall be given under this Article and under Article 3.

Note: *The brackets are to make it optional with the several states whether to require a branch to maintain its own deposit ledgers in order to be considered to be a separate bank for certain purposes under Article 4. In some states "maintaining its own deposit ledgers" is a satisfactory test. In others branch banking practices are such that this test would not be suitable.*

§ 4–107. Time of Receipt of Items.
(1) For the purpose of allowing time to process items, prove balances and make the necessary entries on its books to determine its position for the day, a bank may fix an afternoon hour of two p.m. or later as a cut-off hour for the handling of money and items and the making of entries on its books.
(2) Any item or deposit of money received on any day after a cut-off hour so fixed or after the close of the banking day may be treated as being received at the opening of the next banking day.

§ 4–108. Delays.
(1) Unless otherwise instructed, a collecting bank in a good faith effort to secure payment may, in the case of specific items and with or without the approval of any person involved, waive, modify or extend time limits imposed or permitted by this Act for a period not in excess of an additional banking day without discharge of secondary parties and without liability to its transferor or any prior party.
(2) Delay by a collecting bank or payor bank beyond time limits prescribed or permitted by this Act or by instructions is excused if caused by interruption of communication facilities, suspension of payments by another bank, war, emergency conditions or other circumstances beyond the control of the bank provided it exercises such diligence as the circumstances require.

§ 4–109. Process of Posting.
The "process of posting" means the usual procedure followed by a payor bank in determining to pay an item and in recording the payment including one or more of the following or other steps as determined by the bank:
(a) verification of any signature;
(b) ascertaining that sufficient funds are available;
(c) affixing a "paid" or other stamp;
(d) entering a charge or entry to a customer's account;
(e) correcting or reversing an entry or erroneous action with respect to the item.

Part 2—Collection of Items: Depositary and Collecting Banks
§ 4–201. Presumption and Duration of Agency Status of Collecting Banks and Provisional Status of Credits; Applicability of Article; Item Indorsed "Pay Any Bank".
(1) Unless a contrary intent clearly appears and prior to the time that a settlement given by a collecting bank for an item is or becomes final (subsection (3) of Section 4–211 and Sections 4–212 and 4–213) the bank is an agent or sub-agent of the owner of the item and any settlement given for the item is provisional. This provision applies regardless of the form of indorsement or lack of indorsement and even though credit given for the item is subject to immediate withdrawal as of right or is in fact withdrawn; but the continuance of ownership of an item by its owner and any rights of the owner to proceeds of the item are subject to rights of a collecting bank such as those resulting from outstanding advances on the item and valid rights of setoff. When an item is handled by banks for purposes of presentment, payment and collection, the relevant provisions of this Article apply even though action of parties clearly establishes that a particular bank has purchased the item and is the owner of it.
(2) After an item has been indorsed with the words "pay any bank" or the like, only a bank may acquire the rights of a holder
(a) until the item has been returned to the customer initiating collection; or
(b) until the item has been specially indorsed by a bank to a person who is not a bank.

§ 4–202. Responsibility for Collection; When Action Seasonable.
(1) A collecting bank must use ordinary care in
(a) presenting an item or sending it for presentment; and
(b) sending notice of dishonor or non-payment or returning an item other than a documentary draft to the bank's transferor [or directly to the depositary bank under subsection (2) of Section 4–212] (*see note to Section 4–212*) after learning that the item has not been paid or accepted as the case may be; and
(c) settling for an item when the bank receives final settlement; and
(d) making or providing for any necessary protest; and
(e) notifying its transferor of any loss or delay in transit within a reasonable time after discovery thereof.
(2) A collecting bank taking proper action before its midnight deadline following receipt of an item, notice or payment acts seasonably; taking proper action within a reasonably longer time may be seasonable but the bank has the burden of so establishing.
(3) Subject to subsection (1)(a), a bank is not liable for the insolvency, neglect, misconduct, mistake or default of another bank or person or for loss or destruction of an item in transit or in the possession of others.

§ 4–203. Effect of Instructions.
Subject to the provisions of Article 3 concerning conversion of instruments (Section 3–419) and the provisions of both Article 3 and this Article concerning restrictive indorsements only a collecting bank's transferor can give instructions which affect the bank or constitute notice to it and a collecting bank is not liable to prior parties for any action taken pursuant to such instructions or in accordance with any agreement with its transferor.

§ 4–204. Methods of Sending and Presenting; Sending Direct to Payor Bank.
(1) A collecting bank must send items by reasonably prompt method taking into consideration any relevant instructions, the nature of the item, the number of such items on hand, and the cost of collection involved and the method generally used by it or others to present such items.
(2) A collecting bank may send
(a) any item direct to the payor bank;
(b) any item to any non-bank payor if authorized by its transferor; and

(c) any item other than documentary drafts to any non-bank payor, if authorized by Federal Reserve regulation or operating letter, clearing house rule or the like.

(3) Presentment may be made by a presenting bank at a place where the payor bank has requested that presentment be made.

§ 4–205. Supplying Missing Indorsement; No Notice from Prior Indorsement.

(1) A depositary bank which has taken an item for collection may supply any indorsement of the customer which is necessary to title unless the item contains the words "payee's indorsement required" or the like. In the absence of such a requirement a statement placed on the item by the depositary bank to the effect that the item was deposited by a customer or credited to his account is effective as the customer's indorsement.

(2) An intermediary bank, or payor bank which is not a depositary bank, is neither given notice nor otherwise affected by a restrictive indorsement of any person except the bank's immediate transferor.

§ 4–206. Transfer Between Banks.

Any agreed method which identifies the transferor bank is sufficient for the item's further transfer to another bank.

§ 4–207. Warranties of Customer and Collecting Bank on Transfer or Presentment of Items; Time for Claims.

(1) Each customer or collecting bank who obtains payment or acceptance of an item and each prior customer and collecting bank warrants to the payor bank or other payor who in good faith pays or accepts the item that

(a) he has a good title to the item or is authorized to obtain payment or acceptance on behalf of one who has a good title; and

(b) he has no knowledge that the signature of the maker or drawer is unauthorized, except that this warranty is not given by any customer or collecting bank that is a holder in due course and acts in good faith

(i) to a maker with respect to the maker's own signature; or

(ii) to a drawer with respect to the drawer's own signature, whether or not the drawer is also the drawee; or

(iii) to an acceptor of an item if the holder in due course took the item after the acceptance or obtained the acceptance without knowledge that the drawer's signature was unauthorized; and

(c) the item has not been materially altered, except that this warranty is not given by any customer or collecting bank that is a holder in due course and acts in good faith

(i) to the maker of a note; or

(ii) to the drawer of a draft whether or not the drawer is also the drawee; or

(iii) to the acceptor of an item with respect to an alteration made prior to the acceptance if the holder in due course took the item after the acceptance, even though the acceptance provided "payable as originally drawn" or equivalent terms; or

(iv) to the acceptor of an item with respect to an alteration made after the acceptance.

(2) Each customer and collecting bank who transfers an item and receives a settlement or other consideration for it warrants to his transferee and to any subsequent collecting bank who takes the item in good faith that

(a) he has a good title to the item or is authorized to obtain payment or acceptance on behalf of one who has a good title and the transfer is otherwise rightful; and

(b) all signatures are genuine or authorized; and

(c) the item has not been materially altered; and

(d) no defense of any party is good against him; and

(e) he has no knowledge of any insolvency proceeding instituted with respect to the maker or acceptor or the drawer of an unaccepted item.

In addition each customer and collecting bank so transferring an item and receiving a settlement or other consideration engages that upon dishonor and any necessary notice of dishonor and protest he will take up the item.

(3) The warranties and the engagement to honor set forth in the two preceding subsections arise notwithstanding the absence of indorsement or words of guaranty or warranty in the transfer or presentment and a collecting bank remains liable for their breach despite remittance to its transferor. Damages for breach of such warranties or engagement to honor shall not exceed the consideration received by the customer or collecting bank responsible plus finance charges and expenses related to the item, if any.

(4) Unless a claim for breach of warranty under this section is made within a reasonable time after the person claiming learns of the breach, the person liable is discharged to the extent of any loss caused by the delay in making claim.

§ 4–208. Security Interest of Collecting Bank in Items, Accompanying Documents and Proceeds.

(1) A bank has a security interest in an item and any accompanying documents or the proceeds of either

(a) in case of an item deposited in an account to the extent to which credit given for the item has been withdrawn or applied;

(b) in case of an item for which it has given credit available for withdrawal as of right, to the extent of the credit given whether or not the credit is drawn upon and whether or not there is a right of charge-back; or

(c) if it makes an advance on or against the item.

(2) When credit which has been given for several items received at one time or pursuant to a single agreement is withdrawn or applied in part the security interest remains upon all the items, any accompanying documents or the proceeds of either. For the purpose of this section, credits first given are first withdrawn.

(3) Receipt by a collecting bank of a final settlement for an item is a realization on its security interest in the item, accompanying documents and proceeds. To the extent and so long as the bank does not receive final settlement for the item or give up possession of the item or accompanying documents for purposes other than collection, the security interest continues and is subject to the provisions of Article 9 except that

(a) no security agreement is necessary to make the security interest enforceable (subsection (1)(b) of Section 9–203); and

(b) no filing is required to perfect the security interest; and

(c) the security interest has priority over conflicting perfected security interests in the item, accompanying documents or proceeds.

§ 4–209. When Bank Gives Value for Purposes of Holder in Due Course.

For purposes of determining its status as a holder in due course, the bank has given value to the extent that it has a security interest in an item provided that the bank otherwise complies with the requirements of Section 3–302 on what constitutes a holder in due course.

§ 4–210. Presentment by Notice of Item Not Payable by, Through or at a Bank; Liability of Secondary Parties.

(1) Unless otherwise instructed, a collecting bank may present an item not payable by, through or at a bank by sending to the party to accept or pay a written notice that the bank holds the item for acceptance or payment. The notice must be sent in time to be received on or before the day when presentment is due and the bank must meet any requirement of the party to accept or pay under Section 3–505 by the close of the bank's next banking day after it knows of the requirement.

(2) Where presentment is made by notice and neither honor nor request for compliance with a requirement under Section 3–505 is received by the close of business on the day after maturity or in the case of demand items by the close of business on the third banking day after notice was sent, the presenting bank may treat the item as dishonored and charge any secondary party by sending him notice of the facts.

§ 4–211. Media of Remittance; Provisional and Final Settlement in Remittance Cases.

(1) A collecting bank may take in settlement of an item

(a) a check of the remitting bank or of another bank on any bank except the remitting bank; or

(b) a cashier's check or similar primary obligation of a remitting bank which is a member of or clears through a member of the same clearing house or group as the collecting bank; or

(c) appropriate authority to charge an account of the remitting bank or of another bank with the collecting bank; or

(d) if the item is drawn upon or payable by a person other than a bank, a cashier's check, certified check or other bank check or obligation.

(2) If before its midnight deadline the collecting bank properly dishonors a remittance check or authorization to charge on itself or presents or forwards for collection a remittance instrument of or on another bank which is of a kind approved by subsection (1) or has not been authorized by it, the collecting bank is not liable to prior parties in the event of the dishonor of such check, instrument or authorization.

(3) A settlement for an item by means of a remittance instrument or authorization to charge is or becomes a final settlement as to both the person making and the person receiving the settlement

(a) if the remittance instrument or authorization to charge is of a kind approved by subsection (1) or has not been authorized by the person receiving the settlement and in either case the person receiving the settlement acts seasonably before its midnight deadline in presenting, forwarding for collection or paying the instrument or authorization,—at the time the remittance instrument or authorization is finally paid by the payor by which it is payable;

(b) if the person receiving the settlement has authorized remittance by a non-bank check or obligation or by a cashier's check or similar primary obligation of or a check upon the payor or other remitting bank which is not of a kind approved by subsection (1)(b),—at the time of the receipt of such remittance check or obligation; or

(c) if in a case not covered by sub-paragraphs (a) or (b) the person receiving the settlement fails to seasonably present, forward for collection, pay or return a remittance instrument or authorization to it to charge before its midnight deadline,—at such midnight deadline.

§ 4–212. Right of Charge-Back or Refund.

(1) If a collecting bank has made provisional settlement with its customer for an item and itself fails by reason of dishonor, suspension of payments by a bank or otherwise to receive a settlement for the item which is or becomes final, the bank may revoke the settlement given by it, charge-back the amount of any credit given for the item to its customer's account or obtain refund from its customer whether or not it is able to return the items if by its midnight deadline or within a longer reasonable time after it learns the facts it returns the item or sends notification of the facts. These rights to revoke, charge-back and obtain refund terminate if and when a settlement for the item received by the bank is or becomes final (subsection (3) of Section 4–211 and subsections (2) and (3) of Section 4–213).

(2) Within the time and manner prescribed by this section and Section 4–301, an intermediary or payor bank, as the case may be, may return an unpaid item directly to the depositary bank and may send for collection a draft on the depositary bank and obtain reimbursement. In such case, if the depositary bank has received provisional settlement for the item, it must reimburse the bank drawing the draft and any provisional credits for the item between banks shall become and remain final.]

Note: *Direct returns is recognized as an innovation that is not yet established bank practice, and therefore, Paragraph 2 has been bracketed. Some lawyers have doubts whether it should be included in legislation or left to development by agreement.*

(3) A depositary bank which is also the payor may charge-back the amount of an item to its customer's account or obtain refund in accordance with the section governing return of an item received by a payor bank for credit on its books (Section 4–301).

(4) The right to charge-back is not affected by

(a) prior use of the credit given for the item; or

(b) failure by any bank to exercise ordinary care with respect to the item but any bank so failing remains liable.

(5) A failure to charge-back or claim refund does not affect other rights of the bank against the customer or any other party.

(6) If credit is given in dollars as the equivalent of the value of an item payable in a foreign currency the dollar amount of any charge-back or refund shall be calculated on the basis of the buying sight rate for the foreign currency prevailing on the day when the person entitled to the charge-back or refund learns that it will not receive payment in ordinary course.

§ 4–213. Final Payment of Item by Payor Bank; When Provisional Debits and Credits Become Final; When Certain Credits Become Available for Withdrawal.

(1) An item is finally paid by a payor bank when the bank has done any of the following, whichever happens first:

(a) paid the item in cash; or

(b) settled for the item without reserving a right to revoke the settlement and without having such right under statute, clearing house rule or agreement; or

(c) completed the process of posting the item to the indicated account of the drawer, maker or other person to be charged therewith; or

(d) made a provisional settlement for the item and failed to revoke the settlement in the time and manner permitted by statute, clearing house rule or agreement.

Upon a final payment under subparagraphs (b), (c), or (d) the payor bank shall be accountable for the amount of the item.

(2) If provisional settlement for an item between the presenting and payor banks is made through a clearing house or by debits or credits in an account between them, then to the extent that provisional debits or credits for the item are entered in accounts between the presenting and payor banks or between the presenting and successive prior collecting banks seriatim, they become final upon final payment of the item by the payor bank.

(3) If a collecting bank receives a settlement for an item which is or becomes final (subsection (3) of Section 4–211, subsection (2) of Section 4–213) the bank is accountable to its customer for the amount of the item and any provisional credit given for the item in an account with its customer becomes final.

(4) Subject to any right of the bank to apply the credit to an obligation of the customer, credit given by a bank for an item in an account with its customer becomes available for withdrawal as of right

(a) in any case where the bank has received a provisional settlement for the item,—when such settlement becomes final and the bank has had a reasonable time to learn that the settlement is final;

(b) in any case where the bank is both a depositary bank and a payor bank and the item is finally paid,—at the opening of the bank's second banking day following receipt of the item.

(5) A deposit of money in a bank is final when made but, subject to any right of the bank to apply the deposit to an obligation of the customer, the deposit becomes available for withdrawal as of right at the opening of the bank's next banking day following receipt of the deposit.

§ 4–214. Insolvency and Preference.
(1) Any item in or coming into the possession of a payor or collecting bank which suspends payment and which item is not finally paid shall be returned by the receiver, trustee or agent in charge of the closed bank to the presenting bank or the closed bank's customer.
(2) If a payor bank finally pays an item and suspends payments without making a settlement for the item with its customer or the presenting bank which settlement is or becomes final, the owner of the item has a preferred claim against the payor bank.
(3) If a payor bank gives or a collecting bank gives or receives a provisional settlement for an item and thereafter suspends payments, the suspension does not prevent or interfere with the settlement becoming final if such finality occurs automatically upon the lapse of certain time or the happening of certain events (subsection (3) of Section 4–211, subsections (1)(d), (2) and (3) of Section 4–213).
(4) If a collecting bank receives from subsequent parties settlement for an item which settlement is or becomes final and suspends payments without making a settlement for the item with its customer which is or becomes final, the owner of the item has a preferred claim against such collecting bank.

Part 3—Collection of Items: Payor Banks
§ 4–301. Deferred Posting; Recovery of Payment by Return of Items; Time of Dishonor.
(1) Where an authorized settlement for a demand item (other than a documentary draft) received by a payor bank otherwise than for immediate payment over the counter has been made before midnight of the banking day of receipt the payor bank may revoke the settlement and recover any payment if before it has made final payment (subsection (1) of Section 4–213) and before its midnight deadline it
(a) returns the item; or
(b) sends written notice of dishonor or nonpayment if the item is held for protest or is otherwise unavailable for return.
(2) If a demand item is received by a payor bank for credit on its books it may return such item or send notice of dishonor and may revoke any credit given or recover the amount thereof withdrawn by its customer, if it acts within the time limit and in the manner specified in the preceding subsection.
(3) Unless previous notice of dishonor has been sent an item is dishonored at the time when for purposes of dishonor it is returned or notice sent in accordance with this section.
(4) An item is returned:
(a) as to an item received through a clearing house when it is delivered to the presenting or last collecting bank or to the clearing house or is sent or delivered in accordance with its rules; or
(b) in all other cases, when it is sent or delivered to the bank's customer or transferor or pursuant to his instructions.

§ 4–302. Payor Bank's Responsibility for Late Return of Item.
In the absence of a valid defense such as breach of a presentment warranty (subsection (1) of Section 4–207), settlement effected or the like, if an item is presented on and received by a payor bank the bank is accountable for the amount of
(a) a demand item other than a documentary draft whether properly payable or not if the bank, in any case where it is not also the depositary bank, retains the item beyond midnight of the banking day of receipt without settling for it or, regardless of whether it is also the depositary bank, does not pay or return the item or send notice of dishonor until after its midnight deadline; or
(b) any other properly payable item unless within the time allowed for acceptance or payment of that item the bank either accepts or pays the item or returns it and accompanying documents.

§ 4–303. When Items Subject to Notice, Stop-Order, Legal Process or Setoff; Order in Which Items May Be Charged or Certified.
(1) Any knowledge, notice or stop-order received by, legal process served upon or setoff exercised by a payor bank, whether or not effective under other rules of law to terminate, suspend or modify the bank's right or duty to pay an item or to charge its customer's account for the item, comes too late to so terminate, suspend or modify such right or duty if the knowledge, notice, stop-order or legal process is received or served and a reasonable time for the bank to act thereon expires or the setoff is exercised after the bank has done any of the following:
(a) accepted or certified the item;
(b) paid the item in cash;
(c) settled for the item without reserving a right to revoke the settlement and without having such right under statute, clearing house rule or agreement;
(d) completed the process of posting the item to the indicated account of the drawer, maker, or other person to be charged therewith or otherwise has evidenced by examination of such indicated account and by action its decision to pay the item; or
(e) become accountable for the amount of the item under subsection (1)(d) of Section 4–213 and Section 4–302 dealing with the payor bank's responsibility for late return of items.
(2) Subject to the provisions of subsection (1) items may be accepted, paid, certified or charged to the indicated account of its customer in any order convenient to the bank.

Part 4—Relationship Between Payor Bank and Its Customer
§ 4–401. When Bank May Charge Customer's Account.
(1) As against its customer, a bank may charge against his account any item which is otherwise properly payable from that account even though the charge creates an overdraft.
(2) A bank which in good faith makes payment to a holder may charge the indicated account of its customer according to
(a) the original tenor of his altered item; or
(b) the tenor of his completed item, even though the bank knows the item has been completed unless the bank has notice that the completion was improper.

§ 4–402. Bank's Liability to Customer for Wrongful Dishonor.
A payor bank is liable to its customer for damages proximately caused by the wrongful dishonor of an item. When the dishonor occurs through mistake liability is limited to actual damages proved. If so proximately caused and proved damages may include damages for an arrest or prosecution of the customer or other consequential damages. Whether any consequential damages are proximately caused by the wrongful dishonor is a question of fact to be determined in each case.

§ 4–403. Customer's Right to Stop Payment; Burden of Proof of Loss.
(1) A customer may by order to his bank stop payment of any item payable for his account but the order must be received at such time and in such manner as to afford the bank a reasonable opportunity to act on it prior to any action by the bank with respect to the item described in Section 4–303.
(2) An oral order is binding upon the bank only for fourteen calendar days unless confirmed in writing within that period. A written order is effective for only six months unless renewed in writing.
(3) The burden of establishing the fact and amount of loss resulting from the payment of an item contrary to a binding stop payment order is on the customer.

§ 4–404. Bank Not Obligated to Pay Check More Than Six Months Old.
A bank is under no obligation to a customer having a checking account to pay a check, other than a certified check, which is presented more than six months after its date, but it may charge its customer's account for a payment made thereafter in good faith.

§ 4–405. Death or Incompetence of Customer.
(1) A payor or collecting bank's authority to accept, pay or collect an item or to account for proceeds of its collection if otherwise effective is not rendered ineffective by incompetence of a customer of either

bank existing at the time the item is issued or its collection is undertaken if the bank does not know of an adjudication of incompetence. Neither death nor incompetence of a customer revokes such authority to accept, pay, collect or account until the bank knows of the fact of death or of an adjudication of incompetence and has reasonable opportunity to act on it.

(2) Even with knowledge a bank may for ten days after the date of death pay or certify checks drawn on or prior to that date unless ordered to stop payment by a person claiming an interest in the account.

§ 4–406. Customer's Duty to Discover and Report Unauthorized Signature or Alteration.

(1) When a bank sends to its customer a statement of account accompanied by items paid in good faith in support of the debit entries or holds the statement and items pursuant to a request or instructions of its customer or otherwise in a reasonable manner makes the statement and items available to the customer, the customer must exercise reasonable care and promptness to examine the statement and items to discover his unauthorized signature or any alteration on an item and must notify the bank promptly after discovery thereof.

(2) If the bank establishes that the customer failed with respect to an item to comply with the duties imposed on the customer by subsection (1) the customer is precluded from asserting against the bank

(a) his unauthorized signature or any alteration on the item if the bank also establishes that it suffered a loss by reason of such failure; and

(b) an unauthorized signature or alteration by the same wrongdoer on any other item paid in good faith by the bank after the first item and statement was available to the customer for a reasonable period not exceeding fourteen calendar days and before the bank receives notification from the customer of any such unauthorized signature or alteration.

(3) The preclusion under subsection (2) does not apply if the customer establishes lack of ordinary care on the part of the bank in paying the item(s).

(4) Without regard to care or lack of care of either the customer or the bank a customer who does not within one year from the time the statement and items are made available to the customer (subsection (1)) discover and report his unauthorized signature or any alteration on the face or back of the item or does not within three years from that time discover and report any unauthorized indorsement is precluded from asserting against the bank such unauthorized signature or indorsement or such alteration.

(5) If under this section a payor bank has a valid defense against a claim of a customer upon or resulting from payment of an item and waives or fails upon request to assert the defense the bank may not assert against any collecting bank or other prior party presenting or transferring the item a claim based upon the unauthorized signature or alteration giving rise to the customer's claim.

§ 4–407. Payor Bank's Right to Subrogation on Improper Payment.

If a payor bank has paid an item over the stop payment order of the drawer or maker or otherwise under circumstances giving a basis for objection by the drawer or maker, to prevent unjust enrichment and only to the extent necessary to prevent loss to the bank by reason of its payment of the item, the payor bank shall be subrogated to the rights

(a) of any holder in due course on the item against the drawer or maker; and

(b) of the payee or any other holder of the item against the drawer or maker either on the item or under the transaction out of which the item arose; and

(c) of the drawer or maker against the payee or any other holder of the item with respect to the transaction out of which the item arose.

Part 5—Collection of Documentary Drafts

§ 4–501. Handling of Documentary Drafts; Duty to Send for Presentment and to Notify Customer of Dishonor.

A bank which takes a documentary draft for collection must present or send the draft and accompanying documents for presentment and upon learning that the draft has not been paid or accepted in due course must seasonably notify its customer of such fact even though it may have discounted or bought the draft or extended credit available for withdrawal as of right.

§ 4–502. Presentment of "On Arrival" Drafts.

When a draft or the relevant instructions require presentment "on arrival", "when goods arrive" or the like, the collecting bank need not present until in its judgment a reasonable time for arrival of the goods has expired. Refusal to pay or accept because the goods have not arrived is not dishonor; the bank must notify its transferor of such refusal but need not present the draft again until it is instructed to do so or learns of the arrival of the goods.

§ 4–503. Responsibility of Presenting Bank for Documents and Goods; Report of Reasons for Dishonor; Referee in Case of Need.

Unless otherwise instructed and except as provided in Article 5 a bank presenting a documentary draft

(a) must deliver the documents to the drawee on acceptance of the draft if it is payable more than three days after presentment; otherwise, only on payment; and

(b) upon dishonor, either in the case of presentment for acceptance or presentment for payment, may seek and follow instructions from any referee in case of need designated in the draft or if the presenting bank does not choose to utilize his services it must use diligence and good faith to ascertain the reason for dishonor, must notify its transferor of the dishonor and of the results of its effort to ascertain the reasons therefor and must request instructions.

But the presenting bank is under no obligation with respect to goods represented by the documents except to follow any reasonable instructions seasonably received; it has a right to reimbursement for any expense incurred in following instructions and to prepayment of or indemnity for such expenses.

§ 4–504. Privilege of Presenting Bank to Deal With Goods; Security Interest for Expenses.

(1) A presenting bank which, following the dishonor of a documentary draft, has seasonably requested instructions but does not receive them within a reasonable time may store, sell, or otherwise deal with the goods in any reasonable manner.

(2) For its reasonable expenses incurred by action under subsection (1) the presenting bank has a lien upon the goods or their proceeds, which may be foreclosed in the same manner as an unpaid seller's lien.

ARTICLE 4A: FUNDS TRANSFERS

Part 1—Subject Matter and Definitions

§ 4A–101. Short Title.

This Article may be cited as Uniform Commercial Code—Funds Transfers.

§ 4A–102. Subject Matter.

Except as otherwise provided in Section 4A–108, this Article applies to funds transfers defined in Section 4A–104.

§ 4A–103. Payment Order—Definitions.

(a) In this Article:

(1) "Payment order" means an instruction of a sender to a receiving bank, transmitted orally, electronically, or in writing, to pay, or to cause another bank to pay, a fixed or determinable amount of money to a beneficiary if:

(i) the instruction does not state a condition to payment to the beneficiary other than time of payment,

(ii) the receiving bank is to be reimbursed by debiting an account of, or otherwise receiving payment from, the sender, and

(iii) the instruction is transmitted by the sender directly to the receiving bank or to an agent, funds-transfer system, or communication system for transmittal to the receiving bank.

(2) "Beneficiary" means the person to be paid by the beneficiary's bank.

(3) "Beneficiary's bank" means the bank identified in a payment order in which an account of the beneficiary is to be credited pursuant to the order or which otherwise is to make payment to the beneficiary if the order does not provide for payment to an account.

(4) "Receiving bank" means the bank to which the sender's instruction is addressed.

(5) "Sender" means the person giving the instruction to the receiving bank.

(b) If an instruction complying with subsection (a)(1) is to make more than one payment to a beneficiary, the instruction is a separate payment order with respect to each payment.

(c) A payment order is issued when it is sent to the receiving bank.

§ 4A–104. Funds Transfer—Definitions.

In this Article:

(a) "Funds transfer" means the series of transactions, beginning with the originator's payment order, made for the purpose of making payment to the beneficiary of the order. The term includes any payment order issued by the originator's bank or an intermediary bank intended to carry out the originator's payment order. A funds transfer is completed by acceptance by the beneficiary's bank of a payment order for the benefit of the beneficiary of the originator's payment order.

(b) "Intermediary bank" means a receiving bank other than the originator's bank or the beneficiary's bank.

(c) "Originator" means the sender of the first payment order in a funds transfer.

(d) "Originator's bank" means (i) the receiving bank to which the payment order of the originator is issued if the originator is not a bank, or (ii) the originator if the originator is a bank.

§ 4A–105. Other Definitions.

(a) In this Article:

(1) "Authorized account" means a deposit account of a customer in a bank designated by the customer as a source of payment of payment orders issued by the customer to the bank. If a customer does not so designate an account, any account of the customer is an authorized account if payment of a payment order from that account is not inconsistent with a restriction on the use of that account.

(2) "Bank" means a person engaged in the business of banking and includes a savings bank, savings and loan association, credit union, and trust company. A branch or separate office of a bank is a separate bank for purposes of this Article.

(3) "Customer" means a person, including a bank, having an account with a bank or from whom a bank has agreed to receive payment orders.

(4) "Funds-transfer business day" of a receiving bank means the part of a day during which the receiving bank is open for the receipt, processing, and transmittal of payment orders and cancellations and amendments of payment orders.

(5) "Funds-transfer system" means a wire transfer network, automated clearing house, or other communication system of a clearing house or other association of banks through which a payment order by a bank may be transmitted to the bank to which the order is addressed.

(6) "Good faith" means honesty in fact and the observance of reasonable commercial standards of fair dealing.

(7) "Prove" with respect to a fact means to meet the burden of establishing the fact (Section 1–201(8)).

(b) Other definitions applying to this Article and the sections in which they appear are:

"Acceptance" Section 4A–209
"Beneficiary" Section 4A–103
"Beneficiary's bank" Section 4A–103
"Executed" Section 4A–301
"Execution date" Section 4A–301
"Funds transfer" Section 4A–104
"Funds-transfer system rule" Section 4A–501
"Intermediary bank" Section 4A–104
"Originator" Section 4A–104
"Originator's bank" Section 4A–104
"Payment by beneficiary's bank to beneficiary" Section 4A–405
"Payment by originator to beneficiary" Section 4A–406
"Payment by sender to receiving bank" Section 4A–403
"Payment date" Section 4A–401
"Payment order" Section 4A–103
"Receiving bank" Section 4A–103
"Security procedure" Section 4A–201
"Sender" Section 4A–103

(c) The following definitions in Article 4 apply to this Article:

"Clearing house" Section 4–104
"Item" Section 4–104
"Suspends payments" Section 4–104

(d) In addition Article 1 contains general definitions and principles of construction and interpretation applicable throughout this Article.

§ 4A–106. Time Payment Order Is Received.

(a) The time of receipt of a payment order or communication cancelling or amending a payment order is determined by the rules applicable to receipt of a notice stated in Section 1–201(27). A receiving bank may fix a cut-off time or times on a funds-transfer business day for the receipt and processing of payment orders and communications cancelling or amending payment orders. Different cut-off times may apply to payment orders, cancellations, or amendments, or to different categories of payment orders, cancellations, or amendments. A cut-off time may apply to senders generally or different cut-off times may apply to different senders or categories of payment orders. If a payment order or communication cancelling or amending a payment order is received after the close of a funds-transfer business day or after the appropriate cut-off time on a funds-transfer business day, the receiving bank may treat the payment order or communication as received at the opening of the next funds-transfer business day.

(b) If this Article refers to an execution date or payment date or states a day on which a receiving bank is required to take action, and the date or day does not fall on a funds-transfer business day, the next day that is a funds-transfer business day is treated as the date or day stated, unless the contrary is stated in this Article.

§ 4A–107. Federal Reserve Regulations and Operating Circulars.

Regulations of the Board of Governors of the Federal Reserve System and operating circulars of the Federal Reserve Banks supersede any inconsistent provision of this Article to the extent of the inconsistency.

§ 4A–108. Exclusion of Consumer Transactions Governed by Federal Law.

This Article does not apply to a funds transfer any part of which is governed by the Electronic Fund Transfer Act of 1978 (Title XX, Public Law 95–630, 92 Stat. 3728, 15 U.S.C. § 1693 et seq.) as amended from time to time.

Part 2—Issue and Acceptance of Payment Order

§ 4A–201. Security Procedure.

"Security procedure" means a procedure established by agreement of a customer and a receiving bank for the purpose of (i) verifying that a payment order or communication amending or cancelling a payment order is that of the customer, or (ii) detecting error in the transmission or the content of the payment order or communication. A security procedure may require the use of algorithms or other codes, identifying words or numbers, encryption, callback procedures, or similar security devices. Comparison of a signature on a payment order or communication with an authorized specimen signature of the customer is not by itself a security procedure.

§ 4A–202. Authorized and Verified Payment Orders.

(a) A payment order received by the receiving bank is the authorized order of the person identified as sender if that person authorized the order or is otherwise bound by it under the law of agency.

(b) If a bank and its customer have agreed that the authenticity of payment orders issued to the bank in the name of the customer as sender will be verified pursuant to a security procedure, a payment order received by the receiving bank is effective as the order of the customer, whether or not authorized, if (i) the security procedure is a commercially reasonable method of providing security against unauthorized payment orders, and (ii) the bank proves that it accepted the payment order in good faith and in compliance with the security procedure and any written agreement or instruction of the customer restricting acceptance of payment orders issued in the name of the customer. The bank is not required to follow an instruction that violates a written agreement with the customer or notice of which is not received at a time and in a manner affording the bank a reasonable opportunity to act on it before the payment order is accepted.

(c) Commercial reasonableness of a security procedure is a question of law to be determined by considering the wishes of the customer expressed to the bank, the circumstances of the customer known to the bank, including the size, type, and frequency of payment orders normally issued by the customer to the bank, alternative security procedures offered to the customer, and security procedures in general use by customers and receiving banks similarly situated. A security procedure is deemed to be commercially reasonable if (i) the security procedure was chosen by the customer after the bank offered, and the customer refused, a security procedure that was commercially reasonable for that customer, and (ii) the customer expressly agreed in writing to be bound by any payment order, whether or not authorized, issued in its name and accepted by the bank in compliance with the security procedure chosen by the customer.

(d) The term "sender" in this Article includes the customer in whose name a payment order is issued if the order is the authorized order of the customer under subsection (a), or it is effective as the order of the customer under subsection (b).

(e) This section applies to amendments and cancellations of payment orders to the same extent it applies to payment orders.

(f) Except as provided in this section and in Section 4A–203(a)(1), rights and obligations arising under this section or Section 4A–203 may not be varied by agreement.

§ 4A–203. Unenforceability of Certain Verified Payment Orders.

(a) If an accepted payment order is not, under Section 4A–202(a), an authorized order of a customer identified as sender, but is effective as an order of the customer pursuant to Section 4A–202(b), the following rules apply:

(1) By express written agreement, the receiving bank may limit the extent to which it is entitled to enforce or retain payment of the payment order.

(2) The receiving bank is not entitled to enforce or retain payment of the payment order if the customer proves that the order was not caused, directly or indirectly, by a person (i) entrusted at any time with duties to act for the customer with respect to payment orders or the security procedure, or (ii) who obtained access to transmitting facilities of the customer or who obtained, from a source controlled by the customer and without authority of the receiving bank, information facilitating breach of the security procedure, regardless of how the information was obtained or whether the customer was at fault. Information includes any access device, computer software, or the like.

(b) This section applies to amendments of payment orders to the same extent it applies to payment orders.

§ 4A–204. Refund of Payment and Duty of Customer to Report with Respect to Unauthorized Payment Order.

(a) If a receiving bank accepts a payment order issued in the name of its customer as sender which is (i) not authorized and not effective as the order of the customer under Section 4A–202, or (ii) not enforceable, in whole or in part, against the customer under Section 4A–203, the bank shall refund any payment of the payment order received from the customer to the extent the bank is not entitled to enforce payment and shall pay interest on the refundable amount calculated from the date the bank received payment to the date of the refund. However, the customer is not entitled to interest from the bank on the amount to be refunded if the customer fails to exercise ordinary care to determine that the order was not authorized by the customer and to notify the bank of the relevant facts within a reasonable time not exceeding 90 days after the date the customer received notification from the bank that the order was accepted or that the customer's account was debited with respect to the order. The bank is not entitled to any recovery from the customer on account of a failure by the customer to give notification as stated in this section.

(b) Reasonable time under subsection (a) may be fixed by agreement as stated in Section 1–204(1), but the obligation of a receiving bank to refund payment as stated in subsection (a) may not otherwise be varied by agreement.

§ 4A–205. Erroneous Payment Orders.

(a) If an accepted payment order was transmitted pursuant to a security procedure for the detection of error and the payment order (i) erroneously instructed payment to a beneficiary not intended by the sender, (ii) erroneously instructed payment in an amount greater than the amount intended by the sender, or (iii) was an erroneously transmitted duplicate of a payment order previously sent by the sender, the following rules apply:

(1) If the sender proves that the sender or a person acting on behalf of the sender pursuant to Section 4A–206 complied with the security procedure and that the error would have been detected if the receiving bank had also complied, the sender is not obliged to pay the order to the extent stated in paragraphs (2) and (3).

(2) If the funds transfer is completed on the basis of an erroneous payment order described in clause (i) or (iii) of subsection (a), the sender is not obliged to pay the order and the receiving bank is entitled to recover from the beneficiary any amount paid to the beneficiary to the extent allowed by the law governing mistake and restitution.

(3) If the funds transfer is completed on the basis of a payment order described in clause (ii) of subsection (a), the sender is not obliged to pay the order to the extent the amount received by the beneficiary is greater than the amount intended by the sender. In that case, the receiving bank is entitled to recover from the beneficiary the excess amount received to the extent allowed by the law governing mistake and restitution.

(b) If (i) the sender of an erroneous payment order described in subsection (a) is not obliged to pay all or part of the order, and (ii) the sender receives notification from the receiving bank that the order was

accepted by the bank or that the sender's account was debited with respect to the order, the sender has a duty to exercise ordinary care, on the basis of information available to the sender, to discover the error with respect to the order and to advise the bank of the relevant facts within a reasonable time, not exceeding 90 days, after the bank's notification was received by the sender. If the bank proves that the sender failed to perform that duty, the sender is liable to the bank for the loss the bank proves it incurred as a result of the failure, but the liability of the sender may not exceed the amount of the sender's order.
(c) This section applies to amendments to payment orders to the same extent it applies to payment orders.

§ 4A–209. Acceptance of Payment Order.
(a) Subject to subsection (d), a receiving bank other than the beneficiary's bank accepts a payment order when it executes the order.
(b) Subject to subsections (c) and (d), a beneficiary's bank accepts a payment order at the earliest of the following times:
(1) when the bank (i) pays the beneficiary as stated in Section 4A–405(a) or 4A–405(b), or (ii) notifies the beneficiary of receipt of the order or that the account of the beneficiary has been credited with respect to the order unless the notice indicates that the bank is rejecting the order or that funds with respect to the order may not be withdrawn or used until receipt of payment from the sender of the order;
(2) when the bank receives payment of the entire amount of the sender's order pursuant to Section 4A–403(a)(1) or 4A–403(a)(2); or
(3) the opening of the next funds-transfer business day of the bank following the payment date of the order if, at that time, the amount of the sender's order is fully covered by a withdrawable credit balance in an authorized account of the sender or the bank has otherwise received full payment from the sender, unless the order was rejected before that time or is rejected within (i) one hour after that time, or (ii) one hour after the opening of the next business day of the sender following the payment date if that time is later. If notice of rejection is received by the sender after the payment date and the authorized account of the sender does not bear interest, the bank is obliged to pay interest to the sender on the amount of the order for the number of days elapsing after the payment date to the day the sender receives notice or learns that the order was not accepted, counting that day as an elapsed day. If the withdrawable credit balance during that period falls below the amount of the order, the amount of interest payable is reduced accordingly.
(c) Acceptance of a payment order cannot occur before the order is received by the receiving bank. Acceptance does not occur under subsection (b)(2) or (b)(3) if the beneficiary of the payment order does not have an account with the receiving bank, the account has been closed, or the receiving bank is not permitted by law to receive credits for the beneficiary's account.
(d) A payment order issued to the originator's bank cannot be accepted until the payment date if the bank is the beneficiary's bank, or the execution date if the bank is not the beneficiary's bank. If the originator's bank executes the originator's payment order before the execution date or pays the beneficiary of the originator's payment order before the payment date and the payment order is subsequently canceled pursuant to Section 4A–211(b), the bank may recover from the beneficiary any payment received to the extent allowed by the law governing mistake and restitution.

Part 3—Execution of Sender's Payment Order by Receiving Bank
§ 4A–301. Execution and Execution Date.
(a) A payment order is "executed" by the receiving bank when it issues a payment order intended to carry out the payment order received by the bank. A payment order received by the beneficiary's bank can be accepted but cannot be executed.
(b) "Execution date" of a payment order means the day on which the receiving bank may properly issue a payment order in execution of the sender's order. The execution date may be determined by instruction of the sender but cannot be earlier than the day the order is received and, unless otherwise determined, is the day the order is received. If the sender's instruction states a payment date, the execution date is the payment date or an earlier date on which execution is reasonably necessary to allow payment to the beneficiary on the payment date.

§ 4A–302. Obligations of Receiving Bank in Execution of Payment Order.
(a) Except as provided in subsections (b) through (d), if the receiving bank accepts a payment order pursuant to Section 4A–209(a), the bank has the following obligations in executing the order:
(1) The receiving bank is obliged to issue, on the execution date, a payment order complying with the sender's order and to follow the sender's instructions concerning (i) any intermediary bank or funds-transfer system to be used in carrying out the funds transfer, or (ii) the means by which payment orders are to be transmitted in the funds transfer. If the originator's bank issues a payment order to an intermediary bank, the originator's bank is obliged to instruct the intermediary bank according to the instruction of the originator. An intermediary bank in the funds transfer is similarly bound by an instruction given to it by the sender of the payment order it accepts.
(2) If the sender's instruction states that the funds transfer is to be carried out telephonically or by wire transfer or otherwise indicates that the funds transfer is to be carried out by the most expeditious means, the receiving bank is obliged to transmit its payment order by the most expeditious available means, and to instruct any intermediary bank accordingly. If a sender's instruction states a payment date, the receiving bank is obliged to transmit its payment order at a time and by means reasonably necessary to allow payment to the beneficiary on the payment date or as soon thereafter as is feasible.
(b) Unless otherwise instructed, a receiving bank executing a payment order may (i) use any funds-transfer system if use of that system is reasonable in the circumstances, and (ii) issue a payment order to the beneficiary's bank or to an intermediary bank through which a payment order conforming to the sender's order can expeditiously be issued to the beneficiary's bank if the receiving bank exercises ordinary care in the selection of the intermediary bank. A receiving bank is not required to follow an instruction of the sender designating a funds-transfer system to be used in carrying out the funds transfer if the receiving bank, in good faith, determines that it is not feasible to follow the instruction or that following the instruction would unduly delay completion of the funds transfer.
(c) Unless subsection (a)(2) applies or the receiving bank is otherwise instructed, the bank may execute a payment order by transmitting its payment order by first class mail or by any means reasonable in the circumstances. If the receiving bank is instructed to execute the sender's order by transmitting its payment order by a particular means, the receiving bank may issue its payment order by the means stated or by any means as expeditious as the means stated.
(d) Unless instructed by the sender, (i) the receiving bank may not obtain payment of its charges for services and expenses in connection with the execution of the sender's order by issuing a payment order in an amount equal to the amount of the sender's order less the amount of the charges, and (ii) may not instruct a subsequent receiving bank to obtain payment of its charges in the same manner.

§ 4A–303. Erroneous Execution of Payment Order.
(a) A receiving bank that (i) executes the payment order of the sender by issuing a payment order in an amount greater than the amount of the sender's order, or (ii) issues a payment order in execution of the sender's order and then issues a duplicate order, is entitled to payment of the amount of the sender's order under Section 4A–402(c) if

that subsection is otherwise satisfied. The bank is entitled to recover from the beneficiary of the erroneous order the excess payment received to the extent allowed by the law governing mistake and restitution.

(b) A receiving bank that executes the payment order of the sender by issuing a payment order in an amount less than the amount of the sender's order is entitled to payment of the amount of the sender's order under Section 4A–402(c) if (i) that subsection is otherwise satisfied and (ii) the bank corrects its mistake by issuing an additional payment order for the benefit of the beneficiary of the sender's order. If the error is not corrected, the issuer of the erroneous order is entitled to receive or retain payment from the sender of the order it accepted only to the extent of the amount of the erroneous order. This subsection does not apply if the receiving bank executes the sender's payment order by issuing a payment order in an amount less than the amount of the sender's order for the purpose of obtaining payment of its charges for services and expenses pursuant to instruction of the sender.

(c) If a receiving bank executes the payment order of the sender by issuing a payment order to a beneficiary different from the beneficiary of the sender's order and the funds transfer is completed on the basis of that error, the sender of the payment order that was erroneously executed and all previous senders in the funds transfer are not obliged to pay the payment orders they issued. The issuer of the erroneous order is entitled to recover from the beneficiary of the order the payment received to the extent allowed by the law governing mistake and restitution.

§ 4A–304. Duty of Sender to Report Erroneously Executed Payment Order.

If the sender of a payment order that is erroneously executed as stated in Section 4A–303 receives notification from the receiving bank that the order was executed or that the sender's account was debited with respect to the order, the sender has a duty to exercise ordinary care to determine, on the basis of information available to the sender, that the order was erroneously executed and to notify the bank of the relevant facts within a reasonable time not exceeding 90 days after the notification from the bank was received by the sender. If the sender fails to perform that duty, the bank is not obliged to pay interest on any amount refundable to the sender under Section 4A–402(d) for the period before the bank learns of the execution error. The bank is not entitled to any recovery from the sender on account of a failure by the sender to perform the duty stated in this section.

§ 4A–305. Liability for Late or Improper Execution or Failure to Execute Payment Order.

(a) If a funds transfer is completed but execution of a payment order by the receiving bank in breach of Section 4A–302 results in delay in payment to the beneficiary, the bank is obliged to pay interest to either the originator or the beneficiary of the funds transfer for the period of delay caused by the improper execution. Except as provided in subsection (c), additional damages are not recoverable.

(b) If execution of a payment order by a receiving bank in breach of Section 4A–302 results in (i) noncompletion of the funds transfer, (ii) failure to use an intermediary bank designated by the originator, or (iii) issuance of a payment order that does not comply with the terms of the payment order of the originator, the bank is liable to the originator for its expenses in the funds transfer and for incidental expenses and interest losses, to the extent not covered by subsection (a), resulting from the improper execution. Except as provided in subsection (c), additional damages are not recoverable.

(c) In addition to the amounts payable under subsections (a) and (b), damages, including consequential damages, are recoverable to the extent provided in an express written agreement of the receiving bank.

(d) If a receiving bank fails to execute a payment order it was obliged by express agreement to execute, the receiving bank is liable to the sender for its expenses in the transaction and for incidental expenses and interest losses resulting from the failure to execute. Additional damages, including consequential damages, are recoverable to the extent provided in an express written agreement of the receiving bank, but are not otherwise recoverable.

(e) Reasonable attorney's fees are recoverable if demand for compensation under subsection (a) or (b) is made and refused before an action is brought on the claim. If a claim is made for breach of an agreement under subsection (d) and the agreement does not provide for damages, reasonable attorney's fees are recoverable if demand for compensation under subsection (d) is made and refused before an action is brought on the claim.

(f) Except as stated in this section, the liability of a receiving bank under subsections (a) and (b) may not be varied by agreement.

Part 4—Payment

§ 4A–401. Payment Date.

"Payment date" of a payment order means the day on which the amount of the order is payable to the beneficiary by the beneficiary's bank. The payment date may be determined by instruction of the sender but cannot be earlier than the day the order is received by the beneficiary's bank and, unless otherwise determined, is the day the order is received by the beneficiary's bank.

§ 4A–402. Obligation of Sender to Pay Receiving Bank.

(a) This section is subject to Sections 4A–205 and 4A–207.

(b) With respect to a payment order issued to the beneficiary's bank, acceptance of the order by the bank obliges the sender to pay the bank the amount of the order, but payment is not due until the payment date of the order.

(c) This subsection is subject to subsection (e) and to Section 4A–303. With respect to a payment order issued to a receiving bank other than the beneficiary's bank, acceptance of the order by the receiving bank obliges the sender to pay the bank the amount of the sender's order. Payment by the sender is not due until the execution date of the sender's order. The obligation of that sender to pay its payment order is excused if the funds transfer is not completed by acceptance by the beneficiary's bank of a payment order instructing payment to the beneficiary of that sender's payment order.

(d) If the sender of a payment order pays the order and was not obliged to pay all or part of the amount paid, the bank receiving payment is obliged to refund payment to the extent the sender was not obliged to pay. Except as provided in Sections 4A–204 and 4A–304, interest is payable on the refundable amount from the date of payment.

(e) If a funds transfer is not completed as stated in subsection (c) and an intermediary bank is obliged to refund payment as stated in subsection (d) but is unable to do so because not permitted by applicable law or because the bank suspends payments, a sender in the funds transfer that executed a payment order in compliance with an instruction, as stated in Section 4A–302(a)(1), to route the funds transfer through that intermediary bank is entitled to receive or retain payment from the sender of the payment order that it accepted. The first sender in the funds transfer that issued an instruction requiring routing through that intermediary bank is subrogated to the right of the bank that paid the intermediary bank to refund as stated in subsection (d).

(f) The right of the sender of a payment order to be excused from the obligation to pay the order as stated in subsection (c) or to receive refund under subsection (d) may not be varied by agreement.

§ 4A–403. Payment by Sender to Receiving Bank.

(a) Payment of the sender's obligation under Section 4A–402 to pay the receiving bank occurs as follows:

(1) If the sender is a bank, payment occurs when the receiving bank receives final settlement of the obligation through a Federal Reserve Bank or through a funds-transfer system.

(2) If the sender is a bank and the sender (i) credited an account of the receiving bank with the sender, or (ii) caused an account of the receiving bank in another bank to be credited, payment occurs when the credit is withdrawn or, if not withdrawn, at midnight of the day on which the credit is withdrawable and the receiving bank learns of that fact.

(3) If the receiving bank debits an account of the sender with the receiving bank, payment occurs when the debit is made to the extent the debit is covered by a withdrawable credit balance in the account.

(b) If the sender and receiving bank are members of a funds-transfer system that nets obligations multilaterally among participants, the receiving bank receives final settlement when settlement is complete in accordance with the rules of the system. The obligation of the sender to pay the amount of a payment order transmitted through the funds-transfer system may be satisfied, to the extent permitted by the rules of the system, by setting off and applying against the sender's obligation the right of the sender to receive payment from the receiving bank of the amount of any other payment order transmitted to the sender by the receiving bank through the funds-transfer system. The aggregate balance of obligations owed by each sender to each receiving bank in the funds-transfer system may be satisfied, to the extent permitted by the rules of the system, by setting off and applying against that balance the aggregate balance of obligations owed to the sender by other members of the system. The aggregate balance is determined after the right of setoff stated in the second sentence of this subsection has been exercised.

(c) If two banks transmit payment orders to each other under an agreement that settlement of the obligations of each bank to the other under Section 4A–402 will be made at the end of the day or other period, the total amount owed with respect to all orders transmitted by one bank shall be set off against the total amount owed with respect to all orders transmitted by the other bank. To the extent of the setoff, each bank has made payment to the other.

(d) In a case not covered by subsection (a), the time when payment of the sender's obligation under Section 4A–402(b) or 4A–402(c) occurs is governed by applicable principles of law that determine when an obligation is satisfied.

§ 4A–404. Obligation of Beneficiary's Bank to Pay and Give Notice to Beneficiary.

(a) Subject to Sections 4A–211(e), 4A–405(d), and 4A–405(e), if a beneficiary's bank accepts a payment order, the bank is obliged to pay the amount of the order to the beneficiary of the order. Payment is due on the payment date of the order, but if acceptance occurs on the payment date after the close of the funds-transfer business day of the bank, payment is due on the next funds-transfer business day. If the bank refuses to pay after demand by the beneficiary and receipt of notice of particular circumstances that will give rise to consequential damages as a result of nonpayment, the beneficiary may recover damages resulting from the refusal to pay to the extent the bank had notice of the damages, unless the bank proves that it did not pay because of a reasonable doubt concerning the right of the beneficiary to payment.

(b) If a payment order accepted by the beneficiary's bank instructs payment to an account of the beneficiary, the bank is obliged to notify the beneficiary of receipt of the order before midnight of the next funds-transfer business day following the payment date. If the payment order does not instruct payment to an account of the beneficiary, the bank is required to notify the beneficiary only if notice is required by the order. Notice may be given by first class mail or any other means reasonable in the circumstances. If the bank fails to give the required notice, the bank is obliged to pay interest to the beneficiary on the amount of the payment order from the day notice should have been given until the day the beneficiary learned of receipt of the payment order by the bank. No other damages are recoverable. Reasonable attorney's fees are also recoverable if demand for interest is made and refused before an action is brought on the claim.

(c) The right of a beneficiary to receive payment and damages as stated in subsection (a) may not be varied by agreement or a funds-transfer system rule. The right of a beneficiary to be notified as stated in subsection (b) may be varied by agreement of the beneficiary or by a funds-transfer system rule if the beneficiary is notified of the rule before initiation of the funds transfer.

§ 4A–405. Payment by Beneficiary's Bank to Beneficiary.

(a) If the beneficiary's bank credits an account of the beneficiary of a payment order, payment of the bank's obligation under Section 4A–404(a) occurs when and to the extent (i) the beneficiary is notified of the right to withdraw the credit, (ii) the bank lawfully applies the credit to a debt of the beneficiary, or (iii) funds with respect to the order are otherwise made available to the beneficiary by the bank.

(b) If the beneficiary's bank does not credit an account of the beneficiary of a payment order, the time when payment of the bank's obligation under Section 4A–404(a) occurs is governed by principles of law that determine when an obligation is satisfied.

(c) Except as stated in subsections (d) and (e), if the beneficiary's bank pays the beneficiary of a payment order under a condition to payment or agreement of the beneficiary giving the bank the right to recover payment from the beneficiary if the bank does not receive payment of the order, the condition to payment or agreement is not enforceable.

(d) A funds-transfer system rule may provide that payments made to beneficiaries of funds transfers made through the system are provisional until receipt of payment by the beneficiary's bank of the payment order it accepted. A beneficiary's bank that makes a payment that is provisional under the rule is entitled to refund from the beneficiary if (i) the rule requires that both the beneficiary and the originator be given notice of the provisional nature of the payment before the funds transfer is initiated, (ii) the beneficiary, the beneficiary's bank and the originator's bank agreed to be bound by the rule, and (iii) the beneficiary's bank did not receive payment of the payment order that it accepted. If the beneficiary is obliged to refund payment to the beneficiary's bank, acceptance of the payment order by the beneficiary's bank is nullified and no payment by the originator of the funds transfer to the beneficiary occurs under Section 4A–406.

(e) This subsection applies to a funds transfer that includes a payment order transmitted over a funds-transfer system that (i) nets obligations multilaterally among participants, and (ii) has in effect a loss-sharing agreement among participants for the purpose of providing funds necessary to complete settlement of the obligations of one or more participants that do not meet their settlement obligations. If the beneficiary's bank in the funds transfer accepts a payment order and the system fails to complete settlement pursuant to its rules with respect to any payment order in the funds transfer, (i) the acceptance by the beneficiary's bank is nullified and no person has any right or obligation based on the acceptance, (ii) the beneficiary's bank is entitled to recover payment from the beneficiary, (iii) no payment by the originator to the beneficiary occurs under Section 4A–406, and (iv) subject to Section 4A–402(e), each sender in the funds transfer is excused from its obligation to pay its payment order under Section 4A–402 (c) because the funds transfer has not been completed.

§ 4A–406. Payment by Originator to Beneficiary; Discharge of Underlying Obligation.

(a) Subject to Sections 4A–211(e), 4A–405(d), and 4A–405(e), the originator of a funds transfer pays the beneficiary of the originator's payment order (i) at the time a payment order for the benefit of the beneficiary is accepted by the beneficiary's bank in the funds transfer and (ii) in an amount equal to the amount of the order accepted by the beneficiary's bank, but not more than the amount of the originator's order.

(b) If payment under subsection (a) is made to satisfy an obligation, the obligation is discharged to the same extent discharge would result from payment to the beneficiary of the same amount in money, unless (i) the

payment under subsection (a) was made by a means prohibited by the contract of the beneficiary with respect to the obligation, (ii) the beneficiary, within a reasonable time after receiving notice of receipt of the order by the beneficiary's bank, notified the originator of the beneficiary's refusal of the payment, (iii) funds with respect to the order were not withdrawn by the beneficiary or applied to a debt of the beneficiary, and (iv) the beneficiary would suffer a loss that could reasonably have been avoided if payment had been made by a means complying with the contract. If payment by the originator does not result in discharge under this section, the originator is subrogated to the rights of the beneficiary to receive payment from the beneficiary's bank under Section 4A–404(a).
(c) For the purpose of determining whether discharge of an obligation occurs under subsection (b), if the beneficiary's bank accepts a payment order in an amount equal to the amount of the originator's payment order less charges of one or more receiving banks in the funds transfer, payment to the beneficiary is deemed to be in the amount of the originator's order unless upon demand by the beneficiary the originator does not pay the beneficiary the amount of the deducted charges.
(d) Rights of the originator or of the beneficiary of a funds transfer under this section may be varied only by agreement of the originator and the beneficiary.

ARTICLE 7: WAREHOUSE RECEIPTS, BILLS OF LADING AND OTHER DOCUMENTS OF TITLE

Part 1—General

§ 7–101. Short Title.
This Article shall be known and may be cited as Uniform Commercial Code—Documents of Title.

§ 7–102. Definitions and Index of Definitions.
(1) In this Article, unless the context otherwise requires:

(a) "Bailee" means the person who by a warehouse receipt, bill of lading or other document of title acknowledges possession of goods and contracts to deliver them.
(b) "Consignee" means the person named in a bill to whom or to whose order the bill promises delivery.
(c) "Consignor" means the person named in a bill as the person from whom the goods have been received for shipment.
(d) "Delivery order" means a written order to deliver goods directed to a warehouseman, carrier or other person who in the ordinary course of business issues warehouse receipts or bills of lading.
(e) "Document" means document of title as defined in the general definitions in Article 1 (Section 1–201).
(f) "Goods" means all things which are treated as movable for the purposes of a contract of storage or transportation.
(g) "Issuer" means a bailee who issues a document except that in relation to an unaccepted delivery order it means the person who orders the possessor of goods to deliver. Issuer includes any person for whom an agent or employee purports to act in issuing a document if the agent or employee has real or apparent authority to issue documents, notwithstanding that the issuer received no goods or that the goods were misdescribed or that in any other respect the agent or employee violated his instructions.
(h) "Warehouseman" is a person engaged in the business of storing goods for hire.

(2) Other definitions applying to this Article or to specified Parts thereof, and the sections in which they appear are:

"Duly negotiate". Section 7–501.
"Person entitled under the document". Section 7– 403(4).

(3) Definitions in other Articles applying to this Article and the sections in which they appear are:

"Contract for sale". Section 2–106.
"Overseas". Section 2–323.
"Receipt" of goods. Section 2–103.

(4) In addition Article 1 contains general definitions and principles of construction and interpretation applicable throughout this Article.

§ 7–104. Negotiable and Non-Negotiable Warehouse Receipt, Bill of Lading or Other Document of Title.
(1) A warehouse receipt, bill of lading or other document of title is negotiable

(a) if by its terms the goods are to be delivered to bearer or to the order of a named person; or
(b) where recognized in overseas trade, if it runs to a named person or assigns.

(2) Any other document is non-negotiable. A bill of lading in which it is stated that the goods are consigned to a named person is not made negotiable by a provision that the goods are to be delivered only against a written order signed by the same or another named person.

Part 2—Warehouse Receipts: Special Provisions

§ 7–201. Who May Issue a Warehouse Receipt; Storage Under Government Bond.
(1) A warehouse receipt may be issued by any warehouseman.
(2) Where goods including distilled spirits and agricultural commodities are stored under a statute requiring a bond against withdrawal or a license for the issuance of receipts in the nature of warehouse receipts, a receipt issued for the goods has like effect as a warehouse receipt even though issued by a person who is the owner of the goods and is not a warehouseman.

§ 7–202. Form of Warehouse Receipt; Essential Terms; Optional Terms.
(1) A warehouse receipt need not be in any particular form.
(2) Unless a warehouse receipt embodies within its written or printed terms each of the following, the warehouseman is liable for damages caused by the omission to a person injured thereby:

(a) the location of the warehouse where the goods are stored;
(b) the date of issue of the receipt;
(c) the consecutive number of the receipt;
(d) a statement whether the goods received will be delivered to the bearer, to a specified person, or to a specified person or his order;
(e) the rate of storage and handling charges, except that where goods are stored under a field warehousing arrangement a statement of that fact is sufficient on a non-negotiable receipt;
(f) a description of the goods or of the packages containing them;
(g) the signature of the warehouseman, which may be made by his authorized agent;
(h) if the receipt is issued for goods of which the warehouseman is owner, either solely or jointly or in common with others, the fact of such ownership; and
(i) a statement of the amount of advances made and of liabilities incurred for which the warehouseman claims a lien or security interest (Section 7–209). If the precise amount of such advances made or of such liabilities incurred is, at the time of the issue of the receipt, unknown to the warehouseman or to his agent who issues it, a statement of the fact that advances have been made or liabilities incurred and the purpose thereof is sufficient.

(3) A warehouseman may insert in his receipt any other terms which are not contrary to the provisions of this Act and do not impair his obligation of delivery (Section 7–403) or his duty of care (Section 7–204). Any contrary provisions shall be ineffective.

§ 7–204. Duty of Care; Contractual Limitation of Warehouseman's Liability.
(1) A warehouseman is liable for damages for loss of or injury to the goods caused by his failure to exercise such care in regard to them as a reasonably careful man would exercise under like circumstances but unless otherwise agreed he is not liable for damages which could not have been avoided by the exercise of such care.

(2) Damages may be limited by a term in the warehouse receipt or storage agreement limiting the amount of liability in case of loss or damage, and setting forth a specific liability per article or item, or value per unit of weight, beyond which the warehouseman shall not be liable; provided, however, that such liability may on written request of the bailor at the time of signing such storage agreement or within a reasonable time after receipt of the warehouse receipt be increased on part or all of the goods thereunder, in which event increased rates may be charged based on such increased valuation, but that no such increase shall be permitted contrary to a lawful limitation of liability contained in the warehouseman's tariff, if any. No such limitation is effective with respect to the warehouseman's liability for conversion to his own use.
(3) Reasonable provisions as to the time and manner of presenting claims and instituting actions based on the bailment may be included in the warehouse receipt or tariff.
(4) This section does not impair or repeal . . .

Note: *Insert in subsection (4) a reference to any statute which imposes a higher responsibility upon the warehouseman or invalidates contractual limitations which would be permissible under this Article.*

§ 7–206. Termination of Storage at Warehouseman's Option.
(1) A warehouseman may on notifying the person on whose account the goods are held and any other person known to claim an interest in the goods require payment of any charges and removal of the goods from the warehouse at the termination of the period of storage fixed by the document, or, if no period is fixed, within a stated period not less than thirty days after the notification. If the goods are not removed before the date specified in the notification, the warehouseman may sell them in accordance with the provisions of the section on enforcement of a warehouseman's lien (Section 7–210).
(2) If a warehouseman in good faith believes that the goods are about to deteriorate or decline in value to less than the amount of his lien within the time prescribed in subsection (1) for notification, advertisement and sale, the warehouseman may specify in the notification any reasonable shorter time for removal of the goods and in case the goods are not removed, may sell them at public sale held not less than one week after a single advertisement or posting.
(3) If as a result of a quality or condition of the goods of which the warehouseman had no notice at the time of deposit the goods are a hazard to other property or to the warehouse or to persons, the warehouseman may sell the goods at public or private sale without advertisement on reasonable notification to all persons known to claim an interest in the goods. If the warehouseman after a reasonable effort is unable to sell the goods he may dispose of them in any lawful manner and shall incur no liability by reason of such disposition.
(4) The warehouseman must deliver the goods to any person entitled to them under this Article upon due demand made at any time prior to sale or other disposition under this section.
(5) The warehouseman may satisfy his lien from the proceeds of any sale or disposition under this section but must hold the balance for delivery on the demand of any person to whom he would have been bound to deliver the goods.

§ 7–207. Goods Must Be Kept Separate; Fungible Goods.
(1) Unless the warehouse receipt otherwise provides, a warehouseman must keep separate the goods covered by each receipt so as to permit at all times identification and delivery of those goods except that different lots of fungible goods may be commingled.
(2) Fungible goods so commingled are owned in common by the persons entitled thereto and the warehouseman is severally liable to each owner for that owner's share. Where because of overissue a mass of fungible goods is insufficient to meet all the receipts which the warehouseman has issued against it, the persons entitled include all holders to whom overissued receipts have been duly negotiated.

§ 7–209. Lien of Warehouseman.
(1) A warehouseman has a lien against the bailor on the goods covered by a warehouse receipt or on the proceeds thereof in his possession for charges for storage or transportation (including demurrage and terminal charges), insurance, labor, or charges present or future in relation to the goods, and for expenses necessary for preservation of the goods or reasonably incurred in their sale pursuant to law. If the person on whose account the goods are held is liable for like charges or expenses in relation to other goods whenever deposited and it is stated in the receipt that a lien is claimed for charges and expenses in relation to other goods, the warehouseman also has a lien against him for such charges and expenses whether or not the other goods have been delivered by the warehouseman. But against a person to whom a negotiable warehouse receipt is duly negotiated a warehouseman's lien is limited to charges in an amount or at a rate specified on the receipt or if no charges are so specified then to a reasonable charge for storage of the goods covered by the receipt subsequent to the date of the receipt.
(2) The warehouseman may also reserve a security interest against the bailor for a maximum amount specified on the receipt for charges other than those specified in subsection (1), such as for money advanced and interest. Such a security interest is governed by the Article on Secured Transactions (Article 9).
(3) (a) A warehouseman's lien for charges and expenses under subsection (1) or a security interest under subsection (2) is also effective against any person who so entrusted the bailor with possession of the goods that a pledge of them by him to a good faith purchaser for value would have been valid but is not effective against a person as to whom the document confers no right in the goods covered by it under Section 7–503.

(b) A warehouseman's lien on household goods for charges and expenses in relation to the goods under subsection (1) is also effective against all persons if the depositor was a legal possessor of the goods at the time of deposit. "Household goods" means furniture, furnishings and personal effects used by the depositor in a dwelling.
(4) A warehouseman loses his lien on any goods which he voluntarily delivers or which he unjustifiably refuses to deliver.

Part 3—Bills of Lading: Special Provisions
§ 7–301. Liability for Non-Receipt or Misdescription; "Said to Contain"; "Shipper's Load and Count"; Improper Handling.
(1) A consignee of a non-negotiable bill who has given value in good faith or a holder to whom a negotiable bill has been duly negotiated relying in either case upon the description therein of the goods, or upon the date therein shown, may recover from the issuer damages caused by the misdating of the bill or the non-receipt or misdescription of the goods, except to the extent that the document indicates that the issuer does not know whether any part of all of the goods in fact were received or conform to the description, as where the description is in terms of marks or labels or kind, quantity, or condition or the receipt or description is qualified by "contents or condition of contents of packages unknown", "said to contain", "shipper's weight, load and count" or the like, if such indication be true.
(2) When goods are loaded by an issuer who is a common carrier, the issuer must count the packages of goods if package freight and ascertain the kind and quantity if bulk freight. In such cases "shipper's weight, load and count" or other words indicating that the description was made by the shipper are ineffective except as to freight concealed by packages.
(3) When bulk freight is loaded by a shipper who makes available to the issuer adequate facilities for weighing such freight, an issuer who is a common carrier must ascertain the kind and quantity within a reasonable time after receiving the written request of the shipper to do so. In such cases "shipper's weight" or other words of like purport are ineffective.

(4) The issuer may by inserting in the bill the words "shipper's weight, load and count" or other words of like purport indicate that the goods were loaded by the shipper; and if such statement be true the issuer shall not be liable for damages caused by the improper loading. But their omission does not imply liability for such damages.
(5) The shipper shall be deemed to have guaranteed to the issuer the accuracy at the time of shipment of the description, marks, labels, number, kind, quantity, condition and weight, as furnished by him; and the shipper shall indemnify the issuer against damage caused by inaccuracies in such particulars. The right of the issuer to such indemnity shall in no way limit his responsibility and liability under the contract of carriage to any person other than the shipper.

§ 7–302. Through Bills of Lading and Similar Documents.
(1) The issuer of a through bill of lading or other document embodying an undertaking to be performed in part by persons acting as its agents or by connecting carriers is liable to anyone entitled to recover on the document for any breach by such other persons or by a connecting carrier of its obligation under the document but to the extent that the bill covers an undertaking to be performed overseas or in territory not contiguous to the continental United States or an undertaking including matters other than transportation this liability may be varied by agreement of the parties.
(2) Where goods covered by a through bill of lading or other document embodying an undertaking to be performed in part by persons other than the issuer are received by any such person, he is subject with respect to his own performance while the goods are in his possession to the obligation of the issuer. His obligation is discharged by delivery of the goods to another such person pursuant to the document, and does not include liability for breach by any other such persons or by the issuer.
(3) The issuer of such through bill of lading or other document shall be entitled to recover from the connecting carrier or such other person in possession of the goods when the breach of the obligation under the document occurred, the amount it may be required to pay to anyone entitled to recover on the document therefor, as may be evidenced by any receipt, judgment, or transcript thereof, and the amount of any expense reasonably incurred by it in defending any action brought by anyone entitled to recover on the document therefor.

§ 7–307. Lien of Carrier.
(1) A carrier has a lien on the goods covered by a bill of lading for charges subsequent to the date of its receipt of the goods for storage or transportation (including demurrage and terminal charges) and for expenses necessary for preservation of the goods incident to their transportation or reasonably incurred in their sale pursuant to law. But against a purchaser for value of a negotiable bill of lading a carrier's lien is limited to charges stated in the bill or the applicable tariffs, or if no charges are stated then to a reasonable charge.
(2) A lien for charges and expenses under subsection (1) on goods which the carrier was required by law to receive for transportation is effective against the consignor or any person entitled to the goods unless the carrier had notice that the consignor lacked authority to subject the goods to such charges and expenses. Any other lien under subsection (1) is effective against the consignor and any person who permitted the bailor to have control or possession of the goods unless the carrier had notice that the bailor lacked such authority.
(3) A carrier loses his lien on any goods which he voluntarily delivers or which he unjustifiably refuses to deliver.

§ 7–308. Enforcement of Carrier's Lien.
(1) A carrier's lien may be enforced by public or private sale of the goods, in bloc or in parcels, at any time or place and on any terms which are commercially reasonable, after notifying all persons known to claim an interest in the goods. Such notification must include a statement of the amount due, the nature of the proposed sale and the time and place of any public sale. The fact that a better price could have been obtained by a sale at a different time or in a different method from that selected by the carrier is not of itself sufficient to establish that the sale was not made in a commercially reasonable manner. If the carrier either sells the goods in the usual manner in any recognized market therefor or if he sells at the price current in such market at the time of his sale or if he has otherwise sold in conformity with commercially reasonable practices among dealers in the type of goods sold he has sold in a commercially reasonable manner. A sale of more goods than apparently necessary to be offered to ensure satisfaction of the obligation is not commercially reasonable except in cases covered by the preceding sentence.
(2) Before any sale pursuant to this section any person claiming a right in the goods may pay the amount necessary to satisfy the lien and the reasonable expenses incurred under this section. In that event the goods must not be sold, but must be retained by the carrier subject to the terms of the bill and this Article.
(3) The carrier may buy at any public sale pursuant to this section.
(4) A purchaser in good faith of goods sold to enforce a carrier's lien takes the goods free of any rights of persons against whom the lien was valid, despite noncompliance by the carrier with the requirements of this section.
(5) The carrier may satisfy his lien from the proceeds of any sale pursuant to this section but must hold the balance, if any, for delivery on demand to any person to whom he would have been bound to deliver the goods.
(6) The rights provided by this section shall be in addition to all other rights allowed by law to a creditor against his debtor.
(7) A carrier's lien may be enforced in accordance with either subsection (1) or the procedure set forth in subsection (2) of Section 7–210.
(8) The carrier is liable for damages caused by failure to comply with the requirements for sale under this section and in case of willful violation is liable for conversion.

§ 7–309. Duty of Care; Contractual Limitation of Carrier's Liability.
(1) A carrier who issues a bill of lading whether negotiable or non-negotiable must exercise the degree of care in relation to the goods which a reasonably careful man would exercise under like circumstances. This subsection does not repeal or change any law or rule of law which imposes liability upon a common carrier for damages not caused by its negligence.
(2) Damages may be limited by a provision that the carrier's liability shall not exceed a value stated in the document if the carrier's rates are dependent upon value and the consignor by the carrier's tariff is afforded an opportunity to declare a higher value or a value as lawfully provided in the tariff, or where no tariff is filed he is otherwise advised of such opportunity; but no such limitation is effective with respect to the carrier's liability for conversion to its own use.
(3) Reasonable provisions as to the time and manner of presenting claims and instituting actions based on the shipment may be included in a bill of lading or tariff.

Part 4—Warehouse Receipts and Bills of Lading: General Obligations
§ 7–401. Irregularities in Issue of Receipt or Bill or Conduct of Issuer.
The obligations imposed by this Article on an issuer apply to a document of title regardless of the fact that
(a) the document may not comply with the requirements of this Article or of any other law or regulation regarding its issue, form or content; or
(b) the issuer may have violated laws regulating the conduct of his business; or
(c) the goods covered by the document were owned by the bailee at the time the document was issued; or
(d) the person issuing the document does not come within the definition of warehouseman if it purports to be a warehouse receipt.

§ 7-402. Duplicate Receipt or Bill; Overissue.
Neither a duplicate nor any other document of title purporting to cover goods already represented by an outstanding document of the same issuer confers any right in the goods, except as provided in the case of bills in a set, overissue of documents for fungible goods and substitutes for lost, stolen or destroyed documents. But the issuer is liable for damages caused by his overissue or failure to identify a duplicate document as such by conspicuous notation on its face.

§ 7-403. Obligation of Warehouseman or Carrier to Deliver; Excuse.
(1) The bailee must deliver the goods to a person entitled under the document who complies with subsections (2) and (3), unless and to the extent that the bailee establishes any of the following:

(a) delivery of the goods to a person whose receipt was rightful as against the claimant;

(b) damage to or delay, loss or destruction of the goods for which the bailee is not liable [, but the burden of establishing negligence in such cases is on the person entitled under the document];

Note: *The brackets in (1)(b) indicate that State enactments may differ on this point without serious damage to the principle of uniformity.*

(c) previous sale or other disposition of the goods in lawful enforcement of a lien or on warehouseman's lawful termination of storage;

(d) the exercise by a seller of his right to stop delivery pursuant to the provisions of the Article on Sales (Section 2–705);

(e) a diversion, reconsignment or other disposition pursuant to the provisions of this Article (Section 7–303) or tariff regulating such right;

(f) release, satisfaction or any other fact affording a personal defense against the claimant;

(g) any other lawful excuse.

(2) A person claiming goods covered by a document of title must satisfy the bailee's lien where the bailee so requests or where the bailee is prohibited by law from delivering the goods until the charges are paid.

(3) Unless the person claiming is one against whom the document confers no right under Sec. 7–503(1), he must surrender for cancellation or notation of partial deliveries any outstanding negotiable document covering the goods, and the bailee must cancel the document or conspicuously note the partial delivery thereon or be liable to any person to whom the document is duly negotiated.

(4) "Person entitled under the document" means holder in the case of a negotiable document, or the person to whom delivery is to be made by the terms of or pursuant to written instructions under a non-negotiable document.

§ 7-404. No Liability for Good Faith Delivery Pursuant to Receipt or Bill.
A bailee who in good faith including observance of reasonable commercial standards has received goods and delivered or otherwise disposed of them according to the terms of the document of title or pursuant to this Article is not liable therefor. This rule applies even though the person from whom he received the goods had no authority to procure the document or to dispose of the goods and even though the person to whom he delivered the goods had no authority to receive them.

Part 5—Warehouse Receipts and Bills of Lading: Negotiation and Transfer

§ 7-501. Form of Negotiation and Requirements of "Due Negotiation."
(1) A negotiable document of title running to the order of a named person is negotiated by his indorsement and delivery. After his indorsement in blank or to bearer any person can negotiate it by delivery alone.

(2) (a) A negotiable document of title is also negotiated by delivery alone when by its original terms it runs to bearer.

(b) When a document running to the order of a named person is delivered to him the effect is the same as if the document had been negotiated.

(3) Negotiation of a negotiable document of title after it has been indorsed to a specified person requires indorsement by the special indorsee as well as delivery.

(4) A negotiable document of title is "duly negotiated" when it is negotiated in the manner stated in this section to a holder who purchases it in good faith without notice of any defense against or claim to it on the part of any person and for value, unless it is established that the negotiation is not in the regular course of business or financing or involves receiving the document in settlement or payment of a money obligation.

(5) Indorsement of a non-negotiable document neither makes it negotiable nor adds to the transferee's rights.

(6) The naming in a negotiable bill of a person to be notified of the arrival of the goods does not limit the negotiability of the bill nor constitute notice to a purchaser thereof of any interest of such person in the goods.

§ 7-502. Rights Acquired by Due Negotiation.
(1) Subject to the following section and to the provisions of Section 7–205 on fungible goods, a holder to whom a negotiable document of title has been duly negotiated acquires thereby:

(a) title to the document;

(b) title to the goods;

(c) all rights accruing under the law of agency or estoppel, including rights to goods delivered to the bailee after the document was issued; and

(d) the direct obligation of the issuer to hold or deliver the goods according to the terms of the document free of any defense or claim by him except those arising under the terms of the document or under this Article. In the case of a delivery order the bailee's obligation accrues only upon acceptance and the obligation acquired by the holder is that the issuer and any indorser will procure the acceptance of the bailee.

(2) Subject to the following section, title and rights so acquired are not defeated by any stoppage of the goods represented by the document or by surrender of such goods by the bailee, and are not impaired even though the negotiation or any prior negotiation constituted a breach of duty or even though any person has been deprived of possession of the document by misrepresentation, fraud, accident, mistake, duress, loss, theft or conversion, or even though a previous sale or other transfer of the goods or document has been made to a third person.

§ 7-503. Document of Title to Goods Defeated in Certain Cases.
(1) A document of title confers no right in goods against a person who before issuance of the document had a legal interest or a perfected security interest in them and who neither

(a) delivered or entrusted them or any document of title covering them to the bailor or his nominee with actual or apparent authority to ship, store or sell or with power to obtain delivery under this Article (Section 7–403) or with power of disposition under this Act (Sections 2–403 and 9–307) or other statute or rule of law; nor

(b) acquiesced in the procurement by the bailor or his nominee of any document of title.

(2) Title to goods based upon an unaccepted delivery order is subject to the rights of anyone to whom a negotiable warehouse receipt or bill of lading covering the goods has been duly negotiated. Such a title may be defeated under the next section to the same extent as the rights of the issuer or a transferee from the issuer.

(3) Title to goods based upon a bill of lading issued to a freight forwarder is subject to the rights of anyone to whom a bill issued by the freight forwarder is duly negotiated; but delivery by the carrier in accordance with Part 4 of this Article pursuant to its own bill of lading discharges the carrier's obligation to deliver.

§ 7–504. Rights Acquired in the Absence of Due Negotiation; Effect of Diversion; Seller's Stoppage of Delivery.
(1) A transferee of a document, whether negotiable or non-negotiable, to whom the document has been delivered but not duly negotiated, acquires the title and rights which his transferor had or had actual authority to convey.
(2) In the case of a non-negotiable document, until but not after the bailee receives notification of the transfer, the rights of the transferee may be defeated
(a) by those creditors of the transferor who could treat the sale as void under Section 2–402; or
(b) by a buyer from the transferor in ordinary course of business if the bailee has delivered the goods to the buyer or received notification of his rights; or
(c) as against the bailee by good faith dealings of the bailee with the transferor.
(3) A diversion or other change of shipping instructions by the consignor in a non-negotiable bill of lading which causes the bailee not to deliver to the consignee defeats the consignee's title to the goods if they have been delivered to a buyer in ordinary course of business and in any event defeats the consignee's rights against the bailee.
(4) Delivery pursuant to a non-negotiable document may be stopped by a seller under Section 2–705, and subject to the requirement of due notification there provided. A bailee honoring the seller's instructions is entitled to be indemnified by the seller against any resulting loss or expense.

§ 7–505. Indorser Not a Guarantor for Other Parties.
The indorsement of a document of title issued by a bailee does not make the indorser liable for any default by the bailee or by previous indorsers.

§ 7–506. Delivery Without Indorsement: Right to Compel Indorsement.
The transferee of a negotiable document of title has a specifically enforceable right to have his transferor supply any necessary indorsement but the transfer becomes a negotiation only as of the time the indorsement is supplied.

§ 7–507. Warranties on Negotiation or Transfer of Receipt or Bill.
Where a person negotiates or transfers a document of title for value otherwise than as a mere intermediary under the next following section, then unless otherwise agreed he warrants to his immediate purchaser only in addition to any warranty made in selling the goods
(a) that the document is genuine; and
(b) that he has no knowledge of any fact which would impair its validity or worth; and
(c) that his negotiation or transfer is rightful and fully effective with respect to the title to the document and the goods it represents.

§ 7–508. Warranties of Collecting Bank as to Documents.
A collecting bank or other intermediary known to be entrusted with documents on behalf of another or with collection of a draft of other claim against delivery of documents warrants by such delivery of the documents only its own good faith and authority. This rule applies even though the intermediary has purchased or made advances against the claim or draft to be collected.

Part 6—Warehouse Receipts and Bills of Lading: Miscellaneous Provisions

§ 7–601. Lost and Missing Documents.
(1) If a document has been lost, stolen or destroyed, a court may order delivery of the goods or issuance of a substitute document and the bailee may without liability to any person comply with such order. If the document was negotiable the claimant must post security approved by the court to indemnify any person who may suffer loss as a result of non-surrender of the document. If the document was not negotiable, such security may be required at the discretion of the court. The court may also in its discretion order payment of the bailee's reasonable costs and counsel fees.
(2) A bailee who without court order delivers goods to a person claiming under a missing negotiable document is liable to any person injured thereby, and if the delivery is not in good faith becomes liable for conversion. Delivery in good faith is not conversion if made in accordance with a filed classification or tariff or, where no classification or tariff is filed, if the claimant posts security with the bailee in an amount at least double the value of the goods at the time of posting to indemnify any person injured by the delivery who files a notice of claim within one year after the delivery.

REVISED ARTICLE 9: SECURED TRANSACTIONS

Part 1—General Provisions

§ 9–101. Short Title This article may be cited as Uniform Commercial Code—Secured Transactions.

§ 9–102. Definitions and Index of Definitions.
(a) **[Article 9 definitions.]** In this article:
(1) "Accession" means goods that are physically united with other goods in such a manner that the identity of the original goods is not lost.
(2) "Account", except as used in "account for", means a right to payment of a monetary obligation, whether or not earned by performance, (i) for property that has been or is to be sold, leased, licensed, assigned, or otherwise disposed of, (ii) for services rendered or to be rendered, (iii) for a policy of insurance issued or to be issued, (iv) for a secondary obligation incurred or to be incurred, (v) for energy provided or to be provided, (vi) for the use or hire of a vessel under a charter or other contract, (vii) arising out of the use of a credit or charge card or information contained on or for use with the card, or (viii) as winnings in a lottery or other game of chance operated or sponsored by a State, governmental unit of a State, or person licensed or authorized to operate the game by a State or governmental unit of a State. The term includes health-care-insurance receivables. The term does not include (i) rights to payment evidenced by chattel paper or an instrument, (ii) commercial tort claims, (iii) deposit accounts, (iv) investment property, (v) letter-of-credit rights or letters of credit, or (vi) rights to payment for money or funds advanced or sold, other than rights arising out of the use of a credit or charge card or information contained on or for use with the card.
(3) "Account debtor" means a person obligated on an account, chattel paper, or general intangible. The term does not include persons obligated to pay a negotiable instrument, even if the instrument constitutes part of chattel paper.
(4) "Accounting", except as used in "accounting for", means a record:
(A) authenticated by a secured party;
(B) indicating the aggregate unpaid secured obligations as of a date not more than 35 days earlier or 35 days later than the date of the record; and
(C) identifying the components of the obligations in reasonable detail.
(5) "Agricultural lien" means an interest, other than a security interest, in farm products:
(A) which secures payment or performance of an obligation for:
(i) goods or services furnished in connection with a debtor's farming operation; or
(ii) rent on real property leased by a debtor in connection with its farming operation;
(B) which is created by statute in favor of a person that:
(i) in the ordinary course of its business furnished goods or services to a debtor in connection with a debtor's farming operation; or
(ii) leased real property to a debtor in connection with the debtor's farming operation; and

(C) whose effectiveness does not depend on the person's possession of the personal property.

(6) "As-extracted collateral" means:

(A) oil, gas, or other minerals that are subject to a security interest that:

(i) is created by a debtor having an interest in the minerals before extraction; and

(ii) attaches to the minerals as extracted; or

(B) accounts arising out of the sale at the wellhead or minehead of oil, gas, or other minerals in which the debtor had an interest before extraction.

(7) "Authenticate" means:

(A) to sign; or

(B) to execute or otherwise adopt a symbol, or encrypt or similarly process a record in whole or in part, with the present intent of the authenticating person to identify the person and adopt or accept a record.

(8) "Bank" means an organization that is engaged in the business of banking. The term includes savings banks, savings and loan associations, credit unions, and trust companies.

(9) "Cash proceeds" means proceeds that are money, checks, deposit accounts, or the like.

(10) "Certificate of title" means a certificate of title with respect to which a statute provides for the security interest in question to be indicated on the certificate as a condition or result of the security interest's obtaining priority over the rights of a lien creditor with respect to the collateral.

(11) "Chattel paper" means a record or records that evidence both a monetary obligation and a security interest in specific goods, a security interest in specific goods and software used in the goods, a security interest in specific goods and license of software used in the goods, a lease of specific goods, or a lease of specific goods and license of software used in the goods. In this paragraph, "monetary obligation" means a monetary obligation secured by the goods or owed under a lease of the goods and includes a monetary obligation with respect to software used in the goods. The term does not include (i) charters or other contracts involving the use or hire of a vessel or (ii) records that evidence a right to payment arising out of the use of a credit or charge card or information contained on or for use with the card. If a transaction is evidenced by records that include an instrument or series of instruments, the group of records taken together constitutes chattel paper.

(12) "Collateral" means the property subject to a security interest or agricultural lien. The term includes:

(A) proceeds to which a security interest attaches;

(B) accounts, chattel paper, payment intangibles, and promissory notes that have been sold; and

(C) goods that are the subject of a consignment.

(13) "Commercial tort claim" means a claim arising in tort with respect to which:

(A) the claimant is an organization; or

(B) the claimant is an individual and the claim:

(i) arose in the course of the claimant's business or profession; and

(ii) does not include damages arising out of personal injury to or the death of an individual.

(14) "Commodity account" means an account maintained by a commodity intermediary in which a commodity contract is carried for a commodity customer.

(15) "Commodity contract" means a commodity futures contract, an option on a commodity futures contract, a commodity option, or another contract if the contract or option is:

(A) traded on or subject to the rules of a board of trade that has been designated as a contract market for such a contract pursuant to federal commodities laws; or

(B) traded on a foreign commodity board of trade, exchange, or market, and is carried on the books of a commodity intermediary for a commodity customer.

(16) "Commodity customer" means a person for which a commodity intermediary carries a commodity contract on its books.

(17) "Commodity intermediary" means a person that:

(A) is registered as a futures commission merchant under federal commodities law; or

(B) in the ordinary course of its business provides clearance or settlement services for a board of trade that has been designated as a contract market pursuant to federal commodities law.

(18) "Communicate" means:

(A) to send a written or other tangible record;

(B) to transmit a record by any means agreed upon by the persons sending and receiving the record; or

(C) in the case of transmission of a record to or by a filing office, to transmit a record by any means prescribed by filing-office rule.

(19) "Consignee" means a merchant to which goods are delivered in a consignment.

(20) "Consignment" means a transaction, regardless of its form, in which a person delivers goods to a merchant for the purpose of sale and:

(A) the merchant:

(i) deals in goods of that kind under a name other than the name of the person making delivery;

(ii) is not an auctioneer; and

(iii) is not generally known by its creditors to be substantially engaged in selling the goods of others;

(B) with respect to each delivery, the aggregate value of the goods is $1,000 or more at the time of delivery;

(C) the goods are not consumer goods immediately before delivery; and

(D) the transaction does not create a security interest that secures an obligation.

(21) "Consignor" means a person that delivers goods to a consignee in a consignment.

(22) "Consumer debtor" means a debtor in a consumer transaction.

(23) "Consumer goods" means goods that are used or bought for use primarily for personal, family, or household purposes.

(24) "Consumer-goods transaction" means a consumer transaction in which:

(A) an individual incurs an obligation primarily for personal, family, or household purposes; and

(B) a security interest in consumer goods secures the obligation.

(25) "Consumer obligor" means an obligor who is an individual and who incurred the obligation as part of a transaction entered into primarily for personal, family, or household purposes.

(26) "Consumer transaction" means a transaction in which (i) an individual incurs an obligation primarily for personal, family, or household purposes, (ii) a security interest secures the obligation, and (iii) the collateral is held or acquired primarily for personal, family, or household purposes. The term includes consumer-goods transactions.

(27) "Continuation statement" means an amendment of a financing statement which:

(A) identifies, by its file number, the initial financing statement to which it relates; and

(B) indicates that it is a continuation statement for, or that it is filed to continue the effectiveness of, the identified financing statement.

(28) "Debtor" means:

(A) a person having an interest, other than a security interest or other lien, in the collateral, whether or not the person is an obligor;

(B) a seller of accounts, chattel paper, payment intangibles, or promissory notes; or

(C) a consignee.

(29) "Deposit account" means a demand, time, savings, passbook, or similar account maintained with a bank. The term does not include investment property or accounts evidenced by an instrument.

(30) "Document" means a document of title or a receipt of the type described in Section 7–201(2).

(31) "Electronic chattel paper" means chattel paper evidenced by a record or records consisting of information stored in an electronic medium.

(32) "Encumbrance" means a right, other than an ownership interest, in real property. The term includes mortgages and other liens on real property.

(33) "Equipment" means goods other than inventory, farm products, or consumer goods.

(34) "Farm products" means goods, other than standing timber, with respect to which the debtor is engaged in a farming operation and which are:

(A) crops grown, growing, or to be grown, including:

(i) crops produced on trees, vines, and bushes; and

(ii) aquatic goods produced in aquacultural operations;

(B) livestock, born or unborn, including aquatic goods produced in aquacultural operations;

(C) supplies used or produced in a farming operation; or

(D) products of crops or livestock in their unmanufactured states.

(35) "Farming operation" means raising, cultivating, propagating, fattening, grazing, or any other farming, livestock, or aquacultural operation.

(36) "File number" means the number assigned to an initial financing statement pursuant to Section 9–519(a).

(37) "Filing office" means an office designated in Section 9–501 as the place to file a financing statement.

(38) "Filing–office rule" means a rule adopted pursuant to Section 9–526.

(39) "Financing statement" means a record or records composed of an initial financing statement and any filed record relating to the initial financing statement.

(40) "Fixture filing" means the filing of a financing statement covering goods that are or are to become fixtures and satisfying Section 9–502(a) and (b). The term includes the filing of a financing statement covering goods of a transmitting utility which are or are to become fixtures.

(41) "Fixtures" means goods that have become so related to particular real property that an interest in them arises under real property law.

(42) "General intangible" means any personal property, including things in action, other than accounts, chattel paper, commercial tort claims, deposit accounts, documents, goods, instruments, investment property, letter-of-credit rights, letters of credit, money, and oil, gas, or other minerals before extraction. The term includes payment intangibles and software.

(43) "Good faith" means honesty in fact and the observance of reasonable commercial standards of fair dealing.

(44) "Goods" means all things that are movable when a security interest attaches. The term includes (i) fixtures, (ii) standing timber that is to be cut and removed under a conveyance or contract for sale, (iii) the unborn young of animals, (iv) crops grown, growing, or to be grown, even if the crops are produced on trees, vines, or bushes, and (v) manufactured homes. The term also includes a computer program embedded in goods and any supporting information provided in connection with a transaction relating to the program if (i) the program is associated with the goods in such a manner that it customarily is considered part of the goods, or (ii) by becoming the owner of the goods, a person acquires a right to use the program in connection with the goods. The term does not include a computer program embedded in goods that consist solely of the medium in which the program is embedded. The term also does not include accounts, chattel paper, commercial tort claims, deposit accounts, documents, general intangibles, instruments, investment property, letter-of-credit rights, letters of credit, money, or oil, gas, or other minerals before extraction.

(45) "Governmental unit" means a subdivision, agency, department, county, parish, municipality, or other unit of the government of the United States, a State, or a foreign country. The term includes an organization having a separate corporate existence if the organization is eligible to issue debt on which interest is exempt from income taxation under the laws of the United States.

(46) "Health-care-insurance receivable" means an interest in or claim under a policy of insurance which is a right to payment of a monetary obligation for health-care goods or services provided.

(47) "Instrument" means a negotiable instrument or any other writing that evidences a right to the payment of a monetary obligation, is not itself a security agreement or lease, and is of a type that in ordinary course of business is transferred by delivery with any necessary endorsement or assignment. The term does not include (i) investment property, (ii) letters of credit, or (iii) writings that evidence a right to payment arising out of the use of a credit or charge card or information contained on or for use with the card.

(48) "Inventory" means goods, other than farm products, which:

(A) are leased by a person as lessor;

(B) are held by a person for sale or lease or to be furnished under a contract of service;

(C) are furnished by a person under a contract of service; or

(D) consist of raw materials, work in process, or materials used or consumed in a business.

(49) "Investment property" means a security, whether certificated or uncertificated, security entitlement, securities account, commodity contract, or commodity account.

(50) "Jurisdiction of organization", with respect to a registered organization, means the jurisdiction under whose law the organization is organized.

(51) "Letter-of-credit right" means a right to payment or performance under a letter of credit, whether or not the beneficiary has demanded or is at the time entitled to demand payment or performance. The term does not include the right of a beneficiary to demand payment or performance under a letter of credit.

(52) "Lien creditor" means:

(A) a creditor that has acquired a lien on the property involved by attachment, levy, or the like;

(B) an assignee for benefit of creditors from the time of assignment;

(C) a trustee in bankruptcy from the date of the filing of the petition; or

(D) a receiver in equity from the time of appointment.

(53) "Manufactured home" means a structure, transportable in one or more sections, which, in the traveling mode, is eight body feet or more in width or 40 body feet or more in length, or, when erected on site, is 320 or more square feet, and which is built on a permanent chassis and designed to be used as a dwelling with or without a permanent foundation when connected to the required utilities, and includes the plumbing, heating, air-conditioning, and electrical systems contained therein. The term includes any structure that meets all of the requirements of this paragraph except the size requirements and with respect to which the manufacturer voluntarily files a certification required by the United States Secretary of Housing and Urban Development and complies with the standards established under Title 42 of the United States Code.

(54) "Manufactured-home transaction" means a secured transaction:

(A) that creates a purchase-money security interest in a manufactured home, other than a manufactured home held as inventory; or

(B) in which a manufactured home, other than a manufactured home held as inventory, is the primary collateral.

(55) "Mortgage" means a consensual interest in real property, including fixtures, which secures payment or performance of an obligation.

(56) "New debtor" means a person that becomes bound as debtor under Section 9–203(d) by a security agreement previously entered into by another person.

(57) "New value" means (i) money, (ii) money's worth in property, services, or new credit, or (iii) release by a transferee of an interest in property previously transferred to the transferee. The term does not include an obligation substituted for another obligation.

(58) "Noncash proceeds" means proceeds other than cash proceeds.

(59) "Obligor" means a person that, with respect to an obligation secured by a security interest in or an agricultural lien on the collateral, (i) owes payment or other performance of the obligation, (ii) has provided property other than the collateral to secure payment or other performance of the obligation, or (iii) is otherwise accountable in whole or in part for payment or other performance of the obligation. The term does not include issuers or nominated persons under a letter of credit.

(60) "Original debtor", except as used in Section 9–310(c), means a person that, as debtor, entered into a security agreement to which a new debtor has become bound under Section 9–203(d).

(61) "Payment intangible" means a general intangible under which the account debtor's principal obligation is a monetary obligation.

(62) "Person related to", with respect to an individual, means:

(A) the spouse of the individual;

(B) a brother, brother-in-law, sister, or sister-in-law of the individual;

(C) an ancestor or lineal descendant of the individual or the individual's spouse; or

(D) any other relative, by blood or marriage, of the individual or the individual's spouse who shares the same home with the individual.

(63) "Person related to", with respect to an organization, means:

(A) a person directly or indirectly controlling, controlled by, or under common control with the organization;

(B) an officer or director of, or a person performing similar functions with respect to, the organization;

(C) an officer or director of, or a person performing similar functions with respect to, a person described in subparagraph (A);

(D) the spouse of an individual described in subparagraph (A), (B), or (C); or

(E) an individual who is related by blood or marriage to an individual described in subparagraph (A), (B), (C), or (D) and shares the same home with the individual.

(64) "Proceeds", except as used in Section 9–609(b), means the following property:

(A) whatever is acquired upon the sale, lease, license, exchange, or other disposition of collateral;

(B) whatever is collected on, or distributed on account of, collateral;

(C) rights arising out of collateral;

(D) to the extent of the value of collateral, claims arising out of the loss, nonconformity, or interference with the use of, defects or infringement of rights in, or damage to, the collateral; or

(E) to the extent of the value of collateral and to the extent payable to the debtor or the secured party, insurance payable by reason of the loss or nonconformity of, defects or infringement of rights in, or damage to, the collateral.

(65) "Promissory note" means an instrument that evidences a promise to pay a monetary obligation, does not evidence an order to pay, and does not contain an acknowledgment by a bank that the bank has received for deposit a sum of money or funds.

(66) "Proposal" means a record authenticated by a secured party which includes the terms on which the secured party is willing to accept collateral in full or partial satisfaction of the obligation it secures pursuant to Sections 9–620, 9–621, and 9–622.

(67) "Public-finance transaction" means a secured transaction in connection with which:

(A) debt securities are issued;

(B) all or a portion of the securities issued have an initial stated maturity of at least 20 years; and

(C) the debtor, obligor, secured party, account debtor or other person obligated on collateral, assignor or assignee of a secured obligation, or assignor or assignee of a security interest is a State or a governmental unit of a State.

(68) "Pursuant to commitment", with respect to an advance made or other value given by a secured party, means pursuant to the secured party's obligation, whether or not a subsequent event of default or other event not within the secured party's control has relieved or may relieve the secured party from its obligation.

(69) "Record", except as used in "for record", "of record", "record or legal title", and "record owner", means information that is inscribed on a tangible medium or which is stored in an electronic or other medium and is retrievable in perceivable form.

(70) "Registered organization" means an organization organized solely under the law of a single State or the United States and as to which the State or the United States must maintain a public record showing the organization to have been organized.

(71) "Secondary obligor" means an obligor to the extent that:

(A) the obligor's obligation is secondary; or

(B) the obligor has a right of recourse with respect to an obligation secured by collateral against the debtor, another obligor, or property of either.

(72) "Secured party" means:

(A) a person in whose favor a security interest is created or provided for under a security agreement, whether or not any obligation to be secured is outstanding;

(B) a person that holds an agricultural lien;

(C) a consignor;

(D) a person to which accounts, chattel paper, payment intangibles, or promissory notes have been sold;

(E) a trustee, indenture trustee, agent, collateral agent, or other representative in whose favor a security interest or agricultural lien is created or provided for; or

(F) a person that holds a security interest arising under Section 2–401, 2–505, 2–711(3), 2A–508(5), 4–210, or 5–118.

(73) "Security agreement" means an agreement that creates or provides for a security interest.

(74) "Send", in connection with a record or notification, means:

(A) to deposit in the mail, deliver for transmission, or transmit by any other usual means of communication, with postage or cost of transmission provided for, addressed to any address reasonable under the circumstances; or

(B) to cause the record or notification to be received within the time that it would have been received if properly sent under subparagraph (A).

(75) "Software" means a computer program and any supporting information provided in connection with a transaction relating to the program. The term does not include a computer program that is included in the definition of goods.

(76) "State" means a State of the United States, the District of Columbia, Puerto Rico, the United States Virgin Islands, or any territory or insular possession subject to the jurisdiction of the United States.

(77) "Supporting obligation" means a letter-of-credit right or secondary obligation that supports the payment or performance of an account, chattel paper, a document, a general intangible, an instrument, or investment property.

(78) "Tangible chattel paper" means chattel paper evidenced by a record or records consisting of information that is inscribed on a tangible medium.

(79) "Termination statement" means an amendment of a financing statement which:

(A) identifies, by its file number, the initial financing statement to which it relates; and

(B) indicates either that it is a termination statement or that the identified financing statement is no longer effective.

(80) "Transmitting utility" means a person primarily engaged in the business of:

(A) operating a railroad, subway, street railway, or trolley bus;

(B) transmitting communications electrically, electromagnetically, or by light;

(C) transmitting goods by pipeline or sewer; or

(D) transmitting or producing and transmitting electricity, steam, gas, or water.

(b) [Definitions in other articles.] The following definitions in other articles apply to this article:

"Applicant" Section 5–102.
"Beneficiary" Section 5–102.
"Broker" Section 8–102.
"Certificated security" Section 8–102.
"Check" Section 3–104.
"Clearing corporation" Section 8–102.
"Contract for sale" Section 2–106.
"Customer" Section 4–104.
"Entitlement holder" Section 8–102.
"Financial asset" Section 8–102.
"Holder in due course" Section 3–302.
"Issuer" (with respect to a letter of credit or letter-of-credit right) Section 5–102.
"Issuer" (with respect to a security) Section 8–201.
"Lease" Section 2A–103.
"Lease agreement" Section 2A–103.
"Lease contract" Section 2A–103.
"Leasehold interest" Section 2A–103.
"Lessee" Section 2A–103.
"Lessee in ordinary course of business" Section 2A–103.
"Lessor" Section 2A–103.
"Lessor's residual interest" Section 2A–103.
"Letter of credit" Section 5–102.
"Merchant" Section 2–104.
"Negotiable instrument" Section 3–104.
"Nominated person" Section 5–102.
"Note" Section 3–104.
"Proceeds of a letter of credit" Section 5–114.
"Prove" Section 3–103.
"Sale" Section 2–106.
"Securities account" Section 8–501.
"Securities intermediary" Section 8–102.
"Security" Section 8–102.
"Security certificate" Section 8–102.
"Security entitlement" Section 8–102.
"Uncertificated security" Section 8–102.

(c) [Article 1 definitions and principles.] Article 1 contains general definitions and principles of construction and interpretation applicable throughout this article.

§ 9–103. Purchase-Money Security Interest; Application of Payments; Burden of Establishing.

(a) [Definitions.] In this section:

(1) "purchase-money collateral" means goods or software that secures a purchase-money obligation incurred with respect to that collateral; and

(2) "purchase-money obligation" means an obligation of an obligor incurred as all or part of the price of the collateral or for value given to enable the debtor to acquire rights in or the use of the collateral if the value is in fact so used.

(b) [Purchase-money security interest in goods.] A security interest in goods is a purchase-money security interest:

(1) to the extent that the goods are purchase-money collateral with respect to that security interest;

(2) if the security interest is in inventory that is or was purchase-money collateral, also to the extent that the security interest secures a purchase-money obligation incurred with respect to other inventory in which the secured party holds or held a purchase-money security interest; and

(3) also to the extent that the security interest secures a purchase-money obligation incurred with respect to software in which the secured party holds or held a purchase-money security interest.

(c) [Purchase-money security interest in software.] A security interest in software is a purchase-money security interest to the extent that the security interest also secures a purchase-money obligation incurred with respect to goods in which the secured party holds or held a purchase-money security interest if:

(1) the debtor acquired its interest in the software in an integrated transaction in which it acquired an interest in the goods; and

(2) the debtor acquired its interest in the software for the principal purpose of using the software in the goods.

(d) [Consignor's inventory purchase-money security interest.] The security interest of a consignor in goods that are the subject of a consignment is a purchase-money security interest in inventory.

(e) [Application of payment in non-consumer-goods transaction.] In a transaction other than a consumer-goods transaction, if the extent to which a security interest is a purchase-money security interest depends on the application of a payment to a particular obligation, the payment must be applied:

(1) in accordance with any reasonable method of application to which the parties agree;

(2) in the absence of the parties' agreement to a reasonable method, in accordance with any intention of the obligor manifested at or before the time of payment; or

(3) in the absence of an agreement to a reasonable method and a timely manifestation of the obligor's intention, in the following order:

(A) to obligations that are not secured; and

(B) if more than one obligation is secured, to obligations secured by purchase-money security interests in the order in which those obligations were incurred.

(f) [No loss of status of purchase-money security interest in non-consumer-goods transaction.] In a transaction other than a consumer-goods transaction, a purchase-money security interest does not lose its status as such, even if:

(1) the purchase-money collateral also secures an obligation that is not a purchase-money obligation;
(2) collateral that is not purchase-money collateral also secures the purchase-money obligation; or
(3) the purchase-money obligation has been renewed, refinanced, consolidated, or restructured.

(g) [Burden of proof in non-consumer-goods transaction.] In a transaction other than a consumer-goods transaction, a secured party claiming a purchase-money security interest has the burden of establishing the extent to which the security interest is a purchase-money security interest.

(h) [Non-consumer-goods transactions; no inference.] The limitation of the rules in subsections (e), (f), and (g) to transactions other than consumer-goods transactions is intended to leave to the court the determination of the proper rules in consumer-goods transactions. The court may not infer from that limitation the nature of the proper rule in consumer-goods transactions and may continue to apply established approaches.

§ 9–104. Control of Deposit Account.

(a) [Requirements for control.] A secured party has control of a deposit account if:
(1) the secured party is the bank with which the deposit account is maintained;
(2) the debtor, secured party, and bank have agreed in an authenticated record that the bank will comply with instructions originated by the secured party directing disposition of the funds in the deposit account without further consent by the debtor; or
(3) the secured party becomes the bank's customer with respect to the deposit account.

(b) [Debtor's right to direct disposition.] A secured party that has satisfied subsection (a) has control, even if the debtor retains the right to direct the disposition of funds from the deposit account.

§ 9–105. Control of Electronic Chattel Paper.

A secured party has control of electronic chattel paper if the record or records comprising the chattel paper are created, stored, and assigned in such a manner that:
(1) a single authoritative copy of the record or records exists which is unique, identifiable and, except as otherwise provided in paragraphs (4), (5), and (6), unalterable;
(2) the authoritative copy identifies the secured party as the assignee of the record or records;
(3) the authoritative copy is communicated to and maintained by the secured party or its designated custodian;
(4) copies or revisions that add or change an identified assignee of the authoritative copy can be made only with the participation of the secured party;
(5) each copy of the authoritative copy and any copy of a copy is readily identifiable as a copy that is not the authoritative copy; and
(6) any revision of the authoritative copy is readily identifiable as an authorized or unauthorized revision.

§ 9–106. Control of Investment Property.

(a) [Control under Section 8–106.] A person has control of a certificated security, uncertificated security, or security entitlement as provided in Section 8–106.

(b) [Control of commodity contract.] A secured party has control of a commodity contract if:
(1) the secured party is the commodity intermediary with which the commodity contract is carried; or
(2) the commodity customer, secured party, and commodity intermediary have agreed that the commodity intermediary will apply any value distributed on account of the commodity contract as directed by the secured party without further consent by the commodity customer.

(c) [Effect of control of securities account or commodity account.] A secured party having control of all security entitlements or commodity contracts carried in a securities account or commodity account has control over the securities account or commodity account.

§ 9–107. Control of Letter-of-Credit Right.

A secured party has control of a letter-of-credit right to the extent of any right to payment or performance by the issuer or any nominated person if the issuer or nominated person has consented to an assignment of proceeds of the letter of credit under Section 5–114(c) or otherwise applicable law or practice.

§ 9–108. Sufficiency of Description.

(a) [Sufficiency of description.] Except as otherwise provided in subsections (c), (d), and (e), a description of personal or real property is sufficient, whether or not it is specific, if it reasonably identifies what is described.

(b) [Examples of reasonable identification.] Except as otherwise provided in subsection (d), a description of collateral reasonably identifies the collateral if it identifies the collateral by:
(1) specific listing;
(2) category;
(3) except as otherwise provided in subsection (e), a type of collateral defined in [the Uniform Commercial Code];
(4) quantity;
(5) computational or allocational formula or procedure; or
(6) except as otherwise provided in subsection (c), any other method, if the identity of the collateral is objectively determinable.

(c) [Supergeneric description not sufficient.] A description of collateral as "all the debtor's assets" or "all the debtor's personal property" or using words of similar import does not reasonably identify the collateral.

(d) [Investment property.] Except as otherwise provided in subsection (e), a description of a security entitlement, securities account, or commodity account is sufficient if it describes:
(1) the collateral by those terms or as investment property; or
(2) the underlying financial asset or commodity contract.

(e) [When description by type insufficient.] A description only by type of collateral defined in [the Uniform Commercial Code] is an insufficient description of:
(1) a commercial tort claim; or
(2) in a consumer transaction, consumer goods, a security entitlement, a securities account, or a commodity account.

§ 9–109. Scope.

(a) [General scope of article.] Except as otherwise provided in subsections (c) and (d), this article applies to:
(1) a transaction, regardless of its form, that creates a security interest in personal property or fixtures by contract;
(2) an agricultural lien;
(3) a sale of accounts, chattel paper, payment intangibles, or promissory notes;
(4) a consignment;
(5) a security interest arising under Section 2–401, 2–505, 2–711(3), or 2A–508(5), as provided in Section 9–110; and
(6) a security interest arising under Section 4–210 or 5–118.

(b) [Security interest in secured obligation.] The application of this article to a security interest in a secured obligation is not affected by the fact that the obligation is itself secured by a transaction or interest to which this article does not apply.

(c) [Extent to which article does not apply.] This article does not apply to the extent that:
(1) a statute, regulation, or treaty of the United States preempts this article;

(2) another statute of this State expressly governs the creation, perfection, priority, or enforcement of a security interest created by this State or a governmental unit of this State;
(3) a statute of another State, a foreign country, or a governmental unit of another State or a foreign country, other than a statute generally applicable to security interests, expressly governs creation, perfection, priority, or enforcement of a security interest created by the State, country, or governmental unit; or
(4) the rights of a transferee beneficiary or nominated person under a letter of credit are independent and superior under Section 5–114.

(d) [Inapplicability of article.] This article does not apply to:
(1) a landlord's lien, other than an agricultural lien;
(2) a lien, other than an agricultural lien, given by statute or other rule of law for services or materials, but Section 9–333 applies with respect to priority of the lien;
(3) an assignment of a claim for wages, salary, or other compensation of an employee;
(4) a sale of accounts, chattel paper, payment intangibles, or promissory notes as part of a sale of the business out of which they arose;
(5) an assignment of accounts, chattel paper, payment intangibles, or promissory notes which is for the purpose of collection only;
(6) an assignment of a right to payment under a contract to an assignee that is also obligated to perform under the contract;
(7) an assignment of a single account, payment intangible, or promissory note to an assignee in full or partial satisfaction of a preexisting indebtedness;
(8) a transfer of an interest in or an assignment of a claim under a policy of insurance, other than an assignment by or to a health-care provider of a health-care-insurance receivable and any subsequent assignment of the right to payment, but Sections 9–315 and 9–322 apply with respect to proceeds and priorities in proceeds;
(9) an assignment of a right represented by a judgment, other than a judgment taken on a right to payment that was collateral;
(10) a right of recoupment or set-off, but:
(A) Section 9–340 applies with respect to the effectiveness of rights of recoupment or set-off against deposit accounts; and
(B) Section 9–404 applies with respect to defenses or claims of an account debtor;
(11) the creation or transfer of an interest in or lien on real property, including a lease or rents thereunder, except to the extent that provision is made for:
(A) liens on real property in Sections 9–203 and 9–308;
(B) fixtures in Section 9–334;
(C) fixture filings in Sections 9–501, 9–502, 9–512, 9–516, and 9–519; and
(D) security agreements covering personal and real property in Section 9–604;
(12) an assignment of a claim arising in tort, other than a commercial tort claim, but Sections 9–315 and 9–322 apply with respect to proceeds and priorities in proceeds; or
(13) an assignment of a deposit account in a consumer transaction, but Sections 9–315 and 9–322 apply with respect to proceeds and priorities in proceeds.

§ 9–110. Security Interests Arising under Article 2 or 2A.

A security interest arising under Section 2–401, 2–505, 2–711(3), or 2A–508(5) is subject to this article. However, until the debtor obtains possession of the goods:
(1) the security interest is enforceable, even if Section 9–203(b)(3) has not been satisfied;
(2) filing is not required to perfect the security interest;
(3) the rights of the secured party after default by the debtor are governed by Article 2 or 2A; and
(4) the security interest has priority over a conflicting security interest created by the debtor.

Part 2—Effectiveness of Security Agreement; Attachment of Security Interest; Rights of Parties to Security Agreement

§ 9–201. General Effectiveness of Security Agreement.

(a) [General effectiveness.] Except as otherwise provided in [the Uniform Commercial Code], a security agreement is effective according to its terms between the parties, against purchasers of the collateral, and against creditors.
(b) [Applicable consumer laws and other law.] A transaction subject to this article is subject to any applicable rule of law which establishes a different rule for consumers and [insert reference to (i) any other statute or regulation that regulates the rates, charges, agreements, and practices for loans, credit sales, or other extensions of credit and (ii) any consumer-protection statute or regulation].
(c) [Other applicable law controls.] In case of conflict between this article and a rule of law, statute, or regulation described in subsection (b), the rule of law, statute, or regulation controls. Failure to comply with a statute or regulation described in subsection (b) has only the effect the statute or regulation specifies.
(d) [Further deference to other applicable law.] This article does not:
(1) validate any rate, charge, agreement, or practice that violates a rule of law, statute, or regulation described in subsection (b); or
(2) extend the application of the rule of law, statute, or regulation to a transaction not otherwise subject to it.

§ 9–203. Attachment and Enforceability of Security Interest; Proceeds; Supporting Obligations; Formal Requisites.

(a) [Attachment.] A security interest attaches to collateral when it becomes enforceable against the debtor with respect to the collateral, unless an agreement expressly postpones the time of attachment.
(b) [Enforceability.] Except as otherwise provided in subsections (c) through (i), a security interest is enforceable against the debtor and third parties with respect to the collateral only if:
(1) value has been given;
(2) the debtor has rights in the collateral or the power to transfer rights in the collateral to a secured party; and
(3) one of the following conditions is met:
(A) the debtor has authenticated a security agreement that provides a description of the collateral and, if the security interest covers timber to be cut, a description of the land concerned;
(B) the collateral is not a certificated security and is in the possession of the secured party under Section 9–313 pursuant to the debtor's security agreement;
(C) the collateral is a certificated security in registered form and the security certificate has been delivered to the secured party under Section 8–301 pursuant to the debtor's security agreement; or
(D) the collateral is deposit accounts, electronic chattel paper, investment property, or letter-of-credit rights, and the secured party has control under Section 9–104, 9–105, 9–106, or 9–107 pursuant to the debtor's security agreement.
(c) [Other UCC provisions.] Subsection (b) is subject to Section 4–210 on the security interest of a collecting bank, Section 5–118 on the security interest of a letter-of-credit issuer or nominated person, Section 9–110 on a security interest arising under Article 2 or 2A, and Section 9–206 on security interests in investment property.
(d) [When person becomes bound by another person's security agreement.] A person becomes bound as debtor by a security agreement entered into by another person if, by operation of law other than this article or by contract:

(1) the security agreement becomes effective to create a security interest in the person's property; or

(2) the person becomes generally obligated for the obligations of the other person, including the obligation secured under the security agreement, and acquires or succeeds to all or substantially all of the assets of the other person.

(e) [Effect of new debtor becoming bound.] If a new debtor becomes bound as debtor by a security agreement entered into by another person:

(1) the agreement satisfies subsection (b)(3) with respect to existing or after-acquired property of the new debtor to the extent the property is described in the agreement; and

(2) another agreement is not necessary to make a security interest in the property enforceable.

(f) [Proceeds and supporting obligations.] The attachment of a security interest in collateral gives the secured party the rights to proceeds provided by Section 9–315 and is also attachment of a security interest in a supporting obligation for the collateral.

(g) [Lien securing right to payment.] The attachment of a security interest in a right to payment or performance secured by a security interest or other lien on personal or real property is also attachment of a security interest in the security interest, mortgage, or other lien.

(h) [Security entitlement carried in securities account.] The attachment of a security interest in a securities account is also attachment of a security interest in the security entitlements carried in the securities account.

(i) [Commodity contracts carried in commodity account.] The attachment of a security interest in a commodity account is also attachment of a security interest in the commodity contracts carried in the commodity account.

§ 9–204. After-Acquired Property; Future Advances.

(a) [After-acquired collateral.] Except as otherwise provided in subsection (b), a security agreement may create or provide for a security interest in after-acquired collateral.

(b) [When after-acquired property clause not effective.] A security interest does not attach under a term constituting an after-acquired property clause to:

(1) consumer goods, other than an accession when given as additional security, unless the debtor acquires rights in them within 10 days after the secured party gives value; or

(2) a commercial tort claim.

(c) [Future advances and other value.] A security agreement may provide that collateral secures, or that accounts, chattel paper, payment intangibles, or promissory notes are sold in connection with, future advances or other value, whether or not the advances or value are given pursuant to commitment.

§ 9–205. Use or Disposition of Collateral Permissible.

(a) [When security interest not invalid or fraudulent.] A security interest is not invalid or fraudulent against creditors solely because:

(1) the debtor has the right or ability to:

(A) use, commingle, or dispose of all or part of the collateral, including returned or repossessed goods;

(B) collect, compromise, enforce, or otherwise deal with collateral;

(C) accept the return of collateral or make repossessions; or

(D) use, commingle, or dispose of proceeds; or

(2) the secured party fails to require the debtor to account for proceeds or replace collateral.

(b) [Requirements of possession not relaxed.] This section does not relax the requirements of possession if attachment, perfection, or enforcement of a security interest depends upon possession of the collateral by the secured party.

Part 3—Perfection and Priority

§ 9–301. Law Governing Perfection and Priority of Security Interests. Except as otherwise provided in Sections 9–303 through 9–306, the following rules determine the law governing perfection, the effect of perfection or nonperfection, and the priority of a security interest in collateral:

(1) Except as otherwise provided in this section, while a debtor is located in a jurisdiction, the local law of that jurisdiction governs perfection, the effect of perfection or nonperfection, and the priority of a security interest in collateral.

(2) While collateral is located in a jurisdiction, the local law of that jurisdiction governs perfection, the effect of perfection or nonperfection, and the priority of a possessory security interest in that collateral.

(3) Except as otherwise provided in paragraph (4), while negotiable documents, goods, instruments, money, or tangible chattel paper is located in a jurisdiction, the local law of that jurisdiction governs:

(A) perfection of a security interest in the goods by filing a fixture filing;

(B) perfection of a security interest in timber to be cut; and

(C) the effect of perfection or nonperfection and the priority of a nonpossessory security interest in the collateral.

(4) The local law of the jurisdiction in which the wellhead or minehead is located governs perfection, the effect of perfection or nonperfection, and the priority of a security interest in as-extracted collateral.

§ 9–302. Law Governing Perfection and Priority of Agricultural Liens. While farm products are located in a jurisdiction, the local law of that jurisdiction governs perfection, the effect of perfection or nonperfection, and the priority of an agricultural lien on the farm products.

§ 9–303. Law Governing Perfection and Priority of Security Interests in Goods Covered by a Certificate of Title.

(a) [Applicability of section.] This section applies to goods covered by a certificate of title, even if there is no other relationship between the jurisdiction under whose certificate of title the goods are covered and the goods or the debtor.

(b) [When goods covered by certificate of title.] Goods become covered by a certificate of title when a valid application for the certificate of title and the applicable fee are delivered to the appropriate authority. Goods cease to be covered by a certificate of title at the earlier of the time the certificate of title ceases to be effective under the law of the issuing jurisdiction or the time the goods become covered subsequently by a certificate of title issued by another jurisdiction.

(c) [Applicable law.] The local law of the jurisdiction under whose certificate of title the goods are covered governs perfection, the effect of perfection or nonperfection, and the priority of a security interest in goods covered by a certificate of title from the time the goods become covered by the certificate of title until the goods cease to be covered by the certificate of title.

§ 9–307. Location of Debtor.

(a) ["Place of business."] In this section, "place of business" means a place where a debtor conducts its affairs.

(b) [Debtor's location: general rules.] Except as otherwise provided in this section, the following rules determine a debtor's location:

(1) A debtor who is an individual is located at the individual's principal residence.

(2) A debtor that is an organization and has only one place of business is located at its place of business.

(3) A debtor that is an organization and has more than one place of business is located at its chief executive office.

(c) [Limitation of applicability of subsection (b).] Subsection (b) applies only if a debtor's residence, place of business, or chief executive office, as applicable, is located in a jurisdiction whose law generally requires information concerning the existence of a nonpossessory security interest to be made generally available in a filing, recording, or registration system as a condition or result of the security interest's obtaining priority over the rights of a lien creditor with respect to the collateral. If subsection (b) does not apply, the debtor is located in the District of Columbia.
(d) [Continuation of location: cessation of existence, etc.] A person that ceases to exist, have a residence, or have a place of business continues to be located in the jurisdiction specified by subsections (b) and (c).
(e) [Location of registered organization organized under State law.] A registered organization that is organized under the law of a State is located in that State.
(f) [Location of registered organization organized under federal law; bank branches and agencies.] Except as otherwise provided in subsection (i), a registered organization that is organized under the law of the United States and a branch or agency of a bank that is not organized under the law of the United States or a State are located:

(1) in the State that the law of the United States designates, if the law designates a State of location;
(2) in the State that the registered organization, branch, or agency designates, if the law of the United States authorizes the registered organization, branch, or agency to designate its State of location; or
(3) in the District of Columbia, if neither paragraph (1) nor paragraph (2) applies.

(g) [Continuation of location: change in status of registered organization.] A registered organization continues to be located in the jurisdiction specified by subsection (e) or (f) notwithstanding:

(1) the suspension, revocation, forfeiture, or lapse of the registered organization's status as such in its jurisdiction of organization; or
(2) the dissolution, winding up, or cancellation of the existence of the registered organization.

(h) [Location of United States.] The United States is located in the District of Columbia.
(i) [Location of foreign bank branch or agency if licensed in only one state.] A branch or agency of a bank that is not organized under the law of the United States or a State is located in the State in which the branch or agency is licensed, if all branches and agencies of the bank are licensed in only one State.
(j) [Location of foreign air carrier.] A foreign air carrier under the Federal Aviation Act of 1958, as amended, is located at the designated office of the agent upon which service of process may be made on behalf of the carrier.
(k) [Section applies only to this part.] This section applies only for purposes of this part.

§ 9–308. When Security Interest or Agricultural Lien Is Perfected; Continuity of Perfection.

(a) [Perfection of security interest.] Except as otherwise provided in this section and Section 9–309, a security interest is perfected if it has attached and all of the applicable requirements for perfection in Sections 9–310 through 9–316 have been satisfied. A security interest is perfected when it attaches if the applicable requirements are satisfied before the security interest attaches.
(b) [Perfection of agricultural lien.] An agricultural lien is perfected if it has become effective and all of the applicable requirements for perfection in Section 9–310 have been satisfied. An agricultural lien is perfected when it becomes effective if the applicable requirements are satisfied before the agricultural lien becomes effective.
(c) [Continuous perfection; perfection by different methods.] A security interest or agricultural lien is perfected continuously if it is originally perfected by one method under this article and is later perfected by another method under this article, without an intermediate period when it was unperfected.
(d) [Supporting obligation.] Perfection of a security interest in collateral also perfects a security interest in a supporting obligation for the collateral.
(e) [Lien securing right to payment.] Perfection of a security interest in a right to payment or performance also perfects a security interest in a security interest, mortgage, or other lien on personal or real property securing the right.
(f) [Security entitlement carried in securities account.] Perfection of a security interest in a securities account also perfects a security interest in the security entitlements carried in the securities account.
(g) [Commodity contract carried in commodity account.] Perfection of a security interest in a commodity account also perfects a security interest in the commodity contracts carried in the commodity account.

§ 9–309. Security Interest Perfected Upon Attachment.

The following security interests are perfected when they attach:

(1) a purchase-money security interest in consumer goods, except as otherwise provided in Section 9–311(b) with respect to consumer goods that are subject to a statute or treaty described in Section 9–311(a);
(2) an assignment of accounts or payment intangibles which does not by itself or in conjunction with other assignments to the same assignee transfer a significant part of the assignor's outstanding accounts or payment intangibles;
(3) a sale of a payment intangible;
(4) a sale of a promissory note;
(5) a security interest created by the assignment of a health-care-insurance receivable to the provider of the health-care goods or services;
(6) a security interest arising under Section 2–401, 2–505, 2–711(3), or 2A–508(5), until the debtor obtains possession of the collateral;
(7) a security interest of a collecting bank arising under Section 4–210;
(8) a security interest of an issuer or nominated person arising under Section 5–118;
(9) a security interest arising in the delivery of a financial asset under Section 9–206(c);
(10) a security interest in investment property created by a broker or securities intermediary;
(11) a security interest in a commodity contract or a commodity account created by a commodity intermediary;
(12) an assignment for the benefit of all creditors of the transferor and subsequent transfers by the assignee thereunder; and
(13) a security interest created by an assignment of a beneficial interest in a decedent's estate.

§ 9–310. When Filing Required to Perfect Security Interest or Agricultural Lien; Security Interests and Agricultural Liens to Which Filing Provisions Do Not Apply.

(a) [General rule: perfection by filing.] Except as otherwise provided in subsection (b) and Section 9–312(b), a financing statement must be filed to perfect all security interests and agricultural liens.
(b) [Exceptions: filing not necessary.] The filing of a financing statement is not necessary to perfect a security interest:

(1) that is perfected under Section 9–308(d), (e), (f), or (g);
(2) that is perfected under Section 9–309 when it attaches;
(3) in property subject to a statute, regulation, or treaty described in Section 9–311(a);
(4) in goods in possession of a bailee which is perfected under Section 9–312(d)(1) or (2);
(5) in certificated securities, documents, goods, or instruments which is perfected without filing or possession under Section 9–312(e), (f), or (g);

(6) in collateral in the secured party's possession under Section 9–313;
(7) in a certificated security which is perfected by delivery of the security certificate to the secured party under Section 9–313;
(8) in deposit accounts, electronic chattel paper, investment property, or letter-of-credit rights which is perfected by control under Section 9–314;
(9) in proceeds which is perfected under Section 9–315; or
(10) that is perfected under Section 9–316.

(c) [Assignment of perfected security interest.] If a secured party assigns a perfected security interest or agricultural lien, a filing under this article is not required to continue the perfected status of the security interest against creditors of and transferees from the original debtor.

§ 9–311. Perfection of Security Interests in Property Subject to Certain Statutes, Regulations, and Treaties.

(a) [Security interest subject to other law.] Except as otherwise provided in subsection (d), the filing of a financing statement is not necessary or effective to perfect a security interest in property subject to:
(1) a statute, regulation, or treaty of the United States whose requirements for a security interest's obtaining priority over the rights of a lien creditor with respect to the property preempt Section 9–310(a);
(2) [list any certificate-of-title statute covering automobiles, trailers, mobile homes, boats, farm tractors, or the like, which provides for a security interest to be indicated on the certificate as a condition or result of perfection, and any non-Uniform Commercial Code central filing statute]; or
(3) a certificate-of-title statute of another jurisdiction which provides for a security interest to be indicated on the certificate as a condition or result of the security interest's obtaining priority over the rights of a lien creditor with respect to the property.

(b) [Compliance with other law.] Compliance with the requirements of a statute, regulation, or treaty described in subsection (a) for obtaining priority over the rights of a lien creditor is equivalent to the filing of a financing statement under this article. Except as otherwise provided in subsection (d) and Sections 9–313 and 9–316(d) and (e) for goods covered by a certificate of title, a security interest in property subject to a statute, regulation, or treaty described in subsection (a) may be perfected only by compliance with those requirements, and a security interest so perfected remains perfected notwithstanding a change in the use or transfer of possession of the collateral.

(c) [Duration and renewal of perfection.] Except as otherwise provided in subsection (d) and Section 9–316(d) and (e), duration and renewal of perfection of a security interest perfected by compliance with the requirements prescribed by a statute, regulation, or treaty described in subsection (a) are governed by the statute, regulation, or treaty. In other respects, the security interest is subject to this article.

(d) [Inapplicability to certain inventory.] During any period in which collateral subject to a statute specified in subsection (a)(2) is inventory held for sale or lease by a person or leased by that person as lessor and that person is in the business of selling goods of that kind, this section does not apply to a security interest in that collateral created by that person.

§ 9–312. Perfection of Security Interests in Chattel Paper, Deposit Accounts, Documents, Goods Covered by Documents, Instruments, Investment Property, Letter-of-Credit Rights, and Money; Perfection by Permissive Filing; Temporary Perfection Without Filing or Transfer of Possession.

(a) [Perfection by filing permitted.] A security interest in chattel paper, negotiable documents, instruments, or investment property may be perfected by filing.

(b) [Control or possession of certain collateral.] Except as otherwise provided in Section 9–315(c) and (d) for proceeds:
(1) a security interest in a deposit account may be perfected only by control under Section 9–314;
(2) and except as otherwise provided in Section 9–308(d), a security interest in a letter-of-credit right may be perfected only by control under Section 9–314; and
(3) a security interest in money may be perfected only by the secured party's taking possession under Section 9–313.

(c) [Goods covered by negotiable document.] While goods are in the possession of a bailee that has issued a negotiable document covering the goods:
(1) a security interest in the goods may be perfected by perfecting a security interest in the document; and
(2) a security interest perfected in the document has priority over any security interest that becomes perfected in the goods by another method during that time.

(d) [Goods covered by nonnegotiable document.] While goods are in the possession of a bailee that has issued a nonnegotiable document covering the goods, a security interest in the goods may be perfected by:
(1) issuance of a document in the name of the secured party;
(2) the bailee's receipt of notification of the secured party's interest; or
(3) filing as to the goods.

(e) [Temporary perfection: new value.] A security interest in certificated securities, negotiable documents, or instruments is perfected without filing or the taking of possession for a period of 20 days from the time it attaches to the extent that it arises for new value given under an authenticated security agreement.

(f) [Temporary perfection: goods or documents made available to debtor.] A perfected security interest in a negotiable document or goods in possession of a bailee, other than one that has issued a negotiable document for the goods, remains perfected for 20 days without filing if the secured party makes available to the debtor the goods or documents representing the goods for the purpose of:
(1) ultimate sale or exchange; or
(2) loading, unloading, storing, shipping, transshipping, manufacturing, processing, or otherwise dealing with them in a manner preliminary to their sale or exchange.

(g) [Temporary perfection: delivery of security certificate or instrument to debtor.] A perfected security interest in a certificated security or instrument remains perfected for 20 days without filing if the secured party delivers the security certificate or instrument to the debtor for the purpose of:
(1) ultimate sale or exchange; or
(2) presentation, collection, enforcement, renewal, or registration of transfer.

(h) [Expiration of temporary perfection.] After the 20–day period specified in subsection (e), (f), or (g) expires, perfection depends upon compliance with this article.

§ 9–313. When Possession by or Delivery to Secured Party Perfects Security Interest Without Filing.

(a) [Perfection by possession or delivery.] Except as otherwise provided in subsection (b), a secured party may perfect a security interest in negotiable documents, goods, instruments, money, or tangible chattel paper by taking possession of the collateral. A secured party may perfect a security interest in certificated securities by taking delivery of the certificated securities under Section 8–301.

(b) [Goods covered by certificate of title.] With respect to goods covered by a certificate of title issued by this State, a secured party may perfect a security interest in the goods by taking possession of the goods only in the circumstances described in Section 9–316(d).

(c) [Collateral in possession of person other than debtor.] With respect to collateral other than certificated securities and goods covered by a document, a secured party takes possession of collateral in the possession of a person other than the debtor, the secured party, or a lessee of the collateral from the debtor in the ordinary course of the debtor's business, when:

(1) the person in possession authenticates a record acknowledging that it holds possession of the collateral for the secured party's benefit; or

(2) the person takes possession of the collateral after having authenticated a record acknowledging that it will hold possession of collateral for the secured party's benefit.

(d) [Time of perfection by possession; continuation of perfection.] If perfection of a security interest depends upon possession of the collateral by a secured party, perfection occurs no earlier than the time the secured party takes possession and continues only while the secured party retains possession.

(e) [Time of perfection by delivery; continuation of perfection.] A security interest in a certificated security in registered form is perfected by delivery when delivery of the certificated security occurs under Section 8–301 and remains perfected by delivery until the debtor obtains possession of the security certificate.

(f) [Acknowledgment not required.] A person in possession of collateral is not required to acknowledge that it holds possession for a secured party's benefit.

(g) [Effectiveness of acknowledgment; no duties or confirmation.] If a person acknowledges that it holds possession for the secured party's benefit:

(1) the acknowledgment is effective under subsection (c) or Section 8–301(a), even if the acknowledgment violates the rights of a debtor; and

(2) unless the person otherwise agrees or law other than this article otherwise provides, the person does not owe any duty to the secured party and is not required to confirm the acknowledgment to another person.

(h) [Secured party's delivery to person other than debtor.] A secured party having possession of collateral does not relinquish possession by delivering the collateral to a person other than the debtor or a lessee of the collateral from the debtor in the ordinary course of the debtor's business if the person was instructed before the delivery or is instructed contemporaneously with the delivery:

(1) to hold possession of the collateral for the secured party's benefit; or

(2) to redeliver the collateral to the secured party.

(i) [Effect of delivery under subsection (h); no duties or confirmation.] A secured party does not relinquish possession, even if a delivery under subsection (h) violates the rights of a debtor. A person to which collateral is delivered under subsection (h) does not owe any duty to the secured party and is not required to confirm the delivery to another person unless the person otherwise agrees or law other than this article otherwise provides.

§ 9–314. Perfection by Control.

(a) [Perfection by control.] A security interest in investment property, deposit accounts, letter-of-credit rights, or electronic chattel paper may be perfected by control of the collateral under Section 9–104, 9–105, 9–106, or 9–107.

(b) [Specified collateral: time of perfection by control; continuation of perfection.] A security interest in deposit accounts, electronic chattel paper, or letter-of-credit rights is perfected by control under Section 9–104, 9–105, or 9–107 when the secured party obtains control and remains perfected by control only while the secured party retains control.

(c) [Investment property: time of perfection by control; continuation of perfection.] A security interest in investment property is perfected by control under Section 9–106 from the time the secured party obtains control and remains perfected by control until:

(1) the secured party does not have control; and

(2) one of the following occurs:

(A) if the collateral is a certificated security, the debtor has or acquires possession of the security certificate;

(B) if the collateral is an uncertificated security, the issuer has registered or registers the debtor as the registered owner; or

(C) if the collateral is a security entitlement, the debtor is or becomes the entitlement holder.

§ 9–315. Secured Party's Rights on Disposition of Collateral and in Proceeds.

(a) [Disposition of collateral: continuation of security interest or agricultural lien; proceeds.] Except as otherwise provided in this article and in Section 2–403(2):

(1) a security interest or agricultural lien continues in collateral notwithstanding sale, lease, license, exchange, or other disposition thereof unless the secured party authorized the disposition free of the security interest or agricultural lien; and

(2) a security interest attaches to any identifiable proceeds of collateral.

(b) [When commingled proceeds identifiable.] Proceeds that are commingled with other property are identifiable proceeds:

(1) if the proceeds are goods, to the extent provided by Section 9–336; and

(2) if the proceeds are not goods, to the extent that the secured party identifies the proceeds by a method of tracing, including application of equitable principles, that is permitted under law other than this article with respect to commingled property of the type involved.

(c) [Perfection of security interest in proceeds.] A security interest in proceeds is a perfected security interest if the security interest in the original collateral was perfected.

(d) [Continuation of perfection.] A perfected security interest in proceeds becomes unperfected on the 21st day after the security interest attaches to the proceeds unless:

(1) the following conditions are satisfied:

(A) a filed financing statement covers the original collateral;

(B) the proceeds are collateral in which a security interest may be perfected by filing in the office in which the financing statement has been filed; and

(C) the proceeds are not acquired with cash proceeds;

(2) the proceeds are identifiable cash proceeds; or

(3) the security interest in the proceeds is perfected other than under subsection (c) when the security interest attaches to the proceeds or within 20 days thereafter.

(e) [When perfected security interest in proceeds becomes unperfected.] If a filed financing statement covers the original collateral, a security interest in proceeds which remains perfected under subsection (d)(1) becomes unperfected at the later of:

(1) when the effectiveness of the filed financing statement lapses under Section 9–515 or is terminated under Section 9–513; or

(2) the 21st day after the security interest attaches to the proceeds.

§ 9–316. Continued Perfection of Security Interest Following Change in Governing Law.

(a) [General rule: effect on perfection of change in governing law.] A security interest perfected pursuant to the law of the jurisdiction designated in Section 9–301(1) or 9–305(c) remains perfected until the earliest of:

(1) the time perfection would have ceased under the law of that jurisdiction;

(2) the expiration of four months after a change of the debtor's location to another jurisdiction; or

(3) the expiration of one year after a transfer of collateral to a person that thereby becomes a debtor and is located in another jurisdiction.

(b) [Security interest perfected or unperfected under law of new jurisdiction.] If a security interest described in subsection (a) becomes perfected under the law of the other jurisdiction before the earliest time or event described in that subsection, it remains perfected thereafter. If the security interest does not become perfected under the law of the other jurisdiction before the earliest time or event, it becomes unperfected and is deemed never to have been perfected as against a purchaser of the collateral for value.

(c) [Possessory security interest in collateral moved to new jurisdiction.] A possessory security interest in collateral, other than goods covered by a certificate of title and as-extracted collateral consisting of goods, remains continuously perfected if:

(1) the collateral is located in one jurisdiction and subject to a security interest perfected under the law of that jurisdiction;

(2) thereafter the collateral is brought into another jurisdiction; and

(3) upon entry into the other jurisdiction, the security interest is perfected under the law of the other jurisdiction.

(d) [Goods covered by certificate of title from this state.] Except as otherwise provided in subsection (e), a security interest in goods covered by a certificate of title which is perfected by any method under the law of another jurisdiction when the goods become covered by a certificate of title from this State remains perfected until the security interest would have become unperfected under the law of the other jurisdiction had the goods not become so covered.

(e) [When subsection (d) security interest becomes unperfected against purchasers.] A security interest described in subsection (d) becomes unperfected as against a purchaser of the goods for value and is deemed never to have been perfected as against a purchaser of the goods for value if the applicable requirements for perfection under Section 9–311(b) or 9–313 are not satisfied before the earlier of:

(1) the time the security interest would have become unperfected under the law of the other jurisdiction had the goods not become covered by a certificate of title from this State; or

(2) the expiration of four months after the goods had become so covered.

(f) [Change in jurisdiction of bank, issuer, nominated person, securities intermediary, or commodity intermediary.] A security interest in deposit accounts, letter-of-credit rights, or investment property which is perfected under the law of the bank's jurisdiction, the issuer's jurisdiction, a nominated person's jurisdiction, the securities intermediary's jurisdiction, or the commodity intermediary's jurisdiction, as applicable, remains perfected until the earlier of:

(1) the time the security interest would have become unperfected under the law of that jurisdiction; or

(2) the expiration of four months after a change of the applicable jurisdiction to another jurisdiction.

(g) [Subsection (f) security interest perfected or unperfected under law of new jurisdiction.] If a security interest described in subsection (f) becomes perfected under the law of the other jurisdiction before the earlier of the time or the end of the period described in that subsection, it remains perfected thereafter. If the security interest does not become perfected under the law of the other jurisdiction before the earlier of that time or the end of that period, it becomes unperfected and is deemed never to have been perfected as against a purchaser of the collateral for value.

§ 9–317. Interests That Take Priority over or Take Free of Security Interest or Agricultural Lien.

(a) [Conflicting security interests and rights of lien creditors.] A security interest or agricultural lien is subordinate to the rights of:

(1) a person entitled to priority under Section 9–322; and

(2) except as otherwise provided in subsection (e), a person that becomes a lien creditor before the earlier of the time:

(A) the security interest or agricultural lien is perfected; or

(B) one of the conditions specified in Section 9–203(b)(3) is met and a financing statement covering the collateral is filed.

(b) [Buyers that receive delivery.] Except as otherwise provided in subsection (e), a buyer, other than a secured party, of tangible chattel paper, documents, goods, instruments, or a security certificate takes free of a security interest or agricultural lien if the buyer gives value and receives delivery of the collateral without knowledge of the security interest or agricultural lien and before it is perfected.

(c) [Lessees that receive delivery.] Except as otherwise provided in subsection (e), a lessee of goods takes free of a security interest or agricultural lien if the lessee gives value and receives delivery of the collateral without knowledge of the security interest or agricultural lien and before it is perfected.

(d) [Licensees and buyers of certain collateral.] A licensee of a general intangible or a buyer, other than a secured party, of accounts, electronic chattel paper, general intangibles, or investment property other than a certificated security takes free of a security interest if the licensee or buyer gives value without knowledge of the security interest and before it is perfected.

(e) [Purchase-money security interest.] Except as otherwise provided in Sections 9–320 and 9–321, if a person files a financing statement with respect to a purchase-money security interest before or within 20 days after the debtor receives delivery of the collateral, the security interest takes priority over the rights of a buyer, lessee, or lien creditor which arise between the time the security interest attaches and the time of filing.

§ 9–320. Buyer of Goods.

(a) [Buyer in ordinary course of business.] Except as otherwise provided in subsection (e), a buyer in ordinary course of business, other than a person buying farm products from a person engaged in farming operations, takes free of a security interest created by the buyer's seller, even if the security interest is perfected and the buyer knows of its existence.

(b) [Buyer of consumer goods.] Except as otherwise provided in subsection (e), a buyer of goods from a person who used or bought the goods for use primarily for personal, family, or household purposes takes free of a security interest, even if perfected, if the buyer buys:

(1) without knowledge of the security interest;

(2) for value;

(3) primarily for the buyer's personal, family, or household purposes; and

(4) before the filing of a financing statement covering the goods.

(c) [Effectiveness of filing for subsection (b).] To the extent that it affects the priority of a security interest over a buyer of goods under subsection (b), the period of effectiveness of a filing made in the jurisdiction in which the seller is located is governed by Section 9–316(a) and (b).

(d) [Buyer in ordinary course of business at wellhead or minehead.] A buyer in ordinary course of business buying oil, gas, or other minerals at the wellhead or minehead or after extraction takes free of an interest arising out of an encumbrance.

(e) [Possessory security interest not affected.] Subsections (a) and (b) do not affect a security interest in goods in the possession of the secured party under Section 9–313.

§ 9–322. Priorities among Conflicting Security Interests in and Agricultural Liens on Same Collateral.

(a) [General priority rules.] Except as otherwise provided in this section, priority among conflicting security interests and agricultural liens in the same collateral is determined according to the following rules:

(1) Conflicting perfected security interests and agricultural liens rank according to priority in time of filing or perfection. Priority dates from the earlier of the time a filing covering the collateral is first made or the security interest or agricultural lien is first perfected, if there is no period thereafter when there is neither filing nor perfection.

(2) A perfected security interest or agricultural lien has priority over a conflicting unperfected security interest or agricultural lien.

(3) The first security interest or agricultural lien to attach or become effective has priority if conflicting security interests and agricultural liens are unperfected.

(b) [Time of perfection: proceeds and supporting obligations.] For the purposes of subsection (a)(1):

(1) the time of filing or perfection as to a security interest in collateral is also the time of filing or perfection as to a security interest in proceeds; and

(2) the time of filing or perfection as to a security interest in collateral supported by a supporting obligation is also the time of filing or perfection as to a security interest in the supporting obligation.

(c) [Special priority rules: proceeds and supporting obligations.] Except as otherwise provided in subsection (f), a security interest in collateral which qualifies for priority over a conflicting security interest under Section 9–327, 9–328, 9–329, 9–330, or 9–331 also has priority over a conflicting security interest in:

(1) any supporting obligation for the collateral; and

(2) proceeds of the collateral if:

(A) the security interest in proceeds is perfected;

(B) the proceeds are cash proceeds or of the same type as the collateral; and

(C) in the case of proceeds that are proceeds of proceeds, all intervening proceeds are cash proceeds, proceeds of the same type as the collateral, or an account relating to the collateral.

(d) [First-to-file priority rule for certain collateral.] Subject to subsection (e) and except as otherwise provided in subsection (f), if a security interest in chattel paper, deposit accounts, negotiable documents, instruments, investment property, or letter-of-credit rights is perfected by a method other than filing, conflicting perfected security interests in proceeds of the collateral rank according to priority in time of filing.

(e) [Applicability of subsection (d).] Subsection (d) applies only if the proceeds of the collateral are not cash proceeds, chattel paper, negotiable documents, instruments, investment property, or letter-of-credit rights.

(f) [Limitations on subsections (a) through (e).] Subsections (a) through (e) are subject to:

(1) subsection (g) and the other provisions of this part;

(2) Section 4–210 with respect to a security interest of a collecting bank;

(3) Section 5–118 with respect to a security interest of an issuer or nominated person; and

(4) Section 9–110 with respect to a security interest arising under Article 2 or 2A.

(g) [Priority under agricultural lien statute.] A perfected agricultural lien on collateral has priority over a conflicting security interest in or agricultural lien on the same collateral if the statute creating the agricultural lien so provides.

§ 9–323. Future Advances.

(a) [When priority based on time of advance.] Except as otherwise provided in subsection (c), for purposes of determining the priority of a perfected security interest under Section 9–322(a)(1), perfection of the security interest dates from the time an advance is made to the extent that the security interest secures an advance that:

(1) is made while the security interest is perfected only:

(A) under Section 9–309 when it attaches; or

(B) temporarily under Section 9–312(e), (f), or (g); and

(2) is not made pursuant to a commitment entered into before or while the security interest is perfected by a method other than under Section 9–309 or 9–312(e), (f), or (g).

(b) [Lien creditor.] Except as otherwise provided in subsection (c), a security interest is subordinate to the rights of a person that becomes a lien creditor to the extent that the security interest secures an advance made more than 45 days after the person becomes a lien creditor unless the advance is made:

(1) without knowledge of the lien; or

(2) pursuant to a commitment entered into without knowledge of the lien.

(c) [Buyer of receivables.] Subsections (a) and (b) do not apply to a security interest held by a secured party that is a buyer of accounts, chattel paper, payment intangibles, or promissory notes or a consignor.

(d) [Buyer of goods.] Except as otherwise provided in subsection (e), a buyer of goods other than a buyer in ordinary course of business takes free of a security interest to the extent that it secures advances made after the earlier of:

(1) the time the secured party acquires knowledge of the buyer's purchase; or

(2) 45 days after the purchase.

(e) [Advances made pursuant to commitment: priority of buyer of goods.] Subsection (d) does not apply if the advance is made pursuant to a commitment entered into without knowledge of the buyer's purchase and before the expiration of the 45-day period.

(f) [Lessee of goods.] Except as otherwise provided in subsection (g), a lessee of goods, other than a lessee in ordinary course of business, takes the leasehold interest free of a security interest to the extent that it secures advances made after the earlier of:

(1) the time the secured party acquires knowledge of the lease; or

(2) 45 days after the lease contract becomes enforceable.

(g) [Advances made pursuant to commitment: priority of lessee of goods.] Subsection (f) does not apply if the advance is made pursuant to a commitment entered into without knowledge of the lease and before the expiration of the 45-day period.

§ 9–324. Priority of Purchase-Money Security Interests.

(a) [General rule: purchase-money priority.] Except as otherwise provided in subsection (g), a perfected purchase-money security interest in goods other than inventory or livestock has priority over a conflicting security interest in the same goods, and, except as otherwise provided in Section 9–327, a perfected security interest in its identifiable proceeds also has priority, if the purchase-money security interest is perfected when the debtor receives possession of the collateral or within 20 days thereafter.

(b) [Inventory purchase-money priority.] Subject to subsection (c) and except as otherwise provided in subsection (g), a perfected purchase-money security interest in inventory has priority over a conflicting security interest in the same inventory, has priority over a conflicting security interest in chattel paper or an instrument constituting proceeds of the inventory and in proceeds of the chattel paper, if so provided in Section 9–330, and, except as otherwise provided in Section 9–327, also has priority in identifiable cash proceeds of the inventory to the extent the identifiable cash proceeds are received on or before the delivery of the inventory to a buyer, if:

(1) the purchase-money security interest is perfected when the debtor receives possession of the inventory;

(2) the purchase-money secured party sends an authenticated notification to the holder of the conflicting security interest;

(3) the holder of the conflicting security interest receives the notification within five years before the debtor receives possession of the inventory; and

(4) the notification states that the person sending the notification has or expects to acquire a purchase-money security interest in inventory of the debtor and describes the inventory.

(c) [Holders of conflicting inventory security interests to be notified.] Subsections (b)(2) through (4) apply only if the holder of the conflicting security interest had filed a financing statement covering the same types of inventory:

(1) if the purchase-money security interest is perfected by filing, before the date of the filing; or

(2) if the purchase-money security interest is temporarily perfected without filing or possession under Section 9–312(f), before the beginning of the 20–day period thereunder.

(d) [Livestock purchase-money priority.] Subject to subsection (e) and except as otherwise provided in subsection (g), a perfected purchase-money security interest in livestock that are farm products has priority over a conflicting security interest in the same livestock, and, except as otherwise provided in Section 9–327, a perfected security interest in their identifiable proceeds and identifiable products in their unmanufactured states also has priority, if:

(1) the purchase-money security interest is perfected when the debtor receives possession of the livestock;

(2) the purchase-money secured party sends an authenticated notification to the holder of the conflicting security interest;

(3) the holder of the conflicting security interest receives the notification within six months before the debtor receives possession of the livestock; and

(4) the notification states that the person sending the notification has or expects to acquire a purchase-money security interest in livestock of the debtor and describes the livestock.

(e) [Holders of conflicting livestock security interests to be notified.] Subsections (d)(2) through (4) apply only if the holder of the conflicting security interest had filed a financing statement covering the same types of livestock:

(1) if the purchase-money security interest is perfected by filing, before the date of the filing; or

(2) if the purchase-money security interest is temporarily perfected without filing or possession under Section 9–312(f), before the beginning of the 20–day period thereunder.

(f) [Software purchase-money priority.] Except as otherwise provided in subsection (g), a perfected purchase-money security interest in software has priority over a conflicting security interest in the same collateral, and, except as otherwise provided in Section 9–327, a perfected security interest in its identifiable proceeds also has priority, to the extent that the purchase-money security interest in the goods in which the software was acquired for use has priority in the goods and proceeds of the goods under this section.

(g) [Conflicting purchase-money security interests.] If more than one security interest qualifies for priority in the same collateral under subsection (a), (b), (d), or (f):

(1) a security interest securing an obligation incurred as all or part of the price of the collateral has priority over a security interest securing an obligation incurred for value given to enable the debtor to acquire rights in or the use of collateral; and

(2) in all other cases, Section 9–322(a) applies to the qualifying security interests.

§ 9–325. Priority of Security Interests in Transferred Collateral.

(a) [Subordination of security interest in transferred collateral.] Except as otherwise provided in subsection (b), a security interest created by a debtor is subordinate to a security interest in the same collateral created by another person if:

(1) the debtor acquired the collateral subject to the security interest created by the other person;

(2) the security interest created by the other person was perfected when the debtor acquired the collateral; and

(3) there is no period thereafter when the security interest is unperfected.

(b) [Limitation of subsection (a) subordination.] Subsection (a) subordinates a security interest only if the security interest:

(1) otherwise would have priority solely under Section 9–322(a) or 9–324; or

(2) arose solely under Section 2–711(3) or 2A–508(5).

§ 9–327. Priority of Security Interests in Deposit Account.

The following rules govern priority among conflicting security interests in the same deposit account:

(1) A security interest held by a secured party having control of the deposit account under Section 9–104 has priority over a conflicting security interest held by a secured party that does not have control.

(2) Except as otherwise provided in paragraphs (3) and (4), security interests perfected by control under Section 9–314 rank according to priority in time of obtaining control.

(3) Except as otherwise provided in paragraph (4), a security interest held by the bank with which the deposit account is maintained has priority over a conflicting security interest held by another secured party.

(4) A security interest perfected by control under Section 9–104(a)(3) has priority over a security interest held by the bank with which the deposit account is maintained.

§ 9–328. Priority of Security Interests in Investment Property.

The following rules govern priority among conflicting security interests in the same investment property:

(1) A security interest held by a secured party having control of investment property under Section 9–106 has priority over a security interest held by a secured party that does not have control of the investment property.

(2) Except as otherwise provided in paragraphs (3) and (4), conflicting security interests held by secured parties each of which has control under Section 9–106 rank according to priority in time of:

(A) if the collateral is a security, obtaining control;

(B) if the collateral is a security entitlement carried in a securities account and:

(i) if the secured party obtained control under Section 8–106(d)(1), the secured party's becoming the person for which the securities account is maintained;

(ii) if the secured party obtained control under Section 8–106(d)(2), the securities intermediary's agreement to comply with the secured party's entitlement orders with respect to security entitlements carried or to be carried in the securities account; or

(iii) if the secured party obtained control through another person under Section 8–106(d)(3), the time on which priority would be based under this paragraph if the other person were the secured party; or

(C) if the collateral is a commodity contract carried with a commodity intermediary, the satisfaction of the requirement for control specified in Section 9–106(b)(2) with respect to commodity contracts carried or to be carried with the commodity intermediary.

(3) A security interest held by a securities intermediary in a security entitlement or a securities account maintained with the securities intermediary has priority over a conflicting security interest held by another secured party.

(4) A security interest held by a commodity intermediary in a commodity contract or a commodity account maintained with the commodity intermediary has priority over a conflicting security interest held by another secured party.

(5) A security interest in a certificated security in registered form which is perfected by taking delivery under Section 9–313(a) and not by control under Section 9–314 has priority over a conflicting security interest perfected by a method other than control.

(6) Conflicting security interests created by a broker, securities intermediary, or commodity intermediary which are perfected without control under Section 9–106 rank equally.

(7) In all other cases, priority among conflicting security interests in investment property is governed by Sections 9–322 and 9–323.

§ 9–329. Priority of Security Interests in Letter-of-Credit Right.
The following rules govern priority among conflicting security interests in the same letter-of-credit right:

(1) A security interest held by a secured party having control of the letter-of-credit right under Section 9–107 has priority to the extent of its control over a conflicting security interest held by a secured party that does not have control.

(2) Security interests perfected by control under Section 9–314 rank according to priority in time of obtaining control.

§ 9–330. Priority of Purchaser of Chattel Paper or Instrument.
(a) [Purchaser's priority: security interest claimed merely as proceeds.] A purchaser of chattel paper has priority over a security interest in the chattel paper which is claimed merely as proceeds of inventory subject to a security interest if:

(1) in good faith and in the ordinary course of the purchaser's business, the purchaser gives new value and takes possession of the chattel paper or obtains control of the chattel paper under Section 9–105; and

(2) the chattel paper does not indicate that it has been assigned to an identified assignee other than the purchaser.

(b) [Purchaser's priority: other security interests.] A purchaser of chattel paper has priority over a security interest in the chattel paper which is claimed other than merely as proceeds of inventory subject to a security interest if the purchaser gives new value and takes possession of the chattel paper or obtains control of the chattel paper under Section 9–105 in good faith, in the ordinary course of the purchaser's business, and without knowledge that the purchase violates the rights of the secured party.

(c) [Chattel paper purchaser's priority in proceeds.] Except as otherwise provided in Section 9–327, a purchaser having priority in chattel paper under subsection (a) or (b) also has priority in proceeds of the chattel paper to the extent that:

(1) Section 9–322 provides for priority in the proceeds; or

(2) the proceeds consist of the specific goods covered by the chattel paper or cash proceeds of the specific goods, even if the purchaser's security interest in the proceeds is unperfected.

(d) [Instrument purchaser's priority.] Except as otherwise provided in Section 9–331(a), a purchaser of an instrument has priority over a security interest in the instrument perfected by a method other than possession if the purchaser gives value and takes possession of the instrument in good faith and without knowledge that the purchase violates the rights of the secured party.

(e) [Holder of purchase-money security interest gives new value.] For purposes of subsections (a) and (b), the holder of a purchase-money security interest in inventory gives new value for chattel paper constituting proceeds of the inventory.

(f) [Indication of assignment gives knowledge.] For purposes of subsections (b) and (d), if chattel paper or an instrument indicates that it has been assigned to an identified secured party other than the purchaser, a purchaser of the chattel paper or instrument has knowledge that the purchase violates the rights of the secured party.

§ 9–331. Priority of Rights of Purchasers of Instruments, Documents, and Securities under Other Articles; Priority of Interests in Financial Assets and Security Entitlements under Article 8.
(a) [Rights under Articles 3, 7, and 8 not limited.] This article does not limit the rights of a holder in due course of a negotiable instrument, a holder to which a negotiable document of title has been duly negotiated, or a protected purchaser of a security. These holders or purchasers take priority over an earlier security interest, even if perfected, to the extent provided in Articles 3, 7, and 8.

(b) [Protection under Article 8.] This article does not limit the rights of or impose liability on a person to the extent that the person is protected against the assertion of a claim under Article 8.

(c) [Filing not notice.] Filing under this article does not constitute notice of a claim or defense to the holders, or purchasers, or persons described in subsections (a) and (b).

§ 9–332. Transfer of Money; Transfer of Funds from Deposit Account.
(a) [Transferee of money.] A transferee of money takes the money free of a security interest unless the transferee acts in collusion with the debtor in violating the rights of the secured party.

(b) [Transferee of funds from deposit account.] A transferee of funds from a deposit account takes the funds free of a security interest in the deposit account unless the transferee acts in collusion with the debtor in violating the rights of the secured party.

§ 9–333. Priority of Certain Liens Arising by Operation of Law.
(a) ["Possessory lien."] In this section, "possessory lien" means an interest, other than a security interest or an agricultural lien:

(1) which secures payment or performance of an obligation for services or materials furnished with respect to goods by a person in the ordinary course of the person's business;

(2) which is created by statute or rule of law in favor of the person; and

(3) whose effectiveness depends on the person's possession of the goods.

(b) [Priority of possessory lien.] A possessory lien on goods has priority over a security interest in the goods unless the lien is created by a statute that expressly provides otherwise.

§ 9–334. Priority of Security Interests in Fixtures and Crops.
(a) [Security interest in fixtures under this article.] A security interest under this article may be created in goods that are fixtures or may continue in goods that become fixtures. A security interest does not exist under this article in ordinary building materials incorporated into an improvement on land.

(b) [Security interest in fixtures under real-property law.] This article does not prevent creation of an encumbrance upon fixtures under real property law.

(c) [General rule: subordination of security interest in fixtures.] In cases not governed by subsections (d) through (h), a security interest in fixtures is subordinate to a conflicting interest of an encumbrancer or owner of the related real property other than the debtor.

(d) [Fixtures purchase-money priority.] Except as otherwise provided in subsection (h), a perfected security interest in fixtures has priority over a conflicting interest of an encumbrancer or owner of the real property if the debtor has an interest of record in or is in possession of the real property and:

(1) the security interest is a purchase-money security interest;

(2) the interest of the encumbrancer or owner arises before the goods become fixtures; and

(3) the security interest is perfected by a fixture filing before the goods become fixtures or within 20 days thereafter.

(e) [Priority of security interest in fixtures over interests in real property.] A perfected security interest in fixtures has priority over a conflicting interest of an encumbrancer or owner of the real property if:

(1) the debtor has an interest of record in the real property or is in possession of the real property and the security interest:

(A) is perfected by a fixture filing before the interest of the encumbrancer or owner is of record; and

(B) has priority over any conflicting interest of a predecessor in title of the encumbrancer or owner;

(2) before the goods become fixtures, the security interest is perfected by any method permitted by this article and the fixtures are readily removable:

(A) factory or office machines;

(B) equipment that is not primarily used or leased for use in the operation of the real property; or

(C) replacements of domestic appliances that are consumer goods;

(3) the conflicting interest is a lien on the real property obtained by legal or equitable proceedings after the security interest was perfected by any method permitted by this article; or

(4) the security interest is:

(A) created in a manufactured home in a manufactured-home transaction; and

(B) perfected pursuant to a statute described in Section 9–311(a)(2).

(f) [Priority based on consent, disclaimer, or right to remove.] A security interest in fixtures, whether or not perfected, has priority over a conflicting interest of an encumbrancer or owner of the real property if:

(1) the encumbrancer or owner has, in an authenticated record, consented to the security interest or disclaimed an interest in the goods as fixtures; or

(2) the debtor has a right to remove the goods as against the encumbrancer or owner.

(g) [Continuation of paragraph (f)(2) priority.] The priority of the security interest under paragraph (f)(2) continues for a reasonable time if the debtor's right to remove the goods as against the encumbrancer or owner terminates.

(h) [Priority of construction mortgage.] A mortgage is a construction mortgage to the extent that it secures an obligation incurred for the construction of an improvement on land, including the acquisition cost of the land, if a recorded record of the mortgage so indicates. Except as otherwise provided in subsections (e) and (f), a security interest in fixtures is subordinate to a construction mortgage if a record of the mortgage is recorded before the goods become fixtures and the goods become fixtures before the completion of the construction. A mortgage has this priority to the same extent as a construction mortgage to the extent that it is given to refinance a construction mortgage.

(i) [Priority of security interest in crops.] A perfected security interest in crops growing on real property has priority over a conflicting interest of an encumbrancer or owner of the real property if the debtor has an interest of record in or is in possession of the real property.

(j) [Subsection (i) prevails.] Subsection (i) prevails over any inconsistent provisions of the following statutes:

§ 9-335. Accessions.

(a) [Creation of security interest in accession.] A security interest may be created in an accession and continues in collateral that becomes an accession.

(b) [Perfection of security interest.] If a security interest is perfected when the collateral becomes an accession, the security interest remains perfected in the collateral.

(c) [Priority of security interest.] Except as otherwise provided in subsection (d), the other provisions of this part determine the priority of a security interest in an accession.

(d) [Compliance with certificate-of-title statute.] A security interest in an accession is subordinate to a security interest in the whole which is perfected by compliance with the requirements of a certificate-of-title statute under Section 9–311(b).

(e) [Removal of accession after default.] After default, subject to Part 6, a secured party may remove an accession from other goods if the security interest in the accession has priority over the claims of every person having an interest in the whole.

(f) [Reimbursement following removal.] A secured party that removes an accession from other goods under subsection (e) shall promptly reimburse any holder of a security interest or other lien on, or owner of, the whole or of the other goods, other than the debtor, for the cost of repair of any physical injury to the whole or the other goods. The secured party need not reimburse the holder or owner for any diminution in value of the whole or the other goods caused by the absence of the accession removed or by any necessity for replacing it. A person entitled to reimbursement may refuse permission to remove until the secured party gives adequate assurance for the performance of the obligation to reimburse.

§ 9–336. Commingled Goods.

(a) ["Commingled goods."] In this section, "commingled goods" means goods that are physically united with other goods in such a manner that their identity is lost in a product or mass.

(b) [No security interest in commingled goods as such.] A security interest does not exist in commingled goods as such. However, a security interest may attach to a product or mass that results when goods become commingled goods.

(c) [Attachment of security interest to product or mass.] If collateral becomes commingled goods, a security interest attaches to the product or mass.

(d) [Perfection of security interest.] If a security interest in collateral is perfected before the collateral becomes commingled goods, the security interest that attaches to the product or mass under subsection (c) is perfected.

(e) [Priority of security interest.] Except as otherwise provided in subsection (f), the other provisions of this part determine the priority of a security interest that attaches to the product or mass under subsection (c).

(f) [Conflicting security interests in product or mass] If more than one security interest attaches to the product or mass under subsection (c), the following rules determine priority:

(1) A security interest that is perfected under subsection (d) has priority over a security interest that is unperfected at the time the collateral becomes commingled goods.

(2) If more than one security interest is perfected under subsection (d), the security interests rank equally in proportion to the value of the collateral at the time it became commingled goods.

§ 9–337. Priority of Security Interests in Goods Covered by Certificate of Title.

If, while a security interest in goods is perfected by any method under the law of another jurisdiction, this State issues a certificate of title that does not show that the goods are subject to the security interest or contain a statement that they may be subject to security interests not shown on the certificate:

(1) a buyer of the goods, other than a person in the business of selling goods of that kind, takes free of the security interest if the buyer gives value and receives delivery of the goods after issuance of the certificate and without knowledge of the security interest; and

(2) the security interest is subordinate to a conflicting security interest in the goods that attaches, and is perfected under Section 9–311(b), after issuance of the certificate and without the conflicting secured party's knowledge of the security interest.

Part 5—Filing

§ 9–501. Filing Office.

(a) [Filing offices.] Except as otherwise provided in subsection (b), if the local law of this State governs perfection of a security interest or agricultural lien, the office in which to file a financing statement to perfect the security interest or agricultural lien is:

(1) the office designated for the filing or recording of a record of a mortgage on the related real property, if:

(A) the collateral is as-extracted collateral or timber to be cut; or

(B) the financing statement is filed as a fixture filing and the collateral is goods that are or are to become fixtures; or

(2) the office of [ ] [or any office duly authorized by [ ]], in all other cases, including a case in which the collateral is goods that are or are to become fixtures and the financing statement is not filed as a fixture filing.

(b) [Filing office for transmitting utilities.] The office in which to file a financing statement to perfect a security interest in collateral, including fixtures, of a transmitting utility is the office of [ ]. The financing statement also constitutes a fixture filing as to the collateral indicated in the financing statement which is or is to become fixtures.

§ 9–502. Contents of Financing Statement; Record of Mortgage as Financing Statement; Time of Filing Financing Statement.

(a) [Sufficiency of financing statement.] Subject to subsection (b), a financing statement is sufficient only if it:

(1) provides the name of the debtor;

(2) provides the name of the secured party or a representative of the secured party; and

(3) indicates the collateral covered by the financing statement.

(b) [Real-property-related financing statements.] Except as otherwise provided in Section 9–501(b), to be sufficient, a financing statement that covers as-extracted collateral or timber to be cut, or which is filed as a fixture filing and covers goods that are or are to become fixtures, must satisfy subsection (a) and also:

(1) indicate that it covers this type of collateral;

(2) indicate that it is to be filed [for record] in the real property records;

(3) provide a description of the real property to which the collateral is related [sufficient to give constructive notice of a mortgage under the law of this State if the description were contained in a record of the mortgage of the real property]; and

(4) if the debtor does not have an interest of record in the real property, provide the name of a record owner.

(c) [Record of mortgage as financing statement.] A record of a mortgage is effective, from the date of recording, as a financing statement filed as a fixture filing or as a financing statement covering as-extracted collateral or timber to be cut only if:

(1) the record indicates the goods or accounts that it covers;

(2) the goods are or are to become fixtures related to the real property described in the record or the collateral is related to the real property described in the record and is as-extracted collateral or timber to be cut;

(3) the record satisfies the requirements for a financing statement in this section other than an indication that it is to be filed in the real property records; and

(4) the record is [duly] recorded.

(d) [Filing before security agreement or attachment.] A financing statement may be filed before a security agreement is made or a security interest otherwise attaches.

§ 9–503. Name of Debtor and Secured Party.

(a) [Sufficiency of debtor's name.] A financing statement sufficiently provides the name of the debtor:

(1) if the debtor is a registered organization, only if the financing statement provides the name of the debtor indicated on the public record of the debtor's jurisdiction of organization which shows the debtor to have been organized;

(2) if the debtor is a decedent's estate, only if the financing statement provides the name of the decedent and indicates that the debtor is an estate;

(3) if the debtor is a trust or a trustee acting with respect to property held in trust, only if the financing statement:

(A) provides the name specified for the trust in its organic documents or, if no name is specified, provides the name of the settlor and additional information sufficient to distinguish the debtor from other trusts having one or more of the same settlors; and

(B) indicates, in the debtor's name or otherwise, that the debtor is a trust or is a trustee acting with respect to property held in trust; and

(4) in other cases:

(A) if the debtor has a name, only if it provides the individual or organizational name of the debtor; and

(B) if the debtor does not have a name, only if it provides the names of the partners, members, associates, or other persons comprising the debtor.

(b) [Additional debtor-related information.] A financing statement that provides the name of the debtor in accordance with subsection (a) is not rendered ineffective by the absence of:

(1) a trade name or other name of the debtor; or

(2) unless required under subsection (a)(4)(B), names of partners, members, associates, or other persons comprising the debtor.

(c) [Debtor's trade name insufficient.] A financing statement that provides only the debtor's trade name does not sufficiently provide the name of the debtor.

(d) [Representative capacity.] Failure to indicate the representative capacity of a secured party or representative of a secured party does not affect the sufficiency of a financing statement.

(e) [Multiple debtors and secured parties.] A financing statement may provide the name of more than one debtor and the name of more than one secured party.

§ 9–504. Indication of Collateral.

A financing statement sufficiently indicates the collateral that it covers if the financing statement provides:

(1) a description of the collateral pursuant to Section 9–108; or

(2) an indication that the financing statement covers all assets or all personal property.

§ 9–506. Effect of Errors or Omissions.

(a) [Minor errors and omissions.] A financing statement substantially satisfying the requirements of this part is effective, even if it has minor errors or omissions, unless the errors or omissions make the financing statement seriously misleading.

(b) [Financing statement seriously misleading.] Except as otherwise provided in subsection (c), a financing statement that fails sufficiently to provide the name of the debtor in accordance with Section 9–503(a) is seriously misleading.

(c) [Financing statement not seriously misleading.] If a search of the records of the filing office under the debtor's correct name, using the filing office's standard search logic, if any, would disclose a financing statement that fails sufficiently to provide the name of the debtor in accordance with Section 9–503(a), the name provided does not make the financing statement seriously misleading.

(d) ["Debtor's correct name."] For purposes of Section 9–508(b), the "debtor's correct name" in subsection (c) means the correct name of the new debtor.

§ 9–512. Amendment of Financing Statement.

[Alternative A]

(a) [Amendment of information in financing statement.] Subject to Section 9–509, a person may add or delete collateral covered by, continue or terminate the effectiveness of, or, subject to subsection (e), otherwise amend the information provided in, a financing statement by filing an amendment that:

(1) identifies, by its file number, the initial financing statement to which the amendment relates; and

(2) if the amendment relates to an initial financing statement filed [or recorded] in a filing office described in Section 9–501(a)(1), provides the information specified in Section 9–502(b).

[Alternative B]

(a) [Amendment of information in financing statement.] Subject to Section 9–509, a person may add or delete collateral covered by, continue or terminate the effectiveness of, or, subject to subsection (e), otherwise amend the information provided in, a financing statement by filing an amendment that:

(1) identifies, by its file number, the initial financing statement to which the amendment relates; and

(2) if the amendment relates to an initial financing statement filed [or recorded] in a filing office described in Section 9–501(a)(1), provides the date [and time] that the initial financing statement was filed [or recorded] and the information specified in Section 9–502(b).

[End of Alternatives]

(b) **[Period of effectiveness not affected.]** Except as otherwise provided in Section 9–515, the filing of an amendment does not extend the period of effectiveness of the financing statement.

(c) **[Effectiveness of amendment adding collateral.]** A financing statement that is amended by an amendment that adds collateral is effective as to the added collateral only from the date of the filing of the amendment.

(d) **[Effectiveness of amendment adding debtor.]** A financing statement that is amended by an amendment that adds a debtor is effective as to the added debtor only from the date of the filing of the amendment.

(e) **[Certain amendments ineffective.]** An amendment is ineffective to the extent it:

(1) purports to delete all debtors and fails to provide the name of a debtor to be covered by the financing statement; or

(2) purports to delete all secured parties of record and fails to provide the name of a new secured party of record.

§ 9–515. Duration and Effectiveness of Financing Statement; Effect of Lapsed Financing Statement.

(a) **[Five-year effectiveness.]** Except as otherwise provided in subsections (b), (e), (f), and (g), a filed financing statement is effective for a period of five years after the date of filing.

(b) **[Public-finance or manufactured-home transaction.]** Except as otherwise provided in subsections (e), (f), and (g), an initial financing statement filed in connection with a public-finance transaction or manufactured-home transaction is effective for a period of 30 years after the date of filing if it indicates that it is filed in connection with a public-finance transaction or manufactured-home transaction.

(c) **[Lapse and continuation of financing statement.]** The effectiveness of a filed financing statement lapses on the expiration of the period of its effectiveness unless before the lapse a continuation statement is filed pursuant to subsection (d). Upon lapse, a financing statement ceases to be effective and any security interest or agricultural lien that was perfected by the financing statement becomes unperfected, unless the security interest is perfected otherwise. If the security interest or agricultural lien becomes unperfected upon lapse, it is deemed never to have been perfected as against a purchaser of the collateral for value.

(d) **[When continuation statement may be filed.]** A continuation statement may be filed only within six months before the expiration of the five-year period specified in subsection (a) or the 30-year period specified in subsection (b), whichever is applicable.

(e) **[Effect of filing continuation statement.]** Except as otherwise provided in Section 9–510, upon timely filing of a continuation statement, the effectiveness of the initial financing statement continues for a period of five years commencing on the day on which the financing statement would have become ineffective in the absence of the filing. Upon the expiration of the five-year period, the financing statement lapses in the same manner as provided in subsection (c), unless, before the lapse, another continuation statement is filed pursuant to subsection (d). Succeeding continuation statements may be filed in the same manner to continue the effectiveness of the initial financing statement.

(f) **[Transmitting utility financing statement.]** If a debtor is a transmitting utility and a filed financing statement so indicates, the financing statement is effective until a termination statement is filed.

(g) **[Record of mortgage as financing statement.]** A record of a mortgage that is effective as a financing statement filed as a fixture filing under Section 9–502(c) remains effective as a financing statement filed as a fixture filing until the mortgage is released or satisfied of record or its effectiveness otherwise terminates as to the real property.

§ 9–516. What Constitutes Filing; Effectiveness of Filing.

(a) **[What constitutes filing.]** Except as otherwise provided in subsection (b), communication of a record to a filing office and tender of the filing fee or acceptance of the record by the filing office constitutes filing.

(b) **[Refusal to accept record; filing does not occur.]** Filing does not occur with respect to a record that a filing office refuses to accept because:

(1) the record is not communicated by a method or medium of communication authorized by the filing office;

(2) an amount equal to or greater than the applicable filing fee is not tendered;

(3) the filing office is unable to index the record because:

(A) in the case of an initial financing statement, the record does not provide a name for the debtor;

(B) in the case of an amendment or correction statement, the record:

(i) does not identify the initial financing statement as required by Section 9–512 or 9–518, as applicable; or

(ii) identifies an initial financing statement whose effectiveness has lapsed under Section 9–515;

(C) in the case of an initial financing statement that provides the name of a debtor identified as an individual or an amendment that provides a name of a debtor identified as an individual which was not previously provided in the financing statement to which the record relates, the record does not identify the debtor's last name; or

(D) in the case of a record filed [or recorded] in the filing office described in Section 9–501(a)(1), the record does not provide a sufficient description of the real property to which it relates;

(4) in the case of an initial financing statement or an amendment that adds a secured party of record, the record does not provide a name and mailing address for the secured party of record;

(5) in the case of an initial financing statement or an amendment that provides a name of a debtor which was not previously provided in the financing statement to which the amendment relates, the record does not:

(A) provide a mailing address for the debtor;

(B) indicate whether the debtor is an individual or an organization; or

(C) if the financing statement indicates that the debtor is an organization, provide:

(i) a type of organization for the debtor;

(ii) a jurisdiction of organization for the debtor; or

(iii) an organizational identification number for the debtor or indicate that the debtor has none;

(6) in the case of an assignment reflected in an initial financing statement under Section 9–514(a) or an amendment filed under Section 9–514(b), the record does not provide a name and mailing address for the assignee; or

(7) in the case of a continuation statement, the record is not filed within the six-month period prescribed by Section 9–515(d).

(c) **[Rules applicable to subsection (b).]** For purposes of subsection (b):

(1) a record does not provide information if the filing office is unable to read or decipher the information; and

(2) a record that does not indicate that it is an amendment or identify an initial financing statement to which it relates, as required by Section 9–512, 9–514, or 9–518, is an initial financing statement.

(d) [Refusal to accept record; record effective as filed record.] A record that is communicated to the filing office with tender of the filing fee, but which the filing office refuses to accept for a reason other than one set forth in subsection (b), is effective as a filed record except as against a purchaser of the collateral which gives value in reasonable reliance upon the absence of the record from the files.

§ 9–520. Acceptance and Refusal to Accept Record.

(a) [Mandatory refusal to accept record.] A filing office shall refuse to accept a record for filing for a reason set forth in Section 9–516(b) and may refuse to accept a record for filing only for a reason set forth in Section 9–516(b).

(b) [Communication concerning refusal.] If a filing office refuses to accept a record for filing, it shall communicate to the person that presented the record the fact of and reason for the refusal and the date and time the record would have been filed had the filing office accepted it. The communication must be made at the time and in the manner prescribed by filing-office rule but [, in the case of a filing office described in Section 9–501(a)(2),] in no event more than two business days after the filing office receives the record.

(c) [When filed financing statement effective.] A filed financing statement satisfying Section 9–502(a) and (b) is effective, even if the filing office is required to refuse to accept it for filing under subsection (a). However, Section 9–338 applies to a filed financing statement providing information described in Section 9–516(b)(5) which is incorrect at the time the financing statement is filed.

(d) [Separate application to multiple debtors.] If a record communicated to a filing office provides information that relates to more than one debtor, this part applies as to each debtor separately.

Part 6—Default

§ 9–601. Rights after Default; Judicial Enforcement; Consignor or Buyer of Accounts, Chattel Paper, Payment Intangibles, or Promissory Notes.

(a) [Rights of secured party after default.] After default, a secured party has the rights provided in this part and, except as otherwise provided in Section 9–602, those provided by agreement of the parties. A secured party:

(1) may reduce a claim to judgment, foreclose, or otherwise enforce the claim, security interest, or agricultural lien by any available judicial procedure; and

(2) if the collateral is documents, may proceed either as to the documents or as to the goods they cover.

(b) [Rights and duties of secured party in possession or control.] A secured party in possession of collateral or control of collateral under Section 9–104, 9–105, 9–106, or 9–107 has the rights and duties provided in Section 9–207.

(c) [Rights cumulative; simultaneous exercise.] The rights under subsections (a) and (b) are cumulative and may be exercised simultaneously.

(d) [Rights of debtor and obligor.] Except as otherwise provided in subsection (g) and Section 9–605, after default, a debtor and an obligor have the rights provided in this part and by agreement of the parties.

(e) [Lien of levy after judgment.] If a secured party has reduced its claim to judgment, the lien of any levy that may be made upon the collateral by virtue of an execution based upon the judgment relates back to the earliest of:

(1) the date of perfection of the security interest or agricultural lien in the collateral;

(2) the date of filing a financing statement covering the collateral; or

(3) any date specified in a statute under which the agricultural lien was created.

(f) [Execution sale.] A sale pursuant to an execution is a foreclosure of the security interest or agricultural lien by judicial procedure within the meaning of this section. A secured party may purchase at the sale and thereafter hold the collateral free of any other requirements of this article.

(g) [Consignor or buyer of certain rights to payment.] Except as otherwise provided in Section 9–607(c), this part imposes no duties upon a secured party that is a consignor or is a buyer of accounts, chattel paper, payment intangibles, or promissory notes.

§ 9–607. Collection and Enforcement by Secured Party.

(a) [Collection and enforcement generally.] If so agreed, and in any event after default, a secured party:

(1) may notify an account debtor or other person obligated on collateral to make payment or otherwise render performance to or for the benefit of the secured party;

(2) may take any proceeds to which the secured party is entitled under Section 9–315;

(3) may enforce the obligations of an account debtor or other person obligated on collateral and exercise the rights of the debtor with respect to the obligation of the account debtor or other person obligated on collateral to make payment or otherwise render performance to the debtor, and with respect to any property that secures the obligations of the account debtor or other person obligated on the collateral;

(4) if it holds a security interest in a deposit account perfected by control under Section 9–104(a)(1), may apply the balance of the deposit account to the obligation secured by the deposit account; and

(5) if it holds a security interest in a deposit account perfected by control under Section 9–104(a)(2) or (3), may instruct the bank to pay the balance of the deposit account to or for the benefit of the secured party.

(b) [Nonjudicial enforcement of mortgage.] If necessary to enable a secured party to exercise under subsection (a)(3) the right of a debtor to enforce a mortgage nonjudicially, the secured party may record in the office in which a record of the mortgage is recorded:

(1) a copy of the security agreement that creates or provides for a security interest in the obligation secured by the mortgage; and

(2) the secured party's sworn affidavit in recordable form stating that:

(A) a default has occurred; and

(B) the secured party is entitled to enforce the mortgage nonjudicially.

(c) [Commercially reasonable collection and enforcement.] A secured party shall proceed in a commercially reasonable manner if the secured party:

(1) undertakes to collect from or enforce an obligation of an account debtor or other person obligated on collateral; and

(2) is entitled to charge back uncollected collateral or otherwise to full or limited recourse against the debtor or a secondary obligor.

(d) [Expenses of collection and enforcement.] A secured party may deduct from the collections made pursuant to subsection (c) reasonable expenses of collection and enforcement, including reasonable attorney's fees and legal expenses incurred by the secured party.

(e) [Duties to secured party not affected.] This section does not determine whether an account debtor, bank, or other person obligated on collateral owes a duty to a secured party.

§ 9–608. Application of Proceeds of Collection or Enforcement; Liability for Deficiency and Right to Surplus.

(a) [Application of proceeds, surplus, and deficiency if obligation secured.] If a security interest or agricultural lien secures payment or performance of an obligation, the following rules apply:

(1) A secured party shall apply or pay over for application the cash proceeds of collection or enforcement under Section 9–607 in the following order to:

(A) the reasonable expenses of collection and enforcement and, to the extent provided for by agreement and not prohibited by law, reasonable attorney's fees and legal expenses incurred by the secured party;

(B) the satisfaction of obligations secured by the security interest or agricultural lien under which the collection or enforcement is made; and

(C) the satisfaction of obligations secured by any subordinate security interest in or other lien on the collateral subject to the security interest or agricultural lien under which the collection or enforcement is made if the secured party receives an authenticated demand for proceeds before distribution of the proceeds is completed.

(2) If requested by a secured party, a holder of a subordinate security interest or other lien shall furnish reasonable proof of the interest or lien within a reasonable time. Unless the holder complies, the secured party need not comply with the holder's demand under paragraph (1)(C).

(3) A secured party need not apply or pay over for application noncash proceeds of collection and enforcement under Section 9–607 unless the failure to do so would be commercially unreasonable. A secured party that applies or pays over for application noncash proceeds shall do so in a commercially reasonable manner.

(4) A secured party shall account to and pay a debtor for any surplus, and the obligor is liable for any deficiency.

(b) [No surplus or deficiency in sales of certain rights to payment.] If the underlying transaction is a sale of accounts, chattel paper, payment intangibles, or promissory notes, the debtor is not entitled to any surplus, and the obligor is not liable for any deficiency.

§ 9–609. Secured Party's Right to Take Possession after Default.

(a) [Possession; rendering equipment unusable; disposition on debtor's premises.] After default, a secured party:

(1) may take possession of the collateral; and

(2) without removal, may render equipment unusable and dispose of collateral on a debtor's premises under Section 9–610.

(b) [Judicial and nonjudicial process.] A secured party may proceed under subsection (a):

(1) pursuant to judicial process; or

(2) without judicial process, if it proceeds without breach of the peace.

(c) [Assembly of collateral.] If so agreed, and in any event after default, a secured party may require the debtor to assemble the collateral and make it available to the secured party at a place to be designated by the secured party which is reasonably convenient to both parties.

§ 9–610. Disposition of Collateral after Default.

(a) [Disposition after default.] After default, a secured party may sell, lease, license, or otherwise dispose of any or all of the collateral in its present condition or following any commercially reasonable preparation or processing.

(b) [Commercially reasonable disposition.] Every aspect of a disposition of collateral, including the method, manner, time, place, and other terms, must be commercially reasonable. If commercially reasonable, a secured party may dispose of collateral by public or private proceedings, by one or more contracts, as a unit or in parcels, and at any time and place and on any terms.

(c) [Purchase by secured party.] A secured party may purchase collateral:

(1) at a public disposition; or

(2) at a private disposition only if the collateral is of a kind that is customarily sold on a recognized market or the subject of widely distributed standard price quotations.

(d) [Warranties on disposition.] A contract for sale, lease, license, or other disposition includes the warranties relating to title, possession, quiet enjoyment, and the like which by operation of law accompany a voluntary disposition of property of the kind subject to the contract.

(e) [Disclaimer of warranties.] A secured party may disclaim or modify warranties under subsection (d):

(1) in a manner that would be effective to disclaim or modify the warranties in a voluntary disposition of property of the kind subject to the contract of disposition; or

(2) by communicating to the purchaser a record evidencing the contract for disposition and including an express disclaimer or modification of the warranties.

(f) [Record sufficient to disclaim warranties.] A record is sufficient to disclaim warranties under subsection (e) if it indicates "There is no warranty relating to title, possession, quiet enjoyment, or the like in this disposition" or uses words of similar import.

§ 9–611. Notification Before Disposition of Collateral.

(a) ["Notification date."] In this section, "notification date" means the earlier of the date on which:

(1) a secured party sends to the debtor and any secondary obligor an authenticated notification of disposition; or

(2) the debtor and any secondary obligor waive the right to notification.

(b) [Notification of disposition required.] Except as otherwise provided in subsection (d), a secured party that disposes of collateral under Section 9–610 shall send to the persons specified in subsection (c) a reasonable authenticated notification of disposition.

(c) [Persons to be notified.] To comply with subsection (b), the secured party shall send an authenticated notification of disposition to:

(1) the debtor;

(2) any secondary obligor; and

(3) if the collateral is other than consumer goods:

(A) any other person from which the secured party has received, before the notification date, an authenticated notification of a claim of an interest in the collateral;

(B) any other secured party or lienholder that, 10 days before the notification date, held a security interest in or other lien on the collateral perfected by the filing of a financing statement that:

(i) identified the collateral;

(ii) was indexed under the debtor's name as of that date; and

(iii) was filed in the office in which to file a financing statement against the debtor covering the collateral as of that date; and

(C) any other secured party that, 10 days before the notification date, held a security interest in the collateral perfected by compliance with a statute, regulation, or treaty described in Section 9–311(a).

(d) [Subsection (b) inapplicable: perishable collateral; recognized market.] Subsection (b) does not apply if the collateral is perishable or threatens to decline speedily in value or is of a type customarily sold on a recognized market.

(e) [Compliance with subsection (c)(3)(B).] A secured party complies with the requirement for notification prescribed by subsection (c)(3)(B) if:

(1) not later than 20 days or earlier than 30 days before the notification date, the secured party requests, in a commercially reasonable manner, information concerning financing statements indexed under the debtor's name in the office indicated in subsection (c)(3)(B); and

(2) before the notification date, the secured party:

(A) did not receive a response to the request for information; or

(B) received a response to the request for information and sent an authenticated notification of disposition to each secured party or other lienholder named in that response whose financing statement covered the collateral.

§ 9–615. Application of Proceeds of Disposition; Liability for Deficiency and Right to Surplus.

(a) [Application of proceeds.] A secured party shall apply or pay over for application the cash proceeds of disposition under Section 9–610 in the following order to:

(1) the reasonable expenses of retaking, holding, preparing for disposition, processing, and disposing, and, to the extent provided for by agreement and not prohibited by law, reasonable attorney's fees and legal expenses incurred by the secured party;

(2) the satisfaction of obligations secured by the security interest or agricultural lien under which the disposition is made;

(3) the satisfaction of obligations secured by any subordinate security interest in or other subordinate lien on the collateral if:

(A) the secured party receives from the holder of the subordinate security interest or other lien an authenticated demand for proceeds before distribution of the proceeds is completed; and

(B) in a case in which a consignor has an interest in the collateral, the subordinate security interest or other lien is senior to the interest of the consignor; and

(4) a secured party that is a consignor of the collateral if the secured party receives from the consignor an authenticated demand for proceeds before distribution of the proceeds is completed.

(b) [Proof of subordinate interest.] If requested by a secured party, a holder of a subordinate security interest or other lien shall furnish reasonable proof of the interest or lien within a reasonable time. Unless the holder does so, the secured party need not comply with the holder's demand under subsection (a)(3).

(c) [Application of noncash proceeds.] A secured party need not apply or pay over for application noncash proceeds of disposition under Section 9–610 unless the failure to do so would be commercially unreasonable. A secured party that applies or pays over for application noncash proceeds shall do so in a commercially reasonable manner.

(d) [Surplus or deficiency if obligation secured.] If the security interest under which a disposition is made secures payment or performance of an obligation, after making the payments and applications required by subsection (a) and permitted by subsection (c):

(1) unless subsection (a)(4) requires the secured party to apply or pay over cash proceeds to a consignor, the secured party shall account to and pay a debtor for any surplus; and

(2) the obligor is liable for any deficiency.

(e) [No surplus or deficiency in sales of certain rights to payment.] If the underlying transaction is a sale of accounts, chattel paper, payment intangibles, or promissory notes:

(1) the debtor is not entitled to any surplus; and

(2) the obligor is not liable for any deficiency.

(f) [Calculation of surplus or deficiency in disposition to person related to secured party.] The surplus or deficiency following a disposition is calculated based on the amount of proceeds that would have been realized in a disposition complying with this part to a transferee other than the secured party, a person related to the secured party, or a secondary obligor if:

(1) the transferee in the disposition is the secured party, a person related to the secured party, or a secondary obligor; and

(2) the amount of proceeds of the disposition is significantly below the range of proceeds that a complying disposition to a person other than the secured party, a person related to the secured party, or a secondary obligor would have brought.

(g) [Cash proceeds received by junior secured party.] A secured party that receives cash proceeds of a disposition in good faith and without knowledge that the receipt violates the rights of the holder of a security interest or other lien that is not subordinate to the security interest or agricultural lien under which the disposition is made:

(1) takes the cash proceeds free of the security interest or other lien;

(2) is not obligated to apply the proceeds of the disposition to the satisfaction of obligations secured by the security interest or other lien; and

(3) is not obligated to account to or pay the holder of the security interest or other lien for any surplus.

§ 9–616. Explanation of Calculation of Surplus or Deficiency.

(a) [Definitions.] In this section:

(1) "Explanation" means a writing that:

(A) states the amount of the surplus or deficiency;

(B) provides an explanation in accordance with subsection (c) of how the secured party calculated the surplus or deficiency;

(C) states, if applicable, that future debits, credits, charges, including additional credit service charges or interest, rebates, and expenses may affect the amount of the surplus or deficiency; and

(D) provides a telephone number or mailing address from which additional information concerning the transaction is available.

(2) "Request" means a record:

(A) authenticated by a debtor or consumer obligor;

(B) requesting that the recipient provide an explanation; and

(C) sent after disposition of the collateral under Section 9–610.

(b) [Explanation of calculation.] In a consumer-goods transaction in which the debtor is entitled to a surplus or a consumer obligor is liable for a deficiency under Section 9–615, the secured party shall:

(1) send an explanation to the debtor or consumer obligor, as applicable, after the disposition and:

(A) before or when the secured party accounts to the debtor and pays any surplus or first makes written demand on the consumer obligor after the disposition for payment of the deficiency; and

(B) within 14 days after receipt of a request; or

(2) in the case of a consumer obligor who is liable for a deficiency, within 14 days after receipt of a request, send to the consumer obligor a record waiving the secured party's right to a deficiency.

(c) [Required information.] To comply with subsection (a)(1)(B), a writing must provide the following information in the following order:

(1) the aggregate amount of obligations secured by the security interest under which the disposition was made, and, if the amount reflects a rebate of unearned interest or credit service charge, an indication of that fact, calculated as of a specified date:

(A) if the secured party takes or receives possession of the collateral after default, not more than 35 days before the secured party takes or receives possession; or

(B) if the secured party takes or receives possession of the collateral before default or does not take possession of the collateral, not more than 35 days before the disposition;

(2) the amount of proceeds of the disposition;

(3) the aggregate amount of the obligations after deducting the amount of proceeds;

(4) the amount, in the aggregate or by type, and types of expenses, including expenses of retaking, holding, preparing for disposition, processing, and disposing of the collateral, and attorney's fees secured by the collateral which are known to the secured party and relate to the current disposition;

(5) the amount, in the aggregate or by type, and types of credits, including rebates of interest or credit service charges, to which the obligor is known to be entitled and which are not reflected in the amount in paragraph (1); and

(6) the amount of the surplus or deficiency.

(d) [Substantial compliance.] A particular phrasing of the explanation is not required. An explanation complying substantially with the requirements of subsection (a) is sufficient, even if it includes minor errors that are not seriously misleading.

(e) [Charges for responses.] A debtor or consumer obligor is entitled without charge to one response to a request under this section during any six-month period in which the secured party did not send to the debtor or consumer obligor an explanation pursuant to subsection (b)(1). The secured party may require payment of a charge not exceeding $25 for each additional response.

§ 9–617. Rights of Transferee of Collateral.

(a) [Effects of disposition.] A secured party's disposition of collateral after default:

(1) transfers to a transferee for value all of the debtor's rights in the collateral;

(2) discharges the security interest under which the disposition is made; and

(3) discharges any subordinate security interest or other subordinate lien [other than liens created under [cite acts or statutes providing for liens, if any, that are not to be discharged]].

(b) [Rights of good-faith transferee.] A transferee that acts in good faith takes free of the rights and interests described in subsection (a), even if the secured party fails to comply with this article or the requirements of any judicial proceeding.

(c) [Rights of other transferee.] If a transferee does not take free of the rights and interests described in subsection (a), the transferee takes the collateral subject to:

(1) the debtor's rights in the collateral;

(2) the security interest or agricultural lien under which the disposition is made; and

(3) any other security interest or other lien.

§ 9–620. Acceptance of Collateral in Full or Partial Satisfaction of Obligation; Compulsory Disposition of Collateral.

(a) [Conditions to acceptance in satisfaction.] Except as otherwise provided in subsection (g), a secured party may accept collateral in full or partial satisfaction of the obligation it secures only if:

(1) the debtor consents to the acceptance under subsection (c);

(2) the secured party does not receive, within the time set forth in subsection (d), a notification of objection to the proposal authenticated by:

(A) a person to which the secured party was required to send a proposal under Section 9–621; or

(B) any other person, other than the debtor, holding an interest in the collateral subordinate to the security interest that is the subject of the proposal;

(3) if the collateral is consumer goods, the collateral is not in the possession of the debtor when the debtor consents to the acceptance; and

(4) subsection (e) does not require the secured party to dispose of the collateral or the debtor waives the requirement pursuant to Section 9–624.

(b) [Purported acceptance ineffective.] A purported or apparent acceptance of collateral under this section is ineffective unless:

(1) the secured party consents to the acceptance in an authenticated record or sends a proposal to the debtor; and

(2) the conditions of subsection (a) are met.

(c) [Debtor's consent.] For purposes of this section:

(1) a debtor consents to an acceptance of collateral in partial satisfaction of the obligation it secures only if the debtor agrees to the terms of the acceptance in a record authenticated after default; and

(2) a debtor consents to an acceptance of collateral in full satisfaction of the obligation it secures only if the debtor agrees to the terms of the acceptance in a record authenticated after default or the secured party:

(A) sends to the debtor after default a proposal that is unconditional or subject only to a condition that collateral not in the possession of the secured party be preserved or maintained;

(B) in the proposal, proposes to accept collateral in full satisfaction of the obligation it secures; and

(C) does not receive a notification of objection authenticated by the debtor within 20 days after the proposal is sent.

(d) [Effectiveness of notification.] To be effective under subsection (a)(2), a notification of objection must be received by the secured party:

(1) in the case of a person to which the proposal was sent pursuant to Section 9–621, within 20 days after notification was sent to that person; and

(2) in other cases:

(A) within 20 days after the last notification was sent pursuant to Section 9–621; or

(B) if a notification was not sent, before the debtor consents to the acceptance under subsection (c).

(e) [Mandatory disposition of consumer goods.] A secured party that has taken possession of collateral shall dispose of the collateral pursuant to Section 9–610 within the time specified in subsection (f) if:

(1) 60 percent of the cash price has been paid in the case of a purchase-money security interest in consumer goods; or

(2) 60 percent of the principal amount of the obligation secured has been paid in the case of a non-purchase-money security interest in consumer goods.

(f) [Compliance with mandatory disposition requirement.] To comply with subsection (e), the secured party shall dispose of the collateral:

(1) within 90 days after taking possession; or

(2) within any longer period to which the debtor and all secondary obligors have agreed in an agreement to that effect entered into and authenticated after default.

(g) [No partial satisfaction in consumer transaction.] In a consumer transaction, a secured party may not accept collateral in partial satisfaction of the obligation it secures.

§ 9–621. Notification of Proposal to Accept Collateral.

(a) [Persons to which proposal to be sent.] A secured party that desires to accept collateral in full or partial satisfaction of the obligation it secures shall send its proposal to:

(1) any person from which the secured party has received, before the debtor consented to the acceptance, an authenticated notification of a claim of an interest in the collateral;

(2) any other secured party or lienholder that, 10 days before the debtor consented to the acceptance, held a security interest in or other lien on the collateral perfected by the filing of a financing statement that:

(A) identified the collateral;

(B) was indexed under the debtor's name as of that date; and

(C) was filed in the office or offices in which to file a financing statement against the debtor covering the collateral as of that date; and

(3) any other secured party that, 10 days before the debtor consented to the acceptance, held a security interest in the collateral perfected by compliance with a statute, regulation, or treaty described in Section 9–311(a).

(b) [Proposal to be sent to secondary obligor in partial satisfaction.] A secured party that desires to accept collateral in partial satisfaction of the obligation it secures shall send its proposal to any secondary obligor in addition to the persons described in subsection (a).

§ 9–622. Effect of Acceptance of Collateral.

(a) [Effect of acceptance.] A secured party's acceptance of collateral in full or partial satisfaction of the obligation it secures:

(1) discharges the obligation to the extent consented to by the debtor;

(2) transfers to the secured party all of a debtor's rights in the collateral;

(3) discharges the security interest or agricultural lien that is the subject of the debtor's consent and any subordinate security interest or other subordinate lien; and

(4) terminates any other subordinate interest.

(b) [Discharge of subordinate interest notwithstanding noncompliance.] A subordinate interest is discharged or terminated under subsection (a), even if the secured party fails to comply with this article.

§ 9–623. Right to Redeem Collateral.

(a) [Persons that may redeem.] A debtor, any secondary obligor, or any other secured party or lienholder may redeem collateral.

(b) [Requirements for redemption.] To redeem collateral, a person shall tender:

(1) fulfillment of all obligations secured by the collateral; and

(2) the reasonable expenses and attorney's fees described in Section 9–615(a)(1).

(c) [When redemption may occur.] A redemption may occur at any time before a secured party:

(1) has collected collateral under Section 9–607;

(2) has disposed of collateral or entered into a contract for its disposition under Section 9–610; or

(3) has accepted collateral in full or partial satisfaction of the obligation it secures under Section 9–622.

§ 9–624. Waiver.

(a) [Waiver of disposition notification.] A debtor or secondary obligor may waive the right to notification of disposition of collateral under Section 9–611 only by an agreement to that effect entered into and authenticated after default.

(b) [Waiver of mandatory disposition.] A debtor may waive the right to require disposition of collateral under Section 9–620(e) only by an agreement to that effect entered into and authenticated after default.

(c) [Waiver of redemption right.] Except in a consumer-goods transaction, a debtor or secondary obligor may waive the right to redeem collateral under Section 9–623 only by an agreement to that effect entered into and authenticated after default.

§ 9–625. Remedies for Secured Party's Failure to Comply with Article.

(a) [Judicial orders concerning noncompliance.] If it is established that a secured party is not proceeding in accordance with this article, a court may order or restrain collection, enforcement, or disposition of collateral on appropriate terms and conditions.

(b) [Damages for noncompliance.] Subject to subsections (c), (d), and (f), a person is liable for damages in the amount of any loss caused by a failure to comply with this article. Loss caused by a failure to comply may include loss resulting from the debtor's inability to obtain, or increased costs of, alternative financing.

(c) [Persons entitled to recover damages; statutory damages in consumer-goods transaction.] Except as otherwise provided in Section 9–628:

(1) a person that, at the time of the failure, was a debtor, was an obligor, or held a security interest in or other lien on the collateral may recover damages under subsection (b) for its loss; and

(2) if the collateral is consumer goods, a person that was a debtor or a secondary obligor at the time a secured party failed to comply with this part may recover for that failure in any event an amount not less than the credit service charge plus 10 percent of the principal amount of the obligation or the time-price differential plus 10 percent of the cash price.

(d) [Recovery when deficiency eliminated or reduced.] A debtor whose deficiency is eliminated under Section 9–626 may recover damages for the loss of any surplus. However, a debtor or secondary obligor whose deficiency is eliminated or reduced under Section 9–626 may not otherwise recover under subsection (b) for noncompliance with the provisions of this part relating to collection, enforcement, disposition, or acceptance.

(e) [Statutory damages: noncompliance with specified provisions.] In addition to any damages recoverable under subsection (b), the debtor, consumer obligor, or person named as a debtor in a filed record, as applicable, may recover $500 in each case from a person that:

(1) fails to comply with Section 9–208;

(2) fails to comply with Section 9–209;

(3) files a record that the person is not entitled to file under Section 9–509(a);

(4) fails to cause the secured party of record to file or send a termination statement as required by Section 9–513(a) or (c);

(5) fails to comply with Section 9–616(b)(1) and whose failure is part of a pattern, or consistent with a practice, of noncompliance; or

(6) fails to comply with Section 9–616(b)(2).

(f) [Statutory damages: noncompliance with Section 9–210.] A debtor or consumer obligor may recover damages under subsection (b) and, in addition, $500 in each case from a person that, without reasonable cause, fails to comply with a request under Section 9–210. A recipient of a request under Section 9–210 which never claimed an interest in the collateral or obligations that are the subject of a request under that section has a reasonable excuse for failure to comply with the request within the meaning of this subsection.

(g) [Limitation of security interest: noncompliance with Section 9–210.] If a secured party fails to comply with a request regarding a list of collateral or a statement of account under Section 9–210, the secured party may claim a security interest only as shown in the list or statement included in the request as against a person that is reasonably misled by the failure.

§ 9–626. Action in Which Deficiency or Surplus Is in Issue.

(a) [Applicable rules if amount of deficiency or surplus in issue.] In an action arising from a transaction, other than a consumer transaction, in which the amount of a deficiency or surplus is in issue, the following rules apply:

(1) A secured party need not prove compliance with the provisions of this part relating to collection, enforcement, disposition, or acceptance unless the debtor or a secondary obligor places the secured party's compliance in issue.

(2) If the secured party's compliance is placed in issue, the secured party has the burden of establishing that the collection, enforcement, disposition, or acceptance was conducted in accordance with this part.

(3) Except as otherwise provided in Section 9–628, if a secured party fails to prove that the collection, enforcement, disposition, or acceptance was conducted in accordance with the provisions of this part relating to collection, enforcement, disposition, or acceptance, the liability of a debtor or a secondary obligor for a deficiency is limited to an amount by which the sum of the secured obligation, expenses, and attorney's fees exceeds the greater of:

(A) the proceeds of the collection, enforcement, disposition, or acceptance; or

(B) the amount of proceeds that would have been realized had the noncomplying secured party proceeded in accordance with the provisions of this part relating to collection, enforcement, disposition, or acceptance.

(4) For purposes of paragraph (3)(B), the amount of proceeds that would have been realized is equal to the sum of the secured obligation, expenses, and attorney's fees unless the secured party proves that the amount is less than that sum.

(5) If a deficiency or surplus is calculated under Section 9–615(f), the debtor or obligor has the burden of establishing that the amount of proceeds of the disposition is significantly below the range of prices that a complying disposition to a person other than the secured party, a person related to the secured party, or a secondary obligor would have brought.

(b) [Non-consumer transactions; no inference.] The limitation of the rules in subsection (a) to transactions other than consumer transactions is intended to leave to the court the determination of the proper rules in consumer transactions. The court may not infer from that limitation the nature of the proper rule in consumer transactions and may continue to apply established approaches.

§ 9–627. Determination of Whether Conduct Was Commercially Reasonable.

(a) [Greater amount obtainable under other circumstances; no preclusion of commercial reasonableness.] The fact that a greater amount could have been obtained by a collection, enforcement, disposition, or acceptance at a different time or in a different method from that selected by the secured party is not of itself sufficient to preclude the secured party from establishing that the collection, enforcement, disposition, or acceptance was made in a commercially reasonable manner.

(b) [Dispositions that are commercially reasonable.] A disposition of collateral is made in a commercially reasonable manner if the disposition is made:

(1) in the usual manner on any recognized market;

(2) at the price current in any recognized market at the time of the disposition; or

(3) otherwise in conformity with reasonable commercial practices among dealers in the type of property that was the subject of the disposition.

(c) [Approval by court or on behalf of creditors.] A collection, enforcement, disposition, or acceptance is commercially reasonable if it has been approved:

(1) in a judicial proceeding;

(2) by a bona fide creditors' committee;

(3) by a representative of creditors; or

(4) by an assignee for the benefit of creditors.

(d) [Approval under subsection (c) not necessary; absence of approval has no effect.] Approval under subsection (c) need not be obtained, and lack of approval does not mean that the collection, enforcement, disposition, or acceptance is not commercially reasonable.

APPENDIX C

UNIFORM PARTNERSHIP ACT

Part I. Preliminary Provisions

§ 1. Name of Act

This act may be cited as Uniform Partnership Act.

§ 2. Definition of Terms

In this act, "Court" includes every court and judge having jurisdiction in the case.

"Business" includes every trade, occupation, or profession.

"Person" includes individuals, partnerships, corporations, and other associations.

"Bankrupt" includes bankrupt under the Federal Bankruptcy Act or insolvent under any state insolvent act.

"Conveyance" includes every assignment, lease, mortgage, or encumbrance.

"Real property" includes land and any interest or estate in land.

§ 3. Interpretation of Knowledge and Notice

(1) A person has "knowledge" of a fact within the meaning of this act not only when he has actual knowledge thereof, but also when he has knowledge of such other facts as in the circumstances shows bad faith.

(2) A person has "notice" of a fact within the meaning of this act when the person who claims the benefit of the notice

(a) States the fact to such person, or

(b) Delivers through the mail, or by other means of communication, a written statement of the fact to such person or to a proper person at his place of business or residence.

§ 4. Rules of Construction

(1) The rule that statutes in derogation of the common law are to be strictly construed shall have no application to this act.

(2) The law of estoppel shall apply under this act.

(3) The law of agency shall apply under this act.

(4) This act shall be so interpreted and construed as to effect its general purpose to make uniform the law of those states which enact it.

(5) This act shall not be construed so as to impair the obligations of any contract existing when the act goes into effect, nor to affect any action or proceedings begun or right accrued before this act takes effect.

§ 5. Rules for Cases Not Provided for in This Act

In any case not provided for in this act the rules of law and equity, including the law merchant, shall govern.

Part II. Nature of Partnership

§ 6. Partnership Defined

(1) A partnership is an association of two or more persons to carry on as co-owners a business for profit.

(2) But any association formed under any other statute of this state, or any statute adopted by authority, other than the authority of this state, is not a partnership under this act, unless such association would have been a partnership in this state prior to the adoption of this act; but this act shall apply to limited partnerships except in so far as the statutes relating to such partnerships are inconsistent herewith.

§ 7. Rules for Determining the Existence of a Partnership

In determining whether a partnership exists, these rules shall apply:

(1) Except as provided by Section 16 persons who are not partners as to each other are not partners as to third persons.

(2) Joint tenancy, tenancy in common, tenancy by the entireties, joint property, common property, or part ownership does not of itself establish a partnership, whether such co-owners do or do not share any profits made by the use of the property.

(3) The sharing of gross returns does not of itself establish a partnership, whether or not the persons sharing them have a joint or common right or interest in any property from which the returns are derived.

(4) The receipt by a person of a share of the profits of a business is prima facie evidence that he is a partner in the business, but no such inference shall be drawn if such profits were received in payment:

(a) As a debt by installments or otherwise,

(b) As wages of an employee or rent to a landlord,

(c) As an annuity to a widow or representative of a deceased partner,

(d) As interest on a loan, though the amount of payment vary with the profits of the business.

(e) As the consideration for the sale of a good will of a business or other property by installments or otherwise.

§ 8. Partnership Property

(1) All property originally brought into the partnership stock or subsequently acquired by purchase or otherwise, on account of the partnership, is partnership property.

(2) Unless the contrary intention appears, property acquired with partnership funds is partnership property.

(3) Any estate in real property may be acquired in the partnership name. Title so acquired can be conveyed only in the partnership name.

(4) A conveyance to a partnership in the partnership name, though without words of inheritance, passes the entire estate of the grantor unless a contrary intent appears.

Part III. Relations of Partners to Persons Dealing with the Partnership

§ 9. Partner Agent of Partnership as to Partnership Business

(1) Every partner is an agent of the partnership for the purpose of its business, and the act of every partner, including the execution in the partnership name of any instrument, for apparently carrying on in the usual way the business of the partnership of which he is a member binds the partnership, unless the partner so acting has in fact no authority to act for the partnership in the particular matter, and the person with whom he is dealing has knowledge of the fact that he has no such authority.

(2) An act of a partner which is not apparently for the carrying on of the business of the partnership in the usual way does not bind the partnership unless authorized by the other partners.

(3) Unless authorized by the other partners or unless they have abandoned the business, one or more but less than all the partners have no authority to:

(a) Assign the partnership property in trust for creditors or on the assignee's promise to pay the debts of the partnership,

(b) Dispose of the good will of the business,

(c) Do any other act which would make it impossible to carry on the ordinary business of a partnership,

(d) Confess a judgment,

(e) Submit a partnership claim or liability to arbitration or reference.

(4) No act of a partner in contravention of a restriction on authority shall bind the partnership to persons having knowledge of the restriction.

§ 10. Conveyance of Real Property of the Partnership

(1) Where title to real property is in the partnership name, any partner may convey title to such property by a conveyance executed in the partnership name; but the partnership may recover such property unless the partner's act binds the partnership under the provisions of paragraph (1) of section 9 or unless such property has been conveyed by the grantee or a person claiming through such grantee to a holder for value without knowledge that the partner, in making the conveyance, has exceeded his authority.

(2) Where title to real property is in the name of the partnership, a conveyance executed by a partner, in his own name, passes the equitable interest of the partnership, provided the act is one within the authority of the partner under the provisions of paragraph (1) of section 9.

(3) Where title to real property is in the name of one or more but not all the partners, and the record does not disclose the right of the partnership, the partners in whose name the title stands may convey title to such property, but the partnership may recover such property if the partners' act does not bind the partnership under the provisions of paragraph (1) of section 9, unless the purchaser or his assignee, is a holder for value, without knowledge.

(4) Where the title to real property is in the name of one or more or all the partners, or in a third person in trust for the partnership, a conveyance executed by a partner in the partnership name, or in his own name, passes the equitable interest of the partnership, provided the act is one within the authority of the partner under the provisions of paragraph (1) of section 9.

(5) Where the title to real property is in the names of all the partners a conveyance executed by all the partners passes all their rights in such property.

§ 11. Partnership Bound by Admission of Partner

An admission or representation made by any partner concerning partnership affairs within the scope of his authority as conferred by this act is evidence against the partnership.

§ 12. Partnership Charged With Knowledge of or Notice to Partner

Notice to any partner of any matter relating to partnership affairs, and the knowledge of the partner acting in the particular matter, acquired while a partner or then present to his mind, and the knowledge of any other partner who reasonably could and should have communicated it to the acting partner, operate as notice to or knowledge of the partnership, except in the case of a fraud on the partnership committed by or with the consent of that partner.

§ 13. Partnership Bound by Partner's Wrongful Act

Where, by any wrongful act or omission of any partner acting in the ordinary course of the business of the partnership or with the authority of his co-partners, loss or injury is caused to any person, not being a partner in the partnership, or any penalty is incurred, the partnership is liable therefor to the same extent as the partner so acting or omitting to act.

§ 14. Partnership Bound by Partner's Breach of Trust

The partnership is bound to make good the loss:

(a) Where one partner acting within the scope of his apparent authority receives money or property of a third person and misapplies it; and

(b) Where the partnership in the course of its business receives money or property of a third person and the money or property so received is misapplied by any partner while it is in the custody of the partnership.

§ 15. Nature of Partner's Liability

All partners are liable

(a) Jointly and severally for everything chargeable to the partnership under sections 13 and 14.

(b) Jointly for all other debts and obligations of the partnership; but any partner may enter into a separate obligation to perform a partnership contract.

§ 16. Partner by Estoppel

(1) When a person, by words spoken or written or by conduct, represents himself, or consents to another representing him to any one, as a partner in an existing partnership or with one or more persons not actual partners, he is liable to any such person to whom such representation has been made, who has, on the faith of such representation, given credit to the actual or apparent partnership, and if he has made such representation or consented to its being made in a public manner he is liable to such person, whether the representation has or has not been made or communicated to such person so giving credit by or with the knowledge of the apparent partner making the representation or consenting to its being made.

(a) When a partnership liability results, he is liable as though he were an actual member of the partnership.

(b) When no partnership liability results, he is liable jointly with the other persons, if any, so consenting to the contract or representation as to incur liability, otherwise separately.

(2) When a person has been thus represented to be a partner in an existing partnership, or with one or more persons not actual partners, he is an agent of the persons consenting to such representation to bind them to the same extent and in the same manner as though he were a partner in fact, with respect to persons who rely upon the representation. Where all the members of the existing partnership consent to the representation, a partnership act or obligation results; but in all other cases it is the joint act or obligation of the person acting and the persons consenting to the representation.

§ 17. Liability of Incoming Partner

A person admitted as a partner into an existing partnership is liable for all the obligations of the partnership arising before his admission as though he had been a partner when such obligations were incurred, except that this liability shall be satisfied only out of partnership property.

Part IV. Relations of Partners to One Another

§ 18. Rules Determining Rights and Duties of Partners

The rights and duties of the partners in relation to the partnership shall be determined, subject to any agreement between them, by the following rules:

(a) Each partner shall be repaid his contributions, whether by way of capital or advances to the partnership property and share equally in the profits and surplus remaining after all liabilities, including those to partners, are satisfied; and must contribute towards the losses, whether of capital or otherwise, sustained by the partnership according to his share in the profits.

(b) The partnership must indemnify every partner in respect of payments made and personal liabilities reasonably incurred by him in the ordinary and proper conduct of its business, or for the preservation of its business or property.

(c) A partner, who in aid of the partnership makes any payment or advance beyond the amount of capital which he agreed to contribute, shall be paid interest from the date of the payment or advance.

(d) A partner shall receive interest on the capital contributed by him only from the date when repayment should be made.

(e) All partners have equal rights in the management and conduct of the partnership business.

(f) No partner is entitled to remuneration for acting in the partnership business, except that a surviving partner is entitled to reasonable compensation for his services in winding up the partnership affairs.

(g) No person can become a member of a partnership without the consent of all the partners.

(h) Any difference arising as to ordinary matters connected with the partnership business may be decided by a majority of the partners; but no act in contravention of any agreement between the partners may be done rightfully without the consent of all the partners.

§ 19. Partnership Books

The partnership books shall be kept, subject to any agreement between the partners, at the principal place of business of the partnership, and every partner shall at all times have access to and may inspect and copy any of them.

§ 20. Duty of Partners to Render Information

Partners shall render on demand true and full information of all things affecting the partnership to any partner or the legal representative of any deceased partner or partner under legal disability.

§ 21. Partner Accountable as a Fiduciary

(1) Every partner must account to the partnership for any benefit, and hold as trustee for it any profits derived by him without the consent of the other partners from any transaction connected with the formation, conduct, or liquidation of the partnership or from any use by him of its property.

(2) This section applies also to the representatives of a deceased partner engaged in the liquidation of the affairs of the partnership as the personal representatives of the last surviving partner.

§ 22. Right to an Account

Any partner shall have the right to a formal account as to partnership affairs:

(a) If he is wrongfully excluded from the partnership business or possession of its property by his co-partners,

(b) If the right exists under the terms of any agreement,

(c) As provided by section 21,

(d) Whenever other circumstances render it just and reasonable.

§ 23. Continuation of Partnership Beyond Fixed Term

(1) When a partnership for a fixed term or particular undertaking is continued after the termination of such term or particular undertaking without any express agreement, the rights and duties of the partners remain the same as they were at such termination, so far as is consistent with a partnership at will.

(2) A continuation of the business by the partners or such of them as habitually acted therein during the term, without any settlement or liquidation of the partnership affairs, is prima facie evidence of a continuation of the partnership.

Part V. Property Rights of a Partner

§ 24. Extent of Property Rights of a Partner

The property rights of a partner are (1) his rights in specific partnership property, (2) his interest in the partnership, and (3) his right to participate in the management.

§ 25. Nature of a Partner's Right in Specific Partnership Property

(1) A partner is co-owner with his partners of specific partnership property holding as a tenant in partnership.

(2) The incidents of this tenancy are such that:

(a) A partner, subject to the provisions of this act and to any agreement between the partners, has an equal right with his partners to possess specific partnership property for partnership purposes; but he has no right to possess such property for any other purpose without the consent of his partners.

(b) A partner's right in specific partnership property is not assignable except in connection with the assignment of rights of all the partners in the same property.

(c) A partner's right in specific partnership property is not subject to attachment or execution, except on a claim against the partnership. When partnership property is attached for a partnership debt the partners, or any of them, or the representatives of a deceased partner, cannot claim any right under the homestead or exemption laws.

(d) On the death of a partner his right in specific partnership property vests in the surviving partner or partners, except where the deceased was the last surviving partner, when his right in such property vests in his legal representative. Such surviving partner or partners, or the legal representative of the last surviving partner, has no right to possess the partnership property for any but a partnership purpose.

(e) A partner's right in specific partnership property is not subject to dower, curtesy, or allowances to widows, heirs, or next of kin.

§ 26. Nature of Partner's Interest in the Partnership

A partner's interest in the partnership is his share of the profits and surplus, and the same is personal property.

§ 27. Assignment of Partner's Interest

(1) A conveyance by a partner of his interest in the partnership does not of itself dissolve the partnership, nor, as against the other partners in the absence of agreement, entitle the assignee, during the continuance of the partnership to interfere in the management or administration of the partnership business or affairs, or to require any information or account of partnership transactions, or to inspect the partnership books; but it merely entitles the assignee to receive in accordance with his contract the profits to which the assigning partner would otherwise be entitled.

(2) In case of a dissolution of the partnership, the assignee is entitled to receive his assignor's interest and may require an account from the date only of the last account agreed to by all the partners.

§ 28. Partner's Interest Subject to Charging Order

(1) On due application to a competent court by any judgment creditor of a partner, the court which entered the judgment, order, or decree, or any other court, may charge the interest of the debtor partner with payment of the unsatisfied amount of such judgment debt with interest thereon; and may then or later appoint a receiver of his share of the profits, and of any other money due or to fall due to him in respect of the partnership, and make all other orders, directions, accounts and inquiries which the debtor partner might have made, or which the circumstances of the case may require.

(2) The interest charged may be redeemed at any time before foreclosure, or in case of a sale being directed by the court may be purchased without thereby causing a dissolution:

(a) With separate property, by any one or more of the partners, or

(b) With partnership property, by any one or more of the partners with the consent of all the partners whose interests are not so charged or sold.

(3) Nothing in this act shall be held to deprive a partner of his right, if any, under the exemption laws, as regards his interest in the partnership.

Part VI. Dissolution and Winding Up

§ 29. Dissolution Defined

The dissolution of a partnership is the change in the relation of the partners caused by any partner ceasing to be associated in the carrying on as distinguished from the winding up of the business.

§ 30. Partnership Not Terminated by Dissolution

On dissolution the partnership is not terminated, but continues until the winding up of partnership affairs is completed.

§ 31. Causes of Dissolution

Dissolution is caused:

(1) Without violation of the agreement between the partners,

(a) By the termination of the definite term or particular undertaking specified in the agreement,

(b) By the express will of any partner when no definite term or particular undertaking is specified,

(c) By the express will of all the partners who have not assigned their interests or suffered them to be charged for their separate debts, either before or after the termination of any specified term or particular undertaking,

(d) By the expulsion of any partner from the business bona fide in accordance with such a power conferred by the agreement between the partners;

(2) In contravention of the agreement between the partners, where the circumstances do not permit a dissolution under any other provision of this section, by the express will of any partner at any time;

(3) By any event which makes it unlawful for the business of the partnership to be carried on or for the members to carry it on in partnership;

(4) By the death of any partner;

(5) By the bankruptcy of any partner or the partnership;

(6) By decree of court under section 32.

§ 32. Dissolution by Decree of Court

(1) On application by or for a partner the court shall decree a dissolution whenever:

(a) A partner has been declared a lunatic in any judicial proceeding or is shown to be of unsound mind,

(b) A partner becomes in any other way incapable of performing his part of the partnership contract,

(c) A partner has been guilty of such conduct as tends to affect prejudicially the carrying on of the business,

(d) A partner wilfully or persistently commits a breach of the partnership agreement, or otherwise so conducts himself in matters relating to the partnership business that it is not reasonably practicable to carry on the business in partnership with him,

(e) The business of the partnership can only be carried on at a loss,

(f) Other circumstances render a dissolution equitable.

(2) On the application of the purchaser of a partner's interest under sections 27 or 28:

(a) After the termination of the specified term or particular undertaking,

(b) At any time if the partnership was a partnership at will when the interest was assigned or when the charging order was issued.

§ 33. General Effect of Dissolution on Authority of Partner

Except so far as may be necessary to wind up partnership affairs or to complete transactions begun but not then finished, dissolution terminates all authority of any partner to act for the partnership,

(1) With respect to the partners,

(a) When the dissolution is not by the act, bankruptcy or death of a partner; or

(b) When the dissolution is by such act, bankruptcy or death of a partner, in cases where section 34 so requires.

(2) With respect to persons not partners, as declared in section 35.

§ 34. Right of Partner to Contribution From Copartners After Dissolution

Where the dissolution is caused by the act, death or bankruptcy of a partner, each partner is liable to his copartners for his share of any liability created by any partner acting for the partnership as if the partnership had not been dissolved unless

(a) The dissolution being by act of any partner, the partner acting for the partnership had knowledge of the dissolution, or

(b) The dissolution being by the death or bankruptcy of a partner, the partner acting for the partnership had knowledge or notice of the death or bankruptcy.

§ 35. Power of Partner to Bind Partnership to Third Persons After Dissolution

(1) After dissolution a partner can bind the partnership except as provided in Paragraph (3)

(a) By any act appropriate for winding up partnership affairs or completing transactions unfinished at dissolution;

(b) By any transaction which would bind the partnership if dissolution had not taken place, provided the other party to the transaction.

(I) Had extended credit to the partnership prior to dissolution and had no knowledge or notice of the dissolution; or

(II) Though he had not so extended credit, had nevertheless known of the partnership prior to dissolution, and, having no knowledge or notice of dissolution, the fact of dissolution had not been advertised in a newspaper of general circulation in the place (or in each place if more than one) at which the partnership business was regularly carried on.

(2) The liability of a partner under paragraph (1b) shall be satisfied out of partnership assets alone when such partner had been prior to dissolution

(a) Unknown as a partner to the person with whom the contract is made; and

(b) So far unknown and inactive in partnership affairs that the business reputation of the partnership could not be said to have been in any degree due to his connection with it.

(3) The partnership is in no case bound by any act of a partner after dissolution

(a) Where the partnership is dissolved because it is unlawful to carry on the business, unless the act is appropriate for winding up partnership affairs; or

(b) Where the partner has become bankrupt; or

(c) Where the partner has no authority to wind up partnership affairs; except by a transaction with one who

(I) Had extended credit to the partnership prior to dissolution and had no knowledge or notice of his want of authority; or

(II) Had not extended credit to the partnership prior to dissolution, and, having no knowledge or notice of his want of authority, the fact of his want of authority has not been advertised in the manner provided for advertising the fact of dissolution in paragraph (1bII).

(4) Nothing in this section shall affect the liability under section 16 of any person who after dissolution represents himself or consents to another representing him as a partner in a partnership engaged in carrying on business.

§ 36. Effect of Dissolution on Partner's Existing Liability

(1) The dissolution of the partnership does not of itself discharge the existing liability of any partner.

(2) A partner is discharged from any existing liability upon dissolution of the partnership by an agreement to that effect between himself, the partnership creditor and the person or partnership continuing the business; and such agreement may be inferred from the course of dealing between the creditor having knowledge of the dissolution and the person or partnership continuing the business.

(3) Where a person agrees to assume the existing obligations of a dissolved partnership, the partners whose obligations have been assumed shall be discharged from any liability to any creditor of the partnership who, knowing of the agreement, consents to a material alteration in the nature or time of payment of such obligations.

(4) The individual property of a deceased partner shall be liable for all obligations of the partnership incurred while he was a partner but subject to the prior payment of his separate debts.

§ 37. Right to Wind Up

Unless otherwise agreed the partners who have not wrongfully dissolved the partnership or the legal representative of the last surviving partner, not bankrupt, has the right to wind up the partnership affairs; provided, however, that any partner, his legal representative or his assignee, upon cause shown, may obtain winding up by the court.

§ 38. Rights of Partners to Application of Partnership Property

(1) When dissolution is caused in any way, except in contravention of the partnership agreement, each partner as against his co-partners and all persons claiming through them in respect of their interests in the partnership, unless otherwise agreed, may have the partnership property applied to discharge its liabilities, and the surplus applied to pay in cash the net amount owing to the respective partners. But if dissolution is caused by expulsion of a partner, bona fide under the partnership agreement and if the expelled partner is discharged from all partnership liabilities, either by payment or agreement under section 36(2), he shall receive in cash only the net amount due him from the partnership.

(2) When dissolution is caused in contravention of the partnership agreement the rights of the partners shall be as follows:

(a) Each partner who has not caused dissolution wrongfully shall have,

(I) All the rights specified in paragraph (1) of this section, and

(II) The right, as against each partner who has caused the dissolution wrongfully, to damages for breach of the agreement.

(b) The partners who have not caused the dissolution wrongfully, if they all desire to continue the business in the same name, either by themselves or jointly with others, may do so, during the agreed term for the partnership and for that purpose may possess the partnership property, provided they secure the payment by bond approved by the court, or pay to any partner who has caused the dissolution wrongfully, the value of his interest in the partnership at the dissolution, less any damages recoverable under clause (2aII) of the section, and in like manner indemnify him against all present or future partnership liabilities.

(c) A partner who has caused the dissolution wrongfully shall have:

(I) If the business is not continued under the provisions of paragraph (2b) all the rights of a partner under paragraph (1), subject to clause (2aII), of this section,

(II) If the business is continued under paragraph (2b) of this section the right as against his co-partners and all claiming through them in respect of their interests in the partnership, to have the value of his interest in the partnership, less any damages caused to his co-partners by the dissolution, ascertained and paid to him in cash, or the payment secured by bond approved by the court, and to be released from all existing liabilities of the partnership; but in ascertaining the value of the partner's interest the value of the good will of the business shall not be considered.

§ 39. Rights Where Partnership Is Dissolved for Fraud or Misrepresentation

Where a partnership contract is rescinded on the ground of the fraud or misrepresentation of one of the parties thereto, the party entitled to rescind is, without prejudice to any other right, entitled,

(a) To a lien on, or right of retention of, the surplus of the partnership property after satisfying the partnership liabilities to third persons for any sum of money paid by him for the purchase of an interest in the partnership and for any capital or advances contributed by him; and

(b) To stand, after all liabilities to third persons have been satisfied, in the place of the creditors of the partnership for any payments made by him in respect of the partnership liabilities; and

(c) To be indemnified by the person guilty of the fraud or making the representation against all debts and liabilities of the partnership.

§ 40. Rules for Distribution

In settling accounts between the partners after dissolution, the following rules shall be observed, subject to any agreement to the contrary:

(a) The assets of the partnership are:

(I) The partnership property,

(II) The contributions of the partners necessary for the payment of all the liabilities specified in clause (b) of this paragraph.

(b) The liabilities of the partnership shall rank in order of payment, as follows:

(I) Those owing to creditors other than partners,

(II) Those owing to partners other than for capital and profits,

(III) Those owing to partners in respect of capital,

(IV) Those owing to partners in respect of profits.

(c) The assets shall be applied in the order of their declaration in clause (a) of this paragraph to the satisfaction of the liabilities.

(d) The partners shall contribute, as provided by section 18(a) the amount necessary to satisfy the liabilities; but if any, but not all, of the partners are insolvent, or, not being subject to process, refuse to contribute, the other parties shall contribute their share of the liabilities, and, in the relative proportions in which they share the profits, the additional amount necessary to pay the liabilities.

(e) An assignee for the benefit of creditors or any person appointed by the court shall have the right to enforce the contributions specified in clause (d) of this paragraph.

(f) Any partner or his legal representative shall have the right to enforce the contributions specified in clause (d) of this paragraph, to the extent of the amount which he has paid in excess of his share of the liability.

(g) The individual property of a deceased partner shall be liable for the contributions specified in clause (d) of this paragraph.

(h) When partnership property and the individual properties of the partners are in possession of a court for distribution, partnership creditors shall have priority on partnership property and separate creditors on individual property, saving the rights of lien or secured creditors as heretofore.

(i) Where a partner has become bankrupt or his estate is insolvent the claims against his separate property shall rank in the following order:

(I) Those owing to separate creditors,

(II) Those owing to partnership creditors,

(III) Those owing to partners by way of contribution.

§ 41. Liability of Persons Continuing the Business in Certain Cases

(1) When any new partner is admitted into an existing partnership, or when any partner retires and assigns (or the representative of the deceased partner assigns) his rights in partnership property to two or more of the partners, or to one or more of the partners and one or more third persons, if the business is continued without liquidation of the partnership affairs, creditors of the first or dissolved partnership are also creditors of the person or partnership so continuing the business.

(2) When all but one partner retire and assign (or the representative of a deceased partner assigns) their rights in partnership property to the remaining partner, who continues the business without liquidation of partnership affairs, either alone or with others, creditors of the dissolved partnership are also creditors of the person or partnership so continuing the business.

(3) When any partner retires or dies and the business of the dissolved partnership is continued as set forth in paragraphs (1) and (2) of this section, with the consent of the retired partners or the representative of the deceased partner, but without any assignment of his right in partnership property, rights of creditors of the dissolved partnership and of the creditors of the person or partnership continuing the business shall be as if such assignment had been made.

(4) When all the partners or their representatives assign their rights in partnership property to one or more third persons who promise to pay the debts and who continue the business of the dissolved partnership, creditors of the dissolved partnership are also creditors of the person or partnership continuing the business.

(5) When any partner wrongfully causes a dissolution and the remaining partners continue the business under the provisions of section 38(2b), either alone or with others, and without liquidation of the partnership affairs, creditors of the dissolved partnership are also creditors of the person or partnership continuing the business.

(6) When a partner is expelled and the remaining partners continue the business either alone or with others, without liquidation of the partnership affairs, creditors of the dissolved partnership are also creditors of the person or partnership continuing the business.

(7) The liability of a third person becoming a partner in the partnership continuing the business, under this section, to the creditors of the dissolved partnership shall be satisfied out of partnership property only.

(8) When the business of a partnership after dissolution is continued under any conditions set forth in this section the creditors of the dissolved partnership, as against the separate creditors of the retiring or deceased partner or the representative of the deceased partner, have a prior right to any claim of the retired partner or the representative of the deceased partner against the person or partnership continuing the business, on account of the retired or deceased partner's interest in the dissolved partnership or on account of any consideration promised for such interest or for his right in partnership property.

(9) Nothing in this section shall be held to modify any right of creditors to set aside any assignment on the ground of fraud.

(10) The use by the person or partnership continuing the business of the partnership name, or the name of a deceased partner as part thereof, shall not of itself make the individual property of the deceased partner liable for any debts contracted by such person or partnership.

§ 42. Rights of Retiring or Estate of Deceased Partner When the Business Is Continued

When any partner retires or dies, and the business is continued under any of the conditions set forth in section 41(1, 2, 3, 5, 6), or section 38(2b), without any settlement of accounts as between him or his estate and the person or partnership continuing the business, unless otherwise agreed, he or his legal representative as against such persons or partnership may have the value of his interest at the date of dissolution ascertained, and shall receive as an ordinary creditor an amount equal to the value of his interest in the dissolved partnership with interest, or, at his option or at the option of his legal representative, in lieu of interest, the profits attributable to the use of his right in the property of the dissolved partnership; provided that the creditors of the dissolved partnership as against the separate creditors, or the representative of the retired or deceased partner, shall have priority on any claim arising under this section, as provided by section 41(8) of this act.

§ 43. Accrual of Actions

The right to an account of his interest shall accrue to any partner, or his legal representative, as against the winding up partners or the surviving partners or the person or partnership continuing the business, at the date of dissolution, in the absence of any agreement to the contrary.

Part VII. Miscellaneous Provisions

§ 44. When Act Takes Effect

This act shall take effect on the _______ day of ________one thousand nine hundred and ________.

§ 45. Legislation Repealed

All acts or parts of acts inconsistent with this act are hereby repealed.

APPENDIX D

REVISED UNIFORM PARTNERSHIP ACT (SELECTED PROVISIONS)

SECTION 102. KNOWLEDGE AND NOTICE.

(a) A person knows a fact if the person has actual knowledge of it.
(b) A person has notice of a fact if the person:
(1) knows of it;
(2) has received a notification of it; or
(3) has reason to know it exists from all of the facts known to the person at the time in question.
(c) A person notifies or gives a notification to another by taking steps reasonably required to inform the other person in ordinary course, whether or not the other person learns of it.
(d) A person receives a notification when the notification:
(1) comes to the person's attention; or
(2) is duly delivered at the person's place of business or at any other place held out by the person as a place for receiving communications.
(e) Except as otherwise provided in subsection (f), a person other than an individual knows, has notice, or receives a notification of a fact for purposes of a particular transaction when the individual conducting the transaction knows, has notice, or receives a notification of the fact, or in any event when the fact would have been brought to the individual's attention if the person had exercised reasonable diligence. The person exercises reasonable diligence if it maintains reasonable routines for communicating significant information to the individual conducting the transaction and there is reasonable compliance with the routines. Reasonable diligence does not require an individual acting for the person to communicate information unless the communication is part of the individual's regular duties or the individual has reason to know of the transaction and that the transaction would be materially affected by the information.
(f) A partner's knowledge, notice, or receipt of a notification of a fact relating to the partnership is effective immediately as knowledge by, notice to, or receipt of a notification by the partnership, except in the case of a fraud on the partnership committed by or with the consent of that partner.

SECTION 103. EFFECT OF PARTNERSHIP AGREEMENT; NONWAIVABLE PROVISIONS.

(a) Except as otherwise provided in subsection (b), relations among the partners and between the partners and the partnership are governed by the partnership agreement. To the extent the partnership agreement does not otherwise provide, this [Act] governs relations among the partners and between the partners and the partnership.
(b) The partnership agreement may not:
(1) vary the rights and duties under Section 105 except to eliminate the duty to provide copies of statements to all of the partners;
(2) unreasonably restrict the right of access to books and records under Section 403(b);
(3) eliminate the duty of loyalty under Section 404(b) or 603(b)(3), but:
(i) the partnership agreement may identify specific types or categories of activities that do not violate the duty of loyalty, if not manifestly unreasonable; or
(ii) all of the partners or a number or percentage specified in the partnership agreement may authorize or ratify, after full disclosure of all material facts, a specific act or transaction that otherwise would violate the duty of loyalty;
(4) unreasonably reduce the duty of care under Section 404(c) or 603(b)(3);
(5) eliminate the obligation of good faith and fair dealing under Section 404(d), but the partnership agreement may prescribe the standards by which the performance of the obligation is to be measured, if the standards are not manifestly unreasonable;
(6) vary the power to dissociate as a partner under Section 602(a), except to require the notice under Section 601(1) to be in writing;
(7) vary the right of a court to expel a partner in the events specified in Section 601(5);
(8) vary the requirement to wind up the partnership business in cases specified in Section 801(4), (5), or (6);
(9) vary the law applicable to a limited liability partnership under Section 106(b); or
(10) restrict rights of third parties under this [Act].

SECTION 201. PARTNERSHIP AS ENTITY.

(a) A partnership is an entity distinct from its partners.
(b) A limited liability partnership continues to be the same entity that existed before the filing of a statement of qualification under Section 1001.

SECTION 203. PARTNERSHIP PROPERTY. Property acquired by a partnership is property of the partnership and not of the partners individually.

SECTION 301. PARTNER AGENT OF PARTNERSHIP. Subject to the effect of a statement of partnership authority under Section 303:
(1) Each partner is an agent of the partnership for the purpose of its business. An act of a partner, including the execution of an instrument in the partnership name, for apparently carrying on in the ordinary course the partnership business or business of the kind carried on by the partnership binds the partnership, unless the partner had no authority to act for the partnership in the particular matter and the person with whom the partner was dealing knew or had received a notification that the partner lacked authority.
(2) An act of a partner which is not apparently for carrying on in the ordinary course the partnership business or business of the kind carried on by the partnership binds the partnership only if the act was authorized by the other partners.

SECTION 303. STATEMENT OF PARTNERSHIP AUTHORITY.

(a) A partnership may file a statement of partnership authority, which:

(1) must include:

(i) the name of the partnership;

(ii) the street address of its chief executive office and of one office in this State, if there is one;

(iii) the names and mailing addresses of all of the partners or of an agent appointed and maintained by the partnership for the purpose of subsection (b); and

(iv) the names of the partners authorized to execute an instrument transferring real property held in the name of the partnership; and

(2) may state the authority, or limitations on the authority, of some or all of the partners to enter into other transactions on behalf of the partnership and any other matter.

(b) If a statement of partnership authority names an agent, the agent shall maintain a list of the names and mailing addresses of all of the partners and make it available to any person on request for good cause shown.

(c) If a filed statement of partnership authority is executed pursuant to Section 105(c) and states the name of the partnership but does not contain all of the other information required by subsection (a), the statement nevertheless operates with respect to a person not a partner as provided in subsections (d) and (e).

(d) Except as otherwise provided in subsection (g), a filed statement of partnership authority supplements the authority of a partner to enter into transactions on behalf of the partnership as follows:

(1) Except for transfers of real property, a grant of authority contained in a filed statement of partnership authority is conclusive in favor of a person who gives value without knowledge to the contrary, so long as and to the extent that a limitation on that authority is not then contained in another filed statement. A filed cancellation of a limitation on authority revives the previous grant of authority.

(2) A grant of authority to transfer real property held in the name of the partnership contained in a certified copy of a filed statement of partnership authority recorded in the office for recording transfers of that real property is conclusive in favor of a person who gives value without knowledge to the contrary, so long as and to the extent that a certified copy of a filed statement containing a limitation on that authority is not then of record in the office for recording transfers of that real property. The recording in the office for recording transfers of that real property of a certified copy of a filed cancellation of a limitation on authority revives the previous grant of authority.

(e) A person not a partner is deemed to know of a limitation on the authority of a partner to transfer real property held in the name of the partnership if a certified copy of the filed statement containing the limitation on authority is of record in the office for recording transfers of that real property.

(f) Except as otherwise provided in subsections (d) and (e) and Sections 704 and 805, a person not a partner is not deemed to know of a limitation on the authority of a partner merely because the limitation is contained in a filed statement.

(g) Unless earlier canceled, a filed statement of partnership authority is canceled by operation of law five years after the date on which the statement, or the most recent amendment, was filed with the [Secretary of State].

SECTION 306. PARTNER'S LIABILITY.

(a) Except as otherwise provided in subsections (b) and (c), all partners are liable jointly and severally for all obligations of the partnership unless otherwise agreed by the claimant or provided by law.

(b) A person admitted as a partner into an existing partnership is not personally liable for any partnership obligation incurred before the person's admission as a partner.

(c) An obligation of a partnership incurred while the partnership is a limited liability partnership, whether arising in contract, tort, or otherwise, is solely the obligation of the partnership. A partner is not personally liable, directly or indirectly, by way of contribution or otherwise, for such an obligation solely by reason of being or so acting as a partner. This subsection applies notwithstanding anything inconsistent in the partnership agreement that existed immediately before the vote required to become a limited liability partnership under Section 1001(b).

SECTION 307. ACTIONS BY AND AGAINST PARTNERSHIP AND PARTNERS.

(a) A partnership may sue and be sued in the name of the partnership.

(b) An action may be brought against the partnership and, to the extent not inconsistent with Section 306, any or all of the partners in the same action or in separate actions.

(c) A judgment against a partnership is not by itself a judgment against a partner. A judgment against a partnership may not be satisfied from a partner's assets unless there is also a judgment against the partner.

(d) A judgment creditor of a partner may not levy execution against the assets of the partner to satisfy a judgment based on a claim against the partnership unless the partner is personally liable for the claim under Section 306 and:

(1) a judgment based on the same claim has been obtained against the partnership and a writ of execution on the judgment has been returned unsatisfied in whole or in part;

(2) the partnership is a debtor in bankruptcy;

(3) the partner has agreed that the creditor need not exhaust partnership assets;

(4) a court grants permission to the judgment creditor to levy execution against the assets of a partner based on a finding that partnership assets subject to execution are clearly insufficient to satisfy the judgment, that exhaustion of partnership assets is excessively burdensome, or that the grant of permission is an appropriate exercise of the court's equitable powers; or

(5) liability is imposed on the partner by law or contract independent of the existence of the partnership.

(e) This section applies to any partnership liability or obligation resulting from a representation by a partner or purported partner under Section 308.

SECTION 404. GENERAL STANDARDS OF PARTNER'S CONDUCT.

(a) The only fiduciary duties a partner owes to the partnership and the other partners are the duty of loyalty and the duty of care set forth in subsections (b) and (c).

(b) A partner's duty of loyalty to the partnership and the other partners is limited to the following:

(1) to account to the partnership and hold as trustee for it any property, profit, or benefit derived by the partner in the conduct and winding up of the partnership business or derived from a use by the partner of partnership property, including the appropriation of a partnership opportunity;

(2) to refrain from dealing with the partnership in the conduct or winding up of the partnership business as or on behalf of a party having an interest adverse to the partnership; and

(3) to refrain from competing with the partnership in the conduct of the partnership business before the dissolution of the partnership.

(c) A partner's duty of care to the partnership and the other partners in the conduct and winding up of the partnership business is limited to refraining from engaging in grossly negligent or reckless conduct, intentional misconduct, or a knowing violation of law.

(d) A partner shall discharge the duties to the partnership and the other partners under this [Act] or under the partnership agreement and exercise any rights consistently with the obligation of good faith and fair dealing.
(e) A partner does not violate a duty or obligation under this [Act] or under the partnership agreement merely because the partner's conduct furthers the partner's own interest.
(f) A partner may lend money to and transact other business with the partnership, and as to each loan or transaction the rights and obligations of the partner are the same as those of a person who is not a partner, subject to other applicable law.
(g) This section applies to a person winding up the partnership business as the personal or legal representative of the last surviving partner as if the person were a partner.

SECTION 405. ACTIONS BY PARTNERSHIP AND PARTNERS.

(a) A partnership may maintain an action against a partner for a breach of the partnership agreement, or for the violation of a duty to the partnership, causing harm to the partnership.
(b) A partner may maintain an action against the partnership or another partner for legal or equitable relief, with or without an accounting as to partnership business, to:
(1) enforce the partner's rights under the partnership agreement;
(2) enforce the partner's rights under this [Act], including:
(i) the partner's rights under Sections 401, 403, or 404;
(ii) the partner's right on dissociation to have the partner's interest in the partnership purchased pursuant to Section 701 or enforce any other right under [Article] 6 or 7; or
(iii) the partner's right to compel a dissolution and winding up of the partnership business under Section 801 or enforce any other right under [Article] 8; or
(3) enforce the rights and otherwise protect the interests of the partner, including rights and interests arising independently of the partnership relationship.
(c) The accrual of, and any time limitation on, a right of action for a remedy under this section is governed by other law. A right to an accounting upon a dissolution and winding up does not revive a claim barred by law.

SECTION 501. PARTNER NOT CO-OWNER OF PARTNERSHIP PROPERTY. A partner is not a co-owner of partnership property and has no interest in partnership property which can be transferred, either voluntarily or involuntarily.

SECTION 502. PARTNER'S TRANSFERABLE INTEREST IN PARTNERSHIP. The only transferable interest of a partner in the partnership is the partner's share of the profits and losses of the partnership and the partner's right to receive distributions. The interest is personal property.

SECTION 503. TRANSFER OF PARTNER'S TRANSFERABLE INTEREST.

(a) A transfer, in whole or in part, of a partner's transferable interest in the partnership:
(1) is permissible;
(2) does not by itself cause the partner's dissociation or a dissolution and winding up of the partnership business; and
(3) does not, as against the other partners or the partnership, entitle the transferee, during the continuance of the partnership, to participate in the management or conduct of the partnership business, to require access to information concerning partnership transactions, or to inspect or copy the partnership books or records.
(b) A transferee of a partner's transferable interest in the partnership has a right:
(1) to receive, in accordance with the transfer, distributions to which the transferor would otherwise be entitled;
(2) to receive upon the dissolution and winding up of the partnership business, in accordance with the transfer, the net amount otherwise distributable to the transferor; and
(3) to seek under Section 801(6) a judicial determination that it is equitable to wind up the partnership business.
(c) In a dissolution and winding up, a transferee is entitled to an account of partnership transactions only from the date of the latest account agreed to by all of the partners.
(d) Upon transfer, the transferor retains the rights and duties of a partner other than the interest in distributions transferred.
(e) A partnership need not give effect to a transferee's rights under this section until it has notice of the transfer.
(f) A transfer of a partner's transferable interest in the partnership in violation of a restriction on transfer contained in the partnership agreement is ineffective as to a person having notice of the restriction at the time of transfer.

SECTION 601. EVENTS CAUSING PARTNER'S DISSOCIATION. A partner is dissociated from a partnership upon the occurrence of any of the following events:
(1) the partnership's having notice of the partner's express will to withdraw as a partner or on a later date specified by the partner;
(2) an event agreed to in the partnership agreement as causing the partner's dissociation;
(3) the partner's expulsion pursuant to the partnership agreement;
(4) the partner's expulsion by the unanimous vote of the other partners if:
(i) it is unlawful to carry on the partnership business with that partner;
(ii) there has been a transfer of all or substantially all of that partner's transferable interest in the partnership, other than a transfer for security purposes, or a court order charging the partner's interest, which has not been foreclosed;
(iii) within 90 days after the partnership notifies a corporate partner that it will be expelled because it has filed a certificate of dissolution or the equivalent, its charter has been revoked, or its right to conduct business has been suspended by the jurisdiction of its incorporation, there is no revocation of the certificate of dissolution or no reinstatement of its charter or its right to conduct business; or
(iv) a partnership that is a partner has been dissolved and its business is being wound up;
(5) on application by the partnership or another partner, the partner's expulsion by judicial determination because:
(i) the partner engaged in wrongful conduct that adversely and materially affected the partnership business;
(ii) the partner willfully or persistently committed a material breach of the partnership agreement or of a duty owed to the partnership or the other partners under Section 404; or
(iii) the partner engaged in conduct relating to the partnership business which makes it not reasonably practicable to carry on the business in partnership with the partner;
(6) the partner's:
(i) becoming a debtor in bankruptcy;
(ii) executing an assignment for the benefit of creditors;
(iii) seeking, consenting to, or acquiescing in the appointment of a trustee, receiver, or liquidator of that partner or of all or substantially all of that partner's property; or
(iv) failing, within 90 days after the appointment, to have vacated or stayed the appointment of a trustee, receiver, or liquidator of the partner or of all or substantially all of the partner's property obtained without the partner's consent or

acquiescence, or failing within 90 days after the expiration of a stay to have the appointment vacated;

(7) in the case of a partner who is an individual:

(i) the partner's death;

(ii) the appointment of a guardian or general conservator for the partner; or

(iii) a judicial determination that the partner has otherwise become incapable of performing the partner's duties under the partnership agreement;

(8) in the case of a partner that is a trust or is acting as a partner by virtue of being a trustee of a trust, distribution of the trust's entire transferable interest in the partnership, but not merely by reason of the substitution of a successor trustee;

(9) in the case of a partner that is an estate or is acting as a partner by virtue of being a personal representative of an estate, distribution of the estate's entire transferable interest in the partnership, but not merely by reason of the substitution of a successor personal representative; or

(10) termination of a partner who is not an individual, partnership, corporation, trust, or estate.

SECTION 603. EFFECT OF PARTNER'S DISSOCIATION.

(a) If a partner's dissociation results in a dissolution and winding up of the partnership business, [Article] 8 applies; otherwise, [Article] 7 applies.

(b) Upon a partner's dissociation:

(1) the partner's right to participate in the management and conduct of the partnership business terminates, except as otherwise provided in Section 803;

(2) the partner's duty of loyalty under Section 404(b)(3) terminates; and

(3) the partner's duty of loyalty under Section 404(b)(1) and (2) and duty of care under Section 404(c) continue only with regard to matters arising and events occurring before the partner's dissociation, unless the partner participates in winding up the partnership's business pursuant to Section 803.

SECTION 701. PURCHASE OF DISSOCIATED PARTNER'S INTEREST.

(a) If a partner is dissociated from a partnership without resulting in a dissolution and winding up of the partnership business under Section 801, the partnership shall cause the dissociated partner's interest in the partnership to be purchased for a buyout price determined pursuant to subsection (b).

(b) The buyout price of a dissociated partner's interest is the amount that would have been distributable to the dissociating partner under Section 807(b) if, on the date of dissociation, the assets of the partnership were sold at a price equal to the greater of the liquidation value or the value based on a sale of the entire business as a going concern without the dissociated partner and the partnership were wound up as of that date. Interest must be paid from the date of dissociation to the date of payment.

(c) Damages for wrongful dissociation under Section 602(b), and all other amounts owing, whether or not presently due, from the dissociated partner to the partnership, must be offset against the buyout price. Interest must be paid from the date the amount owed becomes due to the date of payment.

(d) A partnership shall indemnify a dissociated partner whose interest is being purchased against all partnership liabilities, whether incurred before or after the dissociation, except liabilities incurred by an act of the dissociated partner under Section 702.

(e) If no agreement for the purchase of a dissociated partner's interest is reached within 120 days after a written demand for payment, the partnership shall pay, or cause to be paid, in cash to the dissociated partner the amount the partnership estimates to be the buyout price and accrued interest, reduced by any offsets and accrued interest under subsection (c).

(f) If a deferred payment is authorized under subsection (h), the partnership may tender a written offer to pay the amount it estimates to be the buyout price and accrued interest, reduced by any offsets under subsection (c), stating the time of payment, the amount and type of security for payment, and the other terms and conditions of the obligation.

(g) The payment or tender required by subsection (e) or (f) must be accompanied by the following:

(1) a statement of partnership assets and liabilities as of the date of dissociation;

(2) the latest available partnership balance sheet and income statement, if any;

(3) an explanation of how the estimated amount of the payment was calculated; and

(4) written notice that the payment is in full satisfaction of the obligation to purchase unless, within 120 days after the written notice, the dissociated partner commences an action to determine the buyout price, any offsets under subsection (c), or other terms of the obligation to purchase.

(h) A partner who wrongfully dissociates before the expiration of a definite term or the completion of a particular undertaking is not entitled to payment of any portion of the buyout price until the expiration of the term or completion of the undertaking, unless the partner establishes to the satisfaction of the court that earlier payment will not cause undue hardship to the business of the partnership. A deferred payment must be adequately secured and bear interest.

(i) A dissociated partner may maintain an action against the partnership, pursuant to Section 405(b)(2)(ii), to determine the buyout price of that partner's interest, any offsets under subsection (c), or other terms of the obligation to purchase. The action must be commenced within 120 days after the partnership has tendered payment or an offer to pay or within one year after written demand for payment if no payment or offer to pay is tendered. The court shall determine the buyout price of the dissociated partner's interest, any offset due under subsection (c), and accrued interest, and enter judgment for any additional payment or refund. If deferred payment is authorized under subsection (h), the court shall also determine the security for payment and other terms of the obligation to purchase. The court may assess reasonable attorney's fees and the fees and expenses of appraisers or other experts for a party to the action, in amounts the court finds equitable, against a party that the court finds acted arbitrarily, vexatiously, or not in good faith. The finding may be based on the partnership's failure to tender payment or an offer to pay or to comply with subsection (g).

SECTION 702. DISSOCIATED PARTNER'S POWER TO BIND AND LIABILITY TO PARTNERSHIP.

(a) For two years after a partner dissociates without resulting in a dissolution and winding up of the partnership business, the partnership, including a surviving partnership under [Article] 9, is bound by an act of the dissociated partner which would have bound the partnership under Section 301 before dissociation only if at the time of entering into the transaction the other party:

(1) reasonably believed that the dissociated partner was then a partner;

(2) did not have notice of the partner's dissociation; and

(3) is not deemed to have had knowledge under Section 303(e) or notice under Section 704(c).

(b) A dissociated partner is liable to the partnership for any damage caused to the partnership arising from an obligation incurred by the dissociated partner after dissociation for which the partnership is liable under subsection (a).

SECTION 703. DISSOCIATED PARTNER'S LIABILITY TO OTHER PERSONS.

(a) A partner's dissociation does not of itself discharge the partner's liability for a partnership obligation incurred before dissociation. A dissociated partner is not liable for a partnership obligation incurred after dissociation, except as otherwise provided in subsection (b).
(b) A partner who dissociates without resulting in a dissolution and winding up of the partnership business is liable as a partner to the other party in a transaction entered into by the partnership, or a surviving partnership under [Article] 9, within two years after the partner's dissociation, only if the partner is liable for the obligation under Section 306 and at the time of entering into the transaction the other party:
(1) reasonably believed that the dissociated partner was then a partner;
(2) did not have notice of the partner's dissociation; and
(3) is not deemed to have had knowledge under Section 303(e) or notice under Section 704(c).
(c) By agreement with the partnership creditor and the partners continuing the business, a dissociated partner may be released from liability for a partnership obligation.
(d) A dissociated partner is released from liability for a partnership obligation if a partnership creditor, with notice of the partner's dissociation but without the partner's consent, agrees to a material alteration in the nature or time of payment of a partnership obligation.

SECTION 704. STATEMENT OF DISSOCIATION.

(a) A dissociated partner or the partnership may file a statement of dissociation stating the name of the partnership and that the partner is dissociated from the partnership.
(b) A statement of dissociation is a limitation on the authority of a dissociated partner for the purposes of Section 303(d) and (e).
(c) For the purposes of Sections 702(a)(3) and 703(b)(3), a person not a partner is deemed to have notice of the dissociation 90 days after the statement of dissociation is filed.

SECTION 801. EVENTS CAUSING DISSOLUTION AND WINDING UP OF PARTNERSHIP BUSINESS. A partnership is dissolved, and its business must be wound up, only upon the occurrence of any of the following events:
(1) in a partnership at will, the partnership's having notice from a partner, other than a partner who is dissociated under Section 601(2) through (10), of that partner's express will to withdraw as a partner, or on a later date specified by the partner;
(2) in a partnership for a definite term or particular undertaking:
(i) within 90 days after a partner's dissociation by death or otherwise under Section 601(6) through (10) or wrongful dissociation under Section 602(b), the express will of at least half of the remaining partners to wind up the partnership business, for which purpose a partner's rightful dissociation pursuant to Section 602(b)(2)(i) constitutes the expression of that partner's will to wind up the partnership business;
(ii) the express will of all of the partners to wind up the partnership business; or
(iii) the expiration of the term or the completion of the undertaking;
(3) an event agreed to in the partnership agreement resulting in the winding up of the partnership business;
(4) an event that makes it unlawful for all or substantially all of the business of the partnership to be continued, but a cure of illegality within 90 days after notice to the partnership of the event is effective retroactively to the date of the event for purposes of this section;
(5) on application by a partner, a judicial determination that:
(i) the economic purpose of the partnership is likely to be unreasonably frustrated;
(ii) another partner has engaged in conduct relating to the partnership business which makes it not reasonably practicable to carry on the business in partnership with that partner; or
(iii) it is not otherwise reasonably practicable to carry on the partnership business in conformity with the partnership agreement; or
(6) on application by a transferee of a partner's transferable interest, a judicial determination that it is equitable to wind up the partnership business:
(i) after the expiration of the term or completion of the undertaking, if the partnership was for a definite term or particular undertaking at the time of the transfer or entry of the charging order that gave rise to the transfer; or
(ii) at any time, if the partnership was a partnership at will at the time of the transfer or entry of the charging order that gave rise to the transfer.

SECTION 802. PARTNERSHIP CONTINUES AFTER DISSOLUTION.

(a) Subject to subsection (b), a partnership continues after dissolution only for the purpose of winding up its business. The partnership is terminated when the winding up of its business is completed.
(b) At any time after the dissolution of a partnership and before the winding up of its business is completed, all of the partners, including any dissociating partner other than a wrongfully dissociating partner, may waive the right to have the partnership's business wound up and the partnership terminated. In that event:
(1) the partnership resumes carrying on its business as if dissolution had never occurred, and any liability incurred by the partnership or a partner after the dissolution and before the waiver is determined as if dissolution had never occurred; and
(2) the rights of a third party accruing under Section 804(1) or arising out of conduct in reliance on the dissolution before the third party knew or received a notification of the waiver may not be adversely affected.

SECTION 804. PARTNER'S POWER TO BIND PARTNERSHIP AFTER DISSOLUTION. Subject to Section 805, a partnership is bound by a partner's act after dissolution that:
(1) is appropriate for winding up the partnership business; or
(2) would have bound the partnership under Section 301 before dissolution, if the other party to the transaction did not have notice of the dissolution.

SECTION 805. STATEMENT OF DISSOLUTION.

(a) After dissolution, a partner who has not wrongfully dissociated may file a statement of dissolution stating the name of the partnership and that the partnership has dissolved and is winding up its business.
(b) A statement of dissolution cancels a filed statement of partnership authority for the purposes of Section 303(d) and is a limitation on authority for the purposes of Section 303(e).
(c) For the purposes of Sections 301 and 804, a person not a partner is deemed to have notice of the dissolution and the limitation on the partners' authority as a result of the statement of dissolution 90 days after it is filed.
(d) After filing and, if appropriate, recording a statement of dissolution, a dissolved partnership may file and, if appropriate, record a statement of partnership authority which will operate with respect to a person not a partner as provided in Section 303(d) and (e) in any transaction, whether or not the transaction is appropriate for winding up the partnership business.

SECTION 807. SETTLEMENT OF ACCOUNTS AND CONTRIBUTIONS AMONG PARTNERS.

(a) In winding up a partnership's business, the assets of the partnership, including the contributions of the partners required by this section, must be applied to discharge its obligations to creditors, including, to the extent permitted by law, partners who are creditors. Any surplus must be applied to pay in cash the net amount distributable to partners in accordance with their right to distributions under subsection (b).
(b) Each partner is entitled to a settlement of all partnership accounts upon winding up the partnership business. In settling accounts among the partners, profits and losses that result from the liquidation of the partnership assets must be credited and charged to the partners' accounts. The partnership shall make a distribution to a partner in an amount equal to any excess of the credits over the charges in the partner's account. A partner shall contribute to the partnership an amount equal to any excess of the charges over the credits in the partner's account but excluding from the calculation charges attributable to an obligation for which the partner is not personally liable under Section 306.
(c) If a partner fails to contribute the full amount required under subsection (b), all of the other partners shall contribute, in the proportions in which those partners share partnership losses, the additional amount necessary to satisfy the partnership obligations for which they are personally liable under Section 306. A partner or partner's legal representative may recover from the other partners any contributions the partner makes to the extent the amount contributed exceeds that partner's share of the partnership obligations for which the partner is personally liable under Section 306.
(d) After the settlement of accounts, each partner shall contribute, in the proportion in which the partner shares partnership losses, the amount necessary to satisfy partnership obligations that were not known at the time of the settlement and for which the partner is personally liable under Section 306.
(e) The estate of a deceased partner is liable for the partner's obligation to contribute to the partnership.
(f) An assignee for the benefit of creditors of a partnership or a partner, or a person appointed by a court to represent creditors of a partnership or a partner, may enforce a partner's obligation to contribute to the partnership.

SECTION 1001. STATEMENT OF QUALIFICATION.

(a) A partnership may become a limited liability partnership pursuant to this section.
(b) The terms and conditions on which a partnership becomes a limited liability partnership must be approved by the vote necessary to amend the partnership agreement except, in the case of a partnership agreement that expressly considers obligations to contribute to the partnership, the vote necessary to amend those provisions.
(c) After the approval required by subsection (b), a partnership may become a limited liability partnership by filing a statement of qualification. The statement must contain:
  (1) the name of the partnership;
  (2) the street address of the partnership's chief executive office and, if different, the street address of an office in this State, if any;
  (3) if the partnership does not have an office in this State, the name and street address of the partnership's agent for service of process;
  (4) a statement that the partnership elects to be a limited liability partnership; and
  (5) a deferred effective date, if any.
(d) The agent of a limited liability partnership for service of process must be an individual who is a resident of this State or other person authorized to do business in this State.
(e) The status of a partnership as a limited liability partnership is effective on the later of the filing of the statement or a date specified in the statement. The status remains effective, regardless of changes in the partnership, until it is canceled pursuant to Section 105(d) or revoked pursuant to Section 1003.
(f) The status of a partnership as a limited liability partnership and the liability of its partners is not affected by errors or later changes in the information required to be contained in the statement of qualification under subsection (c).
(g) The filing of a statement of qualification establishes that a partnership has satisfied all conditions precedent to the qualification of the partnership as a limited liability partnership.
(h) An amendment or cancellation of a statement of qualification is effective when it is filed or on a deferred effective date specified in the amendment or cancellation.

SECTION 1002. NAME. The name of a limited liability partnership must end with "Registered Limited Liability Partnership", "Limited Liability Partnership", "R.L.L.P.", "L.L.P.", "RLLP," or "LLP".

SECTION 1003. ANNUAL REPORT.

(a) A limited liability partnership, and a foreign limited liability partnership authorized to transact business in this State, shall file an annual report in the office of the [Secretary of State] which contains:
  (1) the name of the limited liability partnership and the State or other jurisdiction under whose laws the foreign limited liability partnership is formed;
  (2) the street address of the partnership's chief executive office and, if different, the street address of an office of the partnership in this State, if any; and
  (3) if the partnership does not have an office in this State, the name and street address of the partnership's current agent for service of process.
(b) An annual report must be filed between [January 1 and April 1] of each year following the calendar year in which a partnership files a statement of qualification or a foreign partnership becomes authorized to transact business in this State.
(c) The [Secretary of State] may revoke the statement of qualification of a partnership that fails to file an annual report when due or pay the required filing fee. To do so, the [Secretary of State] shall provide the partnership at least 60 days' written notice of intent to revoke the statement. The notice must be mailed to the partnership at its chief executive office set forth in the last filed statement of qualification or annual report. The notice must specify the annual report that has not been filed, the fee that has not been paid, and the effective date of the revocation. The revocation is not effective if the annual report is filed and the fee is paid before the effective date of the revocation.
(d) A revocation under subsection (c) only affects a partnership's status as a limited liability partnership and is not an event of dissolution of the partnership.
(e) A partnership whose statement of qualification has been revoked may apply to the [Secretary of State] for reinstatement within two years after the effective date of the revocation. The application must state:
  (1) the name of the partnership and the effective date of the revocation; and
  (2) that the ground for revocation either did not exist or has been corrected.
(f) A reinstatement under subsection (e) relates back to and takes effect as of the effective date of the revocation, and the partnership's status as a limited liability partnership continues as if the revocation had never occurred.

APPENDIX E

REVISED MODEL BUSINESS CORPORATION ACT (SELECTED PROVISIONS)

§ 1.40 Act Definitions

In this Act:

(1) "Articles of incorporation" include amended and restated articles of incorporation and articles of merger.

(2) "Authorized shares" means the shares of all classes a domestic or foreign corporation is authorized to issue.

(3) "Conspicuous" means so written that a reasonable person against whom the writing is to operate should have noticed it. For example, printing in italics or boldface or contrasting color, or typing in capitals or underlined, is conspicuous.

(4) "Corporation" or "domestic corporation" means a corporation for profit, which is not a foreign corporation, incorporated under or subject to the provisions of this Act.

(5) "Deliver" includes mail.

(6) "Distribution" means a direct or indirect transfer of money or other property (except its own shares) or incurrence of indebtedness by a corporation to or for the benefit of its shareholders in respect of any of its shares. A distribution may be in the form of a declaration or payment of a dividend; a purchase, redemption, or other acquisition of shares; a distribution of indebtedness; or otherwise.

(7) "Effective date of notice" is defined in section 1.41.

(8) "Employee" includes an officer but not a director. A director may accept duties that make him also an employee.

(9) "Entity" includes corporation and foreign corporation; not-for-profit corporation; profit and not-for-profit unincorporated association; business trust, estate, partnership, trust, and two or more persons having a joint or common economic interest; and state, United States, and foreign government.

(10) "Foreign corporation" means a corporation for profit incorporated under a law other than the law of this state.

(11) "Governmental subdivision" includes authority, county, district, and municipality.

(12) "Includes" denotes a partial definition.

(13) "Individual" includes the estate of an incompetent or deceased individual.

(14) "Means" denotes an exhaustive definition.

(15) "Notice" is defined in section 1.41.

(16) "Person" includes individual and entity.

(17) "Principal office" means the office (in or out of this state) so designated in the annual report where the principal executive offices of a domestic or foreign corporation are located.

(18) "Proceeding" includes civil suit and criminal, administrative, and investigatory action.

(19) "Record date" means the date established under chapter 6 or 7 on which a corporation determines the identity of its shareholders for purposes of this Act.

(20) "Secretary" means the corporate officer to whom the board of directors has delegated responsibility under section 8.40(c) for custody of the minutes of the meetings of the board of directors and of the shareholders and for authenticating records of the corporation.

(21) "Share" means the unit into which the proprietary interests in a corporation are divided.

(22) "Shareholder" means the person in whose name shares are registered in the records of a corporation or the beneficial owner of shares to the extent of the rights granted by a nominee certificate on file with a corporation.

(23) "State," when referring to a part of the United States, includes a state and commonwealth (and their agencies and governmental subdivisions) and a territory, and insular possession (and their agencies and governmental subdivisions) of the United States.

(24) "Subscriber" means a person who subscribes for shares in a corporation, whether before or after incorporation.

(25) "United States" includes district, authority, bureau, commission, department, and any other agency of the United States.

(26) "Voting group" means all shares of one or more classes or series that under the articles of incorporation or this Act are entitled to vote and be counted together collectively on a matter at a meeting of shareholders. All shares entitled by the articles of incorporation or this Act to vote generally on the matter are for that purpose a single voting group.

§ 2.01 Incorporators

One or more persons may act as the incorporator or incorporators of a corporation by delivering articles of incorporation to the secretary of state for filing.

§ 2.02 Articles of Incorporation

(a) The articles of incorporation must set forth:

- **(1)** a corporate name for the corporation that satisfies the requirements of section 4.01;
- **(2)** the number of shares the corporation is authorized to issue;
- **(3)** the street address of the corporation's initial registered office and the name of its initial registered agent at that office; and
- **(4)** the name and address of each incorporator.

(b) The articles of incorporation may set forth:

- **(1)** the names and addresses of the individuals who are to serve as the initial directors;

(2) provisions not inconsistent with law regarding:

(i) the purpose or purposes for which the corporation is orgainized;

(ii) managing the business and regulating the affairs of the corporation;

(iii) defining, limiting, and regulating the powers of the corporation, its board of directors, and shareholders;

(iv) a par value for authorized shares or classes of shares;

(v) the imposition of personal liability on shareholders for the debts of the corporation to a specified extent and upon specified conditions; and

(3) any provision that under this Act is required or permitted to be set forth in the bylaws.

(4) a provision eliminating or limiting the liability of a director to the corporation or its shareholders for money damages for any action taken, or any failure to take any action, as a director, except liability for (A) the amount of a financial benefit received by a director to which he is not entitled; (B) an intentional infliction of harm on the corporation or the shareholders; (C) a violation of section 8.33; or (D) an intentional violation of criminal law.

(c) The articles of incorporation need not set forth any of the corporate powers enumerated in this Act.

§ 2.03 Incorporation

(a) Unless a delayed effective date is specified, the corporate existence begins when the articles of incorporation are filed.

(b) The secretary of state's filing of the articles of incorporation is conclusive proof that the incorporators satisfied all conditions precedent to incorporation except in a proceeding by the state to cancel or revoke the incorporation or involuntarily dissolve the corporation.

§ 2.04 Liability for Preincorporation Transactions

All persons purporting to act as or on behalf of a corporation, knowing there was no incorporation under this Act, are jointly and severally liable for all liabilities created while so acting.

§ 2.05 Organization of Corporation

(a) After incorporation:

(1) if initial directors are named in the articles of incorporation, the initial directors shall hold an organizational meeting, at the call of a majority of the directors, to complete the organization of the corporation by appointing officers, adopting bylaws, and carrying on any other business brought before the meeting;

(2) if initial directors are not named in the articles, the incorporator or incorporators shall hold an organizational meeting at the call of a majority of the incorporators:

(i) to elect directors and complete the organization of the corporation; or

(ii) to elect a board of directors who shall complete the organization of the corporation.

(b) Action required or permitted by this Act to be taken by incorporators at an organizational meeting may be taken without a meeting if the action taken is evidenced by one or more written consents describing the action taken and signed by each incorporator.

(c) An organizational meeting may be held in or out of this state.

§ 2.06 Bylaws

(a) The incorporators or board of directors of a corporation shall adopt initial bylaws for the corporation.

(b) The bylaws of a corporation may contain any provision for managing the business and regulating the affairs of the corporation that is not inconsistent with law or the articles of incorporation.

§ 3.01 Purposes

(a) Every corporation incorporated under this Act has the purpose of engaging in any lawful business unless a more limited purpose is set forth in the articles of incorporation.

(b) A corporation engaging in a business that is subject to regulation under another statute of this state may incorporate under this Act only if permitted by, and subject to all limitations of, the other statute.

§ 3.02 General Powers

Unless its articles of incorporation provide otherwise, every corporation has perpetual duration and succession in its corporate name and has the same powers as an individual to do all things necessary or convenient to carry out its business and affairs, including without limitation power:

(1) to sue and be sued, complain and defend in its corporate name;

(2) to have a corporate seal, which may be altered at will, and to use it, or a facsimile of it, by impressing or affixing it or in any other manner reproducing it;

(3) to make and amend bylaws, not inconsistent with its articles of incorporation or with the laws of this state, for managing the business and regulating the affairs of the corporation;

(4) to purchase, receive, lease, or otherwise acquire, and own, hold, improve, use, and otherwise deal with, real or personal property, or any legal or equitable interest in property, wherever located;

(5) to sell, convey, mortgage, pledge, lease, exchange, and otherwise dispose of all or any part of its property;

(6) to purchase, receive, subscribe for, or otherwise acquire; own, hold, vote, use, sell, mortgage, lend, pledge, or otherwise dispose of; and deal in and with shares or other interests in, or obligations of, any other entity;

(7) to make contracts and guarantees, incur liabilities, borrow money, issue its notes, bonds, and other obligations, (which may be convertible into or include the option to purchase other securities of the corporation), and secure any of its obligations by mortgage or pledge of any of its property, franchises, or income;

(8) to lend money, invest and reinvest its funds, and receive and hold real and personal property as security for repayment;

(9) to be a promoter, partner, member, associate, or manager of any partnership, joint venture, trust, or other entity;

(10) to conduct its business, locate offices, and exercise the powers granted by this Act within or without this state;

(11) to elect directors and appoint officers, employees, and agents of the corporation, define their duties, fix their compensation, and lend them money and credit;

(12) to pay pensions and establish pension plans, pension trusts, profit sharing plans, share bonus plans, share option plans, and benefit or incentive plans for any or all of its current or former directors, officers, employees, and agents;

(13) to make donations for the public welfare or for charitable, scientific, or educational purposes;

(14) to transact any lawful business that will aid governmental policy;

(15) to make payments or donations, or do any other act, not inconsistent with law, that furthers the business and affairs of the corporation.

§ 3.04 Ultra Vires

(a) Except as provided in subsection (b), the validity of corporate action may not be challenged on the ground that the corporation lacks or lacked power to act.

(b) A corporation's power to act may be challenged:

(1) in a proceeding by a shareholder against the corporation to enjoin the act;

(2) in a proceeding by the corporation, directly, derivatively, or through a receiver, trustee, or other legal representative, against an incumbent or former director, officer, employee, or agent of the corporation; or

(3) in a proceeding by the Attorney General under section 14.30.

(c) In a shareholder's proceeding under subsection (b)(1) to enjoin an unauthorized corporate act, the court may enjoin or set aside the act, if equitable and if all affected persons are parties to the proceeding, and may award damages for loss (other than anticipated profits) suffered by the corporation or another party because of enjoining the unauthorized act.

§ 4.01 Corporate Name

(a) A corporate name:

(1) must contain the word "corporation," "incorporated," "company," or "limited," or the abbreviation "corp.," "inc.," "co.," or "ltd.", or words or abbreviations of like import in another language; and

(2) may not contain language stating or implying that the corporation is organized for a purpose other than that permitted by section 3.01 and its articles of incorporation.

(b) Except as authorized by subsections (c) and (d), a corporate name must be distinguishable upon the records of the secretary of state from:

(1) the corporate name of a corporation incorporated or authorized to transact business in this state;

(2) a corporate name reserved or registered under section 4.02 or 4.03;

(3) the fictitious name adopted by a foreign corporation authorized to transact business in this state because its real name is unavailable; and

(4) the corporate name of a not-for-profit corporation incorporated or authorized to transact business in this state.

(c) A corporation may apply to the secretary of state for authorization to use a name that is not distinguishable upon his records from one or more of the names described in subsection (b). The secretary of state shall authorize use of the name applied for if:

(1) the other corporation consents to the use in writing and submits an undertaking in form satisfactory to the secretary of state to change its name to a name that is distinguishable upon the records of the secretary of state from the name of the applying corporation; or

(2) the applicant delivers to the secretary of state a certified copy of the final judgment of a court of competent jurisdiction establishing the applicant's right to use the name applied for in this state.

(d) A corporation may use the name (including the fictitious name) of another domestic or foreign corporation that is used in this state if the other corporation is incorporated or authorized to transact business in this state and the proposed user corporation:

(1) has merged with the other corporation;

(2) has been formed by reorganization of the other corporation; or

(3) has acquired all or substantially all of the assets, including the corporate name, of the other corporation.

(e) This Act does not control the use of fictitious names.

§ 5.01 Registered Office and Registered Agent

Each corporation must continuously maintain in this state:

(1) a registered office that may be the same as any of its places of business; and

(2) a registered agent, who may be:

(i) an individual who resides in this state and whose business office is identical with the registered office;

(ii) a domestic corporation or not-for-profit domestic corporation whose business office is identical with the registered office; or

(iii) a foreign corporation or not-for-profit foreign corporation authorized to transact business in this state whose business office is identical with the registered office.

§ 6.01 Authorized Shares

(a) The articles of incorporation must prescribe the classes of shares and the number of shares of each class that the corporation is authorized to issue. If more than one class of shares is authorized, the articles of incorporation must prescribe a distinguishing designation for each class, and prior to the issuance of shares of a class the preferences, limitations, and relative rights of that class must be described in the articles of incorporation. All shares of a class must have preferences, limitations, and relative rights identical with those of other shares of the same class except to the extent otherwise permitted by section 6.02.

(b) The articles of incorporation must authorize (1) one or more classes of shares that together have unlimited voting rights, and (2) one or more classes of shares (which may be the same class or classes as those with voting rights) that together are entitled to receive the net assets of the corporation upon dissolution.

(c) The articles of incorporation may authorize one or more classes of shares that:

(1) have special, conditional, or limited voting rights, or no right to vote, except to the extent prohibited by this Act;

(2) are redeemable or convertible as specified in the articles of incorporation (i) at the option of the corporation, the shareholder, or another person or upon the occurrence of a designated event; (ii) for cash, indebtedness, securities, or other property; (iii) in a designated amount or in an amount determined in accordance with a designated formula or by reference to extrinsic data or events;

(3) entitle the holders to distributions calculated in any manner, including dividends that may be cumulative, noncumulative, or partially cumulative;

(4) have preference over any other class of shares with respect to distributions, including dividends and distributions upon the dissolution of the corporation.

(d) The description of the designations, preferences, limitations, and relative rights of share classes in subsection (c) is not exhaustive.

§ 6.02 Terms of Class or Series Determined by Board of Directors

(a) If the articles of incorporation so provide, the board of directors may determine, in whole or part, the preferences, limitations, and relative rights (within the limits set forth in section 6.01) of (1) any class of shares before the issuance of any shares of that class or (2) one or more series within a class before the issuance of any shares of that series.

(b) Each series of a class must be given a distinguishing designation.

(c) All shares of a series must have preferences, limitations, and relative rights identical with those of other shares of the same series and, except to the extent otherwise provided in the description of the series, of those of other series of the same class.

(d) Before issuing any shares of a class or series created under this section, the corporation must deliver to the secretary of state for filing articles of amendment, which are effective without shareholder action, that set forth:

(1) the name of the corporation;

(2) the text of the amendment determining the terms of the class or series of shares;

(3) the date it was adopted; and

(4) a statement that the amendment was duly adopted by the board of directors.

§ 6.03 Issued and Outstanding Shares

(a) A corporation may issue the number of shares of each class or series authorized by the articles of incorporation. Shares that are issued are outstanding shares until they are reacquired, redeemed, converted, or cancelled.

(b) The reacquisition, redemption, or conversion of outstanding shares is subject to the limitations of subsection (c) of this section and to section 6.40.

(c) At all times that shares of the corporation are outstanding, one or more shares that together have unlimited voting rights and one or more shares that together are entitled to receive the net assets of the corporation upon dissolution must be outstanding.

§ 6.20 Subscription for Shares Before Incorporation

(a) A subscription for shares entered into before incorporation is irrevocable for six months unless the subscription agreement provides a longer or shorter period or all the subscribers agree to revocation.

(b) The board of directors may determine the payment terms of subscriptions for shares that were entered into before incorporation, unless the subscription agreement specifies them. A call for payment by the board of directors must be uniform so far as practicable as to all shares of the same class or series, unless the subscription agreement specifies otherwise.

(c) Shares issued pursuant to subscriptions entered into before incorporation are fully paid and nonassessable when the corporation receives the consideration specified in the subscription agreement.

(d) If a subscriber defaults in payment of money or property under a subscription agreement entered into before incorporation, the corporation may collect the amount owed as any other debt. Alternatively, unless the subscription agreement provides otherwise, the corporation may rescind the agreement and may sell the shares if the debt remains unpaid more than 20 days after the corporation sends written demand for payment to the subscriber.

(e) A subscription agreement entered into after incorporation is a contract between the subscriber and the corporation subject to section 6.21.

§ 6.21 Issuance of Shares

(a) The powers granted in this section to the board of directors may be reserved to the shareholders by the articles of incorporation.

(b) The board of directors may authorize shares to be issued for consideration consisting of any tangible or intangible property or benefit to the corporation, including cash, promissory notes, services performed, contracts for services to be performed, or other securities of the corporation.

(c) Before the corporation issues shares, the board of directors must determine that the consideration received or to be received for shares to be issued is adequate. That determination by the board of directors is conclusive insofar as the adequacy of consideration for the issuance of shares relates to whether the shares are validly issued, fully paid, and nonassessable.

(d) When the corporation receives the consideration for which the board of directors authorized the issuance of shares, the shares issued therefor are fully paid and nonassessable.

(e) The corporation may place in escrow shares issued for a contract for future services or benefits or a promissory note, or make other arrangements to restrict the transfer of the shares, and may credit distributions in respect of the shares against their purchase price, until the services are performed, the note is paid, or the benefits received. If the services are not performed, the note is not paid, or the benefits are not received, the shares escrowed or restricted and the distributions credited may be cancelled in whole or part.

§ 6.22 Liability of Shareholders

(a) A purchaser from a corporation of its own shares is not liable to the corporation or its creditors with respect to the shares except to pay the consideration for which the shares were authorized to be issued (section 6.21) or specified in the subscription agreement (section 6.20).

(b) Unless otherwise provided in the articles of incorporation, a shareholder of a corporation is not personally liable for the acts or debts of the corporation except that he may become personally liable by reason of his own acts or conduct.

§ 6.23 Share Dividends

(a) Unless the articles of incorporation provide otherwise, shares may be issued pro rata and without consideration to the corporation's shareholders or to the shareholders of one or more classes or series. An issuance of shares under this subsection is a share dividend.

(b) Shares of one class or series may not be issued as a share dividend in respect of shares of another class or series unless (1) the articles of incorporation so authorize, (2) a majority of the votes entitled to be cast by the class or series to be issued approve the issue, or (3) there are no outstanding shares of the class or series to be issued.

(c) If the board of directors does not fix the record date for determining shareholders entitled to a share dividend, it is the date the board of directors authorizes the share dividend.

§ 6.24 Share Options

A corporation may issue rights, options, or warrants for the purchase of shares of the corporation. The board of directors shall determine the terms upon which the rights, options, or warrants are issued, their form and content, and the consideration for which the shares are to be issued.

§ 6.27 Restriction on Transfer of Shares and Other Securities

(a) The articles of incorporation, bylaws, an agreement among shareholders, or an agreement between shareholders and the corporation may impose restrictions on the transfer or registration of transfer of shares of the corporation. A restriction does not affect shares issued before the restriction was adopted unless the holders of the shares are parties to the restriction agreement or voted in favor of the restriction.

(b) A restriction on the transfer or registration of transfer of shares is valid and enforceable against the holder or a transferee of the holder if the restriction is authorized by this section and its existence is noted conspicuously on the front or back of the certificate or is contained in the information statement required by section 6.26(b). Unless so noted, a restriction is not enforceable against a person without knowledge of the restriction.

(c) A restriction on the transfer or registration of transfer of shares is authorized:

(1) to maintain the corporation's status when it is dependent on the number or identity of its shareholders;

(2) to preserve exemptions under federal or state securities law;

(3) for any other reasonable purpose.

(d) A restriction on the transfer or registration of transfer of shares may:

(1) obligate the shareholder first to offer the corporation or other persons (separately, consecutively, or simultaneously) an opportunity to acquire the restricted shares;

(2) obligate the corporation or other persons (separately, consecutively, or simultaneously) to acquire the restricted shares;

(3) require the corporation, the holders of any class of its shares, or another person to approve the transfer of the restricted shares, if the requirement is not manifestly unreasonable;

(4) prohibit the transfer of the restricted shares to designated persons or classes of persons, if the prohibition is not manifestly unreasonable.

(e) For purposes of this section, "shares" includes a security convertible into or carrying a right to subscribe for or acquire shares.

§ 6.30 Shareholders' Preemptive Rights

(a) The shareholders of a corporation do not have a preemptive right to acquire the corporation's unissued shares except to the extent the articles of incorporation so provide.

(b) A statement included in the articles of incorporation that "the corporation elects to have preemptive rights" (or words of similar import) means that the following principles apply except to the extent the articles of incorporation expressly provide otherwise:

(1) The shareholders of the corporation have a preemptive right, granted on uniform terms and conditions prescribed by the board of directors to provide a fair and reasonable opportunity to exercise the right, to acquire proportional amounts of the corporation's unissued shares upon the decision of the board of directors to issue them.

(2) A shareholder may waive his preemptive right. A waiver evidenced by a writing is irrevocable even though it is not supported by consideration.

(3) There is no preemptive right with respect to:

(i) shares issued as compensation to directors, officers, agents, or employees of the corporation, its subsidiaries or affiliates;

(ii) shares issued to satisfy conversion or option rights created to provide compensation to directors, officers, agents, or employees of the corporation, its subsidiaries or affiliates;

(iii) shares authorized in articles of incorporation that are issued within six months from the effective date of incorporation;

(iv) shares sold otherwise than for money.

(4) Holders of shares of any class without general voting rights but with preferential rights to distributions or assets have no preemptive rights with respect to shares of any class.

(5) Holders of shares of any class with general voting rights but without preferential rights to distributions or assets have no preemptive rights with respect to shares of any class with preferential rights to distributions or assets unless the shares with preferential rights are convertible into or carry a right to subscribe for or acquire shares without preferential rights.

(6) Shares subject to preemptive rights that are not acquired by shareholders may be issued to any person for a period of one year after being offered to shareholders at a consideration set by the board of directors that is not lower than the consideration set for the exercise of preemptive rights. An offer at a lower consideration or after the expiration of one year is subject to the shareholders' preemptive rights.

(c) For purposes of this section, "shares" includes a security convertible into or carrying a right to subscribe for or acquire shares.

§ 6.31 Corporation's Acquisition of Its Own Shares

(a) A corporation may acquire its own shares and shares so acquired constitute authorized but unissued shares.

(b) If the articles of incorporation prohibit the reissue of acquired shares, the number of authorized shares is reduced by the number of shares acquired, effective upon amendment of the articles of incorporation.

(c) Articles of amendment may be adopted by the board of directors without shareholder action, shall be delivered to the secretary of state for filing, and shall set forth:

(1) the name of the corporation;

(2) the reduction in the number of authorized shares, itemized by class and series; and

(3) the total number of authorized shares, itemized by class and series, remaining after reduction of the shares.

§ 6.40 Distributions to Shareholders

(a) A board of directors may authorize and the corporation may make distributions to its shareholders subject to restriction by the articles of incorporation and the limitation in subsection (c).

(b) If the board of directors does not fix the record date for determining shareholders entitled to a distribution (other than one involving a purchase, redemption, or other acquisition of the corporation's shares), it is the date the board of directors authorizes the distribution.

(c) No distribution may be made if, after giving it effect:

(1) the corporation would not be able to pay its debts as they become due in the usual course of business; or

(2) the corporation's total assets would be less than the sum of its total liabilities plus (unless the articles of incorporation permit otherwise) the amount that would be needed, if the corporation were to be dissolved at the time of the distribution, to satisfy the preferential rights upon dissolution of shareholders whose preferential rights are superior to those receiving the distribution.

(d) The board of directors may base a determination that a distribution is not prohibited under subsection (c) either on financial statements prepared on the basis of accounting practices and principles that are reasonable in the circumstances or on a fair valuation or other method that is reasonable in the circumstances.

(e) Except as provided in subsection (g), the effect of a distribution under subsection (c) is measured:

(1) in the case of distribution by purchase, redemption, or other acquisition of the corporation's shares, as of the earlier of (i) the date money or other property is transferred or debt incurred by the corporation or (ii) the date the shareholder ceases to be a shareholder with respect to the acquired shares;

(2) in the case of any other distribution of indebtedness, as of the date the indebtedness is distributed; and

(3) in all other cases, as of (i) the date the distribution is authorized if the payment occurs within 120 days after the date of authorization or (ii) the date the payment is made if it occurs more than 120 days after the date of authorization.

(f) A corporation's indebtedness to a shareholder incurred by reason of a distribution made in accordance with this section is at parity with the corporation's indebtedness to its general, unsecured creditors except to the extent subordinated by agreement.

(g) Indebtedness of a corporation, including indebtedness issued as a distribution, is not considered a liability for purposes of determinations under subsection (c) if its terms provide that payment of principal and interest are made only if and to the extent that payment of a distribution to shareholders could then be made under this section. If the indebtedness is issued as a distribution, each payment of principal or interest is treated as a distribution, the effect of which is measured on the date the payment is actually made.

§ 7.01 Annual Meeting

(a) A corporation shall hold annually at a time stated in or fixed in accordance with the bylaws a meeting of shareholders.

(b) Annual shareholders' meetings may be held in or out of this state at the place stated in or fixed in accordance with the bylaws. If no place is stated in or fixed in accordance with the bylaws, annual meetings shall be held at the corporation's principal office.

(c) The failure to hold an annual meeting at the time stated in or fixed in accordance with a corporation's bylaws does not affect the validity of any corporate action.

§ 7.02 Special Meeting

(a) A corporation shall hold a special meeting of shareholders:

(1) on call of its board of directors or the person or persons authorized to do so by the articles of incorporation or bylaws; or

(2) if the holders of at least 10 percent of all the votes entitled to be cast on any issue proposed to be considered at the proposed special meeting sign, date, and deliver to the corporation's secretary one or more written demands for the meeting describing the purpose or purposes for which it is to be held.

(b) If not otherwise fixed under sections 7.03 or 7.07, the record date for determining shareholders entitled to demand a special meeting is the date the first shareholder signs the demand.

(c) Special shareholders' meetings may be held in or out of this state at the place stated in or fixed in accordance with the bylaws. If no place is stated or fixed in accordance with the bylaws, special meetings shall be held at the corporation's principal office.

(d) Only business within the purpose or purposes described in the meeting notice required by section 7.05(c) may be conducted at a special shareholders' meeting.

§ 7.04 Action Without Meeting

(a) Action required or permitted by this Act to be taken at a shareholders' meeting may be taken without a meeting if the action is taken by all the shareholders entitled to vote on the action. The action must be evidenced by one or more written consents describing the action taken, signed by all the shareholders entitled to vote on the action, and delivered to the corporation for inclusion in the minutes or filing with the corporate records.

(b) If not otherwise determined under sections 7.03 or 7.07, the record date for determining shareholders entitled to take action without a meeting is the date the first shareholder signs the consent under subsection (a).

(c) A consent signed under this section has the effect of a meeting vote and may be described as such in any document.

(d) If this Act requires that notice of proposed action be given to nonvoting shareholders and the action is to be taken by unanimous consent of the voting shareholders, the corporation must give its nonvoting shareholders written notice of the proposed action at least 10 days before the action is taken. The notice must contain or be accompanied by the same material that, under this Act, would have been required to be sent to nonvoting shareholders in a notice of meeting at which the proposed action would have been submitted to the shareholders for action.

§ 7.05 Notice of Meeting

(a) A corporation shall notify shareholders of the date, time, and place of each annual and special shareholders' meeting no fewer than 10 nor more than 60 days before the meeting date. Unless this Act or the articles of incorporation require otherwise, the corporation is required to give notice only to shareholders entitled to vote at the meeting.

(b) Unless this Act or the articles of incorporation require otherwise, notice of an annual meeting need not include a description of the purpose or purposes for which the meeting is called.

(c) Notice of a special meeting must include a description of the purpose or purposes for which the meeting is called.

(d) If not otherwise fixed under sections 7.03 or 7.07, the record date for determining shareholders entitled to notice of and to vote at an annual or special shareholders' meeting is the close of business on the day before the first notice is delivered to shareholders.

(e) Unless the bylaws require otherwise, if an annual or special shareholders' meeting is adjourned to a different date, time, or place, notice need not be given of the new date, time, or place if the new date, time, or place is announced at the meeting before adjournment. If a new record date for the adjourned meeting is or must be fixed under section 7.07, however, notice of the adjourned meeting must be given under this section to persons who are shareholders as of the new record date.

§ 7.06 Waiver of Notice

(a) A shareholder may waive any notice required by this Act, the articles of incorporation, or bylaws before or after the date and time stated in the notice. The waiver must be in writing, be signed by the shareholder entitled to the notice, and be delivered to the corporation for inclusion in the minutes or filing with the corporate records.

(b) A shareholder's attendance at a meeting:

(1) waives objection to lack of notice or defective notice of the meeting, unless the shareholder at the beginning of the meeting objects to holding the meeting or transacting business at the meeting;

(2) waives objection to consideration of a particular matter at the meeting that is not within the purpose or purposes described in the meeting notice, unless the shareholder objects to considering the matter when it is presented.

§ 7.21 Voting Entitlement of Shares

(a) Except as provided in subsections (b) and (c) or unless the articles of incorporation provide otherwise, each outstanding share, regardless of class, is entitled to one vote on each matter voted on at a shareholders' meeting. Only shares are entitled to vote.

(b) Absent special circumstances, the shares of a corporation are not entitled to vote if they are owned, directly or indirectly, by a second corporation, domestic or foreign, and the first corporation owns, directly or indirectly, a majority of the shares entitled to vote for directors of the second corporation.

(c) Subsection (b) does not limit the power of a corporation to vote any shares, including its own shares, held by it in a fiduciary capacity.

(d) Redeemable shares are not entitled to vote after notice of redemption is mailed to the holders and a sum sufficient to redeem the shares has been deposited with a bank, trust company, or other financial institution under an irrevocable obligation to pay the holders the redemption price on surrender of the shares.

§ 7.22 Proxies

(a) A shareholder may vote his shares in person or by proxy.

(b) A shareholder may appoint a proxy to vote or otherwise act for him by signing an appointment form, either personally or by his attorney-in-fact.

(c) An appointment of a proxy is effective when received by the secretary or other officer or agent authorized to tabulate votes. An appointment is valid for 11 months unless a longer period is expressly provided in the appointment form.

(d) An appointment of a proxy is revocable by the shareholder unless the appointment form conspicuously states that it is irrevocable and the appointment is coupled with an interest. Appointments coupled with an interest include the appointment of:

(1) a pledgee;

(2) a person who purchased or agreed to purchase the shares;

(3) a creditor of the corporation who extended it credit under terms requiring the appointment;

(4) an employee of the corporation whose employment contract requires the appointment; or

(5) a party to a voting agreement created under section 7.31.

(e) The death or incapacity of the shareholder appointing a proxy does not affect the right of the corporation to accept the proxy's authority unless notice of the death or incapacity is received by the secretary or other officer or agent authorized to tabulate votes before the proxy exercises his authority under the appointment.

(f) An appointment made irrevocable under subsection (d) is revoked when the interest with which it is coupled is extinguished.

(g) A transferee for value of shares subject to an irrevocable appointment may revoke the appointment if he did not know of its existence when he acquired the shares and the existence of the irrevocable appointment was not noted conspicuously on the certificate representing the shares or on the information statement for shares without certificates.

(h) Subject to section 7.24 and to any express limitation on the proxy's authority appearing on the face of the appointment form, a corporation is entitled to accept the proxy's vote or other action as that of the shareholder making the appointment.

§ 7.25 Quorum and Voting Requirements for Voting Groups

(a) Shares entitled to vote as a separate voting group may take action on a matter at a meeting only if a quorum of those shares exists with respect to that matter. Unless the articles of incorporation or this Act provide otherwise, a majority of the votes entitled to be cast on the matter by the voting group constitutes a quorum of that voting group for action on that matter.

(b) Once a share is represented for any purpose at a meeting, it is deemed present for quorum purposes for the remainder of the meeting and for any adjournment of that meeting unless a new record date is or must be set for that adjourned meeting.
(c) If a quorum exists, action on a matter (other than the election of directors) by a voting group is approved if the votes cast within the voting group favoring the action exceed the votes cast opposing the action, unless the articles of incorporation or this Act require a greater number of affirmative votes.
(d) An amendment of articles of incorporation adding, changing, or deleting a quorum or voting requirement for a voting group greater than specified in subsection (b) or (c) is governed by section 7.27.
(e) The election of directors is governed by section 7.28.

§ 7.27 Greater Quorum or Voting Requirements
(a) The articles of incorporation may provide for a greater quorum or voting requirement for shareholders (or voting groups of shareholders) than is provided for by this Act.
(b) An amendment to the articles of incorporation that adds, changes, or deletes a greater quorum or voting requirement must meet the same quorum requirement and be adopted by the same vote and voting groups required to take action under the quorum and voting requirements then in effect or proposed to be adopted, whichever is greater.

§ 7.28 Voting for Directors; Cumulative Voting
(a) Unless otherwise provided in the articles of incorporation, directors are elected by a plurality of the votes cast by the shares entitled to vote in the election at a meeting at which a quorum is present.
(b) Shareholders do not have a right to cumulate their votes for directors unless the articles of incorporation so provide.
(c) A statement included in the articles of incorporation that "[all] [a designated voting group of] shareholders are entitled to cumulate their votes for directors" (or words of similar import) means that the shareholders designated are entitled to multiply the number of votes they are entitled to cast by the number of directors for whom they are entitled to vote and cast the product for a single candidate or distribute the product among two or more candidates.
(d) Shares otherwise entitled to vote cumulatively may not be voted cumulatively at a particular meeting unless:

(1) the meeting notice or proxy statement accompanying the notice states conspicuously that cumulative voting is authorized; or
(2) a shareholder who has the right to cumulate his votes gives notice to the corporation not less than 48 hours before the time set for the meeting of his intent to cumulate his votes during the meeting, and if one shareholder gives this notice all other shareholders in the same voting group participating in the election are entitled to cumulate their votes without giving further notice.

§ 7.30 Voting Trusts
(a) One or more shareholders may create a voting trust, conferring on a trustee the right to vote or otherwise act for them, by signing an agreement setting out the provisions of the trust (which may include anything consistent with its purpose) and transferring their shares to the trustee. When a voting trust agreement is signed, the trustee shall prepare a list of the names and addresses of all owners of beneficial interests in the trust, together with the number and class of shares each transferred to the trust, and deliver copies of the list and agreement to the corporation's principal office.
(b) A voting trust becomes effective on the date the first shares subject to the trust are registered in the trustee's name. A voting trust is valid for not more than 10 years after its effective date unless extended under subsection (c).
(c) All or some of the parties to a voting trust may extend it for additional terms of not more than 10 years each by signing an extension agreement and obtaining the voting trustee's written consent to the extension. An extension is valid for 10 years from the date the first shareholder signs the extension agreement. The voting trustee must deliver copies of the extension agreement and list of beneficial owners to the corporation's principal office. An extension agreement binds only those parties signing it.

§ 7.31 Voting Agreements
(a) Two or more shareholders may provide for the manner in which they will vote their shares by signing an agreement for that purpose. A voting agreement created under this section is not subject to the provisions of section 7.30.
(b) A voting agreement created under this section is specifically enforceable.

§ 8.01 Requirement for and Duties of Board of Directors
(a) Except as provided in subsection (c), each corporation must have a board of directors.
(b) All corporate powers shall be exercised by or under the authority of, and the business and affairs of the corporation managed under the direction of, its board of directors, subject to any limitation set forth in the articles of incorporation.
(c) A corporation having 50 or fewer shareholders may dispense with or limit the authority of a board of directors by describing in its articles of incorporation who will perform some or all of the duties of a board of directors.

§ 8.03 Number and Election of Directors
(a) A board of directors must consist of one or more individuals, with the number specified in or fixed in accordance with the articles of incorporation or bylaws.
(b) If a board of directors has power to fix or change the number of directors, the board may increase or decrease by 30 percent or less the number of directors last approved by the shareholders, but only the shareholders may increase or decrease by more than 30 percent the number of directors last approved by the shareholders.
(c) The articles of incorporation or bylaws may establish a variable range for the size of the board of directors by fixing a minimum and maximum number of directors. If a variable range is established, the number of directors may be fixed or changed from time to time, within the minimum and maximum, by the shareholders or the board of directors. After shares are issued, only the shareholders may change the range for the size of the board or change from a fixed to a variable-range size board or vice versa.
(d) Directors are elected at the first annual shareholders' meeting and at each annual meeting thereafter unless their terms are staggered under section 8.06.

§ 8.04 Election of Directors by Certain Classes of Shareholders
If the articles of incorporation authorize dividing the shares into classes, the articles may also authorize the election of all or a specified number of directors by the holders of one or more authorized classes of shares. Each class (or classes) of shares entitled to elect one or more directors is a separate voting group for purposes of the election of directors.

§ 8.08 Removal of Directors by Shareholders
(a) The shareholders may remove one or more directors with or without cause unless the articles of incorporation provide that directors may be removed only for cause.
(b) If a director is elected by a voting group of shareholders, only the shareholders of that voting group may participate in the vote to remove him.

(c) If cumulative voting is authorized, a director may not be removed if the number of votes sufficient to elect him under cumulative voting is voted against his removal. If cumulative voting is not authorized, a director may be removed only if the number of votes cast to remove him exceeds the number of votes cast not to remove him.
(d) A director may be removed by the shareholders only at a meeting called for the purpose of removing him and the meeting notice must state that the purpose, or one of the purposes, of the meeting is removal of the director.

§ 8.11 Compensation of Directors
Unless the articles of incorporation or bylaws provide otherwise, the board of directors may fix the compensation of directors.

§ 8.20 Meetings
(a) The board of directors may hold regular or special meetings in or out of this state.
(b) Unless the articles of incorporation or bylaws provide otherwise, the board of directors may permit any or all directors to participate in a regular or special meeting by, or conduct the meeting through the use of, any means of communication by which all directors participating may simultaneously hear each other during the meeting. A director participating in a meeting by this means is deemed to be present in person at the meeting.

§ 8.21 Action Without Meeting
(a) Unless the articles of incorporation or bylaws provide otherwise, action required or permitted by this Act to be taken at a board of directors' meeting may be taken without a meeting if the action is taken by all members of the board. The action must be evidenced by one or more written consents describing the action taken, signed by each director, and included in the minutes or filed with the corporate records reflecting the action taken.
(b) Action taken under this section is effective when the last director signs the consent, unless the consent specifies a different effective date.
(c) A consent signed under this section has the effect of a meeting vote and may be described as such in any document.

§ 8.24 Quorum and Voting
(a) Unless the articles of incorporation or bylaws require a greater number, a quorum of a board of directors consists of:
> **(1)** a majority of the fixed number of directors if the corporation has a fixed board size; or
> **(2)** a majority of the number of directors prescribed, or if no number is prescribed the number in office immediately before the meeting begins, if the corporation has a variable-range size board.

(b) The articles of incorporation or bylaws may authorize a quorum of a board of directors to consist of no fewer than one-third of the fixed or prescribed number of directors determined under subsection (a).
(c) If a quorum is present when a vote is taken, the affirmative vote of a majority of directors present is the act of the board of directors unless the articles of incorporation or bylaws require the vote of a greater number of directors.
(d) A director who is present at a meeting of the board of directors or a committee of the board of directors when corporate action is taken is deemed to have assented to the action taken unless: (1) he objects at the beginning of the meeting (or promptly upon his arrival) to holding it or transacting business at the meeting; (2) his dissent or abstention from the action taken is entered in the minutes of the meeting; or (3) he delivers written notice of his dissent or abstention to the presiding officer of the meeting before its adjournment or to the corporation immediately after adjournment of the meeting. The right of dissent or abstention is not available to a director who votes in favor of the action taken.

§ 8.30 General Standards for Directors
(a) A director shall discharge his duties as a director, including his duties as a member of a committee:
> **(1)** in good faith;
> **(2)** with the care an ordinarily prudent person in a like position would exercise under similar circumstances; and
> **(3)** in a manner he reasonably believes to be in the best interests of the corporation.

(b) In discharging his duties a director is entitled to rely on information, opinions, reports, or statements, including financial statements and other financial data, if prepared or presented by:
> **(1)** one or more officers or employees of the corporation whom the director reasonably believes to be reliable and competent in the matters presented;
> **(2)** legal counsel, public accountants, or other persons as to matters the director reasonably believes are within the person's professional or expert competence; or
> **(3)** a committee of the board of directors of which he is not a member if the director reasonably believes the committee merits confidence.

(c) A director is not acting in good faith if he has knowledge concerning the matter in question that makes reliance otherwise permitted by subsection (b) unwarranted.
(d) A director is not liable for any action taken as a director, or any failure to take any action, if he performed the duties of his office in compliance with this section.

§ 8.33 Liability for Unlawful Distributions
(a) A director who votes for or assents to a distribution made in violation of section 6.40 or the articles of incorporation is personally liable to the corporation for the amount of the distribution that exceeds what could have been distributed without violating section 6.40 or the articles of incorporation if it is established that he did not perform his duties in compliance with section 8.30. In any proceeding commenced under this section, a director has all of the defenses ordinarily available to a director.
(b) A director held liable under subsection (a) for an unlawful distribution is entitled to contribution:
> **(1)** from every other director who could be held liable under subsection (a) for the unlawful distribution; and
> **(2)** from each shareholder for the amount the shareholder accepted knowing the distribution was made in violation of section 6.40 or the articles of incorporation.

(c) A proceeding under this section is barred unless it is commenced within two years after the date on which the effect of the distribution was measured under section 6.40(e) or (g).

§ 8.40 Required Officers
(a) A corporation has the officers described in its bylaws or appointed by the board of directors in accordance with the bylaws.
(b) A duly appointed officer may appoint one or more officers or assistant officers if authorized by the bylaws or the board of directors.
(c) The bylaws or the board of directors shall delegate to one of the officers responsibility for preparing minutes of the directors' and shareholders' meetings and for authenticating records of the corporation.
(d) The same individual may simultaneously hold more than one office in a corporation.

§ 8.41 Duties of Officers
Each officer has the authority and shall perform the duties set forth in the bylaws or, to the extent consistent with the bylaws, the duties prescribed by the board of directors or by direction of an officer authorized by the board of directors to prescribe the duties of other officers.

§ 8.42 Standards of Conduct for Officers

(a) An officer with discretionary authority shall discharge his duties under that authority:

(1) in good faith;

(2) with the care an ordinarily prudent person in a like position would exercise under similar circumstances; and

(3) in a manner he reasonably believes to be in the best interests of the corporation.

(b) In discharging his duties an officer is entitled to rely on information, opinions, reports, or statements, including financial statements and other financial data, if prepared or presented by:

(1) one or more officers or employees of the corporation whom the officer reasonably believes to be reliable and competent in the matters presented; or

(2) legal counsel, public accountants, or other persons as to matters the officer reasonably believes are within the person's professional or expert competence.

(c) An officer is not acting in good faith if he has knowledge concerning the matter in question that makes reliance otherwise permitted by subsection (b) unwarranted.

(d) An officer is not liable for any action taken as an officer, or any failure to take any action, if he performed the duties of his office in compliance with this section.

§ 8.61 Judicial Action

(a) A transaction effected or proposed to be effected by a corporation (or by a subsidiary of the corporation or any other entity in which the corporation has a controlling interest) that is not a director's conflicting interest transaction may not be enjoined, set aside, or give rise to an award of damages or other sanctions, in a proceeding by a shareholder or by or in the right of the corporation, because a director of the corporation, or any person with whom or which he has a personal, economic, or other association, has an interest in the transaction.

(b) A director's conflicting interest transaction may not be enjoined, set aside, or give rise to an award of damages or other sanctions, in a proceeding by a shareholder or by or in the right of the corporation, because the director, or any person with whom or which he has a personal, economic, or other association, has an interest in the transaction, if:

(1) directors' action respecting the transaction was at any time taken in compliance with section 8.62;

(2) shareholders' action respecting the transaction was at any time taken in compliance with section 8.63;

(3) the transaction, judged according to the circumstances at the time of commitment, is established to have been fair to the corporation.

§ 8.62 Directors' Action

(a) Directors' action respecting a transaction is effective for purposes of section 8.61(b)(1) if the transaction received the affirmative vote of a majority (but no fewer than two) of those qualified directors on the board of directors or on a duly empowered committee of the board who voted on the transaction after either required disclosure to them (to the extent the information was not known by them) or compliance with subsection (b); provided that action by a committee is so effective only if (1) all its members are qualified directors, and (2) its members are either all the qualified directors on the board or are appointed by the affirmative vote of a majority of the qualified directors on the board.

(b) If a director has a conflicting interest respecting a transaction, but neither he nor a related person of the director specified in section 8.60(3)(i) is a party to the transaction, and if the director has a duty under law or professional canon, or a duty of confidentiality to another person, respecting information relating to the transaction such that the director may not make the disclosure described in section 8.60(4)(ii), then disclosure is sufficient for purposes of subsection (a) if the director (1) discloses to the directors voting on the transaction the existence and nature of his conflicting interest and informs them of the character and limitations imposed by that duty before their vote on the transaction, and (2) plays no part, directly or indirectly, in their deliberations or vote.

(c) A majority (but no fewer than two) of all the qualified directors on the board of directors, or on the committee, constitutes a quorum for purposes of action that complies with this section. Directors' action that otherwise complies with this section is not affected by the presence or vote of a director who is not a qualified director.

(d) For purposes of this section, "qualified director" means, with respect to a director's conflicting interest transaction, any director who does not have either (1) a conflicting interest respecting the transaction, or (2) a familial, financial, professional, or employment relationship with a second director who does have a conflicting interest respecting the transaction, which relationship would, in the circumstances, reasonably be expected to exert an influence on the first director's judgment when voting on the transaction.

§ 8.63 Shareholders' Action

(a) Shareholders' action respecting a transaction is effective for purposes of section 8.61(b)(2) if a majority of the votes entitled to be cast by the holders of all qualified shares were cast in favor of the transaction after (1) notice to shareholders describing the director's conflicting interest transaction, (2) provision of the information referred to in subsection (d), and (3) required disclosure to the shareholders who voted on the transaction (to the extent the information was not known by them).

(b) For purposes of this section, "qualified shares" means any shares entitled to vote with respect to the director's conflicting interest transaction except shares that, to the knowledge, before the vote, of the secretary (or other officer or agent of the corporation authorized to tabulate votes), are beneficially owned (or the voting of which is controlled) by a director who has a conflicting interest respecting the transaction or by a related person of the director, or both.

(c) A majority of the votes entitled to be cast by the holders of all qualified shares constitutes a quorum for purposes of action that complies with this section. Subject to the provisions of subsections (d) and (e), shareholders' action that otherwise complies with this section is not affected by the presence of holders, or the voting, of shares that are not qualified shares.

(d) For purposes of compliance with subsection (a), a director who has a conflicting interest respecting the transaction shall, before the shareholders' vote, inform the secretary (or other office or agent of the corporation authorized to tabulate votes) of the number, and the identity of persons holding or controlling the vote, of all shares that the director knows are beneficially owned (or the voting of which is controlled) by the director or by a related person of the director, or both.

(e) If a shareholders' vote does not comply with subsection (a) solely because of a failure of a director to comply with subsection (d), and if the director establishes that his failure did not determine and was not intended by him to influence the outcome of the vote, the court may, with or without further proceedings respecting section 8.61(b)(3), take such action respecting the transaction and the director, and give such effect, if any, to the shareholders' vote, as it considers appropriate in the circumstances.

§ 10.01 Authority to Amend

(a) A corporation may amend its articles of incorporation at any time to add or change a provision that is required or permitted in the articles of incorporation or to delete a provision not required in the articles of incorporation. Whether a provision is required or permitted in the articles of incorporation is determined as of the effective date of the amendment.

(b) A shareholder of the corporation does not have a vested property right resulting from any provision in the articles of incorporation, including provisions relating to management, control, capital structure, dividend entitlement, or purpose or duration of the corporation.

§ 10.03 Amendment by Board of Directors and Shareholders

(a) A corporation's board of directors may propose one or more amendments to the articles of incorporation for submission to the shareholders.

(b) For the amendment to be adopted:

(1) the board of directors must recommend the amendment to the shareholders unless the board of directors determines that because of conflict of interest or other special circumstances it should make no recommendation and communicates the basis for its determination to the shareholders with the amendment; and

(2) the shareholders entitled to vote on the amendment must approve the amendment as provided in subsection (e).

(c) The board of directors may condition its submission of the proposed amendment on any basis.

(d) The corporation shall notify each shareholder, whether or not entitled to vote, of the proposed shareholders' meeting in accordance with section 7.05. The notice of meeting must also state that the purpose, or one of the purposes, of the meeting is to consider the proposed amendment and contain or be accompanied by a copy or summary of the amendment.

(e) Unless this Act, the articles of incorporation, or the board of directors (acting pursuant to subsection (c)) require a greater vote or a vote by voting groups, the amendment to be adopted must be approved by:

(1) a majority of the votes entitled to be cast on the amendment by any voting group with respect to which the amendment would create dissenters' rights; and

(2) the votes required by sections 7.25 and 7.26 by every other voting group entitled to vote on the amendment.

§ 10.20 Amendment by Board of Directors or Shareholders

(a) A corporation's board of directors may amend or repeal the corporation's bylaws unless:

(1) the articles of incorporation or this Act reserve this power exclusively to the shareholders in whole or part; or

(2) the shareholders in amending or repealing a particular bylaw provide expressly that the board of directors may not amend or repeal that bylaw.

(b) A corporation's shareholders may amend or repeal the corporation's bylaws even though the bylaws may also be amended or repealed by its board of directors.

§ 11.01 Merger

(a) One or more corporations may merge into another corporation if the board of directors of each corporation adopts and its shareholders (if required by section 11.03) approve a plan of merger.

(b) The plan of merger must set forth:

(1) the name of each corporation planning to merge and the name of the surviving corporation into which each other corporation plans to merge;

(2) the terms and conditions of the merger; and

(3) the manner and basis of converting the shares of each corporation into shares, obligations, or other securities of the surviving or any other corporation or into cash or other property in whole or part.

(c) The plan of merger may set forth:

(1) amendments to the articles of incorporation of the surviving corporation; and

(2) other provisions relating to the merger.

§ 11.02 Share Exchange

(a) A corporation may acquire all of the outstanding shares of one or more classes or series of another corporation if the board of directors of each corporation adopts and its shareholders (if required by section 11.03) approve the exchange.

(b) The plan of exchange must set forth:

(1) the name of the corporation whose shares will be acquired and the name of the acquiring corporation;

(2) the terms and conditions of the exchange;

(3) the manner and basis of exchanging the shares to be acquired for shares, obligations, or other securities of the acquiring or any other corporation or for cash or other property in whole or part.

(c) The plan of exchange may set forth other provisions relating to the exchange.

(d) This section does not limit the power of a corporation to acquire all or part of the shares of one or more classes or series of another corporation through a voluntary exchange or otherwise.

§ 11.04 Merger of Subsidiary

(a) A parent corporation owning at least 90 percent of the outstanding shares of each class of a subsidiary corporation may merge the subsidiary into itself without approval of the shareholders of the parent or subsidiary.

§ 12.01 Sale of Assets in Regular Course of Business and Mortgage of Assets

(a) A corporation may, on the terms and conditions and for the consideration determined by the board of directors:

(1) sell, lease, exchange, or otherwise dispose of all, or substantially all, of its property in the usual and regular course of business,

(2) mortgage, pledge, dedicate to the repayment of indebtedness (whether with or without recourse), or otherwise encumber any or all of its property whether or not in the usual and regular course of business, or

(3) transfer any or all of its property to a corporation all the shares of which are owned by the corporation.

(b) Unless the articles of incorporation require it, approval by the shareholders of a transaction described in subsection (a) is not required.

§ 12.02 Sale of Assets Other Than in Regular Course of Business

(a) A corporation may sell, lease, exchange, or otherwise dispose of all, or substantially all, of its property (with or without the good will), otherwise than in the usual and regular course of business, on the terms and conditions and for the consideration determined by the corporation's board of directors, if the board of directors proposes and its shareholders approve the proposed transaction.

(b) For a transaction to be authorized:

(1) the board of directors must recommend the proposed transaction to the shareholders unless the board of directors determines that because of conflict of interest or other special circumstances it should make no recommendation and communicates the basis for its determination to the shareholders with the submission of the proposed transaction; and

(2) the shareholders entitled to vote must approve the transaction.

§ 13.02 Right to Dissent

(a) A shareholder is entitled to dissent from, and obtain payment of the fair value of his shares in the event of, any of the following corporate actions:

(1) consummation of a plan of merger to which the corporation is a party (i) if shareholder approval is required for the merger by section 11.03 or the articles of incorporation and the shareholder is entitled to vote on the merger or (ii) if the corporation is a subsidiary that is merged with its parent under section 11.04;

(2) consummation of a plan of share exchange to which the corporation is a party as the corporation whose shares will be acquired, if the shareholder is entitled to vote on the plan;

(3) consummation of a sale or exchange of all, or substantially all, of the property of the corporation other than in the usual and regular course of business, if the shareholder is entitled to vote on the sale or exchange, including a sale in dissolution, but not including a sale pursuant to court order or a sale for cash pursuant to a plan by which all or substantially all of the net proceeds of the sale will be distributed to the shareholders within one year after the date of sale;

(4) an amendment of the articles of incorporation that materially and adversely affects rights in respect of a dissenter's shares because it:

(i) alters or abolishes a preferential right of the shares;

(ii) creates, alters, or abolishes a right in respect of redemption, including a provision respecting a sinking fund for the redemption or repurchase, of the shares;

(iii) alters or abolishes a preemptive right of the holder of the shares to acquire shares or other securities;

(iv) excludes or limits the right of the shares to vote on any matter, or to cumulate votes, other than a limitation by dilution through issuance of shares or other securities with similar voting rights; or

(v) reduces the number of shares owned by the shareholder to a fraction of a share if the fractional share so created is to be acquired for cash under section 6.04; or

(5) any corporate action taken pursuant to a shareholder vote to the extent the articles of incorporation, bylaws, or a resolution of the board of directors provides that voting or nonvoting shareholders are entitled to dissent and obtain payment for their shares.

(b) A shareholder entitled to dissent and obtain payment for his shares under this chapter may not challenge the corporate action creating his entitlement unless the action is unlawful or fraudulent with respect to the shareholder or the corporation.

§ 14.30 Grounds for Judicial Dissolution

The [name or describe court or courts] may dissolve a corporation:

(1) in a proceeding by the attorney general if it is established that:

(i) the corporation obtained its articles of incorporation through fraud; or

(ii) he corporation has continued to exceed or abuse the authority conferred upon it by law;

(2) in a proceeding by a shareholder if it is established that:

(i) the directors are deadlocked in the management of the corporate affairs, the shareholders are unable to break the deadlock, and irreparable injury to the corporation is threatened or being suffered, or the business and affairs of the corporation can no longer be conducted to the advantage of the shareholders generally, because of the deadlock;

(ii) the directors or those in control of the corporation have acted, are acting, or will act in a manner that is illegal, oppressive, or fraudulent;

(iii) the shareholders are deadlocked in voting power and have failed, for a period that includes at least two consecutive annual meeting dates, to elect successors to directors whose terms have expired; or

(iv) the corporate assets are being misapplied or wasted;

(3) in a proceeding by a creditor if it is established that:

(i) the creditor's claim has been reduced to judgment, the execution on the judgment returned unsatisfied, and the corporation is insolvent; or

(ii) the corporation has admitted in writing that the creditor's claim is due and owing and the corporation is insolvent; or

(4) in a proceeding by the corporation to have its voluntary dissolution continued under court supervision.

§ 16.01 Corporate Records

(a) A corporation shall keep as permanent records minutes of all meetings of its shareholders and board of directors, a record of all actions taken by the shareholders or board of directors without a meeting, and a record of all actions taken by a committee of the board of directors in place of the board of directors on behalf of the corporation.

(b) A corporation shall maintain appropriate accounting records.

(c) A corporation or its agent shall maintain a record of its shareholders, in a form that permits preparation of a list of the names and addresses of all shareholders, in alphabetical order by class of shares showing the number and class of shares held by each.

(d) A corporation shall maintain its records in written form or in another form capable of conversion into written form within a reasonable time.

(e) A corporation shall keep a copy of the following records at its principal office:

(1) its articles or restated articles of incorporation and all amendments to them currently in effect;

(2) its bylaws or restated bylaws and all amendments to them currently in effect;

(3) resolutions adopted by its board of directors creating one or more classes or series of shares, and fixing their relative rights, preferences, and limitations, if shares issued pursuant to those resolutions are outstanding;

(4) the minutes of all shareholders' meetings, and records of all action taken by shareholders without a meeting, for the past three years;

(5) all written communications to shareholders generally within the past three years, including the financial statements furnished for the past three years under section 16.20;

(6) a list of the names and business addresses of its current directors and officers; and

(7) its most recent annual report delivered to the secretary of state under section 16.22.

§ 16.02 Inspection of Records by Shareholders

(a) Subject to section 16.03(c), a shareholder of a corporation is entitled to inspect and copy, during regular business hours at the corporation's principal office, any of the records of the corporation described in section 16.01(e) if he gives the corporation written notice of his demand at least five business days before the date on which he wishes to inspect and copy.

(b) A shareholder of a corporation is entitled to inspect and copy, during regular business hours at a reasonable location specified by the corporation, any of the following records of the corporation if the shareholder meets the requirements of subsection (c) and gives the corporation written notice of his demand at least five business days before the date on which he wishes to inspect and copy:

(1) excerpts from minutes of any meeting of the board of directors, records of any action of a committee of the board of directors while acting in place of the board of directors on behalf of the corporation, minutes of any meeting of the shareholders, and records of action taken by the shareholders or board of directors without a meeting, to the extent not subject to inspection under section 16.02(a);

(2) accounting records of the corporation; and

(3) the record of shareholders.

(c) A shareholder may inspect and copy the records identified in subsection (b) only if:

(1) his demand is made in good faith and for a proper purpose;

(2) he describes with reasonable particularity his purpose and the records he desires to inspect; and

(3) the records are directly connected with his purpose.

(d) The right of inspection granted by this section may not be abolished or limited by a corporation's articles of incorporation or bylaws.

(e) This section does not affect:

(1) the right of a shareholder to inspect records under section 7.20 or, if the shareholder is in litigation with the corporation, to the same extent as any other litigant;

(2) the power of a court, independently of this Act, to compel the production of corporate records for examination.

APPENDIX F

DICTIONARY OF LEGAL TERMS

abatement Reduction or elimination of gifts by category upon the reduction in value of the estate.

absolute surety Surety liable to a creditor immediately upon the default of the principal debtor.

acceptance *Commercial paper* Acceptance is the drawee's signed engagement to honor the draft as presented. It becomes operative when completed by delivery or notification. UCC § 3–410.

Contracts Compliance by offeree with terms and conditions of offer.

Sale of goods UCC § 2–606 provides three ways a buyer can accept goods: (1) by signifying to the seller that the goods are conforming or that he will accept them in spite of their nonconformity, (2) by failing to make an effective rejection, and (3) by doing an act inconsistent with the seller's ownership.

acceptor Drawee who has accepted an instrument.

accession An addition to one's property by increase of the original property or by production from such property. *E.g.*, A innocently converts the wheat of B into bread. UCC § 9–315 changes the common law where a perfected security interest is involved.

accident and health insurance Provides protection from losses due to accident or sickness.

accommodation An arrangement made as a favor to another, usually involving a loan of money or commercial paper. While a party's intent may be to aid a maker of a note by lending his credit, if he seeks to accomplish thereby legitimate objects of his own and not simply to aid the maker, the act is not for accommodation.

accommodation indorser Signer not in the chain of title.

accommodation party A person who signs commercial paper in any capacity for the purpose of lending his name to another party to an instrument. UCC § 3–415.

accord and satisfaction A method of discharging a claim whereby the parties agree to accept something in settlement, the "accord" being the agreement and the "satisfaction" its execution or performance. It is a new contract that is substituted for an old contract, which is thereby discharged, or for an obligation or cause of action and that must have all of the elements of a valid contract.

account Any account with a bank, including a checking, time, interest or savings account. UCC § 4–194. Also, any right to payment, for goods or services, that is not evidenced by an instrument or chattel paper. *E.g.*, account receivable.

Many of the definitions are abridged and adapted from *Black's Law Dictionary*, 5th edition, West Publishing Company, 1979.

accounting Equitable proceeding for a complete settlement of all partnership affairs.

act of state doctrine Rule that a court should not question the validity of actions taken by a foreign government in its own country.

actual authority Power conferred upon agent by actual consent given by principal.

actual express authority Actual authority derived from written or spoken words of principal.

actual implied authority Actual authority inferred from words or conduct manifested to agent by principal.

actual notice Knowledge actually and expressly communicated.

actus reas Wrongful or overt act.

ademption The removal or extinction of a devise by act of the testator.

adequacy of consideration Not required where parties have freely agreed to the exchange.

adhesion contract Standard "form" contract, usually between a large retailer and a consumer, in which the weaker party has no realistic choice or opportunity to bargain.

adjudication The giving or pronouncing of a judgment in a case; also, the judgment given.

administrative agency Governmental entity (other than courts and legislatures) having authority to affect the rights of private parties.

administrative law Law dealing with the establishment, duties, and powers of agencies in the executive branch of government.

administrative process Entire set of activities engaged in by administrative agencies while carrying out their rulemaking, enforcement, and adjudicative functions.

administrator A person appointed by the court to manage the assets and liabilities of an intestate (a person dying without a will). A person named in the will of a testator (a person dying with a will) is called the executor. Female designations are administratrix and executrix.

adversary system System in which opposing parties initiate and present their cases.

adverse possession A method of acquiring title to real property by possession for a statutory period under certain conditions. The periods of time may differ, depending on whether the adverse possessor has color of title.

affidavit A written statement of facts, made voluntarily, confirmed by oath or affirmation of the party making it, and taken before an authorized officer.

affiliate Person who controls, is controlled by, or is under common control with the issuer.

affirm Uphold the lower court's judgment.

affirmative action Active recruitment of minority applicants.
affirmative defense A response that attacks the plaintiff's legal right to bring an action as opposed to attacking the truth of the claim. *E.g.*, accord and satisfaction; assumption of risk; contributory negligence; duress; estoppel.
affirmative disclosure Requirement that an advertiser include certain information in its advertisement so that the ad is not deceptive.
after-acquired property Property the debtor may acquire at some time after the security interest attaches.
agency Relation in which one person acts for or represents another by the latter's authority.

Actual agency Exists where the agent is really employed by the principal.

Agency by estoppel One created by operation of law and established by proof of such acts of the principal as reasonably lead to the conclusion of its existence.

Implied agency One created by acts of the parties and deduced from proof of other facts.

agent Person authorized to act on another's behalf.
allegation A statement of a party setting out what he expects to prove.
allonge Piece of paper firmly affixed to the instrument.
annuity contract Agreement to pay periodic sums to insured upon reaching a designated age.
annul To annul a judgment or judicial proceeding is to deprive it of all force and operation.
answer The answer is the formal written statement made by a defendant setting forth the ground of his defense.
antecedent debt Preexisting obligation.
anticipatory breach of contract (or **anticipatory repudiation**) The unjustified assertion by a party that he will not perform an obligation that he is contractually obligated to perform at a future time. See UCC §§ 610 & 611.
apparent authority Such principal power that a reasonable person would assume an agent has in light of the principal's conduct.
appeal Resort to a superior (appellate) court to review the decision of an inferior (trial) court or administrative agency.
appeal by right Mandatory review by a higher court.
appellant A party who takes an appeal from one court to another. He may be either the plaintiff or defendant in the original court proceeding.
appellee The party in a cause against whom an appeal is taken; that is, the party who has an interest adverse to setting aside or reversing the judgment. Sometimes also called the "respondent."
appropriation Unauthorized use of another person's name or likeness for one's own benefit.
appurtenances Things appurtenant pass as incident to the principal thing. Sometimes an easement consisting of a right of way over one piece of land will pass with another piece of land as being appurtenant to it.
APR Annual percentage rate.
arbitration The reference of a dispute to an impartial (third) person chosen by the parties, who agree in advance to abide by the arbitrator's award issued after a hearing at which both parties have an opportunity to be heard.
arraignment Accused is informed of the crime against him and enters a plea.
articles of incorporation (or **certificate of incorporation**) The instrument under which a corporation is formed. The contents are prescribed in the particular state's general incorporation statute.
articles of partnership A written agreement by which parties enter into a partnership, to be governed by the terms set forth therein.
as is Disclaimer of implied warranties.
assault Unlawful attempted battery; intentional infliction of apprehension of immediate bodily harm or offensive contact.
assignee Party to whom contract rights are assigned.
assignment A transfer of the rights to real or personal property, usually intangible property such as rights in a lease, mortgage, sale agreement, or partnership.
assignment of rights Voluntary transfer to a third party of the rights arising from a contract.
assignor Party making an assignment.
assumes Delegatee agrees to perform the contractual obligation of the delegator.
assumes the mortgage Purchaser of mortgaged property becomes personally liable to pay the debt.
assumption of risk Plaintiff's express or implied consent to encounter a known danger.
attachment The process of seizing property, by virtue of a writ, summons, or other judicial order, and bringing the same into the custody of the court for the purpose of securing satisfaction of the judgment ultimately to be entered in the action. While formerly the main objective was to coerce the defendant debtor to appear in court, today the writ of attachment is used primarily to seize the debtor's property in the event a judgment is rendered.

Distinguished from execution See **execution**.

Also, the process by which a security interest becomes enforceable. Attachment may occur upon the taking of possession or upon the signing of a security agreement by the person who is pledging the property as collateral.

authority Power of an agent to change the legal status of his principal.
authorized means Any reasonable means of communication.
automatic perfection Perfection upon attachment.
award The decision of an arbitrator.

bad checks Issuing a check with funds insufficient to cover it.
bailee The party to whom personal property is delivered under a contract of bailment.

Extraordinary bailee Absolutely liable for the safety of the bailed property without regard to the cause of loss.

Ordinary bailee Must exercise due care.

bailment A delivery of personal property in trust for the execution of a special object in relation to such goods, beneficial either to the bailor or bailee or both, and upon a contract to either redeliver the goods to the bailor or otherwise dispose of the same in conformity with the purpose of the trust.
bailor The party who delivers goods to another in the contract of bailment.
bankrupt The state or condition of one who is unable to pay his debts as they are, or become, due.
Bankruptcy Code The Act was substantially revised in 1978, effective October 1, 1979. Straight bankruptcy is in the nature of a liquidation proceeding and involves the collection and distribution to creditors of all the bankrupt's nonexempt property by the trustee in the manner provided by the Act. The debtor rehabilitation provisions of the Act (Chapters 11 and 13) differ from straight bankruptcy in that the debtor looks to rehabilitation and reorganization, rather than liquidation, and the creditors look to future earnings of the bankrupt, rather than to property held by the bankrupt, to satisfy their claims.
bargain Negotiated exchange.
bargained exchange Mutually agreed-upon exchange.
basis of the bargain Part of the buyer's assumption underlying the sale.
battery Unlawful touching of another; intentional infliction of harmful or offensive bodily contact.
bearer Person in possession of an instrument.
bearer paper Payable to holder of the instrument.
beneficiary One who benefits from act of another. See also **third-party beneficiary**.

Incidental A person who may derive benefit from performance on contract, though he is neither the promisee nor the one to whom performance is to be rendered. Since the incidental beneficiary is not a donee or creditor beneficiary (see **third-party beneficiary**), he has no right to enforce the contract.

Intended beneficiary Third party intended by the two contracted parties to receive a benefit from their contract.

Trust As it relates to trust beneficiaries, includes a person who has any present or future interest, vested or contingent, and also includes the owner of an interest by assignment or other transfer and, as it relates to a charitable trust, includes any person entitled to enforce the trust.

beyond a reasonable doubt Proof that is entirely convincing and satisfying to a moral certainty; criminal law standard.

bilateral contract Contract in which both parties exchange promises.

bill of lading Document evidencing receipt of goods for shipment issued by person engaged in business of transporting or forwarding goods; includes airbill. UCC § 1–201(6).

Through bill of lading A bill of lading which specifies at least one connecting carrier.

bill of sale A written agreement, formerly limited to one under seal, by which one person assigns or transfers his right to or interest in goods and personal chattels to another.

binder A written memorandum of the important terms of a contract of insurance which gives temporary protection to an insured pending investigation of risk by the insurance company or until a formal policy is issued.

blue law Prohibition of certain types of commercial activity on Sunday.

blue sky laws A popular name for state statutes providing for the regulation and supervision of securities offerings and sales, to protect citizen-investors from investing in fraudulent companies.

bona fide Latin. In good faith.

bond A certificate or evidence of a debt on which the issuing company or governmental body promises to pay the bondholders a specified amount of interest for a specified length of time and to repay the loan on the expiration date. In every case, a bond represents debt—its holder is a creditor of the corporation, not a part owner, as the shareholder is.

boycott Agreement among parties not to deal with a third party.

breach Wrongful failure to perform the terms of a contract.

Material breach Nonperformance which significantly impairs the aggrieved party's rights under the contract.

bribery Offering property to a public official to influence the official's decision.

bulk transfer Transfer not in the ordinary course of the transferor's business of a major part of his inventory.

burglary Breaking and entering the home of another at night with intent to commit a felony.

business judgment rule Protects directors from liability for honest mistakes of judgment.

business trust A trust (managed by a trustee for the benefit of a beneficiary) established to conduct a business for a profit.

but for rule Person's negligent conduct is a cause of an event if the event would not have occurred in the absence of that conduct.

buyer in ordinary course of business Person who buys in ordinary course, in good faith, and without knowledge that the sale to him is in violation of anyone's ownership rights or of a security interest.

by-laws Regulations, ordinances, rules, or laws adopted by an association or corporation for its government.

callable bond Bond that is subject to redemption (reacquisition) by the corporation.

cancellation One party's putting an end to a contract because of a breach by other party.

capital Accumulated goods, possessions, and assets, used for the production of profits and wealth. Owners' equity in a business. Also used to refer to the total assets of a business or to capital assets.

capital surplus Surplus other than earned surplus.

carrier Transporter of goods.

casualty insurance Covers property loss due to causes other than fire or the elements.

cause of action The ground on which an action may be sustained.

caveat emptor Latin. Let the buyer beware. This maxim is more applicable to judicial sales, auctions, and the like than to sales of consumer goods, where strict liability, warranty, and other laws protect.

certificate of deposit A written acknowledgment by a bank or banker of a deposit with promise to pay to depositor, to his order, or to some other person or to his order. UCC § 3–104(2)(c).

certificate of title Official representation of ownership.

certification Acceptance of a check by a drawee bank.

certification of incorporation See **articles of incorporation**.

certification mark Distinctive symbol, word, or design used with goods or services to certify specific characteristics.

certiorari Latin. To be informed of. A writ of common law origin issued by a superior to an inferior court requiring the latter to produce a certified record of a particular case tried therein. It is most commonly used to refer to the Supreme Court of the United States, which uses the writ of certiorari as a discretionary device to choose the cases it wishes to hear.

chancery Equity; equitable jurisdiction; a court of equity; the system of jurisprudence administered in courts of equity.

charging order Judicial lien against a partner's interest in the partnership.

charter An instrument emanating from the sovereign power, in the nature of a grant. A charter differs from a constitution in that the former is granted by the sovereign, while the latter is established by the people themselves.

Corporate law An act of a legislature creating a corporation or creating and defining the franchise of a corporation. Also a corporation's constitution or organic law; that is to say, the articles of incorporation taken in connection with the law under which the corporation was organized.

chattel mortgage A pre-Uniform Commercial Code security device whereby the mortgagee took a security interest in personal property of the mortgagor. Such security device has generally been superseded by other types of security agreements under UCC Article 9 (Secured Transactions).

chattel paper Writings that evidence both a debt and a security interest.

check A draft drawn upon a bank and payable on demand, signed by the maker or drawer, containing an unconditional promise to pay a sum certain in money to the order of the payee. UCC § 3–104(2)(b).

Cashier's check A bank's own check drawn on itself and signed by the cashier or other authorized official. It is a direct obligation of the bank.

C. & F. Cost and freight; a shipping contract.

C.I.F. Cost, insurance, and freight; a shipping contract.

civil law Laws concerned with civil or private rights and remedies, as contrasted with criminal laws.

The system of jurisprudence administered in the Roman empire, particularly as set forth in the compilation of Justinian and his successors, as distinguished from the common law of England and the canon law. The civil law (Civil Code) is followed by Louisiana.

claim A right to payment.

clearinghouse An association of banks for the purpose of settling accounts on a daily basis.

close corporation See **corporation**.

closed-ended credit Credit extended to debtor for a specific period of time.

closed shop Employer can only hire union members.
C.O.D. Collect on delivery; generally a shipping contract.
code A compilation of all permanent laws in force consolidated and classified according to subject matter. Many states have published official codes of all laws in force, including the common law and statutes as judicially interpreted, which have been compiled by code commissions and enacted by the legislatures.
codicil A supplement or an addition to a will; it may explain, modify, add to, subtract from, qualify, alter, restrain, or revoke provisions in an existing will. It must be executed with the same formalities as a will.
cognovit judgment Written authority by debtor for entry of judgment against him in the event he defaults in payment. Such provision in a debt instrument on default confers judgment against the debtor.
collateral Secondarily liable; liable only if the party with primary liability does not perform.
collateral (security) Personal property subject to security interest.
Banking Some form of security in addition to the personal obligation of the borrower.
collateral promise Undertaking to be secondarily liable, that is, liable if the principal debtor does not perform.
collecting bank Any bank, except the payor bank, handling the item for collection. UCC § 4–105(d).
collective mark Distinctive symbol used to indicate membership in an organization.
collision insurance Protects the owner of an automobile against damage due to contact with other vehicles or objects.
commerce power Exclusive power granted by the U.S. Constitution to the federal government to regulate commerce with foreign countries and among the states.
commercial bailment Bailment in which parties derive a mutual benefit.
commercial impracticability Performance can only be accomplished with unforeseen and unjust hardship.
commercial law A phrase used to designate the whole body of substantive jurisprudence (*e.g.*, Uniform Commercial Code; Truth in Lending Act) applicable to the rights, intercourse, and relations of persons engaged in commerce, trade, or mercantile pursuits. See **Uniform Commercial Code**.
commercial paper Bills of exchange (*i.e.*, drafts), promissory notes, bank checks, and other negotiable instruments for the payment of money, which, by their form and on their face, purport to be such instruments. UCC Article 3 is the general law governing commercial paper.
commercial reasonableness Judgment of reasonable persons familiar with the business transaction.
commercial speech Expression related to the economic interests of the speaker and its audience.
common carrier Carrier open to the general public.
common law Body of law originating in England and derived from judicial decisions. As distinguished from statutory law created by the enactment of legislatures, the common law comprises the judgments and decrees of the courts recognizing, affirming, and enforcing usages and customs of immemorial antiquity.
community property Rights of a spouse in property acquired by the other during marriage.
comparable worth Equal pay for jobs of equal value to the employer.
comparative negligence Under comparative negligence statutes or doctrines, negligence is measured in terms of percentage, and any damages allowed shall be diminished in proportion to amount of negligence attributable to the person for whose injury, damage, or death recovery is sought.
complainant One who applies to the courts for legal redress by filing a complaint (*i.e.*, plaintiff).
complaint The pleading which sets forth a claim for relief. Such complaint (whether it be the original claim, counterclaim, cross-claim, or third-party claim) shall contain (1) a short, plain statement of the grounds upon which the court's jurisdiction depends, unless the court already has jurisdiction and the claim needs no new grounds of jurisdiction to support it, (2) a short, plain statement of the claim showing that the pleader is entitled to relief, and (3) a demand for judgment for the relief to which he deems himself entitled. Fed.R. Civil P. 8(a). The complaint, together with the summons, is required to be served on the defendant. Rule 4.
composition Agreement between debtor and two or more of her creditors that each will take a portion of his claim as full payment.
compulsory arbitration Arbitration required by statute for specific types of disputes.
computer crime Crime committed against or through the use of a computer or computer/services.
concealment Fraudulent failure to disclose a material fact.
conciliation Nonbinding process in which a third party acts as an intermediary between disputing parties.
concurrent jurisdiction Authority of more than one court to hear the same case.
condition An uncertain event which affects the duty of performance.
Concurrent conditions The parties are to perform simultaneously.
Express condition Performance is contingent on the happening or nonhappening of a stated event.
condition precedent An event which must occur or not occur before performance is due; event or events (presentment, dishonor, notice of dishonor) which must occur to hold a secondary party liable to commercial paper.
condition subsequent An event which terminates a duty of performance.
conditional acceptance An acceptance of an offer contingent upon the acceptance of an additional or different term.
conditional contract Obligations are contingent upon a stated event.
conditional guarantor of collection Surety liable to creditor only after creditor exhausts his legal remedies against the principal debtor.
confession of judgment Written agreement by debtor authorizing creditor to obtain a court judgment in the event debtor defaults. See also **cognovit judgment**.
confiscation Governmental taking of foreign-owned property without payment.
conflict of laws That branch of jurisprudence, arising from the diversity of the laws of different nations, states, or jurisdictions, that reconciles the inconsistencies, or decides which law is to govern in a particular case.
confusion Results when goods belonging to two or more owners become so intermixed that the property of any of them no longer can be identified except as part of a mass of like goods.
consanguinity Kinship; blood relationship; the connection or relation of persons descended from the same stock or common ancestor.
consensual arbitration Arbitration voluntarily entered into by the parties.
consent Voluntary and knowing willingness that an act should be done.
conservator Appointed by court to manage affairs of incompetent or to liquidate business.
consideration The cause, motive, price, or impelling influence which induces a contracting party to enter into a contract. Some right, interest, profit, or benefit accruing to one party or some forbearance, detriment, loss, or responsibility given, suffered, or undertaken by the other.
consignee One to whom a consignment is made. Person named in bill of lading to whom or to whose order the bill promises delivery. UCC § 7–102(b).
consignment Ordinarily implies an agency; denotes that property is committed to the consignee for care or sale.

consignor One who sends or makes a consignment; a shipper of goods. The person named in a bill of lading as the person from whom the goods have been received for shipment. UCC § 7–102(c).

consolidation In *corporate law*, the combination of two or more corporations into a newly created corporation. Thus, A Corporation and B Corporation consolidate to form C Corporation.

constitution Fundamental law of a government establishing its powers and limitations.

constructive That which is established by the mind of the law in its act of *construing* facts, conduct, circumstances, or instruments. That which has not in its essential nature the character assigned to it, but acquires such character in consequence of the way in which it is regarded by a rule or policy of law; hence, inferred, implied, or made out by legal interpretation; the word "legal" being sometimes used here in lieu of "constructive."

constructive assent An assent or consent imputed to a party from a construction or interpretation of his conduct; as distinguished from one which he actually expresses.

constructive conditions Conditions in contracts which are neither expressed nor implied but rather are imposed by law to meet the ends of justice.

constructive delivery Term comprehending all those acts which, although not truly conferring a real possession of the vendee, have been held by construction of law to be equivalent to acts of real delivery.

constructive eviction Failure by the landlord in any obligation under the lease that causes a substantial and lasting injury to the tenant's enjoyment of the premises.

constructive notice Knowledge imputed by law.

constructive trust Arising by operation of law to prevent unjust enrichment. See also **trustee**.

consumer goods Goods bought or used for personal, family, or household purposes.

consumer product Tangible personal property normally used for family, household, or personal purposes.

contingent remainder Remainder interest, conditional upon the happening of an event in addition to the termination of the preceding estate.

contract An agreement between two or more persons which creates an obligation to do or not to do a particular thing. Its essentials are competent parties, subject matter, a legal consideration, mutuality of agreement, and mutuality of obligation.

Destination contract Seller is required to tender delivery of the goods at a particular destination; seller bears the expense and risk of loss.

Executed contract Fully performed by all of the parties.

Executory contract Contract partially or entirely unperformed by one or more of the parties.

Express contract Agreement of parties that is expressed in words either in writing or orally.

Formal contract Agreement which is legally binding because of its particular form or mode or expression.

Implied-in-fact contract Contract where agreement of the parties is inferred from their conduct.

Informal contract All oral or written contracts other than formal contracts.

Installment contract Goods are delivered in separate lots.

Integrated contract Complete and total agreement.

Output contract A contract in which one party agrees to sell his entire output and the other agrees to buy it; it is not illusory, though it may be indefinite.

Quasi contract Obligation not based upon contract that is imposed to avoid injustice.

Requirements contract A contract in which one party agrees to purchase his total requirements from the other party; hence, such a contract is binding, not illusory.

Substituted contract An agreement between the parties to rescind their old contract and replace it with a new contract.

Unconscionable contract One which no sensible person not under delusion, duress, or in distress would make, and such as no honest and fair person would accept. A contract the terms of which are excessively unreasonable, overreaching, and one-sided.

Unenforceable contract Contract for the breach of which the law does not provide a remedy.

Unilateral and bilateral A unilateral contract is one in which one party makes an express engagement or undertakes a performance, without receiving in return any express engagement or promise of performance from the other. Bilateral (or reciprocal) contracts are those by which the parties expressly enter into mutual engagements.

contract clause Prohibition against the states' retroactively modifying public and private contracts.

contractual liability Obligation on a negotiable instrument, based upon signing the instrument.

contribution Payment from cosureties of their proportionate share.

contributory negligence An act or omission amounting to a want of ordinary care on the part of the complaining party, which, concurring with defendant's negligence, is proximate cause of injury.

The defense of contributory negligence is an absolute bar to any recovery in some states; because of this, it has been replaced by the doctrine of comparative negligence in many other states.

conversion Unauthorized and wrongful exercise of dominion and control over another's personal property, to exclusion of or inconsistent with rights of the owner.

convertible bond Bond that may be exchanged for other securities of the corporation.

copyright Exclusive right granted by federal government to authors of original works including literary, musical, dramatic, pictorial, graphic, sculptural, and film works.

corporation A legal entity ordinarily consisting of an association of numerous individuals. Such entity is regarded as having a personality and existence distinct from that of its several members and is vested with the capacity of continuous succession, irrespective of changes in its membership, either in perpetuity or for a limited term of years.

Closely held or close corporation Corporation that is owned by few shareholders and whose shares are not actively traded.

Corporation de facto One existing under color of law and in pursuance of an effort made in good faith to organize a corporation under the statute. Such a corporation is not subject to collateral attack.

Corporation de jure That which exists by reason of full compliance with requirements of an existing law permitting organization of such corporation.

Domestic corporation Corporation created under the laws of a given state.

Foreign corporation Corporation created under the laws of any other state, government, or country.

Publicly held corporation Corporation whose shares are owned by a large number of people and are widely traded.

Subchapter S corporation A small business corporation which, under certain conditions, may elect to have its undistributed taxable income taxed to its shareholders. I.R.C. § 1371 et seq. Of major significance is the fact that Subchapter S status usually avoids the corporate income tax, and corporate losses can be claimed by the shareholders.

Subsidiary and parent Subsidiary corporation is one in which another corporation (called parent corporation) owns at least a majority of the shares and over which it thus has control.

corrective advertising Disclosure in an advertisement that previous ads were deceptive.

costs A pecuniary allowance, made to the successful party (and recoverable from the losing party), for his expenses in prosecuting or

defending an action or a distinct proceeding within an action. Generally, "costs" do not include attorneys' fees unless such fees are by a statute denominated costs or are by statute allowed to be recovered as costs in the case.
cosureties Two or more sureties bound for the same debt of a principal debtor.
co-tenants Persons who hold title concurrently.
counterclaim A claim presented by a defendant in opposition to or deduction from the claim of the plaintiff.
counteroffer A statement by the offeree which has the legal effect of rejecting the offer and of proposing a new offer to the offeror. However, the provisions of UCC § 2–207(2) modify this principle by providing that the "additional terms are to be construed as proposals for addition to the contract."
course of dealing A sequence of previous acts and conduct between the parties to a particular transaction which is fairly to be regarded as establishing a common basis of understanding for interpreting their expressions and other conduct. UCC § 1–205(1).
course of performance Conduct between the parties concerning performance of the particular contract.
court above—court below In appellate practice, the "court above" is the one to which a cause is removed for review, whether by appeal, writ of error, or certiorari, while the "court below" is the one from which the case is being removed.
covenant Used primarily with respect to promises in conveyances or other instruments dealing with real estate.

Covenants against encumbrances A stipulation against all rights to or interests in the land which may subsist in third persons to the diminution of the value of the estate granted.

Covenant appurtenant A covenant which is connected with land of the grantor, not in gross. A covenant running with the land and binding heirs, executors, and assigns of the immediate parties.

Covenant for further assurance An undertaking, in the form of a covenant, on the part of the vendor of real estate to do such further acts for the purpose of perfecting the purchaser's title as the latter may reasonably require.

Covenant for possession A covenant by which the grantee or lessee is granted possession.

Covenant for quiet enjoyment An assurance against the consequences of a defective title, and against any disturbances thereupon.

Covenants for title Covenants usually inserted in a conveyance of land, on the part of the grantor, and binding him for the completeness, security, and continuance of the title transferred to the grantee. They comprise covenants for seisin, for right to convey, against encumbrances, or quiet enjoyment, sometimes for further assurance, and almost always of warranty.

Covenant in gross Such as do not run with the land.

Covenant of right to convey An assurance by the covenantor that the grantor has sufficient capacity and title to convey the estate which he by his deed undertakes to convey.

Covenant of seisin An assurance to the purchaser that the grantor has the very estate in quantity and quality which he purports to convey.

Covenant of warranty An assurance by the grantor of an estate that the grantee shall enjoy the same without interruption by virtue of paramount title.

Covenant running with land A covenant which goes with the land, as being annexed to the estate, and which cannot be separated from the land or transferred without it. A covenant is said to run with the land when not only the original parties or their representatives, but each successive owner of the land, will be entitled to its benefit, or be liable (as the case may be) to its obligation. Such a covenant is said to be one which "touches and concerns" the land itself, so that its benefit or obligation passes with the ownership. Essentials are that the grantor and grantee must have intended that the covenant run with the land, the covenant must affect or concern the land with which it runs, and there must be privity of estate between the party claiming the benefit and the party who rests under the burden.

covenant not to compete Agreement to refrain from entering into a competing trade, profession, or business.
cover Buyer's purchase of goods in substitution for those not delivered by breaching seller.
credit beneficiary See **third-party beneficiary**.
creditor Any entity having a claim against the debtor.
crime An act or omission in violation of a public law and punishable by the government.
criminal duress Coercion by threat of serious bodily injury.
criminal intent Desired or virtually certain consequences of one's conduct.
criminal law The law that involves offenses against the entire community.
cure The right of a seller under the UCC to correct a nonconforming delivery of goods to buyer within the contract period. § 2–508.
curtesy Husband's estate in the real property of his wife.
cy-pres As near (as possible). Rule for the construction of instruments in equity, by which the intention of the party is carried out *as near as may be,* when it would be impossible or illegal to give it literal effect.

damage Loss, injury, or deterioration caused by the negligence, design, or accident of one person, with respect to another's person or property. The word is to be distinguished from its plural, "damages," which means a compensation in money for a loss or damage.
damages Money sought as a remedy for breach of contract or for tortious acts.

Actual damages Real, substantial, and just damages, or the amount awarded to a complainant in compensation for his actual and real loss or injury, as opposed, on the one hand, to "nominal" damages and, on the other, to "exemplary" or "punitive" damages. Synonymous with "compensatory damages" and "general damages."

Benefit-of-the-bargain damages Difference between the value received and the value of the fraudulent party's performance as represented.

Compensatory damages Compensatory damages are such as will compensate the injured party for the injury sustained, and nothing more; such as will simply make good or replace the loss caused by the wrong or injury.

Consequential damages Such damage, loss, or injury as does not flow directly and immediately from the act of the party, but only from some of the consequences or results of such act. Consequential damages resulting from a seller's breach of contract include any loss resulting from general or particular requirements and needs of which the seller at the time of contracting had reason to know and which could not reasonably be prevented by cover or otherwise, and injury to person or property proximately resulting from any breach of warranty. UCC § 2–715(2).

Exemplary or punitive damages Damages other than compensatory damages which may be awarded against a person to punish him for outrageous conduct.

Expectancy damages Calculable by subtracting the injured party's actual dollar position as a result of the breach from that party's projected dollar position had performance occurred.

Foreseeable damages Loss of which the party in breach had reason to know when the contract was made.

Incidental damages Under UCC § 2–710, such damages include any commercially reasonable charges, expenses, or commissions incurred in stopping delivery, in the transportation, care, and custody of goods after the buyer's breach, in connection with the return or resale of the goods, or otherwise resulting from the breach. Also, such damages, resulting from a seller's breach of contract, include expenses reasonably incurred in inspection, receipt, transportation, and care and custody of goods rightfully rejected, any commercially reasonable charges, expenses, or commissions in connection with effecting cover, and any other reasonable expense incident to the delay or other breach. UCC § 2–715(1).

Irreparable damages In the law pertaining to injunctions, damages for which no certain pecuniary standard exists for measurement.

Liquidated damages and penalties Damages for breach by either party may be liquidated in the agreement but only at an amount which is reasonable in the light of the anticipated or actual harm caused by the breach, the difficulties of proof of loss, and the inconvenience or nonfeasibility of otherwise obtaining an adequate remedy. A term fixing unreasonably large liquidated damages is void as a penalty. UCC § 2–718(1).

Mitigation of damages A plaintiff may not recover damages for the effects of an injury which she reasonably could have avoided or substantially ameliorated. This limitation on recovery is generally denominated as "mitigation of damages" or "avoidance of consequences."

Nominal damages A small sum awarded where a contract has been breached but the loss is negligible or unproven.

Out-of-pocket damages Difference between the value received and the value given.

Reliance damages Contract damages placing the injured party in as good a position as he would have been in had the contract not been made.

Treble damages Three times actual loss.

de facto In fact, in deed, actually. This phrase is used to characterize an officer, a government, a past action, or a state of affairs which must be accepted for all practical purposes but which is illegal or illegitimate. See also **corporation**, *corporation de facto*.

de jure Descriptive of a condition in which there has been total compliance with all requirements of law. In this sense it is the contrary of *de facto*. See also **corporation**, *corporation de jure*.

de novo Anew; afresh; a second time.

debenture Unsecured bond.

debt security Any form of corporate security reflected as debt on the books of the corporation in contrast to equity securities such as stock; *e.g.*, bonds, notes, and debentures are debt securities.

debtor Person who owes payment or performance of an obligation.

deceit A fraudulent and cheating misrepresentation, artifice, or device used to deceive and trick one who is ignorant of the true facts, to the prejudice and damage of the party imposed upon. See also **fraud; misrepresentation.**

decree Decision of a court of equity.

deed A conveyance of realty; a writing, signed by a grantor, whereby title to realty is transferred from one party to another.

deed of trust Interest in real property which is conveyed to a third person as trustee for the creditor.

defamation Injury of a person's reputation by publication of false statements.

default judgment Judgment against a defendant who fails to respond to a complaint.

defendant The party against whom legal action is sought.

definite term Lease that automatically expires at end of the term.

delectus personae Partner's right to choose who may become a member of the partnership.

delegatee Third party to whom the delegator's duty is delegated.

delegation of duties Transferring to another all or part of one's duties arising under a contract.

delegator Party delegating his duty to a third party.

delivery The physical or constructive transfer of an instrument or of goods from one person to another. See also **constructive delivery.**

demand Request for payment made by the holder of the instrument.

demand paper Payable on request.

demurrer An allegation of a defendant that even if the facts as stated in the pleading to which objection is taken be true, their legal consequences are not such as to require the demurring party to answer them or to proceed further with the cause.

The Federal Rules of Civil Procedure do not provide for the use of a demurrer, but provide an equivalent to a general demurrer in the motion to dismiss for failure to state a claim on which relief may be granted. Fed.R. Civil P. 12(b).

deposition The testimony of a witness taken upon interrogatories, not in court, but intended to be used in court. See also **discovery**.

depository bank The first bank to which an item is transferred for collection even though it may also be the payor bank. UCC § 4–105(a).

descent Succession to the ownership of an estate by inheritance or by any act of law, as distinguished from "purchase."

Descents are of two sorts, *lineal* and *collateral*. Lineal descent is descent in a direct or right line, as from father or grandfather to son or grandson. Collateral descent is descent in a collateral or oblique line, that is, up to the common ancestor and then down from him, as from brother to brother, or between cousins.

design defect Plans or specifications inadequate to ensure the product's safety.

devise A testamentary disposition of land or realty; a gift of real property by the last will and testament of the donor. When used as a noun, means a testamentary disposition of real or personal property; when used as a verb, means to dispose of real or personal property by will.

dictum Generally used as an abbreviated form of *obiter dictum*, "a remark by the way"; that is, an observation or remark made by a judge which does not embody the resolution or determination of the court and which is made without argument or full consideration of the point.

directed verdict In a case in which the party with the burden of proof has failed to present a prima facie case for jury consideration, the trial judge may order the entry of a verdict without allowing the jury to consider it because, as a matter of law, there can be only one such verdict. Fed.R. Civil P. 50(a).

disaffirmance Avoidance of a contract.

discharge Termination of certain allowed claims against a debtor.

disclaimer Negation of warranty.

discount A discount by a bank means a drawback or deduction made upon its advances or loans of money, upon negotiable paper or other evidences of debt payable at a future day, which are transferred to the bank.

discovery The pretrial devices that can be used by one party to obtain facts and information about the case from the other party in order to assist the party's preparation for trial. Under the Federal Rules of Civil Procedure, tools of discovery include depositions upon oral and written questions, written interrogatories, production of documents or things, permission to enter upon land or other property, physical and mental examinations, and requests for admission. Rules 26–37.

dishonor To refuse to accept or pay a draft or to pay a promissory note when duly presented. UCC § 3–507(1); § 4–210. See also **protest**.

disparagement Publication of false statements resulting in harm to another's monetary interests.

disputed debt Obligation whose existence or amount is contested.

dissenting shareholder One who opposes a fundamental change and has the right to receive the fair value of her shares.

dissolution The dissolution of a partnership is the change in the relation of the partners caused by any partner's ceasing to be associated with the carrying on, as distinguished from the winding up, of the business. See also **winding up.**

distribution Transfer of partnership property from the partnership to a partner; transfer of property from a corporation to any of its shareholders.

dividend The payment designated by the board of directors of a corporation to be distributed pro rata among a class or classes of the shares outstanding.

document Document of title.
document of title Instrument evidencing ownership of the document and the goods it covers.
domicile That place where a person has his true, fixed, and permanent home and principal establishment, and to which whenever he is absent he has the intention of returning.
dominant Land whose owner has rights in other land.
donee Recipient of a gift.
donee beneficiary See **third-party beneficiary**.
donor Maker of a gift.
dormant partner One who is both a silent and a secret partner.
dower A species of life-estate which a woman is, by law, entitled to claim on the death of her husband, in the lands and tenements of which he was seised in fee during the marriage, and which her issue, if any, might by possibility have inherited.

Dower has been abolished in the majority of the states and materially altered in most of the others.

draft A written order by the first party, called the drawer, instructing a second party, called the drawee (such as a bank), to pay a third party, called the payee. An order to pay a sum certain in money, signed by a drawer, payable on demand or at a definite time, and to order or bearer. UCC § 3–104.
drawee A person to whom a bill of exchange or draft is directed, and who is requested to pay the amount of money therein mentioned. The drawee of a check is the bank on which it is drawn.

When a drawee accepts, he engages that he will pay the instrument according to its tenor at the time of his engagement or as completed. UCC § 3–413(1).

drawer The person who draws a bill or draft. The drawer of a check is the person who signs it.

The drawer engages that upon dishonor of the draft and any necessary notice of dishonor or protest, he will pay the amount of the draft to the holder or to any indorser who takes it up. The drawer may disclaim this liability by drawing without recourse. UCC § 3–413(2).

due negotiation Transfer of a negotiable document in the regular course of business to a holder, who takes in good faith, without notice of any defense or claim, and for value.
duress Unlawful constraint exercised upon a person, whereby he is forced to do some act against his will.

Physical duress Coercion involving physical force or the threat of physical force.

duty Legal obligation requiring a person to perform or refrain from performing an act.

earned surplus Undistributed net profits, income, gains, and losses.
earnest The payment of a part of the price of goods sold, or the delivery of part of such goods, for the purpose of binding the contract.
easement A right in the owner of one parcel of land, by reason of such ownership, to use the land of another for a special purpose not inconsistent with a general property right in the owner. This right is distinguishable from a "license," which merely confers a personal privilege to do some act on the land.

Affirmative easement One where the servient estate must permit something to be done thereon, as to pass over it, or to discharge water on it.

Appurtenant easement An incorporeal right which is attached to a superior right and inheres in land to which it is attached and is in the nature of a covenant running with the land.

Easement by necessity Such arises by operation of law when land conveyed is completely shut off from access to any road by land retained by the grantor or by land of the grantor and that of a stranger.

Easement by prescription A mode of acquiring title to property by immemorial or long-continued enjoyment; refers to personal usage restricted to claimant and his ancestors or grantors.

Easement in gross An easement in gross is not appurtenant to any estate in land or does not belong to any person by virtue of ownership of an estate in other land but is a mere personal interest in or a right to use the land of another; it is purely personal and usually ends with death of grantee.

Easement of access Right of ingress and egress to and from the premises of a lot owner to a street appurtenant to the land of the lot owner.

ejectment An action to determine whether the title to certain land is in the plaintiff or is in the defendant.
electronic funds transfer A transaction with a financial institution by means of computer, telephone, or other electronic instrument.
emancipation The act by which an infant is liberated from the control of a parent or guardian and made his own master.
embezzlement The taking, in violation of a trust, of the property of one's employer.
emergency Sudden, unexpected event calling for immediate action.
eminent domain Right of the people or government to take private property for public use upon giving fair consideration.
employment discrimination Hiring, firing, compensating, promoting, or training of employees based on race, color, sex, religion, or national origin.
employment relationship One in which employer has right to control the physical conduct of employee.
endowment contract Agreement to pay insured a lump sum upon reaching a specified age or in event of death.
entirety Used to designate that which the law considers as a single whole incapable of being divided into parts.
entrapment Induced by a government official into committing a crime.
entrusting Transfer of possession of goods to a merchant who deals in goods of that kind and who may in turn transfer valid title to a buyer in the ordinary course of business.
equal pay Equivalent pay for the same work.
equal protection Requirement that similarly situated persons be treated similarly by government action.
equipment Goods used primarily in business.
equitable Just, fair, and right. Existing in equity; available or sustainable only in equity, or only upon the rules and principles of equity.
equity Justice administered according to fairness, as contrasted with the strictly formulated rules of common law. It is based on a system of rules and principles which originated in England as an alternative to the harsh rules of common law and which were based on what was fair in a particular situation.
equity of redemption The right of the mortgagor of an estate to redeem the same after it has been forfeited, at law, by a breach of the condition of the mortgage, upon paying the amount of debt, interest, and costs.
equity securities Stock or similar security, in contrast to debt securities such as bonds, notes, and debentures.
error A mistake of law, or a false or irregular application of it, such as vitiates legal proceedings and warrants reversal of the judgment.

Harmless error In appellate practice, an error committed in the progress of the trial below which was not prejudicial to the rights of the party assigning it and for which, therefore, the appellate court will not reverse the judgment.

Reversible error In appellate practice, such an error as warrants the appellate court's reversal of the judgment before it.

escrow A system of document transfer in which a deed, bond, or funds is or are delivered to a third person to hold until all conditions in a contract are fulfilled; *e.g.*, delivery of deed to escrow agent under installment land sale contract until full payment for land is made.
estate The degree, quantity, nature, and extent of interest which a person has in real and personal property. An estate in lands, tenements, and hereditaments signifies such interest as the tenant has therein.

Also, the total property of whatever kind that is owned by a decedent prior to the distribution of that property in accordance with the terms of a will or, when there is no will, by the laws of inheritance in the state of domicile of the decedent.

Future estate An estate limited to commence in possession at a future day, either without the intervention of a precedent estate or on the determination by lapse of time, or otherwise, of a precedent estate created at the same time. Examples include reversions and remainders.

estoppel A bar or impediment raised by the law which precludes a person from alleging or from denying a certain fact or state of facts, in consequence of his or her previous allegation, denial, conduct, or admission, or in consequence of a final adjudication of the matter in a court of law. See also **waiver**.

eviction Dispossession by process of law; the act of depriving a person of the possession of lands which he has held, pursuant to the judgment of a court.

evidence Any species of proof or probative matter legally presented at the trial of an issue by the act of the parties and through the medium of witnesses, records, documents, concrete objects, etc., for the purpose of inducing belief in the minds of the court or jury as to the parties' contention.

exception A formal objection to the action of the court, during the trial of a cause, in refusing a request or overruling an objection; implying that the party excepting does not acquiesce in the decision of the court but will seek to procure its reversal, and that he means to save the benefit of his request or objection in some future proceeding.

exclusionary rule Prohibition of illegally obtained evidence.

exclusive dealing Sole right to sell goods in a defined market.

exclusive jurisdiction Such jurisdiction that permits only one court (state or federal) to hear a case.

exculpatory clause Excusing oneself from fault or liability.

execution *Execution of contract* includes performance of all acts necessary to render it complete as an instrument; implies that nothing more need be done to make the contract complete and effective.

Execution upon a money judgment is the legal process of enforcing the judgment, usually by seizing and selling property of the debtor.

executive order Legislation issued by the president or a governor.

executor A person appointed by a testator to carry out the directions and requests in his will and to dispose of the property according to his testamentary provisions after his decease. The female designation is executrix. A person appointed by the court in an intestacy situation is called the administrator(rix).

executory That which is yet to be executed or performed; that which remains to be carried into operation or effect; incomplete; depending upon a future performance or event. The opposite of executed.

executory contract See **contracts**.

executory promise Unperformed obligation.

exemplary damages See **damages**.

exoneration Relieved of liability.

express Manifested by direct and appropriate language, as distinguished from that which is inferred from conduct. The word is usually contrasted with "implied."

express warranty Explicitly made contractual promise regarding property or contract rights transferred; in a sale of goods, an affirmation of fact or a promise about the goods or a description, including a sample, of goods which becomes part of the basis of the bargain.

expropriation Governmental taking of foreign-owned property for a public purpose and with payment.

ex-ship Risk of loss passes to buyer when the goods leaving the ship. See UCC § 2–322. See also **F.A.S.**

extortion Making threats to obtain property.

fact An event that took place or a thing that exists.

false imprisonment Intentional interference with a person's freedom of movement by unlawful confinement.

false light Offensive publicity placing another in a false light.

false pretenses Intentional misrepresentation of fact in order to cheat another.

farm products Crops, livestock, or stock used or produced in farming.

F.A.S. Free alongside. Term used in sales price quotations indicating that the price includes all costs of transportation and delivery of the goods alongside the ship. See UCC § 2–319(2).

federal preemption First right of the federal government to regulate matters within its powers to the possible exclusion of state regulation.

federal question Any case arising under the Constitution, statutes, or treaties of the United States.

fee simple

Absolute A fee simple absolute is an estate that is unlimited as to duration, disposition, and descendibility. It is the largest estate and most extensive interest that can be enjoyed in land.

Conditional Type of transfer in which grantor conveys fee simple on condition that something be done or not done.

Defeasible Type of fee grant which may be defeated on the happening of an event. An estate which may last forever, but which may end upon the happening of a specified event, is a "fee simple defeasible."

Determinable Created by conveyance which contains words effective to create a fee simple and, in addition, a provision for automatic expiration of the estate on occurrence of stated event.

fee tail An estate of inheritance, descending only to a certain class or classes of heirs; *e.g.*, an estate is conveyed or devised "to A. and the heirs of his body," or "to A. and the heirs male of his body," or "to A., and the heirs female of his body."

fellow servant rule Common law defense relieving employer from liability to an employee for injuries caused by negligence of fellow employee.

felony Serious crime.

fiduciary A person or institution who manages money or property for another and who must exercise in such management activity a standard of care imposed by law or contract; *e.g.*, executor of estate; receiver in bankruptcy; trustee.

fiduciary duty Duty of utmost loyalty and good faith, such as that owed by a fiduciary such as an agent to her principal.

field warehouse Secured party takes possession of the goods but the debtor has access to the goods.

final credit Payment of the instrument by the payor bank.

financing statement Under the Uniform Commercial Code, a financing statement is used under Article 9 to reflect a public record that there is a security interest or claim to the goods in question to secure a debt. The financing statement is filed by the security holder with the secretary of state or with a similar public body; thus filed, it becomes public record. See also **secured transaction**.

fire (property) insurance Provides protection against loss due to fire or other related perils.

firm offer Irrevocable offer to sell or buy goods by a merchant in a signed writing which gives assurance that it will not be rescinded for up to three months.

fitness for a particular purpose Goods are fit for a stated purpose, provided that the seller selects the product knowing the buyer's intended use and that the buyer is relying on the seller's judgment.

fixture An article in the nature of personal property which has been so annexed to realty that it is regarded as a part of the land. Examples include a furnace affixed to a house or other building, counters permanently affixed to the floor of a store, and a sprinkler system installed in a building. UCC § 9–313(1)(a).

Trade fixtures Such chattels as merchants usually possess and annex to the premises occupied by them to enable them to store, handle,

and display their goods, which generally are removable without material injury to the premises.
F.O.B. Free on board at some location (for example, F.O.B shipping point; F.O.B destination); the invoice price includes delivery at seller's expense to that location. Title to goods usually passes from seller to buyer at the F.O.B location. UCC § 2–319(1).
foreclosure Procedure by which mortgaged property is sold on default of mortgagor in satisfaction of mortgage debt.
forgery Intentional falsification of a document with intent to defraud.
four unities Time, title, interest, and possession.
franchise A privilege granted or sold, such as to use a name or to sell products or services. The right given by a manufacturer or supplier to a retailer to use his products and name on terms and conditions mutually agreed upon.
fraud Elements include false representation; of a present or past fact; made by defendant; action in reliance thereon by plaintiff; and damage resulting to plaintiff from such misrepresentation.
fraud in the execution Misrepresentation that deceives the other party as to the nature of a document evidencing the contract.
fraud in the inducement Misrepresentation regarding the subject matter of a contract that induces the other party to enter into the contract.
fraudulent misrepresentation False statement made with knowledge of its falsity and intent to mislead.
freehold An estate for life or in fee. It must possess two qualities: (1) immobility, that is, the property must be either land or some interest issuing out of or annexed to land; and (2) indeterminate duration.
friendly fire Fire contained where it is intended to be.
frustration of purpose doctrine Excuses a promisor in certain situations when the objectives of contract have been utterly defeated by circumstances arising after formation of the agreement, and performance is excused under this rule even though there is no impediment to actual performance.
full warranty One under which warrantor will repair the product and, if unsuccessful, will replace it or refund its cost.
fungibles With respect to goods or securities, those of which any unit is, by nature or usage of trade, the equivalent of any other like unit. UCC § 1–201(17); *e.g.*, a bushel of wheat or other grain.
future estate See **estate**.

garnishment A statutory proceeding whereby a person's property, money, or credits in the possession or control of another are applied to payment of the former's debt to a third person.
general intangible Catchall category for collateral not otherwise covered.
general partner Member of either a general or limited partnership with unlimited liability for its debts, full management powers, and a right to share in the profits.
gift A voluntary transfer of property to another made gratuitously and without consideration. Essential requisites of "gift" are capacity of donor, intention of donor to make gift, completed delivery to or for donee, and acceptance of gift by donee.
gift causa mortis A gift in view of death is one which is made in contemplation, fear, or peril of death and with the intent that it shall take effect only in case of the death of the giver.
good faith Honesty in fact in conduct or in a transaction.
good faith purchaser Buyer who acts honestly, gives value, and takes the goods without notice or knowledge of any defect in the title of his transferor.
goods A term of variable content and meaning. It may include every species of personal property, or it may be given a very restricted meaning. Sometimes the meaning of "goods" is extended to include all tangible items, as in the phrase "goods and services."

All things (including specially manufactured goods) which are movable at the time of identification to a contract for sale other than the money in which the price is to be paid, investment securities, and things in action. UCC § 2–105(1).
grantee Transferee of property.
grantor A transferor of property. The creator of a trust is usually designated as the grantor of the trust.
gratuitous promise Promise made without consideration.
group insurance Covers a number of individuals.
guaranty A promise to answer for the payment of some debt, or the performance of some duty, in case of the failure of another person who, in the first instance, is liable for such payment or performance.

The terms *guaranty* and *suretyship* are sometimes used interchangeably; but they should not be confounded. The distinction between contract of suretyship and contract of guaranty is whether or not the undertaking is a joint undertaking with the principal or a separate and distinct contract; if it is the former, it is one of "suretyship," and if the latter, it is one of "guaranty." See also **surety**.
guardianship The relationship under which a person (the guardian) is appointed by a court to preserve and control the property of another (the ward).

heir A person who succeeds, by the rules of law, to an estate in lands, tenements, or hereditaments, upon the death of his ancestor, by descent and right of relationship.
holder Person who is in possession of a document of title or an instrument or an investment security drawn, issued, or indorsed to him or to his order, or to bearer, or in blank. UCC § 1–201(20).
holder in due course A holder who takes an instrument for value, in good faith, and without notice that it is overdue or has been dishonored or of any defense against or claim to it on the part of any person.
holograph A will or deed written entirely by the testator or grantor with his own hand and not witnessed (attested). State laws vary with respect to the validity of the holographic will.
homicide Unlawful taking of another's life.
horizontal privity Who may bring a cause of action.
horizontal restraints Agreements among competitors.
hostile fire Any fire outside its intended or usual place.

identified goods Designated goods as a part of a particular contract.
illegal per se Conclusively presumed unreasonable and therefore illegal.
illusory promise Promise imposing no obligation on the promisor.
implied-in-fact condition Contingencies understood but not expressed by the parties.
implied-in-law condition Contingency that arises from operation of law.
implied warranty Obligation imposed by law upon the transferor of property or contract rights; implicit in the sale arising out of certain circumstances.
implied warranty of habitability Leased premises are fit for ordinary residential purposes.
impossibility Performance that cannot be done.
in personam Against the person. Action seeking judgment against a person involving his personal rights and based on jurisdiction of his person, as distinguished from a judgment against property (*i.e.*, in rem).
in personam jurisdiction Jurisdiction based on claims against a person, in contrast to jurisdiction over his property.
in re In the affair; in the matter of; concerning; regarding. This is the usual method of entitling a judicial proceeding in which there are no adversary parties, but merely some res concerning which judicial action is to be taken, such as a bankrupt's estate, an estate in the probate court, a proposed public highway, etc.

in rem A technical term used to designate proceedings or actions instituted *against the thing*, in contradistinction to personal actions, which are said to be *in personam*.

Quasi in rem A term applied to proceedings which are not strictly and purely *in rem*, but are brought against the defendant personally, though the real object is to deal with particular property or subject property to the discharge of claims asserted; for example, foreign attachment, or proceedings to foreclose a mortgage, remove a cloud from title, or effect a partition.

in rem jurisdiction Jurisdiction based on claims against property.

incidental beneficiary Third party whom the two parties to a contract have no intention of benefiting by their contract.

income bond Bond that conditions payment of interest on corporate earnings.

incontestability clause The prohibition of an insurer to avoid an insurance policy after a specified period of time.

indemnification Duty owed by principal to agent to pay agent for losses incurred while acting as directed by principal.

indemnify To reimburse one for a loss already incurred.

indenture A written agreement under which bonds and debentures are issued, setting forth maturity date, interest rate, and other terms.

independent contractor Person who contracts with another to do a particular job and who is not subject to the control of the other.

indicia Signs; indications. Circumstances which point to the existence of a given fact as probable, but not certain.

indictment Grand jury charge that the defendant should stand trial.

indispensable paper Chattel paper, instruments, and documents.

indorsee The person to whom a negotiable instrument, promissory note, bill of lading, etc., is assigned by indorsement.

indorsement The act of a payee, drawee, accommodation indorser, or holder of a bill, note, check, or other negotiable instrument, in writing his name upon the back of the same, with or without further or qualifying words, whereby the property in the same is assigned and transferred to another. UCC § 3–202 *et seq.*

Blank indorsement No indorsee is specified.

Qualified indorsement Without recourse, limiting one's liability on the instrument.

Restrictive indorsement Limits the rights of the indorser in some manner.

Special indorsement Designates an indorsee to be paid.

infliction of emotional distress Extreme and outrageous conduct intentionally or recklessly causing severe emotional distress.

information Formal accusation of a crime brought by a prosecutor.

infringement Unauthorized use.

injunction An equitable remedy forbidding the party defendant from doing some act which he is threatening or attempting to commit, or restraining him in the continuance thereof, such act being unjust and inequitable, injurious to the plaintiff, and not such as can be adequately redressed by an action at law.

innkeeper Hotel or motel operator.

inquisitorial system System in which the judiciary initiates, conducts, and decides cases.

insider Relative or general partner of debtor, partnership in which debtor is a partner, or corporation in which debtor is an officer, director, or controlling person.

insiders Directors, officers, employees, and agents of the issuer as well as those the issuer has entrusted with information solely for corporate purposes.

insolvency Under the UCC, a person is insolvent who either has ceased to pay his debts in the ordinary course of business or cannot pay his debts as they fall due or is insolvent within the meaning of the Federal Bankruptcy Law. UCC § 1–201(23).

Insolvency (bankruptcy) Total liabilities exceed total value of assets.

Insolvency (equity) Inability to pay debts in ordinary course of business or as they become due.

inspection Examination of goods to determine whether they conform to a contract.

instrument Negotiable instruments, stocks, bonds, and other investment securities.

insurable interest Exists where insured derives pecuniary benefit or advantage by preservation and continued existence of property or would sustain pecuniary loss from its destruction.

insurance A contract whereby, for a stipulated consideration, one party undertakes to compensate the other for loss on a specified subject by specified perils. The party agreeing to make the compensation is usually called the "insurer" or "underwriter"; the other, the "insured" or "assured"; the written contract, a "policy"; the events insured against, "risks" or "perils"; and the subject, right, or interest to be protected, the "insurable interest." Insurance is a contract whereby one undertakes to indemnify another against loss, damage, or liability arising from an unknown or contingent event.

Co-insurance A form of insurance in which a person insures property for less than its full or stated value and agrees to share the risk of loss.

Life insurance Payment of a specific sum of money to a designated beneficiary upon the death of the insured.

Ordinary life Life insurance with a savings component that runs for the life of the insured.

Term life Life insurance issued for a limited number of years that does not have a savings component.

intangible property Protected interests that are not physical.

intangibles Accounts and general intangibles.

intent Desire to cause the consequences of an act or knowledge that the consequences are substantially certain to result from the act.

inter alia Among other things.

inter se or **inter sese** Latin. Among or between themselves; used to distinguish rights or duties between two or more parties from their rights or duties to others.

interest in land Any right, privilege, power, or immunity in real property.

interest in partnership Partner's share in the partnership's profits and surplus.

interference with contractual relations Intentionally causing one of the parties to a contract not to perform the contract.

intermediary bank Any bank, except the depositary or payor bank, to which an item is transferred in the course of collection. UCC § 4–105(c).

intermediate test Requirement that legislation have a substantial relationship to an important governmental objective.

international law Deals with the conduct and relations of nation-states and international organizations.

interpretation Construction or meaning of a contract.

interpretative rules Statements issued by an administrative agency indicating its construction of its governing statute.

intestate A person is said to die intestate when he dies without making a will. The word is also often used to signify the person himself. *Compare* **testator**.

intrusion Unreasonable and highly offensive interference with the seclusion of another.

inventory Goods held for sale or lease or consumed in a business.

invitee A person is an "invitee" on land of another if (1) he enters by invitation, express or implied, (2) his entry is connected with the owner's business or with an activity the owner conducts or permits to be conducted on his land, and (3) there is mutual benefit or a benefit to the owner.

joint liability Liability where creditor must sue all of the partners as a group.
joint and several liability Liability where creditor may sue partners jointly as a group or separately as individuals.
joint stock company A general partnership with some corporate attributes.
joint tenancy See **tenancy**.
joint venture An association of two or more persons to carry on a single business transaction for profit.
judgment The official and authentic decision of a court of justice upon the respective rights and claims of the parties to an action or suit therein litigated and submitted to its determination.
judgment in personam A judgment against a particular person, as distinguished from a judgment against a thing or a right or *status*.
judgment in rem An adjudication pronounced upon the status of some particular thing or subject matter, by a tribunal having competent authority.
judgment n. o. v. Judgment non obstante veredicto in its broadest sense is a judgment rendered in favor of one party notwithstanding the finding of a verdict in favor of the other party.
judgment notwithstanding the verdict A final binding determination on the merits made by the judge after and contrary to the jury's verdict.
judgment on the pleadings Final binding determination on the merits made by the judge after the pleadings.
judicial lien Interest in property that is obtained by court action to secure payment of a debt.
judicial review Power of the courts to determine the constitutionality of legislative and executive acts.
jurisdiction The right and power of a court to adjudicate concerning the subject matter in a given case.
jurisdiction over the parties Power of a court to bind the parties to a suit.
jury A body of persons selected and summoned by law and sworn to try the facts of a case and to find according to the law and the evidence. In general, the province of the jury is to find the facts in a case, while the judge passes upon pure questions of law. As a matter of fact, however, the jury must often pass upon mixed questions of law and fact in determining the case, and in all such cases the instructions of the judge as to the law become very important.
justifiable reliance Reasonably influenced by a misrepresentation.

labor dispute Any controversy concerning terms or conditions of employment or union representation.
laches Based upon maxim that equity aids the vigilant and not those who slumber on their rights. It is defined as neglect to assert a right or claim which, taken together with a lapse of time and other circumstances causing prejudice to the adverse party, operates as a bar in a court of equity.
landlord The owner of an estate in land, or a rental property, who has leased it to another person, called the "tenant." Also called "lessor."
larceny Trespassory taking and carrying away of the goods of another with the intent to permanently deprive.
last clear chance Final opportunity to avoid an injury.
lease Any agreement which gives rise to relationship of landlord and tenant (real property) or lessor and lessee (real or personal property).

The person who conveys is termed the "lessor," and the person to whom conveyed, the "lessee"; and when the lessor conveys land or tenements to a lessee, he is said to lease, demise, or let them.

Sublease, or *underlease* One executed by the lessee of an estate to a third person, conveying the same estate for a shorter term than that for which the lessee holds it.

leasehold An estate in realty held under a lease. The four principal types of leasehold estates are the estate for years, periodic tenancy, tenancy at will, and tenancy at sufferance.
leasehold estate Right to possess real property.
legacy "Legacy" is a gift or bequest by will of personal property, whereas a "devise" is a testamentary disposition of real estate.

Demonstrative legacy A bequest of a certain sum of money, with a direction that it shall be paid out of a particular fund. It differs from a specific legacy in this respect: that, if the fund out of which it is payable fails for any cause, it is nevertheless entitled to come on the estate as a general legacy. And it differs from a general legacy in this: that it does not abate in that class, but in the class of specific legacies.

General legacy A pecuniary legacy, payable out of the general assets of a testator.

Residuary legacy A bequest of all the testator's personal estate not otherwise effectually disposed of by his will.

Specific legacy One which operates on property particularly designated. A legacy or gift by will of a particular specified thing, as of a horse, a piece of furniture, a term of years, and the like.

legal aggregate A group of individuals not having a legal existence separate from its members.
legal benefit Obtaining something to which one had no legal right.
legal detriment Doing an act one is not legally obligated to do or not doing an act one has a legal right to do.
legal entity An organization having a legal existence separate from that of its members.
legal sufficiency Benefit to promisor or detriment to promisee.
legislative rules Substantive rules issued by an administrative agency under the authority delegated to it by the legislature.
letter of credit An engagement by a bank or other person made at the request of a customer that the issuer will honor drafts or other demands for payment upon compliance with the conditions specified in the credit.
letters of administration Formal document issued by probate court appointing one an administrator of an estate.
letters testamentary The formal instrument of authority and appointment given to an executor by the proper court, empowering him to enter upon the discharge of his office as executor. It corresponds to letters of administration granted to an administrator.
levy To assess; raise; execute; exact; tax; collect; gather; take up; seize. Thus, to levy (assess, exact, raise, or collect) a tax; to levy an execution, *i.e.*, to levy or collect a sum of money on an execution.
liability insurance Covers liability to others by reason of damage resulting from injuries to another's person or property.
liability without fault Crime to do a specific act or cause a certain result without regard to the care exercised.
libel Defamation communicated by writing, television, radio, or the like.
liberty Ability of individuals to engage in freedom of action and choice regarding their personal lives.
license License with respect to real property is a privilege to go on premises for a certain purpose, but does not operate to confer on or vest in the licensee any title, interest, or estate in such property.
licensee Person privileged to enter or remain on land by virtue of the consent of the lawful possessor.
lien A qualified right of property which a creditor has in or over specific property of his debtor, as security for the debt or charge or for performance of some act.
lien creditor A creditor who has acquired a lien on the property by attachment.
life estate An estate whose duration is limited to the life of the party holding it or of some other person. Upon the death of the life tenant, the property will go to the holder of the remainder interest or to the grantor by reversion.
limited liability Liability limited to amount invested in a business enterprise.

limited partner Member of a limited partnership with liability for its debts only to the extent of her capital contribution.
limited partnership See **partnership.**
limited partnership association A partnership which closely resembles a corporation.
liquidated Ascertained; determined; fixed; settled; made clear or manifest. Cleared away; paid; discharged.
liquidated damages See **damages**.
liquidated debt Obligation that is certain in amount.
liquidation The settling of financial affairs of a business or individual, usually by liquidating (turning to cash) all assets for distribution to creditors, heirs, etc. To be distinguished from dissolution.
loss of value Value of promised performance minus value of actual performance.
lost property Property with which the owner has involuntarily parted and which she does not know where to find or recover, not including property which she has intentionally concealed or deposited in a secret place for safekeeping. Distinguishable from mislaid property, which has been deliberately placed somewhere and forgotten.

main purpose rule Where object of promisor/surety is to provide an economic benefit for herself, the promise is considered outside of the statute of frauds.
maker One who makes or executes; as the maker of a promissory note. One who signs a check; in this context, synonymous with drawer. See **draft**.
mala in se Morally wrong.
mala prohibita Wrong by law.
mandamus Latin, we command. A legal writ compelling the defendant to do an official duty.
manslaughter Unlawful taking of another's life without malice.
Involuntary manslaughter Taking the life of another by criminal negligence or during the course of a misdemeanor.
Voluntary manslaughter Intentional killing of another under extenuating circumstances.
manufacturing defect Not produced according to specifications.
mark Trade symbol.
market allocations Division of market by customers, geographic location, or products.
marketable title Free from any defects, encumbrances, or reasonable objections to one's ownership.
marshaling of assets Segregating the assets and liabilities of a partnership from the assets and liabilities of the individual partners.
master See **principal**.
material Matters to which a reasonable investor would attach importance in deciding whether to purchase a security.
material alteration Any change that changes the contract of any party to an instrument.
maturity The date at which an obligation, such as the principal of a bond or a note, becomes due.
maxim A general legal principle.
mechanic's lien A claim created by state statutes for the purpose of securing priority of payment of the price or value of work performed and materials furnished in erecting or repairing a building or other structure; as such, attaches to the land as well as buildings and improvements erected thereon.
mediation Nonbinding process in which a third party acts as an intermediary between the disputing parties and proposes solutions for them to consider.
mens rea Criminal intent.
mentally incompetent Unable to understand the nature and effect of one's acts.
mercantile law An expression substantially equivalent to commercial law. It designates the system of rules, customs, and usages generally recognized and adopted by merchants and traders that, either in its simplicity or as modified by common law or statutes, constitutes the law for the regulation of their transactions and the solution of their controversies. The Uniform Commercial Code is the general body of law governing commercial or mercantile transactions.
merchant A person who deals in goods of the kind involved in a transaction or who otherwise by his occupation holds himself out as having knowledge or skill peculiar to the practices or goods involved in the transaction or to whom such knowledge or skill may be attributed by his employment of an agent or broker or other intermediary who by his occupation holds himself out as having such knowledge or skill. UCC § 2–104(1).
merchantability Merchant seller guarantees that the goods are fit for their ordinary purpose.
merger The fusion or absorption of one thing or right into another. In corporate law, the absorption of one company by another, the latter retaining its own name and identity and acquiring the assets, liabilities, franchises, and powers of the former, which ceases to exist as separate business entity. It differs from a consolidation, wherein all the corporations terminate their separate existences and become parties to a new one.
Conglomerate merger An acquisition, which is not horizontal or vertical, by one company of another.
Horizontal merger Merger between business competitors, such as manufacturers of the same type of products or distributors selling competing products in the same market area.
Short-form merger Merger of a 90 percent subsidiary into its parent.
Vertical merger Union with corporate customer or supplier.
midnight deadline Midnight of the next banking day after receiving an item.
mining partnership A specific type of partnership for the purpose of extracting raw minerals.
minor Under the age of legal majority (usually eighteen).
mirror image rule An acceptance cannot deviate from the terms of the offer.
misdemeanor Less serious crime.
mislaid property Property which an owner has put deliberately in a certain place that she is unable to remember, as distinguished from lost property, which the owner has left unwittingly in a location she has forgotten. See also **lost property**.
misrepresentation Any manifestation by words or other conduct by one person to another that, under the circumstances, amounts to an assertion not in accordance with the facts. A "misrepresentation" that justifies the rescission of a contract is a false statement of a substantive fact, or any conduct which leads to a belief of a substantive fact material to proper understanding of the matter in hand. See also **deceit**; **fraud**.
Fraudulent misrepresentation False statement made with knowledge of its falsity and intent to mislead.
Innocent misrepresentation Misrepresentation made without knowledge of its falsity but with due care.
Negligent misrepresentation Misrepresentation made without due care in ascertaining its falsity.
M'Naughten Rule Right/wrong test for criminal insanity.
modify Change the lower court's judgment.
money Medium of exchange issued by a government body.
monopoly Ability to control price or exclude others from the marketplace.
mortgage A mortgage is an interest in land created by a written instrument providing security for the performance of a duty or the payment of a debt.
mortgagor Debtor who uses real estate to secure an obligation.
multinational enterprise Business that engages in transactions involving the movement of goods, information, money, people, or services across national borders.

multiple product order Order requiring an advertiser to cease and desist from deceptive statements on all products it sells.
murder Unlawful and premeditated taking of another's life.
mutual mistake Where the common but erroneous belief of both parties forms the basis of a contract.

necessaries Items needed to maintain a person's station in life.
negligence The omission to do something which a reasonable person, guided by those ordinary considerations which ordinarily regulate human affairs, would do, or the doing of something which a reasonable and prudent person would not do.
Culpable negligence Greater than ordinary negligence but less than gross negligence.
negligence per se Conclusive on the issue of negligence (duty of care and breach).
negotiable Legally capable of being transferred by indorsement or delivery. Usually said of checks and notes and sometimes of stocks and bearer bonds.
negotiable instrument Signed document (such as a check or promissory note) containing an unconditional promise to pay a "sum certain" of money at a definite time to order or bearer.
negotiation Transferee becomes a holder.
net assets Total assets minus total debts.
no arrival, no sale A destination contract, but if goods do not arrive, seller is excused from liability unless such is due to the seller's fault.
no-fault insurance Compensates victims of automobile accidents regardless of fault.
nonconforming use Preexisting use not in accordance with a zoning ordinance.
nonprofit corporation One whose profits must be used exclusively for the charitable, educational, or scientific purpose for which it was formed.
nonsuit Action in form of a judgment taken against a plaintiff who has failed to appear to prosecute his action or failed to prove his case.
note See **promissory note.**
novation A novation substitutes a new party and discharges one of the original parties to a contract by agreement of all three parties. A new contract is created with the same terms as the original one; only the parties have changed.
nuisance Nuisance is that activity which arises from the unreasonable, unwarranted, or unlawful use by a person of his own property, working obstruction or injury to the right of another or to the public, and producing such material annoyance, inconvenience, and discomfort that law will presume resulting damage.

obiter dictum See **dictum.**
objective fault Gross deviation from reasonable conduct.
objective manifestation What a reasonable person under the circumstances would believe.
objective satisfaction Approval based upon whether a reasonable person would be satisfied.
objective standard What a reasonable person under the circumstances would reasonably believe or do.
obligee Party to whom a duty of performance is owed (by delegator and delegatee).
obligor Party owing a duty (to the assignor).
offer A manifestation of willingness to enter into a bargain, so made as to justify another person in understanding that his assent to that bargain is invited and will conclude it. Restatement, Second, Contracts, § 24.
offeree Recipient of the offer.
offeror Person making the offer.
open-ended credit Credit arrangement under which debtor has rights ...ter into a series of credit transactions.
... Belief in the existence of a fact or a judgment as to value.
... Contract providing that an offer will stay open for a specified ...od of time.

order A final disposition made by an agency.
order paper Payable to a named person or to anyone designated by that person.
order to pay Direction or command to pay.
original promise Promise to become primarily liable.
output contract See **contracts.**

palpable unilateral mistake Erroneous belief by one party that is recognized by the other.
parent corporation Corporation which controls another corporation.
parol evidence Literally oral evidence, but now includes prior to and contemporaneous, oral, and written evidence.
parol evidence rule Under this rule, when parties put their agreement in writing, all previous oral agreements merge in the writing and the contract as written cannot be modified or changed by parol evidence, in the absence of a plea of mistake or fraud in the preparation of the writing. But the rule does not forbid a resort to parol evidence not inconsistent with the matters stated in the writing. Also, as regards sales of goods, such written agreement may be explained or supplemented by course of dealing, usage of trade, or course of conduct, and by evidence of consistent additional terms, unless the court finds the writing to have been intended also as a complete and exclusive statement of the terms of the agreement. UCC § 2–202.
part performance In order to establish part performance taking an oral contract for the sale of realty out of the statute of frauds, the acts relied upon as part performance must be of such a character that they reasonably can be naturally accounted for in no other way than that they were performed in pursuance of the contract, and they must be in conformity with its provisions. See UCC § 2–201(3).
partial assignment Transfer of a portion of contractual rights to one or more assignees.
partition The dividing of lands held by joint tenants, copartners, or tenants in common into distinct portions, so that the parties may hold those lands in severalty.
partnership An association of two or more persons to carry on, as co-owners, a business for profit.
Partnerships are treated as a conduit and are, therefore, not subject to taxation. The various items of partnership income (gains and losses, etc.) flow through to the individual partners and are reported on their personal income tax returns.
Limited partnership Type of partnership comprised of one or more general partners who manage business and who are personally liable for partnership debts, and one or more limited partners who contribute capital and share in profits but who take no part in running business and incur no liability with respect to partnership obligations beyond contribution.
Partnership at will One with no definite term or specific undertaking.
partnership capital Total money and property contributed by partners for permanent use by the partnership.
partnership property Sum of all of the partnership's assets.
past consideration An act done before the contract is made.
patent Exclusive right to an invention.
payee The person in whose favor a bill of exchange, promissory note, or check is made or drawn.
payer or **payor** One who pays or who is to make a payment, particularly the person who is to make payment of a check, bill, or note. Correlative to "payee."
payor bank A bank by which an item is payable as drawn or accepted. UCC § 4–105(b). Correlative to "Drawee bank."
per capita This term, derived from the civil law and much used in the law of descent and distribution, denotes that method of dividing an intestate estate by which an equal share is given to each of a number of persons, all of whom stand in equal degree to the decedent, without reference to their stocks or the right of representation. The opposite of *per stirpes*.

per stirpes This term, derived from the civil law and much used in the law of descent and distribution, denotes that method of dividing an intestate estate where a class or group of distributees takes the share to which its deceased would have been entitled, taking thus by its right of representing such ancestor and not as so many individuals. The opposite of *per capita*.
perfect tender rule Seller's tender of delivery must conform exactly to the contract.
perfection of security interest Acts required of a secured party in the way of giving at least constructive notice so as to make his security interest effective at least against lien creditors of the debtor. See UCC §§ 9–302 through 9–306. In most cases, the secured party may obtain perfection either by filing with the secretary of state or by taking possession of the collateral.
performance Fulfillment of one's contractual obligations. See also **part performance; specific performance**.
periodic tenancy Lease with a definite term that is to be continued.
personal defenses Contractual defenses which are good against holders but not holders in due course.
personal property Any property other than an interest in land.
petty crime Misdemeanor punishable by imprisonment of six months or less.
plaintiff The party who initiates a civil suit.
pleadings The formal allegations by the parties of their respective claims and defenses.

Rules or codes of civil procedure Unlike the rigid technical system of common law pleading, pleadings under federal and state rules or codes of civil procedure have a far more limited function, with determination and narrowing of facts and issues being left to discovery devices and pretrial conferences. In addition, the rules and codes permit liberal amendment and supplementation of pleadings.

Under rules of civil procedure, the pleadings consist of a complaint, an answer, a reply to a counterclaim, an answer to a cross-claim, a third-party complaint, and a third-party answer.
pledge A bailment of goods to a creditor as security for some debt or engagement.

Much of the law of pledges has been replaced by the provisions for secured transactions in Article 9 of the UCC.
possibility of reverter The interest which remains in a grantor or testator after the conveyance or devise of a fee simple determinable and which permits the grantor to be revested automatically of his estate on breach of the condition.
possibility test Under the statute of frauds, asks whether performance could possibly be completed within one year.
power of appointment A power of authority conferred by one person by deed or will upon another (called the "donee") to appoint, that is, to select and nominate, the person or persons who is or are to receive and enjoy an estate or an income therefrom or from a fund, after the testator's death, or the donee's death, or after the termination of an existing right or interest.
power of attorney An instrument authorizing a person to act as the agent or attorney of the person granting it.
power of termination The interest left in the grantor or testator after the conveyance or devise of a fee simple on condition subsequent or conditional fee.
precatory Expressing a wish.
precedent An adjudged case or decision of a court, considered as furnishing an example or authority for an identical or similar case afterwards arising or a similar question of law. See also **stare decisis**.
preemptive right The privilege of a stockholder to maintain a proportionate share of ownership by purchasing a proportionate share of any new stock issues.
preference The act of an insolvent debtor who, in distributing his property or in assigning it for the benefit of his creditors, pays or secures to one or more creditors the full amount of their claims or a larger amount than they would be entitled to receive on a *pro rata* distribution. The treatment of such preferential payments in bankruptcy is governed by the Bankruptcy Act, § 547.
preliminary hearing Determines whether there is probable cause.
premium The price for insurance protection for a specified period of exposure.
preponderance of the evidence Greater weight of the evidence; standard used in civil cases.
prescription Acquisition of a personal right to use a way, water, light, and air by reason of continuous usage. See also **easement**.
presenter's warranty Warranty given to any payor or acceptor of an instrument.
presentment The production of a negotiable instrument to the drawee for his acceptance, or to the drawer or acceptor for payment; or of a promissory note to the party liable, for payment of the same. UCC § 3–504(1).
presumption A presumption is a rule of law, statutory or judicial, by which a finding of a basic fact gives rise to the existence of presumed fact, until presumption is rebutted. A presumption imposes on the party against whom it is directed the burden of going forward with evidence to rebut or meet the presumption, but does not shift to such party the burden of proof in the sense of the risk of nonpersuasion, which remains throughout the trial upon the party on whom it was originally cast.
price discrimination Price differential.
price fixing Any agreement for the purpose and effect of raising, depressing, fixing, pegging, or stabilizing prices.
prima facie Latin. At first sight; on the first appearance; on the face of it; so far as can be judged from the first disclosure; presumably; a fact presumed to be true unless disproved by some evidence to the contrary.
primary liability Absolute obligation to pay a negotiable instrument.
principal *Law of agency* The term "principal" describes one who has permitted or directed another (*i.e.*, an agent or a servant) to act for his benefit and subject to his direction and control. Principal includes in its meaning the term "master" or employer, a species of principal who, in addition to other control, has a right to control the physical conduct of the species of agents known as servants or employees, as to whom special rules are applicable with reference to harm caused by their physical acts.

Disclosed principal One whose existence and identity are known.

Partially disclosed principal One whose existence is known but whose identity is not known.

Undisclosed principal One whose existence and identity are not known.
principal debtor Person whose debt is being supported by a surety.
priority Precedence in order of right.
private carrier Carrier which limits its service and is not open to the general public.
private corporation One organized to conduct either a privately owned business enterprise for profit or a nonprofit corporation.
private law The law involving relationships among individuals and legal entities.
privilege Immunity from tort liability.
privity Contractual relationship.
privity of contract That connection or relationship which exists between two or more contracting parties. The absence of privity as a defense in actions for damages in contract and tort actions is generally no longer viable with the enactment of warranty statutes (*e.g.*, UCC § 2–318), acceptance by states of the doctrine of strict liability, and court decisions which have extended the right to sue to third-party beneficiaries and even innocent bystanders.
probable cause Reasonable belief of the offense charged.
probate Court procedure by which a will is proved to be valid or invalid, though in current usage this term has been expanded to include generally all matters and proceedings pertaining to administration of estates, guardianships, etc.

procedural due process Requirement that governmental action depriving a person of life, liberty, or property be done through a fair procedure.
procedural law Rules for enforcing substantive law.
procedural rules Rules issued by an administrative agency establishing its organization, method of operation, and rules of conduct for practice before it.
procedural unconscionability Unfair or irregular bargaining.
proceeds Consideration for the sale, exchange, or other disposition of collateral.
process *Judicial process* In a wide sense, this term may include all the acts of a court from the beginning to the end of its proceedings in a given cause; more specifically, it means the writ, summons, mandate, or other process which is used to inform the defendant of the institution of proceedings against him and to compel his appearance, in either civil or criminal cases.
Legal process This term is sometimes used as equivalent to "lawful process." Thus, it is said that legal process means process not merely fair on its face but valid in fact. But properly it means a summons, writ, warrant, mandate, or other process issuing from a court.
profit corporation One founded for the purpose of operating a business for profit.
profit à prendre Right to make some use of the soil of another, such as a right to mine metals; carries with it the right of entry and the right to remove.
promise to pay Undertaking to pay an existing obligation.
promisee Person to whom a promise is made.
promisor Person making a promise.
promissory estoppel Arises where there is a promise which promisor should reasonably expect to induce action or forbearance on part of promisee and which does induce such action or forbearance, and where injustice can be avoided only by enforcement of the promise.
promissory note An unconditional written promise to pay a specified sum of money on demand or at a specified date. Such a note is negotiable if signed by the maker and containing an unconditional promise to pay a sum certain in money either on demand or at a definite time and payable to order or bearer. UCC § 3–104.
promoters In the law relating to corporations, those persons who first associate themselves for the purpose of organizing a company, issuing its prospectus, procuring subscriptions to the stock, securing a charter, etc.
property Interest that is legally protected.
Abandoned property Intentionally disposed of by the owner.
Lost property Unintentionally left by the owner.
Mislaid property Intentionally placed by the owner but unintentionally left.
prosecute To bring a criminal proceeding.
protest A formal declaration made by a person interested or concerned in some act about to be done, or already performed, whereby he expresses his dissent or disapproval or affirms the act against his will. The object of such a declaration usually is to preserve some right which would be lost to the protester if his assent could be implied, or to exonerate him from some responsibility which would attach to him unless he expressly negatived his assent.
Notice of protest A notice given by the holder of a bill or note to the drawer or indorser that the bill has been protested for refusal of payment or acceptance. UCC § 3–509.
provisional credit Tentative credit for the deposit of an instrument until final credit is given.
proximate cause Where the act or omission played a substantial part in bringing about or actually causing the injury or damage and where the injury or damage was either a direct result or a reasonably probable consequence of the act or omission.
proxy (Contracted from "procuracy.") Written authorization given by one person to another so that the second person can act for the first, such as that given by a shareholder to someone else to represent him and vote his shares at a shareholders' meeting.
public corporation One created to administer a unit of local civil government or one created by the United States to conduct public business.
public disclosure of private facts Offensive publicity given to private information about another person.
public law The law dealing with the relationship between government and individuals.
puffery Sales talk that is considered general bragging or overstatement.
punitive damages Damages awarded in excess of normal compensation to punish a defendant for a serious civil wrong.
purchase money security interest Security interest retained by a seller of goods in goods purchased with the loaned money.

qualified fee Ownership subject to its being taken away upon the happening of an event.
quantum meruit Expression "quantum meruit" means "as much as he deserves"; describes the extent of liability on a contract implied by law. Elements essential to recovery under quantum meruit are (1) valuable services rendered or materials furnished (2) for the person sought to be charged, (3) which services and materials such person accepted, used, and enjoyed, (4) under such circumstances as reasonably notified her that plaintiff, in performing such services, was expected to be paid by the person sought to be charged.
quasi Latin. As if; almost as it were; analogous to. Negatives the idea of identity but points out that the conceptions are sufficiently similar to be classed as equals of one another.
quasi contract Legal fiction invented by common law courts to permit recovery by contractual remedy in cases where, in fact, there is no contract, but where circumstances are such that justice warrants a recovery as though a promise had been made.
quasi in rem See **in rem**.
quasi in rem jurisdiction Jurisdiction over property not based on claims against it.
quiet enjoyment Right of a tenant not to have his physical possession of premises interfered with by the landlord.
quitclaim deed A deed of conveyance operating by way of release; that is, intended to pass any title, interest, or claim which the grantor may have in the premises but neither professing that such title is valid nor containing any warranty or covenants for title.
quorum When a committee, board of directors, meeting of shareholders, legislature, or other body of persons cannot act unless at least a certain number of them are present.

rape Unlawful, nonconsensual sexual intercourse.
ratification In a broad sense, the confirmation of a previous act done either by the party himself or by another; as, for example, confirmation of a voidable act.
In the law of principal and agent, the adoption and confirmation by one person, with knowledge of all material facts, of an act or contract performed or entered into in his behalf by another who at the time assumed without authority to act as his agent.
rational relationship test Requirement that legislation bear a rational relationship to a legitimate governmental interest.
real defenses Defenses that are valid against all holders, including holders in due course.
real property Land, and generally whatever is erected or growing upon or affixed to land. Also, rights issuing out of, annexed to, and exercisable within or about land. See also **fixture**.
reasonable man standard Duty of care required to avoid being negligent; one who is careful, diligent, and prudent.
receiver A fiduciary of the court, whose appointment is incident to other proceedings wherein certain ultimate relief is prayed. He is a

trustee or ministerial officer representing the court, all parties in interest in the litigation, and the property or funds entrusted to him.
recognizance Formal acknowledgment of indebtedness made in court.
redemption The realization of a right to have the title of property restored free and clear of a mortgage, performance of the mortgage obligation being essential for such purpose. (b) Repurchase by corporation of its own shares.
reformation Equitable remedy used to reframe written contracts to reflect accurately real agreement between contracting parties when, either through mutual mistake or unilateral mistake coupled with actual or equitable fraud by the other party, the writing does not embody the contract as actually made.
regulatory license Requirement to protect the public interest.
reimbursement Duty owed by principal to pay back authorized payments agent has made on principal's behalf. Duty owed by a principal debtor to repay surety who pays principal debtor's obligation.
rejection The refusal to accept an offer; manifestation of an unwillingness to accept the goods (sales).
release The relinquishment, concession, or giving up of a right, claim, or privilege, by the person in whom it exists or to whom it accrues, to the person against whom it might have been demanded or enforced.
remainder An estate limited to take effect and be enjoyed after another estate is determined.
remand To send back. The sending by the appellate court of a cause back to the same court out of which it came, for the purpose of having some further action taken on it there.
remedy The means by which the violation of a right is prevented, redressed, or compensated. Though a remedy may be by the act of the party injured, by operation of law, or by agreement between the injurer and the injured, we are chiefly concerned with one kind of remedy, the judicial remedy, which is by action or suit.
rent Consideration paid for use or occupation of property. In a broader sense, it is the compensation or fee paid, usually periodically, for the use of any property, land, buildings, equipment, etc.
replevin An action whereby the owner or person entitled to repossession of goods or chattels may recover those goods or chattels from one who has wrongfully distrained or taken such goods or chattels or who wrongfully detains them.
reply Plaintiff's pleading in response to the defendant's answer.
repudiation Repudiation of a contract means refusal to perform duty or obligation owed to other party.
requirements contract See **contracts.**
res ipsa loquitur "The thing speaks for itself"; permits the jury to infer both negligent conduct and causation.
rescission An equitable action in which a party seeks to be relieved of his obligations under a contract on the grounds of mutual mistake, fraud, impossibility, etc.
residuary Pertaining to the residue; constituting the residue; giving or bequeathing the residue; receiving or entitled to the residue. See also **legacy, residuary legacy**.
respondeat superior Latin. Let the master answer. This maxim means that a master or employer is liable in certain cases for the wrongful acts of his servant or employee, and a principal for those of his agent.
respondent In equity practice, the party who makes an answer to a bill or other proceeding. In appellate practice, the party who contends against an appeal; *i.e.*, the appellee. The party who appeals is called the "appellant."
restitution An equitable remedy under which a person who has rendered services to another seeks to be reimbursed for the costs of his acts (but not his profits) even though there was never a contract between the parties.
restraint on alienation A provision in an instrument of conveyance which prohibits the grantee from selling or transferring the property which is the subject of the conveyance. Many such restraints are unenforceable as against public policy and the law's policy of free alienability of land.
restraint of trade Agreement that eliminates or tends to eliminate competition.
restrictive covenant Private restriction on property contained in a conveyance.
revenue license Measure to raise money.
reverse An appellate court uses the term "reversed" to indicate that it annuls or avoids the judgment, or vacates the decree, of the trial court.
reverse discrimination Employment decisions taking into account race or gender in order to remedy past discrimination.
reversion The term reversion has two meanings. First, it designates the estate left in the grantor during the continuance of a particular estate; second, it denotes the residue left in grantor or his heirs after termination of a particular estate. It differs from a remainder in that it arises by an act of law, whereas a remainder arises by an act of the parties. A reversion, moreover, is the remnant left in the grantor, while a remainder is the remnant of the whole estate disposed of after a preceding part of the same has been given away.
revocation The recall of some power, authority, or thing granted, or a destroying or making void of some deed that had existence until the act of revocation made it void.
revocation of acceptance Rescission of one's acceptance of goods based upon a nonconformity of the goods which substantially impairs their value.
right Legal capacity to require another person to perform or refrain from performing an act.
right of entry The right to take or resume possession of land by entering on it in a peaceable manner.
right of redemption The right (granted by statute only) to free property from the encumbrance of a foreclosure or other judicial sale, or to recover the title passing thereby, by paying what is due, with interest, costs, etc. Not to be confounded with the "equity of redemption," which exists independently of statute but must be exercised before sale. See also **equity of redemption**.
right to work law State statute that prohibits union shop contracts.
rights in collateral Personal property the debtor owns, possesses, or is in the process of acquiring.
risk of loss Allocation of loss between seller and buyer where the goods have been damaged, destroyed, or lost.
robbery Larceny from a person by force or threat of force.
rule Agency statement of general or particular applicability designed to implement, interpret, or process law or policy.
rule against perpetuities Principle that no interest in property is good unless it must vest, if at all, not later than twenty-one years, plus period of gestation, after some life or lives in being at time of creation of interest.
rule of reason Balancing the anticompetitive effects of a restraint against its procompetitive effects.

sale Transfer of title to goods from seller to buyer for a price.
sale on approval Transfer of possession without title to buyer for trial period.
sale or return Sale where buyer has option to return goods to seller.
sanction Means of enforcing legal judgments.
satisfaction The discharge of an obligation by paying a party what is due to him (as on a mortgage, lien, or contract) or what has been awarded to him by the judgment of a court or otherwise. Thus, a judgment is satisfied by the payment of the amount due to the party who has recovered such judgment, or by his levying the amount. See also **accord and satisfaction**.
scienter Latin. Knowingly.
seal Symbol that authenticates a document.

secondary liability Obligation to pay is subject to the conditions of presentment, dishonor, notice of dishonor, and sometimes protest.
secret partner Partner whose membership in the partnership is not disclosed.
Section 402A Strict liability in tort.
secured bond A bond having a lien on specific property.
secured claim Claim with a lien on property of the debtor.
secured party Creditor who possesses a security interest in collateral.
secured transaction A transaction founded on a security agreement. Such agreement creates or provides for a security interest. UCC § 9–105(h).
securities Stocks, bonds, notes, convertible debentures, warrants, or other documents that represent a share in a company or a debt owed by a company.
Certificated security Security represented by a certificate.
Exempt security Security not subject to registration requirements of 1933 Act.
Exempt transaction Issuance of securities not subject to the registration requirements of 1933 Act.
Restricted securities Securities issued under an exempt transaction.
Uncertificated security Security not represented by a certificate.
security agreement Agreement that grants a security interest.
security interest Right in personal property securing payment or performance of an obligation.
seisin Possession with an intent on the part of him who holds it to claim a freehold interest.
self-defense Force to protect oneself against attack.
separation of powers Allocation of powers among the legislative, executive, and judicial branches of government.
service mark Distinctive symbol, word, or design that is used to identify the services of a provider.
servient Land subject to an easement.
setoff A counterclaim demand which defendant holds against plaintiff, arising out of a transaction extrinsic to plaintiff's cause of action.
settlor Creator of a trust.
severance The destruction of any one of the unities of a joint tenancy. It is so called because the estate is no longer a joint tenancy, but is severed.

Term may also refer to the cutting of crops, such as corn, wheat, etc., or to the separation of anything from realty.
share A proportionate ownership interest in a corporation.
Shelley's case, rule in Where a person takes an estate of freehold, legally or equitably, under a deed, will, or other writing, and in the same instrument there is a limitation by way of remainder of any interest of the same legal or equitable quality to his heirs, or heirs of his body, as a class of persons to take in succession from generation to generation, the limitation to the heirs entitles the ancestor to the whole estate.

The rule was adopted as a part of the common law of this country, though it has long since been abolished by most states.
shelter rule Transferee gets rights of transferor.
shipment contract Seller is authorized or required only to bear the expense of placing goods with the common carrier and bears the risk of loss only up to such point.
short-swing profits Profits made by insider through sale or other disposition of corporate stock within six months after purchase.
sight draft An instrument payable on presentment.
signature Any symbol executed with intent to validate a writing.
silent partner Partner who takes no part in the partnership business.
slander Oral defamation.
small claims courts Inferior civil courts with jurisdiction limited by dollar amount.
social security Measures by which the government provides economic assistance to disabled or retired employees and their dependents.
sole proprietorship A form of business in which one person owns all the assets of the business, in contrast to a partnership or a corporation.
sovereign immunity Foreign country's freedom from a host country's laws.
special warranty deed Seller promises that he has not impaired title.
specific performance The doctrine of specific performance is that where damages would compensate inadequately for the breach of an agreement, the contractor or vendor will be compelled to perform specifically what he has agreed to do; *e.g.*, ordered to execute a specific conveyance of land.

With respect to the sale of goods, specific performance may be decreed where the goods are unique or in other proper circumstances. The decree for specific performance may include such terms and conditions as to payment of the price, damages, or other relief as the court may deem just. UCC §§ 2–711(2)(b), 2–716.
standardized business form A preprinted contract.
stare decisis Doctrine that once a court has laid down a principle of law as applicable to a certain state of facts, it will adhere to that principle and apply it to all future cases having substantially the same facts, regardless of whether the parties and property are the same or not.
state action Actions by governments, as opposed to actions taken by private individuals.
state-of-the-art Made in accordance with the level of technology at the time the product is made.
stated capital Consideration, other than that allocated to capital surplus, received for issued stock.
statute of frauds A celebrated English statute, passed in 1677, which has been adopted, in a more or less modified form, in nearly all of the United States. Its chief characteristic is the provision that no action shall be brought on certain contracts unless there be a note or memorandum thereof in writing, signed by the party to be charged or by his authorized agent.
statute of limitation A statute prescribing limitations to the right of action on certain described causes of action; that is, declaring that no suit shall be maintained on such causes of action unless brought within a specified period after the right accrued.
statutory lien Interest in property, arising solely by statute, to secure payment of a debt.
stock "Stock" is distinguished from "bonds" and, ordinarily, from "debentures" in that it gives a right of ownership in part of the assets of a corporation and a right to interest in any surplus after the payment of debt. "Stock" in a corporation is an equity, representing an ownership interest. It is to be distinguished from obligations such as notes or bonds, which are not equities and represent no ownership interest.
Capital stock See **capital**.
Common stock Securities which represent an ownership interest in a corporation. If the company has also issued preferred stock, both common and preferred have ownership rights. Claims of both common and preferred stockholders are junior to claims of bondholders or other creditors of the company. Common stockholders assume the greater risk, but generally exercise the greater control and may gain the greater reward in the form of dividends and capital appreciation.
Convertible stock Stock which may be changed or converted into common stock.
Cumulative preferred Stock having a provision that if one or more dividends are omitted, the omitted dividends must be paid before dividends may be paid on the company's common stock.
Preferred stock is a separate portion or class of the stock of a corporation that is accorded, by the charter or by-laws, a preference or priority in respect to dividends, over the remainder of the stock of the corporation, which in that case is called *common stock*.
Stock warrant A certificate entitling the owner to buy a specified amount of stock at a specified time(s) for a specified price. Differs

from a stock option only in that options are granted to employees and warrants are sold to the public.

Treasury stock Shares reacquired by a corporation.

stock option Contractual right to purchase stock from a corporation.

stop payment Order for a drawee not to pay an instrument.

strict liability A concept applied by the courts in product liability cases in which a seller is liable for any and all defective or hazardous products which unduly threaten a consumer's personal safety. This concept applies to all members involved in the manufacture and sale of any facet of the product.

strict scrutiny test Requirement that legislation be necessary to promote a compelling governmental interest.

subagent Person appointed by agent to perform agent's duties.

subject matter jurisdiction Authority of a court to decide a particular kind of case.

subject to the mortgage Purchaser is not personally obligated to pay the debt, but the property remains subject to the mortgage.

subjective fault Desired or virtually certain consequences of one's conduct.

subjective satisfaction Approval based upon a party's honestly held opinion.

sublease Transfer of less than all of a tenant's interest in a leasehold.

subpoena A subpoena is a command to appear at a certain time and place to give testimony upon a certain matter. A subpoena duces tecum requires production of books, papers, and other things.

subrogation The substitution of one thing for another, or of one person into the place of another with respect to rights, claims, or securities.

Subrogation denotes the putting of a third person who has paid a debt in the place of the creditor to whom he has paid it, so that he may exercise against the debtor all the rights which the creditor, if unpaid, might have exercised.

subscribe Literally, to write underneath, as one's name. To sign at the end of a document. Also, to agree in writing to furnish money or its equivalent, or to agree to purchase some initial stock in a corporation.

subscriber Person who agrees to purchase initial stock in a corporation.

subsidiary corporation Corporation controlled by another corporation.

substantial performance Equitable doctrine protects against forfeiture for technical inadvertence, trivial variations, or omissions in performance.

substantive due process Requirement that governmental action be compatible with individual liberties.

substantive law The basic law of rights and duties (contract law, criminal law, tort law, law of wills, etc.), as opposed to procedural law (law of pleading, law of evidence, law of jurisdiction, etc.).

substantive unconscionability Oppressive or grossly unfair contractual terms.

sue To begin a lawsuit in a court.

suit "Suit" is a generic term of comprehensive signification that applies to any proceeding in a court of justice in which the plaintiff pursues, in such court, the remedy which the law affords him for the redress of an injury or the recovery of a right.

Derivative suit Suit brought by a shareholder on behalf of a corporation to enforce a right belonging to the corporation.

Direct suit Suit brought by a shareholder against a corporation based upon his ownership of shares.

summary judgment Rule of Civil Procedure 56 permits any party to a civil action to move for a summary judgment on a claim, counterclaim, or cross-claim when he believes that there is no genuine issue of material fact and that he is entitled to prevail as a matter of law.

summons Writ or process directed to the sheriff or other proper officer, requiring him to notify the person named that an action has been commenced against him in the court from which the process has issued and that he is required to appear, on a day named, and answer the complaint in such action.

superseding cause Intervening event that occurs after the defendant's negligent conduct and relieves him of liability.

supreme law Law that takes precedence over all conflicting laws.

surety One who undertakes to pay money or to do any other act in event that his principal debtor fails therein.

suretyship A guarantee of debts of another.

surplus Excess of net assets over stated capital.

tangible property Physical objects.

tariff Duty or tax imposed on goods moving into or out of a country.

tenancy Possession or occupancy of land or premises under lease.

Joint tenancy Joint tenants have one and the same interest, accruing by one and the same conveyance, commencing at one and the same time, and held by one and the same undivided possession. The primary incident of joint tenancy is survivorship, by which the entire tenancy on the decease of any joint tenant remains to the survivors, and at length to the last survivor.

Tenancy at sufferance Only naked possession which continues after tenant's right of possession has terminated.

Tenancy at will Possession of premises by permission of owner or landlord, but without a fixed term.

Tenancy by the entirety A tenancy which is created between a husband and wife and by which together they hold title to the whole with right of survivorship so that, upon death of either, the other takes the whole to the exclusion of the deceased's heirs. It is essentially a "joint tenancy," modified by the common law theory that husband and wife are one person.

Tenancy for a period A tenancy for years or for some fixed period.

Tenancy in common A form of ownership whereby each tenant (*i.e.*, owner) holds an undivided interest in property. Unlike the interest of a joint tenant or a tenant by the entirety, the interest of a tenant in common does not terminate upon his or her prior death (*i.e.*, there is no right of survivorship).

tenancy in partnership Type of joint ownership that determines partners' rights in specific partnership property.

tenant Possessor of a leasehold interest.

tender An offer of money; the act by which one produces and offers to a person holding a claim or demand against him the amount of money which he considers and admits to be due, in satisfaction of such claim or demand, without any stipulation or condition.

Also, there may be a tender of performance of a duty other than the payment of money.

tender of delivery Seller makes available to buyer goods conforming to the contract and so notifies the buyer.

tender offer General invitation to all shareholders to purchase their shares at a specified price.

testament Will.

testator One who makes or has made a testament or will; one who dies leaving a will.

third-party beneficiary One for whose benefit a promise is made in a contract but who is not a party to the contract.

Creditor beneficiary Where performance of a promise in a contract will benefit a person other than the promisee, that person is a creditor beneficiary if no purpose to make a gift appears from the terms of the promise, in view of the accompanying circumstances, and performance of the promise will satisfy an actual, supposed, or asserted duty of the promisee to the beneficiary.

Donee beneficiary The person who takes the benefit of the contract even though there is no privity between him and the contracting parties. A third-party beneficiary who is not a creditor beneficiary. See also **beneficiary**.

time paper Payable at definite time.

time-price doctrine Permits sellers to have different prices for cash sales and credit sales.

title The means whereby the owner of lands or of personalty has the just possession of his property.
title insurance Provides protection against defect in title to real property.
tort A private or civil wrong or injury, other than breach of contract, for which a court will provide a remedy in the form of an action for damages.

Three elements of every tort action are the existence of a legal duty from defendant to plaintiff, breach of that duty, and damage as proximate result.
tortfeasor One who commits a tort.
trade acceptance A draft drawn by a seller which is presented for signature (acceptance) to the buyer at the time goods are purchased and which then becomes the equivalent of a note receivable of the seller and the note payable of the buyer.
trade name Name used in trade or business to identify a particular business or manufacturer.
trade secrets Private business information.
trademark Distinctive insignia, word, or design of a good that is used to identify the manufacturer.
transferor's warranty Warranty given by any person who transfers an instrument and receives consideration.
treaty An agreement between or among independent nations.
treble damages Three times actual loss.
trespass At common law, trespass was a form of action brought to recover damages for any injury to one's person or property or relationship with another.

Trespass to chattels or personal property An unlawful and serious interference with the possessory rights of another to personal property.

Trespass to land At common law, every unauthorized and direct breach of the boundaries of another's land was an actionable trespass. The present prevailing position of the courts finds liability for trespass only in the case of intentional intrusion, or negligence, or some "abnormally dangerous activity" on the part of the defendant. *Compare* **nuisance**.

trespasser Person who enters or remains on the land of another without permission or privilege to do so.
trust Any arrangement whereby property is transferred with the intention that it be administered by a trustee for another's benefit.

A trust, as the term is used in the Restatement, when not qualified by the word "charitable," "resulting," or "constructive," is a fiduciary relationship with respect to property, subjecting the person by whom the title to the property is held to equitable duties to deal with the property for the benefit of another person, which arises through a manifestation of an intention to create such benefit. Restatement, Second, Trusts § 2.

Charitable trust To benefit humankind.

Constructive trust Wherever the circumstances of a transaction are such that the person who takes the legal estate in property cannot also enjoy the beneficial interest without necessarily violating some established principle of equity, the court will immediately raise a *constructive trust* and fasten it upon the conscience of the legal owner, so as to convert him into a trustee for the parties who in equity are entitled to the beneficial enjoyment.

Inter vivos trust Established during the settlor's lifetime.

Resulting trust One that arises by implication of law, where the legal estate in property is disposed of, conveyed, or transferred, but the intent appears or is inferred from the terms of the disposition, or from the accompanying facts and circumstances, that the beneficial interest is not to go or be enjoyed with the legal title.

Spendthrift trust Removal of the trust estate from the beneficiary's control.

Testamentary trust Established by a will.

Totten trust A tentative trust which is a joint bank account opened by the settlor.

Voting trust A trust which holds the voting rights to stock in a corporation. It is a useful device when a majority of the shareholders in a corporation cannot agree on corporate policy.

trustee In a strict sense, a "trustee" is one who holds the legal title to property for the benefit of another, while, in a broad sense, the term is sometimes applied to anyone standing in a fiduciary or confidential relation to another, such as agent, attorney, bailee, etc.
trustee in bankruptcy Representative of the estate in bankruptcy who is responsible for collecting, liquidating, and distributing the debtor's assets.
tying arrangement Conditioning a sale of a desired product (tying product) on the buyer's purchasing a second product (tied product).

ultra vires Acts beyond the scope of the powers of a corporation, as defined by its charter or by the laws of its state of incorporation. By the doctrine of ultra vires, a contract made by a corporation beyond the scope of its corporate powers is unlawful.
unconscionable Unfair or unduly harsh.
unconscionable contract See **contracts**.
underwriter Any person, banker, or syndicate that guarantees to furnish a definite sum of money by a definite date to a business or government in return for an issue of bonds or stock. In insurance, the one assuming a risk in return for the payment of a premium.
undisputed debt Obligation whose existence and amount are not contested.
undue influence Term refers to conduct by which a person, through his power over the mind of a testator, makes the latter's desires conform to his own, thereby overmastering the volition of the testator.
unemployment compensation Compensation awarded to workers who have lost their jobs and cannot find other employment.
unenforceable Contract under which neither party can recover.
unfair employer practice Conduct in which an employer is prohibited from engaging.
unfair labor practice Conduct in which an employer or union is prohibited from engaging.
unfair union practice Conduct in which a union is prohibited from engaging.
Uniform Commercial Code One of the Uniform Laws, drafted by the National Conference of Commissioners on Uniform State Laws, governing commercial transactions (sales of goods, commercial paper, bank deposits and collections, letters of credit, bulk transfers, warehouse receipts, bills of lading, investment securities, and secured transactions).
unilateral mistake Erroneous belief on the part of only one of the parties to a contract.
union shop Employer can hire nonunion members, but such employees must then join the union.
universal life Ordinary life divided into two components, a renewable term insurance policy and an investment portfolio.
unliquidated debt Obligation that is uncertain or contested in amount.
unqualified indorsement (see **indorsement**) One that imposes liability upon the indorser.
unreasonably dangerous Danger beyond that which the ordinary consumer contemplates.
unrestrictive indorsement (see **indorsement**) One that does not attempt to restrict the rights of the indorsee.
usage of trade Any practice or method of dealing having such regularity of observance in a place, vocation, or trade as to justify an expectation that it will be observed with respect to the transaction in question.
usury Collectively, the laws of a jurisdiction regulating the charging of interest rates. A usurious loan is one whose interest rates are determined to be in excess of those permitted by the usury laws.

value The performance of legal consideration, the forgiveness of an antecedent debt, the giving of a negotiable instrument, or the giving of an irrevocable commitment to a third party. UCC § 1–201(44).
variance A use differing from that provided in a zoning ordinance in order to avoid undue hardship.
vendee A purchaser or buyer; one to whom anything is sold. See also **vendor.**
vendor The person who transfers property by sale, particularly real estate; "seller" being more commonly used for one who sells personalty. See also **vendee**.
venue "Jurisdiction" of the court means the inherent power to decide a case, whereas "venue" designates the particular county or city in which a court with jurisdiction may hear and determine the case.
verdict The formal and unanimous decision or finding of a jury, impaneled and sworn for the trial of a cause, upon the matters or questions duly submitted to it upon the trial.
vertical privity Who is liable to the plaintiff.
vertical restraints Agreements among parties at different levels of the distribution chain.
vested Fixed; accrued; settled; absolute To be "vested," a right must be more than a mere expectation based on an anticipation of the continuance of an existing law; it must have become a title, legal or equitable, to the present or future enforcement of a demand, or a legal exemption from the demand of another.
vested remainder Unconditional remainder that is a fixed present interest to be enjoyed in the future.
vicarious liability Indirect legal responsibility; for example, the liability of an employer for the acts of an employee or that of a principal for the torts and contracts of an agent.
void Null; ineffectual; nugatory; having no legal force or binding effect; unable, in law, to support the purpose for which it was intended.

This difference separates the words "void" and "voidable": *void* in the strict sense means that an instrument or transaction is nugatory and ineffectual, so that nothing can cure it; *voidable* exists when an imperfection or defect can be cured by the act or confirmation of the person who could take advantage of it.

Frequently, the word "void" is used and construed as having the more liberal meaning of "voidable."
voidable Capable of being made void. See also **void**.
voir dire Preliminary examination of potential jurors.
voluntary Resulting from free choice. The word, especially in statutes, often implies knowledge of essential facts.
voting trust Transfer of corporate shares' voting rights to a trustee.

wager (gambling) Agreement that one party will win or lose depending upon the outcome of an event in which the only interest is the gain or loss.
waiver Terms "estoppel" and "waiver" are not synonymous; "waiver" means the voluntary, intentional relinquishment of a known right, and "estoppel" rests upon principle that, where anyone has done an act or made a statement that would be a fraud on his part to controvert or impair, because the other party has acted upon it in belief that what was done or said was true, conscience and honest dealing require that he not be permitted to repudiate his act or gainsay his statement. See also **estoppel**.
ward An infant or insane person placed by authority of law under the care of a guardian.
warehouse receipt Receipt issued by a person storing goods.
warehouser Storer of goods for compensation.
warrant, *v.* In contracts, to engage or promise that a certain fact or state of facts, in relation to the subject matter, is, or shall be, as it is represented to be.

In conveyancing, to assure the title to property sold, by an express covenant to that effect in the deed of conveyance.
warranty A warranty is a statement or representation made by a seller of goods, contemporaneously with and as a part of a contract of sale, though collateral to express the object of the sale, having reference to the character, quality, or title of goods, and by which the seller promises or undertakes to ensure that certain facts are or shall be as he then represents them.

The general statutory law governing warranties on sales of goods is provided in UCC § 2–312 *et seq*. The three main types of warranties are (1) express warranty; (2) implied warranty of fitness; (3) implied warranty of merchantability.
warranty deed Deed in which grantor warrants good clear title. The usual covenants of title are warranties of seisin, quiet enjoyment, right to convey, freedom from encumbrances, and defense of title as to all claims.

Special warranty deed Seller warrants that he has not impaired title.
warranty liability Applies to persons who transfer an instrument or receive payment or acceptance.
warranty of title Obligation to convey the right to ownership without any lien.
waste Any act or omission that does permanent injury to the realty or unreasonably changes its value.
white-collar crime Corporate crime.
will A written instrument executed with the formalities required by statutes, whereby a person makes a disposition of his property to take effect after his death.
winding up To settle the accounts and liquidate the assets of a partnership or corporation, for the purpose of making distribution and terminating the concern.
without reserve Auctioneer may not withdraw the goods from the auction.
workers' compensation Compensation awarded to an employee who is injured, when the injury arose out of and in the course of his employment.
writ of certiorari Discretionary review by a higher court. See also **certiorari**.
writ of execution Order served by sheriff upon debtor demanding payment of a court judgment against debtor.

zoning Public control over land use.

INDEX

D

E

T